Standard & Poor's
500 Guide

Standard & Poor's
500 Guide

1999 Edition

Standard & Poor's

McGraw-Hill

New York   San Francisco   Washington, D.C.   Auckland   Bogotá
Caracas   Lisbon   London   Madrid   Mexico City   Milan
Montreal   New Delhi   San Juan   Singapore
Sydney   Tokyo   Toronto

FOR STANDARD & POOR'S
Vice President, Index Products & Services: Elliott Shurgin
Managing Editor: Joseph Spiers
Associate Publisher: Frank LoVaglio

McGraw-Hill

A Division of The McGraw-Hill Companies

1 2 3 4 5 6 7 8 9 0   AGM/AGM   9 0 3 2 1 0 9 8

ISBN 0-07-052764-4

*The sponsoring editor for this book was Susan Barry and the
production supervisor was Clare Stanley. The front matter
and introduction were set by North Market Street
Graphics.*

Printed and bound by Quebecor/Martinsburg.

This book is printed on acid-free paper.

The companies contained in this handbook represented the
components of the S&P 500 Index as of September 12, 1998.
Additions to or deletions from the Index will cause its composition to change over time. Company additions and company
deletions from the Standard & Poor's equity indexes do not in
any way reflect an opinion on the investment merits of the
company.

ABOUT THE AUTHOR

Standard & Poor's, a division of The McGraw-Hill Companies, Inc., is the nation's leading securities information company. It provides a broad range of financial services, including the respected Standard & Poor's ratings and stock rankings, advisory services, data guides, and the most closely watched and widely reported gauges of stock market activity—the S&P 500, S&P MidCap 400, S&P SmallCap 600, and the S&P Super Composite 1500 stock price indexes. Standard & Poor's products are marketed around the world and used extensively by financial professionals and individual investors.

Introduction

by Alan J. Miller, C.F.A.

While he was getting dressed one morning, Art Jones heard a news report on the radio saying that the Dow Jones Industrial Average had risen nine points on the previous day. Later he read in his morning newspaper that more stocks had declined than advanced. "How could that be?" he wondered. "Had the market gone up or down?"

Jenny Martin had been interviewing investment advisors to find someone to manage her stock portfolio and it seemed that everyone she spoke to claimed to have outperformed the market. That struck her as hard to believe and, in fact, all the managers she spoke to did seem to be comparing their results to different benchmarks. How could she tell how well those managers really had done?

"I think the market is really going to take off," Mark Johnson thought, "and I'd like to participate. But I'm afraid that even if I'm right, I could end up buying the wrong stocks and the ones I buy could go down while everything else goes up. I can't afford to diversify by buying 1,000 different companies. I just wish there were some way I could buy the whole market. Is there anything I can do?"

Mary Carter had a question for her accountant. "I'd like to invest in a few high-quality, well-established companies that are selling at reasonable prices," she said. "But with thousands and thousands of different companies around—including many that I just wouldn't be interested in because they're too new or too small—I just wouldn't know where to begin. Is there some way I could cut that number down to manageable size and know that the universe I'm looking at consists only of large capitalization, established companies?"

Andrew Perez is the marketing manager for a nationwide computer company whose products and services are used by many of the largest corporations in the country—and he's always on the lookout for even more customers. What he's really looking for are established companies that are in good financial shape and growing, so that they'll be responsive to his suggestions for upgrading their hardware, purchasing additional software, or engaging in more sophisticated networking—and will have the funds to carry out those plans if he convinces them of their value. But where can he find the names of those companies and the information about them which he requires?

Sally Kennedy is the founder and president of a small company in an industry dominated by a dozen or so major competitors. She'd really like to find out how well those larger companies in her industry are doing. Where can she look?

Six different questions, all leading to the same answer: Turn to the Standard & Poor's 500 Index.

What Is the S&P 500?

For sheer longevity, no other stock market indicators compare with the Dow Jones Industrial Average, which has been around since 1884, and the Standard & Poor's 500 Composite Stock Price Index, which was first introduced in 1923. Over the decades, both indicators have been consistently and widely cited as benchmarks of market performance.

Historically, the two indicators were viewed as complementary measures—but in recent years, the key differences between the DJIA and the S&P 500 Index have come into sharper focus. Today, sophisticated investors realize that the DJIA and the S&P 500 Index cannot be used interchangeably: based on different universes and methodologies, they provide very different pictures of market activity.

The DJIA tracks the stock performance of 30 "blue chip" companies, allowing equal weight to a one point move in each stock, notwithstanding substantial differences in stock prices and company capitalizations. As a result, a 5% move, say, in a $200 stock would have ten times the weight of a 5% move in a $20 stock and companies with larger equity capitalizations would not necessarily be weighted any more heavily than companies with smaller capitalizations. Despite these methodological shortcomings, the DJIA has generally been accepted as a reasonable indicator for the "blue chip" market but, because it contains nothing but "blue chip" stocks, by no stretch of the imagination could it be considered representative of the *overall* market.

The S&P 500, on the other hand, covers a far larger and more varied universe of companies, and hence is a more accurate barometer of the overall stock market.

Standard & Poor's 500 composite stock-price index is widely regarded as the most accurate proxy for the stock market and is used by virtually all professional consultants as the benchmark against which to measure money managers' performance. The index contains a representative sample of common stocks that trade on the New York and American Stock Exchanges as well as on the Nasdaq Stock Market (those issues that are part of the Nasdaq National Market). Moreover, because the companies chosen for inclusion in the S&P 500 tend to be the top companies in the U.S., the S&P 500 Index became a component of the U.S. Department of Commerce's Index of Leading Economic Indicators in 1968. Now published by the Conference Board, a private research organization, that widely followed measure is used to signal potential turning points in the U.S. economy. The S&P 500 is also used as the benchmark for $475 billion in passive index funds—such as pension and mutual funds.

As the name indicates, the S&P 500 consists of 500 U.S. stocks, which at the end of the second quarter of 1998 represented about 77% of the total market value of American stocks. Although these are not necessarily the 500 largest companies in the United States, most of the largest companies are included. All of these stocks are widely held and the total market value of the "500" is nearly $7 trillion.

Approximately 92% (459 issues representing 90% of the market value) of the issues in the index are listed on the New York Stock Exchange. Another 8% (38 issues accounting for nearly 10% of the market value) are traded on the Nasdaq Stock Market and the remaining 1% (3 issues with less than 1% of the market value) are listed on the American Stock Exchange.

But let's take another look at the half-dozen questions raised at the beginning of this introduction.

The Six Questions...Answered

1. Art Jones

If the Dow Jones Industrial Average rose nine points but more stocks declined than advanced, had the market really gone up or down?

In a sense, there really is no one answer to that question because it all depends on how you choose to define "the market." But in another sense, it is probably fair to say that the S&P 500 Index provides as good a picture of what the market "really" does as any index around. It is, after all, an average of 500 companies, not just 30, which makes it a better proxy for the overall market than the Dow Jones Industrial Average. And since, unlike advance-decline indices, the 500 stocks are *capitalization* weighted, it wouldn't be distorted by declines in a large number of small companies which might actually have been more than offset (in terms of total dollars gained or lost by investors) by increases in a smaller number of large companies. So if Art wants to know how the market "really" did, he ought to take a look at the S&P 500.

2. Jenny Martin

If all the investment advisors she talks to claim to have outperformed the market (by comparing their results to different benchmarks), how can she tell how well they've truly done?

Now this question turns out to be somewhat easier than it appeared to be at first blush. For if the S&P 500 really is the best proxy for the overall stock market, then an investment advisor who invests in common stocks can reasonably be measured by comparing his performance to that index. Of course, if the advisor invests only in international stocks, or small capitalization stocks, or long-term bonds, or some other mix of assets, a different benchmark would have to be developed to measure his performance fairly. But for the typical common stock manager, the best benchmark probably is the S&P 500.

3. Mark Johnson

How can he invest in the overall market without taking the risk of investing in the stocks of individual companies?

Consider the alternatives. First, Mark might just invest in an actively managed common stock mutual fund which is broadly diversified among hundreds of companies. If the diversification is broad enough, and if the securities owned are selected at random, the law of averages would suggest that the fund's results would approximate those of the overall market (as measured by the S&P 500).

Unfortunately, however, most funds *aren't* that diversified. They might own a couple of hundred stocks, but probably not 500. And for that reason alone, this approach might not work.

But there is another even more important reason why this approach would not work. It is because the portfolios of *actively managed* funds, by definition, are *not* randomized, but rather are consciously structured by their managers to reflect those managers' best judgments regarding the relative attractiveness of alternative investment vehicles. Thus, those managers *intentionally* overweight some companies (which the fund managers expect to be stellar performers) and underweight others (which they expect to fare relatively poorly).

Now, if the fund managers' judgments turn out to be right, terrific. But suppose they're not? In that case, the fund, despite its being broadly diversified, still may perform substantially worse than the market (as measured by the S&P 500). And remember, that risk—the chance of performing poorly as a result of picking the wrong stocks, even though the market on average did well—is precisely the risk that Mark is seeking to avoid.

No, selecting an *actively* managed fund *wouldn't* solve Mark's problem. But suppose Mark could invest in a *passively* managed fund—one whose managers simply tried to replicate the performance of the market as a whole, without trying to add value (and thereby running the risk of subtracting value instead) through individual stock selection. Would that satisfy Mark's need?

In fact, it would. And, fortunately for Mark, *passively* managed mutual funds which merely seek to replicate the performance of the S&P 500 Index (commonly known as index funds) abound. Indeed, these funds have so grown in popularity (in large part because, strange as it may seem, stock market indices actually have tended to *outperform* a majority of mutual funds and pension plans actively managed by professionals) that, as of 1998 mid-year, more than $62.6 billion was invested in mutual funds indexed to the S&P 500.

But passively managed index funds are not the only option open to Mark. He may make an even more direct bet on the direction of the market by investing in "stock index futures" themselves—or, if he is even more speculatively inclined, in *options* on stock index futures.

Stock index futures are, in effect, futures contracts on the value of the theoretical basket of securities which comprise a stock index. Indices on which futures contracts may be written include the New York Stock Exchange Composite Index (traded on the New York Futures Exchange), the Value Line Composite Index (traded on the Kansas City Board of Trade), and, of course, the Standard & Poor's 500 Index and Standard & Poor's MidCap 400 Index (both traded on the Chicago Mercantile Exchange). Since investors in such indices obviously can't deliver an index of stocks to a futures buyer, settlement of such contracts is in cash.

The Chicago Mercantile Exchange also trades options on Standard & Poor's 500 and MidCap 400 futures contracts. Exercise of one of those options establishes a position in the underlying futures contract. Options on the Standard & Poor's 500 Index are traded on the Chicago Board Options Exchange, and options on the Standard & Poor's MidCap 400 Index are traded on the American Stock Exchange. Unlike options on futures contracts, options on stock indices are settled in cash.

Of course, if Mark thought that the market was likely to decline rather than advance, but didn't want to incur the risk of going short the wrong stocks (those that might turn out to rise even in a falling market), trading in Standard & Poor's 500 Index futures contracts and options on those contracts could serve his purposes too. In that event, he would sell short futures contracts or call options on futures contracts or buy put options on futures contracts, rather than buying futures contracts or call options.

Finally, if Mark discovered a stock which he believed would outperform the market substantially but thought that the overall market itself was just as likely to decline as to rise, the futures contracts and options markets could help him too. In that event, he could buy the stock and short the market (by shorting futures contracts or calls on futures contracts on the S&P 500 Composite Index). If he turned out to be right and the stock did substantially outperform the market, he would do well whether the stock market itself rose or fell: if the stock market rose, the stock would rise even more (on a percentage basis), so he'd make more money on his long position in the stock than he would lose on his short positions in the futures or options markets. On the other hand, if the stock market declined, the stock would decline less (or maybe even rise) and he'd make more money on his short positions in futures contracts or options than he'd lose on the stock itself (or maybe, if he got really lucky, even make money on both).

4. Mary Carter

How can she find individual high-quality, well-established companies from which to select, for investment purposes, those that are selling at reasonable prices?

The components of the S&P 500 Composite Index are just what Mary is looking for. Indeed, as of the end of 1998's second quarter, the "average" S&P 500 company boasted a market value of $17.9 billion.

What Mary should do is to turn to the pages of this book, which include extensive data on all 500 companies in the S&P 500 Composite Index. But before doing so, she should be sure to read the final sections of this introduction—"What You'll Find in This Book" and "How to Use This Book to Select Investments"—in order to learn just how to extract the most value from that data.

5. Andrew Perez

How can Andrew find established companies that are in good financial shape, growing, and have the funds to acquire the hardware or software he'll be recommending to them?

The companies in the S&P 500 Composite Index should be Andrew's starting point, too, and the pages of this book are where he'll find the information on those companies which he requires. But before thumbing through these pages, Andrew, like Mary, would be well advised to refer first to the section titled "What You'll Find in This Book," which appears later in this introduction.

6. Sally Kennedy

How can Sally find out how her major competitors, the larger companies in her industry, are doing?

You guessed it: A good place for Sally to start would be with the companies in this book. If Sally's industry is dominated by a number of large competitors, there is little doubt that most, if not all, will show up here. And here's where she's likely to find a lot of the information on those companies too.

But we're at the point now where we really must try to provide Mary, Andrew, and Sally with more guidance. Art, Jenny, and Mark, you will recall, were primarily concerned with using the Standard & Poor's 500 Composite Index in the aggregate, in order to find out how the market's "really" doing (Art), to measure investment managers' performance

(Jenny), or to invest in the market as a whole or hedge individual stock positions (Mark). And we've explained all that.

Mary, Andrew, and Sally, however, are primarily interested in the *components* of the S&P 500, in their quest for companies which might represent good individual investments (Mary), or companies which could turn out to be good potential clients (Andrew), or companies which are important business competitors (Sally). And it is those individual companies which most of this book is about. So it's time to show Mary, Andrew, Sally—and you. . . .

What You'll Find in This Book

In the pages that follow you will find an array of text and statistical data on 500 different companies in 104 industries. This information, dealing with everything from the nature of these companies' basic businesses, recent corporate developments, current outlooks, and select financial information relating to revenues, earnings, dividends, margins, capitalization, and so forth, might initially seem overwhelming. However, it's not that difficult. Just take a few moments to familiarize yourself with what you'll find on these pages.

Following is a glossary of terms and definitions used throughout this book. Please refer to this section as you encounter terms which need further clarification.

Stock Report Terms

Quantitative Evaluations

Standard & Poor's Opinion—Buy, hold or sell recommendations are provided using Standard & Poor's unique STARS (Stock Appreciation Ranking System), which measures short-term (six- to 12-month) appreciation potential of stocks. STARS performance is measured against the performance of the S&P 500 Index.

STARS Rankings are as follows:

***** Buy—Expected to be among the best performers over the next 12 months.
**** Accumulate—Expected to be an above-average performer.
*** Hold—Expected to be an average performer.
** Avoid—Likely to be a below-average performer.
* Sell—Expected to be a well-below-average performer and fall in price.

Outlook—Using Standard & Poor's exclusive proprietary quantitative model, stocks are ranked in one of five Outlook Groups—ranging from Group 5, listing the most undervalued stocks, to Group 1, the most overvalued issues. Group 5 stocks are expected to generally outperform all others. To identify a stock that is in a strengthening or weakening position, a positive (+) or negative (–) Timing Index is placed next to the Outlook ranking. Using these rankings, here's what action should be taken:

5+ = Buy	2+ = Hold if in portfolio
5 = Hold if in portfolio	2– = Sell
4+ = Hold if in portfolio	1+ = Hold if in portfolio
4– = Sell	1– = Sell
3+ = Hold if in portfolio	
3– = Sell	

The Timing Index helps identify the right time to buy stocks, but its most important function is to indicate when it is time to sell. Because Group 5 stocks have historically produced the best results, Standard & Poor's recommends buying only Group 5 stocks with a positive Timing Index. Then, hold onto each one for as long as it remains in a positive trend (positive Timing Index), even if the ranking falls as the stock appreciates toward overvalued status. This will reduce transaction costs and substantially raise your chances of outperforming the market in the long run. It will also raise the number of transactions which qualify as long-term capital gains for tax purposes.

Fair Value—The price at which a stock should sell today as calculated by Standard & Poor's computers using our quantitative model based on the company's earnings, growth potential, return on equity relative to the S&P 500 and its industry group, price to book ratio history, current yield relative to the S&P 500, and other factors. The current fair price is shown given today's S&P 500 level.

Risk—Rates the volatility of the stock's price over the past year.

Technical Evaluation—In researching the past market history of prices and trading volume for each company, Standard & Poor's computer models apply special technical methods and formulas to identify and project price trends for the stock. They analyze how the price of the stock is moving and evaluate the interrelationships between the moving averages to ultimately determine buy or sell signals—and to decide whether they're bullish, neutral or bearish for the stock. The date the signals were initiated is also provided so you can take advantage of a recent or ongoing uptrend in price, or see how a stock has performed over time since our last technical signal was generated.

Relative Strength Rank—Shows, on a scale of 1 to 99, how the stock has performed compared with all other companies in Standard & Poor's universe of companies on a rolling 13-week basis.

Insider Activity—Gives an insight as to insider sentiment by showing whether directors, officers and key employees—who may have proprietary information not available to the general public—are buying or selling the company's stock during the most recent six months.

Key Stock Statistics

Avg. Daily Vol.—The average daily trading volume of the stock for the past 20 days on a rolling basis, shown in millions.

Market Cap.—The price of the stock multiplied by the number of shares outstanding, shown in billions.

Insider Holdings—The percentage of outstanding shares held by directors, officers and key employees of the company, and others who hold a minimum of 10% of the outstanding shares.

Value of $10,000 Invested 5 years ago—The value today of a $10,000 investment in the stock made five years ago, assuming year-end reinvestment of dividends.

Standard & Poor's Ranking

The investment process involves assessment of various factors—such as products and industry position, company resources and financial policy—with results that make some common stocks more highly esteemed than others. In this assessment, Standard & Poor's believes that earnings and dividend performance is the end result of the interplay of these factors and that, over the long run, the record of this performance has a considerable bearing on relative quality. The rankings, however, do not reflect all of the factors that may bear on stock quality.

Growth and stability of earnings and dividends are the key elements in Standard & Poor's earnings and dividend rankings for common stocks, which are designed to capsulize the nature of this record in a single symbol. It should be noted, however, that the process also takes into consideration certain adjustments and modifications deemed desirable in establishing such rankings.

These rankings are derived by means of a computerized scoring system based on per share earnings and dividend records of the most recent ten years. Basic scores are computed for earnings and dividends and then adjusted by a set of predetermined modifiers for growth, stability, and cyclicality. Adjusted scores for earnings and dividends are then combined to yield a final score.

The ranking system also makes allowance for the fact that, in general, corporate size imparts certain recognized advantages from an investment standpoint. Minimum size limits (in terms of corporate sales) are set for the various rankings, but exceptions may be made where a score reflects an outstanding earnings-dividend record.

Final scores are then translated into one of the following rankings:

A+   Highest
A   High
A−   Above Average
B+   Average
B   Below Average
B−   Lower

C   Lowest

D   In Reorganization

NR   No Ranking

In some instances, rankings may be modified by special considerations, such as natural disasters, massive strikes, or nonrecurring accounting adjustments.

It is important to note that a ranking is not a forecast of future market price performance, but is basically an appraisal of past performance of earnings and dividends and relative current standing. Consequently, rankings should not be used as market recommendations: a high-score stock may at times be so overpriced as to justify its sale while a low-score stock may be attractively priced for purchase. Rankings based upon earnings and dividend records are no substitute for complete analysis. They cannot take into account the potential effects of management changes, internal company policies not yet fully reflected in the earnings and dividend record, public relations standings, recent competitive shifts, and a host of other factors that may be relevant in investment decision making.

Beta

The beta coefficient is a measure of the volatility of a stock's price relative to the S&P 500 Index (a proxy for the overall market). An issue with a beta of 1.5 for example, tends to move 50% more than the overall market, in the same direction. An issue with a beta of 0.5 tends to move 50% less. If a stock moved exactly as the market moved, it would have a beta of 1.0. A stock with a negative beta tends to move in a direction opposite to that of the overall market.

Per Share Data ($) Tables

Tangible Book Value; Book Value (See also: "Common Equity" under Industrial)—Indicates the theoretical dollar amount per common share one might expect to receive from a company's tangible "book" assets should liquidation take place. Generally, book value is determined by adding the stated value of the common stock, paid-in capital and retained earnings and then subtracting intangible assets (excess cost over equity of acquired companies, goodwill, and patents), preferred stock at liquidating value and unamortized debt discount. Divide that amount by the outstanding shares to get book value per common share.

Cash Flow—Net income plus depreciation, depletion, and amortization, divided by shares used to calculate earnings per common share. (Also see: "Cash Flow" for Industrial Companies.)

Earnings—The amount a company reports as having been earned for the year on its common stock based on generally accepted accounting standards. Earnings per share are presented on a *"Diluted"* basis pursuant to FASB 128, which became effective December 15, 1997, and are generally reported from continuing operations, before extraordinary items. This reflects a change from previously reported *Primary* earnings per share. INSURANCE companies report *operating earnings* before gains/losses on security transactions and *earnings* after such transactions.

Dividends—Generally total cash payments per share based on the ex-dividend dates over a twelve-month period. May also be reported on a declared basis where this has been established to be a company's payout policy.

Payout Ratio—Indicates the percentage of earnings paid out in dividends. It is calculated by dividing the annual dividend by the earnings. For INSURANCE companies *earnings* after gains/losses on security transactions are used.

Prices High/Low—Shows the calendar year high and low of a stock's market price.

P/E Ratio High/Low—The ratio of market price to earnings—essentially indicates the valuation investors place on a company's earnings. Obtained by dividing the annual earnings into the high and low market price for the year. For INSURANCE companies *operating earnings* before gains/losses on security transactions are used.

Net Asset Value—Appears on investment company reports and reflects the market value of stocks, bonds, and net cash divided by outstanding shares. The % DIFFERENCE indicates the percentage premium or discount of the market price over the net asset value.

Portfolio Turnover—Appears on investment company reports and indicates percentage of total security purchases and sales for the year to overall investment assets. Primarily mirrors trading aggressiveness.

Income/Balance Sheet Data Tables

Banks

Net Interest Income—Interest and dividend income, minus interest expense.

Loan Loss Provision—Amount charged to operating expenses to provide an adequate reserve to cover anticipated losses in the loan portfolio.

Taxable Equivalent Adjustment—Increase to render income from tax-exempt loans and securities comparable to fully taxed income.

Noninterest Income—Service fees, trading and other income, excluding gains/ losses on securities transactions.

% Expenses/Op. Revenues—Noninterest expense as a percentage of taxable equivalent net interest income plus noninterest income (before securities gains/losses). A measure of cost control.

Commercial Loans—Commercial, industrial, financial, agricultural loans and leases, gross.

Other Loans—Gross consumer, real estate and foreign loans.

% Loan Loss Reserve—Contra-account to loan assets, built through provisions for loan losses, which serves as a cushion for possible future loan charge-offs.

% Loans/Deposits—Proportion of loans funded by deposits. A measure of liquidity and an indication of bank's ability to write more loans.

Earning Assets—Assets on which interest is earned.

Money Market Assets—Interest-bearing interbank deposits, federal funds sold, trading account securities.

Investment Securities—Federal, state, and local government bonds and other securities.

Gains/Losses on Securities Transactions—Realized losses on sales of securities, usually bonds.

Net Before Taxes—Amount remaining after operating expenses are deducted from income, including gains or losses on security transactions.

Effective Tax Rate—Actual income tax expense divided by net before taxes.

Net Income—The final profit before dividends (common/preferred) from all sources after deduction of expenses, taxes, and fixed charges, but before any discontinued operations or extraordinary items.

Net Interest Margin—A percentage computed by dividing net interest income, on a taxable equivalent basis, by average earning assets. Used as an analytical tool to measure profit margins from providing credit services.

% Return on Revenues—Net income divided by gross revenues.

% Return on Assets—Net income divided by average total assets. An analytical measure of asset-use efficiency and industry comparison.

% Return on Equity—Net income (minus preferred dividend requirements) divided by average common equity. Generally used to measure performance.

Total Assets—Includes interest-earning financial instruments—principally commercial, real estate, consumer loans and leases; investment securities/trading accounts; cash/money market investments; other owned assets.

Cash—Mainly vault cash, interest-bearing deposits placed with banks, reserves required by the Federal Reserve and items in the process of collection—generally referred to as float.

Government Securities—Includes United States Treasury securities and securities of other U.S. government agencies at book or carrying value. A bank's major "liquid asset."

State and Municipal Securities—State and municipal securities owned at book value.

Loans—All domestic and foreign loans (excluding leases), less unearned discount and reserve for possible losses. Generally considered a bank's principal asset.

Deposits—Primarily classified as either *demand* (payable at any time upon demand of depositor) or *time* (not payable within thirty days).

Deposits/Capital Funds—Average deposits divided by average capital funds. Capital funds include capital notes/debentures, other long-term debt, capital stock, surplus, and undivided profits. May be used as a "leverage" measure.

Long-Term Debt—Total borrowings for terms beyond one year including notes payable, mortgages, debentures, term loans, and capitalized lease obligations.

Common Equity—Includes common/capital surplus, undivided profits, reserve for contingencies and other capital reserves.

% Equity to Assets—Average common equity divided by average total assets. Used as a measure of capital adequacy.

% Equity to Loans—Average common equity divided by average loans. Reflects the degree of equity coverage to loans outstanding.

Industrial Companies

Following data is based on Form 10K Annual Report data as filed with SEC.

Revenues—Net sales and other operating revenues. Includes franchise/leased department income for retailers, and royalties for publishers and oil and mining companies. Excludes excise taxes for tobacco, liquor, and oil companies.

Operating Income—Net sales and operating revenues less cost of goods sold and operating expenses (including research and development, profit sharing, exploration and bad debt, but excluding depreciation and amortization).

% Operating Income of Revenues—Net sales and operating revenues divided into operating income. Used as a measure of operating profitability.

Capital Expenditures—The sum of additions at cost to property, plant and equipment and leaseholds, generally excluding amounts arising from acquisitions.

Depreciation—Includes noncash charges for obsolescence, wear on property, current portion of capitalized expenses (intangibles), and depletion charges.

Interest Expense—Includes all interest expense on short/long-term debt, amortization of debt discount/premium and deferred expenses (e.g., financing costs).

Net Before Taxes—Includes operating and nonoperating revenues (including extraordinary items not net of taxes), less all operating and nonoperating expenses, except income taxes and minority interest, but including equity in nonconsolidated subsidiaries.

Effective Tax Rate—Actual income tax charges divided by net before taxes.

Net Income—Profits derived from all sources after deduction of expenses, taxes, and fixed charges, but before any discontinued operations, extraordinary items, and dividends (preferred/common).

% Net Income of Revenues—Net income divided by sales/operating revenues.

Cash Flow—Net income (before extraordinary items and discontinued operations, and after preferred dividends) plus depreciation, depletion, and amortization.

Cash—Includes all cash and government and other marketable securities.

Current Assets—Those assets expected to be realized in cash or used up in the production of revenue within one year.

Current Liabilities—Generally includes all debts/obligations falling due within one year.

Current Ratio—Current assets divided by current liabilities. A measure of liquidity.

Total Assets—Current assets plus net plant and other noncurrent assets (intangibles and deferred items).

% Return on Assets—Net income divided by average total assets on a per common share basis. Used in industry analysis and as a measure of asset-use efficiency.

Long-Term Debt—Debts/obligations due after one year. Includes bonds, notes payable, mortgages, lease obligations, and industrial revenue bonds. Other Long-Term Debt, when reported as a separate account, is excluded. This account generally includes pension and retirement benefits.

Common Equity (See also: "Book Value" under Per Share Data Table)—Common stock plus capital surplus and retained earnings, less any difference between the carrying value and liquidating value of preferred stock.

Total Invested Capital—The sum of stockholders' equity plus long-term debt, capital lease obligations, deferred income taxes, investment credits, and minority interest.

% Long-Term Debt of Invested Capital—Long-term debt divided by total invested capital. Indicates how highly "lever aged" a business might be.

% Return on Equity—Net income less preferred dividend requirements divided by average common shareholders' equity on a per common share basis. Generally used to measure performance and industry comparisons.

Utilities

Operating Revenues—Represents the amount billed to customers by the utility.

Depreciation—Amounts charged to income to compensate for the decline in useful value of plant and equipment.

Maintenance—Amounts spent to keep plants in good operating condition.

Operating Ratio—Ratio of operating costs to operating revenues or the proportion of revenues absorbed by expenses. Obtained by dividing operating expenses including depreciation, maintenance, and taxes by revenues.

Fixed Charges Coverage—The number of times income before interest charges (operating income plus other income) after taxes covers total interest charges and preferred dividend requirements.

Construction Credits—Credits for interest charged to the cost of constructing new plant. A combination of allowance for equity funds used during construction and allowance for borrowed funds used during construction—credit.

Effective Tax Rate—Actual income tax expense divided by the total of net income and actual income tax expense.

Net Income—Amount of earnings for the year which is available for preferred and common dividend payments.

% Return on Revenues—Obtained by dividing net income for the year by revenues.

% Return on Invested Capital—Percentage obtained by dividing income available for fixed charges by average total invested capital.

% Return on Common Equity—Percentage obtained by dividing income available for common stock (net income less preferred dividend requirements) by average common equity.

Gross Property—Includes utility plant at cost, plant work in progress, and nuclear fuel.

Capital Expenditures—Represents the amounts spent on capital improvements to plant and funds for construction programs.

Net Property—Includes items in gross property less provision for depreciation.

% Earned on Net Property—Percentage obtained by dividing operating income by average net property for the year. A measure of plant efficiency.

Total Invested Capital—Sum of total capitalization (common-preferred-debt), accumulated deferred income taxes, accumulated investment tax credits, minority interest, contingency reserves, and contributions in aid of construction.

Total Capitalization—Combined sum of total common equity, preferred stock and long-term debt.

Long-Term Debt—Debt obligations due beyond one year from balance sheet date.

Capitalization Ratios—Reflect the percentage of each type of debt/equity issues outstanding to total capitalization. % DEBT is obtained by dividing total debt by the sum of debt, preferred, common, paid-in capital and retained earnings. % PREFERRED is obtained by dividing the preferred stocks outstanding by total capitalization. % COMMON, divide the sum of common stocks, paid-in capital and retained earnings by total capitalization.

Finally, at the very bottom of the right-hand page, you'll find general information about the company: its address and telephone number, the names of its senior executive officers and directors (usually including the name of the investor contact), the transfer agent and registrar for the stock, and the state in which the company is incorporated.

How to Use This Book to Select Investments

And so, at last, we come to the $64,000 question: Given this vast array of data, how might a businesswoman seeking to find out about her competition, the marketing manager looking for clients, a job seeker, and the investor use it to best serve their respective purposes?

If you are like one of the first three of these individuals—a businesswoman, the marketing manager, or the job seeker—your task will be arduous, to be sure, but this book will provide you with an excellent starting point and your payoff can make it all worthwhile. You will have to go through this book page by page, looking for those companies that are in the industries in which you are interested, that are of the size and financial strength that appeal to you, that are located geographically in your territory or where you're willing to relocate, that have been profitable and growing, and so forth. And then you will have to read about just what's going on at those companies by referring to the appropriate "Company Overview" and "Business Summary" comments in these reports.

Of course, this book won't do it *all* for you. It is, after all, just a starting point, not a conclusive summary of everything you might need to know. It is designed to educate, not to render advice or provide recommendations. But it will get you pointed in the right direction.

Finally, what about the investor who wants to use this book to find good individual investments from among the 500 stocks in the S&P 500 Index? If you fall into that category, what should you do?

Well, you can approach your quest the same way that the businesswoman looking for information about her competitors, the marketing manager, and the job seeker approached theirs—by thumbing through this book page by page, looking for companies with high historic growth rates, generous dividend payout policies, wide profit margins, A+ Standard & Poor's Rankings, or whatever other characteristics you consider desirable in stocks in which you might invest. In this case, however, we have made your job just a little bit easier.

We have already prescreened the 500 companies in this book for several of the stock characteristics in which investors generally are most interested, including Standard & Poor's Earnings and Dividends Rankings, growth records, and dividend payment histories, and we're pleased to present on the next five pages lists of those companies which score highest on the bases of these criteria. So if you, like most investors, find these characteristics important in potential investments, you might want to turn first to the companies on these lists in your search for attractive investments.

Good luck and happy investment returns!

Companies With Five Consecutive Years of Earnings Increases

This table, compiled from a computer screen of the stocks in this handbook, shows companies that have recorded rising per-share earnings for five consecutive years, have a minimum 10% five-year EPS growth rate based on trailing 12-month earnings, have estimated 1998 EPS at least 10% above those reported for 1997, pay dividends, have an estimated 1998 P/E of less than 25 and have Standard & Poor's earnings and dividend rankings of A– or better. The list is sorted by the five-year EPS growth rate.

Company	Business	Fiscal Year End	5 Yr. EPS Growth Rate %	EPS $ 1997 Act.	EPS $ 1998 Est.	S&P Stock Rank	Price	P/E on 1998 Est.	% Yield
Schlumberger Ltd	Oilfield svs: electronics	Dec	32	2.52	2.95	A-	51.13	17.3	1.5
Rohm & Haas	Mfr specialty chem & plastics	Dec	30	2.13	2.50	A-	28.44	11.4	2.5
MBNA Corp	Bank hldg/credit card svc'g	Dec	26	1.15	1.40	A-	25.56	18.3	1.4
Avery Dennison Corp	Adhesives,labels,office prd	Dec	24	1.93	2.22	A-	48.13	21.7	1.7
MGIC Investment	Provides private mtge insur	Dec	24	2.75	3.30	A-	38.69	11.7	0.3
Air Products & Chem	Indust'l gases,eq,chemicals	Sep	22	1.95	2.43	A	31.50	13.0	2.2
Franklin Resources	Mut'l fd inv advisory & svcs	Sep	22	1.71	2.10	A+	28.94	13.8	0.7
Illinois Tool Works	Fasteners,tools, plastic items	Dec	22	2.33	2.60	A+	45.38	17.5	1.3
State Street Corp	Banking/financial svcs	Dec	18	2.32	2.70	A+	50.38	18.7	1.0
Newell Co	Mfr,mkt consumer products	Dec	17	1.82	2.73	A+	43.50	15.9	1.7
Bemis Co	Packaging,adhesive products	Dec	16	2.00	2.25	A	37.94	16.9	2.3
Bank of New York	Commercial bkg,New York	Dec	15	1.35	1.52	A-	27.75	18.3	2.0
Northern Trust	Comm'l bkg,Chicago, Ill.	Dec	15	2.66	3.00	A	63.97	21.3	1.3
BankAmerica Corp	Commercial bank'g California	Dec	14	4.32	4.85	A-	61.31	12.6	2.3
Federal Home Loan	Provides Residential Mtg fds	Dec	14	1.88	2.25	A+	44.50	19.8	1.1
Norwest Corp	Comm'l banking,Minneapolis	Dec	14	1.75	2.00	A+	32.31	16.2	2.3
Shared Medical Sys	Fin'l/admin hosp computer sv	Dec	14	2.37	2.82	A-	55.19	19.6	1.5
Ecolab Inc	Comm'l cleaning&sanitizing	Dec	13	1.00	1.15	A-	28.50	24.8	1.3
Comerica Inc	Comm'l Bkg,Detroit,Michigan	Dec	12	3.19	3.70	A	56.88	15.4	2.3
Sysco Corp	Food distr & service systems	Jun#	12	0.85	0.95	A+	23.38	24.6	1.5
Federal Natl Mtge	Provides residential mtg fds	Dec	11	2.84	3.20	A	60.38	18.9	1.6
SunTrust Banks	Comm'l bkg,Georgia,FL,Tenn	Dec	11	3.13	3.50	A+	58.00	16.6	1.7
Emerson Electric	Mfr electric/electronic prdts	Sep	10	2.52	2.80	A+	58.50	20.9	2.0

*Actual 1998 EPS & estimated 1999 EPS; P/E based on estimated 1999 EPS. #Actual 1998 EPS; P/E based on 1998 actual EPS.

Chart based on September 11, 1998 prices and data.

NOTE: All earnings estimates are Standard & Poor's projections.

S&P 500 STOCK SCREENS

Stocks With A+ Rankings

Based on the issues in this handbook, this screen shows stocks of all companies with Standard & Poor's earnings and dividend rankings of A+.

Company	Business
Abbott Laboratories	Diversified health care prod
Albertson's, Inc	Food supermkts: food-drug
Amer Home Products	Drugs, food,household prd
Amer Int'l Group	Major int'l insur hldg co
Automatic Data Proc	Computer services
Becton, Dickinson	Health care pr:ind'l safety
Coca-Cola Co	Major soft drink/juice co
ConAgra Inc	Prepared foods:agri-products
Dillard's Inc'A'	Dept stores in southwest US
Dollar General	Self-service discount stores
Electronic Data Systems	Computer systems/svcs
Emerson Electric	Mfr electric/electronic prdts
Federal Home Loan	Provides Residential Mtg fds
Fifth Third Bancorp	Comm'l bkg,Cincinnati,Ohio
Franklin Resources	Mut'l fd inv advisory & svcs
Gap Inc	Apparel specialty stores
Genl Electric	Consumer/ind'l prod,broad'cst
Genl Re Corp	Hldg: reinsur:prop/casual
Genuine Parts	Distrib auto replacement parts
Gillette Co	Shaving, personal care: pens
Home Depot	Bldg mtls,home improv strs
Illinois Tool Works	Fasteners,tools, plastic items
Interpublic Grp Cos	Worldwide advertis'g agencies
Jefferson-Pilot	Insurance hldg co, life
Johnson & Johnson	Health care products
KeyCorp	Commercial bkg,Ohio,Nthn US
May Dept Stores	Large department store chain

Company	Business
MBIA Inc	Insurance for muni bonds
McDonald's Corp	Fast food restaurant:franch'g
Medtronic, Inc	Cardiac pacemakers:med.serv
Merck & Co	Ethical drugs/specialty chem
Minnesota Min'g/Mfg	Scotch tapes: coated abrasives
Motorola, Inc	Semiconductors:communic eq
Newell Co	Mfr,mkt consumer products
Norwest Corp	Comm'l banking,Minneapolis
Omnicom Group	Major int'l advertising co
Philip Morris Cos	Cigarettes,food prod,brew'g
Pitney Bowes	Postage meters: mailing sys
Raytheon Co'B'	Defense&comm'l electr:constr
Regions Financial	Commercial bkg,Alabama
Schering-Plough	Pharmaceut'l/consumer prod
Sherwin-Williams	Large paint & varnish mfr
Sigma-Aldrich	Specialty chem prod
State Street Corp	Banking/financial svcs
SunTrust Banks	Comm'l bkg,Georgia,FL,Tenn
Synovus Financial	Commercial bkg,Georgia
Sysco Corp	Food distr & service systems
Torchmark Corp	Insurance:fin'l services
Travelers Group	Diversified financial svcs
UST Inc	Snuff,tobacco,wine,spirits
Wal-Mart Stores	Operates discount stores
Walgreen Co	Major retail drug chain
Wrigley, (Wm) Jr	Major chewing gum producer

S&P 500 STOCK SCREENS

Rapid Growth Stocks

The stocks listed below have shown strong and consistent earnings growth. Issues of rapidly growing companies tend to carry high price-earnings ratios and offer potential for substantial appreciation. At the same time, though, the stocks are subject to strong selling pressures should growth in earnings slow. Five-year earnings growth rates have been calculated for fiscal years 1993 through 1997 and the most current 12-month earnings.

Company	Business	S&P Stock Rank	Fiscal Year End	EPS $ — 1997 Act.	1998 Est.	5 Yr. EPS % Growth	Price	P/E on 1998 Est.	% Yield
Deere & Co	Lgst mfr farm eq:constr mchy	B+	Oct	3.78	4.40	33	33.19	7.5	2.7
SunAmerica Inc	Life insurance/fin'l svcs	A	Sep	1.80	2.40	31	63.63	26.5	0.9
EMC Corp	Mfr computer storage prod	B	Dec	1.04	1.44	29	53.25	37.0	....
MBNA Corp	Bank hldg/credit card svc'g	A-	Dec	1.15	1.40	26	25.56	18.3	1.4
Dollar General	Self-service discount stores	A+	Jan*	0.84	1.05	25	32.44	30.9	0.5
Avery Dennison Corp	Adhesives,labels,office prd	A-	Dec	1.93	2.22	25	48.13	21.7	1.7
MGIC Investment	Provides private mtge insur	A-	Dec	2.75	3.30	24	38.69	11.7	0.3
Gillette Co	Shaving, personal care: pens	A+	Dec	1.24	1.45	23	41.63	28.7	1.2
AlliedSignal Inc	Aerospace,automotive,fibers	B+	Dec	2.02	2.35	22	33.56	14.3	1.8
Franklin Resources	Mut'l fd inv advisory & svcs	A+	Sep	1.71	2.10	22	28.94	13.8	0.7
United Technologies	Aerospace,climate ctrl sys	B	Dec	4.21	4.85	22	76.69	15.8	1.9
Crane Co	Mfr industrial,consumer prd	B+	Dec	2.44	2.92	21	38.94	13.3	1.5
Gap Inc	Apparel specialty stores	A+	Jan*	1.30	1.85	21	59.75	32.3	0.3
Home Depot	Bldg mtls,home improv strs	A+	Jan*	0.77	1.02	21	40.25	39.5	0.3
Associates First Cap'A'	Consumer/commercial finance	NR	Dec	2.97	3.55	18	61.19	17.2	0.7
AutoZone Inc	Retail auto parts stores	B+	Aug	1.28	1.50	18	24.13	16.1	....
Abbott Laboratories	Diversified health care prod	A+	Dec	1.34	1.51	15	41.06	27.2	1.5
Walgreen Co	Major retail drug chain	A+	Aug	0.88	1.00	15	43.88	43.9	0.6
BankAmerica Corp	Commercial bank'g California	A-	Dec	4.32	4.85	14	61.31	12.6	2.3
Biomet, Inc	Mfr surgical implant devices	B+	May#	0.93	1.11	14	31.75	28.6	0.4
Johnson & Johnson	Health care products	A+	Dec	2.41	2.70	14	76.38	28.3	1.3
Norwest Corp	Comm'l banking,Minneapolis	A+	Dec	1.75	2.00	14	32.31	16.2	2.3
Automatic Data Proc	Computer services	A+	Jun#	1.71	1.98	13	72.00	36.4	0.7
Sysco Corp	Food distr & service systems	A	Jun#	0.85	0.95	12	23.38	24.6	1.5
Household Intl	Finance & banking services	B+	Dec	2.17	2.40	4	39.63	16.5	1.5

*Actual 1998 EPS & estimated 1999 EPS; P/E based on estimated 1999 EPS. #Actual 1998 EPS; P/E based on 1998 actual EPS.

Chart based on September 11, 1998 prices and data.

NOTE: All earnings estimates are Standard & Poor's projections.

S&P 500 STOCK SCREENS

Fast-Rising Dividends

Based on the issues in this handbook, the companies below were chosen on the basis of their five-year annual growth rate in dividends from 1993 to the current 12-month indicated rate. All have increased their dividend payments each calendar year from 1993 to their current 12-month indicated rate.

Company	$ Divd. Paid 1993	$ Divd. Paid 1997	†Ind. Divd. Rate	*Divd. Growth Rate %	Price	% Yield
SunAmerica Inc	0.07	0.30	0.60	51.80	63.63	0.9
Morgan Stan Dean Wittr	0.10	0.67	0.80	48.39	51.00	1.6
BankBoston Corp	0.20	0.98	1.16	38.18	36.38	3.2
Archer-Daniels-Midland	0.05	0.18	0.19	34.38	16.25	1.2
Schwab(Chas)Corp	0.04	0.14	0.16	30.62	34.00	0.5
Medtronic, Inc	0.08	0.22	0.26	29.07	56.88	0.5
Dollar General	0.04	0.13	0.16	28.53	32.44	0.5
Travelers Group	0.16	0.40	0.50	26.47	40.88	1.2
Nucor Corp	0.15	0.38	0.48	26.30	38.25	1.3
Home Depot	0.04	0.10	0.12	25.44	40.25	0.3
Hewlett-Packard	0.23	0.52	0.64	23.73	50.00	1.3
Mattel, Inc	0.11	0.26	0.32	22.95	35.38	0.9
Synovus Financial	0.11	0.23	0.29	21.97	19.56	1.5
Summit Bancorp	0.42	0.99	1.20	21.93	36.75	3.3
Mellon Bank Corp	0.51	1.29	1.44	21.71	56.44	2.6
Bank of New York	0.21	0.49	0.56	21.36	27.75	2.0
Merrill Lynch	0.35	0.75	0.96	21.27	56.00	1.7
Disney (Walt) Co	0.08	0.17	0.21	21.19	25.81	0.8
Intel Corp	0.05	0.11	0.12	20.90	84.94	0.1
Gillette Co	0.20	0.41	0.51	20.15	41.63	1.2
Sysco Corp	0.14	0.30	0.36	20.14	23.38	1.5
Williams Cos	0.26	0.54	0.60	20.13	26.56	2.3
Wal-Mart Stores	0.12	0.26	0.31	19.09	60.63	0.5
Illinois Tool Works	0.24	0.43	0.60	18.69	45.38	1.3
Washington Mutual	0.33	0.71	0.83	18.69	33.03	2.5
Fifth Third Bancorp	0.29	0.55	0.68	17.98	55.94	1.2
Norwest Corp	0.32	0.61	0.74	17.92	32.31	2.3
Pioneer Hi-Bred Intl	0.17	0.33	0.40	17.71	31.19	1.3
Ford Motor	0.80	1.65	1.68	17.57	43.31	3.9
Barrick Gold	0.08	0.16	0.18	17.41	17.88	1.0
Automatic Data Proc	0.24	0.46	0.53	17.20	72.00	0.7
Hasbro Inc	0.15	0.31	0.32	16.95	33.88	0.9
Chase Manhattan	0.65	1.21	1.44	16.83	46.00	3.1
BB&T Corp	0.32	0.58	0.70	16.73	29.50	2.4
Newell Co	0.34	0.64	0.72	16.55	43.50	1.7
Federal Home Loan	0.22	0.40	0.48	16.51	44.50	1.1
Franklin Resources	0.09	0.17	0.20	16.38	28.94	0.7
Philip Morris Cos	0.87	1.60	1.76	16.31	43.00	4.1
U.S. Bancorp	0.33	0.62	0.70	16.20	41.75	1.7
First Union Corp	0.75	1.22	1.68	16.01	50.50	3.3
AlliedSignal Inc	0.29	0.52	0.60	15.64	33.56	1.8
Merck & Co	1.03	1.69	2.16	15.42	128.00	1.7
Goodyear Tire & Rub	0.57	1.14	1.20	15.41	47.56	2.5
Praxair Inc	0.25	0.44	0.50	15.34	33.13	1.5
Computer Assoc Intl	0.04	0.07	0.08	15.20	30.63	0.3
Pitney Bowes	0.45	0.80	0.90	15.02	51.25	1.8
State Street Corp	0.25	0.42	0.52	14.99	50.38	1.0
Schering-Plough	0.43	0.74	0.88	14.84	94.63	0.9
BankAmerica Corp	0.70	1.22	1.38	14.77	61.31	2.3
MBNA Corp	0.18	0.31	0.36	14.71	25.56	1.4
Federal Natl Mtge	0.46	0.84	0.96	14.70	60.38	1.6
Mercantile Bancorp	0.65	1.13	1.24	14.66	45.63	2.7
Johnson & Johnson	0.51	0.85	1.00	14.63	76.38	1.3
Amer Intl Group	0.11	0.19	0.23	14.46	79.00	0.3
ConAgra Inc	0.32	0.56	0.63	14.45	27.00	2.3
Pall Corp	0.32	0.56	0.62	14.39	20.75	3.0
Ecolab Inc	0.19	0.32	0.38	14.38	28.50	1.3
Albertson's, Inc	0.35	0.63	0.68	14.32	51.06	1.3
Fleet Financial Group	0.95	1.80	1.96	14.27	74.94	2.6
Cooper Tire & Rubber	0.20	0.35	0.38	14.07	17.25	2.2
Procter & Gamble	0.58	0.95	1.14	13.95	67.38	1.7
Huntington Bancshares	0.41	0.68	0.80	13.55	24.88	3.2
Genl Electric	0.63	1.04	1.20	13.53	79.25	1.5
Textron, Inc	0.60	0.97	1.14	13.33	61.88	1.8
Avery Dennison Corp	0.45	0.72	0.84	13.25	48.13	1.7
Golden West Finl	0.27	0.46	0.50	13.24	77.38	0.6
Cincinnati Financial	0.33	0.53	0.61	12.98	34.72	1.8
Alberto-Culver Cl'B'	0.13	0.20	0.24	12.92	21.13	1.1
Amer Stores	0.20	0.34	0.36	12.91	29.94	1.2
Republic New York	0.53	0.88	1.00	12.87	42.13	2.4
Pfizer, Inc	0.42	0.68	0.76	12.80	100.63	0.8
Abbott Laboratories	0.33	0.53	0.60	12.64	41.06	1.5
Comerica Inc	0.70	1.12	1.28	12.59	56.88	2.3
Natl City Corp	1.06	1.67	1.92	12.54	66.00	2.9
Bemis Co	0.50	0.80	0.88	12.50	37.94	2.3

†12-month indicated rate. *Five-year annual compounded growth rate. Chart based on September 11, 1998 prices and data.

S&P 500 STOCK SCREENS

Higher Dividends For Ten Years

These companies have all paid higher cash dividends in each of the past ten calendar years and currently yield at least 2%. The ability to increase dividends under the difficult economic conditions that were experienced at times over the past ten years, indicates healthy finances and capable management.

Company	Rank	Price	†Ind. Divd. Rate	% Yield
Air Products & Chem	A	31.50	0.68	2.2
ALLTEL Corp	A	42.12	1.16	2.8
Ameritech Corp	A-	47.62	1.20	2.5
AMP Inc	B+	39.00	1.08	2.8
Anheuser-Busch Cos	A	54.18	1.12	2.1
BB&T Corp	A-	29.50	0.70	2.4
Banc One Corp	A	43.75	1.52	3.5
Bard (C.R.)	B+	37.37	0.76	2.0
Bell Atlantic Corp	B+	44.56	1.54	3.5
Bemis Co	A	37.93	0.88	2.3
Bestfoods	A	45.56	0.90	2.0
Carolina Pwr & Lt	A-	43.43	1.94	4.5
Chevron Corp	B+	82.50	2.44	3.0
Comerica Inc	A	56.87	1.28	2.3
ConAgra Inc	A+	27.00	0.63	2.3
Consolidated Edison	A	47.25	2.12	4.5
Cooper Tire & Rubber	A	17.25	0.38	2.2
Donnelley(RR)& Sons	B+	38.06	0.84	2.2
duPont(EI)deNemours	B	56.62	1.40	2.5
Duke Energy	A-	64.37	2.20	3.4
Emerson Electric	A+	58.50	1.18	2.0
Engelhard Corp	B+	19.37	0.40	2.1
Exxon Corp	A	70.56	1.64	2.3
First Union Corp	A	50.50	1.68	3.3
Fleetwood Enterpr	B+	33.18	0.72	2.2
Fluor Corp	A-	40.62	0.80	2.0
Frontier Corp	B	25.93	0.89	3.4
GPU Inc	B+	38.25	2.06	5.4
Genuine Parts	A+	31.87	1.00	3.1
Heinz (H.J.)	A	55.00	1.37	2.5
Huntington Bancshares	A	24.87	0.80	3.2
Intl Flavors/Fragr	A	37.37	1.48	4.0
Jefferson-Pilot	A+	58.87	1.18	2.0
Johnson Controls	A-	43.56	0.92	2.1
Kellogg Co	A	32.68	0.94	2.9
KeyCorp	A+	29.81	0.94	3.2
Kimberly-Clark	A-	37.87	1.00	2.6
Lincoln Natl Corp	A-	88.50	2.08	2.4
Marsh & McLennan	A	51.37	1.60	3.1
May Dept Stores	A+	56.37	1.27	2.3
McGraw-Hill Companies	NR	75.00	1.56	2.1
Millipore Corp	B	20.37	0.44	2.2
Minnesota Min'g/Mfg	A+	71.56	2.20	3.1
Mobil Corp	A-	78.00	2.28	2.9
Morgan (J.P.)	B+	90.12	3.80	4.2
Natl Service Indus	A	35.75	1.24	3.5
NICOR Inc	A-	39.12	1.48	3.8
Northern States Pwr	A-	27.31	1.43	5.2
Norwest Corp	A+	32.31	0.74	2.3
PPG Indus	A-	52.50	1.44	2.7
Pall Corp	A-	20.75	0.62	3.0
Peoples Energy	B+	35.18	1.92	5.5
Philip Morris Cos	A+	43.00	1.76	4.1
Potlatch Corp	B-	33.25	1.74	5.2
Regions Financial	A+	35.50	0.92	2.6
Republic New York	A-	42.12	1.00	2.4
Rohm & Haas	A	28.43	0.72	2.5
Rubbermaid, Inc	A-	28.31	0.64	2.3
SBC Communications	A-	40.00	0.94	2.3
SAFECO Corp	B+	43.46	1.40	3.2
St. Paul Cos	A-	32.18	1.00	3.1
Sherwin-Williams	A+	22.25	0.45	2.0
Stanley Works	B	38.18	0.86	2.3
Supervalu Inc	A-	21.37	0.53	2.5
V.F. Corp	A-	39.00	0.80	2.1
Wachovia Corp	A+	82.31	1.96	2.4
Winn-Dixie Stores	A	37.62	1.02	2.7

†12-month indicated rate.
Chart based on September 11, 1998 prices and data.

S&P 500 STOCK SCREENS

Stock Reports

In using the Stock Reports in this handbook, please pay particular attention to the dates attached to each evaluation, recommendation, or analysis section. Opinions rendered are as of that date and may change often. It is strongly suggested that before investing in any security you should obtain the current analysis on that issue.

To order the latest Standard & Poor's Stock Report on a company, for as little as $3.00 per report, please call:

S&P Reports On-Demand at 1-800-292-0808.

12-SEP-98 | Industry: Health Care (Diversified)

Summary: This company is a leading maker of pharmaceutical, nutritional, and hospital and laboratory products.

S&P Opinion: Accumulate (★★★)	Recent Price • 41	Yield • 1.5%
	52 Wk Range • 45⅛-28½	12-Mo. P/E • 28.7

Quantitative Evaluations

Outlook
(1 Lowest—5 Highest)
• **2**

Fair Value
• **40¼**

Risk
• **Low**

Earn./Div. Rank
• **A+**

Technical Eval.
• **Bullish** since 10/96

Rel. Strength Rank
(1 Lowest—99 Highest)
• **88**

Insider Activity
• **Favorable**

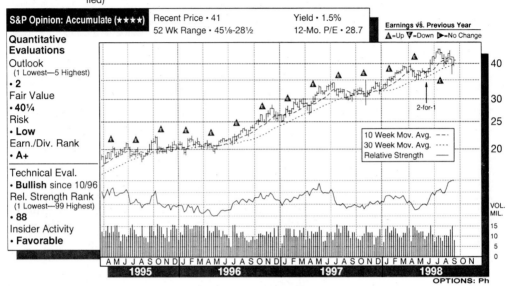

Earnings vs. Previous Year
▲=Up ▼=Down ▶=No Change

10 Week Mov. Avg. ---
30 Week Mov. Avg. ·····
Relative Strength ——

2-for-1

VOL. MIL.

OPTIONS: Ph

Overview - 10-JUL-98

Sales growth for the full year of 1998 is likely to be restricted to mid-single digits, reflecting the effects of negative foreign exchange, as well as weakness in the important Biaxin antibiotic line. However, overall drug sales should rise, aided by growth in Depakote anticonvulsant and Norvir AIDS treatment. Sales of Hytrin to treat enlarged prostates should also hold up, with Abbott retaining market exclusivity on that drug through 1998. Another robust increase is expected in income from Abbott's TAP Japanese drug venture. Infant nutritionals sales are likely to decline somewhat, but adult nutritionals should rise, aided by new products. Gains are indicated for hospital and laboratory products, bolstered by several new diagnostic lines, and by new drug-delivery and anesthesia products. Margins should benefit from the greater volume, and from a slightly lower tax rate.

Valuation - 10-JUL-98

The stock performed well in recent months, buoyed by solid earnings momentum and new product approvals. Abbott should maintain double-digit profit growth in coming years, fortified by dominant positions in growing global health care markets, good cost controls, and proven ability to generate lucrative new cost-saving medical products. This year should mark ABT's 26th year of consecutive double-digit EPS growth. An important source of Abbott's success continues to be its ability to gain access to promising medical products through joint ventures with other firms. Recent new products obtained in this way include TriCor, a drug for high triglyceride levels; and levosimedan, a treatment for congestive heart failure. Abbott also recently arranged a drug co-marketing deal with Boehringer Ingelheim of Germany. The shares are recommended for long-term capital appreciation.

Key Stock Statistics

S&P EPS Est. 1998	1.51	Tang. Bk. Value/Share	2.54
P/E on S&P Est. 1998	27.2	Beta	0.73
S&P EPS Est. 1999	1.69	Shareholders	99,500
Dividend Rate/Share	0.60	Market cap. (B)	$ 63.2
Shs. outstg. (M)	1539.9	Inst. holdings	47%
Avg. daily vol. (M)	2.397		

Value of $10,000 invested 5 years ago: $ 30,246

Fiscal Year Ending Dec. 31

	1998	1997	1996	1995	1994	1993
Revenues (Million $)						
1Q	3,045	3,000	2,672	2,524	2,215	2,046
2Q	3,067	2,900	2,699	2,500	2,204	2,074
3Q	—	2,865	2,646	2,391	2,255	2,060
4Q	—	3,118	2,996	2,597	2,482	2,228
Yr.	—	11,883	11,013	10,012	9,156	8,408
Earnings Per Share ($)						
1Q	**0.38**	**0.34**	0.30	0.26	0.23	0.20
2Q	**0.38**	**0.34**	0.30	0.27	0.23	0.21
3Q	**E0.34**	**0.30**	0.27	0.24	0.21	0.19
4Q	**E0.41**	**0.36**	0.33	0.29	0.27	0.24
Yr.	**E1.51**	**1.34**	**1.21**	1.06	0.94	0.84

Next earnings report expected: early October

Dividend Data (Dividends have been paid since 1926.)

Amount ($)	Date Decl.	Ex-Div. Date	Stock of Record	Payment Date
0.300	Feb. 13	Apr. 13	Apr. 15	May. 15 '98
2-for-1	Feb. 13	Jun. 01	May. 01	May. 29 '98
0.150	Jun. 12	Jul. 13	Jul. 15	Aug. 15 '98
0.150	Sep. 11	Oct. 13	Oct. 15	Nov. 15 '98

A Division of The McGraw-Hill Companies

Business Summary - 10-JUL-98

Abbott Laboratories is a leading player in several growing health care markets, with an outstanding record of long-term sales and earnings growth. The company was founded in the late 19th century by Dr. Wallace C. Abbott, a pioneer in pharmaceutical medicine. Through highly successful acquisition, diversification and R&D programs, Abbott now offers a wide range of prescription pharmaceuticals, infant and adult nutritionals, and hospital and laboratory products. Foreign operations accounted for 32% of sales and 25% of profits in 1997. Sales and earnings in 1997 by product segment were divided:

	Sales	Profits
Pharmaceutical & nutritional	58%	76%
Hospital & laboratory	42%	24%

Accounting for about 30% of total sales, Abbott's pharmaceutical division represents the principal driver of future earnings growth. Key products include Biaxin (sales of $1.3 billion in 1997), the largest selling broad-spectrum antibiotic, which is used for a wide variety of infections including h-pylori (associated with duodenal ulcers); Hytrin ($620 million), a treatment for hypertension and enlarged prostates; and Depakote ($520

million), a leading anti-epileptic agent that is also indicated for the treatment of manic-depressive disorder. Other pharmaceutical products include Norvir protease inhibitor for AIDS, Abbokinase anti-thrombotic agent, Ogen oral estrogen, Survanta lung surfactant and Zyflo asthma treatment. Equity earnings are derived from a 50% interest in TAP Holdings, a joint venture with Takeda Chemical Industries of Japan. Major TAP drugs include Prevacid gastrointestinal agent and Lupron treatment for prostate cancer.

Nutritional businesses (about one quarter of total sales) include leading positions in infant formulas, medical nutritionals for patients with special dietary needs, and enteral feeding items. Leading brands are Similac and Isomil infant formulas, Ensure medical nutritionals, and the Flexiflo enteral feeding device.

Abbott is also a major producer of immunodiagnostics, offering a wide range of tests and diagnostic systems for blood banks, hospitals and laboratories. Products include intravenous and irrigation fluids and related administration equipment. Through its MediSense unit, Abbott provides home glucose monitoring products for diabetics. The Fact line of home pregnancy tests is also offered. Hospital items consist of anesthesia products, specialized electronic drug delivery systems, diagnostic imaging agents and other products.

Per Share Data ($)

(Year Ended Dec. 31)	1997	1996	1995	1994	1993	1992	1991	1990	1989	1988
Tangible Bk. Val.	2.54	2.48	2.79	2.52	2.24	2.00	1.89	1.65	1.54	1.37
Cash Flow	1.81	1.65	1.40	1.25	1.14	0.98	0.86	0.76	0.66	0.57
Earnings	1.34	1.21	1.06	0.94	0.84	0.73	0.64	0.56	0.48	0.42
Dividends	0.53	0.47	0.41	0.37	0.33	0.29	0.24	0.20	0.17	0.14
Payout Ratio	39%	39%	39%	39%	39%	39%	38%	36%	35%	34%
Prices - High	34⅞	28¾	22⅜	17	15½	17⅛	17½	11⅝	8⅞	6⅝
- Low	24⅞	19⅛	15⅜	12¾	11⅜	13⅛	9⅞	7⅞	5¾	5⅜
P/E Ratio - High	26	24	21	18	18	23	27	21	18	16
- Low	19	16	14	14	13	18	15	14	12	13

Income Statement Analysis (Million $)

	1997	1996	1995	1994	1993	1992	1991	1990	1989	1988
Revs.	11,883	11,013	10,012	9,156	8,408	7,852	6,877	6,159	5,380	4,937
Oper. Inc.	3,578	3,303	2,949	2,655	2,442	2,169	1,936	1,762	1,528	1,373
Depr.	728	686	566	511	484	428	379	356	307	271
Int. Exp.	135	95.0	69.0	50.0	54.0	53.0	64.0	91.0	74.0	85.0
Pretax Inc.	2,949	2,670	2,396	2,167	1,943	1,739	1,544	1,351	1,194	1,055
Eff. Tax Rate	29%	30%	30%	30%	28%	29%	30%	29%	28%	29%
Net Inc.	2,094	1,882	1,689	1,517	1,399	1,239	1,089	966	860	752

Balance Sheet & Other Fin. Data (Million $)

	1997	1996	1995	1994	1993	1992	1991	1990	1989	1988
Cash	230	123	316	315	379	258	146	53.0	49.0	583
Curr. Assets	5,038	4,481	4,227	3,876	3,586	3,232	2,891	2,461	2,103	2,353
Total Assets	12,061	11,126	9,413	8,524	7,689	6,941	6,255	5,563	4,852	4,825
Curr. Liab.	5,034	4,344	3,790	3,476	3,095	2,783	2,229	2,001	1,384	1,440
LT Debt	938	933	435	287	307	110	125	135	147	349
Common Eqty.	4,999	4,820	4,397	4,049	3,675	3,348	3,203	2,834	2,726	2,465
Total Cap.	6,074	5,906	4,900	4,392	4,033	3,779	3,675	3,378	3,312	3,213
Cap. Exp.	1,007	949	947	929	953	1,007	771	641	573	521
Cash Flow	2,822	2,568	2,255	2,027	1,883	1,667	1,468	1,322	1,167	1,023
Curr. Ratio	1.0	1.0	1.1	1.1	1.2	1.2	1.3	1.2	1.5	1.6
% LT Debt of Cap.	15.4	15.8	8.9	6.5	7.6	2.9	3.4	4.0	4.4	10.9
% Net Inc.of Revs.	17.6	17.1	16.9	16.6	16.6	15.8	15.8	15.7	16.0	15.2
% Ret. on Assets	18.1	18.3	18.8	18.9	19.3	18.9	18.5	18.8	17.9	16.4
% Ret. on Equity	42.7	40.8	40.0	39.7	40.2	38.1	36.2	35.3	33.4	33.1

Data as orig. reptd.; bef. results of disc. opers. and/or spec. items. Per share data adj. for stk. divs. as of ex-div. date. Bold denotes diluted EPS (FASB 128). E-Estimated. NA-Not Available. NM-Not Meaningful. NR-Not Ranked.

Office—100 Abbott Park Rd., Abbott Park, IL 60064-3500. **Tel**—(847) 937-6100. **Website**—http://www.abbott.com **Chrmn & CEO**—D. L. Burnham. **Pres & COO**—T. R. Hodgson. **SVP & Secy**—J. M. de Lasa. **SVP-Fin & CFO**—G. P. Coughlan. **VP & Treas**—T. C. Freyman. **Investor Contact**—Patricia Bergeron. **Dirs**—F. K. Austen, D. L. Burnham, H. L. Fuller, T. R. Hodgson, D. A. Jones, The Lord Owen CH, B. Powell Jr., A. B. Rand, W. A. Reynolds, W. D. Smithburg, J. R. Walter, W. L. Weiss. **Transfer Agent & Registrar**—BankBoston. **Incorporated**—in Illinois in 1900. **Empl**— 54,487. **S&P Analyst:** H. B. Saftlas

15-SEP-98

Industry: Computer (Software & Services)

Summary: Adobe's software is used to create and print integrated text and graphics for electronic printing and publishing.

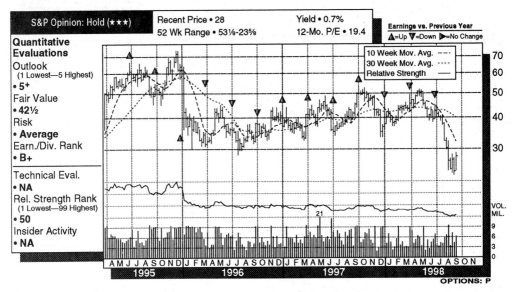

S&P Opinion: Hold (★★★)	Recent Price • 28	Yield • 0.7%
	52 Wk Range • 53⅛-23⅝	12-Mo. P/E • 19.4

Quantitative Evaluations

Outlook (1 Lowest—5 Highest)
• **5+**

Fair Value
• **42½**

Risk
• **Average**

Earn./Div. Rank
• **B+**

Technical Eval.
• **NA**

Rel. Strength Rank (1 Lowest—99 Highest)
• **50**

Insider Activity
• **NA**

Earnings vs. Previous Year
▲=Up ▼=Down ▶=No Change

10 Week Mov. Avg. ----
30 Week Mov. Avg. ......
Relative Strength

OPTIONS: P

Overview - 15-SEP-98

Revenues are expected to decline slightly in FY 98 (Nov.), but should rebound in FY 99. New product introductions will stimulate renewed growth, although this will be offset somewhat by very weak demand in Asian markets, and by declining sales for Macintosh applications. In the third quarter of FY 98, application products on the Windows platform accounted for 56% of total application revenues, while Macintosh products accounted for the remaining 44%. Revenues were helped by the release of Photoshop 5.0 in early May. Operating margins are expected to decline significantly in FY 98, but should also improve next year. Results should be helped by the company's venture investment program. FY 97 EPS included a gain of $0.23 from this program. EPS should also benefit from an aggressive share repurchase plan.

Valuation - 15-SEP-98

The shares have dropped significantly in recent months, reflecting weakness in the Asian market, which accounts for nearly 20% of Adobe's business, as well as a corporate restructuring. The shares were boosted by a bid to acquire the company by Quark, a private company that competes with Adobe. However, Quark recently withdrew its offer. ADBE's results should improve as the company releases several new products. The company's new venture stock dividend program should unlock some of the hidden value of its significant venture investments. Tangible results were seen when ADBE recorded $0.23 in gains from the sale of investments in FY 97. A recent restructuring is expected to lead to annual savings of $60 million. Nevertheless, because of ADBE's high exposure to weak Asian markets, we would not add to positions at this time.

Key Stock Statistics

S&P EPS Est. 1998	1.64	Tang. Bk. Value/Share	10.19
P/E on S&P Est. 1998	17.1	Beta	1.40
S&P EPS Est. 1999	2.30	Shareholders	2,200
Dividend Rate/Share	0.20	Market cap. (B)	$ 1.9
Shs. outstg. (M)	67.2	Inst. holdings	69%
Avg. daily vol. (M)	1.106		

Value of $10,000 invested 5 years ago: NA

Fiscal Year Ending Nov. 30

	1998	1997	1996	1995	1994	1993
Revenues (Million $)						
1Q	197.8	226.5	193.6	188.8	135.9	68.50
2Q	227.3	228.3	204.3	189.5	149.8	79.63
3Q	222.9	230.0	180.9	183.1	146.6	78.76
4Q	—	227.1	207.7	200.9	165.4	86.53
Yr.	—	911.9	786.6	762.3	597.8	313.5
Earnings Per Share ($)						
1Q	**0.38**	0.63	0.44	0.50	0.31	0.34
2Q	**0.41**	0.54	0.29	0.47	0.28	0.31
3Q	Nil	0.72	0.40	0.44	0.29	0.24
4Q	—	0.64	0.92	-0.16	-0.79	0.34
Yr.	—	2.52	2.04	1.26	0.10	1.22

Next earnings report expected: mid December

Dividend Data (Dividends have been paid since 1988.)

Amount ($)	Date Decl.	Ex-Div. Date	Stock of Record	Payment Date
0.050	Dec. 18	Dec. 30	Jan. 02	Jan. 16 '98
0.050	Mar. 26	Apr. 01	Apr. 03	Apr. 17 '98
0.050	Jun. 24	Jul. 01	Jul. 06	Jul. 20 '98
0.050	Sep. 10	Sep. 21	Sep. 23	Oct. 07 '98

A Division of The McGraw-Hill Companies

Business Summary - 15-SEP-98

In 1984, Adobe Systems developed the software that initiated desktop publishing. Today, the company develops and supports computer software used to create, display, print and communicate all forms of electronic documents. Adobe provides graphics products, enterprise products, home and office products and printing system products.

Graphics products primarily include Photoshop, an image enhancement tool; Illustrator, an illustration and page design tool; and PageMaker, a leading desktop publishing product. Others include Premiere, After Effects and Type Library.

Enterprise products include FrameMaker, which is used for authoring and publishing long, complex documents; and Acrobat, which is a tool used to publish and distribute business documents of any kind on corporate e-mail and intranets, the Internet, or CD-ROM.

Home and office products include PageMill, a Web creation tool; and PhotoDeluxe, which allows photographs to be enhanced and personalized.

Adobe's primary printing system product is PostScript, a page description language that delivers high quality output and cross-platform compatibility for graphically rich printing output.

The company sells its application software, and also licenses its technologies to major hardware manufacturers, software developers, and service providers. Application sales accounted for 78% of revenues in FY 97 (Nov.), versus 75% in FY 96. Adobe's software products run on Microsoft Windows, Apple Macintosh and UNIX platforms.

The company has an investment program that includes two venture capital limited partnerships, direct investments, and other activities. These investments introduce ADBE to companies that are strategic to its software business. The program gives ADBE a window on emerging technologies and markets, and funds companies that help make ADBE's products available to its customers. Gross proceeds from the sale of equity securities during 1997 was $40 million. As of November 1997, the program consisted of investments in 22 companies. Adobe had invested about $80 million as of June 1998.

In September 1998, Adobe's directors authorized the repurchase of up to 15 million additional shares of common stock over a two year period. In the third quarter of fiscal 1998, the company repurchased 675,000 shares.

Per Share Data ($)

(Year Ended Nov. 30)	1997	1996	1995	1994	1993	1992	1991	1990	1989	1988
Tangible Bk. Val.	10.40	9.89	9.59	7.47	6.18	5.05	4.13	2.57	1.47	1.07
Cash Flow	3.31	2.78	2.07	0.97	1.51	1.13	1.27	1.02	0.86	0.54
Earnings	2.52	2.04	1.26	0.10	1.22	0.94	1.13	0.92	0.78	0.49
Dividends	0.20	0.20	0.20	0.20	0.19	0.16	0.15	0.12	0.10	0.04
Payout Ratio	8%	10%	16%	NM	15%	17%	13%	13%	11%	8%
Prices - High	53⅛	64¼	74¼	38½	37	34¼	33⅞	25⅜	15	12¾
- Low	32½	28½	27¼	20½	15⅝	12⅝	13⅜	8½	7	5⅞
P/E Ratio - High	21	31	59	NM	30	37	30	28	19	26
- Low	13	14	22	NM	13	14	12	9	9	12

Income Statement Analysis (Million $)

	1997	1996	1995	1994	1993	1992	1991	1990	1989	1988
Revs.	912	787	762	598	313	266	230	169	121	83.0
Oper. Inc.	296	229	242	182	94.5	83.5	84.6	67.0	55.3	36.2
Depr.	59.4	55.6	60.4	53.2	13.6	8.8	6.7	4.9	3.7	2.1
Int. Exp.	Nil	NM	Nil	Nil	Nil	Nil	NA	NA	NA	NA
Pretax Inc.	296	245	164	40.0	91.1	69.5	83.6	66.3	54.9	35.8
Eff. Tax Rate	37%	37%	43%	84%	37%	37%	38%	40%	39%	41%
Net Inc.	187	153	93.5	6.3	57.0	43.6	51.6	40.1	33.7	21.1

Balance Sheet & Other Fin. Data (Million $)

	1997	1996	1995	1994	1993	1992	1991	1990	1989	1988
Cash	268	564	516	400	236	160	116	70.0	50.0	35.0
Curr. Assets	679	737	693	532	304	224	162	109	77.0	52.0
Total Assets	940	1,012	885	626	353	281	221	146	94.0	65.0
Curr. Liab.	225	231	186	169	73.7	56.8	36.9	37.0	34.1	19.0
LT Debt	NA	Nil	Nil	Nil	Nil	Nil	Nil	0.3	0.5	0.9
Common Eqty.	715	707	698	457	279	225	183	108	59.0	44.0
Total Cap.	715	707	698	457	279	225	184	109	60.0	46.0
Cap. Exp.	33.9	45.9	34.1	28.5	14.4	11.9	12.2	7.4	5.2	5.0
Cash Flow	246	209	154	59.5	70.6	52.4	58.3	44.9	37.4	23.2
Curr. Ratio	3.0	3.2	3.7	3.2	4.1	4.0	4.4	2.9	2.3	2.7
% LT Debt of Cap.	Nil	Nil	Nil	Nil	Nil	Nil	Nil	0.2	0.8	1.9
% Net Inc.of Revs.	20.5	19.4	12.3	1.1	18.2	16.4	22.5	23.7	27.8	25.3
% Ret. on Assets	19.1	16.2	11.7	1.1	17.9	17.3	27.5	32.9	42.7	42.9
% Ret. on Equity	26.3	21.8	15.4	1.5	22.5	21.4	34.8	47.4	66.2	61.9

Data as orig. reptd.; bef. results of disc. opers. and/or spec. items. Per share data adj. for stk. divs. as of ex-div. date. Bold denotes diluted EPS (FASB 128). E-Estimated. NA-Not Available. NM-Not Meaningful. NR-Not Ranked.

Office—345 Park Avenue, San Jose, CA 95110-2704. **Tel**—(408) 536-6000. **Fax**—(408) 537-6000. **Website**—http://www.adobe.com **Chrmn & CEO**—J. E. Warnock. **Chrmn & Pres**—C. M. Geschke. **EVP & CFO**—P. J. Bell. **Dirs**—G. P. Carter, C. M. Geschke, W. R. Hambrecht, R. Sedgewick, W. J. Spencer, J. E. Warnock, D. W. Yocam. **Transfer Agent & Registrar**—Chase Bank, SF. **Incorporated**—in California in 1983; reincorporated in Delaware in 1997. **Empl**— 2,702. **S&P Analyst:** Brian Goodstadt

12-SEP-98

Industry: Electronics (Semiconductors)

Summary: This company is a leading producer of semiconductors that are used principally by the computer and telecommunications industries.

S&P Opinion: Hold (★★★)	Recent Price • 17¼	Yield • Nil
	52 Wk Range • 35⅞-12¾	12-Mo. P/E • NM

Earnings vs. Previous Year
▲=Up ▼=Down ▶=No Change

Quantitative Evaluations

Outlook
(1 Lowest—5 Highest)
• **2⁻**

Fair Value
• **14⅛**

Risk
• **High**

Earn./Div. Rank
• **B-**

Technical Eval.
• **Bearish** since 4/98

Rel. Strength Rank
(1 Lowest—99 Highest)
• **87**

Insider Activity
• **Neutral**

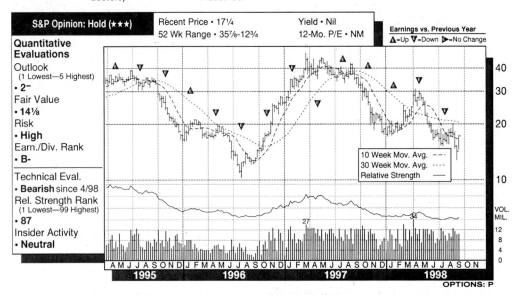

10 Week Mov. Avg. — - -
30 Week Mov. Avg. ·····
Relative Strength —

AMJJASOND J FMAMJJASOND J FMAMJJASOND J FMAMJJASOND J FMAMJJASON N
1995   1996   1997   1998

VOL. MIL.

OPTIONS: P

Overview - 21-JUL-98

We expect 1998 sales to be flat versus a year ago, or about $2.35 billion, although this level is highly dependent upon AMD's ability to ramp up production of its new K6 processor, an alternative solution to Intel's Pentium processor family. AMD has highlighted the attractive price/performance features of the K6, with a goal of offering the chip at a 25% discount to comparable Intel chips. AMD has been successful in achieving design wins with such top-tier PC (personal computer) vendors as Compaq, IBM, Acer and Hewlett Packard. AMD's ability to grow future revenues depends on continued design wins of this Pentium alternative from OEM vendors, its ability to successfully ramp up production of the chip, and, longer term, its timely offering of the next generation chip, the K7. Meanwhile, AMD's non-microprocessor sales, e.g., flash memory, are likely to be lackluster as they continue to reflect aggressive pricing.

Valuation - 21-JUL-98

The shares are likely to remain volatile this year, as AMD focuses on aggressively ramping up production of its new 0.25 micron version of its K6 chip. Undertaking this risky strategy has reduced earnings visibility for 1998. While AMD has stated that it has resolved production difficulties that led it to post recent losses, profitability is still not expected until the fourth quarter of 1998. AMD continues to forecast K6 shipments for the year of 12 million, which was reduced in the first quarter from a prior forecast of 15 million. Despite the risks, based on AMD's ability to garner K6 orders from some high-profile PC vendors and positive reviews of the K6, we believe AMD is well positioned to be the industry's second source for microprocessors after Intel, and therefore believe the shares are worth holding.

Key Stock Statistics

S&P EPS Est. 1998	-1.30	Tang. Bk. Value/Share	13.34
P/E on S&P Est. 1998	NM	Beta	1.07
S&P EPS Est. 1999	0.80	Shareholders	10,000
Dividend Rate/Share	Nil	Market cap. (B)	$ 2.5
Shs. outstg. (M)	143.9	Inst. holdings	56%
Avg. daily vol. (M)	2.540		

Value of $10,000 invested 5 years ago: $ 9,523

Fiscal Year Ending Dec. 31

	1998	1997	1996	1995	1994	1993
Revenues (Million $)						
1Q	540.9	552.0	544.2	620.1	513.1	407.4
2Q	526.5	594.6	455.1	626.2	533.3	409.1
3Q	—	596.6	456.9	590.4	543.1	418.4
4Q	—	613.2	496.9	593.0	545.2	413.4
Yr.	—	2,356	1,953	2,430	2,135	1,648
Earnings Per Share ($)						
1Q	-0.44	0.09	0.18	0.96	0.85	0.63
2Q	-0.45	0.07	-0.26	0.86	0.93	0.65
3Q	E-0.40	-0.22	-0.28	0.52	0.86	0.61
4Q	E-0.01	-0.09	-0.15	0.52	0.39	0.41
Yr.	E-1.30	-0.15	-0.51	2.85	3.02	2.30

Next earnings report expected: early October

Dividend Data

Except for a $0.01-a-share special payment made in 1995, no cash dividends have been paid on the common stock. A "poison pill" stock purchase rights plan was adopted in 1990.

A Division of The McGraw-Hill Companies

Business Summary - 21-JUL-98

Described as the perennial also-ran of the microprocessor world, Advanced Micro Devices (AMD) is currently offering its most attractive alternative to market leader Intel Corp. with its new AMD-K6 chip. The chip began shipping in March 1997, and while touted as "smaller, faster, easier to use, more energy efficient and less expensive than Pentium Pro" by AMD, Intel is expected to be upping the ante with its Pentium II, also targeted for the desktop market for PCs.

To date, the company has based its microprocessor efforts primarily on the X86 architecture, originally developed by Intel Corp. AMD's strategy has been to serve as an alternative source for X86 microprocessors at comparable prices, but with additional customer-driven features. During 1995, a significant portion of AMD's revenues were derived from the company's AM486DX product family. In March 1996, the company began shipping its next generation of microprocessor products known as the K86. AMD's initial K86 product, the 5K86, competed directly with Intel's Pentium family of microprocessors. In March 1997, AMD introduced its K6 family of products, based upon NexGen's sixth-generation NX686 design. AMD acquired fellow chipmaker NexGen Inc. for approximately 33.6 million AMD common shares in January 1996.

In April 1997, AMD said it began shipping its K6 MMX

processor in volume to PC makers. AMD shipped about 350,000 K6 chips in the 1997 second quarter, one million in the third, and 1.5 million in the fourth quarter, just short of its plan for two million. AMD shipped 4.2 million K6 chips during the 1998 first half, and plans to ship a total of 12 million in the full year. There was a shortfall in the first quarter's shipment rate due to AMD's production difficulties related to its aggressive transition to 0.25 micron technology in making the K6 chip. In early 1998, AMD entered into an agreement under which IBM would augment the K6's production, but no quantities have been made public.

In addition to microprocessors for PCs, AMD also makes integrated circuits for memory and logic devices. Memory ICs store data or programs and are characterized as nonvolatile or volatile memory devices. Nonvolatile memories retain data when system power is shut off, while volatile memories do not. AMD does not participate in the market for volatile memories. Nonvolatile memories include erasable programmable read-only memories (EPROMs) and flash memories. In 1997, AMD gained significant market share in the market for flash memories, and has a goal of becoming number one. AMD manufactures flash memories through its joint venture with Fujitsu Ltd., known as FASL (Fujitsu AMD Semiconductor Limited), established in 1993. AMD has a 49.95% equity interest in FASL.

Per Share Data ($)

(Year Ended Dec. 31)	1997	1996	1995	1994	1993	1992	1991	1990	1989	1988
Tangible Bk. Val.	14.28	14.67	20.09	16.38	12.76	9.91	7.27	5.63	6.39	5.91
Cash Flow	2.66	1.94	5.33	5.24	4.14	4.23	3.30	0.79	2.10	2.01
Earnings	-0.15	-0.51	2.85	3.02	2.30	2.57	1.53	-0.78	0.44	0.11
Dividends	Nil	Nil	0.01	Nil	Nil	Nil	Nil	Nil	Nil	Nil
Payout Ratio	Nil	Nil	Nil	Nil	Nil	Nil	Nil	Nil	Nil	Nil
Prices - High	48$\frac{1}{2}$	28$\frac{3}{8}$	39$\frac{1}{4}$	31$\frac{3}{4}$	32$\frac{7}{8}$	21$\frac{1}{2}$	17$\frac{3}{4}$	11$\frac{3}{8}$	10$\frac{1}{2}$	16$\frac{7}{8}$
- Low	17$\frac{1}{8}$	10$\frac{1}{4}$	16$\frac{1}{8}$	16$\frac{3}{4}$	17	7$\frac{3}{8}$	4	3$\frac{1}{2}$	7$\frac{1}{8}$	7$\frac{1}{8}$
P/E Ratio - High	NM	NM	14	11	14	8	12	NM	24	NM
- Low	NM	NM	6	6	7	3	3	NM	16	NM

Income Statement Analysis (Million $)

	1997	1996	1995	1994	1993	1992	1991	1990	1989	1988
Revs.	2,356	1,953	2,430	2,135	1,648	1,514	1,227	1,059	1,105	1,126
Oper. Inc.	304	79.3	611	729	480	422	265	77.0	175	185
Depr.	394	333	263	216	175	152	156	128	136	153
Int. Exp.	45.3	32.5	18.8	10.1	9.8	23.3	25.2	20.2	18.9	18.1
Pretax Inc.	-76.2	-208	378	470	318	272	145	-54.0	50.0	19.0
Eff. Tax Rate	NM	NM	30%	34%	28%	9.80%	NM	NM	7.60%	NM
Net Inc.	-21.1	-69.0	301	305	229	245	145	-54.0	46.0	19.0

Balance Sheet & Other Fin. Data (Million $)

	1997	1996	1995	1994	1993	1992	1991	1990	1989	1988
Cash	241	386	491	378	488	364	301	115	279	287
Curr. Assets	1,175	1,029	1,097	987	964	738	626	397	594	572
Total Assets	3,515	3,145	3,031	2,446	1,929	1,448	1,292	1,112	1,122	1,081
Curr. Liab.	727	583	622	592	455	353	455	318	276	266
LT Debt	663	445	215	46.2	80.0	20.0	42.0	131	126	130
Common Eqty.	2,030	2,022	2,100	1,563	1,180	874	611	464	518	472
Total Cap.	2,789	2,562	2,409	1,854	1,475	1,096	836	794	847	815
Cap. Exp.	685	485	621	549	388	222	111	304	159	133
Cash Flow	373	264	563	511	393	387	291	64.0	172	162
Curr. Ratio	1.6	1.8	1.8	1.7	2.1	2.1	1.4	1.2	2.2	2.2
% LT Debt of Cap.	23.8	17.4	9.0	4.1	5.4	1.8	5.0	16.5	14.9	16.0
% Net Inc.of Revs.	NM	NM	12.4	14.3	13.0	16.2	11.8	NM	4.2	1.7
% Ret. on Assets	NM	NM	11.0	13.8	13.3	17.5	12.0	NM	4.1	1.7
% Ret. on Equity	NM	NM	15.7	21.2	20.8	31.0	24.9	NM	7.2	1.9

Data as orig. reptd.; bef. results of disc. opers. and/or spec. items. Per share data adj. for stk. divs. as of ex-div. date. Bold denotes diluted EPS (FASB 128). E-Estimated. NA-Not Available. NM-Not Meaningful. NR-Not Ranked. Data for 1994 refl. Intel settlement.

Office—One AMD Place, P.O. Box 3453, Sunnyvale, CA 94088-3453. **Tel**—(408) 732-2400. **Website**—http://www.amd.com **Chrmn & CEO**—W. J. Sanders III. **Vice Chrmn**—A. Holbrook. **Pres, COO & Interim CFO**—R. Previte. **VP & Secy**—T. M. McCoy. **Investor Contact**—Toni Beckham (408-749-3127). **Dirs**—F. Baur, C. M. Blalack, R. G. Brown, R. Previte, S. A. Raza, J. L. Roby, W. J. Sanders III, L. Silverman. **Transfer Agent & Registrar**—First National Bank of Boston. **Incorporated**—in Delaware in 1969. **Empl**—12,936. **S&P Analyst**: M. Graham Hackett

STANDARD &POOR'S
STOCK REPORTS

Aeroquip-Vickers

35M

NYSE Symbol **ANV**

In S&P 500

12-SEP-98

Industry: Manufacturing (Diversified)

Summary: This company (formerly Trinova Corp.) is a worldwide maker of engineered components and systems for industry.

S&P Opinion: Accumulate (★★★★)	Recent Price • 39¼	Yield • 2.2%
	52 Wk Range • 72¼-39⅛	12-Mo. P/E • 8.6

Quantitative Evaluations

Outlook (1 Lowest—5 Highest)
• 4

Fair Value
• 55¾

Risk
• Low

Earn./Div. Rank
• B+

Technical Eval.
• NA

Rel. Strength Rank (1 Lowest—99 Highest)
• 35

Insider Activity
• Neutral

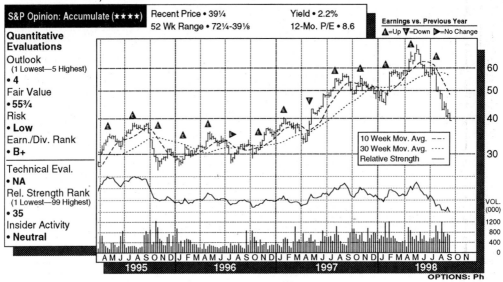

Earnings vs. Previous Year
▲=Up ▼=Down ▶=No Change

10 Week Mov. Avg. – – –
30 Week Mov. Avg. · · · ·
Relative Strength —

OPTIONS: Ph

Overview - 04-AUG-98

For the second quarter of 1998, ANV reported EPS of $1.33, ahead of our estimate, versus $1.15 last year. Aerospace continues to post healthy results as segment operating income rose 22%, on an 18% revenue gain. We continue to see sustainable aerospace growth and profitability, reflecting an extended commercial aircraft delivery cycle, increased sales to the business jet and helicopter markets, retrofit opportunities amid aging commercial fleets, and an expected gradual increase in military spending over the next several years. Segment operating costs should also benefit from the start-up of a new South Carolina machining facility, expected in Q4. While results from automotive were impacted by U.S. start-up costs, the segment has a solid order book of domestic business. Additionally, automotive continues to be well represented among the high end European automakers, and is also winning European transplant business here in the states. Although the industrial segment has seen some softness in in-plant machinery demand, we anticipate an improvement in the air-conditioning market, and continued strength in the European industrial operations. Domestic results should also benefit from improving efficiencies at the Omaha plant, and the start-up of a new cost-efficient piston pump manufacturing facility.

Valuation - 04-AUG-98

We continue to recommend accumulation of the shares, as we see positive fundamentals in place for each segment. The industrial segment should benefit from a strong European economy and improved manufacturing efficiencies. Robust fluid connector sales should continue to drive the streamlined automotive segment, and we see ongoing annualized earnings growth for aerospace in the mid teens. The shares remain attractive at 10X our 1999 EPS estimate of $5.00.

Key Stock Statistics

S&P EPS Est. 1998	4.65	Tang. Bk. Value/Share	15.04
P/E on S&P Est. 1998	8.4	Beta	1.24
S&P EPS Est. 1999	5.00	Shareholders	9,800
Dividend Rate/Share	0.88	Market cap. (B)	$ 1.1
Shs. outstg. (M)	28.2	Inst. holdings	81%
Avg. daily vol. (M)	0.146		

Value of $10,000 invested 5 years ago: $ 20,782

Fiscal Year Ending Dec. 31

	1998	1997	1996	1995	1994	1993
Revenues (Million $)						
1Q	547.1	538.4	512.1	498.6	439.8	429.0
2Q	574.3	556.3	517.9	501.6	460.9	419.8
3Q	—	494.8	493.0	441.4	437.6	393.3
4Q	—	522.8	509.9	442.3	456.4	401.7
Yr.	—	2,112	2,033	1,884	1,795	1,644
Earnings Per Share ($)						
1Q	**1.10**	**0.20**	0.83	0.77	0.46	0.20
2Q	**1.33**	**1.15**	1.11	1.11	0.66	-0.32
3Q	**E1.10**	**1.05**	0.72	0.64	0.52	0.33
4Q	**E1.18**	**1.11**	0.85	0.68	0.62	0.16
Yr.	**E4.65**	**3.51**	3.51	3.20	2.26	0.37

Next earnings report expected: mid October

Dividend Data (Dividends have been paid since 1933.)

Amount ($)	Date Decl.	Ex-Div. Date	Stock of Record	Payment Date
0.200	Oct. 23	Nov. 13	Nov. 17	Dec. 15 '97
0.220	Jan. 22	Feb. 12	Feb. 17	Mar. 13 '98
0.220	Apr. 16	May. 13	May. 15	Jun. 15 '98
0.220	Jul. 23	Aug. 13	Aug. 17	Sep. 15 '98

A Division of The **McGraw·Hill** Companies

Business Summary - 04-AUG-98

Aeroquip-Vickers, Inc. (formerly Trinova Corp.), a diversified manufacturer of engineered components and systems, has a strong worldwide presence in several niche markets. The company's core products are used in the production of mobile equipment, air conditioning and power steering systems, in-plant equipment, commercial aircraft, and marine and defense systems. Foreign operations accounted for 36% of sales and 26% of operating profit in 1997.

Aeroquip industrial products include all pressure ranges of hose and fittings, adapters, self-sealing couplings, molded plastic products and refrigeration and air-conditioning connectors. The Vickers, Inc. unit makes electronic, electrohydraulic, pneumatic and hydraulic control devices; piston and vane pumps and motors; electric motors and drives, and open architecture machine controls. Order backlog in the segment stood at $210.5 million at the end of the first half of 1998, versus $216.1 million a year earlier.

Aeroquip aerospace products include hose, fittings, couplings, swivels, V-band couplings, fuel-handling products, high-pressure tube fittings and marine bearings. Vickers products include fixed and variable-displacement pumps, fuel pumps, hydraulic motors and motor packages, motor pumps and generator packages, electrohydraulic and electromechanical actuators. Order backlog was $395.7 million at the end of the first half of 1998, versus $366.1 million a year earlier.

Aeroquip automotive products include air-conditioning, power steering, oil and transmission cooler and fuel line components and assemblies, exterior trim plastics (spoilers, body side moldings, bumper strips, roof moldings, and rocker panel claddings).

In 1997's first quarter, ANV recorded a special charge of $30 million ($18.5 million, net of tax, or $0.66 a share) related to the divestiture of its automotive interior plastics business. Although this reduced automotive sales in 1997, the strategic decision has benefited results by allowing the segment to focus on its more profitable fluid connector operations.

In the first half of 1998, ANV furthered its international expansion plans with three acquisitions. It purchased Hydrokraft GmbH, a German manufacturer of high pressure axial piston hydraulic pumps, two Italian air conditioning businesses (a producer of valves and accessories and a manufacturer of copper and flexible linesets), and Aerotech South Africa, that country's largest supplier of hose assemblies and fitting products.

The company believes that each of its three segments is well positioned for growth in the upcoming years. The industrial segment should benefit from lower costs related to recent restructuring initiatives. Positive trends are in place for worldwide automotive air conditioning demand, especially from European customers, and aerospace profitability should be sustained over an extended commercial and military aircraft cycle.

Per Share Data ($) (Year Ended Dec. 31)	1997	1996	1995	1994	1993	1992	1991	1990	1989	1988
Tangible Bk. Val.	18.18	15.99	13.91	11.11	8.91	12.34	13.11	21.22	19.75	19.89
Cash Flow	5.93	5.65	5.15	4.11	2.55	2.71	-4.32	3.86	2.84	3.99
Earnings	3.51	3.51	3.20	2.26	0.37	0.51	-6.52	1.51	0.98	2.54
Dividends	0.80	0.80	0.72	0.68	0.68	0.68	0.68	0.68	0.67	0.60
Payout Ratio	23%	23%	22%	30%	184%	133%	NM	42%	67%	23%
Prices - High	57 1/2	37 1/8	38 3/4	40	33 3/4	26 3/4	27 1/2	29 3/8	30 3/8	35
- Low	32 5/8	27 1/4	23 1/2	28 1/2	21	19 1/4	15 3/8	14 7/8	21	24 1/2
P/E Ratio - High	16	11	12	18	91	52	NM	19	31	14
- Low	9	8	7	13	57	38	NM	10	21	10
Income Statement Analysis (Million $)										
Revs.	2,112	2,033	1,884	1,795	1,644	1,696	1,681	1,955	1,942	1,919
Oper. Inc.	295	245	223	202	157	121	73.0	184	224	225
Depr.	73.2	68.7	63.7	60.8	61.8	62.2	62.0	71.2	63.6	56.6
Int. Exp.	27.2	25.8	19.2	21.1	25.5	26.3	26.5	31.7	28.6	31.6
Pretax Inc.	148	153	128	101	17.0	24.0	-194	75.0	63.0	139
Eff. Tax Rate	32%	33%	26%	35%	39%	40%	NM	39%	47%	37%
Net Inc.	101	103	94.9	66.0	11.0	14.0	-183	46.0	33.0	88.0
Balance Sheet & Other Fin. Data (Million $)										
Cash	18.7	23.9	16.2	27.9	20.5	26.0	27.0	25.0	23.0	37.0
Curr. Assets	712	674	616	540	487	547	573	671	738	760
Total Assets	1,377	1,289	1,224	1,001	972	1,017	1,070	1,314	1,361	1,432
Curr. Liab.	441	425	360	289	325	368	450	429	416	384
LT Debt	257	258	302	235	246	239	177	196	204	279
Common Eqty.	510	446	401	320	253	353	375	599	651	679
Total Cap.	767	704	703	703	505	628	583	839	895	997
Cap. Exp.	140	90.6	94.0	55.0	55.0	52.0	86.0	77.0	98.0	115
Cash Flow	174	171	159	127	72.0	77.0	-121	117	97.0	144
Curr. Ratio	1.6	1.6	1.7	1.9	1.5	1.5	1.3	1.6	1.8	2.0
% LT Debt of Cap.	33.5	36.6	43.0	41.8	48.8	38.0	30.4	23.3	22.8	28.0
% Net Inc.of Revs.	4.8	5.1	5.0	3.7	0.6	0.9	NM	2.3	1.7	4.6
% Ret. on Assets	7.6	8.2	8.5	6.6	1.1	1.4	NM	3.7	2.4	6.4
% Ret. on Equity	21.1	24.2	26.3	22.8	3.5	4.0	NM	7.9	5.1	13.6

Data as orig. reptd.; bef. results of disc. opers. and/or spec. items. Per share data adj. for stk. divs. as of ex-div. date. Bold denotes diluted EPS (FASB 128). E-Estimated. NA-Not Available. NM-Not Meaningful. NR-Not Ranked.

Office—3000 Strayer, Maumee, OH 43537-0050. **Tel**—(419) 867-2200. **Fax**—(419) 867-2395. **Website**—http://www.aeroquip-vickers.com **Chrmn, Pres & CEO**—D. F. Allen. **Secy**—J. M. Oathout. **VP & CFO**—D. M. Risley. **VP & Investor Contact**—William R. Ammann (419-867-2215). **Dirs**—D. F. Allen, V. W. Colbert, P. Crawford, J. C. Farrell, D. R. Goode, P. Ormond, J. P. Reilly, W. R. Timken Jr. **Transfer Agent & Registrar**—First Chicago Trust Co. of New York, Jersey City, NJ.**Incorporated**—in Ohio in 1916. **Empl**— 14,780. **S&P Analyst:** Eric J. Hunter

12-SEP-98

Industry:
Insurance (Life & Health)

Summary: This major insurance company sold its property-casualty units and acquired U.S. Healthcare in 1996 to focus on opportunities in managed health care and retirement services.

S&P Opinion: Accumulate (★★★★)	Recent Price • 65¼	Yield • 1.2%
	52 Wk Range • 106⅞-60⅛	12-Mo. P/E • 12.6

Quantitative Evaluations

Outlook
(1 Lowest—5 Highest)
• **4+**

Fair Value
• **83¼**

Risk
• **Average**

Earn./Div. Rank
• **B**

Technical Eval.
• **Bearish** since 7/98

Rel. Strength Rank
(1 Lowest—99 Highest)
• **71**

Insider Activity
• **NA**

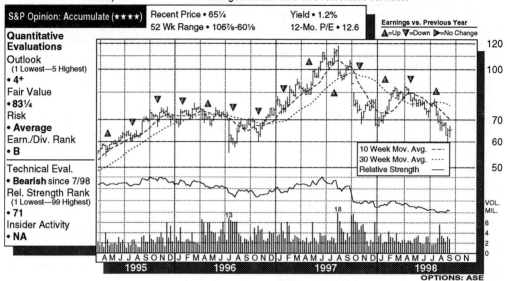

Earnings vs. Previous Year
▲=Up ▼=Down ▶=No Change

10 Week Mov. Avg. – – –
30 Week Mov. Avg. · · · · ·
Relative Strength ——

OPTIONS: ASE

Overview - 12-AUG-98

Operating earnings growth in coming periods is predicated on AET's ability to grapple with rising health care costs as it integrates U.S. Healthcare into its managed care fold. Earnings in this segment in 1997 were hurt by third quarter aftertax charges of $103 million taken to cover an increase in prior-period HMO medical claim reserves. Results in 1996 were impacted by $3.45 a share in unusual charges --including a fourth-quarter charge of $1.86 a share-- to cover certain integration costs related to the $8.9 billion U.S. Healthcare acquisition. As a result of that deal and the sale of its property-casualty unit, AET has transformed itself into a dominant player in the managed health care arena. In July 1998, AET expanded its health care presence even further, by acquiring NYLCare Health Plans from New York Life Insurance Company, for $1.05 billion in cash (and possible future performance-related payments). AET's strategy targets three growth businesses: managed health care, retirement services, and an international segment. To that end, AET agreed in May 1998 to sell its domestic individual life insurance unit to Lincoln National Corp. (NYSE:LNC) for $1 billion in cash. While the shift in business mix leaves AET well positioned in the long term, near-term concerns linger over how smoothly the integration of the U.S. Healthcare acquisition is progressing.

Valuation - 12-AUG-98

After trending steadily upward since late 1996, thanks mainly to positive investor reaction to AET's restructuring moves and expansion into the managed care arena, the shares corrected sharply in late 1997, amid concerns that the integration of the U.S. Healthcare acquisition was running into trouble. Once these fears subsided, the shares began to recover. Despite their recent strength, the shares have additional upside potential.

Key Stock Statistics

S&P EPS Est. 1998	4.25	Tang. Bk. Value/Share	15.18
P/E on S&P Est. 1998	15.4	Beta	1.11
S&P EPS Est. 1999	5.00	Shareholders	29,600
Dividend Rate/Share	0.80	Market cap. (B)	$ 9.4
Shs. outstg. (M)	144.4	Inst. holdings	75%
Avg. daily vol. (M)	0.591		

Value of $10,000 invested 5 years ago: $ 16,868

Fiscal Year Ending Dec. 31

	1998	1997	1996	1995	1994	1993
Revenues (Million $)						
1Q	4,634	4,487	3,330	3,192	4,314	4,294
2Q	4,828	4,628	3,169	3,244	4,405	4,327
3Q	—	4,632	4,174	3,191	4,385	4,303
4Q	—	4,793	4,490	3,351	4,421	4,194
Yr.	—	18,540	15,163	12,978	17,525	17,118
Earnings Per Share ($)						
1Q	**1.05**	1.72	1.43	0.82	0.40	1.26
2Q	**1.69**	1.43	0.21	1.07	1.17	1.36
3Q	—	0.69	0.77	0.99	1.15	2.03
4Q	—	1.71	-0.80	1.28	1.42	-10.09
Yr.	—	**5.60**	1.36	4.16	4.14	-5.54

Next earnings report expected: NA

Dividend Data (Dividends have been paid since 1934.)

Amount ($)	Date Decl.	Ex-Div. Date	Stock of Record	Payment Date
0.200	Sep. 26	Oct. 29	Oct. 31	Nov. 15 '97
0.200	Dec. 05	Jan. 28	Jan. 30	Feb. 15 '98
0.200	Feb. 27	Apr. 22	Apr. 24	May. 15 '98
0.200	Jun. 26	Jul. 29	Jul. 31	Aug. 15 '98

A Division of The McGraw-Hill Companies

Business Summary - 12-AUG-98

In less than 10 years, Aetna has transformed itself from a slow-growing multi-line insurance company saddled with underperforming real estate assets to one of the leading players in the managed health care arena. The company is also focused on the retirement services and large case pension markets domestically and in several international markets. Contributions to revenues (excluding net realized investment gains) in recent years:

	1997	1996
Aetna U.S. Healthcare	70%	64%
Retirement services	10%	12%
International	11%	11%
Large case pensions	9%	13%

Aetna U.S. Healthcare was formed through the July 1996 acquisition of U.S. Healthcare for $8.9 billion in cash and stock. The new entity had total health care enrollment of 13.7 million lives at December 31, 1997. Of that amount, indemnity plans accounted for 19% of enrollment (2.64 million lives), while managed care equaled 81% (11.1 million lives). Managed care enrollment consisted of: HMOs 35% (4.7 million lives), PPOs 26% (3.6 million lives) and POS 20% (2.8 million lives). A net charge of $103 million--taken to cover a higher than expected increase in medical costs--led to lower than expected earnings in 1997's third quarter. Earnings in 1996 were impaired by unusual charges of $3.45 a share--including $1.86 related to the integration of the U.S. Healthcare acquisition.

Retirement services include an array of annuity, pension and life insurance products. At year-end 1997, assets under management totaled $45 billion, up from $32 billion at year-end 1996. The International unit, through subsidiaries and joint ventures, offers life insurance and other financial services in non-U.S. markets. Large case pension assets under management (continuing products) totaled $30 billion at year-end 1997, down from $35 billion at year-end 1996. Property-casualty operations were sold to Travelers Group, Inc. in April 1996 for $4.1 billion in cash.

Per Share Data ($)

(Year Ended Dec. 31)	1997	1996	1995	1994	1993	1992	1991	1990	1989	1988
Tangible Bk. Val.	12.49	10.61	62.11	47.52	62.77	64.07	64.33	61.62	59.33	58.11
Oper. Earnings	NA	0.71	5.89	4.52	-6.07	-0.76	6.28	6.25	4.72	5.85
Earnings	5.60	1.36	4.16	4.14	-5.54	-0.05	4.59	5.52	5.69	6.12
Dividends	0.80	1.78	2.76	2.76	2.76	2.76	2.76	2.76	2.76	2.76
Relative Payout	14%	131%	66%	67%	NM	NM	60%	50%	49%	45%
Prices - High	118⅛	82½	76¾	65¾	66¼	48⅞	49⅛	58⅜	62½	52½
- Low	66¼	55⅜	46¾	42¼	43⅜	38	31⅞	29	46⅝	39½
P/E Ratio - High	21	61	18	16	NM	NM	11	11	11	9
- Low	12	41	11	10	NM	NM	7	5	8	7

Income Statement Analysis (Million $)

	1997	1996	1995	1994	1993	1992	1991	1990	1989	1988
Life Ins. In Force	78,750	76,672	274,429	288,546	299,996	382,542	370,048	347,739	334,029	301,849
Prem. Inc.: Life A & H	2,151	2,243	7,391	6,863	5,818	5,633	5,370	5,296	5,615	10,375
Prem. Inc.: Cas./Prop.	10,384	7,035	41.0	4,430	4,757	5,161	7,005	7,459	7,696	7,803
Net Invest. Inc.	3,378	3,565	3,575	4,464	4,919	5,069	5,735	5,823	5,564	5,826
Oth. Revs.	2,570	2,309	1,972	1,769	1,624	1,634	1,086	442	869	Nil
Total Revs.	15,162	15,163	12,978	17,525	17,118	17,497	19,196	19,020	19,671	24,296
Pretax Inc.	1,511	339	726	658	-1,146	-120	417	624	820	760
Net Oper. Inc.	NA	107	671	510	-673	-84.0	691	696	530	668
Net Inc.	901	205	474	468	-614	-5.0	505	614	639	699

Balance Sheet & Other Fin. Data (Million $)

	1997	1996	1995	1994	1993	1992	1991	1990	1989	1988
Cash & Equiv.	1,806	2,061	2,331	3,731	2,340	3,182	3,997	2,964	3,515	2,747
Premiums Due	1,381	1,190	972	1,723	1,665	2,071	2,977	2,772	2,640	2,597
Invest. Assets: Bonds	34,245	32,336	31,860	37,112	41,545	36,347	35,149	34,227	33,252	31,740
Invest. Assets: Stocks	1,041	1,333	660	1,656	1,659	1,496	1,122	911	1,348	2,178
Invest. Assets: Loans	4,955	7,408	8,957	12,377	15,330	18,515	21,229	23,543	23,425	21,976
Invest. Assets: Total	37,237	43,486	44,050	54,293	61,456	58,797	60,991	63,260	61,191	58,427
Deferred Policy Costs	2,367	2,227	1,953	2,015	1,867	1,706	1,663	1,619	1,536	1,559
Total Assets	96,001	92,913	84,324	94,173	100,037	89,928	91,988	89,301	87,099	81,415
Debt	2,873	2,663	1,379	1,115	1,160	956	1,021	1,012	1,038	1,096
Common Eqty.	10,330	10,024	7,273	5,503	7,043	7,238	7,385	7,072	6,937	6,522
Comb. Loss-Exp. Ratio	NA	NA	108.1	117.7	117.9	131.0	116.7	114.3	112.3	110.9
% Return On Revs.	5.9	1.4	3.7	2.7	NM	NM	2.6	3.2	3.3	2.7
% Ret. on Equity	8.3	2.1	7.5	7.5	NM	NM	7.0	8.8	9.5	10.5
% Invest. Yield	8.4	8.1	8.4	7.7	8.2	8.6	9.2	9.4	9.3	10.3

Data as orig. reptd.; bef. results of disc. opers. and/or spec. items. Per share data adj. for stk. divs. as of ex-div. date. Bold denotes diluted EPS (FASB 128). E-Estimate. NA-Not Available. NM-Not Meaningful. NR-Not Ranked.

Office—151 Farmington Ave., Hartford, CT 06156. **Tel**—(860) 273-0123. **Website**—http://www.Aetna.com **Chrmn & CEO**—R. L. Huber. **Secy**—L. M. Nickerson. **Investor Contact**—Robyn S. Walsh (860) 273-6184 **Dirs**—L. Abramson, B. Z. Cohen, W. H. Donaldson, B. H. Franklin, J. S. Goodman, E. G. Graves, G. Greenwald, E. M. Hancock, R. L. Huber, M. H. Jordan, J. D. Kuehler, F. R. O'Keefe Jr., J. Rodin. **Transfer Agent & Registrar**—First Chicago Trust Co. of New York, NYC. **Incorporated**—in Connecticut in 1853; reincorporated in 1967. **Empl**— 38,600. **S&P Analyst:** Catherine A. Seifert

12-SEP-98

Industry:
Savings & Loan Companies

Summary: In March 1998, Ahmanson, one of the largest thrifts in the U.S., agreed to be acquired by Washington Mutual.

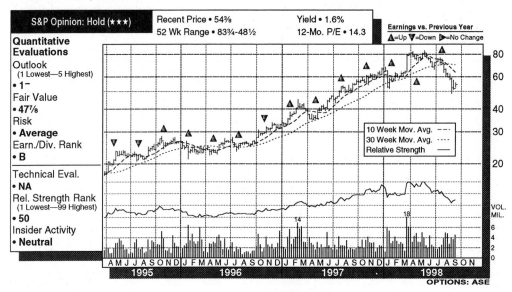

S&P Opinion: Hold (★★★)	Recent Price • 54⅜	Yield • 1.6%
	52 Wk Range • 83¾-48½	12-Mo. P/E • 14.3

Earnings vs. Previous Year
▲=Up ▼=Down ▶=No Change

Quantitative Evaluations

Outlook
(1 Lowest—5 Highest)
• **1⁻**

Fair Value
• **47⅞**

Risk
• **Average**

Earn./Div. Rank
• **B**

Technical Eval.
• **NA**

Rel. Strength Rank
(1 Lowest—99 Highest)
• **50**

Insider Activity
• **Neutral**

10 Week Mov. Avg. — · —
30 Week Mov. Avg. · · · ·
Relative Strength ——

OPTIONS: ASE

Overview - 24-JUL-98

Solid growth in operating earnings is expected for 1998. One positive factor is balance sheet expansion; as part of its strategy of becoming more bank-like, the company plans to increase its consumer and commercial lending operations. In addition to the generally higher yields on these loans, the spread between loan rates and deposit costs could benefit from growth in checking account balances, resulting in part from the purchase of First Interstate branches. Lower credit costs are likely, given the downward trend in nonperforming assets associated the rebound in the California economy, although one concern is the emphasis on diversified lending. Continued gains in fee income are expected with greater sales of alternative investment products. Tight control of costs should further aid comparisons.

Valuation - 24-JUL-98

In March 1998, AHM shares were downgraded to hold, following Washington Mutual's offer to buy the company for about $8 billion. Terms call for shareholders to receive about $73 a share in stock, or about 1.68 WAMU common shares (adjusted) for each AHM common share. As the stock quickly moved close to the offer price, we see little upside potential over the next six months. We also believe that a competing offer is unlikely, because Washington Mutual is paying a full price. At about 17X analyst 1998 EPS estimates, and 4X latest book value, the price is near the upper end of the range of recent S&L mergers. Former rivals during a 1997 hostile takeover battle for Great Western, managements of the two companies apparently found a way to overcome their differences. The motivating factor may have been a desire to create a company of sufficient scale to be a leading player in West Coast markets.

Key Stock Statistics

S&P EPS Est. 1998	4.35	Tang. Bk. Value/Share	17.54
P/E on S&P Est. 1998	12.5	Beta	1.43
S&P EPS Est. 1999	4.60	Shareholders	6,700
Dividend Rate/Share	0.88	Market cap. (B)	$ 5.5
Shs. outstg. (M)	100.9	Inst. holdings	88%
Avg. daily vol. (M)	0.768		

Value of $10,000 invested 5 years ago: $ 33,906

Fiscal Year Ending Dec. 31

	1998	1997	1996	1995	1994	1993
Revenues (Million $)						
1Q	984.5	951.0	955.4	930.0	778.7	827.3
2Q	1,032	963.3	951.0	1,003	774.8	833.9
3Q	—	911.6	925.2	1,510	818.9	819.2
4Q	—	907.1	962.7	954.6	1,009	840.8
Yr.	—	3,733	3,767	4,398	3,381	4.20
Earnings Per Share ($)						
1Q	0.97	0.87	0.45	0.34	0.36	0.23
2Q	**1.12**	1.01	0.51	0.44	0.52	-2.55
3Q	**E1.10**	0.84	-0.85	2.20	0.47	0.50
4Q	**E1.16**	0.89	0.78	0.41	0.23	0.32
Yr.	**E4.35**	3.59	0.92	3.39	1.59	-1.51

Next earnings report expected: mid October

Dividend Data (Dividends have been paid since 1968.)

Amount ($)	Date Decl.	Ex-Div. Date	Stock of Record	Payment Date
0.220	Nov. 04	Nov. 06	Nov. 11	Dec. 01 '97
0.220	Feb. 03	Feb. 06	Feb. 10	Mar. 02 '98
0.220	May. 06	May. 08	May. 12	Jun. 01 '98
0.220	Aug. 04	Aug. 07	Aug. 11	Sep. 01 '98

A Division of The McGraw-Hill Companies

STANDARD
&POOR'S
STOCK REPORTS

H.F. Ahmanson & Company

37M

12-SEP-98

Business Summary - 24-JUL-98

H.F. Ahmanson is one of the largest U.S. savings and loans, based on assets of about $47 billion at December 31, 1997. The company has 370 savings branches in three states, and 126 loan offices in nine states, but operations are to a significant extent concentrated in California. Although AHM is still a traditional thrift, management is intent on giving the company a fresh new look as a high-powered financial services concern. In March 1998, after buying Coast Savings, a large California thrift, the company itself agreed to be acquired by Washington Mutual for about $10 billion in stock.

Loans of $30.8 billion at 1997 year-end (excluding mortgage-backed securities of $12.8 billion) and $32.2 billion ($14.3 billion) a year earlier were divided as follows:

	1997	1996
Single-family	61%	63%
Apartments	32%	30%
Commercial & industrial real estate	4%	4%
Consumer	3%	2%
Other	Nil	1%

Since the early 1980s, AHM has focused almost exclusively on monthly adjustable ARM mortgages tied to the 11th District cost of funds (the average cost of funds for the some 500 thrifts in California, Arizona and Nevada). At year-end 1997, these mortgages comprised 90% of the loan and mortgage-backed securities portfolio. Ahmanson's emphasis on ARMs reflects its aversion to interest rate risk. The yield on the ARMs adjusts upward when funding costs are rising, and it moves down when funding costs are falling. Thus, these instruments help smooth out fluctuations in the spread.

On the deposit side, the company offers a host of traditional S&L products: passbook or regular savings accounts, which pay a low rate but allow the individual access to his funds; and certificates of deposit of various maturities, such as six months or two years, where the customer receives a much higher rate but cannot withdraw the money before maturity without a penalty

Over the past several years, new management led by chairman and CEO Charles Rinehart determined that the traditional thrift business was dying and that, in order to generate satisfactory returns, the company had to diversify into more bank-like operations. Subsequently, AHM expanded lending to include a host of consumer and business products, and, on the savings side, introduced various insurance and investment offerings.

Per Share Data ($)

(Year Ended Dec. 31)	1997	1996	1995	1994	1993	1992	1991	1990	1989	1988
Tangible Bk. Val.	17.54	20.74	25.09	19.70	15.94	17.76	16.63	15.08	14.33	12.80
Earnings	3.59	0.91	3.39	1.59	-1.51	1.19	2.06	1.64	1.95	2.05
Dividends	0.88	0.88	0.88	0.88	0.88	0.88	0.88	0.88	0.88	0.88
Payout Ratio	25%	97%	26%	56%	NM	74%	43%	54%	45%	43%
Prices - High	68	34½	28⅜	22¾	22⅛	19½	20⅞	22½	25	18⅝
- Low	32	21¼	16	15¼	16¾	13	12	10⅝	15¾	13¾
P/E Ratio - High	19	38	8	14	NM	16	10	14	13	9
- Low	9	23	5	10	NM	11	6	6	8	7

Income Statement Analysis (Million $)

	1997	1996	1995	1994	1993	1992	1991	1990	1989	1988
Net Int. Inc.	1,235	1,253	1,227	1,297	1,337	1,359	1,292	1,195	994	875
Loan Loss Prov.	67.1	145	119	177	575	348	195	216	85.0	45.0
Non Int. Inc.	403	252	698	286	97.0	208	205	127	205	235
Non Int. Exp.	769	1,179	981	996	1,079	929	809	807	774	729
Pretax Inc.	655	181	825	411	-219	290	473	298	340	336
Eff. Tax Rate	37%	20%	45%	42%	NM	46%	48%	36%	43%	40%
Net Inc.	414	145	451	237	-137	156	246	191	194	203
% Net Int. Marg.	2.68	2.63	2.41	2.64	2.90	3.02	2.71	2.65	2.51	2.51

Balance Sheet & Other Fin. Data (Million $)

	1997	1996	1995	1994	1993	1992	1991	1990	1989	1988
Total Assets	46,679	49,902	50,530	53,726	50,871	48,141	47,226	51,201	44,652	40,258
Loans	30,029	36,179	36,480	48,791	44,624	42,401	42,318	44,839	38,407	34,260
Deposits	32,268	34,774	34,244	40,655	38,019	39,273	39,147	38,606	33,086	29,506
Capitalization:										
Debt	8,316	9,550	8,717	6,822	3,902	2,662	3,349	7,551	6,186	2,778
Equity	4,260	1,950	2,399	2,309	2,292	2,571	2,481	2,342	2,001	1,886
Total	10,860	12,131	11,774	9,786	6,851	5,408	6,005	9,893	8,187	4,664
% Ret. on Assets	0.9	0.3	0.9	0.5	NM	0.3	0.5	0.4	0.5	0.6
% Ret. on Equity	11.4	3.7	17.0	8.1	NM	5.5	10.0	8.3	10.0	11.1
% Loan Loss Resv.	1.2	1.3	1.2	0.8	1.0	1.0	0.7	0.5	0.3	0.2
% Risk Based Capital	10.8	10.8	12.4	12.2	12.6	13.0	10.4	9.0	7.1	NA
Price Times Book Value:										
Hi	3.9	1.7	1.1	1.2	1.4	1.1	1.3	1.5	1.7	1.5
Low	1.8	1.0	0.6	0.8	1.1	0.7	0.7	0.7	1.1	1.1

Data as orig. reptd.; bef. results of disc. opers. and/or spec. items. Per share data adj. for stk. divs. as of ex-div. date. Bold denotes diluted EPS (FASB 128). E-Estimated. NA-Not Available. NM-Not Meaningful. NR-Not Ranked.

Office—4900 Rivergrade Rd., Irwindale, CA 91706. **Tel**—(818) 960-6311. **Chrmn & CEO**—C. R. Rinehart. **Pres & COO**—B. G. Willison. **EVP & Secy**—M. A. Kleiner. **Vice Chrmn & CFO**—K. M. Twomey. **SVP & Investor Contact**—Stephen A. Swartz (818-814-7986). **Dirs**—B. Allumbaugh, H. A. Black, R. M. Bressler, D. R. Carpenter, P. D. Matthews, R. L. Nolan, D. M. Reyes, C. R. Rinehart, E. A. Sanders, A. W. Schmutz, W. D. Schulte, B. G. Willison. **Transfer Agent & Registrar**—First Chicago Trust Co. of New York, Jersey City, NJ. **Incorporated**—in California in 1928; reincorporated in Delaware in 1985. **Empl**— 9,380. **S&P Analyst:** Paul L. Huberman, CFA

Air Products & Chemicals   39

NYSE Symbol **APD**

In S&P 500

12-SEP-98

Industry:
Chemicals

Summary: This major producer of industrial gases and specialty and intermediate chemicals also has interests in environmental and energy-related businesses.

S&P Opinion: Accumulate (★★★★)	Recent Price • 31½	Yield • 2.2%
	52 Wk Range • 45⅜-30½	12-Mo. P/E • 13.1

Earnings vs. Previous Year
▲=Up ▼=Down ▶=No Change

Quantitative Evaluations

Outlook
(1 Lowest—5 Highest)
• **3+**

Fair Value
• **37¼**

Risk
• **Low**

Earn./Div. Rank
• **A**

Technical Eval.
• **Bullish** since 8/98

Rel. Strength Rank
(1 Lowest—99 Highest)
• **56**

Insider Activity
• **NA**

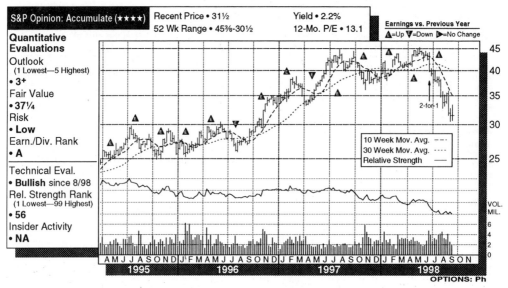

10 Week Mov. Avg. – – –
30 Week Mov. Avg. ·······
Relative Strength ——

2-for-1

VOL.
MIL.

OPTIONS: Ph

Overview - 19-AUG-98

We see earnings in FY 99 (Sep.) benefiting from the moderately growing U.S. and European markets and recent capacity investments, which are resulting in continued volume gains in the industrial gases and specialty chemicals units. Profit margins in gases should rebound to those in FY 98's first half, the highest in several years, on growing volumes as APD continues to fill new capacity, and benefit of recent price increases designed to offset higher power costs. Chemicals earnings should also grow further as volumes grow, though margins in ·FY 98's first quarter were at unusually high level. After record profits in FY 98, the equipment business will have a somewhat lower performance in FY 99 as the order backlog is now more heavily weighted toward lower margin air separation equipment. Unfavorable currency exchange rates, which reduced EPS by $0.11 (adjusted) in FY 98's first half, should have a much smaller impact for the foreseeable future. Earnings for the first nine months of FY 98 included special gains of $0.26 a share, including $0.16 from the sale of APD's 50% interest in the waste-to-energy business in December 1997. The 10% stock buyback program is to be completed by the end of FY 98.

Valuation - 19-AUG-98

As this stock had performed well since mid-1996, we downgraded our opinion in July to accumulate. We still feel APD's growth in operating profits will continue over the next two years. Industrial gases profit margins should rebound to at least the 20% target as major investments and productivity initiatives of the past few years begin to pay off. The new management compensation plan puts great emphasis on near-term EPS growth. The dividend was recently raised for the 16th consecutive year, and the stock split 2-for-1.

Key Stock Statistics

S&P EPS Est. 1998	2.17	Tang. Bk. Value/Share	9.92
P/E on S&P Est. 1998	14.5	Beta	1.13
S&P EPS Est. 1999	2.40	Shareholders	11,400
Dividend Rate/Share	0.68	Market cap. (B)	$ 7.3
Shs. outstg. (M)	231.4	Inst. holdings	75%
Avg. daily vol. (M)	0.604		

Value of $10,000 invested 5 years ago: $ 14,952

Fiscal Year Ending Sep. 30

	1998	1997	1996	1995	1994	1993
Revenues (Million $)						
1Q	1,235	1,121	947.0	920.8	827.3	822.3
2Q	1,209	1,153	1,013	982.9	858.6	833.9
3Q	1,225	1,150	997.0	982.4	868.4	824.8
4Q	—	1,214	1,051	979.2	931.0	855.5
Yr.	—	4,638	4,008	3,865	3,485	3,328
Earnings Per Share ($)						
1Q	**0.72**	0.46	0.40	0.39	0.33	0.30
2Q	**0.55**	0.48	0.60	0.40	0.06	0.33
3Q	**0.63**	0.53	0.43	0.45	0.29	0.31
4Q	—	0.49	0.42	0.42	0.35	-0.07
Yr.	—	1.95	1.86	1.65	1.03	0.88

Next earnings report expected: late October

Dividend Data (Dividends have been paid since 1954.)

Amount ($)	Date Decl.	Ex-Div. Date	Stock of Record	Payment Date
0.300	Nov. 21	Dec. 30	Jan. 02	Feb. 09 '98
0.300	Mar. 19	Mar. 30	Apr. 01	May. 11 '98
2-for-1	May. 06	Jun. 16	May. 15	Jun. 15 '98
0.170	May. 06	Jun. 29	Jul. 01	Aug. 10 '98

A Division of The **McGraw·Hill** *Companies*

Business Summary - 19-AUG-98

Air Products & Chemicals has refocused on its core industrial gases and chemicals businesses since FY 96 (Sep.). The company sold its landfill gas recovery business in November 1996 and in December 1997 sold the 50%-owned American Ref-Fuel waste-to-energy business, which contributed earnings of $0.07 a share in FY 97. As part of its refocusing effort, APD is placing a greater emphasis on near-term financial results.

Contribution by business segment in FY 97 (Sep.):

	Sales	Profits
Industrial gases	58%	68%
Chemicals	31%	27%
Equipment & services	11%	5%

International operations accounted for 29% of sales and 24% of operating income in FY 97.

APD is the fourth largest international producer of industrial, medical and specialty gases, including nitrogen, oxygen, argon, hydrogen, helium, carbon monoxide, synthesis gas and fluorine compounds for both merchant and tonnage (on-site) customers. Sales of atmospheric gases (oxygen, nitrogen and argon) accounted for 24% of total sales in FY 97. The industrial gases industry has historically grown up to two times faster than real economic growth. By the end of FY 97,

APD invested over $2 billion over a three-year period in some 70 major projects and acquisitions, including new hydrogen capacity in the U.S. and Europe. In November 1996, APD completed the acquisition of Carburos Metalicos, S.A., the largest industrial gases company in Spain, with annual sales of about $300 million.

Chemicals include water-based polymers (emulsions, pressure-sensitive adhesives and polyvinyl alcohol) for adhesives, paints, paper and textiles; specialty, polyurethane and epoxy additives for pesticides, plastics, adhesives and coatings; and intermediates (polyurethanes and amines) used in pesticide, coatings, furniture, automotive and construction markets. Over 80% of sales are in product lines with the leading market shares. Commodity chemicals (methanol, ammonia and acetic acid) are also produced as raw materials or coproducts.

Equipment and services consist of cryogenic and process equipment for air separation, gas processing, natural gas liquefaction, hydrogen purification and nitrogen rejection; membranes technology for recovering gases; and ventures in power cogeneration and flue gas desulfurization.

By the end of June 1998, APD had repurchased 14.5 million (adjusted) common shares for a total of $520 million as part of the 10% stock buyback program announced in April 1996.

Per Share Data ($)

(Year Ended Sep. 30)	1997	1996	1995	1994	1993	1992	1991	1990	1989	1988
Tangible Bk. Val.	10.02	10.33	9.51	9.43	8.93	8.94	7.75	7.26	6.24	5.51
Cash Flow	4.04	3.69	3.35	2.61	2.44	2.73	2.56	2.43	2.31	2.15
Earnings	1.95	1.86	1.65	1.03	0.88	1.23	1.11	1.04	1.01	0.97
Dividends	0.57	0.54	0.51	0.47	0.45	0.41	0.38	0.34	0.32	0.28
Payout Ratio	29%	29%	31%	46%	51%	34%	34%	33%	31%	28%
Prices - High	44⅞	35⅜	29⅞	25¼	24¼	24¾	18½	15¼	12¼	13⅜
- Low	33¼	25¼	22	19⅜	18¾	18¼	12⅞	10¾	10	9⅛
P/E Ratio - High	23	19	18	24	28	20	17	15	12	14
- Low	17	14	13	19	20	15	12	10	10	9

Income Statement Analysis (Million $)

	1997	1996	1995	1994	1993	1992	1991	1990	1989	1988
Revs.	4,638	4,008	3,865	3,485	3,328	3,217	2,931	2,895	2,642	2,432
Oper. Inc.	1,160	978	958	840	864	812	729	692	641	621
Depr.	474	412	382	360	353	340	325	308	286	258
Int. Exp.	161	144	118	90.0	86.0	91.0	107	103	88.0	74.0
Pretax Inc.	630	609	553	325	301	407	363	337	321	304
Eff. Tax Rate	32%	32%	33%	28%	33%	32%	31%	32%	31%	30%
Net Inc.	429	416	368	234	201	277	249	230	222	214

Balance Sheet & Other Fin. Data (Million $)

	1997	1996	1995	1994	1993	1992	1991	1990	1989	1988
Cash	52.5	79.0	87.0	100	238	117	104	74.0	50.0	36.0
Curr. Assets	1,624	1,375	1,332	1,178	1,196	998	901	837	757	626
Total Assets	7,244	6,522	5,816	5,036	4,762	4,492	4,228	3,900	3,366	3,000
Curr. Liab.	1,125	1,263	1,311	1,076	874	719	785	623	494	517
LT Debt	2,292	1,739	1,194	923	1,016	956	945	954	854	668
Common Eqty.	2,648	2,574	2,398	2,206	2,102	2,098	1,841	1,688	1,445	1,272
Total Cap.	5,670	4,895	4,070	3,552	3,607	3,556	3,263	3,094	2,716	2,337
Cap. Exp.	870	951	870	614	495	428	506	468	414	409
Cash Flow	903	828	750	594	554	617	574	538	508	473
Curr. Ratio	1.4	1.1	1.0	1.1	1.4	1.4	1.1	1.3	1.5	1.2
% LT Debt of Cap.	40.4	35.6	29.3	26.0	28.2	26.9	29.0	30.8	31.4	28.6
% Net Inc.of Revs.	9.3	10.4	9.5	6.7	6.0	8.6	8.5	7.9	8.4	8.8
% Ret. on Assets	6.2	6.8	6.7	4.8	4.3	6.4	6.1	6.3	7.0	7.5
% Ret. on Equity	16.4	16.8	15.9	10.9	9.5	14.1	14.0	14.6	16.3	17.8

Data as orig. reptd.; bef. results of disc. opers. and/or spec. items. Per share data adj. for stk. divs. as of ex-div. date. Bold denotes diluted EPS (FASB 128). E-Estimated. NA-Not Available. NM-Not Meaningful. NR-Not Ranked.

Office—7201 Hamilton Blvd., Allentown, PA 18195-1501 **Tel**—(610) 481-4911. **Website**—http://www.airproducts.com **Chrmn & Pres**—H. A. Wagner. **VP-Fin**—L. J. Daley. **SVP-Secy**—J. H. Agger. **Investor Contact**—Michael F. Hilton.**Dirs**—T. H. Barrett, L. P. Bremer III, R. Cizik, R. M. Davis, E. E. Hagenlocker, J. F. Hardymon, J. J. Kaminski, T. R. Lautenbach, R. F. M. Lubbers, T. Shiina, L. D. Thomas, H. A. Wagner. **Transfer Agent & Registrar**—First Chicago Trust Co. of New York, Jersey City, NJ. **Incorporated**—in Michigan in 1940; reincorporated in Delaware in 1961. **Empl**— 16,400. **S&P Analyst:** Richard O'Reilly, CFA

12-SEP-98

Industry:
Telecommunications
(Cellular/Wireless)

Summary: This company is the leading stand-alone provider of wireless communications services worldwide.

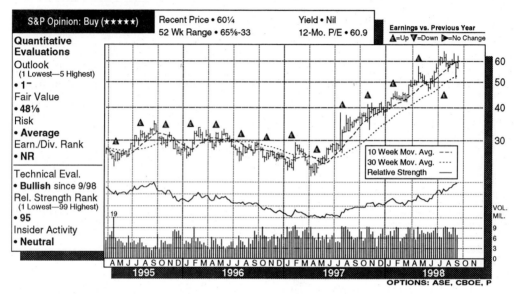

| S&P Opinion: Buy (★★★★) | Recent Price • 60¼ | Yield • Nil |
| | 52 Wk Range • 65⅝-33 | 12-Mo. P/E • 60.9 |

Earnings vs. Previous Year
▲=Up ▼=Down ▶=No Change

Quantitative Evaluations

Outlook
(1 Lowest—5 Highest)
• **1⁻**

Fair Value
• **48⅛**

Risk
• **Average**

Earn./Div. Rank
• **NR**

Technical Eval.
• **Bullish** since 9/98

Rel. Strength Rank
(1 Lowest—99 Highest)
• **95**

Insider Activity
• **Neutral**

10 Week Mov. Avg. – – –
30 Week Mov. Avg. · · · · ·
Relative Strength ——

1995 1996 1997 1998

OPTIONS: ASE, CBOE, P

Overview - 23-JUL-98

Expected industrywide growth in demand for wireless telecommunications services should contribute to strong revenue growth through the addition of three million cellular and PCS customers in 1998. Domestically, this strong growth should offset a continued industrywide decline in the average monthly revenue per subscriber. The acquisition of MediaOne Group's domestic cellular business solidified the company's position as the leading independent provider of global wireless communications. International revenues should continue their strong growth, aided by ATI's position as the largest European cellular provider. The company's extensive international operations make the shares particularly attractive. In addition, ATI has a minority interest in Globalstar, a global satellite network. A $1 billion share buyback was initiated in October 1997.

Valuation - 23-JUL-98

The shares of this worldwide provider of wireless communication services have continued to widely outperform the S&P 500 index, as results continue to exceed industry growth and analyst expectations. ATI has not wilted in the face of increasing PCS (personal communications services) competition, and has proved to be a dominant player, because of significant brand name recognition, and a network that uses cutting edge CDMA digital technology. Operations will benefit from alliances, including the powerful combination of MediaOne Group and ATI's worldwide cellular businesses. International operations should make increasing contributions in future periods, as the market for wireless services abroad continues to expand. This global strength is especially appealing, because ATI beat many of its competitors to these high growth markets.

Key Stock Statistics

S&P EPS Est. 1998	1.10	Tang. Bk. Value/Share	NM
P/E on S&P Est. 1998	54.8	Beta	NA
S&P EPS Est. 1999	1.45	Shareholders	6,300
Dividend Rate/Share	Nil	Market cap. (B)	$ 34.6
Shs. outstg. (M)	573.9	Inst. holdings	52%
Avg. daily vol. (M)	1.753		

Value of $10,000 invested 5 years ago: NA

Fiscal Year Ending Dec. 31

	1998	1997	1996	1995	1994	1993
Revenues (Million $)						
1Q	958.0	836.0	448.9	373.9	257.3	239.0
2Q	1,348	901.0	481.3	403.4	279.2	260.0
3Q	—	916.0	600.7	414.7	290.4	255.0
4Q	—	941.0	720.8	426.6	309.3	235.0
Yr.	—	3,594	2,252	1,619	1,136	988.0
Earnings Per Share ($)						
1Q	**0.30**	**0.13**	0.10	0.07	0.06	--
2Q	**0.25**	**0.21**	0.12	0.08	0.07	--
3Q	**E0.30**	**0.25**	0.10	0.09	0.07	--
4Q	**E0.25**	**0.19**	0.03	0.02	0.01	--
Yr.	**E1.10**	**0.78**	0.36	0.27	0.20	0.09

Next earnings report expected: late October

Dividend Data

No dividends have been paid. The company does not expect to pay cash dividends for the foreseeable future and intends to retain future earnings for the development of its business.

A Division of The McGraw-Hill Companies

Business Summary - 23-JUL-98

This company's cell sites send wireless data that touches the air around the world. Wireless voice services constituted only 5% of total telephone services in 1997, but AirTouch expects their share to surge to 20% by 2004. Its U.S cellular systems interests include markets covering about 43.4 million POPs (as adjusted for percentage ownership) and PCS (personal communications services) markets covering an additional 14.2 million POPs. Following its $5.9 billion acquisition of the cellular and PCS interests of MediaOne Group (UMG; formerly U S West Media Group) in April 1998, ATI is now the largest wireless provider in the U.S., based on the total number of cellular and PCS customers served by its ventures (9 million), and the world's largest multinational wireless company based on total global venture customers (29 million). At June 30, 1998, the company served 7,290,000 cellular subscribers in the U.S.

In April 1998, the company acquired UMG's domestic cellular business, NewVector, and its interest in PrimeCo PCS. The $5.9 billion transaction, which included the assumption of $1.4 billion of debt, expanded ATI's proportionate wireless footprint to cover more than 34 million POPs, through the addition of 2.2 million cellular customers in 12 states, and 62,000 PrimeCo PCS customers. EPS dilution from the transaction is expected to peak at about $0.40 in 1999, and to decline thereafter.

In October 1994, ATI formed a national wireless partnership with U S WEST (UMG), Bell Atlantic (BEL) and NYNEX (NYN); the partnership, which is equally owned by the ATI/USW venture, builds on ATI's joint venture with UMG, BEL and NYN merged their cellular operations, which cover 55 million potential customers on the East Coast and in the Southwest. Under the agreement, the four companies formed a partnership, PrimeCo Personal Communications, which successfully bid for 11 PCS licenses that will complement the four companies' existing cellular assets. As a result of the MediaOne wireless acquisition, ATI increased its ownership in PrimeCo to 50%, from 25%.

ATI has focused its international growth on Europe and Asia, concentrating on countries with favorable demographics such as population growth and per capita income. The company's foreign ventures include Germany, Portugal, Spain, Sweden, Belguim, Italy, Poland, Romania, South Korea, and Japan. AirTouch also holds a 5.7% interest in Globalstar, L.P., a global satellite communications network.

The company is one of the largest providers of paging services in the U.S., offering local, regional and national narrowband data and messaging services in 167 markets in 29 states. At June 30, 1998, domestic paging operations served 3,228,000 customers.

Per Share Data ($)

(Year Ended Dec. 31)	1997	1996	1995	1994	1993	1992	1991	1990	1989	1988
Tangible Bk. Val.	2.33	1.19	6.37	6.05	5.94	6.76	NA	NA	NA	NA
Cash Flow	1.87	1.06	0.71	0.61	0.50	0.31	NA	NA	NA	NA
Earnings	0.78	0.36	0.27	0.20	0.09	0.01	NA	NA	NA	NA
Dividends	Nil	Nil	Nil	Nil	Nil	NA	NA	NA	NA	NA
Payout Ratio	Nil	Nil	Nil	Nil	Nil	NA	NA	NA	NA	NA
Prices - High	42	33⅝	35⅝	30⅝	27¼	NA	NA	NA	NA	NA
- Low	22	24⅞	23⅞	19⅞	24⅜	NA	NA	NA	NA	NA
P/E Ratio - High	54	93	NM	NM	NM	NA	NA	NA	NA	NA
- Low	28	69	NM	NM	NM	NA	NA	NA	NA	NA

Income Statement Analysis (Million $)

	1997	1996	1995	1994	1993	1992	1991	1990	1989	1988
Revs.	3,594	2,252	1,619	1,235	1,058	687	NA	NA	NA	NA
Oper. Inc.	1,255	632	334	278	307	143	NA	NA	NA	NA
Depr.	549	351	222	205	174	130	NA	NA	NA	NA
Int. Exp.	90.0	82.8	28.2	10.7	25.8	6.6	NA	NA	NA	NA
Pretax Inc.	833	443	282	223	154	42.8	NA	NA	NA	NA
Eff. Tax Rate	32%	34%	40%	49%	44%	94%	NA	NA	NA	NA
Net Inc.	448	199	132	98.1	40.1	2.6	NA	NA	NA	NA

Balance Sheet & Other Fin. Data (Million $)

	1997	1996	1995	1994	1993	1992	1991	1990	1989	1988
Cash	1.0	27.7	82.9	840	1,461	NA	NA	NA	NA	NA
Curr. Assets	722	624	506	1,266	1,661	NA	NA	NA	NA	NA
Total Assets	8,970	8,524	5,648	4,488	4,077	3,855	NA	NA	NA	NA
Curr. Liab.	976	761	488	530	314	NA	NA	NA	NA	NA
LT Debt	1,362	1,637	892	120	69.0	69.7	NA	NA	NA	NA
Common Eqty.	4,488	4,021	3,751	3,460	3,337	3,201	NA	NA	NA	NA
Total Cap.	7,602	7,650	5,054	3,919	3,709	NA	NA	NA	NA	NA
Cap. Exp.	683	480	484	383	397	NA	NA	NA	NA	NA
Cash Flow	943	530	354	303	214	133	NA	NA	NA	NA
Curr. Ratio	0.7	0.8	1.0	2.4	5.3	NA	NA	NA	NA	NA
% LT Debt of Cap.	17.9	21.4	17.6	3.1	1.8	NA	NA	NA	NA	NA
% Net Inc.of Revs.	12.5	8.8	8.1	7.9	3.8	0.4	NA	NA	NA	NA
% Ret. on Assets	5.1	2.8	2.6	2.3	1.2	NA	NA	NA	NA	NA
% Ret. on Equity	9.3	4.6	3.7	2.9	1.9	NA	NA	NA	NA	NA

Data as orig. reptd.; bef. results of disc. opers. and/or spec. items. Per share data adj. for stk. divs. as of ex-div. date. Bold denotes diluted EPS (FASB 128). E-Estimated. NA-Not Available. NM-Not Meaningful. NR-Not Ranked.

Office—One California St., San Francisco, CA 94111. **Tel**—(415) 658-2000. **Website**—http://www.airtouch.com **Chrmn & CEO**—S. L. Ginn. **Pres & COO**—A. Sarin.**EVP & CFO**—M. Gyani. **SVP & Secy**—M. G. Gill. **Investor Contact**—Terry D. Kramer.**Dirs**—C. A. Bartz, M. J. Boskin, C. L. Cox, D. G. Fisher, S. L. Ginn, P. Hazen, A. Rock, A. Sarin, C. R. Schwab, G. P. Shultz, C Tien.**Transfer Agent & Registrar**—Bank of New York, Newark, NJ. **Incorporated**—in California in 1984. **Empl**— 8,800. **S&P Analyst:** Philip D. Wohl

12-SEP-98

Industry: Personal Care

Summary: Alberto-Culver produces well-known hair care products and other health and beauty aids, and operates Sally Beauty, the world's largest chain of professional beauty supply stores.

S&P Opinion: Avoid (★★)	Recent Price • 21⅛ Yield • 1.1%
	52 Wk Range • 32½-19¾ 12-Mo. P/E • 14.8

Earnings vs. Previous Year
▲=Up ▼=Down ▶=No Change

Quantitative Evaluations

Outlook
(1 Lowest—5 Highest)
• **1⁻**

Fair Value
• **19¼**

Risk
• **Low**

Earn./Div. Rank
• **A**

Technical Eval.
• **Bullish** since 5/98

Rel. Strength Rank
(1 Lowest—99 Highest)
• **46**

Insider Activity
• **NA**

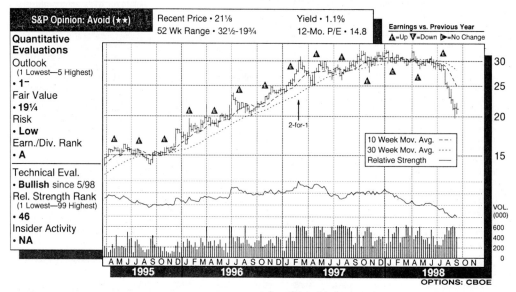

2-for-1

10 Week Mov. Avg. ---
30 Week Mov. Avg. ----
Relative Strength ——

VOL.
(000)

OPTIONS: CBOE

Overview - 28-JUL-98

We expect total sales to advance 3% to 5% in the last quarter of FY 98 (Sep.), primarily driven by new product introductions, international expansion and strategic acquisitions. Sales at Sally Beauty should grow about 10%, driven by new store openings and same-store sales gains in the mid-single-digit range. In FY 99, the company anticipates growing sales by 7.0% per year via focusing on its advertising and promotion areas, without any significant product introductions. As a result of the emphasis on increasing its sales growth rate, ACV believes its profitability will grow more slowly than its 10% expected growth rate in FY 98. Also, the company's fast growing Sally operation may experience weaker profitability as the company aggressively expands this concept. Although gross margins should continue to widen on improved efficiencies, ACV will continue to redeploy savings into increased investment in marketing and advertising for the company's best known and most profitable brands and new products.

Valuation - 28-JUL-98

We recently downgraded ACV shares to avoid from hold based on management's expectation of lower profitability in the next few quarters. Also, it's not apparent that management will be able to readily achieve its goal of 7.0% sales growth in FY 99, as ACV operates in a highly competitive industry. In anticipation of lower profitability, we are lowering our earnings estimates to $1.36 for FY 98 and $1.45 in FY 99. At 19 times our FY 99 EPS estimate, the shares are trading at a multiple nearly twice the company's expected earnings growth rate over the next year, and should be avoided as any recent earnings disappointments have been punished by a skittish market.

Key Stock Statistics

S&P EPS Est. 1998	1.36	Tang. Bk. Value/Share	5.63
P/E on S&P Est. 1998	15.5	Beta	0.78
S&P EPS Est. 1999	1.45	Shareholders	2,300
Dividend Rate/Share	0.24	Market cap. (B)	$0.700
Shs. outstg. (M)	55.1	Inst. holdings	23%
Avg. daily vol. (M)	0.127		

Value of $10,000 invested 5 years ago: $ 17,467

Fiscal Year Ending Sep. 30

	1998	1997	1996	1995	1994	1993
Revenues (Million $)						
1Q	445.4	426.1	347.6	311.5	284.6	269.0
2Q	455.2	439.6	396.1	324.2	302.8	288.5
3Q	467.5	456.2	415.6	357.7	315.0	289.6
4Q	—	453.4	431.1	364.9	313.7	300.5
Yr.	—	1,775	1,590	1,358	1,216	1,148
Earnings Per Share ($)						
1Q	**0.32**	0.30	0.23	0.20	0.20	0.15
2Q	**0.32**	0.31	0.26	0.22	0.17	0.20
3Q	**0.35**	0.33	0.29	0.24	0.22	0.17
4Q	**E0.35**	0.38	0.34	0.28	0.25	0.20
Yr.	**E1.36**	1.32	1.11	0.94	0.79	0.72

Next earnings report expected: late October

Dividend Data (Dividends have been paid since 1967.)

Amount ($)	Date Decl.	Ex-Div. Date	Stock of Record	Payment Date
0.050	Oct. 23	Oct. 30	Nov. 03	Nov. 20 '97
0.060	Jan. 22	Jan. 29	Feb. 02	Feb. 20 '98
0.060	Apr. 23	Apr. 30	May. 04	May. 20 '98
0.060	Jul. 23	Jul. 30	Aug. 03	Aug. 20 '98

Business Summary - 28-JUL-98

Alberto-Culver is best known for its very first product, Alberto VO5 conditioning hairdressing (a formidable weapon in the fight against the "bad hair day"). Today, almost half the company's revenues are generated by its Sally Beauty professional beauty supplies segment. Alberto-Culver's major lines of health and beauty care products include Alberto VO5, TRESemme and CON-SORT hair care, FDS feminine deodorant sprays, and TCB hair care products. Recent new products include Cortexx shampoo and conditioner, Consort Hair Regrowth System, and TCB Relax and Color.

In February 1996, ACV acquired St. Ives Laboratories, makers of Swiss Formula hair and skin care products. The Consumer Products division, which includes heath and beauty products as well as food and household items, accounted for 50% of FY 97 (Sep.) sales. Consumer products also include Mrs. Dash seasonings, Molly McButter, SugarTwin and Static Guard. In July 1996, the company sold its institutional food lines and granted partial market distribution rights to the buyer;

the company continues to own, manufacture and market the brands to retail customers.

Outside the U.S., Alberto-Culver International sells in more than 120 countries; in addition to Alberto VO5 and Swiss Formula, products sold internationally include bandages, antacids, salt substitute and artificial sweetener, liquid soap, anti-perspirants and cologne, shampoo and shower products, home permanents and detergents. Major international markets include the United Kingdom, Europe, Australia, Canada, China, Hong Kong, Italy, Mexico, New Zealand and Puerto Rico.

Sally Beauty stores (50% of FY 97 sales) are self-service cash-and-carry professional beauty supply stores, located primarily in shopping centers. Since 1969, Sally Beauty has grown from a chain of six stores to become the world leader in the distribution of professional beauty supplies with over 1,830 stores in the United States, United Kingdom, Germany and Japan. For the past several years, Sally Beauty has opened approximately 120-150 new stores annually, and expects to continue at this level for the foreseeable future. It also believes that there are significant international opportunities in both existing and new markets.

Per Share Data ($)

(Year Ended Sep. 30)	1997	1996	1995	1994	1993	1992	1991	1990	1989	1988
Tangible Bk. Val.	5.57	4.33	5.08	4.92	4.36	3.96	3.62	3.78	2.77	2.33
Cash Flow	2.02	1.57	1.32	1.09	1.00	0.95	0.73	0.84	0.71	0.64
Earnings	1.32	1.11	0.94	0.79	0.72	0.68	0.53	0.65	0.56	0.50
Dividends	0.20	0.17	0.15	0.14	0.14	0.12	0.11	0.10	0.09	0.07
Payout Ratio	15%	16%	16%	18%	19%	17%	20%	16%	15%	14%
Prices - High	32½	25	18¼	13¾	14⅛	16	17⅛	16⅝	13⅜	9⅝
- Low	23⅝	16¼	13	9¾	10	10⅝	10¼	9⅝	8¼	4⅞
P/E Ratio - High	25	23	19	17	20	24	32	26	24	19
- Low	18	15	14	12	14	16	19	15	15	10

Income Statement Analysis (Million $)

	1997	1996	1995	1994	1993	1992	1991	1990	1989	1988
Revs.	1,775	1,590	1,358	1,216	1,148	1,091	874	796	717	605
Oper. Inc.	159	138	111	94.2	88.7	85.0	61.3	68.8	60.0	50.7
Depr.	30.2	26.0	20.8	17.2	16.2	15.5	11.4	10.1	7.7	7.5
Int. Exp.	11.8	16.0	10.0	8.6	9.7	11.7	6.8	7.9	8.0	5.9
Pretax Inc.	136	100	84.2	71.1	65.1	61.4	48.1	54.7	47.2	44.0
Eff. Tax Rate	37%	37%	37%	38%	37%	37%	37%	36%	38%	39%
Net Inc.	85.4	62.7	52.7	44.1	41.3	38.6	30.1	35.0	29.4	26.9

Balance Sheet & Other Fin. Data (Million $)

	1997	1996	1995	1994	1993	1992	1991	1990	1989	1988
Cash	76.0	71.6	146	50.4	73.9	80.2	84.6	75.0	39.3	34.1
Curr. Assets	580	513	537	402	401	412	404	329	256	217
Total Assets	1,000	909	815	610	593	610	574	437	363	303
Curr. Liab.	311	287	235	216	196	219	192	137	128	122
LT Debt	149	162	183	43.0	80.2	84.5	97.8	60.7	68.9	44.8
Common Eqty.	497	425	371	327	299	286	249	231	160	135
Total Cap.	672	603	567	385	388	378	372	296	233	181
Cap. Exp.	58.2	41.0	31.0	26.2	26.4	21.8	29.7	14.4	17.8	19.7
Cash Flow	116	88.9	73.5	61.3	57.5	54.1	41.5	45.1	37.1	34.4
Curr. Ratio	1.9	1.8	2.3	1.9	2.0	1.9	2.1	2.4	2.0	1.8
% LT Debt of Cap.	22.2	26.9	32.2	11.2	20.7	22.4	26.3	20.5	29.5	24.8
% Net Inc.of Revs.	4.8	4.0	3.9	3.6	3.6	3.5	3.4	4.4	4.1	4.4
% Ret. on Assets	8.9	7.3	7.4	7.4	6.9	6.5	6.0	8.4	8.8	9.6
% Ret. on Equity	18.5	15.8	15.1	14.2	14.2	14.3	12.6	17.3	19.9	20.7

Data as orig. reptd.; bef. results of disc. opers. and/or spec. items. Per share data adj. for stk. divs. as of ex-div. date. Bold denotes diluted EPS (FASB 128). E-Estimated. NA-Not Available. NM-Not Meaningful. NR-Not Ranked.

Office—2525 Armitage Ave., Melrose Park, IL 60160. **Tel**—(708) 450-3000. **Website**—http://www.alberto.com **Chrmn**—L. H. Lavin. **Pres & CEO**—H. B. Bernick. **VP, Secy & Treas**—B. E. Lavin. **Investor Contact**—Daniel B. Stone. **Dirs**—A. R. Abboud, A. G. Atwater, C. L. Bernick, H. B. Bernick, R. P. Gwinn, L. W. Jennings, B. E. Lavin, L. H. Lavin, A. B. Muchin, R. H. Rock, W. C. Stone, H. M. Visotsky, W. W. Wirtz. **Transfer Agent & Registrar**—First National Bank of Boston. **Incorporated**—in Delaware in 1961. **Empl**— 11,000. **S&P Analyst:** Robert J. Izmirlian

Albertson's, Inc.   50

NYSE Symbol **ABS**

In S&P 500

12-SEP-98

Industry:
Retail (Food Chains)

Summary: This operator of supermarkets and combination food-drug stores, the fourth largest U.S. food retailer, operates 930 stores in 24 states.

S&P Opinion: Accumulate (★★★★)

Recent Price • 51	Yield • 1.3%
52 Wk Range • 54⅞-32⅞	12-Mo. P/E • 23.4

Quantitative Evaluations

Outlook
(1 Lowest—5 Highest)
• **2+**

Fair Value
• **52¾**

Risk
• **Average**

Earn./Div. Rank
• **A+**

Technical Eval.
• **Bullish** since 10/97

Rel. Strength Rank
(1 Lowest—99 Highest)
• **91**

Insider Activity
• **Neutral**

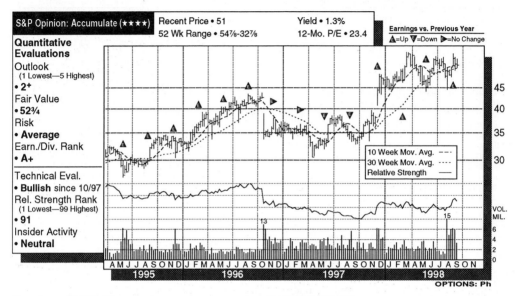

Earnings vs. Previous Year
▲=Up ▼=Down ▶=No Change

10 Week Mov. Avg. – – –
30 Week Mov. Avg. · · · · ·
Relative Strength —

OPTIONS: Ph

Overview - 09-SEP-98

Albertson's strives to grow via a combination of acquisitions and organic store development. To this end, ABS expects to open approximately 60 new stores and remodel another 31 units in FY 99 (Jan.). ABS recently acquired 15 Bruno's stores and is in the process of completing the acquisition of Buttrey Food and Drug Stores Co. In a more significant move, Albertson's recently agreed to acquire American Stores (NYSE: ASC) in a transaction that would result in the creation of the largest U.S. food and drug retailer, with $36 billion in annual sales and over 2,470 stores. The merger should enable ABS to enhance profits via a stronger market position in California, more purchasing power and the elimination of many redundant overhead costs.

Valuation - 09-SEP-98

We continue to rate ABS shares accumulate, and expect its earnings growth rate to increase after the planned merger with American Stores. The combined entities are expected to achieve cost savings of $100 million in the first year, ramping up to $300 million after the third year. Since the merger will not be completed until early 1999, we expect ABS to earn $2.30 in FY 99 (Jan.). However, on a pro forma basis, we estimate that the combined companies would have earned $1.88 in FY 98 and project earnings to grow to $2.25 in FY 99 and $2.50 in FY 2000, giving the merged companies a better than 10% earnings growth rate. We recommend that investors considering ABS for purchase opt for ASC shares (in the merger transaction, ASC shareholders will receive 0.63 ABS shares for each ASC share held) as they were recently trading at a 6.6% discount to their implied takeover price, and see it as a cheaper entry vehicle into ABS stock.

Key Stock Statistics

S&P EPS Est. 1999	2.30	Tang. Bk. Value/Share	10.06
P/E on S&P Est. 1999	22.2	Beta	0.21
S&P EPS Est. 2000	2.50	Shareholders	18,000
Dividend Rate/Share	0.68	Market cap. (B)	$ 12.5
Shs. outstg. (M)	245.5	Inst. holdings	48%
Avg. daily vol. (M)	1.191		

Value of $10,000 invested 5 years ago: $ 22,086

Fiscal Year Ending Jan. 31

	1999	1998	1997	1996	1995	1994
Revenues (Million $)						
1Q	3,848	3,608	3,344	3,083	2,910	2,720
2Q	3,995	3,681	3,481	3,119	2,988	2,768
3Q	—	3,612	3,376	3,104	2,928	2,734
4Q	—	3,789	3,576	3,279	3,069	3,062
Yr.	—	14,690	13,777	12,585	11,895	11,284
Earnings Per Share ($)						
1Q	**0.45**	**0.43**	0.45	0.39	0.34	0.29
2Q	**0.52**	**0.44**	0.48	0.42	0.37	0.30
3Q	**E0.56**	**0.50**	0.42	0.42	0.37	0.25
4Q	**E0.77**	**0.71**	0.61	0.61	0.57	0.50
Yr.	**E2.30**	**2.08**	1.96	1.84	1.65	1.34

Next earnings report expected: late November

Dividend Data (Dividends have been paid since 1960.)

Amount ($)	Date Decl.	Ex-Div. Date	Stock of Record	Payment Date
0.160	Dec. 01	Jan. 28	Jan. 30	Feb. 25 '98
0.170	Mar. 02	Apr. 29	May. 01	May. 25 '98
0.170	May. 21	Jul. 29	Jul. 31	Aug. 25 '98
0.170	Aug. 31	Oct. 28	Oct. 30	Nov. 25 '98

A Division of The McGraw-Hill Companies

Business Summary - 09-SEP-98

In August 1998, Albertson's agreed to acquire American Stores (NYSE: ASC) via an exchange of stock, with ASC shareholders to receive 0.63 of an ABS share for each ASC share. The transaction, initially valued at $11.7 billion, including assumption of debt, is expected to close in early 1999. With more than 910 stores in 22 states in the West, Midwest and South and annual sales approaching $15 billion, ABS is one of the largest U.S. retail food and drug chains.

The majority of the company's stores (878 locations at January 29, 1998) are combination food-drug stores that range in size from 35,000 sq. ft. to 82,000 sq. ft., and offer prescription drugs and an expanded selection of cosmetics and nonfoods in addition to specialty departments such as service seafood and meat, bakery, lobby/video, service delicatessen and floral.

Its 72 conventional supermarkets range in size from 15,000 sq. ft. to 35,000 sq. ft., and offer a full selection of basic grocery, meat, produce and dairy items as well as a limited selection of nonfood merchandise. Many have an in-store bakery and a service delicatessen.

Albertson's also operates 38 warehouse stores under the Max Food and Drug name. These no-frills stores average 17,000 sq. ft. to 73,000 sq. ft., and offer significant savings on meat and produce, and the convenience of bulk packaging.

ABS's long-term aim is to increase net earnings 15% annually. Part of this growth is expected to come from an aggressive store opening and remodeling program. ABS has actively pursued an expansion program of adding new retail stores, enlarging and remodeling existing stores, and replacing smaller ones. About 95% of its retail square footage was opened or remodeled in the past 10 years. In FY 98 (Jan.), ABS opened 64 new stores, including four stores that were acquired, completed 35 remodels, and closed 12 stores, for a net addition of 3 million sq. ft. of retail space. New stores generally consist of combination food-drug stores with 55,000 sq. ft. to 67,000 sq. ft., and a limited number of 40,000 sq. ft. stores for smaller cities or smaller land parcels. Excluding acquisitions, expansion plans for FY 99 call for the addition of 65 new stores and 50 remodels.

In addition to new store development, ABS intends to boost sales by offering a number of customer-focused programs aimed at meeting the changing needs of busy consumers by adding value to their shopping trip. Initiatives include Quick Fixin Ideas, consisting of heat and serve entrees in the service deli and complete meal recipes and value added products in the produce, meat and frozen food departments; expansion of the pharmacy business; and addition of special services such as in-store banking.

Per Share Data ($)

(Year Ended Jan. 31)	1998	1997	1996	1995	1994	1993	1992	1991	1990	1989
Tangible Bk. Val.	9.85	8.95	7.75	6.65	5.48	5.24	4.54	4.06	3.46	2.99
Cash Flow	3.41	0.92	2.83	2.54	2.11	1.70	1.47	1.33	1.14	0.94
Earnings	2.08	1.96	1.84	1.65	1.34	1.04	0.97	0.88	0.73	0.61
Dividends	0.64	0.60	0.52	0.53	0.35	0.31	0.27	0.23	0.18	0.14
Payout Ratio	31%	31%	28%	32%	26%	30%	28%	26%	25%	22%
Cal. Yrs.	1997	1996	1995	1994	1993	1992	1991	1990	1989	1988
Prices - High	48⅝	43¾	34⅝	30⅞	29⅝	26¾	25¾	18⅞	15⅛	9¾
- Low	30½	31½	27¼	25⅛	23⅜	18⅜	16⅜	12¼	9⅛	6
P/E Ratio - High	23	22	19	19	22	26	26	22	21	16
- Low	15	16	15	15	19	18	17	14	13	10

Income Statement Analysis (Million $)

Revs.	14,690	13,777	12,585	11,895	11,284	10,174	8,680	8,219	7,423	6,773
Oper. Inc.	1,221	1,144	1,059	961	826	695	548	498	428	349
Depr.	329	294	251	226	197	172	134	122	108	88.0
Int. Exp.	83.0	71.0	63.1	66.1	55.2	47.7	28.1	29.0	25.8	22.6
Pretax Inc.	827	795	759	679	552	444	406	366	310	257
Eff. Tax Rate	37%	38%	39%	39%	39%	38%	37%	36%	37%	37%
Net Inc.	517	494	465	417	340	276	258	234	197	163

Balance Sheet & Other Fin. Data (Million $)

Cash	108	91.0	69.1	50.0	62.0	40.0	34.0	23.0	44.0	82.0
Curr. Assets	1,628	1,476	1,283	1,190	1,122	1,013	751	677	668	592
Total Assets	5,219	4,715	4,136	3,622	3,295	2,946	2,216	2,014	1,863	1,591
Curr. Liab.	1,276	1,055	1,088	1,095	990	816	652	586	555	488
LT Debt	1,131	1,052	732	512	665	508	152	159	218	177
Common Eqty.	2,462	2,247	1,953	1,688	1,389	1,388	1,199	1,088	929	800
Total Cap.	3,567	3,315	2,686	2,202	2,083	1,917	1,360	1,259	1,170	990
Cap. Exp.	674	673	656	473	456	331	273	255	303	327
Cash Flow	846	788	716	644	536	448	392	356	305	251
Curr. Ratio	1.3	1.4	1.2	1.1	1.1	1.2	1.2	1.2	1.2	1.2
% LT Debt of Cap.	31.7	31.8	27.3	23.3	31.9	26.5	11.1	12.6	18.7	17.9
% Net Inc.of Revs.	3.5	3.6	3.7	3.5	3.0	2.7	3.0	2.8	2.6	2.4
% Ret. on Assets	10.4	11.2	12.0	12.1	11.1	10.7	12.3	12.1	11.4	10.8
% Ret. on Equity	21.8	23.6	25.5	27.1	25.0	21.3	22.7	23.2	22.7	22.1

Data as orig. reptd.; bef. results of disc. opers. and/or spec. items. Per share data adj. for stk. divs. as of ex-div. date. Bold denotes diluted EPS (FASB 128). E-Estimated. NA-Not Available. NM-Not Meaningful. NR-Not Ranked.

Office—250 Parkcenter Blvd., P.O. Box 20, Boise, ID 83726. **Tel**—(208) 385-6200. **Chrmn & CEO**—G. G. Michael. **Pres & COO**—R. L. King. **SVP-Fin & CFO**—A. C. Olson. **VP & Treas**—J. Danielson. **Secy**—Kaye L. O'Riordan. **Investor Contact**—Renee Bergquist. **Dirs**—K. Albertson, A. G. Ames, C. D. Andrus, J. B. Carley, P. I. Corddry, J. B. Fery, C. A. Johnson, C. D. Lein, W. E. McCain, G. G. Michael, B. Rivera, J. B. Scott, T. L. Stevens Jr., W. M. Storey, S. D. Symms. **Transfer Agents & Registrars**—ChaseMellon Shareholder Services, NYC; West One Bank Idaho, Boise. **Incorporated**—in Idaho in 1945; reincorporated in Delaware in 1969. **Empl**— 94,000. **S&P Analyst:** Robert J. Izmirlian

Alcan Aluminium   51

NYSE Symbol **AL**

In S&P 500

12-SEP-98   **Industry:** Aluminum

Summary: Alcan, one of the world's largest aluminum producers from smelting facilities located mainly in Canada, serves a wide geographic range of markets.

S&P Opinion: Hold (★★★)

Recent Price • 22¾	Yield • 2.6%
52 Wk Range • 36-18⅝	12-Mo. P/E • 12.9

Quantitative Evaluations

Outlook (1 Lowest—5 Highest)
• 4

Fair Value
• 27⅝

Risk
• Low

Earn./Div. Rank
• B-

Technical Eval.
• **Bullish** since 5/98

Rel. Strength Rank (1 Lowest—99 Highest)
• 70

Insider Activity
• NA

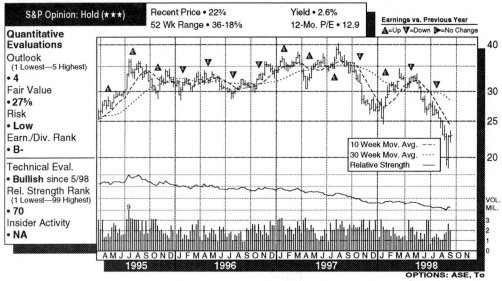

Earnings vs. Previous Year
▲=Up ▼=Down ▶=No Change

10 Week Mov. Avg. ---
30 Week Mov. Avg. ····
Relative Strength ——

VOL. MIL.

OPTIONS: ASE, To

Overview - 11-AUG-98

We project flat revenues in 1998, as gains in volume are offset by lower aluminum prices. As a result of lower aluminum prices and a less favorable product mix, margins are expected to contract and lead to a decline in operating profit and EPS. Assuming a rebound in aluminum prices in 1999, margins and EPS should rebound in 1999.

Valuation - 11-AUG-98

Although Alcan appears very attractive based on valuation, we are maintaining our neutral rating on the shares following second quarter EPS. Among all of the aluminum companies we follow, Alcan was the only company to fall short of the consensus estimate; every other company achieved or exceeded second quarter consensus estimates despite depressed aluminum prices. Lower ingot prices and an unfavorable mix accounted for the poor EPS relative to its peers. Thus, with aluminum prices still under pressure, we would not add to holdings despite the attractiveness of the shares. However, we believe the stock could stage a strong rebound once aluminum prices recover. Aluminum prices appear to be unsustainably low, in view of the supply/ demand fundamentals. As of August 6, 1998, inventories on the London Metal Exchange (LME) totaled 469,250 metric tons, versus 621,975 metric tons in August 1997. Currently, LME inventories are at their lowest level since 1991. Meanwhile, demand appears firm with lower demand in Asia being offset by strength in North America and Europe. Nonetheless, aluminum prices (mid-West delivered) were $0.63/lb. as of early August 1998, versus an average of $0.8275/lb. in August 1997. We expect to see higher prices in 1999 and this will help boost Alcan and the other aluminum stocks. Current owners should maintain positions on that basis.

Key Stock Statistics

S&P EPS Est. 1998	1.90	Tang. Bk. Value/Share	23.05
P/E on S&P Est. 1998	12.0	Beta	1.32
S&P EPS Est. 1999	2.85	Shareholders	22,000
Dividend Rate/Share	0.60	Market cap. (B)	$ 5.2
Shs. outstg. (M)	227.5	Inst. holdings	55%
Avg. daily vol. (M)	0.409		

Value of $10,000 invested 5 years ago: $ 14,292

Fiscal Year Ending Dec. 31

	1998	1997	1996	1995	1994	1993
Revenues (Million $)						
1Q	1,953	1,898	2,015	2,455	1,786	1,731
2Q	1,986	2,011	1,972	2,449	2,059	1,858
3Q	—	1,965	1,881	2,288	2,139	1,813
4Q	—	1,972	1,821	2,195	2,232	1,830
Yr.	—	7,865	7,689	9,387	8,216	7,232
Earnings Per Share ($)						
1Q	0.50	0.62	0.53	0.75	-0.13	-0.11
2Q	0.37	0.50	0.47	0.77	0.01	-0.18
3Q	E0.45	0.34	0.43	0.61	0.27	-0.08
4Q	E0.58	0.56	0.31	0.17	0.19	-0.17
Yr.	E1.90	2.02	1.74	2.30	0.34	-0.54

Next earnings report expected: early October

Dividend Data (Dividends have been paid since 1939.)

Amount ($)	Date Decl.	Ex-Div. Date	Stock of Record	Payment Date
0.150	Oct. 23	Nov. 18	Nov. 20	Dec. 19 '97
0.150	Feb. 12	Feb. 19	Feb. 23	Mar. 20 '98
0.150	Apr. 23	May. 18	May. 20	Jun. 19 '98
0.150	Jul. 23	Aug. 18	Aug. 20	Sep. 21 '98

A Division of The McGraw-Hill Companies

Business Summary - 11-AUG-98

Alcan, the world's second largest aluminum company, is engaged in all aspects of the aluminum industry. Operations include the mining of bauxite, the basic aluminum ore; the refining of bauxite into alumina, an intermediate raw material; the smelting of primary aluminum from alumina; the recycling of aluminum scrap and the transformation of primary aluminum into fabricated and semi-fabricated products.

Operating data (in metric tons) for recent years:

	1997	1996
Fabricated product shipments	1,694,000	1,539,000
Ingot shipments	858,000	810,000
Fabrication of customer owned metal	276,000	258,000
Total aluminum shipments	2,828,000	2,607,000
Alumina shipments	1,679,000	1,585,000
Average aluminum price (lbs.)	$0.73	$0.70
Primary aluminum production	1,429,000	1,407,000
Secondary/recycled production	670,000	639,000

The company's raw materials and chemicals segment consists mostly of alumina production. Alcan is a major supplier of alumina to other aluminum producers.

The primary metals unit produces primary aluminum or ingot for sale to other aluminum makers or fabricators and to the company's own operations.

Fabricated products operations account for the bulk of Alcan's revenues (73% in 1997 and 1996). Flat rolled aluminum sheet and foil comprise 85% of the volume in the fabricated products unit. Beverage can and packaging are the main market for flat roll products. Other important markets are construction, electrical equipment, transportation and independent distributors.

Alcan's main competitors in the aluminum industry are Alcoa, Alumax Inc, Kaiser Aluminum, Pechiney and Reynolds Metals. Aluminum faces stiff competition from plastics (PET) in the beverage can market and from steel, ceramics and glass in other applications. Aluminum's brightest prospects are in motor vehicle applications where demand for weight savings is helping it displace steel. However, competition will remain intense as steelmakers continue to introduce thinner, higher strength steel sheet to compete with aluminum for weight reduction. Global overcapacity is another major challenge to the aluminum industry.

In February 1998, Alcan said that it would construct a 375,000 ton smelter in Alma, Quebec to replace the existing Isle Maligne smelter which is also located in Alma. The total cost of the new smelter is estimated at $1.6 billion, and construction is expected to take a period of 40 months.

Shipments for 1998's second quarter totaled 748,000 metric tons, versus 737,000 metric tons in the 1997 period. Average realized prices for ingot were $0.72/lb., versus $0.80/lb. in 1997; the average realized price for fabricated products was $1.33/lb., versus $1.36/lb. in 1997.

Per Share Data ($)

(Year Ended Dec. 31)	1997	1996	1995	1994	1993	1992	1991	1990	1989	1988
Tangible Bk. Val.	22.35	20.53	19.84	19.17	18.28	19.06	21.17	22.19	20.30	18.06
Cash Flow	3.94	3.72	4.28	2.26	1.43	1.40	1.67	4.08	5.84	6.20
Earnings	2.02	1.74	2.30	0.34	-0.54	-0.60	-0.25	2.33	3.58	3.85
Dividends	0.60	0.60	0.45	0.30	0.30	0.45	0.86	1.12	1.12	0.59
Payout Ratio	30%	34%	20%	88%	NM	NM	NM	48%	31%	15%
Prices - High	40¼	36⅛	36⅝	28⅛	22⅜	22¾	24	24½	25⅛	22¼
- Low	26	28⅜	23⅜	19¾	16⅞	15¼	18	16⅝	20⅛	15⅝
P/E Ratio - High	20	21	16	83	NM	NM	NM	11	7	6
- Low	13	16	10	58	NM	NM	NM	7	6	4

Income Statement Analysis (Million $)

	1997	1996	1995	1994	1993	1992	1991	1990	1989	1988
Revs.	7,777	7,614	9,287	8,216	7,232	7,596	7,748	8,757	8,839	8,529
Oper. Inc.	1,266	1,216	1,494	876	590	575	527	952	1,421	1,800
Depr.	436	431	447	431	443	449	429	393	333	316
Int. Exp.	101	125	206	235	229	267	286	263	180	150
Pretax Inc.	730	636	879	211	-117	-123	-139	670	1,201	1,450
Eff. Tax Rate	35%	35%	39%	53%	NM	NM	NM	19%	29%	34%
Net Inc.	468	410	543	96.0	-103	-111	-36.0	543	835	931

Balance Sheet & Other Fin. Data (Million $)

	1997	1996	1995	1994	1993	1992	1991	1990	1989	1988
Cash	608	546	66.0	27.0	81.0	149	205	200	247	670
Curr. Assets	3,241	3,113	3,005	2,821	2,402	2,655	3,070	3,370	3,471	3,770
Total Assets	9,466	9,325	9,702	9,989	9,810	10,146	10,816	10,649	9,508	8,615
Curr. Liab.	1,424	1,303	1,449	1,384	1,335	1,545	1,960	2,148	2,095	1,655
LT Debt	1,241	1,319	1,711	2,206	2,322	2,287	2,185	1,796	1,079	1,199
Common Eqty.	4,871	4,661	4,482	4,308	4,096	4,266	4,730	4,942	4,610	4,109
Total Cap.	7,327	7,252	7,553	7,809	7,729	7,909	8,337	8,109	7,020	6,598
Cap. Exp.	641	482	390	264	251	389	819	1,255	1,273	660
Cash Flow	894	841	966	506	321	314	373	914	1,147	1,217
Curr. Ratio	2.3	2.4	2.1	2.0	1.8	1.7	1.6	1.6	1.7	2.3
% LT Debt of Cap.	16.9	18.2	22.7	28.2	30.0	28.9	26.2	22.1	15.4	18.2
% Net Inc.of Revs.	6.0	5.4	5.8	1.2	NM	NM	NM	6.2	9.4	10.9
% Ret. on Assets	5.0	4.3	5.5	1.0	NM	NM	NM	5.4	9.2	11.7
% Ret. on Equity	9.6	9.0	11.8	1.8	NM	NM	NM	11.0	18.7	23.9

Data as orig. reptd.; bef. results of disc. opers. and/or spec. items. Per share data adj. for stk. divs. as of ex-div. date. Bold denotes diluted EPS (FASB 128). E-Estimated. NA-Not Available. NM-Not Meaningful. NR-Not Ranked.

Office—1188 Sherbrooke Street West, Montreal, QC, H3A 3G2. **Tel**—(514) 848-8000. **Website**—http://www.alcan.com **Pres & CEO**—J. Bougie. **VP & CFO**—S. Thadhani. **VP & Secy**—P. K. Pal. **Investor Contact**—Alan G. Brown. **Dirs**—J. R. Evans (Chrmn), S. I. Bata, W. R. C. Blundell, J. Bougie, W. Chippindale, D. T. Engen, A. E. Gotlieb, J. E. Newall, P. H. Pearse, G. Russell, G. Saint-Pierre, G. Schulmeyer. **Transfer Agents**—CIBC Mellon Trust Co., Montreal, Winnipeg, Regina, Calgary, Vancouver and Toronto, Canada, and London, England; ChaseMellon Shareholder Services, L.L.C., NYC. **Incorporated**—in Canada in 1928. **Empl**— 33,000. **S&P Analyst:** Leo J. Larkin

Allegheny Teledyne   57K
NYSE Symbol **ALT**
In S&P 500

12-SEP-98

Industry:
Iron & Steel

Summary: ALT, formed via the August 1996 merger of Allegheny Ludlum and Teledyne, produces specialty metals, and aviation, electronics, industrial and consumer products.

S&P Opinion: Avoid (★★)	Recent Price • 15¼	Yield • 4.2%
	52 Wk Range • 32⅞-14	12-Mo. P/E • 11.2

Quantitative Evaluations

Outlook
(1 Lowest—5 Highest)
• **1**⁻

Fair Value
• **14¾**

Risk
• **Low**

Earn./Div. Rank
• **NR**

Technical Eval.
• **Neutral** since 6/98

Rel. Strength Rank
(1 Lowest—99 Highest)
• **33**

Insider Activity
• **NA**

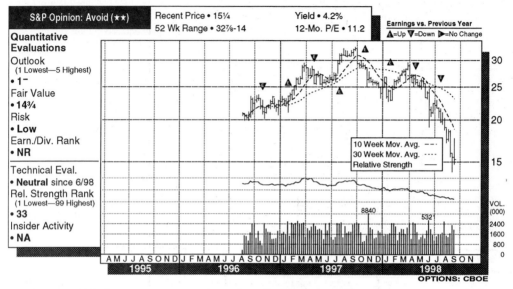

Earnings vs. Previous Year
▲=Up ▼=Down ▶=No Change

10 Week Mov. Avg. ---
30 Week Mov. Avg. ····
Relative Strength —

OPTIONS: CBOE

Overview - 12-AUG-98

Revenues should increase 5% in 1998, reflecting the acquisition of Oregon Metallurgical and Sheffield Forgemasters. Overall operating margins will be down, on persistent weakness in stainless steel and less robust growth from high performance metals. Consequently, both operating and reported EPS will likely trail those of 1997.

Valuation - 12-AUG-98

On August 10, 1998, we downgraded ALT to avoid from hold based on our expectation of continued weakness in stainless steel prices. Stainless prices have been under immense pressure in 1997 and 1998 as a result of rising imports. Through May 1998 (latest available data), stainless steel imports were up 26%. In response to this onslaught, U. S. stainless steelmakers filed anti-dumping suits in early June 1998. Subsequently, on August 5, ALT announced that it would hike prices 4% to 6% on selected products for shipments effective October 5, 1998. Within days of the announcement, two other domestic producers announced similar price hikes. Filing the trade cases will likely lead to a reduced level of imports near term but we doubt the market is strong enough to sustain the proposed hikes. Also, distributor inventories are high and there is a seasonal tendency for distributors to keep inventories low in the last quarter of the year. Thus, we doubt price increases could be sustained until 1999's first quarter at the earliest. Even through recent acquisitions will reduce the amount of stainless steel as a percent of ALT's total sales, the shares are still very sensitive to pricing fluctuations in the stainless steel market. Consequenlty, we think the stock is vulnerable near term despite its attractive yield.

Key Stock Statistics

S&P EPS Est. 1998	1.30	Tang. Bk. Value/Share	5.34
P/E on S&P Est. 1998	11.7	Beta	1.11
S&P EPS Est. 1999	1.70	Shareholders	9,300
Dividend Rate/Share	0.64	Market cap. (B)	$ 3.0
Shs. outstg. (M)	197.0	Inst. holdings	56%
Avg. daily vol. (M)	0.375		

Value of $10,000 invested 5 years ago: NA

Fiscal Year Ending Dec. 31

	1998	1997	1996	1995	1994	1993
Revenues (Million $)						
1Q	1,002	957.9	1,018	1,021	887.0	926.0
2Q	983.4	957.1	997.7	1,097	768.0	904.0
3Q	—	909.2	880.0	967.0	840.0	860.0
4Q	—	920.9	920.3	977.0	973.0	901.0
Yr.	—	3,745	3,816	4,062	3,468	3,592
Earnings Per Share ($)						
1Q	**0.14**	**0.35**	0.46	0.53	—	—
2Q	**0.38**	**0.49**	0.34	0.39	—	—
3Q	**E0.33**	**0.36**	0.11	0.37	—	—
4Q	**E0.45**	**0.47**	0.38	0.28	—	—
Yr.	**E1.30**	**1.67**	1.27	1.57	0.06	0.83

Next earnings report expected: late October

Dividend Data (Dividends have been paid since 1996.)

Amount ($)	Date Decl.	Ex-Div. Date	Stock of Record	Payment Date
0.160	Oct. 23	Nov. 12	Nov. 14	Nov. 28 '97
0.160	Feb. 12	Feb. 26	Mar. 02	Mar. 17 '98
0.160	May. 14	May. 28	Jun. 01	Jun. 16 '98
0.160	Aug. 13	Aug. 27	Aug. 31	Sep. 15 '98

A Division of The McGraw-Hill Companies

Allegheny Teledyne Incorporated

Business Summary - 12-AUG-98

Allegheny Teledyne, Inc. is a diversified manufacturer of specialty metals, aviation, electronics, industrial and consumer products. The company was formed through the merger of Allegheny Ludlum Corp. and Teledyne, Inc. on August 15, 1996. Contributions by segment in 1997 were:

	Revs.	Profits
Specialty metals	53%	59%
Aerospace and electronics	25%	20%
Industrial	15%	13%
Consumer	7%	8%

Foreign sales accounted for 17% of 1997's total, while sales under contract with the U. S. government, including defense, comprised 14%.

Specialty metals operations comprise stainless steel, silicon electrical steels and other specialty metals. Stainless steel products are sold in the form of sheet, strip and plate, as well as stampings and welded tubing. Commodity and premium stainless steel accounted for 24.8% of total sales in 1997. Silicon electrical steel products are used primarily in applications in which electrical conductivity and magnetic properties are important. Other specialty metals include high-speed and

tool steels, high-temperature alloys, zirconium, titanium, tungsten and molybdenum.

Companies in the aerospace and electronics segment produce piston and turbine engines, airframe structures, unmanned aerial vehicles, target drone systems, and equipment and subsystems for spacecraft and avionics. Other products include aircraft-monitoring and control systems, relays and other electronic equipment.

The industrial segment is comprised of companies that are involved in the design and/or manufacture of material handling equipment, machine tools, dies and molds, nitrogen cylinders, specialty valves, pumps and boosters.

The consumer segment manufactures oral hygiene, shower and water purification systems, swimming pool heaters, residential and commercial heating systems, and specialty packaging for consumer products.

Because ALT's operations are so diverse and embrace so many different markets, comparisons with other companies are difficult. Competitors in specialty metals include Armco Inc., J&L Specialty Steel and Lukens Inc. For purposes of comparing overall profitability and price/earnings ratios, ALT could be viewed in relation to other New York Stock Exchange companies with diverse manufacturing operations and broad market exposure. Such companies include Dover Corp., Cooper Industries, Harsco Corp. and Illinois Tool Works.

Per Share Data ($)

(Year Ended Dec. 31)	1997	1996	1995	1994	1993	1992	1991	1990	1989	1988
Tangible Bk. Val.	4.76	3.98	4.46	NA	NA	NA	NA	NA	NA	NA
Cash Flow	2.22	1.90	2.20	0.66	1.43	NA	NA	NA	NA	NA
Earnings	1.67	1.28	1.57	0.06	0.83	NA	NA	NA	NA	NA
Dividends	0.64	0.16	NA	NA	NA	NA	NA	NA	NA	NA
Payout Ratio	38%	12%	NA	NA	NA	NA	NA	NA	NA	NA
Prices - High	32⁷/₈	23³/₄	NA	NA	NA	NA	NA	NA	NA	NA
- Low	21	19⁷/₈	NA	NA	NA	NA	NA	NA	NA	NA
P/E Ratio - High	20	19	NA	NA	NA	NA	NA	NA	NA	NA
- Low	13	16	NA	NA	NA	NA	NA	NA	NA	NA

Income Statement Analysis (Million $)

	1997	1996	1995	1994	1993	1992	1991	1990	1989	1988
Revs.	3,745	3,816	4,062	3,468	3,592	NA	NA	NA	NA	NA
Oper. Inc.	531	504	515	177	313	NA	NA	NA	NA	NA
Depr.	99	105	111	108	103	NA	NA	NA	NA	NA
Int. Exp.	19.6	48.5	NA	NA	NA	NA	NA	NA	NA	NA
Pretax Inc.	475	385	441	29.0	232	NA	NA	NA	NA	NA
Eff. Tax Rate	37%	41%	37%	66%	33%	NA	NA	NA	NA	NA
Net Inc.	298	227	277	10.0	144	NA	NA	NA	NA	NA

Balance Sheet & Other Fin. Data (Million $)

	1997	1996	1995	1994	1993	1992	1991	1990	1989	1988
Cash	50.3	62.5	135	NA	NA	NA	NA	NA	NA	NA
Curr. Assets	1,229	1,200	1,255	NA	NA	NA	NA	NA	NA	NA
Total Assets	2,605	2,606	2,620	NA	NA	NA	NA	NA	NA	NA
Curr. Liab.	562	586	614	NA	NA	NA	NA	NA	NA	NA
LT Debt	326	443	558	NA	NA	NA	NA	NA	NA	NA
Common Eqty.	1,000	872	785	NA	NA	NA	NA	NA	NA	NA
Total Cap.	1,326	1,315	1,343	NA	NA	NA	NA	NA	NA	NA
Cap. Exp.	96.3	88.6	NA	NA	NA	NA	NA	NA	NA	NA
Cash Flow	396	330	388	11.8	247	NA	NA	NA	NA	NA
Curr. Ratio	2.2	2.0	2.0	NA	NA	NA	NA	NA	NA	NA
% LT Debt of Cap.	24.6	33.7	41.5	NA	NA	NA	NA	NA	NA	NA
% Net Inc.of Revs.	7.9	6.0	6.8	0.3	4.0	NA	NA	NA	NA	NA
% Ret. on Assets	11.4	8.7	NA	NA	NA	NA	NA	NA	NA	NA
% Ret. on Equity	31.8	27.1	NA	NA	NA	NA	NA	NA	NA	NA

Data as orig. reptd., pro forma; bef. results of disc. opers. and/or spec. items. Per share data adj. for stk. divs. as of ex-div. date. Balance sheet data for 1995 as of Mar. 31, 1996. Bold denotes diluted EPS (FASB 128). E-Estimated. NA-Not Available. NM-Not Meaningful. NR-Not Ranked.

Office—1000 Six PPG Place, Pittsburgh, PA 15222-5479. **Tel**—(412) 394-2800. **Website**—http://www.alleghenyteledyne.com **Chrmn, Pres & CEO**—R. P. Simmons. **EVP & CFO**—J. L. Murdy. **SVP & Secy**—J. D. Walton. **Investor Contact**—Gary R. Stechmesser (412-394-2813). **Dirs**—A. H. Aronson, R. P. Bozzone, P. S. Brentlinger, F. V. Cahouet, D. C. Creel, C. F. Fetterolf, R. J. Groves, T. Marshall, W. C. McClelland, R. Mehrabian, W. G. Ouchi, C. J. Queenan Jr., G. A. Roberts, J. E. Rohr, R. P. Simmons. **Transfer Agent & Registrar**—ChaseMellon Shareholder Services, Ridgefield Park, NJ. **Incorporated**—in Delaware in 1996. **Empl**— 22,000. **S&P Analyst:** Leo J. Larkin

Allergan, Inc.

61

NYSE Symbol **AGN**

In S&P 500

12-SEP-98

Industry: Health Care (Diversified)

Summary: This company offers a broad line of contact lens care products, ophthalmic drug and surgical products, and treatments for dermatological and neuromuscular disorders.

S&P Opinion: Accumulate (★★★★)	Recent Price • 55¾	Yield • 0.9%
	52 Wk Range • 57⅛-31⅛	12-Mo. P/E • NM

Quantitative Evaluations

Outlook
(1 Lowest—5 Highest)
• **1**

Fair Value
• **49⅛**

Risk
• **Low**

Earn./Div. Rank
• **B+**

Technical Eval.
• **Neutral** since 5/98

Rel. Strength Rank
(1 Lowest—99 Highest)
• **98**

Insider Activity
• **Neutral**

Earnings vs. Previous Year
▲=Up ▼=Down ▶=No Change

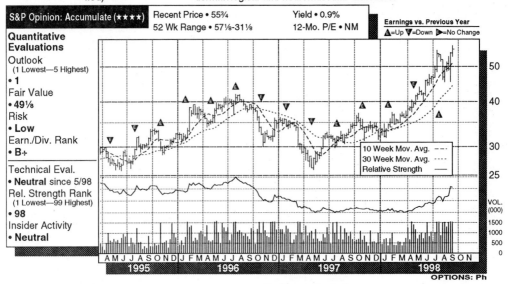

10 Week Mov. Avg. – – –
30 Week Mov. Avg. ·······
Relative Strength ——

VOL. (000)

OPTIONS: Ph

Overview - 24-AUG-98

Sales growth in 1998 is expected to be in low double digits. Despite the impact of generic competition and managed care pressures, overall volume should be helped by further robust gains in new products such as Alphagan for glaucoma, skin care products, and Botox for eye muscle disorders. Skin care product sales are being boosted by strong demand for the new Zorac/Tazorac line of retinoid treatments for psoriasis and acne, while sales of implanted intraocular lenses (IOLs) are being augmented by the new AMO/Array intraocular lens. However, sales of contact lens solutions are likely to remain under pressure as a result of declining usage of hydrogen peroxide solutions and a consumer trend toward disposable lenses. Diluted EPS are projected at $1.95 (before restructuring charges and other nonrecurring items). Further progress to $2.20 a share is projected for 1999.

Valuation - 24-AUG-98

Despite a recent pullback with the selloff in the general market, the shares were still up over 50% from the start of the year, buoyed by strength in health care stocks and significant improvement in operating earnings in recent quarters. Principal factors underlying this growth include strength in sales Botox and Alphagan drugs, new products, and benefits from a major restructuring program. Botox is benefiting from growing off-label usage of the drug as a treatment for neck muscle spasms, lower back pain and migraine, while sales of Alphagan glaucoma drug have recently outpaced those of Merck's rival Trusoft drug. New management is moving aggressively on a major restructuring program aimed at strengthening AGN's core competencies in eye care, skin care, neurological products. The shares, which are often mentioned as a possible takeover, merit accumulation.

Key Stock Statistics

S&P EPS Est. 1998	-0.27	Tang. Bk. Value/Share	7.44
P/E on S&P Est. 1998	NM	Beta	0.67
S&P EPS Est. 1999	2.20	Shareholders	13,000
Dividend Rate/Share	0.52	Market cap. (B)	$ 3.6
Shs. outstg. (M)	65.4	Inst. holdings	83%
Avg. daily vol. (M)	0.353		

Value of $10,000 invested 5 years ago: NA

Fiscal Year Ending Dec. 31

	1998	1997	1996	1995	1994	1993
Revenues (Million $)						
1Q	269.3	256.2	258.1	228.3	210.1	202.8
2Q	325.0	284.5	289.6	262.2	224.7	207.9
3Q	—	287.7	287.5	273.6	242.2	216.9
4Q	—	309.6	311.8	303.1	270.2	231.3
Yr.	—	1,138	1,148	1,067	947.2	858.9
Earnings Per Share ($)						
1Q	-1.87	0.27	0.35	0.34	0.35	0.33
2Q	0.53	0.33	0.01	-0.36	0.37	0.35
3Q	E0.46	0.66	0.26	0.53	0.47	0.43
4Q	E0.61	0.69	0.55	0.61	0.54	0.47
Yr.	E-0.27	1.95	1.17	1.12	1.73	1.58

Next earnings report expected: mid October

Dividend Data (Dividends have been paid since 1989.)

Amount ($)	Date Decl.	Ex-Div. Date	Stock of Record	Payment Date
0.130	Oct. 16	Nov. 13	Nov. 17	Dec. 08 '97
0.130	Jan. 27	Feb. 12	Feb. 17	Mar. 10 '98
0.130	Apr. 21	May. 20	May. 22	Jun. 12 '98
0.130	Jul. 21	Aug. 19	Aug. 21	Sep. 11 '98

A Division of The McGraw-Hill Companies

Business Summary - 24-AUG-98

Allergan is a leading producer of ophthalmic drugs, intraocular lenses and other ophthalmic surgical items and contact lens care solutions. Skin care and Botox drug operations are small but rapidly growing parts of the business. Formerly a division of SmithKline (now SmithKline Beecham plc), AGN became an independent public company in 1989 following a spinoff distribution by SmithKline. International operations accounted for 57% of sales and 52% of operating profits in 1997. Sales by business segment in recent years were:

	1997	1996	1995
Eye care drugs	36%	37%	39%
Optical	33%	35%	35%
Surgical	16%	16%	18%
Botox	8%	6%	4%
Skin care	7%	6%	4%

Eye care drugs include prescription and nonprescription products to treat eye diseases and disorders, including glaucoma, inflammation, infection, allergy and dry eye. Important products include Betagan, a beta adrenergic blocking agent used in the initial treatment of glaucoma; Propine, a drug used when initial drug therapy for glaucoma is inadequate; and Alphagan, a glaucoma drug approved for lowering elevated pressure in the eye after laser surgery. Other drugs include Acular, a treatment for the relief of seasonal conjunctivitis, and several anti-infective agents.

Optical products consist of OTC contact lens care products, including daily cleaners to remove film and deposits from contact lenses; enzymatic cleaners to remove protein deposits; and disinfecting solutions to destroy harmful microorganisms on contact lens surfaces. Lens care products are sold under the Complete, Lens Plus, Ultrazyme and UltraCare names.

Surgical products include intraocular lenses (IOLs) and surgical adjunct products. IOLs are implanted in the eye after the removal of cataracts. Botox is a drug used to treat eye muscle disorders. Skin care items consist of anti-fungal drugs and Zorac/Tazorac, new receptor-selective retinoids to treat acne and psoriasis. Allergan Specialty Therapeutics, Inc. (ASTI) is conducting R&D on new drugs based on AGN's retinoid and neuroprotective technologies. AGN has an option to purchase ASTI, as well as rights on certain ASTI products.

Allergan has several R&D collaborations including one with Cambridge NeuroSciences, Inc. to develop new treatments for glaucoma and other serious ophthalmic disease; an alliance with Sugen, Inc. to develop drugs using Sugen technology to treat ophthalmic neovascular diseases; and a venture with Acadia Pharmaceuticals aimed at developing receptor-selective compounds that may be useful in anesthesia, analgesia and other areas.

Per Share Data ($) (Year Ended Dec. 31)	1997	1996	1995	1994	1993	1992	1991	1990	1989	1988
Tangible Bk. Val.	9.62	7.80	6.09	7.50	6.20	5.61	4.69	4.01	2.78	3.53
Cash Flow	3.00	2.28	2.05	2.55	2.29	2.20	-0.23	1.87	NA	NA
Earnings	1.95	1.17	1.12	1.73	1.58	1.56	-0.92	1.21	0.86	0.88
Dividends	0.52	0.49	0.47	0.42	0.40	0.38	0.33	0.28	0.05	Nil
Payout Ratio	27%	42%	42%	24%	25%	24%	NM	23%	6%	Nil
Prices - High	37 1/8	42	33 3/4	30 7/8	26 3/8	27 1/4	25 1/2	19 3/8	25 1/2	NA
- Low	25 7/8	30	25 3/4	20	20 3/4	20 3/8	16 3/4	12 1/4	15 5/8	NA
P/E Ratio - High	19	36	30	18	17	17	NM	16	30	NA
- Low	13	26	23	12	13	13	NM	10	18	NA
Income Statement Analysis (Million $)										
Revs.	1,138	1,147	1,067	947	859	898	839	884	807	756
Oper. Inc.	207	253	232	209	191	188	184	161	147	174
Depr.	68.8	72.9	60.5	52.3	46.8	42.9	46.2	44.4	42.1	36.3
Int. Exp.	8.9	12.5	13.9	11.3	9.4	14.0	17.4	23.0	24.7	8.6
Pretax Inc.	157	108	125	159	144	144	-48.0	106	75.0	108
Eff. Tax Rate	18%	29%	41%	29%	25%	25%	NM	23%	24%	33%
Net Inc.	128	77.1	72.5	111	105	106	-61.0	81.0	57.0	73.0
Balance Sheet & Other Fin. Data (Million $)										
Cash	181	112	102	131	142	121	127	84.0	84.0	40.0
Curr. Assets	636	600	522	486	444	423	422	431	431	348
Total Assets	1,390	1,350	1,316	1,060	940	886	834	947	936	823
Curr. Liab.	363	375	332	324	276	268	269	256	367	258
LT Debt	143	170	267	84.0	105	82.0	97.0	148	96.0	13.0
Common Eqty.	841	750	669	603	515	500	445	524	445	498
Total Cap.	984	921	936	708	642	595	553	672	542	510
Cap. Exp.	64.4	59.7	62.5	58.3	59.9	65.6	51.0	42.9	63.0	51.4
Cash Flow	197	150	133	163	151	149	-15.0	126	99	109
Curr. Ratio	1.8	1.6	1.6	1.5	1.6	1.6	1.6	1.7	1.2	1.3
% LT Debt of Cap.	14.5	18.5	28.5	11.9	16.3	13.8	17.6	22.0	17.8	2.5
% Net Inc.of Revs.	11.3	6.8	6.8	11.7	12.2	11.8	NM	9.2	7.1	9.6
% Ret. on Assets	9.4	5.8	6.1	11.1	11.7	12.4	NM	8.7	6.5	NA
% Ret. on Equity	16.1	10.9	11.4	19.9	21.0	22.5	NM	16.8	12.1	NA

Data as orig. reptd.; bef. results of disc. opers. and/or spec. items. Per share data adj. for stk. divs. as of ex-div. date. Bold denotes diluted EPS (FASB 128). E-Estimated. NA-Not Available. NM-Not Meaningful. NR-Not Ranked.

Office—2525 Dupont Dr., P.O. Box 19534, Irvine, CA 92713-9534. **Tel**—(714) 246-4500. **Website**—http://www.allergan.com **Chrmn**—H. W. Boyer. **Pres & CEO**—D. Pyott. **CFO & Secy**—F. R. Tunney Jr. **Investor Contact**—Jeffrey Edwards (714-246-4636). **Dirs**—H. W. Boyer, T. J. Erickson, H. E. Evans, W. R. Grant, H. E. Greene Jr., G. S. Herbert, L. J. Kaplan, D. Pyott, L. T. Rosso, L. D. Schaeffer, H. Wendt. **Transfer Agent & Registrar**—First Chicago Trust Co. of New York, Jersey City, NJ. **Incorporated**—in California in 1948. **Empl**— 6,100. **S&P Analyst:** H. B. Saftlas

STANDARD &POOR'S
STOCK REPORTS

AlliedSignal

65T

NYSE Symbol **ALD**

In S&P 500

12-SEP-98

Industry: Manufacturing (Diversified)

Summary: This Fortune 500 company mostly makes hi-tech aircraft components, services aircraft and produces industrial materials.

S&P Opinion: Hold (★★★)	Recent Price • 33½	Yield • 1.8%
	52 Wk Range • 47½-31⅝	12-Mo. P/E • 15.4

Earnings vs. Previous Year
▲=Up ▼=Down ▶=No Change

Quantitative Evaluations

Outlook
(1 Lowest—5 Highest)
• **3**

Fair Value
• **40¼**

Risk
• **Low**

Earn./Div. Rank
• **B+**

Technical Eval.
• **Bearish** since 8/98

Rel. Strength Rank
(1 Lowest—99 Highest)
• **49**

Insider Activity
• **Neutral**

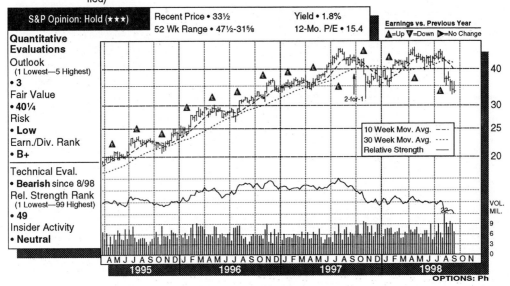

10 Week Mov. Avg. — - —
30 Week Mov. Avg. - - - -
Relative Strength —

2-for-1

VOL. MIL.

1995 1996 1997 1998

OPTIONS: Ph

Overview - 07-AUG-98

On August 4, 1998, ALD made an unsolicited cash bid of $44.50 a share for the approximately 219 million shares of AMP, the world's largest maker of electronic connectors (cables that connect components such as computers, communications equipment and various appliances). The offer reflects ALD's strong desire to expand into faster growing markets, improve profit margins, and reduce earnings cyclicality. ALD would particularly like to counter slowing sales from the company's remaining automotive component and product businesses (25% of 1997 revenues), as well as augment ALD's stronger aerospace (45% of revenues) and industrial materials (30% of revenues) operations. If the company succeeds in acquiring AMP, electronic connectors would become ALD's largest product offering. In 1997, AMP generated revenues of $5.75 billion. Although AMP is the market leader, with a 20% share, since 1993, AMP has been struggling with eroding market share and profits, amid price pressure and high operating costs.

Valuation - 07-AUG-98

Despite ALD's superb history of cost cutting and investment returns, we are chary about its bid for AMP. Although many of AMP's markets have solid growth prospects, these markets are also very competitive and price sensitive. We wonder whether expected cost savings will drop to ALD's bottom line, or into customers' pockets. In addition, we calculate that, based on our $37 to $39 a share valuation of AMP, ALD is paying a 15% premium; we believe this will contribute to expected $0.27 a share dilution in 1998. We are also wary about implications of higher AMP-related debt loads, share buyback suspensions, and possible ALD public stock offerings. At recent levels, we believe ALD share will be only market performers for the long term.

Key Stock Statistics

S&P EPS Est. 1998	2.35	Tang. Bk. Value/Share	3.46
P/E on S&P Est. 1998	14.3	Beta	1.23
S&P EPS Est. 1999	2.70	Shareholders	79,000
Dividend Rate/Share	0.60	Market cap. (B)	$ 18.8
Shs. outstg. (M)	561.3	Inst. holdings	66%
Avg. daily vol. (M)	2.155		

Value of $10,000 invested 5 years ago: $ 24,289

Fiscal Year Ending Dec. 31

	1998	1997	1996	1995	1994	1993
Revenues (Million $)						
1Q	3,646	3,327	3,778	3,419	2,986	2,901
2Q	3,869	3,578	3,347	3,630	3,187	3,055
3Q	—	3,657	3,348	3,499	3,110	2,812
4Q	—	3,910	3,498	3,798	3,534	3,059
Yr.	—	14,472	13,971	14,346	12,817	11,827
Earnings Per Share ($)						
1Q	**0.52**	**0.45**	0.40	0.35	0.30	0.26
2Q	**0.61**	**0.52**	0.48	0.40	0.34	0.29
3Q	**E0.60**	**0.50**	0.45	0.39	0.34	0.29
4Q	**E0.62**	**0.55**	0.48	0.41	0.36	0.31
Yr.	**E2.35**	**2.02**	**1.76**	1.54	1.34	1.16

Next earnings report expected: late October

Dividend Data (Dividends have been paid since 1887.)

Amount ($)	Date Decl.	Ex-Div. Date	Stock of Record	Payment Date
0.130	Oct. 31	Nov. 08	Nov. 20	Dec. 20 '97
0.150	Jan. 28	Feb. 18	Feb. 20	Mar. 10 '98
0.150	Apr. 27	May. 18	May. 20	Jun. 10 '98
0.150	Jul. 24	Aug. 18	Aug. 20	Sep. 10 '98

A Division of The McGraw·Hill Companies

Business Summary - 07-AUG-98

AlliedSignal Inc. is a broadly diversified manufacturer whose operations are conducted under three business segments: aerospace, automotive and engineered materials. The company attempts to balance its business between original equipment and aftermarket sales, as well as geographically. About 40% of sales are tied to aftermarket parts or equipment demand. Similarly, about 40% of sales are derived from foreign markets. In 1997, the company sold its automotive safety restraints business, resulting in a large cash position that it will attempt to deploy in more promising opportunities. Contributions by segment in 1997 were:

	Sales	Net Income
Aerospace	44%	43%
Automotive	26%	24%
Engineered materials	30%	33%

Aerospace products include propulsion and gas turbine engines, environmental control systems, power management and generation systems, landing systems, avionics, wheels, brakes, controls and other products. The division also performs extensive aftermarket activities, providing spare parts, maintenance and repair, and re-trofitting services for the commercial and military markets.

The automotive segment's principal business areas are braking systems, engine components and aftermarket parts and car care products. Within each area, the segment offers a wide range of products for passenger cars and light, medium and heavy trucks. Brand names include Bendix, Fram, Autolite, Garrett and Prestone. After selling its light vehicle conventional braking and anti-lock braking systems (ABS) businesses for $1.5 billion in cash in 1996, ALD sold the safety restraints unit in 1997 to Breed Technologies for $710 million in cash. ALD retained its air brakes and heavy-duty truck ABS businesses. Prestone Products, the well-known supplier of antifreeze and other car care products, was acquired in 1997.

Engineered materials operations comprise four divisions: polymers, fluorine products, specialty chemicals and electronic materials. Other businesses not included in these divisions are carbon materials, specialty films, amorphous metals and the Environmental Catalysts joint venture (supplying the catalyst and substrate used in catalytic converters). In December 1996, ALD acquired the zirconium products business of Cabot Corp.

The company has an active share repurchase program, which was authorized as of December 1997 to buy back 81.4 million common shares.

Per Share Data ($)

(Year Ended Dec. 31)	1997	1996	1995	1994	1993	1992	1991	1990	1989	1988
Tangible Bk. Val.	3.47	4.88	3.56	2.88	2.29	2.12	3.41	6.28	5.88	5.52
Cash Flow	3.07	2.87	2.63	2.26	2.06	1.83	0.36	1.60	1.53	1.41
Earnings	2.02	1.80	1.54	1.34	1.16	0.95	-0.50	0.84	0.89	0.78
Dividends	0.52	0.45	0.39	0.34	0.29	0.25	0.40	0.45	0.45	0.45
Payout Ratio	26%	25%	25%	25%	25%	27%	NM	52%	49%	58%
Prices - High	47⅛	37¼	25	20⅜	20	15½	11¼	9½	10⅛	9¼
- Low	31⅝	23⅝	16¾	15¼	14⅜	10¼	6½	6¼	8	7
P/E Ratio - High	23	21	16	15	17	16	NM	11	11	12
- Low	16	13	11	11	12	11	NM	7	9	9

Income Statement Analysis (Million $)

	1997	1996	1995	1994	1993	1992	1991	1990	1989	1988
Revs.	14,472	13,971	14,346	12,817	11,827	12,042	11,831	12,343	11,942	11,909
Oper. Inc.	2,019	1,456	1,916	1,675	1,452	1,279	1,026	1,156	1,331	1,254
Depr.	609	602	612	523	514	496	470	426	385	376
Int. Exp.	175	186	189	166	186	247	283	300	341	338
Pretax Inc.	1,761	1,553	1,261	1,141	910	702	-389	602	769	639
Eff. Tax Rate	31%	34%	31%	31%	28%	24%	NM	23%	31%	28%
Net Inc.	1,170	1,020	875	759	656	535	-272	462	528	463

Balance Sheet & Other Fin. Data (Million $)

	1997	1996	1995	1994	1993	1992	1991	1990	1989	1988
Cash	611	1,766	540	508	892	931	238	382	525	397
Curr. Assets	5,573	5,839	4,890	4,585	4,567	4,919	4,129	4,316	4,141	4,117
Total Assets	13,707	12,829	12,465	11,321	10,829	10,756	10,382	10,456	10,132	10,005
Curr. Liab.	4,436	3,696	3,804	3,391	3,489	3,505	3,603	3,424	3,227	3,202
LT Debt	1,215	1,317	1,367	1,424	1,602	1,777	1,914	2,051	1,903	2,044
Common Eqty.	4,205	4,180	3,592	2,982	2,390	2,251	2,983	3,380	3,412	3,268
Total Cap.	6,295	6,107	5,509	4,812	4,331	4,440	5,490	6,104	6,037	6,029
Cap. Exp.	717	755	746	639	718	691	668	675	541	602
Cash Flow	1,779	1,622	1,487	1,282	1,170	1,031	197	888	913	839
Curr. Ratio	1.3	1.6	1.3	1.4	1.3	1.4	1.1	1.3	1.3	1.3
% LT Debt of Cap.	19.3	21.6	24.8	29.6	37.0	40.0	34.9	33.6	31.5	33.9
% Net Inc.of Revs.	8.1	7.3	6.1	5.9	5.5	4.4	NM	3.7	4.4	3.9
% Ret. on Assets	8.8	8.1	7.4	6.9	6.1	5.0	NM	4.7	5.3	4.6
% Ret. on Equity	27.9	26.2	26.6	28.3	28.3	20.1	NM	14.1	16.0	14.6

Data as orig. reptd.; bef. results of disc. opers. and/or spec. items. Per share data adj. for stk. divs. as of ex-div. date. Bold denotes diluted EPS (FASB 128). E-Estimated. NA-Not Available. NM-Not Meaningful. NR-Not Ranked.

Office—101 Columbia Rd. (P.O. Box 2245), Morristown, NJ 07962-2245. **Tel**—(201) 455-2000. **Website**—http://www.alliedsignal.com **Chrmn & CEO**—L. A. Bossidy. **EVPs**—J. W. Barter, D. P. Burnham, F. M. Poses. **SVP & CFO**—R. F. Wallman. **VP & Treas**—N. A. Garvey. **Secy**—P. M. Kreindler. **Investor Contact**—James V. Gelly (201-455-2222). **Dirs**—H. W. Becherer, L. A. Bossidy, D. Burnham, A. M. Fudge, P. X. Kelley, R. P. Luciano, R. B. Palmer, R. E. Palmer, F. Poses, I. G. Seidenberg, A. C. Sigler, J. R. Stafford, T. P. Stafford, R. C. Winters, H. T. Yang. **Transfer Agent & Registrar**—Bank of New York, NYC. **Incorporated**—in Delaware in 1985. **Empl**—76,600. **S&P Analyst:** Robert E. Friedman, CPA

Allstate Corp. 67C
NYSE Symbol **ALL**

In S&P 500

12-SEP-98 | **Industry:** Insurance (Property-Casualty)

Summary: Allstate is the second largest property-casualty insurer in the U.S. and a leading provider of auto and homeowners insurance.

S&P Opinion: Accumulate (★★★★)	Recent Price • 39¼ 52 Wk Range • 52⅜-36 Yield • 1.4% 12-Mo. P/E • 9.6

Quantitative Evaluations

Outlook (1 Lowest—5 Highest)
• **2+**

Fair Value
• **37⅜**

Risk
• **Low**

Earn./Div. Rank
• **NR**

Technical Eval.
• **Bearish** since 8/98

Rel. Strength Rank (1 Lowest—99 Highest)
• **67**

Insider Activity
• **Neutral**

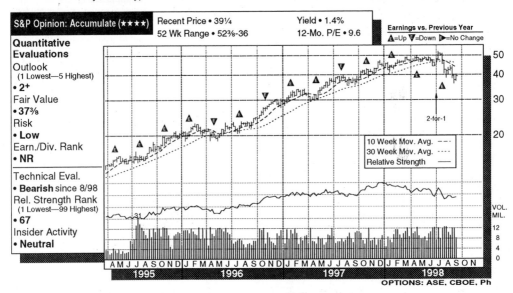

Earnings vs. Previous Year
▲=Up ▼=Down ▶=No Change

10 Week Mov. Avg. ---
30 Week Mov. Avg. ·····
Relative Strength —

2-for-1

OPTIONS: ASE, CBOE, Ph

Overview - 27-JUL-98

Property-casualty premiums should continue to rise moderately (5%) in 1998, as growth in personal auto writings is partly offset by a curtailment of homeowners' writings in catastrophe-prone areas. Since ALL does not utilize catastrophe reinsurance, the company has greater financial risk when catastrophes strike. Partly offsetting this risk is ALL's geographically diverse book of business, strong capital base, and planned expansion into non-standard auto lines. ALL is attempting to reduce its catastrophe exposure in Florida and California, and underwriting results ultimately should benefit from this strategy. While higher industry-wide weather related losses may make year to year comparisons difficult, underlying claim trends remain favorable. Also, life insurance revenues should continue to benefit from pension and annuity product sales, as ALL leverages its customer base and technology.

Valuation - 27-JUL-98

The shares of this leading property-casualty insurer have trended steadily upward in recent years, as investors focused on ALL's franchise value and its ability to produce earnings growth in the midst of an extremely competitive operating environment. Moreover, several pro-active moves -- such as ALL's decisions to boost environmental reserves, more aggressively manage its catastrophe exposure, expand into nonstandard auto and exit the commercial lines business -- have also been viewed favorably by investors. Despite their recent strength, we recommend accumulating the shares. At current levels, there is additional upside in the stock. Note: earnings estimates are for operating earnings (excluding realized investment gains or losses); historical per share data are based on net income.

Key Stock Statistics

S&P EPS Est. 1998	3.00	Tang. Bk. Value/Share	19.79
P/E on S&P Est. 1998	13.1	Beta	1.15
S&P EPS Est. 1999	3.35	Shareholders	220,200
Dividend Rate/Share	0.54	Market cap. (B)	$ 32.6
Shs. outstg. (M)	828.5	Inst. holdings	70%
Avg. daily vol. (M)	2.182		

Value of $10,000 invested 5 years ago: NA

Fiscal Year Ending Dec. 31

	1998	1997	1996	1995	1994	1993
Revenues (Million $)						
1Q	6,450	6,179	5,903	5,573	5,322	—
2Q	6,539	6,073	6,324	5,671	5,318	—
3Q	—	6,384	6,015	5,699	5,394	5,320
4Q	—	6,313	6,057	5,850	5,430	5,283
Yr.	—	25,011	24,299	22,793	21,464	20,946
Earnings Per Share ($)						
1Q	**1.10**	0.86	0.47	0.60	-0.30	0.38
2Q	**1.05**	0.73	0.85	0.57	0.45	0.47
3Q	—	0.94	0.33	0.50	0.21	0.36
4Q	—	1.01	0.67	0.44	0.18	0.28
Yr.	—	3.55	2.31	2.12	0.54	1.50

Next earnings report expected: late October

Dividend Data (Dividends have been paid since 1993.)

Amount ($)	Date Decl.	Ex-Div. Date	Stock of Record	Payment Date
0.270	Feb. 13	Feb. 25	Feb. 27	Apr. 01 '98
0.270	May. 19	May. 27	May. 29	Jul. 01 '98
2-for-1	May. 19	Jul. 02	May. 29	Jul. 01 '98
0.135	Aug. 14	Aug. 27	Aug. 31	Oct. 01 '98

A Division of The McGraw·Hill Companies

STANDARD
&POOR'S
STOCK REPORTS

The Allstate Corporation

67C

12-SEP-98

Business Summary - 27-JUL-98

Established in 1931 by Sears, Roebuck & Co., Allstate -- a.k.a. "The Good Hands People," is the second largest property-liability insurer in the U.S. and one of the 20 largest life insurers. It writes business mainly through more than 15,000 full-time Allstate agents in the U.S. and Canada. On June 30, 1995, Allstate became an independent company when Sears, Roebuck & Co. spun off its 80.3% interest in the company.

The company's primary business is the sale of private passenger automobile and homeowners insurance, and it maintains national market shares of about 12% in each of those lines. ALL is licensed to write policies in all 50 states, the District of Columbia, Puerto Rico and in Canada. ALL is also the largest non-standard auto insurer. One of the company's strategies is to better manage its exposure to catastrophe losses. Another strategy is to increase its presence in the non-standard auto insurance market. During 1997, net written premiums rose 4.5%, to $18.8 billion from $18.6 billion. While this growth was in line with overall industry averages, it reflects varying degrees of written premium growth by product line. Personal auto written premiums rose 4.4%, while homeowners' premiums declined 2.0% during 1997, as ALL continues to pare its exposure to certain storm prone areas. However, nonstandard auto

written premiums advanced about 14.7%, as ALL targets this niche for growth. During 1997, the combined ratio equaled 94.0%, versus 100.5% in 1996.

To better focus on its core personal property-casualty lines of business, Allstate in 1996 sold its commercial lines insurer, Northbrook Holdings Inc., to St. Paul Cos., for $180 million in cash. The company also sold its reinsurance operations.

Allstate Life offers an array of life insurance, annuity and pension products countrywide through various distribution channels, including Allstate agents, financial institutions, independent agents and brokers and direct marketing techniques. Premiums and deposits of $4.9 billion in 1997 were comprised of: fixed annuities 33%, variable annuities 29%, group pension products 12%, universal life insurance 16%, and traditional and other life insurance 10%.

During the six months ended June 30, 1998, property-casualty net written premiums rose 4.2%, year to year. This is about in line with industry averages, and reflects growth in standard and nonstandard auto and homeowners lines. Despite higher storm and catastrophe losses, the combined ratio improved, to 92.9% from 95.2%. Excluding catastrophe losses, the combined ratio was 88.5%, versus 92.7%. Life insurance revenues were up 16.5% during this period, thanks mainly to strong annuity sales.

Per Share Data ($)

(Year Ended Dec. 31)	1997	1996	1995	1994	1993	1992	1991	1990	1989	1988
Tangible Bk. Val.	18.36	15.23	14.17	9.37	11.45	NA	NA	NA	NA	NA
Oper. Earnings	NA	1.78	1.76	0.39	1.33	-0.70	NA	NA	NA	NA
Earnings	3.56	2.31	2.12	0.54	1.50	-0.57	NA	NA	NA	NA
Dividends	0.48	0.42	0.39	0.36	0.18	NA	NA	NA	NA	NA
Relative Payout	14%	18%	18%	67%	12%	NA	NA	NA	NA	NA
Prices - High	47¼	30½	21¼	15	17⅛	NA	NA	NA	NA	NA
- Low	28⅛	18¾	11¾	11⅜	13½	NA	NA	NA	NA	NA
P/E Ratio - High	13	13	10	28	11	NA	NA	NA	NA	NA
- Low	8	8	6	21	9	NA	NA	NA	NA	NA

Income Statement Analysis (Million $)

	1997	1996	1995	1994	1993	1992	1991	1990	1989	1988
Life Ins. In Force	247,192	NA	NA	NA	138,423	124,040	NA	NA	NA	NA
Prem. Inc.: Life A & H	1,502	1,336	1,368	1,053	1,079	1,128	1,197	1,166	NA	NA
Prem. Inc.: Cas./Prop.	18,604	18,366	17,540	16,807	16,323	15,738	15,147	14,281	NA	NA
Net Invest. Inc.	3,861	3,813	3,627	3,401	3,324	3,201	3,001	2,571	2,235	1,781
Oth. Revs.	982	784	258	202	220	162	5.0	181	223	185
Total Revs.	24,949	24,299	22,793	21,464	20,946	20,228	19,350	18,199	16,803	14,924
Pretax Inc.	4,429	2,694	2,477	227	1,376	-1,424	539	301	684	869
Net Oper. Inc.	NA	1,600	1,587	352	1,158	-606	719	571	668	792
Net Inc.	3,105	2,075	1,904	484	1,302	-499	723	691	815	914

Balance Sheet & Other Fin. Data (Million $)

	1997	1996	1995	1994	1993	1992	1991	1990	1989	1988
Cash & Equiv.	220	831	840	778	786	796	NA	NA	NA	NA
Premiums Due	NA	2,691	2,935	2,316	1,964	1,875	NA	NA	NA	NA
Invest. Assets: Bonds	50,860	47,095	45,272	38,041	38,888	32,144	NA	NA	NA	NA
Invest. Assets: Stocks	6,765	5,561	6,150	4,852	4,555	3,837	NA	NA	NA	NA
Invest. Assets: Loans	3,002	3,146	3,280	3,234	3,563	3,701	NA	NA	NA	NA
Invest. Assets: Total	8,000	58,329	56,505	48,179	48,791	41,731	NA	NA	NA	NA
Deferred Policy Costs	2,826	2,614	2,004	2,074	1,511	1,529	NA	NA	NA	NA
Total Assets	80,918	74,508	70,029	61,369	59,358	52,098	NA	NA	NA	NA
Debt	2,446	1,386	1,228	869	850	1,800	NA	NA	NA	NA
Common Eqty.	15,610	13,452	12,680	8,426	10,300	5,383	NA	NA	NA	NA
Comb. Loss-Exp. Ratio	94.0	100.5	100.4	111.0	103.0	120.8	107.5	109.9	107.5	104.6
% Return On Revs.	12.4	8.6	8.4	2.3	6.2	NM	3.7	3.9	4.9	6.1
% Ret. on Equity	21.4	12.3	18.0	5.2	16.6	NM	NM	NM	NM	NM
% Invest. Yield	6.4	6.7	4.8	7.0	7.4	NA	NA	NA	NA	NA

Data as orig. reptd.; bef. results of disc. opers. and/or spec. items. Per share data adj. for stk. divs. as of ex-div. date. Bold denotes diluted EPS (FASB 128). E-Estimate. NA-Not Available. NM-Not Meaningful. NR-Not Ranked.

Office—Allstate Plaza, 2775 Sanders Road, Northbrook, IL 60062. **Tel**—(847) 402-5000. **Website**—http://www.allstate.com **Chrmn & CEO**—J. D. Choate. **Pres & COO**—E. M. Liddy. **VP & CFO**—T. J. Wilson. **VP & Secy**—R. W. Pike. **Dirs**—J. G. Andress, W. L. Batts, E. A. Brennan, J. D. Choate, J. M. Denny, M. A. Miles, J. I. Smith, M. A. Taylor. **Transfer Agent & Registrar**—First Chicago Trust Co. of New York, Jersey City, NJ. **Incorporated**—in Delaware in 1992. **Empl**— 51,400. **S&P Analyst:** Catherine A. Seifert

12-SEP-98   Industry: Telephone

Summary: This company operates one of the largest U.S. telephone systems, serving more than 1.8 million subscriber lines in 14 states.

S&P Opinion: Accumulate (★★★★)	Recent Price • 42⅛	Yield • 2.8%
	52 Wk Range • 48¾-32	12-Mo. P/E • NM

Earnings vs. Previous Year
▲=Up ▼=Down ▷=No Change

Quantitative Evaluations

Outlook
(1 Lowest—5 Highest)
• **2+**

Fair Value
• **41¼**

Risk
• **Low**

Earn./Div. Rank
• **A**

Technical Eval.
• **Bearish** since 8/98

Rel. Strength Rank
(1 Lowest—99 Highest)
• **86**

Insider Activity
• **Neutral**

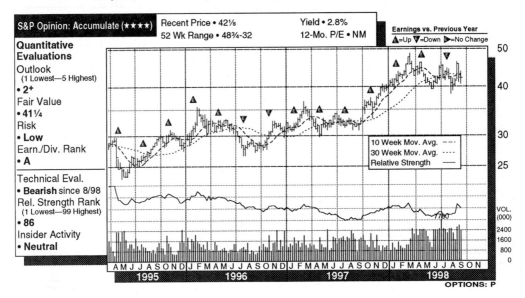

10 Week Mov. Avg. ---
30 Week Mov. Avg. ----
Relative Strength ——

VOL. (000)

OPTIONS: P

Overview - 24-JUL-98

ALLTEL should continue to post earnings gains above the industry average, reflecting growth based on its reduced dependence on communications-related businesses. AT's strategy focuses on diversification into nonregulated businesses, such as information services (IS) and wireless communications, and reaping the one-stop-shopping benefits of combining core telephone and cellular operations. Proprietary technology and software distinguish the IS unit, which accounts for about one-third of total revenues. The wireless unit's customer base continues to grow rapidly, and was recently expanded further through the acquisition of 360 (Degrees) Communications (NYSE: XO). Synergies between the companies are expected to produce $100 million in annual cost savings by 2000, with $20 million and $80 million saved in 1998 and 1999, respectively. Earnings in 1997 included a gain of $0.40 a share on the sale of assets.

Valuation - 24-JUL-98

Information services businesses currently account for about a third of AT's revenues, making its operations much more appealing than those of slower-growing local competitors. The Telecommunications Act's impact on ALLTEL will be softened because new competitors will likely concentrate initially on the larger metropolitan markets, and the company operates in many smaller markets. This is also the primary advantage of acquiring an effective smaller market wireless company like 360 (Degrees) Communications. We project 1999 EPS at $2.55, up from the $2.35 seen for 1998. With growth prospects enhanced by the recent acquisition of XO, we see the shares continuing to outperform the market over the next 12 months.

Key Stock Statistics

S&P EPS Est. 1998	2.35	Tang. Bk. Value/Share	8.67
P/E on S&P Est. 1998	17.9	Beta	0.34
S&P EPS Est. 1999	2.55	Shareholders	92,000
Dividend Rate/Share	1.16	Market cap. (B)	$ 11.5
Shs. outstg. (M)	274.2	Inst. holdings	35%
Avg. daily vol. (M)	0.746		

Value of $10,000 invested 5 years ago: $ 20,992

Fiscal Year Ending Dec. 31

	1998	1997	1996	1995	1994	1993
Revenues (Million $)						
1Q	847.0	784.3	774.3	763.6	709.4	546.7
2Q	934.0	816.9	804.5	786.5	734.6	568.9
3Q	—	813.8	807.4	785.8	745.3	571.7
4Q	—	848.6	806.3	773.9	772.4	654.8
Yr.	—	3,264	3,192	3,110	2,962	2,342
Earnings Per Share ($)						
1Q	**0.66**	**0.54**	0.44	0.41	0.38	0.34
2Q	**0.58**	**0.92**	0.48	0.52	0.40	0.34
3Q	**E0.60**	**0.65**	0.10	0.45	0.42	0.35
4Q	**E0.51**	**0.59**	0.51	0.48	0.23	0.36
Yr.	**E2.35**	**2.70**	1.53	1.86	1.43	1.39

Next earnings report expected: mid October

Dividend Data (Dividends have been paid since 1961.)

Amount ($)	Date Decl.	Ex-Div. Date	Stock of Record	Payment Date
0.290	Oct. 23	Dec. 03	Dec. 05	Jan. 03 '98
0.290	Jan. 29	Feb. 19	Feb. 23	Apr. 03 '98
0.290	Apr. 23	Jun. 03	Jun. 05	Jul. 03 '98
0.290	Jul. 23	Sep. 03	Sep. 08	Oct. 03 '98

A Division of The **McGraw·Hill** *Companies*

Business Summary - 24-JUL-98

ALLTEL Corp. is keeping the channels open to expand its wireless business, while also bundling other offerings such as Internet, local and long-distance telecommunications services. During 1997, the company combined its wireline (telephone) and wireless (cellular) operations in order to establish a one-stop shopping platform. Business segment contributions in 1997 were:

	Revenue	Profits
Wireline	39%	56%
Wireless	16%	23%
Information services	30%	18%
Product distribution	11%	2%
Other	4%	1%

At June 30, 1998, the company provided local telephone service to 1,847,007 access lines in 14 states. 360 (Degrees) Communications (NYSE: XO), a leading independent wireless provider ($4.5 billion in annual revenues), was recently acquired by AT in a $6 billion stock transaction through the exchange of 0.74 of a share of AT common stock for each XO share; AT also assumed $1.8 billion of XO's debt. AT expects to achieve $100 million in annual cost savings by 2000, as a result of operating synergies between the companies.

The information services unit provides outsourcing, software and information processing services to telecommunications, health care and banking companies. AT's cellular operations serve 8.2 million POPs (population adjusted for percent ownership) in 18 states concentrated in the Sun Belt region. Cellular subscribers numbered 1,009,556 at June 30, 1998. Distribution operations include ALLTEL Supply, a leading supplier of telecom equipment; and HWC Distribution, which distributes specialty wire and cable products. Other operations include the publication of telephone directories, paging services, and a 2% interest in WorldCom Inc., a provider of end-to-end telecommunications services.

In January 1997, AT successfully bid for 73 markets in 12 states in a federal Personal Communications Services (PCS) auction. When issued by the FCC, the D and E spectrum blocks licenses will enable the company to increase the size of its potential wireless customer base from 8.4 million to 31.4 million. AT also believes that the licenses will dramatically increase the overlap of its system-wide wireline and wireless territories from 25% to 55%. The company paid about $144 million for the licenses, or approximately $5 per potential customer.

Per Share Data ($)

(Year Ended Dec. 31)	1997	1996	1995	1994	1993	1992	1991	1990	1989	1988
Tangible Bk. Val.	8.67	8.88	7.64	5.96	5.53	4.86	4.58	4.61	4.86	5.14
Cash Flow	5.10	3.77	4.02	3.34	2.84	2.54	2.50	2.34	2.40	2.15
Earnings	2.70	1.53	1.86	1.43	1.39	1.22	1.17	1.18	1.16	0.97
Dividends	1.11	1.05	0.98	0.90	0.82	0.76	0.71	0.66	0.59	0.52
Payout Ratio	41%	69%	53%	63%	59%	62%	61%	56%	51%	54%
Prices - High	41⅝	35⅝	31⅛	31⅜	31¼	25	21⅝	19⅝	21	12⅝
- Low	29¾	26⅝	23¼	24	22⅞	17⅝	15⅞	12⅜	11¾	8⅝
P/E Ratio - High	15	23	17	22	22	20	18	17	18	13
- Low	11	17	12	17	16	14	14	11	10	9

Income Statement Analysis (Million $)

	1997	1996	1995	1994	1993	1992	1991	1990	1989	1988
Revs.	3,264	3,192	3,110	2,962	2,342	2,092	1,748	1,574	1,226	1,068
Depr.	451	424	410	362	272	245	217	192	165	155
Maint.	NA	147	148	151	131	122	109	104	106	101
Constr. Credits	NA	NA	Nil	NA	2.0	2.0	1.9	1.4	1.2	1.4
Eff. Tax Rate	37%	37%	38%	38%	42%	36%	33%	32%	30%	35%
Net Inc.	508	292	355	272	262	229	189	193	154	125

Balance Sheet & Other Fin. Data (Million $)

	1997	1996	1995	1994	1993	1992	1991	1990	1989	1988
Gross Prop.	5,531	5,114	4,842	4,697	4,235	3,297	2,913	2,759	2,486	2,395
Net Prop.	3,190	3,042	2,973	2,963	2,676	2,062	1,825	1,755	1,615	1,553
Cap. Exp.	546	464	523	596	426	367	308	272	231	201
Total Cap.	4,754	4,535	4,270	3,896	3,575	2,643	2,405	2,265	2,057	1,839
Fxd. Chgs. Cov.	5.4	5.2	4.5	4.1	5.4	4.8	4.0	4.5	3.9	3.8
Capitalization:										
LT Debt	1,874	1,756	1,762	1,846	1,596	1,018	992	905	799	675
Pfd.	14.8	15.7	16.3	17.1	18.0	19.1	21.3	23.5	36.1	37.9
Common	2,199	2,088	1,926	1,616	1,545	1,295	1,072	1,005	884	779
% Return On Revs.	15.6	9.1	11.4	9.2	11.2	10.9	10.8	12.3	12.6	11.7
% Return On Invest. Capital	16.6	16.2	16.6	10.9	11.6	12.7	11.4	12.2	11.5	10.4
% Return On Com. Equity	23.6	14.5	20.0	17.1	18.3	18.8	18.0	19.3	18.2	16.3
% Earn. on Net Prop.	24.5	23.4	23.0	16.6	14.0	15.8	14.3	15.2	14.0	11.7
% LT Debt of Cap.	45.8	45.4	47.6	53.1	50.5	43.7	47.6	46.8	46.5	45.2
Capital. % Pfd.	0.4	0.6	0.4	0.5	0.6	0.8	1.0	1.2	2.1	2.6
Capital. % Common	53.8	54.0	52.0	46.4	48.9	55.5	51.4	52.0	51.4	52.2

Data as orig. reptd.; bef. results of disc. opers. and/or spec. items. Per share data adj. for stk. divs. as of ex-div. date. Bold denotes diluted EPS (FASB 128). E-Estimated. NA-Not Available. NM-Not Meaningful. NR-Not Ranked.

Office—One Allied Drive, Little Rock, AR 72202.**Tel**—(501) 905-8000. **Website**—http://www.alltel.com**Chrmn & CEO**—J. T. Ford. **Pres**—S. T. Ford.**SVP & CFO**—D. J. Ferra. **SVP & Secy**—F. X. Frantz. **Treas**—J. M. Green. **VP & Investor Contact**—Shawne S. Leach. **Dirs**—M. D. Andreas, J. R. Belk, J. T. Ford, S. T. Ford, L. L. Gellerstedt III, W. W. Johnson, E. A. Mahony, Jr., J. P. McConnell, J. Natori, R. Townsend, W. H. Zimmer, Jr. **Transfer Agent & Registrar**—First Union National Bank of North Carolina, Charlotte. **Incorporated**—in Delaware. **Empl**— 16,393. **S&P Analyst:** Philip D. Wohl

12-SEP-98   Industry:
Aluminum

Summary: The world's largest aluminum producer, Alcoa makes primary aluminum and fabricated products for the transportation, construction, packaging and other markets.

S&P Opinion: Hold (★★★)	Recent Price • 68	Yield • 1.5%
	52 Wk Range • 84¾-58	12-Mo. P/E • 13.6

Earnings vs. Previous Year
▲=Up ▼=Down ▶=No Change

Quantitative Evaluations

Outlook
(1 Lowest—5 Highest)
• **3⁻**

Fair Value
• **69⅛**

Risk
• **Low**

Earn./Div. Rank
• **B-**

Technical Eval.
• **NA**

Rel. Strength Rank
(1 Lowest—99 Highest)
• **93**

Insider Activity
• **Neutral**

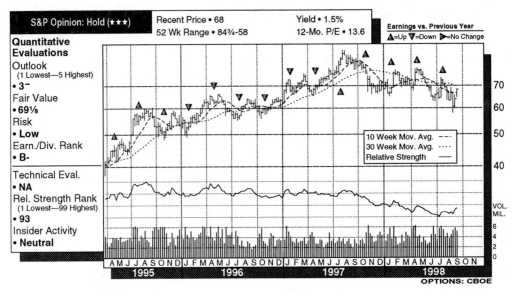

10 Week Mov. Avg. ---
30 Week Mov. Avg. ····
Relative Strength —

VOL.
MIL.

OPTIONS: CBOE

Overview - 09-JUL-98

We project 8% sales growth in 1998, mostly reflecting the acquisition of Inespal, Spain's state owned aluminum manufacturer, and the recently approved acquisition of Alumax Inc. (AMX, NYSE), the world's third largest aluminum producer. Benefiting from higher volume, an improved mix and lower costs, EPS should also rise.

Valuation - 09-JUL-98

Following second quarter EPS, we are maintaining our neutral rating on AA based on our long-term concerns about a glut of aluminum. Second quarter EPS beat the consensus estimate of $1.15, reflecting higher volume, an improved mix and stringent cost control. Recently trading at 13.4X our 1998 EPS estimate versus a 23.2X P/E for the 500 and 13.1X for the other aluminum companies, AA is undervalued. AA warrants a higher multiple given its superior return on equity and better growth prospects vis a vis its competitors. As clearly demonstrated so far in 1998, AA is able to cope with an adverse price environment and still report decent EPS. With its substantial cash flow and strong balance sheet, it can continue to grow via acquisitions. Near-term, AA and the aluminum price appear oversold given that demand appears firm as weakness in Asia is being partially offset by rising demand in Europe. Moreover, supply is favorable. As of early July 1998, London Metal Exchange inventories stood at 521,350 metric tons, down from 662,725 metric tons in early July 1997. We believe that the aluminum price is unduly low in view of near-term fundamentals. However, restart of capacity by several of AA's competitors threatens to cause a glut in the market in 1999. Consequently, we would not add to holdings at this time, notwithstanding our positive longer-term view of the company.

Key Stock Statistics

S&P EPS Est. 1998	4.90	Tang. Bk. Value/Share	22.36
P/E on S&P Est. 1998	13.9	Beta	0.83
S&P EPS Est. 1999	5.75	Shareholders	88,300
Dividend Rate/Share	1.00	Market cap. (B)	$ 12.7
Shs. outstg. (M)	186.8	Inst. holdings	68%
Avg. daily vol. (M)	1.067		

Value of $10,000 invested 5 years ago: $ 21,304

Fiscal Year Ending Dec. 31

	1998	1997	1996	1995	1994	1993
Revenues (Million $)						
1Q	3,473	3,272	3,150	3,010	2,222	2,110
2Q	3,605	3,470	3,413	3,117	2,479	2,405
3Q	—	3,404	3,241	3,265	2,562	2,230
4Q	—	3,335	3,258	3,108	2,642	2,311
Yr.	—	13,482	13,061	12,500	9,904	9,056
Earnings Per Share ($)						
1Q	**1.24**	0.92	1.01	1.08	-0.23	0.15
2Q	**1.24**	1.19	0.76	1.23	0.25	0.20
3Q	**E1.17**	1.32	0.39	1.27	0.39	0.16
4Q	**E1.25**	1.23	0.78	0.85	2.07	-0.50
Yr.	**E4.90**	**4.62**	2.94	4.43	2.48	0.01

Next earnings report expected: early October

Dividend Data (Dividends have been paid since 1939.)

Amount ($)	Date Decl.	Ex-Div. Date	Stock of Record	Payment Date
0.125	Jul. 10	Aug. 05	Aug. 07	Aug. 25 '98
0.250	Jul. 10	Aug. 05	Aug. 07	Aug. 25 '98
.125 Spl.	Sep. 10	Nov. 04	Nov. 06	Nov. 25 '98
0.250	Sep. 10	Nov. 04	Nov. 06	Nov. 25 '98

A Division of The McGraw-Hill Companies

Business Summary - 09-JUL-98

With operations located throughout the world and highly integrated, Alcoa is the largest producer of primary and finished aluminum products. It is also the world's largest supplier of alumina, an intermediate raw material used for production of aluminum.

Operating data for recent years in metric tons:

	1997	1996
Alumina shipments	7,223,000	6,406,000
Primary aluminum shipments	920,000	901,000
Fabricated products	2,036,000	1,940,000
Total aluminum shipments	2,956,000	2,841,000
Average price for aluminum ingot (lbs.)	$0.75	$0.73
Aluminum capacity	2,108,000	2,101,000
Primary aluminum output	1,725,000	1,708,000

The alumina and chemicals segment includes the production and sale of bauxite, alumina and alumina chemicals and transportation services. About two-thirds of revenues in this unit are derived from alumina. Slightly over one-third of alumina shipments are to outside customers.

Aluminum processing includes the manufacture and marketing of molten metal, ingot and aluminum products that are flat-rolled, engineered or finished. Also included are power, transportation and other services.

A substantial portion of sales in aluminum processing is to the packaging, transportation and construction markets. Sales to the packaging market consist mostly of rigid container sheet (RCS) marketed to can companies for production of beverage and food cans and can ends. Other packaging products include sheet and foil products. Processed aluminum products are sold to the aerospace, truck trailer and passenger car markets. Processed aluminum is also widely used for building and construction, particularly for siding, window frames and other residential housing applications.

The principal competitors in aluminum processing are Alcan, Alumax Inc., Commonwealth Aluminum, Kaiser, Pechiney and Quanex Corp. There is substantial excess capacity in the aluminum industry worldwide. Aluminum faces stiff competition from such materials as plastics, steel, glass and ceramics. In recent years, plastic, in the form of polyethylene terephthalate (PET), has been displacing aluminum in the beverage can market. On the other hand, aluminum is gaining market share in passenger car applications, at the expense of steel.

The non-aluminum products segment includes the production and sale of electrical, ceramic, plastic and composite material products, manufacturing equipment, gold, magnesium products and steel and titanium forgings.

Per Share Data ($)

(Year Ended Dec. 31)	1997	1996	1995	1994	1993	1992	1991	1990	1989	1988
Tangible Bk. Val.	22.36	22.23	21.49	19.85	18.95	19.63	27.27	28.96	27.97	24.85
Cash Flow	8.95	7.35	8.54	6.25	4.04	4.25	4.59	5.70	9.04	8.48
Earnings	4.62	2.94	4.43	2.48	0.02	0.12	0.35	1.70	5.33	4.87
Dividends	0.97	1.33	0.90	0.80	0.80	0.80	0.80	0.89	1.50	1.26
Payout Ratio	21%	45%	20%	32%	NM	667%	225%	52%	28%	26%
Prices - High	89⅝	66¼	60¼	45⅛	39¼	40⅜	36⅝	38⅝	39⅞	28¾
- Low	64¼	49⅛	36⅞	32⅛	29½	30½	26⅞	24⅞	27⅝	19⅜
P/E Ratio - High	19	23	14	18	NM	NM	NM	23	7	6
- Low	14	17	8	13	NM	NM	NM	15	5	4

Income Statement Analysis (Million $)

Revs.	13,482	13,061	12,500	9,904	9,056	9,492	9,884	10,710	10,910	9,795
Oper. Inc.	2,238	2,111	2,181	1,193	1,042	1,264	1,507	2,176	2,750	2,509
Depr.	754	764	730	671	705	705	720	690	655	638
Int. Exp.	141	139	122	108	91.0	117	166	205	197	230
Pretax Inc.	1,602	1,082	1,470	823	191	299	400	1,047	2,166	1,635
Eff. Tax Rate	33%	33%	30%	27%	NM	44%	45%	38%	37%	37%
Net Inc.	805	515	791	443	5.0	22.0	63.0	295	945	861

Balance Sheet & Other Fin. Data (Million $)

Cash	801	617	1,063	625	655	548	626	636	805	507
Curr. Assets	4,417	4,281	4,742	4,153	3,703	3,248	3,616	3,744	3,738	3,192
Total Assets	13,071	13,450	13,643	12,353	11,597	11,023	11,178	11,413	11,541	10,538
Curr. Liab.	2,453	2,373	2,652	2,554	2,093	2,165	2,070	2,038	2,143	1,884
LT Debt	1,457	1,690	1,216	1,030	1,433	855	1,131	1,295	1,316	1,525
Common Eqty.	4,363	4,407	4,389	3,943	3,528	3,549	4,882	5,108	5,201	4,570
Total Cap.	6,140	8,080	7,579	6,937	6,637	6,047	8,161	8,803	8,968	8,175
Cap. Exp.	912	996	887	612	747	789	841	851	876	857
Cash Flow	1,557	1,279	1,521	1,112	708	726	781	983	1,598	1,497
Curr. Ratio	1.8	1.8	1.7	1.6	1.8	1.5	1.7	1.8	1.7	1.7
% LT Debt of Cap.	23.7	20.9	16.0	14.8	21.6	14.1	13.9	14.7	14.7	18.7
% Net Inc.of Revs.	6.0	3.9	6.3	4.5	0.1	0.2	0.6	2.8	8.7	8.8
% Ret. on Assets	6.1	3.8	6.1	3.7	Nil	0.2	0.6	2.6	8.6	8.4
% Ret. on Equity	18.3	11.7	18.7	11.7	0.1	0.5	1.2	5.8	19.4	20.4

Data as orig. reptd.; bef. results of disc. opers. and/or spec. items. Per share data adj. for stk. divs. as of ex-div. date. Bold denotes diluted EPS (FASB 128). E-Estimated. NA-Not Available. NM-Not Meaningful. NR-Not Ranked.

Office—425 Sixth Ave., Pittsburgh, PA 15219-1850. **Tel**—(412) 553-4545. **Website**—http://www.alcoa.com **Chrmn & CEO**—P. H. O'Neill. **Pres & COO**—A. L. P. Belda. **Secy**—D. A. Demblowski. **Investor Contact**—Edgar M. Cheely Jr. **Dirs**—K. W. Dam, J. T. Gorman, J. M. Gueron, Sir Ronald Hampel, H. M. Morgan, J. P. Mulroney, P. H. O'Neill, H. B. Schacht, F. A. Thomas, M. v.N. Whitman. **Transfer Agent & Registrar**—First Chicago Trust Co. of New York, Jersey City, NJ. **Incorporated**—in Pennsylvania in 1925. **Empl**— 81,600. **S&P Analyst:** Leo Larkin

ALZA Corp.

76

NYSE Symbol **AZA**

In S&P 500

12-SEP-98

Industry:
Health Care (Specialized Services)

Summary: This company is a leader in the field of controlled release therapeutic drug delivery systems. Earnings are derived from product sales and licensee royalties and fees.

S&P Opinion: Hold (★★★)	

Recent Price • 38¾	Yield • Nil
52 Wk Range • 52⅞-24⅞	12-Mo. P/E • NM

Earnings vs. Previous Year
▲=Up ▼=Down ▷=No Change

Quantitative Evaluations

Outlook
(1 Lowest—5 Highest)
• **1⁻**

Fair Value
• **29¾**

Risk
• **Low**

Earn./Div. Rank
• **B-**

Technical Eval.
• **Bullish** since 3/98

Rel. Strength Rank
(1 Lowest—99 Highest)
• **82**

Insider Activity
• **Neutral**

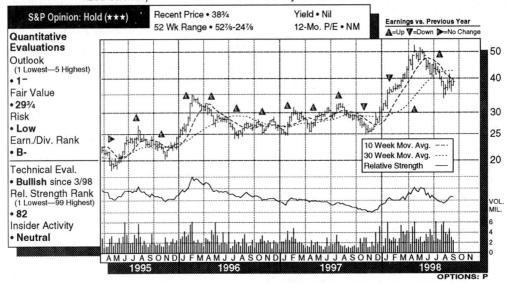

10 Week Mov. Avg. ---
30 Week Mov. Avg. ....
Relative Strength —

VOL. MIL.

AMJJASOND | JFMAMJJASOND | JFMAMJJASOND | JFMAMJJASON
1995 | 1996 | 1997 | 1998

OPTIONS: P

Overview - 10-JUL-98

Revenues should post another impressive gain in 1998, led by a strong rise in sales of ALZA-marketed products. Key proprietary drugs expected to post robust gains include Ethyol, a drug used to prevent kidney damage in patients on chemotherapy; Mycelex, an antifungal agent; and Elmiron treatment for interstitial cystitis and other urological product lines acquired from IVAX Corp. in September 1997. Sales of Testoderm testosterone patch should benefit from the recent launch of a new non-scrotal patch. Although gains are seen in royalties from Nicoderm CQ (marketed by SmithKline Beecham), Glucotrol XL (Pfizer) and Duragesic (Johnson & Johnson), royalties from Procardia XL (Pfizer) are expected to decline. However, margins are expected to be restricted by heavy costs associated with a planned sales force expansion. Earnings for 1998 are projected at $1.31 a share, diluted, with further progress to $1.60 seen for 1999.

Valuation - 10-JUL-98

After peaking in April, the shares have retreated, reflecting disappointing first quarter earnings and anticipated EPS dilution from a sales force expansion. ALZA plans to increase its sales force from 100 to 360, to help promote a growing new drug portfolio. New products include Ditropan XL for urinary incontinence; DUROS leuprolide for prostate cancer; Ethyol prevention of kidney damage; Mycelex antifungal; and Elmiron for interstitial cystitis. Despite heavy near-term SG&A expenses, the beefed up sales force should enable the company to achieve notable sales and earnings growth in coming years. ALZA is currently undergoing a transformation of its business from client-focused product development that relies primarily on royalty income, to a pharmaceutical company marketing its own products. The shares merit retention.

Key Stock Statistics

S&P EPS Est. 1998	1.31	Tang. Bk. Value/Share	4.41
P/E on S&P Est. 1998	29.6	Beta	0.96
S&P EPS Est. 1999	1.60	Shareholders	9,000
Dividend Rate/Share	Nil	Market cap. (B)	$ 3.4
Shs. outstg. (M)	86.6	Inst. holdings	91%
Avg. daily vol. (M)	0.723		

Value of $10,000 invested 5 years ago: NA

Fiscal Year Ending Dec. 31

	1998	1997	1996	1995	1994	1993
Revenues (Million $)						
1Q	130.7	105.5	96.80	80.24	68.17	69.94
2Q	142.3	118.2	128.1	83.01	69.15	57.06
3Q	—	114.5	114.9	85.60	66.23	57.80
4Q	—	126.2	126.2	101.8	75.21	49.39
Yr.	—	464.4	465.9	350.6	278.8	234.2
Earnings Per Share ($)						
1Q	**0.32**	**0.30**	0.24	0.21	0.21	0.26
2Q	**0.34**	**0.27**	0.27	0.21	0.18	0.18
3Q	**E0.32**	**-3.83**	0.27	0.22	0.15	0.18
4Q	**E0.36**	**0.15**	0.30	0.24	0.19	-0.08
Yr.	**E1.31**	**-3.07**	1.08	0.88	0.71	0.54

Next earnings report expected: mid October

Dividend Data

Amount ($)	Date Decl.	Ex-Div. Date	Stock of Record	Payment Date
Stk.	Sep. 08	Oct. 01	Sep. 18	Sep. 30 '97

A Division of The McGraw·Hill Companies

Business Summary - 10-JUL-98

ALZA is a leader in the field of controlled release drug delivery systems. Although initially formed as a research firm deriving all of its revenues from royalties earned on client sales of products based on ALZA technology, the company is now in the midst of transforming itself into a pharmaceutical company marketing its own pharmaceutical products. Revenues in recent years were derived as follows:

	1997	1996	1995
Royalties, fees & other	40%	49%	48%
Product sales	31%	23%	22%
Research revenues	29%	28%	30%

Unlike conventional forms of drug administration such as tablets and injections, the company's drug delivery systems allow the drugs to work at a steady controlled rate, or in a predetermined pattern over extended periods of time. ALZA's drug delivery systems include oral osmotic tablets, transdermal patches, electrotransport systems, and human implantable systems. Drugs produced with controlled release capability generally have better efficacy with less adverse side effects than conventional products.

Most of the company's drugs have been developed through joint ventures with large pharmaceutical compa-

nies. In these joint efforts, clients pay the company product development costs in return for marketing rights to the product; ALZA receives royalties based on the client's product sales. In some cases, the product is manufactured by the company and in others it is produced by the client. Some of the key royalty products include Procardia XL and Minipress XL heart drugs and Glucotrol XL for Type II diabetes, all marketed by Pfizer; NicoDerm CQ, a transdermal patch used for smoking cessation sold by SmithKline Beecham; Catapres-TTS, a treatment for high blood pressure marketed by Boehringer Ingelheim; Duragesic, a pain management drug sold by Johnson & Johnson; and Covera-HS heart drug sold by G.D. Searle.

Products marketed by ALZA include Ethyol, an agent used to reduce kidney toxicity associated with chemotherapy; Testoderm testosterone patch; Mycelex Troche, an antifungal agent used to treat oral thrush; Elmiron, a treatment for interstitial cystitis (a urinary ailment); PolyCitra and BiCitra to treat kidney stones; and Ditropan for urinary incontinence. Co-marketed products consist of Duragesic CII pain management agent, Neu-Trexin for pneumonia, and Hexalen anticancer agent.

R&D outlays equaled 29.1% of total revenues in 1997 and 30.4% in 1996. Funded with $300 million from the company, Crescendo Pharmaceuticals was formed by ALZA in the third quarter of 1997 to develop drugs based on company technologies.

Per Share Data ($)

(Year Ended Dec. 31)	1997	1996	1995	1994	1993	1992	1991	1990	1989	1988
Tangible Bk. Val.	3.52	7.05	5.51	4.44	3.76	5.44	4.48	3.39	2.92	2.53
Cash Flow	-2.68	1.21	1.06	0.87	0.69	1.01	-0.78	0.43	0.34	0.31
Earnings	-3.07	1.08	0.88	0.71	0.54	0.90	-0.88	0.35	0.27	0.26
Dividends	Nil	Nil	Nil	Nil	Nil	Nil	Nil	Nil	Nil	Nil
Payout Ratio	Nil	Nil	Nil	Nil	Nil	Nil	Nil	Nil	Nil	Nil
Prices - High	32½	34⅞	27	30¾	47⅛	55⅛	50⅛	25½	23	15⅛
- Low	24¾	24	18⅛	17	19¼	33½	23⅜	16⅝	11¼	9¾
P/E Ratio - High	NM	32	31	43	87	61	NM	73	83	59
- Low	NM	22	21	24	36	37	NM	48	41	38

Income Statement Analysis (Million $)

	1997	1996	1995	1994	1993	1992	1991	1990	1989	1988
Revs.	464	466	326	261	220	229	140	99	82.0	74.0
Oper. Inc.	196	214	132	109	105	111	60.0	38.0	26.0	21.8
Depr.	33.3	22.0	15.3	13.7	12.3	9.3	6.5	5.6	4.2	3.5
Int. Exp.	55.0	43.0	23.9	19.7	21.1	18.8	18.0	6.4	5.7	5.2
Pretax Inc.	-210	149	117	93.0	66.0	105	-41.4	39.1	29.8	25.0
Eff. Tax Rate	NA	38%	38%	38%	35%	32%	NM	37%	37%	32%
Net Inc.	-260	92.4	72.4	58.1	42.9	72.2	-62.1	24.7	18.8	17.0

Balance Sheet & Other Fin. Data (Million $)

	1997	1996	1995	1994	1993	1992	1991	1990	1989	1988
Cash	65.0	999	419	345	94.0	131	172	302	109	121
Curr. Assets	358	1,175	578	492	198	228	249	354	147	159
Total Assets	1,369	1,614	937	806	622	698	580	531	288	262
Curr. Liab.	105	67.2	68.0	56.0	286	39.1	20.8	18.6	16.5	17.9
LT Debt	903	882	363	346	2.0	232	218	279	77.0	77.0
Common Eqty.	301	597	455	364	307	408	323	220	187	160
Total Cap.	1,204	1,479	817	729	318	646	549	504	266	240
Cap. Exp.	38.8	48.6	46.3	37.2	23.8	41.4	34.1	24.7	44.2	28.2
Cash Flow	-227	114	87.7	71.8	55.1	81.5	-55.6	30.3	22.9	20.5
Curr. Ratio	3.4	17.4	8.5	8.8	0.7	5.8	12.0	19.1	8.9	8.9
% LT Debt of Cap.	75.0	59.6	44.5	47.4	0.6	35.9	39.8	55.5	29.0	32.2
% Net Inc.of Revs.	NA	19.8	22.2	22.3	19.5	31.5	NM	24.8	22.9	23.0
% Ret. on Assets	NA	7.2	8.3	8.1	6.2	11.1	NM	6.0	6.8	6.7
% Ret. on Equity	NA	17.6	17.7	17.3	11.4	19.4	NM	12.1	10.8	11.3

Data as orig. reptd.; bef. results of disc. opers. and/or spec. items. Per share data adj. for stk. divs. as of ex-div. date. Bold denotes diluted EPS (FASB 128). E-Estimated. NA-Not Available. NM-Not Meaningful. NR-Not Ranked.

Office—950 Page Mill Rd. (P.O. Box 10950), Palo Alto, CA 94303-0802. **Tel**—(650) 494-5000. **Website**—http://www.alza.com **Chrmn & CEO**—E. Mario. **VP & CFO**—B. C. Cozadd. **VP & Treas**—D. R. Hoffmann. **Investor Contact**—Karen L. Bergman. **Dirs**—W. R. Brody, W. G. Davis, R. J. Glaser, E. Mario, D. O. Morton, D. M. O'Leary, I. Stein, J. N. Stern. **Transfer Agent & Registrar**—First National Bank of Boston. **Incorporated**—in California in 1968; reincorporated in Delaware in 1987. **Empl**— 1,532. **S&P Analyst:** H. Saftlas

Amerada Hess

80

NYSE Symbol **AHC**

In S&P 500

12-SEP-98

Industry:
Oil (Domestic Integrated)

Summary: This integrated oil and natural gas company has been emphasizing exploration both in the North Sea and the Gulf of Mexico.

S&P Opinion: Avoid (★★)

Recent Price • 53½	Yield • 1.1%
52 Wk Range • 64½-46	12-Mo. P/E • NM

Quantitative Evaluations

Outlook
(1 Lowest—5 Highest)
• **1**

Fair Value
• **44⅜**

Risk
• **Low**

Earn./Div. Rank
• **B-**

Technical Eval.
• **Bullish** since 6/98

Rel. Strength Rank
(1 Lowest—99 Highest)
• **94**

Insider Activity
• **NA**

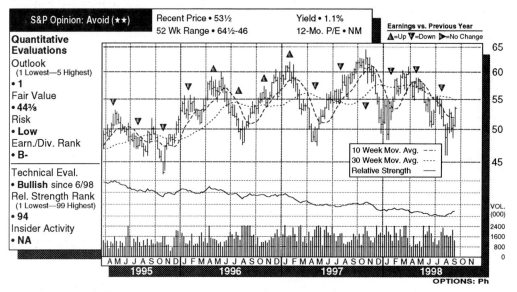

Earnings vs. Previous Year
▲=Up ▼=Down ▶=No Change

10 Week Mov. Avg. - - -
30 Week Mov. Avg. ·····
Relative Strength —

OPTIONS: Ph

Overview - 11-AUG-98

Results in recent periods have been affected by numerous non-operating items, both positive and negative. The loss of $0.38 recorded during the first half of 1998 includes $0.61 in gains from sales of three oil and gas properties in the U.S. and Norway. Share earnings of $0.08 in 1997 include a $0.60 charge for a writedown of North Sea oil and gas properties and a $0.42 refund of U.K. taxes. For 1996, earnings of $7.09 per share included $4.52 of gains on sales of exploration and production properties, including the company's Canadian subsidiary. During 1997, crude oil production declined 7.7%, and natural gas production fell 17%, reflecting the effect of asset sales. Long-term profitability will be enhanced by several strategic moves taken over the past two years, including significant debt reduction, a refocusing of the oil and gas asset base, and the formation of a joint venture with Petroleos de Venezuela (PDVSA) to own and operate AHC's St. Croix, Virgin Islands refinery. However, results for 1998 will be adversely affected by significantly lower oil prices.

Valuation - 11-AUG-98

The recent oil price slide has taken its toll on AHC's shares, which have declined 14% in 1998 to date. The sale of underperforming Canadian and noncore U.S. assets bodes well, as does the recently announced sale of 50% of the St. Croix refinery to Petroleos de Venezuela. However, an unsteady refining margin environment currently prevails, as petroleum product prices have fallen along with the sharp drop in crude oil prices. In addition, the lower oil prices we forecast for 1998 should put some pressure on the shares. We expect the shares to continue underperforming the overall market over the next six to twelve months.

Key Stock Statistics

S&P EPS Est. 1998	0.50	Tang. Bk. Value/Share	34.43
P/E on S&P Est. 1998	NM	Beta	0.68
S&P EPS Est. 1999	2.00	Shareholders	10,200
Dividend Rate/Share	0.60	Market cap. (B)	$ 4.9
Shs. outstg. (M)	91.0	Inst. holdings	62%
Avg. daily vol. (M)	0.348		

Value of $10,000 invested 5 years ago: $ 12,431

Fiscal Year Ending Dec. 31

	1998	1997	1996	1995	1994	1993
Revenues (Million $)						
1Q	1,923	2,416	2,215	1,892	1,858	1,578
2Q	1,644	1,879	2,095	1,773	1,488	1,403
3Q	—	1,901	1,746	1,642	1,494	1,246
4Q	—	2,144	2,216	1,995	1,762	1,645
Yr.	—	8,340	8,272	7,302	6,602	5,873
Earnings Per Share ($)						
1Q	**-0.14**	**0.05**	0.71	0.27	0.90	0.04
2Q	**-0.24**	**0.45**	4.04	-0.43	-0.18	-1.57
3Q	—	**0.25**	1.05	-1.13	-0.02	-0.24
4Q	—	**-0.67**	1.29	-2.95	0.09	-1.45
Yr.	**E0.50**	**0.08**	7.09	-4.24	0.79	-3.22

Next earnings report expected: late October

Dividend Data (Dividends have been paid since 1922.)

Amount ($)	Date Decl.	Ex-Div. Date	Stock of Record	Payment Date
0.150	Dec. 03	Dec. 11	Dec. 15	Jan. 05 '98
0.150	Mar. 04	Mar. 12	Mar. 16	Mar. 31 '98
0.150	Jun. 03	Jun. 11	Jun. 15	Jun. 30 '98
0.150	Sep. 02	Sep. 10	Sep. 14	Sep. 30 '98

A Division of The McGraw-Hill Companies

Business Summary - 11-AUG-98

Amerada Hess (AHC) has undertaken a plan to enhance profitability and increase shareholder returns. During 1996, the company sold $1 billion of exploration and production properties (including its Canadian subsidiary), reduced debt by nearly $800 million, completed the development of high rate of return oil and gas fields, and increased gasoline capacity at its refinery in the Virgin Islands. Additional profit-enhancing steps were taken in 1997.

Almost all of AHC's reserves are now located in its two core areas, the U.S. and the North Sea. Net crude and natural gas liquids production in 1997 averaged 218,572 barrels/day (236,797 in 1996), of which 20% came from the U.S. Natural gas production averaged 569.3 million cubic feet (MMcf) a day (684.7), with 55% in the U.S. The production declines were primarily due to asset sales. Converting the company's gas production to barrels of oil equivalent (6,000 cubic feet of gas equals one barrel), AHC produced 313,448 barrels of oil equivalent/day (BOE/d) in 1997. The company's goal is to produce 500,000 BOE/d by the end of 2000.

Refinery runs averaged 411,000 barrels/day (b/d) in 1997 (396,000 b/d in 1995), and refined products sold totaled 509,000 b/d (495,000 b/d). Refineries are located at St. Croix, U.S. Virgin Islands, and Port Reading, NJ. The St. Croix refinery's fluid catalytic cracking unit, which is responsible for increasing the yield of higher value products, principally gasoline, is now operating at 125,000 b/d, after its capacity was increased from 110/000 b/d during a routine maintenance turnaround in late 1996. Amerada Hess plans to increase the number of company-owned retail stations, and expects to offer more products and services to customers at these locations.

Amerada Hess has for some time stated that it will consider joint ventures involving some or all of its refining and marketing operations. The company undertook such a move in February 1998, when it reached an agreement with state-owned oil giant Petroleos de Venezuela, S.A. (PDVSA), under which PDVSA would acquire a 50% interest in AHC's St. Croix refinery for $625 million, payable over ten years. The two companies will also upgrade the refinery's heavy oil capability, allowing it to process heavy Venezuelan oil. The move is consistent with an emerging trend of industry consolidation that has resulted in several refining and marketing joint ventures and mergers, both in the U.S. and overseas, over the past two years.

Per Share Data ($)

(Year Ended Dec. 31)	1997	1996	1995	1994	1993	1992	1991	1990	1989	1988
Tangible Bk. Val.	35.16	36.35	28.60	33.33	32.71	36.59	38.63	38.34	31.69	27.02
Cash Flow	7.40	15.52	5.37	10.77	5.69	9.63	11.26	15.13	12.60	6.90
Earnings	0.08	7.09	-4.24	0.79	-3.21	0.09	1.04	5.96	5.87	1.51
Dividends	0.60	0.60	0.60	0.60	0.60	0.60	0.60	0.60	0.60	0.60
Payout Ratio	NM	8%	NM	76%	NM	736%	58%	10%	10%	40%
Prices - High	64½	60½	53⅝	52⅝	56⅜	51¼	59⅛	56	51⅞	33¼
- Low	47⅜	47½	43¼	43¾	42⅜	36⅝	42½	42⅞	31	22½
P/E Ratio - High	NM	9	NM	67	NM	NM	57	9	9	22
- Low	NM	7	NM	55	NM	NM	41	7	5	15

Income Statement Analysis (Million $)

	1997	1996	1995	1994	1993	1992	1991	1990	1989	1988
Revs.	8,234	8,272	7,302	6,602	5,852	5,875	6,267	6,948	5,589	4,206
Oper. Inc.	910	1,306	1,149	1,312	737	1,009	973	1,450	1,164	679
Depr.	673	783	893	928	825	833	829	743	546	441
Int. Exp.	136	166	247	245	249	255	238	259	196	145
Pretax Inc.	127	1,014	-351	236	-222	123	116	616	520	150
Eff. Tax Rate	94%	35%	NM	69%	NM	94%	27%	22%	8.50%	17%
Net Inc.	8.0	660	-393	74.0	-297	8.0	84.0	483	476	124

Balance Sheet & Other Fin. Data (Million $)

	1997	1996	1995	1994	1993	1992	1991	1990	1989	1988
Cash	91.0	113	56.0	53.0	80.0	141	120	130	120	213
Curr. Assets	2,204	2,427	1,963	1,722	1,688	2,068	2,476	3,280	1,951	1,570
Total Assets	7,935	7,784	7,756	8,338	8,642	8,722	8,841	9,057	6,867	5,372
Curr. Liab.	1,740	1,737	1,605	1,201	1,443	1,517	1,851	2,677	1,458	1,285
LT Debt	2,003	1,712	2,587	3,235	3,515	3,141	3,023	2,532	2,348	1,314
Common Eqty.	3,216	3,384	2,660	3,100	3,029	3,388	3,132	3,106	2,561	2,215
Total Cap.	5,781	5,712	5,850	6,882	7,006	7,046	6,790	6,198	5,306	3,914
Cap. Exp.	1,346	861	692	596	1,348	1,558	1,712	1,461	1,561	730
Cash Flow	681	1,443	499	1,002	527	841	913	1,226	1,022	566
Curr. Ratio	1.3	1.4	1.2	1.4	1.2	1.4	1.3	1.2	1.3	1.2
% LT Debt of Cap.	34.6	30.0	44.2	47.0	50.2	44.6	44.5	40.9	44.3	33.6
% Net Inc.of Revs.	0.1	8.0	NM	1.1	NM	0.1	1.3	6.9	8.5	3.0
% Ret. on Assets	0.1	8.5	NM	0.9	NM	0.1	0.9	6.1	7.8	2.3
% Ret. on Equity	0.2	21.8	NM	2.4	NM	0.2	2.7	17.0	20.1	5.7

Data as orig. reptd.; bef. results of disc. opers. and/or spec. items. Revenues exclude excise taxes and other income. Per share data adj. for stk. divs. as of ex-div. date. E-Estimated. NA-Not Available. NM-Not Meaningful. NR-Not Ranked.

Office—1185 Avenue of the Americas, New York, NY 10036. **Registrar**—ChaseMellon Shareholder Services, Ridgefield Park, NJ. **Tel**—(212) 997-8500. **Website**—http://www.hess.com **Chrmn & CEO**—J. B. Hess. **Pres & COO**—W. S. H. Laidlaw. **EVP & CFO**—J. Y. Schreyer. **VP, Secy & Investor Contact**—Carl T. Tursi. **Dirs**—N.F. Brady, J. B. Collins II, P. S. Hadley, J. B. Hess, L. Hess, E. E. Holiday, W. R. Johnson, T. H. Kean, W. S. H. Laidlaw, H. W. McCollum, F. A. Olson, R. B. Oresman, J. Y. Schreyer, W. I. Spencer, R. N. Wilson, R. F. Wright. **Transfer Agents**—The Bank of New York, NYC; First Union National Bank, Charlotte, NC; CIBC Mellon Trust Co., Toronto, Ontario, Canada. **Incorporated**—in Delaware in 1920. **Empl**— 9,216. **S&P Analyst:** Norman Rosenberg

12-SEP-98

Industry:
Electric Companies

Summary: Ameren, formed by the December 1997 merger of Union Electric, Missouri's largest electric utility, and CIPSCO, serves about 1.5 million electric and 300,000 natural gas customers.

S&P Opinion: Avoid (★★)	Recent Price • 39½	Yield • 6.4%
	52 Wk Range • 43¾-35½	12-Mo. P/E • 14.1

Quantitative Evaluations

Outlook
(1 Lowest—5 Highest)
• 1⁻

Fair Value
• 36¾

Risk
• **Low**

Earn./Div. Rank
• A-

Technical Eval.
• **NA**

Rel. Strength Rank
(1 Lowest—99 Highest)
• **90**

Insider Activity
• **Neutral**

Earnings vs. Previous Year
▲=Up ▼=Down ▶=No Change

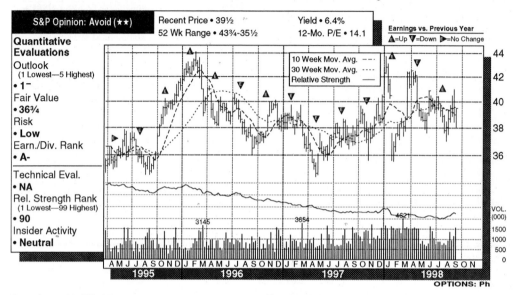

10 Week Mov. Avg. ---
30 Week Mov. Avg. ·····
Relative Strength —

VOL. (000)

OPTIONS: Ph

Overview - 29-JUL-98

Ameren posted second quarter 1998 earnings of $0.61 per share, up from $0.58 a year ago and above the Street consensus. Warm weather drove revenues 4% higher, offsetting greater costs related to the Callaway Nuclear Plant refueling and a $33 million ($0.14 per share) credit to Missouri customers. AEE is in good operating shape, but our prime concern is a high dividend payout. While AEE has enough cash to pay dividends and fund capital investments, we do not see any dividend increases over the next 4-5 years, and we expect little earnings improvement. We expect increased expenses from a recently started marketing segment to offset most of the anticipated merger-related cost savings, at least for the next two years. In addition, revenues will suffer from 5% lower residential electric rates for Ameren's Illinois electric customers, effective August 1, 1998. We could also see legislation deregulating the electric industry in Missouri in 1999, thereby putting greater pressure on earnings and dividends.

Valuation - 29-JUL-98

We continue to recommend avoiding AEE common stock, mainly due to our concerns of a high dividend payout ratio and the probability of downward earnings pressure from future deregulation. While the directors and management have indicated a strong commitment to the present dividend, even a flat dividend over the next few years without a significant increase in earnings growth, which we do not expect, diminishes the stock's value to shareholders. The company's operating fundamentals are sound, but we would wait until the regulatory picture is clearer in Missouri (where the company derives 72% of its revenue). AEE stock should underperform over the next 6-12 months.

Key Stock Statistics

S&P EPS Est. 1998	2.70	Tang. Bk. Value/Share	21.63
P/E on S&P Est. 1998	14.6	Beta	0.40
S&P EPS Est. 1999	2.80	Shareholders	110,100
Dividend Rate/Share	2.54	Market cap. (B)	$ 5.4
Shs. outstg. (M)	137.2	Inst. holdings	32%
Avg. daily vol. (M)	0.291		

Value of $10,000 invested 5 years ago: $ 14,964

Fiscal Year Ending Dec. 31

	1998	1997	1996	1995	1994	1993
Revenues (Million $)						
1Q	700.8	759.7	459.6	447.1	438.9	453.0
2Q	821.8	791.8	545.4	513.6	532.9	512.2
3Q	—	1,043	743.7	713.7	677.2	689.3
4Q	—	731.9	475.7	428.3	407.0	411.5
Yr.	—	3,327	2,260	2,103	2,056	2,066
Earnings Per Share ($)						
1Q	**0.29**	0.32	0.36	0.34	0.34	0.40
2Q	**0.61**	0.58	0.59	0.71	0.92	0.82
3Q	—	1.57	1.78	1.66	1.60	1.54
4Q	—	0.34	0.13	0.24	0.15	0.01
Yr.	**E2.70**	**2.82**	2.86	2.95	3.01	2.77

Next earnings report expected: NA

Dividend Data (Dividends have been paid since 1906.)

Amount ($)	Date Decl.	Ex-Div. Date	Stock of Record	Payment Date
0.635	Oct. 10	Nov. 14	Nov. 18	Dec. 30 '97
0.635	Feb. 13	Mar. 06	Mar. 10	Mar. 31 '98
0.635	Apr. 28	Jun. 08	Jun. 10	Jun. 30 '98
0.635	Aug. 28	Sep. 08	Sep. 10	Sep. 30 '98

A Division of The McGraw-Hill Companies

Business Summary - 29-JUL-98

The merger of Union Electric (now AmerenUE), Missouri's largest electric utility, and CIPSCO Inc. (AmerenCIPS), the holding company for Central Illinois Public Service, was completed on December 31, 1997, creating the 14th largest U.S. electric utility in terms of generating capacity, and the 19th largest in kilowatt-hour (Kwh) sales. UE and CIPS now operate as subsidiaries of Ameren.

Cost savings are expected to be achieved via elimination of duplicate corporate and administrative services, including reduction of the combined staffs of UE and CIPS by more than 300 positions, largely through attrition. Savings will also come from jointly dispatching power, realizing purchasing economies, and decreasing gas reserve margins and pipeline demand charges. Although the company expects to realize most of the savings at the back end of the next 10 years, it looks for some savings as early as 1998. The electric revenue mix for Ameren in 1997 was residential 35%, commercial 30%, industrial 16% and wholesale/other 19%. In 1997, the company sold 43 million dekatherms of natural gas to 294,147 gas customers and 63,981 million Kwh of electricity to 1,471,204 electric customers.

In December 1997, the governor of Illinois signed the Electric Service Customer Choice and Rate Relief Law of 1997, providing for electric utility restructuring in Illinois. The act includes a 5% rate decrease for the company's Illinois residential electric customers, effective August 1, 1998. The company may be subject to additional 5% residential electric rate decreases in each of 2000 and 2002, to the extent that its rates exceed the Midwest utility average at that time. Access for commercial and industrial customers will occur between October 1999 and December 2000, and access to residential customers will occur after May 1, 2002. Other provisions of the act include (1) potential recovery of a portion of stranded costs; (2) an option to eliminate the uniform fuel adjustment clause; and (3) a mechanism to securitize certain future revenues. At December 31, 1997, the company's net investment in generation facilities related to its Illinois retail jurisdiction approximated $836 million.

In Missouri, where approximately 72% of AEE's retail electric revenues are derived, a task force appointed by the Missouri Public Service Commission (MoPSC) is conducting studies of electric industry restructuring and competition, and is expected to issue a report to MoPSC in 1998. At December 31, 1997, the company's net investment in generation facilities related to its Missouri jurisdiction was about $2.7 billion, and net generation-related regulatory assets approximated $462 million.

Per Share Data ($)

(Year Ended Dec. 31)	1997	1996	1995	1994	1993	1992	1991	1990	1989	1988
Tangible Bk. Val.	21.92	22.86	22.18	21.64	20.98	20.75	20.32	19.49	18.84	18.22
Earnings	2.82	2.86	2.95	3.01	2.77	2.83	3.01	2.74	2.61	2.56
Dividends	2.54	2.51	2.46	2.40	2.33	2.26	2.18	2.10	2.02	1.94
Payout Ratio	90%	88%	83%	80%	84%	80%	72%	77%	77%	76%
Prices - High	43¾	44⅛	42	39½	44⅝	38¾	38⅝	30	28⅝	25
- Low	34½	36	34⅝	30¾	35¾	31¾	28½	24⅝	23	21⅜
P/E Ratio - High	16	15	14	13	16	14	11	11	11	10
- Low	12	13	12	10	13	11	9	9	9	8

Income Statement Analysis (Million $)

	1997	1996	1995	1994	1993	1992	1991	1990	1989	1988
Revs.	3,327	2,260	2,103	2,056	2,066	2,015	2,097	2,023	2,010	2,029
Depr.	346	241	233	226	220	214	204	200	196	196
Maint.	310	224	222	198	190	187	170	176	156	163
Fxd. Chgs. Cov.	4.1	4.3	4.3	4.5	4.1	4.1	4.0	3.5	3.5	3.1
Constr. Credits	12.7	13.5	13.0	11.0	12.0	8.0	9.0	14.0	18.0	15.0
Eff. Tax Rate	38%	39%	40%	39%	38%	39%	41%	39%	39%	38%
Net Inc.	387	305	314	321	297	303	322	294	286	292

Balance Sheet & Other Fin. Data (Million $)

	1997	1996	1995	1994	1993	1992	1991	1990	1989	1988
Gross Prop.	12,273	9,040	8,930	8,454	8,344	8,062	7,753	7,512	7,310	7,126
Cap. Exp.	381	376	354	345	304	323	263	256	213	208
Net Prop.	6,987	5,383	5,435	5,345	5,265	5,201	5,119	5,121	5,118	5,152
Capitalization:										
LT Debt	2,506	1,799	1,764	1,823	1,767	1,660	1,730	1,948	2,107	2,189
% LT Debt	44	41	41	42	42	41	43	47	49	50
Pfd.	235	219	219	219	219	219	219	219	228	341
% Pfd.	4.10	5.00	5.10	5.10	5.20	5.40	5.40	5.20	5.30	7.70
Common	3,019	2,355	2,319	2,269	2,206	2,164	2,106	2,021	1,954	1,895
% Common	52	54	54	53	53	54	52	48	46	43
Total Cap.	7,507	5,851	5,826	5,834	5,731	5,071	5,046	5,135	5,202	5,298
% Oper. Ratio	82.5	81.1	79.0	78.1	80.1	79.6	77.0	77.4	76.8	76.1
% Earn. on Net Prop.	8.4	8.0	8.4	8.5	7.9	8.0	9.4	8.9	9.1	9.3
% Return On Revs.	11.6	13.5	14.9	15.6	14.4	15.0	15.3	14.5	14.2	14.4
% Return On Invest. Capital	7.7	7.4	7.6	7.9	7.8	8.6	9.5	9.1	8.5	8.9
% Return On Com. Equity	12.8	12.5	13.1	13.8	13.0	13.7	15.0	14.2	14.0	14.1

Data as orig. reptd.; bef. results of disc. opers. and/or spec. items. Per share data adj. for stk. divs. as of ex-div. date. Bold denotes diluted EPS (FASB 128). E-Estimated. NA-Not Available. NM-Not Meaningful. NR-Not Ranked.

Office—One Ameren Plaza, 1901 Chouteau Ave., St Louis, MO 63103. **Tel**—(314) 621-3222. **Website**—http://www.ameren.com **Chrmn, Pres & CEO**—C. W. Mueller. **Secy**—J. C. Thompson. **Treas**—J. E. Birdsong. **Investor Contact**—Robin Goodwin (314-554-4829). **Dirs**—W. E. Cornelius, C. L. Greenwalt, T. A. Hays, R. A. Liddy, G. R. Lohman, R. A. Lumpkin, J. P. MacCarthy, H. M. Merriman, P. L. Miller Jr., C. W. Mueller, R. H. Quenon, H. Saligman, C. J. Schukai, J. M. Weakley, J. W. Wogsland. **Transfer Agent & Registrar**—Co.'s office. **Incorporated**—in Missouri in 1922. **Empl**—6,035. **S&P Analyst:** J. Robert Cho

12-SEP-98

Industry:
Electric Companies

Summary: This electric utility holding company, operating in Ohio, Indiana, Michigan, Virginia, West Virginia, Kentucky and Tennessee, has agreed to merge with Central and South West.

S&P Opinion: Accumulate (★★★★)	Recent Price • 45⅝	Yield • 5.3%
	52 Wk Range • 52-42	12-Mo. P/E • 14.5

Quantitative Evaluations

Outlook
(1 Lowest—5 Highest)
• **1**

Fair Value
• **34⅞**

Risk
• **Low**

Earn./Div. Rank
• **B+**

Technical Eval.
• **Bearish** since 6/98

Rel. Strength Rank
(1 Lowest—99 Highest)
• **91**

Insider Activity
• **NA**

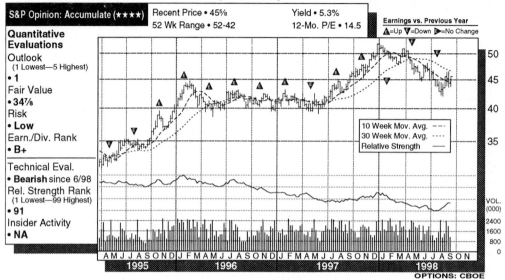

Earnings vs. Previous Year
▲=Up ▼=Down ▶=No Change

10 Week Mov. Avg. - - - -
30 Week Mov. Avg. ‧‧‧‧‧
Relative Strength ——

VOL. (000)

OPTIONS: CBOE

Overview - 11-AUG-98

The proposed merger of AEP and Central and South West (CSR) would result in the largest electric utility in the U.S., serving 4.6 million customers in 11 states, with around $11 billion in annual revenues. The companies expect the merger to realize cost savings of about $2 billion over a 10-year period, to be dilutive by about 3% in the first year after its anticipated completion (around mid-1999), and to become accretive by the end of the third year. We expect earnings to remain essentially flat in 1998. First half results were hurt by mild first quarter weather, snowstorm repair costs, and the shutdown of the Cook nuclear plant. We do not expect to see Unit 1 returned until the turn of the year, with Unit 2 not expected to be back until several months thereafter. Still, we expect AEP to derive long-term benefit from its strength in wholesale energy sales and from the expansion of its international operations.

Valuation - 11-AUG-98

We would continue to accumulate AEP stock. With the shares down about 16% year to date, the stock has become an attractive investment for both the near term and the long term. While the proposed $6.6 billion merger with CSR would be dilutive over the first two years after its anticipated mid-1999 completion, it would provide the new AEP with a regional range that would enable it to become a major marketing force in the U.S. Although we expect the merger to obtain all of the required regulatory approvals, whatever uncertainties are encountered could restrict the performance of the shares. Given the costs related to the proposed merger, we do not expect to see an increase in the dividend. Still, with the dividend now yielding well over 5%, and the shares trading at 12 times our 1999 EPS estimate of $3.50, the stock is attractive for both income and growth oriented investors.

Key Stock Statistics

S&P EPS Est. 1998	3.30	Tang. Bk. Value/Share	24.94
P/E on S&P Est. 1998	13.8	Beta	0.21
S&P EPS Est. 1999	3.50	Shareholders	194,000
Dividend Rate/Share	2.40	Market cap. (B)	$ 8.7
Shs. outstg. (M)	190.9	Inst. holdings	41%
Avg. daily vol. (M)	0.360		

Value of $10,000 invested 5 years ago: $ 19,187

Fiscal Year Ending Dec. 31

	1998	1997	1996	1995	1994	1993
Revenues (Million $)						
1Q	2,171	1,492	1,518	1,416	1,488	1,321
2Q	2,738	1,382	1,401	1,305	1,349	1,210
3Q	—	1,584	1,482	1,523	1,385	1,406
4Q	—	1,703	1,446	1,425	1,283	1,331
Yr.	—	6,167	5,849	5,670	5,505	5,269
Earnings Per Share ($)						
1Q	**0.79**	0.92	0.96	0.80	0.83	0.72
2Q	**0.60**	0.64	0.60	0.52	0.56	0.47
3Q	**E1.09**	1.07	0.87	0.83	0.76	-0.06
4Q	**E0.80**	0.66	0.71	0.70	0.56	0.79
Yr.	**E3.30**	3.28	3.14	2.85	2.71	1.92

Next earnings report expected: late October

Dividend Data (Dividends have been paid since 1909.)

Amount ($)	Date Decl.	Ex-Div. Date	Stock of Record	Payment Date
0.600	Oct. 29	Nov. 06	Nov. 10	Dec. 10 '97
0.600	Jan. 28	Feb. 06	Feb. 10	Mar. 10 '98
0.600	Apr. 22	May. 06	May. 08	Jun. 10 '98
0.600	Jul. 22	Aug. 06	Aug. 10	Sep. 10 '98

A Division of The **McGraw·Hill** *Companies*

Business Summary - 11-AUG-98

In December 1997, AEP and Central and South West (CSR) agreed to merge into a new company that will maintain the name of American Electric Power Company, Inc. Under the terms of the agreement, the shareholders of Central South West will receive 0.6 shares of AEP common stock for each CSR share, with AEP to issue about $6.6 billion in stock. The companies expect the proposed merger to be completed by mid-1999.

American Electric Power provides electricity through its subsidiaries (which began to do business as "American Electric Power" in 1996) to a population of nearly seven million people in portions of Ohio, Indiana, Michigan, Virginia, West Virginia, Kentucky and Tennessee. Electric revenues by customer class in recent years were:

	1997	1996	1995	1994
Residential	31%	33%	34%	33%
Commercial	21%	22%	22%	22%
Industrial	27%	28%	28%	30%
Wholesale	17%	14%	12%	13%
Other	4%	3%	4%	2%

Sources of electric power generation in 1997 were coal 87%, nuclear 9%, and hydro and other 4%.

In February 1997, the company and Public Service of Colorado (NYSE: PSR) made a joint $2.4 billion cash tender offer for Yorkshire Electricity Group, a U.K.-based regional electric company with FY 96 (Mar.) revenues of $2.2 billion and pretax profits of about $311 million. The tender offer was essentially completed in April 1997. AEP and PSR will each invest $360 million in the joint venture, with the remaining $1.7 billion provided by non-recourse loans.

In 1996, one of the company's unregulated subsidiaries, AEP Resources, agreed to participate in the design and construction of two coal-fired, 125 megawatt plants near Nanyang City in the Henan province of China. The plants are expected to be completed by early 1999. The company hopes that its role in the development of the plant, which will be 70%-owned by AEP Resources, will result in a long-term involvement in the building of additional facilities in this rapidly growing market.

In September 1997, AEP shut down Units 1 and 2 of the Cook Nuclear Plant (which constitute around 9% of the company's generating capacity), after questions were raised as to whether the systems used to cool the reactor and containment during a postulated accident would function on a long-term basis. Unit 1 is not expected to be returned to operation until late 1998 or early 1999, while Unit 2 would not be back until at least several months after the return of Unit 1.

In October 1996, the company formed a new subsidiary, AEP Communications Inc., to offer installation, maintenance and engineering services for companies that provide wireless personal communications services and competitive local exchange services.

Per Share Data ($)

(Year Ended Dec. 31)	1997	1996	1995	1994	1993	1992	1991	1990	1989	1988
Tangible Bk. Val.	24.62	23.96	23.08	22.67	22.33	22.87	22.79	22.49	22.60	21.73
Earnings	3.28	3.14	2.85	2.71	1.92	2.54	2.70	2.65	3.25	3.24
Dividends	2.40	2.40	2.40	2.40	2.40	2.40	2.40	2.40	2.36	2.34
Payout Ratio	73%	76%	84%	89%	125%	95%	89%	91%	73%	72%
Prices - High	52	44¾	40⅝	37⅜	40⅜	35¼	34¼	33⅛	33⅜	29¾
- Low	39⅛	38⅝	31¼	27¼	32	30⅜	26⅝	26	25¾	25⅞
P/E Ratio - High	16	14	14	14	21	14	13	13	10	9
- Low	12	12	11	10	17	12	10	10	8	8

Income Statement Analysis (Million $)

	1997	1996	1995	1994	1993	1992	1991	1990	1989	1988
Revs.	6,161	5,849	5,670	5,505	5,269	5,045	5,047	5,167	5,140	4,841
Depr.	591	601	593	572	531	510	508	478	462	451
Maint.	483	503	542	544	523	525	490	502	475	436
Fxd. Chgs. Cov.	3.2	3.1	2.8	2.6	2.5	2.3	2.4	2.5	2.9	2.7
Constr. Credits	NA	NA	NA	NA	NA	9.0	25.0	85.0	184	167
Eff. Tax Rate	32%	34%	33%	26%	32%	26%	25%	25%	29%	27%
Net Inc.	620	587	530	500	354	468	498	496	629	627

Balance Sheet & Other Fin. Data (Million $)

	1997	1996	1995	1994	1993	1992	1991	1990	1989	1988
Gross Prop.	21,181	18,970	18,496	18,175	17,712	17,510	17,148	16,653	16,108	16,651
Cap. Exp.	760	578	606	643	592	629	636	671	838	914
Net Prop.	13,217	11,420	11,385	11,348	11,100	11,228	11,196	11,064	10,843	11,703
Capitalization:										
LT Debt	5,167	4,832	4,920	4,687	4,964	5,126	4,793	4,785	4,516	5,422
% LT Debt	52	48	50	48	50	51	50	50	47	52
Pfd.	174	600	663	824	769	765	673	680	701	746
% Pfd.	1.80	6.00	6.70	8.50	7.80	7.60	6.90	7.00	7.30	7.20
Common	4,677	4,545	4,340	4,230	4,152	4,246	4,222	4,167	4,394	4,226
% Common	47	46	44	43	42	42	44	43	46	41
Total Cap.	13,053	13,024	13,010	12,669	12,841	11,754	11,530	11,638	11,619	12,405
% Oper. Ratio	75.5	82.8	83.0	83.1	82.4	82.5	81.8	83.3	80.5	78.9
% Earn. on Net Prop.	7.6	8.8	8.5	8.3	8.3	7.8	8.2	7.9	8.9	8.9
% Return On Revs.	10.1	10.0	9.3	9.1	6.7	9.3	9.9	9.6	12.2	12.9
% Return On Invest. Capital	7.7	7.8	7.7	7.4	6.7	8.5	8.5	8.2	9.4	9.3
% Return On Com. Equity	13.4	13.2	12.4	11.9	8.4	11.1	11.9	11.6	14.6	15.1

Data as orig. reptd.; bef. results of disc. opers. and/or spec. items. Per share data adj. for stk. divs. as of ex-div. date. Bold denotes diluted EPS (FASB 128). E-Estimated. NA-Not Available. NM-Not Meaningful. NR-Not Ranked.

Office—1 Riverside Plaza, Columbus, OH 43215. **Tel**—(614) 223-1000. **Website**—http://www.aep.com **Chrmn, Pres & CEO**—E. L. Draper Jr. **SVP-Fin, CFO & Treas**—A. A. Pena. **Investor Contact**—John Bilacic. **Dirs**—J. B. DesBarres, E. L. Draper Jr., R. M. Duncan, R. W. Fri, L. A. Hudson Jr., L. J. Kujawa, A. E. Peyton, D. G. Smith, L. G. Stuntz, K. D. Sullivan, M. Tanenbaum. **Transfer Agent & Registrar**—First Chicago Trust Co. of New York, Jersey City, NJ. **Incorporated**—in New York in 1905. **Empl**— 17,844. **S&P Analyst**: Justin McCann

STANDARD &POOR'S
STOCK REPORTS

American Express

112L

NYSE Symbol **AXP**

In S&P 500

12-SEP-98

Industry: Financial (Diversified)

Summary: American Express, a leader in travel-related services, is also active in investment services, expense management services and international banking.

S&P Opinion: Buy (★★★★★)	Recent Price • 78⅜	Yield • 1.1%
	52 Wk Range • 118⅝-68	12-Mo. P/E • 18.0

Quantitative Evaluations

Outlook (1 Lowest—5 Highest)
• **2+**

Fair Value
• **74¼**

Risk
• **Low**

Earn./Div. Rank
• **B+**

Technical Eval.
• **Bearish** since 12/96

Rel. Strength Rank (1 Lowest—99 Highest)
• **36**

Insider Activity
• **Neutral**

Earnings vs. Previous Year
▲=Up ▼=Down ▶=No Change

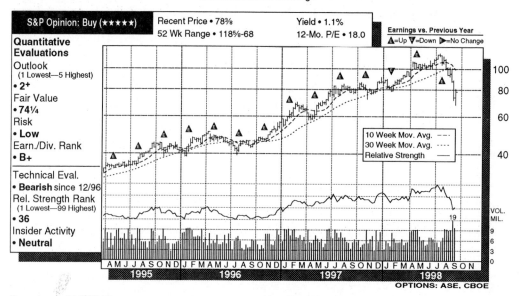

10 Week Mov. Avg. — —
30 Week Mov. Avg. ·····
Relative Strength —

OPTIONS: ASE, CBOE

Overview - 17-AUG-98

Earnings should continue to benefit from growth in charge card volume, reflecting higher spending per cardmember and an increase in cards outstanding. The charge card business is expected to benefit from the introduction of new card products such as co-branded cards and reward innovations targeted to specific market segments. One of AXP's most promising segments is TRS International, where net income is expected to increase 25% annually through at least 2000 as the company focuses on the most affluent markets and builds merchant coverage. An increase in assets under management in the Financial Advisors unit and greater sales of mutual funds should also have a favorable effect. Internal financial targets remain 12% to 15% annual earnings growth and 18% to 20% return on equity. Revenue growth is expected to account for 2/3 of the earnings gain over the next few years, with cost savings and share buybacks for the other 1/3.

Valuation - 17-AUG-98

After a strong performance in the first half of 1998, the shares have since given up some of the gain on concerns about slowing international and travel spending in reaction to comments from management at a recent analyst meeting. We thought the company was no more cautious than usual about its prospects and was merely trying to keep expectations reasonable. The company's growth strategies remain firmly in place, with several new business initiatives expected to keeping earnings momentum going. A substantial ongoing share repurchase program will continue to benefit earnings comparisons. With an expected growth rate well in excess of the broader market and successful long-term strategies working, purchase of the shares is recommended.

Key Stock Statistics

S&P EPS Est. 1998	4.75	Tang. Bk. Value/Share	20.35
P/E on S&P Est. 1998	16.5	Beta	1.41
S&P EPS Est. 1999	5.40	Shareholders	55,800
Dividend Rate/Share	0.90	Market cap. (B)	$ 35.8
Shs. outstg. (M)	456.4	Inst. holdings	63%
Avg. daily vol. (M)	2.813		

Value of $10,000 invested 5 years ago: NA

Fiscal Year Ending Dec. 31

	1998	1997	1996	1995	1994	1993
Revenues (Million $)						
1Q	4,521	4,164	4,257	3,771	3,370	3,360
2Q	4,761	4,422	4,056	3,967	3,506	3,520
3Q	—	4,500	4,044	4,054	3,604	3,580
4Q	—	4,674	3,882	4,048	3,802	3,710
Yr.	—	17,760	16,237	15,841	14,282	14,170
Earnings Per Share ($)						
1Q	0.98	0.94	1.23	0.70	0.62	1.41
2Q	1.24	1.08	0.95	0.81	0.70	0.60
3Q	E1.25	1.10	0.93	0.83	0.71	0.61
4Q	E1.28	1.04	0.80	0.77	0.65	0.57
Yr.	E4.75	4.15	3.89	3.11	2.68	3.17

Next earnings report expected: late October

Dividend Data (Dividends have been paid since 1870.)

Amount ($)	Date Decl.	Ex-Div. Date	Stock of Record	Payment Date
0.225	Sep. 22	Oct. 01	Oct. 03	Nov. 10 '97
0.225	Nov. 24	Dec. 30	Jan. 02	Feb. 10 '98
0.225	Mar. 30	Apr. 07	Apr. 09	May. 08 '98
0.225	May. 27	Jun. 30	Jul. 03	Aug. 10 '98

A Division of The McGraw-Hill Companies

Business Summary - 17-AUG-98

American Express, probably best known for its flagship charge card and travelers cheque products, also offers travel related services, financial advisory services and international banking services. The company's growth strategy is focused on three principal themes: expand its international presence, strengthen the charge card network, and broaden the offering of financial services. Contributions by principal operating segments in 1997 were:

	Revs.	Profits
Travel-related services	71%	62%
Financial Advisors	26%	34%
American Express Bank	3%	4%

Travel Related Services (TRS) markets travelers cheques and the American Express Card, including the Gold Card, the Platinum Card, the Corporate Card and the Optima Card. At year-end 1997, total cards in force worldwide aggregated 42.7 million, up 2.9% from December 31, 1996. Card charge volume in 1997 was $209.2 billion, up 14% from the level of 1996. Travelers cheque sales totaled $25.0 billion in 1997, down from $26.0 billion in 1996. TRS also offers business expense management products and services, corporate and consumer travel products, magazine publishing, database marketing and management, and merchant transaction processing.

In 1997, TRS introduced a number of new revolving credit card products and features designed to meet the needs of specific customer segments and to increase consumer loans outstanding, with a particular focus on international markets. Over the past few years, TRS has expanded its Membership Rewards program to include a broader range of travel rewards and retail merchandise and gourmet gifts. The program remains an important part of TRS's strategy to increase cardmember spending and loyalty.

Financial Advisors provides financial products including financial planning and advice, insurance and annuities, investment products such as certificates, mutual funds and limited partnerships, investment advisory services, trust and employee plan administration services, personal auto and homeowner's insurance, and retail securities brokerage services. At the end of 1997, managed assets totaled $173.4 billion, up from $149.4 billion the year before.

American Express Bank Ltd. offers products designed to meet the financial service needs of corporations, financial institutions, affluent individuals and retail customers. Its primary business lines are corporate banking and finance, correspondent banking, private banking, personal financial services and global trading.

Per Share Data ($)

(Year Ended Dec. 31)	1997	1996	1995	1994	1993	1992	1991	1990	1989	1988
Tangible Bk. Val.	20.53	18.03	16.60	12.57	16.81	14.58	14.43	13.21	12.90	11.39
Earnings	4.15	3.90	3.11	2.68	3.17	0.83	1.59	0.69	2.70	2.31
Dividends	0.90	1.13	0.90	0.93	1.00	1.00	0.96	0.92	0.86	0.76
Payout Ratio	22%	29%	29%	35%	32%	120%	60%	133%	32%	33%
Prices - High	91½	60⅜	45⅛	33⅛	36⅝	25⅜	30⅜	35¼	39⅜	30⅜
- Low	53⅝	38⅝	29	25	22⅜	20	18	17½	26⅜	22⅞
P/E Ratio - High	22	15	15	12	12	31	19	51	15	13
- Low	13	10	9	9	7	24	11	25	10	10

Income Statement Analysis (Million $)

	1997	1996	1995	1994	1993	1992	1991	1990	1989	1988
Cards in Force	42.7	41.5	37.8	36.3	35.4	34.7	36.6	NA	NA	NA
Card Chg Volume	209,200	184,000	163,000	141,000	124,000	118,000	111,000	NA	NA	NA
Premium Inc.	424	395	735	783	702	776	711	597	556	2,527
Commissions	4,386	2,540	2,542	8,591	7,818	13,188	12,006	11,475	11,513	10,375
Int & Div.	4,419	4,357	4,531	4,120	4,914	11,380	11,490	10,936	11,701	9,050
Total Revs.	17,760	16,237	15,841	14,282	14,173	26,961	25,763	24,332	25,047	22,934
Net Bef. Taxes	2,750	2,664	2,183	1,891	2,326	775	759	725	1,527	1,331
Net Inc.	1,991	1,901	1,564	1,380	1,605	436	789	338	1,157	988

Balance Sheet & Other Fin. Data (Million $)

	1997	1996	1995	1994	1993	1992	1991	1990	1989	1988
Total Assets	120,003	108,512	107,405	97,006	94,132	175,752	146,441	137,682	130,855	142,704
Cash Items	4,179	2,677	3,200	3,433	3,312	5,395	4,876	6,400	7,452	10,562
Investment Asset:										
Bonds	Nil	Nil	36,772	23,026	23,026	63,778	49,597	45,670	38,834	42,349
Stocks	Nil	Nil	Nil	Nil	Nil	1,693	1,982	1,968	2,136	3,837
Loans	20,109	18,518	21,595	29,830	29,904	22,782	24,047	18,213	17,963	15,553
Total	59,757	56,857	58,652	54,830	52,930	88,543	76,476	66,100	59,889	63,219
Accounts Receivable	21,774	20,491	19,914	17,147	16,142	32,785	29,882	34,729	34,437	31,710
Cust. Deposits	9,444	9,555	9,885	10,013	11,131	21,360	24,778	27,843	31,191	33,724
Travel Cheques Outst	5,634	5,838	5,697	5,271	4,800	4,729	4,375	4,225	3,834	3,820
Debt	7,873	6,552	7,570	7,162	8,561	15,122	13,292	12,521	14,348	13,508
Common Eqty.	9,574	8,528	8,020	6,233	8,234	6,999	6,815	6,135	5,391	4,748
% Ret. on Assets	1.7	1.8	1.5	1.4	1.7	0.3	0.6	0.3	0.8	0.8
% Ret. on Equity	22.0	22.9	21.3	18.6	20.5	5.7	11.6	5.3	22.5	21.6

Data as orig. reptd.; bef. results of disc. opers. and/or spec. items. Per share data adj. for stk. divs. as of ex-div. date. Bold denotes diluted EPS (FASB 128). E-Estimated. NA-Not Available. NM-Not Meaningful. NR-Not Ranked.

Organized—in Buffalo in 1850; incorporated in 1965. Office—World Financial Center, 200 Vesey St., New York, NY 10285. Tel—(212) 640-2000. Website—http://www.americanexpress.com Chrmn & CEO—H. Golub. Pres & COO—K. I. Chenault. Vice Chrmn & CFO—R. K. Goeltz. Vice Chrmn—G. L. Farr, J. S. Linen. Investor Contact—Susan Miller-Korchak. Dirs—D. F. Akerson, A. L. Armstrong, E. L. Artzt, W. G. Bowen, K. I. Chenault, C. W. Duncan, Jr., H. Golub, B. S. Greenough, F. R. Johnson, V. E. Jordan, Jr., J. Leschly, R. A. McGinn, D. Lewis, A. Papone, F. P. Popoff. Transfer Agent & Registrar—ChaseMellon Shareholder Services, Ridgefield Park, NJ.Incorporated—in New York in 1965; predecessor organized in 1868. Empl—73,620. S&P Analyst: Stephen R. Biggar

12-SEP-98

Industry:
Financial (Diversified)

Summary: American General is a diversified financial services company engaged primarily in the underwriting of life insurance, the sale of annuities and consumer finance lending.

S&P Opinion: Accumulate (★★★★)	Recent Price • 63⅞	Yield • 2.3%
	52 Wk Range • 75⅝-46½	12-Mo. P/E • 16.7

Quantitative Evaluations

Outlook
(1 Lowest—5 Highest)
• **1⁻**

Fair Value
• **58⅝**

Risk
• **Low**

Earn./Div. Rank
• **B+**

Technical Eval.
• **Bearish** since 3/98

Rel. Strength Rank
(1 Lowest—99 Highest)
• **77**

Insider Activity
• **Neutral**

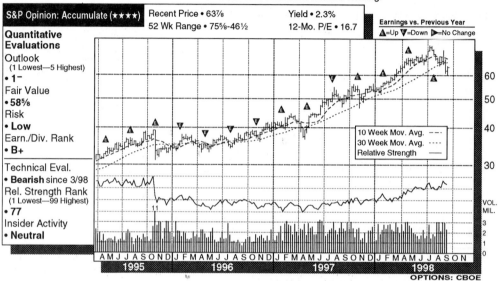

Earnings vs. Previous Year
▲=Up ▼=Down ▷=No Change

10 Week Mov. Avg. ---
30 Week Mov. Avg. ····
Relative Strength —

OPTIONS: CBOE

Overview - 07-AUG-98

Operating earnings growth in 1998 will be aided by continued asset increases, greater market penetration and relatively stable net interest margins in the annuity sector. Results will also be aided by contributions from two recent life insurance acquisitions--Home Beneficial and USLIFE. The February 1998 acquisition of the 55% of Western National it did not already own expanded AGC's presence in the fixed annuities market. So too did the recently completed purchase of Provident Companies' (NYSE: PVT) single premium fixed and tax sheltered annuity business (with $2.4 billion in reserves) for $58 million. Ongoing life insurance profit growth will be aided by contributions from two previous acquisitions (Franklin Life in January 1995 and Independent Life in February 1996) and by expense cuts and productivity gains, which should help offset moderating life insurance policy sales. Consumer finance profits should benefit from recently taken steps, such as slowing receivables growth, selling underperforming assets and shifting the business mix to more real estate-secured loans. Delinquencies were 3.43% of receivables at June 30, 1998, down from 3.60% at year end 1997, and 3.83% at year end 1996. EPS comparisons should be aided by share buybacks.

Valuation - 07-AUG-98

After a mid-1997 runup, sparked by favorable investor reaction to the $1.8 billion acquisition of USLIFE Corp., the shares plateaued. We used this as an opportunity to upgrade our opinion. Despite the shares strength in 1998, we believe there is more upside potential in the stock, particularly since AGC is hitting its targets of 12%-14% operating EPS growth and 15% ROE. EPS estimates are based on operating earnings (which exclude realized investment gains/losses); actual EPS are based on net income.

Key Stock Statistics

S&P EPS Est. 1998	4.00	Tang. Bk. Value/Share	28.27
P/E on S&P Est. 1998	16.0	Beta	0.93
S&P EPS Est. 1999	4.50	Shareholders	27,600
Dividend Rate/Share	1.50	Market cap. (B)	$ 16.2
Shs. outstg. (M)	253.1	Inst. holdings	71%
Avg. daily vol. (M)	0.566		

Value of $10,000 invested 5 years ago: $ 27,026

Fiscal Year Ending Dec. 31

	1998	1997	1996	1995	1994	1993
Revenues (Million $)						
1Q	2,479	2,142	1,711	1,518	1,214	1,960
2Q	2,556	2,226	1,721	1,627	1,232	1,205
3Q	—	2,235	1,725	1,673	1,265	1,222
4Q	—	2,324	1,730	1,677	1,130	1,215
Yr.	—	8,927	6,887	6,495	4,841	4,829
Earnings Per Share ($)						
1Q	0.96	0.85	0.81	0.85	0.75	0.66
2Q	1.01	-0.52	0.79	0.88	0.75	0.70
3Q	—	0.91	0.82	0.86	0.77	0.55
4Q	—	0.92	0.33	0.05	0.18	-0.76
Yr.	—	2.19	2.75	2.64	2.45	1.15

Next earnings report expected: late October

Dividend Data (Dividends have been paid since 1929.)

Amount ($)	Date Decl.	Ex-Div. Date	Stock of Record	Payment Date
0.350	Oct. 23	Oct. 30	Nov. 03	Dec. 01 '97
0.375	Jan. 29	Feb. 10	Feb. 12	Mar. 01 '98
0.375	Apr. 30	May. 07	May. 11	Jun. 01 '98
0.375	Jul. 30	Aug. 06	Aug. 10	Sep. 01 '98

A Division of The McGraw-Hill Companies

Business Summary - 07-AUG-98

American General is one of the largest insurance-based financial services holding companies in the U.S. Its strategy is to focus on three segments of the financial services arena--retirement services, consumer finance and life insurance--and to build a critical mass of market dominance in each segment. Contributions to earnings by business segment in recent years were:

	1997	1996
Life insurance	59%	60%
Retirement annuities	25%	25%
Consumer finance	16%	14%

The life insurance segment underwrites and sells permanent and term life insurance to customers in their homes, through employee agents. Whole, term and interest-sensitive life insurance and annuities are also offered to middle- and upper-middle-income customers through agents, brokers and financial institutions. At December 31, 1997, insurance in force totaled $325 billion. Western National (45% owned) provides annuities marketed through banks and other financial institutions. In recent years, AGC has capitalized on consolidation

sweeping the life insurance industry, making several acquisitions. In April 1997, it acquired Home Beneficial Corp. for $665 million in cash and stock. Home Beneficial, with assets of $1.4 billion and shareholders' equity of $549 million, markets individual life insurance in six mid-Atlantic states and the District of Columbia. Perhaps the most visible acquisition was the June 1997 purchase of USLIFE Corp., for about 40 million AGC common shares, valued at $1.8 billion. This created one of the leading U.S. life insurance-based financial services entities, with combined market value over $12 billion. The pending acquisition of the 55% of Western National that AGC does not already own, for $1.2 billion in cash and stock was to close February 25, 1998.

The retirement annuities segment consists of Variable Annuity Life Insurance Co. (VALIC), one of the largest providers of retirement annuity plans for employees of nonprofit organizations. VALIC provides fixed and variable tax-qualified annuity products on a group and individual basis.

The consumer finance segment offers consumer credit-related products, including home equity loans, retail financing, credit-related insurance and credit cards. At December 31, 1997, receivables outstanding totaled $8.0 billion.

Per Share Data ($)

(Year Ended Dec. 31)	1997	1996	1995	1994	1993	1992	1991	1990	1989	1988
Tangible Bk. Val.	28.07	24.52	25.61	14.09	21.10	17.01	15.52	14.19	13.97	13.14
Oper. Earnings	3.49	3.07	2.57	3.00	1.12	2.41	2.13	1.86	1.55	1.53
Earnings	2.19	2.75	2.64	2.45	1.15	2.45	2.13	2.35	1.67	1.61
Dividends	1.40	1.30	1.24	1.16	1.10	1.04	1.00	1.40	0.75	0.70
Payout Ratio	64%	47%	47%	47%	96%	42%	47%	60%	45%	43%
Prices - High	56¼	41¾	39⅛	30½	36½	29⅜	22⅞	25⅜	19¼	18½
- Low	36½	32⅞	27½	24⅞	26¼	20⅛	14	11¾	14¾	13¾
P/E Ratio - High	26	15	15	12	32	12	11	11	12	11
- Low	17	12	10	10	23	8	7	5	9	9

Income Statement Analysis (Million $)

	1997	1996	1995	1994	1993	1992	1991	1990	1989	1988
Life Ins. In Force	331,676	156,253	149,184	104,751	92,634	101,179	97,534	90,514	90,721	86,490
Prem. Inc.: Life	2,529	1,164	1,064	632	668	703	698	699	724	734
Prem. Inc.: A & H	680	202	195	150	207	189	182	183	188	181
Prem. Inc.: Other	153	128	85.0	71.0	58.0	47.0	41.0	39.0	40.0	40.0
Net Invest. Inc.	NA	3,271	3,095	2,493	2,437	2,327	2,178	2,095	1,919	1,719
Total Revs.	8,873	6,887	6,495	4,841	4,829	4,602	4,395	4,481	4,227	3,823
Pretax Inc.	989	964	850	802	602	775	678	836	603	534
Net Oper. Inc.	NA	NA	537	627	244	524	479	446	383	390
Net Inc.	542	577	545	513	250	533	480	562	413	413

Balance Sheet & Other Fin. Data (Million $)

	1997	1996	1995	1994	1993	1992	1991	1990	1989	1988
Cash & Equiv.	263	149	161	45.0	6.0	17.0	39.0	91.0	108	119
Premiums Due	NA	NA	NA	NA	NA	NA	NA	NA	NA	NA
Invest. Assets: Bonds	47,747	38,490	37,213	25,700	26,546	21,343	17,955	15,954	13,952	12,520
Invest. Assets: Stocks	116	133	186	224	233	390	438	353	1,383	1,120
Invest. Assets: Loans	3,272	4,698	4,646	3,848	4,188	4,784	5,286	5,508	5,175	4,915
Invest. Assets: Total	54,589	44,270	42,904	30,697	31,876	27,814	25,025	23,057	21,548	19,220
Deferred Policy Costs	2,718	2,169	1,625	2,731	1,637	2,083	1,919	1,823	1,725	1,604
Total Assets	80,620	66,254	61,153	46,295	43,982	39,742	36,105	33,808	32,062	30,422
Debt	9,182	9,163	9,193	8,926	7,529	7,471	7,224	7,149	6,864	7,463
Common Eqty.	7,498	5,536	5,801	3,457	5,137	4,614	4,329	4,138	4,090	4,294
% Return On Revs.	6.1	8.4	8.4	10.6	5.2	11.6	10.9	12.5	9.8	10.8
% Ret. on Assets	0.7	0.9	1.0	1.1	0.6	1.4	1.4	1.7	1.3	1.5
% Ret. on Equity	8.2	10.1	11.8	11.9	5.2	11.9	11.3	13.7	9.8	9.7
% Invest. Yield	7.7	8.0	8.4	8.0	8.2	8.8	9.1	9.4	9.4	9.4

Data as orig. reptd.; bef. results of disc. opers. and/or spec. items. Per share data adj. for stk. divs. as of ex-div. date. Bold denotes diluted EPS (FASB 128). E-Estimated. NA-Not Available. NM-Not Meaningful. NR-Not Ranked.

Registrar & Transfer Agent—First Chicago Trust Co. of New York, NYC. **Office**—2929 Allen Parkway, Houston, TX 77019. **Tel**—(713) 522-1111. **Chrmn & CEO**—R. M. Devlin. **Pres**—J. S. D'Agostino. **VP-Treas**—J. L. Gleaves. **VP & Investor Contact**—Robert D. Mrlik (713-831-1137). **Secy**—S. A. Jacobs. **Dirs**—J. E. Attwell, B. F. Carruth, J. S. D'Agostino, W. L. Davis Jr., R. M. Devlin, L. D. Horner, R. J. V. Johnson, M. E. Murphy, J. P. Newton, R. E. Smittcamp, A. M. Tatlock. **Transfer Agent & Registrar**—First Chicago Trust Co. of New York, NYC. **Incorporated**—in Texas in 1926. **Empl**— 15,300. **S&P Analyst:** Catherine A. Seifert

American Greetings

121L

NYSE Symbol **AM**

In S&P 500

12-SEP-98

Industry:
Consumer (Jewelry, Novelties & Gifts)

Summary: American Greetings is the world's largest publicly owned greeting card company, with operations in more than 75 countries.

S&P Opinion: Hold (★★★)	Recent Price • 39¼	Yield • 1.9%
	52 Wk Range • 53¾-34	12-Mo. P/E • 15.0

Quantitative Evaluations

Outlook
(1 Lowest—5 Highest)
• **2+**

Fair Value
• **36¾**

Risk
• **Low**

Earn./Div. Rank
• **A**

Technical Eval.
• **Neutral** since 9/98

Rel. Strength Rank
(1 Lowest—99 Highest)
• **63**

Insider Activity
• **Neutral**

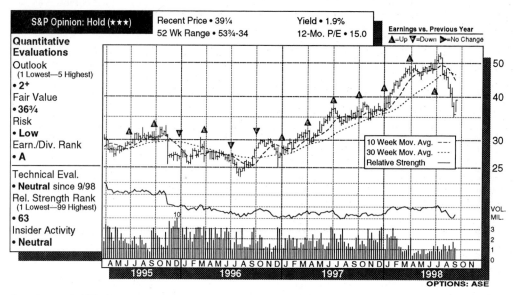

Earnings vs. Previous Year
▲=Up ▼=Down ▶=No Change

10 Week Mov. Avg. ---
30 Week Mov. Avg. ·····
Relative Strength —

OPTIONS: ASE

Overview - 17-AUG-98

Revenues are expected to rise at least 4% in FY 99 (Feb.), aided by continued price and volume growth for everyday greeting cards in the U.S., a small increase in seasonal cards, which declined slightly in FY 98, and a more favorable retail environment. A much improved performance is seen for international operations, aided by several recent acquisitions. Margins will probably widen slightly, as a more favorable product mix and continued cost reduction efforts will be partly offset by costs related to new business initiatives and preparing computer systems for Year 2000 requirements. AM anticipates that it will continue to generate 75% to 80% of its earnings, versus its historical 70%, in the second half, reflecting the shifting of shipments between quarters as it works with retailers to reduce lead times and card inventories.

Valuation - 17-AUG-98

The shares have rebounded significantly from their mid-1996 lows, as results in recent periods met or exceeded expectations. We expect continued moderate improvement in earnings in FY 99, reflecting improving retail traffic, and further growth seen for everyday greeting cards, with consumers continuing to choose the most expensive cards, which generate higher margins. AM's expanding presence in drug chains, supermarkets, and mass merchandisers also enhances prospects. However, with operating earnings growth of about 10% annually seen for the next few years, the stock appears fairly valued at recent levels, and we advise holding the shares for now. Operating EPS in FY 98 equaled $2.37, excluding a one-time gain of $0.18 in the second quarter from the sale of the Acme Frame Products and Wilhold subsidiaries.

Key Stock Statistics

S&P EPS Est. 1999	2.60	Tang. Bk. Value/Share	17.16
P/E on S&P Est. 1999	15.1	Beta	0.55
Dividend Rate/Share	0.76	Shareholders	21,000
Shs. outstg. (M)	70.6	Market cap. (B)	$ 2.6
Avg. daily vol. (M)	0.267	Inst. holdings	79%

Value of $10,000 invested 5 years ago: $ 17,554

Fiscal Year Ending Feb. 28

	1999	1998	1997	1996	1995	1994
Revenues (Million $)						
1Q	487.9	475.1	438.2	438.5	416.0	395.4
2Q	—	484.7	466.5	431.2	401.1	388.4
3Q	—	639.7	647.7	587.6	551.0	522.5
4Q	—	599.3	608.6	545.8	500.4	474.5
Yr.	—	2,199	2,161	2,003	1,869	1,781
Earnings Per Share ($)						
1Q	**0.47**	0.40	0.37	0.50	0.45	0.40
2Q	—	0.35	0.15	0.20	0.18	0.15
3Q	—	1.07	1.00	0.24	0.79	0.70
4Q	—	**0.75**	0.71	0.60	0.58	0.53
Yr.	**E2.60**	2.55	2.23	1.54	2.00	1.77

Next earnings report expected: mid September

Dividend Data (Dividends have been paid since 1950.)

Amount ($)	Date Decl.	Ex-Div. Date	Stock of Record	Payment Date
0.180	Oct. 27	Nov. 24	Nov. 26	Dec. 10 '97
0.180	Jan. 30	Feb. 20	Feb. 24	Mar. 10 '98
0.180	Apr. 07	May. 22	May. 27	Jun. 10 '98
0.190	Jun. 26	Aug. 25	Aug. 27	Sep. 10 '98

A Division of The McGraw-Hill Companies

Business Summary - 17-AUG-98

American Greetings Corporation is believed to be the second largest company in the greeting cards and gift wrap industry and the largest publicly owned company in the industry. It also produces paper party goods, candles and giftware. Contributions to net sales in recent fiscal years (Feb.) were:

	FY 97	FY 96
Everyday greeting cards	44%	44%
Seasonal greeting cards	22%	21%
Gift wrapping & party goods	18%	19%
Other	16%	16%

Products are sold in about 100,000 retail outlets throughout the world, primarily through mass merchandisers, drug stores, supermarkets, card and gift shops, variety stores, combo stores, military post exchanges and department stores. Sales to the five largest customers accounted for 29% of net sales in FY 97. Sales to retail customers are made through 22 sales offices in the U.S., Canada, the U.K., Australia, New Zealand, France, Mexico and South Africa.

The company also operates several smaller business units. Plus Mark produces Christmas gift wrap, boxed cards and accessories. AG Industries designs and manufactures display fixtures. Magnivision is the world's largest manufacturer and distributor of nonprescription reading glasses. Learning Horizons distributes supplemental educational products. AGC Inc. licenses designs, and Those Characters From Cleveland licenses characters. Trademarks include CreataCard, DesignWare, Carlton Cards, Holly Hobbie, Strawberry Shortcake, La Flor, Baobob Tree, L'Chayim To Life, and Yesterday's Treasures. In August 1997, the company sold Acme Frame Products, a manufacturer and distributor of picture frames, and Wilhold, which produces and sells women's hair care products.

The company dramatically increased its presence in the UK during the first quarter of 1998, acquiring the Camden Graphics Group and Hanson White Ltd. Both are London-based greeting card companies that will add about $50 million in revenue and increase UK market share from 11% to 20%. The U.K. has the highest per capita card consumption in the world.

In August 1997, the company sold its Acme Frame Products and Wilhold subsidiaries to Newell Co. (NYSE: NWL). The transaction resulted in a one-time gain of $13.2 million ($0.18 a share) after tax, recorded in the second quarter of FY 98. AM noted that neither of the units fit with its strategic goals.

Per Share Data ($)

(Year Ended Feb. 28)	1998	1997	1996	1995	1994	1993	1992	1991	1990	1989
Tangible Bk. Val.	18.90	18.16	16.53	15.61	14.21	13.06	12.05	10.38	9.45	8.78
Cash Flow	3.43	3.10	2.55	2.92	2.58	2.29	2.13	2.06	2.08	1.59
Earnings	2.55	2.23	1.54	2.00	1.77	1.55	1.40	1.30	1.13	0.69
Dividends	0.71	0.67	0.62	0.55	0.48	0.42	0.38	0.35	0.33	0.33
Payout Ratio	28%	30%	40%	27%	27%	27%	28%	27%	29%	48%
Cal. Yrs.	1997	1996	1995	1994	1993	1992	1991	1990	1989	1988
Prices - High	40⅛	30½	33	34	34¼	26¼	20¾	18¾	18⅝	11¼
- Low	27⅜	23½	25½	25⅞	22½	18⅝	15½	13⅜	10¼	6¾
P/E Ratio - High	16	14	21	17	19	17	15	14	17	16
- Low	11	11	17	13	13	12	11	10	9	10

Income Statement Analysis (Million $)

	1998	1997	1996	1995	1994	1993	1992	1991	1990	1989
Revs.	2,199	2,161	2,003	1,869	1,770	1,672	1,554	1,413	1,287	1,253
Oper. Inc.	346	338	1,318	303	275	245	210	185	162	143
Depr.	65.9	64.6	75.3	68.4	59.6	53.7	45.5	42.2	40.3	39.5
Int. Exp.	23.0	30.7	75.3	16.9	16.9	26.9	30.4	31.4	27.7	33.5
Pretax Inc.	292	254	175	227	209	181	153	131	116	69.0
Eff. Tax Rate	35%	34%	34%	35%	38%	38%	36%	37%	38%	36%
Net Inc.	190	167	115	149	131	112	97.0	82.0	72.0	44.0

Balance Sheet & Other Fin. Data (Million $)

	1998	1997	1996	1995	1994	1993	1992	1991	1990	1989
Cash	47.6	35.1	30.1	87.0	101	235	194	81.0	123	94.0
Curr. Assets	1,023	1,005	970	893	850	912	848	738	681	637
Total Assets	2,146	2,135	2,006	1,762	1,565	1,548	1,438	1,256	1,141	1,088
Curr. Liab.	517	443	454	362	376	330	219	254	201	184
LT Debt	149	220	231	74.0	54.0	169	256	246	235	247
Common Eqty.	1,345	1,362	1,235	1,160	1,053	953	865	657	605	565
Total Cap.	15,365	1,625	1,511	1,291	1,170	1,218	1,219	1,001	940	903
Cap. Exp.	NA	92.8	91.6	97.0	103	77.1	67.3	45.3	42.9	41.9
Cash Flow	256	232	190	217	190	166	143	125	133	102
Curr. Ratio	2.0	2.3	2.1	2.5	2.3	2.1	3.9	2.9	3.4	3.5
% LT Debt of Cap.	9.7	27.2	15.3	5.8	4.6	13.9	21.0	24.6	25.0	27.3
% Net Inc.of Revs.	8.6	7.7	5.7	8.0	7.4	6.7	6.3	5.8	5.6	3.5
% Ret. on Assets	8.9	8.1	6.1	8.9	8.3	7.5	6.8	6.9	6.5	4.0
% Ret. on Equity	14.0	12.9	9.6	13.4	12.9	12.3	11.9	12.1	13.2	8.0

Data as orig. reptd.; bef. results of disc. opers. and/or spec. items. Per share data adj. for stk. divs. as of ex-div. date. Bold denotes diluted EPS (FASB 128). E-Estimated. NA-Not Available. NM-Not Meaningful. NR-Not Ranked.

Office—One American Rd., Cleveland, OH 44144-2398. **Tel**—(216) 252-7300. **Fax**—(216) 252-6777. **Website**—http://www.americangreetings.com **Chrmn & CEO**—M. Weiss. **Pres & COO**—E. Fruchtenbaum. **SVP & CFO**—W. S. Meyer. **SVP & Secy**—J. Groetzinger Jr. **VP, Treas & Investor Contact**—Dale A. Cable. **Dirs**—S. S. Cowen, E. Fruchtenbaum, H. H. Jacobs, H. Mouchly-Weiss, A. B. Ratner, J. S. Spira, H. H. Stone, I. I. Stone, M. Weiss. **Transfer Agent & Registrar**—National City Bank, Cleveland. **Incorporated**—in Ohio in 1944. **Empl**—21,000. **S&P Analyst:** William H. Donald

12-SEP-98

Industry:
Health Care (Diversified)

Summary: This leading maker of prescription drugs also has important interests in over-the-counter medications, medical devices and agricultural products.

S&P Opinion: Hold (★★★)		
Recent Price • 53⅜	Yield • 1.6%	
52 Wk Range • 58¾-33¾	12-Mo. P/E • 28.3	

Quantitative Evaluations

Outlook
(1 Lowest—5 Highest)
• **1‾**

Fair Value
• **40½**

Risk
• **Low**

Earn./Div. Rank
• **A+**

Technical Eval.
• **Bullish** since 10/94

Rel. Strength Rank
(1 Lowest—99 Highest)
• **95**

Insider Activity
• **NA**

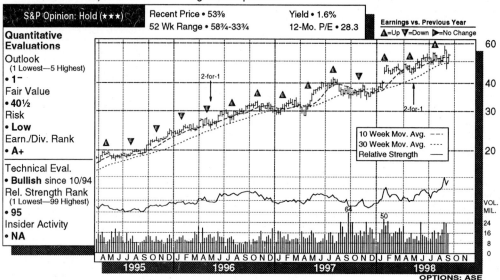

Earnings vs. Previous Year
▲=Up ▼=Down ▶=No Change

10 Week Mov. Avg. ─ ─ ─
30 Week Mov. Avg. ·····
Relative Strength ───

OPTIONS: ASE

Overview - 31-JUL-98

Based on operations as currently constituted (excluding the planned acquisition of Monsanto), AHP's revenues are expected to increase about 5% in 1998. Despite the September 1997 withdrawal of Pondimin and Redux diet pills from the market, drug sales should be bolstered by gains in Prempro/Premphase hormone replacement, Cordarone anti-arrhythmia agent, Effexor antidepressant, Naprelan arthritis treatment and Ziac anti-hypertensive agent. New products such as Zosyn broad spectrum antibiotic and Zoton antiulcer should also augment volume. Another advance is also projected for agricultural products sales, but modest growth at best is seen for consumer health care lines. Diluted EPS are projected at $2.07, including a nonrecurring gain of $0.25 from the sale of medical device businesses in the first quarter.

Valuation - 31-JUL-98

The shares have been significantly affected by merger-related developments thus far in 1998, with the most recent being AHP's planned acquisition of Monsanto (MTC) for nearly 690 million AHP shares. Each MTC share would be exchanged for 1.15 AHP shares. Upon completion of the transaction (expected by the end of 1998), current AHP shareholders will own 65% of the new company, with the balance held by MTC holders. Although the transaction is expected to be dilutive to earnings for the next three years, including dilution of about 15% in the first year, the combination will move AHP into third or fourth place in the global drug market, as well as making it a leading factor in pesticides and other agricultural products. The merger is also expected to yield $1.25 to $1.5 billion in cost savings by 2001. Merger synergies, coupled with a beefed up new drug pipeline, enhance longer term prospects. The shares merit retention.

Key Stock Statistics

S&P EPS Est. 1998	2.07	Tang. Bk. Value/Share	1.08
P/E on S&P Est. 1998	25.8	Beta	0.69
S&P EPS Est. 1999	1.85	Shareholders	67,500
Dividend Rate/Share	0.86	Market cap. (B)	$ 70.3
Shs. outstg. (M)	1315.8	Inst. holdings	64%
Avg. daily vol. (M)	4.532		

Value of $10,000 invested 5 years ago: $ 37,891

Fiscal Year Ending Dec. 31

	1998	1997	1996	1995	1994	1993
Revenues (Million $)						
1Q	3,666	3,603	3,647	3,491	2,144	2,111
2Q	3,342	3,500	3,490	3,299	1,978	1,909
3Q	—	3,482	3,471	3,258	2,259	2,168
4Q	—	3,611	3,481	3,328	2,586	2,116
Yr.	—	14,196	14,088	13,376	8,966	8,305
Earnings Per Share ($)						
1Q	**0.74**	**0.45**	0.39	0.83	0.34	0.32
2Q	**0.39**	**0.35**	0.31	0.24	0.24	0.23
3Q	**E0.46**	**0.33**	0.39	0.22	0.34	0.32
4Q	**E0.48**	**0.43**	0.40	0.07	0.33	0.31
Yr.	**E2.07**	**1.55**	1.48	1.35	1.24	1.18

Next earnings report expected: late October

Dividend Data (Dividends have been paid since 1919.)

Amount ($)	Date Decl.	Ex-Div. Date	Stock of Record	Payment Date
0.430	Jan. 29	Feb. 11	Feb. 13	Mar. 01 '98
2-for-1	Mar. 05	May. 06	Apr. 24	May. 05 '98
0.215	Apr. 23	May. 11	May. 13	Jun. 01 '98
0.215	Jul. 23	Aug. 11	Aug. 13	Sep. 01 '98

Business Summary - 31-JUL-98

This maker of popular consumer medications such as Anacin and Advil pain relievers also produces a wide range of prescription pharmaceuticals, with special emphasis on women's health care. In addition, the company is a leading factor in crop protection products, a business that came with the 1994 acquisition of American Cyanamid. Corporate strategy in recent years has focused on higher-margined pharmaceutical products, with less profitable consumer and medical device lines divested. Under that policy, the company recently sold its Storz Instrument and Sherwood-Davis & Geck medical device businesses for $2.2 billion. The food products business was sold in 1996. Foreign operations are significant, accounting for 42% of sales and 44% of profits in 1997. Contributions by business segment in 1997 were:

	Sales	Profits
Health care products	85%	87%
Agricultural products	15%	13%

Prescription drugs (61% of 1997 sales) are produced by the Wyeth-Ayerst division. This unit is the world's leading maker of women's drugs with its popular line of Premarin and Prempro/Premphase estrogen and progestin replacement products and oral contraceptives such as Triphasal, Lo/Ovral and Alesse. Other important drugs are Cordarone anti-arrhythmia agent; Veralan and Ziac antihypertensives; Lodine, Oruvail and Naprelan anti-arthritics; Suprax, Zosyn and Minocin anti-infectives; Effexor antidepressant; and Duract, a potent non-narcotic analgesic. Vaccines, pediatric products and generic drugs are also produced.

The R&D pipeline includes over 50 experimental compounds encompassing a wide range of therapeutic categories. Products awaiting near-term registration and marketing include Enbrel, a breakthorugh treatment for arthritis developed by Immunex (55% owned); a new pediatric vaccine against meningitis, otitis media and other ailments; Rapamune, used to prevent kidney transplant rejection; and Sonata, a non-benzodiazepine sedative.

The Whitehall and A.H. Robins divisions offer a broad range of OTC medications such as Advil and Anacin analgesics, Dimetapp and Robitussin for coughs and colds, Primatene for asthma, Preparation H for hemorrhoids and Centrum vitamins.

Agricultural products are sold through Cyanamid, a leader in the global crop protection market. Principal products include herbicides such as Raptor, Pursuit and Prowl; insecticides sold under the Counter and other names; and fungicides such as Acrobat and Delan. Animal health products include vaccines, feed additives and related items.

Per Share Data ($)

(Year Ended Dec. 31)	1997	1996	1995	1994	1993	1992	1991	1990	1989	1988
Tangible Bk. Val.	NM	NM	NM	-4.03	2.54	2.28	2.41	1.90	1.12	1.99
Cash Flow	4.18	2.00	1.90	1.49	1.38	1.08	1.22	1.12	1.00	0.90
Earnings	1.55	1.48	1.35	1.24	1.18	0.92	1.09	0.98	0.89	0.80
Dividends	0.83	0.78	0.76	0.73	0.71	0.67	0.59	0.54	0.49	0.45
Payout Ratio	53%	53%	56%	58%	60%	72%	55%	55%	55%	56%
Prices - High	42$\frac{1}{2}$	33$\frac{1}{4}$	25	16$\frac{7}{8}$	17$\frac{1}{4}$	21$\frac{1}{8}$	21$\frac{5}{8}$	13$\frac{3}{4}$	13$\frac{5}{8}$	10$\frac{5}{8}$
- Low	28$\frac{1}{2}$	23$\frac{1}{2}$	15$\frac{1}{2}$	13$\frac{7}{8}$	13$\frac{7}{8}$	15$\frac{5}{8}$	11$\frac{5}{8}$	10$\frac{3}{4}$	10	8$\frac{3}{4}$
P/E Ratio - High	27	22	18	14	15	23	20	14	15	13
- Low	18	16	11	11	3	17	11	11	11	11

Income Statement Analysis (Million $)

	1997	1996	1995	1994	1993	1992	1991	1990	1989	1988
Revs.	14,196	14,088	13,376	8,996	8,305	7,874	7,079	6,775	6,747	5,501
Oper. Inc.	3,946	3,634	3,191	2,484	2,237	2,116	1,884	1,695	1,681	1,460
Depr.	701	658	679	306	241	210	167	180	168	142
Int. Exp.	462	563	605	115	47.0	36.0	31.0	136	40.0	32.0
Pretax Inc.	2,815	2,755	2,439	2,030	1,993	1,724	1,760	1,828	1,414	1,348
Eff. Tax Rate	27%	32%	31%	25%	26%	33%	22%	33%	22%	31%
Net Inc.	2,043	1,883	1,680	1,528	1,469	1,151	1,375	1,231	1,102	932

Balance Sheet & Other Fin. Data (Million $)

	1997	1996	1995	1994	1993	1992	1991	1990	1989	1988
Cash	1,051	1,544	2,020	1,944	2,220	1,982	2,065	1,789	1,208	759
Curr. Assets	7,361	7,470	7,986	7,821	4,808	4,552	4,119	3,826	3,533	2,576
Total Assets	20,825	20,785	21,363	21,675	7,687	7,141	5,939	5,637	5,681	4,611
Curr. Liab.	4,327	4,338	4,556	4,618	1,584	1,493	1,270	1,029	1,109	866
LT Debt	5,032	6,021	7,802	9,973	859	602	105	777	1,896	40.0
Common Eqty.	8,176	6,962	5,543	4,254	3,876	3,560	3,298	2,672	1,967	2,972
Total Cap.	13,415	13,179	13,659	14,551	5,083	4,534	3,595	3,654	3,883	3,012
Cap. Exp.	830	652	638	473	518	428	228	248	251	344
Cash Flow	2,744	2,541	2,359	1,834	1,710	1,361	1,542	1,410	1,248	1,054
Curr. Ratio	1.7	1.7	1.7	1.7	3.0	3.0	3.2	3.7	3.2	3.0
% LT Debt of Cap.	37.5	45.7	57.1	68.5	16.9	13.3	2.9	21.3	48.8	1.3
% Net Inc.of Revs.	14.4	13.4	12.6	17.0	17.7	14.6	19.4	18.2	16.3	16.9
% Ret. on Assets	9.8	8.9	7.8	10.4	19.9	17.7	23.7	21.7	20.8	20.2
% Ret. on Equity	27.0	30.1	34.3	37.8	39.7	33.7	46.0	52.9	42.8	33.8

Data as orig. reptd.; bef. results of disc. opers. and/or spec. items. Per share data adj. for stk. divs. as of ex=div. date. Bold denotes diluted EPS (FASB 128). E-Estimated. NA-Not Available. NM-Not Meaningful. NR-Not Ranked.

Office—Five Giralda Farms, Madison, NJ 07940. **Tel**—(973) 660-5000. **Website**—http://www.ahp.com **Chrmn, Pres & CEO**—J. R. Stafford. **Secy**—Eileen M. Lach. **VP-Fin**—J. R. Considine. **Investor Contact**—Thomas G. Cavanagh. **Dirs**—C. Alexander, F. A. Bennack, Jr., R. G. Blount, R. C. Duke, R. Essner, J. D. Feerick, J. P. Mascotte, M. L. Polan, I. G. Seidenberg, J. R. Stafford, J. R. Torell III, W. Wrigley. **Transfer Agent & Registrar**—ChaseMellon Shareholder Services, Ridgefield Park, NJ. **Incorporated**—in Delaware in 1926. **Empl**— 60,523. **S&P Analyst:** Herman B. Saftlas

12-SEP-98

Industry:
Insurance (Multi-Line)

Summary: One of the world's leading insurance organizations, AIG provides property, casualty and life insurance, as well as other financial services, in 130 countries and territories.

S&P Opinion: Accumulate (★★★★)	Recent Price • 79 Yield • 0.3% 52 Wk Range • 102⅜-64¾ 12-Mo. P/E • 23.5

Quantitative Evaluations

Outlook
(1 Lowest—5 Highest)
• **2**

Fair Value
• **75¼**

Risk
• **Low**

Earn./Div. Rank
• **A+**

Technical Eval.
• **Bearish** since 9/98

Rel. Strength Rank
(1 Lowest—99 Highest)
• **59**

Insider Activity
• **NA**

Earnings vs. Previous Year
▲=Up ▼=Down ▶=No Change

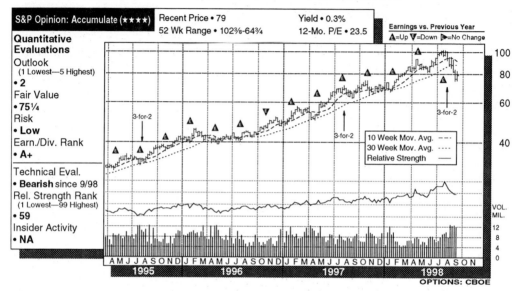

10 Week Mov. Avg. – – –
30 Week Mov. Avg. ·····
Relative Strength ——

VOL. MIL.

OPTIONS: CBOE

Overview - 13-AUG-98

Property-casualty written premium growth will likely be around 5%-6% in 1998, as the effect of a strong U.S. dollar masks otherwise relatively decent underlying premium growth. U.S. market conditions remain competitive, but AIG's expansion into selected personal lines, middle market commercial lines, and specialty coverages should limit the downside from weak commercial lines pricing. Overseas, the outlook is mixed. Near term, the ongoing financial crisis is Asia will limit AIG's growth prospects. We also remain concerned that the "spillover" from Asia extends into other key markets, including Europe. However, in the long term, these markets are important in a global economy, and AIG's unmatched foreign presence gives it an important edge. Assuming a normal level of catastrophe losses, underwriting results should remain profitable, thanks in part to stringent cost controls. Earnings growth will also be aided by continued profit contributions from life insurance and financial services operations. Stock repurchases (including the 5.7 million shares acquired in 1997 for $502 million) will aid EPS comparisons.

Valuation - 13-AUG-98

The shares have generally trended upward since 1994, thanks to a favorable interest rate environment for financial stocks. Despite renewed concerns over extremely competitive conditions in the U.S. property-casualty market, investors have continued to bid up AIG's shares, choosing to focus on AIG's solid long-term underwriting and earnings growth track record and dominant market position. Renewed concerns over the financial turmoil gripping Asia (an important market for AIG) may cause the shares to weaken. We view any near-term pullback in the share price as an opportunity to add to positions.

Key Stock Statistics

S&P EPS Est. 1998	3.45	Tang. Bk. Value/Share	24.50
P/E on S&P Est. 1998	22.9	Beta	1.34
S&P EPS Est. 1999	3.95	Shareholders	18,000
Dividend Rate/Share	0.23	Market cap. (B)	$ 83.0
Shs. outstg. (M)	1050.0	Inst. holdings	53%
Avg. daily vol. (M)	3.455		

Value of $10,000 invested 5 years ago: $ 35,182

Fiscal Year Ending Dec. 31

	1998	1997	1996	1995	1994	1993
Revenues (Million $)						
1Q	7,690	6,483	6,645	6,007	5,226	4,311
2Q	3,909	6,967	6,956	6,458	5,626	5,339
3Q	—	6,810	7,182	6,547	5,675	5,120
4Q	—	6,986	7,422	6,863	5,915	5,360
Yr.	—	27,246	28,205	25,875	22,442	20,130
Earnings Per Share ($)						
1Q	**0.84**	**0.73**	0.63	0.54	0.47	0.44
2Q	**0.89**	**0.79**	0.68	0.60	0.52	0.45
3Q	—	**0.79**	0.69	0.59	0.51	0.42
4Q	—	**0.84**	0.73	0.64	0.54	0.48
Yr.	—	**3.15**	2.73	2.36	2.04	1.79

Next earnings report expected: late October

Dividend Data (Dividends have been paid since 1969.)

Amount ($)	Date Decl.	Ex-Div. Date	Stock of Record	Payment Date
0.075	Mar. 18	Jun. 03	Jun. 05	Jun. 19 '98
0.075	Mar. 18	Jun. 03	Jun. 05	Jun. 19 '98
3-for-2	May. 26	Aug. 03	Jun. 26	Jul. 31 '98
0.056	May. 20	Sep. 02	Sep. 04	Sep. 18 '98

A Division of The McGraw·Hill Companies

Business Summary - 13-AUG-98

New York City-based AIG is one of the world's leading insurance organizations, providing an array of property-casualty and life insurance products through the U.S. and in approximately 129 other countries. It also offers various financial services, including airline leasing and currency trading. While AIG's global franchise is virtually unmatched, its presence in overseas markets renders it vulnerable to foreign currency fluctuations. Revenue contributions in recent years:

	1997	1996	1995
General insurance	47%	48%	50%
Life insurance	42%	42%	40%
Financial services	11%	9%	9%

International operations accounted for 54% of revenues and 57% of pretax profits in 1997. Business in the Far East accounted for 71% of international revenues and 62% international pretax profits.

General insurance written premiums totaling $13.4 billion in 1997 were derived: commercial casualty 52%, international 33%, personal lines 6%, commercial property 4%, pools and associations 3%, and mortgage guaranty 2%.

The Domestic General-Brokerage division deals principally with insurance brokers representing major industrial and commercial clients.

Life insurance subsidiaries offer individual and group life, annuity and accident and health policies. Foreign operations accounted for 92% of the segment's operating income in 1997.

Financial service operations include interest rate and currency swaps, cash management, premium financing, airline leasing and private banking. AIG also owns 50% of Transatlantic Holdings, Inc. (NYSE: TRH), a property-casualty reinsurer.

During the first six months of 1998, competitive property-casualty pricing and the negative impact on foreign businesses from a strong U.S. dollar limited the year-to-year growth in worldwide general insurance premiums to 2.1% (4.7% in original currency). Life premiums advanced 2.2% (16.6% in original currency). AIG has taken a number of steps to offset the tepid growth in its core business and to redeploy some of its excess capital. In addition to numerous transactions overseas, AIG has made several investments in U.S. companies. For example, in mid-July 1998, AIG increased its stake in 20th Century Industries (NYSE:TW), a California-based auto insurer, to over 50%. AIG will likely seek control of TW's board. But, in March 1998, AIG terminated a previously announced bid to acquire American Bankers Insurance Group (ABI) after being locked in a heated battle with Cendant Corp. (NYSE:CD) over ABI.

Per Share Data ($)

(Year Ended Dec. 31)	1997	1996	1995	1994	1993	1992	1991	1990	1989	1988
Tangible Bk. Val.	22.87	20.87	18.58	15.40	14.20	11.79	10.40	8.96	7.84	6.18
Oper. Earnings	NA	2.68	2.31	1.98	1.72	1.45	1.38	1.31	1.24	1.13
Earnings	3.15	2.73	2.36	2.04	1.79	1.51	1.44	1.37	1.31	1.17
Dividends	0.19	0.16	0.15	0.13	0.11	0.10	0.09	0.08	0.07	0.06
Relative Payout	6%	6%	6%	6%	6%	7%	6%	6%	5%	5%
Prices - High	75	51³/₄	42¹/₂	29⁷/₈	29³/₄	24	20¹/₈	16³/₈	17³/₄	10⁷/₈
- Low	47³/₈	39¹/₈	28¹/₂	24¹/₄	21³/₄	16¹/₄	14¹/₄	11¹/₄	10¹/₂	7³/₄
P/E Ratio - High	24	19	18	15	17	16	14	12	14	10
- Low	15	14	12	12	12	11	10	8	8	7

Income Statement Analysis (Million $)

	1997	1996	1995	1994	1993	1992	1991	1990	1989	1988
Life Ins. In Force	436,573	421,983	376,097	333,379	257,162	210,606	193,226	160,373	131,983	118,431
Prem. Inc.: Life A & H	9,926	8,978	8,038	6,724	5,746	4,853	4,059	3,478	2,995	3,459
Prem. Inc.: Cas./Prop.	12,421	11,855	11,406	10,287	9,567	9,209	9,104	9,149	8,529	4,933
Net Invest. Inc.	4,750	4,365	3,811	3,184	2,840	2,566	2,303	2,037	1,760	1,435
Oth. Revs.	688	591	2,620	2,247	1,982	1,761	1,418	1,038	866	3,786
Total Revs.	22,465	25,877	25,875	22,442	20,135	18,389	16,884	15,702	14,150	13,613
Pretax Inc.	4,731	4,013	3,466	2,952	2,601	2,137	2,023	1,812	1,706	1,398
Net Oper. Inc.	NA	NA	2,463	2,119	1,848	1,561	1,492	1,372	1,284	1,175
Net Inc.	3,332	2,897	2,510	2,176	1,918	1,625	1,553	1,442	1,367	1,217

Balance Sheet & Other Fin. Data (Million $)

	1997	1996	1995	1994	1993	1992	1991	1990	1989	1988
Cash & Equiv.	87.0	3,265	3,574	3,402	6,039	5,568	7,880	7,262	5,008	4,687
Premiums Due	10,283	9,617	9,410	8,802	8,364	9,010	9,027	8,793	7,734	6,219
Invest. Assets: Bonds	51,566	48,625	42,901	35,431	30,067	23,613	23,613	20,639	18,049	15,900
Invest. Assets: Stocks	5,209	6,006	5,369	5,099	4,488	2,705	2,291	1,987	2,230	1,627
Invest. Assets: Loans	7,920	7,877	7,861	5,353	3,577	3,080	2,999	2,629	1,612	1,230
Invest. Assets: Total	116,221	103,982	91,627	73,388	60,947	56,977	44,404	34,826	26,593	21,284
Deferred Policy Costs	6,593	6,471	5,768	5,132	4,249	3,658	3,243	2,777	2,350	2,027
Total Assets	163,971	148,431	134,136	114,346	101,015	79,835	69,389	58,143	46,143	37,409
Debt	25,260	23,521	17,990	17,519	15,689	13,464	11,922	10,385	5,860	3,952
Common Eqty.	24,002	22,044	19,827	16,422	15,224	12,632	11,313	9,754	8,255	6,852
Comb. Loss-Exp. Ratio	96.2	96.9	97.0	98.8	100.1	102.4	100.4	99.6	100.0	99.4
% Return On Revs.	14.8	11.2	9.7	9.7	9.5	8.8	9.2	9.2	9.7	8.6
% Ret. on Equity	14.5	13.8	13.9	13.7	13.8	12.6	14.7	15.9	18.0	18.7
% Invest. Yield	4.3	4.5	4.6	4.7	4.4	4.9	5.8	6.6	7.4	7.8

Data as orig. reptd.; bef. results of disc. opers. and/or spec. items. Per share data adj. for stk. divs. as of ex-div. date. Bold denotes diluted EPS (FASB 128). E-Estimate. NA-Not Available. NM-Not Meaningful. NR-Not Ranked.

Office—70 Pine St., New York, NY 10270. **Tel**—(212) 770-7000. **Website**—http://www.aig.com **Chrmn & CEO**—M. R. Greenberg. **Pres**—E. G. Greenberg. **Treas**—W. N. Dooley. **VP & Secy**—K. E. Shannon. **Investor Contact**—Charlene M. Hamrah. **Dirs**—M. B. Aidinoff, L. M. Bentsen, P. Chia, M. A. Cohen, B. B. Conable, Jr., M. Feldstein, L. L. Gonda, E. R. Greenberg, M. R. Greenberg, C. A. Hills, F. J. Hoenemeyer, E. E. Matthews, D. P. Phypers, T. R. Tizzio, E. S. W. Tse, F. G. Wisner. **Transfer Agent & Registrar**—Bank of New York, NYC. **Incorporated**—in Delaware in 1967. **Empl**— 40,000. **S&P Analyst:** Catherine A. Seifert

American Stores   168

NYSE Symbol **ASC**

In S&P 500

12-SEP-98

Industry: Retail (Food Chains)

Summary: This operator of more than 1,550 combination food/drug stores, super drug centers, drug stores and food stores in 26 states has agreed to be acquired by Albertson's, Inc.

S&P Opinion: Accumulate (★★★★)	Recent Price • 29⅞
	52 Wk Range • 32⅛-19⅜

Yield • 1.2%

12-Mo. P/E • 26.5

Quantitative Evaluations

Outlook
(1 Lowest—5 Highest)
• **1**

Fair Value
• **26%**

Risk
• **Low**

Earn./Div. Rank
• **A**

Technical Eval.
• **Bullish** since 8/98

Rel. Strength Rank
(1 Lowest—99 Highest)
• **97**

Insider Activity
• **Neutral**

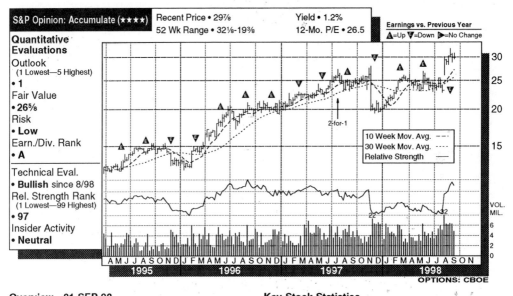

Earnings vs. Previous Year
▲=Up ▼=Down ▶=No Change

10 Week Mov. Avg. - - -
30 Week Mov. Avg. ·····
Relative Strength ——

2-for-1

OPTIONS: CBOE

Overview - 01-SEP-98

In early August 1998, ASC agreed to be acquired by Albertson's, Inc. (NYSE: ABS), with 0.63 of an ABS common share (recent price about $50.56 a share) to be exchanged for each ASC share. ASC's sales grew 3.3% during the first half of FY 99 (Jan.), and are expected to grow at a mid-single digit pace for the remainder of the year. The increase in sales growth should be fueled by a more focused marketing program, the replacement of older stores with new combination stores, and a stepped-up store remodeling program. Over the last few years, ASC has strengthened its capital spending program to bolster its drug store business while focusing on reducing operating costs. These actions, coupled with overhead cost reductions and targeted marketing program should help earnings grow 20% to 30% in the second half of FY 99, to $1.30 for the year.

Valuation - 01-SEP-98

We continue to rate ASC accumulate, based on an improved profitability outlook, as well as longer term synergies expected from the pending Albertson's merger. Excluding one-time charges, the combination is expected to be accretive to Albertson's earnings during the first year, and the combined entities are expected to achieve cost savings of $100 million in the first year, rising to $300 million after the third year. Until the transaction is completed, we expect ASC's operating earnings to rise to $1.30 a share in FY 99 (Jan.), and see the combined companies posting pro forma EPS of $2.25 in FY 99 and $2.50 in FY 2000. In coming periods, we expect ASC shares to closely track the movement of ABS stock, and see them as a cheap entry vehicle into ABS shares, as ASC recently traded at a 9.0% discount to the projeced acquisition price.

Key Stock Statistics

S&P EPS Est. 1999	1.30	Tang. Bk. Value/Share	3.03
P/E on S&P Est. 1999	23.0	Beta	-0.43
S&P EPS Est. 2000	1.50	Shareholders	18,800
Dividend Rate/Share	0.36	Market cap. (B)	$ 8.2
Shs. outstg. (M)	274.5	Inst. holdings	65%
Avg. daily vol. (M)	1.639		

Value of $10,000 invested 5 years ago: $ 30,123

Fiscal Year Ending Jan. 31

	1999	1998	1997	1996	1995	1994
Revenues (Million $)						
1Q	4,873	4,748	4,580	4,362	4,610	4,668
2Q	4,950	4,763	4,625	4,495	4,669	4,693
3Q	—	4,647	4,563	4,361	4,432	4,532
4Q	—	4,981	4,910	5,091	4,647	4,871
Yr.	—	19,139	18,678	18,309	18,355	18,763
Earnings Per Share ($)						
1Q	**0.24**	0.12	0.22	0.18	0.17	0.20
2Q	**0.32**	0.33	0.28	0.25	0.24	0.20
3Q	**E0.29**	0.22	0.26	0.23	0.34	0.16
4Q	**E0.45**	0.35	0.22	0.41	0.46	0.36
Yr.	**E1.30**	1.01	0.98	1.08	1.21	0.93

Next earnings report expected: late November

Dividend Data (Dividends have been paid since 1949.)

Amount ($)	Date Decl.	Ex-Div. Date	Stock of Record	Payment Date
0.090	Sep. 16	Sep. 24	Sep. 26	Oct. 08 '97
0.090	Dec. 09	Dec. 17	Dec. 19	Jan. 02 '98
0.090	Mar. 17	Mar. 25	Mar. 27	Apr. 08 '98
0.090	Jun. 17	Jun. 24	Jun. 27	Jul. 08 '98

A Division of The McGraw·Hill Companies

Business Summary - 01-SEP-98

In August 1998, American Stores agreed to be acquired by Albertson's, Inc. (NYSE: ABS), with each ASC common share to be exchanged for 0.63 of an ABS shares. The transaction, initially valued at $11.7 billion, including the assumption of debt, is expected to close in early 1999. At August 25, 1998, ASC, one of the leading U.S. food and drug retailers, operated a total of 1,558 stores in 26 states, consisting of 535 supermarkets, 754 drug stores, and 269 combination food/drug units. Its stores hold a leading market position in nine of the 25 largest U.S. metropolitan areas.

Food operations (as of early 1997) consist of 182 Acme Markets in four states, 185 Jewel Food Stores in four states, 185 Lucky Stores in the Northern California division, 247 Lucky Stores in the Southern California division, and 13 Jewel Osco stores in the Southwest division. About 153 of the Jewel Food Stores were a combination of Jewel food stores and Osco drug stores.

Drug operations include 576 Osco drug stores (including 153 jointly operated Jewel/Osco combination stores) in 20 states and 306 Sav-on drug stores in two states.

Combination stores average 60,000 sq. ft., and include a pharmacy department as well as an expanded selection of food, drug and general merchandise. The combination stores, and many of the food stores, include other specialty departments such as delicatessens, bakeries, and seafood. Stores sell private label merchandise under such names as President's Choice, American Premier, Value Wise, Lady Lee, Lancaster, Acme, Jewel, Lucky, Osco and Sav-on.

In its effort to spur growth, ASC has doubled its capital expenditures in recent years, to about $1.0 billion. It expects to maintain this aggressive level for the next several years, as it adds 100 to 110 new or replacement stores annually. During FY 98 (Jan.), ASC opened or acquired 96 new stores, completed 65 remodels, and closed or sold 68 stores.

In 1996, ASC began a project known as Delta, designed to move the company from a holding company with seven operating divisions to a centralized operating company, with an ultimate goal of becoming a leading-edge, low cost marketer. The ongoing program has consisted of hundreds of initiatives, including changes in purchasing, warehousing, inventory control and distribution systems.

In April 1997, ASC repurchased about 24.4 million common shares (as adjusted) from the family and certain charitable trusts of L.S. Skaggs, the company's former chairman, for $22.50 a share. Subsequently, shareholders sold 30.8 million additional shares in a public offering at $21.50 a share.

Per Share Data ($)

(Year Ended Jan. 31)	1998	1997	1996	1995	1994	1993	1992	1991	1990	1989
Tangible Bk. Val.	2.55	2.98	2.16	0.98	-0.30	-0.67	-1.51	-2.31	-3.05	-4.04
Cash Flow	2.70	2.49	2.46	2.63	2.21	1.97	2.12	1.95	1.58	1.36
Earnings	1.01	0.98	1.08	1.21	0.93	0.73	0.87	0.66	0.43	0.32
Dividends	0.35	0.32	0.28	0.24	0.40	0.18	0.16	0.14	0.13	0.11
Payout Ratio	35%	32%	26%	20%	43%	25%	18%	21%	31%	35%
Cal. Yrs.	1997	1996	1995	1994	1993	1992	1991	1990	1989	1988
Prices - High	28	21½	15⅜	13⅞	12⅜	11¾	11½	9	9⅛	8⅜
- Low	19⅜	12½	11⅝	10½	9⅛	7⅝	6½	5⅜	6⅝	6
P/E Ratio - High	28	22	14	11	13	16	13	14	21	26
- Low	19	13	11	9	10	10	7	8	15	19

Income Statement Analysis (Million $)

	1998	1997	1996	1995	1994	1993	1992	1991	1990	1989
Revs.	19,139	18,678	18,309	18,355	18,763	19,051	20,823	22,156	22,004	18,478
Oper. Inc.	1,251	1,202	1,112	1,092	1,014	978	955	1,057	894	697
Depr.	469	440	405	407	365	346	345	356	291	253
Int. Exp.	217	183	169	175	193	215	268	361	407	290
Pretax Inc.	524	504	551	606	481	389	451	356	250	207
Eff. Tax Rate	46%	43%	43%	43%	46%	47%	47%	49%	53%	53%
Net Inc.	281	287	318	345	262	206	240	182	118	98.0

Balance Sheet & Other Fin. Data (Million $)

	1998	1997	1996	1995	1994	1993	1992	1991	1990	1989
Cash	48.0	37.0	102	196	59.6	54.0	71.0	77.0	87.0	9.0
Curr. Assets	2,262	2,166	2,084	2,132	1,996	1,999	2,138	2,281	2,261	2,153
Total Assets	8,536	7,881	7,363	7,032	6,927	6,545	6,955	7,245	7,398	7,010
Curr. Liab.	2,121	1,802	1,988	1,931	2,054	1,895	1,975	2,120	2,240	2,188
LT Debt	3,202	2,613	2,105	2,064	2,091	2,176	2,662	3,101	3,399	3,289
Common Eqty.	2,309	2,535	2,354	2,051	1,742	1,692	1,516	1,351	1,202	922
Total Cap.	5,860	5,497	4,825	4,436	4,180	4,012	4,354	4,635	4,707	4,519
Cap. Exp.	996	878	751	538	594	386	355	330	552	1,207
Cash Flow	750	727	722	752	627	553	585	538	400	330
Curr. Ratio	1.1	4.0	1.1	1.1	1.0	1.1	1.1	1.1	1.0	1.0
% LT Debt of Cap.	54.6	47.6	43.7	46.5	50.0	54.2	61.1	66.9	72.2	72.8
% Net Inc.of Revs.	1.5	1.6	1.8	1.9	1.4	1.1	1.2	0.8	0.5	0.5
% Ret. on Assets	3.4	3.8	4.4	4.9	3.9	3.0	3.4	2.5	1.5	1.8
% Ret. on Equity	11.6	11.8	14.4	18.2	15.2	12.7	16.7	14.3	9.7	8.5

Data as orig. reptd.; bef. results of disc. opers. and/or spec. items. Per share data adj. for stk. divs. as of ex-div. date. Bold denotes diluted EPS (FASB 128). E-Estimated. NA-Not Available. NM-Not Meaningful. NR-Not Ranked.

Office—709 East South Temple, Salt Lake City, UT 84102. **Tel**—(801) 539-0112. **Website**—http://www.americanstores.com **Chrmn & CEO**—V. L. Lund. **Vice Chrmn & COO**—D. Maher. **Pres**—T. Beck. **CFO**—N. Rider. **Secy**—J. Lunt. **Investor Contact**—Daniel Zvoneck. **Dirs**—H. I. Bryant, L. H. Callister, A. B. Engebretsen, J. B. Fisher, F. R. Gumucio, L. G. Harmon, D. B. Holbrook, V. L. Lund, J. E. Masline, B. S. Preiskel, J. L. Scott, A. K. Smith. **Transfer Agent & Registrar**—First Chicago Trust Co. of New York, Jersey City, NJ. **Incorporated**— in Utah in 1947; reincorporated in Delaware in 1965. **Empl**— 121,000. **S&P Analyst:** Robert J. Izmirlian

STANDARD &POOR'S
STOCK REPORTS

Ameritech

184T

NYSE Symbol **AIT**

In S&P 500

12-SEP-98

Industry:
Telephone

Summary: Ameritech is one of the largest telephone holding companies in the U.S. It provides service in parts of five upper-midwestern states.

| S&P Opinion: Hold (★★★) | Recent Price • 47⅝ | Yield • 2.5% |
| | 52 Wk Range • 52⅛-30⅛ | 12-Mo. P/E • 15.4 |

Quantitative Evaluations

Outlook
(1 Lowest—5 Highest)
• **1**

Fair Value
• **40¾**

Risk
• **Low**

Earn./Div. Rank
• **A-**

Technical Eval.
• **Bearish** since 3/98

Rel. Strength Rank
(1 Lowest—99 Highest)
• **92**

Insider Activity
• **Neutral**

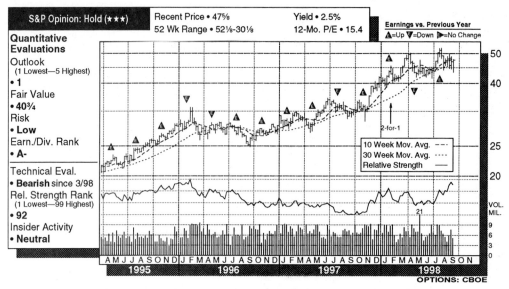

Earnings vs. Previous Year
▲=Up ▼=Down ▶=No Change

2-for-1

10 Week Mov. Avg. -----
30 Week Mov. Avg. ·······
Relative Strength ——

A M J J A S O N D J F M A M J J A S O N D J F M A M J J A S O N D J F M A M J J A S O N
1995   1996   1997   1998

OPTIONS: CBOE

Overview - 23-JUL-98

In May 1998, Ameritech agreed to be acquired by SBC Communications (NYSE: SBC) in a $62 billion stock transaction expected to completed in mid-1999. Under the agreement, AIT shareholders will receive 1.316 SBC shares for each AIT share held, resulting in current SBC shareholders owning about 56% and current AIT shareholders owning about 44% of the combined company. Additionally, Ameritech is moving to position itself for a competitive telephone market; its strategy focuses on entering complementary lines of business such as cable television and long-distance services, while upgrading its network and expanding its security services business. The FCC has turned down the company's applications to offer wireline long-distance services in its region. SBC has begun offering wireless long distance service and has signed up over one-third of its 3.3 million customers.

Valuation - 23-JUL-98

The shares continue to perform in line with the market, and we see this trend continuing over the next 12 months. Over the long term, we believe that Ameritech is very well positioned to take advantage of opportunities to build up new lines of business, such as its security-related unit. We see the company offering long distance services in its own market in late 1998, as it has fulfilled almost all of the 14 points in the FCC's competition check. Many of the RBOCs (regional bell operating companies) continue to have difficulty adjusting to the competitive environment, and AIT is no exception. The shares' above-average yield will be neutralized by regulatory uncertainty over its merger with SBC. We believe the FCC and Justice Department will turn down SBC-Ameritech's request to become a national provider of local telecom services.

Key Stock Statistics

S&P EPS Est. 1998	2.30	Tang. Bk. Value/Share	9.15
P/E on S&P Est. 1998	20.7	Beta	0.66
S&P EPS Est. 1997	2.55	Shareholders	837,500
Dividend Rate/Share	1.20	Market cap. (B)	$ 52.5
Shs. outstg. (M)	1102.4	Inst. holdings	47%
Avg. daily vol. (M)	1.183		

Value of $10,000 invested 5 years ago: $ 32,901

Fiscal Year Ending Dec. 31

	1998	1997	1996	1995	1994	1993
Revenues (Million $)						
1Q	4,133	3,859	3,567	3,146	3,034	2,797
2Q	4,289	3,986	3,744	3,369	3,184	2,951
3Q	—	4,006	3,722	3,381	3,170	2,947
4Q	—	4,147	3,884	3,532	3,181	3,016
Yr.	—	15,998	14,917	13,427	12,570	11,710
Earnings Per Share ($)						
1Q	**0.44**	0.48	0.43	0.53	0.04	0.28
2Q	**1.54**	0.48	0.51	0.46	0.41	0.36
3Q	E0.60	0.56	0.47	0.46	0.23	0.39
4Q	E0.63	**0.55**	0.52	0.37	0.39	0.36
Yr.	**E2.30**	**2.08**	1.94	1.81	1.06	1.39

Next earnings report expected: mid October

Dividend Data (Dividends have been paid since 1984.)

Amount ($)	Date Decl.	Ex-Div. Date	Stock of Record	Payment Date
0.600	Dec. 17	Dec. 29	Dec. 31	Feb. 02 '98
2-for-1	Dec. 17	Jan. 27	Dec. 31	Jan. 26 '98
0.300	Mar. 18	Mar. 27	Mar. 31	May. 01 '98
0.300	Jun. 17	Jun. 26	Jun. 30	Aug. 01 '98

Business Summary - 23-JUL-98

In May 1998, Ameritech agreed to be acquired by SBC Communications (NYSE: SBC) in a $62 billion stock transaction expected to be completed in mid-1999. Under the agreement, AIT shareholders will receive 1.316 SBC shares for each AIT share held, resulting in current SBC shareholders owning about 56% and current AIT shareholders owning about 44% of the combined company.

This Baby Bell has its roots firmly grounded in the Midwest and is one of the largest U.S. telephone holding companies, providing local residential service in five states to over 21.3 million customer access lines.

Ameritech Cellular provides wireless communications services. At December 31, 1997, 3.2 million cellular lines and 1.5 million pagers were in service.

Other units provide directory advertising and publishing; sell, install and maintain business customer premises equipment (CPE) and sell network and central office-based services; arrange financing and leasing of computer and communications products; develop and invest in new products and technology; and develop international business opportunities.

A consortium led by AIT and Bell Atlantic acquired Telecom Corp. of New Zealand for U.S.$2.45 billion in 1990. The companies sold 31% of Telecom Corp.'s share capital in an international public offering in 1991. During 1993, AIT reduced its stake to 24.9%, and recently sold its remaining stake for about $2.1 billion. In January 1998, the company invested $3.1 billion in Tele Danmark (NYSE: TLD) for a 42% stake in the premier Danish telecommucations carrier. AIT also owns 34.5% of MATAV, the telephone company of Hungary, and led a consortium that won the privatization bid for Belgacom, the telephone company of Belgium. AIT is a partner in a venture with The Walt Disney Co., BellSouth, GTE, SBC Communications and SNET; the venture, known as Americast, provides video programming and interactive services in 26 communities, including 14 in Michigan.

In March 1998, Ameritech outlined restructuring plans to reduce operating expenses by $3 billion over the next five years. In conjunction with this action, the company recorded a one-time after-tax charge of $64 million. AIT has also detailed a three-pronged strategy for growth that includes speeding up growth in its telecommunications business, the introduction of new services to customers, and connecting customers around the world.

Per Share Data ($)

(Year Ended Dec. 31)	1997	1996	1995	1994	1993	1992	1991	1990	1989	1988
Tangible Bk. Val.	7.57	6.99	6.33	5.49	7.13	6.41	7.53	7.25	7.05	7.22
Cash Flow	4.38	4.08	3.78	3.08	3.38	3.15	2.90	2.90	2.85	2.81
Earnings	2.08	1.94	1.81	1.06	1.39	1.25	1.10	1.18	1.15	1.14
Dividends	1.15	1.08	1.01	0.97	0.93	0.89	0.86	0.81	0.74	0.69
Payout Ratio	55%	56%	56%	91%	67%	71%	78%	68%	65%	61%
Prices - High	43¹/₈	33¹/₂	29³/₄	21⁵/₈	22³/₄	18¹/₂	17¹/₂	17¹/₂	17¹/₈	12¹/₄
- Low	27⁵/₈	24⁷/₈	20	18¹/₈	17¹/₂	14¹/₈	14	13¹/₈	11³/₄	10¹/₄
P/E Ratio - High	21	17	16	20	16	15	16	15	15	11
- Low	13	13	11	17	13	11	13	11	10	9

Income Statement Analysis (Million $)

	1997	1996	1995	1994	1993	1992	1991	1990	1989	1988
Revs.	15,998	14,917	13,428	12,570	11,710	11,153	10,818	10,663	10,211	9,903
Depr.	2,521	5,870	2,177	2,205	2,162	2,031	1,915	1,825	1,797	1,757
Maint.	NA	NA	NA	NA	1,729	1,737	1,647	1,662	1,590	1,601
Constr. Credits	Nil	Nil	19.7	13.3	11.3	7.6	22.9	20.6	17.8	18.1
Eff. Tax Rate	38%	36%	35%	33%	32%	32%	30%	31%	31%	32%
Net Inc.	2,296	2,134	2,008	1,170	1,513	1,346	1,166	1,254	1,238	1,237

Balance Sheet & Other Fin. Data (Million $)

	1997	1996	1995	1994	1993	1992	1991	1990	1989	1988
Gross Prop.	34,391	32,292	30,874	29,546	29,117	28,370	27,158	26,370	25,092	24,224
Net Prop.	13,873	13,507	13,457	13,455	17,366	17,335	16,986	16,652	16,296	16,078
Cap. Exp.	2,641	3,362	3,015	2,466	2,564	2,267	2,200	2,154	2,015	1,895
Total Cap.	14,208	13,196	12,518	11,370	14,179	14,460	16,187	15,912	16,458	16,058
Fxd. Chgs. Cov.	8.3	6.9	7.6	5.0	5.7	4.9	3.9	4.8	5.4	5.7
Capitalization:										
LT Debt	4,648	4,475	4,513	4,448	4,090	4,586	4,964	5,074	5,069	4,487
Pfd.	Nil	Nil	Nil	Nil	Nil	Nil	Nil	Nil	Nil	Nil
Common	8,308	7,687	7,015	6,055	7,845	6,992	8,097	7,732	7,686	7,844
% Return On Revs.	14.4	14.3	15.0	9.3	12.9	12.1	10.8	11.8	12.1	12.5
% Return On Invest. Capital	30.6	16.5	29.8	12.6	14.1	12.1	10.8	10.7	10.1	10.2
% Return On Com. Equity	28.7	29.0	30.7	14.4	20.4	19.8	14.5	16.3	15.8	15.8
% Earn. on Net Prop.	46.2	43.5	17.5	9.5	11.0	10.0	8.9	9.9	9.9	9.7
% LT Debt of Cap.	35.9	36.8	39.2	42.3	34.3	39.6	38.0	39.6	39.7	36.4
Capital. % Pfd.	Nil	Nil	Nil	Nil	Nil	Nil	Nil	Nil	Nil	Nil
Capital. % Common	58.5	63.2	60.8	57.7	65.7	60.4	62.0	60.4	60.3	63.6

Data as orig. reptd. ; bef. results of disc. opers. and/or spec. items. Per share data adj. for stk divs. as of ex-div. date. Bold denotes diluted EPS (FASB 128). E-Estimated. NA-Not Available. NM-Not Meaningful. NR-Not Ranked.

Office—30 S. Wacker Dr., Chicago, IL 60606. **Tel**—(800) 257-0902. **E-mail**—share.owners@ameritech.com **Website**—http://www.ameritech.com **Chrmn, Pres & CEO**—R. C. Notebaert. **Exec VP & CFO**—O. G. Shaffer. **VP & Treas**—R. W. Pehlke. **Secy**—B. B. Howat. **VP & Investor Contact**—Sari L. Macrie. **Dirs**—D. C. Clark, M. R. Goodes, H. H. Gray, J. A. Henderson, S. B. Lubar, L. M. Martin, A. C. Martinez, J. B. McCoy, R. C. Notebaert, J. D. Ong, A. B. Rand, L. D. Tyson, J. A. Unruh. **Transfer Agent & Registrar**—First Chicago Trust Co. of New York, Jersey City, N.J. **Incorporated**—in Delaware in 1983. **Empl**— 69,056. **S&P Analyst:** Philip D. Wohl

Amgen

3123K
Nasdaq Symbol **AMGN**
In S&P 500

12-SEP-98

Industry: Biotechnology

Summary: This leading biotechnology concern's key products are Epogen and Neupogen, genetically engineered versions of natural hormones that stimulate production of blood components.

S&P Opinion: Accumulate (★★★★)	Recent Price • 72½ 52 Wk Range • 79⅜-44⅞
	Yield • Nil 12-Mo. P/E • 28.9

Quantitative Evaluations

Outlook
(1 Lowest—5 Highest)
• **3+**

Fair Value
• **75¼**

Risk
• **Low**

Earn./Div. Rank
• **B**

Technical Eval.
• **Bullish** since 2/98

Rel. Strength Rank
(1 Lowest—99 Highest)
• **97**

Insider Activity
• **Neutral**

Earnings vs. Previous Year
▲=Up ▼=Down ▶=No Change

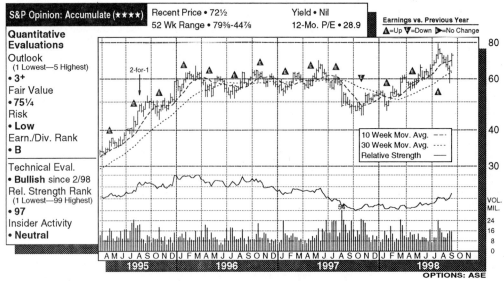

10 Week Mov. Avg. ---
30 Week Mov. Avg. ·····
Relative Strength —

2-for-1

OPTIONS: ASE

Overview - 31-JUL-98

Revenues are expected to advance 6%-7% in 1998, largely reflecting robust sales of Epogen red blood stimulant. Sales of this drug are benefiting from recent government relaxation of restrictive Medicare reimbursement rules for kidney dialysis patients (Epogen's principal market), as well as from expansion in the dialysis patient population and higher dosing. More modest sales gains are seen for Neupogen white blood cell stimulant, as growth in its core oncology market is offset by slowing AIDS sales and softening sales in Europe. Neupogen is used primarily by cancer patients whose immune-fighting white blood cells have been depleted by chemotherapy. Off-label sales of Neupogen to the AIDS market are likely to remain sluggish due to increased usage of protease inhibitors. Despite a projected rise in the tax rate, margins should be relatively well maintained. Diluted EPS should rise to $3.08, with further progress to $3.45 seen for 1999.

Valuation - 31-JUL-98

The shares have been strong performers in recent months, largely on better than expected second quarter earnings and takeover rumors. Earnings growth has been driven chiefly by robust sales of Epogen red blood cell stimulant, reflecting recent easing in Medicare reimbursement standards in the key dialysis patient market. Strength in Epogen has more than offset sluggishness in Neupogen white blood cell stimulant sales. Amgen should retain its premier position in the biotech industry, bolstered by growth in existing products and new products. The R&D pipeline includes new products for obesity, Parkinson's disease, cancer, diabetes, platelet growth and other conditions. Amgen is conservatively valued based on its future earnings potential, and the shares are recommended as a core holding for long-term appreciation in the expanding biotech field.

Key Stock Statistics

S&P EPS Est. 1998	3.08	Tang. Bk. Value/Share	8.65
P/E on S&P Est. 1998	23.5	Beta	1.03
S&P EPS Est. 1999	3.45	Shareholders	14,000
Dividend Rate/Share	Nil	Market cap. (B)	$ 18.4
Shs. outstg. (M)	253.9	Inst. holdings	54%
Avg. daily vol. (M)	2.856		

Value of $10,000 invested 5 years ago: $ 20,534

Fiscal Year Ending Dec. 31

	1998	1997	1996	1995	1994	1993
Revenues (Million $)						
1Q	605.4	575.5	507.9	439.4	364.0	310.2
2Q	656.9	620.5	571.4	493.7	414.7	343.1
3Q	—	598.3	567.0	493.3	426.4	354.9
4Q	—	606.7	593.5	513.5	442.9	365.6
Yr.	—	2,401	2,240	1,940	1,648	1,374
Earnings Per Share ($)						
1Q	0.71	0.65	0.51	0.39	0.33	0.28
2Q	0.82	0.72	0.64	0.49	0.39	0.35
3Q	E0.77	0.31	0.64	0.52	0.41	0.36
4Q	E0.78	0.67	0.64	0.52	0.02	0.32
Yr.	E3.08	2.35	2.42	1.92	1.15	1.30

Next earnings report expected: late October

Dividend Data (Dividends have been paid since 1997.)

No cash dividends have been paid. The company redeemed stock purchase rights in March 1997 for $0.0008 per right. A two-for-one split was effected in August 1995.

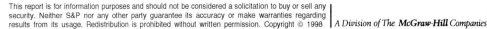

A Division of The **McGraw·Hill** *Companies*

Amgen Inc.

Business Summary - 31-JUL-98

The world's largest independent biotechnology company, Amgen was founded in Thousand Oaks, CA, in 1980 as AMGen (Applied Molecular Genetics). Using the tools of recombinant DNA and molecular biology, the company has developed two of the industry's leading commercial products -- Epogen, which had worldwide sales of $1.16 billion in 1997 ($1.07 billion in 1996), and Neupogen, which had sales of $1.06 billion in 1997 ($1.02 billion in 1996). Foreign operations represented 19% of 1996 sales and 4% of operating profits.

Epogen is a genetically engineered version of human erythropoietin (EPO), a natural hormone that stimulates the production of red blood cells in bone marrow. The drug's primary market is dialysis patients suffering from severe chronic anemia as a result of their failure to produce adequate amounts of natural EPO. Epogen supplements low levels of EPO, eliminating severe and chronic anemia. Amgen has EPO rights to the U.S. dialysis market and has licensed Johnson & Johnson U.S. rights to all other indications.

Neupogen is a recombinant version of human granulocyte colony stimulating factor (G-CSF), a protein that stimulates the production of neutrophils (a type of white blood cell that defends the body against bacterial infection). Its principal use is to build neutrophil levels in cancer patients whose natural neutrophils were destroyed by chemotherapy. Neupogen has an estimated 30% of the U.S. myelosuppressive chemotherapy market. The drug is also being explored as a potential support therapy for pneumonia. An FDA filing is also pending to use Neupogen to treat acute myelogenous leukemia. Amgen has marketing rights to Neupogen in the U.S., Canada and Australia and markets the drug jointly in Europe with F. Hoffmann-La Roche. The latter has rights to the drug in most other areas (rights in Japan are held by Kirin Brewery). In October 1997, the FDA approved Infergen, a new treatment of hepatitis C.

Amgen is committed to investing heavily in R&D to fund future biotech products, with 1997 R&D outlays of $631 million equaling 26.3% of revenues. The company currently has some 12 potential therapeutics in more than 220 clinical trials. Important new products awaiting FDA review or under development include Stemgen, a hematopoietic growth factor used in chemotherapy support programs; GDNF, a treatment for Parkinson's and Lou Gehrig's diseases; Neurotrophin for use in patients with diabetic peripheral neuropathy; IL-1ra and TNF-bp for rheumatoid arthritis; MGDF, a platelet growth factor; KGF, a treatment for mucositis in cancer patients; NESP, a treatment for anemia associated with chronic renal failure; and Leptin, a drug for obesity and Type II diabetes.

Per Share Data ($)

(Year Ended Dec. 31)	1997	1996	1995	1994	1993	1992	1991	1990	1989	1988
Tangible Bk. Val.	8.28	7.20	6.29	4.82	4.37	3.42	2.02	1.57	0.90	0.80
Cash Flow	2.77	2.78	2.22	1.41	1.48	1.32	0.42	0.21	0.16	0.00
Earnings	2.35	2.42	1.92	1.15	1.30	1.22	0.34	0.13	0.10	-0.04
Dividends	0.01	Nil	Nil	Nil	Nil	Nil	Nil	Nil	Nil	Nil
Payout Ratio	NM	Nil	Nil	Nil	Nil	Nil	Nil	Nil	Nil	Nil
Prices - High	69⅜	66½	59¾	30⅛	35⅞	39⅛	38	10⅝	5	3
- Low	44⅞	51⅜	28⅛	17⅜	15½	24⅝	9½	3⅝	2⅝	2⅛
P/E Ratio - High	30	27	31	26	27	32	NM	81	54	NM
- Low	19	21	15	15	12	20	NM	27	28	NM

Income Statement Analysis (Million $)

	1997	1996	1995	1994	1993	1992	1991	1990	1989	1988
Revs.	2,401	2,240	1,940	1,648	1,374	1,093	682	381	190	70.0
Oper. Inc.	1,103	1,058	881	801	619	466	276	123	41.0	3.0
Depr.	117	100	84.2	74.5	48.9	32.5	21.5	17.4	11.9	8.0
Int. Exp.	3.7	10.4	20.0	15.8	10.1	6.2	3.4	4.3	5.3	1.4
Pretax Inc.	861	962	794	588	592	563	158	72.0	29.0	-7.0
Eff. Tax Rate	25%	29%	32%	46%	37%	37%	38%	53%	35%	NM
Net Inc.	644	680	538	320	375	358	97.9	34.3	19.1	-8.2

Balance Sheet & Other Fin. Data (Million $)

	1997	1996	1995	1994	1993	1992	1991	1990	1989	1988
Cash	239	1,077	1,050	697	723	555	378	157	80.0	66.0
Curr. Assets	1,544	1,503	1,454	1,116	1,055	873	590	327	182	98.0
Total Assets	3,110	2,766	2,433	1,994	1,766	1,374	866	514	308	207
Curr. Liab.	742	643	584	536	412	311	295	103	55.0	15.0
LT Debt	229	59.0	177	183	181	130	39.7	12.8	64.7	30.1
Common Eqty.	2,139	1,906	1,672	1,274	1,172	934	531	398	188	162
Total Cap.	2,368	2,122	1,849	1,458	1,353	1,064	571	411	253	192
Cap. Exp.	388	267	163	131	210	219	117	65.0	44.0	44.0
Cash Flow	761	780	622	394	424	390	119	52.0	31.0	Nil
Curr. Ratio	2.1	2.3	2.5	2.1	2.6	2.8	2.0	3.2	3.3	6.5
% LT Debt of Cap.	9.7	2.8	9.6	12.6	13.4	12.2	7.0	3.1	25.6	15.7
% Net Inc.of Revs.	26.8	30.4	27.7	19.4	27.3	32.7	14.3	9.0	10.0	NM
% Ret. on Assets	21.9	26.2	24.3	17.1	24.0	31.5	14.0	7.7	7.3	NM
% Ret. on Equity	30.7	38.0	34.5	26.3	35.8	48.2	20.7	11.0	10.8	NM

Data as orig. reptd.; bef. results of disc. opers. and/or spec. items. Per share data adj. for stk. divs. as of ex-div. date. Bold denotes diluted EPS (FASB 128). E-Estimated. NA-Not Available. NM-Not Meaningful. NR-Not Ranked.

Office—1840 Dehavilland Dr., Thousand Oaks, CA 91320-1789. Tel—(805) 447-1000. Website—http://www.amgen.com Chrmn & CEO—G. M. Binder. Pres & COO—K. W. Sharer. VP & Secy—G. A. Vandeman. SVP-Fin & CFO—R. S. Attiyeh. Investor Contact—Denise Powell. Dirs—G. M. Binder, W. K. Bowes Jr., F. P. Johnson Jr., S. Lazarus, E. Ledder, G. S. Omenn, J. Pelham, K. W. Sharer. Transfer Agent & Registrar—American Stock Transfer & Trust Co., NYC. Incorporated—in California in 1980; reincorporated in Delaware in 1987. Empl— 4,646. S&P Analyst: H. B. Saftlas

STANDARD &POOR'S

STOCK REPORTS

Amoco Corp.

189M

NYSE Symbol **AN**

In S&P 500

12-SEP-98

Industry:
Oil (International Integrated)

Summary: Amoco is a major integrated petroleum and chemicals company.

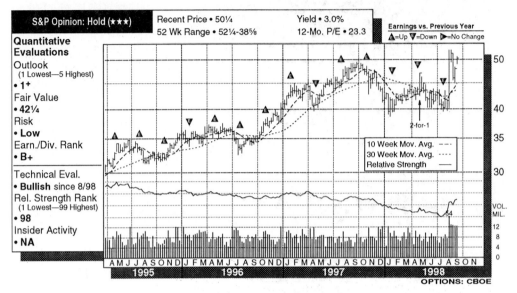

S&P Opinion: Hold (★★★)	Recent Price • 50¼	Yield • 3.0%
	52 Wk Range • 52¼-38⅝	12-Mo. P/E • 23.3

Earnings vs. Previous Year
▲=Up ▼=Down ▶=No Change

Quantitative Evaluations

Outlook
(1 Lowest—5 Highest)
• **1+**

Fair Value
• 42¼

Risk
• **Low**

Earn./Div. Rank
• **B+**

Technical Eval.
• **Bullish** since 8/98

Rel. Strength Rank
(1 Lowest—99 Highest)
• **98**

Insider Activity
• **NA**

2-for-1

10 Week Mov. Avg. ----
30 Week Mov. Avg. ····
Relative Strength ——

VOL.
MIL.

OPTIONS: CBOE

Overview - 27-JUL-98

The company is in the process of streamlining its exploration and production portfolio. In 1997, Amoco sold U.S. oil and gas properties for total proceeds of $1.2 billion. Over the years, the company has reduced the number of countries in which it explores for oil to 20, down from nearly 100 at one point. In the near term, upstream earnings will be restrained by commodity prices that will be much lower than in 1997. Downstream, we believe demand over the next several months will remain healthy, while industry capacity continues to run at high levels in the U.S., benefiting margins in marketing and refining. Margins should also benefit from the lower crude oil prices, which will serve to lower feedstock costs. Chemicals margins were weak in the first half of 1998, and significant improvement will not be seen during the rest of the year, reflecting a current oversupply condition.

Valuation - 27-JUL-98

We expect oil prices to remain sluggish, not rising much from their current levels, which are the lowest seen in over a decade. Prices have declined steadily since November 1997, and are not expected to return to the $18.00/bbl. level until next year at the earliest. Due to the deterioration of oil prices, Amoco has made cuts to its capital spending plan. Over the long term, Amoco, the largest producer of natural gas in North America, will benefit from increasing demand for that commodity. In addition, refining and marketing operations should continue to benefit from healthy domestic industry fundamentals. However, given the current level of oil prices, we remain neutral on the shares, which were recently trading at 20 times estimated 1998 EPS of $2.15.

Key Stock Statistics

S&P EPS Est. 1998	2.15	Tang. Bk. Value/Share	16.50
P/E on S&P Est. 1998	23.4	Beta	0.20
S&P EPS Est. 1999	2.45	Shareholders	134,500
Dividend Rate/Share	1.50	Market cap. (B)	$ 48.0
Shs. outstg. (M)	954.2	Inst. holdings	58%
Avg. daily vol. (M)	3.942		

Value of $10,000 invested 5 years ago: $ 25,123

Fiscal Year Ending Dec. 31

	1998	1997	1996	1995	1994	1993
Revenues (Million $)						
1Q	6,633	8,076	7,394	7,564	6,765	7,564
2Q	7,921	7,756	7,920	7,713	8,035	7,713
3Q	—	8,089	8,150	7,638	7,780	7,638
4Q	—	7,989	8,686	8,089	7,782	8,089
Yr.	—	31,910	32,150	31,004	30,362	31,004
Earnings Per Share ($)						
1Q	**0.40**	0.68	0.73	0.53	0.40	0.23
2Q	**0.30**	0.63	0.60	0.54	0.41	0.49
3Q	—	0.65	0.64	0.60	0.45	0.53
4Q	—	0.81	0.87	0.21	0.54	0.58
Yr.	**E2.15**	2.76	2.83	1.88	1.80	1.83

Next earnings report expected: late October

Dividend Data (Dividends have been paid since 1894.)

Amount ($)	Date Decl.	Ex-Div. Date	Stock of Record	Payment Date
0.750	Jan. 27	Feb. 09	Feb. 11	Mar. 10 '98
2-for-1	Jan. 27	Apr. 29	Mar. 31	Apr. 28 '98
0.375	Apr. 28	May. 11	May. 13	Jun. 10 '98
0.375	Jul. 28	Aug. 10	Aug. 12	Sep. 10 '98

A Division of The McGraw·Hill Companies

STANDARD
&POOR'S
STOCK REPORTS

AMP Incorporated

12L

12-SEP-98

Business Summary - 07-AUG-98

AMP Inc. intends to power its future growth by plugging into the expanding global market for electrical connectors. AMP (not an acronym; it's pronounced just like the unit of electrical measurement) is the world's largest producer of electronic and electrical connection devices. The company has nearly a 20% share of this $25 billion worldwide market.

AMP has a broad offering of over 800,000 parts in more than 450 product lines, giving the company the broadest selection of interconnection devices in the industry. These products are sold to a customer base of nearly 250,000 original electronic equipment makers and service organizations that install and maintain equipment.

Since it became a publicly owned company in 1956, AMP has achieved a solid long-term growth record sparked by the expansion of the electronics and electrical/transportation equipment industries. The company's goal is to outpace the 5%-8% average annual sales growth expected for the connector industry. Other financial goals include achieving pretax margins of 18% or better, and return on equity of 20% or more.

AMP has a three-part strategy to achieve its financial goals. First, the company intends to maintain its leadership in connectors. AMP believes changes in the business environment increasingly favor large, multi-national companies like itself. Second, AMP intends to diversify

into new product and market sectors that utilize its current capabilities. The company believes this would place it in new sectors with potential total market sales of $55 billion, raising its overall potential markets to $80 billion. Third, AMP will continue international expansion. Sales outside the U.S. accounted for approximately 50% of the total in 1997.

The company's products are used in a variety of end-markets. The most important of these markets are consumer and industrial (28% of 1997 revenues), communications (25%), automotive (24%), and personal computers (20%).

In January 1997, AMP announced measures to eliminate or streamline certain product lines and underperforming operations. The company believes these changes will allow it to improve its financial performance without interrupting its three-part growth strategy. Related charges of approximately $195 million were taken in the fourth quarter of 1996. Following weak operating results in the first half of 1998, the company implemented additional measures to reduce costs, including a global work force reduction of 3,500 employees. The company expects to record additional charges of $200 million to $250 million in 1998.

In August 1998, AlliedSignal, a diversified manufacturing and technology company, announced its intention to begin a tender offer for all of AMP's outstanding shares at $44.50 a share in cash.

Per Share Data ($)

(Year Ended Dec. 31)	1997	1996	1995	1994	1993	1992	1991	1990	1989	1988
Tangible Bk. Val.	13.42	12.71	12.72	11.14	9.80	9.26	9.02	8.46	7.63	7.08
Cash Flow	4.08	3.24	3.62	3.19	2.67	2.74	2.35	2.32	2.12	2.20
Earnings	2.08	1.31	1.96	1.76	1.42	1.38	1.23	1.35	1.31	1.48
Dividends	1.04	1.00	0.92	0.84	0.80	0.76	0.72	0.68	0.60	0.50
Payout Ratio	50%	76%	47%	48%	57%	55%	59%	50%	45%	34%
Prices - High	56⅝	46⅛	46¼	39¾	33⅝	34⅜	30	27⅝	24¾	27⅛
- Low	33⅛	32⅞	35⅛	28⅞	27⅜	26⅜	20½	19	20	20¼
P/E Ratio - High	27	35	24	23	24	25	24	20	19	18
- Low	16	25	18	16	19	19	17	14	15	14

Income Statement Analysis (Million $)

	1997	1996	1995	1994	1993	1992	1991	1990	1989	1988
Revs.	5,745	5,468	5,227	4,027	3,451	3,337	3,095	3,044	2,797	2,670
Oper. Inc.	1,185	1,052	1,079	947	787	821	706	694	645	685
Depr.	439	424	361	300	262	288	236	206	170	155
Int. Exp.	51.0	45.1	37.0	20.0	19.5	29.5	41.6	38.3	21.6	16.2
Pretax Inc.	678	438	668	594	486	479	424	462	455	529
Eff. Tax Rate	33%	35%	36%	38%	39%	39%	39%	38%	38%	40%
Net Inc.	458	287	427	369	297	290	260	287	281	319

Balance Sheet & Other Fin. Data (Million $)

	1997	1996	1995	1994	1993	1992	1991	1990	1989	1988
Cash	350	252	271	395	407	478	451	460	334	332
Curr. Assets	2,650	2,356	2,278	2,012	1,644	1,614	1,616	1,618	1,437	1,363
Total Assets	4,848	4,686	4,505	3,771	3,118	3,005	3,007	2,929	2,530	2,376
Curr. Liab.	1,445	1,446	1,266	1,011	752	845	888	953	725	662
LT Debt	160	182	212	211	42.9	53.0	61.1	69.5	82.8
Common Eqty.	2,952	2,790	2,768	2,334	2,056	1,943	1,913	1,793	1,625	1,521
Total Cap.	3,161	3,020	3,026	2,595	2,241	2,061	2,043	1,934	1,767	1,678
Cap. Exp.	481	592	713	457	330	312	313	338	252	220
Cash Flow	897	711	789	669	559	578	496	494	451	474
Curr. Ratio	1.8	1.6	1.8	2.0	2.2	1.9	1.8	1.7	2.0	2.1
% LT Debt of Cap.	5.0	6.0	7.1	8.1	5.8	2.1	2.6	3.2	3.9	4.9
% Net Inc.of Revs.	8.0	5.2	8.2	9.2	8.6	8.7	8.4	9.4	10.0	12.0
% Ret. on Assets	9.6	6.2	10.0	10.7	9.7	9.7	8.7	10.5	11.5	14.3
% Ret. on Equity	15.9	10.3	16.3	16.8	14.8	15.1	14.0	16.8	17.9	22.2

Data as orig. reptd.; bef. results of disc. opers. and/or spec. items. Per share data adj. for stk. divs. as of ex-div. date. Bold denotes diluted EPS (FASB 128). E-Estimated. NA-Not Available. NM-Not Meaningful. NR-Not Ranked.

Office—Friendship Rd., Harrisburg, PA 17105-3608. **Tel**—(717) 564-0100. **Website**—http://www.amp.com **Chrmn**—J. E. Marley. **Pres & CEO**—W. J. Hudson. **VP & CFO**—W.S. Urkiel. **Secy**—D. F. Henschel. **Investor Contact**—Richard Ckaare (717) 592-2323. **Dirs**—R. D. DeNunzio, B. H. Franklin, J. M. Hixon III, W. J. Hudson, J. E. Marley, H. A. McInnes, J. M. Magliochetti, J. J. Meyer, J. C. Morley, P. G. Schloemer, T. Shiina. **Transfer Agent & Registrar**—ChaseMellon Shareholder Services, Ridgefield Park, NJ. **Incorporated**—in Pennsylvania. **Empl**—46,500. **S&P Analyst:** B. McGovern

STANDARD &POOR'S
STOCK REPORTS

AMR Corp.

12Q
NYSE Symbol **AMR**

In S&P 500

12-SEP-98 | Industry: Airlines

Summary: AMR's American Airlines unit in 1998 formed a domestic alliance with US Airways; preliminary regulatory approval was obtained in July for a similar pact with British Airways.

S&P Opinion: Accumulate (★★★★)	Recent Price • 55½	Yield • Nil
	52 Wk Range • 89⅞-48¾	12-Mo. P/E • 8.1

Earnings vs. Previous Year
▲=Up ▼=Down ▶=No Change

Quantitative Evaluations

Outlook
(1 Lowest—5 Highest)
• **4**

Fair Value
• **63⅜**

Risk
• **Low**

Earn./Div. Rank
• **B-**

Technical Eval.
• **NA**

Rel. Strength Rank
(1 Lowest—99 Highest)
• **45**

Insider Activity
• **NA**

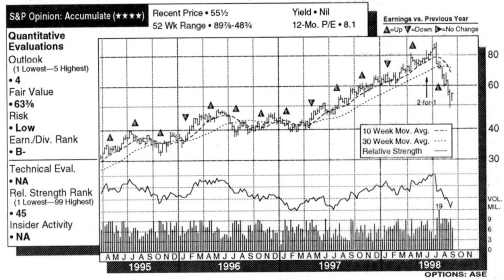

10 Week Mov. Avg. ---
30 Week Mov. Avg. ----
Relative Strength —

2-for-1

VOL. MIL.

A M J J A S O N D | J F M A M J J A S O N D | J F M A M J J A S O N D | J F M A M J J A S O N
1995 | **1996** | **1997** | **1998**

OPTIONS: ASE

Overview - 19-AUG-98

Traffic in 1998 is projected to increase about 2%, versus a 2.3% gain in 1997. Limiting growth will be delays in obtaining aircraft deliveries. International travel should experience faster growth, particularly in Latin American markets, where American has launched new routes to Lima, Peru. Despite economic softness in Asia, AMR's Pacific service will benefit from a new code-share arrangement with JAL and China Eastern, and from the start of new service between the U.S and Japan. Margins will widen, on lower fuel and commission expense, and the absence of costs related to the 1997 pilot strike. Landing fees, food service and jet rentals will be flat. Labor costs will increase, reflecting new labor settlements; maintenance spending will remain heavy, reflecting an older fleet and increased parts costs. Domestic yields will benefit from a greater proportion of business travelers in the mix. International yields will slip. Sabre will benefit from increased bookings and consulting revenue.

Valuation - 19-AUG-98

AMR shares have fallen sharply since July, despite healthy second quarter profits. Investors are worried that a rate war is erupting in American's lucrative Latin American market; that American will lose market share in European markets unless its alliance with British Airways (BA) proceeds; and that domestic markets may be weakening. The European Commission gave preliminary approval to the proposed alliance between American and BA in July 1998, with the provision that slots be divested at two London airports. American began to implement its domestic alliance with US Airways in August; full implementation is subject to labor approval. Despite concerns about international markets, we like AMR at recent levels, as its shares fail to reflect the significant value of its 82% stake in Sabre.

Key Stock Statistics

S&P EPS Est. 1998	7.25	Tang. Bk. Value/Share	28.75
P/E on S&P Est. 1998	7.7	Beta	1.35
S&P EPS Est. 1999	7.35	Shareholders	15,100
Dividend Rate/Share	Nil	Market cap. (B)	$ 10.1
Shs. outstg. (M)	182.3	Inst. holdings	77%
Avg. daily vol. (M)	1.915		

Value of $10,000 invested 5 years ago: $ 16,462

Fiscal Year Ending Dec. 31

	1998	1997	1996	1995	1994	1993
Revenues (Million $)						
1Q	4,737	4,426	4,308	3,970	3,808	3,814
2Q	5,012	4,710	4,550	4,307	4,101	4,212
3Q	—	4,798	4,562	4,445	4,233	4,199
4Q	—	4,636	4,333	4,188	3,995	3,591
Yr.	—	18,570	17,753	16,910	16,137	15,816
Earnings Per Share ($)						
1Q	1.62	0.82	1.01	0.24	-0.15	-0.21
2Q	2.30	1.63	1.68	1.24	0.89	0.20
3Q	E2.05	1.78	1.53	1.50	1.24	0.71
4Q	E1.29	1.17	2.02	-1.77	-0.85	-1.74
Yr.	E7.25	5.39	6.08	1.24	1.13	-1.02

Next earnings report expected: mid October

Dividend Data

Amount ($)	Date Decl.	Ex-Div. Date	Stock of Record	Payment Date
2-for-1	Apr. 15	Jun. 10	May. 26	Jun. 09 '98

A Division of The McGraw·Hill Companies

Business Summary - 19-AUG-98

AMR Corp's American Airlines unit is one of the world's largest airlines. American, which has a dominant position in Latin American travel, hopes to beef up its Atlantic service through a pending alliance with British Airways. American began implementing parts of its domestic alliance with US Airways in August 1998; full implementation is subject to pilot and government approval. A protracted struggle between AMR and its pilots ended in May 1997 with a new contract that lets American's regional affiliate operate small jet aircraft. AMR also holds 82% of the SABRE Group, a leading computer reservations system operator.

American is the second largest U.S. airline, serving 165 destinations worldwide. American operates with hubs in Dallas/Ft. Worth, Chicago, Miami and San Juan (Puerto Rico). Short-haul traffic is fed to American's hubs from its four American Eagle affiliates which is being consolidated into one entity during 1998.

International traffic generated 30% of total passenger revenues in 1997. Latin American service accounts for 53% of its international traffic. Revenues from Pacific travel account for 7% of AMR's international passenger revenue. With the signing of a new aviation accord between the US and Japan in early 1998, AMR's Pacific service should grow at a significantly faster pace; AMR launched new flights to Tokyo and Osaka in 1998.

AMR hopes to fortify its position in the Atlantic market, which accounts for 40% of its international revenues, through an alliance with British Airways (BA). Implementation of the alliance, proposed in June 1996, has met with fierce opposition, because AMR and BA would control 60% of traffic moving between the U.S. and London's Heathrow airport. The European Commission in July 1998 informally approved the alliance subject to the divestiture, without compensation, of 267 slots at two London airports.

The majority of American's employees are represented by labor unions. In May 1997, pilots at American Airlines ratified a new contract through August 2001. A strike by American's pilots in February 1997 cut net income in the 1997 first quarter by $70 million. In return for what is considered a generous compensation package relative to other airline pay scales, AMR got the right to fly up to 67 small scale jets at its American Eagle regional carriers. American Eagle, whose fleet consisted of 199 turboprop aircraft at 1997 year-end, launched regional jet service in the 1998 second quarter. The jets have greater range and capacity and are quieter than turboprop aircraft.

At August 14, 1998, American had on order 34 Boeing 777s, four Boeing 767s, five Boeing 757s, and 100 Boeing 737s.

AMR derived 10% of its total revenues in 1997 from the SABRE Group (82% owned), which operates one of the largest computer reservations systems. AMR's other activities include the transport of cargo and providing a variety of services to unaffiliated airlines.

Per Share Data ($)

(Year Ended Dec. 31)	1997	1996	1995	1994	1993	1992	1991	1990	1989	1988
Tangible Bk. Val.	28.75	23.89	14.89	21.75	11.43	11.03	17.64	24.25	27.52	24.18
Cash Flow	12.25	13.27	9.45	9.35	6.58	3.37	4.29	5.20	8.16	8.29
Earnings	5.39	6.32	1.24	1.13	-1.02	-3.17	-1.77	-0.32	3.58	3.96
Dividends	Nil	Nil	Nil	Nil	Nil	Nil	Nil	Nil	Nil	Nil
Payout Ratio	Nil	Nil	Nil	Nil	Nil	Nil	Nil	Nil	Nil	Nil
Prices - High	66¼	48¾	40⅛	36⅜	36½	40⅛	35⅝	35⅛	53¾	27½
- Low	39⅛	34	26¾	24⅛	27¾	27¼	22⅛	19⅞	26⅛	16⅜
P/E Ratio - High	12	8	32	32	NM	NM	NM	NM	15	7
- Low	7	5	22	21	NM	NM	NM	NM	7	4

Income Statement Analysis (Million $)

	1997	1996	1995	1994	1993	1992	1991	1990	1989	1988
Revs.	18,570	17,753	16,910	16,137	15,701	14,396	12,887	11,720	10,480	8,824
Oper. Inc.	3,170	3,043	2,807	2,537	1,731	955	826	811	1,329	1,318
Depr.	1,244	1,204	1,259	1,253	1,156	980	821	687	585	512
Int. Exp.	399	499	684	637	668	651	508	337	239	233
Pretax Inc.	1,682	1,633	358	370	-112	-696	-339	-33.0	718	741
Eff. Tax Rate	39%	32%	45%	38%	NM	NM	NM	NM	37%	36%
Net Inc.	985	1,105	196	228	-96.0	-474	-239	-40.0	455	477

Balance Sheet & Other Fin. Data (Million $)

	1997	1996	1995	1994	1993	1992	1991	1990	1989	1988
Cash	64.0	1,811	901	777	586	858	1,249	949	601	1,287
Curr. Assets	5,071	4,470	3,137	3,118	2,690	2,868	2,806	2,658	2,091	2,615
Total Assets	20,915	20,497	19,556	19,486	19,326	18,706	16,208	13,354	10,877	9,722
Curr. Liab.	5,617	5,566	4,693	4,914	4,417	4,720	4,742	4,825	3,479	2,796
LT Debt	3,889	4,542	7,052	7,878	7,554	7,838	5,879	3,272	2,306	2,750
Common Eqty.	6,216	5,668	3,642	3,302	3,195	3,349	3,794	3,727	3,766	3,148
Total Cap.	10,715	10,953	11,218	11,537	12,140	11,383	10,214	7,650	6,874	6,715
Cap. Exp.	1,390	547	928	1,114	2,577	3,881	3,918	2,479	1,897	1,111
Cash Flow	2,229	2,309	1,455	1,425	1,000	505	581	648	1,028	979
Curr. Ratio	0.9	0.8	0.7	0.6	0.6	0.6	0.6	0.6	0.6	0.9
% LT Debt of Cap.	36.2	41.5	62.9	68.3	62.2	68.9	57.6	42.8	33.5	40.9
% Net Inc.of Revs.	5.3	6.2	1.2	1.4	NM	NM	NM	NM	4.3	5.4
% Ret. on Assets	4.8	5.5	1.0	1.2	NM	NM	NM	NM	4.3	5.3
% Ret. on Equity	16.6	23.7	5.5	5.3	NM	NM	NM	NM	12.5	16.0

Data as orig. reptd.; bef. results of disc. opers. and/or spec. items. Per share data adj. for stk. divs. as of ex-div. date. Bold denotes diluted EPS (FASB 128). E-Estimated. NA-Not Available. NM-Not Meaningful. NR-Not Ranked.

Office—4333 Amon Carter Blvd., Fort Worth, TX 76155. **Tel**—(817) 963-1234. **Website**—http://www.amrcorp.com **Chrmn & CEO**—D. J. Carty. **SVP & CFO**—G. J. Arpey. **Secy**—C. D. MarLett. **Investor Contact**—Mike Lenz. **Dirs**—D. L. Boren, E. A. Brennan, D. J. Carty, A. M. Codina, C. T. Fisher III, E. G. Graves, D. J. Kelly, A. D. McLaughlin, C. H. Pistor Jr., J. M. Rodgers, J. Rodin, M. Segall. **Transfer Agent & Registrar**—First Chicago Trust Co. of New York, Jersey City, NJ. **Incorporated**—in Delaware in 1934; reincorporated in Delaware in 1982. **Empl**— 114,600. **S&P Analyst:** Stephen R. Klein

STANDARD &POOR'S

STOCK REPORTS

Anadarko Petroleum

194P

NYSE Symbol **APC**

In S&P 500

12-SEP-98

Industry:
Oil & Gas (Exploration & Production)

Summary: Anadarko is one of the leading U.S. independent natural gas and crude oil production companies.

| S&P Opinion: Hold (★★★) | Recent Price • 37⅞ | Yield • 0.5% | Earnings vs. Previous Year |
| | 52 Wk Range • 39½-26½ | 12-Mo. P/E • NM | ▲=Up ▼=Down ▶=No Change |

Quantitative Evaluations

Outlook
(1 Lowest—5 Highest)
• **1+**

Fair Value
• **27**

Risk
• **Average**

Earn./Div. Rank
• **B+**

Technical Eval.
• **NA**

Rel. Strength Rank
(1 Lowest—99 Highest)
• **99**

Insider Activity
• **NA**

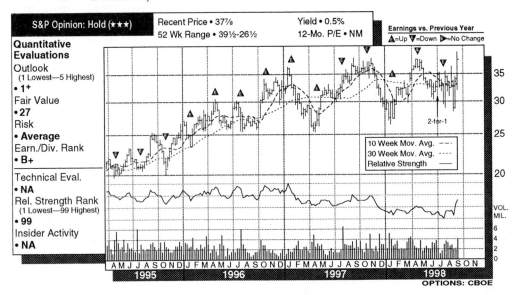

10 Week Mov. Avg. ‒ ‒ ‒
30 Week Mov. Avg. ·····
Relative Strength ‒‒‒

2-for-1

OPTIONS: CBOE

Overview - 11-AUG-98

Earnings in the first half of 1998 were well below the levels recorded in the first six months of 1997, reflecting significantly lower oil and natural gas prices. However, oil production rose 14%, due to the ramp-up of production from the Mahogany field in the Gulf of Mexico, and initial production from Algerian fields. The company's production tends to be higher in the second half of the year, and we do not think that 1998 will be an exception. Significant volume growth, particularly for oil, is projected for the next few years. The company's aggressive exploration program in the Gulf of Mexico sub-salt has yielded positive results. In July, APC announced a major discovery in the Gulf; the company estimates the reservoir's recoverable reserves at some 140 million barrels of oil equivalent. APC's sizable Algerian oil reserves have helped the company achieve a better balance between oil and gas production. Algerian production could represent close to 70% of APC's total oil production by 2000.

Valuation - 11-AUG-98

Oil prices have retreated recently, amid reduced Asian demand, putting a damper on the shares of independent exploration and production companies. However, Anadarko's shares have held up better than those of its peers, as investors have been enthusiastic about the company's latest Gulf of Mexico discovery. The company's excellent reserve replacement history bodes well for increased production over the longer term. APC currently enjoys the lowest reserve replacement costs in the industry. However, given current oil and gas price levels, the shares are trading near their net asset value, and we believe that they will be market performers for the remainder of 1998.

Key Stock Statistics

S&P EPS Est. 1998	0.40	Tang. Bk. Value/Share	9.34
P/E on S&P Est. 1998	94.7	Beta	0.93
S&P EPS Est. 1999	1.00	Shareholders	6,300
Dividend Rate/Share	0.20	Market cap. (B)	$ 4.5
Shs. outstg. (M)	120.1	Inst. holdings	77%
Avg. daily vol. (M)	0.562		

Value of $10,000 invested 5 years ago: $ 26,653

Fiscal Year Ending Dec. 31

	1998	1997	1996	1995	1994	1993
Revenues (Million $)						
1Q	146.4	170.5	135.7	102.8	132.0	129.3
2Q	137.6	138.9	135.1	113.9	119.5	112.5
3Q	—	158.3	128.6	99.3	111.4	103.3
4Q	—	205.5	169.7	118.0	115.3	131.2
Yr.	—	673.2	569.0	434.0	482.5	476.3
Earnings Per Share ($)						
1Q	0.06	0.28	0.17	0.04	0.14	0.14
2Q	0.02	0.12	0.15	0.08	0.10	0.11
3Q	—	0.14	0.21	0.01	0.09	-0.02
4Q	—	0.35	0.32	0.06	0.02	0.12
Yr.	E0.40	0.89	0.85	0.18	0.35	0.35

Next earnings report expected: late October

Dividend Data (Dividends have been paid since 1986.)

Amount ($)	Date Decl.	Ex-Div. Date	Stock of Record	Payment Date
0.075	Jan. 30	Mar. 09	Mar. 11	Mar. 25 '98
0.100	Apr. 30	Jun. 08	Jun. 10	Jun. 24 '98
2-for-1	Apr. 30	Jul. 02	Jun. 15	Jul. 01 '98
0.050	Jul. 29	Sep. 04	Sep. 09	Sep. 23 '98

This report is for information purposes and should not be considered a solicitation to buy or sell any security. Neither S&P nor any other party guarantee its accuracy or make warranties regarding results from its usage. Redistribution is prohibited without written permission. Copyright © 1998

A Division of The McGraw-Hill Companies

Business Summary - 11-AUG-98

Anadarko Petroleum Corporation (APC) is not just in Kansas anymore. In the decade since its spinoff as an independent company in 1986, Anadarko has evolved from a small domestic natural gas producer to one of the world's largest independent oil and gas companies. The company has expanded its domestic holdings, and also has exploration projects under way in Algeria, Eritrea, Jordan and Peru.

The company's drilling program focuses on known petroleum and natural gas areas onshore in North America, primarily in the Anadarko Basin of Oklahoma, the Mid-continent region (Arkoma and Golden Trend Basins) of Arkansas and Oklahoma, the Permian Basin of West Texas and New Mexico, the Rocky Mountain regions of Nevada and Wyoming, and southern Alberta. APC also drills offshore in the Gulf of Mexico, and has 20 sub-salt prospects in the Gulf. On the international front, the company's Algerian acreage is seen as holding great promise. APC spent $120 million for further delineation drilling and development in Algeria in 1997. A significant portion of reserves is located in the Hugoton natural gas field, the largest natural gas field in the U.S. To enhance recovery and marketability of its natural gas reserves, Anadarko owns interests in 16 gas gathering systems and eight gas processing plants in the Mid-continent area.

In the 10 years since it became an independent company, Anadarko has doubled its production volumes. The company aims to double its production volumes again over the next four years. Production in 1997, all of which was U.S.-based, amounted to 9,083,000 bbl. of oil (6,702,000 bbl. in 1996), 178.7 Bcf of natural gas (164.9 Bcf) and 5,467,000 bbl. of natural gas liquids (3,514,000 bbl.). Future production gains will be aided by large Gulf of Mexico and Algerian discoveries.

The company has compiled an impressive reserve replacement record. During 1997, APC replaced 341% of total production with reserves of oil and natural gas, and has more than replaced its production with reserves for 16 consecutive years, dating back to when it was a subsidiary of Panhandle Eastern Corp. (since renamed Panenergy Corp., now a subsidiary of Duke Energy). The company's worldwide finding cost in 1997 was $4.28 per energy equivalent barrel (EEB), and has averaged $3.28 per EEB over the past five years, both numbers far below the industry average.

Anadarko has also achieved a long-desired reserve balance between oil and gas. At year-end 1997, APC had gas reserves of 1.73 trillion cubic feet (Tcf) and 420 million bbl. of oil reserves. On an energy equivalent basis, Anadarko's oil reserves accounted for 59% of total reserves, up from 50% in 1996. By contrast, oil accounted for only 6% of the company's total reserve base in 1986.

Per Share Data ($)

(Year Ended Dec. 31)	1997	1996	1995	1994	1993	1992	1991	1990	1989	1988
Tangible Bk. Val.	9.17	8.38	7.58	7.64	7.37	5.94	5.81	5.63	4.74	4.37
Cash Flow	2.55	2.26	1.58	1.82	1.81	1.45	1.40	1.76	1.68	1.45
Earnings	0.89	0.85	0.18	0.35	0.35	0.24	0.29	0.52	0.46	0.38
Dividends	0.15	0.15	0.15	0.15	0.15	0.15	0.15	0.15	0.15	0.15
Payout Ratio	17%	18%	83%	43%	43%	61%	51%	30%	33%	39%
Prices - High	38³⁄₈	34¹⁄₂	27¹⁄₈	29¹⁄₄	25⁷⁄₈	16¹⁄₂	16⁵⁄₈	20	19¹⁄₄	14
- Low	25³⁄₈	23³⁄₈	17⁷⁄₈	18¹⁄₂	12⁷⁄₈	9¹⁄₄	10³⁄₄	14³⁄₈	12¹⁄₄	11
P/E Ratio - High	43	41	NM	84	74	67	56	38	42	37
- Low	29	27	NM	53	37	38	36	28	27	29

Income Statement Analysis (Million $)

	1997	1996	1995	1994	1993	1992	1991	1990	1989	1988
Revs.	673	569	434	482	476	375	337	388	330	304
Oper. Inc.	402	349	232	267	272	201	194	252	217	202
Depr. Depl. & Amort.	199	167	165	173	168	133	121	132	127	124
Int. Exp.	41.0	56.0	53.0	41.6	38.0	36.6	36.8	42.9	50.9	58.1
Pretax Inc.	164	158	29.3	64.7	77.4	40.0	48.0	84.0	72.0	61.0
Eff. Tax Rate	35%	36%	28%	36%	48%	32%	33%	34%	33%	35%
Net Inc.	107	101	21.0	41.1	40.0	27.3	32.4	55.2	48.0	39.8

Balance Sheet & Other Fin. Data (Million $)

	1997	1996	1995	1994	1993	1992	1991	1990	1989	1988
Cash	8.9	15.0	17.0	6.5	17.8	14.8	15.0	13.0	9.5	6.3
Curr. Assets	219	270	163	139	141	139	107	120	103	109
Total Assets	2,992	2,584	2,267	2,142	2,023	1,905	1,676	1,647	1,553	1,490
Curr. Liab.	252	285	190	128	126	107	104	118	97.0	100
LT Debt	956	731	674	629	543	647	440	427	493	493
Common Eqty.	1,117	1,014	910	900	864	657	641	618	495	455
Total Cap.	2,620	2,244	2,034	1,968	1,831	1,783	1,556	1,512	1,441	1,378
Cap. Exp.	686	427	331	423	265	362	170	213	203	161
Cash Flow	306	268	186	214	208	160	154	187	175	151
Curr. Ratio	0.9	0.9	0.9	1.1	1.1	1.3	1.0	1.0	1.1	1.1
% LT Debt of Cap.	36.5	32.6	33.1	32.0	29.6	36.3	28.2	28.2	34.2	35.8
% Ret. on Assets	3.8	4.2	1.0	2.0	2.0	1.5	1.9	3.4	3.1	2.7
% Ret. on Equity	10.1	10.5	2.3	4.7	5.1	4.2	5.1	9.7	10.1	9.0

Data as orig. reptd.; bef. results of disc opers. and/or spec. items. Per share data adj. for stk. divs. as of ex-div. date. Bold denotes diluted EPS (FASB 128). E-Estimated. NA-Not Available. NM-Not Meaningful. NR-Not Ranked.

Office—Anadarko Tower, 17001 Northchase Dr., P.O. Box 1330, Houston, TX 77060. **Tel**—(713) 875-1101. **Website**—http://www.anadarko.com **Chrmn, Pres & CEO**—R. J. Allison Jr. **SVP-Fin & CFO**—M. E. Rose. **VP & Treas**—A. L. Richey. **VP & Investor Contact**—A. Paul Taylor Jr. **Dirs**—C. P. Albert, R. J. Allison Jr., L. G. Barcus, R. Brown, J. L. Bryan, J. R. Butler, Jr., J. R. Gordon, J. N. Seitz. **Transfer Agent & Registrar**—ChaseMellon Shareholder Services, Ridgefield Park, NJ. **Incorporated**—in Delaware in 1985. **Empl**— 1,386. **S&P Analyst:** Norman Rosenberg

12-SEP-98

Industry:
Communications
Equipment

Summary: This company is a global supplier of communications products and systems to commercial, industrial, government and military customers.

S&P Opinion: Avoid (★★)	Recent Price • 14¼	Yield • Nil
	52 Wk Range • 30-12½	12-Mo. P/E • 11.9

Earnings vs. Previous Year
▲=Up ▼=Down ▶=No Change

Quantitative Evaluations

Outlook
(1 Lowest—5 Highest)
• **5+**

Fair Value
• **21⅝**

Risk
• **Average**

Earn./Div. Rank
• **B**

Technical Eval.
• **NA**

Rel. Strength Rank
(1 Lowest—99 Highest)
• **47**

Insider Activity
• **Neutral**

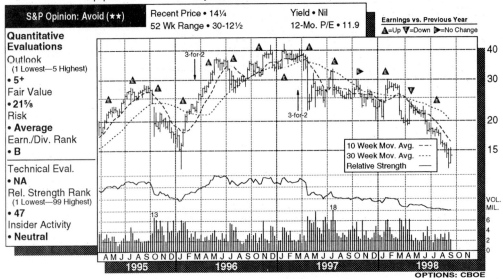

10 Week Mov. Avg. – – –
30 Week Mov. Avg. · · · ·
Relative Strength —

OPTIONS: CBOE

Overview - 23-JUL-98

We expect revenues to be down 2% in FY 98 (Sep.), and to advance about 17% in FY 99, reflecting reported soft demand for wireless infrastructure in the U.S., as well as weakness in Asia. Andrew supplies equipment to primary wireless equipment providers such as Lucent, Motorola and Nortel. These customers have all reported strong growth in the U.S., Latin America and China. Therefore, we are concerned that Andrew may be losing market share to its competitors. For the longer term, Andrew expects revenue growth over the next few years to come from its full line of products for the personal communication systems (PCS) market. PCS networks have begun to effectively compete with cellular service in selected markets. Gross margins narrowed in the FY 98 third quarter, on pricing pressures and due to a larger contribution from low margin wireless accessories. However, operating margins should remain steady as ANDW makes progress in controlling SG&A expenses.

Valuation - 23-JUL-98

The shares are down 6% since our March downgrade to avoid, from hold. Results for the FY 98 third quarter were in line with expectations that had been recently revised downward, with revenues down 2% year to year. Third quarter orders were up 6%, but total backlog remained 11% below the year-ago level. Visibility for the remainder of FY 98 is extremely limited, given the uncertain demand conditions in Asia and the company's guidance for weak demand in the U.S. ANDW's weakness in the U.S. wireless market is particularly troubling, given the solid U.S. order growth posted by wireless equipment manufacturers Lucent, Nortel and QUALCOMM. We would avoid ANDW shares, which were recently trading at about 13X our calendar 1999 EPS estimate of $1.41.

Key Stock Statistics

S&P EPS Est. 1998	1.17	Tang. Bk. Value/Share	5.56
P/E on S&P Est. 1998	12.2	Beta	0.89
S&P EPS Est. 1999	1.37	Shareholders	5,500
Dividend Rate/Share	Nil	Market cap. (B)	$ 1.2
Shs. outstg. (M)	86.1	Inst. holdings	42%
Avg. daily vol. (M)	0.589		

Value of $10,000 invested 5 years ago: $ 29,596

Fiscal Year Ending Sep. 30

	1998	1997	1996	1995	1994	1993
Revenues (Million $)						
1Q	236.8	225.7	177.9	142.6	121.8	101.0
2Q	196.9	202.2	183.2	156.3	142.2	99.9
3Q	204.2	208.9	197.2	161.3	136.0	110.5
4Q	—	232.6	235.3	166.2	158.6	119.4
Yr.	—	869.5	793.6	626.5	558.5	430.8
Earnings Per Share ($)						
1Q	**0.32**	0.28	0.19	0.13	0.08	0.06
2Q	**0.27**	0.29	0.20	0.16	0.10	0.05
3Q	**0.28**	0.27	0.26	0.21	0.12	0.08
4Q	**E0.30**	0.34	0.34	0.27	0.20	0.14
Yr.	**E1.17**	1.18	0.99	0.77	0.50	0.32

Next earnings report expected: late October

Dividend Data

No cash dividends have been paid. Several stock splits have been effected, most recently a three-for-two split in March 1997.

A Division of The **McGraw·Hill** *Companies*

STANDARD
&POOR'S
STOCK REPORTS

Andrew Corporation

3132B
12-SEP-98

Business Summary - 23-JUL-98

Andrew Corporation (ANDW) is positioned to benefit from three trends in global telecommunications: deregulation, privatization and competition. Deregulation creates a less restrictive economic environment and encourages privatization. Investors are increasingly providing the funds needed for newly privatized companies to purchase communications infrastructure. Deregulation also heightens competition by allowing new entrants into the industry. New service providers in turn invest in infrastructure to compete with existing players. ANDW, the successor to a partnership formed in 1937, is a supplier of communications products to commercial, industrial, military and government customers. Its principal products are coaxial cables, antennas and earth stations for satellite communication systems, and radar and communication reconnaissance systems.

Contributions to sales in recent fiscal years (Sep.) were:

	FY 97	FY 96
Coaxial cable systems	54%	52%
Other Products and Services	21%	17%
Terrestrial Microwave	18%	20%
Wireless Accessories	7%	8%

Coaxial cables are used to carry radio-frequency signals, while waveguides (tubular conductors) are used at higher frequencies, although they are also employed in UHF (lower frequency) broadcasting. Semiflexible cables and waveguides are sold under the trademark HELIAX. Microwave antenna systems are used in land-based microwave radio networks by the telecommunications industry. Other users include pipeline companies, electric utilities and railroads.

Earth station antenna systems are used at land-based terminals to receive signals from, and transmit signals to, communication satellites, for distribution of cable signals (CATV), UHF and VHF broadcasts. Defense electronic products, including electronic scanning and communications receiver systems, are used for intelligence gathering in strategic surveillance operations.

ANDW also designs and installs its proprietary distributed communication systems. These systems permit in-building and enclosed area access for all types of wireless communications using semi-flexible coaxial cable sold under the tradename RADIAX.

Network products provide connections between different computing systems and are used by businesses, industries and government customers. Wireless accessories are provided for personal communications systems, cellular handsets and paging devices. Products include portable antennas, batteries, and battery chargers.

Per Share Data ($)

(Year Ended Sep. 30)	1997	1996	1995	1994	1993	1992	1991	1990	1989	1988
Tangible Bk. Val.	5.40	4.56	3.57	2.72	2.10	1.80	1.77	1.56	1.49	1.33
Cash Flow	1.61	1.36	1.05	0.76	0.56	0.44	0.40	0.33	0.29	0.27
Earnings	1.18	0.99	0.77	0.50	0.32	0.26	0.23	0.18	0.16	0.14
Dividends	Nil	Nil	Nil	Nil	Nil	Nil	Nil	Nil	Nil	Nil
Payout Ratio	Nil	Nil	Nil	Nil	Nil	Nil	Nil	Nil	Nil	Nil
Prices - High	42⅝	42⅛	28⅝	15¾	8¾	4⅞	3⅝	2⅝	2⅝	2
- Low	20⅛	12½	15⅛	7⅛	3⅞	2⁹⁄₁₆	2	1½	1¾	1¼
P/E Ratio - High	36	43	37	31	27	19	16	14	16	14
- Low	17	13	20	14	12	9	9	9	11	9

Income Statement Analysis (Million $)

	1997	1996	1995	1994	1993	1992	1991	1990	1989	1988
Revs.	869	794	664	558	431	442	416	366	302	254
Oper. Inc.	208	180	140	98.4	67.3	62.8	57.7	50.1	91.3	35.2
Depr.	39.3	34.3	25.8	21.9	20.7	17.9	17.3	15.1	13.4	13.0
Int. Exp.	5.0	5.2	5.6	5.2	5.5	6.1	6.5	5.2	3.5	2.5
Pretax Inc.	166	141	5.6	69.4	43.6	40.0	35.9	29.2	26.2	21.7
Eff. Tax Rate	35%	36%	36%	36%	36%	38%	38%	39%	38%	36%
Net Inc.	108	90.4	70.0	44.4	27.9	25.0	22.2	18.2	16.2	13.9

Balance Sheet & Other Fin. Data (Million $)

	1997	1996	1995	1994	1993	1992	1991	1990	1989	1988
Cash	93.8	31.3	46.0	40.3	21.7	7.4	17.1	13.8	7.4	9.8
Curr. Assets	460	402	323	261	203	190	210	189	166	148
Total Assets	691	631	505	415	337	314	343	320	266	234
Curr. Liab.	127	117	95.6	91.6	63.9	65.4	59.5	53.2	65.9	48.3
LT Debt	35.7	40.4	45.3	45.5	50.0	52.6	58.3	63.4	15.6	18.8
Common Eqty.	509	456	356	273	220	192	217	199	182	166
Total Cap.	554	496	402	318	270	245	276	262	198	185
Cap. Exp.	49.1	52.5	48.1	27.1	17.9	17.8	25.0	25.2	16.3	12.8
Cash Flow	147	125	95.8	66.3	48.5	42.9	39.4	33.3	29.6	26.9
Curr. Ratio	3.6	3.4	3.4	2.8	3.2	2.9	3.5	3.6	2.5	3.1
% LT Debt of Cap.	6.5	8.1	11.3	14.3	18.5	21.5	21.1	24.2	7.9	10.2
% Net Inc.of Revs.	12.4	11.4	10.8	10.5	6.5	5.7	5.3	5.0	5.4	5.5
% Ret. on Assets	16.3	15.9	NA	11.7	8.4	8.2	6.7	6.3	6.5	6.3
% Ret. on Equity	22.3	22.2	NA	17.9	13.4	13.2	10.7	9.7	9.3	8.8

Data as orig. reptd.; bef. results of disc. opers. and/or spec. items. Per share data adj. for stk. divs. as of ex-div. date. Bold denotes diluted EPS (FASB 128). E-Estimated. NA-Not Available. NM-Not Meaningful. NR-Not Ranked.

Office—10500 West 153rd St., Orland Park, IL 60462. **Tel**—(708) 349-3300. **Website**—http://www.andrew.com **Chrmn, Pres & CEO**—F.L. English. **EVP-Fin, CFO**—Charles R. Nicholas. **Treas and Investor Contact**—Tami Kamarauskas (708-873-2534). **Dirs**—J. G. Bollinger, J. L. Boyes, K. J. Douglas, F. L. English, J. D. Fluno, O. J. Wade. **Transfer Agent & Registrar**—Harris Trust & Savings Bank, Chicago. **Incorporated**—in Illinois in 1947; reincorporated in Delaware in 1987. **Empl**—4,227. **S&P Analyst**: Aydin Tuncer

STANDARD &POOR'S
STOCK REPORTS

Anheuser-Busch

201B

NYSE Symbol **BUD**

In S&P 500

12-SEP-98 | **Industry:** Beverages (Alcoholic) | **Summary:** Parent company of the world's largest brewer, Anheuser-Busch also has interests in entertainment operations.

S&P Opinion: Hold (★★★)

Recent Price • 54⅛	Yield • 2.1%
52 Wk Range • 54⅜-38½	12-Mo. P/E • 22.3

Quantitative Evaluations

Outlook (1 Lowest—5 Highest)
• **2+**

Fair Value
• **50⅝**

Risk
• **Low**

Earn./Div. Rank
• **A**

Technical Eval.
• **Bearish** since 4/98

Rel. Strength Rank (1 Lowest—99 Highest)
• **98**

Insider Activity
• **Neutral**

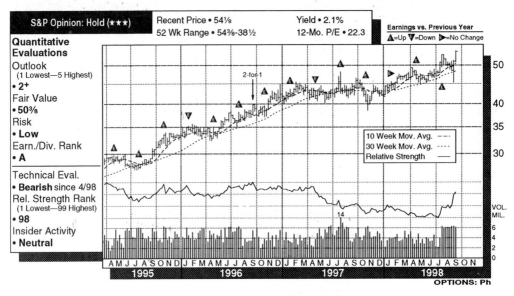

Earnings vs. Previous Year
▲=Up ▼=Down ▶=No Change

10 Week Mov. Avg. ---
30 Week Mov. Avg. ....
Relative Strength —

OPTIONS: Ph

Overview - 31-JUL-98

Net sales (after excise taxes) from ongoing operations should rise at a low single-digit pace in 1998, primarily reflecting a modest 1% to 2% rise in worldwide beer shipments. Operating margins are expected to widen slightly, as increased brewing and packaging costs are more than offset by cost savings accruing from the recent realignment of production facilities. Reflecting the adoption of equity accounting for the company's increased stake in Grupo Modelo, Mexico's largest brewer, net income from continuing operations should rise by 3% to 4%. Excess cash generated from operations should continue to be used primarily for international expansion and for share repurchases. With a modest reduction in shares outstanding, diluted earnings per share are expected to reach $2.52 in 1998, up 7% from 1997's $2.36.

Valuation - 31-JUL-98

Over the past year, the shares have lagged the performance of the broader S&P 500, held by slowing earnings growth stemming from an increasingly competitive domestic beer industry. Intense pricing competition from its closest rivals, combined with a recent rise in popularity for imported beers, has negatively impacted BUD's beer volume growth and profitability in recent quarters. Although this has been mitigated somewhat by quiescent material costs, the company's near-term earnings growth prospects have been reduced by S&P over the past few months. Longer-term prospects remain favorable given the company's wide geographic reach, but the stock's valuation is likely to be pressured until current industry pricing pressures ease. Although recently trading at modest P/E discount to that of the S&P 500 index, the shares are expected to be only market performers over the next 12 months.

Key Stock Statistics

S&P EPS Est. 1998	2.52	Tang. Bk. Value/Share	7.37
P/E on S&P Est. 1998	21.5	Beta	0.61
S&P EPS Est. 1999	2.70	Shareholders	65,100
Dividend Rate/Share	1.12	Market cap. (B)	$ 26.1
Shs. outstg. (M)	482.1	Inst. holdings	62%
Avg. daily vol. (M)	1.651		

Value of $10,000 invested 5 years ago: NA

Fiscal Year Ending Dec. 31

	1998	1997	1996	1995	1994	1993
Revenues (Million $)						
1Q	2,508	2,463	2,372	2,318	2,628	2,503
2Q	3,006	2,994	2,961	2,823	3,169	2,991
3Q	—	3,102	3,064	2,967	3,298	3,157
4Q	—	2,507	2,487	2,233	2,959	2,854
Yr.	—	11,066	10,884	10,341	12,054	11,505
Earnings Per Share ($)						
1Q	**0.54**	0.51	0.54	0.42	0.38	0.34
2Q	**0.80**	0.76	0.70	0.63	0.60	0.56
3Q	**E0.85**	0.79	0.75	0.67	0.63	-0.14
4Q	**E0.33**	0.30	0.30	-0.47	0.34	0.31
Yr.	**E2.52**	2.36	2.28	1.24	1.96	1.08

Next earnings report expected: late October

Dividend Data (Dividends have been paid since 1932.)

Amount ($)	Date Decl.	Ex-Div. Date	Stock of Record	Payment Date
0.260	Oct. 22	Nov. 06	Nov. 10	Dec. 09 '97
0.260	Dec. 17	Feb. 05	Feb. 09	Mar. 09 '98
0.260	Apr. 22	May. 06	May. 08	Jun. 09 '98
0.280	Jul. 22	Aug. 06	Aug. 10	Sep. 09 '98

A Division of The McGraw·Hill Companies

Business Summary - 31-JUL-98

Anheuser-Busch Cos. is the holding company parent of the largest U.S. brewer (Anheuser-Busch, Inc.), whose origins date back to 1875. The company has over the past two years increased its focus on its brewing operations by divesting various of its former non-beer businesses, which included the St. Louis Cardinals baseball team, and its food operations through the spinoff to shareholders of The Earthgrains Company (NYSE-listed) and the divestiture of the assets of Eagle Snacks, Inc. The company retained its beer packaging and entertainment subsidiaries and intends to support the growth of each.

Major beer brands include Budweiser, Bud Light, Bud Dry, Bud Ice, Michelob, Michelob Light, Michelob Dry, Michelob Golden Draft, Busch, Busch Light, Natural Light, Natural Pilsner, King Cobra, Red Wolf, and non-alcoholic malt beverages O'Doul's and Busch NA. During 1997, the company introduced the following brands: Hurricane Ice, Catalina Blonde, Michelob Honey Lager, Michelob Maple Brown, Michelob Pale Ale, Michelob Porter, Michelob Spiced Ale, and Tequiza. The company operates 12 breweries, strategically located across the country, to economically serve its dis-tribution system. Sales in 1997 totaled 96.6 million barrels (up 0.6% from 91.0 million barrels in 1996), or approximately 45% of U.S. industry sales. Through various subsidiaries, the company is involved in a number of beer-related operations that help insulate the company from occasional rises in packaging and ingredient costs. These operations include can manufacturing, metalized paper printing and barley malting.

Through the Busch Entertainment Corp. subsidiary, the company operates nine theme parks, including Busch Gardens in Florida and Virginia; Sea World parks in Florida, Texas, Ohio and California; water parks in Florida and Virginia; an educational play park in Pennsylvania and also the Baseball City Sports Complex in Florida. Through a Spanish affiliate, the company also owns a 19.9% equity interest in Port Aventura S.A., a theme park near Barcelona, Spain. Busch Entertainment contributed 7% of the company's total sales and 13% of operating income in 1997.

In June 1997, the company exercised its remaining options to purchase an additional 13% share in Diblo, Grupo Modelo's operating subsidiary, for $550 million. BUD currently holds a 50.2% direct and indirect interest Modelo and its operating subsidiary, Diblo.

Per Share Data ($)

(Year Ended Dec. 31)	1997	1996	1995	1994	1993	1992	1991	1990	1989	1988
Tangible Bk. Val.	7.37	7.22	7.86	7.64	7.04	7.39	6.88	5.57	4.53	5.29
Cash Flow	3.73	3.46	2.81	3.14	2.18	2.73	2.56	2.35	2.05	1.83
Earnings	2.36	2.28	1.25	1.96	1.08	1.74	1.63	1.48	1.34	1.23
Dividends	1.00	0.92	0.84	0.76	0.68	0.60	0.53	0.47	0.40	0.33
Payout Ratio	42%	40%	67%	39%	63%	34%	32%	32%	30%	26%
Prices - High	48¼	45	34	27¾	30⅛	30⅜	31	22⅝	23	17¼
- Low	38½	32⅜	25⅜	23⅝	21½	25⅞	19⅝	17	15⅜	14½
P/E Ratio - High	20	20	27	14	28	17	19	15	17	14
- Low	16	14	20	12	20	15	12	11	11	12

Income Statement Analysis (Million $)

	1997	1996	1995	1994	1993	1992	1991	1990	1989	1988
Revs.	11,066	10,884	10,341	12,054	11,505	11,394	10,996	10,744	9,481	8,924
Oper. Inc.	2,737	2,623	2,359	2,527	2,385	2,343	2,256	2,080	1,735	1,620
Depr.	684	594	566	628	608	567	534	482	406	356
Int. Exp.	261	233	226	221	208	200	239	283	178	142
Pretax Inc.	1,833	1,893	1,462	1,707	1,050	1,615	1,521	1,352	1,227	1,160
Eff. Tax Rate	38%	39%	39%	40%	43%	38%	38%	38%	38%	38%
Net Inc.	1,179	1,156	887	1,032	595	994	940	842	767	716

Balance Sheet & Other Fin. Data (Million $)

	1997	1996	1995	1994	1993	1992	1991	1990	1989	1988
Cash	147	94.0	94.0	156	127	215	97.0	95.0	36.0	64.0
Curr. Assets	1,584	1,466	1,511	1,862	1,795	1,816	1,628	1,426	1,277	1,194
Total Assets	11,727	10,464	10,591	11,045	10,880	10,538	9,987	9,634	9,026	7,110
Curr. Liab.	1,501	1,431	1,242	1,669	1,816	1,460	1,403	1,412	1,303	1,179
LT Debt	4,366	3,271	3,270	3,078	3,032	2,643	2,645	3,147	3,307	1,615
Common Eqty.	4,042	4,029	4,434	4,415	4,255	4,620	4,438	3,679	3,100	3,103
Total Cap.	9,701	8,508	8,837	8,752	8,458	8,540	8,584	8,222	7,723	5,931
Cap. Exp.	1,199	1,085	953	785	777	737	703	899	1,646	951
Cash Flow	1,863	1,750	1,453	1,660	1,203	1,561	1,474	1,324	1,174	1,072
Curr. Ratio	1.0	1.0	1.2	1.1	1.0	1.2	1.2	1.0	1.0	1.0
% LT Debt of Cap.	45.0	21.4	37.0	35.2	35.8	30.9	30.8	38.3	42.8	27.2
% Net Inc.of Revs.	10.7	10.6	8.6	8.6	5.2	8.7	8.5	7.8	8.1	8.0
% Ret. on Assets	10.6	11.0	8.4	9.6	5.7	9.8	9.5	9.0	9.5	10.7
% Ret. on Equity	29.2	27.3	20.0	24.2	13.7	22.2	23.1	24.9	24.8	24.3

Data as orig. reptd.; bef. results of disc. opers. and/or spec. items. Per share data adj. for stk. divs. as of ex-div. date. Bold denotes diluted EPS (FASB 128). E-Estimated. NA-Not Available. NM-Not Meaningful. NR-Not Ranked.

Office—1 Busch Place, St. Louis, MO 63118. **Tel**—(314) 577-2000. **Website**—http://www.budweiser.com **Chrmn & Pres**—A. A. Busch III. **EVP & CFO**—W. R. Baker.**Secy**—JoBeth G. Brown. **Investor Contact**—David Sauerhoff. **Dirs**—A. A. Busch III, B. A. Edison, C. Fernandez G., A. Fernandez R., P. M. Flanigan, J. R. Jones, J. E. Jacob, C. F. Knight, V. R. Loucks Jr., V. S. Martinez, S. C. Mobley, J. B. Orthwein, W. P. Payne, A. C. Taylor, D. A. Warner III, W. H. Webster, E. E. Whitacre Jr.**Transfer Agent & Registrar**—ChaseMellon Shareholder Services L.L.C., Ridgefield Park, NJ.**Incorporated**—in Missouri in 1925; reincorporated in Delaware in 1979. **Empl**— 24,326. **S&P Analyst:** Richard Joy

STANDARD &POOR'S
STOCK REPORTS

Aon Corp.

201W
NYSE Symbol **AOC**

In S&P 500

12-SEP-98

Industry:
Insurance Brokers

Summary: Following its January 1997 acquisition of Alexander & Alexander, Aon is now the second largest insurance broker in the U.S. It also underwrites an array of insurance products

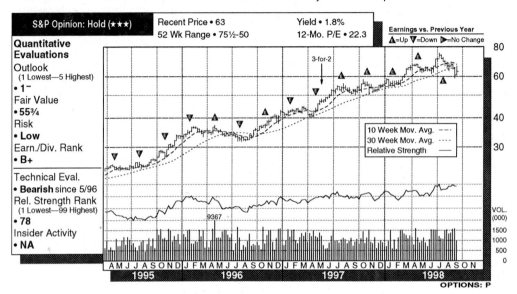

S&P Opinion: Hold (★★★)	Recent Price • 63	Yield • 1.8%
	52 Wk Range • 75½-50	12-Mo. P/E • 22.3

Quantitative Evaluations

Outlook
(1 Lowest—5 Highest)
• **1⁻**

Fair Value
• **55¾**

Risk
• **Low**

Earn./Div. Rank
• **B+**

Technical Eval.
• **Bearish** since 5/96

Rel. Strength Rank
(1 Lowest—99 Highest)
• **78**

Insider Activity
• **NA**

Overview - 07-AUG-98

Revenue growth in 1998 will be aided by contributions from the January 1997 acquisition of Alexander & Alexander Services (AAL). The acquisition of this beleaguered brokerage firm greatly expanded AOC's presence in the brokerage market and, for a brief time, propelled it ahead of rival broker Marsh & McLennan (MMC) to become the largest insurance broker in the U.S. (MMC's March 1997 acquisition of Johnson & Higgins reestablished it as the number one broker.) The rebound in earnings seen in 1998 is skewed by charges totaling $172 million taken during 1997 to cover costs associated with the integration of AAL. But, results in 1998 will be enhanced, as the bulk of the synergies and cost savings associated with this transaction begin to emerge. Additional - but smaller, more opportunistic - acquisitions are also likely. These gains will be partly offset by restrained underlying growth due mainly to ongoing premium price competition in the U.S. insurance market. Contributions from extended warranty lines, especially from appliance and electronics coverages; coupled with an expansion of certain distribution channels, should help insurance underwriting results.

Valuation - 07-AUG-98

The shares climbed steadily upward during much of 1997 and 1998 - as investors reacted favorably to AOC's strategy of repositioning its business mix to one with a higher price-earnings multiple. We applaud this pro-active stance, and believe AOC has done a good job of managing through competitive market conditions. However, at current levels, the shares are fairly valued in the near term.

Key Stock Statistics

S&P EPS Est. 1998	3.25	Tang. Bk. Value/Share	NM
P/E on S&P Est. 1998	19.4	Beta	0.82
S&P EPS Est. 1999	3.75	Shareholders	12,900
Dividend Rate/Share	1.12	Market cap. (B)	$ 10.6
Shs. outstg. (M)	168.9	Inst. holdings	52%
Avg. daily vol. (M)	0.356		

Value of $10,000 invested 5 years ago: $ 30,615

Fiscal Year Ending Dec. 31

	1998	1997	1996	1995	1994	1993
Revenues (Million $)						
1Q	1,562	1,354	942.1	953.2	1,020	950.3
2Q	1,623	1,425	932.4	851.9	1,026	963.0
3Q	—	1,451	944.3	865.7	1,031	954.2
4Q	—	1,521	1,069	894.9	1,080	977.0
Yr.	—	5,751	3,888	3,466	4,157	3,844
Earnings Per Share ($)						
1Q	**0.80**	-0.02	0.56	0.51	0.59	0.52
2Q	**0.81**	0.48	0.37	0.40	0.51	0.46
3Q	—	0.57	0.48	0.44	0.51	0.45
4Q	—	0.65	0.25	0.36	0.49	0.45
Yr.	—	1.68	1.65	1.71	2.09	1.87

Next earnings report expected: NA

Dividend Data (Dividends have been paid since 1950.)

Amount ($)	Date Decl.	Ex-Div. Date	Stock of Record	Payment Date
0.260	Sep. 19	Oct. 31	Nov. 04	Nov. 17 '97
0.260	Jan. 16	Feb. 06	Feb. 10	Feb. 24 '98
0.280	Mar. 23	May. 01	May. 05	May. 18 '98
0.280	Jul. 17	Aug. 03	Aug. 05	Aug. 15 '98

A Division of The McGraw-Hill Companies

Business Summary - 07-AUG-98

In less than five years, Aon Corp. (formerly Combined International) has transformed itself from a multiline insurer with a relatively modest presence in the insurance brokerage arena to the second largest insurance broker in the U.S. AOC accomplished this through an aggressive acquisition plan that included the January 1997 purchase of a beleaguered rival, Alexander & Alexander Services. While Aon's relatively lofty price/earnings multiple is like that of an insurance broker, the company still underwrites an array of insurance products. Contributions to pretax income (in millions, including special charges) in recent years:

	1997	1996
Insurance brokerage & consulting	$348.7	$182.0
Insurance underwriting	278.2	252.4
Corporate & other	-85.3	11.2

At year-end 1997, Aon Group, Inc. was the second largest brokerage and consulting services firm, with more than 400 offices in 60 countries worldwide. Through numerous subsidiaries, it offers insurance placement (both primary and reinsurance), specialized

brokerage services, premium financing services, risk management, loss control, and human resources consulting. This unit's operations were greatly expanded following the January 1997 acquisition of Alexander & Alexander Services, Inc. for about $1.2 billion. AOC has also made subsequent, smaller acquisitions. In February 1998, AOC agreed to acquire a leading Spanish insurance broker for an undisclosed amount. Results of the insurance brokerage unit included $172 million of special charges taken earlier in the year to cover costs associated with the integration of Alexander & Alexander. Earnings here in 1998 should benefit from synergies and cost savings that are beginning to emerge from this acquisition.

Insurance underwriting serves individual consumers throughout the world by providing accident and health coverage, traditional life insurance, extended warranties and credit insurance through global distribution networks.

As part of a plan to shift its focus, the company, in April 1996, sold two key life insurance subsidiaries to GE Capital. AOC sold The Life Insurance Co. of Virginia for $960 million and Union Fidelity Life Insurance Co. for over $400 million.

Per Share Data ($)

(Year Ended Dec. 31)	1997	1996	1995	1994	1993	1992	1991	1990	1989	1988
Tangible Bk. Val.	NA	7.39	8.98	4.32	4.89	9.08	8.92	8.11	8.22	7.41
Oper. Earnings	2.30	1.63	1.70	2.07	1.80	1.27	1.63	1.58	1.55	1.41
Earnings	1.68	1.65	1.71	2.09	1.88	1.28	1.65	1.60	1.57	1.24
Dividends	1.02	0.95	0.89	0.84	0.79	0.74	0.70	0.66	0.61	0.56
Relative Payout	61%	57%	52%	40%	42%	57%	43%	41%	39%	45%
Prices - High	58⅞	43⅛	33⅞	23⅞	26	24	18½	19	19¼	12¾
- Low	40⅛	31⅝	20⅞	19½	20½	17⅜	13¼	11⅞	12	9¾
P/E Ratio - High	35	26	20	11	14	19	11	12	12	9
- Low	24	19	12	9	11	14	8	7	8	7

Income Statement Analysis (Million $)

	1997	1996	1995	1994	1993	1992	1991	1990	1989	1988
Life Ins. In Force	10,438	10,997	NA	75,222	72,161	71,851	71,900	74,791	67,177	65,812
Prem. Inc.: Life A & H	1,081	1,105	1,254	1,684	1,562	1,548	1,487	1,357	1,276	1,785
Prem. Inc.: Cas./Prop.	528	421	173	250	261	278	247	202	170	154
Net Invest. Inc.	494	384	329	760	745	737	713	661	590	503
Oth. Revs.	NA	1,979	1,710	1,464	1,277	773	484	407	338	290
Total Revs.	5,751	3,888	3,466	4,157	3,845	3,337	2,931	2,626	2,325	2,732
Pretax Inc.	542	446	458	538	479	291	332	325	314	278
Net Oper. Inc.	402	283	301	NA	312	203	239	235	229	204
Net Inc.	299	292	304	360	324	206	242	239	232	180

Balance Sheet & Other Fin. Data (Million $)

	1997	1996	1995	1994	1993	1992	1991	1990	1989	1988
Cash & Equiv.	1,085	479	268	642	292	229	183	224	162	141
Premiums Due	863	989	580	2,520	2,101	1,720	822	594	529	473
Invest. Assets: Bonds	4,841	4,092	7,687	7,927	7,858	7,366	6,774	6,038	4,903	4,449
Invest. Assets: Stocks	806	879	1,006	939	933	830	610	628	811	731
Invest. Assets: Loans	NA	87.2	858	782	767	797	852	894	884	824
Invest. Assets: Total	5,922	5,213	10,639	9,783	9,652	9,088	8,360	7,704	6,665	6,065
Deferred Policy Costs	549	599	1,262	1,182	1,005	948	911	868	761	699
Total Assets	18,691	13,723	19,736	17,922	16,279	14,290	11,633	10,432	9,156	8,266
Debt	2,201	475	498	496	521	478	418	430	438	380
Common Eqty.	2,822	2,827	2,666	2,246	2,274	2,089	1,771	1,457	1,421	1,253
Comb. Loss-Exp. Ratio	NA	Nil	NA	NA	NA	NA	NA	NA	NA	NA
% Return On Revs.	5.2	7.6	8.8	8.7	8.4	6.2	8.3	9.1	10.0	7.5
% Ret. on Equity	10.1	11.5	11.4	14.5	14.8	9.9	15.0	16.6	17.2	16.9
% Invest. Yield	8.9	4.9	3.6	7.8	8.0	8.4	8.9	9.2	9.3	9.0

Data as orig. reptd.; bef. results of disc. opers. and/or spec. items. Per share data adj. for stk. divs. as of ex-div. date. Bold denotes diluted EPS (FASB 128). E-Estimate. NA-Not Available. NM-Not Meaningful. NR-Not Ranked.

Office—123 North Wacker Drive, Chicago, IL 60606. **Tel**—(312) 701-3000. **Website**—http://www.aon.com **Chrmn, CEO & Pres**—P. G. Ryan. **EVP, CFO & Treas**—H. N. Medvin. **Investor Contact**—John F. Roskopf. **Dirs**—D. T. Carroll, F. A. Cole, E. D. Jannotta, P. J. Lewis, J. D. Manley, A. J. McKenna, N. N. Minow, P. Pedersen, D. S. Perkins, J. W. Rogers, Jr., P. G. Ryan, G. A. Schaefer, R. I. Skilling, F. L. Turner, A. R. Weber. **Transfer Agent & Registrar**—First Chicago Trust Co. of New York. **Incorporated**—in Illinois in 1949; reincorporated in Delaware in 1980. **Empl**— 28,000. **S&P Analyst:** Catherine A. Seifert

STANDARD &POOR'S
STOCK REPORTS

Apache Corp.

202

NYSE Symbol **APA**

In S&P 500

12-SEP-98

Industry:
Oil & Gas (Exploration & Production)

Summary: This independent energy company explores for and produces and markes oil and natural gas.

S&P Opinion: Accumulate (★★★★)

Recent Price • 28¾	Yield • 1.0%
52 Wk Range • 45-22½	12-Mo. P/E • 26.6

Quantitative Evaluations

Outlook
(1 Lowest—5 Highest)
• **2⁻**

Fair Value
• **26**

Risk
• **Average**

Earn./Div. Rank
• **B+**

Technical Eval.
• **NA**

Rel. Strength Rank
(1 Lowest—99 Highest)
• **96**

Insider Activity
• **Favorable**

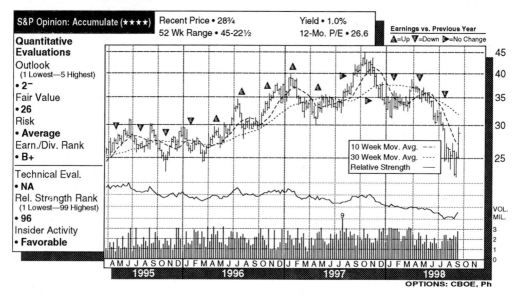

Earnings vs. Previous Year
▲=Up ▼=Down ▶=No Change

10 Week Mov. Avg. - - -
30 Week Mov. Avg. · · · ·
Relative Strength ———

VOL.
MIL.

1995 1996 1997 1998

OPTIONS: CBOE, Ph

Overview - 29-JUL-98

Share earnings advanced to $1.71 in 1997, from $1.42 in 1996, reflecting substantially higher crude oil and natural gas production, and higher North American gas price realizations. Oil prices declined about $1.60 per bbl. for the year. Despite increased production, APA replaced over 200% of production in 1997. This has served to increase APA's reserve life to 9.4 years at the end of 1997. Results in the first half of 1998 were hurt by lower oil and gas prices, although this was partly offset by increased oil and gas production, and by lower operating costs. We expect drilling activity to decline from 1997 levels, although the company has announced plans to take advantage of lower oil services costs, and to increase its spending over the second half of 1998. The May 1996 merger with Phoenix Resources gave APA a stronger foothold in Egypt. During 1997, international operations accounted for 18% of total operating cash flow, 28% of earnings, and 55% of reserve additions. The proportion of oil in the reserve mix has also increased in recent years.

Valuation - 29-JUL-98

The shares were recently down 26% in 1998, and were trading at 5.4X estimated 1998 operating cash flow per share of $4.80, and at a solid discount to their estimated net asset value per share. Given our expectation of weak oil prices for the remainder of 1998, we recommend that investments in the oil sector focus on companies with improving fundamentals, and which will be well positioned to benefit from an eventual recovery in commodity prices. We believe that APA fits this profile, based on its impressive expansion into a leading, geographically diversified, independent energy producer; we recommend accumulation of the shares.

Key Stock Statistics

S&P EPS Est. 1998	0.70	Tang. Bk. Value/Share	19.26
P/E on S&P Est. 1998	41.1	Beta	0.60
S&P EPS Est. 1999	1.70	Shareholders	11,000
Dividend Rate/Share	0.28	Market cap. (B)	$ 2.8
Shs. outstg. (M)	98.6	Inst. holdings	69%
Avg. daily vol. (M)	0.496		

Value of $10,000 invested 5 years ago: $ 16,250

Fiscal Year Ending Dec. 31

	1998	1997	1996	1995	1994	1993
Revenues (Million $)						
1Q	245.9	321.8	206.5	167.7	121.6	108.6
2Q	220.1	258.8	223.7	206.1	134.9	111.3
3Q	—	276.8	242.4	181.3	140.8	122.0
4Q	—	318.9	304.6	195.7	148.3	124.8
Yr.	—	1,176	977.1	750.7	545.6	466.6
Earnings Per Share ($)						
1Q	**0.18**	0.56	0.20	0.06	0.15	0.24
2Q	**0.09**	0.28	0.29	0.01	0.17	0.22
3Q	—	0.33	0.34	0.10	0.17	0.02
4Q	—	0.48	0.59	0.11	0.21	0.22
Yr.	**E0.70**	1.65	1.42	0.28	0.70	0.70

Next earnings report expected: late October

Dividend Data (Dividends have been paid since 1965.)

Amount ($)	Date Decl.	Ex-Div. Date	Stock of Record	Payment Date
0.070	Nov. 19	Dec. 29	Dec. 31	Jan. 30 '98
0.070	Feb. 10	Mar. 27	Mar. 31	Apr. 30 '98
0.070	May. 04	Jun. 26	Jun. 30	Jul. 31 '98
0.070	Jul. 29	Sep. 28	Sep. 30	Oct. 30 '98

A Division of The McGraw·Hill Companies

Business Summary - 29-JUL-98

After spending the first 40 years of its existence as a domestic natural gas producer, Apache Corp. (APA) now has a geographically diversified reserve base almost equally divided between oil and gas. Apache is an independent energy company engaged in the exploration for and development, production, processing and marketing of natural gas and oil. Daily production in 1997 averaged 66,547 bbl. of oil and 608.9 MMcf of gas, versus 53,182 bbl. and 560.9 MMcf in 1996.

The company's operations are still primarily located in North America, with properties located in the Gulf of Mexico, the Anadarko Basin, the Permian Basin, the Gulf Coast, and the Western Sedimentary Basin of Canada. Apache estimates that it is the largest independent producer in Oklahoma. The company also holds international exploration and production acreage in Western Australia and Egypt, and has exploration interests in Indonesia, China, Poland and the Ivory Coast. At December 31, 1997, proved reserves aggregated 273.7 million bbl. of crude oil (235.3 million bbl. at year end 1996) and 1,871.8 Bcf of natural gas (1,625.3 Bcf). On an energy-equivalent basis, natural gas accounted for 53% of total reserves; oil made up 47% of the total. By contrast, oil represented 46% of total reserves in 1996, 40% of total reserves in 1995, and only 34% of total reserves in 1994.

In recent years, Apache has emphasized international

expansion as a key component of its long term growth strategy. While international exploration projects carry much higher risks than those typically associated with domestic programs, the company believes that the potential for reserve additions and profit gains outstrips that of domestic operations. Apache's core international area is Egypt's Western Desert, which accounted for 13% of total proved reserves at year end 1997. In May 1996, APA acquired Phoenix Resources Cos., Inc., which owned a 50% interest in the Qarun Concession in Egypt's Western Desert. Apache now owns a 75% interest in the Qarun Concession, as well its 40% interest in the Khalda Concession. The company's expects its share of oil production to exceed 30,000 bbl. per day in 1998.

Prior to 1996, Apache's acquisition activity generally targeted North American properties. In September 1995, APA acquired substantially all of the oil and gas assets of Aquila Energy Resources Corp., a wholly owned subsidiary of UtiliCorp United Inc., for about $210 million. In May 1995, Apache acquired DEKALB Energy Co., an oil and gas exploration and production company operating in Canada, in exchange for 8.4 million common shares. In March 1995, APA purchased certain oil and gas properties from Texaco Exploration and Production Inc. for an adjusted purchase price of $571 million. In December 1994, it purchased the U.S. oil and gas properties of Crystal Oil Co., for $95.8 million.

Per Share Data ($)

(Year Ended Dec. 31)	1997	1996	1995	1994	1993	1992	1991	1990	1989	1988
Tangible Bk. Val.	18.53	16.86	14.11	13.28	12.86	10.12	9.39	8.65	7.97	6.28
Cash Flow	5.47	5.08	4.43	4.61	4.42	4.63	3.72	3.52	3.41	2.74
Earnings	1.71	1.42	0.28	0.70	0.70	1.02	0.76	0.90	0.64	0.23
Dividends	0.28	0.28	0.28	0.28	0.28	0.28	0.28	0.28	0.28	0.28
Payout Ratio	16%	20%	100%	40%	40%	27%	38%	31%	56%	122%
Prices - High	45	37⅞	31	29¼	33½	22⅛	20¾	20¾	18⅜	8⅞
- Low	30⅛	24⅜	22¼	22¼	17⅝	12	12	13⅜	7⅞	6
P/E Ratio - High	26	27	NM	42	48	22	27	23	29	39
- Low	18	17	NM	32	25	12	16	15	12	26

Income Statement Analysis (Million $)

	1997	1996	1995	1994	1993	1992	1991	1990	1989	1988
Revs.	1,176	977	751	538	463	423	342	261	241	142
Oper. Inc.	712	577	411	327	281	244	201	173	144	84.0
Depr. Depl. & Amort.	388	315	297	240	199	169	136	117	96.0	60.0
Int. Exp.	68.7	89.8	88.1	36.0	32.0	39.2	32.7	15.5	24.8	20.1
Pretax Inc.	259	200	38.1	64.0	58.0	70.0	44.0	57.0	32.0	7.0
Eff. Tax Rate	40%	39%	39%	34%	36%	32%	22%	30%	31%	23%
Net Inc.	155	121	20.2	42.8	37.3	47.8	34.6	40.3	22.1	5.4

Balance Sheet & Other Fin. Data (Million $)

	1997	1996	1995	1994	1993	1992	1991	1990	1989	1988
Cash	9.7	13.2	13.6	15.1	17.1	26.1	6.4	85.2	75.2	34.9
Curr. Assets	348	268	208	135	123	114	91.0	138	133	109
Total Assets	4,139	3,432	2,681	1,879	1,592	1,219	1,209	830	764	702
Curr. Liab.	344	310	230	148	185	158	146	123	108	98.0
LT Debt	150	1,236	1,072	657	453	454	491	195	196	309
Common Eqty.	1,729	1,519	1,092	816	786	475	440	387	350	207
Total Cap.	3,586	3,010	2,345	1,630	1,367	1,013	996	648	599	555
Cap. Exp.	732	124	1,133	494	583	207	686	191	134	288
Cash Flow	543	436	318	283	237	217	170	157	118	65.0
Curr. Ratio	1.0	0.9	0.9	0.9	0.7	0.7	0.6	1.1	1.2	1.1
% LT Debt of Cap.	41.9	41.1	45.7	40.3	33.1	44.9	49.3	30.1	32.7	55.7
% Ret. on Assets	4.1	3.9	0.9	2.5	2.3	3.9	3.3	5.0	2.6	0.7
% Ret. on Equity	9.5	9.3	2.0	5.3	5.3	10.4	8.2	10.8	7.1	2.9

Data as orig. reptd.; bef. results of disc opers. and/or spec. items. Per share data adj. for stk. divs. as of ex-div. date. Revs. in Income Statement Analysis excl. other income. E-Estimated. NA-Not Available. NM-Not Meaningful. NR-Not Ranked.

Office—2000 Post Oak Blvd., Houston, TX 77056-4400. **Tel**—(713) 296-6000.**Website**—http://www.apachecorp.com **Chrmn & CEO**—Raymond Plank. **Pres & COO**—G. S. Farris.**VP & CFO**—Roger B. Plank. **VP & Treas**—M. W. Dundrea.**Secy**—C. L. Peper. **VP & Investor Contact**—Robert Dye. **Dirs**—F. M. Bohen, V. B. Day, G. S. Farris, R. M. Ferlic, E. C. Fiedorek, W. B. Fields, A. D. Frazier, Jr., S. K. Hathaway, J. A. Kocur, G. D. Lawrence, Jr., M. R. Lowe, F. H. Merelli, Raymond Plank, J. A. Rice. **Transfer Agent & Registrar**—Norwest Bank Minnesota, South St. Paul. **Incorporated**—in Delaware in 1954. **Empl**— 1,287. **S&P Analyst:** Norman Rosenberg

12-SEP-98

Industry:
Computers (Hardware)

Summary: This leading maker of personal computers and related products has made a transition to a new line of personal computer products powered by the PowerPC microprocessor.

| S&P Opinion: Hold (★★★) | Recent Price • 37⅞ | Yield • Nil | Earnings vs. Previous Year |
| | 52 Wk Range • 43¾-12¾ | 12-Mo. P/E • NM | ▲=Up ▼=Down ▶=No Change |

Quantitative Evaluations

Outlook
(1 Lowest—5 Highest)
• **1**‾

Fair Value
• **33⅜**

Risk
• **Average**

Earn./Div. Rank
• **B-**

Technical Eval.
• **Bearish** since 3/98

Rel. Strength Rank
(1 Lowest—99 Highest)
• **97**

Insider Activity
• **Neutral**

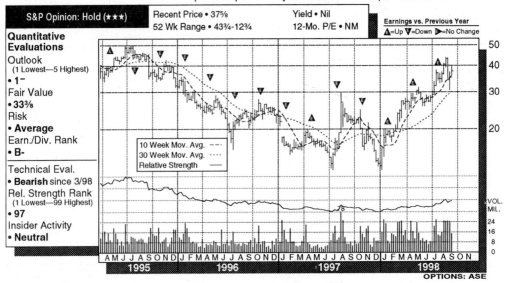

10 Week Mov. Avg. — —
30 Week Mov. Avg. · · · ·
Relative Strength ——

1995   1996   1997   1998

OPTIONS: ASE

Overview - 22-JUL-98

We expect revenues to fall approximately 17% in FY 98 (Sep.), an improvement from the nearly 30% drop in FY 97. The decline reflects Apple's significant loss of market share in recent years. The most precipitous revenue declines were evident in the first half, with the second half of FY 98 enjoying easier comparisons. With FY 98 representing the trough, we project 8% revenue growth in FY 99, as new product offerings should enable Apple to stem further erosion of sales to its traditional strongholds -- creative content and education. However, subsequent revenue growth after Apple has satisfied its installed base with new products could prove challenging, given the price competitiveness of the personal computer industry. Meanwhile, Apple's major turn-arounds in profitability and cash flow have been better than expected. A higher margin product mix has helped gross margins improve, and substantial expense cuts have been implemented. Assuming payment of only modest taxes, we project FY 98 EPS of $1.57.

Valuation - 22-JUL-98

The shares are up strongly since 1997 year end, reflecting the company's earlier than expected return to profitability. Looking forward, although Apple's profit in the first nine months of FY 98 (Sep.) was impressive, we remain cautious. We continue to believe that the company needs to expand its revenue base in order to be considered an attractive investment for the long term. To do this may require accepting somewhat narrower gross margins, in order to compete with other computer makers' lower price points; this could in turn jeopardize the company's sustainability of profits. While the long term outlook is clouded by these risks, the near-term environment appears stable, given the outlook for favorable year-over-year comparisons seen for FY 99's quarterly earnings.

Key Stock Statistics

S&P EPS Est. 1998	1.57	Tang. Bk. Value/Share	9.92
P/E on S&P Est. 1998	24.0	Beta	0.60
S&P EPS Est. 1999	1.75	Shareholders	31,700
Dividend Rate/Share	Nil	Market cap. (B)	$ 5.1
Shs. outstg. (M)	134.6	Inst. holdings	48%
Avg. daily vol. (M)	5.465		

Value of $10,000 invested 5 years ago: $ 6,576

Fiscal Year Ending Sep. 30

	1998	1997	1996	1995	1994	1993
Revenues (Million $)						
1Q	1,578	2,129	3,148	2,832	2,487	2,000
2Q	1,405	1,601	2,185	2,652	2,077	1,974
3Q	1,402	1,737	2,179	2,575	2,150	1,862
4Q	—	1,614	2,321	3,003	2,493	2,141
Yr.	—	7,081	9,833	11,062	9,189	7,977
Earnings Per Share ($)						
1Q	**0.33**	-0.96	-0.56	1.55	0.34	1.33
2Q	**0.38**	-5.64	-5.99	0.59	0.15	0.92
3Q	**0.65**	-0.44	-0.26	0.84	1.16	-1.63
4Q	**E0.36**	-1.25	0.20	0.48	0.95	0.02
Yr.	**E1.57**	-8.29	-6.59	3.45	2.61	0.73

Next earnings report expected: mid October

Dividend Data

Cash payments began in 1987 and were omitted in February 1996.

A Division of The McGraw·Hill Companies

Business Summary - 22-JUL-98

Apple Computer's market share in worldwide personal computer markets has been cut by about two-thirds over the past four years, falling to an estimated 3% in 1997, from 9.4% in 1993. The decline has been linked to the strides made by the Windows platform in narrowing the edge of Apple's products, noted for their ease of use, innovative applications and better stability. Apple Macintosh personal computers were first introduced in 1984.

Under a restructuring program introduced in 1996 and enhanced in March 1997, Apple has outlined a new business model to fix what is wrong with the company, and to restore sustained profitability. Apple is trimming its people and operating cost structure to reflect the fact that it no longer ships one million PCs a quarter (shipments are now about 600,000 to 650,000), and it has refreshed its product line to match the competition in price/performance metrics. These efforts were spearheaded by former chairman and CEO Dr. Gilbert Amelio, who was asked by directors to tender his resignation in July 1997. The company is now searching for a replacement; Apple co-founder Steve Jobs is acting as chairman in the interim.

Apple's hardware strategy is to simplify its product line, focus on key customers and use more standard components. The Power Macintosh family is the most advanced line, intended for businesses and academics. As part of the company's simplification strategy, entry-level Power Macs will supplant the Performa line, targeted at first-time users. In addition, a new low-priced, consumer-oriented platform, the iMac, is scheduled for launch in August, 1998. Rounding out the strategy is the PowerBook portable computer, aimed at the mobile user. In fact, in early 1998, Apple discontinued its Newton hand-held computer to better focus on its core Mac strategy. (All Macs use the PowerPC RISC-based microprocessor developed in an alliance of Apple, IBM and Motorola.)

Apple is also addressing the proprietary nature of its operating system software, Mac OS. In conjunction with updates to its current Mac OS, (7.6 shipped in early 1997, followed later by 8.0), Apple's next generation operating system, Rhapsody, is designed for servers and is more robust, and able to run on multiple platforms, using technology obtained through Apple's February 1997, acquisition of NeXT Software. Steve Jobs was the chairman and CEO of NeXT.

The company has recently effectively discontinued its Mac OS licensee program, which began in 1994 and was intended to expand its installed base via Mac clones. In FY 97 (Sep.), Apple purchased its Mac OS license from Power Computing Corp., its largest licensee.

Other products include servers and a full line of computer peripherals; wholly owned Claris Corp. develops and markets application software.

About half of sales are outside the U.S.

Per Share Data ($) (Year Ended Sep. 30)	1997	1996	1995	1994	1993	1992	1991	1990	1989	1988
Tangible Bk. Val.	8.20	16.53	23.60	19.94	17.45	18.46	14.92	12.54	11.77	8.17
Cash Flow	-7.36	-5.33	4.48	4.03	2.12	6.10	4.28	5.39	4.50	3.68
Earnings	-8.29	-6.59	3.45	2.61	0.73	4.33	2.58	3.77	3.53	3.08
Dividends	Nil	0.12	0.48	0.48	0.48	0.48	0.48	0.44	0.40	0.32
Payout Ratio	Nil	NM	14%	18%	64%	11%	19%	12%	11%	10%
Prices - High	29¾	35½	50⅛	43¾	65¼	70	73¼	47¾	50⅜	47¾
- Low	12¾	16	31⅝	24⅝	22	41½	40¼	24¼	32½	35½
P/E Ratio - High	NM	NM	15	17	89	16	28	13	14	16
- Low	NM	NM	9	9	30	10	16	6	9	12
Income Statement Analysis (Million $)										
Revs.	7,081	9,833	11,062	9,189	7,977	7,087	6,309	5,558	5,284	4,071
Oper. Inc.	-284	-1,047	788	563	597	1,023	876	949	759	698
Depr.	118	156	127	168	166	217	204	203	125	78.0
Int. Exp.	71.0	60.0	48.0	39.7	Nil	Nil	Nil	Nil	Nil	Nil
Pretax Inc.	-1,044	-1,294	674	500	140	855	500	779	744	656
Eff. Tax Rate	NM	NM	37%	38%	38%	38%	38%	39%	39%	39%
Net Inc.	-1,044	-815	424	310	87.0	530	310	475	454	400
Balance Sheet & Other Fin. Data (Million $)										
Cash	1,230	1,745	952	1,258	892	1,436	893	997	809	546
Curr. Assets	3,424	4,515	5,224	4,476	4,338	3,558	2,864	2,403	2,294	1,783
Total Assets	4,233	5,364	6,231	5,303	5,171	4,224	3,494	2,976	2,744	2,082
Curr. Liab.	1,818	2,003	2,325	1,944	2,515	1,426	1,217	1,027	895	827
LT Debt	951	949	303	304	Nil	Nil	Nil	Nil	Nil	Nil
Common Eqty.	1,050	2,058	2,901	2,383	2,026	2,187	1,767	1,447	1,486	1,003
Total Cap.	2,415	3,361	3,906	3,358	2,656	2,798	2,277	1,949	1,849	1,255
Cap. Exp.	53.0	67.0	159	160	213	195	218	224	239	144
Cash Flow	-926	-659	551	478	253	748	514	678	579	478
Curr. Ratio	1.9	2.3	2.2	2.3	1.7	2.5	2.4	2.3	2.6	2.2
% LT Debt of Cap.	39.4	28.2	7.8	9.1	Nil	Nil	Nil	Nil	Nil	Nil
% Net Inc.of Revs.	NM	NM	3.8	3.4	1.1	7.5	4.9	8.5	8.6	9.8
% Ret. on Assets	NM	NM	7.4	5.8	1.9	13.7	9.5	17.3	18.6	22.7
% Ret. on Equity	NM	NM	16.0	13.9	4.2	26.8	19.1	33.9	36.1	44.0

Data as orig. reptd.; bef. results of disc. opers. and/or spec. items. Per share data adj. for stk. divs. as of ex-div. date. Bold denotes diluted EPS (FASB 128). E-Estimated. NA-Not Available. NM-Not Meaningful. NR-Not Ranked.

Office—20525 Mariani Ave., Cupertino, CA 95014. **Tel**—(408) 996-1010. **Website**—http://www.apple.com **Acting Chrmn & CEO**—S. Jobs. **EVP & CFO**—Fred Anderson. **Investor Contact**—Nancy Paxton (408-974-5420). **Dirs**—W. Campbell, G.C.C. Chang, L. Ellison, S. Jobs, E.S. Woolard, Jr., J. York. **Transfer Agent & Registrar**—First National Bank of Boston. **Incorporated**—in California in 1977. **Empl**— 8,437. **S&P Analyst:** Megan Graham Hackett

STANDARD &POOR'S
STOCK REPORTS

Applied Materials

3142

Nasdaq Symbol **AMAT**

In S&P 500

12-SEP-98

Industry: Equipment (Semiconductor)

Summary: This company is the world's largest manufacturer of wafer fabrication equipment for the semiconductor industry.

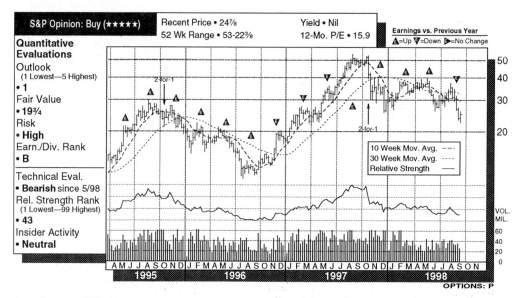

| S&P Opinion: Buy (★★★★) | Recent Price • 24⅞ | Yield • Nil | Earnings vs. Previous Year |
| | 52 Wk Range • 53-22⅜ | 12-Mo. P/E • 15.9 | ▲=Up ▼=Down ▶=No Change |

Quantitative Evaluations

Outlook
(1 Lowest—5 Highest)
• **1**

Fair Value
• **19¾**

Risk
• **High**

Earn./Div. Rank
• **B**

Technical Eval.
• **Bearish** since 5/98

Rel. Strength Rank
(1 Lowest—99 Highest)
• **43**

Insider Activity
• **Neutral**

Legend:
10 Week Mov. Avg. ---
30 Week Mov. Avg. ····
Relative Strength —

OPTIONS: P

Overview - 27-AUG-98

Near-term operating results are likely to trend lower, reflecting the impact of semiconductor overcapacity and the Asian financial crisis. Chip makers have slashed expansion plans and are delaying purchases of production equipment. Still, AMAT is positioned to outperform its peers, largely due to the strength of its products, which enable the production of semiconductors with linewidths (transistor size) of 0.25 micron and below. For the longer term, AMAT is also well positioned to lead a major chip industry technology upgrade to 300 millimeter wafer fabrication. Although lower sales volume will put pressure margins over the next few quarters, proactive cost-saving efforts should cushion the impact somewhat. Based on near-term industrywide challenges, we expect EPS to fall to $0.75 in FY 99 (Oct.), from our FY 98 projection of $1.11 (before extraordinary items).

Valuation - 27-AUG-98

We continue to recommend purchase of AMAT. The shares of this leading semiconductor equipment manufacturer have fallen sharply since last fall, reflecting economic turmoil in Asia and lingering overcapacity in the chip market. While these factors heighten the risk for order push-outs and cancellations in coming quarters, we believe that investor focus will soon shift toward the company's prospects for strong growth in the 1999 to 2000 time frame. The semiconductor industry is in the early stages of a major technology upgrade cycle for 0.25 micron capability. As the industry leader, AMAT is well positioned to benefit from this ongoing technology shift. Although volatile, the shares are attractively valued for aggressive investors with a 12-month or greater investment horizon, at a recent level of 2.6X trailing 12-month sales.

Key Stock Statistics

S&P EPS Est. 1998	1.11	Tang. Bk. Value/Share	7.98
P/E on S&P Est. 1998	22.5	Beta	2.29
S&P EPS Est. 1999	0.75	Shareholders	4,700
Dividend Rate/Share	Nil	Market cap. (B)	$ 9.1
Shs. outstg. (M)	366.3	Inst. holdings	54%
Avg. daily vol. (M)	6.682		

Value of $10,000 invested 5 years ago: $ 59,109

Fiscal Year Ending Oct. 31

	1998	1997	1996	1995	1994	1993
Revenues (Million $)						
1Q	1,308	835.8	1,041	506.1	340.4	216.0
2Q	1,176	900.9	1,128	675.4	411.3	256.0
3Q	884.5	1,057	1,115	897.7	440.2	281.4
4Q	—	1,280	861.0	982.6	467.8	327.4
Yr.	—	4,074	4,145	3,062	1,660	1,080
Earnings Per Share ($)						
1Q	**0.60**	0.08	0.47	0.19	0.11	0.05
2Q	**0.37**	0.27	0.51	0.27	0.16	0.07
3Q	**0.13**	0.49	0.46	0.39	0.17	0.09
4Q	—	0.47	0.20	0.42	0.18	0.10
Yr.	—	1.32	1.63	1.28	0.63	0.30

Next earnings report expected: late November

Dividend Data

Amount ($)	Date Decl.	Ex-Div. Date	Stock of Record	Payment Date
2-for-1	Sep. 11	Oct. 14	Sep. 25	Oct. 13 '97

A Division of The McGraw-Hill Companies

Business Summary - 27-AUG-98

Rapid advances in semiconductor technology, which have allowed computers and other electronic goods to become smaller, faster and cheaper in recent years, are the driving force behind productivity gains in the global economy. While well known semiconductor manufacturers such as Intel have pushed chip technology to a new level, such achievements would not have been possible without the efforts of Applied Materials. As the leading supplier of semiconductor manufacturing equipment, the company provides the enabling technology that is critical for advanced semiconductor production.

In FY 93 (Oct.), AMAT became the first chip-equipment company to post revenues in excess of $1 billion. AMAT is currently the world's largest semiconductor equipment company, with more than $4 billion in annual sales, and the most extensive range of product offerings to the semiconductor market.

The company's products address most of the "front end" equipment market for semiconductor wafer processing. However, the majority of sales come from deposition equipment, where AMAT commands a dominant market share. A fundamental step in fabricating a semiconductor, deposition is a process of layering either electrically insulating (dielectric) or electrically conductive material on the wafer. AMAT currently participates in chemical vapor deposition (CVD), physical vapor deposition (PVD) and epitaxial and polysilicon deposition.

AMAT is also a leader in etch systems. Before etch processing begins, a wafer is patterned with photoresist during photolithography. Etching equipment is then used to selectively remove material from areas not covered by the photoresist.

The company also manufactures ion implantation equipment. During ion implantation, silicon wafers are bombarded by a high-velocity beam of electrically charged ions. These ions penetrate the wafer at selected sites and change the electrical properties of the implanted area.

In an effort to expand its served markets, Applied has begun to aggressively compete in adjacent markets, such as rapid thermal processing (RTP) and chemical mechanical planarization (CMP). In the first quarter of FY 97, AMAT acquired Opal, Inc. and Orbot Instruments, Inc. for $292.5 million in cash. These acquisitions positioned the company to compete in the rapidly growing metrology and wafer/reticle inspection markets.

AMAT is also a 50% shareholder in Applied Komatsu Technology, a joint venture that produces thin film transistors on flat panel displays.

In response to a sharp decline in business volume AMAT announced, in August 1998, that it will reduce its workforce by approximately 2,000 positions, or 15%. In addition, executive salaries will be reduced by 10%.

Per Share Data ($)

(Year Ended Oct. 31)	1997	1996	1995	1994	1993	1992	1991	1990	1989	1988
Tangible Bk. Val.	7.98	6.58	4.97	2.87	1.86	1.52	1.21	1.13	0.98	0.79
Cash Flow	1.90	2.04	1.54	0.80	0.42	0.23	0.18	0.18	0.24	0.20
Earnings	1.32	1.64	1.28	0.63	0.30	0.14	0.10	0.13	0.19	0.15
Dividends	Nil	Nil	Nil	Nil	Nil	Nil	Nil	Nil	Nil	Nil
Payout Ratio	Nil	Nil	Nil	Nil	Nil	Nil	Nil	Nil	Nil	Nil
Prices - High	$54^1/_4$	$22^3/_8$	30	$13^5/_8$	10	$4^7/_8$	$2^3/_8$	$2^1/_2$	$2^1/_{16}$	$2^1/_4$
- Low	$17^3/_8$	$10^7/_8$	$9^1/_4$	$9^1/_8$	4	2	$1^1/_4$	$1^1/_{16}$	$1^3/_8$	$1^1/_{16}$
P/E Ratio - High	41	14	23	22	33	36	25	20	11	15
- Low	13	7	7	14	13	15	13	8	7	7

Income Statement Analysis (Million $)

	1997	1996	1995	1994	1993	1992	1991	1990	1989	1988
Revs.	4,074	4,145	3,062	1,660	1,080	751	639	567	502	363
Oper. Inc.	1,429	1,078	777	396	199	96.1	76.5	74.7	93.6	79.4
Depr.	219	149	83.2	58.5	37.8	27.7	24.5	16.4	11.7	11.4
Int. Exp.	20.7	20.7	21.4	16.0	14.2	15.2	14.0	6.7	2.8	3.2
Pretax Inc.	799	922	699	331	150	58.9	40.4	54.1	84.4	66.7
Eff. Tax Rate	38%	35%	35%	35%	34%	33%	35%	37%	39%	40%
Net Inc.	498	600	454	214	100	39.5	26.2	34.1	51.5	40.0

Balance Sheet & Other Fin. Data (Million $)

	1997	1996	1995	1994	1993	1992	1991	1990	1989	1988
Cash	448	404	769	422	266	223	140	72.0	107	101
Curr. Assets	3,770	2,693	2,312	1,231	776	582	434	367	343	276
Total Assets	5,071	3,638	2,965	1,703	1,120	854	661	558	434	339
Curr. Liab.	1,402	935	862	496	381	248	200	195	143	117
LT Debt	623	275	280	209	121	118	124	54.0	29.0	11.0
Common Eqty.	2,942	2,370	1,784	966	599	474	325	300	254	201
Total Cap.	3,613	2,658	2,075	1,187	727	599	456	362	290	219
Cap. Exp.	339	453	266	186	99	67.0	67.0	111	43.0	20.0
Cash Flow	718	748	547	272	137	67.2	50.7	50.5	63.6	52.0
Curr. Ratio	2.7	2.9	2.7	2.5	2.0	2.3	2.2	1.9	2.4	2.4
% LT Debt of Cap.	17.3	10.3	13.5	17.6	16.7	19.8	27.2	14.8	10.2	5.2
% Net Inc.of Revs.	12.2	14.4	14.8	12.9	9.2	5.3	4.1	6.0	10.3	11.0
% Ret. on Assets	11.4	18.1	19.5	14.9	10.0	4.9	4.3	6.8	13.2	13.9
% Ret. on Equity	18.8	28.9	33.0	26.8	18.4	9.3	8.3	12.1	22.4	22.3

Data as orig. reptd.; bef. results of disc. opers. and/or spec. items. Per share data adj. for stk. divs. as of ex-div. date. Bold denotes diluted EPS (FASB 128). E-Estimated. NA-Not Available. NM-Not Meaningful. NR-Not Ranked.

Office—3050 Bowers Ave., Santa Clara, CA 95054-3299. **Tel**—(408) 727-5555. **Fax**—(408) 986-8352. **Website**—http://www.AppliedMaterials.com **Chrmn & CEO**—J. C. Morgan. **SVP & CFO**—J. R. Bronson. **Investor Contact**—Carolyn Schwartz (800 882-0373). **Dirs**—M. Armacost, D. A. Coleman, H. M. Dwight Jr., P. V. Gerdine, T. Kawanishi, P. R. Low, D. Maydan, J. C. Morgan, A. J. Stein. **Transfer Agent**—Harris Trust Co. of California, Chicago. **Incorporated**—in California in 1967; reincorporated in Delaware in 1987. **Empl**— 13,924. **S&P Analyst**: B. McGovern

12-SEP-98

Industry: Agricultural Products

Summary: This company is a major processor and merchandiser of agricultural commodities, including oilseeds, corn and wheat.

| S&P Opinion: Avoid (★★) | Recent Price • 16¼ | Yield • 1.2% |
| | 52 Wk Range • 23½-14¾ | 12-Mo. P/E • 23.9 |

Earnings vs. Previous Year ▲=Up ▼=Down ▶=No Change

Quantitative Evaluations

Outlook (1 Lowest—5 Highest)
• **2**

Fair Value
• **15⅛**

Risk
• **Low**

Earn./Div. Rank
• **A-**

Technical Eval.
• **Bearish** since 3/98

Rel. Strength Rank (1 Lowest—99 Highest)
• **81**

Insider Activity
• **Neutral**

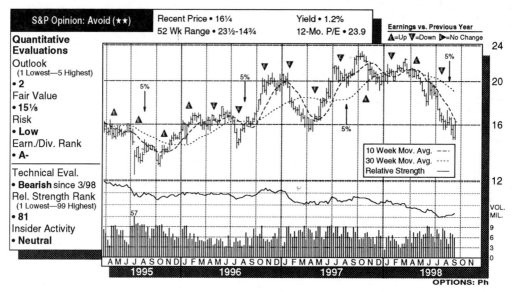

10 Week Mov. Avg. ---
30 Week Mov. Avg. ....
Relative Strength —

OPTIONS: Ph

Overview - 21-JUL-98

Recent company performance has been lackluster, as oversupply in the oilseed market and lower export demand have restricted margins. Exports have been especially hurt by weakness in the Asian markets, which we do not expect to resurface in the immediate future. Additionally, South America has become competitive in the soybean market on account of strong crops there. We continue to expect South America to be a factor in international trade as warm "el nino" weather should provide that region with an above average soybean crop. Reduced demand from Asia, coupled with the expected strong competition from South America will continue to hamper margins at ADM. Although high fructose corn syrup margins have improved, contract prices are sent for the next six months and it is unlikely that better margins will be able to offset weakness in the soybean business. In addition, ADM's cocoa acquisitions have yet to produce desired returns, as the company is still restructuring and consolidating this unit.

Valuation - 21-JUL-98

The shares have been volatile in recent years, reflecting uncertainty stemming from lawsuits related to charges of anti-competitive practices brought against ADM by the U.S. Department of Justice and other parties. Although ADM has settled the most potentially damaging of such litigation, the current trial against three ADM executives regarding price fixing could be a weighing factor on the stock for some time. Additionally, the company is facing a very difficult agricultural market, magnified by the Asian financial crises that have curtailed exports to that region of the world, as well as an increase in competition from other geographic areas. For FY 99 (Jun.), we expect earnings visibility to remain low, especially in the next few quarters. As a result, we anticipate EPS to fall $0.02 from FY 98 to $0.70.

Key Stock Statistics

S&P EPS Est. 1999	0.67	Tang. Bk. Value/Share	10.87
P/E on S&P Est. 1999	24.4	Beta	0.68
Dividend Rate/Share	0.19	Shareholders	33,800
Shs. outstg. (M)	599.1	Market cap. (B)	$ 9.7
Avg. daily vol. (M)	1.222	Inst. holdings	50%

Value of $10,000 invested 5 years ago: $ 12,841

Fiscal Year Ending Jun. 30

	1998	1997	1996	1995	1994	1993
Revenues (Million $)						
1Q	3,651	3,330	3,121	3,015	2,614	2,384
2Q	4,130	3,515	3,415	3,222	2,822	2,547
3Q	4,281	3,415	3,487	3,300	3,010	2,457
4Q	4,047	3,593	3,292	3,135	2,929	2,422
Yr.	16,109	13,853	13,314	12,672	11,374	9,811
Earnings Per Share ($)						
1Q	**0.23**	0.01	0.26	0.25	0.11	0.19
2Q	**0.24**	0.31	0.37	0.35	0.23	0.23
3Q	**0.11**	0.10	0.27	0.31	0.21	0.20
4Q	**0.10**	0.21	0.24	0.36	0.22	0.19
Yr.	**0.69**	0.63	1.15	1.27	0.77	0.82

Next earnings report expected: mid November

Dividend Data (Dividends have been paid since 1927.)

Amount ($)	Date Decl.	Ex-Div. Date	Stock of Record	Payment Date
0.050	Jan. 20	Feb. 04	Feb. 06	Mar. 02 '98
0.050	Apr. 24	May. 06	May. 08	Jun. 01 '98
0.050	Jul. 23	Aug. 05	Aug. 07	Aug. 31 '98
5%	Jul. 23	Aug. 20	Aug. 24	Sep. 21 '98

A Division of The McGraw·Hill Companies

Business Summary - 21-JUL-98

Archer-Daniels-Midland (ADM) calls itself "Supermarket to the world" because it is engaged in the processing and merchandising of many of the most important raw agricultural commodities that are used in the production of food and beverage products consumed by millions of people every day. Most of ADM's business involves converting raw soybeans, corn and wheat into further-processed ingredients for the food manufacturing industry in the U.S. and abroad. Revenue contributions in recent fiscal years (Jun.) were:

	1997	1996
Oilseed	64%	61%
Corn	16%	19%
Wheat flour	12%	13%
Other	8%	7%

Foreign operations accounted for 29% of net sales and 12% of operating profits in FY 97.

Soybeans, cottonseed, sunflower seeds, canola, peanuts, flaxseed and corn germ are processed to provide vegetable oils and meals principally for the food and feed industries. Crude vegetable oil is sold to others or refined and hydrogenated to produce oils for margarine, shortening, salad oils and other food products.

Corn wet milling products include syrup, starch, glucose, dextrose, crystalline dextrose, high-fructose sweeteners, crystalline fructose, corn gluten feed and ethyl alcohol. Dry milled products include ethanol, distilled grains, meal and grits. The most important uses for the company's various corn products are in the food, beverage and pet food industries.

Wheat flour is sold primarily to large bakeries. Durum flour is sold mainly to pasta manufacturers. Bulgur, a gelatinized wheat food, is sold to both domestic and export food markets.

Other operations include: grain merchandising; production of barley malt, cane sugar, animal feeds and various consumer foods; and other products for industrial markets.

ADM reported a 46% decrease in net income in FY 97, as results were hurt principally by high grain costs and a $200 million nonrecurring charge. The charge was to cover the costs of paying criminal fines and settling civil lawsuits that arose from a federal antitrust investigation of ADM's lysine and citric-acid businesses.

Per Share Data ($)

(Year Ended Jun. 30)	1998	1997	1996	1995	1994	1993	1992	1991	1990	1989
Tangible Bk. Val.	NA	10.71	10.85	10.13	8.44	7.45	7.02	6.13	5.41	4.64
Cash Flow	NA	1.38	1.80	1.88	1.33	1.32	1.21	1.10	1.11	0.99
Earnings	0.69	0.64	1.15	1.27	0.77	0.81	0.77	0.71	0.74	0.65
Dividends	0.20	0.18	0.16	0.09	0.05	0.05	0.04	0.04	0.04	0.03
Payout Ratio	29%	28%	14%	7%	7%	6%	6%	6%	5%	4%
Prices - High	22½	23½	21	17¼	17⅜	14⅜	15½	15¾	11⅝	10⅛
- Low	15⅝	15⅜	14⅛	12⅜	11¾	11⅛	10⅝	8¼	7⅞	5⅝
P/E Ratio - High	33	37	18	14	23	18	20	22	16	16
- Low	23	24	12	10	15	13	14	12	11	9

Income Statement Analysis (Million $)

	1998	1997	1996	1995	1994	1993	1992	1991	1990	1989
Revs.	NA	13,853	13,314	12,672	11,374	9,811	9,232	8,468	7,751	7,929
Oper. Inc.	NA	1,071	1,309	1,598	1,121	1,067	1,042	878	923	843
Depr.	NA	446	394	385	354	329	294	261	249	220
Int. Exp.	NA	238	213	203	199	174	137	121	108	97.0
Pretax Inc.	NA	644	1,054	1,182	738	746	760	718	753	668
Eff. Tax Rate	NA	41%	34%	33%	34%	28%	34%	35%	36%	36%
Net Inc.	NA	377	696	796	484	535	504	467	484	425

Balance Sheet & Other Fin. Data (Million $)

	1998	1997	1996	1995	1994	1993	1992	1991	1990	1989
Cash	NA	728	1,355	1,119	1,335	1,868	1,403	891	829	842
Curr. Assets	NA	4,284	4,385	3,713	3,911	3,922	3,213	2,532	2,304	2,106
Total Assets	NA	11,354	10,450	9,757	8,747	8,404	7,525	6,261	5,450	4,728
Curr. Liab.	NA	2,249	1,634	1,172	1,127	960	937	857	676	619
LT Debt	NA	2,345	2,003	2,070	2,021	2,039	1,562	980	751	690
Common Eqty.	NA	6,050	6,145	5,854	5,045	4,883	4,492	3,922	3,573	3,034
Total Cap.	NA	8,993	8,710	8,463	7,499	7,336	6,540	5,355	4,728	4,106
Cap. Exp.	NA	780	754	559	514	394	480	468	327	307
Cash Flow	NA	823	1,090	1,181	839	863	797	728	732	644
Curr. Ratio	NA	1.9	2.7	3.2	3.5	4.1	3.4	3.0	3.4	3.4
% LT Debt of Cap.	NA	26.1	23.0	24.5	27.0	27.8	23.9	18.3	15.9	16.8
% Net Inc.of Revs.	NA	2.7	5.2	6.3	4.3	5.4	5.5	5.5	6.2	5.4
% Ret. on Assets	NA	3.5	6.9	8.7	5.6	6.6	7.3	8.1	9.5	9.3
% Ret. on Equity	NA	6.2	11.6	14.8	9.8	11.3	12.0	12.6	14.6	15.0

Data as orig. reptd.; bef. results of disc. opers. and/or spec. items. Per share data adj. for stk. divs. as of ex-div. date. Bold denotes diluted EPS (FASB 128). E-Estimated. NA-Not Available. NM-Not Meaningful. NR-Not Ranked.

Office—4666 Faries Parkway, Box 1470, Decatur, IL 62525. **Tel**—(217) 424-5200. **Website**—http://www.admworld.com **Chrmn**—D. O. Andreas. **Pres & CEO**—G. A. Andreas. **VP & CFO**—D. J. Schmalz. **VP & Secy**—D. J. Smith. **Dirs**—D. O. Andreas, G. A. Andreas, S. M. Archer Jr., J. R. Block, R. R. Burt, M. H. Carter, G. O. Coan, F. R. Johnson, M. B. Mulrooney, R. S. Strauss, J. K. Vanier, — O. G. Webb, A Young. **Transfer Agent & Registrar**—Harris Trust & Savings Bank, Chicago. **Incorporated**—in Delaware in 1923. **Empl**— 17,160. **S&P Analyst:** Robert J. Izmirlian

STANDARD &POOR'S
STOCK REPORTS
Armco Inc.
216
NYSE Symbol **AS**
In S&P 500

12-SEP-98 | **Industry:** Iron & Steel

Summary: Armco is the second largest U.S. producer of stainless flat rolled steels and the largest producer of electrical steels. It also makes carbon steels and steel products.

S&P Opinion: Buy (★★★★)	Recent Price • 4	Yield • Nil
	52 Wk Range • 7-3	12-Mo. P/E • 5.4

Quantitative Evaluations

Outlook (1 Lowest—5 Highest)
• 1

Fair Value
• 3⅝

Risk
• Average

Earn./Div. Rank
• B-

Technical Eval.
• **Bearish** since 10/96

Rel. Strength Rank (1 Lowest—99 Highest)
• 24

Insider Activity
• NA

Earnings vs. Previous Year
▲=Up ▼=Down ▶=No Change

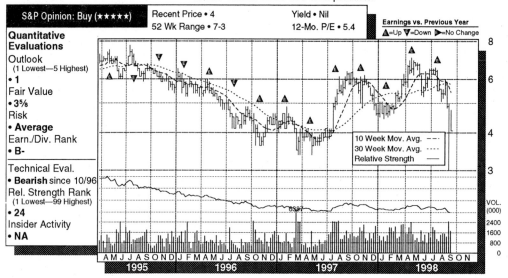

10 Week Mov. Avg. — - —
30 Week Mov. Avg. - - - -
Relative Strength ——

VOL. (000)
2400
1600
800
0

AMJJASOND | JFMAMJJASOND | JFMAMJJASOND | JFMAMJJASON
1995 | 1996 | 1997 | 1998

Overview - 28-JUL-98

We project 2.0% sales growth in 1998, solely reflecting an improved mix in the steel segment; fabricated product sales will approximate 1997's level. An increase in stainless production at the Mansfield plant will lift both revenue and operating profit per ton; operating profit for fabricated products will post a small decline. Aided by lower interest expense, EPS should rise again in 1998.

Valuation - 28-JUL-98

Following second quarter EPS, we are maintaining our buy rating on AS. The company continued to buck industry trends and achieved higher profit per ton despite a decline in stainless steel prices and lower volume. Shipments for the quarter were 318,000 tons, versus 325,000 tons in 1997 but per ton profit rose to $85 from $69 on an improved mix and lower costs. Although AS has made immense progress, it still carries a lower multiple than the other stainless steelmakers. We surmise that the lower multiple reflects AS's very long history of negative surprises and disappointments. Most recently, start-up problems at the Mansfield plant hurt EPS in 1995 and 1996. However, those problems have been resolved and we expect that AS will continue to achieve positive rather than negative EPS surprises in the future. We hasten to add that EPS for 1998's third quarter could be hurt if the current strike at GM extends into August. However, we would regard this as a temporary setback and remain confident that AS will report higher EPS in 1998 and 1999. Besides improving underlying operations, AS has also made great progress in reducing its financial leverage. The pension plan is fully funded and AS now has positive book value. The current turnaround in operations and finances is both genuine and sustainable in our view. As investors become more confident that the improvement is durable, the shares should accelerate their current uptrend.

Key Stock Statistics

S&P EPS Est. 1998	0.70	Tang. Bk. Value/Share	NM
P/E on S&P Est. 1998	5.8	Beta	1.72
S&P EPS Est. 1999	0.90	Shareholders	25,800
Dividend Rate/Share	Nil	Market cap. (B)	$0.438
Shs. outstg. (M)	107.9	Inst. holdings	60%
Avg. daily vol. (M)	0.397		

Value of $10,000 invested 5 years ago: $ 6,017

Fiscal Year Ending Dec. 31

	1998	1997	1996	1995	1994	1993
Revenues (Million $)						
1Q	447.7	441.3	430.4	368.4	379.6	427.0
2Q	450.1	490.3	450.8	390.6	354.9	454.0
3Q	—	461.3	429.2	404.1	368.0	419.8
4Q	—	436.4	413.6	396.8	335.1	363.5
Yr.	—	1,829	1,724	1,560	1,438	1,664
Earnings Per Share ($)						
1Q	0.15	0.05	0.02	-0.03	-0.30	-0.25
2Q	0.23	0.15	-0.08	0.27	0.63	-0.06
3Q	E0.17	0.22	0.06	-0.06	0.20	-1.85
4Q	E0.15	0.13	0.08	-0.12	0.05	-0.48
Yr.	E0.70	0.55	0.08	0.05	0.57	-2.64

Next earnings report expected: late October

Dividend Data

No dividends have been paid on the common shares since 1990.

 A Division of The **McGraw·Hill** *Companies*

Business Summary - 28-JUL-98

Armco is a manufacturer of specialty steels, steel pipe and tubing and snowplows. Following the upgrade of the Mansfield plant in 1996, the company will be able to increase its sales of stainless and electrical steels as a percent of total sales to improve margins. Additionally, the upgrade is intended to help Armco solidify its position as the leading supplier of stainless steel products to the automotive market. Sales and operating profit by segment in 1997:

	Sales	Profits
Specialty flat rolled steel	82%	68%
Other steel & fabricated products	18%	32%

Specialty flat rolled steel consists primarily of chrome stainless, chrome nickel stainless in the form of specialty sheet and strip and electrical steels. Shipments for these three product lines totaled 757,000 tons in 1997, versus 739,000 tons in 1996.

Chrome stainless is a stainless steel product with 10% to 20% chromium content designed for applications where heat and corrosion resistance is important. Chrome stainless is used mostly in automotive emission control systems. Armco is the leading supplier to this market and estimates that U.S. demand for this product totals over 400,000 tons.

Chrome nickel stainless steel contains 18% to 30% chromium and 6% to 20% nickel for enhanced surface quality and corrosion resistance. Chrome nickel is used for automotive trim, kitchen utensils, processing equipment and a variety of industrial applications.

Electrical steel consists of special ferro-magnetic alloys of iron and silicon that increase the efficiency of electric power generation and transmission. Electrical steel is used for making transformers, motors and generators.

Specialty steel also includes semifinished specialty, carbon and galvanized steel. Shipments of semifinished specialty steels totaled 168,000 tons in 1997, up from 97,000 tons in 1996; galvanized and carbon shipments totaled 306,000 tons in 1997, versus 304,000 tons in 1996. Semifinished products are sold to other steelmakers and to converters and processors.

The other steel and fabricated products segment includes Sawhill Tubular, a manufacturer of a wide range of steel pipe and tubular products for the construction, industrial and plumbing markets, and Douglas Dynamics, a manufacturer of snowplows.

In May 1998 Armco and Autokinetics, a Detroit-based design engineering firm, unveiled a project to develop a stainless steel modular automobile frame. The two companies began working on the project in January 1996 and believe that a stainless steel frame could surpass traditional carbon steel or aluminum frames in strength, weight savings and cost. AS and Autokinetics are finishing a Phase I feasibility study. Based on the results of the study, the second phase would involve building a prototype. A full prototype could be completed by as early as mid-1999.

Per Share Data ($)

(Year Ended Dec. 31)	1997	1996	1995	1994	1993	1992	1991	1990	1989	1988
Tangible Bk. Val.	NM	NM	NM	-5.57	-6.59	0.94	5.02	9.31	10.76	9.29
Cash Flow	1.13	0.63	0.43	1.10	-2.06	-3.79	-3.38	-0.26	2.90	2.32
Earnings	0.55	0.08	0.05	0.57	-2.64	-4.37	-3.89	-0.71	2.28	1.40
Dividends	Nil	Nil	Nil	Nil	Nil	Nil	Nil	0.40	0.30	Nil
Payout Ratio	Nil	Nil	Nil	Nil	Nil	Nil	Nil	NM	13%	Nil
Prices - High	6³/₈	6¹/₂	7³/₄	7³/₈	8³/₈	7¹/₂	6¹/₄	11¹/₄	13¹/₂	12¹/₂
- Low	3³/₈	3⁵/₈	5³/₈	4¹/₂	4⁷/₈	4¹/₄	4	3⁷/₈	9¹/₂	9
P/E Ratio - High	12	81	NM	13	NM	NM	NM	NM	6	9
- Low	6	45	NM	8	NM	NM	NM	NM	4	6

Income Statement Analysis (Million $)

	1997	1996	1995	1994	1993	1992	1991	1990	1989	1988
Revs.	1,829	1,724	1,560	1,438	1,664	2,074	1,595	1,735	2,423	3,227
Oper. Inc.	167	142	122	130	80.0	96.0	86.0	126	176	328
Depr.	61.3	58.7	53.0	56.0	60.0	58.0	45.0	40.0	54.0	81.0
Int. Exp.	35.5	37.1	38.0	38.0	44.0	51.0	84.0	140	85.0	119
Pretax Inc.	79.4	27.4	26.0	49.0	-263	-453	-335	-53.0	235	154
Eff. Tax Rate	2.90%	5.10%	7.80%	NM	NM	NM	NM	NM	11%	15%
Net Inc.	77.1	26.0	24.0	78.0	-255	-421	-336	-55.0	210	130

Balance Sheet & Other Fin. Data (Million $)

	1997	1996	1995	1994	1993	1992	1991	1990	1989	1988
Cash	190	169	137	229	184	182	333	189	477	355
Curr. Assets	637	572	614	649	625	784	666	642	884	1,101
Total Assets	1,881	1,868	1,897	1,935	1,905	1,960	1,847	2,294	2,489	2,788
Curr. Liab.	386	358	419	390	353	472	375	479	427	671
LT Debt	307	344	362	364	380	403	355	367	423	552
Common Eqty.	-337	-397	-415	-428	-523	132	484	824	951	815
Total Cap.	155	132	-54.0	145	76.0	763	927	1,290	1,474	1,458
Cap. Exp.	41.9	60.0	143	87.0	54.0	68.0	43.0	70.0	170	120
Cash Flow	121	66.8	55.4	116	-213	-373	-298	-23.0	256	203
Curr. Ratio	1.6	1.6	1.5	1.7	1.8	1.7	1.8	1.3	2.1	1.6
% LT Debt of Cap.	198.1	260.2	NM	250.4	497.6	52.8	38.3	28.4	28.7	37.9
% Net Inc.of Revs.	4.2	1.5	1.5	5.4	NM	NM	NM	NM	8.7	4.0
% Ret. on Assets	4.1	1.4	1.2	4.0	NM	NM	NM	NM	7.9	4.6
% Ret. on Equity	NM	NM	NM	NM	NM	NM	NM	NM	22.8	16.4

Data as orig. reptd.; bef. results of disc. opers. and/or spec. items. Per share data adj. for stk. divs. as of ex-div. date. Bold denotes diluted EPS (FASB 128). E-Estimated. NA-Not Available. NM-Not Meaningful. NR-Not Ranked.

Office—1 Oxford Centre, 301 Grant St., Pittsburgh, PA 15219-1415. **Tel**—(412) 255-9800. **Website**—http://www.armco.com **Chrmn, Pres & CEO**—J. F. Will. **VP-Treas**—J. L. Bertsch. **VP-Secy**—G. R. Hildreth. **Investor Contact**—Frederick P. O'Brien. **Dirs**— D. R. Carmichael, P. H. J. Cholmondeley, D. C. Gilliam, C. J. Hora, Jr., C. Haley, B. E. Robbins, J. H. Suwinski, J. D. Turner, J. F. Will. **Transfer Agent & Registrar**—Fifth Third Bank, Cincinnati. **Incorporated**—in Ohio in 1917. **Empl**— 6,000. **S&P Analyst:** Leo J. Larkin

Armstrong World Industries   222M

NYSE Symbol **ACK**

In S&P 500

12-SEP-98

Industry:
Building Materials

Summary: Armstrong is a leading producer of interior furnishings, including floor coverings and ceiling materials for renovation/remodeling and new construction markets.

S&P Opinion: Hold (★★★)		
Recent Price • 49⅛	Yield • 3.9%	
52 Wk Range • 90-46⅞	12-Mo. P/E • 10.9	

Quantitative Evaluations

Outlook
(1 Lowest—5 Highest)
• **2+**

Fair Value
• **50⅞**

Risk
• **Low**

Earn./Div. Rank
• **B**

Technical Eval.
• **Bearish** since 5/98

Rel. Strength Rank
(1 Lowest—99 Highest)
• **37**

Insider Activity
• **Favorable**

Earnings vs. Previous Year
▲=Up ▼=Down ▶=No Change

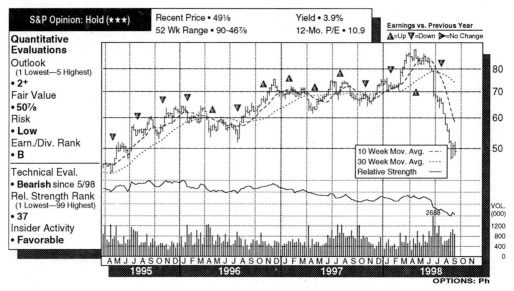

10 Week Mov. Avg. ---
30 Week Mov. Avg. ····
Relative Strength —

OPTIONS: Ph

Overview - 27-JUL-98

Sales from continuing operations in 1998 should benefit from generally higher volume, reflecting increased market share, acquisitions, new products, improved marketing capabilities, focus on developing information technologies and efforts to expand in overseas markets; slowing growth in Southeast Asia will likely restrict the pace of gains. A strong housing market and high confidence levels in the U.S. could aid demand for residential products. Competitive pricing pressures are partly offset by stable to lower raw material prices and efforts to control all expenses. These efforts will include more efficient operations at the flooring business, consolidating operations, reducing corporate overhead, lowering freight and packaging expenses, and renegotiating supply contracts. Results in 1997 benefited from higher sales in North America, lower raw material costs and productivity improvements; Europe's performance was hurt by a strong dollar and highly competitive and generally sluggish economies.

Valuation - 27-JUL-98

We recently downgraded Armstrong World to hold from accumulate as the company announced that second quarter results would not meet expectations. The company projected the quarter's sales and EPS to be below year-ago levels, with earnings of $1.35 to $1.40 per share; it reported $1.38. Armstrong cited economic weakness in Asian and emerging markets and short term domestic pressures. We are skeptical that the company will meet analysts' expectations in the 1998 second half. We reduced our 1998 EPS estimate from $5.75 to $5.40. Low interest rates, a strong housing market, high consumer confidence and an existing multi-million share buyback program should support the stock, despite near-term pressure.

Key Stock Statistics

S&P EPS Est. 1998	5.40	Tang. Bk. Value/Share	18.70
P/E on S&P Est. 1998	9.1	Beta	1.01
Dividend Rate/Share	1.92	Shareholders	7,400
Shs. outstg. (M)	40.0	Market cap. (B)	$ 2.0
Avg. daily vol. (M)	0.184	Inst. holdings	66%

Value of $10,000 invested 5 years ago: $ 17,925

Fiscal Year Ending Dec. 31

	1998	1997	1996	1995	1994	1993
Revenues (Million $)						
1Q	543.1	518.3	501.2	502.2	642.7	611.9
2Q	555.6	577.4	563.2	536.0	689.3	629.0
3Q	—	575.6	563.4	549.0	715.3	660.1
4Q	—	527.4	528.6	497.7	705.4	624.4
Yr.	—	2,199	2,156	2,085	2,753	2,525
Earnings Per Share ($)						
1Q	1.15	1.10	0.88	0.61	1.17	0.21
2Q	1.38	1.43	0.73	1.17	1.31	0.76
3Q	—	0.82	1.06	0.29	1.54	1.04
4Q	—	1.15	1.28	-2.09	1.17	-0.68
Yr.	E5.40	4.50	3.81	-0.02	5.22	1.32

Next earnings report expected: mid October

Dividend Data (Dividends have been paid since 1934.)

Amount ($)	Date Decl.	Ex-Div. Date	Stock of Record	Payment Date
0.440	Oct. 27	Nov. 05	Nov. 07	Dec. 02 '97
0.440	Jan. 26	Feb. 04	Feb. 06	Mar. 03 '98
0.480	Apr. 27	May. 06	May. 08	Jun. 02 '98
0.480	Jul. 27	Aug. 05	Aug. 07	Sep. 02 '98

A Division of The McGraw·Hill Companies

Business Summary - 27-JUL-98

This leading manufacturer of floor coverings, building and industrial products has focused on four interwoven strategies to grow its business: geographic expansion, market share gains, new product introductions, and acquisitions, joint ventures and alliances. These goals, ACK believes, will help it achieve its overriding financial objective of earning in excess of its cost of capital. Armstrong has made strides to meet all of these objectives in the past two years.

For example, its WAVE joint venture with Worthington Industries (Nasdaq: WTHG) has announced new measures to expand its presence in Europe. In midsummer 1997, WAVE bought a privately held Spanish grid manufacturer, Peytesa SA. Currently, Peytesa primarily serves the Portuguese and Spanish markets, but ACK anticipates that it will serve as a base for expansion into Italy, Greece and Turkey; and through its affiliation with ACK, Peytesa will be able to provide additional products. WAVE has also built a new plant in England that will provide grid ceiling products to northern Europe.

Additionally, in March 1997, ACK acquired a controlling interest in a Swedish flooring manufacturer and distributor. Plus, in December 1996, ACK acquired a 30% share of a Polish distributor of floor coverings, and separately agreed to form a joint venture with a Serbian

manufacturer with the intent of selling to Russia and other central and eastern European countries. Similar efforts are being made to expand its distribution in Asia and Latin America.

ACK sells its products to the home improvement and refurbishing, commercial/institutional building, the new residential building, and industrial markets. A broad range of resilient floor covering is manufactured, in both sheet and tile form. Building materials consist of ceiling materials for residential, commercial and institutional uses. Most contain features such as noise reduction, fire protection and ease of installation. Industrial products consist of a variety of products sold to a number of industries.

The floor coverings segment accounted for 51% of ACK's 1997 sales (51% of 1996 sales), building products 34% (33%), and industry products 15% (16%). International sales accounted for 34% of total sales and 27% of the profits in 1997. In late 1995, ACK combined its American Olean Tile ceramic business with Dal-Tile International, forming a new entity called Dal-Tal; it retained a 34% minority interest. In early 1998, ACK expressed its intentions to divest its shares of Dal-Tile stock.

ACK is involved in asbestos-related litigation and in various other lawsuits, which are mostly environmentally related.

Per Share Data ($)

(Year Ended Dec. 31)	1997	1996	1995	1994	1993	1992	1991	1990	1989	1988
Tangible Bk. Val.	18.70	18.07	12.64	17.17	12.88	14.70	16.65	17.01	16.72	21.86
Cash Flow	7.42	7.15	3.98	8.66	4.62	1.51	4.77	6.53	6.11	5.88
Earnings	4.50	3.97	-0.02	5.22	1.32	-2.03	1.11	3.18	3.17	3.51
Dividends	1.72	1.56	1.40	1.26	1.20	1.20	1.19	1.14	1.04	0.97
Payout Ratio	38%	39%	NM	24%	90%	107%	34%	31%	28%
Prices - High	75³/₈	75¹/₄	64¹/₈	57¹/₂	55¹/₄	37¹/₂	34¹/₂	38³/₄	50⁷/₈	44
- Low	61¹/₂	51⁷/₈	38³/₈	36	28³/₄	24¹/₂	22⁷/₈	18	33³/₈	29¹/₂
P/E Ratio - High	17	19	NM	11	42	NM	31	12	16	13
- Low	14	13	NM	7	22	NM	21	6	11	8

Income Statement Analysis (Million $)

	1997	1996	1995	1994	1993	1992	1991	1990	1989	1988
Revs.	2,199	2,156	2,085	2,753	2,525	2,550	2,439	2,531	2,513	2,680
Oper. Inc.	484	407	414	467	348	284	306	365	413	384
Depr.	133	124	136	133	130	137	136	130	133	109
Int. Exp.	28.0	22.6	34.0	28.3	38.0	41.6	45.8	37.5	41.2	26.6
Pretax Inc.	296	240	7.6	306	93.0	-61.0	102	221	241	265
Eff. Tax Rate	38%	31%	NM	31%	29%	NM	39%	34%	35%	37%
Net Inc.	185	165	13.6	210	64.0	-62.5	61.0	143	154	163

Balance Sheet & Other Fin. Data (Million $)

	1997	1996	1995	1994	1993	1992	1991	1990	1989	1988
Cash	57.9	65.4	257	12.0	9.0	15.0	8.0	25.0	17.0	70.0
Curr. Assets	600	565	723	691	640	713	719	727	724	839
Total Assets	2,376	2,136	2,150	2,233	1,929	2,010	2,150	2,146	2,033	2,098
Curr. Liab.	472	321	376	387	436	546	480	545	401	700
LT Debt	223	441	423	483	511	527	566	501	450	186
Common Eqty.	811	790	516	707	547	546	618	631	707	1,011
Total Cap.	1,103	1,274	1,224	1,259	1,110	1,122	1,627	1,575	1,603	1,382
Cap. Exp.	142	221	186	148	118	116	133	195	231	396
Cash Flow	318	280	150	325	174	56.0	177	253	277	272
Curr. Ratio	1.3	1.8	1.9	1.8	1.5	1.3	1.5	1.3	1.8	1.2
% LT Debt of Cap.	20.2	34.7	34.6	38.4	46.0	47.0	34.8	31.8	28.1	13.4
% Net Inc.of Revs.	8.4	7.7	0.6	7.6	2.5	NM	2.5	5.7	6.1	6.1
% Ret. on Assets	8.2	7.7	0.6	10.1	3.2	NM	2.8	7.3	7.8	8.8
% Ret. on Equity	23.1	23.9	NM	30.5	8.1	NM	6.6	19.8	17.7	17.0

Data as orig. reptd.; bef. results of disc. opers. and/or spec. items. Per share data adj. for stk. divs. as of ex-div. date. Bold denotes diluted EPS (FASB 128). E-Estimated. NA-Not Available. NM-Not Meaningful. NR-Not Ranked.

Office—313 W. Liberty St., P.O. Box 3001, Lancaster, PA 17604. **Tel**—(717) 397-0611. **Chrmn, Pres & CEO**—G. A. Lorch. **VP & Treas**—E. R. Case. **VP & Secy**—D. K. Owen. **Investor Contact**—Warren M. Posey. **Dirs**—H. J. Arnelle, V. C. Campbell, D. C. Clark, E. A. Deaver, G. A. Lorch, J. E. Marley, D. W. Raisbeck, J. P. Samper, J. L. Stead. **Transfer Agent & Registrar**—First Chicago Trust Co. of New York, Jersey City, NJ. **Incorporated**—in Pennsylvania in 1891. **Empl**— 10,600. **S&P Analyst:** Efraim Levy

STANDARD &POOR'S
STOCK REPORTS

ASARCO Inc.

231

NYSE Symbol **AR**

In S&P 500

12-SEP-98

Industry:
Metals Mining

Summary: ASARCO is one of the world's largest copper producers. It also mines lead, zinc and silver. Other operations include specialty chemicals, crushed stone and environmental services.

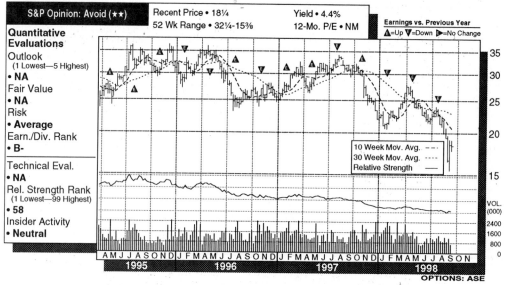

S&P Opinion: Avoid (★★)	Recent Price • 18¼ Yield • 4.4%
	52 Wk Range • 32¼-15⅜ 12-Mo. P/E • NM

Quantitative Evaluations

Outlook
(1 Lowest—5 Highest)
• **NA**

Fair Value
• **NA**

Risk
• **Average**

Earn./Div. Rank
• **B-**

Technical Eval.
• **NA**

Rel. Strength Rank
(1 Lowest—99 Highest)
• **58**

Insider Activity
• **Neutral**

Earnings vs. Previous Year
▲=Up ▼=Down ▶=No Change

10 Week Mov. Avg. – – –
30 Week Mov. Avg. · · · ·
Relative Strength —

OPTIONS: ASE

Overview - 29-JUL-98

We expect a rebound in copper output in 1998 but anticipate that a lower copper price will offset a decline in costs and lead to lower operating profit. Penalized further by the likely absence of large asset sales, AR should incur a loss in 1998. We look for an average copper price of $0.90/lb. in 1998, down from $1.07/lb. in 1997.

Valuation - 29-JUL-98

Following second quarter EPS, we are maintaining our avoid rating on AR. Earlier, on March 10, 1998, we upgraded our investment opinion on AR and two other copper stocks based on our expectation for short-term improvement in copper market fundamentals. Although copper prices set contract lows since our upgrade, the supply picture has improved. As of July 27, 1998, LME inventories stood at 256,525 metric tons, down from 379,235 metric tons as of February 25, 1998; similarly, inventories on the Comex totaled 54,514 metric tons, down from 116,995 metric tons on March 6, 1998. In sum, the combination of strong seasonal demand and some production cutbacks have led to a drop in supply. Also, weakness in Asian demand has been partially offset by strength in North America and Europe. Notwithstanding near-term strength in the metal and a likely rebound in the stocks, we still think AR will underperform the market in 1998 and thus still rate the shares avoid. We anticipate that copper prices will begin another decline by the end of 1998's third quarter as seasonally strong demand ebbs and supply picks up. Moreover, we remain negative on the long-term outlook for copper and copper stocks due to the large expansion of mine production scheduled to come on line between now and 2000. This additional output will depress both the metal and the copper stocks.

Key Stock Statistics

S&P EPS Est. 1998	-1.55	Tang. Bk. Value/Share	40.91
P/E on S&P Est. 1998	NM	Beta	1.35
S&P EPS Est. 1999	-1.30	Shareholders	8,200
Dividend Rate/Share	0.80	Market cap. (B)	$0.726
Shs. outstg. (M)	39.7	Inst. holdings	60%
Avg. daily vol. (M)	0.201		

Value of $10,000 invested 5 years ago: $ 8,562

Fiscal Year Ending Dec. 31

	1998	1997	1996	1995	1994	1993
Revenues (Million $)						
1Q	633.5	715.6	717.2	791.0	443.0	457.0
2Q	602.3	741.0	680.2	787.5	487.8	418.6
3Q	—	661.3	647.8	819.7	513.0	425.2
4Q	—	603.1	651.5	799.6	588.1	435.5
Yr.	—	2,721	2,697	3,198	2,032	1,736
Earnings Per Share ($)						
1Q	-0.80	0.94	0.84	1.56	0.64	-0.74
2Q	-0.37	1.20	1.70	1.34	0.13	-0.58
3Q	E-0.23	1.09	0.14	1.38	-0.39	-0.08
4Q	E-0.15	0.13	0.57	-0.27	1.15	-0.30
Yr.	E-1.55	3.42	3.24	4.00	1.53	-1.70

Next earnings report expected: late October

Dividend Data (Dividends have been paid since 1987.)

Amount ($)	Date Decl.	Ex-Div. Date	Stock of Record	Payment Date
0.200	Oct. 29	Nov. 07	Nov. 12	Dec. 02 '97
0.200	Jan. 28	Feb. 09	Feb. 11	Mar. 03 '98
0.200	Apr. 29	May. 08	May. 12	Jun. 02 '98
0.200	Jul. 29	Aug. 10	Aug. 12	Sep. 02 '98

Business Summary - 29-JUL-98

ASARCO is a major producer of nonferrous metals. Its main business strategy is to expand its mine production in an effort to enhance its smelting and refining businesses. Through subsidiaries, AR produces specialty chemicals and construction aggregates and provides environmental services. These units provide an independent profit base which is used to offset downturns in the core metals businesses. Contributions (profits in millions) in 1997 were:

	Sales	Profits
Copper	73%	$314.2
Lead, zinc & precious metals	12%	-14.7
Specialty chemicals	12%	29.4
Aggregates	2%	13.8
Other	1%	-27.4

Copper production totaled 977.4 million lbs. in 1997, versus 1.02 billion lbs. in 1996, reflecting lower ore grades at the North American mines and partial curtailment of a concentrator. The average price for copper was $1.04 per pound in 1997, versus $1.06 in 1996. On average, about 68% of production comes from U.S.-based mines, with the balance from 53%-owned Southern Peru Copper Corp. (NYSE: SPU).

Lead output was 231 million pounds in 1997, versus 217.9 million pounds in 1996. The average lead price was $0.28 a pound in 1997, versus $0.35 a pound in 1996. Silver production was 6.9 million oz. in 1997, versus 5.8 million oz. The average silver price in 1997 was $4.89 per oz., versus $5.18 in 1996. Zinc output was 145.9 million pounds in 1997, versus 171.9 million pounds in 1996; the average price was $0.60 a pound in 1997, versus $0.47 a pound in 1996. Molybdenum output was 10.1 million pounds in 1997, versus 10.9 million pounds in 1996. the average price was $4.18 per pound in 1997, versus $3.61 in 1996.

ASARCO is the world's fourth largest private-sector producer of copper, with reserves totaling 3.4 billion tons at 1997 year-end. The principal uses of copper are in the construction, electrical and electronic products industries. AR's main competitors include Cyprus Amax Minerals, Freeport McMoRan Copper & Gold and Phelps Dodge.

Copper expansion projects include construction of a SX/EW plant at the Silver Bell Mine, which is expected to produce 36 million pounds of refined copper annually after completion. The Minto Mine is expected to produce 27 million pounds of copper and 10,000 oz. of gold annually after startup in 1998. SPU is expanding the Cuajone mine to increase its output by 130 million pounds and will also modernize the Ilo smelter.

AR recorded asset sale gains of $1.12 a share in 1997 and $1.08 in 1996.

In April 1998 AR announced that it would sell its lead business to the Doe Run Co. The transaction, which is expected to close in 1998's third quarter, will yield some $55 million in cash.

Per Share Data ($) (Year Ended Dec. 31)	1997	1996	1995	1994	1993	1992	1991	1990	1989	1988
Tangible Bk. Val.	42.71	40.56	39.02	36.04	35.27	32.74	36.24	36.78	34.56	30.61
Cash Flow	6.53	6.01	6.81	3.51	0.24	1.39	2.94	5.42	7.03	6.31
Earnings	3.42	3.24	4.00	1.53	-1.70	-0.70	1.12	3.60	5.50	4.92
Dividends	0.80	0.80	0.70	0.40	0.50	0.80	1.60	1.60	1.50	0.70
Payout Ratio	23%	25%	17%	26%	NM	NM	143%	44%	27%	14%
Prices - High	34 1/4	36 1/4	36 5/8	34 7/8	28 5/8	31 3/4	30 1/2	33	35 7/8	29 1/2
- Low	21 3/4	23 1/8	23 5/8	21 3/8	16 1/4	19 3/4	18 1/4	22 1/4	26 1/8	19 3/8
P/E Ratio - High	11	11	9	23	NM	NM	27	9	7	6
- Low	7	7	6	14	NM	NM	16	6	5	4

Income Statement Analysis (Million $)										
Revs.	2,721	2,697	3,198	2,032	1,736	1,908	1,910	2,209	2,211	1,988
Oper. Inc.	426	437	711	148	6.0	149	137	273	330	328
Depr.	131	119	119	83.1	80.6	86.6	74.9	75.1	64.4	58.6
Int. Exp.	74.2	79.2	95.3	62.5	57.3	51.2	46.2	38.0	28.9	27.6
Pretax Inc.	308	327	419	78.0	-106	-66.0	52.0	152	281	274
Eff. Tax Rate	24%	31%	29%	18%	NM	NM	11%	1.70%	18%	24%
Net Inc.	143	138	169	64.0	-71.0	-29.0	46.0	149	231	207

Balance Sheet & Other Fin. Data (Million $)										
Cash	211	193	281	18.0	31.0	33.0	35.0	35.0	23.0	109
Curr. Assets	1,300	1,185	1,217	747	620	687	637	677	579	699
Total Assets	4,110	4,120	4,326	3,291	3,152	2,946	2,937	2,771	2,441	2,223
Curr. Liab.	573	673	652	466	419	421	352	363	338	345
LT Debt	850	759	1,063	915	869	784	748	522	334	253
Common Eqty.	1,694	1,737	1,707	1,517	1,472	1,357	1,495	1,510	1,438	1,331
Total Cap.	2,662	3,164	3,445	2,588	2,488	2,246	2,396	2,160	1,907	1,707
Cap. Exp.	322	286	338	98.0	112	135	283	241	271	97.0
Cash Flow	274	257	288	147	10.0	58.0	121	224	296	266
Curr. Ratio	2.3	1.8	1.9	1.6	1.5	1.6	1.8	1.9	1.7	2.0
% LT Debt of Cap.	32.0	24.0	30.9	35.3	34.9	34.9	31.2	24.2	17.5	14.8
% Net Inc.of Revs.	5.3	5.1	5.3	3.2	NM	NM	2.4	6.8	10.5	10.4
% Ret. on Assets	3.5	3.3	4.5	2.0	NM	NM	1.6	5.8	10.0	9.7
% Ret. on Equity	8.4	8.0	10.5	4.3	NM	NM	3.1	10.2	16.8	16.4

Data as orig. reptd.; bef. results of disc. opers. and/or spec. items. Per share data adj. for stk. divs. as of ex-div. date. Bold denotes diluted EPS (FASB 128). E-Estimated. NA-Not Available. NM-Not Meaningful. NR-Not Ranked.

Office—180 Maiden Lane, New York, NY 10038-4991. **Tel**—(212) 510-2000. **Fax**—(212) 510-1855. **Website**—http://www.asarco.com **Chrmn & Pres**—R. de J. Osborne. **Secy**—R. Ferri. **Exec VP-Fin-CFO**—K. R. Morano. **Treas & Investor Contact**—Christopher F. Schultz. **Dirs**—W. C. Butcher, V. A. Calcarco, J. C. Cotting, D. C. Garfield, E. G. Gee, J. W. Kinnear, F. R. McAllister, K. R. Morano, M. T. Muse, M. T. Nelligan, J. D. Ong, R. de J. Osborne, M. T. Pacheco, J. Wood. **Transfer Agent & Registrar**—Bank of New York, NYC. **Incorporated**—in New Jersey in 1899. **Empl**—11,800. **S&P Analyst:** Leo J. Larkin

Ascend Communications 3155

Nasdaq Symbol **ASND**

In S&P 500

12-SEP-98

Industry: Computers (Networking)

Summary: Ascend develops, manufactures, markets, sells and supports a broad range of high-speed digital wide area network access products.

S&P Opinion: Hold (★★★)	Recent Price • 46 / 52 Wk Range • 55-22
	Yield • Nil / 12-Mo. P/E • 45.1

Quantitative Evaluations

Outlook (1 Lowest—5 Highest)
• **4⁻**

Fair Value
• **57½**

Risk
• **High**

Earn./Div. Rank
• **NR**

Technical Eval.
• **Bearish** since 9/98

Rel. Strength Rank (1 Lowest—99 Highest)
• **92**

Insider Activity
• **Neutral**

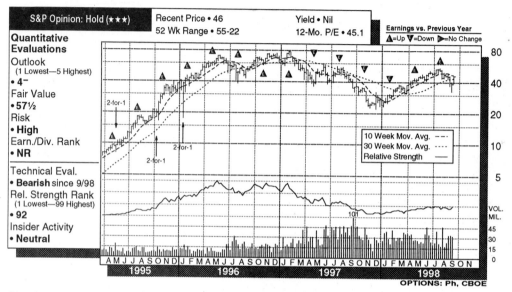

Earnings vs. Previous Year
▲=Up ▼=Down ▶=No Change

10 Week Mov. Avg. – – –
30 Week Mov. Avg. ‥‥‥
Relative Strength —

OPTIONS: Ph, CBOE

Overview - 23-JUL-98

The combination of ASND's expertise in remote access servers and Cascade's (acquired in June 1997) specialization in ATM and Frame Relay switching technologies has begun to offer substantial synergies. While sales growth of Ascend's remote access products has slowed from previously high levels in recent quarters, sales of ATM and Frame Relay products from the Cascade acquisition have taken off as service providers look to increase the capacity of their networks. In fact, Core Systems (ATM and Frame Relay) passed remote access as a percentage of overall corporate sales in the second quarter. We are projecting revenue gains of 19% in 1998 and 33% in 1999. Ascend's MAX WAN access switches have become the products of choice for Internet service providers (ISPs), telecommuters and individuals who need remote access to their networks. We expect EPS growth to slightly lag revenue growth on narrowing gross margins.

Valuation - 23-JUL-98

The shares reacted favorably to steady second quarter results that featured 21% growth in Core Systems sales, which offset seasonally weak remote access revenues. Ascend continues to benefit from the rapid acceptance of Frame Relay and ATM networking technologies for the core of telecommunications services providers' networks. Although gross margins were firm in the second quarter, we expect Cisco Systems' new remote access product to take further market share, and competition from new entrants Nortel and Lucent to put pressure on prices. Given concerns over an increasingly competitive operating environment for Ascend, we view the shares as fairly valued at 32X our $1.57 1999 EPS estimate.

Key Stock Statistics

S&P EPS Est. 1998	1.20	Tang. Bk. Value/Share	6.00
P/E on S&P Est. 1998	38.3	Beta	NA
S&P EPS Est. 1999	1.57	Shareholders	1,100
Dividend Rate/Share	Nil	Market cap. (B)	$ 9.1
Shs. outstg. (M)	197.8	Inst. holdings	63%
Avg. daily vol. (M)	6.325		

Value of $10,000 invested 5 years ago: NA

Fiscal Year Ending Dec. 31

	1998	1997	1996	1995	1994	1993
Revenues (Million $)						
1Q	305.1	292.7	92.03	20.36	6.80	3.10
2Q	327.4	311.7	125.2	125.2	8.20	3.80
3Q	—	270.4	154.6	40.04	10.29	4.00
4Q	—	292.6	177.5	60.61	14.00	5.30
Yr.	—	1,167	549.3	149.6	39.34	16.20
Earnings Per Share ($)						
1Q	0.26	-0.88	0.15	0.04	0.02	NM
2Q	0.29	-0.26	0.22	0.05	0.02	0.00
3Q	E0.31	0.20	0.20	0.07	0.03	0.01
4Q	E0.34	0.24	0.32	0.13	0.03	0.01
Yr.	E1.20	-0.66	0.94	0.28	0.09	0.02

Next earnings report expected: early October

Dividend Data

No cash dividends have been paid.

STANDARD
&POOR'S
STOCK REPORTS

Ascend Communications, Inc.

3155

12-SEP-98

Business Summary - 23-JUL-98

Ascend Communications develops and manufactures high-speed digital remote networking access products that enable its customers to build Internet access systems, extensions and enhancements to corporate backbone networks, and videoconferencing and multimedia access facilities. These systems establish high-speed switched digital connections whose bandwidth, duration and destination can be adjusted to suit user application needs.

The Access Switching business unit produces the MAX family of products, which provide bandwidth-on-demand for wide area network (WAN), Internet and multimedia access over a common set of digital access lines. The MAX can be configured with Multiband cards, providing up to 38 high-speed inverse multiplexing ports, or with Pipeline Ethernet cards and digital modem cards to act as a central-site remote LAN access server, allowing up to 672 remote users. In late 1996, ASND introduced the MAX TNT, a carrier class WAN access switch. Access Switching sales accounted for about 52% and 48% of net sales in 1997 and 1996, respectively.

The Core Systems business offers Frame Relay switches, the CBX 500 family of ATM switches, and the GRF family of IP Switches used to improve the speed,

performance and reliability of backbone carrier networks. Core Systems products accounted for 35% and 36% of net sales in 1997 and 1996, respectively.

The Enterprise Access unit offers the Pipeline family of remote access equipment as well as the Multiband MAX family of inverse multiplexing equipment. The Pipeline product family provides access equipment for remote office, telecommuting and small office/home office (SOHO) and Internet access. ASND's Multiband family of controllers is used for videoconferencing and multimedia networks. Enterprise Access products accounted for 9% and 13% of net sales in 1997 and 1996, respectively.

In June 1998, Ascend announced the first quarter 1998 research findings from Dell'Oro Group, ranking Ascend's MAX family of WAN Access Switches number one in remote access concentrator (RAC) revenue, analog port shipments and ISDN PRI B-channel port shipments. According to Dell'Oro Group, Ascend's MAX family of WAN Access Switches accounted for 30.9% manufacturer revenue market share, topping second and third place 3Com and Cisco. Dell'Oro Group figures show Ascend's continued leadership in analog port shipments, with 35.1% market share. Ascend also leads the RAC ISDN PRI B-channel market segment with more ports shipped than the rest of the industry combined, racking up 53.1% market share.

Per Share Data ($)

(Year Ended Dec. 31)	1997	1996	1995	1994	1993	1992	1991	1990	1989	1988
Tangible Bk. Val.	5.07	9.58	2.69	0.46	0.36	NA	NA	NA	NA	NA
Cash Flow	-0.42	0.95	0.30	0.10	0.02	-0.29	-0.19	NA	NA	NA
Earnings	-0.66	0.89	0.28	0.09	0.02	-0.33	-0.21	-0.27	NA	NA
Dividends	Nil	Nil	Nil	Nil	Nil	Nil	Nil	Nil	Nil	Nil
Payout Ratio	Nil	Nil	Nil	Nil	Nil	Nil	Nil	Nil	Nil	Nil
Prices - High	80¼	75¼	40⅝	5⅝	NA	NA	NA	NA	NA	NA
- Low	22	17½	5	1⁷⁄₁₆	NA	NA	NA	NA	NA	NA
P/E Ratio - High	NM	85	NM	60	NA	NA	NA	NA	NA	NA
- Low	NM	20	NM	15	NA	NA	NA	NA	NA	NA

Income Statement Analysis (Million $)

	1997	1996	1995	1994	1993	1992	1991	1990	1989	1988
Revs.	1,167	549	150	39.3	16.2	7.2	3.2	0.1	NA	NA
Oper. Inc.	359	197	49.0	9.6	1.7	-3.5	-2.4	NA	NA	NA
Depr.	45.7	8.8	2.1	0.6	0.4	0.4	0.2	NA	NA	NA
Int. Exp.	Nil	Nil	0.0	0.1	0.1	0.1	0.1	NA	NA	NA
Pretax Inc.	-45.0	186	49.3	9.9	1.4	-3.8	-2.4	-3.1	NA	NA
Eff. Tax Rate	NM	39%	38%	12%	Nil	Nil	Nil	Nil	Nil	Nil
Net Inc.	-123	113	30.6	8.7	1.4	-3.8	-2.4	-3.1	NA	NA

Balance Sheet & Other Fin. Data (Million $)

	1997	1996	1995	1994	1993	1992	1991	1990	1989	1988
Cash	241	373	211	35.5	6.3	6.6	NA	NA	NA	NA
Curr. Assets	915	572	275	50.9	11.3	9.1	NA	NA	NA	NA
Total Assets	1,138	652	335	53.3	12.4	10.0	5.8	2.2	NA	NA
Curr. Liab.	169	104	39.3	9.6	2.5	1.5	NA	NA	NA	NA
LT Debt	Nil	Nil	Nil	0.1	0.3	0.4	0.3	0.3	NA	NA
Common Eqty.	969	547	296	43.7	9.6	8.1	4.3	1.4	NA	NA
Total Cap.	969	547	296	43.8	9.9	8.5	4.7	1.8	NA	NA
Cap. Exp.	105	58.7	8.9	1.9	0.3	0.4	Nil	NA	NA	NA
Cash Flow	-78.6	122	32.7	9.3	1.8	-3.4	-2.2	NA	NA	NA
Curr. Ratio	5.4	5.5	7.0	5.3	4.5	6.0	NA	NA	NA	NA
% LT Debt of Cap.	Nil	Nil	NM	0.2	3.2	4.6	7.4	17.6	NA	NA
% Net Inc.of Revs.	NM	20.6	20.4	22.1	8.3	NM	NM	NM	NM	NM
% Ret. on Assets	NM	22.1	15.7	10.4	12.1	NM	NM	NM	NM	NM
% Ret. on Equity	NM	25.9	18.0	NM	15.2	NM	NM	NM	NM	NM

Data as orig. reptd.; bef. results of disc. opers. and/or spec. items. Per share data adj. for stk. divs. as of ex-div. date. Bold denotes diluted EPS (FASB 128). E-Estimated. NA-Not Available. NM-Not Meaningful. NR-Not Ranked.

Office—1275 Harbor Bay Parkway, Alameda, CA 94502. **Tel**—(510) 769-6001. **Fax**—(510) 814-2345. **Website**—http://www.ascend.com **Pres & CEO**—M. Ejabat. **VP-Fin & CFO**—M. F. G. Ashby. **Investor Contact**—Paula Cook (510-769-6001). **Dirs**—B. Atkins, R. K. Dahl, M. Ejabat, R. L. Evans, R. E. Hundt, C. R. Kramlich, J. P. Lally, M. Schoffstall. **Transfer Agent & Registrar**—Boston EquiServe, Canton, MA. **Incorporated**—in California in 1989; reincorporated in Delaware in 1994. **Empl**— 1,644. **S&P Analyst:** Aydin Tuncer

Ashland Inc.   232

NYSE Symbol **ASH**

In S&P 500

12-SEP-98

Industry: Oil & Gas (Refining & Marketing)

Summary: This leading independent petroleum refiner and marketer produces lubricants, including Valvoline motor oil, specialty chemicals, plastics and coal.

S&P Opinion: Hold (★★★)	Recent Price • 48¼	Yield • 2.3%
	52 Wk Range • 57⅞–44⅛	12-Mo. P/E • 11.1

Earnings vs. Previous Year
▲=Up ▼=Down ▶=No Change

Quantitative Evaluations

Outlook
(1 Lowest—5 Highest)
• 3⁻

Fair Value
• 51

Risk
• **Low**

Earn./Div. Rank
• B

Technical Eval.
• **Bullish** since 5/98

Rel. Strength Rank
(1 Lowest—99 Highest)
• 78

Insider Activity
• **Neutral**

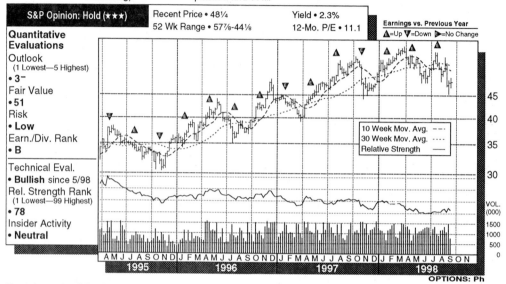

10 Week Mov. Avg. - - -
30 Week Mov. Avg. ·······
Relative Strength —

OPTIONS: Ph

Overview - 29-JUL-98

In the space of a little more than a year, Ashland has taken numerous significant steps aimed at streamlining the company's business focus and enhancing profitability. In July 1997, ASH sold its oil and gas exploration and production unit, and the refining and marketing division was merged with that of USX-Marathon in January, 1998, forming Marathon Ashland Petroleum (MAP). Results from the joint venture, in which ASH has a 38% stake, are now accounted for as equity income, and are not included in consolidated revenues. In addition, the 55% owned Arch Coal subsidiary, formed through the merger of two coal subsidiaries during FY 97 (Sep.), recently acquired Atlantic Richfield's U.S. coal operations. Ashland now plans to reduce its interest in Arch Coal to less than 50%. Looking beyond FY 98, the company plans to focus on integrating recent acquisitions in the Ashland Chemicals, Valvoline and APAC highway construction divisions, with an emphasis on lowering costs.

Valuation - 29-JUL-98

Given the outlook for lower crude oil prices, high industrywide refinery utilization and robust refined product demand, conditions appeared favorable for shares of independent refiners/marketers at the beginning of 1998. However, despite a sharp decline in oil prices, margins, particularly for marketing operations, have not been as strong as expected, as a rapid buildup of product inventories has dampened retail gasoline prices. As a result, shares of independent refiners/marketers have lagged the broader market so far this year; ASH's shares are down about 3% to this point in 1998. The shares, which were recently trading at about 15X estimated FY 98 EPS of $3.50, are expected only to be market performers, despite the company's positive long-term fundamentals.

Key Stock Statistics

S&P EPS Est. 1998	3.50	Tang. Bk. Value/Share	26.09
P/E on S&P Est. 1998	13.8	Beta	1.17
S&P EPS Est. 1999	4.00	Shareholders	22,000
Dividend Rate/Share	1.10	Market cap. (B)	$ 3.7
Shs. outstg. (M)	76.5	Inst. holdings	60%
Avg. daily vol. (M)	0.248		

Value of $10,000 invested 5 years ago: $ 21,275

Fiscal Year Ending Sep. 30

	1998	1997	1996	1995	1994	1993
Revenues (Million $)						
1Q	3,550	3,545	3,173	2,924	2,172	2,555
2Q	1,854	3,346	3,097	2,680	2,200	2,386
3Q	1,877	3,643	3,235	2,998	2,476	2,605
4Q	—	3,665	3,500	3,003	2,609	2,487
Yr.	—	14,319	13,130	11,179	9,457	10,199
Earnings Per Share ($)						
1Q	**0.68**	0.30	1.29	0.50	0.90	0.41
2Q	**0.37**	-0.05	-0.11	-0.55	0.47	0.01
3Q	**1.59**	1.57	1.16	0.69	0.65	0.81
4Q	—	0.62	0.64	-0.55	0.93	1.00
Yr.	**E3.50**	2.57	2.97	0.08	2.94	2.26

Next earnings report expected: mid October

Dividend Data (Dividends have been paid since 1936.)

Amount ($)	Date Decl.	Ex-Div. Date	Stock of Record	Payment Date
0.275	Nov. 06	Nov. 20	Nov. 24	Dec. 15 '97
0.275	Jan. 28	Feb. 20	Feb. 24	Mar. 15 '98
0.275	May. 21	May. 28	Jun. 01	Jun. 15 '98
0.275	Jul. 15	Aug. 21	Aug. 25	Sep. 15 '98

A Division of The **McGraw·Hill** *Companies*

STANDARD
&POOR'S
STOCK REPORTS

Ashland Inc.

232

12-SEP-98

Business Summary - 29-JUL-98

Ashland Inc. (ASH) might not be a household name, but millions of consumers across the U.S. are certainly familiar with some of the company's brand names, such as Valvoline motor oil and SuperAmerica retail gasoline and convenience stores. Ashland is involved in refining and marketing of gasoline, motor oil and other automotive products; the manufacture and distribution of specialty and industrial chemicals; oil exploration; coal mining and highway construction.

Recently, Ashland has made two major moves, aimed at refocusing its business and improving profitability. In July 1997, the company completed the sale of its exploration and production unit, Blazer Energy, to the Eastern Group, a subsidiary of Norwegian oil giant Statoil. Ashland had previously considered a spinoff to shareholders of the Blazer Energy unit. Effective January 1, 1998, Ashland and USX-Marathon Group combined the major elements of their respective refining, marketing and transportation businesses to form Marathon Ashland Petroleum (MAP). Under the terms of the deal, Marathon owns 62% and Ashland 38%, of the new joint venture company, which is one of the largest independent refiner/marketers in the U.S.

During fiscal 1997 (Sep.), ASH processed 358,500 barrels (bbl.) of oil a day and sold 394,400 bbl./day of petroleum products. Valvoline product sales came to 19,100 bbl./day, and SuperAmerica sold some 76,100 bbl./day of gasoline and $600 million of merchandise through its network of 742 stores in 10 states. On July 1, 1997, the company's two coal units, Arch Mineral and Ashland Coal, merged to form a new publicly-traded company, Arch Coal, Inc. (NYSE: ACI) of which ASH is a 54% owner. Arch Coal sold 53.7 million tons of coal in fiscal 1997.

Improving the profitability of the refining segment has proven to be a difficult task. The U.S. refining industry has been forced to deal with the higher costs and excess capacity that resulted from the passage of the Clean Air Act Amendments in 1990. In recent years, high crude oil prices have increased feedstock costs, narrowing margins and reducing profits. However, ASH feels that a slow industry recovery may be at hand. Steady growth in U.S. gasoline demand is forecast over the next decade. Refinery utilization rates currently exceed 90%, as industry participants have cut back on capital spending. ASH has reduced its capital spending as well, with expenditures for refining limited to $100 million in 1997, well below the historical average for this segment. The future direction of the refining industry in the U.S. is sure to have a significant impact on Ashland, one of the nation's largest independent refiners.

Per Share Data ($)

(Year Ended Sep. 30)	1997	1996	1995	1994	1993	1992	1991	1990	1989	1988
Tangible Bk. Val.	25.39	21.89	19.50	19.56	17.90	16.94	23.03	20.94	18.54	17.70
Cash Flow	10.63	9.14	7.94	7.75	7.21	3.79	7.32	8.22	6.97	7.77
Earnings	2.57	2.97	0.08	2.94	2.26	-1.18	2.56	3.27	1.55	3.29
Dividends	1.10	1.10	1.10	1.00	1.00	1.00	1.00	1.00	1.00	0.95
Payout Ratio	43%	37%	NM	34%	44%	NM	41%	32%	67%	30%
Prices - High	54⁷/₈	48⁷/₈	38⁵/₈	44¹/₂	35⁵/₈	34	35¹/₄	40¹/₈	43	38¹/₈
- Low	39¹/₄	34¹/₄	30³/₈	31¹/₄	24¹/₄	22¹/₂	26¹/₈	26³/₈	33¹/₈	26³/₈
P/E Ratio - High	21	16	NM	15	16	NM	14	12	28	12
- Low	15	12	NM	11	11	NM	10	8	21	8

Income Statement Analysis (Million $)

	1997	1996	1995	1994	1993	1992	1991	1990	1989	1988
Revs.	14,319	13,285	12,239	10,382	9,611	9,592	9,303	8,552	8,062	7,826
Oper. Inc.	1,062	858	685	651	587	227	561	606	524	663
Depr.	572	402	487	295	290	290	267	275	301	250
Int. Exp.	170	169	171	117	133	132	125	120	92.0	78.0
Pretax Inc.	335	311	34.0	272	200	-157	193	263	142	271
Eff. Tax Rate	36%	30%	Nil	28%	29%	NM	25%	31%	39%	32%
Net Inc.	192	211	24.0	197	142	-68.0	145	182	86.0	184

Balance Sheet & Other Fin. Data (Million $)

	1997	1996	1995	1994	1993	1992	1991	1990	1989	1988
Cash	268	77.0	52.0	40.0	41.0	53.0	71.0	81.0	70.0	140
Curr. Assets	2,995	2,740	2,575	2,171	1,973	2,110	2,119	2,143	1,778	1,711
Total Assets	7,777	7,269	6,992	5,815	5,552	5,668	5,449	5,118	4,456	4,254
Curr. Liab.	2,261	2,279	2,094	1,688	1,619	2,046	1,823	1,806	1,515	1,489
LT Debt	1,639	1,784	1,828	1,391	1,399	1,445	1,337	1,235	1,074	842
Common Eqty.	2,024	1,527	1,362	1,295	1,155	1,086	1,444	1,280	1,141	1,121
Total Cap.	3,936	3,836	3,239	3,016	2,898	2,590	3,092	2,839	2,494	2,290
Cap. Exp.	431	510	444	376	432	504	445	446	413	343
Cash Flow	755	594	492	473	426	221	412	457	387	434
Curr. Ratio	1.3	1.2	1.2	1.3	1.2	1.0	1.2	1.2	1.2	1.1
% LT Debt of Cap.	41.6	46.5	56.4	46.1	48.3	55.8	43.2	43.5	43.1	36.8
% Net Inc.of Revs.	1.3	1.6	0.2	2.1	1.5	NM	1.6	2.1	1.1	2.3
% Ret. on Assets	2.6	3.0	0.4	3.4	2.5	NM	2.7	3.8	2.0	4.5
% Ret. on Equity	10.3	13.4	0.4	14.4	12.2	NM	10.5	15.1	7.7	17.2

Data as orig. reptd.; bef. results of disc. opers. and/or spec. items. Per share data adj. for stk. divs. as of ex-div. date. Revs in Inc. Statement tbl. incl. excise taxes. Bold denotes diluted EPS (FASB 128). E-Estimated. NA-Not Available. NM-Not Meaningful. NR-Not Ranked.

Registrars—Mellon Securities Trust Co., NYC; Bank One, Lexington, Ky. **Office**—1000 Ashland Dr., Russell, KY 41169.**Registrar**—Mellon Securities Trust Co., NYC; Bank One, Lexington, Ky. **Tel**—(606) 329-3333. **Website**—http://www.ashland.com**Chrmn & CEO**—P. W. Chellgren. **SVP & CFO**—J. M. Quin. **SVP & Secy**—T. L. Feazell.**VP & Investor Contact**—William P. Hartl. **Dirs**—J. S. Blanton, T. E. Bolger, S. C. Butler, F. C. Carlucci, P. W. Chellgren, J. B. Farley, R. E. Gomory, M. L. Jackson, P. F. Noonan, J. C. Pfeiffer, M. D. Rose, W. L. Rouse Jr., R. B. Stobaugh. **Transfer Agent and Registrars**—Harris Trust & Savings Bank, Chicago; Mellon Securities Trust Co., NYC and Bank One, Lexington, Ky. **Incorporated**—in Kentucky in 1936. **Empl**— 37,200. **S&P Analyst:** Norman Rosenberg

12-SEP-98

Industry:
Financial (Diversified)

Summary: This leading diversified finance company provides consumer and commercial finance, leasing and related services in the U.S. and internationally.

S&P Opinion: Accumulate (★★★★)	Recent Price • 61⅛	Yield • 0.7%
	52 Wk Range • 86¾-56⅛	12-Mo. P/E • 18.9

Quantitative Evaluations

Outlook
(1 Lowest—5 Highest)
• **NA**

Fair Value
• **NA**

Risk
• **NA**

Earn./Div. Rank
• **NR**

Technical Eval.
• **NA**

Rel. Strength Rank
(1 Lowest—99 Highest)
• **47**

Insider Activity
• **Neutral**

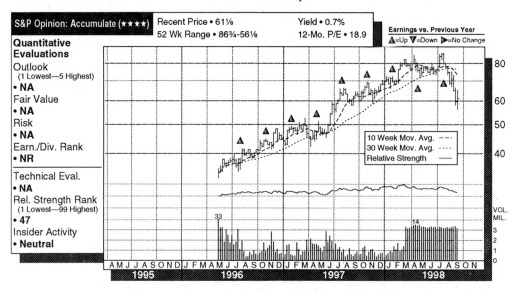

Earnings vs. Previous Year
▲=Up ▼=Down ▷=No Change

10 Week Mov. Avg. ---
30 Week Mov. Avg. ....
Relative Strength —

Overview - 23-JUL-98

Strong internal and well balanced lending growth from an expansion of the branch network, the acquisition of certain credit card portfolios, and expansion of home equity lending markets are expected to result in finance receivable gains of nearly 20% in 1998. Margins have narrowed a bit in recent quarters to the 8.9% level, and are likely to be flat to down in the intermediate term due to competition and a portfolio mix consisting of less unsecured loans. The efficiency ratio, at 43%, is already low when compared to peers and further improvement will be difficult to attain. Increased costs related to ongoing branch expansion, however, should be offset by technological improvements. Reflective of the conservative nature of the company's lending portfolio, which includes a large proportion of secured home equity loans, charge-off rates in the aggregate are not expected to stray much from a low 2.4% level. In line with receivables growth trends, earnings are expected to increase about 20% in 1998.

Valuation - 23-JUL-98

After a particularly strong 1997, the shares have performed about in line with the broader market thus far in 1998. We continue to view the shares as attractive for the long term for investors seeking exposure to the financial sector and who desire relatively stable earnings growth and low associated credit risk. Acquisitions and branch expansion strategies should keep finance receivable growth at nearly 20% in 1998, and the addition of similar portfolio lines will keep interest margins enviably high. With the shares trading at about 21 times our 1999 earnings estimate of $4.10 a share, and earnings growing at a rate well in excess of the overall market, selective accumulation is recommended.

Key Stock Statistics

S&P EPS Est. 1998	3.55	Tang. Bk. Value/Share	13.58
P/E on S&P Est. 1998	17.2	Beta	NA
S&P EPS Est. 1999	4.10	Shareholders	1,600
Dividend Rate/Share	0.40	Market cap. (B)	$ 21.2
Shs. outstg. (M)	346.3	Inst. holdings	39%
Avg. daily vol. (M)	1.494		

Value of $10,000 invested 5 years ago: NA

Fiscal Year Ending Dec. 31

	1998	1997	1996	1995	1994	1993
Revenues (Million $)						
1Q	2,231	1,927	1,645	—	—	—
2Q	2,295	2,050	1,717	—	—	—
3Q	—	2,118	1,844	—	—	—
4Q	—	2,184	1,893	—	—	—
Yr.	—	8,279	7,098	6,107	4,926	4,115
Earnings Per Share ($)						
1Q	**0.81**	0.68	0.55	0.56	0.47	—
2Q	**0.84**	0.71	0.58	0.57	0.47	—
3Q	**E0.92**	0.78	0.66	0.47	0.40	—
4Q	**E0.98**	0.80	0.68	0.49	0.40	—
Yr.	**E3.55**	2.97	2.47	2.09	1.74	—

Next earnings report expected: mid October

Dividend Data (Dividends have been paid since 1996.)

Amount ($)	Date Decl.	Ex-Div. Date	Stock of Record	Payment Date
0.100	Oct. 07	Oct. 30	Nov. 03	Dec. 01 '97
0.100	Jan. 08	Jan. 28	Jan. 30	Mar. 02 '98
0.100	Apr. 08	Apr. 29	May. 01	Jun. 01 '98
0.100	Jul. 07	Jul. 29	Jul. 31	Sep. 01 '98

A Division of The McGraw·Hill Companies

Associates First Capital Corporation

Business Summary - 23-JUL-98

Associates First Capital is a leading diversified consumer and commercial finance organization that provides finance, leasing and related services to individual consumers and businesses in the U.S. and internationally. AFS believes it is the second largest independent finance company in the U.S., based on aggregate net finance receivables outstanding of $55.2 billion at the end of 1997.

Business segment contributions in 1997 were:

	Revs.	Profits
Consumer finance	76%	72%
Commercial finance	24%	28%

The company offers various specialized consumer financing products and services, including home equity lending secured by first mortgages, personal lending, retail sales financing and credit cards. AFS's consumer finance business represented about $37.4 billion, or 68%, of its 1997 year-end net finance receivables. Consumer finance products are distributed through multiple delivery systems, which include more than 2,100 branch offices, a centralized lending operation, and centralized credit card operations. Home equity loans account for the largest portion (50%) of AFS's consumer finance portfolio. Home equity lending activities consist of originating and servicing fixed and variable rate mortgage loans that are primarily secured by single family residential properties. Such loans are made to borrowers mainly for the purpose of debt consolidation and home improvements. The company also offers personal installment loans and purchases consumer retail sales finance contracts. AFS provides revolving credit financing through its credit card business.

AFS's commercial operations mainly provide retail financing, leasing and wholesale financing for heavy-duty and medium-duty trucks and truck trailers, construction, material handling and other industrial and communications equipment, manufactured housing and auto fleet leasing. The commercial finance business represented $17.8 billion, or 32%, of AFS's 1997 year-end net finance receivables.

At the end of 1997, the allowance for losses, or the amount set aside for possible loan defaults, was $1.95 billion (3.53% of net finance receivables), up from $1.56 billion (3.36%) a year earlier. Net credit losses, or the amount actually written off as uncollectible, in 1997 amounted to $1.23 billion (2.40% of average net receivables), versus $885.3 million (2.03%) in 1996.

In April 1998, Ford Motor Co. spun off its 80.7% interest in the company in a tax-free transaction to Ford common and Class B stockholders.

Per Share Data ($)

(Year Ended Dec. 31)	1997	1996	1995	1994	1993	1992	1991	1990	1989	1988
Tangible Bk. Val.	14.88	11.97	14.09	NA	NA	NA	NA	NA	NA	NA
Earnings	2.97	2.47	2.09	1.74	1.43	NA	NA	NA	NA	NA
Dividends	0.40	0.20	Nil	Nil	Nil	Nil	Nil	Nil	Nil	Nil
Payout Ratio	13%	8%	Nil	Nil	Nil	Nil	Nil	Nil	Nil	Nil
Prices - High	72½	48½	NA	NA	NA	NA	NA	NA	NA	NA
- Low	42⅛	29	NA	NA	NA	NA	NA	NA	NA	NA
P/E Ratio - High	24	20	NA	NA	NA	NA	NA	NA	NA	NA
- Low	14	12	NA	NA	NA	NA	NA	NA	NA	NA

Income Statement Analysis (Million $)

	1997	1996	1995	1994	1993	1992	1991	1990	1989	1988
Premium Inc.	421	402	371	329	271	NA	NA	NA	NA	NA
Invest. Inc.	298	215	176	152	134	NA	NA	NA	NA	NA
Oth. Revs.	7,560	6,481	5,561	4,445	3,710	NA	NA	NA	NA	NA
Total Revs.	82.8	7,098	6,107	4,926	4,115	NA	NA	NA	NA	NA
Int. Exp.	2,775	2,456	2,178	1,657	1,422	NA	NA	NA	NA	NA
Exp./Op. Revs.	66%	46%	45%	79%	80%	NA	NA	NA	NA	NA
Pretax Inc.	1,640	1,405	1,198	1,017	821	NA	NA	NA	NA	NA
Eff. Tax Rate	37%	39%	40%	41%	40%	NA	NA	NA	NA	NA
Net Inc.	1,032	857	723	603	494	NA	NA	NA	NA	NA

Balance Sheet & Other Fin. Data (Million $)

	1997	1996	1995	1994	1993	1992	1991	1990	1989	1988
Receivables	55,216	44,950	38,434	32,624	27,402	NA	NA	NA	NA	NA
Cash & Invest.	1,676	1,498	1,413	1,211	NA	NA	NA	NA	NA	NA
Loans	NA	NA	NA	NA	NA	NA	NA	NA	NA	NA
Total Assets	57,233	48,268	41,304	35,283	30,040	NA	NA	NA	NA	NA
Capitalization:										
Debt	49,199	24,029	21,373	17,306	14,826	NA	NA	NA	NA	NA
Equity	6,268	5,437	4,801	4,437	3,774	NA	NA	NA	NA	NA
Total	55,467	29,466	26,173	21,743	18,600	NA	NA	NA	NA	NA
Price Times Bk. Val.: High	4.9	4.1	NA	NA	NA	NA	NA	NA	NA	NA
Price Times Bk. Val.: Low	2.8	2.4	NA	NA	NA	NA	NA	NA	NA	NA
% Return On Revs.	12.9	13.2	11.7	12.2	12.0	NA	NA	NA	NA	NA
% Ret. on Assets	2.0	1.9	1.9	1.9	1.8	NA	NA	NA	NA	NA
% Ret. on Equity	17.6	16.7	15.7	14.7	14.1	NA	NA	NA	NA	NA
Loans/Equity	NA	NA	NA	NA	NA	NA	NA	NA	NA	NA

Data as orig. reptd.; bef. results of disc. opers. and/or spec. items. Per share data adj. for stk. divs. as of ex-div. date. Bold denotes diluted EPS (FASB 128). E-Estimated. NA-Not Available. NM-Not Meaningful. NR-Not Ranked.

Office—250 East Carpenter Freeway, Irving, TX 75062. **Tel**—(972) 652-4000. **Chrmn & CEO**—K. W. Hughes. **Vice-Chrmn**—J. M. McQuillan. **Pres & COO**—H. D. Marshall. **EVP & CFO**—R. A. Guthrie. **Dirs**—J. C. Bacot, J. Devine, E. S. Dobkin, K. W. Hughes., W. M. Issac, H. D. Marshall, H. J. Toffey, Jr., K. Whipple. **Transfer Agent & Registrar**—First Chicago Trust Co. of New York. **Incorporated**—in Delaware in 1918. **Empl**— 22,600.
S&P Analyst: Stephen R. Biggar

STANDARD &POOR'S
STOCK REPORTS

AT&T

15P

NYSE Symbol **T**

In S&P 500

12-SEP-98

Industry:
Telecommunications
(Long Distance)

Summary: AT&T is the largest U.S. long-distance and cellular telephone company.

S&P Opinion: Buy (★★★★)

Recent Price • 55⅞	Yield • 2.4%
52 Wk Range • 68½-43	12-Mo. P/E • 18.2

Quantitative Evaluations

Outlook
(1 Lowest—5 Highest)
• 2⁻

Fair Value
• 54¼

Risk
• Average

Earn./Div. Rank
• B+

Technical Eval.
• **Bearish** since 7/98

Rel. Strength Rank
(1 Lowest—99 Highest)
• 84

Insider Activity
• **Neutral**

Earnings vs. Previous Year
▲=Up ▼=Down ▶=No Change

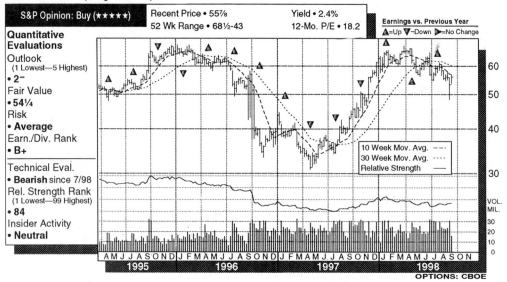

10 Week Mov. Avg. -- --
30 Week Mov. Avg. ········
Relative Strength ——

VOL. MIL.

OPTIONS: CBOE

Overview - 29-JUL-98

AT&T recently took a big step toward entering the local service market through the acquisition of Teleport Communications Group for $11.3 billion in stock. The company also formed a $10 billion alliance with European powerhouse British Telecom (NYSE: BTY), designed to leverage both companies' extensive network assets. In late 1997, AT&T said it would franchise its brand name and marketing rights to affiliated wireless and local phone carriers. This move is expected to save $2 billion to $3 billion in 1998 capital spending, which will be directed at expanding AT&T's national wireless and local footprint (coverage). Separately, the company sold two of its non-core holdings, Universal Card Services and Solutions Customer Care, for a combined $4.1 billion in cash. AT&T's directors recently authorized the repurchase of up to $3 billion of its common stock.

Valuation - 29-JUL-98

The shares recently reacted favorably to the company's second quarter earnings report, which showed the positive impact of cost controls despite only marginal revenue growth. The completion of the Teleport acquisition also signaled the beginning of AT&T's assault on the local market. Teleport will provide AT&T with a national presence in the local market, and will enable it to bundle its services more effectively. We believe Mike Armstrong has been effective in cutting costs in his first nine months as CEO, and has also done an excellent job of setting up a pricing structure that will begin to bear fruit in early 1999. Additionally, we see the company's joint venture with British Telecom as filling a void in international markets. The shares, which have underperformed the market in recent months, should widely beat the market over the next 12 months as revenue growth, margin improvement and an aggressive expansion strategy propel results.

Key Stock Statistics

S&P EPS Est. 1998	3.45	Tang. Bk. Value/Share	8.03
P/E on S&P Est. 1998	16.2	Beta	0.75
S&P EPS Est. 1999	3.80	Shareholders	2,302,300
Dividend Rate/Share	1.32	Market cap. (B)	$101.0
Shs. outstg. (M)	1806.3	Inst. holdings	42%
Avg. daily vol. (M)	5.317		

Value of $10,000 invested 5 years ago: NA

Fiscal Year Ending Dec. 31

	1998	1997	1996	1995	1994	1993
Revenues (Million $)						
1Q	12,631	13,048	12,956	18,262	17,097	15,719
2Q	12,858	13,173	13,032	19,512	18,238	16,316
3Q	—	13,380	13,228	19,704	18,649	16,662
4Q	—	12,828	13,238	22,131	21,110	18,459
Yr.	—	51,319	52,184	79,609	75,094	67,156
Earnings Per Share ($)						
1Q	**0.80**	0.67	0.90	0.76	0.69	0.69
2Q	**0.91**	0.57	0.94	0.85	0.80	0.74
3Q	**E0.85**	0.69	0.84	0.16	0.67	0.78
4Q	**E0.89**	0.81	0.76	-1.67	0.85	0.72
Yr.	**E3.45**	2.74	3.45	0.09	3.01	2.94

Next earnings report expected: mid October

Dividend Data (Dividends have been paid since 1881.)

Amount ($)	Date Decl.	Ex-Div. Date	Stock of Record	Payment Date
0.330	Sep. 22	Sep. 26	Sep. 30	Nov. 01 '97
0.330	Dec. 17	Dec. 29	Dec. 31	Feb. 02 '98
0.330	Mar. 18	Mar. 27	Mar. 31	May. 01 '98
0.330	Jun. 18	Jun. 26	Jun. 30	Aug. 01 '98

A Division of The **McGraw·Hill** *Companies*

STANDARD
&POOR'S
STOCK REPORTS

AT&T Corp.

15P
12-SEP-98

Business Summary - 29-JUL-98

"Ma Bell" spun off its seven "Baby Bells" in 1984; the Baby Bells have since been reduced to five, reflecting mergers between SBC and Pacific Telesis, and Bell Atlantic and NYNEX. The company recently took a big stride to enter the local services market by acquiring Teleport Communications Group (Nasdaq: TCGI) for $11.3 billion in stock. It also entered into a joint venture with British Telecom (NYSE: BTY). The multinational alliance is expected to produce $10 billion in revenues by the year 2000, and will also be accretive to earnings in the first year.

Revenue contributions in recent years were:

	1997	1996
Business long-distance	42%	42%
Consumer long-distance	46%	48%
Wireless services	8%	7%
Local and other	4%	3%

AT&T Wireless Services operates on a TDMA (Time Division Multiple Access) digital technology platform and serves about 6.5 million subscribers.

AT&T WorldNet Internet access service has gone from being a startup in March 1996 to a leading provider of online services, with nearly 1.1 million subscribers at the end of the second quarter of 1998.

The company recently sold its Universal Card Services unit to Citicorp for $3.5 billion in cash. In March 1998, AT&T sold its Solutions Customer Care business to

Cincinnati Bell for $625 million in cash. These moves were part of the company's renewed effort to focus only on businesses that fit into its communications services strategy.

AT&T expects capital expenditures to be about $7 billion in 1998 ($7.6 billion in 1997), with the majority invested to increase investment in its long-distance business markets in order to meet the strong revenue growth offered by the data marketplace.

In late 1996, AT&T completed a plan to split into three separate publicly traded companies. The largest of the three companies consists primarily of core long-distance operations and wireless services, as well as 25% of the Bell Laboratories unit, which designs and develops new products and carries out basic research. This company retained the widely recognized AT&T name. The company provides its long-distance services throughout the U.S. and internationally to virtually all nations and territories, while its wireless operations are the largest of any U.S. carrier. In September 1996, the long-distance giant spun off Lucent Technologies (LU). Lucent's operations include telecommunications equipment manufacturing and the remaining 75% of Bell Labs. The spinoff of the third company, the NCR computer unit, completed the separation strategy.

In 1996, AT&T marketed DirecTV's satellite-to-home television system to its customers, and also acquired a 2.5% interest in DirecTV for $137.5 million, with an option to buy up to 30%.

Per Share Data ($)

(Year Ended Dec. 31)	1997	1996	1995	1994	1993	1992	1991	1990	1989	1988
Tangible Bk. Val.	8.03	6.72	4.69	8.07	9.58	13.55	11.90	12.42	11.45	10.68
Cash Flow	5.09	5.17	3.13	5.66	5.62	5.57	3.42	5.63	5.62	7.64
Earnings	2.74	3.47	0.09	3.01	2.94	2.86	0.40	2.51	2.50	-1.55
Dividends	1.32	1.32	1.32	1.32	1.32	1.32	1.32	1.32	1.20	1.20
Payout Ratio	48%	38%	NM	44%	45%	46%	331%	53%	48%	NM
Prices - High	64	68⁷/₈	68¹/₂	57¹/₈	65	53¹/₈	40³/₈	46⁵/₈	47³/₈	30³/₈
- Low	30³/₄	33¹/₄	47⁵/₈	47¹/₄	50¹/₈	36⁵/₈	29	29	28¹/₈	24¹/₈
P/E Ratio - High	23	20	NM	19	22	19	NM	19	19	NM
- Low	11	10	NM	16	17	13	NM	12	11	NM

Income Statement Analysis (Million $)

	1997	1996	1995	1994	1993	1992	1991	1990	1989	1988
Revs.	51,319	52,184	79,609	75,094	67,156	64,089	63,089	51,321	50,976	51,974
Oper. Inc.	10,795	11,550	13,905	13,137	9,864	9,941	9,451	7,821	7,634	13,543
Depr.	3,827	2,740	4,845	4,136	3,626	3,608	3,897	3,396	3,356	9,886
Int. Exp.	191	527	859	1,520	566	725	805	907	780	700
Pretax Inc.	7,205	8,866	935	7,582	6,204	5,902	883	4,229	3,992	-3,381
Eff. Tax Rate	38%	37%	85%	37%	36%	36%	41%	35%	32%	NM
Net Inc.	4,472	5,608	139	4,710	3,974	3,807	522	2,735	2,697	-1,668

Balance Sheet & Other Fin. Data (Million $)

	1997	1996	1995	1994	1993	1992	1991	1990	1989	1988
Cash	145	134	908	1,208	532	1,310	2,148	1,389	1,183	2,021
Curr. Assets	16,179	18,310	39,509	37,611	29,738	26,514	24,613	17,776	15,291	15,602
Total Assets	58,635	58,635	88,884	79,262	60,766	57,188	53,355	43,775	37,687	35,152
Curr. Liab.	16,942	16,318	39,372	30,930	25,334	21,386	20,991	15,089	12,237	11,225
LT Debt	6,826	7,883	11,635	11,358	6,812	8,604	8,484	9,118	8,144	8,128
Common Eqty.	22,647	20,295	17,274	17,921	13,850	18,921	16,228	14,093	12,738	11,445
Total Cap.	32,184	33,005	35,034	34,517	21,789	32,987	29,123	26,935	23,771	22,129
Cap. Exp.	7,143	6,339	6,411	5,304	3,701	4,183	4,093	3,667	3,757	4,230
Cash Flow	8,299	8,349	4,984	8,846	7,600	7,415	4,419	6,131	6,053	8,216
Curr. Ratio	1.0	1.1	1.0	1.2	1.2	1.2	1.2	1.2	1.2	1.4
% LT Debt of Cap.	21.2	23.9	33.2	32.9	31.3	26.1	29.1	33.9	34.3	36.7
% Net Inc.of Revs.	8.7	10.8	0.2	6.3	5.9	5.9	0.8	5.3	5.3	NM
% Ret. on Assets	7.8	9.5	0.2	6.3	6.7	6.8	1.0	6.7	7.4	NM
% Ret. on Equity	20.8	29.9	0.8	27.7	24.3	21.4	3.2	20.2	22.3	NM

Data as orig. reptd.; bef. results of disc. opers. and/or spec. items. Per share data adj. for stk. divs. as of ex-div. date. Bold denotes diluted EPS (FASB 128). E-Estimated. NA-Not Available. NM-Not Meaningful. NR-Not Ranked.

Office—32 Avenue of the Americas, New York, NY 10013-2412. **Tel**—(212) 387-5400. **Website**—http://www.att.com Chrmn & CEO—C. M. Armstrong.**Pres**—J. Zeglis. **SVP & CFO**—D. Somers. **VP & Treas**—E. M. Dwyer.**VP & Secy**—M. J. Wasser. **Investor Contact**—MaryAnn Nibeojeski. **Dirs**—C. M. Armstrong, K. T. Derr, M. K. Eickhoff, W. Y. Elisha, G. M. C. Fisher, D. V. Fites, R. S. Larsen, D. F. McHenry, M. I. Sovern, T. H. Wyman, J. Zeglis.**Transfer Agent**—First Chicago Trust Co. of New York, Jersey City, NJ. **Incorporated**—in New York in 1885. **Empl**—127,800. **S&P Analyst:** Philip D. Wohl

Atlantic Richfield   244

NYSE Symbol **ARC**

In S&P 500

12-SEP-98

Industry:
Oil (Domestic Integrated)

Summary: This major oil producer in Alaska and leading marketer of gasoline in California and throughout the West also has interests in coal and chemicals.

S&P Opinion: Hold (★★★)	Recent Price • 65¾	Yield • 4.3%
	52 Wk Range • 87¼-56¼	12-Mo. P/E • 17.0

Quantitative Evaluations

Outlook
(1 Lowest—5 Highest)
• **1**

Fair Value
• **55½**

Risk
• **Low**

Earn./Div. Rank
• **B+**

Technical Eval.
• **NA**

Rel. Strength Rank
(1 Lowest—99 Highest)
• **81**

Insider Activity
• **NA**

Earnings vs. Previous Year
▲=Up ▼=Down ▶=No Change

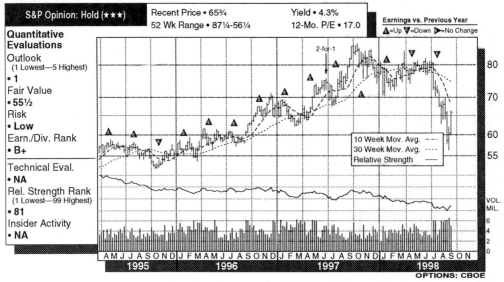

10 Week Mov. Avg. - - -
30 Week Mov. Avg. ....
Relative Strength ——

OPTIONS: CBOE

Overview - 27-MAY-98

Higher worldwide natural gas prices and increased oil and natural gas production boosted exploration and production earnings in 1997, despite lower oil prices. Total production is expected to increase 2% in 1998, though profits will be hindered by lower commodity prices. Refining and marketing earnings rose in 1997, on increased product sales and improved margins. The outlook for refining margins in the company's core west coast market is positive. However, the retail environment in the region remains difficult, and is characterized by frequent price wars. The recently announced acquisition of Union Texas Petroleum will allow ARC to add to its reserve base, primarily in its existing core operating areas. The company recently disposed of its interest in Lyondell Petrochemical, and we have begun to question ARC's commitment to remain in the chemicals business over the long term.

Valuation - 27-MAY-98

The shares have declined about 2.0% in 1998 to date, amid falling oil and gas prices. However, the shares appear fairly valued at this time, trading at about 20X our 1998 EPS forecast, and the outlook for continued oil price weakness over the remainder of 1998 may restrain the shares in the near term. For the long term, repositioning of the asset base overseas, where there are a number of potentially high reward projects under development, should provide above-average return. In January 1997, ARC began production from its Yacheng 13-1 natural gas field in China, that country's largest offshore gas project. The Yadana gas project in Myanmar also holds great promise. We are less optimistic about near-term prospects for the company's investment in LUKoil, despite the region's vast oil and gas reserves, given the political and geological risks associated with Russian joint ventures.

Key Stock Statistics

S&P EPS Est. 1998	4.00	Tang. Bk. Value/Share	25.11
P/E on S&P Est. 1998	16.5	Beta	0.78
S&P EPS Est. 1999	4.55	Shareholders	88,400
Dividend Rate/Share	2.85	Market cap. (B)	$ 21.1
Shs. outstg. (M)	321.1	Inst. holdings	66%
Avg. daily vol. (M)	1.596		

Value of $10,000 invested 5 years ago: $ 14,879

Fiscal Year Ending Dec. 31

	1998	1997	1996	1995	1994	1993
Revenues (Million $)						
1Q	3,550	5,044	4,534	4,244	3,800	4,510
2Q	2,654	4,587	4,960	4,423	4,170	4,670
3Q	—	4,553	4,748	3,872	4,270	4,550
4Q	—	4,500	5,129	4,393	4,244	4,760
Yr.	—	19,272	19,169	16,739	16,550	17,337
Earnings Per Share ($)						
1Q	0.64	1.41	1.13	0.98	0.46	0.80
2Q	0.19	1.55	1.33	1.20	0.07	0.83
3Q	—	1.57	1.47	0.96	1.33	0.21
4Q	—	1.17	1.16	1.06	0.95	-1.03
Yr.	E4.00	5.77	5.09	4.21	2.81	0.83

Next earnings report expected: late October

Dividend Data (Dividends have been paid since 1927.)

Amount ($)	Date Decl.	Ex-Div. Date	Stock of Record	Payment Date
0.713	Oct. 27	Nov. 12	Nov. 14	Dec. 15 '97
0.713	Jan. 26	Feb. 11	Feb. 13	Mar. 13 '98
0.713	May. 04	May. 13	May. 15	Jun. 15 '98
0.713	Jul. 27	Aug. 12	Aug. 14	Sep. 15 '98

A Division of The McGraw·Hill Companies

Business Summary - 27-MAY-98

Atlantic Richfield (ARC), which has traditionally relied upon its state-of-the art oil and gas recovery techniques to prolong the productive lives of older fields, now plans a major acquisition, in an attempt to bolster its reserve base. In May 1998, ARC announced that it had reached an agreement to acquire Union Texas Petroleum (NYSE: UTH), for about $3.3 billion. The acquisition will immediately add 140,000 barrels per day of oil equivalent to ARC's production levels, and 573 million barrels of oil equivalent to ARC's proved reserves. Atlantic Richfield considers UTH to be a particularly good fit, as over 90% of its assets are located in ARC's core operating areas of Alaska, Indonesia, the North Sea and Venezuela.

In 1997, net production of crude oil and natural gas liquids averaged 377,200 bbl. a day in Alaska, 180,700 bbl. a day in the lower 48, and 82,600 b/d international. Total natural gas production was 1.91 Bcf a day. Net proved reserves at 1997 year end stood at 2,699 million bbl. of crude and natural gas liquids (up from 2,521 million bbl. at year end 1996), and 8,472 Bcf of natural gas (8,123). ARC owns 82% of Vastar Resources (NYSE: VRI), an exploration and production company. ARC's capital budget for 1998 has been set at $3.8 billion, up from 1997's actual $3.0 billion, of which more

than 75% was spent on exploration and development. Nearly 70% of the projected 1998 budget is earmarked for exploration and production spending, including expenditures on major development programs in the Gulf of Mexico, Alaska and Indonesia.

The company also participates in crude oil refining and marketing, also known as the downstream. ARC is a leading marketer of gasoline in the five-state region of California, Oregon, Washington, Nevada and Arizona, where the company operates a combined 1,500 retail outlets. In 1997, refinery runs averaged 452,200 b/d and domestic petroleum products sales averaged 543,800 b/d.

The company owns 83% of ARCO Chemical (NYSE: RCM), which makes and markets basic commodity chemicals. ARCO Chemical is a leading producer of propylene oxide (PO), and the co-product tertiary butyl alcohol, which is used to manufacture MTBE, a gasoline additive. PO is a key ingredient in the manufacturing of consumer products. In September 1997, ARC sold its 49.9% interest in Lyondell Petrochemical (NYSE: LYO). In order to focus on its core PO business, ARC sold its U.S.-based plastics business in 1996. In April 1997, ARC announced its plans to exit the coal business; the company is engaged in final discussions for the sale of it U.S. based coal assets.

Per Share Data ($)

(Year Ended Dec. 31)	1997	1996	1995	1994	1993	1992	1991	1990	1989	1988
Tangible Bk. Val.	26.98	24.21	20.84	19.14	18.95	20.91	20.88	21.77	19.48	17.86
Cash Flow	11.11	10.11	9.23	7.92	5.91	9.06	7.45	10.01	10.38	8.80
Earnings	5.77	5.09	4.21	2.81	0.83	3.69	2.19	5.10	5.63	4.39
Dividends	4.22	2.75	2.75	2.75	2.75	2.75	2.75	2.50	2.25	2.00
Payout Ratio	73%	54%	65%	98%	331%	74%	123%	47%	38%	44%
Prices - High	87¼	71¼	59	56¼	63⅞	60⅞	67⅞	71⅛	57¼	45½
- Low	62¼	53¾	50¼	46¼	50¼	49⅛	49⅝	52¾	40¼	33¾
P/E Ratio - High	15	14	14	20	77	16	31	14	10	10
- Low	11	11	12	16	61	13	23	10	7	8

Income Statement Analysis (Million $)

Revs.	18,684	18,592	15,819	15,035	17,189	17,503	17,037	18,008	15,351	17,626
Oper. Inc.	4,074	4,459	3,644	3,039	2,964	3,554	3,491	4,195	3,859	4,715
Depr.	1,746	1,633	1,641	1,671	1,652	1,736	1,701	1,628	1,650	1,597
Int. Exp.	422	690	799	796	771	877	971	914	894	908
Pretax Inc.	2,877	2,709	2,173	1,368	634	1,907	1,160	2,820	3,161	2,820
Eff. Tax Rate	32%	35%	32%	28%	52%	36%	36%	38%	36%	41%
Net Inc.	1,889	1,663	1,376	919	269	1,193	709	1,688	1,953	1,583

Balance Sheet & Other Fin. Data (Million $)

Cash	533	2,244	3,106	4,385	3,747	2,915	2,549	3,031	3,009	1,905
Curr. Assets	3,576	5,433	5,888	6,813	6,231	5,646	5,338	6,048	5,414	4,757
Total Assets	25,322	25,715	23,999	24,563	23,894	24,256	24,492	23,864	22,261	21,514
Curr. Liab.	4,745	5,303	3,963	4,488	4,335	4,821	5,213	4,260	3,437	3,264
LT Debt	4,414	5,593	6,708	7,198	7,089	6,227	5,989	5,997	5,313	5,665
Common Eqty.	8,679	7,801	6,702	6,216	6,061	6,650	6,755	7,065	6,469	6,143
Total Cap.	16,176	16,278	16,580	16,604	16,382	16,258	16,367	16,895	15,551	15,917
Cap. Exp.	2,985	2,141	1,699	1,658	2,070	2,278	3,239	2,718	2,105	3,304
Cash Flow	3,633	3,296	3,017	2,587	1,918	2,926	2,407	3,313	3,599	3,176
Curr. Ratio	0.8	1.0	1.5	1.5	1.4	1.2	1.0	1.4	1.6	1.5
% LT Debt of Cap.	27.3	34.3	40.5	43.4	43.3	38.3	36.6	35.5	34.2	35.6
% Net Inc.of Revs.	9.9	8.8	8.7	6.1	1.6	6.8	4.2	9.4	12.7	9.0
% Ret. on Assets	7.4	6.7	5.7	3.8	1.1	4.9	2.9	7.4	9.1	7.3
% Ret. on Equity	22.9	22.8	21.3	14.9	4.2	17.7	10.3	25.3	31.6	26.9

Data as orig. reptd.; bef. results of disc. opers. and/or spec. items. Per share data adj. for stk. divs. as of ex-div. date. Revs. in qtrly tble. incl. excise taxes and other inc. Bold denotes diluted EPS (FASB 128). E-Estimated. NA-Not Available. NM-Not Meaningful. NR-Not Ranked.

Office—515 South Flower St., Los Angeles, CA 90071-2256. **Tel**—(213) 486-3511. **Website**—http://www.arco.com **Chrmn & CEO**—M. R. Bowlin. **Pres**—W. E. Wade, Jr.**EVP & CFO**—M. L. Knowles. **SVP & Treas**—T. G. Dallas.**SVP & Secy**—B. G. Whitmore.**Investor Contact**—Dennis Schiffel **Dirs**—F. D. Boren, M. R. Bowlin, A. G. Fernandes, J. Gavin, H. H. Gray, M. L. Knowles, K. Kresa, D. T. McLaughlin, J. B. Slaughter, G. L. Tooker, W. E. Wade, Jr., H. Wendt. **Transfer Agent & Registrar**—First Chicago Trust Co. of New York, Jersey City, NJ. **Incorporated**—in Pennsylvania in 1870; reincorporated in Delaware in 1985. **Empl**— 24,000. **S&P Analyst:** Norman Rosenberg

STANDARD &POOR'S
STOCK REPORTS

Autodesk, Inc.

3176J

Nasdaq Symbol **ADSK**

In S&P 500

12-SEP-98

Industry:
Computer (Software & Services)

Summary: Autodesk develops, markets and supports computer-aided design and drafting (CAD) software, including its flagship AutoCAD program, for use on desktop computers and workstations.

S&P Opinion: Accumulate (★★★★)

Recent Price • 25¼
52 Wk Range • 51⅛-22¼

Yield • 0.9%
12-Mo. P/E • 13.8

Earnings vs. Previous Year
▲=Up ▼=Down ▶=No Change

Quantitative Evaluations

Outlook
(1 Lowest—5 Highest)
• **5+**

Fair Value
• **46¼**

Risk
• **Average**

Earn./Div. Rank
• **B+**

Technical Eval.
• **NA**

Rel. Strength Rank
(1 Lowest—99 Highest)
• **32**

Insider Activity
• **Favorable**

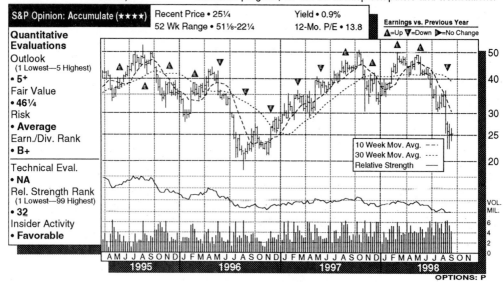

10 Week Mov. Avg. ----
30 Week Mov. Avg. ····
Relative Strength ——

OPTIONS: P

Overview - 27-AUG-98

Revenue growth should slow down in the second half of FY 99 (Jan.), due to continued significant weakness in Asian markets. Revenue growth accelerated following the May 1997 introduction of Release 14, an upgraded version of AutoCAD. Future growth will be aided by the diversification of the company's product line. With 20 new products introduced in FY 98, non-AutoCAD revenues now provide about 30% of the total, and most growth in FY 99 will come from these non-AutoCAD products. Due to the slower revenue growth expected, margins should also narrow in the second half, although they should widen for the full fiscal year. Comparisons will be helped by the absence of the FY 98 first quarter charge of $1.26 a share associated with the acquisition of Softdesk, and for purchased technology. However, the pending acquisition of Discreet Logic should be slightly dilutive to earnings in FY 00.

Valuation - 27-AUG-98

The shares have fallen more than 50% from highs earlier in the year, reflecting concerns about weakness in Asia, as well as potential earnings dilution from the recently announced acquisition of Discreet Logic. However, ADSK's business still appears to be strong across all other geographies. AutoCAD Release 14 was introduced in the FY 98 second quarter, and has spurred a revenue and earnings rebound. We believe the diversification of the company's product line over the past few years will aid future earnings growth. Non-AutoCAD revenues grew 70% in FY 98, and most of the company's growth in FY 99 will come from these products. The next version of AutoCAD should arrive in FY 00. With the successful diversification of its product line with new products targeted at specific industries, we believe the huge sell-off was unwarranted, and recommend accumulating the shares.

Key Stock Statistics

S&P EPS Est. 1999	2.11	Tang. Bk. Value/Share	7.87
P/E on S&P Est. 1999	12.0	Beta	1.55
S&P EPS Est. 2000	2.60	Shareholders	1,600
Dividend Rate/Share	0.24	Market cap. (B)	$ 1.2
Shs. outstg. (M)	47.0	Inst. holdings	79%
Avg. daily vol. (M)	1.478		

Value of $10,000 invested 5 years ago: $ 11,429

Fiscal Year Ending Jan. 31

	1999	1998	1997	1996	1995	1994
Revenues (Million $)						
1Q	187.2	119.0	136.3	138.7	106.6	105.4
2Q	186.6	154.1	128.8	140.7	110.3	106.9
3Q	—	162.2	116.7	128.5	108.2	98.18
4Q	—	181.8	115.0	126.3	129.6	102.1
Yr.	—	617.1	496.7	546.9	454.6	405.6
Earnings Per Share ($)						
1Q	**0.55**	-1.15	0.39	0.51	0.33	0.31
2Q	**0.18**	**0.34**	0.22	0.52	0.34	0.33
3Q	**E0.43**	**0.41**	0.13	0.38	0.32	0.30
4Q	**E0.57**	**0.60**	0.13	0.34	0.15	0.32
Yr.	**E2.11**	**0.31**	0.88	1.76	1.14	1.25

Next earnings report expected: late November

Dividend Data (Dividends have been paid since 1989.)

Amount ($)	Date Decl.	Ex-Div. Date	Stock of Record	Payment Date
0.060	Sep. 25	Oct. 08	Oct. 10	Oct. 24 '97
0.060	Dec. 18	Jan. 07	Jan. 09	Jan. 23 '98
0.060	Mar. 27	Apr. 07	Apr. 10	Apr. 24 '98
0.060	Jul. 01	Jul. 08	Jul. 10	Jul. 24 '98

A Division of The McGraw·Hill Companies

Business Summary - 27-AUG-98

Autodesk designs, develops, markets and supports design automation and multimedia software products for use on personal computers and workstations.

The Design segment includes the company's principal product, AutoCAD, a general-purpose design and drafting tool. AutoCAD, which accounted for about 70% of revenues in FY 98 (Jan.), automates the design and drafting process by enabling users to interactively create, store and edit a wide variety of drawings. The drawing data may be exchanged with other applications software, databases and larger computer-based CAD systems. The company also offers add-on and support software packages for AutoCAD. The most current version, AutoCAD release 14, was introduced in May 1997. AutoCAD has an installed base of over 1.9 million units worldwide.

Other design products include Mechanical Desktop, a mechanical design program; AutoCAD OEM, for creating solutions with scaled feature sets; AutoCAD Map, a CAD-based automated mapping product; Autodesk MapGuide, a Web-based decision support system with a geographic component; and Autodesk World, which allows for the management of geographic-based data.

The Personal Solutions Group develops easy-to-use, affordable tools for professionals, occasional users or consumers who design, draft and diagram. Products include AutoCAD LT, a low-cost CAD package offering 2-D and basic 3-D drafting capabilities; AutoSketch, a low-cost, entry-level 2D drafting package; and Picture This Home! Kitchen & Bath, remodeling programs that help plan and visualize customized designs.

The company's Kinetix division develops 3D content-creation software to computer industry professionals, including visualization, animation and simulation software. Products include: 3D Studio MAX, 3D modeling and animation software for the PC; and 3D Studio VIZ, a design tool that enables users to express ideas on-screen, in 3D.

In March 1997, the company acquired Softdesk, Inc., a supplier of AutoCAD-based application software for the architecture, engineering and construction markets. A charge of $1.26 a share resulted from the transaction. In the second quarter of FY 97, ADSK acquired Teleos Research. The company recorded a charge of $3.2 million ($0.08 a share) related to the acquisition.

In April 1998, ADSK received notice that the Federal Trade Commission (FTC) is investigating its business practices.

In August 1998, ADSK agreed to acquire Discreet Logic, a developer of systems and software used in the creation of digital imagery for video, broadcast, and feature films. ADSK will issue 0.525 of a common share for each Discreet share, giving the deal a value of about $520 million as of August 19.

Per Share Data ($)

(Year Ended Jan. 31)	1998	1997	1996	1995	1994	1993	1992	1991	1990	1989
Tangible Bk. Val.	6.29	5.40	7.39	6.85	6.25	5.58	5.43	4.47	3.28	3.08
Cash Flow	1.19	1.62	2.27	1.48	1.51	1.11	1.38	1.38	1.06	0.74
Earnings	0.31	0.88	1.76	1.14	1.25	0.88	1.16	1.15	0.95	0.68
Dividends	0.24	0.24	0.24	0.24	0.48	0.24	0.23	0.20	0.80	Nil
Payout Ratio	77%	27%	14%	20%	38%	26%	20%	17%	84%	Nil
Cal. Yrs.	1997	1996	1995	1994	1993	1992	1991	1990	1989	1988
Prices - High	51⅛	44¼	53	41½	28⅜	28¼	31⅛	30⅛	21¾	15⅝
- Low	28	18½	31¼	21⅛	18½	11⅝	14¾	16	13¼	8
P/E Ratio - High	NM	50	30	36	23	32	27	26	23	23
- Low	NM	21	18	19	15	13	13	14	14	12

Income Statement Analysis (Million $)

	1998	1997	1996	1995	1994	1993	1992	1991	1990	1989
Revs.	632	510	547	465	419	368	285	238	179	117
Oper. Inc.	147	99	154	130	103	80.0	91.4	93.1	73.4	50.2
Depr.	43.9	34.8	25.2	17.4	13.1	11.3	11.2	11.2	5.4	3.3
Int. Exp.	Nil	Nil	Nil	Nil	NA	NA	NA	NA	NA	NA
Pretax Inc.	55.0	66.5	138	89.1	96.8	69.8	92.3	92.0	76.4	54.2
Eff. Tax Rate	72%	38%	37%	37%	36%	37%	37%	38%	39%	40%
Net Inc.	15.4	41.6	87.8	56.6	62.2	43.9	57.8	56.8	46.4	32.7

Balance Sheet & Other Fin. Data (Million $)

	1998	1997	1996	1995	1994	1993	1992	1991	1990	1989
Cash	96.1	183	193	240	178	153	171	124	106	108
Curr. Assets	308	311	348	373	280	249	248	188	145	133
Total Assets	534	492	518	482	405	358	328	265	194	170
Curr. Liab.	199	150	144	155	102	84.1	57.0	43.8	31.1	18.6
LT Debt	Nil	Nil	Nil	Nil	Nil	Nil	Nil	0.2	0.4	0.3
Common Eqty.	303	244	342	323	297	268	267	218	159	148
Total Cap.	304	247	344	326	302	273	271	221	163	151
Cap. Exp.	15.0	17.4	16.3	20.0	21.5	11.0	9.9	21.1	13.4	9.2
Cash Flow	59.2	76.4	113	74.0	75.3	55.2	68.9	67.9	51.8	36.0
Curr. Ratio	1.5	2.1	2.4	2.4	2.7	3.0	4.3	4.3	4.7	7.2
% LT Debt of Cap.	Nil	Nil	Nil	Nil	Nil	Nil	Nil	0.1	0.2	0.2
% Net Inc.of Revs.	2.4	8.2	16.1	12.2	14.8	11.9	20.3	23.9	26.0	27.9
% Ret. on Assets	3.0	8.3	17.6	12.8	16.4	12.9	19.4	24.6	25.3	22.1
% Ret. on Equity	5.6	14.2	26.4	18.3	22.1	16.6	23.7	30.0	30.1	24.8

Data as orig. reptd.; bef. results of disc. opers. and/or spec. items. Per share data adj. for stk. divs. as of ex-div. date. Bold denotes diluted EPS (FASB 128). E-Estimated. NA-Not Available. NM-Not Meaningful. NR-Not Ranked.

Office—111 McInnis Parkway, San Rafael, CA 94903. **Tel**—(415) 507-5000. **Website**—http://www.autodesk.com **Chrmn & CEO**—C. A. Bartz. **Pres & COO**—E. B. Herr. **VP & CFO**—S. Cakebread. **VP, Treas & Investor Contact**—Christine Tsingos (415-507-6704). **Dirs**—C. Bartz, M. A. Bertelsen, C. W. Beveridge, J. H. Dawson,, P. S. Otellini, M. A. Taylor, M. Topfer. **Transfer Agent**—Harris Trust & Savings Bank, Chicago. **Incorporated**—in California in 1982; reincorporated in Delaware in 1994. **Empl**— 2,470. **S&P Analyst:** Brian Goodstadt

12-SEP-98

Industry: Services (Data Processing)

Summary: This company is the largest independent U.S. computing services firm, and one of the largest in the world.

S&P Opinion: Accumulate (★★★★)	Recent Price • 72	Yield • 0.7%
	52 Wk Range • 75½-46½	12-Mo. P/E • 36.4

Quantitative Evaluations

Outlook (1 Lowest—5 Highest)
• **2⁻**

Fair Value
• **70½**

Risk
• **Low**

Earn./Div. Rank
• **A+**

Technical Eval.
• **Bullish** since 8/96

Rel. Strength Rank (1 Lowest—99 Highest)
• **96**

Insider Activity
• **Unfavorable**

Earnings vs. Previous Year
▲=Up ▼=Down ▶=No Change

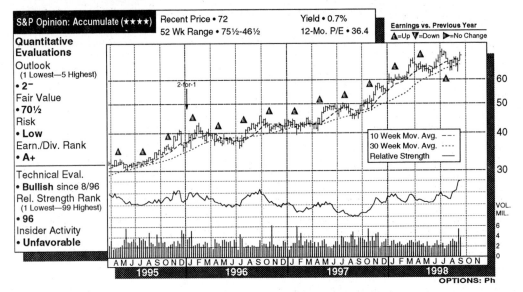

10 Week Mov. Avg. — · —
30 Week Mov. Avg. - - - -
Relative Strength ———

OPTIONS: Ph

Overview - 31-AUG-98

Revenues in FY 99 (Jun.) should grow approximately 15%, aided by gains in each of the company's four major business segments, stemming from its strong competitive position. In addition, revenue growth should be bolstered by contributions from continued acquisitions. The employer services segment should see double-digit growth, aided by robust sales activity and solid client retention rates. Brokerage services growth should be strong, aided by increased terminal count and significantly higher trading volume. Dealer services revenues should be aided by strong repeat business. Claims services are expected to continue to benefit from market share gains. Operating margins should widen, but a higher tax rate and increased shares outstanding should limit EPS growth to 13% to 16%.

Valuation - 31-AUG-98

The shares have been in a long uptrend, reflecting solid, consistent earnings growth. AUD should generate annual earnings growth in the mid-teens over the next several years, driven by continued gains in its four major businesses. Strategic acquisitions should continue to add to the company's business and strengthen its competitive position. The company may eventually add a fifth leg to its business, through acquisition. The stock merits its premium valuation in light of the focused business strategy being executed by AUD's strong management team, as well as the company's record of predictable earnings growth, helped by a client retention rate of over 90%. AUD has posted 148 consecutive quarters of record sales and earnings, and 37 straight years of double-digit earnings per share growth. We expect the shares to outperform the market in the months ahead.

Key Stock Statistics

S&P EPS Est. 1998	NA	Tang. Bk. Value/Share		5.99
P/E on S&P Est. 1998	NA	Beta		0.60
S&P EPS Est. 1999	2.32	Shareholders		28,400
Dividend Rate/Share	0.53	Market cap. (B)		$ 21.7
Shs. outstg. (M)	301.0	Inst. holdings		71%
Avg. daily vol. (M)	0.776			

Value of $10,000 invested 5 years ago: $ 28,528

Fiscal Year Ending Jun. 30

	1998	1997	1996	1995	1994	1993
Revenues (Million $)						
1Q	1,039	910.7	747.1	622.3	552.0	495.0
2Q	1,148	995.6	819.7	672.6	577.7	518.0
3Q	1,309	1,126	1,032	799.0	674.4	613.0
4Q	1,302	1,080	967.9	799.9	664.9	596.6
Yr.	4,798	4,112	3,567	2,894	2,469	2,223
Earnings Per Share ($)						
1Q	0.36	0.32	0.28	0.24	0.21	0.18
2Q	**0.49**	**0.43**	0.39	0.34	0.28	0.25
3Q	**0.62**	0.56	0.49	0.43	0.37	0.33
4Q	**0.52**	0.44	0.42	0.37	0.32	0.28
Yr.	**1.98**	1.76	1.57	1.38	1.19	1.04

Next earnings report expected: mid October

Dividend Data (Dividends have been paid since 1974.)

Amount ($)	Date Decl.	Ex-Div. Date	Stock of Record	Payment Date
0.133	Nov. 11	Dec. 10	Dec. 12	Jan. 01 '98
0.133	Jan. 27	Mar. 11	Mar. 13	Apr. 01 '98
0.133	May. 18	Jun. 10	Jun. 12	Jul. 01 '98
0.133	Aug. 13	Sep. 09	Sep. 11	Oct. 01 '98

STANDARD
&POOR'S
STOCK REPORTS

Automatic Data Processing, Inc.

256

12-SEP-98

Business Summary - 31-AUG-98

AUD provides a broad range of data processing services in four business segments: employer, brokerage, dealer and claims. The company is the largest independent computing services company in the U.S.

Employer services accounted for 55% of revenues in FY 97 (Jun.). Payroll services, with more than 395,000 clients, contributes 85% of the segment's revenue. AUD provides payroll, human resource, benefits administration, time and attendance, and tax filing and reporting services in the U.S., Canada and Europe.

Brokerage services (22% of revenues) include securities processing, real-time market information, and investor communications services to the financial services industry. The company is the largest provider of securities processing services in North America. In FY 97, AUD processed approximately 20% of the retail equity transactions in the U.S. and Canada, handling an average of over 475,000 trades per day.

Dealer services (16% of revenues) provide computing, data and professional services to automobile and truck dealers and manufacturers worldwide. More than

18,000 dealers use ADP's on-site systems and communications networks to manage every area of sales and operations.

Other businesses (7% of revenues) primarily include claims services to the property and casualty insurance industry. AUD offers a broad line of products to help clients accurately estimate auto damage, bodily injury and property claims.

In FY 97, the company acquired Staff Management Systems of Florida, a leading provider of employee leasing services; AT&T's auto dealer management systems business in Europe; and Health Benefits American, a benefits management firm, all for undisclosed amounts.

In FY 97, AUD repurchased approximately 3.2 million shares of its common stock.

The company's capital expenditures were approximately $230 million in FY 98, and its cash flow was about $600 million. Some of this cash flow will be used to continue repurchasing shares of common stock. About $30 million was spent in FY 98 to address the company's year 2000 computer system issues.

Per Share Data ($)

(Year Ended Jun. 30)	1998	1997	1996	1995	1994	1993	1992	1991	1990	1989
Tangible Bk. Val.	NA	4.60	3.71	4.83	3.85	3.25	2.65	3.81	3.82	2.53
Cash Flow	NA	2.53	2.27	1.99	1.71	1.53	1.34	1.23	1.10	0.98
Earnings	1.98	1.80	1.57	1.39	1.19	1.04	0.92	0.81	0.72	0.64
Dividends	0.51	0.45	0.39	0.31	0.27	0.24	0.21	0.18	0.16	0.14
Payout Ratio	26%	25%	25%	22%	23%	23%	23%	22%	22%	21%
Prices - High	75½	62⅝	43⅜	41⅛	29⅞	28½	27⅞	23¼	15⅛	12¾
- Low	57½	39½	35⅝	28¾	23⅞	23½	19⅜	12½	11⅜	9
P/E Ratio - High	38	36	28	30	25	27	30	28	21	20
- Low	29	22	23	21	20	23	21	15	16	14

Income Statement Analysis (Million $)

	1998	1997	1996	1995	1994	1993	1992	1991	1990	1989
Revs.	NA	4,112	3,567	2,894	2,469	2,223	1,941	1,772	1,714	1,678
Oper. Inc.	NA	1,005	867	731	615	547	470	422	411	415
Depr.	NA	223	202	173	148	140	116	114	113	124
Int. Exp.	NA	27.8	29.7	24.3	20.8	19.8	12.3	8.2	12.1	19.7
Pretax Inc.	NA	724	635	534	446	387	342	300	285	272
Eff. Tax Rate	NA	29%	28%	26%	25%	24%	25%	24%	26%	31%
Net Inc.	NA	514	455	395	334	294	256	228	212	188

Balance Sheet & Other Fin. Data (Million $)

	1998	1997	1996	1995	1994	1993	1992	1991	1990	1989
Cash	NA	1,025	636	698	591	368	414	320	396	373
Curr. Assets	NA	1,805	1,454	1,211	985	771	734	622	735	728
Total Assets	NA	4,383	3,840	3,201	2,706	2,439	2,169	1,565	1,692	1,679
Curr. Liab.	NA	1,020	836	543	478	416	367	352	382	377
LT Debt	NA	401	404	390	373	348	333	44.0	53.0	260
Common Eqty.	NA	2,661	2,315	2,097	1,691	1,494	1,297	1,053	1,127	950
Total Cap.	NA	3,165	2,832	2,506	2,098	1,917	1,693	1,164	1,238	1,248
Cap. Exp.	NA	175	164	118	111	87.0	56.0	70.0	82.0	139
Cash Flow	NA	737	656	567	482	434	372	342	325	291
Curr. Ratio	NA	1.8	1.7	2.2	2.1	1.9	2.0	1.8	1.9	1.9
% LT Debt of Cap.	NA	12.7	14.3	15.6	17.8	18.1	19.7	3.8	4.3	20.8
% Net Inc.of Revs.	NA	12.5	12.7	13.6	13.5	13.2	13.2	12.9	12.4	11.2
% Ret. on Assets	NA	12.5	12.9	13.4	13.0	12.7	13.6	14.5	12.5	11.6
% Ret. on Equity	NA	20.6	20.6	20.8	21.0	21.0	21.7	21.6	20.3	20.0

Data as orig. reptd.; bef. results of disc. opers. and/or spec. items. Per share data adj. for stk. divs. as of ex-div. date. Bold denotes diluted EPS (FASB 128). E-Estimated. NA-Not Available. NM-Not Meaningful. NR-Not Ranked.

Office—One ADP Blvd., Roseland, NJ 07068. **Tel**—(201) 994-5000. **Website**—http://www.adp.com **Chrmn, Pres & CEO**—A. F. Weinbach.**CFO**—R. J. Haviland.**VP & Secy**—J. B. Benson. **Dirs**—G. C. Butler, J. A. Califano Jr., L. G. Cooperman, G. H. Heilmeier, A. D. Jordan, H. M. Krueger, C. P. Lazarus, F. V. Malek, H. Taub, L. A. Tisch, A. F. Weinbach, J. S. Weston. **Transfer Agent**—ChaseMellon Shareholder Services, Ridgefield Park, NJ. **Incorporated**—in Delaware in 1961. **Empl**— 30,000. **S&P Analyst**: Brian Goodstadt

AutoZone, Inc.
257M
NYSE Symbol **AZO**

In S&P 500

12-SEP-98

Industry: Retail (Specialty)

Summary: This retailer of automotive parts and accessories operates more than 2,000 outlets, mainly in the Sunbelt and Midwest.

S&P Opinion: Accumulate (★★★★)	Recent Price • 24⅛	Yield • Nil
	52 Wk Range • 38-23	12-Mo. P/E • 17.0

Quantitative Evaluations

Outlook (1 Lowest—5 Highest)
• **3⁻**

Fair Value
• **28¾**

Risk
• **Average**

Earn./Div. Rank
• **B+**

Technical Eval.
• **Bearish** since 8/98

Rel. Strength Rank (1 Lowest—99 Highest)
• **31**

Insider Activity
• **Unfavorable**

Earnings vs. Previous Year
▲=Up ▼=Down ▶=No Change

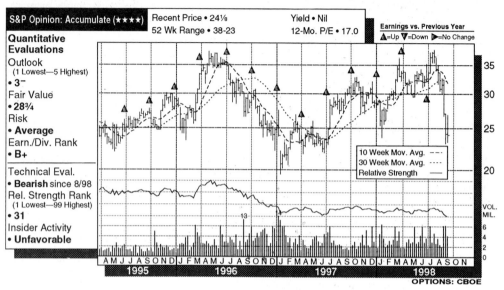

- 10 Week Mov. Avg. – – –
- 30 Week Mov. Avg. ·····
- Relative Strength ——

OPTIONS: CBOE

Overview - 04-JUN-98

Sales should continue to grow an average of 20% annually over the next several years, driven by acquisitions, new store openings, and sales increases at units already in operation. Recent acquisitions have expanded operations into California (Chief Auto Parts) and New England (Auto Palace) and into heavy-duty truck parts (TruckPro). Prospects are enhanced by the rising number and increasing complexity of aging motor vehicles that are in their prime repair years, and by a resumption of growth in domestic vehicle miles traveled. In FY 97 (Aug.), comparable-store sales increased 8%, primarily reflecting a new commercial sales program that targets commercial installers; same-store sales were up 4% in the first nine months of FY 98. AutoZone is one of the few quality, growing public companies in the fragmented automotive parts retailing industry. We expect earnings to increase about 19% in FY 98. Directors recently authorized the repurchase of up to $100 million of common stock.

Valuation - 04-JUN-98

The company is an innovator in the fragmented automotive parts retailing industry, and should continue to rapidly expand its store network, technological supremacy, industry market share and earnings. Shares of automotive parts retailers, including those of AutoZone, have fallen from their peaks, reflecting weakness in the do-it-yourself segment, and fears that sales and margins would shrink permanently, because of intense competition in the auto distribution business. We currently expect AutoZone to ride out this rough patch, which was probably induced by adverse weather and an accelerated commercial program rollout. If we are correct, and AZO maintains annual sales growth of 20% and profit margins of 7% or better, long-term shareholders should be rewarded with higher prices.

Key Stock Statistics

S&P EPS Est. 1998	1.50	Tang. Bk. Value/Share	8.02
P/E on S&P Est. 1998	16.1	Beta	0.80
S&P EPS Est. 1999	1.80	Shareholders	3,300
Dividend Rate/Share	Nil	Market cap. (B)	$ 3.7
Shs. outstg. (M)	152.7	Inst. holdings	64%
Avg. daily vol. (M)	1.088		

Value of $10,000 invested 5 years ago: $ 12,292

Fiscal Year Ending Aug. 31

	1998	1997	1996	1995	1994	1993
Revenues (Million $)						
1Q	675.3	569.1	463.0	389.8	322.9	253.0
2Q	607.1	538.0	425.8	364.1	303.2	242.0
3Q	743.7	637.9	524.2	425.5	358.2	282.8
4Q	—	946.4	829.6	628.8	523.8	439.2
Yr.	—	2,691	2,243	1,808	1,508	1,217
Earnings Per Share ($)						
1Q	0.31	0.25	0.23	0.19	0.15	0.12
2Q	**0.22**	0.19	0.18	0.16	0.14	0.11
3Q	**0.35**	0.30	0.25	0.22	0.19	0.14
4Q	**E0.64**	0.53	0.44	0.37	0.30	0.23
Yr.	**E1.50**	1.28	1.11	0.93	0.78	0.59

Next earnings report expected: late September

Dividend Data

No cash dividends have been paid.

A Division of The **McGraw-Hill** *Companies*

Business Summary - 04-JUN-98

AutoZone is a leading specialty retailer of automotive parts, chemicals and accessories, focusing primarily on "do-it-yourself" consumers. As of late May 1998, the company operated 2,001 stores in 38 states, mostly in the Sunbelt and Midwest. It also sells heavy-duty truck parts through 43 TruckPro stores acquired in May 1998. Key store data for recent fiscal years (Aug.):

	FY 97	FY 96
Number of stores	1,728	1,423
Store square footage (000)	11,611	9,437
Average sales per store (000)	$1,691	$1,702
Average sales per sq. ft.	$253	$258

Each store's product line includes new and remanufactured automotive hard parts, such as alternators, starters, water pumps, brake shoes and pads, carburetors, clutches and engines; maintenance items, such as oil, antifreeze, transmission, brake and power steering fluids, engine additives, protectants and waxes; and accessories, such as car stereos and floor mats. Parts are carried for domestic and foreign cars, vans and light trucks. AZO does not perform repairs or installations.

Stores, generally in high-visibility locations, range in size from 4,000 sq. ft. to 8,100 sq. ft., with new stores increasingly using a larger format. In FY 98, the 6,000 sq. ft. and larger superstores are expected to account for more than 85% of new and replacement units. Of the 1,728 stores in operation at August 31, 1997, 1,063 (62%) were in the 5,400 sq. ft. to 6,600 sq. ft. range. There were 264 stores in Texas, 166 in Ohio, 106 in Tennessee, 96 in Georgia, 70 in Louisiana, 77 in Alabama, 87 in North Carolina, 85 in Indiana, 72 in Missouri, 64 in Arizona, 61 in Mississippi, 60 in Oklahoma, 56 in Illinois, 49 in South Carolina, 82 in Florida, 39 in Arkansas, 48 in Kentucky, and the balance (124) in 10 other states. AZO owns 62% of the stores, with the balance leased.

An everyday low price strategy is used, and AZO attempts to be the price leader in hard parts. Stores carry between 17,000 and 20,000 stock-keeping units. The company also has a commercial sales program that delivers parts to professional repair shops.

In 1996, AZO acquired Alldata Corp., a developer and marketer of proprietary software that provides automotive diagnostic and repair information.

In May 1998, the company acquired TruckPro, which operates 43 stores selling heavy-duty truck parts in 14 states.

Per Share Data ($) (Year Ended Aug. 31)	1997	1996	1995	1994	1993	1992	1991	1990	1989	1988
Tangible Bk. Val.	7.00	5.65	4.54	3.51	2.62	2.02	1.38	0.53	0.33	NA
Cash Flow	1.78	1.52	1.25	1.00	0.74	0.53	0.40	0.26	0.14	0.09
Earnings	1.28	1.11	0.93	0.78	0.59	0.43	0.33	0.19	0.08	0.04
Dividends	Nil	Nil	Nil	Nil	Nil	Nil	Nil	Nil	Nil	Nil
Payout Ratio	Nil	Nil	Nil	Nil	Nil	Nil	Nil	Nil	Nil	Nil
Prices - High	32 3/4	37 5/8	27 3/4	30 3/4	29 1/2	21	17	NA	NA	NA
- Low	19 1/2	22 1/8	22	22	16 7/8	12 5/8	5 3/4	NA	NA	NA
P/E Ratio - High	26	34	30	39	50	48	52	NA	NA	NA
- Low	15	20	24	28	29	29	18	NA	NA	NA
Income Statement Analysis (Million $)										
Revs.	2,691	2,243	1,808	1,508	1,217	1,002	818	672	536	437
Oper. Inc.	399	332	276	224	163	118	89.0	62.0	32.0	24.0
Depr.	77.2	62.9	48.3	33.1	22.0	14.3	10.1	8.3	7.3	6.3
Int. Exp.	8.8	2.0	Nil	NA	NA	NA	7.3	10.9	9.8	8.8
Pretax Inc.	313	267	228	193	143	104	72.0	38.0	15.0	9.0
Eff. Tax Rate	38%	37%	39%	40%	39%	39%	39%	39%	43%	48%
Net Inc.	195	167	139	116	86.9	63.3	44.0	23.3	8.6	4.5
Balance Sheet & Other Fin. Data (Million $)										
Cash	4.7	3.9	6.4	56.2	84.5	57.8	9.0	0.9	0.8	NA
Curr. Assets	779	613	448	424	378	280	235	193	179	138
Total Assets	1,884	1,498	1,112	882	697	502	399	328	298	234
Curr. Liab.	592	613	418	339	286	207	178	165	142	102
LT Debt	198	Nil	Nil	4.0	4.3	6.8	7.0	73.9	93.1	77.1
Common Eqty.	1,075	866	685	528	397	282	209	85.0	59.0	50.0
Total Cap.	1,274	866	686	535	405	291	218	160	154	NA
Cap. Exp.	297	288	258	173	121	70.8	41.1	25.9	32.1	28.2
Cash Flow	272	230	187	149	109	77.6	54.0	31.6	16.0	10.7
Curr. Ratio	1.3	1.0	1.1	1.3	1.3	1.4	1.3	1.2	1.3	1.4
% LT Debt of Cap.	15.5	NM	NM	0.8	1.0	2.3	3.2	46.1	60.4	NA
% Net Inc.of Revs.	7.2	7.5	7.7	7.7	7.1	6.3	5.4	3.5	1.6	1.0
% Ret. on Assets	11.5	20.5	13.9	14.7	14.3	13.9	11.4	7.4	3.2	2.0
% Ret. on Equity	20.1	22.7	22.9	25.1	25.3	25.5	28.9	32.5	15.8	9.3

Data as orig. reptd.; bef. results of disc. opers. and/or spec. items. Per share data adj. for stk. divs. as of ex-div. date. Bold denotes diluted EPS (FASB 128). E-Estimated. NA-Not Available. NM-Not Meaningful. NR-Not Ranked.

Office—123 S. Front St., Memphis, TN 38103-3607. **Tel**—(901) 495-6500. **Fax**—(901) 495-8300. **Website**—http://www.autozone.com **Chrmn & CEO**—J. C. Adams Jr. **Pres & COO**—T. D. Vargo. **EVP & CFO**—R. J. Hunt. **SVP & Secy**—H. L. Goldsmith. **Investor Contact**—Emma Jo Kauffman (901-495-7005). **Dirs**—J. C. Adams Jr., A. M. Clarkson, T. S. Hanemann, G House, J. R. Hyde III, J. F. Keegan, H. R. Kravis, R. I. MacDonnell, M. W. Michelson, J. E. Moll, G. R. Roberts, R. Terry, T. D. Vargo. **Transfer Agent & Registrar**—First Chicago Trust Co. of New York, Jersey City, NJ. **Incorporated**—in Delaware in 1986; reincorporated in Nevada in 1991. **Empl**— 28,700. **S&P Analyst:** Efraim Levy

Avery Dennison 261

NYSE Symbol **AVY**

In S&P 500

12-SEP-98

Industry:
Manufacturing (Specialized)

Summary: This company is a leading worldwide manufacturer of pressure sensitive adhesives and materials, office products, labels, retail systems and specialty chemicals.

S&P Opinion: Accumulate (★★★★)	Recent Price • 48⅛	Yield • 1.7%
	52 Wk Range • 62-37	12-Mo. P/E • 23.1

Quantitative Evaluations

Outlook
(1 Lowest—5 Highest)
• **2+**

Fair Value
• **47¼**

Risk
• **Low**

Earn./Div. Rank
• **A-**

Technical Eval.
• **Bullish** since 9/98

Rel. Strength Rank
(1 Lowest—99 Highest)
• **58**

Insider Activity
• **Neutral**

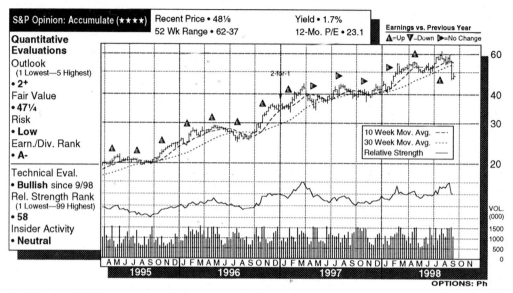

Earnings vs. Previous Year
▲=Up ▼=Down ▶=No Change

10 Week Mov. Avg. – – –
30 Week Mov. Avg. ‑‑‑‑‑
Relative Strength

OPTIONS: Ph

Overview - 11-AUG-98

The company intends to remain focused on its core self-adhesives materials, consumer and office products businesses and grow through internal as well as geographic expansion. Long-term growth is being driven by the widening use of non-impact printing systems for computers and for product tracking and information needs. The proliferation of high quality graphics on packaging and consumer products is also spurring sales of pressure sensitive labels. Sales are expected to continue to advance at a high single digit rate into 1999 on good volume growth as all business segments benefit from growing global economies and strong packaging, durable goods, office, consumer and retail markets. Growth of newer products, such as battery labels, postal stamps and children-related computer games, will also aid sales, boosted by capacity expansions in Germany, Asia and Latin America. Currency exchange rates are expected to become less unfavorable, and paper price deflation may remain modest. Profitability should continue at least at recent record levels as the higher volumes and continuing productivity gains offset higher new product development and marketing costs. The pace of stock buybacks may remain slower than in 1996, which saw the use of proceeds from the sale of assets. Capital spending in 1998 may rise to nearly $200 million from $177 million in 1997.

Valuation - 11-AUG-98

The shares have more than doubled since the end of 1995, reflecting continued good gains in sales and earnings. The dividend has been increased for 22nd consecutive years, a trend that should continue. We feel that the shares are still attractive in view of the positive earnings outlook for the company.

Key Stock Statistics

S&P EPS Est. 1998	2.22	Tang. Bk. Value/Share	6.01
P/E on S&P Est. 1998	21.7	Beta	0.71
S&P EPS Est. 1999	2.50	Shareholders	10,900
Dividend Rate/Share	0.84	Market cap. (B)	$ 5.6
Shs. outstg. (M)	117.0	Inst. holdings	65%
Avg. daily vol. (M)	0.321		

Value of $10,000 invested 5 years ago: $ 37,971

Fiscal Year Ending Dec. 31

	1998	1997	1996	1995	1994	1993
Revenues (Million $)						
1Q	843.0	828.9	796.6	773.2	667.7	666.5
2Q	871.5	844.8	797.7	780.5	718.6	662.2
3Q	—	835.6	819.3	783.5	733.7	638.1
4Q	—	836.4	808.9	776.7	736.7	641.9
Yr.	—	3,346	3,223	3,114	2,857	2,609
Earnings Per Share ($)						
1Q	0.52	0.45	0.38	0.33	0.23	0.19
2Q	0.55	0.47	0.40	0.34	0.25	0.20
3Q	E0.57	0.50	0.45	0.34	0.25	0.17
4Q	E0.58	0.52	0.46	0.35	0.26	0.17
Yr.	E2.22	1.93	1.68	1.35	0.98	0.72

Next earnings report expected: late October

Dividend Data (Dividends have been paid since 1964.)

Amount ($)	Date Decl.	Ex-Div. Date	Stock of Record	Payment Date
0.210	Oct. 23	Dec. 01	Dec. 03	Dec. 17 '97
0.210	Jan. 29	Mar. 02	Mar. 04	Mar. 18 '98
0.210	Apr. 23	Jun. 01	Jun. 03	Jun. 17 '98
0.210	Jul. 23	Aug. 31	Sep. 02	Sep. 16 '98

A Division of The **McGraw·Hill** *Companies*

Business Summary - 11-AUG-98

Avery Dennison Corp. is the leading global manufacturer of pressure sensitive technology and self-adhesive solutions for consumer products and label systems, including office products, product identification and control systems, and specialty tapes and chemicals. It is benefiting from the increasing demand for more informative labels on products, the expanding use of personal computers and printers, accelerating use of bar codes, and the growth of consumer spending in developing countries. AVY achieved record sales and earnings in 1997 for the sixth consecutive year, despite costs of investments in new businesses and products. Excluding the impact of currency, sales rose 6.6% and AVY realized a 24.8% return on equity. AVY was formed through the 1990 merger of Avery International Corp. and Dennison Manufacturing Corp. Segment contributions in 1997 were:

	Sales	Profits
Adhesives and materials	50%	47%
Consumer and converted products	50%	53%

Foreign operations, primarily in Europe, accounted for 36% of sales and 25% of profits in 1997. AVY is investing to build a business base in Asia Pacific, Latin America and Eastern Europe.

The adhesives and materials group includes Fasson-brand pressure sensitive, self-adhesive coated papers, plastic films and metal foils in roll and sheet form, graphic and decoration films and labels, specialty fastening and bonding tapes, and adhesives, protective coatings and electroconductive resins for industrial, automotive, aerospace, appliance, electronic, medical and consumer markets.

Consumer and office products consist of pressure sensitive labels, laser and ink-jet print labels and software, notebooks, binders, presentation and organizing systems, marking devices and numerous other products sold under the Avery, National, and Hi-Liter brands for office, home and school uses.

Converted products include custom labels and application and imprinting machines for the industrial, durable goods, consumer goods and electronic data processing markets; self-adhesive postal stamps; on battery testing labels; automotive decoration films; and Soabar brand tags, labels, printers, marking and coding systems, application devices, and plastic fasteners and cable ties for apparel, retail and industrial markets for use in identification, tracking and control applications.

AVY has bought back nearly 30 million common shares since 1991, for a total of $621 million. In July 1998, directors authorized the repurchase of up to another 5 million shares; about 700,000 shares remained to be acquired under prior authorizations. AVY plans to keep its total debt-to-capital ratio in the 35%-40% range. The ratio was 37.9% at June 30, 1998.

Per Share Data ($)

(Year Ended Dec. 31)	1997	1996	1995	1994	1993	1992	1991	1990	1989	1988
Tangible Bk. Val.	5.91	5.73	6.51	5.54	5.17	5.64	5.54	5.61	4.55	4.22
Cash Flow	3.03	2.76	2.36	1.91	1.54	1.44	1.25	0.78	1.55	1.40
Earnings	1.93	1.68	1.35	0.98	0.72	0.67	0.51	0.05	0.98	0.89
Dividends	0.72	0.62	0.56	0.49	0.45	0.41	0.38	0.32	0.27	0.23
Payout Ratio	37%	37%	41%	50%	62%	60%	74%	672%	28%	26%
Prices - High	45¾	36½	25⅛	18	15¾	14⅝	12⅞	16½	16⅝	13
- Low	33⅜	23¾	16⅝	13¼	12⅝	11⅝	9½	7¾	10½	9⅝
P/E Ratio - High	24	22	19	18	22	22	25	NM	17	15
- Low	17	14	12	13	17	17	19	NM	11	11

Income Statement Analysis (Million $)

	1997	1996	1995	1994	1993	1992	1991	1990	1989	1988
Revs.	3,346	3,223	3,114	2,857	2,609	2,623	2,545	2,590	1,732	1,582
Oper. Inc.	460	419	375	318	271	266	235	245	195	197
Depr.	117	113	108	103	95.4	93.9	92.3	90.1	50.3	45.1
Int. Exp.	31.7	40.9	47.5	45.7	45.5	44.9	42.6	43.3	24.3	26.3
Pretax Inc.	311	271	225	173	132	130	105	16.0	139	128
Eff. Tax Rate	34%	35%	36%	37%	37%	39%	40%	62%	38%	39%
Net Inc.	205	176	144	109	83.3	80.1	63.0	5.9	86.5	77.7

Balance Sheet & Other Fin. Data (Million $)

	1997	1996	1995	1994	1993	1992	1991	1990	1989	1988
Cash	3.3	3.8	27.0	3.1	5.8	3.9	5.3	6.5	3.1	5.9
Curr. Assets	794	805	800	677	615	661	701	847	506	503
Total Assets	2,047	2,037	1,964	1,763	1,639	1,684	1,740	1,890	1,142	1,119
Curr. Liab.	630	694	673	554	473	439	475	548	324	330
LT Debt	404	371	334	347	311	335	330	376	213	215
Common Eqty.	838	832	816	729	719	803	825	846	539	509
Total Cap.	1,292	1,247	1,191	1,116	1,075	1,205	1,235	1,310	818	790
Cap. Exp.	177	188	190	163	101	88.0	123	149	83.0	90.0
Cash Flow	322	289	252	212	179	174	155	96.0	137	123
Curr. Ratio	1.3	1.2	1.2	1.2	1.3	1.5	1.5	1.5	1.6	1.5
% LT Debt of Cap.	31.3	29.8	28.0	31.1	28.9	27.8	26.7	28.7	26.1	27.2
% Net Inc.of Revs.	6.1	5.5	4.6	3.8	3.2	3.1	2.5	0.2	5.0	4.9
% Ret. on Assets	10.0	8.8	7.7	6.6	5.1	4.8	3.5	0.3	7.6	7.1
% Ret. on Equity	24.5	21.4	18.2	15.5	11.2	10.0	7.6	0.7	16.5	15.9

Data as orig. reptd.; bef. results of disc. opers. and/or spec. items. Per share data adj. for stk. divs. as of ex-div. date. Bold denotes diluted EPS (FASB 128). E-Estimated. NA-Not Available. NM-Not Meaningful. NR-Not Ranked.

Office—150 North Orange Grove Blvd., Pasadena, CA 91103. **Tel**—(818) 304-2000. **E-mail**—investorcom@averydennison.com **Website**—http://www.averydennison.com**Chrmn**—C. D. Miller. **Pres & CEO**—P. M. Neal. **SVP-Fin & CFO**—R. M. Calderoni. **SVP & Secy**—R. G. van Schoonenberg. **VP, Treas & Investor Contact**—Wayne H. Smith. **Dirs**—D. L. Allison Jr., J. C. Argue, J. T. Bok, F. V. Cahouet, R. M. Ferry, C. D. Miller, P. W. Mullin, P. M. Neal, S. R. Petersen, J. B. Slaughter. **Transfer Agent & Registrar**—First Chicago Trust Co. of New York, Jersey City, NJ. **Incorporated**—in California in 1946; reincorporated in Delaware in 1977. **Empl**— 16,900. **S&P Analyst:** Richard O'Reilly, CFA

Avon Products

262K

NYSE Symbol **AVP**

In S&P 500

12-SEP-98 **Industry:** Personal Care

Summary: This company is the world's leading direct marketer of cosmetics, toiletries, fashion jewelry and fragrances, with more than two million sales representatives worldwide.

S&P Opinion: Accumulate (★★★★)	Recent Price • 54⅞	Yield • 2.5%
	52 Wk Range • 89-51⅞	12-Mo. P/E • 25.9

Quantitative Evaluations

Outlook (1 Lowest—5 Highest)
• **3**

Fair Value
• **59¼**

Risk
• **Low**

Earn./Div. Rank
• **B+**

Technical Eval.
• **Bearish** since 2/96

Rel. Strength Rank (1 Lowest—99 Highest)
• **21**

Insider Activity
• **Neutral**

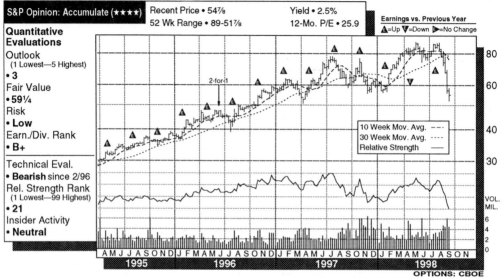

Earnings vs. Previous Year
▲=Up ▼=Down ▶=No Change

10 Week Mov. Avg. ---
30 Week Mov. Avg. ·····
Relative Strength —

OPTIONS: CBOE

Overview - 31-AUG-98

We expect total sales to grow only about 4% to 6% in 1998, reflecting the continued negative impact of foreign currency translations. Sales in the U.S. should rebound, reflecting more sales representatives; new, more profitable products, including high-end skin care products; new licensing contracts; and stepped-up marketing efforts, including improved packaging and increased sampling. Sales in other areas of the world should also advance strongly, especially in Europe and emerging markets. Asia, which was weak during the first half of the year, should begin to benefit from the resumption of business in China. Margins may widen as the company renews its focus on controlling costs, including a comprehensive restructuring program, which is expected to generate $400 million in annual cost savings by 2000. About half of the savings will be reinvested in advertising and promotional efforts to support brand awareness. In September 1998, the shares are set to be split on a two-for-one basis.

Valuation - 31-AUG-98

We recently downgraded AVP to accumulate from buy due to financial problems in some of the emerging markets in which AVP operates. Avon derives about two thirds of its sales and profits from international markets and expects sales from its emerging markets to help fuel future sales growth. However, the recent financial problems in Russia, as well as the continuing financial problems in Japan are likely to slow sales gains. Thus, we lowered our earnings growth expectations to 13% to 15% over the next few years, down from our previous estimate of 16% to 18%, and we cut our 1998 operating EPS estimate to $2.90, from $3.05. Nevertheless, expected cost cutting and a $600 million repurchase program still make the shares an appealing candidate for accumulation.

Key Stock Statistics

S&P EPS Est. 1998	2.90	Tang. Bk. Value/Share	1.72
P/E on S&P Est. 1998	18.9	Beta	1.11
S&P EPS Est. 1999	3.40	Shareholders	24,200
Dividend Rate/Share	1.36	Market cap. (B)	$ 7.2
Shs. outstg. (M)	131.7	Inst. holdings	82%
Avg. daily vol. (M)	1.074		

Value of $10,000 invested 5 years ago: $ 23,098

Fiscal Year Ending Dec. 31

	1998	1997	1996	1995	1994	1993
Revenues (Million $)						
1Q	1,183	1,088	1,016	976.2	886.0	841.9
2Q	1,247	1,225	1,129	1,064	1,007	949.3
3Q	—	1,249	1,177	1,068	1,010	957.1
4Q	—	1,517	1,492	1,384	1,364	1,259
Yr.	—	5,079	4,814	4,492	4,267	4,008
Earnings Per Share ($)						
1Q	-0.24	0.31	0.28	0.25	0.22	0.17
2Q	0.84	0.71	0.64	0.58	0.51	0.46
3Q	—	0.51	0.47	0.41	0.36	0.38
4Q	—	1.01	0.99	0.85	0.80	0.73
Yr.	—	2.54	2.38	2.10	1.88	1.73

Next earnings report expected: late October

Dividend Data (Dividends have been paid since 1919.)

Amount ($)	Date Decl.	Ex-Div. Date	Stock of Record	Payment Date
0.340	Feb. 05	Feb. 12	Feb. 17	Mar. 02 '98
0.340	May. 07	May. 14	May. 18	Jun. 01 '98
0.340	Jul. 22	Aug. 13	Aug. 17	Sep. 01 '98
2-for-1	Jul. 22	Sep. 14	Aug. 24	Sep. 11 '98

A Division of The McGraw Hill Companies

Avon Products, Inc.

Business Summary - 31-AUG-98

Avon Products is calling on a rejuvenated product line to enhance its image and ring up new business for its core beauty care and related products. A major part of its regimen has been the development of a global brand portfolio of products that should appeal to consumers worldwide. Its global brands (Anew, Avon Color, Far Away, Rare Gold, Natori, Josie, Avon Skin Care, and Millennia) stress advanced technology, upscale packaging and consistent imagery. AVP is also reducing the rest of its product portfolio to a smaller but more profitable line-up of cosmetics, fragrances and toiletries.

The company also believes that by consolidating its resources behind select global brands, it can achieve economies of scale that will enable it to reallocate funds to other consumer initiatives such as advertising, public relations and merchandising. Avon embarked upon a major restructuring program at the end of 1997, aimed at reducing annual costs by up to $400 million a year by 2000. Half of the savings are expected to be reinvested in advertising and marketing programs to boost sales, with the company's ultimate goal of increasing annual sales by 8% to 10% and EPS by 16% to 18%.

Avon is the world's leading direct seller of beauty care and related items. More than 2.6 million active representatives (independent contractors who are not employees of Avon) market and sell the company's products by direct contact, either in person or by mail, phone or fax. AVP has operations in 44 countries, and its products are available in 90 more countries through licensing and distribution agreements. Foreign operations accounted for 66% of net sales and 68% of pretax profits in 1997, with 43% of sales and 52% of pretax profits derived from developing markets.

Although 61% of revenues in 1997 were derived from the sale of cosmetics, fragrances and toiletries, the company also offers complementary products such as apparel, jewelry, collectibles, health, home and decorative items.

While Avon has been selling overseas for decades, today it is emphasizing expansion into countries with emerging or developing economies. It has entered 18 new markets since 1990, most recently Croatia, Romania and Ukraine. Its fastest growing international markets include Brazil, Argentina, the Philippines and Malaysia. Other leading expansion markets include China, Central Europe (Poland, Hungary, The Czech Republic and Slovakia) and Russia. Avon's direct sales method has been successful in such emerging markets, which typically have strong demand for Western quality products and an underdeveloped retail infrastructure. Moreover, these areas usually have a large population of entrepreneurial women who are seeking opportunities to earn money.

Per Share Data ($) (Year Ended Dec. 31)	1997	1996	1995	1994	1993	1992	1991	1990	1989	1988
Tangible Bk. Val.	2.16	1.82	1.43	1.29	1.17	1.15	0.74	1.99	-0.83	-0.85
Cash Flow	3.08	2.86	2.52	2.27	2.11	1.59	1.86	1.88	1.60	1.33
Earnings	2.54	2.38	2.10	1.88	1.73	1.22	1.46	1.41	1.05	0.83
Dividends	1.26	1.16	1.05	0.95	0.85	0.75	2.20	0.50	0.50	0.75
Payout Ratio	50%	49%	50%	51%	49%	62%	164%	36%	49%	78%
Prices - High	78	59½	39¼	31⅞	32¼	30⅛	24½	19⅛	20⅝	14¼
- Low	50⅝	36⅜	27	24¼	23⅞	22	13⅛	11⅜	9¾	9⅜
P/E Ratio - High	31	25	19	17	19	25	17	14	20	17
- Low	20	15	13	13	14	18	9	8	9	11
Income Statement Analysis (Million $)										
Revs.	5,079	4,814	4,492	4,267	4,008	3,810	3,593	3,454	3,300	3,063
Oper. Inc.	616	609	566	551	511	513	500	496	463	400
Depr.	72.1	64.5	58.3	55.7	54.7	54.2	52.9	53.6	60.7	63.2
Int. Exp.	41.8	40.0	41.3	51.0	45.0	44.0	97.0	97.0	132	119
Pretax Inc.	535	510	465	434	418	312	372	357	299	228
Eff. Tax Rate	37%	38%	38%	38%	39%	42%	42%	44%	47%	43%
Net Inc.	339	318	286	265	250	175	211	195	152	121
Balance Sheet & Other Fin. Data (Million $)										
Cash	142	185	151	215	232	147	116	380	84.0	164
Curr. Assets	1,344	1,350	1,215	1,150	1,082	903	896	1,174	1,020	1,111
Total Assets	2,273	2,222	2,053	1,978	1,958	1,736	1,729	2,059	2,098	2,460
Curr. Liab.	1,356	1,391	1,245	1,141	1,059	1,003	1,031	1,102	963	1,029
LT Debt	102	105	114	117	124	178	208	335	674	919
Common Eqty.	285	242	193	186	314	311	252	375	210	221
Total Cap.	456	422	387	383	511	548	540	812	989	1,289
Cap. Exp.	169	104	73.0	100	60.0	80.0	65.0	38.0	37.0	51.0
Cash Flow	411	382	344	321	304	229	245	213	177	166
Curr. Ratio	1.0	1.0	1.0	1.0	1.0	0.9	0.9	1.1	1.1	1.1
% LT Debt of Cap.	22.3	24.9	29.5	30.4	24.2	32.4	38.6	41.2	68.1	71.3
% Net Inc.of Revs.	6.7	6.6	6.4	6.2	6.2	4.6	5.9	5.7	4.6	4.0
% Ret. on Assets	15.1	14.9	14.2	13.7	13.5	10.1	9.7	9.4	6.5	5.5
% Ret. on Equity	128.7	146.0	151.3	108.9	79.9	62.2	53.1	54.3	52.6	25.9

Data as orig. reptd.; bef. results of disc. opers. and/or spec. items. Per share data adj. for stk. divs. as of ex-div. date. Bold denotes diluted EPS (FASB 128). E-Estimated. NA-Not Available. NM-Not Meaningful. NR-Not Ranked.

Office—1345 Ave. of the Americas, New York, NY 10105-0196. **Tel**—(212) 282-5320. **Website**—http://www.avon.com **Chrmn & CEO**—J. E. Preston. **Vice Chrmn & COO**—C. R. Perrin. **Pres**—A. Jung. **SVP & CFO**—R. J. Corti. **VP & Secy**—W. M. Miller Jr. **Investor Contact**—Carol Murray-Negron. **Dirs**—B. Barnes, R. S. Barton, E. T. Fogarty, S. C. Gault, G. V. Grune, A. Jung, S. J. Kropf, C. S. Locke, A. S. Moore, R. D. Oliver, C. R. Perrin, J. E. Preston, P. Stern. **Transfer Agent & Registrar**—First Chicago Trust Co. of New York, NYC. **Incorporated**—in New York in 1916. **Empl**— 34,995. **S&P Analyst:** Robert J. Izmirlian

Baker Hughes

266X

NYSE Symbol **BHI**

In S&P 500

12-SEP-98

Industry:
Oil & Gas (Drilling & Equipment)

Summary: This company, a leader in the oil well equipment and services industry, is the world's largest maker of drill bits used by the oil and gas industries.

S&P Opinion: Hold (★★★)	Recent Price • 21½	Yield • 2.1%
	52 Wk Range • 49⅝-17¾	12-Mo. P/E • NM

Quantitative Evaluations

Outlook
(1 Lowest—5 Highest)
• **5**

Fair Value
• **37¾**

Risk
• **Average**

Earn./Div. Rank
• **B**

Technical Eval.
• **Bearish** since 3/98

Rel. Strength Rank
(1 Lowest—99 Highest)
• **41**

Insider Activity
• **Favorable**

Earnings vs. Previous Year
▲=Up ▼=Down ▶=No Change

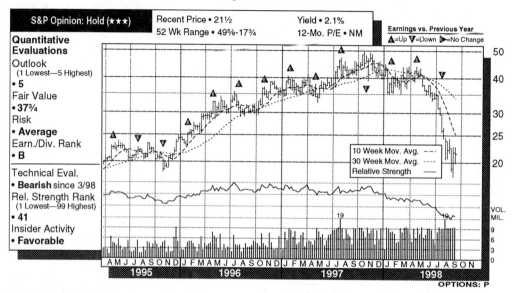

10 Week Mov. Avg. – – –
30 Week Mov. Avg. ·······
Relative Strength ——

VOL.
MIL.

OPTIONS: P

Overview - 05-AUG-98

The planned acquisition of Western Atlas will allow Baker Hughes to offer a wide complement of oilfield products and services, ranging from exploration to production, and including many points in between. The company's ability to gain additional market share in its oilfield services segment reflects new products and acceptance of the integrated solutions unit, and should aid earnings in FY 98 (Sep.). Near-term earnings hinge largely on the level of upstream capital expenditures, which should increase in 1998, despite lower oil prices. However, weak oil prices have resulted in some cutbacks in exploration spending and continued oil price weakness could lead to further cuts. Looking to the longer term, margin expansion, increased outsourcing of wellsite services, and continued robust levels of oil and gas drilling both domestically and outside the U.S. will drive earnings higher. Beyond 1998, we see double-digit average annual EPS growth, assuming some oil price recovery. Share earnings in FY 97 (Sep.) of $0.71 included $1.00 in nonrecurring charges.

Valuation - 05-AUG-98

Although the planned acquisition of Western Atlas appears to be a sound strategic move for the long term, giving Baker Hughes access to the rapidly growing seismic market, we believe that BHI paid a hefty price for Western Atlas, offering a significant premium to WAI's already inflated shares, which had for some time enjoyed a takeover speculation-fueled premium. The recent steep decline in crude oil prices has increased the likelihood that oil producers' actual capital spending will fall short of original budgets. Consequently, shares of oil services providers are likely to be restrained by continued oil price weakness, and we maintain our neutral stance on BHI's shares.

Key Stock Statistics

S&P EPS Est. 1998	1.75	Tang. Bk. Value/Share	9.54
P/E on S&P Est. 1998	12.3	Beta	1.17
S&P EPS Est. 1999	2.05	Shareholders	17,700
Dividend Rate/Share	0.46	Market cap. (B)	$ 6.8
Shs. outstg. (M)	318.5	Inst. holdings	36%
Avg. daily vol. (M)	2.913		

Value of $10,000 invested 5 years ago: $ 12,180

Fiscal Year Ending Sep. 30

	1998	1997	1996	1995	1994	1993
Revenues (Million $)						
1Q	1,133	826.7	694.7	606.9	624.6	684.0
2Q	1,157	850.2	744.8	652.6	650.0	692.0
3Q	1,660	917.3	765.9	668.4	590.5	670.0
4Q	—	1,091	822.4	709.5	639.6	654.8
Yr.	—	3,685	3,028	2,637	2,505	2,702
Earnings Per Share ($)						
1Q	**0.46**	0.35	0.23	0.15	0.10	0.01
2Q	**0.46**	0.40	0.29	0.18	0.14	Nil
3Q	**0.36**	0.56	0.33	0.09	0.22	0.15
4Q	—	-0.49	0.38	0.25	0.39	0.18
Yr.	**E1.75**	0.71	1.23	0.67	0.85	0.34

Next earnings report expected: late October

Dividend Data (Dividends have been paid since 1987.)

Amount ($)	Date Decl.	Ex-Div. Date	Stock of Record	Payment Date
0.115	Oct. 22	Oct. 30	Nov. 03	Nov. 21 '97
0.115	Jan. 28	Feb. 05	Feb. 09	Feb. 27 '98
0.115	Apr. 22	Apr. 30	May. 04	May. 22 '98
0.115	Jul. 22	Jul. 30	Aug. 03	Aug. 21 '98

A Division of The McGraw Hill Companies

Business Summary - 05-AUG-98

Baker Hughes (BHI), the world's largest maker of drill bits used in drilling for oil and gas, seeks to position itself to benefit from the anticipated increase in oil and gas drilling activity. Since its formation in 1987 via the merger of Baker International Corp. and Hughes Tool Co., the company has made a series of acquisitions while disposing of several businesses that were deemed nonessential. The company's most recent. and largest, acquisition was announced in May 1998, when the company signed an agreement to acquire Western Atlas (WAI), a leading seismic and wireline logging services provider. Under terms of the deal, WAI shareholders will receive 2.7 BHI shares per WAI common share held, valuing the transaction at nearly $4 billion. After completing the WAI acquisition, BHI will be able to provide a wide range of equipment and services for the exploration, drilling, completion and production of oil and gas wells. It also makes process equipment for pumping and treating liquids, and specialty chemicals. International sales accounted for 64% of FY 97 (Sep.) revenues. Segment contributions in FY 97 were:

	Revs.	Profits
Oilfield products & services	78%	84%
Chemicals	11%	9%
Process equipment	11%	7%

Oilfield equipment includes a broad range of rolling cutter and diamond drill bits and basic drilling rig equipment. The company believes it is the leading maker of rock drill bits, and is also a major producer of drilling fluids, used to enhance productivity when drilling oil and gas wells. The process equipment segment makes and sells products and provides services used, after oil and gas wells are drilled, to achieve safety and long-term productivity, to provide structural integrity, to protect against pressure and corrosion damage, and to stimulate or rework wells.

The chemicals segment is comprised entirely of one division, Baker Petrolite, which is the result of the combination of Baker Performance Chemicals and Petrolite. Petrolite was acquired in July 1997, for a total consideration of $750 million. Baker Petrolite manufactures specialty chemicals which are sold as part of integrated chemical technology solutions for petroleum production, transportation and refining.

In late 1996, Baker Hughes and oil services industry giant Schlumberger Limited (SLB) announced plans to establish strategic alliances between several of their product lines, in order to enhance product offerings and accelerate new product development. The alliances underscore the emerging trend in the oil services industry toward combinations and cooperation between rivals, in an attempt to develop new technology. Baker Hughes' planned acquisition of Western Atlas is a continuation of this trend.

Per Share Data ($)

(Year Ended Sep. 30)	1997	1996	1995	1994	1993	1992	1991	1990	1989	1988
Tangible Bk. Val.	9.16	6.45	5.21	4.56	10.04	10.43	11.17	10.36	6.95	6.84
Cash Flow	1.93	2.32	1.89	1.94	1.62	1.12	2.27	1.94	1.46	1.37
Earnings	0.71	1.23	0.67	0.85	0.34	Nil	1.26	1.06	0.64	0.45
Dividends	0.46	0.43	0.46	0.46	0.46	0.46	0.46	0.46	0.46	0.46
Payout Ratio	65%	35%	69%	54%	135%	NM	37%	47%	73%	104%
Prices - High	49⅝	38⅞	24⅞	22⅛	29⅝	25⅜	31	34¾	27⅝	19⅞
- Low	32⅝	22¾	16¾	17	18½	15⅞	17⅞	21¾	13⅝	12⅛
P/E Ratio - High	70	32	37	26	87	NM	25	33	43	44
- Low	46	18	25	20	54	NM	14	21	21	27

Income Statement Analysis (Million $)

	1997	1996	1995	1994	1993	1992	1991	1990	1989	1988
Revs.	3,685	3,028	2,637	2,505	2,702	2,539	2,828	2,614	2,328	2,316
Oper. Inc.	616	502	410	361	380	329	434	358	269	251
Depr.	186	156	155	154	179	156	139	113	99	109
Int. Exp.	48.6	55.5	55.6	63.8	64.7	68.1	83.6	77.5	60.0	71.0
Pretax Inc.	213	299	205	226	100	32.0	212	181	119	134
Eff. Tax Rate	49%	41%	42%	42%	41%	84%	18%	21%	29%	53%
Net Inc.	109	176	120	131	59.0	5.0	173	142	83.0	59.0

Balance Sheet & Other Fin. Data (Million $)

	1997	1996	1995	1994	1993	1992	1991	1990	1989	1988
Cash	8.6	7.7	6.8	69.0	7.0	7.0	52.0	125	116	68.0
Curr. Assets	2,221	1,717	1,565	1,400	1,417	1,361	1,358	1,306	1,165	1,202
Total Assets	4,756	3,298	3,167	3,000	3,143	3,213	2,906	2,784	2,066	2,118
Curr. Liab.	936	635	580	545	496	646	705	630	545	610
LT Debt	772	674	798	638	936	812	545	612	417	440
Common Eqty.	2,605	1,689	1,514	1,438	1,411	1,446	1,545	1,424	903	861
Total Cap.	3,652	2,513	2,430	2,334	2,628	2,523	2,155	2,113	1,502	1,486
Cap. Exp.	343	182	139	109	127	138	161	133	145	65.0
Cash Flow	295	332	267	273	225	156	312	248	174	161
Curr. Ratio	2.4	2.7	2.7	2.6	2.9	2.1	1.9	2.1	2.1	2.0
% LT Debt of Cap.	21.1	26.8	32.8	27.3	35.6	32.2	25.3	28.9	27.8	29.6
% Net Inc.of Revs.	3.0	5.8	4.6	5.2	2.2	0.2	6.1	5.4	3.6	2.6
% Ret. on Assets	2.7	5.4	3.9	4.3	1.8	0.2	6.1	5.5	3.9	2.7
% Ret. on Equity	5.1	11.0	7.1	8.4	3.3	NM	11.6	11.1	8.5	6.2

Data as orig. reptd.; bef. results of disc. opers. and/or spec. items. Per share data adj. for stk. divs. as of ex-div. date. Bold denotes diluted EPS (FASB 128). E-Estimated. NA-Not Available. NM-Not Meaningful. NR-Not Ranked.

Office—3900 Essex Lane, Houston, TX 77027-5177. **Tel**—(713) 439-8600. **Chrmn, Pres & CEO**—M. L. Lukens. **SVP & CFO**—E. L. Mattson. **VP & Investor Contact**—Scott B. Gill. **Dirs**—L. M. Alberthal Jr., V. G. Beghini, J. S. Blanton, E. M. Filter, J. B: Foster, R. D. Kinder, M. L. Lukens, J. F. Maher, J. F. McCall, H. J. Riley Jr., D. C. Trauscht. **Transfer Agent & Registrar**—First Chicago Trust Co. of New York, NYC. **Incorporated**—in Delaware in 1987. **Empl**— 21,250. **S&P Analyst:** Norman Rosenberg

STANDARD &POOR'S
STOCK REPORTS

Ball Corp.

272

NYSE Symbol **BLL**

In S&P 500

12-SEP-98

Industry: Containers (Metal & Glass)

Summary: Ball manufactures metal and plastic food and beverage containers, and has interests in aerospace and other technical fields.

S&P Opinion: Accumulate (★★★★)	Recent Price • 29⅛	Yield • 2.1%
	52 Wk Range • 48⅞-28⅝	12-Mo. P/E • 17.9

Quantitative Evaluations

Outlook
(1 Lowest—5 Highest)
• **2**

Fair Value
• **30½**

Risk
• **Low**

Earn./Div. Rank
• **B**

Technical Eval.
• **Bullish** since 9/98

Rel. Strength Rank
(1 Lowest—99 Highest)
• **22**

Insider Activity
• **Neutral**

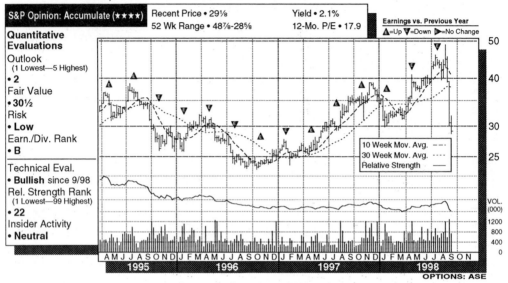

Earnings vs. Previous Year
△=Up ▽=Down ▷=No Change

10 Week Mov. Avg. ----
30 Week Mov. Avg. ······
Relative Strength ——

VOL. (000)

OPTIONS: ASE

Overview - 22-JUL-98

Sales gains should be recorded in 1998. Domestic beverage can and metal food container sales should remain firm, but gains will likely be limited by a mature market. Overall metal container sales should be aided by Ball's ongoing expansion in more vital foreign markets. In addition, BLL's new PET bottle business should generate greater sales. On the downside, tough comparisons should bring a modest sales reduction in the much smaller aerospace and technologies segment. Operating margins should be aided by business transformation efforts of the past few years, production efficiencies, and the maturing PET operation's turn to profitability. While Ball's expansion in Asia has been hampered by overcapacity, growing demand in the region should bring the supply/demand balance more in line. Ball expects its planned takeover of the global can business of Reynolds Metals Co. to be additive in its first full year. It sees combination synergies bringing some $70 million of annual savings within three years. Comparisons will be distorted by $0.14 a share of charges in 1998's first quarter and $0.15 a share of one-time net gains in 1997's second quarter.

Valuation - 22-JUL-98

The shares have rebounded strongly since late 1996, as Ball's actions over the past few years to reposition its business focus started to have a positive impact. We fully agree with Ball's decision to focus on global growth markets and the more popular domestic plastic beverage container market. We also think it will be able to take over the global can business of Reynolds Metals and make it run much more efficiently. Although overcapacity in Asian markets poses a near-term problem, we still think that Ball's initiatives leave it poised for an extended period of EPS growth. Thus, we see the shares outperforming in coming periods.

Key Stock Statistics

S&P EPS Est. 1998	1.95	Tang. Bk. Value/Share	13.67
P/E on S&P Est. 1998	14.9	Beta	0.30
S&P EPS Est. 1999	2.50	Shareholders	8,400
Dividend Rate/Share	0.60	Market cap. (B)	$0.888
Shs. outstg. (M)	30.5	Inst. holdings	68%
Avg. daily vol. (M)	0.251		

Value of $10,000 invested 5 years ago: $ 9,424

Fiscal Year Ending Dec. 31

	1998	1997	1996	1995	1994	1993
Revenues (Million $)						
1Q	549.7	479.8	462.0	605.6	587.3	534.7
2Q	645.6	643.7	600.1	755.2	676.6	665.5
3Q	—	690.2	622.2	760.7	717.5	683.0
4Q	—	574.8	500.1	470.2	613.3	557.7
Yr.	—	2,389	2,184	2,592	2,595	2,441
Earnings Per Share ($)						
1Q	0.14	0.20	0.20	0.52	0.33	0.31
2Q	0.57	0.63	0.42	0.70	0.55	0.43
3Q	E0.85	0.68	0.62	-1.93	0.76	0.10
4Q	E0.39	0.23	-0.90	-0.01	0.71	-2.02
Yr.	E1.95	1.74	0.34	-0.72	2.35	-1.24

Next earnings report expected: late October

Dividend Data (Dividends have been paid since 1958.)

Amount ($)	Date Decl.	Ex-Div. Date	Stock of Record	Payment Date
0.150	Oct. 22	Nov. 26	Dec. 01	Dec. 15 '97
0.150	Jan. 28	Feb. 26	Mar. 02	Mar. 16 '98
0.150	Apr. 22	May. 28	Jun. 01	Jun. 15 '98
0.150	Jul. 22	Aug. 28	Sep. 01	Sep. 15 '98

A Division of The **McGraw-Hill** *Companies*

Business Summary - 22-JUL-98

As 1997 came to an end, Ball Corp. put the finishing touches on a major business transition program adopted in the fall of 1994. This maker of packaging products, primarily for food and beverages, has entered the growing PET plastic container market in North America; significantly increased its position in global growth markets; and reduced its participation in mature North American packaging areas. To top off that effort, in April 1998, Ball agreed to purchase the global beverage can business of Reynolds Metals Co. (NYSE: RLM). In addition to its packaging operations, Ball supplies aerospace and other technologies and services.

Packaging products include aluminum and steel two piece beverage cans, and two and three piece steel food cans. Metal beverage containers and ends represent BLL's largest product line, accounting for 46% of revenues in 1997. Pepsi and Coca-Cola bottlers jointly accounted for 36% of Ball's total sales in 1997.

Ball estimates that it accounted for 17% of all aluminum beverage can shipments in the U.S. and Canada in 1997, and that the combined shipments of its four largest competitors contributed most of the remainder. However, the company will become a much larger factor in this segment following its April 1998 agreement to buy the global beverage can business of Reynolds Metals Co. (NYSE: RLM), the world's third largest aluminum can maker, for a total of $820 million in cash and stock (up to $100 million in stock). In addition to its domestic business, the Reynolds unit holds a one-third stake in a South American beverage can venture. Ball had started taking steps in 1997 to boost its foreign presence. In the second quarter, it bought a 75% interest in Hong Kong-based M.C. Packaging, the largest beverage can maker in China, for U.S.$179 million.

BLL entered the plastic packaging business in 1995, when it began to make polyethylene terephthalate (PET) bottles. All of the company's packaging operations accounted for a total of 83% of its sales in 1997 and 76% of operating profits (excluding certain disposed operations).

Ball exited the mature North American glass container market in October 1996, when it sold its 42% interest in the Ball-Foster Glass Container Co., L.L.C. joint venture, for about $190 million. It also sold its U.S. aerosol can business in that month for $44.3 million.

The aerospace and technologies segment (17% of sales and 24% of operating profits in 1997) provides systems, products and services to the aerospace, defense and commercial markets. U.S. government agencies account for most of the segment's sales.

Ball plans to relocate its corporate headquarters to an existing company-owned building in Colorado by the end of 1998. It sees the move bringing annual pretax savings of more than $4 million.

Per Share Data ($) (Year Ended Dec. 31)	1997	1996	1995	1994	1993	1992	1991	1990	1989	1988
Tangible Bk. Val.	13.78	17.09	16.65	15.80	13.75	20.35	17.16	14.81	14.27	17.92
Cash Flow	5.35	3.42	3.06	6.46	2.59	6.00	6.82	4.47	3.62	3.29
Earnings	1.74	0.34	-0.72	2.35	-1.24	2.21	2.42	2.03	1.44	1.40
Dividends	0.60	0.60	0.60	0.60	1.24	1.22	1.18	1.14	1.10	1.02
Payout Ratio	34%	176%	NM	26%	NM	56%	54%	57%	73%	73%
Prices - High	39	32 1/4	38 3/4	32 1/8	37 1/4	39 1/2	38 1/4	34 1/2	34 3/8	35 7/8
- Low	23 3/4	23 1/8	25 3/4	24 3/8	25 1/8	28	25 5/8	26	25 1/4	25 5/8
P/E Ratio - High	22	95	NM	14	NM	18	16	17	24	26
- Low	14	68	NM	10	NM	13	11	13	18	18
Income Statement Analysis (Million $)										
Revs.	2,389	2,184	2,592	2,595	2,441	2,178	2,267	1,357	1,222	1,073
Oper. Inc.	248	177	254	291	213	238	253	148	110	118
Depr.	118	93.5	114	122	110	99	102	54.0	50.0	44.0
Int. Exp.	53.5	39.9	41.3	44.5	47.6	38.2	42.4	23.5	23.2	15.5
Pretax Inc.	85.2	20.1	-14.1	122	-50.0	103	109	70.0	49.0	48.0
Eff. Tax Rate	38%	36%	NM	37%	NM	35%	37%	28%	26%	32%
Net Inc.	58.3	13.1	-18.6	73.0	-32.5	62.9	66.2	50.2	35.8	32.7
Balance Sheet & Other Fin. Data (Million $)										
Cash	25.5	169	5.1	10.4	8.2	14.5	20.8	30.0	10.4	15.7
Curr. Assets	798	767	593	698	692	619	634	542	374	332
Total Assets	2,090	1,701	1,613	1,760	1,796	1,564	1,559	1,308	938	877
Curr. Liab.	838	511	498	500	451	359	442	323	219	183
LT Debt	366	408	320	377	513	452	334	405	263	196
Common Eqty.	574	587	568	605	549	596	487	337	314	421
Total Cap.	1,113	1,047	937	1,066	1,153	1,159	1,074	944	698	674
Cap. Exp.	97.7	196	206	95.0	141	110	96.0	34.0	56.0	101
Cash Flow	173	104	91.9	192	74.0	156	158	98.0	83.0	77.0
Curr. Ratio	1.0	1.5	1.2	1.4	1.5	1.7	1.4	1.7	1.7	1.8
% LT Debt of Cap.	32.9	39.0	34.2	35.4	44.5	39.0	31.1	42.9	37.6	29.1
% Net Inc.of Revs.	2.4	0.6	NM	2.8	NM	2.9	2.9	3.7	2.9	3.0
% Ret. on Assets	3.1	0.8	NM	4.1	NM	4.1	4.3	4.5	4.1	3.9
% Ret. on Equity	9.9	1.8	NM	12.0	NM	9.9	12.7	13.6	9.3	8.0

Data as orig. reptd.; bef. results of disc. opers. and/or spec. items. Per share data adj. for stk. divs. as of ex-div. date. Bold denotes diluted EPS (FASB 128). E-Estimated. NA-Not Available. NM-Not Meaningful. NR-Not Ranked.

Office—345 South High St., Muncie, IN 47307-0407. **Tel**—(765) 747-6100. **Website**—http://www.ball.com **Chrmn & CEO**—G. A. Sissel. **Pres**—G. A. Matsik. **Vice-Chrmn & CFO**—R. D. Hoover. **Treas**—D. E. Poling. **Secy**—E. A. Overmyer. **Dirs**—F. A. Bracken, H. M. Dean, J. T. Hackett, R. D. Hoover, J. F. Lehman, G. McFadden, R. C. Mercure, Jr., J. Nicholson, G. A. Sissel, W. P. Stiritz. **Transfer Agent & Registrar**—First Chicago Trust Co. of New York, Jersey City, NJ. **Incorporated**—in Indiana in 1922. **Empl**— 10,300. **S&P Analyst:** Robert E. Friedman, CPA

12-SEP-98

Industry: Electric Companies

Summary: This electric and gas utility serves the city of Baltimore and much of central Maryland.

S&P Opinion: Accumulate (★★★★)

Recent Price • 30¼	Yield • 5.5%
52 Wk Range • 34¼-25¾	12-Mo. P/E • 14.2

Quantitative Evaluations

Outlook
(1 Lowest—5 Highest)
• **2**

Fair Value
• **31⅝**

Risk
• **Low**

Earn./Div. Rank
• **B+**

Technical Eval.
• **Bullish** since 8/97

Rel. Strength Rank
(1 Lowest—99 Highest)
• **85**

Insider Activity
• **Neutral**

Earnings vs. Previous Year
▲=Up ▼=Down ▶=No Change

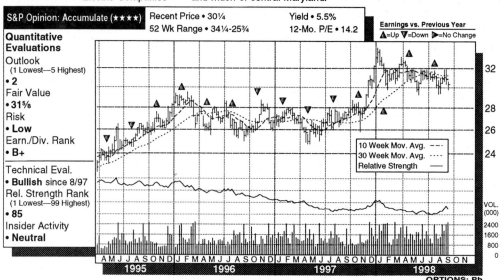

10 Week Mov. Avg. - - -
30 Week Mov. Avg. ......
Relative Strength ——

OPTIONS: Ph

Overview - 18-AUG-98

Following what should be a significant improvement in 1998 earnings, we expect to see only low single-digit EPS growth in 1999. The advance in 1998 is expected to reflect more favorable weather as well as the absence of charges in 1997 of $0.31 and $0.25 a share respectively for real estate writeoffs and costs related to the terminated merger with Potomac Electric Power (NYSE: POM). EPS should also benefit from lower level operation and maintenance expenses, and from increased contributions from non-regulated businesses. In December 1997, BGE and POM terminated a planned merger into Constellation Energy. In July 1998, BGE filed a proposed transition to competition plan with the the Maryland Public Service Commission, in which in exchange for recovery of its stranded costs, BGE would freeze rates from year-end 1998 to July 2002 and apply any increase in earnings to the accelerated write-down of its regulatory-approved investments.

Valuation - 18-AUG-98

We would continue to accumulate BGE stock. With the shares down nearly 10% year to date (versus a 2.7% increase for the S&P index of electric companies and a 1.4% decline for the gas companies), the stock has become attractive. In 1997, the shares rose 27.6% (versus gains of 19.8% and 18.6% for the respective S&P electric and gas indexes). Some of the stock's weakness may reflect doubts about BGE's ability to grow earnings in a competitive environment. However, we expect Maryland to eliminate its prohibition against utilities forming holding companies sometime in 1999. This would enable BGE to directly fund the development and expansion of its non-regulated businesses, which remain the key to its long-term earnings growth. With a dividend yield of well over 5%, and a P/E ratio of about 12X our 1999 EPS estimate of $2.50, the shares remain attractive for long-term total return.

Key Stock Statistics

S&P EPS Est. 1998	2.45	Tang. Bk. Value/Share	17.41
P/E on S&P Est. 1998	12.4	Beta	0.43
S&P EPS Est. 1999	2.50	Shareholders	76,900
Dividend Rate/Share	1.68	Market cap. (B)	$ 4.5
Shs. outstg. (M)	148.7	Inst. holdings	42%
Avg. daily vol. (M)	0.582		

Value of $10,000 invested 5 years ago: $ 18,060

Fiscal Year Ending Dec. 31

	1998	1997	1996	1995	1994	1993
Revenues (Million $)						
1Q	866.1	887.7	861.3	717.8	767.7	683.8
2Q	767.6	746.4	731.7	642.5	651.1	564.7
3Q	—	860.8	826.0	848.8	753.9	774.1
4Q	—	812.6	734.3	725.7	610.3	646.1
Yr.	—	3,308	3,153	2,935	2,783	2,669
Earnings Per Share ($)						
1Q	**0.50**	0.43	0.62	0.41	0.49	0.38
2Q	**0.39**	0.05	0.36	0.28	0.39	0.31
3Q	**E1.17**	1.11	0.93	1.04	0.79	1.01
4Q	**E0.39**	0.12	-0.06	0.29	0.26	0.14
Yr.	**E2.45**	1.72	1.85	2.02	1.93	1.85

Next earnings report expected: late October

Dividend Data (Dividends have been paid since 1910.)

Amount ($)	Date Decl.	Ex-Div. Date	Stock of Record	Payment Date
0.410	Oct. 30	Dec. 08	Dec. 10	Jan. 02 '98
0.410	Feb. 27	Mar. 06	Mar. 10	Apr. 01 '98
0.420	May. 21	Jun. 08	Jun. 10	Jul. 01 '98
0.420	Jul. 17	Sep. 08	Sep. 10	Oct. 01 '98

A Division of The **McGraw·Hill** *Companies*

Business Summary - 18-AUG-98

Following the December 1997 termination of its planned merger with Potomac Electric Power (POM), BGE has redirected its focus to the dramatic changes taking place in the state's electric industry. As it prepares itself for the challenges of a competitive marketplace, the company will continue to seek out the opportunities that will emerge in the non-regulated energy markets.

Baltimore Gas & Electric provides electric and gas service to more than 1.6 million customers in central Maryland. The local economy includes service businesses, heavy industry and the Port of Baltimore. In 1997, electricity accounted for 70% of revenues, gas for 16%, and diversified businesses for 14%. Electric revenues by customer class in recent years were:

	1997	1996	1995	1994
Residential	42%	43%	43%	44%
Commercial	41%	39%	39%	40%
Industrial	10%	9%	9%	10%
Other	7%	8%	9%	6%

In December 1997, the Maryland Public Service Commission ordered that electric competition be phased in over two years, with one-third of the customers provided with the option to choose their electric supplier as of July 1, 2000; another one-third as of July 1, 2001; and all customers as of July 1, 2002.

The company's electric business owns and operates 10 generating plants (including two nuclear units) and has partial ownership in three plants in Pennsylvania, with a total generating capacity of more than 6,200 megawatts. The gas business provides storage and distribution as well as commercial transmission through two gas plants and nine gas stations in and around Baltimore.

BGE is also engaged in diversified businesses through four groups of subsidiaries. Prior to $0.31 a share of real estate writedowns, the diversified businesses contributed $0.34 to 1997 earnings, compared to $0.31 in 1996 and $0.18 ih 1995.

Constellation Holdings, the largest of BGE's diversified businesses, consists of companies involved in the development, ownership and operation of power generation projects; the management of real estate and senior-living facilities; and financial investments.

Other diversified businesses include BGE Corp., which is involved in energy marketing and services; and BGE Home Products and Services, which is engaged in appliance sales and home improvement services.

In February 1997, BGE formed Constellation Power Source, which will sell power products (including risk management for electricity and related fuels) to wholesale customers throughout the U.S.

Per Share Data ($)

(Year Ended Dec. 31)	1997	1996	1995	1994	1993	1992	1991	1990	1989	1988
Tangible Bk. Val.	19.44	19.25	18.96	18.42	17.82	17.57	16.94	16.52	16.55	15.79
Earnings	1.72	1.85	2.02	1.93	1.85	1.63	1.52	1.09	2.03	2.31
Dividends	1.63	1.59	1.55	1.51	1.47	1.43	1.40	1.40	1.38	1.32
Payout Ratio	95%	86%	77%	78%	79%	88%	92%	128%	68%	57%
Prices - High	34¼	29½	29	25½	27½	24⅜	22⅞	23⅛	23¼	22½
- Low	24¾	25	22	20½	22⅜	19¾	17⅛	16¼	19	19⅝
P/E Ratio - High	20	16	14	13	15	15	15	16	11	10
- Low	14	14	11	11	12	12	11	12	9	8

Income Statement Analysis (Million $)

	1997	1996	1995	1994	1993	1992	1991	1990	1989	1988
Revs.	3,308	3,153	2,935	2,783	2,669	2,491	2,459	2,159	2,004	1,864
Depr.	343	330	317	296	237	223	200	171	157	147
Maint.	NA	174	168	165	182	173	174	163	149	133
Fxd. Chgs. Cov.	2.9	2.6	2.6	2.6	2.8	2.4	2.1	1.7	2.8	3.4
Constr. Credits	5.3	10.0	21.8	33.5	22.5	22.1	37.5	53.4	33.2	28.1
Eff. Tax Rate	36%	35%	33%	32%	31%	28%	27%	10%	23%	24%
Net Inc.	283	311	338	324	310	264	234	175	276	303

Balance Sheet & Other Fin. Data (Million $)

	1997	1996	1995	1994	1993	1992	1991	1990	1989	1988
Gross Prop.	8,495	8,196	7,979	7,722	7,359	6,947	6,577	6,207	5,706	5,280
Cap. Exp.	373	361	458	483	478	389	456	535	447	318
Net Prop.	5,652	5,582	5,498	5,417	5,197	4,966	4,774	4,513	4,144	3,853
Capitalization:										
LT Debt	2,989	2,759	2,598	2,585	2,823	2,377	2,390	2,194	2,077	1,769
% LT Debt	49	46	44	45	47	43	47	46	45	44
Pfd.	23.0	345	511	489	552	565	568	534	492	399
% Pfd.	4.87	5.80	8.60	8.40	9.20	10	11	11	11	9.80
Common	2,870	2,857	2,813	2,718	2,621	2,535	2,153	2,073	2,001	1,885
% Common	47	48	47	47	44	46	42	43	44	47
Total Cap.	7,432	7,261	7,234	7,097	7,220	6,626	6,165	5,630	5,326	4,674
% Oper. Ratio	75.4	84.1	82.1	82.7	81.9	82.7	83.2	85.5	80.3	78.3
% Earn. on Net Prop.	11.9	12.1	12.7	9.1	9.5	8.8	8.9	7.2	11.9	10.7
% Return On Revs.	8.6	9.9	11.5	11.6	11.6	10.6	9.5	8.1	13.8	16.3
% Return On Invest. Capital	8.6	9.2	9.6	7.2	7.2	7.1	7.5	6.4	8.5	9.4
% Return On Com. Equity	8.9	9.6	10.8	10.6	10.4	9.5	9.0	6.6	12.6	15.1

Data as orig. reptd.; bef. results of disc opers. and/or spec. items. Per share data adj. for stk. divs. as of ex-div. date. Bold denotes diluted EPS (FASB 128). E-Estimated. NA-Not Available. NM-Not Meaningful. NR-Not Ranked.

Office—39 W. Lexington Street, Baltimore, MD 21201. **Tel**—(410) 783-5920. **Chrmn & CEO**—C. H. Poindexter. **Pres & COO**—E. A. Crooke. **VP, CFO & Secy**—D. A. Brune. **Investor Contact**—Kevin J. Miller. **Dirs**—H. F. Baldwin, B. B. Byron, J. O. Cole, D. A. Colussy, E. A. Crooke, J. R. Curtiss, J. W. Geckle, F. A. Hrabowski III, N. Lampton, C. R. Larson, G. V. McGowan, C. H. Poindexter, G. L. Russell Jr., M. D. Sullivan. **Transfer Agent & Registrar**—Harris Trust & Savings Bank, Chicago. **Incorporated**—in Maryland in 1906. **Empl**— 9,000. **S&P Analyst:** Justin McCann

Banc One   275

NYSE Symbol **ONE**

In S&P 500

12-SEP-98 | **Industry:** Banks (Major Regional) | **Summary:** This Ohio-based bank holding company recently agreed to merge with First Chicago NBD Corp. in a stock transaction.

S&P Opinion: Accumulate (★★★★)	Recent Price • 43¾	Yield • 3.5%
	52 Wk Range • 65⅝-37¾	12-Mo. P/E • NM

Quantitative Evaluations

Outlook
(1 Lowest—5 Highest)
• **2⁻**

Fair Value
• **40⅝**

Risk
• **High**

Earn./Div. Rank
• **A**

Technical Eval.
• **Bearish** since 2/98

Rel. Strength Rank
(1 Lowest—99 Highest)
• **61**

Insider Activity
• **Neutral**

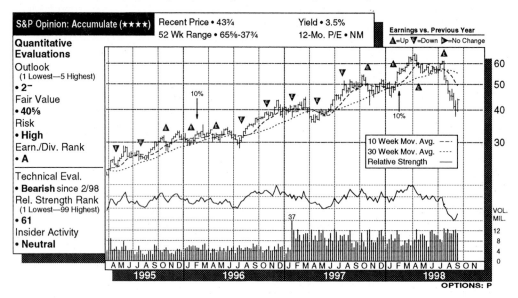

Earnings vs. Previous Year
▲=Up ▼=Down ▶=No Change

10 Week Mov. Avg. — - —
30 Week Mov. Avg. - - - -
Relative Strength ——

OPTIONS: P

Overview - 13-AUG-98

Earnings for the combined Banc One/First Chicago will be more broadly diversified than either component on a stand-alone basis, with an expected 37% from commercial, private banking and investments, 31% from credit cards, 23% from retail and 9% from financial services. Cost savings from the merger, expected at $930 million when phased in over three years, represent 13% of the combined banks' expense base and seem reasonable based on other mergers of equals. Coupled with a revenue enhancement target of $275 million, total synergies are expected at $1.2 billion. This will represent accretion from ONE's stand-alone EPS projections of 1.2% in 1999, 5.9% in 2000 and 6.2% in 2001, making the transaction compelling from a financial standpoint. The company has also set strong performance goals for 1999 of 21% return on equity, a 51% efficiency ratio and 13%-15% earnings growth.

Valuation - 13-AUG-98

Investors reacted enthusiastically to the proposed merger with First Chicago NBD. We view the combined company, which will be the second largest credit card issuer, as having considerable opportunities for cost savings from complementary product sets, as well as revenue enhancements from cross-marketing. Banc One should be able to leverage its highly successful credit model adopted from its early 1997 acquisition of First USA. Key competitive strengths also will be in the retail branch franchise and investment management businesses. With the expectation that the merger will lead to an improved earnings growth rate and risk profile, selective accumulation of the shares is recommended.

Key Stock Statistics

S&P EPS Est. 1998	3.50	Tang. Bk. Value/Share	15.42
P/E on S&P Est. 1998	12.5	Beta	1.49
S&P EPS Est. 1999	4.10	Shareholders	97,100
Dividend Rate/Share	1.52	Market cap. (B)	$ 30.8
Shs. outstg. (M)	704.9	Inst. holdings	56%
Avg. daily vol. (M)	2.625		

Value of $10,000 invested 5 years ago: $ 16,461

Fiscal Year Ending Dec. 31

	1998	1997	1996	1995	1994	1993
Revenues (Million $)						
1Q	3,662	3,131	2,488	2,198	1,965	1,734
2Q	3,767	3,190	2,488	2,229	2,008	1,789
3Q	—	3,490	2,575	2,278	2,113	1,795
4Q	—	3,408	2,737	2,346	1,860	1,828
Yr.	—	13,219	12,147	9,050	7,857	7,227
Earnings Per Share ($)						
1Q	**0.77**	**0.58**	0.70	0.62	0.65	0.58
2Q	**0.68**	**0.03**	0.73	0.64	0.66	0.61
3Q	—	**0.66**	0.74	0.69	0.56	0.62
4Q	—	**0.72**	0.77	0.70	0.12	0.62
Yr.	—	**1.99**	2.52	2.65	2.00	2.42

Next earnings report expected: late October

Dividend Data (Dividends have been paid since 1935.)

Amount ($)	Date Decl.	Ex-Div. Date	Stock of Record	Payment Date
10%	Jan. 20	Feb. 10	Feb. 12	Feb. 26 '98
0.380	Jan. 20	Mar. 11	Mar. 13	Mar. 31 '98
0.380	Apr. 21	Jun. 11	Jun. 15	Jun. 30 '98
0.380	Jul. 21	Sep. 11	Sep. 15	Sep. 30 '98

STANDARD
&POOR'S
STOCK REPORTS

Banc One Corporation

275

12-SEP-98

Business Summary - 13-AUG-98

In a transaction that will create one of the largest banking institutions in the U.S., Banc One reached an agreement to merge with First Chicago NBD Corp. in April 1998. The combined bank would have leading retail branch presence in eight states with 2,000 offices and would be the second largest credit card issuer in the U.S. with $60 billion in managed receivables. As of December 31, 1997, Banc One operated 1,300 banking centers in Ohio, Indiana, Colorado, Wisconsin, Kentucky, Illinois, Texas, Oklahoma, Arizona, Utah, West Virginia and Louisiana. For the past few years, the company has been focused on implementing its Project One program, designed to enhance the effectiveness and efficiency of certain operations by reducing its number of bank charters, combining operations and systems and centralizing various staff and line functions.

In 1997, average earning assets, from which interest income is derived, amounted to $100.7 billion and consisted mainly of loans and leases (82%) and investment securities (16%). Average sources of funds, on which the bank pays interest, included savings and money market accounts (28%), time deposits (23%), interest-bearing demand deposits (1%), noninterest-bearing demand deposits (14%), short-term borrowings (14%), long-term debt (8%), shareholders' equity (9%) and other (3%).

At year-end 1997, nonperforming assets, consisting primarily of non-accrual and other real estate owned, were $476 million (0.56% of loans and related assets), up from $435 million (0.56%) a year earlier. The allowance for loan losses, which is set aside for possible loan defaults, was $1.33 billion (1.62% of loans), versus $1.20 billion (1.51%) a year earlier. Net chargeoffs, or the amount of loans actually written off as uncollectible, were $1.12 billion (1.35% of average loans) in 1997, compared to $820 million (1.08%) in 1996.

In June 1997, ONE acquired First USA, Inc. (NYSE; FUS), the fourth largest VISA/Mastercard issuer in the U.S. with $22.4 billion in managed receivables and 16 million cardholder accounts. Each FUS common share was exchanged for 1.1659 common shares of ONE.

The proposed transaction with First Chicago NBD (NYSE; FCN), which has total assets of $114 billion, calls for each FCN common share to be exchanged for 1.62 ONE common shares and each ONE share to be converted into one share of the new company, which will retain the Banc One name. The merger is expected to be completed in the fourth quarter of 1998.

Per Share Data ($)

(Year Ended Dec. 31)	1997	1996	1995	1994	1993	1992	1991	1990	1989	1988
Tangible Bk. Val.	14.74	16.95	16.36	14.68	14.78	12.23	10.79	9.35	7.98	7.12
Earnings	1.99	2.94	2.65	2.00	2.42	1.97	1.75	1.51	1.38	1.29
Dividends	1.38	1.24	1.13	1.02	0.89	0.73	0.63	0.57	0.52	0.46
Payout Ratio	69%	42%	43%	51%	37%	37%	36%	38%	38%	35%
Prices - High	54³/₈	43¹/₂	33¹/₈	31³/₈	37	32¹/₈	28⁷/₈	18¹/₈	18³/₈	13³/₄
- Low	35⁵/₈	28³/₈	20³/₄	20	26⁵/₈	25³/₈	13⁵/₈	10³/₈	11¹/₈	10¹/₂
P/E Ratio - High	25	15	13	16	15	16	16	12	13	11
- Low	16	10	8	10	11	13	8	7	8	8

Income Statement Analysis (Million $)

	1997	1996	1995	1994	1993	1992	1991	1990	1989	1988
Net Int. Inc.	5,392	4,855	4,129	4,189	4,090	3,165	1,771	1,241	1,116	1,060
Tax Equiv. Adj.	54.0	64.0	80.0	88.0	79.0	75.0	68.0	68.0	77.0	82.0
Non Int. Inc.	3,779	2,135	1,847	1,681	1,492	1,157	844	707	513	452
Loan Loss Prov.	1,211	788	457	242	369	510	424	300	198	183
Exp./Op. Revs.	66%	59%	60%	65%	62%	61%	55%	55%	57%	57%
Pretax Inc.	1,969	2,111	1,910	64.6	1,699	1,161	705	543	463	438
Eff. Tax Rate	34%	32%	33%	34%	34%	33%	25%	22%	25%	22%
Net Inc.	1,306	1,427	1,278	1,005	1,121	781	529	423	348	340
% Net Int. Marg.	5.41	5.59	5.47	5.40	6.29	6.13	6.09	5.27	5.15	5.42

Balance Sheet & Other Fin. Data (Million $)

	1997	1996	1995	1994	1993	1992	1991	1990	1989	1988
Earning Assets:										
Money Mkt	NA	NA	NA	NA	NA	NA	NA	NA	NA	NA
Inv. Securities	15,253	14,635	14,620	15,152	17,408	13,884	7,989	5,272	5,133	4,625
Com'l Loans	25,213	22,559	20,724	17,958	15,064	13,534	11,055	8,530	7,740	7,670
Other Loans	56,840	51,635	45,584	44,035	38,782	25,188	19,142	11,833	10,169	9,654
Total Assets	115,901	101,848	90,454	88,923	79,919	61,417	46,293	30,336	26,552	25,274
Demand Deposits	18,444	16,195	14,767	14,406	13,675	10,316	6,729	3,729	3,545	3,363
Time Deposits	58,970	56,178	52,553	53,684	47,268	38,149	30,328	18,587	17,408	16,139
LT Debt	11,066	4,190	2,720	1,694	1,702	1,173	696	525	356	221
Common Eqty.	10,241	8,440	7,947	7,315	6,784	4,954	3,545	2,876	2,255	2,015
% Ret. on Assets	1.2	1.5	1.4	1.1	1.5	1.3	1.6	1.5	1.4	1.9
% Ret. on Equity	13.9	17.2	16.5	13.8	17.8	17.2	17.4	16.4	16.3	17.8
% Loan Loss Resv.	1.6	1.9	1.4	1.4	1.7	1.9	1.8	1.6	1.4	1.4
% Loans/Deposits	106.0	98.1	97.0	91.1	88.4	79.9	81.5	91.3	85.5	88.8
% Equity to Assets	8.6	8.5	8.5	8.2	8.4	7.6	8.7	9.3	8.3	10.8

Data as orig. reptd.; bef. results of disc. opers. and/or spec. items. Per share data adj. for stk. divs. as of ex-div. date. Bold denotes diluted EPS (FASB 128). E-Estimated. NA-Not Available. NM-Not Meaningful. NR-Not Ranked.

Office—100 E. Broad St., Columbus, OH 43271. **Tel**—(614) 248-5944. **Website**—http://www.bankone.com **Chrmn & CEO**—J. B. McCoy. **Pres & COO**—R. J. Lehmann. **EVP-Fin**—M. J. McMennamin. **Investor Contacts**—Jay S. Gould, Jacqueline R. Spak. **Dirs**—B. Dorrance, C. E. Exley Jr., E. G. Gee, J. R. Hall, L. P. Jackson Jr., J. W. Kessler, R. J. Lehmann, J. B. McCoy, J. G. McCoy, T. R. Shackelford, A. Shumate, F. P. Stratton Jr., J. C. Tolleson, R. D. Walter. **Transfer Agent & Registrar**—Harris Trust & Savings Bank, Chicago. **Incorporated**—in Delaware in 1967; reincorporated in Ohio in 1989.**Empl**— 56,600. **S&P Analyst:** Stephen R. Biggar

STANDARD &POOR'S
STOCK REPORTS

Bank of New York

282

NYSE Symbol **BK**

In S&P 500

12-SEP-98

Industry:
Banks (Major Regional)

Summary: This company is a leader in securities processing and also provides a complete range of banking and other financial services.

| S&P Opinion: Buy (★★★★) | Recent Price • 27¾ | Yield • 2.0% |
| | 52 Wk Range • 34¼-21⅝ | 12-Mo. P/E • 19.1 |

Quantitative Evaluations

Outlook
(1 Lowest—5 Highest)
• **1**

Fair Value
• **19**

Risk
• **Low**

Earn./Div. Rank
• **A-**

Technical Eval.
• **Bullish** since 7/95

Rel. Strength Rank
(1 Lowest—99 Highest)
• **77**

Insider Activity
• **NA**

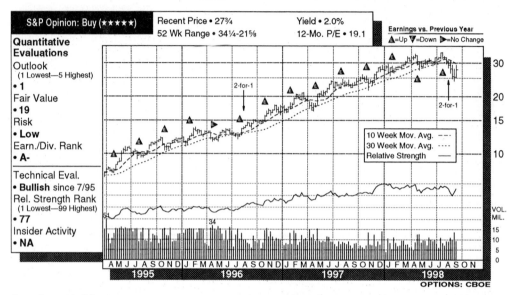

Earnings vs. Previous Year
▲=Up ▼=Down ▶=No Change

10 Week Mov. Avg. ---
30 Week Mov. Avg. ....
Relative Strength —

OPTIONS: CBOE

Overview - 29-JUL-98

Earnings should continue to benefit from strong growth in the securities processing business, BK's principal profit engine, reflecting internal growth of about 15%, and the prospect of acquisitions in this rapidly consolidating industry segment. Meanwhile, new business and ongoing growth in cross-border investing has benefited the global custody business. Net interest income and margins are expected to be lower in 1998 following the 1997 sale of the company's credit card portfolio, which will also result in somewhat lower service charges and fees but substantially reduced loss provisions. The de-emphasis of the credit card business significantly improves both credit quality and the quality of underlying earnings. BK nonetheless remains committed to the future of the retail business, for both diversification and a stable deposit base.

Valuation - 29-JUL-98

BK's unsolicited bid for Mellon Bank put some pressure on the shares in April 1998, although they have since rebounded. Uncertainty about the deal (Mellon flatly rejected the proposed offer) and the premium being paid to Mellon shareholders caused investors to take pause in the valuation of the shares. While Mellon would have been a good fit in many respects, we view the failure of the deal as a non-event, with BK remaining well positioned in all of its target markets. Given the high percentage of income derived from noninterest income activities, we view BK's revenue base as more valuable than that of its regional bank competitors, justifying a premium P/E multiple for its shares. The stock, recently trading at 19X our 1999 EPS estimate of $3.45, is expected to outperform market averages over the next 12 months.

Key Stock Statistics

S&P EPS Est. 1998	1.52	Tang. Bk. Value/Share	6.62
P/E on S&P Est. 1998	18.2	Beta	1.41
S&P EPS Est. 1999	1.73	Shareholders	24,000
Dividend Rate/Share	0.56	Market cap. (B)	$ 20.7
Shs. outstg. (M)	747.3	Inst. holdings	59%
Avg. daily vol. (M)	2.231		

Value of $10,000 invested 5 years ago: $ 47,822

Fiscal Year Ending Dec. 31

	1998	1997	1996	1995	1994	1993
Revenues (Million $)						
1Q	1,387	1,342	1,348	1,255	976.0	955.0
2Q	1,431	1,401	1,756	1,331	1,019	972.0
3Q	—	1,425	1,288	1,352	1,104	963.0
4Q	—	1,528	1,324	1,389	1,151	934.0
Yr.	—	5,697	5,713	5,327	4,251	3,822
Earnings Per Share ($)						
1Q	**0.36**	0.32	0.29	0.28	0.23	0.17
2Q	**0.38**	0.33	0.34	0.28	0.23	0.15
3Q	**E0.39**	0.34	0.30	0.29	0.25	0.20
4Q	**E0.40**	0.38	0.30	0.29	0.27	0.20
Yr.	**E1.52**	1.35	1.20	1.14	0.98	0.72

Next earnings report expected: late October

Dividend Data (Dividends have been paid since 1785.)

Amount ($)	Date Decl.	Ex-Div. Date	Stock of Record	Payment Date
0.260	Jan. 13	Jan. 21	Jan. 23	Feb. 05 '98
0.260	Apr. 14	Apr. 22	Apr. 24	May. 01 '98
0.280	Jul. 14	Jul. 22	Jul. 24	Aug. 06 '98
2-for-1	Jul. 14	Aug. 14	Jul. 24	Aug. 13 '98

A Division of The **McGraw·Hill** *Companies*

The Bank of New York Company, Inc.

Business Summary - 29-JUL-98

The Bank of New York Company (BK) over the past few years has been deriving an increasing percentage of revenues from businesses that provide fee revenues, while traditional interest-revenue generating businesses have been de-emphasized. BK has acquired and integrated a number of corporate trust and custody operations from other large banks that did not have the volume scale to compete successfully in those businesses. BK can probably be more accurately described as a leading global trust bank than as a traditional lending institution.

Principal operations include securities and other processing services (American Depositary Receipts, corporate trust, stock transfer, custody, securities lending, government securities clearance, unit investment trustee services, mutual funds custody, funds transfer, trade finance, cash management); corporate banking (commercial lending, capital markets, leasing and trade finance); and retail banking (363 offices in New York, New Jersey and Connecticut). The company also offers trust, investment management and private banking services, asset-based lending and financial market services such as foreign exchange and interest rate and currency risk management. BK's credit card business, which it believed it did not have the scale to compete, was sold in November 1997.

In 1997, average earning assets, from which interest income is derived, amounted to $48.5 billion and consisted mainly of loans (75%) and investment securities (12%). Average sources of funds included domestic deposits (26%), foreign deposits (25%), noninterest-bearing deposits (16%), short-term borrowings (9%), long-term debt (3%), shareholders' equity (9%) and other (12%).

At year-end 1997, nonperforming assets, consisting primarily of non-accrual loans and other real estate, were $208 million (0.6% of loans and related assets), down from $254 million (0.7%) a year earlier. The allowance for loan losses, which is set aside for possible loan defaults, was $641 million (1.82% of loans), versus $901 million (2.44%) a year earlier. Net chargeoffs, or the amount of loans actually written off as uncollectible, were $354 million (0.97% of average loans) in 1997, versus $455 million (1.24%) in 1996.

In May 1998, the company withdrew an offer to merge with Mellon Bank Corp. (NYSE; MEL) after Mellon rejected the proposed terms of the transaction.

Per Share Data ($) (Year Ended Dec. 31)	1997	1996	1995	1994	1993	1992	1991	1990	1989	1988
Tangible Bk. Val.	6.67	6.50	6.46	5.57	5.08	4.96	4.57	4.57	4.58	4.97
Earnings	1.35	1.24	1.14	0.98	0.72	0.56	0.16	0.50	0.03	0.70
Dividends	0.49	0.42	0.34	0.27	0.21	0.19	0.21	0.27	0.25	0.23
Payout Ratio	36%	34%	30%	28%	30%	34%	130%	53%	821%	33%
Prices - High	29 1/4	18 1/8	12 1/4	8 3/8	7 7/8	6 7/8	4 1/2	5 1/4	6 7/8	4 5/8
- Low	16 3/8	10 7/8	7 1/8	6 1/4	6 3/8	3 3/4	2 1/16	1 11/16	4 5/8	3 1/4
P/E Ratio - High	22	15	11	8	11	12	28	10	NM	7
- Low	12	9	6	6	9	7	13	3	NM	5
Income Statement Analysis (Million $)										
Net Int. Inc.	1,855	1,961	2,029	1,717	1,497	1,224	1,198	1,319	1,253	729
Tax Equiv. Adj.	35.0	38.0	39.0	46.0	53.0	62.0	75.0	79.0	75.0	64.0
Non Int. Inc.	2,001	2,033	1,381	1,274	1,319	1,091	956	894	902	508
Loan Loss Prov.	280	600	330	162	284	427	746	423	783	168
Exp./Op. Revs.	49%	46%	50%	54%	59%	58%	59%	61%	59%	62%
Pretax Inc.	1,773	1,656	1,482	1,198	886	559	177	432	65.0	298
Eff. Tax Rate	38%	38%	38%	37%	37%	34%	31%	29%	22%	29%
Net Inc.	1,104	1,020	914	749	559	369	122	308	51.0	213
% Net Int. Marg.	3.89	4.35	4.53	4.11	3.84	3.55	3.43	3.29	3.09	3.68
Balance Sheet & Other Fin. Data (Million $)										
Earning Assets:										
Money Mkt	7,562	3,249	2,680	4,951	1,630	999	2,402	2,661	2,982	3,023
Inv. Securities	6,628	5,053	4,870	4,651	5,597	4,648	3,773	3,287	3,829	4,274
Com'l Loans	14,429	12,844	14,434	16,085	12,594	12,303	14,484	15,219	16,502	14,405
Other Loans	20,698	24,162	23,253	17,868	18,813	15,928	14,336	18,613	20,135	19,322
Total Assets	59,961	55,765	53,720	48,879	45,546	40,909	39,426	45,390	48,857	47,388
Demand Deposits	12,561	11,812	10,465	8,579	8,690	7,534	6,342	7,355	8,031	8,229
Time Deposits	28,796	27,531	25,453	25,512	23,469	21,915	22,632	26,666	26,896	24,478
LT Debt	1,809	1,816	1,848	1,774	1,590	1,592	1,200	840	866	1,121
Common Eqty.	5,001	5,015	5,119	4,177	3,778	3,210	2,554	2,537	2,489	2,517
% Ret. on Assets	1.9	1.9	1.8	1.5	1.2	0.9	0.3	0.6	0.1	0.8
% Ret. on Equity	21.9	20.0	19.4	19.5	15.0	13.5	4.2	13.0	0.7	18.2
% Loan Loss Resv.	1.8	2.4	2.0	2.4	3.1	3.7	3.6	3.1	3.1	2.8
% Loans/Deposits	84.9	94.1	104.9	97.0	97.6	93.0	96.6	97.0	102.4	101.0
% Equity to Assets	8.7	9.3	9.1	7.5	8.3	5.9	5.0	4.3	4.5	4.3

Data as orig. reptd.; bef. results of disc opers. and/or spec. items. Per share data adj. for stk. divs. as of ex-div. date. Bold denotes diluted EPS (FASB 128). E-Estimated. NA-Not Available. NM-Not Meaningful. NR-Not Ranked.

Office—48 Wall St., New York, NY 10286. **Tel**—(212) 495-1784. **Website**—http://www.bankofny.com **Chrmn & CEO**—T. A. Renyi. **Vice Chrmn**—A. R. Griffith. **SEVP**—D. D. Papageorge. **Secy**—P. C. Miller. **Investor Contacts**—Paul J. Leyden, Nicholas C. Silitch. **Dirs**—J. C. Bacot, R. Barth, F. J. Biondi Jr., W. R. Chaney, R. E. Gomory, A. R. Griffith, E. L. Hennessy Jr., R. J. Kogan, J. A. Luke Jr., J. C. Malone, D. L. Miller, H. B. Morley, D. D. Papageorge, C. A. Rein, T. A. Renyi, H. E. Sells. **Transfer Agent & Registrar**—Bank of New York, NYC. **Incorporated**—in New York in 1968; Bank of New York founded in 1784. **Empl**— 16,494. **S&P Analyst:** Stephen R. Biggar

12-SEP-98

Industry: Banks (Money Center)

Summary: The third largest U.S. bank holding company, BankAmerica recently agreed to merge with North Carolina-based NationsBank.

S&P Opinion: Hold (★★★)

Recent Price • 61¼	Yield • 2.3%
52 Wk Range • 100⅛-52¾	12-Mo. P/E • 13.2

Quantitative Evaluations

Outlook
(1 Lowest—5 Highest)
• **2+**

Fair Value
• **60⅛**

Risk
• **Low**

Earn./Div. Rank
• **A-**

Technical Eval.
• **Bearish** since 8/98

Rel. Strength Rank
(1 Lowest—99 Highest)
• **28**

Insider Activity
• **Neutral**

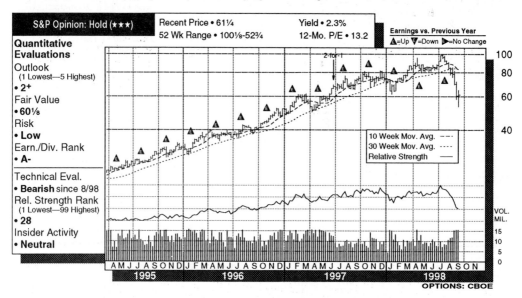

Earnings vs. Previous Year
▲=Up ▼=Down ►=No Change

2-for-1

10 Week Mov. Avg. ---
30 Week Mov. Avg. ····
Relative Strength ——

VOL. MIL.

OPTIONS: CBOE

Overview - 25-AUG-98

Earnings in 1998 should continue to benefit from good internal loan growth, strategic capital redeployment activities, and good expense control. Securitization of consumer loans and narrower interest margins from a less favorable asset mix, however, will limit reported net interest income comparisons. On the noninterest income side of the business, traditional fee income is growing steadily, although trading income has become more volatile, with trading losses in emerging markets expected to continue. The late 1997 Robertson Stephens acquisition has made strong contributions to date, although the unit is being sold in connection with the planned NationsBank merger. Also in light of the merger, a share buyback program has been suspended. The combination with NationsBank is expected to provide long-term financial benefits in the form of operating leverage and stability of earnings.

Valuation - 25-AUG-98

Worries of turmoil overseas and the announced NationsBank merger have made the shares somewhat volatile thus far in 1998. In keeping with recent industry trends, this merger is more about revenue enhancement potential than about cost savings, with most of the incremental earnings benefit built into 2000 projections. In the absence of a significant geographic overlap, the two companies are planning on their complimentary product sets and improved operating leverage to produce strong returns. Although we are positive on the transaction itself for the long term, we expect the shares to track the broader market until merger benefits become tangible and Asia's economic situation is less worrisome.

Key Stock Statistics

S&P EPS Est. 1998	4.85	Tang. Bk. Value/Share	21.78
P/E on S&P Est. 1998	12.6	Beta	1.64
S&P EPS Est. 1999	5.60	Shareholders	139,200
Dividend Rate/Share	1.38	Market cap. (B)	$ 42.0
Shs. outstg. (M)	684.8	Inst. holdings	56%
Avg. daily vol. (M)	3.717		

Value of $10,000 invested 5 years ago: $ 30,706

Fiscal Year Ending Dec. 31

	1998	1997	1996	1995	1994	1993
Revenues (Million $)						
1Q	6,216	5,625	5,363	4,829	3,816	4,014
2Q	6,240	5,801	5,446	5,127	3,957	3,939
3Q	—	6,121	5,525	5,201	4,228	3,952
4Q	—	6,038	5,737	5,229	4,530	3,995
Yr.	—	23,585	22,071	20,386	16,531	15,900
Earnings Per Share ($)						
1Q	**1.17**	1.03	0.90	0.73	0.64	0.59
2Q	**1.24**	1.07	0.92	0.78	0.67	0.60
3Q	—	1.11	0.88	0.86	0.68	0.59
4Q	—	1.12	0.96	0.87	0.70	0.60
Yr.	—	4.32	3.65	3.25	2.68	2.40

Next earnings report expected: mid October

Dividend Data (Dividends have been paid since 1989.)

Amount ($)	Date Decl.	Ex-Div. Date	Stock of Record	Payment Date
0.305	Nov. 03	Nov. 18	Nov. 20	Dec. 12 '97
0.345	Feb. 02	Feb. 18	Feb. 20	Mar. 11 '98
0.345	Apr. 27	May. 18	May. 20	Jun. 11 '98
0.345	Aug. 03	Aug. 18	Aug. 20	Sep. 11 '98

A Division of The McGraw·Hill Companies

Business Summary - 25-AUG-98

In April 1998, BankAmerica agreed to merge with North Carolina-based NationsBank in a transaction that would form the second largest banking institution in the U.S., with $570 billion in assets. Billed as the creation of the first truly national U.S. banking franchise, the combined company would have relationships with 29 million households in 22 states, and would serve two million business in the U.S. and 38 other countries.

BAC currently offers retail deposit, credit card, home mortgage, manufactured housing and auto loan financing to individuals and small businesses through 1,800 full-service branch offices, including 970 offices in California, its largest market. For large public and private sector institutions, the company provides capital-raising services, trade finance, cash management, investment banking, capital markets and credit products, and financial advisory services. It also offers credit and other financial services to real estate market participants, including developers, investors, pension fund advisers, real estate investment trusts and property managers.

In 1997, average earning assets, from which interest income is derived, amounted to $214 billion and consisted mainly of domestic loans (65%), foreign loans (13%) and investment securities (7%). Average sources of funds, used mainly in the lending business, included domestic interest-bearing deposits (34%), foreign interest-bearing deposits (18%), noninterest-bearing deposits (22%), short-term borrowings (12%), long-term debt (6%) and shareholders' equity (8%).

At year-end 1996, nonperforming assets (mainly non-accrual loans) were $899 million (0.42% of assets), down from $1.12 billion (0.59%) a year earlier. The allowance for loan losses, which is set aside for possible loan defaults, was $3.50 billion (2.09% of loans), versus $3.52 billion (2.13%) a year earlier. Net chargeoffs, or the amount of loans actually written off as uncollectible, were $901 million (0.54% of average loans) in 1997, compared to $918 million (0.58%) in 1996.

The pending transaction with NationsBank calls for BAC shareholders to exchange each of their shares for 1.1316 shares of the new BankAmerica Corp., while NationsBank shares would be converted one-for-one into new BankAmerica shares. The merger is expected to close in the fourth quarter of 1998.

Per Share Data ($)

(Year Ended Dec. 31)	1997	1996	1995	1994	1993	1992	1991	1990	1989	1988
Tangible Bk. Val.	20.39	18.18	15.79	12.63	11.18	9.96	15.39	13.61	11.66	9.21
Earnings	4.32	3.65	3.25	2.68	2.40	2.12	2.40	1.93	1.90	1.39
Dividends	1.22	1.08	0.92	0.80	0.70	0.65	0.60	0.50	0.30	Nil
Payout Ratio	28%	30%	28%	30%	29%	31%	25%	26%	16%	Nil
Prices - High	81⅞	52	34¼	25⅛	27¾	24⅞	22⅜	16¾	18¼	9⅝
- Low	47¾	29⅜	19¾	19¼	20¼	17¾	11⅝	8¾	8½	3⅜
P/E Ratio - High	19	14	11	9	12	12	9	9	10	7
- Low	11	8	6	7	8	8	5	5	4	2

Income Statement Analysis (Million $)

	1997	1996	1995	1994	1993	1992	1991	1990	1989	1988
Net Int. Inc.	8,669	8,587	8,462	7,542	7,441	6,718	4,472	4,152	4,023	3,686
Tax Equiv. Adj.	9.0	17.0	NA	24.0	22.0	22.0	9.0	12.0	16.0	17.0
Non Int. Inc.	6,012	5,351	4,512	4,123	4,212	3,638	2,375	2,087	1,830	1,760
Loan Loss Prov.	950	885	440	460	803	990	805	905	770	645
Exp./Op. Revs.	58%	60%	NA	64%	64%	65%	61%	63%	64%	68%
Pretax Inc.	5,326	4,773	4,567	3,717	3,428	2,682	1,873	1,399	1,348	942
Eff. Tax Rate	40%	40%	42%	41%	43%	44%	40%	37%	39%	42%
Net Inc.	3,210	2,873	2,664	2,176	1,954	1,492	1,124	877	820	547
% Net Int. Marg.	4.06	4.23	4.51	4.50	4.71	4.75	4.36	4.29	4.58	4.30

Balance Sheet & Other Fin. Data (Million $)

	1997	1996	1995	1994	1993	1992	1991	1990	1989	1988
Earning Assets:										
Money Mkt	31,292	25,322	20,960	19,211	15,500	10,300	7,600	5,700	4,800	8,100
Inv. Securities	16,453	16,251	16,699	18,016	19,700	15,300	8,400	6,900	7,100	7,700
Com'l Loans	64,470	58,702	40,701	36,869	29,100	28,200	17,600	18,900	18,900	18,700
Other Loans	102,641	106,713	114,672	104,043	97,200	96,300	68,800	66,900	57,000	50,400
Total Assets	260,159	250,753	232,446	215,475	186,900	180,600	115,500	110,700	98,800	94,600
Demand Deposits	35,216	41,150	38,511	36,566	32,900	33,900	18,800	18,700	18,200	17,600
Time Deposits	136,821	126,865	121,983	117,828	108,700	104,000	75,300	73,600	63,000	59,500
LT Debt	13,922	15,430	14,723	13,558	14,100	16,400	3,820	3,930	4,080	3,820
Common Eqty.	19,223	18,471	17,599	15,823	14,200	12,500	6,740	5,810	4,900	3,420
% Ret. on Assets	1.3	1.2	1.2	1.1	1.1	0.9	1.0	0.8	0.8	0.6
% Ret. on Equity	16.5	14.9	14.6	13.1	12.9	12.7	17.3	15.5	18.7	16.9
% Loan Loss Resv.	2.1	2.1	2.3	2.6	2.8	3.1	2.8	3.4	4.5	5.2
% Loans/Deposits	97.1	98.5	96.8	91.3	89.2	90.3	91.8	92.9	93.4	89.5
% Equity to Assets	7.4	7.5	7.5	7.3	7.2	6.3	5.4	5.0	4.2	3.0

Data as orig. reptd.; bef. results of disc opers. and/or spec. items. Per share data adj. for stk. divs. as of ex-div. date. Bold denotes diluted EPS (FASB 128). E-Estimated. NA-Not Available. NM-Not Meaningful. NR-Not Ranked.

Office—Bank of America Center, San Francisco, CA 94104. Tel—(415) 622-3530. Website— http://www.bankamerica.com Chrmn, Pres & CEO—D. A. Coulter. Vice Chrmn & CFO—M. E. O'Neill. EVP & Secy—C. A. Sorokin. Investor Contact—Mike Zampa. Dirs—J. F. Alibrandi, P. B. Bedford, R. A. Clarke, D. A. Coulter, T. F. Crull, K. Feldstein, D. E. Guinn, F. L. Hope Jr., W. E. Massey, J. M. Richman, S. R. Robertson, R. M. Rosenberg, A. M. Spence, S. D. Trujillo. Transfer Agent & Registrar—ChaseMellon Shareholder Services, Ridgefield Park, NJ, and SF. Incorporated—in Delaware in 1968; Bank of America incorporated in California in 1930. Empl— 89,300. S&P Analyst: Stephen R. Biggar

STANDARD &POOR'S
STOCK REPORTS

BankBoston Corp.

283P

NYSE Symbol **BKB**

In S&P 500

12-SEP-98

Industry:
Banks (Major Regional)

Summary: This bank holding company provides consumer banking in southern New England and financing and capital markets services to corporations domestically and abroad.

S&P Opinion: Accumulate (★★★★)	Recent Price • 36⅜	Yield • 3.2%
	52 Wk Range • 59-31½	12-Mo. P/E • 11.7

Quantitative Evaluations

Outlook
(1 Lowest—5 Highest)
• **2+**

Fair Value
• **34⅛**

Risk
• **Low**

Earn./Div. Rank
• **B**

Technical Eval.
• **Bearish** since 7/98

Rel. Strength Rank
(1 Lowest—99 Highest)
• **32**

Insider Activity
• **Neutral**

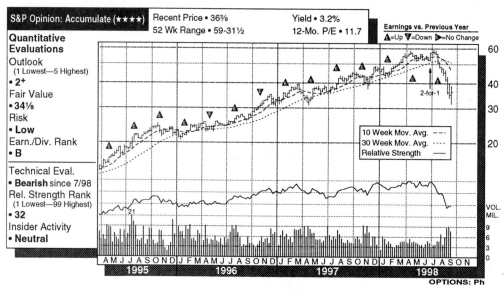

Earnings vs. Previous Year
▲=Up ▼=Down ▶=No Change

10 Week Mov. Avg. ---
30 Week Mov. Avg. ·····
Relative Strength —

2-for-1

VOL. MIL.

OPTIONS: Ph

Overview - 21-AUG-98

Revenue growth remains healthy in the three targeted areas of wholesale banking, retail banking and global banking. The company will add equity underwriting capabilities to its strengths in loan syndications, high-yield debt underwriting and leveraged finance with the upcoming acquisition of Robertson Stephens, which should further improve revenue momentum. On the lending front, double-digit growth in the commercial portfolio has been mitigated by a planned exit of national consumer businesses resulting in lower balances of residential mortgage and credit card loans and modest pressure on the interest margin. Growth is expected to be offset by expenses to support Latin American investment spending, the buildup of corporate banking and global capital markets businesses, and higher compensation costs related to a shift in business mix.

Valuation - 21-AUG-98

After a strong first half performance, the shares rapidly retreated in July and are now about breakeven since the beginning of the year. This most likely reflects renewed concerns about international exposure. The recently announced agreement to purchase the Robertson Stephens investment banking unit of BankAmerica is a good sign that solid efforts are being made to further improve not only revenue growth but diversity of earnings sources. Speculation about a potential takeover or merger will likely continue, reflecting the bank's strong franchise but limited New England retail banking service territory. Trading at only 13 times estimated 1999 earnings of $3.55, the shares should outperform in the year ahead.

Key Stock Statistics

S&P EPS Est. 1998	3.20	Tang. Bk. Value/Share	16.92
P/E on S&P Est. 1998	11.4	Beta	1.56
S&P EPS Est. 1999	3.55	Shareholders	27,700
Dividend Rate/Share	1.16	Market cap. (B)	$ 10.7
Shs. outstg. (M)	294.2	Inst. holdings	65%
Avg. daily vol. (M)	1.624		

Value of $10,000 invested 5 years ago: $ 33,153

Fiscal Year Ending Dec. 31

	1998	1997	1996	1995	1994	1993
Revenues (Million $)						
1Q	1,926	1,605	1,525	1,326	958.8	835.0
2Q	1,848	1,658	1,595	1,339	1,032	848.0
3Q	—	1,715	1,536	1,362	1,285	890.0
4Q	—	1,750	1,590	1,383	1,270	912.0
Yr.	—	6,727	6,237	5,420	4,546	3,485
Earnings Per Share ($)						
1Q	**0.79**	**0.64**	0.47	0.54	0.44	0.24
2Q	**0.80**	**0.68**	0.61	0.56	0.40	0.30
3Q	**E0.81**	**0.73**	0.23	0.58	0.54	0.15
4Q	**E0.80**	**0.78**	0.63	0.59	0.52	0.44
Yr.	**E3.20**	**2.83**	1.97	2.27	1.90	1.14

Next earnings report expected: mid October

Dividend Data (Dividends have been paid since 1784.)

Amount ($)	Date Decl.	Ex-Div. Date	Stock of Record	Payment Date
0.580	Jan. 15	Jan. 29	Feb. 02	Feb. 27 '98
0.580	Apr. 23	Apr. 30	May. 04	May. 29 '98
2-for-1	Apr. 23	Jun. 23	Jun. 01	Jun. 22 '98
0.290	Jul. 22	Jul. 30	Aug. 03	Aug. 28 '98

A Division of The McGraw·Hill Companies

Business Summary - 21-AUG-98

With its corporate motto "Managing for Value," BankBoston (formerly Bank of Boston) intends to increase revenues and earnings by capitalizing on its competitive advantages in target markets. Core disciplines include deploying capital in a way that most effectively creates value, exiting businesses that no longer make strategic sense, and targeted resource allocation through significant investments in talent and technology. Revenues in recent years were:

	1997	1996
Corporate banking/Global capital markets	34%	32%
Regional consumer/Small business	28%	31%
Argentina	9%	8%
Brazil	10%	9%
Global private bank	7%	7%
Other	12%	13%

Corporate banking offers national and regional commercial lending, while global capital markets includes emerging markets sales, trading and research and high yield securities. Regional consumer/small business provides traditional branch banking and deposit products through 468 branches in Massachusetts, Rhode Island, Connecticut and New Hampshire. The Argentina seg-

ment offers products within the large corporate, special industries, middle market and retail businesses. The Brazil segment includes corporate lending, trade financing, treasury and fee-based activities. The global private bank offers asset management, trust, tax and estate planning, loans and deposit products to high-net-worth individuals, professional firms and small businesses.

In 1997, average earning assets, from which interest income is derived, amounted to $57.7 billion and consisted mainly of loans and leases (73%) and investment securities (17%). Average sources of funds included interest-bearing deposits (54%), short-term borrowings (18%), long-term debt (5%), shareholders' equity (7%), noninterest-bearing deposits (12%) and other (4%).

At year-end 1997, nonperforming assets were $356 million (0.87% of loans and related assets), versus $452 million (1.1%) a year earlier. The allowance for loan losses, which is set aside for possible loan defaults, was $712 million (1.62% of loans), versus $883 million (2.15%) a year earlier. Net chargeoffs, or the amount of loans actually written off as uncollectible, were $279 million (0.66% of average loans) in 1997, up from $230 million (0.57%) in 1996.

In May 1998, the company agreed to acquire the investment banking operations of Robertson Stephens from BankAmerica Corp. for $400 million in cash, plus a retention pool of $400 million.

Per Share Data ($)

(Year Ended Dec. 31)	1997	1996	1995	1994	1993	1992	1991	1990	1989	1988
Tangible Bk. Val.	13.71	14.46	13.12	8.88	9.46	7.93	6.61	7.16	10.90	11.39
Earnings	2.83	2.00	2.27	1.90	1.14	1.05	-0.32	-3.10	0.40	2.33
Dividends	0.98	0.84	0.64	0.47	0.20	0.05	0.05	0.41	0.62	0.56
Payout Ratio	35%	42%	28%	25%	18%	5%	NM	NM	155%	24%
Prices - High	48⅞	35⅛	25⅛	14⅝	14⅝	13¼	6½	10	15⅜	15
- Low	31	20¾	12¾	11⅛	10⅛	5⅝	1½	3	7⅞	10½
P/E Ratio - High	17	18	11	8	13	13	NM	NM	38	6
- Low	11	10	6	6	9	5	NM	NM	20	4

Income Statement Analysis (Million $)

	1997	1996	1995	1994	1993	1992	1991	1990	1989	1988
Net Int. Inc.	2,429	2,340	1,741	1,585	1,519	1,098	925	1,013	1,166	1,154
Tax Equiv. Adj.	24.0	20.0	10.0	7.0	8.0	8.0	17.0	26.0	39.0	40.0
Non Int. Inc.	1,483	1,344	1,082	801	572	604	640	677	866	661
Loan Loss Prov.	200	231	250	130	70.0	100	328	620	722	144
Exp./Op. Revs.	59%	63%	56%	62%	74%	76%	84%	86%	58%	64%
Pretax Inc.	1,468	1,133	985	791	490	336	-80.0	-385	120	498
Eff. Tax Rate	40%	43%	45%	44%	44%	43%	NM	NM	41%	35%
Net Inc.	879	65.0	541	442	275	192	-34.0	-437	70.0	322
% Net Int. Marg.	4.25	4.42	4.45	4.17	4.10	3.90	3.26	3.12	3.64	3.86

Balance Sheet & Other Fin. Data (Million $)

	1997	1996	1995	1994	1993	1992	1991	1990	1989	1988
Earning Assets:										
Money Mkt	5,442	4,273	3,709	3,341	2,751	2,539	2,136	2,538	6,389	2,330
Inv. Securities	10,483	8,484	5,627	4,700	3,007	2,911	4,754	3,526	2,784	3,221
Com'l Loans	15,268	13,162	12,848	13,171	18,169	11,003	11,104	11,996	13,753	13,080
Other Loans	28,712	28,279	18,472	18,309	10,613	12,169	11,134	10,601	12,544	13,934
Total Assets	69,268	62,306	47,397	44,630	40,588	32,346	32,700	32,529	39,178	36,061
Demand Deposits	9,592	9,091	5,391	5,469	5,566	4,482	4,003	4,074	4,048	4,553
Time Deposits	36,169	33,740	25,557	25,887	24,049	20,819	20,734	22,435	24,649	19,037
LT Debt	2,941	2,821	2,139	2,169	1,973	1,432	1,103	1,182	1,664	1,719
Common Eqty.	4,332	4,426	3,243	2,634	2,403	1,792	1,406	1,447	1,888	1,877
% Ret. on Assets	1.3	1.1	1.2	1.0	0.8	0.6	NM	NM	0.2	1.0
% Ret. on Equity	19.4	14.5	17.2	16.1	11.8	10.9	NM	NM	2.9	18.3
% Loan Loss Resv.	1.6	2.3	2.4	2.2	2.7	3.6	4.2	4.2	3.6	2.6
% Loans/Deposits	121.6	96.8	100.4	99.5	97.2	90.4	88.6	83.7	89.6	112.2
% Equity to Assets	6.7	7.1	6.4	5.8	5.4	5.0	4.3	4.9	5.3	5.0

Data as orig. reptd.; bef. results of disc opers. and/or spec. items. Per share data adj. for stk. divs. as of ex-div. date. Bold denotes diluted EPS (FASB 128). E-Estimated. NA-Not Available. NM-Not Meaningful. NR-Not Ranked.

Office—100 Federal St., Boston, MA 02110. **Tel**—(617) 434-2200. **Website**—http://www.bankboston.com **Chrmn & CEO**—C. K. Gifford. **Pres & COO**—H. de Campos Meirelles. **CFO & Treas**—S. M. Swihart. **Vice Chrmn**—P. F. Hogan. **Investor Contact**—John A. Kahwaty. **Dirs**—W. A. Budd, J. A. Cervieri Jr., W. F. Connell, G. L. Countryman, W. M. Crozier Jr., A. F. Emerson, C. K. Gifford, T. J. May, D. F. McHenry, H. de Campos Meirelles, P. C. O'Brien, T. R. Piper, F. S. Rodgers, J. W. Rowe, G. P. Strehle, W. C. Van Faasen, T. B. Wheeler, A. M. Zeien. **Transfer Agent & Registrar**—BankBoston. **Incorporated**—in Massachusetts in 1970. **Empl**— 22,500. **S&P Analyst:** Stephen R. Biggar

STANDARD &POOR'S
STOCK REPORTS

Bankers Trust

284

NYSE Symbol **BT**

In S&P 500

12-SEP-98

Industry:
Banks (Money Center)

Summary: This bank holding company focuses on investment banking, risk management, trading and sales, investment management and client processing.

S&P Opinion: Hold (★★★)

Recent Price • 64⅜
52 Wk Range • 136⅜-60⅛

Yield • 6.2%
12-Mo. P/E • 8.6

Earnings vs. Previous Year
▲=Up ▼=Down ▶=No Change

Quantitative Evaluations

Outlook
(1 Lowest—5 Highest)
• **3+**

Fair Value
• **75⅜**

Risk
• **Low**

Earn./Div. Rank
• **B+**

Technical Eval.
• **Bearish** since 7/98

Rel. Strength Rank
(1 Lowest—99 Highest)
• **10**

Insider Activity
• **NA**

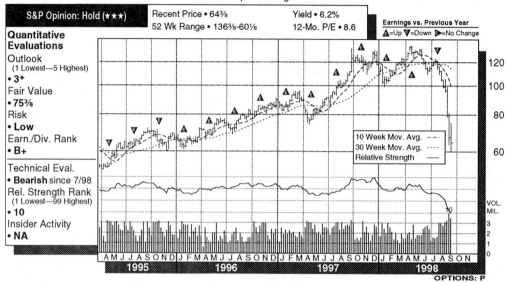

10 Week Mov. Avg. ---
30 Week Mov. Avg. ----
Relative Strength —

OPTIONS: P

Overview - 13-AUG-98

For 1998, the investment banking segment is expected to show good revenue progress, reflecting higher bond and equity underwriting activity, loan syndication fees and merger/acquisition fees following the Alex. Brown acquisition. The acquisition has provided strong cross-selling opportunities, as well as the ability to meet a greater range of client needs. Adverse emerging market results in the first half of 1998 were offset by particular strength in corporate finance and advisory activities. The integration of NatWest's European equities business (acquired in April 1998) is seen as an important expansion of the global investment bank. Control of expense growth has been hurt by higher salary, incentive and employee benefit costs, and this trend is not expected to abate in the near term, given competitive market conditions and greater emphasis on performance-based compensation. Credit quality remains adequate, although Asian uncertainties create the element of additional counterparty credit risk.

Valuation - 13-AUG-98

After recovering from an early selloff, the shares were virtually unchanged year to date in the first seven months of 1998, well below the average money center and the broader market. Concerns over Asian exposure (the company took a $120 million provision in the first half for trading-related credit losses) were most likely the culprit in holding back share gains. Nonetheless, improvement in earnings quality has become apparent as BT shifts to more predictable business lines with longer-term profit potential, such as trust activities, while other more volatile business segments are having less of an impact. Despite trading at somewhat of a valuation discount to its money center peers, we would hold the shares until emerging market troubles are resolved.

Key Stock Statistics

S&P EPS Est. 1998	6.80	Tang. Bk. Value/Share	52.51
P/E on S&P Est. 1998	9.5	Beta	1.44
S&P EPS Est. 1999	8.80	Shareholders	23,100
Dividend Rate/Share	4.00	Market cap. (B)	$ 6.2
Shs. outstg. (M)	96.2	Inst. holdings	58%
Avg. daily vol. (M)	1.374		

Value of $10,000 invested 5 years ago: $ 12,508

Fiscal Year Ending Dec. 31

	1998	1997	1996	1995	1994	1993
Revenues (Million $)						
1Q	3,220	2,513	2,340	1,695	1,716	1,755
2Q	3,487	2,664	2,257	2,107	1,892	1,899
3Q	—	3,254	2,480	2,311	1,914	2,106
4Q	—	3,251	2,488	2,196	1,981	2,040
Yr.	—	12,176	9,565	8,309	7,503	7,800
Earnings Per Share ($)						
1Q	2.01	1.76	1.52	-2.11	1.90	2.64
2Q	1.46	1.89	1.67	0.98	2.09	2.90
3Q	—	2.19	1.99	1.72	1.98	3.60
4Q	—	1.82	1.59	1.36	1.19	3.26
Yr.	—	7.66	6.76	2.03	7.17	12.40

Next earnings report expected: late October

Dividend Data (Dividends have been paid since 1904.)

Amount ($)	Date Decl.	Ex-Div. Date	Stock of Record	Payment Date
1.000	Sep. 16	Sep. 24	Sep. 26	Oct. 25 '97
1.000	Dec. 16	Dec. 23	Dec. 26	Jan. 25 '98
1.000	Mar. 17	Mar. 25	Mar. 27	Apr. 25 '98
1.000	Jun. 16	Jun. 24	Jun. 26	Jul. 25 '98

A Division of The **McGraw·Hill** *Companies*

Bankers Trust New York Corporation

Business Summary - 13-AUG-98

Bankers Trust New York took bold steps in 1997 to increase its presence in the investment banking business with the purchase of Alex. Brown Inc. The company believes that the acquisition has given its clients the benefit of its own expertise in syndicated bank lending and high-yield bonds and Alex. Brown's strength in equities research and underwriting.

BT broadly divides its business into five organizational units. Investment banking offers underwriting, distribution and trading of equity and debt, private placements and structured finance, and merger and acquisition advisory services. Risk management provides interest rate, currency, equity, commodity and credit derivatives. Trading and sales activities involve securities, currency, commodity and derivatives transactions on a proprietary basis. Private Client services include investment management in the global securities markets, financial planning services and market research and investment strategies for high net worth individuals. Global institutional services provides asset management, corporate trust and agency services, cash management and trade finance to financial institutions, corporations and governments. The company also provides various financial services internationally in Australia/New Zealand, Asia and Latin America.

In 1997, average earning assets, from which interest income is derived, amounted to $104.3 billion and consisted mainly of investment securities (41%), trading assets (28%) and loans (18%). Average sources of funds included mainly short-term borrowings (32%), domestic deposits (12%), foreign deposits (15%), long-term debt (8%), noninterest-bearing liabilities (16%) and shareholders' equity.

At year-end 1997, nonperforming assets, including non-accrual loans and real estate owned, were $497 million (2.9% of loans), down from $712 million (5.5%) a year earlier. The allowance for loan losses, which is set aside for possible loan defaults, was $997 million (5.0% of loans), versus $973 million (6.1%) a year earlier. Net chargeoffs, or the amount of loans actually written off as uncollectible, were $23 million (0.13% of average loans) in 1997, compared to $24 million (0.18%) in 1996.

In September 1997, Bankers Trust completed the acquisition of Alex. Brown Inc. (AB) in a transaction whereby each AB common share was exchanged for 0.83 shares of BT. Former AB shareholders now own about 20% of BT's outstanding shares.

Per Share Data ($) (Year Ended Dec. 31)	1997	1996	1995	1994	1993	1992	1991	1990	1989	1988
Tangible Bk. Val.	52.09	55.83	52.09	55.14	53.10	39.90	35.33	31.19	26.29	43.14
Earnings	7.66	6.78	2.03	7.17	12.40	8.82	7.75	7.80	-12.10	8.09
Dividends	4.00	4.00	4.00	3.70	3.24	2.88	2.60	2.38	2.14	1.92
Payout Ratio	52%	59%	197%	52%	26%	33%	34%	31%	NM	24%
Prices - High	133 5/8	90 7/8	72	84 5/8	83 1/2	70 1/8	68	46 3/4	58 1/4	41 1/4
- Low	74	61	49 3/4	54 3/4	65 3/4	50	39 1/2	28 1/2	34 1/2	29 5/8
P/E Ratio - High	17	13	35	12	7	8	9	6	NM	5
- Low	10	9	25	8	5	6	5	4	NM	4

Income Statement Analysis (Million $)	1997	1996	1995	1994	1993	1992	1991	1990	1989	1988
Net Int. Inc.	1,359	966	817	1,172	1,314	1,147	737	793	859	926
Tax Equiv. Adj.	26.0	16.0	41.0	83.0	82.0	52.0	32.0	55.0	89.0	94.0
Non Int. Inc.	4,891	3,124	2,243	2,401	3,351	2,335	2,476	2,307	1,963	1,649
Loan Loss Prov.	30.0	5.0	31.0	25.0	93.0	225	238	194	1,877	50.0
Exp./Op. Revs.	79%	81%	93%	75%	64%	66%	67%	67%	60%	61%
Pretax Inc.	1,239	872	311	869	1,550	906	834	815	-821	914
Eff. Tax Rate	30%	30%	31%	29%	31%	16%	20%	18%	NM	29%
Net Inc.	866	612	215	615	1,070	761	667	665	-979	648
% Net Int. Marg.	1.33	1.05	1.05	1.64	1.82	1.81	1.46	1.48	1.79	2.07

Balance Sheet & Other Fin. Data (Million $)	1997	1996	1995	1994	1993	1992	1991	1990	1989	1988
Earning Assets:										
Money Mkt	27,005	70,714	68,728	63,391	59,842	40,233	35,768	26,466	22,326	19,312
Inv. Securities	81,404	7,920	6,283	7,475	7,073	6,215	6,516	7,030	6,204	4,328
Com'l Loans	6,253	5,053	4,298	4,439	6,004	8,271	7,094	8,316	7,219	9,921
Other Loans	12,605	10,975	8,455	8,164	9,296	9,144	10,043	13,264	14,040	14,314
Total Assets	140,102	120,235	104,002	97,016	92,082	72,448	63,959	63,596	55,658	57,942
Demand Deposits	4,728	3,613	3,292	3,826	3,892	4,206	4,042	7,085	6,262	7,688
Time Deposits	38,102	26,713	22,416	21,113	18,884	20,865	18,792	21,503	19,958	24,803
LT Debt	16,059	11,109	9,294	6,455	5,597	3,992	3,081	2,650	2,435	2,450
Common Eqty.	5,708	4,424	4,119	4,309	4,284	3,309	2,912	2,524	2,136	3,499
% Ret. on Assets	0.7	0.5	0.2	0.6	1.3	1.0	1.1	1.0	NM	1.1
% Ret. on Equity	17.1	13.1	3.9	14.6	29.7	27.4	28.3	31.8	NM	20.3
% Loan Loss Resv.	3.5	4.9	7.9	10.0	8.7	9.3	10.6	10.1	12.9	5.5
% Loans/Deposits	46.6	52.2	49.1	50.1	66.7	69.1	74.7	75.1	80.7	74.2
% Equity to Assets	NA	3.5	4.2	3.9	4.1	3.6	3.7	3.1	5.0	5.5

Data as orig. reptd.; bef. results of disc opers. and/or spec. items. Per share data adj. for stk. divs. as of ex-div. date. Bold denotes diluted EPS (FASB 128). E-Estimated. NA-Not Available. NM-Not Meaningful. NR-Not Ranked.

Office—280 Park Ave., New York, NY 10017. **Tel**—(212) 250-2500. **Website**—http://www.bankerstrust.com **Chrmn, Pres & CEO**—F. N. Newman. **EVP, CFO & Contr**—R. H. Daniel. **VP & Investor Contact**—William McBride (212-250-7961). **Dirs**—L. A. Ault III, N. R. Austrian, G. B. Beitzel, P. A. Griffiths, W. R. Howell, V. E. Jordan Jr., H. Maxwell, F. N. Newman, N. J. Nicholas Jr., R. E. Palmer, D. L. Staheli, P. C. Stewart, G. R. Thoman, G. J. Vojta, P. Volcker. **Transfer Agent & Registrar**—Harris Trust Co. of New York, Chicago. **Incorporated**—in New York in 1966. **Empl**— 18,286. **S&P Analyst:** Stephen R. Biggar

Bard (C. R.)

288

NYSE Symbol **BCR**

In S&P 500

12-SEP-98

Industry:
Health Care (Medical Products & Supplies)

Summary: This company makes and markets a wide range of disposable therapeutic and diagnostic medical devices used in vascular, urological, oncological and surgical procedures.

S&P Opinion: Accumulate (★★★★)	Recent Price • 37⅜	Yield • 2.0%
	52 Wk Range • 41⅝-26½	12-Mo. P/E • 25.1

Quantitative Evaluations

Outlook
(1 Lowest—5 Highest)
• **3**

Fair Value
• **41¾**

Risk
• **Low**

Earn./Div. Rank
• **B+**

Technical Eval.
• **Bullish** since 9/98

Rel. Strength Rank
(1 Lowest—99 Highest)
• **85**

Insider Activity
• **Neutral**

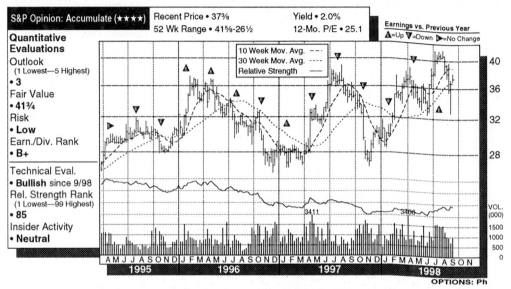

Earnings vs. Previous Year
▲=Up ▼=Down ▶=No Change

- 10 Week Mov. Avg. ----
- 30 Week Mov. Avg. ....
- Relative Strength —

OPTIONS: Ph

Overview - 20-AUG-98

Sales for 1998 are expected to fall short of 1997's $1.2 billion, reflecting declining sales in angioplasty and angiography lines and the planned divestiture of those businesses in the third quarter. In early July, Bard agreed to sell its coronary cath lab business to Arterial Vascular Engineering. However, continuing urology product sales should be helped by new infection control drainage and continence products, while new diagnostics are boosting oncology sales. New specialty access and mesh products are helping surgical products sales. Profitability should benefit from the better volume and cost efficiencies. Diluted EPS are estimated at $2.09 (including a net gain of $0.33 in the second quarter from a patent settlement). Boosted by a better product mix, lower interest expense and reduced shares outstanding, EPS should rise to $2.22 in 1999.

Valuation - 20-AUG-98

The shares moved higher over the past few months, boosted by the company's decision to sell its coronary cath lab business (angioplasty and angiography products) to Arterial Vascular Engineering for $600 million. The cath lab unit had sales of $215 million in 1997, but was only marginally profitable. Bard has been a relatively small player in those markets and the divestiture is expected to have a positive impact on Bard's bottom line. Proceeds from the sale are slated to retire about $100 million in debt and buy back close to 17% of Bard's outstanding common shares. Benefits from these actions coupled with plant consolidations and greater focus on core surgical, oncology and peripheral vascular businesses should generate accelerated earnings growth in the years ahead. The shares are recommended for long-term appreciation.

Key Stock Statistics

S&P EPS Est. 1998	2.09	Tang. Bk. Value/Share	3.37
P/E on S&P Est. 1998	17.9	Beta	1.12
S&P EPS Est. 1999	2.22	Shareholders	7,200
Dividend Rate/Share	0.76	Market cap. (B)	$ 2.1
Shs. outstg. (M)	56.1	Inst. holdings	75%
Avg. daily vol. (M)	0.186		

Value of $10,000 invested 5 years ago: $ 12,740

Fiscal Year Ending Dec. 31

	1998	1997	1996	1995	1994	1993
Revenues (Million $)						
1Q	296.3	300.7	289.2	278.1	247.4	236.0
2Q	300.6	304.0	295.2	291.1	256.3	243.9
3Q	—	297.5	295.8	277.6	251.9	243.5
4Q	—	311.3	314.2	291.0	262.6	247.0
Yr.	—	1,214	1,194	1,138	1,018	970.8
Earnings Per Share ($)						
1Q	**0.44**	0.45	0.48	0.44	0.44	0.51
2Q	**0.71**	0.45	0.48	0.44	0.45	0.39
3Q	**E0.45**	-0.07	0.20	0.25	0.44	-0.48
4Q	**E0.49**	0.42	0.46	0.40	0.11	0.77
Yr.	**E2.09**	1.26	1.61	1.53	1.44	1.19

Next earnings report expected: **late October**

Dividend Data (Dividends have been paid since 1960.)

Amount ($)	Date Decl.	Ex-Div. Date	Stock of Record	Payment Date
0.180	Oct. 08	Oct. 16	Oct. 20	Oct. 31 '97
0.180	Dec. 10	Jan. 22	Jan. 26	Feb. 06 '98
0.180	Apr. 15	Apr. 23	Apr. 27	May. 08 '98
0.190	Jul. 08	Jul. 16	Jul. 20	Jul. 31 '98

Business Summary - 20-AUG-98

C. R. Bard is a leading multinational manufacturer and distributor of medical products. The company, started as a marketer of urethral catheters and other urinary products by Charles Russell Bard in 1907, today offers a wide range of diagnostic and therapeutic medical instruments and devices, sold to hospitals, physicians, nursing homes and other health care markets. Foreign markets are important, accounting for 32% of sales and 21% of operating profits in 1997. In mid-1998 Bard agreed to sell its coronary cath lab business (angioplasty and angiography products) to Arterial Vascular Engineering for $600 million. That business had sales of about $215 million in 1997. Total sales in recent years were divided by principal product segments as follows:

	1997	1996	1995
Vascular	38%	36%	36%
Urological	26%	26%	25%
Oncology	19%	18%	18%
Surgical & other	17%	20%	21%

A wide variety of products are offered to treat peripheral vascular conditions, with a focus on keeping veins and arteries open. Products include electrophysiology products including cardiac mapping andelectrophysiology laboratory systems; diagnostic and temporarypacing electrode catheters; fabrics and meshes forvessel repair; implantable blood vessel replacements;cardiopulmonary support systems; cardiopulmonary support products; vessel grafts; and blood oxygenators and relatedproducts used in open-heart surgery.

Bard is the worldwide market leader in urological diagnostic and interventional products, with a focus on urological drainage, continence, and prostate disease management. Introduced some 60 years ago, the Foley catheter remains one of the most important products in the urological field. Other products in this segment include the Contigen collagen implant used to treat stress urinary incontinence and the Criticore patient monitor that measures a patient's core body temperature and fluid output.

Oncology products are designed for the detection and treatment of various cancers. These include specialty access catheters and ports; gastroenterological products (endoscopic accessories, percutaneous feeding devices and stents); biopsy devices, and tests for the detection and monitoring of bladder and prostate cancer.

Surgical products include meshes for vessel and Hernia repair; irrigation devices for orthopedic and laparoscopic procedures; and topical hemostatic devices. Bard's PerFix plug has allowed hernia procedures to be done in out-patient settings in minutes instead of hours with the older methods. Bard products account for approximately 60% of the hernia repair market.

Per Share Data ($)

(Year Ended Dec. 31)	1997	1996	1995	1994	1993	1992	1991	1990	1989	1988
Tangible Bk. Val.	2.62	2.71	4.36	3.35	4.49	6.45	5.81	5.30	5.00	5.58
Cash Flow	2.26	2.63	2.42	2.20	1.87	1.82	1.63	1.13	1.51	1.67
Earnings	1.26	1.62	1.53	1.44	1.19	1.42	1.08	0.76	1.18	1.38
Dividends	0.70	0.66	0.62	0.58	0.54	0.50	0.46	0.42	0.36	0.28
Payout Ratio	56%	41%	41%	40%	45%	35%	43%	55%	30%	20%
Prices - High	39	37³/₈	32¹/₄	30¹/₂	35¹/₄	35⁷/₈	31³/₄	22¹/₂	26¹/₂	24⁵/₈
- Low	26³/₈	25⁷/₈	25¹/₂	22¹/₄	20¹/₂	22¹/₂	14⁷/₈	12⁷/₈	8³/₄	16⁷/₈
P/E Ratio - High	31	23	21	21	30	25	29	30	22	18
- Low	21	16	17	15	17	16	14	17	16	12

Income Statement Analysis (Million $)

	1997	1996	1995	1994	1993	1992	1991	1990	1989	1988
Revs.	1,214	1,194	1,138	1,018	971	990	876	785	778	758
Oper. Inc.	222	227	208	190	167	144	123	87.0	134	145
Depr.	57.3	57.4	50.6	39.6	35.5	21.2	29.5	19.8	18.1	16.5
Int. Exp.	32.9	26.4	24.2	15.1	11.4	12.6	14.1	14.9	10.9	7.8
Pretax Inc.	105	103	124	103	99	107	77.0	59.0	103	124
Eff. Tax Rate	31%	10%	30%	27%	37%	30%	26%	31%	37%	36%
Net Inc.	72.3	92.5	86.8	74.9	62.1	75.0	57.2	40.3	65.4	78.7

Balance Sheet & Other Fin. Data (Million $)

	1997	1996	1995	1994	1993	1992	1991	1990	1989	1988
Cash	8.0	78.0	51.3	34.2	75.0	49.8	33.8	19.9	11.1	24.3
Curr. Assets	564	577	504	428	422	417	374	341	305	314
Total Assets	1,279	1,333	1,091	958	799	713	658	613	563	531
Curr. Liab.	311	336	273	365	264	215	190	171	123	128
LT Debt	341	343	198	78.3	68.5	68.6	68.9	69.8	70.3	41.2
Common Eqty.	573	602	565	440	383	392	366	342	334	329
Total Cap.	914	945	763	518	452	461	435	412	404	370
Cap. Exp.	32.8	41.6	39.6	34.2	30.7	30.3	31.0	28.2	31.8	26.4
Cash Flow	130	150	137	115	97.6	96.2	86.7	60.1	83.5	95.2
Curr. Ratio	1.8	1.7	1.8	1.2	1.6	1.9	2.0	2.0	2.5	2.4
% LT Debt of Cap.	37.3	36.3	26.0	15.1	15.2	14.9	15.9	16.9	17.4	11.1
% Net Inc.of Revs.	6.0	7.8	7.6	7.4	6.4	7.6	6.5	5.1	8.4	10.4
% Ret. on Assets	5.5	7.7	8.1	8.5	8.3	11.0	9.0	6.9	12.2	15.6
% Ret. on Equity	12.3	15.9	16.4	18.2	16.1	19.8	16.2	12.1	20.1	25.3

Data as orig. reptd.; bef. results of disc. opers. and/or spec. items. Per share data adj. for stk. divs. as of ex-div. date. Bold denotes diluted EPS (FASB 128). E-Estimated. NA-Not Available. NM-Not Meaningful. NR-Not Ranked.

Office—730 Central Ave., Murray Hill, NJ 07974. **Tel**—(908) 277-8000. **Website**—http://www.crbard.com **Chrmn & CEO**—W. H. Longfield. **VP & CFO**—W. C. Bopp. **VP & Secy**—R. A. Flink. **VP, Treas & Investor Contact**—Earle L. Parker. **Dirs**—J. F. Abely, W. C. Bopp, C. Breslawsky, Jr., W. T. Butler, Jr., D. A. Cronin, Jr., T. K. Dunnigan, R. E. Herzlinger, W. H. Longfield, R. P. Luciano, T. L. White. **Transfer Agent & Registrar**—First Chicago Trust Co. of New York, NYC. **Incorporated**—in New York in 1923; reincorporated in New Jersey in 1972. **Empl**—9,550. **S&P Analyst:** H. B. Saftlas

STANDARD &POOR'S
STOCK REPORTS

Barrick Gold

290G
NYSE Symbol **ABX**
In S&P 500

12-SEP-98

Industry:
Gold & Precious Metals
Mining

Summary: Barrick is one of the world's largest gold producers and the second largest in the Americas.

S&P Opinion: Accumulate (★★★★)	
Recent Price • 17⅞	Yield • 1.0%
52 Wk Range • 25⅛-12⅞	12-Mo. P/E • NM

Quantitative Evaluations

Outlook
(1 Lowest—5 Highest)
• **4**

Fair Value
• **21⅛**

Risk
• **Low**

Earn./Div. Rank
• **A-**

Technical Eval.
• **Bearish** since 2/98

Rel. Strength Rank
(1 Lowest—99 Highest)
• **96**

Insider Activity
• **NA**

Earnings vs. Previous Year
△=Up ▽=Down ▷=No Change

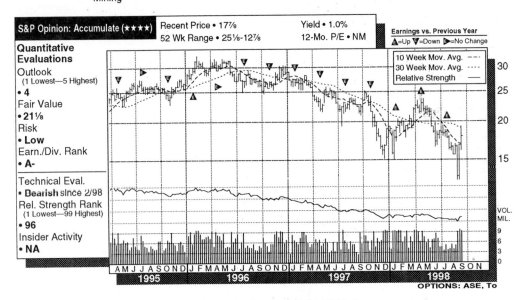

- 10 Week Mov. Avg. — —
- 30 Week Mov. Avg. - - -
- Relative Strength ——

OPTIONS: ASE, To

Overview - 18-AUG-98

EPS in the 1998 second quarter were on target with the analyst estimate of $0.18, as ABX continued to successfully increase output and cut costs. Production in the quarter rose 3.2%, to 754,500 oz., from 731,360 oz. in 1997; cash costs declined to $183/oz., from $206/oz. Total costs declined to $253/oz., from $275/oz. Most of the improvement came from the Meikle mine, which achieved quarterly production of 214,368 oz. at a $75/oz. cash cost, versus $96/oz. ABX remains on track to achieve a cash cost of $170/oz. in 1998, versus 1997's $182/oz. For 1999, the company expects to produce 3.5 million oz. at a cash cost of $150/oz.

Valuation - 18-AUG-98

We are maintaining our accumulate rating on ABX and most other gold stocks, following release of second quarter EPS. While gold stocks have been under pressure through mid-August, we expect the metal and gold stocks to begin an uptrend later in 1998 or in early 1999. Our outlook is based on several factors. First, we anticipate that central bank selling will diminish now that the new European Central Bank has announced its decision to hold 15% of its reserves in gold. Second, the rate of gain on financial investments will decline in 1998 and 1999, offering less competition for gold. Third, gold production will be flat or decline in 1999, boosting prices. Fourth, gold has averaged just $303/oz. through mid-August 1998, versus $331/oz. for all of 1997, but the recent price of about $288/oz. is virtually flat with the 1997 closing price. Also, despite declining fabrication demand and low inflation, gold has remained stable, in contrast to very sharp declines in such base metals as aluminum, copper, lead and zinc. This suggests that there is underlying strength in the metal.

Key Stock Statistics

S&P EPS Est. 1998	0.70	Tang. Bk. Value/Share	9.27
P/E on S&P Est. 1998	25.5	Beta	0.99
S&P EPS Est. 1999	0.95	Shareholders	15,200
Dividend Rate/Share	0.18	Market cap. (B)	$ 6.7
Shs. outstg. (M)	373.0	Inst. holdings	29%
Avg. daily vol. (M)	2.156		

Value of $10,000 invested 5 years ago: $ 11,886

Fiscal Year Ending Dec. 31

	1998	1997	1996	1995	1994	1993
Revenues (Million $)						
1Q	302.0	302.0	329.3	300.0	187.3	144.1
2Q	293.0	312.0	325.5	309.8	207.4	175.2
3Q	—	314.0	313.6	295.2	216.1	178.1
4Q	—	356.0	330.0	376.5	325.2	170.2
Yr.	—	1,284	1,299	1,282	936.1	667.5
Earnings Per Share ($)						
1Q	**0.20**	**0.15**	0.20	0.20	0.21	0.16
2Q	**0.18**	**0.16**	0.19	0.22	0.22	0.20
3Q	**E0.17**	**-0.84**	0.06	0.19	0.20	0.21
4Q	**E0.15**	**0.20**	0.15	0.22	0.18	0.18
Yr.	**E0.70**	**-0.33**	0.60	0.83	0.81	0.75

Next earnings report expected: late October

Dividend Data (Dividends have been paid since 1987.)

Amount ($)	Date Decl.	Ex-Div. Date	Stock of Record	Payment Date
0.080	Nov. 14	Nov. 25	Nov. 28	Dec. 15 '97
0.090	May. 12	May. 27	May. 29	Jun. 15 '98

A Division of The **McGraw·Hill** Companies

STANDARD &POOR'S
STOCK REPORTS

12-SEP-98

Business Summary - 18-AUG-98

Barrick Gold (ABX), the second largest gold producer in North America, has a two-fold strategy: to add high quality reserves, while maintaining low operating costs. ABX entered 1997 with 11 producing mines in the U.S., Canada and Chile, and two more under development. In the 1997 third quarter, ABX incurred a charge of $1.03 a share to write down the value of its highest cost mines. Currently, Barrick plans to produce some 3.0 million oz. in 1998, and 3.5 million oz. in 1999.

Barrick's exploration program focuses on finding and developing new gold reserves in three categories: early exploration stage properties with good potential; development of properties with known mineralization; and acquisition of active producers.

Hedging programs designed to protect against fluctuations in the price of gold are integral to Barrick's operating strategy. The company uses spot deferred contracts, forward sales and options to establish a minimum price for future gold production while maintaining the ability to benefit from rising gold prices.

In 1997, the company realized an average price of $420 per oz. on its sales, versus an average gold price of $332/oz., reflecting the benefits of its hedging program. At the end of 1997, the company had 10.0 million

oz. of production hedged at a minimum average price of $400/oz. through 2000.

The following table presents significant operating, reserve and price data for recent years (reserve data as of year end):

	1997	1996
Gold production (oz.)	3,047,750	3,148,801
Cash operating cost per oz.	$182	$193
Total production cost per oz.	NA	$279
Proven & probable reserves (oz.)	50,318,000	51,100,000
Revenue per oz.	$420	$415
Average spot gold price per oz.	$332	$388

In 1996 the company acquired the Pierina Mine project and 47 other early stage properties throughout Peru as part of its purchase of Arequippa Resources Ltd. for $800 million. Drilling at Pierina began in August 1996, and the company brought 6.5 million oz. of gold into reserves by 1996 year end. The mine is expected to produce at least 500,000 oz. a year at a cost of under $100/oz. beginning in late 1998.

Barrick's exploration at Pascua, its other major development project, added 8.1 million oz. to reserves for a total deposit of over 10 million oz. Pascua is expected to reach 400,000 oz. a year at full production after 2000. The mine's cost is estimated at $200/oz.

Per Share Data ($)

(Year Ended Dec. 31)	1997	1996	1995	1994	1993	1992	1991	1990	1989	1988
Tangible Bk. Val.	8.91	9.39	8.26	7.41	4.16	3.50	2.99	2.41	2.05	1.66
Cash Flow	0.17	1.10	1.34	1.15	1.00	0.86	0.52	0.39	0.32	0.24
Earnings	-0.33	0.60	0.83	0.81	0.75	0.62	0.34	0.23	0.15	0.13
Dividends	0.16	0.14	0.12	0.10	0.08	0.07	0.06	0.04	0.03	0.02
Payout Ratio	NM	23%	14%	14%	11%	11%	17%	20%	23%	16%
Prices - High	28¾	32⅞	27⅝	31	30⅜	16⅜	14	12⅜	8⅝	5¾
- Low	15⅛	24⅝	19¾	19⅞	13⅝	11⅛	9¼	7⅝	4⅛	3¾
P/E Ratio - High	NM	55	33	38	41	26	41	55	57	44
- Low	NM	41	24	25	18	18	27	34	27	28

Income Statement Analysis (Million $)

	1997	1996	1995	1994	1993	1992	1991	1990	1989	1988
Revs.	1,284	1,299	1,282	936	668	540	345	252	206	148
Oper. Inc.	529	509	567	435	337	288	156	107	86.0	60.0
Depr.	188	183	181	106	71.1	69.0	51.3	48.6	40.6	25.7
Int. Exp.	Nil	10.0	21.0	11.4	8.9	9.3	9.4	12.8	12.8	10.7
Pretax Inc.	-80.0	290	390	336	270	223	115	78.0	45.0	39.0
Eff. Tax Rate	NM	25%	25%	25%	21%	22%	20%	25%	21%	23%
Net Inc.	-122	218	292	251	213	175	92.4	58.2	35.8	30.5

Balance Sheet & Other Fin. Data (Million $)

	1997	1996	1995	1994	1993	1992	1991	1990	1989	1988
Cash	292	245	285	458	348	288	252	312	305	51.0
Curr. Assets	446	483	508	656	410	353	328	391	368	87.0
Total Assets	4,306	4,515	3,556	3,472	1,634	1,504	1,306	1,147	1,050	701
Curr. Liab.	193	192	223	289	140	139	112	112	89.0	43.0
LT Debt	500	500	100	285	219	317	306	363	419	256
Common Eqty.	3,324	3,501	2,949	2,617	1,191	993	841	645	526	390
Total Cap.	3,969	4,188	3,222	3,079	1,489	1,360	1,189	1,035	961	658
Cap. Exp.	372	374	385	272	165	255	264	170	224	196
Cash Flow	65.0	401	474	357	284	244	144	107	76.0	56.0
Curr. Ratio	2.3	2.5	2.3	2.3	2.9	2.5	2.9	3.5	4.1	2.0
% LT Debt of Cap.	12.6	11.9	3.1	9.2	14.7	23.3	25.7	35.0	43.6	38.9
% Net Inc.of Revs.	NM	16.7	22.8	26.8	32.0	32.4	26.8	23.1	17.4	20.7
% Ret. on Assets	NM	5.4	8.3	9.1	13.5	12.4	7.4	5.2	3.9	4.4
% Ret. on Equity	NM	6.8	10.5	12.3	19.5	19.0	12.2	9.8	7.5	8.3

Data as orig. reptd.; in US$; bef. results of disc. opers. and/or spec. items. Per share data adj. for stk. divs. as of ex-div. date. Bold denotes diluted EPS (FASB 128). E-Estimated. NA-Not Available. NM-Not Meaningful. NR-Not Ranked.

Office—Royal Bank Plaza, South Tower, 200 Bay St., Suite 2700, Toronto, ON, Canada M5J 2J3. Tel—(416) 861-9911. Fax—(416)-861-0727. Website—http://www.barrick.com Chrmn—P. Munk. Pres & CEO—P. D. Melnuk. Secy—S. E. Veenman. EVP & CFO—R. Oliphant. SVP & Investor Contact—Belle Mulligan. Dirs—H. L. Beck, C. W. D. Birchall, M. A. Cohen, P. A. Crossgrove, J. T. Eyton, D. H. Gilmour, A. A. MacNaughton, B. Mulroney, A. Munk, P. Munk, E. N. Ney, J. L. Rotman, R. M. Smith, G. C. Wilkins. Transfer Agents & Registrars—R-M Trust Co., Toronto; ChaseMellon Shareholder Services, Ridgefield Park, NJ. Incorporated—in Ontario in 1984. Empl— 5,400. S&P Analyst: Leo J. Larkin

12-SEP-98

Industry: Gold & Precious Metals Mining

Summary: In July 1996, this gold mining company acquired Hemlo Gold Mines, a major Canadian producer.

S&P Opinion: Accumulate (★★★★)	Recent Price • 5½	Yield • 0.9%
	52 Wk Range • 7½-3	12-Mo. P/E • NM

Earnings vs. Previous Year
▲=Up ▼=Down ▶=No Change

Quantitative Evaluations

Outlook
(1 Lowest—5 Highest)
• **NA**

Fair Value
• **NA**

Risk
• **Average**

Earn./Div. Rank
• **B-**

Technical Eval.
• **Bearish** since 4/98

Rel. Strength Rank
(1 Lowest—99 Highest)
• **98**

Insider Activity
• **NA**

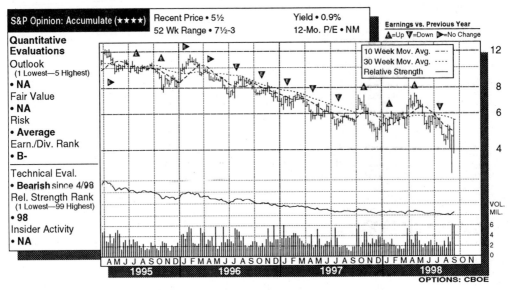

10 Week Mov. Avg. – – –
30 Week Mov. Avg. ······
Relative Strength ——

OPTIONS: CBOE

Overview - 24-AUG-98

Production in 1998 is expected to approximate 1997's level of 876,000 oz. However, assuming the absence of major equipment problems and greater contributions from lower cost mines, cash costs will likely decline to below $175/oz., from $197/oz. in 1997. We believe that gold bottomed in January 1998, and should begin a sustained uptrend in late 1998 or early 1999.

Valuation - 24-AUG-98

On April 21, 1998, we upgraded BMG and most other gold stocks to accumulate, based on a more positive outlook for both the metal and the gold stocks as a group. Our outlook is based several factors. First, we expect central bank selling to diminish now that the new European Central Bank has announced its decision to hold 15% of its reserves in gold. Second, the rate of gain on financial investments will decline in 1998 and 1999, offering less competition for gold. Third, gold production will be flat or even decline in 1999, boosting prices. Fourth, gold has averaged just $303/oz. through mid-August 1998, versus $331/oz. for all of 1997, but the current price of about $288/oz. is virtually dead even with the 1997 closing price. Also, despite declining fabrication demand and low inflation, gold has remained stable, as contrasted with very sharp declines in such base metals as aluminum, copper, lead and zinc. This suggests that there is underlying strength in the metal. Although BMG's reserve and production profile is not as strong as that of some other gold companies that we rate accumulate, the company has a very low cost structure. In the 1998 second quarter, BMG's $166/oz. cash cost was the lowest cash cost of all major North American producers that we follow. Higher gold prices and BMG's very competitive cost structure will lift the shares.

Key Stock Statistics

S&P EPS Est. 1998	-0.10	Tang. Bk. Value/Share	1.72
P/E on S&P Est. 1998	NM	Beta	0.98
S&P EPS Est. 1999	0.05	Shareholders	19,200
Dividend Rate/Share	0.05	Market cap. (B)	$ 1.3
Shs. outstg. (M)	229.8	Inst. holdings	30%
Avg. daily vol. (M)	1.023		

Value of $10,000 invested 5 years ago: $ 11,297

Fiscal Year Ending Dec. 31

	1998	1997	1996	1995	1994	1993
Revenues (Million $)						
1Q	78.90	76.51	105.0	54.08	50.92	53.90
2Q	68.30	91.24	120.4	81.26	57.04	40.52
3Q	—	90.20	90.96	65.49	55.83	50.02
4Q	—	87.00	107.7	83.43	65.89	48.93
Yr.	—	344.9	424.0	284.3	229.7	193.4
Earnings Per Share ($)						
1Q	-0.02	-0.04	0.02	0.01	0.01	-0.04
2Q	-0.05	-0.01	0.01	0.06	0.01	-0.03
3Q	E-0.02	0.09	-0.21	0.01	-0.01	Nil
4Q	E-0.01	-0.09	-0.17	0.01	0.01	-0.03
Yr.	E-0.10	-0.05	-0.36	0.09	0.02	-0.10

Next earnings report expected: early November

Dividend Data (Dividends have been paid since 1985.)

Amount ($)	Date Decl.	Ex-Div. Date	Stock of Record	Payment Date
0.025	Feb. 06	Feb. 17	Feb. 19	Feb. 27 '98
0.025	Jul. 30	Aug. 13	Aug. 17	Aug. 31 '98

A Division of The **McGraw-Hill** *Companies*

STANDARD
&POOR'S
STOCK REPORTS

Battle Mountain Gold Company

292

12-SEP-98

Business Summary - 24-AUG-98

Following its July 1996 merger with Hemlo Gold (in which BMG issued 148,100,000 new common shares), Battle Mountain became North America's fifth largest gold company, in terms of output and reserves. BMG expects to produce 865,000 oz. of gold in 1998, at a cash cost of $180/oz. or less.

BMG has two primary mines: Golden Giant in Canada, and Kori Kollo in Bolivia. In addition, it owns and operates the Holloway mine in Canada, and the Reona mine at the Battle Mountain Complex in Nevada, where evaluation and permitting of the Phoenix project is also under way. BMG has a 50% interest in the Vera Nancy mine at the Pajingo Complex in Australia, and an 8.7% interest in the new Lihir gold mine in Papua New Guinea. Other holdings include a 50% interest in the San Cristobal mine in Chile, and a 54% interest in the Crown Jewel project in Washington State.

BMG's business strategy is to target gold deposits that can add at least 10% to its reserve base and annual production profile and produce at a cash cost of $200 an oz. or less. BMG plans to spend $25 million for exploration in 1998, versus $28 million in 1997. Some $8.1 million will be spent in North America, $6.6 million in South America, $3.9 million in Australia and Africa, and $5.0 million is unallocated. In 1998, BMG planned to operate exploration programs in eight countries, versus 14 countries in 1997.

Major development projects include Crown Jewel, located in the State of Washington. BMG has a 54% stake in the $100 million Crown Jewel project, which could produce 130,000 oz. of gold for BMG's account. The Lihir project in Papua New Guinea, in which BMG owns a net 8.7% stake, is expected to produce 54,000 oz. of gold for BMG's account in 1998.

Production in the 1998 first half totaled 461,000 oz., up from 425,000 oz. in the 1997 period. Cash production costs decreased to $160/oz., from $204/oz. ; total production costs declined to $261/oz., from $295/oz. The average realized price for gold was $309/oz., down from $354/oz. BMG expects to produce about 875,000 oz. in 1998, at an average cash cost of $175/oz. or less.

Significant operating and reserve data for recent years (reserve data as of year end):

	1997	1996
Gold production (oz.)	876,000	916,000
Cash cost per oz.	$197	$210
Total cost per oz.	$288	$310
Proven and probable gold reserves (oz.)	10,140,000	10,600,000
Silver production (oz.)	1,204,000	1,451,000
Contained silver reserves (oz.)	24,515,000	25,250,000
Copper production (lbs.)	4,124,000	4,618,000

Per Share Data ($)

(Year Ended Dec. 31)	1997	1996	1995	1994	1993	1992	1991	1990	1989	1988
Tangible Bk. Val.	1.72	1.86	3.16	3.22	3.17	3.37	3.94	3.58	3.08	2.72
Cash Flow	0.26	0.09	0.91	0.62	0.42	0.07	0.36	0.45	0.79	1.16
Earnings	-0.05	-0.36	0.09	0.02	-0.10	-0.44	-0.02	0.21	0.40	0.91
Dividends	0.05	0.05	0.05	0.05	0.05	0.10	0.10	0.10	0.10	0.10
Payout Ratio	NM	NM	56%	250%	NM	NM	NM	44%	25%	11%
Prices - High	7⅝	11⅝	12⅜	13	11	8⅝	10⅝	19	18¼	19⅛
- Low	4⅜	6⅞	7⅝	8⅞	4⅞	4½	5¾	5½	13	12⅞
P/E Ratio - High	NM	NM	NM	NM	NM	NM	NM	90	46	21
- Low	NM	NM	NM	NM	NM	NM	NM	26	33	14

Income Statement Analysis (Million $)

	1997	1996	1995	1994	1993	1992	1991	1990	1989	1988
Revs.	345	424	284	230	193	182	170	143	131	141
Oper. Inc.	72.2	114	89.0	72.1	35.8	-5.1	22.3	22.9	57.3	78.7
Depr.	72.8	94.2	70.6	51.3	41.5	40.2	28.7	17.5	25.3	15.9
Int. Exp.	9.4	13.3	14.1	13.7	15.1	10.3	8.3	6.8	2.1	Nil
Pretax Inc.	-20.2	-36.9	18.6	16.5	-3.8	-46.0	-5.5	14.1	39.0	70.8
Eff. Tax Rate	NM	NM	15%	15%	NM	NM	NM	18%	32%	16%
Net Inc.	-5.1	-74.3	15.2	9.6	-4.4	-34.9	-1.2	16.0	26.4	59.4

Balance Sheet & Other Fin. Data (Million $)

	1997	1996	1995	1994	1993	1992	1991	1990	1989	1988
Cash	203	103	46.1	76.0	115	45.4	28.7	100	39.6	81.3
Curr. Assets	324	204	116	139	181	86.0	58.0	120	56.0	97.0
Total Assets	1,093	1,037	737	680	668	577	525	449	351	206
Curr. Liab.	106	104	47.0	42.3	40.3	50.1	31.9	28.5	9.7	9.1
LT Debt	241	139	169	166	179	199	125	111	50.0	Nil
Common Eqty.	395	428	260	261	255	270	315	255	204	179
Total Cap.	939	892	541	605	603	505	479	414	338	196
Cap. Exp.	62.4	57.0	12.2	92.0	52.0	114	110	130	173	47.0
Cash Flow	60.2	19.9	78.3	53.4	33.4	5.2	27.5	33.5	51.7	75.3
Curr. Ratio	3.1	8.0	2.5	3.3	4.5	1.7	1.8	4.2	5.8	10.6
% LT Debt of Cap.	25.7	15.6	31.2	27.4	29.7	39.4	26.2	26.9	14.8	Nil
% Net Inc.of Revs.	NM	NM	5.4	4.2	NM	NM	NM	11.2	20.2	42.2
% Ret. on Assets	NM	NM	2.2	1.4	NM	NM	NM	3.9	9.5	34.7
% Ret. on Equity	NM	NM	5.8	0.8	NM	NM	NM	6.7	13.8	40.7

Data as orig. reptd.; bef. results of disc. opers. and/or spec. items. Per share data adj. for stk. divs. as of ex-div. date. Bold denotes diluted EPS (FASB 128). E-Estimated. NA-Not Available. NM-Not Meaningful. NR-Not Ranked.

Office—333 Clay St., 42nd Floor, Houston, TX 77002. **Tel**—(713) 650-6400. **Fax**—(713) 650-3636. **Website**—http//www.bmgold.com **Chrmn**—K. E. Elers. **Pres & CEO**—I.D. Bayer. **VP & Secy**—G. V. Etter. **VP & Investor Contact**—Les Van Dyke. **Dirs**— I. D. Bayer, D. J. Bourne, D. L. Burnstead, D. H. Caspary, C. E. Childers, K. E. Elers, D. Kerr, J. W. McCutcheon, M. Mogford, T. H. Pate, Jr., W. A. Wise. **Transfer Agent & Registrar**—Bank of New York, NYC. **Incorporated**—in Nevada in 1985. **Empl**— 1,600. **S&P Analyst:** Leo J. Larkin

STANDARD &POOR'S
STOCK REPORTS

Bausch & Lomb
293

NYSE Symbol **BOL**

In S&P 500

12-SEP-98

Industry:
Health Care (Medical Products & Supplies)

Summary: This company, the world's leading maker of contact lenses and related solutions, also produces ophthalmic drugs, sunglasses, and biomedical and consumer items.

S&P Opinion: Hold (★★★)	Recent Price • 39⅛	Yield • 2.7%
	52 Wk Range • 52¾-37	12-Mo. P/E • 67.6

Quantitative Evaluations

Outlook
(1 Lowest—5 Highest)
• **2**

Fair Value
• **39¾**

Risk
• **Average**

Earn./Div. Rank
• **B**

Technical Eval.
• **Bearish** since 3/98

Rel. Strength Rank
(1 Lowest—99 Highest)
• **46**

Insider Activity
• **NA**

Earnings vs. Previous Year
▲=Up ▼=Down ▷=No Change

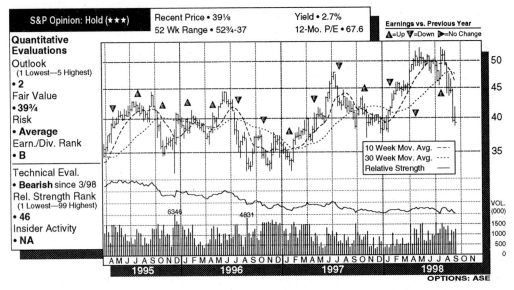

10 Week Mov. Avg. ─ ─ ─
30 Week Mov. Avg. ‧‧‧‧‧‧
Relative Strength ────

VOL. (000)

OPTIONS: ASE

Overview - 17-AUG-98

Sales in 1998 are expected to rise over 20%, bolstered by the inclusion of Chiron Vision and Storz Instrument Co., which were purchased at the end of 1997. Contact lens sales should show gains in both planned replacement and disposable lines, while volume in the lens care solutions business should be augmented by continued growth in the ReNu MultiPlus line for soft contact lenses. New products should bolster both the prescription ophthalmic pharmaceuticals and the over-the-counter eye care medications businesses. Sales of sunglasses should be augmented by new products and more normalized sales to Sunglass Hut (this division's largest customer). Profit comparisons should benefit from the better volume and anticipated improvement in the sunglasses division. EPS are projected at $2.37 (before nonrecurring items), with further progress to $2.80 seen for 1999.

Valuation - 17-AUG-98

After peaking in mid-July, the shares sold off sharply in recent weeks, reflecting the general market slump, sluggishness in the sunglasses business, and the effects of negative foreign exchange. However, more favorable earnings comparisons are projected for the second half, led by improving trends in many key businesses, tight cost controls and contributions from Storz Instrument Co. and Chiron Vision. The December 1997 acqusitions of Storz and Chiron Vision broadened BOL's position in the ophthalmics industry, provided access to high margin cataract and high growth eye surgical businesses, and bolstered BOL's pharmaceuticals business. The company's key strengths include a reputation for high-quality products, and established relationships with eye care professionals throughout the world. The shares merit retention.

Key Stock Statistics

S&P EPS Est. 1998	1.53	Tang. Bk. Value/Share	NM
P/E on S&P Est. 1998	25.6	Beta	0.89
S&P EPS Est. 1999	2.80	Shareholders	9,100
Dividend Rate/Share	1.04	Market cap. (B)	$ 2.2
Shs. outstg. (M)	55.9	Inst. holdings	75%
Avg. daily vol. (M)	0.214		

Value of $10,000 invested 5 years ago: $ 8,353

Fiscal Year Ending Dec. 31

	1998	1997	1996	1995	1994	1993
Revenues (Million $)						
1Q	553.1	451.2	469.3	465.6	438.8	407.6
2Q	635.1	523.2	545.5	535.5	483.3	479.4
3Q	—	468.3	477.2	476.8	449.4	498.8
4Q	—	473.0	434.8	455.1	479.1	486.3
Yr.	—	1,916	1,927	1,933	1,851	1,872
Earnings Per Share ($)						
1Q	**-0.89**	**0.06**	0.39	0.34	0.60	0.54
2Q	**0.98**	**0.36**	0.54	0.89	0.55	0.78
3Q	**E0.66**	**0.33**	0.25	0.75	0.13	0.93
4Q	**E0.78**	**0.13**	0.29	-0.04	-1.05	0.35
Yr.	**E1.53**	**0.89**	1.47	1.94	0.23	2.60

Next earnings report expected: mid October

Dividend Data (Dividends have been paid since 1952.)

Amount ($)	Date Decl.	Ex-Div. Date	Stock of Record	Payment Date
0.260	Oct. 27	Nov. 26	Dec. 01	Jan. 02 '98
0.260	Feb. 24	Mar. 11	Mar. 13	Apr. 01 '98
0.260	Apr. 28	May. 28	Jun. 01	Jul. 01 '98
0.260	Jul. 28	Aug. 28	Sep. 01	Oct. 01 '98

A Division of The McGraw·Hill Companies

Business Summary - 17-AUG-98

This maker of popular Soflens contact lenses, ReNu contact lens solutions and Ray Ban sunglasses, also produces ophthalmic pharmaceuticals, hearing aids, purpose-bred laboratory animals and various other biomedical and consumer products. The company was founded in 1853 by John Jacob Bausch. Foreign business is significant, accounting for 50% of sales and 53% of operating earnings in 1997. Dental products lines were sold in 1996 and the skin care business is now in the process of being divested. Business segment contributions in 1997 were:

	Sales	Profits
Vision care	47%	94%
Eyewear	26%	-29%
Pharmaceuticals	10%	15%
Health care	17%	20%

Bausch & Lomb is the leading player in the global contact lens care market, with its popular ReNu, Sensitive Eyes, and Boston solutions products. Although contact lens solutions is a relatively mature business in the U.S., good growth potential exists overseas. Strong positions are also held in contact lenses with its Soflens 66 and Award brands, which include daily, weekly and monthly wear products. BOL recently expanded its position in the ophthalmic surgical products market with the acquisitions of Storz Instruments and Chiron Vision. Products are marketed through licensed eye care professionals, pharmaceutical retailers and mass merchandisers.

The company is the leading producer of premium-priced (over $30) consumer sunglasses. With demand slipping for its established Ray Ban and Wayfarer brands, BOL has revitalized its line by expanding into more contemporary and sports designs. Some of these products are sold under the Revo, Arnette, Killer Loop, Orb and Sidestreet names. A line of optical thin films is also produced for industrial customers.

Pharmaceuticals include a line of low-cost generic drugs in the highly competitive U.S. market, as well as prescription and over-the-counter eye care pharmaceuticals, sedatives, sleep aids, allergy drugs and other medications sold in the U.S. and Germany. Products are marketed under the Bausch & Lomb, Dr. Mann Pharma, Dr. Winzer and HealthGuard names.

Healthcare products encompass Charles River Laboratories, the world's largest producer of pathogen-free eggs used in vaccine production and a major supplier of purpose-bred rodents for biomedical research; Miracle Ear hearing aids; and various biomedical products and services.

Per Share Data ($)

(Year Ended Dec. 31)	1997	1996	1995	1994	1993	1992	1991	1990	1989	1988
Tangible Bk. Val.	7.41	8.86	9.62	8.79	7.95	11.45	10.18	9.35	7.53	6.20
Cash Flow	2.90	3.47	3.62	1.89	4.01	4.03	2.56	3.23	2.77	2.32
Earnings	0.89	1.47	1.94	0.23	2.60	2.84	1.42	2.19	1.89	1.64
Dividends	1.04	1.04	1.01	0.95	0.88	0.80	0.72	0.66	0.58	0.50
Payout Ratio	117%	71%	52%	NM	34%	28%	50%	30%	30%	30%
Prices - High	47⁷/₈	44¹/₂	44¹/₂	53⁷/₈	57¹/₂	60¹/₂	60	36¹/₂	33	24
- Low	32¹/₂	32¹/₂	30⁷/₈	30⁵/₈	43	44¹/₂	31³/₄	26³/₈	20³/₈	17¹/₄
P/E Ratio - High	54	30	23	NM	22	21	42	17	17	15
- Low	37	22	16	NM	17	16	22	12	11	11

Income Statement Analysis (Million $)

	1997	1996	1995	1994	1993	1992	1991	1990	1989	1988
Revs.	1,916	1,927	1,933	1,851	1,872	1,709	1,520	1,369	1,220	978
Oper. Inc.	332	319	343	268	385	342	316	283	251	199
Depr.	112	113	105	99	84.6	72.0	68.7	63.1	52.6	40.7
Int. Exp.	56.0	51.7	45.8	41.4	34.2	29.5	38.6	39.9	30.8	26.5
Pretax Inc.	118	169	212	90.0	242	263	150	198	174	149
Eff. Tax Rate	39%	38%	37%	59%	33%	32%	40%	33%	33%	34%
Net Inc.	49.4	83.1	112	13.0	157	171	86.0	131	114	98.0

Balance Sheet & Other Fin. Data (Million $)

	1997	1996	1995	1994	1993	1992	1991	1990	1989	1988
Cash	184	168	194	233	546	417	412	386	321	254
Curr. Assets	1,090	948	930	954	1,402	1,082	965	943	778	629
Total Assets	2,773	2,603	2,550	2,458	2,512	1,874	1,770	1,677	1,429	1,211
Curr. Liab.	887	929	859	677	715	567	609	579	444	398
LT Debt	511	236	191	290	321	278	196	215	219	153
Common Eqty.	818	882	929	914	927	898	819	825	713	629
Total Cap.	1,129	1,550	1,551	1,632	1,669	1,196	1,062	1,090	985	813
Cap. Exp.	126	130	95.0	85.0	107	119	89.0	108	100	103
Cash Flow	161	196	217	113	241	243	155	194	167	139
Curr. Ratio	1.2	1.0	1.1	1.4	2.0	1.9	1.6	1.6	1.7	1.6
% LT Debt of Cap.	45.3	15.2	12.4	17.7	19.2	23.2	18.4	19.7	22.2	18.8
% Net Inc.of Revs.	2.6	4.3	5.8	0.7	8.4	10.0	5.7	9.6	9.4	10.0
% Ret. on Assets	1.8	3.2	4.5	0.5	7.2	9.4	5.0	8.5	8.7	9.0
% Ret. on Equity	5.8	9.2	12.2	1.5	17.2	20.0	10.4	17.2	17.0	16.2

Data as orig. reptd.; bef. results of disc. opers. and/or spec. items. Per share data adj. for stk. divs. as of ex-div. date. Bold denotes diluted EPS (FASB 128). E-Estimated. NA-Not Available. NM-Not Meaningful. NR-Not Ranked.

Office—1 Bausch & Lomb Place, Rochester, NY 14604. **Tel**—(716) 338-6000. **Website**—http://www.bausch.com **Chrmn** —W. H. Waltrip. **Pres & CEO**—W. M. Carpenter. **SVP-Fin & CFO**—S. C. McCluski. **Secy**—J. F. Geisel. **Investor Contact**—Angela J. Panzarella. **Dirs**—F. E. Agnew, W. Balderston III, W. M. Carpenter, D. De Sole, J. S. Linen, R. R. McMullin, J. R. Purcell, L. J. Rice, A. W. Trivelpiece, W. H. Waltrip, K. L. Wolfe. **Transfer Agent & Registrar**—First National Bank of Boston. **Incorporated**—in New York in 1908. **Empl**— 13,000. **S&P Analyst:** H. B. Saftlas

Baxter International

293K

NYSE Symbol **BAX**

In S&P 500

12-SEP-98

Industry:
Health Care (Medical Products & Supplies)

Summary: This well known medical products company is a global leader in products and technolgies related to the blood and circulatory system.

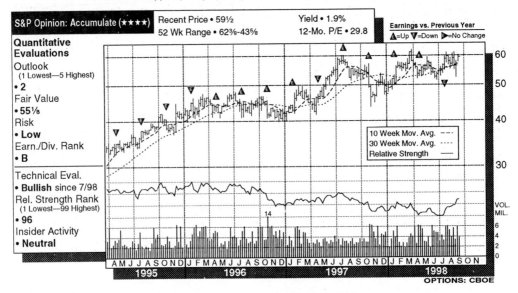

S&P Opinion: Accumulate (★★★★)	Recent Price • 59½	Yield • 1.9%	Earnings vs. Previous Year
	52 Wk Range • 62⅜-43⅝	12-Mo. P/E • 29.8	▲=Up ▼=Down ▶=No Change

Quantitative Evaluations

Outlook
(1 Lowest—5 Highest)
• **2**

Fair Value
• **55⅛**

Risk
• **Low**

Earn./Div. Rank
• **B**

Technical Eval.
• **Bullish** since 7/98

Rel. Strength Rank
(1 Lowest—99 Highest)
• **96**

Insider Activity
• **Neutral**

10 Week Mov. Avg. – – –
30 Week Mov. Avg. ·····
Relative Strength ——

OPTIONS: CBOE

Overview - 26-AUG-98

After factoring in the negative impact of the stronger dollar on foreign sales, revenues in 1998 are expected to rise about 7%. Gains are indicated for renal care products, I.V. systems, tissue heart valves and blood therapies. Growth in the renal area is being helped by expansion in the Latin American market, and by new contracts, such as one with Humana to manage the latter's kidney dialysis patients. I.V. sales are being boosted by BAX's new Colleague electronic infusion pump. Despite growth in the Novacor left ventricular assist system, overall cardiovascular sales are expected to be relatively flat. A new multiyear agreement with the Premier group of hospitals, and the recent acquisition of an anesthesia pharmaceuticals business from The BOC Group will also augment volume. Diluted EPS for 1998 are forecast at $2.55 (before $0.40 in acquisition related charges). Further progress, to $2.87, is seen for 1999.

Valuation - 26-AUG-98

The shares moved higher in recent months, despite increased turbulence in the general market. Baxter's strength reflected robust second quarter earnings, and prospects for more of the same in the second half. Excluding charges related to the May 1998 acquisition of Somatogen and the effects of negative foreign exchange, operating earnings in the second quarter rose 18%. Baxter expects to generate $500 million in operational cash flow for all of 1998, and to maintain at least low double-digit EPS growth over the next few quarters. Long-term prospects are enhanced by recent acquisitions, such as an anesthesia business from The BOC Group and Somatogen (a developer of recombinant hemoglobin technology). The shares merit accumulation for above average long-term total return.

Key Stock Statistics

S&P EPS Est. 1998	2.15	Tang. Bk. Value/Share	3.86
P/E on S&P Est. 1998	27.7	Beta	0.91
S&P EPS Est. 1999	2.87	Shareholders	64,700
Dividend Rate/Share	1.16	Market cap. (B)	$ 17.0
Shs. outstg. (M)	285.4	Inst. holdings	67%
Avg. daily vol. (M)	0.984		

Value of $10,000 invested 5 years ago: NA

Fiscal Year Ending Dec. 31

	1998	1997	1996	1995	1994	1993
Revenues (Million $)						
1Q	1,468	1,443	1,299	1,158	2,193	2,041
2Q	1,646	1,569	1,335	1,275	2,316	2,215
3Q	—	1,494	1,310	1,261	2,315	2,228
4Q	—	1,632	1,494	1,354	2,500	2,395
Yr.	—	6,138	5,438	5,048	9,324	8,879
Earnings Per Share ($)						
1Q	**0.58**	-0.74	0.51	0.35	0.47	0.20
2Q	**0.22**	0.57	0.52	0.41	0.52	0.48
3Q	**E0.63**	0.57	0.50	0.04	0.53	0.49
4Q	**E0.73**	0.64	0.58	0.54	0.61	-2.14
Yr.	**E2.15**	1.06	2.11	1.34	2.13	-0.97

Next earnings report expected: late October

Dividend Data (Dividends have been paid since 1934.)

Amount ($)	Date Decl.	Ex-Div. Date	Stock of Record	Payment Date
0.291	Nov. 18	Dec. 08	Dec. 10	Jan. 02 '98
0.291	Feb. 17	Mar. 10	Mar. 12	Apr. 01 '98
0.291	May. 05	Jun. 09	Jun. 11	Jul. 01 '98
0.291	Aug. 04	Sep. 08	Sep. 10	Oct. 01 '98

A Division of The McGraw-Hill Companies

Business Summary - 26-AUG-98

Founded in 1931 as the first manufacturer of commercially prepared intravenous solutions, Baxter International now ranks as one of the world's leading producers and distributors of medical products and equipment. The company is a global leader in products and technologies associated with the blood and circulatory system. Overseas markets are very significant, accounting for 53% of sales and 69% of operating income in 1997. Baxter's conventional hospital supply business was spun off to shareholders as stock in a new firm called Allegiance Corp. in September 1996. Sales of continuing businesses by product segment in recent years were:

	1997	1996	1995
I.V. systems/medical products	34%	36%	38%
Blood therapies	29%	23%	22%
Renal products	23%	25%	26%
Cardiovascular products	14%	16%	14%

A worldwide leader in intravenous products, Baxter produces more than 800 different I.V. products, as well as other technologies used to deliver medications to patients. The company produces over 100 million I.V. sets each year, which are used in hospitals, nursing homes, and home care settings. Products include solutions and equipment for I.V. nutrition, products for anesthesia and pain management, I.V. antibiotics and other premixed drugs, ambulatory infusion devices for home-based therapies, and automated prescription-filling systems.

The company's blood therapies units are leaders in transfusion products. These encompass systems for collecting, storing and separating blood and its components; clotting factors for people with hemophilia; and immune globulins for patients with immune deficiencies. The 1997 acquisition of Immuno International AG widened the blood therapies line by adding vaccines and specialized blood coagulation products.

Baxter is also a leader in the renal care market, providing dialysis equipment and other products and services for patients suffering from kidney failure. Products are offered for continuous ambulatory peritoneal dialysis (CAPD) and hemodialysis. In CAPD, patients self-infuse dialysis solution several times a day outside hospital settings. In hemodialysis, patients go several times a week to hospitals or clinics where machines filter impurities from their blood. Baxter offers hemodialysis machines and related products for this market.

Cardiovascular products include tissue heart valves, valve-repair products and cardiac monitoring systems. Baxter also produces embolectomy catheters, vascular surgical instruments, and blood filtration devices used in by-pass surgery. Contract perfusion services are also offered.

Per Share Data ($)

(Year Ended Dec. 31)	1997	1996	1995	1994	1993	1992	1991	1990	1989	1988
Tangible Bk. Val.	3.56	4.10	9.58	13.18	11.52	13.59	14.45	13.45	13.49	12.61
Cash Flow	2.48	3.39	2.55	3.73	0.95	3.39	3.55	1.72	2.51	2.23
Earnings	1.06	2.11	1.34	2.13	-0.97	1.99	2.03	-0.05	1.50	1.31
Dividends	1.14	1.17	1.11	1.02	1.00	0.86	0.74	0.64	0.56	0.50
Payout Ratio	107%	55%	83%	48%	NM	43%	36%	NM	36%	38%
Prices - High	60¼	48⅛	44¾	28⅞	32¾	40½	40⅞	29½	25⅞	26⅛
- Low	39⅞	39¾	26¾	21⅝	20	30½	25⅝	20½	17½	16¼
P/E Ratio - High	57	23	33	14	NM	20	20	NM	17	20
- Low	38	19	20	10	NM	15	13	NM	12	12

Income Statement Analysis (Million $)

	1997	1996	1995	1994	1993	1992	1991	1990	1989	1988
Revs.	6,138	5,438	5,048	9,324	8,879	8,471	8,921	8,100	7,399	6,861
Oper. Inc.	1,403	1,259	1,150	1,471	1,525	1,435	1,515	1,374	1,091	971
Depr.	398	348	336	448	531	390	427	446	325	294
Int. Exp.	198	103	96.0	242	232	221	231	264	291	250
Pretax Inc.	523	793	524	810	-318	766	830	128	637	518
Eff. Tax Rate	43%	28%	29%	25%	NM	25%	26%	51%	29%	25%
Net Inc.	300	575	371	596	-267	561	591	40.0	446	388

Balance Sheet & Other Fin. Data (Million $)

	1997	1996	1995	1994	1993	1992	1991	1990	1989	1988
Cash	465	761	476	471	479	32.0	328	40.0	67.0	201
Curr. Assets	3,870	3,480	2,911	4,340	4,422	3,589	4,004	3,443	3,424	3,323
Total Assets	8,707	7,596	9,437	10,002	10,545	9,155	9,340	8,517	8,503	8,550
Curr. Liab.	2,557	2,445	2,154	2,766	2,933	2,368	2,357	2,324	1,859	1,886
LT Debt	2,635	1,695	2,372	2,341	2,800	2,433	2,249	1,729	2,052	2,246
Common Eqty.	2,619	2,504	3,704	3,720	3,185	3,795	4,034	3,753	3,366	3,096
Total Cap.	5,570	4,454	6,249	6,228	6,186	6,402	6,860	6,014	6,563	6,433
Cap. Exp.	403	318	309	502	605	640	627	435	385	499
Cash Flow	698	923	707	1,044	263	946	995	434	709	619
Curr. Ratio	1.5	1.4	1.4	1.6	1.5	1.5	1.7	1.5	1.8	1.8
% LT Debt of Cap.	47.3	38.1	38.0	37.6	45.3	38.0	32.8	28.7	31.3	34.9
% Net Inc.of Revs.	4.9	10.6	7.3	6.4	NM	6.6	6.6	0.5	6.0	5.7
% Ret. on Assets	3.7	6.8	4.0	5.7	NM	6.1	6.6	0.4	5.2	4.7
% Ret. on Equity	11.7	18.5	10.0	17.1	NM	14.2	14.6	NM	11.8	10.9

Data as orig. reptd.; bef. results of disc. opers. and/or spec. items. Per share data adj. for stk. divs. as of ex-div. date. Bold denotes diluted EPS (FASB 128). E-Estimated. NA-Not Available. NM-Not Meaningful. NR-Not Ranked.

Office—One Baxter Parkway, Deerfield, IL 60015. **Tel**—(847) 948-2000. **Website**—http://www.baxter.com **Chrmn & CEO**—V. R. Loucks, Jr. **Pres**—H. M. J. Kraemer, Jr. **SVP & Secy**—D. C. McKee. **Treas**—S. J. Meyer. **Investor Contact**—N. Jeharajah. **Dirs**—W. E. Boomer, P. Chia, J. W. Colloton, S. Crown, M. J. Evans, F. R. Frame, M. R. Ingram, H. M. J. Kraemer, Jr., A. J. Levine, V. R. Loucks, Jr., G. C. St. Laurent, Jr., M. E. Trout, R. V. Tuckson, F. L. Turner. **Transfer Agent & Registrar**—First Chicago Trust Co. of New York, NYC. **Incorporated**—in Delaware in 1931. **Empl**—41,000. **S&P Analyst:** H.B. Saftlas

12-SEP-98

Industry:
Banks (Major Regional)

Summary: BBK (formerly Southern National Corp.) is a bank holding company that, through subsidiaries, operates 527 banking offices in the Carolinas, Virginia, Maryland, and Washington, D.C.

Quantitative Evaluations

Outlook
(1 Lowest—5 Highest)
• 1

Fair Value
• 25

Risk
• Low

Earn./Div. Rank
• A-

Technical Eval.
• NA

Rel. Strength Rank
(1 Lowest—99 Highest)
• 65

Insider Activity
• Unfavorable

Recent Price • 29½
52 Wk Range • 36⅛-25⅞

Yield • 2.4%
12-Mo. P/E • 20.9

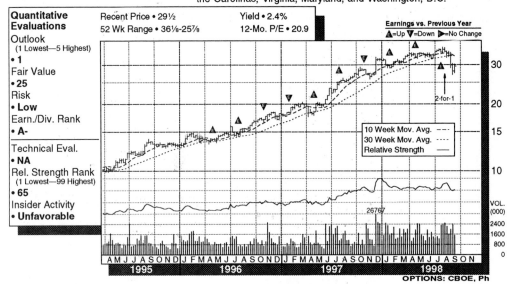

Earnings vs. Previous Year
▲=Up ▼=Down ▶=No Change

10 Week Mov. Avg. - - - -
30 Week Mov. Avg. . . . . .
Relative Strength ———

2-for-1

26767

VOL. (000)

OPTIONS: CBOE, Ph

Business Profile - 24-JUL-98

This $32.3 billion-asset bank holding company is vigorously pursuing a strategy of growth by acquisition from its historic base in the Carolinas into Virginia and Maryland. In early July 1998, BBK entered the metropolitan Washington, DC market by completing acquisition of Franklin Bancorporation, a $659 million-asset bank with six branches in the District of Columbia, one in Bethesda, MD, and two in northern Virginia. BBK plans to acquire Maryland Federal Bancorp of Hyattsville, MD, with $1.2 billion in assets and 28 branches, in the third quarter of 1998. Earlier, in March 1998, BBK completed its merger with Life Bancorp of Norfolk, VA, adding assets of $1.5 billion. BBK is expanding its nonbank product lines through acquisitions in the insurance, employee benefits, and specialty finance fields. On June 13, the company announced a 2-for-1 stock split and a 12.9% increase in the quarterly dividend to $0.35 per pre-split share.

Operational Review - 24-JUL-98

Net interest income in the six months ended June 30, 1998, rose 5.8%, year to year, primarily reflecting 12% growth in average loans and narrower margins. The provision for loan and lease losses was 6.5% lower at $43.0 million. Noninterest income advanced 29%, and after a 14% rise in noninterest expense, pretax income grew 12%. After taxes at 31.5%, versus 34.3%, net income increased 17%, to $235,766,000 ($1.63 a share), from $201,939,000 ($1.40).

Stock Performance - 11-SEP-98

In the past 30 trading days, BBK's shares have declined 16%, compared to a 10% fall in the S&P 500. Average trading volume for the past five days was 378,875 shares, compared with the 40-day moving average of 455,582 shares.

Key Stock Statistics

Dividend Rate/Share	0.70	Shareholders	42,900
Shs. outstg. (M)	286.2	Market cap. (B)	$ 8.4
Avg. daily vol. (M)	0.397	Inst. holdings	19%
Tang. Bk. Value/Share	8.62		
Beta	1.07		

Value of $10,000 invested 5 years ago: $ 35,612

Fiscal Year Ending Dec. 31

	1998	1997	1996	1995	1994	1993
Revenues (Million $)						
1Q	713.3	—	451.4	404.9	—	116.2
2Q	732.9	—	460.7	456.5	—	105.0
3Q	—	1,968	480.4	455.8	—	105.7
4Q	—	682.7	511.4	457.4	—	111.0
Yr.	—	2,598	1,904	1,775	1,544	437.9
Earnings Per Share ($)						
1Q	**0.39**	0.34	0.34	-0.07	—	0.33
2Q	**0.42**	0.35	0.35	0.27	—	0.27
3Q	—	0.23	0.25	0.29	—	0.27
4Q	—	0.38	0.36	0.33	—	0.27
Yr.	—	1.30	1.28	0.83	1.13	1.14

Next earnings report expected: early October

Dividend Data (Dividends have been paid since 1934.)

Amount ($)	Date Decl.	Ex-Div. Date	Stock of Record	Payment Date
0.310	Feb. 24	Apr. 15	Apr. 17	May. 01 '98
0.350	Apr. 29	Jul. 08	Jul. 10	Aug. 03 '98
2-for-1	Jun. 23	Aug. 04	Jul. 10	Aug. 03 '98
0.175	Aug. 25	Oct. 14	Oct. 16	Nov. 02 '98

A Division of The **McGraw-Hill** *Companies*

Business Summary - 24-JUL-98

BB&T Corp. (formerly Southern National Corp.) is a bank holding company, headquartered in Winston-Salem, NC, that, at December 31, 1997, operated 506 banking offices in North and South Carolina and in Virginia, up from 423 a year earlier. Its principal subsidiaries include Branch Banking and Trust Company (NC), Southern National Bank of North Carolina, Southern National Bank of South Carolina, Branch Banking and Trust Company of South Carolina, Lexington State Bank (SC), Community Bank of South Carolina, and Commerce Bank of Virginia Beach.

Gross loans and leases outstanding of $20.52 billion at the end of 1997 broke down as follows:

	1997
Real estate--mortgage	56%
Commercial, financial & agricultural	15%
Consumer	13%
Leases & other	6%
Real estate--construction	10%

The allowance for loan and lease losses at December 31, 1997, was $263.9 million (equal to 1.30% of average loans and leases), versus $230.1 million (1.30%) at year-end 1996. Net chargeoffs in 1997 totaled $73.5 million (0.39% of average loans and leases), versus

$51.5 million (0.30%) in 1996. Nonperforming assets at December 31, 1997, totaled $122.7 million (0.42% of total assets), up from $90.1 million (0.35%) a year earlier.

Total deposits of $20.2 billion at December 31, 1997, consisted of 10% savings and interest checking, 13% noninterest-bearing demand deposits, 24% money rate savings, and 53% other time deposits.

In February, the company announced plans to acquire Maryland Federal Bancorp of Hyattsville, Maryland ($1.2 billion assets, 28 branches) in a deal expected to close in the third quarter of 1998. On March 1, 1998, BB&T completed its merger with Life Bancorp of Norfolk, Virginia ($1.5 billion assets, 20 branches). In July 1998, BB&T completed its acquisition of Franklin Bancorporation of Washington, D.C. ($659 million assets, 9 branches).

In the first quarter of 1998, BB&T took steps towards the acquisition of two insurance agencies in Virginia and one in Charlotte, NC. The company aims to build the largest independent insurance agency in Virginia, as it has in the Carolinas. Other nonbank acquisitions in 1998 include the June purchase of Dealers Credit, a national finance company in Menomonee Falls, WI, that specializes in loans for lawn care equipment, and the July acquisition of W.E. Stanley & Co., an actuarial and employee benefits consulting firm in Greensboro, NC.

Per Share Data ($)

(Year Ended Dec. 31)	1997	1996	1995	1994	1993	1992	1991	1990	1989	1988
Tangible Bk. Val.	8.22	7.91	8.01	6.96	7.84	7.40	5.19	4.74	4.25	3.88
Earnings	1.30	1.28	0.83	1.13	1.14	0.92	0.68	0.51	0.59	0.56
Dividends	0.58	0.50	0.43	0.37	0.32	0.25	0.23	0.21	0.19	0.18
Payout Ratio	45%	39%	52%	33%	28%	27%	34%	42%	33%	32%
Prices - High	32½	18½	14	11	11¾	9⅞	8⅛	7¼	7¾	6½
- Low	17½	12⅞	9⅜	8½	9¼	6½	4⅜	4	6	5½
P/E Ratio - High	25	14	17	10	10	11	12	14	13	12
- Low	13	10	11	7	8	7	6	8	10	9

Income Statement Analysis (Million $)

	1997	1996	1995	1994	1993	1992	1991	1990	1989	1988
Net Int. Inc.	1,100	775	742	737	225	193	151	132	109	97.0
Tax Equiv. Adj.	52.9	34.2	32.5	25.5	10.6	7.7	6.4	6.0	5.8	3.3
Non Int. Inc.	473	294	226	226	66.3	43.1	34.1	33.2	29.3	25.3
Loan Loss Prov.	89.8	53.7	31.4	17.8	5.6	14.4	18.8	21.3	9.3	6.9
Exp./Op. Revs.	60%	74%	67%	59%	60%	60%	66%	66%	67%	69%
Pretax Inc.	547	418	264	362	114	75.8	45.0	31.8	33.3	29.2
Eff. Tax Rate	34%	32%	33%	35%	35%	34%	32%	28%	29%	26%
Net Inc.	360	284	178	237	75.6	50.1	30.8	22.9	23.8	21.6
% Net Int. Marg.	4.55	4.45	4.05	4.29	4.71	5.00	4.90	4.60	4.50	4.60

Balance Sheet & Other Fin. Data (Million $)

	1997	1996	1995	1994	1993	1992	1991	1990	1989	1988
Earning Assets:										
Money Mkt	178	21.0	120	13.0	8.8	49.3	28.7	20.0	NA	NA
Inv. Securities	6,629	5,262	5,355	5,425	1,979	1,386	1,011	851	718	600
Com'l Loans	3,018	2,375	2,098	NA	778	731	641	610	534	576
Other Loans	16,499	12,150	11,783	12,800	2,771	2,120	1,763	1,601	1,363	1,170
Total Assets	29,178	21,247	20,493	19,855	5,898	4,598	3,730	3,342	2,924	2,601
Demand Deposits	2,829	1,990	1,886	1,843	616	487	421	397	409	373
Time Deposits	17,381	12,963	12,798	12,471	3,921	3,304	2,800	2,376	2,019	1,839
LT Debt	3,283	2,052	1,384	911	92.1	33.2	24.2	29.4	35.3	35.0
Common Eqty.	2,238	1,729	1,670	1,493	499	373	235	215	171	148
% Ret. on Assets	1.4	1.4	0.9	1.3	1.4	1.2	0.9	0.7	0.9	0.9
% Ret. on Equity	18.1	16.5	11.6	16.8	18.2	16.4	13.7	10.9	14.8	15.4
% Loan Loss Resv.	1.3	1.3	1.3	1.3	1.1	1.3	1.3	1.2	1.0	1.0
% Loans/Deposits	97.9	97.2	92.4	85.3	76.4	74.4	74.1	79.2	77.5	78.2
% Equity to Assets	7.9	8.1	7.7	7.7	7.3	8.0	6.4	6.4	5.7	5.8

Data as orig. reptd.; bef. results of disc opers. and/or spec. items. Per share data adj. for stk. divs. as of ex-div. date. Bold denotes diluted EPS (FASB 128). E-Estimated. NA-Not Available. NM-Not Meaningful. NR-Not Ranked.

Office—200 West Second Street, Winston-Salem, NC 27101. **Tel**—(910) 733-2000. **Website**—http://www.BBandT.com **Chrmn & CEO**—J. A. Allison. **EVP, CFO & Investor Contact**—Scott E. Reed. **Dirs**—J. A. Allison, P. B. Barringer, A. E. Cleveland, W. R. Cuthbertson Jr., R. E. Deal, A. J. Dooley Sr., T. D. Efird, P. S. Goldsmith, L. V. Hackley, E. F. Hardee, J. Helm, R. Janeway, J. E. Lathem, J. H. Maynard, J. A. McAleer Jr., —A. O. McCauley, R. L. Player Jr., C. E. Pleasants Jr., N. R. Qubein, E. R. Sasser, J. E. Shaw, H. B. Wells. **Transfer Agent**—BB&T Corporate Trust Department, Wilson, North Carolina. **Incorporated**—in North Carolina in 1968. **Empl**— 10,296. **S&P Analyst:** Thomas W. Smith, CFA

STANDARD &POOR'S
STOCK REPORTS

Bear Stearns

295

NYSE Symbol **BSC**

In S&P 500

12-SEP-98

Industry:
Investment Banking/
Brokerage

Summary: This company's Bear, Stearns & Co. unit is a leading investment bank and broker, and is ranked as one of the largest NYSE member firms.

S&P Opinion: No Opinion	Recent Price • 34¾	Yield • 1.7%
	52 Wk Range • 64-32½	12-Mo. P/E • 7.6

Earnings vs. Previous Year
▲=Up ▼=Down ▶=No Change

Quantitative Evaluations

Outlook
(1 Lowest—5 Highest)
• **3+**

Fair Value
• **36¾**

Risk
• **Average**

Earn./Div. Rank
• **A**

Technical Eval.
• **Bearish** since 8/98

Rel. Strength Rank
(1 Lowest—99 Highest)
• **16**

Insider Activity
• **Unfavorable**

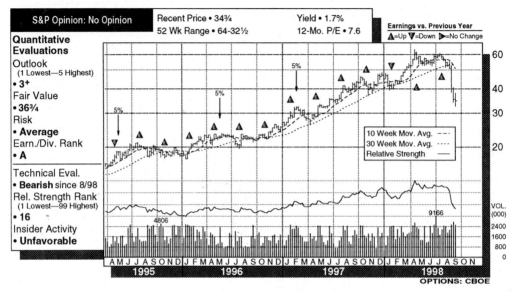

10 Week Mov. Avg. – – –
30 Week Mov. Avg. ·······
Relative Strength ———

VOL.
(000)

2400
1600
800
0

OPTIONS: CBOE

Overview - 22-JUL-98

Profits in FY 99 (Jun.) are expected to retreat from the record level of FY 98. Under a scenario of more typical market conditions, commission revenues are anticipated to decline, although the long-term trend is still positive, due to strong retirement savings flows. Investment banking fees may rise slightly, as restructuring activity in various industries (and thus advisory fees) remains a major growth area. Interest and dividends, which closely track trading volume, are expected to taper off. Principal transactions, or trading income, is highly variable, and accounts for a large component of net income; we project that it will be down modestly in FY 99, although both negative and positive surprises are a distinct possibility. Contributions from the asset management unit, which provides relatively stable fee income, and clearing operations, are expected to improve.

Valuation - 22-JUL-98

The shares, like other brokerage stocks, are down from their recent highs but are still trading near historically high levels, as investors interpret the market's strength as bullish for commission, investment banking and trading lines. Price to book value is the preferred method for valuing shares of securities brokers, because their highly liquid balance sheets are marked to market on a daily basis. The traditional P/E ratio is subject to several distortions: it makes the stocks look undervalued at market tops, when earnings are at their peak, and overvalued at market bottoms, when earnings are depressed. At recent levels, the shares were trading above their average price-to-book-value of the past several years. Bear Stearns has posted a return on equity of about 20% for the past 14 quarters.

Key Stock Statistics

S&P EPS Est. 1999	4.50	Tang. Bk. Value/Share	27.49
P/E on S&P Est. 1999	7.7	Beta	2.02
Dividend Rate/Share	0.60	Shareholders	3,100
Shs. outstg. (M)	113.8	Market cap. (B)	$ 4.0
Avg. daily vol. (M)	0.808	Inst. holdings	61%

Value of $10,000 invested 5 years ago: $ 29,322

Fiscal Year Ending Jun. 30

	1998	1997	1996	1995	1994	1993
Revenues (Million $)						
1Q	1,813	1,236	1,074	808.4	769.4	604.0
2Q	1,993	1,557	1,190	826.7	1,003	631.1
3Q	1,928	1,511	1,296	1,027	899.0	734.1
4Q	2,246	1,773	1,403	1,091	770.2	885.3
Yr.	7,890	6,077	4,964	3,754	3,441	2,857
Earnings Per Share ($)						
1Q	1.11	0.70	0.61	0.22	0.67	0.45
2Q	**1.11**	1.21	0.69	0.19	0.86	0.43
3Q	**1.15**	1.14	0.86	0.54	0.77	0.76
4Q	**1.23**	1.15	1.12	0.59	0.18	0.84
Yr.	**4.60**	4.20	3.27	1.54	2.49	2.47

Next earnings report expected: mid October

Dividend Data (Dividends have been paid since 1986.)

Amount ($)	Date Decl.	Ex-Div. Date	Stock of Record	Payment Date
0.150	Oct. 28	Nov. 12	Nov. 14	Nov. 28 '97
0.150	Jan. 21	Feb. 11	Feb. 13	Feb. 27 '98
0.150	Apr. 15	May. 13	May. 15	May. 29 '98
0.150	Jul. 21	Aug. 12	Aug. 14	Aug. 28 '98

A Division of The McGraw·Hill Companies

STANDARD
&POOR'S
STOCK REPORTS

The Bear Stearns Companies Inc.

295

12-SEP-98

Business Summary - 22-JUL-98

The Bear Stearns Companies Inc. is one of Wall Street's leading firms, with solid representation across the investment banking, sales and trading, research, and asset management areas. A highly profitable subsidiary provides securities clearing and financing services for more than 2,100 broker-dealers, hedge funds, money managers, and other clients worldwide. The firm has avoided layoffs during downturns by carefully planning its staffing needs. Revenue contributions in recent fiscal years (Jun.) were:

	FY 98	FY 97
Commissions	21%	21%
Principal transactions	40%	45%
Investment banking	23%	19%
Interest & dividends, net	15%	14%
Other	1%	1%

Bear Stearns obtains a large part of its net income from trading corporate, government, high yield, emerging markets, mortgage, asset-backed and municipal bonds, with the difference or spread between the bid and ask prices appearing on its income statement under the heading "principal transactions" revenues.

The company will sometimes take modest positions in securities for its own account, in the hope of profiting from a short-term inefficiency. However, the great majority of Bear's inventory positions are to satisfy customer order flow.

Investment banking products such as equities, investment-grade debt, high yield debt, mergers and acquisitions (M & A), and financial restructuring are employed by industry-specific client coverage teams in order to customize solutions for each of the firm's clients. In FY 97, the company managed 107 equity offerings, raising more than $19 billion. It also ranked fifth domestically in the M & A tables in the first half of 1997. Investment banking operations are supported by a large research department. BSC's institutional equity staff, for instance, covers more than 900 companies in 100 industry sectors.

In its retail brokerage operations, Bear Stearn has more than 550 investment professionals who serve private investor needs from seven domestic offices. This division focuses on stock and bonds. It is not a financial supermarket. These account executives keep their clients informed with timely information about their investments, and provide access to every research analyst and expert of the firm.

Per Share Data ($)

(Year Ended Jun. 30)	1998	1997	1996	1995	1994	1993	1992	1991	1990	1989
Tangible Bk. Val.	NA	25.02	19.37	15.46	13.42	11.62	9.49	7.00	6.41	6.04
Cash Flow	NA	4.59	NA	NA	NA	NA	NA	NA	NA	NA
Earnings	4.60	4.20	3.27	1.54	2.50	2.47	2.01	0.92	0.71	0.99
Dividends	0.60	0.58	0.57	0.54	0.49	0.46	0.45	0.36	0.31	0.25
Payout Ratio	13%	14%	17%	35%	20%	19%	22%	39%	44%	25%
Prices - High	64	48½	27	21¼	20⅜	14¾	14¾	12½	8⅞	9¾
- Low	39⅜	25⅝	17⅜	13⅛	13⅞	10½	10⅝	6⅛	4⅞	6¼
P/E Ratio - High	14	12	8	14	8	6	7	12	13	10
- Low	9	6	5	9	6	4	5	6	7	6

Income Statement Analysis (Million $)

	1998	1997	1996	1995	1994	1993	1992	1991	1990	1989
Commissions	NA	732	687	547	483	421	375	339	338	347
Int. Inc.	NA	3,058	2,393	1,970	1,304	902	997	1,279	1,384	1,254
Total Revs.	NA	6,077	4,964	3,754	3,441	2,857	2,677	2,380	2,386	2,365
Int. Exp.	NA	2,551	1,981	1,679	1,020	710	835	1,141	1,217	1,090
Pretax Inc.	NA	1,014	835	388	643	614	508	230	193	287
Eff. Tax Rate	NA	40%	41%	38%	40%	41%	42%	38%	38%	40%
Net Inc.	NA	613	491	241	387	362	295	143	119	172

Balance Sheet & Other Fin. Data (Million $)

	1998	1997	1996	1995	1994	1993	1992	1991	1990	1989
Total Assets	NA	121,434	92,085	74,597	67,392	57,440	45,768	39,285	31,574	36,410
Cash Items	NA	2,698	1,830	2,010	3,285	2,610	2,280	2,331	2,640	1,614
Receivables	NA	79,258	63,221	50,372	49,014	38,840	30,292	27,317	19,504	24,325
Secs. Owned	NA	38,437	26,222	21,509	14,444	15,215	12,162	8,792	8,746	9,733
Sec. Borrowed	NA	53,848	43,222	38,155	34,847	28,743	24,630	24,077	13,439	17,254
Due Brokers & Cust.	NA	32,730	23,753	17,404	17,098	14,634	11,338	9,011	11,864	8,875
Other Liabs.	NA	23,109	16,171	12,475	9,722	10,404	7,483	4,443	4,812	8,831
Capitalization:										
Debt	NA	8,120	6,044	4,060	3,408	1,883	1,040	682	384	385
Equity	NA	2,941	2,307	2,000	1,729	1,439	1,127	1,001	1,001	964
Total	NA	11,746	8,789	6,562	5,725	3,660	2,167	1,754	1,460	1,451
% Return On Revs.	NA	10.1	9.9	6.4	11.2	12.7	11.0	6.0	5.0	7.3
% Ret. on Assets	NA	0.6	0.6	0.3	0.6	0.7	0.7	0.4	0.4	0.5
% Ret. on Equity	NA	22.1	25.6	11.3	22.9	27.7	28.1	13.9	11.8	18.0

Data as orig. reptd.; bef. results of disc. opers. and/or spec. items. Per share data adj. for stk. divs. as of ex-div. date. Bold denotes diluted EPS (FASB 128). E-Estimated. NA-Not Available. NM-Not Meaningful. NR-Not Ranked.

Office—245 Park Ave., New York, NY 10167.**Tel**—(212) 272-2000. **Chrmn**—A. C. Greenberg. **Pres & CEO**—J. E. Cayne. **Secy**—K. L. Edlow. **Treas**—M. Minikes. **SVP-Fin**—S. L. Molinaro Jr. **Investor Contact**—Hannah Burns or Maura Gaenzle (212-272-4445). **Dirs**—E. G. Bewkes III, D. A. Bovin, J. E. Cayne, P. Cherasia, R. R. Cioffi, B. J. Cohen, W. L. deMonchaux, B. E. Geismar, C. D. Glickman, T. R. Green, A. C. Greenberg, D. J. Harrington, R. Harriton, D. L. Keating, M. E. Lehman, — D. A. Liebowitz, B. M. Lisman, R. N. Livney, M. Minikes, W. J. Montgoris, D. R. Mullen Jr., F. T. Nickell, C. M. Overlander, S. E. Raphael, E. J. Rosenwald Jr., L. A. Sachs, F. V. Salerno, A. D. Schwartz, D. M. Solomon, W. J. Spector, R. M. Steinberg, M. L. Tarnopol, V. Tese, M. J. Urfirer, F. Wilpon, U. Zucker. **Transfer Agent & Registrar**—ChaseMellon Shareholder Services, NYC. **Incorporated**—in Delaware in 1985. **Empl**— 9,200. **S&P Analyst:** Paul L. Huberman, CFA

12-SEP-98

Industry:
Health Care (Medical Products & Supplies)

Summary: This company is a major factor in the medical and hospital supply fields, offering a broad range of medical devices and diagnostic products.

S&P Opinion: Buy (★★★★★)	Recent Price • 40⅝	Yield • 0.7%
	52 Wk Range • 43⅞-21	12-Mo. P/E • 44.9

Quantitative Evaluations

Outlook
(1 Lowest—5 Highest)
• **1**

Fair Value
• **31¼**

Risk
• **Low**

Earn./Div. Rank
• **A+**

Technical Eval.
• **Bullish** since 9/98

Rel. Strength Rank
(1 Lowest—99 Highest)
• **92**

Insider Activity
• **Neutral**

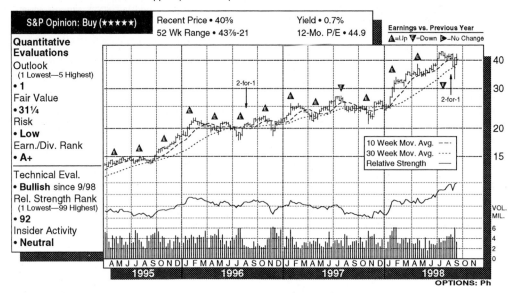

Earnings vs. Previous Year
▲=Up ▼=Down ▶=No Change

10 Week Mov. Avg. ---
30 Week Mov. Avg. ·····
Relative Strength —

VOL.
MIL.

OPTIONS: Ph

Overview - 19-AUG-98

Sales growth in FY 99 (Sep.) is expected to be in the mid-teens, bolstered by the full year inclusion of the medical device division of Ohmeda (part of the BOC Group), which was purchased in April 1998 for $452 million in cash. A leading European marketer of infusion therapy intravenous catheters and critical care products, this unit has annual sales of over $200 million. Higher volume is also projected for BDX's established medical supplies & devices and diagnostic systems lines. Demand for hypodermic and diabetes care lines should continue to benefit from ongoing conversions to safety products, while the flow cytometry business is being boosted by increased T-cell monitoring by persons infected with HIV. Margins should benefit from an improved product mix and cost streamlining measures. EPS are projected at $3.15, up from the $2.74 (before nonrecurring charges) seen for FY 98.

Valuation - 19-AUG-98

The shares have been strong performers thus far in 1998, buoyed by Becton's improving fundamentals and heightened takeover interest in medical stocks. BDX is on track with its stated goal of doubling its size by 2002 and achieving earnings growth of at least 15% per year. Key factors fueling these gains include new product launches, ongoing geographic expansion, tight cost controls and acquisitions. The recent purchase of the Ohmeda business has given BDX a lead position in the European catheter market. Becton also obtained from Endogen licenses to certain T Cell receptor technologies used in diagnostic tests. Major growth areas over the coming years include diabetes products, home health care items, and glucose testing products. The shares, which are being split two for one, are recommended for long-term appreciation.

Key Stock Statistics

S&P EPS Est. 1998	0.88	Tang. Bk. Value/Share	4.11
P/E on S&P Est. 1998	46.1	Beta	0.93
S&P EPS Est. 1999	1.57	Shareholders	9,000
Dividend Rate/Share	0.29	Market cap. (B)	$ 10.0
Shs. outstg. (M)	247.2	Inst. holdings	72%
Avg. daily vol. (M)	0.986		

Value of $10,000 invested 5 years ago: $ 44,170

Fiscal Year Ending Sep. 30

	1998	1997	1996	1995	1994	1993
Revenues (Million $)						
1Q	701.6	655.8	639.9	593.5	554.1	560.0
2Q	738.4	699.2	705.7	692.8	634.8	612.5
3Q	833.6	706.5	693.0	704.1	653.0	625.4
4Q	—	749.0	731.1	722.1	717.6	667.0
Yr.	—	2,811	2,770	2,713	2,559	2,465
Earnings Per Share ($)						
1Q	**0.25**	0.22	0.17	0.12	0.08	0.08
2Q	**0.35**	0.32	0.28	0.23	0.19	0.19
3Q	**-0.05**	0.27	0.28	0.24	0.20	0.19
4Q	**E0.32**	0.34	0.33	0.32	0.29	0.24
Yr.	**E0.88**	1.15	1.05	0.90	0.76	0.68

Next earnings report expected: early November

Dividend Data (Dividends have been paid since 1926.)

Amount ($)	Date Decl.	Ex-Div. Date	Stock of Record	Payment Date
0.145	Nov. 25	Dec. 12	Dec. 16	Jan. 02 '98
0.145	Jan. 27	Mar. 04	Mar. 06	Mar. 31 '98
0.145	May. 19	Jun. 03	Jun. 06	Jun. 30 '98
2-for-1	Jul. 28	Aug. 21	Aug. 10	Aug. 20 '98

A Division of The **McGraw·Hill** *Companies*

STANDARD
&POOR'S
STOCK REPORTS

Becton, Dickinson and Company

301

12-SEP-98

Business Summary - 19-AUG-98

Becton, Dickinson is a leading maker of medical products, offering a broad line of therapeutic and diagnostic items used in hospitals, physicians' offices, research laboratories and other settings. The company traces its roots to a firm started by Maxwell Becton and Fairleigh Dickinson in 1897. One of the first companies to sell U.S. made glass syringes, Becton was also a pioneer in the production of hypodermic needles. Foreign business is significant, accounting for 47% of sales and 30% of profits in FY 97 (Sep.). Contributions by business segment in FY 97 were:

	Sales	Profits
Medical	54%	64%
Diagnostic	46%	36%

Medical products consist of insulin injection systems and infusion therapy and injection systems. The company is the world leader in insulin injection systems and related items for diabetic care, with over 90% of the worldwide market. The infusion therapy business provides products for the continuous delivery of medication to patients in hospitals, clinics and critical care centers. With a solid base of proprietary technology, Becton also holds a leading position in peripheral vascular access

devices. Key products include the Insyte catheter and the Interlink intravenous access system. The company also holds a strong market position in hypodermic needles and syringes. This product line includes disposable and prefillable systems for drug delivery, as well as many safety products that help prevent the spread of disease from accidental needlesticks. Becton is believed to be the world's leading maker of single-use hypodermic needles and syringes, with approximately three-quarters of the total market.

Diagnostic items include flow cytometry products, infectious disease diagnostics, sample collection items and tissue cultures. The company is the world leader in flow cytometry, an innovative technology used in cell analysis. Flow cytometry systems employ laser-based technology to gather cellular diagnostic and research information on a wide range of immune system diseases, including cancer and AIDS. To support physicians and medical researchers in the diagnosis of infectious disease, Becton Dickinson maintains a strong industry position in manual and automated microbiology. The company is also a world leader in the blood sample collection business, led by its Vacutainer line of blood collection equipment. Products in the culture business include the E-Z Culturette, a sampling product able to collect and transport live microorganisms without special growth media.

Per Share Data ($)

(Year Ended Sep. 30)	1997	1996	1995	1994	1993	1992	1991	1990	1989	1988
Tangible Bk. Val.	4.11	4.43	4.46	4.44	4.11	4.32	3.82	3.38	2.97	2.55
Cash Flow	1.97	1.81	1.66	1.29	1.16	1.08	1.09	1.02	0.88	0.80
Earnings	1.15	1.05	0.90	0.76	0.68	0.64	0.61	0.58	0.50	0.46
Dividends	0.26	0.23	0.20	0.18	0.17	0.15	0.14	0.14	0.13	0.11
Payout Ratio	23%	22%	23%	24%	24%	23%	23%	23%	24%	23%
Prices - High	27⅞	22¾	16⅝	12½	10¼	10½	10¼	9⅝	7¾	7¾
- Low	21	17¾	12	8½	8⅛	8	7¼	7	6	5⅞
P/E Ratio - High	24	22	19	16	15	16	17	16	16	17
- Low	18	17	13	11	12	13	12	12	12	13

Income Statement Analysis (Million $)

	1997	1996	1995	1994	1993	1992	1991	1990	1989	1988
Revs.	2,811	2,770	2,713	2,559	2,465	2,365	2,172	2,013	1,811	1,709
Oper. Inc.	661	632	604	511	444	464	438	417	378	348
Depr.	210	200	208	155	146	136	124	111	122	109
Int. Exp.	48.6	64.4	58.7	68.4	74.9	81.8	84.4	85.0	84.4	79.4
Pretax Inc.	423	394	350	296	223	269	267	274	228	206
Eff. Tax Rate	29%	28%	28%	23%	4.50%	26%	29%	34%	31%	28%
Net Inc.	300	283	252	227	213	201	190	182	158	149

Balance Sheet & Other Fin. Data (Million $)

	1997	1996	1995	1994	1993	1992	1991	1990	1989	1988
Cash	113	165	240	179	65.0	100	84.0	73.0	95.0	123
Curr. Assets	1,313	1,277	1,328	1,327	1,151	1,221	1,032	962	869	883
Total Assets	3,080	2,890	3,000	3,160	3,088	3,178	2,780	2,594	2,270	2,068
Curr. Liab.	678	766	720	678	636	713	531	574	568	526
LT Debt	665	468	558	669	681	685	739	649	516	500
Common Eqty.	1,334	1,272	1,344	1,466	1,444	1,536	1,304	1,174	1,071	960
Total Cap.	2,095	1,829	1,935	2,163	2,140	2,403	2,207	1,969	1,650	1,539
Cap. Exp.	170	146	124	123	184	193	215	264	314	278
Cash Flow	507	481	459	378	355	334	312	292	280	258
Curr. Ratio	1.9	1.7	1.8	2.0	1.8	1.7	1.9	1.7	1.5	1.7
% LT Debt of Cap.	31.7	25.6	28.8	30.9	31.8	28.5	33.5	33.0	31.3	32.5
% Net Inc.of Revs.	10.7	10.2	9.3	8.9	8.6	8.5	8.7	9.1	8.7	8.7
% Ret. on Assets	10.1	10.6	8.2	7.5	6.9	6.7	7.1	7.6	7.4	7.6
% Ret. on Equity	22.8	21.5	18.4	15.8	13.9	13.9	15.1	16.2	15.8	16.4

Data as orig. reptd.; bef. results of disc. opers. and/or spec. items. Per share data adj. for stk. divs. as of ex-div. date. Bold denotes diluted EPS (FASB 128). E-Estimated. NA-Not Available. NM-Not Meaningful. NR-Not Ranked.

Office—One Becton Dr., Franklin Lakes, NJ 07417-1880. **Tel**—(201) 847-6800. **Website**—http://www.bd.com **Chrmn, Pres & CEO**—C. Castellini. **VP & CFO**—K. R. Weisshaar. **VP & Secy**—B. M. Healy. **VP & Treas**—G. D. Cheatham. **Investor Contact**—Ronald Jasper. **Dirs**—H. N. Beaty, H. P. Becton, C. Castellini, A. J. Costello, G. M. Edelman, J. W. Galiardo, R. W. Hanselman, F. A. Olson, J. E. Perella, G. M. Shatto, A. Sommer, R. S. Troubh, Baroness Margaretha af Ugglas. **Transfer Agent & Registrar**—First Chicago Trust Co. of New York, NYC. **Incorporated**—in New Jersey in 1906. **Empl**— 18,900. **S&P Analyst:** H. B. Saftlas

STANDARD &POOR'S
STOCK REPORTS

Bell Atlantic

311

NYSE Symbol **BEL**

In S&P 500

12-SEP-98

Industry: Telephone

Summary: This Regional Bell Operating company recently agreed to merge with GTE Corp. in a stock transaction valued at about $53 billion.

S&P Opinion: Hold (★★★)

Recent Price • 44½
52 Wk Range • 53-37⅜

Yield • 3.5%
12-Mo. P/E • 25.3

Earnings vs. Previous Year
▲=Up ▼=Down ▶=No Change

Quantitative Evaluations

Outlook
(1 Lowest—5 Highest)
• **2**

Fair Value
• **42⅛**

Risk
• **Low**

Earn./Div. Rank
• **B+**

Technical Eval.
• **Bullish** since 5/97

Rel. Strength Rank
(1 Lowest—99 Highest)
• **89**

Insider Activity
• **Neutral**

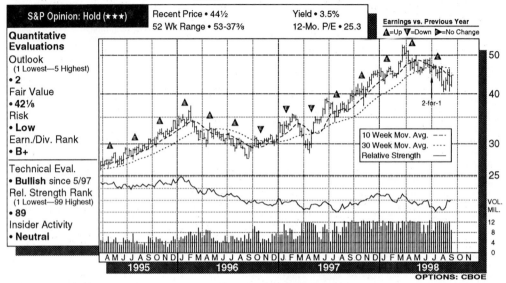

2-for-1

10 Week Mov. Avg. – – –
30 Week Mov. Avg. ·······
Relative Strength ——

VOL.
MIL.

A M J J A S O N D J F M A M J J A S O N D J F M A M J J A S O N D J F M A M J J A S O N
1995   1996   1997   1998

OPTIONS: CBOE

Overview - 14-AUG-98

The company recently agreed to acquire GTE Corp. (NYSE: GTE) by exchanging 1.22 BEL common share for each of GTE's 963 million shares. The transaction, expected to be completed in the second half of 1999, was initially valued at $52.9 billion, and represented a slight discount to GTE's current market price. The merger is expected to produce annual cost savings of $500 million after 2000, and capital savings of $300 million. The August 1997 merger of Bell Atlantic and NYNEX created a global company with over $29 billion in annual revenues. The combined territories cover 25% of the U.S. population; international operations include Europe, Mexico, and Asia. The company's region accounts for nearly 30% of the U.S. long-distance market, and 5% of international long-distance traffic originating in the U.S.

Valuation - 14-AUG-98

The shares, which have sharply underperformed the market, should be aided somewhat by the positive impact of the merger with GTE. However, we see the GTE deal being heavily scrutinized by federal regulators, who continue to be concerned about a lack of competition in BEL's markets. The company is also struggling to deal with limited revenue growth prospects and the potential of a more competitive local telecom environment. Longer-term prospects appear somewhat brighter, as BEL gains strength from access to GTE's long-distance and data networks. Once it can offer long-distance service within its territory (by about 1999 year-end), BEL will exploit the fact that 45% of all long-distance calls made by its customers terminate in its combined region. BEL is likely to perform in line with the market and GTE over the next 12 months, following the recent settlement of a short-lived union strike.

Key Stock Statistics

S&P EPS Est. 1998	2.60	Tang. Bk. Value/Share	8.48
P/E on S&P Est. 1998	17.1	Beta	0.57
S&P EPS Est. 1999	2.85	Shareholders	870,600
Dividend Rate/Share	1.54	Market cap. (B)	$ 69.2
Shs. outstg. (M)	1553.5	Inst. holdings	39%
Avg. daily vol. (M)	2.457		

Value of $10,000 invested 5 years ago: $ 22,092

Fiscal Year Ending Dec. 31

	1998	1997	1996	1995	1994	1993
Revenues (Million $)						
1Q	7,651	3,414	3,220	3,450	3,420	3,163
2Q	7,928	3,441	3,260	3,565	3,430	3,220
3Q	—	7,374	3,267	3,261	3,455	3,290
4Q	—	7,696	3,371	3,154	3,487	3,317
Yr.	—	30,194	13,081	13,430	13,791	12,990
Earnings Per Share ($)						
1Q	**0.57**	**0.45**	0.53	0.47	0.46	0.42
2Q	**0.65**	0.57	0.53	0.51	0.47	0.44
3Q	**E0.70**	0.63	0.53	0.69	0.32	0.45
4Q	**E0.67**	**0.59**	0.40	0.45	0.36	0.39
Yr.	**E2.60**	**1.56**	1.98	2.13	1.60	1.70

Next earnings report expected: late October

Dividend Data (Dividends have been paid since 1984.)

Amount ($)	Date Decl.	Ex-Div. Date	Stock of Record	Payment Date
0.770	Nov. 25	Jan. 07	Jan. 09	Feb. 02 '98
0.770	Mar. 24	Apr. 07	Apr. 10	May. 01 '98
2-for-1	May. 01	Jun. 30	Jun. 01	Jun. 29 '98
0.385	Jun. 23	Jul. 08	Jul. 10	Aug. 03 '98

Business Summary - 14-AUG-98

The company recently agreed to acquire GTE Corp. (NYSE: GTE) via an exchange of stock initially valued at $52.9 billion. The merger is expected to come under severe scrutiny from the FCC and the U.S. Department of Justice, which will focus on its impact on competition in the region. The combined companies would have more than 250,000 employees, and 63 million access lines. The transaction is expected to be accretive to earnings in the first year, and to produce $2 billion in operating cost savings and $2 billion in revenue synergies by the third year.

The August 1997 merger of two of AT&T's Baby Bells, Bell Atlantic and NYNEX, formed the second largest corporate combination in U.S. history. The combined company, also named Bell Atlantic, is headquartered in New York City, and serves more than 40 million telephone access lines and about 6.7 million wireless customers in 25 states, the District of Columbia, and worldwide. BEL's domestic coverage spans the East Coast from Maine to Virginia.

Bell Atlantic is the second largest U.S. provider of local exchange telephone service, based on 1997 U.S. access lines, serving nearly 40 million customer access lines in 13 East Coast states and Washington, DC.

Bell Atlantic Mobile (BAM) has domestic operations in 25 states and international investments in Latin America, Europe and the Pacific Rim. The company also owns a 50% stake in a national wireless partnership, known as PrimeCo Personal Communications L.P., with AirTouch Communications (ATI). PrimeCo reached a level of 598,000 customers during the 1998 second quarter; it added more than 90,000 customers during the quarter.

BEL is a partner with NYNEX and Pacific Telesis in Tele-TV, which will develop video programming and other products and services. BEL also owns a minority interest in Bell Communications Research, which provides technical assistance and consulting services to telephone companies.

International operations include a 24.8% interest in Telecom Corp. of New Zealand; a 42% interest in a Mexican cellular company; and interests in cellular ventures in Italy, Slovakia and the Czech Republic.

The Communications Workers of America recently signed a two-year contract with BEL ending a strike that lasted only three days. Had the strike lasted for an extended period of time it would have cut the company's ability to add customers, services lines and provide directory assistance.

Per Share Data ($)

(Year Ended Dec. 31)	1997	1996	1995	1994	1993	1992	1991	1990	1989	1988
Tangible Bk. Val.	8.23	8.47	7.63	6.93	9.30	8.87	9.74	11.20	10.73	11.47
Cash Flow	5.29	4.92	5.13	NA	NA	NA	NA	NA	NA	NA
Earnings	1.56	1.98	2.13	1.60	1.70	1.61	1.71	1.69	1.36	1.67
Dividends	1.49	1.43	1.40	1.37	1.34	1.29	1.24	1.18	1.10	1.02
Payout Ratio	95%	72%	66%	85%	79%	80%	73%	69%	81%	61%
Prices - High	45⅞	37½	34½	29⅞	34⅝	27	27⅛	28⅝	28⅛	18⅝
- Low	28⅜	27⅝	24¼	24¼	24⅞	20⅛	21½	19¾	17⅜	15⅝
P/E Ratio - High	29	19	16	19	20	17	16	17	21	11
- Low	18	14	11	15	15	12	13	12	13	9

Income Statement Analysis (Million $)

	1997	1996	1995	1994	1993	1992	1991	1990	1989	1988
Revs.	30,194	13,081	13,430	13,791	12,900	12,647	12,280	12,298	11,449	10,880
Depr.	5,864	2,595	2,627	2,652	2,545	2,417	2,299	2,377	2,420	2,354
Maint.	NA	NA	NA	NA	NA	1,875	1,791	1,768	1,718	1,612
Constr. Credits	NA	NA	NA	NA	NA	NA	20.6	24.4	28.5	32.5
Eff. Tax Rate	38%	37%	38%	39%	35%	32%	33%	34%	31%	29%
Net Inc.	2,455	1,739	1,862	1,402	1,482	1,382	1,332	1,313	1,075	1,317

Balance Sheet & Other Fin. Data (Million $)

	1997	1996	1995	1994	1993	1992	1991	1990	1989	1988
Gross Prop.	77,437	34,758	33,554	33,746	32,330	31,046	31,848	30,784	29,312	27,570
Net Prop.	35,039	15,916	15,921	16,938	20,366	20,330	19,962	19,447	18,874	18,174
Cap. Exp.	6,638	2,553	2,627	2,699	2,449	2,547	2,545	2,747	3,008	2,889
Total Cap.	29,522	14,881	14,597	18,228	22,187	21,830	19,444	21,781	20,905	20,121
Fxd. Chgs. Cov.	4.3	6.0	6.0	4.9	4.7	3.9	3.8	4.0	3.8	4.6
Capitalization:										
LT Debt	13,265	5,960	6,407	6,806	7,206	7,348	7,960	8,171	7,721	6,557
Pfd.	200	145	145	85.0	Nil	Nil	Nil	Nil	Nil	Nil
Common	12,789	7,423	6,685	6,081	8,224	7,816	7,831	8,930	8,591	9,177
% Return On Revs.	8.1	13.3	13.9	10.2	11.4	10.9	10.8	10.7	9.4	12.1
% Return On Invest. Capital	NA	19.7	21.0	9.8	9.5	9.5	9.9	9.2	7.9	9.1
% Return On Com. Equity	24.3	24.7	29.2	19.6	17.3	17.4	15.9	14.8	11.7	14.5
% Earn. on Net Prop.	21.0	18.5	18.8	10.2	9.9	9.2	9.4	10.1	8.3	9.6
% LT Debt of Cap.	50.5	44.1	48.4	52.5	46.7	48.5	50.4	47.8	47.3	41.7
Capital. % Pfd.	0.8	1.1	1.1	0.6	Nil	Nil	Nil	Nil	Nil	Nil
Capital. % Common	48.7	54.9	50.5	46.9	53.3	51.5	49.6	52.2	52.7	58.3

Data as orig. reptd. ; bef. results of disc. opers. and/or spec. items. Per share data adj. for stk divs. as of ex-div. date. Bold denotes diluted EPS (FASB 128). E-Estimated. NA-Not Available. NM-Not Meaningful. NR-Not Ranked.

Office—1095 Avenue of the Americas, New York, NY 10036. **Tel**—(212) 395-2121. **Website**—http://www.bellatlantic.com/invest **Chrmn & CEO**—R. W. Smith. **Vice Chrmn, Pres & COO**—I. G. Seidenberg. **SVP & CFO**—F. V. Salerno. **VP & Treas**—E. C. Wolf. **Investor Contact**—Peter D. Crawford. **Dirs**—L. T. Babbio, Jr., R. L. Carrion, J. G. Cullen, L. J. R. de Vink, J. H. Gilliam, Jr., S. P. Goldstein, H. L. Kaplan, E. T. Kennan, T. H. Kean, J. F. Maypole, J. Neubauer, T. H. O'Brien, E. Pfeiffer, H. B. Price, R. L. Ridgway, F. V. Salerno, I. G. Seidenberg, W. V. Shipley, R. W. Smith, J. R. Stafford, M. D. Webb, S. Young. **Transfer Agent**—Boston EquiServe (c/o Bank of Boston). **Incorporated**—in Delaware in 1983. **Empl**—141,401. **S&P Analyst:** Philip D. Wohl

STANDARD &POOR'S
STOCK REPORTS

BellSouth Corp.

314

NYSE Symbol **BLS**

In S&P 500

12-SEP-98

Industry:
Telephone

Summary: BLS, one of the largest U.S. telephone holding companies, provides local service in nine southeastern states, and has also expanded into wireless and international ventures.

| S&P Opinion: Hold (★★★) | Recent Price • 69⅝ | Yield • 2.1% |
| | 52 Wk Range • 73⅜-44⅜ | 12-Mo. P/E • 19.0 |

Earnings vs. Previous Year
▲=Up ▼=Down ▶=No Change

Quantitative Evaluations

Outlook
(1 Lowest—5 Highest)
• 1

Fair Value
• 55½

Risk
• Average

Earn./Div. Rank
• B+

Technical Eval.
• **Bearish** since 7/98

Rel. Strength Rank
(1 Lowest—99 Highest)
• 95

Insider Activity
• NA

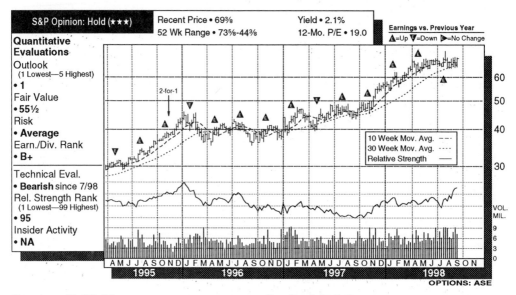

10 Week Mov. Avg. - - -
30 Week Mov. Avg. ·······
Relative Strength ——

OPTIONS: ASE

Overview - 23-JUL-98

The company will continue to encounter increasing pressure as a result of competition in the telecommunications indsutry. Although the 1996 Telecom Act opened BLS's local markets to competition, it also allowed the company to immediately provide long-distance services to its cellular customers. In addition, under the terms of the law, we expect BLS to slowly introduce long-distance services within its own territory sometime in 1999, once it receives the go-ahead (expected in late 1998. The company is continuing to file with the FCC to allow it to offer long-distance services in various states in its operating territory. Sluggish single-digit revenue growth will be augmented by investments in wireless businesses, including strong domestic cellular operations, a 50% stake in a nationwide wireless data provider, and international cellular investments. BLS has also acquired various well-placed international wireless interests.

Valuation - 23-JUL-98

We expect the shares to continue to be only market performers, as the company's wireless and international assets continue to augment sluggish domestic local service growth. BLS must increase even further its emphasis on double-digit growth opportunities, such as wireless and Internet services and international expansion. EPS of $2.87 in 1996 included a $0.35 first quarter gain on the sale of paging assets. We expect 1998 EPS to rise to $3.30 (including a $0.09 one-time gain in the first quarter), from 1997's $3.29 (which included a $0.45 of special income items). The shares offer an above-average yield, but they were recently trading at 20X our 1998 EPS estimate, a level that represents the upper end of the stock's historical P/E range.

Key Stock Statistics

S&P EPS Est. 1998	3.30	Tang. Bk. Value/Share	13.10
P/E on S&P Est. 1998	21.0	Beta	0.52
S&P EPS Est. 1999	3.50	Shareholders	1,084,100
Dividend Rate/Share	1.44	Market cap. (B)	$ 68.2
Shs. outstg. (M)	983.7	Inst. holdings	35%
Avg. daily vol. (M)	1.640		

Value of $10,000 invested 5 years ago: $ 33,099

Fiscal Year Ending Dec. 31

	1998	1997	1996	1995	1994	1993
Revenues (Million $)						
1Q	5,426	4,845	4,541	4,299	4,124	3,834
2Q	5,664	4,923	4,620	4,390	4,128	3,907
3Q	—	5,193	4,928	4,432	4,198	4,015
4Q	—	5,600	5,050	4,765	4,395	4,125
Yr.	—	20,561	19,040	17,886	16,845	15,880
Earnings Per Share ($)						
1Q	**0.89**	**0.70**	0.98	0.55	0.59	0.41
2Q	**0.82**	**0.66**	0.63	0.56	0.52	0.43
3Q	**E0.80**	1.19	0.63	0.56	0.51	0.45
4Q	**E0.79**	**0.74**	0.64	-0.10	0.56	-0.26
Yr.	**E3.30**	**3.29**	2.87	1.57	2.17	1.04

Next earnings report expected: mid October

Dividend Data (Dividends have been paid since 1984.)

Amount ($)	Date Decl.	Ex-Div. Date	Stock of Record	Payment Date
0.360	Sep. 23	Oct. 07	Oct. 09	Nov. 03 '97
0.360	Nov. 24	Jan. 06	Jan. 08	Feb. 02 '98
0.360	Feb. 23	Apr. 07	Apr. 09	May. 01 '98
0.360	Jun. 22	Jul. 06	Jul. 08	Aug. 03 '98

A Division of The McGraw·Hill Companies

Business Summary - 23-JUL-98

BellSouth Corp. has not been answering the bell to provide long-distance service, but it remains the largest U.S. telephone holding company, based on 1997 access lines. The telephone unit provided local exchange telephone service in nine southeastern states to 23,201,000 customer access lines at December 31, 1997. Wireline telephone operations provided 67% of operating revenues in 1997.

The company's wireless operations have consisted primarily of cellular and paging services. At December 31, 1997, BLS served 4,193,000 cellular subscribers in the U.S. Operations also include directory advertising and publishing, wireless data communications services, the sale and service of telecommunications and computer systems and a minority interest in Bell Communications Research.

BellSouth also has interests in international cellular operations covering 57,641,000 POPs (adjusted) in countries including Argentina, Australia, Brazil, Denmark, Germany, India Israel, New Zealand and Venezuela. As of December 31, 1997, international cellular ventures served 1,882,000 subscribers. Other international operations include Optus Communications, which is jointly owned by BellSouth, Cable & Wireless of the U.K., and several leading Australian companies and institutions.

Optus provides a full range of telecommunications services in Australia.

BellSouth estimates that over half the people in the world have never placed a telephone call. In high-growth wireless markets that it serves around the globe, BLS believes it has an even bigger opportunity to bring new services to customers. There are nearly 70 million potential customers in the 13 countries where BLS operates cellular systems, and only one out of every 37 people currently use its service. In comparison, approximately one person in five in the U.S. uses wireless phone service.

In January 1997, BellSouth successfully completed a public tender offer to buy about 57% of Peruvian communications company Tele 2000. The bid was contingent on the acquisition of at least 54% of the shares at the offering price of $1.50 a share. Tele 2000 holds cellular rights to serve Lima and portions of western Peru. It also provides cable TV and paging communications. BLS's acquisition of a 57% ownership of Tele 2000 is worth an estimated $110 million. Separately, the company was the highest bidder ($205 million) for 39 licenses to provide wireless telephone services in 37 southeastern markets. The new licenses fill in BellSouth's wireless telephone coverage throughout its nine-state region: Alabama, Florida, Georgia, Louisiana, Kentucky, Mississippi, North Carolina, South Carolina and Tennessee.

Per Share Data ($)

(Year Ended Dec. 31)	1997	1996	1995	1994	1993	1992	1991	1990	1989	1988
Tangible Bk. Val.	13.33	11.95	10.36	12.96	12.19	12.10	11.73	12.07	12.48	13.35
Cash Flow	7.27	6.62	5.05	5.41	4.17	4.78	4.62	4.76	4.80	4.58
Earnings	3.29	2.88	1.57	2.17	1.04	1.69	1.55	1.69	1.77	1.75
Dividends	1.44	1.44	1.40	1.38	1.38	1.38	1.37	1.34	1.24	1.16
Payout Ratio	44%	50%	89%	63%	133%	82%	88%	79%	70%	66%
Prices - High	58⅛	45⅞	43⅞	31¾	32	27¾	27½	29⅝	29⅛	22
- Low	38⅛	35¼	26⅞	25¼	25¼	21¾	22¾	24½	19½	17⅞
P/E Ratio - High	18	16	28	15	31	16	18	18	16	12
- Low	12	12	17	12	24	13	15	14	11	10

Income Statement Analysis (Million $)

	1997	1996	1995	1994	1993	1992	1991	1990	1989	1988
Revs.	20,561	19,040	17,886	16,845	15,880	15,202	14,446	14,345	13,996	13,597
Depr.	3,964	3,719	3,455	3,206	3,104	3,100	3,016	2,961	2,895	2,682
Maint.	NA	NA	NA	NA	NA	4,662	2,366	2,692	2,449	2,284
Constr. Credits	NA	NA	NA	NA	NA	15.3	18.1	17.6	15.9	22.2
Eff. Tax Rate	39%	38%	40%	37%	36%	36%	33%	32%	31%	32%
Net Inc.	3,270	2,863	1,564	2,160	1,034	1,658	1,507	1,632	1,695	1,666

Balance Sheet & Other Fin. Data (Million $)

	1997	1996	1995	1994	1993	1992	1991	1990	1989	1988
Gross Prop.	53,828	50,059	46,869	44,199	41,975	39,801	38,403	36,812	35,982	34,143
Net Prop.	22,861	21,825	21,092	25,162	24,856	24,273	24,059	23,907	23,742	23,455
Cap. Exp.	NA	4,455	4,203	3,600	3,486	3,189	3,102	3,191	3,223	3,207
Total Cap.	NA	21,365	19,749	25,893	24,856	25,478	25,340	25,335	25,327	24,106
Fxd. Chgs. Cov.	NA	6.8	6.2	6.1	3.3	4.4	3.8	4.1	4.1	4.4
Capitalization:										
LT Debt	NA	8,116	7,924	7,435	7,381	7,360	7,745	7,781	7,055	7,031
Pfd.	NA	Nil	Nil	Nil	Nil	Nil	Nil	Nil	Nil	Nil
Common	15,740	13,249	11,825	14,367	13,494	13,799	13,105	12,666	13,103	11,839
% Return On Revs.	15.9	15.0	8.7	12.8	6.5	10.9	10.4	11.4	12.1	12.2
% Return On Invest. Capital	NA	12.2	19.1	11.1	6.8	9.5	9.1	9.5	10.0	9.9
% Return On Com. Equity	22.2	22.8	11.9	15.4	6.3	11.9	11.3	12.8	13.7	13.8
% Earn. on Net Prop.	41.8	39.6	33.9	11.3	7.0	9.2	8.6	9.5	9.5	9.9
% LT Debt of Cap.	NA	37.9	40.1	34.1	35.4	34.8	37.1	38.1	35.0	37.3
Capital. % Pfd.	NA	Nil	Nil	Nil	Nil	Nil	Nil	Nil	Nil	Nil
Capital. % Common	Nil	66.7	59.9	65.9	64.6	65.2	62.9	61.9	65.0	62.7

Data as orig. reptd.; bef. results of dis. opers. and/or spec. items. Per shar data as adj. for stk. divs. as of ex-div. date. Bold denotes diluted EPS (FASB 128). NA-Not Available. NM-Not Meaningful. NR-Not Ranked.

Office—1155 Peachtree St., N.E., Atlanta, GA 30309-3610. **Tel**—(404) 249-2000. **Website**—http://www.bellsouth.com**Chrmn, Pres & CEO**—F. D. Ackerman. **EVP & CFO**—R. M. Dykes. **VP-Fin & Treas**—M. E. Droege.**SVP & Secy**—A. G. Yokley. **Dirs**—F. D. Ackerman, R. V. Anderson, J. H. Blanchard, J. H. Brown, A. M. Codina, P. B. Davis, J. G. Medlin Jr., L. F. Mullin, R. B. Smith, C. D. Spangler Jr., W. S. Stavropoulos, R. A. Terry, J. T. Wilson.**Transfer Agent & Registrar**—ChaseMellon Shareholder Services, Ridgefield Park, NJ. **Incorporated**—in Georgia in 1983. **Empl**—84,126. **S&P Analyst:** Philip D. Wohl

STANDARD &POOR'S
STOCK REPORTS

Bemis Co.

315

NYSE Symbol **BMS**

In S&P 500

12-SEP-98

Industry:
Containers and Packaging (Paper)

Summary: Bemis has become an important producer of a broad range of flexible packaging, packaging equipment and pressure sensitive materials primarily through internal development.

S&P Opinion: Hold (★★★)	Recent Price • 37⅞	Yield • 2.3%
	52 Wk Range • 46⅞-34⅞	12-Mo. P/E • 18.2

Quantitative Evaluations

Outlook
(1 Lowest—5 Highest)
• **3**

Fair Value
• **43⅞**

Risk
• **Low**

Earn./Div. Rank
• **A**

Technical Eval.
• **Bullish** since 3/98

Rel. Strength Rank
(1 Lowest—99 Highest)
• **81**

Insider Activity
• **NA**

Earnings vs. Previous Year
▲=Up ▼=Down ▶=No Change

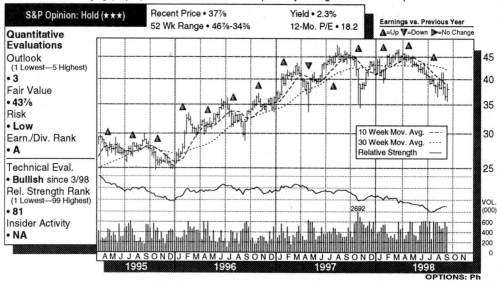

10 Week Mov. Avg. ---
30 Week Mov. Avg. ·····
Relative Strength ——

OPTIONS: Ph

Overview - 31-JUL-98

Despite an almost 4% decline in sales in the first half of 1998, sales for the year are expected to advance modestly, mainly reflecting strength in the plastic packaging segment. Paper packaging results, which have been hurt by inefficiencies related to a reorganization and a weak pricing environment, should begin to improve in the second half of the year, with the trend continuing during 1999. Pressure sensitive materials sales and earnings will continue to be affected by competitive pricing in the roll label area, but should begin to improve sequentially. We see margins widening on better coated and laminated film results, a profitable Paramount business, BMS's focus on higher-margin paper markets and lower SG&A expenses. Cash flow is expected to remain strong, while capital expenditures should continue to decline from the record 1997 level. Long-term results will likely benefit from efforts to boost manufacturing efficiency.

Valuation - 31-JUL-98

The shares, which surged almost 40% from October 1997 to March 1998, have since given back almost 20% of that gain and are trading near their 1998 low. As costs and expenses from the acquired Paramount operations are brought in line with those of comparable operating units, and the new unit is fully integrated into BMS, per share earnings growth should continue to improve. However, although raw material prices have been stabilizing, competitive pricing pressures continue to exist in the paper packaging and pressure sensitive segments, and results remain below management's targets. Despite the shares trading at 17X our 1998 EPS estimate, and only 15X our projection for 1999, both discounts to the market and BMS's peers, with earnings expected to grow at a 13% annual rate, we believe BMS will be no better than a market performer.

Key Stock Statistics

S&P EPS Est. 1998	2.25	Tang. Bk. Value/Share	9.49
P/E on S&P Est. 1998	16.9	Beta	0.81
S&P EPS Est. 1999	2.55	Shareholders	5,900
Dividend Rate/Share	0.88	Market cap. (B)	$ 2.0
Shs. outstg. (M)	53.4	Inst. holdings	52%
Avg. daily vol. (M)	0.110		

Value of $10,000 invested 5 years ago: $ 17,066

Fiscal Year Ending Dec. 31

	1998	1997	1996	1995	1994	1993
Revenues (Million $)						
1Q	451.5	475.5	385.6	368.6	323.3	292.6
2Q	470.6	481.3	411.9	383.2	337.7	303.3
3Q	—	465.5	423.1	372.5	356.2	299.5
4Q	—	454.9	434.9	399.1	373.2	308.1
Yr.	—	1,877	1,655	1,523	1,390	1,203
Earnings Per Share ($)						
1Q	**0.41**	**0.37**	0.41	0.31	0.26	0.21
2Q	**0.56**	**0.52**	0.47	0.41	0.36	0.30
3Q	**E0.58**	**0.47**	0.45	0.40	0.35	0.02
4Q	**E0.70**	**0.64**	0.57	0.51	0.43	0.36
Yr.	**E2.25**	**2.00**	1.90	1.63	1.40	0.89

Next earnings report expected: late October

Dividend Data (Dividends have been paid since 1922.)

Amount ($)	Date Decl.	Ex-Div. Date	Stock of Record	Payment Date
0.200	Oct. 30	Nov. 12	Nov. 14	Dec. 01 '97
0.220	Feb. 05	Feb. 17	Feb. 19	Mar. 02 '98
0.220	May. 07	May. 18	May. 20	Jun. 01 '98
0.220	Jul. 30	Aug. 10	Aug. 12	Sep. 01 '98

A Division of The **McGraw·Hill** *Companies*

Bemis Company, Inc.

Business Summary - 31-JUL-98

With the food industry accounting for 70% of its business, this diversified producer of flexible packaging and pressure-sensitive materials continues to wrap up acquisitions while satisfying its customers' appetites for innovative products and expanding into new markets.

Bemis's (BMS) long-term strategy focuses on targeting product and market segments where there is above average profit potential. The company also has demonstrated confidence in its outlook for potential stock appreciation, having bought back or authorized the repurchase of more than one million of its common shares.

During the past few years, BMS has spent heavily ($170 million in 1997 and $112 million in 1996) to expand its flexible packaging business -- which includes coated and laminated film packaging, polyethylene film packaging, multiwall paper bags and industrial and flexible packaging machinery -- and, to a lesser extent, its pressure sensitive materials segment -- which includes printing products, narrow-web roll label products, graphic films and label applying equipment.

Although Bemis might seem to be all wrapped up in marketing its packaging products in the U.S., Canada and Europe, it has broadened its geographic reach to Southeast Asia, South America and Mexico, where opportunities for growth exist due to strong demand for sophisticated barrier films required to extend the shelf life of perishable foods. In February 1998, BMS agreed to acquire a 33% interest in Brazil's largest flexible packaging concern from Dixie Toga for close to $40 million. The new company, to be called ITAP/Bemis Ltda. has sales of $130 million.

Coated and laminated film products, which include perishable and frozen food packaging, stretch film and carton sealing tape, accounted for 36% of net sales in 1997. Multiwall and consumer-size paper bags for products such as pet food, seed, fertilizers, feed, flour, dairy products, chemicals, sugar and minerals accounted for 12% of sales, while polyethylene packaging products provided 25% of sales. The specialty coated and graphics products segment manufactures pressure-sensitive materials, which accounted for 26% of sales.

In January 1997, BMS acquired Paramount Packaging ($100 million in sales) for $65 million in cash, stock and the assumption of debt. Paramount is a flexible packaging maker, specializing in disposable diaper packaging. In the 1997 second quarter, BMS sold the remainder of its packaging machinery operations.

Per Share Data ($) (Year Ended Dec. 31)	1997	1996	1995	1994	1993	1992	1991	1990	1989	1988
Tangible Bk. Val.	9.24	8.75	8.95	7.58	6.75	6.55	6.51	5.26	5.13	4.64
Cash Flow	3.46	3.14	2.75	2.38	1.78	2.02	1.95	1.82	1.59	1.36
Earnings	2.00	1.90	1.63	1.40	0.89	1.11	1.03	0.99	0.90	0.74
Dividends	0.80	0.72	0.64	0.54	0.50	0.46	0.42	0.36	0.30	0.22
Payout Ratio	40%	38%	39%	39%	56%	42%	37%	36%	32%	28%
Prices - High	47 7/8	37 5/8	30	25 3/4	27 3/8	29 5/8	20 3/4	18 3/4	18 3/4	12 3/4
- Low	33 5/8	25 5/8	23	20 1/2	19 7/8	19 3/4	13 1/2	12 7/8	11 1/4	8
P/E Ratio - High	24	20	18	18	31	27	20	19	21	17
- Low	17	13	14	15	22	18	13	13	13	11
Income Statement Analysis (Million $)										
Revs.	1,877	1,655	1,523	1,390	1,203	1,181	1,142	1,128	1,077	1,069
Oper. Inc.	274	242	206	180	148	147	143	137	130	117
Depr.	78.9	66.2	58.0	50.9	46.2	47.3	47.1	42.3	36.8	33.1
Int. Exp.	18.9	13.4	11.5	8.4	7.2	7.5	12.1	11.7	12.4	11.6
Pretax Inc.	180	163	136	121	76.7	93.7	87.7	84.8	78.7	68.7
Eff. Tax Rate	37%	28%	37%	37%	37%	35%	36%	36%	37%	38%
Net Inc.	108	101	85.2	72.8	46.1	57.3	53.0	50.9	47.0	39.6
Balance Sheet & Other Fin. Data (Million $)										
Cash	13.8	10.2	22.0	12.7	8.9	0.1	1.4	9.2	1.4	1.2
Curr. Assets	516	467	442	419	337	315	308	344	286	303
Total Assets	1,363	1,169	1,031	923	790	743	715	756	632	595
Curr. Liab.	251	214	219	211	184	161	167	194	171	166
LT Debt	317	241	166	172	123	131	129	171	110	120
Common Eqty.	640	567	513	418	371	361	329	296	266	237
Total Cap.	1,055	865	729	654	551	549	527	533	442	419
Cap. Exp.	168	112	93.6	106	91.8	70.7	56.9	73.2	82.6	61.0
Cash Flow	186	167	143	124	92.0	105	100	92.0	83.0	73.0
Curr. Ratio	2.1	2.2	2.0	2.0	1.8	2.0	1.8	1.8	1.7	1.8
% LT Debt of Cap.	30.0	27.9	22.8	26.3	22.4	23.9	24.5	32.1	24.8	28.5
% Net Inc.of Revs.	5.7	6.1	5.6	5.2	3.8	4.8	4.6	4.5	4.4	3.7
% Ret. on Assets	8.5	9.2	8.7	8.5	6.0	7.5	7.5	7.3	7.6	6.9
% Ret. on Equity	17.8	18.8	18.3	18.5	12.6	15.8	17.1	18.1	18.5	17.5

Data as orig. reptd.; bef. results of disc. opers. and/or spec. items. Per share data adj. for stk. divs. as of ex-div. date. Bold denotes diluted EPS (FASB 128). E-Estimated. NA-Not Available. NM-Not Meaningful. NR-Not Ranked.

Office—222 South 9th St., Suite 2300, Minneapolis, MN 55402-4099. **Tel**—(612) 376-3000. **Chrmn & CEO**—J. H. Roe. **Vice Chrmn**—R. F. Mlnarik. **Pres & COO** —J. H. Curler. **SVP & Secy**—S. W. Johnson. **SVP, CFO, Treas & Investor Contact**—Benjamin R. Field III. **Dirs**—W. H. Buxton, J. H. Curler, R. Greenkorn, L. W. Knoblauch, N. P. McDonald, R. F. Mlnarik, R. D. O'Shaughnessy, E. N. Perry, J. H. Roe, C. A. Wurtele. **Transfer Agent & Registrar**—Norwest Bank Minnesota, South St. Paul. **Incorporated**—in Missouri in 1885. **Empl**— 9,300. **S&P Analyst:** Stewart Scharf

Bestfoods

414M

NYSE Symbol **BFO**

In S&P 500

12-SEP-98 Industry: Foods

Summary: This international food processor, which makes a broad line of branded grocery items, spun off its corn refining business to its shareholders at the end of 1997.

S&P Opinion: Accumulate (★★★★)

| Recent Price • 45½ | Yield • 2.0% |
| 52 Wk Range • 60⅞-43¼ | 12-Mo. P/E • 21.9 |

Earnings vs. Previous Year
▲=Up ▼=Down ▷=No Change

Quantitative Evaluations

Outlook
(1 Lowest—5 Highest)
• **1**

Fair Value
• **47⅛**

Risk
• **Low**

Earn./Div. Rank
• **A**

Technical Eval.
• **NA**

Rel. Strength Rank
(1 Lowest—99 Highest)
• **46**

Insider Activity
• **Unfavorable**

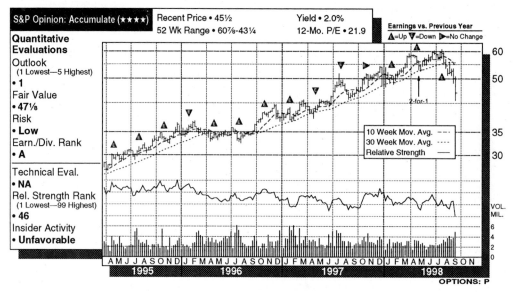

10 Week Mov. Avg. ---
30 Week Mov. Avg. ····
Relative Strength —

2-for-1

VOL. MIL.

OPTIONS: P

Overview - 20-JUL-98

Sales from continuing operations in 1998 are projected to rise at a middle single-digit rate, as increased global consumer food volumes help offset possible unfavorable currency exchange translations. Operating margins in North America and Europe are projected to benefit principally from the increased volumes and cost savings realized from 1997 restructurings, although a significant increase in marketing expenditures on new products could be somewhat offsetting. Latin American profits should remain in a good uptrend, while Asian profit growth will likely remain slow, reflecting high reinvestment into infrastructure. In 1998, we anticipate diluted EPS of $2.23, up nearly 14% from 1997's $1.96 (before restructuring charges amounting to $0.54 per share).

Valuation - 20-JUL-98

Considering the company's improving financial characteristics following the late 1997 spinoff of its volatile corn refining unit, and its status as one of the most international of the world's major branded food companies, the shares are attractive for accumulation. Although trading at a modest P/E premium to that of the S&P 500, the stock was recently selling at a modest discount to most of its closest food company peers. We believe that BFO is well positioned to increase its EPS at a low-teen rate over the next few years, a rate that will exceed the majority of its S&P Food Group peers. With BFO now free of the earnings volatility of the corn refining industry, and better able to focus on extending the reach of its strong portfolio of consumer food brands, we expect the increasing predictability of EPS growth to allow for a gradual expansion in the stock's P/E ratio. We expect BFO to command a 15% to 20% premium to the S&P 500 over time.

Key Stock Statistics

S&P EPS Est. 1998	2.23	Tang. Bk. Value/Share	NM
P/E on S&P Est. 1998	20.4	Beta	0.81
S&P EPS Est. 1999	2.50	Shareholders	28,300
Dividend Rate/Share	0.90	Market cap. (B)	$ 13.1
Shs. outstg. (M)	287.4	Inst. holdings	58%
Avg. daily vol. (M)	0.868		

Value of $10,000 invested 5 years ago: NA

Fiscal Year Ending Dec. 31

	1998	1997	1996	1995	1994	1993
Revenues (Million $)						
1Q	2,121	2,149	2,409	1,955	1,738	1,636
2Q	2,115	2,105	2,514	2,040	1,856	1,690
3Q	—	2,024	2,392	2,046	1,813	1,664
4Q	—	2,123	2,529	2,391	2,019	1,748
Yr.	—	8,400	9,844	8,432	7,425	6,738
Earnings Per Share ($)						
1Q	**0.44**	0.40	0.41	0.36	0.32	0.29
2Q	**0.58**	-0.02	0.52	0.48	-0.06	0.38
3Q	E0.57	0.50	0.50	0.47	0.41	0.40
4Q	E0.65	**0.56**	0.54	0.40	0.45	0.41
Yr.	**E2.23**	**1.43**	1.97	1.72	1.13	1.48

Next earnings report expected: mid October

Dividend Data (Dividends have been paid since 1920.)

Amount ($)	Date Decl.	Ex-Div. Date	Stock of Record	Payment Date
0.450	Nov. 18	Jan. 07	Jan. 09	Jan. 26 '98
0.450	Mar. 17	Mar. 27	Mar. 31	Apr. 24 '98
2-for-1	Mar. 17	Apr. 27	Mar. 31	Apr. 24 '98
0.225	May. 20	Jun. 26	Jun. 30	Jul. 24 '98

A Division of The McGraw-Hill Companies

STANDARD
&POOR'S
STOCK REPORTS

Bestfoods

414M

12-SEP-98

Business Summary - 20-JUL-98

Bestfoods (formerly CPC International) is one of the nation's most international food companies, with operations in more than 60 countries. In order to better focus on its growing array of branded consumer food products, the company divested its corn refining business to BFO shareholders as a new independent publicly owned company, effective at 1997 year-end. The new company, named Corn Products International, Inc., is listed on the NYSE under the symbol CPO. Business segment contributions in 1997 were:

	Sales	Profits
Europe	42%	40%
North America	21%	27%
Latin America	13%	20%
Asia	5%	4%
Baking	19%	9%

Consumer foods include Hellmann's and Best Foods mayonnaise, Mazola corn oil and margarine, Skippy peanut butter, Mueller's pasta, Karo and Golden Griddle syrups, Argo and Maizena corn starches and Knorr soups, bouillons and sauces. Products sold in international markets include Knorr soups, sauces, gravies, desserts and prepared meals; seasonings, condiments and spices; corn starch; quick energy products; cheeses and dairy products; mayonnaise, margarine and corn oil.

BFO's baking business consists of Entenmann's sweet baked products; Thomas' English muffins; Boboli Italian bread shells; and Arnold, Brownberry, Freihofer's and Oroweat breads.

BFO operates approximately 142 plants around the world, consisting of 33 in the United States; 42 in Europe; 23 in Africa/Middle East; 22 in Latin America; 19 in Asia; and three in Canada.

Management's objective is for BFO to continuously rank in the top quartile of its food industry peer group in terms of total return to shareholders. In February 1998, BFO said it expects in 1998 to exceed its 10.6% compound annual growth in operating income (excluding special items) of the past 10 years.

Per Share Data ($)

(Year Ended Dec. 31)	1997	1996	1995	1994	1993	1992	1991	1990	1989	1988
Tangible Bk. Val.	NM	0.82	0.06	2.53	3.19	2.70	2.50	1.75	2.02	2.91
Cash Flow	4.71	3.25	2.85	2.10	2.28	2.17	2.08	1.94	1.71	1.50
Earnings	1.43	1.97	1.72	1.13	1.48	1.39	1.30	1.21	1.05	0.92
Dividends	0.64	0.79	0.74	0.69	0.64	0.59	0.55	0.50	0.44	0.38
Payout Ratio	45%	40%	43%	61%	43%	42%	42%	41%	40%	41%
Prices - High	54⅜	42⅛	37¼	27⅞	25⅝	25⅞	23⅜	21¼	18½	14⅝
- Low	37¾	32½	25⅞	22⅛	20	19⅞	18	15½	12⅜	9⅞
P/E Ratio - High	38	21	22	25	17	19	18	18	17	16
- Low	26	17	15	20	14	14	14	13	12	11

Income Statement Analysis (Million $)

	1997	1996	1995	1994	1993	1992	1991	1990	1989	1988
Revs.	8,400	9,844	8,432	7,425	6,738	6,599	6,189	5,781	5,103	4,700
Oper. Inc.	1,369	1,455	1,370	1,216	1,111	1,076	1,023	954	835	733
Depr.	264	376	322	288	242	238	234	220	202	181
Int. Exp.	172	206	143	107	110	116	128	133	117	96.0
Pretax Inc.	704	918	877	615	790	745	694	638	557	494
Eff. Tax Rate	36%	34%	39%	40%	40%	40%	40%	40%	40%	40%
Net Inc.	429	580	512	345	455	431	404	374	328	289

Balance Sheet & Other Fin. Data (Million $)

	1997	1996	1995	1994	1993	1992	1991	1990	1989	1988
Cash	39.0	163	203	125	166	158	216	48.0	107	87.0
Curr. Assets	2,188	2,751	2,577	2,215	1,972	2,025	1,792	1,714	1,427	1,262
Total Assets	6,100	7,875	7,502	5,668	5,061	5,171	4,510	4,490	3,705	3,342
Curr. Liab.	2,347	2,792	3,066	2,088	1,583	1,706	1,360	1,555	1,197	1,164
LT Debt	1,818	1,869	1,333	879	898	954	1,016	990	845	590
Common Eqty.	862	1,897	1,797	1,696	1,729	1,633	1,432	1,253	1,018	1,195
Total Cap.	2,973	4,256	3,529	2,770	2,804	2,767	2,885	2,706	2,316	2,001
Cap. Exp.	321	540	481	401	363	297	282	336	267	260
Cash Flow	678	941	834	622	685	658	628	584	529	470
Curr. Ratio	0.9	1.0	0.8	1.1	1.2	1.2	1.3	1.1	1.2	1.1
% LT Debt of Cap.	61.1	43.9	37.8	31.7	32.0	34.5	35.2	36.6	36.5	29.5
% Net Inc.of Revs.	5.1	5.9	6.1	4.6	6.7	6.5	6.5	6.5	6.4	6.2
% Ret. on Assets	6.1	7.5	7.8	6.5	8.9	8.9	9.0	9.1	9.5	8.8
% Ret. on Equity	30.0	30.6	30.6	19.7	26.5	26.0	29.3	32.1	30.2	25.6

Data as orig. reptd.; bef. results of disc. opers. and/or spec. items. Per share data adj. for stk. divs. as of ex-div. date. Bold denotes diluted EPS (FASB 128). E-Estimated. NA-Not Available. NM-Not Meaningful. NR-Not Ranked.

Office—International Plaza, Englewood Cliffs, NJ 07632. **Tel**—(201) 894-4000. **Website**—http://www.bestfoods.com**Chrmn & Pres**—C. R. Shoemate. **Treas**—R. S. Gluck. **Secy**—H. A. Heller. **VP & Investor Contact**—B. H. Kastory. **Dirs**—T. H. Black, C. Castellini, A. C. DeCrane, Jr., W. C. Ferguson, R. J. Gillespie, E. R. Gordon, G. V. Grune, L. I. Higdon, Jr., R. G. Holder, E. S. Kraus, A. Labergere, H. de Campos Meirelles, W. S. Norman, C. R. Shoemate. **Transfer Agent & Registrar**—First Chicago Trust Co. of New York, Jersey City, NJ.**Incorporated**—in Delaware in 1959. **Empl**— 44,200. **S&P Analyst:** Richard Joy

STANDARD &POOR'S
STOCK REPORTS

Bethlehem Steel

326

NYSE Symbol **BS**

In S&P 500

12-SEP-98 | **Industry:** Iron & Steel | **Summary:** Bethlehem, the third largest U.S. steel producer, recently acquired Lukens Inc. for $750 million.

S&P Opinion: Hold (★★★)	Recent Price • 7⅝	Yield • Nil
	52 Wk Range • 17⅛-7	12-Mo. P/E • 6.0

Quantitative Evaluations

Outlook
(1 Lowest—5 Highest)
• **5**

Fair Value
• **12**

Risk
• **Average**

Earn./Div. Rank
• **B-**

Technical Eval.
• **Bearish** since 5/98

Rel. Strength Rank
(1 Lowest—99 Highest)
• **27**

Insider Activity
• **NA**

Earnings vs. Previous Year
▲=Up ▼=Down ▶=No Change

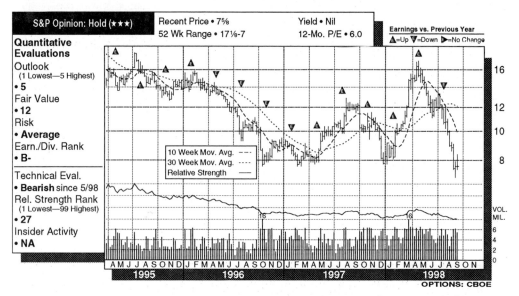

10 Week Mov. Avg. ---
30 Week Mov. Avg. - - -
Relative Strength —

OPTIONS: CBOE

Overview - 07-AUG-98

Excluding the acquisition of Lukens Inc., we project a 1.8% sales decline in 1998, reflecting the absence of non-steel units and a 1.5% decline in average revenue per ton. Volume should at least equal 1997's 8.8 million tons, as demand for steel remains strong in 1998. However, the reentry of Wheeling Pittsburgh Steel into the market, new minimill plants, and continued high levels of imports will result in lower prices. Benefiting from a sharp drop in pension expense, a general cost cutting program, lower depreciation, and the absence of losses from non-steel units, per ton costs should decline by about $15, and lead to a substantial increase in operating income. However, reported EPS will trail 1997 levels, in the absence of a $1.00 gain on an asset sale in 1997, and after a charge for the Lukens merger.

Valuation - 07-AUG-98

After the shares fell 28% since our April 27, 1998, downgrade, we raised our rating on BS to hold, from avoid, based on valuation. Recently trading at 6.0X our 1999 EPS estimate, versus an average of 8.5X for the group, BS is more reasonably valued. Despite its tremendous progress in reducing both operating and financial leverage, BS still has high debt levels in relation to its peers, and its per ton profit still lags the group average. Nevertheless, the company has made great progress in reducing costs, as shown by 1998 first half EPS, which exceeded analyst estimates in each quarter. Now that it has completely divested its non-steel operations, and has appreciably strengthened its product mix with the acquisition of Lukens, BS has strong appeal as a special situation turnaround. However, with steel prices coming under pressure from imports and new minimill production, we would not add to holdings at current levels.

Key Stock Statistics

S&P EPS Est. 1998	1.55	Tang. Bk. Value/Share	5.78
P/E on S&P Est. 1998	4.9	Beta	1.39
S&P EPS Est. 1999	1.65	Shareholders	37,000
Dividend Rate/Share	Nil	Market cap. (B)	$0.988
Shs. outstg. (M)	129.6	Inst. holdings	61%
Avg. daily vol. (M)	1.256		

Value of $10,000 invested 5 years ago: $ 4,765

Fiscal Year Ending Dec. 31

	1998	1997	1996	1995	1994	1993
Revenues (Million $)						
1Q	1,133	1,193	1,119	1,241	1,131	1,020
2Q	1,190	1,207	1,237	1,250	1,231	1,117
3Q	—	1,113	1,175	1,225	1,233	1,055
4Q	—	1,118	1,149	1,152	1,225	1,130
Yr.	—	4,631	4,679	4,868	4,819	4,323
Earnings Per Share ($)						
1Q	**0.49**	**0.25**	-0.09	0.38	0.02	-0.53
2Q	**0.23**	**1.19**	0.14	0.45	0.14	-0.27
3Q	E0.36	0.26	Nil	0.22	Nil	0.22
4Q	E0.47	0.27	-3.19	0.20	0.19	-2.78
Yr.	E1.55	2.03	-3.15	1.24	0.35	-3.37

Next earnings report expected: late October

Dividend Data

Cash dividends were omitted in January 1992. A poison pill stock purchase rights plan was adopted in 1988.

A Division of The McGraw·Hill Companies

STANDARD
&POOR'S
STOCK REPORTS

Bethlehem Steel Corporation

326

12-SEP-98

Business Summary - 07-AUG-98

In October 1996, Bethlehem Steel (BS) began the implementation of an extensive restructuring in an effort to improve profitability and narrow its focus to three core steel businesses. As a result of the restructuring, BS ceased the manufacture of wide flange beams, and no longer operates any non-steel business. Prior to the restructuring, BS was the only integrated steel company making wide flange beams for the construction market, as fierce minimill competition drove all other integrated steelmakers from that arena by 1991. As one indication of a very changed industry landscape, Nucor Corp., the largest U.S. minimill, surpassed BS in total size by the end of 1997.

Operating data (tons) for recent years:

	1997	1996
Shipments	8,790,000	8,764,000
Industry shipments	105,538,000	100,878,000
Production	9,599,000	9,447,000
Operating rate	91%	90%
Operating profit per ton	$30	$16

The Burns Harbor unit is BS's largest and most profitable operation. Products consist mostly of hot rolled, cold rolled and coated steel sheet products. Burns Harbor also produces a substantial amount of plate steel. These products are sold to the distributor, auto, appliance and construction equipment markets.

The Sparrows Point division produces sheet products targeted mostly at the container, distributor, metal building and roofing and machinery markets. Although the unit's profitability has been subpar for a long period of time, the company reaffirmed its intention to maintain Sparrows Point as part of its core operations in May 1997.

Pennsylvania Steel Technologies (PST) makes head hardened rails, standard rails, forging blooms, special sections and large diameter pipe. These products are sold to the rail transportation, machinery, forging and oil and gas transmission markets.

Competition in the steel sheet market is formidable. Besides imported steel, BS's main domestic competitors in the high margin coated products are AKS Steel Holding, Inland Steel Industries, LTV Corp., National Steel, Rouge Steel, USX US Steel Group, Weirton Steel and WHX Corp. In the commodity sheet grades, BS competes with Nucor Corp., Gallatin Steel, Trico Steel and Steel Dynamics. In addition, steel itself faces increased competition in automotive applications from other industrial materials such as aluminum, ceramics, glass and plastic.

BS completed the acquisition of Lukens Inc. on May 29, 1998, for about $565 million, including cash and transaction costs of about $380 million, and the issuance of 15.1 million BS common shares valued at approximately $185 million.

Per Share Data ($)

(Year Ended Dec. 31)	1997	1996	1995	1994	1993	1992	1991	1990	1989	1988
Tangible Bk. Val.	5.78	2.13	1.87	1.45	-5.25	-2.01	2.47	11.96	17.81	19.59
Cash Flow	4.20	-0.74	3.84	2.81	-0.31	0.46	-7.23	-2.41	7.26	9.84
Earnings	2.03	-3.15	1.24	0.35	-3.37	-2.73	-10.41	-6.45	2.93	5.16
Dividends	Nil	Nil	Nil	Nil	Nil	Nil	0.40	0.40	0.20	Nil
Payout Ratio	Nil	Nil	Nil	Nil	Nil	Nil	NM	NM	7%	Nil
Prices - High	12⅞	15⅞	19⅛	24¼	21	17¼	18½	21⅛	28½	25½
- Low	7⅝	7⅝	12⅝	16¼	12⅞	10	10¾	10⅝	15¼	15¼
P/E Ratio - High	6	NM	15	69	NM	NM	NM	NM	10	5
- Low	4	NM	10	46	NM	NM	NM	NM	5	3

Income Statement Analysis (Million $)

	1997	1996	1995	1994	1993	1992	1991	1990	1989	1988
Revs.	4,631	4,679	4,868	4,819	4,323	4,008	4,318	4,899	5,251	5,489
Oper. Inc.	470	405	553	395	332	75.0	86.0	411	697	871
Depr.	231	269	284	261	278	262	240	306	324	332
Int. Exp.	47.0	60.0	65.0	77.0	72.0	75.0	72.0	66.0	73.0	85.0
Pretax Inc.	336	-375	217	95.0	-350	-238	-764	-457	258	391
Eff. Tax Rate	16%	NM	17%	15%	NM	NM	NM	NM	4.70%	NM
Net Inc.	281	-308	180	81.0	-265	-198	-766	-463	246	392

Balance Sheet & Other Fin. Data (Million $)

	1997	1996	1995	1994	1993	1992	1991	1990	1989	1988
Cash	252	137	180	160	229	208	84.0	274	531	507
Curr. Assets	1,464	1,488	1,526	1,569	1,591	961	958	1,203	1,435	1,440
Total Assets	4,803	5,110	5,700	5,782	5,877	5,071	4,128	4,382	4,793	4,448
Curr. Liab.	911	957	1,050	1,011	914	893	931	831	838	870
LT Debt	452	497	547	668	718	727	762	590	656	775
Common Eqty.	1,201	399	669	586	120	58.0	361	1,181	1,683	1,461
Total Cap.	1,667	1,463	1,785	1,824	1,415	1,106	1,436	2,079	2,658	2,565
Cap. Exp.	228	259	267	445	327	329	556	488	421	304
Cash Flow	470	-82.0	442	299	-29.0	38.0	-549	-182	544	698
Curr. Ratio	1.6	1.6	1.4	1.6	1.7	1.1	1.0	1.4	1.7	1.7
% LT Debt of Cap.	27.1	34.0	30.6	36.6	50.8	65.7	53.0	28.4	24.7	30.2
% Net Inc.of Revs.	6.1	NM	3.7	1.7	NM	NM	NM	NM	4.7	7.1
% Ret. on Assets	5.7	NM	3.1	1.3	NM	NM	NM	NM	5.3	7.8
% Ret. on Equity	22.2	NM	22.0	10.2	NM	NM	NM	NM	13.9	28.9

Data as orig. reptd.; bef. results of disc. opers. and/or spec. items. Per share data adj. for stk. divs. as of ex-div. date. Bold denotes diluted EPS (FASB 128). E-Estimated. NA-Not Available. NM-Not Meaningful. NR-Not Ranked.

Office—1170 Eighth Ave., Bethlehem, PA 18016-7699. **Tel**—(610) 694-2424. **Website**—http://www.bethsteel.com **Chrmn & CEO**—C. H. Barnette. **Pres**—R. P. Penny. **EVP, CFO & Treas**—G. L. Millenbruch. **Secy**—W. H. Graham. **Investor Contact**—Blaise E. Derrico. **Dirs**—C. H. Barnette, B. R. Civiletti, W. H. Clark Jr., J. B. Curcio, T. L. Holton, L. B. Kaden, H. P. Kamen, W. Knowlton, R. McClements Jr., G. L. Millenbruch, R. P. Penny, Shirley D. Peterson, D. P. Phypers, W. A. Pogue, J. F. Ruffle. **Transfer Agent & Registrar**—First Chicago Trust Co. of New York, NYC. **Incorporated**—in Delaware in 1936. **Empl**— 17,800. **S&P Analyst:** Leo Larkin

Biomet, Inc.   3277
Nasdaq Symbol **BMET**
In S&P 500

12-SEP-98

Industry:
Health Care (Medical Products & Supplies)

Summary: Biomet makes surgical implants for replacement of hip and knee joints, orthopedic support items, fracture fixation devices, and other related medical devices.

S&P Opinion: Accumulate (★★★★)

| Recent Price • 31¾ | Yield • 0.4% |
| 52 Wk Range • 34¼-20¼ | 12-Mo. P/E • 28.6 |

Earnings vs. Previous Year
▲=Up ▼=Down ▶=No Change

Quantitative Evaluations

Outlook
(1 Lowest—5 Highest)
• 2

Fair Value
• 31⅜

Risk
• Average

Earn./Div. Rank
• B+

Technical Eval.
• **Bullish** since 5/97

Rel. Strength Rank
(1 Lowest—99 Highest)
• 95

Insider Activity
• **Favorable**

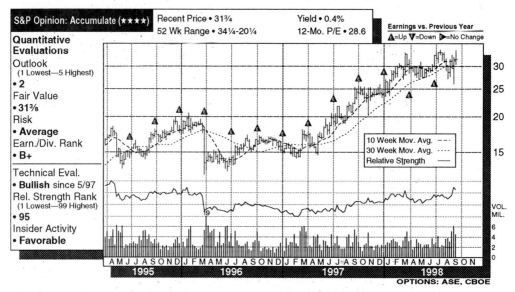

10 Week Mov. Avg. - - - -
30 Week Mov. Avg. ....
Relative Strength ——

OPTIONS: ASE, CBOE

Overview - 10-JUL-98

Revenues in FY 99 (May) are expected to increase about 16%, bolstered by the full-year inclusion of a recently formed joint venture with Merck KGaA (not affiliated with Merck & Co.) and continued gains in established lines. The new venture, called BioMer, is expected to add over $200 million to sales. Reconstructive device sales should benefit from continued market penetration in the U.S. and abroad, led by the Maxim Total Knee System and the Reach Hip System. Gains are also indicated for trauma and fixation products and electrical stimulation devices, aided by new products such as the SpineLink cervical system and the Recovery Protrusio cage. Margins should be well maintained on the higher volume and productivity improvements.

Valuation - 10-JUL-98

The shares rose about 35% during the first half, buoyed by the general market advance, strength in medical issues, and Biomet's improving earnings trend. Bolstered by growth in the replacement market and a robust lineup of new state-of-the-art products, Biomet should be able to continue to grow faster than the overall orthopedic market. The recent formation of BioMer, an orthopedic and biomaterials venture with Merck KGaA, has brought to Biomet a wide array of chemical, biological, drug and orthopedic technologies and products. Biomet also has rights to license Merck's biomaterials-based orthopedic products. Although juries have found Biomet liable for substantial compensatory and punitive damages in two separate lawsuits, the company believes that the judgments will not be upheld on appeal. Biomet has a strong balance sheet, with $134 million in cash and marketable securities, and no long term debt. The shares, which also offer some takeover appeal, merit accumulation.

Key Stock Statistics

S&P EPS Est. 1999	1.29	Tang. Bk. Value/Share	5.41
P/E on S&P Est. 1999	24.6	Beta	0.49
Dividend Rate/Share	0.12	Shareholders	10,200
Shs. outstg. (M)	112.1	Market cap. (B)	$ 3.6
Avg. daily vol. (M)	1.078	Inst. holdings	61%

Value of $10,000 invested 5 years ago: $ 19,826

Fiscal Year Ending May 31

	1998	1997	1996	1995	1994	1993
Revenues (Million $)						
1Q	149.5	137.2	127.2	96.23	86.89	78.10
2Q	156.6	144.0	133.1	106.9	90.31	82.40
3Q	161.0	146.2	133.5	120.7	95.66	84.05
4Q	184.3	153.0	141.4	128.5	100.4	90.77
Yr.	651.4	580.4	535.2	452.3	373.3	353.4
Earnings Per Share ($)						
1Q	**0.26**	0.21	0.18	0.15	0.13	0.13
2Q	**0.28**	0.23	0.20	0.17	0.15	0.14
3Q	**0.28**	0.24	0.20	0.18	0.16	0.14
4Q	**0.30**	0.26	0.24	0.19	0.17	0.15
Yr.	**1.11**	0.94	0.82	0.69	0.61	0.56

Next earnings report expected: mid September

Dividend Data (Dividends have been paid since 1996.)

Amount ($)	Date Decl.	Ex-Div. Date	Stock of Record	Payment Date
0.120	Jul. 01	Jul. 08	Jul. 10	Aug. 07 '98

A Division of The McGraw-Hill Companies

STANDARD
&POOR'S
STOCK REPORTS

Biomet, Inc.

3277

12-SEP-98

Business Summary - 10-JUL-98

Established in 1977, Biomet has grown to become the world's fourth largest orthopedic firm, offering a wide variety of reconstructive implants, electrical bone stimulators and related products. Biomet's products are used primarily by orthopedic medical specialists in the surgical replacement of hip and knee joints and in fracture fixation procedures as an aid to healing. Foreign business is important, accounting for about 29% of sales in FY 98 (May). Sales in recent years were derived:

	FY 98	FY 97	FY 96
Reconstructive devices	60%	61%	61%
EBI products	22%	20%	20%
Other	18%	19%	19%

Reconstructive products are used to replace joints that have deteriorated as a result of disease (principally arthritis and osteoporosis) or injury. Devices include implants for partial or total replacement of hips, knees and shoulders. The company also has the capability of producing other peripheral joints such as ankle and elbow implants. Hip femoral prostheses consist of a femoral head, neck and stem, cast or machined into a single piece. Most hip systems offered use titanium alloy femoral components and ultrahigh-molecular-weight components. Biomet also produces the instruments used by surgeons in orthopedic procedures. The company has

an estimated 10% to 11% share of the total U.S. reconstructive device market.

Acquired in 1988, Electro-Biology, Inc. (EBI) is a leader in the electrical stimulation and external fixation markets. Principal products include both invasive and noninvasive electrical stimulation devices used in the treatment of recalcitrant bone fractures; spinal fusion stimulation systems used as an adjunctive treatment in spinal fusion procedures; external fixation products; and a controlled cold therapy device used to reduce postoperative pain. EBI accounts for half of the domestic electrical stimulation device market.

Other products consist of internal fixation and trauma devices, arthroscopy products, operating room supplies, orthopedic support products, powered surgical equipment, craniomaxillofacial implants, spinal products and instruments.

In January 1998, Biomet formed a joint venture with Merck KGaA, Darmstadt, Germany (not affiliated with Merck & Co.). Biomet and Merck each contributed their existing European orthopedic operations to the venture, called BioMer. Merck brought to the venture an extensive array of chemical, biological, pharmaceutical and orthopedic technologies and products, while Biomet contributed orthopedic products and technologies, especially in total joint replacement. The venture is expected to add over $200 million to Biomet's sales in FY 99 (Biomet books all of BioMer's sales).

Per Share Data ($)

(Year Ended May 31)	1998	1997	1996	1995	1994	1993	1992	1991	1990	1989
Tangible Bk. Val.	5.41	4.74	4.42	3.59	3.12	2.61	2.05	1.54	1.16	0.88
Cash Flow	1.31	1.10	1.00	0.81	0.71	0.66	0.53	0.41	0.32	0.25
Earnings	1.11	0.94	0.82	0.69	0.61	0.56	0.46	0.36	0.27	0.20
Dividends	0.11	0.10	Nil	Nil	Nil	Nil	Nil	Nil	Nil	Nil
Payout Ratio	10%	11%	Nil	Nil	Nil	Nil	Nil	Nil	Nil	Nil
Cal. Yrs.	1997	1996	1995	1994	1993	1992	1991	1990	1989	1988
Prices - High	27	20⅝	19⅞	14¼	16½	30½	32⅜	9⅝	7	4⅛
- Low	14¼	12½	13⅛	9	8⅜	13¾	8⅛	4⅞	4	2⅜
P/E Ratio - High	24	22	24	21	27	54	70	27	26	21
- Low	13	13	16	13	14	25	18	14	15	12

Income Statement Analysis (Million $)

	1998	1997	1996	1995	1994	1993	1992	1991	1990	1989
Revs.	651	580	535	452	373	335	275	210	162	136
Oper. Inc.	204	178	158	133	114	102	78.0	59.5	47.6	35.2
Depr.	23.5	18.5	20.8	14.4	12.0	11.7	8.2	6.5	5.7	5.2
Int. Exp.	0.3	0.7	1.1	1.0	0.6	0.9	0.8	0.5	0.4	0.6
Pretax Inc.	204	169	150	125	107	94.3	76.5	58.6	43.8	32.3
Eff. Tax Rate	39%	37%	37%	37%	35%	32%	32%	33%	32%	33%
Net Inc.	125	106	94.1	79.2	69.8	64.0	51.8	39.5	29.9	21.5

Balance Sheet & Other Fin. Data (Million $)

	1998	1997	1996	1995	1994	1993	1992	1991	1990	1989
Cash	117	123	137	90.0	141	93.6	74.6	50.7	42.9	24.3
Curr. Assets	571	464	463	392	342	271	210	152	115	81.0
Total Assets	849	628	598	539	418	354	279	211	155	119
Curr. Liab.	98.1	72.9	62.0	89.2	53.8	46.7	42.0	33.6	22.6	18.2
LT Debt	Nil	Nil	Nil	Nil	Nil	Nil	Nil	Nil	Nil	Nil
Common Eqty.	667	553	534	445	357	301	232	173	129	98.0
Total Cap.	750	555	536	447	361	304	234	174	130	98.0
Cap. Exp.	44.1	21.4	14.1	28.9	6.5	14.9	14.0	11.1	6.5	7.9
Cash Flow	148	125	115	93.6	81.9	75.6	60.0	46.0	35.6	26.6
Curr. Ratio	5.8	6.4	7.5	4.4	6.4	5.8	5.0	4.5	5.1	4.5
% LT Debt of Cap.	Nil	Nil	Nil	Nil	Nil	Nil	Nil	Nil	Nil	Nil
% Net Inc.of Revs.	19.1	18.3	17.6	17.5	18.7	19.1	18.9	18.8	18.4	15.8
% Ret. on Assets	16.9	17.4	16.5	16.5	18.1	20.0	21.1	21.5	21.8	19.8
% Ret. on Equity	20.4	19.6	19.2	19.8	21.3	23.8	25.5	26.0	26.3	24.6

Data as orig. reptd.; bef. results of disc. opers. and/or spec. items. Per share data adj. for stk. divs. as of ex-div. date. Bold denotes diluted EPS (FASB 128). E-Estimated. NA-Not Available. NM-Not Meaningful. NR-Not Ranked.

Office—Airport Industrial Park, P.O. Box 587, Warsaw, IN 46581-0587. **Tel**—(219) 267-6639. **Website**—http://www.biomet.com **Chrmn**—N. L. Noblitt. **Pres & CEO**—D. A. Miller. **VP-Fin & Treas**—G. D. Hartman. **VP & Secy**—D. P. Hann. **VP & Investor Contact**—Greg W. Sasso (219) 372-1528. **Dirs**—J. L. Ferguson, R. R. Fisher, D. P. Hann, C. S. Harrison, M. R. Harroff, T. F. Kearns Jr., D. A. Miller, J. L. Miller, K. V. Miller, C. E. Niemier, N. L. Noblitt, J. M. Norris, M. T. Quayle, L. G. Tanner. **Transfer Agent**—Lake City Bank, Warsaw. **Incorporated**—in Indiana in 1977. **Empl**—2,550. **S&P Analyst:** H. B. Saftlas

12-SEP-98

Industry: Hardware & Tools

Summary: This company is the world's largest producer of power tools and a leading supplier of household products.

S&P Opinion: Hold (★★★)	Recent Price • 44⅛	Yield • 1.1%
	52 Wk Range • 65½-35¾	12-Mo. P/E • 17.7

Quantitative Evaluations

Outlook (1 Lowest—5 Highest)
• **1**

Fair Value
• **30½**

Risk
• **Average**

Earn./Div. Rank
• **B+**

Technical Eval.
• **Bearish** since 8/98

Rel. Strength Rank (1 Lowest—99 Highest)
• **43**

Insider Activity
• **Neutral**

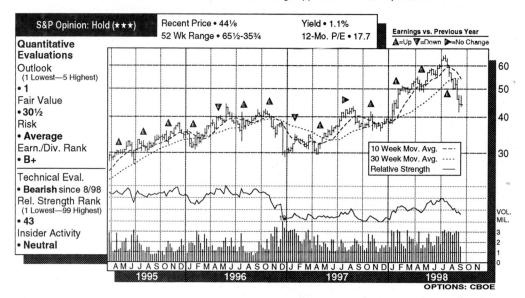

Earnings vs. Previous Year
▲=Up ▼=Down ▶=No Change

10 Week Mov. Avg. – – –
30 Week Mov. Avg. ⋯⋯
Relative Strength ——

OPTIONS: CBOE

Overview - 20-JUL-98

Sales growth in 1997 was restricted by difficult comparisons in the U.S. consumer segment, relatively weak European economies, and the impact of a strong dollar. Sales strengthened in the second half of the year, reflecting a large number of new products; sales improvement in both the near- and long-term will be largely dependent upon the success of new and modified products. A recently announced restructuring plan targets cost reductions in excess of $100 million annually, with most of the benefits beginning in 1999. Consumer price competition is evident in Europe, but an ongoing restructuring program is keeping costs down. An incomplete product line and economic turmoil has hampered sales in new operations in the Far East. A change in goodwill accounting resulted in a first quarter non-cash charge of $900 million ($9.46 a share). Our 1998 EPS estimate of $2.68 excludes non-recurring charges.

Valuation - 20-JUL-98

We recently lowered our recommendation on BDK to hold, from accumulate, on a valuation basis. With the shares trading at over 20X our 1999 EPS estimate of $3.20, we no longer expect the stock to outperform. Operationally, we look favorably at BDK's plans to reposition itself, including the sale of most household operations, Emhart Glass and True Temper Sports, plus such global restructuring steps as employee and plant rationalization. Also positive is a buyback authorization for up to 10% of the company's common stock. BDK expects to offset dilution of about $0.30 a share from divestitures by a $0.28 reduction in goodwill amortization charges. BDK has targeted operating margins of 13% (projected by the company for 1999), sales growth of 4% to 7%, and net income gains of 15%.

Key Stock Statistics

S&P EPS Est. 1998	2.68	Tang. Bk. Value/Share	NM
P/E on S&P Est. 1998	16.5	Beta	1.25
S&P EPS Est. 1999	3.20	Shareholders	19,300
Dividend Rate/Share	0.48	Market cap. (B)	$ 4.1
Shs. outstg. (M)	93.0	Inst. holdings	80%
Avg. daily vol. (M)	0.588		

Value of $10,000 invested 5 years ago: $ 26,519

Fiscal Year Ending Dec. 31

	1998	1997	1996	1995	1994	1993
Revenues (Million $)						
1Q	1,008	1,015	1,065	1,021	1,085	1,100
2Q	1,170	1,182	1,208	1,135	1,221	1,156
3Q	—	1,225	1,187	1,169	1,323	1,190
4Q	—	1,518	1,455	1,440	1,619	1,437
Yr.	—	4,940	4,914	4,766	5,248	4,882
Earnings Per Share ($)						
1Q	**0.30**	**0.27**	-0.40	0.19	0.14	0.13
2Q	**0.61**	**0.47**	0.47	0.29	0.24	0.20
3Q	**E0.67**	**0.60**	0.59	0.33	0.31	0.20
4Q	**E1.10**	**1.00**	0.94	1.51	0.68	0.47
Yr.	**E2.68**	**2.35**	1.66	2.33	1.37	1.00

Next earnings report expected: mid October

Dividend Data (Dividends have been paid since 1937.)

Amount ($)	Date Decl.	Ex-Div. Date	Stock of Record	Payment Date
0.120	Oct. 16	Dec. 10	Dec. 12	Dec. 26 '97
0.120	Feb. 12	Mar. 11	Mar. 13	Mar. 27 '98
0.120	Apr. 28	Jun. 10	Jun. 12	Jun. 26 '98
0.120	Jul. 16	Sep. 09	Sep. 11	Sep. 25 '98

A Division of The **McGraw·Hill** *Companies*

Business Summary - 20-JUL-98

Although best known for its pre-eminent position in power tools, Black & Decker (BDK) makes a wide range of consumer and commercial products. Its products are sold under a number of well known brand names in more than 100 countries. The company has manufacturing operations in 14 countries.

The company is divided into two broad segments: Consumer & Home Improvement (86% of 1997 sales, and 83% of total operating income), and Commercial & Industrial (14%; 17%). U.S. sales accounted for 58% of the total in 1997, Europe 28%, and other countries 14%.

BDK is the world's largest producer of portable electric power tools (such as drills, screwdrivers and saws), residential security hardware (locksets and deadbolts), and electric lawn and garden tools, as well as the largest supplier of power tool accessories and specialized, engineered fastening and assembly systems in the markets it serves. In addition, its household products business is the leader in North America in the small electric appliance (e.g. hand-held vacuums, irons, toasters) and premium portable lighting industries. Its plumbing products business is the third-largest faucet manufacturer in North America, and BDK is the worldwide leader in golf club shafts and glass container-forming and inspection equipment.

Commercial and industrial products include fastening and assembly systems and tools, and high-speed glass container forming and inspection equipment. Market growth in both industries is typically in the low single-digit range. Growth rates in fastening and assembly systems are influenced by the global automotive and other industries, while glass equipment growth rates are influenced by economic cycles for capital goods.

In January 1998, the company announced a restructuring plan, and directors also authorized the repurchase of up to 10% of the common stock over two years. Under the plan, BDK was to divest the majority of its household products operations, plus its Emhart Glass and True Temper Sports divisions. The household products business was sold in June 1998, and the remaining operations are expected to be sold by October or earlier. In addition, labor will be reduced in international markets, and certain assets will be written down. On a pretax basis, the program is expected to cost approximately $225 million. When completed, the restructuring is expected to generate more than $100 million in annual savings.

During 1996, the company also restructured some of its operations, and recorded an after tax charge of $74.8 million, primarily for severance benefits associated with the European consumer business, which had begun to weaken in the latter part of 1995.

BDK reduced its total debt to capitalization ratio to 51.0% in 1997, from 62.3% in 1995. It aims to bring this ratio down to the low 40% range by 1999, through annual free cash flow of $100 million.

Per Share Data ($)

(Year Ended Dec. 31)	1997	1996	1995	1994	1993	1992	1991	1990	1989	1988
Tangible Bk. Val.	NM	NM	NM	NM	NM	NM	NM	NM	NM	11.18
Cash Flow	4.55	4.11	4.34	3.91	2.51	1.52	4.03	4.21	2.18	3.03
Earnings	2.35	1.64	2.33	1.37	1.00	-1.11	0.81	0.84	0.51	1.65
Dividends	0.48	0.48	0.40	0.40	0.40	0.40	0.40	0.40	0.40	0.40
Payout Ratio	20%	29%	17%	29%	40%	NM	50%	48%	78%	24%
Prices - High	43³/₈	44¹/₄	38¹/₈	25³/₄	22¹/₄	26⁷/₈	19⁵/₈	20¹/₈	25¹/₄	24³/₄
- Low	29³/₈	29	22⁷/₈	17	16⁵/₈	14⁵/₈	8¹/₂	8	18¹/₈	17¹/₈
P/E Ratio - High	18	27	16	19	22	NM	24	24	50	15
- Low	13	18	10	12	17	NM	10	10	36	10

Income Statement Analysis (Million $)

	1997	1996	1995	1994	1993	1992	1991	1990	1989	1988
Revs.	4,940	4,914	4,766	5,248	4,882	4,780	4,637	4,832	3,190	2,281
Oper. Inc.	703	572	633	607	455	542	600	693	370	241
Depr.	214	215	207	214	126	201	199	206	99	81.0
Int. Exp.	133	140	193	195	180	228	309	398	198	64.0
Pretax Inc.	349	203	226	190	156	-29.0	108	123	63.0	126
Eff. Tax Rate	35%	22%	4.00%	33%	39%	NM	51%	59%	52%	23%
Net Inc.	227	159	217	127	95.0	-73.0	53.0	51.0	30.0	97.0

Balance Sheet & Other Fin. Data (Million $)

	1997	1996	1995	1994	1993	1992	1991	1990	1989	1988
Cash	247	142	132	66.0	82.0	66.0	75.0	84.0	158	108
Curr. Assets	2,079	1,804	2,107	1,833	1,764	1,783	1,730	1,934	3,105	1,302
Total Assets	5,361	5,154	5,545	5,434	5,311	5,392	5,533	5,890	6,258	1,825
Curr. Liab.	1,373	507	1,787	1,880	1,509	1,490	1,374	1,712	2,426	746
LT Debt	1,624	1,416	1,705	1,723	2,069	2,109	2,626	2,756	2,630	277
Common Eqty.	1,791	1,632	1,273	1,019	899	924	877	921	721	725
Total Cap.	3,473	3,116	3,181	2,938	3,166	3,225	3,693	3,710	3,390	1,031
Cap. Exp.	203	196	203	199	210	184	108	113	112	98.0
Cash Flow	441	374	412	329	210	116	249	257	129	179
Curr. Ratio	1.5	1.2	1.2	1.0	1.2	1.2	1.3	1.1	1.3	1.7
% LT Debt of Cap.	46.8	45.4	53.6	58.7	65.4	65.4	71.1	74.3	77.6	26.9
% Net Inc.of Revs.	4.6	3.2	4.6	2.4	2.0	NM	1.1	1.1	0.9	4.3
% Ret. on Assets	4.3	3.0	4.0	2.4	1.8	NM	0.9	0.8	0.7	5.6
% Ret. on Equity	13.3	10.9	15.8	12.0	9.1	NM	5.5	6.1	4.1	14.1

Data as orig. reptd.; bef. results of disc. opers. and/or spec. items. Per share data adj. for stk. divs. as of ex-div. date. EPS for 1998 1Q excl. nonrecurring charges of $10.51. E-Estimated. NA-Not Available. NM-Not Meaningful. NR-Not Ranked.

Office—701 E. Joppa Rd., Towson, MD 21286. **Tel**—(410) 716-3900. **Website**—http://www.blackanddecker.com **Chrmn, President & CEO**—N. D. Archibald. **SVP & CFO**—T. M. Schoewe. **VP & Treas**—M. M. Rothleitner. **SVP & Secy**—B. B. Lucas. **Director-Investor Relations**—F. Robert Hunter. **Dirs**—N. D. Archibald, N. R. Augustine, B. L. Bowles, M. Candlish, A. G. Decker Jr., A. Luiso, M. H. Willes, M. C. Woodward Jr. **Transfer Agent & Registrar**—First Chicago Trust Co. of New York, NYC. **Incorporated**—in Maryland in 1910. **Empl**— 28,600. **S&P Analyst:** Efraim Levy

STANDARD &POOR'S
STOCK REPORTS

Block (H&R)

336K
NYSE Symbol **HRB**

In S&P 500

12-SEP-98

Industry:
Services (Commercial & Consumer)

Summary: North America's largest tax service company for individuals, HRB recently sold its 80% interest in CompuServe, a major on-line computer information service.

S&P Opinion: Accumulate (★★★★)	Recent Price • 42¼	Yield • 2.4%
	52 Wk Range • 49-33¾	12-Mo. P/E • 11.3

Quantitative Evaluations

Outlook
(1 Lowest—5 Highest)
• **2**

Fair Value
• **39⅝**

Risk
• **Average**

Earn./Div. Rank
• **A-**

Technical Eval.
• **Bullish** since 3/98

Rel. Strength Rank
(1 Lowest—99 Highest)
• **88**

Insider Activity
• **Neutral**

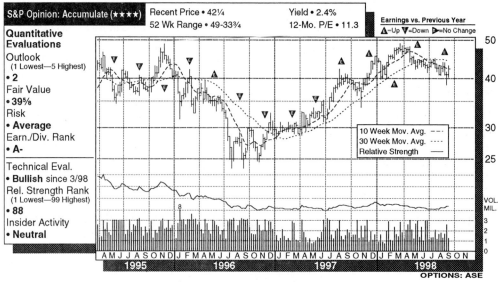

Earnings vs. Previous Year
▲=Up ▼=Down ▶=No Change

10 Week Mov. Avg. — — —
30 Week Mov. Avg. ‑‑‑‑‑
Relative Strength ——

OPTIONS: ASE

Overview - 27-AUG-98

We expect that revenues and earnings for HRB will grow 15% during FY 99 (Apr.). The Option One Mortgage operation (acquired in June 1997) has been performing very well, and we view it as a good fit with the core tax business. The credit card operations are still generating losses, and management is currently investigating opportunities to sell the division, an event we would view favorably. HRB has a very aggressive share repurchase plan in effect and expects to buy back 10 million shares within the next 12 months, which should improve earnings 10%. The international tax preparation business is being expanded overseas, and domestically the firm experienced good margin expansion this past quarter. We are bumping up our FY 99 and FY 00 estimates slightly, from $2.10 to $2.13, and from $2.50 to $2.54.

Valuation - 27-AUG-98

We are encouraged by HRB's mortgage operations and cost reduction efforts. Wall Street should start to revisit its evaluation of HRB now that CompuServe has been divested and with the ailing credit card business likely to be sold. Losses narrowed in the seasonally-slow first quarter, due to tremendous improvement in HRB's mortgage operations. Management's focus on expanding the company as a financial services firm should smooth out earnings from the income-concentrated fourth quarter. New cross-selling initiatives are beginning to show promise in leveraging HRB's brand name and customer base. HRB's balance sheet is pristine, with over $800 million in cash and marketable securities, allowing for great corporate flexibility. With the stock trading at 20X projected FY 99 earnings for a blue chip name with strong potential for upward earnings revisions, we continue to rate the shares accumulate.

Key Stock Statistics

S&P EPS Est. 1999	2.13	Tang. Bk. Value/Share	9.84
P/E on S&P Est. 1999	19.9	Beta	0.98
S&P EPS Est. 2000	2.54	Shareholders	33,100
Dividend Rate/Share	1.00	Market cap. (B)	$ 4.5
Shs. outstg. (M)	106.5	Inst. holdings	77%
Avg. daily vol. (M)	0.355		

Value of $10,000 invested 5 years ago: $ 12,577

Fiscal Year Ending Apr. 30

	1999	1998	1997	1996	1995	1994
Revenues (Million $)						
1Q	78.89	39.21	227.3	33.58	145.4	103.3
2Q	—	82.99	253.4	37.54	172.9	131.2
3Q	—	208.7	363.1	111.0	268.0	229.4
4Q	—	975.9	1,086	712.3	774.0	774.7
Yr.	—	1,307	1,930	894.5	1,360	1,239
Earnings Per Share ($)						
1Q	**-0.26**	**-0.33**	-0.51	-0.51	-0.03	-0.08
2Q	**E-0.22**	**-0.29**	-0.71	-0.21	-0.01	-0.04
3Q	**E-0.10**	**-0.17**	-0.24	-0.15	0.08	-0.17
4Q	**E2.82**	**2.37**	1.90	1.75	0.97	1.83
Yr.	**E2.13**	**1.62**	0.45	1.18	1.01	1.54

Next earnings report expected: mid November

Dividend Data (Dividends have been paid since 1962.)

Amount ($)	Date Decl.	Ex-Div. Date	Stock of Record	Payment Date
0.200	Nov. 24	Dec. 10	Dec. 12	Jan. 02 '98
0.200	Feb. 23	Mar. 09	Mar. 11	Apr. 01 '98
0.200	Jun. 05	Jun. 08	Jun. 10	Jul. 01 '98
0.250	Jun. 17	Sep. 08	Sep. 10	Oct. 01 '98

STANDARD
&POOR'S
STOCK REPORTS

H&R Block, Inc.

336K

12-SEP-98

Business Summary - 27-AUG-98

There's a good chance that you were one of the more than 18 million taxpayers who filed a 1997 tax return either in person, or electronically, through one of H&R Block's (HRB) 10,128 offices worldwide. HRB handled an estimated 13.1% of all individual tax returns filed with the IRS in 1997. Nearly 80% of Americans can find an H&R Block office within 10 miles of home.

In February 1998, Block sold CompuServe (Nasdaq: CSRV), its 80.1%-owned on-line services unit, to WorldCom, Inc. (Nasdaq: WCOM). CSRV shareholders received 0.40625 of a WCOM share for each CSRV share; based on WorldCom's closing price on January 30, 1997, the transaction was valued at about $1.3 billion. HRB will use the after tax proceeds of about $700 million to repurchase its stock, explore expansion opportunities, and strengthen its balance sheet. CompuServe's disappointing results in FY 97 (Apr.) limited Block's earnings performance, driving Block's share price sharply below highs reached in late 1995. As a result, HRB had been pursuing the separation of CSRV, in order to refocus on its core tax and financial services business.

The company has recently been targeting higher income taxpayers who currently do their own taxes or use independent accountants. The number of H&R Block Premium offices increased from 581 in fiscal year 1997, to 598 in 1998. On average, the premium tax service brings in $125 per return, against only $65 for the regular tax service.

HRB is also the market leader in tax preparation in Canada (1,945,000 FY 98 returns filed) and Australia (406,000). In FY 97, the company penetrated the U.K. market with the opening of 12 offices; an additional 16 offices were opened during FY 98.

The rapidly growing Block Financial Corp. unit develops and markets Kiplinger software packages for tax preparation and legal advice. In June 1997, HRB acquired Fleet Financial Group's Option One Mortgage Corp., a mortgage originator with more than 5,000 mortgage brokers in 46 states. Between the acquisition date and April 30, 1998, Option One sold approximately $1.8 billion of mortgage loans through whole-loan sales.

HRB's unprofitable credit card operations have had a negative affect on operations for several years, and management is currently pursuing the sale of the credit card portfolio. In FY 98, the division generated $37.4 million in revenues, but bad debts resulted in a pretax loss of $15.5 million.

In September 1997, as part of its effort to diversify its business portfolio and leverage its large customer base, Block signed an agreement with GEICO insurance companies to provide car insurance information to HRB's tax customers. Other small scale initiatives have been launched, such as financial planning services, in an attempt to maximize HRB's powerful brand name.

Per Share Data ($)

(Year Ended Apr. 30)	1998	1997	1996	1995	1994	1993	1992	1991	1990	1989
Tangible Bk. Val.	9.84	8.83	9.64	5.79	6.03	4.93	4.61	4.28	3.99	3.56
Cash Flow	2.14	2.03	1.49	1.65	2.07	2.19	1.89	1.61	1.43	1.20
Earnings	1.62	0.45	1.18	1.01	1.54	1.68	1.49	1.31	1.16	0.95
Dividends	0.80	1.04	1.27	1.22	1.09	0.97	0.85	0.74	0.61	0.50
Payout Ratio	49%	NM	108%	121%	71%	57%	56%	57%	53%	52%

Cal. Yrs.	1997	1996	1995	1994	1993	1992	1991	1990	1989	1988
Prices - High	45¾	42⅛	48⅞	48¾	42¾	41⅛	38¼	22¾	18¾	17¼
- Low	28	23⅝	33⅜	33	31⅞	30⅛	19⅞	15	13⅛	11⅜
P/E Ratio - High	28	94	41	48	28	24	26	17	16	18
- Low	17	52	28	33	21	18	13	11	11	12

Income Statement Analysis (Million $)

	1998	1997	1996	1995	1994	1993	1992	1991	1990	1989
Revs.	1,307	1,916	861	1,326	1,215	1,495	1,337	1,163	1,028	877
Oper. Inc.	364	171	23.0	258	321	324	282	250	205	165
Depr.	55.8	167	32.4	67.7	57.1	54.7	44.3	33.0	29.2	25.9
Int. Exp.	52.3	11.7	5.5	4.1	3.8	4.9	5.3	10.5	NA	NA
Pretax Inc.	281	62.4	197	220	283	295	264	226	201	162
Eff. Tax Rate	38%	24%	37%	51%	42%	39%	39%	38%	38%	38%
Net Inc.	174	47.8	125	107	164	181	162	140	124	100

Balance Sheet & Other Fin. Data (Million $)

	1998	1997	1996	1995	1994	1993	1992	1991	1990	1989
Cash	901	680	419	353	514	335	274	228	240	252
Curr. Assets	2,143	1,270	1,263	636	700	590	568	648	642	595
Total Assets	2,904	1,906	1,418	1,078	1,075	1,006	963	1,036	942	826
Curr. Liab.	1,277	713	340	359	336	330	328	437	412	357
LT Debt	250	Nil	NM	Nil	Nil	Nil	Nil	Nil	4.9	4.7
Common Eqty.	1,342	999	1,040	686	708	650	614	574	503	446
Total Cap.	1,591	1,025	1,040	686	708	650	614	582	516	461
Cap. Exp.	44.3	165	36.9	173	83.7	71.9	55.8	38.3	28.4	26.6
Cash Flow	230	215	158	175	221	235	207	173	153	126
Curr. Ratio	1.7	1.8	3.7	1.8	2.1	1.8	1.7	1.5	1.6	1.7
% LT Debt of Cap.	15.7	Nil	NM	Nil	Nil	Nil	Nil	Nil	1.0	1.0
% Net Inc.of Revs.	13.3	2.5	14.5	8.1	13.5	12.1	12.1	12.1	12.0	11.4
% Ret. on Assets	7.2	2.6	10.0	10.0	15.8	18.4	16.2	14.1	13.9	13.1
% Ret. on Equity	14.9	4.7	14.4	15.5	24.2	28.6	27.3	25.9	26.0	24.1

Data as orig. reptd.; bef. results of disc. opers. and/or spec. items. Per share data adj. for stk. divs. as of ex-div. date. Bold denotes diluted EPS (FASB 128). E-Estimated. NA-Not Available. NM-Not Meaningful. NR-Not Ranked.

Office—4410 Main St., Kansas City, MO 64111. **Tel**—(816) 753-6900. **Website**—http://www.hrblock.com **Chrmn**—H. W. Bloch. **Pres & CEO**—F. L. Salizzoni. **SVP, CFO & Treas**—O. Wenich. **Secy**—J. H. Ingraham. **Investor Contact**—Brian Schell (816-932-7561). **Dirs**—G. K. Baum, H. W. Bloch, R. E. Davis, D. R. Ecton, H. F. Frigon, R. W. Hale, M. L. Rich, F. L. Salizzoni, L. W. Smith, M. I. Sosland. **Transfer Agent & Registrar**—Boatmen's Trust Co., St. Louis. **Incorporated**—in Missouri in 1955. **Empl**— 2,600. **S&P Analyst:** Jordan Horoschak

STANDARD &POOR'S
STOCK REPORTS

Boeing Co.

340

NYSE Symbol **BA**

In S&P 500

12-SEP-98

Industry:
Aerospace/Defense

Summary: Boeing is the world's leading producer of commercial airplanes, as well as a manufacturer of military aircraft and space systems.

S&P Opinion: Hold (★★★)	Recent Price • 34	Yield • 1.6%
	52 Wk Range • 56¼-29	12-Mo. P/E • NM

Quantitative Evaluations

Outlook (1 Lowest—5 Highest)
• **3**

Fair Value
• **35¼**

Risk
• **Low**

Earn./Div. Rank
• **B**

Technical Eval.
• **NA**

Rel. Strength Rank (1 Lowest—99 Highest)
• **48**

Insider Activity
• **Favorable**

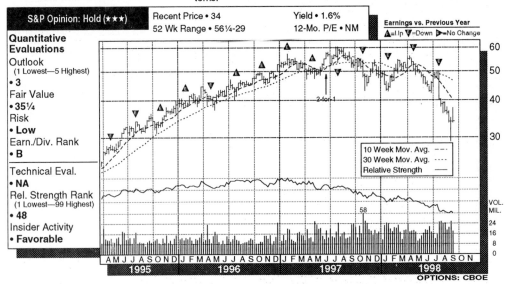

Earnings vs. Previous Year
▲=Up ▼=Down ▶=No Change

10 Week Mov. Avg. ---
30 Week Mov. Avg. ·····
Relative Strength ——

VOL. MIL.

OPTIONS: CBOE

Overview - 24-JUL-98

We believe that Boeing's well publicized production problems are rooted in the company's fierce determination to prevent archrival Airbus Industrie from grabbing market share. In an effort to maintain its 60% share of the $130 billion aerospace industry, BA accepted record aircraft orders. However, worker cutbacks in the early 1990s, and use of just-in-time parts inventory methods, hurt the company's ability to handle the dramatic increases in production capacity needed to meet the order boom. Subsequent worker and parts shortages led to production breakdowns, accounting for $1.9 billion of a $3.3 billion 1997 charge that led to BA's first loss in 50 years. Less publicized, but of equal concern, are narrowing operating profit margins. We believe that the profit declines are being driven by price discounting (as a result of BA's determination to maintain share) and commoditization of commercial aircraft (reflecting airlines' emphasis on cost efficiency rather than on performance, which was BA's historical competitive advantage).

Valuation - 24-JUL-98

Although the shares have declined 30% since mid-1997, we have reservations about BA's ability to materially outperform the market even at recent prices. For the short term, ongoing production problems should force BA to record at least $1.05 billion of additional charges in 1998. In the long term, increasing commoditization of commercial aircraft and intensifying Airbus competition should contribute to a continuing slide in commercial aircraft operating profit margins. Moreover, we are concerned about the potential impact of Asia's economic crisis on BA's long-term profit growth. It is estimated that current Asian orders account for about 40% of BA's backlog of higher-margin 747s, which generate 50% of BA's commercial aircraft operating profits.

Key Stock Statistics

S&P EPS Est. 1998	0.95	Tang. Bk. Value/Share	10.49
P/E on S&P Est. 1998	35.8	Beta	0.95
S&P EPS Est. 1999	2.05	Shareholders	101,200
Dividend Rate/Share	0.56	Market cap. (B)	$ 34.4
Shs. outstg. (M)	1010.7	Inst. holdings	44%
Avg. daily vol. (M)	5.129		

Value of $10,000 invested 5 years ago: $ 18,550

Fiscal Year Ending Dec. 31

	1998	1997	1996	1995	1994	1993
Revenues (Million $)						
1Q	12,941	10,359	4,293	5,037	6,345	6,644
2Q	13,389	12,311	6,275	5,558	5,396	7,985
3Q	—	11,371	5,601	4,381	5,063	5,153
4Q	—	11,727	6,512	4,539	5,120	5,656
Yr.	—	45,800	22,681	19,515	21,924	25,438
Earnings Per Share ($)						
1Q	0.05	0.55	0.17	0.27	0.43	0.48
2Q	0.26	0.48	0.68	-0.34	0.33	0.63
3Q	—	-0.72	0.37	0.33	0.27	0.28
4Q	—	-0.51	0.38	0.32	0.23	0.45
Yr.	E0.95	-0.18	1.85	0.57	1.25	1.83

Next earnings report expected: late October

Dividend Data (Dividends have been paid since 1942.)

Amount ($)	Date Decl.	Ex-Div. Date	Stock of Record	Payment Date
0.140	Oct. 27	Nov. 12	Nov. 14	Dec. 05 '97
0.140	Dec. 08	Feb. 11	Feb. 13	Mar. 06 '98
0.140	Apr. 27	May. 13	May. 15	Jun. 05 '98
0.140	Jun. 29	Aug. 12	Aug. 14	Sep. 04 '98

A Division of The McGraw·Hill Companies

STANDARD
&POOR'S
STOCK REPORTS

The Boeing Company

340

12-SEP-98

Business Summary - 24-JUL-98

Boeing's (BA) fabled past was founded on the company's ability to produce innovative, state-of-the art commercial aircraft. In the late 1950s, Boeing produced the 707, the world's first commercially viable jetliner. In the late 1960s, BA bet the store on the very successful 747, the world's first jumbo jet. In the mid-1990s, BA introduced the high technology 777, the first commercial aircraft designed entirely with the use of computers. In an effort to mitigate earnings cyclicality of the commercial aircraft business, BA greatly expanded its defense and space operations, especially with the 1996 acquisition of Rockwell International's (ROK) defense business and the 1997 purchase of McDonnell Douglas. Important profitability statistics (1997 commercial aircraft profit margins exclude $3.3 billion in special production charges) for recent years were:

	1997	1996	1995
OPERATING PROFIT MARGINS			
Commercial aircraft	5.4%	6.3%	2.8%
Defense and Space	7.3%	7.9%	2.2%
Financing and other	51%	NM	NM
FREE CASH FLOW PER SHARE	$1.25	$0.93	-$2.00

BA's commercial aircraft segment (57% of 1997 reve-

nues) makes a full line of commercial aircraft, ranging from 125-passenger 737 models to giant 500-seat 747 jumbo jets. In 1997, 374 aircraft were delivered, up from 269 in 1996. In 1998, BA expects to deliver 550 aircraft, at a rate of 43 planes per month. Supporting this increase in production is a recently issued forecast by BA that worldwide air passenger traffic will rise an average of 4.9% a year for the next 20 years. During this period, airlines are expected to order 16,160 aircraft to expand their fleets and replace aging planes. BA has been the industry leader, with a 60% share of the commercial aircraft market in recent years. At year-end 1997, backlog stood at $94 billion.

Boeing's defense and space operations (41% of 1997 revenues) include making the E-3 Airborne Warning and Control System (AWACS), the 767-based AWACS, CH-47 helicopters, and B-2 bomber subcontract work. Important development programs are the Joint Strike Fighter, the Airborne Laser, the RAH-66 Comanche helicopter, the F-22 fighter, and the expendable launch vehicle. BA manages NASA's International Space Station program. At year-end 1997, backlog stood at $28 billion.

Higher-margin aircraft financing operations accounted for 2% of 1997 revenues. BA does not intend to materially expand this unit.

Per Share Data ($)

(Year Ended Dec. 31)	1997	1996	1995	1994	1993	1992	1991	1990	1989	1988
Tangible Bk. Val.	10.56	11.75	14.39	14.23	13.21	11.87	11.86	10.15	8.87	7.83
Cash Flow	1.32	3.03	2.00	2.94	3.34	3.69	3.48	2.99	1.89	1.72
Earnings	-0.18	1.59	0.57	1.25	1.83	2.29	2.28	2.00	0.98	0.90
Dividends	0.56	0.55	0.50	0.50	0.50	0.50	0.50	0.47	0.39	0.34
Payout Ratio	NM	34%	87%	40%	27%	22%	22%	24%	40%	39%
Prices - High	60½	53¾	40	25⅛	22⅜	27⅜	26½	31	20⅝	15
- Low	43	37⅛	22¼	21⅛	16¾	16⅝	20⅝	18⅞	12⅞	8¼
P/E Ratio - High	NM	34	70	20	12	12	12	15	21	17
- Low	NM	23	39	17	9	7	9	9	13	9

Income Statement Analysis (Million $)

	1997	1996	1995	1994	1993	1992	1991	1990	1989	1988
Revs.	45,800	22,681	19,515	21,924	25,438	30,184	29,314	27,595	20,276	16,962
Oper. Inc.	2,503	2,212	1,878	2,293	2,716	3,001	2,780	2,208	1,208	1,015
Depr.	1,458	991	976	1,142	1,025	961	826	678	627	567
Int. Exp.	513	203	183	217	189	133	57.0	28.0	24.0	26.0
Pretax Inc.	-340	1,363	360	1,143	1,821	2,256	2,204	1,972	922	820
Eff. Tax Rate	NM	20%	NM	25%	32%	31%	29%	30%	27%	25%
Net Inc.	-177	1,095	393	856	1,244	1,554	1,567	1,385	675	614

Balance Sheet & Other Fin. Data (Million $)

	1997	1996	1995	1994	1993	1992	1991	1990	1989	1988
Cash	4,420	5,258	3,730	2,643	3,108	3,614	3,453	3,326	1,863	3,963
Curr. Assets	19,263	15,080	13,178	10,414	9,175	8,087	8,829	8,770	8,660	8,561
Total Assets	38,024	27,254	22,098	21,463	20,450	18,147	15,784	14,591	13,278	12,608
Curr. Liab.	14,152	8,642	7,415	6,827	6,531	6,140	6,276	7,132	6,673	6,705
LT Debt	6,123	3,980	2,344	2,603	2,613	1,772	1,313	311	275	251
Common Eqty.	12,953	10,941	9,898	9,700	8,983	8,056	8,093	6,973	6,131	5,404
Total Cap.	19,076	14,921	12,242	12,354	11,771	10,003	9,508	7,459	6,605	5,903
Cap. Exp.	1,391	726	629	795	1,348	2,212	1,878	1,609	1,372	709
Cash Flow	1,280	2,086	1,369	1,998	2,269	2,515	2,393	2,063	1,302	1,181
Curr. Ratio	1.4	1.8	1.8	1.5	1.4	1.3	1.4	1.2	1.3	1.3
% LT Debt of Cap.	47.2	26.7	19.1	21.1	22.2	17.7	13.8	4.2	4.2	4.3
% Net Inc.of Revs.	NM	4.8	2.0	3.9	4.9	5.1	5.3	5.0	3.3	3.6
% Ret. on Assets	NM	4.4	1.8	4.1	6.4	9.2	10.4	10.0	5.2	4.9
% Ret. on Equity	NM	10.5	4.0	9.2	14.6	19.3	20.9	21.2	11.7	11.8

Data as orig. reptd.; bef. results of disc. opers. and/or spec. items. Per share data adj. for stk. divs. as of ex-div. date. Bold denotes diluted EPS (FASB 128). E-Estimated. NA-Not Available. NM-Not Meaningful. NR-Not Ranked. Free cash flow: Net income plus depreciation/amortization and decreases in working capital, less net capital expenditures, increases in working capital and preferred dividends.

Office—7755 East Marginal Way South, Seattle, WA 98108. Tel—(206) 655-2121. Website—http://www.boeing.com Chrmn & CEO—P. M. Condit. Pres & COO—H. C. Stonecipher. SVP & CFO—B. E. Givan. Secy—H. Howard. Investor Contact—Larry Bishop (206-655-2608). Dirs—J. H. Biggs, J. E. Bryson, P. M. Condit, K. M. Duberstein, J. B. Fery, P. E. Gray, J. F. McDonnell, W. J. Perry, D. E. Petersen, C. M. Pigott, R. L. Ridgway, H. C. Stonecipher, G. H. Weyerhaeuser. Transfer Agent & Registrar—BankBoston, N.A. Incorporated—in Delaware in 1934. Empl—238,000. S&P Analyst: Robert E. Friedman, CPA

12-SEP-98

Industry: Paper & Forest Products

Summary: This leading forest products company makes paper and paper products, distributes office supplies and produces building materials.

S&P Opinion: Sell (★)	Recent Price • 25	Yield • 2.4%
	52 Wk Range • 45½-23⅛	12-Mo. P/E • NM

Earnings vs. Previous Year
▲=Up ▼=Down ▶=No Change

Quantitative Evaluations

Outlook
(1 Lowest—5 Highest)
• **2⁻**

Fair Value
• **23¾**

Risk
• **Average**

Earn./Div. Rank
• **B-**

Technical Eval.
• **Bearish** since 1/97

Rel. Strength Rank
(1 Lowest—99 Highest)
• **53**

Insider Activity
• **Neutral**

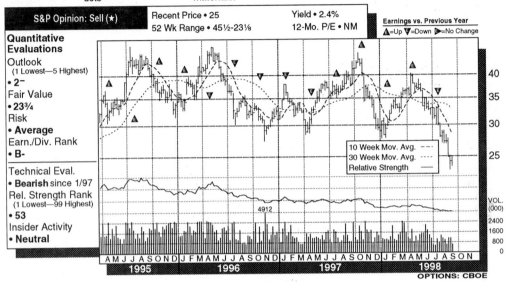

10 Week Mov. Avg. - - - -
30 Week Mov. Avg. · · · ·
Relative Strength —

OPTIONS: CBOE

Overview - 31-JUL-98

We anticipate a moderate sales gain in 1998, on mixed results. We see higher paper and packaging sales, on the maturation of a new paper machine and slightly higher average prices. However, the past year's pricing upturn (after a steep 18 month downturn) seems to have been put on hold. The difficulties stem mostly from the impact of Asia's financial woes and a strong U.S. dollar on foreign trade. Healthy sales gains should persist, however, in the office products area, on continued aggressive takeover, geographic expansion and internal growth programs. On the downside, building products sales will likely fall, as oversupply has dragged down lumber prices. Margins should improve, aided by the ongoing growth in office products and the higher average paper and packaging prices. However, we still see a full year loss, given ongoing troubles in building products and the recent paper recovery setback. Our full-year 1998 forecast excludes a $1.16 a share restructuring charge taken in the second quarter.

Valuation - 31-JUL-98

The shares continued to seesaw over the past year. They headed downward in the fall of 1997, when Asia's financial woes began to cast doubt on the previously expected paper sector recovery. The shares then reversed in early 1998, when a strong U.S. economy led investors to put aside Asian worries. However, they faltered again in the spring, when it became apparent Asia's troubles would not go away too fast. We have been bearish on the forest products industry throughout and remain pessimistic about BCC's upcoming prospects. We see troubles in the global economy continuing to impact commodities markets. As such, we see Boise's paper and wood products businesses stuck in their malaise for an extended period. Given that lack of enthusiasm, we would find a better place for our cash.

Key Stock Statistics

S&P EPS Est. 1998	-0.15	Tang. Bk. Value/Share	17.47
P/E on S&P Est. 1998	NM	Beta	1.03
S&P EPS Est. 1999	0.75	Shareholders	20,400
Dividend Rate/Share	0.60	Market cap. (B)	$ 1.4
Shs. outstg. (M)	56.3	Inst. holdings	80%
Avg. daily vol. (M)	0.182		

Value of $10,000 invested 5 years ago: $ 13,433

Fiscal Year Ending Dec. 31

	1998	1997	1996	1995	1994	1993
Revenues (Million $)						
1Q	1,490	1,274	1,228	1,223	941.0	984.0
2Q	1,538	1,333	1,261	1,270	1,000	974.0
3Q	—	1,442	1,356	1,339	1,090	1,003
4Q	—	1,445	1,263	1,242	1,109	996.9
Yr.	—	5,494	5,108	5,074	4,140	3,958
Earnings Per Share ($)						
1Q	-0.18	-0.51	0.32	0.93	-1.35	-0.56
2Q	-1.20	-0.53	-0.55	1.82	-0.86	-0.72
3Q	—	-0.23	-0.24	2.03	-1.19	-0.91
4Q	—	0.02	-0.16	1.15	0.32	-0.98
Yr.	—	-1.19	-0.63	5.93	-3.08	-3.17

Next earnings report expected: mid October

Dividend Data (Dividends have been paid since 1935.)

Amount ($)	Date Decl.	Ex-Div. Date	Stock of Record	Payment Date
0.150	Dec. 12	Dec. 29	Jan. 01	Jan. 15 '98
0.150	Feb. 06	Mar. 30	Apr. 01	Apr. 15 '98
0.150	Apr. 17	Jun. 29	Jul. 01	Jul. 15 '98
0.150	Jul. 31	Sep. 29	Oct. 01	Oct. 15 '98

A Division of The McGraw-Hill Companies

Business Summary - 31-JUL-98

Boise Cascade produces paper and wood products and distributes office products and building materials. Given the extreme cyclicality of its businesses, BCC has embarked on a program designed to make it consistently profitable and Economic Value Added (EVA)-positive over the course of each business cycle; EVA measures whether income exceeds a company's cost of capital.

In its paper segment, BCC has shifted its focus to uncoated business, printing, forms and converting papers, as well as to packaging grades; uncoated papers now account for about 70% of the segment's sales. The annual capacity of Boise's five pulp and paper mills, which also make market pulp (a raw material in paper) and newsprint, totaled 2.8 million tons at 1997 year-end. The division accounted for 27% of BCC's 1997 sales.

To eliminate some of its highest-cost commodity capacity, in 1995, BCC sold its interest in Rainy River Forest Products, which makes newsprint and certain uncoated grades. In 1996, it sold its coated publication paper business to Mead Corp. for $640 million. BCC also reduced its cost structure through the April 1997 startup of a new 330,000 tons-per-year uncoated paper machine in Jackson, AL. The machine will eliminate the high-cost market pulp produced at the mill. Finally, BCC's commodity cost structure will benefit from a shift in the use of smaller machines to value-added products, including colored and security papers.

Through 81%-owned Boise Cascade Office Products,

BCC distributes a broad line of products for office use which it mostly purchases from others. The products include office and computer supplies, furniture, paper products and promotional items. BCC derived 44% of its sales from this division in 1997.

The building products division (28% of sales in 1997) is a major producer of lumber, plywood, particleboard and specialty wood products. However, BCC plans to shift its strategy toward maintaining commodity plywood and lumber production only where EVA-positive. Boise now wants to focus is growth efforts on the production of engineered wood products such as laminated veneer lumber and oriented strand board. In line with that strategy, BCC announced a restructuring plan in July 1998. The program calls for the closure of three sawmills (used to make lumber) and one plywood plant. The restructuring will reduce Boise's lumber capacity by 28%, all in commodity areas, and plywood capacity by 11%. The company recorded a charge of $1.16 a share in 1998's second quarter for the program.

Boise Cascade owns or controls 2.4 million acres of timberland in North America. Including residuals from its wood products operations, BCC can supply about one-third of its own fiber requirements.

In reporting 1998 second quarter results, Boise said Asian economic turmoil clearly had a negative impact on the near-term outlook for paper and wood products markets. BCC said it expects conditions to worsen in the second half of the year, but remai ns unperturbed about long-term prospects.

Per Share Data ($)

(Year Ended Dec. 31)	1997	1996	1995	1994	1993	1992	1991	1990	1989	1988
Tangible Bk. Val.	17.47	21.88	25.77	18.76	24.83	29.54	37.21	40.06	40.87	37.00
Cash Flow	3.65	4.09	10.78	3.13	3.89	2.22	4.01	7.22	10.99	10.49
Earnings	-1.19	-0.63	5.93	-3.08	-3.17	-4.79	-2.46	1.62	6.19	6.34
Dividends	0.60	0.60	0.60	0.60	0.60	0.60	1.29	1.52	1.43	1.25
Payout Ratio	NM	NM	10%	NM	NM	NM	NM	94%	21%	20%
Prices - High	45½	47¼	47½	30½	27½	25⅜	29¼	46¼	48	50
- Low	27¾	27⅜	26¼	19	19½	16⅜	18⅜	19¾	39¾	36
P/E Ratio - High	NM	NM	8	NM	NM	NM	NM	29	8	8
- Low	NM	NM	4	NM	NM	NM	NM	12	6	6

Income Statement Analysis (Million $)

	1997	1996	1995	1994	1993	1992	1991	1990	1989	1988
Revs.	5,494	5,108	5,074	4,140	3,958	3,716	3,950	4,186	4,338	4,095
Oper. Inc.	365	367	873	350	263	157	194	448	714	758
Depr.	256	233	241	236	268	266	245	213	202	188
Int. Exp.	137	146	137	149	149	170	182	152	112	104
Pretax Inc.	-28.0	31.3	589	-65.0	-125	-252	-127	121	437	478
Eff. Tax Rate	NA	38%	39%	NM	NM	NM	NM	38%	39%	40%
Net Inc.	-30.0	9.1	352	-63.0	-77.0	-153	-79.0	75.0	268	289

Balance Sheet & Other Fin. Data (Million $)

	1997	1996	1995	1994	1993	1992	1991	1990	1989	1988
Cash	64.0	261	52.0	29.5	22.4	20.3	22.0	25.9	25.2	23.3
Curr. Assets	1,354	1,355	1,313	918	887	866	933	998	932	867
Total Assets	4,970	4,711	4,656	4,294	4,513	4,560	4,729	4,785	4,143	3,610
Curr. Liab.	894	933	770	658	688	750	652	758	678	681
LT Debt	1,903	1,526	1,579	1,856	1,840	1,942	2,191	1,935	1,498	925
Common Eqty.	1,251	1,323	1,336	818	969	1,136	1,422	1,556	1,564	1,678
Total Cap.	3,852	3,538	3,295	3,358	3,567	3,578	3,988	3,904	3,380	2,853
Cap. Exp.	280	789	409	271	221	283	299	758	699	430
Cash Flow	190	197	593	119	147	84.0	152	274	463	474
Curr. Ratio	1.5	1.5	1.7	1.4	1.3	1.2	1.4	1.3	1.4	1.3
% LT Debt of Cap.	49.4	43.1	47.9	55.3	51.6	54.3	54.9	49.5	44.3	32.4
% Net Inc.of Revs.	NM	0.2	6.9	NM	NM	NM	NM	1.8	6.2	7.1
% Ret. on Assets	NM	0.2	7.9	NM	NM	NM	NM	1.7	7.4	8.3
% Ret. on Equity	NM	NM	27.8	NM	NM	NM	NM	4.8	19.4	18.3

Data as orig. reptd.; bef. results of disc. opers. and/or spec. items. Per share data adj. for stk. divs. as of ex-div. date. Bold denotes diluted EPS (FASB 128). E-Estimated. NA-Not Available. NM-Not Meaningful. NR-Not Ranked.

Office—1111 W. Jefferson St., P.O. Box 50, Boise, ID 83728-0001.**Tel**—(208) 384-6161. **Website**—http://www.bc.com **Chrmn & CEO**—G. J. Harad. **SVP & CFO**—T. Crumley. **Investor Contact**—Vince Hannity. **Dirs**—A. L. Armstrong, P. J. Carroll, E. E. Hagenlocker, G. J. Harad, R. K. Jaedicke, D. S. Macdonald, G. G. Michael, P. J. Phoenix, A. W. Reynolds, J. E. Shaw, F. A. Shrontz, E. W. Spencer, W. W. Woods Jr. **Transfer Agents**—First Chicago Trust Co. of N.Y., NYC; Co.'s office. **Incorporated**—in Delaware in 1931. **Empl**— 22,514. **S&P Analyst:** Michael W. Jaffe

12-SEP-98

Industry:
Health Care (Medical Products & Supplies)

Summary: This maker of minimally-invasive medical devices for cardiology, radiology and other fields has significantly expanded its sales base through acquisitions and new products.

S&P Opinion: Buy (★★★★)	Recent Price · 66½ 52 Wk Range · 81⅝-41
	Yield · Nil 12-Mo. P/E · 51.6

Quantitative Evaluations

Outlook
(1 Lowest—5 Highest)
· **3**

Fair Value
· **83⅜**

Risk
· **Average**

Earn./Div. Rank
· **NR**

Technical Eval.
· **Bullish** since 3/98

Rel. Strength Rank
(1 Lowest—99 Highest)
· **67**

Insider Activity
· **NA**

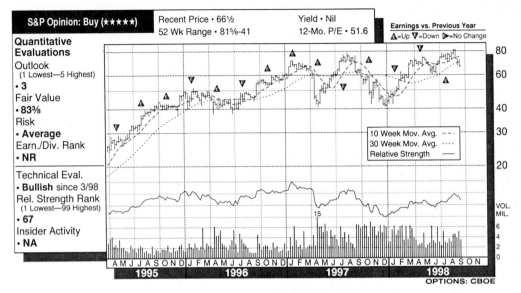

Earnings vs. Previous Year
▲=Up ▼=Down ▶=No Change

10 Week Mov. Avg. – – –
30 Week Mov. Avg. ·······
Relative Strength

VOL.
MIL.

OPTIONS: CBOE

Overview - 10-SEP-98

Sales should post a strong double-digit gain in 1998, spurred by strong demand for established products, new medical devices and greater penetration of foreign markets. Domestic volume over the second half should be augmented by recent FDA approval of BSX's new Radius and Nir stents, which mark the company's entry into the rapidly expanding U.S. coronary stent market. Stents are small wire mesh devices used to prop open coronary arteries to facilitate blood flow to the heart. Sales in Japan should be helped by the launch of the Rotoblator atherectomy device, as well as by the planned introduction of the Nir stent later this year. Margins should be boosted by the better volume and cost containment measures. EPS are projected at $1.88 (before special charges), with further progress to $2.45 seen for 1999.

Valuation - 10-SEP-98

The shares are still up nicely to date in 1998, despite a minor pullback in recent weeks due to turbulence in the general market and concern over economic weakness in Japan (BSX derives about 20% of its sales in Japan). A key positive in the stock has been BSX's growing coronary stent line, supported by the recent U.S. launch of the new state-of-the-art Radius and Nir stents. The planned $2.1 billion purchase of Pfizer's Schneider division will widen BSX's angioplasty line and provide access to valuable rapid exchange technology. Much potential is also seen for BSX's new Vanguard device to treat abdominal aortic aneurysms. BSX maintains formidable positions in most leading growing catheter-based minimally invasive markets, and strong earnings growth should begin in 1999. We continue to recommend purchase of the shares for aggressive investors. The shares are to be split 2-for-1 in November.

Key Stock Statistics

S&P EPS Est. 1998	1.88	Tang. Bk. Value/Share	4.41
P/E on S&P Est. 1998	35.4	Beta	1.42
S&P EPS Est. 1999	2.45	Shareholders	7,200
Dividend Rate/Share	Nil	Market cap. (B)	$ 13.0
Shs. outstg. (M)	195.7	Inst. holdings	46%
Avg. daily vol. (M)	0.882		

Value of $10,000 invested 5 years ago: $ 31,885

Fiscal Year Ending Dec. 31

	1998	1997	1996	1995	1994	1993
Revenues (Million $)						
1Q	470.0	399.2	322.4	257.6	105.3	88.94
2Q	505.7	473.8	357.2	272.1	109.9	94.44
3Q	—	474.8	373.7	277.7	112.2	95.60
4Q	—	493.2	408.7	299.2	121.6	101.1
Yr.	—	1,872	1,462	1,107	448.9	380.1
Earnings Per Share ($)						
1Q	0.34	0.38	-0.01	-0.37	0.18	0.15
2Q	0.39	-0.14	0.13	0.28	0.19	0.17
3Q	E0.52	0.44	0.37	0.28	0.20	0.17
4Q	E0.63	0.12	0.42	-0.16	0.24	0.21
Yr.	E1.88	0.80	0.92	0.05	0.81	0.70

Next earnings report expected: late October

Dividend Data

Dividends have never been paid.

A Division of The McGraw-Hill Companies

STANDARD
&POOR'S
STOCK REPORTS

Boston Scientific Corporation

355

12-SEP-98

Business Summary - 10-SEP-98

Boston Scientific is a leading global maker of medical devices geared for minimally-invasive surgical procedures. The company's history began in the late 1960s when its co-founder, John Abele, acquired an equity interest in Medi-Tech, a maker of steerable catheters. In 1979, John Abele joined Pete Nicholas to form Boston Scientific Corporation, which acquired Medi-Tech. Since then, BSX has expanded significantly through an aggressive acquisition program and internal growth.

The company's products encompass more than 7,500 separate catalog items in more than 50 categories. Products include devices used in cardiology, gastroenterology, pulmonology, radiology, urology and vascular surgery. Generally inserted into the body through natural openings or small skin incisions, these products are then guided to various areas of the anatomy for the diagnosis and treatment of medical problems. Minimally-invasive procedures involve less trauma, risk to the patient, cost and recovery time than conventional surgical methods. Operations outside of North America accounted for 41% of sales and 38% of operating profits in 1997.

BSX sells a broad line of products designed to treat patients with peripheral vascular disease. These include catheters and other items used in coronary and vascular percutaneous transluminal angioplasty, a procedure to enlarge a blocked artery by means of a bal-

loon-tipped catheter; Nir and Radius coronary stents used after angioplasty procedures to prop open arteries; the Greenfield Vena Cava Filter System, a filter permanently implanted in high risk patients to reduce their incidence of pulmonary embolism; a line of surgical and endovascular grafts used to replace impaired arteries; a family of catheter-directed ultrasound imaging systems used to diagnose blood vessels, heart chambers and coronary arteries; the Rotoblator plaque-removing atherectomy device; and electrophysiology (EP) diagnostic systems. Target Therapeutics makes catheter-based disposable and implantable medical devices used to treat neurovascular diseases and disorders.

Non-vascular intervention products consist of catheters and accessories to drain fluid collections from the body, various forms of biopsy products and other accessory devices. The line includes hemostatic catheters and related products used to treat or diagnose gastrointestinal (GI) disorders; biliary intervention products used in endoscopic procedures in the gall bladder and bile ducts; devices used to diagnose and treat polyps and other ailments in the lower GI tract; products designed to treat patients with urinary stone disease; the Dowd Prostate Balloon Dilatation Catheter used to treat benign prostatic hypertrophy; a line of minimally invasive devices to treat female urinary incontinence; and devices used to diagnose and treat chronic bronchitis and lung cancer.

Per Share Data ($)

(Year Ended Dec. 31)	1997	1996	1995	1994	1993	1992	1991	1990	1989	1988
Tangible Bk. Val.	3.47	3.41	3.55	3.14	2.37	2.35	1.48	0.41	NA	NA
Cash Flow	1.24	1.26	0.28	0.91	0.76	0.62	0.48	0.28	0.08	NA
Earnings	0.80	0.92	0.05	0.81	0.70	0.57	0.44	0.25	0.06	-0.01
Dividends	Nil	Nil	Nil	Nil	Nil	Nil	NA	NA	NA	NA
Payout Ratio	Nil	Nil	Nil	Nil	Nil	Nil	NA	NA	NA	NA
Prices - High	78⅜	61½	49⅜	17⅞	23⅝	20⅞	NA	NA	NA	NA
- Low	41	37¾	16⅝	11⅞	9⅜	14	NA	NA	NA	NA
P/E Ratio - High	112	67	NM	22	34	37	NA	NA	NA	NA
- Low	59	41	NM	15	13	25	NA	NA	NA	NA

Income Statement Analysis (Million $)

	1997	1996	1995	1994	1993	1992	1991	1990	1989	1988
Revs.	1,872	1,462	1,107	449	380	315	230	159	116	98.0
Oper. Inc.	502	403	781	139	115	97.2	73.9	42.0	16.0	NA
Depr.	86.7	61.4	39.5	9.1	6.4	4.4	3.4	2.4	2.2	NA
Int. Exp.	14.3	11.2	8.2	2.0	2.1	2.9	2.9	4.6	5.8	NA
Pretax Inc.	259	297	85.8	129	109	91.6	68.8	35.5	8.0	NA
Eff. Tax Rate	38%	44%	90%	38%	36%	38%	39%	34%	34%	NA
Net Inc.	160	167	8.4	79.7	69.7	56.6	41.5	23.5	5.3	-0.9

Balance Sheet & Other Fin. Data (Million $)

	1997	1996	1995	1994	1993	1992	1991	1990	1989	1988
Cash	58.0	75.5	115	118	103	137	66.1	0.3	NA	NA
Curr. Assets	1,064	749	537	264	216	236	149	58.0	NA	NA
Total Assets	1,968	1,512	1,075	432	323	299	208	102	86.0	77.0
Curr. Liab.	808	464	271	73.7	57.1	42.6	29.2	34.1	NA	NA
LT Debt	46.3	Nil	13.2	8.9	6.0	6.1	23.2	19.1	31.6	8.8
Common Eqty.	986	916	752	340	247	249	156	48.0	24.0	18.0
Total Cap.	1,091	976	765	355	266	257	179	67.0	56.0	27.0
Cap. Exp.	220	135	68.6	35.8	35.8	17.6	7.3	3.5	7.3	NA
Cash Flow	247	229	47.9	88.8	76.1	61.0	44.9	25.9	7.5	NA
Curr. Ratio	1.3	1.6	2.0	3.6	3.8	5.6	5.1	1.7	NA	NA
% LT Debt of Cap.	4.2	Nil	1.7	2.5	22.0	2.4	13.0	28.3	56.7	33.1
% Net Inc.of Revs.	8.6	11.4	1.0	17.8	18.3	18.0	18.0	14.8	4.5	NM
% Ret. on Assets	9.2	12.7	1.0	21.1	22.9	25.3	NA	NA	6.5	NM
% Ret. on Equity	16.9	19.8	1.1	27.2	28.8	32.7	NA	NA	25.1	NM

Data as orig. reptd.; bef. results of disc. opers. and/or spec. items. Per share data adj. for stk. divs. as of ex-div. date. Bold denotes diluted EPS (FASB 128). E-Estimated. NA-Not Available. NM-Not Meaningful. NR-Not Ranked.

Office—One Boston Scientific Place, Natick, MA 01760-1537. **Tel**—(508) 650-8000. **Website**—http://www.bsci.com **Chrmn & CEO**—P. M. Nicholas. **SVP-Fin, CFO & Investor Contact**—L. C. Best (508-650-8450). **SVP & Secy**—P. W. Sandman. **Dirs**—J. E. Abele, C. J. Aschauer, Jr., R. F. Bellows, J. A. Ciffolillo, J. L. Fleishman, L. L. Horsch, N. J. Nicholas, Jr., P. M. Nicholas, D. A. Spencer. **Transfer Agent & Registrar**—BankBoston. **Incorporated**—in Delaware in 1979. **Empl**— 11,000. **S&P Analyst:** Herman Saftlas

STANDARD
&POOR'S

STOCK REPORTS

NYSE Symbol **BGG**

In S&P 500

12-SEP-98

Industry:
Manufacturing (Specialized)

Summary: This company is the largest producer of small gasoline engines. More than 80% of its engine sales are to manufacturers of lawn and garden equipment.

S&P Opinion: Avoid (★★)	Recent Price • 37	Yield • 3.1%
	52 Wk Range • 53⅜-33⅜	12-Mo. P/E • 13.0

Quantitative Evaluations

Outlook
(1 Lowest—5 Highest)
• **3+**

Fair Value
• **44½**

Risk
• **Low**

Earn./Div. Rank
• **A-**

Technical Eval.
• **NA**

Rel. Strength Rank
(1 Lowest—99 Highest)
• **77**

Insider Activity
• **Favorable**

Earnings vs. Previous Year
▲=Up ▼=Down ▶=No Change

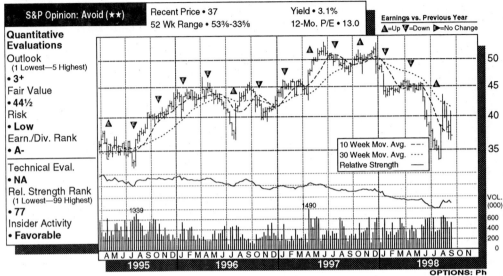

10 Week Mov. Avg. – – –
30 Week Mov. Avg. ·······
Relative Strength ——

VOL. (000)

OPTIONS: Ph

Overview - 06-AUG-98

Sales should rise in low single digits in FY 99 (Jun.), restrained by a lower-margin product mix. The level of growth will depend on whether BGG can boost prices 1% to 2%, while unit volume edges up 2%. Although operating efficiencies will improve, margins should continue to be affected by the strong dollar and weak pricing in Europe. BGG is planning to build inventory earlier in FY 99, which will increase working capital. We expect SG&A expense to be well controlled, at about 9% of sales, versus 9.8% in FY 98, as costs related to work on a software system will be eliminated. EPS could benefit somewhat from an ongoing $300 million share repurchase program, with the remaining $35 million of stock expected to be bought back by December 1998. With new product costs (introducing three new engines) offsetting recent efforts to improve operating efficiencies, long-term growth will depend on BGG's ability to sell higher-margin engines, reduce costs, and reinvest in its core activities.

Valuation - 06-AUG-98

The shares were recently down 20% since early June, and were trading near their lows. We expect the stock to continue to trade in a narrow range, reflecting weak volume and pricing, and uncertainty regarding inventory levels as retailers make their end-of-summer sourcing decisions. Although the company holds a significant worldwide market share for its gasoline engines, the competitive and seasonal nature of the business tends to limit consistent growth. At this stage of the economic cycle, P/E multiples of consumer cyclical companies typically contract, and their shares rarely outperform the broad market. Thus, despite a P/E of only 11X projected FY 99 EPS, we still suggest waiting for signs of sustainable margin improvement before considering the purchase of BGG shares.

Key Stock Statistics

S&P EPS Est. 1999	3.20	Tang. Bk. Value/Share	13.01
P/E on S&P Est. 1999	11.6	Beta	0.22
S&P EPS Est. 2000	3.60	Shareholders	6,800
Dividend Rate/Share	1.16	Market cap. (B)	$0.892
Shs. outstg. (M)	24.1	Inst. holdings	66%
Avg. daily vol. (M)	0.113		

Value of $10,000 invested 5 years ago: NA

Fiscal Year Ending Jun. 30

	1998	1997	1996	1995	1994	1993
Revenues (Million $)						
1Q	170.6	161.7	189.5	227.8	198.6	172.0
2Q	308.5	299.7	329.4	366.7	328.9	305.2
3Q	469.1	476.0	36.50	450.2	30.50	360.9
4Q	379.5	379.1	308.0	294.9	371.8	301.6
Yr.	1,328	1,316	1,287	1,340	1,286	1,139
Earnings Per Share ($)						
1Q	-0.10	-0.18	-0.11	0.40	0.22	-0.07
2Q	**0.41**	0.58	0.82	1.17	0.99	0.81
3Q	**1.45**	1.60	1.57	1.64	1.24	1.06
4Q	**1.13**	0.13	0.91	0.42	1.10	0.63
Yr.	**2.85**	2.16	3.19	3.62	3.54	2.43

Next earnings report expected: mid October

Dividend Data (Dividends have been paid since 1929.)

Amount ($)	Date Decl.	Ex-Div. Date	Stock of Record	Payment Date
0.280	Oct. 14	Nov. 26	Dec. 01	Jan. 02 '98
0.280	Jan. 20	Mar. 26	Mar. 02	Apr. 01 '98
0.280	Apr. 15	Jun. 02	Jun. 04	Jun. 26 '98
0.290	Aug. 05	Aug. 25	Aug. 27	Oct. 01 '98

A Division of The McGraw-Hill Companies

STANDARD
&POOR'S
STOCK REPORTS

Briggs & Stratton Corporation

363

12-SEP-98

Business Summary - 06-AUG-98

For this leading manufacturer of mostly lawn and garden equipment engines, favorable spring weather conditions means favorable results. With 81% BGG's sales derived from mowers and related equipment sales, an early, wet spring is money in the bank.

The company's sales are very seasonal and dependent on weather conditions, with engine sales generally highest in the March quarter, weakest in the September quarter and unpredictable in the June period. A rainy early spring will produce product shortages, resulting in manufacturers building product earlier for the next season. A late, cold spring will postpone retail sales, producing excess inventories and delayed production.

Having spun off its automotive lock business in early 1995, the company is focusing on its power products, such as engines for lawn mowers, garden tractors and tillers. Regarding other kinds of equipment, the category showing the fastest growth is pressure washers, which can be used to clean driveways, patios, lawn furniture, siding, cars and trucks. In FY 97 (Jun.), 19% of sales were to manufacturers of powered equipment for the construction and agricultural industries. Products include generators, pumps and pressure washers.

As the world's largest producer of air-cooled gasoline engines for outdoor power equipment, management refocused its competitive strategy several years ago to recapture its cost leadership position in this market, decentralize its operations for improved product and capital management, and improve its manufacturing processes in order to reduce costs and increase productivity. During FY 96, the company completed construction of three plants in Missouri, Alabama and Georgia. In early FY 97, BGG sold its Menomonee Falls, WI, facility.

BGG has three major customers, with the largest customer, MTD Products, Inc., accounting for 21% of total sales in FY 97. Tomkins PLC accounted for 11%, while A B Electrolux provided 14%. Major competitors include Tecumseh Products Co., Kohler Co., Onan Corp., Honda Motor Co., Ltd., Kawasaki Heavy Industries Ltd., Tecnamotor S.p.A., and Toro Co., Inc.

Export sales, primarily to Europe, accounted for 23% of the total in FY 97, down from 25% in FY 96.

During 1996, BGG sold its Menomonee Falls WI, plant. The company noted that, because it will retain an interest in the warehouse portion of the plant, the gain on the sale will be postponed until that interest ends.

In May 1997, the company completed a self-tender offer for 3,590,223 common shares at $51 each. BGG said it intended to reduce borrowings under a new credit facility pursuant to a $100 million debt offering.

Per Share Data ($)

(Year Ended Jun. 30)	1998	1997	1996	1995	1994	1993	1992	1991	1990	1989
Tangible Bk. Val.	NA	13.82	17.30	15.19	13.96	12.45	10.80	9.84	9.38	8.96
Cash Flow	NA	3.68	4.68	5.17	5.03	4.09	3.23	2.56	2.60	0.71
Earnings	2.85	2.16	3.19	3.62	3.54	2.43	1.78	1.26	1.23	-0.69
Dividends	1.12	1.09	1.05	0.98	0.90	0.85	0.80	0.80	0.80	0.80
Payout Ratio	39%	50%	33%	27%	25%	35%	45%	63%	65%	NM
Prices - High	49	53⅝	46⅞	44⅛	45⅛	44¾	27⅜	22⅜	17	15⅝
- Low	33⅝	42⅝	36½	32¼	30½	23⅜	20⅞	12¼	10¼	12⅛
P/E Ratio - High	17	25	15	12	13	18	15	18	14	NM
- Low	12	20	11	9	9	10	12	10	8	NM

Income Statement Analysis (Million $)

	1998	1997	1996	1995	1994	1993	1992	1991	1990	1989
Revs.	NM	1,316	1,287	1,340	1,286	1,139	1,042	951	1,003	876
Oper. Inc.	NA	147	196	214	215	178	137	101	106	25.0
Depr.	NA	43.4	43.0	44.4	43.0	48.1	42.1	37.7	39.9	40.8
Int. Exp.	NA	9.9	10.1	8.6	9.0	11.3	11.2	11.2	14.2	12.3
Pretax Inc.	NA	99	149	170	170	114	80.2	53.0	53.7	-34.0
Eff. Tax Rate	NA	38%	38%	39%	40%	39%	36%	31%	34%	NM
Net Inc.	NM	61.6	92.4	105	102	70.3	51.5	36.5	35.4	-20.0

Balance Sheet & Other Fin. Data (Million $)

	1998	1997	1996	1995	1994	1993	1992	1991	1990	1989
Cash	NA	113	151	171	221	110	78.9	47.1	9.5	5.7
Curr. Assets	NA	418	456	453	483	353	297	231	202	224
Total Assets	NA	842	838	798	777	656	614	557	535	561
Curr. Liab.	NA	214	190	197	207	158	160	126	118	160
LT Debt	NA	143	60.0	75.0	75.0	75.0	75.0	75.0	75.0	75.0
Common Eqty.	NA	351	501	439	404	360	312	285	271	259
Total Cap.	NA	494	561	514	491	485	441	418	405	389
Cap. Exp.	NA	71.3	77.7	131	40.8	38.1	40.2	32.0	37.8	79.5
Cash Flow	NA	105	135	149	145	118	93.6	74.2	76.8	20.7
Curr. Ratio	NA	1.9	2.4	2.3	2.3	2.2	1.9	1.8	1.7	1.4
% LT Debt of Cap.	NA	28.9	10.7	14.6	15.3	15.5	17.0	17.9	18.5	19.3
% Net Inc.of Revs.	NA	4.7	7.2	7.8	8.0	6.2	4.9	3.8	3.5	NM
% Ret. on Assets	NM	7.3	11.3	13.2	14.3	11.1	8.8	6.7	6.5	NM
% Ret. on Equity	NM	14.5	19.7	24.9	26.8	20.9	17.3	13.1	13.3	NM

Data as orig. reptd.; bef. results of disc. opers. and/or spec. items. Per share data adj. for stk. divs. as of ex-div. date. Bold denotes diluted EPS (FASB 128). E-Estimated. NA-Not Available. NM-Not Meaningful. NR-Not Ranked.

Office—12301 West Wirth St, Wauwatosa, WI 53222. **Tel**—(414) 259-5333. **Chrmn & CEO**—F. P. Stratton, Jr. **Pres & COO**—J. S. Shiely.**EVP, CFO, Secy-Treas & Investor Contact**—Robert H. Eldridge. **Dirs**—M. E. Batten, R. H. Eldridge, P. A. Georgescu, J. L. Murray, R. J. O'Toole, C. B. Rogers, Jr., J. S. Shiely, C. I. Story, F. P. Stratton, Jr., E. J. Zarwell. **Transfer Agent & Registrar**—Firstar Trust Co., Milwaukee. **Incorporated**—in Delaware in 1924; reincorporated in Wisconsin in 1992. **Empl**— 7,560. **S&P Analyst:** Stewart Scharf

12-SEP-98

Industry: Health Care (Diversified)

Summary: BMY, one of the world's largest pharmaceutical concerns. also has interests in infant nutritionals, nonprescription medications, medical devices, and toiletries.

S&P Opinion: Buy (★★★★★)	Recent Price • 103¾	Yield • 1.5%
	52 Wk Range • 125⅞-78¼	12-Mo. P/E • 31.0

Quantitative Evaluations

Outlook
(1 Lowest—5 Highest)
• **1**

Fair Value
• **94⅞**

Risk
• **Low**

Earn./Div. Rank
• **A**

Technical Eval.
• **Bullish** since 9/94

Rel. Strength Rank
(1 Lowest—99 Highest)
• **76**

Insider Activity
• **NA**

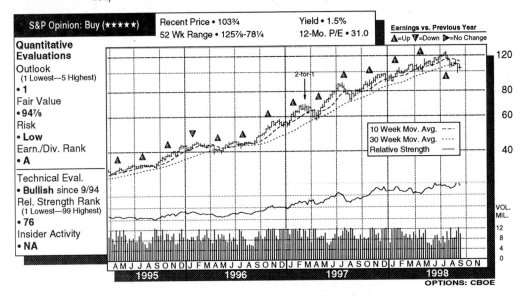

Earnings vs. Previous Year
△=Up ▽=Down ▷=No Change

10 Week Mov. Avg. ---
30 Week Mov. Avg. ·····
Relative Strength —

VOL. MIL.

OPTIONS: CBOE

Overview - 14-AUG-98

Sales growth in 1998 is projected in the 10% range. Despite further generic erosion in the Capoten line, drug sales should be augmented by continued robust gains in Pravachol cholesterol-lowering agent (sales up 18% in the first half of 1998), Taxol anticancer (25%), Glucophage for non-insulin dependent diabetes (55%), Cefzil antibiotic (19%), Zerit AIDS therapy (53%) and Serzone antidepressant (63%). Sales of Pravachol are being boosted by its unique claim that it is effective in reducing the risk of first heart attack, and by stepped-up direct-to-consumer advertising. New products such as Plavix platelet inhibitor for the prevention of stroke and heart attack and Avapro anti-hypertensive should also augment volume. Sales growth is also projected for nutritionals, OTC medications, medical products and toiletries. Margins should benefit from a better product mix and ongoing cost containment measures.

Valuation - 14-AUG-98

The stock has been an outstanding performer in recent years, reflecting strong growth in key drug lines, margin improvement, and enthusiasm over BMY's impressive new drug pipeline. The company has outlined an aggressive R&D program that envisions the development of 15 new drugs in 1998, and 30 by 2003. BMY also plans to increase its total research staff by 50% over the next five years. New drugs in the pipeline include lanotaplase, a clot dissolving agent for heart attack victims that can break up clots with one injection; Omapatrilat for hypertension; UFT for colorectal cancer; GMC skin cancer vaccine; and Lubucavir for hepatitis B. In total, BMY has 50 new drugs in development. The shares are recommended for superior appreciation potential and rising dividend income.

Key Stock Statistics

S&P EPS Est. 1998	3.58	Tang. Bk. Value/Share	5.05
P/E on S&P Est. 1998	29.0	Beta	0.97
S&P EPS Est. 1999	4.05	Shareholders	133,600
Dividend Rate/Share	1.56	Market cap. (B)	$103.3
Shs. outstg. (M)	994.7	Inst. holdings	57%
Avg. daily vol. (M)	2.288		

Value of $10,000 invested 5 years ago: $ 37,172

Fiscal Year Ending Dec. 31

	1998	1997	1996	1995	1994	1993
Revenues (Million $)						
1Q	4,446	4,045	3,669	3,301	2,834	2,755
2Q	4,430	4,064	3,696	3,445	2,970	2,802
3Q	—	4,151	3,745	3,413	2,932	2,862
4Q	—	4,441	3,955	3,608	3,247	2,993
Yr.	—	16,701	15,065	13,767	11,984	11,413
Earnings Per Share ($)						
1Q	**0.91**	**0.79**	0.72	0.65	0.57	0.56
2Q	**0.82**	**0.73**	0.66	0.60	0.54	0.51
3Q	**E0.95**	**0.84**	0.75	0.68	0.61	0.59
4Q	**E0.90**	**0.78**	0.71	-0.14	0.10	0.25
Yr.	**E3.58**	**3.14**	2.80	1.79	1.81	1.90

Next earnings report expected: late October

Dividend Data (Dividends have been paid since 1900.)

Amount ($)	Date Decl.	Ex-Div. Date	Stock of Record	Payment Date
0.380	Sep. 09	Oct. 01	Oct. 03	Nov. 01 '97
0.390	Dec. 02	Dec. 30	Jan. 02	Feb. 01 '98
0.390	Mar. 03	Apr. 01	Apr. 03	May. 01 '98
0.390	Jun. 08	Jun. 30	Jul. 03	Aug. 01 '98

A Division of The **McGraw·Hill** *Companies*

Business Summary - 14-AUG-98

Tracing its roots to companies started during the second half of the 19th century, Bristol-Myers Squibb was formed via the merger of Bristol-Myers and Squibb Corp. in 1989. The company ranks among the world's largest pharmaceutical concerns, with major positions also in OTC medications, medical devices and toiletries. Foreign operations are significant, accounting for 42% of sales and 35% of profits in 1997. Business segment contributions in 1997 were:

	Sales	Profits
Pharmaceuticals	60%	71%
Nutritionals	11%	10%
Consumer medicines	8%	3%
Medical devices	11%	9%
Beauty care	10%	7%

Bristol-Myers Squibb is a global leader in chemotherapy drugs and ranks near the top in ACE inhibitor cardiovasculars, cholesterol-lowering agents and oral cephalosporin antibiotics. Cardiovasculars (18% of total 1997 sales) include Pravachol cholesterol-reducing agent, Capoten/Capozide and Monopril antihypertensives. Pravachol is the only cholesterol drug able to claim the ability to reduce the risk of first heart attack. Principal anticancer drugs (15%) consist of Taxol, Paraplatin, VePesid and Platinol.

A wide variety of of anti-infective drugs (13%) are offered, including Duricef/Ultracef, Cefzil, and Maxipime antibiotics; and Videx and Zerit AIDS therapeutics. Central nervous system agents (6%) consist of Serzone antidepressant, Buspar anti-anxiety agent and Stadol NS analgesic. Other drugs (8%) include Isovue contrast imaging agent, Glucophage for diabetes, Estrace estrogen replacement and dermatological items.

Nutritionals encompass infant formulas such as Enfamil and ProSobee, vitamins and nutritional supplements. Consumer medications include OTC analgesics such as Bufferin and Excedrin, Comtrex cough/cold remedies and skin care items. Medical devices consist of Zimmer, the world leader in orthopedic knee and hip replacements; Convatec, the largest maker of ostomy products; and Linvatec/Hall Surgical, a producer of orthopedic products.

Beauty care items encompass the Clairol, Ultress, Matrix Essentials and Herbal Essence lines of hair care products, Nice 'n Easy and Clairesse hair colorings, Final Net hair spray, Vitalis hair preparation and other products.

R&D expenses totaled $1.4 billion in 1997 (8.3% of sales). The company has some 110 ongoing research programs and 50 drugs in development. Experimental compounds include treatments for cancer, hypertension, dislipidemia, diabetes, obesity, heart failure, coronary thrombosis, stroke, hepatitis, other infectious diseases, migraine, inflammation, pain and skin problems.

Per Share Data ($)

(Year Ended Dec. 31)	1997	1996	1995	1994	1993	1992	1991	1990	1989	1988
Tangible Bk. Val.	5.63	5.06	4.55	4.67	5.45	5.66	5.41	4.99	4.62	5.80
Cash Flow	3.72	3.36	2.23	2.13	2.20	1.77	2.21	1.90	0.90	1.66
Earnings	3.14	2.84	1.79	1.81	1.90	1.49	1.98	1.67	0.71	1.44
Dividends	1.53	1.50	1.49	1.47	1.44	1.40	1.25	1.09	1.01	0.88
Payout Ratio	49%	53%	83%	81%	76%	94%	63%	66%	143%	61%
Prices - High	98¹/₈	58¹/₄	43⁵/₈	30¹/₂	33⁵/₈	45¹/₈	44³/₄	34	29	23¹/₄
- Low	53¹/₄	39	28⁷/₈	25	25¹/₂	30	30⁵/₈	25¹/₄	22	19¹/₈
P/E Ratio - High	31	20	24	17	18	30	23	20	41	16
- Low	17	14	16	14	13	20	15	15	31	13

Income Statement Analysis (Million $)

	1997	1996	1995	1994	1993	1992	1991	1990	1989	1988
Revs.	16,701	15,065	13,767	11,984	11,413	11,156	11,159	10,300	9,189	5,972
Oper. Inc.	5,029	4,472	4,063	3,549	3,211	3,191	3,012	2,633	2,134	1,317
Depr.	591	519	448	328	308	295	246	244	196	128
Int. Exp.	118	93.0	112	83.0	71.0	62.0	68.0	72.0	81.0	37.7
Pretax Inc.	4,482	4,013	2,402	2,555	2,571	1,987	2,887	2,524	1,277	1,285
Eff. Tax Rate	28%	29%	25%	28%	24%	23%	29%	31%	42%	36%
Net Inc.	3,205	2,850	1,812	1,842	1,959	1,538	2,056	1,748	747	829

Balance Sheet & Other Fin. Data (Million $)

	1997	1996	1995	1994	1993	1992	1991	1990	1989	1988
Cash	1,794	2,185	2,178	2,423	2,729	2,385	1,583	1,958	2,282	1,710
Curr. Assets	7,736	7,528	7,018	6,710	6,570	6,621	5,567	5,670	5,552	3,566
Total Assets	14,977	14,685	13,929	12,910	12,101	10,804	9,416	9,215	8,497	5,190
Curr. Liab.	5,032	5,050	4,806	4,274	3,065	3,300	2,752	2,821	2,659	1,164
LT Debt	1,279	966	635	644	588	176	135	231	237	215
Common Eqty.	7,219	6,570	5,821	5,703	5,939	6,019	5,793	5,416	5,081	3,543
Total Cap.	8,498	7,536	6,457	6,348	6,528	6,196	6,042	5,799	5,381	3,851
Cap. Exp.	767	601	513	573	570	647	633	513	555	249
Cash Flow	3,796	3,369	2,260	2,170	2,267	1,833	2,302	1,992	943	957
Curr. Ratio	1.5	1.5	1.5	1.6	2.1	2.0	2.0	2.0	2.1	3.1
% LT Debt of Cap.	15.1	12.8	9.8	10.1	9.0	2.8	2.2	4.0	4.4	5.6
% Net Inc.of Revs.	19.2	18.9	13.2	15.4	17.2	13.8	18.4	17.0	8.1	13.9
% Ret. on Assets	21.6	19.9	13.5	14.8	17.2	15.2	22.2	19.8	8.3	16.7
% Ret. on Equity	46.5	46.0	31.4	31.8	33.0	26.1	36.8	33.4	12.9	24.5

Data as orig. reptd.; bef. results of disc. opers. and/or spec. items. Per share data adj. for stk. divs. as of ex-div. date. Bold denotes diluted EPS (FASB 128). E-Estimated. NA-Not Available. NM-Not Meaningful. NR-Not Ranked.

Office—345 Park Ave., New York, NY 10154-0037. **Tel**—(212) 546-4000. **Website**—http://www.bms.com **Chrmn & CEO**—C. A. Heimbold Jr. **EVP**—K. E. Weg. **SVP & CFO**—M. F. Mee. **VP & Secy**—Alice C. Brennan. **VP & Treas**—H. M. Bains Jr. **Investor Contact**—Tim Cost. **Dirs**—R. E. Allen, V. D. Coffman, E. V. Futter, L. V. Gerstner Jr., I. H. Given, L. H. Glimcher, C. A. Heimbold Jr., J. D. Macomber, J. D. Robinson III, A. C. Sigler, L. W. Sullivan, K. E. Weg. **Transfer Agent & Registrar**—ChaseMellon Shareholder Services, Ridgefield Park, NJ. **Incorporated**—in Delaware in 1933. **Empl**— 53,600. **S&P Analyst:** H. B. Saftlas

12-SEP-98

Industry: Beverages (Alcoholic)

Summary: This leading distiller and importer of alcoholic beverages markets such brands as Jack Daniel's, Southern Comfort, Korbel and Bolla.

S&P Opinion: Hold (★★★)	Recent Price • 60%	Yield • 1.8%
	52 Wk Range • 67-47¼	12-Mo. P/E • 22.4

Quantitative Evaluations

Outlook
(1 Lowest—5 Highest)
• **NA**

Fair Value
• **NA**

Risk
• **NA**

Earn./Div. Rank
• **A**

Technical Eval.
• **Bearish** since 10/97

Rel. Strength Rank
(1 Lowest—99 Highest)
• **85**

Insider Activity
• **NA**

Earnings vs. Previous Year
▲=Up ▼=Down ▶=No Change

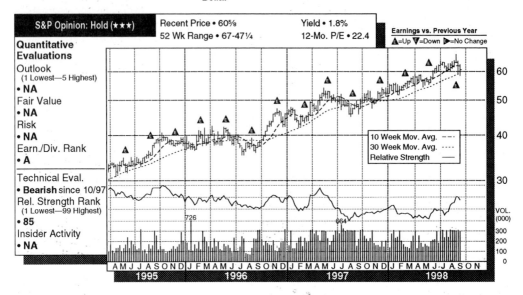

10 Week Mov. Avg. — —
30 Week Mov. Avg. ----
Relative Strength ——

VOL. (000)

1995   1996   1997   1998

Overview - 09-SEP-98

Net sales (excluding excise taxes) in the near term are expected to grow approximately 3% to 5%, driven primarily by improved performance for the consumer durables segment. Unfavorable currency exchange may pressure near-term alcoholic beverage sales. Operating margins should benefit from easing grape cost pressure and recent wine price increases, helping to offset the costs associated with the continued pursuit of marketing and partnership opportunities abroad. Downsizing and cost cutting efforts within the consumer durables division should support profit trends in that segment. A further easing in net interest expense (reflecting lower borrowing levels and interest rates) should allow earnings per share to rise 8% in FY 99 (Apr.), to $2.90.

Valuation - 09-SEP-98

Given our outlook for only modest earnings per share growth through FY 00, the shares are ranked only hold for near-term performance. The company's relatively recession-resistant alcoholic beverage business is a steady generator of cash flow, which could be used to accelerate small acquisitions and/or expand its market presence in developing markets abroad. Although U.S. spirits markets are quite mature, management has shown that it is capable of expanding the company's relatively high-margin sales base through product line extensions and expansion overseas. Meanwhile, downsizing actions within the company's recently ailing consumer nondurables division suggest either gradual segment improvement or its eventual disposal. The company's long record of high returns on shareholders' equity, and its steadily increasing dividend stream, make the relatively low-risk shares a worthwhile long-term holding.

Key Stock Statistics

S&P EPS Est. 1999	2.90	Tang. Bk. Value/Share	8.08
P/E on S&P Est. 1999	20.9	Beta	0.42
S&P EPS Est. 2000	3.15	Shareholders	4,300
Dividend Rate/Share	1.12	Market cap. (B)	$ 2.4
Shs. outstg. (M)	68.7	Inst. holdings	28%
Avg. daily vol. (M)	0.070		

Value of $10,000 invested 5 years ago: $ 25,567

Fiscal Year Ending Apr. 30

	1999	1998	1997	1996	1995	1994
Revenues (Million $)						
1Q	390.1	371.8	365.3	352.1	—	322.5
2Q	—	554.2	456.3	441.9	—	396.0
3Q	—	480.8	393.2	384.5	1,079	348.5
4Q	—	396.6	368.9	366.0	341.8	334.4
Yr.	—	1,670	1,584	1,544	1,420	1,401
Earnings Per Share ($)						
1Q	**0.54**	0.50	0.47	0.46	0.41	0.35
2Q	**E0.96**	0.88	0.80	0.77	0.71	0.76
3Q	**E0.72**	0.66	0.60	0.55	0.54	0.48
4Q	**E0.68**	0.63	0.58	0.52	0.49	0.44
Yr.	**E2.90**	2.67	2.45	2.31	2.15	2.04

Next earnings report expected: late November

Dividend Data (Dividends have been paid since 1960.)

Amount ($)	Date Decl.	Ex-Div. Date	Stock of Record	Payment Date
0.280	Nov. 20	Dec. 03	Dec. 05	Jan. 01 '98
0.280	Jan. 22	Mar. 02	Mar. 04	Apr. 01 '98
0.280	May. 28	Jun. 09	Jun. 11	Jul. 01 '98
0.280	Jul. 23	Aug. 31	Sep. 02	Oct. 01 '98

A Division of The **McGraw-Hill** Companies

Business Summary - 09-SEP-98

Brown-Forman Corp., whose origins date back to 1870, is the world's fourth largest producer of distilled spirits. Among its stable of well-known brands, the company is best known for its popular Jack Daniel's Tennessee Whiskey, which continues to be Brown-Forman's largest sales and profit producer. The company also makes products such as Lenox china, crystal and glassware and Hartmann luggage, which it includes in its consumer durables segment. Contributions in FY 98 (Apr.) were:

	Sales	Profits
Wine & spirits	72%	89%
Consumer durables	28%	11%

While many other alcoholic beverage companies have moved in recent years to reduce their dependence on the highly mature brown spirits market, Brown-Forman has remained defiantly whisky-oriented. Its product line is stocked with whiskies and bourbons such as Jack Daniel's (sales of 5.4 million nine-liter cases in FY 98),

Canadian Mist (2.8 million), Southern Comfort (2.2 million), and Early Times (1.3 million). The company's other major alcoholic beverage lines include brands such as Fetzer wines (2.5 million), Bolla wines (1.5 million), and Korbel Champagnes (1.1 million). The company has also been aggressive in launching new products, such as Jack Daniel's Country Cocktails, a line of low-alcohol beverages; and Tropical Freezes, low-alcohol, pre-blended frozen cocktails.

Brown-Forman added Finlandia vodkas and Michel Picard French wines to its U.S. product portfolio in FY 97. The company's strategy to grow the division is to keep up its international expansion, and continually introduce successful new products.

Consumer durables consist of china, crystal and giftware, marketed under the Lenox and Gorham trademarks, sold through retail outlets and company-operated stores. This segment also includes Dansk, a producer of tableware and giftware, and Hartmann Luggage.

Sales outside the U.S., consisting principally of exports of wines and spirits, amounted to approximately $347 million in FY 98, up 5% from the level of FY 97.

Per Share Data ($)

(Year Ended Apr. 30)	1998	1997	1996	1995	1994	1993	1992	1991	1990	1989
Tangible Bk. Val.	8.08	6.73	5.26	3.94	2.54	6.37	5.78	5.33	4.42	3.03
Cash Flow	3.40	3.16	2.97	2.78	2.63	2.41	2.21	2.13	1.36	2.08
Earnings	2.67	2.45	2.31	2.15	2.04	1.88	1.76	1.74	0.96	1.72
Dividends	1.10	1.06	1.02	0.97	0.93	0.86	0.78	0.72	0.63	0.51
Payout Ratio	41%	43%	44%	45%	45%	46%	44%	41%	65%	30%
Cal. Yrs.	1997	1996	1995	1994	1993	1992	1991	1990	1989	1988
Prices - High	55⅜	47½	40¾	32½	29⅝	30	28⅛	30⅝	29⅜	19⅜
- Low	42	35¼	29⅜	26⅛	24⅜	24	21⅝	18⅝	18¾	11¼
P/E Ratio - High	21	19	18	15	15	16	16	18	31	11
- Low	16	14	13	12	12	13	12	11	20	7

Income Statement Analysis (Million $)

	1998	1997	1996	1995	1994	1993	1992	1991	1990	1989
Revs.	1,669	1,584	1,544	1,420	1,401	1,415	1,260	1,119	1,017	1,006
Oper. Inc.	358	337	320	311	286	299	271	256	259	239
Depr.	51.0	50.0	46.0	43.5	46.0	43.8	37.3	32.4	33.8	21.1
Int. Exp.	14.0	17.0	20.0	22.6	17.2	15.9	13.8	11.1	16.7	24.8
Pretax Inc.	296	273	257	247	257	243	224	220	158	226
Eff. Tax Rate	38%	38%	38%	40%	37%	36%	35%	34%	49%	36%
Net Inc.	185	169	160	149	161	156	146	145	81.0	144

Balance Sheet & Other Fin. Data (Million $)

	1998	1997	1996	1995	1994	1993	1992	1991	1990	1989
Cash	78.0	58.0	54.0	62.0	31.0	93.0	67.0	108	106	96.0
Curr. Assets	869	802	768	698	650	720	651	622	587	517
Total Assets	1,494	1,428	1,381	1,286	1,234	1,311	1,194	1,083	1,021	1,003
Curr. Liab.	382	399	303	286	281	210	214	190	199	204
LT Debt	50.0	63.0	211	247	299	154	114	112	114	115
Common Eqty.	805	718	622	534	452	806	723	649	584	544
Total Cap.	1,005	975	972	907	865	1,082	956	870	806	785
Cap. Exp.	44.0	55.0	59.0	51.1	27.4	33.6	52.1	51.5	50.1	38.0
Cash Flow	235	218	205	192	207	199	183	177	114	175
Curr. Ratio	2.3	2.0	2.5	2.4	2.3	3.4	3.0	3.3	3.0	2.5
% LT Debt of Cap.	4.9	6.4	21.7	27.2	34.6	14.3	11.9	12.9	14.2	14.7
% Net Inc.of Revs.	11.1	10.6	10.4	10.5	11.5	11.0	11.6	13.0	8.0	14.4
% Ret. on Assets	12.7	12.0	12.0	11.8	13.8	12.5	12.9	13.9	8.0	14.9
% Ret. on Equity	24.3	25.2	27.5	30.1	28.6	20.4	21.3	23.6	14.3	29.2

Data as orig. reptd.; bef. results of disc. opers. and/or spec. items. Per share data adj. for stk. divs. as of ex-div. date. Bold denotes diluted EPS (FASB 128). E-Estimated. NA-Not Available. NM-Not Meaningful. NR-Not Ranked.

Office—850 Dixie Highway, Louisville, KY 40210. **Tel**—(502) 585-1100. **Website**—http://www.brown-forman.com **Chrmn & CEO**—O. Brown II. **EVP & CFO**—S. B. Ratoff. **SVP & Secy**—M. B. Crutcher. **Investor Contact**—Steve Rolfs. **Dirs**—B. D. Bramley, G. G. Brown III, O. Brown II, D. G. Calder, O. B. Frazier, R. P. Mayer, S. E. O'Neil, W. M. Street, J. S. Welch. **Transfer Agent & Registrar**—First Chicago Trust Co. of New York, NYC. **Incorporated**—in Delaware in 1933. **Empl**—7,600. **S&P Analyst:** Richard Joy

12-SEP-98 Industry:
Waste Management

Summary: BFI is the second largest U.S. waste hauling and disposal company.

S&P Opinion: Hold (★★★)

| Recent Price • 34¾ | Yield • 2.2% |
| 52 Wk Range • 38⅞-29⅜ | 12-Mo. P/E • 18.2 |

Earnings vs. Previous Year
A=Up ▼=Down ▶=No Change

Quantitative Evaluations

Outlook
(1 Lowest—5 Highest)
• **3+**

Fair Value
• **37¾**

Risk
• **Average**

Earn./Div. Rank
• **B+**

Technical Eval.
• **Bullish** since 8/96

Rel. Strength Rank
(1 Lowest—99 Highest)
• **88**

Insider Activity
• **NA**

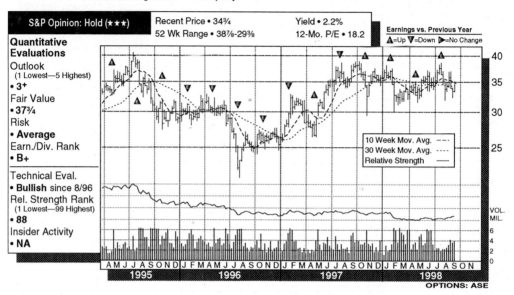

10 Week Mov. Avg. – – –
30 Week Mov. Avg. ·····
Relative Strength —

VOL.
MIL.

1995 1996 1997 1998

OPTIONS: ASE

Overview - 11-AUG-98

This company operates in the fragmented $36.5 billion municipal solid waste (MSW) industry. Although the MSW business has been consolidating over the past several years, the industry is still fragmented and very competitive, with municipal government operations, 25 publicly traded companies and 7,000 privately held outfits controlling 28%, 32% and 40%, respectively, of the MSW industry. Demand for MSW services is primarily driven by GDP and population growth. It is estimated that U.S. GDP and population growth will expand at long-term compound annual growth rates of 2.5% and 1.0%, respectively. In an effort to boost profitability and returns on investment in the slow-growing U.S. MSW industry, BFI has been restructuring its core North American MSW operations, cutting capital spending, reducing debt levels, repurchasing its shares and selling international operations. The company has been particularly focusing on improving landfill internalization rates (percentage of MSW disposed of in BFI landfills rather than in third-party landfills). In general, the higher the internalization rates, the more profitable the landfills become.

Valuation - 11-AUG-98

For several years, BFI shares had been lackluster performers, primarily due to unfavorable industry fundamentals, BFI's over-exposure to the volatile and lower margin recycling business, high levels of capital spending and bloated operating costs. However, in calendar 1997, the stock advanced 40%, bolstered by $800 million in asset sales, $400 million in capital spending cuts and $100 million in restructuring-related annual operating cost savings, as well as an ongoing $1 billion stock buyback program. With the shares only slightly below their 1997 year-end level, they appear to be trading close to their fair market value.

Key Stock Statistics

S&P EPS Est. 1998	1.95	Tang. Bk. Value/Share	6.56
P/E on S&P Est. 1998	17.9	Beta	1.10
S&P EPS Est. 1999	2.20	Shareholders	16,000
Dividend Rate/Share	0.76	Market cap. (B)	$ 6.0
Shs. outstg. (M)	173.8	Inst. holdings	77%
Avg. daily vol. (M)	0.751		

Value of $10,000 invested 5 years ago: $ 15,305

Fiscal Year Ending Sep. 30

	1998	1997	1996	1995	1994	1993
Revenues (Million $)						
1Q	1,345	1,495	1,431	1,293	928.3	848.0
2Q	1,306	1,414	1,374	1,409	984.1	826.0
3Q	1,043	1,471	1,471	1,550	1,161	892.7
4Q	—	1,403	1,503	1,527	1,241	928.5
Yr.	—	5,783	5,779	5,779	4,315	3,495
Earnings Per Share ($)						
1Q	**0.44**	0.36	0.42	0.45	0.34	0.31
2Q	**0.50**	0.35	0.30	0.47	0.34	0.30
3Q	**0.48**	0.21	0.31	0.53	0.41	0.24
4Q	—	0.48	-1.47	0.48	0.42	0.31
Yr.	**E1.95**	1.39	-0.44	1.93	1.52	1.15

Next earnings report expected: NA

Dividend Data (Dividends have been paid since 1950.)

Amount ($)	Date Decl.	Ex-Div. Date	Stock of Record	Payment Date
0.190	Dec. 02	Dec. 17	Dec. 19	Jan. 06 '98
0.190	Mar. 04	Mar. 13	Mar. 17	Apr. 06 '98
0.190	Jun. 03	Jun. 12	Jun. 16	Jul. 06 '98
0.190	Sep. 02	Sep. 16	Sep. 18	Oct. 05 '98

A Division of The **McGraw·Hill** *Companies*

Business Summary - 11-AUG-98

Two years ago, BFI changed its strategic focus from growth in market share to improvement in investment returns. To this end, the company has been restructuring its core North American municipal solid waste (MSW) operations, divesting exotic non-core environmental service businesses, cutting capital spending, reducing debt levels, repurchasing BFI shares and selling international operations.

The company has been particularly focusing on improving landfill internalization rates, or the percentage of MSW disposed of in BFI landfills rather than in third-party landfills. In general, the higher the internalization rates, the more profitable the landfills become.

Profitability performance in recent fiscal years was as follows:

	FY 97	FY 96	FY 95
Gross profit margins	26%	25%	28%
Operating profit margins	10%	2.5%	14%
Free cash flow (000)	$538,000	($403,000)	$6,000
Free cash flow per share	$2.64	($2.01)	$0.03

The company operates in the fragmented $36.5 billion MSW industry. Although the MSW business has been consolidating over the past several years, the industry is still fragmented and very competitive, with municipal government operations, 25 publicly traded companies and 7,000 privately held outfits controlling 28%, 32% and 40%, respectively, of the MSW industry.

Demand for MSW services is primarily driven by GDP and population growth. It is estimated that U.S. GDP and population growth will expand at sustainable compound annual growth rates of 2.5% and 1.0%, respectively.

MSW collection, MSW disposal, recycling, medical waste and other services comprise 60%, 23%, 11%, 4% and 2% of total gross revenues.

North American operations consist of solid waste collection services at some 245 locations in 45 states, Puerto Rico and Canada. The company operates 91 solid waste transfer stations (where waste is compacted for final disposal) and 98 landfills. BFI's 102 North American recyclers serve residential, commercial and industrial customers. The company is the largest provider of medical waste services in North America, operating 29 treatment sites. To a lesser extent, BFI offers street sweeping services; rents and services portable restrooms; and operates several waste-to-energy incinerator plants.

Per Share Data ($) (Year Ended Sep. 30)	1997	1996	1995	1994	1993	1992	1991	1990	1989	1988
Tangible Bk. Val.	5.47	3.43	4.03	6.74	6.24	6.52	4.72	4.65	6.26	5.79
Cash Flow	4.19	2.56	4.71	3.96	3.37	3.42	2.69	3.67	3.20	2.80
Earnings	1.39	-0.44	1.93	1.52	1.15	1.11	0.42	1.68	1.74	1.51
Dividends	0.70	0.68	0.85	0.68	0.68	0.68	0.68	0.64	0.56	0.48
Payout Ratio	50%	NM	44%	45%	59%	65%	159%	38%	32%	31%
Prices - High	38 7/8	32 7/8	40 5/8	32 7/8	28 5/8	27 1/8	30 3/4	49 1/4	42 3/4	29 1/4
- Low	25 3/4	21 3/8	27 1/8	24 1/4	20 7/8	19 1/2	16 7/8	20 3/4	26 7/8	20 7/8
P/E Ratio - High	28	NM	21	22	25	24	73	29	25	19
- Low	19	NM	14	16	18	18	40	12	15	14
Income Statement Analysis (Million $)										
Revs.	5,783	5,779	5,779	4,315	3,495	3,287	3,183	2,967	2,551	2,067
Oper. Inc.	1,251	1,192	1,341	1,003	790	717	782	863	687	579
Depr.	570	603	552	459	380	367	349	305	222	194
Int. Exp.	165	179	160	105	89.6	86.9	83.1	77.9	48.3	37.4
Pretax Inc.	495	27.7	691	499	327	288	117	421	423	360
Eff. Tax Rate	40%	NM	40%	40%	40%	39%	44%	39%	38%	37%
Net Inc.	284	-89.2	385	284	197	176	65.0	257	263	227
Balance Sheet & Other Fin. Data (Million $)										
Cash	78.7	110	198	141	232	389	141	139	133	165
Curr. Assets	1,245	1,388	1,422	1,186	925	1,013	719	772	605	532
Total Assets	6,678	7,601	7,460	5,797	4,296	4,068	3,656	3,574	3,017	2,258
Curr. Liab.	1,435	1,398	1,414	1,179	924	780	715	749	599	386
LT Debt	1,675	2,767	2,411	1,459	1,079	1,094	1,152	1,193	945	630
Common Eqty.	2,661	2,510	2,742	2,392	1,533	1,460	1,114	1,162	1,242	1,043
Total Cap.	4,336	5,277	5,258	3,951	2,634	2,579	2,292	2,380	2,246	1,725
Cap. Exp.	495	935	930	984	665	514	497	481	714	439
Cash Flow	853	514	937	743	577	543	415	562	484	421
Curr. Ratio	0.9	1.0	1.0	1.0	1.0	1.3	1.0	1.0	1.0	1.4
% LT Debt of Cap.	38.6	52.4	45.8	36.9	41.0	42.4	50.3	50.1	42.1	36.5
% Net Inc.of Revs.	4.9	NM	6.6	6.6	5.6	5.3	2.0	8.7	10.3	11.0
% Ret. on Assets	4.0	NM	5.8	5.3	4.7	4.3	1.8	7.7	9.9	10.8
% Ret. on Equity	11.0	NM	14.9	13.8	13.0	13.1	5.7	21.1	22.9	23.6

Data as orig. reptd.; bef. results of disc. opers. and/or spec. items. Per share data adj. for stk. divs. as of ex-div. date. Bold denotes diluted EPS (FASB 128). E-Estimated. NA-Not Available. NM-Not Meaningful. NR-Not Ranked.

Office—Browning-Ferris Bldg., 757 N. Eldridge, P.O. Box 3151, Houston, TX 77253. **Tel**—(281) 870-8100.**Fax**—(281) 870-7844. **Website**—www.bfi.com **Chrmn**—W. D. Ruckelshaus. **Pres & CEO**—B. E. Ranck. **SVP & CFO**—J. E. Curtiss. **VP & Secy**—G. K. Burger. **VP & Investor Contact**—Elizabeth Ivers (281-870-7161).**Dirs**—W. T. Butler, C. J. Grayson Jr., G. Grinstein, N. A. Myers, U. Otto, H. J. Phillips Sr., B. E. Ranck, J. L. Roberts Jr., W. D. Ruckelshaus, M. J. Shapiro, R. M. Teeter, L. A. Waters, M. v. N. Whitman, P. S. Willmott. **Transfer Agent & Registrar**—First Chicago Trust Co. of New York, Jersey City, NJ. **Incorporated**—in Delaware in 1970. **Empl**— 40,000. **S&P Analyst:** Eric J. Hunter

STANDARD &POOR'S
STOCK REPORTS

Brunswick Corp.

382

NYSE Symbol **BC**

In S&P 500

12-SEP-98

Industry:
Leisure Time (Products)

Summary: Brunswick makes outdoor and indoor recreation products, primarily in the pleasure boating, fishing, camping, biking, bowling and billiards markets.

S&P Opinion: Hold (★★★)	Recent Price • 13½	Yield • 3.7%
	52 Wk Range • 37-12¾	12-Mo. P/E • 8.6

Earnings vs. Previous Year
▲=Up ▼=Down ▶=No Change

Quantitative Evaluations

Outlook
(1 Lowest—5 Highest)
• **5**

Fair Value
• **31⅛**

Risk
• **Low**

Earn./Div. Rank
• **B**

Technical Eval.
• **Bullish** since 1/98

Rel. Strength Rank
(1 Lowest—99 Highest)
• **15**

Insider Activity
• **NA**

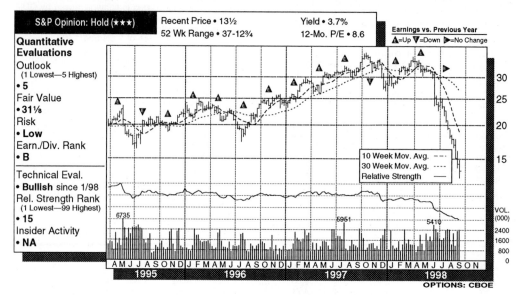

10 Week Mov. Avg. ----
30 Week Mov. Avg. ·····
Relative Strength ——

6735   5951   5410

VOL. (000)
2400
1600
800
0

A M J J A S O N D J F M A M J J A S O N D J F M A M J J A S O N D J F M A M J J A S O N
1995   1996   1997   1998

OPTIONS: CBOE

Overview - 29-JUN-98

We expect BC to generally maintain its strong market position in the marine industry in 1998, although revenues from other recreation-related areas are likely to comprise a larger portion of overall sales, including a boost from acquisitions. BC is expected, during the next few years, to be seeking to increase the sales contribution from its non-marine recreation businesses to about half of the company's total, from 35% in 1997. Meanwhile, we expect 1998 profits from the marine segment to benefit from BC's emphasis on shifting its product mix toward larger, higher-margin cruisers and yachts. In the marine engine business, we look for cost-cutting efforts to help offset costs related to producing lower emission engines. Long term, a federally mandated transition toward more environmentally friendly products may raise consumer prices for some outboard engines. Also, credit restrictions in China are expected to hurt BC's 1998 sales of bowling equipment, including an adverse first quarter impact. Separately, our full-year 1998 earnings estimate includes a $0.09/share benefit from one-time items.

Valuation - 29-JUN-98

We recommend holding the stock of this major recreation company, but do not advise new purchases. This reflects our view that concerns about future profit cyclicality and visibility will limit the stock's performance during the next six to 12 months. Based on estimated 1998 and 1999 earnings, we look for the shares to continue trading at a lower P/E multiple than the overall market. On a more positive note, we view U.S. demographics in the decade ahead as generally favorable for purchases of large pleasure boats.

Key Stock Statistics

S&P EPS Est. 1998	2.25	Tang. Bk. Value/Share	5.86
P/E on S&P Est. 1998	6.0	Beta	1.26
S&P EPS Est. 1999	2.45	Shareholders	18,400
Dividend Rate/Share	0.50	Market cap. (B)	$ 1.3
Shs. outstg. (M)	99.1	Inst. holdings	70%
Avg. daily vol. (M)	0.428		

Value of $10,000 invested 5 years ago: $ 9,524

Fiscal Year Ending Dec. 31

	1998	1997	1996	1995	1994	1993
Revenues (Million $)						
1Q	904.2	841.6	738.9	774.2	634.9	542.8
2Q	1,113	1,008	858.3	839.2	748.2	589.0
3Q	—	876.5	763.6	725.7	662.1	539.4
4Q	—	931.1	799.5	702.3	654.9	535.6
Yr.	—	3,657	3,160	3,041	2,700	2,207
Earnings Per Share ($)						
1Q	**0.59**	**0.53**	0.47	0.42	0.28	0.10
2Q	**0.83**	**0.83**	0.71	0.38	0.58	0.24
3Q	**E0.49**	-0.17	0.41	0.36	0.31	0.16
4Q	**E0.34**	**0.32**	0.29	0.23	0.19	0.07
Yr.	**E2.25**	**1.51**	1.88	1.39	1.35	0.57

Next earnings report expected: mid October

Dividend Data (Dividends have been paid since 1969.)

Amount ($)	Date Decl.	Ex-Div. Date	Stock of Record	Payment Date
0.125	Oct. 21	Nov. 19	Nov. 21	Dec. 15 '97
0.125	Feb. 09	Feb. 23	Feb. 25	Mar. 16 '98
0.125	Apr. 22	May. 20	May. 22	Jun. 15 '98
0.125	Jul. 28	Aug. 21	Aug. 25	Sep. 15 '98

A Division of The McGraw-Hill Companies

Business Summary - 29-JUN-98

Brunswick (BC) is the world's largest manufacturer of pleasure boats and is a leading maker of marine engines. It has also long been a leader in the bowling and billiards markets. Since Peter Larson was named chairman and CEO in 1995, the company has been expanding in the active recreation market, in order to lessen its dependence on the highly cyclical marine business.

In 1997, BC's large marine segment had sales and operating profit (before a one-time charge) totaling $2.4 billion and $269 million, respectively. This segment consists of the Mercury Marine division, which makes outboard and other marine engines, and the Sea Ray and US Marine divisions, which manufacture fiberglass pleasure and offshore fishing boats. BC believes that it has the largest dollar sales volume of recreational marine engines and pleasure boats of any company in the world. BC's engine brand names include Mercury, Mariner, Force, MerCruiser and SportJet. In the boat division, brands include Sea Ray, Baja, Boston Whaler, Bayliner, Maxum and Robalo.

In 1997, BC's sales from its recreation segment totaled $1.3 billion, and operating profit, before an unusual charge, amounted to $141 million. BC is expected to be seeking to increase recreation segment sales to about half of the company's total sales within the next few years, up from 28% in 1996 and 35% in 1997. To spur expansion in this area, Brunswick has made a number of acquisitions since early 1996, spending more than $600 million.

The Brunswick Outdoor Recreation Group includes Zebco and Quantum fishing reels; MotorGuide and Thruster electric trolling motors; American Camper and Remington camping products; Weather-Rite apparel and Realtree rainwear; Mongoose, Ride Hard and Roadmaster bicycles; Flexible Flyer tricycles, wagons and snow goods; Igloo ice chests and coolers; and Hoppe's shooting sports accessories. Also, the Brunswick Indoor Recreation Group is the leading manufacturer of bowling products, including bowling balls and capital equipment; BC owns and operates about 167 recreation centers (including joint ventures), which largely emphasize bowling.

BC's Life Fitness Division designs, markets and manufactures computerized cardiovascular and strength training fitness equipment. BC entered this business with a July 1997 acquisition costing about $315 million, and was expanded with two more acquisitions in November 1997 and February 1998.

BC recorded a charge of $0.63 a share in 1997's third quarter for costs associated with strategic initiatives to streamline operations and improve manufacturing costs. BC expects these moves to generate total pretax savings of $55 million to $60 million over a three-year period.

In June 1998, BC said it intends to appeal an adverse anti-trust verdict related to its marine business.

Per Share Data ($)

(Year Ended Dec. 31)	1997	1996	1995	1994	1993	1992	1991	1990	1989	1988
Tangible Bk. Val.	4.75	7.02	6.51	5.41	4.29	4.31	4.03	4.09	2.90	3.84
Cash Flow	3.07	3.19	2.58	2.60	1.81	1.68	1.24	2.46	1.00	3.88
Earnings	1.51	1.88	1.39	1.35	0.57	0.43	-0.27	0.80	-0.81	2.20
Dividends	0.50	0.50	0.50	0.44	0.44	0.44	0.44	0.44	0.44	0.40
Payout Ratio	33%	27%	36%	33%	77%	102%	NM	55%	NM	18%
Prices - High	37	25⁷/₈	24	25³/₈	18¹/₂	17³/₄	16³/₈	16¹/₈	21¹/₂	24¹/₈
- Low	23¹/₈	17¹/₄	16¹/₄	17	12¹/₂	12¹/₈	8	6³/₈	13	14¹/₂
P/E Ratio - High	25	14	17	19	32	41	NM	20	NM	11
- Low	15	9	12	13	22	28	NM	8	NM	7

Income Statement Analysis (Million $)

	1997	1996	1995	1994	1993	1992	1991	1990	1989	1988
Revs.	3,657	3,160	3,041	2,700	2,207	2,059	2,088	2,478	2,826	3,282
Oper. Inc.	526	435	380	330	218	196	133	234	236	472
Depr.	157	130	121	120	118	116	133	146	160	148
Int. Exp.	51.3	33.4	32.5	28.5	27.2	29.9	32.0	46.3	56.7	40.5
Pretax Inc.	236	290	208	198	87.0	62.0	-22.0	123	-77.0	317
Eff. Tax Rate	36%	36%	36%	35%	37%	36%	NM	42%	NM	39%
Net Inc.	151	186	127	129	55.0	40.0	-24.0	71.0	-71.0	193

Balance Sheet & Other Fin. Data (Million $)

	1997	1996	1995	1994	1993	1992	1991	1990	1989	1988
Cash	85.6	242	356	203	249	196	102	85.0	22.0	32.0
Curr. Assets	1,366	1,242	1,278	1,058	950	865	825	811	779	787
Total Assets	3,241	2,802	2,361	2,122	1,984	1,908	1,857	1,895	1,985	2,092
Curr. Liab.	948	831	680	621	602	503	539	531	563	554
LT Debt	646	455	313	319	325	305	316	302	462	413
Common Eqty.	1,366	1,198	1,044	911	804	823	779	824	776	950
Total Cap.	2,105	1,809	1,515	1,363	1,233	1,302	1,278	1,308	1,384	1,491
Cap. Exp.	191	170	123	105	96.0	89.0	82.0	91.0	128	179
Cash Flow	308	316	248	249	172	156	110	217	89.0	341
Curr. Ratio	1.4	1.5	1.9	1.7	1.6	1.7	1.5	1.5	1.4	1.4
% LT Debt of Cap.	30.7	25.2	20.7	23.4	26.3	23.4	24.7	23.1	33.4	27.7
% Net Inc.of Revs.	4.1	5.9	4.2	4.8	2.5	1.9	NM	2.9	NM	5.9
% Ret. on Assets	5.0	7.2	6.0	6.3	2.8	2.0	NM	3.6	NM	9.8
% Ret. on Equity	11.7	16.6	13.7	15.0	6.7	4.8	NM	8.8	NM	21.8

Data as orig. reptd.; bef. results of disc. opers. and/or spec. items. Per share data adj. for stk. divs. as of ex-div. date. Bold denotes diluted EPS (FASB 128). E-Estimated. NA-Not Available. NM-Not Meaningful. NR-Not Ranked.

Office—1 N. Field Ct., Lake Forest, IL 60045-4811. **Tel**—(847) 735-4700.**Chrmn & CEO**—P. N. Larson. **SVP & CFO**—P. B. Hamilton. **VP & Secy**—M. D. Allen. **VP & Investor Contact**—Kathryn J. Chieger. **VP & Treas**—R. S. O'Brien. **Dirs**—N. D. Archibald, J. L. Bleustein, M. J. Callahan, M. A. Fernandez, P. Harf, P. N. Larson, J. W. Lorsch, R. P. Mark, B. Martin Musham, K. Roman, R. W. Schipke. **Transfer Agent & Registrar**—Co.'s office. **Incorporated**—in Delaware in 1907. **Empl**— 25,300. **S&P Analyst:** Tom Graves, CFA

Burlington Northern Santa Fe 398K

NYSE Symbol **BNI**

In S&P 500

12-SEP-98

Industry: Railroads

Summary: BNI, formed through the 1995 merger of Burlington Northern and Santa Fe Pacific, operates a major U.S. railroad. BNI's pipeline interests were sold in March 1998.

S&P Opinion: Accumulate (★★★★)	Recent Price • 28¾	Yield • 1.7%
	52 Wk Range • 35¾-26⅞	12-Mo. P/E • 13.1

Quantitative Evaluations

Outlook
(1 Lowest—5 Highest)
• **3⁻**

Fair Value
• **34½**

Risk
• **Low**

Earn./Div. Rank
• **NR**

Technical Eval.
• **Bearish** since 8/98

Rel. Strength Rank
(1 Lowest—99 Highest)
• **60**

Insider Activity
• **Neutral**

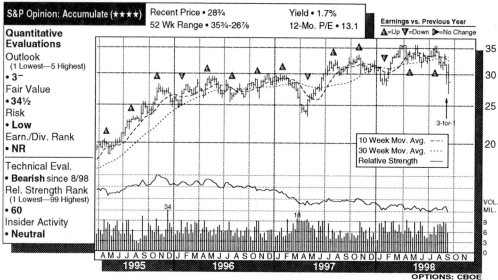

Earnings vs. Previous Year ▲=Up ▼=Down ▶=No Change

10 Week Mov. Avg. - - -
30 Week Mov. Avg. · · · ·
Relative Strength ——

3-for-1

VOL. MIL.

1995 1996 1997 1998

OPTIONS: CBOE

Overview - 04-JUN-98

BNI's purchase of the Bieber to Keddie line in California will let it garner traffic in 1998 from motor carriers. Severe service problems on the Union Pacific since late 1997 have prompted shippers to give BNI more business. BNI also won access to additional UNP customers in early 1998, when the two railroads formed a jointly owned line between Houston and New Orleans. Despite continued mild weather in 1998, coal traffic should rebound, as utilities rebuild stockpiles and BNI wins new contracts. Intermodal will benefit from increased premium LTL business and traffic fed to BNI by its truckload partners. Grain traffic may slip, reflecting weak exports to Asia. Margins will widen, reflecting savings derived from the installation of a new computer system in 1997. The new computer system will permit more efficient routing, thereby cutting labor, fuel and equipment rental charges. Comparisons will benefit from the absence of 1997's difficult weather and restructuring charge, lower fuel and materials costs, and favorable personal injury experience. Offsetting will be increased depreciation charges.

Valuation - 04-JUN-98

BNI's shares have outperformed other rail issues thus far in 1998. Recently, though, BNI has come under pressure as investors are concerned that shippers will succeed in getting Washington to restore industry regulation. Also, investors may see signs that the expansion is slowing. We advise accumulation of BNI because we doubt that the rail industry will be reregulated. Moreover, BNI's traffic should continue to grow faster than other carriers as it is benefiting from the misfortunes of Union Pacific. Additionally, the integration of Burlington's and Santa Fe's information systems is yielding savings from more efficient routing and dispatching and lower fuel, labor and car rental costs.

Key Stock Statistics

S&P EPS Est. 1998	2.42	Tang. Bk. Value/Share	15.49
P/E on S&P Est. 1998	11.9	Beta	0.90
S&P EPS Est. 1999	2.72	Shareholders	74,000
Dividend Rate/Share	0.48	Market cap. (B)	$ 13.6
Shs. outstg. (M)	473.0	Inst. holdings	76%
Avg. daily vol. (M)	1.633		

Value of $10,000 invested 5 years ago: $ 21,946

Fiscal Year Ending Dec. 31

	1998	1997	1996	1995	1994	1993
Revenues (Million $)						
1Q	2,162	2,036	2,027	1,347	1,210	1,170
2Q	2,219	2,073	2,024	1,284	1,192	1,142
3Q	—	2,146	2,044	1,460	1,249	1,141
4Q	—	2,187	2,092	2,092	1,344	1,246
Yr.	—	8,413	8,187	6,183	4,995	4,699
Earnings Per Share ($)						
1Q	0.56	0.32	0.40	0.35	0.30	0.29
2Q	0.58	0.50	0.45	0.44	0.28	0.25
3Q	E0.65	0.60	0.53	0.44	0.41	0.07
4Q	E0.61	0.46	0.52	-0.38	0.50	0.42
Yr.	E2.42	1.88	1.91	0.55	1.49	1.02

Next earnings report expected: late October

Dividend Data (Dividends have been paid since 1940.)

Amount ($)	Date Decl.	Ex-Div. Date	Stock of Record	Payment Date
0.300	Jan. 15	Mar. 06	Mar. 10	Apr. 01 '98
0.300	Apr. 16	Jun. 05	Jun. 09	Jul. 01 '98
3-for-1	Jul. 16	Sep. 02	Aug. 17	Sep. 01 '98
0.120	Jul. 16	Sep. 10	Sep. 14	Oct. 01 '98

A Division of The McGraw-Hill Companies

Business Summary - 04-JUN-98

Burlington Northern Santa Fe Corp., created in September 1995 through the merger of Burlington Northern Inc. and Santa Fe Pacific Corp., operates the second largest U.S. rail system. The merged rail system enjoys a more diversified traffic base and has begun to reap considerable cost savings following the integration of the two lines' computer systems. BNI was a major beneficiary of the merger of Union Pacific and Southern Pacific in late 1996 as the Surface Transportation Board directed UP to grant BNI trackage rights over 3,550 miles of UP lines and sell Burlington another 335 miles. A 44% interest in Santa Fe Pacific Pipeline Partners L.P. was sold in March 1998 for $84 million.

Burlington's merger with Santa Fe Pacific created a 34,000-mile rail system spanning 29 western and midwestern states and two Canadian provinces. Santa Fe's traffic, heavily skewed to intermodal and automobiles, complemented Burlington's largely coal and grain freight base. In 1997 coal accounted for 23% of total rail revenues, agricultural products for 13%, intermodal 27%, and chemicals 9%.

The merger of Burlington and Santa Fe has succeeded in drawing traffic from truckers by creating new long-haul single-system routes. Additionally, significant cost savings are to be derived from the integration of the two railroads' computer systems into a new, more dynamic system, dubbed "Transport Support System"

or TSS. TSS was completed in July 1997 at a cost of $300 million. By more efficiently routing freight, the TSS system will lower labor, fuel and equipment rental costs.

As a condition to the merger of Union Pacific and Southern Pacific in late 1996, BNI was awarded trackage rights over 3,550 miles of those railroads to preserve competition. With these rights, Burlington has been able to offer new service between New Orleans and Houston and Houston and Memphis. In 1998, Burlington Northern is projected to generate some $250 million of revenues from these rights.

The Surface Transportation Board also directed Union Pacific (UP) to sell to BNI 335 miles in Louisiana, Texas and California. In July 1997, BNI completed the purchase of the Bieber to Keddie line in California. The line, which parallels the I-5 truck route, provided the missing link in BNI's system, which is now able to offer single-system rail service from Vancouver to San Diego. In February 1998, to eliminate serious congestion problems with the Gulf region, BNI and UP pooled 342 miles of track between Houston and New Orleans into a jointly owned line. The new track will give BNI access to additional UP shippers generating $40 million in freight revenues.

BNI sold its interests in Santa Fe Pacific Pipeline Partners L.P. to Kinder Morgan Energy Partners L.P. in March 1998 for $84 million, realizing a $32 million net gain ($0.20 a share) in 1998's first quarter.

Per Share Data ($)

(Year Ended Dec. 31)	1997	1996	1995	1994	1993	1992	1991	1990	1989	1988
Tangible Bk. Val.	14.53	12.95	11.22	7.07	5.91	5.24	4.59	5.43	4.78	4.10
Cash Flow	3.52	3.52	2.24	2.83	2.33	2.38	0.17	2.47	2.43	2.52
Earnings	1.88	1.90	0.55	1.49	1.02	1.12	-1.32	0.96	1.06	0.92
Dividends	0.40	0.40	0.40	0.40	0.40	0.40	0.40	0.40	0.40	0.73
Payout Ratio	21%	21%	72%	27%	39%	36%	NM	41%	37%	80%
Prices - High	33⅝	30	28¼	22¼	19⅝	15¾	14	13⅛	10¾	26¾
- Low	23⅜	24½	15⅛	15½	14	11⅛	8¾	7⅜	7⅛	18⅝
P/E Ratio - High	18	16	51	15	19	14	NM	14	10	29
- Low	12	13	27	10	14	10	NM	8	7	20

Income Statement Analysis (Million $)

	1997	1996	1995	1994	1993	1992	1991	1990	1989	1988
Revs.	8,413	8,187	6,183	4,995	4,699	4,630	4,559	4,674	4,606	4,700
Oper. Inc.	2,630	2,508	1,781	1,215	1,013	935	816	941	966	1,039
Depr.	773	760	520	362	352	338	347	346	310	360
Int. Exp.	344	301	220	155	145	186	226	243	277	298
Pretax Inc.	1,404	1,440	334	695	521	452	-489	356	391	354
Eff. Tax Rate	37%	38%	41%	39%	43%	34%	NM	38%	38%	42%
Net Inc.	885	889	198	426	296	299	-305	222	243	207

Balance Sheet & Other Fin. Data (Million $)

	1997	1996	1995	1994	1993	1992	1991	1990	1989	1988
Cash	31.0	47.0	50.0	27.0	17.0	57.0	16.0	56.0	83.0	84.0
Curr. Assets	1,234	1,331	1,264	1,012	891	777	705	625	797	1,065
Total Assets	21,336	19,846	18,269	7,592	7,045	6,537	6,324	6,075	6,148	6,330
Curr. Liab.	2,060	2,311	2,369	1,447	1,529	1,353	1,422	1,170	1,288	1,219
LT Debt	5,181	4,546	4,153	1,697	1,526	1,527	1,834	2,083	2,220	2,723
Common Eqty.	6,812	5,981	5,037	1,892	1,574	1,383	1,202	1,241	1,080	918
Total Cap.	17,168	15,256	13,423	5,390	4,787	4,405	4,123	4,632	4,591	4,841
Cap. Exp.	2,182	2,234	890	698	676	487	509	401	373	415
Cash Flow	1,658	1,649	718	766	626	634	40.0	567	552	566
Curr. Ratio	0.6	0.6	0.5	0.7	0.6	0.6	0.5	0.5	0.6	0.9
% LT Debt of Cap.	30.2	29.8	30.9	31.5	31.9	34.7	44.5	45.0	48.3	56.2
% Net Inc.of Revs.	10.5	10.9	3.2	8.5	6.3	6.5	NM	4.7	5.3	4.4
% Ret. on Assets	4.3	4.7	1.5	5.8	4.3	4.6	NM	3.6	3.9	2.4
% Ret. on Equity	13.8	16.1	4.0	23.3	18.5	22.8	NM	19.0	24.1	8.8

Data as orig. reptd.; bef. results of disc. opers. and/or spec. items. Per share data adj. for stk. divs. as of ex-div. date. Bold denotes diluted EPS (FASB 128). E-Estimated. NA-Not Available. NM-Not Meaningful. NR-Not Ranked.

Office—2650 Lou Menk Drive, Fort Worth, TX 76131-2830. **Tel**—(817) 333-2000. **Website**—http://www.bnsf.com **Chrmn, Pres & CEO**—R. D. Krebs. **SVP & CFO**—D. E. Springer. **VP, Secy & Investor Contact**—Marsha Morgan. **Dirs**—J. F. Alibrandi, J. S. Blanton, J. J. Burns Jr., D, G. Deukmejian, R. D. Krebs, B. M. Lindig, V. S. Martinez, R. S. Roberts, M. J. Shapiro, A. R. Weber, R. H. West, J. S. Whisler, E. E. Whitacre Jr., R. B. Woodard, M. B. Yanney.**Transfer Agent & Registrar**—First Chicago Trust Co. of New York, Jersey City NJ. **Incorporated**—in Delaware in 1961; reincorporated in Delaware in 1995. **Empl**— 44,500. **S&P Analyst:** Stephen R. Klein

STANDARD &POOR'S
STOCK REPORTS

Burlington Resources

398N

NYSE Symbol **BR**

In S&P 500

12-SEP-98

Industry: Oil & Gas (Exploration & Production)

Summary: This company, which acquired Louisiana Land & Exploration Co. in late 1997, is one of the world's largest independent oil and gas exploration and production companies.

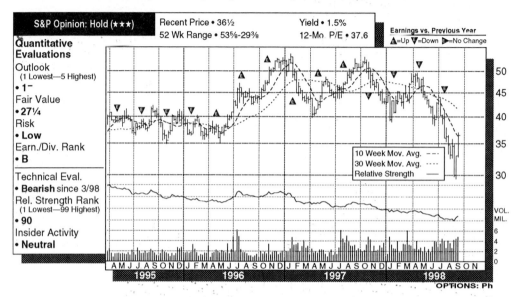

S&P Opinion: Hold (★★★)	Recent Price • 36½	Yield • 1.5%
	52 Wk Range • 53⅝-29⅜	12-Mo P/E • 37.6

Quantitative Evaluations

Outlook (1 Lowest—5 Highest)
• **1⁻**

Fair Value
• **27¼**

Risk
• **Low**

Earn./Div. Rank
• **B**

Technical Eval.
• **Bearish** since 3/98

Rel. Strength Rank (1 Lowest—99 Highest)
• **90**

Insider Activity
• **Neutral**

Earnings vs. Previous Year ▲=Up ▼=Down ▶=No Change

10 Week Mov. Avg. ---
30 Week Mov. Avg. ·····
Relative Strength —

OPTIONS: Ph

Overview - 17-JUL-98

Burlington Resources' (BR) October 1997 acquisition of Louisiana Land & Exploration Co. (LL&E), along with the company's asset divestiture program completed in July 1997, demonstrate that BR is redefining itself as a pure-play exploration and production company, as opposed to an acquisition-oriented firm. Consistent with that approach, the bulk of BR's capital spending program will be used to fund internal development projects, and potential acquisitions will be assessed using conservative pricing assumptions and aggressive hurdle rates. Year to date, the company has not made any acquisitions. Incidentally, BR is one of the few oil companies that has not lowered its capital budget in the wake of current oil price declines. Following the LL&E acquisition, BR identified five operating divisions through which it conducts operations.

Valuation - 17-JUL-98

Though Burlington's shares have traded sideways throughout the past year, the stock has held up well against other exploration and production issues, which have suffered as a result of steep oil price declines. BR's limited exposure to oil should continue to soften the impact on earnings that weak oil prices will have on other firms. Nevertheless, earnings will be affected; we have reduced our EPS estimate for 1998 to $0.55 from $2.00, and maintain a hold rating. With the acquisition of LL&E, the non-core assets sale, and the new organizational structure, Burlington Resources proves that it is very focused. The company should be revisited in the near-term, as the benefits from these changes are realized and commodity prices stabilize.

Key Stock Statistics

S&P EPS Est. 1998	0.55	Tang. Bk. Value/Share	17.28
P/E on S&P Est. 1998	66.4	Beta	0.87
Dividend Rate/Share	0.55	Shareholders	20,100
Shs. outstg. (M)	177.5	Market cap. (B)	$ 6.5
Avg. daily vol. (M)	0.840	Inst. holdings	74%

Value of $10,000 invested 5 years ago: $ 9,886

Fiscal Year Ending Dec. 31

	1998	1997	1996	1995	1994	1993
Revenues (Million $)						
1Q	432.0	568.0	255.5	214.6	275.0	316.5
2Q	412.0	457.0	295.0	211.2	266.0	312.2
3Q	—	464.0	344.0	210.2	273.0	309.5
4Q	—	541.0	399.0	236.5	241.0	310.8
Yr.	—	2,000	1,293	872.5	1,055	1,249
Earnings Per Share ($)						
1Q	**0.27**	**0.73**	0.30	-0.04	0.37	0.35
2Q	**0.13**	**0.49**	0.38	0.02	0.25	1.02
3Q	—	**0.37**	0.47	-2.36	0.16	0.18
4Q	—	**0.20**	0.87	0.18	0.42	0.40
Yr.	**E0.55**	**1.79**	2.02	-2.20	1.20	1.95

Next earnings report expected: early October

Dividend Data (Dividends have been paid since 1988.)

Amount ($)	Date Decl.	Ex-Div. Date	Stock of Record	Payment Date
0.138	Oct. 08	Dec. 10	Dec. 12	Jan. 02 '98
0.138	Jan. 14	Mar. 11	Mar. 13	Apr. 01 '98
0.138	Apr. 08	Jun. 10	Jun. 12	Jul. 01 '98
0.138	Jul. 08	Sep. 09	Sep. 11	Oct. 01 '98

A Division of The **McGraw-Hill** *Companies*

Business Summary - 17-JUL-98

With the $3 billion acquisition of Louisiana Land & Exploration (LL&E) in October 1997, Burlington Resources Inc. (BR) completed its transformation from a pure acquisition and exploitation firm to a more exploration-oriented firm. The purchase followed a two year asset divestiture program in which 27,000 non-strategic wells were sold, along with BR's refinery operations, netting nearly $500 million.

Following the acquisition of LL&E, Burlington conducts operations through five divisions: San Juan, Mid-Continent, Gulf of Mexico, Gulf Coast, and International. Activities of the key San Juan division, which holds 44% of BR's reserves and contributes 49% of the company's gas production, center on the San Juan Basin in northwest New Mexico and southwest Colorado. The Mid-Continent division operates mainly in the Permian Basin in west Texas, the Anadarko Basin in western Oklahoma, and the Williston Basin in western North Dakota and northeast Montana. The Gulf of Mexico division, operating in the shallow and deep waters of the Gulf, employs a strategy of using 3-D seismic technology around existing wells. The Gulf Coast division focuses on south Louisiana, south and east Texas, and the Florida panhandle. International conducts projects in the East Irish Sea, Algeria, and Venezuela. In addition,

BR owns non-operation interests in certain U.K. and Dutch properties. In sum, Burlington owns 14.5 million acres worldwide.

Gas production in 1997 averaged 1.67 Bcf a day, up from 1.60 Bcf a day in 1996. Oil production was 87.2 MBbl. a day (91.1). Burlington drilled 316.6 net wells during 1997 (of which 36.4 were dry), up from 241.0 (24.0) in 1996. Total proved reserves of oil at 1997 year-end were estimated at 253.7 million bbl., down from 305.8 million Bbl. at the end of 1996. Total proved gas reserves totaled 6.4 trillion cubic feet (6.2). In terms of worldwide reserves, BR is second only to Unocal Corp. among all independent oil and gas companies. Burlington's domestic natural gas reserve base is the largest of any independent company, and the third largest of any oil company, including the major oils. During 1997, Burlington replaced 188% of its worldwide production with new reserves - 143% through drill bit additions and 45% through acquisitions.

BR has sharply raised capital spending in recent years; 1997 spending, excluding property acquisitions of approximately $1.0 billion, represented a 45% increase from the 1996 level. In 1998, BR plans to increase capital spending by an additional 15%, to $1.15 billion, excluding acquisitions. Most of the budget will fund exploration and development.

Per Share Data ($)

(Year Ended Dec. 31)	1997	1996	1995	1994	1993	1992	1991	1990	1989	1988
Tangible Bk. Val.	17.07	18.68	17.54	20.30	20.11	18.67	22.11	21.92	22.08	20.19
Cash Flow	4.81	4.75	0.73	3.81	4.13	3.38	3.64	3.43	2.74	2.09
Earnings	1.79	2.02	-2.20	1.20	1.95	1.44	1.48	1.46	0.99	0.46
Dividends	0.55	0.55	0.55	0.55	0.55	0.60	0.70	0.70	0.61	0.29
Payout Ratio	31%	27%	NM	46%	28%	41%	47%	47%	61%	62%
Prices - High	54$\frac{1}{2}$	53$\frac{1}{2}$	42$\frac{1}{4}$	49$\frac{5}{8}$	53$\frac{7}{8}$	43$\frac{1}{2}$	43$\frac{3}{4}$	50$\frac{1}{8}$	53$\frac{5}{8}$	33$\frac{7}{8}$
- Low	39$\frac{3}{4}$	35$\frac{1}{8}$	35$\frac{5}{8}$	33$\frac{1}{8}$	36$\frac{1}{2}$	33	32$\frac{7}{8}$	36$\frac{3}{4}$	32$\frac{1}{8}$	23$\frac{3}{8}$
P/E Ratio - High	30	26	NM	41	28	30	30	34	54	74
- Low	22	17	NM	28	19	23	22	25	32	51

Income Statement Analysis (Million $)

	1997	1996	1995	1994	1993	1992	1991	1990	1989	1988
Revs.	2,000	1,293	873	1,055	1,249	1,141	1,754	1,871	1,715	2,167
Oper. Inc.	1,041	764	-94.6	512	541	496	662	689	553	627
Depr. Depl. & Amort.	538	346	373	337	285	256	289	280	261	244
Int. Exp.	142	113	109	90.0	73.0	79.0	122	116	77.0	89.0
Pretax Inc.	411	307	-576	90.0	307	218	256	282	201	101
Eff. Tax Rate	22%	17%	NM	NM	17%	13%	23%	27%	26%	29%
Net Inc.	319	255	-279	154	255	190	197	208	147	70.0

Balance Sheet & Other Fin. Data (Million $)

	1997	1996	1995	1994	1993	1992	1991	1990	1989	1988
Cash	152	68.0	20.5	20.0	20.0	32.0	17.0	30.0	160	71.0
Curr. Assets	678	442	265	266	277	370	760	1,136	893	1,064
Total Assets	5,821	4,316	4,165	4,809	4,448	4,470	6,290	6,360	6,098	5,589
Curr. Liab.	538	368	322	262	300	346	916	1,070	1,155	826
LT Debt	1,748	1,350	1,350	1,309	819	1,003	1,548	1,378	718	668
Common Eqty.	3,016	2,333	2,220	2,568	2,608	2,406	2,907	3,024	3,223	3,020
Total Cap.	4,967	3,768	3,681	4,358	3,994	3,977	5,135	5,077	4,694	4,339
Cap. Exp.	1,245	554	589	882	553	315	806	1,083	656	588
Cash Flow	857	601	93.0	492	540	446	486	487	408	314
Curr. Ratio	1.3	1.2	0.8	1.0	0.9	1.1	0.8	1.1	0.8	1.3
% LT Debt of Cap.	35.2	35.8	36.7	30.0	20.5	25.2	30.1	27.1	15.3	15.4
% Ret. on Assets	6.3	6.0	NM	3.4	5.7	3.6	3.2	3.4	2.5	NA
% Ret. on Equity	11.9	11.2	NM	6.0	10.1	7.2	6.8	6.8	4.8	NA

Data as orig. reptd.; bef. results of disc opers. and/or spec. items. Per share data adj. for stk. divs. as of ex-div. date. Bold denotes diluted EPS (FASB 128). E-Estimated. NA-Not Available. NM-Not Meaningful. NR-Not Ranked.

Office—5051 Westheimer, Suite 1400, Houston, TX 77056. **Tel**—(713) 624-9500. **Website**—http://www.br-inc.com **Chrmn, Pres & CEO**—B. S. Shackouls. **EVP & CFO**—J. E. Hagale. **Secy**—W. S. Zerwas. **Investor Contact**—John A. Carrara (713 624-9548).**Dirs**—J. V. Byrne, S. P. Gilbert, L. I. Grant, J. T. LaMacchia, J. F. McDonald, K. W. Orce, D. M. Roberts, J. F. Schwarz, W. Scott Jr., B. S. Shackouls, H. L. Steward, W. E. Wall. **Transfer Agent & Registrar**—Boston EquiServe. **Incorporated**—in Delaware in 1988. **Empl**— 1,819. **S&P Analyst:** Ephraim Juskowicz

STANDARD &POOR'S
STOCK REPORTS

Cabletron Systems
417X
NYSE Symbol **CS**
In S&P 500

12-SEP-98

Industry: Computers (Networking)

Summary: CS is a leading provider of intelligent hubs, switching products and management software for Ethernet, Token Ring, FDDI and ATM networking environments.

S&P Opinion: Hold (★★★)	Recent Price • 8⅛	Yield • Nil
	52 Wk Range • 36¼-6⅝	12-Mo. P/E • NM

Quantitative Evaluations

Outlook
(1 Lowest—5 Highest)
• **5**

Fair Value
• **13¾**

Risk
• **Average**

Earn./Div. Rank
• **B+**

Technical Eval.
• **Bearish** since 10/97

Rel. Strength Rank
(1 Lowest—99 Highest)
• **30**

Insider Activity
• **NA**

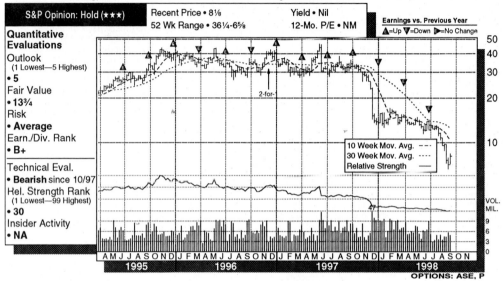

Earnings vs. Previous Year
▲=Up ▼=Down ▷=No Change

10 Week Mov. Avg. - - -
30 Week Mov. Avg. ········
Relative Strength —

2-for-1

OPTIONS: ASE, P

Overview - 25-JUN-98

We now see FY 99 (Feb.) revenues advancing 16%, well below the company's former growth rate, reflecting continued weak demand for older technology equipment (reflecting a transition from shared media hubs to switched technology), as well as weak international markets. Disappointing first quarter FY 99 results point to market share erosion and a lack of revenue visibility for the remainder of FY 99. Gross margins dipped down to the low 40% area, versus CS's former mid-50% level, due to the addition of lower-margin products from the Digital Equipment Corp. (DEC) Network Systems division acquisition, completed in February. Operating costs are expected to come down as a percentage of revenues, reflecting cost cutting and a restructuring effort. Based on these assumptions, we lowered our estimate of calendar 1999 EPS to $0.79, from $1.16.

Valuation - 25-JUN-98

The shares fell sharply following Cabletron's first quarter results of flat revenues and EPS that fell below Street expectations. Without the addition of DEC's sales, the first quarter marked Cabletron's third consecutive quarter of sequential revenue decline. Consolidation among competitors has made the landscape more competitive, and CS has acknowledged that it needs to improve its marketing message to heighten its visibility with new customers. Recent product announcements in the routing switch area, as well as a strategic alliance with Digital Equipment's networking unit, have equipped CS with new technologies that should enable it to participate in industrywide growth expected over the next several years. However, with limited earnings growth in the near term, we believe that the shares are fairly valued at 16X our calendar 1999 EPS estimate of $0.79. First quarter FY 99 EPS includes $0.97 in acquisition related charges.

Key Stock Statistics

S&P EPS Est. 1999	0.46	Tang. Bk. Value/Share	5.78
P/E on S&P Est. 1999	17.7	Beta	1.83
S&P EPS Est. 2000	0.90	Shareholders	3,500
Dividend Rate/Share	Nil	Market cap. (B)	$ 1.3
Shs. outstg. (M)	164.4	Inst. holdings	35%
Avg. daily vol. (M)	1.003		

Value of $10,000 invested 5 years ago: $ 4,836

Fiscal Year Ending Feb. 28

	1999	1998	1997	1996	1995	1994
Revenues (Million $)						
1Q	365.8	362.7	323.5	240.8	180.7	131.5
2Q	—	371.3	340.9	257.3	194.0	141.9
3Q	—	331.8	361.6	275.5	210.0	156.5
4Q	—	311.5	380.5	296.2	226.0	168.2
Yr.	—	1,377	1,407	1,070	810.7	598.1
Earnings Per Share ($)						
1Q	-0.93	0.38	0.37	0.34	0.26	0.19
2Q	—	0.37	0.24	0.37	0.27	0.20
3Q	—	0.13	0.44	0.39	0.29	0.22
4Q	—	-1.67	0.38	0.05	0.32	0.24
Yr.	—	-0.81	1.43	1.14	1.14	0.84

Next earnings report expected: late September

Dividend Data

The company has never paid a cash dividend. A 2.5-for-1 stock split was effected in 1994.

A Division of The McGraw-Hill Companies

Business Summary - 25-JUN-98

Cabletron Systems manufactures hardware and software connectivity solutions for local and wide area networks (LANs and WANs). It derives the majority of its sales from intelligent hubs (MMAC), while software is about 5% of the total. In recent years, the company has posted disappointing results due to heavy pricing pressure and its concentration of older shared media products in its sales, which are rapidly being replaced by switched technology in the networking industry.

CS has been criticized as being slow to adjust to new technologies. Recently, the impact from a sharp falloff in demand for older technology shared media hubs has been exacerbated by production delays for the company's new high-end switches, and by weak international markets.

CS has a networking approach built around its strategy, called Synthesis. This is a blueprint for moving end-users from traditional router-based internetworks to switch-based virtual networks. Synthesis uses CS's hub and management technologies with emerging switching technologies. A key component of Synthesis is the company's MMAC-Plus, an intelligent switching hub that, among other things, provides high-speed switching capabilities for shared-access, packet-based LANs. This product is complemented by CS's Multi Media Access

Center (MMAC), an intelligent hub that allows the integration of multiple network standards such as Ethernet, Token Ring and FDDI. These products are managed by SPECTRUM, a network software product that is regarded as one of the premier network management programs.

In February 1998, CS announced a strategic agreement with Digital Equipment, under which it bought Digital's networking product unit and established reseller and services contracts between the two. The unit operates separately from CS, and serves both CS and Digital customers. Digital provides services for its products and CS products in many geographies. CS has made several other acquisitions to extend its networking technologies. In 1997, it acquired OASys, a developer of management software for telecommunications devices and connections used in fiber-optic networks.

In March 1998 Cabletron acquired Yago Systems, Inc.,aprivately held manufacturer of wire speed routing and layer-4 switching products and solutions. Under the terms of the merger agreement, Cabletron issued 6.1 million shares of Cabletron common stock to the shareholders of Yago in exchange for all of the outstanding shares of stock of Yago. Yago has already had a positive impact on the performance of Cabletron's new high-end SmartSwitch Router.

Per Share Data ($)

(Year Ended Feb. 28)	1998	1997	1996	1995	1994	1993	1992	1991	1990	1989
Tangible Bk. Val.	6.02	6.93	2.65	4.11	2.97	2.04	1.45	1.01	0.51	0.15
Cash Flow	-0.39	1.75	1.36	1.31	0.96	0.68	0.47	0.30	0.19	0.10
Earnings	-0.81	1.43	1.15	1.14	0.84	0.59	0.42	0.27	0.17	0.10
Dividends	Nil	Nil	Nil	Nil	Nil	Nil	Nil	Nil	Nil	Nil
Payout Ratio	Nil	Nil	Nil	Nil	Nil	Nil	Nil	Nil	Nil	Nil
Cal. Yrs.	1997	1996	1995	1994	1993	1992	1991	1990	1989	1988
Prices - High	46½	43⅝	43⅞	26½	23¾	17	11	5⅞	3⅜	NA
- Low	13¼	26½	18¾	16½	14⅞	8⅜	5⅛	1⅜	1⅞	NA
P/E Ratio - High	NM	30	38	23	28	29	27	22	19	NA
- Low	NM	19	16	15	18	14	12	5	11	NA

Income Statement Analysis (Million $)

	1998	1997	1996	1995	1994	1993	1992	1991	1990	1989
Revs.	1,377	1,407	1,070	811	598	418	291	181	105	55.0
Oper. Inc.	244	433	345	265	194	137	95.0	59.3	36.0	19.8
Depr.	65.3	49.7	32.1	26.4	16.9	11.7	7.0	3.6	1.5	0.6
Int. Exp.	Nil	Nil	Nil	Nil	Nil	Nil	Nil	0.0	0.4	0.1
Pretax Inc.	-220	340	245	248	183	130	91.8	57.3	33.0	19.1
Eff. Tax Rate	NM	35%	33%	35%	35%	36%	37%	37%	32%	39%
Net Inc.	-126	222	164	162	119	83.5	58.0	35.9	22.5	11.8

Balance Sheet & Other Fin. Data (Million $)

	1998	1997	1996	1995	1994	1993	1992	1991	1990	1989
Cash	207	215	254	245	164	154	90.9	60.5	15.8	2.3
Curr. Assets	1,034	891	624	471	326	285	193	129	73.0	35.0
Total Assets	1,606	1,307	951	690	499	343	236	154	87.0	40.0
Curr. Liab.	473	214	164	96.3	70.7	51.3	30.7	13.5	19.7	22.0
LT Debt	133	Nil	Nil	Nil	Nil	Nil	Nil	Nil	Nil	0.1
Common Eqty.	989	1,081	778	588	424	289	204	140	67.0	18.0
Total Cap.	1,134	1,092	787	594	428	292	206	140	68.0	18.0
Cap. Exp.	74.2	NA	65.0	63.1	39.4	28.3	25.5	14.5	10.8	4.9
Cash Flow	-61.8	272	196	188	136	95.2	65.1	39.5	24.0	12.4
Curr. Ratio	2.2	4.2	3.8	4.9	4.6	5.5	6.3	9.5	3.7	1.6
% LT Debt of Cap.	11.7	Nil	Nil	Nil	Nil	Nil	Nil	Nil	Nil	0.5
% Net Inc.of Revs.	NM	15.8	15.4	20.0	19.9	20.0	20.0	19.9	21.5	21.5
% Ret. on Assets	NM	19.7	20.0	27.2	28.2	28.7	29.7	29.2	34.5	45.3
% Ret. on Equity	NM	23.9	24.1	32.0	33.3	33.8	33.6	34.0	51.8	113.8

Data as orig. reptd.; bef. results of disc. opers. and/or spec. items. Per share data adj. for stk. divs. as of ex-div. date. Bold denotes diluted EPS (FASB 128). E-Estimated. NA-Not Available. NM-Not Meaningful. NR-Not Ranked.

Office—35 Industrial Way, Rochester, NH 03867-0505. **Tel**—(603) 332-9400. **Website**—http://www.cabletron.com **Chrmn, Pres, CEO & Treas**—C. R. Benson. **Pres, Operations**—J. d'Auguste. **EVP & CFO**—D. J. Kirkpatrick. **Secy**—M. D. Myerow. **Investor Contact**—Jim Caldwell (603-337-4225). **Dirs**—C. R. Benson, P. R. Duncan, D. F. McGuinness, M. D. Myerow, D. B. Reed. **Transfer Agent & Registrar**—State Street Bank & Trust Co., Boston. **Incorporated**—in Delaware in 1988. **Empl**— 6,887. **S&P Analyst:** Aydin Tuncer

12-SEP-98

Industry:
Foods

Summary: Campbell Soup is a major producer of branded soups and other grocery food products. The Dorrance family controls more than 50% of the common stock.

S&P Opinion: Accumulate (★★★★)	Recent Price • 50⅝	Yield • 1.7%
	52 Wk Range • 62⅞-46	12-Mo. P/E • 34.5

Quantitative Evaluations

Outlook
(1 Lowest—5 Highest)
• **2+**

Fair Value
• **48⅝**

Risk
• **Low**

Earn./Div. Rank
• **A-**

Technical Eval.
• **Bearish** since 5/97

Rel. Strength Rank
(1 Lowest—99 Highest)
• **80**

Insider Activity
• **NA**

Earnings vs. Previous Year
▲=Up ▼=Down ▶=No Change

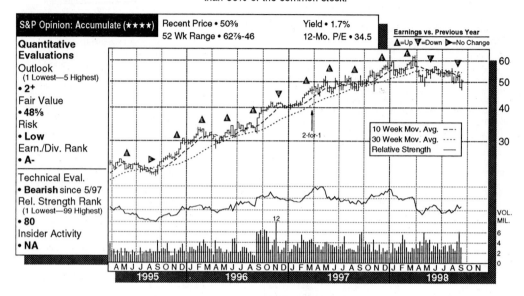

10 Week Mov. Avg. -- -
30 Week Mov. Avg. ·······
Relative Strength ——

2-for-1

Overview - 21-MAY-98

Net sales from current operations are projected to rise at a middle single-digit rate in FY 98 (Jul.), as an even mix of unit volume growth, price increases, and contributions from acquisitions more than offset the impact of recent business divestments and unfavorable currency exchange. The company's relatively high operating profitability is expected to be further enhanced by the increased volumes, improvements in product mix and productivity gains derived from ongoing cost reduction actions. The absence of profits stemming from the March 1998 spin-off of certain "non-core" businesses will likely be more than offset by the proceeds (approximately $500 million) paid from the new entity to Campbell. We expect these proceeds to be used initially for a combination of small international acquisitions and share repurchases.

Valuation - 21-MAY-98

We recently lowered the shares from buy to accumulate, reflecting lower expected growth in wet soup volume for the U.S. in FY 98. Despite this, we continue to view Campbell Soup Co. as among the premier U.S. consumer growth companies, given the company's reliable double-digit EPS gains and high relative returns on shareholders' equity. We also view CPB's move to spin off its "non-core" businesses as positive, since it should enhance margins and returns even more. Therefore, we believe that this equity warrants its current premium valuation relative to its peers and to the S&P 500, and is attractive for purchase at a recent 24.5 times our FY 99 $2.26 EPS estimate. In the near term, earnings growth should be driven by steady volume growth and aggressive cost cutting measures, which will allow for healthy EPS comparisons in FY 98 and beyond.

Key Stock Statistics

S&P EPS Est. 1998	2.00	Tang. Bk. Value/Share	NM
P/E on S&P Est. 1998	25.2	Beta	0.56
S&P EPS Est. 1999	2.26	Shareholders	49,000
Dividend Rate/Share	0.84	Market cap. (B)	$ 22.6
Shs. outstg. (M)	449.1	Inst. holdings	27%
Avg. daily vol. (M)	0.854		

Value of $10,000 invested 5 years ago: NA

Fiscal Year Ending Jul. 31

	1998	1997	1996	1995	1994	1993
Revenues (Million $)						
1Q	2,120	2,052	1,990	1,864	1,763	1,696
2Q	2,342	2,317	2,217	2,040	1,894	1,789
3Q	1,572	1,870	1,831	1,744	1,568	1,632
4Q	1,299	1,725	1,640	1,630	1,465	1,470
Yr.	6,696	7,964	7,678	7,278	6,690	6,586
Earnings Per Share ($)						
1Q	0.58	0.17	0.44	0.40	0.33	0.31
2Q	**0.67**	0.58	0.52	0.47	0.41	-0.23
3Q	**-0.08**	0.34	0.29	0.26	0.23	0.21
4Q	**0.40**	0.42	0.36	0.28	0.28	0.24
Yr.	**1.50**	1.51	1.61	1.40	1.25	0.51

Next earnings report expected: mid November

Dividend Data (Dividends have been paid since 1902.)

Amount ($)	Date Decl.	Ex-Div. Date	Stock of Record	Payment Date
0.210	Nov. 19	Dec. 31	Jan. 05	Jan. 30 '98
Stk.	Feb. 26	Mar. 31	Mar. 09	Mar. 30 '98
0.210	Mar. 26	Apr. 07	Apr. 10	May. 04 '98
0.210	Jun. 25	Jul. 08	Jul. 10	Aug. 03 '98

A Division of The McGraw·Hill Companies

STANDARD
&POOR'S
STOCK REPORTS

Campbell Soup Company

428

12-SEP-98

Business Summary - 21-MAY-98

Probably known best for its ubiquitous red and white soup cans (elevated to icon status by Andy Warhol), Campbell Soup Company is a major force in the U.S. packaged foods industry. The company, which traces its origins in the food business as far back as 1869, manufactures and markets a wide array of branded, prepared convenience food products worldwide. Campbell's operations outside the U.S. accounted for 32% of net sales and 14% of pretax earnings (excluding special charges) in FY 97 (Jul.), mostly in Europe (15% and 4%) and Australia (7% and 4%). Contributions to sales and operating profits by division in FY 97 were:

	Sales	Profits
Soup & Sauces	52%	76%
Biscuit & Confectionery	19%	12%
Foodservice	6%	5%
Other	23%	7%

In September 1997, Campbell announced a plan to spin off numerous "non-core" businesses with revenues of $1.4 billion--including its Swanson frozen foods and Vlasic pickles units. The spinoff (which was completed at the end of March 1998) is consistent with the company's recent initiatives to improve its financial profile. These initiatives have also involved aggressive cost reduction actions, the sale of non-strategic businesses, and share repurchases.

Campbell's major U.S. products include both condensed and ready-to-serve soups (Campbell's, Home Cookin', Chunky, Healthy Request); convenience meals (Hungry Man); beans (Homestyle Pork and Beans); juices (Campbell's Tomato, V8); canned spaghetti and gravies (Franco-American); spaghetti sauce (Prego); and Mexican sauces (Pace). Foodservice operations serve the away-from-home eating market.

The company's Bakery and Confectionery division products include Pepperidge Farm, Inc. in the U.S., a producer of bread, cakes and related products; and Arnotts Biscuits Ltd. of Australia, a maker of biscuit and bakery products. CPB is currenlty negotiating to sell its Belgium-based Biscuits Delacre, a maker of biscuit and chocolate products. Godiva Chocolatier (worldwide) and Lamy-Lutti (Europe) serve the candy market.

International businesses consist of soup, grocery and frozen foods units in Canada, Mexico, Argentina, Europe, Australia and Asia. Major brands include Fray Bentos, Betis, Pleybin, Freshbake and Groko.

Per Share Data ($)

(Year Ended Jul. 31)	1998	1997	1996	1995	1994	1993	1992	1991	1990	1989
Tangible Bk. Val.	NA	NM	1.89	1.51	2.83	2.20	3.15	2.67	2.53	2.53
Cash Flow	NA	2.21	2.27	1.99	1.80	0.95	1.37	1.18	0.36	0.36
Earnings	1.50	1.51	1.61	1.40	1.25	0.51	0.97	0.79	0.01	0.03
Dividends	0.82	0.75	0.67	0.60	0.55	0.46	0.35	0.28	0.24	0.23
Payout Ratio	55%	50%	42%	43%	43%	90%	36%	35%	879%	890%
Prices - High	62⁷/₈	59³/₈	42¹/₈	30⁵/₈	23	22³/₄	22⁵/₈	22	15¹/₂	15¹/₈
- Low	48¹/₈	39³/₈	28	20¹/₂	17¹/₈	17⁵/₈	15³/₄	13¹/₂	11	7⁵/₈
P/E Ratio - High	42	39	26	22	18	44	23	28	NM	NM
- Low	32	26	17	15	14	35	16	17	NM	NM

Income Statement Analysis (Million $)

	1998	1997	1996	1995	1994	1993	1992	1991	1990	1989
Revs.	NM	7,964	7,678	7,278	6,690	6,586	6,263	6,204	6,206	5,672
Oper. Inc.	NA	1,950	1,715	1,504	1,323	1,178	1,093	970	790	711
Depr.	NA	382	326	294	273	223	200	195	184	176
Int. Exp.	NA	167	137	123	85.0	96.0	120	137	122	98.0
Pretax Inc.	NA	1,114	1,197	1,042	963	529	799	675	185	112
Eff. Tax Rate	NA	35%	33%	33%	36%	50%	39%	39%	95%	84%
Net Inc.	NA	713	802	698	630	257	491	402	4.0	13.0

Balance Sheet & Other Fin. Data (Million $)

	1998	1997	1996	1995	1994	1993	1992	1991	1990	1989
Cash	NA	26.0	34.0	53.0	96.0	70.0	118	192	103	147
Curr. Assets	NA	1,583	1,618	1,581	1,601	1,686	1,502	1,519	1,666	1,602
Total Assets	NA	6,459	6,632	6,315	4,992	4,898	4,354	4,149	4,116	3,932
Curr. Liab.	NA	2,981	2,229	2,164	1,665	1,851	1,300	1,278	1,298	1,232
LT Debt	NA	1,153	744	857	560	462	693	773	806	629
Common Eqty.	NA	1,420	2,742	2,468	1,989	1,704	2,028	1,793	1,692	1,778
Total Cap.	NA	2,656	4,028	3,865	2,951	2,435	3,032	2,848	2,789	2,680
Cap. Exp.	NA	331	416	391	421	644	374	361	422	284
Cash Flow	NA	1,095	1,128	992	903	480	691	596	189	189
Curr. Ratio	NA	0.5	0.7	0.7	1.0	0.9	1.2	1.2	1.3	1.3
% LT Debt of Cap.	NA	43.4	18.5	22.2	19.0	19.0	22.9	27.1	28.9	23.5
% Net Inc.of Revs.	NA	9.0	10.5	9.6	9.4	3.9	7.8	6.5	0.1	0.2
% Ret. on Assets	NA	10.9	12.4	11.1	12.7	5.6	11.6	9.8	0.1	0.3
% Ret. on Equity	NA	34.3	30.8	31.3	34.1	13.8	25.8	23.2	0.3	0.7

Data as orig. reptd.; bef. results of disc. opers. and/or spec. items. Per share data adj. for stk. divs. as of ex-div. date. Bold denotes diluted EPS (FASB 128). E-Estimated. NA-Not Available. NM-Not Meaningful. NR-Not Ranked.

Office—Campbell Place, Camden, NJ 08103-1799. **Tel**—(609) 342-4800. **Website**—http://www.campbellsoups.com **Chrmn**—D. W. Johnson. **Pres & CEO**—D. Morrison. **CFO & Treas**—B. L. Anderson. **Secy**—J. J. Furey. **Investor Contact**—Leonard F. Griehs. **Dirs**—A. A. App, E. M. Carpenter, B. Dorrance, T. W. Field Jr., K. B. Foster, H. Golub, D. W. Johnson, D. K. P. Li, P. E. Lippincott, M. A. Malone, C. H. Mott, G. M. Sherman, D. M. Stewart, G. Strawbridge Jr., C. C. Weber. **Transfer Agent & Registrar**—First Chicago Trust Co. of New York, Jersey City, NJ. **Incorporated**—in New Jersey in 1922. **Empl**—37,041. **S&P Analyst:** Richard Joy

Capital One Financial   443

NYSE Symbol **COF**

In S&P 500

12-SEP-98

Industry:
Consumer Finance

Summary: Capital One is one of the largest issuers of Visa and MasterCard credit cards, with 11.7 million cardholders and $14.2 billion in managed loans outstanding at December 31, 1997.

S&P Opinion: Accumulate (★★★★)	Recent Price • 91½	Yield • 0.3%
	52 Wk Range • 127⅞-37¼	12-Mo. P/E • 26.1

Quantitative Evaluations

Outlook
(1 Lowest—5 Highest)
• **3**

Fair Value
• **91⅝**

Risk
• **Average**

Earn./Div. Rank
• **NR**

Technical Eval.
• **Bullish** since 8/97

Rel. Strength Rank
(1 Lowest—99 Highest)
• **50**

Insider Activity
• **Neutral**

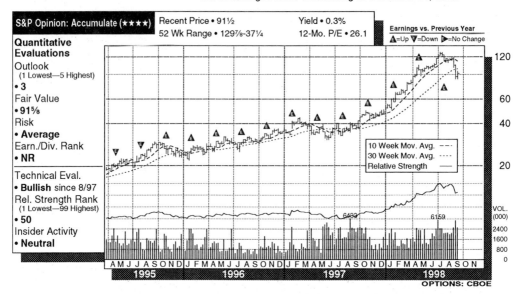

Earnings vs. Previous Year
▲=Up ▼=Down ▶=No Change

10 Week Mov. Avg. ----
30 Week Mov. Avg. ····
Relative Strength —

VOL. (000)

OPTIONS: CBOE

Overview - 29-JUL-98

Favorable industry dynamics, together with the continued success of the company's information-based strategy, which is designed to differentiate among customers and match client characteristics with product offerings, should continue to be the primary earnings drivers. Both account and managed loan growth exceeded expectations in 1998's first half, but a more moderate pace is likely in the second half as a newer generation of products results in lower initial loan balances. Margin contraction from 1998's first quarter reflects lower late fees following a drop in delinquencies, although this has put less pressure on the loss provision. The drop in delinquencies reflects a more cautious approach to underwriting and a somewhat better consumer credit quality environment. The introduction of certain non-credit card lending products and reselling of telecommunications services, as well as expansion of credit card operations into the U.K. and Canada, could provide additional growth opportunities. In line with newer generation product introductions, marketing expenses will increase substantially in 1998.

Valuation - 29-JUL-98

The shares more than doubled in the first half of 1998, reflecting a return to normal earnings growth rates and renewed investor confidence in the company after an earnings shortfall in 1997's first half. Investors have also looked favorably at a management stock option program that bases executive compensation on stock price performance in lieu of salaries. The shares are currently trading at about 25 times expected 1999 earnings of $4.65. While we can not argue for further multiple expansion, the shares are expected to outperform based on an earnings growth rate well in excess of the broader market.

Key Stock Statistics

S&P EPS Est. 1998	3.90	Tang. Bk. Value/Share	16.18
P/E on S&P Est. 1998	23.5	Beta	NA
S&P EPS Est. 1999	4.65	Shareholders	NA
Dividend Rate/Share	0.32	Market cap. (B)	$ 6.0
Shs. outstg. (M)	66.1	Inst. holdings	65%
Avg. daily vol. (M)	0.801		

Value of $10,000 invested 5 years ago: NA

Fiscal Year Ending Dec. 31

	1998	1997	1996	1995	1994	1993
Revenues (Million $)						
1Q	573.9	411.6	304.3	219.2	148.2	—
2Q	600.4	395.9	308.4	308.4	165.5	—
3Q	—	459.9	394.9	265.8	166.4	—
4Q	—	519.6	416.3	286.2	175.4	—
Yr.	—	1,787	1,424	1,010	655.6	469.6
Earnings Per Share ($)						
1Q	**0.96**	0.63	0.57	0.38	0.53	--
2Q	**0.96**	0.58	0.57	0.45	0.52	--
3Q	**E0.98**	0.73	0.58	0.51	-0.02	--
4Q	**E1.00**	0.86	0.60	0.57	0.40	--
Yr.	**E3.90**	2.80	2.32	1.90	1.44	1.37

Next earnings report expected: mid October

Dividend Data (Dividends have been paid since 1995.)

Amount ($)	Date Decl.	Ex-Div. Date	Stock of Record	Payment Date
0.080	Oct. 23	Oct. 31	Nov. 04	Nov. 19 '97
0.080	Jan. 22	Feb. 05	Feb. 09	Feb. 20 '98
0.080	Apr. 23	May. 05	May. 07	May. 21 '98
0.080	Jul. 30	Aug. 11	Aug. 13	Aug. 21 '98

A Division of The **McGraw·Hill** Companies

Capital One Financial Corporation

Business Summary - 29-JUL-98

Capital One Financial, among the largest issuers of Visa and MasterCard credit cards in the U.S. with 8.6 million credit card customers and $14.2 billion in managed loans outstanding as of 1997 year end, attributes its rapid growth rate over the past few years to favorable industry dynamics and the success of its information-based strategy (IBS). Adopted by COF in 1988, IBS is designed to allow Capital One to differentiate among customers and match client characteristics with product offerings. IBS uses vast amounts of data collected on actual and prospective customers to test product ideas before they are launched, allowing the company to ensure a high success rate of individual products. Prior to its November 1994 initial public offering, the company was a wholly owned subsidiary of Signet Banking Corp., which was acquired by First Union Corp. in late 1997.

The company prides itself on its ability to create innovative and profitable products. Capital One was a pioneer of the balance transfer product, which allows consumers to move balances from credit cards with high interest rates to those with low rates. More recently it has begun to offer specialty credit card products, such as secured cards, college student cards and affinity cards, to what it believes are underserved markets in the industry.

At the end of 1997, the company had a total managed consumer loan portfolio of $14.2 billion, (including $9.4 billion of securitized loans), up from $12.8 billion ($8.5 billion) a year earlier. The portfolio consisted of 62% fixed rate and 38% variable interest rate loans at the end of 1997.

At December 31, 1997, the allowance for loan losses, which is set aside for possible loan defaults, stood at $183.0 million (3.76% of total loans), versus $118.5 million (2.73%) a year earlier. Net charge-offs, or the amount of loans written off as uncollectible, in 1997 amounted to $198.2 million (4.83% of average loans), up from $132.6 million (3.63%) in 1996. Noncurrent loans, those on which interest payments are not being received, were $268.1 million (5.51% of total loans) at 1997 year-end, compared with $264.3 million (6.08%) at the end of 1996.

The average yield on interest earning assets was 12.48% in 1997 (13.766% in 1996), while the average rate paid on interest bearing liabilities was 6.31% (6.32%), for a net spread of 6.17% (7.44%).

In July 1998, the company signed an agreement to acquire Summit Acceptance Corp., a subprime automobile finance lender, for $55 million in COF common stock. Completion of the transaction is expected in the third quarter of 1998, with a neutral impact on 1998 earnings.

Per Share Data ($)

(Year Ended Dec. 31)	1997	1996	1995	1994	1993	1992	1991	1990	1989	1988
Tangible Bk. Val.	13.66	11.16	9.06	7.18	6.96	NA	NA	NA	NA	NA
Earnings	2.80	2.30	1.90	1.44	1.37	NA	NA	NA	NA	NA
Dividends	0.32	0.32	0.24	Nil	NA	NA	NA	NA	NA	NA
Payout Ratio	11%	14%	13%	Nil	NA	NA	NA	NA	NA	NA
Prices - High	54¼	36⅞	29⅝	16⅝	NA	NA	NA	NA	NA	NA
- Low	30½	21¾	15⅜	13⅞	NA	NA	NA	NA	NA	NA
P/E Ratio - High	19	16	16	12	NA	NA	NA	NA	NA	NA
- Low	11	9	8	10	NA	NA	NA	NA	NA	NA

Income Statement Analysis (Million $)

	1997	1996	1995	1994	1993	1992	1991	1990	1989	1988
Net Int. Inc.	383	365	208	165	166	NA	NA	NA	NA	NA
Tax Equiv. Adj.	NA	NA	NA	NA	NA	NA	NA	NA	NA	NA
Non Int. Inc.	1,069	763	553	397	197	NA	NA	NA	NA	NA
Loan Loss Prov.	263	167	65.9	30.7	34.0	NA	NA	NA	NA	NA
Non Int. Exp.	884	713	497	384	189	NA	NA	NA	NA	NA
Exp./Op. Revs.	61%	63%	65%	68%	52%	NA	NA	NA	NA	NA
Pretax Inc.	305	248	198	147	140	NA	NA	NA	NA	NA
Eff. Tax Rate	38%	38%	36%	35%	35%	NA	NA	NA	NA	NA
Net Inc.	189	155	129	95.3	90.4	NA	NA	NA	NA	NA
% Net Int. Marg.	8.86	8.16	6.28	6.90	NA	NA	NA	NA	NA	NA

Balance Sheet & Other Fin. Data (Million $)

	1997	1996	1995	1994	1993	1992	1991	1990	1989	1988
Earning Assets:										
Money Mkt	174	450	465	300	Nil	Nil	Nil	Nil	Nil	Nil
Inv. Securities	1,243	895	769	113	785	NA	NA	NA	NA	NA
Earn.Ass. Tot. Loans	4,862	4,225	2,450	2,160	1,790	NA	NA	NA	NA	NA
Total Assets	7,078	6,467	4,759	3,092	3,052	NA	NA	NA	NA	NA
Demand Deposits	796	531	710	687	Nil	Nil	Nil	Nil	Nil	Nil
Time Deposits	1,314	943	696	452	Nil	Nil	Nil	Nil	Nil	Nil
LT Debt	3,633	3,994	2,592	1,376	Nil	Nil	Nil	Nil	Nil	Nil
Common Eqty.	893	740	599	475	460	NA	NA	NA	NA	NA
% Ret. on Assets	2.8	2.8	2.9	3.6	NA	NA	NA	NA	NA	NA
% Ret. on Equity	23.2	22.9	23.3	39.8	NA	NA	NA	NA	NA	NA
% Loan Loss Resv.	3.8	2.7	2.9	3.1	3.5	NA	NA	NA	NA	NA
% Loans/Deposits	370.1	NM	NM	NM	NM	NM	NM	NM	NM	NM
% Loans/Assets	68.0	77.4	64.3	69.8	58.7	NA	NA	NA	NA	NA
% Equity to Assets	12.1	15.7	12.6	15.4	15.1	NA	NA	NA	NA	NA

Data as orig. reptd.; bef. results of disc opers. and/or spec. items. Per share data adj. for stk. divs. as of ex-div. date. Bold denotes diluted EPS (FASB 128). E-Estimated. NA-Not Available. NM-Not Meaningful. NR-Not Ranked.

Office—2980 Fairview Park Dr., Falls Church, VA 22042. **Tel**—(703) 205-1000. **Website**—http://oapitalone.com **Chrmn & CEO**—R. D. Fairbank.**Pres & COO**—N. W. Morris. **SVP & CFO**—J. M. Zinn. **SVP & Secy**—J. G. Finneran Jr. **VP & Investor Contact**—Paul Paquin (703-205-1039). **Dirs**—W. R. Dietz, R. D. Fairbank, J. A. Flick, Jr., P. W. Gross, J. V. Kimsey, N. W. Morris, S. I. Westreich. **Transfer Agent & Registrar**—First Chicago Trust Co. of New York, Jersey City, NJ. **Incorporated**—in Delaware in 1994. **Empl**—5,913. **S&P Analyst:** Stephen R. Biggar

STANDARD &POOR'S
STOCK REPORTS

Cardinal Health

445C

NYSE Symbol **CAH**

In S&P 500

15-SEP-98

Industry:
Distributors (Food & Health)

Summary: Cardinal Health is a wholesale distributor of pharmaceuticals, medical/surgical supplies and related health products.

S&P Opinion: Accumulate (★★★★)	Recent Price • 85¾	Yield • 0.2%
	52 Wk Range • 102½-66¾	12-Mo. P/E • 39.5

Quantitative Evaluations

Outlook
(1 Lowest—5 Highest)
• **4-**

Fair Value
• **102**

Risk
• **Low**

Earn./Div. Rank
• **A-**

Technical Eval.
• **Bullish** since 10/95

Rel. Strength Rank
(1 Lowest—99 Highest)
• **70**

Insider Activity
• **NA**

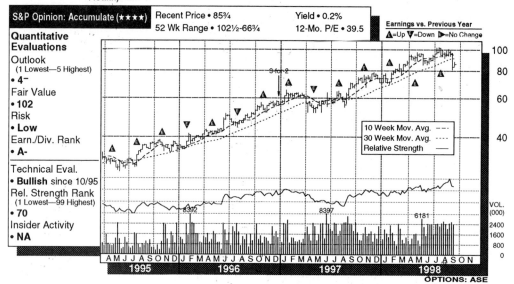

Earnings vs. Previous Year
▲=Up ▼=Down ▶=No Change

10 Week Mov. Avg. - - -
30 Week Mov. Avg. · · · ·
Relative Strength ———

OPTIONS: ASE

Overview - 15-SEP-98

Revenues in FY 99 (Jun.) should approximate $18.0 billion (including bulk deliveries to customer warehouses), reflecting strong internal growth within the core drug distribution business, along with the inclusion of R.P. Scherer (annual revenues of $700 million), one of the leading developers of drug delivery systems and the world's largest manufacturer of soft gelatin (softgel) capsules. The services segment should again provide significant top line growth, on improved performance at Medicine Shoppe International, Pyxis and Owen Healthcare. The planned acquisition of Bergen Brunswig, a deal that was opposed by the FTC, was terminated in early August 1998. However, CAH is likely to pursue smaller acquisitions in order to capture market share and gain economies of scale in this relatively low margin industry. Excluding charges, we see FY 99 and FY 00 EPS of $3.10 and $3.70, respectively.

Valuation - 15-SEP-98

The shares have traded down following the failed merger with Bergen Brunswig, a deal that could have provided significant operating margin expansion opportunities, along with general stock market weakness. Trading at a P/E multiple exceeding both its peer group average and the S&P 500, CAH was vulnerable to any downturn in the market. However, the stock now offers investors an opportunity to purchase one of the premier companies in a sector that offers little foreign exposure, favorable demographics (increased pharmaceutical usage by an aging U.S. population) and defensive characteristics amid a possible domestic economic slowdown. We would recommend that investors add to holdings given the company's reliable earnings prospects and note that CAH was recently trading at only 0.5 times projected FY 99 sales, well below the S&P 500 average.

Key Stock Statistics

S&P EPS Est. 1999	3.10	Tang. Bk. Value/Share	12.91
P/E on S&P Est. 1999	27.7	Beta	0.56
S&P EPS Est. 2000	3.70	Shareholders	2,800
Dividend Rate/Share	0.15	Market cap. (B)	$ 11.8
Shs. outstg. (M)	133.3	Inst. holdings	62%
Avg. daily vol. (M)	0.617		

Value of $10,000 invested 5 years ago: $ 53,764

Fiscal Year Ending Jun. 30

	1998	1997	1996	1995	1994	1993
Revenues (Million $)						
1Q	2,870	2,535	2,097	1,818	1,291	482.0
2Q	3,131	2,816	2,189	1,986	1,398	512.0
3Q	3,381	2,726	2,256	1,988	1,511	499.0
4Q	4,384	2,791	2,320	2,014	1,590	550.0
Yr.	15,918	10,968	8,862	7,806	5,790	--
Earnings Per Share ($)						
1Q	0.49	0.39	0.33	0.26	0.20	0.25
2Q	**0.60**	0.38	0.27	0.33	0.25	0.23
3Q	**0.50**	0.33	0.47	0.41	-0.15	0.29
4Q	**0.58**	0.56	0.08	0.35	0.28	0.22
Yr.	**2.17**	1.66	1.15	1.34	0.57	--

Next earnings report expected: mid October

Dividend Data (Dividends have been paid since 1983.)

Amount ($)	Date Decl.	Ex-Div. Date	Stock of Record	Payment Date
0.025	Nov. 05	Dec. 29	Jan. 01	Jan. 15 '98
0.030	Feb. 11	Mar. 30	Apr. 01	Apr. 15 '98
0.030	May. 13	Jun. 29	Jul. 01	Jul. 15 '98
0.038	Aug. 14	Sep. 29	Oct. 01	Oct. 15 '98

STANDARD
&POOR'S
STOCK REPORTS

Cardinal Health, Inc.

445C
15-SEP-98

Business Summary - 15-SEP-98

Cardinal Health (CAH) is a leading full-service whole-saler distributing a broad line of pharmaceuticals and related health care products to independent and chain drugstores, hospitals, alternate care centers and pharmacy departments of supermarkets and merchandisers throughout the continental U.S. It also provides innovative cost-effective pharmaceutical services that improve the medication use process to a broad base of customers nationwide.

Cardinal distributes a broad line of pharmaceuticals, surgical and hospital supplies, therapeutic plasma and other specialty pharmaceutical products, health and beauty care products, and other items typically sold by hospitals, retail drug stores and other health care providers. As a pharmaceutical wholesaler, Cardinal competes directly with numerous other national and regional wholesalers, direct selling manufacturers, self-warehousing chains, mail-order houses and specialty distributors on the basis of price, breadth of product lines, marketing programs and support services.

In August 1998, CAH acquired R.P. Scherer, a developer and manufacturer of drug delivery systems, including soft gelatin capsules (softgels), that are used to improve the efficacy of drugs by regulating the dosage so as to ease administration, increase absorption, enhance bioavailability and control the time and place of release. Scherer generates about 34% of its sales in the U.S.

Cardinal complements its distribution activities (91% of FY 98 operating revenues) by offering value-added support services (9%) to assist customers and suppliers in maintaining and improving their sales volumes. Services include computerized order entry and order confirmation systems, customized invoicing, generic sourcing programs, product movement and management reports, consultation on store operation and merchandising, and customer training. A software system with customized databases is also available.

The Pyxis Corp. subsidiary develops, manufactures, leases, sells and services point-of-use systems that automate the distribution, management and control of medications and supplies in hospitals and alternate care sites. The PCI Services unit offers integrated drug packaging, while the Medicine Shoppe International division is the largest U.S. franchisor of independent retail pharmacies. Through Allied Pharmacy Services and Owen Healthcare, CAH provides hospitals with pharmacy management and information services.

Other subsidiaries include MediQual Systems, a supplier of clinical data management systems and services to hospitals; and Comprehensive Reimbursement Consultants (acquired in May 1998), a provider of reimbursement consulting services to pharmaceutical, biotechnology and medical products companies.

Per Share Data ($)

(Year Ended Jun. 30)	1998	1997	1996	1995	1994	1993	1992	1991	1990	1989
Tangible Bk. Val.	13.56	11.12	8.74	8.71	5.19	7.13	5.55	4.91	3.62	2.69
Cash Flow	2.79	2.13	1.49	1.67	0.86	1.15	0.87	0.71	0.69	0.69
Earnings	2.17	1.66	1.15	1.34	0.57	0.95	0.71	0.56	0.44	0.41
Dividends	0.11	0.10	0.08	0.08	0.07	0.05	0.04	0.03	0.03	0.02
Payout Ratio	5%	6%	7%	6%	11%	5%	6%	7%	6%	5%
Prices - High	102$\frac{1}{2}$	78$\frac{3}{4}$	58$\frac{1}{2}$	38$\frac{3}{4}$	32$\frac{1}{8}$	18$\frac{1}{8}$	20$\frac{5}{8}$	12$\frac{3}{8}$	8$\frac{3}{8}$	5
- Low	69$\frac{5}{8}$	51$\frac{1}{2}$	35	27$\frac{5}{8}$	22$\frac{1}{8}$	12$\frac{5}{8}$	10$\frac{5}{8}$	6$\frac{3}{4}$	4$\frac{3}{8}$	2$\frac{5}{8}$
P/E Ratio - High	47	47	51	29	50	20	29	22	19	12
- Low	32	31	30	21	39	14	15	12	10	6

Income Statement Analysis (Million $)

	1998	1997	1996	1995	1994	1993	1992	1991	1990	1989
Revs.	15,918	10,968	8,862	7,806	5,790	1,967	1,648	1,184	874	700
Oper. Inc.	538	443	315	185	139	66.3	53.0	39.3	27.9	21.1
Depr.	64.3	51.3	32.0	21.0	17.0	7.2	5.7	4.6	3.1	2.8
Int. Exp.	23.0	28.0	23.9	19.3	18.1	13.4	11.8	10.6	5.9	6.6
Pretax Inc.	403	312	202	147	70.8	54.1	41.0	28.5	20.9	13.6
Eff. Tax Rate	39%	42%	45%	42%	50%	38%	39%	39%	39%	38%
Net Inc.	247	181	112	85.0	35.1	33.6	25.2	17.4	12.8	8.5

Balance Sheet & Other Fin. Data (Million $)

	1998	1997	1996	1995	1994	1993	1992	1991	1990	1989
Cash	305	243	288	41.0	55.0	104	4.7	78.3	11.3	9.3
Curr. Assets	3,229	2,504	2,240	1,687	1,287	579	503	385	213	199
Total Assets	3,961	3,109	2,681	1,842	1,396	656	577	446	251	233
Curr. Liab.	1,844	1,409	1,386	1,073	816	214	168	163	121	115
LT Debt	273	278	265	209	210	185	188	90.0	5.0	50.0
Common Eqty.	1,625	1,332	931	548	368	256	219	193	125	68.0
Total Cap.	1,898	1,610	1,196	757	579	442	408	283	130	118
Cap. Exp.	111	75.2	73.0	43.0	11.2	5.3	8.9	10.9	3.8	8.1
Cash Flow	311	232	144	106	50.9	40.8	30.8	22.0	15.9	11.3
Curr. Ratio	1.8	1.8	1.6	1.6	1.6	2.7	3.0	2.4	1.8	1.7
% LT Debt of Cap.	14.4	17.3	22.2	27.6	36.3	41.9	46.1	31.6	3.6	42.3
% Net Inc.of Revs.	1.6	1.7	1.3	1.1	0.6	1.7	1.5	1.5	1.5	1.2
% Ret. on Assets	7.0	6.1	4.7	5.3	NA	5.4	4.9	4.8	4.2	4.0
% Ret. on Equity	16.7	15.3	13.0	18.5	NA	14.1	12.2	10.4	11.2	13.9

Data as orig. reptd.; bef. results of disc. opers. and/or spec. items. Per share data adj. for stk. divs. as of ex-div. date. Yrs. ended Mar. 31 prior to 1994. Bk. val. incl. intangibles in 1994, 1993. Bold denotes diluted EPS (FASB 128). E-Estimated. NA-Not Available. NM-Not Meaningful. NR-Not Ranked.

Office—5555 Glendon Court, Dublin, OH 43016. **Tel**—(614) 717-5000. **Chrmn & CEO**—R. D. Walter. **Vice Chrmn**—M.G. Whitmire. **Pres & COO**—J. C. Kane. **Acting CFO**—R. J. Miller. **VP & Treas**—Stephanie A. Wagoner. **Secy**—G. H. Bennett Jr. **Investor Contact**—Debra Dendahl Hadley (614-717-7481). **Dirs**—J. F. Finn, R. L. Gerbig, J. F. Havens, R. E. Herzlinger, J. C. Kane, J. M. Losh, G. R. Manser, J. B. McCoy, J. E. Robertson, L. J. Van Fossen, R. D. Walter, M. G. Whitmire. **Transfer Agent**—Bank One, Indianapolis. **Incorporated**—in Ohio in 1971; reincorporated in 1982. **Empl**—11,200. **S&P Analyst:** Robert M. Gold

Carolina Power & Light   450

NYSE Symbol **CPL**

In S&P 500

12-SEP-98

Industry: Electric Companies

Summary: This utility supplies electric power to more than a million customers in a 30,000 sq. mi. area covering east and west North Carolina and central South Carolina.

S&P Opinion: Accumulate (★★★★)	Recent Price • 43⅜	Yield • 4.5%
	52 Wk Range • 46¼-33⅛	12-Mo. P/E • 15.6

Quantitative Evaluations

Outlook
(1 Lowest—5 Highest)
• **2**

Fair Value
• **42½**

Risk
• **Low**

Earn./Div. Rank
• **A-**

Technical Eval.
• **Bullish** since 8/98

Rel. Strength Rank
(1 Lowest—99 Highest)
• **95**

Insider Activity
• **NA**

Earnings vs. Previous Year
▲=Up ▼=Down ▶=No Change

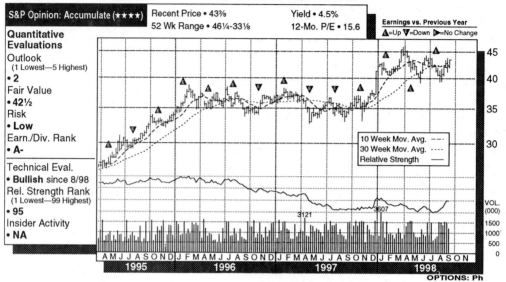

10 Week Mov. Avg. ---
30 Week Mov. Avg. ----
Relative Strength —

OPTIONS: Ph

Overview - 10-AUG-98

CPL should continue to benefit from a strong service area economy and 2% to 3% customer growth. Following an anticipated 11% increase in 1998, we expect EPS to grow an additional 6% to 7% in 1999. Earnings were flat in 1997, with milder weather cutting EPS about $0.20. Results in 1998 will continue to be limited by accelerated amortization of certain regulatory assets in both North and South Carolina, and by amortization of deferred operating and maintenance expenses related to a severe hurricane in September 1996. CPL's location facilitates the purchase and sale of power with a number of other utilities, and it should be able to supply rising demand without adding new generating facilities. Through acquisitions and the development of new businesses, CPL hopes to double its customer base and revenues by 2001.

Valuation - 10-AUG-98

We would continue to accumulate CPL stock. With the shares recently down approximately 5% year to date, the stock is attractive, at a P/E of less than 13X our 1999 EPS estimate of $3.15. When combined with a secure dividend offering a 4.8% yield, it should provide both intermediate and long-term investors with a solid total return. In 1997, the shares were up 16%, somewhat less than the 19.8% increase for the S&P Index of Electric Companies. Reflecting the impact of changing weather patterns, the shares have been volatile over the past 12 months, and were recently trading at about 13% below their period high and 21% above the low. We expect results to continue to benefit from solid economic growth in CPL's service region, and from ongoing efforts to reduce costs. We would also expect any speculation over a possible merger with another utility to provide the stock with an additional degree of support.

Key Stock Statistics

S&P EPS Est. 1998	2.95	Tang. Bk. Value/Share	18.74
P/E on S&P Est. 1998	14.7	Beta	0.40
S&P EPS Est. 1999	3.15	Shareholders	61,800
Dividend Rate/Share	1.94	Market cap. (B)	$ 6.6
Shs. outstg. (M)	151.3	Inst. holdings	36%
Avg. daily vol. (M)	0.328		

Value of $10,000 invested 5 years ago: $ 20,912

Fiscal Year Ending Dec. 31

	1998	1997	1996	1995	1994	1993
Revenues (Million $)						
1Q	752.3	716.1	783.6	728.2	744.5	707.5
2Q	736.1	666.0	686.0	682.0	687.3	674.6
3Q	—	906.8	831.6	875.5	805.5	854.8
4Q	—	735.1	694.6	720.9	639.3	658.6
Yr.	—	3,024	2,996	3,007	2,877	2,895
Earnings Per Share ($)						
1Q	**0.60**	**0.56**	0.81	0.65	0.57	0.57
2Q	**0.45**	**0.37**	0.42	0.36	0.37	0.42
3Q	**E1.25**	**1.15**	0.88	1.02	0.79	0.72
4Q	**E0.65**	**0.58**	0.55	0.45	0.30	0.38
Yr.	**E2.95**	**2.66**	2.66	2.48	2.03	2.10

Next earnings report expected: mid October

Dividend Data (Dividends have been paid since 1937.)

Amount ($)	Date Decl.	Ex-Div. Date	Stock of Record	Payment Date
0.470	Sep. 19	Oct. 08	Oct. 10	Nov. 01 '97
0.485	Dec. 10	Jan. 08	Jan. 12	Feb. 02 '98
0.485	Mar. 18	Apr. 08	Apr. 13	May. 01 '98
0.485	May. 13	Jul. 08	Jul. 10	Aug. 01 '98

A Division of The McGraw-Hill Companies

Business Summary - 10-AUG-98

Located in one of the fastest growing markets in the U.S., Carolina Power & Light serves customers in eastern and western North Carolina and central South Carolina, areas with an estimated population of approximately 3.8 million.

The company provides retail electricity to more than 200 communities (each with an estimated population of 500 or more), and at wholesale to one joint municipal power agency, three municipalities, and two electric membership corporations. Electric revenues by customer class in recent years were:

	1997	1996	1995
Residential	32.6%	33.1%	32.2%
Industrial	21.4%	21.0%	20.6%
Commercial	24.4%	24.1%	24.4%
Other	21.6%	21.8%	22.8%

North Carolina retail customers accounted for 68% of 1996 operating revenues; South Carolina retail customers, 13%; wholesale customers, 13%; and bulk power sales, 6%. The power generating capability of CPL is: coal, 54%; nuclear, 31%; hydro, 2%; and other (including oil, natural gas and propane) 13%.

The company has completed its base load construc-

tion program for the foreseeable future. CPL projects 2.6% average annual growth in system peak demand over the next 10 years, and capacity margins of 9.6% for each of 1998 and 1999, assuming normal weather conditions. It plans construction expenditures of about $398 million (out of total capital spending of $693 million) in 1998, $494 million ($625 million) in 1999, and $526 million ($812 million) in 2000.

CPL has long-term purchase contracts with other utilities (400 mw of generating capacity from Duke Power through mid-1999, and 250 mw from Indiana Michigan Power through 2009). It is also obligated to purchase a percentage of North Carolina Eastern Municipal Power Agency's capacity reserve at Harris plant, in which CPL shares an ownership interest, through 2007.

The company received authorization from both the North Carolina Utility Commission (in December 1996) and the South Carolina Public Service Commission (in March 1997) to accelerate the amortization of certain regulatory assets over a three-year period that began January 1, 1997. The amortization is expected to reduce net income about $56 million in each of the three years. The North Carolina Commission also authorized the amortization of about $40 million of 1996 hurricane-related operation and maintenance expenses over a 40-month period.

Per Share Data ($)

(Year Ended Dec. 31)	1997	1996	1995	1994	1993	1992	1991	1990	1989	1988
Tangible Bk. Val.	18.18	17.16	16.36	15.95	15.86	15.36	14.53	13.68	13.60	14.04
Earnings	2.66	2.66	2.48	2.03	2.10	2.36	2.27	1.58	2.10	1.02
Dividends	1.88	1.82	1.76	1.70	1.64	1.58	1.52	1.46	1.42	1.38
Payout Ratio	71%	68%	71%	84%	78%	67%	67%	92%	68%	135%
Prices - High	42⅝	38¾	34⅝	30	34⅝	28¼	27⅛	23⅞	24	18⅞
- Low	32¾	33¾	26⅛	22½	27	24½	21⅝	19	17½	16
P/E Ratio - High	16	15	14	15	16	12	12	15	11	18
- Low	12	13	11	11	13	10	10	12	8	16

Income Statement Analysis (Million $)

	1997	1996	1995	1994	1993	1992	1991	1990	1989	1988
Revs.	3,024	2,996	3,007	2,877	2,895	2,767	2,686	2,617	2,481	2,273
Depr.	482	387	364	398	414	398	392	417	335	287
Maint.	NA	NA	197	207	235	248	180	199	222	215
Fxd. Chgs. Cov.	4.3	4.1	3.7	3.4	3.2	3.2	3.0	2.1	2.8	1.9
Constr. Credits	4.9	6.4	8.5	9.5	15.0	11.0	9.0	8.0	8.0	8.0
Eff. Tax Rate	38%	41%	39%	35%	35%	37%	36%	33%	31%	37%
Net Inc.	388	391	373	313	346	380	377	280	376	197

Balance Sheet & Other Fin. Data (Million $)

	1997	1996	1995	1994	1993	1992	1991	1990	1989	1988
Gross Prop.	10,977	10,197	9,822	9,546	9,330	9,058	8,798	8,570	8,757	8,484
Cap. Exp.	450	457	344	301	389	334	292	316	322	340
Net Prop.	6,795	6,400	6,329	6,349	6,432	6,426	6,430	6,467	6,676	6,642
Capitalization:										
LT Debt	2,416	2,526	2,610	2,531	2,585	2,675	2,734	2,615	2,524	2,668
% LT Debt	46	47	49	48	48	50	51	50	48	50
Pfd.	59.4	144	144	144	144	144	269	339	350	379
% Pfd.	1.10	2.70	2.70	2.70	2.70	2.70	5.00	6.50	6.60	7.10
Common	2,819	2,690	2,575	2,586	2,632	2,534	2,391	2,254	2,420	2,305
% Common	53	50	48	49	49	47	44	43	46	43
Total Cap.	7,239	7,420	7,288	7,141	7,210	6,673	6,642	6,524	6,658	6,700
% Oper. Ratio	80.6	82.8	82.3	84.7	83.8	80.4	78.8	78.7	76.5	78.1
% Earn. on Net Prop.	7.9	8.1	8.4	7.0	7.3	8.4	8.8	8.5	8.8	7.4
% Return On Revs.	12.8	13.1	12.4	10.9	12.0	13.7	14.0	10.7	15.2	8.7
% Return On Invest. Capital	7.7	7.8	8.0	7.1	8.1	9.2	9.7	9.1	9.3	6.8
% Return On Com. Equity	13.9	14.5	14.1	11.6	13.0	15.4	15.7	15.7	14.6	7.0

Data as orig. reptd.; bef. results of disc opers. and/or spec. items. Per share data adj. for stk. divs. as of ex-div. date. Bold denotes diluted EPS (FASB 128). E-Estimated. NA-Not Available. NM-Not Meaningful. NR-Not Ranked.

Office—411 Fayetteville St., Raleigh, NC 27601. **Tel**—(919) 546-6111. **Website**—www.cplc.com **Chrmn**—S. H. Smith, Jr. **PRES & CEO**—W. Cavanaugh III. **EVP & CFO**—G. E. Harder. **VP & Secy**—W. D. Johnson. **Investor Contact**—Robert F. Drennan, Jr. (919-546-7474). **Dirs**—L. M. Baker, Jr., E. B. Borden, F. J. Capel, W. Cavanaugh III, C. W. Coker, R. L. Daugherty, W. Y. Elisha,, R .L. Jones, E. C. Lee, W. O. McCoy, S. H. Smith, Jr., J. T. Wilson. **Transfer Agent & Registrar**—Wachovia Shareholder Services, Boston. **Incorporated**—in North Carolina in 1926. **Empl**—6,900. **S&P Analyst:** Justin McCann

STANDARD &POOR'S
STOCK REPORTS

Case Corp.

458F

NYSE Symbol **CSE**

In S&P 500

12-SEP-98

Industry: Machinery (Diversified)

Summary: Case is North America's second largest farm equipment manufacturer, and the world's largest manufacturer of light and medium-size construction equipment.

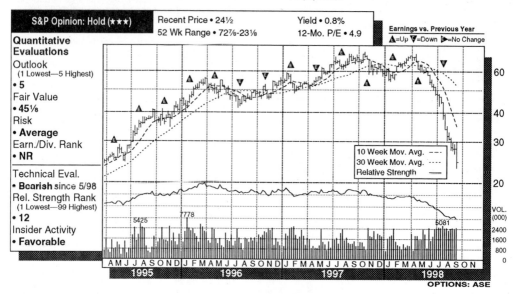

S&P Opinion: Hold (★★★)	Recent Price • 24½	Yield • 0.8%
	52 Wk Range • 72⅞-23⅛	12-Mo. P/E • 4.9

Quantitative Evaluations

Outlook (1 Lowest—5 Highest)
• **5**

Fair Value
• **45⅛**

Risk
• **Average**

Earn./Div. Rank
• **NR**

Technical Eval.
• **Bearish** since 5/98

Rel. Strength Rank (1 Lowest—99 Highest)
• **12**

Insider Activity
• **Favorable**

Earnings vs. Previous Year
▲=Up ▼=Down ▶=No Change

10 Week Mov. Avg. ---
30 Week Mov. Avg. ....
Relative Strength —

OPTIONS: ASE

Overview - 20-JUL-98

We expect revenues to rise 8% in 1998, aided by new products, acquisitions, and growth in financial assets under management. Growth in exports will be limited by the unfavorable impact of foreign exchange rates. The company is continuing a multi-year effort to restrict shipments to dealers, so that dealer inventories can be pared. Case's aim is to manufacture slightly less than dealer sales. Aided by moderating raw material costs and an ongoing productivity effort, gross margins should be flat. With higher interest expense and taxes continuing at a relatively low rate of 32%, net income should increase modestly. Demand for agricultural equipment remains robust, but could be affected by a possible decline in farm income in 1998. The outlook for construction machinery may moderate, due to volatility in capital markets overseas. This may result in reduced development activity in Asia and Latin America; U.S. shipments should remain strong.

Valuation - 20-JUL-98

We downgraded the shares to hold, reflecting concerns that the strengthening of the U.S. dollar would adversely affect demand for farm equipment. The impact of a stronger dollar could be felt not only on direct exports of equipment, but on domestic shipments as well, because of a possible decline in farm income if grain exports fall. Global supplies of corn and soybeans remain low, and changes in U.S. government agricultural policy still favor the continued modernization of farm equipment, but the near-term outlook has been tempered. With the shares recently trading at a P/E multiple close to that of CSE's sustainable EPS growth rate, we continue to maintain a neutral opinion on the shares.

Key Stock Statistics

S&P EPS Est. 1998	5.15	Tang. Bk. Value/Share	27.10
P/E on S&P Est. 1998	4.8	Beta	NA
S&P EPS Est. 1999	5.00	Shareholders	5,200
Dividend Rate/Share	0.20	Market cap. (B)	$ 1.8
Shs. outstg. (M)	74.4	Inst. holdings	85%
Avg. daily vol. (M)	0.609		

Value of $10,000 invested 5 years ago: NA

Fiscal Year Ending Dec. 31

	1998	1997	1996	1995	1994	1993
Revenues (Million $)						
1Q	1,381	1,232	1,171	1,178	1,044	--
2Q	1,672	1,601	1,466	1,377	1,150	--
3Q	--	1,444	1,199	1,182	1,040	--
4Q	—	1,693	1,573	1,282	1,171	--
Yr.	—	6,024	5,409	4,937	4,405	3,890
Earnings Per Share ($)						
1Q	**0.88**	0.82	1.00	0.96	0.48	--
2Q	**1.61**	1.75	1.47	1.53	0.81	--
3Q	**E1.16**	0.98	0.81	1.19	0.37	--
4Q	**E1.50**	1.56	1.33	1.05	0.63	--
Yr.	**E5.15**	5.11	4.49	4.72	2.32	-0.31

Next earnings report expected: mid October

Dividend Data (Dividends have been paid since 1994.)

Amount ($)	Date Decl.	Ex-Div. Date	Stock of Record	Payment Date
0.050	Oct. 01	Dec. 23	Dec. 26	Jan. 27 '98
0.050	Feb. 11	Mar. 25	Mar. 27	Apr. 28 '98
0.050	May. 13	Jun. 24	Jun. 26	Jul. 28 '98
0.050	Aug. 14	Sep. 23	Sep. 25	Oct. 27 '98

A Division of The McGraw-Hill Companies

Business Summary - 20-JUL-98

After years of restructuring efforts while a subsidiary of Tenneco Inc., Case Corp. was spun off by Tenneco in a series of stock offerings that began in 1994 and culminated in 1996 with a final offering of Tenneco's Case common stock. Case is a leading global manufacturer and distributor of farm equipment and of light and medium-size construction equipment. Since its initial public offering, the company has substantially improved profits, and has reinvested them in acquisitions and joint ventures intended to broaden Case's geographical reach and penetrate faster growing overseas markets.

Case distributes products under the Case, Case IH, Case International, and Case Poclain names. Primary markets are North America (58% of 1997 sales) and the European Community (26%). Sales contributions by product line in recent years were:

	1997	1996	1995
Farm equipment	52%	52%	49%
Construction equipment	30%	30%	32%
Replacement parts & finance	18%	18%	19%

Farm equipment consists of a broad line of machinery and implements, including two-wheel- and four-wheel-drive tractors ranging in size from 42 to 425 gross horsepower, combines, cotton pickers, and implements for preparing, planting and cultivating seed beds. CSE's tractor line concentrates on medium- to large-size tractors, which are used by large, high-volume agricultural producers. CSE has equipped combines with monitors that collect and map crop yield data using the guidance of the global positioning satellite system. The data can be used to adjust the application of agricultural chemicals and watering schedules to increase crop yields.

Case construction equipment manufactured is used primarily in light to medium construction work. It includes loader/backhoes, wheel loaders, excavators, skid-steer loaders, crawler dozers, rough-terrain forklifts and trenching equipment. A new fleet management system uses cellular technology to track equipment and schedule repairs.

Products are distributed through a dealer network of about 4,900 independent dealers located in all 50 states and more than 150 countries. Case supplies more than 350,000 parts to dealers and distributors worldwide to support its products. Case Credit provides dealer and customer financing. A $5.2 billion loan portfolio was serviced as of year-end 1997.

Case also has 50% interests in a joint venture with Cummins Engine Co. and a joint venture with AGCO Corp.

Per Share Data ($)

(Year Ended Dec. 31)	1997	1996	1995	1994	1993	1992	1991	1990	1989	1988
Tangible Bk. Val.	25.25	21.67	18.81	13.90	15.31	NA	NA	NA	NA	NA
Cash Flow	7.00	4.71	6.61	4.12	1.40	NA	NA	NA	NA	NA
Earnings	5.11	4.61	4.60	2.26	-0.29	NA	NA	NA	NA	NA
Dividends	0.20	0.20	0.20	0.05	NA	NA	NA	NA	NA	NA
Payout Ratio	4%	4%	4%	2%	NA	NA	NA	NA	NA	NA
Prices - High	72⁷/₈	56¹/₂	45⁷/₈	21¹/₂	NA	NA	NA	NA	NA	NA
- Low	48³/₈	40	20¹/₂	18¹/₄	NA	NA	NA	NA	NA	NA
P/E Ratio - High	14	12	10	10	NA	NA	NA	NA	NA	NA
- Low	9	9	4	8	NA	NA	NA	NA	NA	NA

Income Statement Analysis (Million $)

	1997	1996	1995	1994	1993	1992	1991	1990	1989	1988
Revs.	5,796	5,176	4,937	4,262	3,748	NA	NA	NA	NA	NA
Oper. Inc.	740	624	579	426	163	NA	NA	NA	NA	NA
Depr.	157	138	130	127	118	NA	NA	NA	NA	NA
Int. Exp.	170	160	174	163	171	NA	NA	NA	NA	NA
Pretax Inc.	594	534	427	258	40.0	NA	NA	NA	NA	NA
Eff. Tax Rate	32%	35%	19%	36%	138%	NA	NA	NA	NA	NA
Net Inc.	403	349	346	165	-15.0	NA	NA	NA	NA	NA

Balance Sheet & Other Fin. Data (Million $)

	1997	1996	1995	1994	1993	1992	1991	1990	1989	1988
Cash	252	116	132	68.0	35.0	NA	NA	NA	NA	NA
Curr. Assets	3,600	3,053	2,852	2,542	2,579	NA	NA	NA	NA	NA
Total Assets	6,981	6,059	5,469	5,052	4,746	NA	NA	NA	NA	NA
Curr. Liab.	2,870	2,534	2,466	1,825	1,827	NA	NA	NA	NA	NA
LT Debt	1,404	1,119	889	1,443	1,250	NA	NA	NA	NA	NA
Common Eqty.	2,197	1,904	1,520	1,181	1,072	NA	NA	NA	NA	NA
Total Cap.	3,680	3,100	2,486	2,701	2,402	NA	NA	NA	NA	NA
Cap. Exp.	192	162	115	10.4	NA	NA	NA	NA	NA	NA
Cash Flow	553	480	469	289	98.0	NA	NA	NA	NA	NA
Curr. Ratio	1.3	1.2	1.2	1.4	1.4	NA	NA	NA	NA	NA
% LT Debt of Cap.	38.2	36.1	35.8	53.4	52.0	NA	NA	NA	NA	NA
% Net Inc.of Revs.	7.0	6.7	7.0	3.9	NM	NM	NM	NM	NM	NM
% Ret. on Assets	6.2	6.1	6.6	NA	NA	NA	NA	NA	NA	NA
% Ret. on Equity	19.3	20.4	25.1	NA	NA	NA	NA	NA	NA	NA

Data as orig. reptd.; bef. results of disc. opers. and/or spec. items. Per share data adj. for stk. divs. as of ex-div. date. Bold denotes diluted EPS (FASB 128). E-Estimated. NA-Not Available. NM-Not Meaningful. NR-Not Ranked.

Office—700 State St., Racine, WI 53404. **Tel**—(414) 636-6011. **Website**—http://www.casecorp.com **Chrmn & CEO**—J. P. Rosso. **Pres**—S. G. Lamb. **Secy**—R. S. Brennan. **CFO**—T. R. French. **Investor Contact**—Bryan E. Kneeland. **Dirs**—P. Chia, R. E. Goldsberry, J. T. Grade, T. Hodgson, K. M. Hudson, G. Rosenfeld, J.-P. Rosso, T. R. Tetzlaff, T. N. Urban. **Transfer Agent & Registrar**—First Chicago Trust Co. of New York, Jersey City, NJ. **Incorporated**—in Delaware in 1994. **Empl**— 18,300. **S&P Analyst:** Robert E. Friedman, CPA

12-SEP-98   Industry: Machinery (Diversified)

Summary: This company is the world's largest manufacturer of earthmoving machinery and equipment, and is a major producer of diesel and natural gas engines and turbines.

S&P Opinion: Hold (★★★)		
Recent Price • 45¼	Yield • 2.7%	
52 Wk Range • 60⅞-41⅞	12-Mo. P/E • 9.9	

Earnings vs. Previous Year ▲=Up ▼=Down ▶=No Change

Quantitative Evaluations

Outlook (1 Lowest—5 Highest)
• **3+**

Fair Value
• **53**

Risk
• **Low**

Earn./Div. Rank
• **B**

Technical Eval.
• **Bearish** since 10/96

Rel. Strength Rank (1 Lowest—99 Highest)
• **67**

Insider Activity
• **Neutral**

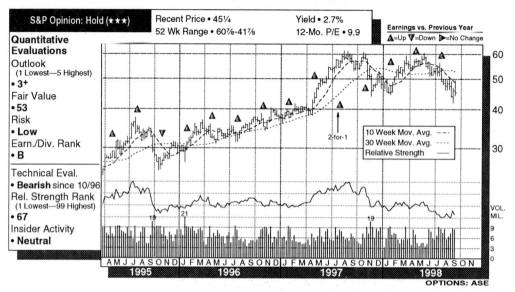

10 Week Mov. Avg. – – –
30 Week Mov. Avg. · · · ·
Relative Strength

2-for-1

OPTIONS: ASE

Overview - 16-JUL-98

Sales should rise in 1998, reflecting the acquisition of Perkins Engines (which extends CAT's range into below 200 horsepower engines), and strengthened demand for heavy duty truck engines. Export sales could decline, as a result of weakness in Asia and the strength of the U.S. dollar. U.S. construction equipment sales should remain stable, as dealers rebuild inventories. A possible decline in farm income could slow demand for new agricultural equipment. Farm equipment sales have been strong for several years, and pent-up demand has been reduced. With stable raw material costs, benefits of a factory modernization program, and higher financial services income, net income could rise slightly. A share repurchase program should boost EPS and help support the stock price. For the longer term, new products and aggressive expansion into the market for mining-related equipment in Russia and China will boost sales and profits. These efforts will develop gradually, and could be supplemented by further opportunistic acquisitions.

Valuation - 16-JUL-98

We are maintaining our neutral rating on the shares of this cyclical capital goods company. Overall sales are flattening, and it is late in the economic cycle. Although demand may hold up in 1998, we think that investors will not award capital goods companies higher P/E multiples at this stage of the cycle. We think that the shares are fairly valued at recent price levels, and expect them to perform only in line with the general stock market. We would view rallies in the shares as opportunities to take profits.

Key Stock Statistics

S&P EPS Est. 1998	4.65	Tang. Bk. Value/Share	11.71
P/E on S&P Est. 1998	9.7	Beta	0.92
S&P EPS Est. 1999	4.70	Shareholders	30,600
Dividend Rate/Share	1.20	Market cap. (B)	$ 16.5
Shs. outstg. (M)	364.8	Inst. holdings	71%
Avg. daily vol. (M)	1.637		

Value of $10,000 invested 5 years ago: $ 37,143

Fiscal Year Ending Dec. 31

	1998	1997	1996	1995	1994	1993
Revenues (Million $)						
1Q	4,794	4,262	3,844	3,913	3,286	2,697
2Q	5,604	4,870	4,008	4,213	3,605	2,905
3Q	—	4,600	4,033	3,733	3,509	2,845
4Q	—	5,193	4,470	4,213	3,928	3,168
Yr.	—	18,925	16,522	16,072	14,328	11,615
Earnings Per Share ($)						
1Q	1.15	1.03	0.77	0.75	0.47	0.09
2Q	1.20	1.13	0.97	0.81	0.59	0.17
3Q	E1.10	1.01	0.81	0.54	0.60	1.06
4Q	E1.20	1.20	0.99	0.77	0.69	0.36
Yr.	E4.65	4.37	3.50	2.86	2.35	1.68

Next earnings report expected: mid November

Dividend Data (Dividends have been paid since 1914.)

Amount ($)	Date Decl.	Ex-Div. Date	Stock of Record	Payment Date
0.250	Oct. 08	Oct. 16	Oct. 20	Nov. 20 '97
0.250	Dec. 10	Jan. 15	Jan. 20	Feb. 20 '98
0.250	Apr. 08	Apr. 16	Apr. 20	May. 20 '98
0.300	Jun. 10	Jul. 16	Jul. 20	Aug. 20 '98

A Division of The **McGraw·Hill** Companies

Business Summary - 16-JUL-98

The world's largest manufacturer of earthmoving and construction machinery, Caterpillar also makes diesel and natural gas engines and turbines. CAT's distinctive yellow machines are in service in nearly every country of the world, and about half of the company's revenues are derived outside the U.S. More than 60% of the company's 197 independent dealers are located outside the U.S. As a major exporter, CAT is exposed to the impact of exchange rate currency fluctuations on both sales and profits. The company must continuously strive to lower costs to maintain its long-term competitiveness. Segment contributions in 1997 were:

	Revs.	Profits
Machinery & equipment	71%	75%
Engines	25%	20%
Financial services	4%	5%

Machinery and equipment produced ranges from small agricultural tractors to the largest mechanical drive mining truck in the world with a payload capacity of 240 tons. With the benefit of breakthrough tire technology, CAT is developing an even larger mining truck whose capacity will be matched to the anticipated sizes for large mining shovels. The product line also includes track and wheel tractors, track and wheel loaders, pipelayers, motor graders, wheel tractor scrapers, track and wheel excavators, backhoe loaders, log skidders, log loaders, off-highway trucks, articulated dump trucks, paving products and related parts. Worldwide machine sales by major end use in 1997 were as follows: transportation 24%; energy 13%; housing and forest products 15%; mining 17%; commercial and industrial construction 15%; food and water 6%; and other 10%.

Diesel and natural gas engines range from 40 hp to 13,600 horsepower, and are used in earthmoving and construction machines, on-highway trucks and marine, petroleum, agricultural, industrial and other applications. CAT also makes turbines ranging from 1,340 horsepower to 15,000 horsepower (1,000 kw to 11,200 kw) primarily for use in electric power generation. The acquisition of Perkins Diesel for $1.325 billion in February 1998 will add sales of about $1.1 billion and expanded CAT's line of sub-200 horsepower reciprocating engines.

Financial services include providing financing for company and noncompetitive equipment sold through dealers, and extending loans to CAT dealers and customers.

Per Share Data ($)

(Year Ended Dec. 31)	1997	1996	1995	1994	1993	1992	1991	1990	1989	1988
Tangible Bk. Val.	11.71	10.16	8.29	6.67	4.53	3.02	9.72	10.81	10.66	9.96
Cash Flow	6.32	5.38	4.59	4.03	3.31	1.08	0.47	1.78	2.38	2.59
Earnings	4.37	3.54	2.86	2.35	1.68	-0.54	-1.00	0.52	1.23	1.52
Dividends	0.90	0.75	0.60	0.23	0.15	0.15	0.30	0.30	0.30	0.19
Payout Ratio	21%	21%	21%	10%	9%	NM	NM	58%	24%	12%
Prices - High	61⅝	40½	37⅝	30⅜	23⅜	15⅝	14½	17⅛	17¼	17⅛
- Low	36¼	27	24⅛	25⅜	13½	10⅜	9½	9⅝	13¼	13½
P/E Ratio - High	14	11	13	13	14	NM	NM	33	14	11
- Low	8	8	8	11	8	NM	NM	18	11	9

Income Statement Analysis (Million $)

	1997	1996	1995	1994	1993	1992	1991	1990	1989	1988
Revs.	18,925	16,522	16,072	14,328	11,615	10,194	10,182	11,436	11,126	10,435
Oper. Inc.	3,529	2,983	2,656	2,321	1,459	685	675	1,055	1,297	1,434
Depr.	738	696	682	680	661	654	593	513	471	434
Int. Exp.	580	510	484	410	440	497	469	406	372	340
Pretax Inc.	2,461	1,974	1,637	1,309	723	-331	-555	288	659	878
Eff. Tax Rate	32%	32%	31%	27%	5.80%	NM	NM	27%	25%	30%
Net Inc.	1,665	1,361	1,136	955	681	-217	-403	210	497	616

Balance Sheet & Other Fin. Data (Million $)

	1997	1996	1995	1994	1993	1992	1991	1990	1989	1988
Cash	292	487	638	419	83.0	119	104	110	148	74.0
Curr. Assets	9,814	8,783	7,647	7,409	6,071	5,537	5,570	5,901	5,708	5,317
Total Assets	20,756	18,728	16,830	16,250	14,807	13,935	12,042	11,951	10,926	9,686
Curr. Liab.	6,379	7,013	6,049	5,498	4,671	4,227	3,859	4,259	3,904	3,435
LT Debt	6,942	4,532	3,964	4,270	3,895	4,119	3,892	2,890	2,288	1,953
Common Eqty.	4,679	4,116	3,388	2,911	2,199	1,575	4,044	4,540	4,474	4,113
Total Cap.	11,679	8,696	7,388	7,181	6,118	5,713	8,022	7,430	6,762	6,251
Cap. Exp.	968	771	679	694	632	640	774	1,039	1,089	793
Cash Flow	2,403	2,057	1,818	1,635	1,342	436	189	723	968	1,050
Curr. Ratio	1.5	1.3	1.3	1.3	1.3	1.3	1.4	1.4	1.5	1.5
% LT Debt of Cap.	59.4	52.1	53.7	59.5	63.7	72.1	48.5	38.9	33.8	31.2
% Net Inc.of Revs.	8.8	8.2	7.1	6.7	5.9	NM	NM	1.8	4.5	5.9
% Ret. on Assets	8.4	7.7	6.9	6.2	4.7	NM	NM	1.8	4.8	7.4
% Ret. on Equity	37.9	36.3	36.1	37.6	36.0	NM	NM	4.7	11.6	16.0

Data as orig. reptd.; bef. results of disc. opers. and/or spec. items. Per share data adj. for stk. divs. as of ex-div. date. Bold denotes diluted EPS (FASB 128). E-Estimated. NA-Not Available. NM-Not Meaningful. NR-Not Ranked.

Office—100 N.E. Adams St., Peoria, IL 61629. Tel—(309) 675-1000. Website—http://www.CAT.com Chrmn & CEO—D. V. Fites. Secy—R. R. Atterbury III. VP & CFO—D. R. Oberhelman. Treas—F. L. McPheeters. Investor Contact—James F. Masterson.Dirs—L. H. Affinito, W. F. Blount, J. T. Dillon, D. V. Fites, J. Gallardo, D. R. Goode, J. P. Gorter, P. A. Magowan, G. R. Parker, G. A. Schaefer, J. I. Smith, C. K. Yeutter. Transfer Agent—First Chicago Trust Co. of New York, Jersey City, NJ. Incorporated—in California in 1925; reincorporated in Delaware in 1986. Empl—64,681. S&P Analyst: Robert E. Friedman, CPA

12-SEP-98

Industry: Broadcasting (Television, Radio & Cable)

Summary: This major media company (formerly Westinghouse Electric) has extensive television and radio operations,

---

S&P Opinion: Hold (★★★)

| Recent Price • 24½ | Yield • Nil |
| 52 Wk Range • 36⅝-23⅜ | 12-Mo. P/E • 21.1 |

Earnings vs. Previous Year
▲=Up ▼=Down ▷=No Change

Quantitative Evaluations

Outlook (1 Lowest—5 Highest)
• 1⁻

Fair Value
• 16⅝

Risk
• **Average**

Earn./Div. Rank
• **B-**

Technical Eval.
• **Bearish** since 8/98

Rel. Strength Rank (1 Lowest—99 Highest)
• 37

Insider Activity
• **Neutral**

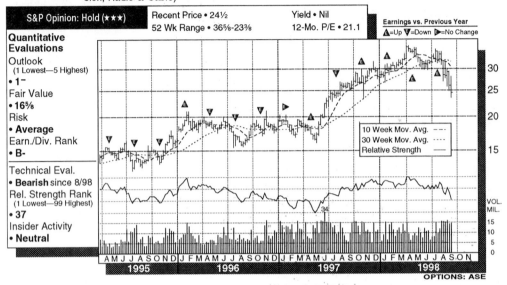

10 Week Mov. Avg. —·—
30 Week Mov. Avg. ·····
Relative Strength ——

OPTIONS: ASE

Overview - 01-MAY-98

In December 1997, this company (formerly Westinghouse Electric Corp.) was renamed CBS Corp., reflecting its increased emphasis on media operations. The company's media businesses include extensive television and radio operations, which came largely from the 1995-97 acquisitions of CBS Inc., Infinity Broadcasting Corp., and full ownership of two cable TV networks. Still pending is the acquisition of American Radio Systems, for $1.6 billion in cash, plus the assumption of about $1 billion of debt. CBS is also in the midst of divesting its industrial operations. This includes the 1997 sale of its Thermo King transport control refrigeration business for more than $2.5 billion, and a recent agreement to sell its power generation business for $1.5 billion. We have restated revenues and EPS for portions of 1997, to reflect a new definition of continuing operations.

Valuation - 01-MAY-98

We have a generally favorable view of CBS's restructuring efforts during the past few years. Investors have responded positively to the transition from a largely industrial company, known as Westinghouse Electric, to a media business now known as CBS Corp. The stock has more than doubled from its 1996 low of $15.38. In our view, CBS remains an okay story stock, especially if U.S. investors are favoring companies with a domestic emphasis. We also expect the stock to get support from a recent authorization for the repurchase of up to $1 billion of common shares. As of April 1998, CBS had purchased about 2.5 million shares under this authorization. However, although we see favorable growth prospects for the company, we consider the stock to be priced at an ample multiple of expected cash flow (net of adjustments related to expected divestitures, tax credits, and various liabilities), and do not advise investors to make new purchases.

Key Stock Statistics

S&P EPS Est. 1998	0.16	Tang. Bk. Value/Share	NM
P/E on S&P Est. 1998	NM	Beta	1.39
S&P EPS Est. 1999	0.33	Shareholders	127,600
Dividend Rate/Share	Nil	Market cap. (B)	$ 17.5
Shs. outstg. (M)	715.9	Inst. holdings	58%
Avg. daily vol. (M)	3.894		

Value of $10,000 invested 5 years ago: $ 19,746

Fiscal Year Ending Dec. 31

	1998	1997	1996	1995	1994	1993
Revenues (Million $)						
1Q	1,949	1,326	1,883	1,294	1,743	2,020
2Q	1,484	1,283	2,148	1,531	2,108	2,154
3Q	—	1,283	1,967	2,229	2,229	2,060
4Q	—	1,471	2,451	2,093	2,768	2,641
Yr.	—	5,363	8,449	6,296	8,848	8,875
Earnings Per Share ($)						
1Q	0.03	-0.18	-1.65	-0.06	0.07	0.14
2Q	0.01	-0.04	-0.20	0.03	0.16	0.20
3Q	E0.04	-0.03	-0.01	0.03	0.15	0.15
4Q	E0.08	-0.01	-0.07	-0.18	-0.30	-1.11
Yr.	E0.16	-0.24	-1.89	-0.19	0.07	-0.64

Next earnings report expected: NA

Dividend Data (Dividends have been paid since 1935.)

Amount ($)	Date Decl.	Ex-Div. Date	Stock of Record	Payment Date
0.050	Nov. 04	Nov. 12	Nov. 14	Dec. 01 '97
0.050	Feb. 04	Feb. 11	Feb. 16	Mar. 01 '98

 A Division of The **McGraw-Hill** *Companies*

Business Summary - 01-MAY-98

Following various acquisitions and divestitures, CBS Corp. emerged in December 1997 as a media company, successor to the old Westinghouse Electric Corp., whose industrial businesses are being divested.

The company's media business was significantly expanded through the acquisitions of CBS Inc. (November 1995) and radio company Infinity Broadcasting Corp. (December 1996), for a total price (excluding debt assumption) of about $9 billion in cash and stock. Current media operations include the CBS television network, about 18 owned television stations, the CBS Radio Network, and more than 70 owned radio stations. The $4.1 billion of media revenues in 1996 excludes any contribution from Infinity.

In September 1997, CBS acquired through an exchange of stock valued at $1.55 billion (59 million shares) ownership of two cable television networks: The Nashville Network (TNN) and Country Music Television (CMT). Based on preliminary estimates, the acquisition was expected to result in additional non-cash charges related to amortization of goodwill totaling about $30 million a year in the future.

Currently pending is a plan to acquire American Radio Systems (AFM) for about $1.6 billion in cash, plus the assumption of approximately $1 billion of debt. The acquisition of AFM, which owns and/or programs and markets about 100 radio stations, is expected to be completed in the 1998 second quarter. In 1997, including a business to be spun off, AFM had revenues of $374.1 million and a net loss of $7.6 million.

CBS's industrial operations are being treated as discontinued. Various businesses have been sold during the past few years, including the October 1997 sale of the Thermo King transport temperature control business for $2.6 billion. Thermo King proceeds were used to repay debt. In November 1997, CBS said it had agreed to sell its power generation unit to Siemens for $1.5 billion. The transaction is expected to completed by mid-1998. CBS expects to reach agreements to divest its other remaining industrial businesses, in the energy systems, process control and government operations areas, by mid-1998. CBS still has sizable obligations related to underfunded pension liabilities and other post-employment benefits, but some of these liabilities could be transferred as part of divesting remaining industrial businesses. In addition, CBS is expected to have tax credits available to shield some future income from cash tax payments.

In February 1998, directors authorized the repurchase of up to $1 billion of common stock, and determined to suspend payment of future cash dividends (beyond the expected March 1, 1998, payment) on the common stock.

Per Share Data ($)

(Year Ended Dec. 31)	1997	1996	1995	1994	1993	1992	1991	1990	1989	1988
Tangible Bk. Val.	NA	NM	-13.99	1.53	-1.10	4.38	7.30	9.35	11.52	11.12
Cash Flow	0.50	-0.98	0.34	0.90	0.24	1.70	-2.25	2.15	4.29	3.93
Earnings	-0.24	-1.89	-0.19	0.07	-0.64	0.93	-3.46	0.91	3.16	2.83
Dividends	0.20	0.20	0.20	0.20	0.40	0.72	1.40	1.35	1.15	0.96
Payout Ratio	NM	NM	NM	NM	NM	78%	NM	146%	36%	34%
Prices - High	32	21⅛	17⅞	15¼	17⅛	21⅛	31	39⅜	38⅛	28¾
- Low	16	15⅜	12⅛	10⅞	12¾	9⅜	13¾	24¼	25⅝	22⅞
P/E Ratio - High	NM	NM	NM	NM	NM	20	NM	43	12	10
- Low	NM	NM	NM	NM	NM	10	NM	27	8	8

Income Statement Analysis (Million $)

	1997	1996	1995	1994	1993	1992	1991	1990	1989	1988
Revs.	5,363	8,449	6,296	8,848	8,875	8,447	12,794	12,915	12,844	12,500
Oper. Inc.	837	628	348	1,010	807	1,017	2,092	1,643	2,389	2,000
Depr.	445	405	218	320	311	270	378	363	334	322
Int. Exp.	386	456	233	177	220	189	998	1,025	912	678
Pretax Inc.	-59.0	-1,297	-40.0	157	-235	536	-1,095	428	1,275	1,066
Eff. Tax Rate	NA	NM	NM	45%	NM	34%	NM	34%	27%	23%
Net Inc.	-130	-837	-44.0	77.0	-174	348	-1,085	268	922	823

Balance Sheet & Other Fin. Data (Million $)

	1997	1996	1995	1994	1993	1992	1991	1990	1989	1988
Cash	8.0	220	213	338	637	739	1,244	1,523	2,281	1,707
Curr. Assets	1,975	4,787	4,306	4,720	4,774	3,965	NA	NA	NA	NA
Total Assets	16,715	19,889	16,752	10,624	10,553	10,398	20,159	22,033	20,314	16,937
Curr. Liab.	1,549	4,300	3,933	3,709	3,925	3,957	NA	NA	NA	NA
LT Debt	3,236	5,149	7,226	1,886	1,885	1,323	5,280	6,091	4,365	3,522
Common Eqty.	8,851	5,738	1,504	1,780	1,037	2,336	3,746	3,897	4,384	3,794
Total Cap.	11,321	10,901	8,745	3,708	2,964	3,700	9,880	10,229	9,320	7,767
Cap. Exp.	121	206	290	259	237	229	363	522	420	420
Cash Flow	314	-432	140	347	86.0	590	-707	631	1,256	1,145
Curr. Ratio	1.3	1.1	1.1	1.3	1.2	1.0	NA	NA	NA	NA
% LT Debt of Cap.	28.6	47.2	83.6	50.9	63.6	35.8	53.4	59.5	46.8	45.3
% Net Inc.of Revs.	NA	NM	NM	0.9	NM	4.1	NM	2.1	7.2	6.6
% Ret. on Assets	NA	NM	NM	0.7	NM	2.2	NM	1.3	4.9	6.1
% Ret. on Equity	NA	NM	NM	1.9	NM	10.4	NM	6.5	22.5	22.3

Data as orig. reptd.; bef. results of disc. opers. and/or spec. items. Per share data adj. for stk. divs. as of ex-div. date. Bold denotes diluted EPS (FASB 128). E-Estimated. NA-Not Available. NM-Not Meaningful. NR-Not Ranked.

Office—51 West 52nd St., New York, NY 10019. **Tel**—(412) 244-2000. **Chrmn & CEO**—M. H. Jordan. **Pres & COO**—M. Karmazin. **EVP & CFO**—F. G. Reynolds.**VP & Secy**—Angeline C. Straka.**VP & Investor Contact**—Mary Stanutz (412-642-4835). **Dirs**—F. C. Carlucci, R. E. Cawthorn, G. H. Conrades, M. C. Dickinson, W. H. Gray, M. H. Jordan, M. Karmazin, J. Leschly, D. K. P. Li, D. T. McLaughlin, R. R. Pivirotto, R. W. Smith P. Stern, R. D. Walter. **Transfer Agent & Registrar**—Bank of New York, NYC. **Incorporated**—in Pennsylvania in 1886. **Empl**— 84,399. **S&P Analyst**: Tom Graves, CFA

Cendant Corp.

417G

NYSE Symbol **CD**

In S&P 500

12-SEP-98

Industry: Services (Commercial & Consumer)

Summary: This major provider of consumer and business services was known as CUC International prior to a December 1997 stock-swap merger with HFS Inc.

S&P Opinion: Accumulate (★★★★)	Recent Price • 11¾	Yield • Nil
	52 Wk Range • 41⅝-10	12-Mo. P/E • 23.2

Quantitative Evaluations

Outlook (1 Lowest—5 Highest)
• **5**

Fair Value
• **16¾**

Risk
• **Average**

Earn./Div. Rank
• **B**

Technical Eval.
• **NA**

Rel. Strength Rank (1 Lowest—99 Highest)
• **17**

Insider Activity
• **NA**

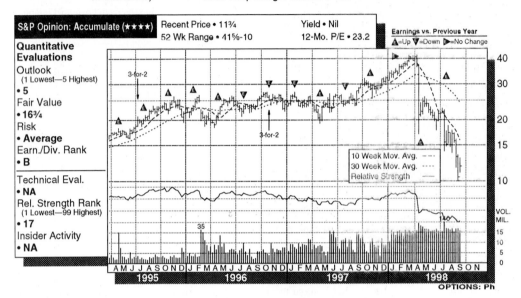

Earnings vs. Previous Year
△=Up ▽=Down ▶=No Change

OPTIONS: Ph

Overview - 01-MAY-98

In April 1998, this company said that it had discovered potential accounting irregularities, and that it expects to restate earnings for 1997, and possibly for other historic periods. Based on currently available information, CD was expecting a downward restatement of about $0.11-to-$0.13 a share for 1997, which would reduce earnings before unusual charges to about $0.87-to-$0.89 a share. Earlier, in December 1997, Cendant (formerly known as CUC International) merged with HFS Inc., a leading franchisor of name brand hotels, real estate and car rental businesses, via a stock-swap transaction. Also, CD recently completed the acquisition of U.K.-based National Parking Corp. Ltd,, which operates parking and auto club businesses. Pending acquisitions by CD include specialty insurance company American Bankers Insurance Group, Inc., and U.K.-based RAC Motoring Service Limited, whose businesses include roadside assistance and the U.K.'s largest driving school company.

Valuation - 01-MAY-98

We advise aggressive investors to accumulate this stock. We raised our opinion on the shares, from "hold," in April 1998, following a plunge in the stock price. News of a prospective downward profit restatement raised concern about the earnings power of some CD businesses, management quality at the company, and the possibility of more accounting issues. Also, we expect that a lower stock price hurts CD's ability to make favorable acquisitions, and CD may face shareholder-related litigation. However, based on our downward revised earnings estimates, and the prospect that the news won't get significantly worse, we view the stock as having some speculative appeal.

Key Stock Statistics

S&P EPS Est. 1998	1.05	Tang. Bk. Value/Share	NM
P/E on S&P Est. 1998	11.2	Beta	1.50
S&P EPS Est. 1999	1.25	Shareholders	9,000
Dividend Rate/Share	Nil	Market cap. (B)	$ 10.1
Shs. outstg. (M)	858.0	Inst. holdings	70%
Avg. daily vol. (M)	7.002		

Value of $10,000 invested 5 years ago: $ 13,746

Fiscal Year Ending Dec. 31

	1998	1997	1996	1995	1994	1993
Revenues (Million $)						
1Q	1,437	1,158	515.5	325.1	245.0	207.0
2Q	1,306	1,301	555.8	347.8	253.0	215.8
3Q	—	1,431	602.2	364.1	263.7	222.1
4Q	—	1,425	674.2	377.9	281.7	234.4
Yr.	—	5,315	2,348	1,415	1,045	879.3
Earnings Per Share ($)						
1Q	0.26	0.19	0.13	0.13	0.10	0.08
2Q	0.24	-0.02	0.10	0.14	0.11	0.08
3Q	—	0.29	-0.04	0.15	0.12	0.09
4Q	—	-0.42	0.22	0.15	0.12	0.10
Yr.	E1.05	0.06	0.41	0.56	0.45	0.34

Next earnings report expected: early December

Dividend Data

A three-for-two stock split was effected in 1995. In June 1989, CD paid special dividends of $1.48 a share (unadjusted) in cash and $2.07 face amount ($0.93 discount amount) of zero-coupon notes due 1996 as part of a recapitalization plan.

A Division of The McGraw·Hill Companies

Business Summary - 01-MAY-98

This large business and consumer services company reflects the December 1997 merger of CUC International (renamed Cendant Corp.) and HFS Inc. Prior to the merger, CUC was a membership-based consumer services company, while HFS was a leading franchisor of name brand hotels, real estate and car rental businesses. Also, Cendant is expected to expand further into new electronic media, combining its existing direct marketing expertise with the technological capabilities of recent acquisitions. However, in April 1998, CD said that had discovered potential accounting irregularities, and that based on currently available information, 1997 earnings per share were expected to be restated downward by about $0.11-to-$0.13.

The merger of CUC and HFS was through an exchange of stock valued at about $14 billion. Excluding unusual charges, and before any future restatement, the pooling-of-interest merger led to 1997 per share earnings of $1.00. Also, in 1996, CUC acquired, in separate transactions, two leading software companies, Davidson & Associates, Inc. and Sierra On-Line Inc., for a total of $2.20 billion of common stock.

Cendant's CUC-related business includes providing customers with access to services such as discount shopping, travel, automobile discounts, dining, home improvement, vacation exchange, credit card and checking account enhancement packages and discount coupon programs. The company also administers insurance package programs that are generally combined with discount shopping and travel memberships for credit union members. Services are provided through individual, wholesale and discount coupon program memberships, at least some of which are marketed through arrangements with financial institutions, retailers, oil companies, credit unions, on-line networks, fund-raisers and others. Major membership services offered include Shoppers Advantage, a discount shopping program; Travelers Advantage, a discount travel service program; and AutoVantage, which offers comprehensive new car summaries and discounts on new domestic and foreign cars purchased through the company's independent dealer network, tire and parts discounts and used car valuations.

On a pro forma basis (assuming the merger with HFS, and before any further restatement), 37% of CD's revenues in 1997 came from what the company calls membership services; 28% were from travel services; 19% were from real estate services; and 16% were from other sources.

Per Share Data ($)

(Year Ended Dec. 31)	1997	1996	1995	1994	1993	1992	1991	1990	1989	1988
Tangible Bk. Val.	0.27	2.28	1.60	1.60	0.42	-0.12	-0.31	-0.52	-0.61	0.31
Cash Flow	0.37	0.49	0.49	0.53	0.43	0.32	0.18	0.17	0.12	-0.02
Earnings	0.06	0.41	0.56	0.44	0.34	0.25	0.12	0.11	0.05	-0.08
Dividends	Nil	Nil	Nil	Nil	Nil	Nil	Nil	Nil	0.66	Nil
Payout Ratio	Nil	Nil	Nil	Nil	Nil	Nil	Nil	Nil	NM	Nil
Prices - High	34³/₈	27¹/₂	26¹/₈	16	17⁵/₈	8⁵/₈	6¹/₂	3	2³/₄	3⁵/₈
- Low	19¹/₄	18³/₈	14¹/₂	11¹/₈	7³/₈	5¹/₈	2⁵/₈	1⁹/₁₆	1³/₈	2³/₁₆
P/E Ratio - High	NM	67	47	36	52	34	59	30	56	NM
- Low	NM	45	26	25	22	21	24	16	28	NM

Income Statement Analysis (Million $)

	1997	1996	1995	1994	1993	1992	1991	1990	1989	1988
Revs.	5,315	2,348	1,415	1,039	875	739	641	451	365	269
Oper. Inc.	1,766	479	286	209	166	122	99	58.5	38.6	44.1
Depr.	257	32.5	15.4	23.3	22.3	17.3	15.7	11.4	10.9	9.1
Int. Exp.	67.0	Nil	Nil	NA	4.8	8.7	16.0	16.5	12.1	1.4
Pretax Inc.	294	276	266	191	142	96.1	45.1	28.8	13.7	-14.6
Eff. Tax Rate	81%	41%	39%	38%	39%	39%	44%	39%	41%	NM
Net Inc.	55.0	164	163	118	87.4	58.8	25.1	17.5	8.1	-11.3

Balance Sheet & Other Fin. Data (Million $)

	1997	1996	1995	1994	1993	1992	1991	1990	1989	1988
Cash	150	553	270	181	117	28.6	14.4	13.3	12.3	38.1
Curr. Assets	2,575	1,430	768	504	377	243	205	143	111	125
Total Assets	14,851	2,473	1,141	768	613	479	322	239	201	216
Curr. Liab.	1,743	481	150	109	123	127	133	103	85.0	68.0
LT Debt	1,348	23.5	14.0	15.0	22.0	37.0	69.0	101	117	14.0
Common Eqty.	4,477	1,255	727	443	285	150	-1.0	-22.0	-41.0	109
Total Cap.	5,892	1,279	741	458	307	187	68.0	80.0	78.0	124
Cap. Exp.	183	59.7	30.2	17.6	9.1	4.6	6.7	4.9	4.1	7.4
Cash Flow	312	197	179	141	110	76.1	40.8	28.9	19.0	-2.3
Curr. Ratio	1.5	3.0	5.1	4.6	3.1	1.9	1.5	1.4	1.3	1.9
% LT Debt of Cap.	22.9	1.8	1.9	3.3	7.2	19.9	101.4	126.5	NM	11.5
% Net Inc.of Revs.	1.0	7.0	11.5	11.3	10.0	8.0	3.9	3.9	2.2	NM
% Ret. on Assets	0.7	9.1	16.2	16.9	15.8	14.1	7.8	8.0	3.7	NM
% Ret. on Equity	2.1	16.6	27.1	32.0	39.7	NM	NM	NM	20.9	NM

Data bef. results of disc. opers. and/or spec. items. Data in quarterly 1998 columns are pro forma for calendar 1997, to reflect pooling-of-interest merger with HFS Inc. and new fiscal year-end. Results for prior fiscal years do not include the HFS merger. Per share data adj. for stk. divs. as of ex-div. date. E-Estimated. NA-Not Available. NM-Not Meaningful. NR-Not Ranked.

Office—707 Summer St., Stamford, CT 06901. **Tel**—(203) 324-9261. **Website**—http:\\www.cendant.com.**Fax**—(203) 977-8501. **Chrmn**—W. A. Forbes. **Pres & CEO**—H. R. Silverman **CFO**—M. P. Monaco. **SVP & Investor Contact**—Laura P. Hamilton (203-965-5114). **Secy**—R. T. Tucker. **Dirs (partial list)**— J. E. Buckman, B. Burnap, L. S. Coleman, T. B. Donnelly, M. L. Edelman, W. A. Forbes, F. D. Green, S. A. Greyser, C. G. Hankin, S. H. Holmes, R. D. Kunisch, C. K. McLeod, M. P. Monaco, B. Mulroney, R. E. Nederlander, B. C. Perfit, A. G. Petrello, R. W. Pittman, E. J. Rosenwald, Jr., E. K. Shelton, H. R. Silverman, J. D. Snodgrass, R. T. Tucker. **Transfer Agent & Registrar**—First National Bank of Boston. **Incorporated**—in Delaware in 1974. **Empl**— 34,000. **S&P Analyst:** Tom Graves, CFA

STANDARD &POOR'S
STOCK REPORTS

Centex Corp.

471

NYSE Symbol **CTX**

In S&P 500

12-SEP-98

Industry:
Homebuilding

Summary: This leading U.S. homebuilder sells homes in 20 states and also engages in mortgage banking, general construction contracting and the manufacture of construction products.

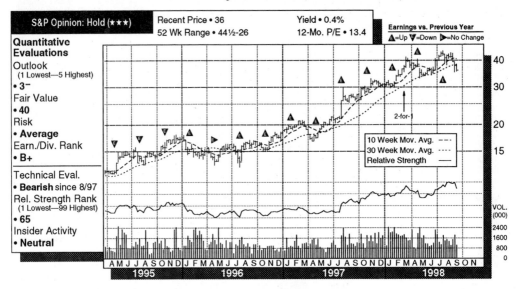

S&P Opinion: Hold (★★★)		
Recent Price • 36	Yield • 0.4%	
52 Wk Range • 44½-26	12-Mo. P/E • 13.4	

Quantitative Evaluations

Outlook
(1 Lowest—5 Highest)
• **3⁻**

Fair Value
• **40**

Risk
• **Average**

Earn./Div. Rank
• **B+**

Technical Eval.
• **Bearish** since 8/97

Rel. Strength Rank
(1 Lowest—99 Highest)
• **65**

Insider Activity
• **Neutral**

Earnings vs. Previous Year
▲=Up ▼=Down ►=No Change

10 Week Mov. Avg. ----
30 Week Mov. Avg. ·····
Relative Strength ——

2-for-1

Overview - 31-AUG-98

With accommodating interest rates leading to better order levels in recent quarters, solid sales growth should be recorded in FY 99 (Mar.). Mortgage originations should mirror home sales, and the sharp drop in interest rates over the past year seems likely to keep refinancings strong. Sales should pick up in contracting, as a solid economy should boost nonresidential construction and outweigh the effects of competitive industry conditions and a recently initiated downsizing. Sales gains should also continue at Centex Construction Products, given good construction markets and tight industry capacity in cement and wallboard. Margins should be aided by a focus on operating efficiencies and cost controls in homebuilding, greater mortgage activity in the financial services area, better construction contracts, and favorable conditions in the construction products business.

Valuation - 31-AUG-98

The shares have moved sharply higher since mid-1996, boosted by investor excitement about Centex's entry into the investment real estate field, along with a downturn in interest rates for much of the past couple of years. Most current factors also point toward interest rates remaining accommodating to home sales over the next year. However, the maturity of the housing cycle and a wide variety of economic uncertainties pose some worries, especially if the summer 1998 stock market correction reduces consumer wealth and consumer confidence. Thus, we would prefer to place our homebuilding investments in firms stressing the recently recovering California market, and those concentrating on strong niche markets (retirement homes, luxury homes). That line of thinking leaves us neutral on the shares.

Key Stock Statistics

S&P EPS Est. 1999	3.20	Tang. Bk. Value/Share	13.81
P/E on S&P Est. 1999	11.3	Beta	1.44
Dividend Rate/Share	0.16	Shareholders	2,200
Shs. outstg. (M)	59.6	Market cap. (B)	$ 2.1
Avg. daily vol. (M)	0.279	Inst. holdings	82%

Value of $10,000 invested 5 years ago: $ 23,239

Fiscal Year Ending Mar. 31

	1999	1998	1997	1996	1995	1994
Revenues (Million $)						
1Q	1,111	861.4	892.4	701.0	832.5	698.3
2Q	—	991.8	1,002	786.9	855.7	813.5
3Q	—	983.1	939.1	790.1	793.2	833.3
4Q	—	1,139	951.9	825.0	796.1	869.5
Yr.	—	3,975	3,785	3,103	3,278	3,214
Earnings Per Share ($)						
1Q	**0.78**	0.45	0.38	0.14	0.83	0.26
2Q	**E0.80**	0.60	0.48	0.25	0.28	0.35
3Q	**E0.80**	**0.60**	0.47	0.26	0.22	0.36
4Q	**E0.82**	**0.71**	0.49	0.27	0.27	0.33
Yr.	**E3.20**	**2.36**	1.81	0.92	1.52	1.30

Next earnings report expected: late October

Dividend Data (Dividends have been paid since 1973.)

Amount ($)	Date Decl.	Ex-Div. Date	Stock of Record	Payment Date
2-for-1	Dec. 18	Mar. 02	Feb. 13	Feb. 27 '98
0.040	Feb. 27	Mar. 13	Mar. 17	Apr. 14 '98
0.040	Jun. 08	Jun. 09	Jun. 11	Jul. 09 '98
0.040	Aug. 07	Sep. 08	Sep. 10	Oct. 01 '98

A Division of The **McGraw·Hill** Companies

Business Summary - 31-AUG-98

Centex Corp. constructs site-built homes in 20 states throughout the U.S. and has ranked among the top 10 homebuilders in the nation in each of the past 28 years. CTX sells homes to both first-time and move-up buyers. In an effort to better serve the growing affordable home market, Centex entered the manufactured housing industry in March 1997 through the acquisition of an 80% stake in Cavco Industries, for $74.3 million. CTX also has operations in a variety of construction and real estate-related businesses.

To reduce exposure to local market volatility, Centex presently builds homes in 260 neighborhoods. The company delivered 12,418 homes in FY 98 (Mar.), off 5.3% from the year-earlier level, which ranks as the highest in its history. Given its diverse grouping of homes, CTX's sales prices fall into a wide range, with the average price amounting to $183,300 in FY 98. Single-family detached homes represent the large majority of Centex's home sales. Conventional homebuilding operations accounted for about 58% of CTX's sales and 60% of operating earnings in FY 98.

Affected by higher interest rates and operating in fewer neighborhoods (as part of a strategy to improve operating efficiencies), CTX recorded a 12% decline in new home unit orders in FY 97. However, orders picked up in FY 98, when a 10% gain was recorded. Positive trends continued in the first quarter of FY 99, with orders up 16%.

Centex's investment real estate division (formed in mid-1996) consists of Centex Real Estate Corp. (CREC), which it obtained in several transactions in FY 96 and FY 97. CREC's property portfolio consists of land in nine states, and CTX conducts major housing operations in all of CREC's principal markets. As a result of the accounting methods used in the transactions, when $125 million of properties contributed to the venture by CTX are developed or sold, proceeds will be reflected as operating margin. In addition, negative goodwill recorded as a result of the combination will be amortized for several years, at an annual rate estimated by CTX at $12 million to $16 million.

To aid in the home selling process, Centex originates mortgage loans through its CTX Mortgage Co. unit. The opening of mortgage offices in most of its housing markets has enabled CTX to provide financing for an average of 71% of its home closings over the past five years (through FY 98); it also originates mortgages on homes sold by others.

Centex's other operations consist of a nationwide construction contracting business and a 56% stake in Centex Construction Products, which makes and distributes portland cement, aggregates, readymix concrete and gypsum wallboard.

Per Share Data ($)

(Year Ended Mar. 31)	1998	1997	1996	1995	1994	1993	1992	1991	1990	1989
Tangible Bk. Val.	14.40	12.62	12.71	11.90	10.56	9.29	8.49	8.04	7.43	6.64
Cash Flow	2.78	2.04	1.13	1.63	1.60	1.21	0.80	0.96	1.15	0.85
Earnings	2.36	1.81	0.92	1.52	1.30	0.95	0.56	0.71	1.00	0.66
Dividends	0.14	0.10	0.10	0.10	0.10	0.10	0.10	0.10	0.09	0.07
Payout Ratio	6%	6%	11%	7%	8%	10%	18%	14%	10%	10%
Cal. Yrs.	1997	1996	1995	1994	1993	1992	1991	1990	1989	1988
Prices - High	33	18⅞	18	22⅞	22⅝	16½	11⅝	11⅛	10½	7⅜
- Low	16¾	12⅝	11	10⅛	13⅜	10	7	4⅞	6⅞	4⅛
P/E Ratio - High	14	10	20	15	17	17	21	16	10	11
- Low	7	7	12	7	10	10	13	7	7	6

Income Statement Analysis (Million $)

Revs.	3,975	3,785	3,103	3,278	3,214	2,503	2,166	2,244	2,073	1,845
Oper. Inc.	334	243	74.7	76.0	155	108	61.0	72.0	90.0	56.0
Depr.	25.6	13.5	12.5	6.4	19.6	16.2	15.4	15.4	8.8	11.3
Int. Exp.	33.3	34.1	40.9	33.0	NA	NA	NA	NA	NA	NA
Pretax Inc.	232	164	87.8	146	135	91.8	45.9	56.6	83.3	58.7
Eff. Tax Rate	38%	35%	39%	37%	37%	34%	25%	23%	26%	32%
Net Inc.	145	107	53.4	92.2	85.2	61.0	34.6	43.6	62.0	40.0

Balance Sheet & Other Fin. Data (Million $)

Cash	98.3	31.3	14.0	24.0	155	136	272	41.0	26.0	22.0
Curr. Assets	NA	NA	NA	NA	NA	NA	NA	NA	NA	NA
Total Assets	3,416	2,679	2,337	2,050	2,580	2,272	2,347	2,032	2,045	1,801
Curr. Liab.	NA	NA	1,277	1,133	1,613	1,366	1,496	1,289	1,354	1,150
LT Debt	238	237	321	221	224	227	230	145	148	152
Common Eqty.	991	836	723	668	669	578	518	484	448	384
Total Cap.	1,464	1,314	1,060	916	944	878	819	708	654	612
Cap. Exp.	36.9	16.1	7.0	10.6	31.9	18.0	18.0	15.0	34.0	28.0
Cash Flow	170	120	65.9	99	105	77.2	50.0	59.0	70.8	51.3
Curr. Ratio	NA	NA	NA	NA	NA	NA	NA	NA	NA	NA
% LT Debt of Cap.	16.2	18.0	30.3	24.2	23.7	25.8	28.1	20.5	22.6	24.9
% Net Inc.of Revs.	3.6	2.8	1.7	2.8	2.6	2.4	1.6	1.9	3.0	2.2
% Ret. on Assets	4.8	4.2	2.4	4.3	3.5	2.6	1.6	2.1	3.2	2.9
% Ret. on Equity	15.9	13.7	7.7	14.6	13.6	11.0	6.8	9.4	14.6	10.9

Data as orig. reptd.; bef. results of disc. opers. and/or spec. items. Per share data adj. for stk. divs. as of ex-div. date. Bold denotes diluted EPS (FASB 128). E-Estimated. NA-Not Available. NM-Not Meaningful. NR-Not Ranked.

Office—2728 N. Harwood, Dallas, TX 75201-1516. **Mailing Address**—P.O. Box 199000, Dallas, TX 75219-9000. **Tel**—(214) 981-5000. **Website**—http://www.centex.com **Chrmn & CEO**—L. E. Hirsch. **Vice Chrmn & CFO**—D. W. Quinn. **VP & Investor Contact**—Sheila E. Gallagher. **Dirs**—A. B. Coleman, D. W. Cook III, J. L. Elek, L. E. Hirsch, C. W. Murchison III, C. H. Pistor, D. W. Quinn, P. R. Seegers, P. T. Stoffel. **Transfer Agent & Registrar**—ChaseMellon, Ridgefield Park, NJ. **Incorporated**—in Nevada in 1968; predecessor organized in Texas in 1950. **Empl**—10,259. **S&P Analyst:** Michael W. Jaffe

12-SEP-98

Industry:
Electric Companies

Summary: This Dallas-based utility holding company, which has four electric utility units in the southwestern U.S. and one in the U.K., has agreed to merge with American Electric Power.

S&P Opinion: Hold (★★★)	Recent Price • 27⅛	Yield • 6.4%
	52 Wk Range • 28-20	12-Mo. P/E • 27.4

Earnings vs. Previous Year
▲=Up ▼=Down ▶=No Change

Quantitative Evaluations

Outlook
(1 Lowest—5 Highest)
• **1**

Fair Value
• **25¼**

Risk
• **Low**

Earn./Div. Rank
• **B+**

Technical Eval.
• **Bullish** since 11/97

Rel. Strength Rank
(1 Lowest—99 Highest)
• **94**

Insider Activity
• **Favorable**

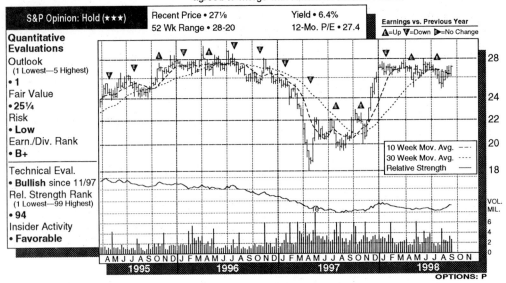

10 Week Mov. Avg. – – –
30 Week Mov. Avg. ·······
Relative Strength ——

VOL. MIL.

A M J J A S O N D | J F M A M J J A S O N D | J F M A M J J A S O N D | J F M A M J J A S O N
1995 | 1996 | 1997 | 1998

OPTIONS: P

Overview - 26-AUG-98

We expect the planned merger of CSR and American Electric Power (AEP) to be completed by mid-1999. The merger would result in the largest electric utility in the U.S., serving 4.6 million customers in 11 states, with around $11 billion in annual revenues. The companies expect the merger to realize cost savings of about $2 billion over a 10-year period, to be dilutive by about 3% in the first year after its anticipated completion, and to become accretive by the end of the third year. Earnings in the first half of 1998 have benefited from more favorable weather and lower O&M expenses. In 1997, earnings were hurt by a one-time charge of $0.76 a share for the U.K.'s windfall profits tax on SEEBOARD, and a charge of nearly $35 million related to the termination of CSR's proposed merger with El Paso Electric Company. On a stand-alone basis, EPS will be essentially flat in 1999, restricted by the rate reduction orders of the Public Utility Commission of Texas (PUCT). In July 1997, the PUCT issued its final order which is expected to decrease the annual net income of CSR's Central Power & Light (CPL) unit by about $33.4 million in 1998, and $42.2 million in 1999.

Valuation - 26-AUG-98

With the planned merger with AEP expected to be completed in mid-1999, we would continue to hold CSR stock. The shares (which are down slightly year to date) should reflect both the price of AEP shares (since the company's shareholders would receive 0.6 AEP shares for each CSR share) and the time lag until the completion of the merger. On its own fundamentals, we have been concerned about CSR's high dividend payout ratio (at 89% of our 1998 EPS estimate of $1.95). However, after the announcement of the proposed merger, the probability of a cut in the dividend (yielding about 6.5%) has been greatly reduced.

Key Stock Statistics

S&P EPS Est. 1998	1.95	Tang. Bk. Value/Share	9.93
P/E on S&P Est. 1998	13.9	Beta	0.35
S&P EPS Est. 1999	1.95	Shareholders	74,000
Dividend Rate/Share	1.74	Market cap. (B)	$ 5.8
Shs. outstg. (M)	212.5	Inst. holdings	57%
Avg. daily vol. (M)	0.537		

Value of $10,000 invested 5 years ago: $ 13,342

Fiscal Year Ending Dec. 31

	1998	1997	1996	1995	1994	1993
Revenues (Million $)						
1Q	1,257	1,278	1,216	659.0	850.0	810.0
2Q	1,344	1,184	1,267	920.0	908.0	892.0
3Q	—	1,477	1,438	1,087	1,070	1,140
4Q	—	1,330	1,235	1,069	795.0	843.0
Yr.	—	5,268	5,155	3,735	3,623	3,688
Earnings Per Share ($)						
1Q	**0.28**	0.12	0.22	0.20	0.23	0.23
2Q	**0.50**	0.39	0.05	0.54	0.55	0.48
3Q	**E0.92**	0.93	0.90	1.04	0.97	0.93
4Q	**E0.25**	0.11	0.26	0.32	0.33	-0.25
Yr.	**E1.95**	1.55	2.07	2.10	2.08	1.39

Next earnings report expected: late October

Dividend Data (Dividends have been paid since 1947.)

Amount ($)	Date Decl.	Ex-Div. Date	Stock of Record	Payment Date
0.435	Oct. 23	Nov. 05	Nov. 07	Dec. 01 '97
0.435	Jan. 21	Feb. 05	Feb. 09	Feb. 27 '98
0.435	Apr. 23	May. 06	May. 08	Jun. 01 '98
0.435	Jul. 22	Aug. 05	Aug. 07	Aug. 31 '98

A Division of The McGraw-Hill Companies

Business Summary - 26-AUG-98

In December 1997, CSR and American Electric Power Co., Inc. (AEP) agreed to merge into a new company that will maintain the AEP name. Under the terms of the agreement, shareholders of Central & South West will receive 0.6 of a share of AEP common stock for each CSR share. The companies expect the proposed merger to be completed by mid-1999.

CSR's U.S. subsidiaries include: Central Power & Light (25% of 1997 revenues, 35% of operating income), Public Service of Oklahoma (13%, 11%), Southwestern Electric Power (17%, 13%) and West Texas Utilities (8%, 12%). In recent years, U.S. electric revenues (which accounted for 64% of total revenues in 1997) were derived as follows:

	1997	1996	1995	1994
Residential	38%	38%	40%	38%
Commercial	27%	27%	28%	27%
Industrial	24%	24%	24%	24%
Other	11%	11%	8%	11%

After the April 1996 acquisition of SEEBOARD plc, a U.K.-based electric company, Central & South West (a Texas-based public utility holding company) now has more customers outside the U.S. than it does with its four electric utilities in the southwestern United States.

SEEBOARD, which accounted for 35% of CSR 's 1997 revenues and 30% of its earnings (second only to Central Power & Light), serves about 2 million customers in an affluent suburban and rural area of southeastern England with above-average economic growth. While distribution and supply represent SEEBOARD's principal regulated businesses, the company is also involved in gas supply, electric generation, and electrical contracting and retailing.

The company's other subsidiaries include CSW Energy, which develops and operates non-utility power projects in the U.S.; EnerShop, which provides energy management analysis and equipment for commercial and government entities; CSW Energy Services, which markets electricity in competitive retail markets; and CSW International, which acquires and operates energy facilities in other countries.

In 1996, CSR secured certification for CSW Communications (later renamed C3 Communications), which develops and operates telecommunication services, as the first exempt company under the 1996 Telecommunications Act. In January 1997, the unit formed a limited partnership (ChoiceCom) with ICG Communications to market telecommunication services to customers in Texas, Oklahoma, Louisiana and Arkansas.

Per Share Data ($)

(Year Ended Dec. 31)	1997	1996	1995	1994	1993	1992	1991	1990	1989	1988
Tangible Bk. Val.	9.20	9.84	9.87	15.90	14.45	14.71	14.30	13.80	13.28	13.75
Earnings	1.55	1.43	2.10	2.08	1.39	2.03	1.99	1.89	1.63	1.72
Dividends	1.74	1.74	1.72	1.70	1.62	1.54	1.46	1.38	1.30	1.22
Payout Ratio	112%	122%	82%	82%	117%	76%	73%	73%	80%	71%
Prices - High	27½	29½	28½	30⅞	34¼	30	27⅛	23	20⅛	17⅜
- Low	18	25⅜	22⅜	20⅛	28¼	24¼	20¾	18⅜	14⅞	14¾
P/E Ratio - High	18	21	14	15	25	15	14	12	12	10
- Low	12	18	11	10	20	12	10	10	9	9

Income Statement Analysis (Million $)

	1997	1996	1995	1994	1993	1992	1991	1990	1989	1988
Revs.	5,268	5,155	3,735	3,623	3,687	3,289	3,047	2,744	2,549	2,512
Depr.	497	464	384	356	330	308	291	284	277	254
Maint.	152	150	161	176	197	170	181	164	155	133
Fxd. Chgs. Cov.	2.1	2.3	2.3	2.8	2.5	2.8	2.8	2.5	2.5	2.7
Constr. Credits	NA	NA	NA	NA	NA	2.0	5.0	4.0	42.0	158
Eff. Tax Rate	30%	42%	20%	28%	29%	26%	28%	31%	29%	24%
Net Inc.	341	315	421	412	281	404	401	386	337	356

Balance Sheet & Other Fin. Data (Million $)

	1997	1996	1995	1994	1993	1992	1991	1990	1989	1988
Gross Prop.	13,846	13,421	13,778	11,868	11,357	11,190	10,788	10,251	9,634	9,370
Cap. Exp.	507	521	474	578	508	425	327	329	331	463
Net Prop.	8,628	8,481	9,017	7,998	7,807	7,903	7,802	7,550	7,186	7,151
Capitalization:										
LT Debt	4,233	4,024	3,914	2,940	2,749	2,647	2,518	2,513	2,537	2,514
% LT Debt	53	49	53	47	46	45	44	45	46	46
Pfd.	202	325	326	327	350	367	389	394	397	396
% Pfd.	2.50	4.00	4.40	5.20	5.80	6.20	6.80	7.00	7.10	7.20
Common	3,556	3,802	3,178	3,052	2,930	2,927	2,834	2,743	2,647	2,594
% Common	45	47	43	48	49	49	49	49	47	47
Total Cap.	10,701	10,714	10,232	8,687	8,299	7,951	7,677	7,528	7,366	7,196
% Oper. Ratio	85.9	84.6	82.4	83.6	87.6	82.0	81.4	82.0	80.7	81.7
% Earn. on Net Prop.	8.6	4.9	4.9	7.5	5.9	7.5	7.4	6.7	6.9	6.5
% Return On Revs.	6.5	6.1	11.3	11.4	7.6	12.3	13.2	14.1	13.2	14.2
% Return On Invest. Capital	8.5	6.9	4.5	8.3	6.8	8.6	8.8	9.5	8.4	8.2
% Return On Com. Equity	8.9	8.5	12.9	13.2	10.6	13.3	13.4	13.2	11.7	12.7

Data as orig. reptd.; bef. results of disc. opers. and/or spec. items. Per share data adj. for stk. divs. as of ex-div. date. Bold denotes diluted EPS (FASB 128). E-Estimated. NA-Not Available. NM-Not Meaningful. NR-Not Ranked.

Office—1616 Woodall Rodgers Freeway, Dallas, TX 75202,1234. **Tel**—(214) 777-1000. **Website**—http://www.csw.com **Chrmn & CEO**—E. R. Brooks. **Pres & COO**—T. V. Shockley III. **EVP & CFO**—G. D. Rosilier. **Secy**—K. C. Raney, Jr. **Investor Contact**—Becky Hall. **Dirs**—M. S. Boren, E. R. Brooks, D. M. Carlton, T. J. Ellis, J. H. Foy, W. R. Howell, R. W. Lawless, J. L. Powell, R. L. Sandor, T. V. Shockley III. **Transfer Agent & Registrar**—Co.'s office. **Incorporated**—in Delaware in 1925. **Empl**— 11,415. **S&P Analyst:** Justin McCann

12-SEP-98

Industry: Services (Data Processing)

Summary: This information services company serves the human resources, transportation and electronic media markets.

| S&P Opinion: Buy (★★★★★) | Recent Price • 56 | Yield • Nil |
| | 52 Wk Range • 64½-33¼ | 12-Mo. P/E • 9.8 |

Quantitative Evaluations

Outlook
(1 Lowest—5 Highest)
• **3+**

Fair Value
• **58⅞**

Risk
• **Average**

Earn./Div. Rank
• **B-**

Technical Eval.
• **Bullish** since 8/98

Rel. Strength Rank
(1 Lowest—99 Highest)
• **90**

Insider Activity
• **NA**

Earnings vs. Previous Year
▲=Up ▼=Down ▶=No Change

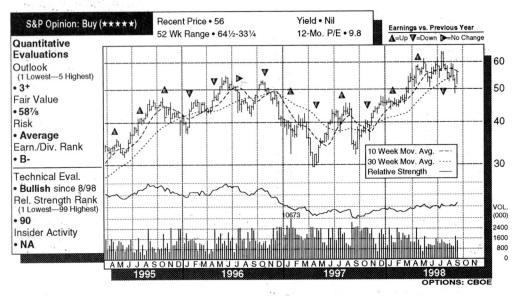

10 Week Mov. Avg. ‑ ‑ ‑
30 Week Mov. Avg. ‑ ‑ ‑ ‑
Relative Strength ———

OPTIONS: CBOE

Overview - 22-JUL-98

Revenues from continuing operations are expected to increase about 15% in 1998. Following the sale of Computing Devices International (CDI), the company's defense electronics business, as well as the sale of its gaming unit, Ceridian has been transformed into a pure information services company. Each of its three businesses should post solid revenue growth in 1998. The Human Resources Group is benefitting from strength in payroll and tax filing services. Comdata is showing strength in the transportation segment. Arbitron is being aided by initiatives to expand its services beyond radio ratings. Margins should widen, on improved operating efficiencies, especially in the payroll area. Earnings shown for the 1997 third quarter are before a $150 million charge ($1.87 a share) for the termination of the CII payroll software development project. Excluding charges and CDI's operations, 1997 EPS would have been $1.55.

Valuation - 22-JUL-98

Ceridian should generate annual operating earnings growth of between 15% and 20% over the next several years, driven by strength in each of its three information services segments. Strategic acquisitions should add incrementally to revenues, and should continue to strengthen the company's competitive position. Cost controls and operating efficiencies should benefit margins. We view favorably the divestiture of non-core businesses, as CEN will now be more of a pure information services company, with steady, recurring revenues, and wider margins. We believe that the shares are undervalued relative to those of the company's payroll competitors, in terms of PE/growth rate and price/sales ratios. We recommend purchasing the shares.

Key Stock Statistics

S&P EPS Est. 1998	1.90	Tang. Bk. Value/Share	3.44
P/E on S&P Est. 1998	29.5	Beta	1.15
S&P EPS Est. 1999	2.30	Shareholders	14,800
Dividend Rate/Share	Nil	Market cap. (B)	$ 4.1
Shs. outstg. (M)	72.5	Inst. holdings	70%
Avg. daily vol. (M)	0.264		

Value of $10,000 invested 5 years ago: $ 36,721

Fiscal Year Ending Dec. 31

	1998	1997	1996	1995	1994	1993
Revenues (Million $)						
1Q	282.3	263.9	369.0	326.2	221.3	224.0
2Q	284.1	261.8	361.5	327.4	218.5	225.9
3Q	—	266.6	361.0	317.9	242.4	208.9
4Q	—	282.5	404.1	361.5	234.1	226.9
Yr.	—	1,075	1,496	1,333	916.3	886.1
Earnings Per Share ($)						
1Q	**0.49**	**0.40**	0.63	0.47	0.42	0.30
2Q	**0.42**	**0.45**	0.53	0.38	0.29	0.20
3Q	**E0.46**	**-1.39**	0.59	0.44	0.35	0.25
4Q	**E0.53**	**1.00**	0.65	-0.06	0.38	-1.24
Yr.	**E1.90**	**0.45**	1.67	1.22	1.43	-0.52

Next earnings report expected: mid October

Dividend Data

Common dividends were omitted in 1985, after having been paid since 1977. In July 1992, the company distributed 0.25 of a Control Data Systems common share for each CEN common share held.

A Division of The **McGraw·Hill** *Companies*

Business Summary - 22-JUL-98

In 1997, Ceridian completed its transformation to a pure information services company. After the sale of Computing Devices International (CDI), its defense electronics segment, the company now provides information services to the human resources, transportation and electronic media markets.

CDI was sold to General Dynamics in late 1997, for $600 million. The proceeds were used to buy back CEN stock. CDI is a provider of mission-critical electronics, software, systems integration and information management, mainly to defense agencies in the U.S. and abroad.

As a company focused entirely on information services, Ceridian believes that it has stronger growth prospects. Its objectives are to boost annual revenues at least 15%, and EPS about 20%.

In the human resources segment (61% of 1997 information services (IS) revenues), CEN serves more than 90,000 customers with services and software designed to help employers more effectively manage their work forces and information that is integral to human resource processes. Its products include payroll processing and tax filing services, human resource information systems, benefits administration software, time and attendance systems and recruiting and skills management software. CEN believes that demand for payroll and tax filing services will remain strong as organizations are forced to adapt to the increasing scope and complexity of laws and regulations governing businesses.

The company's Comdata unit (21% of 1997 IS revenues) provides transaction processing and information services to the transportation industry. Comdata provides trucking companies with fuel cards, as well as fuel management, express cash, permitting, licensing, fuel tax reporting, vehicle escort and other services. It provides services to more than 350,000 drivers and 2,000 truck stop service centers. Comdata sold its gaming services unit to First Data Corp. in January 1998. The unit provided a full range of funds transfers to patrons at gaming properties through credit cards and bank debit cards.

Arbitron (18% of 1997 IS revenues) provides media and marketing research information to broadcasters (primarily in radio) and advertisers. As of December 31, 1997, Arbitron provides quantitative audience research to about 3,000 radio stations and 2,200 advertising agencies nationwide.

In the 1997 first quarter, the company recorded a $12.1 million charge, after tax, to reflect the March 1997 settlement of certain litigation. In the third quarter, CEN recorded a $150 million charge for the termination of the CII payroll software development project.

Per Share Data ($)

(Year Ended Dec. 31)	1997	1996	1995	1994	1993	1992	1991	1990	1989	1988
Tangible Bk. Val.	7.96	0.80	NM	-3.91	-3.63	-2.36	10.09	10.35	9.31	24.97
Cash Flow	1.21	3.44	2.13	2.00	0.07	-0.15	1.66	2.26	-12.53	4.67
Earnings	0.45	2.39	1.22	1.43	-0.52	-0.69	-0.21	0.05	-16.11	0.03
Dividends	Nil	Nil	Nil	Nil	Nil	Nil	Nil	Nil	Nil	Nil
Payout Ratio	Nil	Nil	Nil	Nil	Nil	Nil	Nil	Nil	Nil	Nil
Prices - High	47¾	54⅞	47½	27½	19⅞	17¼	13¾	21⅝	24	30½
- Low	29½	37	26⅛	18½	'13	9⅛	6¾	7⅝	16¼	16⅜
P/E Ratio - High	NM	23	39	19	NM	NM	NM	NM	NM	NM
- Low	NM	15	21	13	NM	NM	NM	NM	NM	NM

Income Statement Analysis (Million $)

	1997	1996	1995	1994	1993	1992	1991	1990	1989	1988
Revs.	1,075	1,496	1,333	916	886	830	1,525	1,691	2,935	3,628
Oper. Inc.	241	276	232	99	79.0	67.0	93.0	131	209	243
Depr.	60.9	73.9	63.0	26.0	26.0	23.0	80.0	94.0	151	194
Int. Exp.	11.2	10.6	31.0	2.0	16.0	16.0	25.0	44.0	94.0	90.0
Pretax Inc.	-138	196	116	85.0	-18.0	-24.0	2.0	16.0	-666	18.0
Eff. Tax Rate	NA	7.30%	16%	7.70%	NM	NM	NM	83%	NM	91%
Net Inc.	35.4	182	97.5	79.0	-22.0	-29.0	-9.0	3.0	-679	2.0

Balance Sheet & Other Fin. Data (Million $)

	1997	1996	1995	1994	1993	1992	1991	1990	1989	1988
Cash	268	169	152	171	216	153	211	351	525	198
Curr. Assets	720	614	571	346	387	346	792	951	1,274	1,675
Total Assets	1,243	1,251	1,126	690	616	530	1,214	1,424	1,861	2,534
Curr. Liab.	479	625	606	307	316	298	467	624	843	919
LT Debt	0.8	142	205	18.0	16.0	187	183	193	352	379
Common Eqty.	588	346	-86.0	-50.0	-124	-100	435	446	401	1,043
Total Cap.	589	496	126	212	134	92.0	636	655	768	1,463
Cap. Exp.	44.2	52.7	53.0	38.0	28.0	19.0	68.0	104	156	257
Cash Flow	96.3	243	148	92.0	3.0	-7.0	71.0	96.0	-529	196
Curr. Ratio	1.5	1.0	0.9	7.1	1.2	1.2	1.7	1.5	1.5	1.8
% LT Debt of Cap.	0.1	28.7	162.4	8.3	12.2	202.9	28.8	29.5	45.9	25.9
% Net Inc.of Revs.	3.3	12.2	7.3	8.6	NM	NM	NM	0.2	NM	NM
% Ret. on Assets	2.8	15.3	9.3	11.9	NM	NM	NM	0.2	NM	0.1
% Ret. on Equity	7.6	NM	NM	NM	NM	NM	NM	0.5	NM	0.1

Data as orig. reptd.; bef. results of disc. opers. and/or spec. items. Per share data adj. for stk. divs. as of ex-div. date. Bold denotes diluted EPS (FASB 128). Tabular revs. and EPS for the first three quarters of 1997 incl. results of discont. ops. E-Estimated. NA-Not Available. NM-Not Meaningful. NR-Not Ranked.

Office—8100 34th Ave. South, Minneapolis, MN 55425. **Tel**—(612) 853-8100. **Website**—http://www.ceridian.com. **Chrmn, Pres & CEO**—L. Perlman. **EVP & CFO**—J. Eickhoff. **VP & Secy**—J. Haveman. **VP & Treas**—J. Grierson. **Investor Contact**—Craig Manson (612-853-6022). **Dirs**—R. M. Davis, R. H. Ewald, R. G. Lareau, R. T. LeMay, G. R. Lewis, C. Marshall, R. A. Matricaria, L. Perlman, C. J. Uhrich, R. W. Vieser, P. S. Walsh. **Transfer Agent & Registrar**—Bank of New York, NYC. **Incorporated**—in Delaware in 1912. **Empl**— 8,000. **S&P Analyst**: Brian Goodstadt

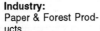
Champion International

490

NYSE Symbol **CHA**

In S&P 500

12-SEP-98

Industry: Paper & Forest Products

Summary: This leading paper maker announced a major reorganization plan in October 1997. When all is said and done, CHA will be focusing on its core coated and uncoated paper lines.

S&P Opinion: Hold (★★★)		
Recent Price • 30⅝	Yield • 0.7%	Earnings vs. Previous Year
52 Wk Range • 66½-29½	12-Mo. P/E • NM	▲=Up ▼=Down ▶=No Change

Quantitative Evaluations

Outlook (1 Lowest—5 Highest)
• **2**

Fair Value
• **30¼**

Risk
• **Low**

Earn./Div. Rank
• **B-**

Technical Eval.
• **NA**

Rel. Strength Rank (1 Lowest—99 Highest)
• **25**

Insider Activity
• **NA**

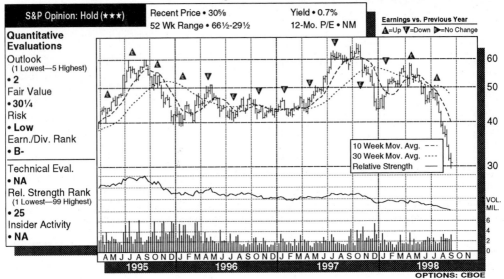

10 Week Mov. Avg. ---
30 Week Mov. Avg. ·······
Relative Strength ——

OPTIONS: CBOE

Overview - 18-AUG-98

Sales from comparable operations should rise modestly in 1998, on mixed results. We expect increased paper sales, on slightly higher average prices for CHA's mainstay coated and uncoated grades. However, Asia's financial woes and a strong U.S. dollar have impacted foreign trade, and led to a recent setback in the modest uncoated pricing recovery seen since early 1997. We expect the paper sales gains to be partly offset by a modest decline in the wood products area, where lumber market oversupply has brought down prices. Margins should widen noticeably, on the maturation of a recently enacted profit enhancement program, which will focus on cost reduction, productivity gains and a better product mix. Slightly higher average full year paper prices should also aid the bottom line. Comparisons will be distorted by a $5.76 a share reorganization charge in 1997's final quarter. One-time gains of $0.07 a share in 1998's second quarter appear in the EPS table, but have been excluded from our forecast.

Valuation - 18-AUG-98

The shares seesawed over the past year. They rebounded strongly in spring and summer 1997, when paper industry conditions began to firm. They have since given back all of the gains (despite a brief early 1998 upturn), as Asia's woes and a strong U.S. dollar set back the paper recovery and also left lumber markets in a bad state. We think Asia's problems will be here for a while, and see them continuing to hinder the forest products industry. On the other hand, we view Champion's recent business reorganization program with enthusiasm. The company's new management team has taken swift actions to address long-running disappointments in operating performance, and we believe CHA will be much better situated for the next industry upturn. As such, we remain neutral on the shares.

Key Stock Statistics

S&P EPS Est. 1998	1.00	Tang. Bk. Value/Share	33.12
P/E on S&P Est. 1998	30.6	Beta	0.90
S&P EPS Est. 1999	1.50	Shareholders	19,600
Dividend Rate/Share	0.20	Market cap. (B)	$ 2.9
Shs. outstg. (M)	95.6	Inst. holdings	91%
Avg. daily vol. (M)	0.548		

Value of $10,000 invested 5 years ago: $ 10,995

Fiscal Year Ending Dec. 31

	1998	1997	1996	1995	1994	1993
Revenues (Million $)						
1Q	1,477	1,367	1,533	1,634	1,226	1,267
2Q	1,474	1,407	1,445	1,756	1,242	1,256
3Q	—	1,478	1,470	1,841	1,385	1,245
4Q	—	1,483	1,432	1,741	1,465	1,300
Yr.	—	5,736	5,880	6,972	5,318	5,069
Earnings Per Share ($)						
1Q	0.20	-0.39	0.88	1.33	-0.41	-0.38
2Q	0.33	-0.12	0.16	1.93	-0.41	-0.31
3Q	—	0.21	0.33	2.47	0.18	-0.65
4Q	—	-5.42	0.11	2.26	1.02	-0.41
Yr.	—	-5.72	1.48	8.01	0.38	-1.75

Next earnings report expected: mid October

Dividend Data (Dividends have been paid since 1940.)

Amount ($)	Date Decl.	Ex-Div. Date	Stock of Record	Payment Date
0.050	Nov. 20	Dec. 17	Dec. 19	Jan. 16 '98
0.050	Feb. 19	Mar. 18	Mar. 20	Apr. 17 '98
0.050	May. 21	Jun. 17	Jun. 19	Jul. 17 '98
0.050	Aug. 20	Sep. 16	Sep. 18	Oct. 16 '98

A Division of The McGraw-Hill Companies

STANDARD
&POOR'S
STOCK REPORTS

Champion International Corporation

490

12-SEP-98

Business Summary - 18-AUG-98

One of the largest U.S. producers of paper and wood products, Champion International has been in transition, with both the chairman and president of the company retiring in 1996. After undertaking an extensive strategic review of the company's businesses, markets, facilities, organizational structure and management processes, CHA's new leaders announced a major business reorganization plan in October 1997. The program will include the divestiture of a variety of non-core assets and the institution of a major profit improvement program.

Champion derived about 83% of sales from its paper division in 1997, with uncoated and coated papers accounting for the large majority. CHA's uncoated papers are used for computer forms, printing and copier paper and envelopes. Its coated papers have uses in catalogs, magazines, textbooks, labels and annual reports. Champion's domestic paper mills have total annual capacity of 3.4 million tons, and it has 571,000 tons of capacity in Brazil; the totals exclude some 1.9 million tons of domestic capacity sold or being offered for sale in CHA's reorganization program.

At the end of 1997, CHA's domestic wood plants had an annual capacity of 922 million sq. ft. of softwood plywood and 475 million board feet of lumber. In Canada, annual capacities stood at 333 million sq. ft. of plywood and 834 million board feet of lumber.

International operations accounted for about 15% of

sales in 1997, but should represent a larger proportion after CHA completes its reorganization.

CHA owns or controls 5.1 million acres of timberlands in the U.S. (excluding 325,000 acres being offered for sale) and 1.5 million acres in Brazil. It also holds cutting rights on 6.4 million acres in Canada. In 1997, CHA harvested about 36% of its domestic fiber requirements from its owned and controlled timberlands.

In June 1998, Champion sold two newsprint mills and three recycling centers, to Donohue Inc., for $459 million. It marked CHA's first divestiture under a reorganization plan announced in October 1997. Champion's program calls for the divestiture of a group of non-core product segments, which in addition to newsprint, include the recycling business, specialty paper grades, premium papers, liquid papers and bleached board. It has also targeted 325,000 acres of timberlands for disposal; businesses slated for disposal accounted for 23% of CHA's revenues in 1997. Initial proceeds have been used mostly to pay down debt. The plan also includes a profit enhancement program aimed at boosting annual pretax profits from ongoing operations by $400 million by the end of 1999. Champion sees those gains coming from cost reductions, productivity increases and changes in product mix; it also implemented a new organizational structure in April 1998, which breaks its operations into seven specialized business groups. As part of the cost cutting program, CHA plans an 11% workforce reduction by 1999 at remaining businesses.

Per Share Data ($)

(Year Ended Dec. 31)	1997	1996	1995	1994	1993	1992	1991	1990	1989	1988
Tangible Bk. Val.	33.39	39.31	38.12	31.74	31.71	34.01	39.51	39.58	38.60	35.06
Cash Flow	-0.31	6.70	12.99	5.31	3.03	4.28	3.83	5.60	7.52	7.53
Earnings	-5.72	1.48	8.01	0.38	-1.75	-0.15	0.14	2.11	4.56	4.80
Dividends	0.20	0.20	0.20	0.20	0.20	0.20	0.20	1.10	1.10	0.95
Payout Ratio	NM	14%	2%	53%	NM	NM	143%	52%	24%	20%
Prices - High	66½	51⅛	60¼	40	34⅝	30¼	30⅝	33¾	37¾	38⅛
- Low	41⅜	39	36⅛	28	27⅛	23½	22¼	23⅛	28⅞	29½
P/E Ratio - High	NM	35	8	NM	NM	NM	NM	16	8	8
- Low	NM	26	5	NM	NM	NM	NM	11	6	6

Income Statement Analysis (Million $)

Revs.	5,736	5,880	6,972	5,318	5,069	4,926	4,786	5,090	5,163	5,129
Oper. Inc.	708	885	1,901	725	510	484	521	857	1,048	1,121
Depr.	518	502	471	459	443	411	342	323	279	260
Int. Exp.	240	233	236	243	258	246	264	227	176	175
Pretax Inc.	-896	205	1,237	106	-157	12.0	74.0	420	735	740
Eff. Tax Rate	NM	31%	38%	23%	NM	NM	51%	47%	40%	37%
Net Inc.	-548	141	772	63.0	-133	14.0	40.0	223	432	456

Balance Sheet & Other Fin. Data (Million $)

Cash	275	175	415	91.0	63.0	92.0	172	103	56.0	54.0
Curr. Assets	1,448	1,316	1,641	1,179	1,114	1,143	1,162	1,104	1,074	986
Total Assets	9,111	9,820	9,543	8,964	9,143	9,381	8,656	8,351	7,531	6,700
Curr. Liab.	1,020	944	1,080	1,034	772	786	794	801	804	699
LT Debt	3,194	3,085	2,829	2,889	3,316	3,291	2,978	2,689	2,025	1,909
Common Eqty.	3,210	3,756	3,647	2,961	2,950	3,159	3,671	3,680	3,589	3,345
Total Cap.	7,398	8,211	7,799	7,258	7,698	7,958	7,678	7,375	6,577	5,776
Cap. Exp.	450	582	624	329	606	718	661	1,047	994	673
Cash Flow	-31.0	643	1,230	494	281	397	354	518	709	716
Curr. Ratio	1.4	1.4	1.5	1.1	1.4	1.5	1.5	1.4	1.3	1.4
% LT Debt of Cap.	43.2	37.6	36.3	39.8	43.1	41.4	38.8	36.5	30.8	33.0
% Net Inc.of Revs.	NM	2.4	11.1	1.2	NM	0.3	0.8	4.4	8.4	8.9
% Ret. on Assets	NM	1.5	8.3	0.7	NM	0.2	0.5	2.8	6.2	7.1
% Ret. on Equity	NM	3.8	23.0	1.2	NM	NM	0.3	5.4	12.6	14.5

Data as orig. reptd.; bef. results of disc. opers. and/or spec. items. Per share data adj. for stk. divs. as of ex-div. date. Bold denotes diluted EPS (FASB 128). E-Estimated. NA-Not Available. NM-Not Meaningful. NR-Not Ranked.

Office—One Champion Plaza, Stamford, CT 06921. **Tel**—(203) 358-7000. **Website**—http://www.championinternational.com **Chrmn & CEO**—R. E. Olson. **SVP-Fin & Investor Contact**—Frank Kneisel. **VP & Secy**—L. A. Fox. **Dirs**—L. A. Bossidy, R. A. Charpie, H. C. Day, A. F. Emerson, A. E. Gotlieb, K. C. Nichols, R. E. Olson, W. V. Shipley, R. E. Walton. **Transfer Agent & Registrar**—ChaseMellon Shareholder Services, Ridgefield Park, NJ. **Incorporated**—in New York in 1937. **Empl**— 23,969. **S&P Analyst:** Michael W. Jaffe

STANDARD &POOR'S
STOCK REPORTS

Chase Manhattan

501V

NYSE Symbol **CMB**

In S&P 500

12-SEP-98

Industry:
Banks (Money Center)

Summary: Following its merger with Chemical Banking, Chase is now the largest U.S. bank holding company, with more than $367 billion in assets.

S&P Opinion: Accumulate (★★★★)	Recent Price • 46	Yield • 3.1%
	52 Wk Range • 77½-40	12-Mo. P/E • 11.4

Quantitative Evaluations

Outlook
(1 Lowest—5 Highest)
• **3**

Fair Value
• **47¾**

Risk
• **NA**

Earn./Div. Rank
• **B**

Technical Eval.
• **NA**

Rel. Strength Rank
(1 Lowest—99 Highest)
• **19**

Insider Activity
• **Neutral**

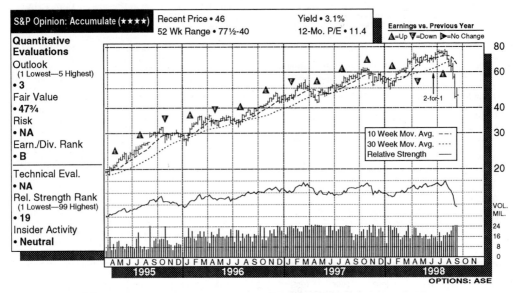

Earnings vs. Previous Year
▲=Up ▼=Down ▷=No Change

10 Week Mov. Avg. ---
30 Week Mov. Avg. ....
Relative Strength —

2-for-1

1995 1996 1997 1998

OPTIONS: ASE

Overview - 30-JUL-98

Revenue growth is expected in the double digits for all three major business units in 1998 with global banking leading the way, reflecting strength in investment banking, global asset management and private banking, and equity-related investments. A plan announced in March 1998 to streamline support functions and realign certain business units is expected to produce annual savings of about $460 million, although the bulk of the savings will be reinvested in higher growth business, such as corporate finance (including underwriting and syndications), credit cards, global services (such as securities processing), and mortgage finance, all of which should generate revenue growth rates of better than 10%. Asia's impact, meanwhile, has been relatively well contained, and total exposure was substantially reduced in 1998's first half. Financial goals include 15% operating earnings growth, an efficiency ratio in the low 50s and a return on equity of 18% or higher by the end of 1998.

Valuation - 30-JUL-98

The shares were up about 38% in 1998's first half, modestly beating the money center bank index and well exceeding the broader market. We attribute the outperformance to a number of factors, including a rebound from a weak fourth quarter following the announcement of trading losses related to adverse overseas markets, and news of a workforce and expense reduction plan in March. The company has made a concerted effort to reallocate expense savings to higher growth businesses, and has an effective capital management program in place. With its far-ranging business lines, we view CMB as having better-than-average revenue generating capabilities and recommend selective accumulation of the shares.

Key Stock Statistics

S&P EPS Est. 1998	4.55	Tang. Bk. Value/Share	25.14
P/E on S&P Est. 1998	10.1	Beta	1.37
S&P EPS Est. 1999	5.30	Shareholders	87,600
Dividend Rate/Share	1.44	Market cap. (B)	$ 39.4
Shs. outstg. (M)	856.5	Inst. holdings	67%
Avg. daily vol. (M)	6.314		

Value of $10,000 invested 5 years ago: $ 28,355

Fiscal Year Ending Dec. 31

	1998	1997	1996	1995	1994	1993
Revenues (Million $)						
1Q	8,258	7,224	6,932	—	3,021	3,049
2Q	8,352	7,491	6,720	—	3,068	3,174
3Q	—	7,858	6,774	—	3,297	3,077
4Q	—	7,808	6,995	—	3,299	3,127
Yr.	—	30,381	27,421	26,368	12,685	12,427
Earnings Per Share ($)						
1Q	0.80	0.98	-0.16	0.69	0.56	0.74
2Q	1.20	1.00	0.90	0.77	0.64	0.68
3Q	—	1.08	0.90	0.79	0.80	0.92
4Q	—	0.97	0.87	0.86	0.32	0.61
Yr.	—	4.02	2.47	3.12	2.32	2.81

Next earnings report expected: late October

Dividend Data (Dividends have been paid since 1827.)

Amount ($)	Date Decl.	Ex-Div. Date	Stock of Record	Payment Date
0.620	Dec. 16	Jan. 02	Jan. 06	Jan. 31 '98
0.720	Mar. 17	Apr. 02	Apr. 06	Apr. 30 '98
2-for-1	Mar. 17	Jun. 15	May. 20	Jun. 12 '98
0.360	Jun. 16	Jul. 01	Jul. 06	Jul. 31 '98

A Division of The **McGraw·Hill** *Companies*

The Chase Manhattan Corporation

Business Summary - 30-JUL-98

Chase Manhattan Corp., formed through the March 1996 merger of Chemical Banking Corp. and Chase Manhattan, is now the largest bank holding company in the U.S., with $366 billion in assets at December 31, 1997. Chase has dubbed itself "the relationship company," with a commitment to understanding its customers, delivering integrated solutions to meet their financial needs and striving to broaden and deepen those relationships.

The company operates in three business segments: global banking, national consumer services and Chase technology solutions. Global banking operates in more than 50 countries and includes global markets (foreign exchange, derivatives, fixed income securities and commodities), global investment banking and corporate lending, Chase capital partners (a private equity organization with $5 billion under management), global asset management and private banking, and middle market banking. National consumer services includes credit cards, where the company is the fourth largest bank credit card issuer in the U.S. with a $32.5 billion managed portfolio, retail payments and investments, mortgage banking, and consumer finance including auto, home equity, student and manufactured housing lending. Chase technology solutions provides information and transaction services globally and includes custody, cash management, trust and other fiduciary services.

In 1997, average earning assets, from which interest income is derived, amounted to $287 billion and consisted mainly of loans (56%) and investment securities (16%). Average sources of funds included interest-bearing deposits (38%), noninterest-bearing deposits (12%), short-term borrowings (26%), long-term debt (4%), shareholders' equity (6%) and other (14%).

At year-end 1997, nonperforming assets, consisting primarily of nonaccrual loans, were $1.02 billion (0.61% of loans), down from $1.15 billion (0.74%) a year earlier. The allowance for loan losses, which is set aside for possible loan defaults, was $3.87 billion (2.15% of loans), versus $3.69 billion (2.29%) a year earlier. Net chargeoffs, or the amount of loans actually written off as uncollectible, were $804 million (0.50% of average loans) in 1997, compared to $897 million (0.67%) in 1996.

Per Share Data ($) (Year Ended Dec. 31)	1997	1996	1995	1994	1993	1992	1991	1990	1989	1988
Tangible Bk. Val.	47.52	21.24	20.91	18.94	18.80	16.21	15.49	16.43	17.00	23.54
Earnings	4.01	2.51	3.12	2.32	2.81	1.95	0.06	1.19	-4.14	6.01
Dividends	1.21	1.09	0.94	0.82	0.69	0.60	0.52	1.15	1.36	1.36
Payout Ratio	30%	43%	30%	35%	24%	31%	NM	96%	NM	23%
Prices - High	63 1/4	48	32 3/8	21 1/8	23 1/4	19 3/4	15 1/8	15 3/4	20 5/8	17
- Low	42 3/8	26 1/8	17 7/8	16 7/8	17 1/2	11	5 1/4	4 7/8	14 1/4	10
P/E Ratio - High	16	19	10	9	8	10	NM	13	NM	3
- Low	11	10	6	7	6	6	NM	4	NM	2
Income Statement Analysis (Million $)										
Net Int. Inc.	8,158	8,340	8,202	4,674	4,636	4,598	4,113	2,051	2,017	2,307
Tax Equiv. Adj.	NA	NA	45.0	24.0	21.0	31.0	47.0	74.0	183	193
Non Int. Inc.	8,313	7,377	6,626	35.3	3,882	2,973	2,736	1,442	1,340	1,396
Loan Loss Prov.	804	897	758	550	1,259	1,365	1,345	537	1,135	364
Exp./Op. Revs.	61%	59%	63%	67%	62%	65%	77%	74%	77%	63%
Pretax Inc.	5,910	3,811	4,812	2,212	2,108	1,329	290	346	-453	908
Eff. Tax Rate	37%	35%	38%	42%	26%	18%	47%	16%	-6.20%	17%
Net Inc.	3,708	2,461	2,970	1,294	1,604	1,086	154	291	-481	754
% Net Int. Marg.	2.86	3.21	3.37	3.61	3.73	3.82	3.33	3.14	3.27	3.72
Balance Sheet & Other Fin. Data (Million $)										
Earning Assets:										
Money Mkt	106,207	97,266	77,966	29,539	28,265	14,009	16,849	6,547	7,821	7,569
Inv. Securities	52,738	48,546	41,769	26,997	25,948	23,426	19,763	10,686	9,708	8,719
Com'l Loans	88,906	70,245	38,738	24,972	33,620	28,015	31,929	18,927	18,167	18,073
Other Loans	79,548	84,847	112,542	54,255	42,238	54,647	52,908	26,682	26,913	24,352
Total Assets	365,521	336,099	303,989	171,423	149,888	139,655	138,930	73,019	71,513	67,349
Demand Deposits	49,808	47,057	39,116	21,399	23,443	22,813	18,025	13,080	13,397	13,348
Time Deposits	143,880	133,864	132,418	75,107	74,834	71,360	74,925	35,871	36,754	34,618
LT Debt	15,127	13,314	12,825	6,753	8,192	6,798	5,738	3,233	2,970	2,805
Common Eqty.	20,002	20,444	18,186	9,262	9,510	8,003	5,683	3,003	2,801	3,063
% Ret. on Assets	1.1	0.8	1.0	0.8	1.1	0.8	0.1	0.4	NM	1.0
% Ret. on Equity	18.4	12.3	16.0	14.8	16.1	16.0	0.4	7.1	NM	28.8
% Loan Loss Resv.	2.2	2.3	2.5	3.1	4.0	3.7	3.9	4.6	5.9	4.9
% Loans/Deposits	87.0	85.7	87.6	81.6	76.7	87.1	90.6	92.2	88.8	86.7
% Equity to Assets	5.5	5.7	5.8	4.7	7.3	4.2	3.4	3.9	3.8	3.1

Data as orig. reptd.; bef. results of disc. opers. and/or spec. items. Per share data adj. for stk. divs. as of ex-div. date. Bold denotes diluted EPS (FASB 128). E-Estimated. NA-Not Available. NM-Not Meaningful. NR-Not Ranked.

Office—270 Park Ave., New York, NY 10017. **Tel**—(212) 270-6000. **Website**—http://www.chase.com **Chrmn & CEO**—W. V. Shipley. **Pres & COO**—T. G. Labrecque. **Investor Contact**—John Borden (212-270-7318). **Dirs**—H. W. Becherer, F. A. Bennack Jr., S. V. Berresford, M. A. Burns, H. L. Fuller, M. R. Goodes, W. H. Gray III, G. V. Grune, W. B. Harrison, Jr., H. S. Hook, H. L. Kaplan, T. G. Labrecque, H. B. Schacht, W. V. Shipley, A. C. Sigler, J. R. Stafford, M. v.N. Whitman. **Transfer Agent & Registrar**—ChaseMellon Shareholder Services, Ridgefield Park. NJ. **Incorporated**—in Delaware in 1968. **Empl**— 70,693. **S&P Analyst:** Stephen R. Biggar

12-SEP-98 Industry: Oil (International Integrated)

Summary: This major integrated oil company has exploration, production, refining and marketing interests throughout the world.

S&P Opinion: Avoid (★★)	Recent Price • 82½	Yield • 3.0%
	52 Wk Range • 90⅛-67¾	12-Mo. P/E • 20.3

Quantitative Evaluations

Outlook
  (1 Lowest—5 Highest)
• **1**

Fair Value
• **65¼**

Risk
• **Low**

Earn./Div. Rank
• **B+**

Technical Eval.
• **NA**

Rel. Strength Rank
  (1 Lowest—99 Highest)
• **94**

Insider Activity
• **Neutral**

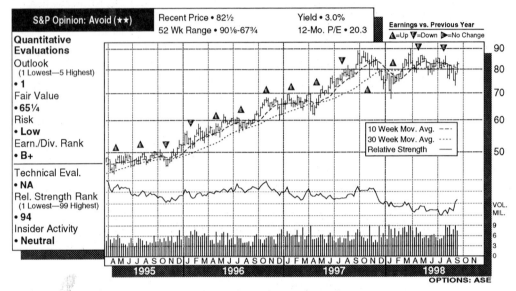

Earnings vs. Previous Year
▲=Up ▼=Down ▷=No Change

10 Week Mov. Avg. ---
30 Week Mov. Avg. ·····
Relative Strength —

VOL. MIL.

OPTIONS: ASE

Overview - 05-AUG-98

Earnings in 1997 benefited from higher oil production and substantial improvement in the refining and marketing division, as lower oil prices led to stronger refining margins. CHV has been divesting nonstrategic businesses, in order to streamline its asset base and lower its cost structure. The program has succeeded, and the company's long-term earnings power has been enhanced by a more focused business profile. CHV's domestic strategy focuses on development of natural gas properties. We expect returns in the gas marketing business to improve, as a result of a new joint venture with NGC Corp. The venture was the second largest gas marketer in North America in 1997, with sales of 8.0 Bcf/day. Overseas, CHV is pioneering exploration and production in the former Soviet Union. Net income fell 35% in the first half of 1998, despite improved petroleum refining and marketing results, as a drop of more than $6.00 per barrel in average oil prices hampered exploration and production profits. Chemicals earnings declined, reflecting lower petrochemicals prices.

Valuation - 05-AUG-98

To this point in 1998, weak oil prices have led to underperformance by the shares of international integrated oils. For CHV, refining and marketing margins continue to benefit from lower crude oil prices seen since early 1997. However, upstream profits will continue to be hampered by a bearish commodity price environment, despite increased production volumes. The outlook for chemicals earnings is negative, despite strong domestic demand, as the Asian economic crisis has reduced export demand, leading to excess supply in the U.S. We expect the shares of the international integrated oil group, and those of Chevron in particular, to underperform the market over the next six to 12 months.

Key Stock Statistics

S&P EPS Est. 1998	3.30	Tang. Bk. Value/Share	27.01
P/E on S&P Est. 1998	25.0	Beta	0.64
S&P EPS Est. 1999	4.10	Shareholders	129,200
Dividend Rate/Share	2.44	Market cap. (B)	$ 54.0
Shs. outstg. (M)	654.4	Inst. holdings	49%
Avg. daily vol. (M)	1.623		

Value of $10,000 invested 5 years ago: $ 29,169

Fiscal Year Ending Dec. 31

	1998	1997	1996	1995	1994	1993
Revenues (Million $)						
1Q	7,653	10,794	10,157	7,635	7,112	8,736
2Q	7,754	9,947	10,514	8,170	7,620	8,400
3Q	—	10,130	10,846	8,024	8,176	8,213
4Q	—	9,712	11,265	7,636	7,432	7,815
Yr.	—	40,583	42,782	31,465	30,340	33,014
Earnings Per Share ($)						
1Q	0.76	1.27	0.94	0.70	0.60	0.77
2Q	0.88	1.25	1.34	0.93	0.39	0.08
3Q	—	1.10	1.00	0.44	0.65	0.65
4Q	—	1.33	0.71	-0.64	0.96	0.46
Yr.	E3.30	4.95	3.98	1.43	2.60	1.94

Next earnings report expected: late October

Dividend Data (Dividends have been paid since 1912.)

Amount ($)	Date Decl.	Ex-Div. Date	Stock of Record	Payment Date
0.580	Oct. 29	Nov. 18	Nov. 20	Dec. 10 '97
0.610	Jan. 28	Feb. 18	Feb. 20	Mar. 10 '98
0.610	Apr. 29	May. 18	May. 20	Jun. 10 '98
0.610	Jul. 29	Aug. 18	Aug. 20	Sep. 10 '98

A Division of The McGraw-Hill Companies

Business Summary - 05-AUG-98

Once a part of John D. Rockefeller's powerful Standard Oil Trust, Chevron Corporation (CHV), formerly Standard Oil of California, is now one of the world's largest oil companies, with international operations including exploration and production of oil and natural gas, crude oil refining, marketing and transportation, and petrochemicals. In 1983, Chevron emerged victorious in a bitter battle for Gulf Oil, paying over $13 billion, in what was at the time the largest cash offer ever made for a company.

Chevron explores for and produces oil and natural gas in 21 countries. In 1997, worldwide production of crude oil and natural gas liquids averaged 1,074,000 barrels (bbl.) a day (32% U.S.), and production of natural gas amounted to 2.43 billion cubic feet (Bcf) a day (76% U.S.). Net proved reserves at 1997 year end were 4,506 million bbl. of crude oil and liquids and 9,963 Bcf of natural gas, ranking Chevron among the top 10 publicly-owned oil companies in the world. Aside from the U.S., CHV has major exploration acreage in Canada, the North Sea, Angola and Nigeria. The company has also made a major investment in the enormous Tengiz oil field in Kazakstan.

CHV has the largest U.S. refining capacity, and ranks among the top 10 in worldwide refining capacity, including its share of affiliates' capacity. Principal refined product markets are in the southeastern, south central and western U.S. Chevron operates over 7,700 service stations throughout the U.S. In November 1996, Chevron announced plans to merge its U.K. refining and marketing subsidiary, Gulf Oil (Great Britain), with those of Murphy Oil and Elf Aquitaine, a France-based international oil company. However, the would-be partners have since bowed out of the merger, citing a lack of significant projected benefits. In early 1996, the company agreed to combine its domestic natural gas gathering, processing and marketing businesses with NGC Corp., creating the largest single player in the domestic market with total combined volumes approaching 10 Bcf/d. The Caltex Group (equally owned with Texaco) markets oil in Africa, Asia and Australia and produces oil in Indonesia.

Chemical products include benzene, styrene, polystyrene, ethylene, polyethylene, paraxylene and normal alpha olefins, as well as fuel additives. Plants are located in 10 states and in France, Brazil and Japan.

CHV's 1997 capital budget came to $5.5 billion, with about 60% spent on exploration and production projects. The company has set its 1998 capital budget at $6.3 billion, of which $4 billion will be spent on exploration and production. About 63% of the exploration and production spending is slated for international projects.

Per Share Data ($) (Year Ended Dec. 31)	1997	1996	1995	1994	1993	1992	1991	1990	1989	1988
Tangible Bk. Val.	26.64	23.93	22.02	22.27	21.41	21.11	21.25	21.14	19.69	21.61
Cash Flow	8.44	7.39	6.61	6.33	5.71	7.08	5.58	6.86	4.12	6.14
Earnings	5.03	3.99	1.43	2.60	1.95	3.26	1.84	3.05	0.36	2.58
Dividends	2.28	2.08	1.93	1.85	1.75	1.65	1.63	1.48	1.40	1.27
Payout Ratio	45%	52%	135%	71%	90%	51%	87%	48%	396%	49%
Prices - High	89 1/8	68 3/8	53 5/8	47 3/8	49 3/8	37 3/4	40 1/8	40 7/8	36 3/4	26
- Low	61 3/4	51	43 3/8	39 7/8	33 3/4	30 1/8	31 3/4	31 5/8	22 3/4	19 1/2
P/E Ratio - High	18	17	37	18	25	12	22	13	NM	10
- Low	12	13	30	15	17	9	17	10	NM	8
Income Statement Analysis (Million $)										
Revs.	40,583	42,782	31,322	30,340	32,123	37,464	36,461	38,607	29,443	25,196
Oper. Inc.	6,747	6,209	4,799	4,925	5,141	5,028	4,562	6,504	3,647	4,828
Depr.	2,300	2,216	3,381	2,431	2,452	2,594	2,616	2,693	2,562	2,436
Int. Exp.	312	472	543	419	371	478	546	635	680	661
Pretax Inc.	5,502	4,740	1,789	2,803	2,426	3,463	2,252	4,213	1,306	2,899
Eff. Tax Rate	41%	45%	48%	40%	48%	36%	43%	49%	81%	39%
Net Inc.	3,256	2,607	930	1,693	1,265	2,210	1,293	2,157	251	1,768
Balance Sheet & Other Fin. Data (Million $)										
Cash	1,015	1,637	1,384	1,306	2,016	1,695	1,485	1,684	1,628	1,815
Curr. Assets	7,006	7,942	7,867	7,591	8,682	8,772	9,031	10,089	8,620	7,941
Total Assets	35,473	34,854	34,330	34,407	34,736	33,970	34,636	35,089	33,884	33,968
Curr. Liab.	6,946	8,907	9,445	9,392	10,606	9,835	9,480	9,017	7,583	7,003
LT Debt	4,431	3,988	4,521	4,128	4,082	4,953	5,991	6,710	7,390	6,833
Common Eqty.	17,472	15,623	14,355	14,596	13,997	13,728	14,739	14,836	13,980	14,788
Total Cap.	25,118	22,462	21,309	21,398	20,995	21,575	23,707	24,702	24,806	25,515
Cap. Exp.	3,899	3,424	3,529	3,112	3,214	3,369	3,665	3,136	3,102	4,911
Cash Flow	5,556	4,823	4,311	4,124	3,717	4,804	3,909	4,850	2,813	4,204
Curr. Ratio	1.0	0.9	0.8	0.8	0.8	0.9	1.0	1.1	1.1	1.1
% LT Debt of Cap.	17.6	17.8	21.2	19.3	19.4	23.0	25.3	27.2	29.8	26.8
% Net Inc.of Revs.	8.0	6.1	29.7	5.6	3.9	5.9	3.5	5.6	0.9	7.0
% Ret. on Assets	9.3	7.6	2.7	4.9	3.7	6.7	3.7	6.3	0.7	5.2
% Ret. on Equity	19.7	17.4	6.4	11.8	9.1	16.0	8.8	15.1	1.7	11.6

Data as orig. reptd.; bef. results of disc. opers. and/or spec. items. Revenues exclude excise taxes and other income. Per share data adj. for stk. divs. as of ex-div. date. E-Estimated. NA-Not Available. NM-Not Meaningful. NR-Not Ranked.

Registrar—First Trust California, SF. **Office**—575 Market St., San Francisco, CA 94105. **Tel**—(415) 894-7700. **Chrmn & CEO**—K. T. Derr. **Vice Chrmn**—J. N. Sullivan. **VP-Fin & CFO**—M. R. Klitten. **Secy**—Lydia I. Beebe. **Investor Contact**—M. J. Foehr. **Dirs**—S. H. Armacost, K. T. Derr, S. Ginn, C. A. Hills, J. B. Johnson, R. H. Matzke, C. M. Pigott, C. Rice, F. A. Shrontz, J. N. Sullivan, C. L. Tien, G. H. Weyerhaeuser, J. A. Young. **Transfer Agent**—Co.'s office. **Incorporated**—in Delaware in 1926. **Empl**— 39,362. **S&P Analyst:** Norman Rosenberg

STANDARD &POOR'S
STOCK REPORTS

Chrysler Corp.

532

NYSE Symbol **C**

In S&P 500

12-SEP-98

Industry:
Automobiles

Summary: The third largest U.S. automaker, Chrysler is the leader in the minivan and sport utility segments of the motor vehicle markets. It recently agreed to merge with Daimler-Benz AG.

S&P Opinion: Hold (★★★)	Recent Price • 51⅜	Yield • 3.1%
	52 Wk Range • 61-31¼	12-Mo. P/E • 10.2

Earnings vs. Previous Year
▲=Up ▼=Down ▶=No Change

Quantitative Evaluations

Outlook
(1 Lowest—5 Highest)
• **1+**

Fair Value
• **45⅞**

Risk
• **Average**

Earn./Div. Rank
• **B**

Technical Eval.
• **Bullish** since 2/98

Rel. Strength Rank
(1 Lowest—99 Highest)
• **78**

Insider Activity
• **Unfavorable**

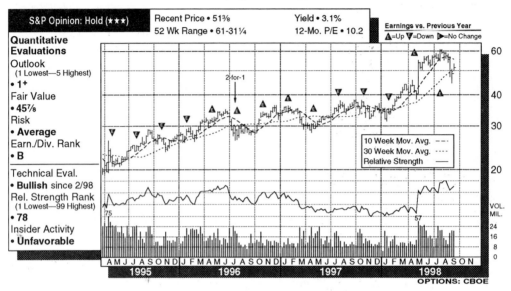

10 Week Mov. Avg. – – –
30 Week Mov. Avg. ·······
Relative Strength —

OPTIONS: CBOE

Overview - 14-JUL-98

In May, Chrysler agreed to merge with Germany's Daimler-Benz AG in a transaction that would create the world's third largest (based on revenues) automobile manufacturer. C stockholders will receive 0.6235 shares of the new company, to be called Daimler-Chrysler, per share held and will own 47% of the new company; Daimler-Benz stockholders will own the balance. The combined firm would have pro-forma 1997 sales of $130 billion and pro-forma net income, exluding non-recurring items, of $4.6 billion. The deal is expected to be accretive to earnings in 1999, as management anticipates $1.4 billion of benefits from higher revenues and costs and operating efficiencies. We expect such benefits to accelerate to more than $3 billion annually within three to five years. The strategic value of the combination is clear as there is little overlap in products and each party has strength in different segments and geographic locations. Daimler-Chrysler will have a strong balance sheet with relatively low debt and significant cash. Chrysler reported record sales and EPS for the 1998 first half. Volume was aided by loyalty coupons and higher incentives. With the expiration of loyalty coupons and an expected moderation of incentives in light of the General Motors strike, volume may decline in the second half of the year.

Valuation - 14-JUL-98

Despite the favorable outlook from the planned merger with Daimler-Benz, in light of the related runup in Chrysler's stock price, we maintain our market performer rating. As the transaction will be accounted for as a pooling of interests, C will be restricted from repurchasing common shares and will reissue 28 million treasury shares. A cash dividend will be paid at a rate comparable to Chrylser's current level.

Key Stock Statistics

S&P EPS Est. 1998	5.24	Tang. Bk. Value/Share	17.39
P/E on S&P Est. 1998	9.8	Beta	1.09
Dividend Rate/Share	1.60	Shareholders	135,000
Shs. outstg. (M)	646.7	Market cap. (B)	$ 33.3
Avg. daily vol. (M)	3.608	Inst. holdings	50%

Value of $10,000 invested 5 years ago: $ 38,306

Fiscal Year Ending Dec. 31

	1998	1997	1996	1995	1994	1993
Revenues (Million $)						
1Q	16,800	16,116	14,956	13,613	13,223	10,904
2Q	17,001	14,388	15,839	12,516	13,082	11,031
3Q	—	13,176	14,356	12,009	11,659	9,713
4Q	—	17,467	16,246	15,057	14,260	11,952
Yr.	—	61,147	61,397	49,333	52,224	43,600
Earnings Per Share ($)						
1Q	**1.60**	**1.45**	1.32	0.80	1.27	0.79
2Q	**1.51**	**0.70**	1.39	0.17	1.30	0.93
3Q	**E0.75**	**0.65**	0.93	0.46	0.88	0.56
4Q	**E1.38**	**1.28**	1.39	1.35	1.60	1.05
Yr.	**E5.24**	**4.09**	4.74	2.77	5.05	3.38

Next earnings report expected: early October

Dividend Data (Dividends have been paid since 1984.)

Amount ($)	Date Decl.	Ex-Div. Date	Stock of Record	Payment Date
0.400	Dec. 04	Dec. 11	Dec. 15	Jan. 15 '98
0.400	Mar. 05	Mar. 11	Mar. 15	Apr. 15 '98
0.400	May. 21	Jun. 11	Jun. 15	Jul. 15 '98
0.400	Sep. 03	Sep. 11	Sep. 15	Oct. 15 '98

A Division of The **McGraw·Hill** *Companies*

Business Summary - 14-JUL-98

In May, Chrysler and Daimler-Benz AG agreed to a merger of the two companies. Chrysler stockholders will receive 0.6235 shares of the new company, to be called Daimler-Chrysler, per share held and will own 47% of the company.

After solid performances in 1996 and 1997, Chrysler's new motto appears to be "Passion, Speed, Growth." The motto indicates a passion for developing great vehicles that exceed customer expectations, and a goal of producing them rapidly (to cut costs), with the two adding up to profitable growth. With its new-found success, Chrysler is balancing shareholder needs with demands of investing in its employees, products and facilities, as well as shoring up its balance sheet.

Chrysler is the third largest U.S. motor vehicle manufacturer. The financial segment consists primarily of Chrysler Financial Corp.'s vehicle financing, insurance and other financing services. The Thrifty Rent-A-Car Systems and Dollar Rent A Car operations were spun off in an initial public offering (IPO) in December 1997. Segment contributions in 1997 were:

	Revs.	Profits
Automotive	96%	87%
Financial services	4%	13%

In 1997, the company had pretax income of $3,853 million in the U.S., $264 million in Canada, and $440 million elsewhere.

Chrysler, Plymouth, Dodge and Eagle (Eagle was discontinued in 1997) car models accounted for 8.9% of total U.S. registrations (including foreign-built cars) in 1997, versus 9.8% in 1996, 9.1% in 1995, 9.0% in 1994, 9.8% in 1993, 8.3% in 1992, 8.6% in 1991 and 9.3% in 1990. Comparable figures for trucks (including Jeeps) were 21.7%, 23.3%, 21.3%, 21.7%, 21.4%, 21.1%, 19.5% and 17.3%. Chrysler's combined share of the North American car and truck market was 15.1% in 1997, 16.1% in 1996, and 14.7% in 1995 and 1994, versus 14.8% in 1993 and 13.4% in 1992. Vehicles are marketed through some 5,100 dealers.

Of the 2,886,981 Chrysler cars and trucks assembled in 1997, 1,826,355 were built in the U.S., 625,079 in Canada, 347,739 in Mexico and 87,808 elsewhere. This compared with a total of 2,958,800 vehicles manufactured in 1996, with 1,825,406 in the U.S., 690,948 in Canada, 359,444 in Mexico and 83,002 elsewhere.

In February 1996, directors made changes in C's governance policies, and entered into a five-year standstill agreement with its largest shareholder, Tracinda Corp., controlled by K. Kerkorian. Directors added a qualifying offer exception to the shareholder rights plan, adopted an anti-greenmail bylaw, voted to pay directors compensation in stock, terminated the directors retirement plan, and mandated higher stock ownership guidelines for directors. The standstill requires Tracinda not to increase its ownership in C, and to sell shares pro rata so as to limit the percentage of shares owned to 13.8%.

From January 1995 through December 1997, C repurchased nearly 175 million common shares at an aggregate cost of $5.2 billion. In light of the planned merger with Daimler-Benz, share repurchases have been suspended.

Per Share Data ($)

(Year Ended Dec. 31)	1997	1996	1995	1994	1993	1992	1991	1990	1989	1988
Tangible Bk. Val.	15.08	13.59	11.65	10.80	2.33	3.48	1.57	3.45	6.32	10.50
Cash Flow	8.03	8.16	5.71	7.76	5.76	3.46	1.91	3.27	3.88	5.28
Earnings	4.09	5.03	2.77	5.05	3.38	0.73	-1.11	0.15	0.68	2.33
Dividends	1.60	1.40	1.00	0.55	0.33	0.30	0.30	0.60	0.60	0.50
Payout Ratio	39%	28%	36%	11%	10%	41%	NM	397%	85%	22%
Prices - High	38½	36⅜	29⅛	31¾	29¼	17	8	10¼	14⅞	14
- Low	28⅛	25⅝	19⅛	21⅝	15⅞	5¾	4⅞	4⅝	9⅛	10¼
P/E Ratio - High	9	8	10	6	9	23	NM	68	22	6
- Low	7	5	7	4	5	8	NM	30	13	4

Income Statement Analysis (Million $)

	1997	1996	1995	1994	1993	1992	1991	1990	1989	1988
Revs.	58,622	59,333	51,190	50,736	42,260	35,501	28,162	29,797	34,922	35,473
Oper. Inc.	5,734	7,347	4,659	7,223	4,977	2,622	720	3,079	5,316	5,535
Depr.	2,696	2,312	2,220	1,944	1,640	1,610	1,465	1,398	1,491	1,325
Int. Exp.	1,200	1,163	1,199	1,114	1,280	1,581	2,031	2,598	2,968	2,592
Pretax Inc.	4,557	6,092	3,449	5,830	3,838	934	-809	147	552	1,692
Eff. Tax Rate	38%	39%	39%	36%	37%	46%	NM	54%	43%	38%
Net Inc.	2,805	3,720	2,121	3,713	2,415	505	-537	68.0	315	1,050

Balance Sheet & Other Fin. Data (Million $)

	1997	1996	1995	1994	1993	1992	1991	1990	1989	1988
Cash	7,848	7,752	8,125	5,145	4,040	2,357	2,041	1,572	1,269	1,644
Total Assets	60,418	56,184	53,756	49,539	43,830	40,653	43,076	46,374	51,038	48,567
LT Debt	9,006	7,184	9,858	7,650	6,871	13,434	14,980	12,750	13,966	14,877
Total Debt	15,485	10,395	14,193	13,106	11,451	15,551	19,438	22,900	27,546	27,147
Common Eqty.	11,362	11,571	10,891	9,831	5,974	6,676	6,109	6,849	7,233	7,582
Cap. Exp.	5,122	4,635	4,109	3,843	3,028	2,916	2,348	2,045	1,922	2,016
Cash Flow	5,500	6,032	4,320	5,577	3,975	2,046	927	1,466	1,806	2,374
% Ret. on Assets	4.8	6.8	4.1	7.9	5.2	1.2	NM	0.1	0.6	3.0
% Ret. on Equity	24.5	33.0	20.3	45.9	33.5	6.8	NM	1.0	4.3	14.5
% LT Debt of Cap.	57.7	47.3	47.4	41.7	50.1	63.3	68.4	60.4	60.7	60.2

Data as orig. reptd.; bef. results of disc. opers. and/or spec. items. Per share data adj. for stk. divs. as of ex-div. date. Bold denotes diluted EPS (FASB 128). E-Estimate. NA-Not Available. NM-Not Meaningful. NR-Not Ranked.

Office—1000 Chrysler Drive, Auburn Hills, MI 48326-2766. **Tel**—(810) 576-5741.**Website**—http://chryslercorp.com **Chrmn, CEO & Pres**—R. J. Eaton. **Vice Chrmn**—R. A. Lutz.**Pres**—T. T. Stallkamp. **EVP & CFO**—G. C. Valade. **VP & Treas**—T. P. Capo. **VP & Secy**—W. J. O'Brien. **Investor Contact**—Sam A. Messina. **Dirs**—L. H. Affinito, J. D. Aljian, R. E. Allen, J. A. Califano Jr., T. G. Denomme, R. J. Eaton, E. G. Graves, K. Kresa, R. J. Lanigan, R. A. Lutz, P. A. Magowan, J. B. Neff, M. T. Stamper, L. R. Wilson.**Transfer Agent & Registrar**—First Chicago Trust Co. of New York, Jersey City, NJ. **Incorporated**—in Delaware in 1925. **Empl**—121,000. **S&P Analyst:** Efraim Levy

STANDARD &POOR'S
STOCK REPORTS

Chubb Corp.

532D

NYSE Symbol **CB**

In S&P 500

12-SEP-98

Industry: Insurance (Property-Casualty)

Summary: This large, broadly based property-casualty insurance organization has divested its interests in life and health insurance and real estate development.

S&P Opinion: Buy (★★★★★)	Recent Price • 64⅞ 52 Wk Range • 88¾-62

Yield • 1.9%

12-Mo. P/E • 14.7

Quantitative Evaluations

Outlook (1 Lowest—5 Highest)
• **2+**

Fair Value
• **61⅝**

Risk
• **Low**

Earn./Div. Rank
• **A-**

Technical Eval.
• **Bearish** since 8/98

Rel. Strength Rank (1 Lowest—99 Highest)
• **60**

Insider Activity
• **Neutral**

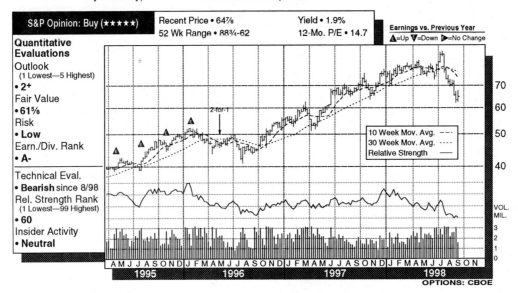

Earnings vs. Previous Year ▲=Up ▼=Down ▶=No Change

10 Week Mov. Avg. ---
30 Week Mov. Avg. ····
Relative Strength —

OPTIONS: CBOE

Overview - 18-JUN-98

Written premiums will likely advance 6%-9% in 1998, reflecting volume growth in several lines, reduced reinsurance coverage, a change in a long-standing pooling arrangement, and international expansion. Improved underwriting trends emerging in several key lines also bode well for the long-term profit picture. Year to year comparisons could be difficult, given the unusually mild weather conditions that existed in 1997. Nevertheless, CB is fundamentally a profitable underwriter. Assuming a "normal" level of catastrophe and weather-related losses, underwriting results should remain profitable. Longer term, margins should be aided by a cost cutting initiative that included a first quarter 1998 restructuring charge of $0.15 a share aimed at producing annual cost savings of $150 million, beginning in 1999. Investment income growth will be modest (6%-8%), amid lower interest rates. The sale of the life insurance unit in May 1997 to Jefferson Pilot Corp. for $875 million is a positive move, since it frees up capital better allocated to buying back shares. CB also divested most of its real estate operations in late 1997 for $737 million.

Valuation - 18-JUN-98

After outperforming the broader market in 1997- thanks to favorable investor reaction to the sale of its underperforming life insurance and real estate units and to its growing personal lines franchise- the shares (along with most of the property-casualty sector) have languished so far in 1998. Renewed concerns over ultra competitive commercial lines pricing and over potentially disappointing second quarter earnings amid higher storm losses have kept the shares under pressure. Despite their near term weakness, the shares are attractively valued in light of CB's solid top line growth prospects and above average underwriting track record.

Key Stock Statistics

S&P EPS Est. 1998	4.15	Tang. Bk. Value/Share	34.46
P/E on S&P Est. 1998	15.6	Beta	1.06
S&P EPS Est. 1999	5.25	Shareholders	8,400
Dividend Rate/Share	1.24	Market cap. (B)	$ 10.8
Shs. outstg. (M)	165.6	Inst. holdings	67%
Avg. daily vol. (M)	0.551		

Value of $10,000 invested 5 years ago: $ 16,517

Fiscal Year Ending Dec. 31

	1998	1997	1996	1995	1994	1993
Revenues (Million $)						
1Q	1,587	1,577	1,482	1,464	1,396	1,238
2Q	1,598	1,510	1,382	1,526	1,415	1,284
3Q	—	1,569	1,357	1,533	1,429	1,570
4Q	—	2,009	1,460	1,566	1,470	1,460
Yr.	—	6,664	5,681	6,089	5,710	5,500
Earnings Per Share ($)						
1Q	**1.12**	1.08	0.85	0.83	0.41	0.82
2Q	**1.08**	1.08	0.98	1.04	0.82	0.94
3Q	—	1.10	0.93	0.96	0.85	-0.71
4Q	—	1.13	1.15	1.08	0.88	0.90
Yr.	—	**4.39**	3.91	3.93	2.98	1.96

Next earnings report expected: late October

Dividend Data (Dividends have been paid since 1902.)

Amount ($)	Date Decl.	Ex-Div. Date	Stock of Record	Payment Date
0.290	Dec. 12	Dec. 26	Dec. 30	Jan. 13 '98
0.310	Mar. 06	Mar. 18	Mar. 20	Apr. 07 '98
0.310	Jun. 12	Jun. 24	Jun. 26	Jul. 14 '98
0.310	Sep. 11	Sep. 23	Sep. 25	Oct. 13 '98

A Division of The **McGraw-Hill** Companies

STANDARD
&POOR'S
STOCK REPORTS

The Chubb Corporation

532D
12-SEP-98

Business Summary - 18-JUN-98

Chubb Corp., recognizing that consolidation in the life insurance industry was resulting in the dominance of that category by much larger competitors, decided in 1996 to focus on its core property-casualty operations. Chubb's management believed that the capital commitment required to stay competitive in the life insurance arena was not in its shareholders' near term interests. For that reason, the company sold its life and health insurance operations to Jefferson-Pilot Corp. (NYSE: JP) in May 1997, for $875 million in cash. Proceeds were earmarked to repurchase common stock. By late 1997, CB had also divested most of its commercial real estate division.

Chubb's property-casualty operations, as a group, constitute the 12th largest U.S. property-casualty (p-c) insurer, based on 1996 (latest available) written premiums. In 1997, Chubb wrote $5.4 billion in net property-casualty premiums (up from $4.8 billion in 1996), of which commercial lines accounted for 76% and personal lines constituted 24%. Written premiums were divided: commercial casualty 17%, executive protection 16%, commercial multi-peril 15%, homeowners 13%, other commercial lines 12%, commercial property

& marine 11%, workers' compensation 5%, personal auto 5%, and other personal lines 6%.

Chubb's underwriting results (as measured by the combined ratio) have typically exceeded industry averages. During 1997, CB's combined ratio was 96.9%, versus an estimated 102% for the entire p-c industry. A combined ratio of under 100% indicates an underwriting profit; while one in excess of 100% points to an underwriting loss. The p-c group operates in the U.S. and abroad through about 3,600 independent agents and some 400 insurance brokers.

During 1997, property-casualty written premiums advanced about 14%. Although some of this growth was due to the termination of a quota share reinsurance agreement, underlying premium growth trends remain robust (up over 9%, despite extremely competitive market conditions. We estimate written premium growth for the overall p-c insurance industry grew less than 5% during 1997, as excess underwriting capacity continued to exert downward pressure on premium prices.

In 1997, most of the commercial real estate assets of Bellemead Development Corp., CB's real estate development unit, were sold for $737. During 1996, CB recorded a net charge of $160 million to write down the carrying value of these assets to their estimated fair value.

Per Share Data ($)

(Year Ended Dec. 31)	1997	1996	1995	1994	1993	1992	1991	1990	1989	1988
Tangible Bk. Val.	33.47	31.24	29.71	24.05	23.92	22.18	19.94	17.13	14.96	13.38
Oper. Earnings	4.00	3.58	3.45	2.75	1.12	2.79	2.92	2.86	2.28	2.21
Earnings	4.39	3.91	3.92	2.98	1.96	3.48	3.16	3.04	2.46	2.13
Dividends	1.16	1.08	0.98	0.92	0.86	0.80	0.74	0.66	0.58	0.54
Relative Payout	26%	39%	25%	31%	44%	23%	23%	22%	24%	25%
Prices - High	78½	56¼	50⅜	41⅝	48¼	45½	39	27⅜	24⅞	15⅞
- Low	51⅛	40⅞	38⅛	34⅜	38	31¼	25	17⅜	14⅜	12⅞
P/E Ratio - High	18	20	13	14	25	13	12	9	10	7
- Low	12	15	10	12	19	9	8	6	6	6

Income Statement Analysis (Million $)

	1997	1996	1995	1994	1993	1992	1991	1990	1989	1988
Life Ins. In Force	NA	NA	66,661	61,701	54,283	46,455	41,502	39,531	38,843	NA
Prem. Inc.: Life A & H	NA	NA	623	836	801	689	634	562	496	NA
Prem. Inc.: Cas./Prop.	5,157	4,569	4,147	3,776	3,505	3,163	3,037	2,836	2,694	3,299
Net Invest. Inc.	785	712	901	829	800	751	701	675	611	526
Oth. Revs.	721	400	418	268	393	337	141	175	222	148
Total Revs.	6,664	5,681	6,089	5,710	5,500	4,941	4,513	4,247	4,023	3,973
Pretax Inc.	973	547	900	639	344	748	684	646	552	470
Net Oper. Inc.	701	434	614	487	193	493	509	492	390	373
Net Inc.	770	486	697	528	344	617	552	522	421	360

Balance Sheet & Other Fin. Data (Million $)

	1997	1996	1995	1994	1993	1992	1991	1990	1989	1988
Cash & Equiv.	12.0	200	257	221	210	207	199	182	174	150
Premiums Due	1,144	985	873	787	720	625	632	633	636	639
Invest. Assets: Bonds	12,454	11,158	12,603	10,722	10,718	10,000	8,660	7,887	7,164	6,271
Invest. Assets: Stocks	871	646	588	642	930	738	1,143	858	869	678
Invest. Assets: Loans	Nil	Nil	212	203	194	193	187	170	161	154
Invest. Assets: Total	14,049	1,281	13,887	12,378	11,842	10,932	9,990	8,914	8,194	7,102
Deferred Policy Costs	677	601	1,171	1,136	1,012	929	886	831	779	719
Total Assets	19,616	19,939	22,997	20,723	19,437	15,019	13,775	12,268	11,179	9,741
Debt	399	1,071	1,344	1,439	1,369	1,361	1,280	1,076	872	544
Common Eqty.	5,657	5,463	5,263	4,247	4,196	3,954	3,542	2,883	2,604	2,255
Comb. Loss-Exp. Ratio	96.9	98.3	96.8	99.5	114.8	101.1	99.5	99.7	101.9	99.7
% Return On Revs.	11.6	8.6	11.4	9.3	5.9	12.5	12.2	12.3	10.5	9.4
% Ret. on Equity	13.8	9.1	14.7	12.5	8.4	16.5	17.2	19.0	17.3	17.7
% Invest. Yield	6.0	6.2	6.9	6.8	7.0	7.1	7.3	7.8	7.9	7.8

Data as orig. reptd.; bef. results of disc. opers. and/or spec. items. Per share data adj. for stk. divs. as of ex-div. date. Bold denotes diluted EPS (FASB 128). E-Estimate. NA-Not Available. NM-Not Meaningful. NR-Not Ranked.

Office—15 Mountain View Rd., Warren, NJ 07061-1615. **Tel**—(908) 903-2000. **Website**—http://www.chubb.com **Chrmn & CEO**—D. R. O'Hare. **Pres**—J. J. Degnan. **VP & Secy**—H. G. Gulick. **VP & Treas**—P. J. Sempier. **VP & Investor Contact**—Gail E. Devlin (908-903-3245). **Dirs**—Z. E. Baird, J. C. Beck, S. P. Burke, J. I. Cash Jr., P. Chubb III, J. J. Cohen, J. M. Cornelius, D. H. Hoag, T. C. MacAvoy,, D. R. O'Hare, W. B. Rudman, Sir David Scholey, R. G. H. Seitz, L. M. Small, R. D. Wood, J. M. Zimmerman. **Transfer Agent & Registrar**—First Chicago Trust Co. of New York, NYC. **Incorporated**—in New Jersey in 1967. **Empl**— 11,000. **S&P Analyst:** Catherine A. Seifert

CIGNA Corp.

532T

NYSE Symbol **CI**

In S&P 500

12-SEP-98

Industry: Insurance (Multi-Line)

Summary: One of the largest insurance-based financial services concerns, CIGNA is a major force in the property-casualty and group life/health insurance fields.

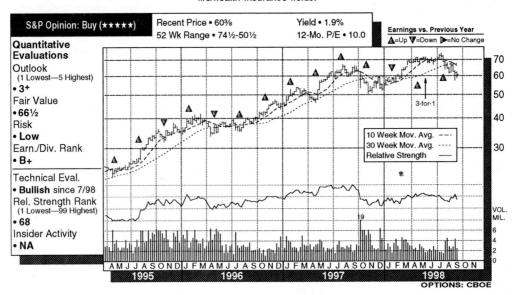

S&P Opinion: Buy (★★★★★)

Recent Price • 60⅜
52 Wk Range • 74½-50½

Yield • 1.9%
12-Mo. P/E • 10.0

Quantitative Evaluations

Outlook
(1 Lowest—5 Highest)
• **3+**

Fair Value
• **66½**

Risk
• **Low**

Earn./Div. Rank
• **B+**

Technical Eval.
• **Bullish** since 7/98

Rel. Strength Rank
(1 Lowest—99 Highest)
• **68**

Insider Activity
• **NA**

Earnings vs. Previous Year
▲=Up ▼=Down ▶=No Change

10 Week Mov. Avg. — - —
30 Week Mov. Avg. - - - -
Relative Strength ——

3-for-1

OPTIONS: CBOE

Overview - 06-AUG-98

Growth in operating earnings seen for 1998 is predicated on CI's ability to integrate recently acquired Healthsource into the fold of its Employee Benefits unit. Earnings at the unit were hurt in 1997 by an uptick in medical cost trends, which exacerbated the impact of Healthsource merger-related expenses on results. That aside, the $1.7 billion acquisition of Healthsource expanded CI's presence in the health care arena, and should be accretive to 1998 earnings. A shift toward lower margin products may offset a higher asset base and limit near-term earnings growth in the Employee Retirement and Savings unit. Property-Casualty (P-C) operating earnings growth will be aided by growth overseas, partly offset by extremely competitive market conditions in the U.S. This unit recorded net charges of $849 million ($11.64 a share) in 1995, to cover an increase in reserves for environmental and asbestos claims. The charges were made to restructure the P-C division into two units (one for ongoing operations, and one responsible for "running off" undesirable business).

Valuation - 06-AUG-98

After trending upward during much of 1997, the shares stumbled in late 1997, when CI (like many of its competitors) said third quarter earnings would be lower than expected, due to higher medical costs in the managed care sector. Since then, the shares have recovered, following several quarters of positive earnings momentum in the managed care sector. The shares should continue to trend upward, as the market rewards CI's shifting business mix and improved earnings outlook with an expansion of the current P/E multiple. Recently trading at less than 13X our 1999 operating EPS estimate of $5.30 (excluding realized investment gains/losses), the stock is undervalued.

Key Stock Statistics

S&P EPS Est. 1998	4.90	Tang. Bk. Value/Share	27.56
P/E on S&P Est. 1998	12.3	Beta	1.29
S&P EPS Est. 1999	5.30	Shareholders	14,000
Dividend Rate/Share	1.15	Market cap. (B)	$ 12.8
Shs. outstg. (M)	212.3	Inst. holdings	81%
Avg. daily vol. (M)	0.617		

Value of $10,000 invested 5 years ago: $ 36,950

Fiscal Year Ending Dec. 31

	1998	1997	1996	1995	1994	1993
Revenues (Million $)						
1Q	5,411	4,645	4,645	4,754	4,531	4,374
2Q	5,321	4,719	4,731	4,753	4,538	4,563
3Q	—	5,182	4,685	4,642	4,600	4,525
4Q	—	5,492	4,889	4,806	4,723	4,940
Yr.	—	20,038	18,950	18,955	18,392	18,402
Earnings Per Share ($)						
1Q	**2.27**	**1.30**	1.03	1.33	0.53	0.21
2Q	**1.42**	**1.25**	1.00	0.94	0.62	0.41
3Q	—	**1.25**	1.23	-2.59	0.57	-0.44
4Q	—	**1.09**	1.36	1.23	0.84	0.90
Yr.	—	**4.88**	4.62	0.95	2.55	1.08

Next earnings report expected: late October

Dividend Data (Dividends have been paid since 1867.)

Amount ($)	Date Decl.	Ex-Div. Date	Stock of Record	Payment Date
0.860	Feb. 25	Mar. 11	Mar. 13	Apr. 10 '98
3-for-1	Feb. 25	May. 18	May. 04	May. 15 '98
0.287	Apr. 22	Jun. 10	Jun. 12	Jul. 10 '98
0.287	Jul. 22	Sep. 09	Sep. 11	Oct. 10 '98

Business Summary - 06-AUG-98

CIGNA Corp. is one of the largest investor-owned insurance organizations. Like many other multi-line insurers, CI has decided to narrow its scope of focus around a few core segments. As part of a plan to concentrate its efforts on its employee benefits and property-casualty segments, in January 1998, CI sold its individual life insurance and annuity business to Lincoln National Corp. (NYSE: LNC), for about $1.4 billion. A second key facet to CI's transformation was its June 1997 purchase of Healthsource, Inc., for about $1.7 billion. Healthsource is a managed care provider, with 1.1 million HMO members, 2.0 million indemnity members, and 2.5 million dental members. Segment contributions (in millions) to operating income in recent years were:

	1997	1996
Employee life & health	$424	$497
Employee retirement & savings	221	201
Individual financial services	200	161
Property-casualty/ongoing	225	211
Property-casualty/runoff	1	2
Other	-100	-70

Total property-casualty written premiums from ongoing operations were $3.3 billion in 1997 ($3.4 billion in 1996), with international (including life and employee benefits) lines providing 55%, workers' compensation 10%, property lines 11%, casualty 9%, commercial packages 5%, marine and aviation 8%, and other lines 2%. Effective at the end of 1995, CI restructured its P-C operations into two separate units. Ongoing operations do not have the financial burden associated with environmental or asbestos claims. Runoff operations contain those operations primarily associated with environmental and asbestos claims.

The employee life and health benefits segment markets a full line of group life and health insurance products, and conducts CI's managed-care operations. Premiums and premium equivalents totaled $20.3 billion in 1997 ($17.9 billion in 1996), of which medical indemnity contributed 39%, medical HMOs 38%, life indemnity 9%, dental indemnity 8%, other indemnity 4%, and dental HMOs 2%. Prepaid medical enrollment at the end of 1997 equaled 5.9 million (up from 4.3 million at year end 1996). The employee retirement and savings benefits segment provides pension, profit-sharing and retirement savings programs to companies of all sizes. At year-end 1997, assets under management in this segment totaled $46.3 billion ($40.6 billion a year earlier). Individual financial services markets disability coverages, investment products, and financial planning services.

Per Share Data ($)

(Year Ended Dec. 31)	1997	1996	1995	1994	1993	1992	1991	1990	1989	1988
Tangible Bk. Val.	24.84	27.66	26.49	21.44	24.59	20.26	20.38	16.81	19.17	17.69
Oper. Earnings	4.72	4.38	0.23	2.42	0.05	0.67	1.87	1.47	1.45	1.63
Earnings	4.88	4.62	0.95	2.55	1.08	1.57	2.11	1.40	1.89	1.66
Dividends	1.11	1.07	1.01	1.01	1.01	1.01	1.01	1.01	0.99	0.99
Relative Payout	23%	23%	106%	40%	94%	65%	48%	72%	52%	59%
Prices - High	66⅞	47¾	38⅜	24⅝	22¾	20¼	20⅝	20¼	22¼	18½
- Low	44¾	35⅝	20¾	19	18⅞	15¾	12	11⅛	15¼	14¼
P/E Ratio - High	14	10	40	10	21	13	10	14	12	11
- Low	9	7	22	7	17	10	6	8	8	9

Income Statement Analysis (Million $)

	1997	1996	1995	1994	1993	1992	1991	1990	1989	1988
Life Ins. In Force	695,272	NA	NA	NA	NA	574,318	508,756	470,957	207,782	182,299
Prem. Inc.: Life A & H	12,251	9,518	9,272	8,869	8,516	9,127	9,019	8,291	5,871	7,657
Prem. Inc.: Cas./Prop.	2,684	4,398	4,640	5,043	5,136	4,797	5,276	5,695	5,623	5,797
Net Invest. Inc.	4,245	4,333	4,296	3,946	3,902	3,914	3,860	3,736	3,540	3,941
Oth. Revs.	858	701	745	534	788	744	595	442	620	495
Total Revs.	20,038	18,950	18,955	18,392	18,402	18,582	18,750	18,164	15,654	17,889
Pretax Inc.	1,650	1,601	251	805	165	179	584	352	592	508
Net Oper. Inc.	971	1,000	50.0	526	NA	145	401	333	354	410
Net Inc.	1,086	1,056	211	554	234	337	453	318	458	418

Balance Sheet & Other Fin. Data (Million $)

	1997	1996	1995	1994	1993	1992	1991	1990	1989	1988
Cash & Equiv.	3,493	2,177	2,467	2,528	1,975	1,745	2,561	1,877	1,420	1,073
Premiums Due	4,265	4,229	4,268	3,986	4,065	3,564	3,931	4,167	3,559	3,274
Invest. Assets: Bonds	36,358	36,253	37,354	31,670	33,112	28,228	26,296	24,918	23,579	22,162
Invest. Assets: Stocks	854	701	661	1,860	1,849	2,321	2,140	1,687	1,316	1,011
Invest. Assets: Loans	18,112	18,223	18,117	15,325	13,684	12,975	13,024	12,544	11,387	10,175
Invest. Assets: Total	56,578	56,534	57,710	50,919	50,728	45,082	42,597	40,092	36,967	33,993
Deferred Policy Costs	1,542	1,230	1,109	1,128	1,085	1,061	1,056	1,001	961	898
Total Assets	108,199	98,932	95,903	86,102	84,975	69,827	66,737	63,691	57,779	55,825
Debt	1,465	1,021	1,066	1,389	1,235	929	848	832	640	643
Common Eqty.	7,932	7,208	7,157	5,811	6,575	5,744	5,863	5,242	5,520	5,238
Comb. Loss-Exp. Ratio	NA	132.0	144.5	123.9	137.4	131.3	117.3	115.9	115.8	109.1
% Return On Revs.	5.4	5.6	1.1	3.0	1.3	1.8	2.4	1.8	2.9	2.3
% Ret. on Equity	14.3	14.7	3.3	8.9	3.8	5.8	8.2	5.9	8.4	7.5
% Invest. Yield	7.5	7.6	15.2	7.8	8.1	8.9	9.4	9.7	9.8	12.0

Data as orig. reptd.; bef. results of disc. opers. and/or spec. items. Per share data adj. for stk. divs. as of ex-div. date. EPS estimate based on op. earns. bef. sec. gains/losses. E-Estimate. NA-Not Available. NM-Not Meaningful. NR-Not Ranked.

Office—One Liberty Place, Philadelphia, PA 19192. **Inc.**—in Delaware in 1981. **Tel**—(215) 761-1000. **Chrmn & CEO**—W. H. Taylor. **VP & CFO**—J. G. Stewart. **Secy**—C. J. Ward. **Investor Contact**—Albert D. Civardelli. **Dirs**—R. P. Bauman, R. H. Campbell, A. C. DeCrane Jr., B. M. Fox, P. N. Larson, M. W. Lewis, P. F. Oreffice, C. R. Shoemate, L. W. Sullivan, W. H. Taylor, H. A. Wagner, C. C. Wait. **Transfer Agent & Registrar**—First Chicago Trust Co. of New York, Jersey City, NJ. **Incorporated**—in Delaware in 1981. **Empl**—47,700. **S&P Analyst:** Catherine A. Seifert

Cincinnati Financial 3533M

Nasdaq Symbol **CINF**

In S&P 500

12-SEP-98

Industry: Insurance (Property-Casualty)

Summary: This insurance holding company markets primarily property and casualty coverage; it also conducts life insurance operations.

S&P Opinion: Hold (★★★)	Recent Price • 34¾	Yield • 1.8%
	52 Wk Range • 47⅛-26¾	12-Mo. P/E • 20.1

Quantitative Evaluations

Outlook (1 Lowest—5 Highest)
• **1**

Fair Value
• **27⅝**

Risk
• **Low**

Earn./Div. Rank
• **A**

Technical Eval.
• **Bearish** since 7/98

Rel. Strength Rank (1 Lowest—99 Highest)
• **79**

Insider Activity
• **Neutral**

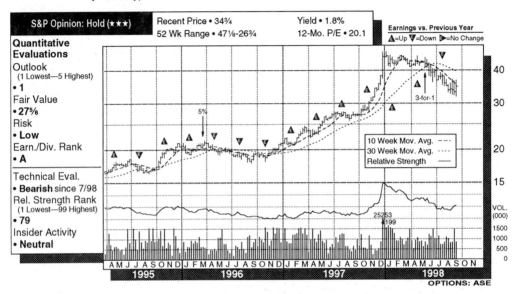

Earnings vs. Previous Year
▲=Up ▼=Down ▶=No Change

10 Week Mov. Avg. – – –
30 Week Mov. Avg. · · · ·
Relative Strength —

3-for-1

OPTIONS: ASE

Overview - 18-JUN-98

Net written premium growth in 1998 will likely be in high single digits (6% to 9%). This is about twice the rate of premium growth of the overall property-casualty industry. CINF's strategy of leveraging the strength of its core network of independent agents has enabled the company to aggressively expand its premium base, both geographically and by product line. Growth rates for personal lines will greatly outpace those of commercial lines, reflecting CINF's decision to expand its writings of core homeowners and personal auto coverage in an attempt to counter the intense price competition that is depressing premium pricng in the commercial lines arena. While underwriting results will continue to be aided by the company's relatively low cost structure, year over year comparisons may be difficult, given the low level of catastrophe losses in 1997. Investment income will be modest in a low interest rate environment, although CINF's aggressive, equity-oriented investment strategy has produced sizable investment gains. Note: EPS estimates are based on operating earnings (which exclude investment gains/losses); actual EPS are based on net income.

Valuation - 18-JUN-98

The shares of this regional property-casualty insurer soared in late 1997 after being added to the S&P 500 on December 17. After remaining in a narrow trading range during early 1998, the shares corrected somewhat in mid-1998 after CINF warned that its second quarter operating earnings would be hurt by heavy storm losses. We expect the shares to recover, and we share the market's positive view of CINF's operating strategy. At current levels, though, most near-term upside is already embedded in the valuation.

Key Stock Statistics

S&P EPS Est. 1998	1.40	Tang. Bk. Value/Share	31.51
P/E on S&P Est. 1998	24.8	Beta	0.42
S&P EPS Est. 1999	1.70	Shareholders	9,900
Dividend Rate/Share	0.61	Market cap. (B)	$ 5.8
Shs. outstg. (M)	167.2	Inst. holdings	36%
Avg. daily vol. (M)	0.204		

Value of $10,000 invested 5 years ago: $ 20,930

Fiscal Year Ending Dec. 31

	1998	1997	1996	1995	1994	1993
Revenues (Million $)						
1Q	512.6	483.7	451.8	414.7	379.7	353.7
2Q	518.6	484.2	442.0	405.0	378.8	371.1
3Q	—	492.0	455.7	416.7	381.7	357.5
4Q	—	482.4	459.2	419.3	372.3	359.9
Yr.	—	1,942	1,809	1,656	1,513	1,442
Earnings Per Share ($)						
1Q	**0.49**	**0.43**	0.35	0.37	0.29	0.34
2Q	**0.35**	**0.44**	0.32	0.32	0.35	0.37
3Q	—	**0.46**	0.27	0.34	0.28	0.21
4Q	—	**0.43**	0.37	0.30	0.27	0.27
Yr.	—	**1.77**	1.31	1.33	1.18	1.19

Next earnings report expected: late October

Dividend Data (Dividends have been paid since 1954.)

Amount ($)	Date Decl.	Ex-Div. Date	Stock of Record	Payment Date
0.410	Nov. 21	Dec. 10	Dec. 12	Jan. 15 '98
0.460	Feb. 07	Mar. 11	Mar. 13	Apr. 15 '98
3-for-1	Feb. 07	May. 18	Apr. 24	May. 15 '98
0.153	May. 22	Jun. 17	Jun. 19	Jul. 15 '98

A Division of The McGraw·Hill Companies

Business Summary - 18-JUN-98

Cincinnati Financial Corp. is a holding company that operates primarily in two industries: property and casualty insurance and life insurance. The company sells insurance primarily in the Midwest and Southeast through a network of independent agents.

Consolidated total revenues and pretax profits in 1997 were derived as follows:

	Revs.	Pretax Profits
Property-casualty insurance	75%	7%
Life & health insurance	3%	1%
Investment income (net)	18%	82%
Realized investment gains & other	4%	10%

The company's principal property-casualty subsidiary, Cincinnati Insurance Co. (CIC), underwrites and sells a broad array of personal and commercial insurance. Operations are conducted in 27 states through a network of 973 independent insurance agents, many of whom own stock in the company. (CIC is licensed in all 50 states, the District of Columbia and Puerto Rico. Plans to expand operations to several other states are under way.) During 1997, net written premiums totaled $1.47

billion, up 6.5% from $1.38 billion of net written premiums in 1996. During 1997, commercial lines coverage accounted for 67% of written premiums, while personal lines (mainly auto and homeowners') accounted for 33%. The combined loss and expense ratio equaled 97.7% (versus an industry average of about 102%), compared with 103% (106%) in 1996. The improved combined ratio largely reflected sharply lower catastrophe losses of $25.5 million versus $64.7 million. This helped offset an uptick in the expense ratio due to costs associated with technology upgrades and expansion efforts.

Life, accident and health insurance is marketed through property-casualty agents and independent life insurance agents. Premium income for Cincinnati Life amounted to $62.9 million in 1997, up from $56.4 million in 1996. During 1997, a new management team was hired and is expanding this unit's worksite marketing activities, introducing a new product line, and exploring expansion opportunities.

Total invested assets of $8.8 billion at 1997 year end (up from $6.3 billion at 1996 year end) were divided: fixed maturities 31%, equity securities 68%, and other invested assets 1%.

Per Share Data ($)

(Year Ended Dec. 31)	1997	1996	1995	1994	1993	1992	1991	1990	1989	1988
Tangible Bk. Val.	28.35	18.95	16.70	11.63	11.70	10.42	8.75	6.16	6.28	5.08
Oper. Earnings	1.54	1.13	1.28	1.11	1.05	0.89	0.86	0.78	0.69	0.78
Earnings	1.77	1.31	1.40	1.18	1.19	1.02	0.89	0.79	0.70	0.80
Dividends	0.55	0.49	0.45	0.39	0.34	0.31	0.27	0.25	0.22	0.18
Relative Payout	31%	38%	31%	33%	28%	30%	31%	31%	31%	22%
Prices - High	47⅛	21⅞	21¼	17⅝	20⅛	19	12⅜	9	8⅜	6⅛
- Low	20⅝	17¾	15⅜	13⅞	15⅛	10¾	7⅞	6½	5⅜	4
P/E Ratio - High	27	17	15	14	17	19	14	12	12	8
- Low	12	14	11	11	13	11	9	8	8	5

Income Statement Analysis (Million $)

	1997	1996	1995	1994	1993	1992	1991	1990	1989	1988
Life Ins. In Force	10,845	9,776	8,329	7,474	6,766	6,111	5,599	5,174	4,572	NA
Prem. Inc.: Life A & H	62.9	56.0	50.9	49.1	48.7	46.4	44.1	43.2	42.1	55.6
Prem. Inc.: Cas./Prop.	1,454	1,367	1,263	1,170	1,092	992	903	828	771	713
Net Invest. Inc.	349	327	300	263	239	219	193	167	149	131
Oth. Revs.	77.4	58.0	41.5	30.8	61.9	46.6	20.9	10.8	11.9	10.4
Total Revs.	1,942	1,809	1,656	1,513	1,442	1,304	1,161	1,049	974	910
Pretax Inc.	395	282	295	249	267	209	177	150	133	147
Net Oper. Inc.	254	193	207	189	NA	148	141	128	111	125
Net Inc.	299	224	227	201	202	171	146	129	114	129

Balance Sheet & Other Fin. Data (Million $)

	1997	1996	1995	1994	1993	1992	1991	1990	1989	1988
Cash & Equiv.	80.2	130	85.1	104	98.0	97.0	100	78.0	71.0	56.0
Premiums Due	159	162	161	142	134	124	116	107	111	98.0
Invest. Assets: Bonds	2,751	2,562	2,447	1,943	1,760	1,636	1,422	1,181	1,098	1,015
Invest. Assets: Stocks	5,999	3,740	3,042	2,231	2,319	1,972	1,605	1,049	1,100	799
Invest. Assets: Loans	Nil	Nil	Nil	Nil	Nil	Nil	Nil	Nil	Nil	Nil
Invest. Assets: Total	8,797	6,344	5,529	4,212	4,117	3,647	3,067	2,268	2,233	1,841
Deferred Policy Costs	135	128	120	110	104	97.3	93.6	88.9	86.8	75.5
Total Assets	9,493	7,046	6,109	4,734	4,602	4,098	3,436	2,590	2,552	2,117
Debt	339	342	301	209	158	147	107	73.0	67.0	65.0
Common Eqty.	4,717	3,163	2,658	1,940	1,947	1,714	1,441	1,007	1,020	816
Comb. Loss-Exp. Ratio	97.7	103.0	NA	NA	100.1	101.8	99.7	99.6	99.7	95.9
% Return On Revs.	15.4	12.4	13.7	13.3	14.0	13.1	12.2	12.2	11.4	13.7
% Ret. on Equity	7.6	7.7	9.9	10.3	11.0	10.8	11.5	12.8	12.1	17.2
% Invest. Yield	4.6	5.5	6.2	6.3	6.2	6.5	7.2	7.4	7.3	7.8

Data as orig. reptd.; bef. results of disc. opers. and/or spec. items. Per share data adj. for stk. divs. as of ex-div. date. Bold denotes diluted EPS (FASB 128). E-Estimate. NA-Not Available. NM-Not Meaningful. NR-Not Ranked.

Office—6200 S. Gilmore Rd., Fairfield, OH 45014-5141. **Tel**—(513) 870-2000. **Website**—http://www.cinfin.com **Chrmn**—J. J. Schiff Jr. **Pres & CEO**—R. B. Morgan. **SVP- CFO, Secy & Treas**—T. F. Elchynski. **Dirs**—W. F. Bahl, M. Brown, R. M. Burridge, J. E. Field, W. R. Johnson, K. C. Lichtendahl, J. G. Miller, R. B. Morgan, J. H. Randolph, J. J. Schiff, J. J. Schiff Jr., R. C. Schiff, T. R. Schiff, F. J. Schultheis, L. R. Webb, A. R. Weiler. **Transfer Agent & Registrar**—Co. itself. **Incorporated**—in Delaware in 1968. **Empl**— 2,670. **S&P Analyst**: C. A. Seifert

12-SEP-98

Industry: Machinery (Diversified)

Summary: This company is a leading maker of plastics machinery, computer controls and software for factory automation.

| S&P Opinion: Hold (★★★) | Recent Price • 17⅞ | Yield • 2.7% |
| | 52 Wk Range • 33¾-17⅜ | 12-Mo. P/E • 8.2 |

Quantitative Evaluations

Outlook
(1 Lowest—5 Highest)
• **5**

Fair Value
• **36¼**

Risk
• **Low**

Earn./Div. Rank
• **B**

Technical Eval.
• **NA**

Rel. Strength Rank
(1 Lowest—99 Highest)
• **31**

Insider Activity
• **NA**

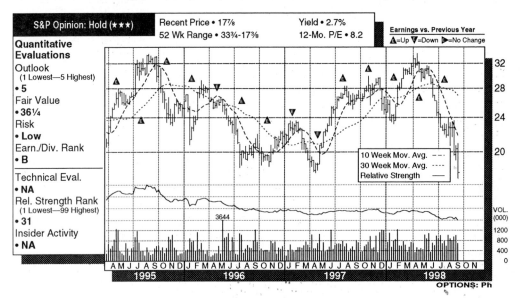

Earnings vs. Previous Year
▲=Up ▼=Down ▶=No Change

10 Week Mov. Avg. ---
30 Week Mov. Avg. ·····
Relative Strength ——

OPTIONS: Ph

Overview - 26-AUG-98

The company's mid-August 1998 agreements to sell its machine tool business and acquire the Uniloy Plastics Machinery division of Johnson Controls, underscores management's desire to expand CMZ's presence in businesses with favorable growth prospects, boost operating profits and reduce earnings volatility. CMZ's machine tool business is low margin, highly cyclical and slow-growing. CMZ is counting on higher margins and reduced earnings volatility from its faster growing plastics machinery unit and recurring "razorblade" sales from its metalcutting unit. However, we believe CMZ's prospects for the next few years will be mixed. Manufacturers are reluctant to expand capacity late in the economic cycle, and order backlog already reflects cautious spending plans. Longer-term, CMZ is boosting efforts to deepen penetration of foreign markets, particularly in Asia and Latin America. It recently announced a joint venture for the production of metalworking machining centers in India.

Valuation - 26-AUG-98

We continue to rate the shares a hold, due to a flat outlook for 1998. This producer of capital goods has had an erratic 10-year earnings record. We think that the volatile earnings will continue, despite efforts to diversify product lines and broaden markets geographically. Although the stock trades at a modest P/E multiple, we do not think that the multiple will expand, since it is late in the economic expansion; the stock will likely be only an average performer over the balance of the cycle. The best time to buy capital goods stocks is early in the cycle, when the economy is clearly in recovery. These stocks typically outperform the stock market for only brief periods over the course of the cycle, and are best traded by nimble investors.

Key Stock Statistics

S&P EPS Est. 1998	2.15	Tang. Bk. Value/Share	5.96
P/E on S&P Est. 1998	8.3	Beta	1.12
S&P EPS Est. 1999	2.50	Shareholders	6,100
Dividend Rate/Share	0.48	Market cap. (B)	$0.704
Shs. outstg. (M)	39.2	Inst. holdings	73%
Avg. daily vol. (M)	0.177		

Value of $10,000 invested 5 years ago: $ 11,981

Fiscal Year Ending Dec. 31

	1998	1997	1996	1995	1994	1993
Revenues (Million $)						
1Q	477.4	377.5	353.4	331.4	245.5	219.0
2Q	490.6	452.1	411.4	413.6	269.3	236.6
3Q	—	452.1	511.1	486.5	361.2	300.7
4Q	—	496.4	453.8	417.8	321.2	272.7
Yr.	—	1,897	1,730	1,649	1,197	1,029
Earnings Per Share ($)						
1Q	**0.44**	**0.32**	0.36	0.38	0.14	0.13
2Q	**0.52**	**0.46**	0.40	0.24	0.23	0.19
3Q	—	**0.56**	0.47	0.46	0.35	-0.23
4Q	—	**0.67**	0.50	1.96	0.38	-1.40
Yr.	**E2.15**	**2.01**	1.73	3.04	1.10	-1.41

Next earnings report expected: early November

Dividend Data (Dividends have been paid since 1923.)

Amount ($)	Date Decl.	Ex-Div. Date	Stock of Record	Payment Date
0.120	Nov. 04	Nov. 25	Nov. 28	Dec. 12 '97
0.120	Feb. 06	Feb. 25	Feb. 27	Mar. 12 '98
0.120	Apr. 28	May. 13	May. 15	Jun. 12 '98
0.120	Jul. 30	Aug. 19	Aug. 21	Sep. 12 '98

A Division of The **McGraw·Hill** *Companies*

STANDARD
&POOR'S
STOCK REPORTS

Cincinnati Milacron Inc.

536

12-SEP-98

Business Summary - 26-AUG-98

Cincinnati Milacron is a leading producer of machine tools, plastics machinery and metal cutting tools. The company has a strong global presence, with about half of its sales from overseas, and a diverse customer base that crosses many industries. The company continues to expand overseas through joint ventures, alliances and acquisitions, and new products play an important role, with about half of sales derived from products designed in the past five years. As of June 30, 1998, the company's backlog totaled $386.5 million, compared with $365 million at the end of 1997. Contributions by segment in 1997 were:

	Sales	Profits
Industrial products	39%	52%
Plastics machinery	37%	38%
Machine tools	24%	9%

Sales by industry: automotive 21%, industrial components & machinery 20%, job shops & custom molders 14%, construction 8%, electrical 8%, aerospace 7%, consumer goods & toys 5%, housewares & appliances 3%, packaging 3%, medical 2% and other 9%.

Industrial products consist of metal cutting tools, metalworking fluids and precision grinding wheels. About 140,000 types, styles and sizes are produced under brand names including Cimcool, Cimform, Valenite, Widia, Weldon, Brubaker, Fastcut and New England Tap. In 1998, the company will invest $15 million to expand round metal cutting tool capacity at three U.S. sites.

Plastics processing machinery includes injection molding machines and extrusion systems. Injection molding includes electric and hydraulic models and reaction injection molding machines. Extrusion systems include twin-screw and single-screw extruders, Sano blown-film and cast-film systems and a variety of blow molding machines. In mid-1998, CMZ agreed to acquire the Uniloy Plastics Machinery Division ($190 million in revenues), from Johnson Controls. Uniloy makes blow molding machines used in the production of beverage containers and industrial components.

Machine tools include Advanced Systems and Standard Machine Tools. Advanced Systems makes five-axis profilers; high-speed routers; milling, die and moldmaking machines; and composite tape-laying and fiber-placement systems. Standard includes vertical and horizontal machining centers; turning centers; mill/turn centers; centerless and chuck grinding machines; and pre-engineered flexible manufacturing cells. In mid-1998, the company agreed to sell Machine Tools to Cincinnati-based UNOVA, Inc. (NYSE: UNA).

Per Share Data ($)

(Year Ended Dec. 31)	1997	1996	1995	1994	1993	1992	1991	1990	1989	1988
Tangible Bk. Val.	5.93	5.28	5.56	3.91	3.52	4.67	4.49	8.85	9.07	9.14
Cash Flow	3.36	3.07	4.31	1.93	-0.60	1.33	-2.17	0.05	1.69	2.05
Earnings	2.01	1.73	3.04	1.10	-1.41	0.58	-3.04	-0.87	0.75	1.02
Dividends	0.42	0.36	0.36	0.36	0.36	0.36	0.63	0.72	0.72	0.72
Payout Ratio	21%	21%	12%	33%	NM	62%	NM	96%	70%	
Prices - High	29⁷/₈	29¹/₄	33⁵/₈	27⁵/₈	29⁵/₈	18¹/₄	15¹/₄	21¹/₄	25¹/₈	26¹/₂
- Low	17⁷/₈	18³/₈	19⁷/₈	18⁵/₈	16¹/₄	10⁷/₈	6⁵/₈	8³/₄	15	17⁷/₈
P/E Ratio - High	15	17	11	25	NM	31	NM	NM	34	26
- Low	9	11	7	17	NM	19	NM	NM	20	16

Income Statement Analysis (Million $)

	1997	1996	1995	1994	1993	1992	1991	1990	1989	1988
Revs.	1,897	1,730	1,649	1,197	1,029	789	754	838	851	858
Oper. Inc.	196	166	153	98.3	72.9	63.9	42.6	56.4	73.2	86.7
Depr.	53.7	50.9	43.6	28.2	26.1	20.9	24.0	23.7	22.9	25.0
Int. Exp.	28.9	34.6	28.0	17.9	15.7	19.1	19.1	19.7	22.5	22.0
Pretax Inc.	105	81.3	137	48.9	-37.2	27.0	-73.4	-17.8	35.2	43.7
Eff. Tax Rate	19%	19%	21%	23%	NM	40%	NM	NM	48%	43%
Net Inc.	80.6	66.3	106	37.7	-45.4	16.1	-83.1	-22.1	18.4	25.0

Balance Sheet & Other Fin. Data (Million $)

	1997	1996	1995	1994	1993	1992	1991	1990	1989	1988
Cash	25.7	27.8	133	21.5	18.8	14.9	16.2	45.2	32.9	17.9
Curr. Assets	752	728	782	515	484	429	443	490	499	528
Total Assets	1,393	1,336	1,197	788	730	579	598	693	686	721
Curr. Liab.	425	410	390	363	369	237	255	236	240	259
LT Debt	304	302	332	143	108	154	156	157	166	182
Common Eqty.	466	440	264	152	118	128	123	242	221	221
Total Cap.	776	748	602	301	232	289	285	414	404	421
Cap. Exp.	795	65.2	52.3	43.0	23.4	17.6	15.5	34.1	33.6	21.5
Cash Flow	134	117	149	65.7	-19.5	36.8	-59.3	1.3	41.1	49.7
Curr. Ratio	1.8	1.8	2.0	1.4	1.3	1.8	1.7	2.1	2.1	2.0
% LT Debt of Cap.	39.2	40.3	55.1	47.5	46.4	53.5	54.7	38.0	41.1	43.3
% Net Inc.of Revs.	4.2	3.8	6.4	3.1	NM	2.0	NM	NM	2.2	2.9
% Ret. on Assets	5.9	5.3	10.6	5.0	NM	2.7	NM	NM	2.6	3.5
% Ret. on Equity	17.7	18.9	50.1	27.7	NM	12.6	NM	NM	8.2	11.5

Data as orig. reptd.; bef. results of disc. opers. and/or spec. items. Per share data adj. for stk. divs. as of ex-div. date. Bold denotes diluted EPS (FASB 128). E-Estimated. NA-Not Available. NM-Not Meaningful. NR-Not Ranked.

Office—4701 Marburg Ave., Cincinnati, OH 45209. **Tel**—(513) 841-8100. **Website**—http://www.milacron.com **Chrmn & CEO**—D. J. Meyer. **Pres & COO**—R. E. Ross. **VP & CFO**—R. D. Brown. **VP & Secy**—W. F. Taylor. **Investor Contact**—Al Beaupre. **Dirs**—D. F. Allen, N. A. Armstrong, B. H. Franklin, H. A. Hammerly, D. J. Meyer, J. E. Perrella, J. A. Pichler, R. E. Ross, J. A. Steger, H. C. Stonecipher. **Transfer Agent & Registrar**—ChaseMellon Shareholder Services, Ridgefield Park, NJ. **Incorporated**—in Ohio in 1922; reincorporated in Delaware in 1983. **Empl**— 12,581.
S&P Analyst: Robert E. Friedman, CPA

STANDARD &POOR'S
STOCK REPORTS

CINergy Corp.

536N

NYSE Symbol **CIN**

In S&P 500

12-SEP-98

Industry: Electric Companies

Summary: This holding company was formed in 1994 via the merger of Cincinnati Gas & Electric Co. and PSI Resources, Inc., the holding company for Indiana's largest electric utility.

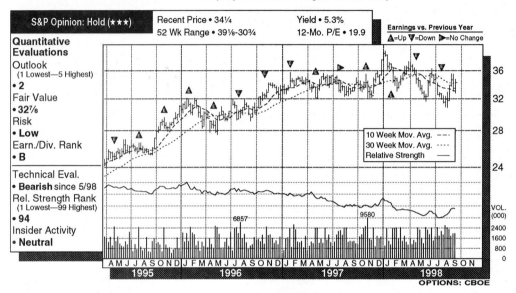

S&P Opinion: Hold (★★★)	Recent Price • 34¼ 52 Wk Range • 39⅛-30¾ Yield • 5.3% 12-Mo. P/E • 19.9

Earnings vs. Previous Year
▲=Up ▼=Down ▷=No Change

Quantitative Evaluations

Outlook
(1 Lowest—5 Highest)
• **2**

Fair Value
• **32⅞**

Risk
• **Low**

Earn./Div. Rank
• **B**

Technical Eval.
• **Bearish** since 5/98

Rel. Strength Rank
(1 Lowest—99 Highest)
• **94**

Insider Activity
• **Neutral**

10 Week Mov. Avg. — — —
30 Week Mov. Avg. - - - -
Relative Strength ———

OPTIONS: CBOE

Overview - 24-AUG-98

We expect EPS in 1998 to decline about 12% from 1997 levels (not including an extraordinary charge of $0.69 a share for U.K. windfall profits tax on 50%-owned Midlands Electricity). The decline mainly reflects one-time second quarter charges of $0.58 a share, including a charge of $0.26 for adding $65 million in reserves for its electricity trading operations. We expect earnings to rebound in 1999 as CIN continues to benefit from cost reductions, modest customer growth, a well positioned gas distribution business, and stable contributions from Midlands. CIN remains an efficient, low-cost electric producer, with rates among the lowest in the Midwest. Profits, however, will be hard earned in the thin margin energy trading operations. CIN is studying strategic alternatives that include the spinoff or sale of its electric generation business. It is also seeking to expand the scale of its organization, and will continue to look at potential partners for a merger, acquisition or alliance.

Valuation - 24-AUG-98

We would continue to hold CIN stock. The shares are down about 13% year to date, as earnings remain restricted by the sharply reduced margins in the power trading operations. In 1997, the shares rose 14.8%, versus a 19.8% gain for the S&P Index of Electric Companies (electricity sales accounted for 89% of 1997 revenues) and an 18.6% increase for the S&P Index of Natural Gas Companies. We believe that CIN is well positioned for a period of rising competition, and it continues to have appeal as a possible merger partner. While the stock appears fairly valued at about 12X our 1999 EPS estimate of $2.70, the shares, with a dividend yield of about 5.4%, remain attractive as a long-term holding for total return.

Key Stock Statistics

S&P EPS Est. 1998	2.00	Tang. Bk. Value/Share	15.79
P/E on S&P Est. 1998	17.1	Beta	0.26
S&P EPS Est. 1999	2.70	Shareholders	77,100
Dividend Rate/Share	1.80	Market cap. (B)	$ 5.4
Shs. outstg. (M)	158.5	Inst. holdings	59%
Avg. daily vol. (M)	0.420		

Value of $10,000 invested 5 years ago: $ 18,957

Fiscal Year Ending Dec. 31

	1998	1997	1996	1995	1994	1993
Revenues (Million $)						
1Q	1,332	1,030	884.0	809.0	866.0	493.5
2Q	1,072	865.3	716.8	668.4	673.0	367.5
3Q	—	1,355	765.7	767.6	692.0	408.6
4Q	—	1,102	876.2	786.0	693.4	482.2
Yr.	—	4,353	3,243	3,031	2,924	1,752
Earnings Per Share ($)						
1Q	**0.67**	**0.72**	0.70	0.65	0.68	0.71
2Q	**-0.16**	0.35	0.35	0.39	0.33	0.38
3Q	**E0.68**	0.53	0.51	0.69	0.39	0.61
4Q	**E0.81**	**0.70**	0.44	0.49	-0.10	-2.08
Yr.	**E2.00**	2.28	2.00	2.22	1.30	-0.39

Next earnings report expected: late October

Dividend Data (Dividends have been paid since 1853.)

Amount ($)	Date Decl.	Ex-Div. Date	Stock of Record	Payment Date
0.450	Oct. 21	Oct. 29	Oct. 31	Nov. 15 '97
0.450	Jan. 28	Feb. 03	Feb. 05	Feb. 15 '98
0.450	Apr. 22	Apr. 29	May. 01	May. 15 '98
0.450	Jul. 29	Aug. 04	Aug. 06	Aug. 15 '98

A Division of The McGraw-Hill Companies

STANDARD
&POOR'S
STOCK REPORTS

CINergy Corp.

536N
12-SEP-98

Business Summary - 24-AUG-98

Formed through the 1994 merger of Cincinnati Gas & Electric Co. and PSI Resources, Inc., CINergy Corp. is a holding company serving 1.4 million electric customers and 450,000 gas customers in a 25,000 square mile area of Ohio, Indiana and Kentucky.

Contributions by business segment in 1997 were:

	Revenues	Profits
Electric	89%	94%
Gas	11%	6%

In its order approving the merger, the SEC reserved jurisdiction over the company's ownership of Cincinnati Gas & Electric's gas operations for three years. At the end of the three-year period, CIN was required to state how its retention of the gas properties met all of the relevant standards of the Public Utility Holding Company Act (PUHCA) of 1935. In February 1998, the company filed with the SEC its rationale on how its retention of the gas operations meets PUHCA requirements.

Cincinnati Gas & Electric (CG&E) and its subsidiaries supply electricity and natural gas in the southwestern portion of Ohio and adjacent areas in Kentucky and Indiana. In December 1996, the Public Utility Commission of Ohio approved an overall average increase in gas revenues of 2.5% ($9.3 million annually) for CG&E.

The primary subsidiary of PSI Resources (formerly PSI Holdings) is PSI Energy (formerly Public Service Co. of Indiana), Indiana's largest electric utility, serving a population of about 1.9 million. In February 1995, regulators approved a settlement that permits CIN a 4.3% rate increase for PSI Energy and apportions savings from the merger between customers and shareholders. Regulators approved an additional 1.9% rate increase for CIN in March 1995. In September 1996, the Indiana Utility Regulatory Commission (IURC) approved an overall retail rate increase of 7.6% ($75.7 million annually) for PSI Energy.

In mid-1996, Avon Energy Partners plc, a newly formed, equally owned joint venture between nonregulated subsidiaries of CIN and GPU, Inc., acquired Midlands Electricity plc, a British regional electric company that distributes and supplies electricity to 2.2 million customers in England, and generates electricity both in England and internationally, for about $2.6 billion.

In September 1997, CINergy, Florida Progess Corp. and New Century Energies formed Cadence Network LLC, a joint venture that will provide energy management services to national accounts. In December 1996, CIN formed Trigen-Cinergy, a joint venture with Trigen Energy Corp. that builds, owns and operates cogeneration and trigeneration facilities.

Per Share Data ($)

(Year Ended Dec. 31)	1997	1996	1995	1994	1993	1992	1991	1990	1989	1988
Tangible Bk. Val.	16.00	16.26	16.17	15.40	17.10	19.01	18.55	17.75	16.59	15.19
Earnings	2.28	2.00	2.22	1.30	-0.39	2.04	2.21	2.75	2.89	2.88
Dividends	1.80	1.74	1.72	1.39	1.68	1.65	1.65	1.60	1.53	1.49
Payout Ratio	79%	87%	77%	107%	NM	81%	75%	58%	53%	52%
Prices - High	39⅛	34¼	31⅛	27¾	29⅝	26⅝	26¾	21⅛	21⅝	19⅜
- Low	32	27½	23⅜	20¾	23⅞	22¼	18⅝	18⅝	16¼	16¼
P/E Ratio - High	17	17	14	21	NM	13	12	8	7	7
- Low	14	14	11	16	NM	11	8	7	6	6

Income Statement Analysis (Million $)

	1997	1996	1995	1994	1993	1992	1991	1990	1989	1988
Revs.	4,353	3,243	3,031	2,924	1,752	1,553	1,518	1,438	1,438	1,386
Depr.	289	283	280	294	152	141	131	94.0	90.0	89.0
Maint.	176	194	182	201	109	105	121	120	115	107
Fxd. Chgs. Cov.	3.1	3.4	2.3	2.3	1.3	2.3	2.9	3.0	3.3	3.4
Constr. Credits	7.4	7.4	10.0	18.5	7.0	18.0	68.0	136	113	92.0
Eff. Tax Rate	37%	40%	39%	44%	NM	25%	19%	16%	21%	24%
Net Inc.	363	335	347	191	-8.7	202	207	235	240	227

Balance Sheet & Other Fin. Data (Million $)

	1997	1996	1995	1994	1993	1992	1991	1990	1989	1988
Gross Prop.	9,914	9,881	9,619	9,363	5,258	5,308	5,110	4,729	4,286	3,865
Cap. Exp.	328	323	325	480	199	230	410	467	441	416
Net Prop.	6,114	6,290	6,251	6,199	3,786	3,945	3,861	3,579	3,203	2,851
Capitalization:										
LT Debt	2,166	2,535	2,531	2,715	1,829	1,810	1,734	1,651	1,348	1,225
% LT Debt	44	48	46	48	50	48	48	49	47	47
Pfd.	178	194	388	478	330	330	330	290	241	243
% Pfd.	3.60	3.70	7.10	8.50	9.00	8.70	9.10	8.70	8.40	9.30
Common	2,539	2,584	2,549	2,414	1,519	1,655	1,584	1,399	1,279	1,146
% Common	52	49	47	43	41	44	43	42	45	44
Total Cap.	6,283	6,636	6,774	6,874	4,553	4,250	4,047	3,717	3,236	2,968
% Oper. Ratio	86.4	82.8	80.8	84.9	81.8	83.3	86.0	84.2	83.3	82.8
% Earn. on Net Prop.	8.8	8.9	9.4	7.2	8.3	6.7	5.7	6.7	7.9	8.8
% Return On Revs.	8.3	10.3	11.5	6.5	NM	13.0	13.6	16.3	16.7	16.4
% Return On Invest. Capital	11.9	8.6	8.9	6.7	3.3	8.7	7.8	9.8	10.9	11.3
% Return On Com. Equity	14.2	13.0	14.0	8.2	NM	10.8	12.2	15.9	18.1	19.8

Data as orig. reptd.; bef. results of disc opers. and/or spec. items. Per share data adj. for stk. divs. as of ex-div. date. Bold denotes diluted EPS (FASB 128). E-Estimated. NA-Not Available. NM-Not Meaningful. NR-Not Ranked.

Registrar—Fifth Third Bank, Cincinnati. **Office**—139 E. Fourth St., Cincinnati, OH 45202. **Tel**—(513) 381-2000. **Chrmn**—J. H. Randolph. **Vice-Chrmn, Pres & CEO**—J. E. Rogers. **VP & CFO**—C. J. Winger. **VP & Secy**—C. M. Foley. **Investor Contact**—Felicia Ferguson (513-287-4348). **Dirs**—N. A. Armstrong, J. K. Baker, M. G. Browning, P. R. Cox, K. M. Duberstein, J. A. Hillenbrand II, G. C. Juilfs, M. Perelman, T. E. Petry, J. H. Randolph, J. E. Rogers, J. J. Schiff Jr., P. R. Sharp, V. P. Smith,— D. S. Taft, O. W. Waddell. **Transfer Agent**—Co.'s office. **Incorporated**—in Ohio in 1837; reincorporated in Delaware in 1994. **Empl**—7,609. **S&P Analyst:** Justin McCann

Circuit City Stores

536V
NYSE Symbol CC
In S&P 500

12-SEP-98

Industry: Retail (Computers & Electronics)

Summary: This large U.S. retailer of brand-name consumer electronics and major appliances also has a majority equity interest in the CarMax auto and truck dealership business.

S&P Opinion: Hold (★★★)	**Recent Price • 32½** / 52 Wk Range • 54½-28⅞
	Yield • 0.4% / 12-Mo. P/E • 28.8

Earnings vs. Previous Year ▲=Up ▼=Down ▶=No Change

Quantitative Evaluations

Outlook (1 Lowest—5 Highest)
• **4+**

Fair Value
• **37⅝**

Risk
• **Average**

Earn./Div. Rank
• **A-**

Technical Eval.
• **NA**

Rel. Strength Rank (1 Lowest—99 Highest)
• **29**

Insider Activity
• **Unfavorable**

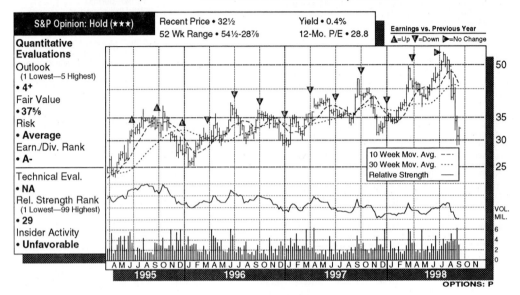

10 Week Mov. Avg. — - —
30 Week Mov. Avg. ------
Relative Strength —

OPTIONS: P

Overview - 29-JUN-98

In FY 99 (Feb.), we expect that CC will get profit growth of more than 20% from its large consumer electronics-related retail business, with help from effective inventory management and higher comparable-unit sales. We look for about 50 new stores to be opened during the year. Also, we estimate that CC's 77.5% ownership of the CarMax used car and truck dealer business will dilute overall earnings by about $0.15/share. In FY 98, the CarMax stake adversely affected CC's earnings by about $0.26, including a writedown in the value of some assets. Over time, we expect that CarMax will get some efficiencies from greater use of smaller format stores, and increased consumer familiarity with the business. Separately, we estimate that CC's investment in a new home video format known as Divx will dilute FY 99 earnings by about $0.20/share. We expect that CC will be seeking to raise additional equity capital for the development of Divx, which is expected to have a national rollout later in 1998.

Valuation - 29-JUN-98

We see some appeal in holding the stock of this aggressive company, but do not advise new purchases. In our view, the stock should be valued primarily on the basis of earnings prospects for CC's large consumer electronic-related business, which we value at about $40 per CC share. In FY 99 (Feb.), we look for this business to generate earnings of about $2.00/share, up approximately 25% from the year before. We value CC's majority ownership of the large but unprofitable CarMax (KMX) auto and truck dealership business at about $6 per CC share, and its partnership investment related to a new home video format known as Divx at no more than $3/share.

Key Stock Statistics

S&P EPS Est. 1999	1.65	Tang. Bk. Value/Share	14.24
P/E on S&P Est. 1999	19.7	Beta	1.16
S&P EPS Est. 2000	2.30	Shareholders	8,100
Dividend Rate/Share	0.14	Market cap. (B)	$ 3.3
Shs. outstg. (M)	100.0	Inst. holdings	80%
Avg. daily vol. (M)	1.008		

Value of $10,000 invested 5 years ago: $ 12,851

Fiscal Year Ending Feb. 28

	1999	1998	1997	1996	1995	1994
Revenues (Million $)						
1Q	1,925	1,857	1,615	1,392	1,049	799.0
2Q	—	2,021	1,767	1,601	1,219	906.7
3Q	—	2,144	1,864	1,783	1,405	1,018
4Q	—	2,850	2,418	2,253	1,910	1,407
Yr.	—	8,871	7,664	7,029	5,583	4,130
Earnings Per Share ($)						
1Q	**0.13**	0.13	0.17	0.25	0.20	0.18
2Q	**E0.29**	0.28	0.32	0.42	0.37	0.29
3Q	**E0.28**	0.14	0.20	0.32	0.29	0.20
4Q	**E0.95**	0.58	0.68	0.83	0.86	0.70
Yr.	**E1.65**	**1.13**	1.37	1.82	1.72	1.36

Next earnings report expected: mid September

Dividend Data (Dividends have been paid since 1979.)

Amount ($)	Date Decl.	Ex-Div. Date	Stock of Record	Payment Date
0.035	Sep. 15	Sep. 26	Sep. 30	Oct. 15 '97
0.035	Dec. 15	Dec. 29	Dec. 31	Jan. 15 '98
0.035	Mar. 16	Mar. 27	Mar. 31	Apr. 15 '98
0.035	Jun. 22	Jun. 26	Jun. 30	Jul. 15 '98

A Division of The McGraw-Hill Companies

Business Summary - 29-JUN-98

Circuit City Stores, Inc. is a large retailer of brand-name consumer electronics, major appliances, personal computers and music software. Also, CC owns about 77.5% of the CarMax Group, which is a large retailer of used cars and light trucks, and has been investing in a new home video medium known as Divx.

In FY 98 (Feb.), the Circuit City consumer electronics-related retail business had operatng revenues of $8.0 billion, up 12% from the year before. At April 30, 1998, this business included the operation of 558 stores throughout the U.S., with most of them having a "superstore" format. Revenue sources in recent fiscal years were:

	FY 98	FY 97	FY 96
Television	18%	18%	17%
VCR/Camcorders	13%	14%	13%
Audio	17%	18%	19%
Home office	25%	24%	26%
Appliances	15%	15%	14%
Other	12%	11%	11%

At the end of FY 98 (Feb.), CC's consumer electronics-related business had four superstore formats with square footage and merchandise assortments tailored to population size and volume expectations. In FY 98, CC opened 57 superstores, including entries into the New York, Dayton, Columbus and Indianapolis metropoitan markets. Also, Circuit City operated 52 mall-based Circuit City Express units, which averaged about 2,000 to 3,000 sq. ft. In FY 98, there was a net increase of seven Express units. In addition, at the end of FY 98, CC operated four "electronics-only" stores.

Circuit City Stores, Inc.-- CarMax Group (NYSE: KMX; 77.5% owned) is a leading retailer of used cars and light trucks in the U.S. At April 30, 1998, CarMax operated 19 superstores in 11 markets. At two of these locations, CarMax was also selling new vehicles, under franchise agreements with Chrysler. In FY 98, CarMax had operating revenues of $874 million, up 71% from the prior year. In a public offering completed in February 1997, CC sold 21.9 million shares of KMX common stock. The KMX stock is intended to track separately the performance of CarMax's operations.

CC owns about two-thirds of Digital Video Express, LP, a partnership formed to develop a video disc technology (Divx), which was recently introduced to consumers in Richmond, VA, and San Francisco. Divx offers consumers a no-return rental-like system for viewing videos on disc.

Per Share Data ($)

(Year Ended Feb. 28)	1998	1997	1996	1995	1994	1993	1992	1991	1990	1989
Tangible Bk. Val.	14.24	13.45	10.93	9.10	7.39	6.02	4.78	3.96	3.92	3.03
Cash Flow	2.22	2.37	2.63	2.41	1.92	1.58	1.21	0.92	1.09	0.95
Earnings	1.13	1.37	1.82	1.72	1.36	1.15	0.82	0.61	0.85	0.77
Dividends	0.14	0.14	0.12	0.10	0.08	0.06	0.05	0.05	0.04	0.03
Payout Ratio	8%	9%	6%	6%	6%	5%	6%	8%	4%	4%
Cal. Yrs.	1997	1996	1995	1994	1993	1992	1991	1990	1989	1988
Prices - High	45½	38¾	38	27	33⅞	26⅛	13	14½	13½	11⅜
- Low	28⅝	25	21	16½	19¾	11⅛	5⅝	4½	8⅞	4¾
P/E Ratio - High	33	28	21	16	25	23	16	24	16	15
- Low	21	18	12	10	15	10	7	7	10	6

Income Statement Analysis (Million $)

	1998	1997	1996	1995	1994	1993	1992	1991	1990	1989
Revs.	8,871	7,664	7,029	5,583	4,130	3,270	2,790	2,367	2,097	1,721
Oper. Inc.	311	-8.0	392	345	269	221	169	132	159	140
Depr.	116	99	79.8	66.9	55.0	41.7	35.7	29.1	21.9	17.0
Int. Exp.	36.5	6.3	32.2	13.9	7.4	6.8	10.7	14.2	11.7	10.0
Pretax Inc.	168	15.9	287	269	209	175	124	91.0	128	115
Eff. Tax Rate	38%	42%	38%	38%	37%	37%	37%	38%	39%	39%
Net Inc.	104	136	179	168	132	110	78.2	56.7	78.1	69.5

Balance Sheet & Other Fin. Data (Million $)

	1998	1997	1996	1995	1994	1993	1992	1991	1990	1989
Cash	117	203	43.7	47.0	75.2	141	71.5	25.2	91.7	46.1
Curr. Assets	2,146	2,163	1,736	1,387	997	791	597	450	442	367
Total Assets	3,232	3,081	2,526	2,004	1,555	1,263	1,000	874	714	587
Curr. Liab.	906	837	831	706	546	373	279	261	222	192
LT Debt	424	430	399	179	30.0	82.0	85.0	94.0	94.0	95.0
Common Eqty.	1,730	1,615	1,064	877	710	576	448	367	359	274
Total Cap.	2,181	2,078	1,481	1,056	740	658	533	461	453	368
Cap. Exp.	588	542	518	375	252	190	110	160	69.0	82.0
Cash Flow	221	235	259	235	187	152	114	86.0	100	86.0
Curr. Ratio	2.4	2.6	2.1	2.0	1.8	2.1	2.1	1.7	2.0	1.9
% LT Debt of Cap.	24.5	20.7	27.0	16.9	4.0	12.5	16.0	20.5	20.7	25.7
% Net Inc.of Revs.	1.2	1.8	2.6	3.0	3.2	3.4	2.8	2.4	3.7	4.0
% Ret. on Assets	3.3	4.9	18.5	9.4	9.4	9.7	8.3	7.1	11.9	13.6
% Ret. on Equity	6.2	10.2	21.4	21.1	20.6	21.4	19.1	15.5	24.5	29.1

Data as orig. reptd.; bef. results of disc. opers. and/or spec. items. Per share data adj. for stk. divs. as of ex-div. date. Bold denotes diluted EPS (FASB 128). E-Estimated. NA-Not Available. NM-Not Meaningful. NR-Not Ranked.

Office—9950 Mayland Dr., Richmond, VA 23233-1464. **Tel**—(804) 527-4000. **Chrmn & CEO**—R. L. Sharp.**Vice Chrmn**—A. L. Wurtzel. **Pres & COO**—W. A. McCollough. **EVP, CFO & Secy**—M. T. Chalifoux. **VP & Treas**—P. J. Dunn. **Investor Contact**—Ann M. Collier (804-527-4058).**Dirs**—M. T. Chalifoux, R. N. Cooper, B. S. Feigin, R. S. Jepson, Jr., H. G. Robinson, W. J. Salmon, M. Salovaara, R. L. Sharp, J. W. Snow, E. Villanueva, A. L. Wurtzel. **Transfer Agent & Registrar**—Norwest Bank Minnesota, South St. Paul. **Incorporated**—in Virginia in 1949. **Empl**— 41,742. **S&P Analyst:** Tom Graves, CFA

STANDARD &POOR'S
STOCK REPORTS

Cisco Systems

3536C

Nasdaq Symbol **CSCO**

In S&P 500

12-SEP-98

Industry: Computers (Networking)

Summary: Cisco offers a complete line of routers and switching products that connect and manage communications among local and wide area computer networks employing a variety of protocols.

S&P Opinion: Buy (★★★★★)	Recent Price • 92¾
	52 Wk Range • 105¼-45⅜

Yield • Nil

12-Mo. P/E • 73.6

Quantitative Evaluations

Outlook
(1 Lowest—5 Highest)
• **4⁻**

Fair Value
• **115**

Risk
• **Average**

Earn./Div. Rank
• **B+**

Technical Eval.
• **Bullish** since 5/97

Rel. Strength Rank
(1 Lowest—99 Highest)
• **90**

Insider Activity
• **NA**

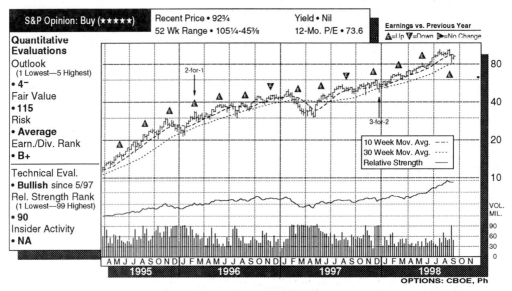

Earnings vs. Previous Year
▲=Up ▼=Down ▶=No Change

10 Week Mov. Avg. - - -
30 Week Mov. Avg. - - - -
Relative Strength ———

OPTIONS: CBOE, Ph

Overview - 06-AUG-98

We project revenue growth of slightly more than 30% for FY 99 (Jul.), similar to the FY 98 rate. Growth should be fueled by continued benefits from CSCO's broad product line of networking gear, and by a shift in customer preferences to favor a single vendor able to provide complete end-to-end networking solutions. New opportunities for Cisco in the service provider market should also boost revenue momentum. Gross margins have been maintained at approximately 65%, as an adverse mix shift (as the high growth of CSCO's lower priced access and switching products outpaces the growth of its more mature, high-end core router products) is being partly offset by cost cutting efforts and steady introductions of new products. Operating expenses should run at a rate of 35% of revenues, as CSCO builds its sales and marketing infrastructure, and invests heavily in R&D to stay ahead of the technology curve. Based on these assumptions, we forecast EPS of $2.16 for FY 99.

Valuation - 06-AUG-98

We continue to recommend buying the shares, in light of consistent evidence that Cisco's market position continues to strengthen. While the networking industry remains highly competitive, and consolidation in the industry is likely to continue to produce rivals to Cisco's dominant market share, we believe that the company's large installed base and reputation should enable it to continue to thrive. The company has consistently posted solid earnings growth, and continues to look for growth within the industry average of 30% to 50% for the next several years. With the shares trading at a P/E multiple (based on our forecast for FY 2000 EPS) that is attractive relative to Cicso's long-term earnings growth rate, we recommend purchase.

Key Stock Statistics

S&P EPS Est. 1998	NA	Tang. Bk. Value/Share	6.09
P/E on S&P Est. 1998	NA	Beta	1.17
S&P EPS Est. 1999	2.16	Shareholders	8,300
Dividend Rate/Share	Nil	Market cap. (B)	$ 96.1
Shs. outstg. (M)	1036.5	Inst. holdings	60%
Avg. daily vol. (M)	15.734		

Value of $10,000 invested 5 years ago: $ 141,558

Fiscal Year Ending Jul. 31

	1998	1997	1996	1995	1994	1993
Revenues (Million $)						
1Q	1,869	1,435	710.2	392.9	248.5	126.4
2Q	2,016	1,592	826.5	454.9	302.2	145.1
3Q	2,184	1,648	985.1	509.9	331.2	172.4
4Q	2,390	2,390	1,292	621.2	361.2	205.2
Yr.	8,459	6,440	4,096	1,979	1,243	649.0
Earnings Per Share ($)						
1Q	0.32	0.17	0.20	0.12	0.08	0.04
2Q	**0.43**	0.33	0.22	0.06	0.10	0.05
3Q	**0.45**	0.37	0.26	0.15	0.11	0.06
4Q	**0.45**	0.15	0.27	0.17	0.11	0.07
Yr.	**1.26**	1.01	0.91	0.51	0.40	0.22

Next earnings report expected: NA

Dividend Data

Amount ($)	Date Decl.	Ex-Div. Date	Stock of Record	Payment Date
3-for-2	Nov. 03	Dec. 17	Nov. 18	Dec. 16 '97
3-for-2	Aug. 04	Sep. 16	Aug. 14	Sep. 15 '98

 A Division of The **McGraw·Hill** *Companies*

Business Summary - 06-AUG-98

Cisco Systems is the world's largest supplier of high-performance computer internetworking systems. Its routers and other communication products connect and manage local and wide area networks (LANs and WANs) that employ a variety of protocols, media interfaces, network topologies and cabling systems, enabling customers to connect different computer networks using different hardware and software across offices, countries and continents.

Key to Cisco's growth is its position as the provider offering the industry's broadest line of networking products. This is critical, as customers prefer complete end-to-end networking solutions. Demand for switches is being led by the need for greater bandwidth by corporate users--Cisco dominates in this market. However, the market for networking equipment for the regional telephone companies and Internet-service providers is proving to be another strong growth area, Cisco faces several strong competitors in this market, including Ascend Communications and Lucent Technologies.

Cisco's product family includes backbone and remote access routers, LAN and asynchronous transfer mode (ATM) switches, dial-up access servers and network management software. High-performance, intelligent routers interconnect networks using different protocols and media. Access routers extend the network to regional sales groups, small satellite offices and individual telecommuters. All products support multiprotocol multiple media connectivity in multivendor environments. CSCO's Internetwork Operating System (IOS) provides a common software platform across networks.

To answer criticisms that routers create bottlenecks in the Internet backbone, the network core, Cisco has introduced its Gigabit Switch Router (GSR), or the Cisco 12000 Series, providing Internet routing and switching at gigabit speeds. Targeted at the Internet-service provider market, the GSR competes against Ascend's high-speed router. Other Cisco product offerings include CSCO's 3800 multiservice access concentrator, which integrates switched voice, multiprotocol data and routing over Frame Relay and ATM, and the TGX 8750 core switch integrates IP and ATM technologies through Tag Switching for the WAN. In addition, Cisco has introduced its Cisco Broadband DSL Product Line which enables network providers (like RBOCs and CLECs) to offer high-speed data and voice services to the fast-growing residential and work at home markets.

Cisco has had an active acquisition strategy, acquiring some key technologies. The largest and most successful was the July 1996 acquisition of StrataCom Inc., a leading maker of high speed ATM and Frame Relay switching technologies, in a $4 billion stock deal. Increasingly Cisco is making acquisitions that further its technological capabilities in the new area of voice/video/data integration on a single network.

Per Share Data ($)

(Year Ended Jul. 31)	1998	1997	1996	1995	1994	1993	1992	1991	1990	1989
Tangible Bk. Val.	NA	6.39	2.89	1.69	1.10	0.64	0.34	0.19	0.11	0.02
Cash Flow	NA	1.83	1.07	0.58	0.43	0.24	0.12	0.06	0.02	0.01
Earnings	1.26	1.01	0.91	0.51	0.40	0.22	0.11	0.06	0.02	0.01
Dividends	Nil	Nil	Nil	Nil	Nil	Nil	Nil	Nil	Nil	Nil
Payout Ratio	Nil	Nil	Nil	Nil	Nil	Nil	Nil	Nil	Nil	Nil
Prices - High	104¹/₂	60⁵/₈	46¹/₈	29³/₄	13⁵/₈	9⁷/₈	6³/₄	2⁷/₈	¹⁵/₁₆	NA
- Low	51¹/₂	30¹/₈	21¹/₄	10³/₄	6¹/₄	5¹/₂	2³/₄	¹³/₁₆	³/₈	NA
P/E Ratio - High	83	60	50	60	34	45	58	40	45	NA
- Low	41	30	23	21	16	25	24	14	18	NA

Income Statement Analysis (Million $)

	1998	1997	1996	1995	1994	1993	1992	1991	1990	1989
Revs.	NA	6,440	4,096	1,979	1,243	649	340	183	70.0	28.0
Oper. Inc.	NA	1,839	1,533	701	519	277	136	69.0	22.0	7.0
Depr.	NA	212	133	58.5	30.8	13.3	6.5	3.0	0.8	0.1
Int. Exp.	NA	NM	NM	NA	NA	NA	NA	NA	0.0	NA
Pretax Inc.	NA	1,889	1,465	679	509	275	136	71.0	23.0	7.0
Eff. Tax Rate	NA	44%	38%	38%	38%	38%	38%	39%	41%	40%
Net Inc.	NA	1,049	913	421	315	172	84.4	43.2	13.9	4.2

Balance Sheet & Other Fin. Data (Million $)

	1998	1997	1996	1995	1994	1993	1992	1991	1990	1989
Cash	NA	270	1,038	440	183	89.0	156	91.0	57.0	4.0
Curr. Assets	NA	3,101	2,160	996	508	268	247	141	78.0	16.0
Total Assets	NA	5,452	3,630	1,757	1,054	595	324	154	83.0	17.0
Curr. Liab.	NA	1,120	769	338	206	120	78.3	26.3	13.2	8.8
LT Debt	NA	NM	NM	Nil	Nil	Nil	Nil	Nil	0.1	0.2
Common Eqty.	NA	4,290	2,820	1,379	848	475	246	128	69.0	8.0
Total Cap.	NA	4,332	2,852	1,420	848	475	246	128	69.0	8.0
Cap. Exp.	NA	330	283	112	59.6	33.9	21.6	11.3	4.1	0.3
Cash Flow	NA	1,261	1,046	480	346	185	90.8	46.2	14.7	4.3
Curr. Ratio	NA	2.8	2.8	2.9	2.5	2.2	3.2	5.4	5.9	1.8
% LT Debt of Cap.	NA	NM	NM	Nil	Nil	Nil	Nil	Nil	0.2	2.7
% Net Inc.of Revs.	NA	16.3	22.3	21.3	25.3	26.5	24.8	23.6	19.9	15.1
% Ret. on Assets	NA	23.1	32.5	30.0	38.2	37.0	34.7	36.5	23.2	39.2
% Ret. on Equity	NA	29.5	41.7	37.8	47.6	47.2	44.4	43.9	34.8	78.9

Data as orig. reptd.; bef. results of disc. opers. and/or spec. items. Per share data adj. for stk. divs. as of ex-div. date. Bold denotes diluted EPS (FASB 128). E-Estimated. NA-Not Available. NM-Not Meaningful. NR-Not Ranked.

Office—170 W. Tasman Drive, San Jose, CA 95134-1706. **Tel**—(408) 526-4000. **Website**—http://www.cisco.com **Chrmn**—J. P. Morgridge. **Vice Chrmn**—D. T. Valentine. **Pres & CEO**—J. Chambers. **CFO, SVP-Fin & Admin, Secy**—L. R. Carter.**Investor Contact**—M. Thurber (408-526-8893). **Dirs**— C. Bartz, J. T. Chambers, M. S. Frankel, J. F. Gibbons, E. R. Kozel, R. M. Moley, J. P. Morgridge, R. L. Puette, M. Son, D. T. Valentine, S. M. West. **Transfer Agent & Registrar**—First National Bank of Boston. **Incorporated**—in California in 1984. **Empl**— 14,800. **S&P Analyst:** Megan Graham Hackett

Citicorp

537M

NYSE Symbol **CCI**

In S&P 500

12-SEP-98

Industry: Banks (Money Center)

Summary: This company, the parent of Citibank and the second largest U.S. bank holding company, recently agreed to merge with Travelers Group.

S&P Opinion: Buy (★★★★)	Recent Price • 96	Yield • 2.4%
	52 Wk Range • 182-83½	12-Mo. P/E • 12.4

Earnings vs. Previous Year
▲=Up ▼=Down ▶=No Change

Quantitative Evaluations

Outlook (1 Lowest—5 Highest)
• 3+

Fair Value
• 105

Risk
• **Low**

Earn./Div. Rank
• **B**

Technical Eval.
• **Bearish** since 8/98

Rel. Strength Rank (1 Lowest—99 Highest)
• 16

Insider Activity
• **Neutral**

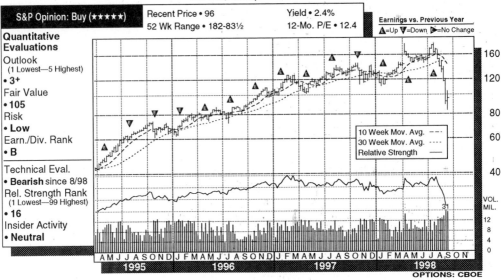

10 Week Mov. Avg. —-—
30 Week Mov. Avg. ……
Relative Strength ——

OPTIONS: CBOE

Overview - 27-JUL-98

The global corporate banking segment, where both emerging markets and global relationship banking divisions remain strong, should continue to be the primary earnings growth driver for 1998. The global consumer business has been hurt in recent periods by higher costs to support marketing, technology initiatives and investment in new markets, as well as greater credit costs, although lower loss rates seen recently in the U.S. bankcard business are encouraging. The acquisition of AT&T's Universal credit card business should provide operating advantages (e.g. funding costs) and cross-selling opportunities going forward. Asia has remained a weak area for the company, particularly with respect to credit costs, but strong foreign exchange and derivatives volume has provided an offset. Longer term, the pending merger with Travelers is expected to create vast opportunities for cross marketing of products, increased revenue diversity, strong capital levels and enhanced global presence.

Valuation - 27-JUL-98

The shares jumped considerably in April in connection with the announced merger with Travelers Group. We view the combination positively for the long term and maintained our buy recommendation on the shares, while noting that considerable hurdles remain, including regulatory issues and the integration of a merger of this magnitude. Clearly, the transaction is more about revenue growth than cost cutting, and the combined 100 million customer base of the merged company will create considerable opportunities for cross marketing of products. For the near term, we expect earnings improvements from a better domestic credit quality environment and benefits from a restructuring announced in late 1997. Accordingly, the shares remain attractive for superior capital appreciation in the year ahead.

Key Stock Statistics

S&P EPS Est. 1998	9.00	Tang. Bk. Value/Share	41.94
P/E on S&P Est. 1998	10.7	Beta	1.67
S&P EPS Est. 1999	10.60	Shareholders	60,000
Dividend Rate/Share	2.30	Market cap. (B)	$ 43.4
Shs. outstg. (M)	451.9	Inst. holdings	65%
Avg. daily vol. (M)	5.956		

Value of $10,000 invested 5 years ago: $ 46,744

Fiscal Year Ending Dec. 31

	1998	1997	1996	1995	1994	1993
Revenues (Million $)						
1Q	9,069	8,249	7,919	7,715	8,234	7,907
2Q	9,865	8,589	8,016	7,934	8,788	7,795
3Q	—	8,860	8,116	7,954	7,036	8,095
4Q	—	8,999	8,554	8,087	7,592	8,399
Yr.	—	34,697	32,605	31,690	31,650	32,196
Earnings Per Share ($)						
1Q	**2.23**	2.01	1.82	1.71	1.24	0.71
2Q	**2.30**	2.10	1.86	1.76	1.83	0.88
3Q	**E2.00**	1.01	1.85	1.79	1.87	1.06
4Q	**E2.47**	2.20	1.97	1.89	2.20	1.16
Yr.	**E9.00**	7.33	7.43	7.21	7.15	3.82

Next earnings report expected: late October

Dividend Data (Dividends have been paid since 1994.)

Amount ($)	Date Decl.	Ex-Div. Date	Stock of Record	Payment Date
0.525	Oct. 21	Oct. 29	Oct. 31	Nov. 19 '97
0.575	Jan. 20	Jan. 28	Jan. 31	Feb. 19 '98
0.575	Apr. 21	Apr. 28	Apr. 30	May. 19 '98
0.575	Jul. 20	Jul. 29	Jul. 31	Aug. 19 '98

A Division of The **McGraw-Hill** *Companies*

STANDARD
&POOR'S
STOCK REPORTS

Citicorp

537M
12-SEP-98

Business Summary - 27-JUL-98

With about 3,000 locations sporting its familiar blue and white colors in 98 countries and territories, Citicorp (CCI) believes it is distinguished from its competitors by the breadth of its reach and depth of its presence in markets around the world. In a bold move designed to enhance its position as a global leader in financial services, CCI agreed to merge with Travelers Group in April 1998 in the largest corporate merger in history. The combined company, to be named Citigroup Inc., will have principal focus on traditional banking, consumer finance, credit cards, investment banking, securities brokerage and asset management, and property casualty and life insurance.

Principal Citicorp businesses are focused on global consumer and global corporate banking. Global consumer (39% of net income in 1997) operates a full-service consumer franchises including branch and electronic banking, credit and charge cards, and personalized wealth management services for high net-worth clients. Global corporate banking serves corporations, financial institutions, governments, investors

and other participants in developed and emerging markets throughout the world.

Average earning assets, from which interest income is derived, amounted to $252 billion at the end of 1997, up from $232 billion a year earlier. About 69% of these assets consisted of consumer and commercial loans, with the balance securities held for investment or short term assets. Sources of funds, which the bank uses in its lending business, included mostly interest-bearing deposits (57%), debt, shareholders' equity and various non-interest bearing deposits.

Credit quality was relatively stable in 1997. Credit loss reserves, which are held in case of loan defaults, totaled $6.00 billion (3.16% of loans) at the end of 1997, up slightly from $5.98 billion (3.15%) the year before. Net write-offs, or the amount of loans actually charged off as uncollectible, were $1.81 billion (1.71% of average loans) in 1997, versus $1.73 billion (1.64%) in 1996.

The transaction with Travelers Group, expected to close in the third quarter of 1998, calls for each CCI share to be exchanged for 2.5 shares of the new Citigroup, with Travelers shares converted on a one-for-one basis into Citigroup shares.

Per Share Data ($)

(Year Ended Dec. 31)	1997	1996	1995	1994	1993	1992	1991	1990	1989	1988
Tangible Bk. Val.	41.94	39.65	38.01	33.58	25.09	20.41	19.51	21.63	22.37	22.54
Earnings	7.33	7.50	7.21	7.15	3.82	1.35	-3.22	0.57	1.16	4.87
Dividends	2.10	1.80	1.20	0.45	Nil	Nil	0.75	1.74	1.58	1.45
Payout Ratio	29%	24%	17%	6%	Nil	Nil	NM	305%	137%	30%
Prices - High	145¼	109¾	74	47¾	39¾	22½	17½	29⅝	35½	27
- Low	99⅝	62	38½	36⅛	20½	10⅜	8½	10¾	24⅝	18
P/E Ratio - High	20	15	10	7	10	17	NM	52	31	6
- Low	14	8	5	5	5	8	NM	19	21	4

Income Statement Analysis (Million $)

	1997	1996	1995	1994	1993	1992	1991	1990	1989	1988
Net Int. Inc.	11,402	10,940	9,951	8,911	7,690	7,456	7,265	7,185	7,358	7,605
Tax Equiv. Adj.	52.0	40.0	33.0	26.0	15.0	19.0	35.0	62.0	85.0	92.0
Non Int. Inc.	9,305	9,046	8,595	7,637	8,385	8,153	7,155	7,350	6,214	5,305
Loan Loss Prov.	1,907	1,926	1,991	1,881	2,600	4,146	3,890	2,662	2,521	1,330
Exp./Op. Revs.	68%	61%	60%	62%	66%	64%	77%	76%	71%	69%
Pretax Inc.	5,722	6,073	5,585	4,611	2,860	1,418	-236	826	1,533	2,707
Eff. Tax Rate	37%	38%	38%	26%	33%	49%	-285.70%	62%	68%	37%
Net Inc.	3,591	3,788	3,464	3,422	1,919	722	-913	318	498	1,698
% Net Int. Marg.	4.55	NM	NM	NA	3.88	3.76	3.72	3.51	3.77	4.14

Balance Sheet & Other Fin. Data (Million $)

	1997	1996	1995	1994	1993	1992	1991	1990	1989	1988
Earning Assets:										
Money Mkt	63,638	53,566	49,234	52,732	29,702	30,020	23,310	19,140	30,490	21,070
Inv. Securities	33,361	28,186	20,067	20,703	15,530	15,060	14,710	14,080	14,700	15,220
Com'l Loans	75,947	12,799	13,113	13,836	12,931	14,340	16,450	19,650	19,840	21,220
Other Loans	108,066	162,820	153,614	139,670	127,139	126,700	136,400	138,900	142,600	131,200
Total Assets	310,897	281,018	256,853	250,489	217,000	214,000	217,000	217,000	230,600	207,700
Demand Deposits	26,528	24,758	21,552	20,860	20,100	18,800	17,300	16,100	17,700	16,300
Time Deposits	172,593	160,197	145,579	134,866	125,000	125,400	129,200	126,300	120,200	107,800
LT Debt	19,785	18,850	18,488	17,877	18,100	20,100	23,300	23,200	24,000	24,000
Common Eqty.	19,293	18,644	16,510	13,582	10,066	7,970	7,350	8,190	8,240	8,270
% Ret. on Assets	1.2	1.4	1.4	1.5	0.9	0.3	NM	0.1	0.2	0.8
% Ret. on Equity	18.2	20.6	20.7	NA	17.8	6.8	NM	2.1	4.3	21.5
% Loan Loss Resv.	3.2	3.1	3.2	3.4	3.1	2.8	2.2	2.9	3.0	2.8
% Loans/Deposits	106.6	97.2	99.1	97.9	95.8	96.9	103.1	109.7	116.1	120.3
% Equity to Assets	6.4	6.5	5.9	NA	4.2	3.3	3.8	3.7	3.9	3.6

Data as orig. reptd.; bef. results of disc opers. and/or spec. items. Per share data adj. for stk. divs. as of ex-div. date. Bold denotes diluted EPS (FASB 128). E-Estimated. NA-Not Available. NM-Not Meaningful. NR-Not Ranked.

Office—399 Park Ave., New York, NY 10043. **Tel**—(212) 559-1000. **Website**—http://www.citibank.com **Chrmn & CEO**—J. S. Reed. **EVP**—T. E. Jones. **EVP & CFO**—V. J. Menezes. **Vice Chrmn & Secy**—C. E. Long. **Investor Contact**—Frederick A. Roesch. **Dirs**—A. J. P. Belda, D. W. Calloway, P. J. Collins, K. T. Derr, J. M. Deutch, R. Mark, R. D. Parsons, J. S. Reed, W. R. Rhodes, R. L. Ridgway, H. O. Ruding, R. B. Shapiro, F. A. Shrontz, F. A. Thomas, E. S. Woolard Jr. **Transfer Agents & Registrars**—Citibank, N.A., NYC; ChaseMellon Shareholder Services, Los Angeles; First Chicago Trust Co., Jersey City, NJ; Montreal Trust Co., Toronto. **Incorporated**—in Delaware in 1967; bank founded in 1812. **Empl**—93,700. **S&P Analyst:** Stephen R. Biggar

Clear Channel Communications 548T
NYSE Symbol **CCU**
In S&P 500

12-SEP-98

Industry: Broadcasting (Television, Radio & Cable)

Summary: This company owns or programs 194 radio stations and 18 television stations, and owns 88,000 billboards.

S&P Opinion: Buy (★★★★)	Recent Price • 40⅜	Yield • Nil	Earnings vs. Previous Year
	52 Wk Range • 62⅜-27¾	12-Mo. P/E • NM	▲=Up ▼=Down ▶=No Change

Quantitative Evaluations

Outlook
(1 Lowest—5 Highest)
• **1⁻**

Fair Value
• **31⅞**

Risk
• **Average**

Earn./Div. Rank
• **B**

Technical Eval.
• **Bullish** since 1/97

Rel. Strength Rank
(1 Lowest—99 Highest)
• **32**

Insider Activity
• **Neutral**

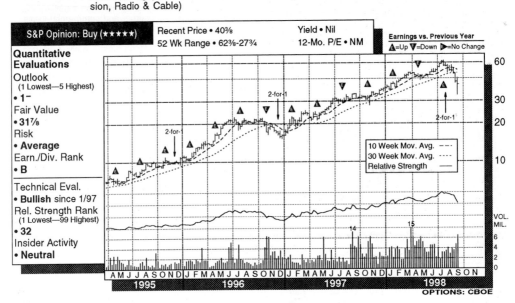

10 Week Mov. Avg. ---
30 Week Mov. Avg. ----
Relative Strength

VOL. MIL.

OPTIONS: CBOE

Overview - 04-JUN-98

Clear Channel is a company in transition, having for several years been an aggressive acquirer of radio and TV stations throughout the U.S., as well as investing in radio properties in Australia, New Zealand and Mexico. The company has forged a strong franchise in Spanish-language broadcast properties, and, through acquisitions beginning in April 1997, it has become largest billboard advertising company as a means to capitalize on synergies between that business and radio. Boosted by recent and pending acquisitions, including Paxson Communications, revenues and cash flow will again advance in 1998. Individual station performance is expected to benefit from healthy advertising demand, aggressive marketing, sales and promotions, as well as operating efficiencies through 1998 and beyond. Reported share earnings will be diluted by stock issued in acquisitions.

Valuation - 04-JUN-98

The shares have climbed over 32% since the beginning of 1998, after having gained 90% over the course of 1997. CCU's strong performance is indicative of the company's successful growth through accretive acquisitions. A favorable outlook for radio advertising, plus management's proven skill in boosting the profitability of acquired stations, have made it a favorite among investors. With the Hispanic population the fastest-growing segment in the U.S., CCU's prominent position in Spanish-language stations places it in a strong position for future growth. CCU's foray into billboard advertising also enhances the outlook for future growth and profitability. Thus, although the shares are already richly priced, selling at 91X the $1.05 EPS we are projecting for 1998, they remain an attractive accumulation for long-term capital gains.

Key Stock Statistics

S&P EPS Est. 1998	0.36	Tang. Bk. Value/Share	NM
P/E on S&P Est. 1998	NM	Beta	0.76
S&P EPS Est. 1999	0.57	Shareholders	6,400
Dividend Rate/Share	Nil	Market cap. (B)	$ 10.0
Shs. outstg. (M)	248.3	Inst. holdings	65%
Avg. daily vol. (M)	1.240		

Value of $10,000 invested 5 years ago: $ 247,699

Fiscal Year Ending Dec. 31

	1998	1997	1996	1995	1994	1993
Revenues (Million $)						
1Q	203.6	98.29	62.21	58.65	38.87	24.02
2Q	320.0	186.8	81.37	72.34	48.11	31.55
3Q	—	184.1	94.84	68.13	47.57	32.23
4Q	—	227.9	113.3	84.24	66.14	47.88
Yr.	—	697.1	351.7	283.4	200.7	135.7
Earnings Per Share ($)						
1Q	0.02	0.05	0.05	0.02	0.02	0.00
2Q	0.22	0.08	0.09	0.07	0.04	0.02
3Q	—	0.10	0.02	0.06	0.04	0.02
4Q	—	0.11	0.10	0.09	0.06	0.04
Yr.	E0.36	0.33	0.25	0.23	0.16	0.07

Next earnings report expected: early November

Dividend Data

Amount ($)	Date Decl.	Ex-Div. Date	Stock of Record	Payment Date
2-for-1	Jul. 13	Jul. 29	Jul. 21	Jul. 28 '98

A Division of The McGraw-Hill Companies

Clear Channel Communications, Inc.

548T
12-SEP-98

Business Summary - 04-JUN-98

Clear Channel Communications, a diversified communications company, and one of the country's largest radio broadcasters, is clearly a company in transition, having for several years been an aggressive acquirer of broadcasting and outdoor billboard properties in the U.S. and abroad. Excluding pending acquisitions, CCU owned or programmed 194 radio stations and 18 television stations in 39 markets in the U.S. as of the end of April 1998. CCU has also forged a strong franchise in Spanish-language broadcast properties through its 32.3% ownership of Heftel Broadcasting, the largest Spanish-language radio broadcaster in the U.S. With the April 1997 purchase of Eller Media, Clear Channel became one of the largest U.S. outdoor advertising companies. On April 1, 1998, CCU acquired Universal Outdoor Holdings, whose inventory of over 34,000 display faces in 23 markets gave CCU a total advertising display inventory of over 88,000 display faces in 31 major metropolitan markets across the U.S.

In the four months through April 1998, CCU acquired 21 radio stations and entered agreements to acquire an additional 12 stations. In April, CCU purchased 40% of Grupo Acir, a Mexico City-based owner of 164 radio stations. As of June 1, 1998, CCU had acquired about 30% of More Group Plc, an outdoor advertiser in the U.K. In 1997, Clear Channel purchased over 60 U.S. radio stations including Paxson Communications Corp.'s 46 radio stations (42 located in Florida) and other properties for $600 million. CCU acquired more than 50 U.S. radio stations in 1996. The company's radio stations are located primarily in the South, Southwest, Midwest and Northeast.

The Australian Radio Network (50% owned) owns 12 radio stations in major markets and a radio sales representation company. The New Zealand Radio Network (33.3% owned) owns more than 50 radio stations. Heftel Broadcasting (32.3%) owns or programs 38 Spanish-language radio stations in 11 markets, including stations in the top 10 Hispanic markets in the U.S.

CCU owns and operates five radio networks: Clear Channel Sports, which provides sports coverage in Oklahoma, Texas and Iowa; Oklahoma News Network; Kentucky News Network; Virginia News Network; and the Voice of Southwest Agriculture. Each network has from 50 to 100 affiliated stations. Television stations are in Alabama, Oklahoma, Florida, Arizona, Rhode Island, Tennessee, Minnesota, Kansas and New York. The company added six more networks to its stable upon completion of the Paxson acquisition in 1997.

L. Lowry Mays and B. J. McCombs together own about 21% of Clear Channel's equity.

Per Share Data ($)

(Year Ended Dec. 31)	1997	1996	1995	1994	1993	1992	1991	1990	1989	1988
Tangible Bk. Val.	NA	NM	-1.00	-0.56	-0.04	-0.29	-0.11	-0.40	0.03	0.17
Cash Flow	0.97	0.56	0.47	0.34	0.21	0.14	0.09	0.07	0.03	0.03
Earnings	0.34	0.25	0.23	0.16	0.07	0.04	0.01	0.00	0.00	0.02
Dividends	Nil	Nil	Nil	Nil	Nil	Nil	Nil	Nil	0.13	Nil
Payout Ratio	Nil	Nil	Nil	Nil	Nil	Nil	Nil	Nil	NM	Nil
Prices - High	40	22^5/$_8$	11^1/$_8$	6^1/$_2$	4^5/$_8$	1^{13}/$_{16}$	1	^{3}/$_4$	^{11}/$_{16}$	^{5}/$_8$
- Low	16^7/$_8$	10^1/$_4$	6^1/$_4$	3^7/$_8$	1^5/$_8$	^{7}/$_8$	^{11}/$_{16}$	^{1}/$_2$	^{7}/$_{16}$	^{7}/$_{16}$
P/E Ratio - High	NM	90	49	41	64	50	86	NM	NM	32
- Low	NM	41	28	25	22	24	60	NM	NM	22

Income Statement Analysis (Million $)

	1997	1996	1995	1994	1993	1992	1991	1990	1989	1988
Revs.	697	352	244	173	118	82.2	74.1	60.3	45.7	35.1
Oper. Inc.	282	145	105	67.6	38.7	25.8	17.0	15.0	10.9	8.0
Depr.	114	45.8	33.8	24.7	17.4	12.3	7.6	6.6	3.0	1.3
Int. Exp.	75.1	30.1	20.8	7.7	5.4	4.7	5.4	8.0	6.4	3.5
Pretax Inc.	111	76.4	52.7	36.4	15.7	7.6	2.5	NM	0.3	3.3
Eff. Tax Rate	43%	37%	39%	40%	42%	43%	55%	NM	240%	44%
Net Inc.	63.6	37.7	32.0	22.0	9.1	4.3	1.1	-0.3	-0.4	1.8

Balance Sheet & Other Fin. Data (Million $)

	1997	1996	1995	1994	1993	1992	1991	1990	1989	1988
Cash	24.7	16.7	5.4	6.8	5.5	2.8	3.8	1.7	1.2	1.5
Curr. Assets	199	113	70.5	53.9	38.2	24.8	20.5	20.6	16.9	8.5
Total Assets	3,456	1,325	563	412	228	147	92.0	102	95.0	65.0
Curr. Liab.	86.9	43.5	36.0	27.7	26.1	10.1	10.0	8.9	15.5	4.0
LT Debt	1,540	725	334	238	87.8	97.0	48.1	80.9	69.0	43.5
Common Eqty.	1,747	513	164	131	98.3	31.1	24.8	2.7	2.3	14.8
Total Cap.	3,318	1,256	510	371	190	132	75.8	86.1	73.1	59.2
Cap. Exp.	31.0	19.7	15.1	5.7	2.7	27.7	1.9	7.2	15.5	8.8
Cash Flow	178	83.5	65.8	46.7	26.6	16.5	8.8	6.3	2.6	3.1
Curr. Ratio	2.3	2.6	2.0	1.9	1.5	2.5	2.1	2.3	1.1	2.1
% LT Debt of Cap.	46.4	57.7	65.5	64.1	46.3	73.7	63.5	94.1	94.4	73.4
% Net Inc.of Revs.	9.1	10.7	13.2	12.7	7.7	5.2	1.5	NM	NM	5.2
% Ret. on Assets	2.7	4.0	6.6	6.9	4.6	3.5	1.0	NM	NM	3.1
% Ret. on Equity	5.6	11.1	21.8	19.1	13.6	15.1	8.0	NM	NM	13.2

Data as orig. reptd.; bef. results of disc. opers. and/or spec. items. Q revs. incl. agency commissions prior to 1996. Per share data adj. for stk. divs. as of ex-div. date. Bold denotes diluted EPS (FASB 128). E-Estimated. NA-Not Available. NM-Not Meaningful. NR-Not Ranked.

Office—200 Concord Plaza, Suite 600, San Antonio, TX 78216-6940. **Tel**—(210) 822-2828. **Website**—http://www.clearchannel.com **Chrmn & CEO**—L. L. Mays. **Pres**—M. P. Mays. **EVP & CFO**—R. T. Mays. **VP-Fin**—H. Lane. **SVP & Investor Contact**—Herbert W. Hill Jr. **Dirs**—K. Eller, A. D. Feld, L. L. Mays, B. J. McCombs, T. H. Strauss, J. H. Williams. **Transfer Agent & Registrar**—Bank of New York, NYC. **Incorporated**—in Texas in 1974. **Empl**—3,219. **S&P Analyst:** William H. Donald

STANDARD &POOR'S
STOCK REPORTS

Clorox Co.

556

NYSE Symbol **CLX**

In S&P 500

12-SEP-98

Industry:
Household Products
(Nondurables)

Summary: This company is a diversified producer of household cleaning, grocery and specialty food products.

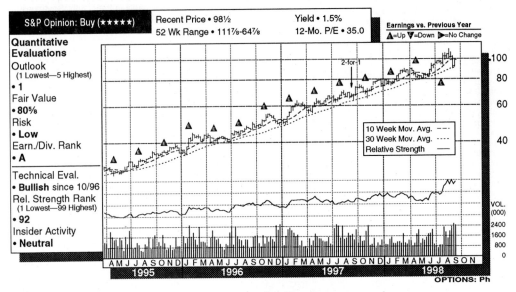

S&P Opinion: Buy (★★★★)	Recent Price • 98½	Yield • 1.5%
	52 Wk Range • 111⅞-64⅞	12-Mo. P/E • 35.0

Earnings vs. Previous Year
▲=Up ▼=Down ▶=No Change

Quantitative Evaluations

Outlook
(1 Lowest—5 Highest)
• **1**

Fair Value
• **80%**

Risk
• **Low**

Earn./Div. Rank
• **A**

Technical Eval.
• **Bullish** since 10/96

Rel. Strength Rank
(1 Lowest—99 Highest)
• **92**

Insider Activity
• **Neutral**

10 Week Mov. Avg. — - —
30 Week Mov. Avg. ·······
Relative Strength ———

OPTIONS: Ph

Overview - 05-AUG-98

We expect sales to increase 12% annually for the next two years, as the company strives to meet its $3.5 billion sales target for 2000. The increase will be propelled by higher sales of existing products, contributions from new products (especially in overseas markets), line extensions of existing products, and acquisitions. Likely acquisitions would come internationally, particularly in Latin America, where CLX has had recent success with acquisitions of Arela cleaners and bleach in Chile, and X-14 kitchen cleaner in Brazil. The company expects 20% of revenues to be derived from overseas markets by 2000, up from 18% in FY 98 (Jun.). Margins are likely to widen, as efforts to cut overhead and operating costs (by an estimated $25 million in the next two years), as well as selective price increases should offset aggressive new product spending, continued competitive pricing, and costs of overseas expansion.

Valuation - 05-AUG-98

We recently upgraded the shares to buy, from accumulate, based on stronger profitability. CLX surprised the market with a much lower tax rate in FY 98, with a drop to 37.0%, from 40.0%. As the company increases its overseas business, it is likely that the tax rate will fall even further. As a result of the improved profit outlook, we recently increased our EPS estimate $0.20, to $3.30, for FY 99. It is likely that the company will be able to increase earnings 15% to 18% over the next few years, paced by aggressive international expansion, volume gains, selective price increases, acquisition synergies, and cost cutting strategies. Although the shares were recently trading at a premium valuation, they deserve this premium, and we recommend that investors accumulate the stock for long-term capital gains.

Key Stock Statistics

S&P EPS Est. 1999	3.30	Tang. Bk. Value/Share	NM
P/E on S&P Est. 1999	29.9	Beta	0.76
Dividend Rate/Share	1.44	Shareholders	13,400
Shs. outstg. (M)	103.9	Market cap. (B)	$ 10.2
Avg. daily vol. (M)	0.571	Inst. holdings	52%

Value of $10,000 invested 5 years ago: $ 48,677

Fiscal Year Ending Jun. 30

	1998	1997	1996	1995	1994	1993
Revenues (Million $)						
1Q	649.3	590.8	518.5	476.4	449.7	394.7
2Q	591.8	530.2	466.8	414.4	370.8	327.4
3Q	680.5	649.2	560.1	499.1	481.9	435.6
4Q	819.6	762.5	672.8	594.3	534.4	476.6
Yr.	2,741	2,533	2,218	1,984	1,837	1,634
Earnings Per Share ($)						
1Q	0.72	0.64	0.56	0.50	0.42	0.41
2Q	**0.47**	**0.42**	0.36	0.32	0.28	0.25
3Q	**0.72**	0.64	0.57	0.51	0.47	0.41
4Q	**0.93**	0.72	0.64	0.56	0.50	0.50
Yr.	**2.82**	2.41	2.14	1.89	1.68	1.53

Next earnings report expected: mid October

Dividend Data (Dividends have been paid since 1968.)

Amount ($)	Date Decl.	Ex-Div. Date	Stock of Record	Payment Date
0.320	Sep. 18	Oct. 22	Oct. 24	Nov. 14 '97
0.320	Jan. 21	Jan. 28	Jan. 30	Feb. 13 '98
0.320	Mar. 18	Apr. 22	Apr. 24	May. 15 '98
0.360	Jul. 14	Jul. 29	Jul. 31	Aug. 19 '98

A Division of The **McGraw·Hill** *Companies*

Business Summary - 05-AUG-98

Over the years, the name Clorox has become nearly synonymous with household bleach. No wonder. Since it introduced its first pint of Clorox bleach in the 1920s, The Clorox Company has come to dominate the U.S. bleach market, with nearly a 70% share.

Today, the company has become a diversified consumer products company whose domestic retail products include many of the best-known brands of laundry additives, home cleaning and automotive appearance products, cat litter, insecticides, charcoal briquets, salad dressings, sauces and water filtration systems. CLX believes that a great majority of its brands either lead or are a strong second in their categories. In addition to its household products, the company also operates a Professional Products division to serve the needs of professional cleaning and sanitizing businesses.

New products and acquisitions have been drivers of growth for CLX. FY 97 (Jun.) saw a record pace of new product introductions, with 15 new items in the U.S. and 24 in international markets. CLX's acquisition strategy is to obtain strong brands in core categories that add power to its lineup and that provide entry to new and growing markets internationally. The most significant acquisition in FY 97 was of Armor All Products (auto cleaning products) for $360 million.

CLX has also identified insecticides as a key growth area, and has secured exclusive rights to Fipronil, a powerful new bug-killing ingredient which received U.S. federal regulatory approval in August 1997.

CLX is investing heavily to expand business internationally in the areas of laundry additives, home cleaning products and insecticides. Now, with a product presence in more than 70 countries, special emphasis is being placed on Latin America and the Pacific Rim. In FY 97, CLX significantly expanded its presence in Latin America by acquiring four separate businesses including the Shell Group's non-core line of household products in Chile, the Pinoluz brand of pine cleaner in Argentina, and the Limpido brand of liquid bleach and an increased ownership stake in Tecnoclor S.A., both in Colombia. The total cost of these four acquisitions was approximately $110 million. These acquisitions boosted Clorox's international exposure to 16% of net sales for FY 97, up from 4% in FY 92. The company's goal is to have 20% of revenues from overseas markets by 2000.

In the first nine months of FY 98, net sales grew 9%, to $1.92 billion from $1.77 billion in FY 97. Strong showings were reported at the company's home cleaning, food, and cat litter units. In addition, shipments of Brita water filtration systems set an all-time record and Armor All was additive to earnings during the third quarter. Net earnings outpaced sales, growing 14%, to $199.8 million, from $175.0 million.

Per Share Data ($)

(Year Ended Jun. 30)	1998	1997	1996	1995	1994	1993	1992	1991	1990	1989
Tangible Bk. Val.	NA	NM	2.23	3.35	3.65	3.79	3.06	2.68	6.56	6.20
Cash Flow	NA	3.64	3.26	2.87	2.85	2.21	1.82	1.24	1.83	1.69
Earnings	2.82	2.41	2.14	1.89	1.68	1.53	1.08	0.49	1.40	1.31
Dividends	1.28	1.16	1.06	0.96	0.90	0.85	0.80	0.73	0.65	0.55
Payout Ratio	45%	48%	50%	51%	54%	56%	74%	151%	45%	41%
Prices - High	104¼	80⅜	55⅛	39⅝	29¾	27¾	26	21¼	22¾	22¼
- Low	74⅜	48⅝	35	27⅝	23½	22	19¾	17½	16⅛	15⅛
P/E Ratio - High	37	33	23	21	18	18	24	43	16	17
- Low	26	20	16	15	14	14	18	36	11	11

Income Statement Analysis (Million $)

	1998	1997	1996	1995	1994	1993	1992	1991	1990	1989
Revs.	NA	2,533	2,218	1,984	1,837	1,634	1,717	1,646	1,484	1,356
Oper. Inc.	NA	593	532	463	420	348	311	295	260	243
Depr.	NA	126	117	104	94.1	73.6	80.5	81.4	47.8	41.3
Int. Exp.	NA	55.6	38.3	25.1	18.4	18.9	24.7	28.2	3.9	7.2
Pretax Inc.	NA	416	370	338	307	275	211	86.0	244	230
Eff. Tax Rate	NA	40%	40%	41%	41%	39%	44%	39%	37%	37%
Net Inc.	NA	249	222	201	180	168	118	53.0	154	146

Balance Sheet & Other Fin. Data (Million $)

	1998	1997	1996	1995	1994	1993	1992	1991	1990	1989
Cash	NA	101	90.8	137	NA	116	69.0	114	125	233
Curr. Assets	NA	673	574	600	504	532	418	467	418	615
Total Assets	NA	2,778	2,179	1,907	1,698	1,649	1,615	1,603	1,138	1,213
Curr. Liab.	NA	893	624	479	376	372	421	348	226	331
LT Debt	NA	566	356	253	216	204	257	400	8.0	7.0
Common Eqty.	NA	1,036	933	944	909	879	814	784	811	786
Total Cap.	NA	1,773	1,438	1,342	1,258	1,227	1,188	1,247	912	882
Cap. Exp.	NA	95.2	84.8	62.9	36.6	78.0	125	132	157	92.0
Cash Flow	NA	376	339	305	306	242	198	134	201	187
Curr. Ratio	NA	0.8	0.9	1.3	1.3	1.4	1.0	1.3	1.9	1.9
% LT Debt of Cap.	NA	31.9	24.8	18.9	17.1	16.6	21.6	32.1	0.8	0.8
% Net Inc.of Revs.	NA	9.8	10.0	10.1	9.7	10.3	6.9	3.2	10.4	10.7
% Ret. on Assets	NA	10.1	10.9	11.1	10.7	10.3	7.3	3.8	13.2	12.1
% Ret. on Equity	NA	25.1	23.7	21.7	20.1	19.8	14.7	6.6	19.5	19.2

Data as orig. reptd.; bef. results of disc. opers. and/or spec. items. Per share data adj. for stk. divs. as of ex-div. date. Bold denotes diluted EPS (FASB 128). E-Estimated. NA-Not Available. NM-Not Meaningful. NR-Not Ranked.

Office—1221 Broadway, Oakland, CA 94612. **Tel**—(510) 271-7000. **Website**—http://www.clorox.com **Chrmn, Pres & CEO**—G. C. Sullivan. **VP & CFO**—K. M. Rose. **VP & Secy**—E. A. Cutter. **VP, Treas & Investor Contact**—Scott House. **Dirs**—W. F. Ausfahl, D. Boggan Jr., J. W. Collins, U. Fairchild, J. Manchot, D. O. Morton, K. Morwind, E. L. Scarff, L. R. Scott, G. C. Sullivan, J. A. Vohs, C. A. Wolfe. **Transfer Agent & Registrar**—First Chicago Trust Co. of New York. **Incorporated**—in Ohio in 1957; reincorporated in Delaware in 1986. **Empl**— 5,500. **S&P Analyst**: Robert J. Izmirlian

STANDARD &POOR'S
STOCK REPORTS

Coastal Corp.

560K

NYSE Symbol **CGP**

In S&P 500

12-SEP-98

Industry: Natural Gas

Summary: Coastal operates one of the largest U.S. natural gas pipeline systems. Activities also include exploration and production, oil refining and chemicals.

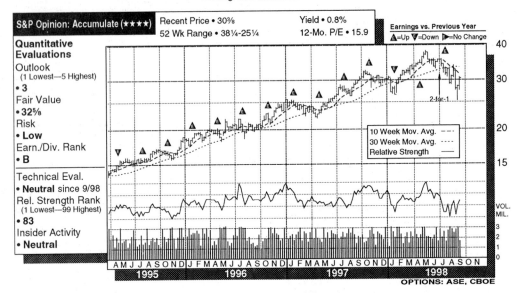

S&P Opinion: Accumulate (★★★★)

Recent Price • 30⅜
52 Wk Range • 38¼-25¼

Yield • 0.8%
12-Mo. P/E • 15.9

Quantitative Evaluations

Outlook
(1 Lowest—5 Highest)
• **3**

Fair Value
• **32⅝**

Risk
• **Low**

Earn./Div. Rank
• **B**

Technical Eval.
• **Neutral** since 9/98

Rel. Strength Rank
(1 Lowest—99 Highest)
• **83**

Insider Activity
• **Neutral**

Earnings vs. Previous Year
▲=Up ▼=Down ▶=No Change

10 Week Mov. Avg.
30 Week Mov. Avg.
Relative Strength

2-for-1

VOL. MIL.

OPTIONS: ASE, CBOE

Overview - 20-MAY-98

As expected, Coastal posted first quarter 1998 EPS of $1.10, up from $0.90 the previous year. Greater crude oil throughput at refineries, natural gas pipeline throughput and profit from the power segment helped offset 28% and 32% drops in realized natural gas and oil prices, respectively. First quarter results in Natural Gas were down primarily due to the gain from the equalization payment associated with the formation of Engage Energy in the first quarter of 1997. Refining margins should continue to benefit from a successful restructuring, pipelines will provide a steady earnings stream, and although the power segment is still small, it should continue to make a positive contribution. We are keeping our 1998 and 1999 earnings estimates at $3.85 and $4.25, respectively, and believe CGP can increase earnings at an average 13% per year for the next 4-5 years. The company has one of the highest rates of return on equity in its peer group and a reasonable debt to capitalization ratio of 44%.

Valuation - 20-MAY-98

CGP achieved 21% earnings growth in 1997, and we believe 13% annual earnings growth is achievable going forward. The company's diversification efforts, including domestic and overseas expansions, are enabling it to advance toward this objective. Yet growth may not be as robust in the near term. Lower commodity prices will act as an ongoing drag on oil and exploration activities, while the power segment is at an early stage and not likely to be a major contributor. However, refining margins have been good recently and should continue to be so in a lower cost environment for crude oil, and the pipelines will provide a steady earnings stream. The shares may be accumulated for above-average performance.

Key Stock Statistics

S&P EPS Est. 1998	1.93	Tang. Bk. Value/Share	12.18
P/E on S&P Est. 1998	15.8	Beta	0.94
S&P EPS Est. 1999	2.13	Shareholders	60,800
Dividend Rate/Share	0.25	Market cap. (B)	$ 6.5
Shs. outstg. (M)	212.6	Inst. holdings	66%
Avg. daily vol. (M)	0.550		

Value of $10,000 invested 5 years ago: $ 27,132

Fiscal Year Ending Dec. 31

	1998	1997	1996	1995	1994	1993
Revenues (Million $)						
1Q	1,957	3,206	3,095	2,618	2,701	2,647
2Q	1,924	2,080	2,938	2,614	2,487	2,632
3Q	—	2,143	2,785	2,546	2,676	2,308
4Q	—	2,225	3,349	2,670	2,352	2,549
Yr.	—	9,653	12,167	10,448	10,215	10,136
Earnings Per Share ($)						
1Q	**0.55**	**0.45**	0.37	0.26	0.36	0.12
2Q	**0.43**	**0.35**	0.29	0.25	0.18	0.13
3Q	—	**0.35**	0.26	0.19	0.10	-0.08
4Q	—	**0.59**	1.35	0.51	0.37	0.34
Yr.	**E1.93**	**1.74**	2.26	1.20	1.02	0.51

Next earnings report expected: late October

Dividend Data (Dividends have been paid since 1977.)

Amount ($)	Date Decl.	Ex-Div. Date	Stock of Record	Payment Date
0.100	Feb. 05	Feb. 25	Feb. 27	Apr. 01 '98
0.063	May. 07	May. 27	May. 29	Jul. 01 '98
2-for-1	May. 07	Jul. 02	May. 27	Jul. 01 '98
0.063	Aug. 06	Aug. 27	Aug. 31	Oct. 01 '98

A Division of The McGraw-Hill Companies

STANDARD
&POOR'S
STOCK REPORTS

The Coastal Corporation

560K

12-SEP-98

Business Summary - 20-MAY-98

With a reliable stream of earnings from its gas pipeline business to steady its course, this diversified energy company is rapidly expanding in such higher-growth areas as oil and gas production and the generation of power in foreign markets. Coastal Corp. (CGP) also operates refineries and mines coal.

CGP believes its Natural Gas Group (21% of revenues and 61% of operating profit in 1997) will continue in its traditional role as a dependable contributor to the company's bottom line. ANR Pipeline provides transportation, storage, gathering and balancing of natural gas to customers through 10,611 miles of pipeline and 75 compressor stations throughout the Midwest. The peak delivery capacity at December 31, 1997, was 5.9 Bcf per day. The Colorado Interstate Gas (CIG) transmission system extends from gas production areas in the Texas Panhandle, western Oklahoma and western Kansas to the Denver area, and from production areas in Montana, Wyoming and Utah, also to the Denver area. CIG's principal transmission and storage pipeline facilities at December 31, 1997, consisted of 4,160 miles of pipeline and 59 compressor stations, and the design peak day gas delivery capacity was approximately 2.0 Bcf per day.

The company's Exploration and Production Group (6% and 23%) continued to grow in 1997, as CGP has fo-cused its drilling efforts on such areas as South Texas, the Texas/Louisiana coastal plains and the Gulf of Mexico, where it believes the potential for hydrocarbon production is the strongest. As of December 31, 1997, the company had 1,752,514 MMcf of estimated proved reserves of natural gas and 40,143,000 barrels of estimated proved reserves of oil, condensate and natural gas liquids (NGL). Natural gas production averaged 540 MMcf daily in 1997, compared to 461 MMcf daily in 1996. Crude oil, condensate and NGL production averaged 13,736 barrels daily in 1997, down from 13,893 barrels daily in 1996.

CGP also sees growth opportunities for its Power business (1% and 1%) as it boosts spending for power projects in selected areas across the globe.

Operating profit of CGP's Refining, Marketing and Chemicals Group (70% and 11%) was hit by narrow margins on sales of refined products and the chemical paraxylene. CGP believes that the group's recent restructuring will allow it to benefit from any future upturn in margins. Throughput at CGP's refineries averaged 414,000 barrels per day in 1997.

The sale of CGP's Utah-based coal operations for $610 million in 1996 shifted the focus of the Coal Group (2% and 3%) to the eastern U.S., where the company controls 540 million recoverable tons of bituminous coal reserves.

Per Share Data ($)

(Year Ended Dec. 31)	1997	1996	1995	1994	1993	1992	1991	1990	1989	1988
Tangible Bk. Val.	12.15	10.90	9.24	8.13	7.20	6.82	9.58	9.29	8.37	6.76
Cash Flow	3.76	4.50	3.10	2.75	2.21	1.21	1.90	2.55	2.38	2.79
Earnings	1.75	2.27	1.20	1.02	0.51	-0.61	0.46	1.07	0.95	0.90
Dividends	0.20	0.20	0.20	0.20	0.20	0.20	0.20	0.20	0.15	0.13
Payout Ratio	11%	9%	17%	20%	39%	NM	43%	18%	17%	16%
Prices - High	32½	25¾	18⅞	16⅞	15¾	15	18⅜	19⅞	16⅝	11⅞
- Low	22	17½	12⅝	12⅜	11¾	11	11⅞	14⅝	11	8⅞
P/E Ratio - High	19	11	16	16	31	NM	40	18	17	13
- Low	13	8	10	12	23	NM	26	14	12	10

Income Statement Analysis (Million $)

	1997	1996	1995	1994	1993	1992	1991	1990	1989	1988
Revs.	9,653	12,167	10,448	10,215	10,136	10,063	9,549	9,381	8,271	8,186
Oper. Inc.	1,170	1,402	1,067	1,034	931	734	846	1,028	937	968
Depr.	437	456	382	363	356	378	301	309	269	312
Int. Exp.	308	368	421	416	451	496	460	462	463	452
Pretax Inc.	527	663	323	325	202	-198	158	380	290	255
Eff. Tax Rate	26%	25%	16%	28%	41%	NM	39%	41%	38%	38%
Net Inc.	392	500	270	233	118	-126	96.0	226	178	157

Balance Sheet & Other Fin. Data (Million $)

	1997	1996	1995	1994	1993	1992	1991	1990	1989	1988
Cash	20.0	106	59.0	74.0	159	44.0	24.0	71.0	149	11.0
Curr. Assets	2,529	3,196	2,250	2,428	2,574	3,028	3,028	3,244	3,194	2,479
Total Assets	11,625	11,613	10,659	10,535	10,227	10,580	9,487	9,230	8,773	7,865
Curr. Liab.	2,501	2,947	2,207	2,514	2,390	2,612	2,772	2,974	2,879	2,533
LT Debt	3,663	3,526	3,662	3,720	3,813	4,306	3,866	3,436	3,248	3,100
Common Eqty.	3,280	3,034	2,470	2,248	2,068	1,999	2,030	1,969	1,774	1,256
Total Cap.	8,511	7,967	7,815	7,652	7,457	7,692	6,562	6,072	5,727	5,080
Cap. Exp.	997	881	627	543	393	574	729	587	428	197
Cash Flow	812	956	652	578	463	250	397	535	447	460
Curr. Ratio	1.0	1.1	1.0	1.0	1.1	1.2	1.1	1.1	1.1	1.0
% LT Debt of Cap.	43.0	44.3	46.9	47.0	51.1	56.0	58.9	56.6	56.7	61.0
% Net Inc.of Revs.	4.1	4.1	2.6	2.3	1.2	NM	1.0	2.4	2.2	1.9
% Ret. on Assets	3.4	4.5	2.6	2.2	1.1	NM	1.0	2.5	2.0	1.7
% Ret. on Equity	11.9	18.2	10.7	10.0	5.2	NM	4.8	12.0	11.0	13.5

Data as orig. reptd.; bef. results of disc. opers. and/or spec. items. Per share data adj. for stk. divs. as of ex-div. date. Bold denotes diluted EPS (FASB 128). E-Estimated. NA-Not Available. NM-Not Meaningful. NR-Not Ranked.

Office—Coastal Tower, Nine Greenway Plaza, Houston, TX 77046-0995. **Tel**—(713) 877-1400. **Chrmn, Pres, CEO & CFO**—D. A. Arledge. **SVP & Secy**—A. M. O'Toole. **VP & Controller**—J. B. Levos. **Treas**—R. D. Matthews. **Investor Contact**—Stirling D. Pack Jr. **Dirs**—D. A. Arledge, J. M. Bissell, G. L. Brundrett Jr., H. Burrow, R. D. Chapin Jr., J. F. Cordes, R. L. Gates, K. O. Johnson, J. S. Katzin, J. C. MacNeil Jr., T. R. McDade, L. D. Wooddy Jr., O. S. Wyatt Jr. **Transfer Agents & Registrars**—Bank of New York, NYC; Co.'s office. **Incorporated**—in Delaware in 1972. **Empl**—13,200. **S&P Analyst:** J. Robert Cho

STANDARD &POOR'S
STOCK REPORTS

Coca-Cola

562

NYSE Symbol **KO**

In S&P 500

12-SEP-98

Industry:
Beverages
(Non-Alcoholic)

Summary: Coca-Cola is the world's largest soft-drink company and has a sizable fruit juice business. Its bottling interests include a 44% stake in NYSE-listed Coca-Cola Enterprises.

S&P Opinion: Accumulate (★★★★)	Recent Price • 62⅜	Yield • 1.0%
	52 Wk Range • 88⅞-50	12-Mo. P/E • 40.3

Quantitative Evaluations

Outlook
(1 Lowest—5 Highest)
• 1

Fair Value
• 55⅛

Risk
• Low

Earn./Div. Rank
• A+

Technical Eval.
• **Bullish** since 12/97

Rel. Strength Rank
(1 Lowest—99 Highest)
• 39

Insider Activity
• **Neutral**

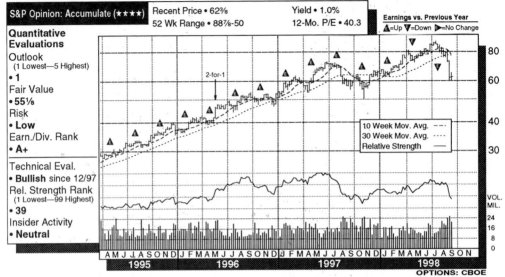

Earnings vs. Previous Year
▲=Up ▼=Down ▶=No Change

2-for-1

10 Week Mov. Avg. ---
30 Week Mov. Avg. ----
Relative Strength ——

VOL.
MIL.

OPTIONS: CBOE

Overview - 22-JUL-98

Revenues are projected to rise approximately 10% in 1998, as a high single-digit increase in gallon shipments, and higher concentrate prices, help to offset unfavorable currency exchange translations (principally in Europe and Asia). Operating margins should continue to widen, aided by operating efficiencies and a favorable business mix shift toward more-profitable soft drink concentrate sales and away from capital-intensive bottling operations. Higher equity income is seen, reflecting anchor bottler internal growth, as well as reduced costs associated with bottler consolidations. High levels of free cash flow should help to reduce debt, while still allowing for share repurchases on the order of about 1% to 2% annually. We anticipate diluted EPS to rise to $1.62 in 1998, up 15% from 1997's $1.41 (excluding $0.23 in transaction gains). In 1999, EPS of $1.90 are anticipated.

Valuation - 22-JUL-98

After an uncharacteristic underperformance in 1997, the shares have outpaced the S&P 500 in 1998 to date, despite a slowing of the EPS growth rate. Reported EPS comparison in recent quarters have been affected by difficult foreign currency exchange translations, and, to a lesser degree, by a number of unusual events, including the sale of certain minority equity interests, and restructuring charges taken to enhance manufacturing efficiencies in North America. S&P expects such transactions to help raise the level of company operating efficiencies, and better enable it to achieve a high-teen rate of EPS growth over time. Earnings should also benefit from continued strong worldwide case volume growth, and from a moderating foreign currency environment. KO's bright prospects, dominant market position, and sound finances make the shares attractive despite their premium valuation.

Key Stock Statistics

S&P EPS Est. 1998	1.62	Tang. Bk. Value/Share	2.99
P/E on S&P Est. 1998	38.5	Beta	1.10
S&P EPS Est. 1999	1.90	Shareholders	22,600
Dividend Rate/Share	0.60	Market cap. (B)	$153.9
Shs. outstg. (M)	2465.5	Inst. holdings	49%
Avg. daily vol. (M)	5.413		

Value of $10,000 invested 5 years ago: $ 31,885

Fiscal Year Ending Dec. 31

	1998	1997	1996	1995	1994	1993
Revenues (Million $)						
1Q	4,457	4,138	4,194	3,854	3,352	3,060
2Q	5,151	5,075	5,253	4,936	4,342	3,899
3Q	—	4,954	4,656	4,895	4,461	3,629
4Q	—	4,701	4,443	4,333	4,017	3,373
Yr.	—	18,868	18,546	18,018	16,172	13,957
Earnings Per Share ($)						
1Q	**0.34**	0.39	0.28	0.25	0.20	0.17
2Q	**0.48**	0.52	0.42	0.35	0.29	0.26
3Q	**E0.43**	0.40	0.39	0.32	0.28	0.23
4Q	**E0.37**	0.33	0.31	0.26	0.22	0.18
Yr.	**E1.62**	1.64	1.38	1.18	0.99	0.84

Next earnings report expected: mid October

Dividend Data (Dividends have been paid since 1893.)

Amount ($)	Date Decl.	Ex-Div. Date	Stock of Record	Payment Date
0.140	Oct. 17	Nov. 26	Dec. 01	Dec. 15 '97
0.150	Feb. 20	Mar. 11	Mar. 15	Apr. 01 '98
0.150	Apr. 15	Jun. 11	Jun. 15	Jul. 01 '98
0.150	Jul. 16	Sep. 11	Sep. 15	Oct. 01 '98

A Division of The **McGraw·Hill** *Companies*

Business Summary - 22-JUL-98

The Coca-Cola Company is the world's largest producer of soft drink concentrates and syrups, as well as the world's largest producer of juice and juice-related products. Finished soft drink products bearing the company's trademarks have been sold in the U.S. since 1886, and are now sold in nearly 200 countries. Sales and operating profit in 1997 were distributed as follows:

	Sales	Profits
North America	34%	24%
Greater Europe	29%	27%
Middle & Far East	23%	28%
Latin America	11%	18%
Africa	3%	3%

The company's business may be the most focused and efficient of any in the world, and is, quite simply, the production and sale of soft drink and non-carbonated beverage concentrates and syrups. These products are sold to the company's authorized independent and company-owned bottling/canning operations, and fountain wholesalers. These customers then either combine the syrup with carbonated water, or combine the concentrate with sweetener, water and carbonated water to produce finished soft drinks. The finished soft drinks are packaged in authorized containers bearing the company's well-known trademarks, which include Coca-Cola (best-selling soft drink in the world, including Coca-Cola classic), caffeine free Coca-Cola (classic), diet Coke (sold as Coke light in many markets outside the U.S.), Cherry Coke, diet Cherry Coke, Fanta, Sprite, diet Sprite, Barq's, Surge, Mr. PiBB, Mello Yello, TAB, Fresca, PowerAde, Minute Maid, Hi-C, Fruitopia, and other products developed for specific markets, including Georgia ready to drink coffees. KO has equity positions in approximately 42 unconsolidated bottling, canning and distribution operations for its products worldwide, including bottlers representing about 54% of the company's U.S. unit case volume in 1997.

The company enters into forward exchange contracts, and purchases currency options (principally European currencies and Japanese yen) to reduce the risk that the company's eventual dollar net cash inflows resulting from sales outside the U.S. will be adversely affected by changes in exchange rates.

Per Share Data ($)

(Year Ended Dec. 31)	1997	1996	1995	1994	1993	1992	1991	1990	1989	1988
Tangible Bk. Val.	2.67	2.18	1.77	1.79	1.55	1.34	1.55	1.31	1.09	1.05
Cash Flow	1.89	1.59	1.36	1.14	0.97	0.83	0.70	0.60	0.49	0.41
Earnings	1.64	1.40	1.19	0.99	0.84	0.71	0.60	0.51	0.42	0.36
Dividends	0.56	0.50	0.44	0.39	0.34	0.28	0.24	0.20	0.17	0.15
Payout Ratio	34%	36%	37%	39%	40%	39%	39%	39%	39%	41%
Prices - High	72⅝	54¼	40¼	26¾	22⅝	22¾	20½	12¼	10⅛	5⅝
- Low	51⅛	36⅛	24⅜	19½	18¾	17¾	10¾	8⅛	5⅜	4⅜
P/E Ratio - High	44	39	34	27	27	32	34	24	24	16
- Low	31	26	21	20	22	25	18	16	13	12

Income Statement Analysis (Million $)

	1997	1996	1995	1994	1993	1992	1991	1990	1989	1988
Revs.	18,868	18,546	18,018	16,172	13,957	13,074	11,572	10,236	8,966	8,338
Oper. Inc.	5,627	4,394	4,546	4,090	3,485	3,080	2,586	2,237	1,910	1,768
Depr.	626	479	454	382	333	310	254	236	184	170
Int. Exp.	258	286	272	199	178	171	185	231	315	239
Pretax Inc.	6,055	4,596	4,328	3,728	3,185	2,746	2,383	2,014	1,764	1,582
Eff. Tax Rate	32%	24%	31%	32%	31%	31%	32%	31%	32%	34%
Net Inc.	4,129	3,492	2,986	2,554	2,188	1,884	1,618	1,382	1,193	1,045

Balance Sheet & Other Fin. Data (Million $)

	1997	1996	1995	1994	1993	1992	1991	1990	1989	1988
Cash	1,737	1,658	1,315	1,531	1,078	1,063	1,117	1,492	1,182	1,231
Curr. Assets	5,969	5,910	5,450	5,205	4,434	4,248	4,144	4,143	3,604	3,245
Total Assets	16,940	16,161	15,041	13,873	12,021	11,052	10,222	9,278	8,283	7,451
Curr. Liab.	7,379	7,416	7,348	6,177	5,171	5,303	4,118	4,296	3,658	2,869
LT Debt	801	1,116	1,141	1,426	1,428	1,120	985	536	549	761
Common Eqty.	7,311	6,156	5,392	5,235	4,584	3,888	4,426	3,774	3,185	3,045
Total Cap.	8,560	7,573	6,727	6,841	6,125	5,090	5,611	4,650	4,330	4,376
Cap. Exp.	1,093	990	937	878	808	1,083	792	642	462	387
Cash Flow	4,755	3,971	3,440	2,936	2,521	2,194	1,872	1,600	1,355	1,208
Curr. Ratio	0.8	0.8	0.7	0.8	0.9	0.8	1.0	1.0	1.0	1.1
% LT Debt of Cap.	9.4	14.7	17.0	20.8	23.3	22.0	17.6	11.5	12.7	17.4
% Net Inc.of Revs.	21.9	18.8	16.6	15.8	15.7	14.4	14.0	13.5	13.3	12.5
% Ret. on Assets	24.9	22.4	20.7	19.9	19.0	17.9	16.6	15.8	15.5	13.6
% Ret. on Equity	61.3	60.5	56.2	52.4	51.8	45.7	39.6	39.3	38.5	33.9

Data as orig. reptd.; bef. results of disc. opers. and/or spec. items. Per share data adj. for stk. divs. as of ex-div. date. Bold denotes diluted EPS (FASB 128). E-Estimated. NA-Not Available. NM-Not Meaningful. NR-Not Ranked.

Office—1 Coca-Cola Plaza, N.W., Atlanta, GA 30313. **Tel**—(404) 676-2121. **Website**—http://www.cocacola.com **Chrmn & CEO**—M. D. Ivester. **CFO**—J. E. Chesnut. **Secy**—Susan E. Shaw. **Investor Contact**—Nancy W. Ford. **Dirs**—H. A. Allen, R. W. Allen, C. P. Black, W. E. Buffett, C. W. Duncan, Jr., M. D. Ivester, S. B. King, D. F. McHenry, S. Nunn, P. F. Oreffice, J. D. Robinson III, P. V. Ueberroth, J. B. Williams. **Transfer Agent & Registrar**—First Chicago Trust Co. of New York, Jersey City, NJ. **Incorporated**—in Delaware in 1919. **Empl**— 29,500. **S&P Analyst:** Richard Joy

12-SEP-98

Industry:
Household Products
(Nondurables)

Summary: This major consumer products company markets oral care, body care, household surface care, fabric care and animal dietary care products in more than 210 countries and territories.

S&P Opinion: Accumulate (★★★★)	Recent Price • 69¾	Yield • 1.6%
	52 Wk Range • 98⅞-61¾	12-Mo. P/E • 28.7

Quantitative Evaluations

Outlook
(1 Lowest—5 Highest)
• **1**

Fair Value
• **58⅞**

Risk
• **Low**

Earn./Div. Rank
• **B+**

Technical Eval.
• **Bearish** since 8/98

Rel. Strength Rank
(1 Lowest—99 Highest)
• **41**

Insider Activity
• **Favorable**

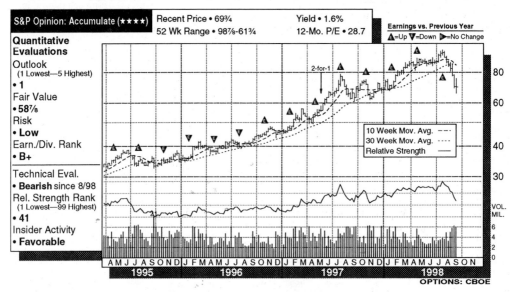

Earnings vs. Previous Year
▲=Up ▼=Down ▶=No Change

10 Week Mov. Avg. ‐ ‐ ‐
30 Week Mov. Avg. ‐ ‐ ‐ ‐
Relative Strength ———

OPTIONS: CBOE

Overview - 28-JUL-98

Consolidated sales, excluding currency translations, should advance about 3% to 5% in 1998, aided by new products, particularly the U.S. launch of Colgate Total toothpaste. For the first half of 1998, Total toothpaste has garnered a 10% market share. Sales should also benefit from further overseas expansion and acquisitions. Unit volume is likely to rise about 4.0% to 5% in 1998 and in the mid-single digits in 1999. Gross margins should widen about 100 basis points, on a more profitable mix, especially in the oral care area, higher sales in more profitable developing countries, investment in technology to improve communications among all aspects of the business, and continued cost savings and more efficient manufacturing as a result of a 1995 restructuring and the European rollout of SAP. Cost savings are likely to be reinvested in marketing efforts to boost market share and brand awareness.

Valuation - 28-JUL-98

CL shares should continue to appreciate, as CL continues to record strong earnings momentum given its successful new products, cost cutting and intensive marketing initiatives. More recently, gross margins have begun to benefit from the company's efforts to control costs. A 1995 restructuring resulted in savings of about $50 million in 1997 and is expected to result in savings of $108 and $135 million in 1998 and 1999, respectively. These savings are being used to boost advertising expenditures, create new products and pay down debt. Earnings per share are likely to grow 14% to 16% annually for the foreseeable future. Given CL's strong brand franchise, growth prospects, and increased global share, we believe that the stock, recently trading at 33X estimated 1999 EPS of $3.00, merits a premium market value and remains an attractive portfolio addition.

Key Stock Statistics

S&P EPS Est. 1998	2.60	Tang. Bk. Value/Share	NM
P/E on S&P Est. 1998	26.8	Beta	1.30
S&P EPS Est. 1999	3.00	Shareholders	45,900
Dividend Rate/Share	1.10	Market cap. (B)	$ 20.6
Shs. outstg. (M)	295.7	Inst. holdings	61%
Avg. daily vol. (M)	1.304		

Value of $10,000 invested 5 years ago: $ 28,107

Fiscal Year Ending Dec. 31

	1998	1997	1996	1995	1994	1993
Revenues (Million $)						
1Q	2,160	2,147	2,054	1,980	1,770	1,703
2Q	2,257	2,301	2,167	2,091	1,891	1,775
3Q	—	2,297	2,231	2,134	1,931	1,823
4Q	—	2,312	2,297	2,153	1,996	1,840
Yr.	—	9,057	8,749	8,358	7,588	7,141
Earnings Per Share ($)						
1Q	**0.60**	**0.52**	0.47	0.53	0.49	0.42
2Q	**0.62**	**0.54**	0.49	0.47	0.47	0.43
3Q	**E0.66**	**0.58**	0.53	-0.88	0.50	0.45
4Q	**E0.72**	**0.63**	0.60	0.40	0.46	0.39
Yr.	**E2.60**	**2.27**	2.09	0.52	1.91	1.69

Next earnings report expected: mid October

Dividend Data (Dividends have been paid since 1895.)

Amount ($)	Date Decl.	Ex-Div. Date	Stock of Record	Payment Date
0.275	Oct. 09	Oct. 23	Oct. 27	Nov. 17 '97
0.275	Jan. 08	Jan. 23	Jan. 27	Feb. 17 '98
0.275	Mar. 05	Apr. 23	Apr. 27	May. 15 '98
0.275	Jul. 09	Jul. 23	Jul. 27	Aug. 17 '98

 A Division of The McGraw·Hill Companies

Business Summary - 28-JUL-98

With more than 70% of its sales from international markets, Colgate-Palmolive is a leading global consumer products company in the oral, personal and household care and pet food markets. Its products are marketed to 5.7 billion people in more than 210 countries and territories worldwide, under such internationally recognized brand names as Colgate, Palmolive, Mennen, Ajax, Fab, Sorriso and Protex, as well as Hill's Science Diet and Hill's Prescription Diet.

Oral, personal and household care products consist of toothpastes, oral rinses and toothbrushes, bar and liquid soaps, shampoos, conditioners, deodorants and antiperspirants, baby and shave products, laundry and dishwashing detergents, fabric softeners, cleansers and cleaners, bleaches and other similar items. Pet nutrition products include pet food products manufactured and marketed by Hill's Pet Nutrition.

About 31% of sales in 1997 were from products introduced in the past five years. More new products were introduced in 1997 than in any previous year.

While Colgate believes that new products, creative advertising and consumer research are the cornerstone of long-term growth, its marketing strategy takes different paths in the high-growth emerging markets and in developed regions.

In the developing nations of Latin America, Asia, Africa and Central Europe, Colgate seeks to build product awareness and usage by introducing its brands to consumers and actively encouraging them to improve personal hygiene and thereby increase consumption of basic personal and household products. The company also offers its products in more affordable formulas and sizes. On the other hand, in the highly competitive, more established markets of North America and Western Europe, it tries to gain market share by emphasizing innovative value-added new products with wider margins.

Worldwide, Colgate is reducing costs by standardizing product formulas and sizes, and limiting the number of suppliers, and capitalizing on regional economies of scale with local manufacturing. It also hope to reduce costs through the rollout of SAP management software.

In September 1995, CL embarked on a major worldwide restructuring of its manufacturing and administrative operations aimed at generating significant efficiencies and improving competitiveness. The program resulted in a 1995 third-quarter pretax charge of $460.5 million. To date, 20 factories have been closed or reconfigured; the realignments are expected to be completed in 1998. Savings from this program began to be realized in late 1996 and are expected to reach $100 million annually by 1998.

Per Share Data ($)

(Year Ended Dec. 31)	1997	1996	1995	1994	1993	1992	1991	1990	1989	1988
Tangible Bk. Val.	NA	NM	NM	0.44	0.87	3.64	3.46	2.96	4.20	4.12
Cash Flow	3.20	3.17	1.63	2.71	2.36	2.07	0.93	1.61	1.35	0.85
Earnings	2.27	2.10	0.52	1.91	1.69	1.46	0.39	1.14	0.99	0.56
Dividends	1.06	0.94	0.88	0.77	0.67	0.57	0.51	0.45	0.39	0.37
Payout Ratio	47%	45%	169%	40%	40%	40%	144%	40%	38%	67%
Prices - High	78⅝	48¼	38¾	32¾	33⅝	30⅜	24⅝	18⅞	16¼	12⅜
- Low	45	34½	29	24¾	23⅜	22⅝	16⅞	13¼	11	9⅝
P/E Ratio - High	35	23	74	17	20	21	64	17	16	22
- Low	20	16	56	13	14	15	44	12	11	17

Income Statement Analysis (Million $)

	1997	1996	1995	1994	1993	1992	1991	1990	1989	1988
Revs.	9,057	8,749	8,358	7,588	7,141	7,007	6,060	5,691	5,039	4,734
Oper. Inc.	1,591	1,470	1,337	1,228	1,113	943	744	663	523	441
Depr.	320	316	300	235	210	193	146	126	97.0	82.0
Int. Exp.	232	244	251	131	81.0	87.0	114	109	97.0	116
Pretax Inc.	1,131	955	364	918	864	728	218	511	447	250
Eff. Tax Rate	32%	34%	53%	33%	33%	35%	43%	37%	37%	39%
Net Inc.	740	635	172	580	548	477	125	321	280	153

Balance Sheet & Other Fin. Data (Million $)

	1997	1996	1995	1994	1993	1992	1991	1990	1989	1988
Cash	183	308	257	218	211	221	245	276	524	366
Curr. Assets	2,196	2,372	2,360	2,178	2,070	1,995	1,858	1,813	1,897	1,783
Total Assets	7,539	7,902	7,642	6,142	5,761	5,434	4,511	4,158	3,536	3,218
Curr. Liab.	1,959	1,904	1,753	1,529	1,394	1,360	1,262	1,297	989	1,072
LT Debt	2,341	2,787	2,992	1,752	1,532	947	851	1,068	1,059	674
Common Eqty.	1,793	1,641	1,272	1,799	1,851	2,598	1,847	1,348	1,110	1,138
Total Cap.	4,805	5,055	4,909	3,870	3,674	3,738	2,928	2,694	2,406	2,008
Cap. Exp.	479	459	432	401	364	416	285	385	211	303
Cash Flow	1,039	930	472	794	736	649	250	428	367	234
Curr. Ratio	1.1	1.3	1.3	1.4	1.5	1.5	1.5	1.4	1.9	1.7
% LT Debt of Cap.	48.7	55.2	60.9	45.3	41.7	25.3	29.1	39.7	44.0	33.6
% Net Inc.of Revs.	8.2	7.3	2.1	7.6	7.7	6.8	2.1	5.6	5.6	3.2
% Ret. on Assets	9.6	7.9	2.5	9.9	10.1	9.2	2.7	8.3	8.5	4.7
% Ret. on Equity	41.9	42.1	11.2	31.1	24.7	19.8	6.2	24.4	24.5	14.7

Data as orig. reptd.; bef. results of disc. opers. and/or spec. items. Per share data adj. for stk. divs. as of ex-div. date. Bold denotes diluted EPS (FASB 128). E-Estimated. NA-Not Available. NM-Not Meaningful. NR-Not Ranked.

Office—300 Park Ave., New York, NY 10022-7499. **Tel**—(212) 310-2000. **Website**—http://www.colgate.com **Chrmn & CEO**—R. Mark. **Pres**—W. S. Shanahan. **CFO**—S. Patrick. **SVP & Secy**—A. D. Hendry. **Investor Contact**—Bina Thompson (212-310-3072). **Dirs**—J. K. Conway, R. E. Ferguson, E. M. Hancock, D. W. Johnson, R. J. Kogan, J. P. Kendall, D. E. Lewis, R. Mark, H. B. Wentz Jr. **Transfer Agent & Registrar**—First Chicago Trust Co. of New York, Jersey City, NJ. **Incorporated**—in Delaware in 1923. **Empl**— 37,800. **S&P Analyst:** Robert J. Izmirlian

Columbia Energy Group   580

NYSE Symbol **CG**

12-SEP-98

Industry: Natural Gas

Summary: This company (formerly Columbia Gas System) is engaged in the production, transmission and distribution of natural gas.

S&P Opinion: Hold (★★★)	Recent Price • 52	Yield • 1.5%
	52 Wk Range • 57⅞-45⅝	12-Mo. P/E • 17.8

Quantitative Evaluations

Outlook
(1 Lowest—5 Highest)
• **1**

Fair Value
• **42⅛**

Risk
• **Low**

Earn./Div. Rank
• **B-**

Technical Eval.
• **Bullish** since 5/97

Rel. Strength Rank
(1 Lowest—99 Highest)
• **84**

Insider Activity
• **Neutral**

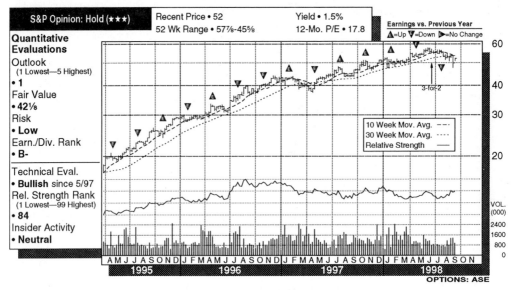

Earnings vs. Previous Year
▲=Up ▼=Down ▶=No Change

10 Week Mov. Avg. – – –
30 Week Mov. Avg. ·····
Relative Strength —

3-for-2

OPTIONS: ASE

Overview - 17-JUL-98

Columbia Energy again managed to beat the Street estimate with EPS of $0.27 in the second quarter of 1998, down from $0.42 a year ago. The year to year drop in earnings was caused primarily by weather that was 38% warmer than last year. The acquisition of an Appalachian supplier and the subsequent increase in the E&P business, aggressive expansion of CG's marketing activities and lower operation and maintenance expanses partially offset the loss in gas distribution income. We are maintaining our respective 1998 and 1999 estimates (adjusted for the 3-for-2 split) at $3.60 and $3.93. The company intends to increase operating income derived from the unregulated segment from the present 10% to 30% by 2002 by expanding the energy marketing and exploration and production segments. In the traditional distribution and transmission businesses, demand for natural gas should continue to grow over the long term, but a decrease in economic growth would dampen CG's prospects in the near term, as would expected flat natural gas prices. Otherwise, the company is in good shape, with a 54% debt to capitalization ratio, and a dividend payout of just 22% of our 1998 earnings estimate.

Valuation - 17-JUL-98

We still recommend holding CG common stock for the near term. Continued weakness in oil and gas prices will likely stymie the exploration and production segment, and a slowing economy will cut into demand growth for natural gas. While the long-term outlook for CG is still strong, and we still expect annual earnings growth of close to 10%, the short term uncertainty in the gas and oil market will limit CG stock's appreciation. CG is fairly valued as a multiple of our 1998 and 1999 estimates of $3.60 and $3.93, adjusted for a 3-for-2 stock split.

Key Stock Statistics

S&P EPS Est. 1998	3.60	Tang. Bk. Value/Share	23.21
P/E on S&P Est. 1998	14.5	Beta	0.64
S&P EPS Est. 1999	3.93	Shareholders	40,800
Dividend Rate/Share	0.80	Market cap. (B)	$ 4.3
Shs. outstg. (M)	83.4	Inst. holdings	62%
Avg. daily vol. (M)	0.226		

Value of $10,000 invested 5 years ago: $ 42,143

Fiscal Year Ending Dec. 31

	1998	1997	1996	1995	1994	1993
Revenues (Million $)						
1Q	1,593	1,528	1,203	1,031	1,157	1,223
2Q	1,322	810.7	582.4	454.6	520.5	592.9
3Q	—	995.0	450.8	366.3	386.5	565.5
4Q	—	1,720	1,118	783.6	769.0	1,010
Yr.	—	5,054	3,354	2,635	2,833	3,391
Earnings Per Share ($)						
1Q	1.77	1.95	1.99	1.70	1.85	1.85
2Q	0.27	0.42	0.10	0.41	0.63	-0.04
3Q	—	Nil	-0.07	0.25	-0.20	-0.71
4Q	—	0.90	0.83	-8.11	0.97	0.91
Yr.	E3.60	3.27	2.75	-5.71	3.25	2.01

Next earnings report expected: **early October**

Dividend Data (Dividends have been paid since 1996.)

Amount ($)	Date Decl.	Ex-Div. Date	Stock of Record	Payment Date
0.250	Feb. 18	Feb. 26	Mar. 02	Mar. 16 '98
0.200	May. 20	May. 28	Jun. 01	Jun. 15 '98
0.300	May. 20	May. 28	Jun. 01	Jun. 15 '98
0.200	Aug. 19	Aug. 27	Aug. 31	Sep. 15 '98

A Division of The McGraw·Hill Companies

Columbia Energy Group

Business Summary - 17-JUL-98

In order to compete in an environment of rapid deregulation, Columbia Energy Group (CG) reorganized its operations to emphasize innovation and customer service. The changes included implementing re-engineering programs; beginning residential customer choice programs; setting up a common effort with The SABRE Group, an American Airlines subsidiary, to facilitate industrywide natural gas transportation transactions; and establishing a mass-market-oriented energy services unit, Columbia Energy Services. CG's subsidiaries are principally engaged in the production, transmission and distribution of natural gas, but the company intends to rapidly expand the energy marketing unit and the exploration and productions segment.

In the more traditional gas transmission segment (17% of revenues, but 52% of operating profits in 1997), CG is looking to expand rapidly. In January 1997, the FERC (Federal Energy Regulatory Commission) approved the nonenvironmental aspects of a project that, according to the company, would increase service levels more than 7%, or about 500 million cubic feet (MMcf) of gas per day. To help keep costs down, the company is using alternatives to new construction, including enhancements to existing facilities and alliances with other pipelines. In April 1997, CG announced the launching of a $600 million pipeline project to carry at least 650 MMcf a day of natural gas to eastern markets by the 1999 heating season. The project involves CMS Energy, MCN Energy, and Westcoast Energy. CG's transmission subsidiaries currently operate a 23,100 mile pipeline network serving 15 states and DC.

Columbia's five distribution subsidiaries, which accounted for 43% of revenues and 44% of profits in 1997, provide natural gas service to nearly 2 million customers in Ohio, Pennsylvania, Virginia, Kentucky and Maryland, and sold 313.2 billion cubic feet of gas (Bcf) in 1997, versus 316.2 Bcf in 1996. Gas transported for others totaled 258.9 Bcf, up from 248.8 Bcf. In all of these service areas, CG is moving to bring choice and better service to residential and industrial customers. CG has already begun pilot programs that allow some of its customers in Pennsylvania, Ohio and Virginia to purchase natural gas from suppliers other than Columbia Gas.

Other CG operations include Columbia Natural Resources Inc., which manages more than 6,200 gas and oil wells; Columbia Energy Service Corp., which markets more than 1 Bcf of natural gas per day and started marketing electricity in December 1997; Commonwealth Propane Inc. and Columbia Propane Corp., which sold a combined 71 million gallons of propane in 1997, down 6.7% from 1996; and TriStar Ventures Corp., which develops, owns and operates natural gas-fueled cogeneration power plants.

Per Share Data ($) (Year Ended Dec. 31)	1997	1996	1995	1994	1993	1992	1991	1990	1989	1988
Tangible Bk. Val.	21.51	18.74	15.09	19.35	16.18	14.08	13.18	23.11	23.56	22.69
Cash Flow	5.92	5.41	-2.03	6.70	5.17	6.05	-6.73	4.98	5.57	4.78
Earnings	3.27	2.75	-5.71	3.25	2.01	1.19	-10.48	1.47	2.14	1.64
Dividends	0.60	0.40	Nil	Nil	Nil	Nil	0.77	1.47	1.33	1.53
Payout Ratio	18%	15%	Nil	Nil	Nil	Nil	NM	100%	62%	93%
Prices - High	52 3/8	44 1/8	29 3/8	20 1/2	18 3/8	15 7/8	31 5/8	36 1/2	35 1/8	29 7/8
- Low	37 3/8	27 7/8	15 3/8	14 3/8	12 1/8	9 3/8	8 5/8	27 5/8	22 1/2	17 7/8
P/E Ratio - High	16	16	NM	6	9	13	NM	25	16	18
- Low	11	10	NM	4	6	8	NM	19	11	11
Income Statement Analysis (Million $)										
Revs.	5,054	3,354	2,635	2,833	3,391	2,927	2,577	2,358	3,204	3,129
Oper. Inc.	509	478	390	635	613	531	-800	511	595	530
Depr.	221	215	270	262	240	368	285	249	234	213
Int. Exp.	161	164	1,041	15.0	102	14.0	140	181	208	176
Pretax Inc.	392	338	-642	392	288	161	-1,205	163	215	170
Eff. Tax Rate	30%	34%	NM	37%	47%	44%	NM	36%	32%	30%
Net Inc.	273	222	-422	246	152	91.0	-794	105	146	119
Balance Sheet & Other Fin. Data (Million $)										
Cash	28.7	49.8	8.0	1,482	1,340	821	408	8.0	14.0	6.0
Curr. Assets	1,708	1,436	1,276	2,485	2,487	2,129	1,825	1,462	1,645	1,438
Total Assets	6,612	6,005	6,057	7,165	6,958	6,531	6,332	6,196	5,878	5,641
Curr. Liab.	1,718	1,452	1,579	860	1,094	863	829	1,933	1,886	1,547
LT Debt	2,004	2,004	2,005	4.3	4.8	5.4	6.1	1,429	1,196	1,338
Common Eqty.	1,791	1,554	1,114	1,468	1,227	1,075	1,007	1,758	1,620	1,553
Total Cap.	4,448	4,152	2,666	1,855	1,526	1,312	5,176	4,196	3,832	3,900
Cap. Exp.	421	316	411	434	355	295	377	628	467	282
Cash Flow	495	437	-152	508	392	459	-509	353	380	324
Curr. Ratio	1.0	1.0	0.8	2.9	2.3	2.5	2.2	0.8	0.9	0.9
% LT Debt of Cap.	45.1	48.3	75.2	0.2	0.3	0.4	0.5	44.8	42.5	46.3
% Net Inc.of Revs.	5.4	6.6	NM	8.7	4.5	3.1	NM	4.4	4.6	3.8
% Ret. on Assets	NA	3.7	NM	3.5	2.3	1.4	NM	1.6	2.5	2.1
% Ret. on Equity	NA	16.6	NM	18.3	13.2	8.7	NM	5.9	9.2	7.2

Data as orig. reptd.; bef. results of disc. opers. and/or spec. items. Per share data adj. for stk. divs. as of ex-div. date. Bold denotes diluted EPS (FASB 128). E-Estimated. NA-Not Available. NM-Not Meaningful. NR-Not Ranked.

Office—12355 Sunrise Valley Dr., Ste. 300, Reston, VA 20191-3420. **Tel**—(703) 295-0300. **Fax**—(703) 758-9042. **Website**—http://www.columbiaenergy.com **Chrmn, Pres & CEO**—O. G. Richard III. **SVP & CFO**—M. W. O'Donnell. **Investor Contact**—Thomas L. Hughes (703-295-0429). **Dirs**—R. F. Albosta, R. H. Beeby, W. K. Cadman, J. P. Heffernan, K. L. Hendricks, D. P. Hodel, M. T. Hopkins, J. B. Johnston, M. Jozoff, W. E. Lavery, G. E. Mayo, D. E. Olesen, O. G. Richard III, J. R. Thomas II, W. R. Wilson. **Transfer Agent & Registrar**—Harris Trust Co. of New York, NYC. **Incorporated**—in Delaware in 1926. **Empl**— 8,529. **S&P Analyst:** J. Robert Cho

Columbia/HCA Healthcare 580R

NYSE Symbol **COL**

In S&P 500

12-SEP-98

Industry:
Health Care (Hospital Management)

Summary: Columbia/HCA operates 309 hospitals and 105 freestanding outpatient surgery centers. Home healthcare and other businesses are being sold as part of a broad restructuring program.

S&P Opinion: Hold (★★★)	Recent Price • 21¾	Yield • 0.4%
	52 Wk Range • 34⅝-21	12-Mo. P/E • NM

Earnings vs. Previous Year
▲=Up ▼=Down ▶=No Change

Quantitative Evaluations

Outlook
(1 Lowest—5 Highest)
• **3+**

Fair Value
• **25¾**

Risk
• **Low**

Earn./Div. Rank
• **NR**

Technical Eval.
• **Bearish** since 7/98

Rel. Strength Rank
(1 Lowest—99 Highest)
• **37**

Insider Activity
• **Neutral**

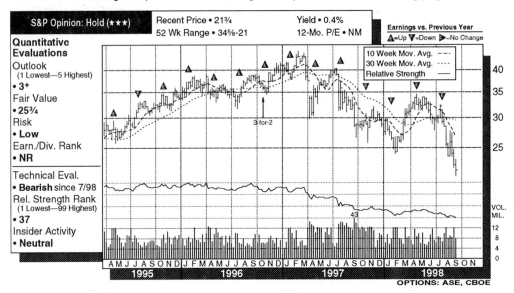

10 Week Mov. Avg. ----
30 Week Mov. Avg. ·····
Relative Strength ——

3-for-2

43

VOL. MIL.

OPTIONS: ASE, CBOE

Overview - 26-AUG-98

Revenues from continuing operations are not likely to expand materially in 1998, reflecting soft same-store in-patient admissions, an increased proportion of dis-counted HMO business (38% of admissions), and lower Medicare rates. Operating margins will suffer from the weakened revenue line, and substantial earnings gains are not expected at least for several more quarters, as management's primary focus remains operational re-structuring. During 1998, COL has sold or agreed to sell all of its home healthcare operations, as well as a significant portion of its outpatient surgery centers and most of the businesses acquired from Value Health. The company is also seeking IRS approval to create two spinoff companies; the Pacific Group, consisting of 42 hospitals (revenues of $950 million in the first half of 1998); and the America Group, consisting of 22 hospi-tals ($260 million).

Valuation - 26-AUG-98

The stock continues to be negatively affected by lack of earnings visibility, as management pursues a compre-hensive restructuring program, while grappling with lower Medicare inpatient reimbursement rates, weak ad-mission trends, and continued negative media publicity. For the longer term, however, we envision a more streamlined and geographically focused company, with about 200 acute care hospitals and annual revenues of about $12 billion. The single most important hurdle will remain the resolution of the federal probe of COL's Medicare billing practices. Assuming that the situation is resolved and the IRS approves COL's asset spinoff plans, the shares offer substantial upside prospects, and are worth holding at recent levels. Excluding charges, we see 1998 EPS of $1.30, and look for a gain in 1999 to $1.50.

Key Stock Statistics

S&P EPS Est. 1998	1.30	Tang. Bk. Value/Share	6.47
P/E on S&P Est. 1998	16.8	Beta	0.85
S&P EPS Est. 1999	1.50	Shareholders	18,400
Dividend Rate/Share	0.08	Market cap. (B)	$ 13.6
Shs. outstg. (M)	645.3	Inst. holdings	69%
Avg. daily vol. (M)	2.043		

Value of $10,000 invested 5 years ago: $ 15,627

Fiscal Year Ending Dec. 31

	1998	1997	1996	1995	1994	1993
Revenues (Million $)						
1Q	4,901	4,988	4,951	4,380	2,778	2,654
2Q	4,781	4,845	4,933	4,361	2,689	2,536
3Q	—	14,445	4,887	4,371	2,728	2,491
4Q	—	4,374	5,138	4,583	2,937	2,571
Yr.	—	18,819	19,909	17,695	11,132	10,252
Earnings Per Share ($)						
1Q	**0.34**	**0.66**	0.61	0.53	0.27	0.41
2Q	**0.27**	**0.58**	0.54	0.11	0.40	0.33
3Q	**E0.32**	**0.15**	0.46	0.41	0.33	0.05
4Q	**E0.37**	**-1.16**	0.61	0.53	0.41	0.35
Yr.	**E1.30**	**0.27**	2.22	1.58	1.42	1.13

Next earnings report expected: late October

Dividend Data (Dividends have been paid since 1993.)

Amount ($)	Date Decl.	Ex-Div. Date	Stock of Record	Payment Date
0.020	Nov. 13	Jan. 28	Feb. 01	Mar. 01 '98
0.020	Mar. 06	Apr. 29	May. 01	Jun. 01 '98
0.020	Jul. 17	Jul. 29	Aug. 01	Sep. 01 '98
0.020	Sep. 10	Oct. 28	Nov. 01	Dec. 01 '98

Business Summary - 26-AUG-98

Columbia/HCA generated impressive growth in past years by aggressively acquiring hospitals and developing integrated service networks that offer HMO and other customers a full continuum of care. By expanding volume and gaining economies of scale, COL was able to steadily lower its cost structure while capturing market share from its non-profit competitors. However, during 1997, the company became the target of an investigation focused on its Medicare business (34% of 1997 revenues), including allegedly fraudulent billing practices. This development significantly disrupted hospital operations, and resulted in a complete overhaul of COL's management. Aside from resolving the federal probe, new management has embarked on an asset divestiture program, including freestanding outpatient surgery centers, home healthcare operations, and most of the businesses acquired from Value Health. COL will also seek to restructure the acute care hospitals along geographic lines.

At the end of 1997, COL owned and operated 309 acute care hospitals with 60,643 licensed beds, 22 psychiatric hospitals with 2,476 licensed beds, more than 135 outpatient surgery centers, and about 550 home health care locations in 37 U.S. states, the U.K., and Switzerland. The company also operated through equally owned joint ventures 27 hospitals that are not consolidated in its financial statements.

Most of the acute-care hospitals provide a range of medical and surgical services, including inpatient care, intensive and cardiac care, diagnostic services and emergency services. Outpatient and ancillary health care services are provided by these hospitals, as well as at freestanding facilities operated by Columbia, including outpatient surgery and diagnostic centers, rehabilitation centers and home health agencies.

The psychiatric hospitals provide therapeutic programs tailored to child psychiatric, adolescent psychiatric, adult psychiatric, adolescent alcohol or drug abuse and adult alcohol or drug abuse patients.

Hospital admissions in 1997 totaled 1,915,100 (up from 1,895,400 in 1996); average length of stay was 5.0 days (5.1); patient days were 9,492,300 (9,712,900); surgery cases totaled 1,976,900 (1,945,500); and the occupancy rate was 43% (42%). Outpatient revenues as a percentage of patient revenues were 37% (36.0%).

In July 1997, Dr. Thomas Frist Jr. replaced Richard Scott as the company's chairman and CEO. David Vandewater, the company's president and COO, also resigned, as did several other high level managers. The management shake-up was attributed largely to director concern about the company's operating strategies, amid the government's investigation of COL facilities and business practices in Texas, Florida, Tennessee, Utah, North Carolina, Oklahoma and Georgia.

Per Share Data ($)

(Year Ended Dec. 31)	1997	1996	1995	1994	1993	1992	1991	1990	1989	1988
Tangible Bk. Val.	5.81	7.30	5.43	5.07	4.43	6.83	4.27	0.87	NA	NA
Cash Flow	2.14	3.92	3.03	2.58	2.22	1.66	1.35	1.10	1.01	NA
Earnings	0.27	2.22	1.58	1.42	1.13	0.79	0.61	0.55	0.32	NA
Dividends	0.07	0.08	0.08	0.06	0.04	Nil	Nil	Nil	NA	NA
Payout Ratio	26%	4%	5%	4%	4%	Nil	Nil	Nil	NA	NA
Prices - High	44⁷/₈	41⁷/₈	36	30¹/₈	22⁵/₈	14⁵/₈	12¹/₂	10³/₈	NA	NA
- Low	25³/₄	31⁵/₈	23⁵/₈	22¹/₈	10⁷/₈	9¹/₈	6¹/₂	6⁵/₈	NA	NA
P/E Ratio - High	NM	19	23	21	20	19	20	19	NA	NA
- Low	NM	14	15	16	10	12	11	12	NA	NA

Income Statement Analysis (Million $)

	1997	1996	1995	1994	1993	1992	1991	1990	1989	1988
Revs.	18,819	19,909	17,695	11,132	10,252	807	499	290	153	NA
Oper. Inc.	2,783	4,136	3,620	2,214	1,938	115	77.0	44.0	25.0	NA
Depr.	1,238	1,155	981	609	554	28.7	18.4	9.6	3.8	NA
Int. Exp.	493	498	460	260	333	49.1	23.9	17.4	10.9	NA
Pretax Inc.	538	2,656	1,892	12.6	978	52.5	34.3	17.4	9.9	NA
Eff. Tax Rate	38%	38%	38%	39%	40%	32%	28%	21%	0.60%	NA
Net Inc.	182	1,505	1,064	745	575	25.9	15.2	9.8	6.3	NA

Balance Sheet & Other Fin. Data (Million $)

	1997	1996	1995	1994	1993	1992	1991	1990	1989	1988
Cash	110	113	232	13.0	224	76.1	29.4	7.9	1.1	NA
Curr. Assets	4,423	4,413	4,200	2,550	2,488	338	166	103	41.0	NA
Total Assets	22,022	21,272	19,892	12,339	10,216	1,072	485	322	138	NA
Curr. Liab.	2,773	2,946	2,738	1,767	1,915	203	98.0	80.0	32.0	NA
LT Debt	9,276	6,781	7,137	3,853	3,335	539	230	172	90.0	NA
Common Eqty.	7,250	8,609	7,129	5,022	3,471	265	118	41.0	5.0	NA
Total Cap.	17,362	17,490	16,247	9,612	7,420	851	380	233	108	NA
Cap. Exp.	1,422	1,400	1,527	975	1,042	344	96.0	108	10.0	NA
Cash Flow	1,420	2,660	2,045	1,354	1,129	54.6	33.6	19.5	10.0	NA
Curr. Ratio	1.6	1.5	1.5	1.4	1.3	1.7	1.7	1.3	1.3	NA
% LT Debt of Cap.	53.4	38.8	43.9	40.1	44.9	63.3	60.5	74.0	83.3	NA
% Net Inc.of Revs.	1.0	7.6	6.0	6.7	5.6	3.2	3.0	3.4	4.1	NA
% Ret. on Assets	0.8	7.3	5.9	6.4	4.8	3.0	3.4	4.3	NA	NA
% Ret. on Equity	2.3	19.0	16.1	17.0	14.1	12.0	17.6	41.7	NA	NA

Data as orig. reptd.; bef. results of disc. opers. and/or spec. items. Per share data adj. for stk. divs. as of ex-div. date. Revs. & EPS for 3Q 1997 are for nine mos. ended Sep. 30. E-Estimated. NA-Not Available. NM-Not Meaningful. NR-Not Ranked.

Registrar & Transfer Agent—National City Bank, Cleveland. **Office**—One Park Plaza, Nashville, TN 37203. **Tel**—(615) 344-9551. **Website**—http://www.columbia.net **Chrmn & CEO**—T. F. Frist Jr. **Pres & COO**—J. O. Bovande Jr. **SVP & CFO**—R. B. Stearns. **Investor Contact**—W. M. Kimbrough (615-344-1129). **Dirs**—M. Averhoff, M. Feldstein, T. F. Frist Jr., F. W. Gluck, J. A. Karam, T. M. Long, D. S. MacNaughton, J. H. McArthur, R. C. McWhorter, , T. S. Murphy, K. C. Nelson, C. E. Reichardt, F. S. Royal, W. T. Young. **Transfer Agent & Registrar**—National City Bank, Cleveland. **Incorporated**—in Nevada in 1990. **Empl**— 285,000. **S&P Analyst:** Robert M. Gold

Comcast Corp. 3571

Nasdaq Symbol **CMCSK**

In S&P 500

12-SEP-98

Industry:
Broadcasting (Television, Radio & Cable)

Summary: This company, now the fourth largest cable TV system operator in the U.S., is also a major provider of cellular telephone services in the Northeast.

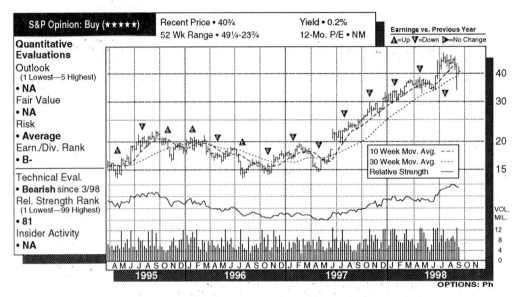

| S&P Opinion: Buy (★★★★) | Recent Price • 40¾ | Yield • 0.2% | Earnings vs. Previous Year |
| | 52 Wk Range • 49¼-23¾ | 12-Mo. P/E • NM | ▲=Up ▼=Down ►=No Change |

Quantitative Evaluations

Outlook
(1 Lowest—5 Highest)
• **NA**

Fair Value
• **NA**

Risk
• **Average**

Earn./Div. Rank
• **B-**

Technical Eval.
• **Bearish** since 3/98

Rel. Strength Rank
(1 Lowest—99 Highest)
• **81**

Insider Activity
• **NA**

10 Week Mov. Avg. -- --
30 Week Mov. Avg. ......
Relative Strength ——

OPTIONS: Ph

Overview - 14-AUG-98

Double digits advances in revenues and cash flow should continue at least through 1999, boosted by acquisitions, higher monthly rates charged to subscribers, growth in the number of cable and cellular subscribers, and growing demand for a la carte cable services. Electronic retailing revenues will also advance. High levels of book charges and interest expense, stemming from acquisitions, will lead to further net losses. Cost cutting and noncore asset sales are continuing, providing further strength to ongoing operations. Microsoft Corp.'s $1 billion capital infusion in June 1997 supports the cable division's forays into high-speed data and video transmission technologies. The aggressive deployment of new technologies and services across each business line expands Comcast's reach to consumers.

Valuation - 14-AUG-98

We upgraded our opinion on CMCSK to strong buy from accumulate in mid August. CMCSK was recently trading at less than 9X estimated 1999 cash flow, which was higher than its peers, but less than the 14X multiple that Microsoft co-founder Paul Allen agreed to pay in a recent cable deal. In addition to takeover appeal and discounted valuation, the shares' market prospects are enhanced by a minority interest held by MSFT, consistent double-digit growth in cash flow, as well as other favorable cable industry developments. The company agreed in August to accelerate its purchase of a 35% ownership and 75% voting stake in Jones Intercable at less than 9X cash flow. Growth in cellular revenues and cash flows should also remain at healthy levels. Continuing investment in new technologies, programming and other ventures offers strong promise for future growth and profitability.

Key Stock Statistics

S&P EPS Est. 1998	-0.37	Tang. Bk. Value/Share	NM
P/E on S&P Est. 1998	NM	Beta	1.12
Dividend Rate/Share	0.09	Shareholders	4,500
Shs. outstg. (M)	369.2	Market cap. (B)	$ 13.4
Avg. daily vol. (M)	2.240	Inst. holdings	59%

Value of $10,000 invested 5 years ago: $ 34,570

Fiscal Year Ending Dec. 31

	1998	1997	1996	1995	1994	1993
Revenues (Million $)						
1Q	1,360	1,131	950.7	663.6	328.7	325.2
2Q	1,322	1,185	945.6	823.6	340.6	340.1
3Q	—	1,204	974.6	870.3	345.7	335.4
4Q	—	1,393	1,168	1,006	360.2	337.5
Yr.	—	4,913	4,038	3,363	1,375	1,338
Earnings Per Share ($)						
1Q	-0.24	-0.20	-0.14	Nil	-0.07	-0.11
2Q	-0.25	-0.05	0.07	-0.12	-0.05	-0.08
3Q	—	-0.17	-0.04	-0.01	-0.07	-0.17
4Q	—	-0.24	-0.10	-0.03	-0.13	-0.10
Yr.	E-0.37	-0.66	-0.21	-0.16	-0.32	-0.46

Next earnings report expected: mid November

Dividend Data (Dividends have been paid since 1987.)

Amount ($)	Date Decl.	Ex-Div. Date	Stock of Record	Payment Date
0.023	Sep. 25	Dec. 02	Dec. 04	Dec. 25 '97
0.023	Dec. 23	Mar. 03	Mar. 05	Mar. 26 '98
0.023	Apr. 01	Jun. 02	Jun. 04	Jun. 25 '98
0.023	Jun. 18	Sep. 01	Sep. 03	Sep. 24 '98

A Division of The McGraw-Hill Companies

Business Summary - 14-AUG-98

Comcast has expanded beyond the "wired world" defined by its traditional cable TV business. In addition to providing wired telecommunications such as cable TV and telephone services, Comcast also offers wireless telecommunications, including cellular telephone services, personal communications services, and direct-to-home satellite TV; and content, through principal ownership of QVC, and ownership interests in Comcast-Spectacor, E! Entertainment, and through other programming investments. The company's consolidated and affiliated operations serve over ten million customers worldwide.

CMCSK serves over 4.8 million cable subscribers, making it the fourth largest U.S. cable system operator. Cable operations were boosted considerably by the November 1996 purchase of W.E. Scripps systems serving about 805,000 subscribers. During 1997, the company sold its equity interests in Teleport Communications Group, as well as its U.K. cable business. In June 1997, Microsoft invested $1 billion in CMCSK through the purchase of common and convertible preferred stock. The investment provided Comcast with needed funds to deploy high-speed data and video services, as well as access to MSFT's expertise. In August 1998, Comcast agreed to accelerate its planned

purchase of Bell Canada International's 37% ownership stake and 75% vote in Jones Intercable (the eighth largest cable company with 1.4 million subscribers) for $700 million.

Through Comcast Cellular Corp., cellular telephone services are provided in Pennsylvania (Philadelphia area), New Jersey, Delaware, and Illinois, to a population of more than 8.2 million. At December 31, 1997, cellular subscribers totaled over 783,000. Other wireless interests include a minority stake in Sprint PCS, a provider of wireless "personal communications" services. A joint venture, @Home, offers high-speed cable modems and Internet access to cable subscribers. Direct broadcast satellite (DBS) operations include an investment in Primestar Partners.

Content consists largely of a 57% interest in QVC, an electronic retailing business. Comcast has a 50.1% ownership in a joint venture which owns 68.8% of E! Entertainment. Interests are also held in a number of cable TV program suppliers, including Viewer's Choice, The Golf Channel, Speedvision, Outdoor Life, Music Choice, Lightspan and the Sunshine Network.

Comcast-Spectacor owns 66% of the Philadelphia 76ers basketball team, the Philadelphia Flyers hockey team, and two sports arenas. In October 1997, the company launched Comcast-SportsNet, a 24-hour regional sports network.

Per Share Data ($)

(Year Ended Dec. 31)	1997	1996	1995	1994	1993	1992	1991	1990	1989	1988
Tangible Bk. Val.	NM	NM	NM	-3.04	-3.93	-0.89	0.10	-0.13	0.99	1.37
Cash Flow	2.10	2.61	2.72	1.11	1.13	0.07	0.05	-0.10	-0.09	0.07
Earnings	-0.66	-0.21	-0.16	-0.32	-0.46	-1.08	-0.87	-1.05	-0.93	-0.31
Dividends	0.09	0.09	0.09	0.09	0.09	0.09	0.09	0.08	0.06	0.05
Payout Ratio	NM	NM	NM	NM	NM	NM	NM	NM	NM	NM
Prices - High	33	21³/₈	22³/₈	24	28¹/₈	13¹/₈	12¹/₈	11³/₄	13¹/₄	8¹/₄
- Low	14⁵/₈	13³/₄	13³/₄	14	11⁵/₈	9	7¹/₄	5¹/₈	7¹/₄	5⁷/₈
P/E Ratio - High	NM	NM	NM	NM	NM	NM	NM	NM	NM	NM
- Low	NM	NM	NM	NM	NM	NM	NM	NM	NM	NM

Income Statement Analysis (Million $)

	1997	1996	1995	1994	1993	1992	1991	1990	1989	1988
Revs.	4,913	4,038	3,363	1,375	1,338	900	721	657	562	450
Oper. Inc.	1,469	1,207	1,019	576	606	397	309	271	224	123
Depr.	936	698	689	336	342	232	164	161	134	58.0
Int. Exp.	565	541	525	313	347	268	205	203	205	116
Pretax Inc.	-228	-16.1	-45.4	-85.0	-84.0	-157	-98.0	-144	-114	-39.0
Eff. Tax Rate	NM	NM	NM	NM	NM	NM	NM	NM	NM	NM
Net Inc.	-208	-52.5	-37.8	-75.0	-99.0	-217	-155	-177	-148	-48.0

Balance Sheet & Other Fin. Data (Million $)

	1997	1996	1995	1994	1993	1992	1991	1990	1989	1988
Cash	578	540	910	465	680	348	596	206	273	197
Curr. Assets	1,560	1,406	1,654	609	777	429	645	251	314	242
Total Assets	12,804	12,089	9,580	6,763	4,948	4,272	2,794	2,457	2,583	2,371
Curr. Liab.	1,418	1,365	1,122	661	595	392	264	187	157	122
LT Debt	6,559	7,103	6,944	4,811	4,163	3,974	2,165	2,002	1,998	1,811
Common Eqty.	1,101	520	-827	-726	-869	-181	19.0	-22.0	168	206
Total Cap.	10,317	9,796	6,116	5,475	3,292	3,792	2,472	2,226	2,376	2,197
Cap. Exp.	926	670	623	270	NA	NA	NA	92.0	90.0	99
Cash Flow	712	646	651	261	243	14.0	9.0	-17.0	-15.0	10.0
Curr. Ratio	1.1	1.0	1.5	0.9	1.3	1.1	2.4	1.3	2.0	2.0
% LT Debt of Cap.	63.4	72.5	113.5	87.9	126.4	104.8	87.6	89.9	84.1	82.4
% Net Inc.of Revs.	NM	NM	NM	NM	NM	NM	NM	NM	NM	NM
% Ret. on Assets	NM	NM	NM	NM	NM	NM	NM	NM	NM	NM
% Ret. on Equity	NM	NM	NM	NM	NM	NM	NM	NM	NM	NM

Data as orig. reptd.; bef. results of disc. opers. and/or spec. items. Per share data adj. for stk. divs. as of ex-div. date. Bold denotes diluted EPS (FASB 128). E-Estimated. NA-Not Available. NM-Not Meaningful. NR-Not Ranked.

Office—1500 Market St., Philadelphia, PA 19102-2148. **Tel**—(215) 665-1700. **Website**—http://www.comcast.com. **Chrmn**—R. J. Roberts. **Vice Chrmn**—J. A. Brodsky. **Pres**—B. L. Roberts. **SVP-Treas**—John R. Alchin. **SVP & Secy**—D. L. Wang. **Investor Contact**—Marlene Dooner (215-981-7537).**Dirs**—D. Aaron, G. G. Amsterdam, S. M. Bonovitz, J. A. Brodsky, J. L. Castle, B. L. Roberts, R. J. Roberts, B. C. Watson, I. A. Wechsler, A. Wexler. **Transfer Agent**—Bank of New York, NYC. **Incorporated**—in Pennsylvania in 1969. **Empl**— 17,600. **S&P Analyst:** William H. Donald

Comerica Inc. 591F

NYSE Symbol **CMA**

In S&P 500

12-SEP-98

Industry: Banks (Major Regional)

Summary: This Detroit-based bank holding company operates banking affiliates in Michigan, Texas, California and Florida.

S&P Opinion: Hold (★★★)

Recent Price • 56⅞	Yield • 2.3%
52 Wk Range • 73-50⅛	12-Mo. P/E • 16.4

Quantitative Evaluations

Outlook
(1 Lowest—5 Highest)
• **1+**

Fair Value
• **43¼**

Risk
• **Low**

Earn./Div. Rank
• **A**

Technical Eval.
• **Bearish** since 8/98

Rel. Strength Rank
(1 Lowest—99 Highest)
• **66**

Insider Activity
• **Neutral**

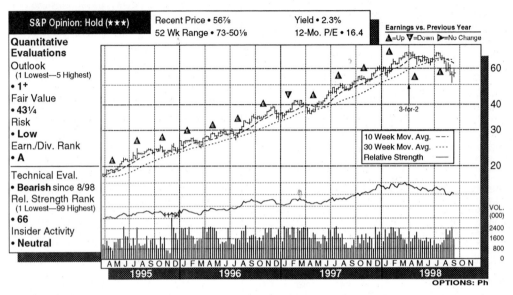

Earnings vs. Previous Year
▲=Up ▽=Down ▷=No Change

3-for-2

10 Week Mov. Avg. - - -
30 Week Mov. Avg. - - - -
Relative Strength ——

OPTIONS: Ph

Overview - 04-AUG-98

Reported loan growth in 1998 is likely to be relatively flat, as healthy commercial lending activity is offset by the recent sale of certain indirect consumer loans and credit card receivables. Net interest margins should remain in the 4.5% to 4.6% range, though some erosion from a less favorable asset mix following the consumer loan sale is possible in the near term. Reflecting a more conservative lending strategy, the loan loss provision will likely continue to exceed net charge-offs by a wide margin, leading to a build up of loss reserves. Noninterest income is expected to register ongoing gains in trust income and service charges. Overall, earnings growth should continue to benefit from improvements inherent in the Direction 2000 program, which is aimed at increasing efficiency and enhancing revenues.

Valuation - 04-AUG-98

The shares, up 10% in the first half of 1998, modestly lagged both the major regional bank average and the S&P 500 index. Nonetheless, the shares continue to trade at a premium valuation to other major regionals, at least in part due to speculation that the bank is a potential takeover target. However, with a current valuation of roughly four times the company's book value, a large takeover premium from current levels is unlikely. Fundamentally, we view the shares as fairly priced at 18 times our 1998 earnings estimate of $3.70 a share and would not commit to new positions at this time. The shares remain a good long-term value based on the company's diversified and growing service territory and strong credit quality.

Key Stock Statistics

S&P EPS Est. 1998	3.70	Tang. Bk. Value/Share	16.59
P/E on S&P Est. 1998	15.4	Beta	1.38
S&P EPS Est. 1999	4.15	Shareholders	17,500
Dividend Rate/Share	1.28	Market cap. (B)	$ 8.8
Shs. outstg. (M)	155.5	Inst. holdings	54%
Avg. daily vol. (M)	0.436		

Value of $10,000 invested 5 years ago: $ 31,804

Fiscal Year Ending Dec. 31

	1998	1997	1996	1995	1994	1993
Revenues (Million $)						
1Q	808.7	756.6	791.9	736.9	557.3	543.9
2Q	800.0	784.8	763.0	778.4	629.5	557.5
3Q	—	811.0	749.8	786.1	657.6	548.1
4Q	—	822.9	765.1	811.2	704.2	595.8
Yr.	—	3,175	3,070	3,113	2,559	2,245
Earnings Per Share ($)						
1Q	0.88	0.74	0.65	0.57	0.53	0.46
2Q	0.92	0.78	0.67	0.57	0.55	0.47
3Q	E0.93	0.83	0.69	0.61	0.56	0.47
4Q	E0.97	0.85	0.35	0.61	0.55	0.51
Yr.	E3.70	3.19	1.59	2.36	2.19	1.90

Next earnings report expected: mid October

Dividend Data (Dividends have been paid since 1936.)

Amount ($)	Date Decl.	Ex-Div. Date	Stock of Record	Payment Date
0.430	Nov. 21	Dec. 11	Dec. 15	Jan. 01 '98
0.320	May. 15	Jun. 11	Jun. 15	Jul. 01 '98
0.320	Jul. 17	Sep. 11	Sep. 15	Oct. 01 '98
3-for-2	Jan. 05	Apr. 02	Mar. 15	Apr. 01 '98

A Division of The McGraw-Hill Companies

Business Summary - 04-AUG-98

Comerica Inc. is a Detroit-based bank holding company that operates banking subsidiaries in Michigan, California, Texas and Florida, including a network of some 350 branch offices. For the past three years, the company has been focused on its Direction 2000 program, which is aimed at realigning and consolidating certain operations to better achieve financial performance targets. Phase III of the program, fully implemented as of the first quarter of 1998, is expected to reduce overhead costs and increase revenues, although the full effect will not be realized until 1999.

Operations are broadly divided into three lines of business: the Business Bank, the Individual Bank and the Investment Bank. The Business Bank is comprised of middle-market lending, asset-based lending, large corporate banking and international financial services. The Individual Bank includes consumer lending and deposit gathering, mortgage loan origination and servicing, small business banking and private banking. The Investment Bank is responsible for the sale of mutual fund and annuity products, as well as life, disability and

long-term care insurance products. Core businesses are tailored to each of the company's four primary geographic markets: Michigan, Texas, California and Florida.

In 1997, average earning assets, from which interest income is derived, amounted to $32.0 billion and consisted mainly of loans and leases (85%) and investment securities (15%). Average sources of funds, used in the lending business, included interest-bearing deposits (46%), noninterest-bearing deposits (17%), short-term borrowings (11%), long-term debt (17%), shareholders' equity (8%) and other (1%).

At year-end 1997, nonperforming assets, consisting primarily of nonaccrual loans and other real estate owned, were $103 million (0.36% of loans and related assets), down from $140 million (0.53%) a year earlier. The allowance for loan losses, which is set aside for possible loan defaults, was $424 million (1.47% of loans), versus $367 million (1.40%) a year earlier. Net chargeoffs, or the amount of loans actually written off as uncollectible, were $89 million (0.33% of average loans) in 1997, compared to $85 million (0.33%) in 1996.

Per Share Data ($)

(Year Ended Dec. 31)	1997	1996	1995	1994	1993	1992	1991	1990	1989	1988
Tangible Bk. Val.	16.02	14.70	15.17	12.21	12.66	10.31	9.01	8.52	7.55	7.43
Earnings	3.19	2.37	2.36	2.19	1.90	1.28	1.68	1.68	1.03	1.51
Dividends	1.15	1.01	0.91	0.83	0.71	0.64	0.61	0.58	0.51	0.42
Payout Ratio	36%	43%	39%	38%	38%	50%	37%	34%	49%	28%
Prices - High	61⅞	39⅝	28½	20⅞	23½	21⅞	17⅞	10⅞	13⅛	11½
- Low	34⅛	24⅛	16⅛	16⅛	16¾	17½	9¼	7⅛	10⅛	8¾
P/E Ratio - High	19	17	12	10	12	17	11	6	13	8
- Low	11	10	7	7	9	14	6	4	10	6

Income Statement Analysis (Million $)

	1997	1996	1995	1994	1993	1992	1991	1990	1989	1988
Net Int. Inc.	1,443	1,412	1,300	1,230	1,134	1,086	595	492	447	396
Tax Equiv. Adj.	9.0	15.0	21.0	24.1	30.0	37.3	21.0	24.3	24.5	26.8
Non Int. Inc.	522	493	487	463	463	395	182	158	134	126
Loan Loss Prov.	146	114	86.5	56.0	69.0	113	58.0	57.0	103	39.0
Exp./Op. Revs.	51%	56%	60%	62%	64%	70%	63%	63%	63%	61%
Pretax Inc.	817	646	626	582	489	313	217	171	96.0	148
Eff. Tax Rate	35%	35%	34%	33%	30%	28%	29%	25%	19%	24%
Net Inc.	530	417	413	387	341	226	153	128	78.0	112
% Net Int. Marg.	4.53	4.54	4.19	4.32	4.65	4.75	4.87	4.59	4.54	4.46

Balance Sheet & Other Fin. Data (Million $)

	1997	1996	1995	1994	1993	1992	1991	1990	1989	1988
Earning Assets:										
Money Mkt	203	65.5	238	429	2,122	1,481	722	706	666	1,421
Inv. Securities	4,006	4,800	6,859	7,876	6,300	4,749	3,115	3,145	2,519	1,841
Com'l Loans	16,323	13,926	12,371	10,892	9,296	8,184	4,049	4,638	4,349	3,327
Other Loans	12,572	12,281	12,071	11,408	9,804	9,859	5,464	3,833	3,721	3,711
Total Assets	36,292	34,206	35,470	33,430	30,295	26,587	14,451	13,300	12,150	11,146
Demand Deposits	6,761	6,713	5,580	5,257	4,939	4,366	1,920	1,806	1,742	1,670
Time Deposits	15,825	15,654	17,587	17,175	16,011	16,029	9,521	8,949	8,141	7,580
LT Debt	7,286	4,242	4,644	1,742	1,461	737	239	264	274	276
Common Eqty.	2,512	2,366	2,608	2,392	2,182	1,988	1,010	749	663	595
% Ret. on Assets	1.5	1.2	1.2	1.2	1.3	0.9	1.1	1.1	0.7	1.1
% Ret. on Equity	21.1	16.4	16.5	16.7	15.9	12.0	16.6	17.8	12.0	19.2
% Loan Loss Resv.	1.5	1.4	1.4	1.5	1.6	1.6	1.3	1.3	2.5	1.8
% Loans/Deposits	127.9	117.2	105.5	99.4	91.2	88.5	81.9	77.6	80.4	74.8
% Equity to Assets	6.9	7.1	7.3	7.3	7.8	7.3	6.6	5.8	5.5	5.4

Data as orig. reptd.; bef. results of disc opers. and/or spec. items. Per share data adj. for stk. divs. as of ex-div. date. Bold denotes diluted EPS (FASB 128). E-Estimated. NA-Not Available. NM-Not Meaningful. NR-Not Ranked.

Office—Comerica Tower at Detroit Center, 500 Woodward Ave., Detroit, MI 48226. **Tel**—(313) 222-3300. **Website**—http://www.comerica.com **Chrmn & CEO**—E. A. Miller.**Vice Chrmn**—J. D. Lewis. **Pres**—M. T. Monahan. **Exec VP & CFO**—R. W. Babb Jr.**Investor Contact**—Allison T. McFerren (313) 222-6317. **Dirs**—E. P. Casey, J. F. Cordes, J. P. DiNapoli, M. M. Fisher, J. D. Lewis, P. Shontz Longe, W. B. Lyon, G. V. MacDonald, E. A. Miller, M. T. Monahan, A. A. Piergallini, H. F. Sims, M. D. Walker.**Transfer Agent & Registrar**—Norwest Shareowner Services, St. Paul. **Incorporated**—in Delaware in 1972.**Empl**— 10,877. **S&P Analyst:** Stephen R. Biggar

12-SEP-98

Industry: Computers (Hardware)

Summary: Compaq is the second largest computer company and the leading manufacturer of desktop and portable computers and PC servers. It recently acquired Digital Equipment Corp.

S&P Opinion: Accumulate (★★★★)	Recent Price • 31⅞	Yield • 0.2%
	52 Wk Range • 39¾-23⅛	12-Mo. P/E • NM

Quantitative Evaluations

Outlook (1 Lowest—5 Highest)
• **3⁻**

Fair Value
• **33¼**

Risk
• **Average**

Earn./Div. Rank
• **B**

Technical Eval.
• **Bullish** since 7/98

Rel. Strength Rank (1 Lowest—99 Highest)
• **89**

Insider Activity
• **Neutral**

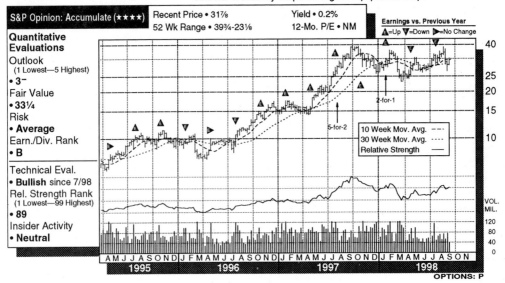

Earnings vs. Previous Year
▲=Up ▼=Down ▶=No Change

2-for-1

5-for-2

10 Week Mov. Avg. -- -
30 Week Mov. Avg. ·······
Relative Strength ——

VOL. MIL.

OPTIONS: P

Overview - 21-JUL-98

We project revenues of some $33 billion for CPQ in 1998, benefiting from its combination with Digital Equipment, effective June 11, 1998. Through the second quarter, revenues were under pressure as CPQ worked off an inventory buildup. However, we believe that underlying demand remains robust for CPQ's personal computers (PCs) and PC Servers, and that results should benefit in the second half as CPQ optimizes its distribution model. Upside to our estimates could come from better than expected synergies between CPQ's leading share in computing hardware and Digital's strong services capabilities. We expect CPQ to focus on aggressively reducing overhead and redundancies, but savings from the combination are not expected to materialize until the fourth quarter. We caution investors that risk to our 1998 estimate of $0.60 (before nonrecurring charges) includes issues that may arise in Compaq's relationship with channel partners and the integration of Digital's and CPQ's sales forces.

Valuation - 21-JUL-98

We continue to recommend accumulating the shares. CPQ's strong revenue growth and asset management were impressive in 1997, and while 1998 first half results showed limited revenue growth, we believe that CPQ remains one of the best positioned companies to capitalize on the PC industry's 15% to 20% projected growth. Moreover, through the acquisition of Digital Equipment, CPQ can now compete for the largest computing customers, utilizing Digital's global sales and service capabilities and high end UNIX operating system. While the benefits of the largest merger in the computer industry's history may take some time to be fully realized, CPQ's strong track record of streamlining operations and effective execution should help CPQ shares outperform the market.

Key Stock Statistics

S&P EPS Est. 1998	0.60	Tang. Bk. Value/Share	6.20
P/E on S&P Est. 1998	53.1	Beta	1.13
S&P EPS Est. 1999	1.70	Shareholders	8,700
Dividend Rate/Share	0.06	Market cap. (B)	$ 53.3
Shs. outstg. (M)	1671.0	Inst. holdings	42%
Avg. daily vol. (M)	14.427		

Value of $10,000 invested 5 years ago: $ 98,261

Fiscal Year Ending Dec. 31

	1998	1997	1996	1995	1994	1993
Revenues (Million $)						
1Q	5,687	5,272	4,205	2,959	2,278	1,611
2Q	5,832	5,515	4,001	3,501	2,499	1,632
3Q	—	6,474	4,481	3,594	2,838	1,746
4Q	—	7,323	5,422	4,701	3,251	2,202
Yr.	—	24,584	18,109	14,755	10,866	7,191
Earnings Per Share ($)						
1Q	**0.01**	**0.27**	0.17	0.16	0.16	0.08
2Q	**-2.33**	**0.17**	0.19	0.18	0.16	0.08
3Q	**E0.18**	**0.33**	0.25	0.18	0.15	0.08
4Q	**E0.39**	**0.43**	0.33	0.06	0.18	0.12
Yr.	**E0.60**	**1.19**	**0.87**	0.58	0.65	0.36

Next earnings report expected: mid October

Dividend Data (Dividends have been paid since 1998.)

Amount ($)	Date Decl.	Ex-Div. Date	Stock of Record	Payment Date
0.015	Oct. 16	Dec. 29	Dec. 31	Jan. 20 '98
2-for-1	Oct. 16	Jan. 21	Dec. 31	Jan. 20 '98
0.015	Mar. 12	Mar. 27	Mar. 31	Apr. 20 '98
0.015	Jun. 12	Jun. 26	Jun. 30	Jul. 20 '98

STANDARD
&POOR'S
STOCK REPORTS

Compaq Computer Corporation

596C

12-SEP-98

Business Summary - 21-JUL-98

On June 11, 1998, in a move to gain the second position in the computing industry, Compaq acquired Digital Equipment Corp. (DEC) in a cash and stock transaction valued at about $8 billion, making it the largest acquisition in computer industry history. DEC, with revenues of $13 billion in FY 97 (Jun.), provides CPQ with a global service organization and a high-end 64-bit UNIX offering. The transaction, accounted for under purchase accounting, is expected to be accretive to CPQ earnings per share by the fourth quarter of 1998.

While the Digital acquisition makes Compaq the number two computer company worldwide, Compaq remains the leader in worldwide market share in the market for personal computers and servers. CPQ products are sold and supported in more than 100 countries through a broad network of CPQ authorized partners.

CPQ continues to be a revolutionary in the PC industry. In 1997, CPQ basically introduced the sub-$1,000 price point to the PC market. These PCs include attractive features and CPQ has been able to meet these competitive price points partly because of lower component prices but also as a result of new manufacturing efficiencies yielded through its new manufacturing strategy, BTO (Build To Order). This strategy is part of a larger, new business model CPQ launched, called ODM (Optimized Distribution Model), to offer customers better

support and services at better prices, to compete head-to-head with direct-seller Dell Computer.

The Digital acquisition furthers CPQ's goal of increasing its presence in the enterprise market for computers, and complements its 1997 acquisition of Tandem Computer, a leader in complex enterprise-class networks. Prior to these acquisitions, CPQ had broadened its product offering to this market, and introduced new clustering and internetworking solutions. In 1996, CPQ entered the workstation market with its Professional Workstation line, featuring Intel's Pentium Pro (and now also Pentium II) processor and Windows NT operating system.

Under its Presario line, CPQ offers consumers and home office users PCs rich with multimedia capabilities.

CPQ also has offerings in the fast-growing networking products arena. CPQ's Internetworking Products Group includes NetWorth Inc. (acquired in 1995), a provider of Fast Ethernet networking products, and Thomas-Conrad Corp., a maker of network interface cards and hubs. In 1997, Compaq centered its efforts on its Netelligent product line in developing switches, repeaters and options that lower the cost and complexity of migrating from Ethernet to Fast Ethernet. CPQ has in the past targeted its networking products at smaller businesses and work groups in larger corporations, but the addition of Microcom (acquired in 1997) also added WAN (wide area network) products through Microcom's modem and remote access technology.

Per Share Data ($)

(Year Ended Dec. 31)	1997	1996	1995	1994	1993	1992	1991	1990	1989	1988
Tangible Bk. Val.	6.21	4.49	3.46	2.81	2.10	1.68	1.53	1.44	0.99	0.70
Cash Flow	1.53	1.15	0.73	0.77	0.49	0.30	0.22	0.44	0.32	0.24
Earnings	1.19	0.94	0.58	0.65	0.36	0.17	0.10	0.34	0.26	0.21
Dividends	0.02	Nil	Nil	Nil	Nil	Nil	Nil	Nil	Nil	Nil
Payout Ratio	2%	Nil	Nil	Nil	Nil	Nil	Nil	Nil	Nil	Nil
Prices - High	39¾	17⅜	11⅜	8⅜	5	3⅜	5	4½	3¾	2⁹⁄₁₆
- Low	14¼	7⅛	6¼	4⅞	2¾	1½	1½	2⅜	2	1⅜
P/E Ratio - High	34	18	20	13	14	19	50	13	14	12
- Low	12	8	11	7	8	9	15	7	8	7

Income Statement Analysis (Million $)

	1997	1996	1995	1994	1993	1992	1991	1990	1989	1988
Revs.	24,584	18,109	14,755	10,866	7,191	4,100	3,271	3,599	2,876	2,066
Oper. Inc.	3,532	2,162	1,738	1,434	847	482	469	784	573	408
Depr.	545	285	214	168	155	159	164	135	84.0	48.0
Int. Exp.	168	91.0	106	74.0	63.0	47.5	43.9	54.9	46.8	27.7
Pretax Inc.	2,758	1,876	1,188	1,172	616	311	174	671	498	375
Eff. Tax Rate	33%	30%	34%	26%	25%	31%	25%	32%	33%	32%
Net Inc.	1,855	1,313	789	867	462	213	131	455	333	255

Balance Sheet & Other Fin. Data (Million $)

	1997	1996	1995	1994	1993	1992	1991	1990	1989	1988
Cash	6,418	3,993	745	471	627	357	452	435	161	281
Curr. Assets	12,017	9,169	6,527	5,158	3,291	2,319	1,783	1,688	1,312	1,115
Total Assets	14,631	10,526	7,818	6,166	4,084	3,142	2,826	2,718	2,090	1,590
Curr. Liab.	5,202	3,852	2,680	2,013	1,244	960	639	644	564	480
LT Debt	Nil	300	300	300	Nil	Nil	73.0	73.0	274	275
Common Eqty.	9,429	6,144	4,614	3,674	2,654	2,007	1,931	1,859	1,172	815
Total Cap.	9,429	6,674	5,138	4,153	2,840	2,183	2,188	2,074	1,526	1,110
Cap. Exp.	729	342	391	357	145	159	160	325	362	286
Cash Flow	2,400	1,598	1,003	1,035	617	372	295	590	417	304
Curr. Ratio	2.3	2.4	2.4	2.6	2.6	2.4	2.8	2.6	2.3	2.3
% LT Debt of Cap.	Nil	4.5	5.8	7.2	Nil	Nil	3.3	3.5	17.9	24.8
% Net Inc.of Revs.	7.5	7.3	5.3	8.0	6.4	5.2	4.0	12.6	11.6	12.4
% Ret. on Assets	14.7	14.5	11.3	16.7	12.5	7.3	4.8	18.2	18.0	19.6
% Ret. on Equity	23.8	24.4	19.0	27.0	19.4	11.1	7.0	28.9	33.3	40.3

Data as orig. reptd.; bef. results of disc. opers. and/or spec. items. Per share data adj. for stk. divs. as ex-div. date. Bold denotes diluted EPS (FASB 128). E-Estimated. NA-Not Available. NM-Not Meaningful. NR-Not Ranked.

Office—20555 SH 249, Houston, TX 77070. **Tel**—(713) 370-0670. **Website**— http://www.compaq.com **Pres & CEO**—E. Pfeiffer. **SVP-Fin & CFO**—E. Mason. **SVP & Secy**—J. D. Cabello. **Dirs**—B. M. Rosen (Chrmn), L. T. Babbio, R. T. Enloe III, G. H. Heilmeier, G. E. R. Kinnear II, P. N. Larson, K. L. Lay, T. J. Perkins, E. Pfeiffer, K. Roman, L. Salhany. **Transfer Agents & Registrars**—Co. itself; BancBoston Trust Co. of New York. **Incorporated**—in Delaware in 1982. **Empl**— 31,627. **S&P Analyst:** Megan Graham Hackett

STANDARD &POOR'S
STOCK REPORTS

Computer Associates Int'l **597**

NYSE Symbol **CA**

In S&P 500

12-SEP-98

Industry:
Computer (Software & Services)

Summary: This company develops, markets and supports standardized software products, including systems software, database management systems and applications software.

S&P Opinion: Accumulate (★★★★)

Recent Price • 30⅝	Yield • 0.3%
52 Wk Range • 61⅞-26	12-Mo. P/E • 33.7

Quantitative Evaluations

Outlook
(1 Lowest—5 Highest)
• 4

Fair Value
• 40½

Risk
• Average

Earn./Div. Rank
• B+

Technical Eval.
• **Bearish** since 7/98

Rel. Strength Rank
(1 Lowest—99 Highest)
• 26

Insider Activity
• Neutral

Earnings vs. Previous Year
▲=Up ▼=Down ▶=No Change

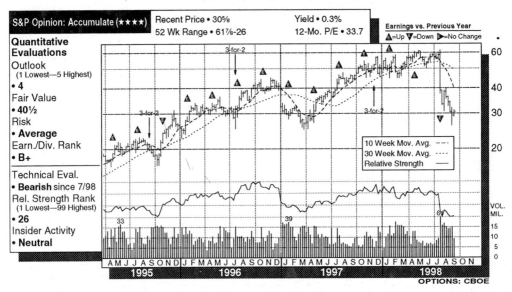

10 Week Mov. Avg. — - —
30 Week Mov. Avg. - - - -
Relative Strength ——

OPTIONS: CBOE

Overview - 28-JUL-98

We are lowering our revenue projection for FY 99 (Mar.), as we expect continued strong growth in the company's client/server revenues to be somewhat offset by slower mainframe revenues. CA is making a product transition from the slower growth mainframe software market to faster growing client/server software products. Its flagship product, Unicenter TNG, the company's popular systems management offering, is exhibiting strong momentum. Client/server revenues continue to show strength, with a 35% increase in the most recent quarter, while mainframe revenues rose 3%. Service revenues could add to revenue growth, although they may hamper continued margin improvement. FY 98 comparisons benefited from the absence of a FY 97 charge of $598 million ($1.61 a share) related to the acquisition of Cheyenne Software.

Valuation - 28-JUL-98

The share price fell sharply in July, after CA reported strong results but warned that revenue growth may slow for the remainder of the year. Although less than 5% of revenues come from Asia, some large multinational customers with Asian exposure are becoming more cautious in their spending. In addition, some customers may defer spending on new technologies until they resolve their Year 2000 problems. Nevertheless, we remain positive on the company's long-term growth prospects. CA's new services segment should provide significant revenues, as it expands this group internally and through strategic acquisitions. For the longer term, the new Jasmine object database could provide a lucrative revenue stream. The flagship systems management product, Unicenter TNG, continues to gain momentum. Its successor version, Unicenter TND, will be introduced in 1999.

Key Stock Statistics

S&P EPS Est. 1999	2.31	Tang. Bk. Value/Share	2.99
P/E on S&P Est. 1999	13.3	Beta	1.42
S&P EPS Est. 2000	2.68	Shareholders	8,500
Dividend Rate/Share	0.08	Market cap. (B)	$ 17.2
Shs. outstg. (M)	561.3	Inst. holdings	52%
Avg. daily vol. (M)	2.859		

Value of $10,000 invested 5 years ago: $ 51,791

Fiscal Year Ending Mar. 31

	1999	1998	1997	1996	1995	1994
Revenues (Million $)						
1Q	1,047	890.7	792.1	577.5	476.6	423.4
2Q	—	1,122	990.1	812.3	623.3	517.0
3Q	—	1,239	1,053	1,004	721.0	574.4
4Q	—	1,467	1,205	1,110	802.0	633.7
Yr.	—	4,719	4,040	3,505	2,623	2,148
Earnings Per Share ($)						
1Q	-0.87	0.28	0.21	0.16	-0.16	0.05
2Q	E0.51	0.48	0.39	-1.17	0.23	0.15
3Q	E0.63	0.60	-0.57	0.40	0.31	0.21
4Q	E0.81	0.71	0.61	0.47	0.38	0.28
Yr.	E2.31	2.06	0.65	-0.10	0.76	0.69

Next earnings report expected: late October

Dividend Data (Dividends have been paid since 1990.)

Amount ($)	Date Decl.	Ex-Div. Date	Stock of Record	Payment Date
3-for-2	Oct. 21	Nov. 28	Nov. 05	Nov. 26 '97
0.040	Dec. 15	Dec. 17	Dec. 19	Jan. 05 '98
0.040	May. 19	Jun. 17	Jun. 19	Jul. 07 '98

A Division of The **McGraw·Hill** Companies

Business Summary - 28-JUL-98

Computer Associates International designs, develops and markets more than 500 enterprise systems management, information management and business applications software solutions to a broad spectrum of organizations.

Systems management software enables customers to more efficiently utilize data processing hardware, software and personnel resources, by providing tools to measure and improve computer performance and programmer productivity. In FY 97 (Mar.), CA released its latest systems management platform, Unicenter TNG (The Next Generation), an object-oriented solution that lets organizations visualize and control their entire information technology infrastructure. The next version, Unicenter TND (The Next Dimension) will be introduced in 1999. This version will include a time element that can not only look back in time, but can help predict potential system problems in the future.

The company's new Harmony strategy integrates three major information management products. Jasmine, introduced in FY 98, is a pure object-oriented database that provides the foundation to store, manage, and maintain multimedia and business objects. Ingres is CA's more traditional relational database offering. Opal

helps customers modernize existing applications by migrating from older legacy mainframe solutions to newer, more modern applications.

Business management applications are used in financial, human resource, manufacturing, distribution and banking applications systems.

In 1998, CA introduced CA-Fix/2000, an automated date correction tool that helps companies tackle their Year 2000-related problems.

In the first quarter of FY 99, the company recorded a $1.1 billion charge for stock issuance under a 1995 executive compensation plan.

In early 1998, CA made an unsuccessful bid to acquire Computer Sciences Corp. for about $9 billion. The company then started its own services organization, which it plans to expand internally and through selective acquisitions.

In the third quarter of FY 97, the company recorded a charge of $598 million ($1.61 a share), related to the acquisition of Cheyenne Software, a leading vendor of storage management software and provider of antivirus and communications software products.

In August 1995, CA acquired Legent Corp., which provides a broad range of computer software products for the management of information systems across several platforms and operating systems.

Per Share Data ($)

(Year Ended Mar. 31)	1998	1997	1996	1995	1994	1993	1992	1991	1990	1989
Tangible Bk. Val.	2.53	0.95	1.28	2.36	1.89	1.43	1.32	1.67	1.48	1.21
Cash Flow	2.68	2.08	0.64	1.18	1.03	0.76	0.51	0.43	0.42	0.45
Earnings	2.06	0.65	-0.10	0.76	0.69	0.43	0.27	0.25	0.25	0.30
Dividends	0.07	0.06	0.06	0.04	0.04	0.03	0.03	0.03	Nil	Nil
Payout Ratio	3%	10%	NM	5%	6%	7%	11%	12%	Nil	Nil
Cal. Yrs.	1997	1996	1995	1994	1993	1992	1991	1990	1989	1988
Prices - High	57½	45¼	31⅜	15⅛	13⅛	6⅛	3½	5	6½	4⅞
- Low	24⅞	22½	13⅞	8⅛	6	3¼	1⅞	1⁵/₁₆	3⅛	3½
P/E Ratio - High	28	70	NM	20	19	14	13	20	26	16
- Low	12	35	NM	11	9	8	7	5	12	12

Income Statement Analysis (Million $)

Revs.	4,719	4,040	3,505	2,623	2,148	1,841	1,509	1,348	1,296	1,030
Oper. Inc.	2,366	2,056	1,678	1,190	821	579	405	364	369	345
Depr.	349	424	404	236	192	191	144	109	107	79.0
Int. Exp.	147	104	81.0	23.6	13.1	16.9	9.8	6.2	8.0	10.2
Pretax Inc.	1,874	932	-100	697	627	384	267	261	236	268
Eff. Tax Rate	38%	61%	NM	38%	36%	36%	39%	39%	33%	39%
Net Inc.	1,169	366	-56.0	432	401	246	163	159	158	164

Balance Sheet & Other Fin. Data (Million $)

Cash	251	143	201	301	368	229	282	248	110	53.0
Curr. Assets	2,255	1,780	1,448	1,148	999	869	904	888	725	528
Total Assets	6,706	6,084	5,016	3,269	2,492	2,349	2,169	1,599	1,453	1,167
Curr. Liab.	1,876	1,727	1,501	848	549	528	593	361	329	285
LT Debt	1,027	1,663	945	50.0	71.0	167	41.0	25.0	26.0	44.0
Common Eqty.	2,481	1,503	1,482	1,578	1,243	1,055	988	1,090	990	748
Total Cap.	4,460	4,019	3,148	2,089	1,613	1,478	1,255	1,238	1,124	882
Cap. Exp.	84.0	41.4	21.0	35.0	29.0	22.2	15.1	19.2	22.8	22.4
Cash Flow	1,518	790	348	668	593	437	307	268	265	243
Curr. Ratio	1.2	1.0	1.0	1.4	1.8	1.6	1.5	2.5	2.2	1.9
% LT Debt of Cap.	23.0	43.0	30.0	2.4	4.4	11.3	3.3	2.0	2.3	5.0
% Net Inc.of Revs.	24.8	9.1	NM	16.5	18.7	13.3	10.8	11.8	12.2	15.9
% Ret. on Assets	18.3	6.6	NM	15.1	16.8	11.2	8.7	10.6	11.5	15.9
% Ret. on Equity	58.7	24.5	NM	30.9	35.4	24.7	15.9	15.5	17.3	25.6

Data as orig. reptd.; bef. results of disc. opers. and/or spec. items. Per share data adj. for stk. divs. as of ex-div. date. Bold denotes diluted EPS (FASB 128). E-Estimated. NA-Not Available. NM-Not Meaningful. NR-Not Ranked.

Office—One Computer Associates Plaza, Islandia, NY 11788. **Tel**—(516) 342-5224. **Website**—http://www.cai.com **Chrmn & CEO**—C. B. Wang. **Pres**—S. Kumar. **SVP & CFO**—P. A. Schwartz. **SVP & Secy**—B. A. Frease. **SVP & Treas**—I. Zar. **Investor Contact**—Douglas Robinson. **Dirs**—R. M. Artzt, I. Goldstein, R. A. Grasso, S. S. Kenny, S. Kumar, E. C. Lord III, G. E. Martinelli, W. F. P. de Vogel, C. B. Wang. **Transfer Agent**—ChaseMellon Shareholder Services, Ridgefield Park, NJ. **Incorporated**—in Delaware in 1974. **Empl**— 11,400. **S&P Analyst:** Brian Goodstadt

12-SEP-98

Industry:
Computer (Software & Services)

Summary: This leading vendor in the computer services industry provides management consulting, systems development, integration and operations, and other information technology services.

S&P Opinion: Accumulate (★★★★)

Recent Price • 65
52 Wk Range • 70-33⅝

Yield • Nil
12-Mo. P/E • 38.0

Quantitative Evaluations

Outlook
(1 Lowest—5 Highest)
• **3⁻**

Fair Value
• **64¼**

Risk
• **Average**

Earn./Div. Rank
• **B+**

Technical Eval.
• **Bullish** since 11/97

Rel. Strength Rank
(1 Lowest—99 Highest)
• **97**

Insider Activity
• **Neutral**

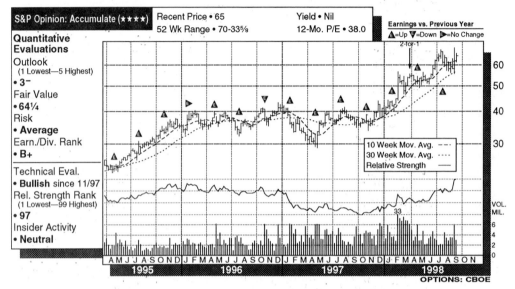

Earnings vs. Previous Year
▲=Up ▼=Down ▷=No Change

10 Week Mov. Avg. ---
30 Week Mov. Avg. ....
Relative Strength ——

VOL. MIL.

OPTIONS: CBOE

Overview - 31-JUL-98

Revenue growth should accelerate in FY 99 (Mar.), following 18% growth in FY 98. Revenues are expected to advance 18% to 20% in FY 99, aided by internal growth and acquisitions. The company has made more than 50 acquisitions since 1986. Commercial revenues have risen to over 75% of total revenues, and should continue to be boosted by strong consulting and systems integration outsourcing. CSC is also addressing new business opportunities in the federal market. Margins are expected to widen on the higher volume, a better product mix, and well controlled costs. Earnings should benefit from the higher revenues and expected improvement in margins. Fourth quarter FY 98 EPS included a charge of $20.7 million ($0.09 a share) related to the company's response to a failed takeover attempt by Computer Associates.

Valuation - 31-JUL-98

The shares of this leading computer services company climbed sharply after Computer Associates (CA) bid to acquire CSC for $54 a share (adjusted), but fell after CA dropped its bid. Now free of the hostile offer, CSC can pursue its own strong growth prospects. As a result, the stock has rebounded strongly. CSC's earnings are highly predictable, aided by a visible revenue stream associated with multi-year contracts. Selective acquisitions should continue to strengthen the company's competitive position. We believe that CSC should benefit from the vast market for fixing Year 2000 computer problems. Demand is also strengthened by growing markets for client/server, electronic commerce, data warehousing and enterprise resource planning solutions. The stock merits a premium valuation in light of the strong, predictable and accelerating sales and earnings growth that we project.

Key Stock Statistics

S&P EPS Est. 1999	2.09	Tang. Bk. Value/Share	9.86
P/E on S&P Est. 1999	31.1	Beta	1.02
S&P EPS Est. 2000	2.70	Shareholders	10,900
Dividend Rate/Share	Nil	Market cap. (B)	$ 10.3
Shs. outstg. (M)	157.9	Inst. holdings	70%
Avg. daily vol. (M)	0.837		

Value of $10,000 invested 5 years ago: $ 49,840

Fiscal Year Ending Mar. 31

	1999	1998	1997	1996	1995	1994
Revenues (Million $)						
1Q	1,754	1,489	1,304	966.8	738.1	608.1
2Q	—	1,579	1,355	1,005	788.5	622.3
3Q	—	1,664	1,422	1,110	827.9	621.4
4Q	—	1,869	1,535	1,161	1,018	730.9
Yr.	—	6,601	5,616	4,242	3,373	2,583
Earnings Per Share ($)						
1Q	0.40	0.33	0.29	0.24	0.21	0.18
2Q	E0.46	0.37	0.09	0.27	0.22	0.18
3Q	E0.54	0.43	0.36	0.32	0.32	0.21
4Q	E0.70	0.50	0.48	0.41	0.36	0.32
Yr.	E2.09	1.64	1.23	1.24	1.04	0.89

Next earnings report expected: late October

Dividend Data (Dividends have been paid since 1998.)

Amount ($)	Date Decl.	Ex-Div. Date	Stock of Record	Payment Date
2-for-1	Feb. 02	Mar. 24	Mar. 02	Mar. 23 '98
0.002	Mar. 04	Mar. 26	Mar. 30	Apr. 13 '98

A Division of The McGraw·Hill Companies

Business Summary - 31-JUL-98

Computer Sciences is one of the largest computer services companies in the U.S., providing a variety of information technology consulting, systems integration and outsourcing to industry and government. The company expects robust worldwide demand to continue in each of these segments over the next few years.

In the U.S. commercial market (42% of FY 98 revenues, versus 39% in FY 97), CSC provides outsourcing services, including systems analysis, applications development, network operations, and desktop and data center management. The company also provides consulting and technical services in the development and integration of computer and communications systems. In FY 98 (Mar.), CSC entered into a technology alliance with DuPont, under which CSC now operates DuPont's global information systems and technology infrastructure and provides selected applications and software services.

The company's international operations (33%; 32%), with major offices in eight countries, provide a wide range of information technology services to commercial and public sector clients. Services include consulting and professional services, systems integration and outsourcing.

Serving the U.S. federal government market (25%; 29%) for more than three decades, the company provides IT services, such as the development of software for mission-critical systems for defense and civil agency applications. CSC also provides systems engineering and technical assistance in network management, satellite communications, intelligence, aerospace, logistics and related high-technology fields.

CSC has formed groups that focus on specific technical solutions, including CSC Lynx, a framework for rapid systems development; data warehousing; electronic commerce; enterprise resource planning; information security; supply chain management; and Year 2000 compliance.

In the second quarter of FY 97, the company recorded a charge of $48,929,000 ($0.45 a share) for expenses and write-offs related to the acquisition of The Continuum Co., Inc., an international consulting and computer services firm. As adjusted for its March 1996 acquisition of Hogan Systems, Continuum had pro forma revenues of about $490 million in the 12 months ended December 31, 1995.

In the fourth quarter of FY 98, Computer Associates dropped a bid to acquire the company. CSC recorded a charge of $20.7 million ($0.09 a share), related to the company's response to the takeover attempt.

Per Share Data ($)

(Year Ended Mar. 31)	1998	1997	1996	1995	1994	1993	1992	1991	1990	1989
Tangible Bk. Val.	9.32	7.23	7.68	6.18	4.46	3.83	2.94	3.26	2.99	2.93
Cash Flow	4.08	3.36	3.58	2.67	2.15	1.96	1.51	1.08	1.03	0.87
Earnings	1.64	1.23	1.24	1.04	0.89	0.78	0.69	0.67	0.68	0.55
Dividends	0.00	Nil	Nil	Nil	Nil	Nil	Nil	Nil	Nil	Nil
Payout Ratio	NM	Nil	Nil	Nil	Nil	Nil	Nil	Nil	Nil	Nil
Cal. Yrs.	1997	1996	1995	1994	1993	1992	1991	1990	1989	1988
Prices - High	43$7/8$	43$1/4$	37$5/8$	26$3/8$	16$3/4$	14	13$1/2$	9$5/8$	9$3/4$	9
- Low	29	32$1/8$	23$1/4$	15$7/8$	11$3/4$	9$1/2$	8	6$1/8$	7$3/4$	6$3/8$
P/E Ratio - High	27	35	30	25	19	18	20	14	14	16
- Low	18	26	19	15	13	12	12	9	11	12

Income Statement Analysis (Million $)

Revs.	6,601	5,616	4,242	3,373	2,583	2,480	2,113	1,738	1,500	1,304
Oper. Inc.	849	718	514	376	291	263	210	146	130	119
Depr.	387	333	252	173	131	119	81.7	40.2	34.0	31.1
Int. Exp.	51.0	40.3	35.0	28.8	17.2	20.5	21.2	14.0	11.7	8.1
Pretax Inc.	191	303	231	174	149	128	109	104	105	86.0
Eff. Tax Rate	NM	37%	39%	36%	39%	39%	38%	36%	36%	37%
Net Inc.	260	192	142	111	90.9	78.1	68.2	65.0	65.5	52.5

Balance Sheet & Other Fin. Data (Million $)

Cash	275	110	105	155	127	155	130	137	119	76.0
Curr. Assets	1,983	1,612	1,144	1,082	857	748	666	618	557	428
Total Assets	4,047	3,581	2,596	2,334	1,806	1,454	1,375	1,007	918	715
Curr. Liab.	1,215	1,087	760	778	661	445	401	355	343	245
LT Debt	736	631	405	310	273	295	349	109	108	75.0
Common Eqty.	2,001	1,670	1,306	1,149	806	695	607	526	458	389
Total Cap.	2,737	2,416	1,783	1,511	1,115	991	956	635	566	464
Cap. Exp.	349	322	260	193	119	95.4	52.7	27.0	33.8	39.4
Cash Flow	647	526	394	283	222	197	150	105	100	84.0
Curr. Ratio	1.6	1.5	1.5	1.4	1.3	1.7	1.7	1.7	1.6	1.7
% LT Debt of Cap.	26.9	26.1	22.7	20.5	24.5	29.8	36.5	17.1	19.1	16.2
% Net Inc.of Revs.	3.9	3.4	3.3	3.3	3.5	3.2	3.2	3.7	4.4	4.0
% Ret. on Assets	6.8	5.9	5.7	5.1	5.5	5.5	5.7	6.7	8.0	7.6
% Ret. on Equity	14.2	12.5	11.5	10.9	12.0	11.9	11.9	13.1	15.4	14.5

Data as orig. reptd.; bef. results of disc. opers. and/or spec. items. Per share data adj. for stk. divs. as of ex-div. date. Bold denotes diluted EPS (FASB 128). E-Estimated. NA-Not Available. NM-Not Meaningful. NR-Not Ranked.

Office—2100 E. Grand Ave., El Segundo, CA 90245. **Tel**—(310) 615-0311. **Website**—http://www.csc.com **Chrmn**—W. R. Hoover.**Pres & CEO**—V. B. Honeycutt. **VP & CFO**—L. J. Level. **VP & Secy**—H. D. Fisk. **Investor Contact**—Spencer Davis.**Dirs**—H. P. Allen, I. W. Bailey II, V. B. Honeycutt, W. R. Hoover, R. C. Lawton, L. J. Level, T. A. McDonnell, F. W. McFarlan, J. R. Mellor, W. P. Rutledge. **Transfer Agent & Registrar**—ChaseMellon Shareholder Services, NYC. **Incorporated**—in Nevada in 1959. **Empl**— 45,000. **S&P Analyst:** Brian Goodstadt

12-SEP-98   Industry: Foods

Summary: ConAgra is the largest independent U.S. food processor, with interests in branded dry grocery and frozen food products, processed meats, flour milling, and grain merchandising.

S&P Opinion: Hold (★★★)

Recent Price • 27	Yield • 2.3%
52 Wk Range • 38¾-22½	12-Mo. P/E • 19.9

Quantitative Evaluations

Outlook
(1 Lowest—5 Highest)
• **3**

Fair Value
• **28½**

Risk
• **Low**

Earn./Div. Rank
• **A+**

Technical Eval.
• **Bullish** since 7/98

Rel. Strength Rank
(1 Lowest—99 Highest)
• **92**

Insider Activity
• **Neutral**

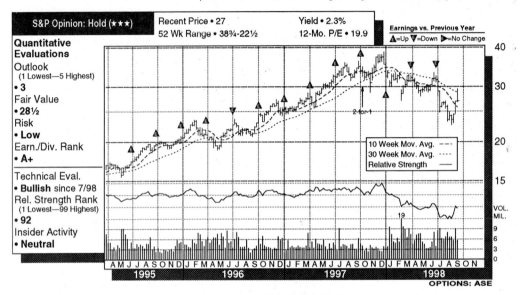

Earnings vs. Previous Year
▲=Up ▼=Down ▶=No Change

10 Week Mov. Avg. ‑ ‑ ‑
30 Week Mov. Avg. ·····
Relative Strength —

OPTIONS: ASE

Overview - 06-JUL-98

Sales through FY 99 (May) are projected to remain relatively flat, as lower selling prices for the company's meat and poultry products offset internal growth at other divisions and contributions from acquisitions. Grocery/Diversified profits should continue to generate annual operating profit growth of about 10%, as continued good growth in the frozen foods division outweighs higher new product expense at Hunt-Wesson. Inputs & Ingredients should post modest earnings growth, with gains for specialty food ingredients partly offset by soft international demand for grain and fertilizer. Refrigerated Products profits are expected to remain weak, hurt by current over-supplied meat and poultry market conditions. Overall, we look for EPS growth of only 6.6% in FY 99, to $1.45, from FY 98's $1.36. We anticipate that improved market conditions will fuel a 14% rise in FY 2000, to $1.65.

Valuation - 06-JUL-98

The shares have been weak performers thus far in 1998, reflecting a significant slowing of earnings growth, caused principally by a current market glut of meat and poultry products. With market conditions unlikely to improve materially over the next few quarters, near-term EPS growth will be restricted, despite ConAgra's substantial business diversity. Importantly, we believe that recent difficulties faced by the fresh meats and poultry businesses may be the catalyst to divest these operations, in order for management to better focus on more lucrative branded packaged foods operations. The relatively low-risk shares, recently trading at a modest P/E discount to the shares of CAG's major food company peers and to the S&P 500 Index, are a worthwhile holding for long-term capital gains.

Key Stock Statistics

S&P EPS Est. 1999	1.45	Tang. Bk. Value/Share	0.81
P/E on S&P Est. 1999	18.6	Beta	0.77
S&P EPS Est. 2000	1.65	Shareholders	31,000
Dividend Rate/Share	0.63	Market cap. (B)	$ 13.0
Shs. outstg. (M)	480.3	Inst. holdings	51%
Avg. daily vol. (M)	1.438		

Value of $10,000 invested 5 years ago: $ 18,420

Fiscal Year Ending May 31

	1998	1997	1996	1995	1994	1993
Revenues (Million $)						
1Q	6,140	6,158	6,436	6,246	5,687	5,520
2Q	6,434	6,590	6,630	6,289	6,355	5,560
3Q	5,385	5,459	5,773	5,758	5,581	5,060
4Q	5,882	5,795	5,983	5,817	5,888	5,378
Yr.	23,841	24,002	24,822	24,109	23,512	21,519
Earnings Per Share ($)						
1Q	0.24	0.21	0.18	0.15	0.14	0.14
2Q	0.47	0.41	0.36	0.32	0.28	0.26
3Q	**0.30**	0.32	0.28	0.24	0.21	0.18
4Q	**0.36**	0.41	-0.42	0.32	0.28	0.21
Yr.	**1.36**	1.34	0.40	1.03	0.91	0.79

Next earnings report expected: mid September

Dividend Data (Dividends have been paid since 1976.)

Amount ($)	Date Decl.	Ex-Div. Date	Stock of Record	Payment Date
0.156	Sep. 25	Nov. 05	Nov. 07	Dec. 01 '97
0.156	Dec. 04	Jan. 28	Jan. 30	Mar. 01 '98
0.156	Apr. 10	Apr. 29	May. 01	Jun. 01 '98
0.156	Jul. 10	Jul. 29	Jul. 31	Sep. 01 '98

A Division of The **McGraw·Hill** *Companies*

STANDARD
&POOR'S
STOCK REPORTS

ConAgra, Inc.

601

12-SEP-98

Business Summary - 06-JUL-98

Measured by sales, ConAgra is the largest independent food company in the U.S. ConAgra's business interests are far reaching, giving it a sizable participation in virtually all areas of the U.S. food processing industry. Sales and operating profit contributions by business segment in FY 98 (May) were:

	Sales	Profits
Grocery/Diversified Products	24%	59%
Refrigerated Foods	51%	15%
Food Inputs & Ingredients	25%	26%

The Grocery/Diversified Products segment consists of those companies that produce branded shelf-stable and frozen food products. Major shelf-stable grocery brands include Hunt's and Healthy Choice tomato products; Wesson oils; Healthy Choice soups; Orville Redenbacher's and Act II popcorn; Peter Pan peanut butter; and Van Camp's canned beans. Major frozen grocery brands include Healthy Choice, Banquet, Marie Callender's, Kid Cuisine, Morton, Chun King, and La Choy. Diversified products companies include

Lamb-Weston (frozen potatoes); Arrow Industries (maker of private label products); and business interests in seafood, pet products, and frozen microwave products in the U.K.

Refrigerated Foods consists of beef, pork and lamb products (Monfort, Armour); branded processed meats (Armour, Swift Premium, Eckrich, Healthy Choice); poultry (Butterball, Country Pride); cheeses (County Line); and refrigerated dessert toppings (Reddi-Wip);

Food Inputs & Ingredients businesses include crop protection chemicals and fertilizers; grain processing (flour, oat and dry corn milling; barley processing); and worldwide commodity trading (grains, oilseeds, edible beans and peas, and other commodities).

ConAgra's long-stated objectives include increasing EPS at least 14% per year, on average; and increasing the common stock dividend in line with earnings growth. The company's earnings have increased for 18 consecutive years, with EPS rising at an approximate 14.9% average annual rate during that period. In FY 98, the common dividend was increased 15%, marking the 23rd consecutive annual increase of at least 14%. A two-for-one stock split was effected October 1, 1997.

Per Share Data ($)

(Year Ended May 31)	1998	1997	1996	1995	1994	1993	1992	1991	1990	1989
Tangible Bk. Val.	0.81	0.08	NM	0.15	-0.81	-1.23	-1.06	-2.13	2.29	2.31
Cash Flow	2.33	2.23	1.30	1.85	1.71	1.53	1.44	1.17	0.95	0.81
Earnings	1.36	1.34	0.40	1.03	0.91	0.79	0.75	0.71	0.63	0.55
Dividends	0.60	0.53	0.46	0.39	0.35	0.30	0.26	0.22	0.19	0.17
Payout Ratio	44%	39%	116%	38%	38%	41%	35%	32%	31%	30%
Cal. Yrs.	1997	1996	1995	1994	1993	1992	1991	1990	1989	1988
Prices - High	38³/₄	27³/₈	20⁷/₈	16⁵/₈	16⁷/₈	17⁷/₈	18¹/₄	12³/₄	10¹/₈	7⁵/₈
- Low	24¹/₂	18⁷/₈	14⁷/₈	12³/₄	11³/₈	12¹/₄	11¹/₄	7⁵/₈	6¹/₂	5¹/₄
P/E Ratio - High	28	20	53	16	19	23	24	18	16	14
- Low	18	14	38	12	13	16	15	11	10	10

Income Statement Analysis (Million $)

	1998	1997	1996	1995	1994	1993	1992	1991	1990	1989
Revs.	23,841	24,022	24,822	24,109	23,512	21,519	21,219	19,505	15,501	11,340
Oper. Inc.	1,767	1,709	1,629	1,476	1,337	1,213	1,207	1,040	623	538
Depr.	446	414	408	376	368	349	319	251	120	94.0
Int. Exp.	338	332	352	311	289	283	356	329	192	149
Pretax Inc.	1,021	1,081	409	826	720	631	588	515	357	312
Eff. Tax Rate	38%	40%	54%	40%	39%	38%	37%	40%	35%	37%
Net Inc.	628	615	189	496	437	392	372	311	232	198

Balance Sheet & Other Fin. Data (Million $)

	1998	1997	1996	1995	1994	1993	1992	1991	1990	1989
Cash	95.0	106	114	60.0	452	447	536	967	333	607
Curr. Assets	5,487	5,205	5,567	5,140	5,143	4,487	4,371	4,343	3,348	3,160
Total Assets	11,703	11,277	11,197	10,801	10,722	9,989	9,759	9,420	4,804	4,278
Curr. Liab.	5,070	4,990	5,194	3,965	4,753	4,273	4,081	4,087	2,968	2,651
LT Debt	2,487	2,356	2,263	2,520	2,207	2,159	2,124	2,093	635	560
Common Eqty.	2,779	2,472	2,256	2,495	2,227	2,055	2,232	1,817	1,096	950
Total Cap.	5,791	5,352	5,044	5,895	4,889	4,570	4,713	4,266	1,837	1,627
Cap. Exp.	569	670	669	428	395	341	370	332	349	253
Cash Flow	1,074	1,029	597	847	782	716	667	543	350	291
Curr. Ratio	1.1	1.0	1.1	1.3	1.1	1.1	1.1	1.1	1.1	1.2
% LT Debt of Cap.	42.9	44.0	44.9	42.7	45.1	47.3	45.1	49.1	34.6	34.4
% Net Inc.of Revs.	2.6	2.6	0.8	2.1	1.9	1.8	1.8	1.6	1.5	1.7
% Ret. on Assets	5.5	5.5	1.7	4.6	4.2	3.8	3.7	4.2	5.1	5.3
% Ret. on Equity	23.9	26.0	7.6	20.0	19.4	16.4	16.4	19.0	22.3	22.0

Data as orig. reptd.; bef. results of disc. opers. and/or spec. items. Per share data adj. for stk. divs. as of ex-div. date. Bold denotes diluted EPS (FASB 128). E-Estimated. NA-Not Available. NM-Not Meaningful. NR-Not Ranked.

Office—One ConAgra Dr., Omaha, NE 68102-5001. **Tel**—(402) 595-4000. **Chrmn**—P. B. Fletcher. **Vice Chrmn, Pres & CEO**—B. Rohde. **VP & Investor Contact**—Walter H. Casey. **Dirs**—M. C. Bay, P. B. Fletcher, C. M. Harper, R. A. Krane, G. Rauenhorst, C. E. Reichardt, B. Rohde, R. W. Roskens, M. R. Scardino, W. Scott, Jr., K. E. Stinson, J. J. Thompson, F. B. Wells, T. R. Williams, C. K. Yeutter. **Transfer Agent & Registrar**—ChaseMellon Shareholder Services, L.L.C., Ridgefield Park, NJ. **Incorporated**—in Nebraska in 1919; reincorporated in Delaware in 1975. **Empl**—82,169. **S&P Analyst:**   Richard Joy

Conseco, Inc.   609

NYSE Symbol **CNC**

In S&P 500

12-SEP-98   **Industry:** Insurance (Life & Health)

Summary: This holding company engages in the acquisition, owner-ship and management of annuity, life, and supplemental health insur-ance companies.

S&P Opinion: Accumulate (★★★★)	Recent Price • 28⅞	Yield • 1.9%
	52 Wk Range • 58⅛-26⅜	12-Mo. P/E • 23.1

Earnings vs. Previous Year
▲=Up ▼=Down ▶=No Change

Quantitative Evaluations

Outlook
(1 Lowest—5 Highest)
• **3**

Fair Value
• **33⅝**

Risk
• **Average**

Earn./Div. Rank
• **B+**

Technical Eval.
• **Bearish** since 8/98

Rel. Strength Rank
(1 Lowest—99 Highest)
• **19**

Insider Activity
• **Favorable**

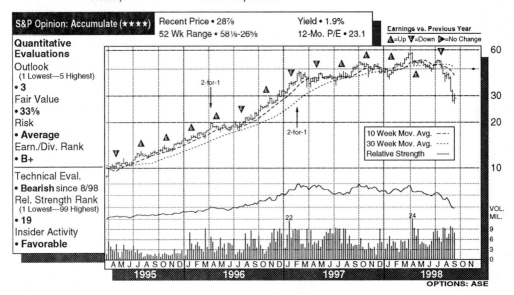

2-for-1

2-for-1

10 Week Mov. Avg. ----
30 Week Mov. Avg. ·····
Relative Strength ——

VOL.
MIL.

1995   1996   1997   1998

OPTIONS: ASE

Overview - 14-AUG-98

Operating earnings growth in coming periods will be aided by contributions from an ongoing acquisition plan, assuming CNC chooses acquisition candidates with complementary products and distribution systems, and is able to smoothly integrate them into its fold. On June 30, 1998, CNC acquired Green Tree Financial Corp. (NYSE: GNT) for stock valued at around $6 billion. CNC expects the deal to be accretive to earnings, beginning in the third quarter of 1998. But, the second quarter net loss largely reflected a $498 million ($1.61 a share) nonrecurring charge to cover $148 million in merger related expenses and a $350 million asset writedowns. That aside, profit gains from internal sources are predicated on strong deposit growth and favorable interest rate spreads in the life insurance and annuity areas. Cross selling opportunities and expense savings from 1997's acquisitions also enhance the profit outlook. The resumption of stock repurchases following the GNT deal will aid EPS growth. During 1997, CNC repurchased 12.1 million common shares. Estimates are based on operating earnings (before special charges); actual EPS are based on net income.

Valuation - 14-AUG-98

After rebounding from a sharp correction in late 1994 that was sparked by CNC's failed attempt to acquire NYSE-listed Kemper Corp., the shares have recently plateaued. We attribute this to concerns over CNC's somewhat aggressive "growth through acquisition" strategy, and to negative investor reaction to the Green-tree deal. Although we share some of these concerns, CNC is a well run company with a well defined growth strategy. For investors with a long term time horizon, we recommend using any near term weakness to accu-mulate the shares.

Key Stock Statistics

S&P EPS Est. 1998	3.25	Tang. Bk. Value/Share	0.96
P/E on S&P Est. 1998	8.9	Beta	1.49
S&P EPS Est. 1999	4.00	Shareholders	7,000
Dividend Rate/Share	0.56	Market cap. (B)	$ 9.0
Shs. outstg. (M)	312.4	Inst. holdings	68%
Avg. daily vol. (M)	2.393		

Value of $10,000 invested 5 years ago: $ 25,954

Fiscal Year Ending Dec. 31

	1998	1997	1996	1995	1994	1993
Revenues (Million $)						
1Q	1,699	1,099	691.8	652.3	490.2	751.6
2Q	1,839	1,361	672.5	737.1	413.9	619.0
3Q	—	1,484	834.3	676.7	423.9	628.7
4Q	—	1,625	866.5	789.2	534.0	636.7
Yr.	—	5,568	3,067	2,855	1,862	2,636
Earnings Per Share ($)						
1Q	0.81	0.51	0.59	0.23	0.69	1.17
2Q	-0.88	0.62	0.43	1.12	0.28	0.39
3Q	—	0.73	0.55	0.46	0.30	0.40
4Q	—	0.91	0.54	0.58	-0.03	0.50
Yr.	—	2.67	2.12	2.37	1.28	2.46

Next earnings report expected: late October

Dividend Data (Dividends have been paid since 1988.)

Amount ($)	Date Decl.	Ex-Div. Date	Stock of Record	Payment Date
0.125	Oct. 11	Dec. 17	Dec. 19	Jan. 02 '98
0.125	Feb. 25	Mar. 18	Mar. 20	Apr. 01 '98
0.125	May. 14	Jun. 17	Jun. 19	Jul. 01 '98
0.140	Jul. 30	Sep. 16	Sep. 18	Oct. 01 '98

Business Summary - 14-AUG-98

Conseco, Inc. (CNC) is a holding company engaged in the acquisition, ownership and operation of annuity, life and health insurance companies. Its strategy has been to acquire companies with profitable product niches and strong distribution systems; to consolidate and streamline the management and administrative functions; to realize superior investment returns through active asset management; to eliminate any unprofitable products and distribution channels; and to expand the profitable distribution channels and products.

Premiums collected in 1997 equaled $5.4 billion, of which annuities accounted for 31%, supplemental health insurance 36%, major medical 16%, life insurance 15%, and other 2%.

During 1997 CNC completed the following acquisitions: In March, CNC acquired Capitol American Financial Corp. for $650 million in cash and stock. In April, the company purchased Pioneer Financial Services for approximately $477 million in stock. On October 1, 1997, CNC acquired Colonial Penn Life Insurance from Leucadia National Corp. (NYSE: LUK) for $460 million in

cash and notes. On December 5, 1997 CNC acquired Washington National Corp. (NYSE: WNT) for $410 million. CNC's results in 1997 continued to benefit from its ongoing acquisition efforts and from internal growth. Operating earnings (net income before realized investment gains/losses and nonrecurring and extraordinary charges) in the twelve months ended December 31, 1997, rose to $2.74 a share, diluted, up from $1.93 in 1996. During 1996, CNC completed the following acquisitions: Life Partners Group, Inc., for $850 million (August); the 62% of American Life Holdings it did not already own, for $165 million in cash (September); American Travellers Corp., for $793 million in stock (December); Transport Holdings, Inc., for $311 million in stock (December); and the 10% of Bankers Life Holding it did not already own, for $117 million in cash (December). From 1982 through the end of 1995, CNC completed 12 acquisitions, with the first seven as wholly owned subsidiaries and the last five through acquisition partnerships. In September 1996, CNC dissolved its acquisition partnership, Conseco Capital Partners II, because of regulatory changes.

Per Share Data ($)

(Year Ended Dec. 31)	1997	1996	1995	1994	1993	1992	1991	1990	1989	1988
Tangible Bk. Val.	0.73	3.69	NM	-2.52	5.28	3.96	2.57	NM	0.52	0.03
Oper. Earnings	2.74	1.89	1.26	1.48	2.42	1.29	0.72	0.31	0.20	0.14
Earnings	2.67	2.12	2.37	1.29	2.46	1.40	1.07	0.34	0.44	0.27
Dividends	0.31	0.08	0.02	0.13	0.08	0.02	0.02	0.01	0.01	0.01
Payout Ratio	12%	4%	1%	10%	3%	2%	2%	4%	3%	2%
Prices - High	50	33⅛	15¾	16⅝	19	11⅞	8½	1⅞	1¾	¹⁵⁄₁₆
- Low	30¾	14⅞	8⅛	9	11⅛	5⅛	1½	1¹⁄₁₆	¹¹⁄₁₆	⁹⁄₁₆
P/E Ratio - High	19	16	7	13	8	8	8	5	4	3
- Low	12	7	3	7	5	4	1	3	2	2

Income Statement Analysis (Million $)

	1997	1996	1995	1994	1993	1992	1991	1990	1989	1988
Life Ins. In Force	104,145	80,150	NA	NA	NA	23,025	24,216	29,025	14,370	12,941
Prem. Inc.: Life	3,411	1,654	1,465	1,286	1,294	379	281	153	197	240
Prem. Inc.: A & H	Nil	Nil	Nil	NA	NA	NA	NA	NA	NA	NA
Prem. Inc.: Other	65.8	80.2	59.0	191	446	258	139	12.0	32.0	3.0
Net Invest. Inc.	1,825	1,303	1,143	386	896	889	972	588	430	345
Total Revs.	5,568	3,067	2,855	1,862	2,636	1,526	1,392	753	659	588
Pretax Inc.	1,003	494	419	324	610	330	223	65.0	70.0	46.0
Net Oper. Inc.	575	268	131	175	302	163	84.0	39.0	32.0	26.0
Net Inc.	574	252	223	154	309	175	121	42.0	47.0	30.0

Balance Sheet & Other Fin. Data (Million $)

	1997	1996	1995	1994	1993	1992	1991	1990	1989	1988
Cash & Equiv.	379	297	208	126	168	157	172	575	408	143
Premiums Due	849	504	84.8	46.0	511	892	NA	NA	NA	NA
Invest. Assets: Bonds	23,764	17,589	13,153	7,067	9,822	8,331	8,174	5,703	3,716	2,916
Invest. Assets: Stocks	229	100	36.6	39.6	30.3	71.6	48.2	43.8	34.5	29.7
Invest. Assets: Loans	1,767	1,346	907	387	675	362	1,107	735	418	446
Invest. Assets: Total	29,929	19,631	14,415	8,159	11,689	9,450	10,427	6,900	4,379	3,553
Deferred Policy Costs	3,382	2,559	1,427	1,322	862	934	768	613	278	248
Total Assets	35,915	25,613	17,298	10,812	13,749	11,773	11,596	8,284	5,176	4,031
Debt	1,306	1,095	871	192	703	555	497	527	308	331
Common Eqty.	3,774	2,818	828	463	855	544	382	120	108	41.0
% Return On Revs.	0.6	9.1	7.8	8.3	11.7	11.5	8.7	5.5	7.2	5.2
% Ret. on Assets	1.9	1.3	1.6	1.3	2.2	1.5	1.2	0.6	1.0	0.8
% Ret. on Equity	17.2	12.0	34.1	20.6	36.1	36.6	45.5	31.6	52.0	53.2
% Invest. Yield	7.8	7.7	11.8	4.0	8.5	8.9	10.9	10.4	10.8	10.8

Data as orig. reptd.; bef. results of disc. opers. and/or spec. items. Per share data adj. for stk. divs. as of ex-div. date. Bold denotes diluted EPS (FASB 128). E-Estimated. NA-Not Available. NM-Not Meaningful. NR-Not Ranked.

Office—11825 N. Pennsylvania St., Carmel, IN 46032. **Tel**—(317) 817-6100. **Website**—http://www.conseco.com **Chrmn, CEO & Pres**—S. C. Hilbert. **Exec VP & CFO**—R. M. Dick. **Exec VP & Secy**—J. J. Sabl. **VP & Investor Contact**—James W. Rosensteele (317) 817-2893. **Dirs**—N. E. Cuneo, D. R. Decatur, R. M. Dick, D. F. Gongaware, M. P. Hathaway, S. C. Hilbert, J. D. Massey, D. E. Murray Sr., J. M. Mutz. **Transfer Agent & Registrar**—First Union National Bank, Indianapolis. **Incorporated**—in Indiana in 1979. **Empl**— 6,500. **S&P Analyst:** Catherine A. Seifert

12-SEP-98

Industry: Electric Companies

Summary: This electric and gas utility, which serves the commercial and residential economy of New York City, has agreed to acquire Orange and Rockland Utilities.

S&P Opinion: Hold (★★★)	Recent Price • 47¼	Yield • 4.5%
	52 Wk Range • 48¾-32¼	12-Mo. P/E • 15.4

Quantitative Evaluations

Outlook
(1 Lowest—5 Highest)
• **2**

Fair Value
• **46¼**

Risk
• **Low**

Earn./Div. Rank
• **A**

Technical Eval.
• **Bullish** since 7/97

Rel. Strength Rank
(1 Lowest—99 Highest)
• **96**

Insider Activity
• **NA**

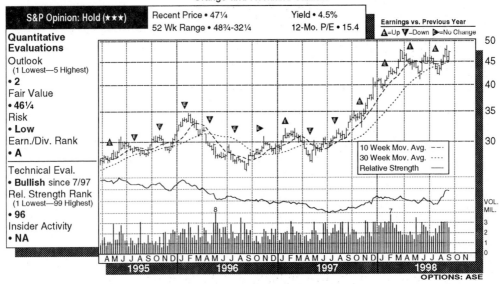

Earnings vs. Previous Year
△=Up ▽–Down ▷=No Change

10 Week Mov. Avg. — - —
30 Week Mov. Avg. - - - -
Relative Strength —

OPTIONS: ASE

Overview - 17-AUG-98

The planned $790 million acquisition of Orange and Rockland Utilities, which would increase ED's customer base by 380,000, is expected to result in annual savings of about $50 million a year, and to be accretive after the first year. While EPS in 1998 will be essentially flat, we expect to see low single-digit EPS growth in 1999. A September 1997 settlement agreement with the New York State Public Service Commission provides for a five-year transition period during which ED will continue to recover its stranded costs through customer rates. The agreement called for the sale to unaffiliated parties of at least 50% of ED's New York City electric fossil-fueled generating capacity, with the remaining generating capacity transferred to an unregulated company affiliate. The auction process was commenced in August 1998 and is expected to be completed in early 1999. Over the transition period, generation-related revenues will be reduced by about $1 billion. In December 1997, ED announced the authorization (subject to state approval) of a $1 billion share repurchase program.

Valuation - 17-AUG-98

We recommend holding ED stock. After a 41% advance in 1997 (more than double the 20% rise in the S&P Index of Electric Companies), the shares are up more than 10% year to date. The strong performance has been aided by a settlement agreement that will enable the company to recover more than 90% of its stranded costs (estimated at about $6 billion). It also reflects ED's improved operational efficiencies and the benefits being derived from a still strong local economy. Following its recent gains, the stock seems fairly valued at nearly 15X our 1999 EPS estimate of $3.05. Still, with a secure dividend offering a 4.7% yield, ED remains an attractive vehicle for income.

Key Stock Statistics

S&P EPS Est. 1998	2.95	Tang. Bk. Value/Share	24.08
P/E on S&P Est. 1998	16.0	Beta	0.36
S&P EPS Est. 1999	3.05	Shareholders	143,800
Dividend Rate/Share	2.12	Market cap. (B)	$ 11.0
Shs. outstg. (M)	233.8	Inst. holdings	37%
Avg. daily vol. (M)	0.737		

Value of $10,000 invested 5 years ago: $ 20,505

Fiscal Year Ending Dec. 31

	1998	1997	1996	1995	1994	1993
Revenues (Million $)						
1Q	1,853	1,886	1,867	1,669	1,698	1,586
2Q	1,561	1,504	1,540	1,460	1,392	1,396
3Q	—	2,011	1,920	1,880	1,822	1,800
4Q	—	1,720	1,632	1,528	1,461	1,484
Yr.	—	7,121	6,960	6,537	6,373	6,265
Earnings Per Share ($)						
1Q	0.73	0.69	0.78	0.82	0.77	0.62
2Q	0.26	0.18	0.28	0.29	0.33	0.23
3Q	E1.45	1.49	1.38	1.38	1.41	1.35
4Q	E0.51	0.59	0.49	0.44	0.47	0.46
Yr.	E2.95	2.95	2.93	2.93	2.98	2.66

Next earnings report expected: late October

Dividend Data (Dividends have been paid since 1885.)

Amount ($)	Date Decl.	Ex-Div. Date	Stock of Record	Payment Date
0.525	Oct. 28	Nov. 17	Nov. 19	Dec. 15 '97
0.530	Jan. 27	Feb. 13	Feb. 18	Mar. 15 '98
0.530	Apr. 28	May. 11	May. 13	Jun. 15 '98
0.530	Jul. 28	Aug. 17	Aug. 19	Sep. 15 '98

A Division of The McGraw-Hill Companies

STANDARD
&POOR'S
STOCK REPORTS

Consolidated Edison, Inc.

612

12-SEP-98

Business Summary - 17-AUG-98

Serving a territory with a population of more than 8 million, Consolidated Edison supplies electricity to all of New York City (except part of Queens) and most of Westchester County. Gas and steam services are provided in certain parts of the service area. In 1997, electric sales accounted for 79.1% of revenues, gas 15.4%. and steam 5.5%. Electric revenues in recent years by customer class were:

	1997	1996	1995	1994
Residential	29%	29%	33%	34%
Commercial-industrial	69%	69%	61%	62%
Other	2%	2%	6%	4%

In May 1998, ED announced plans to acquire Orange and Rockland Utilities (ORU), an electric/gas utility with 1996 revenues of $649 million, for $790 million. ORU serves about 273,600 electric customers and 107,000 gas customers in an area of 1,350 square miles in southwestern New York State, northern New Jersey, and northeastern Pennsylvania. The transaction is expected to be completed in the spring of 1999.

On January 1, 1998, ED was restructured into a new holding company, Consolidated Edison, Inc., with four subsidiaries: Consolidated Edison Company of New York, which will continue to provide regulated electricity, natural gas and steam services; Consolidated Edison

Solutions, a non-regulated provider of energy sales and services; Consolidated Edison Development, an investor in energy infrastructure development projects; and Consolidated Edison Energy, a marketer of energy generation services to the wholesale electric market.

In 1997, 22.7% of the electricity supplied to ED's customers was obtained through economy purchases of energy produced by a variety of fuels. Of the remaining 77.3%, oil was used to generate 7.6%; natural gas, 57.9%; nuclear power, 8.5%; hydroelectric, 2.4%; and refuse, 0.9%.

In September 1997, the New York Public Service Commission (PSC) approved a restated settlement agreement that authorized (subject to shareholder approval) the establishment of a holding company, and the implementation of a five-year rate plan in which base rates would immediately be lowered by 25% for the company's largest industrial customers and, by the final year of the transition, 10% for all of the company's industrial, residential and commercial customers. Under the agreement, the company would divest by December 2002 (unless the PSC authorizes a delay) at least 50% of its New York City fossil-fueled generating capacity to unaffiliated third parties.

In August 1998, the company announced the beginning of the auction process for its fossil-fuel electric generating stations. The auction is expected to be completed in early 1999.

Per Share Data ($)

(Year Ended Dec. 31)	1997	1996	1995	1994	1993	1992	1991	1990	1989	1988
Tangible Bk. Val.	24.52	23.69	22.81	21.90	20.89	20.58	20.00	19.56	19.07	18.35
Earnings	2.95	2.93	2.93	2.98	2.66	2.46	2.32	2.34	2.49	2.47
Dividends	2.10	2.08	2.04	2.00	1.94	1.90	1.86	1.82	1.72	1.60
Payout Ratio	71%	71%	70%	67%	73%	77%	80%	78%	69%	65%
Prices - High	41½	34¾	32¼	32⅜	37¾	32⅞	28¾	29¼	29⅞	23¾
- Low	27	25⅞	25½	23	30¼	25	22½	19¾	22¼	20½
P/E Ratio - High	14	12	11	11	14	13	12	13	12	10
- Low	9	9	9	8	11	10	10	8	9	8

Income Statement Analysis (Million $)

	1997	1996	1995	1994	1993	1992	1991	1990	1989	1988
Revs.	7,121	6,960	6,537	6,373	6,265	5,933	5,873	5,739	5,551	5,109
Depr.	503	496	456	422	404	381	360	343	325	308
Maint.	475	459	512	506	571	529	521	510	483	447
Fxd. Chgs. Cov.	4.0	4.3	4.0	4.3	3.9	3.6	3.5	3.8	4.2	4.5
Constr. Credits	7.0	5.0	5.6	18.9	10.6	13.8	14.4	9.0	13.1	12.1
Eff. Tax Rate	35%	36%	35%	37%	36%	35%	34%	34%	34%	33%
Net Inc.	713	694	724	734	659	604	567	571	606	599

Balance Sheet & Other Fin. Data (Million $)

	1997	1996	1995	1994	1993	1992	1991	1990	1989	1988
Gross Prop.	15,659	15,352	14,851	14,390	13,750	13,191	12,521	11,922	11,366	10,868
Cap. Exp.	669	724	706	805	803	830	784	736	630	629
Net Prop.	11,267	11,067	10,814	10,561	10,156	9,730	9,263	8,815	8,411	8,071
Capitalization:										
LT Debt	4,229	4,281	3,962	4,078	3,694	3,494	3,420	3,371	3,150	2,890
% LT Debt	40	41	39	41	39	39	40	40	39	37
Pfd.	233	323	640	640	641	641	633	636	639	642
% Pfd.	3.00	3.10	6.30	6.40	6.80	7.10	7.30	7.50	7.80	8.30
Common	5,930	5,728	5,523	5,313	5,069	4,887	4,608	4,502	4,382	4,205
% Common	57	55	55	53	54	54	53	53	54	54
Total Cap.	12,949	12,793	12,603	12,562	11,965	10,252	9,751	9,517	9,116	8,626
% Oper. Ratio	85.3	85.4	84.1	83.7	84.8	85.2	86.2	86.0	85.9	84.9
% Earn. on Net Prop.	9.4	9.3	51.4	10.0	9.6	9.3	9.0	9.3	9.5	9.8
% Return On Revs.	10.0	10.0	11.1	11.5	10.5	10.2	9.7	10.0	10.9	11.7
% Return On Invest. Capital	8.1	8.0	11.5	8.5	8.5	9.0	8.9	8.9	9.5	9.6
% Return On Com. Equity	11.9	12.2	12.7	13.5	12.5	12.0	11.6	12.0	13.2	13.7

Data as orig. reptd.; bef. results of disc opers. and/or spec. items. Per share data adj. for stk. divs. as of ex-div. date. Bold denotes diluted EPS (FASB 128). E-Estimated. NA-Not Available. NM-Not Meaningful. NR-Not Ranked.

Registrar—ChaseMellon Shareholder Services, Ridgefield Park, NJ. **Office**—4 Irving Place, New York, NY 10003. **Tel**—(212) 460-3900. **Website**—http://www.coned.com **Chrmn, Pres & CEO**—E. R. McGrath. **EVP & CFO**—J. S. Freilich. **Secy**—A. M. Bankston. **VP & Controller**—H. Schoenblum. **VP & Treas**—R. P. Stelben. **Investor Contact**—William J. Clifford. **Directors**—E. V. Conway, G. J. Davis, R. M. Davis, J. S. Frelich, E. V. Futter, A. Hauspurg, S. Hernandez-Pinero, P. W. Likins, E. R. McGrath, D. K. Ross, R. G. Schwartz, R. A. Voell, S. R. Volk. **Transfer Agent**—Co.'s office. **Incorporated**—in New York in 1884. **Empl**— 15,029. **S&P Analyst:** Justin McCann

Consolidated Natural Gas   626

NYSE Symbol **CNG**

In S&P 500

12-SEP-98   Industry:
Natural Gas

Summary: One of the largest U.S. integrated natural gas companies, CNG operates mainly in Ohio, Pennsylvania, West Virginia and New York and other Northeastern and Mid-Atlantic states.

S&P Opinion: Hold (★★★)	Recent Price • 43⅛	Yield • 4.5%
	52 Wk Range • 60⅞-41⅝	12-Mo. P/E • 17.9

Earnings vs. Previous Year
▲=Up ▼=Down ▶=No Change

Quantitative Evaluations

Outlook
(1 Lowest—5 Highest)
• **2**

Fair Value
• **43**

Risk
• **Low**

Earn./Div. Rank
• **B+**

Technical Eval.
• **Bearish** since 8/97

Rel. Strength Rank
(1 Lowest—99 Highest)
• **51**

Insider Activity
• **Neutral**

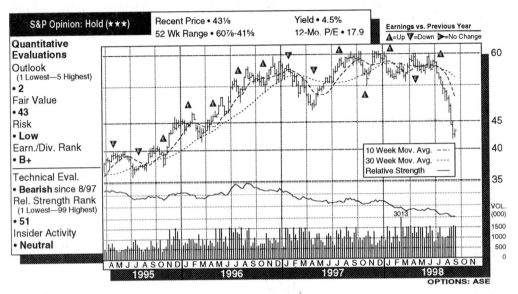

10 Week Mov. Avg. ———
30 Week Mov. Avg. ......
Relative Strength ———

OPTIONS: ASE

Overview - 25-AUG-98

We expect EPS to advance around 20% in 1999. This will follow an essentially flat performance in 1998, which has been hurt by the mild winter weather, and lower gas and oil wellhead prices. After significant first quarter losses, CNG has sold its wholesale energy trading and marketing operations. The company will retain its retail energy marketing operations, but will no longer report it as a separate segment. While CNG is still looking for an acquisition and/or alliance, it has shifted its focus from the distribution sector to the exploration and production (E&P) sector. Although core gas distribution profits will continue to benefit from a diverse service territory and a competitive rate structure, earnings growth will mainly come from the strength of E&P operations, which should continue to be bolstered by increased production and lower operating expenses.

Valuation - 25-AUG-98

We would continue to hold CNG stock. While the shares are down 20% year to date, weakened by substantially reduced expectations for 1998, we see the potential for a solid recovery in 1999. The shares were up only 9.5% in 1997 (compared with an 18.6% increase for the S&P Index of Natural Gas Companies), but had recovered a strong 28% from their sharp drop during the first four months of the year. We expect the dividend, which is yielding about 4.0%, to remain at its current level, with cash directed toward E&P expansion and a potential acquisition. After discontinuing its wholesale energy marketing operations, CNG will pursue growth opportunities in other nonregulated markets. This should provide support for the stock, which, trading at a P/E of less than 13 times our 1999 EPS estimate of $3.80, remains attractive for long-term total return.

Key Stock Statistics

S&P EPS Est. 1998	3.15	Tang. Bk. Value/Share	25.15
P/E on S&P Est. 1998	13.7	Beta	0.87
S&P EPS Est. 1999	3.80	Shareholders	38,500
Dividend Rate/Share	1.94	Market cap. (B)	$ 4.1
Shs. outstg. (M)	95.9	Inst. holdings	52%
Avg. daily vol. (M)	0.365		

Value of $10,000 invested 5 years ago: $ 12,128

Fiscal Year Ending Dec. 31

	1998	1997	1996	1995	1994	1993
Revenues (Million $)						
1Q	999	1,699	1,315	1,192	1,214	1,132
2Q	530.4	1,031	655.0	665.0	582.0	549.0
3Q	—	1,130	595.1	515.1	452.0	473.0
4Q	—	1,850	1,229	935.6	789.0	1,030
Yr.	—	5,701	3,794	3,307	3,036	3,184
Earnings Per Share ($)						
1Q	**1.45**	**1.74**	1.92	-0.23	1.41	1.36
2Q	**0.43**	**0.41**	0.37	-0.36	0.03	0.07
3Q	**E0.09**	**0.05**	-0.05	-0.12	-0.26	-0.32
4Q	**E1.18**	**0.92**	0.93	0.94	0.79	0.93
Yr.	**E3.15**	**3.15**	3.16	0.23	1.97	2.03

Next earnings report expected: late October

Dividend Data (Dividends have been paid since 1944.)

Amount ($)	Date Decl.	Ex-Div. Date	Stock of Record	Payment Date
0.485	Dec. 09	Jan. 13	Jan. 15	Feb. 14 '98
0.485	Mar. 10	Apr. 13	Apr. 15	May. 15 '98
0.485	Jun. 09	Jul. 13	Jul. 15	Aug. 15 '98
0.485	Sep. 08	Oct. 13	Oct. 15	Nov. 16 '98

A Division of The McGraw-Hill Companies

Business Summary - 25-AUG-98

As one of the largest natural gas companies in the United States, Consolidated Natural Gas is engaged in all aspects of the business, including exploration and production, purchasing, gathering, transmission, storage and distribution. Revenues and profits (in million $) by segment in 1997 were:

	Revenues	Profits
Distribution	31.7%	$266.6
Transmission	7.6%	178.4
Exploration & production	11.1%	142.8
Energy marketing services	48.6%	-17.1
Other	1.0%	-9.3

CNG supplies gas to about 1.78 million retail customers in Ohio, Pennsylvania, Virginia and West Virginia through five gas distribution subsidiaries. CNG Transmission operates an interstate pipeline system serving CNG's distribution units and nonaffiliated utilities in the Midwest, the Mid-Atlantic states and the Northeast.

Exploration and production activities are conducted by CNG Producing, primarily in the Gulf of Mexico, the Southwest, the Appalachian region and Canada. Total gas production in 1997 was 158 billion cubic feet (bcf), up from 148 bcf in 1996. Oil production was 7.3 million barrels (bbl.), up from 4.8 million bbl. in 1996. In March 1997, CNG commenced production at Neptune, a 50%-owned deep-water oil and natural gas project in the Gulf of Mexico that has added 190 bcf of proved gas reserves. The company also has a 37.5% interest in Popeye, a deep-water natural gas discovery in the Gulf of Mexico that began production in January 1996.

In March 1998, CNG International (CNGI) acquired a one-third interest in the AlintaGas Dampier-to-Bunbury Natural Gas Pipeline in Western Australia. El Paso Energy also owns one-third, with the remaining one-third equally held among three other Australian investors. In December 1996, CNGI and El Paso Energy entered into a similar joint venture in which each acquired a 30% interest in Epic Energy, an Australian entity formed to hold the Australian pipeline assets formerly held by Tenneco Energy, with the remaining 40% held equally among four Australian investors.

In December 1997, CNGI acquired 12.5% interests in two gas utility holding companies in Argentina, as well as a 20% interest in an electric utility holding company in Buenos Aires.

In July 1998, Consolidated Natural Gas sold its wholesale energy trading and marketing operations to Sempre Energy for approximately $48 million. Earlier, in April 1998, CNG announced that it would no longer report financial results for energy marketing services as a separate segment. It would, however, maintain its retail energy marketing operations aimed at residential and small business customers.

Per Share Data ($)

(Year Ended Dec. 31)	1997	1996	1995	1994	1993	1992	1991	1990	1989	1988
Tangible Bk. Val.	24.66	23.06	21.66	23.48	23.30	22.96	21.57	21.28	20.20	19.81
Cash Flow	6.34	6.38	2.98	4.97	5.21	5.42	5.22	5.20	5.54	5.28
Earnings	3.15	3.16	0.23	1.97	2.03	2.19	1.94	1.91	2.20	2.34
Dividends	1.94	1.94	1.94	1.94	1.92	1.90	1.88	1.84	1.76	1.64
Payout Ratio	62%	61%	NM	98%	95%	87%	97%	96%	80%	70%
Prices - High	$60^7/_8$	$59^5/_8$	$46^1/_4$	47	$55^3/_8$	$48^5/_8$	45	$52^7/_8$	$51^1/_2$	$41^3/_4$
- Low	$47^3/_8$	$41^1/_2$	$33^5/_8$	$33^7/_8$	$42^5/_8$	$33^1/_2$	$37^7/_8$	41	$37^1/_8$	$33^3/_4$
P/E Ratio - High	19	19	NM	24	27	22	23	28	23	18
- Low	15	13	NM	17	21	15	20	21	17	14

Income Statement Analysis (Million $)

	1997	1996	1995	1994	1993	1992	1991	1990	1989	1988
Revs.	5,710	3,794	3,307	3,036	3,184	2,521	2,607	2,715	2,802	2,468
Oper. Inc.	398	392	147	623	652	630	570	582	598	535
Depr.	330	304	257	279	295	288	285	282	275	243
Int. Exp.	114	109	111	97.0	90.0	101	111	117	100	74.0
Pretax Inc.	451	454	24.0	266	288	264	223	216	251	264
Eff. Tax Rate	33%	42%	13%	31%	35%	26%	25%	24%	28%	27%
Net Inc.	304	298	21.3	183	188	195	169	164	182	193

Balance Sheet & Other Fin. Data (Million $)

	1997	1996	1995	1994	1993	1992	1991	1990	1989	1988
Cash	65.0	44.5	36.3	31.9	27.1	43.4	25.0	70.0	27.8	20.9
Curr. Assets	1,454	1,393	1,069	1,065	1,043	1,197	1,094	1,235	1,087	952
Total Assets	6,314	6,001	5,418	5,519	5,410	5,242	5,011	5,006	4,601	4,109
Curr. Liab.	1,386	1,364	1,111	1,211	1,113	1,238	1,185	1,239	1,245	1,066
LT Debt	1,553	1,426	1,292	1,152	1,159	1,112	1,159	1,129	891	662
Common Eqty.	2,359	2,205	2,046	2,184	2,176	2,133	1,890	1,845	1,672	1,635
Total Cap.	4,650	4,342	4,041	4,128	4,154	3,953	3,789	3,714	3,317	3,030
Cap. Exp.	521	439	435	416	341	439	484	402	631	399
Cash Flow	634	602	278	462	483	483	453	446	457	435
Curr. Ratio	1.0	1.0	1.0	0.9	0.9	1.0	0.9	1.0	0.9	0.9
% LT Debt of Cap.	33.4	32.8	32.0	27.9	27.9	28.1	30.6	30.4	26.8	21.8
% Net Inc.of Revs.	5.3	7.9	0.7	6.0	5.9	7.7	6.5	6.0	6.5	7.8
% Ret. on Assets	4.9	5.2	0.4	3.4	3.5	3.7	3.3	3.3	4.2	4.8
% Ret. on Equity	13.3	14.0	1.0	8.4	8.7	9.4	9.0	9.1	11.0	12.0

Data as orig. reptd.; bef. results of disc. opers. and/or spec. items. Per share data adj. for stk. divs. as of ex-div. date. Bold denotes diluted EPS (FASB 128). E-Estimated. NA-Not Available. NM-Not Meaningful. NR-Not Ranked.

Office—CNG Tower, 625 Liberty Ave., Pittsburgh, PA 15222-3199. **Tel**—(412) 690-1000. **Website**—http://www.cng.com **Chrmn & CEO**—G. A. Davidson Jr. **SVP & CFO**—D. M. Westfall. **Secy**—L. J. McKeown. **Investor Contacts**—James W. Garrett / Daniel J. Zajdel. **Dirs**—W. S. Barrack, J. W. Connolly, G. A. Davidson Jr., R. E. Galvin, R. J. Groves, P. E. Lego, M. A. McKenna, S. A. Minter, R. P. Simmons. **Transfer Agent & Registrar**—First Chicago Trust Company of New York, Jersey City, NJ. **Incorporated**—in Delaware in 1942. **Empl**— 6,412. **S&P Analyst:** Justin McCann

STANDARD &POOR'S
STOCK REPORTS

Consolidated Stores
628

NYSE Symbol **CNS**

In S&P 500

12-SEP-98

Industry: Retail (Discounters)

Summary: This retailer, which operates more than 2,300 stores, places an emphasis on selling discounted closeout merchandise and toys.

S&P Opinion: Accumulate (★★★★)	Recent Price • 32½	Yield • Nil	Earnings vs. Previous Year
	52 Wk Range • 50-28	12-Mo. P/E • 41.2	△=Up ▽=Down ▶=No Change

Quantitative Evaluations

Outlook
(1 Lowest—5 Highest)
• **4⁻**

Fair Value
• **43**

Risk
• **Average**

Earn./Div. Rank
• **B**

Technical Eval.
• **Bearish** since 5/98

Rel. Strength Rank
(1 Lowest—99 Highest)
• **74**

Insider Activity
• **NA**

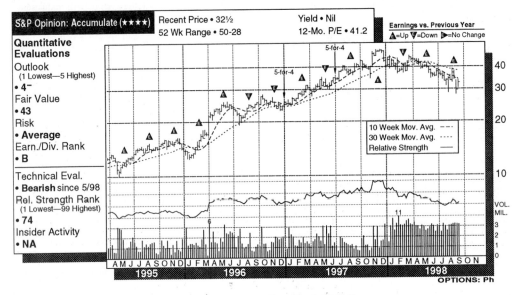

10 Week Mov. Avg. – – –
30 Week Mov. Avg. ·······
Relative Strength ——

OPTIONS: Ph

Overview - 24-AUG-98

In January 1998, this retailer acquired Mac Frugal's Bargains Close-outs Inc. (MFI) in a stock-swap transaction valued at about $1 billion. Including restatements to reflect the acquisition, CNS's FY 98 revenues totaled $4.1 billion, and full-year earnings per share, before a fourth quarter one-time charge of $0.74, amounted to $1.51. Prior to acquiring MFI, CNS was operating, under the Odd Lots and Big Lots names, more than 600 closeout stores, which primarily sell new, name-brand products obtained from manufacturers' excess inventories. Earlier, in May 1996, CNS significantly expanded its toy operations when it acquired the Kay-Bee (or K*B) toy business, which includes both currently promoted and closeout merchandise. In the year ahead, we expect that CNS's overall earnings will benefit from economies of scale, improved product offerings at some of the close-out stores, cost controls, and synergy from owning related businesses. Long term, we expect that furniture sales will increasingly be a growth driver for CNS.

Valuation - 24-AUG-98

In mid-August 1998, we lowered our opinion on this stock to "accumulate," from "buy." The shares had moved up sharply from their recent low, and we were increasingly concerned that the seasonality of CNS's business (i.e. heavily weighted toward the fourth quarter) and some wariness about EPS visibility would restrain the valuation given to the stock. However, while we are concerned about the risk of an earnings disappointment in FY 99's fourth quarter, we look for prospects of sizable profit growth in the fiscal year ending January 2000 to enable the stock to outperform the S&P 500 in the next six-to-12 months.

Key Stock Statistics

S&P EPS Est. 1999	1.90	Tang. Bk. Value/Share	9.76
P/E on S&P Est. 1999	17.1	Beta	0.85
S&P EPS Est. 2000	2.30	Shareholders	1,300
Dividend Rate/Share	Nil	Market cap. (B)	$ 3.6
Shs. outstg. (M)	109.3	Inst. holdings	90%
Avg. daily vol. (M)	1.115		

Value of $10,000 invested 5 years ago: $ 28,265

Fiscal Year Ending Jan. 31

	1999	1998	1997	1996	1995	1994
Revenues (Million $)						
1Q	823.2	778.3	322.0	291.8	242.3	210.2
2Q	823.9	801.3	533.0	325.1	272.8	234.4
3Q	—	859.6	597.0	357.5	310.1	261.1
4Q	—	1,616	1,196	537.9	453.4	349.6
Yr.	—	4,055	2,648	1,512	1,279	1,055
Earnings Per Share ($)						
1Q	**0.01**	-0.01	0.10	0.04	0.03	0.02
2Q	**0.06**	0.05	-0.05	0.12	0.09	0.09
3Q	**E0.14**	0.12	0.02	0.13	0.11	0.09
4Q	**E1.69**	0.60	1.26	0.56	0.51	0.38
Yr.	**E1.90**	0.77	1.35	0.85	0.74	0.58

Next earnings report expected: mid November

Dividend Data

No cash dividends have been paid. Five-for-four stock splits were effected in December 1996 and June 1997.

A Division of The McGraw·Hill Companies

Business Summary - 24-AUG-98

Here's a big company that's looking to attract customers with small prices and merchandise for little people. Consolidated Stores is a large U.S. retailer of closeout merchandise and is also one of the biggest toy retailers in the U.S. As of August 1998, CNS was operating more than 2,317 stores in all 50 states and Puerto Rico. Also, CNS sells some merchandise wholesale.

CNS is growing through both acquisitions and internal development. In January 1998, CNS acquired Mac Frugal's Bargains Close-outs Inc. (MFI), in a stock-swap transaction valued at about $1 billion. With restatements to account for the pooling-of-interests acquisition, CNS's FY 98 revenues (with MFI) were up 19% from those of the prior year. Excluding one-time charges, earnings per share from continuing operations increased 20% from the year earlier pro forma level of $1.26. As of January 1998, Mac Frugal's was operating 326 closeout stores in 18 states, doing business under the Pic 'N' Save and Mac Frugal's Bargains Close-outs names. In the acquisition of MFI, CNS issued 23.4 million common shares.

As of August 1998, including the MFI acquisition, there were 1,050 stores operating in CNS's Close-out Division. Prior to acquiring MFI, CNS already had a sizable close-out division, with merchandise largely sold at

more than 600 Big Lots and Odd Lots stores. Much of the closeout merchandise provided by CNS is likely to be new, name-brand products obtained from manufacturers' excess inventories. Such inventories have generally resulted from manufacturers having production overruns, package changes, discontinued products and returns. The MFI acquisition may lead (or already have led to) some FY 99 store closings.

Also, as of August 1998, CNS was operating 1,267 toy stores, most of which were part of the May 1996 acquisition of the Kay-Bee Toys division from Melville Corp. for about $285 million (adjusted). The acquired Kay-Bee (or K*B) stores generally offer a combination of currently promoted and closeout merchandise. CNS also has toy stores that carry primarily closeout toys.

In the fiscal year ending January 1999, CNS is expected to open about 265 stores (excluding toy units added for the holiday season), of which roughly 110 would be close-out units, about 115 would be toy stores, and 30-to-40 would be furniture stores. Roughly 50 units may be closed. Also, CNS's existing store base is expected to be placing greater emphasis on frozen food and furniture. Earlier, in FY 97, CNS's earnings from continuing operations were boosted by CNS's decision to close an unprofitable closeout division that included the All for One and iTZADEAL! chains.

Per Share Data ($)

(Year Ended Jan. 31)	1998	1997	1996	1995	1994	1993	1992	1991	1990	1989
Tangible Bk. Val.	9.60	8.15	5.22	4.31	3.56	2.91	2.37	2.10	2.04	2.13
Cash Flow	1.47	1.93	1.24	1.09	0.89	0.76	0.51	0.28	0.11	0.50
Earnings	0.77	1.35	0.84	0.74	0.58	0.50	0.28	0.06	-0.10	0.32
Dividends	Nil	Nil	Nil	Nil	Nil	Nil	Nil	Nil	Nil	Nil
Payout Ratio	Nil	Nil	Nil	Nil	Nil	Nil	Nil	Nil	Nil	Nil
Cal. Yrs.	1997	1996	1995	1994	1993	1992	1991	1990	1989	1988
Prices - High	50	28³⁄₈	16³⁄₈	13	14¹⁄₄	12	7³⁄₄	3⁵⁄₈	5³⁄₈	4¹⁄₂
- Low	24¹⁄₂	12³⁄₈	10¹⁄₈	7³⁄₈	9	6³⁄₈	2³⁄₁₆	1³⁄₁₆	2³⁄₁₆	2¹⁄₂
P/E Ratio - High	65	21	19	18	25	24	28	58	NM	14
- Low	32	9	12	10	16	13	8	19	NM	8

Income Statement Analysis (Million $)

Revs.	4,055	2,648	1,512	1,275	1,055	929	771	679	609	627
Oper. Inc.	268	245	142	12.5	100	83.9	54.5	30.8	26.2	54.4
Depr.	79.2	48.4	30.0	26.5	23.7	19.5	16.1	15.5	14.8	12.8
Int. Exp.	25.7	16.8	8.0	8.0	6.3	5.7	6.3	9.6	10.0	7.6
Pretax Inc.	162	180	102	92.0	71.7	60.3	32.4	6.6	-14.5	37.1
Eff. Tax Rate	47%	37%	37%	40%	40%	38%	38%	32%	NM	39%
Net Inc.	85.9	113	64.4	55.2	43.0	37.1	20.1	4.5	-7.0	22.6

Balance Sheet & Other Fin. Data (Million $)

Cash	41.7	30.0	13.0	40.4	24.9	35.3	39.1	3.9	7.5	16.8
Curr. Assets	1,107	927	452	381	311	262	219	178	190	184
Total Assets	1,746	1,331	640	552	468	391	329	288	308	286
Curr. Liab.	525	457	198	171	136	119	99	78.0	63.4	75.2
LT Debt	115	151	25.0	40.0	50.0	50.0	50.0	50.1	91.1	53.3
Common Eqty.	1,035	682	390	315	259	209	171	150	145	151
Total Cap.	1,106	870	434	372	325	272	230	210	245	211
Cap. Exp.	146	93.6	48.1	41.6	46.0	40.4	18.1	7.9	32.0	13.7
Cash Flow	165	162	94.5	81.7	66.7	56.7	36.2	20.1	7.8	35.4
Curr. Ratio	2.1	2.0	2.3	2.2	2.3	2.2	2.2	2.3	3.0	2.4
% LT Debt of Cap.	11.1	17.4	5.8	10.7	15.4	18.4	21.7	23.9	37.2	25.3
% Net Inc.of Revs.	2.1	4.2	4.3	4.3	4.1	4.0	4.0	0.7	NM	3.6
% Ret. on Assets	5.6	11.5	10.9	10.8	10.0	10.3	6.5	1.5	NM	8.5
% Ret. on Equity	10.0	21.2	18.3	19.2	18.3	19.5	12.5	3.1	NM	16.2

Data largely as orig. reptd.; bef. results of disc. opers. and/or spec. items. Per share data adj. for stk. divs. as of ex-div. date. Bold denotes diluted EPS (FASB 128). E-Estimated. NA-Not Available. NM-Not Meaningful. NR-Not Ranked.

Office—300 Phillipi Rd., Columbus, OH 43228. **Tel**—(614) 278-6800. **Fax**—(614) 278-6666. **Website**—http://www.cnstores.com **Chrmn & CEO**—W. G. Kelley.**Pres**—M. L. Glazer.**EVP & CFO**—Michael J. Potter.**SVP-Secy**—A. J. Bell.**Investor Contact**—Michael J. Wagner.**Dirs**—S. M. Berman, W. E. Carlborg, M. L. Glazer, W. G. Kelley, D. T. Kollat, B. J. Lauderback, N. P. Morton, D. B. Tishkoff, W. A. Wickham. **Transfer Agent & Registrar**—National City Bank, Cleveland. **Incorporated**—in Delaware 1983.**Empl**— 50,324. **S&P Analyst:** Tom Graves, CFA

Cooper Industries   660

NYSE Symbol **CBE**

In S&P 500

12-SEP-98

Industry:
Machinery (Diversified)

Summary: Cooper Industries, a diversified, worldwide manufacturer of electrical products, tools and hardware, has agreed to sell its automotive products segment.

S&P Opinion: Hold (★★★)

Recent Price • 44
52 Wk Range • 70%-40%

Yield • 3.0%
12-Mo. P/E • 13.0

Earnings vs. Previous Year
▲=Up ▼=Down ►=No Change

Quantitative Evaluations

Outlook
(1 Lowest—5 Highest)
• **4+**

Fair Value
• **54¼**

Risk
• **Low**

Earn./Div. Rank
• **A-**

Technical Eval.
• **Bullish** since 6/98

Rel. Strength Rank
(1 Lowest—99 Highest)
• **54**

Insider Activity
• **Neutral**

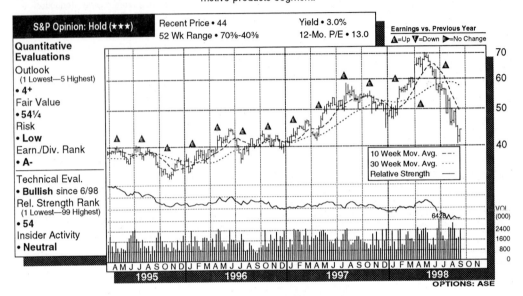

- 10 Week Mov. Avg. ---
- 30 Week Mov. Avg. ·····
- Relative Strength —

VOL (000)
2400
1600
800
0

AMJJASOND J FMAMJ JASOND J FMAMJ J ASOND J FMAMJ J A S O N
1995   1996   1997   1998

OPTIONS: ASE

Overview - 21-AUG-98

CBE recently agreed to sell its automotive products segment ($1.9 billion in 1997 sales), to Federal-Mogul Corp. for $1.9 billion. We would like to see the company use the proceeds for a combination of share repurchases, debt reduction and strategic or accretive acquisitions. Revenues from continuing operations should rise in the mid-single digits in 1998, led by gains in Tools & Hardware and Electrical Products, aided by global expansion and acquisitions. All segments will be negatively impacted by soft economic conditions in Asia and the strike at General Motors. CBE hopes to benefit from slightly better pricing (aided by its products' market-share-leading positions), a leveling of raw material prices, and product line extensions via complementary acquisitions that leverage its overhead cost structure.

Valuation - 21-AUG-98

We recently upgraded the shares from avoid to hold, as CBE agreed to sell its automotive operations. Although second quarter earnings were lower-than-expected and CBE warned of reduced visibility for the second half of the year, the recent share decline largely reflects the discounting of that news. Long term, margins should widen on acquisitions, which are helping to grow the top line, and improved information technology, which is poised to cut overhead costs and improve working capital turnover. CBE has stated a preference for making acquisitions rather than buying back shares or boosting the dividend. However, CBE is willing to repurchase shares if appropriate acquisitions are not found. Accretive acquisitions should supplement the moderate growth expected from the current business mix and help Cooper realize its goal of annual 8% sales and 12% EPS growth, along with improved margins and asset utilization.

Key Stock Statistics

S&P EPS Est. 1998	3.40	Tang. Bk. Value/Share	NM
P/E on S&P Est. 1998	12.9	Beta	0.86
S&P EPS Est. 1999	3.75	Shareholders	31,300
Dividend Rate/Share	1.32	Market cap. (B)	$ 5.1
Shs. outstg. (M)	116.4	Inst. holdings	80%
Avg. daily vol. (M)	0.481		

Value of $10,000 invested 5 years ago: NA

Fiscal Year Ending Dec. 31

	1998	1997	1996	1995	1994	1993
Revenues (Million $)						
1Q	1,343	1,319	1,292	1,123	1,038	1,471
2Q	1,429	1,385	1,351	1,268	1,174	1,612
3Q	—	1,297	1,308	1,206	1,136	1,592
4Q	—	1,288	1,333	1,288	1,240	1,599
Yr.	—	5,289	5,284	4,886	4,588	6,274
Earnings Per Share ($)						
1Q	**0.76**	**0.67**	0.58	0.48	0.34	0.44
2Q	**0.88**	**0.86**	0.82	0.71	0.58	0.79
3Q	—	**0.84**	0.72	0.65	0.55	0.75
4Q	—	**0.90**	0.81	0.68	0.63	0.78
Yr.	**E3.40**	**3.26**	2.77	2.51	2.10	2.75

Next earnings report expected: late October

Dividend Data (Dividends have been paid since 1947.)

Amount ($)	Date Decl.	Ex-Div. Date	Stock of Record	Payment Date
0.330	Nov. 04	Dec. 03	Dec. 05	Jan. 02 '98
0.330	Feb. 11	Feb. 26	Mar. 02	Apr. 01 '98
0.330	Apr. 28	Jun. 09	Jun. 11	Jul. 01 '98
0.330	Aug. 04	Sep. 10	Sep. 14	Oct. 01 '98

A Division of The **McGraw·Hill** *Companies*

Business Summary - 21-AUG-98

Cooper Industries, a diversified, worldwide manufacturer of electrical products, tools and hardware, and automotive products, is focused on leveraging its strong brand name recognition by broadening its product line; strengthening its manufacturing and distribution systems to lower costs and improve customer service; expanding globally via acquisitions and joint ventures to participate in growing economies; and improving working capital efficiency and increasing cash flow to fuel future growth.

The company recently agreed to sell its automotive operations ($1.9 billion in 1997 revenues) to Federal-Mogul Corp. for $1.9 billion in cash. Proceeds could be used for funding internal growth and acquisitions for the remaining segments, share repurchases or general corporate purposes.

Electrical products contributed 49% of revenues in 1997, tools & hardware 16% and automotive products 35%.

The electrical products segment makes electrical and electronic distribution and circuit protection products and lighting fixtures for use in residential, commercial and industrial construction, maintenance and repair. It also makes products for use by utilities and industries for primary power distribution and control. Products are marketed under the Arrow Hart, Buss, Edison,

Crouse-Hinds, CEAG, McGraw-Edison, Fail-Safe, halo, Kyle, Metalux and RTE names. About 24% of electrical products shipments were to international destinations. In June 1997, CBE acquired Kearney Co., a manufacturer of electrical power equipment; the acquisition broadened Cooper's systems automation product line with utilities.

Tools and hardware items are made for use in residential, commercial and industrial construction, maintenance and repair, and for general industrial and consumer use. Product lines include a variety of hand and power tool brands as well as chain and fittings. Some 38% of tools and hardware segment sales were to international markets. In May 1997, CBE sold its Kirsch drapery hardware and custom window coverings business for $216 million.

The automotive products segment manufactures spark plugs, wiper blades, lamps, brake system components and other products for use by the automotive aftermarket and in automobile assemblies. It also makes suspension, steering, temperature control and driveline components for the automotive aftermarket. Brand names include Apex, Anco, Belden, Champion, Wagner and Zanxx. International shipments accounted for 29% of automotive sales. In March 1998, CBE swapped its temperature control product lines (1997 revenues of $120 million) for the brake business ($160 million) of Standard Motor Products, Inc. (NYSE: SMP).

Per Share Data ($)

(Year Ended Dec. 31)	1997	1996	1995	1994	1993	1992	1991	1990	1989	1988
Tangible Bk. Val.	1.60	NM	-4.71	5.02	-3.14	-6.12	0.93	-2.34	-2.23	5.02
Cash Flow	5.26	5.08	4.46	4.31	5.40	5.25	5.34	4.96	3.84	3.40
Earnings	3.26	2.93	2.51	2.10	2.75	2.71	3.04	2.81	2.51	2.21
Dividends	1.32	1.32	1.32	1.32	1.32	1.24	1.16	1.08	1.00	0.90
Payout Ratio	40%	45%	53%	63%	48%	46%	38%	38%	41%	41%
Prices - High	58⅝	44⅝	40½	52¼	54¾	59⅜	58	46	40	31⅜
- Low	40	34⅛	32⅞	31⅝	45⅝	41¾	38½	31¼	26⅞	25⅛
P/E Ratio - High	18	15	16	25	20	22	19	16	16	14
- Low	12	12	13	15	17	15	13	11	11	11

Income Statement Analysis (Million $)

	1997	1996	1995	1994	1993	1992	1991	1990	1989	1988
Revs.	5,289	5,284	4,886	4,588	6,253	6,119	6,155	6,206	5,115	4,250
Oper. Inc.	939	869	848	777	1,006	945	1,080	1,065	783	610
Depr.	220	234	219	199	303	289	258	238	141	121
Int. Exp.	90.0	142	151	73.0	99	116	161	214	183	112
Pretax Inc.	627	558	478	505	625	580	669	629	475	386
Eff. Tax Rate	37%	44%	41%	42%	41%	38%	41%	43%	44%	42%
Net Inc.	395	315	281	293	367	361	393	361	268	224

Balance Sheet & Other Fin. Data (Million $)

	1997	1996	1995	1994	1993	1992	1991	1990	1989	1988
Cash	30.0	16.0	18.0	25.3	13.0	17.8	19.4	13.5	28.5	7.0
Curr. Assets	2,137	2,098	2,127	2,100	2,582	2,837	2,909	2,908	2,799	1,963
Total Assets	6,053	6,053	6,064	6,401	7,148	7,576	7,149	7,168	6,745	4,384
Curr. Liab.	1,385	1,381	1,382	1,333	1,703	1,650	1,711	1,866	1,782	1,163
LT Debt	1,272	1,738	1,865	1,362	1,816	1,816	1,479	1,684	1,829	1,170
Common Eqty.	2,577	1,890	1,717	2,741	2,231	2,117	2,648	2,353	1,979	1,771
Total Cap.	3,849	3,628	3,582	4,103	4,239	4,683	5,167	5,020	4,743	2,942
Cap. Exp.	196	202	188	209	275	274	266	240	191	128
Cash Flow	615	549	500	492	617	598	600	550	404	346
Curr. Ratio	1.5	1.5	1.5	1.6	1.5	1.7	1.7	1.6	1.6	1.7
% LT Debt of Cap.	33.0	47.9	52.1	33.2	29.6	38.8	28.6	33.6	38.6	39.8
% Net Inc.of Revs.	7.5	6.0	5.8	6.4	5.9	5.9	6.4	5.8	5.2	5.3
% Ret. on Assets	6.6	5.2	4.5	4.6	5.0	4.9	5.4	5.2	4.7	5.5
% Ret. on Equity	17.7	17.5	12.6	10.2	14.4	12.9	13.5	14.3	13.6	13.3

Data as orig. reptd.; bef. results of disc. opers. and/or spec. items. Per share data adj. for stk. divs. as of ex-div. date. Bold denotes diluted EPS (FASB 128). E-Estimated. NA-Not Available. NM-Not Meaningful. NR-Not Ranked.

Office—600 Travis, Suite 5800, Houston, TX 77002. **Tel**—(713) 209-8400. **E-mail**—info@cooperindustries.com **Website**—http://www.cooperindustries.com **Chrmn, Pres & CEO**—H. J. Riley Jr. **SVP-Fin & CFO**—D. B. McWilliams. **VP & Treas**—A. J. Hill. **SVP & Secy**—D. K. Schumacher. **Investor Contact**—Richard J. Bajenski (713-209-8610). **Dirs**—W. L. Batts, A. J. P. Belda, R. M. Devlin, C. J. Grum, L. A. Hill, H. S. Hook, C. S. Nicandros, F. A. Olson, J. D. Ong, H. J. Riley Jr., Sir Ralph H. Robins, J. R. Wilson. **Transfer Agent & Registrar**—First Chicago Trust Co. of New York, Jersey City, NJ. **Incorporated**—in Ohio in 1929. **Empl**—41,200. **S&P Analyst:** Efraim Levy

Cooper Tire & Rubber
661K
NYSE Symbol **CTB**

In S&P 500

12-SEP-98

Industry:
Auto Parts & Equipment

Summary: The fourth largest U.S. tire maker, Cooper supplies tires exclusively for the replacement market. It also manufactures original equipment automotive components.

S&P Opinion: Avoid (★★)	Recent Price • 17¼	Yield • 2.2%	Earnings vs. Previous Year
	52 Wk Range • 28⅜-15¾	12-Mo. P/E • 10.8	▲=Up ▼=Down ▶=No Change

Quantitative Evaluations

Outlook
(1 Lowest—5 Highest)
• **2**

Fair Value
• **16¾**

Risk
• **Low**

Earn./Div. Rank
• **A**

Technical Eval.
• **Bearish** since 6/90

Rel. Strength Rank
(1 Lowest—99 Highest)
• **65**

Insider Activity
• **NA**

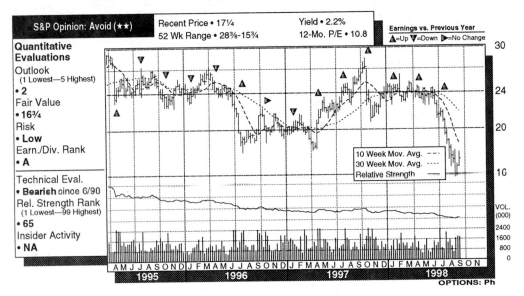

10 Week Mov. Avg. -----
30 Week Mov. Avg. ·····
Relative Strength ——

VOL.
(000)

OPTIONS: Ph

Overview - 31-JUL-98

Sales should rise in 1998, reflecting stronger demand from Pep Boys and other customers, and new engineered products contracts. Efforts to raise prices continue to be thwarted by competitive market conditions. Meanwhile, raw material costs, which ran up sharply in 1995, have generally been declining since the fourth quarter of 1996, and we anticipated further decreases in 1998. Nevertheless, margins will continue under severe pressure, as selling prices decline. Over the long term, results should be aided by the company's strong relationships with its independent dealers, acquisitions, and major investments aimed at boosting operating efficiencies. Favorable long-term trends include a growing vehicle population, a continuing rise in miles driven per vehicle, and efforts to expand export sales. Local production of engineered rubber products in Europe is possible if demand is sufficient. CTB expects to continue high levels of spending to boost productivity and efficiency.

Valuation - 31-JUL-98

The shares have been under pressure from competitive market conditions. Despite the depressed price, we think that the stock will continue to underperform the market, reflecting what we expect to be only a gradual earnings recovery, as raw material prices decrease and contributions from the Avon Tyres acquisition begin to have a positive impact on earnings. The benefits of cost cutting efforts will be offset by CTB's continued inability to institute price increases; this will also slow its efforts to improve profitability. The balance sheet remains strong, and the company should be able to finance capital spending planned for the future without issuing additional equity.

Key Stock Statistics

S&P EPS Est. 1998	1.85	Tang. Bk. Value/Share	10.26
P/E on S&P Est. 1998	9.3	Beta	1.07
Dividend Rate/Share	0.38	Shareholders	6,000
Shs. outstg. (M)	77.4	Market cap. (B)	$ 1.3
Avg. daily vol. (M)	0.297	Inst. holdings	67%

Value of $10,000 invested 5 years ago: $ 5,467

Fiscal Year Ending Dec. 31

	1998	1997	1996	1995	1994	1993
Revenues (Million $)						
1Q	437.6	379.5	381.0	365.4	329.1	280.1
2Q	461.7	464.0	398.9	371.4	329.3	292.6
3Q	—	480.6	423.2	375.0	383.5	326.1
4Q	—	488.9	416.3	381.9	361.3	294.9
Yr.	—	1,813	1,619	1,494	1,403	1,194
Earnings Per Share ($)						
1Q	0.34	0.31	0.28	0.33	0.32	0.30
2Q	0.41	0.40	0.30	0.29	0.33	0.29
3Q	—	0.40	0.32	0.32	0.42	0.30
4Q	—	0.44	0.40	0.41	0.47	0.33
Yr.	E1.85	1.55	1.30	1.35	1.54	1.22

Next earnings report expected: mid October

Dividend Data (Dividends have been paid since 1950.)

Amount ($)	Date Decl.	Ex-Div. Date	Stock of Record	Payment Date
0.095	Nov. 13	Nov. 25	Nov. 28	Dec. 23 '97
0.095	Feb. 10	Mar. 05	Mar. 09	Mar. 31 '98
0.095	May. 13	May. 29	Jun. 02	Jun. 30 '98
0.095	Jul. 21	Sep. 04	Sep. 09	Sep. 30 '98

A Division of The McGraw-Hill Companies

Business Summary - 31-JUL-98

Cooper Tire & Rubber (CTB) is treading foreign territory in an effort to become a more global company. In March 1997, CTB, the fourth largest producer of tires in the U.S., and the ninth largest in the world, acquired the tire operations of Avon Rubber p.l.c. of the U.K., for $97 million. Although CTB markets its products in more than 100 countries worldwide, Avon gave the company manufacturing and distribution facilities located closer to overseas customers. With the acquisition, CTB acquired a manufacturing plant in England, as well as tire distribution companies and facilities in France, Germany and Switzerland.

CTB, founded in 1914, and based in Findlay, OH, sells tires exclusively to the replacement market and also makes inner tubes and engineered rubber automotive components for original equipment manufacturers.

CTB makes both automobile and truck tires which are sold through independent dealers and distributors under the Cooper, Mastercraft, Starfire and now Cooper-Avon brandnames as well as under private-label brands. Independent tire dealers account for about 71% of the replacement tires sold in the U.S. CTB's 1997 sales of automobile and truck tires represented 13% of all domestic, original equipment and replacement tire sales. In 1996, the company added six new passenger tire lines focusing on the performance-oriented driver, in-

cluding extensions and new additions to its Cobra line of performance tires.

The company supplies its engineered rubber products to nearly every automobile maker in the U.S. and Canada. CTB makes vibration control products for increased riding comfort and to reduce vehicle noise; rubber seals for doors, trunks, windows and hoods; and reinforced hoses used mainly to transport fluids, fuels and gases. In 1996, CTB introduced major new products for General Motors and Chrysler including tradional door and glass seals and a new plastic veneer door opening weather strip.

Tires are made at four domestic plants and five U.S. plants produce engineered rubber products. The company also has one plant in Mexico that manufactures engineered products and inner tubes and one U.S. plant that makes inner tubes.

Despite intense industry conditions in the replacement tire market and a decline in sales to a major customer, CTB posted record revenues in 1997 of $1.8 billion (up 12% from 1996). Earnings rebounded 13% to $122.4 million from the previous year as improved efficiencies and product mix offset pricing pressures and a weak UK market.

In May 1997, directors authorized the repurchase of an additional 5 million shares, but the company has said it does not expect to retire stock at recent price levels of about $24 a share.

Per Share Data ($) (Year Ended Dec. 31)	1997	1996	1995	1994	1993	1992	1991	1990	1989	1988
Tangible Bk. Val.	10.22	9.67	8.95	7.65	6.30	5.52	5.14	4.47	3.77	3.15
Cash Flow	2.74	2.22	2.11	2.20	1.78	1.75	1.35	1.14	1.00	0.75
Earnings	1.55	1.30	1.35	1.54	1.22	1.30	0.96	0.81	0.71	0.51
Dividends	0.35	0.31	0.27	0.23	0.20	0.17	0.13	0.10	0.09	0.07
Payout Ratio	23%	24%	20%	15%	16%	13%	14%	13%	12%	14%
Prices - High	28⅜	27⅜	29⅝	29½	39⅝	35⅝	26⅜	10½	9¾	6⅞
- Low	18	17⅞	22¼	21⅝	20	22⅛	7⅞	6¼	5⅝	3⅝
P/E Ratio - High	18	21	22	19	32	27	27	13	14	14
- Low	12	14	16	14	16	17	8	8	8	7

Income Statement Analysis (Million $)

	1997	1996	1995	1994	1993	1992	1991	1990	1989	1988
Revs.	1,813	1,619	1,494	1,403	1,194	1,175	1,001	896	867	748
Oper. Inc.	304	250	240	264	212	209	160	136	118	86.0
Depr.	94.5	76.8	63.6	55.6	46.4	38.1	32.0	27.6	23.4	19.9
Int. Exp.	15.7	6.0	3.4	3.9	4.7	5.0	8.3	7.3	6.3	6.4
Pretax Inc.	195	172	180	208	164	170	124	105	93.0	65.0
Eff. Tax Rate	37%	37%	37%	38%	38%	36%	36%	37%	37%	37%
Net Inc.	122	108	113	129	102	108	79.4	66.5	58.2	41.1

Balance Sheet & Other Fin. Data (Million $)

	1997	1996	1995	1994	1993	1992	1991	1990	1989	1988
Cash	52.9	19.0	23.0	103	25.8	55.1	24.4	10.1	49.6	38.7
Curr. Assets	555	444	431	455	332	315	262	268	249	229
Total Assets	1,496	1,273	1,144	1,040	890	797	671	616	520	443
Curr. Liab.	200	187	158	152	127	140	117	101	99	86.0
LT Debt	206	69.5	28.6	33.6	38.7	48.1	53.5	91.0	65.7	67.8
Common Eqty.	834	787	749	662	550	471	440	369	310	258
Total Cap.	1,047	909	814	725	608	526	532	494	405	350
Cap. Exp.	108	194	194	78.0	117	110	86.0	100	73.0	71.0
Cash Flow	217	185	176	184	149	146	111	94.0	82.0	61.0
Curr. Ratio	2.8	2.4	2.7	3.0	2.6	2.3	2.2	2.7	2.5	2.7
% LT Debt of Cap.	19.6	7.7	3.5	4.6	6.4	9.1	10.1	18.4	16.2	19.4
% Net Inc.of Revs.	6.8	6.7	7.6	9.2	8.6	9.2	7.9	7.4	6.7	5.5
% Ret. on Assets	8.8	9.0	10.3	13.3	12.1	14.7	12.3	11.7	12.1	9.6
% Ret. on Equity	15.1	14.1	16.0	21.2	20.0	23.7	19.6	19.5	20.5	17.1

Data as orig. reptd.; bef. results of disc. opers. and/or spec. items. Per share data adj. for stk. divs. as of ex-div. date. Bold denotes diluted EPS (FASB 128). E-Estimated. NA-Not Available. NM-Not Meaningful. NR-Not Ranked.

Office—701 Lima Ave., Findlay, OH 45840. **Tel**—(419) 423-1321. **Website**—http://www.coopertire.com **Chrmn, CEO, & Pres**—P. W. Rooney. **EVP, CFO & Investor Contact**—J. Alec Reinhardt. **VP & Treas**—W. C. Hattendorf. **Secy**—S. C. Kaiman. **Dirs**—A. H. Aronson, E. D. Dunford, J. Fahl, D. M. Fretz, D. J. Gormley, J. F. Meier, B. O. Pond., J. A. Reinhardt, P. W. Rooney, J. H. Shuey. **Transfer Agent & Registrar**—Fifth Third Bank, Cincinnati. **Incorporated**—in Delaware in 1930. **Empl**— 10,456. **S&P Analyst:** Efraim Levy

Coors (Adolph) Co.   3621M

Nasdaq Symbol **ACCOB**

In S&P 500

12-SEP-98

Industry: Beverages (Alcoholic)

Summary: Adolph Coors Co. is the parent company of the third largest U.S. brewer, with an approximate 10% market share.

S&P Opinion: Accumulate (★★★★)	Recent Price • 49⅜	Yield • 1.2%
	52 Wk Range • 49⅞-29¼	12-Mo. P/E • 25.6

Earnings vs. Previous Year
▲=Up ▼=Down ▶=No Change

Quantitative Evaluations

Outlook (1 Lowest—5 Highest)
• **2+**

Fair Value
• **43⅞**

Risk
• **Average**

Earn./Div. Rank
• **B**

Technical Eval.
• **Neutral** since 9/98

Rel. Strength Rank (1 Lowest—99 Highest)
• **99**

Insider Activity
• **Neutral**

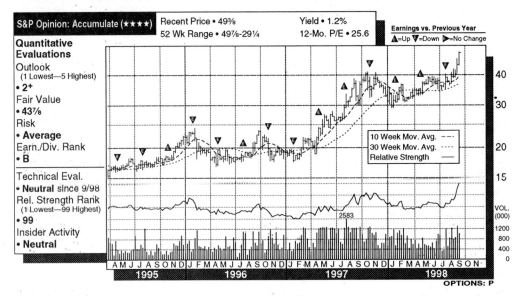

10 Week Mov. Avg. - - - -
30 Week Mov. Avg. - - - -
Relative Strength —

2583

VOL. (000)
1200
800
400
0

1995 1996 1997 1998

OPTIONS: P

Overview - 31-JUL-98

Net sales (after excise taxes) are expected to grow at a low to mid-single-digit annual rate through 1998, led primarily by positive domestic and export sales volume of the company's most important product, Coors Light. Gross margins should continue to benefit from the increased sales volume and a favorable packaging raw material environment. Marketing outlays are expected to remain at a high level, to combat a high level of competitive pressures, but modest operating margin expansion is seen. Helped by a $71.5 million legal award from Molson Breweries in 1997's second quarter, further reductions in net interest expense is seen. Assuming also an annual 2% reduction in shares outstanding, we look for EPS to reach $2.00 in 1998, up from 1997's $1.79 (before special credits of $0.37). The quarterly dividend was boosted by 20% in September 1997, to $0.60 annually.

Valuation - 31-JUL-98

A favorable packaging cost environment in the mature U.S. beer industry has led to aggressive multi-pack and pricing activity among the major brewers in recent months. However, Coors has been successful in combating such pressures on profitability with effective promotional activity, cost control, and good performance in its key export markets, such as Canada and the Caribbean. Strong sales and earnings momentum seen in the first half of 1998, should provide good momentum for the remainder of the peak summer selling season. The shares remain attractively valued, at a modest P/E discount to that of the S&P 500 index, and at a very low price/sales ratio of approximately 0.8. We expect the company's improving fundamentals and low relative valuation to drive above average gains over the next 12 months.

Key Stock Statistics

S&P EPS Est. 1998	2.00	Tang. Bk. Value/Share	20.80
P/E on S&P Est. 1998	24.7	Beta	0.22
S&P EPS Est. 1999	2.15	Shareholders	4,900
Dividend Rate/Share	0.60	Market cap. (B)	$ 1.7
Shs. outstg. (M)	36.3	Inst. holdings	41%
Avg. daily vol. (M)	0.242		

Value of $10,000 invested 5 years ago: $ 34,198

Fiscal Year Ending Dec. 31

	1998	1997	1996	1995	1994	1993
Revenues (Million $)						
1Q	414.1	399.0	370.0	326.6	318.4	296.0
2Q	541.9	520.8	503.5	399.5	432.2	412.9
3Q	—	489.7	454.6	567.9	555.6	535.6
4Q	—	412.6	404.1	381.4	356.4	337.3
Yr.	—	1,822	1,732	1,675	1,663	1,582
Earnings Per Share ($)						
1Q	0.26	0.21	-0.08	Nil	0.18	0.12
2Q	1.06	1.34	0.63	0.40	0.63	0.50
3Q	E0.51	0.46	0.49	0.59	0.45	0.25
4Q	E0.20	0.15	0.10	0.14	0.26	-1.97
Yr.	E2.00	2.16	1.14	1.13	1.52	-1.10

Next earnings report expected: NA

Dividend Data (Dividends have been paid since 1970.)

Amount ($)	Date Decl.	Ex-Div. Date	Stock of Record	Payment Date
0.150	Nov. 13	Nov. 25	Nov. 30	Dec. 15 '97
0.150	Feb. 13	Feb. 25	Feb. 28	Mar. 16 '98
0.150	May. 15	May. 27	May. 31	Jun. 15 '98
0.150	Aug. 14	Aug. 27	Aug. 31	Sep. 15 '98

A Division of The McGraw-Hill Companies

Adolph Coors Company

Business Summary - 31-JUL-98

Founded in 1873, Adolph Coors Co., through its Coors Brewing Co. subsidiary, is the third-largest U.S. brewer. In 1997, the company sold 20.6 million barrels of beer and other malt beverage products, up 3.0% from the level of 1996.

The relatively modest sales volume growth for 1997 was yet another indication that Coors, like all of the major U.S. brewers, competes in a very mature U.S. market which offers little pricing flexibility. To make matters worse, Coors remains at a competitive disadvantage on the cost front, given its small size relative to its two much larger rivals, Anheuser-Busch and Miller Brewing. The company's strategy in recent years has been to innovate via unique brews and beer packaging, and to increase its exposure in less developed, international markets.

The company's stable of well-known brands includes Coors Light (accounting for more than two-thirds of total sales volume), Original Coors, Coors Extra Gold, Coors Dry, Coors Non-Alcoholic , Keystone, Keystone Light, Keystone Dry, Keystone Ice and Keystone Amber Light, sold in all 50 states and the District of Columbia. Coors also sells premium-priced brews such as Winterfest and Blue Moon, , as well as import or licensed products such as George Killian's Irish Red and Steinlager. The company also produces Zima Clearmalt, a malt-based beverage. Premium and above-premium beers accounted for some 88% of total sales volume in 1997.

Coors has three domestic production facilities: the first, the world's largest single-site brewery, is in Golden, CO; the second, a packaging and brewing facility, is in Memphis, TN; the third facility, which currently operates as a packaging plant and distribution facility, is near Elkton, VA. Significant portions of the company's aluminum can, glass bottle and malt requirements are produced in its own facilities.

Through its U.S. and foreign production facilities, Coors markets its products to approximately 40 international markets and to U.S. military bases worldwide. Original Coors and Coors Light are brewed and distributed by Molson Breweries of Canada Limited under agreement.

In April 1997, the company settled certain legal disputes involving Molson Breweries of Canada, and signed a conditional agreement for a new venture to manage Coors brands in Canada. Under the settlement terms, Molson paid Coors approximately $72 million, which was reflected in the company's second quarter results. In January 1998, Coors Canada began operations.

Per Share Data ($) (Year Ended Dec. 31)	1997	1996	1995	1994	1993	1992	1991	1990	1989	1988
Tangible Bk. Val.	19.36	18.30	17.59	17.06	16.21	17.81	28.64	28.59	28.12	28.37
Cash Flow	5.24	4.33	4.30	4.67	2.02	4.00	4.45	4.56	3.66	4.32
Earnings	2.16	1.14	1.13	1.52	-1.10	0.95	0.64	1.05	0.36	1.28
Dividends	0.55	0.50	0.50	0.50	0.50	0.50	0.50	0.50	0.50	0.50
Payout Ratio	25%	44%	44%	33%	NM	53%	78%	48%	140%	39%
Prices - High	41 1/4	24 1/4	23 1/4	20 7/8	22 1/2	22 7/8	24 1/4	27 3/8	24 3/8	21
- Low	17 1/2	16 3/4	15 1/8	14 3/4	15	15 1/2	17 3/8	17 1/8	17 3/8	16 7/8
P/E Ratio - High	19	21	21	14	NM	24	38	26	68	16
- Low	8	15	13	10	NM	16	27	16	48	13
Income Statement Analysis (Million $)										
Revs.	1,822	1,732	1,675	1,663	1,582	1,551	1,917	1,863	1,764	1,522
Oper. Inc.	233	208	188	215	196	188	194	235	197	181
Depr.	117	121	123	121	119	114	142	130	121	111
Int. Exp.	13.6	17.1	18.4	17.8	20.6	21.6	17.6	4.8	5.4	3.4
Pretax Inc.	147	75.0	73.0	104	57.0	59.0	23.0	64.0	26.0	77.0
Eff. Tax Rate	44%	42%	41%	44%	NM	39%	NM	39%	49%	39%
Net Inc.	82.3	43.4	43.2	58.1	-41.9	35.7	23.9	38.9	13.1	46.9
Balance Sheet & Other Fin. Data (Million $)										
Cash	169	111	32.4	27.0	82.0	40.0	15.0	64.0	44.0	72.0
Curr. Assets	517	417	363	355	384	382	543	522	456	481
Total Assets	1,412	1,363	1,387	1,372	1,351	1,373	1,986	1,762	1,531	1,571
Curr. Liab.	359	292	324	380	377	269	432	321	262	284
LT Debt	145	176	195	131	175	220	220	110	Nil	Nil
Common Eqty.	737	715	695	674	632	685	1,099	1,092	1,061	1,062
Total Cap.	958	968	960	872	860	985	1,479	1,383	1,252	1,267
Cap. Exp.	60.3	65.0	146	160	122	115	355	302	150	178
Cash Flow	199	165	166	179	77.0	150	166	169	135	158
Curr. Ratio	1.4	1.4	1.1	0.9	1.0	1.4	1.3	1.6	1.7	1.7
% LT Debt of Cap.	15.1	18.2	20.3	14.9	20.3	22.3	14.9	8.0	Nil	Nil
% Net Inc.of Revs.	4.5	2.5	2.6	3.5	NM	2.3	1.2	2.1	0.7	3.1
% Ret. on Assets	5.9	3.2	3.1	4.3	NM	2.1	1.3	2.3	0.8	3.1
% Ret. on Equity	11.3	6.2	6.3	8.9	NM	4.0	2.2	3.6	1.2	4.5

Data as orig. reptd.; bef. results of disc. opers. and/or spec. items. Per share data adj. for stk. divs. as of ex-div. date. Bold denotes diluted EPS (FASB 128). E-Estimated. NA-Not Available. NM-Not Meaningful. NR-Not Ranked.

Office—Golden, CO 80401. **Tel**—(303) 279-6565. **Chrmn & Pres**—W. K. Coors. **Vice Chrmn**—J. Coors. **VPs**—P. H. Coors, W. L. Kiely III. **Secy**—P. J. Smith. **Treas**—K. L. MacWilliams. **Investor Contact**—Dave Dunnewald. **Dirs**—J. Coors, P. H. Coors, W. K. Coors, J. B. Llewellyn, L. G. Nogales, P. A. Patsley, W. R. Sanders. **Transfer Agent**—Boston EquiServe, Canton, MA. **Incorporated**—in Colorado in 1913. **Empl**— 5,800. **S&P Analyst:** Richard Joy

Corning Inc.

672

NYSE Symbol **GLW**

In S&P 500

12-SEP-98

Industry:
Manufacturing (Diversified)

Summary: Corning makes fiber optics, specialty materials and consumer products. Health care operations were spun off in 1996, and consumer products operations were sold in 1998.

S&P Opinion: Hold (★★★)	Recent Price • 25½	Yield • 2.8%
	52 Wk Range • 49½-22⅞	12-Mo. P/E • 14.5

Earnings vs. Previous Year
▲=Up ▼=Down ▶=No Change

Quantitative Evaluations

Outlook
(1 Lowest—5 Highest)
• **3**

Fair Value
• **25⅛**

Risk
• **Average**

Earn./Div. Rank
• **B+**

Technical Eval.
• **Bullish** since 9/97

Rel. Strength Rank
(1 Lowest—99 Highest)
• **44**

Insider Activity
• **Neutral**

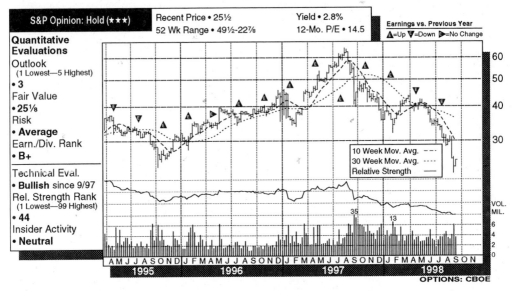

10 Week Mov. Avg. – – –
30 Week Mov. Avg. ·······
Relative Strength ——

VOL.
MIL.

OPTIONS: CBOE

Overview - 22-JUL-98

Following the April 1998 divestiture of its consumer products unit, GLW is focusing on its high technology glass and ceramics businesses. Primary products are optical fiber for communications, and ceramic catalytic converter substrates for auto emission controls. These activities will be supplemented by a series of partnerships in related businesses. The communications division will continue to benefit from growth in demand for fiber optic cable, although at a slower rate in 1998, due to a slowdown in Asia. Growth in substrates is being driven by overseas demand. The consumer products divestiture leaves GLW strategically better focused on high growth markets. Gross margins should improve, in the absence of the low-margin consumer business, but operating margins could deteriorate, due to higher selling expense. Equity income may flatten, on weakness in some international markets. GLW's long-term goals include increasing earnings at least 15% a year, and achieving return on equity of over 20%. GLW expects to build on its leadership in glass, ceramics and photonics, is extending its capabilities in polymers and surfaces, and expects to be a leader in developing new technologies. Foreign markets will remain important to long-term sales growth.

Valuation - 22-JUL-98

We are maintaining our hold recommendation on the shares, despite GLW's recent steps to streamline the conglomerate. We view the shares as adequately valued at a recent level of 22X our 1998 EPS estimate of $1.50 (excluding the consumer products unit). Following the spinoffs, we think that GLW has adequate earnings and cash flow to maintain the dividend at its recent rate. Nevertheless, shareholders should not add to positions until the valuation is more reasonable.

Key Stock Statistics

S&P EPS Est. 1998	1.50	Tang. Bk. Value/Share	4.31
P/E on S&P Est. 1998	17.0	Beta	0.63
S&P EPS Est. 1999	1.90	Shareholders	18,000
Dividend Rate/Share	0.72	Market cap. (B)	$ 5.9
Shs. outstg. (M)	231.9	Inst. holdings	56%
Avg. daily vol. (M)	0.932		

Value of $10,000 invested 5 years ago: NA

Fiscal Year Ending Dec. 31

	1998	1997	1996	1995	1994	1993
Revenues (Million $)						
1Q	794.8	955.9	845.6	1,123	956.6	827.6
2Q	855.9	1,041	920.7	1,307	1,109	912.8
3Q	—	1,048	919.2	1,578	1,453	1,207
4Q	—	1,085	999	1,339	1,281	1,091
Yr.	—	4,129	3,685	5,346	4,799	4,039
Earnings Per Share ($)						
1Q	**0.27**	**0.39**	0.27	0.27	0.28	0.26
2Q	**0.24**	**0.53**	0.41	-1.32	0.54	0.47
3Q	—	**0.47**	0.42	0.37	0.36	-0.18
4Q	—	**0.46**	0.40	0.37	0.14	-0.64
Yr.	—	**1.85**	1.48	-0.23	1.32	-0.09

Next earnings report expected: mid October

Dividend Data (Dividends have been paid since 1881.)

Amount ($)	Date Decl.	Ex-Div. Date	Stock of Record	Payment Date
0.180	Dec. 03	Dec. 11	Dec. 15	Dec. 31 '97
0.180	Feb. 04	Feb. 26	Mar. 02	Mar. 31 '98
0.180	Apr. 30	May. 28	Jun. 01	Jun. 30 '98
0.180	Jul. 24	Aug. 28	Sep. 01	Sep. 30 '98

A Division of The McGraw-Hill Companies

STANDARD
&POOR'S
STOCK REPORTS

Corning Incorporated

672

12-SEP-98

Business Summary - 22-JUL-98

Following the December 31, 1996, spinoff to shareholders of its clinical laboratories and pharmaceutical services businesses, Corning remained in three businesses: communications products, specialty materials and consumer products. In 1997, a further step in the deconglomeration of this S&P 500 company was taken with a plan to sell GLW's original business, Corning's consumer products segment, for $800 million and an 11% equity interest in the acquirer, AEA Investors. However, the agreement was terminated, and GLW subsequently sold the unit in 1998 to Borden, for $603 million and an 8% interest in the unit. In earlier spinoffs, GLW shareholder received all of the shares of Quest Diagnostics (clinical laboratories) and Covance (pharmaceutical services), two newly created, independent, publicly traded companies. Shareholders received one Quest share for every eight GLW shares, and one Covance share for every four shares. These businesses contributed $3.3 billion in revenues in 1995, and pretax income of $406 million.

The two segments that Corning now considers to be core segments are Corning Communications and Corning Technologies. Communications primarily manufactures optical fiber, cable, hardware and components for the global telecommunications industry. GLW is believed to be the world's highest volume and lowest cost producer in the industry. The company is in the forefront of technology in this area, operating through various subsidiaries. GLW is also a leader in flat glass for liquid-crystal displays and large-screen 40 inch or larger projection TV lenses and, through two international alliances, components for television tube manufacturing.

Corning Technologies produces ceramic emission control substrates used in automobile catalytic converters and other pollution-control devices. Demand for these substrates continues to grow as motor vehicle emission regulations are implemented worldwide. The company also produces plastic and glass laboratory products for the life sciences market and specialty glass material components.

The divested consumer products division made the ubiquitous Corning and Corelle houseware products, as well as Steuben crystal. The unit had 1997 sales of $601 million, and income of $57.0 million.

GLW recorded equity income from various investments totaling $79.2 million in 1997. In 1995, GLW wrote off its investment in, and no longer recognizes income from, 50%-owned Dow Corning, a producer of silicones, which filed for bankruptcy protection.

Per Share Data ($)

(Year Ended Dec. 31)	1997	1996	1995	1994	1993	1992	1991	1990	1989	1988
Tangible Bk. Val.	3.83	2.76	2.99	3.75	3.37	8.16	9.40	9.01	9.08	8.78
Cash Flow	3.10	2.77	-1.43	2.92	1.37	2.72	2.90	2.93	2.31	2.48
Earnings	1.85	1.50	-0.23	1.32	-0.09	1.40	1.66	1.54	1.40	1.63
Dividends	0.72	0.72	0.72	0.69	0.68	0.62	0.68	0.46	0.53	0.48
Payout Ratio	39%	48%	NM	52%	NM	44%	42%	30%	38%	29%
Prices - High	65⅛	46¼	37⅜	35	39	40⅜	43⅛	25⅞	21¾	17½
- Low	33¾	27⅞	24⅛	27⅝	24	28¾	21	17⅜	16	11¼
P/E Ratio - High	35	31	NM	27	NM	29	26	17	16	11
- Low	18	19	NM	21	NM	21	13	11	11	7

Income Statement Analysis (Million $)

Revs.	4,090	3,652	5,313	4,799	4,035	3,744	3,287	2,980	2,469	2,152
Oper. Inc.	1,084	850	1,032	1,028	763	730	654	603	433	370
Depr.	322	288	377	338	280	248	248	260	171	154
Int. Exp.	99	87.0	128	122	94.0	68.9	60.4	58.6	53.0	43.9
Pretax Inc.	743	559	183	508	37.0	380	439	436	381	398
Eff. Tax Rate	31%	29%	85%	34%	96%	24%	25%	31%	31%	26%
Net Inc.	440	343	-51.0	281	-15.0	266	311	289	259	292

Balance Sheet & Other Fin. Data (Million $)

Cash	65.0	223	215	161	161	133	208	133	353	157
Curr. Assets	1,424	1,419	1,834	1,726	1,472	1,289	1,229	1,098	1,169	930
Total Assets	4,811	4,321	5,987	6,023	5,232	4,286	3,853	3,512	3,361	2,898
Curr. Liab.	1,018	808	1,165	1,074	1,020	824	708	640	682	509
LT Debt	1,134	1,208	1,393	1,406	1,586	816	700	611	625	499
Common Eqty.	1,246	961	2,103	2,263	1,686	1,804	2,019	1,850	1,711	1,561
Total Cap.	3,016	2,867	3,768	4,305	3,543	2,888	2,935	2,667	2,466	2,166
Cap. Exp.	775	598	495	387	443	377	345	417	377	288
Cash Flow	760	629	-323	618	263	512	557	547	430	446
Curr. Ratio	1.4	1.8	1.6	1.6	1.4	1.6	1.7	1.7	1.7	1.8
% LT Debt of Cap.	37.6	42.1	66.2	32.7	44.8	28.2	23.9	22.9	25.3	23.0
% Net Inc.of Revs.	10.8	9.4	Nil	5.9	NM	7.1	9.5	9.7	10.5	13.6
% Ret. on Assets	9.6	7.0	Nil	4.7	NM	6.5	8.2	8.5	8.1	10.6
% Ret. on Equity	39.7	22.3	Nil	13.4	NM	13.8	15.6	16.3	15.4	19.0

Data as orig. reptd.; bef. results of disc. opers. and/or spec. items. Per share data adj. for stk. divs. as of ex-div. date. Bold denotes diluted EPS (FASB 128). E-Estimated. NA-Not Available. NM-Not Meaningful. NR-Not Ranked.

Office—One Riverfront Plaza, Corning, NY 14831. **Tel**—(607) 974-9000. **Fax**—(607) 974-8551. **Website**—http://www.corning.com **Chrmn & CEO**—R. G. Ackerman. **Vice Chrmn**—V. C. Campbell. **VP & CFO**—J. B. Flaws.**Secy**—A. J. Peck Jr.**Investor Contact**—Richard B. Klein (607-974-8313). **Dirs**—R. G. Ackerman, R. Barker, J. S. Brown, V. C. Campbell, L. S. Eagleburger, J. H. Foster, N. E. Garrity, G. Gund, J. M. Hennessy, J. R. Houghton, J. W. Kinnear, J. W. Loose, J. J. O'Connor, C. A. Rein, H. Rosovsky, H. O. Ruding, W. D. Smithburg.**Transfer Agent & Registrar**—Harris Trust & Savings Bank, Chicago. **Incorporated**—in New York in 1936. **Empl**— 20,000. **S&P Analyst:** Robert E. Friedman, CPA

Costco Companies 3628R

Nasdaq Symbol **COST**

In S&P 500

12-SEP-98

Industry:
Retail (General Merchandise)

Summary: Costco (formerly Price/Costco) operates more than 275 membership warehouses in the U.S. and Canada. It also has units in the U.K., Taiwan and Mexico.

S&P Opinion: Accumulate (★★★★)	Recent Price • 51¾	Yield • Nil	Earnings vs. Previous Year
	52 Wk Range • 65¾-33⅞	12-Mo. P/E • 27.1	▲=Up ▼=Down ▶=No Change

Quantitative Evaluations

Outlook
(1 Lowest—5 Highest)
• **2⁻**

Fair Value
• **49½**

Risk
• **Low**

Earn./Div. Rank
• **B-**

Technical Eval.
• **NA**

Rel. Strength Rank
(1 Lowest—99 Highest)
• **68**

Insider Activity
• **Unfavorable**

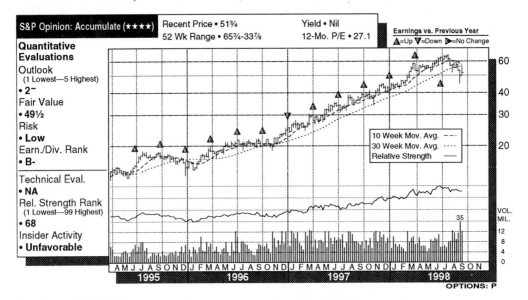

10 Week Mov. Avg. — — —
30 Week Mov. Avg. · · · · ·
Relative Strength ———

OPTIONS: P

Overview - 25-AUG-98

Sales should increase moderately in FY 99 (Aug.), reflecting 3% growth in same-store sales and some 16 to 18 new warehouses; membership fees should be up only slightly. Gross margins should widen marginally, reflecting the increased volume from a larger unit base. Price increases should be controlled as low prices remain COST's competitive advantage in the overcrowded retail marketplace. Selling, general and administrative expenses should increase slightly as a percentage of sales. Interest expense could rise, as borrowings are used to fund the store expansion program. Over the long term, a larger base of warehouse clubs and expansion overseas should continue to boost earnings. Consolidation in the warehouse club sector has resulted in the concentration of business in the hands of fewer players, resulting in a decline in the head-to-head competition that plagued the industry in the past. Earnings in FY 97 reflected a $0.17 a share charge for SFAS No. 121 (impairment of long-lived assets).

Valuation - 25-AUG-98

We have upgraded the shares of this successful and growing warehouse club operator to accumulate. Same-store sales have remained strong in FY 98, increasing by 8% in the first 36 weeks. Ample opportunities to open new units domestically and abroad, a lessening of competition through store closures, industry consolidation and a more rational pricing environment favor the outlook. The company's expanding array of more profitable perishables, its growing higher-margin ancillary businesses and aggressive expansion plans bode well for the long term. The company's core earnings growth rate is in the 15% to 16% range.

Key Stock Statistics

S&P EPS Est. 1998	2.00	Tang. Bk. Value/Share	13.05
P/E on S&P Est. 1998	25.9	Beta	NA
S&P EPS Est. 1999	2.30	Shareholders	7,600
Dividend Rate/Share	Nil	Market cap. (B)	$ 11.2
Shs. outstg. (M)	216.5	Inst. holdings	78%
Avg. daily vol. (M)	3.552		

Value of $10,000 invested 5 years ago: NA

Fiscal Year Ending Aug. 31

	1998	1997	1996	1995	1994	1993
Revenues (Million $)						
1Q	5,430	4,883	4,384	4,030	3,681	3,423
2Q	5,795	5,239	4,689	4,307	4,098	3,736
3Q	5,338	4,836	4,311	3,896	3,616	3,348
4Q	—	6,916	6,183	6,014	5,086	4,648
Yr.	—	21,874	19,566	19,566	16,481	15,155
Earnings Per Share ($)						
1Q	0.44	0.16	0.25	0.22	-0.17	0.20
2Q	**0.56**	0.46	0.35	0.31	0.27	0.31
3Q	0.38	0.31	0.21	0.17	0.14	0.16
4Q	E0.62	0.54	0.42	0.35	0.27	0.34
Yr.	E2.00	1.46	1.24	1.06	0.51	1.01

Next earnings report expected: mid October

Dividend Data

No cash dividends have been paid since 1989, and the company does not intend to pay any in the foreseeable future.

A Division of The McGraw·Hill Companies

Business Summary - 25-AUG-98

Costco Companies (formerly Price/Costco, Inc.) began as the pioneering "I can get it for you wholesale" membership warehouse concept in 1976 in San Diego, California, known as The Price Co. In 1993, Price merged with Costco Wholesale Corp. of Seattle, Washington, creating a $15 billion company with over 200 membership warehouses in the U.S. and Canada. The company spun off Price Enterprises, Inc. to shareholders in 1994, consisting of commercial real estate operations and certain other assets.

Low prices on a limited selection of national brand merchandise and selected private-label products in a wide range of merchandise categories produce high sales volume and rapid inventory turnover. Rapid inventory turnover, combined with operating efficiencies achieved by volume purchasing in a no-frills, self-service warehouse facility, enables the company to operate profitably at significantly lower gross margins than traditional retailers and even discounters and supermarkets. Costco buys virtually all of its merchandise directly from manufacturers for shipment either directly to the warehouse clubs or to a consolidation point (depot) where various shipments are combined so as to minimize freight and handling costs. COST generally re-

ceives cash from the sale of a substantial portion of its inventory at mature warehouse operations before it is required to pay vendors, even though the company often pays early to obtain payment discounts.

The company has two primary types of membership: Business and Gold Star (individual) members. Businesses (including individuals) with a resale or business license may become Business members by paying an annual $30 fee. Gold Star membership is $35 annually. As of August 31, 1997, Costco had 3.5 million Business memberships and 7.8 million Gold Star memberships.

A typical warehouse format averages about 127,000 sq. ft. Floor plans are designed for economy and efficiency in the use of selling space, in the handling of merchandise and in the control of inventory. Merchandise is generally stored on racks above the sales floor and displayed on pallets containing large quantities of each item, reducing labor required for handling and stocking. Specific items in each product line are limited to fast-selling models, sizes and colors. COST carries only an average of about 3,500 to 4,500 stockkeeping units (SKUs) per warehouse. Typically, a discount retailer or supermarket stocks 40,000 to 60,000 SKUs. Many products are offered for sale in case, carton or multiple-pack quantities only.

Per Share Data ($)

(Year Ended Aug. 31)	1997	1996	1995	1994	1993	1992	1991	1990	1989	1988
Tangible Bk. Val.	11.31	9.07	7.84	7.56	8.08	16.29	14.58	12.49	10.55	9.53
Cash Flow	2.31	2.00	1.71	1.14	NA	3.37	3.35	2.78	2.51	2.23
Earnings	1.46	1.24	1.05	0.51	1.01	2.61	2.68	2.47	2.30	1.93
Dividends	Nil	Nil	Nil	Nil	Nil	Nil	Nil	Nil	1.50	Nil
Payout Ratio	Nil	Nil	Nil	Nil	Nil	Nil	Nil	Nil	64%	Nil
Prices - High	45⅛	26	18¾	21⅝	42¼	55	58½	48¼	49½	42¼
- Low	23¾	14⅝	12	12½	17⅛	29½	37¾	26½	34¾	31
P/E Ratio - High	31	21	18	42	NM	21	22	20	22	22
- Low	16	12	11	25	12	11	14	11	15	16

Income Statement Analysis (Million $)

	1997	1996	1995	1994	1993	1992	1991	1990	1989	1988
Revs.	21,874	19,567	17,906	16,476	15,464	14,097	12,042	9,531	8,002	4,140
Oper. Inc.	838	663	582	503	477	465	407	NA	NA	160
Depr.	182	162	142	139	112	89.0	72.0	NA	NA	14.7
Int. Exp.	76.0	78.0	67.9	57.6	46.1	35.5	26.0	18.8	24.6	11.5
Pretax Inc.	520	423	368	204	370	401	361	287	235	157
Eff. Tax Rate	40%	41%	41%	46%	40%	40%	39%	39%	39%	40%
Net Inc.	312	249	217	111	223	242	219	175	144	95.0

Balance Sheet & Other Fin. Data (Million $)

	1997	1996	1995	1994	1993	1992	1991	1990	1989	1988
Cash	176	102	45.7	63.0	210	376	NA	NA	NA	290
Curr. Assets	2,110	1,828	1,702	1,534	1,389	1,388	NA	NA	NA	528
Total Assets	5,476	4,912	4,437	4,236	3,940	3,577	2,986	2.0	1,740	993
Curr. Liab.	1,964	1,772	1,693	1,647	1,258	1,106	NA	NA	NA	306
LT Debt	917	1,229	1,095	795	813	814	500	200	234	200
Common Eqty.	2,468	1,778	1,531	1,685	1,797	1,594	1,430	988	778	480
Total Cap.	3,507	3,136	2,690	2,581	2,674	2,461	NA	NA	NA	687
Cap. Exp.	553	507	531	477	533	636	342	NA	NA	82.0
Cash Flow	494	4.1	359	250	335	332	291	NA	NA	109
Curr. Ratio	1.1	1.0	1.0	0.9	1.1	1.3	NA	NA	NA	1.7
% LT Debt of Cap.	26.1	39.2	40.1	30.8	30.4	33.1	NA	NA	NA	29.1
% Net Inc.of Revs.	1.4	1.3	1.2	0.7	1.4	1.7	1.8	1.8	1.8	2.3
% Ret. on Assets	6.0	5.3	5.0	2.7	5.9	7.4	8.7	9.3	9.0	10.3
% Ret. on Equity	14.7	15.1	13.5	6.4	13.2	16.0	18.1	27.6	21.1	22.0

Data as orig. reptd.; bef. results of disc. opers. and/or spec. items. Per share data adj. for stk. divs. as of ex-div. date. Bold denotes diluted EPS (FASB 128). E-Estimated. NA-Not Available. NM-Not Meaningful. NR-Not Ranked.

Office—999 Lake Dr., Issaquah, WA 98027. **Tel**—(425) 313-8100. **Website**—www.cost.com **Chrmn**—J. H. Brotman. **Pres & CEO**—J. D. Sinegal. **EVP, CFO & Investor Contact**—Richard A. Galanti (425-313-8203). **Dirs**—J. H. Brotman, R. D. DiCerchio, R. A. Galanti, H. E. James, R. M. Libenson, J. W. Meisenbach, C. T. Munger, F. O. Paulsell, J. S. Ruckelshaus, J. D. Sinegal. **Transfer Agent & Registrar**—ChaseMellon Shareholder Services. **Incorporated**—in Delaware in 1993. **Empl**— 57,000. **S&P Analyst:** Karen J. Sack, CFA

12-SEP-98

Industry:
Consumer Finance

Summary: A leading mortgage banker, Countrywide originates, purchases, sells and services mortgage loans.

S&P Opinion: Hold (★★★)	Recent Price • 38½	Yield • 0.8%
	52 Wk Range • 56¼-31⅜	12-Mo. P/E • 11.9

Quantitative Evaluations

Outlook
(1 Lowest—5 Highest)
• 1⁻

Fair Value
• 34¼

Risk
• **Low**

Earn./Div. Rank
• **A-**

Technical Eval.
• **NA**

Rel. Strength Rank
(1 Lowest—99 Highest)
• **49**

Insider Activity
• **Neutral**

Earnings vs. Previous Year
△=Up ▽=Down ▷=No Change

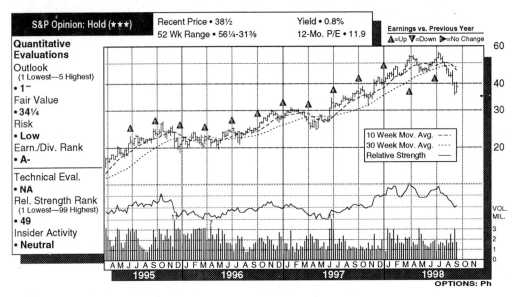

10 Week Mov. Avg. ——
30 Week Mov. Avg. ----
Relative Strength ——

VOL.
MIL.

OPTIONS: Ph

Overview - 19-JUN-98

Profits before nonrecurring gains are expected to improve in FY 99 (Feb.). One positive factor is increased mortgage loan production, reflecting expansion of the branch network, an ongoing recovery in housing, and projections for relatively stable interest rates, which should encourage homebuying activity. The high-margin home equity and sub-prime categories should experience the fastest growth. Margins are likely to be flat, reflecting costs associated with expansion of the office network and new lending initiatives. Costs or benefits of hedging activities are uncertain, although they typically account for a large percentage of net income. Impairment of servicing assets, also unpredictable, can have a major effect on net income. Fee income from the mortgage servicing portfolio is likely to increase.

Valuation - 19-JUN-98

The shares are expected to perform only in line with market averages. An industry leader, CCR is fairly valued at a P/E ratio on projected FY 99 EPS that is below the market P/E. We believe that this discount is justified, because the company's fortunes are tied to a significant extent to the cyclical mortgage industry, a business characterized by few barriers to entry, intense competition, and narrow margins. Historically, Countrywide has experienced difficulty in adjusting staffing levels during both downturns and expansions. Another of our concerns about Countrywide is its earnings quality. In many quarters, gains on the sale of loans or income from recovery of the servicing hedge, which we view as nonrecurring, account for a significant portion of pretax income. Nevertheless, the company has managed to achieve earnings growth over the past several years.

Key Stock Statistics

S&P EPS Est. 1999	3.20	Tang. Bk. Value/Share	19.99
P/E on S&P Est. 1999	12.1	Beta	1.54
Dividend Rate/Share	0.32	Shareholders	2,800
Shs. outstg. (M)	111.0	Market cap. (B)	$ 4.3
Avg. daily vol. (M)	0.470	Inst. holdings	80%

Value of $10,000 invested 5 years ago: $ 26,038

Fiscal Year Ending Feb. 28

	1999	1998	1997	1996	1995	1994
Revenues (Million $)						
1Q	450.3	318.6	263.3	179.0	177.1	166.7
2Q	—	405.2	270.8	209.3	151.1	188.3
3Q	—	375.1	281.5	225.6	133.7	196.4
4Q	—	410.0	296.8	246.9	140.7	204.2
Yr.	—	1,509	1,113	860.7	602.7	755.6
Earnings Per Share ($)						
1Q	**0.78**	0.64	0.58	0.39	0.37	0.49
2Q	**E0.83**	0.99	0.60	0.49	0.21	0.51
3Q	**E0.79**	0.71	0.62	0.51	0.18	0.46
4Q	**E0.80**	0.74	0.63	0.55	0.21	0.51
Yr.	**E3.20**	3.09	2.44	1.95	0.96	1.97

Next earnings report expected: mid September

Dividend Data (Dividends have been paid since 1978.)

Amount ($)	Date Decl.	Ex-Div. Date	Stock of Record	Payment Date
0.080	Sep. 16	Oct. 10	Oct. 15	Oct. 31 '97
0.080	Dec. 16	Jan. 13	Jan. 15	Feb. 02 '98
0.080	Mar. 18	Apr. 09	Apr. 14	Apr. 30 '98
0.080	Jun. 17	Jul. 13	Jul. 15	Jul. 31 '98

Business Summary - 19-JUN-98

Countrywide Credit Industries (CCR) originates, purchases, sells and services loans for single family homes. As a mortgage banker, CCR basically originates mortgages on single-family homes. However, instead of holding the mortgage in its portfolio like a thrift, the company sells the loan to the Federal National Mortgage Association or another investor. Countrywide also receives fees for servicing mortgages--that is, collecting the principal and interest from the borrower, counseling delinquent borrowers, supervising the foreclosure process if necessary, and performing other related services. In FY 98 (Feb.), Countrywide's loan production totaled some $48.8 billion, about 5% of the single family mortgage origination market. Pretax profits were obtained as follows in recent fiscal years:

	FY 98	FY 97
Mortgage banking	75%	87%
Other	25%	13%

About 75% of the loans that Countrywide makes are to finance the purchase of a home. Typically, the company will make a loan for about 80% of the appraised value of the home, although it has programs to accommodate people who wish to put down as little as 5%. Borrowers are required to provide information on their employment history, bank accounts, debts owed, etc in order for the company to assess their creditworthiness.

The other area in which CCR is involved is refinancing, which occurs when an existing homeowner takes out a new mortgage at a lower interest rate and repays the older mortgage. During periods of very low mortgage rates, homeowners refinance their mortgages in droves The last major refinancing wave occurred in 1993. Other activities include insurance, escrow services, brokering service contracts, and trading mortgage-backed securities.

Countrywide has a complex income statement. The most straightforward line item is the fees or points it charges borrowers when they take out a loan. Gain on sale refers to the appreciation a loan experiences between the time it is originated and then sold. Amortization and impairment/recovery of mortgage servicing rights refers to the noncash writedown or writeup the company makes to its loan servicing portfolio in response to such things as increased prepayments or "runoff." The servicing hedge gain or loss derives from price changes in the various financial instruments (options on Treasury futures, CMO tranches, etc.) CCR holds to offset changes in the value of its mortgage servicing portfolio.

Per Share Data ($)

(Year Ended Feb. 28)	1998	1997	1996	1995	1994	1993	1992	1991	1990	1989
Tangible Bk. Val.	19.12	15.19	12.91	10.32	9.67	8.29	7.00	3.22	2.89	2.69
Cash Flow	3.09	2.82	2.26	2.28	4.80	3.54	1.76	1.10	0.88	NA
Earnings	3.09	2.44	1.95	0.96	1.97	1.65	0.88	0.47	0.31	0.27
Dividends	0.32	0.32	0.32	0.32	0.28	0.24	0.16	0.12	0.11	0.12
Payout Ratio	10%	13%	16%	33%	14%	16%	18%	25%	36%	45%
Cal. Yrs.	1997	1996	1995	1994	1993	1992	1991	1990	1989	1988
Prices - High	43¼	30¼	26¾	19⅛	23⅜	20	17¾	4⅛	4¼	4
- Low	24⅜	19¾	12½	12⅜	15¼	10⅞	3¾	2⁵⁄₁₆	2⅝	2³⁄₁₆
P/E Ratio - High	14	12	14	20	12	12	20	8	14	14
- Low	8	8	6	13	8	7	4	5	8	8

Income Statement Analysis (Million $)

	1998	1997	1996	1995	1994	1993	1992	1991	1990	1989
Loan Fees	1,209	967	632	471	518	342	150	79.9	68.4	53.9
Int. Inc.	440	350	354	343	376	212	115	83.6	78.5	60.8
Total Revs.	1,882	1,656	1,142	870	1,031	654	328	208	179	142
Int. Exp.	424	317	282	268	276	149	82.0	73.4	74.7	57.5
Exp./Op. Revs.	73%	75%	72%	83%	71%	64%	69%	82%	88%	88%
Pretax Inc.	566	422	326	147	299	234	100	37.2	21.8	16.9
Eff. Tax Rate	39%	39%	40%	40%	40%	40%	40%	40%	40%	36%
Net Inc.	345	257	196	88.4	180	140	60.2	22.3	13.1	10.8

Balance Sheet & Other Fin. Data (Million $)

	1998	1997	1996	1995	1994	1993	1992	1991	1990	1989
Net Prop.	226	274	141	146	146	95.0	54.0	45.0	45.0	NA
Cash & Secs.	5,303	18.3	16.4	17.6	4.0	12.6	14.5	6.6	2.1	NA
Loans	5,292	2,580	4,740	2,899	3,714	2,343	1,585	714	456	NA
Total Assets	12,219	8,089	8,658	5,580	5,586	3,299	2,410	1,122	839	829
Capitalization:										
Debt	7,975	2,368	1,912	1,499	1,197	735	430	209	127	245
Equity	2,088	1,612	1,320	943	880	693	557	132	117	109
Total	6,284	3,980	3,145	2,442	2,077	1,428	1,026	341	244	353
Price Times Bk. Val.: High	2.3	2.0	2.1	1.9	2.0	2.8	2.8	5.5	1.4	NA
Price Times Bk. Val.: Low	1.3	1.6	1.0	1.2	1.3	1.8	2.2	1.2	0.8	NA
Cash Flow	345	298	227	210	437	300	120	52.0	37.0	NA
% Return On Revs.	18.3	15.6	17.2	10.2	17.4	21.4	18.3	10.7	7.3	7.6
% Ret. on Assets	3.4	3.1	2.8	1.6	4.0	4.9	3.4	2.3	1.6	1.3
% Ret. on Equity	18.7	17.6	17.3	9.7	22.8	21.8	16.4	16.0	11.6	10.4

Data as orig. reptd.; bef. results of disc. opers. and/or spec. items. Per share data adj. for stk. divs. as of ex-div. date. Bold denotes diluted EPS (FASB 128). E-Estimated. NA-Not Available. NM-Not Meaningful. NR-Not Ranked.

Office—4500 Park Granada Blvd., Calabasas, CA 91302. **Tel**—(818) 225-3550. **Website**—http://www.countrywide.com **Chrmn & Pres**—D. S. Loeb. **COO**—S. L. Kurland. **CFO**—C. M. Garcia. **Secy**—S. E. Samuels. **Dirs**—J. M. Cunningham, R. J. Donato, B. M. Enis, E. Heller, D. S. Loeb, A. R. Mozilo, H. W. Snyder. **Transfer Agent & Registrar**—Bank of New York, NYC. **Incorporated**—in New York in 1969; reincorporated in Delaware in 1987. **Empl**— 8,000. **S&P Analyst:** Paul L. Huberman, CFA

Crane Co.

680

NYSE Symbol **CR**

In S&P 500

12-SEP-98

Industry: Manufacturing (Diversified)

Summary: Crane is a diversified manufacturer of engineered products for the aerospace, fluid handling, automatic merchandising and construction industries.

S&P Opinion: Hold (★★★)		
Recent Price • 38⅞		Yield • 1.5%
52 Wk Range • 56⅜-37⅝		12-Mo. P/E • 14.1

Quantitative Evaluations

Outlook
(1 Lowest—5 Highest)
• **3**

Fair Value
• **42¼**

Risk
• **Low**

Earn./Div. Rank
• **B+**

Technical Eval.
• **Neutral** since 9/98

Rel. Strength Rank
(1 Lowest—99 Highest)
• **45**

Insider Activity
• **Neutral**

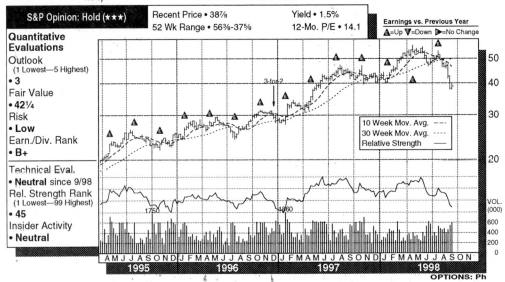

Earnings vs. Previous Year
▲=Up ▼=Down ▶=No Change

10 Week Mov. Avg. ---
30 Week Mov. Avg. ....
Relative Strength —

OPTIONS: Ph

Overview - 21-JUL-98

Crane reported favorable results for the second quarter of 1998, on continued strength in its aerospace division. Net sales in the segment were up 18%, and operating profits rose 43%, year to year, aided by acquisitions. We expect further aerospace gains for the remainder of 1998 reflecting a growing backlog, and operational improvements at Interpoint, which was acquired in late 1996. While the Interpoint integration has been challenged by systems, manufacturing and control problems, we see the potential for significant margin expansion as these issues are addressed by a new management team. Fluid Handling operating profit was off 9% for the quarter partially reflecting delays related to the integration of the Stockham bronze and iron valve businesses; however, these problems should be remedied by year end. Wholesale Distribution should continue to benefit from a strong Canadian industrial economy. While solid engineered materials results should persist reflecting robust demand for Kemlite products, Crane Controls and Merchandising Systems experienced slowing sales growth in the second quarter.

Valuation - 21-JUL-98

We continue to recommend holding the shares, which have outperformed the Manufacturing (Diversified) index year to date through July 10. Although the aerospace segment was responsible for only 17% of revenues in 1997, it accounted for 41% of profits. With a booming aircraft market, the segment should continue to be the main driver of CR's growth. Fluid Handling and Engineered Materials should also post gains. With a strong balance sheet and healthy cash flow, CR has considerable financial flexibility; however, with slower growth operations in its business portfolio, we view the shares as fairly valued at 15 times our 1999 EPS estimate of $3.30.

Key Stock Statistics

S&P EPS Est. 1998	2.92	Tang. Bk. Value/Share	6.79
P/E on S&P Est. 1998	13.3	Beta	1.12
S&P EPS Est. 1999	3.30	Shareholders	6,000
Dividend Rate/Share	0.60	Market cap. (B)	$ 1.8
Shs. outstg. (M)	45.8	Inst. holdings	51%
Avg. daily vol. (M)	0.104		

Value of $10,000 invested 5 years ago: $ 27,770

Fiscal Year Ending Dec. 31

	1998	1997	1996	1995	1994	1993
Revenues (Million $)						
1Q	526.8	467.3	436.5	432.6	331.7	312.3
2Q	563.4	518.8	466.2	451.5	428.7	337.7
3Q	—	534.8	481.1	453.3	451.1	337.9
4Q	—	515.9	463.9	444.9	441.9	322.3
Yr.	—	2,037	1,848	1,782	1,653	1,310
Earnings Per Share ($)						
1Q	**0.65**	**0.50**	0.40	0.29	0.17	0.24
2Q	**0.79**	**0.64**	0.48	0.44	0.35	0.35
3Q	**E0.78**	**0.68**	0.59	0.47	0.35	0.28
4Q	**E0.70**	**0.64**	0.54	0.46	0.37	0.21
Yr.	**E2.92**	**2.44**	2.01	1.67	1.24	1.08

Next earnings report expected: mid October

Dividend Data (Dividends have been paid since 1939.)

Amount ($)	Date Decl.	Ex-Div. Date	Stock of Record	Payment Date
0.125	Feb. 23	Mar. 04	Mar. 06	Mar. 13 '98
0.125	Apr. 20	Jun. 03	Jun. 05	Jun. 12 '98
0.100	Aug. 17	Aug. 28	Sep. 01	Sep. 14 '98
3-for-2	Aug. 17	Sep. 15	Sep. 01	Sep. 14 '98

A Division of The McGraw·Hill Companies

STANDARD
&POOR'S
STOCK REPORTS

Crane Co.

680

12-SEP-98

Business Summary - 21-JUL-98

Crane Co., a well diversified manufacturer of engineered products and distributor of doors, windows and millwork, has enjoyed a successful five year growth record by effectively penetrating niche markets, through both internal growth and acquisitions. CR believes it can achieve optimal performance in each operating segment by employing a decentralized management approach, and using incentive based compensation plans. Operations outside the U.S. accounted for 18% of sales and 11% of operating profits in 1997.

Recently, the company's growth has been driven by the aerospace business, its most profitable segment. Aerospace manufactures numerous products and systems for the aircraft industry including: electronically controlled anti-skid braking systems; position indication and control systems; fuel and hydraulic pumps; hydraulic and pneumatic valves; and power conditioning products and systems.

In October 1996, the aerospace segment nearly doubled its revenue generating capabilities with the acquisition of Interpoint, a leading producer of miniature DC-to-DC power converters and microcircuits.

The fluid handling unit consists of a valve business that serves the global market and pumps used in the chemical, general industrial and commercial industries.

Engineered materials makes fiberglass-reinforced plastic panels, corrosion-resistant, plastic-lined pipes, fittings and valves used in process industries, high-pressure fittings and hoses, high-voltage, high-frequency capacitors, and plumbing products.

Crane Controls produces pressure and temperature switches, directional valve controls, balancing and shower valves, electronic and rotational speed sensors.

Merchandising systems makes vending machines for the automated merchandising industry in the U.S., and coin validation systems for the automatic vending market in Europe.

Wholesale distribution consists mostly of Huttig Sash & Door, the largest U.S. distributor of doors, windows, molding and trim, and related building products.

Other recent acquisitions include the March 1997 purchase of the transportation products business of Sequentia, Inc., a maker of fiberglass reinforced plastic panels for truck bodies, trailers and containers. Polyvend, a maker of snack and food vending machines, was also acquired in March 1997.

In April 1997, CR acquired ITI Movats, a supplier of nuclear valve diagnostic equipment, from Westinghouse. In July 1997, MALLCO lumber and building material, Inc., an Arizona wholesale distributor of lumber, doors, and engineered wood products, was acquired. In December 1997, Stockham Valves & Fittings was acquired for integration into the fluid handling segment.

Per Share Data ($)

(Year Ended Dec. 31)	1997	1996	1995	1994	1993	1992	1991	1990	1989	1988
Tangible Bk. Val.	5.71	4.43	3.21	2.07	6.49	6.04	6.51	6.76	4.98	4.55
Cash Flow	3.64	3.08	2.73	2.02	1.61	1.04	1.45	1.79	1.58	1.37
Earnings	2.44	2.01	1.67	1.24	1.08	0.53	0.95	1.31	1.15	0.97
Dividends	0.50	0.50	0.50	0.50	0.50	0.50	0.50	0.50	0.47	0.41
Payout Ratio	20%	25%	30%	40%	46%	95%	53%	38%	40%	43%
Prices - High	47¼	31½	26⅜	19⅝	20⅝	18⅝	20	18½	16⅝	15⅛
- Low	27½	24	17¼	16⅛	15⅛	14½	12½	11⅞	10	9
P/E Ratio - High	19	16	16	16	19	35	21	14	15	16
- Low	11	12	10	13	14	28	13	9	9	9

Income Statement Analysis (Million $)

	1997	1996	1995	1994	1993	1992	1991	1990	1989	1988
Revs.	2,037	1,848	1,782	1,653	1,310	1,307	1,303	1,438	1,456	1,313
Oper. Inc.	252	216	192	145	110	108	103	136	126	115
Depr.	55.4	49.4	48.8	35.5	24.3	23.7	23.7	23.1	21.3	19.7
Int. Exp.	23.8	23.4	26.9	24.2	11.4	14.5	11.5	16.7	19.2	18.8
Pretax Inc.	176	145	122	91.0	80.0	NA	72.0	102	91.6	81.5
Eff. Tax Rate	36%	37%	37%	39%	39%	37%	38%	39%	39%	40%
Net Inc.	113	92.1	76.3	55.9	48.9	24.3	45.0	62.7	55.9	49.2

Balance Sheet & Other Fin. Data (Million $)

	1997	1996	1995	1994	1993	1992	1991	1990	1989	1988
Cash	7.0	11.6	5.5	2.1	12.6	49.0	23.0	8.0	6.0	42.0
Curr. Assets	608	540	498	480	394	379	377	392	398	432
Total Assets	1,186	1,089	998	1,008	744	630	630	665	655	682
Curr. Liab.	296	254	241	244	272	174	170	174	184	195
LT Debt	261	268	281	331	106	111	84.0	104	119	143
Common Eqty.	533	463	375	328	291	271	300	317	284	275
Total Cap.	816	760	684	692	403	386	404	470	450	462
Cap. Exp.	40.6	50.5	26.6	28.0	64.0	23.0	21.0	33.0	33.0	18.0
Cash Flow	168	142	125	91.4	73.2	48.0	68.7	86.0	77.2	68.9
Curr. Ratio	2.1	2.1	2.1	2.0	1.4	2.2	2.2	2.2	2.2	2.2
% LT Debt of Cap.	31.9	35.2	41.1	47.9	26.2	28.8	20.8	22.1	26.5	31.0
% Net Inc.of Revs.	5.5	5.0	4.3	3.4	3.7	1.9	3.5	4.4	3.8	3.7
% Ret. on Assets	9.9	8.8	7.6	6.4	7.1	3.9	7.0	9.6	8.5	7.4
% Ret. on Equity	22.7	22.0	21.7	18.0	17.4	8.6	14.7	21.1	20.3	18.8

Data as orig. reptd.; bef. results of disc. opers. and/or spec. items. Per share data adj. for stk. divs. as of ex-div. date. Bold denotes diluted EPS (FASB 128). E-Estimated. NA-Not Available. NM-Not Meaningful. NR-Not Ranked.

Office—100 First Stamford Place, Stamford, CT 06902. **Tel**—(203) 363-7300. **Chrmn & CEO**—R. S. Evans. **Pres & COO**—L. Hill Clark. **VP-Fin, CFO & Investor Contact**—David S. Smith. **VP & Secy**—A. I. duPont. **Crane Shareholders Direct**—(888-272-6327). **Dirs**—M. Anathan III, E. T. Bigelow, Jr., R. S. Evans, R. S. Forte, D. R. Gardner, J. Gaulin, D. C. Minton, C. J. Queenan, Jr., B. Yavitz. **Transfer Agent & Registrar**—First Chicago Trust Co. of New York, Jersey City, NJ. **Incorporated**—in Illinois in 1865; reincorporated in Delaware in 1985. **Empl**— 11,000. **S&P Analyst:** Eric J. Hunter

12-SEP-98

Industry:
Containers (Metal & Glass)

Summary: This leading packaging company makes metal food, beverage and aerosol cans, plastic containers, health and beauty product packaging, and closures, pumps and dispensing systems.

S&P Opinion: Hold (★★★)	Recent Price • 35⅛	Yield • 2.8%
	52 Wk Range • 55⅛-30½	12-Mo. P/E • 16.2

Earnings vs. Previous Year
▲=Up ▼=Down ▶=No Change

Quantitative Evaluations

Outlook
(1 Lowest—5 Highest)
• **4+**

Fair Value
• **48⅞**

Risk
• **Low**

Earn./Div. Rank
• **B**

Technical Eval.
• **NA**

Rel. Strength Rank
(1 Lowest—99 Highest)
• **53**

Insider Activity
• **NA**

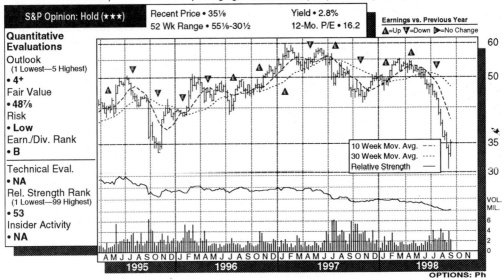

10 Week Mov. Avg. ---
30 Week Mov. Avg. ·····
Relative Strength —

1995   1996   1997   1998

VOL. MIL.

OPTIONS: Ph

Overview - 20-JUL-98

Sales should be modestly higher in 1998, as the likelihood of higher raw material costs should enable CCK to pass through price hikes in certain areas. The sales forecast also assumes that exchange rate comparisons will be more favorable than in 1997, when the strength of the U.S. dollar against European currencies restricted results. Volume trends will likely be mixed among product categories and geographic regions. Margins should widen, on benefits of ongoing cost containment programs, the restructuring of domestic businesses over the past few years, and a sharp reduction in overhead costs generated through the integration of CarnaudMetalbox (CMB). A better product pricing environment should also help. Longer term, the CMB deal should bring major competitive advantages, provide CCK with greater ability to serve global customers and give it more leverage in areas such as materials purchasing. Comparisons will be distorted by $0.31 a share of restructuring charges and $0.20 a share of gains on asset sales recorded in 1997 (both diluted). Crown's March 1998 repurchase of 5.3% of its voting securities from Compagnie Generale d'Industrie et Participations, for $369 million, will have little impact on 1998 EPS.

Valuation - 20-JUL-98

After rising sharply between the fall of 1995 and early 1997, mostly on excitement about CCK's merger with CMB, the shares have since underperformed. The weakness has been largely related to earnings disappointments, as European operations have battled a strong U.S. dollar. Crown's dominant position in global packaging would cause us to hold the shares in their recent trading range of 17 to 18 times our 1998 EPS forecast. However, still competitive industry conditions would stop us from adding to our position at this time.

Key Stock Statistics

S&P EPS Est. 1998	2.70	Tang. Bk. Value/Share	NM
P/E on S&P Est. 1998	13.0	Beta	0.62
S&P EPS Est. 1999	3.05	Shareholders	5,700
Dividend Rate/Share	1.00	Market cap. (B)	$ 4.4
Shs. outstg. (M)	124.4	Inst. holdings	61%
Avg. daily vol. (M)	0.540		

Value of $10,000 invested 5 years ago: $ 9,345

Fiscal Year Ending Dec. 31

	1998	1997	1996	1995	1994	1993
Revenues (Million $)						
1Q	1,892	1,937	1,551	1,127	943.0	913.1
2Q	2,245	2,287	2,354	1,386	1,135	1,169
3Q	—	2,341	2,462	1,427	1,283	1,146
4Q	—	1,929	1,965	1,114	1,091	935.2
Yr.	—	8,495	8,332	5,054	4,452	4,163
Earnings Per Share ($)						
1Q	0.29	0.26	0.28	0.41	0.38	0.35
2Q	0.95	0.98	0.77	0.58	0.73	0.65
3Q	E1.09	0.62	0.81	-0.22	-0.08	0.68
4Q	E0.37	0.31	0.26	0.07	0.45	0.40
Yr.	E2.70	2.15	2.16	0.83	1.47	2.08

Next earnings report expected: late October

Dividend Data (Dividends have been paid since 1996.)

Amount ($)	Date Decl.	Ex-Div. Date	Stock of Record	Payment Date
0.250	Oct. 23	Oct. 31	Nov. 04	Nov. 20 '97
0.250	Jan. 09	Jan. 30	Feb. 03	Feb. 20 '98
0.250	Apr. 01	Apr. 29	May. 01	May. 20 '98
0.250	Jul. 24	Aug. 04	Aug. 06	Aug. 20 '98

A Division of The **McGraw·Hill** *Companies*

STANDARD
&POOR'S
STOCK REPORTS

Crown Cork & Seal Company, Inc.

690

12-SEP-98

Business Summary - 20-JUL-98

Crown Cork & Seal became the world's leading maker of packaging products for consumer goods through its February 1996 purchase of CarnaudMetalbox (CMB), a major European packaging producer. The transaction also drastically reduced its proportion of domestic revenues. In 1997, more than 60% of CCK's sales were derived outside of the U.S., with Europe accounting for more than three-quarters of its non-U.S. sales. Domestic sales had accounted for 67% of CCK's revenue base before the takeover.

The company's products include metal cans and plastic containers for food, beverage, household, personal care and other products; packaging for health and beauty care applications; closures (including bottle caps and metal can closures), pumps and dispensing systems; and composite containers. During 1997, CCK derived 82% of sales from metal packaging and other operations and the rest from plastic packaging.

The company estimates that its capital expenditures will approximate $2.25 billion (exclusive of potential acquisitions) for the five-year period from 1998 through 2002. Over the near term, Crown will continue to focus on projects to enhance productivity and contain costs, as well as those that provide growth opportunities.

Under current management, Crown has pursued a strategy of growth through acquisition within the global packaging industry. From 1989 through 1996, CCK completed 20 acquisitions of companies with total net sales of about $8 billion (certain businesses have also been divested over that period). This aggressive strategy was capped by the February 1996 takeover of CMB, which added nearly $5 billion to Crown's sales base. The total cost of the takeover, excluding liabilities assumed, was $4.0 billion in cash and stock.

Crown's operating performance tends to be skewed by seasonal factors. Beverage products tend to be consumed in greater amounts during warmer months of the year, so CCK's sales and earnings have generally been higher in the second and third quarters of the year. The 1996 acquisition of CMB should further increase the seasonality, as the takeover lifted food packaging products to 31% of CCK's sales in 1997, from 19% in 1995. Food can sales tend to be highest in the third quarter of the year due to the agricultural harvest.

CCK recorded $0.31 a diluted share of restructuring charges in 1997's third quarter. The charges covered Crown's restructuring actions in its PET plastic container business, which have included the closing and reorganization of six plants, and certain restructuring activities in other product areas, mostly in Europe. When fully implemented, CCK sees the programs bringing about $20 million of annual cost savings.

Per Share Data ($)

(Year Ended Dec. 31)	1997	1996	1995	1994	1993	1992	1991	1990	1989	1988
Tangible Bk. Val.	NM	NM	4.03	2.60	1.48	1.59	6.69	10.99	7.24	7.79
Cash Flow	5.83	6.21	3.67	3.92	4.28	3.43	2.83	2.42	1.98	1.81
Earnings	2.15	2.16	0.83	1.47	2.08	1.79	1.48	1.24	1.19	1.12
Dividends	1.00	1.00	Nil	Nil	Nil	Nil	Nil	Nil	Nil	Nil
Payout Ratio	47%	46%	Nil	Nil	Nil	Nil	Nil	Nil	Nil	Nil
Prices - High	59³/₄	55¹/₂	50⁵/₈	41⁷/₈	41⁷/₈	41¹/₈	31	22³/₈	19	15³/₄
- Low	43¹/₂	40⁵/₈	33¹/₂	33¹/₂	33¹/₄	27³/₈	18¹/₄	16¹/₂	14⁵/₈	10¹/₈
P/E Ratio - High	28	26	61	28	20	23	21	18	16	14
- Low	20	19	40	23	16	15	12	13	12	9

Income Statement Analysis (Million $)

Revs.	8,495	8,332	5,054	4,452	4,163	3,781	3,807	3,072	1,910	1,834
Oper. Inc.	1,373	1,212	604	617	562	471	401	325	206	214
Depr.	540	496	256	218	192	142	118	95.0	62.0	57.0
Int. Exp.	340	306	149	99	89.8	77.4	76.6	59.9	12.0	10.0
Pretax Inc.	457	418	111	199	285	261	215	178	148	161
Eff. Tax Rate	32%	32%	23%	28%	34%	39%	39%	40%	36%	42%
Net Inc.	302	284	75.0	131	181	155	128	107	94.0	93.0

Balance Sheet & Other Fin. Data (Million $)

Cash	206	160	68.1	43.5	54.2	26.9	20.2	21.8	14.4	18.0
Curr. Assets	3,147	3,292	1,709	1,606	1,325	1,302	1,149	983	656	504
Total Assets	12,306	12,590	5,052	4,781	4,217	3,825	2,983	2,596	1,655	1,073
Curr. Liab.	4,049	3,663	1,279	1,483	1,281	1,135	761	736	594	321
LT Debt	3,301	3,924	1,490	1,090	892	940	585	484	94.0	Nil
Common Eqty.	3,025	3,563	1,461	1,365	1,252	1,144	1,084	951	811	648
Total Cap.	7,113	7,731	3,070	2,566	2,217	2,326	1,863	1,562	1,037	743
Cap. Exp.	515	631	434	440	271	151	185	506	342	104
Cash Flow	818	760	331	349	373	298	246	209	156	151
Curr. Ratio	0.8	0.9	1.3	1.1	1.0	1.1	1.5	1.1	1.1	1.6
% LT Debt of Cap.	46.4	50.8	48.5	42.5	40.2	404.0	31.4	31.0	9.1	Nil
% Net Inc.of Revs.	3.6	3.4	1.5	2.9	4.3	4.1	3.4	3.5	4.9	5.1
% Ret. on Assets	2.4	3.3	1.5	2.9	4.4	4.6	4.6	5.0	6.7	9.0
% Ret. on Equity	9.1	10.6	5.3	10.0	14.9	14.0	12.6	12.1	12.6	14.8

Data as orig. reptd.; bef. results of disc. opers. and/or spec. items. Per share data adj. for stk. divs. as of ex-div. date. Bold denotes diluted EPS (FASB 128). E-Estimated. NA-Not Available. NM-Not Meaningful. NR-Not Ranked.

Office—One Crown Way, Philadelphia, PA 19154-4599. **Tel**—(215) 698-5100. **Website**—http://www.crowncork.com **Chrmn & CEO**—W. J. Avery. **Pres & COO**—J. W. Conway. **EVP & CFO**—A. W. Rutherford. **SVP, Treas & Investor Contact**—Craig R. L. Calle. **Dirs**—W. J. Avery, H. E. Butwel, C. F. Casey, J. W. Conway, F. X. Dalton, G. de Wouters, T. H. Karlsson, R. L. Krzyzanowski, J. C. Mandeville, M. J. McKenna, J.-P. Rosso, A. W. Rutherford, H. A. Sorgenti. **Transfer Agent & Registrar**—First Chicago Trust Co. of New York, Jersey City, NJ. **Incorporated**—in New York in 1927; reincorporated in Pennsylvania in 1989. **Empl**—40,985. **S&P Analyst:** Robert E. Friedman, CPA

STANDARD &POOR'S
STOCK REPORTS

CSX Corp.

416N

NYSE Symbol **CSX**

In S&P 500

12-SEP-98

Industry:
Railroads

Summary: CSX has interests in rail, shipping, barge and logistics services. CSX's bid to operate a portion of Conrail could win regulatory clearance by July 1998.

S&P Opinion: Accumulate (★★★★)	Recent Price • 40⅛ 52 Wk Range • 61⅝-36½	Yield • 3.0% 12-Mo. P/E • 13.4

Earnings vs. Previous Year
▲=Up ▼=Down ►=No Change

Quantitative Evaluations

Outlook
(1 Lowest—5 Highest)
• **3**

Fair Value
• **43⅜**

Risk
• **Low**

Earn./Div. Rank
• **B+**

Technical Eval.
• **Bearish** since 5/98

Rel. Strength Rank
(1 Lowest—99 Highest)
• **76**

Insider Activity
• **NA**

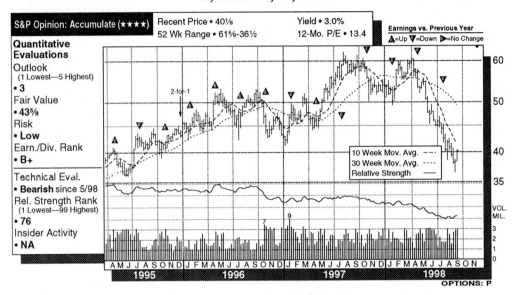

10 Week Mov. Avg. – – –
30 Week Mov. Avg. ·······
Relative Strength ——

OPTIONS: P

Overview - 04-JUN-98

A moderate profit gain is anticipated in 1998 from CSX's rail operation. The integration of the Conrail routes could begin as early as the third quarter. Coal traffic may remain soft reflecting mild winter weather and slack demand overseas. Moderate growth is projected for industrial commodities, with chemicals benefiting from a diversion of truck traffic. Margins will be flat, despite lower fuel costs, as labor productivity initially suffers as CSX faces added costs to recruit and train new personnel and mesh the Conrail lines into its system. Moderate volume growth is projected for intermodal operations, mainly on the international side. Shipping profits will drop, as rates remain under pressure in all markets. Growth for container loads could slow to about 2% to 4%, from 7% in 1997, as Sea-Land loses market share in Asia to non-dollar based shipping lines. While barge profits will fall, proceeds from the sale of that unit will be applied to cut interest expense. Solid growth is projected for CSX's logistics unit. Equity contributions from Conrail will exceed 1997 levels.

Valuation - 04-JUN-98

After a run for new highs in early 1998, shares of this transportation concern slumped in mid-1998. Troubles at Union Pacific have spooked rail investors. While CSX does not anticipate problems integrating Conrail's operations, it could face additional regulatory conditions as the government adopts a more cautious posture with this rail transaction. CSX sees $410 million in net revenue and cost savings from Conrail by the third year of full ownership. Another weight on CSX's shares is the slump in Asian shipping traffic which is hitting its Sea-Land unit. We think CSX is worth accumulating, as the shares trade at a large discount to the P/E multiple of the S&P 500.

Key Stock Statistics

S&P EPS Est. 1998	3.65	Tang. Bk. Value/Share	26.85
P/E on S&P Est. 1998	11.0	Beta	0.95
S&P EPS Est. 1999	4.50	Shareholders	55,100
Dividend Rate/Share	1.20	Market cap. (B)	$ 8.8
Shs. outstg. (M)	218.6	Inst. holdings	60%
Avg. daily vol. (M)	0.528		

Value of $10,000 invested 5 years ago: $ 13,317

Fiscal Year Ending Dec. 31

	1998	1997	1996	1995	1994	1993
Revenues (Million $)						
1Q	2,580	2,567	2,514	2,468	2,227	2,123
2Q	2,642	2,678	2,672	2,600	2,371	2,264
3Q	—	2,649	2,647	2,665	2,470	2,238
4Q	—	2,727	2,703	2,771	2,540	2,315
Yr.	—	10,621	10,536	10,504	9,608	8,940
Earnings Per Share ($)						
1Q	**0.41**	**0.69**	0.69	0.57	0.35	-0.05
2Q	**0.68**	**1.03**	1.11	0.09	0.78	0.74
3Q	**E1.05**	**0.93**	1.04	0.96	0.84	0.30
4Q	**E1.19**	**0.97**	1.17	1.31	1.15	0.73
Yr.	**E3.65**	**3.62**	**3.96**	2.94	3.11	1.73

Next earnings report expected: late October

Dividend Data (Dividends have been paid since 1922.)

Amount ($)	Date Decl.	Ex-Div. Date	Stock of Record	Payment Date
0.300	Oct. 21	Nov. 21	Nov. 25	Dec. 15 '97
0.300	Feb. 11	Feb. 23	Feb. 25	Mar. 13 '98
0.300	Apr. 28	May. 20	May. 22	Jun. 15 '98
0.300	Jul. 08	Aug. 21	Aug. 25	Sep. 15 '98

A Division of The **McGraw·Hill** *Companies*

Business Summary - 04-JUN-98

After fighting a bitter battle against Norfolk Southern to acquire Conrail, this major transportation company decided a little less than half a loaf was better than none. CSX Corp. and Norfolk agreed in early 1997 to divide Conrail, and in June, CSX completed the acquisition of 42% of Conrail for $4.1 billion. CSX also provides shipping, intermodal and logistics services. In April 1998 CSX agreed to sell its barge unit for $850 million while retaining a 34% stake in the new entity.

CSX Transportation (47% of 1997 revenues) operates the third largest U.S. railroad, with 18,300 miles of track extending from the eastern seaboard to western gateways of Chicago, St. Louis and Memphis. Shipment of coal accounts for 33% of rail revenues, followed by chemicals (15%) and automobiles (11%).

Spurred by consolidation in the western rail market, in October 1996, CSX bid $9.1 billion for Conrail, an eastern U.S. railroad. Norfolk, another Eastern railroad, then forced CSX into a bidding war for Conrail. A truce was reached, under which CSX agreed to take 42% of Conrail. Pending regulatory clearance, anticipated by July 1998, CSX's Conrail holdings have been placed in a voting trust. While CSX cannot control its portion of Conrail until then, it will report equity income from Conrail. CSX's investment in Conrail reduced EPS by $0.43 in 1997 and $0.19 in 1998's first quarter.

The acquired Conrail routes will expand CSX Transportation's network to 22,000 miles of track in 22 states, plus two Canadian provinces. CSX will get 3,500 miles of track and share another 1,200 miles with Norfolk. CSX estimates that the Conrail lines will add some $1.7 billion to its revenue base in the first year. By the third full year of operation, CSX projects that it will derive $264 million in annual cost savings by improving asset utilization, reducing empty movements, and rationalizing administrative tasks and facilities.

Sea-Land Service (37% of revenues) is the largest U.S. flag container ship operator. Sea-Land's fleet of 98 vessels serves 120 ports in 80 nations. Since 1996, Sea-Land has had an alliance with Maersk Lines, a Danish carrier, which involves the sharing of vessels and equipment in certain markets. In late 1996 Congress passed a new Maritime Security Program under which Sea-Land will receive $31.5 million annually to defray the cost of operating 15 ships with U.S. crews.

In June 1998 CSX expects to complete the sale of its American Commercial Lines unit (6% of revenues) for $850 million to a joint venture with Vectura Group. CSX will own 34% of the venture, which will operate a fleet of 4,500 barges and 195 towboats.

CSX Intermodal (6% of revenues) provides transcontinental intermodal services, employing most national railroads. Logistics and warehousing services (4% of revenues) are provided by Customized Transportation Inc.

Per Share Data ($)

(Year Ended Dec. 31)	1997	1996	1995	1994	1993	1992	1991	1990	1989	1988
Tangible Bk. Val.	26.45	23.02	20.15	16.61	13.89	13.27	15.40	17.88	16.52	15.20
Cash Flow	6.73	6.89	5.80	5.87	4.48	2.66	2.12	4.22	4.25	1.43
Earnings	3.62	4.00	2.94	3.12	1.73	0.10	-0.38	1.81	2.04	-0.17
Dividends	1.08	1.04	0.92	0.88	0.79	0.76	0.71	0.70	0.64	0.62
Payout Ratio	30%	26%	31%	28%	46%	NM	NM	39%	30%	NM
Prices - High	62³/₈	53¹/₈	46¹/₈	46¹/₄	44¹/₈	36⁷/₈	29	19¹/₈	19³/₈	16¹/₄
- Low	41¹/₄	42¹/₈	34³/₄	31⁵/₈	33¹/₄	27¹/₄	14⁷/₈	13	14⁷/₈	12¹/₄
P/E Ratio - High	17	13	16	15	25	NM	NM	11	9	NM
- Low	11	11	12	10	19	NM	NM	7	7	NM

Income Statement Analysis (Million $)

	1997	1996	1995	1994	1993	1992	1991	1990	1989	1988
Revs.	10,621	10,536	10,504	9,608	8,940	8,734	8,636	8,205	7,745	7,592
Oper. Inc.	2,271	2,142	2,029	1,809	1,578	1,492	1,355	1,341	1,316	1,376
Depr.	688	620	600	577	572	527	501	473	447	467
Int. Exp.	451	249	270	310	298	276	306	319	349	358
Pretax Inc.	1,224	1,316	974	1,027	647	8.0	-88.0	552	716	-40.0
Eff. Tax Rate	31%	35%	37%	35%	42%	NM	NM	31%	37%	NM
Net Inc.	799	855	618	652	359	20.0	-76.0	365	427	-38.0

Balance Sheet & Other Fin. Data (Million $)

	1997	1996	1995	1994	1993	1992	1991	1990	1989	1988
Cash	690	682	660	535	499	530	465	609	591	625
Curr. Assets	2,175	2,072	1,935	1,665	1,571	1,421	1,535	1,725	1,711	2,435
Total Assets	19,957	19,957	14,282	13,724	13,420	13,049	12,798	12,804	12,298	13,026
Curr. Liab.	2,707	2,757	2,991	2,505	2,275	2,280	2,477	2,303	2,331	3,061
LT Debt	6,416	4,331	2,222	2,618	3,133	3,245	2,804	3,025	2,727	3,032
Common Eqty.	5,766	4,995	4,242	3,731	3,180	2,975	3,182	3,541	3,247	3,242
Total Cap.	15,121	12,046	9,024	8,919	8,654	8,302	8,207	9,100	8,626	8,716
Cap. Exp.	1,125	1,223	1,156	875	768	1,041	864	927	815	1,151
Cash Flow	1,487	1,475	1,218	1,229	931	547	425	830	862	419
Curr. Ratio	0.8	0.8	0.6	0.7	0.7	0.6	0.6	0.7	0.7	0.8
% LT Debt of Cap.	42.4	36.0	24.6	29.4	36.7	39.1	34.2	33.2	31.6	34.8
% Net Inc.of Revs.	7.5	8.1	5.9	6.8	4.0	0.2	NM	4.4	5.5	NM
% Ret. on Assets	4.3	5.5	4.4	4.8	2.7	0.2	NM	2.9	3.5	NM
% Ret. on Equity	14.8	18.5	15.5	18.8	11.7	0.6	NM	10.5	13.3	NM

Data as orig. reptd.; bef. results of disc. opers. and/or spec. items. Per share data adj. for stk. divs. as of ex-div. date. Bold denotes diluted EPS (FASB 128). E-Estimated. NA-Not Available. NM-Not Meaningful. NR-Not Ranked.

Office—One James Center, 901 E. Cary St., Richmond, VA 23219-4031. **Tel**—(804) 782-1400. **Website**—http://www.csx.com **Chrmn & Pres**—J. W. Snow. **EVP & CFO**—P. R. Goodwin. **VP-Treas**—G. R. Weber. **VP & Secy**—A. A. Rudnick. **Investor Contact**—Joseph C. Wilkinson. **Dirs**—E. E. Bailey, R. L. Burrus Jr., B. C. Gottwald, J. R. Hall, R. D. Kunisch, J. W. McGlothlin, S. J. Morcott, C. E. Rice, W. C. Richardson, F. S. Royal, J. W. Snow. **Transfer Agent & Registrar**—Harris Trust Co., Chicago. **Incorporated**—in Virginia in 1978. **Empl**— 46,911. **S&P Analyst**: Stephen R. Klein

STANDARD &POOR'S
STOCK REPORTS

Cummins Engine 701
NYSE Symbol **CUM**

In S&P 500

12-SEP-98

Industry: Trucks & Parts

Summary: Cummins is the leading manufacturer of diesel engines for heavy-duty trucks and has a growing midrange engine business.

S&P Opinion: Avoid (★★)

Recent Price • 42½	Yield • 2.6%
52 Wk Range • 82½-40½	12-Mo. P/E • 9.3

Earnings vs. Previous Year
▲=Up ▼=Down ▶=No Change

Quantitative Evaluations

Outlook (1 Lowest—5 Highest)
• 4

Fair Value
• 56⅛

Risk
• **Low**

Earn./Div. Rank
• **B**

Technical Eval
• **Neutral** since 9/98

Rel. Strength Rank (1 Lowest—99 Highest)
• 51

Insider Activity
• **NA**

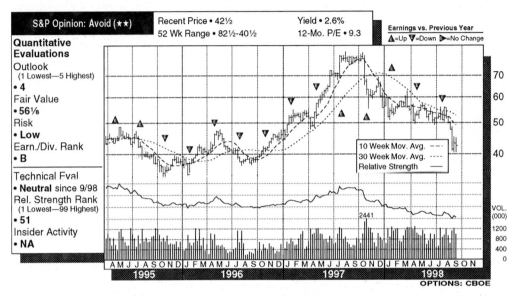

10 Week Mov. Avg.
30 Week Mov. Avg.
Relative Strength

OPTIONS: CBOE

Overview - 22-JUL-98

Industrywide heavy-duty truck shipments are expected to rise 3% in 1998, after recovering slightly in 1997 to about 201,000 units in North America. This follows a 20% drop in 1996 from the industry's all-time peak of 246,000. Heavy-duty engine shipments should mirror heavy truck demand. Midrange engine sales will be flat at best, on flat to lower North American vehicle demand and lower overseas shipments owing to the strength of the U.S. dollar and near term weakness in Asian markets. Earnings will be down, due to the weakness in Asia and a $30 million first quarter 1998 charge for excess warranty costs related to midrange engines sold in prior years. We remain concerned that any slowdown in the economy would provoke a resumption of the slide in demand that occurred in 1996, when shipments fell 20% in the heavy-duty segment, to 176,000. Longer term, the company should continue to benefit from a broadened product line and expanding global distribution, particularly in the Asia-Pacific region, where several joint ventures have been formed. These joint ventures gain entry into faster-growing emerging markets for CUM.

Valuation - 22-JUL-98

Although earnings held up well in 1997, we expect 1998 to be a more difficult year. We still think there is little pent-up demand, following the strong years experienced in the first half of the decade. Thus, we expect this near-term recovery in heavy-truck demand to be vulnerable to any slowdown in the domestic economy. In addition, recent instability in Asia will delay the progress of CUM's Asian ventures. Despite the recent collapse of the stock, we would still avoid the shares, which were recently trading at 14 times expected earnings for 1998.

Key Stock Statistics

S&P EPS Est. 1998	4.35	Tang. Bk. Value/Share	20.21
P/E on S&P Est. 1998	9.8	Beta	1.27
S&P EPS Est. 1999	4.75	Shareholders	500
Dividend Rate/Share	1.10	Market cap. (B)	$ 1.6
Shs. outstg. (M)	38.5	Inst. holdings	66%
Avg. daily vol. (M)	0.216		

Value of $10,000 invested 5 years ago: $ 12,078

Fiscal Year Ending Dec. 31

	1998	1997	1996	1995	1994	1993
Revenues (Million $)						
1Q	1,500	1,304	1,316	1,334	1,099	1,048
2Q	1,635	1,396	1,316	1,361	1,205	1,093
3Q	—	1,366	1,264	1,219	1,156	988.3
4Q	—	1,559	1,361	1,331	1,278	1,118
Yr.	—	5,625	5,257	5,245	4,737	4,248
Earnings Per Share ($)						
1Q	0.18	1.06	1.21	1.63	1.35	1.12
2Q	1.38	1.40	1.10	1.69	1.58	1.32
3Q	E1.30	1.38	0.67	1.14	1.48	1.11
4Q	E1.49	1.66	1.03	1.05	1.68	1.42
Yr.	E4.35	5.48	4.01	5.52	6.11	4.95

Next earnings report expected: mid October

Dividend Data (Dividends have been paid since 1948.)

Amount ($)	Date Decl.	Ex-Div. Date	Stock of Record	Payment Date
0.275	Oct. 14	Nov. 26	Dec. 01	Dec. 15 '97
0.275	Feb. 10	Feb. 26	Mar. 02	Mar. 16 '98
0.275	Apr. 06	May. 28	Jun. 01	Jun. 15 '98
0.275	Jul. 09	Aug. 28	Sep. 01	Sep. 15 '98

A Division of The McGraw-Hill Companies

Business Summary - 22-JUL-98

After surviving a difficult decade marked by frequent, sizable losses, Cummins Engine Co. emerged in the 1990s as a leader in the intensely competitive global market for diesel engines. Cummins is the leading maker of heavy-duty and midrange diesel engines, engine components and power systems for use in truck, bus, marine, power generation, military vehicle, construction, mining, logging, agriculture and rail applications. Steps taken in the 1980s to hone the company's competitiveness included plant restructuring, job layoffs and a financial recapitalization that included equity investments by three large customers and the company's founders, the Miller family.

To ensure better performance in future heavy-duty truck industry downturns, the company diversified its product line in the first half of the 1990s by developing a successful line of midrange diesel engines, and globally through formation of numerous foreign joint ventures that could make use of the company's engine technology. Today, about 47% of sales are derived from the automotive markets. Heavy-duty truck engines account for about half of the automotive shipments with

midrange engines and bus and light commercial vehicles the rest. Meanwhile, power generation market sales have grown to 21% of total sales and industrial markets contribute 19%. The remaining 13% of sales is derived from sales of Fleetguard filtration products, Holset turbochargers and other components.

Every major U.S. truck manufacturer offers Cummins engines as standard or optional equipment. Sales of heavy-duty, midrange and high-horsepower engines were 369,800 in 1997, compared with 332,300 in 1996, 338,900 in 1995, and 200,600 in 1991. CUM's share of the North American heavy-duty diesel truck engine market has drifted down to about 32% in recent years from 46% in 1990 and over 50% in the prior nine years. This reduction in market share reflects several factors, including the rapid expansion of the heavy-duty truck market from 1991 to 1995, CUM's focus on markets other than heavy-duty trucks and a decision by management to pursue profits instead of market share. While the company has continued to take aggressive action in recent years when necessary to further reduce operating costs, several years of strong profits have permitted the company to chart a course for international growth.

Per Share Data ($)

(Year Ended Dec. 31)	1997	1996	1995	1994	1993	1992	1991	1990	1989	1988
Tangible Bk. Val.	29.57	28.12	24.73	25.78	18.41	11.21	17.14	18.68	19.89	27.52
Cash Flow	9.49	7.92	9.18	9.19	8.40	5.54	1.81	-1.43	5.54	2.57
Earnings	5.48	4.01	5.52	6.11	4.95	1.77	-2.48	-7.24	-0.76	-3.35
Dividends	1.07	1.00	1.00	0.63	0.28	0.10	0.35	1.10	1.10	1.10
Payout Ratio	20%	25%	18%	10%	6%	6%	NM	NM	NM	NM
Prices - High	83	47³⁄₄	48⁵⁄₈	57⁵⁄₈	54³⁄₈	40¹⁄₂	27¹⁄₄	27³⁄₄	36¹⁄₈	34
- Low	44¹⁄₄	34¹⁄₂	34	35⁷⁄₈	37³⁄₈	26⁵⁄₈	16¹⁄₄	15⁵⁄₈	24	21⁵⁄₈
P/E Ratio - High	15	12	9	9	11	23	NM	NM	NM	NM
- Low	8	9	6	6	8	15	NM	NM	NM	NM

Income Statement Analysis (Million $)

	1997	1996	1995	1994	1993	1992	1991	1990	1989	1988
Revs.	5,625	5,257	5,245	4,737	4,248	3,749	3,406	3,462	3,511	3,310
Oper. Inc.	434	357	459	435	370	253	137	116	190	192
Depr.	158	149	143	128	122	123	127	143	135	132
Int. Exp.	26.0	18.0	13.0	17.5	36.3	41.0	42.5	43.9	51.8	52.6
Pretax Inc.	286	214	177	294	205	76.0	-46.0	-141	21.0	-47.0
Eff. Tax Rate	26%	25%	NM	14%	11%	12%	NM	NM	108%	NM
Net Inc.	212	160	224	253	183	67.0	-66.0	-164	-6.0	-63.0

Balance Sheet & Other Fin. Data (Million $)

	1997	1996	1995	1994	1993	1992	1991	1990	1989	1988
Cash	49.0	108	60.0	147	77.0	54.0	52.0	80.0	73.0	59.0
Curr. Assets	1,710	1,553	1,388	1,298	1,072	996	908	991	975	1,027
Total Assets	3,765	3,369	3,056	2,706	2,391	2,231	2,041	2,086	2,031	2,064
Curr. Liab.	1,055	1,021	1,053	840	700	724	689	728	750	721
LT Debt	522	283	117	155	190	412	443	411	406	409
Common Eqty.	1,422	1,312	1,183	1,073	709	386	509	554	407	587
Total Cap.	1,997	1,595	1,300	1,248	1,028	929	1,137	1,145	1,095	1,169
Cap. Exp.	405	304	223	238	184	139	124	147	138	151
Cash Flow	370	309	367	381	297	182	54.0	-35.0	116	55.0
Curr. Ratio	1.6	1.5	1.3	1.5	1.5	1.4	1.3	1.4	1.3	1.4
% LT Debt of Cap.	26.1	17.7	9.0	12.4	18.4	44.4	39.0	35.9	37.1	35.0
% Net Inc.of Revs.	3.8	3.0	4.3	5.3	4.3	1.8	NM	NM	NM	NM
% Ret. on Assets	5.9	5.0	7.8	9.6	7.5	2.9	NM	NM	NM	NM
% Ret. on Equity	15.5	12.8	19.9	27.5	30.6	12.1	NM	NM	NM	NM

Data as orig. reptd.; bef. results of disc. opers. and/or spec. items. Per share data adj. for stk. divs. as of ex-div. date. Bold denotes diluted EPS (FASB 128). E-Estimated. NA-Not Available. NM-Not Meaningful. NR-Not Ranked.

Office—500 Jackson St., Columbus, IN 47202. **Tel**—(812) 377-5000. **Website**—http://cummins.com **Chrmn & CEO**—J. A. Henderson. **Pres & COO**—T. Solso. **VP & CFO**—K. M. Patel. **Secy**—M. R. Gerstle. **Investor Contact**—Linda Hall. **Dirs**—H. Brown, R. J. Darnall, J. Deutch, W. Y. Elisha, H. H. Gray, J. A. Henderson, W. I. Miller, D. S. Perkins, W. D. Ruckelshaus, H. B. Schacht, T. M. Solso, F. A. Thomas, J. L. Wilson. **Transfer Agent & Registrar**—First Chicago Trust Co. of New York, Jersey City, NJ. **Incorporated**—in Indiana in 1919. **Empl**— 26,300. **S&P Analyst**: Robert E. Friedman, CPA

STANDARD &POOR'S
STOCK REPORTS

CVS Corp.

417J

NYSE Symbol **CVS**

In S&P 500

12-SEP-98

Industry:
Retail (Drug Stores)

Summary: CVS, the largest U.S. retail drugstore chain in terms of store count, operates about 4,100 stores in 24 states.

S&P Opinion: Buy (★★★★★)	Recent Price • 41¾	Yield • 0.6%
	52 Wk Range • 47⅞-25½	12-Mo. P/E • 49.1

Quantitative Evaluations

Outlook
(1 Lowest—5 Highest)
• 1⁻

Fair Value
• 33⅞

Risk
• Average

Earn./Div. Rank
• B-

Technical Eval.
• NA

Rel. Strength Rank
(1 Lowest—99 Highest)
• 91

Insider Activity
• Neutral

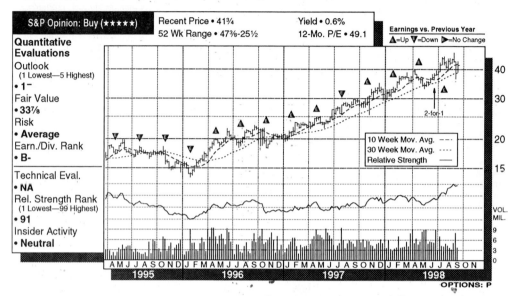

Earnings vs. Previous Year
▲=Up ▼=Down ▶=No Change

10 Week Mov. Avg. ---
30 Week Mov. Avg. ----
Relative Strength ―

VOL. MIL.

OPTIONS: P

Overview - 30-JUL-98

We expect sales to grow in the 8.0% to 10% range in 1999, reflecting improvement at Revco, the recent acquisition of Arbor Drugs, the addition of about 320 new stores, and same-store sales gains in upper-single to low double digits. Same-store sales growth at old Revco locations should outpace that of core CVS units, as the company completes the reconfiguration of the stores to CVS's more profitable mix. Reconfigured Revco stores should also benefit as the percentage of customers that purchase general merchandise in Revco reconfigured stores rises from its current level of 21% to the 42% seen for the average CVS store. In addition, efforts to control costs, and increased operating leverage arising from a larger store base, particularly from the continued relocation of stores from strip shopping centers to more profitable free-standing locations, should also boost earnings.

Valuation - 30-JUL-98

We continue to recommend purchase of the shares, based on expected synergies from the Revco and Arbor Drugs acquisitions. By the end of 1998, CVS expects to complete the conversion of the remaining 400 Revco stores not yet converted, as well as the conversion of Arbor stores recently acquired. These stores represent untapped revenue growth, as acquired stores converted to the CVS format typically experience a 10% to 14% gain in revenues. We project earnings growth in the 18% to 20% range over the next several years, but this could accelerate, as the company has indicated a possible increase in the number of stores it plans to open in the next few years. Despite its premium valuation of 34X our 1998 EPS estimate of $1.25 (excluding charges for the Arbor acquisition), we believe that the stock continues to provide a strong value.

Key Stock Statistics

S&P EPS Est. 1998	1.25	Tang. Bk. Value/Share	4.78
P/E on S&P Est. 1998	33.4	Beta	0.75
S&P EPS Est. 1999	1.48	Shareholders	5,700
Dividend Rate/Share	0.23	Market cap. (B)	$ 16.3
Shs. outstg. (M)	389.3	Inst. holdings	81%
Avg. daily vol. (M)	1.024		

Value of $10,000 invested 5 years ago: NA

Fiscal Year Ending Dec. 31

	1998	1997	1996	1995	1994	1993
Revenues (Million $)						
1Q	3,334	1,515	1,258	2,125	2,380	2,033
2Q	3,756	3,161	1,364	2,292	2,507	2,537
3Q	—	3,080	1,356	2,351	2,737	2,355
4Q	—	3,337	1,550	2,921	3,661	3,510
Yr.	—	12,738	5,528	9,689	11,286	10,435
Earnings Per Share ($)						
1Q	0.34	0.26	0.17	-0.13	-0.03	-0.12
2Q	0.03	-0.69	0.41	0.05	0.20	0.34
3Q	—	0.20	0.20	-0.11	0.23	0.17
4Q	—	0.30	0.28	-2.81	0.98	1.11
Yr.	—	0.07	1.06	-3.01	1.38	1.50

Next earnings report expected: late October

Dividend Data (Dividends have been paid since 1916.)

Amount ($)	Date Decl.	Ex-Div. Date	Stock of Record	Payment Date
0.110	Jan. 14	Jan. 21	Jan. 24	Feb. 02 '98
0.110	Mar. 12	Apr. 21	Apr. 23	May. 01 '98
2-for-1	May. 13	Jun. 16	May. 25	Jun. 15 '98
0.058	May. 13	Jul. 21	Jul. 23	Aug. 01 '98

A Division of The McGraw-Hill Companies

Business Summary - 30-JUL-98

Following the May 1997 acquisition of Revco, D.S., Inc, CVS became the largest U.S. drugstore chain, based on store count, with approximately 4,000 stores in 24 states and the District of Columbia, and annual revenues approaching $13 billion. CVS is the leader in the Northeast, Mid-Atlantic, Midwest and Southeast. The stores are well positioned, operating in 48 of the 100 leading U.S. drugstore markets, with the first or second position in approximately 80% of these markets.

On March 31, 1998, CVS acquired Arbor Drugs Inc., the leading regional drugstore chain in southern Michigan, with 207 stores, and annual revenues of nearly $1 billion. The merger provided entry for CVS into Detroit, the fourth largest U.S. drugstore market.

The company's stores are located primarily in strip shopping centers or free-standing locations, with the typical store ranging in size from 8,000 sq. ft. to 10,000 sq. ft. In addition to prescription drugs, the stores offer a broad selection of over-the-counter drugs, health and beauty aids, cosmetics, greeting cards, photo processing services, convenience foods, and seasonal items, including more than 1,300 CVS private label products.

Since 1992, sales have grown at a compound annual rate of 11%, and CVS's $573 in sales per sq. ft. places

it among the top performers in its industry. Its productivity is driven by its use of point-of-sale data and its move toward category management, which enables it to refine and tailor store merchandise selection market-by-market, based on local demographics.

Pharmacy operations, which accounted for 54% of sales in 1997, will continue to be a key focus of the company's business, reflecting its ability to succeed in the rapidly growing managed care arena and its ongoing purchase of prescription files from independent pharmacies. During 1997, CVS dispensed more than 225 million prescriptions, making it the largest U.S. drugstore chain in terms of prescriptions filled and pharmacy sales.

The addition of new stores will continue to play a big role in the company's growth. It is actively seeking to relocate many of its strip center locations to freestanding sites. During 1997, CVS opened 287 new stores, including 116 relocations, and also began the process of converting all Revco stores to the CVS format. It expects to open 300 new stores in 1998, and more than 350 annually in 1999 and beyond. Much of the planned store openings will be based on CVS's 10,125 sq. ft. freestanding prototype that includes a drive-thru pharmacy.

Per Share Data ($)

(Year Ended Dec. 31)	1997	1996	1995	1994	1993	1992	1991	1990	1989	1988
Tangible Bk. Val.	3.97	3.93	4.79	9.09	8.47	7.78	6.11	4.92	4.68	6.42
Cash Flow	0.71	1.43	2.00	2.35	2.41	1.64	2.33	2.40	2.27	2.02
Earnings	0.07	1.06	-3.00	1.38	1.50	0.67	1.60	1.79	1.78	1.63
Dividends	0.22	0.22	0.76	0.76	0.76	0.74	0.72	0.71	0.65	0.53
Payout Ratio	NM	21%	NM	55%	51%	111%	45%	40%	35%	32%
Prices - High	35	23	20	$20^7/_8$	$27^3/_8$	$27^1/_2$	$27^5/_8$	$28^7/_8$	$26^7/_8$	$19^1/_4$
- Low	$19^1/_2$	$13^5/_8$	$14^3/_8$	$14^3/_4$	$19^1/_2$	$21^1/_4$	$19^1/_4$	$16^3/_8$	$18^1/_2$	$13^3/_8$
P/E Ratio - High	NM	22	NM	15	18	41	17	16	15	12
- Low	NM	13	NM	11	13	32	12	9	10	8

Income Statement Analysis (Million $)

Revs.	12,738	5,528	8,689	11,286	10,435	10,433	9,886	8,687	7,554	6,780
Oper. Inc.	864	376	391	817	809	909	822	779	759	672
Depr.	222	76.0	197	206	192	201	152	124	106	87.0
Int. Exp.	45.0	31.0	55.0	34.1	25.8	26.7	31.2	25.8	10.9	4.2
Pretax Inc.	155	403	-797	578	600	335	640	633	649	586
Eff. Tax Rate	76%	41%	NM	38%	37%	38%	38%	32%	32%	32%
Net Inc.	37.0	239	-615	307	332	156	347	385	398	355

Balance Sheet & Other Fin. Data (Million $)

Cash	169	424	130	117	81.0	145	79.0	111	369	298
Curr. Assets	3,685	1,973	2,560	2,650	2,398	2,442	2,370	2,113	1,875	1,694
Total Assets	5,637	2,832	3,962	4,735	4,272	4,214	4,085	3,662	3,032	2,736
Curr. Liab.	2,855	1,182	1,798	1,643	1,328	1,381	1,330	1,202	855	824
LT Debt	273	304	328	350	365	375	384	395	390	48.0
Common Eqty.	2,077	946	1,212	2,369	2,228	2,060	1,735	1,495	1,261	1,706
Total Cap.	2,634	1,569	1,644	2,924	2,790	2,575	2,662	2,427	2,176	1,913
Cap. Exp.	312	224	395	421	387	304	253	231	203	189
Cash Flow	245	301	-418	497	507	341	483	493	490	441
Curr. Ratio	1.3	1.7	1.4	1.6	1.8	1.8	1.8	1.8	2.2	2.1
% LT Debt of Cap.	10.4	19.4	20.0	12.0	13.1	14.6	14.4	16.3	17.9	2.5
% Net Inc.of Revs.	0.3	4.3	NM	2.7	3.2	1.5	3.5	4.4	5.3	5.2
% Ret. on Assets	0.9	7.1	NM	6.8	7.8	3.7	8.9	11.5	14.2	14.3
% Ret. on Equity	1.5	20.8	NM	12.6	14.7	6.8	20.4	26.8	26.7	22.4

Data as orig. reptd.; bef. results of disc. opers. and/or spec. items. Per share data adj. for stk. divs. as of ex-div. date. Bold denotes diluted EPS (FASB 128). E-Estimated. NA-Not Available. NM-Not Meaningful. NR-Not Ranked.

Office—One CVS Drive, Woonsocket, RI 02895. **Tel**—(401) 765-1500. **Website**—http://www.cvs.com **Chrmn**—S. P. Goldstein. **Pres. & CEO**—T. M. Ryan. **EVP & CFO**—C. C. Conaway. **VP & Investor Contact**—Nancy Christal. **Secy**—Z. P. Lankowsky. **Dirs**—A. J. Bloostein, W. D. Cornwell, T. P. Gerrity, S. P. Goldstein, W. H. Joyce, T. R. Lautenbach, T. Murray, S. Z. Rosenberg, T. M. Ryan, I. G. Seidenberg, P. C. Stewart, T. O. Thorsen, M. C. Woodward Jr. **Transfer Agent & Registrar**—ChaseMellon Shareholder Services, So. Hackensack, NJ. **Incorporated**—in New York in 1914; reincorporated in Delaware in 1996. **Empl**— 90,000. **S&P Analyst:** Robert J. Izmirlian

STANDARD &POOR'S
STOCK REPORTS

Cyprus Amax Minerals

709W

NYSE Symbol **CYM**

In S&P 500

12-SEP-98 Industry: Metals Mining

Summary: CYM is a leading U.S. copper and coal producer, the world's largest producer of molybdenum and lithium, and explores for copper.

S&P Opinion: Hold (★★★)	Recent Price • 11⅝	Yield • 6.9%
	52 Wk Range • 25-9⅛	12-Mo. P/E • NM

Quantitative Evaluations

Outlook (1 Lowest—5 Highest)
• **NA**

Fair Value
• **NA**

Risk
• **Low**

Earn./Div. Rank
• **B-**

Technical Eval.
• **Neutral** since 6/98

Rel. Strength Rank (1 Lowest—99 Highest)
• **78**

Insider Activity
• **NA**

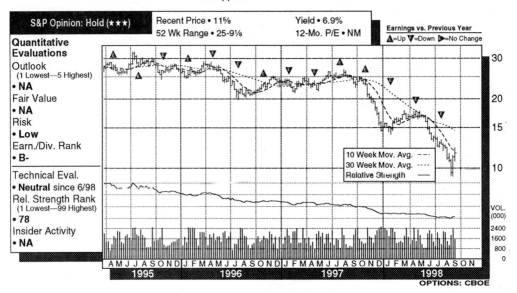

Earnings vs. Previous Year
▲=Up ▼=Down ▶=No Change

10 Week Mov. Avg. ---
30 Week Mov. Avg. ·····
Relative Strength —

VOL. (000)

OPTIONS: CBOE

Overview - 26-AUG-98

Copper production will decline to about 970 million lbs. in 1998, from 1997's 1.02 billion lbs., as a result of CYM's decision to curtail high cost production in response to lower copper prices. The cuts are expected to occur at the Bagdad and Sierrita mines in Arizona. Coal production will decline, as a result of the pending sale of several properties; margins should exceed those of 1997. As a result of depressed copper prices, we project a loss for 1998.

Valuation - 26-AUG-98

Following release of second quarter EPS, we are maintaining our hold rating on CYM. Earlier, in March 1998, we upgraded our rating on CYM and two other copper stocks, based on our expectation of short-term improvement in copper market fundamentals. It appears that a build-up on both commodity exchanges has plateaued. As of August 25, 1998, London Metal Exchange inventories were 295,675 metric tons, versus 379,325 metric tons at February 25, 1998; Comex inventories currently total 57,997 metric tons, versus 116,995 metric tons on March 6. Strong seasonal demand and production cutbacks will keep copper prices from slipping below the $0.70 level. We remain negative on the long-term outlook for copper, due to a large expansion of mine production scheduled to come on line by 2000. We rate CYM as a hold, due to its appeal as a potential merger candidate. If our assumption about weak secular copper market conditions proves accurate, there will be consolidation in the industry. CYM has recently divested some gold and coal assets, and plans to sell its lithium unit. This will generate substantial cash flow that will be used to reduce debt, narrows CYM's focus to copper, and helps increase its potential as a merger partner for another copper producer.

Key Stock Statistics

S&P EPS Est. 1998	-0.60	Tang. Bk. Value/Share	24.12
P/E on S&P Est. 1998	NM	Beta	0.85
S&P EPS Est. 1999	-0.40	Shareholders	45,000
Dividend Rate/Share	0.80	Market cap. (B)	$ 1.1
Shs. outstg. (M)	93.7	Inst. holdings	58%
Avg. daily vol. (M)	0.370		

Value of $10,000 invested 5 years ago: $ 4,698

Fiscal Year Ending Dec. 31

	1998	1997	1996	1995	1994	1993
Revenues (Million $)						
1Q	732.0	888.0	684.0	807.0	588.4	374.7
2Q	619.0	842.0	740.0	875.0	697.0	453.6
3Q	—	860.0	665.0	786.0	771.0	393.6
4Q	—	757.0	754.0	739.0	732.0	541.7
Yr.	—	3,346	2,843	3,207	2,788	1,764
Earnings Per Share ($)						
1Q	Nil	0.56	0.62	1.00	0.15	0.24
2Q	-0.44	0.65	0.52	1.39	0.30	1.73
3Q	E-0.10	0.42	0.10	-2.23	0.47	0.30
4Q	E-0.06	-1.09	-0.62	0.98	0.68	-0.14
Yr.	E-0.60	0.54	0.62	1.13	1.59	1.85

Next earnings report expected: late October

Dividend Data (Dividends have been paid since 1988.)

Amount ($)	Date Decl.	Ex-Div. Date	Stock of Record	Payment Date
0.200	Dec. 11	Jan. 07	Jan. 09	Feb. 02 '98
0.200	Feb. 12	Apr. 07	Apr. 09	May. 01 '98
0.200	Jun. 18	Jul. 08	Jul. 10	Aug. 03 '98
0.200	Aug. 20	Oct. 07	Oct. 09	Nov. 02 '98

Cyprus Amax Minerals Company

Business Summary - 26-AUG-98

This diversified mining company is one of the world's largest and lowest-cost copper producers. Cyprus Amax Minerals (CYM) is also a leading producer of molybdenum (used mainly in steelmaking, as well as in paint and oil refining), coal and lithium. Operating profits by segment (in millions) in recent years were:

	1997	1996	1995
Copper/molybdenum	$314	$151	$584
Coal	-15	90	-308
Other	2	-32	-37

The copper/molybdenum unit operates three major copper mines in Arizona, one in Chile, one in Peru and one primary molybdenum mine in Colorado. In 1997, copper output was 1.018 billion lbs., versus 768 million lbs., in 1996 and 687 million lbs. in 1995. The average copper sales price was unchanged at $1.04/lb; the average price was $1.33/lb in 1995. CYM's copper/molybdenum reserves at year-end 1996 were 3.6 billion tons, versus 3.7 billion tons at the end of 1995.

In 1996, CYM completed two major copper projects in South America; this was expected to make significant additions to future production, and to lower costs. The company completed the expansion of Cerro Verde, its 82%-owned copper mine in Peru, and, in December

1996, 51%-owned El Abra in Chile began startup. CYM expected El Abra to produce about 250 million lbs. for its account in 1997.

CYM is the world's largest producer of molybdenum. Production totaled 63 million lbs. in 1997, versus 56 million lbs. in 1996. The average price increased to $5.50/lb. from $5.25/lb. in 1996.

Coal production was 88 million tons in 1997, versus 82 million tons in 1996 and 81 million in 1995. Most of the coal is produced in the U.S. and is sold to electric utilities under long-term contracts. Due partly to changes in the electric utility industry, CYM had to re-negotiate several long-term contracts, leading to lower prices and profits. In February 1998, CYM announced plans to sell several coal properties to AEI Holding Co.; subject to certain conditions, the sale was expected to close in the 1998 second quarter.

In February 1998, 59%-owned Amax Gold agreed to be acquired by Kinross Gold Corp. (KGC, NYSE). Each Amax Gold share will be exchanged for 0.8 of a KGC share. The new company will be North America's fifth largest gold producer, and its costs would be in the lowest quartile of world producers.

Through the 1998 second quarter, CYM eliminated more than $600 million in long-term obligations, thereby reducing its debt to capital ratio by five percentage points. CYM has also concluded a definitive agreement to sell its lithium unit, following regulatory approvals.

Per Share Data ($)

(Year Ended Dec. 31)	1997	1996	1995	1994	1993	1992	1991	1990	1989	1988
Tangible Bk. Val.	24.92	25.32	25.38	22.64	24.16	19.52	28.02	27.94	30.92	25.62
Cash Flow	4.80	4.27	4.51	4.31	4.58	-3.17	3.60	5.03	8.46	6.08
Earnings	0.54	0.62	1.13	1.59	1.85	-6.31	0.72	2.38	6.06	4.21
Dividends	0.80	0.80	0.80	0.90	0.80	0.85	0.80	0.80	0.60	0.13
Payout Ratio	148%	129%	71%	57%	43%	NM	112%	32%	10%	3%
Prices - High	26³/₄	29¹/₈	32¹/₈	33³/₈	36⁷/₈	32	25³/₈	28¹/₂	33	24
- Low	14³/₈	19⁷/₈	24¹/₄	23¹/₈	21	18¹/₂	17¹/₂	13⁷/₈	21³/₈	13¹/₈
P/E Ratio - High	50	47	28	21	20	NM	35	12	5	6
- Low	27	32	21	15	11	NM	24	6	4	3

Income Statement Analysis (Million $)

	1997	1996	1995	1994	1993	1992	1991	1990	1989	1988
Revs.	3,346	2,843	3,207	2,788	1,764	1,641	1,657	1,866	1,790	1,327
Oper. Inc.	918	607	923	583	336	-65.0	174	346	426	264
Depr.	444	339	296	253	145	128	112	107	93.0	73.0
Int. Exp.	198	189	137	107	41.6	19.8	22.4	19.7	12.5	14.7
Pretax Inc.	40.0	77.0	120	221	131	-328	54.0	124	327	219
Eff. Tax Rate	NA	14%	2.50%	25%	24%	NM	20%	11%	24%	23%
Net Inc.	69.0	77.0	124	166	100	-245	43.0	111	250	170

Balance Sheet & Other Fin. Data (Million $)

	1997	1996	1995	1994	1993	1992	1991	1990	1989	1988
Cash	250	193	191	139	96.0	90.0	79.0	39.0	44.0	163
Curr. Assets	1,132	1,049	1,090	1,041	1,008	584	578	565	503	562
Total Assets	6,459	6,786	6,196	5,407	5,625	1,683	1,966	1,919	1,841	1,651
Curr. Liab.	835	745	798	618	967	258	279	229	252	219
LT Debt	2,202	2,554	1,877	1,391	1,347	232	239	246	108	120
Common Eqty.	2,325	2,355	2,360	2,096	2,212	923	1,094	1,088	1,183	1,007
Total Cap.	4,758	5,110	4,468	3,845	3,735	1,175	1,595	1,614	1,528	1,364
Cap. Exp.	391	856	929	359	266	156	190	208	349	364
Cash Flow	494	397	420	401	243	-128	140	203	329	237
Curr. Ratio	1.4	1.4	1.4	1.7	1.0	2.3	2.1	2.5	2.0	2.6
% LT Debt of Cap.	46.3	50.0	42.0	36.2	36.1	19.8	15.0	15.2	7.1	8.8
% Net Inc.of Revs.	2.1	2.7	3.9	6.0	5.7	NM	2.6	5.9	14.0	12.8
% Ret. on Assets	1.0	1.9	2.2	3.0	2.3	NM	2.2	5.9	14.5	12.1
% Ret. on Equity	2.1	3.3	4.5	7.2	4.9	NM	2.6	8.4	21.8	17.5

Data as orig. reptd.; bef. results of disc. opers. and/or spec. items. Per share data adj. for stk. divs. as of ex-div. date. Bold denotes diluted EPS (FASB 128). E-Estimated. NA-Not Available. NM-Not Meaningful. NR-Not Ranked.

Office—9100 E. Mineral Circle, Englewood, CO 80112. **Tel**—(303) 643-5000. **Website**—http://www.cyprusamax.com**Chrmn, Pres & CEO**—M. H. Ward. **SVP & Secy**—P. C. Wolf. **SVP & CFO**—G. J. Malys. **VP, Treas & Investor Contact**—Frank J. Kane. **Dirs**—A. Born, L. G. Alvarado, G. S. Ansell, W. C. Bousquette, T. V. Falkie, A. M. Gray, R. A. Schnabel, T. M. Solso, J. H. Stookey, J. A. Todd Jr., B. B. Turner, M. H. Ward.**Transfer Agent & Registrar**—Bank of New York, NYC. **Incorporated**—in Delaware in 1969. **Empl**— 10,500. **S&P Analyst:** Leo J. Larkin

12-SEP-98

Industry:
Auto Parts & Equipment

Summary: Dana manufactures truck and car components as well as parts both for OEMs and for distribution in the automotive aftermarket.

S&P Opinion: Buy (★★★★)	Recent Price • 40½ Yield • 2.9%
	52 Wk Range • 61½-37½ 12-Mo. P/E • 10.7

Quantitative Evaluations

Outlook
(1 Lowest—5 Highest)
• **3⁻**

Fair Value
• **45½**

Risk
• **Low**

Earn./Div. Rank
• **B+**

Technical Eval.
• **NA**

Rel. Strength Rank
(1 Lowest—99 Highest)
• **46**

Insider Activity
• **Neutral**

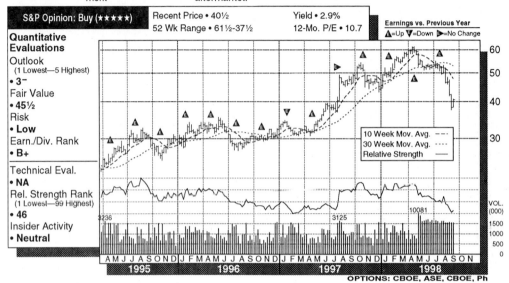

Earnings vs. Previous Year
▲=Up ▼=Down ▶=No Change

10 Week Mov. Avg. ---
30 Week Mov. Avg. ·····
Relative Strength —

OPTIONS: CBOE, ASE, CBOE, Ph

Overview - 10-AUG-98

Sales should grow in 1998, as contributions from acquisitions, including Echlin Inc., outweigh revenues lost as a result of divestitures. Demand for replacement parts has been sluggish, but should ultimately rebound, with continued use of aging vehicles, as well as a return to more normal weather patterns in North America. For the long term, international operations should continue to grow, fueled by acquisitions and a continuing trend to outsourcing by global vehicle producers. DCN is increasing its investment in Europe, India and the Asia-Pacific Rim. Its long-term goals remain to derive 50% of sales from foreign markets and 50% from domestic sales, and also to derive 50% from vehicle original equipment (OE) and 50% from aftermarket parts distribution, off-highway OE and industrial equipment OE. DCN believes that by balancing its exposure to these broad categories it can reduce earnings volatility.

Valuation - 10-AUG-98

Sales and earnings should grow steadily, as DCN continues to rationalize operations, increase systems content per vehicle, and expand market share via strategic acquisitions, improved engineering, and global ventures. The company's focus on core operations should help it achieve its January 1999 targets of 10% top-line growth (one-third through acquisitions), after tax return on sales of at least 5%, and 20% ROE. DCN's strategy appears to be working. The company posted record sales in each quarter of 1997, and in the first quarter of 1998, with year to year growth accelerating since the 1997 second half. DCN's valuation should benefit from improving operating performance, and from expanding market share in a consolidating industry. Despite negative sentiment toward auto parts stocks, we see the recent decline in the shares as providing an attractive purchase opportunity.

Key Stock Statistics

S&P EPS Est. 1998	3.85	Tang. Bk. Value/Share	10.99
P/E on S&P Est. 1998	10.5	Beta	1.07
S&P EPS Est. 1999	4.58	Shareholders	32,500
Dividend Rate/Share	1.16	Market cap. (B)	$ 6.7
Shs. outstg. (M)	164.9	Inst. holdings	51%
Avg. daily vol. (M)	0.445		

Value of $10,000 invested 5 years ago: $ 20,323

Fiscal Year Ending Dec. 31

	1998	1997	1996	1995	1994	1993
Revenues (Million $)						
1Q	2,350	2,115	1,973	1,924	1,597	1,324
2Q	2,340	2,141	2,020	1,969	1,712	1,418
3Q	—	1,961	1,816	1,727	1,610	1,291
4Q	—	2,074	1,877	1,977	1,695	1,428
Yr.	—	8,291	7,686	7,598	6,614	5,460
Earnings Per Share ($)						
1Q	**1.00**	0.90	0.78	0.59	0.48	0.26
2Q	**1.08**	0.90	0.90	0.88	0.69	0.40
3Q	—	0.93	0.64	0.60	0.54	0.36
4Q	—	**0.79**	0.69	0.77	0.60	0.38
Yr.	**E3.85**	3.49	2.99	2.84	2.31	1.39

Next earnings report expected: late October

Dividend Data (Dividends have been paid since 1936.)

Amount ($)	Date Decl.	Ex-Div. Date	Stock of Record	Payment Date
0.270	Oct. 20	Nov. 26	Dec. 01	Dec. 15 '97
0.270	Feb. 09	Feb. 25	Feb. 27	Mar. 13 '98
0.290	Apr. 20	May. 28	Jun. 01	Jun. 15 '98
0.290	Jul. 20	Aug. 28	Sep. 01	Sep. 15 '98

A Division of The **McGraw·Hill** Companies

Business Summary - 10-AUG-98

To assure a place among a rapidly consolidating group of top tier automotive component manufacturers, Dana is building critical mass by focusing on core businesses, while divesting units that do not meet its goals. It defines a core business as one with leading or second place market share, global sales over $500 million, at least 10% sales annual growth, and net return on sales of 6% or better (unleveraged). Since 1990, DCN has completed more than 40 acquisitions and joint ventures, with about 75% internationally based. In 1997 alone, it announced or completed seven acquisitions and joint ventures, as well as nine divestitures. It recently completed the purchase of Echlin Inc. (1997 sales of $3.6 billion) for about $3.9 billion.

DCN makes components and systems for the worldwide vehicular, industrial and off-highway original equipment (OE) markets, and is a major supplier to the related aftermarkets. Dana Credit Corp. provides leasing and financial services through subsidiaries. In 1997, vehicular products accounted for 76% of revenues, and industrial lines for 24%. International operations contributed 28% of revenues in each of 1996 and 1997.

Consolidated sales by market in 1997 were: 41% light trucks and cars OE, 18% medium and heavy trucks OE, 12% automotive distribution, 10% mobile off-highway/industrial distribution, 6% truck parts distri-

bution, 11% mobile off-highway OE, and 3% industrial equipment OE.

Vehicular products consist of drivetrain components, such as axles and driveshafts; engine parts, such as piston rings, seals, filters and gaskets; structural products, such as vehicular frames, engine cradles and rails; and industrial products, such as electrical and mechanical brakes and clutches, drives and motion control devices and fluid power components, such as pumps, cylinders and control valves.

In September 1997, DCN sold its clutch business (annual sales of about $179 million) to Eaton for $180 million. Separately, it sold its transmission business ($104 million) to a 49%-owned Mexican affiliate. Effective January 1, 1998, DCN bought Eaton's axle and brake business ($660 million) for $287 million.

As part of its strategy to concentrate on core businesses and divest underperforming assets, in the fourth quarter of 1997, the company sold its French distribution operation, its flat rubber product business, and its 49% interest in Korea Spicer Corp.

In 1997, DCN acquired Clark-Hurth Components, a leading global supplier of off-highway drivetrain components and systems. Separately, it acquired the piston ring and cylinder liner business of SPX Corp.; this should enhance DCN's global position in engine hard parts for OE and aftermarket applications.

Per Share Data ($)

(Year Ended Dec. 31)	1997	1996	1995	1994	1993	1992	1991	1990	1989	1988
Tangible Bk. Val.	10.99	11.11	8.08	6.77	5.63	5.09	9.45	12.79	12.46	11.80
Cash Flow	6.77	5.73	5.27	4.45	3.50	2.67	2.51	2.67	3.21	3.54
Earnings	3.49	3.01	2.84	2.31	1.39	0.49	0.17	0.93	1.62	2.00
Dividends	1.04	0.98	0.90	0.83	0.80	0.80	0.80	0.80	0.80	0.77
Payout Ratio	30%	33%	32%	36%	58%	163%	487%	86%	50%	39%
Prices - High	54⅜	35½	32⅝	30¾	30⅛	24⅛	18¼	19⅛	21½	20¼
- Low	30⅝	27¼	21⅜	19⅝	22	13⅜	12⅜	10	16½	16¼
P/E Ratio - High	16	12	11	13	22	49	NM	21	13	10
- Low	9	9	8	8	16	27	NM	11	10	8

Income Statement Analysis (Million $)

	1997	1996	1995	1994	1993	1992	1991	1990	1989	1988
Revs.	8,291	7,686	7,598	6,763	5,588	5,036	4,591	5,225	5,157	5,190
Oper. Inc.	705	725	709	738	585	411	372	601	647	666
Depr.	335	278	246	211	196	192	193	143	129	125
Int. Exp.	196	159	146	113	137	168	200	271	255	232
Pretax Inc.	686	416	509	416	244	58.0	NM	182	246	279
Eff. Tax Rate	43%	32%	36%	38%	37%	NM	NM	48%	37%	35%
Net Inc.	369	306	288	228	129	43.0	13.0	76.0	132	162

Balance Sheet & Other Fin. Data (Million $)

	1997	1996	1995	1994	1993	1992	1991	1990	1989	1988
Cash	93.0	228	66.0	48.2	50.0	42.0	50.0	42.0	71.0	54.0
Curr. Assets	NA	NA	NA	NA	NA	NA	NA	NA	NA	NA
Total Assets	7,119	7,119	5,694	5,111	4,632	4,343	4,179	4,513	5,225	4,786
Curr. Liab.	NA	NA	NA	NA	NA	NA	NA	NA	NA	NA
LT Debt	2,178	1,698	1,315	870	846	1,043	1,207	1,152	1,165	1,009
Common Eqty.	1,701	1,429	1,165	940	801	707	989	1,049	1,020	960
Total Cap.	4,033	3,127	2,634	1,962	1,789	1,878	2,512	2,572	2,560	2,328
Cap. Exp.	426	357	204	337	178	114	150	228	235	226
Cash Flow	704	584	534	439	324	235	206	219	262	287
Curr. Ratio	NA	NA	NA	NA	NA	NA	NA	NA	NA	NA
% LT Debt of Cap.	54.0	54.3	49.9	44.3	47.3	55.5	48.1	44.8	45.5	43.3
% Net Inc.of Revs.	4.5	39.8	37.9	3.4	2.3	0.9	0.3	1.4	2.6	3.1
% Ret. on Assets	5.6	5.2	5.3	4.7	2.8	1.0	0.3	1.6	2.6	4.3
% Ret. on Equity	23.6	23.6	27.4	26.2	16.5	4.8	1.3	7.3	13.3	17.6

Data as orig. reptd.; bef. results of disc. opers. and/or spec. items. Per share data adj. for stk. divs. as of ex-div. date. Bold denotes diluted EPS (FASB 128). E-Estimated. NA-Not Available. NM-Not Meaningful. NR-Not Ranked.

Office—4500 Dorr St., Toledo, OH 43697. **Tel**—(419) 535-4500. **Website**—http://www.dana.com **Chrmn & CEO**—S. J. Morcott. **President & COO**—J. Magliochetti. **VP & CFO**—J. S. Simpson. **Treas**—A. G. Paton. **Secy**—M. J. Strobel. **Investor Contact**—Steve Superits (419-535-4636). **Dirs**—B. F. Bailar, A. C. Baillie, E. M. Carpenter, E. Clark, G. H. Hiner, J.M. Magliochetti, M. R. Marks, S. J. Morcott, R. P. Priory, J. D. Stevenson, T. B. Sumner Jr. **Transfer Agent & Registrar**—ChaseMellon Shareholder Services, Ridgefield Park, NJ. **Incorporated**—in Virginia in 1916. **Empl**—79,000. **S&P Analyst:** Efraim Levy

12-SEP-98

Industry: Restaurants

Summary: This restaurant company operates the Red Lobster and Olive Garden chains.

S&P Opinion: Accumulate (★★★★)	Recent Price • 15⅝	Yield • 0.5%
	52 Wk Range • 18⅛-9	12-Mo. P/E • 23.3

Quantitative Evaluations

Outlook
(1 Lowest—5 Highest)
• **4+**

Fair Value
• **19⅜**

Risk
• **Average**

Earn./Div. Rank
• **NR**

Technical Eval.
• **Bullish** since 8/98

Rel. Strength Rank
(1 Lowest—99 Highest)
• **80**

Insider Activity
• **Neutral**

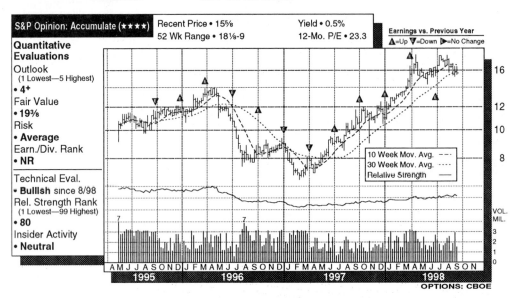

Earnings vs. Previous Year
▲=Up ▼=Down ▶=No Change

10 Week Mov. Avg. – – –
30 Week Mov. Avg. ————
Relative Strength ————

OPTIONS: CBOE

Overview - 10-JUL-98

Sales in FY 99 (May) should increase only modestly, reflecting fewer units in operation. The company has pruned its store base, closing underperforming units. Same-store sales at Olive Garden should continue to increase, while Red Lobster's same-unit sales should improve and remain positive. The total cost of sales ratio should remain about level with that of FY 98. Food and beverage prices should remain tame, but labor costs will increase. Selling, general and administrative expenses should be well controlled. Operating income should increase significantly. Depreciation should decline, with fewer units in operation. Interest expense should decline slightly. Earnings per share should climb about 19%, benefiting from a share buyback program. The company is expanding its Bahama Breeze concept, opening its third unit. DRI repurchased 13.5 million of its common shares in FY 98, under a 15.8 million share authorization.

Valuation - 10-JUL-98

We recommend accumulating the stock of this restaurant company, as earnings growth is back on track. For the near term, we expect continued improvement in customer satisfaction at the Red Lobster chain to lead to favorable word-of-mouth and more repeat visits. The long-term demographics of the U.S. population should generally be favorable for operators of casual dining restaurants. As consumers age, they are likely to increasingly appreciate and be able to afford the type of food offerings and amenities offered by chains such as Red Lobster and Olive Garden. Somewhat offsetting this is a very crowded marketplace, which is keenly competitive. However, new restaurant concepts aid the company's long-term outlook.

Key Stock Statistics

S&P EPS Est. 1999	0.80	Tang. Bk. Value/Share	7.03
P/E on S&P Est. 1999	19.5	Beta	NA
Dividend Rate/Share	0.08	Shareholders	28,000
Shs. outstg. (M)	139.2	Market cap. (B)	$ 2.2
Avg. daily vol. (M)	0.381	Inst. holdings	58%

Value of $10,000 invested 5 years ago: NA

Fiscal Year Ending May 31

	1998	1997	1996	1995	1994	1993
Revenues (Million $)						
1Q	809.3	805.6	836.0	788.0	742.0	677.0
2Q	745.3	748.8	731.2	733.0	674.0	623.0
3Q	811.3	800.9	795.1	803.0	755.0	711.0
4Q	921.2	816.6	829.5	838.0	791.0	727.0
Yr.	3,287	3,172	3,192	3,162	2,963	2,737
Earnings Per Share ($)						
1Q	0.16	0.13	-0.08	0.20	--	--
2Q	0.05	-0.07	0.10	0.07	--	--
3Q	**0.20**	0.10	0.22	-0.07	--	--
4Q	**0.27**	0.19	-0.76	0.11	--	--
Yr.	**0.67**	0.35	0.47	0.31	0.75	0.56

Next earnings report expected: late September

Dividend Data (Dividends have been paid since 1995.)

Amount ($)	Date Decl.	Ex-Div. Date	Stock of Record	Payment Date
0.040	Sep. 26	Oct. 08	Oct. 10	Nov. 01 '97
0.040	Mar. 27	Apr. 07	Apr. 10	May. 01 '98

A Division of The McGraw·Hill Companies

STANDARD
&POOR'S
STOCK REPORTS

Darden Restaurants, Inc.

717

12-SEP-98

Business Summary - 10-JUL-98

Darden Restaurants is a leader in the casual dining segment of the restaurant industry, with about a 9% market share. This highly fragmented industry is characterized by thousands of independent operators and small chains. Chains account for just 23% in the full-service segment of eating out, while they dominate the fast-food segment, with 63% market share. The company was spun off from General Mills, Inc. in May 1995. DRI is named after William B. Darden, who founded the Red Lobster chain in 1968.

Red Lobster is the largest U.S. chain of full-service, seafood specialty restaurants. As of February 22, 1998, DRI was operating 684 units, of which about 649 were in the U.S., with the balance in Canada. The restaurants feature fresh fish, shrimp, crab, lobster, scallops, and other seafood, served in a casual atmosphere. In September 1996, Red Lobster introduced a new menu that places greater emphasis on lower-priced items. The menu included 15 entrees priced at under $10. In FY 97, the average check per person was between $12.75 and $14.25; alcoholic beverages accounted for about 8% of sales.

Olive Garden is the largest U.S. chain of casual, full-service Italian-food restaurants. As of February 22, 1998, there were 465 units in operation, most of which were in the U.S. The Olive Garden menu offers recipes from northern and southern Italy. Dinner entree prices at Olive Garden restaurants range from about $6.95 to $13.95, and lunch entree prices range from about $4.75 to $7.95. DRI has also been testing a limited-menu Olive Garden Cafe concept in foodcourt settings at seven regional shopping malls. In February 1996, DRI opened the first unit of a new Caribbean-themed restaurant concept, called Bahama Breeze. A second Bahama Breeze opened in May 1997, and the company plans up to three new units in FY 98.

After completing a two-year market optimization study, the company restructured its operations. It closed a total of 50 Red Lobster and Olive Garden restaurants in the third and fourth quarters of FY 97, recording a related $230 million pretax charge in the third quarter. Red Lobster's FY 97 sales of $1.87 billion were down 2% from the FY 96 level. Operating profits were below prior-year levels; average store sales were $2.6 million. Annual sales at Olive Garden totaled $1.3 billion, a 3% increase. Double-digit gains were recorded in operating profit; average store sales were $2.6 million.

Per Share Data ($)

(Year Ended May 31)	1998	1997	1996	1995	1994	1993	1992	1991	1990	1989
Tangible Bk. Val.	7.03	7.22	7.58	7.37	6.61	NA	NA	NA	NA	NA
Cash Flow	1.51	0.30	1.32	1.17	1.54	NA	NA	NA	NA	NA
Earnings	0.67	0.35	0.47	0.31	0.75	NA	NA	NA	NA	NA
Dividends	0.08	0.08	0.08	Nil	NA	NA	NA	NA	NA	NA
Payout Ratio	12%	23%	17%	Nil	NA	NA	NA	NA	NA	NA
Cal. Yrs.	1997	1996	1995	1994	1993	1992	1991	1990	1989	1988
Prices - High	12½	14	12⅛	NA	NA	NA	NA	NA	NA	NA
- Low	6¾	7½	9⅛	NA	NA	NA	NA	NA	NA	NA
P/E Ratio - High	19	40	26	NA	NA	NA	NA	NA	NA	NA
- Low	10	21	19	NA	NA	NA	NA	NA	NA	NA

Income Statement Analysis (Million $)

	1998	1997	1996	1995	1994	1993	1992	1991	1990	1989
Revs.	3,287	3,172	3,192	3,163	2,963	NA	NA	NA	NA	NA
Oper. Inc.	300	235	345	316	331	NA	NA	NA	NA	NA
Depr.	126	137	135	135	125	NA	NA	NA	NA	NA
Int. Exp.	20.5	23.3	24.9	26.1	22.6	NA	NA	NA	NA	NA
Pretax Inc.	154	27.6	114	59.8	188	NA	NA	NA	NA	NA
Eff. Tax Rate	34%	NM	35%	18%	36%	NA	NA	NA	NA	NA
Net Inc.	102	-91.0	74.4	49.2	120	NA	NA	NA	NA	NA

Balance Sheet & Other Fin. Data (Million $)

	1998	1997	1996	1995	1994	1993	1992	1991	1990	1989
Cash	33.5	25.5	30.3	20.1	17.7	NA	NA	NA	NA	NA
Curr. Assets	398	337	288	308	250	NA	NA	NA	NA	NA
Total Assets	1,985	1,964	2,089	2,113	1,859	NA	NA	NA	NA	NA
Curr. Liab.	559	481	445	517	403	NA	NA	NA	NA	NA
LT Debt	311	313	301	304	304	NA	NA	NA	NA	NA
Common Eqty.	1,020	1,081	1,223	1,174	1,052	NA	NA	NA	NA	NA
Total Cap.	1,408	1,464	1,625	1,580	1,447	NA	NA	NA	NA	NA
Cap. Exp.	112	160	214	358	335	NA	NA	NA	NA	NA
Cash Flow	228	45.8	209	185	245	NA	NA	NA	NA	NA
Curr. Ratio	0.7	0.7	0.6	0.6	0.6	NA	NA	NA	NA	NA
% LT Debt of Cap.	22.0	21.4	18.5	19.2	21.0	NA	NA	NA	NA	NA
% Net Inc.of Revs.	3.1	NM	2.3	1.6	4.0	NA	NA	NA	NA	NA
% Ret. on Assets	5.2	NM	3.5	NA	NA	NA	NA	NA	NA	NA
% Ret. on Equity	9.7	NM	6.2	NA	NA	NA	NA	NA	NA	NA

Data as orig. reptd.; bef. results of disc. opers. and/or spec. items. Per share data adj. for stk. divs. as of ex-div. date. Bold denotes diluted EPS (FASB 128). E-Estimated. NA-Not Available. NM-Not Meaningful. NR-Not Ranked.

Office—5900 Lake Ellenor Dr., Orlando, FL 32809.**Tel**—(407) 245-4000. **Chrmn & CEO**—J. R. Lee.**SVP-Fin**—J. D. Smith.**SVP, Treas & Investor Contact**—Clarence Otis, Jr.**Dirs**—H. B. Atwater, J. P. Birkelund, D. B. Burke, O. C. Donald, J. R. Lee, B. S. Murphy, R. E. Rivera, M. D. Rose, J. A. Smith, B. Sweatt.**Transfer Agent & Registrar**—Norwest Bank, St. Paul, MN.**Incorporated**—in Florida in 1995.**Empl**— 114,582. **S&P Analyst:** Karen J. Sack, CFA

STANDARD &POOR'S
STOCK REPORTS

Data General

717M

NYSE Symbol **DGN**

In S&P 500

12-SEP-98

Industry: Computers (Hardware)

Summary: This company provides enterprise servers, storage systems and services primarily based on industry standard technology.

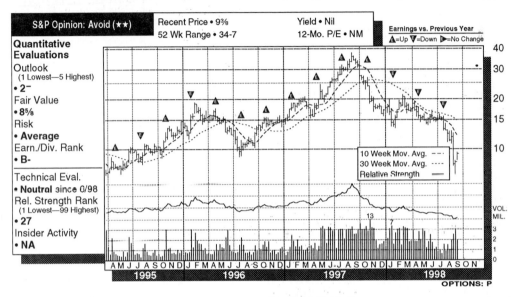

S&P Opinion: Avoid (★★)	Recent Price • 9⅜ Yield • Nil
	52 Wk Range • 34-7 12-Mo. P/E • NM

Quantitative Evaluations

Outlook
(1 Lowest—5 Highest)
• **2⁻**

Fair Value
• **8⅝**

Risk
• **Average**

Earn./Div. Rank
• **B-**

Technical Eval.
• **Neutral** since 0/98

Rel. Strength Rank
(1 Lowest—99 Highest)
• **27**

Insider Activity
• **NA**

OPTIONS: P

Overview - 24-JUL-98

In June 1998, DGN announced that it would take a $125 million charge to restructure its AViiON division, discontinue its THiiN Line Internet appliance line and cut about 400 jobs. The company hopes to see $50-55 million in annual cost savings from the restructuring, of which $10 million will be reinvested in CLARiiON. We now expect revenues to decline for full year FY 98 (Sep.), as demand for Data General's CLARiiON disk array products remains weak, reflecting lower demand for the storage industry as a whole, as well as a slower-than-expected industrywide transition to fibre-channel technology. Gross margins will continue to be under pressure due to price competition, as well as lower unit volumes, which will not allow the company to leverage fixed costs. The outlook for DGN is clouded by uncertainty as to when the market for fibre-channel technology will finally pick up. DGN should have sufficient operating loss carryforwards left to keep its effective tax rate near its current low level throughout FY 98.

Valuation - 24-JUL-98

Data General reported a loss of $3.15 a share (incl. a $2.74 a share restructuring charge) for the third quarter of FY 98 (Sep.) - worse than expected. Total revenues declined 10%, as demand for the company's CLARiiON disk array products continues to be weak. DGN is continuing to be hurt by the transition to fibre-channel technology, and the company is reporting low volumes in this area at the same time that many competitors, particularly EMC, are reporting volume increases. DGN has responded to its problems with yet another restructuring, and there is no timetable for a return to profitability. With revenue and earnings visibility limited, we recommend the shares be avoided.

Key Stock Statistics

S&P EPS Est. 1998	-3.18	Tang. Bk. Value/Share	7.70
P/E on S&P Est. 1998	NM	Beta	1.54
S&P EPS Est. 1999	0.65	Shareholders	12,500
Dividend Rate/Share	Nil	Market cap. (B)	$0.464
Shs. outstg. (M)	49.5	Inst. holdings	83%
Avg. daily vol. (M)	0.521		

Value of $10,000 invested 5 years ago: $ 8,064

Fiscal Year Ending Sep. 30

	1998	1997	1996	1995	1994	1993
Revenues (Million $)						
1Q	365.3	348.4	327.6	282.2	261.2	280.0
2Q	361.8	389.4	335.2	283.8	282.9	267.5
3Q	351.3	391.3	323.2	280.5	283.8	252.4
4Q	—	404.1	336.3	312.8	292.6	278.4
Yr.	—	1,533	1,322	1,159	1,121	1,078
Earnings Per Share ($)						
1Q	**0.07**	0.25	0.12	0.63	-0.60	0.02
2Q	**-0.09**	0.32	0.15	-0.30	-1.35	-0.22
3Q	**-3.15**	0.34	0.17	-1.65	-0.34	-0.47
4Q	E-0.01	0.35	0.24	0.04	-0.17	-1.06
Yr.	E-3.18	1.26	0.68	-1.23	-2.45	-1.73

Next earnings report expected: late October

Dividend Data

No dividends have been paid. A "poison pill" stock purchase rights plan was adopted in 1986.

A Division of The **McGraw·Hill** *Companies*

STANDARD
&POOR'S
STOCK REPORTS

Data General Corporation

717M
12-SEP-98

Business Summary - 24-JUL-98

Data General (DGN) has completed a transition from proprietary minicomputers to computer systems and related technologies serving open systems. The transition has been a painful one, as DGN returned to profitability in FY 96 (Sep.) after posting losses for most of the past decade. Results have been hurt by restructuring charges taken in the preceding five fiscal years aggregating $222 million, brought on by DGN's need to move along with the rest of the industry away from minicomputers toward more powerful and less expensive PCs. On top of all this, the company announced in June 1998, that it would take a $125 million restructuring charge to cut 400 jobs, restructure its AViiON division and discontinue its THiiN Line Internet appliance.

Product sales contributed 75% of revenues in FY 97, up from 70% in FY 96 and 65% in FY 95. DGN's two main product lines are AViiON servers (42% of total revenues) and CLARiiON storage products (33%). The remainder of revenues are derived from sales of older product lines; peripheral equipment, such as monitors, printers, multiplexors, disk storage, magnetic tape equipment and modems; and services and support, which include systems installation, consulting, design and maintenance services provided worldwide.

AViiON computers function as servers or multi-user systems for a wide range of applications to large enterprises that need high-availability systems to support large numbers of users, large volumes of transactions, and vast databases. Intel-based AViiON systems, launched in October 1995, use a Pentium Pro processor and generated the majority of AViiON revenues in FY 97. Intel systems should continue to grow as a percentage of revenues as clients migrate away from older machines.

CLARiiON mass storage subsystems range from disk arrays for the PC/local area network to high-capacity, high-availability arrays for enterprise storage applications. During 1997, the company began delivering a new generation of CLARiiON products based on fibre-channel technology, which has increased bandwidth, enabling the movement of up to five times more data, and greater scalability, permitting the use of much larger disk arrays. The majority of CLARiiON systems are sold to original equipment manufacturers (OEMs), who can package CLARiiON with their own systems. Hewlett-Packard is the largest CLARiiON customer and accounted for 16% of total company revenues in FY 97. Systems are also sold to systems integrators and distributors.

DGN's THiiN Line business unit was formed to develop products for the Internet/intranet market. The company's first THiiN Line product was introduced in October 1997. DGN recently announced it would discontinue this business.

Per Share Data ($)

(Year Ended Sep. 30)	1997	1996	1995	1994	1993	1992	1991	1990	1989	1988
Tangible Bk. Val.	10.68	8.31	7.36	8.47	10.51	13.27	15.50	13.21	17.68	21.51
Cash Flow	3.06	2.65	0.74	-0.30	0.52	0.66	5.40	-1.45	-0.62	2.96
Earnings	1.26	0.68	-1.23	-2.45	-1.73	-1.91	2.62	-4.65	-4.10	-0.55
Dividends	Nil	Nil	Nil	Nil	Nil	Nil	Nil	Nil	Nil	Nil
Payout Ratio	Nil	Nil	Nil	Nil	Nil	Nil	Nil	Nil	Nil	Nil
Prices - High	37$7/8$	19$1/8$	14$3/4$	12	13$7/8$	18$1/8$	22$1/2$	13$1/4$	19$1/2$	28$1/8$
- Low	14$1/8$	9	6$5/8$	6$5/8$	7$3/4$	7$1/8$	3$3/4$	3$1/2$	11$3/4$	16$3/4$
P/E Ratio - High	30	28	NM	NM	NM	NM	9	NM	NM	NM
- Low	11	13	NM	NM	NM	NM	1	NM	NM	NM

Income Statement Analysis (Million $)

	1997	1996	1995	1994	1993	1992	1991	1990	1989	1988
Revs.	1,533	1,322	1,159	1,121	1,078	1,116	1,229	1,216	1,314	1,365
Oper. Inc.	142	118	41.9	32.0	55.0	76.0	174	35.0	54.0	141
Depr.	79.2	80.4	74.8	77.0	79.0	84.0	91.0	96.0	102	98.0
Int. Exp.	15.4	13.1	13.8	14.0	14.8	14.5	12.6	10.6	11.3	16.2
Pretax Inc.	58.3	31.6	-38.1	-86.0	-55.0	-59.0	92.0	-136	-113	-7.0
Eff. Tax Rate	4.12%	11%	NM	NM	NM	NM	6.40%	NM	NM	NM
Net Inc.	55.9	28.1	-46.7	-88.0	-60.0	-63.0	86.0	-139	-119	-16.0

Balance Sheet & Other Fin. Data (Million $)

	1997	1996	1995	1994	1993	1992	1991	1990	1989	1988
Cash	217	179	189	190	192	216	241	75.0	129	141
Curr. Assets	858	617	591	598	612	684	691	596	710	670
Total Assets	1,135	860	832	822	866	940	944	909	1,040	1,078
Curr. Liab.	392	366	370	327	303	328	285	444	442	390
LT Debt	213	150	153	157	158	162	165	57.0	71.0	66.0
Common Eqty.	519	329	280	309	377	450	494	405	522	612
Total Cap.	732	479	433	466	535	612	659	462	593	678
Cap. Exp.	111	94.7	96.5	93.0	95.0	94.0	83.0	85.0	91.0	97.0
Cash Flow	135	109	28.1	-11.0	18.0	22.0	176	-43.0	-18.0	83.0
Curr. Ratio	2.2	1.7	1.6	1.8	2.0	2.1	2.4	1.3	1.6	1.7
% LT Debt of Cap.	29.1	31.3	35.3	33.7	29.6	26.5	25.0	12.3	11.9	9.7
% Net Inc.of Revs.	3.6	2.1	NM	NM	NM	NM	7.0	NM	NM	NM
% Ret. on Assets	5.6	3.3	NM	NM	NM	NM	9.1	NM	NM	NM
% Ret. on Equity	13.2	9.2	NM	NM	NM	NM	18.7	NM	NM	NM

Data as orig. reptd.; bef. results of disc. opers. and/or spec. items. Per share data adj. for stk. divs. as of ex-div. date. Bold denotes diluted EPS (FASB 128). E-Estimated. NA-Not Available. NM-Not Meaningful. NR-Not Ranked.

Office—4400 Computer Dr., Westboro, MA 01580. **Tel**—(508) 898-5000. **Website**—http://www.dg.com **Chrmn**—F. R. Adler. **Pres & CEO**—R. L. Skates. **SVP & CFO**—A. W. DeMelle. **Secy**—C. E. Kaplan. **Investor Contact**—David P. Roy. **Dirs**—F. R. Adler, F. Colloredo-Mansfeld, J. G. McElwee, R. L. Skates, W. N. Thorndike, D. H. Trautlein, R. L. Tucker. **Transfer Agent & Registrar**—Bank of New York, NYC. **Incorporated**—in Delaware in 1968. **Empl**—5,100. **S&P Analyst:** Jim Corridore

STANDARD &POOR'S
STOCK REPORTS

Dayton Hudson

720

NYSE Symbol **DH**

In S&P 500

12-SEP-98

Industry:
Retail (General Merchandise)

Summary: This diversified retailer derives most of its operating income from its 796 Target discount stores. It also operates 269 Mervyn's and 65 department stores.

S&P Opinion: Hold (★★★)	
Recent Price • 39⅝	Yield • 0.9%
52 Wk Range • 53½-26⅛	12-Mo. P/E • 21.5

Quantitative Evaluations

Outlook
(1 Lowest—5 Highest)
• **2**

Fair Value
• **38**

Risk
• **Average**

Earn./Div. Rank
• **A**

Technical Eval.
• **Bullish** since 8/98

Rel. Strength Rank
(1 Lowest—99 Highest)
• **54**

Insider Activity
• **Neutral**

Earnings vs. Previous Year
▲=Up ▼=Down ▶=No Change

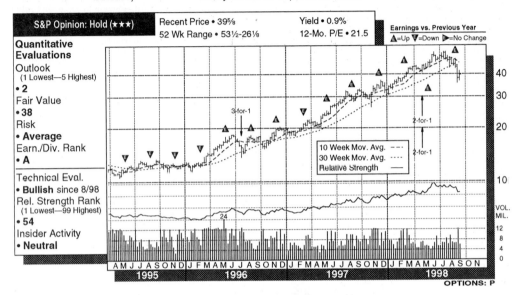

10 Week Mov. Avg. – – –
30 Week Mov. Avg. ·····
Relative Strength —

OPTIONS: P

Overview - 08-JUN-98

Revenues should increase 12% in FY 99 (Jan.), mostly reflecting about 65 new Target stores; same-store sales should rise about 4% at Target, with modest gains at Mervyn's and a moderate increase at the department stores. Operating profit gains at all divisions should reflect the company's efforts to control operating expenses. Target is clearly DH's strongest retail franchise and its growth vehicle for the future. The Mervyn's division has been a weak performer for the past few years, having lost its focus in an overcrowded apparel market. However, new merchandising strategies and a cost reduction program should result in operating income gains. The department store division is benefiting from the company's strategy of improving the merchandise assortment, boosting customer service, and eliminating frequent promotions and excessive markdowns.

Valuation - 08-JUN-98

The share price has been in a steady uptrend since January 1997, and has broken through its 52-week high. The company posted solid sales gains and earnings in the first quarter of FY 99. However, we remain neutral on the stock at this time, since we believe that the shares amply reflect all the good news. The management team has successfully led a turnaround at Mervyn's, lowered the cost structure at Target, and improved sales and operating profit at the department stores. The company is generating enough cash flow to reduce its debt, while funding a $1.5 billion capital expenditure program. Also, from time to time, the shares get a boost from speculation that the company plans to sell its department store division, although management has denied this on numerous occasions.

Key Stock Statistics

S&P EPS Est. 1999	1.90	Tang. Bk. Value/Share	9.52
P/E on S&P Est. 1999	20.9	Beta	1.07
S&P EPS Est. 2000	2.20	Shareholders	10,800
Dividend Rate/Share	0.36	Market cap. (B)	$ 17.4
Shs. outstg. (M)	439.1	Inst. holdings	80%
Avg. daily vol. (M)	1.729		

Value of $10,000 invested 5 years ago: $ 34,761

Fiscal Year Ending Jan. 31

	1999	1998	1997	1996	1995	1994
Revenues (Million $)						
1Q	6,468	5,889	5,380	4,757	4,470	4,040
2Q	7,056	6,293	5,751	5,236	4,802	4,287
3Q	—	6,622	6,073	5,573	5,046	4,625
4Q	—	8,953	8,167	7,950	6,998	6,281
Yr.	—	27,757	25,371	23,516	21,311	19,233
Earnings Per Share ($)						
1Q	**0.34**	0.28	0.08	0.02	0.08	0.06
2Q	**E0.36**	0.30	0.22	0.05	0.10	0.05
3Q	**E0.39**	0.40	0.26	0.09	0.14	0.09
4Q	**E0.82**	0.76	0.48	0.51	0.64	0.64
Yr.	**E1.90**	**1.70**	1.03	0.67	0.96	0.83

Next earnings report expected: mid November

Dividend Data (Dividends have been paid since 1965.)

Amount ($)	Date Decl.	Ex-Div. Date	Stock of Record	Payment Date
0.180	Jan. 14	Feb. 18	Feb. 20	Mar. 10 '98
2-for-1	Mar. 11	May. 01	Apr. 10	Apr. 30 '98
0.090	Apr. 08	May. 18	May. 20	Jun. 10 '98
0.090	Jun. 10	Aug. 18	Aug. 20	Sep. 10 '98

A Division of The McGraw-Hill Companies

STANDARD
&POOR'S
STOCK REPORTS

Dayton Hudson Corporation

720

12-SEP-98

Business Summary - 08-JUN-98

Dayton Hudson, the fourth largest U.S. general merchandise retailer, was formed in 1969 through the merger of two old-line department store companies, Dayton Corp. and J. L. Hudson Co. In 1990, DH acquired another venerable retailer, Marshall Field & Co. The department stores (once run separately, but now operated under the Dayton Hudson Department Store Co. umbrella) have since been eclipsed by DH's fast-growing Target division, which now accounts for the bulk of its revenues and profits.

.DH's retailing segments contributed to its FY 98 (Jan.) results as follows:

	Revs.	Profits
Target	73%	71%
Mervyn's	15%	15%
Department stores	11%	13%

Target is an upscale discount store that offers low prices on a broad assortment of mid-range fashion and basic hardlines. According to DH, Target should provide the majority of the company's growth in the years ahead, with annual square footage increases of 10% to 12%. At FY 98 year end, DH operated 796 Target stores in 38 states, with a total of 87.2 million retail sq. ft.

Mervyn's is a moderate-priced promotional family department store chain specializing in apparel and other soft goods. At the end of FY 98, there were 269 Mervyn's stores in 16 states; total retail square footage amounted to 21.8 million. In the spring of 1995, the division embarked on a new strategy to gain market share and to improve its financial performance. The company's strategy includes increasing its assortment of national brands and infusing a California theme into its merchandising and advertising.

Dayton Hudson Department Store Co. operated 21 Hudson's, 20 Dayton's and 24 Marshall Field's stores at the end of FY 98; retail area totaled 14.1 million sq. ft. The company significantly reduced the frequency and duration of store-wide promotional events in FY 97. While comparable-store sales declined, as a result of lost promotional volume, sales of regular-priced merchandise and better lines of merchandise showed healthy sales gains. In FY 98, the department store division focused on increasing sales, while reducing expenses and improving overall profitability.

Capital expenditures in FY 98 were about $1.5 billion for new stores, remodeling of existing units and other capital support. The majority of new store growth came from 65 new Target units.

Per Share Data ($)

(Year Ended Jan. 31)	1998	1997	1996	1995	1994	1993	1992	1991	1990	1989
Tangible Bk. Val.	9.55	8.10	7.29	7.08	6.38	5.80	5.22	4.80	4.12	4.00
Cash Flow	3.22	2.57	2.10	2.19	1.99	1.90	1.60	1.76	1.58	1.16
Earnings	1.70	1.03	0.67	0.96	0.83	0.84	0.64	0.90	0.90	0.57
Dividends	0.33	0.31	0.29	0.28	0.27	0.25	0.24	0.22	0.19	0.17
Payout Ratio	19%	30%	43%	29%	32%	30%	37%	24%	19%	28%
Cal. Yrs.	1997	1996	1995	1994	1993	1992	1991	1990	1989	1988
Prices - High	37	20⅜	13⅜	14½	14⅛	13¼	13⅜	13¼	11⅛	7⅝
- Low	18	11½	10½	10⅞	10½	9⅝	9	7¾	6½	4¾
P/E Ratio - High	22	20	20	15	17	16	21	15	12	13
- Low	11	11	16	11	13	12	14	9	7	8

Income Statement Analysis (Million $)

	1998	1997	1996	1995	1994	1993	1992	1991	1990	1989
Revs.	27,757	25,371	23,516	21,311	19,233	17,927	16,115	14,739	13,644	12,204
Oper. Inc.	2,435	2,009	1,537	1,671	1,573	1,507	1,276	1,352	1,259	980
Depr.	693	650	594	531	498	459	410	369	314	290
Int. Exp.	416	442	442	439	453	446	407	344	283	231
Pretax Inc.	1,326	783	501	714	607	611	472	659	678	472
Eff. Tax Rate	40%	40%	38%	39%	38%	37%	36%	38%	40%	39%
Net Inc.	802	474	311	434	375	383	301	410	410	287

Balance Sheet & Other Fin. Data (Million $)

	1998	1997	1996	1995	1994	1993	1992	1991	1990	1989
Cash	211	201	175	147	321	117	96.0	92.0	103	53.0
Curr. Assets	5,561	5,440	4,955	4,959	4,511	4,414	4,032	3,658	3,107	2,981
Total Assets	14,191	13,389	12,570	11,697	10,778	10,337	9,485	8,524	6,684	6,523
Curr. Liab.	4,556	4,111	3,523	3,390	3,075	2,964	2,580	2,422	2,195	2,003
LT Debt	4,425	4,808	4,959	4,488	4,279	4,330	4,227	3,682	2,510	2,383
Common Eqty.	4,180	3,519	3,146	3,043	2,737	2,486	2,231	2,048	1,753	1,861
Total Cap.	9,635	9,278	9,047	7,725	7,167	6,923	6,524	5,755	4,264	4,244
Cap. Exp.	1,354	1,301	1,505	1,095	978	938	1,009	678	603	678
Cash Flow	1,495	1,124	905	946	856	818	686	754	723	577
Curr. Ratio	1.2	1.3	1.4	1.5	1.5	1.5	1.6	1.5	1.4	1.5
% LT Debt of Cap.	45.9	51.8	54.9	58.1	59.7	62.5	64.8	64.0	58.9	56.1
% Net Inc.of Revs.	2.9	1.9	1.4	2.0	1.9	2.1	1.9	2.8	3.0	2.4
% Ret. on Assets	6.0	3.7	2.6	3.9	3.9	3.3	3.3	5.4	6.5	4.8
% Ret. on Equity	20.8	14.2	9.5	14.3	13.7	15.2	12.9	20.2	23.7	15.7

Data as orig. reptd.; bef. results of disc. opers. and/or spec. items. Per share data adj. for stk. divs. as of ex-div. date. Bold denotes diluted EPS (FASB 128). E-Estimated. NA-Not Available. NM-Not Meaningful. NR-Not Ranked.

Office—777 Nicollet Mall, Minneapolis, MN 55402. **Tel**—(612) 370-6948. **Website**—http://www.dhc.com **Chrmn & CEO**—R. J. Ulrich. **VP & Secy**—J. T. Hale. **SVP & Treas**—D. A. Scovanner. **Investor Contact**—Susan Kahn (612-370-6735). **Dirs**—L. D. DeSimone, R. A. Enrico, W. W. George, R. L. Hale, B. R. Hollander, M. J. Hooper, J. A. Johnson, R. M. Kovacevich, S. W. Sanger, S. D. Trujillo, R. J. Ulrich. **Transfer Agent & Registrar**—First Chicago Trust Co. of New York, NYC. **Incorporated**—in Minnesota in 1902. **Empl**— 230,000. **S&P Analyst:** Karen J. Sack, CFA

STANDARD &POOR'S
STOCK REPORTS

Deere & Co.

728

NYSE Symbol **DE**

In S&P 500

12-SEP-98

Industry:
Machinery (Diversified)

Summary: The world's largest producer of farm equipment, Deere is also an important maker of construction machinery and lawn and garden equipment.

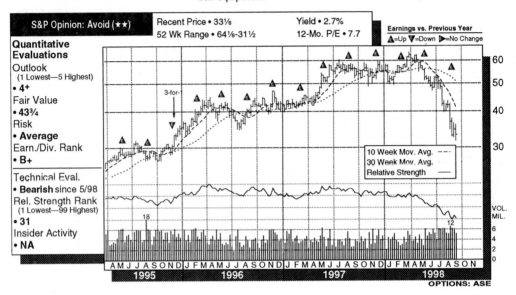

| S&P Opinion: Avoid (★★) | Recent Price • 33⅛ | Yield • 2.7% |
| | 52 Wk Range • 64⅛-31½ | 12-Mo. P/E • 7.7 |

Quantitative Evaluations

Outlook
(1 Lowest—5 Highest)
• **4+**

Fair Value
• **43¾**

Risk
• **Average**

Earn./Div. Rank
• **B+**

Technical Eval.
• **Bearish** since 5/98

Rel. Strength Rank
(1 Lowest—99 Highest)
• **31**

Insider Activity
• **NA**

Earnings vs. Previous Year
▲=Up ▼=Down ▶=No Change

3-for-

10 Week Mov. Avg. - - -
30 Week Mov. Avg. ———
Relative Strength ·······

VOL. MIL.

OPTIONS: ASE

Overview - 19-AUG-98

We expect a single-digit revenue increase in FY 99 (Oct.), reflecting higher volume and prices, and acquisitions. However, agricultural equipment demand growth may slow, due to the strengthening of the U.S. dollar, which may reduce export demand for equipment. In addition, U.S. farmers' income may decline in 1999, due to weaker exports of grains. This may lead to lower equipment purchases by U.S. farmers in FY 99. Sales of construction equipment may also lag, due to flattening export markets and a leveling off of purchases by domestic fleet operators. Despite reasonably high capacity utilization, only modest increases in raw material costs, and overhead cost reductions, operating profit from equipment segments should flatten. Even with continued growth in income from financial services, earnings should decline slightly in FY 99. For the longer term, we expect a resumption of the rise in overseas demand for U.S. wheat and corn crops.

Valuation - 19-AUG-98

We recently downgraded DE to avoid, from hold. We believe that earnings may decline modestly in FY 99, as the farm equipment cycle matures. In addition, export sales could turn down, on the impact of foreign currency exchange shifts. Cyclical farm equipment company shares trade in cycles that focus on prospective earnings growth. With little improvement expected, we expect DE's relative price performance to continue to deteriorate. We believe that the lion's share of price appreciation in the current cycle has been realized, and expect DE to underperform as the cycle ages. Based in part on DE's normalized average ROE of 14% (adjusted for a 210% debt-to-equity ratio), our intrinsic valuations calculate that DE is trading above its long-term fair value.

Key Stock Statistics

S&P EPS Est. 1998	4.40	Tang. Bk. Value/Share	16.65
P/E on S&P Est. 1998	7.5	Beta	1.18
S&P EPS Est. 1999	4.10	Shareholders	29,300
Dividend Rate/Share	0.88	Market cap. (B)	$ 7.9
Shs. outstg. (M)	238.5	Inst. holdings	78%
Avg. daily vol. (M)	1.673		

Value of $10,000 invested 5 years ago: $ 26,112

Fiscal Year Ending Oct. 31

	1998	1997	1996	1995	1994	1993
Revenues (Million $)						
1Q	2,846	2,396	2,318	2,088	1,727	1,424
2Q	4,070	3,521	3,089	2,812	2,460	2,105
3Q	3,693	3,430	2,905	2,673	2,327	2,049
4Q	—	3,444	2,917	2,719	2,516	2,176
Yr.	—	12,791	11,229	10,291	9,030	7,754
Earnings Per Share ($)						
1Q	**0.81**	0.69	0.63	0.53	0.34	-0.16
2Q	**1.45**	1.25	1.04	0.91	0.73	0.09
3Q	**1.19**	1.00	0.79	0.69	0.61	0.40
4Q	**E0.94**	0.84	0.68	0.57	0.66	0.47
Yr.	**E4.40**	3.78	3.14	2.71	2.34	0.80

Next earnings report expected: late November

Dividend Data (Dividends have been paid since 1937.)

Amount ($)	Date Decl.	Ex-Div. Date	Stock of Record	Payment Date
0.220	Dec. 03	Dec. 29	Dec. 31	Feb. 02 '98
0.220	Feb. 25	Mar. 27	Mar. 31	May. 01 '98
0.220	May. 27	Jun. 26	Jun. 30	Aug. 03 '98
0.220	Aug. 26	Sep. 28	Sep. 30	Nov. 02 '98

A Division of The McGraw·Hill Companies

STANDARD
&POOR'S
STOCK REPORTS

Deere & Company

728

12-SEP-98

Business Summary - 19-AUG-98

From Kalamazoo to Kazakhstan, and at many places in between, the ubiquitous green and yellow John Deere logo is seen on Deere & Co.'s agricultural, industrial and lawn and garden equipment. Since its invention of the original self-scouring steel plow in 1837, Deere grew to become the global leader in agricultural equipment since 1963. In 1918, Deere produced its first tractors and engines, and in the 1920s, manufacturing of industrial equipment began. Lawn and garden equipment was added to the product line in 1963. Through subsidiaries, Deere finances the sale and leasing of equipment and also provides credit, insurance and health care products. Contributions in FY 97 (Oct.) (profits in million $) were:

	Revs.	Profits
Farm equipment	56%	$1,072
Construction equipment	18%	216
Commercial & consumer equipment	14%	114
Financial services	12%	214

With products manufactured in 10 countries and marketed in more than 160 countries, operations outside the U.S. and Canada accounted for 28% of revenues in FY 97 (25% in 1996), and 21% of operating income (18%). New product development is an important part of the company's strategy; $412 million was spent on research and development in 1997.

Farm equipment includes a full range of agricultural equipment for the farming industry, including tractors; tillage, soil preparation, planting and harvesting machinery; and crop handling equipment. Sales and profits have been in an upswing since mid-FY 93, reflecting a healthy farm economy. However, farm incomes in North America are projected to decline modestly in 1998, due to lower exports of crops to weakening Asian markets.

Industrial equipment includes a broad range of machines used in earthmoving and forestry, including wheel and crawler tractors and attachments; crawler dozers and loaders; four-wheel-drive loaders; elevating scrapers; motor graders; excavators; log skidders; and tree harvesting equipment.

Lawn and grounds care equipment includes smaller tractors for lawn, garden and utility purposes; riding and walk-behind mowers; and other outdoor power products. More than two dozen new hand-held and ride-on products have been introduced since 1996, and DE is becoming a force in the lawn and garden market.

Through subsidiaries, DE finances the sale and lease of equipment and provides credit, insurance and health care products. Credit operations had receivables under management of $6.4 billion as of October 31, 1997.

Per Share Data ($)

(Year Ended Oct. 31)	1997	1996	1995	1994	1993	1992	1991	1990	1989	1988
Tangible Bk. Val.	15.96	12.72	10.61	8.77	6.97	10.10	10.78	12.12	11.94	10.97
Cash Flow	5.30	4.39	3.79	3.35	1.90	1.24	0.89	2.72	2.56	2.23
Earnings	3.78	3.14	2.71	2.34	0.80	0.16	-0.09	1.81	1.69	1.35
Dividends	0.80	0.80	0.75	0.68	0.67	0.67	0.67	0.67	0.43	0.22
Payout Ratio	21%	25%	28%	29%	84%	408%	NM	37%	26%	17%
Prices - High	60½	47⅛	36	30¼	26⅛	18	19⅛	26⅛	21⅜	16⅞
- Low	39⅞	33	21⅝	20⅜	14⅛	12¼	13¼	12½	14⅝	11⅛
P/E Ratio - High	16	15	12	13	33	NM	NM	14	13	12
- Low	11	11	8	9	18	NM	NM	7	9	8

Income Statement Analysis (Million $)

	1997	1996	1995	1994	1993	1992	1991	1990	1989	1988
Revs.	12,791	11,229	10,291	8,934	7,654	6,847	6,926	7,759	7,113	5,365
Oper. Inc.	2,295	1,999	1,768	1,390	904	589	701	1,110	1,036	472
Depr.	366	311	283	262	255	246	224	209	198	185
Int. Exp.	422	402	392	303	369	415	452	435	407	161
Pretax Inc.	1,511	1,298	1,104	936	282	52.0	-25.0	593	547	320
Eff. Tax Rate	36%	37%	36%	36%	35%	28%	NM	31%	31%	10%
Net Inc.	960	817	706	604	184	37.0	-20.0	411	380	287

Balance Sheet & Other Fin. Data (Million $)

	1997	1996	1995	1994	1993	1992	1991	1990	1989	1988
Cash	330	1,161	364	245	338	217	279	185	204	49.0
Curr. Assets	NA	NA	NA	NA	NA	NA	NA	NA	NA	3,115
Total Assets	16,320	14,653	13,847	12,781	11,352	11,446	11,649	10,664	9,145	5,245
Curr. Liab.	NA	NA	NA	NA	NA	NA	NA	NA	NA	1,728
LT Debt	2,623	2,425	2,176	2,054	2,549	2,477	2,217	1,799	1,696	817
Common Eqty.	4,148	3,557	3,085	2,558	2,085	2,650	2,836	3,008	2,780	2,456
Total Cap.	6,792	5,991	5,277	4,625	4,642	5,152	5,128	4,978	4,622	3,288
Cap. Exp.	485	687	383	331	313	349	352	376	272	204
Cash Flow	1,326	1,128	989	866	439	283	204	620	578	472
Curr. Ratio	NA	NA	NA	NA	NA	NA	NA	NA	NA	1.8
% LT Debt of Cap.	38.6	40.5	41.2	44.4	54.9	48.1	43.2	36.1	36.6	24.8
% Net Inc.of Revs.	7.5	7.3	6.9	6.8	2.4	0.5	NM	5.3	5.3	5.3
% Ret. on Assets	6.2	5.7	5.3	5.0	1.5	0.3	NM	4.1	5.3	5.5
% Ret. on Equity	24.9	24.6	25.0	25.9	7.3	1.4	NM	14.2	14.4	12.6

Data as orig. reptd.; bef. results of disc. opers. and/or spec. items. Per share data adj. for stk. divs. as of ex-div. date. Bold denotes diluted EPS (FASB 128). E-Estimated. NA-Not Available. NM-Not Meaningful. NR-Not Ranked.

Office—John Deere Rd., Moline, IL 61265. **Tel**—(309) 765-8000. **Website**—http://www.deere.com Chrmn & CEO—H. W. Becherer. CFO—N. J. Jones. **Treas**—J. Jabanoski. **Secy**—F. S. Cottrell. **Investor Contact**—Heather L. Robinson. **Dirs**—H. W. Becherer, J. R. Block, L. A. Hadley, R. E. Herzlinger, S. C. Johnson, A. L. Kelly, A. Madero, A. Santamarina, W. A. Schreyer, J. R. Stafford, D. H. Stowe Jr., J. R. Walter, A. R. Weber. **Transfer Agent & Registrar**—Bank of New York, NYC. **Incorporated**—in Delaware in 1958; business estd. in 1837. **Empl**— 33,919. **S&P Analyst:** Robert E. Friedman, CPA

STANDARD &POOR'S
STOCK REPORTS

Dell Computer

3665T

Nasdaq Symbol **DELL**

In S&P 500

12-SEP-98

Industry: Computers (Hardware)

Summary: Dell is the leading direct marketer and one of the world's top 10 manufacturers of personal computers compatible with industry standards established by IBM.

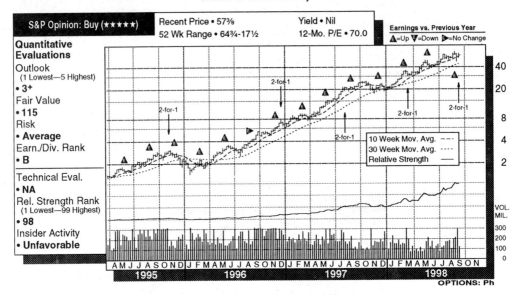

| S&P Opinion: Buy (★★★★) | Recent Price • 57⅜ | Yield • Nil |
| | 52 Wk Range • 64¾-17½ | 12-Mo. P/E • 70.0 |

Quantitative Evaluations

Outlook (1 Lowest—5 Highest)
• 3+

Fair Value
• 115

Risk
• Average

Earn./Div. Rank
• B

Technical Eval.
• NA

Rel. Strength Rank (1 Lowest—99 Highest)
• 98

Insider Activity
• Unfavorable

Earnings vs. Previous Year
▲=Up ▼=Down ▶=No Change

10 Week Mov. Avg. ---
30 Week Mov. Avg. ----
Relative Strength —

OPTIONS: Ph

Overview - 24-AUG-98

We project revenue growth of approximately 50% in FY 99 (Jan.), after FY 98's stellar 59% gain. Through the second quarter, Dell's revenues grew at a better than 50% pace, and we believe this is sustainable through the remainder of the year. Dell's direct model lets it offer feature rich PCs (personal computers) at attractive price points. Because of its direct relationship with users, Dell's inventories of key components, such as microprocessors and hard disk drives, are closely matched to user demand, and this enables Dell to benefit both by keeping inventories low, and from having components reflect the latest technology. Dell is leveraging this advantage to boost market share in notebooks, servers and international markets. Gross margins should be about 22%, roughly in line with FY 98 levels, as benefits from lower component costs are passed on to customers and Dell grows in the higher-margin notebook and server markets.

Valuation - 24-AUG-98

We continue to recommend buying the shares. Dell has consistently reported revenue and EPS growth exceeding the industry's rate, and we expect this to continue, reflecting the strength of Dell's direct sales model, a strong brand name, and superior execution and cash flow management. We project revenue and EPS growth on the order of 40% and more ahead as a result of healthy PC demand, as Dell further penetrates high-margin server, workstation and notebook markets, and as it continues to execute on a superior business model. While Dell's stock price appreciation has resulted in a valuation that exceeds the high end of the range for PC vendors, its EPS growth has also been superior, and we expect the shares to outperform the market over the next 12 months.

Key Stock Statistics

S&P EPS Est. 1999	1.05	Tang. Bk. Value/Share	1.11
P/E on S&P Est. 1999	54.7	Beta	1.55
S&P EPS Est. 2000	1.45	Shareholders	3,700
Dividend Rate/Share	Nil	Market cap. (B)	$ 72.7
Shs. outstg. (M)	1265.9	Inst. holdings	45%
Avg. daily vol. (M)	53.166		

Value of $10,000 invested 5 years ago: $ 382,913

Fiscal Year Ending Jan. 31

	1999	1998	1997	1996	1995	1994
Revenues (Million $)						
1Q	3,920	2,588	1,638	1,136	767.0	672.4
2Q	4,331	2,814	1,690	1,206	791.5	700.6
3Q	—	3,188	2,019	1,416	884.5	757.3
4Q	—	3,737	2,412	1,539	1,033	743.0
Yr.	—	12,327	7,759	5,296	3,475	2,873
Earnings Per Share ($)						
1Q	0.22	0.14	0.05	0.03	0.01	0.01
2Q	0.25	0.15	0.07	0.07	0.02	-0.06
3Q	E0.27	0.17	0.10	0.05	0.03	0.01
4Q	E0.31	0.20	0.13	0.04	0.04	0.01
Yr.	E1.05	0.64	0.34	0.17	0.11	-0.03

Next earnings report expected: late November

Dividend Data

Amount ($)	Date Decl.	Ex-Div. Date	Stock of Record	Payment Date
2-for-1	Feb. 18	Mar. 09	Feb. 27	Mar. 06 '98
2-for-1	Aug. 18	Sep. 08	Aug. 28	Sep. 04 '98

A Division of The McGraw·Hill Companies

Business Summary - 24-AUG-98

In July 1994, Dell discontinued retail channel sales to focus exclusively on its direct business. Since then the company has witnessed explosive growth. As of the second quarter of calendar 1998, Dell was the world's second largest PC maker (growing at nearly four times the rate of the industry), and neck and neck with Compaq Computer for the number two spot in the U.S., according to market researcher International Data Corp. (IDC).

Dell Computer Corp. is a direct marketer of personal computers, including desktops, notebooks and servers, and most recently introduced workstations to its product line. The company has effectively leveraged its direct approach to increase its penetration in corporate accounts, consumer markets and internationally. International sales accounted for 31% of the total in FY 98 (Jan.). Part of Dell's strategy includes providing customers with the ability to electronically design, price and purchase computer systems and to obtain online support through Dell's Internet site. As of the end of second quarter calendar 1998, Dell said that sales generated from its Internet site were roughly $6 million a day.

Dell's line of enterprise systems (9% of FY 98 system revenue) includes workstations and servers sold under the PowerEdge name. These servers are used in a networked environment to distribute files, database information, applications and communication products. After entering the workstation market in early 1997, as of the end of the year, Dell had already become the third largest supplier worldwide, according to market researcher IDC.

Dell's desktop computer systems remain the largest segment (71% of FY 98 system revenues) and include the OptiPlex line, which is targeted at corporate and other major account customers and offers advanced features and high reliability; Dell Dimension XPS, a line aimed at technologically sophisticated business and individual users; and Dell Dimension, which is targeted at small-to-medium-sized businesses and individual users.

Dell's higher margin notebooks, or portables, were 20% of system revenues in FY 98, and include the Latitude product lines, for corporate users, and the Inspiron line for consumers and small businesses.

Dell also offers thousands of software packages and peripheral products through its DellWare program. Dell services include software integration and network installation and support.

The company's manufacturing facilities are located in Austin, TX; Limerick, Ireland; and Penang, Malaysia. Dell recently added a manufacturing plant in China, and plans to participate in that region's 28.5% annual growth in PCs forecast for the next five years, according to IDC.

Per Share Data ($)

(Year Ended Jan. 31)	1998	1997	1996	1995	1994	1993	1992	1991	1990	1989
Tangible Bk. Val.	1.00	0.58	0.65	0.41	0.28	0.31	0.24	0.12	0.09	0.08
Cash Flow	0.69	0.38	0.20	0.13	-0.01	0.10	0.06	0.04	0.01	0.02
Earnings	0.64	0.35	0.17	0.11	-0.03	0.08	0.04	0.03	0.01	0.02
Dividends	Nil	Nil	Nil	Nil	Nil	Nil	Nil	Nil	Nil	Nil
Payout Ratio	Nil	Nil	Nil	Nil	Nil	Nil	Nil	Nil	Nil	Nil
Cal. Yrs.	1997	1996	1995	1994	1993	1992	1991	1990	1989	1988
Prices - High	26	8	$3^{1}/_{8}$	$1^{1}/_{2}$	$1^{9}/_{16}$	$1^{1}/_{2}$	$^{3}/_{4}$	$^{3}/_{8}$	$^{1}/_{4}$	$^{1}/_{4}$
- Low	$6^{1}/_{4}$	$1^{7}/_{16}$	$1^{1}/_{4}$	$^{5}/_{8}$	$^{7}/_{16}$	$^{1}/_{2}$	$^{5}/_{16}$	$^{1}/_{8}$	$^{1}/_{8}$	$^{3}/_{16}$
P/E Ratio - High	41	23	18	14	NM	19	17	14	39	16
- Low	10	4	7	6	NM	6	8	3	19	10

Income Statement Analysis (Million $)

Revs.	12,327	7,759	5,296	3,475	2,873	2,014	890	546	389	258
Oper. Inc.	1,383	761	415	282	83.0	159	82.5	53.3	18.4	24.9
Depr.	67.0	47.0	38.0	33.1	30.6	19.6	13.8	7.9	5.4	2.1
Int. Exp.	3.0	7.0	15.0	12.2	8.3	7.9	1.8	1.5	3.4	1.3
Pretax Inc.	1,368	747	383	213	-39.0	143	73.4	43.6	8.3	21.2
Eff. Tax Rate	31%	29%	29%	30%	NM	29%	31%	38%	38%	32%
Net Inc.	944	531	272	149	-36.0	102	50.9	27.2	5.1	14.4

Balance Sheet & Other Fin. Data (Million $)

Cash	1,844	1,352	646	527	337	95.0	155	37.0	Nil	36.0
Curr. Assets	3,912	2,747	1,957	1,470	1,048	853	512	236	143	149
Total Assets	4,268	2,993	2,148	1,594	1,140	927	560	264	172	167
Curr. Liab.	2,697	1,658	939	751	538	494	230	141	85.0	86.0
LT Debt	17.0	18.0	113	113	100	48.4	41.5	4.2	6.0	5.5
Common Eqty.	1,293	806	967	527	344	369	274	112	80.0	75.0
Total Cap.	1,310	824	1,080	765	571	418	316	116	86.0	81.0
Cap. Exp.	187	114	101	63.7	48.1	47.3	32.6	9.5	13.6	6.6
Cash Flow	1,011	578	310	174	-9.0	121	64.7	35.1	10.6	16.6
Curr. Ratio	1.5	1.7	2.1	2.0	1.9	1.7	2.2	1.7	1.7	1.7
% LT Debt of Cap.	1.3	2.2	10.5	14.8	17.5	11.6	13.1	3.6	7.0	6.8
% Net Inc.of Revs.	7.7	6.8	5.1	4.3	NM	5.0	5.7	5.0	1.3	5.6
% Ret. on Assets	26.0	20.7	14.5	10.9	NM	13.5	11.5	12.3	3.0	11.0
% Ret. on Equity	89.9	59.9	36.3	32.2	NM	31.2	24.7	28.1	6.6	32.4

Data as orig. reptd.; bef. results of disc. opers. and/or spec. items. Per share data adj. for stk. divs. as of ex-div. date. Bold denotes diluted EPS (FASB 128). E-Estimated. NA-Not Available. NM-Not Meaningful. NR-Not Ranked.

Office—2214 W. Braker Lane, Suite D, Austin, TX 78758-4053. **Tel**—(512) 338-4400. **Website**—http://www.dell.com **Chrmn & CEO**—M. S. Dell. **Vice-Chrmn**—K. B. Rollins. **SVP-Fin & CFO**—T. J. Meredith. **VP & Treas**—A. Smith. **Secy**—T. B. Green. **Dirs**—D. J. Carty, M. S. Dell, P. O. Hirschbiel, Jr., M. H. Jordan, T. W. Luce III, K. Luft, C. B. Malone, A. J. Mandl, M. A. Miles. **Transfer Agent & Registrar**—American Stock Transfer & Trust Co., NYC. **Incorporated**—in Delaware in 1987. **Empl**— 20,800. **S&P Analyst:** Megan Graham Hackett

Delta Air Lines

734

NYSE Symbol **DAL**

In S&P 500

12-SEP-98

Industry:
Airlines

Summary: DAL, the third largest U.S. airline, extends its global reach via an alliance with Swissair, Sabena and Austrian Airlines. An alliance with United Airlines has been proposed.

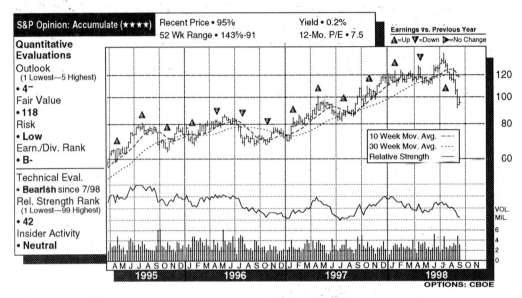

S&P Opinion: Accumulate (★★★★)	Recent Price • 95⅞	Yield • 0.2%
	52 Wk Range • 143⅝-91	12-Mo. P/E • 7.5

Earnings vs. Previous Year
▲=Up ▼=Down ▶=No Change

Quantitative Evaluations

Outlook
(1 Lowest—5 Highest)
• **4⁻**

Fair Value
• **118**

Risk
• **Low**

Earn./Div. Rank
• **B-**

Technical Eval.
• **Bearish** since 7/98

Rel. Strength Rank
(1 Lowest—99 Highest)
• **42**

Insider Activity
• **Neutral**

10 Week Mov. Avg. ---
30 Week Mov. Avg. .....
Relative Strength —

OPTIONS: CBOE

Overview - 24-JUN-98

Traffic in FY 99 (Jun.) could increase some 4%-5%, following an estimated 3% gain in FY 98. Traffic growth will be paced by gains on the international side. DAL has sharply expanded its offerings to Latin America including new routes to Venezuela, Peru, Panama and San Salvador. In Asia, a new aviation treaty with Japan is enabling Delta to increase the frequency on existing routes and add new destinations. Domestically, growth in FY 99 will approximate that of FY 98 as the economy remains robust and DAL benefits from more feeder traffic from Comair. Delta Express will continue to grow at a rapid pace. Margins could widen slightly. Fuel costs and agents' commissions will fall, while aircraft rents, marketing expense, landing fees and facilities rents will be flat. Offsetting, DAL faces higher labor costs, increased spending for food service and information technology and heavier depreciation charges. Yields on trans-Atlantic routes will be firm, while low-fare competition could depress yields domestically. Interest costs will fall.

Valuation - 24-JUN-98

The shares of this leading airline continue to perform well as investors apply higher P/E multiples to all airline issues. The proposed alliance with United Airlines would be a plus if it can be implemented without government interference. The alliance follows the rejection of DAL's bid in January 1998 to acquire Continental Airlines. A major push to expand Latin American service is underway. A new aviation accord between the U.S. and Japan is enabling DAL to substantially expand its service to Asia. We think that the shares of this well-positioned carrier continue to merit accumulation, as it trades at lower multiples than its peers.

Key Stock Statistics

S&P EPS Est. 1999	13.00	Tang. Bk. Value/Share	35.50
P/E on S&P Est. 1999	7.3	Beta	1.11
Dividend Rate/Share	0.20	Shareholders	22,900
Shs. outstg. (M)	75.7	Market cap. (B)	$ 7.2
Avg. daily vol. (M)	0.745	Inst. holdings	66%

Value of $10,000 invested 5 years ago: $ 19,046

Fiscal Year Ending Jun. 30

	1998	1997	1996	1995	1994	1993
Revenues (Million $)						
1Q	3,552	3,432	3,188	3,157	3,220	3,064
2Q	3,433	3,197	2,944	2,919	3,017	2,875
3Q	3,389	3,420	2,964	2,902	2,943	2,927
4Q	3,760	3,541	3,359	3,216	3,179	3,132
Yr.	14,133	13,590	12,455	12,194	12,359	11,997
Earnings Per Share ($)						
1Q	3.34	3.09	3.47	1.00	0.65	-3.07
2Q	**2.40**	1.66	0.93	-0.79	-3.36	-3.46
3Q	**2.45**	2.52	-5.77	-0.66	-2.10	-3.61
4Q	**4.52**	3.98	2.69	4.49	-5.50	-0.41
Yr.	**12.68**	11.30	1.42	4.07	-10.32	-10.54

Next earnings report expected: late October

Dividend Data (Dividends have been paid since 1949.)

Amount ($)	Date Decl.	Ex-Div. Date	Stock of Record	Payment Date
0.050	Jan. 22	Feb. 09	Feb. 11	Mar. 01 '98
0.050	Apr. 24	May. 11	May. 13	Jun. 01 '98
0.050	Jul. 23	Aug. 10	Aug. 12	Sep. 01 '98
2-for-1	Jul. 14	Nov. 17	Nov. 02	Nov. 16 '98

A Division of The **McGraw-Hill** Companies

Delta Air Lines, Inc.

Business Summary - 24-JUN-98

Delta Air Lines operates the third largest U.S. airline. Since 1991, DAL has significantly increased its international service through acquisitions, strategic alliances and the receipt of operating rights. With a labor force that is some 85% non-union, Delta enjoys one of the industry's lowest cost structures. Recent competitive assaults by no-frills, startup carriers have been beaten back through the company's Delta Express offering. Following the rejection of its bid to acquire Continental Airlines in January 1998, DAL sought to fortify its domestic position via a proposed alliance with United Airlines.

Delta provides service to 149 U.S. cities via hubs in Atlanta, Cincinnati, Dallas/Ft. Worth and Salt Lake City. Short haul traffic is fed to DAL's hubs by four Delta Connection carriers: Atlantic Southeast Airlines (26% owned), Comair (21% owned), SkyWest (15% owned) and Business Express.

DAL's international passenger operations accounted for 20% of total revenues in FY 97 (Jun.). DAL serves 68 foreign destinations directly and through code-sharing partners. In FY 97, DAL took a $52 million pretax charge to cover costs to restructure its European operations. Profits from international traffic are also benefiting from the Atlantic Excellence alliance formed in June 1996 with Swissair, Sabena Belgian World Airlines and Austrian Airlines. During 1997, Delta launched a major drive to expand its presence in Latin America (only 2% of FY 97 revenues). Since 1997 service has been initiated to Brazil, Venezuela, Peru, Panama and other destinations. A 35% stake in AeroPeru was acquired in early 1998.

Delta is one of the industry's lowest cost carriers. DAL's non-union employees, representing some 85% of its work force, received wage increases of 2% to 5% in July 1997. In 1996, Delta's pilots signed a four-year contract providing for a 2% wage cut and reduced benefits, in return for options on 10,000,000 DAL common shares. The 1996 pilot contract also paved the way for the formation of Delta Express, by allowing pilots at Express to earn 32% less than mainline pilots. In early 1998 two unions were vying for representation of DAL's flight attendants.

Delta Express, launched in late 1996, is designed to check competitive inroads from discount airlines. Delta Express keeps costs down with lower pilot salaries, a simplified fleet, and all-coach seating. Delta Express only flies point-to-point routes, between 14 cities primarily in the Northeast, Midwest and five cities in Florida.

In April 1998 Delta and United Airlines announced plans to form a marketing alliance, subject to pilot approval. The two airlines contemplate combining their frequent flyer programs, code-sharing on domestic routes and sharing of airport facilities. DAL believes that no government clearance for the alliance is required.

Per Share Data ($) (Year Ended Jun. 30)	1998	1997	1996	1995	1994	1993	1992	1991	1990	1989
Tangible Bk. Val.	NA	35.50	21.19	NM	NM	25.28	16.01	33.49	39.25	46.72
Cash Flow	NA	20.73	15.34	17.96	5.38	4.55	2.22	4.02	15.18	17.23
Earnings	12.68	11.30	1.42	4.07	-10.32	-10.54	-10.60	-7.73	5.79	9.37
Dividends	0.20	0.20	0.20	0.20	0.20	0.70	1.20	1.20	1.70	1.20
Payout Ratio	2%	2%	14%	5%	NM	NM	NM	NM	28%	13%
Prices - High	143 5/8	120 5/8	87	79 7/8	57 7/8	61 3/8	75 1/4	78 3/4	80 7/8	85 3/4
- Low	109	69 1/4	66 7/8	50 1/4	39 1/2	45 3/4	47 3/4	55 1/2	52 1/2	48 3/4
P/E Ratio - High	11	11	61	20	NM	NM	NM	NM	NM	14
- Low	9	6	47	12	NM	NM	NM	NM	NM	9
Income Statement Analysis (Million $)										
Revs.	NA	13,590	12,455	12,194	12,359	11,997	10,837	9,171	8,582	8,089
Oper. Inc.	NA	2,292	1,926	1,283	757	259	-33.0	71.0	881	1,065
Depr.	NA	710	634	622	678	752	635	521	462	387
Int. Exp.	NA	207	269	292	304	239	221	163	84.0	71.0
Pretax Inc.	NA	1,415	276	494	-659	-650	-785	-499	468	711
Eff. Tax Rate	NA	40%	44%	NM	NM	NM	NM	NM	35%	35%
Net Inc.	NA	854	156	294	-408	-414	-505	-323	303	461
Balance Sheet & Other Fin. Data (Million $)										
Cash	NA	1,170	1,652	1,233	1,302	1,180	50.0	764	68.0	530
Curr. Assets	NA	2,867	3,282	3,014	3,223	2,822	1,698	1,892	1,018	1,475
Total Assets	NA	12,741	12,226	12,143	11,896	11,871	10,162	8,411	7,227	6,484
Curr. Liab.	NA	4,083	3,638	3,441	3,536	2,973	3,543	2,155	1,833	1,763
LT Debt	NA	1,797	2,175	3,121	3,228	3,717	2,833	2,059	1,315	703
Common Eqty.	NA	3,007	2,540	1,827	1,467	1,863	1,466	2,006	2,118	2,620
Total Cap.	NA	4,804	4,715	5,068	4,797	5,714	5,047	4,956	4,466	3,890
Cap. Exp.	NA	1,948	936	626	1,032	1,714	2,481	2,059	1,538	1,244
Cash Flow	NA	1,555	790	916	269	227	110	178	747	848
Curr. Ratio	NA	0.7	0.9	0.9	0.9	0.9	0.5	0.9	0.6	0.8
% LT Debt of Cap.	NA	37.4	46.1	61.5	67.3	65.1	56.1	41.5	29.4	18.1
% Net Inc.of Revs.	NA	6.3	1.3	2.4	NM	NM	NM	NM	3.5	5.7
% Ret. on Assets	NA	6.8	12.8	2.4	NM	NM	NM	NM	4.6	7.5
% Ret. on Equity	NA	30.5	71.4	17.8	NM	NM	NM	NM	12.5	19.1

Data as orig. reptd.; bef. results of disc. opers. and/or spec. items. Per share data adj. for stk. divs. as of ex-div. date. Bold denotes diluted EPS (FASB 128). E-Estimated. NA-Not Available. NM-Not Meaningful. NR-Not Ranked.

Office—Hartsfield Atlanta International Airport, Atlanta, GA 30320. **Tel**—(404) 715-2600. **Website**—http://www.delta-air.com **Chrmn**—G. Grinstein. **Pres & CEO**—L. F. Mullin. **EVP & CFO**—W. C. Jenson. **SVP & Secy**—R. S. Harkey. **Investor Contact**—Brenda Barnes (404-715-6679). **Dirs**—E. L. Artzt, H. A. Biedenharn III, J. L. Broadhead, E. H. Budd, R. E. Cartledge, M. J. Evans, G. Grinstein, J. Hill, Jr., L. F. Mullin, A. J. Young. **Transfer Agent & Registrar**—First Chicago Trust Co. of New York, Jersey City, NJ. **Incorporated**—in Louisiana in 1930; reincorporated in Delaware in 1967. **Empl**— 63,441. **S&P Analyst:** Stephen R. Klein

STANDARD &POOR'S
STOCK REPORTS
Deluxe Corp.
735
NYSE Symbol **DLX**
In S&P 500

12-SEP-98

Industry:
Specialty Printing

Summary: This major printer of bank checks also produces computer forms, provides software and services to financial institutions, and is a direct marketer of consumer products.

S&P Opinion: Hold (★★★)	Recent Price • 29⅞	Yield • 4.9%
	52 Wk Range • 38⅛-27¾	12-Mo. P/E • 46.1

Quantitative Evaluations

Outlook
(1 Lowest—5 Highest)
• **4+**

Fair Value
• **35½**

Risk
• **Low**

Earn./Div. Rank
• **B**

Technical Eval.
• **Bullish** since 8/98

Rel. Strength Rank
(1 Lowest—99 Highest)
• **66**

Insider Activity
• **NA**

Earnings vs. Previous Year
▲=Up ▼=Down ▶=No Change

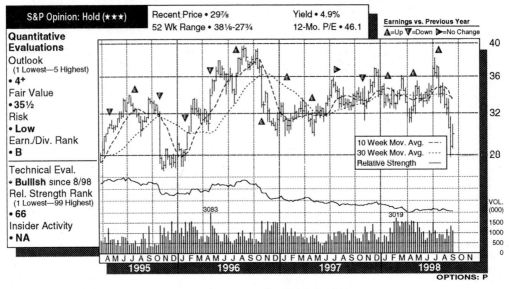

10 Week Mov. Avg. — —
30 Week Mov. Avg. - - - -
Relative Strength ——

3083   3019

VOL. (000)
1500
1000
500
0

OPTIONS: P

Overview - 24-AUG-98

As part of a major effort to reposition itself from being largely a check printing company into an electronic payments and information services concern, DLX is at the midpoint of a major restructuring program begun in late 1995 that involves closing and consolidating 26 of its 41 printing and warehousing facilities, consolidating other operations, and divesting a number of slow-growth, low-margin businesses. DLX plans to boost the revenue generating capabilities of its ongoing businesses through a number of measures. Although it expects to eliminate $150 million in annual operating costs by the end of the restructuring, it will continue to incur unspecified charges in the effort. DLX's results for 1997 included $1.60 in charges related to writedowns, write-offs, legal proceedings, plant closings, elimination of some job functions, and other balance sheet adjustments. Non-recurring charges in 1996 totaled $1.10.

Valuation - 24-AUG-98

Spurred by a massive ongoing restructuring, operating earnings have recovered from a three-year downturn. The shares were recently trading at a relatively generous 15X the $2.25 a share EPS we are projecting for 1998 (before nonrecurring charges), versus 1997's $2.15 (before charges). Although the company's dominance in the check printing market, its strong cash flow, and its aggressive new management leadership put it in a favorable position to serve the financial institutions market, the outlook for that segment is clouded by recent announcements of major mergers in the financial institutions sector. Nevertheless, we are fairly confident management can deliver on its stated goal of 5% to 9% average annual earnings growth going forward

Key Stock Statistics

S&P EPS Est. 1998	2.25	Tang. Bk. Value/Share	5.21
P/E on S&P Est. 1998	13.3	Beta	0.53
S&P EPS Est. 1999	2.55	Shareholders	300
Dividend Rate/Share	1.48	Market cap. (B)	$ 2.4
Shs. outstg. (M)	80.8	Inst. holdings	69%
Avg. daily vol. (M)	0.225		

Value of $10,000 invested 5 years ago: $ 8,445

Fiscal Year Ending Dec. 31

	1998	1997	1996	1995	1994	1993
Revenues (Million $)						
1Q	489.0	490.1	488.1	465.4	430.0	406.0
2Q	474.8	463.8	446.6	442.3	412.3	362.9
3Q	—	466.9	460.5	449.2	478.9	372.0
4Q	—	498.6	480.5	501.1	478.9	441.2
Yr.	—	1,919	1,896	1,858	1,748	1,582
Earnings Per Share ($)						
1Q	**0.54**	**0.50**	0.23	0.42	0.46	0.62
2Q	**0.52**	**0.46**	0.46	0.37	0.36	0.03
3Q	**E0.59**	**-0.82**	0.41	0.37	0.40	0.45
4Q	**E0.60**	**0.41**	-0.30	-0.01	0.49	0.61
Yr.	**E2.25**	**0.55**	0.79	1.15	1.71	1.71

Next earnings report expected: mid October

Dividend Data (Dividends have been paid since 1921.)

Amount ($)	Date Decl.	Ex-Div. Date	Stock of Record	Payment Date
0.370	Oct. 31	Nov. 13	Nov. 17	Dec. 01 '97
0.370	Jan. 30	Feb. 12	Feb. 17	Mar. 02 '98
0.370	May. 05	May. 14	May. 18	Jun. 01 '98
0.370	Aug. 07	Aug. 20	Aug. 24	Sep. 08 '98

A Division of The McGraw·Hill Companies

Business Summary - 24-AUG-98

Deluxe Corp., formerly known as Deluxe Check Printers, has moved well beyond printing checks for a living, but the company still accounts for nearly 55% of the U.S. check printing market. It is also the largest third-party processor of automated teller machine (ATM) transactions; the leading processor of interchange transactions for shared ATM networks; the leading provider of account verification to financial institutions; and the largest check authorization service for retailers.

Payment systems and methods have been changing in the U.S. in recent years as banking and other industries have introduced alternatives to the traditional check, including charge cards, credit cards, debit cards and electronic payments, among others. Check sales and prices have also been pressured by increased competition. In addition, the direct mail segment of the check market is growing as a lower-priced alternative to financial institution checks, and now represents about 20% of the personal check market. The company believes that checks will remain an important payment option, but in recent years management has focused on controlling expenses and increasing efficiency, and on higher margin products and services. In late 1995 and early 1996, the company announced the start of a major consolidation program that included closing of 26 of

its 41 printing and warehousing facilities over the 1996-1997 period, and significantly reducing staff and production employees.

Deluxe Financial Services (DFS) provides check printing, direct marketing, customer database management, and related services. It also provides payment systems protection services, including check authorization, account verification, and collection services. Its major customers are financial institutions and retailers. Small businesses also rely on DFS for short-run computer and business forms. DFS also sells personalized ATM cards and credit and debit cards to financial institutions and retailers, and driver's licenses and other identification cards to government agencies.

Deluxe Electronic Payment Systems (DEPS) provides electronic funds transfer processing and software. It also provides services in emerging debit markets, including electronic benefit transfer and retail point-of-sale (POS) transaction processing. These programs use ATM and POS terminals to deliver food stamps and welfare assistance in nine states. Medicaid verification services are provided in New York State.

Deluxe Direct (DD) markets specialty papers and other products to small businesses, provides tax forms and electronic tax filing services to tax preparers, and sells direct mail greeting cards, gift wrap and related products to consumers.

Per Share Data ($)

(Year Ended Dec. 31)	1997	1996	1995	1994	1993	1992	1991	1990	1989	1988
Tangible Bk. Val.	6.36	6.54	4.96	5.90	6.15	7.77	6.93	5.88	5.47	4.61
Cash Flow	1.71	2.09	2.40	2.76	2.58	3.21	3.08	2.64	2.31	2.13
Earnings	0.55	0.80	1.15	1.71	1.71	2.42	2.18	2.03	1.79	1.68
Dividends	1.48	1.48	1.48	1.46	1.42	1.34	1.22	1.10	0.98	0.86
Payout Ratio	NM	185%	129%	85%	83%	55%	56%	54%	55%	51%
Prices - High	37	39¾	34	38	47⅞	49	48½	35⅞	35¾	28⅜
- Low	29¾	27	25¾	25⅝	31¾	38⅛	32⅝	26⅝	24	21
P/E Ratio - High	67	50	30	22	28	20	22	18	20	17
- Low	54	34	22	15	19	16	15	13	13	13

Income Statement Analysis (Million $)

	1997	1996	1995	1994	1993	1992	1991	1990	1989	1988
Revs.	1,919	1,896	1,858	1,748	1,582	1,534	1,474	1,414	1,316	1,196
Oper. Inc.	253	306	287	320	353	389	364	326	289	265
Depr.	97.0	107	103	86.4	72.3	66.6	76.0	74.1	44.9	38.1
Int. Exp.	8.8	10.6	13.1	11.3	10.3	15.4	8.2	1.4	2.2	5.1
Pretax Inc.	115	119	169	241	236	325	295	283	246	227
Eff. Tax Rate	61%	45%	44%	42%	40%	38%	38%	39%	38%	37%
Net Inc.	44.7	65.5	94.4	141	142	203	183	172	153	143

Balance Sheet & Other Fin. Data (Million $)

	1997	1996	1995	1994	1993	1992	1991	1990	1989	1988
Cash	179	143	19.9	78.0	222	381	317	114	45.0	22.0
Curr. Assets	513	450	381	421	522	611	539	344	263	220
Total Assets	1,148	1,176	1,295	1,256	1,252	1,200	1,099	924	847	786
Curr. Liab.	382	341	369	290	298	224	208	199	168	167
LT Debt	110	109	111	111	111	116	111	12.0	10.0	11.0
Common Eqty.	610	713	780	814	801	830	748	676	631	568
Total Cap.	726	835	926	966	954	975	891	725	679	619
Cap. Exp.	110	92.0	125	126	62.1	71.6	76.0	64.0	88.4	78.9
Cash Flow	142	172	198	227	214	269	259	223	198	182
Curr. Ratio	1.3	1.3	1.0	1.4	1.8	2.7	2.6	1.7	1.6	1.3
% LT Debt of Cap.	15.2	13.1	12.0	11.5	11.6	11.8	12.4	1.6	1.5	1.8
% Net Inc.of Revs.	2.3	3.5	5.1	8.1	9.0	13.2	12.4	12.2	11.6	12.0
% Ret. on Assets	3.8	9.3	7.4	11.2	11.7	17.7	18.1	19.6	18.7	17.3
% Ret. on Equity	6.8	8.8	11.8	17.5	17.5	25.7	25.7	26.5	25.5	27.0

Data as orig. reptd.; bef. results of disc. opers. and/or spec. items. Per share data adj. for stk. divs. as of ex-div. date. E-Estimated. NA-Not Available. NM-Not Meaningful. NR-Not Ranked.

Office—3680 Victoria St. N., St. Paul, MN 55126-2966. **Tel**—(612) 483-7111. **Website**—http://www.deluxe.com **Chrmn**—H. V. Haverty.**Pres & CEO**—J. A. Blanchard III. **EVP & COO**—J. K. Twogood. **SVP & Secy**—J. H. LeFevre. **SVP, CFO & Investor Contact**—Thomas W. VanHimbergen (612-483-7355). **Dirs**—C. W. Aurand Jr., J. A. Blanchard III, B. B. Grogan, H. V. Haverty, D. R. Hollis, A. F. Jacobson, W. MacMillan, S. Nachtsheim, J. J. Renier, R. C. Salipante.**Transfer Agent & Registrar**—Norwest Bank Minnesota, South St. Paul. **Incorporated**—in Minnesota in 1920. **Empl**—19,600. **S&P Analyst:** William H. Donald

STANDARD &POOR'S
STOCK REPORTS

Dillard's, Inc.

757F
NYSE Symbol **DDS**

In S&P 500

12-SEP-98 | **Industry:** Retail (Department Stores) | **Summary:** This company operates more than 260 department stores located primarily in the Southwest and Midwest.

S&P Opinion: Hold (★★★)	Recent Price • 30⅛	Yield • 0.5%
	52 Wk Range • 44¾-28½	12-Mo. P/E • 12.4

Quantitative Evaluations

Outlook
(1 Lowest—5 Highest)
• **3**

Fair Value
• **34¼**

Risk
• **Low**

Earn./Div. Rank
• **A+**

Technical Eval.
• **Bearish** since 7/98

Rel. Strength Rank
(1 Lowest—99 Highest)
• **49**

Insider Activity
• **Neutral**

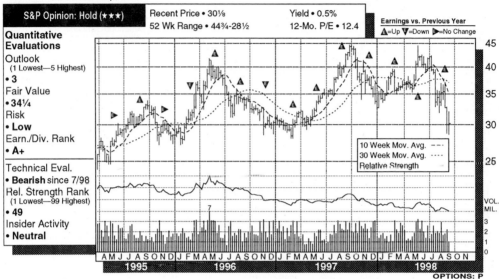

Earnings vs. Previous Year
▲=Up ▼=Down ▶=No Change

10 Week Mov. Avg. - - -
30 Week Mov. Avg. ······
Relative Strength

VOL. MIL.

OPTIONS: P

Overview - 28-MAY-98

The company has agreed to acquire Mercantile Stores Company Inc., (MST), with $3 billion in annual revenues and 103 traditional department stores. On May 22, 1998, DDS began a cash tender offer for all MST shares at $80 a share (a total of about $2.9 billion). Mercantile's stores span 17 states (mainly in the South, Southeast and Midwest), contiguous with many DDS department stores. As a result, DDS plans to sell 20% to 25% of the overlapping stores. Proceeds would be used to pay down debt incurred to finance the acquisition. The combined company would have annual revenues of about $10 billion. Expense ratios should benefit from consolidation of the two companies, leading to the elimination of many duplicative functions. DDS has a strong history of successful growth via acquisitions, and has shown that it can benefit from economies of scale. The company's strong balance sheet leaves ample room for borrowing to finance the purchase of Mercantile. Members of the Dillard family control the supervoting Class B common stock.

Valuation - 28-MAY-98

Investors applauded the Mercantile acquisition announcement. A larger store base, increased buying clout, and lower expense ratios should put earnings on a solid growth track in coming years. Acquisitions have been an important part of Dillard's growth strategy, and Mercantile is one of the last large public department store chains available for merger. Dillard, with its strong MIS capabilities, squeezes excess costs from an acquired department store chain, and acquisitions become additive to earnings early on. Our EPS estimate of $2.60 for FY 99 (Jan.) is subject to change as details of the timing of the merger, one-time charges, and proceeds from asset sales become known. We recommend holding the shares for capital gains.

Key Stock Statistics

S&P EPS Est. 1999	2.60	Tang. Bk. Value/Share	25.76
P/E on S&P Est. 1999	11.6	Beta	0.53
Dividend Rate/Share	0.16	Shareholders	6,900
Shs. outstg. (M)	110.9	Market cap. (B)	$ 3.2
Avg. daily vol. (M)	0.357	Inst. holdings	70%

Value of $10,000 invested 5 years ago: $ 6,204

Fiscal Year Ending Jan. 31

	1999	1998	1997	1996	1995	1994
Revenues (Million $)						
1Q	1,730	1,515	1,453	1,327	1,284	1,163
2Q	1,552	1,453	1,340	1,265	1,184	1,105
3Q	—	1,592	1,543	1,406	1,334	1,228
4Q	—	2,071	1,980	1,921	1,744	1,635
Yr.	—	6,632	6,412	5,918	5,546	5,131
Earnings Per Share ($)						
1Q	**0.58**	**0.52**	0.50	0.43	0.43	0.43
2Q	**0.45**	**0.40**	0.35	0.34	0.30	0.35
3Q	**E0.45**	**0.40**	0.28	0.45	0.45	0.38
4Q	**E1.15**	**1.00**	0.98	0.26	1.05	0.99
Yr.	**E2.60**	**2.31**	2.09	1.48	2.23	2.14

Next earnings report expected: mid November

Dividend Data (Dividends have been paid since 1969.)

Amount ($)	Date Decl.	Ex-Div. Date	Stock of Record	Payment Date
0.040	Sep. 19	Sep. 26	Sep. 30	Nov. 03 '97
0.040	Dec. 05	Dec. 29	Dec. 31	Feb. 02 '98
0.040	Mar. 20	Mar. 27	Mar. 31	May. 01 '98
0.040	Jun. 02	Jun. 26	Jun. 30	Aug. 03 '98

*A Division of The **McGraw·Hill** Companies*

Dillard's, Inc.

Business Summary - 28-MAY-98

Dillard's, Inc. (formerly Dillard Department Stores, Inc.) is an outgrowth of the department store founded in 1938 by William Dillard, the company's current chairman. Dillard's operated 263 traditional department stores and seven clearance centers in 27 states in the South and Midwest at the end of January 1998. The heaviest concentrations of stores were in Texas, Florida, Louisiana, Missouri, Oklahoma, Ohio, North Carolina and Arizona.

Much of Dillard's growth has been through acquisitions. Its strategy is to enter or further penetrate markets where it can become the dominant conventional department store operator. Over the past 10 years, the company has more than tripled its store base, with much of the growth coming from acquisitions. Stores with low occupancy costs, where there is an opportunity to generate higher profits on lower volumes, have been emphasized. The company also acquires stores that are successful, but not dominant in their markets, and expands their operations to establish a dominant position.

In FY 98, the company acquired a total of 20 stores: seven in Virginia (from Proffitt's, Inc.); 10 in Florida (from Dayton Hudson Corp.); and three Macy's stores in Texas. DDS added 12 new stores, entering two new markets (Cheyenne, WY, and Stockton, CA), and expanded four stores. It also closed three stores, of which two were clearance centers. Square footage totaled 43.3 million at the end of FY 98, up 8.3% from the level a year earlier. The company planned to open eight new stores and expand nine in FY 99. Total capital expenditures for FY 99 should approximate $320 million (before the Mercantile Stores acquisition). The company continues to finance the growth of its business primarily through operating earnings.

In February 1997, directors authorized the repurchase of up to $300 million of Class A common stock. Through May 2, 1998, the company had purchased $275 million of Class A shares.

Per Share Data ($)

(Year Ended Jan. 31)	1998	1997	1996	1995	1994	1993	1992	1991	1990	1989
Tangible Bk. Val.	25.76	23.83	21.93	20.55	18.42	16.28	14.19	12.31	10.23	7.80
Cash Flow	4.09	3.80	3.18	3.91	3.65	3.31	2.85	2.57	2.29	1.94
Earnings	2.31	2.09	1.48	2.23	2.14	2.11	1.84	1.67	1.45	1.18
Dividends	0.16	0.14	0.12	0.12	0.08	0.08	0.07	0.07	0.06	0.05
Payout Ratio	7%	7%	8%	5%	4%	4%	4%	4%	4%	5%
Cal. Yrs.	1997	1996	1995	1994	1993	1992	1991	1990	1989	1988
Prices - High	44¾	41¾	37⅞	37⅝	52⅞	51½	45⅝	32	24¾	15½
- Low	28	27⅛	24	25½	33⅛	30	27½	20⅝	13¾	8⅜
P/E Ratio - High	19	20	23	17	25	24	25	19	17	13
- Low	12	13	16	11	15	14	15	12	9	7

Income Statement Analysis (Million $)

	1998	1997	1996	1995	1994	1993	1992	1991	1990	1989
Revs.	6,632	6,228	6,097	5,729	5,312	4,883	4,184	3,734	3,160	2,655
Oper. Inc.	554	511	529	721	702	633	544	477	405	327
Depr.	200	194	192	190	171	136	113	99	85.7	73.3
Int. Exp.	129	121	120	124	131	122	113	99	93.0	83.0
Pretax Inc.	410	380	270	406	400	375	322	281	228	173
Eff. Tax Rate	37%	37%	38%	38%	40%	37%	36%	35%	35%	34%
Net Inc.	258	239	167	252	241	236	206	183	148	114

Balance Sheet & Other Fin. Data (Million $)

	1998	1997	1996	1995	1994	1993	1992	1991	1990	1989
Cash	42.0	64.0	58.4	51.1	51.2	92.6	41.6	38.2	54.1	41.5
Curr. Assets	2,998	2,761	2,658	2,525	2,457	2,367	2,089	1,855	1,526	1,220
Total Assets	5,592	5,060	4,779	4,578	4,430	4,107	3,499	3,008	2,496	2,068
Curr. Liab.	1,099	895	870	759	796	690	737	663	533	582
LT Debt	1,378	1,187	1,179	1,201	1,270	1,414	1,038	871	772	646
Common Eqty.	2,807	2,716	2,478	2,323	2,081	1,832	1,583	1,364	1,094	752
Total Cap.	4,493	4,165	3,909	3,819	3,634	3,418	2,761	2,345	1,963	1,485
Cap. Exp.	509	350	347	253	317	344	288	292	207	181
Cash Flow	458	433	359	442	412	372	319	281	234	187
Curr. Ratio	2.7	3.1	3.1	3.3	3.1	3.4	2.8	2.8	2.9	2.1
% LT Debt of Cap.	30.6	28.5	30.2	31.4	34.9	41.4	37.6	37.1	39.4	43.5
% Net Inc.of Revs.	3.9	3.8	2.8	4.4	4.5	4.8	4.9	4.9	4.7	4.3
% Ret. on Assets	4.8	4.9	3.6	5.6	5.6	6.2	6.3	6.5	6.2	6.4
% Ret. on Equity	9.3	9.2	7.0	11.4	12.3	13.8	13.9	14.6	15.4	16.3

Data as orig. reptd.; bef. results of disc. opers. and/or spec. items. Per share data adj. for stk. divs. as of ex-div. date. Bold denotes diluted EPS (FASB 128). E-Estimated. NA-Not Available. NM-Not Meaningful. NR-Not Ranked.

Office—1600 Cantrell Rd. (P.O. Box 486), Little Rock, AR 72203. **Tel**—(501) 376-5200. **Chrmn & CEO**—W. Dillard. **Pres & COO**—W. Dillard II. **VP, CFO & Investor Contact**—James I. Freeman. **Dirs**—C. N. Clyde Jr., R. C. Connor, D. Corbusier, W. D. Davis, A. Dillard, M. Dillard, W. Dillard, W. Dillard II, J. I. Freeman, J. P. Hammerschmidt, W. B. Harrison Jr., J. M. Hessels, J. H. Johnson, E. R. Kemp, W. Sutton. **Transfer Agent & Registrar**—ChaseMellon Shareholder Services, Ridgefield Park, NJ. **Incorporated**—in Delaware in 1964. **Empl**—45,000. **S&P Analyst:** Karen J. Sack, CFA

STANDARD &POOR'S
STOCK REPORTS

Disney (Walt)

758M

NYSE Symbol **DIS**

In S&P 500

12-SEP-98

Industry: Entertainment

Summary: This major filmed entertainment and theme park company acquired broadcaster and publisher Capital Cities/ABC in February 1996.

S&P Opinion: Hold (★★★)	Recent Price • 25¾	Yield • 0.8%
	52 Wk Range • 42¾-25	12-Mo. P/E • 27.2

Quantitative Evaluations

Outlook
(1 Lowest—5 Highest)
• **2⁻**

Fair Value
• **28¼**

Risk
• **Low**

Earn./Div. Rank
• **A**

Technical Eval.
• **NA**

Rel. Strength Rank
(1 Lowest—99 Highest)
• **28**

Insider Activity
• **NA**

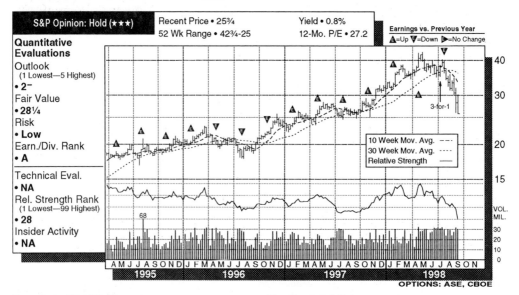

Earnings vs. Previous Year
▲=Up ▼=Down ▶=No Change

10 Week Mov. Avg. - - -
30 Week Mov. Avg. · · · ·
Relative Strength ——

3-for-1

OPTIONS: ASE, CBOE

Overview - 25-AUG-98

With its strong franchise in family entertainment, DIS is well situated for the coming multimedia age. The operations of this diversified company include filmed entertainment, broadcasting, theme parks, and retail stores. In 1996, DIS acquired broadcaster and publisher Capital Cities/ABC, in exchange for cash and stock valued at about $20 billion. Disney's new Animal Kingdom theme park opened in Florida in April 1998. DIS's earnings for the first half of FY 98 (Sep.) included asset sale gains of about $0.05 a share (as adjusted). Recent and estimated earnings include non-cash expense from amortization of acquisition-related intangibles.

Valuation - 25-AUG-98

We advise holding the stock of this major entertainment company, but do not recommend new purchases. We believe that DIS's premium valuation is due in part to affection by consumers for the company's products. We expect the stock to be bolstered by anticipation and success from the release of five new animated theatrical films over the next 16 months, and by expectations related to the debut of a second California theme park in 2001. In part, our hold opinion on the shares reflects our view that expected earnings and cash flow for the coming year are adequately reflected in the stock price. For the long term, we expect growing income levels in foreign markets to boost future demand for Disney-related products. However, economic problems in Asia are likely to restrict spending in that region in the near term. We believe that investors should view DIS's EPS on an adjusted basis, i.e., adding back the large amount of noncash amortization related to acquisitions. In the coming year, we look for amortization to total about $0.20 a share (as adjusted). The stock was split three for one in July 1998.

Key Stock Statistics

S&P EPS Est. 1998	0.98	Tang. Bk. Value/Share	1.62
P/E on S&P Est. 1998	26.3	Beta	1.07
S&P EPS Est. 1999	1.15	Shareholders	588,000
Dividend Rate/Share	0.21	Market cap. (B)	$ 52.9
Shs. outstg. (M)	2048.7	Inst. holdings	45%
Avg. daily vol. (M)	6.893		

Value of $10,000 invested 5 years ago: $ 18,641

Fiscal Year Ending Sep. 30

	1998	1997	1996	1995	1994	1993
Revenues (Million $)						
1Q	6,339	6,278	3,837	3,302	2,727	2,391
2Q	5,242	5,481	4,543	2,923	2,276	2,026
3Q	5,248	5,194	5,087	2,764	2,354	1,937
4Q	—	5,520	5,272	3,124	2,698	2,175
Yr.	—	22,473	18,739	12,112	10,055	8,529
Earnings Per Share ($)						
1Q	**0.37**	**0.36**	0.31	0.30	0.23	0.17
2Q	**0.18**	0.16	-0.01	0.20	0.15	0.13
3Q	**0.20**	0.23	0.20	0.20	0.16	0.16
4Q	**E0.23**	0.20	0.16	0.17	0.14	-0.05
Yr.	**E0.98**	0.95	0.65	0.87	0.68	0.41

Next earnings report expected: mid November

Dividend Data (Dividends have been paid since 1957.)

Amount ($)	Date Decl.	Ex-Div. Date	Stock of Record	Payment Date
0.133	Nov. 24	Jan. 07	Jan. 09	Feb. 20 '98
0.158	Jan. 27	Apr. 07	Apr. 10	May. 22 '98
3-for-1	Apr. 22	Jul. 10	Jun. 19	Jul. 09 '98
0.053	Jun. 24	Jul. 22	Jul. 24	Aug. 21 '98

Business Summary - 25-AUG-98

With operations ranging from theme parks and retail stores to movies and broadcasting, The Walt Disney Co. is looking to combine imaginative material with masterful marketing, as it delivers popular culture around the world. DIS's principal competitors include Time Warner, Viacom Inc., News Corp. and Sony Corp. In FY 97 (Sep.), business segment contributions (excluding a gain from the sale of a TV station) were:

	Revs.	Profits
Creative content	49%	44%
Broadcasting	29%	30%
Theme parks & resorts	22%	26%

In 1996, DIS acquired broadcaster/publisher Capital Cities/ABC (CCB) in a transaction valued at about $20 billion. DIS divested much of CCB's publishing operations in 1997.

DIS's creative content segment includes production and distribution of theatrical motion pictures, television shows and home videos. Other operations include The Disney Channel on cable TV, merchandise licensing, and a chain of more than 600 Disney retail stores.

DIS's broadcasting segment includes ownership and operation of about 10 television stations, the ABC TV network, and various radio stations. The company also owns and operates The Disney Channel, which is dis-

tributed through cable TV systems; and has 80% ownership of various ESPN cable channels, 50% ownership of the Lifetime cable channel, a 39.6% interest in the E! Entertainment cable channel, and 37.5% ownership of the Arts & Entertainment cable network.

Theme parks/resorts include the Walt Disney World Complex in Florida, which contains the Magic Kingdom, Epcot Center, the Disney-MGM Studio Theme Park, the newly opened (April 1998) Animal Kingdom, and at least 15 hotels owned by DIS. The company is also planning a $1.4 billion expansion of the Disneyland theme park resort in Anaheim, CA. The expansion, expected to be completed in 2001, would include a new theme park, called Disney's California Adventure, and a 750-room hotel. In Japan, Tokyo Disneyland is owned and operated by Oriental Land Co., Ltd., pursuant to a licensing agreement. Oriental Land Co. plans to open a second theme park, called Tokyo DisneySea, in 2001. DIS's theme park segment also includes ownership interests in two professional sports teams: The Mighty Ducks and the California Angels. Other DIS businesses include Disney Cruise Line, whose first ship was officially launched in July 1998. In June 1998, the company agreed to a transaction that would result in DIS owning 43% of Internet company Infoseek Corp.

DIS also owns about 39% of Euro Disney S.C.A., a French company that operates the Disneyland Paris theme park business.

Per Share Data ($)

(Year Ended Sep. 30)	1997	1996	1995	1994	1993	1992	1991	1990	1989	1988
Tangible Bk. Val.	0.63	NM	4.23	3.31	2.89	2.75	2.27	1.99	1.65	1.40
Cash Flow	3.36	2.78	2.03	1.66	1.04	0.98	0.90	0.83	0.71	0.52
Earnings	0.95	0.65	0.87	0.68	0.41	0.51	0.40	0.50	0.43	0.32
Dividends	0.16	0.13	0.11	0.09	0.08	0.06	0.05	0.04	0.04	0.03
Payout Ratio	17%	20%	13%	13%	19%	13%	13%	8%	8%	10%
Prices - High	33³/₈	25³/₄	21³/₈	16¹/₄	16¹/₄	15¹/₈	10⁷/₈	11³/₈	11³/₈	5³/₄
- Low	22¹/₈	17³/₄	15	12⁵/₈	12	9¹/₂	7³/₄	7¹/₈	5³/₈	4¹/₂
P/E Ratio - High	35	39	25	24	40	39	27	23	27	18
- Low	23	27	17	19	29	19	20	14	13	14

Income Statement Analysis (Million $)

	1997	1996	1995	1994	1993	1992	1991	1990	1989	1988
Revs.	22,473	18,739	12,112	10,055	8,529	7,504	6,182	5,844	4,594	3,438
Oper. Inc.	8,903	6,968	4,115	3,412	2,589	2,047	1,799	1,825	1,573	1,127
Depr.	4,958	3,944	1,853	1,608	1,028	760	795	538	464	338
Int. Exp.	741	545	236	172	184	152	142	91.0	76.0	38.0
Pretax Inc.	3,387	2,061	2,117	1,703	1,074	1,302	1,019	1,325	1,153	842
Eff. Tax Rate	42%	41%	35%	35%	38%	37%	38%	38%	39%	38%
Net Inc.	1,966	1,214	1,380	1,110	671	817	637	824	703	522

Balance Sheet & Other Fin. Data (Million $)

	1997	1996	1995	1994	1993	1992	1991	1990	1989	1988
Cash	317	732	1,943	187	363	765	886	820	381	428
Curr. Assets	NA	NA	NA	NA	NA	NA	NA	NA	NA	NA
Total Assets	37,776	37,777	14,606	12,826	11,751	10,862	9,429	8,022	6,657	5,109
Curr. Liab.	NA	NA	NA	NA	NA	NA	NA	NA	NA	915
LT Debt	11,068	12,342	2,984	2,107	1,131	1,608	1,818	1,330	375	424
Common Eqty.	17,285	16,086	6,651	5,508	5,030	4,705	3,871	3,489	3,044	2,359
Total Cap.	30,032	29,172	10,702	8,554	6,834	7,201	6,443	5,822	4,482	3,371
Cap. Exp.	1,922	1,745	897	1,026	814	599	954	727	785	835
Cash Flow	6,924	5,158	3,233	2,719	1,700	1,576	1,431	1,362	1,167	860
Curr. Ratio	NA	NA	NA	NA	NA	NA	NA	NA	NA	NA
% LT Debt of Cap.	36.9	42.3	27.9	24.6	16.5	22.3	28.2	27.2	19.2	12.6
% Net Inc.of Revs.	8.7	6.5	11.4	11.0	7.9	10.9	10.3	14.1	15.3	15.2
% Ret. on Assets	5.2	4.7	10.1	9.1	5.9	8.0	7.3	11.4	11.9	11.7
% Ret. on Equity	11.8	10.7	22.7	21.3	13.7	19.0	17.4	25.5	25.9	24.7

Data as orig. reptd.; bef. results of disc. opers. and/or spec. items. Per share data adj. for stk. divs. as of ex-div. date. Bold denotes diluted EPS (FASB 128). E-Estimated. NA-Not Available. NM-Not Meaningful. NR-Not Ranked.

Office—500 S. Buena Vista St., Burbank, CA 91521. **Tel**—(818) 560-1000. **Website**—http://www.disney.com/investors **Chrmn & CEO**—M. D. Eisner.**Vice Chrmn**—R. E. Disney.**SEVP**—S. M. Litvack. **EVP & CFO**—T. O. Staggs.**Investor Contact**—W. M. Webb. **Dirs**—R. F. Bowers, R. E. Disney, M. D. Eisner, S. P. Gold, S. M. Litvack, I. E. Lozano Jr., G. J. Mitchell, T. S. Murphy, R. A. Nunis, L. J. O'Donovan, S. Poitier, I. E. Russell, R. A. M. Stern, E. C. Walker, R. L. Watson, G. L. Wilson. **Transfer Agent & Registrar**—Co.'s office. **Incorporated**—in California in 1938; reincorporated in Delaware in 1987. **Empl**— 100,000. **S&P Analyst:** Tom Graves, CFA

Dollar General

763M

NYSE Symbol **DG**

In S&P 500

12-SEP-98

Industry: Retail (Discounters)

Summary: This discount retailer sells inexpensive soft and hard goods to low-, middle- and fixed-income families through more than 3,100 stores in small communities in 24 states.

S&P Opinion: Hold (★★★)	Recent Price • 32⅜	Yield • 0.5%
	52 Wk Range • 47¼-23	12-Mo. P/E • 34.5

Quantitative Evaluations

Outlook
(1 Lowest—5 Highest)
• **4⁻**

Fair Value
• **38⅛**

Risk
• **Average**

Earn./Div. Rank
• **A+**

Technical Eval.
• **Bearish** since 8/98

Rel. Strength Rank
(1 Lowest—99 Highest)
• **60**

Insider Activity
• **Unfavorable**

Earnings vs. Previous Year
▲=Up ▼=Down ▶=No Change

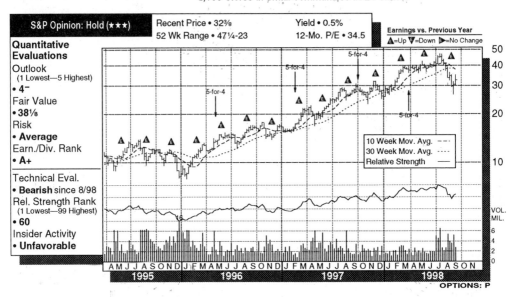

10 Week Mov. Avg. ----
30 Week Mov. Avg. ·····
Relative Strength —

OPTIONS: P

Overview - 08-JUL-98

Total sales in FY 99 (Jan.) should rise about 25%, reflecting 400 to 450 new units. Same-store sales should advance about 8%. Gross margins should narrow, reflecting a reduction in prices. An improved distribution system should boost the company's in-stock position. SG&A expenses should decline as a percentage of sales, aided by tight control of costs, offset somewhat by increased operating expenses from a larger store base. Interest expense should decline, reflecting lower debt levels. Favorable consumer response to better merchandise selection and to DG's commitment to everyday low pricing, accelerated new store development, aggressive overhead cost controls, and increased use of cost-effective information technology should fuel continued 20%-plus annual sales and earnings growth for the foreseeable future. Despite an aggressive capital expenditure program, the company has excess cash flow, and has completed a two million share repurchase program. Additional repurchase programs are a possibility.

Valuation - 08-JUL-98

The share price has been rising fairly consistently since early 1997. With decidedly less retail square footage devoted to this segment of retailing, the low- priced, bargain sector will continue to outpace the moderate-priced group. We believe that the stock is fairly valued at recent levels. Same-store sales should remain strong in FY 99. We are projecting a 25% increase in EPS for FY 99. The company is conservatively financed, generating solid gains in cash flow. The shares are a solid holding for long-term appreciation. A five-for-four stock split was completed in late March 1998.

Key Stock Statistics

S&P EPS Est. 1999	1.05	Tang. Bk. Value/Share	3.57
P/E on S&P Est. 1999	30.9	Beta	1.27
S&P EPS Est. 2000	1.35	Shareholders	3,500
Dividend Rate/Share	0.16	Market cap. (B)	$ 5.4
Shs. outstg. (M)	167.2	Inst. holdings	55%
Avg. daily vol. (M)	0.816		

Value of $10,000 invested 5 years ago: $ 70,883

Fiscal Year Ending Jan. 31

	1999	1998	1997	1996	1995	1994
Revenues (Million $)						
1Q	705.3	520.0	455.9	343.4	287.0	221.8
2Q	741.4	596.8	494.4	408.2	317.3	255.6
3Q	—	649.4	509.0	437.2	359.4	272.6
4Q	—	861.1	675.2	575.4	484.8	383.1
Yr.	—	2,627	2,134	1,764	1,449	1,133
Earnings Per Share ($)						
1Q	**0.18**	0.11	0.09	0.07	0.06	0.04
2Q	**0.19**	0.15	0.13	0.10	0.08	0.06
3Q	**E0.24**	0.19	0.15	0.12	0.10	0.07
4Q	**E0.45**	**0.38**	0.30	0.23	0.19	0.13
Yr.	**E1.05**	**0.84**	0.66	0.51	0.44	0.29

Next earnings report expected: mid November

Dividend Data (Dividends have been paid since 1975.)

Amount ($)	Date Decl.	Ex-Div. Date	Stock of Record	Payment Date
0.040	Feb. 24	Mar. 05	Mar. 09	Mar. 23 '98
0.040	Apr. 27	May. 07	May. 11	May. 25 '98
0.032	Aug. 25	Sep. 02	Sep. 07	Sep. 21 '98
5-for-4	Aug. 25	Sep. 22	Sep. 07	Sep. 21 '98

A Division of The McGraw-Hill Companies

Business Summary - 08-JUL-98

Dollar General Corporation focuses on customers that most other retailers ignore. The company operates a chain of more than 3,100 stores, with nearly half of the merchandise priced at a dollar or less; the most expensive items are generally priced at $35. Serving small towns, some 70% of the stores are located in communities with populations of 20,000 or fewer.

Contributions to sales in recent fiscal years (Jan.) were:

	FY 98	FY 97
Soft goods (mainly apparel)	82%	25%
Hard goods	18%	75%

The company's stores are located in 24 states, with the greatest concentrations (as of January 30, 1998) in Texas (432), Tennessee (214), Florida (185), Kentucky (173), Missouri (169), Virginia (168), Indiana (166), Ohio (159), Georgia (158) and Illinois (155). The typical store is relatively small (6,400 sq. ft. average). About 67% of the stores are located in strip shopping centers, with the remainder in freestanding and downtown buildings. The company negotiates low-cost, short-term leases, usually of three to five years, with multiple renewal op-

tions. In FY 98, rent costs averaged $4.04 per square foot.

Dollar General seeks to serve the consumable basic merchandise needs of low, middle and fixed income customers. The company's typical customer is a female living in a household of three to four individuals with a household income of less than $30,000 per year; 37% of U.S. household income for the year 1995 were under $25,000. In 1998, the average customer transaction was about $8. The company limits its stockkeeping units to 3,000 items per store. In FY 98, hardlines represented more than 80% of net sales. About 97% consisted of first-run merchandise, with the remainder manufacturers' overruns, closeouts and irregular merchandise. The company keeps store rental and operating costs low. DG has become more efficient by accelerating delivery of merchandise to stores to every week from every two weeks. With lower inventory levels and point-of-sale scanners in all stores in FY 98, shrinkage (theft of merchandise) has been reduced.

In FY 98, the company opened over 400 new stores within its current 24-state market. Some 67% of the company's store base consists of new or remodeled stores. In 1999, the company plans to open about 500 to 525 new stores. New store growth is targeted at 15% annually over the next few years.

Per Share Data ($)

(Year Ended Jan. 31)	1998	1997	1996	1995	1994	1993	1992	1991	1990	1989
Tangible Bk. Val.	4.14	3.47	2.97	2.34	1.49	1.22	0.99	0.88	0.80	0.75
Cash Flow	1.05	1.04	0.81	0.54	0.37	0.27	0.18	0.14	0.12	0.11
Earnings	0.84	0.67	0.51	0.44	0.29	0.22	0.14	0.10	0.08	0.07
Dividends	0.13	0.12	0.10	0.06	0.04	0.03	0.03	0.02	0.02	0.02
Payout Ratio	15%	18%	19%	14%	14%	14%	19%	25%	30%	36%
Cal. Yrs.	1997	1996	1995	1994	1993	1992	1991	1990	1989	1988
Prices - High	32	17⅞	13⅞	10	8⅞	5¼	3¼	1⁷⁄₁₆	1⁹⁄₁₆	1⅜
- Low	15¼	7⅞	8	6⅜	4⅜	2⅞	¹⁵⁄₁₆	⅞	1¹⁄₁₆	¹¹⁄₁₆
P/E Ratio - High	38	27	27	23	31	24	24	14	19	20
- Low	18	12	16	15	15	13	7	9	13	10

Income Statement Analysis (Million $)

	1998	1997	1996	1995	1994	1993	1992	1991	1990	1989
Revs.	2,627	2,134	1,765	1,449	1,133	921	754	653	615	613
Oper. Inc.	274	221	174	138	91.9	69.1	44.5	34.7	32.3	28.4
Depr.	38.7	31.0	25.2	17.3	11.7	8.2	6.7	6.7	6.0	6.0
Int. Exp.	3.8	4.7	7.4	2.8	2.2	2.6	3.1	5.0	5.8	6.3
Pretax Inc.	232	185	142	118	75.0	58.2	34.7	23.1	20.3	16.2
Eff. Tax Rate	38%	38%	38%	38%	38%	39%	38%	37%	39%	38%
Net Inc.	145	115	87.8	73.6	48.6	35.6	21.5	14.6	12.4	10.0

Balance Sheet & Other Fin. Data (Million $)

	1998	1997	1996	1995	1994	1993	1992	1991	1990	1989
Cash	7.1	6.6	4.3	33.0	35.4	25.0	7.9	3.9	6.5	5.7
Curr. Assets	667	505	516	410	315	256	192	168	155	183
Total Assets	915	718	680	541	397	316	237	208	194	210
Curr. Liab.	308	224	254	209	148	117	62.4	55.1	45.1	52.4
LT Debt	1.3	2.6	3.3	4.8	5.7	7.0	21.2	19.1	26.8	45.6
Common Eqty.	583	485	419	323	241	190	151	132	121	112
Total Cap.	607	494	426	332	249	199	175	153	149	158
Cap. Exp.	108	84.4	60.5	65.8	35.0	24.7	12.8	8.9	17.0	4.5
Cash Flow	180	144	111	90.1	60.3	43.8	28.2	21.3	18.4	16.0
Curr. Ratio	2.2	2.2	2.0	2.0	2.1	2.2	3.1	3.1	3.4	3.5
% LT Debt of Cap.	0.2	0.5	0.8	1.4	2.3	3.5	12.1	12.5	18.0	28.9
% Net Inc.of Revs.	5.5	5.4	5.0	5.1	4.3	3.9	2.9	2.2	2.0	1.6
% Ret. on Assets	17.7	16.5	14.4	16.7	13.4	12.7	9.6	7.3	6.1	4.6
% Ret. on Equity	26.5	24.9	23.1	27.5	22.3	20.6	15.1	11.6	10.6	9.1

Data as orig. reptd.; bef. results of disc. opers. and/or spec. items. Per share data adj. for stk. divs. as of ex-div. date. Bk. Val. incl. intangibles. Bold denotes diluted EPS (FASB 128). E-Estimated. NA-Not Available. NM-Not Meaningful. NR-Not Ranked.

Office—104 Woodmont Blvd., Suite 500, Nashville, TN 37205. **Tel**—(615) 783-2000. **Website**—www.dollargeneral.com **Chrmn & CEO**—C. Turner, Jr. **VP & CFO**—P. Richards. **Investor Contact**—Kiley Fleming. **Dirs**—J. L. Clayton, R. D. Dickson, J. B. Holland, B. M. Knuckles, W. N. Rasmussen, C. Turner, C. Turner Jr., D. M. Wilds, W. S. Wire II. **Transfer Agent**—Registrar & Transfer Co. Cranford, NJ. **Incorporated**—in Kentucky in 1955. **Empl**— 25,400. **S&P Analyst:** Karen J. Sack, CFA

Dominion Resources 766J

NYSE Symbol **D**

In S&P 500

12-SEP-98

Industry:
Electric Companies

Summary: This utility holding company's main unit, Virginia Electric & Power Co., provides electric service in Virginia and, to a lesser extent, in North Carolina.

S&P Opinion: Hold (★★★)

Recent Price • 42
52 Wk Range • 42⅞-34⅞

Yield • 6.1%
12-Mo. P/E • 38.5

Quantitative Evaluations

Outlook
(1 Lowest—5 Highest)
• **1⁻**

Fair Value
• **39**

Risk
• **Low**

Earn./Div. Rank
• **B**

Technical Eval.
• **Bullish** since 10/97

Rel. Strength Rank
(1 Lowest—99 Highest)
• **94**

Insider Activity
• **NA**

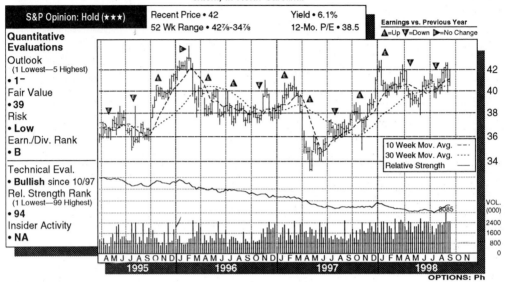

Earnings vs. Previous Year
△=Up ▽=Down ▷=No Change

10 Week Mov. Avg. —-
30 Week Mov. Avg. ----
Relative Strength —

VOL. (000)

8085

2400
1600
800
0

OPTIONS: Ph

Overview - 19-AUG-98

With the August 1998 sale of its U.K.-based East Midlands Electricity, D has significantly re-ordered its strategic priorities. The sale, which resulted in a gain estimated at $216 million, provided the company with $650 million in after-tax cash proceeds. We expect this cash to be used for the acquisition of more domestic power generation assets (with the primary focus on Northeast markets), the expansion of its foreign operations (particularly in Latin America), and the repurchase of common stock (with more than $100 million expected to be bought back within the next year). Virginia Power is among the lowest-cost U.S. generators, and its ongoing restructuring and cost cutting activities are expected to yield annual savings of $55 million to $65 million through the end of the decade. The August 1998 rate settlement approval has removed regulatory uncertainty and should enable D to position itself for a more competitive market environment.

Valuation - 19-AUG-98

We would continue to hold the shares of Dominion Resources. Although the stock is down slightly year to date, it has rebounded about 20% from its recent low. Earlier in the year, the shares had been hurt by the impact of an exceptionally mild winter (subsequently offset by a period of abnormally hot weather) and uncertainties as to the impact the move to a more competitive market could have on Virginia Power's ability to recover its stranded costs, which include a significant level of high cost purchased power contracts. The August 1998 rate settlement approval by the Virginia State Corporation Commission has essentially removed this uncertainty. The stock should also be supported by the high dividend yield and D's $650 million share repurchase program, with more than $100 million expected to be bought back within the next year.

Key Stock Statistics

S&P EPS Est. 1998	1.95	Tang. Bk. Value/Share	16.55
P/E on S&P Est. 1998	21.5	Beta	0.29
S&P EPS Est. 1999	2.90	Shareholders	248,900
Dividend Rate/Share	2.58	Market cap. (B)	$ 8.3
Shs. outstg. (M)	196.5	Inst. holdings	37%
Avg. daily vol. (M)	0.886		

Value of $10,000 invested 5 years ago: $ 15,105

Fiscal Year Ending Dec. 31

	1998	1997	1996	1995	1994	1993
Revenues (Million $)						
1Q	2,158	1,855	1,239	1,129	1,167	1,106
2Q	2,067	1,635	1,121	1,043	1,110	1,005
3Q	—	2,060	1,287	1,345	1,210	1,287
4Q	—	1,887	1,195	1,135	1,005	1,036
Yr.	—	7,678	4,842	4,652	4,491	4,434
Earnings Per Share ($)						
1Q	0.72	0.93	0.85	0.63	0.84	0.74
2Q	-0.42	0.43	0.53	0.45	0.80	0.63
3Q	E1.07	1.12	0.91	1.14	0.94	1.20
4Q	E0.58	0.53	0.36	0.23	0.23	0.55
Yr.	E1.95	2.15	2.65	2.45	2.81	3.12

Next earnings report expected: mid October

Dividend Data (Dividends have been paid since 1925.)

Amount ($)	Date Decl.	Ex-Div. Date	Stock of Record	Payment Date
0.645	Oct. 17	Nov. 25	Nov. 28	Dec. 20 '97
0.645	Feb. 20	Feb. 27	Mar. 03	Mar. 20 '98
0.645	Apr. 17	May. 27	May. 29	Jun. 20 '98
0.645	Jul. 29	Aug. 26	Aug. 28	Sep. 20 '98

A Division of The **McGraw·Hill** *Companies*

Business Summary - 19-AUG-98

Dominion Resources is a utility holding company whose main U.S. subsidiary, Virginia Electric & Power Co., provides electric service in Virginia and to a lesser extent in North Carolina. The company also owns two other subsidiaries: Dominion Energy, an independent power and natural gas company, and Dominion Capital, a financial services and real estate firm.

In August 1998, D sold U.K.-based East Midlands Electricity (acquired in January 1997 for $2.2 billion) to PowerGen (a U.K.-based power generator) for about $3.2 billion. Based in Nottingham, England, East Midlands, which had 1997 revenues of $1.97 billion, is primarily an electric distribution and supply company that owns and operates the 41,600 mile distribution network in the East Midlands region of England.

Contributions by business segment in 1997 were:

	Revenues	Net income
Virginia Power	66%	76%
East Midlands	26%	8%
Non-utility	8%	16%

Virginia Power's service territory in Virginia and North Carolina is characterized by government installations, high-technology centers and financial services businesses. It has one of the strongest economies in the nation. Ranked among the lowest-cost producers of electricity in the U.S., Virginia Power had as its sources of electric generation in 1997: coal, 40% (38% in 1996); nuclear, 34% (32%); net purchased power, 23% (27%); oil, 1% (1%); and other, 2% (2%).

In August 1998, the Virginia State Corporation Commission (SCC) approved settlement of Virginia Power's pending rate case. The settlement, which establishes certainty in Virginia Power's rates through February 28, 2002, provides: an immediate $150 million one-time refund to customers within 90 days of the SCC order; a two-phased rate reduction - a $100 million annual reduction retroactive to March 1, 1998, with an additional $50 million annual reduction beginning March 1, 1999; the write-off of $220 million in regulatory assets; and an incentive mechanism that allows the company to grow its earnings and benefit from future efficiency gains.

Dominion Energy provides non-utility electric power generation outside of Virginia Power's service territory and is active in the development, exploration and operation of oil and natural gas reserves. The company has ownership and operating interests in power projects in six states, Argentina, Bolivia, Belize and Peru.

Dominion Capital is a diversified investment and financial services company that is engaged in a variety of debt and equity investments, including the origination, servicing and securitization of residential mortgages.

Per Share Data ($)

(Year Ended Dec. 31)	1997	1996	1995	1994	1993	1992	1991	1990	1989	1988
Tangible Bk. Val.	16.55	27.21	26.73	26.51	26.38	25.21	24.41	23.41	22.67	21.91
Earnings	2.15	2.65	2.45	2.81	3.12	2.66	2.94	2.92	2.76	3.01
Dividends	2.58	2.58	2.58	2.55	2.48	2.40	2.31	2.23	2.15	2.07
Payout Ratio	120%	97%	105%	91%	79%	92%	79%	78%	79%	70%
Prices - High	42⁷/₈	44³/₈	41⁵/₈	45³/₈	49¹/₂	41	38¹/₈	32⁵/₈	32	31¹/₂
- Low	33¹/₄	36⁷/₈	34⁷/₈	34⁷/₈	38¹/₄	34¹/₈	29⁷/₈	27⁵/₈	27	27¹/₄
P/E Ratio - High	20	17	17	16	16	15	13	11	12	10
- Low	15	14	14	12	12	13	10	9	10	9

Income Statement Analysis (Million $)

	1997	1996	1995	1994	1993	1992	1991	1990	1989	1988
Revs.	7,678	4,842	4,652	4,491	4,434	3,791	3,786	3,533	3,700	3,344
Depr.	819	615	551	533	510	450	450	423	463	492
Maint.	1,238	251	261	263	279	281	305	281	295	272
Fxd. Chgs. Cov.	2.4	3.1	2.4	2.6	2.8	2.5	2.4	2.3	2.2	2.4
Constr. Credits	Nil	Nil	6.7	6.4	5.1	9.5	11.8	5.1	6.2	3.5
Eff. Tax Rate	34%	31%	30%	26%	29%	32%	31%	31%	29%	22%
Net Inc.	399	472	425	478	559	475	511	504	470	491

Balance Sheet & Other Fin. Data (Million $)

	1997	1996	1995	1994	1993	1992	1991	1990	1989	1988
Gross Prop.	19,520	16,816	15,977	15,415	15,009	14,147	13,388	12,684	12,148	11,360
Cap. Exp.	649	484	578	721	1,127	941	815	827	938	827
Net Prop.	12,533	10,509	10,322	10,245	10,207	9,687	9,278	8,959	8,733	8,218
Capitalization:										
LT Debt	7,196	4,728	4,612	4,711	4,751	4,404	4,393	4,396	4,547	4,177
% LT Debt	49	45	45	47	48	47	49	50	52	51
Pfd.	1,074	824	824	816	829	829	735	758	782	750
% Pfd.	7.30	7.90	8.10	8.10	8.20	8.90	8.20	8.60	9.00	9.20
Common	5,040	4,924	4,742	4,586	4,436	4,131	3,878	3,624	3,421	3,224
% Common	34	47	47	45	44	44	43	41	39	40
Total Cap.	14,658	12,474	12,111	12,016	11,897	11,173	10,237	10,013	10,023	9,376
% Oper. Ratio	83.6	81.6	80.0	76.9	79.3	78.2	76.6	75.8	77.1	76.2
% Earn. on Net Prop.	13.0	11.5	11.2	10.2	9.2	8.8	9.7	9.7	9.9	9.7
% Return On Revs.	5.2	9.8	9.1	10.6	12.6	12.5	13.5	14.3	12.7	14.8
% Return On Invest. Capital	7.6	9.8	8.6	8.8	9.9	9.8	11.2	11.3	10.8	10.9
% Return On Com. Equity	8.0	9.8	9.1	10.6	11.9	10.5	12.1	12.5	12.2	13.9

Data as orig. reptd.; bef. results of disc. opers. and/or spec. items. Per share data adj. for stk. divs. as of ex-div. date. Bold denotes diluted EPS (FASB 128). E-Estimated. NA-Not Available. NM-Not Meaningful. NR-Not Ranked.

Office—901 East Byrd St., Suite 1700, Richmond, VA 23219-6111. **Tel**—(804) 775-5700. **Chrmn, Pres & CEO**—T. E. Capps.**EVP & CFO**—E. M. Roach, Jr. **VP & Treas**—G. S. Hetzer. **Secy**—P. A. Wilkerson. **Investor Contacts**—Fred G. Wood III (5813) / Mark C. Stevens (5745). **Dirs**—J. B. Adams, Jr., N. Askew, J. B. Bernhardt, J. F. Betts, T. E. Capps, T. N. Chewning, J. E. Clary, R. J. Davies, J. W. Harris, D. L. Heavenridge, B. J. Lambert III, R. L. Leatherwood, H. L. Lindsay, Jr., K. A. Randall, W. T. Roos, F. S. Royal, J. W. Sack, S. D. Simmons, R. H. Spilman, W. G. Thomas, D. A. Wollard. **Transfer Agent & Registrar**—Company's office.**Incorporated**—in Virginia in 1909. **Empl**— 15,700. **S&P Analyst**: Justin McCann

12-SEP-98

Industry:
Specialty Printing

Summary: The largest commercial printer in the U.S., Donnelley specializes in the production of catalogs, inserts, magazines, books, directories, and financial and computer documentation.

S&P Opinion: Hold (★★★)

Recent Price • 38
52 Wk Range • 48-32⅜

Yield • 2.2%
12-Mo. P/E • 33.1

Quantitative Evaluations

Outlook
(1 Lowest—5 Highest)
• **3+**

Fair Value
• **40**

Risk
• **Low**

Earn./Div. Rank
• **B+**

Technical Eval.
• **NA**

Rel. Strength Rank
(1 Lowest—99 Highest)
• **66**

Insider Activity
• **NA**

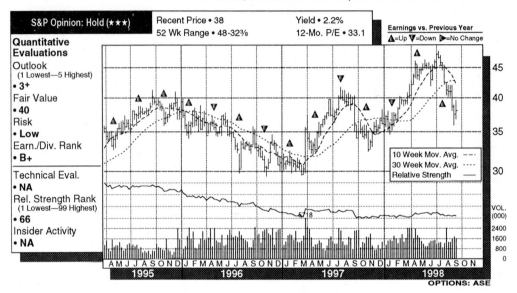

Earnings vs. Previous Year
▲=Up ▼=Down ▶=No Change

10 Week Mov. Avg. - - -
30 Week Mov. Avg. ......
Relative Strength ——

VOL. (000)

OPTIONS: ASE

Overview - 17-AUG-98

Operating earnings in the second quarter of 1998 advanced 22%, on a 0.5% rise in revenues from continuing operations, helped by volume gains at most business units, productivity measures, restructuring actions take over the last 18 months, and a turnaround in the logistics business. Net income climbed 56%, to $59 million, from $38 million; results included losses from discontinued operations of $80 million and $7 million in the respective periods. Return on invested capital rose 12.6%, from 10.9%, and inventory and accounts receivables continued to decline. The outlook for the remainder of 1998 is favorable; excluding a gain of $0.61 a share in the second quarter, from the sale of the remaining interest in Metromail Corp., we are projecting EPS of $1.95 for 1998, up 39% from 1997's $1.40; higher EPS will reflect in part an 8% share buyback program. We project another advance, to $2.30, in 1999.

Valuation - 17-AUG-98

Despite possible short-lived market setbacks in coming periods, the general long-term outlook for the stock is good. Earnings comparisons, helped by the absence of money-losing operations (including the sale of part of Stream International) and improving margins, are recovering rapidly, and should nearly match the record set in 1995. Further gains are anticipated in 1999 and beyond. The market views favorably DNY's retrenchment efforts, as well as the appointment of William L. Davis, formerly a senior executive at Emerson Electric, as chairman and CEO, as exhibited by the stock's rebound to a 52-week high after the appointment in late March. Although, the shares are richly valued at a recent level of 21X estimated 1998 EPS, and 18X projected 1999 EPS, they may be held for long-term capital gains.

Key Stock Statistics

S&P EPS Est. 1998	1.95	Tang. Bk. Value/Share	7.21
P/E on S&P Est. 1998	19.5	Beta	0.81
S&P EPS Est. 1999	2.30	Shareholders	11,500
Dividend Rate/Share	0.84	Market cap. (B)	$ 5.3
Shs. outstg. (M)	139.2	Inst. holdings	82%
Avg. daily vol. (M)	0.320		

Value of $10,000 invested 5 years ago: $ 13,030

Fiscal Year Ending Dec. 31

	1998	1997	1996	1995	1994	1993
Revenues (Million $)						
1Q	1,161	1,475	1,547	1,318	1,071	960.0
2Q	1,144	1,505	1,578	1,491	1,117	994.0
3Q	—	1,557	1,603	1,705	1,243	1,124
4Q	—	1,402	1,872	1,998	1,458	1,310
Yr.	—	4,850	6,599	6,512	4,889	4,388
Earnings Per Share ($)						
1Q	**0.31**	0.24	-2.45	0.31	0.28	-0.14
2Q	**0.97**	0.31	0.35	0.42	0.38	0.34
3Q	—	0.56	0.45	0.60	0.52	0.45
4Q	—	0.31	0.66	0.62	0.57	0.51
Yr.	—	**1.40**	-0.47	1.95	1.75	1.16

Next earnings report expected: late October

Dividend Data (Dividends have been paid since 1911.)

Amount ($)	Date Decl.	Ex-Div. Date	Stock of Record	Payment Date
0.200	Sep. 25	Nov. 05	Nov. 07	Nov. 29 '97
0.200	Jan. 22	Feb. 02	Feb. 04	Feb. 28 '98
0.200	Mar. 26	May. 07	May. 11	Jun. 02 '98
0.210	Jul. 27	Aug. 06	Aug. 10	Sep. 01 '98

Business Summary - 17-AUG-98

R. R. Donnelley & Sons, also known as The Lakeside Press, provides a wide range of services in print and digital media in 19 countries on four continents. It is the largest U.S. commercial printer.

DNY is a major supplier of print and digital media services in the U.K. and also provides services in Latin America, other locations in Europe and in Asia. International operations provided 17% of 1997 revenues.

The company provides printing and related services to the merchandising, magazine, book, directory and financial markets. The commercial print industry is large and fragmented with over 52,000 firms, with over 1 million employees in the U.S. and generating about $140 billion in revenue. Donnelley has market leading positions in five categories of the market served by its business units: Merchandise Media, which serves the catalog, retail insert and direct-mail markets; Magazine Publishing Services, which serves the consumer and the trade and specialty magazine markets; Book Publishing Services, which serves the trade and educational book markets; Telecommunications, which serves the domestic and international directory markets; and Financial Services, which serves the communication needs of the capital markets and the mutual fund and healthcare industries.

The commercial print marketplace continues to be competitive. Consolidation in Donnelley's customer base and in the printing market has resulted in pressure on pricing and increased competition for market share. These industry trends are expected to continue. Donnelley plans to manage these trends by capitalizing on its market-leading positions, by leveraging its capabilities and by controlling costs.

For most of 1997, DNY owned about 80% of Stream International Holdings Inc. (SIH), which included three business units: Modus Media International (software replication, documentation, and kitting and assembly); Corporate Software & Technology (licensing and fulfillment, customized documentation, license administration and user training); and Stream International (technical and help-line support). In December 1997, SIH was reorganized into three separate businesses, and DNY's interest was restructured so that it now owns 87% of the common stock of Stream, 86% of the common stock of CS&T, and non-voting preferred stock of MMI. As a result of the restructuring and DNY's intention to dispose of its interest in CS&T, it now reports its interests in CS&T and MMI as discontinued operations.

Per Share Data ($) (Year Ended Dec. 31)	1997	1996	1995	1994	1993	1992	1991	1990	1989	1988
Tangible Bk. Val.	8.31	7.22	7.46	7.13	8.76	9.03	8.25	7.32	7.73	6.81
Cash Flow	3.91	1.53	4.53	3.78	2.94	3.17	2.88	2.71	2.42	2.29
Earnings	1.40	-1.04	1.95	1.75	1.16	1.51	1.32	1.46	1.43	1.32
Dividends	0.78	0.74	0.68	0.60	0.54	0.51	0.50	0.48	0.44	0.39
Payout Ratio	56%	NM	35%	34%	47%	34%	38%	33%	31%	30%
Prices - High	41 3/4	39 7/8	41 1/4	32 1/2	32 3/4	33 3/4	25 5/8	26 3/8	25 5/8	19 3/8
- Low	29 1/2	29 3/8	28 7/8	26 7/8	26 1/8	23 3/4	19 1/2	17 1/8	17 1/8	15
P/E Ratio - High	30	NM	21	19	28	22	19	18	18	15
- Low	21	NM	15	15	23	16	15	12	12	11
Income Statement Analysis (Million $)										
Revs.	4,850	6,599	6,512	4,889	4,388	4,193	3,915	3,498	3,122	2,878
Oper. Inc.	811	813	958	773	690	664	605	542	487	463
Depr.	371	389	398	313	275	258	210	180	154	150
Int. Exp.	91.0	95.0	121	63.7	51.9	43.9	55.9	25.3	11.3	15.1
Pretax Inc.	304	-109	440	39.5	277	361	320	360	352	317
Eff. Tax Rate	32%	NM	32%	32%	35%	35%	36%	37%	37%	35%
Net Inc.	207	-157	299	269	179	235	205	226	222	205
Balance Sheet & Other Fin. Data (Million $)										
Cash	48.0	31.1	33.0	21.0	11.0	12.0	99	123	110	118
Curr. Assets	1,147	1,753	1,908	1,353	1,110	1,022	NA	NA	726	692
Total Assets	4,134	4,849	5,385	4,452	3,654	3,410	3,404	3,343	2,507	2,346
Curr. Liab.	813	1,148	1,130	802	685	612	727	677	412	376
LT Debt	1,153	1,431	1,561	1,212	673	523	528	647	63.0	121
Common Eqty.	1,592	1,631	2,173	1,978	1,844	1,849	1,730	1,596	1,446	1,296
Total Cap.	2,974	3,316	4,035	3,478	2,790	2,772	2,640	2,624	1,874	1,771
Cap. Exp.	360	403	456	425	307	228	288	425	237	184
Cash Flow	578	232	697	582	454	493	415	406	376	355
Curr. Ratio	1.4	1.5	1.7	1.7	1.6	1.7	NA	NA	1.8	1.8
% LT Debt of Cap.	38.8	43.1	38.7	34.9	24.1	18.8	20.0	24.7	3.3	6.8
% Net Inc.of Revs.	4.3	NM	4.6	5.5	4.1	5.6	5.2	6.5	7.1	7.1
% Ret. on Assets	4.6	NM	6.1	6.6	5.1	6.9	6.1	7.7	9.1	9.3
% Ret. on Equity	12.8	NM	14.4	14.1	9.7	13.1	12.3	14.9	16.2	16.7

Data as orig. reptd.; bef. results of disc. opers. and/or spec. items. Per share data adj. for stk. divs. as of ex-div. date. Bold denotes diluted EPS (FASB 128). E-Estimated. NA-Not Available. NM-Not Meaningful. NR-Not Ranked.

Office—77 West Wacker Drive, Chicago, IL 60601-1696. **Tel**—(312) 326-8000. **Website**—http://www.rrdonnelley.com. **Chrmn & CEO**—W. L. Davis. **Vice Chrmn**—J. R. Donnelley. **Secy**—Monica M. Fohrman. **CFO**—Cheryl A. Francis. **VP & Treas**—G. A. Stoklosa. **VP & Investor Contact**—Jonathon M. Singer (312-326-7754). **Dirs**—J. B. Anderson Jr., M. L. Collins, W. L. Davis, J. R. Donnelley, C. C. Haffner III, J. H. Hamilton, T. S. Johnson, G. A. Lorch, M. B. Puckett, J. M. Richman, W. D. Sanders, B. L. Thomas, H. B. White, S. M. Wolf. **Transfer Agent & Registrar**—First Chicago Trust Co. of New York, Jersey City, NJ. **Incorporated**—in Delaware in 1956. **Empl**— 26,000. **S&P Analyst:** William H. Donald

STANDARD &POOR'S
STOCK REPORTS

Dover Corp.
769

NYSE Symbol **DOV**

In S&P 500

12-SEP-98

Industry:
Machinery (Diversified)

Summary: Dover makes a broad variety of products, ranging from elevators to electronic circuitry assembly equipment, for the electronic, building, petroleum, aerospace and other industries.

S&P Opinion: Hold (★★★)	Recent Price • 27½	Yield • 1.4%
	52 Wk Range • 39⅞-25½	12-Mo. P/E • 15.8

Earnings vs. Previous Year
▲=Up ▼=Down ▶=No Change

Quantitative Evaluations

Outlook
(1 Lowest—5 Highest)
• **4**

Fair Value
• **34¼**

Risk
• **Average**

Earn./Div. Rank
• **A**

Technical Eval.
• **Bearish** since 7/98

Rel. Strength Rank
(1 Lowest—99 Highest)
• **61**

Insider Activity
• **Favorable**

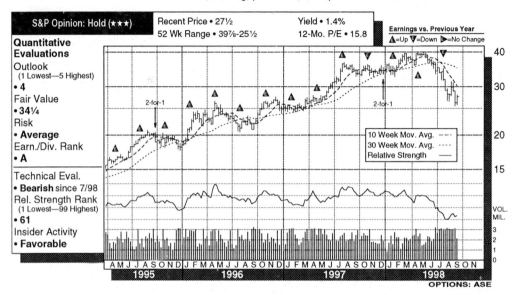

10 Week Mov. Avg. ----
30 Week Mov. Avg. ······
Relative Strength ——

OPTIONS: ASE

Overview - 21-JUL-98

We expect sales to rise 8% in 1998, mainly reflecting acquisitions. Excluding acquisitions, several areas of weakness have emerged, including technologies that may be affected by the Asian economic and currency problems. Heil Trailers has recovered from a 1996 downturn, but Heil Refuse is suffering from lower capital spending by waste companies. Demand at Belvac (can-making equipment) is turning down again, after a flat 1997. Margins should benefit from management's mid-1998 decision to spin off DOV's less profitable elevator operations. With higher interest expense expected, earnings should flatten in 1998. Over the long term, Dover should continue to benefit from an entrepreneurial style that is characterized by an operating structure featuring 50 stand-alone companies. This structure places responsibility on managers close to actual operations, and permits greater flexibility and responsiveness to a dynamic environment. The success of this approach is shown by the company's high returns on equity and assets earned over a long period.

Valuation - 21-JUL-98

Although we have a positive long-term view of the company, we are maintaining our hold recommendation on the shares for the near term. We believe that the stock is fairly valued at a recent level of 22X our 1998 EPS estimate. The 1998 estimate reflects a relatively flat earnings projection, excluding a net nonrecurring gain of $0.11 a share in 1997. Based on Dover's excellent financial results over the years, as well as projected future growth, current owners should continue to hold for long-term gains. The shares should be supported by steady share repurchases, funded by strong cash flow from operations.

Key Stock Statistics

S&P EPS Est. 1998	1.75	Tang. Bk. Value/Share	1.68
P/E on S&P Est. 1998	15.7	Beta	0.63
S&P EPS Est. 1999	2.00	Shareholders	3,000
Dividend Rate/Share	0.38	Market cap. (B)	$ 6.1
Shs. outstg. (M)	223.1	Inst. holdings	70%
Avg. daily vol. (M)	0.680		

Value of $10,000 invested 5 years ago: $ 26,158

Fiscal Year Ending Dec. 31

	1998	1997	1996	1995	1994	1993
Revenues (Million $)						
1Q	1,149	1,009	999	854.1	680.7	567.0
2Q	1,235	1,154	1,023	948.2	761.2	594.5
3Q	—	1,164	1,009	934.5	804.5	642.2
4Q	—	1,221	1,044	1,009	838.9	680.5
Yr.	—	4,548	4,076	3,746	3,085	2,484
Earnings Per Share ($)						
1Q	**0.40**	**0.35**	0.34	0.27	0.18	0.15
2Q	**0.45**	**0.55**	0.39	0.35	0.23	0.17
3Q	—	**0.44**	0.64	0.32	0.23	0.18
4Q	—	**0.45**	0.36	0.30	0.24	0.18
Yr.	**E1.75**	**1.79**	1.72	1.23	0.89	0.69

Next earnings report expected: mid October

Dividend Data (Dividends have been paid since 1947.)

Amount ($)	Date Decl.	Ex-Div. Date	Stock of Record	Payment Date
2-for-1	Nov. 06	Dec. 16	Nov. 28	Dec. 15 '97
0.095	Feb. 05	Feb. 25	Feb. 27	Mar. 13 '98
0.095	May. 07	May. 27	May. 29	Jun. 15 '98
0.095	Aug. 06	Aug. 27	Aug. 31	Sep. 15 '98

A Division of The McGraw-Hill Companies

Business Summary - 21-JUL-98

The prototypical industrial conglomerate, Dover Corporation manufactures a broad variety of specialized industrial products that are marketed to the building, petroleum, electronics, aerospace and other industries. The company utilizes a decentralized management style and relies on frequent acquisitions to supplement the moderate growth typical of the mature markets in which it competes. Segment contributions in 1997 were:

	Sales	Profits
Dover Technologies	29%	30%
Dover Elevator International	19%	14%
Dover Industries	19%	20%
Dover Diversified	17%	18%
Dover Resources	16%	18%

International business accounted for 20% of sales and 14% of operating profit in 1996 (latest available).

Dover Technologies makes a variety of electronic equipment and components, including electronic circuitry assembly equipment, automated soldering and board handling equipment, continuous ink jet printers, microwave and R.F. filters and coaxial switches.

Dover Elevator International makes geared and gearless traction elevators, hydraulic elevators and replacement parts and provides installation and repair services. New elevators accounted for about half of the segment's 1996 sales and were profitable for the first time since 1990. Service sales, by contrast, are steady and highly profitable.

Dover Diversified makes can production equipment, plate/frame heat exchangers, industrial/marine fluid film bearings, air conditioning compressors, commercial refrigeration and display cases, electrical distribution systems and flexographic presses.

Dover Industries businesses include producers of automotive lifts and alignment racks, food preparation equipment, solid-waste compaction equipment, waste collection vehicles, machine tools, and auto collision measuring and repair systems.

Dover Resources makes pumps for the delivery of fuel oil, equipment for natural gas compressors, sucker rods, pumps, valves and fittings, gasoline nozzles and fittings, and liquid filtration systems.

Acquisition investment totaled $261 million in 1997, versus $282 million in 1996. Of the 17 separate transactions in 1997, 15 were add-ons to existing businesses. Dover also invested $86 million to repurchase 3.2 million common shares (as adjusted) during the first half of 1997.

Per Share Data ($)

(Year Ended Dec. 31)	1997	1996	1995	1994	1993	1992	1991	1990	1989	1988
Tangible Bk. Val.	2.81	2.29	1.78	1.85	1.42	1.95	2.24	1.84	1.88	1.67
Cash Flow	2.54	2.27	1.70	1.30	1.03	0.89	0.89	0.95	0.88	0.83
Earnings	1.79	1.73	1.23	0.89	0.69	0.56	0.54	0.64	0.57	0.56
Dividends	0.36	0.32	0.29	0.24	0.23	0.21	0.20	0.19	0.17	0.15
Payout Ratio	20%	19%	24%	28%	32%	38%	38%	29%	30%	28%
Prices - High	36¾	27⅝	20⅞	16¾	15½	11⅞	11	10⅜	9⅞	9⅛
- Low	24⅛	18⅜	12⅞	12½	11¼	9⅝	8⅝	6⅞	6⅞	6⅝
P/E Ratio - High	20	16	17	19	22	21	20	16	17	16
- Low	13	11	11	14	16	17	16	11	12	12

Income Statement Analysis (Million $)

	1997	1996	1995	1994	1993	1992	1991	1990	1989	1988
Revs.	4,548	4,076	3,746	3,085	2,484	2,272	2,196	2,210	2,120	1,954
Oper. Inc.	783	664	546	421	331	281	249	331	314	301
Depr.	171	125	108	95.8	77.0	77.5	85.4	77.5	78.8	73.8
Int. Exp.	46.9	42.0	40.1	36.5	22.3	20.1	23.2	30.7	29.6	21.3
Pretax Inc.	617	589	417	307	246	200	204	244	227	225
Eff. Tax Rate	34%	34%	33%	34%	36%	36%	37%	36%	37%	35%
Net Inc.	405	390	278	202	158	129	128	156	144	146

Balance Sheet & Other Fin. Data (Million $)

	1997	1996	1995	1994	1993	1992	1991	1990	1989	1988
Cash	125	218	149	145	96.0	101	127	152	176	85.0
Curr. Assets	1,591	1,490	1,384	1,133	904	774	756	815	823	739
Total Assets	3,278	2,993	2,667	2,071	1,774	1,426	1,357	1,468	1,406	1,366
Curr. Liab.	1,197	1,139	95.0	772	596	572	475	608	577	541
LT Debt	263	253	256	254	252	1.2	6.3	21.0	26.7	27.8
Common Eqty.	1,778	1,490	1,228	996	870	805	828	788	747	741
Total Cap.	2,007	1,797	1,530	1,252	1,142	828	870	846	810	799
Cap. Exp.	146	126	104	84.9	48.7	47.8	50.4	52.7	70.4	60.5
Cash Flow	576	515	386	298	235	207	214	233	223	220
Curr. Ratio	1.3	1.3	2.1	1.5	1.5	1.4	1.6	1.3	1.4	1.4
% LT Debt of Cap.	13.1	14.1	16.8	20.3	22.1	0.1	0.7	2.5	3.3	3.5
% Net Inc.of Revs.	8.9	9.6	7.5	6.6	6.4	5.7	5.8	7.0	6.8	7.5
% Ret. on Assets	12.9	13.8	11.8	10.6	9.9	9.4	9.2	11.0	10.6	11.7
% Ret. on Equity	24.4	28.7	25.1	21.8	18.9	16.1	16.0	20.7	19.8	20.8

Data as orig. reptd.; bef. results of disc. opers. and/or spec. items. Per share data adj. for stk. divs. as of ex-div. date. Bold denotes diluted EPS (FASB 128). E-Estimated. NA-Not Available. NM-Not Meaningful. NR-Not Ranked.

Office—280 Park Ave., New York, NY 10017-1292. **Tel**—(212) 922-1640. **Website**—http://www.dovercorporation.com **Chrmn**—G. L. Roubos. **Pres & CEO**—T. L. Reece. **Secy**—R. G. Kuhbach. **VP-Fin & Investor Contact**—John F. McNiff. **Dirs**—D. H. Benson, M. O. Bryant, J. M. Ergas, R. Fleming, J. F. Fort, J. L. Koley, J. F. McNiff, A. J. Ormsby, T. L. Reece, G. L. Roubos. **Transfer Agent & Registrar**—Harris Trust & Savings Bank, Chicago. **Incorporated**—in Delaware in 1947. **Empl**— 26,234. **S&P Analyst:** Robert E. Friedman, CPA

Dow Chemical — 770

NYSE Symbol **DOW**

In S&P 500

12-SEP-98

Industry: Chemicals

Summary: The second largest chemical company in the U.S., DOW produces basic chemicals and plastics, industrial specialties, and agricultural products.

S&P Opinion: Hold (★★★)	Recent Price • 79⅝	Yield • 4.4%
	52 Wk Range • 102⅝-74⅝	12-Mo. P/E • 11.3

Quantitative Evaluations

Outlook (1 Lowest—5 Highest)
• **2+**

Fair Value
• **77¼**

Risk
• **Low**

Earn./Div. Rank
• **B**

Technical Eval.
• **Neutral** since 9/98

Rel. Strength Rank (1 Lowest—99 Highest)
• **63**

Insider Activity
• **Neutral**

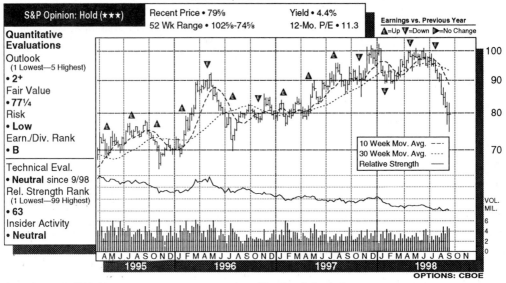

Earnings vs. Previous Year
▲=Up ▼=Down ▶=No Change

10 Week Mov. Avg. - - -
30 Week Mov. Avg. ·······
Relative Strength ——

OPTIONS: CBOE

Overview - 19-AUG-98

We expect DOW's basic plastics and chemicals businesses to show unfavorable profit comparisons for the rest of 1998 and into 1999 due to a cyclical downturn in industry selling prices, partly as a result of the Asian economic crisis. Feedstock costs should be stable to modestly higher over the balance of 1998. Polyethylene prices and margins may continue to drop as a result of the addition of new industry capacity, while polystyrene pricing continues to be under pressure from low styrene costs. Caustic soda profits should continue to improve greatly as a result of the surge in selling prices since mid-1997, helping to offset much lower prices for glycol and vinyl monomer. Specialty chemicals and plastics will likely continue to grow on strong demand, though the agricultural sciences unit should have a seasonal downturn in the second half after a strong first half performance. Cost reductions implemented in recent years will help dampen the cyclical downturn in overall results. An ongoing stock buyback program will aid EPS comparisons. A first quarter gain from the sale of the consumer products business was largely offset by non-recurring restructuring and environmental charges. Earnings in 1997's second quarter included a $0.43 gain from the sale of a business.

Valuation - 19-AUG-98

We continue to recommend "hold" in view of expectations of a downturn in EPS in 1998 and 1999, as a result of increasing industry capacity for ethylene and plastics, and despite a P/E that is below that of the overall market based on projected 1998 EPS. The dividend provides a yield well above that of the overall market. A recent proposal to settle the breast implant claims involving 50%-owned Dow Corning Co. would remove a cloud over DOW, though claims may continue to be filed against DOW.

Key Stock Statistics

S&P EPS Est. 1998	6.40	Tang. Bk. Value/Share	26.06
P/E on S&P Est. 1998	12.5	Beta	0.86
S&P EPS Est. 1999	6.00	Shareholders	103,800
Dividend Rate/Share	3.48	Market cap. (B)	$ 17.9
Shs. outstg. (M)	224.1	Inst. holdings	61%
Avg. daily vol. (M)	0.965		

Value of $10,000 invested 5 years ago: $ 17,580

Fiscal Year Ending Dec. 31

	1998	1997	1996	1995	1994	1993
Revenues (Million $)						
1Q	4,829	4,992	4,982	5,205	4,541	4,363
2Q	4,857	5,366	5,176	5,517	4,934	4,822
3Q	—	4,857	4,992	4,884	5,046	4,370
4Q	—	4,803	4,903	4,594	5,494	4,505
Yr.	—	20,018	20,053	20,200	20,015	18,060
Earnings Per Share ($)						
1Q	1.84	1.88	1.90	2.03	0.62	1.47
2Q	1.86	2.45	2.20	1.22	0.91	0.54
3Q	E1.40	1.82	1.92	2.15	1.04	0.50
4Q	E1.30	1.55	1.69	1.63	0.80	-0.18
Yr.	E6.40	7.70	7.71	7.03	3.37	2.33

Next earnings report expected: late October

Dividend Data (Dividends have been paid since 1911.)

Amount ($)	Date Decl.	Ex-Div. Date	Stock of Record	Payment Date
0.870	Dec. 11	Dec. 29	Dec. 31	Jan. 30 '98
0.870	Feb. 12	Mar. 27	Mar. 31	Apr. 30 '98
0.870	May. 14	Jun. 26	Jun. 30	Jul. 30 '98
0.870	Sep. 03	Sep. 28	Sep. 30	Oct. 30 '98

A Division of The **McGraw·Hill** *Companies*

Business Summary - 19-AUG-98

Over the past several years, DOW, the second largest domestic chemicals company, ended an effort to diversify and has refocused on chemistry-related businesses. Businesses sold in recent years included pharmaceuticals, personal care, and household products units. Meanwhile, DOW has expanded geographically in Latin America, Eastern Europe and Asia, and entered new businesses such as polypropylene, PET polyester, and elastomers. It has also reduced its annual costs by more than $900 million a year since 1992. The company has repurchased 24% of its common stock since 1994, for $5.3 billion. Segment contributions in 1997 were:

	Sales	Profits
Chemicals & Metals	14%	23%
Performance Chemicals	23%	23%
Plastics	21%	31%
Performance Plastics	26%	34%
Hydrocarbons	11%	-1%
Diversified/not allocated	5%	-10%

Foreign operations accounted for 56% of sales and 62% of operating income in 1997.

Chemicals and metals include inorganics (chlorine, caustic soda, chlorinated solvents, ethylene dichloride, vinyl chloride, magnesium metals) and organics (phenols, acetone, ethylene oxide/glycol, propylene oxide/glycol, and glycerine) used primarily as raw materials in the manufacture of customers' products. DOW is the world's largest maker of chlorine and caustic soda. Performance chemicals consist of latex coatings and binders, surfactants, superabsorbent polymers, cellulose ethers, ion exchange resins, heat transfer fluids, lubricants, and solvents. In June 1997, DOW bought for $1.2 billion the remaining 40% interest in DowElanco (renamed Dow AgroSciences), a maker of herbicides and insecticides with annual sales of over $2 billion. Dow owns 68% of Mycogen Corp., an agribusiness and biotechnology company.

DOW is the world's largest producer of polyethylene and polystyrene resins which are used in a broad variety of applications. It also makes polypropylene, PET polyester, polycarbonates, ABS, adhesives, polyurethanes, polyols, isocyanates, epoxy resins, and fabricated products (foams and films).

Hydrocarbons and energy includes olefins, aromatics, styrene, and power and steam. In June 1997, DOW sold its 80% interest in Destec Energy, Inc., an independent power producer, for $974 million.

Other businesses include environmental services (sold August 1998) and advanced materials. DOW in January 1998 sold its consumer products business (plastic films, Ziploc bags, Fantastik cleaner) for $1.2 billion.

Per Share Data ($)

(Year Ended Dec. 31)	1997	1996	1995	1994	1993	1992	1991	1990	1989	1988
Tangible Bk. Val.	26.06	29.20	26.52	13.71	13.09	13.46	18.95	16.81	14.70	26.35
Cash Flow	13.37	13.00	12.94	8.77	7.89	6.47	8.76	9.91	13.03	12.01
Earnings	7.70	7.71	7.03	3.37	2.33	0.99	3.46	5.10	9.20	8.55
Dividends	3.36	3.00	2.90	2.60	2.60	2.60	2.60	2.60	2.37	1.73
Payout Ratio	44%	39%	41%	77%	112%	263%	75%	51%	26%	20%
Prices - High	102⅝	92½	78	79¼	62	62⅞	58	75¾	72¼	62⅝
- Low	76⅜	68¼	61⅜	56½	49	51	44⅛	37	55½	51⅛
P/E Ratio - High	13	12	11	24	27	64	17	15	8	7
- Low	10	9	9	17	21	52	13	7	6	6

Income Statement Analysis (Million $)

	1997	1996	1995	1994	1993	1992	1991	1990	1989	1988
Revs.	20,018	20,053	20,200	20,015	18,060	18,971	18,807	19,773	17,600	16,682
Oper. Inc.	4,013	4,385	5,333	3,795	3,044	3,197	3,391	4,049	4,987	5,174
Depr.	1,287	1,298	1,442	1,490	1,522	1,489	1,435	1,296	1,036	976
Int. Exp.	471	529	462	603	666	773	704	740	513	400
Pretax Inc.	2,948	3,288	3,529	2,052	1,525	872	1,688	2,563	3,935	3,867
Eff. Tax Rate	35%	36%	41%	38%	40%	31%	30%	38%	37%	38%
Net Inc.	1,808	1,907	2,078	938	644	276	942	1,384	2,487	2,410

Balance Sheet & Other Fin. Data (Million $)

	1997	1996	1995	1994	1993	1992	1991	1990	1989	1988
Cash	235	2,302	3,450	1,134	837	606	536	299	289	225
Curr. Assets	8,640	9,830	10,554	8,693	7,652	7,443	7,719	8,019	7,340	6,363
Total Assets	24,040	24,673	23,582	26,545	25,505	25,360	24,727	23,953	22,166	16,239
Curr. Liab.	7,340	6,004	5,601	6,618	5,651	5,641	6,135	5,754	6,484	4,175
LT Debt	4,196	4,196	4,705	5,303	5,902	6,191	6,079	5,209	3,855	3,338
Common Eqty.	7,626	7,954	7,361	8,212	8,034	8,034	9,441	8,728	7,957	7,255
Total Cap.	13,196	15,280	14,841	16,687	16,763	16,515	17,053	15,499	13,187	11,207
Cap. Exp.	1,198	1,344	1,417	1,183	1,414	1,608	1,931	2,228	2,066	1,959
Cash Flow	3,089	3,198	3,520	2,421	2,159	1,758	2,370	2,674	3,522	3,386
Curr. Ratio	1.2	1.6	1.9	1.3	1.4	1.3	1.3	1.4	1.1	1.5
% LT Debt of Cap.	31.7	15.0	31.7	31.8	35.2	37.5	35.6	33.6	29.2	29.8
% Net Inc.of Revs.	9.0	9.5	10.3	4.7	3.6	1.5	5.0	7.0	14.1	14.4
% Ret. on Assets	7.4	7.9	8.3	5.6	2.5	1.1	3.9	6.0	13.1	16.0
% Ret. on Equity	23.1	24.8	26.7	11.4	7.9	3.1	10.3	16.5	33.0	37.5

Data as orig. reptd.; bef. results of disc. opers. and/or spec. items. Per share data adj. for stk. divs. as of ex-div. date. Bold denotes diluted EPS (FASB 128). E-Estimated. NA-Not Available. NM-Not Meaningful. NR-Not Ranked.

Registrar—Boston EquiServe. **Office**—2030 Dow Center, Midland, MI 48674. **Tel**—(517) 636-1000. **Website**—http://www.dow.com **Chrmn**—F. P. Popoff. **Pres & CEO**—W. S. Stavropoulos. **EVP & CFO**—J. P. Reinhard. **Secy**—J. Scriven. **Investor Contact**—Teri S. LeBeau. **Dirs**—A. A. Allemang, J. K. Barton, D. T. Buzzelli, A. J. Carbone, F. P. Corson, J. C. Danforth, W. D. Davis, M. L. Dow, J. L. Downey, E. C. Falla, B. H. Franklin, A. D. Gilmour, M. D. Parker, F. P. Popoff, J. P. Reinhard, H. T. Shapiro, W. S. Stavropoulos, P. G. Stern. **Transfer Agent & Registrar**—Boston EquiServe, Boston. **Incorporated**—in Delaware in 1947. **Empl**— 42,900. **S&P Analyst:** Richard O'Reilly, CFA

12-SEP-98

Industry: Publishing

Summary: Dow Jones publishes The Wall Street Journal and Barron's, provides newswire, news retrieval and financial information services, and publishes general circulation newspapers.

S&P Opinion: Hold (★★★)	Recent Price • 48½ Yield • 2.0% 52 Wk Range • 59-42¾ 12-Mo. P/E • NM

Quantitative Evaluations

Outlook
(1 Lowest—5 Highest)
• **1⁻**

Fair Value
• **31**

Risk
• **Average**

Earn./Div. Rank
• **B+**

Technical Eval.
• **Bullish** since 3/98

Rel. Strength Rank
(1 Lowest—99 Highest)
• **70**

Insider Activity
• **Unfavorable**

Earnings vs. Previous Year
▲=Up ▼=Down ▶=No Change

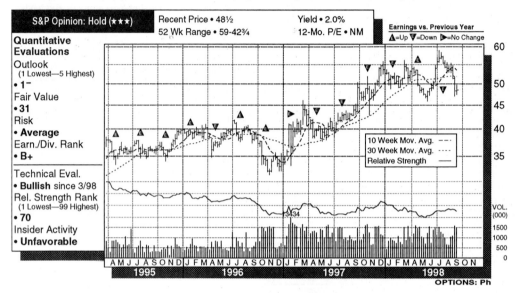

10 Week Mov. Avg. ---
30 Week Mov. Avg. ···
Relative Strength —

OPTIONS: Ph

Overview - 30-JUL-98

Revenue growth through 1998 at the company's publishing operations will reflect higher advertising rates and some improvement in linage anticipated at the newspapers, as well as modest gains in circulation revenue. Rising newsprint costs will put some pressure on profit margins. Revenues and operating profits from electronic information services will no longer be negatively affected by the troubled Telerate unit, which was sold in May 1998. Dow Jones incurred a $98 million loss on the sale in addition to 1998 operating losses of $23.3 million. On a pro forma basis, excluding Telerate, Q2 EPS was $0.56 and first half EPS was $1.07. EPS should approximate $2.08 before such charges in 1998. We are tentatively projecting EPS of $2.30 in 1999.

Valuation - 30-JUL-98

On May 30, 1998, DJ completed the previously announced sale of Dow Jones Markets (DJM) to Bridge Information Systems for $510 million in cash and convertible stock. The sale of money-losing DJM (formerly Telerate) allows management to concentrate its energies and resources on the profitable publishing and financial information businesses. Although the sale resulted in substantial charges to 1998 earnings, the market's valuation of the now-liberated Dow Jones reflects the generally favorable prospects for its continuing operations. Notwithstanding cyclical fluctuations in business conditions and paper prices, the publishing and information segments should enjoy healthy long-term growth. Thus, while the shares of Dow Jones are still richly valued based on improved earnings prospects going forward, the shares remain an attractive investment for long-term value investors.

Key Stock Statistics

S&P EPS Est. 1998	2.08	Tang. Bk. Value/Share	5.07
P/E on S&P Est. 1998	23.3	Beta	0.74
S&P EPS Est. 1999	2.30	Shareholders	17,300
Dividend Rate/Share	0.96	Market cap. (B)	$ 3.5
Shs. outstg. (M)	93.7	Inst. holdings	58%
Avg. daily vol. (M)	0.312		

Value of $10,000 invested 5 years ago: $ 20,499

Fiscal Year Ending Dec. 31

	1998	1997	1996	1995	1994	1993
Revenues (Million $)						
1Q	621.5	606.0	584.8	545.4	499.2	463.0
2Q	601.1	640.7	630.6	577.0	524.1	487.0
3Q	—	636.3	594.9	549.3	501.0	468.7
4Q	—	689.5	671.3	612.1	566.6	512.6
Yr.	—	2,573	2,482	2,284	2,091	1,932
Earnings Per Share ($)						
1Q	**0.35**	**0.26**	0.39	0.48	0.43	0.31
2Q	**-0.54**	**0.36**	0.54	0.51	0.46	0.40
3Q	—	**0.28**	0.42	0.35	0.34	0.30
4Q	—	**-9.22**	0.62	0.62	0.60	0.47
Yr.	—	**-8.36**	1.96	1.96	1.83	1.48

Next earnings report expected: early October

Dividend Data (Dividends have been paid since 1906.)

Amount ($)	Date Decl.	Ex-Div. Date	Stock of Record	Payment Date
0.240	Oct. 15	Oct. 30	Nov. 03	Dec. 01 '97
0.240	Jan. 21	Jan. 29	Feb. 02	Mar. 02 '98
0.240	Apr. 16	Apr. 29	May. 01	Jun. 01 '98
0.240	Jun. 17	Sep. 02	Aug. 03	Sep. 01 '98

A Division of The McGraw-Hill Companies

Business Summary - 30-JUL-98

Dow Jones & Co., a venerable name in its own right, is the parent of two equally venerable publications -- The Wall Street Journal, and Barron's National Business and Financial Weekly. In addition, the company provides information services and publishes general circulation newspapers. International operations accounted for 27% of consolidated revenues and 84% of the operating loss in 1997.

On May 30, 1998, DJ completed the previously announced sale of unprofitable Dow Jones Markets (formerly Telerate) to Bridge Information Systems for $360 million cash and $150 million in five-year, 4% preferred stock of Bridge, which is convertible into 10% of Bridge's common equity. Dow Jones Markets (DJM) is a major supplier of computerized financial information and transaction systems and services to financial professionals. DJ incurred a $98 million loss on the sale in addition to 1998 operating losses of $23.3 million through the date of sale. In 1997, DJ incurred substantial charges totaling $1.03 billion related to the writedown of DJM's carrying value to $550 million, from $1.4 billion, as well as other restructuring charges.

The Wall Street Journal, a financial and business daily, is the largest-circulation daily newspaper in the U.S. In March 1998, The Wall Street Journal added a "Week-

end" section on Fridays. In September 1997, the Journal began publishing daily television listings as an advertising page in the Marketplace section. An advertiser-sponsored Sports USA listing was added on Fridays, and paid listings under the banner "Theatre USA" now appear on Wednesdays. The moves were made to widen circulation appeal and add new sources of advertising. DJ also publishes two international editions -- The Asian Wall Street Journal, with year-end 1997 circulation of over 56,000 daily, and The Wall Street Journal/Europe, with daily circulation of over 66,000 in 1997 -- and The Wall Street Journal Interactive Edition. The company publishes Barron's, a weekly magazine covering business and finance, and several other periodicals including the Dow Jones Business and Financial Weekly, and SmartMoney magazine in partnership with Hearst Corp.

Information services include newswires, index services, radio and TV programming, and interactive services, including Dow Jones Interactive, which provides users with online access to the contents of over 5,000 publications, including 1,200 non-U.S. sources.

Ottaway Newspapers publishes 19 daily and 17 weekly community newspapers. Total circulation is more than 725,000. DJ also holds equity or other interests in international business and financial wire services, newspapers, and other publications.

Per Share Data ($)

(Year Ended Dec. 31)	1997	1996	1995	1994	1993	1992	1991	1990	1989	1988
Tangible Bk. Val.	4.07	3.89	3.01	1.83	1.45	0.58	0.14	-0.37	-1.04	1.95
Cash Flow	-5.74	4.22	4.08	3.90	3.37	2.94	2.53	2.91	4.72	3.79
Earnings	-8.36	1.96	1.96	1.83	1.48	1.17	0.71	1.06	3.15	2.35
Dividends	0.96	0.96	0.92	0.84	0.80	0.76	0.76	0.76	0.72	0.68
Payout Ratio	NM	49%	47%	46%	54%	65%	106%	72%	23%	29%
Prices - High	55⅞	41⅞	40⅛	41⅞	39	35⅜	30⅝	33¾	42½	36½
- Low	33⅜	31⅞	30⅝	28⅛	26¾	24½	21⅝	18⅛	29¼	26¾
P/E Ratio - High	NM	21	20	23	26	30	43	32	13	16
- Low	NM	16	16	15	18	21	30	17	9	11

Income Statement Analysis (Million $)

	1997	1996	1995	1994	1993	1992	1991	1990	1989	1988
Revs.	2,573	2,482	2,284	2,091	1,932	1,818	1,725	1,720	1,688	1,603
Oper. Inc.	510	555	510	564	505	460	424	415	494	492
Depr.	251	218	206	205	189	179	183	186	158	140
Int. Exp.	19.4	18.8	18.3	16.9	22.6	30.4	41.2	55.5	20.7	28.6
Pretax Inc.	-763	331	323	339	286	234	159	182	561	449
Eff. Tax Rate	NM	45%	43%	47%	49%	50%	55%	41%	40%	41%
Net Inc.	-801	190	190	181	148	118	72.0	107	317	228

Balance Sheet & Other Fin. Data (Million $)

	1997	1996	1995	1994	1993	1992	1991	1990	1989	1988
Cash	23.8	6.8	14.0	11.0	6.0	16.0	36.0	18.0	46.0	61.0
Curr. Assets	507	404	371	310	268	249	272	248	269	265
Total Assets	1,920	2,760	2,599	2,446	2,350	2,372	2,471	2,591	2,688	2,112
Curr. Liab.	672	601	582	531	471	462	457	404	411	402
LT Debt	229	332	254	296	261	335	448	608	719	290
Common Eqty.	781	1,644	1,602	1,482	1,493	1,449	1,436	1,435	1,405	1,161
Total Cap.	1,010	1,976	1,856	1,777	1,759	1,798	1,963	2,143	2,238	1,674
Cap. Exp.	348	232	219	222	161	126	106	123	175	184
Cash Flow	-550	408	396	386	336	298	255	293	475	368
Curr. Ratio	0.8	0.7	0.6	0.6	0.6	0.5	0.6	0.6	0.7	0.7
% LT Debt of Cap.	22.7	16.8	13.7	16.6	14.8	18.6	22.8	28.4	32.1	17.3
% Net Inc.of Revs.	NM	7.7	8.3	8.7	7.6	6.5	4.2	6.2	18.8	14.2
% Ret. on Assets	NM	7.1	7.5	7.7	6.3	4.9	2.8	4.0	13.2	11.0
% Ret. on Equity	NM	11.7	12.3	12.4	10.1	8.2	5.0	7.5	24.7	22.3

Data as orig. reptd.; bef. results of disc. opers. and/or spec. items. Per share data adj. for stk. divs. as of ex-div. date. Bold denotes diluted EPS (FASB 128). E-Estimated. NA-Not Available. NM-Not Meaningful. NR-Not Ranked.

Office—200 Liberty St., New York, NY 10281. **Tel**—(212) 416-2000. **Website**—http://www.dowjones.com **Chrmn & CEO**—P. R. Kann. **Pres & COO**—K. L. Burenga. **SVP & Secy**—P. G. Skinner. **VP-Fin & CFO**—K. J. Roche. **Investor Contact**— Jan Abernathy. **Dirs**—R. V. Araskog, C. Bancroft, K. L. Burenga, W. C. Cox, Jr., H. Golub, L. Hill, I. O. Hockaday, Jr., V. E. Jordan, Jr., P. R. Kann, D. K. P. Li, J. C. MacElree, F. N. Newman, J. A. Ottaway, Jr., J. Q. Riordan, W. C. Steere, Jr.**Transfer Agent & Registrar**—ChaseMellon Shareholder Services, L.L.C., Ridgefield Park, NJ. **Incorporated**—in Delaware in 1949. **Empl**— 12,309. **S&P Analyst:** William H. Donald

12-SEP-98

Industry:
Oil & Gas (Drilling &
Equipment)

Summary: Dresser supplies products and services primarily to the oil
and natural gas exploration and refined product manufacturing industries.

| S&P Opinion: Hold (★★★) | Recent Price • 32 | Yield • 2.4% |
| | 52 Wk Range • 55⅛-25 | 12-Mo. P/E • 15.1 |

**Quantitative
Evaluations**

Outlook
(1 Lowest—5 Highest)
• 2

Fair Value
• 28%

Risk
• Average

Earn./Div. Rank
• B+

Technical Eval.
• Bearish since 3/98

Rel. Strength Rank
(1 Lowest—99 Highest)
• 69

Insider Activity
• NA

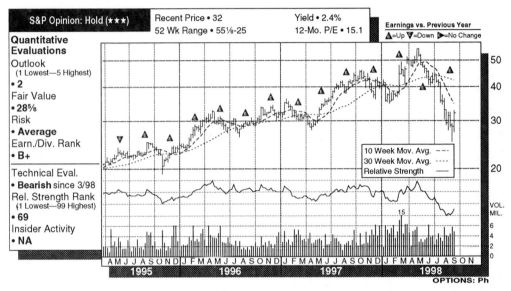

Earnings vs. Previous Year
▲=Up ▼=Down ▶=No Change

10 Week Mov. Avg. ---
30 Week Mov. Avg. ----
Relative Strength ——

VOL.
MIL.

1995　1996　1997　1998

OPTIONS: Ph

Overview - 11-JUN-98

DI recently announced an agreement to be acquired by
Halliburton. This will create the world's largest oil services company, with an unparalleled range of product
and services offerings. Earnings should continue to rise
in FY 98 (Oct.) and beyond, as a result of increased
market penetration for a number of new products, despite sluggish commodity prices. A pick-up in West African and Gulf of Mexico exploration activities will be the
major contributor to cash flow and earnings growth,
which remain impressive. Important product lines, such
as directional drilling and measurement-while-drilling,
provide access to high-growth segments in the upstream sector. Growing backlogs, which reached $5.8
billion at the end of FY 97, will flow to the bottom line in
1998 and 1999, and with still-healthy U.S. natural gas
prices and robust demand sparking a surge in gas drilling activity, bookings are expected to remain strong.

Valuation - 11-JUN-98

The shares surged in February 1998 on the announcement of the acquisition by Halliburton, but have since
fallen off, amid a general weakness in oil services providers' shares, and were recently up 3.7% in 1998. The
sustained slump in oil prices has raised fears of an industrywide cutback in exploration and production capital
expenditures, which would negatively affect the earnings of oil services companies such as Dresser. However, natural gas fundamentals still appear positive, and
a continued upturn in refining margins expected in 1998
should provide a lift, with wider margins likely to translate into increased demand for oil pumps and valves.
The opening of Latin American, West African and Far
East markets to oil and natural gas exploration offers
positive long-term benefits for the Dresser-Halliburton
combination.

Key Stock Statistics

S&P EPS Est. 1998	2.05	Tang. Bk. Value/Share	5.44
P/E on S&P Est. 1998	15.6	Beta	1.42
Dividend Rate/Share	0.76	Shareholders	20,000
Shs. outstg. (M)	175.8	Market cap. (B)	$ 5.6
Avg. daily vol. (M)	0.968	Inst. holdings	68%

Value of $10,000 invested 5 years ago: $ 20,609

Fiscal Year Ending Oct. 31

	1998	1997	1996	1995	1994	1993
Revenues (Million $)						
1Q	1,736	1,705	1,463	1,300	1,396	924.0
2Q	2,008	1,771	1,630	1,261	1,325	1,067
3Q	2,106	1,872	1,638	1,437	1,194	1,065
4Q	—	2,110	1,831	1,630	1,416	1,160
Yr.	—	7,458	6,562	5,629	5,331	4,216
Earnings Per Share ($)						
1Q	**0.35**	0.30	0.26	0.21	1.08	0.14
2Q	**0.53**	0.42	0.31	0.25	0.29	0.02
3Q	**0.61**	0.47	0.38	0.25	0.21	0.26
4Q	—	0.62	0.49	0.46	0.40	0.50
Yr.	**E2.05**	1.81	1.44	1.17	1.98	0.92

Next earnings report expected: early December

Dividend Data (Dividends have been paid since 1948.)

Amount ($)	Date Decl.	Ex-Div. Date	Stock of Record	Payment Date
0.190	Nov. 20	Nov. 26	Dec. 01	Dec. 22 '97
0.190	Jan. 15	Feb. 26	Mar. 02	Mar. 20 '98
0.190	May. 06	May. 28	Jun. 01	Jun. 22 '98
0.190	Aug. 21	Aug. 28	Sep. 01	Sep. 21 '98

A Division of The McGraw-Hill Companies

Business Summary - 11-JUN-98

Formed by Solomon R. Dresser nearly 120 years ago in the oil boom town of Bradford, PA, Dresser Industries (DI) has grown into a multibillion-dollar industrial giant. In February 1998, the company announced that it has agreed to be acquired by fellow oil services industry stalwart Halliburton Co. (HAL) in a transaction that will create the world's largest oil services concern, with $17 billion in annual revenues, and 100,000 employees. Under terms of the transaction, expected to close in late 1998, Dresser shareholders will receive one HAL share for each DI common share. The combined company will operate under the Halliburton name.

Dresser's three main operating divisions are petroleum products and services, engineering services and energy equipment. Segment revenue and operating profit contributions in FY 97 (Oct.) were:

	Revs.	Profits
Petroleum products & services	36%	46%
Engineering services	26%	15%
Energy equipment	38%	39%

The petroleum products and services segment provides a broad range of products and technical services for oil and gas well exploration, development, production and drilling. Major operating units include Sperry-Sun, which provides directional and measure-ment-while-drilling services and equipment; Security, which makes drill bits, including polycrystalline diamond cutter (PDC) and natural diamond drill bits; Baroid, a supplier of drilling fluids used primarily to lubricate and cool the drill bit and facilitate the removal of cuttings; Wheatley TXT Corp., a maker of pumps, valves and metering equipment; and Bredero-Shaw, an international pipecoating operation.

The engineering segment, consisting of the operations of the M.W. Kellogg subsidiary, participates in the design and construction of facilities used by all segments of the hydrocarbon industry. M.W. Kellogg's largest markets, based on contribution to revenue, are petrochemicals and refining. Other major markets include oil and gas, liquid natural gas (LNG) and fertilizers.

The energy equipment segment makes electrical generator systems, turbines, compressors, valves and controls, pumps, power systems, and measure and control devices. The Dresser-Rand unit, 51% owned, makes compressors, electric motors and turbines; 49%-owned Ingersoll-Dresser makes pumps. Dresser's Wayne division manufactures and markets fully integrated vehicle fueling systems for the retail petroleum industry, including gasoline pumps and dispensers and point-of-sale credit and debit card machines. Thus, through its three major operating divisions, Dresser Industries is truly involved in every segment of the petroleum industry, from the wellhead to the gas tank.

Per Share Data ($)

(Year Ended Oct. 31)	1997	1996	1995	1994	1993	1992	1991	1990	1989	1988
Tangible Bk. Val.	5.29	4.05	4.45	5.30	2.77	4.17	10.45	10.43	10.03	9.32
Cash Flow	3.26	2.73	2.30	3.16	2.08	1.24	1.80	1.96	1.89	1.59
Earnings	1.81	1.44	1.17	1.98	0.92	0.52	1.04	1.29	1.21	0.89
Dividends	0.70	0.68	0.68	0.68	0.60	0.60	0.60	0.55	0.45	0.28
Payout Ratio	39%	47%	58%	34%	65%	115%	58%	43%	37%	30%
Prices - High	$46\frac{1}{8}$	$34\frac{3}{8}$	$25\frac{1}{8}$	$24\frac{7}{8}$	$25\frac{3}{8}$	$23\frac{5}{8}$	$28\frac{1}{2}$	$28\frac{1}{8}$	24	$17\frac{7}{8}$
- Low	$27\frac{3}{4}$	$23\frac{1}{4}$	$18\frac{1}{2}$	$18\frac{1}{2}$	$17\frac{1}{4}$	$17\frac{1}{4}$	$16\frac{1}{4}$	$16\frac{1}{2}$	$14\frac{1}{2}$	$11\frac{1}{4}$
P/E Ratio - High	25	24	21	13	28	45	27	22	20	20
- Low	15	16	16	9	19	33	16	13	12	13

Income Statement Analysis (Million $)

	1997	1996	1995	1994	1993	1992	1991	1990	1989	1988
Revs.	7,419	6,533	5,613	5,307	4,216	3,797	4,670	4,480	3,982	3,942
Oper. Inc.	824	687	552	555	391	214	298	292	288	248
Depr.	255	230	207	216	159	99	101	92.0	91.0	97.0
Int. Exp.	68.6	60.5	47.4	49.3	27.4	29.7	39.4	39.4	46.4	46.6
Pretax Inc.	547	427	342	619	251	144	239	280	259	193
Eff. Tax Rate	35%	34%	32%	36%	33%	45%	36%	34%	34%	33%
Net Inc.	318	258	213	362	127	70.0	140	174	163	123

Balance Sheet & Other Fin. Data (Million $)

	1997	1996	1995	1994	1993	1992	1991	1990	1989	1988
Cash	163	232	249	515	239	155	285	361	455	188
Curr. Assets	2,472	2,470	2,201	2,197	1,615	1,407	1,608	1,757	1,766	1,647
Total Assets	5,099	5,150	4,707	4,324	3,642	3,188	3,251	3,309	3,056	2,899
Curr. Liab.	1,687	1,862	1,712	1,367	1,433	1,318	1,063	1,099	972	928
LT Debt	758	756	460	461	308	25.0	222	232	238	255
Common Eqty.	1,732	1,582	1,657	1,632	944	949	1,761	1,764	1,608	1,505
Total Cap.	2,490	2,494	2,195	2,177	1,403	1,125	2,087	2,094	1,927	1,838
Cap. Exp.	303	335	288	187	140	89.0	147	124	80.0	63.0
Cash Flow	573	488	420	578	285	169	241	266	255	220
Curr. Ratio	1.5	1.3	1.3	1.6	1.1	1.1	1.5	1.6	1.8	1.8
% LT Debt of Cap.	30.4	30.3	20.9	21.2	22.0	2.2	10.7	11.1	12.4	13.9
% Net Inc.of Revs.	4.3	3.9	3.8	6.8	3.0	1.8	3.0	3.9	4.1	3.1
% Ret. on Assets	6.2	5.2	4.7	7.9	3.7	2.2	4.3	5.5	5.5	4.4
% Ret. on Equity	19.2	15.9	13.0	25.0	13.4	5.1	8.0	10.3	10.5	8.3

Data as orig. reptd.; bef. results of disc. opers. and/or spec. items. Per share data adj. for stk. divs. as of ex-div. date. Bold denotes diluted EPS (FASB 128). E-Estimated. NA-Not Available. NM-Not Meaningful. NR-Not Ranked.

Office—2001 Ross Ave., Dallas, TX 75201. **Tel**—(214) 740-6000. **Chrmn & CEO**— W. E. Bradford. **Pres & COO**— D. C. Vaughn. **SVP & CFO**—G. H. Juetten. **VP & Secy**—R. Morris. **Investor Contact**—Donald R. Galletly (214-740-6757). **Dirs**—W. E. Bradford, S. B. Casey Jr., L. S. Eagleburger, S. A. Earle, R. Fulgham, J. A. Gavin, R. L. Hunt, J. L. Martin, L. H. Olmer, J. A. Precourt, D. C. Vaughn, R. W. Vieser. **Transfer Agent & Registrar**—The Bank of New York, NYC. **Incorporated**—in Delaware in 1956. **Empl**— 31,300. **S&P Analyst:** Norman Rosenberg

DTE Energy

711R
NYSE Symbol DTE
In S&P 500

12-SEP-98

Industry:
Electric Companies

Summary: This electric utility serves southeastern Michigan, an area that contains 20% of U.S. automakers and many other heavy industrial producers.

S&P Opinion: Hold (★★★)

Recent Price • 42⅞
52 Wk Range • 43⅝-28

Yield • 4.9%
12-Mo. P/E • 13.2

Quantitative Evaluations

Outlook
(1 Lowest—5 Highest)
• **2**

Fair Value
• **42¼**

Risk
• **Low**

Earn./Div. Rank
• **A-**

Technical Eval.
• **Neutral** since 6/98

Rel. Strength Rank
(1 Lowest—99 Highest)
• **95**

Insider Activity
• **Neutral**

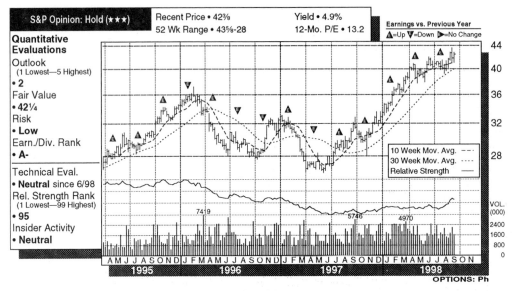

Earnings vs. Previous Year
▲=Up ▼=Down ▶=No Change

10 Week Mov. Avg. ---
30 Week Mov. Avg. ·····
Relative Strength —

OPTIONS: Ph

Overview - 20-AUG-98

Following mid-single-digit growth in 1998, EPS should see only low single-digit growth in 1999. As Michigan moves toward restructuring legislation (which will not take place until after the November elections), DTE is working for the passage of its revised consumer choice plan, which would involve a gradual five-stage phase-in to full competition in 2002. We expect kwh sales to increase only fractionally in 1999. Long-term contracts that reduce rates to automakers and other industrial customers secure more than 20% of DTE's kwh sales through 2004. While the lower rates will reduce revenues, the contracts will provide a certain stability to earnings. Still, DTE's primary growth will come from non-regulated businesses, which could account for 20% of earnings by 2000, with Edison Energy Services (which is involved in capital intensive projects for large industrial and institutional customers) contributing about two-thirds of the increase.

Valuation - 20-AUG-98

We would continue to hold DTE stock. After rising only 7.1% in 1997 (compared with a 19.8% gain for the S&P Index of Electric Companies), the shares are up about 18.7% year to date (versus a 4.1% increase for its industry peers). For the near term, we expect EPS gains to be relatively modest. Longer term, earnings growth will come from continued cost reduction, and from the non-regulated businesses. DTE intends to cut its debt level, now at 51% of total capital, to 48%. Dividend growth, however, will be restricted by a high level of planned retirements and internally funded capital projects. While the shares seem fairly valued at a P/E of 13X our 1999 EPS estimate of $3.10, a dividend yield of 5.0% makes it a solid long-term holding for income-oriented investors.

Key Stock Statistics

S&P EPS Est. 1998	3.05	Tang. Bk. Value/Share	24.92
P/E on S&P Est. 1998	13.9	Beta	0.38
S&P EPS Est. 1999	3.10	Shareholders	132,800
Dividend Rate/Share	2.06	Market cap. (B)	$ 6.2
Shs. outstg. (M)	145.1	Inst. holdings	49%
Avg. daily vol. (M)	0.360		

Value of $10,000 invested 5 years ago: $ 18,693

Fiscal Year Ending Dec. 31

	1998	1997	1996	1995	1994	1993
Revenues (Million $)						
1Q	945.0	868.6	909.6	880.3	899.6	874.9
2Q	1,064	892.3	871.3	856.0	872.7	835.2
3Q	—	1,030	977.3	1,032	944.4	976.3
4Q	—	973.9	887.2	867.0	802.7	869.0
Yr.	—	3,764	3,645	3,636	3,519	3,555
Earnings Per Share ($)						
1Q	**0.72**	**0.49**	0.75	0.73	0.72	0.86
2Q	**0.69**	**0.59**	0.54	0.58	0.54	0.64
3Q	**E0.90**	**0.91**	0.31	0.98	0.80	0.99
4Q	**E0.74**	**0.89**	0.54	0.51	0.61	0.84
Yr.	**E3.05**	**2.88**	2.13	2.80	2.67	3.34

Next earnings report expected: late October

Dividend Data (Dividends have been paid since 1909.)

Amount ($)	Date Decl.	Ex-Div. Date	Stock of Record	Payment Date
0.515	Nov. 24	Dec. 17	Dec. 19	Jan. 15 '98
0.515	Feb. 23	Mar. 18	Mar. 20	Apr. 15 '98
0.515	May. 27	Jun. 18	Jun. 22	Jul. 15 '98
0.515	Jul. 21	Sep. 17	Sep. 21	Oct. 15 '98

A Division of The McGraw·Hill Companies

Business Summary - 20-AUG-98

Formed on January 1, 1996, DTE Energy is the holding company for Detroit Edison Co., the largest electric utility in Michigan, serving some two million customers in the southeastern part of the state.

Revenues by customer class in recent years were:

	1997	1996	1995
Residential	31.3%	32.9%	33.3%
Commercial	39.9%	41.3%	41.1%
Industrial	19.3%	20.0%	20.0%
Other	6.7%	5.7%	5.5%
Non-regulated	2.8%	0.1%	0.1%

DTE owns and operates a coal-transshipment facility in Superior, WI, that delivers low sulphur Western coal to Detroit Edison and other utility and industrial customers. Sources of electric energy in 1997 were coal and other fossil fuel, 78.3% (80.9% in 1996), nuclear 10.3% (9.2%) and purchased power 11.4% (9.9%).

In 1997, sales to automotive and auto-related customers accounted for about 10% of Detroit Edison's operating revenues. In 1995, DTE obtained special contracts that will secure automakers' business within its service area through 2004, in exchange for annual rate reductions of $30 to $50 million.

In its non-regulated businesses, DTE develops and owns capital-intensive energy projects for large industrial and institutional customers. The company also offers industrial and utility clients a variety of specialty engineering services as well as project management for customers building, expanding or renovating their high-voltage electrical distribution systems. Other businesses include the operation of landfill gas-to-energy facilities, providing its expertise in the application of new energy technologies, power marketing, real estate development and the retail marketing of energy and communications convenience products.

The company has engaged in extensive debt refinancing in recent years and expects to continue to refinance its higher-cost debt and equity securities.

The Fermi 2 nuclear power plant was returned to operation in early May 1997. The plant had been shut down in January 1997 for an inspection of the generator after the failure of an electrical component in the switchyard outside the plant.

In January 1998, the Michigan Public Service Commission (MPSC) adopted a phase-in schedule that would enable Michigan customers to select their electricity suppliers as early as 1998, with full customer choice provided by 2002. The MPSC also estimated DTE's stranded costs at $2.48 billion, which could potentially be recovered through the use of a transition surcharge.

Per Share Data ($)

(Year Ended Dec. 31)	1997	1996	1995	1994	1993	1992	1991	1990	1989	1988
Tangible Bk. Val.	24.55	23.41	23.40	22.66	21.24	20.78	18.96	17.19	15.79	14.87
Earnings	2.88	2.13	2.80	2.67	3.34	3.79	3.64	3.26	2.65	-1.95
Dividends	2.06	2.06	2.06	2.06	2.06	1.98	1.88	1.78	1.68	1.68
Payout Ratio	72%	97%	74%	77%	62%	52%	52%	55%	63%	NM
Prices - High	34³/₄	37¹/₄	34⁷/₈	30¹/₄	37¹/₈	35¹/₄	35³/₈	30¹/₄	25⁷/₈	17¹/₂
- Low	26¹/₈	27⁵/₈	25³/₄	24¹/₄	29⁷/₈	30¹/₄	27³/₄	23¹/₂	17¹/₂	12
P/E Ratio - High	12	17	12	11	11	9	10	9	10	NM
- Low	9	13	9	9	9	8	8	7	6	NM

Income Statement Analysis (Million $)

	1997	1996	1995	1994	1993	1992	1991	1990	1989	1988
Revs.	3,764	3,645	3,635	3,519	3,555	3,558	3,592	3,307	3,203	3,102
Depr.	660	527	501	476	433	423	412	406	365	325
Maint.	Nil	278	240	262	251	263	290	280	291	276
Fxd. Chgs. Cov.	3.2	3.2	3.2	3.0	3.1	3.0	2.7	2.4	2.1	0.2
Constr. Credits	Nil	5.4	3.7	3.7	3.0	3.0	4.0	3.0	4.0	5.0
Eff. Tax Rate	38%	42%	41%	39%	37%	35%	32%	30%	26%	NM
Net Inc.	417	309	406	420	522	588	568	514	426	-234

Balance Sheet & Other Fin. Data (Million $)

	1997	1996	1995	1994	1993	1992	1991	1990	1989	1988
Gross Prop.	14,495	13,777	13,304	13,046	12,717	13,223	12,791	12,487	11,700	11,406
Cap. Exp.	456	531	454	378	399	416	272	230	243	235
Net Prop.	8,934	8,501	8,519	8,586	8,651	9,014	8,992	9,053	8,678	8,770
Capitalization:										
LT Debt	3,914	3,895	3,756	3,951	3,972	4,129	4,388	5,050	4,692	4,378
% LT Debt	51	52	50	53	52	55	58	63	63	62
Pfd.	144	144	327	380	381	334	353	376	399	416
% Pfd.	1.80	1.90	4.30	5.00	5.00	4.40	4.70	4.70	5.30	5.90
Common	3,562	3,444	3,436	3,326	3,296	3,114	2,848	2,588	2,370	2,227
% Common	47	46	46	44	43	41	38	32	32	32
Total Cap.	9,904	9,822	9,902	10,019	9,994	9,265	9,202	9,525	8,860	8,329
% Oper. Ratio	80.2	79.1	79.7	79.6	76.3	73.2	74.0	73.4	76.6	76.5
% Earn. on Net Prop.	8.4	7.2	8.6	8.3	9.8	10.6	10.3	9.9	8.6	7.7
% Return On Revs.	11.1	8.5	11.2	11.9	14.7	16.5	15.8	15.6	13.3	NM
% Return On Invest. Capital	9.9	6.2	7.4	7.1	9.0	10.7	10.8	10.8	10.4	2.7
% Return On Com. Equity	11.9	8.9	12.0	11.8	15.2	18.6	19.5	19.1	16.8	NM

Data as orig. reptd.; bef. results of disc opers. and/or spec. items. Per share data adj. for stk. divs. as of ex-div. date. Bold denotes diluted EPS (FASB 128). E-Estimated. NA-Not Available. NM-Not Meaningful. NR-Not Ranked.

Office—2000 Second Ave., Detroit, MI 48226-1279. **Tel**—(313) 235-4000. **Website**—http://www.detroitedison.com. **Chrmn, Pres, CEO & COO**—A. F. Earley, Jr.**EVP & CFO**—L. G. Garberding. **Secy**—S. M. Beale.**Investor Contacts**—Lisa Consiglio/Susan Hennessey (313-235-8030). **Dirs**—T. E. Adderley, L. Bauder, D. Bing, W. C. Brooks, A. F. Earley, Jr., L. G. Garberding, A. D. Gilmour, T. S. Leipprandt, J. E. Lobbia, E. A. Miller, D. E. Richardson, A. E. Schwartz, W. Wegner. **Transfer Agent & Registrar**—Co.'s office. **Incorporated**—in New York in 1903; reincorporated in Michigan in 1967.**Empl**— 8,732. **S&P Analyst:** Justin McCann

STANDARD &POOR'S
STOCK REPORTS

Duke Energy

779

NYSE Symbol **DUK**

In S&P 500

12-SEP-98

Industry: Electric Companies

Summary: DUK provides electric service to 1.8 million customers in North and South Carolina, and is one of the largest U.S. transporters and marketers of natural gas.

S&P Opinion: Accumulate (★★★★)	Recent Price • 64⅜	Yield • 3.4%
	52 Wk Range • 64⅜-44½	12-Mo. P/E • 22.4

Quantitative Evaluations

Outlook (1 Lowest—5 Highest)
• **2**

Fair Value
• **61**

Risk
• **Low**

Earn./Div. Rank
• **A-**

Technical Eval.
• **Bullish** since 6/97

Rel. Strength Rank (1 Lowest—99 Highest)
• **97**

Insider Activity
• **Neutral**

Earnings vs. Previous Year
▲=Up ▼=Down ▶=No Change

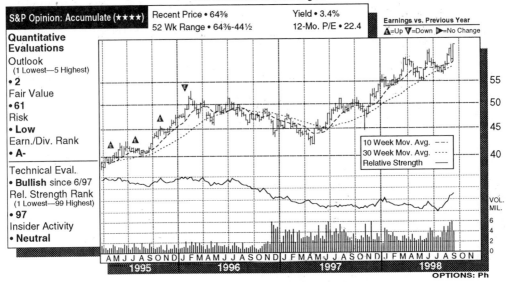

10 Week Mov. Avg. — — —
30 Week Mov. Avg. - - - -
Relative Strength ——

VOL. MIL.

OPTIONS: Ph

Overview - 12-AUG-98

Aided by the hot summer weather, EPS in 1998 should advance more than 35% from 1997's EPS, which was hurt by costs related to the June 1997 merger with Pan Energy. As a result of the merger, which is expected to become accretive around mid-1999, DUK is now the third largest marketer of natural gas in North America; the fourth largest natural gas liquids producer in the U.S.; the owner of a network of more than 22,000 miles of interstate natural gas pipeline; and one of the largest and lowest-cost U.S. electric utilities. DUK should continue to benefit from expansion into non-regulated businesses. The acquisition of three generating plants from PG&E Corp. will enhance its operations in the California power market, while its acquisition of PG&E's Queensland State Gas Pipeline will provide electric generation opportunities in Australia.

Valuation - 12-AUG-98

We would continue to accumulate DUK stock. The shares are up 4.5% year to date, compared with a 2.7% increase for the S&P Index of Electric Companies and a 1.4% decline in the S&P Index of Natural Gas Companies. In 1997, the shares rose 19.7%, roughly matching the 19.8% and 18.6% increases for the respective electric and gas indexes. However, after the sharp drop that followed the November 1996 announcement of the planned merger with PanEnergy (reflecting its dilutive impact), the stock has gained more than 38% since bottoming in the 1997 second quarter. In the merger, Duke issued about $7.7 billion in stock to PanEnergy shareholders, and there was an approximate $200 million increase in annual dividends. While the merger will not be accretive until the second half of 1999, we believe that it is already providing significant competitive advantages in an increasingly integrated energy market.

Key Stock Statistics

S&P EPS Est. 1998	3.45	Tang. Bk. Value/Share	19.67
P/E on S&P Est. 1998	18.7	Beta	0.23
S&P EPS Est. 1999	3.70	Shareholders	130,700
Dividend Rate/Share	2.20	Market cap. (B)	$ 23.2
Shs. outstg. (M)	361.1	Inst. holdings	49%
Avg. daily vol. (M)	1.086		

Value of $10,000 invested 5 years ago: $ 22,666

Fiscal Year Ending Dec. 31

	1998	1997	1996	1995	1994	1993
Revenues (Million $)						
1Q	4,115	3,786	—	1,111	1,099	1,008
2Q	4,014	3,113	—	1,052	1,083	987.0
3Q	—	4,821	—	1,380	1,273	1,290
4Q	—	4,590	—	1,133	1,034	996.9
Yr.	—	16,309	4,758	4,677	4,489	4,282
Earnings Per Share ($)						
1Q	0.87	0.84	—	0.92	0.79	0.63
2Q	0.76	0.43	—	0.61	0.56	0.53
3Q	E1.15	0.83	—	1.33	1.13	1.12
4Q	E0.67	0.41	—	0.39	0.40	0.52
Yr.	E3.45	2.50	3.37	3.25	2.88	2.80

Next earnings report expected: late October

Dividend Data (Dividends have been paid since 1926.)

Amount ($)	Date Decl.	Ex-Div. Date	Stock of Record	Payment Date
0.550	Oct. 28	Nov. 12	Nov. 14	Dec. 16 '97
0.550	Jan. 05	Feb. 11	Feb. 13	Mar. 16 '98
0.550	Apr. 16	May. 13	May. 15	Jun. 16 '98
0.550	Jun. 17	Aug. 12	Aug. 14	Sep. 16 '98

A Division of The McGraw-Hill Companies

Business Summary - 12-AUG-98

Duke Energy was formed on June 18, 1997, through the merger of Duke Power and PanEnergy. With the electricity and natural gas operations of the two companies combined, DUK hopes to become the premier provider of energy products and services in North America. Segment contributions in 1997 were:

	Revs.	Oper. Inc.
Electric Operations	27%	60%
Natural Gas Transmission	9%	31%
Energy Services	63%	11%
Other	1%	-2%

The Electric Operations segment provides for the generation, transmission, distribution and sale of electricity in central and western North Carolina and the western portion of South Carolina. Through its Duke Power and Nantahala Power and Light Company subsidiaries, the company serves around two million customers in this 20,000-square mile service territory. The company operates three nuclear power generating stations and eight coal-fired stations, as well as hydroelectric and combustion turbine stations. In July 1998, DUK acquired three generating plants in California from PG&E Corporation, for $501 million.

In June 1998, the company's Duke Energy International subsidiary acquired the Australian energy hold-

ings of PG&E, which include a 627-kilometer gas pipeline in the state of Queensland, the pipeline operations, and the trading and marketing operations

The Natural Gas Transmission segment is involved in the interstate transportation and storage of natural gas. The operations include four interstate pipeline units (Texas Eastern Transmission Corporation, Algonquin Gas Transmission Company, Panhandle Eastern Pipe Line Company, and Trunkline Gas Company) that deliver, through a 22,000-mile pipeline system connected to all major U.S. supply basins, about 12% of the natural gas consumed in the U.S. to markets throughout the midwestern, mid-Atlantic and New England states.

The Energy Services segment is comprised of several business units: The Field Services unit gathers and processes natural gas, produces and markets natural gas liquids, and transports and trades crude oil; the Global Asset Development unit develops, owns and operates energy-related facilities around the world; the Other Energy Services unit provides engineering consulting, construction and integrated energy solutions; and the Trading and Marketing unit markets natural gas, electricity and other energy-related products. In June 1997, DUK purchased the remaining 50% interest in its Duke/Louis Dreyfus power marketing joint venture.

Through subsidiaries, DUK is also involved in communication services and real estate operations.

Per Share Data ($)

(Year Ended Dec. 31)	1997	1996	1995	1994	1993	1992	1991	1990	1989	1988
Tangible Bk. Val.	18.72	23.13	22.17	20.91	19.91	19.52	19.30	18.35	17.60	15.63
Earnings	2.50	3.37	3.25	2.88	2.80	2.21	2.60	2.40	2.56	1.95
Dividends	2.16	2.08	2.00	1.92	1.84	1.76	1.68	1.60	1.52	1.44
Payout Ratio	86%	62%	62%	67%	66%	80%	65%	67%	59%	74%
Prices - High	56½	53	47⅞	43	44⅞	37½	35	32⅜	28¼	24½
- Low	41⅞	43⅜	37⅜	32⅞	35⅜	31⅜	26¾	25½	21⅜	21⅛
P/E Ratio - High	23	16	15	15	16	17	13	13	11	13
- Low	17	13	11	11	12	14	10	11	8	11

Income Statement Analysis (Million $)

	1997	1996	1995	1994	1993	1992	1991	1990	1989	1988
Revs.	16,309	4,758	4,677	4,489	4,282	3,961	3,817	3,681	3,639	3,627
Depr.	841	492	458	460	488	491	432	406	411	418
Maint.	NA	NA	NA	NA	375	403	355	404	349	383
Fxd. Chgs. Cov.	3.7	4.2	4.3	4.1	4.2	3.1	3.5	3.4	3.8	3.2
Constr. Credits	109	112	23.1	27.4	27.1	21.2	70.0	109	80.0	68.0
Eff. Tax Rate	39%	40%	40%	38%	40%	37%	34%	32%	34%	32%
Net Inc.	974	730	715	639	626	508	584	538	572	448

Balance Sheet & Other Fin. Data (Million $)

	1997	1996	1995	1994	1993	1992	1991	1990	1989	1988
Gross Prop.	25,448	14,946	14,937	14,489	13,760	14,953	14,337	13,617	12,689	11,698
Cap. Exp.	1,323	646	713	772	655	588	807	1,052	1,060	949
Net Prop.	15,736	9,386	9,361	9,264	8,924	8,882	8,699	8,450	7,917	7,374
Capitalization:										
LT Debt	6,530	3,538	3,711	3,567	3,285	3,202	3,160	3,103	2,822	2,729
% LT Debt	45	39	40	40	39	39	40	41	40	40
Pfd.	489	684	684	780	781	780	731	742	675	684
% Pfd.	3.40	7.50	7.50	8.80	9.30	9.60	9.20	9.70	9.40	10
Common	7,540	4,889	4,785	4,533	4,338	4,151	4,066	3,817	3,657	3,444
% Common	52	54	52	51	52	51	51	50	51	50
Total Cap.	18,673	11,737	11,824	11,501	10,895	9,798	9,558	9,241	8,685	8,306
% Oper. Ratio	91.8	81.4	91.1	82.6	81.0	81.7	81.5	82.5	80.6	82.6
% Earn. on Net Prop.	15.4	14.5	14.5	8.6	9.2	8.2	8.2	7.9	9.2	8.8
% Return On Revs.	6.0	15.3	15.3	14.2	14.6	12.8	15.3	14.6	15.7	12.4
% Return On Invest. Capital	11.2	16.9	12.6	7.9	8.5	8.4	9.1	8.8	9.5	8.3
% Return On Com. Equity	14.1	14.2	14.3	13.3	12.5	11.1	13.5	13.1	14.7	13.4

Data as orig. reptd.; bef. results of disc. opers. and/or spec. items. Per share data adj. for stk. divs. as of ex-div. date. Bold denotes diluted EPS (FASB 128). E-Estimated. NA-Not Available. NM-Not Meaningful. NR-Not Ranked.

Office—422 S. Church St., Charlotte, NC 28202-1904. **Registrar**—First Union National Bank of North Carolina, Charlotte. **Tel**—(704) 594-6200. **Website**—http://www.duke-energy.com **Chrmn & CEO**—R. B. Priory. **Pres & COO**—P. M. Anderson. **EVP & CFO**—R. J. Osborne. **Secy**—W. E. Poe, Jr. **SVP & Treas**—P. F. Ferguson, Jr. **VP & Investor Contact**—Sue A. Becht. **Dirs**—P. M. Anderson, A. Bernhardt, Sr., R. J. Brown, W. A. Coley, W. T. Esrey, A. M. Gray, D. R. Hendrix, H. S. Hook, G. D. Johnson Jr., W. W. Johnson, M. Lennon, L. E. Linbeck Jr., J. G. Martin, B. Mickel, R. B. Priory, R. M. Robinson II. **Transfer Agent and Registrar**—Company's office. **Incorporated**—in New Jersey in 1917; reincorporated in North Carolina in 1964. **Empl**— 22,726. **S&P Analyst:** Justin McCann

STANDARD
&POOR'S
STOCK REPORTS

Dun & Bradstreet Corp.

780B

NYSE Symbol **DNB**

In S&P 500

12-SEP-98

Industry:
Services (Commercial
& Consumer)

Summary: This company is the world's largest provider of commercial credit and business marketing information, and debt rating services.

| S&P Opinion: Hold (★★★) | Recent Price • 22¾ | Yield • 3.3% |
| | 52 Wk Range • 36⅝-2⅝ | 12-Mo. P/E • NM |

Quantitative Evaluations

Outlook
(1 Lowest—5 Highest)
• 4

Fair Value
• 27¾

Risk
• High

Earn./Div. Rank
• NR

Technical Eval.
• NA

Rel. Strength Rank
(1 Lowest—99 Highest)
• 97

Insider Activity
• Favorable

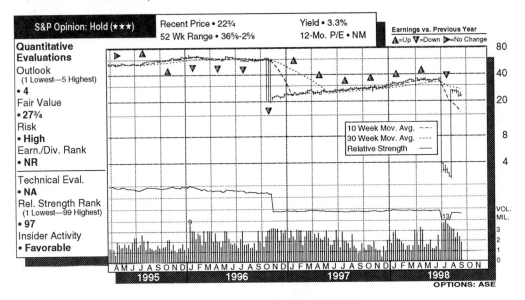

Earnings vs. Previous Year
▲=Up ▼=Down ▶=No Change

10 Week Mov. Avg. ---
30 Week Mov. Avg. ----
Relative Strength —

OPTIONS: ASE

Overview - 01-SEP-98

Revenus for the six months ended June 30, 1998, rose 8.9%, year to year, on an adjusted basis, reflecting the operations of DNB on a standalone basis, separate from Reuben H. Donnelley. Operating income rose 2.6%, but after sharply reduced non-operating costs and other items, income from continuing operations was up 8.1%, despite second quarter transaction costs of $22.6 million, or $0.14 a share. The business outlook remains positive, but year-to-year comparisons will be up against strong year-earlier results in the second half of 1998 and in 1999. We estimate 1998 EPS, boosted by a 7% stock buyback program, will advance roughly 24% to $1.58 from $1.27. An 11% rise in EPS to $1.75 is tentatively projected for 1999.

Valuation - 01-SEP-98

Effective July 1, 1998, Reuben H. Donnelley Co. was separated from The Dun & Bradstreet Corp., as part of management's continuing efforts to boost shareholder value. One long-term benefit of the strategy is that it provides DNB with greater managerial and operational flexibility to respond to changing market conditions. With $450 million in debt shifted to Donnelley's balance sheet, the new DNB is provided with additional financial flexibility. We expect EPS to rise roughly 11% in 1999, after an estimated 15% advance in 1998. The shares appear reasonably priced at this time, selling for about 16X our 1998 estimate. Although DNB's business is subject to the cyclicality of economic and financial markets worldwide, given the fairly stable outlook over the long term, we consider the stock an attractive holding for the long-term value investor. The quarterly cash dividend payout for the new DNB was initiated at $0.185 per share.

Key Stock Statistics

S&P EPS Est. 1998	1.58	Tang. Bk. Value/Share	NM
P/E on S&P Est. 1998	14.4	Beta	0.25
S&P EPS Est. 1999	1.75	Shareholders	12,700
Dividend Rate/Share	0.74	Market cap. (B)	$ 3.9
Shs. outstg. (M)	170.9	Inst. holdings	80%
Avg. daily vol. (M)	0.497		

Value of $10,000 invested 5 years ago: NA

Fiscal Year Ending Dec. 31

	1998	1997	1996	1995	1994	1993
Revenues (Million $)						
1Q	471.1	436.4	450.4	1,220	1,099	1,071
2Q	484.0	440.9	505.1	1,307	1,185	1,162
3Q	—	447.8	509.8	1,333	1,203	1,158
4Q	—	485.9	693.9	1,555	1,408	1,319
Yr.	—	1,811	2,159	5,415	4,896	4,710
Earnings Per Share ($)						
1Q	**0.32**	0.21	0.13	0.64	0.64	0.59
2Q	**0.23**	0.28	-0.26	0.86	0.85	0.78
3Q	E0.39	0.31	0.14	1.01	0.98	0.89
4Q	E0.64	**0.46**	-0.17	-0.62	1.23	0.15
Yr.	**E1.58**	**1.27**	-0.16	1.89	3.70	2.42

Next earnings report expected: mid September

Dividend Data (Dividends have been paid since 1934.)

Amount ($)	Date Decl.	Ex-Div. Date	Stock of Record	Payment Date
0.220	Apr. 15	May. 18	May. 20	Jun. 10 '98
Stk.	Jun. 03	Jul. 01	Jun. 17	Jun. 30 '98
0.185	Jul. 20	Aug. 18	Aug. 20	Sep. 10 '98

A Division of The McGraw-Hill Companies

Business Summary - 01-SEP-98

On July 1, 1998, Reuben H. Donnelley Co. (directory services) was separated from Dun & Bradstreet Corp. In 1996, in another major strategic move in an effort to enhance shareholder value, Dun & Bradstreet divested itself of all non-core businesses, and split itself into three separate entities: 1) The Dun & Bradstreet Corp. (which kept the original company's name), consisting of the flagship Dun & Bradstreet (D&B) commercial credit and business marketing information service, Moody's Investors Service, and Reuben H. Donnelley; 2) AC-Nielsen Corp., a leading market research organization; and 3) Cognizant Corp., consisting of IMS International, Gartner Group, Nielsen Media Research, Pilot Software, Cognizant Technology Solutions, Cognizant Enterprises, and Erisco. In connection with the reorganization, Dun & Bradstreet Software, NCH Promotional Services, and American Credit Indemnity were divested. On July 1, 1998, Nielsen Media Research was spun off from Cognizant.

Excluding R. H. Donnelley, the businesses making up the new Dun & Bradstreet (DNB) contributed to 1997 revenues as follows: D&B 75%, and Moody's 25%.

Dun & Bradstreet is the world's largest provider of business information and decision-support services that help customers in marketing, commercial credit and collections reduce risk, improve cash flow, increase sales and revenues and speed payments. The company has operations in 37 countries, and a worldwide database covering more than 44 million businesses. D&B also provides receivables management services worldwide.

Moody's Investors Service is a leading global provider of financial analysis, opinion, research and information. Moody's publishes credit opinions on investment securities, assigning ratings to fixed-income securities and other credit obligations. The company also provides a broad range of business and financial information in print or electronic formats. Founded in 1900, Moody's employs 600 analysts, and has a total of more than 1,500 associates located throughout the world. Moody's provides ratings and information on governmental and commercial entities in over 70 countries; its customers include investors, banks, and a wide range of corporate and governmental issuers of securities in more than 120 countries.

Per Share Data ($)

(Year Ended Dec. 31)	1997	1996	1995	1994	1993	1992	1991	1990	1989	1988
Tangible Bk. Val.	NM	NM	-0.04	-0.28	-0.27	6.14	5.79	5.24	5.62	6.56
Cash Flow	2.03	0.15	4.68	5.61	4.01	4.72	4.35	4.34	4.44	3.90
Earnings	1.27	-0.16	1.89	3.70	2.42	3.10	2.85	2.80	3.14	2.67
Dividends	0.88	1.82	2.63	2.56	2.40	2.25	2.15	2.09	1.94	1.68
Payout Ratio	1%	NM	139%	69%	99%	73%	75%	73%	61%	63%
Prices - High	31¼	69	65½	64	68½	59⅛	58	48⅝	60¼	57½
- Low	23⅛	19¼	48½	51⅞	55¾	50⅝	39⅛	36⅛	41¼	45⅞
P/E Ratio - High	36	NM	35	17	28	19	20	17	19	22
- Low	18	NM	26	14	23	16	14	13	13	17

Income Statement Analysis (Million $)

	1997	1996	1995	1994	1993	1992	1991	1990	1989	1988
Revs.	1,811	1,783	5,415	4,896	4,710	4,751	4,643	4,818	4,322	4,267
Oper. Inc.	536	198	876	1,249	1,111	1,075	1,020	1,051	1,109	1,032
Depr.	132	141	475	324	282	289	268	280	244	231
Int. Exp.	53.0	37.0	53.0	39.0	24.7	32.8	52.7	44.7	11.8	6.6
Pretax Inc.	332	-14.0	444	879	588	795	731	752	915	791
Eff. Tax Rate	34%	NM	28%	28%	27%	30%	30%	32%	36%	37%
Net Inc.	219	-115	321	630	429	554	509	508	586	499

Balance Sheet & Other Fin. Data (Million $)

	1997	1996	1995	1994	1993	1992	1991	1990	1989	1988
Cash	82.0	128	439	362	669	540	311	338	760	1,069
Curr. Assets	806	760	2,299	1,981	2,122	1,930	1,767	1,786	2,013	2,717
Total Assets	2,225	2,294	5,516	5,464	5,170	4,915	4,777	4,754	5,184	5,024
Curr. Liab.	1,497	2,008	2,834	2,187	2,044	1,645	1,527	1,676	1,721	1,919
LT Debt	Nil	Nil	Nil	Nil	Nil	Nil	Nil	Nil	Nil	Nil
Common Eqty.	-489	-454	1,183	1,319	1,111	2,156	2,161	2,080	2,185	2,093
Total Cap.	-187	-454	1,351	1,528	1,197	2,156	2,161	2,090	2,580	2,093
Cap. Exp.	51.0	58.0	286	273	236	197	226	300	311	319
Cash Flow	351	25.0	796	953	710	842	776	789	830	729
Curr. Ratio	0.5	0.4	0.8	0.9	1.0	1.2	1.2	1.1	1.2	1.4
% LT Debt of Cap.	Nil	Nil	Nil	Nil	Nil	Nil	Nil	Nil	Nil	Nil
% Net Inc.of Revs.	12.1	NM	6.0	12.9	9.1	11.7	11.0	10.5	13.6	11.7
% Ret. on Assets	10.2	NM	5.9	11.9	8.7	11.4	10.7	10.4	11.6	11.0
% Ret. on Equity	NM	NM	25.7	51.9	27.0	25.7	24.0	24.3	27.6	24.1

Data as orig. reptd.; bef. results of disc opers. and/or spec. items. Per share data adj. for stk. divs. as of ex-div. date. Bold denotes diluted EPS (FASB 128). E-Estimated. NA-Not Available. NM-Not Meaningful. NR-Not Ranked.

Office—One Diamond Hill Rd., Murray Hill, NJ 07974. **Tel**—(908) 665-5000. **Website**—http://www.dnb.com **Chrmn & CEO**—V. Taylor. **SVP & CFO**—F. S. Sowinski. **VP**—N. L. Henry. **Investor Contact**—Sandy Parker. **Dirs**—H. Adams Jr., C. L. Alexander Jr., M. J. Evans, R. R. Glauber, R. L. Kuehn Jr., R. J. Lanigan, V. R. Loucks Jr., H. A. McKinnell, F. R. Noonan, M. R. Quinlan, V. Taylor. **Transfer Agent & Registrar**—First Chicago Trust Co. of New York, NYC. **Incorporated**—in Delaware in 1930. **Empl**— 16,000. **S&P Analyst:** W. H. Donald

12-SEP-98

Industry:
Chemicals

Summary: This broadly diversified company is the largest U.S. chemicals manufacturer; it plans to sell Conoco, a large international integrated petroleum company.

S&P Opinion: Hold (★★★)	Recent Price • 56⅝	Yield • 2.5%
	52 Wk Range • 84⅜-50⅛	12-Mo. P/E • 31.1

Earnings vs. Previous Year
▲=Up ▼=Down ▶=No Change

Quantitative Evaluations

Outlook
(1 Lowest—5 Highest)
• **1+**

Fair Value
• **50½**

Risk
• **Low**

Earn./Div. Rank
• **B**

Technical Eval.
• **Neutral** since 7/98

Rel. Strength Rank
(1 Lowest—99 Highest)
• **62**

Insider Activity
• **NA**

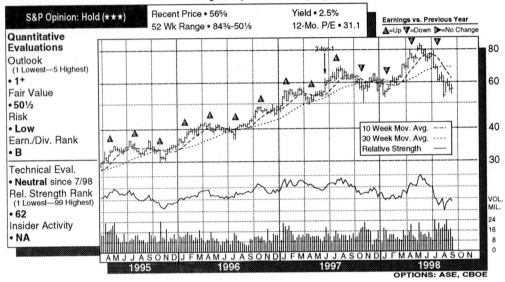

10 Week Mov. Avg. ----
30 Week Mov. Avg. ·····
Relative Strength ——

VOL.
MIL.

OPTIONS: ASE, CBOE

Overview - 17-AUG-98

DuPont plans to sell its Conoco oil unit, using the proceeds to invest in life sciences businesses. DD will sell publicly up to a 20% of Conoco by the end of 1998, and intends to divest its remaining interest as soon as practical, through further stock offerings or a spin-off to DD shareholders. Analysts value Conoco at nearly $25 billion. In early July, DD acquired for $2.6 billion, Merck's 50% interest in a pharmaceutical joint venture with DD. The company will take a pretax charge of up to $1.6 billion related to the purchase. Operating EPS will decline in 1998. Volumes in DD's chemicals related units will grow modestly in 1998, reflecting slower growth in world economies, largely as a result of the Asian financial crisis. There will also be the negative impact of the auto strike and softer demand for apparel fibers and pesticides. Despite the negative impact of the strong U.S. dollar, overall selling prices should soon turn positive, led by recoveries in titanium pigment and nylon. Conoco's earnings will be reduced by sharply lower oil prices, outweighing modestly higher production and better refining margins. New oil and natural gas reserves that will begin production during 1998's second half include those in the North Sea and in Venezuela. There will be higher interest expense from acquisitions. DD recorded special charges totaling $1.49 a share in the second half of 1997.

Valuation - 17-AUG-98

After outperforming the overall stock market for the past few years, reflecting favorable earnings and DD's strategy of expanding its life sciences operations, the stock dived during the summer on lower EPS. Investors will likely now focus on difficult conditions in DD's core chemicals units, discounting longer term growth prospects of life sciences (20% of pro forma income). The dividend may be reduced following the Conoco IPO.

Key Stock Statistics

S&P EPS Est. 1998	3.00	Tang. Bk. Value/Share	8.66
P/E on S&P Est. 1998	18.9	Beta	0.94
S&P EPS Est. 1999	3.50	Shareholders	158,100
Dividend Rate/Share	1.40	Market cap. (B)	$ 64.1
Shs. outstg. (M)	1131.7	Inst. holdings	55%
Avg. daily vol. (M)	3.962		

Value of $10,000 invested 5 years ago: $ 28,140

Fiscal Year Ending Dec. 31

	1998	1997	1996	1995	1994	1993
Revenues (Million $)						
1Q	11,378	11,211	10,769	10,502	9,190	9,070
2Q	11,140	11,402	11,148	11,076	10,161	9,550
3Q	—	11,136	10,486	10,200	9,845	9,231
4Q	—	11,330	11,407	10,385	10,137	9,251
Yr.	—	45,079	43,810	42,163	39,333	37,098
Earnings Per Share ($)						
1Q	**0.79**	0.89	0.79	0.70	0.47	0.36
2Q	**0.83**	0.99	0.89	0.85	0.58	0.38
3Q	**E0.65**	-0.02	0.80	0.69	0.47	-0.51
4Q	**E0.73**	0.23	0.76	0.56	0.47	0.17
Yr.	**E3.00**	2.08	3.18	2.81	2.00	0.41

Next earnings report expected: late October

Dividend Data (Dividends have been paid since 1904.)

Amount ($)	Date Decl.	Ex-Div. Date	Stock of Record	Payment Date
0.315	Oct. 29	Nov. 12	Nov. 14	Dec. 13 '97
0.315	Jan. 28	Feb. 11	Feb. 13	Mar. 14 '98
0.350	Apr. 29	May. 13	May. 15	Jun. 12 '98
0.350	Jul. 28	Aug. 12	Aug. 14	Sep. 12 '98

A Division of The McGraw·Hill Companies

Business Summary - 17-AUG-98

DuPont, the largest domestic chemicals producer, plans to divest Conoco, a major oil company, using the proceeds to invest in life sciences businesses. As part of that strategy, it acquired in late 1997 a 20% interest in Pioneer Hi-Bred International for $1.7 billion, and bought Ralston Purina's Protein Technologies unit for $1.5 billion. In July 1998, DD purchased the other 50% interest in a pharmaceutical joint venture held by Merck for $2.6 billion. In addition, DD, since the end of 1997, has purchased the polyester (intermediates, films, and PET resins) businesses of Imperial Chemical Industries, making it a leading integrated polyester producer. It also plans to buy ICI's titanium pigments unit, expanding its world leadership and giving it manufacturing sites in Europe. It will pay a total of $3 billion for these businesses. Total debt at June 30, 1998 was $16.0 billion.

Contributions by industry segment in 1997 were:

	Sales	Net Income
Chemicals	9%	13%
Fibers	17%	22%
Polymers	15%	21%
Life sciences	6%	14%
Diversified businesses	6%	6%
Petroleum expl. & production	12%	17%
Petroleum ref., mkt. & trans.	35%	7%

Foreign operations accounted for 45% of sales and 52% of net income in 1997.

Commodity and specialty chemicals include titanium pigments, fluoroproducts, acids, peroxygens and polymer intermediates. DD is a leading producer of man-made fibers (Dacron polyester, Lycra spandex, Stainmaster nylon, Kevlar aramid) for textiles, carpets and industrial uses; and polymers, elastomers, films, finishes, and fabricated and automotive products. Life sciences consists of agricultural pesticides and the recently consolidated pharmaceuticals business. Diversified businesses include electronic materials (photoresists, semiconductor materials), polyester resins and films, printing systems, and a 50%-owned coal operation.

Conoco is a major international integrated petroleum company, with proved developed reserves at 1997 year end of 600 million bbl. of oil and 3,061 Bcf of natural gas. Production is mainly from the U.S., the Gulf of Mexico, the North Sea, Dubai, Russia and Indonesia. Oil production in 1997 was 367,000 bbl. a day, up slightly versus 1996, while natural gas output declined 1%. In 1997, proved reserves increased 38% as Conoco replaced 450% of its oil and natural gas produced during the year. Refinery capacity is 733,000 bbl. a day at four refineries in the U.S., one in England, and a 19% interest in one in Germany. A new 100,000 bbl. per day joint venture refinery in Malaysia is to start up in the second half of 1998.

Per Share Data ($) (Year Ended Dec. 31)	1997	1996	1995	1994	1993	1992	1991	1990	1989	1988
Tangible Bk. Val.	8.66	8.85	6.59	9.07	7.91	8.20	11.90	11.48	10.71	10.29
Cash Flow	4.16	5.58	5.14	4.18	2.93	2.81	3.20	3.79	3.69	3.23
Earnings	2.08	3.23	2.81	2.00	0.41	0.71	1.04	1.70	1.76	1.52
Dividends	1.23	1.11	1.01	0.91	0.88	0.87	0.84	0.81	0.72	0.62
Payout Ratio	59%	34%	36%	45%	212%	122%	81%	47%	41%	41%
Prices - High	69¾	49¾	36½	31¼	27	27½	25	21¼	21⅛	15½
- Low	46⅜	34⅞	26⅜	24⅛	22¼	21¾	16⅜	15¾	14⅜	12⅝
P/E Ratio - High	34	15	13	16	65	38	24	12	12	10
- Low	22	11	9	12	54	30	16	9	8	8
Income Statement Analysis (Million $)										
Revs.	45,079	43,810	42,163	39,333	37,098	37,208	38,151	39,709	35,099	32,917
Oper. Inc.	8,118	7,975	7,675	6,944	6,166	4,837	6,200	7,160	7,020	6,280
Depr.	2,385	2,621	2,722	2,976	3,411	2,818	2,901	2,625	2,530	2,466
Int. Exp.	642	857	929	702	788	837	949	980	731	553
Pretax Inc.	4,680	5,981	5,390	4,382	958	1,811	2,818	4,154	4,324	3,824
Eff. Tax Rate	49%	39%	39%	38%	41%	46%	50%	44%	43%	43%
Net Inc.	2,405	3,636	3,293	2,727	566	975	1,403	2,310	2,480	2,190
Balance Sheet & Other Fin. Data (Million $)										
Cash	1,004	1,319	1,455	1,109	1,240	1,674	468	611	692	603
Curr. Assets	11,874	11,103	10,955	11,108	10,899	12,228	10,874	12,233	11,344	10,238
Total Assets	42,942	37,987	37,312	36,892	37,053	38,870	36,117	38,128	34,715	30,719
Curr. Liab.	14,070	10,987	12,731	7,565	9,439	10,226	7,493	10,023	9,348	6,696
LT Debt	5,929	5,087	5,678	6,376	6,531	7,193	6,456	5,663	4,149	3,232
Common Eqty.	11,033	10,472	8,199	12,585	10,993	11,528	16,502	16,181	15,561	15,343
Total Cap.	19,953	17,929	15,897	20,889	19,414	20,937	26,363	25,523	23,107	21,820
Cap. Exp.	4,768	3,303	3,240	3,050	3,655	4,397	5,026	5,383	4,285	4,004
Cash Flow	4,780	6,257	6,015	5,693	3,967	3,783	4,294	5,120	5,178	4,646
Curr. Ratio	0.8	1.0	0.9	1.5	1.2	1.2	1.5	1.2	1.2	1.5
% LT Debt of Cap.	29.7	28.4	35.7	30.5	33.6	34.4	24.5	22.2	18.0	14.8
% Net Inc.of Revs.	5.3	8.3	7.8	8.0	1.7	2.6	3.7	5.8	7.1	6.7
% Ret. on Assets	5.9	9.7	8.9	7.4	1.5	2.6	3.8	6.4	7.7	7.4
% Ret. on Equity	22.3	38.8	31.6	23.0	4.9	6.9	8.5	14.7	16.4	14.8

Data as orig. reptd.; bef. results of disc. opers. and/or spec. items. Per share data adj. for stk. divs. as of ex-div. date. Bold denotes diluted EPS (FASB 128). E-Estimated. NA-Not Available. NM-Not Meaningful. NR-Not Ranked.

Office—1007 Market St., Wilmington, DE 19898. **Registrar**—Wilmington Trust Co. **Tel**—(302) 774-1000. **Website**—http://www.dupont.com**Chrmn**—J. A. Krol. **Pres & CEO**—C. O. Holliday, Jr. **Secy**—L. B. Lancaster. **SVP & CFO**—G. M. Pfeiffer. **VP & Investor Contact**—John W. Himes. **Dirs**— P. N. Barnevik, C. J. Crawford, E. B. du Pont, L. C. Duemling, A. W. Dunham, C. O. Holliday, Jr., L. D. Juliber, J. A. Krol, W. K. Reilly, H. R. Sharp III, C. M. Vest, G. Watanabe, S. I. Weill, E. S. Woolard, Jr. **Transfer Agent & Registrar**—First Chicago Trust Co. of New York, Jersey City, NJ. **Incorporated**—in Delaware in 1915. **Empl**— 98,000. **S&P Analyst:** Richard O'Reilly, CFA

12-SEP-98

Industry:
Natural Gas

Summary: Through subsidiaries, this company distributes natural gas to 530,000 customers in the Boston area and also provides barge transportation services.

S&P Opinion: Hold (★★★)	Recent Price • 40¾	Yield • 4.0%
	52 Wk Range • 45⅝-36⅜	12-Mo. P/E • 15.8

Earnings vs. Previous Year
▲=Up ▼=Down ▶=No Change

Quantitative Evaluations

Outlook
(1 Lowest—5 Highest)
• **2**

Fair Value
• **38¾**

Risk
• **Low**

Earn./Div. Rank
• **B**

Technical Eval.
• **Bullish** since 8/98

Rel. Strength Rank
(1 Lowest—99 Highest)
• **89**

Insider Activity
• **NA**

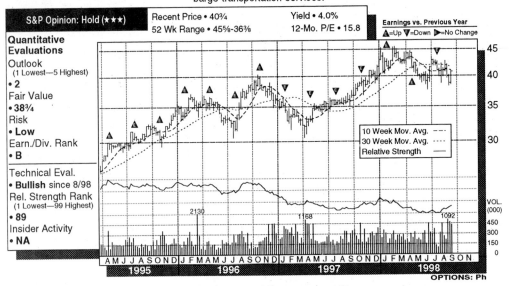

10 Week Mov. Avg. ---
30 Week Mov. Avg. ----
Relative Strength —

VOL. (000)

2130   1168   1092

OPTIONS: Ph

Overview - 28-JUL-98

Despite temperatures that were 23% warmer than last year, Eastern Enterprises's Boston Gas unit managed to improve its year to year earnings contribution by 14% in the second quarter of 1998. Overall, the company earned $0.36 per share, versus $0.38 in the year ago period. This excludes an extraordinary gain of $2.35 per share for the reversal of the company's Coal Act reserves following the Supreme Court's decision that the Coal Act was unconstitutional as applied to EFU. The company was hurt by weak commodity prices and their effect on barge operations, and by start-up costs for ServicEdge. We are maintaining our 1998 and 1999 EPS estimates at $2.60 and $3.00, respectively. Over the long term, the company expects ServicEdge to contribute to earnings by the end of 1999, and a rebound in Asia should help to improve conditions for commodity markets. On the utility front, Boston Gas continues to improve its operating efficiency, and the merger with Essex County Gas was approved by its shareholders and will help the company increase its customer base and further improve operating margins.

Valuation - 28-JUL-98

We are maintaining our neutral stance on EFU stock. Although EFU's long-term prospects are strong, with increasing demand for natural gas in New England, the stock is fairly valued based on our respective 1998 and 1999 earnings estimates of $2.60 and $3.00. The creation of ServicEdge provides unregulated growth opportunities, but Midland will continue to drag down earnings in the near term as economic problems in Asia dampen grain demand, and the strong U.S. dollar continues to hurt coal exports. However, the annual dividend of $1.64 provides a good yield, and it will likely be raised toward the end of 1998 making EFU stock attractive for total return.

Key Stock Statistics

S&P EPS Est. 1998	2.60	Tang. Bk. Value/Share	25.33
P/E on S&P Est. 1998	15.7	Beta	0.37
S&P EPS Est. 1999	3.00	Shareholders	5,100
Dividend Rate/Share	1.64	Market cap. (B)	$0.833
Shs. outstg. (M)	20.4	Inst. holdings	79%
Avg. daily vol. (M)	0.124		

Value of $10,000 invested 5 years ago: $ 19,487

Fiscal Year Ending Dec. 31

	1998	1997	1996	1995	1994	1993
Revenues (Million $)						
1Q	342.9	376.9	419.2	367.0	372.5	368.4
2Q	192.6	207.9	214.6	198.9	191.8	259.8
3Q	—	125.5	133.9	133.4	139.2	195.9
4Q	—	259.9	240.7	250.1	221.4	275.8
Yr.	—	970.2	1,007	949.4	924.9	1,100
Earnings Per Share ($)						
1Q	**1.50**	**1.38**	1.61	1.51	1.38	1.02
2Q	**0.36**	**0.44**	0.49	0.35	0.24	0.14
3Q	—	**-0.20**	0.03	-0.13	-0.27	-0.93
4Q	—	**0.92**	0.84	1.25	0.52	-1.66
Yr.	**E2.60**	**2.54**	2.98	2.98	1.87	-1.43

Next earnings report expected: late October

Dividend Data (Dividends have been paid since 1974.)

Amount ($)	Date Decl.	Ex-Div. Date	Stock of Record	Payment Date
0.410	Oct. 23	Nov. 26	Dec. 01	Jan. 05 '98
0.410	Feb. 25	Mar. 05	Mar. 09	Apr. 02 '98
0.410	May. 27	Jun. 04	Jun. 08	Jul. 02 '98
0.410	Jul. 22	Aug. 31	Sep. 02	Oct. 02 '98

A Division of The McGraw·Hill Companies

Business Summary - 28-JUL-98

Eastern Enterprises's (EFU) strategy no longer includes its 50% interest in AllEnergy Marketing Co., a joint venture with New England Electric System (NEES) that the company sold in December 1997, but the company continues to pursue growth opportunities in unregulated areas of the energy business. EFU started two new businesses in 1997 to actively seek new opportunities. ServicEdge Partners, Inc. offers heating, ventilation and air conditioning equipment installation and services to gas, oil and electric customers. AMR Data Corp. provides customized meter services primarily to municipal utilities in the Northeast. On the traditional gas distribution front, the planned acquisition of Essex County Gas Co. (Nasdaq: ECGC) is proceeding on schedule and is expected to be completed by mid-1998; ECGC shareholders approved the merger in June. ECGC has about 42,000 customers north of Boston, an area that the company believes has greater growth potential than Boston Gas's (BG) operating area.

BG is New England's largest gas distributor, transporting natural gas to 530,000 residential, commercial and industrial customers in Boston and 73 other communities. As BG relinquishes its function of purchase and resale of natural gas to independent energy marketers, management intends to turn BG into primarily a provider of local distribution services, i.e., transporting gas that marketers sell to their customers. During this unbundling process, Boston Gas will transition from a full-service utility to a distribution company and, conse-

quently, revenues associated with the sale of gas, according to the company, will decline.

BG's revenues will get a slight boost from a May 1997 Massachusetts Department of Public Utilities ruling, in which Boston Gas was granted an additional $1.9 million in revenues (a $6.3 million increase was granted in a November 1996 order) and a reduction in the productivity factor portion of the performance-based rate formula established in the November 1996 order by 50 basis points, from 2% to 1.5%. The company expects the adjustment to the productivity factor to add about $1.3 million to revenues each year over the five-year life of the plan, which began November 1997.

EFU's Midland segment is the leading carrier of coal and a major carrier of other dry bulk cargoes on the nation's inland waterways, with a fleet of 2,302 barges and 87 towboats. The company plans to continue participating modestly in grain transportation markets, but it will focus on increasing its market share for the transportation of other commodities, including steel/scrap, alumina, fertilizer, etc. Midland transported 123.2 million tons in 1997, down from 140.0 million in 1996.

In June 1998, the Supreme Court declared the Coal Act unconstitutional as applied to Eastern Enterprises. The company had established reserves totaling $80 billion to fund a possible liability in health benefits to retired coal miners. As a result of this decision, EFU reversed that charge, less associated expenses, to its second quarter 1998 earnings, resulting in an extraordinary gain of $75 million.

Per Share Data ($)

(Year Ended Dec. 31)	1997	1996	1995	1994	1993	1992	1991	1990	1989	1988
Tangible Bk. Val.	22.03	21.08	19.60	18.33	16.75	18.88	18.19	19.79	18.81	20.41
Cash Flow	5.86	6.12	6.01	4.70	1.19	4.04	3.36	4.51	4.00	3.61
Earnings	2.54	2.97	2.98	1.87	-1.43	1.67	1.30	2.77	2.43	2.18
Dividends	1.61	1.51	1.42	1.40	1.40	1.40	1.40	1.40	1.40	1.30
Payout Ratio	63%	51%	48%	75%	NM	84%	107%	49%	57%	59%
Prices - High	45⅜	40⅜	35½	28	30	28⅝	30	35	35¼	26¾
- Low	30½	30½	25¼	22¼	25½	23½	22	23⅛	22¾	21¾
P/E Ratio - High	18	14	12	15	NM	17	23	13	15	12
- Low	12	10	8	12	NM	14	17	8	9	10

Income Statement Analysis (Million $)

	1997	1996	1995	1994	1993	1992	1991	1990	1989	1988
Revs.	970	1,007	949	925	1,100	1,091	993	950	840	672
Oper. Inc.	174	186	175	156	136	150	121	129	113	98.0
Depr.	67.9	64.5	61.5	58.9	59.0	53.6	46.5	40.3	36.4	33.1
Int. Exp.	34.3	35.0	39.0	37.5	35.1	35.2	34.9	32.2	30.6	26.4
Pretax Inc.	76.6	96.2	84.9	65.3	-15.2	63.4	47.1	88.6	74.2	63.1
Eff. Tax Rate	32%	37%	29%	38%	NM	40%	38%	28%	24%	20%
Net Inc.	52.0	60.7	60.4	38.9	-32.2	37.9	29.4	64.0	56.6	50.7

Balance Sheet & Other Fin. Data (Million $)

	1997	1996	1995	1994	1993	1992	1991	1990	1989	1988
Cash	175	160	191	61.0	52.0	105	107	158	38.0	112
Curr. Assets	412	400	425	343	363	387	340	386	256	317
Total Assets	1,434	1,434	1,377	1,339	1,380	1,425	1,333	1,199	1,149	1,087
Curr. Liab.	215	234	225	212	285	206	208	178	177	146
LT Debt	342	403	403	419	388	406	359	332	309	308
Common Eqty.	446	428	396	374	364	518	503	513	498	473
Total Cap.	916	953	917	914	872	1,075	993	976	933	903
Cap. Exp.	82.3	111	78.0	58.0	64.0	83.0	112	97.0	90.0	63.0
Cash Flow	120	125	122	98.0	27.0	91.0	76.0	104	93.0	84.0
Curr. Ratio	1.9	1.7	1.9	1.6	1.3	1.9	1.6	2.2	1.4	2.2
% LT Debt of Cap.	37.3	42.3	43.9	45.9	44.5	37.8	36.1	34.0	33.1	34.1
% Net Inc.of Revs.	5.4	6.1	6.4	4.2	NM	3.5	3.0	6.7	6.7	7.5
% Ret. on Assets	3.6	4.4	4.4	2.9	NM	2.7	2.3	5.5	5.1	4.8
% Ret. on Equity	11.9	14.8	15.7	10.7	NM	7.4	5.8	12.8	11.6	11.0

Data as orig. reptd.; bef. results of disc. opers. and/or spec. items. Per share data adj. for stk. divs. as of ex-div. date. Bold denotes diluted EPS (FASB 128). E-Estimated. NA-Not Available. NM-Not Meaningful. NR-Not Ranked.

Office—9 Riverside Rd., Weston, MA 02193. **Tel**—(781) 647-2300. **Website**—http://www.efu.com **C̱hrmn & CEO**—J. A. Ives.**Pres**—R. R. Clayton. **SVP & CFO**—W. J. Flaherty. **SVP & Secy**—L. W. Law Jr. **Investor Contact**—Jane W. McCahon. **Trustees**—J. R. Barker, R. R. Clayton, J. D. Curtin Jr., S. Frankenheim, J. A. Ives, L. R. Jaskol, W. J. Knox, R. K. Spence, D. B. Stone. **Transfer Agent & Registrar**—BankBoston, N.A., Boston. **Established**—in Massachusetts in 1929. **Empl**— 2,867. **S&P Analyst**: J. Robert Cho

12-SEP-98   Industry: Chemicals

Summary: This major international producer of plastics, chemicals and fibers is the largest producer of polyester resins.

S&P Opinion: Hold (★★★)

Recent Price • 51⅝	Yield • 3.4%
52 Wk Range • 72⅞-49	12-Mo. P/E • 13.9

Earnings vs. Previous Year
▲=Up ▼=Down ▶=No Change

Quantitative Evaluations

Outlook (1 Lowest—5 Highest)
• **2⁻**

Fair Value
• **51⅜**

Risk
• **Low**

Earn./Div. Rank
• **NR**

Technical Eval.
• **Bullish** since 11/97

Rel. Strength Rank (1 Lowest—99 Highest)
• **61**

Insider Activity
• **NA**

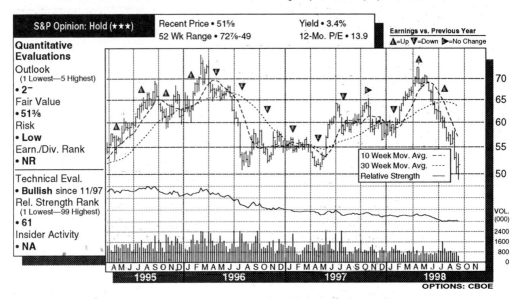

10 Week Mov. Avg.
30 Week Mov. Avg.
Relative Strength

VOL. (000)

1995 1996 1997 1998

OPTIONS: CBOE

Overview - 19-MAY-98

After a 2% revenue decline in 1997, on lower selling prices, we see modest sales growth for 1998, on continued good volume gains, aided by major capital programs of the past two years. EMN will have about 20% more PET capacity, thanks to the full-year addition of a plant in Spain and the startup of two other plants during 1998. The coatings, fine chemicals, and specialty plastics units should see good volume growth. Lower prices for polyethylene, oxo chemicals and filter tow will offset greater capacity for these products. While PET in 1997 recovered much of the 1996 drop in prices and margins, we expect this material to experience renewed downward pressure in 1998. The container plastics segment could return to the black in the second half, as plant startup costs decline. Filter tow sales and profits will likely decline in 1998, as lower prices outweigh expected favorable volume comparisons; inventory reductions and new industry supplies in China hurt results in 1997. The company is targeting another $100 million of labor and material productivity gains in 1998, following $150 million achieved in 1997. Capital spending will decline to under $600 million, from 1997's $749 million. EMN could resume repurchasing stock.

Valuation - 19-MAY-98

We are maintaining our hold opinion on the stock, in view of the unfavorable intermediate-term outlook for PET. EMN is looking at strategies to return the PET business to above its cost of capital, and will explore all options. We think that PET will be kept, as EMN has the leading share of the PET market, which is seeing double-digit volume growth. EMN should still post relatively healthy earnings in 1998, as higher volumes for major products will be largely offset by lower prices. The dividend provides an above-average yield.

Key Stock Statistics

S&P EPS Est. 1998	4.25	Tang. Bk. Value/Share	24.05
P/E on S&P Est. 1998	12.1	Beta	NA
S&P EPS Est. 1999	4.50	Shareholders	94,200
Dividend Rate/Share	1.76	Market cap. (B)	$ 4.1
Shs. outstg. (M)	79.2	Inst. holdings	73%
Avg. daily vol. (M)	0.143		

Value of $10,000 invested 5 years ago: NA

Fiscal Year Ending Dec. 31

	1998	1997	1996	1995	1994	1993
Revenues (Million $)						
1Q	1,148	1,171	1,261	1,232	983.0	941.0
2Q	1,165	1,208	1,241	1,321	1,047	1,012
3Q	—	1,145	1,167	1,266	1,130	970.0
4Q	—	1,154	1,113	1,221	1,169	980.0
Yr.	—	4,678	4,782	5,040	4,329	3,903
Earnings Per Share ($)						
1Q	0.94	0.92	1.39	1.58	0.68	0.71
2Q	1.21	1.14	1.41	1.90	1.00	0.90
3Q	E1.15	1.22	1.22	1.81	1.12	0.57
4Q	E0.95	0.35	0.70	1.50	1.25	0.28
Yr.	E4.25	3.63	4.79	6.78	4.05	2.46

Next earnings report expected: late October

Dividend Data (Dividends have been paid since 1994.)

Amount ($)	Date Decl.	Ex-Div. Date	Stock of Record	Payment Date
0.440	Nov. 07	Dec. 11	Dec. 15	Jan. 02 '98
0.440	Feb. 03	Mar. 06	Mar. 10	Apr. 01 '98
0.440	May. 07	Jun. 11	Jun. 15	Jul. 01 '98
0.440	Aug. 06	Sep. 11	Sep. 15	Oct. 01 '98

Business Summary - 19-MAY-98

This major international producer of chemicals, plastics and fibers plans to expand its foreign sales and manufacturing assets over the next few years. Eastman Chemical (EMN) also intends to reduce its cost structure by a total of $500 million by 2000, through labor productivity and better raw material usage. Business segment contributions (profits in millions) in 1997 were:

	Sales	Profits
Specialty & performance	56%	$450
Plastics	28%	-38
Chemicals intermediates	16%	156

International operations accounted for 25% of sales and reported $88 million of operating losses in 1997.

The specialty & performance segment includes acetate cigarette filter tow and textile yarn (28% of segment sales in 1997). Worldwide demand for filter tow is projected to grow 2% to 3% annually over the long term. EMN also produces chemicals for coatings, inks and resins (26%), including solvents, alcohols, glycols and resins; and fine chemicals (15%) used in photographic products, pharmaceuticals, home care products and custom chemicals. The segment also includes performance chemicals (12%), including polymer and fiber additives, adhesives, and food ingredients; and specialty

plastics (19%), including polyolefins, modified polyesters, cellulosics and alloys for value-added uses.

EMN is the world's largest producer of polyester plastics (62% of plastics segment's 1997 sales), which are used for packaging applications, including polyethylene terephthalate (PET) for containers such as soft-drink bottles; it also makes polyethylene resins (38%) used in films, extrusion coatings, fibers and injection-molding applications. EMN began production in May 1997 at a PET plant in Spain with annual capacity of 130,000 tons. The company will complete and start up PET plants in the Netherlands and Argentina during 1998, increasing its total annual PET capacity to 3 billion lbs. It has delayed plans to build a PET plant in the U.S. Plastics earnings fell sharply in 1996, followed by a loss in 1997, reflecting lower PET prices. Overcapacity worldwide continue to pressure PET prices. EMN has introduced two new specialty polyethylene resins, which are expected to be more profitable than its other products, and to reduce the cyclicality of this business.

The chemical intermediates segment includes acetyl, oxo chemicals and plasticizers used for polymers, agricultural chemicals, industrial chemicals and additives, and pharmaceuticals. Volume growth of these chemicals tend to follow the growth in the world economy. EMN is building a new oxo chemicals plant in Singapore, with production expected to begin in 1999.

Per Share Data ($)

(Year Ended Dec. 31)	1997	1996	1995	1994	1993	1992	1991	1990	1989	1988
Tangible Bk. Val.	22.40	21.28	19.10	15.59	NA	NA	NA	NA	NA	NA
Cash Flow	7.86	9.01	10.52	8.04	NA	6.86	NA	NA	NA	NA
Earnings	3.63	4.80	6.78	4.05	2.46	2.72	3.69	3.91	NA	NA
Dividends	1.76	1.72	1.64	1.60	Nil	NA	NA	NA	NA	NA
Payout Ratio	48%	36%	24%	40%	Nil	NA	NA	NA	NA	NA
Prices - High	65⅜	76¼	69½	56	48⅛	NA	NA	NA	NA	NA
- Low	50¾	50¾	48½	39½	42⅞	NA	NA	NA	NA	NA
P/E Ratio - High	18	16	10	14	20	NA	NA	NA	NA	NA
- Low	14	11	7	10	17	NA	NA	NA	NA	NA

Income Statement Analysis (Million $)

	1997	1996	1995	1994	1993	1992	1991	1990	1989	1988
Revs.	4,678	4,782	5,040	4,329	3,903	3,811	3,614	3,433	NA	NA
Oper. Inc.	895	977	1,272	965	NA	814	NA	NA	NA	NA
Depr.	327	314	308	329	NA	337	NA	NA	NA	NA
Int. Exp.	87.0	67.0	79.0	98.0	84.0	100	NA	NA	NA	NA
Pretax Inc.	446	607	899	550	336	355	NA	NA	NA	NA
Eff. Tax Rate	36%	37%	38%	39%	39%	38%	NA	NA	NA	NA
Net Inc.	286	380	559	336	204	221	300	317	NA	NA

Balance Sheet & Other Fin. Data (Million $)

	1997	1996	1995	1994	1993	1992	1991	1990	1989	1988
Cash	29.0	24.0	100	90.0	141	16.0	NA	NA	NA	NA
Curr. Assets	1,490	1,345	1,469	1,273	1,103	1,089	NA	NA	NA	NA
Total Assets	5,778	5,266	4,854	4,375	4,341	4,319	4,010	3,760	NA	NA
Curr. Liab.	954	787	873	800	469	2,212	NA	NA	NA	NA
LT Debt	1,714	1,523	1,217	1,195	1,801	Nil	NA	NA	NA	NA
Common Eqty.	1,753	1,639	1,528	1,295	1,061	1,101	1,165	948	NA	NA
Total Cap.	3,864	3,510	3,075	2,815	2,862	1,395	NA	NA	NA	NA
Cap. Exp.	749	789	446	281	NA	NA	NA	NA	NA	NA
Cash Flow	613	694	867	665	NA	558	NA	NA	NA	NA
Curr. Ratio	1.6	1.7	1.7	1.6	2.4	0.5	NA	NA	NA	NA
% LT Debt of Cap.	44.4	43.3	39.6	42.5	62.9	Nil	NA	NA	NA	NA
% Net Inc.of Revs.	6.1	7.9	11.1	7.8	5.2	5.8	8.3	9.2	NA	NA
% Ret. on Assets	5.6	7.5	12.1	7.7	NA	NA	7.7	NA	NA	NA
% Ret. on Equity	16.9	24.0	39.6	28.5	NA	NA	28.4	NA	NA	NA

Data as orig. reptd.; bef. results of disc. opers. and/or spec. items. Per share data adj. for stk. divs. as of ex-div. date. Statistical data pro forma prior to 1994. E-Estimated. NA-Not Available. NM-Not Meaningful. NR-Not Ra

Office—100 North Eastman Rd., Kingsport, TN 37660-5075. **Tel**—(423) 229-2000. **Website**—http://www.eastman.com **Chrmn & CEO**—E. W. Deavenport Jr. **SVP & CFO**—A.R. Rothwell. **VP & Secy**—T. K. Lee. **Investor Contact**—Albert J. Wargo. **Dirs**—H. J. Arnelle, R. W. Bourne Jr., C. A. Campbell Jr., E. W. Deavenport Jr., J. E. Dempsey, J. W. Donehower, L. Liu, M. R. Marks, G. B. Mitchell, J. A. White. **Transfer Agent & Registrar**—First Chicago Trust Co. of New York, Jersey City, NJ. **Incorporated**—in Delaware in 1993. **Empl**— 16,100. **S&P Analyst:** Richard O'Reilly, CFA

STANDARD &POOR'S
STOCK REPORTS

Eastman Kodak

802

NYSE Symbol **EK**

In S&P 500

12-SEP-98

Industry: Photography/Imaging

Summary: This major imaging company has a large international presence.

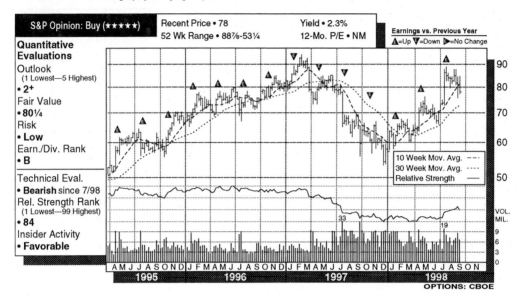

S&P Opinion: Buy (★★★★★)

Recent Price • 78

52 Wk Range • 88⅞-53¼

Yield • 2.3%

12-Mo. P/E • NM

Earnings vs. Previous Year
▲=Up ▼=Down ▶=No Change

Quantitative Evaluations

Outlook
(1 Lowest—5 Highest)
• **2+**

Fair Value
• **80¼**

Risk
• **Low**

Earn./Div. Rank
• **B**

Technical Eval.
• **Bearish** since 7/98

Rel. Strength Rank
(1 Lowest—99 Highest)
• **84**

Insider Activity
• **Favorable**

10 Week Mov. Avg. - - -
30 Week Mov. Avg. ·····
Relative Strength —

VOL. MIL.

OPTIONS: CBOE

Overview - 14-AUG-98

This large imaging company is in the midst of its latest restructuring program, through which EK is expected to reduce its cost structure by at least a net $500 million (about $1.00 a share, after tax) in 1998, and an additional amount in 1999, which would bring the two-year net savings total to at least $1 billion. However, a portion of the savings may be offset by price reductions or other marketing activity. Although EK is facing a difficult competitive environment, as well as an adverse impact from economic problems in Asia, recent earnings improvement has been impressive. Excluding a $0.13 a share asset sale gain, 1998's second quarter earnings were up about 24% from the year-ago level, helped by manufacturing productivity gains, and lower expenses in other categories. Before one-time items, we estimate full-year 1998 earnings of $4.44 a share, which is comparable to $3.52 in 1997 and $4.50 in 1996.

Valuation - 14-AUG-98

In July 1998, after EK reported better-than-expected second quarter earnings, we raised our opinion on the stock to "buy," from "hold." We look for the this brand name stock to benefit from higher earnings estimates for 1998 and 1999, and, with improved investor sentiment, an expansion of the stock's P/E multiple. Over the long term, we look for electronic imaging products to be of growing significance and value to EK. However, at least for the next few years, we expect products based on silver halide film to remain very important. For the longer term, we look for EK's results to benefit from development of overseas markets and greater effectiveness in translating research efforts into new products.

Key Stock Statistics

S&P EPS Est. 1998	4.53	Tang. Bk. Value/Share	8.30
P/E on S&P Est. 1998	17.2	Beta	0.35
S&P EPS Est. 1999	5.00	Shareholders	137,100
Dividend Rate/Share	1.76	Market cap. (B)	$ 25.2
Shs. outstg. (M)	322.8	Inst. holdings	57%
Avg. daily vol. (M)	1.481		

Value of $10,000 invested 5 years ago: $ 22,682

Fiscal Year Ending Dec. 31

	1998	1997	1996	1995	1994	1993
Revenues (Million $)						
1Q	2,911	3,133	3,388	3,137	2,755	3,540
2Q	3,541	3,853	4,117	3,938	3,425	4,265
3Q	—	3,773	4,149	3,813	3,529	4,133
4Q	—	3,779	4,314	4,092	3,848	4,480
Yr.	—	14,538	15,968	14,980	13,557	16,364
Earnings Per Share ($)						
1Q	**0.69**	**0.44**	0.80	0.77	0.44	0.29
2Q	**1.51**	**1.11**	1.30	1.11	0.88	0.93
3Q	**E1.10**	**0.71**	1.22	0.99	0.57	-0.39
4Q	**E1.23**	**0.76**	-0.34	0.80	-0.23	0.62
Yr.	**E4.53**	**0.01**	2.93	3.67	1.65	1.44

Next earnings report expected: mid October

Dividend Data (Dividends have been paid since 1902.)

Amount ($)	Date Decl.	Ex-Div. Date	Stock of Record	Payment Date
0.440	Oct. 10	Nov. 26	Dec. 01	Jan. 02 '98
0.440	Feb. 12	Feb. 26	Mar. 02	Apr. 01 '98
0.440	Apr. 17	May. 28	Jun. 01	Jul. 01 '98
0.440	Jul. 21	Aug. 28	Sep. 01	Oct. 01 '98

A Division of The **McGraw·Hill** *Companies*

STANDARD
&POOR'S
STOCK REPORTS

Eastman Kodak Company

802

12-SEP-98

Business Summary - 14-AUG-98

With cost-savings benefits from its latest restructuring program, this large imaging company should be better positioned to face a difficult competitive environment and an adverse impact from economic problems in Asia. We expect EK to reduce its cost structure by at least a net $500 million (about $1.00 a share, after tax) in 1998, and an additional amount in 1999, which would bring the two-year net savings total to at least $1 billion. However, a portion of the savings may be offset by price reductions or other marketing activity.

Since 1994, EK has divested billions of dollars of non-core businesses, participated in the introduction of a new consumer photo system, and has continued to work on products that enable customers to store and manipulate images in a digital format. EK is now led by former Motorola executive George Fisher, who joined the company in December 1993. Traditional chemical-based photography remains very important for EK, but digital technology, in which information is stored in a binary format of on-off signals, is of growing significance as a means of creating and transmitting images. However, in 1997, we believe that EK had a sizable loss related to digital products.

Sales to customers outside the U.S. accounted for 53% of sales in 1997.

Largely based on the markets it serves, EK reports its results in two business segments: Consumer and Com-

mercial. Contributions from continuing operations in 1997 (profit before restructuring charge) were:

	Sales	Profit
Consumer	43%	69%
Commercial	47%	31%

The consumer imaging segment includes films, photographic papers, processing services, photographic chemicals, cameras and projectors. Since 1996, EK has been participating in the roll-out of the Advanced Photo System (APS), through its Advantix line of products. Although incompatible with existing cameras, APS should offer additional features and ease-of-use that are attractive to consumers.

Commercial-oriented businesses include films, photographic papers and plates, chemicals, processing equipment, audiovisual equipment, copiers, microfilm products, applications software, printers and other business equipment.

Excluding charges related to such items as restructuring and asset writedowns, EK's earnings per share in 1997 and 1996 totaled $3.52 and $4.50, respectively. Earlier, in 1994, 1993 and 1992, EK had restructuring charges of $0.75, $1.16 and $0.43 a share, respectively (excluding Eastman Chemical Co.). Also, as of approximately mid-1998, EK had authorization to spend up to about $430 million to repurchase its common stock. In January 1997, directors announced the first dividend boost since about 1988.

Per Share Data ($)

(Year Ended Dec. 31)	1997	1996	1995	1994	1993	1992	1991	1990	1989	1988
Tangible Bk. Val.	8.09	12.51	13.25	10.01	-2.89	6.60	5.40	7.05	6.36	6.69
Cash Flow	2.51	5.68	6.34	4.28	4.83	7.79	4.60	6.20	5.72	7.96
Earnings	0.01	3.00	3.67	1.65	1.44	3.06	0.05	2.17	1.63	4.31
Dividends	1.76	1.60	1.60	1.60	2.00	2.00	2.00	2.00	2.00	1.90
Payout Ratio	NM	53%	44%	97%	139%	65%	823%	92%	123%	44%
Prices - High	94¾	85	70⅜	56¾	65	50¾	49¾	43⅞	52⅜	53¼
- Low	53¼	65⅛	47⅛	40⅝	40¼	37¾	37⅝	33¾	40	39⅛
P/E Ratio - High	NM	28	19	34	45	17	NM	20	32	12
- Low	NM	22	13	25	28	12	NM	16	25	9

Income Statement Analysis (Million $)

	1997	1996	1995	1994	1993	1992	1991	1990	1989	1988
Revs.	14,538	15,967	14,980	13,557	16,364	20,183	19,419	18,908	18,398	17,034
Oper. Inc.	2,431	3,107	2,841	2,545	3,122	3,874	3,852	4,153	3,792	4,121
Depr.	828	903	916	883	1,111	1,539	1,477	1,309	1,326	1,183
Int. Exp.	98.0	83.0	78.0	177	635	907	931	925	963	760
Pretax Inc.	53.0	1,556	1,926	1,002	856	1,601	11.0	1,257	925	2,236
Eff. Tax Rate	91%	35%	35%	45%	45%	38%	NM	44%	43%	38%
Net Inc.	5.0	1,011	1,252	554	475	994	17.0	703	529	1,397

Balance Sheet & Other Fin. Data (Million $)

	1997	1996	1995	1994	1993	1992	1991	1990	1989	1988
Cash	728	1,796	1,811	2,068	1,966	560	924	916	1,279	1,075
Curr. Assets	5,475	6,965	7,309	7,683	8,021	7,405	8,258	8,608	8,591	8,684
Total Assets	13,145	14,438	14,477	14,968	20,325	23,138	24,170	24,125	23,652	22,964
Curr. Liab.	5,177	5,417	4,643	5,735	4,910	5,998	6,899	7,163	6,573	5,850
LT Debt	585	559	665	660	6,853	7,202	7,597	6,989	7,376	7,779
Common Eqty.	3,161	4,734	5,121	4,017	3,356	6,557	6,104	6,737	6,642	6,780
Total Cap.	3,746	5,395	5,812	4,772	10,288	14,828	15,191	15,556	15,708	16,124
Cap. Exp.	1,485	1,341	1,034	1,153	1,082	2,092	2,135	2,037	2,118	2,764
Cash Flow	833	1,914	2,168	1,437	1,586	2,533	1,494	2,012	1,855	2,580
Curr. Ratio	1.1	1.3	1.6	1.3	1.6	1.2	1.2	1.2	1.3	1.5
% LT Debt of Cap.	15.6	10.4	11.5	13.8	66.6	48.6	50.0	44.9	47.0	48.2
% Net Inc.of Revs.	0.0	6.4	8.4	4.1	2.9	4.9	0.1	3.7	2.9	8.2
% Ret. on Assets	0.0	7.0	8.5	3.1	2.2	4.2	0.1	2.9	2.3	7.5
% Ret. on Equity	0.1	20.6	27.4	14.8	9.5	15.7	0.3	10.5	7.9	21.8

Data as orig. reptd.; bef. results of disc. opers. and/or spec. items. Per share data adj. for stk. divs. as of ex-div. date. Bold denotes diluted EPS (FASB 128). E-Estimated. NA-Not Available. NM-Not Meaningful. NR-Not Ranked.

Office—343 State St., Rochester, NY 14650. **Tel**—(716) 724-4000. **Website**—http://www.kodak.com **Chrmn & CEO**—G. M. C. Fisher. **Pres & COO**—D. A. Carp. **EVP & CFO**—H. L. Kavetas. **Treas**—D. M. Pollock. **Secy**—J. P. Haag. **Investor Contact**—Don Flick. **Dirs**—R. S. Braddock, D. A. Carp, M. L. Collins, L. D'Andrea, A. F. Emerson, G. M. C. Fisher, P. E. Gray, D. I. Jager, H. L. Kavetas, D. E. Lewis, P. H. O'Neill, J. J. Phelan Jr., R. A. Zimmerman. **Transfer Agent & Registrar**—First Chicago Trust Co., NYC. **Incorporated**—in New Jersey in 1901. **Empl**—91,500. **S&P Analyst:** Tom Graves, CFA

Eaton Corp.

804

NYSE Symbol **ETN**

In S&P 500

12-SEP-98

Industry:
Manufacturing (Diversified)

Summary: Eaton, a leading producer of auto and truck parts, also makes equipment for the semiconductor industry.

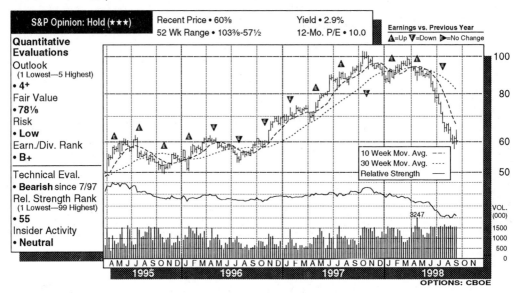

| S&P Opinion: Hold (★★★) | Recent Price • 60⅜ | Yield • 2.9% |
| | 52 Wk Range • 103⅜-57½ | 12-Mo. P/E • 10.0 |

Earnings vs. Previous Year
▲=Up ▼=Down ▶=No Change

Quantitative Evaluations

Outlook
(1 Lowest—5 Highest)
• **4+**

Fair Value
• **78⅛**

Risk
• **Low**

Earn./Div. Rank
• **B+**

Technical Eval.
• **Bearish** since 7/97

Rel. Strength Rank
(1 Lowest—99 Highest)
• **55**

Insider Activity
• **Neutral**

10 Week Mov. Avg.
30 Week Mov. Avg. - - - -
Relative Strength —

3247

VOL. (000)

OPTIONS: CBOE

Overview - 15-JUL-98

Sales should rise in 1998, on strength in the heavy truck market, but there is little pent-up demand to sustain sales, and a renewed slowdown would be felt quickly. Light vehicle markets are flat, but a focus on new products and systems will increase dollar content per vehicle assembled. With the recent sale of the appliance controls unit, the remaining controls business focuses on more lucrative power, automotive, aerospace and manufacturing equipment devices. Demand for distribution and control products should be spurred by new products that improve the quality of electricity. Semiconductor equipment demand has slowed, reflecting financial troubles in Asia, but the market may be stabilizing. Productivity gains, together with lower interest expense as long term debt is pared, should lead to higher net income in 1998. For the longer term, Eaton is focusing expansion plans on the Far East and Latin America, expected to be leading growth areas over the next decade, despite recent turmoil. Eaton also recently sold its axle and brake business to Dana Corp., and bought Dana's Spicer clutch business.

Valuation - 15-JUL-98

Despite the diversification of sales resulting from ETN's acquisition of the distribution and controls business from Westinghouse, the company remains heavily exposed to the cyclical vehicular, consumer durables, and capital goods markets. This exposure has traditionally led to an earnings multiple below that of the S&P 500. Although the company's volatile end markets are currently reasonably stable, it is still late in the economic cycle, and we do not think that the stock's historical discount to the S&P 500 will be eliminated. We expect the stock to be an average performer during the next 12 months.

Key Stock Statistics

S&P EPS Est. 1998	6.30	Tang. Bk. Value/Share	14.79
P/E on S&P Est. 1998	9.6	Beta	0.76
S&P EPS Est. 1999	6.95	Shareholders	22,100
Dividend Rate/Share	1.76	Market cap. (B)	$ 4.3
Shs. outstg. (M)	71.4	Inst. holdings	61%
Avg. daily vol. (M)	0.481		

Value of $10,000 invested 5 years ago: $ 17,000

Fiscal Year Ending Dec. 31

	1998	1997	1996	1995	1994	1993
Revenues (Million $)						
1Q	1,687	1,789	1,736	1,731	1,371	1,086
2Q	1,712	1,909	1,782	1,758	1,545	1,147
3Q	—	1,931	1,719	1,672	1,531	1,053
4Q	—	1,934	1,724	1,661	1,605	1,115
Yr.	—	7,563	6,961	6,822	6,052	4,401
Earnings Per Share ($)						
1Q	1.42	1.29	1.23	1.39	1.01	0.76
2Q	1.57	1.61	1.32	1.41	1.13	0.77
3Q	—	0.69	1.11	1.18	1.10	0.63
4Q	—	2.35	0.85	1.16	1.15	0.41
Yr.	E6.30	5.93	4.46	5.13	4.40	2.57

Next earnings report expected: mid October

Dividend Data (Dividends have been paid since 1923.)

Amount ($)	Date Decl.	Ex-Div. Date	Stock of Record	Payment Date
0.440	Oct. 22	Oct. 30	Nov. 03	Nov. 25 '97
0.440	Jan. 28	Feb. 05	Feb. 09	Feb. 25 '98
0.440	Apr. 22	Apr. 30	May. 04	May. 22 '98
0.440	Jul. 22	Jul. 30	Aug. 03	Aug. 25 '98

A Division of The **McGraw·Hill** Companies

Business Summary - 15-JUL-98

Well known for its dominant position in heavy duty truck transmissions, Eaton Corp. is also either the leader or second in most of the products manufactured for the electrical and electronic controls and vehicular components markets. ETN's goals are to boost sales to $10 billion by 2000, and to generate internal earnings growth of 10% a year. To achieve these goals, ETN is focused on entering emerging markets with its major products and maintaining technological leadership and cost competitiveness. The company augments internal growth through acquisitions.

Segment operating profit margins for recent years were:

	1997	1996	1995
Electrical and Electronic Controls	5.9%	8.0%	7.9%
Vehicles	13%	9.6%	13%
Defense Systems (sold late 1997)	Def.	3.6%	1.7%

The Electronic and Electrical Controls segment (53% of 1997 revenues) consists of industrial and commercial, automotive, and specialty. Cutler-Hammer produces industrial and commercial controls and includes the Westinghouse business. Products include a broad range of electromechanical and electronic controls such as sensors, panelboards, switchboards and relays; counters; electrical adjustable speed drives; and low-voltage distribution equipment. Eaton controls are used in nearly every kind of automotive application, ranging from remote keyless entry systems to dashboard and door controls. In recent years, semiconductor wafer fabrication equipment has become an important line for ETN, as demand for ion implantation equipment has boomed. Several years ago, a group was formed to develop products for the $9.2 billion flat panel manufacturing industry. The group will apply ETN's ion implantation technology to flat panel manufacturing. This new process is expected to provide tremendous growth potential because it will lower production costs and improve resolution quality. Other opportunities include VORAD vehicular collision warning and intelligent cruise control systems.

The Vehicle Components segment (46% of 1997 revenues), makes parts and equipment for heavy trucks (61% of 1997 VC revenues), automobiles and light trucks (23%), and off-highway vehicles (16%). The principal line is truck transmissions, but ETN also holds strong positions in engine valves, valve lifters, superchargers, locking differentials, viscous fan drives, fans, and fan shrouds. Promising areas for growth include the automation of heavy duty truck transmissions which are now mostly manually shifted, and the "Fleet Advisor" on-board transportation logistics management system for use by commercial fleets.

Per Share Data ($) (Year Ended Dec. 31)	1997	1996	1995	1994	1993	1992	1991	1990	1989	1988
Tangible Bk. Val.	14.73	14.31	12.67	10.49	11.61	9.71	12.56	12.36	10.64	11.47
Cash Flow	10.33	8.69	8.72	7.26	5.19	4.45	3.19	4.45	4.54	4.63
Earnings	5.93	4.50	5.13	4.40	2.57	1.99	0.92	2.38	2.79	3.06
Dividends	1.72	1.60	1.50	1.20	1.15	1.10	1.10	1.05	1.00	0.83
Payout Ratio	29%	36%	29%	27%	45%	55%	121%	42%	35%	26%
Prices - High	103 3/8	70 7/8	62 1/2	62 1/8	55 3/8	41 5/8	33 1/8	32 1/4	33 3/4	28 3/4
- Low	67 1/4	50 3/8	45 1/4	43 7/8	38 1/4	30 7/8	23 3/8	20 3/8	26 1/2	22 3/8
P/E Ratio - High	17	16	12	14	22	21	36	13	12	9
- Low	11	11	9	10	15	16	25	9	9	7
Income Statement Analysis (Million $)										
Revs.	7,563	6,961	6,822	6,052	4,401	3,869	3,381	3,639	3,671	3,469
Oper. Inc.	1,042	854	921	776	563	399	329	439	506	518
Depr.	342	320	281	216	182	170	155	146	131	117
Int. Exp.	86.0	93.0	96.0	101	87.0	90.0	86.0	88.0	81.3	81.9
Pretax Inc.	668	485	592	488	262	178	82.0	250	336	367
Eff. Tax Rate	31%	28%	33%	32%	31%	23%	24%	32%	38%	38%
Net Inc.	464	349	399	333	180	137	62.0	169	210	228
Balance Sheet & Other Fin. Data (Million $)										
Cash	53.0	60.0	84.0	41.0	300	216	122	217	193	192
Curr. Assets	2,055	2,017	1,967	1,846	1,466	1,318	1,186	1,296	1,291	1,305
Total Assets	5,465	5,307	5,053	4,682	3,268	3,096	3,087	3,013	3,052	3,034
Curr. Liab.	1,357	1,230	1,145	1,102	787	655	699	633	616	827
LT Debt	1,272	1,062	1,084	1,053	649	833	795	755	836	655
Common Eqty.	2,071	2,160	1,975	1,680	1,105	948	1,153	1,140	1,145	1,159
Total Cap.	3,343	3,222	3,059	2,733	1,754	1,795	2,084	2,060	2,148	1,938
Cap. Exp.	438	347	399	267	227	172	170	202	212	209
Cash Flow	806	669	680	549	362	307	217	315	341	345
Curr. Ratio	1.5	1.6	1.7	1.7	1.9	2.0	1.7	2.0	2.1	1.6
% LT Debt of Cap.	38.0	33.0	35.5	38.5	37.0	46.4	38.1	36.7	38.9	33.8
% Net Inc.of Revs.	6.1	5.1	5.9	5.5	4.1	3.5	1.8	4.6	5.7	6.6
% Ret. on Assets	8.6	6.8	8.2	8.1	5.6	4.4	2.0	5.8	6.9	7.8
% Ret. on Equity	21.9	16.9	21.9	23.1	17.3	12.9	5.4	15.4	18.3	21.2

Data as orig. reptd.; bef. results of disc. opers. and/or spec. items. Per share data adj. for stk. divs. as of ex-div. date. Bold denotes diluted EPS (FASB 128). E-Estimated. NA-Not Available. NM-Not Meaningful. NR-Not Ranked.

Office—Eaton Center, Cleveland, OH 44114-2584. **Tel**—(216) 523-5000. **Website**—http://www.eaton.com **Chrmn & CEO**—S. R. Hardis. **Pres & COO**—A. M. Cutler. **CFO**—A. T. Dillon. **Treas**—R. E. Parmenter.**Secy**—E. R. Franklin. **Investor Contact**—William C. Hartman. **Dirs**—N. A. Armstrong, A. M. Cutler, P. B. Davis, E. Green, S. R. Hardis, N. C. Lautenbach, J. R. Miller, F. C. Moseley, V. A. Pelson, A. W. Reynolds, G. L. Tooker. **Transfer Agent & Registrar**—First Chicago Trust Co., Jersey City, NJ.**Incorporated**—in Ohio in 1916. **Empl**— 54,000. **S&P Analyst:** Robert E. Friedman, CPA

STANDARD &POOR'S
STOCK REPORTS
Ecolab Inc.
805M
NYSE Symbol **ECL**
In S&P 500

12-SEP-98

Industry: Chemicals (Specialty)

Summary: Ecolab is the leading worldwide marketer of cleaning, sanitizing and maintenance products and services for the hospitality, institutional and industrial markets.

S&P Opinion: Accumulate (★★★★)	Recent Price • 28½	Yield • 1.3%
	52 Wk Range • 33⅛-23⅛	12-Mo. P/E • 26.6

Quantitative Evaluations

Outlook (1 Lowest—5 Highest)
• **2**

Fair Value
• **27¼**

Risk
• **Low**

Earn./Div. Rank
• **A-**

Technical Eval.
• **Bearish** since 8/98

Rel. Strength Rank (1 Lowest—99 Highest)
• **78**

Insider Activity
• **Neutral**

Earnings vs. Previous Year
△=Up ▽=Down ▷=No Change

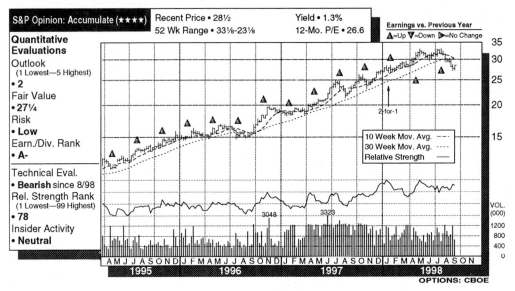

10 Week Mov. Avg. — — —
30 Week Mov. Avg. ‑‑‑‑‑
Relative Strength ——

2-for-1

3048   3323

OPTIONS: CBOE

Overview - 07-AUG-98

S&P projects that sales and earnings will continue to advance going into 1999 on continued worldwide gains in most core businesses, aided by sales force, product line and market share expansions. Hospitality and food service markets are generally healthy and a modestly positive pricing environment will also add to the gains. International sales growth will be boosted by ongoing growth in Latin America and Canada, though the strong U.S. dollar and the economic crisis in Asia (10% of sales) will limit gains. Acquisitions made since 1997 will contribute to the gains. Profitability will likely be maintained through the contribution of an improved product mix, achieved on a high level of new products, volume gains, and by stable raw material costs. Gibson Chemical (Australia), acquired in late 1997 with annual sales of about $120 million, will be neutral to profits in 1998 and accretive in 1999. Interest expense will climb sharply, due to the Gibson acquisition and a more active stock buyback program. Earnings of the European joint venture should post further increases as a result of actions taken in the past two years to streamline the organization and the introduction of new products, though second half comparisons will be difficult as a result of sluggish key European markets and unfavorable exchange rates.

Valuation - 07-AUG-98

S&P's "accumulate" opinion on ECL reflects the company's attractive long term growth prospects and strong cash flow. We view the shares as still attractive, despite their strong performance since 1994 and their premium P/E multiple compared to the overall market. The dividend has been raised steadily for many years; the shares were split 2-for-1 in January 1998.

Key Stock Statistics

S&P EPS Est. 1998	1.15	Tang. Bk. Value/Share	4.38
P/E on S&P Est. 1998	24.8	Beta	0.83
S&P EPS Est. 1999	1.30	Shareholders	5,000
Dividend Rate/Share	0.38	Market cap. (B)	$ 3.7
Shs. outstg. (M)	129.6	Inst. holdings	48%
Avg. daily vol. (M)	0.183		

Value of $10,000 invested 5 years ago: $ 34,065

Fiscal Year Ending Dec. 31

	1998	1997	1996	1995	1994	1993
Revenues (Million $)						
1Q	436.4	373.8	333.7	309.6	274.9	240.8
2Q	468.5	411.8	373.2	333.4	299.2	257.8
3Q	—	432.9	392.1	348.5	320.4	275.6
4Q	—	421.9	391.0	349.4	313.1	267.4
Yr.	—	1,640	1,490	1,341	1,208	1,042
Earnings Per Share ($)						
1Q	**0.23**	0.20	0.15	0.14	0.13	0.10
2Q	**0.28**	0.25	0.21	0.19	0.17	0.15
3Q	**E0.34**	0.30	0.28	0.23	0.21	0.18
4Q	**E0.30**	0.26	0.23	0.20	0.12	0.17
Yr.	**E1.15**	1.00	0.87	0.75	0.63	0.60

Next earnings report expected: late October

Dividend Data (Dividends have been paid since 1936.)

Amount ($)	Date Decl.	Ex-Div. Date	Stock of Record	Payment Date
2-for-1	Dec. 15	Jan. 16	Dec. 26	Jan. 15 '98
0.095	Feb. 20	Mar. 13	Mar. 17	Apr. 15 '98
0.095	May. 08	Jun. 12	Jun. 16	Jul. 15 '98
0.095	Aug. 14	Sep. 11	Sep. 15	Oct. 15 '98

A Division of The McGraw-Hill Companies

STANDARD
&POOR'S
STOCK REPORTS

Ecolab Inc.

805M
12-SEP-98

Business Summary - 07-AUG-98

Using its "Circle the Customer-Circle the Globe" strategy, this leading global supplier of cleaning, sanitizing and maintenance products and services for hospitality, institutional and industrial markets has been successful in leveraging its customer base by providing all the services and products to meet their needs and in expanding its products and services worldwide. ECL achieved record sales, net income and share earnings for the sixth consecutive year in 1997. Geographic contributions in 1997 were:

	Sales	Profits
U.S.	78%	88%
International	22%	12%

In the U.S., Ecolab is the leading supplier of institutional cleaners and sanitizers (55% of domestic sales in 1997) for warewashing, laundry, kitchen cleaning and general housekeeping, product dispensing equipment and dishwashing racks and related kitchen sundries to the foodservice, lodging and health care industries. The Kay division (6%) supplies cleaning and sanitizing products for the quick-service restaurant industry. The Food and Beverage division (16%) provides cleaning and sanitizing products and services to farms, dairy plants, and food and beverage processors. ECL also provides

institutional and commercial pest elimination and prevention services (8%), janitorial products (floor care, disinfectants, odor control and hand care products, 8%), textile care products (5%) for large institutional and commercial laundries, and water treatment products (2%) for commercial, institutional, and industrial markets.

Ecolab also provides institutional cleaning, textile, janitorial and food and beverage products and services in Canada, Latin America and the Asia/Pacific region.

As part of a strategy of growing partly through acquisitions, in December 1997 ECL acquired (for $150 million) Gibson Chemical, an Australian maker of cleaning products with annual sales of about $120 million. In July 1998, ECL purchased GCS Service, Inc., a provider of commercial kitchen equipment repair services with sales of $48 million in 1997. The February 1996 purchase of Huntington Laboratories, Inc., a manufacturer of janitorial products with annual sales of $50 million, doubled the size of ECL's janitorial operations, making it the second largest supplier in North America.

The 50%-owned Henkel-Ecolab joint venture provides cleaning and sanitizing services for European institutional and industrial markets. Sales were $845 million in 1997, down from $906 million in 1996. Equity income in the venture was a record $13.4 million in 1997, versus $13.0 million in 1996, aided by cost savings. Henkel KGaA owns 23.9% of ECL.

Per Share Data ($)

(Year Ended Dec. 31)	1997	1996	1995	1994	1993	1992	1991	1990	1989	1988
Tangible Bk. Val.	2.59	3.27	3.13	3.13	2.67	2.51	2.12	0.30	0.64	0.69
Cash Flow	1.75	1.57	1.33	1.12	1.00	0.89	0.88	1.36	0.69	1.03
Earnings	1.00	0.88	0.75	0.63	0.60	0.52	0.48	0.49	0.03	0.41
Dividends	0.34	0.29	0.26	0.23	0.20	0.18	0.17	0.17	0.17	0.16
Payout Ratio	34%	33%	34%	36%	33%	35%	42%	34%	NM	40%
Prices - High	28	19³/₄	15⁷/₈	11³/₄	11⁷/₈	9⁵/₈	8³/₈	7³/₄	9	7
- Low	18¹/₈	14⁵/₈	10	9⁵/₈	9¹/₈	6⁵/₈	4⁷/₈	4¹/₈	6¹/₄	5³/₈
P/E Ratio - High	28	23	21	19	20	19	18	16	NM	17
- Low	18	17	13	15	15	13	10	9	NM	13

Income Statement Analysis (Million $)

	1997	1996	1995	1994	1993	1992	1991	1990	1989	1988
Revs.	1,640	1,490	1,341	1,208	1,042	1,005	918	1,390	1,306	1,212
Oper. Inc.	319	275	239	212	172	165	154	204	165	179
Depr.	101	89.5	76.3	66.9	50.2	47.7	43.6	82.9	72.8	69.9
Int. Exp.	12.6	14.4	11.5	16.2	25.2	39.7	36.2	33.5	35.4	34.3
Pretax Inc.	219	184	159	135	109	91.6	84.7	93.4	13.8	78.1
Eff. Tax Rate	39%	39%	38%	37%	31%	30%	34%	43%	77%	44%
Net Inc.	134	113	99	84.6	75.9	64.3	55.7	53.7	3.1	44.1

Balance Sheet & Other Fin. Data (Million $)

	1997	1996	1995	1994	1993	1992	1991	1990	1989	1988
Cash	61.2	69.3	24.7	98.0	48.0	36.0	78.0	28.0	122	19.0
Curr. Assets	510	436	358	401	298	254	284	249	400	286
Total Assets	1,416	1,208	1,061	1,020	863	832	922	926	1,043	943
Curr. Liab.	404	328	311	254	196	188	238	234	257	229
LT Debt	259	149	89.4	105	126	208	319	205	225	254
Common Eqty.	552	520	457	462	374	344	298	343	406	433
Total Cap.	811	669	546	567	500	552	617	657	741	687
Cap. Exp.	122	112	110	88.0	68.0	57.0	53.0	64.0	63.0	66.0
Cash Flow	235	203	175	151	126	112	95.0	129	76.0	112
Curr. Ratio	1.3	1.3	1.1	1.6	1.5	1.4	1.2	1.1	1.6	1.3
% LT Debt of Cap.	31.9	22.2	16.4	18.6	25.1	37.8	51.7	31.1	30.4	36.9
% Net Inc.of Revs.	8.2	7.6	7.4	7.0	7.3	6.4	6.1	3.9	0.2	3.6
% Ret. on Assets	10.2	10.0	9.6	8.7	9.0	7.3	5.2	5.9	0.3	4.6
% Ret. on Equity	25.0	23.2	21.6	19.6	21.1	19.9	13.7	13.2	0.7	10.6

Data as orig. reptd.; bef. results of disc. opers. and/or spec. items. Per share data adj. for stk. divs. as of ex-div. date. Bold denotes diluted EPS (FASB 128). E-Estimated. NA-Not Available. NM-Not Meaningful. NR-Not Ranked.

Office—Ecolab Center, St. Paul, MN 55102. **Tel**—(612) 293-2233. **E-Mail**—ecolab@shareholder.com **Website**—http://www.ecolab.com **Chrmn & CFO**—M. E. Shannon. **Pres & CEO**—A. L. Schuman. **VP & Secy**—K. A. Iverson. **VP & Treas**—S. L. Fritze. **VP & Investor Contact**—Michael J. Monahan. **Dirs**—L. S. Biller, R. S. Block, J. J. Howard, J.W. Johnson, J. W. Levin, F. Richards, R. L. Schall, R. Schulz, A. L. Schuman, M. E. Shannon, P. L. Smith, H. Uytterhoeven, A. Woeste. **Transfer Agent & Registrar**—First Chicago Trust Co. of New York, Jersey City, NJ. **Incorporated**—in Delaware in 1924. **Empl**— 9,573. **S&P Analyst**: Richard O'Reilly, CFA

STANDARD &POOR'S
STOCK REPORTS

Edison International

806M

NYSE Symbol **EIX**

In S&P 500

12-SEP-98 | **Industry:** Electric Companies

Summary: Edison International is the holding company for Southern California Edison. Other businesses include electric power generation, financial investments and real estate development.

S&P Opinion: Accumulate (★★★★)

Recent Price • 26½
52 Wk Range • 31-24¾

Yield • 3.9%
12-Mo. P/E • 14.2

Quantitative Evaluations

Outlook (1 Lowest—5 Highest)
• **2+**

Fair Value
• **26¾**

Risk
• **Low**

Earn./Div. Rank
• **B**

Technical Eval.
• **NA**

Rel. Strength Rank (1 Lowest—99 Highest)
• **74**

Insider Activity
• **Neutral**

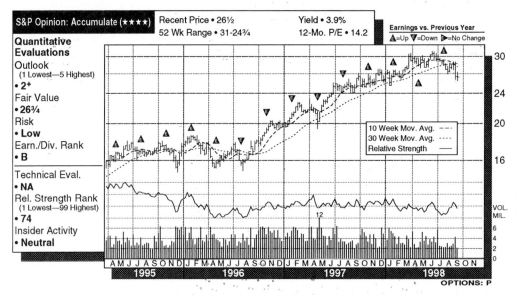

Earnings vs. Previous Year
▲=Up ▼=Down ▷=No Change

10 Week Mov. Avg. −·−·
30 Week Mov. Avg. ·····
Relative Strength —

OPTIONS: P

Overview - 10-AUG-98

We expect high single-digit EPS growth in 1999, as the company benefits from the continuing growth of its non-regulated businesses. The planned acquisition of the Homer City Generating Station, which will enable EIX to compete in the the mid-Atlantic power markets, is expected to be neutral to 1999 earnings, and accretive thereafter. Utility earnings in 1998 will be restricted by lower rates resulting from Assembly Bill 1890, which opened (in March 1998) the retail market to direct competition, reducing rates for residential and small customers by 10%. This will be partially offset, however, by EIS's reduced costs and shares outstanding. The company sold its 12 gas-fired generating plants for $1.188 billion, which was more than double their stated book value of $569 million. EIX should gain from the growth (close to 20% a year) in its non-regulated operations and, with these businesses expected to account for close to 40% of revenues within the next 5 years, there is the potential for significant EPS growth.

Valuation - 10-AUG-98

Although the performance of the stock has been flat year to date, we would continue to accumulate EIX shares. Given the growth potential of the non-regulated operations, the stock is attractive at less than 14X our 1999 EPS estimate of $2.00. In 1997, the shares surged 37%, outperforming the 31% gain of the S&P 500 and the 19.8% advance of the S&P Index of Electric Companies. The shares will also be buoyed by the company's share repurchase program, as well as from a PUC provision allowing full recovery of its stranded generating plant costs. Despite a recent 4% increase in the dividend, the payout ratio of 56% (on our 1998 EPS estimate) remains well below the industry average.

Key Stock Statistics

S&P EPS Est. 1998	1.85	Tang. Bk. Value/Share	14.73
P/E on S&P Est. 1998	14.3	Beta	0.55
S&P EPS Est. 1999	2.00	Shareholders	102,200
Dividend Rate/Share	1.04	Market cap. (B)	$ 9.4
Shs. outstg. (M)	353.6	Inst. holdings	41%
Avg. daily vol. (M)	0.599		

Value of $10,000 invested 5 years ago: $ 16,532

Fiscal Year Ending Dec. 31

	1998	1997	1996	1995	1994	1993
Revenues (Million $)						
1Q	1,910	2,001	1,968	1,822	1,747	1,785
2Q	2,243	2,167	1,814	1,861	1,878	1,768
3Q	—	2,738	2,568	2,670	2,678	2,424
4Q	—	2,329	2,195	2,030	2,042	1,845
Yr.	—	9,235	8,544	8,383	8,345	7,821
Earnings Per Share ($)						
1Q	**0.38**	0.35	0.38	0.34	0.30	0.33
2Q	**0.40**	0.34	0.35	0.36	0.32	0.32
3Q	**E0.69**	0.70	0.63	0.65	0.61	0.47
4Q	**E0.38**	0.36	0.27	0.31	0.30	0.31
Yr.	**E1.85**	1.73	1.63	1.66	1.52	1.43

Next earnings report expected: late October

Dividend Data (Dividends have been paid since 1909.)

Amount ($)	Date Decl.	Ex-Div. Date	Stock of Record	Payment Date
0.250	Sep. 18	Oct. 01	Oct. 03	Oct. 31 '97
0.250	Nov. 25	Dec. 31	Jan. 05	Jan. 31 '98
0.260	Feb. 19	Apr. 01	Apr. 03	Apr. 30 '98
0.260	May. 21	Jun. 30	Jul. 02	Jul. 31 '98

A Division of The McGraw·Hill Companies

Business Summary - 10-AUG-98

Edison International is the parent corporation of Southern California Edison (the second largest electric utility in the United States) and eight non-utility subsidiaries. Revenues in recent years were:

	1997	1996	1995
Electric Utility	86.1%	88.7%	93.7%
Diversified operations	13.9%	11.3%	6.3%

Edison International's main subsidiary, Southern California Edison (SCE), provides electric service to 4.2 million customers in a 50,000 square-mile area of central and southern California (excluding Los Angeles and certain other cities). In 1997, residential customers accounted for 38% of SCE's operating revenues; commercial customers, 38%; industrial customers, 12%; and other customers, 12%.

Between November 1997 and March 1998, SCE sold its 12 gas-fired generating plants for a total price of $1,188,000,000. The company continues to own one diesel fueled generating plant and 38 hydro electric plants. It also has a 75% interest in the San Onofre 2 and 3 nuclear generating units and a 15.8% interest in the three-unit Palo Verde nuclear station. SCE's power sources in 1997 were: purchased, 49%; nuclear, 17%; natural gas, 16%; coal, 12%; and hydro, 6%. Purchased power will likely represent a similar portion of power sources in the future.

Non-utility units include Edison Mission Energy (EME), which develops, owns and operates independent power facilities; Edison Capital, a provider of capital and financial services to support the growth of energy and infrastructure projects; Edison EV, which provides charging equipment for electric vehicles; Edison Source, a retail provider of energy services and energy marketing; and Edison Select, a provider of consumer products and services that build on the Edison brand.

In August 1998, EME agreed to acquire the coal-fired Homer City Generating Station in western Pennsylvania for $1.8 billion. The facility has access to power pools in Pennsylvania, New Jersey, Maryland and New York. The transaction is expected to close in early 1999.

On March 31, 1998, the right to direct access to choice of electric supplier was provided for all California customers. This was one of the byproducts of Assembly Bill 1890, which through legislation passed in September 1996, restructured the California power market. Key elements of the bill include a nonbypassable competitive transition charge for recovery of stranded costs; a 10% rate reduction for residential and small commercial customers starting in 1998, to be financed by rate reduction bonds; a rate freeze for industrial, agricultural and large commercial customers through March 31, 2002; the formation of a generation power exchange and an independent system operator to manage and control the transmission system and ensure reliability.

Per Share Data ($)

(Year Ended Dec. 31)	1997	1996	1995	1994	1993	1992	1991	1990	1989	1988
Tangible Bk. Val.	13.65	14.12	13.40	12.76	12.45	12.49	12.12	11.85	11.39	10.86
Earnings	1.73	1.64	1.66	1.52	1.43	1.66	1.60	1.80	1.78	1.75
Dividends	1.00	1.25	1.00	1.10	1.42	1.39	1.35	1.31	1.27	1.23
Payout Ratio	58%	76%	60%	73%	99%	84%	84%	73%	71%	70%
Prices - High	27³/₄	20³/₈	18	20¹/₂	25³/₄	23⁷/₈	23³/₄	20¹/₈	20¹/₂	18⁵/₈
- Low	19³/₈	15	14³/₈	12³/₈	19⁷/₈	20¹/₈	18	16³/₄	15¹/₂	14⁵/₈
P/E Ratio - High	16	12	11	13	18	14	15	11	12	11
- Low	11	9	9	8	14	12	11	9	9	8

Income Statement Analysis (Million $)

	1997	1996	1995	1994	1993	1992	1991	1990	1989	1988
Revs.	9,235	8,545	8,405	8,345	7,821	7,984	7,502	7,199	6,904	6,253
Depr.	1,362	1,173	1,014	945	922	807	764	716	690	647
Maint.	406	331	359	332	363	362	382	375	378	375
Fxd. Chgs. Cov.	2.3	3.2	3.3	2.9	2.6	3.1	2.9	3.1	3.2	3.3
Constr. Credits	17.0	26.0	33.0	28.0	36.0	37.0	28.0	23.0	22.0	30.0
Eff. Tax Rate	40%	44%	42%	40%	36%	39%	38%	39%	43%	41%
Net Inc.	700	717	739	681	639	739	703	786	778	762

Balance Sheet & Other Fin. Data (Million $)

	1997	1996	1995	1994	1993	1992	1991	1990	1989	1988
Gross Prop.	24,661	21,134	20,717	20,127	19,441	18,652	17,523	16,916	16,376	16,840
Cap. Exp.	783	744	NA	1,137	1,259	844	986	905	838	835
Net Prop.	14,117	11,703	12,148	12,417	12,303	11,937	11,184	11,220	11,281	11,395
Capitalization:										
LT Debt	8,871	7,475	7,195	6,347	6,459	6,320	5,745	5,291	5,283	5,422
% LT Debt	59	51	50	48	50	49	48	47	47	49
Pfd.	609	709	709	721	634	637	558	569	583	598
% Pfd.	4.05	4.80	5.00	5.50	4.90	4.90	4.70	5.00	5.20	5.40
Common	5,527	6,397	6,360	6,144	5,948	5,954	5,681	5,503	5,289	5,065
% Common	37	44	45	47	46	46	47	48	47	46
Total Cap.	19,452	19,943	19,638	18,305	17,476	15,618	13,260	12,532	12,234	12,029
% Oper. Ratio	87.8	82.7	83.6	84.4	84.4	83.2	83.6	82.6	83.1	82.5
% Earn. on Net Prop.	10.2	12.4	11.2	10.5	10.0	11.0	11.0	11.1	10.3	9.6
% Return On Revs.	7.6	8.4	8.8	8.2	8.2	9.3	9.4	10.9	11.3	12.2
% Return On Invest. Capital	10.5	7.1	7.9	7.0	7.1	8.6	10.1	11.3	11.5	11.3
% Return On Com. Equity	11.7	11.2	11.8	11.3	10.7	12.5	12.5	14.5	15.0	15.3

Data as orig. reptd.; bef. results of disc opers. and/or spec. items. Per share data adj. for stk. divs. as of ex-div. date. Bold denotes diluted EPS (FASB 128). E-Estimated. NA-Not Available. NM-Not Meaningful. NR-Not Ranked.

Office—2244 Walnut Grove Ave., Rosemead, CA 91770. **Tel**—(626) 302-2222. **Website**—http://edisonx.com **Chrmn & CEO**—J. E. Bryson. **EVP & CFO**—A. J. Fohrer. **Secy**—B. P. Ryder. **Investor Contacts**—Jo Ann Goddard (2515) / Joy Kedroski (2062). **Dirs**—J. E. Bryson, W. H. Chen, W. Christopher, S. E. Frank, C. C. Frost, J. C. Hanley, C. F. Huntsinger, C. D. Miller, L. G. Nogales, R. L. Olson, J. J. Pinola, J. M. Rosser, E. L. Shannon, Jr., R. H. Smith, T. C. Sutton, D. M. Tellep, J. D. Watkins, E. Zapanta. **Transfer Agent & Registrar**—Company's office. **Incorporated**—in California in 1909. **Empl**— 14,105. **S&P Analyst:** Justin McCann

STANDARD &POOR'S
STOCK REPORTS

EG&G Inc.

789

NYSE Symbol **EGG**

In S&P 500

12-SEP-98

Industry: Electronics (Instrumentation)

Summary: This technologically diversified company provides advanced scientific and technical products and services worldwide.

S&P Opinion: Hold (★★★)	Recent Price • 23¼	Yield • 2.4%
	52 Wk Range • 33¾-18	12-Mo. P/E • 10.5

Quantitative Evaluations

Outlook
(1 Lowest—5 Highest)
• 2

Fair Value
• 23¼

Risk
• **Average**

Earn./Div. Rank
• **B+**

Technical Eval.
• **Bullish** since 3/98

Rel. Strength Rank
(1 Lowest—99 Highest)
• 51

Insider Activity
• **Neutral**

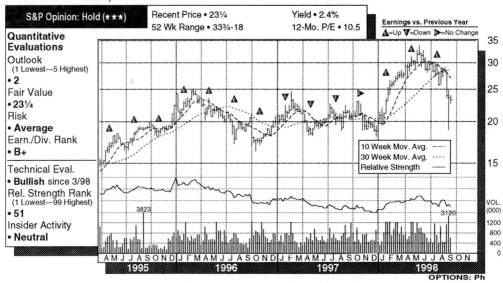

Earnings vs. Previous Year
▲=Up ▼=Down ▶=No Change

10 Week Mov. Avg. ----
30 Week Mov. Avg. ....
Relative Strength ——

VOL. (000)
1200
800
400
0

OPTIONS: Ph

Overview - 28-JUL-98

Revenues are expected to continue to increase modestly through much of 1998, and into 1999, reflecting growth in all segments. Technical services sales should rise on new contracts and demand for automotive testing services. Mechanical components profits are seen benefiting from strong aerospace bookings and the April 1998 acquisition of Belfab-a maker of bellows instruments. Double-digit operating margins are expected to continue in the instruments group as the product mix improves. In optoelectronics, IC Sensors reached breakeven in the second quarter, and should be profitable for the balance of this year. Additional restructuring charges are likely in the second half of 1998, following charges of $0.49 and $0.47 a share in the first and second quarters, respectively. The second quarter charges were offset by an $0.88 gain from the sale of the Sealol division. Gains from the restructuring should add $0.05 a share to earnings in 1999.

Valuation - 28-JUL-98

The shares were recently off their highs, following a roller-coaster ride during 1997 and a 68% climb in the first half of 1998. EGG continues to streamline its operations, and results for the balance of 1998 and beyond will depend on the market acceptance of new products, the extent to which improved operating efficiencies will be able to offset increased pricing pressure, and the effect of foreign currency fluctuations. EGG, which has been repurchasing stock, plans to continue its buyback program, which should aid EPS somewhat. However, with the shares trading at 21X our recently raised EPS projection for 1998 (before one-time gains from the sale of Rotron and Sealol, and restructuring charges), and 17X our 1999 estimate, and EPS growth projected at 18%, we view the stock as no better than a market performer.

Key Stock Statistics

S&P EPS Est. 1998	1.35	Tang. Bk. Value/Share	6.01
P/E on S&P Est. 1998	17.2	Beta	0.61
S&P EPS Est. 1999	1.60	Shareholders	11,300
Dividend Rate/Share	0.56	Market cap. (B)	$ 1.1
Shs. outstg. (M)	46.0	Inst. holdings	66%
Avg. daily vol. (M)	0.267		

Value of $10,000 invested 5 years ago: $ 14,011

Fiscal Year Ending Dec. 31

	1998	1997	1996	1995	1994	1993
Revenues (Million $)						
1Q	355.9	347.0	346.8	338.2	325.7	648.9
2Q	356.3	368.7	355.9	342.3	329.9	662.0
3Q	—	358.4	354.8	361.6	336.9	746.3
4Q	—	386.8	369.8	377.5	340.1	640.7
Yr.	—	1,461	1,427	1,420	1,333	2,698
Earnings Per Share ($)						
1Q	0.75	0.10	0.25	0.17	0.14	0.34
2Q	0.68	-0.29	0.30	0.23	0.16	0.37
3Q	—	0.30	0.30	0.27	-1.03	0.27
4Q	—	0.45	0.30	0.40	0.15	0.43
Yr.	—	0.67	1.15	1.05	-0.58	1.41

Next earnings report expected: late October

Dividend Data (Dividends have been paid since 1965.)

Amount ($)	Date Decl.	Ex-Div. Date	Stock of Record	Payment Date
0.140	Oct. 22	Jan. 14	Jan. 16	Feb. 06 '98
0.140	Jan. 21	Apr. 15	Apr. 17	May. 08 '98
0.140	May. 21	Jul. 22	Jul. 24	Aug. 10 '98
0.140	Jul. 22	Oct. 21	Oct. 23	Nov. 10 '98

A Division of The McGraw·Hill Companies

Business Summary - 28-JUL-98

Studying high-speed photographic and stroboscopic techniques and their applications beginning in 1931 wasn't a bad idea for two of EG&G's (EGG) founders. They became the basis for several of this technologically diversified company's current core areas. Contributions by segment in 1997 were:

	Sales	Profits
Technical services	41%	32%
Instruments	21%	29%
Mechanical components	20%	31%
Optoelectronics	18%	8%

EGG's strategic objective is to enhance shareholder value through the introduction of new products and technology into new and existing markets. In the instruments segment, where the company develops and manufactures hardware and associated software for applications in medical diagnostics, biochemical and medical research, EGG has identified several markets in which its core technologies provide a competitive advantage, including X-ray imaging applied to food monitoring and airport security. It will continue to seek acquisitions focused on the clinical and diagnostics markets and the bioanalytical research market, and expects this segment to be the largest contributor to income in 1999.

The company's technical services segment supplies

engineering, scientific, management and technical support services to a broad range of governmental and industrial customers. The largest contributors in this segment are automotive testing and the operation of the Kennedy Space Center. In May 1998, the division received a $113 million U.S. Navy contract.

Mechanical components include high-reliability advanced seals and bellows products, and precision components for aerospace applications. In early 1998, EGG sold Rotron ($70 million in sales), a maker of fans, blowers and motors, to AMETEK, Inc., for $103 million. A net gain of $1.00 a share was recorded on the sale in the 1998 first quarter. In April 1998, EGG sold its Sealol Industrial Seals division ($88 million in sales) to TI Group plc., for $100 million. EGG simultaneously purchased TI's Belfab division ($30 million in sales), a producer of specialty bellows devices, for $45 million.

The optoelectronics segment designs and manufactures optical sensors ranging from simple photo cells to sophisticated imaging systems and light sources that include flashlamps and laser diodes. The company is also designing medical imaging devices based on amorphous silicon technology that are expected to replace the film in many X-ray applications.

During 1997, EGG repurchased 1,332,000 of its common shares for an average cost of $21.09 each. Through the first half of 1998, it bought back 447,000 shares for $11.4 million. Also, capital expenditures for 1998 are seen at $40 million to $50 million.

Per Share Data ($)

(Year Ended Dec. 31)	1997	1996	1995	1994	1993	1992	1991	1990	1989	1988
Tangible Bk. Val.	5.50	5.50	5.12	5.77	6.03	6.11	5.34	4.28	3.96	4.89
Cash Flow	1.64	2.02	1.82	0.08	2.08	2.20	2.06	1.83	1.64	1.56
Earnings	0.67	1.15	1.05	-0.58	1.41	1.56	1.46	1.30	1.20	1.15
Dividends	0.56	0.56	0.56	0.56	0.52	0.50	0.42	0.38	0.34	0.30
Payout Ratio	84%	49%	53%	NM	37%	32%	29%	29%	28%	26%
Prices - High	24⅝	25⅛	24½	19	24½	26¾	25	20½	18¼	19½
- Low	18	16¼	13	13¾	15¾	17⅞	15½	14	14¼	13⅜
P/E Ratio - High	37	22	23	NM	17	17	17	16	15	17
- Low	27	14	12	NM	11	11	11	11	12	12

Income Statement Analysis (Million $)

	1997	1996	1995	1994	1993	1992	1991	1990	1989	1988
Revs.	1,461	1,427	1,420	1,333	2,698	2,789	2,689	2,474	1,650	1,406
Oper. Inc.	132	129	122	97.0	159	166	159	138	124	123
Depr.	44.6	40.9	39.4	36.8	37.8	36.3	33.7	29.9	25.5	24.6
Int. Exp.	12.5	13.4	8.5	5.4	6.3	7.2	8.8	10.5	9.1	7.5
Pretax Inc.	54.0	80.4	86.1	-17.0	122	121	120	107	100	97.0
Eff. Tax Rate	43%	32%	37%	NM	35%	28%	33%	31%	30%	30%
Net Inc.	30.6	54.5	54.3	-32.1	79.6	87.8	81.2	74.0	69.9	68.7

Balance Sheet & Other Fin. Data (Million $)

	1997	1996	1995	1994	1993	1992	1991	1990	1989	1988
Cash	57.9	47.8	76.0	75.7	72.2	69.8	63.0	34.2	28.6	41.9
Curr. Assets	488	455	469	481	465	483	456	408	407	364
Total Assets	832	823	804	793	769	750	698	675	643	539
Curr. Liab.	286	260	250	282	237	235	241	258	256	173
LT Debt	114	115	115	0.8	1.5	2.0	2.3	7.0	8.9	14.8
Common Eqty.	328	365	367	445	478	474	421	370	349	332
Total Cap.	443	480	482	446	479	476	423	381	361	356
Cap. Exp.	48.7	80.5	61.8	37.3	27.9	22.4	26.6	19.8	23.3	27.9
Cash Flow	75.3	95.4	93.7	5.0	117	124	115	104	95.0	93.0
Curr. Ratio	1.7	1.8	1.9	1.7	2.0	2.1	1.9	1.6	1.6	2.1
% LT Debt of Cap.	25.9	24.0	23.9	0.2	0.3	0.4	0.5	1.8	2.5	4.2
% Net Inc.of Revs.	2.1	3.8	3.8	NM	2.9	3.1	3.0	3.0	4.2	4.9
% Ret. on Assets	3.7	6.7	6.8	NM	10.5	12.1	11.8	11.4	12.0	12.5
% Ret. on Equity	8.8	14.9	13.4	NM	16.8	19.6	20.5	20.9	20.8	21.9

Data as orig. reptd.; bef. results of disc. opers. and/or spec. items. Per share data adj. for stk. divs. as of ex-div. date. Bold denotes diluted EPS (FASB 128). E-Estimated. NA-Not Available. NM-Not Meaningful. NR-Not Ranked.

Office—45 William St., Wellesley, MA 02181. **Tel**—(781) 237-5100.**Fax**—(617) 431-4255.**Website**—http://www.egginc.com **Chrmn & CEO**—J. M. Kucharski.**Pres & COO**—G. L. Summe. **SVP & CFO**—J. F. Alexander, II. **SVP & Clerk**—M. Gross. **Investor Contact**—Deborah S. Lorenz. **Dirs**—T. J. Erickson, J. B. Gray, K. F. Hansen, J. J. F. Keane, M. Kucharski, N. A. Lopardo, G. E. Marshall, M. C. Ruettgers, J. L. Thompson, G. R. Tod. **Transfer Agent**—Bank of Boston. **Incorporated**—in Massachusetts in 1947. **Empl**— 14,000. **S&P Analyst:** Stewart Scharf

Electronic Data Systems   817M

NYSE Symbol **EDS**

In S&P 500

12-SEP-98

Industry:
Services (Computer Systems)

Summary: This company, split off from General Motors in June 1996, is a leading provider of a full range of information technology services.

S&P Opinion: Hold (★★★)	Recent Price • 34	Yield • 1.8%
	52 Wk Range • 50⅞-25½	12-Mo. P/E • 18.3

Earnings vs. Previous Year
▲=Up ▼=Down ▶=No Change

Quantitative Evaluations

Outlook
(1 Lowest—5 Highest)
• **4**

Fair Value
• **44¾**

Risk
• **NA**

Earn./Div. Rank
• **A+**

Technical Eval.
• **NA**

Rel. Strength Rank
(1 Lowest—99 Highest)
• **65**

Insider Activity
• **NA**

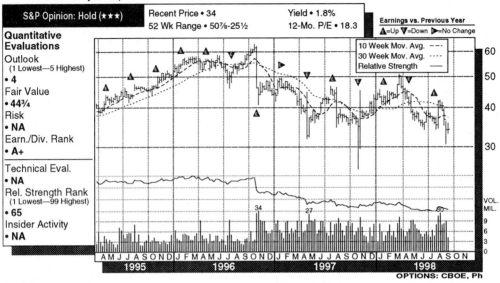

OPTIONS: CBOE, Ph

Overview - 04-AUG-98

Revenue growth has been restricted due to lower revenues from General Motors and the write-down of problem contracts. Growth has improved recently, aided by strong sales activity in non-GM business. However, this summer's prolonged strike at GM should further hamper revenue growth, as GM focuses more on its cost structure. The company signed $16.3 billion of new business in 1997, compared with only $8.4 billion in 1996. While GM business should continue to decline, base revenues should rise at a double-digit rate in 1998. As of July 1998, the pipeline of business opportunities over the next 12 months was about $60 billion worth of multi-year contracts. Margins should improve as massive cost cutting efforts take effect and revenues reaccelerate. However, near-term margins will be hurt by the declining GM business. Excluding one-time restructuring charges and write-downs, EPS would have been $1.92 in 1997, and $2.07 in 1996.

Valuation - 04-AUG-98

The shares declined sharply several times in the past year and a half, reflecting slower revenue growth, restructuring charges and disappointing earnings results. However, the company is cutting costs and signing new business. EDS is also investing in high potential growth areas, including electronic business, Internet applications and direct and database marketing services. Debt has been declining, due to strong free cash flow, and as a result, interest expense continues to decline. EDS booked $6.5 billion in new business contracts in the first half of the year. However, we believe the company needs to get a better handle on its cost structure, and improve its lagging GM business. With the computer services market remaining strong and the pipeline of new business opportunities large, we recommend holding the shares for long-term growth.

Key Stock Statistics

S&P EPS Est. 1998	1.78	Tang. Bk. Value/Share	8.15
P/E on S&P Est. 1998	19.1	Beta	0.60
S&P EPS Est. 1999	2.16	Shareholders	260,500
Dividend Rate/Share	0.60	Market cap. (B)	$ 16.7
Shs. outstg. (M)	492.2	Inst. holdings	49%
Avg. daily vol. (M)	1.589		

Value of $10,000 invested 5 years ago: $ 11,163

Fiscal Year Ending Dec. 31

	1998	1997	1996	1995	1994	1993
Revenues (Million $)						
1Q	3,942	3,592	3,367	2,776	2,239	2,073
2Q	4,186	3,682	3,498	2,950	2,334	2,091
3Q	—	3,734	3,570	3,074	2,565	2,084
4Q	—	4,228	4,006	3,622	2,914	2,314
Yr.	—	15,236	14,441	12,422	10,052	8,562
Earnings Per Share ($)						
1Q	**0.37**	**0.39**	0.45	0.42	0.36	0.32
2Q	**0.45**	**0.05**	-0.67	0.47	0.41	0.37
3Q	—	**0.47**	0.55	0.51	0.45	0.40
4Q	—	**0.57**	0.56	0.56	0.49	0.42
Yr.	—	**1.48**	0.89	1.96	1.71	1.51

Next earnings report expected: late October

Dividend Data (Dividends have been paid since 1984.)

Amount ($)	Date Decl.	Ex-Div. Date	Stock of Record	Payment Date
0.150	Oct. 09	Nov. 10	Nov. 13	Dec. 10 '97
0.150	Feb. 05	Feb. 12	Feb. 17	Mar. 10 '98
0.150	Apr. 02	Apr. 13	Apr. 15	Jun. 10 '98
0.150	Aug. 06	Aug. 14	Aug. 18	Sep. 10 '98

A Division of The McGraw-Hill Companies

Business Summary - 04-AUG-98

Electronic Data Systems (EDS), split off from General Motors Corp. in June 1996, is a leading provider of a full range of information technology (IT) services to enterprises, government entities and individuals worldwide. Services are provided in the categories of systems and technology services, business process management, management consulting and electronic markets.

The systems and technology services segment is EDS's traditional outsourcing business. It includes systems development, systems integration, systems management, desktop services, year 2000 conversions and enterprise software solutions.

In the business process management area, EDS may manage an entire business function within the client's organization, which may include IT operations, remittance processing, procurement logistics, enterprise customer management, customer service and training.

Management consulting services, provided through the A.T. Kearney subsidiary, include business and market strategy. Services focus on strategic consulting, operations consulting and technology consulting.

The company's electronic markets offerings include interactive marketing and payment services, Internet and online services and advertising, electronic commerce, smart cards, multimedia and home shopping, and the design of Internet web sites, intranets and extranets.

EDS focuses its business on specific industries. Revenues by business segment in 1997 were divided: manufacturing 44%, financial services 15%, government 14%, communications 6%, health 6%, transportation 4%, energy 3%, and other 8%.

Revenues derived from contracts with General Motors were approximately 28% of 1997 total revenues, down from 30% in 1996. In April 1996, EDS entered into a 10-year agreement under which it would continue to be GM's principal provider of information technology services.

In the second quarter of 1996, EDS recorded nonrecurring charges of $1.18 a share, consisting of an $850 million restructuring charge and $45.5 million in costs related to the company's split-off from GM.

In the second quarter of 1997, EDS recorded a charge of $265 million ($0.35 a share) for employee reductions and asset writedowns. A pretax charge of $38.7 million ($0.05 a share) was recorded in the fourth quarter of 1997 for asset writedowns.

Per Share Data ($) (Year Ended Dec. 31)	1997	1996	1995	1994	1993	1992	1991	1990	1989	1988
Tangible Bk. Val.	8.15	7.54	7.87	7.01	11.28	10.66	10.36	9.68	8.17	5.73
Cash Flow	3.95	3.32	3.65	2.91	2.48	2.28	2.11	1.91	1.71	1.60
Earnings	1.48	0.89	1.96	1.71	1.51	1.33	1.17	1.04	0.91	0.79
Dividends	0.60	0.60	0.52	0.48	0.40	0.36	0.32	0.28	0.24	0.17
Payout Ratio	41%	67%	27%	28%	26%	27%	27%	27%	27%	22%
Prices - High	49⅝	63⅜	52⅝	39½	35⅞	34	33	20⅛	14½	11¼
- Low	25½	40¾	36⅞	27½	26	25¼	17½	12¼	10⅝	8⅜
P/E Ratio - High	34	71	27	23	24	26	28	19	16	14
- Low	17	46	19	16	17	19	15	12	12	11
Income Statement Analysis (Million $)										
Revs.	15,236	14,441	12,422	9,960	8,507	8,155	7,029	6,022	5,374	4,745
Oper. Inc.	2,753	2,767	2,337	1,821	1,577	1,438	1,297	1,137	982	887
Depr.	1,210	1,181	808	578	466	458	446	417	382	392
Int. Exp.	176	153	121	52.9	39.9	61.1	43.8	30.1	24.0	18.3
Pretax Inc.	1,142	674	1,467	1,284	1,131	1,001	894	789	680	589
Eff. Tax Rate	36%	36%	36%	36%	36%	37%	37%	37%	36%	35%
Net Inc.	731	432	939	822	724	636	563	497	435	384
Balance Sheet & Other Fin. Data (Million $)										
Cash	677	963	639	758	608	588	416	715	681	728
Curr. Assets	5,169	5,008	4,382	3,354	2,507	2,157	1,946	1,716	1,458	1,339
Total Assets	11,174	11,174	10,832	8,787	6,942	6,124	5,703	4,565	3,918	3,416
Curr. Liab.	3,258	3,163	3,261	2,873	2,160	1,903	2,397	1,654	1,495	1,377
LT Debt	1,791	2,324	1,853	1,021	523	561	276	263	211	89.0
Common Eqty.	5,310	4,783	4,979	4,232	3,617	3,063	2,610	2,182	1,764	1,404
Total Cap.	7,575	8,030	7,571	5,913	4,782	4,220	3,301	2,889	2,308	1,723
Cap. Exp.	769	1,158	1,262	1,121	799	639	673	515	383	301
Cash Flow	1,941	1,613	1,747	1,399	1,190	1,093	1,009	914	817	777
Curr. Ratio	1.6	1.6	1.3	1.2	1.2	1.1	0.8	1.0	1.0	1.0
% LT Debt of Cap.	23.6	28.9	24.5	17.3	10.9	13.3	8.4	9.1	9.1	5.1
% Net Inc.of Revs.	4.8	3.0	7.6	8.3	8.5	7.8	8.0	8.3	8.1	8.1
% Ret. on Assets	6.5	3.9	9.6	10.4	10.7	9.9	10.8	11.6	12.1	12.2
% Ret. on Equity	14.5	8.9	20.4	20.9	20.8	20.8	23.1	24.9	27.9	31.5

Data as orig. reptd.; bef. results of disc. opers. and/or spec. items. Per share data adj. for stk. divs. as of ex-div. date. Bold denotes diluted EPS (FASB 128). E-Estimated. NA-Not Available. NM-Not Meaningful. NR-Not Ranked.

Office—5400 Legacy Dr., Plano, TX 75024. **Tel**—(972) 604-6000. **E-mail**—info@eds.com **Website**—http://www.eds.com **Chrmn & CEO**—L. M. Alberthal Jr. **Pres & COO**—J. M. Heller. **EVP & CFO**—J. M. Grant. **EVP & Secy**—J. R. Castle Jr. **VP & Treas**—A. E. Weynand. **Investor Contact**—Myrna Vance. **Dirs**—L. M. Alberthal Jr., J. A. Baker III, R. B. Cheney, G. J. Fernandes, W. H. Gray III, R. J. Groves, J. M. Heller, R. L. Hunt, C. R. Kidder, J. Rodin, E. J. Sosa. **Transfer Agent & Registrar**—Bank of New York. **Empl**— 110,000. **S&P Analyst:** Brian Goodstadt

STANDARD &POOR'S
STOCK REPORTS

EMC Corp.

789D

NYSE Symbol **EMC**

In S&P 500

12-SEP-98

Industry:
Computers (Peripherals)

Summary: This company is the leading supplier of enterprise storage systems and software for mainframe and open systems environments.

S&P Opinion: Buy (★★★★)

| Recent Price • 53¼ | Yield • Nil |
| 52 Wk Range • 59⅜-23½ | 12-Mo. P/E • 44.0 |

Quantitative Evaluations

Outlook
(1 Lowest—5 Highest)
• **4**

Fair Value
• 62¾

Risk
• **Average**

Earn./Div. Rank
• **B**

Technical Eval.
• **NA**

Rel. Strength Rank
(1 Lowest—99 Highest)
• **97**

Insider Activity
• **Neutral**

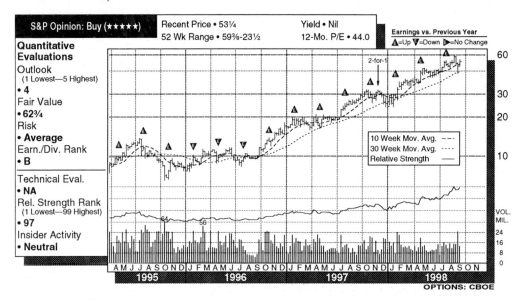

Earnings vs. Previous Year
▲=Up ▼=Down ▶=No Change

10 Week Mov. Avg. – – –
30 Week Mov. Avg. · · · ·
Relative Strength —

OPTIONS: CBOE

Overview - 22-JUL-98

Revenues are expected to advance over 30% in 1998, reflecting particularly strong demand for the company's Symmetrix enterprise data storage systems for both client/server and mainframe environments. The proliferation of data across companies is creating tremendous demand for systems and software to help store and manage this data. Software revenues, which now contribute 10% of total revenues, should more than double in 1998, to a projected $400 million, from 1997's $177 million. Revenues have been strong recently across all geographic regions, including Asia. Contributions from alliances and relationships with major computer industry players continue to boost revenues. Margins are expected to widen, due to EMC's rapidly growing software business, as well as rapidly declining component costs. Earnings should climb over 40% in 1998.

Valuation - 22-JUL-98

The shares of this leading supplier of storage solutions have surged in 1998, reflecting the company's steadily growing market share, strong demand, and widening margins. We expect EMC's market share to continue to increase in 1998. The company also holds a substantial technology lead over its competitors, due to its focus solely on storage, and to heavy investments in research and development over the past several years. The continuing focus on storage software products will help both sales and margins. About 80% of research and development spending is for software, providing a competitive advantage for EMC. Results are also being boosted by additional sales related to Year 2000 compliance testing. We believe that EMC is well positioned as the leader in a rapidly growing industry, and recommend purchasing the shares.

Key Stock Statistics

S&P EPS Est. 1998	1.44	Tang. Bk. Value/Share	4.79
P/E on S&P Est. 1998	37.0	Beta	1.32
S&P EPS Est. 1999	1.85	Shareholders	4,500
Dividend Rate/Share	Nil	Market cap. (B)	$ 26.6
Shs. outstg. (M)	499.5	Inst. holdings	73%
Avg. daily vol. (M)	3.685		

Value of $10,000 invested 5 years ago: $ 179,368

Fiscal Year Ending Dec. 31

	1998	1997	1996	1995	1994	1993
Revenues (Million $)						
1Q	828.4	618.4	521.5	448.1	267.1	138.8
2Q	952.0	713.5	545.0	478.6	308.1	179.5
3Q	—	732.6	550.8	475.5	215.8	215.8
4Q	—	873.4	656.4	519.1	430.7	248.6
Yr.	—	2,938	2,274	1,921	1,377	782.6
Earnings Per Share ($)						
1Q	**0.28**	0.22	0.17	0.17	0.12	0.04
2Q	**0.36**	0.25	0.18	0.19	0.13	0.07
3Q	**E0.36**	0.25	0.18	0.17	0.16	0.10
4Q	**E0.44**	0.32	0.25	0.13	0.18	0.12
Yr.	**E1.44**	1.04	0.78	0.68	0.59	0.33

Next earnings report expected: late October

Dividend Data

Amount ($)	Date Decl.	Ex-Div. Date	Stock of Record	Payment Date
2-for-1	Oct. 21	Nov. 18	Oct. 21	Nov. 17 '97

A Division of The **McGraw·Hill** Companies

Business Summary - 22-JUL-98

EMC Corp. is the leader in the enterprise storage industry. The company designs and manufactures storage-related hardware, software and service products for the open systems, mainframe and network attached information storage and retrieval system market.

In 1997, enterprise storage was approximately a $10.2 billion industry. EMC held a 50% market share in the mainframe segment, and a 27% share in the faster-growing open systems market. Overall, the storage industry is expected to grow about 35% annually, reaching $35 billion industry by 2001.

The company's principal hardware products are based on Integrated Cached Disk Array (ICDA) technology, which combines high speed semiconductor cache memory with an array of industry standard disk drives. Products include the Symmetrix series of high-speed ICDA-based storage system for the mainframe computer markets, first introduced in 1991. Product sales to the mainframe storage market accounted for 41%, 55% and 74% of 1997, 1996 and 1995 product revenues, respectively.

EMC's Symmetrix 3000 family of ICDA products, first introduced in 1995, serves the open systems storage market. Revenues from the open systems market represented about 50%, 33% and 11%, respectively, of total product revenues in 1997, 1996 and 1995.

Network attached storage systems connect directly to local and wide area networks without the use of a host computer. Since 1996, products include the EMC Celerra File Server and the EMC Celerra Media Server.

EMC Enterprise Storage software allows companies to capture, move and protect, share and manage, and ultimately leverage their huge volumes of information into profitability and competitive advantage. With more than 70% of the company's engineers working on software, EMC expects its software revenues to reach $400 million in 1998, up from $177 million in 1997, and $75 million in 1996, which would make EMC one of the top 25 software companies in the world.

In 1997, EMC launched its Enterprise Storage Professional Services business to deliver professional services to its global customer base.

The company believes that its products are well suited for sale by resellers and OEMs in partnership with EMC, and that its revenues from these channels will continue to increase. Resellers and OEMs accounted for 27% of 1997 revenues, up from 19% in 1996.

In 1997, EMC derived 57% of revenues from North America, 33% from Europe, the Middle East and Africa, 9% from the Asia Pacific region, and 1% from South America.

Per Share Data ($) (Year Ended Dec. 31)	1997	1996	1995	1994	1993	1992	1991	1990	1989	1988
Tangible Bk. Val.	4.77	3.33	2.48	1.78	1.12	0.50	0.40	0.37	0.34	0.41
Cash Flow	1.28	0.95	0.78	0.65	0.38	0.14	0.07	0.06	-0.05	-0.02
Earnings	1.04	0.79	0.68	0.59	0.33	0.09	0.04	0.03	-0.07	-0.03
Dividends	Nil	Nil	Nil	Nil	Nil	Nil	Nil	Nil	Nil	Nil
Payout Ratio	Nil	Nil	Nil	Nil	Nil	Nil	Nil	Nil	Nil	Nil
Prices - High	$32\frac{5}{8}$	$18\frac{1}{4}$	$13\frac{3}{4}$	12	$9\frac{3}{4}$	3	$1\frac{1}{8}$	$\frac{13}{16}$	$\frac{1}{2}$	$1\frac{9}{16}$
- Low	$15\frac{7}{8}$	$7\frac{5}{8}$	$6\frac{1}{2}$	$6\frac{1}{4}$	$2\frac{5}{8}$	$\frac{15}{16}$	$\frac{7}{16}$	$\frac{5}{16}$	$\frac{1}{4}$	$\frac{5}{16}$
P/E Ratio - High	31	23	20	20	30	34	26	27	NM	NM
- Low	15	10	10	11	8	11	10	9	NM	NM
Income Statement Analysis (Million $)										
Revs.	2,938	2,274	1,878	1,377	783	349	232	171	132	123
Oper. Inc.	798	583	489	383	202	63.9	30.1	16.7	-15.9	-7.2
Depr.	136	86.9	53.6	32.7	21.7	17.4	9.3	7.5	5.1	3.1
Int. Exp.	15.5	12.0	12.9	15.3	6.0	4.8	1.9	1.9	2.9	0.9
Pretax Inc.	718	519	451	355	180	42.3	20.1	12.5	-26.1	-7.6
Eff. Tax Rate	25%	26%	28%	30%	29%	32%	35%	29%	NM	NM
Net Inc.	539	386	327	251	127	28.7	13.0	8.9	-18.6	-7.8
Balance Sheet & Other Fin. Data (Million $)										
Cash	955	727	380	241	345	55.1	16.8	35.5	17.8	10.1
Curr. Assets	2,627	1,754	1,319	902	650	217	112	104	88.0	111
Total Assets	3,490	2,294	1,746	1,318	830	321	190	157	137	153
Curr. Liab.	506	418	359	301	133	76.3	44.1	28.2	14.0	25.9
LT Debt	559	191	246	286	274	75.7	15.7	15.8	15.4	6.3
Common Eqty.	2,376	1,637	1,140	728	419	158	126	108	98.0	115
Total Cap.	2,980	1,874	1,386	1,014	693	239	146	128	117	127
Cap. Exp.	211	126	92.0	109	51.3	28.5	19.6	16.2	9.0	15.3
Cash Flow	675	473	380	283	149	46.1	22.3	16.3	-13.5	-4.7
Curr. Ratio	5.2	4.2	3.7	3.0	4.9	2.8	2.5	3.7	6.3	4.3
% LT Debt of Cap.	18.8	10.2	17.7	28.2	39.5	31.7	10.8	12.3	13.2	5.0
% Net Inc.of Revs.	18.3	17.0	17.4	18.2	16.2	8.2	5.6	5.2	NM	NM
% Ret. on Assets	18.6	19.1	21.3	22.8	20.9	11.2	7.4	6.0	NM	NM
% Ret. on Equity	26.8	27.8	35.0	42.7	41.6	20.0	11.0	8.5	NM	NM

Data as orig. reptd.; bef. results of disc. opers. and/or spec. items. Per share data adj. for stk. divs. as of ex-div. date. Bold denotes diluted EPS (FASB 128). E-Estimated. NA-Not Available. NM-Not Meaningful. NR-Not Ranked.

Office—171 South St., Hopkinton, MA 01748-9103. **Tel**—(508) 435-1000. **Website**—http://www.emc.com **Chrmn**—R. J. Egan. **Pres & CEO**—M. C. Ruettgers. **VP & CFO**—W. J. Teuber, Jr. **Dirs**—M. J. Cronin, J. F. Cunningham, J. R. Egan, M. E. Egan, R. J. Egan, W. P. Fitzgerald, J. Oliveri, M. C. Ruettgers. **Transfer Agent & Registrar**—State Street Bank & Trust Co., Boston. **Incorporated**—in Massachusetts in 1979. **Empl**— 6,400. **S&P Analyst:** Brian Goodstadt

STANDARD &POOR'S
STOCK REPORTS

Emerson Electric

824

NYSE Symbol **EMR**

In S&P 500

12-SEP-98

Industry:
Electrical Equipment

Summary: This company is a diversified manufacturer of electrical and electronic products, including motors, controls and tools.

S&P Opinion: Hold (★★★)

Recent Price • 58½	Yield • 2.0%
52 Wk Range • 67⅜-49¾	12-Mo. P/E • 21.4

Quantitative Evaluations

Outlook
(1 Lowest—5 Highest)
• **2**

Fair Value
• **56⅜**

Risk
• **Low**

Earn./Div. Rank
• **A+**

Technical Eval.
• **Bullish** since 10/95

Rel. Strength Rank
(1 Lowest—99 Highest)
• **81**

Insider Activity
• **Neutral**

Earnings vs. Previous Year
▲=Up ▼=Down ▷=No Change

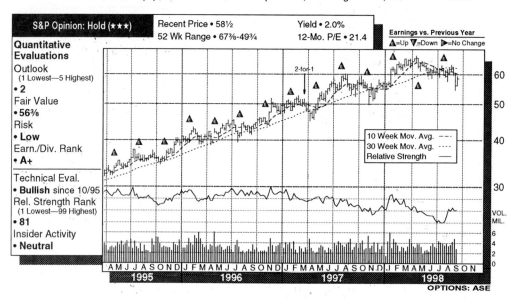

10 Week Mov. Avg. - - -
30 Week Mov. Avg. · · · ·
Relative Strength ——

2-for-1

OPTIONS: ASE

Overview - 07-AUG-98

Sales in FY 98 (Sep.) are expected to advance about 10%, reflecting continued growth in worldwide demand for EMR's products, and benefits from acquisitions. Domestic gains should be driven by continued economic growth, although at a slower pace. International sales and exports are likely to flatten, with a downturn in Asia/Pacific businesses being offset by strength in Europe. Additional acquisitions and new product introductions should support 10% average annual sales growth through 2000. Of particular note is that 32% of FY 97 sales were derived from products introduced in the past five years. Margins should widen, as volume continues to rise, and with the continued migration of production to low-cost labor regions of the world such as Southeast Asia. Strong cash flow should support capital expenditures, significant share repurchases, and higher dividend payments.

Valuation - 07-AUG-98

Emerson is one of only a few companies that consistently post improved earnings year after year. Proactive management is quick to adapt to changing markets, identify new markets and successful products, and minimize the cost of unsuccessful ventures. This strategic success, combined with strong cost reduction and productivity enhancement activities, makes EMR's shares a core long-term holding. However, we think that the company's favorable long-term track record is already reflected in the stock price. EMR's earnings are unlikely to grow at more than 10% a year on average, and, with a P/E multiple of 20X our FY 99 estimate, the shares appear fully priced. Strong cash flow and a share repurchase program should support the stock, but we think the shares will be only average performers.

Key Stock Statistics

S&P EPS Est. 1998	2.80	Tang. Bk. Value/Share	5.48
P/E on S&P Est. 1998	20.9	Beta	0.88
S&P EPS Est. 1999	3.10	Shareholders	35,900
Dividend Rate/Share	1.18	Market cap. (B)	$ 25.8
Shs. outstg. (M)	440.5	Inst. holdings	67%
Avg. daily vol. (M)	0.803		

Value of $10,000 invested 5 years ago: $ 24,144

Fiscal Year Ending Sep. 30

	1998	1997	1996	1995	1994	1993
Revenues (Million $)						
1Q	3,172	2,831	2,566	2,285	2,010	1,984
2Q	3,382	3,104	2,820	2,514	2,117	2,057
3Q	3,465	3,208	2,897	2,630	2,244	2,092
4Q	—	3,156	2,868	2,585	2,238	2,041
Yr.	—	12,299	11,150	10,013	8,607	8,174
Earnings Per Share ($)						
1Q	**0.64**	0.57	0.52	0.46	0.66	0.36
2Q	**0.69**	0.63	0.57	0.51	0.43	0.40
3Q	**0.73**	0.67	0.59	0.54	0.47	0.41
4Q	**E0.74**	0.65	0.59	0.53	0.47	0.40
Yr.	**E2.80**	2.52	2.27	2.08	2.02	1.57

Next earnings report expected: early November

Dividend Data (Dividends have been paid since 1947.)

Amount ($)	Date Decl.	Ex-Div. Date	Stock of Record	Payment Date
0.295	Nov. 04	Nov. 19	Nov. 21	Dec. 10 '97
0.295	Feb. 03	Feb. 18	Feb. 20	Mar. 10 '98
0.295	May. 05	May. 13	May. 15	Jun. 10 '98
0.295	Aug. 04	Aug. 12	Aug. 14	Sep. 10 '98

A Division of The McGraw-Hill Companies

STANDARD
&POOR'S
STOCK REPORTS

Emerson Electric Co.

824

05-SEP-98

Business Summary - 07-AUG-98

Emerson Electric is a diversified manufacturer of a broad range of electrical and electronic products. The company has become renowned for one of the longest running records of consecutive annual increases in earnings, EPS, and dividends per share, extending to 40 years as of 1997. Several strategies have contributed to this record of success, including a strong new product development effort. About 32% of sales in FY 97 (Sep.) were generated by new products, and the company has a long-term target of 35% of sales from new products. The new product effort is supported by investing over 3.5% of sales into engineering and development. The company focuses on being the low-cost producer in its markets, and excess cash flow is returned to shareholders via share repurchases.

EMR's more than 50 divisions produce a wide variety of products for commercial, industrial and consumer markets. These divisions are grouped in seven focused business organizations: electronics and computer support products, HVAC components, industrial components and equipment, industrial motors and drives, motors and appliance components, process control, and tools. For reporting purposes, these seven groups are combined into two segments: commercial and industrial (60% of sales; 55% of profits) and appliance and construction-related (40%; 45%). International operations

accounted for 34% of sales and 27% of operating income in FY 97.

The commercial and industrial segment includes process control instrumentation, valves and systems, industrial motors and drives, industrial machinery, equipment and components, and electronic products. These products are sold to commercial and industrial distributors and end-users for manufacturing and heavy commercial applications.

Products used in process industries include various types of instrumentation, valves and control systems for measurement and control of fluid flow. The company also makes electronic measurement and data acquisition equipment for use in industrial processing. Beginning with a line of electric motors for industrial and heavy commercial applications, Emerson's products for industrial automation include certain kinds of integral horsepower motors, gear drives, pump motors, alternators and electronic variable-speed drives.

The appliance and construction-related components segment consists of fractional-horsepower motors, appliance components, heating, ventilating and air-conditioning components, and tools. These products are sold to distributors and OEMs for inclusion in end-products and systems that are ultimately sold through commercial and residential building construction channels.

Per Share Data ($)

(Year Ended Sep. 30)	1997	1996	1995	1994	1993	1992	1991	1990	1989	1988
Tangible Bk. Val.	5.23	5.77	5.54	5.54	4.63	5.84	4.92	4.37	5.12	4.40
Cash Flow	3.67	3.31	2.98	2.83	2.33	2.04	1.98	1.89	1.76	1.58
Earnings	2.52	2.27	2.03	2.02	1.57	1.48	1.42	1.38	1.31	1.16
Dividends	1.08	0.98	0.89	0.78	0.72	0.69	0.66	0.63	0.56	0.50
Payout Ratio	43%	43%	44%	39%	46%	47%	47%	46%	43%	43%
Prices - High	60⅜	51¾	40⅞	33	31⅛	29	27½	22¼	20	18
- Low	45	38¾	30¾	28⅛	26⅜	23⅜	18½	15⅜	14¾	13⅝
P/E Ratio - High	24	23	20	16	20	20	19	16	15	16
- Low	18	17	15	14	17	16	13	11	11	12

Income Statement Analysis (Million $)

	1997	1996	1995	1994	1993	1992	1991	1990	1989	1988
Revs.	12,298	11,150	10,013	8,607	8,174	7,706	7,427	7,573	7,071	6,651
Oper. Inc.	2,494	2,259	2,009	1,739	1,618	1,444	1,405	1,374	1,273	1,191
Depr.	512	465	409	365	341	253	254	231	200	195
Int. Exp.	121	127	111	89.0	119	91.0	113	117	78.0	76.0
Pretax Inc.	1,784	1,609	1,460	1,428	1,112	1,044	1,003	989	954	860
Eff. Tax Rate	37%	37%	36%	37%	36%	37%	37%	38%	38%	39%
Net Inc.	1,122	1,019	929	904	708	663	632	613	588	529

Balance Sheet & Other Fin. Data (Million $)

	1997	1996	1995	1994	1993	1992	1991	1990	1989	1988
Cash	221	149	117	113	102	80.0	102	98.0	113	108
Curr. Assets	4,717	4,187	3,784	3,338	3,074	2,977	2,989	3,139	2,851	2,764
Total Assets	11,463	10,481	9,399	8,215	7,815	6,627	6,364	6,376	5,408	5,027
Curr. Liab.	3,842	3,021	3,281	2,617	2,693	1,812	2,094	2,336	1,533	1,438
LT Debt	571	773	209	280	438	448	450	496	419	481
Common Eqty.	5,420	5,353	4,871	4,342	3,915	3,730	3,257	2,990	3,073	2,820
Total Cap.	5,992	6,126	5,080	4,622	4,536	4,178	3,707	3,486	3,492	3,302
Cap. Exp.	575	514	421	332	306	346	311	310	286	236
Cash Flow	1,634	1,484	1,338	1,269	1,049	916	886	845	788	724
Curr. Ratio	1.2	1.4	1.2	1.3	1.1	1.6	1.4	1.3	1.9	1.9
% LT Debt of Cap.	9.6	12.6	4.1	6.1	9.7	10.7	12.1	14.2	12.0	14.6
% Net Inc.of Revs.	9.1	9.1	9.2	10.5	8.7	8.6	8.5	8.1	8.3	8.0
% Ret. on Assets	10.2	10.3	10.5	11.3	9.8	10.2	9.9	10.4	11.3	10.8
% Ret. on Equity	20.8	19.9	20.1	22.0	18.5	19.0	20.2	20.2	20.1	19.4

Data as orig. reptd.; bef. results of disc. opers. and/or spec. items. Per share data adj. for stk. divs. as of ex-div. date. Bold denotes diluted EPS (FASB 128). E-Estimated. NA-Not Available. NM-Not Meaningful. NR-Not Ranked.

Office—8000 W. Florissant Ave., St. Louis, MO 63136. **Tel**—(314) 553-2000. **Chrmn & CEO**—C. F. Knight. **Pres & COO**—G. W. Tamke. **SVP & CFO**—W. J. Galvin. **SVP & Secy**—W. W. Withers. **Investor Contact**—Nancy L. Wulf (314-553-2197). **Dirs**—J. G. Berges, L. L. Browning Jr., A. A. Busch III, D. C. Farrell, J. A. Frates, R. B. Horton, C. F. Knight, G. A. Lodge, V. R. Loucks Jr., R. B. Loynd, R. L. Ridgway, R. W. Staley, A. E. Suter, G. W. Tamke, W. M. Van Cleave, E. E. Whitacre Jr. **Transfer Agent & Registrar**—ChaseMellon Shareholder Services, South Hackensack, NJ. **Incorporated**—in Missouri in 1890. **Empl**— 86,400. **S&P Analyst:** Robert E. Friedman, CPA

Engelhard Corp.

829M

NYSE Symbol **EC**

In S&P 500

12-SEP-98

Industry: Chemicals (Diversified)

Summary: Engelhard is a leading producer of catalysts, pigments and additives, and engineered materials. It also provides precious and base metals management services.

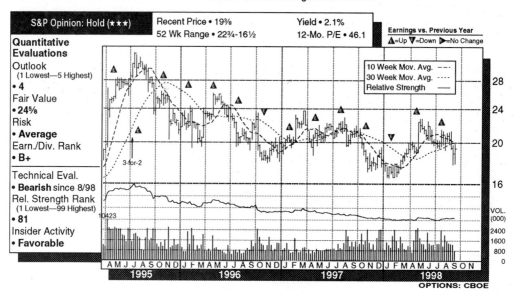

S&P Opinion: Hold (★★★)	Recent Price • 19⅜	Yield • 2.1%
	52 Wk Range • 22¾-16½	12-Mo. P/E • 46.1

Quantitative Evaluations

Outlook (1 Lowest—5 Highest)
• **4**

Fair Value
• **24%**

Risk
• **Average**

Earn./Div. Rank
• **B+**

Technical Eval.
• **Bearish** since 8/98

Rel. Strength Rank (1 Lowest—99 Highest)
• **81**

Insider Activity
• **Favorable**

Earnings vs. Previous Year ▲=Up ▼=Down ▶=No Change

10 Week Mov. Avg. – – –
30 Week Mov. Avg. ⋯⋯
Relative Strength ——

3-for-2

OPTIONS: CBOE

Overview - 22-MAY-98

The fourth quarter 1997 loss included special charges totaling $96 million after taxes ($0.66 a share) for recent restructuring actions at its CLAL metal fabricating venture, stationary source emission control business, and in petroleum cracking catalysts. EC has also restructured its ICC desiccant venture. These businesses had aggregate losses of $0.10 in 1997. Results also include a pretax charge of $39 million ($0.15 a share) related to fraud against EC's Japanese metal trading unit. EC could have additional pretax losses of up to $16 million in 1998. Sales and net income before any impact of the fraud are expected to continue to increase in 1998. Auto emission catalysts will advance on growing volumes, as EC began to supply General Motors in late 1997. Sales to GM will grow rapidly over the next two years. Petroleum catalysts will benefit from aggressive manufacturing cost reductions, including the recent closing of the European FCC plant. Pigments may improve on stronger demand in key paper markets; the plastics and paint markets for specialty minerals should continue to grow. Results for metals management should be at least at 1997's strong level due to unusually high volatility in precious metals markets. The tax rate will climb by one percentage point.

Valuation - 22-MAY-98

We have a "hold" opinion on EC. The stock is up about 24% year to date, reflecting better than expected first quarter EPS and outlook for rest of 1998. New management is taking steps to improve results. We expect EC to post an eighth consecutive year of record earnings (excluding special items) in 1998. Dividends, raised for 15 consecutive years, should continue to grow over the long term.

Key Stock Statistics

S&P EPS Est. 1998	1.30	Tang. Bk. Value/Share	3.22
P/E on S&P Est. 1998	14.9	Beta	0.92
S&P EPS Est. 1999	1.45	Shareholders	8,500
Dividend Rate/Share	0.40	Market cap. (B)	$ 2.8
Shs. outstg. (M)	144.5	Inst. holdings	46%
Avg. daily vol. (M)	0.252		

Value of $10,000 invested 5 years ago: $ 14,146

Fiscal Year Ending Dec. 31

	1998	1997	1996	1995	1994	1993
Revenues (Million $)						
1Q	970.5	884.2	774.7	694.5	557.7	490.2
2Q	1,075	896.7	783.9	721.1	633.4	563.2
3Q	—	836.1	800.9	724.6	578.6	558.1
4Q	—	1,014	824.9	699.9	616.1	539.4
Yr.	—	3,631	3,184	2,840	2,386	2,151
Earnings Per Share ($)						
1Q	**0.30**	**0.26**	0.23	0.19	0.16	0.15
2Q	**0.35**	**0.30**	0.28	0.26	0.22	0.20
3Q	**E0.31**	**0.27**	0.24	0.26	0.21	0.19
4Q	**E0.34**	**-0.50**	0.30	0.25	0.23	-0.43
Yr.	**E1.30**	**0.33**	1.05	0.96	0.82	0.11

Next earnings report expected: late October

Dividend Data (Dividends have been paid since 1981.)

Amount ($)	Date Decl.	Ex-Div. Date	Stock of Record	Payment Date
0.100	Oct. 02	Dec. 10	Dec. 12	Dec. 31 '97
0.100	Mar. 05	Mar. 11	Mar. 13	Mar. 31 '98
0.100	May. 07	Jun. 10	Jun. 12	Jun. 30 '98
0.100	Jul. 08	Sep. 11	Sep. 15	Sep. 30 '98

STANDARD
&POOR'S
STOCK REPORTS

Engelhard Corporation

829M
12-SEP-98

Business Summary - 22-MAY-98

Since commercializing the first automotive catalyst (for emission control) in the mid-1970s, Engelhard (EC) has been a leader in catalyst development for environmental, transportation and industrial applications, as well as in pigments and colorants for paper and other materials. Contributions by product segment in 1997 were:

	Sales	Profits
Catalysts & chemicals	26%	44%
Pigments & additives	16%	36%
Engineered materials & commodities management	58%	20%

International operations accounted for 32% of sales and 24% of operating profits in 1997.

EC is a major supplier of catalysts and process technologies for the petroleum refining, chemical, petrochemical, pharmaceutical, food processing, automobile, truck, aircraft, power generation and process industries. EC in 1997 began selling the first urban-bus emission system certified by the U.S. EPA for urban bus retrofit. As a result, EC has succeeded in capturing a major share of this market. The chemical catalyst business has grown in recent years as EC has taken over production of catalysts from customers that formerly made their own, as well as formed alliances to sell catalysts. In late 1996, EC began shipping catalysts

for use in an improved process for ammonia production developed by M.W. Kellogg. Through another alliance, EC is selling catalysts to plastics producers that use technology licensed by Geon, a leading producer of PVC plastic. In 1997, EC and Dow Chemical began to sell catalysts for styrene production. The May 1998 acquisition of Mallinckrodt Inc.'s catalyst business ($100 million in annual sales) for $210 million expanded EC into polymerization catalysts.

Pigments and additives consist of kaolin-based coatings and extender pigments for a wide variety of papers, including printing, writing, newsprint and paperboard; and pigments and additives, thickeners and absorbents used in plastics, paints, inks and rubber. In May 1996, the company acquired Mearl Corp., a leading manufacturer of pearlescent pigments and iridescent film, expanding EC's presence in automobile and cosmetic pigments.

Engineered materials consist of fabricated precious metal (platinum, gold and silver) products and coatings for industrial markets. In June 1995, the majority of this business was transferred to a joint venture, Engelhard-CLAL, whose results are now included in equity earnings. The Industrial Commodities Management business purchases and sells precious metals, base metals and energy and related products. EC is also engaged in secondary refining to recover precious metals.

Per Share Data ($)

(Year Ended Dec. 31)	1997	1996	1995	1994	1993	1992	1991	1990	1989	1988
Tangible Bk. Val.	3.95	5.79	5.13	4.31	3.69	4.38	5.00	4.72	4.24	5.04
Cash Flow	0.66	1.57	1.41	1.30	0.57	1.15	1.09	0.96	-0.06	0.80
Earnings	0.33	1.05	0.96	0.82	0.11	0.67	0.58	0.47	-0.51	0.42
Dividends	0.38	0.36	0.32	0.31	0.35	0.25	0.22	0.20	0.17	0.16
Payout Ratio	115%	34%	33%	37%	NM	37%	38%	43%	NM	38%
Prices - High	23³/₄	26¹/₈	32¹/₂	21	20	16¹/₄	10¹/₈	7	7⁵/₈	6¹/₂
- Low	17	17⁷/₈	14⁷/₈	13⁷/₈	12⁷/₈	9¹/₄	5	5	5¹/₈	4⁷/₈
P/E Ratio - High	72	25	34	26	NM	24	17	15	NM	15
- Low	52	17	16	17	NM	14	9	11	NM	12

Income Statement Analysis (Million $)

	1997	1996	1995	1994	1993	1992	1991	1990	1989	1988
Revs.	3,631	3,184	2,840	2,385	2,149	2,397	2,430	2,937	2,403	2,351
Oper. Inc.	320	332	281	247	207	214	206	187	166	154
Depr.	47.8	74.8	65.5	69.1	65.9	73.8	77.8	74.4	68.8	56.7
Int. Exp.	52.8	45.0	31.3	22.0	13.7	16.6	22.2	27.1	38.6	27.0
Pretax Inc.	85.8	210	185	157	-5.0	134	118	94.0	-125	87.0
Eff. Tax Rate	44%	28%	26%	25%	NM	25%	25%	25%	NM	27%
Net Inc.	47.8	150	138	118	17.0	100	87.9	70.3	-77.5	63.7

Balance Sheet & Other Fin. Data (Million $)

	1997	1996	1995	1994	1993	1992	1991	1990	1989	1988
Cash	28.8	39.6	40.0	26.0	26.0	31.0	36.0	47.0	41.0	49.0
Curr. Assets	1,255	1,184	601	574	517	569	576	618	653	657
Total Assets	2,586	2,495	1,646	1,441	1,279	1,279	1,256	1,320	1,340	1,413
Curr. Liab.	1,240	1,069	495	549	463	366	378	482	475	355
LT Debt	374	375	212	112	112	114	115	119	220	221
Common Eqty.	785	833	738	615	531	647	757	710	637	760
Total Cap.	1,159	1,208	950	726	646	773	878	838	865	1,059
Cap. Exp.	137	128	148	98.0	NA	54.0	46.0	80.0	87.0	125
Cash Flow	95.6	225	203	187	83.0	174	166	145	-9.0	120
Curr. Ratio	1.0	1.1	1.2	1.0	1.1	1.6	1.5	1.3	1.4	1.9
% LT Debt of Cap.	32.2	31.0	22.4	15.4	17.4	14.7	13.0	14.3	25.5	20.9
% Net Inc. of Revs.	1.3	4.7	4.9	4.9	0.8	42.0	3.6	2.4	NM	2.7
% Ret. on Assets	1.9	6.8	9.0	8.7	1.3	8.0	6.8	5.3	NM	4.8
% Ret. on Equity	5.9	19.1	20.4	20.7	2.9	14.4	12.0	10.4	NM	8.5

Data as orig. reptd.; bef. results of disc. opers. and/or spec. items. Per share data adj. for stk. divs. as of ex-div. date. Bold denotes diluted EPS (FASB 128). E-Estimated. NA-Not Available. NM-Not Meaningful. NR-Not Ranked.

Office—101 Wood Ave., Iselin, NJ 08830-0770. **Tel**—(732) 205-6000. **Website**—http://www.engelhard.com **Chrmn & CEO**—O. R. Smith. **Pres**—B. W. Perry. **SVP & CFO**—T. P. Fitzpatrick. **VP & Secy**—A. A. Dornbusch II. **VP & Investor Contact**—Peter B. Martin. **Dirs**—L. Alvarado, M. H. Antonini, A. W. Lea, W. R. Loomis, Jr., J. V. Napier, N. T. Pace, B W. Perry, R. F. Richards, H. R. Slack, O. R. Smith, D. G. Watson. **Transfer Agent & Registrar**—ChaseMellon Shareholder Services, Ridgefield Park, NJ. **Incorporated**—in Delaware in 1938. **Empl**— 6,400. **S&P Analyst**: Richard O'Reilly, CFA

Enron Corp.

830J
NYSE Symbol ENE
In S&P 500

12-SEP-98

Industry:
Natural Gas

Summary: ENE, the largest U.S. marketer of natural gas and the largest independent marketer of wholesale electricity, completed the acquisition of NYSE-listed Portland General in mid-1997.

S&P Opinion: Accumulate (★★★★)

Recent Price • 45⅞	Yield • 2.1%
52 Wk Range • 58⅜-35¼	12-Mo. P/E • 20.8

Quantitative Evaluations

Outlook
(1 Lowest—5 Highest)
• **2⁻**

Fair Value
• **43⅜**

Risk
• **Low**

Earn./Div. Rank
• **A-**

Technical Eval.
• **Bullish** since 1/98

Rel. Strength Rank
(1 Lowest—99 Highest)
• **75**

Insider Activity
• **Unfavorable**

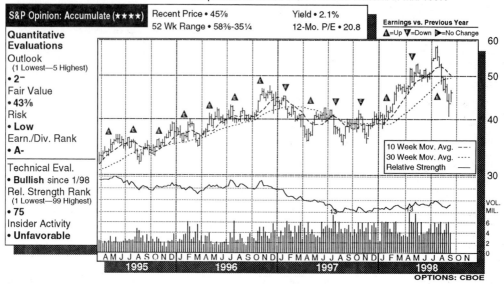

Earnings vs. Previous Year
▲=Up ▼=Down ▶=No Change

10 Week Mov. Avg. ---
30 Week Mov. Avg. ....
Relative Strength —

OPTIONS: CBOE

Overview - 24-JUL-98

Enron Corp. (ENE) continues to impress with its very broad range of international energy operations. The $3 billion acquisition of Portland General Electric appears to be well absorbed, and the company's aggressive stance suggests future expansion into other regulated electricity markets. The company added to its expanding presence in Brazil with the July 16, 1998 purchase of Elektro, that country's sixth largest electricity distributor, emerging as the successful bidder by paying nearly double the asking price. Led by its premier operation, the Wholesale Energy division, Enron posted second quarter 1998 earnings of $0.42 per share, versus $0.38 (excluding non-recurring items) in the same period in 1997; results were slightly higher than the Street estimate. Worldwide commodity deliveries increased substantially. The company has been touting its new Retail Energy Services division, a segment which focuses on end-users in the commercial and light industrial sectors. Though the division is still experiencing start-up costs, it secured $650 million in new contracts during the second quarter.

Valuation - 24-JUL-98

Enron's shares are trading near their 52-week high, a rare occurrence among energy stocks in today's weak oil price environment. This is because Enron's diverse energy-related businesses insulate it against temporary commodity price declines. We have upgraded ENE to an accumulate rating, as the company consistently demonstrates its ability to perform efficiently in all energy areas. Additionally, shares should benefit medium term, as nine international projects are expected to be completed before 2000. These projects when added to the company's numerous existing projects in Europe and emerging countries, confirm that Enron is well prepared for future growth outside the U.S.

Key Stock Statistics

S&P EPS Est. 1998	2.05	Tang. Bk. Value/Share	20.20
P/E on S&P Est. 1998	22.4	Beta	0.76
S&P EPS Est. 1999	2.50	Shareholders	25,600
Dividend Rate/Share	0.95	Market cap. (B)	$ 15.1
Shs. outstg. (M)	329.5	Inst. holdings	57%
Avg. daily vol. (M)	1.104		

Value of $10,000 invested 5 years ago: $ 22,493

Fiscal Year Ending Dec. 31

	1998	1997	1996	1995	1994	1993
Revenues (Million $)						
1Q	5,682	5,344	3,054	2,304	2,450	1,857
2Q	6,557	3,240	2,961	2,149	1,898	1,907
3Q	—	5,806	3,225	2,186	1,997	1,934
4Q	—	5,872	4,049	2,550	2,560	2,274
Yr.	—	20,273	13,289	9,189	8,905	7,972
Earnings Per Share ($)						
1Q	**0.65**	0.81	0.86	0.79	0.70	0.60
2Q	**0.42**	-1.71	0.46	0.37	0.30	0.24
3Q	—	0.42	0.48	0.40	0.38	0.07
4Q	—	0.53	0.51	0.52	0.43	0.42
Yr.	**E2.05**	0.32	2.16	2.07	1.80	1.32

Next earnings report expected: mid October

Dividend Data (Dividends have been paid since 1935.)

Amount ($)	Date Decl.	Ex-Div. Date	Stock of Record	Payment Date
0.237	Oct. 14	Nov. 26	Dec. 01	Dec. 22 '97
0.237	Feb. 10	Feb. 26	Mar. 02	Mar. 20 '98
0.237	May. 05	May. 28	Jun. 01	Jun. 22 '98
0.237	Aug. 11	Aug. 28	Sep. 01	Sep. 22 '98

A Division of The McGraw-Hill Companies

Business Summary - 24-JUL-98

This Houston-based integrated natural gas and electricity giant is powering ahead at home and abroad with boundless energy. Not satisfied with its status as the largest U.S. marketer of natural gas and unregulated electricity, Enron Corp. (ENE) forayed into the regulated electricity business with its $3 billion purchase of Portland General Electric (PGE) in July 1997. The company has operations in numerous countries, and is pushing for further market share. International projects under construction include eight power plants and one pipeline system, which are expected to be completed by 2000. Enron added to its foreign portfolio with its July 16, 1998 acquisition of Elektro, Brazil's sixth largest electricity distributor, for $1.3 billion, paying a 98% premium over the asking price.

Enron's businesses are organized under several divisions. The Transportation and Distribution division operates a 32,000 mile natural gas pipeline, transporting 18% of the natural gas consumed in the U.S. Enron owns and operates four major pipelines in North America: Northern Natural Gas, Transwestern, Florida Gas Transmission (50% interest), and Northern Border (8%). Collectively, about 9 Bcfe of gas are transported to 21 states per day through the pipelines; efforts to expand capacity are currently underway. In addition, this division is responsible for electricity transmission and distribution through the PGE subsidiary, which serves mostly residential customers in Oregon.

The Exploration and Production division conducts activities through 55%-owned Enron Oil & Gas Co. (EOG). At year-end 1997, EOG had estimated net proved reserves of 4,001 Bcf of natural gas and 78.7 MBbls of oil, condensate and natural gas liquids. Most of EOG's reserves and production are domestic; however, the company has expanded operations in such areas as Trinidad and India, and sees future growth primarily from its international efforts.

Wholesale Energy Operations and Services, Enron's largest and most profitable division, provides integrated energy-related products and services to wholesale customers worldwide, including the development, construction and operation of power plants, natural gas pipelines and other energy-related assets, energy commodity sales and services, risk management products, and financial services. Through this division, the company has interests in existing and future power plants and gas pipelines in numerous European and emerging countries, and arranges debt and equity financing for exploration and production companies. Lastly, Retail Energy Services offers direct sales of energy products and services to end-use customers, particularly in the commercial and light industrial sectors.

Per Share Data ($)

(Year Ended Dec. 31)	1997	1996	1995	1994	1993	1992	1991	1990	1989	1988
Tangible Bk. Val.	11.38	14.01	11.99	10.89	9.93	9.96	8.43	8.02	7.69	7.38
Cash Flow	2.48	4.24	3.84	3.61	3.24	3.06	2.88	2.65	2.77	2.56
Earnings	0.32	2.31	2.07	1.80	1.32	1.43	1.07	0.88	1.01	0.50
Dividends	0.91	0.86	0.81	0.76	0.71	0.66	0.63	0.62	0.62	0.62
Payout Ratio	NM	37%	39%	42%	54%	50%	59%	71%	62%	125%
Prices - High	45$\frac{1}{8}$	47$\frac{1}{2}$	39$\frac{3}{8}$	34$\frac{5}{8}$	37	25$\frac{1}{8}$	19$\frac{1}{4}$	15$\frac{3}{4}$	15$\frac{1}{4}$	10$\frac{3}{4}$
- Low	35	34$\frac{5}{8}$	28	26$\frac{3}{4}$	22$\frac{1}{4}$	15$\frac{3}{8}$	12$\frac{3}{8}$	12$\frac{5}{8}$	8$\frac{7}{8}$	8$\frac{3}{4}$
P/E Ratio - High	NM	21	19	19	28	18	18	18	15	22
- Low	NM	15	14	15	17	11	12	14	9	18

Income Statement Analysis (Million $)

	1997	1996	1995	1994	1993	1992	1991	1990	1989	1988
Revs.	20,273	13,289	9,189	8,984	7,972	6,325	13,520	13,165	9,836	5,708
Oper. Inc.	690	690	1,050	1,157	1,076	981	864	787	688	695
Depr.	600	474	432	441	458	361	366	356	351	389
Int. Exp.	470	308	284	273	300	327	391	395	398	433
Pretax Inc.	95.0	930	881	671	498	446	344	267	295	165
Eff. Tax Rate	NA	29%	32%	25%	27%	21%	27%	22%	23%	21%
Net Inc.	105	584	520	453	333	336	242	202	226	130

Balance Sheet & Other Fin. Data (Million $)

	1997	1996	1995	1994	1993	1992	1991	1990	1989	1988
Cash	170	256	115	132	140	142	217	214	109	131
Curr. Assets	4,669	3,979	2,727	1,909	2,019	2,126	1,805	2,137	1,632	1,357
Total Assets	23,422	16,137	13,239	11,966	11,504	10,664	10,072	9,849	9,105	8,695
Curr. Liab.	4,412	3,708	2,432	2,297	2,676	2,642	2,280	2,421	1,606	1,363
LT Debt	6,287	3,363	3,065	2,805	2,661	2,459	3,109	2,983	3,184	3,335
Common Eqty.	5,484	3,586	3,028	2,740	2,474	2,364	1,706	1,619	1,548	1,399
Total Cap.	16,051	9,994	6,588	8,246	7,555	6,966	6,339	6,789	6,924	6,895
Cap. Exp.	1,413	855	731	661	688	589	707	629	480	294
Cash Flow	688	1,042	936	880	774	675	583	533	551	483
Curr. Ratio	1.1	1.1	1.1	0.8	0.8	0.8	0.8	0.9	1.0	1.0
% LT Debt of Cap.	39.2	33.7	46.5	34.0	35.2	35.3	44.7	43.9	46.0	48.4
% Net Inc.of Revs.	0.5	4.4	5.7	5.0	4.2	5.3	1.8	1.5	2.3	2.3
% Ret. on Assets	0.5	4.0	4.4	3.8	2.9	2.9	2.4	2.1	2.5	1.4
% Ret. on Equity	1.9	17.7	17.5	16.7	12.7	14.4	13.0	11.2	13.2	6.8

Data as orig. reptd.; bef. results of disc. opers. and/or spec. items. Per share data adj. for stk. divs. as of ex-div. date. Bold denotes diluted EPS (FASB 128). E-Estimated. NA-Not Available. NM-Not Meaningful. NR-Not Ranked.

Office—1400 Smith St., Houston, TX 77002-7369. **Tel**—(713) 853-6161. **Website**—http://www.enron.com **Chrmn & CEO**—K. L. Lay. **Vice Chrmn**—K. L. Harrison. **Pres & COO**—J. K. Skilling. **VP & Secy**—P. B. Menchaca. **VP & Treas**—W. D. Gathmann. **Investor Contacts**—Mark E. Koenig, Edmund P. Segner III. **Dirs**—R. A. Belfer, N. P. Blake Jr., R. C. Chan, J. H. Duncan, J. H. Foy, W. L. Gramm, K. L. Harrison, R. K. Jaedicke, K. L. Lay, C. A. LeMaistre, J. J. Meyer, J. K. Skilling, J. A. Urquhart, J. Wakeham, C. E. Walker, B. G. Willison, H. S. Winokur Jr. **Transfer Agent & Registrar**—First Chicago Trust Co. of New York, Jersey City, NJ. **Incorporated**—in Delaware in 1930. **Empl**— 15,500. **S&P Analyst:** Ephraim Juskowicz.

STANDARD &POOR'S
STOCK REPORTS

Entergy Corp.

831M
NYSE Symbol **ETR**

In S&P 500

12-SEP-98

Industry:
Electric Companies

Summary: This electric utility holding company, which provides service to customers in Arkansas, Louisiana, Mississippi and Texas, intends to sell its international distribution operations.

S&P Opinion: Hold (★★★)	Recent Price • 29½ Yield • 6.1%
	52 Wk Range • 30¼-23 12-Mo. P/E • 30.1

Quantitative Evaluations

Outlook
(1 Lowest—5 Highest)
• **2⁻**

Fair Value
• **28⅜**

Risk
• **Low**

Earn./Div. Rank
• **B**

Technical Eval.
• **Bullish** since 6/98

Rel. Strength Rank
(1 Lowest—99 Highest)
• **96**

Insider Activity
• **Neutral**

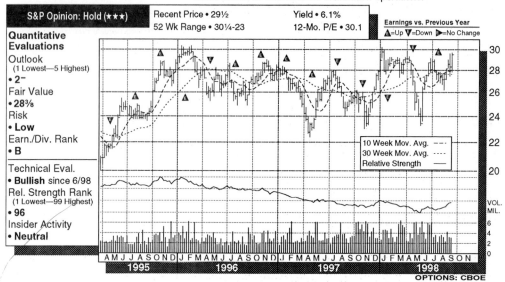

Earnings vs. Previous Year
▲=Up ▼=Down ▶=No Change

10 Week Mov. Avg. — · —
30 Week Mov. Avg. - - - -
Relative Strength —

OPTIONS: CBOE

Overview - 02-SEP-98

With the August 1998 announcement of its dramatic restructuring, Entergy has become a different company. In addition to implementing a 33% cut in its dividend (effective with the September 1 payment), ETR will divest its international distribution operations (including London Electricity and the Australian-based CitiPower) and some of its non-core U.S. operations. The asset sales and the savings from the dividend cut (which will reduce ETR's payout ratio from nearly 90% to less than 60%) should realize around $4 billion, and Entergy has targeted 70% of it for debt reduction, 20% for investments and 10% for either of the two. The divestiture of these operations will enable ETR to focus on significantly improving the customer service of its U.S. utilities and to expand its nuclear, global power generation and power marketing operations. While rate reductions in Arkansas, Louisiana and Texas will result in lower revenues from the utilities, ETR intends to achieve earnings growth through reducing its annual costs by around $200 million by the end of 1999.

Valuation - 02-SEP-98

We recommend holding Entergy stock. Although the 33% cut in the dividend has reduced the yield from around 6.4% to about 4.3%, it was essential for long-term shareholder value. Confronted with rate reductions and a more moderate level of growth in the regional economy, ETR intends to grow earnings by building on its strengths in nuclear operations, international power generation projects, and power marketing. After only an 8.4% increase in 1997 (compared to a 19.6% gain for the S&P Index of Electric Companies), the shares are down 6.7% year to date (versus a 7.7% increase for its industry peers). Still, the restructuring initiated by new top management should result in improved shareholder returns.

Key Stock Statistics

S&P EPS Est. 1998	2.05	Tang. Bk. Value/Share	19.72
P/E on S&P Est. 1998	14.4	Beta	0.54
S&P EPS Est. 1999	2.10	Shareholders	92,200
Dividend Rate/Share	1.80	Market cap. (B)	$ 7.3
Shs. outstg. (M)	246.6	Inst. holdings	75%
Avg. daily vol. (M)	0.676		

Value of $10,000 invested 5 years ago: $ 12,498

Fiscal Year Ending Dec. 31

	1998	1997	1996	1995	1994	1993
Revenues (Million $)						
1Q	2,313	2,046	1,604	1,346	1,406	926.4
2Q	2,509	2,178	1,853	1,572	1,586	1,070
3Q	—	2,798	2,138	1,937	1,806	1,411
4Q	—	2,540	1,569	1,426	1,165	1,078
Yr.	—	9,562	7,164	6,274	5,963	4,485
Earnings Per Share ($)						
1Q	**0.20**	0.47	-0.38	0.25	0.31	0.33
2Q	**0.83**	0.61	0.83	0.71	0.63	0.75
3Q	**E0.98**	0.33	1.22	1.16	0.63	1.34
4Q	**E0.04**	-0.36	0.16	0.02	-0.07	0.21
Yr.	**E2.05**	1.03	1.83	2.13	1.49	2.62

Next earnings report expected: early November

Dividend Data (Dividends have been paid since 1988.)

Amount ($)	Date Decl.	Ex-Div. Date	Stock of Record	Payment Date
0.450	Sep. 26	Nov. 07	Nov. 12	Dec. 01 '97
0.450	Jan. 23	Feb. 09	Feb. 11	Mar. 01 '98
0.450	Mar. 25	May. 11	May. 13	Jun. 01 '98

A Division of The **McGraw·Hill** *Companies*

STANDARD
&POOR'S
STOCK REPORTS

Entergy Corporation

831M
12-SEP-98

Business Summary - 02-SEP-98

This New Orleans-based public utility holding company (formerly Middle South Utilities) was reorganized in April 1996 into five operating subsidiaries under a single corporate identity and adopted the Entergy name and logo.

As the holding company for Entergy Arkansas, Entergy Gulf States, Entergy Louisiana, Entergy Mississippi and Entergy New Orleans, ETR provides electricity to around 2.5 million U.S. retail customers. The company also owns System Energy Resources, which has a 90% interest in the Grand Gulf 1 nuclear plant. Revenues by segment in recent years were:

	1997	1996	1995
Electric	68.4%	90.1%	96.8%
Non-regulated & foreign	29.7%	7.2%	0.7%
Natural gas & steam	1.9%	2.7%	2.4%

Power sources for domestic utilities and System Energy in 1997 were: nuclear 41% (41% in 1996); natural gas 39% (42%); coal 16% (16%); and fuel oil 4% (1%).

In August 1998, ETR announced that it would divest its international distribution operations, including London Electricity in the U.K. and CitiPower in Australia. It also plans to sell Entergy Security, Entergy Integrated Solutions, and some of its telecommunications interests.

In February 1997, Entergy acquired for $2.1 billion London Electricity plc, an electric distribution company serving around 2 million customers in the greater London area. In January 1996, ETR acquired CitiPower, an electric distribution utility serving 242,000 customers in Melbourne, Australia, for about $1.2 billion. ETR also has an indirect 5% interest in Edesur, S.A., which supplies electricity to 1.9 million customers in Buenos Aires, Argentina.

The company entered into telecommunications-based businesses in 1996, mainly security monitoring firms operating in North and South Carolina, Alabama, Florida, Georgia, Mississippi, Louisiana and Texas.

In December 1993, ETR acquired Entergy Gulf States (formerly Gulf States Utilities), which serves parts of Louisiana and Texas and owns 70% of the River Bend nuclear plant, for $2.3 billion. In 1988, the Public Utility Commission in Texas (PUCT) placed in abeyance, with no finding as to prudence, about $1.4 billion of River Bend plant investment and $157 million of deferred operating and carrying costs. As of December 31, 1997, River Bend plant costs held in abeyance totaled $264 million. In January 1997, the Texas Supreme Court remanded the case to the PUCT for further proceedings. In January 1998, the PUCT voted to disallow recovery of the $1.4 billion of abeyed plant costs.

Per Share Data ($)

(Year Ended Dec. 31)	1997	1996	1995	1994	1993	1992	1991	1990	1989	1988
Tangible Bk. Val.	19.72	25.77	28.25	27.74	27.16	24.23	23.31	22.01	20.50	23.70
Earnings	1.03	1.83	2.13	1.49	2.62	2.48	2.64	2.44	-2.31	2.01
Dividends	1.80	1.80	1.80	1.80	1.65	1.45	1.25	1.05	0.90	0.20
Payout Ratio	175%	98%	85%	121%	63%	58%	47%	43%	NM	10%
Prices - High	30¼	30⅜	29¼	37⅜	39⅞	33⅝	29⅞	23⅝	23¼	16⅛
- Low	22⅜	24⅞	20	21¼	32½	26⅛	21⅞	18	15½	8½
P/E Ratio - High	29	17	14	25	15	14	11	10	NM	8
- Low	22	14	9	14	12	11	8	7	NM	4

Income Statement Analysis (Million $)

	1997	1996	1995	1994	1993	1992	1991	1990	1989	1988
Revs.	9,562	7,164	6,274	5,963	4,485	4,116	4,051	3,982	3,724	3,565
Depr.	980	791	691	657	444	425	399	393	406	391
Maint.	NA	NA	NA	NA	307	302	283	278	279	238
Fxd. Chgs. Cov.	1.9	2.5	2.3	1.6	2.4	2.1	2.1	2.1	0.4	1.8
Constr. Credits	18.0	18.3	18.0	21.8	14.0	12.0	15.0	11.0	11.0	16.0
Eff. Tax Rate	59%	50%	41%	24%	36%	34%	34%	37%	NM	32%
Net Inc.	301	420	485	342	458	438	482	478	-472	411

Balance Sheet & Other Fin. Data (Million $)

	1997	1996	1995	1994	1993	1992	1991	1990	1989	1988
Gross Prop.	29,102	25,109	24,080	23,557	23,180	15,051	14,813	14,591	14,297	14,101
Cap. Exp.	847	572	618	676	512	427	397	400	370	346
Net Prop.	19,517	16,223	15,821	15,917	16,022	10,736	10,812	10,928	10,998	11,111
Capitalization:										
LT Debt	9,304	7,838	7,081	7,367	7,679	5,326	5,493	6,072	6,347	6,448
% LT Debt	55	51	49	49	50	52	53	56	56	53
Pfd.	1,003	928	954	1,001	900	705	690	642	681	794
% Pfd.	5.80	6.00	6.60	6.90	5.90	6.80	6.60	5.90	6.10	6.50
Common	6,693	6,641	6,472	6,351	6,536	4,279	4,208	4,121	4,220	4,901
% Common	39	43	45	44	43	42	41	38	38	40
Total Cap.	22,156	19,876	18,897	19,959	19,917	12,088	12,348	12,677	12,893	13,808
% Oper. Ratio	81.3	82.4	80.6	82.1	77.9	76.7	73.7	73.7	73.1	70.0
% Earn. on Net Prop.	10.1	7.9	7.7	6.7	7.4	8.9	9.8	9.6	9.0	9.6
% Return On Revs.	3.1	5.9	7.7	5.7	10.2	10.6	11.9	12.0	NM	11.5
% Return On Invest. Capital	7.7	6.2	6.3	5.5	6.3	8.7	9.3	9.2	1.9	9.0
% Return On Com. Equity	3.7	6.3	7.6	5.3	12.6	10.3	11.6	11.5	NM	8.7

Data as orig. reptd.; bef. results of disc. opers. and/or spec. items. Per share data adj. for stk. divs. as of ex-div. date. Bold denotes diluted EPS (FASB 128). E-Estimated. NA-Not Available. NM-Not Meaningful. NR-Not Ranked.

Office—639 Loyola Ave., New Orleans, LA 70113. **Tel**—(504) 529-5262. **Website**—http://www.entergy.com **Chrmn & Acting CEO**—R. v.d. Luft. **Pres & COO**—J. W. Leonard. **Vice Chrmn**—J. L. Maulden. **EVP & CFO**—C. J. Wilder. **Investor Contact**—Paul LaRosa. **SVP & Treas**—N. A. Nakagama. **VP & Secy**—M. G. Thompson. **Dirs**—W. F. Blount, J. A. Cooper, Jr., L. J. Fjeldstad, N. C. Francis, R. v.d. Luft, K. R. McKee, P. W. Murrill, J. R. Nichols, E. H. Owen, J. N. Palmer, Sr., R. D. Pugh, W. C. Smith, B. A. Steinhagen. **Transfer Agent & Registrar**—ChaseMellon Shareholder Services, LLC, Ridgefield Park, NJ. **Incorporated**— in Delaware in 1994; in Florida in 1949. **Empl**— 17,288. **S&P Analyst:** Justin McCann

Equifax Inc.

835Q

NYSE Symbol **EFX**

In S&P 500

12-SEP-98

Industry:
Services (Data Processing)

Summary: This company provides information, processing, consulting and software solutions that facilitate buyer-seller transactions worldwide.

S&P Opinion: Accumulate (★★★★)

Recent Price • 32¼
52 Wk Range • 44⅛-28½

Yield • 1.1%
12-Mo. P/E • 26.1

Earnings vs. Previous Year
▲=Up ▼=Down ▶=No Change

Quantitative Evaluations

Outlook
(1 Lowest—5 Highest)
• **1**‾

Fair Value
• **28¾**

Risk
• **Average**

Earn./Div. Rank
• **A-**

Technical Eval.
• **Bearish** since 7/97

Rel. Strength Rank
(1 Lowest—99 Highest)
• **42**

Insider Activity
• **Favorable**

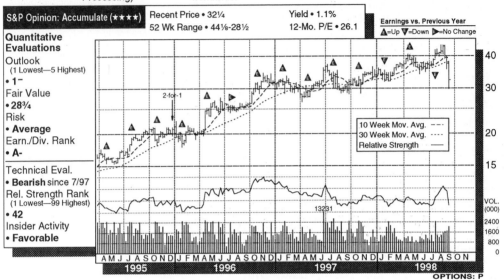

10 Week Mov. Avg. ---
30 Week Mov. Avg. ....
Relative Strength —

OPTIONS: P

Overview - 21-JUL-98

Equifax is a premier provider of credit card processing, credit reporting and check services. The company spun off its Insurance Services Group, Choicepoint, in 1997, in order to focus its resources on its core businesses. The spinoff accounts for the apparent revenue drop in 1997, over 1996. The company's 1998 second quarter results were in line with analyst expectations. International operations were again particularly strong, both in terms of revenue growth and in terms of margin improvement. Equifax recently announced an alliance with IBM, with the purpose of developing and marketing services to ensure safe and secure transactions over the Internet through the offering of a broad range of digital certificates. While the deal will have no immediate impact, we are optimistic about the long-term prospects for this joint venture.

Valuation - 21-JUL-98

We continue to recommend accumulation of Equifax. We are forecasting 1998 EPS of $1.45, representing growth of only 15% from 1997 levels, versus management's targeted goal of 18% to 20% annual growth, including possible acquisitions. The reason for the apparent slowdown in earnings growth is the company's spending related to the Year 2000 problem. Management has estimated that these necessary expenses will amount to about $11 million, or $0.07 to $0.08 a share, after tax, in 1998. Looking past 1998, the company should be able to boost revenues at about 15% a year, and to utilize its operating leverage to enhance EPS by 18% to 20% a year. The stock has underperformed the overall market, year to date, and was recently trading at a reasonable multiple of 22X our 1999 EPS estimate of $1.75. We believe that the stock's current valuation is attractive based on the company's substantial free cash flow, shareholder focus and earnings visibility.

Key Stock Statistics

S&P EPS Est. 1998	1.45	Tang. Bk. Value/Share	NM
P/E on S&P Est. 1998	22.3	Beta	0.96
S&P EPS Est. 1999	1.75	Shareholders	9,000
Dividend Rate/Share	0.35	Market cap. (B)	$ 4.8
Shs. outstg. (M)	148.0	Inst. holdings	58%
Avg. daily vol. (M)	0.355		

Value of $10,000 invested 5 years ago: NA

Fiscal Year Ending Dec. 31

	1998	1997	1996	1995	1994	1993
Revenues (Million $)						
1Q	353.1	312.1	423.0	384.2	319.4	276.0
2Q	393.5	343.0	445.6	407.4	342.7	298.0
3Q	—	344.1	455.0	412.0	359.3	312.0
4Q	—	367.0	487.6	419.3	400.7	331.0
Yr.	—	1,366	1,811	1,623	1,422	1,217
Earnings Per Share ($)						
1Q	**0.31**	**0.26**	0.25	0.19	0.17	0.12
2Q	**0.35**	**0.41**	0.28	0.23	0.20	0.15
3Q	**E0.37**	**0.32**	0.32	0.25	0.21	-0.05
4Q	**E0.42**	**0.26**	0.37	0.30	0.24	0.19
Yr.	**E1.45**	**1.25**	1.03	0.98	0.81	0.42

Next earnings report expected: mid October

Dividend Data (Dividends have been paid since 1913.)

Amount ($)	Date Decl.	Ex-Div. Date	Stock of Record	Payment Date
0.088	Oct. 29	Nov. 20	Nov. 24	Dec. 15 '97
0.088	Jan. 28	Feb. 18	Feb. 20	Mar. 13 '98
0.088	Apr. 29	May. 20	May. 22	Jun. 15 '98
0.088	Jul. 29	Aug. 21	Aug. 25	Sep. 15 '98

A Division of The **McGraw·Hill** Companies

Equifax Inc.

Business Summary - 21-JUL-98

Through the utilization of its vast expertise in providing information, processing, consulting and software solutions, Equifax (EFX) facilitates and enhances buyer-seller transactions worldwide. In 1997, EFX handled over 10 million transactions per day for its 300,000 worldwide customers. The company plans to continue to focus on geographic expansion, and deploying advanced technologies, two strategies that have proved successful in the past. Equifax serves the information and processing needs of financial services and other industries through its four primary divisions: North American Information Services, Payment Services, Equifax Europe, and Equifax Latin America.

North American Information Services (52% of 1997 sales) assists clients in managing risk, scoring credit performance, analyzing trends and predicting outcomes. This division serves various industries, including banking, finance, retail, telecommunications, utilities and healthcare administration. In the 1997 first quarter, the company acquired two risk management services businesses, the credit files of five credit bureaus in the U.S., and the remaining 50% interest in DICOM S.A. in Chile, for an aggregate of $69,045,000.

Payment Services (32%) provides check authorization and risk management processes along with credit card processing. Payment Services serves more than 38,000 clients and 21 million cardholders. The division also includes an ownership position in Equifax Venture Infotex, India's first third-party card processing company.

Through an alliance with IBM, EFX entered Hong Kong and mainland China for the first time, supplying credit card processing services to three leading Pacific Rim banks.

Equifax Europe (13%) consists of operations primarily in the U.K., as well as joint ventures in Spain and Portugal. Equifax Europe handles credit card processing, risk management, as well as marketing services.

Equifax Latin America (2%) consists of leading credit information companies in Chile and Argentina, and a developing operation in Mexico. Mexican operations are not expected to make significant contributions for the near term, and will require continued moderate investment over the next few years.

In July 1998, EFX acquired The Decisioneering Group, a recognized leader in knowledge engineering and strategic consulting solutions. The acquisition will result in the establishment of a new business unit to deliver strategic-level business and decision analytics across a variety of industries.

Per Share Data ($)

(Year Ended Dec. 31)	1997	1996	1995	1994	1993	1992	1991	1990	1989	1988
Tangible Bk. Val.	NA	NM	Nil	0.20	0.89	0.96	1.49	1.63	1.49	1.48
Cash Flow	1.78	1.81	1.48	1.25	0.79	0.85	0.67	0.61	0.67	0.63
Earnings	1.26	1.03	0.98	0.81	0.42	0.52	0.33	0.40	0.36	0.37
Dividends	0.34	0.33	0.32	0.30	0.28	0.26	0.26	0.24	0.21	0.20
Payout Ratio	27%	32%	32%	37%	66%	50%	79%	61%	59%	56%
Prices - High	37⅛	34½	21¾	15¼	13¾	10⅜	10⅝	11¼	10	8¼
- Low	26½	17¾	12⅝	11	8¾	7¼	6¾	6¾	6½	6⅛
P/E Ratio - High	30	33	22	19	32	20	32	28	27	22
- Low	21	17	13	14	20	14	20	17	18	17

Income Statement Analysis (Million $)

	1997	1996	1995	1994	1993	1992	1991	1990	1989	1988
Revs.	1,366	1,811	1,623	1,422	1,217	1,134	1,094	1,079	840	743
Oper. Inc.	401	401	340	281	222	195	181	173	111	87.0
Depr.	77.1	85.9	77.0	66.5	54.9	53.8	55.9	36.0	29.4	24.3
Int. Exp.	20.8	23.0	21.0	15.6	10.9	4.0	7.3	14.0	12.6	4.4
Pretax Inc.	323	304	249	207	112	145	94.0	113	60.0	58.0
Eff. Tax Rate	43%	42%	41%	42%	43%	41%	42%	43%	41%	42%
Net Inc.	186	178	148	120	63.5	85.3	54.1	63.9	35.7	34.0

Balance Sheet & Other Fin. Data (Million $)

	1997	1996	1995	1994	1993	1992	1991	1990	1989	1988
Cash	52.3	49.9	26.0	79.0	86.0	87.0	105	115	14.0	6.0
Curr. Assets	401	437	367	376	303	279	304	324	178	149
Total Assets	1,177	1,303	1,054	1,021	731	709	716	754	551	421
Curr. Liab.	328	375	251	300	154	129	153	154	137	118
LT Debt	339	306	303	212	200	192	77.0	143	89.0	30.0
Common Eqty.	349	425	353	362	254	258	350	373	247	225
Total Cap.	688	731	656	581	461	464	447	570	384	295
Cap. Exp.	34.5	56.0	31.7	20.2	39.8	34.6	23.6	45.9	55.7	59.5
Cash Flow	263	264	225	187	118	139	110	100	65.0	58.0
Curr. Ratio	1.2	1.2	1.5	1.3	2.0	2.2	2.0	2.1	1.3	1.3
% LT Debt of Cap.	49.2	41.9	46.1	36.5	43.4	41.3	17.2	25.1	23.1	10.2
% Net Inc.of Revs.	13.6	9.8	9.1	8.5	5.2	7.5	4.9	5.9	4.2	4.6
% Ret. on Assets	15.0	15.1	14.2	13.7	8.9	12.5	7.3	7.7	7.3	9.3
% Ret. on Equity	47.9	45.6	41.3	38.8	25.0	29.4	14.9	16.4	15.1	18.4

Data as orig. reptd.; bef. results of disc. opers. and/or spec. items. Per share data adj. for stk. divs. as of ex-div. date. Bold denotes diluted EPS (FASB 128). E-Estimated. NA-Not Available. NM-Not Meaningful. NR-Not Ranked.

Office—1600 Peachtree St., N.W., P.O. Box 4081, Atlanta, GA 30302 Tel—(404) 885-8000. Website—http://www.equifax.com Chrmn—C. B. Rogers, Jr. Pres & CEO—T. F. Chapman. VP & CFO—D. A. Post. VP, Secy & Investor Contact—Marietta E. Zakas. Dirs—L. A. Ault III, T. F. Chapman, J. L. Clendenin, A. W. Dahlberg, R. P. Forrestal, L. P. Humann, D. W. McGlaughlin, L. L. Prince, D. R. Riddle, C. B. Rogers, Jr., B. L. Siegel, L. W. Sullivan. Transfer Agent & Registrar—Suntrust Bank, Atlanta. Incorporated—in Georgia in 1913. Empl— 10,000. S&P Analyst: Mark Cavallone

12-SEP-98

Industry:
Oil (International Integrated)

Summary: Exxon is a major factor in the world crude oil, natural gas and chemical industries.

S&P Opinion: Hold (★★★)	Recent Price • 70½	Yield • 2.3%
	52 Wk Range • 76-54¾	12-Mo. P/E • 22.5

Quantitative Evaluations

Outlook
(1 Lowest—5 Highest)
• **1+**

Fair Value
• **42¾**

Risk
• **Low**

Earn./Div. Rank
• **A**

Technical Eval.
• **Bullish** since 9/98

Rel. Strength Rank
(1 Lowest—99 Highest)
• **93**

Insider Activity
• **Neutral**

Earnings vs. Previous Year
▲=Up ▼=Down ▶=No Change

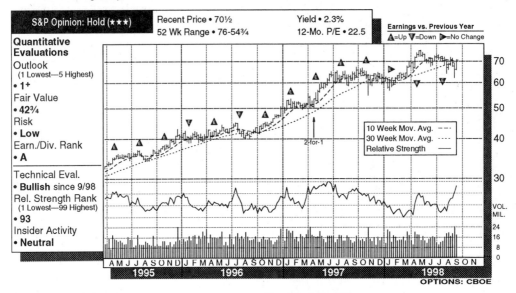

10 Week Mov. Avg. -----
30 Week Mov. Avg. ······
Relative Strength ——

2-for-1

OPTIONS: CBOE

Overview - 27-JUL-98

Over the long term, XON should benefit from increased natural gas sales to Latin America and the Pacific Rim, a result of expanding economies in those areas. Results for 1997 included gains of $0.13 per share from nonrecurring items. Debt service is modest, and debt accounts for only 18% of total capital, while internal cash generation exceeded capital spending (mainly internationally focused) in 1997. Exploration and production earnings declined in 1997, on lower oil and gas production and lower crude oil prices. However, refining and marketing profits more than doubled, as petroleum product sales increased and refining margins improved. We expect downstream profits to remain strong in 1998, as lower crude oil prices will lead to healthier margins. Chemical profits rose 14% in 1997, on higher volumes and margins. However, we expect weak petrochemicals margins in 1998.

Valuation - 27-JUL-98

Ignoring the recent oil price weakness, investors have instead been focusing on XON's excellent long-term earnings power. Although natural gas fundamentals in Europe do not make us optimistic about short-term prices, we forecast significant (2.5%-4%) long-term growth in international volumes. Meanwhile, the average world oil price has fallen significantly in recent months, due to increased worldwide production, and the near-term oil price outlook remains bearish. Downstream margins will firm in Europe, where nearly 43% of XON's refining capacity is situated, due to lower crude oil prices and reduced industry capacity. However, the shares appear fairly valued on a cash-flow basis, trading at a premium to other international oils, and are expected to be market performers over the remainder of 1998.

Key Stock Statistics

S&P EPS Est. 1998	2.80	Tang. Bk. Value/Share	17.78
P/E on S&P Est. 1998	25.2	Beta	0.68
S&P EPS Est. 1999	3.10	Shareholders	610,000
Dividend Rate/Share	1.64	Market cap. (B)	$172.1
Shs. outstg. (M)	2438.4	Inst. holdings	42%
Avg. daily vol. (M)	4.226		

Value of $10,000 invested 5 years ago: $ 28,279

Fiscal Year Ending Dec. 31

	1998	1997	1996	1995	1994	1993
Revenues (Million $)						
1Q	26,211	29,556	30,474	29,779	25,624	26,900
2Q	25,525	28,673	31,625	31,667	27,102	27,600
3Q	—	28,765	32,938	30,969	29,237	27,400
4Q	—	33,275	32,120	15,478	30,165	27,700
Yr.	—	120,279	116,728	107,893	112,128	109,500
Earnings Per Share ($)						
1Q	**0.76**	**0.86**	0.76	0.67	0.46	0.47
2Q	**0.65**	**0.78**	0.63	0.65	0.35	0.49
3Q	—	**0.73**	0.63	0.60	0.46	0.55
4Q	—	**1.00**	1.00	0.63	0.77	0.60
Yr.	**E2.80**	**3.37**	**2.99**	2.59	2.04	2.10

Next earnings report expected: late October

Dividend Data (Dividends have been paid since 1882.)

Amount ($)	Date Decl.	Ex-Div. Date	Stock of Record	Payment Date
0.410	Oct. 29	Nov. 07	Nov. 12	Dec. 10 '97
0.410	Jan. 28	Feb. 06	Feb. 10	Mar. 10 '98
0.410	Apr. 29	May. 11	May. 13	Jun. 10 '98
0.410	Jul. 29	Aug. 11	Aug. 13	Sep. 10 '98

A Division of The **McGraw·Hill** Companies

Business Summary - 27-JUL-98

Every day, millions of motorists "put a tiger in their tanks" at some 32,000 Exxon or Esso service stations around the world, a testament to this energy giant's global reach. One of the world's largest companies by a number of measures, Exxon is involved in every phase of the petroleum industry, from exploring for and producing oil and natural gas in 26 countries to refining and marketing operations carried out in 76 countries. The company traces its roots to Standard Oil and its founder John D. Rockefeller, the archetypal oil tycoon.

Exxon is not only about oil, however. The company operates the world's third largest petrochemical company and is the world's largest independent (nonutility) power producer. It also has a major presence in coal and minerals. The following table shows the breakdown in operating profits in recent years. Given the cyclical nature of these businesses, the relative contributions can vary widely from year to year.

	1997	1996
Exploration/production	55%	67%
Refining & marketing	24%	12%
Chemicals	16%	16%
Coal & other	5%	5%

Exxon is second only to Royal Dutch/Shell in terms of the size of its oil and gas reserves: 6.2 billion barrels of crude oil and 26.1 trillion cubic feet of natural gas as of the end of 1997. This represents about a 14-year supply of production, a total well above the industry average and showing XON's strength relative to its major competitors. During 1997, average crude oil and natural gas liquids production was 1.0% lower than in 1996. Natural gas production in 1997 declined 3.6%, due primarily to lower European gas production. Worldwide refinery throughput rose 5.8%, and petroleum product sales were up 4.2%.

Results in 1997 were mixed. Lower oil and gas production and lower oil prices led to a 7.2% decline in exploration and production profits. However, refining and marketing earnings more than doubled, aided by the company's highest petroleum product sales volumes in 23 years and improved margins. Chemicals profits rose 14%, on higher volumes and improved margins. Overall, net income rose 13% in 1997.

Despite its massive capital budget, which exceeded $8.8 billion in 1997 and is projected at the same level for 1998, Exxon has shown a willingness to share its cash with its stockholders, having raised the dividend in each of the past 14 years. The dividend yield was 2.3% as of late July 1998, compared to the benchmark S&P 500 yield of about 1.4%.

Per Share Data ($)

(Year Ended Dec. 31)	1997	1996	1995	1994	1993	1992	1991	1990	1989	1988
Tangible Bk. Val.	17.37	16.64	15.32	14.84	14.03	13.62	14.08	13.26	12.09	12.32
Cash Flow	5.63	5.16	4.76	4.05	4.02	3.94	4.21	4.18	3.13	3.77
Earnings	3.37	3.01	2.59	2.04	2.10	1.91	2.23	1.98	1.16	1.98
Dividends	1.63	1.56	1.50	1.46	1.44	1.42	1.34	1.24	1.15	1.07
Payout Ratio	48%	52%	58%	71%	68%	74%	60%	62%	99%	53%
Prices - High	67¼	50⅝	43	33¾	34½	32¾	31	27⅝	25⅞	23⅞
- Low	48¼	38⅞	30⅛	28⅛	28⅞	26⅞	24⅞	22½	20¼	16
P/E Ratio - High	20	17	17	17	16	17	14	14	22	12
- Low	14	13	12	14	14	14	11	11	17	8

Income Statement Analysis (Million $)

	1997	1996	1995	1994	1993	1992	1991	1990	1989	1988
Revs.	135,142	131,543	121,804	99,683	97,825	103,160	102,847	105,519	86,656	79,557
Oper. Inc.	16,993	15,387	14,584	11,942	12,063	11,928	13,006	14,099	12,932	13,077
Depr.	5,474	5,329	5,386	5,015	4,759	5,044	4,935	5,493	4,968	4,794
Int. Exp.	415	984	1,104	1,178	1,055	1,148	1,141	1,510	1,378	1,042
Pretax Inc.	13,204	11,916	10,442	8,037	8,302	7,534	8,685	8,452	5,266	8,654
Eff. Tax Rate	33%	37%	38%	34%	33%	33%	34%	38%	39%	36%
Net Inc.	8,460	7,510	6,470	5,100	5,280	4,810	5,600	5,010	2,975	5,260

Balance Sheet & Other Fin. Data (Million $)

	1997	1996	1995	1994	1993	1992	1991	1990	1989	1988
Cash	4,047	2,969	1,789	1,775	1,652	1,515	1,587	1,379	2,016	2,409
Curr. Assets	21,192	19,910	17,318	16,460	14,859	16,424	17,012	18,336	16,576	14,846
Total Assets	96,064	95,527	91,296	87,862	84,145	85,030	87,560	87,707	83,219	74,293
Curr. Liab.	19,654	19,505	18,736	19,493	18,590	19,663	20,854	24,025	21,984	17,479
LT Debt	7,050	7,236	7,778	8,831	8,506	8,637	8,582	7,687	9,275	4,689
Common Eqty.	43,470	43,239	39,982	36,861	34,840	33,824	34,974	33,025	30,238	31,767
Total Cap.	66,533	66,167	62,815	59,849	56,632	56,523	58,925	56,260	54,735	50,583
Cap. Exp.	7,393	7,209	7,128	6,643	6,919	7,225	7,262	6,474	12,002	5,927
Cash Flow	13,915	12,812	11,818	10,069	9,985	9,793	10,466	10,428	7,909	10,054
Curr. Ratio	1.1	2.1	0.9	0.8	0.8	0.8	0.8	0.8	0.8	0.8
% LT Debt of Cap.	10.6	10.9	12.4	14.8	15.0	15.3	14.6	13.7	16.9	9.3
% Net Inc.of Revs.	6.3	5.7	5.3	5.1	5.4	4.7	5.4	4.7	3.4	6.6
% Ret. on Assets	8.8	8.0	7.2	5.9	6.2	5.8	6.4	5.9	3.8	7.3
% Ret. on Equity	19.5	18.0	16.8	14.1	15.2	13.8	16.3	15.6	9.6	16.7

Data as orig. reptd.; bef. results of disc. opers. and/or spec. items. Per share data adj. for stk. divs. as of ex-div. date. Revs. in Income Statement Analysis table excl. excise taxes prior to 1995. Bold denotes diluted EPS (FASB 128). E-Estimated. NA-Not Available. NM-Not Meaningful. NR-Not Ranked.

Office—5959 Las Colinas Blvd., Irving, TX 75039-2298. **Tel**—(972) 444-1000. **Website**—http://www.exxon.com **Chrmn & CEO**—L. R. Raymond. **Secy & VP-Investor Relations**—T. P. Townsend. **VP & Treas**—E. A. Robinson.**Dirs**—M. J. Boskin, D. W. Calloway, R. Dahan, J. Hay, J. R. Houghton, W. R. Howell, R. C. King, P. E. Lippincott, H. J. Longwell, M. C. Nelson, L. R. Raymond, R. E. Wilhelm. **Transfer Agent**—Bank of Boston. **Incorporated**—in New Jersey in 1882. **Empl**— 80,000. **S&P Analyst:** Norman Rosenberg

FDX Corp.

865M

NYSE Symbol **FDX**

In S&P 500

12-SEP-98

Industry:
Air Freight

Summary: FDX, formed in early 1998, is a holding company for Federal Express Corp. and Caliber System, Inc.

S&P Opinion: Hold (★★★)	Recent Price • 47⅞	Yield • Nil	Earnings vs. Previous Year
	52 Wk Range • 84½-47⅛	12-Mo. P/E • 14.2	▲=Up ▼=Down ▶=No Change

Quantitative Evaluations

Outlook
(1 Lowest—5 Highest)
• 4⁻

Fair Value
• 61¾

Risk
• **Low**

Earn./Div. Rank
• **B-**

Technical Eval.
• **Bearish** since 3/98

Rel. Strength Rank
(1 Lowest—99 Highest)
• **44**

Insider Activity
• **NA**

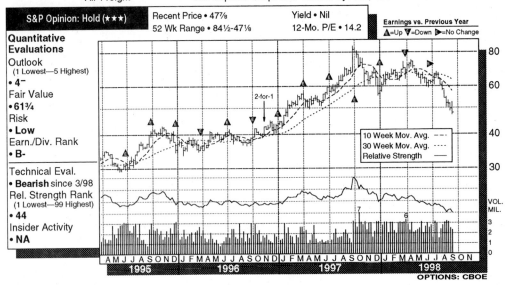

10 Week Mov. Avg. — – –
30 Week Mov. Avg. ········
Relative Strength ——

2-for-1

VOL. MIL.

OPTIONS: CBOE

Overview - 22-JUL-98

FedEx's domestic Priority Overnight service is projected to grow 4% in FY 99 (May), down from 6.3% in FY 98. Growth for deferred delivery services will be cut sharply, as comparisons are hurt by the loss of most of the volume obtained during a strike at rival UPS in August 1997. In addition, FedEX's deferred delivery product will see a diversion of business to its RPS unit, as that carrier initiates a delivery guarantee for its ground-based service. Double-digit gains are seen for international priority packages, although the rate will be down from FY 98's 23% pace. Despite softness in Asia, a new aviation treaty with Japan allows FedEx to expand aggressively. While RPS's volumes will benefit from its date-specific guarantee, margins may suffer, as it needs to increase spending on technology. Viking will see moderate volume growth and firm rates. Comparisons will benefit from the absence of merger-related expenses in FY 98.

Valuation - 22-JUL-98

After peaking in mid-1997, the shares have been stuck in a basebuilding mode. Investors remain concerned about the situation in Asia, although weakness in that area has not significantly hurt profits. Also weighing down the shares is a slowing of growth for FedEx domestic express business after it switched to distance-based pricing. Still unresolved is what the FAA's final policy on B727 freighters will be, since it could force FedEx to cut payloads. Also, to remain competitive with UPS, FDX's RPS is offering a money-back guarantee for its service, which could prompt FedEx customers to switch to the lower-cost RPS ground service. Finally, FedEx faces increasing competition from the Postal Service's Priority Mail offering. On the positive side, in 1998, FedEx won unrestricted access to fly to Japan and points beyond. Weighing the pros and cons, we advise a neutral position.

Key Stock Statistics

S&P EPS Est. 1999	4.25	Tang. Bk. Value/Share	24.52
P/E on S&P Est. 1999	11.3	Beta	1.09
S&P EPS Est. 2000	5.00	Shareholders	9,600
Dividend Rate/Share	Nil	Market cap. (B)	$ 7.1
Shs. outstg. (M)	147.4	Inst. holdings	69%
Avg. daily vol. (M)	0.727		

Value of $10,000 invested 5 years ago: $ 17,591

Fiscal Year Ending May 31

	1998	1997	1996	1995	1994	1993
Revenues (Million $)						
1Q	3,297	2,692	2,453	2,231	2,016	1,865
2Q	3,299	2,852	2,547	2,359	2,122	1,965
3Q	3,986	2,907	2,535	2,333	2,077	1,940
4Q	4,078	3,068	2,738	2,470	2,265	2,039
Yr.	15,873	11,520	10,274	9,392	8,479	7,808
Earnings Per Share ($)						
1Q	1.22	0.54	0.67	0.54	0.30	0.10
2Q	0.91	0.90	0.79	0.77	0.54	0.33
3Q	**0.09**	0.54	0.23	0.56	0.28	0.08
4Q	**1.14**	1.14	1.00	0.77	0.71	0.51
Yr.	**3.34**	3.12	2.69	2.63	1.82	1.00

Next earnings report expected: early October

Dividend Data

No dividends have been paid on the common stock.

A Division of The **McGraw·Hill** *Companies*

STANDARD
&POOR'S
STOCK REPORTS

FDX Corporation

865M
12-SEP-98

Business Summary - 22-JUL-98

FDX Corp. was formed in January 1998, via the merger of Caliber System, Inc. and Federal Express Corp. It provides worldwide time-definite transportation services. Caliber's RPS provides ground-based business-to-business delivery for small packages. Other businesses acquired with Caliber were Viking Freight, which provides regional freight service; Roberts Express (time-critical courier services); and Caliber Logistics (integrated transportation/distribution management services).

FDX provides same-day, overnight and deferred delivery services for documents, packages and freight, through 38,500 ground vehicles and 613 aircraft. The FAA is currently considering requiring operators of B727s (FDX has 163) to cut maxmium payloads or to make modifications to strengthen the aircraft floor.

FDX's most important service is Priority Overnight, which generated 40% of FY 98 (May) revenues. The service guarantees delivery of packages up to 150 lbs. to most communities in the U.S. by 10:30 AM. Priority Overnight's growth fell sharply in FY 98, after FDX adopted distance-based pricing. The move, designed to better match prices with costs, did lead to an improvement in yields.

FDX's fastest growing domestic services are deferred delivery services, FedEx 2Day and Express Saver. Express Saver, launched in July 1997, provides guaranteed delivery of shipments in most of the U.S. within three business days. Volumes surged in FY 98, when rival United Parcel Service (UPS) was struck for two weeks. FDX, which believes it has retained 15% of the strike-related business, said profits from UPS business added $0.25 a share in FY 98.

International delivery services for documents and freight have been growing faster than domestic business in recent years. In FY 98, international shipments (23% of total revenues) accounted for 8.6% of volume, up from 6.6% in FY 91. In February 1998, Japan and the U.S. signed a new aviation pact that lets FDx fly anywhere in Japan, and to pick up shipments there for other parts of Asia. The pact clears the way for FDX to accelerate development of its Subic Bay hub in the Philippines, to support intra-Asia traffic and shipments to and from China.

The acquisition of Caliber was undertaken primarily to obtain RPS, the second largest U.S. carrier of small shipments. This let FDX deepen its penetration of the deferred delivery market, and positioned it for an assault on UPS. RPS's 1998 decision to offer guaranteed delivery for deferred shipments could prompt shippers to move some FDX business to RPS.

Per Share Data ($)

(Year Ended May 31)	1998	1997	1996	1995	1994	1993	1992	1991	1990	1989
Tangible Bk. Val.	24.52	22.58	19.25	16.51	13.51	11.32	10.09	10.70	9.97	8.61
Cash Flow	9.81	9.82	9.02	8.40	7.03	6.13	4.29	5.07	5.59	5.29
Earnings	3.34	3.12	2.69	2.63	1.82	1.00	-1.05	0.06	1.09	1.59
Dividends	Nil	Nil	Nil	Nil	Nil	Nil	Nil	Nil	Nil	Nil
Payout Ratio	Nil	Nil	Nil	Nil	Nil	Nil	Nil	Nil	Nil	Nil
Cal. Yrs.	1997	1996	1995	1994	1993	1992	1991	1990	1989	1988
Prices - High	84½	45	43	40⅜	36¼	28	22¼	29	29	25½
- Low	42	33½	29¼	26¾	22¼	17¼	15¾	14¾	21⅛	17¾
P/E Ratio - High	25	14	16	15	20	28	NM	NM	27	16
- Low	13	11	11	10	12	17	NM	NM	19	11

Income Statement Analysis (Million $)

	1998	1997	1996	1995	1994	1993	1992	1991	1990	1989
Revs.	15,873	11,520	10,274	9,392	8,479	7,808	7,550	7,688	7,015	5,167
Oper. Inc.	2,047	1,477	1,344	1,244	1,113	926	834	935	893	812
Depr.	964	778	720	652	583	562	577	535	479	387
Int. Exp.	124	91.0	135	142	182	200	203	232	216	140
Pretax Inc.	899	628	540	522	378	204	-146	41.0	218	298
Eff. Tax Rate	45%	43%	43%	43%	46%	46%	NM	86%	47%	44%
Net Inc.	498	361	308	298	204	110	-113	6.0	116	166

Balance Sheet & Other Fin. Data (Million $)

	1998	1997	1996	1995	1994	1993	1992	1991	1990	1989
Cash	230	122	93.0	358	393	155	78.0	118	98.0	157
Curr. Assets	2,880	2,133	1,728	1,869	1,762	1,440	1,206	1,283	1,315	1,100
Total Assets	9,686	7,625	6,699	6,433	5,992	5,793	5,463	5,672	5,675	5,293
Curr. Liab.	2,804	1,963	1,618	1,779	1,536	1,449	1,385	1,494	1,240	1,089
LT Debt	1,385	1,398	1,325	1,325	1,632	1,882	1,798	1,827	2,148	2,139
Common Eqty.	3,961	2,962	2,576	2,246	1,925	1,671	1,580	1,669	1,649	1,494
Total Cap.	5,620	4,520	3,965	3,627	3,560	3,626	3,501	3,713	4,096	3,632
Cap. Exp.	1,880	1,471	1,412	1,061	1,089	867	771	986	1,145	1,687
Cash Flow	1,462	1,139	1,028	950	787	672	443	540	595	554
Curr. Ratio	1.0	1.1	1.1	1.1	1.1	1.0	0.9	0.9	1.1	1.0
% LT Debt of Cap.	24.6	31.0	33.4	36.5	45.8	51.9	51.3	49.2	56.6	58.9
% Net Inc.of Revs.	3.1	3.1	3.0	3.2	2.4	1.4	NM	0.1	1.7	3.2
% Ret. on Assets	5.8	5.0	4.7	4.8	3.4	1.9	NM	0.1	2.1	4.0
% Ret. on Equity	14.4	13.0	12.8	14.3	11.3	6.7	NM	0.4	7.3	11.9

Data as orig. reptd.; bef. results of disc. opers. and/or spec. items. Per share data adj. for stk. divs. as of ex-div. date. Bold denotes diluted EPS (FASB 128). E-Estimated. NA-Not Available. NM-Not Meaningful. NR-Not Ranked.

Office—2005 Corporate Ave., Memphis, TN 38132. **Tel**—(901) 369-3600. **Website**—http://www.fedex.com **Chrmn, Pres & CEO**—F. W. Smith. **EVP & CFO**—A. B. Graf. **EVP & Secy**—K. R. Masterson. **Investor Contact**—Elizabeth Allen (901-395-3653). **Dirs**—R. H. Allen, H. H. Baker Jr., R. L. Cox, R. D. DeNunzio, J. L. Estrin, P. Greer, J. R. Hyde III, C. T. Manatt, G. J. Mitchell, J. W. Smart Jr., F. W. Smith, J. I. Smith, P. S. Walsh, P. S. Willmott. **Transfer Agent & Registrar**—First Chicago Trust Co. of New York, Jersey City, NJ. **Incorporated**—in Delaware in 1971. **Empl**— 170,000.
S&P Analyst: Stephen R. Klein

Federal Home Loan Mortgage   865T

NYSE Symbol **FRE**

In S&P 500

12-SEP-98

Industry:
Financial (Diversified)

Summary: Federal Home Loan Mortgage ("Freddie Mac"), a corporate instrumentality of the U.S. government, buys mortgages from lenders in order to increase the supply of funds for housing.

S&P Opinion: Accumulate (★★★★)

| Recent Price • 44½ | Yield • 1.1% |
| 52 Wk Range • 51⅜-33½ | 12-Mo. P/E • 21.3 |

Earnings vs. Previous Year
▲=Up ▼=Down ▶=No Change

Quantitative Evaluations

Outlook
(1 Lowest—5 Highest)
• **1+**

Fair Value
• **38⅛**

Risk
• **Low**

Earn./Div. Rank
• **A+**

Technical Eval.
• **Bullish** since 9/95

Rel. Strength Rank
(1 Lowest—99 Highest)
• **84**

Insider Activity
• **NA**

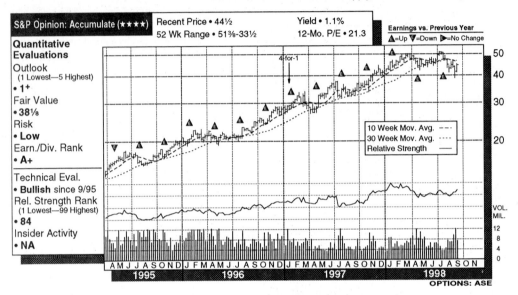

OPTIONS: ASE

Overview - 17-JUL-98

Share earnings are projected to grow steadily at percentages in the low teens over the next three to five years. The main factor expected to benefit earnings is expansion of the retained mortgage portfolio Freddie Mac holds for its own account, although there will be cyclically slow periods. FRE should continue to expand this portfolio through new mortgage purchases due to growth in the level of mortgage debt outstanding, its access to low-cost financing by virtue of its quasi-agency status, and the fact that it only owns a small share of total mortgage debt. Only modest gains are seen in the company's securitization operations, reflecting the large balance of mortgages already securitized and a reduced need by well-capitalized thrifts to hold MBS in their portfolios. Lower credit losses also aid the outlook.

Valuation - 17-JUL-98

Freddie Mac shares are a solid, long-term core holding. Although the stock was recently trading at a P/E on projected 1998 EPS in line with market averages, we expect the company to boost earnings at low double-digit rates on average for the foreseeable future, above the growth rate of the overall market. We attach a high degree of confidence to our growth outlook, as FRE enjoys competitive endowments such as access to financing only modestly above Treasury rates (because of its quasi-agency status) and a low cost structure, resulting from economies of scale inherent in its businesses. In addition, total mortgage debt outstanding is increasing. The company typically generates an impressive return on equity of over 20%, much better than that of other financial concerns. Lastly, credit quality trends are positive.

Key Stock Statistics

S&P EPS Est. 1998	2.25	Tang. Bk. Value/Share	8.74
P/E on S&P Est. 1998	19.8	Beta	1.28
S&P EPS Est. 1999	2.60	Shareholders	1,900
Dividend Rate/Share	0.48	Market cap. (B)	$ 30.2
Shs. outstg. (M)	678.6	Inst. holdings	72%
Avg. daily vol. (M)	1.886		

Value of $10,000 invested 5 years ago: $ 39,845

Fiscal Year Ending Dec. 31

	1998	1997	1996	1995	1994	1993
Revenues (Million $)						
1Q	4,495	3,844	2,749	2,143	1,574	1,165
2Q	4,854	4,014	2,995	2,305	1,626	1,318
3Q	—	3,589	3,137	2,489	1,779	1,382
4Q	—	2,902	3,235	2,582	1,944	1,591
Yr.	—	14,399	12,116	9,519	6,923	5,456
Earnings Per Share ($)						
1Q	**0.54**	0.44	0.40	0.34	0.36	0.27
2Q	**0.56**	0.46	0.43	0.34	0.32	0.23
3Q	**E0.57**	0.49	0.41	0.36	0.32	0.26
4Q	**E0.58**	0.51	0.43	0.38	0.33	0.26
Yr.	**E2.25**	1.88	1.67	1.42	1.33	1.02

Next earnings report expected: mid October

Dividend Data (Dividends have been paid since 1989.)

Amount ($)	Date Decl.	Ex-Div. Date	Stock of Record	Payment Date
0.100	Sep. 05	Sep. 11	Sep. 15	Sep. 30 '97
0.100	Dec. 05	Dec. 11	Dec. 15	Dec. 31 '97
0.120	Mar. 06	Mar. 12	Mar. 16	Mar. 31 '98
0.120	Jun. 05	Jun. 11	Jun. 15	Jun. 30 '98

A Division of The McGraw·Hill Companies

Business Summary - 17-JUL-98

The Federal Home Loan Mortgage Corp., better known as Freddie Mac, is one of two public govern-ment-sponsored enterprises (the other being rival Fan-nie Mae) formed to promote home ownership by in-creasing the availability of mortgage financing. The company was originally part of the Federal Home Loan Bank Board, which was dismantled under the S&L bailout law of 1989. Of its 18 directors, 13 are elected by stockholders and five are picked by the President. Freddie Mac has two principal business segments.

In its portfolio business, Freddie Mac functions quite similarly to a savings and loan, which originates home mortgage loans to hold for its own account. The major differences are that (1) Freddie Mac uses capital mar-ket borrowings to finance its mortgage purchases, whereas the thrift uses retail savings, and (2) Freddie Mac purchases mortgages from various lenders, while the thrift actually issues the homebuyer a mortgage.

The term "retained mortgage portfolio" is intended to indicate that these mortgages are "warehoused" (i.e. held) as a long-term investment for their valuable inter-est income. This business is quite profitable for Freddie because its cost of funds is in one sense subsidized by its quasi-agency status. The retained portfolio business generates the majority of the company's profits. At De-

cember 31, 1997, Freddie Mac's retained mortgage portfolio totaled some $164.4 billion, up from $137.5 bil-lion a year ago.

The company's mortgage-backed security (MBS) oper-ation is best illustrated by an example. Typically, a bank or thrift will decide it prefers to hold MBS as opposed to originated loans. The institution then gives the loan, or more often a pool of loans, to Freddie Mac, which gives the lender MBS in return. Both parties win. Freddie Mac receives a fee of about one-fifth of 1% to guarantee the principal and interest on the MBS. And the lender has a nearly risk-free instrument on which it receives principal and interest payments. Freddie Mac makes money in this business because its loss rate is very low--people will default on all sorts of bills but the basic need for shelter provides a powerful incentive to keep the mort-gage more or less current.

Nonperforming single-family loans amounted to 0.57% of the total portfolio at December 31, 1997, down from 0.58% a year earlier. Apartment delinquencies and fore-closures were 1.18% of the total portfolio, based on principal balances, versus 1.96% a year earlier.

According to a study by the Office of Management and Budget, mortgage rates are about 0.25-0.50% lower be-cause Freddie Mac and its rival Fannie Mae exist in the form and size they do.

Per Share Data ($)

(Year Ended Dec. 31)	1997	1996	1995	1994	1993	1992	1991	1990	1989	1988
Tangible Bk. Val.	8.74	9.63	7.38	6.45	4.95	4.17	3.56	2.96	2.66	NA
Earnings	1.88	1.67	1.42	1.33	1.02	0.82	0.77	0.57	0.55	0.48
Dividends	0.40	0.35	0.30	0.26	0.22	0.19	0.17	0.13	0.13	NA
Payout Ratio	21%	21%	21%	20%	22%	23%	22%	23%	24%	NA
Prices - High	44½	29¼	20⅞	15¾	14¼	12⅜	11⅝	6⅞	8¾	4⅜
- Low	26¾	19⅛	12½	11¾	11⅜	8½	3¾	2½	4⅛	3¾
P/E Ratio - High	24	18	15	12	14	15	15	12	16	9
- Low	14	11	9	9	11	10	5	4	7	8

Income Statement Analysis (Million $)

	1997	1996	1995	1994	1993	1992	1991	1990	1989	1988
Interest On: Mtges.	11,030	9,038	6,505	4,528	3,296	2,608	2,332	2,053	2,016	1,569
Interest On: Invest.	1,971	1,745	1,888	1,287	1,127	917	1,095	1,258	1,169	833
Int. Exp.	11,119	8,241	6,997	4,703	3,571	2,830	2,744	2,692	2,668	1,910
Guaranty Fees	0.0	1,249	1,087	1,108	1,033	936	792	654	572	465
Loan Loss Prov.	310	320	255	200	300	473	431	474	260	204
Admin. Exp.	495	440	395	379	361	329	287	243	217	194
Pretax Inc.	2,215	1,797	1,586	1,482	1,128	901	800	587	628	554
Eff. Tax Rate	26%	30%	31%	31%	30%	31%	31%	30%	30%	31%
Net Inc.	1,395	1,243	1,091	1,027	786	622	555	414	437	381

Balance Sheet & Other Fin. Data (Million $)

	1997	1996	1995	1994	1993	1992	1991	1990	1989	1988
Mtges.	164,250	137,520	107,411	72,295	55,732	33,523	26,537	21,395	21,329	16,815
Invest.	13,402	16,331	13,962	17,808	18,223	12,542	9,956	11,012	5,765	9,107
Cash & Equiv.	438	9,141	7,483	11,442	3,216	6,453	7,987	4,859	5,397	5,525
Total Assets	194,597	173,866	137,181	106,199	83,880	59,502	46,860	40,579	35,462	34,352
ST Debt	85,128	80,105	62,141	47,303	17,999	12,854	17,239	19,959	16,673	18,847
LT Debt	83,446	76,386	57,820	48,984	31,994	16,777	13,023	10,982	9,474	8,035
Equity	5,934	6,685	5,000	4,300	3,574	3,008	2,566	2,136	1,916	1,584
% Ret. on Assets	0.8	0.8	0.9	1.1	1.1	1.2	1.3	1.1	1.3	1.3
% Ret. on Equity	20.6	18.5	22.1	24.4	21.4	21.2	23.6	20.4	25.0	27.5
Equity/Assets Ratio	3.1	4.0	3.8	4.2	4.6	5.2	5.4	5.3	5.0	4.6
Price Times Book Value:										
Hi	5.1	3.0	2.8	2.4	2.9	2.5	3.3	2.3	3.3	NA
Low	4.1	2.0	1.7	1.8	2.3	1.7	1.0	0.9	1.5	NA

Data as orig. reptd.; bef. results of disc. opers. and/or spec. items. Per share data adj. for stk. divs. as of ex-div. date. Bold denotes diluted EPS (FASB 128). E-Estimated. NA-Not Available. NM-Not Meaningful. NR-Not Ranked.

Office—8200 Jones Branch Dr., McLean, VA 22102. **Tel**—(703) 903-2000. **Website**—http://www.freddiemac.com **Chrmn & CEO**—L. C. Brendsel. **Pres**—D. W. Glenn. **VP & Secy**—M. E. Mater. **Investor Contact**—Cindy Gertz (703-903-2798). **Dirs**—L. C. Brendsel, D. DeConcini, D. W. Glenn, G. D Gould, N. F. Hartigan, T. W. Jones, H. Kaufman, M. E. Mater, J. B. McCoy, J. F. Montgomery, R. E. Palmer, R. F. Poe, D. J. Schuenke, C. Seix, J. Serna, Jr., W. J. Turner, H. F. Woods. **Transfer Agent & Registrar**—First Chicago Trust Co. of New York, Jersey City, N. J. **Incorporated**—under the laws of the United States in 1970. **Empl**— 3,134. **S&P Analyst:** Paul L. Huberman, CFA

12-SEP-98

Industry:
Financial (Diversified)

Summary: "Fannie Mae," a U.S. government-sponsored company, uses mostly borrowed funds to buy a variety of mortgages, thereby creating a secondary market for mortgage lenders.

S&P Opinion: Accumulate (★★★★)	

Recent Price • 60⅜	Yield • 1.6%
52 Wk Range • 68¼-44⅜	12-Mo. P/E • 19.8

Quantitative Evaluations

Outlook
(1 Lowest—5 Highest)
• **1+**

Fair Value
• **50⅞**

Risk
• **Average**

Earn./Div. Rank
• **A**

Technical Eval.
• **Bullish** since 3/96

Rel. Strength Rank
(1 Lowest—99 Highest)
• **86**

Insider Activity
• **NA**

Earnings vs. Previous Year
▲=Up ▼=Down ▶=No Change

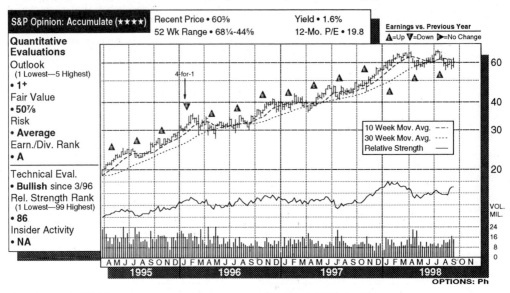

10 Week Mov. Avg. — — —
30 Week Mov. Avg. · · · ·
Relative Strength ——

OPTIONS: Ph

Overview - 17-JUL-98

Fannie Mae should increase its earnings per share 10% to 15% a year for the foreseeable future (excluding nonrecurring expenses, such as a charitable contribution in 1995). This outlook reflects projected growth in the mortgage portfolio that Fannie Mae holds for its own account (accounting for about two-thirds of profits). FNM should expand this portfolio about 9% to 13% in 1999, based on projected growth of 7% to 9% in mortgage debt, home price inflation, and the company's plans to increase its purchases of mortgage-backed securities. The mortgage-backed securities segment (which provides about one-third of net income) is growing less rapidly, partly reflecting the fact that a high percentage of mortgages has already been securitized, as well as reduced demand for MBS on the part of certain financial institutions. No major increase in credit provisioning is likely, given the company's strong reserve position. Long-term prospects are further enhanced by share repurchases.

Valuation - 17-JUL-98

The shares of Fannie Mae, which we regard as a solid core holding, carry an accumulate recommendation. The company enjoys favorable long-term growth prospects, as a result of projected increases in mortgage debt outstanding, continued gains in its securitization activities, new housing initiatives, and its access to low-cost financing by virtue of its quasi-agency status. Another positive factor is the fact that Fannie Mae faces only one competitor in its major markets. The company typically generates a high return on shareholders' equity. For instance, in the second quarter of 1998, FNM's ROE was over 25%, well above the average for a financial company. The stock merits a premium P/E valuation to that of the overall market.

Key Stock Statistics

S&P EPS Est. 1998	3.20	Tang. Bk. Value/Share	12.34
P/E on S&P Est. 1998	18.9	Beta	1.04
S&P EPS Est. 1999	3.60	Shareholders	19,000
Dividend Rate/Share	0.96	Market cap. (B)	$ 62.6
Shs. outstg. (M)	1036.9	Inst. holdings	77%
Avg. daily vol. (M)	2.930		

Value of $10,000 invested 5 years ago: $ 35,786

Fiscal Year Ending Dec. 31

	1998	1997	1996	1995	1994	1993
Revenues (Million $)						
1Q	7,401	6,672	6,065	5,290	4,304	2,863
2Q	—	6,862	6,146	5,452	4,496	3,897
3Q	—	7,004	6,317	5,631	4,735	4,071
4Q	—	7,237	6,526	5,866	5,038	4,222
Yr.	—	27,777	25,054	22,250	18,573	16,053
Earnings Per Share ($)						
1Q	**0.78**	0.67	0.61	0.52	0.50	0.44
2Q	**0.80**	0.69	0.61	0.53	0.49	0.45
3Q	**E0.80**	0.72	0.63	0.55	0.49	0.48
4Q	**E0.82**	0.75	0.65	0.37	0.47	0.48
Yr.	**E3.20**	2.84	2.50	1.96	1.95	1.86

Next earnings report expected: early October

Dividend Data (Dividends have been paid since 1956.)

Amount ($)	Date Decl.	Ex-Div. Date	Stock of Record	Payment Date
0.210	Oct. 21	Oct. 29	Oct. 31	Nov. 25 '97
0.240	Jan. 20	Jan. 28	Jan. 30	Feb. 25 '98
0.240	Apr. 21	Apr. 28	Apr. 30	May. 25 '98
0.240	Jul. 21	Jul. 29	Jul. 31	Aug. 25 '98

A Division of The **McGraw·Hill** *Companies*

Business Summary - 17-JUL-98

The Federal National Mortgage Association, more commonly known as Fannie Mae, is a government-sponsored enterprise, chartered by Congress to increase the availability of mortgage credit for homebuyers. Its mission, in essence, is to increase the rate of home ownership--which in turn makes American society more stable. The company's predecessor was formed during the Great Depression, to make home ownership possible during a time when it was nearly impossible for people in certain parts of the country to obtain a mortgage. The company basically operates in two business segments.

In its retained portfolio business, which accounts for about two-thirds of profits, the company buys a variety of mortgages from banks, thrifts, mortgage bankers and others for its own account. The term retained is intended to indicate that Fannie Mae holds these mortgages for investment, just as an S&L, which originates mortgages, holds mortgages in its own portfolio. The company finances its mortgage purchases by debt offerings of various maturities. This business activity is especially profitable, because FNM enjoys access to low-cost funds by virtue of its quasi-agency status: investors believe that there is a very low risk of default on the company's bonds, because, in the event of

trouble, the government would probably step in and make good on the obligations. Fannie Mae is an extremely large company. As an indication of the company's size, at the end of 1996, Fannie Mae owned $287.1 billion of mortgages, equal to 6.8% of the total mortgages outstanding nationwide.

In its securitization operations, which account for much of the remaining profits, the company swaps mortgage-backed securities (MBSs) for mortgages with various lending institutions, and in the process earns a fee of about 0.23%. One reason lenders swap loans for MBSs is that the latter add to liquidity. Fannie Mae essentially functions as a mortgage insurer, to the extent that it accepts the risk of default on the mortgage in exchange for a fee or a premium.

Finally, the company earns a small amount for guaranteeing complex mortgage-backed securities that are put together by Wall Street firms.

Although FNM is highly profitable in a variety of interest rate environments, Congress is constantly concerned about its risk exposure on the $900 billion plus of mortgages and mortgage-backed securities outstanding, since the U. S. government would ultimately have to make good on large-scale defaults. Congress has therefore established capital standards, which the company meets.

Per Share Data ($)

(Year Ended Dec. 31)	1997	1996	1995	1994	1993	1992	1991	1990	1989	1988
Tangible Bk. Val.	12.34	11.10	10.04	8.74	7.39	6.20	5.08	4.13	3.13	2.39
Earnings	2.84	2.50	1.94	1.95	1.86	1.50	1.33	1.13	0.79	0.54
Dividends	0.84	0.76	0.68	0.60	0.46	0.34	0.26	0.18	0.11	0.06
Payout Ratio	30%	30%	35%	31%	25%	23%	20%	16%	14%	11%
Prices - High	57¼	41⅝	31½	22⅝	21½	19⅜	17⅜	11⅛	11⅝	4⅜
- Low	36⅛	27½	17¼	17	18¼	13¾	8⅛	6¼	4¼	2⁷⁄₁₆
P/E Ratio - High	20	17	16	12	12	13	13	10	15	8
- Low	13	11	9	9	10	9	6	6	5	5

Income Statement Analysis (Million $)

	1997	1996	1995	1994	1993	1992	1991	1990	1989	1988
Interest On: Mtges.	22,716	20,560	18,154	15,851	13,957	12,651	11,603	10,958	10,103	9,629
Interest On: Invest.	3,662	3,212	2,917	1,496	876	884	990	1,111	977	597
Int. Exp.	22,429	20,180	18,024	14,524	12,300	11,476	10,815	10,476	9,889	9,389
Guaranty Fees	0.0	1,196	0.0	1,083	961	834	675	536	408	328
Loan Loss Prov.	NA	195	140	155	175	320	370	310	310	365
Admin. Exp.	636	560	546	525	443	381	319	286	254	218
Pretax Inc.	4,337	3,905	2,995	3,146	3,005	2,382	2,081	1,647	1,104	663
Eff. Tax Rate	29%	30%	28%	32%	32%	31%	30%	29%	27%	24%
Net Inc.	3,068	2,754	2,155	2,141	2,042	1,649	1,455	1,173	807	507

Balance Sheet & Other Fin. Data (Million $)

	1997	1996	1995	1994	1993	1992	1991	1990	1989	1988
Mtges.	313,316	286,259	252,588	220,525	189,892	156,021	126,486	113,875	107,756	99,867
Invest.	64,596	56,606	57,273	46,335	21,396	14,786	10,999	9,868	6,656	5,289
Cash & Equiv.	2,205	850	318	231	977	5,193	3,194	4,178	5,214	2,859
Total Assets	391,673	351,041	316,550	272,508	216,979	180,978	147,072	133,113	124,315	112,258
ST Debt	175,400	159,900	146,153	112,602	71,950	56,404	34,608	38,453	36,346	36,599
LT Debt	194,374	171,370	153,021	144,628	129,162	109,896	99,329	84,950	79,718	68,860
Equity	13,793	12,773	10,959	9,541	8,052	6,774	5,547	3,941	2,991	2,260
% Ret. on Assets	0.8	0.8	0.7	0.9	1.0	1.0	1.0	0.9	0.7	0.5
% Ret. on Equity	24.4	23.9	21.0	24.3	27.5	26.8	30.7	33.8	30.7	24.9
Equity/Assets Ratio	NA	3.4	3.5	3.6	3.7	3.8	3.4	2.7	2.2	1.9
Price Times Book Value:										
Hi	4.6	3.8	3.1	2.6	2.9	3.1	3.4	2.7	3.7	1.8
Low	2.9	2.5	1.7	1.9	2.5	2.2	1.6	1.5	1.3	1.0

Data as orig. reptd.; bef. results of disc opers. and/or spec. items. Per share data adj. for stk. divs. as of ex-div. date. Bold denotes diluted EPS (FASB 128). E-Estimated. NA-Not Available. NM-Not Meaningful. NR-Not Ranked.

Office—3900 Wisconsin Ave. N.W., Washington, DC 20016. **Tel**—(202) 752-7000. **Website**—http://www.fanniemae.com **Chrmn & CEO**—J. A. Johnson. **Pres**—L. M. Small. **EVP & CFO**—J. T. Howard. **EVP & Secy**—J. Gorelick. **Investor Contact**—Jayne Shontell (202-752-7115). **Dirs**—F. M. Beck, R. E. Birk, E. Broad, W. M. Daley, T. P. Gerrity, J. A. Johnson, T. A. Leonard, V. A. Mai, A. McLaughlin, R. D. Parsons, F. D. Raines, J. R. Sasso, A. Shusta, L. M. Small, C. J. Sumner, J. H. Villarreal, K. H. Williams. **Incorporated**—under the laws of the United States in 1938. **Empl**— 3,400. **S&P Analyst:** Paul L. Huberman, CFA

12-SEP-98

Industry: Retail (Department Stores)

Summary: Federated operates more than 400 department stores and 160 specialty stores in 36 states. It acquired R. H. Macy & Co. in 1994.

S&P Opinion: Buy (★★★★★)	Recent Price • 43¼	Yield • Nil
	52 Wk Range • 56⅛-39¼	12-Mo. P/E • 14.9

Quantitative Evaluations

Outlook
(1 Lowest—5 Highest)
• 3

Fair Value
• 45¼

Risk
• **Average**

Earn./Div. Rank
• **NR**

Technical Eval.
• **Bullish** since 8/98

Rel. Strength Rank
(1 Lowest—99 Highest)
• **54**

Insider Activity
• **NA**

Earnings vs. Previous Year
▲=Up ▼=Down ▷=No Change

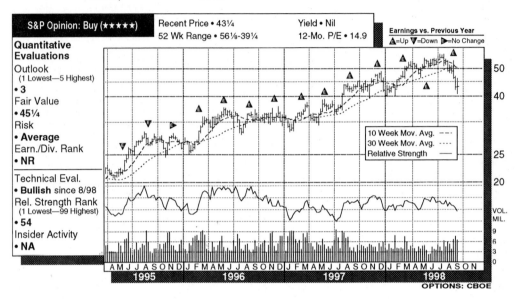

10 Week Mov. Avg. ---
30 Week Mov. Avg. ····
Relative Strength —

OPTIONS: CBOE

Overview - 01-JUN-98

Net sales should increase only moderately in FY 99 (Jan.), reflecting store closings; same-store sales should increase about 2.5% to 3.0%. The company has closed a number of underperforming units in an effort to better utilize its asset base. Gross margins should widen somewhat, as Federated increases emphasis on private-label apparel with its higher margins. As expense ratios continue to decline, the company will pass the savings on to customers in the form of lower prices. As a result, expense ratios should decline only modestly, as most available expense savings were realized in past years. Earnings before interest, depreciation and amortization, and taxes should increase about 10%. Depreciation and amortization charges will be about the same as in FY 98. Aided by a decline in interest expense, earnings could increase strongly, to $3.00 a share. Further acquisitions are a possibility.

Valuation - 01-JUN-98

First quarter FY 99 earnings met our expectations with slightly wider gross margins and lower expense ratios; operating income rose 22%. The company's strong management team has continued to meet and even exceed its stated goals for cost reduction and profitability. Benefits from economies of scale should continue to boost profitability over the next few years, as will greater emphasis on private brands, with their wider margins. The company's strong cash flow should allow Federated to continue to pay down debt in FY 99. Also, it plans to repurchase as much $500 million common shares. We see the company's core earnings growth rate at 15% to 16%. We recommend purchasing the shares of this strong player in the rapidly consolidating department store sector of retailing.

Key Stock Statistics

S&P EPS Est. 1999	3.05	Tang. Bk. Value/Share	21.74
P/E on S&P Est. 1999	14.2	Beta	1.00
S&P EPS Est. 2000	3.55	Shareholders	NA
Dividend Rate/Share	Nil	Market cap. (B)	$ 9.1
Shs. outstg. (M)	210.9	Inst. holdings	93%
Avg. daily vol. (M)	1.258		

Value of $10,000 invested 5 years ago: $ 21,898

Fiscal Year Ending Jan. 31

	1999	1998	1997	1996	1995	1994
Revenues (Million $)						
1Q	8,456	3,409	3,301	2,988	1,650	1,590
2Q	3,523	3,453	3,284	3,047	1,596	1,502
3Q	—	3,746	3,609	3,748	1,927	1,789
4Q	—	5,060	5,035	5,265	3,139	2,348
Yr.	—	15,668	15,229	15,049	8,316	7,229
Earnings Per Share ($)						
1Q	0.27	0.11	-0.18	-0.31	0.25	0.17
2Q	0.47	0.31	-0.13	-0.37	0.03	0.07
3Q	E0.53	0.47	0.20	-0.24	-0.24	0.16
4Q	E1.78	1.66	1.39	1.21	0.71	1.16
Yr.	E3.05	2.58	1.25	0.39	1.41	1.56

Next earnings report expected: mid November

Dividend Data

FD does not anticipate paying dividends in the foreseeable future. A poison pill stock purchase rights plan was adopted in 1992.

A Division of The **McGraw-Hill** *Companies*

STANDARD
&POOR'S
STOCK REPORTS

Federated Department Stores, Inc.

874

12-SEP-98

Business Summary - 01-JUN-98

Federated Department Stores and its predecessors have been operating department stores in the U.S. since 1830. The company is one of the leading U.S. department store operators, with 400 stores in 33 states as of January 31, 1998. Operations are conducted under the names Jordan Marsh, Bloomingdale's, The Bon Marche, Broadway, Burdine's, Goldsmith's, Lazarus, Rich's, Stern's, Weinstock's and Macy's. In May, 1998 the company agreed to sell its more than 160 specialty stores, operating under the names Aeropostale and Charter Club, with annual sales of $185 million. FD operates a mail-order catalog business, Bloomingdale's By Mail. The company merged with R. H. Macy & Co. on December 19, 1994. On October 1, 1995, Federated acquired the 82-store chain Broadway Stores, Inc.; a number of stores acquired at that time are being disposed of.

Each Federated department store division is well established in its operating areas. The department stores sell a wide variety of merchandise, including women's, men's and children's apparel, cosmetics, home furnishings and other consumer goods.

The company provides a number of support functions to its retail operating divisions on an integrated, companywide basis. Federated Merchandising/Federated Product Development, a division of the company based in New York City, provides centralized buying services for the company's retail operating divisions and private-label design and sourcing for planned growth in merchandise brands. Financial and Credit Services Group, Federated Systems Group and Federated Logistics have expanded their roles to achieve greater efficiencies.

Federated opened six new department stores in 1997, two new furniture galleries and closed 19 stores. FD plans to open three new units in 1998. Budgeted capital expenditures are about $2.3 billion from 1998 through 2000. Management anticipates funding these expenditures from operations. Management believes that the department store industry will continue to consolidate, and intends to consider acquisitions of department store assets and companies

The company has off-balance-sheet financing of up to $300 million of non-proprietary credit card receivables from accounts owned by Federated. At January 31, 1998, $243 million of borrowings were outstanding under this arrangement.

Per Share Data ($)

(Year Ended Jan. 31)	1998	1997	1996	1995	1994	1993	1992	1991	1990	1989
Tangible Bk. Val.	21.74	19.00	17.38	14.39	22.64	13.64	13.61	NA	NA	NA
Cash Flow	5.22	3.91	3.07	3.54	3.35	3.39	NA	NA	NA	NA
Earnings	2.58	1.28	0.39	1.41	1.56	1.19	NA	NA	NA	NA
Dividends	Nil	Nil	Nil	Nil	Nil	Nil	NA	NA	NA	NA
Payout Ratio	Nil	Nil	Nil	Nil	Nil	Nil	NA	NA	NA	NA
Cal. Yrs.	1997	1996	1995	1994	1993	1992	1991	1990	1989	1988
Prices - High	48⁷/₈	37	30¹/₈	25¹/₄	25	20¹/₈	NA	NA	NA	NA
- Low	30	25	17⁷/₈	18	17³/₈	11¹/₄	NA	NA	NA	NA
P/E Ratio - High	19	29	77	18	16	17	NA	NA	NA	NA
- Low	12	20	46	13	11	9	NA	NA	NA	NA

Income Statement Analysis (Million $)

	1998	1997	1996	1995	1994	1993	1992	1991	1990	1989
Revs.	15,668	15,229	15,049	8,636	7,473	7,305	7,158	7,137	NA	NA
Oper. Inc.	1,951	1,760	1,498	919	735	676	528	NA	NA	NA
Depr.	610	558	515	283	227	246	261	NA	NA	NA
Int. Exp.	418	499	509	263	214	258	504	365	NA	NA
Pretax Inc.	958	441	202	331	368	232	-1,849	-155	NA	NA
Eff. Tax Rate	40%	40%	63%	43%	47%	43%	NM	NM	NM	NM
Net Inc.	575	266	75.0	188	197	133	-1,235	-0.4	NA	NA

Balance Sheet & Other Fin. Data (Million $)

	1998	1997	1996	1995	1994	1993	1992	1991	1990	1989
Cash	142	149	173	206	222	567	1,002	615	NA	NA
Curr. Assets	6,194	6,429	6,360	5,190	3,298	3,390	3,841	3,726	NA	NA
Total Assets	13,738	14,264	14,295	12,380	7,419	7,020	7,501	7,357	NA	NA
Curr. Liab.	3,060	3,596	3,098	2,712	1,330	1,163	1,917	1,800	NA	NA
LT Debt	3,919	4,606	5,632	4,529	2,787	2,810	3,177	3,274	NA	NA
Common Eqty.	5,256	4,669	4,274	3,640	2,278	2,075	1,454	1,425	NA	NA
Total Cap.	10,114	10,106	10,639	9,162	5,869	5,636	5,377	4,699	NA	NA
Cap. Exp.	696	846	696	387	313	208	202	NA	NA	NA
Cash Flow	1,185	824	590	471	423	378	-974	NA	NA	NA
Curr. Ratio	2.0	1.8	2.0	1.9	2.5	2.9	2.0	2.1	NA	NA
% LT Debt of Cap.	38.7	45.6	52.9	49.4	47.5	49.9	59.1	69.7	NA	NA
% Net Inc.of Revs.	3.7	1.8	0.5	2.2	2.6	1.8	NM	NM	NM	NM
% Ret. on Assets	4.1	1.9	0.6	1.6	3.2	1.4	NM	NM	NM	NM
% Ret. on Equity	11.6	6.0	1.9	5.4	10.7	6.1	NM	NM	NM	NM

Data as orig. reptd.; bef. results of disc. opers. and/or spec. items. Per share data adj. for stk. divs. as of ex-div. date. Bold denotes diluted EPS (FASB 128). E-Estimated. NA-Not Available. NM-Not Meaningful. NR-Not Ranked.

Office—7 West Seventh St., Cincinnati, OH 45202. **Tel**—(513) 579-7000. **Website**—http://www.federated-fds.com **Chrmn & CEO**—J. M. Zimmerman. **SVP & CFO**—K. M. Hoguet. **SVP & Secy**—D. J. Broderick. **Investor Contact**—Susan Robinson. **Dirs**—M. Feldberg, E. G. Graves, Sr., G. V. Grune, S. Levinson, T. J. Lundgren, J. Neubauer, J. A. Pichler, R. W. Tysoe, K. M. von der Heyden, C. E. Weatherup, M. C. Whittington, J. M. Zimmerman. **Transfer Agent**—Bank of New York, NYC. **Incorporated**—in Delaware in 1929. **Empl**— 114,700. **S&P Analyst:** Karen J. Sack, CFA

Fifth Third Bancorp 3869

Nasdaq Symbol **FITB**

In S&P 500

12-SEP-98

Industry: Banks (Major Regional)

Summary: This regional bank holding company, with about $28 billion in assets, operates about 480 full service banking centers in Ohio, Indiana, Kentucky, Arizona and Florida.

S&P Opinion: Hold (★★★)

Recent Price • 57⅞	Yield • 1.2%
52 Wk Range • 67¼–41⅛	12-Mo. P/E • 36.3

Quantitative Evaluations

Outlook
(1 Lowest—5 Highest)
• **1**

Fair Value
• **42⅜**

Risk
• **Average**

Earn./Div. Rank
• **A+**

Technical Eval.
• **Bearish** since 12/96

Rel. Strength Rank
(1 Lowest—99 Highest)
• **84**

Insider Activity
• **Neutral**

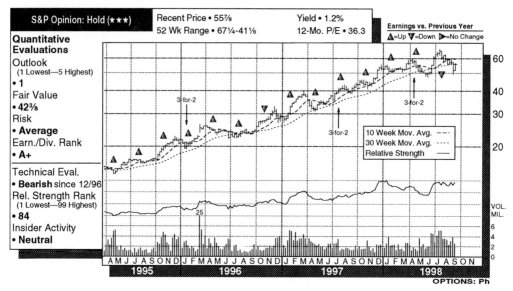

Earnings vs. Previous Year
⒜=Up ▼=Down ▷=No Change

10 Week Mov. Avg. – – –
30 Week Mov. Avg. ·····
Relative Strength ——

VOL. MIL.

OPTIONS: Ph

Overview - 31-JUL-98

Near double-digit growth in earning assets is expected in 1998, with particular strength in the direct sales channel, such as home equity, through banking centers and commercial lease and real estate segments. Together with relative stability in interest margins, net interest income should be in the high single-digits. Good loan charge-off trends and adequate loss reserves will likely result in only a nominal increase in the loan loss provision to account for loan growth. Much healthier growth is projected on the fee-based income side of the business, with continued gains in core service charges, investment advisory income and mortgage banking income driving a better than 20% increase in noninterest income. Expense growth may be hurt in the intermediate term on Year 2000 issues and a greater proportion of compensation-based revenues, although efficiency will remain among the best in the industry. Overall earnings growth is predicted at 18% for 1998 and 15% for 1999.

Valuation - 31-JUL-98

With solid, ROE, ROA and efficiency levels, Fifth Third remains one of the industry's most profitable institutions. The shares easily outperformed the broader market in the past two calendar years but were up only in line with our major regional bank average in the first half of 1998. Nonetheless, the shares are trading at about 27X our 1999 EPS estimate of $2.30 and over 5X tangible book value per share. Both measures are at the high end of FITB's historical valuation and in comparison with peer banking companies. Although much of the premium valuation afforded the shares can be justified by the company's financial performance, we expect further appreciation from current levels to be limited to tracking the broader market.

Key Stock Statistics

S&P EPS Est. 1998	2.00	Tang. Bk. Value/Share	8.47
P/E on S&P Est. 1998	28.0	Beta	1.24
S&P EPS Est. 1999	2.30	Shareholders	15,600
Dividend Rate/Share	0.68	Market cap. (B)	$ 15.0
Shs. outstg. (M)	267.9	Inst. holdings	46%
Avg. daily vol. (M)	0.636		

Value of $10,000 invested 5 years ago: $ 38,515

Fiscal Year Ending Dec. 31

	1998	1997	1996	1995	1994	1993
Revenues (Million $)						
1Q	646.9	461.3	406.7	339.5	273.4	231.4
2Q	661.6	475.0	435.4	360.4	280.2	237.6
3Q	—	486.1	454.4	383.1	290.4	241.5
4Q	—	565.5	456.8	395.9	334.2	243.4
Yr.	—	1,924	1,754	1,479	1,178	953.9
Earnings Per Share ($)						
1Q	**0.46**	**0.39**	0.35	0.30	0.26	0.22
2Q	**0.22**	**0.41**	0.36	0.31	0.28	0.24
3Q	—	**0.44**	0.33	0.33	0.29	0.25
4Q	—	**0.45**	0.39	0.35	0.30	0.26
Yr.	—	**1.69**	1.41	1.29	1.12	0.97

Next earnings report expected: mid October

Dividend Data (Dividends have been paid since 1952.)

Amount ($)	Date Decl.	Ex-Div. Date	Stock of Record	Payment Date
0.220	Sep. 16	Sep. 26	Sep. 30	Oct. 15 '97
0.220	Dec. 16	Dec. 29	Dec. 31	Jan. 15 '98
3-for-2	Mar. 17	Apr. 16	Mar. 31	Apr. 15 '98
0.170	Jun. 16	Jun. 26	Jun. 30	Jul. 15 '98

A Division of The **McGraw·Hill** *Companies*

STANDARD
&POOR'S
STOCK REPORTS

Fifth Third Bancorp

3869

12-SEP-98

Business Summary - 31-JUL-98

Headquartered in Cincinnati, Fifth Third Bancorp has about 480 branches located throughout Ohio, Indiana, Kentucky, Arizona and Florida. The company is consistently ranked as one the most efficient in the U.S., as measured by the efficiency ratio. Fifth Third's loan and lease portfolio is almost evenly divided between the commercial and consumer segments.

Operations are divided into the Retail Banking, Commercial Banking, Investment Advisory Services and Data Processing segments. Retail Banking provides a full range of deposit products and consumer loans and leases. Commercial Banking offers services to business, government and professional customers. Investment Advisory provides a full range of investment alternatives for individuals, companies and not-for-profit organizations. Data Processing, through Midwest Payment Systems, provides electronic funds transfer services, merchant transaction processing, operates an ATM network and provides other data processing services to affiliated and unaffiliated customers.

In 1997, average earnings assets, from which interest income is derived, amounted to $19.2 billion and consisted mainly of loans (67%) and investment securities

(33%). Average sources of funds included interest, savings and money market deposits 26%, time and certificates of deposit 31%, foreign deposits 2%, short-term borrowings 16%, long-term debt 2%, non-interest bearing demand deposits 10%, stockholders' equity 10% and other 3%.

At year-end 1997, nonperforming assets, consisting primarily of non-accrual loans, renegotiated loans and other real estate owned, were $85.2 million (0.29% of total loans and related assets), up from $73.3 million (0.28%) a year earlier. The allowance for loan losses, which is set aside for possible loan defaults, was $200.9 million (1.50% of total loans), versus $187.3 million (1.50%). Net charge-offs, or the amount actually written off as uncollectible, were $68.4 million ($0.54% of average loans) in 1997, compared to $60.0 million (0.49%) in 1996.

In June 1998, Fifth Third completed the acquisition of Columbus, Ohio-based State Savings Company (assets of $2.8 billion) and Dayton, Ohio-based CitFed Bancorp ($3.5 billion). Also in June, the company acquired The Ohio Company, which has retail brokerage, public finance, corporate finance and money management lines of business.

Per Share Data ($)

(Year Ended Dec. 31)	1997	1996	1995	1994	1993	1992	1991	1990	1989	1988
Tangible Bk. Val.	8.47	7.79	7.19	6.27	5.78	4.70	4.21	3.93	3.50	3.07
Earnings	1.69	1.43	1.29	1.13	0.97	0.81	0.69	0.61	0.55	0.52
Dividends	0.57	0.49	0.43	0.36	0.30	0.27	0.23	0.20	0.18	0.15
Payout Ratio	33%	34%	33%	32%	31%	33%	33%	33%	32%	30%
Prices - High	55⁵/₈	33	22⁵/₈	16¹/₄	17¹/₂	16	13¹/₂	7¹/₄	7⁷/₈	6
- Low	27	19³/₈	13⁷/₈	13³/₄	14⁵/₈	11³/₄	5⁷/₈	4⁵/₈	5⁷/₈	4¹/₈
P/E Ratio - High	33	23	18	14	18	20	20	12	14	12
- Low	16	14	11	12	15	14	8	8	11	8

Income Statement Analysis (Million $)

	1997	1996	1995	1994	1993	1992	1991	1990	1989	1988
Net Int. Inc.	745	689	563	517	436	394	332	293	275	189
Tax Equiv. Adj.	NA	6.2	7.9	24.6	20.4	17.2	19.1	14.4	15.1	14.8
Non Int. Inc.	439	364	301	256	227	199	168	138	118	91.0
Loan Loss Prov.	80.3	64.0	43.0	35.8	44.5	65.3	55.7	39.9	36.5	26.1
Exp./Op. Revs.	43%	45%	44%	47%	48%	47%	48%	50%	51%	48%
Pretax Inc.	604	500	431	365	295	240	199	168	150	112
Eff. Tax Rate	34%	33%	33%	33%	33%	32%	30%	29%	28%	25%
Net Inc.	401	335	288	244	196	164	138	120	108	84.0
% Net Int. Marg.	4.11	3.99	3.90	4.16	4.51	4.73	4.58	4.56	4.74	4.80

Balance Sheet & Other Fin. Data (Million $)

	1997	1996	1995	1994	1993	1992	1991	1990	1989	1988
Earning Assets:										
Money Mkt	750	854	635	1,129	3.0	1.0	192	336	274	226
Inv. Securities	6,469	6,401	4,338	2,531	1,487	1,933	2,064	1,355	1,059	767
Com'l Loans	5,684	5,903	5,209	4,345	3,933	3,223	2,684	2,696	2,547	2,004
Other Loans	7,555	7,060	6,808	5,586	4,878	4,371	3,228	2,912	2,736	1,845
Total Assets	21,375	20,549	17,053	14,957	11,966	10,213	8,826	7,956	7,143	5,246
Demand Deposits	2,426	2,496	6,103	1,680	1,463	1,307	1,151	989	961	784
Time Deposits	12,488	11,879	6,383	8,951	7,165	6,225	5,536	5,396	4,822	3,310
LT Debt	458	278	425	179	283	254	13.0	14.0	13.0	12.0
Common Eqty.	2,277	2,144	1,725	1,399	1,198	1,005	879	783	699	509
% Ret. on Assets	1.9	1.8	1.8	1.8	1.8	1.7	1.7	1.6	1.6	1.8
% Ret. on Equity	18.1	17.3	18.4	18.6	18.2	17.3	16.6	16.2	16.5	18.0
% Loan Loss Resv.	1.5	1.5	1.5	1.5	1.5	1.5	1.6	1.6	1.6	1.6
% Loans/Deposits	90.1	87.1	93.6	95.3	100.5	99.2	86.8	86.1	89.3	91.7
% Equity to Assets	10.5	10.3	9.9	9.9	9.9	10.1	10.1	10.1	9.8	10.0

Data as orig. reptd.; bef. results of disc opers. and/or spec. items. Per share data adj. for stk. divs. as of ex-div. date. Bold denotes diluted EPS (FASB 128). E-Estimated. NA-Not Available. NM-Not Meaningful. NR-Not Ranked.

Office—Fifth Third Center, Cincinnati, OH 45263. **Tel**—(513) 579-5300. **Website**—http://www.53.com **Pres & CEO**—G. A. Schaefer Jr. **Sr VP, CFO & Treas**—N. E. Arnold. **Sr VP & Secy**—M. K. Keating. **Dirs**—D. F. Allen, J. F. Barrett, M. C. Boesel Jr., G. V. Dirvin, T. B. Donnell, R. T. Farmer, I. W. Gorr, J. H. Head Jr., J. R. Herschede, W. G. Kagler, J. D. Kiggen, M. D. Livingston, R. B. Morgan, J.E. Rogers, B. H. Rowe, G. A. Schaefer, Jr., J. J. Schiff Jr., D. J. Sullivan Jr., D. S. Taft. **Transfer Agent & Registrar**—Fifth Third Bank, Cincinnati. **Incorporated**—in Ohio in 1975. **Empl**— 6,787.
S&P Analyst: Stephen R. Biggar

First Chicago NBD 891K

NYSE Symbol **FCN**

In S&P 500

12-SEP-98

Industry: Banks (Money Center)

Summary: This bank holding company recently agreed to merge with Columbus, Ohio-based Banc One.

S&P Opinion: Accumulate (★★★★)

Recent Price • 71	Yield • 2.5%
52 Wk Range • 101-60⅝	12-Mo. P/E • 13.6

Quantitative Evaluations

Outlook (1 Lowest—5 Highest)
• **2+**

Fair Value
• **63⅜**

Risk
• **Average**

Earn./Div. Rank
• **B-**

Technical Eval.
• **NA**

Rel. Strength Rank (1 Lowest—99 Highest)
• **64**

Insider Activity
• **Favorable**

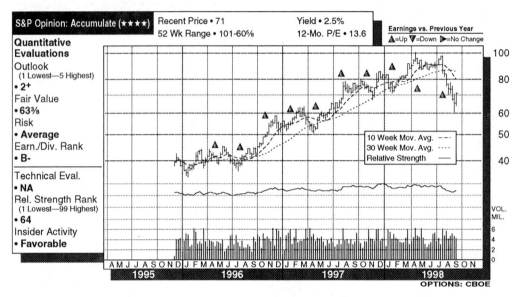

Earnings vs. Previous Year
▲=Up ▼=Down ▶=No Change

10 Week Mov. Avg. ---
30 Week Mov. Avg. ....
Relative Strength —

VOL. MIL.

OPTIONS: CBOE

Overview - 20-JUL-98

Net interest income is expected to be relatively flat in 1998, reflecting modest loan growth and continued pressure on margins. Loan growth has been impacted by the company's selectivity in the large capitalization sector, while margin compression reflects a less favorable earning asset mix due to lower credit card balances and ongoing competition for fees and pricing. Loss provisions are expected to approximate the level of charge-offs, which have shown modest increases over the last few quarters. Noninterest income should provide much of the expected earnings growth, led by healthy rises in services charges and commissions, although market-driven revenue could remain volatile. The balance of the expected 12% earnings growth in 1998 is expected in the form of good expense control. The company is projecting benefits from the Banc One merger of $1.2 billion, including $930 million of cost savings and $275 million in revenue enhancements, to be phased in beginning with 1999.

Valuation - 20-JUL-98

The shares have been rated accumulate since the announced merger with Banc One. We view the combined company, which will be the second largest credit card issuer, as having considerable opportunities for cost savings from overlapping branch networks and product sets, as well as revenue enhancements from cross-marketing abilities. Banc One should be able to leverage its highly successful credit model adopted from its acquisition of First USA in early 1997. Key competitive strengths also will be in the retail branch franchise and investment management businesses. With the expectation that the merger will lead to an improved earnings growth rate and risk profile, selective accumulation of the shares is recommended.

Key Stock Statistics

S&P EPS Est. 1998	5.50	Tang. Bk. Value/Share	28.24
P/E on S&P Est. 1998	12.9	Beta	1.45
S&P EPS Est. 1999	6.15	Shareholders	39,400
Dividend Rate/Share	1.76	Market cap. (B)	$ 20.4
Shs. outstg. (M)	287.7	Inst. holdings	54%
Avg. daily vol. (M)	0.984		

Value of $10,000 invested 5 years ago: NA

Fiscal Year Ending Dec. 31

	1998	1997	1996	1995	1994	1993
Revenues (Million $)						
1Q	2,603	2,413	2,618	2,562	--	2,562
2Q	2,753	2,504	2,565	2,642	--	2,642
3Q	—	2,582	2,505	2,756	--	2,756
4Q	—	2,599	2,429	2,721	--	2,721
Yr.	—	10,098	10,117	10,681	8,556	10,681
Earnings Per Share ($)						
1Q	1.30	1.17	1.04	1.01	--	--
2Q	1.38	1.20	1.10	0.99	--	--
3Q	E1.39	1.26	1.09	1.07	--	--
4Q	E1.43	1.28	1.15	0.37	--	--
Yr.	E5.50	4.90	4.33	3.45	3.67	3.90

Next earnings report expected: mid October

Dividend Data (Dividends have been paid since 1996.)

Amount ($)	Date Decl.	Ex-Div. Date	Stock of Record	Payment Date
0.440	Nov. 14	Dec. 03	Dec. 05	Jan. 01 '98
0.440	Feb. 13	Mar. 04	Mar. 06	Apr. 01 '98
0.440	May. 08	Jun. 03	Jun. 05	Jul. 01 '98
0.440	Jul. 10	Sep. 02	Sep. 04	Oct. 01 '98

A Division of The McGraw·Hill Companies

Business Summary - 20-JUL-98

In a transaction that will create the second largest credit card issuer in the U.S. with $60 billion in managed receivables, First Chicago NBD Corp. agreed in April 1998 to merge with Columbus, Ohio-based Banc One. Having earlier merged with NBD Bancorp in late 1995, the company continues to strive to be the leading bank for consumers and businesses in the Midwest, a leading provider of credit card and other consumer financial services nationally, and a premier provider of focused financial services to corporate and institutional customers in the U.S. and in major international markets.

Operations are broadly divided into four lines of business: regional banking, corporate banking, corporate investments and credit card. Regional banking includes retail banking serving metropolitan Chicago, Michigan and Indiana through more than 650 branch offices, private banking and investments, small business and middle market banking. Corporate banking targets commercial and investment banking products and services. Corporate investments focuses on growth equity, tax-advantaged, value-oriented, and funding and liquidity investments. Credit card operations develop and market credit card products and related services to individuals nationwide. With about $18.3 billion in credit card receivables under management, the company is one of the largest bank card issuers in the U.S.

In 1997, average earning assets, from which interest income is derived, amounted to $108 billion and consisted mainly of loans (71%) and investment securities (9%). Average sources of funds, used in the lending business, included interest-bearing deposits (47%), non-interest-bearing deposits (13%), short-term borrowings (17%), long-term debt (9%), shareholders' equity (7%) and other (7%).

At year-end 1997, nonperforming assets, consisting primarily of non-accrual loans and other real estate owned, were $326 million (0.5% of loans and related assets), up from $290 million (0.4%) a year earlier. The allowance for loan losses, which is set aside for possible loan defaults, was $1.41 billion (2.0% of loans), versus $1.41 billion (2.1%) a year earlier. Net chargeoffs, or the amount of loans actually written off as uncollectible, were $724 million (1.1% of average loans) in 1997, compared to $670 million (1.0%) in 1996.

The merger with Banc One (NYSE; ONE) calls for each FCN common share to be exchanged for 1.62 common shares of ONE; the new company will retain the Banc One name. The transaction is expected to be completed in the fourth quarter of 1998.

Per Share Data ($)

(Year Ended Dec. 31)	1997	1996	1995	1994	1993	1992	1991	1990	1989	1988
Tangible Bk. Val.	26.87	27.32	25.25	NA	NA	NA	NA	NA	NA	NA
Earnings	4.90	4.39	3.45	3.67	3.90	0.60	NA	NA	NA	NA
Dividends	1.64	1.48	1.35	NA	NA	NA	NA	NA	NA	NA
Payout Ratio	33%	34%	39%	NA	NA	NA	NA	NA	NA	NA
Prices - High	85⅞	58⅞	42½	NA	NA	NA	NA	NA	NA	NA
- Low	50½	34¾	38	NA	NA	NA	NA	NA	NA	NA
P/E Ratio - High	18	13	12	NA	NA	NA	NA	NA	NA	NA
- Low	10	8	11	NA	NA	NA	NA	NA	NA	NA

Income Statement Analysis (Million $)

	1997	1996	1995	1994	1993	1992	1991	1990	1989	1988
Net Int. Inc.	3,572	3,620	3,208	2,956	2,784	2,693	NA	NA	NA	NA
Tax Equiv. Adj.	95.0	102	103	88.0	110	115	NA	NA	NA	NA
Non Int. Inc.	2,445	2,208	2,144	2,193	2,298	1,711	NA	NA	NA	NA
Loan Loss Prov.	725	735	510	276	390	1,145	NA	NA	NA	NA
Exp./Op. Revs.	55%	55%	65%	62%	61%	73%	NA	NA	NA	NA
Pretax Inc.	2,266	2,162	1,754	1,877	2,002	272	NA	NA	NA	NA
Eff. Tax Rate	33%	34%	34%	34%	36%	18%	NA	NA	NA	NA
Net Inc.	1,525	1,436	1,150	1,237	1,286	224	NA	NA	NA	NA
% Net Int. Marg.	3.95	3.83	3.14	NA	NA	NA	NA	NA	NA	NA

Balance Sheet & Other Fin. Data (Million $)

	1997	1996	1995	1994	1993	1992	1991	1990	1989	1988
Earning Assets:										
Money Mkt	19,603	14,483	30,089	32,325	NA	NA	NA	NA	NA	NA
Inv. Securities	9,330	7,178	9,449	13,675	NA	NA	NA	NA	NA	NA
Com'l Loans	31,083	29,538	27,139	NA	NA	NA	NA	NA	NA	NA
Other Loans	37,641	37,640	37,905	58,484	NA	NA	NA	NA	NA	NA
Total Assets	114,096	104,619	122,002	123,379	NA	NA	NA	NA	NA	NA
Demand Deposits	16,069	15,702	15,234	13,746	NA	NA	NA	NA	NA	NA
Time Deposits	52,420	47,967	53,872	52,572	NA	NA	NA	NA	NA	NA
LT Debt	10,088	8,454	8,163	5,283	NA	NA	NA	NA	NA	NA
Common Eqty.	7,770	8,563	7,961	7,616	NA	NA	NA	NA	NA	NA
% Ret. on Assets	1.4	1.3	1.0	NA	NA	NA	NA	NA	NA	NA
% Ret. on Equity	18.4	17.0	15.5	NA	NA	NA	NA	NA	NA	NA
% Loan Loss Resv.	2.0	2.1	2.1	2.0	NA	NA	NA	NA	NA	NA
% Loans/Deposits	100.3	104.3	93.2	NA	NA	NA	NA	NA	NA	NA
% Equity to Assets	7.5	7.3	6.5	NA	NA	NA	NA	NA	NA	NA

Data as orig. reptd.; bef. results of disc opers. and/or spec. items. Per share data adj. for stk. divs. as of ex-div. date. Bold denotes diluted EPS (FASB 128). E-Estimated. NA-Not Available. NM-Not Meaningful. NR-Not Ranked.

Office—One First National Plaza, Chicago, IL 60670. **Tel**—(312) 732-4000. **Website**—http://www.fcnbd.com **Chrmn, Pres & CEO**—V. G. Istock. **EVP & CFO**—R. A. Rosholt. **Investor Contact**—Harry Hallowell (312) 732-4812. **Dirs**—T. E. Adderley, J. K. Baker, J. H. Bryan, S. Buschmann, J. S. Crown, M. A. Fay, C. T. Fisher III, V. G. Istock, T. H. Jeffs II, W. G. Lowrie, R. A. Manoogian, W. T. McCormick, Jr, A. J. McKenna, E. L. Neal, J. J. O'Connor, T. E. Reilly, Jr., J. W. Rogers, Jr., A. Simmons, R. L. Thomas, D. J. Vitale. **Transfer Agent & Registrar**—First Chicago Trust Co. of New York, Jersey City, NJ.**Incorporated**—in Delaware in 1969; Bank chartered in 1863.**Empl**— 33,962. **S&P Analyst:** Stephen R. Biggar

STANDARD &POOR'S
STOCK REPORTS

First Data

893H
NYSE Symbol **FDC**

In S&P 500

12-SEP-98 | Industry: Services (Data Processing)

Summary: FDC provides information processing and related services to the transaction card, mutual fund, teleservices and information management industries.

S&P Opinion: Accumulate (★★★★)

Recent Price • 23¾
52 Wk Range • 41⅜-20

Yield • 0.3%
12-Mo. P/E • 25.3

Earnings vs. Previous Year
▲=Up ▼=Down ▶=No Change

Quantitative Evaluations

Outlook
(1 Lowest—5 Highest)
• **3**

Fair Value
• **23¾**

Risk
• **Low**

Earn./Div. Rank
• **B+**

Technical Eval.
• **Bearish** since 7/98

Rel. Strength Rank
(1 Lowest—99 Highest)
• **50**

Insider Activity
• **Neutral**

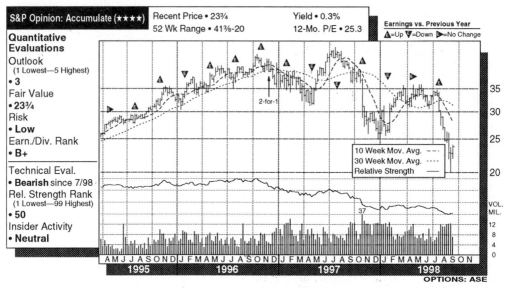

10 Week Mov. Avg. — — -
30 Week Mov. Avg. - - - -
Relative Strength —

OPTIONS: ASE

Overview - 28-JUL-98

Following divestitures of slower growing businesses, First Data now relies on three core operating divisions: Issuer Processing, Merchant Processing and Payment Instruments. The Payment Instruments unit has been the most consistent performer of late, while the Issuer Processing business has slowed. The struggling Merchant Processing division has been affected by a transition to bank alliances, in which FDC and banks combine resources and share profits in order to achieve greater operating efficiencies. The transition should eventually lead to improved operating margins, as greater economies of scale are realized. In July 1998, the company reported second quarter results that were in line with expectations, after excluding nonrecurring charges. Revenues were down slightly, but were up 11% after accounting for divestitures.

Valuation - 28-JUL-98

Second quarter results contained a $160 million charge related to delays in the conversion of Hong-Kong credit card accounts. We are currently forecasting EPS of $1.64 in 1998, excluding charges, with a gain to $1.85 in 1999. While the earnings growth rate is not that impressive, First Data generates over $1 billion in cash annually, and deserves a premium valuation to its growth rate. The company could also employ some of its cash for accretive acquisitions that would add to its growth rate. One potential risk for the stock involves the recent spate of bank mergers, and the pricing power that larger banks will have. However, these mergers could also be a positive factor, as certain FDC clients merge with non-clients, thus contributing more accounts to FDC. We continue to recommend accumulation of the stock, in light of the company's leadership position and electronic commerce initiatives.

Key Stock Statistics

S&P EPS Est. 1998	1.64	Tang. Bk. Value/Share	NM
P/E on S&P Est. 1998	14.5	Beta	1.27
S&P EPS Est. 1999	1.85	Shareholders	4,900
Dividend Rate/Share	0.08	Market cap. (B)	$ 10.6
Shs. outstg. (M)	446.8	Inst. holdings	80%
Avg. daily vol. (M)	2.580		

Value of $10,000 invested 5 years ago: $ 14,009

Fiscal Year Ending Dec. 31

	1998	1997	1996	1995	1994	1993
Revenues (Million $)						
1Q	1,232	1,243	1,130	903.4	376.0	347.0
2Q	1,305	1,318	1,200	1,093	410.0	379.0
3Q	—	1,278	1,258	1,071	432.0	381.0
4Q	—	1,380	1,350	1,119	434.4	383.0
Yr.	—	5,235	4,934	4,186	1,652	1,490
Earnings Per Share ($)						
1Q	**0.29**	**0.29**	0.23	0.20	0.20	0.17
2Q	**0.10**	**-0.06**	0.30	0.23	0.21	0.17
3Q	—	**0.42**	0.36	0.27	0.24	0.20
4Q	—	**0.13**	0.48	-0.88	0.29	0.24
Yr.	—	**0.79**	1.37	-0.19	0.94	0.78

Next earnings report expected: late October

Dividend Data (Dividends have been paid since 1992.)

Amount ($)	Date Decl.	Ex-Div. Date	Stock of Record	Payment Date
0.020	Sep. 17	Sep. 29	Oct. 01	Oct. 15 '97
0.020	Dec. 10	Dec. 30	Jan. 02	Jan. 15 '98
0.020	Mar. 11	Mar. 30	Apr. 01	Apr. 15 '98
0.020	May. 13	Jun. 29	Jul. 01	Jul. 15 '98

Business Summary - 28-JUL-98

The numbers are staggering: more than 180 million card accounts on file, 5.4 billion merchant transcations processed in 1997, and 50,000 Western Union agent locations. With sales of $5.2 billion in 1997, First Data Corp. (FDC) has transformed itself from a small credit-card processing operation within American Express into the world's second largest independent data services company. The company provides high-quality, high-volume information processing and related services and is involved in nearly every part of the burgeoning credit-card business except for actually issuing cards.

Domestic Card Issuer Services (22% of 1997 revenue from continuing operations) provides a variety of processing and related services to financial institutions issuing VISA and MasterCard credit cards and oil company and retail store credit cards. Services include transaction reporting, settlement and billing, and certain security and related services. In 1997, FDC added consumer credit information products and decision-making tools for credit and risk management.

Domestic Merchant Processing Services (25%) uses bank alliances to contract directly with merchants to provide processing services related to the merchant's

acceptance of cards and checks at the point of sale. The Telecheck system is one of the world's largest check acceptance services. International Card Services (5%) operates in the U.K. and Australia and encompasses the company's principal processing facilities outside of the U.S. Payment Instruments (26%), primarily operating through Western Union, represents the leading nonbank money transfer and bill payment services provider. In August 1997, FDC acquired Orlandi Valuta, a U.S.-Mexico money transfer business.

Investment Processing Services (5%) provides back-office processing services to the mutual fund industry. Specialty services (7%) complement transaction processing and include data capture, and electronic database management.

By leveraging its size, economies of scale and market leadership, FDC is winning significant contracts. In February 1997, the company announced a seven-year agreement to provide credit card processing services to four members of the HSBC (Hong Kong and Shanghai Banking Corp.) Group in Hong Kong, the U.K. and the U.S. In addition, FDC signed an agreement with Banc One to provide bank card processing for six million accounts. In the second quarter of 1997, the company formed MSFDC, a joint venture with Microsoft that will facilitate electronic bill presentation and payment.

Per Share Data ($)

(Year Ended Dec. 31)	1997	1996	1995	1994	1993	1992	1991	1990	1989	1988
Tangible Bk. Val.	NA	NM	NM	4.71	4.33	3.61	NA	NA	NA	NA
Cash Flow	1.91	2.23	0.57	1.58	1.31	1.09	0.96	0.81	0.73	NA
Earnings	0.79	1.37	-0.20	0.94	0.78	0.65	0.56	0.49	0.47	0.30
Dividends	0.08	0.07	0.06	0.06	0.06	0.03	NA	NA	NA	NA
Payout Ratio	10%	5%	NM	6%	8%	5%	NA	NA	NA	NA
Prices - High	46⅛	44	35⅝	25⅜	21⅛	17¼	NA	NA	NA	NA
- Low	25	30⅜	23	20¼	15⅝	10⅝	NA	NA	NA	NA
P/E Ratio - High	58	32	NM	27	27	26	NA	NA	NA	NA
- Low	32	22	NM	22	20	16	NA	NA	NA	NA

Income Statement Analysis (Million $)

	1997	1996	1995	1994	1993	1992	1991	1990	1989	1988
Revs.	5,235	4,934	4,081	1,652	1,490	1,205	1,026	845	672	466
Oper. Inc.	1,726	1,548	1,162	526	450	329	274	217	177	NA
Depr.	534	424	347	144	118	97.5	82.7	67.5	53.7	NA
Int. Exp.	117	110	106	41.3	41.4	34.0	30.6	19.9	21.2	NA
Pretax Inc.	706	1,032	168	356	291	232	191	167	162	103
Eff. Tax Rate	50%	38%	NM	42%	41%	39%	38%	38%	39%	39%
Net Inc.	357	637	-84.0	208	173	141	118	103	98.0	63.0

Balance Sheet & Other Fin. Data (Million $)

	1997	1996	1995	1994	1993	1992	1991	1990	1989	1988
Cash	411	272	231	1,188	698	329	335	154	NA	NA
Curr. Assets	NA	NA	NA	NA	NA	NA	NA	NA	NA	NA
Total Assets	15,315	14,340	12,218	5,419	4,148	3,916	3,172	2,376	2,035	1,591
Curr. Liab.	NA	NA	NA	NA	NA	NA	NA	NA	NA	NA
LT Debt	1,751	1,709	886	429	521	351	444	165	200	18.0
Common Eqty.	3,657	3,710	3,145	1,015	954	794	567	499	476	378
Total Cap.	5,408	5,417	4,031	1,444	1,476	1,145	1,010	664	676	396
Cap. Exp.	297	393	262	155	84.9	62.2	59.1	58.2	49.9	NA
Cash Flow	891	106	263	352	291	239	201	170	152	NA
Curr. Ratio	NA	NA	NA	NA	NA	NA	NA	NA	NA	NA
% LT Debt of Cap.	32.4	31.5	22.0	29.7	35.3	30.7	43.9	24.8	29.5	4.6
% Net Inc.of Revs.	6.8	12.9	NM	12.6	11.6	11.7	11.5	12.1	14.6	13.5
% Ret. on Assets	2.4	4.8	NM	4.4	4.3	3.9	4.3	4.7	5.4	4.3
% Ret. on Equity	9.7	18.6	NM	21.4	19.8	20.3	22.1	21.1	23.0	18.0

Data as orig. reptd.; bef. results of disc. opers. and/or spec. items. Per share data adj. for stk. divs. as of ex-div. date. Bold denotes diluted EPS (FASB 128). E-Estimated. NA-Not Available. NM-Not Meaningful. NR-Not Ranked.

Office—401 Hackensack Ave., Hackensack, NJ 07601. **Tel**—(201) 525-4700. **Website**—www.firstdatacorp.com **Chrmn & CEO**—H. C. Duques. **EVP & CFO**—L. Adrean. **Investor Contact**—Donald Y. Sharp. **Dirs**—B. Burdetsky, H. C. Duques, C. F. Jones, J. D. Robinson III, C. T. Russell, B. L. Schwartz, J. E. Spero, G. K. Staglin. **Transfer Agent & Registrar**—Norwest Bank Minnesota, South St. Paul. **Incorporated**—in Delaware in 1992. **Empl**— 36,000. **S&P Analyst:** Mark Cavallone

First Union Corp.

901K

NYSE Symbol **FTU**

In S&P 500

12-SEP-98

Industry:
Banks (Money Center)

Summary: This North Carolina-based bank holding company operates full-service branches along the East Coast from Florida to Connecticut.

S&P Opinion: Buy (★★★★)	Recent Price • 50½	Yield • 3.3%
	52 Wk Range • 65⅞-44½	12-Mo. P/E • 19.2

Quantitative Evaluations

Outlook
(1 Lowest—5 Highest)
• **1⁻**

Fair Value
• **43¾**

Risk
• **Low**

Earn./Div. Rank
• **A**

Technical Eval.
• **Bearish** since 9/98

Rel. Strength Rank
(1 Lowest—99 Highest)
• **67**

Insider Activity
• **Unfavorable**

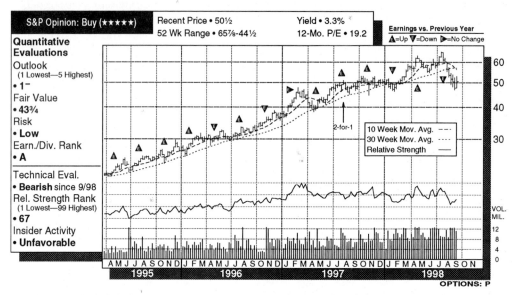

Earnings vs. Previous Year
▲=Up ▼=Down ▶=No Change

2-for-1

10 Week Mov. Avg. ---
30 Week Mov. Avg. ·····
Relative Strength —

OPTIONS: P

Overview - 20-JUL-98

Net interest income will likely be down in 1998, as internal growth in the loan portfolio from a healthy service territory is mitigated by asset securitization strategies. Margins are expected to narrow on a change in the asset mix following the sale of consumer loans, with offsets to be found in a lower loan loss provision. The main earnings growth driver will be increased contributions from noninterest income sources, particularly capital management (mutual funds, trust and brokerage services), due to a higher level of assets under management, and capital markets (underwriting, loan syndication and asset securitization) are expected. This follows significant investments in these areas over the past three years, as part of a corporate strategy to have fee-based businesses account for at least 40% of the total revenue base by 2000. The recent acquisition of CoreStates Financial offers opportunities to streamline expenses and leverage FTU's expansive product array to a broad set of customers. Internal financial targets include a return on equity of 20% to 22%, earnings growth of 10% to 14% and an efficiency ratio of 50% to 54%.

Valuation - 20-JUL-98

The shares remain in a long term uptrend. Already exceptional growth in noninterest income could accelerate further into 1998, as investment banking operations are leveraged. We remain impressed with FTU's efforts to greatly increase noninterest income sources, which diversifies risk, provides a larger base for future revenue growth and provides reduced interest-rate sensitivity. The stability that such revenues bring should also allow a further expansion of the P/E multiple in the market.

Key Stock Statistics

S&P EPS Est. 1998	3.80	Tang. Bk. Value/Share	13.29
P/E on S&P Est. 1998	13.3	Beta	1.09
S&P EPS Est. 1999	4.40	Shareholders	103,500
Dividend Rate/Share	1.68	Market cap. (B)	$ 50.0
Shs. outstg. (M)	989.4	Inst. holdings	40%
Avg. daily vol. (M)	3.076		

Value of $10,000 invested 5 years ago: $ 27,901

Fiscal Year Ending Dec. 31

	1998	1997	1996	1995	1994	1993
Revenues (Million $)						
1Q	4,956	3,442	2,865	1,753	1,443	1,371
2Q	5,289	3,586	2,977	1,882	1,509	1,424
3Q	—	3,638	3,023	2,044	1,610	1,465
4Q	—	4,496	3,120	2,146	1,691	1,495
Yr.	—	14,329	11,985	7,825	6,254	5,755
Earnings Per Share ($)						
1Q	0.90	0.79	0.42	0.66	0.64	0.58
2Q	0.26	0.77	0.78	0.72	0.66	0.66
3Q	—	0.87	0.65	0.75	0.68	0.56
4Q	—	0.56	0.83	0.79	0.52	0.56
Yr.	—	2.99	2.58	2.92	2.49	2.37

Next earnings report expected: mid October

Dividend Data (Dividends have been paid since 1914.)

Amount ($)	Date Decl.	Ex-Div. Date	Stock of Record	Payment Date
0.320	Oct. 21	Nov. 25	Nov. 28	Dec. 15 '97
0.370	Dec. 16	Feb. 25	Feb. 27	Mar. 16 '98
0.370	Apr. 21	May. 27	May. 29	Jun. 15 '98
0.420	Jun. 16	Aug. 27	Aug. 31	Sep. 15 '98

A Division of The **McGraw-Hill** *Companies*

Business Summary - 20-JUL-98

Having completed its April 1998 merger with Philadelphia-based CoreStates Financial Corp., First Union has the largest domestic deposit share from Florida to Connecticut and has nationwide presence as the 8th largest securities brokerage company, 18th largest mutual fund provider, 2nd largest home equity lender and 12th largest mortgage servicing company. Its goal is to complement its traditional banking products with a complete selection of fully integrated investment banking products and a lifetime array of asset management offerings. The company has strengths in commercial mortgage securitizations, leveraged finance and loan syndication transactions, and also has sizable small business and cash management operations.

In 1997, average earning assets, from which interest income is derived, amounted to $133.5 billion and consisted mainly of loans and leases (75%) and investment securities (16%). Average sources of funds, on which the bank pays interest, included savings and NOW accounts (20%), time deposits (23%), money market accounts (10%), foreign deposits (1%), noninterest-bearing demand deposits (13%), short-term

borrowings (19%), long-term debt (5%), shareholders' equity (7%) and other (2%).

At year-end 1997, nonperforming assets, consisting primarily of nonaccrual loans and other real estate owned, were $723 million (0.75% of loans and related assets), versus $802 million (0.78%) a year earlier. The allowance for loan losses, which is set aside for possible loan defaults, was $1.21 billion (1.25% of loans), against $1.50 billion (1.47%) a year earlier. Net charge-offs, or the amount of loans actually written off as uncollectible, were $635 million (0.63% of average loans) in 1997, equal to $635 million (0.65%) in 1996.

In April 1998, the company completed the acquisition of Philadelphia-based CoreStates Financial (NYSE; CFL) in a transaction whereby each CFL share was exchanged for 1.62 FTU common shares. CoreStates had about $48 billion in assets.

In June 1998, the company completed the acquisition of The Money Store, creating the nation's largest national provider of home equity and SBA loans and the 3rd largest provider of student loans. Holders of Money Store common stock received 0.5851 shares of FTU common stock for each of their shares, valuing the transaction at $2.1 billion.

Per Share Data ($)

(Year Ended Dec. 31)	1997	1996	1995	1994	1993	1992	1991	1990	1989	1988
Tangible Bk. Val.	14.71	12.46	13.14	11.52	11.85	10.31	8.04	7.27	7.75	7.10
Earnings	2.99	2.67	2.92	2.49	2.37	1.86	1.27	1.26	1.20	1.38
Dividends	1.22	1.10	0.98	0.86	0.75	0.64	0.56	0.54	0.50	0.43
Payout Ratio	41%	41%	34%	35%	32%	34%	44%	43%	42%	31%
Prices - High	53	38⅞	29¾	24	26⅝	22½	15½	11	13½	12
- Low	36⅜	25⅝	20¾	19½	18⅝	14⅝	6¾	6⅞	9⅞	9⅝
P/E Ratio - High	18	15	10	10	11	12	12	9	11	9
- Low	12	10	7	8	8	8	5	5	8	7

Income Statement Analysis (Million $)

	1997	1996	1995	1994	1993	1992	1991	1990	1989	1988
Net Int. Inc.	5,743	4,996	3,263	3,034	2,766	2,008	1,476	1,278	1,030	1,038
Tax Equiv. Adj.	Nil	84.0	82.3	92.7	101	91.0	107	120	129	135
Non Int. Inc.	3,362	2,322	1,429	1,166	1,165	843	746	542	394	410
Loan Loss Prov.	840	375	180	100	222	250	482	178	81.0	61.0
Exp./Op. Revs.	61%	63%	62%	62%	63%	64%	63%	65%	68%	67%
Pretax Inc.	2,710	2,310	1,559	1,415	1,221	722	396	400	308	362
Eff. Tax Rate	30%	35%	35%	35%	33%	29%	20%	24%	17%	18%
Net Inc.	1,896	1,499	1,013	925	818	515	319	304	256	297
% Net Int. Marg.	4.36	4.21	4.41	4.78	4.78	4.98	4.27	4.06	4.23	4.72

Balance Sheet & Other Fin. Data (Million $)

	1997	1996	1995	1994	1993	1992	1991	1990	1989	1988
Earning Assets:										
Money Mkt	13,907	11,274	5,971	3,523	1,716	1,945	1,357	1,683	452	522
Inv. Securities	23,590	16,683	15,171	11,482	14,437	9,934	6,595	8,055	6,120	5,509
Com'l Loans	28,111	23,639	21,289	17,521	14,196	10,120	10,260	9,220	7,347	7,099
Other Loans	72,148	72,219	45,513	37,181	33,014	23,529	22,160	17,316	14,668	11,974
Total Assets	157,274	157,274	96,740	77,314	70,787	51,327	46,085	40,781	32,131	28,978
Demand Deposits	21,753	18,632	11,788	10,524	10,861	8,053	6,662	5,140	3,964	4,231
Time Deposits	81,136	76,183	53,212	48,435	42,881	31,337	29,936	22,540	17,535	15,802
LT Debt	8,042	7,660	6,444	3,429	3,062	2,522	2,039	1,191	872	634
Common Eqty.	12,032	10,008	6,152	5,398	5,176	3,800	2,981	2,532	2,076	1,923
% Ret. on Assets	1.3	1.1	1.2	1.3	1.2	1.1	0.8	0.8	0.8	1.1
% Ret. on Equity	17.2	16.5	17.4	16.5	16.5	14.2	10.8	11.1	12.8	16.2
% Loan Loss Resv.	1.3	1.4	1.5	1.8	2.2	2.1	2.0	1.7	1.2	1.3
% Loans/Deposits	94.2	101.1	101.0	91.6	87.2	84.7	87.7	94.8	101.6	94.5
% Equity to Assets	7.4	6.6	6.6	7.5	7.1	7.1	6.4	6.3	6.6	6.6

Data as orig. reptd.; bef. results of disc opers. and/or spec. items. Per share data adj. for stk. divs. as of ex-div. date. Bold denotes diluted EPS (FASB 128). E-Estimated. NA-Not Available. NM-Not Meaningful. NR-Not Ranked.

Office—One First Union Center, Charlotte, NC 28288-0570. **Tel**—(704) 374-6161. **Website**—http://www.firstunion.com **Chrmn & CEO**—E. E. Crutchfield Jr. **Pres**—J. R. Georgius. **EVP & CFO**—R. T. Atwood. **EVP & Secy**—M. A. Cowell Jr. **Investor Contact**—Alice Lehman. **Dirs**—E. E. Barr, G. A. Bernhardt, W. W. Bradley, R. J. Brown, E. E. Crutchfield Jr., R. D. Davis, R. S. Dickson, B. F. Dolan, R. Dowd Sr., J. R. Georgius, A. M. Goldberg, W. H. Goodwin Jr., H. H. Haworth, F. M. Henry, L. G. Herring,—J. A. Laughery, M. Lennon, R. D. Lovett, M. J. McDonald, M. S. McDonald, J. Neubauer, R. N. Reynolds, R. G. Shaw, C. M. Shelton Sr., L. L. Smith, A. P. Terracciano, D. L. Trogdon, J. D. Uible, B. J. Walker. **Transfer Agent & Registrar**—First Union National Bank of North Carolina, Charlotte. **Incorporated**—in North Carolina in 1967; bank chartered in 1908. **Empl**— 44,536. **S&P Analyst**: Stephen R. Biggar

STANDARD &POOR'S
STOCK REPORTS

FirstEnergy Corp.

902K

NYSE Symbol **FE**

In S&P 500

12-SEP-98

Industry:
Electric Companies

Summary: This newly merged electric utility holding company provides service to 2.1 million customers in northern and central Ohio and western Pennsylvania.

S&P Opinion: Hold (★★★)	Recent Price • 29⅛	Yield • 5.2%
	52 Wk Range • 31⅞-22½	12-Mo. P/E • 16.7

Quantitative Evaluations

Outlook
(1 Lowest—5 Highest)
• **3⁻**

Fair Value
• **30**

Risk
• **Low**

Earn./Div. Rank
• **B**

Technical Eval.
• **NA**

Rel. Strength Rank
(1 Lowest—99 Highest)
• **89**

Insider Activity
• **Neutral**

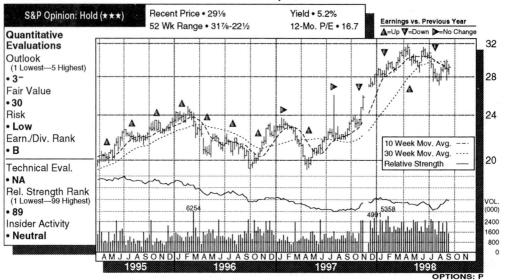

Earnings vs. Previous Year
▲=Up ▼=Down ▶=No Change

10 Week Mov. Avg. – – –
30 Week Mov. Avg. ·····
Relative Strength ——

OPTIONS: P

Overview - 27-AUG-98

EPS in 1998 will increase about 3% from 1997 levels (before non-recurring charges of $0.22 a share), which reflected Ohio Edison's results up to the November 7, 1997 completion of the merger with Centerior Energy, and the combined contributions thereafter. Results in 1998 have been hurt by the extreme pricing volatility of the power markets in June, with second quarter EPS reduced $0.22 by purchased power costs and $0.11 from a power trading credit loss. FE subsequently tightened its credit and risk management policies, and we expect EPS to rebound about 20% in 1999. FE expects to yield annual savings of about $90 million from its recently implemented work force reduction program. In January 1997, the Public Utilities Commission of Ohio approved a plan that would reduce Centerior's rates by nearly $500 million, and would prohibit it from filing for a rate increase before 2006. As part of the merger plan, FE will seek to reduce its debt by $2.5 billion through 2000.

Valuation - 27-AUG-98

We would continue to hold FirstEnergy stock. Despite a decline of about 7% from their early 1998 high, the shares have remained fairly strong, at 36% above their 52 week low. While the merger is expected to yield about $1 billion in savings over the next 10 years, EPS gains will be modest, restricted by rate discounts to large industrial customers, and by a freeze on rate increases until 2006. In addition, as a high-cost utility with the highest electric rates in the region, FE will find it difficult to gain a competitive edge. However, we expect to see FE make significant progress in reducing its $7.0 billion in debt. The stock appears fairly valued at about 12X our 1999 EPS estimate of $2.40, but a dividend yield of about 5.1% makes the shares attractive for long-term income-oriented investors.

Key Stock Statistics

S&P EPS Est. 1998	2.00	Tang. Bk. Value/Share	8.91
P/E on S&P Est. 1998	14.6	Beta	0.40
S&P EPS Est. 1999	2.40	Shareholders	127,000
Dividend Rate/Share	1.50	Market cap. (B)	$ 6.9
Shs. outstg. (M)	237.1	Inst. holdings	44%
Avg. daily vol. (M)	0.408		

Value of $10,000 invested 5 years ago: $ 17,977

Fiscal Year Ending Dec. 31

	1998	1997	1996	1995	1994	1993
Revenues (Million $)						
1Q	1,200	604.8	611.6	587.7	601.3	593.2
2Q	1,277	593.3	599.3	593.8	585.4	563.4
3Q	—	652.7	646.9	667.0	614.4	624.5
4Q	—	973.3	611.9	617.3	567.1	588.9
Yr.	—	2,821	2,470	2,466	2,368	2,370
Earnings Per Share ($)						
1Q	**0.56**	0.51	0.49	0.46	0.44	0.40
2Q	**0.27**	0.51	0.51	0.50	0.48	0.45
3Q	**E0.68**	0.61	0.62	0.61	0.58	0.54
4Q	**E0.49**	0.36	0.48	0.48	0.47	-1.38
Yr.	**E2.00**	1.94	2.10	2.05	1.97	0.01

Next earnings report expected: mid October

Dividend Data (Dividends have been paid since 1930.)

Amount ($)	Date Decl.	Ex-Div. Date	Stock of Record	Payment Date
0.375	Jan. 20	Feb. 04	Feb. 06	Mar. 01 '98
0.375	Apr. 21	May. 05	May. 07	Jun. 01 '98
0.375	Jul. 21	Aug. 05	Aug. 07	Sep. 01 '98
0.375	Nov. 04		Nov. 07	Dec. 01 '97

A Division of The McGraw-Hill Companies

STANDARD
&POOR'S
STOCK REPORTS

FirstEnergy Corp.

902K
12-SEP-98

Business Summary - 27-AUG-98

FirstEnergy was formed November 8, 1997, through the merger of Ohio Edison and Centerior Energy. With combined revenues of about $5 billion, assets of $18 billion, and 56 billion kilowatt-hour (kwh) sales, FE is the 12th largest (based on annual kwh sales) U.S. investor-owned electric utility system.

Ohio Edison (OE) and its wholly owned subsidiary Pennsylvania Power Co. (Penn) serve more than one million customers in the highly industrialized areas of central and northeastern Ohio and western Pennsylvania. Centerior Energy, formed through the 1986 merger of Cleveland Electric Illuminating (CEI) and Toledo Edison (TE), supplies electricity to more than one million people in northern Ohio.

Rate plans for Ohio Edison and Penn Power maintain current base rates through December 31, 2005, and June 20, 2006, respectively. As part of OE's regulatory plan, transition rate credits implemented for customers are expected to reduce operating revenues about $600 million during the plan period. OE has been authorized to recognize depreciation expenses of more than $2.36 billion over the life of the plan.

In April 1996, the Public Utility Commission of Ohio (PUCO) granted the operating subsidiaries an aggre-gate rate increase of $119 million ($84 million for Cleveland Electric and $35 million for Toledo Edison). The rate order provides for recovery of all costs to provide regulated services, including the amortization of regulatory assets. PUCO also recommended the writedown of certain assets for regulatory purposes by an aggregate of $1.25 billion through 2001.

All of OE's regulatory assets (costs which may be recovered from customers) and CEI's and TE's regulatory assets related to their non-nuclear operations are being recovered under provisions of these plans. In October 1997, CEI and TE respectively reduced their regulatory assets related to their nuclear assets by $499 million and $295 million.

In January 1997, PUCO approved FirstEnergy's rate reduction and economic development plan for Centerior's subsidiaries, providing its customers with rate reductions of $400 million over the next eight years and, beginning in 2006, a base rate for customers that would be15% below the existing level.

In March 1998, in a joint venture with Belden & Blake Corp., the company formed FE Holdings, LLC, so as to acquire natural gas properties. The joint venture then acquired Marble Energy Corp., a privately held and intergrated natural gas company with about $125 million in 1997 revenues.

Per Share Data ($)

(Year Ended Dec. 31)	1997	1996	1995	1994	1993	1992	1991	1990	1989	1988
Tangible Bk. Val.	8.91	16.41	15.78	15.13	14.63	15.11	15.01	16.15	16.28	15.97
Earnings	1.94	2.10	2.05	1.97	0.01	1.70	1.60	1.67	2.18	1.22
Dividends	1.50	1.50	1.50	1.50	1.50	1.50	1.50	1.73	1.96	1.96
Payout Ratio	77%	71%	73%	76%	NM	88%	94%	104%	90%	161%
Prices - High	29	24⁷/₈	23³/₄	22³/₄	26	24	20¹/₂	23⁷/₈	24	21
- Low	19¹/₄	19¹/₄	18¹/₂	16¹/₂	21	18³/₄	16³/₈	15⁷/₈	18⁵/₈	17¹/₄
P/E Ratio - High	15	12	12	12	NM	14	13	14	11	17
- Low	10	9	9	8	NM	11	10	10	9	14

Income Statement Analysis (Million $)

	1997	1996	1995	1994	1993	1992	1991	1990	1989	1988
Revs.	2,821	2,470	2,466	2,368	2,370	2,332	2,359	2,226	2,155	2,143
Depr.	475	356	256	221	218	226	236	224	213	224
Maint.	NA	NA	NA	NA	NA	NA	NA	208	190	150
Fxd. Chgs. Cov.	2.6	2.9	2.7	2.5	2.4	2.4	2.2	2.6	3.1	2.3
Constr. Credits	3.5	3.1	5.7	5.2	5.0	6.0	11.0	20.0	26.0	18.0
Eff. Tax Rate	40%	39%	39%	38%	69%	34%	39%	37%	29%	32%
Net Inc.	306	315	317	304	24.5	277	265	282	361	219

Balance Sheet & Other Fin. Data (Million $)

	1997	1996	1995	1994	1993	1992	1991	1990	1989	1988
Gross Prop.	17,516	8,733	8,747	8,745	8,610	8,489	8,346	8,239	8,052	7,862
Cap. Exp.	204	148	198	258	257	253	236	271	258	222
Net Prop.	11,880	5,418	5,695	5,835	5,878	5,938	5,985	6,049	6,082	6,048
Capitalization:										
LT Debt	6,970	2,713	2,786	3,167	3,039	3,122	3,243	3,105	3,074	3,209
% LT Debt	58	49	50	54	54	53	54	51	51	52
Pfd.	995	367	372	368	302	414	420	417	444	451
% Pfd.	8.20	6.60	6.70	6.30	5.00	7.00	7.00	6.90	7.30	7.30
Common	4,160	2,503	2,408	2,317	2,243	2,408	2,372	2,545	2,566	2,531
% Common	34	45	43	40	40	41	39	42	42	41
Total Cap.	14,754	7,560	7,552	7,875	7,687	6,787	6,878	6,854	6,794	6,764
% Oper. Ratio	81.2	78.5	77.0	76.5	77.8	77.6	76.7	77.1	74.8	76.8
% Earn. on Net Prop.	6.0	9.5	9.8	9.5	8.9	8.8	9.1	8.4	9.0	8.0
% Return On Revs.	10.8	12.8	12.9	12.8	1.0	11.9	11.2	12.7	16.8	10.2
% Return On Invest. Capital	5.5	7.5	7.5	7.4	4.1	8.2	8.3	7.5	8.3	5.9
% Return On Com. Equity	9.2	12.3	12.5	12.4	11.4	10.8	9.9	9.9	13.0	7.0

Data as orig. reptd.; bef. results of disc. opers. and/or spec. items. Data pr. to Nov. 7, 1997 are for Ohio Edison before the merger. Per share data adj. for stk. divs. as of ex-div. date. Bold denotes diluted EPS (FASB 128). E-Estimated. NA-Not Available. NM-Not Meaningful. NR-Not Ranked.

Office—76 South Main St., Akron, OH 44308.Tel—(330) 384-5100. Website—http://www.firstenergycorp.com Chrmn & CEO—W. R. Holland. Pres & COO—H. P. Burg. VP & CFO—R. H. Marsh. Treas—T. F. Struck, II. Secy—N. C. Ashcom. Investor Relations—R. E. Seeholzer. Dirs—H. P. Burg, R. M. Carter, C. A. Cartwright, W. F. Conway, W. R. Holland, R. L. Loughhead, R. W. Maier, G. H. Meadows, P. J. Powers, C. W. Rainger, R. C. Savage, G. M. Smart, J. T. Williams Sr. Transfer Agent & Registrar—Co.'s office. Incorporated—in Ohio in 1997. Empl— 10,020. S&P Analyst: Justin McCann

Fleet Financial

903A

NYSE Symbol **FLT**

In S&P 500

12-SEP-98

Industry: Banks (Major Regional)

Summary: This company operates general commercial banking and trust businesses in Rhode Island, New York, Connecticut, Massachusetts, New Jersey, Maine and New Hampshire.

S&P Opinion: Accumulate (★★★★)

Recent Price • 74⅞

52 Wk Range • 90¾-60

Yield • 2.6%

12-Mo. P/E • 15.5

Quantitative Evaluations

Outlook (1 Lowest—5 Highest)
• **1⁻**

Fair Value
• **65⅛**

Risk
• **NA**

Earn./Div. Rank
• **B+**

Technical Eval.
• **NA**

Rel. Strength Rank (1 Lowest—99 Highest)
• **79**

Insider Activity
• **Neutral**

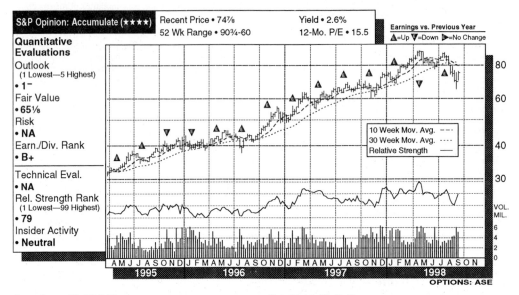

Earnings vs. Previous Year
▲=Up ▼=Down ▶=No Change

10 Week Mov. Avg. ---
30 Week Mov. Avg. ....
Relative Strength —

OPTIONS: ASE

Overview - 26-AUG-98

Fleet made substantial progress in 1997 on its strategy to exit businesses not meeting profitability requirements and invest in businesses that broaden its product mix and distribution capabilities. Acquisitions in the past year included Columbia Management (an investment management company), Quick & Reilly (a large national discount broker) and Advanta's credit card business, all of which serve to increase operations geographically, improve the proportion of revenues from fee-based businesses and expand the product line. On the lending side of the business, high single-digit loan growth is expected, although an increase in funding costs to support the Advanta business and its effect on margins will limit the contribution to net interest income. Aided by cost control efforts, noninterest expense growth should be held to the low single-digits, despite spending on Year 2000 issues. A conservative 10% gain in earnings is projected for 1998.

Valuation - 26-AUG-98

Fleet continues to prove itself to be a savvy acquirer, far exceeding expense savings projections when combining operations and maintaining acquisition pricing discipline. Recent acquisitions have also substantially improved revenue growth opportunities in relatively high margin businesses. With the expectation that financial benefits from recent acquisitions will continue to become more apparent in earnings, selective accumulation of the shares is recommended. Merger rumors continue to circulate, which should provide continued upside momentum for the shares.

Key Stock Statistics

S&P EPS Est. 1998	5.20	Tang. Bk. Value/Share	19.06
P/E on S&P Est. 1998	14.4	Beta	1.12
S&P EPS Est. 1999	5.75	Shareholders	38,200
Dividend Rate/Share	1.96	Market cap. (B)	$ 21.3
Shs. outstg. (M)	283.9	Inst. holdings	55%
Avg. daily vol. (M)	1.047		

Value of $10,000 invested 5 years ago: $ 27,651

Fiscal Year Ending Dec. 31

	1998	1997	1996	1995	1994	1993
Revenues (Million $)						
1Q	2,289	1,951	1,838	1,851	1,067	1,124
2Q	2,525	1,974	2,006	2,015	1,090	1,193
3Q	—	1,990	2,094	1,988	1,137	1,246
4Q	—	2,002	2,062	2,021	1,134	1,114
Yr.	—	8,095	8,000	7,875	4,445	4,677
Earnings Per Share ($)						
1Q	**1.06**	1.10	0.94	0.82	0.79	0.67
2Q	**1.29**	1.19	0.96	0.91	0.90	0.72
3Q	—	1.21	1.02	0.96	1.01	0.78
4Q	—	1.23	1.05	-1.17	1.05	0.85
Yr.	—	4.74	3.98	1.57	3.75	3.01

Next earnings report expected: mid October

Dividend Data (Dividends have been paid since 1791.)

Amount ($)	Date Decl.	Ex-Div. Date	Stock of Record	Payment Date
0.490	Oct. 15	Dec. 01	Dec. 03	Jan. 01 '98
0.490	Feb. 18	Feb. 27	Mar. 03	Apr. 01 '98
0.490	Apr. 15	Jun. 01	Jun. 03	Jul. 01 '98
0.490	Aug. 19	Sep. 01	Sep. 03	Oct. 01 '98

A Division of The **McGraw-Hill** Companies

STANDARD
&POOR'S
STOCK REPORTS

Fleet Financial Group, Inc.

903A

12-SEP-98

Business Summary - 26-AUG-98

Fleet Financial Group took further steps in 1997 to transform itself into diversified financial services company while keeping a strategy of shifting its revenue stream toward a better balance of interest-based and fee-based revenues. In that regard, in 1997 it made acquisitions complimentary to traditional banking operations. These included Quick & Reilly Group, the third largest discount brokerage firm in the U.S., Columbia Management, an investment management company, and the credit card business of Advanta Corp. These acquisitions are expected to double the number of customers Fleet serves to more than 13 million.

The company is organized around several business lines. Commercial finance provides credit and banking services to corporate, middle-market, real estate, government and leasing customers as well as cash management, trade services, foreign exchange, interest-rate protection and investment products. Consumer banking consists mainly of retail banking (1,200 branches in New England, New York and New Jersey) and small business banking. The financial services segment offers student loan processing, credit card services and technology banking. Investment services includes the private client group, retirement plans services, discount brokerage, retail investment and institutional asset services. Other units include treasury, which offers interest-rate risk management and foreign exchange services, and mortgage banking/venture capital, which originates, sells and services first mortgage products and provides private equity capital.

In 1997, average earning assets, from which interest income is derived, amounted to $70.4 billion and consisted mainly of loans and leases (84%) and investment securities (12%). Average sources of funds included interest-bearing deposits (58%), noninterest-bearing deposits (19%), short-term borrowings (6%), long-term debt (6%), shareholders' equity (9%) and other (2%).

At year-end 1997, nonperforming assets (non-accrual loans and other real estate owned) were $416 million (0.68% of loans), down from $723 million (1.23%) a year earlier. The allowance for loan losses, which is set aside for possible loan defaults, was $1.43 billion (2.34% of loans), versus $1.49 billion (2.53%) a year earlier. Net chargeoffs, or the amount of loans actually written off as uncollectible, were $376 million (0.65% of average loans) in 1997, compared to $370 million (0.66%) in 1996.

Per Share Data ($)

(Year Ended Dec. 31)	1997	1996	1995	1994	1993	1992	1991	1990	1989	1988
Tangible Bk. Val.	19.94	18.18	18.46	13.55	20.27	12.06	13.33	10.85	13.64	12.41
Earnings	4.74	3.95	1.57	3.75	3.01	1.78	0.67	-0.75	3.34	3.07
Dividends	1.84	1.74	1.60	1.40	1.02	0.82	0.80	1.25	1.31	1.20
Payout Ratio	39%	44%	102%	37%	34%	46%	119%	NM	39%	39%
Prices - High	75$^1/_8$	56$^1/_4$	43$^1/_4$	41$^3/_8$	37$^7/_8$	33$^7/_8$	26$^3/_8$	27$^5/_8$	30$^7/_8$	27$^7/_8$
- Low	48$^3/_4$	37$^5/_8$	29$^7/_8$	29$^7/_8$	28$^1/_4$	24$^1/_4$	9$^5/_8$	8$^7/_8$	23$^3/_4$	22$^3/_8$
P/E Ratio - High	16	14	28	11	13	19	39	NM	9	9
- Low	10	10	19	8	9	14	14	NM	7	7

Income Statement Analysis (Million $)

	1997	1996	1995	1994	1993	1992	1991	1990	1989	1988
Net Int. Inc.	3,627	3,043	3,020	1,982	2,051	1,954	1,404	1,153	1,252	1,148
Tax Equiv. Adj.	40.0	36.0	44.0	40.0	33.0	29.8	46.0	94.0	90.0	85.0
Non Int. Inc.	2,214	2,158	1,818	1,174	1,465	1,229	933	791	564	487
Loan Loss Prov.	322	213	101	62.0	271	486	509	762	160	107
Exp./Op. Revs.	58%	66%	77%	65%	68%	74%	78%	64%	60%	62%
Pretax Inc.	2,171	1,931	1,034	1,023	821	518	153	-162	539	478
Eff. Tax Rate	40%	41%	41%	39%	40%	44%	36%	NM	31%	30%
Net Inc.	1,303	1,139	610	613	488	280	98.0	-74.0	371	336
% Net Int. Marg.	5.21	4.81	4.12	4.65	5.02	4.81	4.05	3.92	4.96	5.11

Balance Sheet & Other Fin. Data (Million $)

	1997	1996	1995	1994	1993	1992	1991	1990	1989	1988
Earning Assets:										
Money Mkt	498	1,772	61.0	NA	Nil	NM	463	2,264	1,081	402
Inv. Securities	9,362	8,680	19,331	11,244	14,123	12,660	10,624	5,270	5,524	4,656
Com'l Loans	35,614	31,889	25,474	12,675	12,333	12,517	12,199	12,117	12,765	10,782
Other Loans	25,565	26,955	26,051	15,355	13,977	16,217	16,751	10,121	11,535	10,335
Total Assets	85,535	85,518	84,432	48,757	47,923	46,939	45,445	32,507	33,441	29,052
Demand Deposits	13,148	17,903	12,305	6,890	6,473	6,483	6,517	3,433	3,613	3,962
Time Deposits	50,587	49,168	44,817	27,916	24,612	26,252	28,729	19,758	18,063	16,739
LT Debt	4,500	5,114	6,481	3,457	3,444	3,812	2,511	2,314	1,649	1,495
Common Eqty.	7,343	6,462	5,966	3,001	3,138	2,397	2,460	1,941	2,160	1,914
% Ret. on Assets	1.5	1.3	0.7	1.3	1.1	0.6	0.3	NM	1.3	1.2
% Ret. on Equity	18.0	18.3	7.6	19.0	16.1	10.4	3.9	NM	17.7	18.1
% Loan Loss Resv.	2.3	2.5	2.6	3.4	3.8	3.6	3.6	3.3	1.5	1.6
% Loans/Deposits	200.7	85.5	90.2	80.5	84.6	87.8	80.2	92.5	107.8	98.2
% Equity to Assets	8.1	7.3	6.6	6.5	7.5	5.8	5.6	6.0	6.9	6.7

Data as orig. reptd.; bef. results of disc opers. and/or spec. items. Per share data adj. for stk. divs. as of ex-div. date. Bold denotes diluted EPS (FASB 128). E-Estimated. NA-Not Available. NM-Not Meaningful. NR-Not Ranked.

Office—One Federal St., Boston, MA 02110. **Tel**—(617) 292-2000. **Website**—http://www.fleet.com **Chrmn & CEO**—T. Murray. **Pres & COO**—R. J. Higgins. **Vice-Chrmn & CFO**—E. M. McQuade. **EVP & Secy**—W. C. Mutterperl. **Investor Contact**—Thomas R. Rice. **Dirs**—J. B. Alvord, W. Barnet III, B. R. Boss, S. B. Brown, P. J. Choquette, Jr., K. B. Clark, J. T. Collins, J. F. Hardymon, M. L. Heard, R. M. Kavner, R. C. Kennedy, R. J. Matura, A. C. Milot, T. Murray, T. D. O'Connor, M. B. Picotte, T. C. Quick, L. D. Rice, J. R. Riedman, T. M. Ryan, S. O. Thier, P. R. Tregurtha. **Transfer Agent & Registrar**—Fleet National Bank, Hartford, CT. **Incorporated**—in Delaware in 1968. **Empl**— 34,000. **S&P Analyst:** Stephen R. Biggar

12-SEP-98

Industry: Homebuilding

Summary: Fleetwood is the largest U.S. manufacturer of recreational vehicles and manufactured housing.

S&P Opinion: Hold (★★★)	Recent Price • 33⅛	Yield • 2.2%
	52 Wk Range • 48-28⅛	12-Mo. P/E • 11.0

Quantitative Evaluations

Outlook
(1 Lowest—5 Highest)
• **3+**

Fair Value
• **36½**

Risk
• **Average**

Earn./Div. Rank
• **B+**

Technical Eval.
• **Bearish** since 6/97

Rel. Strength Rank
(1 Lowest—99 Highest)
• **66**

Insider Activity
• **Neutral**

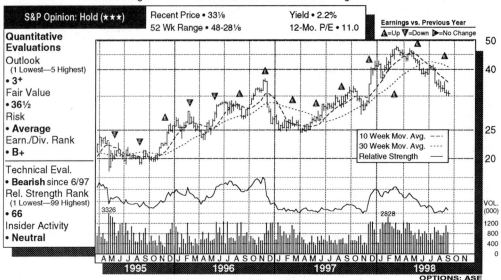

Earnings vs. Previous Year
▲=Up ▼=Down ▶=No Change

10 Week Mov. Avg. - - -
30 Week Mov. Avg. ·····
Relative Strength ——

OPTIONS: ASE

Overview - 09-JUL-98

Sales should rise somewhat in FY 99 (Apr.). We expect slightly higher sales in the manufactured home division, as FLE's expansion program (seven plants were added between FY 96 and early FY 98) eliminated capacity constraints, and inventories at retailers seem to be coming into better balance (excess inventories slowed industry trends during the past year). On the downside, however, with competitors buying up retailers who feature FLE homes, the company's distribution channel has been threatened. In response, FLE has decided to set up its own retail channel. We also see RV sales up a little, with good economic conditions and lower oil prices outweighing FLE's smaller market share of recent years. Margins should widen a bit, on better efficiencies in manufactured homes, and the elimination of difficulties related to the realignment of motor home production. Comparisons will be distorted by a gain of $0.28 a share in the FY 98 first quarter.

Valuation - 09-JUL-98

The shares surged between the spring of 1997 and early 1998. Initial gains came when lower interest rates and a lack of inflationary pressure made investors more enthusiastic about business prospects. The shares really took flight when margin recovery in the manufactured home segment let EPS far exceed forecasts in the FY 98 second and third quarters. However, the shares have posted a lackluster performance since the spring of 1998, limited by investor worries about the economy and the possible elimination of pent-up demand for housing. We disagree with these beliefs, and think that Asian financial woes will leave us with a Goldilocks economy. We also think that FLE has gotten its operations in better order, and agree with its move to become a force in manufactured home retailing. However, given the likely learning curve to be faced, we remain neutral on the shares.

Key Stock Statistics

S&P EPS Est. 1999	3.15	Tang. Bk. Value/Share	11.13
P/E on S&P Est. 1999	10.5	Beta	1.13
Dividend Rate/Share	0.72	Shareholders	1,600
Shs. outstg. (M)	32.0	Market cap. (B)	$ 1.1
Avg. daily vol. (M)	0.178	Inst. holdings	92%

Value of $10,000 invested 5 years ago: $ 15,489

Fiscal Year Ending Apr. 30

	1999	1998	1997	1996	1995	1994
Revenues (Million $)						
1Q	840.2	728.5	751.3	704.7	764.3	537.4
2Q	—	769.1	748.8	707.1	710.4	567.5
3Q	—	710.6	628.0	625.4	661.4	548.6
4Q	—	842.4	746.4	772.0	719.5	715.9
Yr.	—	3,051	2,874	2,809	2,856	2,369
Earnings Per Share ($)						
1Q	0.86	0.84	0.64	0.44	0.63	0.33
2Q	E0.89	0.77	0.68	0.47	0.45	0.37
3Q	E0.60	0.57	0.38	0.32	0.39	0.26
4Q	E0.80	0.81	0.58	0.27	0.34	0.50
Yr.	E3.15	3.01	2.30	1.50	1.82	1.46

Next earnings report expected: late November

Dividend Data (Dividends have been paid since 1965.)

Amount ($)	Date Decl.	Ex-Div. Date	Stock of Record	Payment Date
0.170	Sep. 09	Oct. 01	Oct. 03	Nov. 12 '97
0.170	Dec. 09	Dec. 30	Jan. 02	Feb. 11 '98
0.170	Mar. 10	Apr. 01	Apr. 03	May. 13 '98
0.180	Jun. 09	Jul. 02	Jul. 07	Aug. 12 '98

A Division of The McGraw·Hill Companies

STANDARD
&POOR'S
STOCK REPORTS

Fleetwood Enterprises, Inc.

903E
12-SEP-98

Business Summary - 09-JUL-98

Fleetwood Enterprises is the largest U.S. producer of both recreational vehicles (RVs) and manufactured homes. Results have been volatile, reflecting the cyclical nature of its businesses. FLE's RVs include motor homes, travel trailers, folding trailers and slide-in truck campers. Primary uses for the self-propelled vehicles include vacations, camping trips and other leisure activities. FLE is also a long-established producer of manufactured homes, whose low prices and easy maintenance make them popular. In FY 98 (Apr.), 50% of revenues and 46% of operating profits came from the RV segment, 49% and 45% from manufactured housing, and the rest from a supply division.

FLE offers bus-like motor homes, with an interior that usually includes the driver area, kitchen, bathroom, dining and sleeping areas. Its conventional motor homes are fully self-contained, sleep four to eight people, and range in length from 24 ft. to 40 ft. The company also sells compact motor homes, with basically the same features as full-size models, ranging in size from 19 ft. to 31 ft. FLE's motor home brand names include Bounder, Southwind and Tioga.

FLE designs its travel trailers to be towed by pickup trucks, vans or other vehicles. The trailers have uses and features similar to motor homes. FLE also produces slide-in truck campers, which fit in the bed of

pickup trucks, and makes folding trailers. During FY 98, FLE sold a total of 69,494 RVs (20% motor homes, 50% travel trailers, and 30% folding trailers).

With many U.S. households priced out of the site-built single family home market, manufactured homes have become a growing residential source. Manufactured homes are built in factories, transported to homesites in one or more sections, and installed using their own chassis on either temporary or permanent foundations. While transportable, the homes are rarely moved after placement. FLE's homes range in size from 820 sq. ft. to 2,650 sq. ft., with retail prices ranging from $11,000 to $120,000; most sell for under $25,000. In FY 98, FLE shipped a total of 65,544 manufactured homes (65,354 in FY 97).

In February 1998, FLE reached a definitive agreement to acquire HomeUSA, Inc. (1996 pro forma revenues of $202 million), the leading independent retailer of manufactured homes, for $162 million in cash and stock. It simultaneously bought Pulte Corp.'s 51% interest in a venture formed by Pulte and FLE in October 1997, and subsequently agreed to buy or purchased several modest sized manufactured homes retailers. This marks a major strategy change for FLE, which has decided to set up its own retail channel and become a vertically integrated manufacturer. However, Fleetwood will also keep up its relationship with its independent retailer network.

Per Share Data ($)

(Year Ended Apr. 30)	1998	1997	1996	1995	1994	1993	1992	1991	1990	1989
Tangible Bk. Val.	11.96	12.40	14.22	13.20	11.88	11.01	10.26	9.78	9.51	8.75
Cash Flow	3.69	3.00	2.30	2.34	1.90	1.61	1.26	1.08	1.54	1.79
Earnings	3.01	2.30	1.50	1.82	1.46	1.23	0.88	0.69	1.21	1.53
Dividends	0.68	0.64	0.60	0.56	0.50	0.47	0.44	0.42	0.38	0.32
Payout Ratio	23%	28%	40%	31%	34%	38%	49%	60%	31%	21%
Cal. Yrs.	1997	1996	1995	1994	1993	1992	1991	1990	1989	1988
Prices - High	42¾	37¼	26⅜	27¼	26⅞	24⅝	18⅜	14⅝	15⅜	13⅜
- Low	24⅜	23⅛	17¾	17⅞	16½	12¾	10¼	7⅞	11	8½
P/E Ratio - High	14	16	18	15	18	20	21	21	13	9
- Low	8	10	12	10	11	10	12	11	9	6

Income Statement Analysis (Million $)

Revs.	3,051	2,874	2,809	2,856	2,369	1,942	1,589	1,401	1,549	1,619
Oper. Inc.	198	167	159	183	140	116	116	66.0	105	119
Depr.	27.8	27.5	27.1	24.1	20.4	17.3	17.1	17.5	14.8	12.0
Int. Exp.	3.6	4.0	1.4	25.6	18.2	17.0	16.8	16.7	16.1	6.8
Pretax Inc.	175	147	111	142	112	91.3	64.1	47.0	87.0	114
Eff. Tax Rate	38%	39%	38%	41%	41%	38%	37%	35%	37%	38%
Net Inc.	109	90.0	69.9	69.9	67.4	56.6	40.2	30.4	55.0	70.5

Balance Sheet & Other Fin. Data (Million $)

Cash	28.1	37.8	15.8	40.6	37.3	34.8	28.0	15.0	19.0	25.0
Curr. Assets	683	NA	NA	NA	NA	NA	NA	NA	NA	NA
Total Assets	1,129	872	1,109	1,345	1,224	1,062	915	765	817	718
Curr. Liab.	326	NA	NA	NA	NA	NA	409	302	364	NA
LT Debt	55.0	55.0	80.0	145	180	150	Nil	Nil	Nil	Nil
Common Eqty.	376	443	649	608	546	503	468	428	424	401
Total Cap.	719	498	729	752	726	653	468	428	424	401
Cap. Exp.	37.8	56.1	32.9	68.0	72.9	42.2	25.7	19.2	33.1	32.7
Cash Flow	136	118	107	109	87.8	73.9	57.4	47.9	69.9	82.5
Curr. Ratio	2.1	NA	NA	NA	NA	NA	NA	NA	NA	NA
% LT Debt of Cap.	7.6	11.0	11.0	19.3	24.8	23.0	Nil	Nil	Nil	Nil
% Net Inc.of Revs.	3.6	3.1	2.5	3.0	2.8	2.9	2.5	2.2	3.6	4.4
% Ret. on Assets	10.8	9.0	10.3	6.6	5.9	5.7	4.7	3.9	7.3	11.4
% Ret. on Equity	21.5	16.4	11.2	14.7	12.8	11.6	8.8	7.2	13.5	18.9

Data as orig. reptd.; bef. results of disc. opers. and/or spec. items. Per share data adj. for stk. divs. as of ex-div. date. Bold denotes diluted EPS (FASB 128). E-Estimated. NA-Not Available. NM-Not Meaningful. NR-Not Ranked.

Office—3125 Myers St., Riverside, CA 92503-5527. **Tel**—(909) 351-3500. **Website**—http://www.fleetwood.com **Chrmn & CEO**—G. F. Kummer. **Pres**—N. W. Potter. **VP & Secy**—W. H. Lear. **SVP, CFO & Investor Contact**—Paul M. Bingham. **Dirs**—W. F. Beran, A. Crean, J. L. Doti, T. A. Fuentes, G. F. Kummer, D. M. Lawson, N. W. Potter, W. W. Weide. **Transfer Agent & Registrar**—First National Bank of Boston. **Incorporated**—in California in 1950; reincorporated in Delaware in 1977. **Empl**— 18,000. **S&P Analyst:** Michael W. Jaffe

STANDARD &POOR'S
STOCK REPORTS

Fluor Corp.

911

NYSE Symbol **FLR**

In S&P 500

12-SEP-98 Industry: Engineering & Construction

Summary: One of the largest international engineering, construction and related services companies, Fluor also has investments in coal.

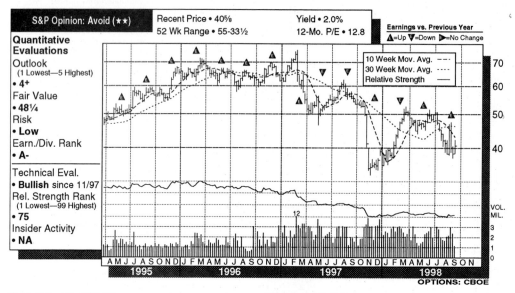

S&P Opinion: Avoid (★★)	Recent Price • 40⅝	Yield • 2.0%
	52 Wk Range • 55-33½	12-Mo. P/E • 12.8

Quantitative Evaluations

Outlook (1 Lowest—5 Highest)
• **4+**

Fair Value
• **48¼**

Risk
• **Low**

Earn./Div. Rank
• **A-**

Technical Eval.
• **Bullish** since 11/97

Rel. Strength Rank (1 Lowest—99 Highest)
• **75**

Insider Activity
• **NA**

Earnings vs. Previous Year
▲=Up ▼=Down ▶=No Change

10 Week Mov. Avg. – – –
30 Week Mov. Avg. ·····
Relative Strength —

OPTIONS: CBOE

Overview - 24-AUG-98

Fluor is a company in transition. In July 1998, Philip Carroll, FLR's new CEO, took over the reigns of the company. Fluor has reversed course, embarking on an aggressive multi-year expansion, due to weak results in FY 97 (Oct.). It became apparent in 1997 that a commitment to aggressive revenue growth in recent years had encumbered FLR with lower margin engineering and construction (E&C) contracts. Many E&C offices were closed, and the business was reorganized. In addition, the company now aims to accept only higher-margin contracts. FLR is also evaluating the sale of non-core businesses, including the equipment leasing division, American Equipment Co. FLR has indicated that it is still committed to the E&C business and to A. T. Massey Coal. Capital spending for 1998 has been pared to $450 million, from $650 million in 1997. Directors have authorized the repurchase of up to 10 million shares on the open market in 1998; some 950,000 shares were bought in 1997.

Valuation - 24-AUG-98

We continue our avoid recommendation, primarily due to below-average long-term industry fundamentals. The global engineering and construction business is highly sensitive to the vagaries of the global economy, and operates in very competitive markets. As a result, industry operating profit margins and returns on equity (ROE) are typically well below those of the S&P 500 average. Although new management may eventually be able to boost FLR's ROE from 8.6% to its 15% historic average, this would still be below the S&P 500 average of 18% to 20%. Moreover, with the stock recently trading at 15X our FY 98 EPS estimate of $2.65, the shares were selling at a premium to FLR's 8% sustainable EPS growth rate.

Key Stock Statistics

S&P EPS Est. 1998	2.65	Tang. Bk. Value/Share	16.65
P/E on S&P Est. 1998	15.3	Beta	1.06
S&P EPS Est. 1999	3.00	Shareholders	15,600
Dividend Rate/Share	0.80	Market cap. (B)	$ 3.2
Shs. outstg. (M)	79.0	Inst. holdings	65%
Avg. daily vol. (M)	0.446		

Value of $10,000 invested 5 years ago: $ 10,543

Fiscal Year Ending Oct. 31

	1998	1997	1996	1995	1994	1993
Revenues (Million $)						
1Q	3,399	3,434	2,402	2,060	2,058	1,807
2Q	3,282	3,186	2,582	2,229	2,080	2,006
3Q	3,529	3,676	2,703	2,437	1,963	1,844
4Q	—	4,003	3,328	2,576	2,385	2,193
Yr.	—	14,299	11,015	9,301	8,485	7,850
Earnings Per Share ($)						
1Q	**0.66**	0.73	0.68	0.61	0.53	0.43
2Q	**0.67**	-0.83	0.75	0.66	0.58	0.51
3Q	**0.81**	0.79	0.81	0.72	0.58	0.50
4Q	—	1.04	0.93	0.79	0.63	0.59
Yr.	—	1.73	3.17	2.78	2.32	2.03

Next earnings report expected: mid November

Dividend Data (Dividends have been paid since 1974.)

Amount ($)	Date Decl.	Ex-Div. Date	Stock of Record	Payment Date
0.200	Dec. 10	Dec. 19	Dec. 23	Jan. 13 '98
0.200	Mar. 10	Mar. 20	Mar. 24	Apr. 14 '98
0.200	Jun. 09	Jun. 19	Jun. 23	Jul. 14 '98
0.200	Sep. 08	Sep. 18	Sep. 22	Oct. 13 '98

A Division of The McGraw-Hill Companies

Business Summary - 24-AUG-98

Through its Fluor Daniel division, Fluor Corp. is one of the largest providers of engineering, construction and other services to a broad range of clients worldwide. Fluor's A. T. Massey unit mines low-sulfur steam and metallurgical coal. Contributions in recent fiscal years (Oct.) were:

	FY 97	FY 96
Revenues		
Engineering & construction	92%	91%
Coal	8%	9%
Profits		
Engineering & construction	44%	70%
Coal	56%	30%

Fluor Daniel provides engineering, construction and related services worldwide to clients in four business groups: process, industrial, power and government, and diversified services. Process serves customers in the chemicals, plastics and fibers, petroleum and petrochemicals and production and pipeline industries. Industrial serves the automotive and general manufacturing, consumer products, commercial and institutional facilities, electronics, food and beverage, infrastructure, mining and metals, pharmaceuticals and biotechnology, pulp and paper and telecommunications industries. Power and government includes power generation and

services. Diversified services includes construction equipment sales and services, environmental, facility and plant services, procurement, technology and temporary staffing services. Services provided include feasibility studies, conceptual design, engineering and procurement, project and construction management, technical services, quality control, site evaluation and project financing.

Contracts range from a few million to several billion dollars. Success in this industry depends on proper bidding and execution of contracts to realize adequate profits on jobs undertaken. Fluor Daniel's stated backlog was $14.4 billion at October 31, 1997, versus $15.8 billion at October 31, 1996. The value of signed contracts is actually somewhat higher, but portions of contracts, usually government work, are excluded from backlog until funding is approved and the contracts become firm. The 1997 backlog was 44% process, 36% industrial, 15% power and government, and 5% diversified services. The geographic division of the backlog was 39% U.S., 17% Asia Pacific, 27% Europe and Middle East, 11% Australia, and 6% Americas.

A.T. Massey Coal Co. produces, processes and sells steam and metallurgical grade coal from 17 mining complexes. In FY 97, Massey produced 19,300,000 tons of steam coal and 16,343,000 tons of metallurgical coal (17,520,000 and 13,571,000 tons, respectively, in FY 96). At the end of FY 97, total recoverable reserves were estimated at 1,764,000,000 short tons.

Per Share Data ($)

(Year Ended Oct. 31)	1997	1996	1995	1994	1993	1992	1991	1990	1989	1988
Tangible Bk. Val.	18.84	18.86	16.80	14.79	12.72	10.81	12.58	10.75	9.03	7.61
Cash Flow	4.64	5.46	4.57	3.70	3.28	3.22	3.21	2.93	2.38	1.63
Earnings	1.73	3.17	2.78	2.32	2.03	1.65	1.83	1.71	1.35	0.71
Dividends	0.76	0.68	0.60	0.52	0.48	0.40	0.32	0.24	0.14	0.02
Payout Ratio	44%	21%	22%	22%	24%	24%	17%	14%	10%	3%
Prices - High	75⅞	71⅞	68	56¼	46⅛	48⅛	54¾	49¼	37¾	23⅞
- Low	33½	57¾	42¾	40⅛	38	36⅝	32⅛	29	21⅝	12¾
P/E Ratio - High	44	23	24	24	23	29	30	29	28	34
- Low	19	18	15	17	19	22	18	17	16	18

Income Statement Analysis (Million $)

	1997	1996	1995	1994	1993	1992	1991	1990	1989	1988
Revs.	14,299	11,015	9,301	8,485	7,850	6,601	6,742	7,446	6,278	5,132
Oper. Inc.	511	596	489	413	346	343	271	267	242	164
Depr.	248	194	147	114	103	127	114	100	83.0	73.0
Int. Exp.	31.0	16.0	13.0	17.0	20.0	24.0	13.0	15.0	20.0	27.0
Pretax Inc.	255	413	362	303	242	215	228	190	175	91.0
Eff. Tax Rate	43%	35%	36%	37%	31%	37%	35%	27%	38%	38%
Net Inc.	146	268	232	192	167	135	149	139	108	56.0

Balance Sheet & Other Fin. Data (Million $)

	1997	1996	1995	1994	1993	1992	1991	1990	1989	1988
Cash	299	316	292	492	312	343	370	271	235	165
Curr. Assets	2,226	1,797	1,412	1,258	1,309	1,139	1,160	1,223	1,036	999
Total Assets	4,698	3,952	3,229	2,825	2,589	2,365	2,421	2,476	2,154	2,073
Curr. Liab.	1,991	1,646	1,239	1,021	931	845	848	984	798	844
LT Debt	301	3.0	3.0	30.0	67.0	72.0	88.0	72.0	76.0	109
Common Eqty.	1,741	1,670	1,430	1,220	1,044	881	1,020	864	720	602
Total Cap.	2,108	1,713	1,477	1,296	1,162	1,016	1,218	1,040	885	790
Cap. Exp.	NA	392	319	237	172	287	160	156	139	86.0
Cash Flow	394	462	379	307	270	262	263	238	192	130
Curr. Ratio	1.1	1.1	1.1	1.2	1.4	1.3	1.4	1.2	1.3	1.2
% LT Debt of Cap.	14.3	0.2	0.2	2.3	5.7	7.1	7.2	6.9	8.6	13.8
% Net Inc.of Revs.	1.0	2.4	2.4	2.3	2.1	2.0	2.2	1.9	1.7	1.1
% Ret. on Assets	3.4	7.5	7.7	7.1	6.7	5.6	6.1	6.0	5.1	2.7
% Ret. on Equity	8.6	17.3	NA	17.0	17.3	14.2	15.8	17.5	16.3	9.9

Data as orig. reptd.; bef. results of disc. opers. and/or spec. items. Per share data adj. for stk. divs. as of ex-div. date. Bold denotes diluted EPS (FASB 128). E-Estimated. NA-Not Available. NM-Not Meaningful. NR-Not Ranked.

Office—3353 Michelson Dr., Irvine, CA 92698. **Tel**—(714) 975-2000. **Website**—http://www.fluor.com **Chrmn & CEO**—Philip J. Carroll (effective 7/98). **SVP & Secy**—L. N. Fisher. **SVP & CFO**—J. M. Conaway. **Investor Contact**—Lila J. Churney (714-975-3909). **Dirs**—D. L. Blankenship, C. A. Campbell Jr., P. J. Fluor, D. P. Gardner, T. L. Gossage, B. R. Inman, V. S. Martinez, D. R. O'Hare, R. Renwick, J. O. Rollans, M. A. Seger, J. C. Stein. **Transfer Agent & Registrar**—ChaseMellon Shareholder Services, Los Angeles, CA & Ridgefield Park, NJ. **Incorporated**—in California in 1924; reincorporated in Delaware in 1978. **Empl**— 52,461. **S&P Analyst:** Robert E. Friedman, CPA

STANDARD &POOR'S

STOCK REPORTS

FMC Corp.

846K

NYSE Symbol **FMC**

In S&P 500

12-SEP-98

Industry: Chemicals (Diversified)

Summary: FMC is a major producer of industrial, specialty and agri-cultural chemicals, and petroleum, food and transportation machinery.

S&P Opinion: Hold (★★★)	Recent Price • 53½	Yield • Nil
	52 Wk Range • 91⅜-51¼	12-Mo. P/E • 12.7

Earnings vs. Previous Year
▲=Up ▼=Down ▶=No Change

Quantitative Evaluations

Outlook
(1 Lowest—5 Highest)
• **3+**

Fair Value
• **64**

Risk
• **Low**

Earn./Div. Rank
• **B**

Technical Eval.
• **Bearish** since 3/98

Rel. Strength Rank
(1 Lowest—99 Highest)
• **53**

Insider Activity
• **NA**

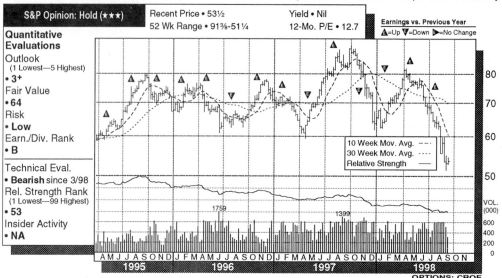

10 Week Mov. Avg. ---
30 Week Mov. Avg. ····
Relative Strength —

1759   1399

VOL.
(000)
600
400
200
0

A M J J A S O N D | J F M A M J J A S O N D | J F M A M J J A S O N D | J F M A M J J A S O N
1995   1996   1997   1998

OPTIONS: CBOE

Overview - 20-JUL-98

We see earnings for the performance chemicals recovering in 1998 on a strong rebound in the pesticide business, assuming a more normal summer level of pest infestations in U.S. markets, boosted by cost reductions initiated at the start of 1998 and greater supplies of the first product of a new family of herbicides as production difficulties at a new plant were resolved early in the year. Machinery will achieve another record year on strong increases for energy and airline equipment. Demand for subsea oil production equipment should remain strong, though low oil prices may result in softened demand for other products. Weak market conditions in industrial chemicals will persist for the rest of 1998, resulting in lower average selling prices for hydrogen peroxide and phosphorus. Domestic soda ash prices will not improve over 1997's reduced levels, while Asian demand and prices are sharply lower. The fourth quarter 1997 loss included after-tax charges of $181 million ($5.03 a share) for asset writedowns in phosphorus and process additives, and cost reductions primarily in pesticides. These charges may result in annual cost savings of about $0.50 per share. FMC plans to repurchase about $150 million of stock each year in 1998 and 1999, completing a $500 million buyback program announced in 1997, helping to offset dilution from the absence of profits from the defense business sold in 1997.

Valuation - 20-JUL-98

The stock is virtually unchanged year to date, and well below its record high at the end of September 1997. We continue to have a "hold" recommendation. While favorable earnings comparisons are likely in 1998, concerns regarding weak fundamentals in certain industrial chemicals, low oil prices, and difficulties achieving acceptable returns from some investment projects (lithium, peroxide) may limit the stock's performance.

Key Stock Statistics

S&P EPS Est. 1998	5.40	Tang. Bk. Value/Share	10.80
P/E on S&P Est. 1998	9.9	Beta	0.94
S&P EPS Est. 1999	6.00	Shareholders	11,300
Dividend Rate/Share	Nil	Market cap. (B)	$ 1.8
Shs. outstg. (M)	34.5	Inst. holdings	72%
Avg. daily vol. (M)	0.112		

Value of $10,000 invested 5 years ago: $ 10,808

Fiscal Year Ending Dec. 31

	1998	1997	1996	1995	1994	1993
Revenues (Million $)						
1Q	1,022	992.9	1,094	1,016	908.0	901.7
2Q	1,155	1,134	1,251	1,128	1,063	979.0
3Q	—	1,059	1,262	1,156	1,015	926.5
4Q	—	1,072	1,363	1,209	1,039	946.5
Yr.	—	4,313	5,081	4,510	4,011	3,754
Earnings Per Share ($)						
1Q	0.75	0.56	1.45	1.40	1.24	1.23
2Q	1.89	1.84	1.51	2.06	1.82	1.69
3Q	E1.60	1.43	1.56	1.51	0.93	0.95
4Q	E1.16	-4.50	1.17	0.75	0.68	-2.77
Yr.	E5.40	-0.67	4.28	5.72	4.66	1.11

Next earnings report expected: mid October

Dividend Data

Dividends, paid since 1935, were eliminated as part of a 1986 recapitalization in which each public stockholder received $80 cash and one share of the recapitalized company for each FMC share held. FMC financed the plan with $2 billion of debt. A "poison pill" stock purchase rights plan was adopted in 1988.

 A Division of The **McGraw·Hill** *Companies*

Business Summary - 20-JUL-98

FMC is concentrating on plans to increase earnings, while continuing to improve working capital efficiency. (FMC reduced working capital in 1997 by more than its $100 million goal). While investments in the machinery and equipment business paid off with record profits in 1997, major projects in the chemicals businesses have not yet achieved expected returns. In October 1997, as part of a portfolio review, FMC and Harsco Corp. sold their United Defense joint venture (sales in 1996 of $1 billion; 60% owned by FMC) for $850 million. Directors subsequently authorized a $500 million stock repurchase program. Sales and operating profits in 1997 were derived as follows:

	Sales	Profits
Performance chemicals	29%	29%
Industrial chemicals	24%	35%
Machinery & equipment	47%	36%

International operations accounted for 40% of sales and 48% of pretax income in 1997.

Performance chemicals include pesticides (insecticides and herbicides for crop protection and pest control) and specialty chemicals. FMC is the world's leading producer of carrageenan pharmaceutical ingredients and food stabilizers and thickeners, as well as lithium compounds and phosphate flame retardants. It also pro-

duces water additives. A new soybean herbicide (Authority), the first of two new products, was launched in the U.S. in 1997. Quantities were limited in 1997 due to startup problems at a new manufacturing facility. Process changes completed in early 1998 doubled the plant's capacity. The second product was introduced in Europe during 1997, with the U.S. planned in 1999. Startup of a new low-cost lithium plant in Argentina was completed in late 1997.

FMC is the world's largest producer of natural soda ash and derivatives and a leading producer of peroxides, phosphorus, zeolites, silicates and sulfur derivatives. Segment profits declined in 1997 primarily as a result of lower prices for soda ash and hydrogen peroxide.

Machinery and equipment include energy (wellhead completion equipment, subsea equipment, metering systems, valves, pumps and loading arms, and marine terminals) and transportation equipment (airline loading and de-icing equipment, conveyor equipment, and bulk and unit material-handling equipment and systems); and food machinery (harvesting, preparation, processing, packaging and handling equipment and systems). In June 1996, the company acquired Frigoscandia Equipment Holding AB, Sweden, a producer of freezing equipment, for $165 million. Backlog at June 30, 1998, was $1.3 billion, up from $989 million at year-end 1997, reflecting increases in the energy, transportation and food equipment businesses.

Per Share Data ($)

(Year Ended Dec. 31)	1997	1996	1995	1994	1993	1992	1991	1990	1989	1988
Tangible Bk. Val.	9.76	9.60	8.39	8.08	5.99	6.10	8.79	4.30	-2.05	-6.53
Cash Flow	5.76	12.42	12.24	10.59	7.13	11.62	10.97	10.16	9.85	9.16
Earnings	-0.67	5.73	5.72	4.66	1.11	5.23	4.77	4.30	4.35	3.60
Dividends	Nil	Nil	Nil	Nil	Nil	Nil	Nil	Nil	Nil	Nil
Payout Ratio	Nil	Nil	Nil	Nil	Nil	Nil	Nil	Nil	Nil	Nil
Prices - High	91³/₈	78	80	65¹/₈	54	53¹/₄	51⁵/₈	38³/₄	49	39¹/₈
- Low	59³/₈	60⁷/₈	57¹/₈	45¹/₂	41¹/₂	42¹/₂	29¹/₂	25³/₈	31⁵/₈	24³/₈
P/E Ratio - High	NM	14	14	14	49	10	11	9	11	11
- Low	NM	11	10	10	37	8	6	6	7	7

Income Statement Analysis (Million $)

	1997	1996	1995	1994	1993	1992	1991	1990	1989	1988
Revs.	4,313	4,970	4,567	4,011	3,754	3,974	3,899	3,722	3,415	3,287
Oper. Inc.	561	727	666	535	452	542	550	518	499	480
Depr.	238	254	249	221	222	235	225	211	198	199
Int. Exp.	118	119	102	73.0	74.0	97.0	128	157	169	194
Pretax Inc.	-51.0	380	247	314	40.0	283	259	219	225	198
Eff. Tax Rate	NM	28%	13%	25%	NM	31%	32%	26%	27%	31%
Net Inc.	-25.0	218	216	173	41.0	193	173	155	157	129

Balance Sheet & Other Fin. Data (Million $)

	1997	1996	1995	1994	1993	1992	1991	1990	1989	1988
Cash	63.0	75.0	71.0	98.0	78.0	24.0	44.0	93.0	95.0	131
Curr. Assets	1,716	2,193	1,805	1,376	1,160	1,123	1,180	1,295	1,312	1,317
Total Assets	4,113	4,990	4,301	3,352	2,813	2,827	2,816	2,959	2,819	2,749
Curr. Liab.	1,465	2,021	1,793	1,269	1,156	1,124	1,193	1,255	1,194	1,089
LT Debt	1,140	1,268	975	901	750	844	929	1,159	1,326	1,468
Common Eqty.	760	856	653	417	217	219	310	150	-71.0	-223
Total Cap.	1,959	2,263	1,785	1,417	1,010	1,118	1,424	1,475	1,369	1,390
Cap. Exp.	317	533	566	356	215	314	217	380	281	186
Cash Flow	213	472	465	394	263	428	398	366	355	329
Curr. Ratio	1.2	1.1	1.0	1.1	1.0	1.0	1.0	1.0	1.1	1.2
% LT Debt of Cap.	58.1	56.0	54.6	63.6	74.2	75.4	65.3	78.5	96.8	NM
% Net Inc.of Revs.	NM	4.3	4.7	4.3	1.1	4.8	4.4	4.2	4.6	3.9
% Ret. on Assets	NM	4.7	5.6	5.6	1.4	6.8	6.0	5.4	5.6	4.8
% Ret. on Equity	NM	28.9	40.4	54.6	18.7	72.1	75.0	NM	NM	NM

Data as orig. reptd.; bef. results of disc. opers. and/or spec. items. Per share data adj. for stk. divs. as of ex-div. date. Bold denotes diluted EPS (FASB 128). E-Estimated. NA-Not Available. NM-Not Meaningful. NR-Not Ranked.

Office—200 E. Randolph Dr., Chicago, IL 60601. **Tel**—(312) 861-6000. **Website**—http://www.fmc.com **Chrmn & CEO**—R. N. Burt. **Pres**—L. D. Brady. **EVP & CFO**—M. J. Callahan. **Secy**—J. P. McGrath.**Investor Contact**—Randy Woods (312-861-6160). **Dirs**—L. D. Brady, B. A. Bridgewater Jr., P. A. Buffler, R. N. Burt, A. J. Costello, P. L. Davies Jr., J. A. Francois-Poncet, E. C. Meyer, E. J. Mooney, W. F. Reilly, J. R. Thompson, C. Yeutter. **Transfer Agent & Registrar**—Harris Trust & Savings Bank, Chicago. **Incorporated**—in Delaware in 1928. **Empl**— 16,805. **S&P Analyst:** Richard O'Reilly, CFA

STANDARD &POOR'S
STOCK REPORTS

Ford Motor

917

NYSE Symbol **F**

In S&P 500

12-SEP-98 **Industry:** Automobiles

Summary: Ford is the world's second largest producer of cars and trucks and has a rapidly growing financial services operation.

S&P Opinion: Hold (★★★)	Recent Price • 43¼	Yield • 3.9%
	52 Wk Range • 65⅞-37½	12-Mo. P/E • 7.8

Quantitative Evaluations

Outlook (1 Lowest—5 Highest)
• **2⁻**

Fair Value
• **42**

Risk
• **Low**

Earn./Div. Rank
• **B**

Technical Eval.
• **Bearish** since 8/98

Rel. Strength Rank (1 Lowest—99 Highest)
• **47**

Insider Activity
• **Favorable**

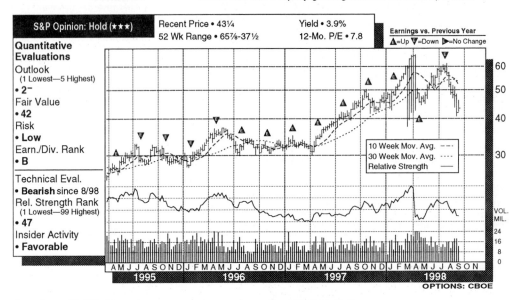

Earnings vs. Previous Year
▲=Up ▼=Down ▶=No Change

10 Week Mov. Avg. – – –
30 Week Mov. Avg. ·······
Relative Strength

VOL.
MIL.

OPTIONS: CBOE

Overview - 27-JUL-98

Ford's vehicle sales in 1998 will be hindered by the discontinuation of certain weak selling models and the impact of a higher dollar. Overall industry demand could be flat to slightly higher. Profit margins could remain under pressure, despite strenuous efforts to reduce operating costs and streamline model development costs under the Ford 2000 project. As of June 1998, Ford had already met its 1998 target to eliminate over $1 billion of costs (assuming constant vehicle production volume and mix); in 1997 it reduced costs by $3 billion, while holding capital expenditures at 1996 levels. However, marketing costs could restrict sales and profits, as Ford has consistently priced vehicles higher than similar competitive products. This has forced it to use marketing incentives to sell its most popular lines such as the Taurus and Sable midsize cars. In a successful attempt to better allow Ford's stock price to reflect the financial services units, the company has spun off all of its Associates First Capital unit and part of its Hertz car rental unit; it also sold most of USL Capital to help unlock the hidden value of that segment.

Valuation - 27-JUL-98

Most consumer economic indicators remain favorable, including job reports that point toward moderate economic growth in 1998. Assuming no major economic shocks, we see Ford's earnings declining in 1998 on increased incentives and reduced production, offset by cost reductions and an improved product mix. As it is late in the economic cycle, we do not expect auto stocks to enjoy a multiple expansion, and we thus rate Ford a hold. A larger dividend, and efforts to unlock hidden value, such as the recently completed spinoff and sale of financial services and rental car operations, should help support the stock price.

Key Stock Statistics

S&P EPS Est. 1998	5.00	Tang. Bk. Value/Share	21.03
P/E on S&P Est. 1998	8.7	Beta	0.92
S&P EPS Est. 1999	4.90	Shareholders	252,200
Dividend Rate/Share	1.68	Market cap. (B)	$ 49.4
Shs. outstg. (M)	1211.6	Inst. holdings	48%
Avg. daily vol. (M)	3.359		

Value of $10,000 invested 5 years ago: NA

Fiscal Year Ending Dec. 31

	1998	1997	1996	1995	1994	1993
Revenues (Million $)						
1Q	36,584	36,202	36,261	34,783	30,400	26,760
2Q	37,289	40,265	37,937	36,389	33,770	29,420
3Q	—	36,096	33,960	31,418	30,660	24,500
4Q	—	39,952	38,833	34,547	33,643	27,840
Yr.	—	153,627	146,991	137,137	128,439	108,520
Earnings Per Share ($)						
1Q	**1.36**	**1.20**	0.54	1.44	0.83	0.51
2Q	**1.91**	**2.06**	1.60	1.45	1.63	0.72
3Q	—	**0.91**	0.57	0.28	1.04	0.40
4Q	—	**1.45**	1.00	0.49	1.47	0.65
Yr.	**E5.00**	5.62	3.72	3.58	4.97	2.27

Next earnings report expected: mid October

Dividend Data (Dividends have been paid since 1983.)

Amount ($)	Date Decl.	Ex-Div. Date	Stock of Record	Payment Date
0.420	Jan. 08	Jan. 28	Jan. 30	Mar. 02 '98
Stk.	Mar. 03	Apr. 08	Mar. 12	Apr. 07 '98
0.420	Apr. 09	Apr. 29	May. 01	Jun. 01 '98
0.420	Jul. 09	Jul. 29	Jul. 31	Sep. 01 '98

A Division of The McGraw-Hill Companies

Business Summary - 27-JUL-98

Ford is the world's second largest motor vehicle manufacturer. It produces cars and trucks, many of the vehicles' plastic, glass and electronic components, and replacement parts. Ford also owns 33.4% of Mazda Motor Corp. Financial services include Ford Motor Credit (automotive financing and insurance), American Road Insurance Co., Hertz Corp. (car rental), and Granite Management. Granite manages a portfolio of real estate loans retained following the 1994 sale of First Nationwide Financial, a savings and loan subsidiary. In the third quarter of 1996, Ford sold most of the assets of USL Capital (formerly U.S. Leasing). The company took a $233 million aftertax charge in 1996 to write down its investment in Budget Rent a Car. In April 1997, Ford spun off 18.5% of Hertz Corp. in a public offering.

In April 1998, the company distributed its 80.7% interest in Associates First Capital Corp. to Ford common and class B shareholders. Earlier, Ford sold its heavy-truck business to Freightliner Corp.

In 1997, automotive net income was a record $4.7 billion. U.S. income was $3.7 billion, versus $2.0 billion in 1996. Outside the U.S., Ford recorded net income of $1.0 billion, versus a net loss of $352 million. The foreign improvement reflected greater efficiencies and lower separation costs. Financial services net income was $2.2 billion in 1997 versus a record $2.8 billion in 1996.

Various Ford, Mercury, Lincoln and Jaguar models accounted for a 19.7% share of cars sold in U.S. markets (including foreign-built) in 1997, compared with 20.6% in 1996, 20.9% in 1995, 21.8% in 1994, 22.3% in 1993, 21.8% in 1992, 20.1% in 1991, 21.1% in 1990, 22.3% in 1989, 21.7% in 1988 and 20.2% in 1987. Comparable figures for trucks were 31.2%, 31.1%, 31.9%, 30.1%, 30.5%, 29.7%, 28.9%, 29.3%, 28.8% and 29.0%. Vehicle factory sales totaled 6,943,000 in 1997, of which 4,016,000 were in the U.S., versus 6,653,000 and 3,897,000, respectively in 1996, and 6,606,000 and 3,993,000, respectively, in 1995.

In January 1998, Ford reported that it had eliminated $3.0 billion (at constant volume and mix) of costs in 1997; in July 1998, it announced that it had exceeded its 1998 target of an additional $1.0 billion in cost savings.

At June 30, 1998, the company's net cash position was a record $14.1 billion, compared to $12.7 billion at December 31, 1997, and $9.9 billion at June 30, 1997.

For its automotive business, for 1998, Ford has targeted a 5% return on sales for North America, profitability in Europe, a breakeven position in South America, and a reduction in capital spending.

Ford recently submitted a letter of intent to bid to acquire a controlling interest in South Korea's Kia Motor Inc. Kia, which is in receivership, with debts exceeding assets, is 30% owned by the South Korean government, 9.4% by Ford and 7.0% by Ford's Mazda Motor Corp. affiliate.

Per Share Data ($)

(Year Ended Dec. 31)	1997	1996	1995	1994	1993	1992	1991	1990	1989	1988
Tangible Bk. Val.	21.01	17.52	15.53	17.85	12.20	4.68	14.21	16.59	17.55	21.94
Cash Flow	11.86	9.60	9.93	14.21	9.85	6.21	3.68	6.20	8.64	9.40
Earnings	5.62	3.72	3.58	4.97	2.28	-0.73	-2.40	0.93	4.11	5.48
Dividends	1.65	1.47	1.23	0.91	0.80	0.80	0.97	1.50	1.50	1.15
Payout Ratio	29%	40%	34%	18%	35%	NM	NM	165%	37%	21%
Prices - High	50¼	37¼	32⅞	35⅛	33⅛	24½	18⅞	24⅝	28⅜	27½
- Low	30	27¼	24⅝	25⅝	21½	13⅞	11¾	12½	20¾	19⅛
P/E Ratio - High	9	10	9	7	15	NM	NM	26	7	5
- Low	5	7	7	5	9	NM	NM	13	5	3

Income Statement Analysis (Million $)

Revs.	153,731	146,991	137,137	128,439	108,448	100,132	88,286	97,650	96,146	92,446
Oper. Inc.	31,017	25,267	24,423	25,408	18,228	13,877	11,762	15,420	18,209	17,240
Depr.	7,645	6,875	6,500	9,336	7,468	6,756	5,778	4,880	4,229	3,792
Int. Exp.	10,500	10,399	10,046	7,744	7,289	7,917	9,219	9,573	8,598	6,138
Pretax Inc.	10,939	6,793	6,705	8,789	4,003	-126	-2,586	1,495	6,030	8,342
Eff. Tax Rate	34%	32%	36%	38%	34%	NM	NM	36%	35%	36%
Net Inc.	6,920	4,446	4,139	5,308	2,529	-501	-2,257	860	3,835	5,300

Balance Sheet & Other Fin. Data (Million $)

Cash	20,835	15,414	12,406	13,822	12,307	12,217	12,928	8,247	11,932	14,770
Total Assets	279,097	262,867	243,283	219,354	198,938	180,545	174,429	173,662	160,893	143,366
LT Debt	80,245	77,136	73,734	65,207	54,984	49,436	50,218	45,332	38,921	32,113
Total Debt	168,925	150,239	141,354	123,868	111,976	98,504	97,413	95,519	82,871	69,948
Common Eqty.	30,734	26,068	23,547	18,259	12,174	11,353	20,390	23,238	22,728	21,529
Cap. Exp.	8,717	8,651	8,997	9,470	6,814	5,790	5,847	7,163	6,767	4,782
Cash Flow	14,511	11,321	10,639	14,357	9,709	6,044	3,498	5,740	8,064	9,092
% Ret. on Assets	2.6	1.8	1.8	2.5	1.3	NM	NM	0.5	2.6	5.7
% Ret. on Equity	23.9	17.7	16.6	32.7	18.9	NM	NM	3.7	17.6	26.9
% LT Debt of Cap.	68.5	71.3	72.1	70.3	72.8	72.3	65.5	62.4	59.0	55.6

Data as orig. reptd.; bef. results of disc. opers. and/or spec. items. Per share data adj. for stk. divs. as of ex-div. date. Bold denotes diluted EPS (FASB 128). E-Estimate. NA-Not Available. NM-Not Meaningful. NR-Not Ranked.

Office—The American Rd., Dearborn, MI 48121. **Tel**—(313) 322-3000. **E-mail**—stockinfo@ford.com.**Website**—http://www.ford.com.**Chrmn, Pres. & CEO**—A. Trotman. **Vice Chrmn**—W. W. Booker, E. E. Hagenlocker.**EVP & CFO**—J. M. Devine. **Secy**—J. M. Rintamaki. **Investor Contact**—Mel Stephens. **Dirs**— M. D. Dingman, E. B. Ford II, W. C. Ford, W. C. Ford, Jr., I. O. Hockaday, Jr., M-J Kravis, E. R. Marram, H. A. Neal, C. E. Reichardt, J. L. Thornton, A. J. Trotman.**Transfer Agent & Registrar**—First Chicago Trust Co. of New York, NYC. **Incorporated**—in Delaware in 1919. **Empl**— 371,702. **S&P Analyst:** Efraim Levy

STANDARD &POOR'S
STOCK REPORTS

Fort James

919P

NYSE Symbol **FJ**

In S&P 500

12-SEP-98

Industry:
Household Products
(Nondurables)

Summary: This leading producer of consumer and commercial tissue products was formed through the August 1997 merger of James River and Fort Howard.

S&P Opinion: Accumulate (★★★★)	Recent Price • 27⅛	Yield • 2.2%
	52 Wk Range • 53-26½	12-Mo. P/E • 69.6

Earnings vs. Previous Year
▲=Up ▼=Down ▶=No Change

Quantitative Evaluations

Outlook
(1 Lowest—5 Highest)
• **3⁻**

Fair Value
• **32¾**

Risk
• **Low**

Earn./Div. Rank
• **B-**

Technical Eval.
• **NA**

Rel. Strength Rank
(1 Lowest—99 Highest)
• **27**

Insider Activity
• **Neutral**

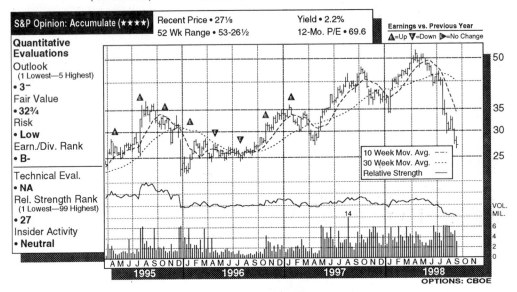

10 Week Mov. Avg. - - -
30 Week Mov. Avg. · · · ·
Relative Strength —

VOL.
MIL.

OPTIONS: CBOE

Overview - 27-JUL-98

Sales from comparable operations will likely be unchanged in 1998. FJ's retail tissue businesses should see decent demand, but conditions have been challenging in North American away-from-home markets. We also expect average tissue and towel prices to be a bit higher. However, the slight sales gain we see in tissue should be offset by some troubles in flexible packaging and weak business paper markets. Operating margins should widen on savings related to the August 1997 combination of James River and Fort Howard to form Fort James. The merger had been slightly accretive on a pro forma basis in 1997 and should eventually bring $200 million of annual savings, with some $150 million to be seen in 1998. However, those gains will be partly offset by the impact of FJ's weaker product areas and spending to protect market share in North American tissue. Interest charges should also be lower, on FJ's October 1997 refinancing of $2.3 billion of debt and reduced borrowing levels. Comparisons will be distorted by $1.62 a share of restructuring charges in 1997.

Valuation - 27-JUL-98

The shares have weakened in recent days, on a somewhat less positive profit outlook. The modified prospects stem from FJ's inability to pass through a price hike in North American away-from-home tissue, spending to protect the company's North American towel and tissue turf, and troubles in business paper markets. With those factors having a larger than expected impact, we downgraded the shares from a buy recommendation in July. However, we still see the company recording solid EPS gains through 1999. As such, while we would be less aggressive buyers of FJ shares, we still find them attractive in their recent trading range of about 12 times our revised 1999 forecast.

Key Stock Statistics

S&P EPS Est. 1998	2.50	Tang. Bk. Value/Share	0.64
P/E on S&P Est. 1998	10.8	Beta	1.04
S&P EPS Est. 1999	2.85	Shareholders	11,100
Dividend Rate/Share	0.60	Market cap. (B)	$ 6.0
Shs. outstg. (M)	220.6	Inst. holdings	77%
Avg. daily vol. (M)	0.921		

Value of $10,000 invested 5 years ago: NA

Fiscal Year Ending Dec. 31

	1998	1997	1996	1995	1994	1993
Revenues (Million $)						
1Q	1,796	1,818	1,487	1,668	1,106	1,114
2Q	1,857	1,854	1,497	1,818	1,198	1,198
3Q	—	1,825	1,407	1,735	1,445	1,184
4Q	—	1,762	1,300	1,579	1,669	1,155
Yr.	—	7,259	5,691	6,800	5,417	4,650
Earnings Per Share ($)						
1Q	**0.53**	--	0.07	0.14	-0.19	-0.22
2Q	**0.62**	1.12	0.18	0.32	0.06	0.06
3Q	—	0.29	0.62	0.27	-0.18	-0.08
4Q	—	-1.05	0.24	0.08	-0.41	-0.16
Yr.	—	0.35	1.15	0.81	-0.72	-0.40

Next earnings report expected: late October

Dividend Data (Dividends have been paid since 1973.)

Amount ($)	Date Decl.	Ex-Div. Date	Stock of Record	Payment Date
0.150	Oct. 15	Dec. 15	Dec. 17	Dec. 31 '97
0.150	Feb. 19	Mar. 13	Mar. 17	Mar. 31 '98
0.150	Apr. 23	Jun. 12	Jun. 16	Jun. 30 '98
0.150	Aug. 20	Sep. 14	Sep. 16	Sep. 30 '98

A Division of The McGraw-Hill Companies

Business Summary - 27-JUL-98

Formed through the August 1997 merger of James River Corp. (JR) and Fort Howard Corp. (FORT), Fort James believes it took the number one spot in the overall U.S. tissue market (with a 30% share) from Kimberly-Clark and holds the number two position worldwide. In the merger, FORT shareholders received 1.375 shares of the new firm for each share held, and JR shareholders maintained their shares. The merger combined JR's strong brand names, marketing capabilities and global reach, and Fort Howard's leading share in the domestic commercial tissue market and low-cost production capabilities. FJ's management team included key executives from both firms, but M.T. Riordan (former chairman and CEO of Fort Howard) left his presidential post in July 1998 to seek other opportunities.

The company's North American Consumer Products division (59% of FJ's sales in 1997) supplies both retail and commercial products. In the retail area, it provides consumers with a broad array of bath and facial tissue products, paper towels, napkins, plates and cups. Some of its leading retail brands include Mardi Gras, Vanity Fair, Dixie, Quilted Northern and Brawny. Fort James also ranks as the largest North American producer of private label towel, tissue and napkin products, accounting for more than 40% of the U.S. market. In addition, FJ offers a complete line of commercial products

used by hotels, restaurants, office buildings and institutions; also ranked number one in this area, FJ has an estimated 40% market share. In May 1998, the company announced plans to divide the North American Consumer Products division into two parts: Dixie (its disposable cups and plates business) and North American Consumer Towel and Tissue.

Fort James also has a significant position in the European consumer products market, where it believes it holds the number two spot in tissue sales. The division represented 25% of sales in 1997.

The company also produces paper-based packaging for food and pharmaceuticals, and communications papers; combining for 16% of FJ's sales in 1997.

With most of its tissue capacity based on virgin pulp-based products, James River had focused its product offerings in the near-premium to premium end. Conversely, Fort Howard used wastepaper for almost all of its fiber requirements, and focused its product offerings in the value and economy end. The combination gives Fort James a more complete grouping of products and a better geographical balance of mills.

Between September 1997 and April 1998, FJ made three separate redemption calls for all remaining shares of its preferred stock (in several series). The calls resulted in the conversion of those shares into about 24.8 million FJ common shares and $98.1 million in cash. In October 1997, FJ also refinanced $2.1 billion of debt.

Per Share Data ($)

(Year Ended Dec. 31)	1997	1996	1995	1994	1993	1992	1991	1990	1989	1988
Tangible Bk. Val.	NM	9.76	8.73	7.48	16.30	18.00	24.76	24.99	24.65	22.46
Cash Flow	2.68	6.73	6.30	4.16	3.97	2.54	4.22	2.34	6.13	5.89
Earnings	0.35	1.15	0.81	-0.72	-0.40	-1.82	0.66	-0.08	2.45	2.87
Dividends	0.60	0.60	0.60	0.60	0.60	0.60	0.70	0.30	0.60	0.48
Payout Ratio	171%	52%	74%	NM	NM	NM	106%	NM	24%	17%
Prices - High	47⅛	35	37⅜	24¾	23⅜	23⅜	29¼	29¼	34⅜	29¾
- Low	27¼	22⅜	20¼	15⅝	16¼	17	17	18½	25¾	21⅛
P/E Ratio - High	NM	30	46	NM	NM	NM	44	NM	14	10
- Low	NM	19	25	NM	NM	NM	26	NM	11	7

Income Statement Analysis (Million $)

	1997	1996	1995	1994	1993	1992	1991	1990	1989	1988
Revs.	7,259	5,691	6,800	5,417	4,650	4,728	4,562	5,416	5,950	5,872
Oper. Inc.	1,552	866	936	566	472	406	536	NA	827	826
Depr.	495	422	461	398	358	356	292	NA	301	246
Int. Exp.	352	171	233	189	143	161	170	169	208	190
Pretax Inc.	273	289	237	-10.0	17.0	-187	133	166	372	441
Eff. Tax Rate	60%	44%	47%	NM	114%	NM	41%	53%	39%	41%
Net Inc.	105	157	126	-13.0	Nil	-121	78.0	78.0	222	255

Balance Sheet & Other Fin. Data (Million $)

	1997	1996	1995	1994	1993	1992	1991	1990	1989	1988
Cash	34.0	33.8	66.0	59.0	24.0	375	85.0	32.0	76.0	24.0
Curr. Assets	1,917	1,520	1,871	1,976	1,282	1,697	1,533	1,911	1,454	1,456
Total Assets	7,733	6,542	7,259	7,924	5,851	6,336	5,627	5,741	5,818	5,558
Curr. Liab.	1,584	1,220	1,099	1,569	781	928	705	789	812	735
LT Debt	4,156	1,854	2,503	2,668	1,943	2,154	1,758	1,802	1,771	1,918
Common Eqty.	232	1,568	1,514	1,421	1,514	1,659	2,221	2,212	2,203	2,046
Total Cap.	5,391	4,603	5,411	5,579	4,341	4,713	4,808	4,813	4,886	4,739
Cap. Exp.	506	426	441	352	331	470	467	NA	575	685
Cash Flow	557	579	529	340	325	208	345	NA	501	479
Curr. Ratio	1.2	1.3	1.7	1.3	1.6	1.8	2.2	2.4	1.8	2.0
% LT Debt of Cap.	77.1	40.2	46.3	47.8	44.8	45.7	36.6	37.4	36.3	40.5
% Net Inc.of Revs.	1.4	2.8	1.9	NM	NM	NM	1.7	1.4	3.7	4.3
% Ret. on Assets	1.5	2.3	1.7	NM	NM	NM	1.4	1.4	3.9	4.8
% Ret. on Equity	6.9	10.2	8.7	NM	NM	NM	2.4	2.4	9.4	11.9

Data as orig. reptd. for James River; bef. results of disc. opers. and/or spec. items. Per share data adj. for stk. divs. as of ex-div. date. Bold denotes diluted EPS (FASB 128). E-Estimated. NA-Not Available. NM-Not Meaningful. NR-Not Ranked.

Office—P.O. Box 89, Deerfield, IL 60015.**Tel**—(847) 317-5000. **Website**—http://www.fortjames.com **Chrmn & CEO**—M. L. Marsh. **Investor Contact**—C. C. Gunter (804) 649-4307. **Dirs**—B. L. Bowles, W. T. Burgin, J. L. Burke, W. H. Clark Jr., W. T. Comfort Jr., G. P. Coughlan, W. V. Daniel, B. C. Gottwald, M. L. Marsh, R. H. Niehaus, R. M. O'Neil, M. T. Riordan, R. L. Sharp, F. V. Sica, A. M. Whittemore. **Transfer Agent & Registrar**—Norwest Bank Minnesota, St. Paul. **Incorporated**—in Virginia in 1969. **Empl**— 29,000. **S&P Analyst:** Michael W. Jaffe

STANDARD &POOR'S
STOCK REPORTS

Fortune Brands

919W
NYSE Symbol **FO**

In S&P 500

12-SEP-98

Industry:
Housewares

Summary: This diversified holding company has interests in a wide variety of consumer businesses, including home improvement, distilled spirits, and office and golf-related products.

S&P Opinion: Buy (★★★★)	Recent Price • 28½	Yield • 2.9%
	52 Wk Range • 42¼-25¼	12-Mo. P/E • 35.2

Earnings vs. Previous Year
▲=Up ▼=Down ▶=No Change

Quantitative Evaluations

Outlook
(1 Lowest—5 Highest)
• **2**

Fair Value
• **27¼**

Risk
• **Low**

Earn./Div. Rank
• **B**

Technical Eval.
• **NA**

Rel. Strength Rank
(1 Lowest—99 Highest)
• **47**

Insider Activity
• **Neutral**

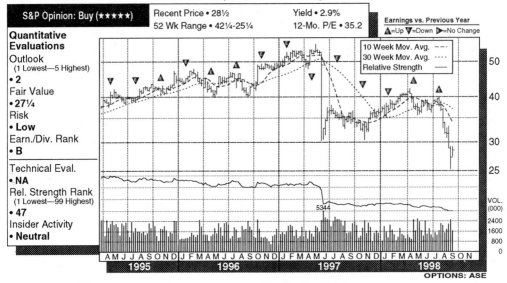

10 Week Mov. Avg. – – –
30 Week Mov. Avg. · · · · ·
Relative Strength ——

OPTIONS: ASE

Overview - 29-JUL-98

We expect 1998 sales to rise in the 6% to 8% range, as better than 10% growth in both the golf and leisure and office products divisions helps offset more modest growth for the hardware and home improvement and distilled spirits segments. Gains are likely to continue to be tempered by the negative effect of a strong dollar on foreign sales. FO's diverse portfolio of market-leading businesses should continue to generate a high level of free cash (mostly reflecting relatively low capital requirements for liquor operations), which will be used for potential acquisitions and modest debt reduction. In July 1998, the company acquired the Geyser Peak wine business to help boost its distilled spirits operations. It is likely that the company will continue to use excess cash to make selective acquisitions to leverage its core business lines.

Valuation - 29-JUL-98

Although the company's unusual business mix of both consumer cyclical and consumer noncyclical products offers few synergies, most of the businesses are market leaders in their respective fields and, as such, command a relatively high degree of pricing flexibility. FO has been successful in making acquisitions to leverage its core businesses by integrating distribution capabilities and consolidating overhead expenses. This should enable the company to generate 6% to 8% annual operating profit growth. With FO benefiting from a strong balance sheet and steady cash generation, which is actively used to repurchase shares, we see EPS growing at a faster rate, seen in the range of 13% to 15% over time. In light of the company's growing sales momentum and better than expected savings from its 1997 restructuring program, we believe the shares, recently trading at 23 times our 1998 EPS estimate of $1.70, are undervalued.

Key Stock Statistics

S&P EPS Est. 1998	1.70	Tang. Bk. Value/Share	1.84
P/E on S&P Est. 1998	16.8	Beta	0.63
S&P EPS Est. 1999	1.95	Shareholders	51,900
Dividend Rate/Share	0.84	Market cap. (B)	$ 4.9
Shs. outstg. (M)	172.8	Inst. holdings	54%
Avg. daily vol. (M)	0.482		

Value of $10,000 invested 5 years ago: NA

Fiscal Year Ending Dec. 31

	1998	1997	1996	1995	1994	1993
Revenues (Million $)						
1Q	1,204	1,105	1,339	1,258	2,033	2,090
2Q	1,326	1,236	1,389	1,274	--	2,020
3Q	—	1,186	1,437	1,341	--	1,980
4Q	—	1,318	1,617	1,482	5,457	2,200
Yr.	—	4,845	5,776	5,355	7,490	8,290
Earnings Per Share ($)						
1Q	**0.30**	0.20	0.70	0.60	0.64	1.22
2Q	**0.50**	0.03	0.69	0.63	0.75	0.75
3Q	**E0.34**	0.16	0.80	0.82	0.65	0.42
4Q	**E0.56**	-0.15	0.67	0.85	2.34	0.91
Yr.	**E1.70**	0.23	2.86	2.90	4.38	3.30

Next earnings report expected: late October

Dividend Data (Dividends have been paid since 1905.)

Amount ($)	Date Decl.	Ex-Div. Date	Stock of Record	Payment Date
0.210	Sep. 30	Nov. 07	Nov. 12	Dec. 01 '97
0.210	Jan. 27	Feb. 09	Feb. 11	Mar. 02 '98
0.210	Apr. 28	May. 11	May. 13	Jun. 01 '98
0.210	Jul. 28	Aug. 10	Aug. 12	Sep. 01 '98

A Division of The **McGraw-Hill** *Companies*

Business Summary - 29-JUL-98

Fortune Brands, Inc. (formerly American Brands, Inc.) is a holding company with subsidiaries engaged in various consumer-related businesses. On May 30, 1997, American Brands divested its remaining tobacco operations to AMB shareholders via a tax-free spinoff of the shares of Gallaher Group Plc, a newly formed English company. Both Gallaher ADRs (symbol GLH) and Fortune Brands common stock began trading on the NYSE on June 2. Fortune Brands' remaining operating companies have some of the world's best known consumer brands, with approximately 80% of 1997 sales coming from brands that were number one or two in their categories. Pro forma sales and profit contributions in 1997 were:

	Revs.	Profits
Hardware & home improvement	28.7%	28.0%
Office products	26.7%	5.6%
Distilled spirits	25.7%	46.2%
Golf & leisure	18.8%	20.3%

Hardware and home improvement products are sold through the company's MasterBrand Industries subsidiary, whose major units include Moen, Master Lock, Aristokraft and Waterloo. Moen is a leading producer of faucets, sinks and plumbing accessories in the U.S. and Asia. Master Lock produces various types of key-controlled and combination locks, and door locksets and related hardware. Aristokraft produces kitchen cabinets and bathroom vanities. Waterloo manufactures tool storage products, which consist mainly of steel tool boxes, tool chests, workbenches and related products for both private-label sale and for Sears.

Distilled spirits are sold through the company's JBB Worldwide subsidiary. Leading brands include Jim Beam Bourbon whiskey, DeKuyper cordials, Gilbey's gin and Kamchatka vodka. Principal markets are the U.S., the U.K. and Australia, which combined account for approximately 85% of JBB's total sales.

Office products are sold through the company's ACCO World Corporation. ACCO sells a wide variety of traditional and computer-related office products and supplies, personal computer accessory products, time management products and presentation aids.

Golf and leisure products operations are conducted through the company's Acushnet unit, which is a leading producer of golf balls (Titleist, Pinnacle), shoes (Classics, DryJoys), clubs (Cobra, DCI, Titleist Titanium, Scotty Cameron by Titleist, Bulls Eye) and gloves (Sta-Sof, Weather-Sof). Other products include bags, carts, dress and athletic shoes, as well as socks and accessories.

Per Share Data ($)

(Year Ended Dec. 31)	1997	1996	1995	1994	1993	1992	1991	1990	1989	1988
Tangible Bk. Val.	1.93	-1.55	3.13	5.33	2.51	5.33	3.87	2.83	5.29	2.14
Cash Flow	1.64	4.46	4.28	5.94	4.83	5.78	5.30	4.28	4.35	3.82
Earnings	0.23	2.86	2.90	4.38	3.30	4.29	3.91	2.99	3.26	2.72
Dividends	1.41	2.00	2.00	1.99	1.97	1.80	1.59	1.41	1.25	1.13
Payout Ratio	NM	70%	69%	45%	60%	42%	41%	48%	39%	40%
Prices - High	56	50⅛	47¼	38⅜	40⅝	49⅞	47⅝	41⅝	41	35⅞
- Low	30¼	39⅞	36⅝	29⅜	28½	39	35⅝	30⅞	30⅝	21⅛
P/E Ratio - High	NM	18	16	9	12	12	12	14	13	13
- Low	NM	14	13	7	9	9	9	10	9	8

Income Statement Analysis (Million $)

	1997	1996	1995	1994	1993	1992	1991	1990	1989	1988
Revs.	4,845	5,776	5,355	7,490	8,288	8,840	8,379	8,270	7,265	7,236
Oper. Inc.	723	1,363	1,293	1,557	1,670	1,970	1,777	1,730	1,536	1,454
Depr.	243	275	258	314	309	304	281	251	206	212
Int. Exp.	117	179	160	212	244	270	264	279	281	267
Pretax Inc.	140	824	894	1,351	1,076	1,398	1,238	1,048	1,062	984
Eff. Tax Rate	70%	40%	39%	35%	38%	37%	35%	43%	41%	45%
Net Inc.	42.0	497	543	885	668	884	806	596	631	541

Balance Sheet & Other Fin. Data (Million $)

	1997	1996	1995	1994	1993	1992	1991	1990	1989	1988
Cash	54.0	120	140	110	142	140	129	154	149	116
Curr. Assets	2,096	3,873	3,164	4,671	NA	NA	NA	NA	NA	NA
Total Assets	6,943	9,504	8,021	9,794	16,339	14,963	15,116	13,835	11,394	12,201
Curr. Liab.	1,769	3,695	2,411	3,116	NA	NA	NA	NA	NA	NA
LT Debt	739	1,598	1,155	1,512	2,492	2,407	2,552	2,434	1,717	2,359
Common Eqty.	4,006	3,671	3,863	4,622	4,254	4,283	4,163	3,633	2,938	2,492
Total Cap.	4,795	5,402	5,160	6,283	6,888	6,947	7,118	6,483	5,042	5,180
Cap. Exp.	197	240	208	201	250	289	234	297	257	235
Cash Flow	284	771	800	1,198	976	1,178	1,073	832	822	738
Curr. Ratio	1.2	1.1	1.3	1.5	NA	NA	NA	NA	NA	NA
% LT Debt of Cap.	15.4	29.6	22.4	24.1	36.2	34.6	35.9	37.5	34.1	45.5
% Net Inc.of Revs.	0.9	8.6	10.1	11.8	8.1	10.0	9.6	7.2	8.7	7.5
% Ret. on Assets	0.5	5.7	6.1	6.8	4.3	5.9	5.5	4.6	5.3	5.9
% Ret. on Equity	1.1	13.2	12.8	19.9	15.6	20.8	20.2	17.3	22.4	21.1

Data as orig. reptd.; bef. results of disc. opers. and/or spec. items. Per share data adj. for stk. divs. as of ex-div. date. Bold denotes diluted EPS (FASB 128). E-Estimated. NA-Not Available. NM-Not Meaningful. NR-Not Ranked.

Office—1700 E. Putnam Ave., Old Greenwich, CT 06870-0811.**Tel**—(203) 698-5000. **Website**—http://www.fortunebrands.com **Chrmn & CEO**—T. C. Hays. **Pres & COO**—J. T. Ludes. **Secy**—L. F. Femous Jr. **Treas**—M. Hausberg. **SVP & CFO**—D. L. Bauerlein Jr. **Investor Contact**—Daniel A. Conforti. **Dirs**—E. R. Anderson, P. O. Ewers, T. C. Hays, J. W. Johnstone Jr., W. J. Kelley, S. Kirschner, G. R. Lohman, J. T. Ludes, C. H. Pistor Jr., A. M. Tatlock, J. W. Thompson, P. M. Wilson. **Transfer Agent & Registrar**—Co. itself. **Incorporated**—in New Jersey in 1904. **Empl**— 25,000. **S&P Analyst**: Robert J. Izmirlian

STANDARD &POOR'S
STOCK REPORTS

Foster Wheeler

920

NYSE Symbol **FWC**

In S&P 500

12-SEP-98

Industry:
Engineering & Construction

Summary: This global engineering and construction concern also operates U.S. and foreign power plants.

S&P Opinion: Hold (★★★)	Recent Price • 12⅝	Yield • 6.6%
	52 Wk Range • 45¾-11¾	12-Mo. P/E • 48.8

Earnings vs. Previous Year
▲=Up ▼=Down ▶=No Change

Quantitative Evaluations

Outlook
(1 Lowest—5 Highest)
• **5**

Fair Value
• **24⅛**

Risk
• **Low**

Earn./Div. Rank
• **A-**

Technical Eval.
• **NA**

Rel. Strength Rank
(1 Lowest—99 Highest)
• **24**

Insider Activity
• **Favorable**

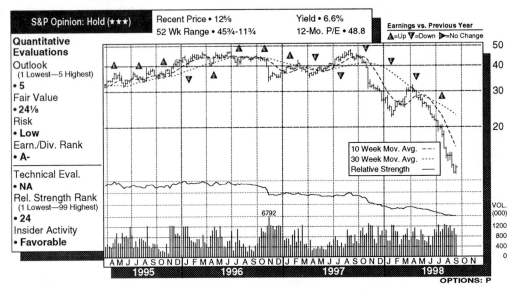

10 Week Mov. Avg. – – –
30 Week Mov. Avg. · · · ·
Relative Strength —

6792

VOL.
(000)

OPTIONS: P

Overview - 04-AUG-98

We project a 3% rise in operating revenues in 1998, reflecting a flat backlog. Earnings should rebound in the absence of 1997's nonrecurring charges of $98.5 million, which outweighed a gain of $56.4 million on the sale of the company's Glitsch International subsidiary. Bookings slowed in the fourth quarter of 1997 but total backlog was maintained at $7.2 billion at the end of 1997. Over the longer term, the company's fortunes will be influenced by overall capital spending in industries and countries in which the company offers its services, and its ability to successfully bid on important contracts. Despite the recent volatility in Asian capital markets, a growing presence in the developing regions of the world, including China, Singapore and Thailand, should ensure FWC's ability to compete where growth opportunities may be the most impressive, and will aid the company in diversifying out of slower growing and more mature markets. The impact on profit margins of the recent strength in the U.S. dollar is of concern, but use of local labor around the world should help control costs.

Valuation - 04-AUG-98

Although earnings should rebound in 1998, we think the stock will not benefit as a result, because the economic cycle is aging and order backlogs may turn down. In addition, there is concern regarding recent events in Asia. Shares of cyclical companies tend to trade at low multiples of peak earnings and at a discount to the market as measured by the S&P 500. Although FWC's shares are trading near their 12 month low, we think it is still too early to increase holdings in the company.

Key Stock Statistics

S&P EPS Est. 1998	2.05	Tang. Bk. Value/Share	7.95
P/E on S&P Est. 1998	6.2	Beta	1.16
S&P EPS Est. 1999	2.20	Shareholders	7,000
Dividend Rate/Share	0.84	Market cap. (B)	$0.517
Shs. outstg. (M)	40.7	Inst. holdings	72%
Avg. daily vol. (M)	0.223		

Value of $10,000 invested 5 years ago: $ 5,163

Fiscal Year Ending Dec. 31

	1998	1997	1996	1995	1994	1993
Revenues (Million $)						
1Q	1,028	965.1	843.9	636.0	469.6	587.0
2Q	1,054	1,031	977.6	678.7	571.2	970.5
3Q	—	1,030	968.5	779.9	533.6	616.4
4Q	—	1,034	1,240	947.5	660.0	1,230
Yr.	—	4,060	4,041	3,042	2,234	4,006
Earnings Per Share ($)						
1Q	0.43	0.50	0.58	0.50	0.43	0.36
2Q	0.50	-0.09	0.62	0.53	0.47	0.41
3Q	—	-0.72	0.59	0.48	0.41	0.34
4Q	—	0.06	0.24	-0.67	0.52	0.51
Yr.	E2.05	-0.26	2.02	0.79	1.83	1.62

Next earnings report expected: late October

Dividend Data (Dividends have been paid since 1960.)

Amount ($)	Date Decl.	Ex-Div. Date	Stock of Record	Payment Date
0.210	Oct. 28	Nov. 12	Nov. 14	Dec. 15 '97
0.210	Jan. 27	Feb. 11	Feb. 16	Mar. 16 '98
0.210	Apr. 27	May. 13	May. 15	Jun. 15 '98
0.210	Jul. 28	Aug. 12	Aug. 14	Sep. 15 '98

A Division of The McGraw·Hill Companies

Business Summary - 04-AUG-98

Formed in 1927 via a consolidation of companies controlled by the Foster and Wheeler families, Foster Wheeler has been a leader in providing design, engineering and construction services to the chemical, petroleum refining, power generating and environmental control industries for much of the century.

Segment operating profit margins in recent years were as follows:

	1997	1996	1995
OPERATING PROFIT MARGINS			
Engineering & construction	6.0%	8.1%	9.2%
Energy equipment	8.3%	17%	10%
Power systems	Def.	42%	38%

Foreign operations, which account for about 60% of revenues, remain the focus of growth opportunities as there is great demand for new power generating facilities in emerging growth regions of the world such as Asia, Latin America and the Middle East.

The Engineering and Construction Group (69% of 1997 revenues) designs, engineers and constructs petroleum, chemical, petrochemical and alternative fuel facilities and related infrastructure. It also provides environmental services for hazardous and mixed waste investigation and remediation, pollution control systems, wastewater treatment and other environmental services. The group captured $3.6 billion of new orders in 1997 and had a backlog of $5.3 billion at year end.

The Energy Equipment Group (26%) designs and fabricates steam generators and condensers, mass transfer equipment, tower packings and industrial wire mesh for the power generation and chemical separations industries worldwide. It also provides natural gas processing engineering and construction. This segment received $1.3 billion of new orders in 1997 and ended the year with $1.6 billion of backlog.

The Power Systems Group (5%) includes the owning/leasing for third parties of solid waste-to-energy and cogeneration plants. Waste-to-energy projects take approximately two to three years from award of a contract and the signing of a service agreement with a community to the beginning of construction. The company operates 14 U.S. and foreign facilities throughout the U.S., all of which produce and sell electric power. Foster Wheeler is also developing six new facilities: three in Italy, one in Chile, one in Portugal and one in Minnesota. The group's new orders amounted to $159 million in 1997, with year-end backlog at $255 million.

Per Share Data ($) (Year Ended Dec. 31)	1997	1996	1995	1994	1993	1992	1991	1990	1989	1988
Tangible Bk. Val.	7.89	8.80	9.03	10.83	11.10	10.52	14.72	14.11	12.86	12.63
Cash Flow	1.27	3.59	2.31	3.05	2.84	2.49	2.20	1.76	1.44	1.38
Earnings	-0.26	2.03	0.79	1.83	1.62	1.28	1.22	1.08	0.95	0.81
Dividends	0.83	0.81	0.77	0.72	0.65	0.58	0.53	0.48	0.44	0.44
Payout Ratio	NM	40%	97%	39%	40%	46%	44%	45%	46%	54%
Prices - High	48 1/8	47 1/4	43 1/2	45 1/8	35 7/8	32 7/8	34	28 3/4	22	17 1/4
- Low	26 1/8	33 1/2	29 3/8	26 5/8	25 7/8	23	20 1/4	17 3/4	14 1/4	11 1/2
P/E Ratio - High	NM	23	55	25	22	26	28	27	23	21
- Low	NM	17	37	15	16	18	17	16	15	14
Income Statement Analysis (Million $)										
Revs.	4,060	4,006	3,042	2,234	2,583	2,495	1,992	1,661	1,243	1,054
Oper. Inc.	37.2	239	204	165	132	134	92.0	65.0	37.0	57.0
Depr.	62.0	63.6	54.6	43.7	43.7	43.3	34.7	24.1	17.2	20.0
Int. Exp.	54.7	61.3	49.1	35.4	33.8	35.9	32.4	27.7	30.1	25.6
Pretax Inc.	-2.3	127	74.0	112	99	70.3	63.8	50.1	42.3	43.2
Eff. Tax Rate	NM	35%	55%	37%	39%	32%	28%	20%	21%	34%
Net Inc.	-10.5	82.2	28.5	65.4	57.7	45.5	43.3	38.3	33.6	28.5
Balance Sheet & Other Fin. Data (Million $)										
Cash	167	404	280	354	377	271	233	191	221	165
Curr. Assets	1,545	1,762	1,439	1,113	983	925	838	750	671	633
Total Assets	3,366	3,510	2,776	2,063	1,806	1,763	1,635	1,441	1,181	1,109
Curr. Liab.	1,437	1,442	1,240	891	779	721	572	565	404	376
LT Debt	886	796	554	467	397	427	441	282	241	216
Common Eqty.	619	689	626	456	400	387	538	514	467	451
Total Cap.	1,532	1,528	1,202	953	824	841	1,006	823	727	691
Cap. Exp.	190	159	59.4	39.0	28.0	56.0	119	154	170	94.0
Cash Flow	51.5	146	83.1	109	101	88.8	78.0	62.4	50.9	48.5
Curr. Ratio	1.1	1.2	1.2	1.2	1.3	1.3	1.5	1.3	1.7	1.7
% LT Debt of Cap.	57.8	52.1	46.1	49.0	48.2	50.8	43.9	34.2	33.2	31.2
% Net Inc.of Revs.	NM	2.1	1.0	2.9	2.2	1.8	2.2	2.3	2.7	2.7
% Ret. on Assets	NM	2.5	1.2	3.4	3.2	2.7	2.8	2.9	2.9	2.6
% Ret. on Equity	NM	12.5	5.3	15.2	14.6	9.8	8.2	7.8	7.3	6.3

Data as orig. reptd.; bef. results of disc. opers. and/or spec. items. Per share data adj. for stk. divs. as of ex-div. date. Bold denotes diluted EPS (FASB 128). E-Estimated. NA-Not Available. NM-Not Meaningful. NR-Not Ranked.

Office—Perryville Corporate Park, Clinton, NJ 08809-4000. **Tel**—(908) 730-4000. **Chrmn, Pres & CEO**—R. J. Swift. **CFO**—D. J. Roberts. **Treas**—R. D. Iseman. **Dirs**—E. D. Atkinson, L. E. Azzato, D. J. Farris, E. J. Ferland, M. C. Goss, C. J. Horner, J. J. Melone, F. E. Perkins, J. E. Stuart, C. Y. C. Tse. **Transfer Agent & Registrar**—ChaseMellon Shareholder Services, Ridgefield Park, NJ. **Incorporated**—in New York in 1927. **Empl**— 11,100. **S&P Analyst:** Robert E. Friedman, CPA

STANDARD &POOR'S
STOCK REPORTS

FPL Group

846N
NYSE Symbol **FPL**

In S&P 500

12-SEP-98

Industry:
Electric Companies

Summary: This electric utility holding company's primary unit is Florida Power & Light Co., which provides electricity to most of the territory along Florida's east and lower west coasts.

S&P Opinion: Accumulate (★★★★)	Recent Price • 67⅛	Yield • 3.0%	Earnings vs. Previous Year
	52 Wk Range • 68-48¼	12-Mo. P/E • 18.2	▲=Up ▼=Down ■=No Change

Quantitative Evaluations

Outlook
(1 Lowest—5 Highest)
• **1**

Fair Value
• **57**

Risk
• **Low**

Earn./Div. Rank
• **B**

Technical Eval.
• **Bullish** since 5/97

Rel. Strength Rank
(1 Lowest—99 Highest)
• **97**

Insider Activity
• **Neutral**

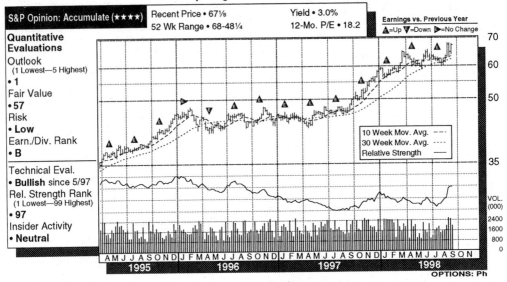

10 Week Mov. Avg. — — —
30 Week Mov. Avg. ....
Relative Strength ———

VOL. (000)
2400
1600
800
0

AMJJASOND|JFMAMJJASOND|JFMAMJJASOND|JFMAMJJASON
1995 1996 1997 1998

OPTIONS: Ph

Overview - 22-JUL-98

Following an anticipated 5% increase in 1998, EPS should grow over 6% in 1999. While FPL continues to benefit from the expansion of its non-regulated operations and from production costs that are among the lowest in the U.S., earnings growth remains restricted by its plan to accelerate the depreciation of its high cost nuclear units and to amortize a regulatory asset. Utility revenues, which rose 5.5% in 1997, should see similar increases in 1998 and 1999, aided by growth rates in regional population and customer demand that are well above the industry average. Results for this low-cost electric utility should also be enhanced by reduced fuel and purchased power expenses. FPL's planned acquisition (agreed to in January 1998) of 35 power generation plants in Maine is expected to give a modest lift to near-term earnings. The balance sheet is sound, with long term debt at less than 40% of total capital.

Valuation - 22-JUL-98

We would continue to accumulate FPL stock. The shares (which gained nearly 29% in 1997) are up about 5% year to date, compared to a 1% increase for the S&P Index of Electric Companies. To position itself for a competitive market environment, FPL cut its dividend 32% in May 1994. Dividend increases have since resumed. In March 1998, the payment was increased 4.2% and we expect it to grow at a rate well above the electric utility industry average for the next several years. The payout ratio, at 53% of our 1998 EPS estimate, is well below the industry average, and provides FPL with the financial flexibility essential to the expansion of its non-regulated operations. With the shares, which have more than doubled in value over the past five years, trading at less than 16 times our 1999 EPS estimate of $4.00, FPL's stock is attractive for both intermediate and long-term total return.

Key Stock Statistics

S&P EPS Est. 1998	3.75	Tang. Bk. Value/Share	26.62
P/E on S&P Est. 1998	17.9	Beta	0.14
S&P EPS Est. 1999	4.00	Shareholders	66,200
Dividend Rate/Share	2.00	Market cap. (B)	$ 12.2
Shs. outstg. (M)	181.2	Inst. holdings	52%
Avg. daily vol. (M)	0.585		

Value of $10,000 invested 5 years ago: $ 23,652

Fiscal Year Ending Dec. 31

	1998	1997	1996	1995	1994	1993
Revenues (Million $)						
1Q	1,338	1,445	1,358	1,177	1,178	1,132
2Q	1,692	1,587	1,474	1,467	1,442	1,350
3Q	—	1,859	1,770	1,587	1,512	1,603
4Q	—	1,478	1,435	1,361	1,290	1,231
Yr.	—	6,369	6,037	5,592	5,423	5,316
Earnings Per Share ($)						
1Q	**0.63**	**0.58**	0.54	0.57	0.53	0.50
2Q	**1.02**	**0.95**	0.86	0.79	0.70	0.60
3Q	**E1.56**	1.52	1.44	1.37	1.25	0.75
4Q	**E0.54**	**0.52**	0.49	0.43	0.43	0.45
Yr.	**E3.75**	3.57	3.33	3.16	2.91	2.30

Next earnings report expected: mid October

Dividend Data (Dividends have been paid since 1944.)

Amount ($)	Date Decl.	Ex-Div. Date	Stock of Record	Payment Date
0.480	Nov. 17	Nov. 25	Nov. 28	Dec. 15 '97
0.500	Feb. 16	Feb. 25	Feb. 27	Mar. 16 '98
0.500	May. 18	May. 27	May. 29	Jun. 15 '98
0.500	Aug. 17	Aug. 26	Aug. 28	Sep. 15 '98

A Division of The **McGraw·Hill** *Companies*

STANDARD
&POOR'S
STOCK REPORTS

FPL Group, Inc.

846N
12-SEP-98

Business Summary - 22-JUL-98

FPL Group is the holding company for Florida Power & Light Co., which serves, through 3.6 million customer accounts, more than 7 million people (about half the population of Florida) in an area covering nearly all of the eastern seaboard and southern part of the state. Given the area's attractive climate and quality of life, the region should continue to see strong growth. In recent years, electric revenues by class of customer were:

	1997	1996	1995	1994
Residential	56%	57%	56%	56%
Commercial	37%	36%	35%	36%
Industrial	3%	3%	4%	4%
Wholesale/Other	4%	4%	5%	4%

The Florida Power & Light Co., which accounts for substantially all of FPL's revenues, continues to focus on the reduction of its costs and improved plant performance. Since 1990, operating and maintenance costs have been reduced by 30%.

Sources of power in 1997 were: natural gas, 29%; nuclear, 25%; oil, 18%; purchases from other utilities, 12%; other purchases, 8%; and coal, 8%.

FPL owns and operates four nuclear units, two at Turkey Point and two at St. Lucie. While Turkey Point has been cited by the Nuclear Regulatory Commission (NRC) as one of the country's superior performers, the St. Lucie plant had received increased attention and fines from the NRC, reflecting a series of mechanical and operational problems. In 1997, FPL implemented corrective actions at the St. Lucie plant that resulted in improved operations and regulatory performance.

FPL Group Capital is a wholly owned subsidiary that owns and funds FPL's independent power projects and agricultural operations. In January 1998, it formed FPL Energy, to manage existing non-regulated investments and to pursue new investments in the domestic and international energy markets. FPL Energy consolidated the operations and assets of FPL Group International and ESI Energy Inc., which participated in non-utility, environmentally favored alternative energy projects. In January 1998, FPL Energy agreed to acquire 35 electric power generation plants from Central Maine Power for $846 million. The deal, which needs to be approved by Maine regulators, should close in the fall of 1998. FPL Group Capital also owns Turner Foods, a leading citrus grove operator.

In order to strengthen its financial position, FPL retired more than $560 million of debt and preferred stock in 1997. Over the past three years, the company has reduced its debt, preferred stock and commercial paper balances by more than $1.5 billion.

Per Share Data ($)

(Year Ended Dec. 31)	1997	1996	1995	1994	1993	1992	1991	1990	1989	1988
Tangible Bk. Val.	26.62	24.61	24.06	22.50	21.58	19.84	18.60	19.48	24.47	23.44
Earnings	3.57	3.33	3.16	2.91	2.30	2.65	2.31	-2.86	3.12	3.42
Dividends	1.92	1.84	1.76	1.88	2.47	2.43	2.39	2.34	2.26	2.18
Payout Ratio	54%	55%	56%	65%	107%	92%	103%	NM	72%	64%
Prices - High	60	48⅛	46½	39⅛	41	38⅜	37¼	36½	36¾	32½
- Low	42⅝	41½	34	26⅞	35½	32	28⅛	26⅛	29	27¾
P/E Ratio - High	17	14	15	13	18	14	16	NM	12	10
- Low	12	12	11	9	15	12	12	NM	9	8

Income Statement Analysis (Million $)

	1997	1996	1995	1994	1993	1992	1991	1990	1989	1988
Revs.	6,369	6,037	5,592	5,423	5,316	5,193	5,249	6,289	6,180	5,853
Depr.	1,061	960	918	724	598	554	518	617	758	616
Maint.	NA	NA	NA	NA	NA	358	405	408	385	373
Fxd. Chgs. Cov.	4.0	4.0	3.6	3.2	3.0	3.1	2.5	NM	2.6	2.8
Constr. Credits	Nil	2.0	15.0	24.0	66.2	57.8	34.0	25.0	22.0	16.0
Eff. Tax Rate	33%	34%	37%	37%	37%	36%	29%	16%	30%	31%
Net Inc.	618	579	553	519	429	467	276	-390	410	448

Balance Sheet & Other Fin. Data (Million $)

	1997	1996	1995	1994	1993	1992	1991	1990	1989	1988
Gross Prop.	17,820	17,034	16,725	16,390	15,881	14,972	13,771	12,962	12,167	11,534
Cap. Exp.	551	488	671	906	1,248	1,270	1,197	1,038	783	668
Net Prop.	9,354	9,384	9,852	10,203	10,289	9,866	9,081	8,456	8,079	7,940
Capitalization:										
LT Debt	2,949	3,144	3,377	4,050	4,020	4,280	3,948	3,863	3,465	3,412
% LT Debt	37	39	42	47	46	49	51	51	47	47
Pfd.	226	332	340	545	548	551	496	521	519	535
% Pfd.	2.80	4.10	4.20	6.30	6.30	6.40	6.40	6.90	7.00	7.40
Common	4,845	4,592	4,392	4,197	4,101	3,836	3,354	3,161	3,452	3,265
% Common	60	57	54	49	47	44	43	42	46	45
Total Cap.	9,493	10,201	10,299	10,917	10,722	10,732	9,674	9,516	9,384	9,151
% Oper. Ratio	85.5	85.5	84.5	84.5	86.4	85.1	86.6	100.8	88.0	87.7
% Earn. on Net Prop.	13.1	9.1	11.9	8.2	7.2	8.2	8.1	NM	9.3	9.2
% Return On Revs.	9.7	9.6	9.9	9.6	8.1	9.0	7.2	NM	6.6	7.6
% Return On Invest. Capital	9.4	8.5	NM	7.8	7.0	8.0	7.8	NM	10.2	9.0
% Return On Com. Equity	13.1	12.9	12.9	12.5	10.8	13.0	11.5	NM	12.2	14.1

Data as orig. reptd.; bef. results of disc. opers. and/or spec. items. Per share data adj. for stk. divs. as of ex-div. date. Bold denotes diluted EPS (FASB 128). E-Estimated. NA-Not Available. NM-Not Meaningful. NR-Not Ranked.

Office—700 Universe Blvd., Juno Beach, FL 33408. **Tel**—(561) 694-4000. **Website**—http://www.fpl.com **Chrmn, Pres & CEO**—J. L. Broadhead. **CFO**—K. M. Davis. **Secy**—D. P. Coyle. **Investor Contact**—Scott Dudley (561-694-4697) / Max Kuniansky (561-694-4699). **Dirs**—H. J. Arnelle, S. S. Barrat, R. M. Beall II, J. L. Broadhead, J. H. Brown, A. M. Codina, M. M. Criser, B. F. Dolan, W. D. Dover, A. W. Dreyfoos, Jr., P. J. Evanson, D. Lewis, F. V. Malek, P. R. Tregurtha. **Transfer Agent & Registrar**—Boston EquiServe. **Incorporated**—in Florida in 1925; reincorporated in Florida in 1984. **Empl**— 10,039. **S&P Analyst:** Justin McCann

Franklin Resources

922Q

NYSE Symbol **BEN**

In S&P 500

12-SEP-98

Industry:
Investment Management

Summary: Franklin Resources is one of the world's largest publicly traded independent asset managers.

S&P Opinion: Buy (★★★★★)	Recent Price • 28⅞	Yield • 0.7%
	52 Wk Range • 57⅞-25¾	12-Mo. P/E • 14.3

Earnings vs. Previous Year
▲=Up ▼=Down ▶=No Change

Quantitative Evaluations

Outlook
(1 Lowest—5 Highest)
• **4**

Fair Value
• **36½**

Risk
• **Average**

Earn./Div. Rank
• **A+**

Technical Eval.
• **NA**

Rel. Strength Rank
(1 Lowest—99 Highest)
• **16**

Insider Activity
• **Unfavorable**

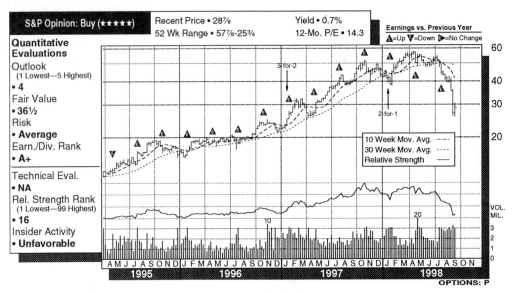

10 Week Mov. Avg. ---
30 Week Mov. Avg. ·····
Relative Strength —

VOL. MIL.

OPTIONS: P

Overview - 28-JUL-98

Solid earnings-per-share growth in the double-digit range is expected for FY 99 (Sep.). Contributors to the anticipated profit growth include the ongoing reinvestment of dividends and interest by existing fundholders, greater retirement savings by the baby boomer generation, and improved sales of international funds, mainly in Europe. Domestic stock funds have been the company's best selling product in recent periods. Margins, which are extremely wide compared to industrial and other financial concerns, could expand further, based on anticipated growth in assets under management. Because of goodwill resulting from the Heine deal, cash flow will be considerably greater than net income. The major risk is the direction of domestic and overseas financial markets. If, for example, Asian and other emerging markets weakened further, assets under management and thus advisory fees would also fall.

Valuation - 28-JUL-98

The shares carry a buy recommendation. Franklin Resources enjoys a favorable long-term growth outlook, aided by the purchase of Heine Securities, which broadens its range of product offerings, adds mutual funds with excellent track records, and opens up a new channel of distribution. Other contributors to the projected growth include increased retirement savings by the baby boomer generation, and the highly attractive economics of the investment management business. Valuation levels are attractive. The stock trades at a P/E ratio on projected FY 99 earnings per share in line with market averages, but deserves a premium multiple given its impressive pretax margins and return on equity in excess of 20%. One risk is the level of the stock market, as fees are computed as a percentage of assets under management.

Key Stock Statistics

S&P EPS Est. 1998	2.10	Tang. Bk. Value/Share	3.84
P/E on S&P Est. 1998	13.8	Beta	1.91
S&P EPS Est. 1999	2.60	Shareholders	2,000
Dividend Rate/Share	0.20	Market cap. (B)	$ 7.3
Shs. outstg. (M)	253.0	Inst. holdings	32%
Avg. daily vol. (M)	0.829		

Value of $10,000 invested 5 years ago: $ 25,774

Fiscal Year Ending Sep. 30

	1998	1997	1996	1995	1994	1993
Revenues (Million $)						
1Q	632.4	440.0	342.6	208.2	198.5	126.9
2Q	673.7	521.9	393.8	199.8	213.6	153.6
3Q	672.6	577.9	395.4	212.7	204.9	162.7
4Q	—	643.1	390.8	225.1	209.9	197.5
Yr.	—	2,183	1,523	845.3	826.9	640.7
Earnings Per Share ($)						
1Q	**0.52**	0.38	0.30	0.25	0.23	0.14
2Q	**0.50**	0.40	0.30	0.25	0.27	0.17
3Q	**0.52**	0.44	0.33	0.28	0.24	0.18
4Q	**E0.56**	0.49	0.34	0.30	0.25	0.21
Yr.	**E2.10**	1.71	1.26	1.08	1.00	0.71

Next earnings report expected: late October

Dividend Data (Dividends have been paid since 1981.)

Amount ($)	Date Decl.	Ex-Div. Date	Stock of Record	Payment Date
0.050	Dec. 12	Dec. 29	Dec. 31	Jan. 15 '98
2-for-1	Dec. 12	Jan. 16	Dec. 31	Jan. 15 '98
0.050	Mar. 18	Mar. 27	Mar. 31	Apr. 15 '98
0.050	Jun. 18	Jun. 26	Jun. 30	Jul. 15 '98

A Division of The McGraw-Hill Companies

Business Summary - 28-JUL-98

Franklin Resources is one of the largest mutual fund management companies in the U.S., with some $226 billion in assets under management at September 30, 1997. In essence, the company manages assets for individuals who have sent in their money. Franklin is an extremely profitable company, owing mainly to the attractive economics of the investment management business. The company receives a fee of some 0.68% on a huge balance of funds, or $1.3 billion in FY 97 (Sep.), but its costs amount to little more than renting office space and paying its employees. Assets under management broke down as follows at the end of the last two fiscal years:

	9/97	9/96
Fixed Income:		
Tax-free income	20%	28%
U.S. government fixed income	7%	10%
Money fund	1%	2%
Global/int'l fixed income	2%	2%
Equity and Income:		
Global/int'l equity	33%	31%
U.S. equity/income	23%	13%
Institutional	14%	14%

The company has a leading share of fixed-income mutual funds, particularly California municipal bonds. Franklin was one of the first mutual fund organizations to offer investors a California muni fund. Investors in municipal bond funds are often wealthy people in high tax brackets.

The company's international equity funds were acquired in 1992 with the purchase of Templeton Galbraith Hansberger, a firm run by legendary investor Sir John Templeton, who pioneered international investing. These funds boast excellent long-term performance records, although John Templeton has retired from active duty. In November 1996, the company acquired Heine Securities, which owns the Short Hills, NJ-based Mutual Series of mutual funds run by famed value investor Michael Price. This deal rounded out the company's fund offering to include a domestic equity line-up. The company paid $618 million for the complex, which had $17 billion of assets under management.

Two important facts about Franklin are that Charles and Rupert Johnson, the Chairman and Executive Vice President, respectively, own some 34.5% of the stock outstanding, and that the funds, prior to the Heine deal, had been sold with a load charge primarily through the broker-dealer community.

Per Share Data ($)

(Year Ended Sep. 30)	1997	1996	1995	1994	1993	1992	1991	1990	1989	1988
Tangible Bk. Val.	5.00	3.15	2.06	1.03	0.10	2.00	1.55	1.23	0.92	0.64
Cash Flow	4.40	1.42	1.27	NA	NA	NA	NA	NA	NA	NA
Earnings	1.72	1.26	1.08	1.00	0.71	0.53	0.42	0.38	0.33	0.28
Dividends	0.17	0.15	0.13	0.13	0.09	0.09	0.08	0.07	0.05	0.05
Payout Ratio	10%	12%	12%	11%	13%	16%	18%	18%	15%	17%
Prices - High	51⅞	24⅞	19⅜	17	17¼	13	9⅜	6	5	2⅝
- Low	22⅛	15½	11	11¼	10⅝	7⅝	4⅞	3¾	2½	1⅞
P/E Ratio - High	30	20	18	17	24	25	23	16	15	10
- Low	13	12	10	11	15	14	12	10	8	7

Income Statement Analysis (Million $)

Commissions	NA	NA	37.1	96.6	87.1	30.3	24.4	23.0	20.4	18.8
Int. Inc.	16.1	NA	NA	NA	NA	NA	NA	NA	NA	NA
Total Revs.	2,163	1,523	874	827	641	385	318	288	253	203
Int. Exp.	25.3	36.9	39.8	9.4	9.4	12.7	11.6	NA	NA	NA
Pretax Inc.	616	456	387	363	274	205	163	144	130	109
Eff. Tax Rate	30%	31%	31%	31%	36%	39%	40%	38%	39%	39%
Net Inc.	434	315	269	251	175	124	98.2	89.4	78.6	66.3

Balance Sheet & Other Fin. Data (Million $)

Total Assets	3,095	2,374	2,245	1,738	1,582	834	579	479	394	177
Cash Items	435	502	246	210	303	2.8	3.9	1.7	1.1	1.0
Receivables	438	188	149	51.7	248	171	119	83.0	85.0	23.0
Secs. Owned	190	199	233	189	217	598	408	351	277	120
Sec. Borrowed	Nil	Nil	Nil	Nil	Nil	Nil	Nil	Nil	Nil	Nil
Due Brokers & Cust.	Nil	Nil	118	127	91.7	34.6	35.9	32.0	28.4	6.6
Other Liabs.	37.8	574	584	297	355	177	174	154	143	18.0
Capitalization:										
Debt	612	400	382	384	455	156	5.6	4.2	6.1	2.6
Equity	1,854	1,401	1,161	931	720	467	363	289	217	150
Total	2,347	1,800	1,543	1,314	1,175	623	369	293	223	153
% Return On Revs.	20.1	20.3	30.8	30.4	27.4	32.2	30.9	31.1	31.0	32.7
% Ret. on Assets	15.9	13.6	12.8	15.1	14.5	17.6	18.6	20.5	21.9	42.1
% Ret. on Equity	26.7	24.6	25.8	30.4	29.6	29.9	30.1	35.4	42.9	52.0

Data as orig. reptd.; bef. results of disc opers. and/or spec. items. Per share data adj. for stk. divs. as of ex-div. date. Bold denotes diluted EPS (FASB 128). E-Estimated. NA-Not Available. NM-Not Meaningful. NR-Not Ranked.

Office—777 Mariners Island Blvd., San Mateo, CA 94404. **Tel**—(415) 312-2000. **Website**—http://www.frk.com **Pres & CEO**—C. B. Johnson. **Exec VP & Secy**—H. E. Burns. **Sr VP, Treas & CFO**—M. L. Flanagan. **Investor Contact**—Bijan Modanlou (650)525-7584. **Dirs**—H. E. Burns, J. R. Grosvenor, F. W. Hellman, C. B. Johnson, C. E. Johnson, R. H. Johnson Jr., H. O. Kline, P. M. Sacerdote, L. E. Woodworth. **Transfer Agent & Registrar**—Bank of New York, NYC. **Incorporated**—in Delaware in 1969. **Empl**—6,400. **S&P Analyst:** Paul L. Huberman, CFA

12-SEP-98

Industry: Metals Mining

Summary: This company explores for, mines and mills copper, gold and silver in Indonesia. It also has a copper smelting and refining operation in Spain.

S&P Opinion: Avoid (★★)	Recent Price • 13⅜	Yield • 1.5%
	52 Wk Range • 29⅞-11¼	12-Mo. P/E • 19.5

Quantitative Evaluations

Outlook (1 Lowest—5 Highest)
• **1+**

Fair Value
• **10¼**

Risk
• **Average**

Earn./Div. Rank
• **B+**

Technical Eval.
• **NA**

Rel. Strength Rank (1 Lowest—99 Highest)
• **75**

Insider Activity
• **NA**

Earnings vs. Previous Year
▲=Up ▼=Down ▷=No Change

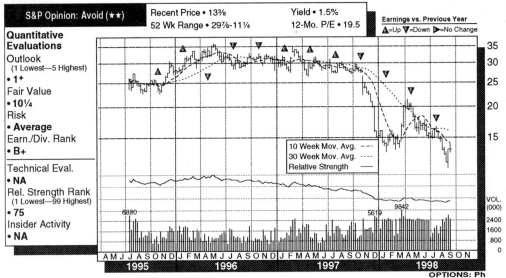

10 Week Mov. Avg. — - —
30 Week Mov. Avg. - - - -
Relative Strength

VOL. (000)

OPTIONS: Ph

Overview - 06-AUG-98

A breakout from current copper and gold production levels will occur in 1998, after startup of the fourth concentrator mill. By the 1998 second quarter, mill output should average 200,000 tons a day, up from 128,600 metric tons in 1997. However, with lower copper and gold prices, as well as higher interest expense and depreciation charges, EPS in 1998 will trail those of 1997.

Valuation - 06-AUG-98

Despite FCX's operational excellence and appeal as an exploration play, we still rate the shares avoid, following release of second quarter EPS. As part of FCX's "Hunker Down & Go" program to increase output and reduce costs, mill throughput rose to 201,200 tons a day in the quarter, up from 166,000 tons a day in 1998's first quarter and 130,800 tons in 1997, in part reflecting the successful startup of the fourth concentrator mill. Cash costs declined to $0.17/lb., from $0.19/lb. in 1998's first quarter and $0.29/lb. in 1997. A large rise in global mine production scheduled to occur between now and 2000 will depress copper prices. As of early August 1998 copper is up from a 12 year low in early July. This is partly the result of a decline in London Metal Exchange inventories to 260,700 metric tons as of August 3, 1998 from a high of 379,325 metric tons on February 25, 1998. We consider this temporary, and expect prices to decline by the end of the third quarter, as seasonal strength ebbs. Despite successful expansion and cost cutting, EPS will continue to decline or stagnate at best. For the long term, we have a favorable view of FCX, given its enviable cost position and reserve growth potential. Viewed on existing gold reserves, FCX appears extremely undervalued. However, our near-term avoid rating reflects concern over continued weakness in copper and the negative implications for EPS.

Key Stock Statistics

S&P EPS Est. 1998	0.60	Tang. Bk. Value/Share	NM
P/E on S&P Est. 1998	22.4	Beta	1.14
S&P EPS Est. 1999	0.80	Shareholders	27,800
Dividend Rate/Share	0.20	Market cap. (B)	$ 1.4
Shs. outstg. (M)	179.9	Inst. holdings	41%
Avg. daily vol. (M)	0.843		

Value of $10,000 invested 5 years ago: NA

Fiscal Year Ending Dec. 31

	1998	1997	1996	1995	1994	1993
Revenues (Million $)						
1Q	396.1	523.8	388.4	408.8	266.1	133.5
2Q	433.9	567.0	424.4	421.5	281.4	215.0
3Q	—	489.5	474.7	469.8	313.4	261.5
4Q	—	420.6	617.6	534.3	351.3	315.9
Yr.	—	2,001	1,905	1,834	1,212	925.9
Earnings Per Share ($)						
1Q	0.15	0.31	0.11	0.21	0.07	0.02
2Q	0.14	0.35	0.15	0.20	0.05	-0.11
3Q	E0.15	0.19	0.24	0.30	0.07	0.10
4Q	E0.16	0.21	0.39	0.27	0.20	0.15
Yr.	E0.60	1.06	0.89	0.98	0.38	0.16

Next earnings report expected: late October

Dividend Data (Dividends have been paid since 1995.)

Amount ($)	Date Decl.	Ex-Div. Date	Stock of Record	Payment Date
0.225	Oct. 03	Oct. 10	Oct. 15	Nov. 01 '97
0.050	Jan. 06	Jan. 14	Jan. 16	Feb. 01 '98
0.050	Apr. 07	Apr. 14	Apr. 16	May. 01 '98
0.050	Jul. 07	Jul. 14	Jul. 16	Aug. 01 '98

A Division of The McGraw·Hill Companies

Business Summary - 06-AUG-98

Freeport-McMoRan Copper & Gold is unique among major natural resources companies: it has substantial reserves of both precious metals (i.e., gold and silver) and copper. One of the world's largest and lowest-cost copper and gold producers, FCX conducts mining operations in Indonesia through majority-owned subsidiaries, P.T. Freeport Indonesia Co. and P.T. IRJA Eastern Minerals Corp. FCX is also engaged in copper smelting and refining through Atlantic Copper Holding, S.A. and has a joint-venture interest in a copper smelter being constructed in Gresik, East Java, Indonesia.

FCX's principal near-term goal is to complete the construction of a fourth concentrator mill by mid-1998. Upon completion, the company's total mill throughput is expected to reach 190,000 metric tons to 200,000 metric tons per day, a significant jump from 1997 mill throughput that averaged 128,600 metric tons a day. Copper cash production costs were $0.22 a lb. in 1997, up from $0.17 in 1996. Total production costs were $0.37 a lb. in 1997, versus $0.30 in 1996.

Copper sales in 1997 totaled 1,166,500 lbs.in 1997 at an average realized price of $0.94/lb., versus 1,118,800 lbs. in 1996 at an average realized price of $1.02/lb. Gold sales were 1,888,100 oz. at $346.14/oz., versus 1,698,900 oz. at an average realized price of $390.96/oz. Silver sales totaled 2,724,300 oz. at $4.68/oz., versus 2,532,000 oz. at $4.95/oz. in 1996.

At year-end 1997, proved and probable reserves were 47.1 billion lbs. of copper, 62.7 million oz. of gold, and 138.4 million oz. of silver. At year-end 1996, proved and probable reserves were 43.2 billion lbs. of copper, 55.3 million oz. of gold, and 118.7 million oz. of silver. FCX conducts most of its exploration at its Grasberg property. The Grasberg deposit contains extensive gold reserves and has one of the three largest open-pit copper reserves of any mine in the world.

The company's principal competitors in copper include Asarco Inc., Cyprus Amax Minerals and Phelps Dodge. Copper is used mostly in the construction, electrical and electronic industries. According the World Bureau of Metal Statistics, global mine production increased to 11.4 million metric tons in 1997 from 11.0 million in 1996; world refined production rose to 13.4 million metric tons from 12.7 million metric tons in 1996 while consumption advanced to 12.6 million metric tons from 12.4 million metric tons in 1996.

The company purchased 1.1 million shares of its common stock during 1998's second quarter for $17.4 million, or about $16 a share on average. As of July 20, 1998, approximately 5.4 million shares of remain under the company's 40 million open market share purchase programs. During 1997, FCX purchased 18.3 million of its common shares for $493.8 million, or an average of $24.07 a share.

Per Share Data ($)

(Year Ended Dec. 31)	1997	1996	1995	1994	1993	1992	1991	1990	1989	1988
Tangible Bk. Val.	NM	1.61	1.55	1.68	1.86	2.16	0.95	1.15	0.84	0.82
Cash Flow	2.32	2.03	1.84	0.75	0.50	0.91	0.77	0.74	0.72	0.68
Earnings	1.06	0.89	0.98	0.38	0.16	0.66	0.56	0.54	0.58	0.55
Dividends	0.90	0.90	0.68	0.60	0.60	0.60	0.55	0.69	0.56	0.16
Payout Ratio	85%	101%	69%	158%	379%	91%	98%	128%	96%	29%
Prices - High	34⅞	36⅛	30¾	NA	NA	NA	NA	NA	NA	NA
- Low	14⅞	27⅜	22⅝	NA	NA	NA	NA	NA	NA	NA
P/E Ratio - High	33	41	31	NA	NA	NA	NA	NA	NA	NA
- Low	14	31	23	NA	NA	NA	NA	NA	NA	NA

Income Statement Analysis (Million $)

	1997	1996	1995	1994	1993	1992	1991	1990	1989	1988
Revs.	2,001	1,905	1,834	1,212	926	714	468	434	368	335
Oper. Inc.	878	812	718	323	244	325	216	240	228	221
Depr.	24.0	174	124	75.1	67.9	48.3	38.4	35.5	24.6	20.9
Int. Exp.	175	140	97.7	35.1	39.8	42.9	39.8	21.7	7.3	5.4
Pretax Inc.	517	522	545	279	137	265	160	192	206	200
Eff. Tax Rate	45%	47%	43%	44%	49%	39%	29%	45%	44%	45%
Net Inc.	245	226	254	130	61.0	130	102	93.0	99	94.0

Balance Sheet & Other Fin. Data (Million $)

	1997	1996	1995	1994	1993	1992	1991	1990	1989	1988
Cash	9.0	37.1	26.9	44.0	14.0	372	80.8	44.4	60.3	64.2
Curr. Assets	463	661	653	603	428	661	510	156	136	135
Total Assets	4,152	3,866	3,582	3,040	2,117	1,694	1,158	675	415	291
Curr. Liab.	476	598	527	432	288	169	41.7	67.5	62.5	61.4
LT Debt	2,308	1,426	1,080	526	212	645	632	294	130	40.0
Common Eqty.	-71.1	325	882	346	373	422	173	209	144	140
Total Cap.	3,551	3,066	2,267	2,396	1,641	1,510	964	605	351	229
Cap. Exp.	595	490	308	743	760	437	246	188	138	66.0
Cash Flow	459	400	378	154	100	171	140	128	123	115
Curr. Ratio	1.0	1.1	1.2	1.4	1.5	3.9	12.2	2.3	2.2	2.2
% LT Debt of Cap.	65.0	46.5	47.6	21.9	12.9	42.7	65.6	48.6	37.0	17.5
% Net Inc.of Revs.	12.2	11.9	13.8	10.7	6.6	18.2	21.8	21.3	26.8	28.1
% Ret. on Assets	6.1	7.1	7.7	5.0	3.1	8.9	11.1	16.6	28.0	NA
% Ret. on Equity	NM	56.7	27.0	21.5	7.9	40.5	53.5	51.1	69.6	NA

Data as orig. reptd.; bef. results of disc. opers. and/or spec. items. Per share data adj. for stk. divs. as of ex-div. date. Divs. on the Cl. B shs. were initiated in Oct. 95; divs. pr. to 1995 are payments on Cl. A shs. E-Estimated. NA-Not Available. NM-Not Meaningful. NR-Not Ranked.

Office—1615 Poydras St. New Orleans, LA 70112.**Tel**—(504) 582-4000. **Website**—http://www.fcx.com **Chrmn & CEO**—J. R. Moffett. **Vice Chrmn**—R. L. Latiolais. **Pres, COO & CFO**—R. C. Adkerson. **Secy**—M. C. Kilanowski, Jr. **Investor Contact**—Christopher D. Sammons. **Dirs**—R. W. Bruce III, L. A. Davis, R. A. Day, W. B. Harrison, J. B. Johnston, H. A. Kissinger, B. L. Lackey, R. L. Latiolais, J. C. A. Leslie, G. K. McDonald, G. A. Mealey, J. R. Moffett, G. Putnam, B. M. Rankin,Jr., J. T. Wharton. — **Transfer Agent & Registrar**—ChaseMellon Shareholder Services, LLC, Ridgefield Park, NJ. **Incorporated**—in Delaware in 1987. **Empl**— 6,300. **S&P Analyst:** Leo J. Larkin

STANDARD &POOR'S
STOCK REPORTS

Frontier Corp.

926H
NYSE Symbol **FRO**

In S&P 500

12-SEP-98

Industry:
Telephone

Summary: Frontier, the fifth largest U.S. long-distance carrier, provides long-distance, local telephone and wireless services.

S&P Opinion: Hold (★★★)	Recent Price • 25⅞	Yield • 3.4%
	52 Wk Range • 37⅛-20	12-Mo. P/E • 39.3

Quantitative Evaluations

Outlook
(1 Lowest—5 Highest)
• **2⁻**

Fair Value
• **26¼**

Risk
• **Average**

Earn./Div. Rank
• **B**

Technical Eval.
• **Bullish** since 10/97

Rel. Strength Rank
(1 Lowest—99 Highest)
• **40**

Insider Activity
• **Favorable**

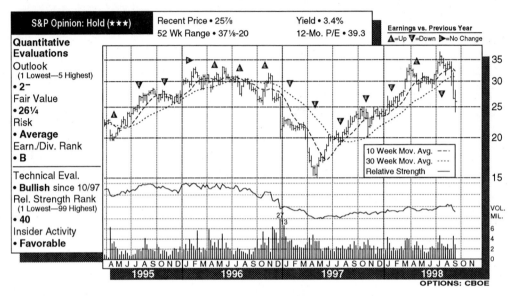

Earnings vs. Previous Year
▲=Up ▼=Down ▶=No Change

10 Week Mov. Avg. ---
30 Week Mov. Avg. ····
Relative Strength —

VOL. MIL.

OPTIONS: CBOE

Overview - 24-JUL-98

Frontier is currently the fifth largest U.S. long-distance carrier, deriving more than two-thirds of its revenues from this segment. The company has eliminated 700 positions as part of a restructuring plan that includes the sale of its prepaid calling card business. In response to this action, FRO recorded a one-time charge of $40.5 million, or $0.24 a share, in the fourth quarter of 1997. Separately, the company is investing $450 million to build a nationwide fiber-optic network. The network, which is expected to be completed in 1999, should reduce FRO's network transmission costs, increase capacity, and improve performance. In the first quarter of 1997, the company recorded $62.8 million in after-tax charges to write off certain network costs. Growth in local and Internet services should supplement mid-single-digit long-distance increases.

Valuation - 24-JUL-98

Future results should benefit from operating efficiencies from line improvements and bundling of services. Many other telecommunications companies are also positioning to build out existing networks to capitalize on the opportunities presented by industry legislation. We see the winners in this industry not only maximizing the efficiencies of a larger network but also driving revenue growth beyond industry averages. We believe the shares will be market performers over the next year, reflecting our bullish stance on the long-distance industry, as well as the company's growth into local and Internet service businesses. Tempering that enthusiasm is the fact that the shares are trading at 33x our 1998 EPS estimate of $1.10, which represents a significant premium to our projected five-year annualized growth rate of 15%.

Key Stock Statistics

S&P EPS Est. 1998	1.10	Tang. Bk. Value/Share	2.49
P/E on S&P Est. 1998	23.6	Beta	0.64
S&P EPS Est. 1999	1.35	Shareholders	30,200
Dividend Rate/Share	0.89	Market cap. (B)	$ 4.4
Shs. outstg. (M)	171.5	Inst. holdings	54%
Avg. daily vol. (M)	0.584		

Value of $10,000 invested 5 years ago: $ 17,884

Fiscal Year Ending Dec. 31

	1998	1997	1996	1995	1994	1993
Revenues (Million $)						
1Q	632.0	573.4	655.1	459.0	241.8	211.0
2Q	648.3	584.7	670.3	506.9	251.8	222.9
3Q	—	601.6	669.1	571.4	243.1	230.5
4Q	—	593.2	581.1	606.4	248.8	242.1
Yr.	—	2,353	2,576	2,144	985.5	906.5
Earnings Per Share ($)						
1Q	0.20	-0.08	0.40	0.32	0.32	0.27
2Q	0.01	0.26	0.42	0.33	0.47	0.29
3Q	E0.35	0.24	0.45	-0.12	0.35	0.28
4Q	E0.29	-0.09	0.06	0.36	0.36	0.38
Yr.	E1.10	0.33	1.32	0.89	1.50	1.21

Next earnings report expected: late October

Dividend Data (Dividends have been paid since 1926.)

Amount ($)	Date Decl.	Ex-Div. Date	Stock of Record	Payment Date
0.223	Dec. 15	Jan. 13	Jan. 15	Feb. 02 '98
0.223	Mar. 23	Apr. 13	Apr. 15	May. 01 '98
0.223	Jun. 15	Jul. 13	Jul. 15	Aug. 03 '98
0.223	Aug. 24	Oct. 13	Oct. 15	Nov. 02 '98

A Division of The McGraw·Hill Companies

STANDARD
&POOR'S
STOCK REPORTS

Frontier Corporation

926H
12-SEP-98

Business Summary - 24-JUL-98

This diversified telecommunications company spans the current landscape by providing local, long-distance and wireless services. It is one of the few companies capable of bundling these services through an end-to-end system architecture. Segment contributions (profits in millions) in 1997 were:

	Revs.	Profits
Long-distance	70%	-$118.1
Local	28%	238.3
Corporate and other	2%	-11.7

Frontier provides long-distance services to customers throughout nearly all of the U.S. and in the U.K. The company also provides local telephone service in Rochester, NY, and adjacent areas, and owns 34 small local telephone companies operating in 13 states. As of December 31, 1997, Frontier had a total of 998,467 access lines.

The company also provides cellular telephone services, primarily in upstate New York and Pennsylvania. Following the July 1994 formation of an equally owned joint venture with Bell Atlantic Mobile (formerly NYNEX Mobile Communications), FRO manages cellular operations covering 2.7 million POPs (adjusted for ownership). During the 1997 first quarter, FRO sold its 69.5%

interest in the South Alabama Cellular Communications Partnership to Alltel, for an undisclosed amount.

In October 1996, Frontier said it would join with Qwest Communications to build the industry's most technologically advanced fiber optic network. The $2 billion network, which should be completed during 1999, will be the largest single fiber build in U.S. telecommunications history. Frontier plans to invest a total of nearly $450 million in the project.

FRO recorded an after-tax charge of $40.5 million, or $0.24 a share, in the 1997 fourth quarter, related to a restructuring effort that includes the divestiture of noncore product lines and businesses. The company recorded $62.8 million of after-tax charges in the first quarter of 1997, related to the writeoff of certain network costs.

The company recently completed the acquisition of GlobalCenter, a leading Internet, data and digital distribution services provider, for 6.4 million shares of FRO stock. The transaction, expected to be accretive to earnings in the first half of 1999 (but dilutive by about $0.05 a share in 1998), will further leverage the company's investment in its SONET fiber-optic network. Separately, Frontier has significantly expanded the number of states in which it provides local service, to 29, and is close to reaching its goal of having local service in 35 states, or about 70% of the population, by the end of 1998.

Per Share Data ($)

(Year Ended Dec. 31)	1997	1996	1995	1994	1993	1992	1991	1990	1989	1988
Tangible Bk. Val.	5.79	3.06	2.13	9.03	7.11	6.89	6.53	6.73	7.78	7.25
Cash Flow	1.59	2.48	1.95	NA	NA	NA	NA	NA	NA	NA
Earnings	0.33	1.32	0.89	1.50	1.21	1.04	1.18	0.86	1.00	1.08
Dividends	0.87	0.85	0.83	0.81	0.79	0.77	0.75	0.73	0.71	0.68
Payout Ratio	NM	64%	93%	54%	65%	74%	64%	85%	71%	63%
Prices - High	25	33⅜	30	25¼	25⅛	17⅞	17	20¾	22⅞	12⅞
- Low	15¼	19⅞	19¼	20¼	17⅜	14⅝	13	12⅜	12⅞	10¼
P/E Ratio - High	76	25	34	17	21	17	14	24	23	12
- Low	46	15	22	13	14	14	11	14	13	9

Income Statement Analysis (Million $)

	1997	1996	1995	1994	1993	1992	1991	1990	1989	1988
Revs.	2,353	2,576	2,144	985	906	804	703	600	562	479
Depr.	207	190	170	117	115	114	97.0	80.0	65.0	62.0
Maint.	Nil	Nil	Nil	NA	NA	NA	NA	NA	NA	NA
Constr. Credits	Nil	Nil	Nil	1.1	1.3	1.3	1.6	2.0	1.9	1.9
Eff. Tax Rate	45%	40%	41%	34%	35%	34%	35%	36%	32%	34%
Net Inc.	54.6	218	145	110	82.7	70.5	73.3	49.7	51.5	50.9

Balance Sheet & Other Fin. Data (Million $)

	1997	1996	1995	1994	1993	1992	1991	1990	1989	1988
Gross Prop.	2,427	2,276	2,097	1,591	1,594	1,615	1,514	1,190	1,025	903
Net Prop.	1,038	971	881	877	942	957	928	767	685	617
Cap. Exp.	277	247	164	87.0	102	124	106	106	105	106
Total Cap.	1,912	1,741	1,551	1,514	1,288	1,269	1,290	981	898	734
Fxd. Chgs. Cov.	6.1	9.8	7.4	3.8	2.7	3.1	3.5	3.2	3.7	4.1
Capitalization:										
LT Debt	931	678	623	579	493	526	591	363	338	244
Pfd.	19.9	22.6	22.8	22.8	22.8	22.8	22.8	22.8	22.8	22.8
Common	950	1,038	889	800	652	599	564	449	395	333
% Return On Revs.	2.3	8.5	6.8	11.2	9.1	8.8	10.4	8.3	9.2	10.6
% Return On Invest. Capital	16.4	26.6	8.9	15.6	10.1	9.3	10.4	8.7	9.4	10.0
% Return On Com. Equity	5.4	22.5	16.0	14.0	13.0	11.6	15.0	11.2	18.9	15.4
% Earn. on Net Prop.	29.1	47.2	41.6	17.5	15.3	14.1	11.7	11.7	12.5	12.5
% LT Debt of Cap.	48.7	39.0	41.1	40.6	42.2	45.8	50.2	43.5	44.8	40.7
Capital. % Pfd.	1.1	1.3	1.5	1.6	2.0	2.0	1.9	2.7	3.0	3.8
Capital. % Common	49.7	59.7	57.4	57.8	55.9	52.2	47.9	53.8	52.2	55.5

Data as orig. reptd.; bef. results of disc. opers. and/or spec. items. Per share data adj. for stk. divs. as of ex-div. date. Bold denotes diluted EPS (FASB 128). E-Estimated. NA-Not Available. NM-Not Meaningful. NR-Not Ranked.

Office—180 S. Clinton Ave., Rochester, NY 14646-0700. **Tel**—(716) 777-1000. **Website**—http://www.frontiercorp.com **Pres & CEO**—J. P. Clayton. **EVP & CFO**—L. L. Massaro. **Treas**—J. Enis. **Secy**—J. S. Trubek. **Investor Contact**—Philip Yawman. **Dirs**—P. C. Barron, R. Cesan, J. P. Clayton, B. Evans Edgerton, J. A. Estrada, M. Faherty, D. E. Gill, A. C. Hasselwander, R. Holland Jr., D. H. McCorkindale, L. J. Thomas.**Transfer Agent & Registrar**—Boston EquiServ Shareowner Services.**Incorporated**—in New York in 1920. **Empl**— 7,444. **S&P Analyst:** Philip D. Wohl

Fruit of the Loom   927H

NYSE Symbol **FTL**

In S&P 500

12-SEP-98   **Industry:** Textiles (Apparel)

Summary: This leading international basic apparel maker emphasizes value-priced branded products for consumers of all ages.

S&P Opinion: Accumulate (★★★★)

Recent Price • 18¼	Yield • Nil
52 Wk Range • 38⅛-18	12-Mo. P/E • NM

Quantitative Evaluations

Outlook (1 Lowest—5 Highest)
• **3+**

Fair Value
• **24¼**

Risk
• **Average**

Earn./Div. Rank
• **C**

Technical Eval.
• **Bearish** since 8/98

Rel. Strength Rank (1 Lowest—99 Highest)
• **11**

Insider Activity
• **NA**

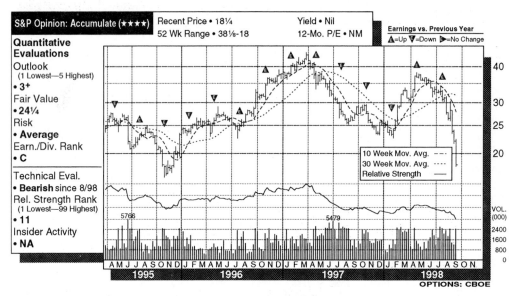

Earnings vs. Previous Year
▲=Up ▼=Down ▶=No Change

10 Week Mov. Avg. - - -
30 Week Mov. Avg. ·······
Relative Strength —

OPTIONS: CBOE

Overview - 20-JUL-98

Sales and earnings in 1997 for this apparel manufacturer were disappointing, reflecting competitive pricing, sluggish consumer demand, nonrecurring charges and excessive inventories. In order to address these issues, FTL accelerated its plan to move sewing operations offshore, but this resulted in severance costs, inefficiencies, high inventory levels, and sporadic plant shutdowns. However, we expect to see 6% - 7% sales growth and significantly better margins in 1998, driven by new products, a focus on higher margin products, reduction of inventory, a lessening of pricing pressures, particularly on T-shirts, and benefits from the completion of the offshore move. Typically, FTL generates strong cash flow in the second half of the year, and has been using the proceeds to repurchase stock.

Valuation - 20-JUL-98

In the first half of 1998, earnings benefited from significant margin expansion and a lower effective tax rate. We expect to see this trend continue in the latter half of the year due to an increase in sales and improved expenses as a result of the manufacturing and distribution move offshore and reduced promotional activity. In February 1998, FTL announced its intention to relocate to the Cayman Islands, a tax haven. If the decision is approved, the company's effective tax rate could be slashed to about 10% beginning in the second half of 1998. Fruit of the Loom, Inc. would be owned by a holding company based in the Cayman Islands, and FTL shareholders would become shareholders of the new entity. With expanding margins and the tax benefits from the proposed reorganization, we believe the stock is undervalued at under 14X our 1998 estimate of $2.46.

Key Stock Statistics

S&P EPS Est. 1998	2.46	Tang. Bk. Value/Share	NM
P/E on S&P Est. 1998	7.4	Beta	0.78
S&P EPS Est. 1999	3.00	Shareholders	1,800
Dividend Rate/Share	Nil	Market cap. (B)	$ 1.2
Shs. outstg. (M)	72.1	Inst. holdings	70%
Avg. daily vol. (M)	0.441		

Value of $10,000 invested 5 years ago: $ 3,753

Fiscal Year Ending Dec. 31

	1998	1997	1996	1995	1994	1993
Revenues (Million $)						
1Q	457.2	501.0	506.2	528.2	438.2	429.0
2Q	628.0	640.7	732.2	724.8	635.2	523.0
3Q	—	569.7	628.0	641.3	640.4	484.2
4Q	—	428.5	581.0	508.8	584.0	448.3
Yr.	—	2,140	2,447	2,403	2,298	1,884
Earnings Per Share ($)						
1Q	**0.43**	0.28	0.16	0.22	0.33	0.58
2Q	**0.90**	0.31	0.63	0.52	0.51	0.77
3Q	**E0.66**	-0.52	0.63	0.32	0.53	0.64
4Q	**E0.47**	-5.66	0.56	-4.05	-0.58	0.81
Yr.	**E2.46**	-5.18	1.98	-2.99	0.79	2.80

Next earnings report expected: late October

Dividend Data

The company does not anticipate paying dividends for the foreseeable future.

Business Summary - 20-JUL-98

Fruit of the Loom (FTL) has recently undergone a metamorphosis from a manufacturing-oriented business to a marketing-driven company. Traditionally, FTL was one of the world's leading apparel manufacturers. The company is a vertically integrated producer of basic, value-priced apparel, emphasizing branded products for consumers ranging from infants to senior citizens. Being vertically integrated means that FTL is one of the few manufacturers in the industry capable of turning yarn into a packaged product all under the same roof, controlling every step of the manufacturing process along the way. As a result, management believes that it is the low cost producer in the industry.

Perhaps best known for its underwear apparel, in which it holds a 34% share of the U.S. men's and boy's market, FTL also offers women's and girls underwear, infant and toddler apparel, activewear for the imprint market, and casualwear. FTL has expanded into the licensed sports apparel segment with its Pro Player and Fans Gear brands, and the jeanswear market through its acquisition of The Gitano Group. The company's easily recognizable portfolio of brand names includes Fruit of the Loom, BVD, Best, Screen Stars, Munsingwear and Wilson.

The company's transition to a marketing focus is continuing in 1998. New advertising campaigns were initially launched in 1996. Miami Dolphins coach Jimmy Johnson was signed as a spokesperson for Pro Player, and Miami's Joe Robbie Stadium was renamed Pro Player Stadium. In addition, the company sponsored CountryFest 97, which, with more than a quarter million fans, was one of the largest events in music history.

In addition to its marketing initiatives, FTL has also focused on controlling expenses, after recording restructuring charges of nearly $300 million in late 1995. A key strategy has been to increase offshore sourcing. At the end of 1996, about 58% of production was done offshore; and the company anticipates that over 95% of all sewing operations will be done offshore in 1998. This should lead to cost savings and margin enhancement in 1998. However, this move has not been smooth, as FTL's manufacturing operations have experienced inefficiencies that resulted in steep margin erosion during 1997.

In February 1998, the company announced its intention to relocate to the Cayman Islands, a tax haven. If the decision is approved, FTL's effective tax rate could be slashed to about 10% beginning in the second half of 1998. Shareholders will vote on the matter early in the third quarter of 1998. Fruit of the Loom, Inc. would become owned by a holding company based in the Cayman Islands, and FTL shareholders would become shareholders of the new entity.

Per Share Data ($)

(Year Ended Dec. 31)	1997	1996	1995	1994	1993	1992	1991	1990	1989	1988
Tangible Bk. Val.	NM	4.18	1.64	2.11	2.00	0.59	-1.97	-7.18	-9.04	-10.57
Cash Flow	-3.08	4.02	-0.77	2.67	4.25	3.71	2.81	2.47	2.27	2.16
Earnings	-5.18	1.98	-2.99	0.79	2.80	2.48	1.60	1.25	1.17	1.19
Dividends	Nil	Nil	Nil	Nil	Nil	Nil	Nil	Nil	Nil	Nil
Payout Ratio	Nil	Nil	Nil	Nil	Nil	Nil	Nil	Nil	Nil	Nil
Prices - High	44⅞	39	27¾	33	49¼	49⅝	28	15⅜	16	7⅝
- Low	23⅛	22½	16½	23	22⅞	26½	7⅝	6⅛	6⅛	4¼
P/E Ratio - High	NM	20	NM	42	18	20	18	12	14	6
- Low	NM	11	NM	29	8	11	5	5	5	4

Income Statement Analysis (Million $)

	1997	1996	1995	1994	1993	1992	1991	1990	1989	1988
Revs.	2,140	2,447	2,403	2,298	1,884	1,855	1,628	1,427	1,321	1,005
Oper. Inc.	-282	481	218	436	492	503	403	376	333	291
Depr.	154	156	169	143	110	93.2	83.8	76.0	68.1	65.9
Int. Exp.	84.7	104	117	104	73.0	82.0	115	129	124	105
Pretax Inc.	-451	185	-246	134	367	320	201	149	131	95.0
Eff. Tax Rate	NM	18%	NM	548%	42%	41%	45%	48%	45%	23%
Net Inc.	-384	151	-226	60.0	213	189	111	77.0	72.0	73.0

Balance Sheet & Other Fin. Data (Million $)

	1997	1996	1995	1994	1993	1992	1991	1990	1989	1988
Cash	16.1	18.7	26.5	49.4	74.2	57.4	31.4	59.6	16.7	15.4
Curr. Assets	1,016	842	1,060	1,077	943	744	656	629	453	411
Total Assets	2,483	2,547	2,920	3,164	2,734	2,282	2,115	2,151	1,878	1,830
Curr. Liab.	525	327	304	332	251	434	370	495	350	467
LT Debt	1,193	867	1,427	1,440	1,194	756	811	1,014	988	905
Common Eqty.	422	1,065	896	1,126	1,047	855	689	418	327	258
Total Cap.	1,615	1,949	2,323	2,609	2,292	1,611	1,500	1,432	1,445	1,290
Cap. Exp.	55.4	44.5	126	246	263	189	74.0	158	85.0	160
Cash Flow	-230	307	-58.3	203	323	282	195	153	140	133
Curr. Ratio	1.9	2.6	3.5	3.2	3.8	1.7	1.8	1.3	1.3	0.9
% LT Debt of Cap.	73.9	44.4	61.4	55.2	52.1	46.9	54.1	70.8	68.4	70.1
% Net Inc.of Revs.	NM	6.2	NM	2.6	11.3	10.2	6.8	5.4	5.5	7.3
% Ret. on Assets	NM	5.5	NM	2.0	8.5	8.5	4.7	3.8	3.9	4.2
% Ret. on Equity	NM	15.4	NM	5.5	22.4	24.3	18.6	20.7	24.6	32.4

Data as orig. reptd.; bef. results of disc. opers. and/or spec. items. Per share data adj. for stk. divs. as of ex-div. date. Bold denotes diluted EPS (FASB 128). E-Estimated. NA-Not Available. NM-Not Meaningful. NR-Not Ranked.

Office—233 S. Wacker Dr., 5000 Sears Tower, Chicago, IL 60606. **Tel**—(312) 876-1724. **Website**—http://www.fruit.com **Chrmn & CEO**—W. Farley. **Pres & COO**—R. C. Lappin. **SEVP & CFO**—L. K. Switzer. **Investor Contact**—Mark A. Steinkrauss (312-993-1889). **Dirs**—O. A. Al Askari, D. S. Bookshester, W. Farley, J. B. Holland, L. W. Jennings, H. A. Johnson, R. C. Lappin, A. L. Weil, B. G. Wolfson. **Incorporated**—in Delaware in 1985. **Empl**— 28,500. **S&P Analyst:** Kathleen J. Fraser

STANDARD &POOR'S
STOCK REPORTS

Gannett Co.

936B

NYSE Symbol **GCI**

In S&P 500

12-SEP-98

Industry:
Publishing (Newspapers)

Summary: This leading newspaper publisher also owns TV stations and cable television systems, and produces syndicated TV programming.

S&P Opinion: Hold (★★★)	Recent Price • 58	Yield • 1.4%
	52 Wk Range • 75⅛-49	12-Mo. P/E • 17.5

Quantitative Evaluations

Outlook
(1 Lowest—5 Highest)
• **3**

Fair Value
• **59⅜**

Risk
• **Low**

Earn./Div. Rank
• **A**

Technical Eval.
• **NA**

Rel. Strength Rank
(1 Lowest—99 Highest)
• **65**

Insider Activity
• **Neutral**

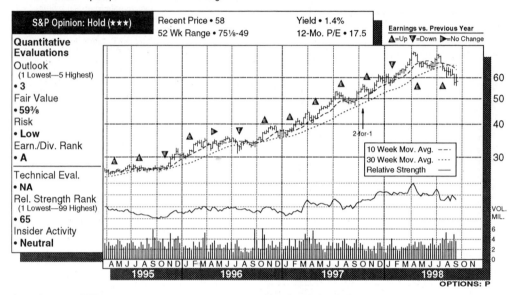

Earnings vs. Previous Year
▲=Up ▼=Down ▶=No Change

10 Week Mov. Avg. – – –
30 Week Mov. Avg. ·······
Relative Strength —

2-for-1

VOL.
MIL.

OPTIONS: P

Overview - 11-JUN-98

Revenues from continuing operations should increase about 8% in 1998 after a rise of 7% in 1997, aided by favorable contributions from each major business segment. Demand for newspaper and television advertising will remain strong. Year-to-year comparisons will be affected by several station-trading transactions and acquisitions. Operating margins will narrow in 1998, due to moderately higher newsprint prices, versus 15% lower prices in 1997. The impact will be partly mitigated by operating efficiencies, and improving profitability in Detroit. GCI plans to pay down debt by over $400 million annually, thereby cutting interest expense by roughly $40 million each year. We expect earnings rise 14% in 1998, to $2.85, before a $0.64 Q1 gain from sales of radio stations and the alarm security business.

Valuation - 11-JUN-98

The shares, recently selling some 10% below their all-time high, are priced at 24X the $2.85 EPS we are projecting for 1998, excluding a $0.64 nonrecurring gain. Year-to-date in 1998, GCI has performed about in line with other newspaper companies and the general market. For these reasons, we advise against buying more shares at present, but we consider GCI a good foundation stock for the long-term investor, given the favorable outlook for the company's operations. The December 1995 purchase of Multimedia, Inc. boosted GCI's broadcast media properties and gave it entry into cable operations, television programming and syndication. Multimedia's assets provide needed diversity and a more profitable and faster-growing business mix. The purchase also gives GCI operations some insulation from the cyclical swings inherent in the newspaper business. We expect earnings gains to average in the mid teens over the next several years.

Key Stock Statistics

S&P EPS Est. 1998	3.49	Tang. Bk. Value/Share	0.29
P/E on S&P Est. 1998	16.6	Beta	0.75
S&P EPS Est. 1999	3.30	Shareholders	14,000
Dividend Rate/Share	0.80	Market cap. (B)	$ 16.5
Shs. outstg. (M)	284.6	Inst. holdings	72%
Avg. daily vol. (M)	0.823		

Value of $10,000 invested 5 years ago: $ 25,608

Fiscal Year Ending Dec. 31

	1998	1997	1996	1995	1994	1993
Revenues (Million $)						
1Q	1,200	1,077	1,024	913.8	876.6	844.7
2Q	1,304	1,188	1,109	1,014	966.9	937.8
3Q	—	1,146	1,093	932.3	932.4	876.5
4Q	—	1,319	1,195	1,147	1,049	982.6
Yr.	—	4,729	4,421	4,007	3,825	3,642
Earnings Per Share ($)						
1Q	**1.20**	**0.48**	0.31	0.31	0.27	0.23
2Q	**0.78**	**0.68**	0.49	0.50	0.45	0.39
3Q	**E0.61**	**0.53**	0.40	0.34	0.37	0.30
4Q	**E0.88**	**0.80**	1.02	0.56	0.54	0.44
Yr.	**E3.49**	**2.50**	2.21	1.71	1.61	1.36

Next earnings report expected: mid October

Dividend Data (Dividends have been paid since 1929.)

Amount ($)	Date Decl.	Ex-Div. Date	Stock of Record	Payment Date
0.190	Oct. 21	Dec. 10	Dec. 12	Jan. 02 '98
0.190	Feb. 24	Mar. 04	Mar. 06	Apr. 01 '98
0.190	Apr. 28	Jun. 03	Jun. 05	Jul. 01 '98
0.200	Aug. 18	Sep. 09	Sep. 11	Oct. 01 '98

*A Division of The **McGraw·Hill** Companies*

Business Summary - 11-JUN-98

Extra! Extra! Read all about it! The nation's largest newspaper publisher is alive and well two years after swallowing whole a major multimedia company, namely Multimedia, Inc. Gannett substantially boosted its presence in broadcasting and newspapers with that December 1995 purchase which included 11 dailies and 49 nondaily newspapers, five TV stations, two radio stations, cable TV systems now serving 478,000 subscribers, security monitoring services, and a TV programming and syndication business.

That feeding frenzy cost Gannett about $2.24 billion ($1.71 billion in cash plus the assumption of $530 million of Multimedia's old outstanding debts). GCI's long-term debt (due after one year) shot up to nearly $2.8 billion, from less than $800 million at the end of 1995. Long term debt as a percentage of capital mushroomed to an unpalatable 53%, a leverage ratio much too high for the American stomach! Big appetite or not, Gannett needed to slim down, so on August 22, 1996, it shed its outdoor advertising business (billboards, bus shelters, stuff like that). Gannett Outdoor was sold for $713 million in cash, with most of the net proceeds earmarked to pay down debt. Gannett had said earlier that it would slim its debt load down at the rate of at least $400 million a year.

Multimedia Entertainment, once the undisputed king

of the talk show producers (Donahue, Sally Jessy Raphael, Rush Limbaugh, Susan Powter, Jerry Springer, Dennis Prager), has in recent years seen its portion of the talk show pie nibbled away by hungry competitors. The company fought back by adding new onscreen talent of its own, such as Powter, Springer and Prager. Nevertheless, in order to raise money and ease the strain on the resources, Gannett sold Sally Jessy Raphael, Jerry Springer, Pat Bullard and several international programs to MCA in December 1996 for $40-$45 million.

Newspaper operations (which accounted for 80% of Gannett's total revenues in 1997 and 73% of operating income) comprise 89 daily newspapers, including USA TODAY, with a total average daily circulation of about 6.7 million copies in 1997, making it the largest newspaper publisher in the U.S. The company also publishes a number of nondaily local publications and USA WEEKEND, a weekend newspaper magazine. Papers are published in 38 states, as well as Guam and the U.S. Virgin Islands.

Broadcasting (15% and 24%) is represented by 20 TV stations and 5 radio stations. The five radio stations were sold in January 1998, however. Other businesses (5% and 3%) consisted of the cable television operations acquired with Multimedia, and the alarm security business. In March 1998, GCI sold the alarm security business.

Per Share Data ($)

(Year Ended Dec. 31)	1997	1996	1995	1994	1993	1992	1991	1990	1989	1988
Tangible Bk. Val.	NM	NM	NM	1.25	1.39	0.74	0.46	1.90	1.61	0.81
Cash Flow	3.55	4.37	2.45	2.33	2.08	1.89	1.67	1.78	1.82	1.68
Earnings	2.50	2.21	1.71	1.61	1.36	1.20	1.00	1.18	1.24	1.13
Dividends	0.74	0.71	0.69	0.67	0.65	0.63	0.62	0.60	0.56	0.51
Payout Ratio	30%	32%	40%	41%	48%	53%	59%	51%	45%	45%
Prices - High	61¾	39⅜	32½	29½	29⅛	27	23½	22¼	25	20
- Low	35¾	29½	24¾	23⅛	23⅜	20⅝	17⅝	14¾	17¼	14⅝
P/E Ratio - High	25	18	19	18	21	23	24	19	20	18
- Low	14	13	15	14	17	17	18	13	14	13

Income Statement Analysis (Million $)

	1997	1996	1995	1994	1993	1992	1991	1990	1989	1988
Revs.	4,729	4,421	4,007	3,825	3,642	3,469	3,382	3,442	3,518	3,314
Oper. Inc.	1,617	1,354	1,062	1,022	924	815	759	873	947	865
Depr.	301	193	210	209	210	198	200	194	190	177
Int. Exp.	98.2	136	52.2	46.2	51.5	53.3	76.0	77.1	93.6	91.5
Pretax Inc.	1,209	1,087	803	782	668	574	503	618	648	607
Eff. Tax Rate	41%	43%	41%	47%	41%	40%	40%	39%	39%	40%
Net Inc.	713	624	477	465	398	346	302	377	398	364

Balance Sheet & Other Fin. Data (Million $)

	1997	1996	1995	1994	1993	1992	1991	1990	1989	1988
Cash	45.1	27.0	47.0	44.3	75.5	73.3	70.7	56.2	55.6	48.7
Curr. Assets	885	767	854	651	758	631	636	669	671	665
Total Assets	6,890	6,350	6,504	3,707	3,824	3,609	3,684	3,826	3,783	3,793
Curr. Liab.	768	719	813	527	455	432	444	500	478	501
LT Debt	1,741	1,880	2,768	767	851	1,081	1,335	849	922	1,135
Common Eqty.	3,480	2,931	2,146	1,822	1,908	1,580	1,539	2,063	1,996	1,786
Total Cap.	5,623	4,811	5,241	2,754	2,964	2,754	3,129	3,177	3,167	3,148
Cap. Exp.	221	260	184	151	182	173	213	205	210	209
Cash Flow	1,014	1,230	687	674	607	544	501	571	588	542
Curr. Ratio	1.2	1.1	1.1	1.2	1.7	1.5	1.4	1.3	1.4	1.3
% LT Debt of Cap.	30.9	39.0	52.8	27.9	28.7	39.2	42.7	26.7	29.1	36.0
% Net Inc.of Revs.	15.1	14.1	11.9	12.2	10.9	10.0	8.9	11.0	11.3	11.0
% Ret. on Assets	10.8	9.7	9.3	12.7	10.6	9.5	8.4	10.0	10.5	10.0
% Ret. on Equity	22.2	24.6	24.1	25.6	22.6	22.1	17.7	18.7	21.0	21.5

Data as orig. reptd.; bef. results of disc. opers. and/or spec. items. Per share data adj. for stk. divs. as of ex-div. date. Bold denotes diluted EPS (FASB 128). E-Estimated. NA-Not Available. NM-Not Meaningful. NR-Not Ranked.

Office—1100 Wilson Blvd., Arlington, VA 22234. **Tel**—(703) 284-6000. **Website**—http://www.gannett.com **Chrmn, Pres & CEO**—J. J. Curley. **Vice Chrmn & Pres**—D. H. McCorkindale. **EVP-CFO**—L. F. Miller**SVP & Secy**—T. L. Chapple. **SVP & Treas**—J. L. Thomas. **VP-Investor Contact**—Gracia Martore (703-284-6918). **Dirs**—M. A. Brockaw, P. B. Clark, J. J. Curley, S. T. K. Ho, D. Lewis, J. P. Louis, D. H. McCorkindale, T. A. Reynolds Jr, K. H. Williams. **Transfer Agent & Registrar**—Norwest Bank Minnesota. **Incorporated**—in New York in 1923; reincorporated in Delaware in 1972. **Empl**—39,000. **S&P Analyst:** William H. Donald

12-SEP-98

Industry: Retail (Special-ty-Apparel)

Summary: This specialty apparel retailer operates The Gap Stores, Banana Republic, and Old Navy Clothing Co., offering casual clothing to upper, moderate and value-oriented market segments.

S&P Opinion: Hold (★★★)		
Recent Price • 59¾	Yield • 0.3%	
52 Wk Range • 68-32	12-Mo. P/E • 37.3	

Earnings vs. Previous Year
▲=Up ▼=Down ▶=No Change

Quantitative Evaluations

Outlook
(1 Lowest—5 Highest)
• **2+**

Fair Value
• **53¾**

Risk
• **Average**

Earn./Div. Rank
• **A+**

Technical Eval.
• **Bullish** since 2/97

Rel. Strength Rank
(1 Lowest—99 Highest)
• **92**

Insider Activity
• **Neutral**

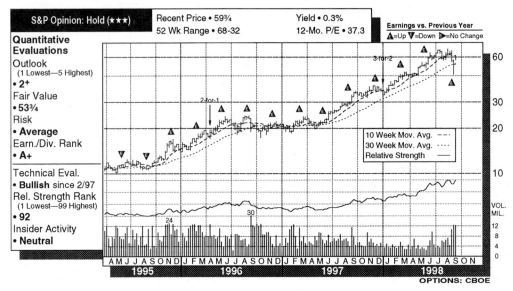

10 Week Mov. Avg. ----
30 Week Mov. Avg. ·······
Relative Strength ——

OPTIONS: CBOE

Overview - 06-JUL-98

Same-store sales should advance in the 3% range in FY 99 (Jan.), and with a 16% increase in square foot-age and strong sales gains at Old Navy stores, total sales could increase 14%. Gross margins should widen, with improved inventory management resulting in a bet-ter mix of fashion and basic merchandise. This should boost margins overall. Expense ratios should increase, reflecting higher depreciation charges from new larger stores. Operating income should increase 14%. The ag-gressive rollout of Old Navy Clothing Co. value priced stores enhances the company's earnings prospects. However, since Old Navy operates with lower margins, as it contributes a larger portion of Gap's business it will lower overall company gross margins. International expansion should also aid long-term growth. The com-pany has taken on a moderate amount of long term debt (about 31% of equity) to fund its unit expansion and its 30 million common share repurchase program, of which it has completed 57%. The company com-pleted a 3-for-2 stock split in December 1997.

Valuation - 06-JUL-98

The shares of this fast growing, well managed retailer should be held for capital appreciation. The stock's pre-mium valuation is justified given Gap's strong consumer franchise and healthy financial performance, but the shares appear fairly valued at these levels. In a se-verely overstored retail environment, GPS continues to gain market share. The company's aggressive expan-sion of 300 new stores in FY 99, a new Banana Repub-lic catalog and expansion of its Gap on-line business bode well for future earnings gains. We believe the company's core growth rate is about 16% to 19%.

Key Stock Statistics

S&P EPS Est. 1999	1.85	Tang. Bk. Value/Share	4.31
P/E on S&P Est. 1999	32.3	Beta	0.83
S&P EPS Est. 2000	2.15	Shareholders	6,800
Dividend Rate/Share	0.20	Market cap. (B)	$ 23.5
Shs. outstg. (M)	392.8	Inst. holdings	47%
Avg. daily vol. (M)	2.329		

Value of $10,000 invested 5 years ago: $ 57,330

Fiscal Year Ending Jan. 31

	1999	1998	1997	1996	1995	1994
Revenues (Million $)						
1Q	1,720	1,231	1,113	848.7	752.0	643.6
2Q	1,905	1,345	1,120	868.5	773.1	693.2
3Q	—	1,766	1,383	1,156	988.4	898.7
4Q	—	2,165	1,668	1,522	1,210	1,060
Yr.	—	6,508	5,284	4,395	3,723	3,296
Earnings Per Share ($)						
1Q	**0.34**	**0.20**	0.19	0.12	0.15	0.10
2Q	**0.34**	**0.17**	0.15	0.07	0.10	0.07
3Q	E0.51	**0.40**	0.32	0.27	0.21	0.18
4Q	E0.65	**0.53**	0.41	0.36	0.27	0.25
Yr.	E1.85	**1.30**	1.07	0.82	0.73	0.59

Next earnings report expected: mid November

Dividend Data (Dividends have been paid since 1976.)

Amount ($)	Date Decl.	Ex-Div. Date	Stock of Record	Payment Date
3-for-2	Nov. 24	Dec. 23	Dec. 08	Dec. 22 '97
0.050	Feb. 24	Mar. 04	Mar. 06	Mar. 16 '98
0.050	May. 19	Jun. 03	Jun. 05	Jun. 15 '98
0.050	Sep. 09	Sep. 17	Sep. 21	Oct. 01 '98

The Gap, Inc.

Business Summary - 06-JUL-98

The Gap, Inc. is synonymous with casual clothing for women, men and children, sold through its Gap, GapKids, babyGap, Banana Republic and Old Navy Clothing Co. concepts. Since its inception in 1969, the company has built retail concepts into brand names. At May 2, 1998, it operated 2,196 stores (1,040 Gap, 265 Banana Republic, 586 GapKids and 305 Old Navy stores).

The Gap format is the company's original concept, started in 1969 in San Francisco. At that time, jeans dominated the stores. The company still emphasizes denim clothing but khakis and other casual staples are now important product categories. With higher margins than staple items, the merchandising mix has shifted toward the addition of fashion items, such as skirts and dresses, and accessories. Complementary product lines, such as shoes and personal care products, have also been added to the store assortment.

Banana Republic was acquired in 1983, with two stores and a mail order catalog. The company expanded its merchandise to feature trendy travel and safari clothing and accessories in a theatrical environment, including jeeps and banana trees. By 1988, the safari look was stale. The catalog was discontinued, and Banana developed a new merchandising strategy offering high quality sophisticated sportswear for men and women.

Targeting low-income customers, The Old Navy Clothing Co. is Gap's fastest growing division. Almost double the size of Gap stores, at 15,000 sq. ft., these stores sell clothing for the entire family. In an attempt to make shopping more fun and to differentiate these stores from others, old cars and gumball machines have been added to the merchandise display. Many Old Navy units also have a place to grab a snack or sit down to eat a light meal.

GapKids was introduced in 1986 to provide parents and gift-givers well-designed clothing for children from two to twelve. The babyGap line of newborn, infant and toddler clothing is available in virtually all GapKids stores.

Gap has moved across the Atlantic with stores in the U.K. and France, and also operates in Japan. Ninety-one stores are located in Canada.

The Gap, Inc. continually tests new products and new product categories in its stores. The company has its own product development and design teams. Gap employs more than 1,000 suppliers located domestically and overseas to manufacture goods to the company's specifications.

Per Share Data ($)										
(Year Ended Jan. 31)	**1998**	**1997**	**1996**	**1995**	**1994**	**1993**	**1992**	**1991**	**1990**	**1989**
Tangible Bk. Val.	4.03	4.02	3.80	3.17	2.59	2.05	1.59	1.05	0.76	0.66
Cash Flow	1.96	1.57	1.27	1.12	0.87	0.71	0.70	0.46	0.32	0.24
Earnings	1.30	1.07	0.82	0.73	0.59	0.49	0.54	0.34	0.23	0.17
Dividends	0.20	0.20	0.16	0.15	0.13	0.11	0.10	0.07	0.06	0.04
Payout Ratio	15%	19%	20%	21%	21%	22%	19%	22%	24%	25%
Cal. Yrs.	1997	1996	1995	1994	1993	1992	1991	1990	1989	1988
Prices - High	38 5/8	24 3/8	17	16 1/2	19 3/4	19 3/4	18 3/4	6	5 1/8	3 1/2
- Low	18 5/8	14	9 7/8	9 5/8	9 3/8	9 3/8	5 1/2	3 1/4	3	1 9/16
P/E Ratio - High	30	23	21	22	40	40	35	18	22	21
- Low	14	13	12	13	19	19	10	10	13	9
Income Statement Analysis (Million $)										
Revs.	6,508	5,284	4,395	3,723	3,296	2,960	2,519	1,934	1,587	1,252
Oper. Inc.	1,121	944	767	687	547	438	444	290	214	167
Depr.	270	215	197	168	122	94.2	70.1	51.3	37.9	31.4
Int. Exp.	Nil	NA	NA	NA	0.8	3.8	3.5	1.4	2.8	3.4
Pretax Inc.	854	749	585	529	425	340	371	237	163	126
Eff. Tax Rate	38%	39%	40%	40%	39%	38%	38%	39%	40%	41%
Net Inc.	534	453	354	320	258	211	230	145	98.0	74.0
Balance Sheet & Other Fin. Data (Million $)										
Cash	913	622	669	588	544	243	193	67.0	39.0	46.0
Curr. Assets	1,831	1,329	1,280	1,056	956	691	566	365	317	258
Total Assets	3,338	2,627	2,343	2,004	1,763	1,379	1,147	777	579	481
Curr. Liab.	992	775	552	500	462	335	330	264	187	152
LT Debt	496	Nil	Nil	Nil	75.0	75.0	77.5	5.0	17.5	20.0
Common Eqty.	1,584	1,654	1,640	1,375	1,126	888	678	466	338	276
Total Cap.	2,080	1,654	1,640	1,375	1,201	963	755	471	355	296
Cap. Exp.	466	372	302	233	223	211	245	208	93.0	67.0
Cash Flow	804	668	551	488	380	305	300	196	136	106
Curr. Ratio	1.8	1.7	2.3	2.1	2.1	2.1	1.7	1.4	1.7	1.7
% LT Debt of Cap.	23.8	Nil	Nil	Nil	6.2	7.8	10.3	1.1	4.9	6.7
% Net Inc.of Revs.	8.2	8.6	8.1	8.6	7.8	7.1	9.1	7.5	6.2	5.9
% Ret. on Assets	17.9	18.2	16.3	17.0	16.4	16.6	23.8	21.3	18.4	16.4
% Ret. on Equity	33.0	27.5	23.5	25.6	25.6	26.8	40.1	35.9	31.8	27.3

Data as orig. reptd.; bef. results of disc. opers. and/or spec. items. Per share data adj. for stk. divs. as of ex-div. date. Bold denotes diluted EPS (FASB 128). E-Estimated. NA-Not Available. NM-Not Meaningful. NR-Not Ranked.

Office—One Harrison St., San Francisco, CA 94105. **Tel**—(415) 952-4400. **Website**—http://www.gap.com **Chrmn**—D. G. Fisher. **Pres & CEO**—M. S. Drexler. **EVP & COO**— R. J. Fisher. **SVP, CFO & Investor Contact**—Warren R. Hashagen. **Secy**—Anne B. Gust. **Dirs**—A. D. P. Bellamy, J. G. Bowes, M. S. Drexler, D. F. Fisher, D. G. Fisher, R. J. Fisher, L. J. Fjeldstad, W. A. Hasler, J. M. Lillie, C. R. Schwab, B. Walker Jr., S. S. Zyman.**Transfer Agent & Registrar**—Harris Trust Co. of California, Chicago. **Incorporated**—in California in 1969. **Empl**— 81,000. **S&P Analyst:** Karen J. Sack, CFA

12-SEP-98

Industry: Computers (Hardware)

Summary: Gateway 2000 is a leading direct marketer of personal computers in the U.S.

S&P Opinion: Accumulate (★★★★)

| Recent Price • 49¾ | Yield • Nil |
| 52 Wk Range • 68¾-25 | 12-Mo. P/E • 64.6 |

Quantitative Evaluations

Outlook
(1 Lowest—5 Highest)
• **4⁻**

Fair Value
• **61¼**

Risk
• **High**

Earn./Div. Rank
• **NR**

Technical Eval.
• **NA**

Rel. Strength Rank
(1 Lowest—99 Highest)
• **72**

Insider Activity
• **Neutral**

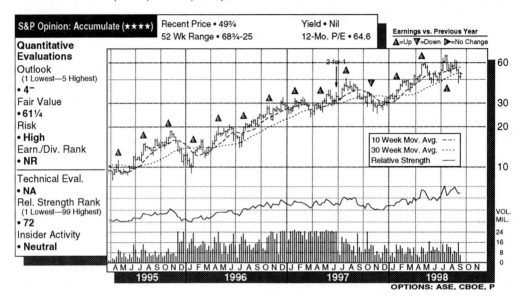

Earnings vs. Previous Year
▲=Up ▼=Down ▷=No Change

10 Week Mov. Avg. ---
30 Week Mov. Avg. ·····
Relative Strength ——

OPTIONS: ASE, CBOE, P

Overview - 27-JUL-98

Revenues should grow over 20% in 1998, on strong underlying PC unit demand and new products, offset somewhat by lower average selling prices in a competitive environment. Demand for PCs is being driven by falling prices, and by upgrades reflecting the new release of Windows NT software and Windows 98 from Microsoft and new Intel microprocessors. Furthermore, GTW's new Your:);Ware selling program, in which software, Internet service and financing can be bundled with a PC purchase, is helping the company to broaden its addressable market. We believe that gross margins will remain in the 19% to 20% range, helped in part by this bundling approach, but this will likely be at least partly offset by the company's greater spending in the areas of marketing and support staff. We project 1998 EPS of $2.15, marking a sharp increase from 1997's $0.70, when results suffered from inventory issues and execution problems that led to third quarter charges of $0.61 a share.

Valuation - 27-JUL-98

We continue to recommend accumulating the shares. GTW has a strong niche position in the PC industry, and enjoys the inherent advantages of the direct business model. Although the company posted disappointing earnings in the 1997 second half, as it invested aggressively in infrastructure to bring its direct business model to the next level, its PC shipment volumes continue to outpace the industry average, as it boosts market share. In addition, the acquisition of Advanced Logic Research broadens GTW's product line to the market for high-end servers, which also now includes workstations. We believe that GTW's solid market position and new avenues of growth should lead to future EPS surprises.

Key Stock Statistics

S&P EPS Est. 1998	2.15	Tang. Bk. Value/Share	6.60
P/E on S&P Est. 1998	23.1	Beta	NA
S&P EPS Est. 1999	2.80	Shareholders	2,200
Dividend Rate/Share	Nil	Market cap. (B)	$ 7.7
Shs. outstg. (M)	155.8	Inst. holdings	28%
Avg. daily vol. (M)	2.010		

Value of $10,000 invested 5 years ago: NA

Fiscal Year Ending Dec. 31

	1998	1997	1996	1995	1994	1993
Revenues (Million $)						
1Q	1,728	1,418	1,142	776.0	615.9	421.0
2Q	1,619	1,393	1,137	766.4	616.5	364.7
3Q	—	1,505	1,203	888.7	644.4	400.1
4Q	—	1,977	1,553	1,245	824.3	545.9
Yr.	—	6,294	5,035	3,676	2,701	1,732
Earnings Per Share ($)						
1Q	0.48	0.43	0.33	0.24	0.16	0.18
2Q	0.38	0.36	0.33	0.22	0.03	0.14
3Q	E0.49	-0.68	0.39	0.26	0.17	0.17
4Q	E0.80	0.59	0.56	0.37	0.25	0.21
Yr.	E2.15	0.70	1.60	1.09	0.61	0.70

Next earnings report expected: late October

Dividend Data

No cash dividends have been paid. The shares were split two for one in June 1997.

A Division of The McGraw·Hill Companies

Gateway 2000, Inc.

943G
12-SEP-98

Business Summary - 27-JUL-98

Gateway is among the largest PC (personal computer) suppliers in the U.S. Like Dell Computer, the company sells directly to users, primarily targeting experienced PC users willing to buy a computer unseen, provided that the price is right. GTW is also progressing in efforts to increase major account sales, which has helped it boost market share over the past year. Its share of the U.S. market for PCs in 1997 rose to 7% (according to market researcher Dataquest), on a 35% increase in its U.S. PC shipments, versus 21% for the industry on average. GTW has a smaller share of the global market, but plans to expand its international operations. The U.S. accounted for about 86% of 1997 revenues.

During 1997, the company extended its traditional business model. Instead of relying on customers happy buying PCs "unseen", by the end of 1997, GTW had opened 37 Gateway Country stores in which customers could "test drive" PCs in the store. By the end of 1998, the company plans to double that figure. Also, in 1997, GTW acquired Advanced Logic Research, giving it access to the server market, thereby enabling the company access to larger customers that required a broad product offering in the high-end computing space.

GTW retains a strong niche position with PC enthusiasts. It advertises mainly through computer trade publications, and maintains a close relationship with customers to achieve greater responsiveness and better service. Customers can have their PCs custom-configured by GTW, with a choice of microprocessors of varying clock speeds, memory and storage capacities, as well as other options. GTW estimates that over 50% of its business comes from repeat buyers, or based on word-of-mouth from previous buyers.

The company believes that the direct selling business model, versus indirect (or using the retail channel), helps promote customer loyalty and brand awareness. Other advantages of the direct model include the ability to offer product at a more competitive price, since the vendor is able to avoid the traditional markups and the inventory and occupancy costs associated with traditional retail channels; in addition, the risk of inventory obsolescence is reduced.

GTW also stands out as one of the first PC makers to incorporate Intel's latest and greatest microprocessor into its product line. In fact, GTW's recently announced new additions to its product line based on Intel's latest processor, the Pentium II, the same day that Intel launched the new processor.

In April 1998, GTW changed its name from Gateway 2000 to Gateway (its legal name remains Gateway 2000). This initiative was part of a new branding campaign under which GTW also changed its logo to one that combines its trademark black-and-white spotted cow design with the Gateway name in green, to represent growth.

Per Share Data ($)

(Year Ended Dec. 31)	1997	1996	1995	1994	1993	1992	1991	1990	1989	1988
Tangible Bk. Val.	5.50	5.32	3.73	2.60	1.94	1.15	NA	NA	NA	NA
Cash Flow	1.26	2.00	1.33	0.72	0.76	0.55	NA	NA	NA	NA
Earnings	0.70	1.60	1.09	0.61	0.70	0.52	NA	NA	NA	NA
Dividends	Nil	Nil	Nil	Nil	Nil	Nil	Nil	Nil	Nil	Nil
Payout Ratio	Nil	Nil	Nil	Nil	Nil	Nil	Nil	Nil	Nil	Nil
Prices - High	46¼	33⅛	18¾	12⅜	10¾	NA	NA	NA	NA	NA
- Low	23⅝	9	8	4⅝	7½	NA	NA	NA	NA	NA
P/E Ratio - High	66	21	17	20	15	NA	NA	NA	NA	NA
- Low	34	6	7	8	11	NA	NA	NA	NA	NA

Income Statement Analysis (Million $)

	1997	1996	1995	1994	1993	1992	1991	1990	1989	1988
Revs.	6,294	5,035	3,676	2,701	1,732	1,107	NA	NA	NA	NA
Oper. Inc.	377	418	287	159	157	108	NA	NA	NA	NA
Depr.	86.8	61.8	38.1	18.0	8.0	4.9	NA	NA	NA	NA
Int. Exp.	NA	Nil	Nil	NA	NA	NA	NA	NA	NA	NA
Pretax Inc.	204	383	262	146	154	106	NA	NA	NA	NA
Eff. Tax Rate	46%	35%	34%	34%	35%	34%	NA	NA	NA	NA
Net Inc.	110	251	173	96.0	100	70.0	NA	NA	NA	NA

Balance Sheet & Other Fin. Data (Million $)

	1997	1996	1995	1994	1993	1992	1991	1990	1989	1988
Cash	594	516	169	244	132	NA	NA	NA	NA	NA
Curr. Assets	1,545	1,318	866	659	501	247	NA	NA	NA	NA
Total Assets	2,039	1,673	1,124	771	564	269	NA	NA	NA	NA
Curr. Liab.	1,004	800	525	349	255	137	NA	NA	NA	NA
LT Debt	7.2	7.2	10.8	27.1	29.1	11.8	NA	NA	NA	NA
Common Eqty.	930	816	555	376	280	129	NA	NA	NA	NA
Total Cap.	937	823	573	410	309	143	NA	NA	NA	NA
Cap. Exp.	162	86.0	77.5	29.0	35.9	14.3	NA	NA	NA	NA
Cash Flow	197	312	211	114	108	75.0	NA	NA	NA	NA
Curr. Ratio	1.5	1.6	1.6	1.9	2.0	1.8	NA	NA	NA	NA
% LT Debt of Cap.	0.8	0.9	1.9	6.7	9.4	9.6	NA	NA	NA	NA
% Net Inc.of Revs.	1.7	5.0	4.7	3.6	5.8	6.3	NA	NA	NA	NA
% Ret. on Assets	NA	17.9	18.3	14.4	24.0	35.4	NA	NA	NA	NA
% Ret. on Equity	NA	36.6	37.2	29.3	48.8	72.5	NA	NA	NA	NA

Data as orig. reptd.; bef. results of disc. opers. and/or spec. items. Per share data adj. for stk. divs. as of ex-div. date. Bold denotes diluted EPS (FASB 128). E-Estimated. NA-Not Available. NM-Not Meaningful. NR-Not Ranked.

Office—610 Gateway Drive, N. Sioux City, SD 57049-2000. **Tel**—(605) 232-2000.**Website**—http://www.gateway.com **Chrmn. & CEO**—T. W. Waitt. **Pres & COO**—J. Weitzen. **SVP, CFO & Treas**—D. J. McKittrick. **Investor Contact**—Marlys Johnson (605-232-2709). **Dirs**—C. G. Carey, G. H. Krauss, D. L. Lacey, J. F. McCann, R. D. Snyder, T. W. Waitt, J. Weitzen. **Transfer Agent & Registrar**—Norwest Bank Minnesota, N.A. **Incorporated**—in Iowa in 1986, reincorporated in South Dakota in 1989 and Delaware in 1991. **Empl**— 13,300. **S&P Analyst:** Megan Graham Hackett

STANDARD &POOR'S
STOCK REPORTS

General Dynamics

964

NYSE Symbol **GD**

In S&P 500

12-SEP-98

Industry:
Aerospace/Defense

Summary: This defense contractor designs and manufactures ocean vessels and armored ground vehicles for the military.

| S&P Opinion: Hold (★★★) | Recent Price • 46½ | Yield • 1.9% |
| | 52 Wk Range • 49⅜-38 | 12-Mo. P/E • 17.5 |

Quantitative Evaluations

Outlook
(1 Lowest—5 Highest)
• 1⁻

Fair Value
• 42⅞

Risk
• **Low**

Earn./Div. Rank
• **B+**

Technical Eval.
• **Bullish** since 5/97

Rel. Strength Rank
(1 Lowest—99 Highest)
• **91**

Insider Activity
• **Neutral**

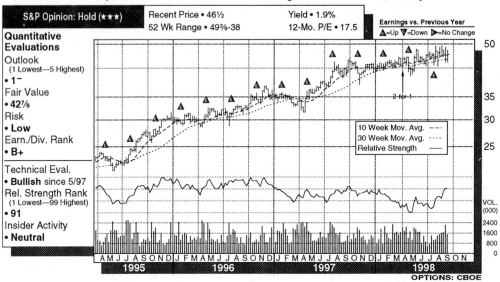

Earnings vs. Previous Year
▲=Up ▼=Down ▶=No Change

10 Week Mov. Avg. — - -
30 Week Mov. Avg. ......
Relative Strength ——

2 for 1

VOL.
(000)
2400
1600
800
0

OPTIONS: CBOE

Overview - 16-JUL-98

Revenues in 1998 should increase robustly from those of 1997, aided by recent acquisitions, including a defense electronics business acquired from Lucent Technologies and Ceridian Corp.'s Computing Devices International unit. The marine group should be boosted by work on projects to develop several prototype ships, including the LPD-17 Amphibious Assault Ship for the Navy. Increased activity on the Seawolf and development work on the NSSN New Attack Submarine -- a 30-submarine follow-on program to Seawolf -- will boost revenues. Design work on the Marine Corps' Advanced Amphibious Assault Vehicle and a multi-year U.S. Army contract to upgrade 580 Abrams tanks will continue to boost armored vehicle revenues. GD continues a cost-cutting program, with savings shared with customers. GD has little debt, with more than $800 million in cash, and is generating over $200 million a year in free cash flow. These resources will facilitate further strategic additions to expand GD's capabilities in marine vessels, armored vehicles and systems integration.

Valuation - 16-JUL-98

Despite the fact that General Dynamics maintains a dominant position in many of its niche defense markets, generates solid cash flow and possesses among the strongest balance sheets in the defense industry, we are generally cautious about companies that derive a majority of revenues from unpredictable U.S. and foreign military markets. Moreover, although General Dynamics has posted respectable seven-year average returns on equity of about 15%, it has posted lackluster per share book value growth, which we view as a proxy for per share instrinsic value growth. Based on projected 17% average ROE and 13% sustainable EPS growth, our relative and intrinsic valuations indicate GD stock should perform in line with the broader market over the long term.

Key Stock Statistics

S&P EPS Est. 1998	2.75	Tang. Bk. Value/Share	6.75
P/E on S&P Est. 1998	16.9	Beta	0.68
S&P EPS Est. 1999	2.95	Shareholders	22,200
Dividend Rate/Share	0.88	Market cap. (B)	$ 5.9
Shs. outstg. (M)	126.6	Inst. holdings	55%
Avg. daily vol. (M)	0.356		

Value of $10,000 invested 5 years ago: $ 31,481

Fiscal Year Ending Dec. 31

	1998	1997	1996	1995	1994	1993
Revenues (Million $)						
1Q	1,154	941.0	893.0	753.0	800.0	858.0
2Q	1,178	1,032	930.0	703.0	820.0	774.0
3Q	—	988.0	862.0	718.0	714.0	776.0
4Q	—	1,101	896.0	893.0	724.0	779.0
Yr.	—	4,062	3,581	3,067	3,058	3,187
Earnings Per Share ($)						
1Q	**0.65**	**0.56**	0.52	0.47	0.43	0.53
2Q	**0.72**	**0.64**	0.53	0.48	0.44	0.50
3Q	—	**0.65**	0.54	0.49	0.42	0.60
4Q	—	**0.66**	0.56	0.51	0.46	0.51
Yr.	**E2.75**	**2.49**	2.13	1.96	1.75	2.13

Next earnings report expected: mid October

Dividend Data (Dividends have been paid since 1979.)

Amount ($)	Date Decl.	Ex-Div. Date	Stock of Record	Payment Date
2-for-1	Mar. 04	Apr. 03	Mar. 13	Apr. 02 '98
0.220	Mar. 04	Apr. 07	Apr. 09	May. 08 '98
0.220	May. 06	Jul. 15	Jul. 17	Aug. 14 '98
0.220	Aug. 05	Oct. 07	Oct. 09	Nov. 13 '98

A Division of The McGraw-Hill Companies

Business Summary - 16-JUL-98

Once the most diverse defense contractor, General Dynamics streamlined its business by shedding missiles, aviation and space products units to focus on marine vessels and combat vehicles. Now, the company is seeking acquisitions that extend its capabilities within those two sectors. More than 90% of GD's revenues are derived from supplying weapons systems and services to the U.S. government.

GD's Marine group (57% of 1997 sales) is comprised of Electric Boat and Bath Iron Works (acquired in 1995). Electric Boat is the U.S. Navy's lead supplier of nuclear submarines, having designed 15 classes of submarines, including the Trident ballistic missile and Seawolf attack submarines. Seawolf, the first of which was delivered in mid-1997, is the fastest, quietest and most heavily armed attack submarine ever built; two more are to be built for the U.S. Navy. Electric Boat is also the lead designer on the New Attack Submarine, a 30-vessel program that calls for joint construction of the first four submarines beginning in 1998 with Newport News Shipbuilding. Bath designs and builds surface combat ships, including the Navy's only such ship under construction today: the Arleigh Burke class DDG 51 Aegis guided missile destroyer. Bath is competing on the LPD 17 Amphibious Assault Ship and the Arse-

nal ship programs as a prelude to competition for the SC 21 surface combatant for the 21st century, which will succeed the Arleigh Burke ships. The AMSEA division operates 16 ready-reserve and prepositioning ships for the Navy.

Combat Systems (37% of 1997 sales) is the sole producer of the M1 Abrams main battle tank and its derivatives, as well as sole-source designer on the U.S. Marine Corps' high-priority, 1,000-unit Advanced Amphibious Assault Vehicle. The U.S. Army plans to upgrade more than 1,000 older M1 tanks to the M1A2 configuration. Other combat vehicles and mobility systems are also produced, following the 1996 purchase of Teledyne Vehicle Systems. In addition, Land Systems is the second-source producer of the Single Channel Ground and Airborne Radio System (SINCGARS) for the U.S. Army.

In 1997, GD acquired Lockheed Martin's Defense Systems and Armament Systems businesses for $450 million. Defense Systems' major products are light wheeled scout and armored vehicles, transmissions for Crusader and Bradley armored personnel carriers, turret drive systems for the Bradley and the Light Armored Vehicle. Armament Systems is principally a supplier of high-speed Gatling guns.

Other activities are the Freeman Energy coal mining company and Patriots LNG tanker leasing subsidiaries.

Per Share Data ($)

(Year Ended Dec. 31)	1997	1996	1995	1994	1993	1992	1991	1990	1989	1988
Tangible Bk. Val.	5.65	13.58	12.39	10.45	9.40	15.15	11.81	9.06	12.57	11.13
Cash Flow	1.61	2.67	2.26	2.06	2.58	2.01	4.04	-1.77	3.91	4.20
Earnings	2.50	2.13	1.96	1.75	2.13	1.64	2.23	-3.83	1.75	2.26
Dividends	0.82	0.80	0.74	0.68	0.45	0.36	0.25	0.25	0.25	0.25
Payout Ratio	33%	38%	38%	38%	21%	22%	11%	NM	14%	11%
Prices - High	45¾	37¾	31½	23⅞	30	27	13⅝	11½	15⅛	14¾
- Low	31⅝	28½	21¼	19	20⅛	13⅜	5⅛	4¾	10⅝	11¾
P/E Ratio - High	18	18	16	14	14	16	6	NM	9	7
- Low	13	13	11	11	9	8	2	NM	6	5

Income Statement Analysis (Million $)

	1997	1996	1995	1994	1993	1992	1991	1990	1989	1988
Revs.	4,062	3,581	3,067	3,058	3,187	3,472	8,751	10,173	10,043	9,551
Oper. Inc.	549	434	353	360	365	231	692	-466	944	848
Depr.	91.0	67.0	38.0	39.0	56.0	56.0	303	344	360	326
Int. Exp.	12.0	14.0	4.0	5.0	4.0	10.0	58.0	72.0	94.0	62.5
Pretax Inc.	479	409	375	343	413	227	331	-987	448	455
Eff. Tax Rate	34%	34%	34%	35%	35%	NM	NM	NM	35%	17%
Net Inc.	316	270	247	223	270	248	374	-638	293	379

Balance Sheet & Other Fin. Data (Million $)

	1997	1996	1995	1994	1993	1992	1991	1990	1989	1988
Cash	336	894	1,095	1,059	585	945	820	115	14.0	228
Curr. Assets	1,689	1,858	2,013	1,797	1,654	3,655	4,319	3,927	3,990	3,636
Total Assets	4,091	3,299	3,164	2,673	2,635	4,222	6,207	6,537	6,549	6,118
Curr. Liab.	1,291	833	859	626	775	1,948	3,109	2,918	2,078	2,046
LT Debt	257	156	170	196	201	38.0	365	900	906	975
Common Eqty.	1,915	1,714	1,567	1,316	1,177	1,874	1,980	1,510	2,126	1,922
Total Cap.	2,172	1,870	1,737	1,512	1,378	1,912	2,345	2,414	3,671	3,367
Cap. Exp.	83.0	75.0	32.0	23.0	14.0	18.0	82.0	321	419	496
Cash Flow	407	337	285	262	326	304	674	-294	653	705
Curr. Ratio	1.3	2.2	2.3	2.9	2.1	1.9	1.4	1.3	1.9	1.8
% LT Debt of Cap.	11.8	8.3	9.8	13.0	14.6	2.0	15.6	37.3	24.7	29.0
% Net Inc.of Revs.	7.8	7.5	8.1	7.3	8.5	7.1	4.3	NM	2.9	4.0
% Ret. on Assets	8.6	8.3	8.5	8.4	7.8	5.6	5.8	NM	4.6	6.8
% Ret. on Equity	17.4	16.5	17.2	17.8	17.6	14.9	21.4	NM	14.5	21.6

Data as orig. reptd.; bef. results of disc. opers. and/or spec. items. Per share data adj. for stk. divs. as of ex-div. date. Bold denotes diluted EPS (FASB 128). E-Estimated. NA-Not Available. NM-Not Meaningful. NR-Not Ranked.

Office—3190 Fairview Park Dr., Falls Church, VA 22042.**Tel**—(703) 876-3000. **Chrmn & CEO**—N. D. Chabraja. **Pres & COO**—J. E. Turner. **VP & CFO**—M. J. Mancuso. **Secy**—P. A. Hesse. **Investor Contact**—W. Raymond A. Lewis (703-876-3195). **Dirs**—F. C. Carlucci, N. D. Chabraja, J. S. Crown, L. Crown, C. H. Goodman, G. R. Sullivan, C. A. H. Trost. **Transfer Agent & Registrar**—First Chicago Trust Co. of New York, Jersey City, NJ. **Incorporated**—in Delaware in 1952. **Empl**— 22,100. **S&P Analyst:** Robert E. Friedman, CPA

STANDARD &POOR'S
STOCK REPORTS

General Electric

966

NYSE Symbol **GE**

In S&P 500

12-SEP-98

Industry:
Electrical Equipment

Summary: GE's major businesses include aircraft engines, medical systems, power systems, broadcasting, appliances, lighting and financial services.

S&P Opinion: Hold (★★★)	Recent Price • 79¼	Yield • 1.5%
	52 Wk Range • 96⅞-59	12-Mo. P/E • 30.2

Quantitative Evaluations

Outlook
(1 Lowest—5 Highest)
• **1**

Fair Value
• **69¾**

Risk
• **Low**

Earn./Div. Rank
• **A+**

Technical Eval.
• **Bullish** since 10/96

Rel. Strength Rank
(1 Lowest—99 Highest)
• **68**

Insider Activity
• **Neutral**

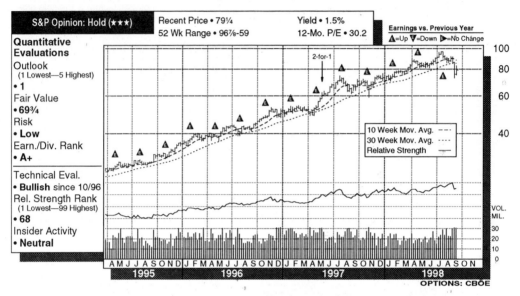

Earnings vs. Previous Year
▲=Up ▼=Down ▶=No Change

- 10 Week Mov. Avg. ----
- 30 Week Mov. Avg. ....
- Relative Strength ——

OPTIONS: CBOE

Overview - 10-JUL-98

Revenues are expected to rise 10% in 1998 from those of 1997, reflecting favorable trends in aerospace and financial businesses, and a continued emphasis on international expansion, acquisitions, and on broadening of the aftermarket repair and services businesses. The focus on service will be most visible in the aircraft engine, medical equipment, and power generation businesses. At the original equipment end of the business, aircraft engines will benefit from a sharp increase in market share. NBC is expected to grow earnings by 20%, even with the loss of Seinfeld and professional football broadcasts. Financial services should continue to expand at a 15% to 20% annual rate, aided by aggressive marketing and acquisitions. GE's consolidated earnings should benefit from improved margins on greater volume, improved manufacturing efficiencies, and strong cost control programs.

Valuation - 10-JUL-98

We are maintaining our hold recommendation on the shares, based on price. While this diversified powerhouse has long established itself as a well managed company that delivers consistent earnings growth, we think that the price of the stock has reached levels consistent with the company's financial performance. While we still view the shares as a core long-term holding, we think that they will only be average performers over the next year, as the company's earnings catch up to its premium valuation. Substantial share repurchases and a rising dividend will improve the value of the stock over time, but we would defer additional purchases until a more reasonable P/E is reached.

Key Stock Statistics

S&P EPS Est. 1998	2.85	Tang. Bk. Value/Share	4.81
P/E on S&P Est. 1998	27.8	Beta	1.16
S&P EPS Est. 1999	3.20	Shareholders	493,000
Dividend Rate/Share	1.20	Market cap. (B)	$257.9
Shs. outstg. (M)	3253.7	Inst. holdings	49%
Avg. daily vol. (M)	7.070		

Value of $10,000 invested 5 years ago: $ 41,872

Fiscal Year Ending Dec. 31

	1998	1997	1996	1995	1994	1993
Revenues (Million $)						
1Q	22,626	20,157	17,098	15,126	12,657	12,900
2Q	25,070	21,997	19,066	17,809	14,768	14,761
3Q	—	21,991	20,021	17,341	14,481	14,858
4Q	—	26,695	22,994	19,752	17,791	18,087
Yr.	—	90,840	79,179	70,028	60,108	60,562
Earnings Per Share ($)						
1Q	**0.57**	**0.50**	0.46	0.41	0.35	0.32
2Q	**0.74**	**0.65**	0.57	0.51	0.46	0.19
3Q	**E0.75**	**0.60**	0.54	0.48	0.42	0.35
4Q	**E0.78**	**0.70**	0.63	0.56	0.49	0.43
Yr.	**E2.85**	**2.46**	2.16	1.95	1.73	1.29

Next earnings report expected: early October

Dividend Data (Dividends have been paid since 1899.)

Amount ($)	Date Decl.	Ex-Div. Date	Stock of Record	Payment Date
0.300	Dec. 19	Dec. 29	Dec. 31	Jan. 26 '98
0.300	Feb. 13	Mar. 05	Mar. 09	Apr. 27 '98
0.300	Jun. 26	Jul. 06	Jul. 08	Jul. 27 '98
0.300	Sep. 11	Sep. 28	Sep. 30	Oct. 26 '98

A Division of The McGraw·Hill Companies

STANDARD
&POOR'S

STOCK REPORTS

General Electric Company

966

12-SEP-98

Business Summary - 10-JUL-98

This diverse company has the highest market capitalization of any public company. GE's interests include a broad range of services, technology and manufacturing industries. GE's senior management has proven adept at defining broad themes which lower level managers implement. Key to GE's business plan is the requirement that businesses be first or second in market share in their industries. Businesses that aren't leaders are divested.

Six themes are currently being pursued: quality, globalization, service, information technology and consumer wealth accumulation and protection. Quality involves a company-wide initiative to boost quality and lower costs. The company believes that this should boost margins in 1998 and beyond as hundreds of projects underway mature. Globalization is the pursuit of rapid growth in overseas markets. Already more than 40% of GE's revenues (including exports) and 32% of profits are derived overseas.

Service aims to capture a larger part of the recurring revenue stream tied to aftermarket service of manufactured products. This strategy is having the largest impact on aircraft engines, medical equipment, power generation and locomotives. Information technology is developing information services units such as GE's media and satellite leasing businesses, as well as applying information technology in all units to improve their competitiveness. Consumer wealth accumulation addresses the growing demand for financial, insurance, health care and other needs of aging baby-boomers.

Segment contributions in 1997 (profits in million $):

	Revs.	Profits
Aircraft engines	8.3%	$1,051
Appliances	7.1%	458
Broadcasting	5.5%	1,002
Industrial products & systems	11.6%	1,490
Materials	7.1%	1,476
Power generation	7.9%	758
Technical products/services	5.2%	828
Financial services	42.3%	4,422
Other	5.0%	3,558

GE operates in two groups: product, service and media businesses and GE Capital Services (GECS). Product, service and media includes 11 businesses: aircraft engines, appliances, lighting, medical systems, NBC, plastics, power systems, electrical distribution and control, information services, motors and industrial systems, and transportation systems. GECS operates 27 financial businesses clustered in equipment management, specialty insurance, consumer services, specialized financing and mid-market financing.

Per Share Data ($)

(Year Ended Dec. 31)	1997	1996	1995	1994	1993	1992	1991	1990	1989	1988
Tangible Bk. Val.	4.69	4.09	4.88	4.40	4.53	4.08	3.44	3.54	3.33	2.75
Cash Flow	3.67	3.35	3.02	2.67	2.25	2.08	2.09	1.92	1.71	1.57
Earnings	2.46	2.20	1.95	1.73	1.29	1.25	1.27	1.21	1.09	0.94
Dividends	1.08	0.95	0.84	0.74	0.63	0.58	0.52	0.48	0.42	0.36
Payout Ratio	44%	43%	43%	43%	38%	46%	41%	39%	39%	39%
Prices - High	76½	53⅛	36⅝	27½	26¾	21⅞	19½	18⅞	16¼	12
- Low	48	34¾	25	22½	20¼	18¼	13¼	12½	10⅞	9⅝
P/E Ratio - High	31	24	19	16	21	17	15	16	15	13
- Low	19	16	13	13	16	14	10	10	10	10

Income Statement Analysis (Million $)

Revs.	90,840	79,179	70,028	59,316	59,827	56,274	59,379	57,662	53,884	49,414
Oper. Inc.	NA	22,764	20,821	16,194	16,241	15,205	15,887	15,377	13,944	11,190
Depr.	4,082	3,785	3,594	3,207	3,261	2,818	2,832	2,508	2,256	2,266
Int. Exp.	8,384	7,904	7,327	5,024	7,057	6,943	7,504	7,544	6,812	5,129
Pretax Inc.	11,419	10,806	9,737	8,831	6,726	6,326	6,508	6,229	5,787	4,782
Eff. Tax Rate	26%	33%	33%	31%	32%	31%	31%	30%	31%	28%
Net Inc.	8,203	7,280	6,573	5,915	4,424	4,305	4,435	4,303	3,939	3,386

Balance Sheet & Other Fin. Data (Million $)

Cash	5,861	64,080	43,890	33,556	3,218	3,129	1,971	1,975	2,258	2,187
Curr. Assets	NA	NA	NA	NA	NA	NA	NA	NA	NA	NA
Total Assets	304,012	272,402	228,035	194,484	251,506	192,876	168,259	153,884	128,344	110,865
Curr. Liab.	NA	NA	82,001	72,854	155,729	120,475	102,611	93,022	73,902	61,800
LT Debt	46,603	49,246	51,027	36,979	28,270	25,376	22,682	21,043	16,110	15,082
Common Eqty.	34,438	31,125	29,609	26,387	25,824	23,459	21,683	21,680	20,890	18,466
Total Cap.	93,374	91,651	90,972	70,418	60,859	54,719	49,392	47,746	41,544	37,902
Cap. Exp.	8,388	7,760	6,447	7,492	4,739	4,824	5,000	4,523	5,474	3,681
Cash Flow	12,285	11,065	10,162	9,122	7,685	7,123	7,267	6,811	6,195	5,652
Curr. Ratio	NA	NA	NA	NA	NA	NA	NA	NA	NA	NA
% LT Debt of Cap.	50.0	53.7	56.1	52.5	46.5	46.4	45.9	44.1	38.8	39.8
% Net Inc.of Revs.	9.0	9.2	9.4	10.0	7.4	7.7	7.5	7.5	7.3	6.9
% Ret. on Assets	2.8	2.9	3.2	2.7	2.0	2.4	2.8	3.1	3.3	4.5
% Ret. on Equity	25.0	24.0	23.5	22.7	18.0	19.2	20.6	20.6	20.0	19.4

Data as orig. reptd.; bef. results of disc. opers. and/or spec. items. Per share data adj. for stk. divs. as of ex-div. date. Bold denotes diluted EPS (FASB 128). E-Estimated. NA-Not Available. NM-Not Meaningful. NR-Not Ranked.

Office—3135 Easton Turnpike, Fairfield, CT 06431. **Tel**—(203) 373-2211. **Website**—http://www.ge.com **Chrmn & CEO**—J. F. Welch Jr. **VP & Secy**—B. W. Heineman Jr. **SVP-Fin & CFO**—D. D. Dammerman. **Investor Contact**—Mark L. Vachon (203-373-2816). **Dirs**—D. W. Calloway, J. I. Cash, Jr., S. S. Cathcart, D. D. Dammerman, P. Fresco, C. X. Gonzalez, G. G. Michelson, E. F. Murphy, S. Nunn, J. D. Opie, R. S. Penske, B. S. Preiskel, F. H. T. Rhodes, A. C. Sigler, D. A. Warner III, J. F. Welch Jr. **Transfer Agent & Registrar**—Bank of New York, NYC. **Incorporated**—in New York in 1892. **Empl**— 239,000. **S&P Analyst:** Robert E. Friedman, CPA

12-SEP-98

Industry:
Communications
Equipment

Summary: This company (formerly NextLevel Systems) is a leading supplier of broadband and satellite communications systems and equipment.

S&P Opinion: Hold (★★★)	Recent Price • 19	Yield • Nil
	52 Wk Range • 29½-12⅝	12-Mo. P/E • NM

Quantitative Evaluations

Outlook
(1 Lowest—5 Highest)
• **4⁻**

Fair Value
• **25**

Risk
• **NA**

Earn./Div. Rank
• **NR**

Technical Eval.
• **NA**

Rel. Strength Rank
(1 Lowest—99 Highest)
• **31**

Insider Activity
• **NA**

Earnings vs. Previous Year
▲=Up ▼=Down ▶=No Change

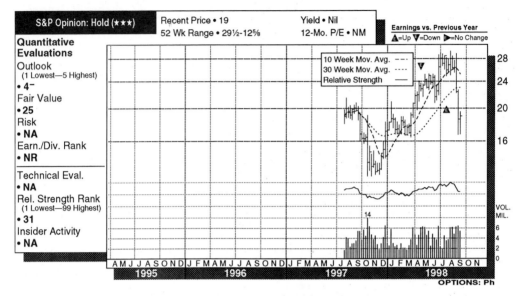

10 Week Mov. Avg. ---
30 Week Mov. Avg. ·····
Relative Strength ——

OPTIONS: Ph

Overview - 20-AUG-98

We expect revenues to increase about 11% in 1998, as accelerating digital system sales outwiegh slower analog equipment sales. In December 1997, GIC announced a restructuring plan to cut costs; this is expected to add $0.05 to $0.07 to 1998 EPS. Separately, the company signed long-term agreements with leading cable operators to provide about $4.5 billion worth of digital set-top boxes over the next three to five years. In January 1998, GIC formed a strategic alliance with Sony Corp., to jointly develop digital TV technologies. Sony planned to purchase 7.5 million GIC common shares (approximately 5% of the shares currently outstanding) at $25 each. We expect EPS to climb significantly in 1998, on wider gross margins and cost reduction efforts. The company changed its name back to General Instrument, from NextLevel Systems, effective February 1998.

Valuation - 20-AUG-98

The shares were recently up over 30% in 1998, on the heels of GIC's December 1997 announcement that it had received orders totaling $4.5 billion over the next three to five years to supply at least 15 million advanced digital set-top devices to nine leading cable system operators. Although we do not foresee a substantial increase in sales growth from these orders until the end of 1999, GIC appears to have solidified its competitive position going into the digital rollout. We are encouraged by GIC's divestiture of non-core business units. Based on a recent valuation of 33X our 1999 EPS estimate of $0.91, and a 25% growth rate, we view the shares as fairly valued. EPS for the first two quarters of 1997 are pro forma. EPS in the 1998 first quarter include $0.53 in restructuring charges.

Key Stock Statistics

S&P EPS Est. 1998	0.73	Tang. Bk. Value/Share	4.31
P/E on S&P Est. 1998	26.0	Beta	1.14
S&P EPS Est. 1999	0.91	Shareholders	NA
Dividend Rate/Share	Nil	Market cap. (B)	$ 2.9
Shs. outstg. (M)	150.9	Inst. holdings	74%
Avg. daily vol. (M)	1.546		

Value of $10,000 invested 5 years ago: NA

Fiscal Year Ending Dec. 31

	1998	1997	1996	1995	1994	1993
Revenues (Million $)						
1Q	416.9	408.0	—	—	—	—
2Q	488.5	450.4	—	—	—	—
3Q	—	464.6	—	—	—	—
4Q	—	441.1	—	—	—	—
Yr.	—	1,764	1,756	—	—	—
Earnings Per Share ($)						
1Q	-0.40	0.03	—	—	—	—
2Q	0.19	0.01	—	—	—	—
3Q	—	0.16	—	—	—	—
4Q	—	-0.31	—	—	—	—
Yr.	—	-0.11	-0.68	—	—	—

Next earnings report expected: late October

Dividend Data

No cash dividends have been paid.

A Division of The McGraw-Hill Companies

Business Summary - 20-AUG-98

This company (GIC) is one of three publicly traded companies that were spun off from General Instrument Corp. (old) in July 1997. The company changed its name back to General Instrument Corp., from NextLevel Systems, in February 1998. GIC is a worldwide supplier of systems and equipment for high-performance networks delivering video, voice, and data/Internet services. The company is the market share leader for U.S. analog set-top terminals used to access cable service.

Sales of analog and digital television systems accounted for 51% of net sales in 1997. The principal analog products of the company's Broadband Networks Group accounted for 58% of broadband sales in 1997. Subscriber products include addressable systems, which permit control, through a set-top terminal, of a subscriber's cable television services from a central headend computer without requiring access to the subscriber's premises. Transmission products include signal processing equipment, amplifiers, fiber optic equipment, and passive components for wired television distribution systems. The Digital Networks Systems business unit is deploying digital television systems that enable satellite programmers and cable operators to deliver four to 10 times as much information over their existing networks.

Satellite Data Networks (20% of 1997 sales) was a pioneer in digital satellite television with its DigiCipher system, the first digital access control system designed for video entertainment signals. The satellite group is the sole supplier of digital satellite receivers to PRIMESTAR, a consortium of cable television operators and GE Americom. In addition, GIC is the sole supplier of digital satellite encoders to DIRECTV, USSB, Galaxy Latin America, and DIRECTV Japan.

High-speed data networks are viewed by management as an emerging growth opportunity for the Satellite Group. The SURFboard cable modem provides Internet and multimedia services to homes and business at speeds up to nearly 1,000 times those of conventional modems. The modem features a telephone return path that is optimal for existing cable infrastructure because only a small percentage of cable systems are currently offering "two-way" cable service.

In January 1998, GIC placed its advanced telephony business, Next Level Communications, into a limited partnership with General instrument as limited partner with an 80% stake. GIC is now a pure-play cable and satellite TV systems business.

TCI, including its affiliates, and Time Warner each accounted for 14% of consolidated net sales in 1996.

In May 1998, GIC said that TCI.NET, the broadband data division of Tele-Communications, Inc., had committed to purchase its SURFboard cable modems.

Per Share Data ($)

(Year Ended Dec. 31)	1997	1996	1995	1994	1993	1992	1991	1990	1989	1988
Tangible Bk. Val.	4.46	2.46	NA	NA	NA	NA	NA	NA	NA	NA
Cash Flow	NA	NA	NA	NA	NA	NA	NA	NA	NA	NA
Earnings	-0.11	-0.68	NA	NA	NA	NA	NA	NA	NA	NA
Dividends	Nil	Nil	Nil	Nil	Nil	Nil	Nil	Nil	Nil	Nil
Payout Ratio	Nil	Nil	Nil	Nil	Nil	Nil	Nil	Nil	Nil	Nil
Prices - High	21½	NA	NA	NA	NA	NA	NA	NA	NA	NA
- Low	12⅝	NA	NA	NA	NA	NA	NA	NA	NA	NA
P/E Ratio - High	NM	NM	NM	NM	NM	NM	NM	NM	NM	NM
- Low	NM	NM	NM	NM	NM	NM	NM	NM	NM	NM

Income Statement Analysis (Million $)

	1997	1996	1995	1994	1993	1992	1991	1990	1989	1988
Revs.	1,764	1,756	NA	NA	NA	NA	NA	NA	NA	NA
Oper. Inc.	79.7	NA	NA	NA	NA	NA	NA	NA	NA	NA
Depr.	89.9	NA	NA	NA	NA	NA	NA	NA	NA	NA
Int. Exp.	5.2	NA	NA	NA	NA	NA	NA	NA	NA	NA
Pretax Inc.	-9.6	-148	NA	NA	NA	NA	NA	NA	NA	NA
Eff. Tax Rate	NM	NM	NM	NM	NM	NM	NM	NM	NM	NM
Net Inc.	-16.1	-95.8	NA	NA	NA	NA	NA	NA	NA	NA

Balance Sheet & Other Fin. Data (Million $)

	1997	1996	1995	1994	1993	1992	1991	1990	1989	1988
Cash	65.6	18.3	NA	NA	NA	NA	NA	NA	NA	NA
Curr. Assets	825	740	NA	NA	NA	NA	NA	NA	NA	NA
Total Assets	1,675	1,626	NA	NA	NA	NA	NA	NA	NA	NA
Curr. Liab.	389	376	NA	NA	NA	NA	NA	NA	NA	NA
LT Debt	Nil	280	NA	NA	NA	NA	NA	NA	NA	NA
Common Eqty.	1,215	914	NA	NA	NA	NA	NA	NA	NA	NA
Total Cap.	1,220	1,201	NA	NA	NA	NA	NA	NA	NA	NA
Cap. Exp.	79.8	NA	NA	NA	NA	NA	NA	NA	NA	NA
Cash Flow	73.7	NA	NA	NA	NA	NA	NA	NA	NA	NA
Curr. Ratio	2.1	2.0	NA	NA	NA	NA	NA	NA	NA	NA
% LT Debt of Cap.	NM	23.3	NA	NA	NA	NA	NA	NA	NA	NA
% Net Inc.of Revs.	NM	NM	NM	NM	NM	NM	NM	NM	NM	NM
% Ret. on Assets	NM	NM	NM	NM	NM	NM	NM	NM	NM	NM
% Ret. on Equity	NM	NM	NM	NM	NM	NM	NM	NM	NM	NM

Data as orig. reptd.; bef. results of disc. opers. and/or spec. items. Per share data adj. for stk. divs. as of ex-div. date. EPS for 1997 1Q & 2Q, and all data for 1996, are pro forma. Bk. Val. & Bal. Sheet data for 1996 are as of Mar. 31, 1997, pro forma. E-Estimated. NA-Not Available. NM-Not Meaningful. NR-Not Ranked.

Office—101 Tournament Drive, Horsham, PA 19044 **Tel**—(215) 323-1000. **Website**—http://www.gi.com **Chmn & CEO**—E. D. Breen. **VP & CFO**—E. M. Pillmore. **VP & Secy**—S. M. Meyer. **Investor Contact**—Dario Santana (215 323-1213). **Dirs**—E. D. Breen, J. S. Brown, F. M. Drendel, L. Forester, T. J. Forstmann, A. M. Mandl, J. T. O'Rourke. **Transfer Agent**—ChaseMellon Shareholder Services, Ridgefield Park, NJ. **Incorporated**—in Delaware in 1997. **Empl**— 7,350. **S&P Analyst:** Aydin Tuncer

STANDARD &POOR'S
STOCK REPORTS

General Mills

976

NYSE Symbol **GIS**

In S&P 500

12-SEP-98

Industry:
Foods

Summary: This company is a major producer of packaged consumer food products, including Big G cereals and Betty Crocker desserts/baking mixes.

S&P Opinion: Hold (★★★)	Recent Price • 65⅜	Yield • 3.2%
	52 Wk Range • 78¼-59⅛	12-Mo. P/E • 25.2

Quantitative Evaluations

Outlook
(1 Lowest—5 Highest)
• **2+**

Fair Value
• **64⅞**

Risk
• **Low**

Earn./Div. Rank
• **B+**

Technical Eval.
• **Bullish** since 5/98

Rel. Strength Rank
(1 Lowest—99 Highest)
• **88**

Insider Activity
• **Neutral**

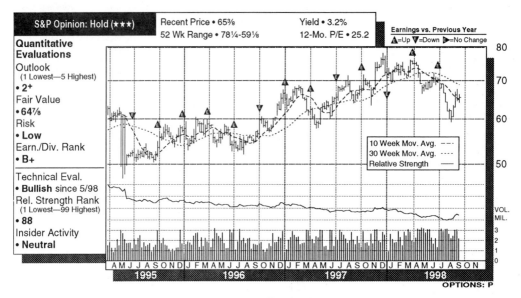

Earnings vs. Previous Year
▲=Up ▼=Down ▶=No Change

10 Week Mov. Avg. – – –
30 Week Mov. Avg. · · · · ·
Relative Strength —

OPTIONS: P

Overview - 09-JUL-98

Sales from continuing operations through FY 99 (May) are expected to rise at a middle single-digit rate, led by a projected 3%-4% increase in unit volumes and very modest price inflation. Operating margins are expected to benefit from a combination of volume-based efficiencies, further productivity gains arising from the recent realignment of manufacturing facilities, and from anticipated profit contributions from international joint ventures in FY 99; Operating profits are expected to rise at a high single-digit rate through FY 99. Assuming a steady easing in net interest expense, a modestly lower effective tax rate and a modest reduction in shares outstanding, diluted earnings per share are expected to reach $3.55 in FY 99, up 9% from FY 98's $3.22 (excluding unusual charges).

Valuation - 09-JUL-98

In the face of intensely competitive conditions within the U.S. ready-to-eat cereal market, GIS has sustained its approximate 26% market share (including the recently acquired Chex and Cookie Crisp brands) while increasing profits--a testament to its effective brand management skills. Although such pressures are likely to remain in coming periods, the company's diversification into other consumer packaged food categories and an increasing exposure in international markets should be mitigating factors. The shares, which have sharply lagged the ascent of both its food company peers and that of the S&P 500 index over the past year, should rise more in tandem with both in the near term. Valued at a modest discount to the level of the P/E of the S&P 500, the relatively low-risk shares are a worthwhile holding at current levels for long-term capital gains.

Key Stock Statistics

S&P EPS Est. 1999	3.55	Tang. Bk. Value/Share	NM
P/E on S&P Est. 1999	18.4	Beta	0.40
Dividend Rate/Share	2.12	Shareholders	25,000
Shs. outstg. (M)	154.8	Market cap. (B)	$ 10.1
Avg. daily vol. (M)	0.573	Inst. holdings	63%

Value of $10,000 invested 5 years ago: NA

Fiscal Year Ending May 31

	1998	1997	1996	1995	1994	1993
Revenues (Million $)						
1Q	1,417	1,316	1,276	1,157	2,090	2,020
2Q	1,638	1,560	1,448	1,417	2,182	2,097
3Q	1,425	1,290	1,309	1,224	2,101	2,011
4Q	1,554	1,444	1,382	1,229	2,144	2,007
Yr.	6,033	5,609	5,416	5,027	8,517	8,135
Earnings Per Share ($)						
1Q	**0.82**	0.62	0.86	0.75	1.04	0.97
2Q	**0.40**	1.00	0.92	0.85	0.88	0.85
3Q	**0.81**	0.78	0.73	0.13	0.91	0.86
4Q	**0.57**	0.42	0.49	-0.09	0.12	0.42
Yr.	**2.60**	2.82	3.00	1.64	2.95	3.10

Next earnings report expected: mid September

Dividend Data (Dividends have been paid since 1898.)

Amount ($)	Date Decl.	Ex-Div. Date	Stock of Record	Payment Date
0.530	Sep. 22	Oct. 08	Oct. 10	Nov. 01 '97
0.530	Dec. 08	Jan. 07	Jan. 09	Feb. 02 '98
0.530	Feb. 23	Apr. 07	Apr. 10	May. 01 '98
0.530	Jun. 22	Jul. 08	Jul. 10	Aug. 01 '98

A Division of The McGraw·Hill Companies

STANDARD
&POOR'S
STOCK REPORTS

General Mills, Inc.

976

12-SEP-98

Business Summary - 09-JUL-98

General Mills (GIS) is the second-largest U.S. producer of ready-to-eat breakfast cereals and a leading producer of other highly advertised consumer packaged foods. Major cereal brands, most of which bear the Big G label, include Cheerios, Wheaties, Lucky Charms, Total and the recently acquired Chex line of cereals. Other consumer packaged food products include baking mixes (Betty Crocker, Bisquick); convenience foods (Betty Crocker dry packaged dinner mixes, Potato Buds instant mashed potatoes); snack products and beverages (Pop Secret microwave popcorn, Bugles snacks, grain and fruit snack products, Squeezit single-serving fruit juice drinks); and other products, including Yoplait and Colombo yogurt. The company also engages in grain merchandising, produces its own ingredient flour requirements and sells flour to bakeries. Products are also made and sold in Canada and Europe, Japan, Korea and Latin America. Sales and operating earnings (before unusual charges) generated outside the U.S. in FY 97 accounted for only 4% and 3%, respectively, of the company's total.

GIS is involved in three joint ventures, consisting of a 50% equity interest in Cereal Partners Worldwide, a joint venture with Nestle that manufactures and markets breakfast cereals in more than 60 countries outside North America, including France, Spain, Portugal, Italy, Ireland, Germany, the U.K., Mexico and the Philippines; a 40.5% equity interest in Snack Ventures Europe, a joint venture with PepsiCo that manufactures and markets snack foods in continental Europe; and a 50% equity interest in International Dessert Partners, a joint venture with CPC International that manufactures and markets baking mixes and desserts in Latin America. The joint ventures are reflected in GIS's financial statements on an equity accounting basis and have in the aggregate resulted in charges of $2.9 million, $6.3 million, and $2.8 million in FY 98, FY 97 and FY 96, respectively.

Capital investment for fixed assets and joint-venture development totaled $200 million in FY 98, down from $209 million in FY 97. For FY 99 and FY 2000, the company expects capital investment needs (including joint-venture funding) to average $225 million annually.

Per Share Data ($)

(Year Ended May 31)	1998	1997	1996	1995	1994	1993	1992	1991	1990	1989
Tangible Bk. Val.	NM	NM	1.24	0.13	6.27	7.15	7.79	6.26	4.57	4.19
Cash Flow	3.81	3.98	4.17	2.86	4.86	4.76	4.51	4.15	3.37	2.83
Earnings	2.60	2.82	3.00	1.64	2.95	3.10	3.05	2.82	2.28	1.93
Dividends	2.12	2.03	1.91	1.88	1.88	1.68	1.48	1.28	1.10	0.94
Payout Ratio	82%	72%	64%	115%	63%	43%	49%	46%	48%	48%
Cal. Yrs.	1997	1996	1995	1994	1993	1992	1991	1990	1989	1988
Prices - High	78¼	67½	64⅝	62¼	74⅛	75⅞	73⅝	52	38⅜	29
- Low	57¾	52	47¼	49⅜	56⅞	58¾	43½	31⅜	25⅛	21½
P/E Ratio - High	30	24	22	38	25	24	24	18	17	15
- Low	22	18	16	30	19	19	14	11	11	11

Income Statement Analysis (Million $)

	1998	1997	1996	1995	1994	1993	1992	1991	1990	1989
Revs.	6,033	5,609	5,416	5,027	8,517	8,135	7,778	7,153	6,448	5,621
Oper. Inc.	1,145	1,042	1,046	881	1,303	1,188	1,145	1,040	821	694
Depr.	195	183	187	191	304	271	242	213	176	149
Int. Exp.	129	117	117	126	122	100	89.5	94.0	75.5	63.7
Pretax Inc.	664	703	756	405	753	844	845	766	613	518
Eff. Tax Rate	36%	37%	37%	36%	38%	40%	40%	39%	39%	39%
Net Inc.	422	445	476	260	470	506	506	464	374	315

Balance Sheet & Other Fin. Data (Million $)

	1998	1997	1996	1995	1994	1993	1992	1991	1990	1989
Cash	6.0	13.0	21.0	13.0	Nil	100	1.0	40.0	71.0	11.0
Curr. Assets	1,035	1,011	100	897	1,129	1,077	1,035	1,082	910	841
Total Assets	3,861	3,902	3,295	3,358	5,198	4,651	4,305	3,902	3,290	2,888
Curr. Liab.	1,444	1,293	1,192	1,221	1,832	1,559	1,372	1,272	1,173	1,038
LT Debt	1,640	1,530	1,221	1,401	1,417	1,268	921	879	689	536
Common Eqty.	191	495	308	141	1,151	1,219	1,371	1,114	810	732
Total Cap.	2,244	2,441	1,936	1,960	3,178	2,944	2,726	2,448	1,926	1,668
Cap. Exp.	184	163	129	157	560	624	695	555	540	442
Cash Flow	617	628	663	451	774	777	748	678	550	464
Curr. Ratio	0.7	0.8	0.8	0.7	0.6	0.8	0.8	0.9	0.8	0.8
% LT Debt of Cap.	73.1	62.7	63.1	71.5	44.6	43.1	33.8	35.9	35.8	32.2
% Net Inc.of Revs.	7.0	8.0	8.8	5.2	5.5	6.2	6.5	6.5	5.8	5.6
% Ret. on Assets	10.9	12.4	14.3	6.4	9.6	11.5	12.3	12.8	12.0	11.5
% Ret. on Equity	123.2	110.7	212.0	40.2	39.9	39.7	40.7	48.0	48.2	46.5

Data as orig. reptd.; bef. results of disc. opers. and/or spec. items. Per share data adj. for stk. divs. as of ex-div. date. Bold denotes diluted EPS (FASB 128). E-Estimated. NA-Not Available. NM-Not Meaningful. NR-Not Ranked.

Office—Number One General Mills Blvd., Minneapolis, MN 55426. **Tel**—(612) 540-2311. **Website**—http://www.genmills.com **Chrmn & CEO**—S. W. Sanger. **Vice Chrmn**—R. G. Viault. **Pres**—C. W. Gaillard. **Investor Contact**—Eric Larson. **Dirs**—R. M. Bressler, L. D. DeSimone, W. T. Esrey, C. W. Gaillard, J. R. Hope, K. A. Macke, M. D. Rose, S. W. Sanger, A. M. Spence, D. A. Terrell, R. G. Viault, C. A. Wurtele. **Transfer Agent & Registrar**—Norwest Stock Transfer, St. Paul, MN. **Incorporated**—in Delaware in 1928. **Empl**— 10,200. **S&P Analyst:** Richard Joy

12-SEP-98   Industry: Automobiles

Summary: GM is the world's largest producer of cars and trucks, and has significant finance, aerospace, defense and electronics operations.

S&P Opinion: Hold (★★★)	Recent Price • 56⅜	Yield • 3.5%
	52 Wk Range • 76⅞-54⅜	12-Mo. P/E • 8.7

Quantitative Evaluations

Outlook
(1 Lowest—5 Highest)
• **4+**

Fair Value
• **72⅞**

Risk
• **Low**

Earn./Div. Rank
• **B**

Technical Eval.
• **Bearish** since 6/98

Rel. Strength Rank
(1 Lowest—99 Highest)
• **48**

Insider Activity
• **Neutral**

Earnings vs. Previous Year
▲=Up ▼=Down ▶=No Change

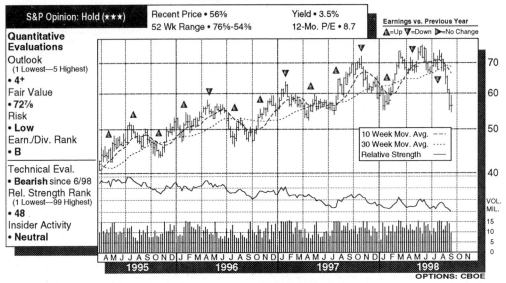

10 Week Mov. Avg. – – –
30 Week Mov. Avg. ·····
Relative Strength —

OPTIONS: CBOE

Overview - 15-JUL-98

Sales and profits in 1998 should benefit from a larger than usual number of restyled vehicles introduced in 1997, offset by the impact of strikes that temporarily shut down most North American plants. GM said the strike cost it $1.18 billion in the second quarter. Still, assuming a quick resolution of the strike, North American operations should again be profitable in 1998, but Delphi Automotive Systems margins will likely continue under pressure, reflecting competitive price reductions and manufacturing startup costs associated with a high level of turnover stemming from OEM new model introductions. GM finished 1997 with its lowest combined car/truck market share in history (30.8%). In the absence of a deep cyclical downturn and an extended strike, GM should continue to accumulate a large cash cushion. Marketing expenses have risen, due to intensifying competition.

Valuation - 15-JUL-98

In anticipation of a favorable resolution of the parts plant strikes and in light of the overall positive economic environment, we have restored our hold recommendation on GM. Strike costs, which reduced second quarter EPS by $1.79, will accelerate as inventory disappears, unless a settlement is reached. However, as the shares are already trading several dollars below pre-strike levels, and we believe Wall Street will be generally sympathetic, due to the need of the company to stand firm to obtain necessary productivity gains, we do not see significant further downside. In addition, as we expect a rebound when an agreement is announced, we believe it is okay to hold the shares in anticipation of such news. As we expect competitive pressures, already intense, to increase in coming periods, with industrywide sales flat to down in the second half of the year, we would not recommend adding to positions.

Key Stock Statistics

S&P EPS Est. 1998	5.95	Tang. Bk. Value/Share	5.80
P/E on S&P Est. 1998	9.5	Beta	1.00
Dividend Rate/Share	2.00	Shareholders	592,500
Shs. outstg. (M)	654.2	Market cap. (B)	$ 36.9
Avg. daily vol. (M)	2.704	Inst. holdings	59%

Value of $10,000 invested 5 years ago: NA

Fiscal Year Ending Dec. 31

	1998	1997	1996	1995	1994	1993
Revenues (Million $)						
1Q	41,571	42,241	39,240	43,285	37,495	35,000
2Q	38,901	45,146	44,772	44,146	40,392	36,658
3Q	—	41,890	39,109	37,463	34,510	30,138
4Q	—	48,897	40,948	43,935	42,553	37,268
Yr.	—	178,174	164,069	168,829	154,951	138,220
Earnings Per Share ($)						
1Q	2.27	2.28	0.93	2.51	1.86	0.93
2Q	0.52	2.67	2.65	2.39	2.23	0.92
3Q	—	1.34	1.57	0.42	0.40	-0.49
4Q	—	2.33	0.92	1.98	1.74	1.28
Yr.	E5.95	8.62	6.01	7.28	6.20	6.07

Next earnings report expected: mid October

Dividend Data (Dividends have been paid since 1915.)

Amount ($)	Date Decl.	Ex-Div. Date	Stock of Record	Payment Date
Stk.	Dec. 15	Dec. 19	Dec. 17	Dec. 18 '97
0.500	Feb. 09	Feb. 17	Feb. 19	Mar. 10 '98
0.500	May. 04	May. 12	May. 14	Jun. 10 '98
0.500	Apr. 15	Aug. 11	Aug. 13	Sep. 10 '98

A Division of The McGraw-Hill Companies

Business Summary - 15-JUL-98

General Motors is the world's largest manufacturer of cars and trucks. Net income by segment in recent years was divided as follows ($ in millions):

	1997	1996	1995
North American Automotive	$2,297	1,246	$2,396
International Automotive	1,139	1,532	1,644
GM Acceptance Corp.	1,301	1,240	1,031
GM Hughes Electronics	1,276	1,151	1,108
Other	-355	-216	-198
Discontinued ops. (EDS)	Nil	10	900

Chevrolet, Buick, Cadillac, Oldsmobile, Pontiac, Saturn and GEO models accounted for 32.4% of total new U.S. car registrations (including imports) in 1997, versus 32.7% in 1996, 34.2% in 1995, 34.3% in 1994, 34.4% in 1993, 34.6% in 1992 and 35.6% in 1991 and 1990. Comparable figures for Chevrolet, GMC, Pontiac and Oldsmobile trucks were 28.8%, 29.0%, 29.9%, 30.9%, 31.4%, 33.3%, 34.0% and 35.7%, respectively. Worldwide wholesale sales were 8,776,000 vehicles in 1997, 8,263,000 in 1996, and 8,567,000 in 1995. GM's market share in Western Europe was 11.3% in 1997 and 11.7% in 1996.

General Motors Acceptance Corp. provides vehicle financing, insurance and other financial services. GM Hughes Electronics produces automotive and defense electronics, and operates a direct broadcast satellite television system called DIRECTV, which had 3.3 million household subscribers at year-end 1997. GM sold a 2.5% interest in DIRECTV to AT&T for $138 million; this values the DIRECTV unit at $5.5 billion.

In January 1997, GM announced a series of actions intended to unlock shareholder value in the Hughes business segments. In December 1997, Hughes defense operations were spun off to shareholders and merged into Raytheon Co. in a $9.8 billion transaction. GM Class H common stock was recapitalized into a new class of GM common stock that will track Hughes' telecommunications and space business (Hughes Telecom). GM also transferred Hughes' automotive electronics subsidiary, Delco Electronics, to the Delphi Automotive Systems unit. In addition, GM is exploring a partial public offering of Delphi Automotive, the world's largest auto parts supplier.

Other GM products include locomotives; drilling, marine and stationary engines; heavy-duty automatic transmissions; and automated production and test equipment. In June 1996, GM received $500 million related to the completion of the splitoff of Electronic Data Systems, which provides computer services.

In November 1996, GM and the United Auto Workers agreed to a 3-year contract guaranteeing 95% of union work force levels, but gave GM some flexibility to outsource to non-union suppliers. However, about 18 local union contracts, which expired in September 1996, have yet to be renewed. Several strikes by local unions in 1997 impaired new vehicle launches.

In February 1998, directors authorized a new $4 billion share repurchase program; since January 1997, the company has bought $6.3 billion of stock.

Per Share Data ($)

(Year Ended Dec. 31)	1997	1996	1995	1994	1993	1992	1991	1990	1989	1988
Tangible Bk. Val.	5.80	7.30	7.68	12.14	-16.55	-11.48	25.86	29.52	43.48	46.93
Cash Flow	31.97	22.11	24.99	20.72	16.26	9.00	4.64	8.87	18.80	18.98
Earnings	8.62	6.07	7.28	6.20	2.13	-4.85	-8.85	-4.09	6.33	6.82
Dividends	2.00	1.60	1.10	0.80	0.80	1.40	1.60	3.00	3.00	2.50
Payout Ratio	23%	26%	15%	13%	38%	NM	NM	NM	47%	33%
Prices - High	72³/₈	59³/₈	53¹/₈	65³/₈	57¹/₈	44³/₈	44³/₈	50¹/₂	50¹/₂	44¹/₈
- Low	52¹/₄	45³/₄	37¹/₄	36¹/₈	32	28⁵/₈	26³/₄	33¹/₈	39¹/₈	30
P/E Ratio - High	8	10	7	11	27	NM	NM	NM	8	6
- Low	6	8	5	6	15	NM	NM	NM	6	4

Income Statement Analysis (Million $)

	1997	1996	1995	1994	1993	1992	1991	1990	1989	1988
Revs.	167,970	158,015	163,861	152,172	135,696	131,590	122,081	123,276	124,993	120,387
Oper. Inc.	20,225	19,513	23,811	21,565	17,059	13,143	12,257	15,862	20,443	19,291
Depr.	16,616	11,840	12,022	10,025	9,442	8,959	7,916	7,362	7,168	7,081
Int. Exp.	6,113	5,744	5,352	5,466	5,718	7,349	8,346	8,870	8,859	7,298
Pretax Inc.	7,714	6,676	9,776	8,353	2,575	-3,332	5,892	-2,216	6,398	6,735
Eff. Tax Rate	14%	26%	29%	32%	4.30%	NM	NM	NM	34%	31%
Net Inc.	6,698	4,953	6,933	5,659	2,466	-2,620	-4,991	-1,985	4,224	4,632

Balance Sheet & Other Fin. Data (Million $)

	1997	1996	1995	1994	1993	1992	1991	1990	1989	1988
Cash	11,262	22,262	16,643	10,939	13,791	7,790	4,282	3,689	5,170	5,800
Total Assets	228,888	222,142	217,123	198,598	188,200	191,012	184,325	180,236	173,297	164,063
LT Debt	41,472	39,040	36,675	38,123	33,846	39,956	40,683	38,510	36,969	31,909
Total Debt	93,249	86,266	83,324	73,730	70,441	82,592	94,022	95,634	93,425	88,425
Common Eqty.	17,505	23,168	2,961	9,155	1,191	1,399	26,238	28,736	33,464	34,153
Cap. Exp.	10,320	9,949	10,077	17,465	15,175	12,874	12,897	10,932	10,647	7,312
Cash Flow	23,242	16,712	18,745	15,363	11,551	6,032	2,853	5,338	11,358	11,687
% Ret. on Assets	3.0	2.3	3.3	2.9	1.3	NM	NM	NM	2.5	3.7
% Ret. on Equity	32.4	21.1	38.3	102.6	161.3	NM	NM	NM	12.5	14.1
% LT Debt of Cap.	69.5	59.7	61.1	74.2	84.8	84.2	53.8	53.9	49.6	46.4

Data as orig. reptd.; bef. results of disc. opers. and/or spec. items. Per share data adj. for stk. divs. as of ex-div. date. Quarterly tables reflect total revenues. Bold denotes diluted EPS (FASB 128). E-Estimate. NA-Not Available. NM-Not Meaningful. NR-Not Ranked

Office—3044 West Grand Blvd., Detroit, MI 48202-3091. **Tel**—(313) 556-5000. **Website**—http://www.gm.com **Chrmn, Pres & CEO**—J. F. Smith, Jr. **EVP & CFO**—J. M. Losh. **VP & Treas**—J. D. Finnegan. **Secy**—Nancy E. Polis. **Institutional Contact**—Paul Johnson (212-418-6270). **Stockholder Contact**—(313-556-2044). **Dirs**—A. L. Armstrong, P. Barnevik, J. H. Bryan, T. E. Everhart, C. T. Fisher III, G. M. C. Fisher, J. W. Marriott, Jr., A. D. McLaughlin, H. J. Pearce, E. Pfeiffer, E. T. Pratt, Jr., J. G. Smale, J. F. Smith, Jr., L. W. Sullivan, D. Weatherstone, T. H. Wyman. **Transfer Agent & Registrar**—Boston EquiServe.**Incorporated**—in Delaware in 1916. **Empl**— 647,000. **S&P Analyst**: Efraim Levy

General Re   993

NYSE Symbol **GRN**

In S&P 500

12-SEP-98

Industry:
Insurance (Property-Casualty)

Summary: General Re, the largest property-casualty reinsurer in the U.S., agreed in late June 1998 to merge with Berkshire Hathaway Inc.

S&P Opinion: Hold (★★★)	Recent Price • 197⅞	Yield • 1.2%	Earnings vs. Previous Year
	52 Wk Range • 275-191	12-Mo. P/E • 15.6	▲=Up ▼=Down ▶=No Change

Quantitative Evaluations

Outlook
(1 Lowest—5 Highest)
• **2+**

Fair Value
• **198**

Risk
• **Low**

Earn./Div. Rank
• **A+**

Technical Eval.
• **Bearish** since 9/95

Rel. Strength Rank
(1 Lowest—99 Highest)
• **51**

Insider Activity
• **Favorable**

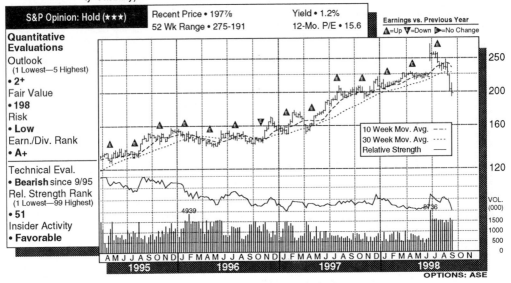

10 Week Mov. Avg. ---
30 Week Mov. Avg. ·····
Relative Strength ——

OPTIONS: ASE

Overview - 04-AUG-98

GRN's long term outlook is enhanced by its pending merger with Berkshire Hathaway Inc. (BRK). Terms of the deal call for GRN shareholders to receive either 0.0035 Class A shares or 0.105 Class B shares of Berkshire Hathaway stock. Based on July 31, 1998 closing prices, the offer was worth approximately $245.37 a share. The transaction is set to close by year end 1998. Meanwhile, GRN's written premium growth in 1998 will be under 5%, as contributions from an acquisition and faster growth in its relatively small life/health reinsurance unit are offset by weakness in GRN's core U.S. commercial lines market. Premium growth here is being stymied by an intensely competitive pricing environment, brought on by an overabundance of underwriting capacity. Moreover, the large case commercial casualty lines market -- a core market for the company -- is probably the most price competitive. While the near term erosion in GRN's premium base appears to be a negative, GRN's refusal to write subpar, inadequately priced business for the sake of near term premium growth actually leaves it better positioned in the long run. Assuming "normal" catastrophe loss experience, underwriting results should remain at about breakeven, which is above the industry average.

Valuation - 04-AUG-98

After a mixed performance during 1997, this reinsurer's shares trended upward in early 1998. The shares recently got a boost from the BRK deal. We view the deal positively. Partnering with Berkshire Hathaway will enable GRN to accept a greater deal of near term earnings volatility and more aggressively grow its business, particularly overseas. Based on July 31, 1998 closing prices, the all-stock deal was worth approximately $245.37, or approximately 3.5% more than GRN's closing price of $237.

Key Stock Statistics

S&P EPS Est. 1998	13.00	Tang. Bk. Value/Share	99.61
P/E on S&P Est. 1998	15.2	Beta	0.93
S&P EPS Est. 1999	14.50	Shareholders	4,000
Dividend Rate/Share	2.36	Market cap. (B)	$ 15.0
Shs. outstg. (M)	75.7	Inst. holdings	82%
Avg. daily vol. (M)	0.379		

Value of $10,000 invested 5 years ago: $ 18,478

Fiscal Year Ending Dec. 31

	1998	1997	1996	1995	1994	1993
Revenues (Million $)						
1Q	1,890	2,061	1,942	1,200	1,024	925.4
2Q	1,903	2,080	2,074	1,943	896.0	843.4
3Q	—	2,076	2,022	2,004	935.0	904.2
4Q	—	2,031	2,258	2,070	982.6	887.0
Yr.	—	8,251	8,296	7,210	3,837	3,560
Earnings Per Share ($)						
1Q	**3.40**	2.91	2.87	2.20	1.15	1.89
2Q	**3.22**	2.81	2.80	2.58	2.12	2.20
3Q	—	2.98	2.31	2.39	2.29	2.03
4Q	—	3.05	3.00	2.75	2.41	2.00
Yr.	—	11.76	11.00	9.92	7.97	8.11

Next earnings report expected: early November

Dividend Data (Dividends have been paid since 1934.)

Amount ($)	Date Decl.	Ex-Div. Date	Stock of Record	Payment Date
0.550	Dec. 10	Dec. 18	Dec. 22	Dec. 31 '97
0.590	Feb. 11	Mar. 20	Mar. 24	Mar. 31 '98
0.590	Jun. 10	Jun. 19	Jun. 23	Jun. 30 '98
0.590	Sep. 09	Sep. 17	Sep. 21	Sep. 30 '98

A Division of The McGraw-Hill Companies

Business Summary - 04-AUG-98

As the parent of General Reinsurance Group, the largest reinsurance organization in the U.S., GRN is well positioned to capitalize on the consolidation and "flight to quality" trends driving the reinsurance market today. GRN surprised many when, on June 19, 1998, it agreed to be acquired by Berkshire Hathaway Inc. Operating in the U.S., Canada and more than 30 other countries, GRN increased its presence in the global reinsurance market in 1994 when it acquired a controlling interest in German reinsurer Cologne Re. Contributions to pretax operating income, before equity earnings:

	1997	1996
U.S. Property-Casualty	66%	61%
International Property-Casualty	23%	26%
Life/Health	6%	5%
Financial Services	5%	8%

Net premiums written in 1997 totaled $6.5 billion ($6.7 billion in 1996), of which domestic property-casualty operations accounted for 47%, international property-casualty equaled 35% and life/health amounted to 18%. The combined (loss and expense) ratio for do-

mestic operations was 99.2% in 1997, versus 99.1% in 1996. The combined ratio for international operations was 102.4% in 1997, versus 102.1% in 1996. A combined ratio of 100% or less indicates an underwriting profit.

During 1996, GRN capitalized on the consolidation trend in the reinsurance market and acquired National Re for about $940 million in cash and stock. This acquisition, which was not dilutive to 1997 earnings, expanded GRN's presence in the reinsurance market for regional, midsize and specialty companies. A direct writer, National Re had 1996 gross premiums of about $364 million. By using reinsurance, primary insurers can limit their exposure to risk and usually write more business than their surplus levels would normally permit. Most of GRN's business is written on an excess of loss basis, which means that its liability arises only after the loss incurred by the primary insurer exceeds a specified amount.

To a lesser degree, GRN also offers life and health reinsurance. During 1997, written premiums were $1.2 billion ($1.1 billion in 1996), of which life reinsurance accounted for 70% and health 30%. General Re Financial Products offers interest rate and cross currency swaps and fixed-income option products.

Per Share Data ($)

(Year Ended Dec. 31)	1997	1996	1995	1994	1993	1992	1991	1990	1989	1988
Tangible Bk. Val.	92.89	76.92	80.22	59.35	56.68	49.90	45.16	37.50	34.31	29.04
Oper. Earnings	11.72	10.79	9.47	7.43	7.01	5.30	6.37	6.35	6.08	5.44
Earnings	11.76	11.00	9.92	7.97	8.11	6.84	7.46	6.89	6.52	5.39
Dividends	2.20	2.04	1.96	1.92	1.88	1.80	1.68	1.52	1.36	1.20
Payout Ratio	19%	19%	20%	24%	23%	26%	23%	22%	21%	22%
Prices - High	221¼	170¼	158¼	129⅛	133⅜	123½	102¾	93¼	96¼	59⅜
- Low	151	138¾	121⅝	101¾	104¾	77½	83¾	69	54⅜	45½
P/E Ratio - High	19	15	16	16	16	18	14	14	15	11
- Low	13	13	12	13	13	11	11	10	8	8

Income Statement Analysis (Million $)

	1997	1996	1995	1994	1993	1992	1991	1990	1989	1988
Premium Inc.	6,607	6,678	5,837	2,788	2,446	2,319	2,241	2,102	1,908	2,044
Net Invest. Inc.	1,288	1,205	1,017	749	755	755	752	706	673	570
Oth. Revs.	356	413	346	300	359	313	214	186	190	122
Total Revs.	6,963	8,296	7,210	3,837	3,560	3,387	3,207	2,993	2,771	2,736
Pretax Inc.	1,327	1,297	1,117	794	885	721	793	738	733	571
Net Oper. Inc.	965	877	788	621	604	465	562	566	559	519
Net Inc.	968	894	82.5	665	697	596	657	614	599	513

Balance Sheet & Other Fin. Data (Million $)

	1997	1996	1995	1994	1993	1992	1991	1990	1989	1988
Cash & Equiv.	352	770	648	514	300	245	244	228	219	183
Premiums Due	NA	2,832	2,368	1,421	798	670	588	551	577	503
Invest. Assets: Bonds	20,799	21,402	17,304	14,174	11,441	9,376	9,015	8,224	7,458	6,829
Invest. Assets: Stocks	5,789	4,464	3,944	2,977	2,726	2,157	1,827	1,286	1,342	1,037
Invest. Assets: Loans	Nil	Nil	Nil	Nil	Nil	Nil	Nil	Nil	Nil	Nil
Invest. Assets: Total	31,669	26,562	23,494	18,898	14,167	11,532	10,842	9,510	8,799	7,866
Deferred Policy Costs	476	457	434	324	153	155	157	149	139	136
Total Assets	41,459	40,161	35,946	29,597	18,469	13,280	12,416	11,033	10,390	9,394
Debt	2,750	430	155	188	453	209	316	277	278	127
Common Eqty.	8,019	7,326	6,587	4,859	4,761	4,227	3,911	3,270	3,084	2,695
Prop. & Cas. Loss Ratio	NA	71.5	71.7	70.7	70.6	78.8	72.5	68.2	70.6	70.0
Prop. & Cas. Expense Ratio	NA	33.3	32.7	30.6	30.9	29.6	29.7	30.8	29.0	29.1
Prop. & Cas. Combined Ratio	NA	104.8	104.4	101.3	101.5	108.4	102.2	99.0	99.6	99.1
% Return On Revs.	13.9	10.8	11.4	17.3	19.6	17.6	20.5	20.5	21.6	19.0
% Ret. on Equity	12.6	12.7	14.3	15.5	14.7	14.7	18.1	19.0	20.7	19.7

Data as orig. reptd.; bef. results of disc. opers. and/or spec. items. Per share data adj. for stk. divs. as of ex-div. date. EPS estimates are based on operating earnings before securities gains/losses. Bold denotes diluted EPS (FASB 128). E-Estimated. NM-Not Meaningful. NR-Not Ranked.

Office—Financial Centre, 695 E. Main St., P.O. Box 10351, Stamford, CT 06904. **Tel**—(203) 328-5000. **Chrmn & CEO**—R. E. Ferguson. **Pres & COO**—J. E. Gustafson. **VP-Secy**—C. F. Barr. **VP-CFO**—J. P. Brandon. **Investor Contacts**—Katherine Stallfort & Deborah Tracy. **Dirs**—L. W. Benson, W. M. Cabot, R. E. Ferguson, W. C. Ferguson, D. J. Kirk, K. Koplovitz, E. H. Malone, A. W. Mathieson, M. G. McGuinn, D. E. McKinney, S. A. Ross, W. F. Williams. **Transfer Agent & Registrar**—American Stock Transfer & Trust Co., NYC. **Incorporated**—in New York in 1921; reincorporated in Delaware in 1972. **Empl**— 3,700. **S&P Analyst:** Catherine A. Seifert

General Signal

996A

NYSE Symbol **GSX**

In S&P 500

12-SEP-98

Industry: Electrical Equipment

Summary: General Signal makes a variety of industrial and electrical equipment. In July 1998, it agreed to be acquired by SPX Corp.

S&P Opinion: Hold (★★★)	Recent Price • 36⅜	Yield • 3.0%	Earnings vs. Previous Year
	52 Wk Range • 47¼-35½	12-Mo. P/E • 13.5	▲=Up ▼=Down ▶=No Change

Quantitative Evaluations

Outlook
(1 Lowest—5 Highest)
• **3+**

Fair Value
• **42½**

Risk
• **Low**

Earn./Div. Rank
• **B**

Technical Eval.
• **Bearish** since 3/98

Rel. Strength Rank
(1 Lowest—99 Highest)
• **73**

Insider Activity
• **NA**

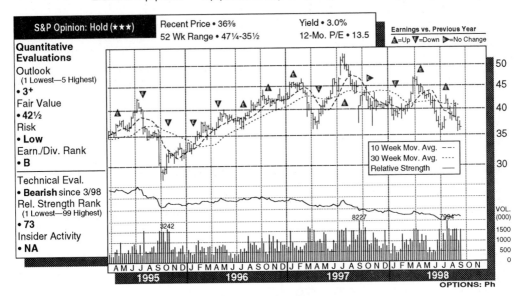

```
10 Week Mov. Avg.  ---
30 Week Mov. Avg.  ....
Relative Strength  —
```

OPTIONS: Ph

Overview - 21-JUL-98

On July 20, 1998, General Signal agreed to be acquired by SPX Corp. (NYSE: SPW), an acquisitive auto parts maker with $1 billion in revenues, for $45 a share in stock and cash. We believe SPW wants to diversify its acquisition platform utilizing GSX's industrial controls and electrical equipment businesses. SPW wants to enter new businesses that are more reasonably priced than the available crop of automotive businesses. Separately, in the last several years, General Signal has been trying to get its "sea legs", by streamlining and restructuring operations. Since 1989, the company has reduced operations from 44 to 14 businesses. However, challenges still remain. Recent problems in ongoing businesses involved a slowdown at Kayex, which makes crystal growing furnaces for semiconductor manufacturers, and delayed new product introductions in 1997 at two units which hampered sales. Those products have now been released. The company now plans to merge two units, Lightnin and DeZurik, to reduce combined operating costs. A long-term effort to reduce inventories, lower purchasing costs, raise productivity and step up product development continues.

Valuation - 21-JUL-98

In light of the proposed SPW/GSX merger, we upgraded General Signal to a "hold" rating. Although we remain cautious about the long-term prospects of the combined company, we believe it would be advantageous, from a capital tax savings viewpoint, for General Signal shareholders to convert GSX stock to SPW shares. Moreover, restructuring efforts may be bearing fruit for the company. In the second quarter of 1998, the company posted per-share earnings of $0.70, versus $0.68 a year ago.

Key Stock Statistics

S&P EPS Est. 1998	2.50	Tang. Bk. Value/Share	7.55
P/E on S&P Est. 1998	14.6	Beta	0.76
S&P EPS Est. 1999	2.75	Shareholders	10,400
Dividend Rate/Share	1.08	Market cap. (B)	$ 1.6
Shs. outstg. (M)	43.7	Inst. holdings	69%
Avg. daily vol. (M)	0.370		

Value of $10,000 invested 5 years ago: $ 13,870

Fiscal Year Ending Dec. 31

	1998	1997	1996	1995	1994	1993
Revenues (Million $)						
1Q	374.4	505.6	481.7	411.0	342.4	377.0
2Q	401.6	539.6	515.0	421.4	378.6	387.0
3Q	—	475.7	521.6	455.5	390.0	373.0
4Q	—	433.7	546.7	501.6	416.7	393.8
Yr.	—	1,955	2,065	1,863	1,528	1,530
Earnings Per Share ($)						
1Q	0.50	0.47	0.51	0.58	0.47	0.42
2Q	0.70	0.68	0.64	0.50	0.53	0.44
3Q	—	0.73	0.75	0.54	0.58	0.52
4Q	—	0.75	0.78	0.41	0.62	0.10
Yr.	—	2.60	2.68	2.03	2.20	1.47

Next earnings report expected: late October

Dividend Data (Dividends have been paid since 1940.)

Amount ($)	Date Decl.	Ex-Div. Date	Stock of Record	Payment Date
0.255	Sep. 18	Oct. 07	Oct. 09	Oct. 17 '97
0.270	Dec. 11	Jan. 06	Jan. 12	Jan. 21 '98
0.270	Mar. 19	Apr. 07	Apr. 09	Apr. 20 '98
0.270	Jun. 18	Jul. 07	Jul. 09	Jul. 17 '98

 A Division of The **McGraw-Hill** Companies

Business Summary - 21-JUL-98

General Signal (GSX) is a broadly diversified manufacturer with 14 businesses grouped in three segments. The businesses, which as a group derive only 13% of sales and 8% of earnings from foreign operations, operate in a decentralized fashion in an effort to foster an entrepreneurial organizational style. Presently, management is focused on maximizing the performance of the 15 business units. GSX expects to spin off GS Networks to shareholders in 1998; three other unidentified businesses may be sold. In addition, the DeZurik and Lightnin units will be merged in 1998.

Business segment contributions in 1997 were:

	Sales	Profits
Process controls	34%	53%
Electrical controls	47%	24%
Industrial technology	19%	23%

Process controls include DeZurik, Kayex, Lightnin, Revco/Lindberg and Stock Equipment. The process control divisions produce industrial fluid mixers, agitators, coal feeder equipment, industrial valves, consistency transmitters, ultra-low-temperature laboratory freezers, special refrigerators, CO_2 incubators, industrial and laboratory ovens and furnaces, and crystal growing furnaces for the semiconductor wafer manufacturing industry. In the 1997 third quarter, GSX sold its GS Pump unit for $200 million to Pentair.

Electrical control products include several well-known brands, including Best Power (uninterruptible power systems), Edwards Systems Technology (fire detection systems) and Waukesha Electric Systems (medium-power transformers, remanufacturing and decommissioning services). Other products include power conditioners/regulators, electrical conduit and cable fittings, enclosures and controls, industrial lighting, heat-trace systems, firestop products, low-voltage systems service, emergency lighting, exit signs, signaling devices, flexible wiring systems, fractional-horsepower electric motors, radio frequency transmission and pressurization equipment and systems.

The industrial technology segment includes GS Networks, GFI Genfare and Metal Forge. GFI Genfare and Metal Forge manufacture metal components and assemblies for automobiles and bicycles, electronic fareboxes, turnstiles, vending equipment, performance monitoring and test equipment for telecommunications and other industries. GS Networks, which will be spun off in 1998, provides network matrix switching systems, host networking products and fiber management systems.

Per Share Data ($)

(Year Ended Dec. 31)	1997	1996	1995	1994	1993	1992	1991	1990	1989	1988
Tangible Bk. Val.	7.77	7.05	3.51	7.51	7.20	4.79	6.70	5.89	8.89	8.65
Cash Flow	3.90	4.04	3.35	3.08	2.35	1.36	2.88	0.97	3.71	1.57
Earnings	2.60	2.68	2.03	2.20	1.47	0.23	1.66	-0.34	2.06	0.46
Dividends	1.02	0.96	0.72	0.92	0.90	0.90	0.90	0.90	0.90	0.90
Payout Ratio	39%	36%	35%	42%	61%	387%	54%	NM	44%	198%
Prices - High	53	44¹/₂	42¹/₂	38	36³/₄	32⁵/₈	27	29³/₄	29	28¹/₄
- Low	36¹/₈	32	28	30¹/₈	30¹/₈	25⁷/₈	17⁵/₈	15³/₄	22⁷/₈	20
P/E Ratio - High	20	17	21	17	25	NM	16	NM	14	62
- Low	14	12	14	14	20	NM	11	NM	11	44

Income Statement Analysis (Million $)

	1997	1996	1995	1994	1993	1992	1991	1990	1989	1988
Revs.	1,954	2,065	1,863	1,528	1,530	1,618	1,611	1,695	1,918	1,760
Oper. Inc.	245	292	264	168	160	164	158	177	196	136
Depr.	64.0	69.0	64.0	41.7	39.6	44.0	47.2	50.6	63.1	61.8
Int. Exp.	13.0	22.0	24.0	11.8	16.5	27.1	32.2	37.6	45.1	12.4
Pretax Inc.	253	222	156	160	94.0	14.0	89.0	-25.0	106	53.0
Eff. Tax Rate	48%	40%	36%	35%	30%	32%	29%	NM	26%	52%
Net Inc.	131	133	36.0	104	67.0	9.0	64.0	-13.0	78.0	25.0

Balance Sheet & Other Fin. Data (Million $)

	1997	1996	1995	1994	1993	1992	1991	1990	1989	1988
Cash	50.0	18.0	Nil	Nil	1.0	16.0	18.0	8.0	24.0	109
Curr. Assets	568	692	721	717	595	678	602	714	774	892
Total Assets	1,388	1,551	1,613	1,343	1,225	1,226	1,180	1,295	1,324	1,397
Curr. Liab.	377	439	432	357	326	336	358	403	445	396
LT Debt	208	201	429	269	191	358	290	398	331	492
Common Eqty.	630	744	578	548	525	365	476	450	506	461
Total Cap.	888	962	1,007	817	717	723	809	879	870	989
Cap. Exp.	56.5	59.0	49.0	74.8	55.1	49.3	48.1	68.8	62.0	38.8
Cash Flow	195	202	164	146	106	53.0	111	37.0	142	87.0
Curr. Ratio	1.5	1.6	1.7	2.0	1.8	2.0	1.7	1.8	1.7	2.3
% LT Debt of Cap.	23.4	20.9	42.6	32.9	26.7	49.5	35.8	45.2	38.1	49.7
% Net Inc.of Revs.	6.7	6.4	1.9	6.8	4.4	0.6	4.0	NM	4.1	1.4
% Ret. on Assets	8.9	8.4	2.4	8.1	4.9	0.8	5.2	5.8	5.8	2.1
% Ret. on Equity	19.1	20.2	6.4	19.5	13.8	2.2	13.8	NM	16.2	4.6

Data as orig. reptd.; bef. results of disc. opers. and/or spec. items. Per share data adj. for stk. divs. as of ex-div. date. Bold denotes diluted EPS (FASB 128). E-Estimated. NA-Not Available. NM-Not Meaningful. NR-Not Ranked.

Offices—One High Ridge Park, P.O. Box 10010, Stamford, CT 06904. **Tel**—(203) 329-4100. **Website**—http://www.generalsignal.com **Chrmn & CEO**—M. D. Lockhart. **EVP & CFO**—T. D. Martin. **VP & Secy**—J. L. Bober. **VP & Investor Contact**—Nino J. Fernandez. **Dirs**—H. K. Bowen, V. C. Campbell, M. A. Carpenter, U. F. Fairbairn, R. E. Ferguson, R. D. Kennedy, M. D. Lockhart, J. R. Selby. **Transfer Agent**—First Chicago Trust Co. of New York, Jersey City, NJ. **Incorporated**—in New York in 1904. **Empl**—13,000. **S&P Analyst**: Robert E. Friedman, CPA

12-SEP-98

Industry: Auto Parts & Equipment

Summary: This company is a leading wholesale distributor of automotive replacement parts, industrial parts and supplies, and office products.

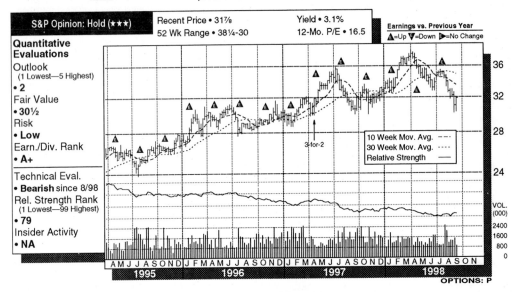

S&P Opinion: Hold (★★★)	Recent Price • 31⅞	Yield • 3.1%
	52 Wk Range • 38¼-30	12-Mo. P/E • 16.5

Earnings vs. Previous Year
▲=Up ▼=Down ▶=No Change

Quantitative Evaluations

Outlook (1 Lowest—5 Highest)
• **2**

Fair Value
• **30½**

Risk
• **Low**

Earn./Div. Rank
• **A+**

Technical Eval.
• **Bearish** since 8/98

Rel. Strength Rank (1 Lowest—99 Highest)
• **79**

Insider Activity
• **NA**

3-for-2

10 Week Mov. Avg. -- ---
30 Week Mov. Avg. ......
Relative Strength ———

VOL. (000)

OPTIONS: P

Overview - 23-JUL-98

Despite strong marketing programs, GPC's sales growth has moderated, reflecting soft industry-wide conditions in the automotive parts aftermarket, and a competitive environment in the office products segment. In 1997, auto parts revenues were up 2%, and office products gained 4%. This relatively weak performance was partly offset by gains at the industrial parts group, where sales rose 10%. Longer term prospects for GPC's auto parts segment are enhanced by the rising number and increasing complexity of vehicles. The average vehicle in the U.S. is currently more than eight years old. Despite the improved quality of new vehicles, the growing number of older vehicles, together with an increase in the percentage of those vehicles that will be subject to emissions inspection, will fuel increased demand for parts needed to return them to original specifications. GPC also benefits from expansion of its market share, as long-term consolidation in the industry drives out smaller participants. GPC is known for its excellent, conservative management.

Valuation - 23-JUL-98

We continue our hold recommendation on the shares. Although an ongoing consolidation in the aftermarket presents an opportunity for market share growth, GPC's conservative management practices will serve as a restraint on its growth rate. The stock now trades at about 17X expected 1998 EPS, and we do not expect much expansion of the multiple without evidence of a sustainable, faster growth rate. In recent years, earnings growth has averaged 10%. We expect only average performance for the near term, but a solid balance sheet, low debt level, and strong cash flow are resources that could be used to accelerate earnings growth.

Key Stock Statistics

S&P EPS Est. 1998	2.10	Tang. Bk. Value/Share	10.76
P/E on S&P Est. 1998	15.2	Beta	0.59
Dividend Rate/Share	1.00	Shareholders	7,800
Shs. outstg. (M)	178.7	Market cap. (B)	$ 5.7
Avg. daily vol. (M)	0.260	Inst. holdings	69%

Value of $10,000 invested 5 years ago: $ 16,753

Fiscal Year Ending Dec. 31

	1998	1997	1996	1995	1994	1993
Revenues (Million $)						
1Q	1,533	1,458	1,400	1,281	1,162	1,038
2Q	1,619	1,510	1,445	1,309	1,220	1,106
3Q	—	1,556	1,475	1,362	1,268	1,145
4Q	—	1,481	1,401	1,309	1,208	1,095
Yr.	—	6,005	5,720	5,262	4,858	4,384
Earnings Per Share ($)						
1Q	**0.45**	**0.42**	0.41	0.37	0.34	0.30
2Q	**0.48**	**0.46**	0.45	0.41	0.38	0.35
3Q	—	**0.47**	0.45	0.42	0.39	0.34
4Q	—	**0.55**	0.51	0.48	0.44	0.39
Yr.	**E2.10**	**1.90**	1.82	1.68	1.55	1.39

Next earnings report expected: late October

Dividend Data (Dividends have been paid since 1948.)

Amount ($)	Date Decl.	Ex-Div. Date	Stock of Record	Payment Date
0.240	Nov. 17	Dec. 03	Dec. 05	Jan. 02 '98
0.250	Feb. 16	Mar. 04	Mar. 06	Apr. 01 '98
0.250	Apr. 22	Jun. 03	Jun. 05	Jul. 01 '98
0.250	Aug. 17	Sep. 02	Sep. 04	Oct. 01 '98

A Division of The **McGraw·Hill** Companies

Genuine Parts Company

Business Summary - 23-JUL-98

Genuine Parts Company is the leading independent distributor of automotive replacement parts. As of December 1997, it was operating 62 NAPA warehouse distribution centers in the U.S., about 750 company-owned jobbing stores, five Rayloc auto parts rebuilding plants, and three Balkamp distribution centers. It also directly owns 49% of UAP/NAPA, a Canadian automotive parts distributor, plus a 23% interest in UAP Inc., the owner of the remaining 51% of UAP/NAPA. Contributions by segment in 1997 were:

	Sales	Profits
Automotive parts & supplies	51%	54%
Industrial parts & supplies	31%	28%
Office products	18%	18%

Automotive parts serves 5,600 NAPA Auto Parts jobbing stores, including about 750 company-owned stores, which sell to garages, service stations, car and truck dealers, fleet operators, leasing companies, bus and truck lines, etc. About 200,000 items are stocked. Rebuilt parts are distributed under the Rayloc brand name. Balkamp is a majority-owned subsidiary that distributes service and supply items to NAPA distribution centers.

Motion Industries, the industrial parts segment, distributes more than 200,000 parts and related supply items, including bearings, fluid transmission equipment, hydraulic and pneumatic products, material handling components, agricultural and irrigation equipment, and related items from locations in 46 states, with approximately 420 branches, 27 service centers, and seven distribution centers.

S.P. Richards Co. distributes more than 20,000 office products items, including information processing supplies and office furniture, machines and supplies to office suppliers, from 46 facilities in 31 states, including 40 distribution centers, five furniture centers and one Horizon Data Supplies facility.

GPC said that market conditions in all three distribution groups remained favorable in 1996, with all three enjoying higher sales. Price increases were minimal, with unit sales increases accounting for most of the revenue expansion. The situation was similar in 1997, except that sales slowed in the auto parts and office products segments. In 1997, auto parts sales were up 2.1%, while industrial parts advanced 10% and office products sales increased 4.5%. Mild winter weather hurt auto parts sales, and a competitive and rapidly changing environment constrained office products.

In July 1998, GPC completed the acquisition of EIS, Inc. for cash and stock aggregating approximately $200 million. EIS is a wholesale distributor of material and supplies to the electrical and electronic industries. The company expects EIS sales of about $500 million in 1998.

Per Share Data ($) (Year Ended Dec. 31)	1997	1996	1995	1994	1993	1992	1991	1990	1989	1988
Tangible Bk. Val.	10.39	6.41	6.02	8.30	7.75	7.19	6.57	6.01	5.57	4.96
Cash Flow	2.23	2.09	1.91	1.75	1.57	1.46	1.39	1.35	1.29	1.18
Earnings	1.90	1.82	1.68	1.55	1.39	1.28	1.21	1.19	1.15	1.05
Dividends	0.96	0.89	0.84	0.77	0.71	0.66	0.64	0.61	0.53	0.46
Payout Ratio	51%	49%	50%	49%	51%	52%	53%	51%	47%	44%
Prices - High	35⅞	31⅝	28	26¼	26	23⅛	21⅞	19	19⅜	18⅛
- Low	28⅝	26⅝	23⅝	22⅜	21⅞	19⅜	15½	14¾	15½	14⅜
P/E Ratio - High	19	17	17	17	19	18	18	16	17	17
- Low	15	15	14	14	16	15	13	12	14	14
Income Statement Analysis (Million $)										
Revs.	6,005	5,720	5,262	4,858	4,384	3,669	3,435	3,319	3,161	2,942
Oper. Inc.	624	596	554	502	453	379	359	353	339	312
Depr.	58.9	50.4	43.2	37.4	34.4	31.1	29.8	28.8	24.6	24.3
Int. Exp.	NA	NM	NM	1.3	1.6	1.8	5.4	5.1	5.4	1.8
Pretax Inc.	566	545	511	477	428	356	337	335	323	292
Eff. Tax Rate	39%	40%	40%	39%	39%	38%	38%	38%	38%	37%
Net Inc.	342	330	309	289	259	220	208	207	199	181
Balance Sheet & Other Fin. Data (Million $)										
Cash	72.8	67.4	44.3	82.0	188	173	186	145	170	123
Curr. Assets	2,094	1,938	1,764	1,596	1,506	1,277	1,179	1,099	1,056	968
Total Assets	2,754	2,522	2,274	2,029	1,871	1,597	1,467	1,352	1,292	1,141
Curr. Liab.	557	568	476	422	353	309	291	269	245	231
LT Debt	210	110	60.6	11.4	12.3	13.0	12.7	16.4	43.1	18.2
Common Eqty.	1,859	1,732	1,651	1,526	1,445	1,235	1,127	1,033	972	863
Total Cap.	2,198	1,953	1,770	1,607	1,517	1,288	1,176	1,083	1,047	910
Cap. Exp.	90.4	95.2	91.0	66.0	57.5	31.2	27.9	44.5	53.2	35.0
Cash Flow	401	380	352	326	293	251	238	235	224	206
Curr. Ratio	3.8	3.4	3.7	3.8	4.3	4.1	4.1	4.1	4.3	4.2
% LT Debt of Cap.	9.5	5.6	3.4	0.7	0.8	1.0	1.1	1.5	4.1	2.0
% Net Inc.of Revs.	5.7	5.8	5.9	5.9	5.9	6.0	6.0	6.2	6.3	6.2
% Ret. on Assets	13.0	13.8	14.4	14.9	14.4	14.3	14.7	15.7	16.4	16.7
% Ret. on Equity	19.1	19.5	19.5	19.5	18.6	18.6	19.2	20.8	21.7	22.3

Data as orig. reptd.; bef. results of disc. opers. and/or spec. items. Per share data adj. for stk. divs. as of ex-div. date. Bold denotes diluted EPS (FASB 128). E-Estimated. NA-Not Available. NM-Not Meaningful. NR-Not Ranked.

Office—2999 Circle 75 Pkwy, Atlanta, GA 30339. **Tel**—(770) 953-1700. **Website**—http://www.genpt.com **Chrmn & CEO**—L. L. Prince. **Pres & COO**—T. C. Gallagher. **Secy**—C. Yancey. **SVP-Fin & Investor Contact**—Jerry W. Nix. **Dirs**—R. W. Courts III, B. Currey, Jr., J. Douville, R. P. Forrestal, T. C. Gallagher, J. H. Lanier, Jr., L. L. Prince, A. S. Shepherd, L. G. Steiner, J. B. Williams. **Transfer Agent & Registrar**—SunTrust Bank, Atlanta. **Incorporated**—in Georgia in 1928. **Empl**— 24,500. **S&P Analyst:** Efraim Levy

Georgia-Pacific (Georgia-Pacific Group) 1006

NYSE Symbol **GP**

In S&P 500

12-SEP-98

Industry:
Paper & Forest Products

Summary: Georgia-Pacific Corp. separated its businesses into two distinct classes of common stock in late 1997. Georgia-Pacific Group represents its paper and building products operations.

S&P Opinion: Avoid (★★)	Recent Price • 37¾	Yield • 2.6%
	52 Wk Range • 108½-37⅜	12-Mo. P/E • NM

Quantitative Evaluations

Outlook
(1 Lowest—5 Highest)
• **3 –**

Fair Value
• **47½**

Risk
• **Low**

Earn./Div. Rank
• **B-**

Technical Eval.
• **Bullish** since 12/95

Rel. Strength Rank
(1 Lowest—99 Highest)
• **21**

Insider Activity
• **Neutral**

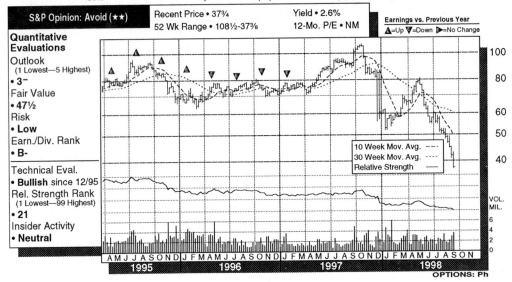

Earnings vs. Previous Year
▲=Up ▼=Down ▶=No Change

10 Week Mov. Avg. - - -
30 Week Mov. Avg. · · · ·
Relative Strength ——

OPTIONS: Ph

Overview - 04-AUG-98

Sales from comparable operations should be about flat in 1998, on mixed results. Sales should be a bit higher in the paper sector, on a slight gain in average paper and packaging prices. However, with Asia's financial woes and a strong U.S. dollar affecting foreign trade, a modest pricing recovery seen between early 1997 and early 1998 (after a severe downturn since late 1995) has been put on hold. The paper sector gains should be offset by lower building products sales, as oversupply has dragged down lumber prices, and wood panels markets still battle excess capacity (despite some recent strength in oriented strand board). We see operating margins widening, despite the lackluster sales picture. We see gains resulting from higher average paper and board pricing, savings from an aggressive cost reduction program (initiated in mid-1996), and the ongoing reorganization of the building products distribution business. Comparisons will be distorted by major write-offs in the 1997 fourth quarter.

Valuation - 04-AUG-98

Georgia-Pacific Group shares opened for trading at $64 in December 1997, and have seesawed since inception. The shares initially moved sharply higher, as investors put aside worries about the Asian financial crisis, and started to believe that a solid forest products recovery was at hand. They gave back these gains since the spring of 1998, when it began to look as if Asia's troubles would have a greater impact and last longer than previously expected. We have been bearish on the forest products industry throughout, and maintain our negative investment stance on GP. Given our belief that troubles in the global economy will limit industry prospects for an extended period, we see little chance of a major profit recovery at Georgia-Pacific in coming periods. We would therefore still avoid the shares.

Key Stock Statistics

S&P EPS Est. 1998	1.20	Tang. Bk. Value/Share	20.86
P/E on S&P Est. 1998	31.5	Beta	1.06
S&P EPS Est. 1999	1.40	Shareholders	39,800
Dividend Rate/Share	1.00	Market cap. (B)	$ 3.5
Shs. outstg. (M)	93.3	Inst. holdings	65%
Avg. daily vol. (M)	0.521		

Value of $10,000 invested 5 years ago: NA

Fiscal Year Ending Dec. 31

	1998	1997	1996	1995	1994	1993
Revenues (Million $)						
1Q	3,193	—	3,053	3,477	2,942	2,944
2Q	3,275	—	3,324	3,700	3,187	3,205
3Q	—	9,747	3,451	3,705	3,267	2,982
4Q	—	3,221	3,196	3,410	3,342	3,199
Yr.	—	12,968	13,024	14,292	12,738	12,330
Earnings Per Share ($)						
1Q	0.17	—	0.55	2.59	0.63	0.47
2Q	0.33	—	0.11	2.95	0.16	0.06
3Q	E0.35	0.19	1.09	3.57	0.98	-0.33
4Q	E0.35	-1.13	0.02	2.17	1.89	-0.41
Yr.	E1.20	-0.94	1.78	11.29	3.66	-0.21

Next earnings report expected: early October

Dividend Data (Dividends have been paid since 1927.)

Amount ($)	Date Decl.	Ex-Div. Date	Stock of Record	Payment Date
Stk.	Dec. 08	Dec. 17	Dec. 16	Dec. 17 '97
0.250	Jan. 26	Feb. 02	Feb. 04	Feb. 13 '98
0.250	May. 05	May. 12	May. 14	May. 22 '98
0.250	Jul. 30	Aug. 06	Aug. 10	Aug. 19 '98

A Division of The McGraw·Hill Companies

Business Summary - 04-AUG-98

Effective December 17, 1997, Georgia-Pacific Corp. separated its businesses for trading under two distinct classes of common stock. The company's previously existing common stock was designated as Georgia-Pacific Group shares (NYSE: GP), reflecting the performance of the pulp, paper and building products businesses. The company's timber business is represented by a new class of shares, trading as The Timber Co. (NYSE: TGP). In recent years, Georgia-Pacific also restructured its building products distribution business and established an aggressive cost cutting program. GP derives most of its sales in the U.S.

GP ranks as the largest U.S. producer of structural and other wood panels, including plywood, oriented strand board and industrial panels. The company accounts for about 20% of U.S. structural panel capacity. Georgia-Pacific also holds the number two spot in lumber output, and produces gypsum products and chemicals. The segment's distribution division sells products made by both GP and third parties.

In the pulp and paper area, GP holds the number two spot in containerboard (about 65% of GP's containerboard is used in its corrugated box plants), uncoated free sheet and market pulp (the primary raw material in many grades of paper). It also produces tissue.

At 1997 year end, GP had the capacity to produce 9.4 million tons of pulp, paper and paperboard.

During 1996, GP set a goal of lifting pretax earnings by $400 million over a three-year period, through reduction of overhead costs and improvement of operating efficiencies. It expects to reduce costs by over $200 million by eliminating lower-value activities and streamlining its processes and organizations. GP thought it could achieve the other $200 million in combined savings and revenue enhancements from information systems improvements and a restructuring of its building products distribution business. In January 1998, GP announced an extension of the restructuring, under which it will seek to sell most of its millwork fabrication plants (which assemble doors, windows and other moulding products) and certain distribution warehouses in the western U.S. A material writeoff related to these latest actions was recorded in the fourth quarter of 1997.

Georgia-Pacific separated its timber business in December 1997, through the distribution of one TGP share for each GP share held. Georgia-Pacific (The Timber Co.) owns or controls some 5.8 million acres of timberlands in North America. Georgia-Pacific Corp. undertook this recapitalization because it believed that the highly cyclical nature of its paper and building products businesses had been limiting the valuation of its more stable timber operation. The timber business makes most of its sales to GP's manufacturing operations.

Per Share Data ($)

(Year Ended Dec. 31)	1997	1996	1995	1994	1993	1992	1991	1990	1989	1988
Tangible Bk. Val.	20.86	20.38	19.77	9.03	5.98	7.00	9.00	10.76	30.30	27.79
Cash Flow	9.05	12.07	19.78	12.70	9.18	9.12	8.74	13.06	13.30	9.44
Earnings	-0.94	1.78	11.29	3.66	-0.21	-0.69	-0.40	4.28	7.42	4.76
Dividends	2.00	2.00	1.90	1.60	1.60	1.60	1.60	1.60	1.45	1.25
Payout Ratio	NM	112%	17%	44%	NM	NM	NM	38%	19%	25%
Prices - High	108$^{1}/_{2}$	81	95$^{3}/_{4}$	79	75	72	60$^{1}/_{4}$	52$^{1}/_{8}$	62	42$^{7}/_{8}$
- Low	56	63	65$^{3}/_{4}$	56$^{3}/_{4}$	55	48$^{1}/_{4}$	36$^{1}/_{4}$	25$^{3}/_{8}$	36$^{5}/_{8}$	30$^{3}/_{4}$
P/E Ratio - High	NM	46	8	22	NM	NM	NM	12	8	9
- Low	NM	35	6	16	NM	NM	NM	6	5	6

Income Statement Analysis (Million $)

	1997	1996	1995	1994	1993	1992	1991	1990	1989	1988
Revs.	12,968	13,024	14,292	12,738	12,330	11,847	11,524	12,665	10,171	9,509
Oper. Inc.	1,159	1,672	2,854	1,773	1,385	1,339	1,283	2,026	1,871	1,434
Depr.	910	937	762	805	823	848	784	749	524	459
Int. Exp.	381	470	434	460	516	567	598	645	272	222
Pretax Inc.	-117	296	1,697	572	23.0	-74.0	259	719	1,087	778
Eff. Tax Rate	45%	46%	40%	43%	178%	NM	113%	49%	39%	40%
Net Inc.	-86.0	161	1,018	326	-18.0	-60.0	-34.0	365	661	467

Balance Sheet & Other Fin. Data (Million $)

	1997	1996	1995	1994	1993	1992	1991	1990	1989	1988
Cash	8.0	10.0	11.0	53.0	41.0	55.0	48.0	58.0	23.0	62.0
Curr. Assets	2,911	2,615	2,595	1,862	1,646	1,607	1,562	1,766	1,829	1,892
Total Assets	11,779	12,818	12,335	10,728	10,545	10,890	10,622	12,060	7,056	7,115
Curr. Liab.	2,698	2,490	1,762	2,325	2,064	2,452	2,722	2,535	924	1,013
LT Debt	3,057	4,371	4,704	3,904	4,157	4,019	3,743	5,218	2,336	2,514
Common Eqty.	-3,522	3,521	3,519	2,620	2,402	2,508	2,736	2,975	2,717	2,635
Total Cap.	7,539	9,053	9,370	7,578	7,654	7,729	7,274	9,121	5,894	5,937
Cap. Exp.	731	1,059	1,339	894	467	384	528	3,789	499	1,552
Cash Flow	824	1,098	1,780	1,131	805	788	750	1,114	1,185	926
Curr. Ratio	1.1	1.1	1.5	0.8	0.8	0.7	0.6	0.7	2.0	1.9
% LT Debt of Cap.	40.5	48.3	50.2	51.5	54.3	52.0	51.5	57.2	39.6	42.3
% Net Inc.of Revs.	1.0	1.2	7.2	2.6	NM	NM	NM	2.9	6.5	4.9
% Ret. on Assets	1.0	1.3	8.8	3.1	NM	NM	NM	3.8	9.8	7.5
% Ret. on Equity	3.7	4.6	33.2	13.0	NM	NM	NM	12.8	25.8	18.5

Data as orig. reptd.; bef. results of disc. opers. and/or spec. items. Per share data adj. for stk. divs. as of ex-div. date. Bold denotes diluted EPS (FASB 128). E-Estimated. NA-Not Available. NM-Not Meaningful. NR-Not Ranked.

Office—133 Peachtree St., N.E., Atlanta, GA 30303. **Tel**—(404) 652-4000. **Website**—http://www.gp.com **Chrmn, Pres & CEO**—A. D. Correll. **EVP & CFO**—J. F. McGovern. **VP & Secy**—K. F. Khoury. **Dirs**—R. Carswell, A. D. Correll, J. Evans, D. V. Fites, H. C. Fruehauf Jr., R. V. Giordano, D. R. Goode, T. M. Hahn Jr., M. D. Ivester, F. Jungers, L. W. Sullivan, J. B. Williams. **Transfer Agent & Registrar**—First Chicago Trust Co. of New York, Jersey City, NJ. **Incorporated**—in Georgia. in 1927. **Empl**— 46,500. **S&P Analyst:** Michael W. Jaffe

12-SEP-98

Industry: Personal Care

Summary: Gillette is a global manufacturer of razors and blades, hair care products, toiletries, writing instruments, small appliances and alkaline batteries.

S&P Opinion: Accumulate (★★★★)	Recent Price • 41⅞	Yield • 1.2%
	52 Wk Range • 62⅝-38⅞	12-Mo. P/E • 32.0

Quantitative Evaluations

Outlook
(1 Lowest—5 Highest)
• **1**

Fair Value
• **36⅝**

Risk
• **Low**

Earn./Div. Rank
• **A+**

Technical Eval.
• **Bearish** since 8/98

Rel. Strength Rank
(1 Lowest—99 Highest)
• **40**

Insider Activity
• **Neutral**

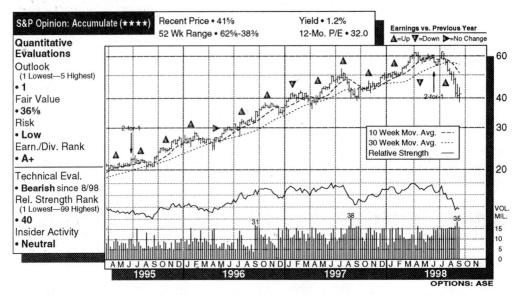

Earnings vs. Previous Year
▲=Up ▼=Down ▶=No Change

10 Week Mov. Avg. ---
30 Week Mov. Avg. ·····
Relative Strength

OPTIONS: ASE

Overview - 22-JUL-98

We expect consolidated sales will rise 3% to 5% in 1998, aided by new product introductions, particularly the mid-year launch of the new Mach3 shaving system, and the new Duracell Ultra battery line. Sales gains will be somewhat limited by the continued negative effect of a strong dollar overseas. It is likely that operating margins will contract a bit in 1998 as the start-up costs for the Mach3 shaver and destocking of older Gillette shavers will crimp profitability. This will be partly offset by stronger battery margins given the introduction of the Duracell Ultra line and the expansion of G's international battery business. Longer term, the introduction of the higher-margin Mach3 product line should help accelerate earnings growth to 16% to 18%.

Valuation - 22-JUL-98

Gillette's stock has been a stellar performer in recent years, reflecting strong, stable earnings growth and high returns on equity and sales. However, the shares, recently trading at 39X estimated 1998 EPS of $1.45, are priced substantially above both the company's expected earnings growth rate and the P/E ratio of the S&P 500. Although we believe that this price is warranted, given Gillette's well-known and growing global brand franchise, leading positions in nearly all of its markets, and high overseas exposure, we believe the shares are vulnerable in the event of earnings disappointments. For this reason, we recommend that investors with a short time horizon use caution when adding the stock to a portfolio. For the longer term, we recommend that investors accumulate the stock for above-average appreciation.

Key Stock Statistics

S&P EPS Est. 1998	1.45	Tang. Bk. Value/Share	2.54
P/E on S&P Est. 1998	28.7	Beta	1.10
S&P EPS Est. 1999	1.70	Shareholders	55,700
Dividend Rate/Share	0.51	Market cap. (B)	$ 46.7
Shs. outstg. (M)	1122.9	Inst. holdings	61%
Avg. daily vol. (M)	5.352		

Value of $10,000 invested 5 years ago: $ 31,174

Fiscal Year Ending Dec. 31

	1998	1997	1996	1995	1994	1993
Revenues (Million $)						
1Q	2,025	2,180	2,059	1,536	1,361	1,217
2Q	2,325	2,285	2,272	1,601	1,407	1,237
3Q	—	2,437	2,366	1,670	1,503	1,340
4Q	—	3,160	3,001	1,988	1,799	1,617
Yr.	—	10,062	9,698	6,795	6,070	5,411
Earnings Per Share ($)						
1Q	**0.23**	**0.25**	0.23	0.22	0.18	0.16
2Q	**0.33**	**0.28**	0.25	0.21	0.18	0.15
3Q	**E0.43**	**0.31**	0.28	0.23	0.19	0.16
4Q	**E0.45**	**0.41**	0.10	0.26	0.23	0.01
Yr.	**E1.45**	1.24	**0.83**	0.93	0.79	0.48

Next earnings report expected: mid October

Dividend Data (Dividends have been paid since 1906.)

Amount ($)	Date Decl.	Ex-Div. Date	Stock of Record	Payment Date
0.215	Dec. 18	Jan. 29	Feb. 02	Mar. 05 '98
0.255	—	Apr. 29	May. 01	Jun. 05 '98
2-for-1	Feb. 19	Jun. 08	May. 15	Jun. 05 '98
0.128	Jul. 16	Jul. 30	Aug. 03	Sep. 04 '98

A Division of The **McGraw·Hill** Companies

Business Summary - 22-JUL-98

Although best known for its core Gillette and Sensor blades and razors, the company enjoys a market-leading share in most of its businesses. Other legs of the business include Braun electric shavers and appliances, toiletries and cosmetics (Right Guard and Soft & Dri), Oral-B dental products, and stationery products (Parker, Paper Mate and Waterman). The businesses all share several common traits. They are number one worldwide in their markets, profitable, fast growing, and anchored by a strong technological base.

Climaxing a five-year search for a business that could become a solid sixth leg, in September 1996, Gillette acquired Duracell International Inc., the world's leading manufacturer and marketer of high-performance alkaline batteries, with about 40% of the world market. The merger united two successful companies, forging a $10 billion consumer products giant whose stable of powerful global brands makes it a formidable player in the world's consumer marketplace.

Segment contributions in 1997 were:

	Sales	Profits
Blades & razors	29%	50%
Braun products	17%	13%
Toiletries & cosmetics	14%	5%
Stationery products & other	9%	7%
Oral-B dental items	6%	4%
Duracell Products	25%	22%

Gillette's mission is to achieve or enhance a clear worldwide leadership position in the core consumer product categories in which it competes. In 1997, nearly 75% of its sales came from the product categories in which it holds the number one worldwide position. Its success hinges on a continuing commitment to innovation. During 1996, the company introduced more than 20 new products, keeping with its goal of having at least 40% of sales coming from items introduced in the past five years. Gillette surpassed this goal in 1997, with a record 49% of sales coming from products introduced in the past five years.

To drive future growth, Gillette expects spending on research and development, capital projects and advertising to rise at least as fast as sales. The bulk of expenditures in 1997 principally reflected signficant expenditures in the blade and razor and Duracell and Braun product segments.

Geographic expansion has played an important role in the company's success, with businesses in developing markets showing especially significant growth. Manufacturing operations are conducted at 64 facilities in 26 countries, and products are distributed through wholesalers, retailers and agents in over 200 countries and territories. International operations provided 63% of 1997 sales and 62% of profits.

Per Share Data ($)

(Year Ended Dec. 31)	1997	1996	1995	1994	1993	1992	1991	1990	1989	1988
Tangible Bk. Val.	2.08	1.57	1.34	1.22	0.58	1.17	0.75	-0.10	-0.24	-0.46
Cash Flow	1.61	1.20	1.21	1.03	0.69	0.82	0.71	0.61	0.51	0.45
Earnings	1.25	0.85	0.93	0.79	0.48	0.58	0.48	0.40	0.34	0.31
Dividends	0.41	0.34	0.29	0.24	0.20	0.17	0.15	0.13	0.12	0.11
Payout Ratio	33%	40%	31%	31%	42%	30%	32%	33%	35%	31%
Prices - High	53¼	38⅞	27¾	19⅛	16	15⅜	14	8⅛	6¼	6⅛
- Low	36	24⅛	17¾	14½	11⅞	11	7	5½	4⅛	3⅝
P/E Ratio - High	43	45	30	24	33	26	29	20	18	20
- Low	29	28	19	18	25	19	15	14	12	12

Income Statement Analysis (Million $)

	1997	1996	1995	1994	1993	1992	1991	1990	1989	1988
Revs.	10,062	9,698	6,795	6,070	5,411	5,163	4,684	4,345	3,819	3,581
Oper. Inc.	2,746	2,431	1,620	1,442	1,276	1,178	1,054	950	799	741
Depr.	422	381	249	215	189	211	193	177	135	127
Int. Exp.	78.0	77.0	59.0	61.0	60.0	83.0	115	169	146	138
Pretax Inc.	2,221	1,525	1,297	1,104	683	830	694	593	474	449
Eff. Tax Rate	36%	38%	37%	37%	38%	38%	38%	38%	40%	40%
Net Inc.	1,427	949	824	698	427	513	427	368	285	269

Balance Sheet & Other Fin. Data (Million $)

	1997	1996	1995	1994	1993	1992	1991	1990	1989	1988
Cash	105	84.0	48.0	46.0	39.0	40.0	57.0	81.0	137	175
Curr. Assets	4,690	4,732	3,105	2,747	2,528	2,336	2,178	2,094	1,855	1,740
Total Assets	10,864	10,435	6,340	5,494	5,102	4,190	3,887	3,671	3,114	2,868
Curr. Liab.	2,641	2,935	2,124	1,783	1,760	1,561	1,485	1,308	1,061	965
LT Debt	1,476	1,490	691	715	840	554	742	1,046	1,041	1,675
Common Eqty.	4,748	4,396	2,416	1,963	1,434	1,462	1,057	165	70.0	-85.0
Total Cap.	6,715	6,310	3,296	2,937	2,507	2,169	2,020	2,037	1,807	1,681
Cap. Exp.	973	830	471	400	352	321	286	255	223	189
Cash Flow	1,849	1,330	1,068	909	611	720	602	488	396	396
Curr. Ratio	1.8	1.6	1.5	1.5	1.4	1.5	1.5	1.6	1.7	1.8
% LT Debt of Cap.	22.0	23.6	21.0	24.4	33.5	25.5	36.7	51.3	57.6	99.6
% Net Inc.of Revs.	14.2	9.8	12.1	11.5	7.9	9.9	9.1	8.5	7.5	7.5
% Ret. on Assets	13.4	9.8	14.1	13.2	9.2	12.7	10.7	10.8	9.5	10.4
% Ret. on Equity	31.2	23.0	37.6	40.8	29.1	39.1	65.8	263.6	NM	128.6

Data as orig. reptd.; bef. results of disc. opers. and/or spec. items. Per share data adj. for stk. divs. as of ex-div. date. Bold denotes diluted EPS (FASB 128). E-Estimated. NA-Not Available. NM-Not Meaningful. NR-Not Ranked.

Office—Prudential Tower Bldg., Boston, MA 02199. **Tel**—(617) 421-7000. **Chrmn & CEO**—A. M. Zeien.**Pres & COO**—M.C. Hawley. **SVP-Fin & CFO**—C. W. Cramb. **Secy**—J. C. Richardson.**Investor Contact**—Everett Howell. **Dirs**—W. E. Buffett, W. H. Gantz, M. B. Gifford, C. R. Goldberg, M. C. Hawley, H. H. Jacobi, H. R. Kravis, R. R. Pivirotto, A. B. Trowbridge, A. M. Zeien. **Transfer Agent & Registrar**—First National Bank of Boston. **Incorporated**—in Delaware in 1917.**Empl**— 44,000. **S&P Analyst:** Robert J. Izmirlian

12-SEP-98

Industry: Savings & Loan Companies

Summary: Golden West is the holding company for World Savings & Loan, one of the largest U.S. savings and loan associations.

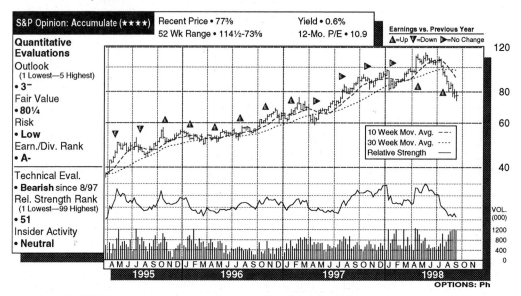

S&P Opinion: Accumulate (★★★★)

| Recent Price • 77⅞ | Yield • 0.6% |
| 52 Wk Range • 114½-73⅝ | 12-Mo. P/E • 10.9 |

Quantitative Evaluations

Outlook
(1 Lowest—5 Highest)
• **3⁻**

Fair Value
• **80¼**

Risk
• **Low**

Earn./Div. Rank
• **A-**

Technical Eval.
• **Bearish** since 8/97

Rel. Strength Rank
(1 Lowest—99 Highest)
• **51**

Insider Activity
• **Neutral**

Earnings vs. Previous Year
▲=Up ▼=Down ▶=No Change

10 Week Mov. Avg. – – –
30 Week Mov. Avg. ·····
Relative Strength ——

VOL. (000)

OPTIONS: Ph

Overview - 11-AUG-98

Profits are expected to improve in 1999 from 1998's anticipated level. Modest loan growth appears likely, reflecting the continued strong California economy which stimulates home buying activity and aggressive pricing on the company's ARMs, partially offset by a high level of refinancing activity. We see total mortgage originations of $7.2 billion for 1999, versus the $8.0 billion expected for 1998. A lower provision for loan losses is highly probable. GDW is selling its foreclosed properties for better prices, and non-performing assets are trending down, partly due to the strong housing market. Some contraction in the spread between loan rates and funding costs may occur, resulting primarily from the tight yield curve. Continued low general and administrative costs are likely. Share buybacks will continue to bolster EPS comparisons.

Valuation - 11-AUG-98

In August 1998, the stock was downgraded to accumulate from buy. The main factor behind the opinion change relates to the extremely challenging interest rate environment. With only a minimal difference between long term and short term interest rates, the company's spread is likely to come under pressure. Also, with low long-term interest rates, originations of adjustable rate mortgages, GDW's principal product, could decline. The foregoing nothwithstanding, Golden West is one of the thrift industry's lowest cost providers, with a ratio of overhead costs to average assets of less than one half the industry average. We also see the company as a long-term takeover target, reflecting management's large stock holdings and the company's status as one of the few large California franchises remaining.

Key Stock Statistics

S&P EPS Est. 1998	7.90	Tang. Bk. Value/Share	50.76
P/E on S&P Est. 1998	9.8	Beta	1.26
S&P EPS Est. 1999	8.65	Shareholders	1,600
Dividend Rate/Share	0.50	Market cap. (B)	$ 4.5
Shs. outstg. (M)	57.6	Inst. holdings	66%
Avg. daily vol. (M)	0.250		

Value of $10,000 invested 5 years ago: $ 18,523

Fiscal Year Ending Dec. 31

	1998	1997	1996	1995	1994	1993
Revenues (Million $)						
1Q	781.2	693.5	655.9	562.9	463.1	474.9
2Q	783.7	710.0	646.3	613.4	468.9	485.5
3Q	—	738.6	664.3	642.3	477.9	488.3
4Q	—	771.6	684.6	651.5	504.0	483.5
Yr.	—	2,914	2,656	2,470	1,914	1,932
Earnings Per Share ($)						
1Q	**1.89**	1.43	1.34	0.87	1.02	1.12
2Q	**2.01**	1.51	1.35	0.91	0.98	1.10
3Q	**E1.96**	1.56	2.32	1.08	0.91	1.00
4Q	**E2.04**	1.62	1.32	1.14	0.79	1.06
Yr.	**E7.90**	6.13	6.33	4.00	3.71	4.28

Next earnings report expected: mid October

Dividend Data (Dividends have been paid since 1977.)

Amount ($)	Date Decl.	Ex-Div. Date	Stock of Record	Payment Date
0.125	Oct. 29	Nov. 12	Nov. 14	Dec. 10 '97
0.125	Feb. 06	Feb. 11	Feb. 16	Mar. 10 '98
0.125	May. 06	May. 13	May. 15	Jun. 10 '98
0.125	Jul. 28	Aug. 12	Aug. 14	Sep. 10 '98

A Division of The McGraw·Hill Companies

STANDARD
&POOR'S
STOCK REPORTS

Golden West Financial Corporation

1025

12-SEP-98

Business Summary - 11-AUG-98

Golden West Financial is a plain-vanilla thrift that focuses on traditional thrift activities of using retail savings to fund investment in one- to four-family mortgage loans. Because of this emphasis, Golden West avoided many of the credit quality problems that affected its peers in the 1980s. The company ranks as one of the largest thrifts in the U.S., based on total assets of $40 billion. Branch operations are concentrated in California, although the company has a minor presence in seven other states. Golden West basically offers one loan product: a monthly adjustable-rate mortgage indexed to thrift cost of funds in California, Arizona and Nevada (the Federal Home Loan Bank's 11th District). Although not perfect, this instrument helps smooth out earnings fluctuations across interest rate environments. The company is run by the husband and wife team of Herbert and Marion Sandler, who are astute and somewhat tight-fisted business people.

Management's strategy is three-pronged: to keep costs as low as possible, to lend only to the most creditworthy homebuyers and to capture the high-end saver's dollar. As an indication of the company's operating efficiency, overhead costs are less than 1% of its assets, about one-half the industry average and 50% better than direct competitors such as H. F. Ahmanson.

Golden West's low cost structure was achieved through the following: a spare branch office design, reliance on part-time branch personnel, who for the most part do not receive benefits, a high degree of automation, and a light support staff at headquarters. Visitors to headquarters will find no receptionist. They must use a telephone to announce themselves.

Regarding loan operations, the company typically generates a high volume of new loans through a combination of frequent media advertising, aggressive pricing, and high-level marketing to realtors' associations. New loans originated in 1997 totaled $7.5 billion, up from $7.0 billion in 1996. Despite the high volume, credit losses have historically been low. Golden West keeps losses down by requiring down payments slightly higher than average, and by using outside appraisers, who assess a property's marketability, in addition to its value based on comparable sales. The property's marketability would be important if the company had to foreclose.

On the deposit side, the average savings customer maintains far larger balances than is typical, and also receives a higher interest rate. Management believes that this focus on the well-to-do shopper, when properly executed, leads to improved operating efficiencies, which partially compensate for the higher rate that the company pays out to attract the funds.

Per Share Data ($)

(Year Ended Dec. 31)	1997	1996	1995	1994	1993	1992	1991	1990	1989	1988
Tangible Bk. Val.	47.20	40.89	36.22	31.81	30.17	24.45	19.88	14.41	11.50	8.90
Earnings	6.13	6.33	4.00	3.71	4.28	4.46	3.76	2.87	2.51	2.20
Dividends	0.46	0.40	0.35	0.31	0.27	0.23	0.19	0.17	0.15	0.13
Payout Ratio	7%	6%	9%	8%	6%	5%	5%	6%	6%	6%
Prices - High	$97^{7}/_{8}$	$68^{3}/_{4}$	$57^{1}/_{2}$	46	$50^{3}/_{8}$	$46^{1}/_{4}$	$44^{1}/_{4}$	$35^{1}/_{4}$	$33^{3}/_{4}$	$17^{3}/_{8}$
- Low	$58^{7}/_{8}$	49	$34^{3}/_{4}$	$34^{1}/_{4}$	$37^{1}/_{8}$	$35^{1}/_{2}$	$22^{1}/_{4}$	$17^{5}/_{8}$	$15^{3}/_{8}$	$11^{3}/_{8}$
P/E Ratio - High	16	11	14	12	12	10	12	12	13	8
- Low	10	8	9	9	9	8	6	6	6	5

Income Statement Analysis (Million $)

	1997	1996	1995	1994	1993	1992	1991	1990	1989	1988
Net Int. Inc.	890	831	723	721	733	717	632	497	421	377
Loan Loss Prov.	57.6	84.3	61.0	63.0	65.8	43.2	30.2	13.6	6.7	1.9
Non Int. Inc.	73.1	74.9	43.0	37.5	62.0	41.1	26.9	28.9	34.6	27.3
Non Int. Exp.	327	453	319	303	273	252	242	229	182	187
Pretax Inc.	587	368	385	390	457	464	387	283	246	215
Eff. Tax Rate	40%	NM	39%	41%	40%	39%	38%	36%	36%	36%
Net Inc.	354	370	235	230	274	284	239	181	158	138
% Net Int. Marg.	2.32	2.39	2.13	2.43	2.61	2.83	2.66	2.36	2.25	2.60

Balance Sheet & Other Fin. Data (Million $)

	1997	1996	1995	1994	1993	1992	1991	1990	1989	1988
Total Assets	39,590	37,731	35,118	31,684	28,829	25,890	24,298	22,562	19,521	16,721
Loans	33,261	34,179	34,380	28,265	25,435	23,760	22,088	20,216	16,990	14,265
Deposits	24,110	22,100	20,848	19,219	17,422	16,486	16,819	14,372	11,787	10,496
Capitalization:										
Debt	9,737	10,712	9,367	8,874	8,178	6,515	4,973	5,234	5,889	4,071
Equity	2,698	2,350	2,278	2,000	2,066	1,727	1,449	1,220	1,046	896
Total	12,435	13,062	11,645	10,874	10,244	8,242	6,422	6,455	6,935	4,967
% Ret. on Assets	0.9	1.1	0.7	0.8	1.0	1.1	1.0	0.9	0.9	1.0
% Ret. on Equity	14.0	16.0	11.0	11.1	14.4	17.9	17.9	16.0	16.3	16.7
% Loan Loss Resv.	0.7	0.1	0.1	0.4	0.4	0.3	0.2	0.1	0.1	0.1
% Risk Based Capital	NA	10.0	13.4	13.5	17.4	16.3	15.0	11.6	11.6	NA
Price Times Book Value:										
Hi	2.1	1.7	1.6	1.4	1.7	1.9	2.2	2.4	2.9	2.0
Low	1.2	1.2	1.0	1.1	1.2	1.5	1.1	1.2	1.3	1.3

Data as orig. reptd.; bef. results of disc opers. and/or spec. items. Per share data adj. for stk. divs. as of ex-div. date. Bold denotes diluted EPS (FASB 128). E-Estimated. NA-Not Available. NM-Not Meaningful. NR-Not Ranked.

Reincorporated—in Delaware in 1975.**Office**—1901 Harrison St., Oakland, CA 94612. **Tel**—(510) 446-3420. **Co-Chrmn & Co-CEO**—H. M. Sandler. **Co-Chrmn & Co-CEO**—M. O. Sandler. **Pres**—R. W. Kettell. **EVP & Investor Contact**—J. L. Helvey (510-446-3405). **VP & Secy**—R. C. Rowe. **Dirs**—M. B. Cattani, L. J. Galen, A. Hernandez, P. A. King, B. A. Osher, K. T. Rosen, H. M. Sandler, M. O. Sandler. L. Tang Schilling. **Transfer Agent & Registrar**—ChaseMellon Shareholder Services, SF. **Empl**— 5,000. **S&P Analyst:** Paul L. Huberman, CFA

12-SEP-98

Industry: Chemicals (Diversified)

Summary: This company provides aircraft systems, components and services and manufactures a wide range of specialty chemicals.

S&P Opinion: Hold (★★★)	Recent Price • 29⅛ Yield • 3.8%
	52 Wk Range • 56-26½ 12-Mo. P/E • 15.0

Earnings vs. Previous Year
▲=Up ▼=Down ▶=No Change

Quantitative Evaluations

Outlook
(1 Lowest—5 Highest)
• **2⁻**

Fair Value
• **30¼**

Risk
• **Low**

Earn./Div. Rank
• **B-**

Technical Eval.
• **Neutral** since 7/98

Rel. Strength Rank
(1 Lowest—99 Highest)
• **24**

Insider Activity
• **NA**

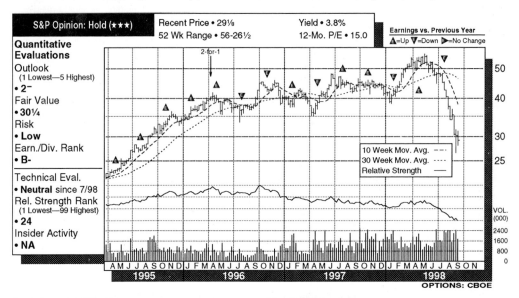

10 Week Mov. Avg. ─ ─ ─
30 Week Mov. Avg. ∙ ∙ ∙ ∙
Relative Strength ──

OPTIONS: CBOE

Overview - 20-JUL-98

Sales in 1998 should rise about 17%, reflecting growth in aerospace and specialty chemicals. The acquisition of Rohr Inc., a major producer of nacelle systems, accounted for about $1.07 billion of 1997 sales, and extended the range of products offered by GR to the commercial and military aviation industries. GR also divested several commodity chemical units in recent years, and is now focusing on high margin specialty chemicals. The aerospace segment should continue to benefit from an upturn in commercial aircraft output. Specialty chemical revenues should grow 14%, on strong volume in additives, and contributions by recent acquisitions. Chemical margins are projected to widen, on the greater volume in ongoing operations, aided by favorable raw materials prices. Aerospace segment margins are widening, as productivity gains are achieved. In addition, consolidation of overhead administrative functions should boost operating margins. Over the long term, GR will continue to focus on aerospace and specialty chemicals, and to pursue internal growth opportunities, as well as additional acquisitions.

Valuation - 20-JUL-98

We upgraded the shares to hold after the release of GR's first quarter earnings report. GR has made good progress in consolidating Rohr and several chemicals acquisitions. Margins widened impressively in the first quarter. We expect continued strong performance, due to further overhead cost reductions. We now expect the shares to keep pace with the market in the months ahead. The company's stock price should reflect an earnings multiple that is a blend of the aerospace and specialty chemical industries in which it competes.

Key Stock Statistics

S&P EPS Est. 1998	3.00	Tang. Bk. Value/Share	9.29
P/E on S&P Est. 1998	9.7	Beta	1.53
S&P EPS Est. 1999	3.50	Shareholders	10,400
Dividend Rate/Share	1.10	Market cap. (B)	$ 2.2
Shs. outstg. (M)	74.0	Inst. holdings	66%
Avg. daily vol. (M)	0.429		

Value of $10,000 invested 5 years ago: $ 14,739

Fiscal Year Ending Dec. 31

	1998	1997	1996	1995	1994	1993
Revenues (Million $)						
1Q	937.7	764.2	531.2	594.0	502.4	376.5
2Q	1,011	846.4	550.2	600.6	540.5	452.7
3Q	—	870.2	567.6	606.0	561.5	500.8
4Q	—	892.1	589.8	608.0	594.8	488.3
Yr.	—	3,373	2,239	2,409	2,199	1,818
Earnings Per Share ($)						
1Q	**0.72**	0.40	0.45	0.30	0.06	-0.17
2Q	**0.74**	0.87	0.56	0.81	0.32	0.08
3Q	**E0.75**	0.50	0.47	0.59	0.41	0.27
4Q	**E0.75**	-0.26	0.49	0.44	0.33	-0.03
Yr.	**E3.00**	**1.53**	1.97	2.15	1.12	0.14

Next earnings report expected: mid October

Dividend Data (Dividends have been paid since 1939.)

Amount ($)	Date Decl.	Ex-Div. Date	Stock of Record	Payment Date
0.275	Oct. 20	Dec. 04	Dec. 08	Jan. 02 '98
0.275	Feb. 16	Mar. 05	Mar. 09	Apr. 01 '98
0.275	Apr. 20	Jun. 04	Jun. 08	Jul. 01 '98
0.275	Jul. 20	Sep. 03	Sep. 08	Oct. 01 '98

Business Summary - 20-JUL-98

The B.F.Goodrich Company provides aircraft systems, components and services, and makes a wide range of specialty chemicals. The company has been evolving in recent years and has bought and sold a number of businesses in the chemical and aerospace segment. In 1997, the company sold its chlor-alkali and olefins business and the sealants, coating and adhesives business unit. In December 1997, GR merged with Rohr Inc., a maker of engine nacelles, in a pooling of interests transaction valued at $1.3 billion in stock and assumption of debt. Segment contributions in 1997 (profit in million $, restated for the Rohr acquisition) were:

	Sales	Profits
Aerospace products	73%	$260.3
Specialty chemicals	27%	128.2

The aerospace segment consists of four business groups: aerostructures (42% of segment sales), landing systems (21%), sensors and integrated systems (22%), and maintenance, repair and overhaul (15%). The acquisition of Rohr accounted for about $1.07 billion of

sales in 1997 and $42 million of operating income. The operations of Rohr account for most of the aerostructures group. This business provides some of the nacelle systems for about 90% of the world's commercial transport aircraft fleet. Landing systems includes aircraft landing gear and evacuation products, wheels and brakes. Sensors and integrated systems produces a variety of sensors and systems for aircraft, engines, space vehicles and launch vehicles. The aerospace segment is expected to benefit in 1998 from a combined 35% increase in commercial aircraft deliveries by Boeing and Airbus, the two leading commercial aircraft producers.

Specialty chemicals include the specialty plastics group (65% of segment sales), which makes thermoplastic polyurethanes, low-combustibility plastics and thermoset resins; the specialty additives group (35%), manufactures synthetic thickeners and emulsifiers, controlled-release and suspension agents, rubber and lubricant additives and plastic and adhesive modifiers. Additives are provided to a variety of industries ranging from personal-care products and cosmetics to automotive, tires and petroleum products. Specialty plastics markets range from apparel and medical to communications, electronics and construction.

Per Share Data ($)

(Year Ended Dec. 31)	1997	1996	1995	1994	1993	1992	1991	1990	1989	1988
Tangible Bk. Val.	11.35	8.53	6.58	4.14	4.00	9.22	17.16	21.34	19.95	19.02
Cash Flow	3.38	4.16	4.42	3.29	2.08	2.16	0.71	4.17	5.17	5.90
Earnings	1.53	1.97	2.15	1.12	0.14	-0.34	-1.75	2.12	3.21	4.00
Dividends	1.10	1.10	1.10	1.10	1.10	1.10	1.10	1.06	1.00	0.86
Payout Ratio	72%	56%	51%	98%	NM	NM	NM	50%	31%	22%
Prices - High	48¼	45⅞	36⅜	24¼	27⅛	29⅛	23⅞	23¾	34½	30⅜
- Low	35⅛	33⅜	20⅞	19½	19¾	19½	18	14¾	19¼	18¾
P/E Ratio - High	32	23	17	22	NM	NM	NM	11	11	8
- Low	23	17	10	17	NM	NM	NM	7	6	5

Income Statement Analysis (Million $)

	1997	1996	1995	1994	1993	1992	1991	1990	1989	1988
Revs.	3,373	2,239	2,409	2,199	1,818	2,526	2,472	2,433	2,420	2,417
Oper. Inc.	501	361	357	292	196	201	188	256	376	402
Depr.	139	118	114	112	100	128	125	104	99	96.0
Int. Exp.	73.0	40.4	58.0	48.0	43.0	49.0	46.0	37.0	41.0	45.0
Pretax Inc.	207	178	198	109	15.0	-16.0	-109	132	244	255
Eff. Tax Rate	45%	35%	38%	40%	Nil	NM	NM	13%	30%	18%
Net Inc.	113	106	118	66.0	15.0	-9.0	-81.0	116	171	210

Balance Sheet & Other Fin. Data (Million $)

	1997	1996	1995	1994	1993	1992	1991	1990	1989	1988
Cash	47.0	48.7	60.0	36.0	33.0	97.0	61.0	154	276	314
Curr. Assets	1,401	912	950	879	794	797	776	857	1,040	1,003
Total Assets	3,494	2,663	2,490	2,469	2,360	2,452	2,271	2,366	2,274	2,073
Curr. Liab.	935	663	601	638	469	566	530	610	486	491
LT Debt	564	400	422	427	487	403	344	207	289	308
Common Eqty.	1,423	1,050	879	813	784	718	1,104	1,249	1,167	1,045
Total Cap.	2,110	1,573	1,423	1,350	1,386	1,252	1,566	1,635	1,638	1,508
Cap. Exp.	160	184	148	129	232	204	211	244	266	185
Cash Flow	252	225	232	170	107	111	36.0	211	261	297
Curr. Ratio	1.5	1.4	1.6	1.4	1.7	1.4	1.5	1.4	2.1	2.0
% LT Debt of Cap.	26.7	25.5	29.7	31.6	35.1	32.2	22.0	12.7	17.6	20.4
% Net Inc.of Revs.	3.4	4.8	4.9	3.0	0.8	NM	NM	4.8	7.1	8.7
% Ret. on Assets	3.7	4.2	4.8	2.7	0.6	NM	NM	5.0	7.9	10.5
% Ret. on Equity	9.2	11.1	14.0	7.2	0.9	NM	NM	8.9	14.7	20.9

Data as orig. reptd.; bef. results of disc. opers. and/or spec. items. Per share data adj. for stk. divs. as of ex-div. date. Bold denotes diluted EPS (FASB 128). E-Estimated. NA-Not Available. NM-Not Meaningful. NR-Not Ranked.

Office—4020 Kinross Lakes Parkway, Richfield, OH 44286-9368. **Tel**—(216) 659-7789. **Website**—http://www.bfgoodrich.com **Chrmn, Pres & CEO**—D. L. Burner. **EVP & CFO**—D. L. Tobler. **VP & Secy**—N. J. Calise. **Investor Contact**—John T. Bingle (216-659-7788). **Dirs**—J. G. Brown, D. L. Burner, D. C. Creel, G. A. Davidson, Jr., R. K. Davidson, J. J. Glasser, J. K. Glore, D. E. Olesen, R. de J. Osborne, J. A. Pichler, A. M. Rankin, Jr., R. H. Rau, I. M. Ross, D. L. Tobler, J. R. Wilson, A. T. Young. **Transfer Agent & Registrar**—Bank of New York, NYC. **Incorporated**—in New York in 1912. **Empl**— 15,809. **S&P Analyst:** Robert E. Friedman, CPA

12-SEP-98

Industry:
Auto Parts & Equipment

Summary: Goodyear is the largest U.S. manufacturer of tires, and one of the largest worldwide. Operations also include rubber and plastic products and chemicals.

S&P Opinion: Hold (★★★)		
Recent Price • 47½	Yield • 2.5%	
52 Wk Range • 76¾-45⅞	12-Mo. P/E • 13.2	

Quantitative Evaluations

Outlook
(1 Lowest—5 Highest)
• **4**

Fair Value
• **56¾**

Risk
• **Low**

Earn./Div. Rank
• **B+**

Technical Eval.
• **Bearish** since 6/98

Rel. Strength Rank
(1 Lowest—99 Highest)
• **43**

Insider Activity
• **NA**

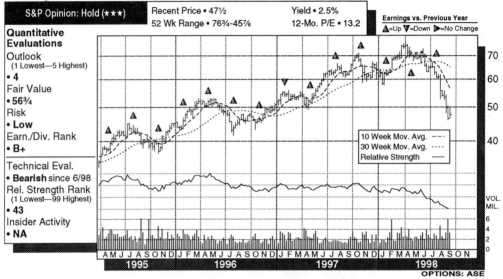

Earnings vs. Previous Year
▲=Up ▼=Down ▶=No Change

10 Week Mov. Avg. ---
30 Week Mov. Avg. ······
Relative Strength —

VOL. MIL.

OPTIONS: ASE

Overview - 27-JUL-98

Unit sales should rise modestly in 1998, on increases in worldwide demand for both original equipment and re-placement tires. While pricing remains competitive, thereby restricting margins, raw material costs have de-clined. In fact, lower raw material costs, an improved product mix, and continued aggressive efforts to lower SG&A expenses and generate further productivity gains are having a substantial positive impact on margins and earnings. Moreover, GT expects ultimately to reap $200 million in annual savings from restructuring plans an-nounced in the 1997 fourth quarter; GT recorded a re-lated $265 million charge in the quarter. Revenues and operating profits generated by the All-American Pipeline decreased in 1997, on lower throughput; in March 1998, GT agreed to sell this non-core business for ap-proximately $420 million.

Valuation - 27-JUL-98

The shares have retreated from their high, in part due to strikes at GM, even as Goodyear continues to ration-alize costs, improve margins, and invest in new technol-ogies. We expect GT to exploit its large foreign market position and leading market share of the U.S. replace-ment tire market, as well as the relative financial weak-ness of some competitors. Earnings in 1998 could be hurt by a stronger U.S. dollar and the impact of the GM strike, but should benefit from diminished raw material cost pressures. The stock, recently trading at about 12X projected 1998 EPS of $5.10, is among the most under-valued of the automotive suppliers. GT is less suscepti-ble to deep cyclical downturns, given its primary focus on the replacement market (as opposed to the original equipment market). With a steadily strengthening bal-ance sheet, commitment to a healthy dividend payout, and a $600 million stock buyback program, the shares are an attractive addition to long-term holdings.

Key Stock Statistics

S&P EPS Est. 1998	5.10	Tang. Bk. Value/Share	22.78
P/E on S&P Est. 1998	9.3	Beta	1.13
Dividend Rate/Share	1.20	Shareholders	30,300
Shs. outstg. (M)	157.0	Market cap. (B)	$ 7.5
Avg. daily vol. (M)	0.753	Inst. holdings	77%

Value of $10,000 invested 5 years ago: $ 15,555

Fiscal Year Ending Dec. 31

	1998	1997	1996	1995	1994	1993
Revenues (Million $)						
1Q	3,094	3,233	3,246	3,243	2,910	2,814
2Q	3,138	3,316	3,330	3,351	3,052	3,000
3Q	—	3,322	3,268	3,305	3,116	2,913
4Q	—	3,284	3,270	3,267	3,211	2,916
Yr.	—	13,155	13,113	13,166	12,288	11,643
Earnings Per Share ($)						
1Q	1.33	1.08	0.98	0.88	0.77	0.60
2Q	1.25	1.22	1.22	1.15	1.08	1.05
3Q	—	1.22	1.09	1.03	1.00	0.92
4Q	—	1.14	-2.63	0.96	0.90	0.76
Yr.	E5.10	3.53	0.66	4.02	3.75	3.33

Next earnings report expected: late October

Dividend Data (Dividends have been paid since 1937.)

Amount ($)	Date Decl.	Ex-Div. Date	Stock of Record	Payment Date
0.300	Oct. 07	Nov. 13	Nov. 17	Dec. 15 '97
0.300	Feb. 03	Feb. 12	Feb. 17	Mar. 16 '98
0.300	Apr. 06	May. 13	May. 15	Jun. 15 '98
0.300	Aug. 04	Aug. 13	Aug. 17	Sep. 15 '98

A Division of The **McGraw·Hill** *Companies*

Business Summary - 27-JUL-98

In the consolidating global rubber fabrication and tire industry, Goodyear Tire & Rubber Co. (GT) should emerge as one of a handful of clear winners. It is creatively and aggressively rationalizing operations, divesting non-core operations, and exploring international growth opportunities, such as its recent investments in Poland and South Africa. Currently with the top market share in North America, Latin America, China and India, GT is likely to continue to make fill-out acquisitions in the $200 million to $400 million range to strengthen its distribution, and explore strategic alliances that help address potential manufacturing overcapacity issues.

In early 1998, Goodyear articulated its financial goals. These targets include: growing sales at twice the industry rate, generating $20 billion to $23 billion in revenues by the end of the year 2003, reducing selling, general and administrative expenses to below 12% of sales, producing a return on sales of 6.5% to 7.0%.

In 1997, GT obtained 86% of sales and 75% of profits from tire products; 14% (20%) from general rubber, chemical, and plastic products; and less than 1% (5%) from its oil transportation segment.

The U.S. accounted fcr 53% of sales in 1997, while foreign operations contributed 47% of sales. U.S. operations recorded an operating profit of $377.6 million. International operating income of $553.2 million was de-

rived from Europe (39%), Latin America (40%), Asia (12%) and Canada (9%).

Tires and related products include new tires and inner tubes, retreads, repair/maintenance items, and auto repairs and services. Replacement volume is significantly higher than sales to the original equipment market.

General products include automotive and industrial belts and hoses, molded products, foam cushioning accessories, tank track, organic chemicals for rubber and plastic processing, synthetic rubber and rubber lattices.

The All-American Pipeline is a common carrier crude oil pipeline extending from California to Texas. In March 1998, Goodyear agreed to sell its pipeline assets for approximately $420 million.

In January 1997, GT re-entered the South African market by acquiring a 60% interest in Contred (sales of $400 million) for $121 million. Contred is also South Africa's largest manufacturer of heavy-duty conveyor belts and power transmission products. In March 1998, GT purchased the remaining 40% interest in Contred for $59 million.

In May 1997, GT settled an 18-day strike with the United Steelworkers of America, and signed a new six-year contract (twice as long as usual) that contained a no strike clause, and granted flexibility to outsource and run plants 24 hours a day. Also in May, GT and Sumitomo Rubber agreed to test an arrangement that could help GT penetrate the Japanese market.

Per Share Data ($)

(Year Ended Dec. 31)	1997	1996	1995	1994	1993	1992	1991	1990	1989	1988
Tangible Bk. Val.	21.68	21.03	21.38	16.44	13.90	11.21	17.87	17.94	18.55	17.65
Cash Flow	6.51	3.63	6.88	6.46	5.99	5.70	4.31	3.23	4.96	6.17
Earnings	3.53	0.66	4.02	3.75	3.33	2.57	0.62	-0.33	1.64	3.06
Dividends	1.14	1.03	0.95	0.75	0.57	0.28	0.20	0.90	0.90	0.85
Payout Ratio	32%	156%	24%	20%	18%	11%	38%	NM	55%	28%
Prices - High	71¼	53	45⅜	49¼	47¼	38⅛	27⅛	23¼	29⅞	34
- Low	49¼	41½	33	31⅝	32⅝	26	8⅜	6½	21⅛	23½
P/E Ratio - High	20	80	11	13	14	15	44	NM	18	11
- Low	14	63	8	8	10	10	14	NM	13	8

Income Statement Analysis (Million $)

	1997	1996	1995	1994	1993	1992	1991	1990	1989	1988
Revs.	13,155	13,113	13,166	12,288	11,643	11,785	10,907	11,273	10,869	10,810
Oper. Inc.	1,689	1,657	1,570	1,492	1,431	1,312	1,063	883	1,154	1,131
Depr.	469	461	435	410	393	446	442	415	384	357
Int. Exp.	119	134	140	135	167	237	326	363	390	364
Pretax Inc.	845	122	926	890	812	653	290	70.0	490	557
Eff. Tax Rate	29%	17%	34%	34%	37%	40%	68%	135%	58%	34%
Net Inc.	559	102	611	567	489	367	75.0	-38.0	189	350

Balance Sheet & Other Fin. Data (Million $)

	1997	1996	1995	1994	1993	1992	1991	1990	1989	1988
Cash	259	239	268	266	228	304	235	277	215	234
Curr. Assets	4,164	4,025	3,842	3,623	3,263	3,310	3,119	3,324	3,272	3,558
Total Assets	9,917	9,672	9,790	9,123	8,436	8,564	8,511	8,964	8,460	8,618
Curr. Liab.	3,251	2,766	2,736	2,572	2,524	2,646	2,393	2,294	2,200	2,459
LT Debt	845	1,132	1,320	1,109	1,066	1,471	2,038	3,286	2,963	3,045
Common Eqty.	3,395	3,279	3,282	2,803	2,301	1,930	2,731	2,098	2,144	2,027
Total Cap.	4,240	4,652	4,765	4,056	3,489	3,530	5,488	6,120	5,895	5,724
Cap. Exp.	699	618	616	523	432	367	346	575	783	747
Cash Flow	1,028	563	1,046	977	882	813	516	377	573	707
Curr. Ratio	1.3	1.5	1.4	1.4	1.3	1.3	1.3	1.4	1.5	1.4
% LT Debt of Cap.	19.9	24.3	27.7	27.3	30.5	41.7	37.1	53.7	50.3	53.2
% Net Inc.of Revs.	4.2	0.8	4.6	4.6	4.2	3.1	0.7	NM	1.7	3.2
% Ret. on Assets	5.7	1.0	6.5	6.4	5.6	4.3	0.8	NM	2.2	4.1
% Ret. on Equity	16.7	3.1	20.1	22.2	22.7	15.6	2.8	NM	9.1	18.1

Data as orig. reptd.; bef. results of disc. opers. and/or spec. items. Per share data adj. for stk. divs. as of ex-div. date. Bold denotes diluted EPS (FASB 128). E-Estimated. NA-Not Available. NM-Not Meaningful. NR-Not Ranked.

Office--1144 East Market St., Akron, OH 44316-0001. Tel—(330) 796-2121. Website—http://www.goodyear.com Chrmn, Pres & CEO—S. F. Gibara. EVP & CFO—R. W. Tieken. VP & Secy—J. Boyazis. VP & Treas—R. W. Hauman. Director, Investor Relations—Holly K. Ash. Dirs—J. G. Breen, W. E. Butler, T. H. Cruikshank, K. G. Farley, S. F. Gibara, W. J. Hudson, G. G. Michelson, S. A. Minter, A. Pytte, G. H. Schofield, W. C. Turner, M. D. Walker. Transfer Agent & Registrar—First Chicago Trust Co. of New York, Jersey City, NJ. Incorporated—in Ohio in 1898. Empl—95,302. S&P Analyst: Efraim Levy

STANDARD &POOR'S
STOCK REPORTS

GPU, Inc.

933T

NYSE Symbol **GPU**

In S&P 500

12-SEP-98

Industry:
Electric Companies

Summary: This New Jersey-based energy holding company serves more than 4.3 million customers in New Jersey, Pennsylvania, Australia and the U.K.

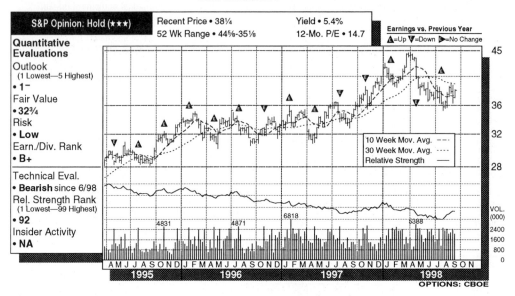

| S&P Opinion: Hold (★★★) | Recent Price • 38¼ | Yield • 5.4% |
| | 52 Wk Range • 44⅝-35⅛ | 12-Mo. P/E • 14.7 |

Earnings vs. Previous Year
▲=Up ▼=Down ▶=No Change

Quantitative Evaluations

Outlook
(1 Lowest—5 Highest)
• **1⁻**

Fair Value
• **32¾**

Risk
• **Low**

Earn./Div. Rank
• **B+**

Technical Eval.
• **Bearish** since 6/98

Rel. Strength Rank
(1 Lowest—99 Highest)
• **92**

Insider Activity
• **NA**

10 Week Mov. Avg. — — —
30 Week Mov. Avg. - - - -
Relative Strength ———

OPTIONS: CBOE

Overview - 20-AUG-98

Results in 1998 will be hurt by a second quarter charge of $2.16 a share to cover stranded costs not recognized by the Pennsylvania Public Utility Commission (PPUC). However, after GPU filed a suit challenging the order, the PPUC agreed to enter into settlement talks that could increase the level of stranded costs GPU will be allowed to recover. The planned $1.9 billion acquisition of PowerNet, the electrical transmission company for the Australian state of Victoria, is expected to dilute 1998 EPS by $0.06, due to the related issuance in early 1998 of 7 million new shares, with proceeds used to reduce acquisition debt. Having reached agreements to sell its Three Mile Island Unit-1 nuclear facility and 50%-owned, coal-fired Homer City Generating Station, GPU will continue to exit the domestic generation business and focus on its transmission and distribution operations.

Valuation - 20-AUG-98

Although the shares were recently down about 10% in 1998 (reflecting the PPUC order restricting the level of recoverable stranded costs), we would continue to hold the stock. We believe that settlement talks with the PPUC will result in at least a moderately higher level of recoverable costs. In addition, proceeds that GPU will receive from the sale of its generation assets will let it significantly reduce acquisiton-related debt and expand other non-regulated operations. We also expect long-term benefits from the PowerNet acquisition. A dividend payout below the industry average has allowed dividend increases of 3.0% in 1998, 3.1% in 1997, and 3.2% in 1996, well above the industry average. The shares, recently yielding 5.4% and trading at 12X our 1999 EPS estimate of $3.10, remain an attractive holding for long-term total return.

Key Stock Statistics

S&P EPS Est. 1998	1.15	Tang. Bk. Value/Share	22.92
P/E on S&P Est. 1998	33.3	Beta	0.41
S&P EPS Est. 1999	3.10	Shareholders	43,400
Dividend Rate/Share	2.06	Market cap. (B)	$ 4.9
Shs. outstg. (M)	127.9	Inst. holdings	69%
Avg. daily vol. (M)	0.457		

Value of $10,000 invested 5 years ago: $ 18,910

Fiscal Year Ending Dec. 31

	1998	1997	1996	1995	1994	1993
Revenues (Million $)						
1Q	1,043	1,051	1,023	914.0	937.2	881.1
2Q	1,015	942.8	912.3	864.6	873.5	863.2
3Q	—	1,117	1,058	1,095	994.7	990.2
4Q	—	1,032	924.7	931.0	844.1	861.5
Yr.	—	4,143	3,918	3,805	3,650	3,596
Earnings Per Share ($)						
1Q	**1.07**	**1.28**	0.90	0.65	1.07	0.72
2Q	**0.62**	**0.58**	0.61	0.53	-1.09	0.52
3Q	**E1.09**	0.14	0.29	2.02	0.97	1.14
4Q	**E0.53**	0.77	0.67	0.59	0.47	0.27
Yr.	**E1.15**	**2.77**	**2.47**	3.79	1.42	2.65

Next earnings report expected: mid October

Dividend Data (Dividends have been paid since 1987.)

Amount ($)	Date Decl.	Ex-Div. Date	Stock of Record	Payment Date
0.500	Oct. 08	Oct. 29	Oct. 31	Nov. 26 '97
0.500	Dec. 04	Jan. 28	Jan. 30	Feb. 25 '98
0.515	Apr. 02	Apr. 22	Apr. 24	May. 27 '98
0.515	Jun. 03	Jul. 29	Jul. 31	Aug. 26 '98

A Division of The **McGraw·Hill** *Companies*

STANDARD
&POOR'S
STOCK REPORTS

GPU, Inc.

933T
12-SEP-98

Business Summary - 20-AUG-98

New Jersey-based electric utility holding company GPU Inc. (GPU) completed a restructuring in 1996 that resulted in its Jersey Central Power & Light (JCP&L), Metropolitan Edison (Met-Ed) and Pennsylvania Electric (Penelec) subsidiaries being combined into a single subsidiary, GPU Energy, which serves nearly 2 million customers in New Jersey and Pennsylvania. Domestic electric revenues by customer class in 1997 were:

	Total	JCP&L	Met-Ed	Penelec
Residential	42%	45%	41%	35%
Commercial	35%	39%	29%	33%
Industrial	21%	15%	28%	28%
Other	2%	1%	2%	4%

Sources of domestic power requirements in 1997 were: coal 62% (60% in 1996), nuclear 38% (35%), gas 2% (1%), and oil 1% (1%).

In June 1996, GPU and Cinergy formed an equally owned joint venture, Avon Energy Partners plc, a U.K. limited liability corporation, to acquire Midlands Electricity plc, one of the 12 British regional electric companies, for about $2.6 billion. Midlands provides electricity to 2.2 million customers. It also owns domestic and international generation projects and is pursuing additional international generation and transmission projects.

In November 1997, GPU acquired PowerNet, the electric transmission company for the Australian state of Victoria, for $1.88 billion. It also announced plans to sell all of its domestic non-nuclear generation assets, which have a book value of $1.1 billion.

In August 1998, 50%-owned NGE Generation announced the sale of its Pennsylvania-based Homer City Generating Station to Edison International, for $1.8 billion. The transaction is expected to close in early 1999.

In July 1998, GPU agreed to sell its Three Mile Island Unit 1 (TMI-1) nuclear plant to AmerGen Energy (a joint venture of Peco Energy and British Energy PLC) for $100 million, with payments to be made over five years. The agreement will let GPU purchase the energy and capacity from Unit 1 from January 1, 2000, through December 31, 2001. In addition to TMI-1, GPU Energy companies have invested in two other major nuclear facilities: Oyster Creek (owned by JCP&L) and Three Mile Island Unit 2, which, like TMI-1, is jointly owned by Met-Ed (50%), JCP&L (25%) and Penelec (25%).

In 1979, an accident shut down the 880 mw TMI-2 unit, causing significant damage to, and contamination of, the plant, and a release of radioactivity into the environment. GPU's recoverable investment in TMI-2 was $275 million. It completed the cleanup of TMI-2 in 1990, at a cost of $973 million, and the unit was entered into long-term monitored storage in 1993. In June 1996, a federal judge dismissed 2,100 lawsuits claiming personal injury as a result of the accident. GPU expects the plaintiffs to appeal.

Per Share Data ($)

(Year Ended Dec. 31)	1997	1996	1995	1994	1993	1992	1991	1990	1989	1988
Tangible Bk. Val.	20.82	25.16	24.55	22.33	22.65	21.44	20.77	19.79	18.58	17.41
Earnings	2.77	2.47	3.79	1.42	2.65	2.27	1.96	2.51	2.51	2.38
Dividends	1.99	1.93	1.86	1.77	1.65	1.57	1.45	1.25	1.00	0.68
Payout Ratio	72%	78%	49%	125%	62%	69%	74%	50%	40%	28%
Prices - High	42¾	35¼	34	31⅝	34¾	27⅞	27¼	23⅝	23⅝	19¼
- Low	30¾	30⅛	26¼	23¾	25¾	24¼	21¾	19¼	18⅛	13⅝
P/E Ratio - High	15	14	9	22	13	12	14	9	9	8
- Low	11	12	7	17	10	11	11	8	7	6

Income Statement Analysis (Million $)

	1997	1996	1995	1994	1993	1992	1991	1990	1989	1988
Revs.	4,143	3,918	3,805	3,650	3,596	3,434	3,372	2,996	2,911	2,834
Depr.	467	400	378	354	360	340	389	320	287	256
Maint.	NA	NA	NA	NA	NA	NA	239	233	254	261
Fxd. Chgs. Cov.	2.7	3.3	2.9	2.6	3.0	2.9	2.5	3.0	3.2	3.5
Constr. Credits	5.6	10.7	14.7	11.8	9.9	12.6	14.4	19.1	19.6	17.9
Eff. Tax Rate	37%	38%	37%	32%	38%	38%	35%	34%	37%	36%
Net Inc.	335	298	440	164	296	252	218	278	282	284

Balance Sheet & Other Fin. Data (Million $)

	1997	1996	1995	1994	1993	1992	1991	1990	1989	1988
Gross Prop.	13,098	10,092	9,802	9,415	8,923	8,546	8,094	7,909	7,968	7,495
Cap. Exp.	356	404	462	586	496	460	467	491	487	441
Net Prop.	9,048	6,388	6,369	6,267	5,994	5,829	5,572	5,512	5,307	5,056
Capitalization:										
LT Debt	4,326	3,177	2,568	2,345	2,320	2,222	1,992	1,936	1,889	1,751
% LT Debt	55	47	42	44	44	44	42	42	43	42
Pfd.	488	510	562	453	308	465	465	500	400	400
% Pfd.	6.20	7.60	9.20	8.40	5.90	9.20	9.80	11	9.20	9.60
Common	3,100	3,048	3,065	2,573	2,610	2,379	2,306	2,197	2,063	2,024
% Common	39	45	49	48	50	47	48	47	47	49
Total Cap.	9,603	8,432	7,716	6,966	6,798	6,037	5,734	5,578	5,393	5,155
% Oper. Ratio	83.5	87.0	85.3	86.6	85.3	86.9	87.6	84.6	84.5	84.7
% Earn. on Net Prop.	7.6	8.0	8.9	8.0	9.0	7.9	7.6	8.5	8.7	8.8
% Return On Revs.	8.1	7.6	11.6	4.5	8.2	7.3	6.5	9.3	9.7	10.0
% Return On Invest. Capital	9.7	6.7	10.6	5.9	8.2	8.1	7.9	9.0	9.3	9.1
% Return On Com. Equity	10.9	9.6	15.9	6.3	11.9	10.7	9.7	12.3	13.8	14.2

Data as orig. reptd.; bef. results of disc opers. and/or spec. items. Per share data adj. for stk. divs. as of ex-div. date. Bold denotes diluted EPS (FASB 128). E-Estimated. NA-Not Available. NM-Not Meaningful. NR-Not Ranked.

Office—300 Madison Avenue, Morristown, NJ 07962-1911. **Tel**—(973) 455-8200. **Chrmn, Pres & CEO**—F. D. Hafer. **SVP & CFO**—J. G. Graham. **VP & Treas**—T. G. Howson. **Secy**—M. A. Nalewako. **Investor Contact**—Joanne M. Barbieri. **Dirs**—T. H. Black, T. B. Hagen, H. F. Henderson Jr., J. R. Leva, J. M. Pietruski, C. A. Rein, P. R. Roedel, B. S. Townsend, C. A. H. Trost, P. K. Woolf. **Transfer Agent**—ChaseMellon Shareholder Services, Ridgefield Park, NJ. **Incorporated**—in New York; reincorporated in Pennsylvania in 1969. **Empl**—9,387. **S&P Analyst:** Justin McCann

12-SEP-98

Industry: Chemicals (Specialty)

Summary: This major global specialty chemicals company recently merged its packaging business with Sealed Air Corp.

S&P Opinion: Hold (★★★)	
Recent Price • 12⅞	Yield • Nil
52 Wk Range • 86⅞-11¾	12-Mo. P/E • 7.4

Quantitative Evaluations

Outlook (1 Lowest—5 Highest)
• 3⁻

Fair Value
• 14⅞

Risk
• NA

Earn./Div. Rank
• B-

Technical Eval.
• NA

Rel. Strength Rank (1 Lowest—99 Highest)
• 24

Insider Activity
• NA

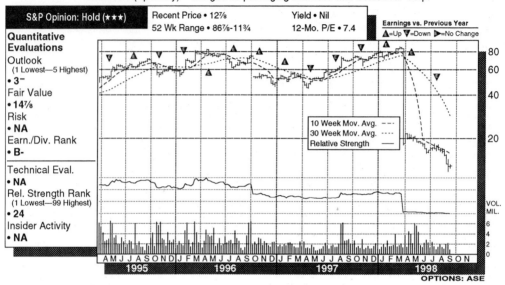

Earnings vs. Previous Year
▲=Up ▼=Down ▶=No Change

10 Week Mov. Avg. ---
30 Week Mov. Avg. ·····
Relative Strength ——

OPTIONS: ASE

Overview - 22-MAY-98

GRA at the end of March 1998 merged its Cryovac packaging materials business (sales of $1.8 billion) into Sealed Air Corp. (SEE) in a tax-free transaction worth over $6.0 billion in stock and cash. GRA shareholders now own a 63% fully diluted interest in the new Sealed Air (sales of more than $2.5 billion). Prior to the merger, GRA completed the spin-off of its specialty chemicals businesses (catalysts, construction products, container products) as a separate company with annual sales of about $1.5 billion and retaining the Grace name. The new Grace also received $1.25 billion, which it used to repay most of its debt. GRA may sell its container products unit (annual sales of $260 million). GRA will use its healthy balance sheet to make acquisitions and repurchase up to 20% of its common stock. We see sales for the new Grace advancing in 1998, despite the negative impact of the strong U.S. dollar and economic problems in Asia. The catalysts business should show some recovery with firmer FCC pricing and higher volumes. GRA is implementing overhead cost reductions, and also hopes to sell a biomedical unit that had losses of $0.11 a share in 1997. The pending purchase of the Crosfield business will be accretive to EPS in 1999.

Valuation - 22-MAY-98

Since 1995, GRA has created shareholder value, both from operational improvements and creative transactions. These have included the 1996 spin-off of its health care business and the sale of several businesses. A significant portion of the total proceeds of $3.5 billion from asset sales was used to buy back 25% of its stock. GRA holders received about $65 in Sealed Air common and convertible preferred stock from the sale of GRA's packaging unit. The shares are fairly valued at the current EPS estimate for 1998; GRA does not intend to pay a dividend.

Key Stock Statistics

S&P EPS Est. 1998	1.15	Tang. Bk. Value/Share	3.28
P/E on S&P Est. 1998	11.2	Beta	1.04
S&P EPS Est. 1999	1.40	Shareholders	18,500
Dividend Rate/Share	Nil	Market cap. (B)	$0.966
Shs. outstg. (M)	75.0	Inst. holdings	32%
Avg. daily vol. (M)	0.309		

Value of $10,000 invested 5 years ago: NA

Fiscal Year Ending Dec. 31

	1998	1997	1996	1995	1994	1993
Revenues (Million $)						
1Q	340.8	362.0	889.8	853.4	1,077	986.2
2Q	383.3	379.0	920.0	862.0	1,237	1,094
3Q	—	372.0	821.0	946.4	1,307	1,136
4Q	—	366.0	851.0	933.4	1,473	1,192
Yr.	—	1,480	3,454	3,666	5,093	4,408
Earnings Per Share ($)						
1Q	0.15	0.14	0.42	0.27	0.41	0.35
2Q	0.32	1.08	2.41	0.51	-1.43	0.60
3Q	E0.33	0.20	0.61	0.20	0.81	-2.56
4Q	E0.35	-0.26	-1.44	-2.92	1.10	3.05
Yr.	E1.15	1.17	2.32	-2.05	0.88	1.46

Next earnings report expected: NA

Dividend Data (Dividends have been paid since 1934.)

Amount ($)	Date Decl.	Ex-Div. Date	Stock of Record	Payment Date
0.145	Jul. 10	Aug. 26	Aug. 28	Sep. 09 '97
0.145	Nov. 06	Nov. 24	Nov. 26	Dec. 09 '97

A Division of The McGraw-Hill Companies

Business Summary - 22-MAY-98

This large global supplier of specialty chemicals has made numerous changes since early 1995; it divested non-core assets for $3.5 billion, repurchased 25% of its outstanding common stock for $1.6 billion, and implemented significant cost savings. In the latest development, GRA in March 1998 merged its Cryovac packaging business with Sealed Air Corp. (SEE) in a transaction valued at over $6 billion. GRA shareholders now own 63% of SEE. GRA now has annual sales of about $1.5 billion. While the new Grace is much smaller in sales than historically, it is a more focused and profitable company, with a healthier balance sheet and positive cash flow. Ongoing segment contributions in 1997 were:

	Revs.	Profits
Catalysts & silica	48%	57%
Construction	32%	25%
Container products	18%	14%
Other	2%	4%

International operations accounted for 46% of sales in 1997.

The Davidson division makes catalysts (28% of total sales in 1997) used in petroleum refining and polyolefin processing, and silica and zeolite adsorbents (14%) for use in a variety of industrial and consumer applications.

Davidson is the world's leading supplier of fluid cracking catalysts (FCC) for petroleum refining. In April 1998, GRA announced an agreement to buy the Crosfield business of Imperial Chemical Industries for $455 million. Crosfield, with sales in 1997 of $270 million, is a major producer of silica, silicate and zeolite products and hydroprocessing and specialty catalysts.

Construction products include cement and concrete additives (19% of total sales in 1997) and building materials (13%), consisting of waterproofing products and fireproofing products used for steel. Darex Container Products consists of container and closure sealants, and coatings for metal packaging. In April 1998, GRA said it was continuing a strategic review of Darex and that a conclusion would be reached in 1998.

The Cryovac business (sales of $1.83 billion in 1997, classified as a discontinued operation) consists of flexible multi-layer plastic laminates and shrinkable films and bags, as well as foam trays and rigid plastic containers.

As part of its plan to focus on its core businesses, GRA in 1996 and 1997 sold its water treatment and process chemicals business (annual sales of about $400 million), the Amicon separation unit, the cocoa business, and the specialty polymers unit. In September 1996, GRA merged its National Medical Care, Inc. unit with the dialysis business of Fresenius AG, forming Fresenius Medical Care (FMS).

Per Share Data ($)

(Year Ended Dec. 31)	1997	1996	1995	1994	1993	1992	1991	1990	1989	1988
Tangible Bk. Val.	5.69	7.58	11.53	6.06	8.54	11.73	17.10	15.68	14.12	13.41
Cash Flow	2.38	4.23	-0.12	3.66	3.53	3.58	5.95	5.75	5.97	4.91
Earnings	1.17	2.32	-2.05	0.88	1.46	0.88	2.51	2.36	3.01	2.26
Dividends	0.56	0.50	1.18	1.40	1.40	1.40	1.40	1.40	1.40	1.40
Payout Ratio	48%	22%	NM	159%	96%	159%	57%	60%	47%	62%
Prices - High	81⅛	83	71⅝	46¾	41¼	45	40¾	33⅝	39⅛	29⅞
- Low	44⅜	45⅝	38¼	35¼	34⅜	32	23⅜	17	25⅛	23½
P/E Ratio - High	69	36	NM	53	16	51	16	14	13	13
- Low	38	20	NM	40	13	36	9	7	8	10

Income Statement Analysis (Million $)

	1997	1996	1995	1994	1993	1992	1991	1990	1989	1988
Revs.	1,480	3,454	3,666	5,093	4,408	5,518	6,049	6,754	6,115	5,786
Oper. Inc.	155	577	357	775	608	632	742	765	625	615
Depr.	93.0	184	186	261	189	241	300	292	252	224
Int. Exp.	19.0	72.0	92.0	119	89.0	134	202	239	223	176
Pretax Inc.	143	349	-311	139	221	224	359	329	385	317
Eff. Tax Rate	39%	39%	NM	40%	39%	65%	39%	35%	33%	39%
Net Inc.	88.0	214	-196	83.0	134	79.0	219	203	257	192

Balance Sheet & Other Fin. Data (Million $)

	1997	1996	1995	1994	1993	1992	1991	1990	1989	1988
Cash	48.0	68.0	41.0	78.0	48.0	63.0	207	116	109	133
Curr. Assets	2,176	1,775	1,681	2,229	1,975	2,091	1,990	2,380	2,166	2,014
Total Assets	3,773	4,946	6,298	6,231	6,109	5,599	6,007	6,227	5,619	5,310
Curr. Liab.	1,358	1,487	2,214	2,232	1,993	1,640	1,622	1,680	1,589	1,484
LT Debt	659	1,073	1,296	1,099	1,174	1,355	1,793	1,964	1,638	1,509
Common Eqty.	468	632	1,225	1,492	1,510	1,538	2,018	1,905	1,723	1,544
Total Cap.	1,147	1,705	2,573	2,696	2,789	3,293	4,068	4,144	3,611	3,145
Cap. Exp.	259	457	538	445	310	398	489	554	515	586
Cash Flow	181	398	-11.0	344	323	320	519	494	509	416
Curr. Ratio	1.6	1.2	0.8	1.0	1.0	1.3	1.2	1.4	1.4	1.4
% LT Debt of Cap.	57.5	62.9	50.4	40.8	42.1	41.1	44.1	47.4	45.4	48.0
% Net Inc.of Revs.	5.9	6.2	NM	1.6	3.0	1.4	3.6	3.0	4.2	3.3
% Ret. on Assets	2.0	3.8	NM	1.3	2.3	1.4	3.5	3.4	4.7	3.9
% Ret. on Equity	16.0	23.0	NM	5.5	8.6	4.4	11.0	11.1	15.6	12.7

Data as orig. reptd.; bef. results of disc. opers. and/or spec. items. Per share data adj. for stk. divs. as of ex-div. date. Bold denotes diluted EPS (FASB 128). E-Estimated. NA-Not Available. NM-Not Meaningful. NR-Not Ranked.

Office—One Town Center Rd., Boca Raton, FL 33486-1010. **Tel**—(561) 362-2000. **Website**—http://www.grace.com **Chrmn, Pres & CEO**—A. J. Costello. **SVP & CFO**—L. Ellberger. **Secy**—R. B. Lamm. **Investor Contact**—Susan G. Eccher. **Dirs**—J. F. Akers, A. J. Costello, M. A. Fox, J.J. Murphy, T. A. Vanderslice. **Transfer Agent**—ChaseMellon Shareholder Services, NYC. **Incorporated**—in Connecticut in 1899; reincorporated in Delaware in 1996. **Empl**— 6,300. **S&P Analyst:** Richard O'Reilly, CFA

12-SEP-98

Industry: Electronics (Component Distributors)

Summary: Grainger is a leading distributor of equipment, components and supplies to commercial, industrial, contractor and institutional markets.

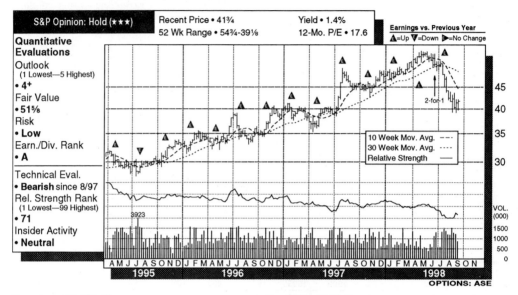

| S&P Opinion: Hold (★★★) | Recent Price • 41¾ | Yield • 1.4% |
| | 52 Wk Range • 54¾-39⅛ | 12-Mo. P/E • 17.6 |

Earnings vs. Previous Year
▲=Up ▼=Down ▶=No Change

Quantitative Evaluations

Outlook (1 Lowest—5 Highest)
• **4+**

Fair Value
• **51⅝**

Risk
• **Low**

Earn./Div. Rank
• **A**

Technical Eval.
• **Bearish** since 8/97

Rel. Strength Rank (1 Lowest—99 Highest)
• **71**

Insider Activity
• **Neutral**

10 Week Mov. Avg. - - -
30 Week Mov. Avg. ·····
Relative Strength —

2-for-1

OPTIONS: ASE

Overview - 16-JUL-98

Sales are expected to rise 7% in 1998, reflecting our projections of a 4% volume rise and 3% average price increase. Grainger's national accounts program targeting large OEMs should continue to aid sales growth. Gross margins may widen slightly, as sales to national accounts require a lower level of selling, general and administrative expenses. In addition, comparisons will benefit from the absence of excess costs of $0.06 a share in 1997 to contend with the United Parcel Service strike. Warehousing and administrative costs will benefit from the company's continuing efforts to upgrade its computerized order entry/processing and inventory management systems. These programs are yielding positive results, in the form of better customer service and lower overhead and freight costs. Partly offsetting these factors are increased costs to expand the integrated supply business, and increased marketing efforts through a variety of distribution channels. For the long term, Grainger will continue to grow in line with the economy, in the absence of any further substantial acquisitions.

Valuation - 16-JUL-98

We continue our neutral rating on the stock. The shares were recently trading at about 20X expected 1998 EPS, a rich multiple in light of the modest growth envisioned. With their high P/E multiple, we think that the shares will only be average performers over the next year. We think that the shares should be held by current owners, due to their S&P earnings/dividend ranking of A, which reflects steady growth of earnings and dividends over an extended period of time, but new purchases should be delayed until the valuation becomes more compelling.

Key Stock Statistics

S&P EPS Est. 1998	2.50	Tang. Bk. Value/Share	14.02
P/E on S&P Est. 1998	16.7	Beta	0.81
S&P EPS Est. 1999	2.80	Shareholders	2,000
Dividend Rate/Share	0.60	Market cap. (B)	$ 4.1
Shs. outstg. (M)	97.7	Inst. holdings	61%
Avg. daily vol. (M)	0.258		

Value of $10,000 invested 5 years ago: $ 14,960

Fiscal Year Ending Dec. 31

	1998	1997	1996	1995	1994	1993
Revenues (Million $)						
1Q	1,057	985.6	842.6	806.8	706.4	606.2
2Q	1,119	1,051	888.6	813.5	768.5	660.4
3Q	—	1,067	901.9	850.0	779.3	698.8
4Q	—	1,033	904.1	806.6	768.9	663.0
Yr.	—	4,137	3,537	3,277	3,023	2,628
Earnings Per Share ($)						
1Q	**0.58**	0.52	0.49	0.46	0.41	0.33
2Q	**0.60**	0.56	0.48	0.39	0.41	0.34
3Q	—	0.56	0.51	0.48	0.42	0.38
4Q	—	0.63	0.54	0.49	0.01	0.40
Yr.	**E2.50**	2.27	2.02	1.82	1.25	1.44

Next earnings report expected: mid October

Dividend Data (Dividends have been paid since 1965.)

Amount ($)	Date Decl.	Ex-Div. Date	Stock of Record	Payment Date
0.270	Jan. 28	Feb. 05	Feb. 09	Mar. 01 '98
0.300	Apr. 29	May. 07	May. 11	Jun. 01 '98
2-for-1	Apr. 29	Jun. 15	May. 11	Jun. 12 '98
0.150	Jul. 29	Aug. 06	Aug. 10	Sep. 01 '98

A Division of The McGraw·Hill Companies

Business Summary - 16-JUL-98

W.W. Grainger is a nationwide distributor of maintenance, repair and operating supplies, and a provider of related information, serving the commercial, industrial, contractor and institutional markets. The company operates multiple distribution channels including branch stores, distribution centers, direct sales, catalog sales and electronic sales via the Internet. The company's customer base is diverse, both by industry and by geographic location.

Important profitability statistics for recent years:

	1997	1996	1995
Gross profit margins	36%	36%	36%
Operating profit margins	9.5%	9.8%	9.7%
Free cash flow (000)	$261,366	$143,154	$36,617
Free cash flow per share	$2.56	$1.39	$0.36

The company's core branch-based business, Grainger, is a nationwide distributor of industrial and commercial equipment and supplies. It distributes motors, HVAC equipment, lighting, hand and power tools, pumps and electrical equipment, as well as many other items. Grainger sells principally to contractors, service shops, industrial and commercial maintenance departments, manufacturers, hotels, and health care and educational facilities. The division has a customer base numbering

more than 1,300,000. Products are offered through a network of approximately 350 Grainger stores located in 50 states and Puerto Rico and one in Mexico. The company conducts its Canadian industrial distribution business through GWW's Acklands-Grainger unit. Acklands-Grainger is Canada's largest industrial supplies distributor, with 170 branches and five distribution centers throughout Canada.

The company's massive general catalog is an important selling tool listing over 78,000 items. About 25% of the division's 1997 sales consisted of items bearing Grainger's registered trademarks. The company's largest customer, GM, accounted for about 1% of 1997 sales. Products are purchased from more than 1,000 suppliers, the largest of which accounted for nearly 11% of 1997 purchases.

Grainger's businesses also include Lab Safety Supply and Parts Company of America. Wisconsin-based Lab Safety is a leading national marketer of safety products, serving customers through a catalog of 40,000 items. Products include respiratory systems, protective clothing, and other equipment used in the workplace and in environmental clean-up operations. Parts Company of America distributes some 230,000 spare and replacement parts for most products found in the Grainger General Catalog. Orders are taken 24 hours a day, 365 days a year, and in-stock items are shipped within 24 hours.

Per Share Data ($)

(Year Ended Dec. 31)	1997	1996	1995	1994	1993	1992	1991	1990	1989	1988
Tangible Bk. Val.	11.13	11.64	10.87	9.32	8.05	7.55	8.13	7.54	6.71	5.85
Cash Flow	3.05	2.74	2.52	1.90	2.01	1.75	1.53	1.46	1.41	1.24
Earnings	2.27	2.02	1.82	1.25	1.44	1.29	1.19	1.16	1.10	0.98
Dividends	0.53	0.49	0.45	0.39	0.35	0.33	0.30	0.28	0.25	0.21
Payout Ratio	23%	24%	24%	31%	24%	25%	25%	24%	23%	21%
Prices - High	49⅞	40¾	33⅞	34⅝	33⅜	30½	27¾	19⅝	16⅝	16⅞
- Low	35¼	31⅜	27¾	25¾	25⅞	19½	15⅛	13⅝	13⅛	12⅜
P/E Ratio - High	22	20	19	28	23	24	23	17	15	17
- Low	16	16	15	21	18	15	13	12	12	13

Income Statement Analysis (Million $)

	1997	1996	1995	1994	1993	1992	1991	1990	1989	1988
Revs.	4,137	3,537	3,277	3,023	2,628	2,364	2,077	1,935	1,727	1,535
Oper. Inc.	473	420	387	368	311	278	242	237	224	206
Depr.	79.7	74.3	70.9	66.7	59.2	49.1	37.8	33.1	33.3	28.5
Int. Exp.	5.5	3.0	6.4	3.8	3.0	3.4	3.2	2.8	2.4	3.5
Pretax Inc.	390	349	312	229	250	227	209	208	197	180
Eff. Tax Rate	41%	40%	40%	44%	40%	40%	39%	39%	39%	39%
Net Inc.	232	209	187	128	149	137	128	127	120	109

Balance Sheet & Other Fin. Data (Million $)

	1997	1996	1995	1994	1993	1992	1991	1990	1989	1988
Cash	46.9	127	11.4	15.0	3.0	45.0	141	147	81.0	79.0
Curr. Assets	1,183	1,320	1,063	964	824	794	854	829	755	620
Total Assets	1,998	2,119	1,669	1,535	1,377	1,311	1,217	1,162	1,065	936
Curr. Liab.	534	616	444	459	381	315	280	269	262	237
LT Debt	131	6.2	8.7	1.0	6.2	6.9	11.3	14.5	2.8	16.5
Common Eqty.	1,295	1,463	1,179	1,033	942	931	860	815	732	635
Total Cap.	1,429	1,471	1,188	1,049	971	979	921	881	793	699
Cap. Exp.	108	62.1	112	120	99	77.4	32.8	35.0	35.2	87.1
Cash Flow	311	283	258	195	208	186	166	160	153	137
Curr. Ratio	2.2	2.1	2.4	2.1	2.2	2.5	3.0	3.1	2.9	2.6
% LT Debt of Cap.	9.2	0.4	0.7	0.1	0.6	0.7	1.2	1.6	0.4	2.4
% Net Inc.of Revs.	5.6	5.9	5.7	4.2	5.7	5.8	6.1	6.6	6.9	7.1
% Ret. on Assets	11.3	11.0	11.7	8.8	11.3	10.9	10.9	11.4	11.9	12.4
% Ret. on Equity	16.8	15.8	16.4	12.9	16.2	15.4	15.4	16.4	17.5	18.1

Data as orig. reptd.; bef. results of disc. opers. and/or spec. items. Per share data adj. for stk. divs. as of ex-div. date. Bold denotes diluted EPS (FASB 128). Free cash flow: Net income plus depreciation/amortization and declines in working capital, less net capital expenditures, increases in working capital and preferred stock dividends. E-Estimated. NA-Not Available. NM-Not Meaningful. NR-Not Ranked.

Office—455 Knightsbridge Pkwy., Lincolnshire, IL 60069-3620. **Tel**—(847) 793-9030. **Website**—http://www.grainger.com **Chrmn, Pres & CEO**—R. L. Keyser. **CFO**—P. O. Loux. **Investor Contact**—Robert D. Pappano. **Secy**—J. M. Baisley. **Dirs**—G. R. Baker, R. E. Elberson, J. D. Fluno, W. H. Gantz, D. W. Grainger, R. L. Keyser, J. W. McCarter, Jr., F. L. Turner, J. S. Webb. **Transfer Agent & Registrar**—First National Bank of Boston. **Incorporated**—in Illinois in 1928. **Empl**— 15,300. **S&P Analyst:** Robert E. Friedman, CPA.

12-SEP-98

Industry: Retail (Food Chains)

Summary: This company operates more than 900 conventional supermarkets and larger superstores throughout the U.S. and in Ontario.

S&P Opinion: Hold (★★★)	Recent Price • 24⅜	Yield • 1.6%
	52 Wk Range • 36-23	12-Mo. P/E • 15.6

Quantitative Evaluations

Outlook
(1 Lowest—5 Highest)
• **2**

Fair Value
• **26¼**

Risk
• **Average**

Earn./Div. Rank
• **B-**

Technical Eval.
• **NA**

Rel. Strength Rank
(1 Lowest—99 Highest)
• **48**

Insider Activity
• **Favorable**

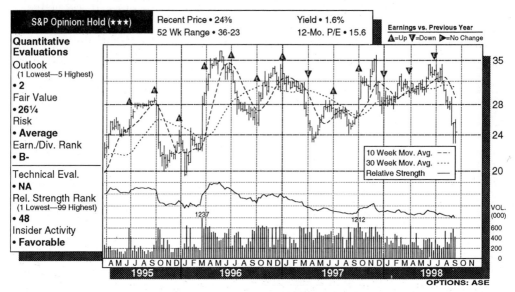

Earnings vs. Previous Year
▲=Up ▼=Down ▶=No Change

10 Week Mov. Avg. – – –
30 Week Mov. Avg. - - - -
Relative Strength ——

VOL. (000)

OPTIONS: ASE

Overview - 10-JUL-98

We expect sales to rise approximately 3% to 5% in FY 99 (Feb.), as contributions from new stores help to offset flat same-store sales. GAP has accelerated the conversion of its units to a new superstore format that typically ranges from 50,000 sq. ft. to 65,000 sq. ft. Response to the new stores has been positive, although comparable-store sales at existing GAP units have been hurt by the cannibalizing effect of the newer, larger stores. Margins will continue under pressure, due to a lack of food price inflation, as well as intense competition in most of the company's operating regions. However, GAP will continue to increase its offerings of private label product lines, Master Choice and America's Choice, which are among its highest margin products. Over the long term, a more extensive offering of these higher-margin products, should boost earnings growth.

Valuation - 10-JUL-98

We continue to maintain a neutral opinion on GAP shares. In the past year, the stock has underperformed both the S&P Retail (Food Chains) Index and the broader market. Sales and earnings comparisons in recent periods have been hurt by an exceptionally competitive and promotional retail environment, particularly in the Northeast. EPS in the fourth quarter of FY 98 were also reduced about $0.26 a share for costs due to the company's deferral of certain cash payments from suppliers. These payments will be reflected in FY 99 earnings. Based on the recent and ongoing aggressive growth of superstores by GAP's major competitors, and the company's low return on sales in comparison to that of other industry participants, we believe that the shares are adequately valued at a recent level of 18X our estimated FY 99 EPS of $1.75.

Key Stock Statistics

S&P EPS Est. 1999	1.75	Tang. Bk. Value/Share	24.47
P/E on S&P Est. 1999	13.9	Beta	1.29
S&P EPS Est. 2000	2.00	Shareholders	8,800
Dividend Rate/Share	0.40	Market cap. (B)	$0.932
Shs. outstg. (M)	38.3	Inst. holdings	36%
Avg. daily vol. (M)	0.092		

Value of $10,000 invested 5 years ago: $ 11,410

Fiscal Year Ending Feb. 28

	1999	1998	1997	1996	1995	1994
Revenues (Million $)						
1Q	3,078	3,105	3,093	3,136	3,225	3,279
2Q	—	2,336	2,330	2,341	2,391	2,399
3Q	—	2,319	2,319	2,294	2,346	2,343
4Q	—	2,503	2,348	2,331	2,370	2,363
Yr.	—	10,262	10,089	10,101	10,332	10,384
Earnings Per Share ($)						
1Q	**0.50**	0.60	0.57	0.38	0.19	0.45
2Q	**E0.42**	0.42	0.37	0.25	0.16	0.15
3Q	**E0.37**	0.29	0.37	0.20	-4.86	0.01
4Q	**E0.46**	0.35	0.60	0.67	0.15	-0.51
Yr.	**E1.75**	1.66	1.91	1.50	-4.36	0.10

Next earnings report expected: NA

Dividend Data (Dividends have been paid since 1986.)

Amount ($)	Date Decl.	Ex-Div. Date	Stock of Record	Payment Date
0.100	Oct. 02	Oct. 14	Oct. 16	Nov. 03 '97
0.100	Dec. 09	Jan. 08	Jan. 12	Feb. 02 '98
0.100	Mar. 24	Apr. 07	Apr. 09	May. 01 '98
0.100	Jul. 14	Jul. 22	Jul. 24	Aug. 10 '98

A Division of The **McGraw·Hill** *Companies*

Business Summary - 10-JUL-98

With nearly $10.3 billion in sales in FY 98 (Feb.), The Great Atlantic and Pacific Tea Company (GAP) operates one of the 10 largest retail food chains in the U.S., with market leading positions in New York and Detroit.

The company has conventional supermarkets and larger superstores selling food and general merchandise in 20 U.S. states, the District of Columbia, and Ontario, under trade names that include A&P, Waldbaum's, Food Emporium, Super Fresh, Farmer Jack, Kohl's, Sav-A-Center, Super Food Mart, Ultra Mart, Dominion, and Food Basics.

At July 7, 1998, GAP operated 919 stores, averaging about 35,000 sq. ft., and serviced 53 franchised Food Basics stores in Canada. Through its Compass Foods division, it also manufactures and distributes a line of coffees under the Eight O'clock, Bokar and Royale labels.

GAP's U.S. stores offer America's Choice and Master Choice, private premium label merchandise, which are strong contributors to operating margins, and which the company believes will play an important role in its future growth. The company anticipates that these two brands will account for up to 20% of the company's future sales.

GAP has historically expanded and diversified geographically mainly through the acquisition of other supermarkets. The company has closed more than 600 outmoded stores in the past 10 years, including 74 stores in FY 98. At the same time, its development program calls for opening new stores and expanding or remodeling certain existing stores. In FY 98, GAP spent $268 million on capital improvements, with the major part used to open 33 new supermarkets, three new liquor stores, and four new Food Basics franchised stores in Canada, and remodel or expand 45 units. The company plans to spend $300 million on capital improvements in FY 99, primarily to open 45 new stores and expand or remodel 80 stores.

For the next several years, GAP plans to open about 50 to 55 new stores a year and remodel an additional 50 units, with an attendant annual increase in square footage of about 3%. Newer stores are expected to range in size from 50,000 sq. ft. to 65,000 sq. ft.

In support of its retail operations, the company operates two coffee roasting plants, two bakeries, one delicatessen food kitchen and an ice cream plant. It also sells coffee and ice cream products to other retailers. To improve customer service, store operations and merchandising, GAP also intends to focus on the use of technology, such as scanning and other technological advances.

Per Share Data ($)

(Year Ended Feb. 28)	1998	1997	1996	1995	1994	1993	1992	1991	1990	1989
Tangible Bk. Val.	24.22	23.27	21.53	20.28	26.02	27.06	32.79	31.96	27.49	24.50
Cash Flow	7.84	8.00	7.42	1.80	6.11	3.27	7.65	9.15	8.54	7.29
Earnings	1.66	1.91	1.50	-4.36	0.10	-2.58	1.85	3.95	3.84	3.34
Dividends	0.40	0.20	0.20	0.65	0.80	0.80	0.80	0.78	0.68	0.57
Payout Ratio	24%	10%	13%	NM	NM	NM	43%	20%	18%	17%
Cal. Yrs.	1997	1996	1995	1994	1993	1992	1991	1990	1989	1988
Prices - High	36	36³/₄	29	27³/₈	35	35¹/₄	57³/₄	61³/₄	65³/₈	48¹/₈
- Low	23¹/₈	19¹/₂	17⁵/₈	17³/₈	22¹/₂	21³/₈	25¹/₂	37³/₄	44¹/₄	31⁷/₈
P/E Ratio - High	22	19	19	NM	NM	NM	31	16	17	14
- Low	14	10	12	NM	NM	NM	14	10	12	10

Income Statement Analysis (Million $)

Revs.	10,262	10,089	10,101	10,332	10,384	10,499	11,591	11,391	11,148	10,068
Oper. Inc.	389	401	376	349	298	341	426	534	488	418
Depr.	234	231	225	235	230	224	222	199	180	151
Int. Exp.	80.0	73.0	73.0	73.0	63.3	66.4	81.4	79.7	73.5	48.5
Pretax Inc.	83.0	101	81.0	-128	7.0	-171	124	262	251	224
Eff. Tax Rate	23%	27%	29%	NM	40%	NM	43%	43%	42%	43%
Net Inc.	64.0	73.0	57.0	-166	4.0	-99.0	71.0	151	147	128

Balance Sheet & Other Fin. Data (Million $)

Cash	71.0	99	100	129	124	110	55.7	28.5	35.1	44.5
Curr. Assets	1,217	1,231	1,184	1,194	1,230	1,221	1,175	1,212	1,076	1,069
Total Assets	2,995	3,003	2,877	2,895	3,099	3,091	3,213	3,307	2,832	2,640
Curr. Liab.	955	1,016	1,006	1,096	1,151	1,165	1,002	1,096	996	978
LT Debt	816	840	780	759	707	596	692	753	563	507
Common Eqty.	926	890	823	775	994	1,034	1,253	1,221	1,092	971
Total Cap.	1,864	1,843	1,733	1,652	1,802	1,772	2,114	2,127	1,744	1,552
Cap. Exp.	268	297	236	215	261	252	168	467	221	369
Cash Flow	298	304	282	69.0	234	125	292	350	326	278
Curr. Ratio	1.3	1.2	1.2	1.1	1.1	1.0	1.2	1.1	1.1	1.1
% LT Debt of Cap.	43.7	45.6	45.0	45.9	39.2	33.7	32.7	35.4	32.3	32.7
% Net Inc.of Revs.	0.6	0.7	0.6	NM	Nil	NM	0.6	1.3	1.3	1.3
% Ret. on Assets	2.1	2.5	2.0	NM	0.1	NM	2.2	4.9	5.4	5.2
% Ret. on Equity	7.0	8.5	7.1	NM	0.4	NM	5.7	13.0	14.2	14.0

Data as orig. reptd.; bef. results of disc. opers. and/or spec. items. Per share data adj. for stk. divs. as of ex-div. date. Bold denotes diluted EPS (FASB 128). E-Estimated. NA-Not Available. NM-Not Meaningful. NR-Not Ranked.

Office—2 Paragon Drive, Montvale, NJ 07645. **Tel**—(201) 573-9700. **Website**—http://www.aptea.com. **Chrmn** —J. Wood. **Pres & CEO**—C. W. E. Haub. **Vice Chrmn & CFO**—Fred Corrado. **VP & Secy**—P. R. Brooker. **Investor Contact**—Michael Rourke (201-930-4236). **Dirs**—J. D. Barline, R. Baumeister, F. Corrado, C. F. Edley, C. W. E. Haub, H. Haub, B. B. Hauptfuhrer, W. A. Liffers, F. Teelen, R. L. Wetzel, J. Wood. **Transfer Agent & Registrar**—American Stock Transfer & Trust Co., NYC. **Incorporated**—in Maryland in 1925. **Empl**— 80,000. **S&P Analyst:** Maureen C. Carini

12-SEP-98

Industry: Chemicals (Specialty)

Summary: This company, the world's leading producer of certain specialty chemicals, recently completed the spinoff of its petroleum additives business.

S&P Opinion: Hold (★★★)	Recent Price • 38⅞	Yield • 0.8%
	52 Wk Range • 54⅛-36⅝	12-Mo. P/E • 74.9

Quantitative Evaluations

Outlook
(1 Lowest—5 Highest)
• **2+**

Fair Value
• **38¾**

Risk
• **Low**

Earn./Div. Rank
• **A**

Technical Eval.
• **Bearish** since 5/98

Rel. Strength Rank
(1 Lowest—99 Highest)
• **79**

Insider Activity
• **Favorable**

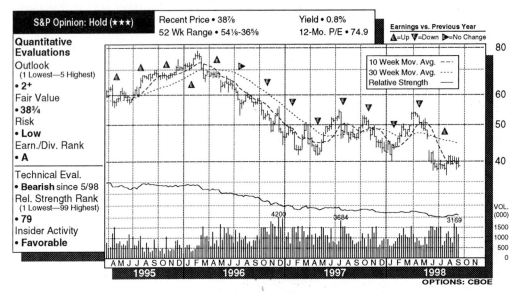

Earnings vs. Previous Year
▲=Up ▼=Down ▶=No Change

10 Week Mov. Avg. ---
30 Week Mov. Avg. ······
Relative Strength ——

4200   3684   3169

VOL. (000)

OPTIONS: CBOE

Overview - 22-MAY-98

As a means to increase shareholder value, GLK completed the spinoff of its petroleum additives business as Octel Corp. (OTL; sales of $531 million and net income of $119 million in 1997) in May 1998. GLK shareholders received one share of OTL for every four GLK shares held. GLK also plans to dispose of its discontinued furfural, European trading, and environmental services businesses (sales of $237 million; minimal profits). The new GLK, with sales of $1.3 billion and net income $119 million in 1997 before special charges, consists primarily of specialty chemical businesses. GLK received from Octel Corp. a special cash dividend of about $300 million (net of taxes and transaction costs). GLK will use the funds to build its specialty chemicals business and to buy back common stock. GLK may undertake other restructurings, including selling other specialty chemicals units. We estimate EPS for the new GLK in 1998 at $2.25, before a nonrecurring charge of $0.19 in the first quarter related to management changes. GLK earned $1.97 a share in 1997 before special charges of $0.78. Comparisons in 1998 should be favorable, due to price increases in flame retardants and volume gains in polymer stabilizers and water chemicals. Octel Corp. had estimated pro forma EPS of $1.60 in 1997.

Valuation - 22-MAY-98

The stock has been a poor performer in the past few years, largely reflecting disappointing earnings. The spinoff of Octel Corp. removes the cloud of declining lead antiknocks hanging over GLK's potentially faster growing specialty chemicals businesses. Investors welcomed the appointment in April of a new CEO from outside the company. We feel that the new GLK is fairly valued at the current price to ongoing EPS.

Key Stock Statistics

S&P EPS Est. 1998	2.25	Tang. Bk. Value/Share	16.45
P/E on S&P Est. 1998	17.3	Beta	0.68
S&P EPS Est. 1999	2.50	Shareholders	4,100
Dividend Rate/Share	0.32	Market cap. (B)	$ 2.3
Shs. outstg. (M)	59.1	Inst. holdings	79%
Avg. daily vol. (M)	0.342		

Value of $10,000 invested 5 years ago: NA

Fiscal Year Ending Dec. 31

	1998	1997	1996	1995	1994	1993
Revenues (Million $)						
1Q	334.8	319.6	537.0	569.0	449.0	430.0
2Q	401.9	356.4	595.0	640.9	526.0	462.0
3Q	—	309.6	564.4	586.2	525.0	470.0
4Q	—	325.7	515.4	565.0	565.0	430.0
Yr.	—	1,311	2,212	2,361	2,065	1,792
Earnings Per Share ($)						
1Q	**0.29**	**0.43**	1.03	1.02	0.94	0.90
2Q	**0.64**	**0.55**	1.20	1.20	0.96	0.98
3Q	—	**0.48**	1.09	1.15	1.05	0.96
4Q	—	**-0.28**	0.62	1.15	1.05	0.98
Yr.	—	**1.19**	3.94	4.52	4.00	3.82

Next earnings report expected: late October

Dividend Data (Dividends have been paid since 1973.)

Amount ($)	Date Decl.	Ex-Div. Date	Stock of Record	Payment Date
0.160	Nov. 21	Dec. 29	Jan. 01	Feb. 03 '98
0.160	Feb. 17	Mar. 30	Apr. 01	May. 05 '98
Stk.	May. 08	May. 26	May. 15	May. 22 '98
0.080	Jun. 11	Jun. 29	Jul. 01	Aug. 04 '98

A Division of The McGraw-Hill Companies

Business Summary - 22-MAY-98

As a means to increase shareholder value, this specialty chemicals producer in May 1998 completed the spinoff of its Octel Corp. (OTL) petroleum additives business (reported as discontinued operations in 1997, with sales of $531 million and net income of $119 million before special charges). GLK also plans to dispose its discontinued furfural, European trading, and environmental services businesses (total sales of $237 million). The remainder of GLK had net income of $119 million (before charges of $47 million) in 1997 on sales of $1.3 billion. GLK received $300 million from Octel in the form of a special distribution prior to the spinoff. GLK will use the funds to build its specialty chemicals businesses and to repurchase common stock. Segment sales contributions in recent years were:

	1997	1996
Water treatment chemicals	27%	32%
Flame retardants	23%	22%
Polymer stabilizers	19%	18%
Intermediates/fine chemicals	16%	14%
Specialized services/manufacturing	15%	14%

Foreign operations accounted for 30% of sales and 9% of pretax income in 1997.

GLK is the world's leading supplier of bromine and chlorine-based specialty biocides for recreational and industrial water treatment, sold under the BioGuard, OMNI, Hydrotech, and AQUA CHEM brand names.

GLK is the world's leading producer of bromine-based flame retardants, which together with polymer stabilizers (anti-oxidants, UV absorbers, light stabilizers) are used to enhance the performance of a wide variety of polymer systems. In late 1997, GLK acquired Cookson Group's Anzon unit, the leading global maker of antimony products used as flame retardants.

Specialty chemicals include bromine and derivative products, fine chemicals and various agricultural products, and custom chemical manufacturing.

The specialized services and manufacturing segment includes fluorine chemicals (including fire extinguishants); OSCA oilfield completion services; and toxicological services.

GLK has repurchased approximately 11.7 million of its common shares since 1993, for about $700 million, including 2.8 million shares in 1997. About 6.5 million shares remain authorized to be purchased.

U.K.-based Octel Corp. (OTL) is the world's leading producer of a wide range of transportation fuel additives, including lead antiknock octane boosters, cetane improvers, detergents, anti-oxidants, stabilizers and corrosion inhibitors. Octel is the world's major supplier of lead antiknock compounds. Lead antiknocks had higher profitability than do most of GLK's other products.

Per Share Data ($)

(Year Ended Dec. 31)	1997	1996	1995	1994	1993	1992	1991	1990	1989	1988
Tangible Bk. Val.	20.23	17.07	15.52	13.37	12.84	10.55	9.47	7.65	6.11	6.19
Cash Flow	2.41	5.89	5.80	5.47	5.09	4.32	3.13	2.73	2.36	1.95
Earnings	1.19	3.94	4.52	4.00	3.82	3.27	2.23	2.00	1.76	1.49
Dividends	0.63	0.57	0.44	0.39	0.35	0.31	0.27	0.23	0.20	0.17
Payout Ratio	53%	14%	10%	10%	9%	10%	12%	12%	11%	12%
Prices - High	54⁷/₈	78⁵/₈	74⁵/₈	82	84	71³/₈	58	34	24	16¹/₂
- Low	41¹/₂	44¹/₄	55³/₄	48³/₄	64¹/₂	50¹/₄	30³/₈	20³/₈	14¹/₈	12¹/₈
P/E Ratio - High	46	20	17	20	22	22	26	17	14	11
- Low	35	11	12	12	17	15	14	10	8	8

Income Statement Analysis (Million $)

	1997	1996	1995	1994	1993	1992	1991	1990	1989	1988
Revs.	1,311	2,212	2,361	2,065	1,792	1,496	1,308	1,066	792	558
Oper. Inc.	265	570	581	541	515	438	360	314	201	125
Depr.	73.7	124	83.4	102	90.0	74.9	63.8	50.6	41.7	32.3
Int. Exp.	56.3	26.0	21.2	11.9	8.2	12.4	12.3	13.1	12.6	4.4
Pretax Inc.	117	379	438	436	415	361	320	290	202	144
Eff. Tax Rate	39%	34%	32%	28%	27%	28%	21%	24%	22%	28%
Net Inc.	71.8	250	296	279	273	233	157	141	123	103

Balance Sheet & Other Fin. Data (Million $)

	1997	1996	1995	1994	1993	1992	1991	1990	1989	1988
Cash	73.7	202	181	145	180	141	81.0	60.6	30.4	12.2
Curr. Assets	669	1,177	1,125	980	857	773	641	608	447	223
Total Assets	2,270	2,661	2,469	2,111	1,901	1,732	1,649	1,406	1,097	664
Curr. Liab.	304	434	465	428	368	431	303	307	210	123
LT Debt	561	504	340	144	61.0	46.0	140	76.0	114	19.0
Common Eqty.	1,307	1,487	1,416	1,311	1,257	1,053	900	744	591	482
Total Cap.	1,936	2,119	1,876	1,557	1,410	1,182	1,230	1,001	841	541
Cap. Exp.	133	237	247	123	79.3	69.4	90.7	73.6	80.1	47.0
Cash Flow	145	375	379	381	363	308	221	191	165	136
Curr. Ratio	2.2	2.7	2.4	2.3	2.3	1.8	2.1	2.0	2.1	1.8
% LT Debt of Cap.	29.0	23.7	18.1	9.2	4.3	3.9	11.4	7.6	13.5	3.6
% Net Inc.of Revs.	5.5	11.3	12.5	13.5	15.2	15.6	12.0	13.2	15.5	18.5
% Ret. on Assets	2.9	4.8	12.9	14.3	15.0	13.7	10.3	11.2	13.9	16.6
% Ret. on Equity	5.1	17.2	21.7	22.3	23.6	23.8	19.1	21.1	22.8	23.6

Data as orig. reptd.; bef. results of disc. opers. and/or spec. items. Per share data adj. for stk. divs. as of ex-div. date. Bold denotes diluted EPS (FASB 128). E-Estimated. NA-Not Available. NM-Not Meaningful. NR-Not Ranked.

Office—One Great Lakes Blvd., West Lafayette, IN 47906-0200. **Tel**—(765) 497-6100. **Website**—http://www.greatlakeschem.com **Chrmn**—M. M. Hale. **Pres & CEO**—M. Bulriss. **EVP-Fin & CFO**—R. T. Jeffares. **Secy**—M. P. McClanahan. **Investor Contact**—Jeffrey Potrzebowski. **Dirs**—E. Bayh, T. M. Fulton, M. M. Hale, L. E. Lataif, R. H. Leet, R. B. McDonald, M. G. Nichols, J. D. Proops. **Transfer Agent & Registrar**—Harris Trust & Savings Bank, Chicago. **Incorporated**—in Michigan in 1933; reincorporated in Delaware in 1970. **Empl**— 5,100. **S&P Analyst**: Richard O'Reilly, CFA

STANDARD &POOR'S
STOCK REPORTS

GTE Corp.

934P
NYSE Symbol **GTE**

In S&P 500

12-SEP-98

Industry:
Telephone

Summary: GTE, one of the largest U.S.-based local telephone holding companies, has agreed to merge with Bell Atlantic via an exchange of stock.

S&P Opinion: Hold (★★★)	

Recent Price • 49½	Yield • 3.8%
52 Wk Range • 64⅜-40½	12-Mo. P/E • 21.1

Quantitative Evaluations

Outlook
(1 Lowest—5 Highest)
• **2**

Fair Value
• **48¾**

Risk
• **Low**

Earn./Div. Rank
• **B+**

Technical Eval.
• **Bearish** since 8/98

Rel. Strength Rank
(1 Lowest—99 Highest)
• **74**

Insider Activity
• **Neutral**

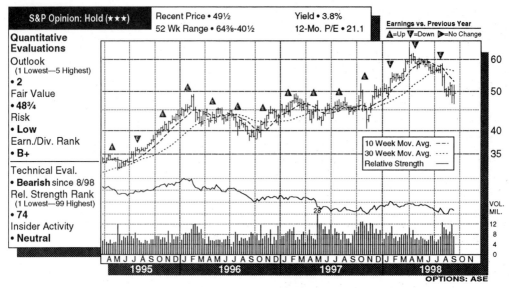

Earnings vs. Previous Year
▲=Up ▼=Down ▷=No Change

10 Week Mov. Avg. – – –
30 Week Mov. Avg. · · · ·
Relative Strength ——

OPTIONS: ASE

Overview - 29-JUL-98

The company recently agreed to merge with Bell Atlantic (NYSE: BEL). Each GTE common share would be exchanged for 1.22 BEL common shares (recent price about $45.6875). The transaction, which is expected to be completed in the second half of 1999, was initially valued at $52.9 billion. In early 1998, the company announced plans to divest non-strategic properties, in a move expected to generate proceeds of $2 billion to $3 billion. GTE also expects to reduce annual expenses by $500 million over the next two years, through the reduction of 1,500 employees and concentration on more efficient assets. In connection with these actions, the company recorded an after tax charge of $802 million ($0.83 a share) in the first quarter of 1998. Unlike the Baby Bells, GTE is free to offer long-distance services in its own regions. The acquisition of BBN Corp. gave GTE key strategic access to the lucrative, high-margin Internet business services market.

Valuation - 29-JUL-98

We question GTE's motivation in its planned merger with Bell Atlantic. While many of its competitors have paired with high growth companies, GTE has made a commitment to a mature Regional Bell Operating Company that produces only marginal gains in sales and earnings. The shares have widely underperformed the market over the past six months, and we now see them as fairly valued, as most of the negative reaction is already built into the stock. We also viewed the company's unsuccessful attempt to purchase MCI as a lack of timely decision making on the part of management. This rock solid company has committed to going in an opposite direction to that of industry leaders AT&T and WorldCom, which have made efforts to pursue opportunities in more attractive markets.

Key Stock Statistics

S&P EPS Est. 1998	2.50	Tang. Bk. Value/Share	4.92
P/E on S&P Est. 1998	19.8	Beta	0.61
S&P EPS Est. 1999	3.50	Shareholders	516,000
Dividend Rate/Share	1.88	Market cap. (B)	$ 47.7
Shs. outstg. (M)	964.0	Inst. holdings	45%
Avg. daily vol. (M)	1.852		

Value of $10,000 invested 5 years ago: $ 18,658

Fiscal Year Ending Dec. 31

	1998	1997	1996	1995	1994	1993
Revenues (Million $)						
1Q	5,885	5,281	4,951	4,665	4,750	4,830
2Q	0.02	5,692	5,293	4,932	4,960	4,920
3Q	—	5,940	5,344	4,996	5,000	4,940
4Q	—	6,347	5,751	5,364	5,250	5,060
Yr.	—	23,260	21,339	19,957	19,940	19,750
Earnings Per Share ($)						
1Q	**0.15**	**0.69**	0.63	0.56	0.52	0.48
2Q	**0.69**	**0.70**	0.66	0.60	0.62	0.46
3Q	**E0.85**	**0.79**	0.78	0.72	0.69	0.59
4Q	**E0.81**	**0.73**	0.82	0.74	0.72	-0.50
Yr.	**E2.50**	**2.90**	2.88	2.62	2.55	1.03

Next earnings report expected: mid October

Dividend Data (Dividends have been paid since 1936.)

Amount ($)	Date Decl.	Ex-Div. Date	Stock of Record	Payment Date
0.470	Nov. 06	Nov. 19	Nov. 21	Jan. 01 '98
0.470	Jan. 15	Feb. 18	Feb. 20	Apr. 01 '98
0.470	Apr. 15	May. 20	May. 22	Jul. 01 '98
0.470	Aug. 06	Aug. 20	Aug. 24	Oct. 01 '98

A Division of The **McGraw·Hill** *Companies*

GTE Corporation

934P

12-SEP-98

Business Summary - 29-JUL-98

GTE Corp. is one of the largest U.S.-based telephone holding companies. Its operations include interests in everything from wireless and defense communications to finance, insurance and leasing. Segment contributions in recent years were:

	1997	1996
Local services	28%	29%
Network access services	21%	22%
Toll services	12%	12%
Cellular services	12%	12%
Directory services	6%	7%
Other services and sales	21%	18%

The company recently agreed to merge with Bell Atlantic (NYSE: BEL), with each GTE share to be exchange for 1.22 BEL shares, in a transaction expected to be completed in the second half of 1999.

In early 1998, the company announced plans to divest itself of non-strategic properties and reduce costs. GTE expects to generate proceeds of $2-$3 billion from the sale of underperforming operations, and will reduce annual expenses by $500 million over two years primarily through the reduction of 1,500 employees.

In the U.S., GTE provides local exchange telephone service through more than 22.3 million access lines in portions of 28 states. It is selling or trading non-strategic operations. Through a 26% interest in the Venezuelan national telephone company, it provides local, national and international long-distance services in that country. Subsidiaries also provide telephone service through about 3.5 million access lines in Canada, Argentina and the Dominican Republic.

The telecommunications products and services segment provides directory advertising; intelligence and electronic defense systems; specialized telecommunications services and systems; aircraft-passenger telecommunications; and cellular telephone service in the U.S., Canada, Venezuela, Argentina and the Dominican Republic.

GTE currently provides cellular service to more than 4.6 million U.S. subscribers (5.2 million internationally). It offers wireless service to 17 states, with major markets including Birmingham, Cincinnati, Cleveland, Houston, Indianapolis, Louisville, Memphis, Nashville, Richmond, San Francisco, San Diego, Seattle, Tampa/St. Petersburg and Honolulu. GTE has also launched digital wireless service in six U.S. markets, using code division multiple access technology, the most advanced digital technology available. It has made significant progress on the Internet front, becoming the first local telephone company to sign more than 100,000 active subscribers.

In June 1997, GTE acquired BBN Corp., the leading U.S. provider of Internet access and value-added services for businesses.

Per Share Data ($)

(Year Ended Dec. 31)	1997	1996	1995	1994	1993	1992	1991	1990	1989	1988
Tangible Bk. Val.	5.02	5.01	4.21	8.63	7.75	8.30	9.75	11.52	12.01	12.46
Cash Flow	6.94	6.78	6.41	6.13	4.65	5.58	5.38	6.40	6.04	5.68
Earnings	2.90	2.89	2.62	2.55	1.03	1.95	1.69	2.26	2.08	1.79
Dividends	1.88	1.88	1.88	1.88	1.83	1.76	1.64	1.52	1.40	1.30
Payout Ratio	65%	65%	72%	74%	178%	94%	98%	68%	68%	72%
Prices - High	52¼	49¼	45⅛	35¼	39⅞	35¾	35	36	35⅝	23
- Low	40½	37¾	30	29½	34⅛	28⅞	27½	23½	21½	16⅞
P/E Ratio - High	18	17	17	14	39	18	21	16	17	13
- Low	14	13	11	12	33	15	16	10	10	9

Income Statement Analysis (Million $)

	1997	1996	1995	1994	1993	1992	1991	1990	1989	1988
Revs.	23,260	21,339	19,957	19,944	19,748	19,984	19,621	18,374	17,424	16,460
Depr.	3,886	3,770	3,675	3,432	3,419	3,289	3,254	2,753	2,621	2,559
Maint.	NA	NA	NA	NA	2,136	2,097	2,206	NA	NA	NA
Constr. Credits	Nil	Nil	Nil	28.0	40.0	43.0	56.0	59.0	NA	NA
Eff. Tax Rate	37%	37%	37%	37%	34%	34%	29%	29%	30%	32%
Net Inc.	2,794	2,798	2,538	2,451	990	1,787	1,529	1,541	1,417	1,225

Balance Sheet & Other Fin. Data (Million $)

	1997	1996	1995	1994	1993	1992	1991	1990	1989	1988
Gross Prop.	56,490	53,481	50,947	44,287	43,099	43,354	41,846	34,890	NA	NA
Net Prop.	24,080	22,902	22,437	26,631	26,362	27,300	26,969	22,327	NA	NA
Cap. Exp.	5,128	4,088	4,034	4,192	3,893	3,909	3,965	3,453	NA	NA
Total Cap.	26,567	24,336	23,048	27,899	27,002	28,994	33,807	26,787	24,986	23,904
Fxd. Chgs. Cov.	4.3	4.7	4.3	4.4	3.4	2.8	2.5	2.7	NA	NA
Capitalization:										
LT Debt	14,494	13,210	12,744	12,163	13,019	14,182	16,049	NA	NA	NA
Pfd.	Nil	Nil	Nil	1,741	1,373	1,363	1,785	1,818	NA	NA
Common	8,038	7,336	6,871	10,473	9,482	9,964	10,854	8,647	NA	NA
% Return On Revs.	12.0	13.1	12.7	12.3	5.0	8.9	7.8	8.4	8.1	7.4
% Return On Invest. Capital	22.0	23.4	14.1	13.9	8.2	10.4	9.6	10.5	NA	NA
% Return On Com. Equity	36.3	39.4	29.2	23.3	10.0	16.9	14.5	18.1	NA	NA
% Earn. on Net Prop.	16.9	17.1	33.7	12.5	7.4	12.0	11.5	12.5	NA	NA
% LT Debt of Cap.	64.3	64.3	65.0	37.4	54.5	55.6	56.0	53.4	NA	NA
Capital. % Pfd.	Nil	Nil	Nil	5.3	5.8	5.3	6.2	8.1	NA	NA
Capital. % Common	35.7	35.7	45.6	32.1	39.7	39.1	37.8	38.5	NA	NA

Data as orig. reptd. ; bef. results of disc. opers. and/or spec. items. Per share data adj. for stk divs. as of ex-div. date. Bold denotes diluted EPS (FASB 128). E-Estimated. NA-Not Available. NM-Not Meaningful. NR-Not Ranked.

Office—One Stamford Forum, Stamford, CT 06904. **Tel**—(203) 965-2000. **Website**—http://www.gte.com **Chrmn & CEO**—C. R. Lee. **Pres**—K. B. Foster. **SVP-Fin & CFO**—J. M. Kelly. **Secy**—M. Drost. **VP & Treas**—D. P. O'Brien. **Dirs**—E. L. Artzt, J. R. Barker, E. H. Budd, R. F. Daniell, K. B. Foster, J. L. Johnson, R. W. Jones, J. L. Ketelson, C. R. Lee, M. T. Masin, S. O. Moose, R. E. Palmer, R. D. Storey. **Transfer Agent & Registrar**—BankBoston, N.A. **Incorporated**—in New York in 1935. **Empl**—102,000. **S&P Analyst:** Philip D. Wohl

STANDARD &POOR'S
STOCK REPORTS

Guidant Corp.

1072M
NYSE Symbol **GDT**
In S&P 500

12-SEP-98

Industry:
Health Care (Medical Products & Supplies)

Summary: This leading maker of devices used in cardiac rhythm management and coronary artery disease intervention also offers minimally invasive surgical products.

S&P Opinion: Buy (★★★★)	Recent Price • 74⅜	Yield • 0.1%
	52 Wk Range • 90-46⅞	12-Mo. P/E • 46.5

Quantitative Evaluations

Outlook
(1 Lowest—5 Highest)
• **2⁻**

Fair Value
• **68¾**

Risk
• **Average**

Earn./Div. Rank
• **NR**

Technical Eval.
• **Bullish** since 11/96

Rel. Strength Rank
(1 Lowest—99 Highest)
• **93**

Insider Activity
• **NA**

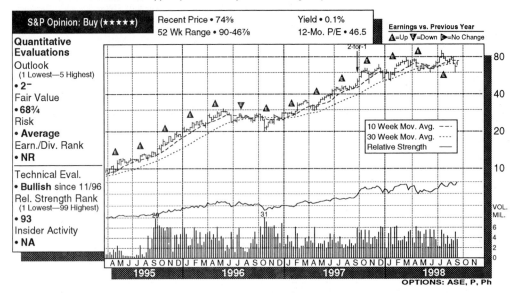

Earnings vs. Previous Year
▲=Up ▼=Down ▶=No Change

10 Week Mov. Avg. ---
30 Week Mov. Avg. ····
Relative Strength —

OPTIONS: ASE, P, Ph

Overview - 30-JUN-98

Sales in 1998 could reach $1.8 billion, up from 1997's $1.0 billion, bolstered by rapid growth in GDT's new Multi-Link coronary stent line (a leading product in the U.S. stent market). Coronary stents are small mesh-like catheters, used to prevent reocclusion of arterial walls following angioplasty. Robust sales advances are also indicated for implantable cardioverter defibrillators (ICDs), led by the new Ventak AV II DR. This device is the world's first ICD able to treat life-threatening cardiac arrhythmias and also provide pacing capability in both the upper and lower chambers of the heart. Healthy gains are also seen for angioplasty and cardiac pacing products. Despite ongoing dilution from the 1997 acquisition of Endovascular Technologies, margins should widen, on the greater volume, an improved product mix, and cost efficiencies.

Valuation - 30-JUN-98

Following a strong uptrend through early March, the shares have moved in a more erratic pattern in recent months, as investors showed concern over new competition in the coronary stent market. Although GDT is still a leader with its Multi-Link stent, its market share has eroded somewhat in recent months, due to the launch of a rival stent from Arterial Vascular Engineering. Another competing stent from Boston Scientific is expected in the near term. Despite the competition, GDT should remain a major player in the rapidly expanding stent market. Much potential is also seen for GDT's implantable cardioverter defibrillator line, as well as from new angioplasty products. The R&D pipeline includes vascular grafts to treat abdominal aortic aneurysms, pacemakers for congestive heart failure, and catheter systems to prevent restenosis. The shares are recommended for aggressive investors.

Key Stock Statistics

S&P EPS Est. 1998	1.95	Tang. Bk. Value/Share	3.19
P/E on S&P Est. 1998	38.1	Beta	NA
S&P EPS Est. 1999	2.50	Shareholders	3,300
Dividend Rate/Share	0.05	Market cap. (B)	$ 11.2
Shs. outstg. (M)	150.8	Inst. holdings	82%
Avg. daily vol. (M)	0.817		

Value of $10,000 invested 5 years ago: NA

Fiscal Year Ending Dec. 31

	1998	1997	1996	1995	1994	1993
Revenues (Million $)						
1Q	470.3	265.5	252.1	224.8	204.1	187.4
2Q	487.8	281.0	265.5	224.1	206.6	193.2
3Q	—	283.3	260.1	234.1	217.4	199.4
4Q	—	495.8	270.8	248.3	234.3	214.7
Yr.	—	1,328	1,049	931.3	862.4	797.4
Earnings Per Share ($)						
1Q	**0.37**	0.30	0.20	0.14	0.12	--
2Q	**0.52**	0.06	-0.32	0.15	0.10	--
3Q	**E0.49**	0.32	0.28	0.20	0.17	--
4Q	**E0.53**	0.41	0.29	0.21	0.15	--
Yr.	**E1.95**	**1.00**	0.45	0.70	0.53	0.19

Next earnings report expected: mid October

Dividend Data (Dividends have been paid since 1995.)

Amount ($)	Date Decl.	Ex-Div. Date	Stock of Record	Payment Date
0.013	Oct. 23	Nov. 28	Dec. 02	Dec. 16 '97
0.013	Feb. 16	Feb. 27	Mar. 03	Mar. 17 '98
0.013	May. 18	May. 29	Jun. 02	Jun. 16 '98
0.013	Jul. 30	Aug. 28	Sep. 01	Sep. 15 '98

A Division of The **McGraw·Hill** *Companies*

Guidant Corporation

Business Summary - 30-JUN-98

Guidant Corp. is a leader in medical devices designed for use in cardiac rhythm management and coronary artery disease intervention. A line of minimally invasive specialty surgical products is also offered. The company was formed in September 1994 via the combination of five medical device companies that had formerly been subsidiaries of Eli Lilly & Co. Foreign operations are important, accounting for 32% of 1997 sales. Much of Guidant's success in recent years stemmed from an ambitious R&D program, which continues to spawn innovative medical devices. R&D expenditures in 1997 equaled 15.7% of sales, considerably higher than the industry average. Sales by major product segments in recent years were divided as follows:

	1997	1996	1995
Cardiac rhythm management	50%	55%	49%
Vascular intervention	45%	40%	48%
Cardiac & vascular surgery	5%	5%	3%

Cardiac rhythm management products consist of implantable devices used to detect and treat abnormal heart rhythms or arrhythmias. Guidant is believed to have over 45% of the market for implantable cardioverter defibrillators (ICDs) used to treat tachyarrhythmia or rapid heart beating. Principal products include the Ventak line of multi-tiered defibrillators that provide antitachycardia pacing, cardioversion, defibrillation and bradycardia pacing to meet individual patient needs; and Endotak endocardial leads that are inserted through a vein into the heart, allowing arrhythmias to be detected and treated by ICDs. The company is also developing electrophysiology catheters used to diagnose and treat cardiac arrhythmias.

Guidant also has about a 10% share of the cardiac pacemaker or bradycardia pacing market. Pacemakers are used to manage slow or irregular heartbeating caused by disorders which disrupt the heart's normal electrical conduction system. The line includes pacers that treat one or both chambers of the heart, as well as sensor-driven rate response devices that adjust pacing frequency to patient activity levels.

The company is a world market leader in vascular intervention products for both PTCA (percutaneous transluminal coronary angioplasty) and DCA (directional coronary atherectomy). Its broad product line includes PCTA perfusion systems, rapid exchange systems, guide wires, DCA systems, and stents. GDT holds nearly half of the U.S. stent market with its state-of-the-art Multi-Link stent.

Cardiac and vascular surgical products include devices used in bypass surgery, products for laparoscopic surgeries, and related items. Laparoscopic procedures are performed through small incisions in the body, and involve much less trauma than conventional surgery.

Per Share Data ($)

(Year Ended Dec. 31)	1997	1996	1995	1994	1993	1992	1991	1990	1989	1988
Tangible Bk. Val.	2.61	1.68	0.61	-0.27	-0.70	NA	NA	NA	NA	NA
Cash Flow	1.44	0.92	1.18	1.09	0.63	NA	NA	NA	NA	NA
Earnings	1.00	0.46	0.70	0.64	0.19	NA	NA	NA	NA	NA
Dividends	0.06	0.05	0.03	Nil	NA	NA	NA	NA	NA	NA
Payout Ratio	5%	11%	4%	Nil	NA	NA	NA	NA	NA	NA
Prices - High	69½	30¾	21⅜	8⅛	NA	NA	NA	NA	NA	NA
- Low	26⅞	19¾	7¾	7¼	NA	NA	NA	NA	NA	NA
P/E Ratio - High	70	67	30	15	NA	NA	NA	NA	NA	NA
- Low	27	43	11	14	NA	NA	NA	NA	NA	NA

Income Statement Analysis (Million $)

	1997	1996	1995	1994	1993	1992	1991	1990	1989	1988
Revs.	1,328	1,049	931	862	795	NA	NA	NA	NA	NA
Oper. Inc.	353	301	266	236	214	NA	NA	NA	NA	NA
Depr.	66.0	66.2	67.8	64.4	61.4	NA	NA	NA	NA	NA
Int. Exp.	19.5	24.2	33.1	18.8	34.7	NA	NA	NA	NA	NA
Pretax Inc.	249	150	170	156	43.9	NA	NA	NA	NA	NA
Eff. Tax Rate	40%	56%	41%	41%	40%	NA	NA	NA	NA	NA
Net Inc.	150	65.8	101	92.1	26.5	NA	NA	NA	NA	NA

Balance Sheet & Other Fin. Data (Million $)

	1997	1996	1995	1994	1993	1992	1991	1990	1989	1988
Cash	17.7	1.5	3.0	113	30.8	NA	NA	NA	NA	NA
Curr. Assets	625	419	389	458	368	NA	NA	NA	NA	NA
Total Assets	1,225	1,004	1,057	1,104	980	NA	NA	NA	NA	NA
Curr. Liab.	541	308	279	341	185	NA	NA	NA	NA	NA
LT Debt	80.0	234	385	473	533	NA	NA	NA	NA	NA
Common Eqty.	582	448	384	264	209	NA	NA	NA	NA	NA
Total Cap.	662	682	769	737	742	NA	NA	NA	NA	NA
Cap. Exp.	76.8	62.1	64.7	51.1	NA	NA	NA	NA	NA	NA
Cash Flow	216	132	169	157	87.9	NA	NA	NA	NA	NA
Curr. Ratio	1.2	1.4	1.4	1.3	2.0	NA	NA	NA	NA	NA
% LT Debt of Cap.	13.7	34.3	50.1	64.1	71.9	NA	NA	NA	NA	NA
% Net Inc.of Revs.	11.3	6.3	10.9	10.7	3.3	NA	NA	NA	NA	NA
% Ret. on Assets	13.5	6.4	9.4	NM	NA	NA	NA	NA	NA	NA
% Ret. on Equity	29.1	15.8	31.2	NM	NA	NA	NA	NA	NA	NA

Data as orig. reptd.; bef. results of disc. opers. and/or spec. items. Per share data adj. for stk. divs. as of ex-div. date. Bold denotes diluted EPS (FASB 128). E-Estimated. NA-Not Available. NM-Not Meaningful. NR-Not Ranked.

Office—111 Monument Circle, 29th Floor, Indianapolis, IN 46204. **Tel**—(317) 971-2000. **Website**—http//www.guidant.com **Chrmn**—J. M. Cornelius. **Pres & CEO**—R. W. Dollens. **VP-Fin & CFO**—K. E. Brauer. **Investor Contact**—Todd McKinney. **VP & Secy**—J. B. King. **Dirs**—J. M. Cornelius, M. A. Cox, R. W. Dollens, E. C. Falla, J. B. King, S. B. King, J. K. Moore, M. Novitch, E. L. Step, R. E. Wager. **Transfer Agent & Registrar**—First Chicago Trust Co. of New York, Jersey City, NJ. **Incorporated**—in Indiana in 1994. **Empl**— 5,100. **S&P Analyst:** Herman Saftlas

Halliburton Co.

1088

NYSE Symbol **HAL**

In S&P 500

12-SEP-98

Industry:
Oil & Gas (Drilling & Equipment)

Summary: Halliburton provides products used in oil and natural gas development and production; through its Brown & Root subsidiary, it offers engineering and construction services.

S&P Opinion: Hold (★★★)

Recent Price • 32¾	Yield • 1.5%
52 Wk Range • 63¼-25½	12-Mo. P/E • 16.6

Quantitative Evaluations

Outlook
(1 Lowest—5 Highest)
• **4⁻**

Fair Value
• **36**

Risk
• **Average**

Earn./Div. Rank
• **B**

Technical Eval.
• **Bearish** since 6/98

Rel. Strength Rank
(1 Lowest—99 Highest)
• **70**

Insider Activity
• **NA**

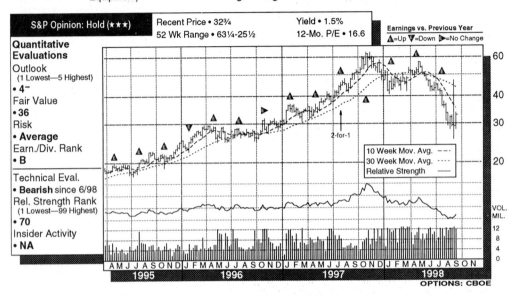

Earnings vs. Previous Year
△=Up ▽=Down ▷=No Change

10 Week Mov. Avg. ----
30 Week Mov. Avg. ·····
Relative Strength ——

2-for-1

VOL. MIL.

OPTIONS: CBOE

Overview - 28-JUL-98

HAL's recently announced merger with Dresser Industries will create an oil services powerhouse capable of offering an unparalleled range of products and services to all sectors of the petroleum business. HAL, which returned to profitability in 1994, saw a 47% increase in 1997 share earnings, reflecting strong demand for the company's products, the result of increased capital spending, higher levels of outsourcing, and market share gains. Halliburton has succeeded in cutting costs, resulting in higher after tax margins and increased profitability. With nearly 80% of its revenues tied to the energy industry, we believe that the company will see benefits from long term growth in worldwide demand. A joint venture in China to produce flow measurement equipment, as well as a major North Sea subsea construction project, will also aid future results

Valuation - 28-JUL-98

After advancing 72% in 1997, the shares have declined 31% in 1998, as slumping oil prices have triggered a slump in oil service company stocks. In response to these lower prices, oil companies have begun to curtail their exploration spending, dampening the outlook for the oil services industry. Commodity price weakness aside, the company has put together an impressive string of contract wins. The recent acquisition of NUMAR Corp., coupled with the 1996 acquisition of Landmark Graphics, gives HAL major exposure to the rapidly growing seismic and logging markets. And the merger with Dresser, expected to close by year-end, will make HAL the most powerful name in the oil services industry. However, with oil prices expected to remain weak, we are now neutral on the shares, which were recently trading at 18X projected 1998 EPS.

Key Stock Statistics

S&P EPS Est. 1998	1.95	Tang. Bk. Value/Share	9.44
P/E on S&P Est. 1998	16.8	Beta	1.01
S&P EPS Est. 1999	2.70	Shareholders	16,200
Dividend Rate/Share	0.50	Market cap. (B)	$ 8.6
Shs. outstg. (M)	263.2	Inst. holdings	74%
Avg. daily vol. (M)	2.972		

Value of $10,000 invested 5 years ago: $ 25,674

Fiscal Year Ending Dec. 31

	1998	1997	1996	1995	1994	1993
Revenues (Million $)						
1Q	2,355	1,898	1,705	1,274	1,376	1,559
2Q	2,476	2,231	1,831	1,398	1,425	1,597
3Q	—	2,305	1,860	1,490	1,405	1,541
4Q	—	2,385	1,990	1,537	1,533	1,653
Yr.	—	8,819	7,385	5,699	5,741	6,351
Earnings Per Share ($)						
1Q	**0.44**	0.32	0.18	0.17	0.08	0.09
2Q	**0.51**	0.40	0.28	0.24	-0.09	0.10
3Q	—	0.47	0.30	0.30	0.23	-0.70
4Q	—	0.56	0.42	0.32	0.56	-0.18
Yr.	**E1.95**	1.75	1.19	1.02	0.78	-0.71

Next earnings report expected: late October

Dividend Data (Dividends have been paid since 1947.)

Amount ($)	Date Decl.	Ex-Div. Date	Stock of Record	Payment Date
0.125	Oct. 30	Nov. 28	Dec. 02	Dec. 23 '97
0.125	Feb. 19	Mar. 02	Mar. 04	Mar. 25 '98
0.125	May. 19	Jun. 01	Jun. 03	Jun. 24 '98
0.125	Jul. 16	Sep. 01	Sep. 03	Sep. 24 '98

A Division of The McGraw-Hill Companies

Business Summary - 28-JUL-98

Halliburton (HAL), already a major factor in the oilfield services business and a major participant in the engineering and construction industry, now plans to merge with Dresser Industries (DI) to form the undisputed oil services leader. In February 1998, the companies announced plans to merge, with each Dresser shareholder receiving one newly issued share of Halliburton common stock. The merger will create an oil services and engineering and construction powerhouse with some $16 billion in annual revenues. The combined company will operate under the Halliburton name.

Halliburton's business units are grouped in two main divisions, the Energy Group and the Construction and Engineering Group. Revenue contributions in recent years were:

	1997	1996
Energy Group	65%	58%
Engineering & Construction Group	35%	42%

The Energy Group consists of Halliburton Energy Services, which provides a wide range of products and services for oil and gas exploration, development and production; Brown & Root Energy Services, which supplies engineering and construction services to the oil and gas industry; Landmark Graphics, which supplies informa-

tion systems and software that help companies find and produce oil and gas. Landmark Graphics was acquired in October 1996 in a stock transaction valued at about $557 million. Halliburton Energy Development is a newly formed division of the Energy Group that will integrate the products, services and technologies of the other three Energy Group units to provide solutions in the development and management of oil and gas fields.

In recent years, oil and gas producers have been outsourcing an increasing number of oilfield services to oil services providers, such as Halliburton. Recently, the trend has been toward "one stop shop" providers, companies that are capable of offering an entire range of products and services for oil and gas producers, aiding them in exploring for oil and gas, developing oil and gas fields and producing from those fields. With its unparalleled range of oilfield product and service offerings, the new Halliburton will be well positioned to benefit from this trend.

The Engineering and Construction Group consists of two units, Brown & Root Engineering and Construction and Brown & Root Government Services. Brown & Root Engineering and Construction offers a wide variety of services to several markets, including refining, chemicals and manufacturing industries. Brown & Root Government Services provides construction, engineering and maintenance services to federal, state and local governments.

Per Share Data ($)

(Year Ended Dec. 31)	1997	1996	1995	1994	1993	1992	1991	1990	1989	1988
Tangible Bk. Val.	8.63	7.70	6.76	7.58	7.29	8.30	9.49	9.94	9.36	9.46
Cash Flow	2.94	2.25	2.08	1.93	0.56	0.78	1.26	1.88	1.61	1.41
Earnings	1.75	1.19	1.02	0.78	-0.71	-0.57	0.13	0.93	0.63	0.41
Dividends	0.50	0.50	0.50	0.50	0.50	0.50	0.50	0.50	0.50	0.50
Payout Ratio	29%	42%	49%	64%	NM	NM	402%	54%	80%	126%
Prices - High	63¼	31⅞	25½	18⅝	22	18½	27⅝	29⅜	22¼	18¼
- Low	29¾	22⅜	16½	14	12⅞	10⅞	12¾	19⅜	13¾	12¼
P/E Ratio - High	36	27	25	24	NM	NM	NM	32	35	45
- Low	17	19	16	18	NM	NM	NM	21	22	30

Income Statement Analysis (Million $)

	1997	1996	1995	1994	1993	1992	1991	1990	1989	1988
Revs.	8,819	7,385	5,699	5,648	6,275	6,525	6,976	6,905	5,659	4,826
Oper. Inc.	1,117	772	627	446	448	412	296	518	446	353
Depr.	310	269	244	262	288	289	244	202	209	213
Int. Exp.	43.0	24.0	46.0	47.0	50.0	54.0	53.0	34.0	37.0	59.0
Pretax Inc.	766	404	367	291	-188	-130	93.0	354	246	152
Eff. Tax Rate	39%	26%	36%	39%	NM	NM	69%	43%	46%	45%
Net Inc.	454	300	234	178	-160	-123	27.0	197	134	85.0

Balance Sheet & Other Fin. Data (Million $)

	1997	1996	1995	1994	1993	1992	1991	1990	1989	1988
Cash	221	214	175	507	133	256	331	168	402	345
Curr. Assets	2,972	2,398	2,050	NA	NA	NA	NA	NA	NA	NA
Total Assets	5,603	4,437	3,647	5,268	5,403	4,736	5,017	4,544	4,263	4,722
Curr. Liab.	1,773	1,505	1,156	950	1,067	1,017	999	897	715	592
LT Debt	NA	200	200	623	598	603	651	190	198	199
Common Eqty.	2,585	2,159	1,750	1,942	1,888	1,907	2,165	2,247	2,119	2,107
Total Cap.	NA	2,359	1,950	2,570	2,489	2,522	2,875	2,544	2,421	2,479
Cap. Exp.	NA	396	289	235	247	316	426	332	202	169
Cash Flow	764	568	478	439	127	166	270	400	342	297
Curr. Ratio	1.7	1.6	1.8	NA	NA	NA	NA	NA	NA	NA
% LT Debt of Cap.	NA	8.5	10.3	24.2	24.0	23.9	22.6	7.4	8.2	8.0
% Net Inc.of Revs.	5.1	4.1	4.1	3.1	NM	NM	0.4	2.9	2.4	1.8
% Ret. on Assets	9.0	7.3	6.1	3.3	NM	NM	0.6	4.5	3.0	1.9
% Ret. on Equity	19.1	14.7	12.7	9.3	NM	NM	1.2	9.0	6.3	4.0

Data as orig. reptd.; bef. results of disc. opers. and/or spec. items. Per share data adj. for stk. divs. as of ex-div. date. Bold denotes diluted EPS (FASB 128). E-Estimated. NA-Not Available. NM-Not Meaningful. NR-Not Ranked.

Office—3600 Lincoln Plaza, 500 N. Akard St., Dallas, TX 75201-3391. Tel—(214) 978-2600. Website—http://www.halliburton.comChrmn, CEO & Pres—R. B. Cheney. Vice Chrmn—D. P. Jones. Pres & COO—D. J. Lesar. EVP & CFO—G. V. Morris. VP & Investor Contact—Guy T. Marcus. Dirs—A. L. Armstrong, R. B. Cheney, Lord Clitheroe, R. L. Crandall, C. J. DiBona, W. R. Howell, D. P. Jones, D. E. Lewis, C. J. Silas, R. T. Staubach, R. J. Stegemeier. Transfer Agent & Registrar—ChaseMellon Shareholder Services, Ridgefield, NJ. Incorporated—in Delaware in 1924. Empl— 70,750. S&P Analyst: Norman Rosenberg

STANDARD &POOR'S
STOCK REPORTS

Harcourt General

1096G

NYSE Symbol **H**

In S&P 500

12-SEP-98

Industry:
Retail (Department Stores)

Summary: This major publisher and owner of 53% of The Neiman Marcus Group, acquired National Education Corp. (NEC) in June 1997.

| S&P Opinion: Accumulate (★★★★) | Recent Price • 48 | Yield • 1.6% |
| | 52 Wk Range • 61⅞-46 | 12-Mo. P/E • 39.7 |

Earnings vs. Previous Year
▲=Up ▼=Down ▷=No Change

Quantitative Evaluations

Outlook
(1 Lowest—5 Highest)
• **1**

Fair Value
• **44½**

Risk
• **Average**

Earn./Div. Rank
• **B**

Technical Eval.
• **Bullish** since 9/97

Rel. Strength Rank
(1 Lowest—99 Highest)
• **59**

Insider Activity
• **NA**

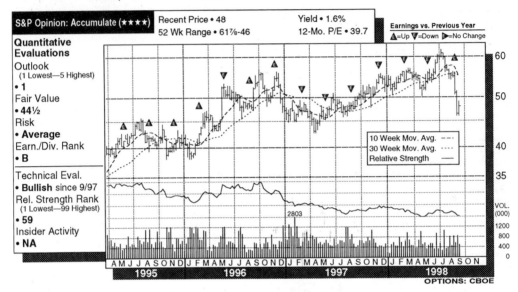

10 Week Mov. Avg. ---
30 Week Mov. Avg. ·····
Relative Strength —

2803

VOL. (000)

OPTIONS: CBOE

Overview - 21-MAY-98

We expect EPS of $2.05 in FY 98 (Oct.), up from FY 97's $1.78 before nonrecurring charges totaling about $242.1 million, or $3.42 a share (net), related to the June 1997 acquisition of National Education Corp. (NEC). In FY 98, we expect continued healthy revenue and profits from publishing. Although state adoptions will be lower than in FY 97, el-hi textbook sales should be healthy nonetheless. Strong college and professional sales will be augmented by the purchase (pending) of Mosby Inc. We expect operating profit to rise 8% to 10% at 53%-owned Neiman Marcus. The acquisition of NEC will dilute FY 98 EPS by 10% to 15%, reflecting amortization charges. However, H expects the acquisition to be accretive in following years, as the contribution to operating cash flow will likely offset the amortization charges, the loss of interest income, and the cost of debt used to finance the purchase.

Valuation - 21-MAY-98

Based on H's favorable long-term record of building asset value, the shares are attractive for capital appreciation. The June 1997 purchase of National Education (NEC) and the planned purchase of Mosby Inc. are viewed favorably for the long term in spite of initial dilution. NEC and Mosby provide additional operating diversity through their markets, and NEC accelerates H's entry into high-growth distance learning, supplemental publishing, and computer-based training markets. H's management has an excellent record of boosting shareholder value through acquisitions. For the long term, we expect H to find growth opportunities for its publishing assets in the evolving multi-media world. We also expect The Neiman Marcus Group (NMG; 53% owned) to continue to build on its franchise in the high-end retailing business.

Key Stock Statistics

S&P EPS Est. 1998	2.05	Tang. Bk. Value/Share	NM
P/E on S&P Est. 1998	23.4	Beta	0.74
Dividend Rate/Share	0.76	Shareholders	8,400
Shs. outstg. (M)	70.9	Market cap. (B)	$ 2.4
Avg. daily vol. (M)	0.139	Inst. holdings	64%

Value of $10,000 invested 5 years ago: $ 14,361

Fiscal Year Ending Oct. 31

	1998	1997	1996	1995	1994	1993
Revenues (Million $)						
1Q	900.6	768.7	698.4	663.3	703.8	810.0
2Q	1,037	880.0	844.3	774.5	832.7	930.0
3Q	1,162	1,052	879.2	813.3	815.1	1,010
4Q	—	991.3	867.9	783.7	802.7	907.2
Yr.	—	3,692	3,290	3,035	3,154	3,656
Earnings Per Share ($)						
1Q	**-0.21**	0.20	0.23	0.17	0.07	0.34
2Q	**-0.25**	0.04	0.14	0.16	0.04	0.07
3Q	**1.54**	-2.00	1.45	1.29	0.57	1.28
4Q	—	0.11	0.81	0.74	0.54	0.39
Yr.	**E2.05**	-1.64	2.62	2.31	1.22	2.08

Next earnings report expected: early December

Dividend Data (Dividends have been paid since 1953.)

Amount ($)	Date Decl.	Ex-Div. Date	Stock of Record	Payment Date
0.190	Sep. 05	Oct. 09	Oct. 14	Oct. 31 '97
0.190	Dec. 16	Jan. 13	Jan. 15	Jan. 31 '98
0.190	Mar. 13	Apr. 07	Apr. 10	Apr. 30 '98
0.190	Jun. 19	Jul. 10	Jul. 14	Jul. 31 '98

A Division of The McGraw·Hill Companies

STANDARD
&POOR'S
STOCK REPORTS

Harcourt General, Inc.

1096G
12-SEP-98

Business Summary - 21-MAY-98

This diversified company (formerly General Cinema Corp.) includes publishing, retailing and professional services. Like a chameleon, H has drastically changed its identity over the past decade. The company sold its insurance businesses in 1994, and its theater business was spun off to shareholders in 1993. Former operations also included soft drink bottling. Most recently, H agreed (in May 1998) to acquire Mosby, Inc., a professional health sciences publisher, from Times Mirror Inc. for $415 million. Mosby, with annual revenues of $225 million, publishes in 31 languages and sells in 41 countries. In June 1997, H acquired National Education Corp. (NEC) for $854 million. NEC adds new distribution channels to H's existing lineup of educational businesses, and it accelerates H's entry into several non-traditional educational growth markets. NEC's operations include ICS Learning Systems, a leading worldwide provider of distance education in vocational, academic and professional studies; National Education Training Group, a global leader in Information Technology interactive media-based learning products; and Steck-Vaughn Publishing (STEK), a major U.S. publisher of supplemental education materials.

H's publishing business (including NEC) had FY 97

(Oct.) revenues of $1.4 billion and a net operating loss of $139 million. The business largely comes from the 1991 acquisition of Harcourt Brace & Co. Major educational imprints include Harcourt Brace; Holt, Rinehard and Winston; and Steck-Vaughn. The learning and assessment group includes the operations of NETg, ICS, The Psychological Corporation, Harcourt Professional Education Group, and Archipelago Productions. The worldwide scientific, technical and medical group includes W.B. Saunders, Academic Press, Churchill Livingstone, and Harcourt Brace Publishers International.

H has a 53% equity interest (51% voting power) in The Neiman-Marcus Group (NMG), which includes the 30-store Neiman-Marcus retail chain, the NM Direct mail order business, and two Bergdorf Goodman stores in New York City. In FY 97, NMG's revenues were $2.2 billion, and operating profit was $195 million. Operating results of NMG are consolidated with those of Harcourt with a three-month lag. NMG common stock is traded on the NYSE under the ticker symbol "NMG".

The professional services segment had FY 97 revenue of $105 million and an operating loss of $25 million. It includes Drake Beam Morin, which provides career transition, employee outplacement and consulting services.

Per Share Data ($)

(Year Ended Oct. 31)	1997	1996	1995	1994	1993	1992	1991	1990	1989	1988
Tangible Bk. Val.	NM	8.03	6.77	7.93	8.30	6.49	0.34	20.36	19.52	6.65
Cash Flow	3.22	5.10	4.51	3.27	4.20	3.64	0.12	2.33	2.20	2.26
Earnings	-1.64	2.62	2.31	1.22	2.08	1.44	-3.88	1.51	1.43	1.12
Dividends	0.73	0.69	0.65	0.61	0.57	0.53	0.49	0.45	0.41	0.37
Payout Ratio	NM	26%	28%	50%	27%	37%	NM	29%	27%	31%
Prices - High	55⅝	57	45¾	39½	46⅛	36⅝	24¾	27	28½	25¾
- Low	42⅝	38	32⅜	30¼	31¼	18	16½	16½	23⅛	15¾
P/E Ratio - High	NM	22	20	32	22	25	NM	18	20	23
- Low	NM	15	14	25	15	13	NM	11	16	14

Income Statement Analysis (Million $)

	1997	1996	1995	1994	1993	1992	1991	1990	1989	1988
Revs.	3,692	3,290	3,035	3,209	3,692	3,715	3,616	2,177	1,937	2,346
Oper. Inc.	512	525	494	436	484	415	248	123	121	229
Depr.	343	180	176	163	169	174	315	63.0	59.0	85.0
Int. Exp.	94.3	82.9	88.7	86.0	85.0	86.0	349	104	89.0	93.0
Pretax Inc.	-71.0	289	269	152	262	187	-359	176	180	133
Eff. Tax Rate	NM	34%	34%	36%	37%	39%	NM	35%	39%	35%
Net Inc.	-114	191	178	98.0	165	114	-292	111	106	83.0

Balance Sheet & Other Fin. Data (Million $)

	1997	1996	1995	1994	1993	1992	1991	1990	1989	1988
Cash	82.6	775	607	820	619	566	1,859	1,634	1,688	23.0
Curr. Assets	1,485	1,933	1,610	2,021	NA	NA	NA	2,197	2,208	571
Total Assets	3,781	3,326	2,884	3,242	5,977	5,287	6,208	3,068	3,404	1,898
Curr. Liab.	993	948	785	875	NA	NA	NA	581	1,082	344
LT Debt	1,290	714	749	1,123	924	902	870	747	680	820
Common Eqty.	844	1,032	940	1,040	1,042	910	453	1,609	1,528	581
Total Cap.	2,644	2,190	1,889	2,367	2,175	2,032	1,481	2,431	2,264	1,477
Cap. Exp.	195	243	220	196	179	202	172	106	138	123
Cash Flow	228	371	353	261	335	288	9.0	172	163	166
Curr. Ratio	1.5	2.0	2.1	2.3	NA	NA	NA	3.8	2.0	1.7
% LT Debt of Cap.	48.8	32.6	39.7	47.5	42.5	44.4	58.7	30.7	30.0	55.5
% Net Inc.of Revs.	NM	5.8	5.9	3.0	4.5	3.0	NM	5.1	5.5	3.5
% Ret. on Assets	NM	6.2	5.8	2.1	2.9	2.0	NM	3.4	4.0	4.7
% Ret. on Equity	NM	19.3	17.9	9.3	16.9	16.7	NM	7.0	9.8	14.7

Data as orig. reptd.; bef. results of disc. opers. and/or spec. items. Per share data adj. for stk. divs. as of ex-div. date. Bold denotes diluted EPS (FASB 128). E-Estimated. NA-Not Available. NM-Not Meaningful. NR-Not Ranked.

Office—27 Boylston St., Chestnut Hill, MA 02167. **Tel**—(617) 232-8200. **Chrmn & CEO**—Richard A. Smith. **SVP & CFO**—J. R. Cook. **SVP & Secy**—E. P. Geller. **VP & Investor Contact**—Peter Farwell. **Dirs**—W. F. Connell, G. L. Countryman, J. M. Greenberg, B. J. Knez, J. R. Lurie, L. M. Martin, M. Segall, Richard A. Smith, Robert A. Smith, P. Stern, H. Uyterhoeven, C. R. Wharton, Jr. **Transfer Agent & Registrar**—BankBoston, N. A. **Incorporated**—in Delaware in 1950. **Empl**— 20,200. **S&P Analyst:** William H. Donald

12-SEP-98

Industry:
Machinery (Diversified)

Summary: This leading maker of large mining excavators, buckets and drilling equipment is exploring the option of selling its papermaking machinery business.

S&P Opinion: Hold (★★★)	Recent Price • 15	Yield • 2.7%
	52 Wk Range • 44¾-14⅛	12-Mo. P/E • 11.4

Quantitative Evaluations

Outlook
(1 Lowest—5 Highest)
• **3+**

Fair Value
• **17½**

Risk
• **Average**

Earn./Div. Rank
• **B+**

Technical Eval.
• **Bullish** since 11/97

Rel. Strength Rank
(1 Lowest—99 Highest)
• **10**

Insider Activity
• **NA**

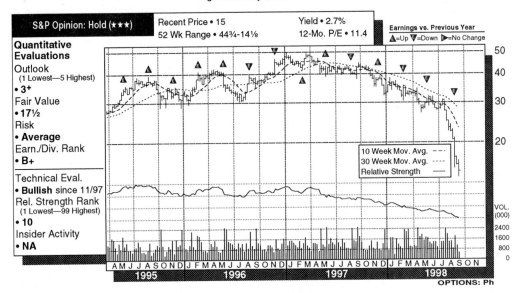

Earnings vs. Previous Year
▲=Up ▼=Down ▷=No Change

10 Week Mov. Avg. — – –
30 Week Mov. Avg. – – – –
Relative Strength —

VOL. (000)

OPTIONS: Ph

Overview - 28-AUG-98

Harnischfeger primarily sells its papermaking machinery (52% of revenues) to pulp and paper mills. HPH sells much of its mining equipment (36% of revenues) to the coal-mining industry. We believe the company's papermaking machinery and mining equipment businesses operate in very challenging market environments. Demand for HPH products tend to move in long cycles, with lead times of up to two years. Moreover, demand for HPH's products is highly sensitive to volatile coal, metals and paper commodity prices. Weakening commodity prices typically spur order deferrals and cancellations, which in turn, can translate into dramatic revenue and profit declines. Currently, HPH is incurring the wrath of collapsing Asian economies. Ongoing weak Asian demand for coal and paper is causing declines coal and paper commodity prices, which in turn, is forcing mining and paper mills to defer capital equipment purchases.

Valuation - 28-AUG-98

We continue our "hold" rating on Harnischfeger, due to our cautious outlook for HPH's near- and long-term prospects. We expect HPH to post weak FY 98 Asia-related per-share earnings, despite recent company efforts to cut operating expenses dramatically (including workforce reductions of 20%). Revenue and earnings growth should rebound in FY 99, because it's believed many of HPH's customers are operating equipment at or beyond its useful lives. Our intrinsic value calculations indicate HPH shares are trading slightly below HPH's fair value; however, because of the currently unstable global economic climate and unfavorable long-term industry economics of HPH's primary businesses, we remain cautious about the stock.

Key Stock Statistics

S&P EPS Est. 1998	0.60	Tang. Bk. Value/Share	6.31
P/E on S&P Est. 1998	25.0	Beta	0.88
S&P EPS Est. 1999	1.70	Shareholders	2,000
Dividend Rate/Share	0.40	Market cap. (B)	$0.717
Shs. outstg. (M)	47.8	Inst. holdings	90%
Avg. daily vol. (M)	0.217		

Value of $10,000 invested 5 years ago: $ 8,254

Fiscal Year Ending Oct. 31

	1998	1997	1996	1995	1994	1993
Revenues (Million $)						
1Q	634.3	699.4	632.7	449.4	248.0	282.0
2Q	709.7	794.6	739.5	541.0	260.5	321.1
3Q	503.6	786.0	779.8	547.7	285.3	310.1
4Q	—	808.5	712.0	614.0	345.8	321.5
Yr.	—	3,089	2,864	2,152	1,140	1,235
Earnings Per Share ($)						
1Q	**0.46**	0.65	0.50	0.06	0.08	0.02
2Q	**-1.57**	0.94	0.71	0.46	0.11	0.13
3Q	**-0.83**	0.75	0.80	0.81	0.17	-1.78
4Q	—	0.86	0.41	0.65	0.37	0.91
Yr.	—	3.20	2.42	1.99	0.74	-0.67

Next earnings report expected: mid November

Dividend Data (Dividends have been paid since 1988.)

Amount ($)	Date Decl.	Ex-Div. Date	Stock of Record	Payment Date
0.100	Dec. 10	Dec. 23	Dec. 26	Jan. 06 '98
0.100	Feb. 09	Mar. 23	Mar. 25	Apr. 07 '98
0.100	Jun. 09	Jun. 23	Jun. 25	Jul. 07 '98
0.100	Aug. 25	Sep. 23	Sep. 25	Oct. 06 '98

A Division of The McGraw-Hill Companies

Business Summary - 28-AUG-98

The only U.S. producer of papermaking machinery, Harnischfeger is also a leader in mining machinery and equipment, and in material handling equipment, a business which the company may sell. Segment contributions in FY 97 (Oct.) were:

	Sales	Profits
Papermaking machinery	52%	59%
Mining equipment	36%	28%
Material handling equip.	12%	13%

Foreign operations accounted for 41% of sales and 40% of operating profits in FY 97.

Beloit Corp. (80% owned) manufactures papermaking machinery systems and related products for the pulp and paper industries. Beloit operates on a global basis, with manufacturing facilities in the U.S. and nine other countries. Activities are divided into three categories: manufacture and installation of equipment, rebuilds and servicing and sale of ancillary equipment and replacement parts. Beloit has the industry's largest installed equipment base, consisting of about 1,200 machines. In FY 96, Beloit recorded a $43 million charge for a plan to create an organization that would increase customer satisfaction while reducing costs and cycle times. Customers will benefit from optimized productivity and up-

time at pulp and paper mills. Further charges are expected in FY 98 due to a downturn in demand.

Mining equipment consists of P&H Mining, Joy Mining and Longwall International and Dobson Park Industries plc. P&H makes electric mining shovels, electric and diesel electric draglines, buckets, hydraulic mining excavators, large rotary blasthole drilling equipment and related replacement parts for the surface mining and quarrying industries. P&H makes some of the largest mobile units in existence such as draglines with buckets the size of a four-car garage. With the addition of Longwall International, Joy offers integrated underground longwall mining systems as well as continuous mining systems. Systems include shearers, roof supports and armored face conveyors, continuous miners, shuttle cars, articulated battery and chain haulage and flexible conveyor trains. There are more than 120 Joy longwall installations worldwide, used to mine coal and other minerals. These units deliver up to 6,000 tons of coal per hour with eight workers. Joy also makes a highwall mining system for coal extraction from exposed surface seams in the walls of surface coal mines.

In January 1998, HPH sold 80% of P & H Material Handling, for $340 million. P&H makes industrial cranes including overhead, portal, dockside and container cranes, and electric wire, rope and chain hoists for a variety of uses. Industrial cranes are used in steel mills, factories, shipyards, loading docks and woodyards.

Per Share Data ($)

(Year Ended Oct. 31)	1997	1996	1995	1994	1993	1992	1991	1990	1989	1988
Tangible Bk. Val.	4.59	2.42	7.09	12.03	12.69	16.55	16.21	14.99	12.51	10.61
Cash Flow	5.17	4.30	3.61	2.41	0.89	3.20	3.16	3.12	2.37	1.91
Earnings	3.20	2.42	1.99	0.74	-0.67	1.95	2.08	2.18	1.66	1.15
Dividends	0.40	0.40	0.40	0.40	0.40	0.40	0.40	0.20	0.20	0.15
Payout Ratio	12%	17%	20%	54%	NM	21%	19%	9%	12%	15%
Prices - High	49¼	50	39⅜	28⅜	25½	22⅞	22	25	22⅜	24
- Low	32⅛	29⅜	26	18½	17⅛	16⅛	16	12⅜	15	14⅜
P/E Ratio - High	15	21	20	38	NM	12	11	11	13	21
- Low	10	12	13	25	NM	8	8	6	9	13

Income Statement Analysis (Million $)

	1997	1996	1995	1994	1993	1992	1991	1990	1989	1988
Revs.	3,089	2,864	2,152	1,139	1,243	1,391	1,601	1,776	1,483	1,209
Oper. Inc.	384	352	220	89.0	86.0	148	152	153	130	91.0
Depr.	94.4	89.2	70.5	43.6	41.3	36.6	33.6	30.4	23.2	21.5
Int. Exp.	76.0	68.8	51.7	26.4	27.7	19.5	15.9	18.4	15.8	26.8
Pretax Inc.	247	182	146	27.0	-27.0	102	125	132	109	60.0
Eff. Tax Rate	34%	35%	37%	20%	NM	35%	36%	34%	35%	28%
Net Inc.	153	114	92.1	19.1	-17.7	56.7	64.6	70.0	53.8	32.5

Balance Sheet & Other Fin. Data (Million $)

	1997	1996	1995	1994	1993	1992	1991	1990	1989	1988
Cash	29.4	36.9	239	153	126	171	220	240	216	147
Curr. Assets	1,589	1,410	1,213	719	656	880	943	1,010	895	730
Total Assets	2,925	2,690	2,041	1,439	1,334	1,508	1,507	1,576	1,370	1,195
Curr. Liab.	1,662	1,077	723	468	424	463	567	644	534	458
LT Debt	713	658	459	243	243	245	112	115	121	84.0
Common Eqty.	764	673	559	486	503	591	594	583	514	461
Total Cap.	1,658	1,480	1,053	827	866	979	847	827	747	627
Cap. Exp.	100	66.6	61.8	35.1	63.0	53.1	46.7	60.7	51.6	35.4
Cash Flow	247	203	163	63.0	24.0	93.0	98.0	100	77.0	54.0
Curr. Ratio	1.0	1.3	1.7	1.5	1.5	1.9	1.7	1.6	1.7	1.6
% LT Debt of Cap.	43.0	44.4	43.6	29.4	28.1	25.0	13.2	13.9	16.2	13.4
% Net Inc.of Revs.	4.9	4.0	4.3	1.7	NM	4.1	4.0	3.9	3.6	2.7
% Ret. on Assets	5.4	4.3	4.6	1.3	NM	3.9	4.3	4.8	4.2	2.6
% Ret. on Equity	21.3	18.5	17.3	3.7	NM	9.9	11.3	12.9	11.1	7.5

Data as orig. reptd.; bef. results of disc. opers. and/or spec. items. Per share data adj. for stk. divs. as of ex-div. date. Bold denotes diluted EPS (FASB 128). E-Estimated. NA-Not Available. NM-Not Meaningful. NR-Not Ranked.

Office—3600 South Lake Drive, St. Francis, WI 53235. **Tel**—(414) 486-6400. **Website**—http://www.hii.com **Chrmn, & CEO**—J. T. Grade. **EVP & COO**—J. N. Hanson. **EVP-Fin & CFO**—F. M. Corby Jr. **EVP & Secy**—K. T. Lundgren. **Investor Contact**—Susan DeBorg (414-486-6626).**Dirs**—D. M. Alvarado, L. Brady, F. M. Corby, Jr., J. D. Correnti, H. L. Davis, R. M. Gerrity, J. T. Grade, J. N. Hanson, R. B. Hoffman, R. C. Joynes, J. Labruyere, L. D. LaTorre, L. E. Redon, D. Taylor. **Transfer Agent & Registrar**— Bank of Boston. **Incorporated**—in Wisconsin in 1910; reincorporated in Delaware in 1971. **Empl**— 15,500. **S&P Analyst:** Robert E. Friedman, CPA

STANDARD &POOR'S
STOCK REPORTS

Harrah's Entertainment

1099H

NYSE Symbol **HET**

In S&P 500

12-SEP-98

Industry: Gaming, Lottery & Pari-mutuel Cos.

Summary: This company, which operates about 19 gaming properties, acquired casino company Showboat, Inc., in mid-1998.

S&P Opinion: Accumulate (★★★★)	Recent Price • 15	Yield • Nil
	52 Wk Range • 26⅜-14⅛	12-Mo. P/E • 12.0

Quantitative Evaluations

Outlook
(1 Lowest—5 Highest)
• **5**

Fair Value
• **33½**

Risk
• **Average**

Earn./Div. Rank
• **B**

Technical Eval.
• **Bearish** since 6/98

Rel. Strength Rank
(1 Lowest—99 Highest)
• **28**

Insider Activity
• **NA**

Earnings vs. Previous Year
▲=Up ▼=Down ▷=No Change

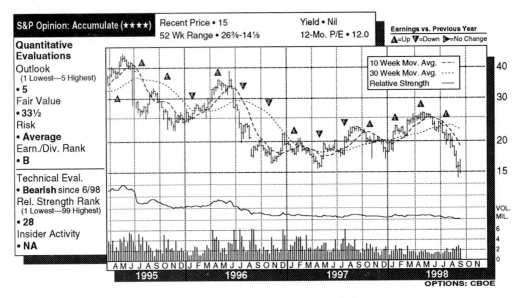

10 Week Mov. Avg. ----
30 Week Mov. Avg. ·····
Relative Strength ——

OPTIONS: CBOE

Overview - 06-JUL-98

On about June 1, 1998, this large gaming company acquired the casino company Showboat, Inc., for about $519 million, and also assumed approximately $635 million of Showboat debt. HET now operates approximately 19 gaming properties, including six in Nevada and two in Atlantic City, and a pair of riverboats in the Chicago area. In 1997, HET's "normalized" earnings totaled $1.07 a share, including an adverse impact from construction disruptions in Las Vegas. Excluded from the $1.07 are various items, including a gain on HET equity interest in a New Zealand casino, some charges or costs related to a New Orleans casino project, and openings costs related to various new facilities. In 1998, we look for HET's profit comparisons to get some help from a renovation/expansion of the Harrah's casino/hotel in Las Vegas; a new gambler rewards program; and the presence of two new HET managed casinos, on Indian land in North Carolina and Kansas.

Valuation - 06-JUL-98

We generally like HET's acquisition of Showboat, Inc. (SBO). In December 1997, we raised our opinion on the stock to accumulate, from avoid. The acquisition of SBO should expand the company's cross-marketing opportunities, and aid HET's gambler rewards program. Moreve, in the U.S., the addition of SBO will significantly increase HET's presence in the Atlantic City and Chicago-area gaming markets. Excluding one-time items, and helped by cost cutting, we look for no more than modest first-year EPS dilution from the SBO acquisition. However, following the $519 million acquisition, we do not expect much, if any, in the way of HET stock repurchase activity in 1998.

Key Stock Statistics

S&P EPS Est. 1998	1.30	Tang. Bk. Value/Share	6.85
P/E on S&P Est. 1998	11.5	Beta	1.38
S&P EPS Est. 1999	1.50	Shareholders	13,200
Dividend Rate/Share	Nil	Market cap. (B)	$ 1.5
Shs. outstg. (M)	101.3	Inst. holdings	70%
Avg. daily vol. (M)	0.484		

Value of $10,000 invested 5 years ago: NA

Fiscal Year Ending Dec. 31

	1998	1997	1996	1995	1994	1993
Revenues (Million $)						
1Q	414.4	374.1	383.1	356.5	290.3	269.2
2Q	478.6	408.9	401.2	389.3	338.8	316.3
3Q	—	438.3	429.2	425.8	366.8	346.7
4Q	—	398.0	545.6	378.4	343.6	319.7
Yr.	—	1,619	1,588	1,550	1,339	1,252
Earnings Per Share ($)						
1Q	**0.25**	**0.17**	0.30	0.28	0.22	0.12
2Q	**0.36**	**0.25**	0.29	0.35	0.30	0.22
3Q	**E0.50**	**0.52**	0.41	0.50	0.29	0.39
4Q	**E0.24**	**0.12**	-0.05	-0.35	-0.31	0.19
Yr.	**E1.30**	**1.06**	0.95	0.76	0.49	0.89

Next earnings report expected: late October

Dividend Data

In mid-1995, shareholders of Promus Cos. received one share of Promus Hotel Corp.

A Division of The McGraw·Hill Companies

STANDARD &POOR'S
STOCK REPORTS

Harrah's Entertainment, Inc.

1099H
12-SEP-98

Business Summary - 06-JUL-98

Harrah's Entertainment, Inc., is the most geographically diversified casino company in North America. Following the recent acquisition of Showboat, Inc. (SBO), HET operates approximately 19 gaming properties in 10 states, including six in Nevada and two in Atlantic City. The SBO acquisition, for which HET paid about $519 million, and assumed approximately $635 million of debt, also included equity interests related to a casino in Sydney, Australia.

Contributions to HET's operating profit (in millions of dollars, including depreciation charges, but before pre-opening or opening costs, equity income (or losses), writedowns and reserves, venture restructuring costs, and corporate expense) from divisions or areas in recent years (prior to the SBO acquisition) were:

	1997	1996
Riverboats	$124.2	$141.2
Northern Nevada	44.5	59.8
Southern Nevada	41.9	68.0
Atlantic City	73.3	75.0
Other	6.2	-1.2
Total	290.1	342.8

Including a 55%-owned East Chicago, IN, gaming project that was part of the SBO acquisition, HET's Riverboat division would now include the operation of

casinos on boats or barges in five states. In addition to the SBO Indiana casino, this includes gaming projects in Joliet, IL, Vicksburg and Tunica, MS, Shreveport, LA, North Kansas City, MO, and Maryland Heights, MO. HET has joint venture partners in some of these gaming projects, and some of the projects include two HET casinos.

In northern Nevada, HET operates Harrah's Reno, Harrah's Lake Tahoe, and Bill's Lake Tahoe Casino. In southern Nevada, it operates Harrah's Las Vegas, recently being expanded, an SBO casino/hotel, and Harrah's Laughlin. HET also recently expanded its Harrah's casino/hotel in Atlantic City, NJ.

Operations also include management of Indian casinos in Arizona, Washington, and North Carolina. A HET-managed casino on Indian land in Kansas opened in January 1998. In June 1998, a management contract related to a New Zealand casino is expected to be bought out by another party. In addition, HET owns about 14% of Sodak Gaming Inc., a distributor of gaming machines.

In November 1997, HET expressed support for a proposed reorganization plan for a land-based New Orleans casino project that is in bankruptcy proceedings. A temporary casino there closed in November 1995, but the project may still be revived, at a better and more permanent site. A HET subsidiary owns an equity interest in a partnership that was formed to develop, own and operate the New Orleans project.

Per Share Data ($)

(Year Ended Dec. 31)	1997	1996	1995	1994	1993	1992	1991	1990	1989	1988
Tangible Bk. Val.	6.79	6.43	5.11	6.09	4.75	3.68	3.16	1.96	NA	NM
Cash Flow	2.27	1.94	1.69	1.17	1.68	1.22	1.05	1.03	NA	NA
Earnings	1.06	0.95	0.76	0.49	0.89	0.51	0.33	0.30	0.33	0.24
Dividends	Nil	Nil	Nil	Nil	Nil	Nil	Nil	10.00	NM	NM
Payout Ratio	Nil	Nil	Nil	Nil	Nil	Nil	Nil	NM	NM	NM
Prices - High	23	38⅞	45⅞	55¼	55	18¾	9⅛	10⅝	NM	NM
- Low	15½	16⅜	22⅛	25⅞	17½	7⅜	3⅞	3	NM	NM
P/E Ratio - High	22	41	60	NM	62	37	27	36	NM	NM
- Low	15	17	29	NM	20	15	12	10	NM	NM

Income Statement Analysis (Million $)

	1997	1996	1995	1994	1993	1992	1991	1990	1989	1988
Revs.	1,619	1,588	1,550	1,339	1,252	1,113	1,031	1,004	945	871
Oper. Inc.	385	392	419	340	356	281	246	210	NA	182
Depr.	122	102	95.4	70.6	80.7	71.7	65.3	57.0	NA	44.8
Int. Exp.	79.1	70.9	98.0	82.0	110	121	137	129	132	122
Pretax Inc.	184	172	152	139	170	88.0	52.0	44.1	45.0	26.1
Eff. Tax Rate	37%	39%	40%	54%	43%	42%	43%	47%	44%	33%
Net Inc.	108	99	78.8	50.0	92.0	51.0	30.0	23.4	25.6	17.5

Balance Sheet & Other Fin. Data (Million $)

	1997	1996	1995	1994	1993	1992	1991	1990	1989	1988
Cash	116	105	96.3	85.0	62.0	43.8	34.6	40.3	NA	33.9
Curr. Assets	212	202	189	172	164	137	103	110	109	128
Total Assets	2,006	1,974	1,637	1,738	1,793	1,597	1,523	1,433	1,342	1,334
Curr. Liab.	211	205	202	295	252	157	223	204	173	135
LT Debt	924	889	754	727	840	877	835	904	914	895
Common Eqty.	736	720	586	623	536	428	375	213	176	222
Total Cap.	1,696	1,654	1,363	1,376	1,454	1,352	1,244	1,174	1,123	1,153
Cap. Exp.	230	314	186	219	239	118	174	173	NA	NA
Cash Flow	230	201	174	121	173	123	95.0	80.0	NA	NA
Curr. Ratio	1.0	1.0	0.9	0.6	0.6	0.9	0.5	0.5	0.6	0.9
% LT Debt of Cap.	54.5	53.7	55.3	52.9	57.7	64.9	67.1	76.9	81.4	77.6
% Net Inc.of Revs.	6.6	6.2	5.1	3.7	7.3	4.6	2.9	2.3	2.7	2.0
% Ret. on Assets	5.4	9.1	4.7	2.8	5.4	3.3	1.8	NA	NA	NA
% Ret. on Equity	14.8	15.1	13.0	8.6	19.0	12.8	9.3	NA	NA	NA

Data as orig. reptd.; bef. results of disc. opers. and/or spec. items. Per share data adj. for stk. divs. as of ex-div. date. Bold denotes diluted EPS (FASB 128). E-Estimated. NA-Not Available. NM-Not Meaningful. NR-Not Ranked.

Office—1023 Cherry Rd., Memphis, TN 38117. **Tel**—(901) 762-8600. **Website**—http://www.harrahs.com **Chrmn, Pres & CEO**—P. G. Satre. **EVP & CFO**—C. V. Reed. **VP, Treas & Investor Contact**—Charles Atwood (901-762-8852). **Dirs**—S. Clark-Jackson, J. B. Farley, J. M. Henson, R. Horn, R. B. Martin, W. J. Salmon, P. G. Satre, B. A. Sells, E. N. Williams. **Transfer Agent & Registrar**—Bank of New York, NYC. **Incorporated**—in Delaware in 1989. **Empl**— 22,000. **S&P Analyst:** Tom Graves, CFA

Harris Corp.

1099M

NYSE Symbol **HRS**

In S&P 500

12-SEP-98

Industry:
Communications
Equipment

Summary: Harris makes advanced electronic systems, semiconductors, communications equipment and systems, and office equipment.

S&P Opinion: Accumulate (★★★★)	Recent Price • 33⅛ 52 Wk Range • 55¼-31⅞

Yield • 2.9%
12-Mo. P/E • 20.0

Earnings vs. Previous Year
▲=Up ▼=Down ▶=No Change

Quantitative Evaluations

Outlook
(1 Lowest—5 Highest)
• **3**

Fair Value
• **38¼**

Risk
• **Low**

Earn./Div. Rank
• **A-**

Technical Eval.
• **Neutral** since 6/98

Rel. Strength Rank
(1 Lowest—99 Highest)
• **46**

Insider Activity
• **NA**

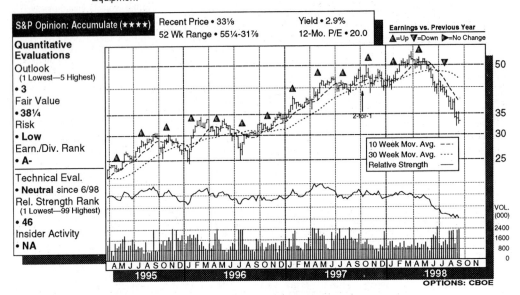

2-for-1

10 Week Mov. Avg. - - - -
30 Week Mov. Avg. ·······
Relative Strength ——

VOL.
(000)
2400
1600
800
0

A M J J A S O N D J F M A M J J A S O N D J F M A M J J A S O N D J F M A M J J A S O N
1995   1996   1997   1998

OPTIONS: CBOE

Overview - 04-AUG-98

We expect sales to rise approximately 5% to 7% in FY 99 (Jun.). The communication sector will pace the advance, reflecting growth in the segment's digital switch business, coupled with higher sales for microwave systems, broadcast products, and telephone test equipment. Longer term, this sector will benefit from the emergence of digital television in the U.S., a potential $6 billion market. The semiconductor sector's revenues have been negatively impacted by pricing pressures. In response, HRS has taken action to reduce its cost structure, including an 8% reduction in headcount. In connection with these actions the company recorded a $90 million charge in the fourth quarter of FY 98. Additional charges of $52 million were taken in the Lanier, Communications and Electronic Systems groups, representing one-time measures to reduce overhead and to exit non-strategic product lines. Overall, we look for earnings per share to advance to $3.07 in FY 99, from the $2.84 reported in FY 98 (before charges).

Valuation - 04-AUG-98

Following a sharp advance early in the year, the shares have retreated, reflecting weak semiconductor industry conditions and fears that the strong dollar would crimp revenue and earnings growth. However, we are maintaining our accumulate recommendation, as we believe the shares are attractively valued at 13X our FY 99 (Jun.) EPS estimate of $3.07. The company's diversified business units have solid growth prospects, and a demonstrated ability to generate cash. While the first half of FY 99 is likely to show slower revenue growth, we expect earnings momentum to continue over the course of the fiscal year. As such, we believe the shares will outperform the broader market over the next six to 12 months.

Key Stock Statistics

S&P EPS Est. 1999	3.07	Tang. Bk. Value/Share	18.29
P/E on S&P Est. 1999	10.8	Beta	0.98
Dividend Rate/Share	0.96	Shareholders	10,600
Shs. outstg. (M)	80.0	Market cap. (B)	$ 2.7
Avg. daily vol. (M)	0.412	Inst. holdings	68%

Value of $10,000 invested 5 years ago: NA

Fiscal Year Ending Jun. 30

	1998	1997	1996	1995	1994	1993
Revenues (Million $)						
1Q	979.6	883.4	816.7	807.3	769.1	728.0
2Q	970.0	945.9	916.6	863.1	807.5	767.0
3Q	961.6	921.4	875.9	850.4	838.3	744.0
4Q	993.8	1,047	1,012	923.3	921.2	859.0
Yr.	3,939	3,797	3,621	3,444	3,336	3,099
Earnings Per Share ($)						
1Q	0.55	0.49	0.43	0.36	0.31	0.55
2Q	**0.66**	0.58	0.52	0.44	0.38	0.32
3Q	**0.75**	0.70	0.57	0.49	0.41	0.41
4Q	**-0.29**	0.86	0.78	0.68	0.43	0.47
Yr.	**1.66**	2.63	2.29	1.98	1.53	1.41

Next earnings report expected: late October

Dividend Data (Dividends have been paid since 1941.)

Amount ($)	Date Decl.	Ex-Div. Date	Stock of Record	Payment Date
0.220	Oct. 24	Nov. 19	Nov. 21	Dec. 05 '97
0.220	Feb. 27	Mar. 06	Mar. 10	Mar. 18 '98
0.220	Apr. 27	May. 28	Jun. 01	Jun. 12 '98
0.240	Aug. 31	Sep. 10	Sep. 14	Sep. 23 '98

A Division of The McGraw-Hill Companies

STANDARD
&POOR'S
STOCK REPORTS

Harris Corporation

1099M
12-SEP-98

Business Summary - 04-AUG-98

Harris Corp. (HRS) has posted solid earnings gains since the economy emerged from a recession in the early part of the decade. It is a diversified company that operates four business segments in growing industries: electronic systems, semiconductors, communications and office equipment distribution. Each segment, with the exception of electronic systems, has contributed to the growth in profits. Segment contributions in FY 97 (Jun.) were:

	Sales	Net income
Electronic systems	26%	19%
Semiconductors	18%	28%
Communications	25%	22%
Lanier Worldwide	31%	32%

Sales in FY 97 of products exported from the U.S. or manufactured abroad were 29% of total revenues, compared with 33% in FY 96. Approximately 49% of these sales were to Europe and Asia.

While each segment is distinct, HRS believes it can exploit synergies that exist between segments. For instance, the semiconductor segment developed new devices with the benefit of the electronic systems segment's vast defense technologies.

The electronic systems segment is engaged in research, development, design and production of a broad range of high-technology systems for government and commercial organizations in the U.S. and overseas. Applications include defense, air traffic control, avionics, satellite communications, space exploration, mobile radio networks, simulation, energy management, law enforcement, electronic systems testing and newspaper composition.

The semiconductor segment produces digital and analog integrated circuits and discrete semiconductors for power, signal processing, data acquisition and logic applications.

The communications segment makes products characterized by three principal communication technologies: broadcast, including radio and television products and transmission systems; two-way radio and complete turnkey communication systems; and telecommunications. Harris has secured commitments from major broadcast customers to supply equipment for the conversion to digital television that will occur over the next six to eight years. The company believes the potential domestic market approximates $6 billion.

Lanier Worldwide, Inc. sells and services office equipment and business communication products. This segment has benefited recently from new top-end product introductions and a national accounts program.

Per Share Data ($)

(Year Ended Jun. 30)	1998	1997	1996	1995	1994	1993	1992	1991	1990	1989
Tangible Bk. Val.	NA	16.96	14.92	13.92	13.01	12.36	11.76	11.29	11.78	10.68
Cash Flow	NA	4.97	4.47	4.08	3.37	3.31	3.23	2.60	3.98	2.99
Earnings	1.66	2.63	2.29	1.98	1.53	1.41	1.12	0.25	1.65	1.50
Dividends	0.88	0.76	0.68	0.62	0.56	0.52	0.52	0.52	0.48	0.44
Payout Ratio	53%	29%	30%	31%	36%	37%	46%	208%	29%	29%
Prices - High	38⅜	50	35¾	30¾	26⅛	23¾	17¾	14½	18⅛	19¾
- Low	39½	33¾	24½	20¼	18⅞	16⅞	13⅜	9⅛	6⅞	13¼
P/E Ratio - High	33	19	16	16	17	17	16	58	11	13
- Low	23	13	11	10	12	12	12	37	4	9

Income Statement Analysis (Million $)

Revs.	NA	3,797	3,621	3,444	3,336	3,099	3,004	3,040	3,053	2,214
Oper. Inc.	NA	498	475	445	376	333	314	331	400	280
Depr.	NA	184	171	165	146	150	165	184	184	116
Int. Exp.	NA	69.0	64.0	65.4	58.6	60.2	66.1	77.5	74.1	36.9
Pretax Inc.	NA	312	274	238	194	170	125	10.0	190	167
Eff. Tax Rate	NA	33%	35%	35%	37%	35%	30%	NM	31%	31%
Net Inc.	NA	208	178	155	122	111	87.0	19.0	131	116

Balance Sheet & Other Fin. Data (Million $)

Cash	NA	162	99	142	139	132	124	59.0	138	189
Curr. Assets	NA	2,064	1,941	1,811	1,698	1,571	1,533	1,496	1,585	1,534
Total Assets	NA	3,638	3,207	2,836	2,677	2,542	2,484	2,486	2,625	2,558
Curr. Liab.	NA	1,289	1,183	1,055	805	778	764	853	1,194	1,238
LT Debt	NA	687	589	476	662	612	613	563	301	315
Common Eqty.	NA	1,578	1,373	1,249	1,188	1,141	1,068	1,028	1,083	947
Total Cap.	NA	2,354	2,024	1,781	1,872	1,764	1,719	1,633	1,431	1,320
Cap. Exp.	NA	350	363	195	135	149	122	133	193	110
Cash Flow	NA	391	349	320	268	261	252	204	314	232
Curr. Ratio	NA	1.6	1.6	1.7	2.1	2.0	2.0	1.8	1.3	1.2
% LT Debt of Cap.	NA	29.1	29.1	26.7	35.3	34.7	35.6	34.5	21.0	23.8
% Net Inc.of Revs.	NA	5.4	4.9	4.5	3.7	3.6	2.9	0.6	4.3	5.2
% Ret. on Assets	NA	6.0	5.9	5.6	4.7	4.4	3.5	0.8	5.0	5.5
% Ret. on Equity	NA	14.0	13.6	12.7	10.5	10.0	8.3	1.9	12.7	12.1

Data as orig. reptd.; bef. results of disc. opers. and/or spec. items. Per share data adj. for stk. divs. as of ex-div. date. Bold denotes diluted EPS (FASB 128). E-Estimated. NA-Not Available. NM-Not Meaningful. NR-Not Ranked.

Office—1025 West NASA Blvd., Melbourne, FL 32919. **Tel**—(407) 727-9100. **Website**—http://www.harris.com **Chrmn, Pres & CEO**—P. W. Farmer. **SVP & CFO**—B. R. Roub. **VP & Secy**—R. L. Ballantyne. **Investor Contact**—P. Padgett. **Dirs**—R. Cizik, L. E. Coleman, A. C. DeCrane, R. D. DeNunzio, J. L. Dionne, P. W. Farmer, J. T. Hartley, K. Katen, A. Trowbridge. **Transfer Agent & Registrar**—ChaseMellon Shareholder Services, Ridgefield Park, NJ.**Incorporated**—in Delaware in 1926. **Empl**— 29,000. **S&P Analyst**: B. McGovern

12-SEP-98 **Industry:** Insurance (Multi-Line)

Summary: HIG, spun off in December 1995 from old ITT Corp., is one of the largest U.S. multi-line insurance holding companies, with a growing international presence.

S&P Opinion: Buy (★★★★)	Recent Price • 47⅝	Yield • 1.8%
	52 Wk Range • 60-39¼	12-Mo. P/E • 10.8

Quantitative Evaluations

Outlook (1 Lowest—5 Highest)
• 3

Fair Value
• 47¼

Risk
• **Low**

Earn./Div. Rank
• **NR**

Technical Eval.
• **NA**

Rel. Strength Rank (1 Lowest—99 Highest)
• 71

Insider Activity
• **Neutral**

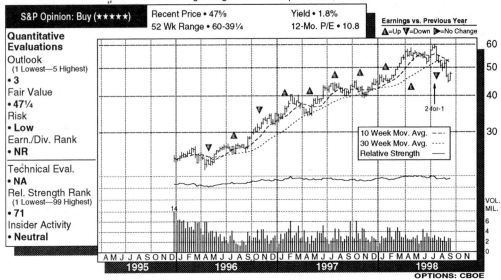

Earnings vs. Previous Year
▲=Up ▼=Down ▶=No Change

10 Week Mov. Avg. ----
30 Week Mov. Avg. ·····
Relative Strength ——

2-for-1

VOL. MIL.

OPTIONS: CBOE

Overview - 14-AUG-98

Operating earnings growth in coming periods will be driven primarily by growth in the annuity line. A rebound in 1997 operating earnings was skewed by charges of $593 million ($2.96 a share) recorded in 1996, mainly to cover an increase in environmental and asbestos reserves. Excluding this, property-casualty written premiums in the U.S. will likely advance 5%-6% in 1998, as expanded distribution efforts are limited by a competitive pricing environment. Favorable underlying claim trends are being masked by higher catastrophe losses. During the first six months of 1998, catastrophe losses of $86 million (versus $19 million in the year earlier period) led to a mere 7.3% rise in per share operating earnings, to $1.62 versus $1.51. Longer term, margins will be aided by tighter underwriting standards and cost containment efforts. But, profitability overseas may be hurt by difficult conditions in the U.K. motor insurance market. Life insurance operations will continue to be driven by strong sales of annuities, though the robust growth seen recently may be hard to sustain, long term. Still, HIG will likely retain its position as the leading writer of variable annuities. Finally, net income in 1997 includes a gain of $368 million (about $1.56 a share) from the initial public offering of 18.6% of Hartford Life stock.

Valuation - 14-AUG-98

After the December 1995 three-way spinoff of old ITT Corp., HIG shares have generally trended higher. Despite their strength, the shares remain undervalued. Recently trading at less than 13X our 1999 operating EPS estimate of $4.00 a share (excluding realized investment gains or losses), the shares have additional upside potential, particularly in light of the promising growth prospects that will likely emerge from HIG's expanded distribution efforts.

Key Stock Statistics

S&P EPS Est. 1998	3.40	Tang. Bk. Value/Share	27.51
P/E on S&P Est. 1998	14.0	Beta	NA
S&P EPS Est. 1999	4.00	Shareholders	60,000
Dividend Rate/Share	0.84	Market cap. (B)	$ 11.1
Shs. outstg. (M)	233.4	Inst. holdings	71%
Avg. daily vol. (M)	0.525		

Value of $10,000 invested 5 years ago: NA

Fiscal Year Ending Dec. 31

	1998	1997	1996	1995	1994	1993
Revenues (Million $)						
1Q	3,728	3,118	3,278	3,005	—	—
2Q	3,493	3,142	3,026	2,914	—	—
3Q	—	3,306	2,836	3,058	—	—
4Q	—	3,739	3,333	3,173	—	—
Yr.	—	13,305	12,473	12,150	11,102	—
Earnings Per Share ($)						
1Q	1.10	0.85	0.41	0.59	--	--
2Q	0.99	2.40	0.61	0.45	--	--
3Q	--	1.25	-2.31	0.74	--	--
4Q	--	1.07	0.88	0.60	--	--
Yr.	—	5.58	-0.42	2.38	2.65	2.25

Next earnings report expected: late October

Dividend Data (Dividends have been paid since 1996.)

Amount ($)	Date Decl.	Ex-Div. Date	Stock of Record	Payment Date
0.420	Feb. 17	Feb. 26	Mar. 02	Apr. 01 '98
0.420	May. 21	May. 28	Jun. 01	Jul. 01 '98
2-for-1	May. 21	Jul. 16	Jun. 24	Jul. 15 '98
0.210	Jul. 16	Aug. 28	Sep. 01	Oct. 01 '98

A Division of The McGraw-Hill Companies

Business Summary - 14-AUG-98

This leading insurance company recently changed its name (from ITT Hartford Group) to better reflect its current ownership structure. Prior to its December 1995 spinoff, HIG was a subsidiary of ITT Corp. From its founding in 1810 as a local fire insurance company, HIG has grown to become one of the ten largest insurers in both the property-casualty and life insurance industries. HIG's strategy is to focus on five core areas: life insurance, reinsurance, commercial lines property-casualty insurance, personal lines property-casualty insurance, and international operations.

Contributions to pretax operating earnings (in million $ in recent years) were:

	1997	1996
North American P&C	$727	-$399
International	162	210
Life	480	378
Runoff and other	-34	-507

The North American property-casualty operations, with $5.7 billion in earned premiums in 1997, provide a wide range of commercial, personal, specialty and reinsur-

ance coverages. HIG also ranks among the 10 largest personal lines carriers, is the endorsed provider of automobile and homeowners coverages to members of the American Association of Retired Persons; and is also a major reinsurer. The February 1998, acquisition of Omni Insurance Group (for $187 million) expanded HIG's presence in the nonstandard auto insurance market. Results in 1997 rebounded amid the absence of charges of $510 million ($4.35 a share) taken to cover an increase in reserves for asbestos and environmental claims in 1996.

HIG's life insurance operations provide individual and group life and disability insurance, asset accumulation products, and financial services for individuals, corporations and governmental entities. This unit is a leading writer of variable annuities in the U.S., with an 11% market share in 1995. Account values at year-end 1997 totaled $70.8 billion, of which individual annuities accounted for $56.3 billion. In May 1997, HIG sold approximately 17% of its life unit, Hartford Life Inc. (NYSE: HLI), in an initial public offering.

ITT Hartford also offers an array of insurance products in Europe. International written premiums totaled $1.6 billion in 1997.

Per Share Data ($)

(Year Ended Dec. 31)	1997	1996	1995	1994	1993	1992	1991	1990	1989	1988
Tangible Bk. Val.	25.79	19.23	20.07	13.38	16.86	NA	NA	NA	NA	NA
Oper. Earnings	4.70	-1.35	3.17	2.90	2.68	NA	NA	NA	NA	NA
Earnings	5.58	-0.42	2.38	2.65	2.25	-1.15	1.81	1.38	NA	NA
Dividends	0.80	0.80	Nil	NA	NA	NA	NA	NA	NA	NA
Relative Payout	14%	NM	Nil	NA	NA	NA	NA	NA	NA	NA
Prices - High	47¼	35	25⅛	NA	NA	NA	NA	NA	NA	NA
- Low	32½	22¼	23¾	NA	NA	NA	NA	NA	NA	NA
P/E Ratio - High	8	NM	11	NA	NA	NA	NA	NA	NA	NA
- Low	6	NM	10	NA	NA	NA	NA	NA	NA	NA

Income Statement Analysis (Million $)

	1997	1996	1995	1994	1993	1992	1991	1990	1989	1988
Life Ins. In Force	407,860	312,176	339,291	246,138	182,784	126,447	NA	NA	NA	NA
Prem. Inc.: Life A & H	3,323	3,185	2,738	2,173	1,812	1,340	NA	NA	NA	NA
Prem. Inc.: Cas./Prop.	7,000	6,891	6,890	6,580	6,338	6,094	NA	NA	NA	NA
Net Invest. Inc.	2,655	2,523	2,420	2,259	2,033	1,985	NA	NA	NA	NA
Oth. Revs.	327	-125	102	90.0	155	443	NA	NA	NA	NA
Total Revs.	13,305	12,473	12,150	11,102	10,338	9,862	9,242	8,836	NA	NA
Pretax Inc.	1,703	-317	742	852	687	-500	NA	NA	NA	NA
Net Oper. Inc.	1,117	-317	742	691	638	NA	NA	NA	NA	NA
Net Inc.	1,332	-99.0	559	632	537	-273	431	328	NA	NA

Balance Sheet & Other Fin. Data (Million $)

	1997	1996	1995	1994	1993	1992	1991	1990	1989	1988
Cash & Equiv.	140	112	95.0	55.0	61.0	NA	NA	NA	NA	NA
Premiums Due	1,873	1,797	1,890	2,000	1,788	NA	NA	NA	NA	NA
Invest. Assets: Bonds	35,053	31,449	31,168	27,418	26,870	NA	NA	NA	NA	NA
Invest. Assets: Stocks	1,922	1,865	1,342	1,350	1,302	NA	NA	NA	NA	NA
Invest. Assets: Loans	3,759	3,839	3,380	2,614	1,402	NA	NA	NA	NA	NA
Invest. Assets: Total	37,363	33,800	36,675	32,453	30,582	NA	NA	NA	NA	NA
Deferred Policy Costs	4,181	3,535	2,945	2,525	2,024	NA	NA	NA	NA	NA
Total Assets	131,743	108,840	93,855	76,765	66,179	54,180	37,771	NA	NA	NA
Debt	1,773	1,532	1,022	596	579	576	594	NA	NA	NA
Common Eqty.	6,085	4,520	4,702	3,184	4,012	3,679	3,816	NA	NA	NA
Comb. Loss-Exp. Ratio	102.3	105.2	104.5	102.8	105.9	114.8	111.3	109.7	NA	NA
% Return On Revs.	10.0	NM	4.6	5.7	5.2	NM	4.7	3.7	NA	NA
% Ret. on Equity	25.1	NM	14.2	15.4	14.2	NM	NA	NA	NA	NA
% Invest. Yield	6.7	6.8	7.0	7.0	7.0	7.6	NA	NA	NA	NA

Data as orig. reptd.; bef. results of disc. opers. and/or spec. items. Per share data adj. for stk. divs. as of ex-div. date. Bold denotes diluted EPS (FASB 128). E-Estimate. NA-Not Available. NM-Not Meaningful. NR-Not Ranked.

Office—Hartford Plaza, Hartford, CT 06115. **Tel**—(860) 547-5000. **Website**—http://www.itthartford.com **Chrmn, CEO & Pres**—R. Ayer. **EVP & COO**—L. A. Smith (Life operations). **EVP & CFO**—D. K. Zwiener. **EVP & Chief Investment Officer**—J. H. Gareau. **VP & Secy**—M. O'Halloran. **Wilder. SVP & Controller**—J. J. Westervelt. **Investor Contact**—Stephen P. Minihan (860-547-2403). **Dirs**—B. B. Anderson, R. V. Araskog, R. Ayer, R. A. Burnett, D. R. Frahm, A. A. Hartman, P. G. Kirk, R. W. Selander, L. A. Smith, D. C. Thomas, G. I. Ulmer, D. K. Zwiener. **Transfer Agent**—Bank of New York, NYC. **Incorporated**—in Delaware in 1995. **Empl**— 21,000. **S&P Analyst:** Catherine A. Seifert

STANDARD &POOR'S
STOCK REPORTS

Hasbro Inc.
8088
ASE Symbol **HAS**
In S&P 500

12-SEP-98

Industry: Leisure Time (Products)

Summary: Hasbro, one of the world's largest toy companies, has a broadly diversified line sold under the Kenner, Milton Bradley, Parker Brothers and Playskool brand names.

S&P Opinion: Accumulate (★★★★)	Recent Price • 33⅞	Yield • 0.9%
	52 Wk Range • 40⅞-25¾	12-Mo. P/E • 41.3

Quantitative Evaluations

Outlook
(1 Lowest—5 Highest)
• **2⁻**

Fair Value
• **30⅞**

Risk
• **Low**

Earn./Div. Rank
• **B+**

Technical Eval.
• **Bullish** since 5/97

Rel. Strength Rank
(1 Lowest—99 Highest)
• **73**

Insider Activity
• **Neutral**

Earnings vs. Previous Year
△=Up ▽=Down ▶=No Change

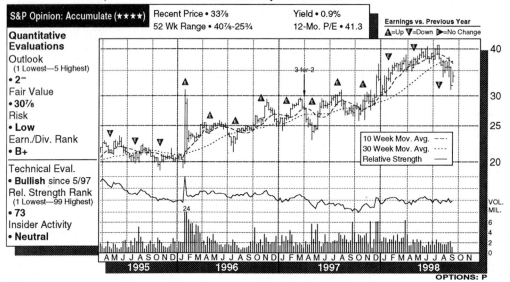

10 Week Mov. Avg. ---
30 Week Mov. Avg. ····
Relative Strength —

3-for-2

1995 1996 1997 1998

VOL. MIL.

OPTIONS: P

Overview - 24-AUG-98

Hasbro is the second largest U.S. toy supplier, surpassed only by Mattel Inc. Its strongest categories include products for boys and games, including items related to Batman and Star Wars movies, Tonka vehicles and Monopoly. Various games, including Boggle and Candy Land, are marketed under the Milton Bradley and Parker Brothers names. Other HAS products include G.I. Joe, Play-Doh, Nerf, Playskool items for younger children, and Raggedy Ann dolls. Also, HAS has agreed to acquire MicroProse, Inc., a provider of personal computer games, and in April 1998, acquired assets of Tiger Electronics, Inc. Earlier, in March 1998, HAS acquired rights to various Atari video games, at least some of which HAS is expected to update. Also, HAS's earnings in 1998's first half were limited, in part, by a reduction and change in purchasing patterns by retailer Toys 'R Us. Our 1998 earnings estimates exclude an expected one-time charge related to the MicroProse acquisition. In 1997, HAS's EPS included about $0.68 (diluted) of charges related to restructuring activity.

Valuation - 24-AUG-98

In mid-July 1998, we raised our opinion on the stock of this major toy company to "accumulate," from "hold." We look for interest in HAS's new Teletubbies products, and future Star Wars-related products to help the stock. Also, we expect earnings visibility during at least the next few years to be helped by restructuring activity. We generally like HAS's recent efforts to expand its presence in electronic or computer-based products, as we expect that a growing portion of overall future toy spending will be going to these categories. Also, unless HAS is expecting to make a sizable acquisition, we look for the shares to get at least some support from stock repurchases.

Key Stock Statistics

S&P EPS Est. 1998	1.85	Tang. Bk. Value/Share	3.22
P/E on S&P Est. 1998	18.3	Beta	0.81
S&P EPS Est. 1999	2.25	Shareholders	5,000
Dividend Rate/Share	0.32	Market cap. (B)	$ 4.5
Shs. outstg. (M)	131.5	Inst. holdings	76%
Avg. daily vol. (M)	0.369		

Value of $10,000 invested 5 years ago: $ 16,444

Fiscal Year Ending Dec. 31

	1998	1997	1996	1995	1994	1993
Revenues (Million $)						
1Q	482.8	555.8	538.6	526.5	489.1	487.0
2Q	572.1	583.9	511.6	481.9	444.3	515.5
3Q	—	915.8	845.1	826.2	796.2	812.4
4Q	—	1,133	1,107	1,024	940.6	932.2
Yr.	—	3,189	3,002	2,858	2,670	2,747
Earnings Per Share ($)						
1Q	**0.06**	0.20	0.19	0.17	0.20	0.20
2Q	**0.04**	0.10	0.05	-0.11	0.01	0.20
3Q	—	0.57	0.54	0.48	0.57	0.56
4Q	—	0.14	0.75	0.65	0.57	0.52
Yr.	**E1.85**	1.02	1.52	1.17	1.34	1.48

Next earnings report expected: mid October

Dividend Data (Dividends have been paid since 1981.)

Amount ($)	Date Decl.	Ex-Div. Date	Stock of Record	Payment Date
0.080	Dec. 11	Jan. 29	Feb. 02	Feb. 16 '98
0.080	Feb. 24	Apr. 29	May. 01	May. 15 '98
0.080	May. 19	Jul. 30	Aug. 03	Aug. 17 '98
0.080	Jul. 23	Oct. 29	Nov. 02	Nov. 16 '98

A Division of The **McGraw·Hill** Companies

Hasbro Inc.

Business Summary - 24-AUG-98

With products ranging from Batman and Raggedy Ann to Monopoly and Tonka trucks, this leading toymaker opens windows of imagination around the world. Based on annual sales, Hasbro is second only to Mattel among U.S. toy suppliers. In December 1997, HAS announced a restructuring program, as well as an authorization to repurchase $500 million of common stock. The company recorded about $0.68 a share of one-time charges in the 1997 fourth quarter.

In the game category, where Hasbro is particularly strong, the company markets products under the Milton Bradley and Parker Brothers brand names. Hasbro's games include Monopoly, Boggle, The Game of Life, Stratego, Lucky Ducks, and Candy Land, as well as jigsaw puzzles. We expect that HAS's presence in hand-held electronic games was sharply increased by the April 1998 acquisition of the operating assets of Tiger Electronics, Inc., and its affiliates. Also, HAS has agreed to acquire MicroProse, Inc., a provider of personal computer games.

In boys' toys, Hasbro offers a wide range of products, some of which are licensed and tied to entertainment properties, including Batman and Star Wars. In 1997, HAS had products linked to the movie sequel to Jurassic Park. Other boys' toys include G.I. Joe, the Tonka line of trucks and vehicles, and the Super Soaker line of water products.

Hasbro's infant and preschool items are principally marketed under the Playskool brand. The preschool line includes such well known products as Lincoln Logs, Tinkertoy, and Mr. Potato Head.

Girls' items include Raggedy Ann and Raggedy Andy, Baby Go Bye Bye, the Littlest Pet Shop, and Sleep Over Club activity kits. HAS also offers various other activity items, including Play-Doh, Easy Bake Oven, and the Nerf line of products.

Other HAS products include CD-ROM titles related to some of the company's brands. New HAS products for 1996 included various game and activity items related to the popular series of Goosebumps books, and new Playskool Magic Touch Talking Books. In May 1997, HAS acquired the assets of Cap Toys and OddzOn Products from Russ Berrie and Co., Inc.

In 1997, international operations accounted for 46% of HAS's net revenues and 34% of operating profit.

In 1997, HAS spent $135 million to buy back 4.8 million of its common shares. Also, in October 1997, HAS issued warrants to purchase 6.5 million common shares at an exercise price of $28/share. This was likely related to HAS receiving an expanded licensing agreement for products related to Star Wars movies. Also, as of early 1998, HAS and some other toy-related companies were defendants in one or more cases related to alleged violations of antitrust law.

Per Share Data ($)

(Year Ended Dec. 31)	1997	1996	1995	1994	1993	1992	1991	1990	1989	1988
Tangible Bk. Val.	6.54	6.41	5.41	4.72	4.67	3.17	2.35	4.97	4.14	4.18
Cash Flow	1.80	2.26	1.87	1.97	1.97	1.81	1.03	0.99	1.13	1.01
Earnings	1.02	1.51	1.17	1.34	1.48	1.34	0.63	0.69	0.69	0.55
Dividends	0.34	0.38	0.21	0.18	0.15	0.13	0.10	0.08	0.07	0.05
Payout Ratio	33%	25%	18%	13%	10%	9%	16%	12%	10%	8%
Prices - High	36½	31⅛	23½	24⅜	26¾	23⅞	18⅛	9⅝	10⅞	7⅝
- Low	22⅞	19¼	18⅞	18⅝	18¾	15⅜	6¾	5	6¾	5⅜
P/E Ratio - High	36	21	20	18	18	18	29	14	16	14
- Low	22	13	16	14	13	12	11	7	10	10

Income Statement Analysis (Million $)

	1997	1996	1995	1994	1993	1992	1991	1990	1989	1988
Revs.	3,189	3,002	2,858	2,670	2,747	2,541	2,141	1,520	1,410	1,358
Oper. Inc.	473	430	365	394	432	387	290	223	230	217
Depr.	113	98.2	91.4	85.4	65.3	62.1	52.5	39.7	59.9	63.0
Int. Exp.	27.5	31.5	37.6	30.8	29.8	35.9	42.6	16.5	24.3	29.9
Pretax Inc.	205	307	253	292	325	292	146	152	157	131
Eff. Tax Rate	34%	35%	38%	39%	39%	39%	44%	42%	41%	45%
Net Inc.	135	200	156	179	200	179	81.7	89.2	92.2	72.4

Balance Sheet & Other Fin. Data (Million $)

	1997	1996	1995	1994	1993	1992	1991	1990	1989	1988
Cash	362	219	161	137	186	126	121	289	278	232
Curr. Assets	1,574	1,487	1,425	1,252	1,301	1,117	1,025	862	807	736
Total Assets	2,900	2,702	2,616	2,378	2,293	2,083	1,950	1,285	1,246	1,112
Curr. Liab.	1,004	831	870	764	748	701	594	358	384	273
LT Debt	Nil	149	150	150	201	206	380	57.0	58.0	127
Common Eqty.	1,838	1,652	1,526	1,395	1,277	1,106	955	868	802	700
Total Cap.	1,838	1,801	1,747	1,545	1,477	1,312	1,336	925	860	830
Cap. Exp.	99	102	101	111	100	90.4	56.0	36.2	50.3	54.4
Cash Flow	248	298	247	265	265	241	134	129	150	133
Curr. Ratio	1.6	1.8	1.6	1.6	1.7	1.6	1.7	2.4	2.1	2.7
% LT Debt of Cap.	Nil	8.3	8.6	9.7	13.6	15.7	28.5	6.2	6.7	15.3
% Net Inc.of Revs.	4.2	6.7	5.5	6.7	7.3	7.0	3.8	5.9	6.5	5.3
% Ret. on Assets	4.8	7.5	6.3	7.7	9.1	8.8	5.0	7.2	7.4	6.6
% Ret. on Equity	7.7	12.6	10.7	13.4	16.7	17.3	8.9	10.9	11.4	10.8

Data as orig. reptd.; bef. results of disc. opers. and/or spec. items. Per share data adj. for stk. divs. as of ex-div. date. Bold denotes diluted EPS (FASB 128). E-Estimated. NA-Not Available. NM-Not Meaningful. NR-Not Ranked.

Office—1027 Newport Ave., P.O. Box 1059, Pawtucket, RI 02862-1059. Tel—(401) 431-8697. Website—http://www.hasbro.com Chrmn & CEO—A. G. Hassenfeld. Vice Chrmn—H. P. Gordon. EVP & CFO—John T. O'Neill. Investor Contact—Renita E. O'Connell.SVP & Secy—S. P. Waldoks. Dirs—A. R. Batkin, H. P. Gordon, A. Grass, A. G. Hassenfeld, S. Hassenfeld, M. J. Kravis, C. Malone, M. W. Offit, N. T. Pace, E. J. Rosenwald, Jr., C. Spielvogel, P. R. Tisch, A. J. Verrecchia, P. Wolfowitz. Transfer Agent & Registrar—BankBoston, N.A. Incorporated—in Rhode Island in 1926. Empl— 12,000. S&P Analyst: Tom Graves, CFA

12-SEP-98

Industry:
Computer (Software & Services)

Summary: This company is a leading provider of information systems for the health care industry.

S&P Opinion: Accumulate (★★★★)	Recent Price • 26⅞	Yield • 0.3%
	52 Wk Range • 38⅜-18⅜	12-Mo. P/E • 53.8

Quantitative Evaluations

Outlook
(1 Lowest—5 Highest)
• **4−**

Fair Value
• **34¾**

Risk
• **Average**

Earn./Div. Rank
• **B**

Technical Eval.
• **Bullish** since 5/97

Rel. Strength Rank
(1 Lowest—99 Highest)
• **74**

Insider Activity
• **Neutral**

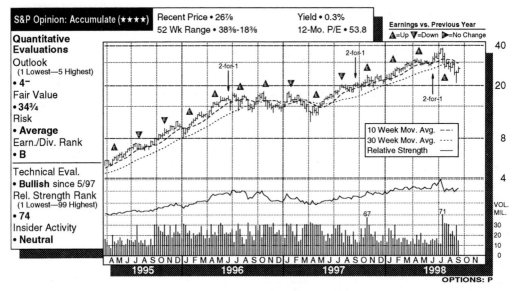

Earnings vs. Previous Year
▲=Up ▼=Down ▶=No Change

10 Week Mov. Avg. ---
30 Week Mov. Avg. ····
Relative Strength —

OPTIONS: P

Overview - 15-JUL-98

Revenues are expected to rise 25% to 30% in 1998, following a 27% increase in 1997, aided by continued strong demand for the company's software products and remote processing, maintenance and other services, aided by a growing installed base. The cost-effective and productivity enhancing nature of the company's products make them particularly attractive to the cost-conscious health care industry. Operating margins reached 31.6% in the 1998 second quarter, up from 30.0% in the first quarter, and from 25.6% in the 1997 quarter. Margins are expected to continue to widen, on volume efficiencies, a more favorable revenue mix, and well controlled costs. A large and growing business pipeline ($1.8 billion as of June 30, 1998) adds to the predictability of sales and earnings growth. Earnings comparisons should benefit from the strong sales growth and wider margins.

Valuation - 15-JUL-98

The shares of this leading provider of computer-based information systems to health care organizations have advanced rapidly for the past several years, far outpacing the broader stock market. Continued strong earnings gains and increased predictability associated with earnings have fueled the rise in the share price. The company continues to strengthen its competitive position, releasing new products, enhancing existing products, making strategic acquisitions and adding to its sales force. Earnings are expected to grow much faster than the market, and the balance sheet is very strong, with nearly $500 million in cash and short-term investments. The shares deserve their premium valuation. In light of the rapid earnings growth that we project, the shares are expected to outperform the market in coming months.

Key Stock Statistics

S&P EPS Est. 1998	0.66	Tang. Bk. Value/Share	1.98
P/E on S&P Est. 1998	40.7	Beta	1.46
S&P EPS Est. 1999	0.84	Shareholders	2,500
Dividend Rate/Share	0.08	Market cap. (B)	$ 11.6
Shs. outstg. (M)	431.0	Inst. holdings	80%
Avg. daily vol. (M)	4.577		

Value of $10,000 invested 5 years ago: $ 169,985

Fiscal Year Ending Dec. 31

	1998	1997	1996	1995	1994	1993
Revenues (Million $)						
1Q	342.9	263.3	172.5	99.2	67.51	52.31
2Q	376.7	291.5	193.3	109.9	78.34	57.47
3Q	—	307.2	206.4	137.9	85.94	62.20
4Q	—	341.2	224.3	148.6	95.41	65.16
Yr.	—	1,203	796.6	495.6	327.2	237.1
Earnings Per Share ($)						
1Q	**0.15**	**0.09**	0.06	0.04	0.02	0.01
2Q	**0.17**	**0.06**	0.07	-0.21	0.02	0.02
3Q	**E0.17**	**0.13**	0.04	0.03	0.03	0.02
4Q	**E0.18**	**0.06**	0.03	0.05	0.03	0.03
Yr.	**E0.66**	**0.33**	0.20	-0.08	0.11	0.07

Next earnings report expected: NA

Dividend Data (Dividends have been paid since 1982.)

Amount ($)	Date Decl.	Ex-Div. Date	Stock of Record	Payment Date
0.020	Feb. 10	Mar. 27	Mar. 31	Apr. 22 '98
2-for-1	May. 12	Jun. 10	May. 27	Jun. 09 '98
0.020	May. 12	Jun. 26	Jun. 30	Jul. 21 '98
0.020	Aug. 11	Sep. 28	Sep. 30	Oct. 21 '98

A Division of The McGraw-Hill Companies

STANDARD
&POOR'S
STOCK REPORTS

HBO & Company

4071

12-SEP-98

Business Summary - 15-JUL-98

Health care service providers and insurers have tuned into HBO in increasing numbers. No, we're not referring to the famed pay-TV service. HBO & Co. (Nasdaq: HBOC), which is not at all related to the cable network, has developed computer-based information systems tailored to manage the complex requirements of today's health care service providers and payers. HBOC's offerings help keep track of patient records through the disparate locations in which healthcare services are provided. In addition, its products and services address the increasing information needs of employers, insurance companies and government agencies as they seek data regarding the delivery and cost of health care services.

HBOC provides products and services in three distinct segments: software (36% of 1997 revenues; 34% in 1996), hardware (15%; 16%) and services (49%; 50%).

Software products consist of applications for several areas of information access and delivery: acute-care (hospital), infrastructure, and community health, clinical, practice, access, resource and enterprise management.

HBOC offers installation and implementation services for these software products. It also offers software maintenance and enhancement services, as well as custom programming and system modifications to meet special customer requirements.

The company's customers include integrated delivery networks, managed care organizations, physician practices and clinics, payors (insurance companies, HMOs, PPOs, etc.), home health agencies and hospitals. As of December 31, 1997, HBOC serves more than 9,000 customers worldwide (96% in North America; 4% international). One or more of the company's products are installed in approximately 52% of the community hospitals in the U.S.

The company continues to make strategic acquisitions to bolster its presence in niche areas. HBOC made five acquisitions in 1997, including AMISYS Managed Care Systems Inc. (June), Enterprise Systems Inc. (June), AT&T's UK Specialist Healthcare Services division (October), HPR Inc. (December), and National Health Enhancement Systems, Inc. (December).

Per Share Data ($)

(Year Ended Dec. 31)	1997	1996	1995	1994	1993	1992	1991	1990	1989	1988
Tangible Bk. Val.	1.72	0.96	0.42	0.13	0.21	0.17	0.10	0.12	0.14	0.12
Cash Flow	0.48	0.33	0.02	0.15	0.10	0.08	0.03	0.08	0.11	0.11
Earnings	0.34	0.20	-0.09	0.11	0.07	0.05	-0.01	0.03	0.06	0.05
Dividends	0.03	0.02	0.02	0.02	0.02	0.02	0.02	0.02	0.02	0.02
Payout Ratio	9%	7%	11%	19%	25%	34%	NM	60%	30%	36%
Prices - High	24³/₈	18¹/₈	10⁷/₈	4⁵/₈	2⁷/₈	1⁵/₈	³/₄	¹⁵/₁₆	1¹/₁₆	³/₄
- Low	10⁵/₈	8¹/₄	4¹/₈	2³/₈	1¹/₁₆	⁵/₈	⁵/₁₆	¹/₄	⁹/₁₆	³/₈
P/E Ratio - High	73	61	60	43	39	30	NM	30	17	14
- Low	32	28	23	22	14	11	NM	8	9	7

Income Statement Analysis (Million $)

	1997	1996	1995	1994	1993	1992	1991	1990	1989	1988
Revs.	1,203	797	496	327	237	202	171	201	204	187
Oper. Inc.	380	229	126	59.9	37.3	26.1	17.9	27.4	37.6	35.6
Depr.	62.4	49.2	30.2	11.9	6.1	5.7	10.2	12.0	12.5	14.5
Int. Exp.	Nil	Nil	NA	NA	1.5	1.2	2.3	3.4	2.4	2.9
Pretax Inc.	239	122	-42.0	47.0	30.5	19.9	-4.3	10.7	23.5	19.0
Eff. Tax Rate	40%	40%	NM	40%	40%	34%	NM	33%	34%	34%
Net Inc.	144	74.0	-25.2	28.2	18.3	13.1	-2.9	7.1	15.5	12.5

Balance Sheet & Other Fin. Data (Million $)

	1997	1996	1995	1994	1993	1992	1991	1990	1989	1988
Cash	432	160	65.3	5.8	23.2	7.6	2.7	2.3	4.7	4.5
Curr. Assets	924	520	252	123	73.2	69.2	70.7	70.2	58.1	44.3
Total Assets	1,313	849	535	234	119	103	103	123	114	101
Curr. Liab.	405	316	205	131	59.6	54.6	53.2	51.0	63.0	49.8
LT Debt	1.0	0.2	0.6	Nil	Nil	Nil	20.0	37.5	6.8	10.0
Common Eqty.	901	525	319	91.5	50.0	40.8	22.6	26.7	32.5	28.5
Total Cap.	902	525	320	101	59.0	48.0	50.0	72.0	51.0	51.0
Cap. Exp.	63.1	20.8	11.2	5.7	8.6	4.4	6.4	10.6	7.6	13.4
Cash Flow	206	123	5.0	40.1	24.4	18.8	7.3	19.1	28.0	27.0
Curr. Ratio	2.3	1.6	1.2	0.9	1.2	1.3	1.3	1.4	0.9	0.9
% LT Debt of Cap.	0.1	Nil	0.2	Nil	Nil	Nil	40.0	52.0	13.3	19.7
% Net Inc.of Revs.	11.9	9.3	NM	8.6	7.7	6.5	NM	3.5	7.6	6.7
% Ret. on Assets	13.3	9.9	NM	15.6	16.7	12.3	NM	6.2	14.6	12.3
% Ret. on Equity	20.1	15.8	NM	38.8	40.8	40.4	NM	24.9	51.6	52.0

Data as orig. reptd.; bef. results of disc. opers. and/or spec. items. Per share data adj. for stk. divs. as of ex-div. date. Bold denotes diluted EPS (FASB 128). E-Estimated. NA-Not Available. NM-Not Meaningful. NR-Not Ranked.

Office—301 Perimeter Center North, Atlanta, GA 30346. **Tel**—(770) 393-6000. **Website**—http://www.hboc.com **Chrmn**—H. T. Green, Jr. **Pres & CEO**—C. W. McCall. **SVP-Fin & CFO**—J. P. Gilbertson. **VP & Secy**—J. M. Lapine. **Investor Contact**—Beth Dalton. **Dirs**— A. C. Eckert III, H. T. Green, Jr., P. A. Incarnati, A. F. Irby III, G. E. Mayo, C. W. McCall, J. V. Napier, C. E. Thoele, D. Wegmiller. **Transfer Agent & Registrar**—Trust Co. Bank, Atlanta. **Incorporated**—in Delaware in 1974. **Empl**— 6,300. **S&P Analyst:** Brian Goodstadt

12-SEP-98

Industry:
Health Care
(Long-Term Care)

Summary: Healthsouth is the largest provider of outpatient surgery and rehabilitation services in the U.S..

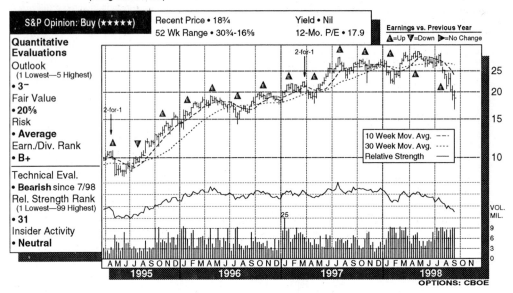

S&P Opinion: Buy (★★★★)	Recent Price • 18¾	Yield • Nil	**Earnings vs. Previous Year**
	52 Wk Range • 30¾-16⅝	12-Mo. P/E • 17.9	▲=Up ▼=Down ▶=No Change

Quantitative Evaluations

Outlook
(1 Lowest—5 Highest)
• **3⁻**

Fair Value
• **20⅝**

Risk
• **Average**

Earn./Div. Rank
• **B+**

Technical Eval.
• **Bearish** since 7/98

Rel. Strength Rank
(1 Lowest—99 Highest)
• **31**

Insider Activity
• **Neutral**

2-for-1

10 Week Mov. Avg. — - —
30 Week Mov. Avg. - - - -
Relative Strength ——

VOL. MIL.

OPTIONS: CBOE

Overview - 23-JUL-98

Following HRC's recent acquisition of 34 outpatient surgery centers from Columbia/HCA, and with the inclusion of National Surgery Centers Inc. (acquired in July 1998), strong internal growth in the existing base of rehabilitative and outpatient surgery facilities, and greater penetration of markets such as occupational medicine and diagnostic imaging, we see 1998 revenues approaching $4 billion. The company has clearly established itself as the dominant U.S. provider of outpatient rehab and surgery services, with facilities in all 50 states. Operating margins will continue to benefit from HRC's extensive network and ability to smoothly absorb acquisitions, and EBITDA margins should approach 34% in 1998. We look for 1998 EPS to rise about 32%, to $1.20. Our 1999 estimate remains at $1.50, before an expected upward adjustment for the National Surgery transaction.

Valuation - 23-JUL-98

We remain bullish on the stock, and feel that HRC represents one of the more compelling investments in the healthcare services group. Including expected accretion from the purchase of outpatient facilities from Columbia/HCA, we see 1998 EPS at $1.20. Assuming some accretion from the National Surgery purchase, we expect to revise our 1999 projection upward about 5%, but need more details about the integration process before making specific adjustments. Based on HRC's bright earnings prospects, relatively low Medicare exposure, and strong cash flow generation, we continue to view the stock as underpriced, and believe that it will significantly outperform the S&P 500 during the second half of 1998. Assuming that the P/E moves toward our projected long-term EPS growth target, we have a nine-month price target of $34 to $35.

Key Stock Statistics

S&P EPS Est. 1998	1.20	Tang. Bk. Value/Share	2.77
P/E on S&P Est. 1998	15.6	Beta	1.46
S&P EPS Est. 1999	1.50	Shareholders	3,700
Dividend Rate/Share	Nil	Market cap. (B)	$ 7.9
Shs. outstg. (M)	422.6	Inst. holdings	77%
Avg. daily vol. (M)	1.804		

Value of $10,000 invested 5 years ago: $ 28,436

Fiscal Year Ending Dec. 31

	1998	1997	1996	1995	1994	1993
Revenues (Million $)						
1Q	907.7	691.6	581.2	347.4	231.3	116.2
2Q	942.5	723.0	595.6	390.0	247.4	119.6
3Q	—	748.4	616.9	402.2	261.1	121.3
4Q	—	854.3	642.8	417.1	301.6	125.3
Yr.	—	3,017	2,437	1,557	1,127	482.3
Earnings Per Share ($)						
1Q	**0.27**	0.19	0.12	0.12	0.10	0.08
2Q	**0.28**	0.23	0.18	-0.01	0.10	0.08
3Q	**E0.32**	0.24	0.18	0.15	0.11	0.08
4Q	**E0.33**	0.25	0.19	0.17	0.05	-0.17
Yr.	**E1.20**	0.91	0.68	0.42	0.35	0.06

Next earnings report expected: late October

Dividend Data

No cash dividends have been paid. A two-for-one stock split was effected in march 1997.

A Division of The McGraw-Hill Companies

Business Summary - 23-JUL-98

Driven by its visionary leader, Richard Scrushy, Healthsouth Corp. has grown from its humble origins as a provider of orthopaedic and musculoskelatal rehabilitation services on an outpatient basis, to the largest U.S. provider of outpatient surgery and rehabilitative healthcare services. At 1997 year-end, HRC had more than 1,750 patient locations in 50 states, the U.K., and Australia. By payor source, revenues in 1997 came from Medicare (37%), commercial insurance or managed care (35%), workers' compensation (11%) and other (17%).

The company operates the largest group of affiliated proprietary outpatient rehabilitation facilities in the U.S., offering a range of services, including physical and occupational therapy, with a primary focus on orthopedic injuries, sports injuries, work injuries, hand and upper extremity injuries, back injuries and various neurological/neuromuscular conditions. At December 31, 1997, services were provided through 1,150 locations, including freestanding outpatient centers and their satellites, outpatient satellites of inpatient facilities and outpatient facilities managed under contract.

At 1997 year-end, HRC operated 132 inpatient rehabilitation facilities with a total of 7,682 beds, representing the largest group of affiliated proprietary inpatient rehabilitation sites in the U.S. It also operated a 71-bed rehabilitation hospital in Australia. The facilities provide medical, nursing, therapy and ancillary services to patients suffering significant physical disabilities due to various conditions such as head injury, spinal cord injury, stroke, certain orthopedic problems and neuromuscular disease.

As an outgrowth of its rehabilitative healthcare services business, HRC has acquired medical centers in certain markets in which it already had a presence. As of December 31, 1997, it operated four medical centers with 800 licensed beds which provide general and specialty medical and surgical healthcare services, emphasizing orthopaedics, sports medicine and rehabilitation.

Largely as a result of an aggressive acquisition program in recent years, Healthsouth is also the largest operator of outpatient surgery centers in the U.S., with 172 freestanding surgery centers, including five mobile lithotripsy units, in 35 states. More than 80% of these facilities are located in markets served by the company's outpatient and rehabilitative service facilities, allowing HRC to generate significant cross-selling opportunities and to centralize administrative functions.

One of the areas targeted for future growth is diagnostic imaging, where the company provides outpatient diagnostic imaging services such as magnetic resonance imaging (MRI), X-ray, ultrasound, mammography, nuclear medicine and flouroscopy. At 1997 year-end, HRC operated 101 diagnostic centers in 21 states and the U.K.

Per Share Data ($) (Year Ended Dec. 31)	1997	1996	1995	1994	1993	1992	1991	1990	1989	1988
Tangible Bk. Val.	2.31	1.46	1.03	3.12	2.54	2.52	2.49	1.68	1.07	0.95
Cash Flow	1.59	1.26	0.80	0.85	0.36	0.41	0.32	0.29	0.20	0.14
Earnings	0.91	0.67	0.41	0.35	0.06	0.25	0.21	0.18	0.13	0.09
Dividends	Nil	Nil	Nil	Nil	Nil	Nil	Nil	Nil	Nil	Nil
Payout Ratio	Nil	Nil	Nil	Nil	Nil	Nil	Nil	Nil	Nil	Nil
Prices - High	$28\frac{7}{8}$	$19\frac{7}{8}$	$16\frac{1}{4}$	$9\frac{7}{8}$	$6\frac{5}{8}$	$9\frac{3}{8}$	$8\frac{3}{4}$	$4\frac{1}{4}$	$3\frac{1}{4}$	$2\frac{5}{16}$
- Low	$17\frac{3}{4}$	$13\frac{1}{2}$	$8\frac{1}{4}$	$5\frac{7}{8}$	3	$3\frac{7}{8}$	$3\frac{5}{8}$	$2\frac{5}{16}$	$1\frac{9}{16}$	$1\frac{5}{16}$
P/E Ratio - High	32	30	39	28	NM	37	41	24	25	25
- Low	20	20	20	17	NM	15	17	13	12	14
Income Statement Analysis (Million $)										
Revs.	3,017	2,437	1,557	1,127	482	407	225	180	114	75.0
Oper. Inc.	975	730	537	234	107	75.6	50.3	36.5	21.9	14.8
Depr.	250	189	143	75.6	36.5	18.9	10.5	8.0	4.9	3.1
Int. Exp.	112	97.3	102	59.0	15.1	12.8	11.9	12.4	8.6	4.3
Pretax Inc.	602	270	212	87.3	10.9	46.5	35.4	21.1	13.0	9.8
Eff. Tax Rate	34%	34%	36%	39%	37%	33%	33%	34%	34%	33%
Net Inc.	331	221	92.5	53.2	6.7	29.7	22.4	12.9	8.1	5.7
Balance Sheet & Other Fin. Data (Million $)										
Cash	148	152	156	83.0	62.0	86.0	107	71.0	32.0	18.0
Curr. Assets	1,083	848	704	396	262	213	185	128	87.0	52.0
Total Assets	5,401	3,372	2,230	1,552	1,168	642	472	301	219	134
Curr. Liab.	516	304	297	177	90.1	42.4	19.9	17.2	14.9	13.8
LT Debt	1,555	1,451	1,356	930	780	300	164	150	133	57.0
Common Eqty.	3,157	1,516	1,186	426	295	290	279	128	66.0	57.0
Total Cap.	4,883	3,065	2,624	1,362	1,078	599	444	279	200	117
Cap. Exp.	346	173	172	124	111	133	104	39.0	43.0	22.0
Cash Flow	581	410	236	129	43.2	48.7	32.8	20.9	13.0	8.9
Curr. Ratio	2.1	2.8	2.0	2.2	2.9	5.0	9.3	7.4	5.8	3.8
% LT Debt of Cap.	31.9	47.3	51.7	68.3	72.3	50.0	37.0	53.7	66.3	49.2
% Net Inc.of Revs.	11.0	9.1	4.6	4.7	1.4	7.3	9.9	7.2	7.1	7.6
% Ret. on Assets	7.5	7.0	3.6	3.6	0.7	5.3	4.9	4.5	4.6	4.9
% Ret. on Equity	14.1	16.3	9.5	13.8	2.3	10.3	9.6	12.3	13.1	10.5

Data as orig. reptd.; bef. results of disc. opers. and/or spec. items. Per share data adj. for stk. divs. as of ex-div. date. Bold denotes diluted EPS (FASB 128). E-Estimated. NA-Not Available. NM-Not Meaningful. NR-Not Ranked.

Office—Two Perimeter Park South, Birmingham, AL 35243. **Tel**—(205) 967-7116. **Website**—http://www.healthsouth.com **Chrmn & CEO**—R. M. Scrushy. **Pres & COO**—J. P. Bennett. **EVP, CFO & Treas**—M. D. Martin. **EVP & Secy**—A. J. Tanner. **Dirs**—J. P. Bennett, P. D. Brown, J. S. Chamberlin, C. S. Givens, J. C. Gordon, L. R. House, M. D. Martin, C. W. Newhall III, R. M. Scrushy, G. H. Strong, A. J. Tanner, P. C. Watkins. **Transfer Agent & Registrar**—Chase Bank, NYC. **Incorporated**—in Delaware in 1984. **Empl**— 56,281. **S&P Analyst:** Robert M. Gold

Heinz (H.J.)

1126M

NYSE Symbol **HNZ**

In S&P 500

12-SEP-98

Industry: Foods

Summary: H.J. Heinz Co. produces a wide variety of food products worldwide, with major presence in the U.S. in condiments, canned tuna, pet food and frozen potatoes and meals.

S&P Opinion: Hold (★★★)	Recent Price • 55	Yield • 2.5%
	52 Wk Range • 59⅞-43⅜	12-Mo. P/E • 26.4

Quantitative Evaluations

Outlook (1 Lowest—5 Highest)
• **1+**

Fair Value
• **42¾**

Risk
• **Low**

Earn./Div. Rank
• **A**

Technical Eval.
• **Bearish** since 1/97

Rel. Strength Rank (1 Lowest—99 Highest)
• **92**

Insider Activity
• **Favorable**

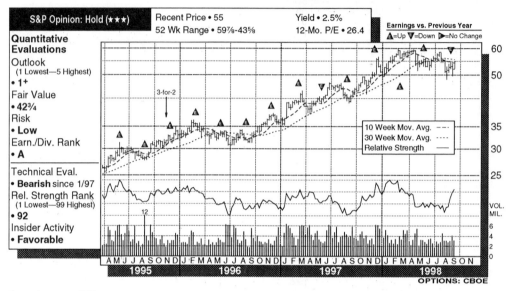

Earnings vs. Previous Year
▲=Up ▼=Down ▶=No Change

10 Week Mov. Avg. – – –
30 Week Mov. Avg. ······
Relative Strength ——

OPTIONS: CBOE

Overview - 17-JUN-98

Sales through FY 99 (Apr.) are expected to rise only modestly, as broad-based unit volume growth for continuing operations is offset by recent divestitures and possible unfavorable currency exchange translations. Operating margins are expected to widen as a result of an improved sales mix and from the anticipated cost savings accruing from facility consolidations and employee reductions announced in March 1997. Net interest expense comparisons will ease as acquisition-related debt is paid down. Favorable tax legislation in Italy and the United Kingdom may allow for an easing in the effective tax rate near term. In all, we anticipate earnings per share of $2.40 in FY 99, up nearly 12% from FY 98's $2.15 (excluding special items).

Valuation - 17-JUN-98

In March 1997, management launched its largest-ever reorganization plan, designed to strengthen the company's six core businesses and improve its profitability and global growth. This is to be accomplished by a combination of non-strategic business and other asset divestments, the closure or sale of at least 25 of its 104 plants around the world, and the elimination of about 6% of its 43,000 person work force. The company believes that the moves will yield pretax savings of some $120 million in FY 98 (and $200 million in FY 99 and beyond), which will allow greater marketing spending and increased cash flow. While still in the early stages of implementation, we expect these actions to support the company's goal to increase EPS by 10% to 12% annually over the next few years. However, at a recent 23 times our FY 99 EPS estimate of $2.40, the shares trade at par to other leading consumer staples companies and appear to be poised only for near-term market performance.

Key Stock Statistics

S&P EPS Est. 1999	2.40	Tang. Bk. Value/Share	NM
P/E on S&P Est. 1999	22.9	Beta	0.70
S&P EPS Est. 2000	2.60	Shareholders	59,400
Dividend Rate/Share	1.37	Market cap. (B)	$ 19.9
Shs. outstg. (M)	362.1	Inst. holdings	60%
Avg. daily vol. (M)	0.667		

Value of $10,000 invested 5 years ago: $ 22,276

Fiscal Year Ending Apr. 30

	1999	1998	1997	1996	1995	1994
Revenues (Million $)						
1Q	2,228	2,233	2,209	2,094	1,736	1,583
2Q	—	2,264	2,394	2,288	1,975	1,808
3Q	—	2,236	2,308	2,193	1,954	1,710
4Q	—	2,476	2,447	2,537	2,421	1,945
Yr.	—	9,209	9,357	9,112	8,087	7,047
Earnings Per Share ($)						
1Q	**0.58**	0.65	0.48	0.46	0.41	0.39
2Q	—	0.51	0.47	0.42	0.37	0.50
3Q	—	**0.50**	0.47	0.42	0.37	0.33
4Q	—	**0.49**	-0.61	0.45	0.43	0.34
Yr.	—	**2.15**	0.81	1.75	1.59	1.57

Next earnings report expected: early December

Dividend Data (Dividends have been paid since 1911.)

Amount ($)	Date Decl.	Ex-Div. Date	Stock of Record	Payment Date
0.315	Dec. 02	Dec. 17	Dec. 19	Jan. 10 '98
0.315	Mar. 11	Mar. 19	Mar. 23	Apr. 10 '98
0.315	Jun. 10	Jun. 18	Jun. 22	Jul. 10 '98
0.343	Sep. 08	Sep. 17	Sep. 21	Oct. 10 '98

A Division of The McGraw·Hill Companies

STANDARD
&POOR'S
STOCK REPORTS

H.J. Heinz Company

1126M
12-SEP-98

Business Summary - 17-JUN-98

Although largely known for its familiar ketchup, H.J. Heinz boasts many other branded food products, ranging from StarKist tuna to Weight Watchers frozen dinners, that are consumed by millions of people every day. The company's current operating strategy rests upon three pillars: renewed focus on core competencies, acquisitions, and cost control. Sales are geographically broadly based, with contributions by major region derived in FY 97 (Apr.) as follows:

	Sales	Profits
North America	60%	28%
Europe	24%	42%
Asia/Pacific	12%	22%
Other	4%	8%

The company is looking to increase its leadership, both through internal growth and via acquisitions, in six core businesses around the world: foodservice, baby foods, ketchup and condiments, pet food, tuna and weight control. In particular, developing international markets should provide significant opportunities for Heinz's portfolio of consumer products. Its stable of products already includes 26 global brands with annual sales of $100 million or more. The company also indicated recently that it would rid itself of non-core operations that do not fit well with this strategy.

The company's extensive product line includes Heinz-brand ketchup, sauces and other condiments (18% of FY 97 sales); pet food (13%), with products such as 9Lives cat food, Kibbles N' Bits and Ken-L-Ration dog food, Jerky Treats and Meat Bones dog snacks; StarKist tuna and other seafood products; lower-calorie products (Weight Watchers frozen entrees and desserts); soup (Chef Francisco); sauces/pastes, condiments and pickles, beans full-calorie frozen entrees, and many other related food products.

HNZ also operates and franchises weight control classes, and operates other related programs and activities through its Weight Watchers International subsidiary. Although the entire domestic weight-loss industry continues to exhibit weakness, the U.S. market share of the Weight Watchers meetings program exceeds 50%. As a result of an improved cost structure and an established infrastructure, Weight Watchers meeting operations would benefit if the percentage of dieters using weight-loss services increases.

Per Share Data ($)

(Year Ended Apr. 30)	1998	1997	1996	1995	1994	1993	1992	1991	1990	1989
Tangible Bk. Val.	NM	0.02	0.87	0.34	2.67	2.49	3.11	3.92	3.26	3.04
Cash Flow	2.99	1.72	2.66	2.43	2.21	1.95	2.13	1.91	1.69	1.48
Earnings	2.15	0.81	1.75	1.59	1.57	1.36	1.57	1.42	1.27	1.11
Dividends	1.24	1.14	1.03	0.94	0.86	0.78	0.70	0.62	0.54	0.46
Payout Ratio	57%	140%	59%	59%	55%	56%	42%	42%	41%	41%
Cal. Yrs.	1997	1996	1995	1994	1993	1992	1991	1990	1989	1988
Prices - High	56⅝	38⅜	34⅞	26	30⅛	30⅜	32⅜	24⅝	23⅞	16⅝
- Low	35¼	29¾	24¼	20½	22¾	23⅜	21	18⅜	15	12½
P/E Ratio - High	26	47	20	16	19	22	20	17	19	15
- Low	16	37	14	13	15	17	13	13	12	11

Income Statement Analysis (Million $)

Revs.	9,209	9,357	9,112	8,087	7,047	7,103	6,582	6,647	6,086	5,801
Oper. Inc.	1,834	1,096	1,631	1,471	1,189	1,285	1,097	1,230	1,087	949
Depr.	314	340	344	315	248	232	212	193	165	146
Int. Exp.	259	274	278	211	149	146	144	146	120	78.0
Pretax Inc.	1,255	479	1,024	938	922	716	984	903	811	725
Eff. Tax Rate	36%	37%	36%	37%	35%	26%	35%	37%	38%	39%
Net Inc.	802	302	659	591	603	530	638	568	504	440

Balance Sheet & Other Fin. Data (Million $)

Cash	96.0	189	108	207	142	224	273	314	241	238
Curr. Assets	2,687	3,013	3,047	2,823	2,292	2,623	2,280	2,120	2,014	1,775
Total Assets	8,023	8,438	8,624	8,247	6,381	6,821	5,932	4,935	4,487	4,002
Curr. Liab.	2,164	2,880	2,715	2,564	1,692	2,866	2,844	1,430	1,280	1,116
LT Debt	2,769	2,284	2,282	2,327	1,727	1,009	178	717	875	693
Common Eqty.	2,216	2,440	2,707	2,472	2,338	2,321	2,367	2,274	1,886	1,776
Total Cap.	5,276	4,989	5,308	5,148	4,314	3,526	2,881	3,337	3,072	2,752
Cap. Exp.	374	377	335	342	275	431	331	345	355	323
Cash Flow	1,116	642	1,003	906	850	762	850	761	669	586
Curr. Ratio	1.2	1.1	1.1	1.1	1.4	0.9	0.8	1.5	1.6	1.6
% LT Debt of Cap.	52.5	45.8	43.0	45.2	40.0	28.6	6.2	21.5	28.5	25.2
% Net Inc.of Revs.	8.7	3.2	7.2	7.3	8.6	7.5	9.7	8.5	8.3	7.6
% Ret. on Assets	9.7	3.5	7.8	8.1	9.2	8.3	11.9	11.9	12.0	11.5
% Ret. on Equity	34.5	11.7	25.4	24.6	26.2	22.6	27.8	27.0	27.7	26.0

Data as orig. reptd.; bef. results of disc. opers. and/or spec. items. Per share data adj. for stk. divs. as of ex-div. date. Bold denotes diluted EPS (FASB 128). E-Estimated. NA-Not Available. NM-Not Meaningful. NR-Not Ranked.

Office—600 Grant St., Pittsburgh, PA 15219. **Tel**—(412) 456-5700. **Chrmn & CEO**—A. J. F. O'Reilly. **Pres**—W. R. Johnson. **Vice Chrmn**—J. J. Bogdanovich. **EVP & CFO**—P. F. Renne. **Secy**—B. E. Thomas, Jr. **Dirs**—J. J. Bogdanovich, N. F. Brady, R. M. Cyert, T. S. Foley, E. E. Holiday, S. C. Johnson, W. R. Johnson, D. R. Keough, A. Lippert, L. J. McCabe, A. J. F. O'Reilly, P. F. Renne, L. Ribolla, H. J. Schmidt, E. B. Sheldon, W. P. Snyder III, W. C. Springer, S. D. Wiley, D. R. Williams.**Transfer Agent & Registrar**—ChaseMellon Shareholder Services, Ridgefield Park, NJ. **Incorporated**—in Pennsylvania in 1900. **Empl**— 44,700. **S&P Analyst:**   Richard Joy

Helmerich & Payne   1128

NYSE Symbol **HP**

In S&P 500

12-SEP-98

Industry:
Oil & Gas (Drilling & Equipment)

Summary: This leading contract driller in the U.S. and in Latin America is also engaged in the production of oil and natural gas.

S&P Opinion: Hold (★★★)	Recent Price • 21	Yield • 1.3%
	52 Wk Range • 45⅝-16⅛	12-Mo. P/E • 10.5

Earnings vs. Previous Year
▲=Up ▼=Down ▷=No Change

Quantitative Evaluations

Outlook
(1 Lowest—5 Highest)
• **4**

Fair Value
• **25⅝**

Risk
• **Average**

Earn./Div. Rank
• **B**

Technical Eval.
• **Neutral** since 5/98

Rel. Strength Rank
(1 Lowest—99 Highest)
• **87**

Insider Activity
• **Neutral**

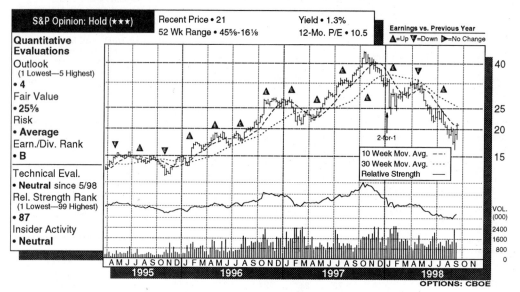

2-for-1

10 Week Mov. Avg. – – –
30 Week Mov. Avg. · · · · ·
Relative Strength ——

VOL.
(000)
2400
1600
800
0

1995 1996 1997 1998

OPTIONS: CBOE

Overview - 04-AUG-98

Improved utilization rates and higher dayrates for the company's rig fleet contributed to earnings gains in the first nine months of FY 98 (Sep.). However, lower oil and gas prices hampered exploration and production earnings. Due to the recent deterioration of commodity prices, there has been some softening in onshore drilling markets, both in the U.S. and abroad, but the long term supply/demand picture for drilling rigs is still favorable. The company is highly leveraged to natural gas markets, where robust demand should keep prices north of $2.00 per Mcf in 1998. Near-term natural gas price fundamentals still look healthy, with lower than normal storage levels, and increased demand from storage owners and electric utilities. However, average crude oil and natural gas price realizations should be somewhat lower in FY 98. HP has a strong balance sheet, with no long term debt, and a $258 million investment securities portfolio that could be used to fund its FY 98 and FY 99 capital budgets.

Valuation - 04-AUG-98

Like those of HP's industry peers, the company's shares have slumped since last fall, as oil prices have retreated amid a worldwide oversupply. This has led to a decline in drilling activity, and drilling contractors, particularly those operating land rigs, are beginning to feel the pinch. Dayrates are beginning to weaken, and we expect further declines in onshore dayrates over the rest of 1998. In addition, Venezuela, a major operating area for HP, and once considered the world's hottest land drilling market, is experiencing some decline in drilling activity, reflecting cutbacks in government spending. Given the deteriorating industry fundamentals, we maintain our neutral opinion on the shares, despite HP's positive long-term outlook.

Key Stock Statistics

S&P EPS Est. 1998	2.10	Tang. Bk. Value/Share	16.47
P/E on S&P Est. 1998	10.0	Beta	1.02
S&P EPS Est. 1999	2.50	Shareholders	1,500
Dividend Rate/Share	0.28	Market cap. (B)	$ 1.1
Shs. outstg. (M)	50.3	Inst. holdings	67%
Avg. daily vol. (M)	0.327		

Value of $10,000 invested 5 years ago: $ 18,537

Fiscal Year Ending Sep. 30

	1998	1997	1996	1995	1994	1993
Revenues (Million $)						
1Q	151.8	118.3	88.43	79.94	82.19	83.00
2Q	142.4	132.5	95.21	79.30	87.88	83.35
3Q	177.1	129.8	101.4	78.76	78.70	73.61
4Q	—	137.3	108.3	87.78	80.23	75.14
Yr.	—	517.9	387.5	325.8	329.0	315.1
Earnings Per Share ($)						
1Q	**0.58**	0.41	0.19	0.09	0.15	0.15
2Q	**0.38**	0.45	0.20	0.12	0.13	0.15
3Q	**0.67**	0.47	0.26	0.10	0.06	0.10
4Q	—	0.36	0.28	-0.10	0.09	0.10
Yr.	**E2.10**	1.69	0.92	0.20	0.43	0.51

Next earnings report expected: early November

Dividend Data (Dividends have been paid since 1959.)

Amount ($)	Date Decl.	Ex-Div. Date	Stock of Record	Payment Date
0.070	Dec. 03	Feb. 11	Feb. 13	Mar. 02 '98
0.070	Mar. 04	May. 13	May. 15	Jun. 01 '98
0.070	Jun. 03	Aug. 12	Aug. 14	Sep. 01 '98
0.070	Sep. 02	Nov. 10	Nov. 13	Dec. 01 '98

Business Summary - 04-AUG-98

While the booming offshore market has grabbed most of the oil and gas drilling industry's recent headlines, the land drilling segment has also shown significant improvement in recent years, despite some recent weakness resulting from sharply lower oil prices. As one of the industry's leading land drillers, Helmerich & Payne (HP) has shared in the land market's bounty and believes it is well positioned to participate in the segment's continued improvement. The company is also involved in oil and gas exploration and production, natural gas marketing and real estate development, and has equity investments in other publicly held firms. The chemicals manufacturing division was sold in August 1996. Segment contributions in FY 97 (Sep.), with profits in millions, were:

	Revs.	Profits
Contract drilling	61%	$67.6
Oil/gas exploration & production	22%	57.9
Natural gas marketing	13%	3.4
Real estate	2%	5.6
Other	2%	-0.3

As of July 1998, HP's drilling segment had a fleet of 73 land rigs, of which 33 are located in the U.S. and 40 outside the U.S., primarily in Venezuela, as well as in Colombia, Bolivia, Ecuador and Peru. The company also participates in the offshore segment, with 11 off-

shore platform rigs. Nine of these rigs are located in the Gulf of Mexico; one is offshore California and another in South America. Average U.S. rig utilization rate in FY 97 was 88% (up from 82% in FY 96). International rig utilization averaged 91% in FY 97 (85%).

Oil and gas properties are in Louisiana, Kansas, Texas and Oklahoma. The company also explores in the Rocky Mountain area, New Mexico, Alabama, Florida, Michigan and Mississippi. Net oil production in FY 97 amounted to 2,700 bbl./day (b/d) (for an average sales price of $20.77 a bbl.), up from 2,218 b/d ($19.00 a bbl.) in FY 96. Net natural gas sales were 110,900 Mcf/d (for an average sales price of $2.23 Mcf), versus 94,617 Mcf/d ($1.75 Mcf). Proved developed oil reserves at September 30, 1997, were 5.8 million bbl., versus 6.4 million bbl. a year earlier. Gas reserves were 256.4 Bcf, down from 261.5 Bcf.

The chemical division, Natural Gas Odorizing, Inc., which makes warning odorants used in natural and liquefied gas, was sold to a subsidiary of Occidental Petroleum in August 1996. HP received about two million Occidental common shares in the transaction.

The company conducts natural gas marketing operations through its Helmerich & Payne Energy Services subsidiary. Helmerich & Payne Properties is one of the largest owners and managers of industrial and commercial real estate in Tulsa, OK. The company also held a portfolio of stocks valued at about $258 million as of June 30, 1998.

Per Share Data ($)

(Year Ended Sep. 30)	1997	1996	1995	1994	1993	1992	1991	1990	1989	1988
Tangible Bk. Val.	15.60	12.98	11.36	10.61	10.33	10.04	10.03	9.79	9.17	8.91
Cash Flow	3.13	2.13	1.77	1.67	1.58	1.25	1.33	1.92	1.36	1.21
Earnings	1.69	0.92	0.20	0.43	0.51	0.23	0.44	0.98	0.47	0.41
Dividends	0.26	0.25	0.25	0.24	0.24	0.23	0.23	0.22	0.21	0.20
Payout Ratio	15%	27%	125%	56%	48%	103%	53%	23%	45%	48%
Prices - High	45⁵/₈	27³/₈	15⁵/₈	15³/₄	18³/₄	14	14⁵/₈	18⁷/₈	17¹/₄	12⁷/₈
- Low	20³/₄	13¹/₂	12¹/₈	12³/₈	11¹/₈	9⁵/₈	9	12	10¹/₄	9¹/₂
P/E Ratio - High	27	30	78	36	37	62	33	19	37	31
- Low	12	15	61	29	22	43	20	12	22	23

Income Statement Analysis (Million $)

Revs.	506	387	315	323	306	230	190	199	151	139
Oper. Inc.	200	132	90.5	84.8	86.8	65.0	55.0	74.0	61.0	54.0
Depr.	71.7	59.4	77.1	60.4	52.6	49.6	43.1	45.3	43.3	38.0
Int. Exp.	4.2	0.7	0.4	0.4	0.9	0.6	0.4	1.1	5.9	6.3
Pretax Inc.	132	71.2	14.8	31.2	41.9	20.0	34.0	70.0	33.0	26.0
Eff. Tax Rate	34%	36%	34%	33%	41%	44%	37%	32%	30%	24%
Net Inc.	84.2	45.4	9.8	21.0	24.6	10.8	21.2	47.6	22.7	20.2

Balance Sheet & Other Fin. Data (Million $)

Cash	28.0	17.9	28.7	38.0	71.0	51.0	70.0	134	121	117
Curr. Assets	158	114	115	123	150	133	142	201	168	162
Total Assets	1,034	822	710	625	611	586	575	583	591	576
Curr. Liab.	95.2	62.6	69.6	46.7	46.4	35.9	34.0	53.9	53.9	26.5
LT Debt	Nil	Nil	Nil	Nil	3.6	8.0	6.0	6.0	49.0	71.0
Common Eqty.	781	646	562	524	509	493	491	479	443	431
Total Cap.	922	744	628	569	557	541	539	526	535	545
Cap. Exp.	162	110	111	103	50.6	81.0	99	41.0	56.0	50.0
Cash Flow	156	105	86.9	81.4	77.1	60.5	64.0	93.0	66.0	58.2
Curr. Ratio	1.7	1.8	1.7	2.6	3.2	3.7	4.2	3.7	3.1	6.1
% LT Debt of Cap.	Nil	Nil	Nil	Nil	0.6	1.5	1.1	1.1	9.2	13.0
% Net Inc.of Revs.	16.6	11.7	3.1	6.5	8.0	4.7	11.2	23.9	15.1	14.5
% Ret. on Assets	9.1	5.9	1.5	3.4	4.1	1.9	3.7	8.0	3.9	3.5
% Ret. on Equity	11.8	7.5	1.8	4.1	4.9	2.2	4.4	10.2	5.2	4.7

Data as orig. reptd.; bef. results of disc. opers. and/or spec. items. Per share data adj. for stk. divs. as of ex-div. date. Bold denotes diluted EPS (FASB 128). E-Estimated. NA-Not Available. NM-Not Meaningful. NR-Not Ranked.

Office—Utica at 21st St., Tulsa, OK 74114. **Tel**—(918) 742-5531. **Chrmn**—W. H. Helmerich III. **Pres & CEO**—H. Helmerich. **VP & Secy**—S. R. Mackey. **VP-Fin & Investor Contact**—Doug Fears.**Dirs**—W. L. Armstrong, G. A. Cox, G. S. Dotson, H. Helmerich, W. H. Helmerich III, L. F. Rooney III, G. A. Schaefer, J. D. Zeglis. **Transfer Agent & Registrar**—Liberty National Bank & Trust Co. of Oklahoma City.**Incorporated**—in Delaware in 1940.**Empl**— 3,627. **S&P Analyst:** Norman Rosenberg

STANDARD &POOR'S
STOCK REPORTS
Hercules Inc.
1130
NYSE Symbol **HPC**
In S&P 500

12-SEP-98

Industry: Chemicals (Specialty)

Summary: This producer of specialty chemicals plans to acquire BetzDearborn for a total of $3.1 billion in cash and assumption of debt.

S&P Opinion: Hold (★★★)	Recent Price • 28⅝	Yield • 3.8%
	52 Wk Range • 51⅝-24⅝	12-Mo. P/E • 11.4

Quantitative Evaluations

Outlook (1 Lowest—5 Highest)
• **2+**

Fair Value
• **28½**

Risk
• **Low**

Earn./Div. Rank
• **A-**

Technical Eval.
• **Bearish** since 5/98

Rel. Strength Rank (1 Lowest—99 Highest)
• **42**

Insider Activity
• **NA**

Earnings vs. Previous Year
▲=Up ▼=Down ▶=No Change

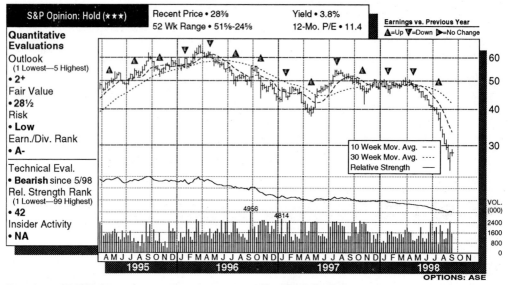

10 Week Mov. Avg. ----
30 Week Mov. Avg. ····
Relative Strength ——

4956 · 4814

VOL. (000)

OPTIONS: ASE

Overview - 07-AUG-98

On July 30, 1998, Hercules agreed to acquire BetzDearborn (BTL) for a total of about $2.4 billion plus the assumption of $700 million in BTL debt. This merger is part of HPC's strategy to more than double its sales by early next decade. Following the merger, which is planned for the fourth quarter of 1998, annual sales for HPC will be about $3.5 billion. The deal, which combines HPC's paper chemicals business with BTL's paper process chemicals operations, will make HPL the leading supplier of paper chemicals with sales of nearly $1 billion. BTL is also the second largest supplier of water treatment chemicals, adding a new business line for HPC. Hercules expects to achieve annual cost savings from the merger of over $100 million. Pro forma debt to capital ratio will climb to about 86%, and HPC has indicated that it could issue equity linked securities as part of the debt refinancing. The merger will be dilutive to earnings in 1999 and is projected to become accretive in the year 2000. We see sales growth for ongoing businesses in the mid-single digit range over the near term, boosted by recent small acquisitions and partly offset by the negative impact of the strong U.S. dollar and economic crisis in Asia. First quarter 1998 EPS included a $0.41 nonrecurring charge for litigation settlement.

Valuation - 07-AUG-98

After striking out three times, HPC has finally hit the big one with the proposed acquisition of BetzDearborn. While HPC is paying a 100% premium over BTL's closing price the day before the announcement, the multiple to cash flow is below other recent industry transactions. The merger is projected to be dilutive to EPS in 1999 before turning accretive in 2000. We remain neutral on the shares and would not recommend adding to current holdings.

Key Stock Statistics

S&P EPS Est. 1998	3.05	Tang. Bk. Value/Share	6.85
P/E on S&P Est. 1998	9.3	Beta	1.10
S&P EPS Est. 1999	3.25	Shareholders	20,300
Dividend Rate/Share	1.08	Market cap. (B)	$ 2.7
Shs. outstg. (M)	94.6	Inst. holdings	75%
Avg. daily vol. (M)	0.385		

Value of $10,000 invested 5 years ago: $ 15,153

Fiscal Year Ending Dec. 31

	1998	1997	1996	1995	1994	1993
Revenues (Million $)						
1Q	430.0	495.1	502.6	693.0	680.0	672.0
2Q	445.0	501.9	544.9	614.3	706.0	710.7
3Q	—	448.1	518.1	570.3	681.0	676.0
4Q	—	421.0	494.7	549.6	754.1	714.7
Yr.	—	1,866	2,060	2,427	2,821	2,773
Earnings Per Share ($)						
1Q	**0.29**	**1.03**	0.70	0.76	0.43	0.34
2Q	**0.77**	**0.73**	0.81	0.70	0.54	0.42
3Q	—	**0.81**	0.80	0.72	0.55	0.40
4Q	—	**0.61**	0.73	0.75	0.77	0.46
Yr.	—	**3.18**	3.04	2.93	2.29	1.62

Next earnings report expected: late October

Dividend Data (Dividends have been paid since 1913.)

Amount ($)	Date Decl.	Ex-Div. Date	Stock of Record	Payment Date
0.250	Oct. 24	Dec. 03	Dec. 05	Dec. 22 '97
0.270	Dec. 17	Mar. 04	Mar. 06	Mar. 25 '98
0.270	Apr. 30	Jun. 03	Jun. 05	Jun. 25 '98
0.270	Jul. 29	Sep. 02	Sep. 04	Sep. 25 '98

A Division of The McGraw·Hill Companies

Business Summary - 07-AUG-98

Hercules, after completing a portfolio and capital redeployment program that generated proceeds of over $1.5 billion, now has a vision to be a substantially larger company, with sales of $4 billion to $5 billion by early in the next decade. To achieve this vision, HPC intends to grow its core specialty chemicals businesses through both acquisitions and internal growth. In July 1998, HPC agreed to acquire BetzDearborn Inc. (BTL) for $2.4 billion plus assumption of $700 million in debt. BTL, with annual sales of $1.3 billion, is a leading supplier of water treatment (62% of total sales) and process treatment (38%) chemicals. After the acquisition, HPC will then have annual revenues of $3.5 billion. HPC also expects to increase the revenue contribution from new products to 30% (it was only 16% in 1997), while making significant productivity gains. Since 1990, HPC has repurchased more than 66 million common shares (46% of shares then outstanding) for $2.48 billion. Segment contributions in 1997 were:

	Sales	Profits
Chemical specialties	52%	31%
Food & functional products	48%	69%

International operations contributed 56% of sales and 84% of profits in 1997.

Specialty chemicals consist of paper chemicals (sizing agents, emulsions, defoamers) and resins (rosin and hydrocarbon resins, peroxides and cross-linkers used in adhesives, packaging, inks and toners, plastics, and rubbers; and terpene aroma chemicals for consumer products). In July 1998 HPC acquired the remaining 49% interest in a polypropylene fibers venture (annual sales of $300 million) formed in 1997 with the Danaklon Group of Jacob Holms & Sons A/S.

Food ingredients include food gums (the world's largest maker of pectin and agar, and the second largest producer of carrageenan), used in foods and beverages. Aqualon is HPC's largest business and a global leader in water-soluble polymers and coatings used in paints, adhesives, paper, personal care products, drugs, foods and beverages, inks and oil well drilling.

Over the five years through 2002, HPC expects capital spending to be about $700 million, or about 28% higher for the average year compared with the previous five-year period. Two major expansion projects are scheduled to be completed in 1998: hydrocarbon resins in the Netherlands, to bring worldwide annual hydrocarbon capacity to over 175,000 metric tons; and a carrageenan project in the Philippines, to produce 2,400 metric tons using new cost-saving technology. The latter project will replace existing capacity in Denmark and add 600 tons of annual capacity.

Per Share Data ($)

(Year Ended Dec. 31)	1997	1996	1995	1994	1993	1992	1991	1990	1989	1988
Tangible Bk. Val.	7.18	8.75	9.97	11.10	11.17	13.38	13.70	13.78	13.59	14.86
Cash Flow	3.88	4.03	3.98	3.52	2.94	2.48	1.91	2.00	2.17	1.85
Earnings	3.18	3.04	2.93	2.29	1.62	1.23	0.67	0.68	-0.70	0.85
Dividends	1.00	0.92	0.84	0.75	0.75	0.75	0.75	0.75	0.75	0.67
Payout Ratio	31%	30%	29%	32%	46%	61%	110%	110%	NM	76%
Prices - High	54½	66¼	62¼	40½	38¼	21¼	16¾	13⅞	17⅜	18
- Low	37¾	42¾	38¼	32⅛	21⅛	14⅞	10⅝	8½	12¾	14¼
P/E Ratio - High	17	22	21	18	24	17	25	20	NM	22
- Low	12	14	13	14	13	12	16	13	NM	17

Income Statement Analysis (Million $)

	1997	1996	1995	1994	1993	1992	1991	1990	1989	1988
Revs.	1,866	2,060	2,427	2,813	2,773	2,865	2,929	3,200	3,092	2,802
Oper. Inc.	466	528	531	578	564	503	455	433	383	300
Depr.	73.0	106	133	148	169	172	180	191	179	145
Int. Exp.	39.0	40.0	33.0	36.0	41.9	49.0	69.3	85.0	65.6	49.2
Pretax Inc.	593	485	505	408	305	256	166	163	-115	163
Eff. Tax Rate	45%	33%	34%	33%	32%	35%	43%	41%	NM	26%
Net Inc.	324	325	333	274	208	168	95.0	96.0	-96.0	120

Balance Sheet & Other Fin. Data (Million $)

	1997	1996	1995	1994	1993	1992	1991	1990	1989	1988
Cash	17.0	30.0	73.0	112	155	54.0	179	225	70.0	200
Curr. Assets	689	739	867	1,152	1,227	1,232	1,411	1,600	1,534	1,479
Total Assets	2,411	2,386	2,493	2,941	3,162	3,228	3,467	3,700	3,653	3,325
Curr. Liab.	799	694	687	767	884	757	764	908	918	529
LT Debt	799	345	298	307	317	431	483	601	576	429
Common Eqty.	690	887	1,082	1,295	1,368	1,746	1,918	1,942	1,897	2,045
Total Cap.	1,649	1,361	1,475	1,731	1,811	2,302	2,555	2,660	2,615	2,673
Cap. Exp.	119	120	117	164	149	150	214	272	293	251
Cash Flow	397	431	466	422	378	340	275	287	300	267
Curr. Ratio	0.9	1.1	1.3	1.5	1.4	1.6	1.8	1.8	1.7	2.8
% LT Debt of Cap.	48.5	25.3	20.2	17.7	17.5	18.7	18.9	22.6	22.0	16.0
% Net Inc.of Revs.	17.4	15.8	13.7	9.7	7.5	5.9	3.2	3.0	NM	4.3
% Ret. on Assets	13.5	13.3	12.3	9.2	6.7	5.2	2.7	2.6	NM	3.6
% Ret. on Equity	41.1	32.9	28.0	21.1	13.9	9.5	4.9	5.0	NM	5.9

Data as orig. reptd.; bef. results of disc. opers. and/or spec. items. Per share data adj. for stk. divs. as of ex-div. date. Bold denotes diluted EPS (FASB 128). E-Estimated. NA-Not Available. NM-Not Meaningful. NR-Not Ranked.

Office—Hercules Plaza, 1313 N. Market St., Wilmington, DE 19894-0001. **Tel**—(302) 594-5000. **Website**—http://www.herc.com **Chrmn & CEO**—R. K. Elliott. **Pres**—V. J. Corbo. **Secy**—I. J. Floyd. **Sr VP & CFO**—G. MacKenzie. **Treas**—J. M. King. **VP & Investor Contact**—Robert E. Gallant. **Dirs**—V. J. Corbo, R. K. Elliott, R. M. Fairbanks III, E. E. Holiday, R. G. Jahn, G. N. Kelley, R. L. MacDonald Jr., H. E. McBrayer, P. McCausland, P. A. Sneed. **Transfer Agents & Registrars**—ChaseMellon Shareholder Services, Ridgefield Park, NJ. **Incorporated**—in Delaware in 1912. **Empl**—6,221. **S&P Analyst:** Richard O'Reilly, CFA

STANDARD &POOR'S
STOCK REPORTS

Hershey Foods

1132

NYSE Symbol **HSY**

In S&P 500

12-SEP-98

Industry:
Foods

Summary: Hershey is the leading U.S. producer of chocolate and confectionery products. Through its Hershey Pasta Group, it is also the leading U.S. producer of dry pasta products.

S&P Opinion: Accumulate (★★★★)	Recent Price • 66⅜ Yield • 1.4% 52 Wk Range • 76⅜-50% 12-Mo. P/E • 28.7

Quantitative Evaluations

Outlook
(1 Lowest—5 Highest)
• **1+**

Fair Value
• **60½**

Risk
• **Low**

Earn./Div. Rank
• **A**

Technical Eval.
• **Bullish** since 8/98

Rel. Strength Rank
(1 Lowest—99 Highest)
• **88**

Insider Activity
• **NA**

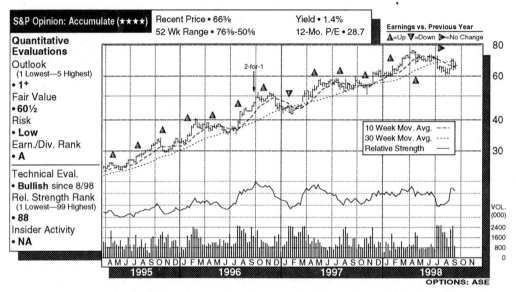

Earnings vs. Previous Year
▲=Up ▼=Down ▶=No Change

10 Week Mov. Avg. – – –
30 Week Mov. Avg. - - - -
Relative Strength ———

VOL. (000)

OPTIONS: ASE

Overview - 04-AUG-98

Sales are projected to rise by approximately 6% in 1998, led by unit volume growth for new (Classic Caramels, ReeseSticks) and existing confectionery products. Operating margins are expected to widen, led by efficiencies realized from the higher volumes and by the integration of the recently acquired Leaf North America operations. An easing in important raw material costs (milk, flour) may also help to offset the effects of increased marketing support behind new products, and a more aggressive promotional stance. With capital spending levels likely to rise only modestly over the next few years, significant levels of free cash will be available to repurchase shares on an ongoing basis. We anticipate that diluted EPS will increase nearly 10% in 1998, to $2.45 from 1997's $2.23. In 1999 and beyond, an approximate 12% to 15% rate of annual EPS growth is seen.

Valuation - 04-AUG-98

We lowered our recommendation on the shares in early July to accumulate, from buy, reflecting a reduction in our earnings growth expectations for 1998. The shares remain attractive, given the company's strengthening fundamentals and dominant position (34% U.S. market share) in the relatively high-margin, expanding, $12 billion U.S. confectionery market. In addition, a return to a mid-teen earnings growth rate and possible share repurchases are likely to keep the shares in favor amid a possible slowdown in U.S. economic growth in late 1998 and early 1999. Given continued competitive pressures facing the company's pasta operations (HSY is the leading U.S. producer), a spin-off of the unit is possible in 1998. The low-risk shares are suited for virtually all accounts.

Key Stock Statistics

S&P EPS Est. 1998	2.45	Tang. Bk. Value/Share	2.59
P/E on S&P Est. 1998	27.1	Beta	0.24
S&P EPS Est. 1999	2.80	Shareholders	42,300
Dividend Rate/Share	0.96	Market cap. (B)	$ 7.5
Shs. outstg. (M)	143.1	Inst. holdings	38%
Avg. daily vol. (M)	0.392		

Value of $10,000 invested 5 years ago: $ 31,557

Fiscal Year Ending Dec. 31

	1998	1997	1996	1995	1994	1993
Revenues (Million $)						
1Q	1,098	1,002	931.5	867.5	883.9	897.8
2Q	890.4	905.7	796.3	722.3	676.0	618.4
3Q	—	1,152	1,072	981.1	966.5	935.7
4Q	—	1,242	1,189	1,120	1,080	1,036
Yr.	—	4,302	3,989	3,691	3,606	3,488
Earnings Per Share ($)						
1Q	**0.52**	**0.45**	0.39	0.35	0.30	0.58
2Q	**0.33**	**0.33**	0.27	0.19	0.14	0.14
3Q	**E0.73**	**0.67**	0.61	0.51	0.47	0.41
4Q	**E0.87**	**0.80**	0.51	0.69	0.14	0.52
Yr.	**E2.45**	**2.23**	**1.75**	1.70	1.06	1.66

Next earnings report expected: late October

Dividend Data (Dividends have been paid since 1930.)

Amount ($)	Date Decl.	Ex-Div. Date	Stock of Record	Payment Date
0.220	Nov. 04	Nov. 19	Nov. 21	Dec. 15 '97
0.220	Feb. 03	Feb. 20	Feb. 24	Mar. 13 '98
0.220	Apr. 07	May. 20	May. 22	Jun. 15 '98
0.240	Aug. 04	Aug. 21	Aug. 25	Sep. 15 '98

A Division of The McGraw·Hill Companies

Business Summary - 04-AUG-98

Hershey Foods Corporation, primarily through its Hershey Chocolate U.S.A., Hershey International and Hershey Pasta Group divisions and its Hershey Canada Inc. subsidiary, produces and distributes a broad line of chocolate, confectionery, grocery and pasta products. Financial results over the past few years have strengthened, driven mainly by a rationalization of product lines that offered subpar investment returns, the integration of a number of complementary acquisitions, and an extraordinarily high rate of new product success.

The company makes chocolate and confectionery products in various packaged forms and markets them under more than 50 brands. Principal chocolate and confectionery products in the U.S. are: Hershey's, Hershey's with almonds, and Cookies 'N' Mint bars; Hugs and Kisses (both also with almonds) chocolates; Kit Kat wafer bars; Mr. Goodbar chocolate bars; Reese's Pieces candies; Rolo caramels in milk chocolate; Skor toffee bars; Y&S Twizzlers licorice; and Amazin' Fruit gummy bears fruit candy. HSY significantly increased its participation in the non-chocolate side of the confec-

tionery industry through its late 1996 acquisition of Leaf North America, whose major brands include Jolly Rancher, Whoppers, Milk Duds, and Good & Plenty. Grocery products include Hershey's chocolate chips, cocoa and syrup; and Reese's peanut butter and peanut butter chips. Hershey's chocolate milk is produced and sold under license by independent dairies throughout the U.S., using a chocolate milk mix manufactured by HSY. The most significant raw material used in the production of the company's chocolate and confectionery products is cocoa beans.

HSY also makes pasta products throughout most of the U.S. and markets its products on a regional basis under several brand names, including San Giorgio, Ronzoni, Skinner, P&R, Light 'n Fluffy and American Beauty.

The company has various international arrangements, the investment in which changes from time to time, but which in the aggregate are not material to HSY.

In September 1997, the dividend paid on the common stock was increased 10%, marking the 23rd consecutive annual increase.

Per Share Data ($)

(Year Ended Dec. 31)	1997	1996	1995	1994	1993	1992	1991	1990	1989	1988
Tangible Bk. Val.	2.11	3.89	4.24	5.70	5.36	5.91	5.07	4.58	4.13	3.52
Cash Flow	3.24	2.64	2.51	1.80	2.21	1.81	1.62	1.54	1.25	1.04
Earnings	2.23	1.77	1.70	1.06	1.66	1.34	1.22	1.20	0.95	0.80
Dividends	0.84	0.76	0.69	0.63	0.57	0.52	0.47	0.49	0.37	0.33
Payout Ratio	38%	43%	40%	59%	34%	38%	39%	41%	39%	41%
Prices - High	63⅞	51¾	34	26¾	28	24¼	22¼	19⅞	18½	14⅜
- Low	42⅛	32	24	20⅝	21¾	19⅛	17⅝	14⅛	12⅜	11
P/E Ratio - High	29	29	20	25	17	18	18	17	19	18
- Low	19	18	14	19	13	14	14	12	13	14

Income Statement Analysis (Million $)

	1997	1996	1995	1994	1993	1992	1991	1990	1989	1988
Revs.	4,302	3,989	3,691	3,606	3,488	3,220	2,899	2,716	2,421	2,168
Oper. Inc.	783	697	645	604	557	513	463	412	365	310
Depr.	153	133	134	129	100	84.4	72.7	61.7	54.5	43.7
Int. Exp.	79.1	53.6	50.0	40.3	34.9	41.8	39.7	32.2	30.1	35.4
Pretax Inc.	554	480	466	333	511	401	363	362	290	236
Eff. Tax Rate	39%	43%	40%	45%	42%	40%	40%	40%	41%	39%
Net Inc.	336	273	282	184	297	243	220	216	171	145

Balance Sheet & Other Fin. Data (Million $)

	1997	1996	1995	1994	1993	1992	1991	1990	1989	1988
Cash	54.2	61.4	32.0	27.0	16.0	203	71.0	27.0	52.0	70.0
Curr. Assets	1,035	986	922	949	889	940	744	662	568	619
Total Assets	3,291	3,185	2,831	2,891	2,855	2,673	2,342	2,079	1,814	1,765
Curr. Liab.	796	817	864	796	814	737	471	341	286	345
LT Debt	1,029	655	357	157	166	174	283	273	216	233
Common Eqty.	853	1,161	1,083	1,441	1,412	1,465	1,335	1,244	1,117	1,006
Total Cap.	2,149	2,040	1,632	1,792	1,751	1,843	1,790	1,671	1,475	1,371
Cap. Exp.	173	159	141	139	212	250	226	179	162	102
Cash Flow	489	407	416	313	397	327	292	278	226	188
Curr. Ratio	1.3	1.2	1.1	1.2	1.1	1.3	1.6	1.9	2.0	1.8
% LT Debt of Cap.	47.9	32.1	21.9	8.8	9.5	9.5	15.8	16.4	14.7	17.0
% Net Inc.of Revs.	7.8	6.9	7.6	5.1	8.5	7.5	7.6	7.9	7.1	6.7
% Ret. on Assets	10.4	9.1	9.9	6.4	10.9	9.7	9.9	11.1	9.6	8.5
% Ret. on Equity	33.4	24.4	22.3	13.0	21.0	17.3	17.0	18.3	16.1	15.7

Data as orig. reptd.; bef. results of disc. opers. and/or spec. items. Per share data adj. for stk. divs. as of ex-div. date. Bold denotes diluted EPS (FASB 128). E-Estimated. NA-Not Available. NM-Not Meaningful. NR-Not Ranked.

Office—100 Crystal A Drive, Hershey, PA 17033. **Tel**—(717) 534-6799. **Website**—http://www.hersheys.com **Chrmn & CEO**—K. L. Wolfe. **Pres**—J. P. Viviano. **SVP-Fin & Treas**—W. F. Christ. **Investor Contact**—James A. Edris. **Dirs**—W. H. Alexander, R. H. Campbell, C. McCollister Evarts, B. Guiton Hill, J. C. Jamison, M. J. McDonald, J. M. Pietruski, V. A. Sami, J. P. Viviano, K. L. Wolfe. **Transfer Agent & Registrar**—ChaseMellon Shareholder Services, Ridgefield Park, NJ. **Incorporated**—in Delaware in 1927. **Empl**— 14,900. **S&P Analyst:** Richard Joy

STANDARD &POOR'S
STOCK REPORTS

Hewlett-Packard

1137

NYSE Symbol **HWP**

In S&P 500

12-SEP-98

Industry: Computers (Hardware)

Summary: Hewlett-Packard is a leading manufacturer of computer products, including printers, servers, workstations and PCs. The company also offers a vast service and support network.

S&P Opinion: Hold (★★★)	

Recent Price • 50
52 Wk Range • 82⅜-47¾

Yield • 1.3%
12-Mo. P/E • 17.6

Quantitative Evaluations

Outlook
(1 Lowest—5 Highest)
• 1⁻

Fair Value
• 46¼

Risk
• Average

Earn./Div. Rank
• A

Technical Eval.
• **Bearish** since 6/98

Rel. Strength Rank
(1 Lowest—99 Highest)
• 62

Insider Activity
• NA

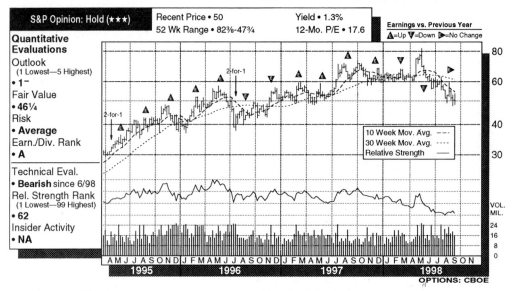

Earnings vs. Previous Year
▲=Up ▼=Down ▶=No Change

10 Week Mov. Avg. – – –
30 Week Mov. Avg. - - - -
Relative Strength —

2-for-1

VOL.
MIL.

OPTIONS: CBOE

Overview - 20-AUG-98

We recently reduced our revenue growth forecast for FY 98 (Oct.) to 11%, from 13%. While HP has been enjoying strength in its high-end servers, including the successful introduction of its V-class servers, this has been offset by cost competition in the personal computer (PC) and printer markets. Coupled with weakness in demand from Asia's financially distressed economies, HP has witnessed a substantial slowing in its typical revenue growth rate of roughly 15%. Gross margins pressures due to mix are likely to continue, as a greater proportion of sales is coming from less profitable PC and printer sales. In response, HP has targeted cost reductions to help maintain earnings growth. In fact, the company recently announced a goal of achieving operating expense growth rate roughly 10 percentage points below that of revenue growth for FY 99. A FY 98 fourth quarter restructuring charge of about $100 million is anticipated as part of this effort.

Valuation - 20-AUG-98

We continue to believe that the shares will perform in line with the overall stock market. While HP's strong product offerings give the company a healthy competitive position in the industry, pressure on margins from pricing pressures and the adverse impact of weak Asian markets and a strong U.S. dollar have reduced earnings visibility. For the long term, however, we believe that HP's results will reflect the benefits of its strong new product lineup and the company's steady market share gains. Moreover, the company's aggressive actions in asset management and supply chain and distribution programs bode well for these revenue gains to flow more easily to the bottom line. We believe that these long-term positive factors, coupled with HP's strong market position, make the shares worth holding.

Key Stock Statistics

S&P EPS Est. 1998	2.85	Tang. Bk. Value/Share	16.57
P/E on S&P Est. 1998	17.5	Beta	1.35
S&P EPS Est. 1999	3.65	Shareholders	92,100
Dividend Rate/Share	0.64	Market cap. (B)	$ 52.0
Shs. outstg. (M)	1039.5	Inst. holdings	49%
Avg. daily vol. (M)	3.869		

Value of $10,000 invested 5 years ago: $ 30,402

Fiscal Year Ending Oct. 31

	1998	1997	1996	1995	1994	1993
Revenues (Million $)						
1Q	11,816	10,295	9,288	7,304	5,682	4,573
2Q	12,040	10,340	9,880	7,428	6,254	5,096
3Q	10,979	10,471	9,105	7,739	6,053	4,961
4Q	—	11,789	10,147	9,048	7,002	5,687
Yr.	—	42,895	38,420	31,519	24,991	20,317
Earnings Per Share ($)						
1Q	**0.86**	0.87	0.75	0.57	0.35	0.26
2Q	**0.65**	0.75	0.69	0.55	0.39	0.34
3Q	**0.58**	0.58	0.40	0.55	0.33	0.27
4Q	**E0.76**	0.75	0.62	0.65	0.46	0.29
Yr.	**E2.85**	2.95	2.46	2.31	1.53	1.16

Next earnings report expected: mid November

Dividend Data (Dividends have been paid since 1965.)

Amount ($)	Date Decl.	Ex-Div. Date	Stock of Record	Payment Date
0.140	Nov. 21	Dec. 22	Dec. 24	Jan. 14 '98
0.140	Jan. 23	Mar. 23	Mar. 25	Apr. 15 '98
0.160	May. 15	Jun. 22	Jun. 24	Jul. 15 '98
0.160	Jul. 16	Sep. 21	Sep. 23	Oct. 14 '98

A Division of The McGraw-Hill Companies

Business Summary - 20-AUG-98

Hewlett-Packard's broad technology portfolio has served the company well: revenue growth has averaged nearly 20% during its past two fiscal years (Oct.). However, factors such as a strong U.S. dollar; greater competition in the printer market as well as in servers, workstations and personal computers (PCs); and seasonal weakness has resulted in a slowdown in revenue growth in recent reporting periods compared with stronger levels in years prior to FY 97. Industry market researchers rank HP among the top five vendors in the U.S. in terms of PC shipments, and as a leading global supplier of PC servers and workstations.

HP's computer business (roughly 83% of revenues) includes PCs, servers, workstations and printers. HP has a two-pronged strategy, with product offerings in competing UNIX and Windows NT markets. HP's computer lines include workstations and multiuser systems for both technical and commercial users; the HP Vectra series of IBM-compatible personal computers for businesses; and the HP Pavilion family of home computers. HWP's newest 9000 family of workstations and servers run on the 64-bit-PA-8000 Precision Architecture reduced instruction set computing (PA-RISC) microprocessors. HP is also codeveloping Intel's next generation 64-bit Merced chip, to be available in 1999.

HP is well known for its position in the printer market with its popular HP LaserJet and DeskJet families. There has been aggressive pricing from Lexmark in the printer market, but HWP still dominates, and has a series of new products planned. Printers and related products are roughly 35% of HWP sales.

HWP has begun consolidating its sales and channel management activities to focus on emerging markets to better capitalize on their growth. Specifically, in the area of electronic commerce, HWP has merged with Verifone in a $1.3 billion stock-for-stock deal to add to this capability, and it has stated that leveraging the power of the Internet will be the basis of its new products.

The company is well regarded for its service capabilities--it offers software programming services, network services, distributed systems services and data management services. Services contribute approximately 16% of HWP total revenues.

HP's diverse product line also includes electronic test and measurement devices (voltmeters and multimeters, counters, oscilloscopes and logic analyzers, signal generators and specialized communications test equipment); medical electronic equipment (monitoring systems); chemical analysis (gas and liquid chromatographs, mass spectrometers, spectrophotometers); and electronic components (microwave semiconductor and optoelectronic devices). These lines account for some 17% of HP's revenues.

Per Share Data ($)

(Year Ended Oct. 31)	1997	1996	1995	1994	1993	1992	1991	1990	1989	1988
Tangible Bk. Val.	15.52	13.25	11.61	9.22	7.80	6.86	7.22	6.52	5.30	4.84
Cash Flow	4.42	3.69	3.40	2.50	1.90	1.54	1.31	1.27	1.34	1.20
Earnings	2.95	2.46	2.31	1.53	1.16	0.87	0.76	0.77	0.88	0.84
Dividends	0.52	0.46	0.38	0.28	0.23	0.18	0.12	0.10	0.09	0.07
Payout Ratio	18%	19%	16%	18%	19%	21%	16%	14%	10%	8%
Prices - High	72⅞	57¾	48⅜	25⅝	22⅜	21¼	14⅜	12⅝	15⅜	16⅜
- Low	48⅛	36⅞	24½	18	16⅛	12⅝	7½	6¼	10⅛	11
P/E Ratio - High	25	23	21	17	19	24	19	16	17	19
- Low	16	15	11	12	14	14	10	8	11	13

Income Statement Analysis (Million $)

	1997	1996	1995	1994	1993	1992	1991	1990	1989	1988
Revs.	42,895	38,420	31,519	24,991	20,317	16,410	14,494	13,233	11,899	9,831
Oper. Inc.	5,895	5,023	4,707	3,555	2,622	2,183	1,890	1,650	1,630	1,572
Depr.	1,556	1,297	1,139	1,006	743	673	555	488	435	353
Int. Exp.	215	327	206	155	121	96.0	130	172	126	77.0
Pretax Inc.	4,445	3,694	3,632	2,423	1,783	1,325	1,127	1,056	1,151	1,142
Eff. Tax Rate	30%	30%	33%	34%	34%	34%	33%	30%	28%	29%
Net Inc.	3,119	2,586	2,433	1,599	1,177	881	755	739	829	816

Balance Sheet & Other Fin. Data (Million $)

	1997	1996	1995	1994	1993	1992	1991	1990	1989	1988
Cash	4,569	3,327	2,616	2,478	1,644	1,035	1,120	1,106	926	918
Curr. Assets	20,947	17,991	16,239	12,509	10,236	7,679	6,716	6,510	5,731	4,420
Total Assets	31,749	27,699	24,427	19,567	16,736	13,700	11,973	11,395	10,075	7,497
Curr. Liab.	11,219	10,623	10,944	8,230	6,868	5,094	4,063	4,443	3,743	2,570
LT Debt	3,158	2,579	663	547	667	425	188	139	474	61.0
Common Eqty.	16,155	13,438	11,839	9,926	8,511	7,499	7,269	6,363	5,446	4,533
Total Cap.	19,313	16,017	12,502	10,473	9,209	7,973	7,700	6,763	6,168	4,770
Cap. Exp.	2,338	2,201	1,601	1,257	1,489	1,032	862	955	915	648
Cash Flow	4,675	3,883	3,572	2,605	1,920	1,554	1,310	1,305	1,264	1,169
Curr. Ratio	1.9	1.7	1.5	1.5	1.5	1.5	1.7	1.5	1.5	1.7
% LT Debt of Cap.	16.4	16.1	5.3	5.2	7.2	5.3	2.4	2.1	7.7	1.3
% Net Inc.of Revs.	7.3	6.7	7.7	6.4	5.8	5.4	5.2	5.6	7.0	8.3
% Ret. on Assets	10.5	9.9	11.1	8.8	7.7	6.9	6.4	6.8	9.4	11.0
% Ret. on Equity	14.5	20.5	22.4	17.3	14.7	11.9	10.9	12.4	16.5	17.9

Data as orig. reptd.; bef. results of disc. opers. and/or spec. items. Per share data adj. for stk. divs. as of ex-div. date. Bold denotes diluted EPS (FASB 128). E-Estimated. NA-Not Available. NM-Not Meaningful. NR-Not Ranked.

Office—3000 Hanover St., Palo Alto, CA 94304. **Tel**—(650) 857-1501. **Website**—http://www.hp.com **Chrmn, Pres & CEO**—L. E. Platt. **EVP-Fin & CFO**—R. P. Wayman. **Secy**—D. C. Nordlund.**Investor Contact**—Steve Pavlovich. **Dirs**—T. E. Everhart, J. B. Fery, J.-P. G. Gimon, S. Ginn, R. A. Hackborn, W. B. Hewlett, G. A. Keyworth II, D. M. Lawrence, M.D., P. F. Miller Jr., S. P. Orr, D.W. Packard, L. E. Platt, R. P. Wayman. **Transfer Agent & Registrar**—Harris Trust & Savings Bank, Chicago. **Incorporated**—in California in 1947. **Empl**— 127,200. **S&P Analyst:** Megan Graham Hackett

STANDARD &POOR'S
STOCK REPORTS

Hilton Hotels

1140

NYSE Symbol **HLT**

In S&P 500

12-SEP-98

Industry: Lodging - Hotels

Summary: Hilton Hotels has a large gaming business, and owns, manages or franchises about 220 non-casino hotels.

S&P Opinion: Accumulate (★★★★)	Recent Price • 19⅛	Yield • 1.7%
	52 Wk Range • 35¾-17½	12-Mo. P/E • 18.8

Quantitative Evaluations

Outlook (1 Lowest—5 Highest)
• **5+**

Fair Value
• **39¼**

Risk
• **Average**

Earn./Div. Rank
• **B+**

Technical Eval.
• **Bearish** since 3/98

Rel. Strength Rank (1 Lowest—99 Highest)
• **27**

Insider Activity
• **NA**

Earnings vs. Previous Year
▲=Up ▼=Down ▶=No Change

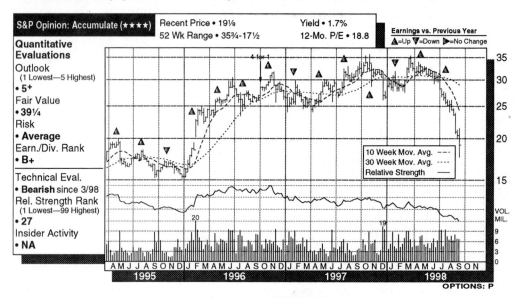

10 Week Mov. Avg. ----
30 Week Mov. Avg. ----
Relative Strength ——

OPTIONS: P

Overview - 06-JUL-98

In June 1998, the company said it plans to split itself, on a tax-free basis, into two separate businesses. Stock of a new publicly owned gaming company, whose assets would include a large casino/hotel presence in Nevada and Atlantic City, would be spun off to HLT shareholders. HLT also anticipates that the newly created gaming company will merge with the Mississippi gaming operations of Grand Casinos (NYSE: GND), which include three casino/hotels. After the spinoff, the remainder of HLT would consist primarily of a large hotel business that would own, manage or franchise more than 250 lodging properties. Our earnings estimates are for HLT as currently constituted. Earlier, in 1997, an effort by HLT to acquire hotel and gaming company ITT Corp. was unsuccessful. In December 1996, HLT acquired gaming company Bally Entertainment Co. Excluding nonrecurring charges, HLT's 1997 basic earnings per share were $1.23, up from $1.01 in 1996.

Valuation - 06-JUL-98

We like HLT's plan for a tax-free division of itself into two separate cosmpanies. This separation should better enable potential investors to focus on either HLT's non-casino hotel operations, or on a large gaming business, whose ownership is to be spun off. We are less enthusiastic about the prospects of the new gaming company acquiring Grand Casinos (GND) through a stock swap. However, the GND transaction may have been motivated, in part, by tax considerations related to the HLT split-up. Based on estimated cash flow of HLT and of the spun-off gaming company, we expect HLT's stock (or the combined value of HLT stock and that of the spinoff) to reach at least the mid-$30s in the next six to 12 months.

Key Stock Statistics

S&P EPS Est. 1998	1.40	Tang. Bk. Value/Share	8.61
P/E on S&P Est. 1998	13.7	Beta	0.97
S&P EPS Est. 1999	1.65	Shareholders	16,200
Dividend Rate/Share	0.32	Market cap. (B)	$ 4.7
Shs. outstg. (M)	246.9	Inst. holdings	55%
Avg. daily vol. (M)	1.406		

Value of $10,000 invested 5 years ago: $ 19,319

Fiscal Year Ending Dec. 31

	1998	1997	1996	1995	1994	1993
Revenues (Million $)						
1Q	1,396	1,303	957.0	381.9	338.8	331.6
2Q	1,413	1,360	1,004	424.2	381.2	345.2
3Q	—	1,314	943.0	385.7	380.9	346.7
4Q	—	1,339	1,036	457.6	405.3	370.0
Yr.	—	5,316	3,940	1,649	1,506	1,394
Earnings Per Share ($)						
1Q	0.29	0.26	0.18	0.17	0.12	0.12
2Q	0.39	0.34	0.30	0.27	0.17	0.14
3Q	E0.36	0.35	0.28	0.13	0.14	0.11
4Q	E0.36	-0.03	0.03	0.33	0.20	0.17
Yr.	E1.40	0.94	0.79	0.89	0.63	0.54

Next earnings report expected: late October

Dividend Data (Dividends have been paid since 1946.)

Amount ($)	Date Decl.	Ex-Div. Date	Stock of Record	Payment Date
0.080	Nov. 13	Dec. 03	Dec. 05	Dec. 19 '97
0.080	Jan. 22	Mar. 04	Mar. 06	Mar. 20 '98
0.080	May. 07	Jun. 03	Jun. 05	Jun. 19 '98
0.080	Jul. 09	Sep. 02	Sep. 04	Sep. 18 '98

A Division of The **McGraw-Hill** *Companies*

Business Summary - 06-JUL-98

In June 1998, this large hotel and gaming company announced a plan to divide itself into two separate companies. Ownership of most of HLT's gaming assets would be spun off to shareholders, through a tax-free distribution, and the spun-off company would then acquire the Mississippi gaming operations of Grand Casinos (NYSE: GND). HLT expects both transactions, which are subject to shareholder and regulatory approvals, to be completed by the end of 1998. After the spinoff, the remainder of HLT would primarily consist of a hotel business that owns, manages or franchises more than 250 lodging properties.

HLT's gaming business currently includes six Nevada casino/hotels, with a total of about 14,235 hotel rooms or suites, and 479,000 sq. ft. of casino space. Three of the properties are in Las Vegas, including the Las Vegas Hilton, where a new Star Trek attraction recently opened. A fourth Las Vegas HLT casino/hotel, featuring a Paris, France, theme, may open in the third quarter of 1999. HLT also has two casino/hotels in Reno, NV, and one in Laughlin, NV.

In Atlantic City, HLT owns and operates two casino/hotels, with a total of about 2,070 rooms and 215,000 sq. ft. of gaming space. This includes a casino annex with a Wild West theme; the annex opened in

mid-1997. Other HLT gaming interests include water-based casino projects in Missouri, Louisiana and Mississippi; two casino/hotels in Australia; and a gaming project in Uruguay. The company operates and has at least a minority ownership interest in each of these facilities. A joint venture interest in a Windsor, ON, gaming business is not expected to be part of the spun-off gaming company.

As of year-end 1997, HLT's large non-casino hotel business included about 239 properties with 84,670 rooms. Of these, the company had ownership interests in 32 (23,799 rooms), managed 27 (15,779), and was the franchisor of 180 (45,092). Owned hotels include the Waldorf-Astoria in New York City and the Palmer House Hilton in Chicago. In January 1997, HLT and British company Ladbroke Group PLC signed agreements that should increasingly unite Hilton hotels around the world. HLT and Ladbroke, which has rights to the Hilton name outside of the U.S., plan to take such steps as expanding a customer loyalty program to all Hilton hotels worldwide, and developing common advertising for the Hilton brand.

Since Stephen F. Bollenbach became CEO of HLT in early 1996, HLT has completed acquisitions valued at over $2 billion, including the December 1996 acquisition of gaming company Bally Entertainment company. HLT also made an unsuccessful effort to acquire ITT Corp.

Per Share Data ($)

(Year Ended Dec. 31)	1997	1996	1995	1994	1993	1992	1991	1990	1989	1988
Tangible Bk. Val.	8.25	7.63	6.49	5.86	5.53	5.25	5.01	4.86	4.60	4.26
Cash Flow	2.21	1.34	1.62	1.28	1.12	1.06	0.99	1.03	0.95	1.00
Earnings	0.94	0.79	0.89	0.63	0.54	0.54	0.44	0.58	0.57	0.68
Dividends	0.32	0.30	0.30	0.30	0.30	0.30	0.30	0.29	0.25	0.24
Payout Ratio	34%	39%	34%	48%	56%	55%	68%	49%	44%	36%
Prices - High	35¾	31¾	20	18½	15¼	13⅜	12½	21⅛	28⅞	13⅞
- Low	24	15¼	15⅛	12½	10⅜	10	8⅝	6⅝	12⅛	8½
P/E Ratio - High	38	40	22	29	29	25	28	36	51	20
- Low	26	19	17	20	19	18	19	11	21	13

Income Statement Analysis (Million $)

	1997	1996	1995	1994	1993	1992	1991	1990	1989	1988
Revs.	5,316	3,940	1,649	1,456	1,358	1,203	1,082	1,087	954	915
Oper. Inc.	896	507	496	354	316	294	249	274	236	246
Depr.	300	178	142	127	112	100	94.0	86.0	74.0	61.0
Int. Exp.	190	106	113	92.7	82.4	71.8	63.3	68.9	81.2	58.7
Pretax Inc.	448	267	280	201	161	159	123	167	159	185
Eff. Tax Rate	42%	40%	37%	39%	36%	35%	31%	33%	31%	29%
Net Inc.	250	156	173	122	103	104	84.0	113	110	131

Balance Sheet & Other Fin. Data (Million $)

	1997	1996	1995	1994	1993	1992	1991	1990	1989	1988
Cash	330	438	409	393	479	511	350	100	445	434
Curr. Assets	1,011	1,151	717	674	727	676	502	285	610	586
Total Assets	7,826	7,577	3,060	2,926	2,675	2,659	2,187	1,927	2,216	1,893
Curr. Liab.	941	998	535	328	278	365	195	241	587	307
LT Debt	2,709	2,606	1,070	1,252	1,113	1,087	789	527	487	569
Common Eqty.	3,368	3,196	1,254	1,128	1,057	1,003	953	923	883	814
Total Cap.	6,695	6,415	2,447	2,504	2,310	2,237	1,912	1,624	1,555	1,562
Cap. Exp.	531	242	187	254	157	221	78.0	202	332	317
Cash Flow	550	334	315	249	215	204	178	198	184	192
Curr. Ratio	1.1	1.1	1.3	2.1	2.6	1.9	2.6	1.2	1.0	1.9
% LT Debt of Cap.	40.5	40.6	43.8	50.0	48.2	48.6	41.3	32.4	31.3	36.4
% Net Inc.of Revs.	4.7	3.9	10.5	8.4	7.6	8.6	7.8	10.3	11.5	14.3
% Ret. on Assets	3.2	2.8	5.8	4.3	3.8	4.3	4.1	5.5	5.3	8.0
% Ret. on Equity	7.6	7.0	14.6	11.1	10.0	10.6	9.0	12.5	12.9	16.7

Data as orig. reptd.; bef. results of disc. opers. and/or spec. items. Per share data adj. for stk. divs. as of ex-div. date. E-Estimated. NA-Not Available. NM-Not Meaningful. NR-Not Ranked.

Office—9336 Civic Center Dr., Beverly Hills, CA 90210. **Tel**—(310) 278-4321. **Website**—http://www.hilton.com **Chrmn**—B. Hilton. **Pres & CEO**—S. F. Bollenbach. **EVP & CFO**—M. J. Hart. **SVP & Treas**—S. A. LaPorta. **VP & Secy**—C. L. Marsh. **Investor Contacts**—Marc A. Grossman (SVP), Geoffrey A. Davis. **Dirs**—S. F. Bollenbach, A. S. Crown, P. M. George, A. M. Goldberg, B. Hilton, E. M. Hilton, D. H. Huckestein, R. L. Johnson, D. R. Knab, B. V. Lambert, D. F. Tuttle, S. D. Young Jr. **Transfer Agent & Registrar**—ChaseMellon Shareholder Services, Ridgefield Park, NJ. **Incorporated**—in Delaware in 1946. **Empl**—61,000. **S&P Analyst:** Tom Graves, CFA

STANDARD &POOR'S
STOCK REPORTS

Home Depot

1149

NYSE Symbol **HD**

In S&P 500

12-SEP-98

Industry:
Retail (Building Supplies)

Summary: HD operates a chain of more than 620 retail warehouse-type stores, selling a wide variety of home improvement products for the do-it-yourself and home remodeling markets.

S&P Opinion: Accumulate (★★★★)	Recent Price • 40¼	Yield • 0.3%
	52 Wk Range • 49-25⅛	12-Mo. P/E • 45.2

Quantitative Evaluations

Outlook
(1 Lowest—5 Highest)
• **2**

Fair Value
• **39⅛**

Risk
• **Average**

Earn./Div. Rank
• **A+**

Technical Eval.
• **Bullish** since 3/97

Rel. Strength Rank
(1 Lowest—99 Highest)
• **80**

Insider Activity
• **Unfavorable**

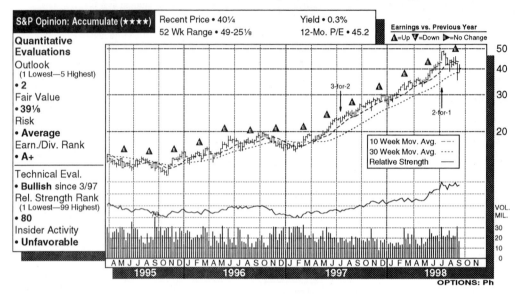

Earnings vs. Previous Year
▲=Up ▼=Down ►=No Change

10 Week Mov. Avg. ‒ ‒ ‒
30 Week Mov. Avg. · · · ·
Relative Strength —

OPTIONS: Ph

Overview - 08-JUN-98

Revenue growth of this leading home improvement retailer should be about 25% in FY 99 (Jan.), mainly fueled by the company's ongoing aggressive expansion program. About 140 new units are planned for FY 99. Same-unit sales should rise about 5% to 6%. Operating income should increase about 24%, reflecting wider margins and improved expense ratios. HD has additional room for growth in the highly fragmented, $140 billion do-it-yourself home improvement industry, with only a 14% share of the market. The industry is projected to grow at an annual 5% rate through the end of the decade. The bulk of the growth should come from the estimated 75 million older homes that will need to be repaired. HD plans to operate 1,300 stores by the end of 2000. As of February 1, 1998, the company had $173.8 million in cash and short-term investments.

Valuation - 08-JUN-98

The shares have risen dramatically, in tandem with the market and, importantly, with solid earnings gains in FY 98 and in the first quarter of FY 99. Although the shares warrant a premium P/E multiple to that of the market, reflecting HD's outstanding earnings record and well defined growth prospects, the stock price appears already to reflect most of the good news anticipated over the next year. However, with plans to expand the company's store base by 21% annually over the next few years, Home Depot is building substantially on its already dominant position in the do-it-yourself market. We also anticipate an easing of the competitive landscape, as small regional players fall by the wayside. EPS should continue to grow 23% to 25% annually for the next few years; the shares should be accumulated for capital gains.

Key Stock Statistics

S&P EPS Est. 1999	1.02	Tang. Bk. Value/Share	5.19
P/E on S&P Est. 1999	39.3	Beta	0.65
S&P EPS Est. 2000	1.25	Shareholders	77,700
Dividend Rate/Share	0.12	Market cap. (B)	$ 59.2
Shs. outstg. (M)	1470.5	Inst. holdings	59%
Avg. daily vol. (M)	5.195		

Value of $10,000 invested 5 years ago: $ 24,332

Fiscal Year Ending Jan. 31

	1999	1998	1997	1996	1995	1994
Revenues (Million $)						
1Q	7,123	5,657	4,362	3,569	2,872	2,180
2Q	8,139	6,550	5,293	4,152	3,287	2,454
3Q	—	6,217	4,922	3,998	3,240	2,317
4Q	—	5,731	4,959	3,752	3,077	2,287
Yr.	—	24,156	19,536	15,470	12,477	9,239
Earnings Per Share ($)						
1Q	**0.23**	**0.17**	0.14	0.11	0.10	0.11
2Q	**0.31**	**0.24**	0.19	0.15	0.13	0.10
3Q	**E0.25**	**0.16**	0.15	0.12	0.10	0.08
4Q	**E0.25**	**0.20**	0.17	0.13	0.11	0.08
Yr.	**E1.02**	**0.77**	0.65	0.51	0.44	0.34

Next earnings report expected: mid November

Dividend Data (Dividends have been paid since 1987.)

Amount ($)	Date Decl.	Ex-Div. Date	Stock of Record	Payment Date
0.050	Feb. 26	Mar. 03	Mar. 05	Mar. 19 '98
0.060	May. 27	Jun. 09	Jun. 11	Jun. 25 '98
2-for-1	May. 27	Jul. 06	Jun. 11	Jul. 02 '98
0.030	Aug. 20	Sep. 01	Sep. 03	Sep. 17 '98

A Division of The McGraw·Hill Companies

Business Summary - 08-JUN-98

Home Depot is a do-it-yourselfer's paradise. Founded in 1978, The Home Depot is the world's largest home improvement retailer and currently has garnered about 14% of the U.S. $140 billion home improvement industry. The company operates retail warehouse-type stores selling a wide assortment of building materials and home improvement products, primarily to the do-it-yourself and home remodeling markets. At February 1, 1998, it was operating 624 stores in 44 states, mostly in California, Florida and Texas, and 32 stores in Canada.

Stores average 105,000 sq. ft., plus 20,000 sq. ft. to 28,000 sq. ft. of garden center and storage space. They stock 40,000 to 50,000 product items. HD aims to provide a broad range of merchandise, consisting of many different kinds of building and home improvement materials, at competitive prices. The company trains employees to be knowledgeable about the products in the stores; they may also have trade skills or direct experience in using the products.

Growth opportunities remain in existing and as yet untapped markets in the U.S. HD plans to expand its square footage base by 21% to 22% annually, which will take the company to over 1,300 stores by the end of 2001.

The EXPO Design Centers, with about 144,000 sq. ft. of selling space, are a test concept, marketing upscale interior design products. The company currently operates five units and plans to add two design centers in FY 99.

In 1994, HD acquired a 75% interest in Canada's Aikenhead's Home Improvement Warehouse chain from Molson Cos. Ltd., for $160 million. Beginning in 2000, it has the right to acquire the remaining 25%. The chain, known as Home Depot Canada, currently operates 32 warehouse-style stores in Canada. In an attempt to strengthen its position in the $10 billion market for direct mail marketing of maintenance, repair and operations products to the U.S. building and facilities management markets, in March 1997, the company acquired Maintenance Warehouse/America Corp. ($130 million in revenues). The company believes that the Home Depot concept is ripe for global expansion. In mid-1998, a Home Depot store is planned for Santiago, Chile, as a prelude to expansion in Latin America. The company has formed a joint venture with S.A.C.I. Falabella, the largest department store chain in Chile.

Per Share Data ($)

(Year Ended Jan. 31)	1998	1997	1996	1995	1994	1993	1992	1991	1990	1989
Tangible Bk. Val.	4.75	4.07	3.42	2.47	2.07	1.72	1.32	0.62	0.47	0.35
Cash Flow	0.95	0.80	0.64	0.51	0.40	0.32	0.24	0.18	0.13	0.09
Earnings	0.78	0.65	0.51	0.44	0.34	0.27	0.20	0.15	0.10	0.08
Dividends	0.10	0.08	0.06	0.05	0.04	0.03	0.02	0.01	0.01	0.01
Payout Ratio	12%	12%	12%	11%	12%	10%	9%	8%	8%	7%
Cal. Yrs.	1997	1996	1995	1994	1993	1992	1991	1990	1989	1988
Prices - High	30¼	19⁷/₈	16⁵/₈	16¹/₈	17	17¹/₈	11³/₄	4⁷/₈	2⁷/₈	1⁹/₁₆
- Low	15⁷/₈	13⁷/₈	12¼	12¹/₈	11⁵/₈	9⁷/₈	3⁷/₈	2¹/₂	1⁷/₁₆	⁷/₈
P/E Ratio - High	39	31	32	48	50	63	58	32	27	21
- Low	21	21	24	36	35	36	19	17	13	12

Income Statement Analysis (Million $)

	1998	1997	1996	1995	1994	1993	1992	1991	1990	1989
Revs.	24,156	19,536	15,470	12,477	9,239	7,148	5,137	3,815	2,759	2,000
Oper. Inc.	2,299	1,766	1,361	1,117	793	615	434	300	205	141
Depr.	283	232	181	130	85.9	65.6	52.3	34.4	20.5	14.4
Int. Exp.	42.0	39.0	25.0	53.5	44.6	48.6	24.0	31.1	18.3	4.5
Pretax Inc.	1,914	1,543	1,195	980	737	576	396	260	182	126
Eff. Tax Rate	39%	39%	39%	38%	38%	37%	37%	37%	39%	39%
Net Inc.	1,160	938	732	605	457	363	249	163	112	77.0

Balance Sheet & Other Fin. Data (Million $)

	1998	1997	1996	1995	1994	1993	1992	1991	1990	1989
Cash	172	558	108	58.0	431	414	395	137	135	16.0
Curr. Assets	4,460	3,709	2,672	2,133	1,967	1,562	1,158	714	566	337
Total Assets	11,229	9,342	7,354	5,778	4,701	3,932	2,510	1,640	1,118	699
Curr. Liab.	2,456	1,842	1,416	1,214	973	755	534	413	292	194
LT Debt	1,303	1,247	720	983	882	844	271	531	303	108
Common Eqty.	7,098	5,955	4,988	3,442	2,814	2,304	1,691	683	512	383
Total Cap.	8,595	7,366	5,822	4,496	3,724	3,164	1,969	1,222	825	504
Cap. Exp.	1,525	1,194	1,278	1,101	900	437	432	398	205	105
Cash Flow	1,443	1,170	913	734	543	428	301	196	132	91.0
Curr. Ratio	1.8	2.0	1.9	1.8	2.0	2.1	2.2	1.7	1.9	1.7
% LT Debt of Cap.	15.2	16.9	16.9	21.9	23.7	26.7	13.7	43.4	36.7	21.3
% Net Inc.of Revs.	4.8	4.8	4.7	4.8	5.0	5.1	4.9	4.3	4.1	3.8
% Ret. on Assets	11.3	11.2	11.1	11.5	10.5	11.0	11.2	11.7	12.2	12.4
% Ret. on Equity	17.8	17.1	17.4	19.2	17.8	17.8	19.9	27.0	24.8	21.7

Data as orig. reptd.; bef. results of disc. opers. and/or spec. items. Per share data adj. for stk. divs. as of ex-div. date. Bold denotes diluted EPS (FASB 128). E-Estimated. NA-Not Available. NM-Not Meaningful. NR-Not Ranked.

Office—2727 Paces Ferry Rd., Atlanta, GA 30339. **Tel**—(770) 433-8211. **Website**—http://www.HomeDepot.com **Chrmn, CEO & Secy**—B. Marcus. **Pres**—A. M. Blank. **EVP & CAO**—R. M. Brill. **CFO**—M. L. Day. **Investor Contact**—Kim Schreckengost. **Dirs**—A. M. Blank, F. Borman, R. M. Brill, J. L. Clendenin, B. R. Cox, M. A. Hart III, J. W. Inglis, D. R. Keough, K. G. Langone, B. Marcus, M. F. Wilson. **Transfer Agent & Registrar**—BankBoston, N.A , Bostom, MA. **Incorporated**—in Delaware in 1978. **Empl**— 125,000. **S&P Analyst:** Karen J. Sack, CFA

Homestake Mining

1152

NYSE Symbol **HM**

In S&P 500

12-SEP-98

Industry:
Gold & Precious Metals Mining

Summary: On April 30, 1998, HM, one of the world's largest gold producers, completed the acquisition of Plutonic Resources Limited for some 64.4 million common shares.

S&P Opinion: Accumulate (★★★★)	Recent Price • 11¾	Yield • 1.7%
	52 Wk Range • 15½-7⅞	12-Mo. P/E • NM

Quantitative Evaluations

Outlook
(1 Lowest—5 Highest)
• **NA**

Fair Value
• **NA**

Risk
• **Average**

Earn./Div. Rank
• **B-**

Technical Eval.
• **Bearish** since 4/98

Rel. Strength Rank
(1 Lowest—99 Highest)
• **98**

Insider Activity
• **Neutral**

Earnings vs. Previous Year
▲=Up ▼=Down ▷=No Change

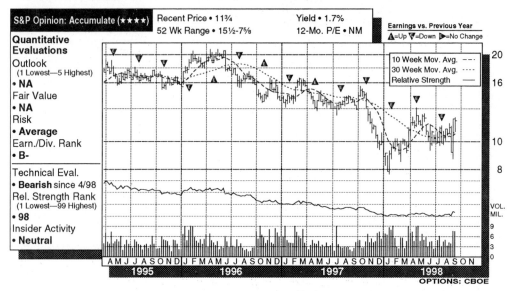

10 Week Mov. Avg. — · —
30 Week Mov. Avg. · · · ·
Relative Strength ———

OPTIONS: CBOE

Overview - 14-AUG-98

HM's gold production in 1998 should increase to about 2.5 million oz. from 1.9 million oz. in 1997, mostly reflecting the acquisition of Plutonic Resources Ltd. Second quarter 1998 losses, excluding unusual charges, totaled $0.06, versus a $0.08 consensus loss estimate. The better-than-projected results reflected sharply lower costs and higher production.

Valuation - 14-AUG-98

On April 21, 1998, we upgraded HM and most other gold stocks to accumulate, based on a more positive outlook both for the metal and the gold stocks as a group. While gold stocks have been under pressure through mid-August, we expect gold and gold stocks to begin an uptrend later in 1998 or in early 1999. Our outlook is based several different factors. First, we expect that central bank selling will diminish now that the new European Central Bank has announced its decision to hold 15% of its reserves in gold. Second, the rate of gain on financial investments will decline in 1998 and 1999 and become less competition for gold. Third, gold production will plateau or even decline in 1999 and this should boost prices. HM lags the other major North American gold companies in costs and reserve growth but we elected to raise HM to accumulate from avoid based on our belief that the Plutonic acquisition will materially expand HM's long-term reserve growth. Near term, there will be some dilution from the issuance of so many HM common to pay for the acquisition, but the company had to take dramatic steps to break the long-standing logjam in its production and reserve profile. With a better gold environment, we believe the acquisition will pay off. Through 1998's first half, HM has significantly narrowed the cost gap with its peers, partly reflecting the merger with Plutonic.

Key Stock Statistics

S&P EPS Est. 1998	-0.25	Tang. Bk. Value/Share	2.86
P/E on S&P Est. 1998	NM	Beta	0.67
S&P EPS Est. 1999	0.10	Shareholders	22,800
Dividend Rate/Share	0.20	Market cap. (B)	$ 2.5
Shs. outstg. (M)	211.2	Inst. holdings	33%
Avg. daily vol. (M)	1.167		

Value of $10,000 invested 5 years ago: $ 11,430

Fiscal Year Ending Dec. 31

	1998	1997	1996	1995	1994	1993
Revenues (Million $)						
1Q	174.3	250.2	202.8	179.9	172.4	170.0
2Q	195.3	168.7	201.5	195.6	202.1	187.1
3Q	—	158.2	183.7	181.4	167.0	180.4
4Q	—	146.8	178.9	189.4	164.0	184.7
Yr.	—	723.8	766.9	746.4	705.5	722.2
Earnings Per Share ($)						
1Q	**-0.03**	**0.34**	0.09	0.05	0.18	0.04
2Q	**-0.15**	**-0.11**	0.05	0.08	0.24	0.08
3Q	**E-0.04**	**-1.12**	0.05	0.04	0.08	0.16
4Q	**E-0.03**	**-0.26**	0.02	0.05	0.07	0.09
Yr.	**E-0.25**	**-1.15**	0.21	0.22	0.57	0.38

Next earnings report expected: mid October

Dividend Data (Dividends have been paid since 1946.)

Amount ($)	Date Decl.	Ex-Div. Date	Stock of Record	Payment Date
0.050	Sep. 26	Oct. 29	Oct. 31	Nov. 21 '97
0.050	Mar. 27	Apr. 24	Apr. 28	May. 21 '98

A Division of The McGraw·Hill Companies

Homestake Mining Company

Business Summary - 14-AUG-98

Homestake Mining is one of the world's largest gold producers. The company's chief business objective is to regain its growth momentum in an effort to close the valuation gap between itself and the other major North American gold producers. Specifically, HM seeks to eliminate the difference between its market capitalization per ounce of proven and probable reserves and that of the average of the S&P Precious Metals Index.

On April 29, 1998, HM acquired Plutonic Resources Limited of Australia for $770 million in stock or about 64.4 million common shares. The addition of Plutonic will enable HM to achieve a 30% increase in output over a five year period at a cash cost of about $227/oz. Plutonic will add 2.2 million oz. to reserves and some 8.5 million oz. to resources. HM believes that areas contiguous to Plutonic's existing mines as well as its 6,000 square miles of property in Western Australia have excellent exploration potential.

Following the combination, HM is North America's third largest gold producer. The merged company has a total of 18 mines in four countries, consisting of 10 underground mines and 8 surface mines. The acquisition will increase HM's 1998 gold output by some 450,000 oz. and boost its 1999 production by 600,000 oz. HM expects to realize about $20 million in annual cost savings by combining Plutonic's operations and exploration with HM's existing Australian operations. Excluding one-time transaction costs, the merger is expected to be accretive to 1998 EPS and cash flow.

In 1997 HM adopted a formal hedging policy which permits the sale of 30% of the following 10 year's gold production at specified price levels. In 1998, HM will deliver 120,000 oz. of gold at an average gold price of $339/oz. as part of its forward sales program.

The following table presents significant operating and reserve data for recent years (reserve data as of year end).

	1997	1996
Gold production (oz.)	1,996,000	1,968,000
Cash cost per oz.	$237	$248
Total cost per oz.	$291	$306
Average realized gold price (oz.)	$333	$389
Proven and probable reserves (oz.)	17,000,000	20,400,000

In 1997's third quarter, HM incurred a $0.99 charge to write down the value of its investment in the Main Pass sulfur mine, provide for future reclamation expenses, recognize foreign exchange losses and the reduction of carrying values of short-lived mining projects and other investments.

Cash costs for 1998's first half were $207/oz., versus $256/oz. in 1997; total costs for the same period were $263/oz., down from $315/oz. Production for 1998's first half increased to 1,303,000 oz. from 1,237,200 oz. in 1997.

Per Share Data ($) (Year Ended Dec. 31)	1997	1996	1995	1994	1993	1992	1991	1990	1989	1988
Tangible Bk. Val.	3.62	5.24	4.52	4.27	3.74	3.40	6.72	8.14	8.15	7.76
Cash Flow	-0.39	0.97	0.94	1.12	1.14	-0.43	-0.29	0.56	0.88	1.26
Earnings	-1.15	0.21	0.22	0.57	0.38	-1.31	-1.01	-0.19	0.18	0.65
Dividends	0.15	0.20	0.20	0.17	0.10	0.20	0.20	0.20	0.20	0.20
Payout Ratio	NM	95%	91%	31%	26%	NM	NM	NM	112%	31%
Prices - High	16⅝	20⅞	19⅛	24⅞	22⅞	16⅝	19⅝	23⅝	20⅝	19
- Low	8¼	13⅝	14¾	16⅛	9⅝	10	13⅞	15¼	12	12⅛
P/E Ratio - High	NM	99	87	44	60	NM	NM	NM	NM	29
- Low	NM	65	67	28	25	NM	NM	NM	NM	19
Income Statement Analysis (Million $)										
Revs.	660	743	716	659	704	660	387	482	398	346
Oper. Inc.	97.5	185	169	141	168	-27.8	-61.7	74.0	54.9	57.0
Depr.	112	112	100	76.0	103	117	71.3	74.5	68.4	59.1
Int. Exp.	11.3	10.6	11.3	10.8	9.1	16.9	5.6	11.8	14.2	4.1
Pretax Inc.	-167	71.7	85.5	95.0	61.0	-188	-130	-14.0	26.0	81.0
Eff. Tax Rate	NM	37%	46%	8.10%	9.40%	NM	NM	NM	34%	21%
Net Inc.	-168	30.3	30.2	78.0	52.0	-175	-99	-19.0	18.0	63.0
Balance Sheet & Other Fin. Data (Million $)										
Cash	94.7	220	212	205	135	71.0	158	312	262	222
Curr. Assets	376	379	369	343	238	179	265	412	388	307
Total Assets	1,305	1,482	1,322	1,202	1,121	1,145	927	1,081	1,094	984
Curr. Liab.	109	117	98.4	97.0	104	156	83.2	95.8	89.4	64.4
LT Debt	264	185	185	185	189	205	48.2	72.4	93.1	60.3
Common Eqty.	532	769	636	589	515	465	669	807	800	757
Total Cap.	1,053	1,251	1,103	994	923	901	770	940	972	887
Cap. Exp.	131	106	81.0	89.0	58.0	63.0	138	112	86.0	112
Cash Flow	-56.5	143	130	1.5	156	-58.0	-29.0	56.0	86.0	122
Curr. Ratio	3.5	3.2	3.8	3.5	2.3	1.2	3.2	4.3	4.3	4.8
% LT Debt of Cap.	25.0	14.8	16.8	18.6	20.5	22.8	6.3	7.7	9.6	6.8
% Net Inc.of Revs.	NM	8.2	4.2	11.8	7.5	NM	NM	NM	4.4	18.3
% Ret. on Assets	NM	4.3	2.4	6.7	4.6	NM	NM	NM	1.7	6.7
% Ret. on Equity	NM	8.6	5.0	14.1	10.7	NM	NM	NM	2.2	8.7

Data as orig. reptd.; bef. results of disc. opers. and/or spec. items. Per share data adj. for stk. divs. as of ex-div. date. Bold denotes diluted EPS (FASB 128). E-Estimated. NA-Not Available. NM-Not Meaningful. NR-Not Ranked.

Office—650 California St., San Francisco, CA 94108-2788. **Tel**—(415) 981-8150. **Fax**—(415) 397-5038. **Website**—http://www.homestake.com **Chrmn,Pres & CEO**—J. E. Thompson. **VP-Fin & CFO**—G. G. Elam. **VP & Secy**—W. Kirk.**Investor Contact**—Michael A. Stevens. **Dirs**—M. N. Anderson, R. H. Clark Jr., H. M. Conger, G. R. Durham, D. W. Fuerstenau, H. G. Grundstedt, W. A. Humphrey, R. K. Jaedicke, J. Neerhout Jr., S. T. Peeler, C. A. Rae, B. A. Schepman, J. E. Thompson. **Transfer Agent & Registrar**—First National Bank of Boston. **Incorporated**—in California in 1877; reincorporated in Delaware in 1984. **Empl**— 1,734. **S&P Analyst:** Leo J. Larkin

STANDARD &POOR'S
STOCK REPORTS

Honeywell Inc.

1154

NYSE Symbol **HON**

In S&P 500

12-SEP-98

Industry: Electrical Equipment

Summary: Honeywell is a major manufacturer of automation and control systems for homes, buildings, industry and aerospace.

S&P Opinion: Hold (★★★)	Recent Price • 66⅜	Yield • 1.7%
	52 Wk Range • 96⅜-61¾	12-Mo. P/E • 16.5

Quantitative Evaluations

Outlook
(1 Lowest—5 Highest)
• **3+**

Fair Value
• **73¼**

Risk
• **Low**

Earn./Div. Rank
• **A-**

Technical Eval.
• **Bearish** since 3/98

Rel. Strength Rank
(1 Lowest—99 Highest)
• **47**

Insider Activity
• **Neutral**

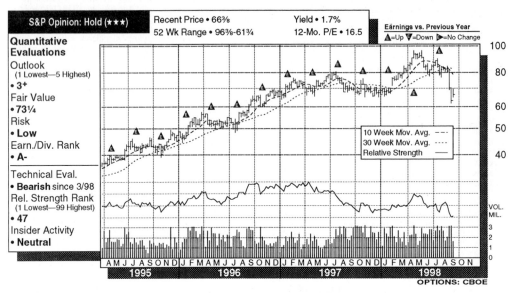

Earnings vs. Previous Year
▲=Up ▼=Down ▶=No Change

10 Week Mov. Avg. ----
30 Week Mov. Avg. ....
Relative Strength ——

OPTIONS: CBOE

Overview - 21-JUL-98

Sales in 1998 are forecast to rise about 8% from those of 1997, led by gains in space and aviation controls. Growth in the home and building segment may resume, aided by efforts to redesign product lines for the residential markets and expand penetration in the commercial market segments for building controls. Gains in industrial controls sales could be slowed by moderation in international demand. The aviation segment should achieve robust growth, on continued strength in the business/commuter aircraft market and increased activity for the International Space Station. The segment should also benefit from increased deliveries of large commercial aircraft and from modernization of navigation systems on existing jets. Margins are projected to widen on productivity improvement and cost reduction initiatives. The share repurchase program should be resumed once debt levels are reduced following the recent Measurex deal. Free cash flow of between $400 million and $450 million is expected in 1998.

Valuation - 21-JUL-98

We maintain a hold recommendation on the shares as we expect the stock to perform in line with the market. The stock is trading at a PE reflective of its peer group of electrical equipment companies. Although HON's prospects for 1998 are generally favorable, there are uncertainties which warrant caution. Prime concerns are the impact that changes in foreign currency exchange values and slowing industrial activity will have on earnings. Increased income in the home and building controls unit is dependent on the success of efforts to cut costs. The shares, which have historically traded at a discount to the S&P 500, now trade at about 19 times estimated 1998 earnings. While we would avoid further purchases, the shares merit holding by long-term investors.

Key Stock Statistics

S&P EPS Est. 1998	4.45	Tang. Bk. Value/Share	9.68
P/E on S&P Est. 1998	14.9	Beta	1.10
S&P EPS Est. 1999	4.85	Shareholders	32,500
Dividend Rate/Share	1.12	Market cap. (B)	$ 8.4
Shs. outstg. (M)	126.1	Inst. holdings	69%
Avg. daily vol. (M)	0.625		

Value of $10,000 invested 5 years ago: $ 22,653

Fiscal Year Ending Dec. 31

	1998	1997	1996	1995	1994	1993
Revenues (Million $)						
1Q	1,923	1,686	1,620	1,479	1,348	1,440
2Q	2,035	1,977	1,772	1,656	1,464	1,452
3Q	—	2,039	1,803	1,680	1,508	1,452
4Q	—	2,326	2,117	1,917	1,738	1,620
Yr.	—	8,028	7,312	6,731	6,057	5,963
Earnings Per Share ($)						
1Q	**0.75**	**0.59**	0.51	0.43	0.36	0.42
2Q	**0.98**	**0.76**	0.66	0.54	0.44	0.53
3Q	**E1.14**	**0.92**	0.80	0.66	0.54	0.60
4Q	**E1.58**	**1.38**	1.21	0.99	0.81	0.85
Yr.	**E4.45**	**3.65**	3.18	2.62	2.15	2.40

Next earnings report expected: mid October

Dividend Data (Dividends have been paid since 1928.)

Amount ($)	Date Decl.	Ex-Div. Date	Stock of Record	Payment Date
0.280	Oct. 21	Nov. 25	Nov. 28	Dec. 15 '97
0.280	Feb. 17	Feb. 25	Feb. 27	Mar. 16 '98
0.280	Apr. 21	May. 27	May. 29	Jun. 15 '98
0.280	Jul. 21	Aug. 26	Aug. 28	Sep. 14 '98

A Division of The McGraw·Hill Companies

STANDARD
&POOR'S
STOCK REPORTS

Honeywell Inc.

1154

12-SEP-98

Business Summary - 21-JUL-98

Honeywell, best known for its residential thermostats and climate controls, is turning up the heat in its efforts to grow annual sales to $10 billion by 2000 and further expand its margins. Products cover a broad range of automation and control systems for residential, commercial, industrial, space and aviation purposes.

In recent years, HON has attempted to assert itself in retail distribution by acquiring companies that extend its line of consumer products. HON's industrial automation business was greatly expanded by the 1997 addition of Measurex, a supplier of process controls for manufacturing of flat products. HON's avionics business should benefit in the next few years from the development of an advanced cockpit design for the new Boeing 777 widebody aircraft which can be adapted for use in numerous other aircraft. The ability to standardize cockpit design among different planes could provide a significant competitive advantage in the next decade. Another promising opportunity is HON's partnership with Trimble Navigation to provide Global Positioning System (GPS) navigation systems in aviation.

International operations are important to HON, accounting for 39% of sales and 37% of operating profits in recent years. Growth in international operations in 1998 could be hurt by a 15% average appreciation of the U.S. dollar versus the foreign currencies in which HON transacts business.

Home and building controls (42% of 1997 sales; 33% of 1997 operating profit) makes over 3,500 products including environmental control systems, security and fire alarm systems, home automation systems, energy-efficient lighting controls and building management systems. The 1996 acquisitions of Duracraft (humidifiers and portable electric heaters) and Filtercold (water filtration systems) extended the line of Honeywell branded residential products.

Industrial controls (32%; 35%) provides computer-based systems, sensors and various automation and control products for industrial automation. The division also furnishes services, including product and component testing and instrument maintenance, repair and calibration. Measurex was acquired for $600 million in cash in early 1997, strengthening HON's position in products for pulp and paper manufacturing and other flat product process industries.

Space and aviation controls (24%, 29%) include control and guidance systems for commercial and military aircraft and space satellite applications. Besides the GPS navigation opportunities, recent new products include Primus Epic integrated business jet avionics, TCAS 2000 enhanced airborne collision avoidance, and Pegasus flight management systems. HON participates in defense programs including the Space Based Infrared System (SBIRS).

Per Share Data ($)

(Year Ended Dec. 31)	1997	1996	1995	1994	1993	1992	1991	1990	1989	1988
Tangible Bk. Val.	9.66	11.97	11.16	14.57	13.48	13.10	13.26	11.99	11.99	10.04
Cash Flow	6.13	5.44	4.90	3.97	4.15	4.64	4.05	4.01	4.69	-0.89
Earnings	3.71	3.18	2.62	2.15	2.40	2.88	2.35	2.45	3.23	-2.56
Dividends	1.09	1.06	1.00	0.97	0.91	0.84	0.77	0.70	0.57	0.53
Payout Ratio	29%	33%	38%	45%	38%	29%	32%	27%	16%	NM
Prices - High	80⅞	69⅞	49½	36⅞	39⅜	38	32¾	28⅛	22⅞	19
- Low	63⅞	44⅜	30¾	28¼	31	30¼	20½	17¾	14⅞	13⅝
P/E Ratio - High	22	22	19	17	16	13	14	11	7	NM
- Low	17	14	12	13	13	10	9	7	5	NM

Income Statement Analysis (Million $)

	1997	1996	1995	1994	1993	1992	1991	1990	1989	1988
Revs.	8,028	7,312	6,731	6,057	5,963	6,223	6,193	6,309	6,059	7,148
Oper. Inc.	1,117	958	853	717	766	761	795	787	722	406
Depr.	320	288	293	235	235	243	239	236	248	283
Int. Exp.	102	81.0	83.0	76.0	68.0	90.0	89.0	106	135	254
Pretax Inc.	703	610	506	370	479	635	509	516	676	-200
Eff. Tax Rate	33%	34%	34%	25%	33%	37%	35%	28%	19%	NM
Net Inc.	471	666	334	279	322	400	331	372	550	-434

Balance Sheet & Other Fin. Data (Million $)

	1997	1996	1995	1994	1993	1992	1991	1990	1989	1988
Cash	134	127	301	275	256	346	508	368	254	180
Curr. Assets	3,258	2,981	2,767	2,649	2,550	2,708	2,699	2,582	2,801	2,764
Total Assets	6,411	5,493	5,060	4,886	4,598	4,870	4,807	4,746	5,258	5,089
Curr. Liab.	2,319	2,067	2,023	2,072	1,856	1,969	2,095	2,175	2,416	2,394
LT Debt	1,177	715	481	502	504	512	640	616	693	801
Common Eqty.	2,389	2,205	2,040	1,855	1,773	1,790	1,851	1,697	1,918	1,731
Total Cap.	3,617	2,966	2,560	2,396	2,305	2,450	2,543	2,349	2,638	2,569
Cap. Exp.	298	297	238	262	232	244	240	252	268	328
Cash Flow	791	691	627	514	558	643	570	608	798	-151
Curr. Ratio	1.4	1.4	1.4	1.3	1.4	1.4	1.3	1.2	1.2	1.2
% LT Debt of Cap.	32.5	24.1	13.0	20.9	21.9	20.9	25.2	26.2	26.3	31.2
% Net Inc.of Revs.	5.9	5.5	5.0	4.6	5.4	6.4	5.3	5.9	9.1	NM
% Ret. on Assets	7.9	7.6	6.7	6.0	6.8	8.4	7.0	7.9	11.0	NM
% Ret. on Equity	20.5	19.0	17.1	15.6	18.4	22.2	18.8	21.9	31.2	NM

Data as orig. reptd.; bef. results of disc. opers. and/or spec. items. Per share data adj. for stk. divs. as of ex-div. date. Bk. val. includes intangibles prior to 1995. Bold denotes diluted EPS (FASB 128). E-Estimated. NA-Not Available. NM-Not Meaningful. NR-Not Ranked.

Office—Honeywell Plaza, Minneapolis, MN 55408. **Tel**—(612) 951-1000. **Website**—http://www.honeywell.com **Chrmn & CEO**—M. R. Bonsignore. **Pres & COO**—G. Ferrari.**VP & CFO**—L. W. Stranghoener. **VP & Secy**—K. M. Gibson.**VP & Investor Contact**—Scott Clements (612-951-2122).**Dirs**—A. J. Baciocco Jr., E. E. Bailey, M. R. Bonsignore, W. H. Donaldson, G. Ferrari, R. D. Fullerton, J. J. Howard III, B. Karatz, A. B. Rand, S. G. Rothmeier, M. W. Wright. **Transfer Agent & Registrar**—ChaseMellon Shareholder Services, NYC. **Incorporated**—in Delaware in 1927. **Empl**— 57,500. **S&P Analyst:** Robert E. Friedman, CPA

12-SEP-98

Industry:
Consumer Finance

Summary: This company is a major provider of consumer financial services in the U.S., Canada and the U.K.

S&P Opinion: Accumulate (★★★★)

Recent Price • 39⅝	Yield • 1.5%
52 Wk Range • 53⅝-35¼	12-Mo. P/E • 45.5

Quantitative Evaluations

Outlook
(1 Lowest—5 Highest)
• **3⁻**

Fair Value
• **37⅞**

Risk
• **Low**

Earn./Div. Rank
• **B+**

Technical Eval.
• **Bullish** since 10/95

Rel. Strength Rank
(1 Lowest—99 Highest)
• **64**

Insider Activity
• **Favorable**

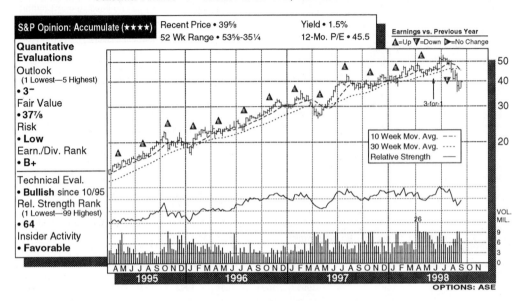

Earnings vs. Previous Year
▲=Up ▼=Down ▷=No Change

10 Week Mov. Avg. ---
30 Week Mov. Avg. ....
Relative Strength —

3-for-1

26

VOL. MIL.

1995 1996 1997 1998

OPTIONS: ASE

Overview - 10-SEP-98

Managed receivables growth for the now combined Household/Beneficial is expected in the high single-digit range in 1998, led by strength in the home equity and auto lending segments. The net interest margin, which was 7.75% in 1998's second quarter, is expected to widen to about 8.0% by the end of the year on modest improvements to both asset yields and funding costs. Near-term efforts will be focused on fully integrating Beneficial. In particular, substantial opportunities exist for improving the efficiency ratio of the combined company. Household (with an efficiency ratio of 34%) was much more efficient on a stand alone basis than Beneficial (53%) prior to the merger and should be able to leverage this on the combined company. Other benefits from the merger are expected to include expanded distribution, leveraging strengths in the private label credit card portfolios and a combining of U.K. businesses. Absent merger charges, earnings are expected to reach $2.40 a share in 1998.

Valuation - 10-SEP-98

The shares declined about 13% in the first eight months of 1998, with most of the drop coming in August alone on international financial turmoil. The company has proven itself to be a savvy acquirer, and has kept a close eye on credit quality in a particularly difficult credit environment. We view the Beneficial Corp. merger as favorable and see HI as a winner in the longer-term trend of consolidation in the diversified financial services industry. Good receivables growth, healthy margins and efficiency improvements are expected to allow for continued earnings momentum. Trading at only 12 times our 1999 per-share earnings estimate of $3.15, the shares are expected to outperform the broader market in the year ahead.

Key Stock Statistics

S&P EPS Est. 1998	2.40	Tang. Bk. Value/Share	8.44
P/E on S&P Est. 1998	16.5	Beta	1.46
S&P EPS Est. 1999	3.15	Shareholders	10,900
Dividend Rate/Share	0.60	Market cap. (B)	$ 19.5
Shs. outstg. (M)	492.4	Inst. holdings	54%
Avg. daily vol. (M)	1.844		

Value of $10,000 invested 5 years ago: $ 45,749

Fiscal Year Ending Dec. 31

	1998	1997	1996	1995	1994	1993
Revenues (Million $)						
1Q	2,772	1,336	1,175	1,246	1,129	1,076
2Q	2,760	1,293	1,307	1,341	1,132	1,080
3Q	—	1,423	1,242	1,313	1,143	1,156
4Q	—	1,451	1,335	1,245	1,200	1,143
Yr.	—	5,503	5,059	5,144	4,603	4,455
Earnings Per Share ($)						
1Q	**0.71**	**0.43**	0.36	0.30	0.25	0.21
2Q	**-1.03**	**0.49**	0.41	0.33	0.27	0.22
3Q	—	**0.57**	0.46	0.37	0.30	0.24
4Q	—	**0.66**	0.54	0.43	0.36	0.30
Yr.	—	**2.17**	1.77	1.44	1.17	0.97

Next earnings report expected: late October

Dividend Data (Dividends have been paid since 1926.)

Amount ($)	Date Decl.	Ex-Div. Date	Stock of Record	Payment Date
0.450	Mar. 10	Mar. 27	Mar. 31	Apr. 15 '98
3-for-1	Mar. 10	Jun. 02	May. 14	Jun. 01 '98
0.150	May. 13	Jun. 24	Jun. 26	Jul. 15 '98
0.150	Sep. 11	Sep. 28	Sep. 30	Oct. 15 '98

A Division of The **McGraw·Hill** Companies

STANDARD
&POOR'S
STOCK REPORTS

Household International, Inc.

1160

12-SEP-98

Business Summary - 10-SEP-98

This major provider of consumer financial services in the U.S., Canada and the U.K. merged with Beneficial Corp. in June 1998. This follows the 1997 acquisition of Transamerica's consumer finance business. Receivables growth remains a primary focus in 1998. With this in mind, the company plans to focus on its two largest businesses: Household Finance, where it intends to concentrate on its branch network; and MasterCard/Visa, where it plans to increase marketing spending with programs targeted toward affinity, co-branded and proprietary cards.

Managed receivables of $45.4 billion at 1997 year end, up from $42.6 billion a year earlier, were divided:

	1997	1996
First mortgage	1%	2%
Home equity	24%	19%
Auto finance	2%	--
Visa/Mastercard	40%	44%
Private label	13%	13%
Other unsecured	18%	20%
Commercial	2%	2%

Household Finance Corp., the oldest and largest independent consumer finance company in the U.S., offers a variety of secured and unsecured lending products to middle-income customers through a network of 644 branch lending offices throughout the U.S. Operations are focused primarily on home equity loans and unsecured credit products.

Household Retail Services (HRS) is a revolving credit merchant participation business that purchases and services merchants' revolving charge accounts resulting from consumer purchases of electronics, furniture and home improvement products. HRS believes that it is the second largest U.S. provider of private-label credit cards.

Household Credit Services markets Visa/Mastercard credit cards, with $16.8 billion of receivables owned and serviced at 1997 year end. The company issues co-branded cards, affinity cards and its own branded card. Major card programs include the GM Card and the AFL-CIO's Union Privilege card.

Other units include HFC Bank plc, a major provider of consumer loans and credit cars in the U.K.; Household Financial Corp. Ltd., one of the largest providers of consumer loans and private label credit cards in Canada; Household Automotive Finance, a leading provider of indirect automobile financing in the U.S.; and Household Life Insurance, which provides credit life, accident, disability and unemployment insurance to customers in the U.S. and Canada.

The Beneficial merger (NYSE; BNL), which closed on June 30, 1998, called for each BNL common share to be exchanged for 1.0222 shares of HI, for an indicated value of about $8.6 billion. BNL provides consumer finance, credit card, banking and insurance products in the U.S., the U.K. and Ireland.

Per Share Data ($)

(Year Ended Dec. 31)	1997	1996	1995	1994	1993	1992	1991	1990	1989	1988
Tangible Bk. Val.	8.58	6.74	7.23	5.12	5.59	4.51	4.24	4.18	5.64	5.60
Earnings	2.17	1.77	1.44	1.17	0.97	0.66	0.53	1.01	0.98	0.83
Dividends	0.54	0.49	0.44	0.41	0.39	0.38	0.37	0.36	0.36	0.34
Payout Ratio	25%	28%	30%	35%	40%	58%	71%	36%	36%	42%
Prices - High	43⅜	32¾	22¾	13¼	13½	10⅛	10½	8⅞	10⅞	10⅛
- Low	26¼	17⅜	12	9½	9	6⅞	4⅝	3¼	7¾	6⅝
P/E Ratio - High	20	19	16	11	14	15	20	9	11	12
- Low	12	10	8	8	9	11	9	3	8	8

Income Statement Analysis (Million $)

	1997	1996	1995	1994	1993	1992	1991	1990	1989	1988
Total Revs.	5,503	5,058	5,144	4,603	4,455	4,181	4,594	4,320	3,490	2,637
Int. Exp.	1,503	1,521	1,557	1,243	1,150	1,420	1,887	2,026	1,708	1,219
Exp./Op. Revs.	81%	84%	85%	89%	90%	93%	96%	92%	91%	89%
Pretax Inc.	1,029	822	754	528	451	278	200	349	333	292
Eff. Tax Rate	33%	35%	40%	30%	34%	31%	25%	33%	34%	37%
Net Inc.	687	539	453	368	299	191	150	235	218	184

Balance Sheet & Other Fin. Data (Million $)

	1997	1996	1995	1994	1993	1992	1991	1990	1989	1988
Cash & Secs.	2,566	2,521	4,909	9,546	9,113	7,646	6,710	5,332	4,367	3,359
Loans	23,811	24,067	21,732	20,556	19,563	18,961	18,987	22,194	20,017	16,123
Total Assets	30,303	29,595	29,219	34,338	32,961	31,128	29,982	29,455	26,163	21,032
ST Debt	6,081	6,428	6,659	4,372	5,642	5,253	4,142	5,681	6,865	5,702
Capitalization:										
Debt	20,930	14,802	11,228	10,274	9,114	9,015	9,595	9,561	7,916	6,560
Equity	4,691	2,941	2,691	2,200	2,078	1,608	1,525	1,344	1,194	1,174
Total	19,690	17,538	14,124	13,117	11,531	10,959	11,624	11,374	9,490	7,734
Price Times Bk. Val.: High	5.0	4.9	3.2	2.6	2.4	2.2	2.5	2.1	1.9	1.8
Price Times Bk. Val.: Low	3.0	2.6	1.7	1.9	1.6	1.5	1.1	0.8	1.4	1.2
% Return On Revs.	12.5	10.6	8.8	8.0	6.7	4.6	3.3	5.4	6.3	7.0
% Ret. on Assets	2.3	1.8	1.4	1.1	0.9	0.6	0.5	0.8	0.9	1.0
% Ret. on Equity	17.3	19.1	17.5	16.0	14.2	10.6	9.0	17.7	18.4	15.9
Loans/Equity	6.4	12.2	11.6	9.4	10.5	11.8	14.2	16.6	15.3	13.5

Data as orig. reptd.; bef. results of disc opers. and/or spec. items. Per share data adj. for stk. divs. as of ex-div. date. Bold denotes diluted EPS (FASB 128). E-Estimated. NA-Not Available. NM-Not Meaningful. NR-Not Ranked.

Office—2700 Sanders Rd., Prospect Heights, IL 60070-2799. **Tel**—(847) 564-5000. **Website**—http://www.household.com **Chrmn & CEO**—W. F. Aldinger. **EVP & CFO**—D. A. Schoenholz. **Investor Contact**—Craig A. Streem (847-564-6053). **Dirs**—W. F. Aldinger, R. J. Darnall, G. G. Dillon, J. A. Edwardson, M. J. Evans, D. Fishburn, C. F. Freidheim Jr., L. E. Levy, G. A. Lorch, J. D. Nichols, J. B. Pitblado, S. J. Stewart, L. W. Sullivan. **Transfer Agent & Registrar**—Harris Trust & Savings Bank, Chicago. **Incorporated**—in Delaware in 1925. **Empl**— 14,700. **S&P Analyst:** Stephen R. Biggar

STANDARD &POOR'S
STOCK REPORTS
Houston Industries
1162
NYSE Symbol **HOU**
In S&P 500

12-SEP-98 | Industry: Electric Companies

Summary: This international energy holding company is one of the largest U.S. electric and natural gas companies.

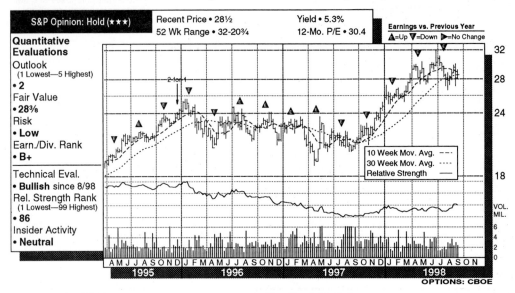

S&P Opinion: Hold (★★★)	Recent Price • 28½	Yield • 5.3%
	52 Wk Range • 32-20¾	12-Mo. P/E • 30.4

Earnings vs. Previous Year
▲=Up ▼=Down ▶=No Change

Quantitative Evaluations

Outlook (1 Lowest—5 Highest)
• **2**

Fair Value
• **28⅜**

Risk
• **Low**

Earn./Div. Rank
• **B+**

Technical Eval.
• **Bullish** since 8/98

Rel. Strength Rank (1 Lowest—99 Highest)
• **86**

Insider Activity
• **Neutral**

10 Week Mov. Avg. – – –
30 Week Mov. Avg. ----
Relative Strength —

OPTIONS: CBOE

Overview - 31-AUG-98

We expect HOU to realize high single-digit growth in 1999 operating income. While operating income in 1998 will remain essentially flat 1997's $1.83 (adjusted for nonrecurring charges), reported EPS will be down, due to non-cash, unrealized accounting losses related to the ownership of uniquely structured securities. In the first half of 1998, these losses came to $288 million ($1.01 a share). The recent purchase of four generating plants from Southern California Edison will enable HOU to play a significant role in the California power market. Based on proposed legislation, HOU expects its HL&P unit to become a wires only company, with net income declining from about $460 million in 1997 to about $280 million in 2002. However, earnings of the overall company should see long-term annual growth of 5% to 6%, fueled by significant operating synergies, a greater percentage of earnings from higher-growth gas operations, and increased contributions from international projects and investments.

Valuation - 31-AUG-98

We recommend holding the stock. The shares were recently up more than 9% year to date, reflecting continuing expansion of HOU's international and non-regulated operations. In 1997, the shares rose 18.2%, in line with respective gains of 19.8% and 18.6% for the S&P Indexes of Electric and Natural Gas Companies. However, they had recovered nearly 42% from a sharp decline earlier in the year, which was mainly the result of the uncertainties about the regulatory environment and restructuring legislation (now put off until 1999) in Texas. Despite a high payout ratio, the dividend is secure. With natural gas companies historically commanding higher multiples than electric utilities, we expect the P/E to increasingly reflect potential earnings contribution from NorAm and the non-regulated operations.

Key Stock Statistics

S&P EPS Est. 1998	1.05	Tang. Bk. Value/Share	15.89
P/E on S&P Est. 1998	27.2	Beta	0.43
S&P EPS Est. 1999	2.00	Shareholders	66,000
Dividend Rate/Share	1.50	Market cap. (B)	$ 8.5
Shs. outstg. (M)	296.1	Inst. holdings	44%
Avg. daily vol. (M)	0.594		

Value of $10,000 invested 5 years ago: $ 18,061

Fiscal Year Ending Dec. 31

	1998	1997	1996	1995	1994	1993
Revenues (Million $)						
1Q	2,637	878.1	824.4	755.2	882.0	866.0
2Q	2,739	1,064	1,114	989.8	1,067	1,068
3Q	—	2,159	1,246	1,185	1,216	1,417
4Q	—	2,772	906.0	800.1	837.1	974.0
Yr.	—	6,873	4,095	3,730	4,002	4,324
Earnings Per Share ($)						
1Q	-0.11	0.26	-0.07	0.10	0.14	0.10
2Q	0.16	0.52	0.58	0.54	0.51	0.39
3Q	E0.94	0.93	0.98	0.95	0.96	1.00
4Q	E0.06	-0.01	0.15	0.02	0.05	0.11
Yr.	E1.05	1.66	1.66	1.60	1.66	1.60

Next earnings report expected: late October

Dividend Data (Dividends have been paid since 1922.)

Amount ($)	Date Decl.	Ex-Div. Date	Stock of Record	Payment Date
0.375	Dec. 11	Feb. 11	Feb. 16	Mar. 10 '98
0.375	Mar. 10	May. 13	May. 15	Jun. 10 '98
0.375	Jun. 03	Aug. 12	Aug. 14	Sep. 10 '98
0.375	Sep. 02	Nov. 12	Nov. 16	Dec. 10 '98

A Division of The **McGraw·Hill** *Companies*

Business Summary - 31-AUG-98

In August 1997, Houston Industries, the holding company for Houston Lighting & Power Co. (HL&P), acquired NorAm Energy, the third largest natural gas utility in the U.S. The transaction increased HOU's customer base by 2.1 million, to (excluding overlapping customers) about 3.6 million customers in six states.

HL&P supplies electricity to around 1.6 million customers along the Texas Gulf Coast. HL&P's fuel sources in 1997 were coal and lignite, 41%; gas, 30%; nuclear, 9%; and purchased power, 20%.

Electric operations accounted for 61% of revenues (89% of operating income) in 1997; energy marketing, 23% (1%); natural gas distribution, 13% (5%); interstate pipeline, 2% (3%); and international, 1% (2%).

The Arkla, Entex and Minnegasco units acquired in the merger with NorAm provide gas distribution services in six central states extending from the Gulf Coast to Minnesota. Together, they serve over 2.8 million customers in 1,366 communities, including the metropolitan areas of Houston, Minneapolis, Little Rock and Shreveport.

The acquisition of NorAm provided HOU with a growing energy trading business and significant midstream gas assets in the form of interstate pipelines, gathering systems and storage facilities. The pipeline business is conducted though NGT (located primarily in Arkansas and Oklahoma), which operates 6,200 miles of trans-

mission lines; and MRT, which operates a 2,000 mile interstate pipeline system with access to the St. Louis and southeastern Illinois markets. NorAm's energy marketing division markets natural gas and electric power. It also provides services in price risk management, natural gas gathering, and retail energy marketing.

In March 1997, HOU formed Houston Industries Power Generation (HIPG), which acquires, develops and operates domestic non-regulated power generation facilities. In April 1998, HIPG acquired four natural gas-fired generating plants from Southern California Edison, for $237 million.

International operations are conducted though HI Energy, which participates in foreign power generation projects and invests in the privatization of foreign electric utilities. In August 1998, HI Energy and its Venezuelan partner, CEDC (the holding company for Electricidad de Caracas), acquired, for $550 million, a 65% interest in two electric distribution systems serving 1.2 million customers in Colombia. Earlier, in May 1997, HI Energy and CEDC acquired, for $498 million, a 57% interest in Empresa de Energia del Pacifico S.A., an integrated utility that serves 270,000 customers in the Valle del Cauca Province of Colombia. In May 1996, the unit acquired, for $392 million, 11.4% of Light-Servicos de Eletricidade, which operates an integrated electric system serving the city (and portions of the state) of Rio de Janeiro, Brazil.

Per Share Data ($)

(Year Ended Dec. 31)	1997	1996	1995	1994	1993	1992	1991	1990	1989	1988
Tangible Bk. Val.	16.57	14.88	15.08	8.90	8.12	8.15	8.81	9.53	9.59	14.02
Earnings	1.66	1.66	1.60	1.66	1.60	1.31	1.64	1.33	1.66	1.67
Dividends	1.50	1.50	1.50	1.50	1.50	1.49	1.48	1.48	1.48	1.47
Payout Ratio	90%	90%	94%	90%	94%	113%	90%	111%	89%	88%
Prices - High	27¼	25⅝	24½	23⅞	24⅞	23½	22¼	18⅝	18	17
- Low	18⅞	20½	17¾	15	21¼	20⅛	17⅜	15⅜	13⅜	13⅜
P/E Ratio - High	16	15	15	14	16	14	14	14	11	10
- Low	11	12	11	9	13	12	11	11	8	8

Income Statement Analysis (Million $)

	1997	1996	1995	1994	1993	1992	1991	1990	1989	1988
Revs.	6,873	4,095	3,730	4,002	4,324	4,596	4,444	4,179	3,790	3,649
Depr.	652	550	478	484	465	465	435	407	381	321
Maint.	NA	NA	250	248	290	257	231	213	185	188
Fxd. Chgs. Cov.	2.6	3.3	2.1	2.5	2.4	2.1	2.3	2.2	3.0	2.9
Constr. Credits	3.0	6.7	12.0	10.0	7.0	12.0	16.0	13.0	55.0	211
Eff. Tax Rate	33%	33%	33%	33%	34%	30%	31%	31%	33%	25%
Net Inc.	421	405	398	407	416	340	417	339	413	395

Balance Sheet & Other Fin. Data (Million $)

	1997	1996	1995	1994	1993	1992	1991	1990	1989	1988
Gross Prop.	16,039	13,015	12,781	13,018	12,554	12,282	12,018	11,682	11,537	11,466
Cap. Exp.	329	318	301	418	333	336	376	358	389	582
Net Prop.	11,269	8,756	8,865	9,329	9,198	9,190	9,279	9,254	9,433	9,383
Capitalization:										
LT Debt	5,218	3,026	3,338	4,223	4,243	4,441	4,869	4,612	4,758	3,411
% LT Debt	50	43	43	52	53	54	56	52	53	47
Pfd.	10.0	135	402	473	519	558	460	568	568	440
% Pfd.	0.10	1.40	5.10	5.90	6.50	6.70	5.20	6.40	6.30	6.10
Common	4,887	3,828	4,124	3,369	3,274	3,285	3,449	3,647	3,676	3,407
% Common	47	40	52	42	41	40	39	41	41	47
Total Cap.	13,619	9,628	10,324	10,560	10,458	10,529	10,602	10,531	10,659	8,822
% Oper. Ratio	87.5	80.7	81.1	80.2	81.7	83.1	81.6	81.4	85.3	84.6
% Earn. on Net Prop.	10.6	4.6	7.9	8.6	8.6	8.4	8.8	8.3	5.9	6.1
% Return On Revs.	6.1	9.9	10.7	10.2	9.6	7.4	9.4	8.1	10.9	10.8
% Return On Invest. Capital	7.9	10.3	7.0	7.3	8.0	7.4	8.5	7.3	7.5	7.9
% Return On Com. Equity	9.7	10.2	10.6	12.3	12.8	12.8	12.0	9.4	11.7	11.8

Data as orig. reptd.; bef. results of disc. opers. and/or spec. items. Per share data adj. for stk. divs. as of ex-div. date. Bold denotes diluted EPS (FASB 128). E-Estimated. NA-Not Available. NM-Not Meaningful. NR-Not Ranked.

Office—1111 Louisiana, Houston, TX 77002. **Tel**—(713) 207-3000. **Chrmn & CEO**—D. D. Jordan. **Pres & COO**—R. S. Letbetter. **EVP & CFO**—S. W. Naeve. **EVP & Secy**—H. R. Kelly. **Investor Contact**—J. R. (Randy) Burkhalter (3115). **Dirs**—J. A. Baker III, R. E. Balzhiser, M. Carroll, J. T. Cater, O. H. Crosswell, R. J. Cruikshank, L. F. Deily, J. M. Grant, R. C. Hanna, L. W. Hogan, T. M. Honea, D. D. Jordan, R. S. Letbetter, A. F. Schilt, B. Wolfe. **Transfer Agent & Registrar**—Co.'s office. **Incorporated**—in Texas in 1906; reincorporated in Texas in 1976. **Empl**— 12,714. **S&P Analyst:** Justin McCann

STANDARD &POOR'S
STOCK REPORTS

Humana Inc.

1175M

NYSE Symbol **HUM**

In S&P 500

12-SEP-98

Industry:
Health Care (Managed Care)

Summary: This leading provider of managed healthcare services recently terminated an agreement to merge with rival HMO operator United Healthcare.

S&P Opinion: Hold (★★★)	Recent Price • 14	Yield • Nil
	52 Wk Range • 32⅛-12¼	12-Mo. P/E • 12.0

Quantitative Evaluations

Outlook
(1 Lowest—5 Highest)
• 5

Fair Value
• 28⅞

Risk
• Average

Earn./Div. Rank
• B

Technical Eval.
• **Bearish** since 7/98

Rel. Strength Rank
(1 Lowest—99 Highest)
• 13

Insider Activity
• **Neutral**

Earnings vs. Previous Year
▲=Up ▼=Down ▶=No Change

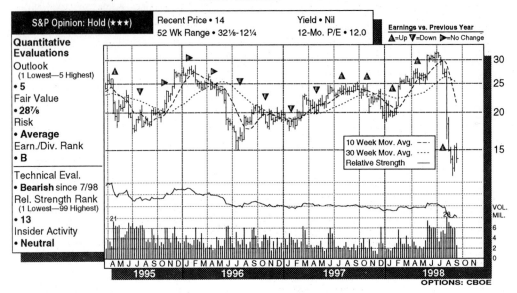

10 Week Mov. Avg. ----
30 Week Mov. Avg. ·····
Relative Strength ——

VOL. MIL.

1995   1996   1997   1998

OPTIONS: CBOE

Overview - 19-AUG-98

The company recently terminated it's planned merger with United Healthcare (UNH) following a surprising second quarter loss by United which precipitated a sharp decline in UNH share price. Humana was to be purchased by UNH in a tax-free exchange of stock initially valued at $5.5 billion. On a stand-alone basis, we still look for Humana to generate premium revenues in 1998 of about $10.5 billion, reflecting commercial rate hikes upwards of 4%, Medicare rate increases of about 2%, the inclusion of former Physician Corp. of America and ChoiceCare members, and higher Medicare enrollment. Same-store commercial enrollment growth will moderate on the impact of the 1998 rate hikes. The medical loss ratio may push towards 84% in 1998 as pharmaceutical cost inflation remains above 10%, and we see EPS of $1.30 in 1998 and $1.60 in 1999.

Valuation - 19-AUG-98

We lowered our opinion from accumulate to hold following the collapse of the merger agreement with United Healthcare. The proposed deal was viewed as a long term positive for Humana as it explores methods to bolster profit margins and expand geographically. Absent the combination and given the modest enrollment growth outlook for 1998 and 1999, we now see long term EPS growth in the 18% to 19% range and feel that the stock is amply priced at recent levels. During the second quarter of 1998, EPS of $0.31 fell a few cents below our estimate on a higher-than-anticipated medical loss ratio. Given that HUM has been eliminating its less-profitable contracts, we were surprised that the medical loss ratio remained above 83%, and have lowered our 1998 estimate by $0.05 to $1.30. Assuming no further enrollment slowdown, we see 1999 EPS of $1.60.

Key Stock Statistics

S&P EPS Est. 1998	1.30	Tang. Bk. Value/Share	2.63
P/E on S&P Est. 1998	10.8	Beta	1.71
S&P EPS Est. 1999	1.60	Shareholders	10,400
Dividend Rate/Share	Nil	Market cap. (B)	$ 2.3
Shs. outstg. (M)	166.9	Inst. holdings	73%
Avg. daily vol. (M)	1.368		

Value of $10,000 invested 5 years ago: $ 6,915

Fiscal Year Ending Dec. 31

	1998	1997	1996	1995	1994	1993
Revenues (Million $)						
1Q	2,402	1,803	1,588	1,048	853.0	786.0
2Q	2,446	1,805	1,605	1,070	897.0	778.0
3Q	—	1,968	1,784	1,094	926.0	782.0
4Q	—	2,337	1,811	1,490	920.0	791.0
Yr.	—	7,880	6,788	4,702	3,576	3,137
Earnings Per Share ($)						
1Q	**0.30**	**0.24**	0.32	0.32	0.20	0.11
2Q	**0.31**	**0.25**	-0.58	0.28	0.33	0.12
3Q	**E0.34**	**0.27**	0.20	0.27	0.27	0.15
4Q	**E0.35**	**0.29**	0.13	0.30	0.30	0.18
Yr.	**E1.30**	**1.05**	0.07	1.17	1.10	0.56

Next earnings report expected: NA

Dividend Data

Cash dividend payments were suspended in 1993.

A Division of The **McGraw·Hill** *Companies*

Business Summary - 19-AUG-98

Humana ranks among the largest providers of managed healthcare services in the U.S., offering a wide range of products to employer groups, as well as to Medicare and Medicaid-eligible individuals. As of June 30, 1998, fully insured medical membership totaled 5.6 million, comprised of commercial (3,260,700), Medicare risk (501,000), TRICARE (1,096,300), Medicaid (630,200) and Medicare supplement (61,800). The majority of enrollment is centered in Florida, with more recent expansion efforts focused on Texas, Ohio and Puerto Rico.

The company offers a full range of health care products in virtually all of its markets. Its principal product is the HMO (health maintenance organization), in which the company charges its members a fixed annual premium in return for an agreement to use only those doctors included in the network. Its other managed care plan, the preferred provider organization (PPO), also offers a fixed annual premium but allows the member the option of going to physicians outside of the network. In return, the member may be required to pay a portion of the provider's fees.

The company's HMO plans generally reimburse providers on a "capitated" basis, under an actuarially determined, fixed, per-member per-month fee. This fee does not vary with the nature or extent of services provided to the member, and is generally designed to shift a portion of the HMO's financial risk to the primary care physician. Providers participating in the company's PPO plans are generally reimbursed on a negotiated fee-for-service basis. At 1997 year-end, Humana's 18 owned and operated HMOs contracted with about 73,500 physicians (including roughly 21,500 primary care) and about 1,100 hospitals, and had contracts with approximately 7,000 other providers. In addition, about 55,000 physicians and 750 hospitals were contracted directly with the company to provide services to PPO members, and 5,500 contracts (including some contracts to also serve HMO members) were in place with other providers to service PPO members.

Specialty and administrative service products include dental, group life, workers' compensation and pharmacy benefit management services. Specialty product membership at June 30, 1998, totaled 3,171,200, including 693,400 utilizing an administrative service only product.

Per Share Data ($) (Year Ended Dec. 31)	1997	1996	1995	1994	1993	1992	1991	1990	1989	1988
Tangible Bk. Val.	1.68	4.93	4.64	5.60	5.17	2.89	12.70	11.18	8.99	7.87
Cash Flow	1.69	0.68	1.60	1.40	0.85	-0.32	3.76	3.49	2.88	2.65
Earnings	1.05	0.07	1.17	1.10	0.56	-0.63	2.26	2.05	1.71	1.53
Dividends	Nil	Nil	Nil	Nil	Nil	0.90	0.82	0.72	0.63	0.55
Payout Ratio	Nil	Nil	Nil	Nil	Nil	NM	37%	35%	32%	36%
Prices - High	25¼	28⅞	28	25⅜	21⅜	29½	35⅛	34	29⅜	19⅛
- Low	17⅜	15	17	15⅞	5⅞	17	22¾	23½	16¼	12¾
P/E Ratio - High	24	NM	24	23	38	NM	16	17	17	12
- Low	17	NM	15	14	10	NM	10	11	10	8
Income Statement Analysis (Million $)										
Revs.	7,880	6,677	4,605	3,654	3,195	2,778	5,865	4,852	4,088	3,435
Oper. Inc.	242	112	272	300	197	89.0	825	749	670	636
Depr.	108	98.0	70.0	50.0	47.0	49.0	236	215	194	183
Int. Exp.	20.0	11.0	11.0	4.0	7.0	12.0	103	115	142	148
Pretax Inc.	270	18.0	288	257	143	-142	555	499	399	354
Eff. Tax Rate	36%	33%	24%	32%	38%	NM	36%	36%	36%	36%
Net Inc.	173	12.0	190	176	89.0	-99.0	355	318	256	227
Balance Sheet & Other Fin. Data (Million $)										
Cash	627	1,584	1,338	881	799	284	161	155	184	247
Curr. Assets	2,750	2,002	1,593	1,038	1,002	477	1,169	1,055	1,015	928
Total Assets	5,418	3,153	2,878	1,957	1,731	1,174	4,427	3,936	3,697	3,422
Curr. Liab.	2,263	1,500	1,192	816	771	561	1,105	975	777	634
LT Debt	1,486	225	250	Nil	71.0	21.0	826	717	1,140	1,211
Common Eqty.	1,501	1,292	1,287	1,058	889	528	2,009	1,750	1,327	1,155
Total Cap.	2,987	1,517	1,537	1,058	960	549	3,055	2,702	2,706	2,625
Cap. Exp.	73.0	72.0	54.0	39.0	28.0	NA	586	452	287	222
Cash Flow	281	110	260	226	136	-50.0	591	549	450	410
Curr. Ratio	1.2	1.3	1.4	1.3	1.3	0.9	1.1	1.1	1.3	1.5
% LT Debt of Cap.	49.7	14.8	16.3	Nil	7.4	3.8	27.0	26.5	42.1	46.1
% Net Inc.of Revs.	2.2	0.2	4.1	4.8	2.8	NM	6.1	6.6	6.3	6.6
% Ret. on Assets	4.0	0.4	7.9	9.5	6.5	NA	8.4	8.1	7.2	6.8
% Ret. on Equity	12.4	1.0	16.2	18.0	14.1	NA	18.8	20.2	20.6	20.9

Data as orig. reptd.; bef. results of disc. opers. and/or spec. items. Per share data adj. for stk. divs. as of ex-div. date. Bold denotes diluted EPS (FASB 128). E-Estimated. NA-Not Available. NM-Not Meaningful. NR-Not Ranked.

Office—Humana Bldg., 500 West Main St., Louisville, KY 40202. **Tel**—(502) 580-1000. **Website**—http://www.Humana.com **Pres & CEO**—G. H. Wolf. **VP & Treas**—J. W. Doucette. **VP & CFO**—J. E. Murray. **Investor Contact**—Laurie G. Scarborough. **Dirs**—K. F. Austen, M. E. Gellert, J. R. Hall, D. A. Jones, D. A. Jones Jr., I. Lerner, W. A. Reynolds, G. H. Wolf. **Transfer Agent**—Bank of Louisville. **Incorporated**—in Delaware in 1964. **Empl**— 19,500. **S&P Analyst:** Robert M. Gold

Huntington Bancshares   4211
Nasdaq Symbol **HBAN**
In S&P 500

12-SEP-98 **Industry:** Banks (Major Regional) **Summary:** This $28 billion regional bank holding company has a net-work of branches throughout the Midwest and the East Coast.

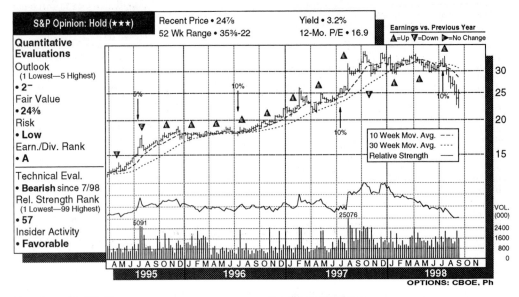

S&P Opinion: Hold (★★★)

Recent Price • 24⅞
52 Wk Range • 35⅜-22

Yield • 3.2%
12-Mo. P/E • 16.9

Quantitative Evaluations

Outlook
(1 Lowest—5 Highest)
• **2⁻**

Fair Value
• **24⅜**

Risk
• **Low**

Earn./Div. Rank
• **A**

Technical Eval.
• **Bearish** since 7/98

Rel. Strength Rank
(1 Lowest—99 Highest)
• **57**

Insider Activity
• **Favorable**

OPTIONS: CBOE, Ph

Overview - 24-JUL-98

Loan growth is expected in the mid single digits in 1998, as demand for lending products remains healthy in virtually all markets. The net interest margin has been impacted by competition for commercial loans and a decline in higher-yielding installment loans, but should rebound in 1998's second half to around the 4.35% range, reflecting better deposit growth following the acquisition of Barnett's Florida branches and the sale of lower-yielding assets. On the noninterest income side of the business, the company is benefiting from particularly strong fee growth from mortgage banking and brokerage and insurance sales. Noninterest expense growth, which was high in 1997 on spending for an advertising brand campaign, should trend down with a longer range goal to bring the efficiency ratio to 50%, from 54.9% in 1997. Credit quality is strong, with an aggregate charge-off rate of only 0.41% and the loan loss allowance at 1.50% of total loans at June 30, 1998. An aggressive acquisition program, designed to increase market penetration in areas where the company has a presence, is expected to continue.

Valuation - 24-JUL-98

With business trends benefiting from a relatively healthy regional territory, core earnings growth of about 10% is expected in the near term, about average for our major regional bank group. Acquisitions should continue to provide better market penetration and longer term scale advantages, but may be dilutive near term. Fundamentally, the shares, trading at 18 times our estimate for 1998 earnings of $1.75, appear fairly valued, but remain worthwhile for long-term investors seeking stable growth with relatively low risk and a good dividend yield.

Key Stock Statistics

S&P EPS Est. 1998	1.75	Tang. Bk. Value/Share	10.08
P/E on S&P Est. 1998	14.2	Beta	0.88
S&P EPS Est. 1999	2.00	Shareholders	29,300
Dividend Rate/Share	0.80	Market cap. (B)	$ 5.3
Shs. outstg. (M)	211.7	Inst. holdings	22%
Avg. daily vol. (M)	0.324		

Value of $10,000 invested 5 years ago: $ 25,098

Fiscal Year Ending Dec. 31

	1998	1997	1996	1995	1994	1993
Revenues (Million $)						
1Q	599.2	471.0	442.5	401.4	362.9	314.9
2Q	612.5	498.7	442.3	420.1	359.5	348.8
3Q	—	502.8	449.4	439.1	359.1	388.7
4Q	—	588.3	419.3	449.8	373.6	489.7
Yr.	—	2,324	1,783	1,710	1,455	1,542
Earnings Per Share ($)						
1Q	**0.42**	**0.36**	0.35	0.29	0.37	0.31
2Q	**0.43**	**0.39**	0.37	0.32	0.37	0.33
3Q	**E0.44**	**0.19**	0.38	0.36	0.31	0.34
4Q	**E0.46**	**0.43**	0.35	0.37	0.29	0.35
Yr.	**E1.75**	**1.38**	1.49	1.34	1.34	1.32

Next earnings report expected: mid October

Dividend Data (Dividends have been paid since 1912.)

Amount ($)	Date Decl.	Ex-Div. Date	Stock of Record	Payment Date
0.200	Feb. 26	Mar. 13	Mar. 17	Apr. 01 '98
0.200	May. 20	Jun. 11	Jun. 15	Jul. 01 '98
10%	May. 20	Jul. 13	Jul. 15	Jul. 31 '98
0.200	Aug. 19	Sep. 14	Sep. 16	Oct. 01 '98

A Division of The **McGraw·Hill** *Companies*

STANDARD
&POOR'S
STOCK REPORTS

Huntington Bancshares Incorporated

4211
12-SEP-98

Business Summary - 24-JUL-98

As competition among banks has become increasingly intense, Huntington Bancshares (HBAN) has distinguished itself as a financial institution that consistently provides its retail and commercial clients the highest level of customer service. This $28 billion regional bank holding company, headquartered in Columbus, OH, is able to service its clients by providing an array of differentiated products through subsidiaries that operate a network of over 600 branches in 12 states in the Midwest and along the East Coast.

The company segments its operations into five distinct lines of business. These are: retail banking- which provides credit cards, equity loans, mortgage loans, installment loans and deposit products to retail and community business banking customers; corporate banking-representing small, middle-market and large corporate banking relationships; dealer sales- relating mainly to the automotive sector and including floor plan financing, indirect loans and leases; private financial group- which provides personal trust, asset management, investment advisory and other wealth management services; and treasury/other- which includes managing the company's $6 billion investment portfolio.

Net interest income, the largest component of total revenues, is the excess of the interest a bank receives on loans and other investments over the interest it pays on the funds it borrows. The key factors fueling growth of net interest income are a bank's level of earning assets and its ability to maximize the spread between the yield it receives and the interest it must pay, as it carefully manages the riskiness of the assets into which it invests. At 1997 year-end, about 66% of HBAN's total assets were invested in loans, most of which were concentrated in the consumer (45% of total loans), commercial (30%), and real estate mortgage (20%) segments.

At the end of 1997, nonperforming assets, consisting of non-accrual loans, renegotiated loans and other real estate, were $87.1 million (0.49% of total loans and other assets), up from $76.7 million (0.46%) a year earlier. The allowance for loan losses, which is set aside for possible loan defaults, was $258.2 million (1.46% of total loans), versus $230.8 million (1.38%) the year before. Net charge-offs, or the amount of loans actually written off as uncollectible, were $88.2 million (0.50% of average loans) in 1997, up from $70.0 million (0.44%) in 1996.

In June 1998, the company completed the acquisition of 60 former Barnett Banks banking offices from NationsBank Corp., adding $2.3 billion in deposits and $1.3 billion in loans and more than doubling its existing banking offices in Florida.

Per Share Data ($)

(Year Ended Dec. 31)	1997	1996	1995	1994	1993	1992	1991	1990	1989	1988
Tangible Bk. Val.	9.60	8.76	8.58	7.76	7.26	6.35	5.78	5.32	5.07	4.74
Earnings	1.38	1.49	1.34	1.34	1.32	0.94	0.79	0.57	0.76	0.73
Dividends	0.69	0.63	0.59	0.52	0.43	0.35	0.33	0.29	0.25	0.22
Payout Ratio	50%	42%	44%	39%	32%	38%	41%	51%	33%	30%
Prices - High	35³/₈	23⁷/₈	19¹/₈	15⁷/₈	15³/₄	12¹/₈	8⁷/₈	7³/₈	8¹/₈	6¹/₂
- Low	20⁵/₈	16⁷/₈	12¹/₈	11⁷/₈	11¹/₈	8	4³/₈	3⁵/₈	5⁵/₈	4³/₄
P/E Ratio - High	26	16	14	12	12	13	10	13	11	9
- Low	15	11	9	9	8	9	6	6	7	7

Income Statement Analysis (Million $)

	1997	1996	1995	1994	1993	1992	1991	1990	1989	1988
Net Int. Inc.	1,027	759	725	756	796	610	478	424	389	328
Tax Equiv. Adj.	11.9	5.1	6.8	9.5	11.7	11.6	14.5	17.7	20.9	20.8
Non Int. Inc.	335	255	248	233	279	201	167	153	139	107
Loan Loss Prov.	108	65.0	28.7	15.3	79.3	75.7	56.7	71.0	39.9	26.3
Exp./Op. Revs.	59%	56%	58%	61%	61%	69%	67%	66%	63%	65%
Pretax Inc.	459	399	378	366	364	200	166	115	144	112
Eff. Tax Rate	36%	34%	35%	34%	35%	31%	30%	26%	25%	22%
Net Inc.	293	262	244	243	237	139	117	85.0	108	88.0
% Net Int. Marg.	4.44	4.11	4.15	4.96	5.20	5.27	4.63	4.17	4.31	4.48

Balance Sheet & Other Fin. Data (Million $)

	1997	1996	1995	1994	1993	1992	1991	1990	1989	1988
Earning Assets:										
Money Mkt	556	12.0	495	18.0	76.0	265	84.0	84.0	141	417
Inv. Securities	5,743	4,804	4,789	3,780	4,199	3,564	2,756	2,606	2,918	1,916
Com'l Loans	5,271	4,463	4,190	4,257	3,916	3,188	2,903	3,010	3,073	2,608
Other Loans	12,468	9,798	9,072	8,146	8,070	5,724	5,390	4,880	4,239	3,322
Total Assets	26,731	20,852	20,255	17,771	17,619	13,895	12,333	11,809	11,680	9,506
Demand Deposits	2,550	5,050	4,861	4,816	2,069	1,729	1,531	1,470	1,412	1,349
Time Deposits	3,768	8,336	7,776	7,149	9,976	8,223	7,980	7,645	7,177	5,758
LT Debt	2,886	1,556	2,103	1,023	684	270	137	141	153	153
Common Eqty.	2,025	1,512	1,519	1,412	1,325	941	853	786	721	570
% Ret. on Assets	1.2	1.3	1.3	1.4	1.4	1.1	1.0	0.7	1.0	1.0
% Ret. on Equity	16.5	17.3	16.7	17.3	19.5	15.5	14.3	11.1	15.8	16.2
% Loan Loss Resv.	1.5	1.4	1.5	1.6	1.8	1.6	1.5	1.5	1.1	1.1
% Loans/Deposits	98.6	106.5	104.9	103.7	99.5	89.6	87.2	86.6	85.1	83.4
% Equity to Assets	7.4	7.4	7.7	8.4	7.2	7.0	7.0	6.6	6.5	6.2

Data as orig. reptd.; bef. results of disc opers. and/or spec. items. Per share data adj. for stk. divs. as of ex-div. date. Bold denotes diluted EPS (FASB 128). E-Estimated. NA-Not Available. NM-Not Meaningful. NR-Not Ranked.

Office—41 S. High St., Columbus, OH 43287.**Tel**—(614) 480-8300. **Website**—http://www.huntington.com **Chrmn & CEO**—F. Wobst. **Vice Chrmn**—P. E. Geier, W. L. Hoskins, R. J. Seiffert. **Pres, Treas & COO**—Z. Sofia. **EVP & CFO**—G. R. Williams. **Secy**—R. K. Frasier. **Investor Contact**—Anne Creek (614) 480-3954. **Dirs**—D. M. Casto III, D. Conrad, P. T. Hayot, W. J. Lhota, R. H. Schottenstein, G. A. Skestos, L. R. Smoot, Sr., T. P. Smucker, Z. Sofia, W. J. Williams, F. Wobst. **Transfer Agent**—Huntington National Bank, Columbus. **Incorporated**—in Maryland in 1966. **Empl**— 9,485. **S&P Analyst:** Stephen R. Biggar

STANDARD &POOR'S
STOCK REPORTS

IKON Office Solutions

1184K

NYSE Symbol **IKN**

In S&P 500

12-SEP-98

Industry: Photography/Imaging

Summary: This leading distributor of office equipment has expanded into outsourcing and network services in recent years. The company spun off its paper distribution unit at 1996 year-end.

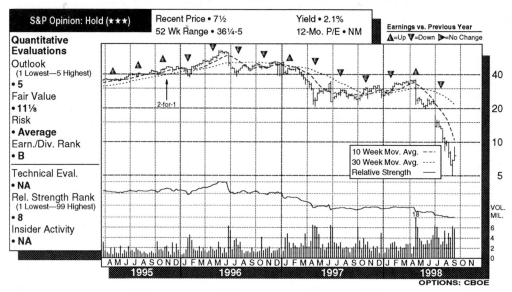

S&P Opinion: Hold (★★★)	Recent Price • 7½	Yield • 2.1%
	52 Wk Range • 36¼-5	12-Mo. P/E • NM

Quantitative Evaluations

Outlook (1 Lowest—5 Highest)
• **5**

Fair Value
• **11⅛**

Risk
• **Average**

Earn./Div. Rank
• **B**

Technical Eval.
• **NA**

Rel. Strength Rank (1 Lowest—99 Highest)
• **8**

Insider Activity
• **NA**

Earnings vs. Previous Year
▲=Up ▼=Down ▷=No Change

2-for-1

10 Week Mov. Avg. - - -
30 Week Mov. Avg. · · · ·
Relative Strength —

VOL. MIL.

OPTIONS: CBOE

Overview - 29-APR-98

IKON should record moderate sales growth in FY 98 (Sep.), fueled by an ongoing acquisition program, internal growth, and aggressive expansion in outsourcing and office equipment networking. These factors will be partly offset by difficulties stemming from IKON's efforts to create a new company-wide business infrastructure, as well as competitive pricing pressure. Margins will likely narrow, dragged down by the business transformation and pricing troubles. Our estimates include $0.20 a share of charges recorded in the first half of FY 98 for costs of the business transformation program; additional charges to be recorded through the end of FY 98 have not been included in our forecast. FY 97 EPS included $0.61 a share of transformation costs.

Valuation - 29-APR-98

The shares have performed dismally since mid-1996, hurt mostly by IKON's extremely poor implementation of a new operating structure. The shares began to stage a bit of a recovery between the fall of 1997 and the spring of 1998, when it appeared that IKN's restructuring problems had been ironed out. However, when the company's FY 98 second quarter earnings report showed that to be untrue (with competitive pricing pressures also thrown into the mix), the shares got crushed again. While IKON's management has done a horrible job implementing its business transformation program, we agree with its expansion and restructuring actions. In addition, the initiatives should be nearing conclusion around FY 98 year-end, and IKN has also finally acknowledged the need to add to its management pool. Based on these factors, and with the shares now trading at only 14X to 15X our reduced FY 99 EPS forecast, we would be inclined to hold onto positions, although IKN's miscues will be difficult to forget.

Key Stock Statistics

S&P EPS Est. 1998	1.20	Tang. Bk. Value/Share	NM
P/E on S&P Est. 1998	6.3	Beta	1.48
S&P EPS Est. 1999	1.65	Shareholders	15,000
Dividend Rate/Share	0.16	Market cap. (B)	$ 1.0
Shs. outstg. (M)	135.6	Inst. holdings	57%
Avg. daily vol. (M)	1.280		

Value of $10,000 invested 5 years ago: NA

Fiscal Year Ending Sep. 30

	1998	1997	1996	1995	1994	1993
Revenues (Million $)						
1Q	1,374	1,140	900.6	2,182	1,922	1,444
2Q	1,439	1,278	1,015	2,446	1,969	1,491
3Q	1,395	1,316	1,059	2,596	2,001	1,547
4Q	—	1,394	1,125	2,669	2,104	1,962
Yr.	—	1,439	4,100	9,892	7,996	6,445
Earnings Per Share ($)						
1Q	**0.24**	0.30	0.25	0.39	0.30	0.26
2Q	**0.25**	0.07	0.28	0.41	0.32	0.28
3Q	**-0.69**	0.19	0.30	0.49	-0.47	0.29
4Q	**E0.33**	0.21	0.30	0.52	0.41	-0.85
Yr.	**E1.20**	0.77	1.12	1.81	0.55	-0.02

Next earnings report expected: mid October

Dividend Data (Dividends have been paid since 1965.)

Amount ($)	Date Decl.	Ex-Div. Date	Stock of Record	Payment Date
0.040	Nov. 06	Nov. 20	Nov. 24	Dec. 10 '97
0.040	Jan. 22	Feb. 19	Feb. 23	Mar. 10 '98
0.040	May. 08	May. 21	May. 26	Jun. 10 '98
0.040	Jul. 30	Aug. 20	Aug. 24	Sep. 10 '98

A Division of The McGraw·Hill Companies

STANDARD
&POOR'S
STOCK REPORTS

IKON Office Solutions, Inc.

1184K

12-SEP-98

Business Summary - 29-APR-98

IKON Office Solutions (formerly Alco Standard Corp.) is a leading office technology company. In recent years, the company conducted operations through its IKON Office Solutions unit, which distributes office equipment, and Unisource Worldwide, which distributes paper and supply systems. However, when the IKON unit's outsourcing business began to encounter major competitive battles with Unisource's printing customers, the company decided that the two should operate as independent, publicly owned companies. As such, effective December 31, 1996, Unisource was spun off to IKN shareholders, with the name of the parent company changed to IKON Office Solutions on January 27, 1997.

IKON sells, rents and leases photocopiers, fax machines, digital printers and other automated office equipment for use in both traditional and integrated office environments. In recent years, IKON has expanded into outsourcing, imaging and networking services. IKON views leasing as an important customer retention tool, and derived nearly 70% of FY 97 (Sep.) revenues through leasing and servicing contracts (61% in FY 96).

The company has locations throughout the U.S. and Canada, as well as in Europe (mostly in the U.K.); a total of about 1,100 facilities at FY 97 year-end. Foreign operations account for a modest proportion of IKON's business, but it expects to rapidly expand in selected global markets, and sees annual foreign sales tripling, to about $2 billion, by 2000.

With operations hurt by poorly implemented business transformation programs, IKON's internal revenue growth since the second quarter of FY 97 has fallen far short of the 15% growth rate it seeks. Competitive pricing pressure has been added to the mix, and IKN's internal revenue gains were held to 5% in the FY 98 second quarter; at the end of the quarter, IKON said it expected only 5% to 7% internal revenue gains in the second half of the year. Given its current situation, in April 1998, the company said that its earlier EPS growth estimate for FY 98 had been too ambitious (it had expected 20% EPS gains, before transformation charges). IKON now sees EPS of $0.72 to $0.76 in the second half of the year, versus $0.65 in FY 97 period (both before transformation expenses).

IKN purchased 89 companies in FY 97; the acquisitions recorded $528 million of revenues in the year preceding their purchase. In line with its new operating strategy, IKON acquired 28 technology services companies and 27 outsourcing and imaging firms, with only 34 purchases falling into its core traditional office equipment business; it purchased 27 more companies in the first half of FY 98.

Per Share Data ($)

(Year Ended Sep. 30)	1997	1996	1995	1994	1993	1992	1991	1990	1989	1988
Tangible Bk. Val.	NM	6.68	2.84	3.84	1.32	3.85	5.09	5.04	4.70	5.55
Cash Flow	1.93	2.04	2.78	1.45	0.81	1.79	1.74	1.75	1.92	1.55
Earnings	0.77	1.12	1.81	0.55	-0.02	1.11	0.97	1.09	1.34	1.06
Dividends	0.26	0.56	0.52	0.50	0.48	0.46	0.44	0.42	0.38	0.34
Payout Ratio	34%	50%	28%	91%	NM	41%	45%	38%	26%	32%
Prices - High	46⅝	66	47⅛	32¾	27⅜	21⅜	18	19	18⅜	14
- Low	20⅝	37⅜	31	24¾	17⅞	16⅝	14½	13⅞	12¾	10⅛
P/E Ratio - High	61	59	26	60	NM	19	18	17	14	13
- Low	27	33	17	45	NM	15	15	13	9	10

Income Statement Analysis (Million $)

	1997	1996	1995	1994	1993	1992	1991	1990	1989	1988
Revs.	5,128	4,100	9,794	7,993	6,438	4,922	4,752	4,309	4,139	3,810
Oper. Inc.	516	496	468	439	339	278	260	233	221	191
Depr.	157	118	110	96.8	79.4	64.1	68.5	54.6	50.6	47.5
Int. Exp.	146	105	96.1	71.8	63.9	51.2	48.3	37.2	33.6	22.8
Pretax Inc.	213	273	360	157	25.0	173	144	145	149	132
Eff. Tax Rate	43%	40%	39%	55%	69%	40%	39%	37%	22%	23%
Net Inc.	122	165	219	71.0	8.0	104	88.0	91.0	116	100

Balance Sheet & Other Fin. Data (Million $)

	1997	1996	1995	1994	1993	1992	1991	1990	1989	1988
Cash	21.0	46.0	90.0	53.0	36.0	24.0	120	27.0	38.0	37.0
Curr. Assets	2,126	1,509	2,161	NA	NA	NA	NA	NA	NA	839
Total Assets	5,324	5,385	4,738	3,502	3,349	2,445	2,021	1,738	1,479	1,399
Curr. Liab.	1,374	1,258	1,390	1,057	1,020	762	611	576	539	443
LT Debt	1,984	1,535	1,143	806	1,003	697	464	357	227	171
Common Eqty.	1,192	1,965	1,376	1,166	819	860	821	686	594	659
Total Cap.	3,797	3,982	3,108	2,205	2,049	1,587	1,310	1,086	875	879
Cap. Exp.	193	147	99	108	84.0	58.0	55.0	67.0	75.0	49.0
Cash Flow	259	261	314	156	77.0	168	156	145	166	147
Curr. Ratio	1.5	1.2	1.6	NA	NA	NA	NA	NA	NA	1.9
% LT Debt of Cap.	52.3	38.6	36.8	36.5	49.0	43.9	35.4	32.8	25.9	19.4
% Net Inc.of Revs.	2.4	4.1	2.2	0.9	0.1	2.1	1.8	2.1	2.8	2.6
% Ret. on Assets	2.3	3.5	5.3	1.9	0.3	4.6	4.5	5.6	8.7	7.4
% Ret. on Equity	6.5	8.0	16.0	5.6	NM	12.2	11.2	14.1	20.0	15.8

Data as orig. reptd.; bef. results of disc. opers. and/or spec. items. Per share data adj. for stk. divs. as of ex-div. date. Bold denotes diluted EPS (FASB 128). E-Estimated. NA-Not Available. NM-Not Meaningful. NR-Not Ranked.

Office—70 Valley Stream Pkwy., Malverne, PA 19355 (P.O. Box 834), Valley Forge, PA 19482-0834. **Tel**—(610) 296-8000. **Website**—http://www.ikon.com **Chrmn & CEO**—J. E. Stuart. **EVP & CFO**—K. E. Dinkelacker. **Investor Contact**—Suzanne Shenk. **Dirs**—J. R. Birle, P. E. Cushing, K. E. Dinkelacker, W. F. Drake Jr., F. S. Hammer, B. B. Hauptfuhrer, R. A. Jalkut, J. E. Stuart. **Transfer Agent & Registrar**—National City Bank. Cleveland. **Incorporated**—in Ohio in 1952. **Empl**— 41,000. **S&P Analyst:** Michael W. Jaffe

Illinois Tool Works

1186M

NYSE Symbol **ITW**

In S&P 500

12-SEP-98

Industry: Manufacturing (Diversified)

Summary: This company makes industrial components and other specialty products for high-volume manufacturing. Primary markets include the auto, food and construction industries.

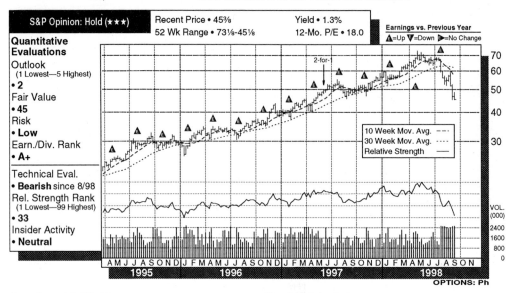

S&P Opinion: Hold (★★★)

Recent Price • 45⅜
52 Wk Range • 73⅛-45⅛

Yield • 1.3%
12-Mo. P/E • 18.0

Quantitative Evaluations

Outlook
(1 Lowest—5 Highest)
• **2**

Fair Value
• **45**

Risk
• **Low**

Earn./Div. Rank
• **A+**

Technical Eval.
• **Bearish** since 8/98

Rel. Strength Rank
(1 Lowest—99 Highest)
• **33**

Insider Activity
• **Neutral**

OPTIONS: Ph

Overview - 24-JUL-98

We anticipate revenue growth of about 5% in 1998, with moderate economic growth in North America and Europe. Continued high capacity utilization, firm pricing and stable raw material costs should aid margins and lift gross profits. Aided by lower interest costs, well controlled SG&A expenses, increased nonoperating income, lower costs for integrating acquisitions and a flat tax rate, earnings should continue to advance in 1998. Further acquisitions, perhaps increasingly focused on foreign markets, along with continued improvement in core businesses, increased nonoperating income, gains in market share and the introduction of new products should boost long-term sales and earnings. Over the long term, the company will continue to make frequent, modest acquisitions to boost its growth rate and continue to run them as stand-alone operations to foster flexibility and maintain an entrepreneurial organization with local management that is held accountable for the performance of their units. The company's two reporting segments operate 365 separate business units in 34 countries.

Valuation - 24-JUL-98

We are maintaining our hold opinion on Illinois Tool Works, as we believe that the shares are fully valued and that potential upside from current levels is limited. The shares, recently trading at about 23 times our 1998 earnings estimate of $2.60, are at a level above that of most other diversified manufacturers we follow. We think the premium valuation accorded the shares reflects the company's successful long-term track record of expansion by both internal growth and by acquisition and a record of regular dividend increases. While the shares are a worthwhile long-term holding, we think this is not the time to add to positions.

Key Stock Statistics

S&P EPS Est. 1998	2.60	Tang. Bk. Value/Share	8.79
P/E on S&P Est. 1998	17.5	Beta	1.19
S&P EPS Est. 1999	3.00	Shareholders	4,500
Dividend Rate/Share	0.60	Market cap. (B)	$ 11.3
Shs. outstg. (M)	250.0	Inst. holdings	70%
Avg. daily vol. (M)	0.657		

Value of $10,000 invested 5 years ago: $ 29,602

Fiscal Year Ending Dec. 31

	1998	1997	1996	1995	1994	1993
Revenues (Million $)						
1Q	1,341	1,230	1,137	929.1	771.4	750.0
2Q	1,420	1,326	1,325	1,091	881.0	829.3
3Q	—	1,315	1,238	1,045	870.9	779.5
4Q	—	1,349	1,297	1,087	937.9	800.3
Yr.	—	5,220	4,997	4,152	3,461	3,159
Earnings Per Share ($)						
1Q	**0.59**	**0.49**	0.41	0.33	0.23	0.19
2Q	**0.70**	**0.61**	0.53	0.46	0.31	0.24
3Q	—	**0.59**	0.49	0.42	0.32	0.23
4Q	—	**0.64**	0.54	0.45	0.38	0.26
Yr.	**E2.60**	2.33	1.95	1.65	1.23	0.92

Next earnings report expected: mid October

Dividend Data (Dividends have been paid since 1933.)

Amount ($)	Date Decl.	Ex-Div. Date	Stock of Record	Payment Date
0.120	Oct. 22	Dec. 29	Dec. 31	Jan. 23 '98
0.120	Feb. 20	Mar. 27	Mar. 31	Apr. 24 '98
0.120	May. 08	Jun. 17	Jun. 20	Jul. 24 '98
0.150	Aug. 07	Sep. 28	Sep. 30	Oct. 23 '98

A Division of The **McGraw·Hill** Companies

STANDARD
&POOR'S
STOCK REPORTS

Illinois Tool Works Inc.

1186M
12-SEP-98

Business Summary - 24-JUL-98

As a whole, Illinois Tool Works can be categorized as a producer of highly engineered fasteners, components, assemblies and systems, but the categorization stops right there. This company operates 365 small industrial businesses in a highly decentralized structure that places responsibility on managers at the lowest level possible in order to focus each of these business units on the needs of its particular customers. Each business unit manager is responsible for and is held strictly accountable for the results of his or her individual business. The company grows by developing new products and makes numerous acquisitions of small to mid-sized businesses. The company is diversified not only by customer and industry, but by geographic region, with some 36% of revenues and 29% of operating profits derived overseas.

Segment operating profit margins in recent years were as follows:

	1997	1996	1995
Engineered components	19%	17%	16%
Industrial systems and consumables	16%	15%	14%
Leasing and investments	39%	37%	73%

The engineered components segment (42% of reve-

nues and 45% of operating profits in 1997) produces short lead time plastic and metal components, fasteners and assemblies, industrial fluids and adhesives, fastening tools, and welding products. The largest markets served are automotive (39% of segment revenues), construction (29%), general industrial (14%), consumer durables (9%) and electronics (4%).

The industrial systems and consumables segment (56% of revenues, 51% of operating profits in 1997) produces longer lead time systems and related consumables for consumer and industrial packaging; marking, labeling and identification systems; industrial spray coating equipment and systems; and quality assurance equipment and systems. Important markets are general industrial (27% of segment revenues), food and beverage (16%), construction (13%), automotive (11%) and industrial capital goods (7%). Among ITW's more important divisions are Signode, which makes packaging application equipment and steel and plastic protective strap, and Hi-Cone, which makes plastic multipack ring carriers.

The company also has a leasing and investment segment, which accounts for 2% of revenues and 4% of operating profits. This segment holds almost $1.2 billion of investments in commercial mortgage loans and real estate, equipment leasing, affordable housing and property development.

Per Share Data ($)

(Year Ended Dec. 31)	1997	1996	1995	1994	1993	1992	1991	1990	1989	1988
Tangible Bk. Val.	8.14	6.80	5.66	4.73	3.67	4.13	3.59	3.40	2.56	2.51
Cash Flow	3.07	2.69	2.29	1.81	1.50	1.41	1.31	1.29	1.15	1.02
Earnings	2.33	1.97	1.65	1.23	0.92	0.86	0.81	0.84	0.77	0.67
Dividends	0.46	0.36	0.32	0.34	0.24	0.23	0.20	0.17	0.14	0.11
Payout Ratio	20%	18%	19%	28%	27%	26%	25%	20%	18%	17%
Prices - High	60⅛	43⅝	32¾	22¾	20¼	17⅝	17⅜	14⅜	11⅞	11
- Low	37⅜	26	19⅞	18½	16¼	14¼	11⅜	9⅞	8¼	7⅝
P/E Ratio - High	26	22	20	19	22	21	21	17	16	16
- Low	16	13	12	15	18	17	14	12	11	11

Income Statement Analysis (Million $)

	1997	1996	1995	1994	1993	1992	1991	1990	1989	1988
Revs.	5,220	4,997	4,152	3,461	3,159	2,812	2,640	2,544	2,173	1,930
Oper. Inc.	1,113	979	785	624	510	463	414	428	372	335
Depr.	185	178	152	132	132	122	111	99	83.0	74.0
Int. Exp.	19.4	27.8	31.6	26.9	35.0	42.9	44.3	39.2	31.0	26.1
Pretax Inc.	924	770	624	450	336	310	288	300	269	233
Eff. Tax Rate	37%	37%	38%	38%	39%	38%	37%	39%	39%	40%
Net Inc.	587	486	388	278	207	192	181	182	164	140

Balance Sheet & Other Fin. Data (Million $)

	1997	1996	1995	1994	1993	1992	1991	1990	1989	1988
Cash	186	138	117	76.9	35.4	31.2	93.1	46.8	30.9	26.7
Curr. Assets	1,859	1,701	1,532	1,263	1,094	1,005	1,088	1,143	824	714
Total Assets	5,395	4,806	3,613	2,580	2,337	2,204	2,257	2,150	1,688	1,380
Curr. Liab.	1,158	1,219	851	628	546	513	646	528	384	321
LT Debt	854	819	616	273	376	252	307	431	334	226
Common Eqty.	2,806	2,396	1,924	1,542	1,259	1,340	1,212	1,092	871	745
Total Cap.	3,660	3,215	2,540	1,884	1,727	1,646	1,578	1,585	1,278	1,038
Cap. Exp.	179	169	150	131	120	115	170	192	162	84.0
Cash Flow	772	665	540	410	338	314	291	282	247	214
Curr. Ratio	1.6	1.4	1.8	2.0	2.0	2.0	1.7	2.2	2.1	2.2
% LT Debt of Cap.	23.3	25.4	24.2	14.5	21.8	15.3	19.5	27.2	26.2	21.8
% Net Inc.of Revs.	11.3	9.7	9.3	8.0	6.5	6.8	6.8	7.2	7.5	7.3
% Ret. on Assets	11.5	11.6	12.5	11.3	9.1	8.6	8.1	9.4	10.6	10.4
% Ret. on Equity	22.6	22.5	22.4	19.8	15.8	15.0	15.6	18.4	20.1	20.5

Data as orig. reptd.; bef. results of disc. opers. and/or spec. items. Per share data adj. for stk. divs. as of ex-div. date. Bold denotes diluted EPS (FASB 128). E-Estimated. NA-Not Available. NM-Not Meaningful. NR-Not Ranked.

Office—3600 W. Lake Ave., Glenview, IL 60025-5811. **Tel**—(847) 724-7500. **Website**—http://www.itwbrands.com **Chrmn & CEO**—W. J. Farrell. **CFO**—J. C. Kinney. **Secy**—S. S. Hudnut. **Investor Contact**—Linda Williams. **Dirs**—M. J. Birck, M. D. Brailsford, S. Crown, H. R. Crowther, W. J. Farrell, L. R. Flury, J. C. Kinney, R. C. McCormack, P. B. Rooney, H. B. Smith Jr., O. J. Wade. **Transfer Agent & Registrar**—Harris Trust & Savings Bank, Chicago. **Incorporated**—in Delaware in 1961. **Empl**— 25,700. **S&P Analyst:** Robert E. Friedman, CPA

STANDARD &POOR'S
STOCK REPORTS

IMS Health

1179W
NYSE Symbol **RX**

In S&P 500

12-SEP-98

Industry:
Services (Commercial & Consumer)

Summary: This company integrates information systems, technology and services for the pharmaceutical and health care industries.

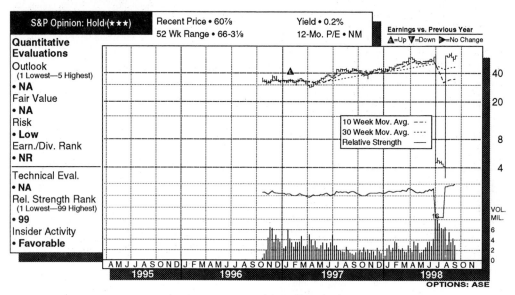

| S&P Opinion: Hold (★★★) | Recent Price • 60⅞ | Yield • 0.2% | Earnings vs. Previous Year |
| | 52 Wk Range • 66-3⅛ | 12-Mo. P/E • NM | ▲=Up ▼=Down ▶=No Change |

Quantitative Evaluations

Outlook
(1 Lowest—5 Highest)
• **NA**

Fair Value
• **NA**

Risk
• **Low**

Earn./Div. Rank
• **NR**

Technical Eval.
• **NA**

Rel. Strength Rank
(1 Lowest—99 Highest)
• **99**

Insider Activity
• **Favorable**

10 Week Mov. Avg. – – –
30 Week Mov. Avg. - - - -
Relative Strength ———

OPTIONS: ASE

Overview - 04-AUG-98

IMS (formerly part of Cognizant Corp.) reported a 33% advance in pro forma Q2 EPS on a 14% rise in revenues, reflecting healthy growth in North American sales management products and services, increased usage of the Global Services MIDAS database by international pharmaceutical companies, and gains in Japan reflecting greater usage of pharmaceutical market data with the launch of weekly delivery of the data rather than monthly as in the past . The strong Q2 results prompted the company to report that it expects to be at, or above, the high end of its 21%-24% EPS growth target for 1998. We recently raised our 1998, 1999 and 2000 EPS estimates by roughly $0.10 each to $1.73, $2.15 and $2.65, respectively. IMS's prospects will be bolstered well into the next century by strong growth anticipated in the pharmaceutical industry.

Valuation - 04-AUG-98

The shares of RX are trading at P/E multiples in the high 20s, and we believe they will continue to warrant high-growth status. The separation of IMS Health from Nielsen Media Research, which became effective on June 30, 1998, allows each to pursue growth strategies particularly suited to its business. IMS has a long track record of earnings growth, driven in part by renewable revenues based on multi-year or annually renewable contracts. Underlying the sound financial outlook for IMS are positive developments in the global pharmaceutical and health care industries. Sustained growth anticipated for the pharmaceutical industry well into the next century should translate into excellent growth opportunities for IMS. We expect EPS growth to average in the mid- to high 20s over the next 5 to 10 years.

Key Stock Statistics

S&P EPS Est. 1998	NA	Tang. Bk. Value/Share	4.94
P/E on S&P Est. 1998	NA	Beta	NA
Dividend Rate/Share	0.12	Shareholders	NA
Shs. outstg. (M)	166.8	Market cap. (B)	$ 10.2
Avg. daily vol. (M)	0.847	Inst. holdings	3%

Value of $10,000 invested 5 years ago: NA

Fiscal Year Ending Dec. 31

	1998	1997	1996	1995	1994	1993
Revenues (Million $)						
1Q	96.06	—	370.0	347.5	—	—
2Q	270.5	—	415.7	362.2	—	—
3Q	—	—	424.2	374.5	—	—
4Q	—	—	520.7	458.1	—	—
Yr.	—	1,060	1,731	1,542	—	—
Earnings Per Share ($)						
1Q	**0.07**	—	0.24	0.15	—	—
2Q	**0.07**	—	0.30	0.22	—	—
3Q	—	—	0.37	0.09	—	—
4Q	—	—	0.58	0.06	—	—
Yr.	—	1.39	1.49	0.52	—	—

Next earnings report expected: mid November

Dividend Data (Dividends have been paid since 1997.)

Amount ($)	Date Decl.	Ex-Div. Date	Stock of Record	Payment Date
0.030	Apr. 21	May. 01	May. 05	Jun. 12 '98
Stk.	Jun. 15	Jul. 01	Jun. 25	Jun. 30 '98
0.030	Jul. 22	Jul. 29	Jul. 31	Sep. 11 '98
1-for-3 REV.	—	Aug. 26		Aug. 26 '98

STANDARD
&POOR'S
STOCK REPORTS

IMS Health Inc.

1179W
12-SEP-98

Business Summary - 04-AUG-98

IMS Health is the world's leading provider of information solutions to the pharmaceutical and health care industries, with operations in over 90 countries. IMS was spun off on July 1, 1998, from Cognizant Corp., itself a 1996 spinoff from Dun & Bradstreet Corp. IMS is one of five companies created from Dun & Bradstreet Corp. as part of a strategy to significantly improve shareholder value. IMS retained a 49% interest in Gartner Group Inc., the world's leading supplier of research and analysis to the information and technology industry. IMS also owns Cognizant Technology Solutions, an outsourcer of software applications and development services specializing in Year 2000 conversion services. CTS completed an IPO of 2.9 million shares of Class A common stock in mid-June 1998. Walsh International, which develops and markets sales force automation systems for pharmaceutical companies, was acquired in June 1998. PMSI, which provides information services to pharmaceutical and health care companies in the U.S., Europe and Japan, was acquired in July 1998.

IMS operates through five major business units serving the health care industry: market research to measure worldwide product volumes, trends and market share; sales management services, which enable client companies to measure the impact of their sales force activity; technology-enabled selling involving sales automation; over-the-counter tracking services of non-prescription pharmaceutical products; and software-based services for the managed care industry.

As the largest information partner to the pharmaceutical industry for over 40 years, IMS is integral to both strategic and day-to-day decision-making. Underlying the sound financial outlook for IMS are positive developments in the global pharmaceutical and health care industries. These developments include a growing number of products being brought to market by the pharmaceutical industry, an increase in sales due to changing demographics, the recognition of the cost-saving benefits of drug treatment, and the growing importance of over-the-counter products and pharmaceutical marketing efforts to consumers.

Based on the billions of dollars invested in research and development by pharmaceutical companies, several factors make this the "golden age" for new drug development. Such factors include record volumes of new drug compounds in trial phases, the quality of these pipeline drugs inasmuch as they largely represent breakthrough drugs in critical research areas rather than copycat drugs, and explosive consumer demand for lifestyle drugs such as Viagra.

Per Share Data ($)

(Year Ended Dec. 31)	1997	1996	1995	1994	1993	1992	1991	1990	1989	1988
Tangible Bk. Val.	4.41	3.67	3.43	NA	NA	NA	NA	NA	NA	NA
Cash Flow	2.57	1.94	1.31	NA	NA	NA	NA	NA	NA	NA
Earnings	1.86	1.49	0.52	NA	NA	NA	NA	NA	NA	NA
Dividends	0.12	Nil	NA	NA	NA	NA	NA	NA	NA	NA
Payout Ratio	6%	Nil	NA	NA	NA	NA	NA	NA	NA	NA
Prices - High	45½	38	NA	NA	NA	NA	NA	NA	NA	NA
- Low	28	30½	NA	NA	NA	NA	NA	NA	NA	NA
P/E Ratio - High	24	26	NA	NA	NA	NA	NA	NA	NA	NA
- Low	15	21	NA	NA	NA	NA	NA	NA	NA	NA

Income Statement Analysis (Million $)

	1997	1996	1995	1994	1993	1992	1991	1990	1989	1988
Revs.	1,418	1,731	1,542	NA	NA	NA	NA	NA	NA	NA
Oper. Inc.	453	477	300	NA	NA	NA	NA	NA	NA	NA
Depr.	117	134	133	NA	NA	NA	NA	NA	NA	NA
Int. Exp.	2.3	1.3	0.5	NA	NA	NA	NA	NA	NA	NA
Pretax Inc.	430	349	163	NA	NA	NA	NA	NA	NA	NA
Eff. Tax Rate	27%	44%	45%	NA	NA	NA	NA	NA	NA	NA
Net Inc.	312	195	88.9	NA	NA	NA	NA	NA	NA	NA

Balance Sheet & Other Fin. Data (Million $)

	1997	1996	1995	1994	1993	1992	1991	1990	1989	1988
Cash	318	429	545	NA	NA	NA	NA	NA	NA	NA
Curr. Assets	694	994	NA	NA	NA	NA	NA	NA	NA	NA
Total Assets	1,580	1,875	NA	NA	NA	NA	NA	NA	NA	NA
Curr. Liab.	441	680	NA	NA	NA	NA	NA	NA	NA	NA
LT Debt	Nil	Nil	65.5	NA	NA	NA	NA	NA	NA	NA
Common Eqty.	802	873	799	NA	NA	NA	NA	NA	NA	NA
Total Cap.	915	978	865	NA	NA	NA	NA	NA	NA	NA
Cap. Exp.	72.0	75.0	77.0	NA	NA	NA	NA	NA	NA	NA
Cash Flow	430	329	221	NA	NA	NA	NA	NA	NA	NA
Curr. Ratio	1.6	1.5	NA	NA	NA	NA	NA	NA	NA	NA
% LT Debt of Cap.	Nil	Nil	7.6	NA	NA	NA	NA	NA	NA	NA
% Net Inc.of Revs.	22.0	11.3	5.8	NA	NA	NA	NA	NA	NA	NA
% Ret. on Assets	18.1	11.8	NA	NA	NA	NA	NA	NA	NA	NA
% Ret. on Equity	37.3	26.5		NA	NA	NA	NA	NA	NA	NA

Data as orig. reptd.; bef. results of disc. opers. and/or spec. items. Per share data adj. for stk. divs. as of ex-div. date. Bold denotes diluted EPS (FASB 128). E-Estimated. NA-Not Available. NM-Not Meaningful. NR-Not Ranked.

Office—200 Nyala Farms Rd., Westport, CT 06880. **Tel**—(203) 222-4200. **Website**—http://www.imshealth.com **Chrmn & CEO**—R. E. Weissman. **Pres & COO**—Victoria R. Fash. **SVP-Fin**—A. J. Klutch. **VP & Investor Contact**—Susan V. Watson (203-222-4238). **Dirs**—C. L. Alexander Jr., J. P. Imlay Jr., R. J. Kamerschen, R. L. Lanigan, H. E. Lockhart, J. R. Peterson, M. B. Puckett, R. E. Weissman, W. C. VanFaasen. **Transfer Agent & Registrar**—First Chicago Trust Co. of New York, Jersey City, NJ. **Incorporated**—in Delaware in 1996. **Empl**— 8,000. **S&P Analyst:** William H. Donald

STANDARD &POOR'S
STOCK REPORTS

Inco Ltd.

1187P

NYSE Symbol **N**

In S&P 500

12-SEP-98 | Industry: Metals Mining | **Summary:** This leading nickel producer announced a comprehensive restructuring in February 1998.

S&P Opinion: Hold (★★★)	Recent Price • 10⅛	Yield • 1.0%
	52 Wk Range • 26-8¼	12-Mo. P/E • NM

Quantitative Evaluations

Outlook
(1 Lowest—5 Highest)
• **NA**

Fair Value
• **NA**

Risk
• **Average**

Earn./Div. Rank
• **B-**

Technical Eval.
• **Bullish** since 10/97

Rel. Strength Rank
(1 Lowest—99 Highest)
• **59**

Insider Activity
• **NA**

Earnings vs. Previous Year
▲=Up ▼=Down ▶=No Change

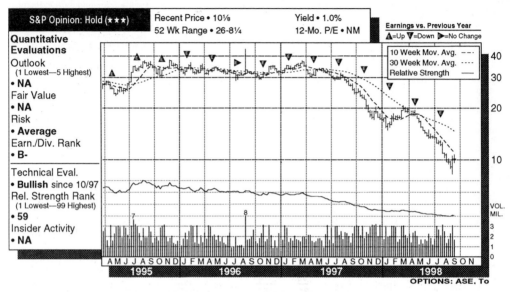

10 Week Mov. Avg. ---
30 Week Mov. Avg. ····
Relative Strength ——

OPTIONS: ASE, To

Overview - 05-AUG-98

We project losses for Inco in 1998 as sharply lower prices for nickel offset strenuous cost reduction efforts. Cost reductions include permanent work force reductions at the Ontario and Manitoba divisions, consolidation of various functions, reductions in exploration and capital spending and divestiture of $85 million of non-core assets. As a result of these actions, Inco expects to realize sustainable annual savings of $165 million, beginning in 1999. However, we see no signs that pricing for nickel will improve anytime soon and expect Inco to report a loss in 1998, excluding charges. As of early August 1998, nickel was trading at $1.97 per pound, versus $3.33 a pound in August 1997.

Valuation - 05-AUG-98

Although Inco's second quarter 1998 results showed dramatic improvement from the first quarter, we are maintaining our avoid rating on the stock. We believe that nickel prices will remain weak and that this will exert downward pressure on the stock. Barring a dramatic improvement in Asian economies in 1999 and an increase in stainless steel production, nickel prices will stay depressed for the rest of 1998 and much of 1999. Besides anemic demand, nickel prices will be hurt by increased supply from several new projects coming on stream in late 1998. Combined with sluggish demand, we see little in the way of relief for nickel prices even though inventories on the London Metal Exchange (LME) totaled 61,050 metric tons as of July 31, 1998, down from a high of 66,510 metric tons on February 11, 1998. The other major negative for Inco is the continued impasse with the provincial government of Newfoundland over the construction of a smelter and refinery at the Voisey's Bay nickel project. The uncertainty over the timing and ultimate development of the project will continue to weigh on the stock price.

Key Stock Statistics

S&P EPS Est. 1998	-0.15	Tang. Bk. Value/Share	19.56
P/E on S&P Est. 1998	NM	Beta	1.11
S&P EPS Est. 1999	0.20	Shareholders	24,800
Dividend Rate/Share	0.10	Market cap. (B)	$ 1.7
Shs. outstg. (M)	166.1	Inst. holdings	56%
Avg. daily vol. (M)	0.489		

Value of $10,000 invested 5 years ago: $ 4,920

Fiscal Year Ending Dec. 31

	1998	1997	1996	1995	1994	1993
Revenues (Million $)						
1Q	500.0	795.0	834.0	881.0	524.0	542.8
2Q	494.0	655.0	822.0	856.1	590.0	603.9
3Q	—	567.0	688.0	830.1	603.3	468.0
4Q	—	541.0	761.0	903.7	766.8	515.7
Yr.	—	2,367	3,105	3,471	2,484	2,130
Earnings Per Share ($)						
1Q	**-0.32**	**0.29**	0.49	0.57	-0.53	-0.22
2Q	**-0.09**	**0.05**	0.47	0.47	-0.07	-0.03
3Q	**E0.35**	**-0.02**	0.21	0.33	0.02	0.83
4Q	**E-0.09**	**-0.09**	0.08	0.45	0.73	-0.36
Yr.	**E-0.15**	**-0.10**	1.09	1.82	0.15	0.22

Next earnings report expected: late October

Dividend Data (Dividends have been paid since 1934.)

Amount ($)	Date Decl.	Ex-Div. Date	Stock of Record	Payment Date
0.100	Oct. 27	Nov. 05	Nov. 07	Dec. 01 '97
0.025	Feb. 11	Feb. 19	Feb. 23	Mar. 13 '98
0.025	Apr. 22	Apr. 30	May. 04	Jun. 01 '98
0.025	Jul. 27	Aug. 05	Aug. 07	Sep. 01 '98

A Division of The McGraw-Hill Companies

STANDARD
&POOR'S
STOCK REPORTS

Inco Limited

1187P
12-SEP-98

Business Summary - 05-AUG-98

Inco is one of the world's largest nickel producers, as well as a producer of copper and other metals and metal products.

On February 11, 1998, Inco announced that it would incur pretax charges for restructuring and writedowns, in order to increase cash flow and cope with the current low nickel price. As a result of delays in the environmental review process, as well as inability to resolve differences with various parties, initial concentrate production from Voisey Bay will not begin until late 2000 at the earliest. The main reason for the delay is the current impasse with the provincial government of Newfoundland over the construction of a smelter and refinery.

Nickel is a hard, malleable metal used mostly in the production of stainless steel. Inco estimates that the global stainless steel industry accounts for about two-thirds of primary nickel consumption. Global output of stainless steel rose to 16.1 million metric tons in 1997, from 14.9 million metric tons in 1996. Production of low alloy steel, non-ferrous alloys, foundry industry castings and non-alloying uses such as electroplating account for the balance of nickel consumption.

Primary nickel accounted for 77% of total sales in 1997, copper 14%, precious metals 4%, cobalt 3%, and other products 2%. Inco's average realized price for nickel in 1997 was $3.36/lb., versus $3.61 in 1996. Average copper price realizations in 1997 were $1.07/lb., versus $1.12 in 1996. Nickel production in 1997 totaled 395 million lbs., versus 412 million lbs. in 1996. At year-end 1997, proven and probable reserves in Canada totaled 356 million metric tons, versus 364 million metric tons a year earlier. Inco owns 59% of P.T. International Nickel Indonesia, which produces nickel in matte, an intermediate product. At the end of 1997, reserves of P.T. Inco were 108 million metric tons.

Inco's principal competitors are RAO Norilsk Nickel, Falconbridge Ltd., ERAMET, WMC Ltd. (Western Mining) and QNI Ltd. Inco estimates that the company and its five main competitors accounted for 65% of total world primary nickel production in 1997; the balance of the market is supplied by more than 30 producers worldwide. Inco estimates that it maintained its world market share of nickel at about 27% in 1997. It also estimates that primary nickel demand in 1997 was 997,000 metric tons and primary supply was 1,000,000 metric tons.

On July 9, 1998, Inco announced the execution of a definitive agreement to sell its Alloys International unit. The company expects to receive cash proceeds of $408 million before fees and expenses, and will realize an after-tax gain of some $73 million. The transaction is expected to close in 1998's third quarter.

Per Share Data ($)

(Year Ended Dec. 31)	1997	1996	1995	1994	1993	1992	1991	1990	1989	1988
Tangible Bk. Val.	19.56	28.25	13.65	15.08	14.57	14.71	15.70	15.78	12.33	6.51
Cash Flow	1.30	3.19	9.03	2.32	2.46	2.13	2.96	6.19	8.95	8.18
Earnings	-0.10	1.09	1.82	0.15	0.22	-0.21	0.74	4.18	7.11	6.50
Dividends	0.40	0.40	0.40	0.40	0.40	0.85	1.00	1.00	0.85	10.70
Payout Ratio	NM	37%	22%	NM	182%	NM	137%	24%	12%	165%
Prices - High	37⅝	36¾	38	31¼	27¾	34⅜	38	31⅞	37⅝	35⅛
- Low	17	28¾	23½	21⅜	17⅜	19⅛	23⅞	22⅛	25⅝	17⅜
P/E Ratio - High	NM	34	21	NM	NM	NM	51	8	5	5
- Low	NM	26	13	NM	NM	NM	32	5	4	3

Income Statement Analysis (Million $)

	1997	1996	1995	1994	1993	1992	1991	1990	1989	1988
Revs.	2,367	3,105	3,471	2,484	2,130	2,559	2,999	3,108	3,948	3,263
Oper. Inc.	367	632	811	310	164	366	478	798	1,546	1,473
Depr.	226	259	255	252	246	253	235	209	194	177
Int. Exp.	81.0	95.0	88.0	89.0	99	113	120	112	138	92.0
Pretax Inc.	60.0	322	460	-13.0	25.0	22.0	122	693	1,314	1,268
Eff. Tax Rate	50%	37%	NM	NM	NM	94%	12%	33%	39%	46%
Net Inc.	17.0	168	227	22.0	28.0	-18.0	83.0	441	753	691

Balance Sheet & Other Fin. Data (Million $)

	1997	1996	1995	1994	1993	1992	1991	1990	1989	1988
Cash	40.0	78.0	154	164	47.0	35.0	31.0	70.0	115	657
Curr. Assets	1,296	1,434	1,478	1,418	1,184	1,140	1,432	1,354	1,350	1,921
Total Assets	7,772	7,642	4,693	4,016	3,890	4,161	4,478	4,058	3,666	4,079
Curr. Liab.	606	629	712	498	492	542	924	720	759	2,052
LT Debt	1,495	1,241	840	922	946	1,081	991	893	925	674
Common Eqty.	3,247	3,290	1,601	1,767	1,607	1,608	1,668	1,648	1,289	689
Total Cap.	6,502	6,386	3,370	2,977	2,814	3,026	3,006	2,828	2,398	1,507
Cap. Exp.	535	449	326	139	186	234	440	573	389	229
Cash Flow	217	427	1,066	270	270	230	312	645	942	862
Curr. Ratio	2.1	2.3	2.1	2.8	2.4	2.1	1.5	1.9	1.8	0.9
% LT Debt of Cap.	23.0	37.7	25.0	31.0	33.6	35.7	33.0	31.6	38.6	44.7
% Net Inc.of Revs.	0.7	5.4	6.6	0.9	1.3	NM	2.8	14.2	19.1	21.2
% Ret. on Assets	0.2	2.7	5.2	0.5	0.7	NM	1.9	11.4	19.6	19.5
% Ret. on Equity	NM	6.9	14.9	1.0	1.5	NM	4.6	29.7	75.9	76.8

Data as orig. reptd.; bef. results of disc. opers. and/or spec. items. Per share data adj. for stk. divs. as of ex-div. date. Bold denotes diluted EPS (FASB 128). E-Estimated. NA-Not Available. NM-Not Meaningful. NR-Not Ranked.

Offices—145 King Street West, Suite 1500, Toronto, ON, Canada, M5H 487; One New York Plaza, New York, NY 10004. **Tel**—(416) 361-7511; NYC (212) 612-5500. **Website**—http://www.incoltd.com **Chrmn & CEO**—M. D. Sopko. **Pres**—S. M. Hand. **EVP & Secy**—S. T. Feiner.**VP & Treas**—A. J. Sabatino. **Investor Contact**—N. Kurt Barnes.**Dirs**—G. A. Barton, J. M. Y. Boulle, A. A. Bruneau, P. Crawford, J. A. Erola, W. F. Glavin, S. M. Hand, C. H. Hantho, E. L. Mercaldo, D. P. O'Brien, R. J. Richardson, M. D. Sopko, R. M. Thomson. **Transfer Agents & Registrars**—CIBC Mellon Trust Co., Toronto; ChaseMellon Shareholder Services, L. L. C., NYC. **Incorporated**—in Canada in 1916. **Empl**—14,278. **S&P Analyst:** Leo Larkin

STANDARD &POOR'S
STOCK REPORTS

Ingersoll-Rand

1196

NYSE Symbol **IR**

In S&P 500

12-SEP-98

Industry: Machinery (Diversified)

Summary: This major producer of air compressors also has an important stake in other nonelectrical machinery, including equipment for the construction and auto industries.

S&P Opinion: Hold (★★★)	Recent Price • 38¼	Yield • 1.6%
	52 Wk Range • 54-34⅝	12-Mo. P/E • 14.7

Quantitative Evaluations

Outlook
(1 Lowest—5 Highest)
• **3⁻**

Fair Value
• **43¼**

Risk
• **Low**

Earn./Div. Rank
• **B+**

Technical Eval.
• **Bullish** since 6/98

Rel. Strength Rank
(1 Lowest—99 Highest)
• **58**

Insider Activity
• **NA**

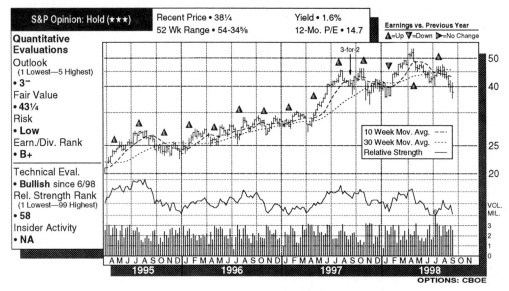

Earnings vs. Previous Year
▲=Up ▼=Down ▶=No Change

10 Week Mov. Avg. ----
30 Week Mov. Avg. ......
Relative Strength ——

OPTIONS: CBOE

Overview - 27-JUL-98

Sales should rise 15% in 1998, reflecting 5% internal growth, as well as the addition of Thermo King, which was acquired from Westinghouse on October 31, 1997, for $2.56 billion cash. The inclusion of Thermo King extends IR's market for compressor products into the transport temperature control market. Construction and general industrial markets should remain firm but flat in 1998. Automotive markets could decline, on a further shift in demand to foreign vehicles, resulting from the recent strength of the U.S. dollar versus the Japanese yen. Even without a market shift, demand may be flat, because the economic cycle is mature. Housing markets should remain strong, aided by a favorable interest rate environment. Clark will continue to boost the machinery business, and engineered equipment will be aided by a continuing upturn in pump industry demand and firming of prices. For the long term, we expect acquisitions and international initiatives to continue to play an important role in the company's growth, as many of its markets are mature, and tend toward slow and cyclical growth.

Valuation - 27-JUL-98

We continue to rate the stock a hold, based on valuation. The shares, recently trading at 18X our 1998 EPS estimate, are adequately valued. Although they may continue to trend higher with the stock market, we expect them to perform only in line with market averages. As the economic cycle continues to lengthen, the shares may eventually begin to underperform, as cyclical stocks usually do. We would not add to positions, and would use rallies in the shares as opportunities to take profits.

Key Stock Statistics

S&P EPS Est. 1998	2.70	Tang. Bk. Value/Share	NM
P/E on S&P Est. 1998	14.2	Beta	1.25
S&P EPS Est. 1999	3.05	Shareholders	13,000
Dividend Rate/Share	0.60	Market cap. (B)	$ 6.3
Shs. outstg. (M)	165.2	Inst. holdings	73%
Avg. daily vol. (M)	0.575		

Value of $10,000 invested 5 years ago: $ 21,794

Fiscal Year Ending Dec. 31

	1998	1997	1996	1995	1994	1993
Revenues (Million $)						
1Q	2,003	1,639	1,605	1,186	1,010	952.1
2Q	2,186	1,837	1,762	1,392	1,144	1,007
3Q	—	1,694	1,596	1,521	1,114	973.5
4Q	—	1,934	1,704	1,630	1,240	1,089
Yr.	—	7,103	6,703	5,729	4,507	4,021
Earnings Per Share ($)						
1Q	**0.60**	0.48	0.47	0.29	0.21	0.16
2Q	**0.85**	0.68	0.57	0.42	0.33	0.23
3Q	—	0.58	0.51	0.39	0.31	0.22
4Q	—	0.57	0.67	0.60	0.49	0.43
Yr.	**E2.70**	2.31	2.22	1.70	1.33	1.04

Next earnings report expected: late October

Dividend Data (Dividends have been paid since 1910.)

Amount ($)	Date Decl.	Ex-Div. Date	Stock of Record	Payment Date
0.150	Nov. 05	Nov. 14	Nov. 18	Dec. 01 '97
0.150	Feb. 04	Feb. 12	Feb. 17	Mar. 02 '98
0.150	May. 06	May. 14	May. 18	Jun. 01 '98
0.150	Aug. 05	Aug. 14	Aug. 18	Sep. 01 '98

Business Summary - 27-JUL-98

Ingersoll-Rand (IR) is a diversified producer of capital goods. Its primary business involves the design and manufacture of compressed air systems, but other products range from industrial production equipment to door locks to golf cars. Segment operating profit margins in recent years were as follows:

	1997	1996	1995
Standard machinery	12%	10%	9.8%
Bearings, locks & tools	14%	13%	12%
Engineered equipment	4.5%	8.3%	4.1%
Thermo King (acq. in 1997)	NM	---	---

In 1997, international operations accounted for 35% of revenues and almost 20% of operating profits.

Standard machinery (44% of 1997 revenues) includes a broad line of portable and packaged air compressors, vacuum pumps, air drying and filtering systems. This segment also manufactures pavement millers, rock drills, blasthole drills, skid steel loaders, compact hydraulic excavators, vibratory compactors, asphalt pavers, jackhammers, golf cars, utility vehicles, mining machinery, agricultural sprayers. These products are used in construction, mining, agriculture, process industries, service stations and by electric utilities. Standard machinery operates 11 U.S. and 10 international plants.

Bearings, locks and tools (41% of 1997 revenues) include needle bearings, tapered roller bearings, precision components, air-powered tools, hoists and winches, air motors and air starters, automated assembly and test systems, door locks, electronic access systems, door closers and exit devices. These products are principally used in the automotive and aerospace industries. This segment operates 37 U.S. and 28 international plants.

Engineered equipment (13% of 1997 revenues) consists of centrifugal and reciprocating pumps, pulp & paper processing equipment, pelletizing equipment, filters, aerators and dewatering systems. This equipment is used in the pulp & paper industry, food and agricultural and minerals processing industries. In 1997, IR sold Clark-Hurth a producer of axles and transmissions for off-highway vehicles to Dana Corp., after determining that it did not fit into IR's long-term business profile. Clark-Hurth had generated revenues of sales of $350 million. Engineered equipment operates seven U.S. and 15 international plants.

In late 1997, IR acquired Thermo King Corp. (2% of 1997 revenues) from CBS, Inc. for about $2.6 billion in cash. Thermo King is the largest maker of refrigerators used in truck trailers, seagoing containers and railcars. At CBS, Thermo King generated 14% operating profit margins on about $1 billion in revenues. The newly acquired business derives more than of half of its revenues from international sales. Thermo King operates six U.S. and 10 international plants.

Per Share Data ($) (Year Ended Dec. 31)	1997	1996	1995	1994	1993	1992	1991	1990	1989	1988
Tangible Bk. Val.	NM	5.56	3.32	8.89	7.88	7.52	9.83	10.03	8.91	8.07
Cash Flow	3.60	3.48	2.83	2.17	1.82	1.49	1.79	1.87	1.89	1.50
Earnings	2.31	2.22	1.70	1.33	1.04	0.74	0.97	1.19	1.26	1.00
Dividends	0.57	0.52	0.49	0.48	0.47	0.46	0.44	0.42	0.39	0.35
Payout Ratio	25%	23%	29%	36%	45%	62%	45%	36%	31%	34%
Prices - High	46 1/4	31 3/4	28 1/4	27 3/4	26 5/8	22 7/8	18 3/8	20 1/8	16 3/4	14 7/8
- Low	27 7/8	23 3/8	18 7/8	19 5/8	19 1/8	16 5/8	11 5/8	9 1/2	11 1/4	10 3/8
P/E Ratio - High	20	14	17	21	26	31	19	17	13	15
- Low	12	11	11	15	18	23	12	8	9	10
Income Statement Analysis (Million $)										
Revs.	7,103	6,703	5,729	4,507	4,021	3,784	3,586	3,738	3,447	3,021
Oper. Inc.	973	886	676	510	420	372	393	464	458	362
Depr.	212	203	179	133	124	117	127	107	96.3	76.8
Int. Exp.	140	120	90.0	47.0	54.8	57.6	63.5	70.8	43.0	36.0
Pretax Inc.	614	568	429	343	265	148	235	285	311	231
Eff. Tax Rate	38%	37%	37%	35%	34%	46%	36%	35%	35%	30%
Net Inc.	381	358	270	211	164	116	151	185	202	162
Balance Sheet & Other Fin. Data (Million $)										
Cash	112	192	147	211	234	230	138	52.0	139	256
Curr. Assets	2,545	2,536	2,346	2,003	1,902	1,968	1,682	1,697	1,599	1,662
Total Assets	8,416	5,622	5,563	3,597	3,375	3,388	2,980	2,983	2,595	2,483
Curr. Liab.	2,328	1,290	1,329	1,040	1,024	1,080	778	964	676	685
LT Debt	2,528	1,164	1,304	316	314	356	376	265	280	301
Common Eqty.	2,341	2,091	1,796	1,531	1,350	1,293	1,633	1,556	1,377	1,243
Total Cap.	4,997	3,368	3,271	2,001	1,810	1,795	2,146	1,952	1,886	1,764
Cap. Exp.	186	195	212	159	132	132	185	195	155	110
Cash Flow	593	561	450	344	287	232	277	290	291	232
Curr. Ratio	1.1	2.0	1.8	1.9	1.9	1.8	2.2	1.8	2.4	2.4
% LT Debt of Cap.	50.5	34.5	39.9	15.8	17.4	19.8	17.5	13.6	14.8	17.0
% Net Inc.of Revs.	5.4	5.3	4.7	4.7	4.1	3.1	4.2	5.0	5.9	5.3
% Ret. on Assets	5.4	6.4	5.9	6.1	4.8	3.6	5.0	6.6	8.0	6.9
% Ret. on Equity	17.2	18.4	16.2	14.6	12.3	7.9	9.4	12.5	14.8	13.1

Data as orig. reptd.; bef. results of disc. opers. and/or spec. items. Per share data adj. for stk. divs. as of ex-div. date. Bold denotes diluted EPS (FASB 128). E-Estimated. NA-Not Available. NM-Not Meaningful. NR-Not Ranked.

Office—200 Chestnut Ridge Rd., Woodcliff Lake, NJ 07675. **Tel**—(201) 573-0123. **Chrmn, Pres & CEO**—J. E. Perrella. **CFO**—D. W. Devonshire. **Treas**—W. J. Armstrong. **Secy**—R. G. Heller. **Investor Contact**—Joseph Fimbianti (201-573-3486). **Dirs**—J. P. Flannery, C. J. Horner, H. W. Lichtenberger, T. E. Martin, J. E. Perrella, O. R. Smith, R. J. Swift, J. F. Travis, T. L. White. **Transfer Agent & Registrar**—Bank of New York, NYC. **Incorporated**—in New Jersey in 1905. **Empl**— 46,600. **S&P Analyst:** Robert E. Friedman, CPA

STANDARD &POOR'S
STOCK REPORTS

Intel Corp.

4249H

Nasdaq Symbol **INTC**

In S&P 500

14-SEP-98

Industry:
Electronics (Semiconductors)

Summary: Intel is the world's largest manufacturer of microprocessors, the central processing unit of a PC. Various other products that enhance a PC's capabilities are also produced.

S&P Opinion: Accumulate (★★★★)	Recent Price • 84⅞	Yield • 0.1%
	52 Wk Range • 99¼-65⅝	12-Mo. P/E • 26.3

Quantitative Evaluations

Outlook (1 Lowest—5 Highest)
• **1⁻**

Fair Value
• **74¾**

Risk
• **Average**

Earn./Div. Rank
• **A-**

Technical Eval.
• **Neutral** since 9/98

Rel. Strength Rank (1 Lowest—99 Highest)
• **96**

Insider Activity
• **Neutral**

Earnings vs. Previous Year
▲=Up ▼=Down ▶=No Change

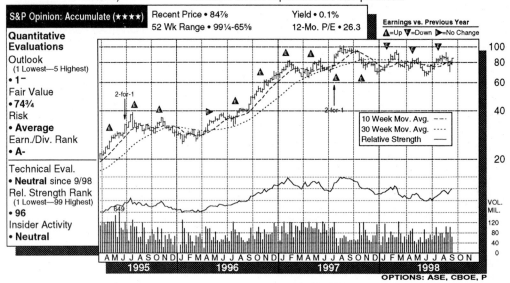

10 Week Mov. Avg. — ⋅ —
30 Week Mov. Avg. ⋅⋅⋅⋅⋅
Relative Strength ——

VOL. MIL.

OPTIONS: ASE, CBOE, P

Overview - 14-SEP-98

We project 1998 revenues will be up modestly (2.2%), reflecting pricing pressure on microprocessors, reduced demand from OEM vendors as they work off excess inventories of personal computers (PCs), and weak demand from Asia. We expect stronger revenue growth in the second half of the year, as the excess inventory situation is corrected. The pace of this reacceleration will also depend upon the rate of acceptance and pricing power that Intel has with its new Mendecino chip (for low end PCs) and Xeon chip (for servers and workstations). Meanwhile, Intel has been shifting to the Pentium II (which now accounts for over 50% of production), which carries lower gross margins, due to the greater amount of packaged components that it requires. However, cost cutting, the higher priced Xeon chip, and Intel's push to 0.18 micron production will help to alleviate margin pressure further out in 1998 and in 1999. We forecast EPS of $3.15 for 1998, with improvement to $3.95 in 1999.

Valuation - 14-SEP-98

We continue to recommend accumulating the shares, based on our positive long-term view of Intel's strong fundamentals. For the near-term, however, we see continued volatility likely in the shares, given concerns over the demand and aggressive pricing environment for microprocessors. We project that pricing pressures for Intel should begin to ease in the 1998 second half, as Intel's new products help it regain share from rival chip makers and enable it to further penetrate the market for higher-end platforms, thus reviving revenue growth. Given Intel's dominance in the microprocessor industry, and our assumption that earnings momentum will be restored, we recommend accumulating the shares, which are trading at an attractive price-to-earnings ratio based on our 1999 estimate.

Key Stock Statistics

S&P EPS Est. 1998	3.15	Tang. Bk. Value/Share	12.94
P/E on S&P Est. 1998	27.0	Beta	1.15
S&P EPS Est. 1999	3.95	Shareholders	124,000
Dividend Rate/Share	0.12	Market cap. (B)	$142.7
Shs. outstg. (M)	1680.0	Inst. holdings	43%
Avg. daily vol. (M)	21.721		

Value of $10,000 invested 5 years ago: $ 79,140

Fiscal Year Ending Dec. 31

	1998	1997	1996	1995	1994	1993
Revenues (Million $)						
1Q	6,001	6,448	4,644	3,557	2,660	2,024
2Q	5,927	5,960	4,621	3,894	2,770	2,130
3Q	—	6,155	5,142	4,171	2,863	2,240
4Q	—	6,507	6,440	4,580	3,228	2,389
Yr.	—	25,070	20,847	16,202	11,521	8,782
Earnings Per Share ($)						
1Q	**0.72**	1.10	0.51	0.51	0.35	0.31
2Q	**0.66**	0.92	0.58	0.49	0.36	0.33
3Q	**E0.78**	0.88	0.74	0.53	0.38	0.33
4Q	**E0.90**	0.98	1.06	0.49	0.21	0.34
Yr.	**E3.15**	3.87	2.90	2.02	1.31	1.30

Next earnings report expected: mid October

Dividend Data (Dividends have been paid since 1992.)

Amount ($)	Date Decl.	Ex-Div. Date	Stock of Record	Payment Date
0.030	Sep. 17	Oct. 29	Nov. 01	Dec. 01 '97
0.030	Nov. 12	Jan. 28	Feb. 01	Mar. 01 '98
0.030	Mar. 26	Apr. 29	May. 01	Jun. 01 '98
0.030	Jul. 22	Aug. 05	Aug. 07	Sep. 01 '98

A Division of The **McGraw-Hill** *Companies*

Business Summary - 14-JUL-98

With an overwhelming market share of about 85% in 1997, as measured by International Data Corp., Intel is by far the leader in sales of microprocessors for PCs (personal computers).

INTC's product strategy is twofold: the company offers OEMs (original equipment manufacturers) a wide range of PC building-block products to meet their needs, and also offers PC users products that expand the capability of their systems and networks.

Intel introduced the first microprocessor in 1971. A microprocessor constitutes the "brains" (the central processing unit) of a PC, processing system data and controlling the other devices in the system. Intel has led the introduction of new microprocessor technology. In 1997, Intel made one of its most significant product transitions, as its sixth-generation Pentium line, the P6, faced the steepest production ramp-up in company history; the P6 is slated to hit the crossover point in the 1998 second quarter, outshipping the P5 (fifth-generation Pentium line) chips. While Intel introduced its first product based on P6 architecture in late 1995, the Pentium Pro, it is targeted for use in workstations and servers (and is currently being replaced by the high-performance Xeon chip). The Pentium II, a P6 offering in the volume desktop market, was launched in May 1997.

The Pentium II uses a Dual Independent Bus (DIB)

architecture that addresses the bandwidth constraint that limits microprocessor performance. The Pentium II was initially offered at speeds up to 300 MHz, but, by 2000, a combination of DIB architecture, Pentium II processor systems, and a new feature called an Accelerator Graphics Port should let bandwidth scale with the processor to reach clock speeds of 500 MHz. In 1999, Intel and Hewlett-Packard plan to have sample volumes of a next generation microprocessor, the 64-bit Merced chip, raising microprocessor speeds to 900 MHz. Planned production volume of the chip, originally expected in late 1999, has been postponed to mid-2000.

Intel also produces chipsets that support and extend the graphic and other capabilities of microprocessors; embedded chips, which provide devices like wireless communications devices, printers, copiers and fax machines with computing power; and flash memory chips used to store computer data.

INTC is offering a growing number of networking products, to help proliferate the use and lower the cost of networked computing. These products include EtherExpress adapters, Express Switching Hubs and Stackable Hubs, and LANDesk network management products.

Domestic manufacturing and test facilities are located in Arizona, Oregon, California and New Mexico. Outside the U.S., most wafer production occurs at plants in Israel and Ireland, while test and assembly are conducted in Malaysia and the Philippines. More than half of sales are outside the U.S.

Per Share Data ($)

(Year Ended Dec. 31)	1997	1996	1995	1994	1993	1992	1991	1990	1989	1988
Tangible Bk. Val.	11.85	10.28	7.39	5.61	4.49	3.25	2.71	2.25	1.73	1.44
Cash Flow	5.09	3.96	2.79	1.90	1.71	0.92	0.74	0.58	0.42	0.46
Earnings	3.87	2.90	2.02	1.31	1.30	0.62	0.49	0.40	0.26	0.32
Dividends	0.11	0.09	0.07	0.06	0.09	0.01	Nil	Nil	Nil	Nil
Payout Ratio	3%	3%	3%	4%	7%	2%	Nil	Nil	Nil	Nil
Prices - High	102	70¾	39¼	18⅜	18⅝	11½	7⅜	6½	4½	4⅝
- Low	62⅞	24⅞	15¾	14	10¾	5⅞	4¾	3½	2⅞	2⁷/₁₆
P/E Ratio - High	26	24	19	14	14	18	15	16	17	15
- Low	16	9	8	11	8	9	10	9	11	8

Income Statement Analysis (Million $)

	1997	1996	1995	1994	1993	1992	1991	1990	1989	1988
Revs.	25,070	20,847	16,202	11,521	8,782	5,844	4,779	3,921	3,127	2,875
Oper. Inc.	12,079	9,441	6,623	4,863	4,109	2,043	1,498	1,151	794	805
Depr.	2,192	1,888	1,371	1,028	717	518	418	292	237	211
Int. Exp.	27.0	58.0	75.0	84.0	58.0	66.0	88.0	102	102	78.0
Pretax Inc.	10,659	7,934	5,638	3,603	3,530	1,569	1,195	986	583	629
Eff. Tax Rate	35%	35%	37%	37%	35%	32%	32%	34%	33%	28%
Net Inc.	6,945	5,157	3,566	2,288	2,295	1,067	819	650	391	453

Balance Sheet & Other Fin. Data (Million $)

	1997	1996	1995	1994	1993	1992	1991	1990	1989	1988
Cash	4,102	7,907	2,458	2,410	3,136	2,835	2,277	1,785	1,090	971
Curr. Assets	15,867	13,684	8,097	6,167	5,802	4,691	3,604	3,119	2,163	1,970
Total Assets	28,880	23,765	17,504	13,816	11,344	8,089	6,292	5,376	3,994	3,550
Curr. Liab.	6,020	4,863	3,619	3,024	2,433	1,842	1,228	1,314	921	934
LT Debt	448	728	400	392	426	2.5	363	345	412	479
Common Eqty.	19,295	16,872	12,140	9,267	7,500	5,445	4,418	3,592	2,549	2,080
Total Cap.	20,819	18,597	13,160	10,048	8,223	5,874	4,924	4,063	3,073	2,616
Cap. Exp.	4,501	3,024	3,550	2,441	1,933	1,228	948	680	422	477
Cash Flow	9,137	7,045	4,937	3,316	3,012	1,584	1,237	943	628	664
Curr. Ratio	2.6	2.8	2.2	2.0	2.4	2.5	2.9	2.4	2.3	2.1
% LT Debt of Cap.	2.2	3.9	3.0	3.9	5.2	4.2	7.4	8.5	13.4	18.3
% Net Inc.of Revs.	27.7	24.7	22.0	19.9	26.1	18.3	17.1	16.6	12.5	15.8
% Ret. on Assets	26.4	25.0	22.8	18.3	23.6	14.7	13.9	13.4	10.3	14.3
% Ret. on Equity	36.1	35.6	33.3	27.4	35.5	35.5	20.2	20.5	16.7	26.0

Data as orig. reptd.; bef. results of disc. opers. and/or spec. items. Per share data adj. for stk. divs. as of ex-div. date. Bold denotes diluted EPS (FASB 128). E-Estimated. NA-Not Available. NM-Not Meaningful. NR-Not Ranked.

Office—2200 Mission College Blvd., Santa Clara, CA 95052-8119. **Tel**—(408) 765-8080. **Chrmn Emeritus**—G. E. Moore. **Chrmn & CEO**—A. S. Grove. **Pres**—C. R. Barrett. **Investor Contact**—Gordon Casey. **VP & CFO**—A. D. Bryant. **VP & Secy**—F. T. Dunlap, Jr. **Dirs**—C. R. Barrett, J. P. Browne, W. H. Chen, A. S. Grove, D. J. Guzy, R. Hodgson, S. Kaplan, G. E. Moore, M. Palevsky, A. Rock, J. E. Shaw, L. L. Vadasz, D. B. Yoffie, C. E. Young. **Transfer Agent & Registrar**—Harris Trust and Savings Bank. **Incorporated**—in California in 1968. **Empl**— 63,700. **S&P Analyst:** Megan Graham Hackett

12-SEP-98

Industry: Computers (Hardware)

Summary: The world's largest technology company, IBM offers a diversified line of computer hardware equipment, application and system software, and related services.

S&P Opinion: Accumulate (★★★★)	Recent Price • 126½	Yield • 0.7%
	52 Wk Range • 138⅛-88⅝	12-Mo. P/E • 21.1

Quantitative Evaluations

Outlook
(1 Lowest—5 Highest)
• **2+**

Fair Value
• **120**

Risk
• **Average**

Earn./Div. Rank
• **B**

Technical Eval.
• **Bearish** since 12/97

Rel. Strength Rank
(1 Lowest—99 Highest)
• **95**

Insider Activity
• **Neutral**

Earnings vs. Previous Year
▲=Up ▼=Down ▶=No Change

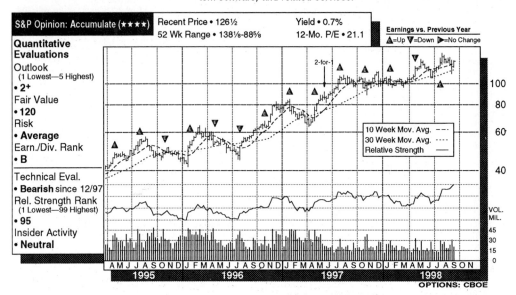

10 Week Mov. Avg. ---
30 Week Mov. Avg. ····
Relative Strength —

OPTIONS: CBOE

Overview - 06-AUG-98

Revenues in 1998 should grow in the high single digits, on a constant-currency basis, as gains in services are tempered by slower growth in hardware, software, rentals and financing, and maintenance. Hardware growth should be helped by improving personal computer (PC) sales, new server offerings and hard disk drives (storage). While PC sales were weaker in the first half of the year, reflecting excess inventory and pricing pressures, we believe that underlying PC demand remains healthy, and results should improve noticeably in the second half of the year. Growth in services should remain at about 20%, and software revenues should continue to rise. We expect gross margins to narrow from 1997 levels, on pricing pressures and sales mix issues. Operating expenses should rise less rapidly than revenues, aided by expense controls. EPS, boosted by a lower tax rate and fewer shares outstanding, are estimated at $6.55 in 1998.

Valuation - 06-AUG-98

We continue to recommend accumulating IBM shares. The stock has continued to strengthen in 1998, with IBM's outlook the most positive it has been in recent memory, reflecting impressive new product introductions, sounder businesses, and signs that investment in faster-growing segments is paying off. Still, a good portion of IBM's EPS growth continues to be fueled by a lower tax rate and fewer shares outstanding, rather than top-line growth. We believe that IBM's ability to reach double-digit revenue growth will remain challenged by the slower growth of its hardware businesses. Despite our near-term revenue concerns, we expect IBM's turnaround to continue, reflecting its strategies in software and services, Internet solutions, storage products, and new hardware products.

Key Stock Statistics

S&P EPS Est. 1998	6.55	Tang. Bk. Value/Share	19.23
P/E on S&P Est. 1998	19.3	Beta	1.09
S&P EPS Est. 1999	7.35	Shareholders	615,600
Dividend Rate/Share	0.88	Market cap. (B)	$118.1
Shs. outstg. (M)	933.1	Inst. holdings	49%
Avg. daily vol. (M)	4.734		

Value of $10,000 invested 5 years ago: $ 54,050

Fiscal Year Ending Dec. 31

	1998	1997	1996	1995	1994	1993
Revenues (Million $)						
1Q	17,618	17,308	16,559	15,735	13,373	13,058
2Q	18,823	18,872	18,183	17,531	15,351	15,519
3Q	—	18,605	18,062	16,754	15,431	14,743
4Q	—	23,723	23,143	21,920	19,897	19,396
Yr.	—	78,508	75,947	71,940	64,052	62,716
Earnings Per Share ($)						
1Q	**1.06**	1.19	0.70	1.06	0.32	-0.25
2Q	**1.50**	1.46	1.25	1.49	0.57	-7.05
3Q	**E1.66**	1.38	1.23	-0.48	0.59	-0.06
4Q	**E2.33**	2.11	1.97	1.54	1.03	0.31
Yr.	**E6.55**	6.01	5.01	3.62	2.51	-7.01

Next earnings report expected: late October

Dividend Data (Dividends have been paid since 1916.)

Amount ($)	Date Decl.	Ex-Div. Date	Stock of Record	Payment Date
0.200	Oct. 28	Nov. 06	Nov. 10	Dec. 10 '97
0.200	Jan. 27	Feb. 06	Feb. 10	Mar. 10 '98
0.220	Apr. 28	May. 06	May. 08	Jun. 10 '98
0.220	Jul. 28	Aug. 06	Aug. 10	Sep. 10 '98

A Division of The McGraw-Hill Companies

Business Summary - 06-AUG-98

IBM is the world's largest computer concern. Once viewed mostly as a hardware company, it has refocused to target faster-growing markets. While hardware accounted for 50% of revenues in 1994 (server hardware alone was 17%), it now provides about 40%. IBM's fast-growing Services group now provides 28% of revenues, versus 15% in 1994. IBM also acquired software pioneer Lotus in 1995, and Tivoli Systems, a provider of management software for client/server environments, in 1996, to benefit from the higher growth rate of distributed software. Software represents about 17% of IBM revenues.

Despite IBM's strategic turnaround, sales growth is still likely to be limited to single digits, reflecting the adverse impact of a strong U.S. dollar, as more than half (67%) of revenues are from non-U.S. operations; and because of its sheer size. For IBM to grow 10% means adding $8 billion in revenues a year to its nearly $80 billion base.

IBM's hardware, once thought of as principally mainframes (System/390) and minicomputers (AS/400), has made a transition to more open systems. IBM has refurbished its line of PCs (personal computers) and is now ranked number two worldwide, behind Compaq Computer. Storage products, primarily hard disk drives, have reflected strong revenue growth in recent

quarters, as IBM leverages its technological edge and expertise in the high end of the market.

IBM's Services segment has grown between 25% and 30% over the past three years. IBM Services includes consulting, education, systems integration design and development, managed operations of systems and networks and availability services. While software growth has not been as strong, this reflects the dampening effect of slowing demand for host software business, versus strong growth in distributed software business (spurred by the Lotus and Tivoli acquisitions).

Revenues from maintenance have been declining, reflecting an industrywide phenomenon. In 1994, maintenance revenues were 11% of the total, and are now down to 8%. Other IBM revenues include rentals and financing (6%): financing for purchasing and leasing its products.

IBM has made important strides in embracing open systems. In March 1997, it announced new, high-powered workstations, based on Intel processors for the first time, and running the popular Windows NT. In September 1997, IBM announced a new technology, called CMOS 7S, under which it would lead the use of copper instead of aluminum to create the circuitry on silicon wafers. Copper, a better electrical conductor than aluminum, has not been used in making microprocessors because of its corrosive properties, making its use difficult in semiconductor manufacturing.

Per Share Data ($)

(Year Ended Dec. 31)	1997	1996	1995	1994	1993	1992	1991	1990	1989	1988
Tangible Bk. Val.	19.23	19.99	19.45	18.60	15.45	23.93	32.20	37.15	33.16	32.89
Cash Flow	9.98	8.61	7.14	6.10	-2.90	-1.81	4.01	8.94	6.88	7.90
Earnings	6.01	5.12	3.62	2.51	-7.01	-6.01	-0.49	5.25	3.23	4.63
Dividends	0.78	0.65	0.50	0.50	0.79	2.42	2.42	2.42	2.37	2.20
Payout Ratio	13%	13%	14%	20%	NM	NM	NM	46%	72%	47%
Prices - High	113½	83	57⅜	38¼	30	50¼	69⅞	61⅝	65½	64¾
- Low	63⅝	41⅝	35⅛	25¾	20⅜	24⅜	41¾	47¼	46¾	52⅛
P/E Ratio - High	19	16	16	15	NM	NM	NM	12	20	14
- Low	11	8	10	10	NM	NM	NM	9	14	11

Income Statement Analysis (Million $)

	1997	1996	1995	1994	1993	1992	1991	1990	1989	1988
Revs.	78,508	75,947	71,940	64,052	62,716	64,523	64,792	69,018	62,710	59,681
Oper. Inc.	13,116	12,272	11,546	9,202	5,018	8,199	9,489	15,249	13,553	12,617
Depr.	4,018	3,676	3,955	4,197	4,710	4,793	5,149	4,217	4,240	3,871
Int. Exp.	760	747	748	1,247	1,319	1,461	1,566	1,446	1,118	802
Pretax Inc.	9,027	8,587	7,813	5,155	-8,796	-9,025	121	10,203	6,645	9,033
Eff. Tax Rate	33%	37%	47%	41%	NM	NM	566%	41%	43%	39%
Net Inc.	6,093	5,429	4,178	3,021	-7,986	-6,864	-563	6,020	3,758	5,491

Balance Sheet & Other Fin. Data (Million $)

	1997	1996	1995	1994	1993	1992	1991	1990	1989	1988
Cash	7,553	8,137	7,701	10,554	7,133	5,649	5,151	4,551	4,961	6,123
Curr. Assets	40,418	40,695	40,691	41,338	39,202	39,692	40,969	38,920	35,875	35,343
Total Assets	81,499	81,132	80,292	81,091	81,113	86,705	92,473	87,568	77,734	73,037
Curr. Liab.	33,507	34,000	31,648	29,226	33,150	36,737	33,624	25,276	21,700	17,387
LT Debt	13,696	9,872	10,060	12,548	15,245	12,853	13,231	11,943	10,825	8,518
Common Eqty.	19,564	21,375	22,170	22,288	18,613	27,624	37,006	42,832	38,509	39,509
Total Cap.	34,999	33,127	34,290	37,842	36,786	42,507	52,164	58,636	52,614	52,650
Cap. Exp.	6,793	5,883	4,744	3,078	3,154	4,751	6,502	6,548	6,410	5,431
Cash Flow	10,091	9,085	8,133	7,134	-3,323	-2,071	4,385	10,237	7,998	9,362
Curr. Ratio	1.2	1.2	1.3	1.4	1.2	1.1	1.2	1.5	1.7	2.0
% LT Debt of Cap.	39.1	29.8	29.3	53.2	41.4	30.2	25.4	20.4	20.6	16.2
% Net Inc.of Revs.	7.8	7.2	5.8	4.7	NM	NM	NM	8.7	6.0	9.2
% Ret. on Assets	7.5	6.8	5.2	3.7	NM	NM	NM	7.3	5.0	8.1
% Ret. on Equity	29.8	24.9	18.5	14.3	NM	NM	NM	14.8	9.8	14.2

Data as orig. reptd.; bef. results of disc. opers. and/or spec. items. Per share data adj. for stk. divs. as of ex-div. date. Bold denotes diluted EPS (FASB 128). E-Estimated. NA-Not Available. NM-Not Meaningful. NR-Not Ranked.

Office—New Orchard Rd., Armonk, NY 10504. **Tel**—(914) 499-1900. **Chrmn & CEO**—L. V. Gerstner Jr. **SVP & General Counsel**—L. R. Ricciardi. **CFO**—D. Maine. **Treas**—J. Serkes. **Secy**—J. E. Hickey. **Investor Contact**—H. Parke III. **Stockholder Relations Dept**—Tel: (914-499-7777). **Dirs**—C. Black, J. Dormann, L. V. Gerstner Jr., N. O. Keohane, C. F. Knight, M. Makihara, L. A. Noto, J. B. Slaughter, A. Trotman, L. C. van Wachem, C. M. Vest. **Transfer Agent & Registrar**—First Chicago Trust Co. of New York, Jersey City, NJ. **Incorporated**—in N.Y. in 1911. **Empl**—269,465. **S&P Analyst:** M. Graham Hackett

12-SEP-98 | Industry: Chemicals (Specialty)

Summary: This leading producer of flavors and fragrances used in a wide variety of consumer goods derives over two-thirds of sales and earnings from operations outside the U.S.

| S&P Opinion: Hold (★★★) | Recent Price • 37⅜ | Yield • 4.0% |
| | 52 Wk Range • 53-35⅜ | 12-Mo. P/E • 19.3 |

Earnings vs. Previous Year
▲=Up ▼=Down ▷=No Change

Quantitative Evaluations

Outlook (1 Lowest—5 Highest)
• **2+**

Fair Value
• **38¼**

Risk
• **Low**

Earn./Div. Rank
• **A**

Technical Eval.
• **Bearish** since 3/98

Rel. Strength Rank (1 Lowest—99 Highest)
• **60**

Insider Activity
• **Neutral**

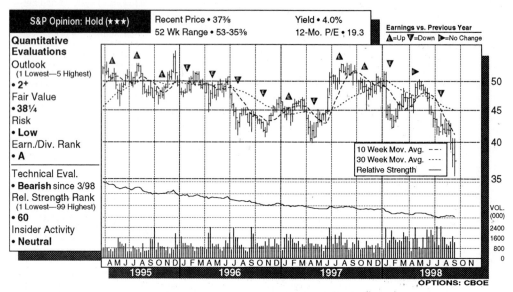

10 Week Mov. Avg. – – –
30 Week Mov. Avg. ·····
Relative Strength ——

VOL. (000)
2400
1600
800
0

A M J J A S O N D | J F M A M J J A S O N D | J F M A M J J A S O N D | J F M A M J J A S O N
1995 | 1996 | 1997 | 1998

OPTIONS: CBOE

Overview - 11-AUG-98

Sales in the 1998 first half declined 3.4%, year to year, reflecting unfavorable currency exchange rates and economic problems in Asia. We expect sales and earnings to show favorable comparisons in the second half of 1998, with full year sales flat versus 1997. There will be rising volumes of flavors, fragrances and aromas in most parts of the world, reflecting growing consumer demand for personal care, detergent, household, food and beverage products. A very high level of new product introductions by customers will be beneficial. The North American and European fine fragrance sales are picking up as a result of the return to normal ordering patterns. However, economic downturns in Southeast Asia are expected to continue for the rest of the year, reducing growth in consumer spending. A strong U.S. dollar should continue to modestly restrict sales growth, while price softness for certain flavors and aroma chemicals will likely continue to restrict results. IFF will realize most of the full annual cost savings of about $0.12 a share from the completed streamlining of worldwide aroma chemical production facilities, including the closing of a plant at 1997 year end. EPS comparisons will benefit from a continuing stock repurchase program.

Valuation - 11-AUG-98

The stock has been a lackluster performer over the past three years, due to a sluggish trend in sales and earnings. On disappointing EPS, the shares fell nearly 20%, year to date. We view the shares, selling at a slight discount to the market, as an attractive long-term holding, as company fundamentals remain sound, with high levels of new product development projects. The dividend has been raised for 37 consecutive years, and increases should continue in the future.

Key Stock Statistics

S&P EPS Est. 1998	2.00	Tang. Bk. Value/Share	8.82
P/E on S&P Est. 1998	18.7	Beta	0.66
S&P EPS Est. 1999	2.25	Shareholders	5,600
Dividend Rate/Share	1.48	Market cap. (B)	$ 4.0
Shs. outstg. (M)	107.2	Inst. holdings	61%
Avg. daily vol. (M)	0.271		

Value of $10,000 invested 5 years ago: $ 12,230

Fiscal Year Ending Dec. 31

	1998	1997	1996	1995	1994	1993
Revenues (Million $)						
1Q	373.4	382.8	382.8	373.6	323.5	309.0
2Q	365.3	381.5	374.4	394.3	345.2	321.3
3Q	—	356.2	354.9	360.1	341.7	298.6
4Q	—	306.3	324.0	311.5	304.8	259.6
Yr.	—	1,427	1,436	1,439	1,315	1,189
Earnings Per Share ($)						
1Q	**0.58**	**0.58**	0.60	0.63	0.53	0.49
2Q	**0.52**	**0.57**	0.26	0.68	0.58	0.53
3Q	**E0.52**	**0.52**	0.48	0.57	0.53	0.44
4Q	**E0.38**	**0.32**	0.37	0.36	0.39	0.32
Yr.	**E2.00**	**1.99**	1.71	2.24	2.03	1.78

Next earnings report expected: late October

Dividend Data (Dividends have been paid since 1956.)

Amount ($)	Date Decl.	Ex-Div. Date	Stock of Record	Payment Date
0.370	Dec. 09	Dec. 19	Dec. 23	Jan. 09 '98
0.370	Feb. 10	Mar. 24	Mar. 26	Apr. 10 '98
0.370	May. 14	Jun. 24	Jun. 26	Jul. 10 '98
0.370	Sep. 08	Sep. 23	Sep. 25	Oct. 09 '98

A Division of The **McGraw·Hill** *Companies*

Business Summary - 11-AUG-98

Founded in 1909, International Flavors & Fragrances (IFF) is the leading maker of products used by other manufacturers to enhance the aromas and taste of consumers' everyday life.

IFF already receives over two-thirds of its sales from outside the U.S. Future opportunities for growth include markets in Asia, Latin America and Eastern Europe, where rising consumer incomes are likely to boost demand for manufactured products that use the types of ingredients provided by IFF. Sales and profits in 1997 by geographic area were:

	Sales	Profits
U.S.	31%	21%
Western Europe	40%	53%
Other	29%	26%

Fragrance products accounted for 58% of IFF's sales in 1997. Fragrances are used in the manufacture of soaps, detergents, cosmetic creams, lotions and powders, lipsticks, aftershave lotions, deodorants, hair preparations, air fresheners, perfumes and colognes and other consumer products. Most of the major U.S. companies in these industries are customers of IFF. Cosmetics (including perfumes and toiletries) and household products (soaps and detergents) are the company's two largest customer groups.

Flavor products account for IFF's remaining sales.

Flavors are sold principally to the food, beverage and other industries for use in such consumer products as soft drinks, candies, cake mixes, desserts, prepared foods, dietary foods, dairy products, drink powders, pharmaceuticals, oral care products, alcoholic beverages and tobacco. Two of the company's largest customers for flavors products are major producers of prepared foods and beverages in the U.S.

IFF uses both synthetic and natural ingredients in its compounds. It has had a consistent commitment to research and development, spending 6% to 7% of annual sales on R&D for over the past three decades. R&D is conducted in 30 laboratories in 24 countries.

For a decade, until 1996, the company achieved steady sales and earnings growth. However, it was hurt during 1996 by slow customer reordering of fine fragrances, while flavor sales were limited by the impact of consolidation among food customers and unusual cool summer weather. Results in 1997 were further restricted by a stronger U.S. dollar. A completed streamlining of IFF's aroma chemicals production should generate pretax annual cost savings of $20 million.

IFF is financially strong, with almost no long term debt. The cash dividend was increased in 1997, for the 37th consecutive year. In September 1996, directors approved a new stock buyback program for an additional 7.5 million common shares. As of March 31, 1998, about 2.5 million were acquired under the new buyback program.

Per Share Data ($)

(Year Ended Dec. 31)	1997	1996	1995	1994	1993	1992	1991	1990	1989	1988
Tangible Bk. Val.	9.17	9.79	10.06	9.04	7.96	8.48	8.39	7.84	6.70	6.11
Cash Flow	2.45	2.15	2.61	2.35	2.09	1.83	1.73	1.62	1.43	1.33
Earnings	1.99	1.71	2.24	2.03	1.78	1.53	1.47	1.37	1.22	1.13
Dividends	1.45	1.38	1.27	1.12	1.02	0.93	0.83	0.73	0.66	0.56
Payout Ratio	73%	81%	57%	55%	57%	61%	56%	54%	54%	50%
Prices - High	53³/₈	51⁷/₈	55⁷/₈	47⁷/₈	39⁷/₈	38³/₄	35	25	25⁷/₈	18¹/₈
- Low	39⁷/₈	40³/₄	45¹/₄	35⁵/₈	33	31¹/₂	22⁷/₈	18¹/₄	16¹/₈	14³/₈
P/E Ratio - High	27	30	25	24	22	25	24	18	21	16
- Low	20	24	20	18	19	20	16	13	13	13

Income Statement Analysis (Million $)

	1997	1996	1995	1994	1993	1992	1991	1990	1989	1988
Revs.	1,427	1,436	1,439	1,315	1,189	1,126	1,017	963	870	840
Oper. Inc.	382	388	425	385	341	318	284	268	238	234
Depr.	50.3	47.7	40.7	36.4	35.1	34.0	29.4	28.2	24.3	22.7
Int. Exp.	2.4	2.7	3.2	13.5	17.4	12.4	9.5	22.1	7.5	8.2
Pretax Inc.	340	299	394	360	324	282	269	252	223	209
Eff. Tax Rate	36%	37%	35%	37%	38%	37%	37%	38%	38%	39%
Net Inc.	218	190	249	226	202	177	169	157	139	129

Balance Sheet & Other Fin. Data (Million $)

	1997	1996	1995	1994	1993	1992	1991	1990	1989	1988
Cash	217	318	297	302	311	430	410	376	289	236
Curr. Assets	935	1,006	1,036	964	879	965	918	853	724	646
Total Assets	1,422	1,507	1,534	1,400	1,225	1,268	1,217	1,129	970	882
Curr. Liab.	265	280	276	260	227	195	181	158	140	126
LT Debt	5.1	8.3	11.6	14.3	Nil	Nil	Nil	Nil	Nil	Nil
Common Eqty.	1,000	1,077	1,117	1,008	892	977	960	898	765	695
Total Cap.	1,029	1,102	1,142	1,037	903	984	982	919	782	714
Cap. Exp.	58.2	79.4	94.4	101	82.3	51.1	53.3	41.2	33.4	40.2
Cash Flow	269	238	290	262	238	211	198	185	163	151
Curr. Ratio	3.5	3.6	3.8	3.7	3.9	5.0	5.1	5.4	5.2	5.1
% LT Debt of Cap.	0.5	0.8	1.0	1.4	Nil	Nil	Nil	Nil	Nil	Nil
% Net Inc.of Revs.	15.3	13.2	17.3	17.2	17.0	15.7	16.6	16.3	15.9	15.3
% Ret. on Assets	14.9	12.5	17.0	17.3	16.5	14.2	14.4	14.9	14.9	14.6
% Ret. on Equity	21.0	17.3	23.4	23.9	22.0	18.2	18.2	18.8	18.9	19.0

Data as orig. reptd.; bef. results of disc. opers. and/or spec. items. Per share data adj. for stk. divs. as of ex-div. date. Bold denotes diluted EPS (FASB 128). E-Estimated. NA-Not Available. NM-Not Meaningful. NR-Not Ranked.

Office—521 W. 57th St., New York, NY 10019-2960. **Tel**—(212) 765-5500. **Chrmn & Pres**—E. P. Grisanti. **VP & Secy**—S. A. Block. **VP-CFO & Investor Contact**—Douglas J. Wetmore.**Dirs**—M. Hayes Adame, D. G. Bluestein, B. D. Chadbourne, R. Chandler Duke, R. M. Furlaud, E. P. Grisanti, H. G. Reid, G. Rowe Jr., S. M. Rumbough Jr., H. P. van Ameringen, W. D. Van Dyke III. **Transfer Agent & Registrar**—Bank of New York, NYC. **Incorporated**—in New York in 1909. **Empl**— 4,639. **S&P Analyst**: Richard O'Reilly, CFA

STANDARD &POOR'S
STOCK REPORTS

International Paper

1222

NYSE Symbol **IP**

In S&P 500

12-SEP-98

Industry:
Paper & Forest Products

Summary: This worldwide producer of printing papers, packaging and forest products also operates specialty businesses and a broadly based paper distribution network.

S&P Opinion: Hold (★★★)

Recent Price • 41⅝	Yield • 2.4%
52 Wk Range • 61¾-35½	12-Mo. P/E • 31.8

Quantitative Evaluations

Outlook
(1 Lowest—5 Highest)
• **1⁻**

Fair Value
• **36**

Risk
• **NA**

Earn./Div. Rank
• **B-**

Technical Eval.
• **Neutral** since 6/98

Rel. Strength Rank
(1 Lowest—99 Highest)
• **81**

Insider Activity
• **Neutral**

Earnings vs. Previous Year
▲=Up ▼=Down ▶=No Change

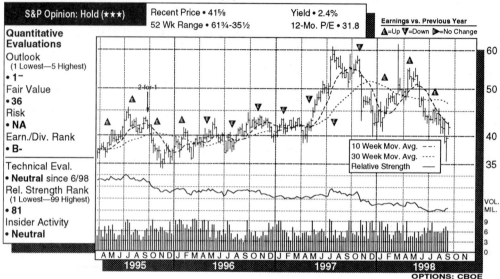

10 Week Mov. Avg. — - —
30 Week Mov. Avg. - - - -
Relative Strength ——

OPTIONS: CBOE

Overview - 13-AUG-98

Sales from comparable operations should be modestly higher in 1998, boosted by slightly higher average paper and packaging prices. However, Asia's financial woes and a strong U.S. dollar have hurt foreign trade, and the modest pricing recovery seen between early 1997 and early 1998 recently suffered a setback. We see wider operating margins despite the dimming sales outlook. We see those gains driven largely by benefits from an early 1996 restructuring program. Given our forecast of higher average full year paper and packaging prices, pricing should also give some modest bottom line assistance. Comparisons will be distorted by net one-time charges of $1.53 a share in 1997, stemming mainly from a new restructuring program. IP's latest business improvement program will reduce its sales base, but should further aid the bottom line in 1998, after being slightly accretive in 1997. The August 1998 purchase of Mead's distribution business should have little impact on 1998 EPS, but should aid future results after IP completes its plan to close over 25 facilities and eliminate $100 million in redundant costs.

Valuation - 13-AUG-98

The shares rebounded strongly in the spring and summer of 1997, on a combination of firming paper industry conditions and investor enthusiasm for a business reorganization program announced in July. They have since given back all of those gains (despite a brief early 1998 upturn), as Asia's financial woes dampened the outlook for forest products markets. Asia's crisis has played a major part in the recent setback of the industry's modest recovery, and leaves us pessimistic about upcoming prospects. However, given our belief that IP's recent business improvement efforts will leave it better situated for the next industry upturn, we have a neutral investment stance on the shares.

Key Stock Statistics

S&P EPS Est. 1998	1.25	Tang. Bk. Value/Share	21.13
P/E on S&P Est. 1998	33.3	Beta	1.09
S&P EPS Est. 1999	1.75	Shareholders	33,900
Dividend Rate/Share	1.00	Market cap. (B)	$ 12.8
Shs. outstg. (M)	307.2	Inst. holdings	67%
Avg. daily vol. (M)	1.389		

Value of $10,000 invested 5 years ago: $ 14,332

Fiscal Year Ending Dec. 31

	1998	1997	1996	1995	1994	1993
Revenues (Million $)						
1Q	4,868	4,862	4,798	4,492	3,414	3,362
2Q	4,707	5,034	5,093	5,084	3,633	3,506
3Q	—	5,119	5,108	5,145	3,792	3,405
4Q	—	5,081	5,144	5,076	4,127	3,412
Yr.	—	20,096	20,143	19,797	14,966	13,685
Earnings Per Share ($)						
1Q	**0.25**	0.11	0.36	0.97	0.30	0.26
2Q	**0.28**	-1.39	0.33	1.25	0.36	0.31
3Q	**E0.32**	0.34	0.37	1.27	0.45	0.20
4Q	**E0.40**	0.44	-0.02	1.01	0.61	0.41
Yr.	**E1.25**	-0.50	1.04	4.50	1.73	1.17

Next earnings report expected: mid October

Dividend Data (Dividends have been paid since 1946.)

Amount ($)	Date Decl.	Ex-Div. Date	Stock of Record	Payment Date
0.250	Nov. 11	Nov. 19	Nov. 21	Dec. 15 '97
0.250	Feb. 11	Feb. 18	Feb. 20	Mar. 16 '98
0.250	May. 12	May. 20	May. 22	Jun. 15 '98
0.250	Aug. 11	Aug. 19	Aug. 21	Sep. 15 '98

A Division of The McGraw-Hill Companies

Business Summary - 13-AUG-98

One of the world's largest paper, paperboard and packaging producers, IP is also active in a variety of other forest and non-forest products areas. Living up to its name, International Paper serves customers in over 130 nations; sales outside the U.S., including exports, accounted for 35% of the total in 1997. IP also initiated a business reorganization plan in July 1997.

The printing papers division (26% of sales in 1997) makes a wide variety of uncoated grades, including copier and printing paper, and papers used for books, index cards, envelopes, and artist and other needs. Coated grades include papers used in magazines and other publications; and bristols for book covers and commercial printing. It also makes pulp products, the basic raw material for papers, paperboard, disposable diapers and some fabrics.

The packaging sector (23% of sales) produces containerboard (used to make corrugated boxes) and corrugated boxes. It also makes premium bleached board for use in folding cartons, liquid packaging and food service products, and aseptic packaging systems to help keep perishable liquids fresh without refrigeration.

IP distributes printing, packaging, graphic arts and industrial supply products (22% of sales), mostly made by others, through over 300 centers (mostly in the U.S.). In August 1998, IP acquired Mead Corp.'s Zellerbach distribution business (annual sales of about $1.2 billion), for $263 million.

Specialty products (16% of sales) include panels; industrial papers; tissue; and chemicals. IP also explores for oil and gas.

The forest products division (13% of sales) controls 6.3 million acres of timberland in the U.S., including 5.6 million acres held through a majority interest in IP Timberlands, Ltd. IP also controls 845,000 acres of timberland in New Zealand and has a presence in Chile. In addition, the segment sells lumber and panels.

In May 1998, IP announced it will reorganize into seven more specialized business groups. The new groups will be: Building Materials, Consumer Packaging, Distribution, European Papers, Industrial Packaging, Printing Papers, and Specialty Businesses.

In August 1998, IP completed its plan to sell $1 billion in nonstrategic assets, under a July 1997 reorganization program. It also reported plans to make another $500 million of asset sales over the next year. The company concluded its initial plan through the $282 million sale of its Veratec nonwovens business. Other major transactions included the October 1997 sale of IP's multiwall kraft packaging business; the shutdown or sale of various small mills and paper machines; and the sale of the photographics and pressroom chemicals divisions of the imaging products business. The reorganization also called for the restructuring of IP's printing papers business and a 10% reduction in workforce (mostly from the business sales). The revamping of printing papers operations has consisted of the reduction of 400,000 tons of uncoated paper and pulp capacity through shutdowns and conversions to different grades.

Per Share Data ($) (Year Ended Dec. 31)	1997	1996	1995	1994	1993	1992	1991	1990	1989	1988
Tangible Bk. Val.	20.36	21.99	24.68	22.84	22.08	22.07	21.84	22.54	21.52	19.20
Cash Flow	3.68	5.12	8.50	5.27	4.82	4.08	4.97	5.66	6.37	5.46
Earnings	-0.50	1.04	4.50	1.73	1.17	0.58	1.80	2.60	3.86	3.29
Dividends	1.00	1.00	0.92	0.84	0.84	0.84	0.84	0.84	0.77	0.64
Payout Ratio	NM	96%	20%	49%	72%	145%	47%	32%	20%	19%
Prices - High	61	44⅝	45¾	40¼	35	39¼	39⅛	29⅞	29⅜	24¾
- Low	38⅝	35⅝	34⅛	30⅜	28⅜	29¼	25¼	21⅜	22⅝	18¼
P/E Ratio - High	NM	43	10	23	30	67	22	11	8	8
- Low	NM	34	8	18	24	50	14	8	6	6
Income Statement Analysis (Million $)										
Revs.	20,096	20,143	19,797	14,966	13,685	13,598	12,703	12,960	11,378	9,533
Oper. Inc.	2,404	2,614	3,552	1,898	1,708	1,701	1,713	2,088	2,159	1,824
Depr.	1,258	1,194	1,031	885	898	850	700	653	549	485
Int. Exp.	490	530	551	367	322	289	351	303	216	171
Pretax Inc.	16.0	802	1,872	664	500	206	638	946	1,405	1,222
Eff. Tax Rate	238%	41%	36%	35%	42%	31%	38%	40%	39%	36%
Net Inc.	-150	303	1,153	432	289	142	399	569	864	754
Balance Sheet & Other Fin. Data (Million $)										
Cash	398	352	312	270	242	225	238	256	102	122
Curr. Assets	5,945	5,998	5,873	4,830	4,401	4,366	4,131	3,939	3,096	2,343
Total Assets	26,754	28,252	23,977	17,836	16,631	16,459	14,941	13,669	11,582	9,462
Curr. Liab.	4,880	5,894	4,863	4,034	4,009	4,531	3,727	3,155	2,730	1,562
LT Debt	7,154	6,691	5,946	4,464	3,601	3,096	3,351	3,096	2,324	1,853
Common Eqty.	8,710	9,344	7,797	6,514	6,225	6,189	5,739	5,632	5,147	4,557
Total Cap.	20,188	20,668	15,717	12,590	11,440	10,702	10,134	9,863	8,493	7,624
Cap. Exp.	1,111	1,394	1,518	1,114	954	1,368	1,197	1,409	1,345	899
Cash Flow	1,107	1,497	2,184	1,317	1,187	992	1,099	1,222	1,394	1,218
Curr. Ratio	1.2	1.0	1.2	1.2	1.1	1.0	1.1	1.2	1.1	1.5
% LT Debt of Cap.	35.4	32.3	37.8	35.5	31.5	28.9	33.1	31.4	27.4	24.3
% Net Inc.of Revs.	NM	1.5	5.8	2.9	2.1	1.0	3.1	4.4	7.6	7.9
% Ret. on Assets	NM	1.2	5.5	2.5	1.7	0.9	2.8	4.5	8.3	8.3
% Ret. on Equity	NM	3.5	16.1	6.7	4.6	2.3	6.9	10.5	17.6	17.1

Data as orig. reptd.; bef. results of disc. opers. and/or spec. items. Per share data adj. for stk. divs. as of ex-div. date. Bold denotes diluted EPS (FASB 128). E-Estimated. NA-Not Available. NM-Not Meaningful. NR-Not Ranked.

Office—Two Manhattanville Rd., Purchase, NY 10577. **Tel**—(914) 397-1500. **Website**—http://www.ipaper.com **Chrmn & CEO**—J. T. Dillon. **SVP & CFO**—M. M. Parrs. **Investor Contact**—Carol Tutundgy. **Dirs**—P. I. Bijur, W. C. Butcher, J. T. Dillon, R. J. Eaton, J. A. Georges, T. C. Graham, J. R. Kennedy, D. F. McHenry, P. F. Noonan, J. C. Pfeiffer, E. T. Pratt Jr., C. R. Shoemate, C. W. Smith. **Transfer Agent & Registrar**—ChaseMellon, Ridgefield Park, NJ. **Incorporated**—in New York in 1941. **Empl**— 82,000. **S&P Analyst:** Michael W. Jaffe

STANDARD &POOR'S
STOCK REPORTS

Interpublic Group

1236S

NYSE Symbol **IPG**

In S&P 500

12-SEP-98

Industry: Services (Advertising & Marketing)

Summary: Interpublic is one of the world's largest organizations of advertising agencies and marketing communications companies.

S&P Opinion: Accumulate (★★★★)	Recent Price • 52⅜

Recent Price • 52⅜	Yield • 1.1%	
52 Wk Range • 65¼-44¼	12-Mo. P/E • 25.2	

Quantitative Evaluations

Outlook (1 Lowest—5 Highest)
• **3⁻**

Fair Value
• **55¾**

Risk
• **Low**

Earn./Div. Rank
• **A+**

Technical Eval.
• **Bullish** since 8/95

Rel. Strength Rank (1 Lowest—99 Highest)
• **60**

Insider Activity
• **NA**

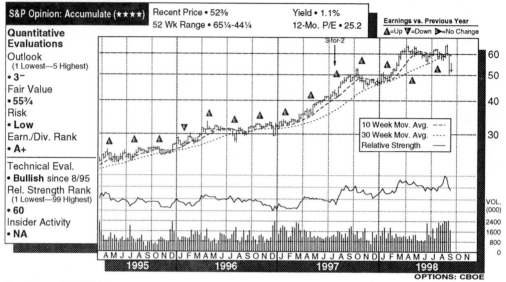

Earnings vs. Previous Year
▲=Up ▼=Down ▷=No Change

10 Week Mov. Avg. ---
30 Week Mov. Avg. ·····
Relative Strength —

VOL. (000)

OPTIONS: CBOE

Overview - 29-MAY-98

Gross income, which advanced 25% in the first quarter, should continue to improve on a year-to-year basis through each quarter of 1998 (after currency translations), following a 23% advance for 1997. The gains reflect strong growth in net new business as well as from acquisitions. In addition to a robust U.S. market, growth will come from expanding Latin American and other markets. Margins will benefit from ongoing cost-control measures. An ongoing share buyback program, which is currently limited to two million shares per year, will also benefit the bottom line because most acquisitions are for stock. Aided by continuing advertising health in most major geographical markets and by acquisitions, gross income should again advance in 1999. Net income will benefit from operating efficiencies, as well as the healthy revenue gains.

Valuation - 29-MAY-98

The stock is selling near its all-time high, up more than 75% over the past 52 weeks. We recently upgraded our near-term opinion on IPG to accumulate from hold following release of Q1 earnings, based on our renewed confidence that IPG will sustain its outstanding growth record. We estimate a 17% earnings gain for 1998, aided by a robust advertising climate, acquisitions (including Hill, Holliday, Connors, Cosmopulos, Inc.) and operating efficiencies, and tentatively project a 19% advance for 1999. The company is aggressively diversifying its business base, seeking to increase the proportion of revenues derived from direct marketing, new media and other sources. These efforts also brighten the longer-term prospects for revenue growth and operating margins. Longer term, IPG is favored for dependable earnings and dividend growth prospects and, thus, total return. The dividend has been raised in each of the past 12 years.

Key Stock Statistics

S&P EPS Est. 1998	2.22	Tang. Bk. Value/Share	0.32
P/E on S&P Est. 1998	23.6	Beta	0.65
S&P EPS Est. 1999	2.65	Shareholders	7,500
Dividend Rate/Share	0.60	Market cap. (B)	$ 7.1
Shs. outstg. (M)	136.2	Inst. holdings	74%
Avg. daily vol. (M)	0.522		

Value of $10,000 invested 5 years ago: $ 24,413

Fiscal Year Ending Dec. 31

	1998	1997	1996	1995	1994	1993
Revenues (Million $)						
1Q	733.5	597.2	506.2	460.4	421.0	389.8
2Q	972.4	812.3	675.4	557.1	497.5	483.8
3Q	—	723.5	567.7	492.5	440.5	411.0
4Q	—	992.8	788.3	669.7	625.3	509.3
Yr.	—	3,126	2,538	2,180	1,984	1,794
Earnings Per Share ($)						
1Q	**0.21**	**0.18**	0.15	0.13	0.11	0.10
2Q	**0.84**	**0.71**	0.69	0.55	0.48	0.43
3Q	**E0.33**	**0.28**	0.23	0.19	0.15	0.13
4Q	**E0.85**	**0.71**	0.63	0.24	0.27	0.45
Yr.	**E2.22**	**1.90**	1.71	1.11	1.02	1.11

Next earnings report expected: late October

Dividend Data (Dividends have been paid since 1971.)

Amount ($)	Date Decl.	Ex-Div. Date	Stock of Record	Payment Date
0.130	Oct. 26	Nov. 24	Nov. 26	Dec. 15 '97
0.130	Dec. 18	Feb. 24	Feb. 26	Mar. 16 '98
0.150	May. 18	May. 26	May. 28	Jun. 15 '98
0.150	Jul. 30	Aug. 26	Aug. 28	Sep. 15 '98

A Division of The McGraw-Hill Companies

The Interpublic Group of Companies, Inc.

Business Summary - 29-MAY-98

The Interpublic Group of Companies is one of the world's largest organizations of advertising agencies and marketing communications companies. Some of its agencies' more famous campaigns include: "Pardon me, would you have any Grey Poupon?," for Grey Poupon mustard, and "It takes a tough man to make a tender chicken," for Perdue. The advertising agency functions of the company are conducted in more than 120 countries through McCann-Erickson Worldwide, Ammirati Puris Lintas, The Lowe Group, Campbell Mithun Esty (75%-owned), Western International Media and other affiliated companies.

The principal functions of the company's advertising agencies are to plan and create advertising programs for clients and to place the advertising in various media. The usual advertising agency commission is 13% of the gross charge (billings) for advertising space or time, but discounting is common. During 1997, the three largest clients together accounted for over 25% of income from commissions and fees.

Interpublic recently acquired Hill, Holliday, Connors, Cosmopulos, Inc., one of the top 25 agencies in the country with about $600 million in annual billings. IPG completed a number of major takeovers in the past two years, including Draft Worldwide, the largest independent global direct marketing company, with billings of $655 million. It also acquired New York-based Media Incorporated and its affiliate Media Direct Partners, Inc., rapidly growing media planning and buying companies; William Douglas McAdams, Inc., the sixth largest medical agency in the U.S., with billings of roughly $170 million; and Jay Advertising, a Rochester, NY-based agency with annual billings of $50 million. In 1997, IPG acquired a majority interest in Addis-Wechsler & Associates, one of Hollywood's leading personal management/production firms. IPG also purchased Adler, Boschetto Peebles & Partners, a direct marketer with annual billings of $135 million, and Marketing Corp. of America, with annual billings of nearly $300 million.

Operations outside the U.S. accounted for 53% of income from commissions and fees in 1997.

In addition to advertising agency activities, IPG is involved in publishing, market research, direct marketing, sales promotion, public relations, product development and other related services. IPG owns a minority interest in CKS Group, a leading marketing communications and new media firm. It also has an ownership interest in Atlantis Communications, a TV and feature film producer and distributor based in Canada.

Per Share Data ($) (Year Ended Dec. 31)	1997	1996	1995	1994	1993	1992	1991	1990	1989	1988
Tangible Bk. Val.	0.64	1.01	0.93	0.41	0.65	1.00	1.20	1.18	2.37	3.30
Cash Flow	2.42	2.21	1.77	1.58	1.65	1.52	1.36	1.17	1.00	0.86
Earnings	1.90	1.71	1.11	1.02	1.11	1.00	0.87	0.79	0.70	0.61
Dividends	0.50	0.44	0.40	0.36	0.33	0.30	0.27	0.25	0.21	0.17
Payout Ratio	26%	26%	36%	36%	29%	30%	33%	34%	31%	30%
Prices - High	53	33½	28⅞	23⅞	23¾	23⅞	19⅛	12⅝	12⅝	8¼
- Low	31⅜	26⅜	21⅛	18⅜	15⅞	17⅛	11¼	9¾	8⅛	6½
P/E Ratio - High	28	20	26	23	21	24	22	16	18	14
- Low	16	15	19	18	14	17	13	12	12	11
Income Statement Analysis (Million $)										
Revs.	2,997	2,431	2,094	1,916	1,740	1,804	1,635	1,329	1,218	1,153
Oper. Inc.	437	351	322	278	265	248	230	168	144	124
Depr.	75.0	60.5	77.6	63.9	61.3	59.2	53.9	37.8	30.3	24.9
Int. Exp.	49.4	40.7	38.0	32.9	26.4	33.2	33.5	18.9	15.0	10.2
Pretax Inc.	448	370	260	205	233	210	187	156	144	133
Eff. Tax Rate	41%	41%	47%	42%	43%	44%	47%	47%	47%	51%
Net Inc.	239	205	130	115	125	112	94.6	80.1	70.6	60.1
Balance Sheet & Other Fin. Data (Million $)										
Cash	715	504	457	442	322	291	276	216	123	180
Curr. Assets	4,026	3,353	2,974	2,675	2,003	1,915	2,032	1,915	1,373	1,297
Total Assets	5,703	4,765	4,260	3,793	2,870	2,623	2,784	2,584	1,741	1,600
Curr. Liab.	3,752	3,199	2,827	2,595	1,836	1,690	1,854	1,769	1,210	1,117
LT Debt	453	346	284	242	226	200	170	144	37.0	43.0
Common Eqty.	1,355	872	750	649	564	511	587	510	368	333
Total Cap.	1,592	1,241	1,048	904	803	728	774	668	417	390
Cap. Exp.	96.9	79.1	69.6	55.9	78.8	36.9	46.6	37.2	45.6	44.1
Cash Flow	314	266	207	179	187	171	148	118	101	85.0
Curr. Ratio	1.1	1.1	1.0	1.0	1.1	1.1	1.1	1.1	1.1	1.2
% LT Debt of Cap.	28.4	27.9	27.1	26.8	28.1	27.5	22.0	21.6	8.8	10.9
% Net Inc.of Revs.	8.0	8.4	6.2	6.0	7.2	6.2	5.8	6.0	5.8	5.2
% Ret. on Assets	4.6	4.5	3.2	3.4	4.6	4.1	3.5	3.6	4.2	4.0
% Ret. on Equity	19.6	25.3	31.8	18.7	23.3	20.4	17.0	17.8	20.3	19.1

Data as orig. reptd.; bef. results of disc. opers. and/or spec. items. Quarterly revs. incl. other inc. Per share data adj. for stk. divs. as of ex-div. date. Bold denotes diluted EPS (FASB 128). E-Estimated. NA-Not Available. NM-Not Meaningful. NR-Not Ranked.

Office—1271 Ave. of the Americas, New York, NY 10020. **Tel**—(212) 399-8000. **Website**—http://www.interpublic.com **Chrmn, Pres & CEO**—P. H. Geier Jr. **VP-Secy**—N. Camera. **Vice Chrmn-Fin & Operations & Investor Contact**—Eugene P. Beard. **Dirs**—E. P. Beard, F. J. Borelli, R. K. Brack, J. M. Considine, J. J. Dooner Jr., P. H. Geier Jr., F. B. Lowe, L. H. Olsen, M. F. Puris, A. Questrom, J. P. Samper. **Transfer Agent & Registrar**—First Chicago Trust Co. of New York, NYC. **Incorporated**—in Delaware in 1930. **Empl**— 27,100. **S&P Analyst:** William H. Donald

ITT Industries

1181R

NYSE Symbol **IIN**

In S&P 500

12-SEP-98

Industry:
Auto Parts & Equipment

Summary: This diversified industrial manufacturer is the legal successor to the old ITT Corp.

S&P Opinion: Hold (★★★)	Recent Price • 32	Yield • 1.9%
	52 Wk Range • 38⅞-28⅛	12-Mo. P/E • 35.2

Quantitative Evaluations

Outlook
(1 Lowest—5 Highest)
• **3**

Fair Value
• **33⅞**

Risk
• **Low**

Earn./Div. Rank
• **NR**

Technical Eval.
• **NA**

Rel. Strength Rank
(1 Lowest—99 Highest)
• **74**

Insider Activity
• **Neutral**

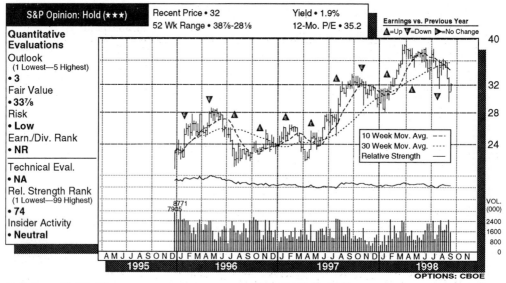

Earnings vs. Previous Year
▲=Up ▼=Down ▶=No Change

10 Week Mov. Avg. ---
30 Week Mov. Avg. ·····
Relative Strength ——

OPTIONS: CBOE

Overview - 28-JUL-98

With the spinoff of its nonindustrial pieces complete, IIN recently announced separate agreements for the sale of its two major automotive businesses. Expected net proceeds of approximately $2.6 billion would be used to repurchase up to $1 billion of IIN common stock, reduce debt and expand core businesses. The company intends to improve its operating margin toward its 1999 target of 9%, based on cost reductions and improved efficiencies. Beginning in 1999, the outlook brightens as certain cost reductions kick in, and pricing pressures ease on new product introductions. However, the absence of automotive profits could dilute EPS by up to 10% in 1999, before the impact of any acquisitions, but should be neutral to 2000 results. Ultimately, the absence of the pricing pressure and foreign currency translation in the automotive business should allow for incremental improvement to double-digit earnings gains. Defense and electronics, with its highest order input in 10 years, is benefiting from new technologies with commercial applications, a trend in government outsourcing, and improved margins. Fluid Technology, with its May 1997 acquisition of Goulds Pumps, Inc. for $934 million in cash and assumed debt, is the world's largest pump manufacturer, with revenues that should exceed $2 billion annually. Strong cash flow supports a modest cash dividend, debt reduction, and global expansion and other capital spending plans.

Valuation - 28-JUL-98

Although trading at just 13X our downward revised 1999 earnings per share estimate of $2.50, the impact of reduced expectations for 1999 may pressure the shares in the near term. With solid prospects for continued earnings growth via new business, joint ventures and acquisitions, IIN remains an attractive portfolio holding.

Key Stock Statistics

S&P EPS Est. 1998	2.35	Tang. Bk. Value/Share	NM
P/E on S&P Est. 1998	13.6	Beta	0.92
S&P EPS Est. 1999	2.50	Shareholders	57,000
Dividend Rate/Share	0.60	Market cap. (B)	$ 3.8
Shs. outstg. (M)	118.4	Inst. holdings	76%
Avg. daily vol. (M)	0.470		

Value of $10,000 invested 5 years ago: NA

Fiscal Year Ending Dec. 31

	1998	1997	1996	1995	1994	1993
Revenues (Million $)						
1Q	2,144	2,167	2,201	2,248	5,210	2,248
2Q	2,154	2,251	2,241	2,337	6,000	2,337
3Q	—	2,060	2,045	2,048	5,670	2,048
4Q	—	2,299	2,231	2,251	6,700	2,251
Yr.	—	8,777	8,718	8,884	23,620	22,760
Earnings Per Share ($)						
1Q	0.46	0.37	0.33	0.34	1.39	0.34
2Q	0.57	0.69	0.56	0.35	1.84	0.35
3Q	—	-0.77	0.36	-0.47	1.75	-0.47
4Q	—	0.65	0.59	-0.14	2.12	-0.14
Yr.	E2.35	0.94	1.85	0.03	7.10	7.29

Next earnings report expected: mid October

Dividend Data (Dividends have been paid since 1996.)

Amount ($)	Date Decl.	Ex-Div. Date	Stock of Record	Payment Date
0.150	Oct. 14	Nov. 25	Nov. 28	Jan. 01 '98
0.150	Jan. 20	Feb. 25	Feb. 27	Apr. 01 '98
0.150	May. 14	May. 27	May. 29	Jul. 01 '98
0.150	Jul. 28	Aug. 26	Aug. 28	Oct. 01 '98

A Division of The McGraw·Hill Companies

STANDARD
&POOR'S
STOCK REPORTS

ITT Industries, Inc.

1181R
12-SEP-98

Business Summary - 28-JUL-98

ITT Industries (formerly ITT Corp.) is the legal successor to the old ITT Corp. In December 1995, the company completed a restructuring announced in June 1995, which divided old ITT Corp. into three separate, publicly owned entities. ITT Industries retains old ITT's industrial units. Two spinoff companies were formed: ITT Hartford Group (insurance) and New ITT Corp. (hotels, gaming, entertainment and education). Old ITT shares were converted into ITT Industries shares on a one-for-one basis. One share each of New ITT and ITT Hartford were distributed to shareholders for each IIN share. After the discontinuation and spinoff of ITT Hartford Group (insurance) and New ITT Corp. (hotels, gaming and entertainment), IIN produces automotive components, defense and electronics and fluid technology products. Segment contributions (profits in millions) in 1997 were:

	Revs.	Profits
Automotive	59%	$311
Defense & electronics	19%	127
Fluid technology	20%	157
Dispositions & other	2%	-9.4

The U.S. accounted for nearly 54% of 1997 sales, Western Europe 40%, and Canada and other 6%.

Automotive (1997 sales of $5.5 billion) supplies original equipment and replacement brake and chassis systems and body and electrical systems. Brake and chassis includes antilock brake, traction control and chassis systems, foundation brakes, fluid handling products and Koni shock absorbers. Body and electrical includes door and window assemblies, wiper modules, seat and air management systems, switches and fractional-horsepower motors. GM and Ford accounted for 21% and 13% of segment sales in 1997. Automotive is developing integrated components such as complete axles and vehicle stability management systems that combine chassis parts, antilock brakes, and traction and engine torque control. The company recently reached separate agreements to sell automotive businesses.

Defense and electronics (1997 sales of $1.7 billion) includes tactical communications and electronic warfare systems, night vision devices, radar, space payloads and operations/management services. Commercial items include connectors, switches, cable assemblies and night vision devices. Some 66% of segment sales are to government entities, of which 85% are to the U.S. government.

Fluid Technology (1997 sales of $1.8 billion) supplies pumps, valves, heat exchangers, mixers and fluid measuring instruments and controls. Markets include water and wastewater treatment, industrial and process, and construction. Fluid Technology has become the world's largest pump manufacturer (formerly third largest) following its May 1997 acquisition of Goulds Pumps, Inc., with expected revenues of over $2 billion.

Per Share Data ($)

(Year Ended Dec. 31)	1997	1996	1995	1994	1993	1992	1991	1990	1989	1988
Tangible Bk. Val.	NM	3.81	2.26	50.41	64.08	59.93	69.47	64.01	55.42	56.33
Cash Flow	4.07	5.66	3.83	12.30	12.08	2.38	10.65	11.97	9.88	9.34
Earnings	0.94	1.85	0.03	7.10	7.29	-2.47	6.42	8.06	6.52	5.99
Dividends	0.60	0.60	0.99	1.98	1.98	1.84	1.72	1.63	1.51	1.31
Payout Ratio	64%	32%	NM	28%	27%	NM	26%	19%	21%	21%
Prices - High	33⅝	28⅝	24¼	104¼	94⅞	72⅛	63	60⅞	64½	54⅞
- Low	22⅛	21½	21¼	77	69	53¾	44⅞	40¼	49¾	43¼
P/E Ratio - High	36	15	NM	15	13	NM	10	8	10	9
- Low	24	12	NM	11	9	NM	7	5	8	7

Income Statement Analysis (Million $)

	1997	1996	1995	1994	1993	1992	1991	1990	1989	1988
Revs.	8,777	8,718	8,884	23,620	22,762	21,651	20,421	20,604	20,054	19,355
Oper. Inc.	904	941	869	2,678	2,502	1,374	2,288	2,274	2,560	2,369
Depr.	378	433	423	592	576	553	535	506	485	500
Int. Exp.	133	169	175	413	920	1,050	1,073	1,079	1,105	949
Pretax Inc.	187	371	71.0	1,259	1,282	-497	990	1,385	1,237	1,117
Eff. Tax Rate	39%	40%	71%	31%	27%	NM	12%	19%	20%	19%
Net Inc.	114	223	21.0	852	910	-269	817	1,056	922	858

Balance Sheet & Other Fin. Data (Million $)

	1997	1996	1995	1994	1993	1992	1991	1990	1989	1988
Cash	192	122	94.0	4,816	4,321	5,659	2,853	3,017	2,927	3,443
Curr. Assets	2,377	2,289	2,502	NA	NA	NA	NA	NA	NA	NA
Total Assets	6,221	5,491	5,879	100,854	70,560	58,764	53,867	49,043	45,503	41,941
Curr. Liab.	3,545	2,538	2,661	NA	NA	NA	NA	NA	NA	NA
LT Debt	532	583	961	3,340	9,561	9,517	9,539	7,245	6,875	4,638
Common Eqty	822	799	627	5,326	7,534	7,136	7,949	7,308	6,803	7,527
Total Cap.	1,386	1,492	1,709	8,979	17,407	17,013	18,712	15,791	14,932	12,673
Cap. Exp.	460	406	450	727	505	646	791	742	604	524
Cash Flow	492	656	429	1,414	1,450	279	1,299	1,508	1,364	1,336
Curr. Ratio	0.7	0.9	0.9	NA	NA	NA	NA	NA	NA	NA
% LT Debt of Cap.	38.4	39.1	56.3	37.2	54.9	55.9	51.0	45.9	46.0	36.6
% Net Inc.of Revs.	1.3	2.6	0.3	3.6	4.0	NM	4.0	5.1	4.6	4.4
% Ret. on Assets	1.9	3.9	0.3	1.0	1.4	NM	1.6	2.3	2.2	3.1
% Ret. on Equity	14.1	31.3	0.2	13.5	12.0	NM	10.0	14.7	12.8	11.4

Data as orig. reptd. (for old ITT prior to 1995); bef. results of disc. opers. and/or spec. items. Per share data adj. for stk. divs. as of ex-div. date. Bold denotes diluted EPS (FASB 128). E-Estimated. NA-Not Available. NM-Not Meaningful. NR-Not Ranked.

Office—4 W. Red Oak Lane, White Plains, NY 10604. **Tel**—(914) 641-2000. **Fax**—(914) 696-2950. **Website**—http://www.ittind.com **Chrmn, Pres & CEO**—D. T. Engen. **CFO**—H. Kunz. **VP-Secy**—G. L. Carr. **VP-Investor Contact**—Ralph D. Allen (914-641-2030). **Dirs**—R. V. Araskog, R. A. Burnett, C. J. Crawford, M. David-Weill, D. T. Engen, S. P. Gilbert, C. A. Gold, E. C. Meyer, S. Taurel. **Transfer Agent and Registrar**—Bank of New York, NYC. **Incorporated**—in Maryland in 1920; reincorporated in Delaware in 1968 and Indiana in 1995. **Empl**— 58,497. **S&P Analyst:** Efraim Levy

STANDARD &POOR'S
STOCK REPORTS

Jefferson-Pilot

1260

NYSE Symbol **JP**

In S&P 500

12-SEP-98

Industry:
Insurance (Life & Health)

Summary: Jefferson-Pilot provides an array of insurance and communications products and services. The bulk of revenues and income is derived from life and health insurance operations.

S&P Opinion: Hold (★★★)	Recent Price • 58⅞	Yield • 2.0%
	52 Wk Range • 62⅛-47⅞	12-Mo. P/E • 16.9

Quantitative Evaluations

Outlook
(1 Lowest—5 Highest)
• **1**

Fair Value
• **42½**

Risk
• **Low**

Earn./Div. Rank
• **A+**

Technical Eval.
• **Bullish** since 6/94

Rel. Strength Rank
(1 Lowest—99 Highest)
• **92**

Insider Activity
• **NA**

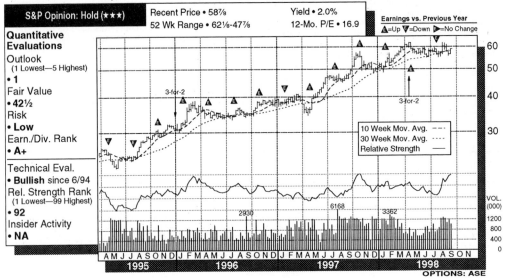

Earnings vs. Previous Year
▲=Up ▼=Down ▶=No Change

- 10 Week Mov. Avg. ---
- 30 Week Mov. Avg. —
- Relative Strength —

OPTIONS: ASE

Overview - 13-AUG-98

Operating earnings growth in coming periods is predicated on continued strong individual life insurance premium growth. JP's recent growth here has been aided by robust sales of individual annuities and interest-sensitive life insurance products. Although many of these products increase the company's exposure to interest rate changes, this risk is manageable. The recent acquisition of Chubb Life will strengthen JP's core life insurance offerings. Steps taken to increase agent productivity and reduce expenses are also aiding profit margins. Revenues and margins in the group insurance area may come under continued pressure from adverse disability claim trends and increased price competition in traditional medical coverages. JP's decision to focus on its group life and disability lines and de-emphasize the sale of new group medical products until certain profit targets are met leaves that unit better positioned, long term. An continued strong advertising market bodes well for the communications group. Investment income growth will be modest, reflecting a relatively low interest rate environment.

Valuation - 13-AUG-98

The shares of this life and health insurer trended upward during most of 1997 and into early 1998. Much of this strength was tied to favorable investor reaction to several pro-active moves JP has taken to narrow its scope of focus in an attempt to build shareholder value. After receiving a fairly generous expansion to their price/earnings (p/e) multiple, the shares plateaued in mid-1998, as the market's focus shifted back to JP's underlying fundamentals and prospects for only modest growth in operating earnings. Nevertheless, at current levels, the shares are trading at the upper end of their historical p/e multiple range and are fairly valued for the near term.

Key Stock Statistics

S&P EPS Est. 1998	3.25	Tang. Bk. Value/Share	25.52
P/E on S&P Est. 1998	18.1	Beta	0.52
S&P EPS Est. 1999	3.60	Shareholders	10,000
Dividend Rate/Share	1.18	Market cap. (B)	$ 6.2
Shs. outstg. (M)	106.1	Inst. holdings	43%
Avg. daily vol. (M)	0.269		

Value of $10,000 invested 5 years ago: $ 31,782

Fiscal Year Ending Dec. 31

	1998	1997	1996	1995	1994	1993
Revenues (Million $)						
1Q	697.0	591.0	534.2	315.2	307.3	306.7
2Q	650.0	665.0	528.5	328.9	314.5	308.1
3Q	—	657.0	515.0	381.6	312.5	302.7
4Q	—	665.0	548.6	543.7	334.6	329.2
Yr.	—	2,578	2,125	1,569	1,269	1,247
Earnings Per Share ($)						
1Q	**1.04**	1.02	0.65	0.48	0.48	0.44
2Q	**0.94**	0.96	0.68	0.48	0.52	0.46
3Q	—	0.74	0.60	0.61	0.52	0.46
4Q	—	0.75	0.70	0.81	0.59	0.58
Yr.	—	3.47	2.73	2.37	2.10	1.94

Next earnings report expected: late October

Dividend Data (Dividends have been paid since 1913.)

Amount ($)	Date Decl.	Ex-Div. Date	Stock of Record	Payment Date
3-for-2	Feb. 09	Apr. 14	Mar. 20	Apr. 13 '98
0.295	Feb. 09	May. 13	May. 15	Jun. 05 '98
0.295	May. 04	Aug. 12	Aug. 14	Sep. 05 '98
0.295	Aug. 12	Nov. 10	Nov. 13	Dec. 05 '98

A Division of The McGraw-Hill Companies

Business Summary - 13-AUG-98

Jefferson-Pilot Corp. has been narrowing its scope of focus around the life and health insurance area; and disposing its non-core assets. To that end, the company sold Jefferson-Pilot Title Insurance Co. and Jefferson-Pilot Fire & Casualty Co. in 1995. To help build critical mass in its core life insurance unit, the company has made some strategic acquisitions recently. JP also owns and operates radio and television stations, and produces televised sports programs. Segment contributions from continuing operations in 1997 were:

	Revs.	Net Income
Individual life insurance	50%	58%
Annuities & investment products	20%	19%
Group insurance	19%	3%
Communications & other (incl. inv. gains)	11%	20%

Jefferson Pilot Life Insurance Co. underwrites an array of life insurance products, including whole life, term life, annuity and endowment policies, on an individual and group basis. Products are marketed through a general agency system that utilizes the services of career agents, home service agents, and independent marketing organizations. Accident and health insurance is also offered, mostly on a group basis.

As of year-end 1997, Jefferson-Pilot Communication Co. owned and operated three television and 17 radio stations, in North Carolina, South Carolina, Virginia, Georgia, Florida, Colorado and California. Other operations include a sports production company.

In May 1995, JP acquired the life insurance and annuity business of Kentucky Central Life and Health Insurance Co. (KC). It assumed assets of $869 million, and recorded a liability of $1.1 billion in connection with the acquisition of KC, which was seized by state regulators in 1993. In late 1995, JP acquired Alexander Hamilton Life Insurance Co. of America from Household International, for $575 million. Perhaps the company's most visible acquisition was the May 1997 purchase of the life insurance unit of Chubb Corp. (NYSE: CB) for $875 million, consisting of $775 million in cash paid by JP to CB, and a $100 million dividend that Chubb Life paid to CB. The Jefferson Pilot Financial Insurance Co. (formerly Chubb Life) and its subsidiaries offer a broad range of individual life insurance products, including variable universal and term life insurance.

Per Share Data ($) (Year Ended Dec. 31)	1997	1996	1995	1994	1993	1992	1991	1990	1989	1988
Tangible Bk. Val.	35.38	20.83	19.53	15.39	15.22	14.61	13.26	11.32	11.41	10.00
Oper. Earnings	2.78	2.44	2.06	1.75	1.61	1.49	1.33	1.15	0.99	0.74
Earnings	3.47	2.73	2.37	2.10	1.94	1.77	1.52	1.31	1.08	0.77
Dividends	1.04	0.93	0.83	0.75	0.67	0.58	0.49	0.44	0.40	0.37
Relative Payout	30%	34%	35%	36%	35%	33%	32%	34%	37%	49%
Prices - High	57 7/8	39 3/4	32 1/8	24 1/2	25 3/4	22	17 3/8	13 1/4	13 1/2	11 1/8
- Low	34 3/8	30 1/8	22 1/2	19 1/4	20 1/4	14 7/8	10 1/8	9 5/8	8 7/8	7 5/8
P/E Ratio - High	17	15	14	12	13	12	11	10	12	15
- Low	10	11	9	9	10	8	7	7	8	10
Income Statement Analysis (Million $)										
Life Ins. In Force	162,096	109,407	111,383	45,049	41,591	40,843	38,460	38,465	36,977	36,291
Prem. Inc.: Life A & H	1,135	994	810	655	627	NA	NA	NA	NA	NA
Prem. Inc.: Cas./Prop.	Nil	Nil	Nil	Nil	Nil	Nil	Nil	Nil	Nil	Nil
Net Invest. Inc.	1,103	893	541	375	370	361	353	342	333	314
Oth. Revs.	340	238	218	238	250	NA	NA	NA	NA	NA
Total Revs.	2,578	2,125	1,569	1,269	1,247	1,202	1,173	1,163	1,140	1,223
Pretax Inc.	591	443	381	348	322	286	245	222	198	139
Net Oper. Inc.	323	263	222	190	158	171	153	139	126	98.0
Net Inc.	396	294	255	230	219	206	176	158	138	101
Balance Sheet & Other Fin. Data (Million $)										
Cash & Equiv.	9.0	271	279	90.0	101	223	226	185	232	211
Premiums Due	Nil	96.0	134	64.2	60.5	42.6	40.1	39.3	44.4	38.5
Invest. Assets: Bonds	13,945	10,550	9,986	3,547	3,222	2,816	2,580	2,341	2,243	2,101
Invest. Assets: Stocks	893	929	863	718	833	838	784	610	780	618
Invest. Assets: Loans	3,138	2,535	2,201	887	798	782	769	767	743	747
Invest. Assets: Total	14,881	14,143	13,168	5,220	4,917	4,493	4,189	3,774	3,818	3,518
Deferred Policy Costs	1,364	934	835	329	278	260	249	236	221	215
Total Assets	23,131	17,562	16,478	6,140	5,641	5,236	4,925	4,455	4,530	4,174
Debt	916	370	137	Nil	Nil	Nil	Nil	Nil	Nil	Nil
Common Eqty.	2,732	2,297	2,156	1,733	1,733	1,687	1,563	1,353	1,475	1,336
Comb. Loss-Exp. Ratio	NA	NA	NA	95.4	96.5	NA	NA	NA	NA	NA
% Return On Revs.	15.4	13.8	16.3	18.1	17.6	16.9	15.0	13.6	12.1	8.0
% Ret. on Equity	14.7	13.2	13.1	13.3	12.9	12.5	12.1	11.1	9.9	7.6
% Invest. Yield	6.8	6.5	5.9	7.4	7.9	NA	NA	NA	NA	NA

Data as orig. reptd.; bef. results of disc. opers. and/or spec. items. Per share data adj. for stk. divs. as of ex-div. date. Bold denotes diluted EPS (FASB 128). E-Estimate. NA-Not Available. NM-Not Meaningful. NR-Not Ranked.

Office—100 North Greene St., Greensboro, NC 27401. **Tel**—(910) 691-3000. **Pres & CEO**—D. A. Stonecipher. **VP & CFO & Treas**—D. R. Glass. **VP & Secy**—J. D. Hopkins. **Dirs**— T. M. Belk, W. E. Blackwell, E. B. Borden, W. H. Cunningham, C. R. Ferguson, R. G. Greer, G. W. Henderson, III, H. L. McColl Jr., E. S. Melvin, K. Mlekush, W. P. Payne, D. S. Russell Jr., R. H. Spilman, D. A. Stonecipher, M. A. Walls. **Transfer Agent & Registrar**—First Union National Bank, Charlotte. **Incorporated**—in North Carolina in 1968. **Empl**— 12,650. **S&P Analyst:** Catherine A. Seifert

12-SEP-98

Industry: Manufacturing (Diversified)

Summary: This company supplies building controls and energy management systems, automotive seating and batteries.

S&P Opinion: Accumulate (★★★★)	Recent Price • 43½	Yield • 2.1%
	52 Wk Range • 61⅞-42⅛	12-Mo. P/E • 13.1

Quantitative Evaluations

Outlook (1 Lowest—5 Highest)
• **2⁻**

Fair Value
• **43⅞**

Risk
• **Low**

Earn./Div. Rank
• **A-**

Technical Eval.
• **Bearish** since 8/98

Rel. Strength Rank (1 Lowest—99 Highest)
• **49**

Insider Activity
• **Neutral**

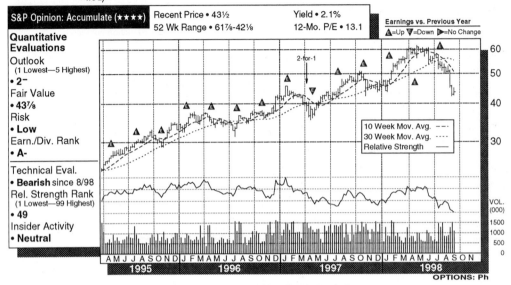

Earnings vs. Previous Year
△=Up ▽=Down ▷=No Change

10 Week Mov. Avg. ---
30 Week Mov. Avg. ·····
Relative Strength ——

OPTIONS: Ph

Overview - 27-JUL-98

Sales from continuing operations should continue to rise in FY 98 (Sep.), reflecting continued growth in automotive seating, retrofit controls, and the facility management business. JCI expects to continue to expand its share of the automotive seating and interior business in Europe and North America as it wins new contracts and demand grows for vehicles that it supplies. Facilities management should benefit from new customers, as outsourcing trends continue. This business offers lower building operating costs to its customers through its facility management services. In October 1997, JCI was chosen to provide the energy management and environmental control system for the Pentagon in Washington, D.C.; this contract represents one of the largest control system projects in the company's history. Battery sales are improving with the addition of new accounts; and with ongoing cost reductions in the battery unit, and the sale of a major part of the volatile and underperforming plastic segment, operating income should rise. Sales and profitability were restricted in FY 97 and the first half of FY 98 by the appreciating value of the U.S. dollar against the currencies of many key trading partners as well as a strike at a leading auto manufacturer.

Valuation - 27-JUL-98

The company is executing important strategic steps that position it to become an important Tier 1 global automotive interiors supplier. This enhances the likelihood of further strong gains in earnings in future years. Earnings should grow modestly even in a cyclical downturn in North America, as JCI benefits from global expansion and accretive acquisitions. We expect the stock to be an above-average performer over the near term, and it is a worthwhile addition to portfolios seeking stable dividend growth and long-term capital appreciation.

Key Stock Statistics

S&P EPS Est. 1998	3.40	Tang. Bk. Value/Share	3.70
P/E on S&P Est. 1998	12.8	Beta	0.95
S&P EPS Est. 1999	3.95	Shareholders	46,300
Dividend Rate/Share	0.92	Market cap. (B)	$ 3.7
Shs. outstg. (M)	84.7	Inst. holdings	61%
Avg. daily vol. (M)	0.251		

Value of $10,000 invested 5 years ago: $ 22,221

Fiscal Year Ending Sep. 30

	1998	1997	1996	1995	1994	1993
Revenues (Million $)						
1Q	3,056	2,761	2,186	1,858	1,585	1,511
2Q	3,007	2,744	2,440	2,051	1,682	1,445
3Q	3,190	2,879	2,706	2,181	1,758	1,594
4Q	—	2,761	2,677	2,241	1,846	1,632
Yr.	—	11,145	10,009	8,330	6,871	6,182
Earnings Per Share ($)						
1Q	**0.70**	0.63	0.54	0.47	0.43	0.37
2Q	**0.56**	-0.06	0.41	0.36	0.28	0.21
3Q	**0.90**	0.85	0.80	0.64	0.53	0.47
4Q	**E1.24**	1.06	0.95	0.79	0.66	0.53
Yr.	**E3.40**	2.48	2.69	2.27	1.90	1.58

Next earnings report expected: late October

Dividend Data (Dividends have been paid since 1901.)

Amount ($)	Date Decl.	Ex-Div. Date	Stock of Record	Payment Date
0.230	Nov. 19	Dec. 10	Dec. 12	Jan. 02 '98
0.230	Jan. 28	Mar. 11	Mar. 13	Mar. 31 '98
0.230	May. 20	Jun. 10	Jun. 12	Jun. 30 '98
0.230	Jul. 22	Sep. 09	Sep. 11	Sep. 30 '98

A Division of The **McGraw·Hill** *Companies*

STANDARD
&POOR'S
STOCK REPORTS

Johnson Controls, Inc.

1267
12-SEP-98

Business Summary - 27-JUL-98

Founded in 1885, Johnson Controls is a leading manufacturer of automotive interior systems, automotive batteries and automated building control systems. It also provides facility management services for commercial buildings. Contributions by segment in FY 97 (Sep.) were:

	Sales	Income
Automotive	72%	84%
Controls & facility management	28%	16%

The automotive segment manufactures complete seats and seating components for North American and European car and light-truck manufacturers. The company offers customers complete design, manufacturing and just-in-time delivery capabilities. This segment has expanded rapidly in recent years by gaining contracts to produce seats previously manufactured in-house by automakers and by expansion in Europe. The battery unit, the largest automotive battery operation in North America, makes lead-acid batteries primarily for the automotive replacement market and for original equipment manufacturers.

The controls segment manufactures, installs and services controls and control systems, principally for non-residential buildings, that are used for temperature and energy management, fire safety and security maintenance. The segment also includes custom engineering, installation and servicing of process control systems and a growing facilities management business that provides operations and maintenance services for more than 600 million square feet of building space around the world.

In February 1997, JCI sold its Plastic Container division to Schmalbach-Lubeca AG/Continental Can Europe (a member of the VIAG Group) for about $650 million. This transaction allowed it to avoid a secondary stock issuance it had been considering to partially finance the $1.35 billion acquisition of Prince Automotive. Prince, based in Holland, Michigan, was acquired in October. It supplies overhead systems and consoles, door panels, floor consoles, visors and armrests for 80 mostly domestic vehicle platforms.

JCI believes current government building trends promoting facility management outsourcing and energy efficiency programs have created additional opportunity. The "Big Three" U.S. auto manufacturers -- Ford, General Motors and Chrylser -- accounted for 17%, 11% and 11%, respectively, of total sales in FY 97.

Per Share Data ($)

(Year Ended Sep. 30)	1997	1996	1995	1994	1993	1992	1991	1990	1989	1988
Tangible Bk. Val.	NM	9.38	8.47	12.76	11.24	12.76	11.26	10.93	10.19	9.13
Cash Flow	6.66	6.62	5.92	5.05	4.50	4.09	3.58	3.37	3.21	3.00
Earnings	2.48	2.69	2.27	1.90	1.58	1.43	1.09	1.06	1.27	1.42
Dividends	0.86	0.82	0.78	0.72	0.68	0.64	0.62	0.60	0.58	0.55
Payout Ratio	35%	30%	34%	38%	43%	45%	57%	56%	48%	39%
Prices - High	51	42¾	34⅞	30⅞	29⅝	23⅛	18⅜	16⅛	23⅜	19¼
- Low	35⅜	31¼	22⅞	22½	21½	17⅜	11	8⅝	14	12⅜
P/E Ratio - High	21	16	15	16	19	16	17	15	18	14
- Low	14	12	10	12	14	12	10	8	11	9

Income Statement Analysis (Million $)

	1997	1996	1995	1994	1993	1992	1991	1990	1989	1988
Revs.	11,145	10,009	8,330	6,871	6,182	5,157	4,559	4,504	3,684	3,100
Oper. Inc.	951	830	737	624	537	479	426	409	349	326
Depr.	355	330	289	258	238	213	197	181	144	116
Int. Exp.	122	85.0	68.0	46.6	50.7	52.6	60.4	56.1	42.5	33.3
Pretax Inc.	425	443	388	326	251	228	176	173	179	187
Eff. Tax Rate	42%	41%	42%	43%	45%	46%	46%	47%	46%	45%
Net Inc.	221	235	196	165	138	123	95.0	92.0	98.0	104

Balance Sheet & Other Fin. Data (Million $)

	1997	1996	1995	1994	1993	1992	1991	1990	1989	1988
Cash	112	164	104	133	87.7	96.0	92.0	54.0	27.0	20.0
Curr. Assets	2,529	2,594	2,064	1,779	1,532	1,524	1,376	1,291	1,101	959
Total Assets	6,049	5,123	4,321	3,807	3,231	3,180	2,841	2,799	2,415	2,013
Curr. Liab.	2,973	2,302	1,910	1,516	1,285	1,245	1,105	1,099	838	696
LT Debt	806	757	630	670	500	503	491	483	445	342
Common Eqty.	1,545	1,353	1,180	1,039	911	1,023	891	861	803	853
Total Cap.	2,494	2,264	1,970	1,873	1,591	1,761	1,636	1,609	1,502	1,267
Cap. Exp.	371	370	451	348	298	237	156	298	224	230
Cash Flow	566	556	485	414	367	328	284	266	238	219
Curr. Ratio	0.9	1.1	1.1	1.2	1.2	1.2	1.2	1.2	1.3	1.4
% LT Debt of Cap.	32.3	33.5	31.9	35.8	31.5	28.6	30.0	30.0	29.6	27.0
% Net Inc.of Revs.	2.0	2.4	2.3	2.4	2.2	2.4	2.1	2.1	2.6	3.3
% Ret. on Assets	4.0	5.0	4.8	4.7	4.3	4.1	3.4	3.5	4.2	5.6
% Ret. on Equity	14.6	16.5	16.8	16.0	13.2	11.9	9.9	10.1	11.0	12.8

Data as orig. reptd.; bef. results of disc. opers. and/or spec. items. Per share data adj. for stk. divs. as of ex-div. date. Bold denotes diluted EPS (FASB 128). E-Estimated. NA-Not Available. NM-Not Meaningful. NR-Not Ranked.

Office—5757 N. Green Bay Ave., P.O. Box 591, Milwaukee, WI 53201-0591. **Tel**—(414) 228-1200. **Website**—http://www.johnsoncontrols.com **Chrmn, Pres & CEO**—J. H. Keyes. **Secy**—J. P. Kennedy. **VP & CFO**—S. A. Roell. **Investor Contact**—Denise M. Zutz. **Dirs**—W. F. Andrews, R. L. Barnett, F. L. Brengel, P. A. Brunner, R. A. Cornog, W. D. Davis, J. H. Keyes, S. J. Morcott, R. F. Teerlink, G. R. Whitaker Jr. **Transfer Agent & Registrar**—Firstar Trust Co., Milwaukee. **Incorporated**—in Wisconsin in 1900. **Empl**— 65,800. **S&P Analyst:** Efraim Levy

STANDARD &POOR'S
STOCK REPORTS

Johnson & Johnson

NYSE Symbol **JNJ**

1268

In S&P 500

12-SEP-98

Industry:
Health Care (Diversified)

Summary: The world's largest and most comprehensive health care company, J&J offers a broad line of drugs, consumer products and other medical and dental items.

S&P Opinion: Buy (★★★★★)	Recent Price • 76⅝	Yield • 1.3%
	52 Wk Range • 79⅞-53	12-Mo. P/E • 30.0

Quantitative Evaluations

Outlook
(1 Lowest—5 Highest)
• **2**

Fair Value
• **77⅜**

Risk
• **Low**

Earn./Div. Rank
• **A+**

Technical Eval.
• **Bullish** since 11/97

Rel. Strength Rank
(1 Lowest—99 Highest)
• **93**

Insider Activity
• **Neutral**

Earnings vs. Previous Year
▲=Up ▼=Down ▶=No Change

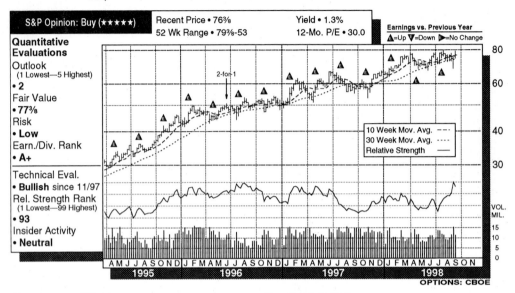

10 Week Mov. Avg. ---
30 Week Mov. Avg. ·····
Relative Strength ——

OPTIONS: CBOE

Overview - 20-JUL-98

Sales growth in 1998 is expected only in the low single digits, largely due to negative foreign exchange and intensified competition in the coronary stent market. JNJ has seen its dominance of the coronary stent market erode in the face of more advanced products from Guidant and Arterial Vascular Engineering. Consumer products sales are also likely to slip modestly. However, pharmaceutical volume should hold up well, augmented by gains in Risperdal anti-psychotic agent, Procrit treatment of anemia, Duragesic transdermal patch for chronic pain, Levaquin anti-infective and Ultram analgesic. In the device area, gains are seen for sales of Ethicon's laparoscopy and wound closure instruments. Margins should be well maintained on better volume and productivity gains.

Valuation - 20-JUL-98

The shares moved generally higher over the past nine months, buoyed by the general market advance and particular strength in medical issues. Despite a very modest sales gain, EPS for the second quarter rose 10.6%, reflecting JNJ's tight rein on operating costs. Although negative foreign exchange and competition in the stent market will probably continue to restrict sales growth over the next few quarters, longer-range prospects remain bright, in view of J&J's dominant positions in growing global health care markets, contributions from new drugs, and renewed focus on innovative medical devices. Promising pipeline drugs include Pariet for heartburn, Reminyl for Alzheimer's disease and Cladribine for multiple sclerosis. New consumer items include Acuvue bifocal lenses, Toric contact lenses for patients with astigmatism, Sucralose artificial sweetener and Benecol cholesterol-lowering margarine. We continue to recommend purchase of the shares.

Key Stock Statistics

S&P EPS Est. 1998	2.70	Tang. Bk. Value/Share	7.46
P/E on S&P Est. 1998	28.3	Beta	0.98
S&P EPS Est. 1999	3.05	Shareholders	138,500
Dividend Rate/Share	1.00	Market cap. (B)	$102.7
Shs. outstg. (M)	1344.9	Inst. holdings	54%
Avg. daily vol. (M)	2.618		

Value of $10,000 invested 5 years ago: $ 33,242

Fiscal Year Ending Dec. 31

	1998	1997	1996	1995	1994	1993
Revenues (Million $)						
1Q	5,783	5,715	5,334	4,496	3,690	3,560
2Q	5,783	5,698	5,382	4,762	3,916	3,541
3Q	—	5,586	5,402	4,738	4,038	3,506
4Q	—	5,630	5,502	4,846	4,090	3,531
Yr.	—	22,629	21,620	18,842	15,734	14,138
Earnings Per Share ($)						
1Q	**0.73**	**0.66**	0.59	0.51	0.42	0.39
2Q	**0.74**	**0.67**	0.60	0.51	0.43	0.38
3Q	**E0.68**	**0.63**	0.56	0.48	0.41	0.35
4Q	**E0.55**	**0.45**	0.42	0.36	0.29	0.26
Yr.	**E2.70**	**2.41**	2.17	1.86	1.56	1.37

Next earnings report expected: mid October

Dividend Data (Dividends have been paid since 1944.)

Amount ($)	Date Decl.	Ex-Div. Date	Stock of Record	Payment Date
0.220	Oct. 20	Nov. 14	Nov. 18	Dec. 09 '97
0.220	Jan. 02	Feb. 12	Feb. 17	Mar. 10 '98
0.250	Apr. 23	May. 15	May. 19	Jun. 09 '98
0.250	Jul. 20	Aug. 14	Aug. 18	Sep. 08 '98

A Division of The McGraw·Hill Companies

STANDARD
&POOR'S
STOCK REPORTS

Johnson & Johnson

1268

12-SEP-98

Business Summary - 20-JUL-98

Well known for household names like Tylenol and Band-Aid adhesive bandages, Johnson & Johnson ranks as the largest and most diversified health care company in the world. J&J traces its roots to James Johnson and Edward Mead Johnson, who formed the company over 110 years ago. Today, J&J offers an impressive list of blockbuster prescription drugs, professional products and the broadest line of health-related consumer products. Foreign business accounted for 48% of sales and 38% of profits in 1997. Sales and earnings in 1997 were divided:

	Sales	Profits
Pharmaceuticals	34%	56%
Professional	37%	32%
Consumer	29%	12%

Despite its immense size, J&J continues to generate robust earnings growth. While helped by an expanding health care marketplace, J&J's outstanding success also reflects proficient management who directed the company's growth through well-planned, strategic acquisitions, aggressive R&D spending, and a policy of decentralized management. New product launches and products introduced in new foreign markets over the past five years accounted for 36% of total sales in 1997

Some of the more noteworthy fast-growing product lines developed in recent years have been Risperdal anti-psychotic and Sporanox antifungal drugs, the LifeScan home glucose monitoring system and the Palmaz-Schatz coronary stent used after angioplasty procedures. These and similar products enabled J&J to chalk up compound EPS growth of over 14% over the 1992-97 period.

Although usually thought of as a medical products and hospital supplies firm, J&J derives close to 60% of its profits from a growing list of drugs. Over 80 different prescription drug, contraceptive and veterinary products are sold, 20 of which each generate revenues in excess of $100 million. Some of the big sellers include Procrit red blood stimulant, Propulsid gastrointestinal, Risperdal anti-psychotic and Ortho-Novum oral contraceptive.

Leading positions are also maintained in growing professional and consumer products lines. Professional items include older items such as sutures, wound closure products and surgical accessories, as well as newer products such as coronary stents, angioplasty catheters and disposable contact lenses. Albeit slower growing, J&J's wide list of consumer products such as Tylenol, bandages, toiletries and other items provides a solid base of stability and cash flow.

Per Share Data ($)

(Year Ended Dec. 31)	1997	1996	1995	1994	1993	1992	1991	1990	1989	1988
Tangible Bk. Val.	6.76	5.80	4.71	3.67	3.61	3.40	3.67	3.15	2.58	2.17
Cash Flow	3.19	2.93	2.52	2.13	1.84	1.66	1.47	1.22	1.08	0.96
Earnings	2.47	2.17	1.86	1.56	1.37	1.23	1.10	0.86	0.81	0.71
Dividends	0.85	0.74	0.64	0.56	0.51	0.45	0.39	0.33	0.28	0.24
Payout Ratio	35%	34%	34%	36%	37%	36%	35%	38%	34%	33%
Prices - High	67¼	54	46¼	28¼	25¼	29⅜	29⅜	18½	14⅞	11
- Low	48⅝	41⅝	26⅞	18	17⅞	21½	16⅜	12¾	10⅜	8⅝
P/E Ratio - High	27	25	25	18	18	24	26	22	18	15
- Low	20	19	14	12	13	17	15	15	13	12

Income Statement Analysis (Million $)

	1997	1996	1995	1994	1993	1992	1991	1990	1989	1988
Revs.	22,629	21,620	18,842	15,734	14,138	13,753	12,447	11,232	9,757	9,000
Oper. Inc.	5,689	5,312	6,002	3,531	3,011	2,837	2,657	2,399	2,019	1,741
Depr.	1,067	1,009	857	724	617	560	493	474	358	337
Int. Exp.	120	180	213	186	174	177	175	206	182	135
Pretax Inc.	4,576	4,033	3,317	2,681	2,332	2,207	2,038	1,623	1,514	1,396
Eff. Tax Rate	28%	28%	28%	25%	23%	26%	28%	30%	29%	30%
Net Inc.	3,303	2,887	2,403	2,006	1,787	1,625	1,461	1,143	1,082	974

Balance Sheet & Other Fin. Data (Million $)

	1997	1996	1995	1994	1993	1992	1991	1990	1989	1988
Cash	2,753	2,136	1,364	704	476	878	792	931	583	660
Curr. Assets	10,563	9,370	7,938	6,680	5,217	5,423	4,933	4,664	3,776	3,503
Total Assets	21,453	20,010	17,873	15,668	12,242	11,884	10,513	9,506	7,919	7,119
Curr. Liab.	5,283	5,184	4,388	4,266	3,212	3,427	2,689	2,623	1,927	1,868
LT Debt	1,126	1,410	2,107	2,199	1,493	1,365	1,301	1,316	1,170	1,166
Common Eqty.	12,359	10,836	9,045	7,122	5,568	5,171	5,626	4,900	4,148	3,503
Total Cap.	13,660	12,416	11,308	9,451	7,183	6,627	6,927	6,216	5,318	4,669
Cap. Exp.	1,391	1,373	1,256	937	975	1,103	987	830	750	664
Cash Flow	4,370	3,896	3,260	2,730	2,404	2,185	1,954	1,617	1,440	1,311
Curr. Ratio	2.0	1.8	1.8	1.6	1.6	1.6	1.8	1.8	2.0	1.9
% LT Debt of Cap.	8.2	11.4	18.6	23.3	20.8	20.6	18.8	21.2	22.0	25.0
% Net Inc.of Revs.	14.6	13.3	12.8	12.7	12.6	11.8	11.7	10.2	11.1	10.8
% Ret. on Assets	15.9	15.2	14.3	14.4	15.0	14.6	14.6	13.1	14.4	14.5
% Ret. on Equity	28.5	29.0	29.7	31.6	33.6	30.4	27.8	25.3	28.3	28.3

Data as orig. reptd.; bef. results of disc. opers. and/or spec. items. Per share data adj. for stk. divs. as of ex-div. date. Bold denotes diluted EPS (FASB 128). E-Estimated. NA-Not Available. NM-Not Meaningful. NR-Not Ranked.

Office—One Johnson & Johnson Plaza, New Brunswick, NJ 08933. **Tel**—(732) 524-0400. **Website**—http://www.jnj.com **Chrmn & CEO**—R. S. Larsen. **Vice Chrmn**—R. N. Wilson. **VP-Fin & CFO**—R. J. Darretta. **Secy**—P. S. Galloway. **Treas**—J. A. Papa. **Investor Contact**—David R. Sheffield (800-950-5089). **Dirs**—G. N. Burrow, J. G. Cooney, J. G. Cullen, M. J. Folkman, A. D. Jordan, A. G. Langbo, R. S. Larsen, J. S. Mayo, P. J. Rizzo, H. B. Schacht, M. F. Singer, J. W. Snow, R. N. Wilson. **Transfer Agent & Registrar**—First Chicago Trust Co. of New York, Jersey City, NJ. **Incorporated**—in New Jersey in 1887. **Empl**— 90,500. **S&P Analyst:** H. B. Saftlas

STANDARD &POOR'S
STOCK REPORTS

Jostens, Inc.

1271K

NYSE Symbol **JOS**

In S&P 500

12-SEP-98

Industry:
Consumer (Jewelry, Novelties & Gifts)

Summary: Jostens produces class rings, yearbooks and recognition products for schools and businesses. It also offers school photography.

| S&P Opinion: Hold (★★★) | Recent Price • 20⅝ | Yield • 4.3% | Earnings vs. Previous Year |
| | 52 Wk Range • 28¼-19⅜ | 12-Mo. P/E • 13.7 | ▲=Up ▼=Down ▶=No Change |

Quantitative Evaluations

Outlook
(1 Lowest—5 Highest)
• **3+**

Fair Value
• **21⅞**

Risk
• **Low**

Earn./Div. Rank
• **B**

Technical Eval.
• **Bearish** since 5/98

Rel. Strength Rank
(1 Lowest—99 Highest)
• **67**

Insider Activity
• **Neutral**

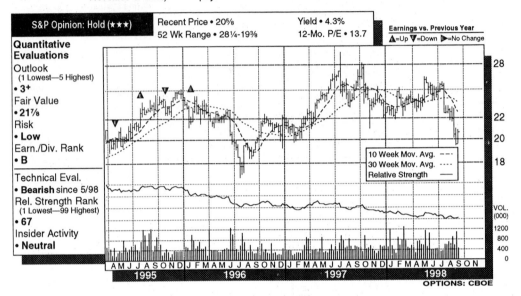

10 Week Mov. Avg. – –
30 Week Mov. Avg. - - -
Relative Strength —

VOL. (000)
1200
800
400
0

1995   1996   1997   1998

OPTIONS: CBOE

Overview - 27-JUL-98

The company's long-term goals are to boost revenue and net income in the low single-digits and high double-digits, respectively. Revenues should get a boost from sales of millennium (Year 2000) commemoratives, aided by favorable demographics for school products. Recognition products sales are expected to develop in coming years, as JOS has become more focused on developing new corporate contracts. We expect modest single-digit revenue growth, and about 10% EPS growth in 1998. Although gross margins will widen, SG&A costs from increased technology investments and sales force restructuring charges will restrict overall financial performance. Results could perk up in 1999 and 2000, as the company expects to slow the pace of capital expenditure investment. During the first half of 1998, JOS repurchased about $55 million of common stock, and has another $45 million available under a current authorization.

Valuation - 27-JUL-98

We continue to rate the shares a hold. It seems that the company has been restructuring and making operations more efficient for the past two years. Its most recent black eye was the loss of its largest independent high school sales representative firm; this should shave $4 million to $6 million from top line growth in the second half of 1998. Nevertheless, gross margins should begin to expand, as JOS streamlined its photography unit. Much of the gross margin improvement will be offset by information service and marketing investments which will likely peak in 2000 to 2001. Meanwhile, the company's aggressive share repurchase program and above average dividend yield should provide support for the shares.

Key Stock Statistics

S&P EPS Est. 1998	1.55	Tang. Bk. Value/Share	2.60
P/E on S&P Est. 1998	13.3	Beta	0.67
S&P EPS Est. 1999	1.80	Shareholders	7,900
Dividend Rate/Share	0.88	Market cap. (B)	$0.760
Shs. outstg. (M)	36.8	Inst. holdings	78%
Avg. daily vol. (M)	0.157		

Value of $10,000 invested 5 years ago: $ 9,806

Fiscal Year Ending Dec. 31

	1998	1997	1996	1995	1994	1993
Revenues (Million $)						
1Q	168.3	150.4	—	97.75	98.02	149.0
2Q	298.9	297.3	—	165.8	157.6	198.0
3Q	—	109.1	105.4	141.9	139.0	158.7
4Q	—	185.7	171.7	289.8	270.4	321.9
Yr.	—	742.5	277.1	695.2	665.1	827.3
Earnings Per Share ($)						
1Q	0.28	0.26	—	0.06	0.08	0.03
2Q	1.01	0.98	—	0.31	0.27	0.13
3Q	—	-0.16	-0.13	0.18	0.21	-0.20
4Q	—	0.39	0.11	0.79	0.67	-0.54
Yr.	—	1.47	-0.02	1.28	1.23	-0.58

Next earnings report expected: late October

Dividend Data (Dividends have been paid since 1960.)

Amount ($)	Date Decl.	Ex-Div. Date	Stock of Record	Payment Date
0.220	Oct. 22	Nov. 13	Nov. 17	Dec. 01 '97
0.220	Feb. 09	Feb. 11	Feb. 16	Mar. 02 '98
0.220	Apr. 23	May. 13	May. 15	Jun. 01 '98
0.220	Jul. 23	Aug. 13	Aug. 17	Sep. 01 '98

A Division of The McGraw·Hill Companies

STANDARD
&POOR'S
STOCK REPORTS

Jostens, Inc.

1271K
12-SEP-98

Business Summary - 27-JUL-98

Jostens (JOS) is a provider of products and services that help people recognize achievements and affiliations throughout their lives. Products and services include class rings, yearbooks, graduation products, student photography packages, customized business performance and service awards, sports awards and customized affinity products.

The company's operations are classified into two business segments: school-based recognition products and services (School Products) and longevity and performance recognition products and services for businesses (Recognition). More than 85% of sales are derived the the School Products division, while the remaining revenues are attributed to the recognition products and services segment. These two business divisions sell their products in elementary schools, high schools, colleges and businesses in the U.S. and some foreign countries via a sales force of approximately 950 representatives.

The School Products segment manufactures and markets products that recognize individual and group achievement and affiliation primarily in the academic market. School products is comprised of five businesses: Printing & Publishing, Jewelry, Graduation

Products, U.S. Photography, and Jostens Canada. School products include class rings; graduation products such as announcements, diplomas, caps and gowns; student yearbooks; school photography; Jostens Canada; and other businesses, including commercial printing and the direct marketing of customized products to university alumni and members of sororities, fraternities and other affinity groups.

The Recognition segment makes motivation and recognition products, including specialized jewelry, rings, watches, plaques and engraved certificates.

Results are highly seasonal, experiencing strong seasonal business swings concurrent with the school year as 40% to 45% of full-year sales and 65% to 70% of full-year profits occur in the period from April to June.

The company expects results over the next several years to benefit from favorable demographics for school products, new corporate contracts, and the rollout of products related to the coming millennium (Year 2000) that will commemorate the classes of 1999, 2000 and 2001.

In 1997, the company switched from a fiscal year ending June 30 to a December 31 year end, in an effort to better facilitate budgeting and planning.

Per Share Data ($)

(Year Ended Dec. 31)	1997	1996	1995	1994	1993	1992	1991	1990	1989	1988
Tangible Bk. Val.	2.51	2.21	2.42	5.27	4.59	5.97	6.60	5.85	4.94	4.29
Cash Flow	2.04	0.24	1.70	1.85	0.28	0.59	2.02	2.14	1.98	1.89
Earnings	1.46	-0.02	1.28	1.23	-0.58	-0.18	1.50	1.58	1.51	1.39
Dividends	0.88	0.88	0.88	0.88	0.88	0.87	0.83	0.78	0.70	0.62
Payout Ratio	60%	NM	69%	72%	NM	NM	56%	50%	47%	45%
Prices - High	29⅝	24⅜	24⅜	23¾	20	29	37⅜	38⅝	33	30⅜
- Low	19¾	16⅞	16⅞	17¾	15⅛	16½	23¾	28½	22½	18⅛
P/E Ratio - High	20	NM	19	19	NM	NM	25	24	22	22
- Low	14	NM	13	14	NM	NM	16	18	15	13

Income Statement Analysis (Million $)

	1997	1996	1995	1994	1993	1992	1991	1990	1989	1988
Revs.	742	277	695	665	827	915	876	860	788	696
Oper. Inc.	122	14.1	111	123	61.0	106	128	135	122	113
Depr.	22.1	9.9	16.6	28.3	38.9	34.9	21.3	23.0	18.9	19.6
Int. Exp.	6.9	4.3	9.4	5.5	6.8	5.7	8.7	10.2	10.6	10.0
Pretax Inc.	93.4	NM	87.5	93.9	-34.0	-5.0	98.0	102	94.0	87.0
Eff. Tax Rate	39%	3188%	41%	41%	NM	NM	37%	37%	36%	37%
Net Inc.	57.2	-0.8	51.6	55.9	-26.3	-7.9	61.4	64.2	60.2	54.4

Balance Sheet & Other Fin. Data (Million $)

	1997	1996	1995	1994	1993	1992	1991	1990	1989	1988
Cash	Nil	Nil	13.3	173	108	14.0	45.0	16.0	27.0	68.0
Curr. Assets	253	248	251	402	396	379	370	336	296	290
Total Assets	391	381	384	548	570	583	565	530	473	453
Curr. Liab.	246	243	242	196	223	199	164	191	158	154
LT Debt	Nil	3.9	3.9	53.9	54.0	55.0	55.0	32.0	53.0	75.0
Common Eqty.	127	113	122	271	257	313	327	296	257	222
Total Cap.	127	116	126	325	317	385	401	340	316	299
Cap. Exp.	24.4	9.9	15.4	19.1	15.2	20.9	19.6	23.4	18.7	17.8
Cash Flow	79.3	9.1	68.2	84.2	12.6	26.9	82.7	87.1	79.1	74.0
Curr. Ratio	1.0	1.0	1.0	2.1	1.8	1.9	2.3	1.8	1.9	1.9
% LT Debt of Cap.	Nil	3.3	3.1	16.6	17.1	14.3	13.8	9.3	16.9	25.1
% Net Inc.of Revs.	7.7	NM	7.4	8.4	NM	NM	7.0	7.5	7.6	7.8
% Ret. on Assets	14.8	NM	11.1	10.0	NM	NM	11.2	12.7	12.9	12.0
% Ret. on Equity	47.7	NM	26.3	21.2	NM	NM	19.6	23.0	24.9	26.1

Data as orig. reptd.; bef. results of disc. opers. and/or spec. items. Per share data adj. for stk. divs. as of ex-div. date. Prior to 1996, yrs. ended Jun. 30 of foll. cal. yr. Data for 1996 is for six mos. ended Dec. 31. E-Estimated. NA-Not Available. NM-Not Meaningful. NR-Not Ranked.

Office—5501 Norman Center Dr., Minneapolis, MN 55437. **Tel**—(612) 830-3300. **Fax**—(612) 897-4116. **Website**—http://www.jostens.com **Chrmn, Pres & CEO**—R. C. Buhrmaster. **EVP & COO**—D. J. Larkin. **Secy**—B. K. Beutner. **SVP & CFO**—W. N. Priesmeyer. **Treas**—L. U. McGrath. **Investor Contact**—Kevin Whalen (612-380-3251). **Dirs**—L. H. Affinito, R. C. Buhrmaster, J. W. Eugster, M. L. Jackson, R. P. Jensen, W. Lewis, K. B. Melrose, R. A. Zona. **Transfer Agent & Registrar**—Norwest Bank Minnesota, South St. Paul. **Incorporated**—in Minnesota in 1906. **Empl**—6,500. **S&P Analyst:** Robert J. Izmirlian

STANDARD &POOR'S
STOCK REPORTS

Kmart Corp.

1273J
NYSE Symbol **KM**
In S&P 500

12-SEP-98

Industry: Retail (General Merchandise)

Summary: Kmart operates more than 2,000 discount stores in the U.S. and Puerto Rico, and also operates stores in Canada.

S&P Opinion: Hold (★★★)	Recent Price • 13⅝	Yield • Nil
	52 Wk Range • 20⅞-10½	12-Mo. P/E • 20.0

Quantitative Evaluations

Outlook (1 Lowest—5 Highest)
• **3⁻**

Fair Value
• **13¼**

Risk
• **Average**

Earn./Div. Rank
• **B+**

Technical Eval.
• **Bearish** since 3/98

Rel. Strength Rank (1 Lowest—99 Highest)
• **39**

Insider Activity
• **NA**

Earnings vs. Previous Year
▲=Up ▼=Down ▶=No Change

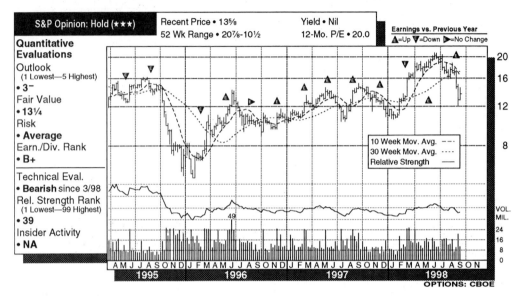

10 Week Mov. Avg. — — —
30 Week Mov. Avg. - - - -
Relative Strength ———

OPTIONS: CBOE

Overview - 07-JUL-98

This discount retailer is making a number of strategic moves to stem a loss of market share to competitors such as Wal-Mart and Target, and to deal with excess industry retail square footage. It has closed underperforming stores, cut corporate overhead and sold nonstrategic assets. KM has also implemented new inventory systems and is upgrading its distribution system. To improve its balance sheet and cash position, it has sold over $3.5 billion in assets. Recent sales trends have improved slightly, although some gains were generated by promotions and markdowns, particularly in women's apparel. Sharp expense reductions have boosted operating income, and earnings improvement in FY 99 (Jan.) should mainly reflect the continuation of expense reductions and lower interest charges. However, the worst is behind, and Kmart has returned to stable, albeit modest, earnings growth over the near term.

Valuation - 07-JUL-98

We remain neutral on the shares of this discount retailer for the near term. The management team has taken the right steps in an attempt to restore the company's competitive position. However, retailing continues to be a battle for market share, with too many stores vying for the same consumer dollar for undifferentiated merchandise. This means that price has become the magnet to draw customers. It remains unclear whether KM has a viable long-term strategy to gain enough market share to sustain earnings growth beyond the next few years. With the shares recently trading at a healthy 20X estimated FY 99 EPS, improved earnings for the company are already reflected in the share price.

Key Stock Statistics

S&P EPS Est. 1999	0.95	Tang. Bk. Value/Share	11.22
P/E on S&P Est. 1999	14.3	Beta	1.00
S&P EPS Est. 2000	1.15	Shareholders	900
Dividend Rate/Share	Nil	Market cap. (B)	$ 6.7
Shs. outstg. (M)	492.3	Inst. holdings	67%
Avg. daily vol. (M)	2.483		

Value of $10,000 invested 5 years ago: $ 6,760

Fiscal Year Ending Jan. 31

	1999	1998	1997	1996	1995	1994
Revenues (Million $)						
1Q	7,515	7,263	6,975	7,443	7,276	9,027
2Q	8,117	7,846	7,566	8,440	8,340	10,198
3Q	—	7,315	7,212	7,975	8,170	9,768
4Q	—	9,759	9,684	10,531	10,527	10,267
Yr.	—	32,183	31,437	34,389	34,313	34,557
Earnings Per Share ($)						
1Q	**0.10**	0.03	-0.08	-0.26	0.03	0.11
2Q	**0.16**	0.06	0.05	0.05	0.18	0.22
3Q	**E0.11**	0.04	0.02	-0.26	0.06	0.20
4Q	**E0.59**	0.35	0.45	-0.80	0.27	-1.35
Yr.	**E0.95**	0.51	0.48	-1.08	0.55	-0.73

Next earnings report expected: mid November

Dividend Data

Cash dividends on the common stock, paid each year since 1913, were omitted in late 1995. A poison pill stock purchase rights plan was adopted in 1988.

A Division of The McGraw-Hill Companies

STANDARD
&POOR'S
STOCK REPORTS

Kmart Corporation

1273J

12-SEP-98

Business Summary - 07-JUL-98

Kmart is synonymous with discount store retailing. Its 2,136 mass merchandise discount stores are the successor to the business developed by S.S. Kresge, who opened his first store in 1899. After operating Kresge department stores for over 45 years, the Kmart store program began with its first store in March 1962.

In 1994, following several quarters of disappointing results, the company began a review of its long-term strategy and short-term needs. As a result, it took a number of steps to improve operating results and strengthen its balance sheet. KM sold its 21.5% interest in Coles Meyer Ltd., an Australian retailer, for $928 million. It also sold its OfficeMax Inc., Sports Authority, Inc. and Borders Group specialty retailing concepts through IPOs and sold its PACE Membership Warehouse unit and PayLess Drug stores. In 1995, the company closed 214 underperforming stores and eliminated $700 million in unproductive inventory and $540 million in expenses. During 1997, the company sold its interest in Kmart Mexico for about $74 million; sold its Canadian operations for about $54 million and a Canadian $109 million note, retaining a 12.5% interest in Kmart Canada; and

sold its Builders Square subsidiary for about $10 million cash and other consideration.

KM's general merchandise retail operations are located in 311 of the 316 Metropolitan Statistical Areas (MSAs) in the U.S. and in each of the three MSAs in Puerto Rico. Stores range from 40,000 to 120,000 square feet with the majority of modernized stores 80,000 to 120,000 square feet. There were a total of 670 Big Kmart stores at the end of FY 98. Super Kmart centers range from 135,000 to 194,000 square feet and feature a full line of general merchandise and grocers as well as ancillary services, such as video rentals, dry cleaning, hair care, optical and floral shops. Full-size stores are located in the most densely populated urban centers. In order to boost square per square foot and profitability the company has also begun stocking market-leader brands, upgrading and streamlining private-label products, improving merchandise presentation, adjusting pricing strategy, and increasing merchandise in-stock position.

All U.S. Kmart footwear departments are operated under license agreements with the Meldisco subsidiary of Footstar Inc. (formerly Melville Corp.).

Per Share Data ($)

(Year Ended Jan. 31)	1998	1997	1996	1995	1994	1993	1992	1991	1990	1989
Tangible Bk. Val.	11.13	10.50	10.99	12.25	10.40	13.16	12.65	11.74	11.35	12.56
Cash Flow	1.85	1.82	0.52	2.05	0.59	3.37	3.21	3.13	1.96	3.09
Earnings	0.51	0.48	-1.08	0.55	-0.73	2.06	2.02	1.89	0.81	2.00
Dividends	Nil	Nil	0.60	0.96	0.95	0.91	0.88	0.85	0.78	0.64
Payout Ratio	Nil	Nil	NM	175%	NM	43%	43%	45%	96%	32%
Cal. Yrs.	**1997**	**1996**	**1995**	**1994**	**1993**	**1992**	**1991**	**1990**	**1989**	**1988**
Prices - High	15¼	14¼	16¼	22	25¾	28⅛	24¾	18⅝	22½	19⅞
- Low	10⅛	5¾	5⅞	12½	19½	20⅞	12⅞	11¾	16¼	14½
P/E Ratio - High	30	30	NM	40	NM	14	12	10	28	10
- Low	20	12	NM	23	NM	10	6	6	20	7

Income Statement Analysis (Million $)

Revs.	32,183	31,437	34,654	34,025	34,353	37,942	34,792	32,281	29,736	27,496
Oper. Inc.	1,555	1,427	1,427	1,344	1,755	2,361	2,077	1,871	1,810	1,835
Depr.	660	654	729	724	684	685	552	497	461	437
Int. Exp.	363	453	453	511	501	460	401	416	388	351
Pretax Inc.	369	262	-711	294	-549	1,426	1,301	1,146	515	1,244
Eff. Tax Rate	33%	NM	NM	39%	NM	34%	34%	34%	37%	36%
Net Inc.	249	231	-489	260	-327	941	859	756	323	803

Balance Sheet & Other Fin. Data (Million $)

Cash	498	406	1,095	480	449	611	565	278	353	948
Curr. Assets	7,476	7,733	8,822	9,187	9,847	10,509	8,990	7,896	7,984	7,146
Total Assets	13,558	14,286	15,397	17,029	17,504	18,931	15,999	13,899	13,145	12,126
Curr. Liab.	3,274	3,602	3,264	5,626	5,724	5,495	4,308	4,377	4,299	3,492
LT Debt	2,904	3,599	5,564	3,778	3,947	4,935	3,925	3,299	3,029	2,946
Common Eqty.	5,434	5,092	5,280	5,900	4,950	6,393	5,905	5,384	4,972	5,009
Total Cap.	9,319	9,681	10,844	9,810	10,040	12,739	11,050	8,840	8,101	8,175
Cap. Exp.	678	343	578	1,259	1,208	1,435	1,329	974	689	694
Cash Flow	909	885	239	936	269	1,545	1,367	1,253	784	1,240
Curr. Ratio	2.3	2.1	2.7	1.6	1.7	1.9	2.1	1.8	1.9	2.0
% LT Debt of Cap.	31.1	37.2	51.3	38.5	39.3	38.7	35.5	37.3	37.4	36.0
% Net Inc.of Revs.	0.8	0.7	NM	0.8	NM	2.5	2.5	2.3	1.1	2.9
% Ret. on Assets	1.8	1.6	NM	1.5	NM	5.4	5.7	5.6	2.6	6.9
% Ret. on Equity	4.7	4.5	NM	3.9	NM	13.9	14.4	14.6	6.5	17.1

Data as orig. reptd.; bef. results of disc. opers. and/or spec. items. Per share data adj. for stk. divs. as of ex-div. date. Bold denotes diluted EPS (FASB 128). E-Estimated. NA-Not Available. NM-Not Meaningful. NR-Not Ranked.

Office—3100 W. Big Beaver Rd., Troy, MI 48084-3163. **Tel**—(810) 643-1000.**Chrmn, Pres & CEO**—F. Hall. **COO**—W. Flick.**SVP & CFO**—M. E. Welch III. **VP & Secy**—Nancy W. LaDuke. **Investor Contact**—Robert M. Burton. **Dirs**—J. B. Adamson, L. H. Affinito, S. F. Bollenbach, J. A. Califano, R. G. Cline, W. D. Davis, E. C. Falla, J. P. Flannery, F. Hall, R. D. Kennedy, J. R. Munro, R. B. Smith, W. P. Weber, J. O. Welch, Jr. **Transfer Agent & Registrar**—First National Bank of Boston. **Incorporated**—in Michigan in 1916. **Empl**— 261,000. **S&P Analyst:** Karen J. Sack, CFA

Kaufman & Broad Home   1286H

NYSE Symbol **KBH**

In S&P 500

12-SEP-98   **Industry:** Homebuilding

Summary: KBH, the leading homebuilder in California, has been aggressively expanding into other areas of the U.S. in recent years. It also has operations in France.

S&P Opinion: Accumulate (★★★★)	Recent Price • 19¾	Yield • 1.5%
	52 Wk Range • 35-19	12-Mo. P/E • 11.7

Quantitative Evaluations

Outlook
(1 Lowest—5 Highest)
• **2⁻**

Fair Value
• **21**

Risk
• **Average**

Earn./Div. Rank
• **B-**

Technical Eval.
• **Bearish** since 7/98

Rel. Strength Rank
(1 Lowest—99 Highest)
• **21**

Insider Activity
• **NA**

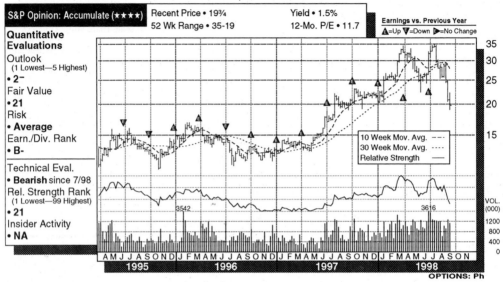

Earnings vs. Previous Year ▲=Up ▼=Down ▶=No Change

10 Week Mov. Avg. — — —
30 Week Mov. Avg. ·······
Relative Strength —

VOL. (000)

OPTIONS: Ph

Overview - 22-JUL-98

A strengthening California economy and KBH's new emphasis on pre-selling homes allowed order backlog at May 31, 1998 ($1.1 billion) to rise 68% from a year earlier. Sales should be further aided by a large menu of new community openings, and comparisons will benefit from measurement against a period slowed by a new business strategy implementation (KB 2000 communities). Those factors should far outweigh a small reduction in the average price of homes sold, as non-California homes (which carry lower prices) will likely account for a bigger share of sales. All told, solid revenue gains from comparable operations should be seen in FY 98 (Nov.); assuming that interest rates stay accommodating. A larger proportion of KB2000 deliveries should bring wider operating margins, as the pre-selling of homes will allow Kaufman to sell more options and hold down production and overhead costs. KBH's reduced level of speculative building should also aid the bottom line. Several spring 1998 takeovers will have little bottom line impact in FY 98, but should add significantly to EPS in the following year.

Valuation - 22-JUL-98

After a lackluster performance for several years, when KBH's mainstay California homebuilding market was plagued by a weak state economy and interest rates seesawed, the shares have surged since spring 1997 (outside of a brief, but sharp downturn in spring 1998). The gains reflect a period of lower rates, indications of the success of KBH's new operating strategy, and California's economic recovery. These factors play a big part in our forecast of better EPS in FY 98 and FY 99. When combined with our enthusiasm for KBH's expansion strategy, and our belief that rates will stay buyer friendly for some time, we think the shares will outperform over the coming year.

Key Stock Statistics

S&P EPS Est. 1998	2.05	Tang. Bk. Value/Share	11.54
P/E on S&P Est. 1998	9.7	Beta	1.78
S&P EPS Est. 1999	2.60	Shareholders	2,200
Dividend Rate/Share	0.30	Market cap. (B)	$0.790
Shs. outstg. (M)	39.9	Inst. holdings	82%
Avg. daily vol. (M)	0.257		

Value of $10,000 invested 5 years ago: $ 13,516

Fiscal Year Ending Nov. 30

	1998	1997	1996	1995	1994	1993
Revenues (Million $)						
1Q	426.3	346.4	302.5	229.8	256.9	224.9
2Q	537.5	414.2	482.4	315.5	326.0	320.0
3Q	—	468.8	481.4	372.3	348.9	319.9
4Q	—	646.9	520.8	478.9	404.5	373.1
Yr.	—	1,876	1,787	1,397	1,336	1,238
Earnings Per Share ($)						
1Q	**0.20**	0.11	0.10	0.01	0.22	0.12
2Q	**0.42**	0.27	-2.47	0.10	0.28	0.22
3Q	**E0.57**	0.38	0.33	0.17	0.27	0.26
4Q	**E0.86**	0.69	0.50	0.45	0.39	0.34
Yr.	**E2.05**	1.45	-1.54	0.73	1.16	0.96

Next earnings report expected: mid September

Dividend Data (Dividends have been paid since 1986.)

Amount ($)	Date Decl.	Ex-Div. Date	Stock of Record	Payment Date
0.075	Sep. 30	Nov. 07	Nov. 12	Nov. 26 '97
0.075	Dec. 04	Feb. 09	Feb. 11	Feb. 25 '98
0.075	Apr. 02	May. 11	May. 13	May. 27 '98
0.075	Jul. 10	Aug. 11	Aug. 13	Aug. 27 '98

A Division of The **McGraw·Hill** *Companies*

Business Summary - 22-JUL-98

Kaufman and Broad Home is the largest single-family homebuilder in California, and prompted by a prolonged economic downturn in that state (which subsequently came to an end), since 1993 has expanded into Nevada, Arizona, Colorado, Utah, New Mexico and Texas. After accounting for 25% of domestic unit volume in FY 95 (Nov.), non-California U.S. home shipments rose to 45% of the FY 96 total, and to 54% in FY 97. The gains mostly stem from KBH's March 1996 purchase of Rayco Ltd., the leading builder in San Antonio, with an amazing share of about 40% of the city's new home market in recent years. KBH also ranks as one of the largest builders in Paris, France, and delivered its first homes in Mexico in FY 96. Building contributions (profits in millions) in FY 97 were:

	Sales	Profits
California	54%	$65.6
Other U.S.	36%	34.2
France	10%	2.0

KBH delivered 11,443 homes in FY 97 at an average price of $159,700, versus 10,249 in FY 96 ($163,300); its average home sale price in FY 97 was $208,500 in California and $118,700 in other U.S. areas.

KBH mostly sells single-family detached homes. It generally constructs the homes in medium-size developments close to major metropolitan areas, catering to first-time buyers. Like most major builders, the company acts as the general contractor for its communities and hires subcontractors for all production activities.

The company also provides mortgage banking services to domestic home buyers. It views this as an important factor in its ability to complete sales.

During FY 98, KBH plans to maintain its focus on the two primary strategic objectives it established for the prior year--acceleration of growth and the implementation of the KB2000 business model. The company expects to step up its growth pace by focusing on its more vital current markets, as well as undertaking new market entry. It views Texas and other western states as primary areas for potential growth. In addition to acquiring Rayco in March 1996, the company began operations in Dallas in FY 96, Austin in early 1997, and entered Houston in March 1998 through the purchase of Hallmark Residential Group. Also in March 1998, KBH acquired Denver-based builder PrideMark Homes, and in April 1998, it bought Tucson, AZ-based Estes Homebuilding Co. KBH has also been implementing its KB2000 business model, emphasizing elements such as pre-selling homes, with construction of any given home delayed until the sale is under contract. Advantages of pre-selling include the ability to personalize the home to specific customer needs; and the capacity to minimize production and overhead costs through the use of even-flow production techniques, where a set number of homes is targeted for completion on any given day.

Per Share Data ($)

(Year Ended Nov. 30)	1997	1996	1995	1994	1993	1992	1991	1990	1989	1988
Tangible Bk. Val.	9.02	7.75	12.37	12.46	12.76	9.20	8.97	8.45	6.76	8.49
Cash Flow	1.75	-1.27	0.89	1.00	0.90	0.87	0.89	1.37	2.57	1.92
Earnings	1.45	-1.54	0.73	1.16	0.96	0.78	0.80	1.25	2.44	1.76
Dividends	0.30	0.30	0.30	0.30	0.30	0.30	0.30	0.30	4.80	0.30
Payout Ratio	21%	NM	41%	26%	31%	37%	33%	21%	166%	17%
Prices - High	23⅛	16⅞	16	25½	24¾	25	18¼	15¼	21¾	13½
- Low	12¾	11¼	10⅞	12⅛	16	11⅜	8¾	5⅜	9⅞	8¼
P/E Ratio - High	16	NM	22	22	26	32	23	12	9	8
- Low	9	NM	15	10	17	15	11	4	4	5

Income Statement Analysis (Million $)

Revs.	1,876	1,787	1,397	1,336	1,238	1,094	1,221	1,366	1,265	903
Oper. Inc.	141	136	96.0	115	122	100	120	159	208	99
Depr.	11.9	10.8	6.3	3.4	2.6	3.5	3.3	3.9	4.3	4.3
Int. Exp.	42.5	77.1	79.5	62.6	66.4	73.8	82.2	93.2	85.0	16.9
Pretax Inc.	91.5	-95.8	45.5	75.0	74.0	57.0	65.0	101	154	98.0
Eff. Tax Rate	36%	NM	36%	37%	33%	30%	26%	30%	40%	43%
Net Inc.	58.2	-61.2	29.0	46.6	39.9	28.2	26.5	39.9	81.4	48.0

Balance Sheet & Other Fin. Data (Million $)

Cash	68.2	9.8	43.4	55.0	75.0	66.0	51.0	28.0	117	37.0
Curr. Assets	NA	NA	NA	NA	NA	NA	NA	NA	NA	NA
Total Assets	1,419	1,243	1,574	1,454	1,339	1,432	1,373	1,544	1,487	603
Curr. Liab.	NA	NA	NA	NA	NA	NA	NA	NA	NA	NA
LT Debt	698	578	791	677	476	727	582	600	726	110
Common Eqty.	383	340	414	403	443	318	258	234	187	232
Total Cap.	1,083	919	1,233	1,115	964	1,132	949	937	968	383
Cap. Exp.	Nil	Nil	Nil	Nil	Nil	Nil	Nil	Nil	Nil	Nil
Cash Flow	70.1	-50.4	35.3	40.1	37.6	31.6	29.8	43.8	84.2	52.4
Curr. Ratio	NA	NA	NA	NA	NA	NA	NA	NA	NA	NA
% LT Debt of Cap.	64.5	62.9	64.1	60.7	49.4	64.2	61.3	64.0	74.9	28.8
% Net Inc.of Revs.	3.1	NM	2.1	3.5	3.2	2.6	2.2	2.9	6.4	5.3
% Ret. on Assets	4.4	NM	2.0	3.4	2.9	1.8	1.8	2.6	7.8	8.3
% Ret. on Equity	16.1	NM	4.7	9.0	9.2	9.0	10.6	18.9	37.9	22.7

Data as orig. reptd.; bef. results of disc. opers. and/or spec. items. Per share data adj. for stk. divs. as of ex-div. date. Bold denotes diluted EPS (FASB 128). E-Estimated. NA-Not Available. NM-Not Meaningful. NR-Not Ranked.

Office—10990 Wilshire Blvd., Los Angeles, CA 90024. **Tel**—(310) 231-4000. **Website**—http://kaufmanandbroad.com **Chrmn, Pres & CEO**—B. Karatz. **SVP & CFO**—M. F. Henn. **VP, Treas & Investor Contact**—Dennis Welsch (310-231-4010). **Dirs**—S. Bartlett, R. W. Burkle, J. Evans, R. R. Irani, J. A. Johnson, B. Karatz, G. Nafilyan, L. G. Nogales, C. R. Rinehart, S. C. Sigoloff. **Transfer Agent & Registrar**—ChaseMellon Shareholder Services, Los Angeles. **Incorporated**—in Delaware in 1981. **Empl**— 2,040. **S&P Analyst:** Michael W. Jaffe

STANDARD &POOR'S
STOCK REPORTS

Kellogg Co.

1289

NYSE Symbol **K**

In S&P 500

12-SEP-98 Industry: Foods

Summary: Kellogg is the world's leading producer of ready-to-eat cereal products, with a dominant 40% global market share. The W.K. Kellogg Foundation Trust holds 34% of the stock.

S&P Opinion: Avoid (★★)

Recent Price • 32⅝
52 Wk Range • 50⅜-28½

Yield • 2.9%
12-Mo. P/E • 24.2

Quantitative Evaluations

Outlook (1 Lowest—5 Highest)
• **1**

Fair Value
• **26⅜**

Risk
• **Low**

Earn./Div. Rank
• **A**

Technical Eval.
• **Bearish** since 2/98

Rel. Strength Rank (1 Lowest—99 Highest)
• **78**

Insider Activity
• **Neutral**

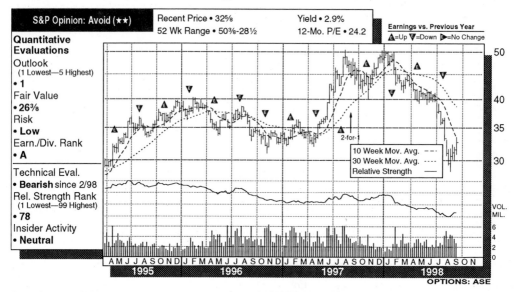

Earnings vs. Previous Year
▲=Up ▼=Down ▶=No Change

10 Week Mov. Avg. – – –
30 Week Mov. Avg. ·······
Relative Strength —

OPTIONS: ASE

Overview - 04-AUG-98

Net sales in 1998 are projected to be essentially unchanged, as very modest unit volume growth and price increases are largely offset by negative currency exchange translations. Near-term results will be affected by recently stepped-up marketing spending behind additional promotional activity and accelerated expansion of its convenience foods into international markets. For the longer term, cost saving benefits from a continuing streamlining of manufacturing facilities should allow for margin stability. Interest expense is expected to be higher, reflecting increased borrowings for share repurchases. Overall, we anticipate 1998 EPS (before non-recurring items) of only $1.45, down 15% from 1997's $1.70 (before unusual charges). Over the next few years, annual EPS growth of approximately 5% to 10% is seen, buoyed mostly by share repurchases.

Valuation - 04-AUG-98

As a result of the intensely competitive state of the U.S. ready-to-eat cereal industry, we remain cautious on Kellogg's near-term prospects. Competition in the ready-to-eat cereal industry remains fierce, stemming mainly from a greater number of low-price competitors over the past few years, despite soft cereal demand. Nevertheless, with cereal category margins still high relative to those of other grocery products, more price competition is possible in the future. Kellogg is somewhat insulated from domestic pressures by its large overseas presence, but near-term earnings could still suffer. The shares have commanded a large valuation premium relative to the S&P 500 over the years, because of K's financial strength and its relatively wide margins. However, this premium could narrow in coming periods, reflecting rising investor concern about the company's future prospects.

Key Stock Statistics

S&P EPS Est. 1998	1.45	Tang. Bk. Value/Share	2.43
P/E on S&P Est. 1998	22.5	Beta	0.51
S&P EPS Est. 1999	1.60	Shareholders	26,800
Dividend Rate/Share	0.94	Market cap. (B)	$ 13.3
Shs. outstg. (M)	407.1	Inst. holdings	74%
Avg. daily vol. (M)	0.774		

Value of $10,000 invested 5 years ago: $ 11,095

Fiscal Year Ending Dec. 31

	1998	1997	1996	1995	1994	1993
Revenues (Million $)						
1Q	1,643	1,689	1,786	1,716	1,611	1,518
2Q	1,714	1,720	1,651	1,780	1,617	1,542
3Q	—	1,804	1,682	1,845	1,742	1,669
4Q	—	1,618	1,558	1,663	1,592	1,566
Yr.	—	6,830	6,677	7,004	6,562	6,295
Earnings Per Share ($)						
1Q	**0.42**	**0.38**	0.48	0.45	0.41	0.38
2Q	**0.35**	**0.39**	0.18	0.31	0.34	0.31
3Q	**E0.37**	**0.50**	0.38	0.53	0.48	0.45
4Q	**E0.31**	**0.04**	0.21	-0.17	0.35	0.33
Yr.	**E1.45**	**1.32**	1.25	1.12	1.57	1.47

Next earnings report expected: early November

Dividend Data (Dividends have been paid since 1923.)

Amount ($)	Date Decl.	Ex-Div. Date	Stock of Record	Payment Date
0.225	Oct. 31	Dec. 25	Dec. 28	Dec. 15 '97
0.225	Feb. 20	Feb. 26	Mar. 02	Mar. 13 '98
0.225	Apr. 24	May. 27	May. 29	Jun. 15 '98
0.235	Jul. 31	Aug. 26	Aug. 28	Sep. 15 '98

A Division of The McGraw-Hill Companies

Business Summary - 04-AUG-98

Kellogg Co., incorporated in 1922, is the world's leading producer of ready-to-eat cereal products, with an approximate 34% market share in North America and 40% globally (both measured by volume). In recent years, the company has expanded its operations from ready-to-eat cereals to also include other grain-based convenience food products, such as Pop-Tarts toaster pastries, Eggo frozen waffles, Nutri-Grain cereal bars, Rice Krispies Treats squares, and Lender's bagels. Sales and profit contributions by geographic region in 1997 were:

	Sales	Profits
U.S.	58%	70%
Europe	25%	16%
Other	17%	14%

Products are manufactured in 19 countries and distributed in more than 160. Ready-to-eat cereals include Corn Flakes, Rice Krispies, Special K, Frosted Flakes, All-Bran, Corn Pops, Raisin Bran, Frosted Mini-Wheats, Bran Flakes, and Low Fat Granola. Cereals are generally marketed under the Kellogg's name and are sold principally to the grocery trade through direct sales forces for resale to consumers and through broker and distribution arrangements in less developed market areas.

The company's U.S. manufacturing facilities include four cereal plants and warehouses, in Battle Creek, MI; Lancaster, PA; Memphis, TN; and Omaha, NE. Other non-cereal foods are also manufactured in the U.S. at various plant locations. Manufacturing facilities outside the U.S. are in Argentina, Australia, Brazil, Canada, China, Colombia, Ecuador, Germany, Great Britain, Guatemala, India, Italy, Japan, Mexico, South Africa, South Korea, Spain, Thailand and Venezuela. The principal ingredients in K's products include corn grits, oats, rice, various fruits, sweeteners, wheat and wheat derivatives.

During 1997, Kellogg incurred non-recurring charges and other unusual items totaling $140.5 million, after tax ($0.34 a share), primarily for streamlining initiatives related to management's plan to optimize the company's pan-European operations, as well as continuing productivity programs in the U.S. and Australia. Charges consisted of manufacturing asset production redeployment, associated management consulting and similar costs.

The W. K. Kellogg Foundation Trust holds 34% of the common shares.

Per Share Data ($)

(Year Ended Dec. 31)	1997	1996	1995	1994	1993	1992	1991	1990	1989	1988
Tangible Bk. Val.	2.42	2.15	3.67	4.07	3.63	3.98	4.38	3.81	3.28	2.91
Cash Flow	2.07	1.86	1.72	2.15	2.04	1.92	1.72	1.46	1.21	1.26
Earnings	1.32	1.25	1.12	1.57	1.47	1.43	1.25	1.04	0.86	0.97
Dividends	0.87	0.81	0.75	0.70	0.66	0.60	0.54	0.48	0.43	0.38
Payout Ratio	66%	65%	67%	44%	45%	42%	43%	46%	50%	39%
Prices - High	50½	40⅜	39¾	30⅜	34	37¾	33½	19⅜	20⅜	17⅛
- Low	32	31	26¼	23¾	23⅝	27¼	17½	14¾	14½	12¼
P/E Ratio - High	38	32	35	19	23	26	27	19	24	18
- Low	24	25	23	15	16	19	14	14	17	13

Income Statement Analysis (Million $)

	1997	1996	1995	1994	1993	1992	1991	1990	1989	1988
Revs.	6,830	6,677	7,004	6,562	6,295	6,191	5,787	5,181	4,652	4,349
Oper. Inc.	1,480	1,347	1,519	1,419	1,334	1,294	1,251	1,086	900	934
Depr.	287	252	259	256	265	232	223	200	168	140
Int. Exp.	108	70.0	70.0	52.3	40.4	33.6	60.7	84.5	72.6	60.4
Pretax Inc.	905	860	796	1,130	1,034	1,070	984	815	667	775
Eff. Tax Rate	38%	38%	38%	38%	34%	36%	38%	38%	37%	38%
Net Inc.	564	531	490	705	681	683	606	503	422	480

Balance Sheet & Other Fin. Data (Million $)

	1997	1996	1995	1994	1993	1992	1991	1990	1989	1988
Cash	173	244	222	266	98.0	126	178	101	80.0	185
Curr. Assets	1,467	1,529	1,429	1,434	1,245	1,237	1,173	1,041	906	1,063
Total Assets	4,877	5,051	4,415	4,467	4,237	4,015	3,926	3,749	3,390	3,298
Curr. Liab.	1,657	2,199	1,265	1,185	1,215	1,071	1,324	1,110	1,037	1,184
LT Debt	1,416	727	718	719	522	315	15.0	296	371	272
Common Eqty.	998	1,282	1,591	1,808	1,713	1,945	2,160	1,902	1,634	1,483
Total Cap.	2,414	2,235	2,511	2,725	2,424	2,445	2,514	2,544	2,295	2,048
Cap. Exp.	312	307	316	354	450	474	334	321	509	538
Cash Flow	851	783	749	962	946	914	829	703	590	620
Curr. Ratio	0.9	0.7	1.1	1.2	1.0	1.2	0.9	0.9	0.9	0.9
% LT Debt of Cap.	58.7	32.5	28.6	26.4	21.5	12.9	0.6	11.6	16.2	13.3
% Net Inc.of Revs.	8.3	8.0	7.0	10.7	10.8	11.0	10.5	9.7	9.1	11.0
% Ret. on Assets	11.4	11.2	11.1	16.4	16.8	17.3	15.8	14.2	12.7	16.1
% Ret. on Equity	49.5	37.0	28.8	40.6	38.0	33.5	29.9	28.6	27.2	35.7

Data as orig. reptd.; bef. results of disc. opers. and/or spec. items. Per share data adj. for stk. divs. as of ex-div. date. Bold denotes diluted EPS (FASB 128). E-Estimated. NA-Not Available. NM-Not Meaningful. NR-Not Ranked.

Office—One Kellogg Square, P.O. Box 3599, Battle Creek, MI 49016-3599. **Tel**—(616) 961-2000. **Website**—http://www.kelloggs.com **Chrmn & CEO**—A. G. Langbo. **Vice Chrmn**—W. A. Camstra. **Pres & COO**—C. M. Gutierrez. **Treas & Investor Contact**—John Bolt. **Dirs**—B. S. Carson, C. S. Fiorina, C. X. Gonzalez, G. Gund, W. E. LaMothe, A. G. Langbo, R. G. Mawby, A. McLaughlin, J. R. Munro, H. A. Poling, W. C. Richardson, D. Rumsfeld, J. L. Zabriskie. **Transfer Agent & Registrar**—Harris Trust & Savings Bank, Chicago. **Incorporated**—in Delaware in 1922. **Empl**—14,339. **S&P Analyst:** Richard Joy

STANDARD &POOR'S
STOCK REPORTS

Kerr-McGee

1295

NYSE Symbol **KMG**

In S&P 500

12-SEP-98

Industry:
Oil & Gas (Exploration & Production)

Summary: This oil and natural gas exploration and production company also engages in chemical production.

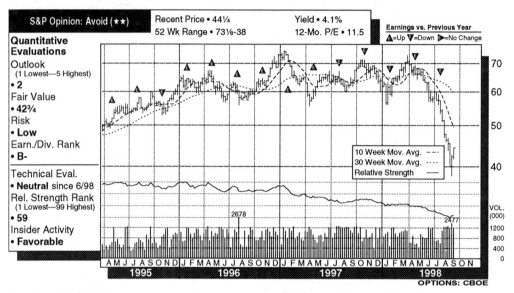

S&P Opinion: Avoid (★★)		
Recent Price • 44¼	Yield • 4.1%	
52 Wk Range • 73⅛-38	12-Mo. P/E • 11.5	

Quantitative Evaluations

Outlook
(1 Lowest—5 Highest)
• **2**

Fair Value
• **42¾**

Risk
• **Low**

Earn./Div. Rank
• **B-**

Technical Eval.
• **Neutral** since 6/98

Rel. Strength Rank
(1 Lowest—99 Highest)
• **59**

Insider Activity
• **Favorable**

Earnings vs. Previous Year
▲=Up ▼=Down ▶=No Change

10 Week Mov. Avg. - - -
30 Week Mov. Avg. ·····
Relative Strength —

VOL. (000)
OPTIONS: CBOE

Overview - 05-AUG-98

A restructuring of the oil and gas exploration and production segment has focused on the divestiture of non-strategic and high-cost properties, including the merger of North American onshore properties into Devon Energy, and will result in a stronger portfolio of assets and more efficient operations. Core exploration and production areas now include the Gulf of Mexico, the North Sea and offshore China. Profitability on a per barrel of oil basis will also benefit from lower depreciation levels. The company recently divested its coal division, and will focus on its core oil and gas and chemicals businesses. Chemicals operations will focus on the production of titanium dioxide pigment, with capacity expansions and selective acquisitions planned. Results in the first half of 1998 were hampered by sharply lower oil and gas prices. Oil production rose 8%, while natural gas output was essentially unchanged.

Valuation - 05-AUG-98

The shares were recently down about 21% in 1998, reflecting lower oil prices. With the weak oil price environment expected to prevail throughout 1998, we expect the shares to continue to underperform the broader market during the second half of the year. During 1997, exploration and production operating profits were 14% lower, due primarily to lower oil and gas production and weaker oil prices. Prices have continued to decline thus far in 1998, and it will be difficult for KMG to match its 1997 upstream earnings. Earnings in the near term will benefit from improved chemical segment profits, resulting from higher titanium dioxide pigment sales prices and increased volumes. Plans for exploration in the North Sea, China and the Gulf of Mexico, as well as recent sale of the underperforming coal business, offer long-term upside potential.

Key Stock Statistics

S&P EPS Est. 1998	1.85	Tang. Bk. Value/Share	27.93
P/E on S&P Est. 1998	24.0	Beta	0.94
S&P EPS Est. 1999	2.75	Shareholders	11,500
Dividend Rate/Share	1.80	Market cap. (B)	$ 2.1
Shs. outstg. (M)	47.7	Inst. holdings	73%
Avg. daily vol. (M)	0.367		

Value of $10,000 invested 5 years ago: $ 11,774

Fiscal Year Ending Dec. 31

	1998	1997	1996	1995	1994	1993
Revenues (Million $)						
1Q	369.0	468.0	454.8	463.9	800.9	783.5
2Q	394.6	412.0	470.2	456.7	864.8	845.8
3Q	—	402.0	487.6	456.0	858.2	819.2
4Q	—	429.0	518.5	424.6	829.5	832.6
Yr.	—	1,711	1,931	1,801	3,353	3,281
Earnings Per Share ($)						
1Q	**0.50**	1.45	0.94	0.71	0.42	0.50
2Q	**0.55**	0.87	1.01	0.68	0.58	0.70
3Q	—	0.77	1.27	-2.56	0.35	0.39
4Q	—	0.95	1.21	0.70	0.39	Nil
Yr.	E1.85	4.04	4.43	-0.47	1.74	1.57

Next earnings report expected: late October

Dividend Data (Dividends have been paid since 1941.)

Amount ($)	Date Decl.	Ex-Div. Date	Stock of Record	Payment Date
0.450	Nov. 18	Dec. 03	Dec. 05	Jan. 02 '98
0.450	Jan. 13	Mar. 04	Mar. 06	Apr. 01 '98
0.450	May. 12	Jun. 03	Jun. 05	Jul. 01 '98
0.450	Jul. 14	Sep. 02	Sep. 04	Oct. 01 '98

A Division of The McGraw·Hill Companies

STANDARD
&POOR'S
STOCK REPORTS

Kerr-McGee Corporation

1295

12-SEP-98

Business Summary - 05-AUG-98

Kerr-McGee's longtime chairman and CEO Frank Mc-Pherson retired in February 1997, but not before he and other members of senior management of the domestic integrated oil company had made several moves to strengthen its long-term competitive position. During 1995, KMG disposed of the majority of its refining and marketing assets (classified as discontinued since April 1995). A restructuring of the exploration and production segment was begun in late 1995. Effective December 31, 1996, Kerr-McGee merged its North American onshore exploration and production operations into Devon Energy (NYSE: DVN). In return, KMG received a 31% ownership interest in Devon. In January 1998, KMG announced its intent to exit the coal business.

After all of these moves, Kerr-McGee will focus on its core exploration and production area of the Gulf of Mexico and its portfolio of international prospects, as well as its principal chemicals business, titanium dioxide pigments. In 1997, crude oil and condensate production averaged 56,900 bbl. a day (68,600 bbl./day in 1996); natural gas sales were 184 MMcf per day (281 MMcf). The average crude oil price received by the company in 1997 was $18.51 per bbl., down from $19.16 in 1996. KMG's average natural gas price rose to $2.56 per Mcf in 1997 from $2.12 in 1996. Net proved reserves at the

end of 1997 were 164 million bbl. of crude oil and condensate (168 million bbl. at year end 1996) and 500 Bcf of natural gas (523 Bcf). Much of the decline in the company's production and reserves since 1996 is attributable to the Devon Energy transaction; reserves and production from these properties are no longer accounted for on Kerr-McGee's financial statements.

Major initiatives in the chemicals segment include leveraging upon the strong worldwide growth in pigment demand. The segment's largest and most profitable product is titanium dioxide pigment, accounting for the majority of chemicals operating profits in 1997. The pigment is used to impart whiteness to products in the paint, paper and cosmetics industries. KMG is the world's third largest producer of titanium dioxide using chloride technology. The company believes that most of the future growth in titanium dioxide pigment demand will be for chloride titanium dioxide. In 1997, titanium dioxide capacity reached 265,000 tons, up from 1996 capacity of 248,000 tons. A large capacity expansion is planned for 1998.

KMG's coal business, which will be sold, is the seventh largest U.S. coal producer. The company sold 36,192,000 tons of coal in 1997 (35,259,000 in 1996), marking a company record for annual production. The majority of coal sales have traditionally been to electric utilities under long-term contracts.

Per Share Data ($)

(Year Ended Dec. 31)	1997	1996	1995	1994	1993	1992	1991	1990	1989	1988
Tangible Bk. Val.	27.93	26.01	27.72	29.73	29.27	27.96	31.43	30.77	29.44	29.42
Cash Flow	9.52	10.41	6.13	8.41	8.08	5.92	8.40	8.83	9.00	8.47
Earnings	4.04	4.43	-0.47	1.74	1.57	-0.53	2.10	2.26	2.58	2.11
Dividends	1.80	1.64	1.55	1.52	1.52	1.52	1.50	1.41	1.26	1.10
Payout Ratio	45%	37%	NM	87%	97%	NM	71%	60%	50%	52%
Prices - High	75	74¹/₈	64	51	56	46³/₈	46⁷/₈	53⁵/₈	52	42⁷/₈
- Low	55¹/₂	55³/₄	44	40	41³/₄	35⁵/₈	35¹/₈	42³/₈	37³/₈	32³/₄
P/E Ratio - High	19	17	NM	29	36	NM	22	24	20	20
- Low	14	13	NM	23	27	NM	17	19	14	16

Income Statement Analysis (Million $)

	1997	1996	1995	1994	1993	1992	1991	1990	1989	1988
Revs.	1,711	1,931	1,801	3,353	3,281	3,382	3,274	3,683	3,087	2,689
Oper. Inc.	496	565	600	513	467	272	488	636	572	506
Depr.	263	297	341	345	321	312	304	327	313	308
Int. Exp.	46.0	61.0	72.0	69.0	67.0	81.0	94.0	105	84.0	74.0
Pretax Inc.	277	323	-67.0	132	118	-64.0	166	156	205	157
Eff. Tax Rate	30%	32%	NM	38%	35%	NM	39%	28%	39%	35%
Net Inc.	194	220	-24.0	90.0	77.0	-26.0	102	113	126	102

Balance Sheet & Other Fin. Data (Million $)

	1997	1996	1995	1994	1993	1992	1991	1990	1989	1988
Cash	183	121	87.0	82.0	94.0	57.0	192	453	86.0	128
Curr. Assets	689	805	766	963	866	917	951	1,192	878	844
Total Assets	3,096	3,124	3,232	3,698	3,547	3,521	3,421	3,473	3,332	3,123
Curr. Liab.	523	485	580	890	787	707	608	720	550	614
LT Debt	660	737	745	673	590	792	926	805	858	615
Common Eqty.	1,440	1,367	1,416	1,543	1,512	1,350	1,516	1,491	1,476	1,422
Total Cap.	2,259	2,508	2,266	2,395	2,274	2,308	2,609	2,541	2,596	2,306
Cap. Exp.	341	392	485	411	451	373	514	506	506	409
Cash Flow	457	517	317	435	398	286	406	440	439	410
Curr. Ratio	1.3	1.7	1.3	1.1	1.1	1.3	1.6	1.7	1.6	1.4
% LT Debt of Cap.	29.2	29.4	32.8	28.1	25.9	34.3	35.5	31.7	33.1	26.7
% Net Inc.of Revs.	11.3	11.4	NM	2.7	2.3	NM	3.1	3.1	4.1	3.8
% Ret. on Assets	6.2	6.9	NM	2.5	2.1	NM	3.0	3.4	3.8	3.3
% Ret. on Equity	13.9	15.8	NM	5.9	5.2	NM	6.8	7.7	8.5	7.3

Data as orig. reptd.; bef. results of disc. opers. and/or spec. items. Per share data adj. for stk. divs. as of ex-div. date. Bold denotes diluted EPS (FASB 128). E-Estimated. NA-Not Available. NM-Not Meaningful. NR-Not Ranked.

Office—Kerr-McGee Center (P.O. Box 25861), Oklahoma City, OK 73125. Tel—(405) 270-1313. Chrmn & CEO—L. R. Corbett. Vice Chrmn—T.J. McDaniel. EVP & CFO—J. C. Linehan. SVP & Secy—R.G. Horner, Jr. VP & Investor Contact—Richard C. Buterbaugh (405-270-3125). Dirs—P. M. Anderson, B. E. Bidwell, L. R. Corbett, M. C. Jischke, T. J. McDaniel, W. C. Morris, J. J. Murphy, L. C. Richie, R. M. Rompala, F. M. Walters. Transfer Agent & Registrar—Bank One Trust Co., Oklahoma City. Incorporated—in Delaware in 1932. Empl—3,746. S&P Analyst: Norman Rosenberg

STANDARD &POOR'S
STOCK REPORTS

KeyCorp

1295M
NYSE Symbol **KEY**

In S&P 500

12-SEP-98 | **Industry:** Banks (Major Regional) | **Summary:** This multiregional bank holding company, headquartered in Cleveland, operates more than 1,000 branch offices in 13 states.

S&P Opinion: Hold (★★★)	Recent Price • 29¾	Yield • 3.2%
	52 Wk Range • 44⅞-24¾	12-Mo. P/E • 13.7

Earnings vs. Previous Year
▲=Up ▼=Down ▶=No Change

Quantitative Evaluations

Outlook (1 Lowest—5 Highest)
• **2**

Fair Value
• **26¾**

Risk
• **Low**

Earn./Div. Rank
• **A+**

Technical Eval.
• **Bearish** since 7/97

Rel. Strength Rank (1 Lowest—99 Highest)
• **67**

Insider Activity
• **Neutral**

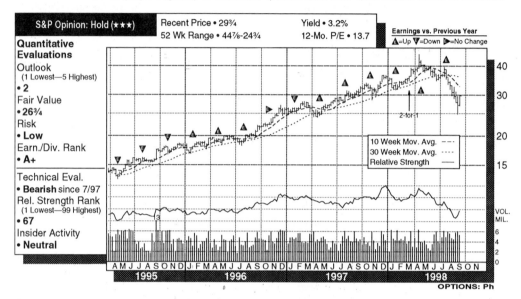

2-for-1

10 Week Mov. Avg. ---
30 Week Mov. Avg. ·····
Relative Strength —

OPTIONS: Ph

Overview - 19-AUG-98

KEY is expected to post loan growth in targeted areas in the double-digits in 1998 (excluding the effect of securitizations), similar to trends seen in 1997, with particular strength in commercial lending. Net interest margins are likely to narrow a bit further in 1998 on higher funding costs, competitive pressures and the repricing of existing loan portfolios. Late 1997 acquisitions of an equipment leasing firm and home equity finance concern Champion Mortgage show a dedication to improving the revenue growth rate, as does the pending acquisition of McDonald & Co., an investment banking and securities brokerage company. Return on equity should continue to improve as KEY targets for divestiture lines of business that do not meet its 20% ROE goal. Earnings growth of about 10% is expected in 1998.

Valuation - 19-AUG-98

The shares have declined about 13% thus far in 1998, most likely reflecting disappointment in the quality of earnings. While hitting consensus EPS estimates, earnings in recent quarters have been helped by branch sale gains. Nonetheless, KEY is taking steps to improve its growth rate, with acquisitions pending or recently completed in the equipment leasing, home equity finance and investment banking areas. Coupled with a stabilizing net interest margin and healthy commercial lending volume, future results should begin to improve. For now, the shares are ranked hold based on a belief that gains will be held back until investors see tangible improvement in operating results.

Key Stock Statistics

S&P EPS Est. 1998	2.28	Tang. Bk. Value/Share	10.02
P/E on S&P Est. 1998	13.1	Beta	1.33
S&P EPS Est. 1999	2.55	Shareholders	35,900
Dividend Rate/Share	0.94	Market cap. (B)	$ 13.1
Shs. outstg. (M)	439.9	Inst. holdings	46%
Avg. daily vol. (M)	1.138		

Value of $10,000 invested 5 years ago: $ 22,721

Fiscal Year Ending Dec. 31

	1998	1997	1996	1995	1994	1993
Revenues (Million $)						
1Q	1,683	1,514	1,485	1,416	1,272	1,270
2Q	1,752	1,583	1,498	1,522	1,330	1,318
3Q	—	1,740	1,527	1,534	1,374	1,340
4Q	—	1,731	1,528	1,582	1,397	1,288
Yr.	—	6,568	6,038	6,054	5,373	5,216
Earnings Per Share ($)						
1Q	0.53	0.47	0.44	0.35	0.42	0.39
2Q	0.56	0.51	0.46	0.41	0.45	0.41
3Q	E0.58	0.53	0.45	0.45	0.46	0.41
4Q	E0.61	0.56	0.34	0.43	0.40	0.24
Yr.	E2.28	2.07	1.69	1.65	1.73	1.45

Next earnings report expected: mid October

Dividend Data (Dividends have been paid since 1963.)

Amount ($)	Date Decl.	Ex-Div. Date	Stock of Record	Payment Date
0.420	Nov. 20	Nov. 28	Dec. 02	Dec. 15 '97
2-for-1	Jan. 15	Mar. 09	Feb. 18	Mar. 06 '98
0.235	May. 07	May. 29	Jun. 02	Jun. 15 '98
0.235	Jul. 16	Aug. 28	Sep. 01	Sep. 15 '98

A Division of The **McGraw·Hill** Companies

Business Summary - 19-AUG-98

With a corporate motto "The Key Difference," KeyCorp has transformed itself over the past few years with an objective of becoming a leader in the national financial services industry. The Key Difference refers to the company's national operating structure, customer-friendly technology, sophisticated sales culture and high-energy marketing strategies. Operations are broadly organized into four main operating groups, with contributions to net income (in $ million) and return on equity in 1997 as follows:

	Net Inc.	Return on equity
Corporate capital	$232	26.6%
Consumer finance	$102	10.7%
Community banking	$569	20.8%
Capital partners	$31	12.1%

Corporate capital offers a complete range of financing, transaction processing and financial advisory services to corporations throughout the U.S., including specialized services such as international banking, corporate finance advisory services, capital markets products, and 401(k) and trust custody products. Consumer finance is responsible for non-branch-based consumer loan and deposit products such as credit cards, automobile loans and leases, marine and recreational vehicle loans. Community banking delivers branch-based retail financial products and services to small business and consumers through over 1,000 KeyBank Centers in 13 states. Capital partners, formed in late 1997, offers asset management, investment banking, insurance and brokerage services.

During 1997, average earning assets, from which interest income is derived, were $61.3 billion and consisted mainly of loans (84%) and investment securities (15%). Average sources of funds included interest-bearing deposits (51%), short-term borrowings (17%), long-term debt (9%), shareholders' equity (7%), noninterest-bearing deposits (12%) and other (4%).

Nonperforming assets, which included mainly non-accrual loans, at December 31, 1997, were $431 million (0.81% of loans and other real estate owned), up from $400 million (0.81%) a year earlier. The allowance for loan losses, which is held in anticipation of loan losses, amounted to $900 million (1.69% of loans) at the end of 1997, versus $870 million (1.77) a year before. Net charge-offs, or the amount of loans actually written off as uncollectible, were $293 million (0.57% of average loans) in 1997, up from $195 million (0.40%) in 1996.

In 1998, the company reached an agreement to acquire McDonald & Co. Investments, a full-service investment banking and securities brokerage company, for $653 million in common stock.

Per Share Data ($)

(Year Ended Dec. 31)	1997	1996	1995	1994	1993	1992	1991	1990	1989	1988
Tangible Bk. Val.	9.14	8.95	8.39	7.62	7.24	7.88	8.46	7.67	8.29	7.49
Earnings	2.07	1.69	1.65	1.73	1.45	1.25	1.23	1.16	1.16	1.05
Dividends	0.84	0.76	0.72	0.64	0.56	0.49	0.46	0.44	0.40	0.34
Payout Ratio	41%	45%	44%	37%	39%	39%	38%	38%	35%	32%
Prices - High	36⅝	27⅛	18⅝	16⅞	18⅝	16¾	13⅛	8⅞	10⅛	9½
- Low	24	16¾	12⅜	11⅞	13⅝	12⅛	7⅝	6	8¼	7¾
P/E Ratio - High	18	16	11	10	13	13	11	8	9	9
- Low	12	10	7	7	9	10	6	5	7	7

Income Statement Analysis (Million $)

	1997	1996	1995	1994	1993	1992	1991	1990	1989	1988
Net Int. Inc.	2,794	2,717	2,637	2,693	2,679	1,130	687	624	426	360
Tax Equiv. Adj.	44.0	50.0	57.3	58.8	63.1	27.6	21.4	25.3	17.0	19.3
Non Int. Inc.	1,305	1,086	974	897	973	492	218	231	161	144
Loan Loss Prov.	320	197	101	125	212	147	79.9	94.7	51.6	24.9
Exp./Op. Revs.	59%	72%	63%	59%	64%	63%	65%	69%	65%	67%
Pretax Inc.	1,345	1,143	1,158	1,283	1,084	439	234	162	146	130
Eff. Tax Rate	32%	31%	32%	34%	35%	31%	30%	4.40%	24%	23%
Net Inc.	919	783	789	853	710	301	163	155	110	100
% Net Int. Marg.	4.62	4.78	4.47	4.84	5.31	5.33	5.19	4.66	4.93	4.50

Balance Sheet & Other Fin. Data (Million $)

	1997	1996	1995	1994	1993	1992	1991	1990	1989	1988
Earning Assets:										
Money Mkt	NA	NA	NA	NA	NA	779	761	347	846	1,005
Inv. Securities	8,938	9,329	9,748	12,797	12,849	5,607	3,563	3,165	1,868	1,646
Com'l Loans	18,013	14,980	14,422	12,498	10,668	5,354	3,382	3,487	2,634	2,662
Other Loans	35,367	34,255	33,270	34,082	30,729	10,848	6,275	6,587	4,175	3,600
Total Assets	73,699	67,621	66,339	66,798	59,631	24,978	15,405	15,110	10,903	10,010
Demand Deposits	9,368	9,524	9,281	9,136	8,826	3,659	1,967	2,023	1,583	1,505
Time Deposits	35,705	35,793	38,001	39,428	37,673	14,999	9,568	10,095	6,841	6,171
LT Debt	7,446	4,213	4,004	3,570	1,764	886	177	183	122	182
Common Eqty.	5,223	4,881	4,993	4,538	4,234	1,808	1,117	1,005	721	665
% Ret. on Assets	1.3	1.1	1.2	1.4	1.2	1.3	1.1	1.0	1.1	1.1
% Ret. on Equity	18.1	15.6	16.2	19.6	17.8	18.2	15.4	16.1	16.1	16.2
% Loan Loss Resv.	1.7	1.8	1.8	1.8	1.9	3.1	1.7	1.8	1.3	1.3
% Loans/Deposits	118.4	94.9	100.9	95.9	89.0	86.8	83.7	83.1	80.8	81.6
% Equity to Assets	7.2	7.5	7.2	6.8	6.8	6.8	7.1	6.3	6.8	6.5

Data as orig. reptd.; bef. results of disc opers. and/or spec. items. Per share data adj. for stk. divs. as of ex-div. date. Bold denotes diluted EPS (FASB 128). E-Estimated. NA-Not Available. NM-Not Meaningful. NR-Not Ranked.

Office—127 Public Square, Cleveland, OH 44114-1306.**Tel**—(216) 689-6300. **Website**—http://www.key.com **Chrmn & CEO**—R. W. Gillespie. **Pres & COO**—H. L. Meyer III. **Sr EVP-CFO**—K. B. Somers. **Investor Contact**—Lee Irving. **Dirs**—C. D. Andrus, W. G. Bares, A. C. Bersticker, C. A. Cartwright, T. A. Commes, K. M. Curtis, J. C. Dimmer, R. W. Gillespie, S. R. Hardis, H. S. Hemingway, C. R. Hogan, D. J. McGregor, H. L. Meyer III, S. A. Minter, M. T. Moore, R. W. Pogue, R. B. Stafford, D. W. Sullivan, P. G. Ten Eyck II, N. B. Veeder.**Transfer Agent & Registrar**—Harris Trust and Savings Bank, Chicago. **Incorporated**—in Ohio in 1958.**Empl**— 24,711. **S&P Analyst:** Stephen R. Biggar

Kimberly-Clark

1298

NYSE Symbol **KMB**

In S&P 500

12-SEP-98

Industry:
Household Products
(Nondurables)

Summary: KMB makes consumer and personal care products, including Huggies diapers and Kleenex tissues. Operations were substantially expanded by the late 1995 purchase of Scott Paper.

S&P Opinion: Accumulate (★★★★)		
Recent Price • 37⅞	Yield • 2.6%	
52 Wk Range • 59⅜-35⅞	12-Mo. P/E • 27.4	

Quantitative Evaluations

Outlook
(1 Lowest—5 Highest)
• **3**

Fair Value
• **42⅝**

Risk
• **Low**

Earn./Div. Rank
• **A-**

Technical Eval.
• **Bearish** since 7/98

Rel. Strength Rank
(1 Lowest—99 Highest)
• **56**

Insider Activity
• **Neutral**

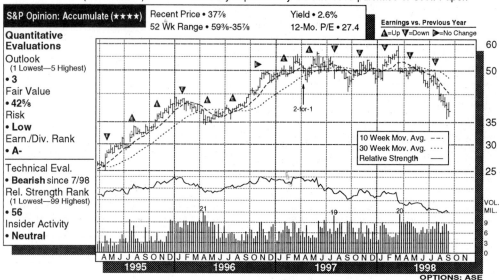

Earnings vs. Previous Year
▲=Up ▼=Down ▶=No Change

10 Week Mov. Avg. ---
30 Week Mov. Avg. ····
Relative Strength —

OPTIONS: ASE

Overview - 06-AUG-98

We expect slightly higher sales from comparable operations in 1998. Sales should be aided by the ongoing expansion of the personal care products business. Despite a competitive environment, KMB should also see some recovery in the North American away-from-home business, which was slowed in 1997 by a program to shift Scott Paper's (acquired in late 1995) commercial business to larger distributors. In addition, we see slightly higher average prices for KMB's overall products roster. Those positives will be mostly offset by lower sales volumes of consumer tissue in highly competitive European markets and in North America. Margins should be about flat. Profitability should benefit from cost and capacity reductions under a November 1997 restructuring program; the program should bring $200 million of annual savings by 2000, with about $100 million expected in 1998. Lessening troubles in away-from-home operations should also help, but European difficulties and higher interest charges will offset the improvement. Comparisons will be distorted by $0.82 a share of one-time charges in 1997. One-time charges of $0.07 a share taken in the first half of 1998 have been left out of our full-year EPS estimate.

Valuation - 06-AUG-98

The shares have lagged since late 1996, on disappointments in KMB's operating performance. The shortfalls have been mostly related to competitive pressures in Europe and a transition in the away-from-home tissue business. The slowdown has been discouraging, but we have been enthused about KMB's corrective efforts. They include a late 1997 restructuring program, and the March 1998 assignment of top North American managers to head up the European effort. We also have a positive outlook for KMB's business sectors. As such, we would still accumulate the shares.

Key Stock Statistics

S&P EPS Est. 1998	2.50	Tang. Bk. Value/Share	5.28
P/E on S&P Est. 1998	15.2	Beta	0.70
S&P EPS Est. 1999	2.95	Shareholders	56,200
Dividend Rate/Share	1.00	Market cap. (B)	$ 20.7
Shs. outstg. (M)	547.4	Inst. holdings	66%
Avg. daily vol. (M)	1.641		

Value of $10,000 invested 5 years ago: NA

Fiscal Year Ending Dec. 31

	1998	1997	1996	1995	1994	1993
Revenues (Million $)						
1Q	3,049	3,238	3,202	3,255	1,777	1,702
2Q	3,041	3,124	3,348	3,484	1,830	1,726
3Q	—	3,095	3,276	3,607	1,837	1,781
4Q	—	3,089	3,324	3,443	1,921	1,764
Yr.	—	12,547	13,149	13,789	7,364	6,973
Earnings Per Share ($)						
1Q	**0.53**	**0.64**	0.56	0.35	0.42	0.39
2Q	**0.54**	**0.63**	0.65	0.55	0.47	0.41
3Q	—	**0.57**	0.66	0.66	0.44	0.34
4Q	—	**-0.26**	0.61	-1.50	0.33	0.44
Yr.	—	**1.58**	2.49	0.06	1.67	1.59

Next earnings report expected: late October

Dividend Data (Dividends have been paid since 1935.)

Amount ($)	Date Decl.	Ex-Div. Date	Stock of Record	Payment Date
0.240	Nov. 20	Dec. 03	Dec. 05	Jan. 05 '98
0.250	Feb. 26	Mar. 04	Mar. 06	Apr. 02 '98
0.250	Apr. 30	Jun. 03	Jun. 05	Jul. 02 '98
0.250	Aug. 03	Sep. 02	Sep. 04	Oct. 02 '98

A Division of The McGraw-Hill Companies

Business Summary - 06-AUG-98

Best known for brand names such as Kleenex, Scott, Huggies and Kotex, Kimberly-Clark sells consumer products in some 150 countries. After operating as a broadly diversified enterprise, KMB underwent a major transition over the past few years. Kimberly now focuses strictly on global consumer products. After reaching its business strategy decision, KMB greatly expanded its consumer products operations through the December 1995 acquisition of Scott Paper for 238 million common shares (adjusted). KMB has also actively divested its non-core operations.

Operations outside of North America contributed 34% of sales and 14% of operating profits (before one-time charges) in 1997. KMB has operations in Europe, the Far East, Latin America, Africa and the Middle East.

The company's personal care products include disposable diapers, training and youth pants; feminine and adult incontinence care products; wet wipes; health care products; and related products. Tissue-based products include facial and bathroom tissue, paper towels and wipers for household and away-from-home use; pulp; and related products. Kimberly ranks as the second largest household and personal care products company in the U.S. and the world's largest tissue maker.

KMB became a major player in professional health care products when it acquired Tecnol Medical Products in December 1997, for $428 million in stock.

Kimberly spun off its tobacco-related paper businesses

in late 1995, and sold its air transportation services unit in 1995 and 1996. KMB has also been divesting its pulp and commodities paper operations. Internal pulp operations have met about 80% of Kimberly's virgin fiber needs, but because pulp is a capital-intensive business given to price and profit swings, KMB has taken actions to reduce its level of pulp integration. In March 1997, Kimberly sold its Alabama pulp and newsprint mill, for $602.7 million.

Given its disappointment with recent operating results, KMB announced a major restructuring plan in November 1997, which will be geared toward streamlining operations and tightening industry capacity. Under the plan, KMB will sell, close or downsize 18 manufacturing plants and reduce its workforce by about 5,000.

Kimberly recorded a 1.7% year to year EPS decline in the second quarter of 1998 (before one-time items), as ongoing weakness in its European business and adverse foreign currency effects outweighed better earnings in its North American consumer tissue and away-from-home businesses. The company noted that it had taken aggressive actions to address its difficulties in Europe, and believed that a turnaround was underway. One of KMB's largest initiatives has been its March 1998, naming of three top North American managers to head up the European effort. Kimberly also said that its previously announced restructuring plan for its overall business, and its aggressive productivity and cost reduction programs, led it to expect year-to-year operating pr ofit gains in the second half of the year.

Per Share Data ($)

(Year Ended Dec. 31)	1997	1996	1995	1994	1993	1992	1991	1990	1989	1988
Tangible Bk. Val.	6.35	7.96	6.50	8.10	7.63	6.82	7.87	7.07	6.46	5.79
Cash Flow	2.46	3.48	1.10	2.69	2.50	1.98	2.42	2.10	1.97	1.76
Earnings	1.58	2.49	0.06	1.67	1.59	1.07	1.59	1.35	1.31	1.18
Dividends	0.96	0.92	0.90	0.88	0.86	0.82	0.76	0.68	0.65	0.40
Payout Ratio	61%	37%	NM	53%	54%	76%	48%	50%	49%	34%
Prices - High	56⅞	49⅞	41½	30	30	31	31⅝	26⅛	21½	18⅞	16½
- Low	43¼	34⅜	23⅝	23½	22⅜	23⅛	19	15⅜	14⅜	11½
P/E Ratio - High	36	20	NM	18	19	29	16	16	14	14
- Low	27	14	NM	14	14	22	12	11	11	10

Income Statement Analysis (Million $)

	1997	1996	1995	1994	1993	1992	1991	1990	1989	1988
Revs.	12,547	13,149	13,789	7,364	6,973	7,091	6,777	6,407	5,734	5,393
Oper. Inc.	2,276	2,615	2,235	1,149	1,096	1,082	1,007	994	884	828
Depr.	491	561	582	330	296	289	266	240	211	188
Int. Exp.	165	201	254	139	132	118	117	108	88.0	88.0
Pretax Inc.	1,345	2,154	186	828	811	545	757	719	680	630
Eff. Tax Rate	32%	33%	18%	33%	35%	34%	31%	39%	36%	37%
Net Inc.	884	1,404	33.0	535	511	345	508	432	424	379

Balance Sheet & Other Fin. Data (Million $)

	1997	1996	1995	1994	1993	1992	1991	1990	1989	1988
Cash	91.0	83.0	222	24.0	35.0	41.0	43.0	60.0	164	84.0
Curr. Assets	3,489	3,539	3,814	1,810	1,675	1,683	1,475	1,397	1,443	1,236
Total Assets	11,266	11,846	11,439	6,716	6,381	6,029	5,650	5,284	4,923	4,268
Curr. Liab.	3,706	3,687	3,870	2,059	1,909	1,823	1,433	1,466	1,293	979
LT Debt	1,804	1,739	1,985	930	933	995	875	729	745	743
Common Eqty.	4,125	4,483	3,650	2,596	2,457	2,191	2,520	2,260	2,086	1,866
Total Cap.	6,673	7,233	6,594	4,218	4,042	3,797	4,128	3,711	3,580	3,288
Cap. Exp.	944	884	818	485	655	691	537	659	696	438
Cash Flow	1,375	1,965	615	865	807	634	774	672	635	566
Curr. Ratio	0.9	1.0	1.0	0.9	0.9	0.9	1.0	1.0	1.1	1.3
% LT Debt of Cap.	27.0	24.0	30.1	22.0	23.1	26.2	21.2	19.6	20.8	22.6
% Net Inc.of Revs.	7.0	10.7	1.0	7.3	7.3	4.9	7.5	6.7	7.4	7.0
% Ret. on Assets	7.6	12.1	1.0	8.2	8.2	5.9	9.3	8.5	9.2	9.3
% Ret. on Equity	20.5	34.5	1.0	21.2	22.0	14.6	21.3	20.0	21.4	22.0

Data as orig. reptd.; bef. results of disc. opers. and/or spec. items. Per share data adj. for stk. divs. as of ex-div. date. Bold denotes diluted EPS (FASB 128). E-Estimated. NA-Not Available. NM-Not Meaningful. NR-Not Ranked.

Office—P.O. Box 619100, Dallas, TX 75261-9100. **Tel**—(214) 830-1200. **Website**—http://www.kimberly-clark.com **Chrmn & CEO**—W. R. Sanders. **SVP & CFO**—J. W. Donehower. **Investor Contact**—Mike Masseth. **Dirs**—J. F. Bergstrom, P. S. J. Cafferty, P. J. Collins, R. W. Decherd, W. O. Fifield, C. X. Gonzalez, L. E. Levy, F. A. McPherson, L. Johnson Rice, W. R. Sanders, W. R. Schmitt, R. L. Tobias. **Transfer Agent & Registrar**—BankBoston N.A. **Incorporated**—in Delaware in 1928. **Empl**— 57,000. **S&P Analyst:** Michael W. Jaffe

12-SEP-98

Industry: Entertainment

Summary: This company is a leading distributor of first-run syndicated television programs, including "Wheel of Fortune," "Jeopardy!" and "The Oprah Winfrey Show."

S&P Opinion: Accumulate (★★★★)	Recent Price • 23⅛	Yield • Nil
	52 Wk Range • 30¾-20⅜	12-Mo. P/E • 12.7

Quantitative Evaluations

Outlook
(1 Lowest—5 Highest)
• **3**

Fair Value
• **25¼**

Risk
• **Low**

Earn./Div. Rank
• **B+**

Technical Eval.
• **Bearish** since 12/96

Rel. Strength Rank
(1 Lowest—99 Highest)
• **65**

Insider Activity
• **Unfavorable**

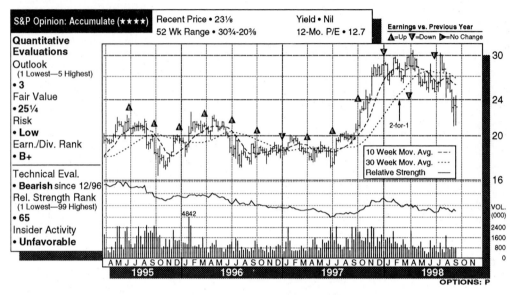

Earnings vs. Previous Year
▲=Up ▼=Down ▶=No Change

10 Week Mov. Avg. - - -
30 Week Mov. Avg. · · · ·
Relative Strength ——

2-for-1

VOL. (000)

OPTIONS: P

Overview - 24-AUG-98

This major distributor of first-run television shows receives most of its revenues and earnings from three programs: "Wheel of Fortune," "Jeopardy!" and "The Oprah Winfrey Show." KWP's operations also include producing and distributing a magazine show called "Inside Edition." In the fiscal year ending August 1998, earnings per share are expected to be down moderately from FY 97's level, but we look for FY 99 results to be boosted by the two new KWP-distributed shows that are slated to premiere around September 1998: a talk show that features TV star Roseanne Barr and a new version of the "Hollywood Squares" game show. Also, a new KWP-distributed variety/talk show starring Martin Short is planned for a fall 1999 debut. In May 1997, KWP paid a special dividend of $1.00 a share (adjusted for a 2-for-1 stock split in February 1998).

Valuation - 24-AUG-98

We recommend accumulating the stock of this television show distributor. We look for the shares to benefit from expectations for three new KWP shows which would begin airing within the next 13 months. Also, we are impressed by KWP's strong balance sheet and cash flow generation. The stock's below-market P/E is at least partly due to KWP's current profit dependence on three older TV shows, and uncertainty about the future use of KWP's cash and investments, which totaled about $725 million as of May 1998 (excluding about $130 million of recoupable advances). We expect that KWP is looking for attractive acquisition opportunities, but it's not clear what will result. Also, there could be further stock repurchase activity. As of early July 1998, KWP had authorization to buy back up to approximately seven million additional shares.

Key Stock Statistics

S&P EPS Est. 1998	1.80	Tang. Bk. Value/Share	10.71
P/E on S&P Est. 1998	12.8	Beta	0.88
S&P EPS Est. 1999	2.10	Shareholders	600
Dividend Rate/Share	Nil	Market cap. (B)	$ 1.7
Shs. outstg. (M)	73.2	Inst. holdings	71%
Avg. daily vol. (M)	0.160		

Value of $10,000 invested 5 years ago: $ 14,231

Fiscal Year Ending Aug. 31

	1998	1997	1996	1995	1994	1993
Revenues (Million $)						
1Q	172.9	164.3	162.1	147.1	193.1	169.7
2Q	173.9	175.2	176.8	143.7	137.1	113.1
3Q	168.0	166.8	165.8	142.6	111.9	87.94
4Q	—	165.1	158.7	140.7	38.62	103.6
Yr.	—	671.3	663.4	574.2	480.7	474.3
Earnings Per Share ($)						
1Q	**0.46**	0.47	0.58	0.38	0.51	0.49
2Q	**0.44**	0.48	0.47	0.40	0.32	0.31
3Q	**0.45**	0.47	0.46	0.39	0.26	0.24
4Q	**E0.46**	0.48	0.47	0.41	0.08	0.28
Yr.	**E1.80**	1.91	1.99	1.57	1.17	1.32

Next earnings report expected: late October

Dividend Data (Dividends have been paid since 1997.)

Amount ($)	Date Decl.	Ex-Div. Date	Stock of Record	Payment Date
2-for-1	Dec. 16	Feb. 18	Feb. 03	Feb. 17 '98

A Division of The **McGraw·Hill** Companies

Business Summary - 24-AUG-98

This television show distributor is looking to expand its already formidable presence in program syndication. Two new KWP-distributed shows are slated to debut around September 1998. One of them would be a talk show featuring Roseanne Barr, and the other would be a new version of the game show "Hollywood Squares." Also, a new KWP-distributed variety/talk show, starring Martin Short, is planned for a debut in September or the fall of 1999. We expect that each of these three new shows would be co-produced by KWP. Other uses for the company's cash equivalents and investments, which had a total value of about $725 million at the end of May 1998, may include one or more acquisitions. In May 1997, KWP paid a special dividend of $1.00 a share (adj.).

Three popular KWP-distributed programs -- "The Oprah Winfrey Show," "Wheel of Fortune" and "Jeopardy!" -- accounted for 77% of the company's revenues in FY 97 (Aug.). KWP distributes (markets) these shows to individual TV stations around the U.S., through a process known as syndication. It has presold each of these hits to TV stations covering most of the U.S. through at least the 1998-99 season. The company's long-term approach is indicated by its April 1997 announcement that commitments had been received from TV stations in all 25 of the top U.S. television markets to carry "Wheel"

and "Jeopardy" through the 2001-02 television season. KWP also produces and distributes a syndicated magazine show called "Inside Edition." Another magazine show, called "American Journal," was to be discontinued after the 1997-98 season.

Merv Griffin Enterprises is producer of "Wheel of Fortune" and "Jeopardy!," and KWP has exclusive distribution rights for these shows as long as it has sufficient broadcast commitments to cover their production and distribution costs. The agreements have prohibited KWP from distributing, on a similar basis, game shows of other producers while it is distributing "Wheel of Fortune" and "Jeopardy!." "The Oprah Winfrey Show" is produced by a business controlled by Ms. Winfrey, who has agreed to continue hosting and producing this program through the 1999-2000 broadcast season..

Revenues from distribution of first-run syndicated programs come from two sources. KWP typically receives license fees from individual TV stations and receives an amount of commercial time that it sells to advertisers. The company also distributes a library of movies and other TV programs to domestic TV stations. These include various Sherlock Holmes and Charlie Chan films and "The Little Rascals."

As of November 1997, officers and directors owned or had exercisable options to acquire more than 17 million KWP common shares (adjusted for a 1998 2-for-1 stock split).

Per Share Data ($)

(Year Ended Aug. 31)	1997	1996	1995	1994	1993	1992	1991	1990	1989	1988
Tangible Bk. Val.	10.71	9.89	7.83	6.25	5.29	4.49	3.17	1.94	0.82	-0.10
Cash Flow	1.93	2.00	1.57	1.18	1.34	1.23	1.25	1.15	1.02	0.78
Earnings	1.91	1.99	1.57	1.17	1.32	1.22	1.19	1.07	0.97	0.76
Dividends	1.00	Nil	Nil	Nil	Nil	Nil	Nil	Nil	Nil	Nil
Payout Ratio	52%	Nil	Nil	Nil	Nil	Nil	Nil	Nil	Nil	Nil
Prices - High	29¼	22⅝	22¼	22⅛	21⅞	17⅝	17¼	15	13½	8⅞
- Low	17	17⅛	16¼	16⅝	15⅞	11⅛	10¾	9⅛	7⅝	5¼
P/E Ratio - High	15	11	14	19	17	15	14	14	14	12
- Low	9	9	10	14	12	9	9	8	8	7

Income Statement Analysis (Million $)

	1997	1996	1995	1994	1993	1992	1991	1990	1989	1988
Revs.	671	663	574	481	474	503	476	454	396	280
Oper. Inc.	193	192	163	128	152	154	159	148	136	105
Depr.	1.2	0.8	0.6	0.5	1.4	1.1	5.1	5.5	3.9	1.1
Int. Exp.	NM	NM	NM	Nil	Nil	Nil	11.7	11.3	9.5	3.9
Pretax Inc.	222	232	183	141	163	157	154	140	125	102
Eff. Tax Rate	35%	35%	36%	37%	37%	40%	40%	40%	41%	41%
Net Inc.	143	150	117	88.0	102	94.9	93.2	84.1	73.2	60.7

Balance Sheet & Other Fin. Data (Million $)

	1997	1996	1995	1994	1993	1992	1991	1990	1989	1988
Cash	318	345	447	342	300	311	242	153	47.0	21.0
Curr. Assets	704	636	589	405	428	428	364	269	156	90.0
Total Assets	902	854	687	570	536	498	501	407	302	117
Curr. Liab.	118	116	111	110	141	155	238	144	123	92.0
LT Debt	NM	NM	NM	Nil	Nil	Nil	Nil	90.7	89.5	30.0
Common Eqty.	784	738	576	459	394	343	242	146	62.0	-7.0
Total Cap.	784	738	576	459	394	343	263	261	177	25.0
Cap. Exp.	8.1	0.4	2.3	0.6	1.7	0.3	4.3	4.2	2.9	0.4
Cash Flow	145	151	118	89.0	103	96.0	98.3	89.6	77.1	61.8
Curr. Ratio	6.0	5.5	5.3	3.7	3.0	2.8	1.5	1.9	1.3	1.0
% LT Debt of Cap.	NM	NM	NM	Nil	Nil	Nil	Nil	34.7	50.6	NM
% Net Inc.of Revs.	21.4	22.7	20.4	18.4	21.5	18.9	19.6	18.5	18.5	21.7
% Ret. on Assets	16.3	19.5	17.0	16.1	19.9	19.0	20.5	23.7	35.0	53.8
% Ret. on Equity	18.8	22.9	20.4	20.8	28.0	32.4	47.9	80.6	265.6	454.8

Data as orig. reptd.; bef. results of disc. opers. and/or spec. items. Per share data adj. for stk. divs. as of ex-div. date. Bold denotes diluted EPS (FASB 128). E-Estimated. NA-Not Available. NM-Not Meaningful. NR-Not Ranked.

Office—12400 Wilshire Blvd., Suite 1200, Los Angeles, CA 90025.**Tel**—(310) 826-1108. **Chrmn**—Roger King. **Vice Chrmn & CEO**—M. King. **Pres & COO**—J. Haimovitz. **VP & Secy**—D. King. **SVP & CFO**—S. A. LoCascio. **Dirs**—R. G. Chambers, J. Chaseman, D. King, M. King, Richard King, Roger King, F. D. Rosen **Transfer Agent**—First Chicago Trust Co. of New York, Jersey City, NJ. **Incorporated**—in Delaware in 1984.**Empl**— 487.
S&P Analyst: Tom Graves, CFA

STANDARD &POOR'S
STOCK REPORTS

KLA-Tencor Corp.

4318C

Nasdaq Symbol **KLAC**

In S&P 500

12-SEP-98

Industry: Equipment (Semiconductor)

Summary: KLA-Tencor is the world's leading manufacturer of yield monitoring and process control systems for the semiconductor industry.

S&P Opinion: Buy (★★★★★)	Recent Price • 24½	Yield • Nil
	52 Wk Range • 75¼-21¼	12-Mo. P/E • 16.1

Quantitative Evaluations

Outlook (1 Lowest—5 Highest)
• **5**

Fair Value
• **38¼**

Risk
• **High**

Earn./Div. Rank
• **B-**

Technical Eval.
• **Bearish** since 11/97

Rel. Strength Rank (1 Lowest—99 Highest)
• **53**

Insider Activity
• **NA**

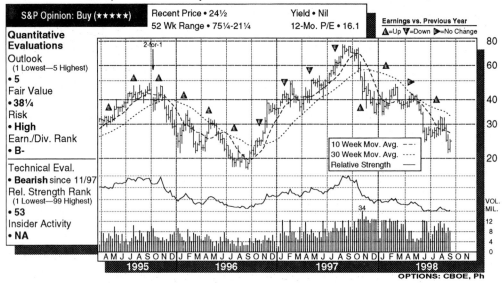

Earnings vs. Previous Year ▲=Up ▼=Down ▶=No Change

10 Week Mov. Avg. – – –
30 Week Mov. Avg. – – –
Relative Strength ——

OPTIONS: CBOE, Ph

Overview - 30-JUL-98

Near-term operating results are likely to trend lower, reflecting the impact of the Asian financial crisis. Chip makers in that region have cut capital spending plans and pushed out orders for equipment. Despite signs of an industry-wide slowdown, we expect KLAC to outperform its peers, on the strength of its yield management and process control systems. Sales of these products are not as dependent on new fab construction as other semiconductor manufacturing equipment and, therefore, the company has better visibility than many of its peers. Furthermore, KLAC has a healthy backlog of orders to sustain it during this period of uncertainty. We expect margins to come under pressure on the anticipated decline in volume, though favorable changes in the product mix should dampen the impact. Overall, however, we look for EPS of $0.96 in FY 99 (Jun.), down from the $1.76 recorded in FY 98 (excluding non-recurring charges).

Valuation - 30-JUL-98

The shares of this semiconductor equipment maker have fallen sharply in recent months, reflecting economic turmoil in Asia and industry-wide overcapacity. While these factors increase the risk of continued order pushouts and cancellations, we believe investors' focus will soon shift toward the company's prospects for strong growth in the latter part of 1999 and into 2000. Thus, we recommend purchase of the shares. KLAC holds a dominant position in yield monitoring and process control, and it is extremely well positioned to realize strong revenue and earnings gains as chip makers convert capacity to leading edge 0.25 micron technology. Despite near-term uncertainty in the overall chip equipment market, we believe the shares are attractively valued for aggressive investors, at 2.1X trailing 12 month sales.

Key Stock Statistics

S&P EPS Est. 1999	0.96	Tang. Bk. Value/Share	11.68
P/E on S&P Est. 1999	25.5	Beta	1.83
Dividend Rate/Share	Nil	Shareholders	1,200
Shs. outstg. (M)	86.9	Market cap. (B)	$ 2.1
Avg. daily vol. (M)	1.919	Inst. holdings	69%

Value of $10,000 invested 5 years ago: $ 40,000

Fiscal Year Ending Jun. 30

	1998	1997	1996	1995	1994	1993
Revenues (Million $)						
1Q	312.4	261.1	149.1	83.18	51.90	38.40
2Q	326.4	242.2	165.8	104.7	57.09	38.70
3Q	274.2	252.3	187.5	118.1	62.67	42.24
4Q	253.4	276.2	192.6	136.4	72.08	47.88
Yr.	1,166	1,032	694.9	442.4	243.7	167.2
Earnings Per Share ($)						
1Q	0.56	0.40	0.52	0.27	0.10	0.02
2Q	**0.59**	0.40	0.57	0.02	0.15	0.04
3Q	**0.43**	0.43	0.61	0.43	0.20	0.05
4Q	**0.04**	0.01	0.61	0.47	0.23	0.08
Yr.	**1.52**	1.24	2.31	1.20	0.68	0.17

Next earnings report expected: late October

Dividend Data

No cash has been paid. A two-for-one stock split was effected in 1995.

A Division of The McGraw-Hill Companies

KLA-Tencor Corporation

Business Summary - 30-JUL-98

Formed through the April 1997 merger of two 20-year-old companies, KLA Instruments and Tencor instruments, KLA-Tencor (KLAC) is the world's leading manufacturer of yield management and process monitoring systems for the semiconductor industry. The company is one of a handful of U.S. semiconductor equipment companies whose revenues exceed $1 billion a year -- KLAC's reached $1.03 billion in FY 97 (Jun.).

Maximizing yields, or the number of good die per wafer, is a key goal in manufacturing integrated circuits (ICs). Higher yields increase revenues obtained for each semiconductor wafer processed. As IC linewidths decrease, yields become more sensitive to the size and density of defects. KLAC's systems are used to improve yields by identifying defects, analyzing them to determine process problems, and, after corrective action has been taken, monitoring subsequent results to ensure that the problem has been contained. Monitoring and analysis often take place at several points in the fabrication process, as wafers move through a production cycle consisting of hundreds of processing steps. With in-line systems, corrections can be made while the wafer is still in the production line, rather than waiting days for end-of-process testing and feedback.

The company's wafer inspection systems include un-patterned and patterned wafer inspection tools used to find, count and characterize particles and pattern defects on wafers both in engineering applications and in-line at various stages during the semiconductor manufacturing process. In 1997, KLAC introduced the 2138, a new patterned wafer inspection system designed to address chemical mechanical planarization and other inspection applications. The 2138 extends the company's full line of in-line monitoring systems and is based on KLAC's 2135, which was introduced in 1996.

The Reticle Inspection Business (RAPID) Unit's 351 Inspection System manages the quality of photomasks and reticles (used in copying circuit designs onto an IC during the photolithography process) throughout their useful lives.

The company's film measurement division produces both film thickness and resistivity measurement tools. KLAC's metrology products measure the widths of circuit lines and the alignment of patterns from layer to layer in the process. The optical metrology product line is known as the 5000 series. To meet the need for measuring sub-half micron features, KLAC introduced an electron-beam metrology system, the 8100 CD-SEM, in June 1996.

The company sells its systems to virtually all of the world's semiconductor manufacturers. International sales accounted for about 65% of KLAC's revenues in FY 97.

Per Share Data ($)

(Year Ended Jun. 30)	1998	1997	1996	1995	1994	1993	1992	1991	1990	1989
Tangible Bk. Val.	NA	12.10	10.55	8.07	4.99	2.93	2.77	3.10	3.40	3.11
Cash Flow	NA	1.85	2.62	1.42	0.93	0.42	-0.16	0.31	0.50	0.51
Earnings	1.52	1.24	2.31	1.20	0.69	0.17	-0.45	0.07	0.26	0.33
Dividends	Nil	Nil	Nil	Nil	Nil	Nil	Nil	Nil	Nil	Nil
Payout Ratio	Nil	Nil	Nil	Nil	Nil	Nil	Nil	Nil	Nil	Nil
Prices - High	48	76⁷/₈	40	48³/₄	27	14¹/₈	6⁷/₈	7¹/₄	6¹/₄	6⁷/₈
- Low	24¹/₄	33⁵/₈	17¹/₂	23¹/₄	12¹/₄	5¹/₈	3	4	2⁷/₈	3³/₄
P/E Ratio - High	32	62	17	41	40	81	NM	NM	24	21
- Low	16	27	8	19	18	29	NM	NM	11	12

Income Statement Analysis (Million $)

Revs.	NA	1,032	695	442	244	167	156	148	168	165
Oper. Inc.	NA	259	194	118	50.8	20.4	5.3	14.1	22.7	24.5
Depr.	NA	52.3	16.3	10.6	10.7	9.6	10.7	9.1	8.7	6.4
Int. Exp.	NA	Nil	1.4	2.4	2.0	3.4	3.9	3.3	0.6	1.0
Pretax Inc.	NA	174	189	88.8	40.2	9.3	-16.3	3.5	14.0	18.0
Eff. Tax Rate	NA	39%	36%	34%	25%	25%	NM	31%	33%	35%
Net Inc.	NA	105	121	58.6	30.2	7.0	-16.6	2.4	9.4	11.7

Balance Sheet & Other Fin. Data (Million $)

Cash	NA	279	124	119	139	52.4	23.7	31.3	42.1	26.9
Curr. Assets	NA	860	494	361	278	152	135	141	145	126
Total Assets	NA	1,343	713	546	322	199	188	198	179	161
Curr. Liab.	NA	325	169	133	66.0	58.0	50.8	49.6	45.7	42.3
LT Debt	NA	Nil	Nil	Nil	20.0	20.0	24.0	24.0	Nil	Nil
Common Eqty.	Nil	1,015	537	404	227	114	103	113	122	111
Total Cap.	NA	1,019	544	413	256	141	138	148	134	118
Cap. Exp.	NA	56.8	39.1	19.0	10.5	5.8	5.1	33.6	11.3	10.7
Cash Flow	NA	158	137	69.3	40.9	16.6	-5.9	11.5	18.1	18.1
Curr. Ratio	NA	2.6	2.9	2.7	4.2	2.6	2.7	2.8	3.2	3.0
% LT Debt of Cap.	NA	Nil	NM	NM	7.8	14.2	17.4	16.2	Nil	Nil
% Net Inc.of Revs.	Nil	10.2	17.5	13.2	12.3	4.2	NM	1.6	5.6	7.1
% Ret. on Assets	NA	11.5	19.2	13.5	11.5	3.5	NM	1.3	5.5	7.9
% Ret. on Equity	NA	15.3	25.7	18.5	17.6	6.3	NM	2.0	8.0	11.2

Data as orig. reptd.; bef. results of disc. opers. and/or spec. items. Per share data adj. for stk. divs. as of ex-div. date. Bold denotes diluted EPS (FASB 128). E-Estimated. NA-Not Available. NM-Not Meaningful. NR-Not Ranked.

Office—160 Rio Robles, San Jose, CA 95134. Tel—(408) 434-4200. Website—http://www.kla-tencor.com Chrmn & CEO—K. Levy. Pres & COO—K. L. Schroeder. VP-Fin & CFO—R. J. Boehlke. Secy—P. E. Kreutz. Dirs—E. W. Barnholt, L. J. Chamberlain, K. Levy, R. E. Lorenzini, Y. Nishi, S. Rubinovitz, K. L. Schroeder, D. Tellefsen. Transfer Agent & Registrar—First National Bank of Boston. Incorporated—in Delaware in 1975. Empl— 2,500. S&P Analyst: B. McGovern

Knight Ridder

1308

NYSE Symbol **KRI**

In S&P 500

12-SEP-98

Industry:
Publishing (Newspapers)

Summary: Knight Ridder is the nation's second largest newspaper publisher, with products in print and online, and has equity holdings in newsprint mills.

S&P Opinion: Hold (★★★)	Recent Price • 47¼	Yield • 1.7%
	52 Wk Range • 59⅝-44⅞	12-Mo. P/E • 11.9

Quantitative Evaluations

Outlook (1 Lowest—5 Highest)
• **3+**

Fair Value
• **54⅜**

Risk
• **Low**

Earn./Div. Rank
• **A-**

Technical Eval.
• **Bullish** since 7/98

Rel. Strength Rank (1 Lowest—99 Highest)
• **69**

Insider Activity
• **Neutral**

Earnings vs. Previous Year
▲=Up ▼=Down ▶=No Change

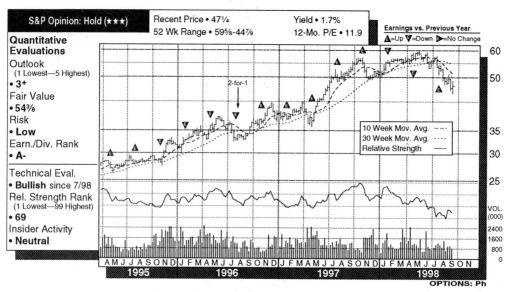

- 10 Week Mov. Avg. ----
- 30 Week Mov. Avg. ·····
- Relative Strength —

2-for-1

OPTIONS: Ph

Overview - 23-JUN-98

Higher revenues from continuing operations in 1998 will largely reflect newspaper acquisitions and healthy advertising demand. Moderately higher average newsprint prices in 1998 will be more than offset by a smaller rise in labor and other costs, stemming from widespread cost-cutting and productivity measures undertaken earlier, and strong improvement in Philadelphia and Detroit. Comparisons will also benefit from the recent sales of five lower-margined newspapers. Equity earnings from newsprint should advance in 1998. Dilution from the purchase of the four Disney newspapers is expected to be less than 10%. Helped by a 15-million share buyback program, we expect 1998 EPS to rise nonetheless, to $2.60, from the $2.30 reported for 1997, excluding one-time gains aggregating $1.61.

Valuation - 23-JUN-98

We recently downgraded our opinion on KRI to "hold" from "accumulate." The shares, which slightly outperformed other newspaper stocks and the general market in the five months through the end of May, are expected to be market performers in upcoming months. A generally favorable operating environment, characterized by moderately improving advertising revenues, reasonable newsprint price hikes anticipated, and strong numbers coming out of Detroit, should continue through 1999. KRI management is taking many steps to boost business and profitability over the longer term. Divestitures during 1997 of cable operations and financial services have transformed the company almost exclusively into a newspaper publisher. Although that strategy subjects the company to the cyclical vagaries of newspaper publishing, the newspapers are located in a wide cross-section of U.S. markets, providing some insulation from regional economic differences.

Key Stock Statistics

S&P EPS Est. 1998	2.60	Tang. Bk. Value/Share	NM
P/E on S&P Est. 1998	18.2	Beta	0.79
S&P EPS Est. 1999	2.90	Shareholders	11,300
Dividend Rate/Share	0.80	Market cap. (B)	$ 3.7
Shs. outstg. (M)	78.8	Inst. holdings	72%
Avg. daily vol. (M)	0.188		

Value of $10,000 invested 5 years ago: $ 18,416

Fiscal Year Ending Dec. 31

	1998	1997	1996	1995	1994	1993
Revenues (Million $)						
1Q	743.9	600.8	697.7	674.6	630.9	583.9
2Q	779.3	711.6	717.0	687.5	661.5	621.7
3Q	—	748.8	653.8	638.0	642.6	593.1
4Q	—	815.6	706.4	751.8	713.9	652.6
Yr.	—	2,877	2,775	2,752	2,649	2,451
Earnings Per Share ($)						
1Q	**1.02**	**1.85**	0.24	0.34	0.28	0.21
2Q	**0.68**	**0.60**	0.43	0.94	0.46	0.39
3Q	—	**0.69**	1.31	0.07	0.34	0.28
4Q	—	**0.84**	0.77	0.32	0.49	0.47
Yr.	**E2.60**	**3.91**	1.90	1.67	1.57	1.34

Next earnings report expected: late October

Dividend Data (Dividends have been paid since 1941.)

Amount ($)	Date Decl.	Ex-Div. Date	Stock of Record	Payment Date
0.200	Oct. 28	Nov. 07	Nov. 12	Nov. 24 '97
0.200	Jan. 27	Feb. 09	Feb. 11	Feb. 23 '98
0.200	Apr. 28	May. 11	May. 13	May. 25 '98
0.200	Jul. 28	Aug. 10	Aug. 12	Aug. 24 '98

A Division of The McGraw-Hill Companies

Business Summary - 23-JUN-98

At a time when most newspaper publishers see fit to diversify, Knight Ridder (formerly Knight-Ridder Inc.) narrowed its focus in 1997 with the sales of virtually all non-newspaper businesses, and a major purchase of four newspapers from the Walt Disney Company. With those moves, the company became the largest publicly-owned, pure-play newspaper publisher in the U.S.

Based on circulation, KRI is the second largest newspaper publisher in the U.S. The company publishes 31 daily newspapers in 28 U.S. markets, with 9.2 million readers daily and 12.8 million on Sunday. It also maintains 33 associated Web sites and has investments in two newsprint mills. The larger papers include the Miami Herald, Philadelphia Inquirer, Philadelphia Daily News, Detroit Free Press, The Kansas City Star, Forth Worth Star-Telegram, San Jose Mercury and San Jose News.

KRI sold its Business Information Services (BIS) division to M.A.I.D plc on November 12, 1997, for $420 million. The operations of BIS included the Dialog and Data-Star information retrieval services; and real-time financial news and pricing information through such products as FuturesCenter, MoneyCenter and TradeCenter. Technimetrics, a creator of global financial marketing databases and consulting services for investor relations, is also up for sale.

In May 1997, KRI acquired four newspapers from Walt Disney Co. for $1.65 billion, comprised of 1,754,930 shares of Series B convertible preferred stock and the assumption of $990 million of bank debt. Combined circulation of the papers, located in Kansas City, Fort Worth, Belleville (Illinois), and Wilkes-Barre, is about 630,000 daily and 898,000 Sunday. KRI also acquired three additional newspapers over the course of 1997.

During 1997, the company purchased more than 13.8 million shares of its common stock on the open market. In the three months through March 1998, Knight Ridder purchased an additional 3.7 million shares.

KRI posted a net after-tax gain of $0.45 a share in the first quarter of 1998 from the sale of the remainder of its TKR Cable Co. interests to its joint-venture partner, Tele-Communications Inc., and from the sale of a newspaper.

KRI posted a net after-tax gain of $1.36 a share in the first quarter of 1997 from the sale of most of its TKR Cable Co. interests to its joint-venture partner, Tele-Communications Inc.; a gain of $0.24 in the third quarter on the exchange of the Daily Camera in Boulder, Colo; and a $0.10 gain on the sale of four newspapers in the fourth quarter.

Per Share Data ($) (Year Ended Dec. 31)	1997	1996	1995	1994	1993	1992	1991	1990	1989	1988
Tangible Bk. Val.	NM	2.29	1.51	4.79	4.81	4.38	4.08	1.66	1.67	0.59
Cash Flow	5.46	4.45	3.18	2.75	2.46	2.35	2.33	2.55	2.75	2.13
Earnings	3.91	2.75	1.67	1.57	1.34	1.32	1.27	1.47	1.72	1.29
Dividends	0.80	0.79	0.74	0.73	0.70	0.70	0.70	0.67	0.62	0.57
Payout Ratio	20%	29%	44%	46%	52%	53%	57%	44%	36%	41%
Prices - High	57 1/8	42	33 3/8	30 1/2	32 1/2	32 1/8	28 3/4	29	29 1/4	23 7/8
- Low	35 3/4	29 7/8	25 1/4	23 1/4	25 3/8	25 3/4	21 7/8	18 1/2	21 1/2	17 7/8
P/E Ratio - High	15	15	20	19	24	24	23	20	17	18
- Low	9	11	15	15	19	19	17	13	13	14
Income Statement Analysis (Million $)										
Revs.	2,877	2,775	2,752	2,649	2,451	2,330	2,237	2,305	2,268	2,083
Oper. Inc.	663	501	391	459	409	402	353	410	430	366
Depr.	157	166	152	128	124	113	110	110	108	95.0
Int. Exp.	97.3	73.2	60.0	44.6	45.1	52.4	68.8	71.8	84.6	62.5
Pretax Inc.	705	467	288	300	249	245	210	252	300	240
Eff. Tax Rate	42%	43%	42%	40%	38%	38%	37%	39%	38%	37%
Net Inc.	397	268	167	171	148	146	132	149	180	147
Balance Sheet & Other Fin. Data (Million $)										
Cash	160	22.9	26.0	9.3	23.0	97.1	26.2	26.2	60.6	32.2
Curr. Assets	641	566	503	423	401	461	370	389	416	687
Total Assets	4,355	2,900	3,006	2,447	2,431	2,458	2,333	2,270	2,135	2,357
Curr. Liab.	599	555	438	421	406	405	336	314	346	603
LT Debt	1,599	771	1,001	412	410	496	557	804	661	727
Common Eqty.	1,550	1,132	1,111	1,225	1,243	1,182	1,149	895	917	822
Total Cap.	3,432	2,079	2,278	1,776	1,793	1,795	1,908	1,886	1,737	1,692
Cap. Exp.	107	127	121	67.0	71.0	101	167	246	125	115
Cash Flow	553	434	319	299	272	259	242	259	288	242
Curr. Ratio	1.1	1.0	1.1	1.0	1.0	1.1	1.1	1.2	1.2	1.1
% LT Debt of Cap.	46.6	37.9	43.9	23.2	22.9	27.6	29.2	42.6	38.0	43.0
% Net Inc.of Revs.	13.8	9.7	6.1	6.5	6.0	6.3	5.9	6.5	7.9	7.0
% Ret. on Assets	10.9	9.1	6.1	7.1	6.1	6.0	5.5	6.9	8.1	7.0
% Ret. on Equity	29.6	23.9	14.3	14.1	12.2	12.4	12.5	16.8	21.0	17.6

Data as orig. reptd.; bef. results of disc. opers. and/or spec. items. Per share data adj. for stk. divs. as of ex-div. date. Bold denotes diluted EPS (FASB 128). E-Estimated. NA-Not Available. NM-Not Meaningful. NR-Not Ranked.

Office—One Herald Plaza, Miami, FL 33132. **Tel**—(305) 376-3800. **Chrmn & CEO**—P. A. Ridder. **VP & Secy**—D. C. Harris. **Sr VP & CFO**—R. Jones. **VP & Investor Contact**—Polk Laffoon IV (305) 376-3838. **Dirs**—J. I. Cash Jr., J. R. Challinor, A. H. Chapman Jr.,K. F. Fieldstein, T. P. Gerrity, P. C. Goldmark Jr., B. B. Hauptfuhrer, J. Hill Jr., M. K. Oshman, T. L. Phillips, P. A. Ridder, R. L. Tobias, G. F. Valdes-Fauli, J. L. Weinberg.**Transfer Agent & Registrar**—Chase Bank, NYC. **Incorporated**—in Ohio in 1974. **Empl**— 22,000. **S&P Analyst:** William H. Donald

STANDARD &POOR'S
STOCK REPORTS

Kohl's Corp.

1309J

NYSE Symbol **KSS**

In S&P 500

12-SEP-98

Industry: Retail (Department Stores)

Summary: This company operates more than 190 specialty department stores, primarily in the Midwest, featuring moderately priced apparel, shoes, accessories and products for the home.

S&P Opinion: Hold (★★★)	Recent Price • 45	Yield • Nil
	52 Wk Range • 58⅞-29	12-Mo. P/E • 43.8

Earnings vs. Previous Year
▲=Up ▼=Down ▶=No Change

Quantitative Evaluations

Outlook
(1 Lowest—5 Highest)
• **3⁻**

Fair Value
• **52¾**

Risk
• **Average**

Earn./Div. Rank
• **NR**

Technical Eval.
• **Bullish** since 8/95

Rel. Strength Rank
(1 Lowest—99 Highest)
• **61**

Insider Activity
• **Neutral**

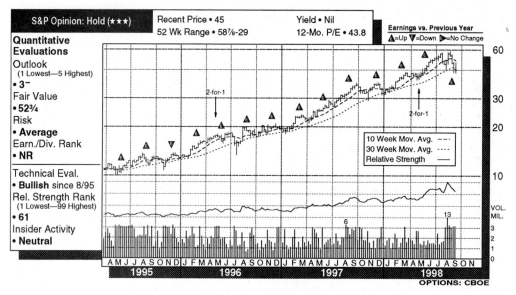

10 Week Mov. Avg. ---
30 Week Mov. Avg. ····
Relative Strength —

VOL. MIL.

1995   1996   1997   1998

OPTIONS: CBOE

Overview - 08-JUN-98

Sales should increase about 24% in FY 99 (Jan.), boosted by moderate same-store sales growth of about 5% and by the planned opening of 32 new stores. Gross margins should widen slightly on the higher volume, partly offset by competitive pricing. With a growing store base, the company's expense ratios will be better leveraged. Operating income should increase more than 20%. Interest expense will be higher, on increased debt to fund the company's aggressive capital expenditure program. The company is plowing its strong cash flow and expanded borrowings into expansion. Current working capital, cash flows from operations and revolving credit will be able to satisfy current capital expenditure programs. Capital expenditures in FY 99 should total about $220 million. The company plans to have a total of 300 stores by the end of the year 2000. The shares were split 2-for-1 in April 1998.

Valuation - 08-JUN-98

The shares of this well-managed regional retailer appear fairly valued at current lofty levels. Over the past three years, Kohl's has continued to gain market share, with strong same-store sales gains, and to outperform most other family apparel retailers by a wide margin. The company's aggressive store opening program, particularly its entry into the Northeast, its low cost structure and its conservative balance sheet continue to bode well for earnings gains over the next few years. The company's core earnings growth rate is in the range of 20% to 22%, and this appears to be already reflected in the stock price. Nevertheless, the shares are a worthwhile holding for long-term capital gains.

Key Stock Statistics

S&P EPS Est. 1999	1.10	Tang. Bk. Value/Share	5.94
P/E on S&P Est. 1999	41.0	Beta	0.84
S&P EPS Est. 2000	1.35	Shareholders	4,500
Dividend Rate/Share	Nil	Market cap. (B)	$ 7.1
Shs. outstg. (M)	158.0	Inst. holdings	74%
Avg. daily vol. (M)	1.035		

Value of $10,000 invested 5 years ago: $ 60,082

Fiscal Year Ending Jan. 31

	1999	1998	1997	1996	1995	1994
Revenues (Million $)						
1Q	744.6	600.5	468.6	368.4	308.0	250.3
2Q	758.8	623.9	474.6	363.5	292.4	257.4
3Q	—	757.8	598.0	486.8	389.5	341.0
4Q	—	1,078	846.9	707.0	564.3	457.1
Yr.	—	3,060	2,388	1,926	1,554	1,306
Earnings Per Share ($)						
1Q	**0.17**	**0.10**	0.10	0.08	0.08	0.05
2Q	**0.19**	0.14	0.10	0.08	0.07	0.05
3Q	**E0.25**	0.21	0.15	0.05	0.10	0.09
4Q	**E0.51**	**0.45**	0.35	0.28	0.23	0.19
Yr.	**E1.10**	**0.91**	0.69	0.49	0.47	0.38

Next earnings report expected: mid November

Dividend Data

Amount ($)	Date Decl.	Ex-Div. Date	Stock of Record	Payment Date
2-for-1	Mar. 10	Apr. 28	Apr. 10	Apr. 27 '98

Business Summary - 08-JUN-98

One of the fastest-growing family department store chains in the U.S., Kohl's has expanded from 40 stores in 1986 to 197 as of May 1998. From its midwestern roots, Kohl's now operates stores in the mid-Atlantic as far south as Charlotte, North Carolina. By the end of 1998, it expects to operate 214 units. Most stores are in strip shopping centers, but the company operates stores in malls and freestanding units as well.

The stores feature quality, moderately priced national brand merchandise, including apparel, shoes, accessories, soft home products and housewares. Stores are designed to help customers shop without assistance, and feature simple layouts and in-store signs. The middle-income customer is the company's target market. Stores offer dominant assortments of merchandise in complete selections of styles, colors and sizes. As a complement to its national brands, KSS offers private-label merchandise under several names. It plans to increase private-label sales to about 20%. The company phased out its low-margin electronics business in 1996 in order to add higher-margin apparel lines.

The company's strategy is to maintain a low cost structure, enabling it to keep prices low and to boost profitability. Central to this are lean staffing levels, sophisticated management systems and operating efficiencies from centralized buying, advertising and distribution.

The company planned to open about 32 stores in 1998. The company's store expansion emphasizes existing markets, where it can leverage advertising, purchasing, transportation and other regional expenses, and contiguous markets, where it can extend regional facilities.

In August 1997, the company issued 9.1 million (adjusted) new shares of its common stock; net proceeds of about $282.9 million were earmarked for financing store growth. The company anticipates that current working capital, cash flows from operations, its revolving credit facility, short-term trade credit and other lending facilities will be able to satisfy its current operating needs, planned capital expenditures and debt service requirements.

Net sales increased 24% in the first quarter of FY 99, reflecting the addition of new stores, and same-store sales gains of 12.0%. Operating income increased 31%, reflecting the increased sales and improved gross margin.

Per Share Data ($)

(Year Ended Jan. 31)	1998	1997	1996	1995	1994	1993	1992	1991	1990	1989
Tangible Bk. Val.	5.76	3.13	2.37	1.80	1.44	1.03	0.54	0.20	NA	NA
Cash Flow	1.27	0.99	0.72	0.65	0.54	0.35	0.31	NA	NA	NA
Earnings	0.90	0.69	0.49	0.47	0.38	0.22	0.15	0.17	NA	NA
Dividends	Nil	Nil	Nil	Nil	Nil	Nil	Nil	NA	NA	NA
Payout Ratio	Nil	Nil	Nil	Nil	Nil	Nil	Nil	NA	NA	NA
Cal. Yrs.	1997	1996	1995	1994	1993	1992	1991	1990	1989	1988
Prices - High	37¾	21	13¾	13⅞	13	8	NA	NA	NA	NA
- Low	18⅛	12⅝	9½	9¾	6½	3⅜	NA	NA	NA	NA
P/E Ratio - High	42	30	28	30	34	36	NA	NA	NA	NA
- Low	20	18	19	21	17	15	NA	NA	NA	NA

Income Statement Analysis (Million $)

	1998	1997	1996	1995	1994	1993	1992	1991	1990	1989
Revs.	3,060	2,388	1,926	1,554	1,306	1,097	1,006	863	NA	NA
Oper. Inc.	316	233	184	151	126	99	73.9	75.1	NA	NA
Depr.	57.4	44.0	34.0	27.4	23.2	16.7	18.7	18.7	NA	NA
Int. Exp.	24.6	17.9	13.5	7.4	6.7	14.7	20.2	NA	NA	NA
Pretax Inc.	235	171	123	117	96.7	50.1	31.7	NA	NA	NA
Eff. Tax Rate	40%	40%	41%	42%	42%	43%	45%	NA	NA	NA
Net Inc.	141	102	72.7	68.5	55.7	28.7	17.5	22.9	NA	NA

Balance Sheet & Other Fin. Data (Million $)

	1998	1997	1996	1995	1994	1993	1992	1991	1990	1989
Cash	44.2	8.9	2.8	30.4	8.5	4.2	0.9	NA	NA	NA
Curr. Assets	811	465	300	286	202	211	179	465	NA	NA
Total Assets	1,620	1,122	805	659	469	445	398	NA	NA	NA
Curr. Liab.	286	236	155	172	115	106	139	NA	NA	NA
LT Debt	310	312	188	109	52.0	95.0	89.0	108	NA	NA
Common Eqty.	955	517	411	334	263	207	134	121	NA	NA
Total Cap.	1,310	868	629	463	329	314	232	NA	NA	NA
Cap. Exp.	203	NA	132	108	58.8	46.3	27.5	11.3	NA	NA
Cash Flow	199	146	107	95.9	78.9	45.4	36.2	41.6	NA	NA
Curr. Ratio	2.8	2.0	1.9	1.7	1.8	2.0	1.3	NA	NA	NA
% LT Debt of Cap.	23.6	35.9	29.8	23.5	15.7	30.3	38.5	NA	NA	NA
% Net Inc.of Revs.	4.6	4.3	3.8	4.4	4.3	2.6	1.7	2.6	NA	NA
% Ret. on Assets	10.3	10.6	9.9	12.1	12.2	6.1	4.0	NA	NA	NA
% Ret. on Equity	19.2	23.0	19.5	22.9	23.7	26.5	24.6	NA	NA	NA

Data as orig. reptd.; bef. results of disc. opers. and/or spec. items. Per share data adj. for stk. divs. as of ex-div. date. Bold denotes diluted EPS (FASB 128). E-Estimated. NA-Not Available. NM-Not Meaningful. NR-Not Ranked.

Office—N54 W13600 Woodale Drive, Menomonee Falls, WI 53051. **Tel**—(414) 783-5800. **Chrmn & CEO**—W. S. Kellogg. **Pres**—J. H. Baker. **VP, CFO & Investor Contact**—Arlene Meier (414-783-1646). **VP & Secy**—J. F. Herma. **Dirs**—J. H. Baker, J. D. Ericson, J. F. Herma, W. S. Kellogg, L. Montgomery, F. V. Sica, H. Simon, P. M. Sommerhauser, R. E. White. **Transfer Agent & Registrar**—Bank of New York, NYC. **Incorporated**—in Delaware in 1988; reincorporated in Wisconsin in 1993. **Empl**—32,200. **S&P Analyst:** Karen J. Sack, CFA

STANDARD & POOR'S
STOCK REPORTS

Kroger Co.

1314C

NYSE Symbol **KR**

In S&P 500

12-SEP-98

Industry:
Retail (Food Chains)

Summary: This operator of supermarkets and convenience stores is one of the largest chains in the U.S., with over 1,400 supermarkets and more than 815 convenience stores.

S&P Opinion: Buy (★★★★★)

Recent Price • 49¾	Yield • Nil
52 Wk Range • 54⅛-27⅞	12-Mo. P/E • 33.7

Quantitative Evaluations

Outlook
(1 Lowest—5 Highest)
• **2**

Fair Value
• **47⅞**

Risk
• **Low**

Earn./Div. Rank
• **B+**

Technical Eval.
• **Bullish** since 6/97

Rel. Strength Rank
(1 Lowest—99 Highest)
• **96**

Insider Activity
• **Neutral**

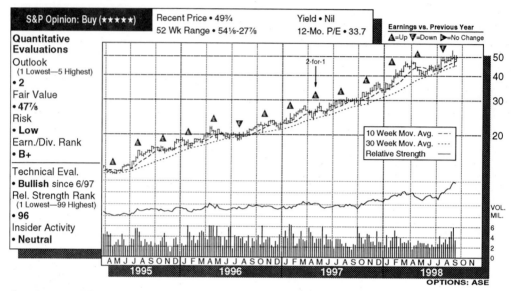

Earnings vs. Previous Year
▲=Up ▼=Down ▶=No Change

- 10 Week Mov. Avg. ---
- 30 Week Mov. Avg. ······
- Relative Strength —

OPTIONS: ASE

Overview - 21-JUL-98

Sales should rise about 8%-10% in 1998, bolstered by new and remodeled stores, which will increase retail square footage by about 4.5% to 5%. Identical-store sales are likely to be flat to slightly higher tempered by continuing grocery price deflation and intense competition in many markets. Gross margins should widen, however, reflecting increased sales of higher-margin private-label products, improved buying clout and lower transportation costs. Operating margins should also benefit from an increased use of technology and the company's ongoing success at controlling costs and reducing debt. In particular, KR's recently announced merger of its two Texas retail divisions into one operating unit should reduce costs and improve overall efficiency. Although we expect net income to grow in the 18% to 20% range, EPS gains are likely to be held to about 15% to 17%, restrained by more shares outstanding, reflecting increased employee ownership.

Valuation - 21-JUL-98

Despite an intensely competitive retail food industry and a deflationary market, KR continued to post solid sales gains and healthy increases in operating income during the first half of 1998. The company, which is still highly leveraged, has proved that it can generate strong cash flow to pay down debt in a timely fashion. KR is now in a position to generate consistent increases in cash flow and income. In light of KR's strong consistent performance, coupled with our belief that food prices will once again begin to trend upward, boosting same-store sales comparisons, we continue to rate KR shares as strong "buy". The defensive quality of the supermarket industry makes the shares, recently selling at 21 times estimated 1999 earnings of $2.25, even more attractive for purchase.

Key Stock Statistics

S&P EPS Est. 1998	1.95	Tang. Bk. Value/Share	NM
P/E on S&P Est. 1998	25.5	Beta	0.42
S&P EPS Est. 1999	2.25	Shareholders	47,100
Dividend Rate/Share	Nil	Market cap. (B)	$ 12.8
Shs. outstg. (M)	256.5	Inst. holdings	52%
Avg. daily vol. (M)	0.974		

Value of $10,000 invested 5 years ago: $ 68,118

Fiscal Year Ending Dec. 31

	1998	1997	1996	1995	1994	1993
Revenues (Million $)						
1Q	6,389	6,139	5,784	5,465	5,329	5,174
2Q	6,442	6,232	5,844	5,653	5,394	5,329
3Q	—	7,687	7,343	6,959	6,650	6,479
4Q	—	6,510	6,199	5,861	5,586	5,402
Yr.	—	26,567	25,171	23,938	22,959	22,384
Earnings Per Share ($)						
1Q	**0.41**	0.34	0.29	0.28	0.25	0.15
2Q	**0.36**	0.41	0.30	0.35	0.31	0.14
3Q	—	0.36	0.28	0.26	0.23	0.12
4Q	—	**0.56**	0.47	0.42	0.40	0.40
Yr.	—	**1.69**	**1.36**	1.32	1.19	0.80

Next earnings report expected: late October

Dividend Data

No cash dividends have been paid since 1988. A 2-for-1 stock split was effected in April 1997.

A Division of The McGraw·Hill Companies

STANDARD
&POOR'S
STOCK REPORTS

The Kroger Co.

1314C
12-SEP-98

Business Summary - 21-JUL-98

With more than 1,400 stores in 24 states and annual sales of nearly $27 billion, The Kroger Co. owns and operates the nation's largest supermarket chain.

Through a mixture of new square footage, increased profitability at existing stores, and better technology and logistics systems, KR hopes to grow earnings per share at least 13% to 15% annually over the next three years.

Most Kroger stores are located in the Midwest, South, Southeast and Southwest. The company's subsidiary, Dillon Companies Inc., also operates 260 stores mainly in Colorado, Kansas, Arizona and Missouri, under the names Dillon, King Soopers, Fry's Food, Gerbes, City Market and Sav-Mor. The subsidiary also operates 816 convenience stores in 15 states, under such names as Kwik Shop, Quik Stop, Tom Thumb, Turkey Hill, Loaf 'N Jug and Mini Mart.

Management's ability to take advantage of Kroger's number one or number two position in virtually every market it serves has translated into solid and consistent operating performance over the past several years. Furthermore, KR has significantly improved its profitability through investments in technology and logistics, as well as a continued emphasis on expense controls. Over the past few years, Kroger has focused on streamlining its distribution network and reducing transportation and storage costs. In early 1997, KR also coordinated certain grocery purchases across marketing areas, resulting in additional buying efficiencies. It can now use its tremendous clout to negotiate national promotions and reduce product costs.

KR's food and drug combination store, accounting for 67% of the store base and 80% of food store sales in 1997, is the driving force behind the company's growth. In addition to traditional grocery items, these stores offer a pharmacy plus a variety of service-oriented specialty departments, such as floral, service meat, seafood, bakeries, cheese, expanded health and beauty care, video rental, book stores, photofinishing and seasonal non-food general merchandise. Combination stores averaged 54,173 square feet at the end of 1997. Smaller superstores, which average 33,420 square feet and do not contain these specialty departments, accounted for 18% of 1997 food store sales.

KR also operates 36 food processing facilities to supply over 4,000 private-label products to its stores.

Over the next two years, KR expects to invest $775 million-$850 million annually to add approximately 100 new stores, both through new store openings and acquisitions, resulting in an annual compounded retail square footage gain of about 5%. Its strategy is to invest in existing markets or adjacent geographic regions where it has a strong franchise and can leverage marketing, distribution and overhead dollars.

Per Share Data ($)

(Year Ended Dec. 31)	1997	1996	1995	1994	1993	1992	1991	1990	1989	1988
Tangible Bk. Val.	NA	NM	NM	-9.95	-11.66	-15.06	-16.02	-17.09	-18.03	-18.45
Cash Flow	3.13	2.66	2.19	2.40	1.99	1.87	1.85	1.86	1.33	1.66
Earnings	1.69	1.34	1.32	1.19	0.80	0.56	0.56	0.48	-0.12	0.12
Dividends	Nil	Nil	Nil	Nil	Nil	Nil	Nil	Nil	Nil	20.41
Payout Ratio	Nil	Nil	Nil	Nil	Nil	Nil	Nil	Nil	Nil	NM
Prices - High	$37^1/4$	$23^3/4$	$18^7/8$	$13^1/2$	$10^7/8$	$10^5/8$	$12^1/4$	$8^1/2$	$9^7/8$	$29^1/2$
- Low	$22^3/4$	$16^3/4$	$11^3/4$	$9^3/4$	7	$5^5/8$	$6^3/8$	$5^3/8$	$4^1/4$	$3^5/8$
P/E Ratio - High	22	18	14	11	14	19	22	18	NM	NM
- Low	13	12	9	8	9	10	11	11	NM	NM

Income Statement Analysis (Million $)

	1997	1996	1995	1994	1993	1992	1991	1990	1989	1988
Revs.	26,567	25,171	23,938	22,959	22,384	22,145	21,351	20,261	19,104	19,053
Oper. Inc.	1,377	1,212	1,134	1,027	954	889	934	912	842	689
Depr.	380	344	311	278	253	241	234	238	236	245
Int. Exp.	285	300	313	331	392	475	535	564	651	210
Pretax Inc.	712	568	510	421	284	173	169	142	-9.0	52.0
Eff. Tax Rate	38%	38%	37%	36%	40%	42%	40%	41%	NM	33%
Net Inc.	444	353	319	269	171	101	101	83.0	-16.0	35.0

Balance Sheet & Other Fin. Data (Million $)

	1997	1996	1995	1994	1993	1992	1991	1990	1989	1988
Cash	65.0	Nil	Nil	27.0	121	104	4.0	55.0	115	211
Curr. Assets	2,641	2,353	2,107	2,152	2,226	2,168	1,992	1,950	2,048	2,470
Total Assets	6,301	5,825	5,045	4,708	4,480	4,303	4,114	4,119	4,242	4,614
Curr. Liab.	2,944	2,713	2,565	2,395	2,251	2,174	2,087	2,062	2,069	2,165
LT Debt	3,493	3,479	3,490	3,889	4,135	4,473	4,408	4,558	4,724	4,724
Common Eqty.	-783	-1,181	-1,602	-2,153	-2,459	-2,699	-2,748	-2,859	-2,964	-2,927
Total Cap.	2,874	2,629	2,040	1,908	1,858	2,051	1,928	1,970	2,053	2,348
Cap. Exp.	612	734	726	534	395	245	226	229	131	378
Cash Flow	824	697	614	547	424	342	335	322	217	263
Curr. Ratio	0.9	0.9	0.8	0.9	1.0	1.0	1.0	0.9	1.0	1.1
% LT Debt of Cap.	121.5	103.2	171.1	203.8	222.5	218.1	228.6	231.4	NM	NM
% Net Inc.of Revs.	1.7	1.4	1.3	1.2	0.8	0.5	0.5	0.4	NM	0.2
% Ret. on Assets	7.3	6.5	6.2	5.8	3.6	2.4	2.4	2.0	NM	0.8
% Ret. on Equity	NM	NM	NM	NM	NM	NM	NM	NM	NM	NM

Data as orig. reptd.; bef. results of disc. opers. and/or spec. items. Per share data adj. for stk. divs. as of ex-div. date. Bold denotes diluted EPS (FASB 128). E-Estimated. NA-Not Available. NM-Not Meaningful. NR-Not Ranked.

Office—1014 Vine St., Cincinnati, OH 45202. **Tel**—(513) 762-4000. **Chrmn & CEO**—J. A. Pichler. **Pres & COO**—D. B. Dillon. **VP & Secy**—P. W. Heldman. **VP, Treas & Investor Contact**—L. Turner. **Dirs**—R. V. Anderson, J. L. Clendenin, D. B. Dillon, R. W. Dillon, J. T. LaMacchia, E. M. Liddy, P. Shontz Longe, C. R. Moore, T. B. Morton Jr., T. H. O'Leary, J. D. Ong, K. D. Ortega, J. A. Pichler, M. R. Seger, J. D. Woods. **Transfer Agent & Registrar**—Bank of New York, NYC. **Incorporated**—in Ohio in 1902. **Empl**—212,000. **S&P Analyst:** Maureen C. Carini

STANDARD &POOR'S
STOCK REPORTS

Laidlaw Inc.
1321M
NYSE Symbol **LDW**

In S&P 500

12-SEP-98

Industry:
Services (Commercial & Consumer)

Summary: This Canadian company is the leading North American provider of school transportation and emergency healthcare services.

S&P Opinion: Avoid (★★)

Recent Price • 9⅛
52 Wk Range • 16⅝-8⅝

Yield • 2.0%
12-Mo. P/E • 8.9

Earnings vs. Previous Year
▲=Up ▼=Down ▶=No Change

Quantitative Evaluations

Outlook
(1 Lowest—5 Highest)
• **5**

Fair Value
• **15¼**

Risk
• **NA**

Earn./Div. Rank
• **B**

Technical Eval.
• **NA**

Rel. Strength Rank
(1 Lowest—99 Highest)
• **61**

Insider Activity
• **NA**

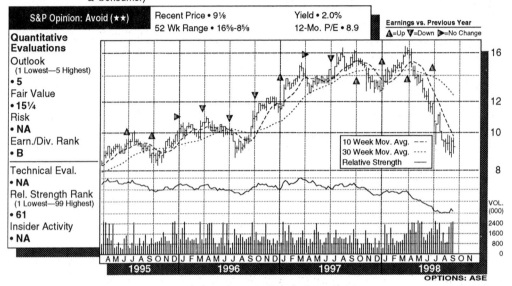

10 Week Mov. Avg. ---
30 Week Mov. Avg. ····
Relative Strength —

VOL. (000)
2400
1600
800
0

OPTIONS: ASE

Overview - 16-JUL-98

Revenues in FY 98 (Aug.) are expected to climb nearly 40%, fueled by acquisitions during fiscal 1997. Top-line growth over the next few quarters should slow to about 20%, as acquisition activity moderates and organic growth remains negligible. Profitability in the passenger services unit should improve, driven by synergies from recent purchases. However, margins will be squeezed in the emergency healthcare division, reflecting pricing pressure, increased scrutiny related to Medicare reimbursements and weakness in certain markets. In addition, the bottom-line will be limited by a higher tax rate and more shares outstanding. We expect FY 98 income from continuing operations (excluding nonrecurring charges) to rise 25%, to $0.79 a share, from $0.63 in FY 97. Results in FY 97 exclude a $0.49 restructuring charge and income of $1.78 from discontinued operations.

Valuation - 16-JUL-98

In early July, we downgraded Laidlaw to an avoid from neutral. News of an unfavorable U.S. tax court ruling could disallow deductions taken by Laidlaw during the 1986 to 1988 time frame. If the ruling stands up to an appeal, LDW would owe approximately $140 million in taxes and interest. Additional potential liability exists for the 1989 to 1994 period. Total liabilities, both claimed and potentially claimed, could reach $500 million, or $1.50 per share. Margins in the firm's healthcare segment are under pressure and we have concerns about the company's ability to effectively integrate acquisitions. We are encouraged by Laidlaw's exit from the solid waste industry and its efforts to focus on its bus transportation and emergency healthcare businesses. However, we feel the stock will underperform the overall market as investors steer clear of the uncertainty surrounding the company.

Key Stock Statistics

S&P EPS Est. 1998	0.79	Tang. Bk. Value/Share	NM
P/E on S&P Est. 1998	11.6	Beta	1.03
S&P EPS Est. 1999	0.95	Shareholders	6,400
Dividend Rate/Share	0.28	Market cap. (B)	$ 3.0
Shs. outstg. (M)	329.8	Inst. holdings	30%
Avg. daily vol. (M)	0.485		

Value of $10,000 invested 5 years ago: $ 11,429

Fiscal Year Ending Aug. 31

	1998	1997	1996	1995	1994	1993
Revenues (Million U.S. $)						
1Q	1,094	702.9	618.8	569.7	546.2	513.0
2Q	1,026	694.5	575.8	597.0	520.4	469.0
3Q	896.3	897.8	622.9	733.4	579.1	543.8
4Q	—	735.5	478.5	617.3	482.6	467.6
Yr.	—	3,031	2,296	2,517	2,128	1,993
Earnings Per Share (U.S. $)						
1Q	0.25	0.18	0.14	0.14	0.14	0.18
2Q	**0.21**	0.08	0.08	0.10	0.06	0.10
3Q	**0.51**	-0.20	0.16	0.18	0.14	-0.12
4Q	**E0.07**	0.08	0.02	0.06	-0.01	-1.21
Yr.	**E0.79**	0.14	0.40	0.48	0.33	-1.05

Next earnings report expected: mid October

Dividend Data (Dividends have been paid since 1969.)

Amount (Can. $)	Date Decl.	Ex-Div. Date	Stock of Record	Payment Date
0.050	Oct. 16	Oct. 29	Oct. 31	Nov. 15 '97
0.070	Jan. 12	Jan. 28	Jan. 30	Feb. 15 '98
0.070	Apr. 08	Apr. 29	May. 01	May. 15 '98
0.070	Jul. 10	Jul. 29	Jul. 31	Aug. 15 '98

A Division of The McGraw-Hill Companies

Business Summary - 16-JUL-98

Over the past several years, Laidlaw has essentially completed a make-over and is now the leading North American provider of student, municipal transit, and health care transportation services.

The company is the largest school bus operator in North America, providing daily transportation for more than two million students using 37,000 vehicles. In February 1997, LDW purchased Vancom Inc., the third largest U.S. school bus company, expanding its business by 10%. During the fourth quarter of FY 97 (Aug.), LDW purchased The DAVE Companies, which operates over 1,700 vehicles and has annualized revenues of roughly $88 million. In October 1997, LDW acquired, for $75 million, Greyhound Canada Transportation Corporation. Greyhound Canada operates nearly 400 coaches, serves over two million customers and has annualized revenues of $135 million.

With the purchase of American Medical Response in February 1997, for $1.1 billion, LDW is now the largest provider of health care transportation services, with annual sales of $1.3 billion and 4,700 vehicles in operation. In July 1997, LDW acquired, for $400 million, Emcare Holdings Inc. (Nasdaq: EMCR), dramatically increasing the scope of its emergency physician services. Emcare, with over $260 million in annualized rev-

enues, operates in 21 states and contracts with 1,800 physicians. In October 1997, the company acquired Spectrum Healthcare Services Inc., a provider of emergency room services with revenues of $160 million.

In May 1997, LDW merged its hazardous waste management company with Rollins Environmental Services, Inc. for $400 million and 120 million REN common shares, forming 67%-owned Laidlaw Environmental Services (LLE). LDW recorded a $133 million charge related to the merger in the third quarter of FY 97.

In December 1996, LDW sold its Laidlaw Waste Systems to Allied Waste Industries, Inc. for a total of $1.6 billion, including a 20% interest in Allied. Earnings for the FY 97 second quarter included an after-tax gain of $549.7 million from the transaction. LDW sold its interest in Allied in May 1997 for $376 million, completing its exit from the solid waste industry.

In July 1998, LDW received an unfavorable ruling from the U.S. Tax Court. The judgement, could cause a reassessment of the company's 1986, 1987 and 1988 tax returns. Interest deductions taken during that time period would be disallowed and, as a result, tax and interest of about $141 million would be payable. In addition, the Internal Revenue Service has asserted similar claims against LDW for the tax years 1989, 1990 and 1991, amounting to about $289 million in taxes and interest. The company intends to appeal the decision.

Per Share Data (U.S. $)

(Year Ended Aug. 31)	1997	1996	1995	1994	1993	1992	1991	1990	1989	1988
Tangible Bk. Val.	0.84	3.02	3.50	3.90	3.86	5.40	4.82	6.23	4.82	2.74
Cash Flow	1.04	1.07	1.42	1.17	-0.22	1.38	-0.48	1.92	1.70	1.37
Earnings	0.14	0.40	0.48	0.33	-1.05	0.52	-1.35	1.10	1.00	0.76
Dividends	0.15	0.14	0.16	0.12	0.12	0.14	0.27	0.23	0.19	0.15
Payout Ratio	107%	35%	33%	36%	NM	28%	NM	21%	21%	21%
Prices - High	16½	12¼	10⅛	8½	9½	11¼	20¼	24⅝	23¾	17½
- Low	11½	8⅝	7⅝	5½	5⅜	6⅞	7¼	15½	12⅝	11¼
P/E Ratio - High	NM	31	21	26	NM	22	NM	22	24	23
- Low	NM	22	16	17	NM	13	NM	14	13	15

Income Statement Analysis (Million U.S. $)

	1997	1996	1995	1994	1993	1992	1991	1990	1989	1988
Revs.	3,031	2,296	2,517	2,128	1,993	1,926	1,882	1,738	1,413	1,183
Oper. Inc.	617	430	541	459	435	467	463	482	390	314
Depr.	286	197	260	235	232	230	216	190	143	109
Int. Exp.	138	108	133	117	106	122	133	113	65.0	28.0
Pretax Inc.	-109	147	168	121	-317	169	-303	309	258	198
Eff. Tax Rate	NM	21%	21%	25%	NM	18%	NM	14%	18%	25%
Net Inc.	45.2	117	133	91.0	-291	138	-328	265	211	147

Balance Sheet & Other Fin. Data (Million U.S. $)

	1997	1996	1995	1994	1993	1992	1991	1990	1989	1988
Cash	241	226	147	200	212	132	125	208	70.0	110
Curr. Assets	1,107	774	719	614	654	524	520	540	305	292
Total Assets	6,117	4,932	4,286	3,633	3,575	3,659	3,595	3,895	2,651	1,637
Curr. Liab.	624	480	552	392	407	349	316	318	211	172
LT Debt	2,192	1,929	1,669	1,403	1,377	1,261	1,508	1,435	899	514
Common Eqty.	2,785	2,128	1,688	1,576	1,544	1,950	1,672	1,907	1,330	755
Total Cap.	5,149	4,189	3,412	3,037	2,974	3,310	3,279	3,577	2,440	1,464
Cap. Exp.	237	289	317	329	319	229	248	597	442	416
Cash Flow	331	314	393	326	-61.0	368	-117	447	346	243
Curr. Ratio	1.8	1.6	1.3	1.6	1.6	1.5	1.6	1.7	1.4	1.7
% LT Debt of Cap.	42.6	46.1	48.9	46.2	46.3	38.1	46.0	40.1	36.8	35.1
% Net Inc.of Revs.	1.5	5.1	5.3	4.3	NM	7.2	NM	15.3	14.9	12.5
% Ret. on Assets	0.8	2.6	3.3	2.5	NM	3.6	NM	7.8	9.3	9.9
% Ret. on Equity	1.8	8.5	8.1	5.8	NM	7.3	NM	15.3	18.4	18.8

Data as orig. reptd.; in U.S. funds; based on Canadian GAAP; bef. results of disc. opers. and/or spec. items. Per share data adj. for stk. divs. as of ex-div. date. E-Estimated. NA-Not Available. NM-Not Meaningful. NR-Not Ranked.

Office—3221 N. Service Rd., Burlington, ON L7R 3Y8, Canada. **Tel**—(905) 336-1800. **Fax**—(416) 336-3976. **Website**—http://www.laidlaw.com **Chrmn**—P. N. T. Widdrington. **Pres & CEO**—J. R. Bullock. **SVP & CFO**—L. W. Haworth. **VP & Investor Contact**—T. A. G. Watson. **Secy**—W. R. Cottick. **Dirs**—J. R. Bullock, W. P. Cooper, J. P. Edwards, W. A. Farlinger, R. K. Gamey, D. M. Green, M. Q. Hesse, D. P. O'Brien, G. Ritchie, W. W. Stinson, S. M. Thompson, P. N. T. Widdrington. **Transfer Agents & Registrars**—R-M Trust Co., Toronto; ChaseMellon Shareholder Services, Ridgefield Park, NJ. **Incorporated**—in Ontario in 1966. **Empl**— 72,225. **S&P Analyst**: Jordan Horoschak

12-SEP-98

Industry: Investment Banking/ Brokerage

Summary: Lehman Brothers is a major global investment bank serving institutional, corporate and government clients and high net worth individuals.

S&P Opinion: No Opinion	Recent Price • 35¾	Yield • 0.8%
	52 Wk Range • 85-32⅜	12-Mo. P/E • 5.8

Quantitative Evaluations

Outlook
(1 Lowest—5 Highest)
• **3⁻**

Fair Value
• **42¼**

Risk
• **Average**

Earn./Div. Rank
• **NR**

Technical Eval.
• **Neutral** since 9/98

Rel. Strength Rank
(1 Lowest—99 Highest)
• **6**

Insider Activity
• **Neutral**

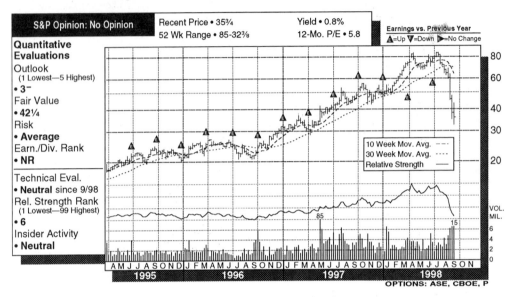

Earnings vs. Previous Year
▲=Up ▼=Down ▶=No Change

10 Week Mov. Avg. ---
30 Week Mov. Avg. ····
Relative Strength ——

OPTIONS: ASE, CBOE, P

Overview - 19-JUN-98

Profits for the fiscal year ending November 30, 1998, are expected to increase from FY 97's level. LEH has made a commitment to expand in higher-margin areas like equities and high yield. Also, the stock market is off to a good start, which should help commission revenues, and rapid consolidation in a number of industries implies an improved mergers and acquisitions contribution. Principal transactions income, which is hard to predict, is assumed to be flat. Given large merchant banking gains realized last year, this year's comparisons could be unfavorable. Overseas, LEH's business is expected to recover slightly, as nations in Asia work to solve some of their fiscal problems. A level tax rate is anticipated, as is an increase in shares outstanding. The company is required to share a portion of its profits with American Express when net income exceeds $400 million.

Valuation - 19-JUN-98

Price to book value, a rough proxy for liquidation worth, is the preferred measure to use in valuing securities brokers, because their highly liquid balance sheets can be marked to market to arrive at a meaningful shareholders' equity balance. In addition, the traditional price/earnings ratio is subject to distortions. At market tops, the P/E ratio makes the stocks appear too inexpensive. At market bottoms, the P/E ratio makes the shares appear unduly expensive. The shares are currently trading at more than twice book value, the high end of their range since the spinoff from American Express. We attribute this to a high level of merger and acquisition activity in the brokerage industry, with numerous deals involving both private and public firms being announced or completed in the past six months.

Key Stock Statistics

S&P EPS Est. 1998	NA	Tang. Bk. Value/Share	36.50
P/E on S&P Est. 1998	NA	Beta	NA
Dividend Rate/Share	0.30	Shareholders	27,300
Shs. outstg. (M)	118.3	Market cap. (B)	$ 4.2
Avg. daily vol. (M)	2.012	Inst. holdings	58%

Value of $10,000 invested 5 years ago: NA

Fiscal Year Ending Nov. 30

	1998	1997	1996	1995	1994	1993
Revenues (Million $)						
1Q	4,580	3,999	3,386	3,112	--	--
2Q	5,554	3,806	3,476	3,298	—	--
3Q	--	4,469	3,585	3,453	—	--
4Q	--	4,609	3,813	3,613	—	--
Yr.	--	16,883	14,260	13,471	9,190	8,692
Earnings Per Share ($)						
1Q	**1.44**	1.16	0.79	0.31	--	--
2Q	**2.12**	0.95	0.89	0.43	0.39	--
3Q	—	1.30	0.60	0.52	0.10	--
4Q	—	1.30	0.96	0.49	0.32	--
Yr.	—	4.72	3.24	1.76	0.81	3.08

Next earnings report expected: early October

Dividend Data (Dividends have been paid since 1994.)

Amount ($)	Date Decl.	Ex-Div. Date	Stock of Record	Payment Date
0.060	Nov. 03	Nov. 12	Nov. 14	Nov. 28 '97
0.075	Jan. 27	Feb. 06	Feb. 10	Feb. 27 '98
0.075	May. 05	May. 13	May. 15	May. 29 '98
0.075	Aug. 04	Aug. 12	Aug. 15	Aug. 31 '98

A Division of The **McGraw·Hill** *Companies*

Business Summary - 19-JUN-98

Lehman Brothers is a major global investment bank serving institutional, corporate, government and high net worth individual clients and customers. Its worldwide headquarters in New York and regional headquarters in London and Tokyo are complemented by offices in the U.S., Europe, the Middle East, and Latin and South America and the Asia Pacific region. Revenue contributions in FY 97 (Nov.) and FY 96 were:

	1997	1996
Principal transactions	37%	46%
Investment banking	34%	28%
Commissions	11%	11%
Interest & dividends (net)	16%	14%
Other	2%	1%

Since 1990 Lehman Brothers has focused on a "client/customer-driven" strategy. Under this strategy, the company concentrates on serving the needs of major issuing and advisory clients and investing customers worldwide to build a flow of business that leverages its research, underwriting and distribution capabilities. Customer flow is the company's primary source of net revenues. In addition, Lehman also takes proprietary positions based upon expected movements in interest rate, foreign exchange, equity and commodity markets in both the short- and long-term.

As an investment banker, Lehman raises debt or equity capital for corporations, governments and other organizations, typically earning a fee representing the difference between what the company buys the offering for from the company and what it sells the securities for in the open market. Investment banking revenues also include fees the company receives for advising companies on mergers and acquisitions, divestitures and other restructuring moves. In 1997, Lehman was again among the leaders in global mergers and acquisitions, serving as financial adviser in over $180 billion of announced transactions, of which 150 transactions totaling over $69 billion were completed in 1997, with the remainder targeted for 1998 closure. The company advised in 45 cross-border transactions. The company is a member of all principal securities and commodities exchanges in the U.S., and holds memberships or associate memberships on principal international securities and commodities exchanges.

The company's businesses are subject to volatility, primarily due to changes in interest and foreign exchange rates and security valuations, global economic and political trends and industry competition. As a result, revenues and earnings may vary significantly from quarter to quarter and from year to year.

Per Share Data ($)

(Year Ended Nov. 30)	1997	1996	1995	1994	1993	1992	1991	1990	1989	1988
Tangible Bk. Val.	33.02	31.62	26.87	23.91	21.93	NA	NA	NA	NA	NA
Cash Flow	5.44	NA	NA	NA	NA	NA	NA	NA	NA	NA
Earnings	4.72	3.24	1.76	0.81	3.08	NA	NA	NA	NA	NA
Dividends	0.24	0.20	0.20	0.17	NA	NA	NA	NA	NA	NA
Payout Ratio	5%	6%	11%	22%	NA	NA	NA	NA	NA	NA
Prices - High	56½	32½	24⅝	20⅞	NA	NA	NA	NA	NA	NA
- Low	28½	20⅝	14½	13¾	NA	NA	NA	NA	NA	NA
P/E Ratio - High	12	10	14	26	NA	NA	NA	NA	NA	NA
- Low	6	6	8	17	NA	NA	NA	NA	NA	NA

Income Statement Analysis (Million $)

	1997	1996	1995	1994	1993	1992	1991	1990	1989	1988
Commissions	423	362	450	445	488	NA	NA	NA	NA	NA
Int. Inc.	13,635	11,298	10,788	6,761	5,679	NA	NA	NA	NA	NA
Total Revs.	15,053	14,260	13,476	9,190	8,692	NA	NA	NA	NA	NA
Int. Exp.	13,010	10,816	10,405	6,452	5,203	NA	NA	NA	NA	NA
Pretax Inc.	937	637	369	193	587	NA	NA	NA	NA	NA
Eff. Tax Rate	31%	35%	34%	35%	37%	NA	NA	NA	NA	NA
Net Inc.	647	416	242	126	368	NA	NA	NA	NA	NA

Balance Sheet & Other Fin. Data (Million $)

	1997	1996	1995	1994	1993	1992	1991	1990	1989	1988
Total Assets	151,705	128,596	115,303	109,947	80,474	NA	NA	NA	NA	NA
Cash Items	2,834	2,837	1,819	2,384	2,406	NA	NA	NA	NA	NA
Receivables	12,838	9,944	60,694	58,597	40,816	NA	NA	NA	NA	NA
Secs. Owned	76,862	61,453	51,322	47,473	35,699	NA	NA	NA	NA	NA
Sec. Borrowed	93,284	82,483	67,236	69,853	50,319	NA	NA	NA	NA	NA
Due Brokers & Cust.	21,703	14,882	8,824	5,657	5,515	NA	NA	NA	NA	NA
Other Liabs.	11,934	11,435	22,780	19,721	11,439	NA	NA	NA	NA	NA
Capitalization:										
Debt	99,129	15,922	12,765	11,321	9,899	NA	NA	NA	NA	NA
Equity	4,015	3,366	2,990	2,687	2,594	NA	NA	NA	NA	NA
Total	24,276	19,796	16,463	14,716	13,201	NA	NA	NA	NA	NA
% Return On Revs.	4.3	3.0	1.8	1.4	4.2	NA	NA	NA	NA	NA
% Ret. on Assets	0.5	0.3	0.2	NA	NA	NA	NA	NA	NA	NA
% Ret. on Equity	15.5	11.9	7.0	NA	NA	NA	NA	NA	NA	NA

Data as orig. reptd.; bef. results of disc. opers. and/or spec. items. Per share data adj. for stk. divs. as of ex-div. date. Yr. ended Dec. 31 in 1993. Pro forma pr. to 1995. Bold denotes diluted EPS (FASB 128). E-Estimated. NA-Not Available. NM-Not Meaningful. NR-Not Ranked.

Office—3 World Financial Center, New York, NY 10285. **Tel**—(212) 526-7000. **Website**—http://www.lehman.com **Chrmn & CEO**—R. S. Fuld Jr. **CFO**—C. Hintz. **Investor Contact**—Shaun Butler (212-526-8381). **Dirs**—M. L. Ainslie, J. F. Akers, R. S. Berlind, T. H. Cruikshank, R. S. Fuld Jr., H. Kaufman, H. Kobayashi, J. D. Macomber, D. Merrill, M. Yamada. **Transfer Agent & Registrar**—Bank of Boston. **Incorporated**—in Delaware in 1983. **Empl**— 8,387. **S&P Analyst:** Paul Huberman, CFA

STANDARD &POOR'S
STOCK REPORTS

Lilly (Eli)

1354K

NYSE Symbol **LLY**

In S&P 500

12-SEP-98

Industry:
Health Care (Drugs - Major Pharmaceuticals)

Summary: This major worldwide prescription drugmaker produces Prozac antidepressant, Ceclor and other antibiotics, diabetic care items and animal health products.

S&P Opinion: Buy (★★★★★)	Recent Price • 74⅞	Yield • 1.1%	Earnings vs. Previous Year
	52 Wk Range • 77⅝-54⅞	12-Mo. P/E • 43.0	▲=Up ▼=Down ▶=No Change

Quantitative Evaluations

Outlook
(1 Lowest—5 Highest)
• **1**

Fair Value
• **62¼**

Risk
• **Average**

Earn./Div. Rank
• **A-**

Technical Eval.
• **NA**

Rel. Strength Rank
(1 Lowest—99 Highest)
• **97**

Insider Activity
• **Unfavorable**

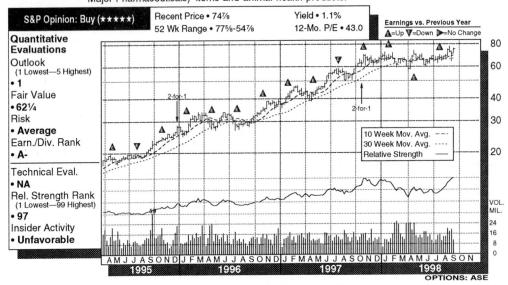

10 Week Mov. Avg. - - - -
30 Week Mov. Avg. ....
Relative Strength ——

OPTIONS: ASE

Overview - 31-JUL-98

Driven by strong gains in new drugs, sales in 1998 are expected to rise 17% to 18%. Despite likely continued slippage in older Ceclor/cefaclor and Vancocin antibiotic and Axid antiulcer lines, volume should be augmented by further gains in Prozac antidepressant, Zyprexa for schizophrenia, ReoPro antiplatelet agent, Gemzar anti-cancer and Humulin human insulin. Sales of Zyprexa are expected to increase more than 75%, to $1.3 billion, aided by its high efficacy profile and anticipated expansion of its label to include bipolar disorder. Re-opro has emerged as a leading therapeutic agent for preventing adverse events following angioplasty procedures, while Gemzar should benefit from a recent FDA panel recommendation to use the drug in treating lung cancer. Margins should benefit from the better volume and productivity improvements.

Valuation - 31-JUL-98

The shares traded in a fairly narrow range in recent months, reflecting disappointing sales of the new Evista osteoporosis drug, and concern over looming expiration of Prozac patents in 2001 and 2003. However, we do not expect generic competition against Prozac before 2003, by which time Lilly should have a portfolio of new drugs to offset any falloff in Prozac sales. Newer products such as Zyprexa anti-psychotic, ReoPro cardiovascular, and Gemzar anticancer should all continue to show robust growth in coming years. Despite a slow start, Lilly is also very positive about Evista. Evista, which was approved to treat osteoporosis, is also believed to be able to reduce the risks of breast and uterine cancers. The R&D pipeline also includes new compounds for endocrine and infectious diseases, Parkinson's disease, cancer, and cardiovascular conditions. The shares are recommended for superior total return.

Key Stock Statistics

S&P EPS Est. 1998	1.90	Tang. Bk. Value/Share	2.85
P/E on S&P Est. 1998	39.4	Beta	0.80
S&P EPS Est. 1999	2.25	Shareholders	54,500
Dividend Rate/Share	0.80	Market cap. (B)	$ 82.5
Shs. outstg. (M)	1101.3	Inst. holdings	60%
Avg. daily vol. (M)	3.501		

Value of $10,000 invested 5 years ago: $ 56,390

Fiscal Year Ending Dec. 31

	1998	1997	1996	1995	1994	1993
Revenues (Million $)						
1Q	2,269	1,953	1,783	1,717	1,309	1,560
2Q	2,341	1,989	1,698	1,615	1,347	1,561
3Q	—	2,160	1,804	1,632	1,507	1,531
4Q	—	2,416	2,061	1,800	1,548	1,801
Yr.	—	8,518	7,347	6,764	5,712	6,452
Earnings Per Share ($)						
1Q	**0.47**	**0.38**	0.35	0.33	0.26	0.32
2Q	**0.44**	**-1.57**	0.32	0.27	0.28	0.29
3Q	**E0.49**	**0.40**	0.38	0.27	0.26	0.25
4Q	**E0.50**	**0.40**	0.34	0.28	0.23	-0.44
Yr.	**E1.90**	**-0.35**	1.39	1.15	1.02	0.42

Next earnings report expected: mid October

Dividend Data (Dividends have been paid since 1885.)

Amount ($)	Date Decl.	Ex-Div. Date	Stock of Record	Payment Date
0.200	Sep. 15	Nov. 12	Nov. 14	Dec. 10 '97
0.200	Dec. 15	Feb. 11	Feb. 13	Mar. 10 '98
0.200	Apr. 20	May. 13	May. 15	Jun. 10 '98
0.200	Jul. 20	Aug. 12	Aug. 14	Sep. 10 '98

A Division of The **McGraw·Hill** *Companies*

Business Summary - 31-JUL-98

This leading maker of prescription drugs is well known for its popular Prozac antidepressant drug. It also produces other ethical drugs and animal health products, and operates one of the largest U.S. pharmacy benefit management firms. The company traces its history to Colonel Eli Lilly, a Union officer in the Civil War, who invented a process for coating pills with gelatin. Foreign operations accounted for 36% of sales in 1997. Lilly completed the divestiture of its medical device businesses in 1995.

Prozac, which accounted for 30% of total sales in 1997, is Lilly's most important product. A selective serotonin reuptake inhibitor (SSRI), Prozac is also prescribed in many countries for bulimia and obsessive-compulsive disorder. A decade after its first launch, Prozac remains the world's most widely prescribed antidepressant with about 20% of the U.S. market. Another growing central nervous system drug is Zyprexa, a new breakthrough treatment for schizophrenia and bipolar illness (9% of 1997 sales).

Endocrine agents (16%) are another key business. Lilly was a pioneer in the early commercialization of animal-based insulin, as well as genetically engineered human insulin. Licensed from Genentech, recombinant insulin is sold as Humulin. Other endocrine products include Humatrope, a recombinant human growth hormone, and Humalog, a rapid-acting recombinant insulin.

Lilly's sales of anti-infectives (15%) declined in 1997, largely due to generic erosion in older antibiotic lines. Principal products include Ceclor/cefaclor, Vancocin HCl, Keflex and Keftab, and Lorabid. Other drugs (17%) include Evista, a new treatment for osteoporosis; Axid antiulcer; ReoPro, a drug used to prevent adverse effects from angioplasty procedures; Dobutrex, a treatment for congestive heart failure; anticancer agents such as Oncovin and Gemzar; Darvocet-N analgesic; and Permax for Parkinson's disease.

Animal health products (7%) include cattle feed additives, antibiotics and related items. PCS Health Systems (6%) provides computer-based prescription drug claims processing, pharmacy benefit management services and related services for health care plan sponsors. More than 51 million persons are members in PCS-affiliated plans. In July 1997, the company sold its 40% interest in DowElanco, a maker of herbicides and other plant science products, to Dow Chemical, for about $900 million.

Lilly's ratio of R&D to sales (16.2% in 1997) ranks among the industry's highest. The R&D pipeline includes new compounds for endocrine and infectious diseases, diabetes, Parkinson's disease, cancer, and cardiovascular conditions.

Per Share Data ($)

(Year Ended Dec. 31)	1997	1996	1995	1994	1993	1992	1991	1990	1989	1988
Tangible Bk. Val.	2.83	1.87	1.21	0.81	3.56	3.79	3.88	2.81	2.96	2.57
Cash Flow	0.11	1.89	1.64	1.40	0.76	1.01	1.38	1.17	0.98	0.83
Earnings	-0.35	1.39	1.15	1.02	0.42	0.70	1.13	0.97	0.80	0.67
Dividends	0.74	0.69	0.66	0.63	0.60	0.55	0.50	0.41	0.34	0.29
Payout Ratio	NM	49%	57%	61%	145%	78%	44%	42%	42%	41%
Prices - High	70⅜	40¼	28½	16⅝	15½	22	21¼	22⅝	17⅛	11½
- Low	35⅝	24¾	15⅝	11¾	10⅞	14½	16⅞	14¾	10⅝	8⅞
P/E Ratio - High	NM	29	25	16	37	31	19	23	21	17
- Low	NM	18	14	11	26	21	15	15	13	13

Income Statement Analysis (Million $)

	1997	1996	1995	1994	1993	1992	1991	1990	1989	1988
Revs.	8,518	7,347	6,764	5,712	6,452	6,167	5,726	5,192	4,176	4,070
Oper. Inc.	2,968	2,591	2,536	2,227	2,224	2,089	2,079	1,764	1,360	1,220
Depr.	510	544	554	432	398	368	311	224	196	173
Int. Exp.	234	325	324	129	97.0	109	88.9	93.8	57.1	55.7
Pretax Inc.	510	2,032	1,756	1,699	702	1,182	1,879	1,599	1,330	1,116
Eff. Tax Rate	175%	25%	26%	30%	30%	30%	30%	30%	29%	32%
Net Inc.	-384	1,524	1,307	1,185	491	828	1,315	1,127	940	761

Balance Sheet & Other Fin. Data (Million $)

	1997	1996	1995	1994	1993	1992	1991	1990	1989	1988
Cash	1,948	955	1,084	747	987	728	782	751	652	762
Curr. Assets	5,321	3,891	4,139	3,962	3,697	3,006	2,939	2,501	2,274	2,415
Total Assets	12,577	14,307	14,413	14,507	9,624	8,673	8,299	7,143	5,848	5,263
Curr. Liab.	4,192	4,222	4,967	5,670	2,928	2,399	2,272	2,818	1,329	1,289
LT Debt	2,326	2,517	2,593	2,126	835	582	396	277	270	388
Common Eqty.	4,645	6,100	5,433	5,356	4,569	4,892	4,966	3,467	3,757	3,225
Total Cap.	7,187	8,993	8,321	7,670	5,531	5,644	5,777	4,096	4,327	3,848
Cap. Exp.	366	444	551	577	634	913	1,142	1,007	555	372
Cash Flow	125	2,068	1,861	1,617	889	1,106	1,625	1,352	1,135	934
Curr. Ratio	1.3	0.9	0.8	0.7	1.3	1.3	1.3	0.9	1.7	1.9
% LT Debt of Cap.	32.4	28.0	31.2	27.7	15.1	10.3	6.8	6.8	6.2	10.1
% Net Inc.of Revs.	NA	20.7	19.3	20.7	7.6	13.4	23.0	21.7	22.5	18.7
% Ret. on Assets	NA	10.6	9.0	9.8	5.4	9.8	16.3	17.7	16.8	14.6
% Ret. on Equity	NA	26.4	24.2	23.9	10.4	16.8	30.0	31.9	26.7	24.5

Data as orig. reptd.; bef. results of disc. opers. and/or spec. items. Per share data adj. for stk. divs. as of ex-div. date. Bold denotes diluted EPS (FASB 128). E-Estimated. NA-Not Available. NM-Not Meaningful. NR-Not Ranked.

Office—Lilly Corporate Center, Indianapolis, IN 46285. **Tel**—(317) 276-2000. **Website**—http://www.lilly.com **Chrmn & CEO**—R. L. Tobias. **Pres & COO**—S. Taurel. **EVP & CFO**—C. E. Golden. **VP & Treas**—E. A. Miller. **Secy**—D. P. Carmichael. **Investor Contact**—T. W. Grein (317-276-2506). **Dirs**—E. Bayh, S. C. Beering, A. G. Gilman, C. E. Golden, K. N. Horn, C. La Force, Jr., K. L. Lay, F. G. Prendergast, K. P. Siefert, R. L. Tobias, S. Taurel, A. M. Watanabe, A. O. Way. **Transfer Agent & Registrar**—First Chicago Trust Co. of New York. **Incorporated**—in Indiana in 1901. **Empl**—31,100. **S&P Analyst**: H. B. Saftlas

STANDARD &POOR'S
STOCK REPORTS

Limited (The)

1354T

NYSE Symbol **LTD**

In S&P 500

12-SEP-98

Industry: Retail (Specialty-Apparel)

Summary: This specialty retailer of women's apparel in the U.S. has more than 3,600 stores, and also owns an 83% stake in Intimate Brands, Inc.

S&P Opinion: Hold (★★★)	Recent Price • 23¾	Yield • 2.2%
	52 Wk Range • 36½-20⅛	12-Mo. P/E • 30.1

Quantitative Evaluations

Outlook (1 Lowest—5 Highest)
• **4+**

Fair Value
• **30**

Risk
• **Low**

Earn./Div. Rank
• **A-**

Technical Eval.
• **NA**

Rel. Strength Rank (1 Lowest—99 Highest)
• **52**

Insider Activity
• **Neutral**

Earnings vs. Previous Year
▲=Up ▼=Down ▶=No Change

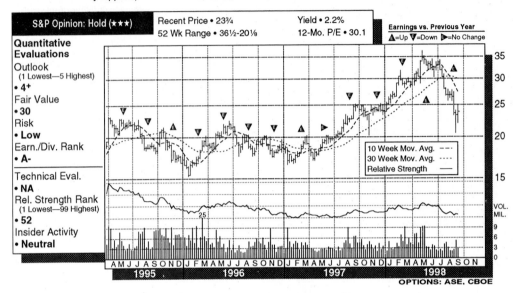

10 Week Mov. Avg. -----
30 Week Mov. Avg. .....
Relative Strength ——

OPTIONS: ASE, CBOE

Overview - 04-JUN-98

The Limited is taking a number of steps to boost shareholder value and to build a franchise in its women's businesses. In May 1998, the company completed an exchange offer allowing shareholders to exchange some or all of their LTD shares for 43 million shares of Abercrombie & Fitch (ANF). The company thereby divested its ownership of ANF, in which it had held an 84% stake. The exchange reduced the number of LTD shares outstanding by about 17%. The company will continue to retain its 83% stake in Intimate Brands (IBI), and to expand Victoria's Secret and Bath & Body Works stores. LTD is closing five of its six Henri Bendel stores, and is also closing the least productive of its Limited, Lerner, Lane Bryant, and Express units. Earnings in the first quarter of FY 99 (Jan.) were $0.09 a share before non-recurring gains. For the past few years, the company's earnings have mostly been derived from its stakes in IBI and ANF.

Valuation - 04-JUN-98

Investors have regained some confidence in LTD's earnings power, based on restructuring steps taken, and on an 8% rise in same-store sales in the first quarter of FY 99. However, the company still operates too many specialty apparel stores selling similar merchandise in an overstored environment, and seems unable to gain consistent sales momentum in all of its divisions. LTD has not yet proved itself able to turn these businesses around to deliver sustained profitability. We are encouraged, however, by the store closures and new management at Express, but anticipate only modest improvement in operating earnings from the women's businesses in coming periods.

Key Stock Statistics

S&P EPS Est. 1999	1.62	Tang. Bk. Value/Share	7.49
P/E on S&P Est. 1999	14.7	Beta	0.68
S&P EPS Est. 2000	1.70	Shareholders	74,900
Dividend Rate/Share	0.52	Market cap. (B)	$ 5.4
Shs. outstg. (M)	227.9	Inst. holdings	64%
Avg. daily vol. (M)	0.648		

Value of $10,000 invested 5 years ago: NA

Fiscal Year Ending Jan. 31

	1999	1998	1997	1996	1995	1994
Revenues (Million $)						
1Q	2,008	1,830	1,788	1,588	1,482	1,519
2Q	2,083	2,020	1,896	1,719	1,585	1,689
3Q	—	2,071	1,995	1,803	1,715	1,617
4Q	—	3,268	2,966	2,771	2,539	2,421
Yr.	—	9,189	8,645	7,881	7,321	7,245
Earnings Per Share ($)						
1Q	**0.28**	0.09	0.09	0.11	0.13	0.12
2Q	**0.13**	0.10	0.12	0.14	0.15	0.19
3Q	**E0.18**	0.29	0.59	1.83	0.25	0.23
4Q	**E1.05**	0.31	0.78	0.60	0.72	0.54
Yr.	**E1.62**	**0.79**	1.54	2.68	1.25	1.08

Next earnings report expected: NA

Dividend Data (Dividends have been paid since 1970.)

Amount ($)	Date Decl.	Ex-Div. Date	Stock of Record	Payment Date
0.130	Jan. 30	Mar. 04	Mar. 06	Mar. 17 '98
Stk.	May. 22	Jun. 02	May. 29	Jun. 01 '98
0.130	May. 18	Jun. 03	Jun. 05	Jun. 16 '98
0.130	Aug. 21	Sep. 02	Sep. 04	Sep. 15 '98

A Division of The **McGraw·Hill** *Companies*

The Limited, Inc.

Business Summary - 04-JUN-98

This specialty retailer has grown in 35 years from three stores to 3,684 stores (as of May 1998), and has spawned a host of new retailing formats. The Limited operates its own group of women's and "emerging" apparel stores (including its well-known namesake), and also owns 83% of Intimate Brands, Inc. (IBI). IBI consists of Victoria's Secret Stores, Victoria's Secret catalogue, and Bath & Body Works.

As a result of an ongoing review of the company's retail businesses and investments, LTD incurred total charges of $289 million ($0.60 a share) in the fourth quarter of FY 98 (Jan.). The charges included $68 million for the closing of the 118-store Cacique chain, part of Intimate Brands, $95 million in charges related to the closing of five Henri Bendel stores, $86 million related to the women's businesses, $28 million for closing or downsizing 80 stores in the women's businesses, and a $12 million writedown of a real estate investment..

The women's businesses include Express, Lerner New York, Lane Bryant, Limited Stores, and Henri Bendel. These stores accounted for 45% of total sales in FY 98, amounting to $3.9 billion, down 9.7% from the level of

FY 97. There was an operating loss of $268 million at the women's businesses, versus income of $64 million.

The emerging businesses include Structure, Limited Too, and Galyan's Trading (sporting goods and related apparel). Sales of these businesses totaled $1.1 billion in FY 98, up 11%. Operating profit increased 72% to $117 million, before non-recurring gains.

In October 1995, the company sold 40 million Intimate Brands common shares at $17 a share in an initial public offering. The Limited retained 83% of the shares. The spinoff was part of a reconfiguring of the company, announced in March 1995, that would include the spinoff of other divisions over time. In March 1996, The Limited repurchased 85 million of its common shares at $19 each through a tender offer. Funds for the repurchase were derived from the spinoff of Intimate Brands and the sale of 60% ownership in World Financial Network, the company's credit card processing venture. In September 1996, the company sold a 16% stake in its Abercrombie & Fitch (ANF) unit in an initial public offering. Following a May 1998 exchange offer to shareholders, LTD no longer has a stake in ANF.

The company also owns Mast Industries, a contract manufacturer and importer of women's apparel.

Per Share Data ($)

(Year Ended Jan. 31)	1998	1997	1996	1995	1994	1993	1992	1991	1990	1989
Tangible Bk. Val.	7.49	7.09	9.01	7.72	6.82	6.25	5.19	4.33	3.45	2.64
Cash Flow	1.93	2.57	3.48	2.00	1.79	1.93	1.72	1.61	1.40	1.07
Earnings	0.79	1.54	2.68	1.25	1.08	1.25	1.11	1.10	0.96	0.68
Dividends	0.48	0.40	0.40	0.36	0.36	0.28	0.28	0.24	0.16	0.12
Payout Ratio	61%	26%	15%	29%	33%	22%	25%	22%	17%	18%
Cal. Yrs.	1997	1996	1995	1994	1993	1992	1991	1990	1989	1988
Prices - High	25¾	22½	23¼	22⅜	30	32⅞	31⅝	25⅝	20	14
- Low	16½	15¼	15⅞	16¾	16⅝	19¼	17⅝	11¾	12⅝	8¼
P/E Ratio - High	33	15	9	18	28	26	28	23	21	20
- Low	21	10	6	13	15	15	16	11	13	12

Income Statement Analysis (Million $)

Revs.	9,189	8,645	7,881	7,545	7,420	7,086	6,281	5,376	4,750	4,155
Oper. Inc.	1,006	938	897	1,067	957	1,036	935	882	785	606
Depr.	313	290	286	268	258	247	223	184	160	139
Int. Exp.	69.0	75.4	77.0	65.4	63.9	62.4	63.9	56.6	58.1	63.4
Pretax Inc.	457	675	1,185	744	645	745	660	653	574	396
Eff. Tax Rate	40%	36%	19%	40%	39%	39%	39%	39%	40%	38%
Net Inc.	217	434	962	448	391	455	403	398	347	245

Balance Sheet & Other Fin. Data (Million $)

Cash	1,098	313	1,646	243	321	41.2	33.7	13.2	21.7	15.3
Curr. Assets	2,031	1,545	2,800	2,548	2,221	1,784	1,604	1,365	1,164	1,024
Total Assets	4,301	4,120	5,267	4,570	4,135	3,846	3,419	2,872	2,418	2,146
Curr. Liab.	1,093	907	717	798	707	721	520	481	478	456
LT Debt	650	650	650	650	650	542	714	540	446	518
Common Eqty.	2,044	1,923	3,201	2,761	2,441	2,268	1,877	1,560	1,240	946
Total Cap.	2,797	2,810	4,148	3,717	3,366	3,084	2,858	2,355	1,901	1,663
Cap. Exp.	405	409	374	320	296	430	523	429	320	327
Cash Flow	530	724	1,248	716	649	702	626	581	507	384
Curr. Ratio	1.9	1.7	3.9	3.2	3.1	2.5	3.1	2.8	2.4	2.2
% LT Debt of Cap.	23.2	23.1	15.7	17.5	19.3	17.6	25.0	23.0	23.4	31.1
% Net Inc.of Revs.	2.4	5.0	12.2	5.9	5.3	6.4	6.4	7.4	7.3	5.9
% Ret. on Assets	5.2	9.2	19.6	10.3	9.9	12.5	12.8	15.0	15.2	13.1
% Ret. on Equity	10.9	16.9	32.3	17.2	16.7	22.0	23.4	28.4	31.7	29.2

Data as orig. reptd.; bef. results of disc. opers. and/or spec. items. Per share data adj. for stk. divs. as of ex-div. date. Bold denotes diluted EPS (FASB 128). E-Estimated. NA-Not Available. NM-Not Meaningful. NR-Not Ranked.

Office—Two Limited Parkway, Columbus, OH 43216; P.O. Box 16000, Columbus 43230. **Tel**—(614) 479-7000. **Chrmn & Pres**—L. H. Wexner. **Secy**—Bella Wexner. **VP & CFO**—K. B. Gilman. **VP & Investor Contact**—Tom Katzenmeyer. **Dirs**—E. M. Freedman, E. G. Gee, K. B. Gilman, D. T. Kollat, C. Malone, L. A. Schlesinger, D. B. Shackelford, A. R. Tessler, M. Trust, A. Wexner, B. Wexner, L. H. Wexner, R. Z. Zimmerman. **Transfer Agent & Registrar**—First Chicago Trust Co. of New York, NYC. **Incorporated**—in Ohio in 1967; reincorporated in Delaware in 1982. **Empl**—131,000. **S&P Analyst:** Karen J. Sack, CFA

12-SEP-98

Industry:
Insurance (Multi-Line)

Summary: LNC sold its property-casualty unit in late 1997, in order to focus on core life insurance, annuity and asset management operations.

S&P Opinion: Hold (★★★)	Recent Price • 88½	Yield • 2.4%	
	52 Wk Range • 98⅞-64⅝	12-Mo. P/E • 8.5	

Quantitative Evaluations

Outlook
(1 Lowest—5 Highest)
• **2+**

Fair Value
• **81⅝**

Risk
• **Low**

Earn./Div. Rank
• **A-**

Technical Eval.
• **Bearish** since 12/96

Rel. Strength Rank
(1 Lowest—99 Highest)
• **84**

Insider Activity
• **Neutral**

Earnings vs. Previous Year
▲=Up ▼=Down ▶=No Change

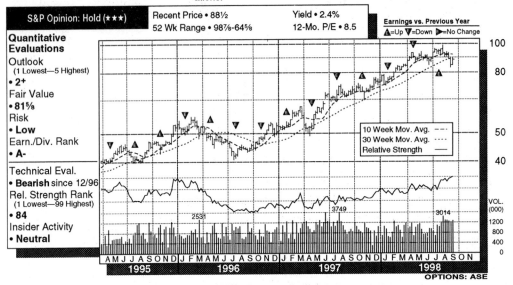

10 Week Mov. Avg. ----
30 Week Mov. Avg. ······
Relative Strength ——

OPTIONS: ASE

Overview - 31-JUL-98

A rebound in operating earnings seen for 1998, to $5.00 a share, versus 1997's operating loss of $0.49 a share, is skewed by $287 million of nonrecurring charges (about $2.76 a share) recorded in the 1997 fourth quarter to boost reserves in two U.K. lines of business. The move followed a 1997 second quarter charge of $1.24 a share, to boost individual disability reserves. That aside, operating earnings growth in 1998 will continue to be driven by strong life insurance and annuity results. For the longer term, growth will be aided by the January 2, 1998, acquisition of CIGNA Corp.'s individual life and annuity division for $1.4 billion in cash. However, a 1998 first quarter pretax charge of $30 million to consolidate this unit will mask near-term EPS contributions. Reinsurance profits will also likely continue to trend upward, assuming that favorable mortality trends continue. Strong underlying asset growth and the absence of further expansion-related costs bode well for the asset management unit. Growth here in recent years has been enhanced by acquisitions. Further acquisitions are likely, as LNC seeks to build critical mass here.

Valuation - 31-JUL-98

After bottoming in mid-1996, amid disappointment over LNC's first half results (due mainly to higher property-casualty weather-related losses), the shares have trended steadily upward, despite a correction in early 1997 that was driven mainly by concerns over higher interest rates. Recent strength was tied to favorable investor response to changes made by LNC in its business mix, such as selling its property-casualty unit. The change leaves LNC better positioned for the long term. However, most of the upside is already included in the stock's recent valuation. As a result, we believe that the shares are adequately valued for the near term.

Key Stock Statistics

S&P EPS Est. 1998	5.00	Tang. Bk. Value/Share	27.13
P/E on S&P Est. 1998	17.7	Beta	0.80
S&P EPS Est. 1999	5.75	Shareholders	13,100
Dividend Rate/Share	2.08	Market cap. (B)	$ 8.9
Shs. outstg. (M)	100.5	Inst. holdings	73%
Avg. daily vol. (M)	0.389		

Value of $10,000 invested 5 years ago: $ 29,209

Fiscal Year Ending Dec. 31

	1998	1997	1996	1995	1994	1993
Revenues (Million $)						
1Q	1,448	1,701	1,641	1,484	2,007	2,003
2Q	1,507	1,128	1,644	1,646	1,544	1,902
3Q	—	1,267	1,685	1,668	1,562	2,327
4Q	—	1,305	1,752	1,835	1,871	2,121
Yr.	—	4,898	6,721	6,633	6,984	8,297
Earnings Per Share ($)						
1Q	**1.20**	1.27	1.34	1.30	1.46	0.69
2Q	**1.46**	-0.46	1.07	1.13	0.45	1.23
3Q	—	1.22	1.14	1.48	0.56	1.82
4Q	—	-1.34	1.37	0.72	0.90	0.31
Yr.	—	0.21	4.91	4.63	3.37	4.06

Next earnings report expected: late October

Dividend Data (Dividends have been paid since 1920.)

Amount ($)	Date Decl.	Ex-Div. Date	Stock of Record	Payment Date
0.520	Nov. 13	Jan. 01	Jan. 09	Feb. 01 '98
0.520	Mar. 12	Apr. 07	Apr. 09	May. 01 '98
0.520	May. 14	Jul. 08	Jul. 10	Aug. 01 '98
0.520	Aug. 13	Oct. 07	Oct. 09	Nov. 01 '98

A Division of The McGraw-Hill Companies

Business Summary - 31-JUL-98

By focusing on six key areas (annuities, 401(k) retirement plans, life insurance, life reinsurance, institutional investment management, and retail mutual funds), LNC is transforming itself from a staid, slow-growing multiline insurance company into a leading provider of financial services. Segment contributions (in millions) to operating income (from continuing operations, before restructuring charges) in recent years were:

	1997	1995
Life insurance/annuities	$255.8	$212.6
Lincoln UK	-108.3	66.1
Reinsurance	-151.6	74.0
Investment management	4.5	10.2
Other operations	-51.1	-64.1

Life insurance is offered by three companies, including Lincoln National Life, the 12th largest life insurer in the U.S. At year-end 1997, annuity, 401(k) retirement plan, life insurance and pension accounts totaled $53.7 billion. Fixed and variable annuities, traditional and interest-sensitive life insurance, and pension products are marketed through agents, securities brokers, banks and financial planners. Strength in the annuity area fueled a 20% rise in the unit's 1997 operating profits. The January 2, 1998, acquisition of CIGNA Corp's. individual life insurance and annuity business added $41 billion of life insurance in force.

Lincoln UK offers life insurance, investment and retirement planning products through 1,800 sales representatives and agents in the United Kingdom. At year end 1997, individual life insurance in force totaled $25 billion, and unit-linked assets under management (similar to variable life insurance) equaled $5.6 billion..

LNC's reinsurance unit, Lincoln Re, is a leading life/health reinsurer, offering life, accident, and disability programs to insurance companies, HMOs, and self-funded employer-sponsored plans worldwide.

Investment management activities consist of institutional investment management ($31.5 billion of assets under management at year-end 1997) and retail mutual funds ($22.5 billion under management, mostly through the Delaware family of retail mutual funds). Operating profits have come under pressure from expenses to expand the retail mutual fund business, an area targeted for growth. In May 1997, LNC acquired the Voyager mutual fund group for $70 million in stock. Further acquisitions are likely.

Property-casualty insurance operations, conducted by 83%-owned American States Financial, were sold in October 1997 to SAFECO Corp., for $2.82 billion.

Per Share Data ($)

(Year Ended Dec. 31)	1997	1996	1995	1994	1993	1992	1991	1990	1989	1988
Tangible Bk. Val.	38.69	31.93	32.45	27.34	37.48	28.22	25.31	22.58	21.51	19.61
Oper. Earnings	-0.49	4.15	2.95	3.75	3.36	2.63	1.89	2.56	2.31	2.06
Earnings	0.21	4.91	4.63	3.37	4.06	3.90	2.30	2.15	3.03	1.60
Dividends	1.96	1.84	1.72	1.64	1.52	1.46	1.36	1.30	1.24	1.18
Relative Payout	NM	37%	37%	49%	37%	37%	59%	61%	41%	74%
Prices - High	78¹/₈	57	53³/₄	44³/₈	48¹/₄	38¹/₈	27⁵/₈	30⁵/₈	31¹/₂	26³/₄
- Low	49	40³/₄	34⁵/₈	34⁵/₈	34³/₄	25¹/₄	19	15³/₈	21³/₈	20¹/₈
P/E Ratio - High	NM	12	12	13	12	10	12	14	10	17
- Low	NM	8	7	10	9	6	8	7	7	13

Income Statement Analysis (Million $)

	1997	1996	1995	1994	1993	1992	1991	1990	1989	1988
Life Ins. In Force	212,500	218,900	194,400	NA	233,766	217,985	255,557	257,471	259,543	216,812
Prem. Inc.: Life A & H	1,329	2,193	2,098	NA	3,515	3,216	4,488	4,036	3,641	3,518
Prem. Inc.: Cas./Prop.	832	1,617	1,679	NA	1,841	2,083	2,242	2,292	2,321	2,197
Net Invest. Inc.	2,251	2,366	2,286	2,011	2,147	1,987	1,799	1,653	1,580	1,439
Oth. Revs.	487	545	570	514	786	748	640	509	539	158
Total Revs.	2,893	6,721	6,633	6,984	8,289	8,034	9,169	8,490	8,081	7,312
Pretax Inc.	34.0	712	627	376	588	425	199	200	330	180
Net Oper. Inc.	257	434	307	390	344	241	NA	NA	NA	NA
Net Inc.	21.0	514	482	350	415	363	208	191	269	147

Balance Sheet & Other Fin. Data (Million $)

	1997	1996	1995	1994	1993	1992	1991	1990	1989	1988
Cash & Equiv.	3,795	1,715	2,036	1,471	1,123	1,452	972	1,142	1,014	1,274
Premiums Due	621	651	538	565	602	792	926	1,008	828	771
Invest. Assets: Bonds	24,066	27,906	25,834	21,644	23,964	20,331	17,849	14,211	13,077	10,463
Invest. Assets: Stocks	660	993	1,165	1,039	1,080	923	1,025	834	868	570
Invest. Assets: Loans	4,051	4,031	3,790	3,406	3,896	3,699	3,675	3,715	3,511	3,325
Invest. Assets: Total	25,212	34,045	31,936	26,971	29,732	25,525	22,987	19,112	17,782	14,878
Deferred Policy Costs	1,624	1,892	1,437	2,444	2,011	2,118	1,972	1,594	1,402	1,030
Total Assets	77,175	71,713	63,258	49,330	48,380	39,672	34,095	27,597	25,070	20,964
Debt	808	626	659	420	335	423	253	379	379	477
Common Eqty.	4,983	4,467	4,375	2,730	3,761	2,636	2,461	2,236	2,185	2,037
Comb. Loss-Exp. Ratio	NM	105.8	104.9	105.7	107.5	112.7	111.9	109.2	106.7	100.5
% Return On Revs.	0.7	7.6	7.3	5.0	5.0	4.5	2.3	2.3	3.3	2.5
% Ret. on Equity	0.4	11.6	13.3	10.3	13.0	13.6	8.3	8.2	12.2	8.6
% Invest. Yield	7.5	7.2	7.3	7.1	7.8	8.2	8.5	9.0	9.7	8.8

Data as orig. reptd.; bef. results of disc. opers. and/or spec. items. Per share data adj. for stk. divs. as of ex-div. date. Bold denotes diluted EPS (FASB 128). E-Estimate. NA-Not Available. NM-Not Meaningful. NR-Not Ranked.

Office—200 E. Berry St., Fort Wayne, IN 46802-2706. **Tel**—(219) 455-2000.**Website**—http://www.lnc.com **Chrmn & CEO**—I. M. Rolland.**Pres**—J. A. Boscia.**EVP & CFO**—R. C. Vaughan.**Secy**—C. S. Womack.**VP & Investor Contact**—Daniel W. Weber. **Dirs**—J. P. Barrett, T. D. Bell Jr., J. A. Boscia, D. R. Efroymson, E. G. Johnson, H. L. Kavetas, M. L. Lachman, R. Pieper, J. M. Pietruski, I. M. Rolland, J. S. Ruckelshaus, G. R. Whitaker Jr. **Transfer Agent & Registrar**—First National Bank of Boston. **Incorporated**—in Indiana in 1905; reincorporated in 1968.**Empl**— 8,120. **S&P Analyst:** C. Seifert

STANDARD &POOR'S
STOCK REPORTS

Liz Claiborne

1363W

NYSE Symbol **LIZ**

In S&P 500

12-SEP-98

Industry:
Textiles (Apparel)

Summary: Liz Claiborne designs and markets men's and women's apparel that is made by independent suppliers and sold through department and specialty stores throughout the world.

S&P Opinion: Hold (★★★)	Recent Price • 26¼	Yield • 1.7%
	52 Wk Range • 57⅞-25⅞	12-Mo. P/E • 9.4

Earnings vs. Previous Year
▲=Up ▼=Down ▶=No Change

Quantitative Evaluations

Outlook
(1 Lowest—5 Highest)
• **4+**

Fair Value
• **41¼**

Risk
• **Average**

Earn./Div. Rank
• **A-**

Technical Eval.
• **Bearish** since 7/98

Rel. Strength Rank
(1 Lowest—99 Highest)
• **15**

Insider Activity
• **NA**

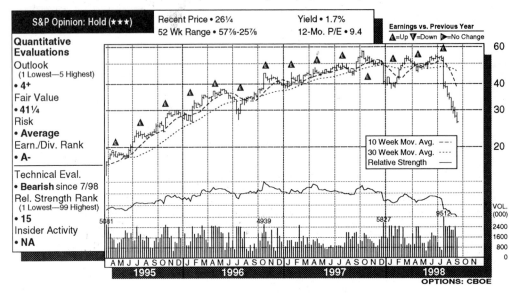

10 Week Mov. Avg. ---
30 Week Mov. Avg. ·····
Relative Strength ——

VOL. (000)
OPTIONS: CBOE

Overview - 28-JUL-98

Sales should advance about 8% in the second half of 1998, primarily driven by the launch of DKNY jeans in early 1998. The addition of DKNY has already contributed to the 7.6% sales growth in the first half of 1998 and will continue to boost sales. The introduction of DKNY Active clothing is slated for 1999. Sales of larger size clothing, accessories and menswear should also continue to contribute modestly to the sales increase, as should the special markets division, which includes Emma James (a budget label), the First Issue brand in Sears, the Russ brand in Wal-Mart, and the Crazy Horse label in J.C. Penney. Higher SG&A expenses related to the start-up of the DKNY line and J.H. Collectibles restricted the bottom line in the first half of the year, and additional costs related to DKNY will hurt margins in the second half. Considering these factors and the company's aggressive share repurchase program, we expect EPS in 1998 to grow approximately 7%, to $2.82.

Valuation - 28-JUL-98

Shares of LIZ have fallen recently due to lower bookings for the holiday season, less favorable pricing in discount retail stores and higher costs associated with a new distribution center. As a result, we have lowered our earnings estimates for the latter half of 1998, and have downgraded the stock to hold, from accumulate. Although sales rose 5.1% in the second quarter of 1998, inventory levels were up 15%; therefore, we remain cautious. Earnings will continue to benefit from the company's aggressive share repurchase program; however, with the stock recently trading at 14X our revised 1998 EPS estimate of $2.82, and 12X our 1999 estimate of $3.25, we believe shares of LIZ are fairly valued.

Key Stock Statistics

S&P EPS Est. 1998	2.82	Tang. Bk. Value/Share	14.73
P/E on S&P Est. 1998	9.3	Beta	1.11
S&P EPS Est. 1999	3.25	Shareholders	10,100
Dividend Rate/Share	0.45	Market cap. (B)	$ 1.7
Shs. outstg. (M)	65.4	Inst. holdings	85%
Avg. daily vol. (M)	0.467		

Value of $10,000 invested 5 years ago: $ 6,975

Fiscal Year Ending Dec. 31

	1998	1997	1996	1995	1994	1993
Revenues (Million $)						
1Q	656.0	596.6	556.6	527.1	541.4	531.0
2Q	565.2	537.9	500.6	474.9	490.0	506.9
3Q	—	685.9	622.1	582.6	616.8	621.9
4Q	—	592.2	538.3	497.1	514.7	544.1
Yr.	—	2,413	2,218	2,082	2,163	2,204
Earnings Per Share ($)						
1Q	**0.69**	**0.59**	0.49	0.37	0.35	0.50
2Q	**0.47**	**0.41**	0.31	0.23	0.20	0.38
3Q	**E1.00**	**0.95**	0.78	0.64	0.55	0.47
4Q	**E0.68**	**0.70**	0.57	0.45	-0.04	0.19
Yr.	**E2.82**	**2.63**	2.15	1.69	1.06	1.54

Next earnings report expected: late October

Dividend Data (Dividends have been paid since 1984.)

Amount ($)	Date Decl.	Ex-Div. Date	Stock of Record	Payment Date
0.113	Oct. 09	Nov. 06	Nov. 11	Dec. 03 '97
0.113	Jan. 23	Feb. 12	Feb. 17	Mar. 06 '98
0.113	Mar. 12	Apr. 30	May. 04	Jun. 01 '98
0.113	Jun. 26	Aug. 05	Aug. 07	Sep. 04 '98

A Division of The McGraw·Hill Companies

Business Summary - 28-JUL-98

With brand names recognized by nearly 99% of all female consumers in the U.S., Liz Claiborne is one of the largest "better" women's sportswear and dress companies in the U.S. LIZ designs and markets an extensive range of high-quality fashion apparel and accessories, with selections appropriate for a range of casual to dressy occasions. Although career apparel continues to be the driving force behind LIZ's fashion image, it has begun to increase emphasis on casual clothing to be consistent with trends in the market.

Liz Claiborne recently adopted a multi-brand portfolio strategy to offer a wide range of products across all consumer channels, and to all price points. To that end, the company offers the Dana Buchman and dana b. & karen labels at "bridge" prices, Liz Claiborne, Claiborne and Elisabeth at "better" prices and Emma James in the "upper moderate" zone, to department and specialty stores. The company's First Issue brand for Sears, as well as its Villager line for other regional department stores, are available at more popular price points, while the budget-priced Russ line is made for customers of Wal-Mart and other mass merchandisers. Recently, LIZ acquired the license for DKNY Jeans which was launched in early 1998, and DKNY Activewear which is scheduled to launch in the first quarter of 1999. Additionally, the company plans to reintroduce the JH Collectibles line in the Spring of 1999. The company also licenses the Liz Claiborne name for a number of additional products including women's shoes, home furnishings, optics, sunglasses, watches, and men's tailored clothing.

Products are manufactured in the U.S. and abroad, and are sold through leading department and specialty stores. Approximately 87% of 1997 sales were made to the company's 100 largest customers, with Dillard Department Stores the largest customer (12% of sales). LIZ products are also sold in 117 stores in and department stores in 24 countries outside the U.S.

Following several years of lackluster sales growth and declining earnings, the company in 1995 embarked upon a major restructuring and transformation program to focus on quality, improve product innovation and development, reduce costs, and use technology as a competitive tool. Several initiatives to heighten its brand image include the LizView fixturing program, designed to enhance the presentation of products on retail selling floors, and the LizEdge in-store servicing and maintenance program. The company also consolidated its sourcing base to increase leverage with regard to cost quality and delivery, reduced excess inventories by over 50%, and implemented in-stock reorder programs. In the fourth quarter of 1997, LIZ reached its goal of reducing operating expenses by $100 million.

Per Share Data ($) (Year Ended Dec. 31)	1997	1996	1995	1994	1993	1992	1991	1990	1989	1988
Tangible Bk. Val.	13.94	14.37	13.41	12.77	12.41	12.05	10.67	8.39	6.94	5.22
Cash Flow	3.29	2.74	2.21	1.50	1.93	2.95	2.92	2.62	2.05	1.40
Earnings	2.63	2.15	1.69	1.06	1.54	2.61	2.61	2.37	1.87	1.26
Dividends	0.45	0.45	0.45	0.45	0.44	0.39	0.33	0.24	0.19	0.17
Payout Ratio	17%	21%	27%	42%	28%	15%	12%	10%	10%	14%
Prices - High	57⅞	45⅛	30	26⅝	42⅞	47⅞	50¾	35	27¾	20
- Low	38⅛	26¼	14⅜	15⅜	18	31⅞	28¼	20¼	16½	12¾
P/E Ratio - High	22	21	18	25	28	18	19	15	15	16
- Low	14	12	9	15	12	12	11	9	9	10
Income Statement Analysis (Million $)										
Revs.	2,413	2,218	2,082	2,163	2,204	2,194	2,007	1,729	1,411	1,184
Oper. Inc.	323	278	229	186	215	351	361	326	263	183
Depr.	46.0	42.9	39.0	35.0	32.3	28.5	27.0	21.2	15.7	12.5
Int. Exp.	Nil	Nil	NA	NA	NA	NA	NA	1.5	1.3	1.3
Pretax Inc.	293	249	203	131	199	342	351	329	270	182
Eff. Tax Rate	37%	38%	38%	37%	37%	36%	37%	38%	39%	40%
Net Inc.	185	156	127	83.0	125	219	223	206	165	110
Balance Sheet & Other Fin. Data (Million $)										
Cash	138	529	438	330	309	426	472	432	373	278
Curr. Assets	1,057	1,142	1,065	1,023	1,004	1,110	1,014	853	746	549
Total Assets	1,305	1,383	1,329	1,290	1,236	1,285	1,175	985	849	629
Curr. Liab.	328	326	307	303	254	270	250	244	209	147
LT Debt	Nil	1.0	1.1	1.2	1.3	1.4	1.6	15.1	15.6	14.1
Common Eqty.	922	1,020	988	983	978	998	910	713	612	458
Total Cap.	932	1,030	997	986	982	1,015	925	740	639	482
Cap. Exp.	34.0	23.3	34.4	70.6	91.4	34.7	56.0	38.1	38.2	32.5
Cash Flow	231	199	166	118	158	247	250	227	180	123
Curr. Ratio	3.2	3.5	3.5	3.4	3.9	4.1	4.1	3.5	3.6	3.7
% LT Debt of Cap.	Nil	0.1	0.1	0.1	0.1	0.1	0.2	2.0	2.4	2.9
% Net Inc.of Revs.	7.7	7.1	6.1	3.8	5.7	10.0	11.1	11.9	11.7	9.3
% Ret. on Assets	13.7	11.5	9.8	6.6	10.2	18.0	20.6	22.8	22.2	19.8
% Ret. on Equity	19.0	15.5	12.9	8.5	13.0	23.3	27.4	31.6	30.7	27.0

Data as orig. reptd.; bef. results of disc. opers. and/or spec. items. Per share data adj. for stk. divs. as of ex-div. date. Bold denotes diluted EPS (FASB 128). E-Estimated. NA-Not Available. NM-Not Meaningful. NR-Not Ranked.

Office—1441 Broadway, New York, NY 10018. **Registrar & Transfer Agent**—First Chicago Trust Co. of New York, NYC. **Tel**—(212) 354-4900. **Website**—www.lizclaiborne.com **Chrmn & CEO**—P. R. Charron. **Pres**—D. V. Seegal. **SVP-Fin & CFO**—S. M. Miller. **Secy**—K. P. Kopelman. **Investor Contact**—Walter Krieger. **Dirs**—B. W. Aronson, E. H. Bedell, P. R. Charron, J. A. Chazen, A. M. Fudge, J. J. Gordon, K. P. Kopelman, K. Koplovitz, L. Lowenstein, P. E. Tierney Jr. **Transfer Agent & Registrar**—First Chicago Trust Co. of New York, NYC. **Incorporated**—in Delaware in 1981; predecessor incorporated in New York in 1976. **Empl**— 7,400. **S&P Analyst:** Kathleen J. Fraser

Lockheed Martin

1364H

NYSE Symbol **LMT**

In S&P 500

12-SEP-98

Industry: Aerospace/Defense

Summary: LMT is one of the largest makers of military aircraft, missiles and radar systems.

S&P Opinion: Hold (★★★)

Recent Price • 95⅜	Yield • 1.7%
52 Wk Range • 117⅞-87¼	12-Mo. P/E • 15.2

Quantitative Evaluations

Outlook
(1 Lowest—5 Highest)
• **2**

Fair Value
• **94½**

Risk
• **Low**

Earn./Div. Rank
• **NR**

Technical Eval.
• **Bearish** since 7/98

Rel. Strength Rank
(1 Lowest—99 Highest)
• **80**

Insider Activity
• **NA**

Earnings vs. Previous Year
▲=Up ▼=Down ▷=No Change

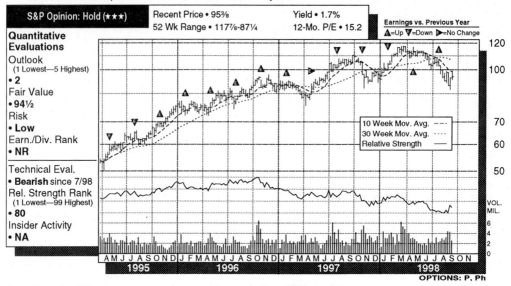

OPTIONS: P, Ph

Overview - 27-JUL-98

With revenues of about $28 billion, Lockheed Martin lies between Boeing (BA), the world's largest aerospace/defense company (revenues of $50 billion), and number three Raytheon (RTN.B; revenues of $20 billion). Recently, LMT ended its merger pact with Northrop Grumman (NOC), the fourth largest aerospace/defense concern (revenues of $9 billion), due to pressure from the Pentagon. It feared the merger would overly curtail competition. The failed merger doesn't help LMT's competitive position. According to a Wall Street Journal citing of LMT documents, LMT believes BA and RTN.B are twice as large as LMT in military aircraft and defense electronics, respectively. In efforts to reduce its dependence on unpredictable military demand, LMT has been expanding into commercial markets. LMT especially sees opportunities in the commercial satellite industry. Industry observers estimate industrywide satellite launches will total more than 500 over the next several years, as burgeoning demand for satellite-based telecommunications systems begins to accelerate.

Valuation - 27-JUL-98

In the last several years, LMT has outpaced the S&P 500, mostly aided by EPS gains from acquisition-related cost-cuttings. Now that the large-scale, defense industry consolidation appears to be over, we wonder whether LMT will be able outpace the market going forward. We believe the defense industry itself is very capital- and R&D-intensive, highly dependent upon very unpredictable U.S. and foreign government sales and faces intensifying competition (from Boeing, Raytheon, and the probable consolidation of the fragmented European defense industry). So, based on average defense industry business economics and our projections of average LMT debt-adjusted ROE and EPS growth rates, we don't believe LMT will consistently outperform the market, long-term.

Key Stock Statistics

S&P EPS Est. 1998	6.70	Tang. Bk. Value/Share	NM
P/E on S&P Est. 1998	14.2	Beta	0.86
S&P EPS Est. 1999	7.40	Shareholders	42,600
Dividend Rate/Share	1.60	Market cap. (B)	$ 18.7
Shs. outstg. (M)	195.7	Inst. holdings	94%
Avg. daily vol. (M)	0.731		

Value of $10,000 invested 5 years ago: NA

Fiscal Year Ending Dec. 31

	1998	1997	1996	1995	1994	1993
Revenues (Million $)						
1Q	6,217	6,674	5,109	5,644	5,036	3,649
2Q	6,520	6,898	7,076	5,606	5,562	5,935
3Q	—	6,619	7,028	5,551	5,704	5,913
4Q	—	7,878	7,662	6,052	6,604	6,900
Yr.	—	28,069	26,875	22,853	22,906	22,397
Earnings Per Share ($)						
1Q	**1.42**	1.35	1.35	0.65	1.38	—
2Q	**1.52**	1.42	1.50	-0.36	1.31	—
3Q	—	1.51	1.55	1.43	1.28	—
4Q	—	**1.83**	2.40	1.56	1.35	—
Yr.	**E6.70**	**6.09**	**6.09**	3.28	5.32	3.99

Next earnings report expected: late October

Dividend Data (Dividends have been paid since 1995.)

Amount ($)	Date Decl.	Ex-Div. Date	Stock of Record	Payment Date
0.400	Oct. 23	Nov. 26	Dec. 01	Dec. 31 '97
0.400	Feb. 26	Mar. 05	Mar. 09	Mar. 31 '98
0.400	Apr. 24	May. 28	Jun. 01	Jun. 30 '98
0.400	Aug. 14	Aug. 28	Sep. 01	Sep. 30 '98

A Division of The McGraw-Hill Companies

Business Summary - 27-JUL-98

The largest and most broadly diversified space and defense contractor, Lockheed operates the famed Skunk Works, which has since 1943 designed and produced the most advanced top-secret aircraft for the U.S. government including the SR-71 and U-2 spy planes, and the F-117A Stealth fighter. LMT's current iteration was formed by merger with Martin Marietta in 1995, and the addition of Loral's defense electronics and systems integration units in 1996. Segment data for 1997 (profits based on $2,779 million) were:

	Sales	Profit
Space and strategic missiles	29.6%	37.9%
Aeronautics	21.5%	22.0%
Electronics	25.2%	21.4%
Information & services	23.0%	5.9%
Energy & other	0.6%	12.8%

Even in the current environment of declining defense spending, the U.S. government remains LMT's main customer, accounting for 65% of 1997 sales; foreign governments represented 17% of sales.

The space and strategic missiles sector produces spacecraft, launch vehicles, missiles and communications systems. Major programs include Titan and Atlas expendable launch vehicles, Trident submarine-launched fleet ballistic missiles, MILSTAR communications satellites and THAAD ground-based theater air defense systems. LMT is part of teams developing various next generation systems including the Space Based Infrared System for missile detection and the Airborne Laser, which will be aircraft-mounted and capable of destroying enemy missiles shortly after launch.

Major aeronautics programs include the F-16 and F-22 fighters, the C-130 military transport aircraft, and the P-3 maritime patrol aircraft. In 1996, LMT was awarded a contract to develop one of two competing versions of the Joint Strike Fighter for use by all branches of the U.S. and U.K. militaries. The next round of competition will conclude in 1999, with the winner expected to receive a revenue stream exceeding $750 billion over 40 years.

Information and services include information processing, simulation/training and automation systems; and commercial electronics. Other includes project management and systems integration for the Department of Energy. In 1996, LMT swapped the 81% of Martin Marietta Materials shares it owned for 7.9 million LMT shares. Space Shuttle processing operations were transferred to United States Space Alliance, a joint venture with Boeing, in 1997.

LMT produces undersea, shipboard, land-based and airborne electronic systems. Major programs include the AEGIS cruiser and destroyer air defense system, the LANTIRN aircraft targeting system, and the helicopter-borne Hellfire and Longbow missiles.

Per Share Data ($)

(Year Ended Dec. 31)	1997	1996	1995	1994	1993	1992	1991	1990	1989	1988
Tangible Bk. Val.	NA	NM	4.06	1.43	-3.15	NA	NA	NA	NA	NA
Cash Flow	10.74	13.46	8.48	10.33	8.75	6.34	NA	NA	NA	NA
Earnings	6.09	6.80	3.28	5.32	3.99	3.31	3.05	2.97	NA	NA
Dividends	1.60	1.55	0.70	NA	NA	NA	NA	NA	NA	NA
Payout Ratio	26%	23%	21%	NA	NA	NA	NA	NA	NA	NA
Prices - High	113⅜	96⅝	79½	NA	NA	NA	NA	NA	NA	NA
- Low	78¼	73	50	NA	NA	NA	NA	NA	NA	NA
P/E Ratio - High	19	14	24	NA	NA	NA	NA	NA	NA	NA
- Low	13	11	15	NA	NA	NA	NA	NA	NA	NA

Income Statement Analysis (Million $)

	1997	1996	1995	1994	1993	1992	1991	1990	1989	1988
Revs.	28,069	26,875	22,853	22,906	22,397	16,030	NA	NA	NA	NA
Oper. Inc.	3,349	3,478	2,893	2,716	2,476	1,733	NA	NA	NA	NA
Depr.	1,052	1,197	921	937	936	594	NA	NA	NA	NA
Int. Exp.	842	700	288	304	278	177	NA	NA	NA	NA
Pretax Inc.	1,937	2,033	1,089	1,675	1,306	1,004	NA	NA	NA	NA
Eff. Tax Rate	33%	34%	37%	37%	37%	35%	NA	NA	NA	NA
Net Inc.	1,300	1,347	682	1,055	829	649	NA	NA	NA	NA

Balance Sheet & Other Fin. Data (Million $)

	1997	1996	1995	1994	1993	1992	1991	1990	1989	1988
Cash	NA	Nil	653	639	366	NA	NA	NA	NA	NA
Curr. Assets	10,105	9,940	8,177	8,143	6,961	5,157	NA	NA	NA	NA
Total Assets	28,361	29,257	17,648	18,049	17,108	10,827	NA	NA	NA	NA
Curr. Liab.	9,189	8,704	5,291	5,635	5,191	3,139	NA	NA	NA	NA
LT Debt	10,528	10,188	3,010	3,594	4,026	1,803	NA	NA	NA	NA
Common Eqty.	5,176	5,856	5,433	5,086	4,201	3,482	NA	NA	NA	NA
Total Cap.	15,704	16,044	9,433	9,680	9,227	5,285	NA	NA	NA	NA
Cap. Exp.	750	737	531	509	536	498	NA	NA	NA	NA
Cash Flow	2,299	2,544	1,603	1,932	1,720	1,243	NA	NA	NA	NA
Curr. Ratio	1.1	1.1	1.5	1.4	1.3	1.6	NA	NA	NA	NA
% LT Debt of Cap.	67.0	63.5	31.9	37.1	43.6	34.1	NA	NA	NA	NA
% Net Inc.of Revs.	4.6	5.0	3.0	4.6	3.7	4.0	NA	NA	NA	NA
% Ret. on Assets	4.5	4.8	3.8	6.0	5.9	6.1	NA	NA	NA	NA
% Ret. on Equity	22.6	22.8	11.8	21.4	20.4	16.8	NA	NA	NA	NA

Data as orig. reptd.; bef. results of disc. opers. and/or spec. items. Per share data adj. for stk. divs. as of ex-div. date. Bold denotes diluted EPS (FASB 128). E-Estimated. NA-Not Available. NM-Not Meaningful. NR-Not Ranked.

Office—6801 Rockledge Dr., Bethesda, MD 20817. **Tel**—(301) 897-6000. **Website**—http://www.lmco.com **Chrmn**—N. R. Augustine. **Pres & CEO Elect**—V. D. Coffman. **SVP & CFO**—M. C. Bennett. **Secy**—L. M. Trippett. **VP & Investor Contact**—James R. Ryan (301-897-6584). **Dirs**—N. R. Augustine, M. C. Bennett, L. V. Cheney, V. D. Coffman, H. I. Flournoy, J. F. Gibbons, E. E. Hood Jr., C. B. Hurtt, G. S. King, V. N. Marafino, E. F. Murphy, A. E. Murray, F. Savage, P. B. Teets, D. M. Tellep, C. A. H. Trost, J. R. Ukropina, D. C. Yearley. **Transfer Agent & Registrar**—First Chicago Trust Co. of New York. **Incorporated**—in Delaware in 1995. **Empl**— 173,000. **S&P Analyst:** Robert E. Friedman, CPA

12-SEP-98

Industry: Insurance (Multi-Line)

Summary: This conglomerate derives most of its revenues from life and property-casualty insurance (through 84%-owned CNA Financial Corp.) and the sale of cigarettes (through Lorillard).

S&P Opinion: Hold (★★★)	Recent Price • 83⅞	Yield • 1.2%
	52 Wk Range • 115⅝-78	12-Mo. P/E • 14.8

Earnings vs. Previous Year
▲=Up ▼=Down ▶=No Change

Quantitative Evaluations

Outlook (1 Lowest—5 Highest)
• **NA**

Fair Value
• **NA**

Risk
• **Low**

Earn./Div. Rank
• **B**

Technical Eval.
• **Bearish** since 4/98

Rel. Strength Rank (1 Lowest—99 Highest)
• **83**

Insider Activity
• **Unfavorable**

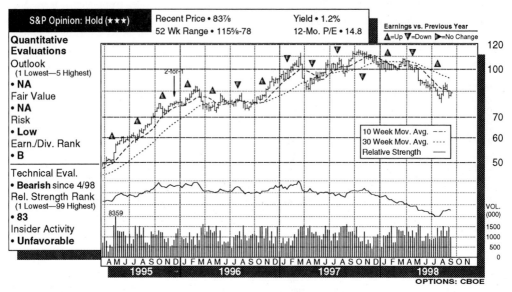

10 Week Mov. Avg. – – –
30 Week Mov. Avg. · · · ·
Relative Strength ——

OPTIONS: CBOE

Overview - 13-AUG-98

Written premiums at 84%-owned CNA Financial Corp. (NYSE: CNA) will likely rise 5%-6% in 1998. This rather tepid rate of premium growth is due to an industry-wide weak pricing environment brought on by an oversupply of underwriting capacity. Underwriting results may deteriorate, as adverse claim trends in certain commercial accounts and higher year to year catastrophe losses offset expense savings from the May 1995 acquisition (for $1.1 billion) of Continental Corp. CNA is also restructuring in an attempt to better combat the competitive insurance market conditions. CNA plans to take a third quarter 1998 pretax charge of $175 million to $260 million to cover restructuring costs. The outlook for Lorillard is mixed. As a result of its ownership in the fourth largest U.S. producer of tobacco products, Loews has been named a defendant in many lawsuits seeking damages for the health effects of tobacco products. Charges related to tobacco settlement litigation, such as the $122 million ($1.06 a share) recorded during 1997, will likely continue.

Valuation - 13-AUG-98

After trending upward during much of early 1997, the shares corrected, reflecting concerns over continuing tobacco litigation and weak property-casualty insurance pricing. Despite their relatively modest valuation (less than 10X our 1999 operating earnings estimate), the shares will likely be only average performers in the near term, due to the negative outlook for tobacco stocks and to mediocre property-casualty fundamentals.

Key Stock Statistics

S&P EPS Est. 1998	9.00	Tang. Bk. Value/Share	78.86
P/E on S&P Est. 1998	9.3	Beta	0.67
S&P EPS Est. 1999	10.50	Shareholders	3,500
Dividend Rate/Share	1.00	Market cap. (B)	$ 9.6
Shs. outstg. (M)	114.7	Inst. holdings	46%
Avg. daily vol. (M)	0.269		

Value of $10,000 invested 5 years ago: $ 14,822

Fiscal Year Ending Dec. 31

	1998	1997	1996	1995	1994	1993
Revenues (Million $)						
1Q	4,795	4,939	5,045	3,703	3,205	3,543
2Q	5,405	4,749	5,045	4,519	3,393	3,375
3Q	—	5,111	5,216	4,960	3,545	3,417
4Q	—	5,339	5,137	5,495	3,371	3,352
Yr.	—	20,139	20,442	18,677	13,515	13,687
Earnings Per Share ($)						
1Q	-0.73	2.08	3.13	1.82	-0.05	2.63
2Q	2.15	0.55	3.25	3.56	0.50	1.58
3Q	—	1.72	3.37	3.28	1.12	-0.70
4Q	—	2.55	2.15	6.32	0.67	1.10
Yr.	—	6.90	11.91	14.98	2.23	4.63

Next earnings report expected: NA

Dividend Data (Dividends have been paid since 1967.)

Amount ($)	Date Decl.	Ex-Div. Date	Stock of Record	Payment Date
0.250	Oct. 20	Oct. 30	Nov. 03	Dec. 01 '97
0.250	Jan. 20	Feb. 04	Feb. 06	Mar. 02 '98
0.250	Apr. 21	Apr. 29	May. 01	Jun. 01 '98
0.250	Jul. 21	Jul. 30	Aug. 03	Sep. 01 '98

Business Summary - 13-AUG-98

Loews Corporation is one of the few remaining true conglomerates, with interests in insurance, tobacco, oil and gas drilling, hotels, and watches. Segment contributions (in million $) in 1997 were:

	Revs.	Profits
Property-casualty ins.	$12,943	$1,288
Life insurance	4,132	314
Cigarettes	2,417	578
Hotels	223	39
Watches/timing devices	129	17
Drilling	978	440
Investment loss & other	-682	-687

Based on aggregate industry written premium data, 84%-owned CNA Financial Corp. is the third largest U.S. property-casualty insurer. CNA expanded its presence in the property-casualty insurance arena during 1995, when it acquired Continental Corp. for $1.1 billion. During 1997, earned premiums from voluntary business amounted to $10.1 billion ($9.9 billion in 1996), of which professional and specialty lines accounted for 17%, general liability and commercial auto 17%, work-

ers' compensation 18%, personal lines 17%, reinsurance and other 11%, commercial multi-peril 10%, and accident and health 10%. During 1997, CNA's combined (loss, expense, and dividend) ratio was 108.9%, versus an industry average of about 102%. The combined ratio is a measure of underwriting performance whereby a ratio of 100% or under indicates an underwriting profit, while one in excess of 100% points to an underwriting loss. CNA's life insurance unit is the 22nd largest in the U.S. Earned premiums totaled $3.4 billion in 1997 (unchanged from 1996), of which group accident and health accounted for 74%, individual life and annuities 19%, and other (mainly group life) 7%. CNA also owns 62% of CNA Surety corp. (NYSE:SUR), formed in September 1997 through the merger of CNA's surety business with Capsure Holdings Corp.

Lorillard, Inc. is the fourth largest U.S. producer of tobacco products, with a market share of 8.7%. Its flagship brand, Newport, accounted for 76% of unit sales in 1997.

The hotel division operates 14 hotels in the U.S., Canada and Monaco. Bulova Corp. (97% owned) distributes and sells watches, clocks, and components. Diamond Offshore Drilling Inc. (50.3% owned) owns offshore drilling rigs and related equipment.

Per Share Data ($)

(Year Ended Dec. 31)	1997	1996	1995	1994	1993	1992	1991	1990	1989	1988
Tangible Bk. Val.	77.51	71.03	65.50	45.62	49.54	40.84	40.78	34.88	30.73	25.80
Oper. Earnings	NA	NA	NA	4.35	1.03	-1.86	5.09	5.38	5.39	4.91
Earnings	6.90	11.91	14.98	2.23	4.63	-0.17	6.57	5.50	6.04	5.85
Dividends	1.00	1.00	1.00	0.50	0.50	0.50	0.50	0.50	0.50	0.50
Relative Payout	14%	8%	7%	22%	11%	NM	8%	9%	8%	9%
Prices - High	115⅝	95⅞	79⅞	51⅜	60⅛	63¼	56½	63½	67½	41⅝
- Low	85½	72½	43⅜	42¼	43⅜	51¾	44¼	37½	38½	31
P/E Ratio - High	17	8	5	23	13	NM	9	12	11	7
- Low	12	6	3	19	9	NM	7	7	6	5

Income Statement Analysis (Million $)

	1997	1996	1995	1994	1993	1992	1991	1990	1989	1988
Life Ins. In Force	311,598	237,009	166,047	127,433	112,248	105,212	98,678	89,262	85,919	NA
Prem. Inc.: Life A & H	3,431	3,347	3,007	2,616	2,392	2,393	2,269	2,082	2,037	NA
Prem. Inc.: Cas./Prop.	NA	10,127	8,724	6,837	6,274	6,352	6,654	6,295	5,394	NA
Net Invest. Inc.	2,442	2,476	2,212	1,671	1,378	1,992	2,149	1,666	1,625	1,549
Oth. Revs.	4,339	4,492	4,735	2,390	3,643	2,955	2,548	2,594	2,381	NA
Total Revs.	20,193	20,442	18,677	13,515	13,687	13,691	13,620	12,637	11,437	10,865
Pretax Inc.	1,593	2,408	2,839	266	689	-517	1,231	932	952	1,322
Net Oper. Inc.	NA	NA	NA	NA	132	-243	701	788	811	NA
Net Inc.	794	1,384	1,766	268	594	-22.0	904	805	907	890

Balance Sheet & Other Fin. Data (Million $)

	1997	1996	1995	1994	1993	1992	1991	1990	1989	1988
Cash & Equiv.	498	306	242	161	156	105	102	83.0	63.0	40.0
Premiums Due	NA	NA	NA	NA	4,077	4,223	4,318	4,579	3,885	2,598
Invest. Assets: Bonds	30,723	29,478	30,468	20,852	17,658	23,127	22,740	18,615	18,918	14,362
Invest. Assets: Stocks	1,163	1,136	1,214	1,438	1,240	860	653	880	609	466
Invest. Assets: Loans	NA	NA	309	244	295	330	373	403	431	473
Invest. Assets: Total	41,618	39,917	39,631	31,076	27,290	24,376	23,919	19,931	19,282	15,335
Deferred Policy Costs	2,142	1,854	1,493	1,025	979	887	853	826	762	663
Total Assets	69,577	67,683	65,058	50,336	45,850	40,492	39,195	34,736	32,451	25,830
Debt	5,906	4,371	4,248	2,144	2,196	1,760	1,945	1,826	1,866	1,393
Common Eqty.	9,664	8,731	8,239	5,405	6,127	5,527	5,667	5,041	4,810	4,028
Comb. Loss-Exp. Ratio	108.2	108.4	107.0	110.0	123.5	141.9	113.8	112.9	113.6	NA
% Return On Revs.	4.5	6.8	9.5	2.0	4.3	NM	6.6	6.4	7.9	8.2
% Ret. on Equity	8.6	16.3	25.9	4.6	10.2	NM	16.9	16.3	20.5	24.5
% Invest. Yield	5.9	6.2	5.5	5.7	5.3	8.2	9.8	8.7	9.4	10.9

Data as orig. reptd.; bef. results of disc. opers. and/or spec. items. Per share data adj. for stk. divs. as of ex-div. date. Bold denotes diluted EPS (FASB 128). E-Estimate. NA-Not Available. NM-Not Meaningful. NR-Not Ranked.

Office—667 Madison Ave., New York, NY 10021-8087. **Tel**—(212) 545-2000. **Co-Chrmn & Co-CEO**—L. A. Tisch, P. R. Tisch. **COO & Pres**—J. S. Tisch. **SVP & CFO**—P. W. Keegan. **SVP & Secy**—B. Hirsh. **Treas**—J. J. Kenny. **Dirs**—C. B. Benenson, J. Brademas, D. H. Chookaszian, P. J. Fribourg, B. Myerson, E. J. Noha, G. R. Scott, A. H. Tisch, J. M. Tisch, J. S. Tisch, L. A. Tisch, P. R. Tisch. **Transfer Agent & Registrar**—ChaseMellon Shareholder Services, Ridgefield Park, NJ. **Incorporated**—in New York in 1954; reincorporated in Delaware in 1970. **Empl**—35,900. **S&P Analyst:** Catherine A. Seifert

STANDARD &POOR'S
STOCK REPORTS

Longs Drug Stores
1375

NYSE Symbol **LDG**

In S&P 500

12-SEP-98

Industry:
Retail (Drug Stores)

Summary: This company operates one of the largest drug store chains in North America, with 373 stores in the western U.S. and Hawaii.

S&P Opinion: Hold (★★★)		
Recent Price • 38½	Yield • 1.5%	
52 Wk Range • 39⅛-23⅞	12-Mo. P/E • 25.0	

Quantitative Evaluations

Outlook
(1 Lowest—5 Highest)
• **1**

Fair Value
• **30½**

Risk
• **Low**

Earn./Div. Rank
• **B+**

Technical Eval.
• **Neutral** since 8/98

Rel. Strength Rank
(1 Lowest—99 Highest)
• **99**

Insider Activity
• **NA**

Earnings vs. Previous Year
▲=Up ▼=Down ▶=No Change

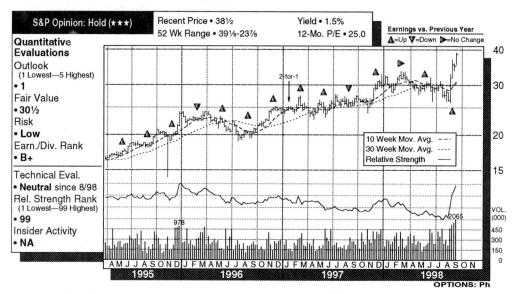

10 Week Mov. Avg. — - —
30 Week Mov. Avg. - - - -
Relative Strength ——

OPTIONS: Ph

Overview - 27-AUG-98

We expect sales to increase nearly 10% during FY 99 (Jan.), primarily reflecting new store openings, a half-year contribution from the acquisition of Western Drug Distributors, and same-store sales growth of approximately 6.0%. Gross margins may benefit from an improved product mix, marketing initiatives, and better inventory management. It appears that the company is making progress in improving margins through the implementation of automatic inventory replenishment and increased category management aimed at improving product display and assortment. However, this improvement is likely to be offset by a higher percentage of third-party plan sales, and increased pricing pressure from supermarkets on some of LDG's front end products. Higher investment levels in technology, particularly for Year 2000 initiatives, and increased marketing costs, may also limit gains.

Valuation - 27-AUG-98

We continue to rate the shares a hold. Although the company is making strides in sales growth and margin improvement, results will be limited by increased spending necessary to make its technology systems compliant for Y2K initiatives. In addition, LDG continues to face increasing competitive pressure in its markets, both from other drug stores and from supermarkets and mass merchandisers. Although the company would be an attractive takeover candidate, Longs continues to reiterate its intention to remain independent. A stock purchase rights plan makes it less likely that LDG will become a takeover candidate. We believe that the shares, recently trading at 20X our EPS estimate of $1.65 for FY 99, are amply valued, based on an expected earnings growth rate of 8.0% to 11% for the foreseeable future.

Key Stock Statistics

S&P EPS Est. 1999	1.65	Tang. Bk. Value/Share	15.02
P/E on S&P Est. 1999	23.4	Beta	0.20
S&P EPS Est. 2000	1.80	Shareholders	15,400
Dividend Rate/Share	0.56	Market cap. (B)	$ 1.5
Shs. outstg. (M)	38.9	Inst. holdings	41%
Avg. daily vol. (M)	0.278		

Value of $10,000 invested 5 years ago: $ 24,952

Fiscal Year Ending Jan. 31

	1999	1998	1997	1996	1995	1994
Revenues (Million $)						
1Q	752.8	752.8	665.4	639.8	622.3	608.0
2Q	786.8	718.3	681.5	646.4	626.3	609.4
3Q	—	714.6	666.9	628.9	614.5	597.2
4Q	—	809.1	814.5	729.3	695.2	684.7
Yr.	—	2,953	2,828	2,644	2,558	2,499
Earnings Per Share ($)						
1Q	**0.37**	0.36	0.35	0.33	0.32	0.27
2Q	**0.38**	0.31	0.34	0.31	0.29	0.32
3Q	**E0.30**	0.26	0.24	0.22	0.15	0.21
4Q	**E0.60**	0.56	0.56	0.29	0.41	0.41
Yr.	**E1.65**	1.49	1.49	1.14	1.18	1.21

Next earnings report expected: mid November

Dividend Data (Dividends have been paid since 1961.)

Amount ($)	Date Decl.	Ex-Div. Date	Stock of Record	Payment Date
0.140	Nov. 19	Nov. 28	Dec. 02	Jan. 09 '98
0.140	Feb. 24	Mar. 06	Mar. 10	Apr. 10 '98
0.140	May. 22	May. 29	Jun. 02	Jul. 10 '98
0.140	Aug. 18	Aug. 28	Sep. 01	Oct. 09 '98

A Division of The **McGraw·Hill** *Companies*

STANDARD
&POOR'S
STOCK REPORTS

Longs Drug Stores Corporation

1375

12-SEP-98

Business Summary - 27-AUG-98

At January 28, 1998, this leading West Coast drug store chain was operating 349 stores, located primarily in California (297), with the balance in Hawaii (32), Nevada (12) and Colorado (8). Most stores range in size from 15,000 sq. ft. to 25,000 sq. ft., of which 68% is devoted to selling space. In addition to prescription drugs, stores sell the core categories of cosmetics, over-the-counter health care products, photo and photo processing, greeting cards and convenience foods. The majority of the merchandise consists of nationally advertised brands, but more than 1,200 items are offered under the company's private label.

Although pharmacy operations accounted for only 34% of the company's nearly $3.0 billion in sales in FY 98 (Jan.), versus an industry average of nearly 50%, they continue to be the cornerstone of LDG's business. Longs believes that the increased traffic associated with its stores' large front-end business has allowed it to fill more prescriptions per store per day than any other drugstore operator in its markets.

Together with pharmacy, a major driver of sales is LDG's new centralized category management system. The company's four-year-old point-of-sale system, backed by a rapid replenishment program, has enabled the chain to tighten inventory, avoid running out of stock on items and increase inventory turns. In 1996, Longs expanded its category management program to 63 merchandise categories. The final targeted category, cosmetics, was completed in FY 98. Although store managers are still encouraged to customize about 10% of their store's inventory mix for local market conditions, the introduction of category management has limited their autonomy in these key categories, replaced by chainwide merchandising and consistent core categories.

To fortify itself against intensifying competition, Longs added 14 new stores in FY 98, including one store in the new market of Denver. The company also agreed to acquire Western Drug Distributors, a chain of 20 stores in Washington and Oregon.

Adding stores also means adding doors for Longs' own pharmacy network and for other pharmacy networks in which it participates. In FY 98, LDG merged its year-old pharmacy benefit management subsidiary, Integrated Health Concepts. (IHC) with the PBM of American Stores Corp. (NYSE: ASC). The equally owned joint venture, operating under the name Rx America, now serves approximately 400 HMO and insurance provider clients that manage more than 3 million lives.

Per Share Data ($)

(Year Ended Jan. 31)	1998	1997	1996	1995	1994	1993	1992	1991	1990	1989
Tangible Bk. Val.	15.12	14.21	13.19	12.74	12.10	11.22	10.35	9.40	8.34	7.73
Cash Flow	2.66	2.61	2.15	2.09	2.01	1.98	1.93	2.00	1.95	1.78
Earnings	1.49	1.49	1.15	1.18	1.21	1.29	1.35	1.47	1.50	1.38
Dividends	0.56	0.56	0.56	0.56	0.56	0.56	0.54	0.51	0.47	0.43
Payout Ratio	38%	38%	49%	48%	46%	43%	39%	35%	31%	31%
Cal. Yrs.	1997	1996	1995	1994	1993	1992	1991	1990	1989	1988
Prices - High	32¾	25¼	24⅛	20	19	20	22¼	22½	24¼	18¾
- Low	22⅝	19	15¼	15⅛	15⅝	16¼	15½	16⅝	17¼	14¾
P/E Ratio - High	22	17	21	17	16	16	16	15	16	14
- Low	15	13	13	13	13	13	11	11	11	11

Income Statement Analysis (Million $)

	1998	1997	1996	1995	1994	1993	1992	1991	1990	1989
Revs.	2,953	2,828	2,644	2,558	2,499	2,475	2,366	2,334	2,111	1,925
Oper. Inc.	141	141	131	119	115	116	115	120	119	109
Depr.	45.2	43.9	40.3	37.8	33.0	28.4	23.3	21.3	18.2	16.2
Int. Exp.	NA	NA	NA	NA	NA	NA	NA	NA	NA	NA
Pretax Inc.	95.0	97.0	77.0	81.0	82.0	87.0	91.0	98.0	101	93.0
Eff. Tax Rate	39%	40%	40%	40%	40%	39%	39%	39%	39%	40%
Net Inc.	57.7	59.0	46.2	48.7	49.8	53.0	55.4	59.6	61.3	55.9

Balance Sheet & Other Fin. Data (Million $)

	1998	1997	1996	1995	1994	1993	1992	1991	1990	1989
Cash	48.6	22.8	49.3	57.5	42.5	16.1	12.0	9.7	24.6	21.8
Curr. Assets	481	451	447	427	390	343	326	313	286	250
Total Assets	946	880	854	828	795	709	673	623	567	508
Curr. Liab.	313	287	287	258	247	206	205	198	185	180
LT Debt	14.2	5.2	8.3	11.2	13.8	16.3	18.5	20.5	22.4	Nil
Common Eqty.	589	554	523	524	500	458	423	379	336	309
Total Cap.	631	559	531	570	548	503	468	426	381	328
Cap. Exp.	78.0	70.0	49.1	39.2	61.7	55.4	59.7	52.0	43.4	37.6
Cash Flow	103	103	86.6	86.5	82.7	81.4	78.7	81.0	79.5	72.1
Curr. Ratio	1.5	1.6	1.6	1.7	1.6	1.7	1.6	1.6	1.5	1.4
% LT Debt of Cap.	2.3	0.9	1.6	2.0	2.5	3.2	4.0	4.8	5.9	Nil
% Net Inc.of Revs.	2.0	2.1	1.7	1.9	2.0	2.1	2.3	2.6	2.9	2.9
% Ret. on Assets	6.3	6.8	5.5	6.0	6.6	7.7	8.5	10.0	11.4	11.5
% Ret. on Equity	10.0	10.9	16.5	9.5	10.3	12.0	13.7	16.7	18.9	18.6

Data as orig. reptd.; bef. results of disc. opers. and/or spec. items. Per share data adj. for stk. divs. as of ex-div. date. Bold denotes diluted EPS (FASB 128). E-Estimated. NA-Not Available. NM-Not Meaningful. NR-Not Ranked.

Office—141 N. Civic Dr., Walnut Creek, CA 94596. **Tel**—(510) 937-1170. **Website**—http://www.longs.com **Chrmn & CEO**—R. M. Long. **Pres**—S. D. Roath. **SVP & CFO**—R. A. Plomgren. **VP & Secy**—G. L. White. **VP, Treas & Investor Contact**—Clay E. Selland. **Dirs**—R. M. Brooks, W. G. Combs, D. G. DeSchane, E. E. Johnston, R. M. Long, M. S. Metz, R. A. Plomgren, S. D. Roath, G. H. Saito, H. R. Somerset, D. L. Sorby, T. R. Sweeney, F. E. Trotter. **Transfer Agent & Registrar**—ChaseMellon Shareholder Services, SF. **Incorporated**—in California in 1946; reincorporated in Maryland in 1985. **Empl**— 17,300. **S&P Analyst**: Robert J. Izmirlian

STANDARD &POOR'S
STOCK REPORTS

Louisiana-Pacific

1381

NYSE Symbol **LPX**

In S&P 500

12-SEP-98

Industry:
Paper & Forest Products

Summary: This major forest products company produces oriented strand board, plywood, lumber, other building products and pulp.

| S&P Opinion: Sell (★) | Recent Price • 20⅛ | Yield • 2.8% |
| | 52 Wk Range • 25⅞-16⅝ | 12-Mo. P/E • 49.2 |

Quantitative Evaluations

Outlook
(1 Lowest—5 Highest)
• **1**

Fair Value
• **18**

Risk
• **Low**

Earn./Div. Rank
• **B-**

Technical Eval.
• **Bearish** since 6/98

Rel. Strength Rank
(1 Lowest—99 Highest)
• **91**

Insider Activity
• **Neutral**

Earnings vs. Previous Year
▲=Up ▼=Down ▶=No Change

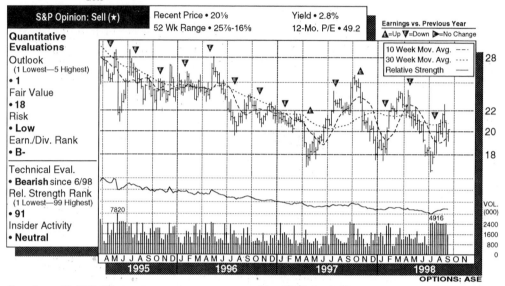

10 Week Mov. Avg. ---
30 Week Mov. Avg. ·····
Relative Strength ——

OPTIONS: ASE

Overview - 17-AUG-98

Sales from comparable operations will likely be flat in 1998, on mixed results. We see much lower lumber sales, as oversupply seems likely to cause ongoing pricing troubles. We see that weakness offset by higher sales in the panels sector, where strong housing markets and growing user familiarity boosted OSB prices considerably in recent days. However, given the very high levels of industry capacity added over the past few years, we still expect pricing weakness in that volatile grade as the year goes on. Margins should improve, aided mostly by the fall 1997 restructuring program, under which LPX has disposed of money-losing non-core assets and put various cost reduction initiatives in place. Despite those positives, we still see troubles in lumber and panel markets limiting LPX's performance. Comparisons will be distorted by $0.19 a share of net one-time charges recorded in 1997. Net one-time gains of $1.79 a share from asset sales and charges for legal matters appear in the EPS table, but have been excluded from our full year 1998 estimate.

Valuation - 17-AUG-98

The shares have fallen sharply over the past few years, with recent year weakness related to significant industry capacity expansion in OSB markets and lumber oversupply. LPX has taken positive steps since the fall of 1996 by closing its money-losing Alaskan pulp mill and certain other non-competitive plants, and under a restructuring program announced in October 1997, has aggressively disposed of other non-core assets. However, we maintain a dim view about prospects. Although OSB markets have experienced a resurgence over the past few months, we still think high OSB capacity will hinder LPX's mainstay panels business in coming periods. With lumber markets also reeling, we would still sell our LPX shares.

Key Stock Statistics

S&P EPS Est. 1998	0.20	Tang. Bk. Value/Share	11.09
P/E on S&P Est. 1998	NM	Beta	0.90
S&P EPS Est. 1999	0.75	Shareholders	23,900
Dividend Rate/Share	0.56	Market cap. (B)	$ 2.2
Shs. outstg. (M)	109.8	Inst. holdings	60%
Avg. daily vol. (M)	0.543		

Value of $10,000 invested 5 years ago: $ 7,664

Fiscal Year Ending Dec. 31

	1998	1997	1996	1995	1994	1993
Revenues (Million $)						
1Q	548.3	554.6	584.1	686.8	698.0	649.0
2Q	623.2	633.3	658.3	709.3	774.7	596.6
3Q	—	619.5	676.3	776.8	818.4	629.4
4Q	—	595.1	567.3	670.3	748.4	636.1
Yr.	—	2,403	2,486	2,843	3,040	2,511
Earnings Per Share ($)						
1Q	**-0.23**	**0.39**	-0.03	0.50	0.77	0.80
2Q	**-1.87**	**-0.10**	0.19	0.25	0.75	0.60
3Q	—	**-1.03**	-1.89	-1.48	0.86	0.38
4Q	—	**-0.20**	-0.14	0.25	0.77	0.54
Yr.	—	**-0.94**	-1.87	-0.48	3.15	2.32

Next earnings report expected: late October

Dividend Data (Dividends have been paid since 1973.)

Amount ($)	Date Decl.	Ex-Div. Date	Stock of Record	Payment Date
0.140	Oct. 27	Nov. 14	Nov. 18	Dec. 02 '97
0.140	Jan. 26	Feb. 11	Feb. 13	Mar. 02 '98
0.140	May. 04	May. 13	May. 15	Jun. 01 '98
0.140	Jul. 27	Aug. 17	Aug. 19	Sep. 01 '98

A Division of The McGraw-Hill Companies

Business Summary - 17-AUG-98

Louisiana-Pacific produces panels, lumber, and other building products, and to a much lesser extent, pulp. The company's very poor operating performance in recent days prompted it to recruit an aggressive new management team over the past two years. That team has closed a large number of unprofitable, outdated mills, and settled many outstanding legal issues (mostly related to defects in siding products installed prior to 1996). Topping off its effort, LPX initiated a major restructuring program in October 1997, under which it further divested non-core operations.

Panel products include plywood and various reconstituted panel products such as oriented strand board (OSB), industrial particleboard, medium-density fiberboard and hardboard. LPX ranks as the largest North American OSB producer, operating 16 plants with an aggregate annual capacity of 4.5 billion sq. ft. at 1997 year end; it also operates one overseas plant. The company additionally operates five plywood plants in the South, with a combined annual capacity of 1.3 billion sq. ft. Panel products accounted for 44% of sales in 1997. In recent years, environmental pressure on timber harvesting (especially in the West) led to reduced supplies and higher costs, causing many of the industry's plywood mills to close permanently. The lost volume has been replaced by reconstituted panels.

Lumber operations (28% of 1997 sales) include 14 western sawmills (annual production capacity of 1.1BBF) and 15 southern sawmills (0.5 BBF).

Other building products (23%) include hardwood veneers, engineered I-joists and cellulose insulation.

LPX has two pulp mills located in California (attempting to sell in restructuring effort) and British Columbia; 5% of sales in 1997. A third mill in Alaska was permanently closed in March 1997.

LPX distributes its products mainly through distributors and home centers. Export sales accounted for 10% of the total in 1997.

At December 31, 1997, LPX owned 1,368,400 acres of timberland; including over 300,000 acres in California since sold in restructuring.

In June 1998, LPX sold its California timberlands and associated operations to Simpson Investment Co. and Samsone Partners, L.P. in separate transactions. Total consideration amounted to $615 million. When combined with the sales of LPX's window and door division and other non-strategic assets in the second quarter, the company had raised about $800 million under the restructuring effort announced in October 1997. The program called for Louisiana-Pacific to sell $800 million to $1 billion of non-strategic assets (certain other desired sales not yet accomplished), with its subsequent focus placed on growing and improving its core building products businesses. LPX plans to use proceeds to reduce debt and build shareholder value.

In July 1998, directors authorized the repurchase of up to 20 million common shares, which if completed, would represent close to 20% of LPX's shares.

Per Share Data ($) (Year Ended Dec. 31)	1997	1996	1995	1994	1993	1992	1991	1990	1989	1988
Tangible Bk. Val.	11.09	12.70	15.12	16.33	14.26	12.46	11.14	10.85	10.31	10.17
Cash Flow	0.76	-0.08	1.41	4.94	3.99	3.13	1.91	2.19	2.92	2.44
Earnings	-0.94	-1.87	-0.48	3.15	2.32	1.63	0.52	0.82	1.68	1.18
Dividends	0.56	0.56	0.55	0.48	0.43	0.39	0.36	0.35	0.33	0.30
Payout Ratio	NM	NM	NM	15%	19%	24%	70%	41%	19%	25%
Prices - High	25⁷/₈	28¹/₈	30¹/₂	48	42¹/₈	31¹/₂	15¹/₈	15¹/₈	14¹/₂	12¹/₂
- Low	17	19⁵/₈	20⁷/₈	25³/₄	28³/₄	14⁵/₈	8⁷/₈	6³/₄	9³/₈	8¹/₂
P/E Ratio - High	NM	NM	NM	15	18	19	30	18	9	11
- Low	NM	NM	NM	8	12	9	17	8	6	7

Income Statement Analysis (Million $)

	1997	1996	1995	1994	1993	1992	1991	1990	1989	1988
Revs.	2,403	2,486	2,843	3,040	2,511	2,185	1,702	1,793	2,010	1,799
Oper. Inc.	95.4	223	472	756	616	461	256	279	425	349
Depr.	184	192	203	197	183	163	150	134	121	128
Int. Exp.	30.9	21.3	16.2	14.5	16.3	26.6	43.8	47.1	44.9	36.0
Pretax Inc.	-149	-326	-94.8	560	428	283	87.0	137	292	214
Eff. Tax Rate	NM	NM	NM	38%	41%	38%	36%	34%	34%	37%
Net Inc.	-101	-200	-51.7	347	254	177	56.0	91.0	193	135

Balance Sheet & Other Fin. Data (Million $)

	1997	1996	1995	1994	1993	1992	1991	1990	1989	1988
Cash	31.9	27.8	75.4	316	262	228	191	209	353	256
Curr. Assets	597	579	619	694	614	539	461	509	654	536
Total Assets	2,578	2,589	2,805	2,716	2,466	2,206	2,107	2,104	2,032	1,796
Curr. Liab.	319	345	449	345	317	296	260	196	180	163
LT Debt	572	459	201	210	289	386	493	589	530	370
Common Eqty.	1,286	1,428	1,656	1,849	1,571	1,361	1,204	1,167	1,177	1,137
Total Cap.	2,037	2,050	2,065	2,329	2,125	1,902	1,837	1,897	1,842	1,624
Cap. Exp.	205	266	413	352	290	202	202	375	260	183
Cash Flow	82.1	-9.0	151	544	438	340	206	225	313	263
Curr. Ratio	1.9	1.7	1.4	2.0	1.9	1.8	1.8	2.6	3.6	3.3
% LT Debt of Cap.	28.1	22.4	9.8	9.0	13.6	20.3	26.8	31.0	28.7	22.8
% Net Inc.of Revs.	NM	NM	NM	11.4	10.1	8.1	3.3	5.1	9.6	7.5
% Ret. on Assets	NM	NM	NM	13.3	10.8	8.2	2.7	4.5	10.0	7.3
% Ret. on Equity	NM	NM	NM	20.1	17.3	13.7	4.7	8.0	16.5	12.6

Data as orig. reptd.; bef. results of disc. opers. and/or spec. items. Per share data adj. for stk. divs. as of ex-div. date. Bold denotes diluted EPS (FASB 128). E-Estimated. NA-Not Available. NM-Not Meaningful. NR-Not Ranked.

Office—111 S.W. Fifth Ave., Portland, OR 97204-3699. **Tel**—(503) 221-0800. **Website**—www.lpcorp.com **Chrmn & CEO**—M. A. Suwyn. **VP & CFO**—C. M. Stevens. **Investor Contact**—Russ S. Pattee. **Dirs**—J. W. Barter, W. C. Brooks, A. W. Dunham, P. S. du Pont IV, B. G. Hill, D. R. Kayser, P. F. McCartan, L. C. Simpson, M. A. Suwyn. **Transfer Agent & Registrar**—First Chicago Trust Co. of New York, Jersey City, NJ. **Incorporated**—in Delaware in 1972. **Empl**—12,000. **S&P Analyst:** Michael W. Jaffe

STANDARD &POOR'S
STOCK REPORTS

Lowe's Companies
1386D
NYSE Symbol **LOW**

In S&P 500

12-SEP-98

Industry:
Retail (Building Supplies)

Summary: This company retails building materials and supplies, lumber, hardware and appliances through more than 445 stores in 25 states.

S&P Opinion: Hold (★★★)	Recent Price • 36⅞ Yield • 0.3%
	52 Wk Range • 46⅛-18⅝ 12-Mo. P/E • 31.0

Quantitative Evaluations

Outlook
(1 Lowest—5 Highest)
• **3⁻**

Fair Value
• **38¼**

Risk
• **Average**

Earn./Div. Rank
• **A-**

Technical Eval.
• **Bearish** since 10/97

Rel. Strength Rank
(1 Lowest—99 Highest)
• **81**

Insider Activity
• **NA**

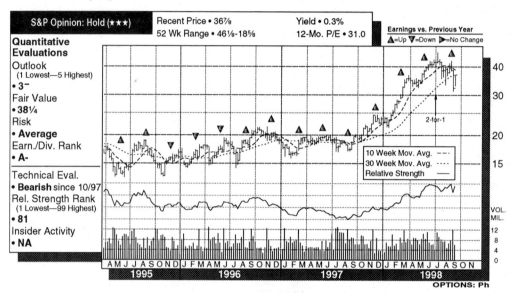

Earnings vs. Previous Year
▲=Up ▼=Down ▷=No Change

10 Week Mov. Avg. ---
30 Week Mov. Avg. ·····
Relative Strength —

2-for-1

VOL. MIL.

OPTIONS: Ph

Overview - 08-JUN-98

Continued healthy consumer demand should boost same-store sales in FY 99 (Jan.) about 4%, with total company sales up about 15%, benefiting from newer and larger stores that offer a broader selection of merchandise, with wider overall margins. SG&A expenses will increase as a percentage of sales, reflecting higher staffing levels and training necessary in larger stores. Depreciation charges will also increase, as the company opened 60 new units in FY 98, and continues to execute an aggressive capital expenditure program approximating $1.4 billion; 80% of capital spending is for new store expansion. Interest expense should rise, in part as a result of the increased capital expenditure program. With store expansion of 15% annually for the next five years, together with emphasis on larger, more productive stores, earnings should continue on a growth track. In April 1998, the company announced plans for expansion into California; the plans call for investing over $1.5 billion to open more than 100 new stores in western markets over the next three to four years.

Valuation - 08-JUN-98

Given the sharp appreciation in the stock price thus far in 1998, we rate the shares only as a hold. We believe that the recent P/E multiple of 32X FY 99 estimated EPS reflects the good news anticipated in the year ahead. Strong comparable-store sales should be boosted by a strong housing market and penetration into new markets, as well as by the company's shift to larger, more productive units. The more favorable merchandise mix of the larger units boosts profitability. The shares of this growth company warrant a premium multiple to that of the market.

Key Stock Statistics

S&P EPS Est. 1999	1.25	Tang. Bk. Value/Share	7.72
P/E on S&P Est. 1999	29.5	Beta	0.53
S&P EPS Est. 2000	1.50	Shareholders	7,400
Dividend Rate/Share	0.12	Market cap. (B)	$ 13.0
Shs. outstg. (M)	351.8	Inst. holdings	61%
Avg. daily vol. (M)	1.721		

Value of $10,000 invested 5 years ago: $ 62,892

Fiscal Year Ending Jan. 31

	1999	1998	1997	1996	1995	1994
Revenues (Million $)						
1Q	2,900	2,401	1,907	1,635	1,397	992.1
2Q	3,426	2,808	2,459	1,978	1,647	1,242
3Q	—	2,530	2,193	1,766	1,579	1,158
4Q	—	2,398	2,042	1,697	1,487	1,146
Yr.	—	10,137	8,600	7,075	6,111	4,538
Earnings Per Share ($)						
1Q	**0.27**	**0.20**	0.14	0.18	0.17	0.10
2Q	**0.47**	**0.36**	0.35	0.27	0.23	0.15
3Q	**E0.30**	**0.25**	0.21	0.14	0.17	0.11
4Q	**E0.23**	**0.20**	0.16	0.12	0.14	0.09
Yr.	**E1.25**	**1.02**	0.87	0.70	0.72	0.45

Next earnings report expected: mid November
Dividend Data (Dividends have been paid since 1961.)

Amount ($)	Date Decl.	Ex-Div. Date	Stock of Record	Payment Date
0.055	Dec. 16	Jan. 14	Jan. 17	Jan. 31 '98
0.055	Apr. 07	Apr. 15	Apr. 17	Apr. 30 '98
2-for-1	May. 29	Jun. 29	Jun. 12	Jun. 26 '98
0.030	May. 29	Jul. 15	Jul. 17	Jul. 31 '98

A Division of The McGraw-Hill Companies

Business Summary - 08-JUN-98

Lowe's Companies is the second largest U.S. do-it-yourself and home improvement retailer; Home Depot is the leader, with annual revenues more than double those of Lowe's. Capitalizing on a growing number of U.S. households (now 100 million) and on historically high rates of home ownership, LOW has grown from 15 stores in FY 62 (Jan.) to more than 446 at the end of FY 98. The company operates in 25 states, mainly in the East. According to the Home Improvement Research Institute, the size of the home improvement market was about $142 billion in 1997, and was growing at about 5% annually.

Contributions to sales by product line in recent fiscal years were:

	FY 98	FY 97
Lumber & building materials	28%	30%
Kitchen, bath & laundry	11%	12%
Paint & sundries	8%	8%
Plumbing & electrical	18%	17%
Yard, patio & garden	16%	15%
Power tools & hardware	12%	12%
Home decoration	7%	6%

In FY 98, an average Lowe's store had sales of $22.2 million. The company's largest stores, over 80,000 sq. ft., averaged sales of $26.1 million. LOW has been increasing the size of its stores over the past few years. Large stores (over 80,000 sq. ft.) provided 70% of sales in FY 98, up from 61% in FY 97. These units contributed 64% of operating profits in FY 98, up from 53% in FY 97.

The company's FY 98 capital expenditure budget totaled $860 million, and increased to $1.0 billion in FY 99. The expansion was to be funded with cash from operations. More than 80% of the budget was earmarked for store expansion, consisting of about 60 new stores. About 70% were in new markets, with the balance consisting of relocations of existing stores, with increases in sales floor square footage of 20%.

Sales in the first quarter of FY 99 rose 21%, and comparable-store sales increased 5.0%. Net income rose 34%. Sales have grown at an annual compound rate of 20% over the past seven years, and earnings have advanced at 26% annually during the same period.

Per Share Data ($)

(Year Ended Jan. 31)	1998	1997	1996	1995	1994	1993	1992	1991	1990	1989
Tangible Bk. Val.	7.42	6.39	5.15	4.45	2.96	2.51	2.29	2.34	2.17	1.98
Cash Flow	1.72	1.46	1.17	1.07	0.72	0.53	0.22	0.41	0.41	0.36
Earnings	1.02	0.87	0.70	0.72	0.45	0.29	0.02	0.24	0.25	0.23
Dividends	0.11	0.10	0.10	0.09	0.16	0.07	0.07	0.07	0.06	0.06
Payout Ratio	11%	12%	13%	12%	36%	25%	305%	27%	24%	25%
Cal. Yrs.	1997	1996	1995	1994	1993	1992	1991	1990	1989	1988
Prices - High	24⅝	21¾	19½	20¾	15	6⅜	4⅝	6¼	4	3
- Low	15⅞	14⅜	13	13¼	6	4	2⅞	2⁵⁄₁₆	2⅝	2¹⁄₁₆
P/E Ratio - High	24	25	28	29	34	22	NM	26	16	13
- Low	15	16	18	18	13	14	NM	10	10	9

Income Statement Analysis (Million $)

Revs.	10,137	8,600	7,075	6,111	4,538	3,846	3,056	2,833	2,651	2,517
Oper. Inc.	865	701	540	481	297	211	151	169	174	168
Depr.	241	198	150	110	80.5	69.8	58.3	51.4	46.1	41.2
Int. Exp.	73.3	65.1	54.7	44.8	26.6	19.4	19.9	23.0	22.4	24.2
Pretax Inc.	559	454	352	344	198	126	5.0	100	109	106
Eff. Tax Rate	36%	36%	35%	35%	34%	33%	NM	29%	31%	35%
Net Inc.	357	292	226	224	132	84.7	6.5	71.1	74.9	69.2

Balance Sheet & Other Fin. Data (Million $)

Cash	195	70.0	171	268	108	54.8	30.8	50.1	55.6	60.3
Curr. Assets	2,110	1,851	1,604	1,557	1,084	746	770	616	596	578
Total Assets	5,219	4,435	3,556	3,106	2,202	1,609	1,441	1,203	1,147	1,086
Curr. Liab.	1,449	1,349	950	946	681	500	589	338	308	286
LT Debt	1,046	767	866	681	592	314	114	159	168	190
Common Eqty.	2,601	2,217	1,657	1,420	874	733	669	683	646	587
Total Cap.	3,771	3,086	2,607	2,150	1,492	1,063	788	865	840	800
Cap. Exp.	773	677	520	414	337	243	140	91.0	92.0	82.0
Cash Flow	598	490	376	333	212	155	65.0	123	121	110
Curr. Ratio	1.5	1.4	1.7	1.6	1.6	1.5	1.3	1.8	1.9	2.0
% LT Debt of Cap.	27.7	24.9	33.3	31.7	39.7	29.5	14.4	18.4	20.0	23.8
% Net Inc.of Revs.	3.5	3.4	3.2	3.7	2.9	2.2	0.2	2.5	2.8	2.7
% Ret. on Assets	7.4	7.3	6.8	8.2	6.9	5.6	0.5	6.1	6.7	6.7
% Ret. on Equity	14.8	15.1	14.7	18.9	16.3	12.1	1.0	10.8	12.1	12.2

Data as orig. reptd.; bef. results of disc. opers. and/or spec. items. Per share data adj. for stk. divs. as of ex-div. date. Bold denotes diluted EPS (FASB 128). E-Estimated. NA-Not Available. NM-Not Meaningful. NR-Not Ranked.

Office—State Highway 268 East (P.O. Box 1111), North Wilkesboro, NC 28656. **Tel**—(910) 651-4000. **Website**—http://www.lowes.com **Chrmn., Pres & CEO**—R. L. Tillman. **SVP & Secy**—W. C. Warden Jr. **SVP, CFO & Treas**—T. E. Whiddon. **Investor Contact**—Robert A. Niblock. **Dirs**—W. A. Andres, J. M. Belk, L. L. Berry, P. C. Browning, C. A. Farmer, P. Fulton, J. F. Halpin, L. G. Herring, R. K. Lochridge, R. B. Long, C. B. Malone, R. G. Schwartz, R. L. Strickland, R. L. Tillman. **Transfer Agent & Registrar**—Wachovia Shareholder Services Boston. **Incorporated**—in North Carolina in 1952. **Empl**— 65,000. **S&P Analyst**: Karen J. Sack, CFA

STANDARD &POOR'S
STOCK REPORTS

LSI Logic

1319D
NYSE Symbol **LSI**
In S&P 500

12-SEP-98

Industry: Electronics (Semiconductors)

Summary: This company is a leading supplier of custom performance semiconductors.

S&P Opinion: Hold (★★★)	Recent Price • 11¾	Yield • Nil
	52 Wk Range • 33¾-11½	12-Mo. P/E • 12.2

Quantitative Evaluations

Outlook
(1 Lowest—5 Highest)
• **4**

Fair Value
• **16⅜**

Risk
• **High**

Earn./Div. Rank
• **B-**

Technical Eval.
• **Bearish** since 7/98

Rel. Strength Rank
(1 Lowest—99 Highest)
• **11**

Insider Activity
• **NA**

Earnings vs. Previous Year
▲=Up ▼=Down ▶=No Change

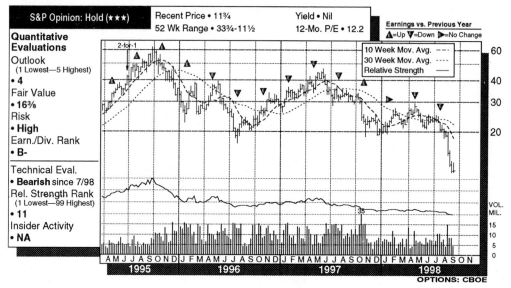

OPTIONS: CBOE

Overview - 24-AUG-98

We expect total sales to be flat to moderately lower in 1998, as weak demand continues to plague the global semiconductor industry. While the company's communications and consumer related businesses have performed well, softness in the computer sector has restricted revenue growth. Furthermore, top-line growth has been limited by the persistent strength of the dollar versus the yen, although lower wafer costs have reduced the impact on EPS. Gross margins are likely to narrow in the fourth quarter and into 1999, reflecting startup costs at a new wafer fab. Margins could improve thereafter, provided unit volumes begin to ramp up. Overall, we look for EPS to fall in 1998 to $0.75, from 1997's $1.12.. We look for EPS to rebound in 1999, to about $1.20. In August 1998, LSI acquired Symbios, Inc., from Hyundai Electronics, for $760 million in cash, including assumed liabilities. The transaction, expected to be accretive to 1999 EPS, broadened LSI's served markets to include the storage segment.

Valuation - 24-AUG-98

Despite the challenging near-term operating environment in the semiconductor industry, we are maintaining our hold opinion on the shares. Near-term operating results are likely to trend lower, reflecting soft demand and a generally weak order outlook. In addition, we remain concerned that the company's plans to add production capacity in late 1998 will put near-term pressure on profitability. On a positive note, LSI has shown strength in design wins, and it is well positioned for growth in consumer areas such as digital cameras, set top boxes, and digital video disk. Although sluggish near-term prospects add a degree of risk, we expect the share price to be buoyed by emerging growth prospects for 1999.

Key Stock Statistics

S&P EPS Est. 1998	0.75	Tang. Bk. Value/Share	11.47
P/E on S&P Est. 1998	15.7	Beta	1.80
S&P EPS Est. 1999	1.20	Shareholders	1,700
Dividend Rate/Share	Nil	Market cap. (B)	$ 1.7
Shs. outstg. (M)	140.9	Inst. holdings	38%
Avg. daily vol. (M)	1.851		

Value of $10,000 invested 5 years ago: $ 21,975

Fiscal Year Ending Dec. 31

	1998	1997	1996	1995	1994	1993
Revenues (Million $)						
1Q	324.9	308.4	311.4	280.2	193.8	168.9
2Q	330.1	332.0	325.4	307.1	212.1	177.1
3Q	—	326.9	300.2	330.8	240.2	183.8
4Q	—	323.0	301.8	349.6	255.7	189.0
Yr.	—	1,290	1,239	1,268	901.8	718.8
Earnings Per Share ($)						
1Q	**0.22**	**0.28**	0.32	0.38	0.18	0.11
2Q	**0.23**	**0.32**	0.35	0.44	0.22	0.14
3Q	**E0.13**	**0.31**	0.21	0.50	0.26	0.14
4Q	**E0.17**	**0.23**	0.23	0.54	0.31	0.15
Yr.	**E0.75**	**1.12**	**1.07**	1.86	0.99	0.55

Next earnings report expected: mid October

Dividend Data

LSI has never paid cash dividends. A poison pill stock purchase rights plan was adopted in 1988. A two-for-one stock split was effected in 1995.

A Division of The **McGraw·Hill** *Companies*

Business Summary - 24-AUG-98

LSI Logic, "the system-on-a-chip company," is in the business of integrating the key functions of an electronic system on a single customized chip. This enables the company's customers, who are generally electronic original equipment manufacturers (OEMs), to reduce component design costs, improve product performance, retain control over proprietary logic, and shorten product development cycles.

LSI creates its system-on-a-chip products with its CoreWare design methodology. Using sophisticated electronic design automation tools, customers add unique product features around pre-wired cores of industry-standard architecture protocols and algorithms that are electronically stitched together on a single chip. CoreWare methodology is based upon application-specific integrated circuit (ASIC) technology--that is, semiconductors designed to satisfy a customer's particular requirement. LSI is a market share leader in the global ASIC market.

LSI directs its marketing and selling efforts toward selected customers in the consumer, communications, and computer industries. LSI Logic targets high-growth end markets that are characterized by increasingly shortened product life cycles and ongoing changes in technological standards and performance requirements.

As a result, customers in these markets tend to benefit from the flexibility of the company's customized ASIC design methodology to help differentiate their products while still complying with existing and emerging global industry standards.

The end markets served by the company's customers include digital video (DVD), digital broadcasting (set-top box) and personal entertainment applications for the consumer market segment, networking and wireless communication for the communications market, and desktop, personal computer and office automation applications for the computer products market.

The company sells its products on a worldwide basis through direct sales and marketing and field engineering organizations and through independent sales representatives and distributors. Sony Corporation accounted for approximately 22% of the company's 1997 revenues, up from 14% in 1996.

In August 1998, LSI acquired Symbios, Inc., a wholly owned subsidiary of Hyundai Electronics America, for $760 million in cash, including assumed liabilities. Symbios designs, manufactures and markets client/server integrated circuits, cell-based application specific integrated circuits, host adaptor boards, and storage subsystems. LSI believes that the transaction will be accretive to earnings in 1999.

Per Share Data ($)

(Year Ended Dec. 31)	1997	1996	1995	1994	1993	1992	1991	1990	1989	1988
Tangible Bk. Val.	11.17	10.18	9.41	4.72	2.94	2.17	3.35	3.28	3.62	4.10
Cash Flow	2.27	2.25	2.92	1.93	1.21	-0.08	1.00	0.80	0.76	0.94
Earnings	1.12	1.12	1.86	0.99	0.55	-1.24	0.10	-0.40	-0.30	0.29
Dividends	Nil	Nil	Nil	Nil	Nil	Nil	Nil	Nil	Nil	Nil
Payout Ratio	Nil	Nil	Nil	Nil	Nil	Nil	Nil	Nil	Nil	Nil
Prices - High	46$^7/_8$	39$^5/_8$	62$^1/_2$	22$^3/_4$	9$^5/_8$	5$^5/_8$	6$^1/_4$	6$^1/_2$	6$^1/_4$	6$^7/_8$
- Low	18$^5/_8$	17	18$^1/_4$	7$^3/_4$	5$^1/_8$	2$^7/_{16}$	2$^3/_4$	2$^5/_8$	3$^1/_8$	3$^5/_8$
P/E Ratio - High	42	35	34	23	18	NM	66	NM	NM	23
- Low	17	15	10	8	9	NM	28	NM	NM	13

Income Statement Analysis (Million $)

	1997	1996	1995	1994	1993	1992	1991	1990	1989	1988
Revs.	1,290	1,239	1,268	902	719	617	698	655	547	379
Oper. Inc.	362	340	454	261	150	104	101	136	101	79.0
Depr.	166	147	136	104	66.0	103	79.0	101	88.0	53.0
Int. Exp.	1.5	13.6	16.3	18.5	15.4	14.7	19.4	21.3	17.3	11.3
Pretax Inc.	224	205	335	156	80.7	-99	12.3	-18.5	-34.9	31.2
Eff. Tax Rate	28%	28%	28%	28%	30%	NM	50%	NM	NM	42%
Net Inc.	161	144	238	109	54.0	-109	8.3	-34.0	-24.9	23.8

Balance Sheet & Other Fin. Data (Million $)

	1997	1996	1995	1994	1993	1992	1991	1990	1989	1988
Cash	105	717	686	429	202	153	157	159	153	204
Curr. Assets	870	1,051	1,137	731	426	350	386	439	392	425
Total Assets	2,127	1,953	1,850	1,270	853	736	748	784	765	787
Curr. Liab.	438	345	396	308	189	211	161	193	151	130
LT Debt	67.3	281	222	263	220	192	166	190	204	192
Common Eqty.	1,566	1,316	1,216	545	292	198	293	276	297	332
Total Cap.	1,689	1,607	1,453	937	638	525	587	591	614	657
Cap. Exp.	513	362	233	166	90.0	142	78.0	71.0	121	110
Cash Flow	327	294	374	212	120	-7.3	87.1	67.4	62.9	77.2
Curr. Ratio	2.0	3.0	2.9	2.4	2.3	1.7	2.4	2.3	2.6	3.3
% LT Debt of Cap.	4.0	17.5	15.3	28.0	34.5	36.5	28.3	32.1	33.3	29.2
% Net Inc.of Revs.	12.5	11.9	18.8	12.1	7.5	NM	1.2	NM	NM	6.3
% Ret. on Assets	7.9	7.7	15.3	9.7	6.5	NM	1.1	NM	NM	3.2
% Ret. on Equity	11.2	11.6	27.0	24.7	21.1	NM	2.9	NM	NM	7.4

Data as orig. reptd.; bef. results of disc. opers. and/or spec. items. Per share data adj. for stk. divs. as of ex-div. date. Bold denotes diluted EPS (FASB 128). E-Estimated. NA-Not Available. NM-Not Meaningful. NR-Not Ranked.

Office—1551 McCarthy Blvd., Milpitas, CA 95035. **Tel**—(408) 433-4365. **Website**—http://www.lsilogic.com **Chrmn & CEO**—W. J. Corrigan. **SVP & CFO**—R. D. Norby. **VP & Secy**—D. E. Sanders. **Investor Contact**—Diana Matley. **Dirs**—T. Z. Chu, W. J. Corrigan, M. R. Currie, J. H. Keyes, R. D. Norby. **Transfer Agent & Registrar**—Bank of Boston. **Incorporated**—in California in 1980; reincorporated in Delaware in 1986. **Empl**—4,443. **S&P Analyst:** B. McGovern

Lucent Technologies

1387A

NYSE Symbol **LU**

In S&P 500

12-SEP-98

Industry:
Communications
Equipment

Summary: This former division of AT&T is one of the world's leading designers, developers and manufacturers of telecommunications equipment, software and products.

| S&P Opinion: Hold (★★★) | Recent Price • 78⅜ | Yield • 0.2% |
| | 52 Wk Range • 108½-36¼ | 12-Mo. P/E • NM |

Earnings vs. Previous Year
▲=Up ▼=Down ▶=No Change

Quantitative Evaluations

Outlook
(1 Lowest—5 Highest)
• **1⁻**

Fair Value
• **66¼**

Risk
• **Average**

Earn./Div. Rank
• **NR**

Technical Eval.
• **NA**

Rel. Strength Rank
(1 Lowest—99 Highest)
• **77**

Insider Activity
• **Neutral**

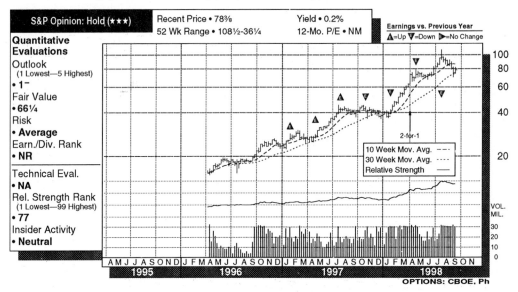

10 Week Mov. Avg. ---
30 Week Mov. Avg. ·····
Relative Strength —

2-for-1

OPTIONS: CBOE, Ph

Overview - 20-AUG-98

Revenue growth is expected to be 13% in FY 98 (Sep.), on increased sales of systems for network operators, business communications systems and microelectronic products. Lucent is benefiting from continued demand for second lines in businesses and residences, for uses such as Internet services and data traffic. The company has acquired a number of businesses to fill in key positions in its messaging and data networking portfolio. In late 1997, LU acquired Livingston Enterprises, a provider of remote access networking equipment, for $610 million, and Prominet Corp., a maker of Gigabit Ethernet equipment, for $200 million. In April 1998, LU acquired Yurie Systems for $1 billion in cash. Yurie is a technology leader in the high growth wide area network asynchronous transfer mode (ATM) access market. We expect significant cost reductions over the next year, and are looking for EPS growth of about 42% in FY 98.

Valuation - 20-AUG-98

The shares were recently up over 115% in 1998, as investors have cheered Lucent's targeted acquisition strategy for rounding out its data networking portfolio. In addition, Lucent is leveraging the R&D expertise of Bell Labs to introduce industry leading semiconductors and optical networking products. The April 1998 acquisition of Yurie Systems filled a key space in Lucent's data networking portfolio. Yurie's addressable market in ATM WAN access equipment is growing at over 50% a year. The shares were recently trading at about 42X our calendar 1999 EPS estimate of $2.00. We view the stock as fairly valued at these levels, based on Lucent's 20% growth rate and solid fundamentals. FY 98 third quarter EPS included $0.49 in acquisition-related charges.

Key Stock Statistics

S&P EPS Est. 1998	1.66	Tang. Bk. Value/Share	3.75
P/E on S&P Est. 1998	47.3	Beta	NA
S&P EPS Est. 1999	1.90	Shareholders	1,760,000
Dividend Rate/Share	0.16	Market cap. (B)	$103.1
Shs. outstg. (M)	1315.0	Inst. holdings	38%
Avg. daily vol. (M)	8.598		

Value of $10,000 invested 5 years ago: NA

Fiscal Year Ending Sep. 30

	1998	1997	1996	1995	1994	1993
Revenues (Million $)						
1Q	8,724	7,938	7,427	—	—	—
2Q	6,157	5,149	4,577	—	—	—
3Q	7,228	6,340	5,364	—	—	--
4Q	--	6,933	5,918	—	—	—
Yr.	—	26,360	23,286	21,413	—	—
Earnings Per Share ($)						
1Q	**0.61**	0.68	0.65	—	—	—
2Q	**0.02**	0.05	-0.08	—	—	—
3Q	**-0.18**	0.17	0.06	—	—	—
4Q	—	-0.46	0.20	—	—	—
Yr.	—	0.42	0.82	-0.68	—	—

Next earnings report expected: late October

Dividend Data (Dividends have been paid since 1996.)

Amount ($)	Date Decl.	Ex-Div. Date	Stock of Record	Payment Date
0.075	Dec. 17	Jan. 28	Jan. 31	Mar. 01 '98
2-for-1	Feb. 18	Apr. 02	Mar. 06	Apr. 01 '98
0.040	Apr. 15	Apr. 28	Apr. 30	Jun. 01 '98
0.040	Jul. 15	Jul. 29	Jul. 31	Sep. 01 '98

A Division of The McGraw·Hill Companies

Business Summary - 20-AUG-98

Lucent Technologies Inc., formerly a unit of AT&T, was spun off from the long-distance giant in September 1996. The company is one of the world's leading designers, developers and manufacturers of telecommunications systems, software and products. It is a global market leader in the sale of public telecommunications systems and is a supplier of systems or software to most of the world's largest network operators. LU is also a global market leader in the sale of business communications systems and in the sale of microelectronic components for communications applications to manufacturers of communications systems and computers. In addition, Lucent has provided engineering, installation and operations support services to more than 250 network operators in 75 countries, 1.4 million business locations in the U.S. and approximately 100,000 business locations in over 90 other countries.

Revenues in FY 97 (Sep.) were generated from the sale of systems for network operators (59%), business communications systems (24%), microelectronic products (11%), consumer products (4%) and other systems and products (2%), including systems for the U.S. government. Some 24% of total revenues were from international sales, up from 16% the level in FY 86.

LU's systems and software enable network operators to provide wireline and wireless local, long-distance and international voice, data and video communications services. LU has a wireline local access installed base of about 120 million lines, representing about 10% of the worldwide installed base.

R&D activities are conducted through Bell Laboratories, which consists of approximately three-quarters of the total resources of AT&T's former Bell Laboratories division. One recent result of these R&D efforts was the introduction by LU's Optical Networking group of a new dense wavelength division multiplexing (DWDM) system that supports up to 80 optical channels at 2.5 gigabits per second over a single optical fiber. The WaveStar OLS 400G system has a capacity of 400 gigabits per second and will be available in the fourth quarter of FY 98.

In July 1998, the company announced a series of contract wins valued at over $3 billion. Lucent won a five-year, $2.4 billion contract to expand SBC Communications' digital network. In addition, it was awarded two contracts with Saudi Telecommunications, valued at $810 million, to modernize telephone switch systems serving 900,000 telephone lines, and to expand Saudi Arabia's GSM mobile phone network.

Per Share Data ($)

(Year Ended Sep. 30)	1997	1996	1995	1994	1993	1992	1991	1990	1989	1988
Tangible Bk. Val.	2.64	2.11	1.66	NA	NA	NA	NA	NA	NA	NA
Cash Flow	1.54	0.97	0.50	NA	NA	NA	NA	NA	NA	NA
Earnings	0.42	0.19	-0.68	NA	NA	NA	NA	NA	NA	NA
Dividends	0.15	0.04	NA	NA	NA	NA	NA	NA	NA	NA
Payout Ratio	35%	21%	NA	NA	NA	NA	NA	NA	NA	NA
Prices - High	45³/₈	26⁵/₈	NA	NA	NA	NA	NA	NA	NA	NA
- Low	22³/₈	13¹/₂	NA	NA	NA	NA	NA	NA	NA	NA
P/E Ratio - High	NM	NM	NA	NA	NA	NA	NA	NA	NA	NA
- Low	NM	NM	NA	NA	NA	NA	NA	NA	NA	NA

Income Statement Analysis (Million $)

	1997	1996	1995	1994	1993	1992	1991	1990	1989	1988
Revs.	26,360	15,859	21,413	NA	NA	NA	NA	NA	NA	NA
Oper. Inc.	3,081	1,424	493	NA	NA	NA	NA	NA	NA	NA
Depr.	1,450	937	1,493	NA	NA	NA	NA	NA	NA	NA
Int. Exp.	305	230	302	NA	NA	NA	NA	NA	NA	NA
Pretax Inc.	1,502	388	-1,137	NA	NA	NA	NA	NA	NA	NA
Eff. Tax Rate	62%	37%	NM	NM	NM	NM	NM	NM	NM	NM
Net Inc.	541	224	-866	NA	NA	NA	NA	NA	NA	NA

Balance Sheet & Other Fin. Data (Million $)

	1997	1996	1995	1994	1993	1992	1991	1990	1989	1988
Cash	1,350	2,241	3,843	NA	NA	NA	NA	NA	NA	NA
Curr. Assets	12,501	12,784	12,074	NA	NA	NA	NA	NA	NA	NA
Total Assets	23,811	22,626	21,117	NA	NA	NA	NA	NA	NA	NA
Curr. Liab.	10,738	10,713	11,563	NA	NA	NA	NA	NA	NA	NA
LT Debt	1,665	1,634	123	NA	NA	NA	NA	NA	NA	NA
Common Eqty.	3,387	3,387	2,329	NA	NA	NA	NA	NA	NA	NA
Total Cap.	5,052	4,320	2,452	NA	NA	NA	NA	NA	NA	NA
Cap. Exp.	1,635	939	1,277	NA	NA	NA	NA	NA	NA	NA
Cash Flow	1,991	1,161	626	NA	NA	NA	NA	NA	NA	NA
Curr. Ratio	1.2	1.2	1.8	NA	NA	NA	NA	NA	NA	NA
% LT Debt of Cap.	33.0	37.8	5.0	NA	NA	NA	NA	NA	NA	NA
% Net Inc.of Revs.	2.1	1.4	NM	NM	NM	NM	NM	NM	NM	NM
% Ret. on Assets	2.3	1.1	NA	NA	NA	NA	NA	NA	NA	NA
% Ret. on Equity	17.8	10.9	NA	NA	NA	NA	NA	NA	NA	NA

Data as orig. reptd. (9 mos. in 1996; 12 mos. ended Dec. in 1995); bef. results of disc. opers. and/or spec. items. Per share data adj. for stk. divs. as of ex-div. date. E-Estimated. NA-Not Available. NM-Not Meaningful. NR-Not Ranked. Bold denotes diluted EPS (FASB 128).

Office—600 Mountain Ave., Murray Hill, NJ 07974. **Tel**—(908) 582-8500. **Website**—http://www.lucent.com **Chmn, Pres & CEO**—R. A. McGinn. **EVP & COO-Domestic**—D. Stanzione. **EVP & COO-International**—B. Verwaayen. **SVP & Secy**—R. J. Rawson. **Dirs**—P. A. Allaire, C. A. Hills, D. Lewis, R. A. McGinn, P. H. O'Neill, D. S. Perkins, H. B. Schacht, F. A. Thomas, J. A. Young. **Incorporated**—in Delaware in 1995. **Empl**—131,000. **S&P Analyst:** Aydin Tuncer

12-SEP-98

Industry:
Health Care (Diversi-fied)

Summary: Following the 1997 acquisition of Nellcor Puritan Bennett, this company is now a leading producer of respiratory products, as well as imaging agents and pharmaceutical products.

S&P Opinion: Avoid (★★)	Recent Price • 20¾	Yield • 3.2%	
	52 Wk Range • 40-20⅜	12-Mo. P/E • NM	

Earnings vs. Previous Year
▲=Up ▼=Down ▶=No Change

Quantitative Evaluations

Outlook
(1 Lowest—5 Highest)
• **1**

Fair Value
• **16¾**

Risk
• **Low**

Earn./Div. Rank
• **B**

Technical Eval.
• **Bullish** since 6/98

Rel. Strength Rank
(1 Lowest—99 Highest)
• **30**

Insider Activity
• **Neutral**

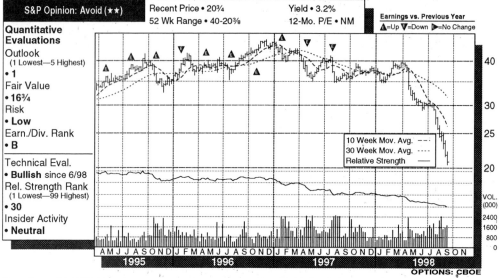

10 Week Mov. Avg. ---
30 Week Mov. Avg. ----
Relative Strength —

VOL.
(000)
2400
1600
800
0

AMJJASOND JFMAMJJASOND JFMAMJJASOND JFMAMJJASON
1995   1996   1997   1998

OPTIONS: CBOE

Overview - 24-AUG-98

In August 1997, the company completed its $1.9 billion, or $28.50 per share, all-cash acquisition of Nellcor Puritan Bennett, making it a premier worldwide health care supplier with approximately $2.4 billion in combined revenues. The acquisition is expected to aid long-term growth as more health care providers shift to larger suppliers with broad and deep product lines to meet their needs. The combined entity should benefit from enhanced revenue growth, consolidation synergies and cost reductions. MKG expects the transaction to be accretive to earnings in FY 99 (Jun.), with revenue growth of 8%-9% and EPS growth of 10%-12%. In addition, synergies should reduce costs by $75 to $80 million in FY 99. MKG expects FY 99 EPS of $2.25 to $2.35.

Valuation - 24-AUG-98

Revenues should continue to grow, due to strength in respiratory care sales. However, weaker x-ray contrast media revenue, reflecting greater pricing pressure in the U.S. and the negative impact of a stronger dollar, may offset these increases. Pricing of imaging agents should improve in FY 99, boosting MKG's bottom line. Although the Nellcor acquisition broadens MKG's product portfolio and creates cross-selling opportunities, management faces continued pricing pressures in the healthcare market, while continuing to integrate operations and grow the company. Overall, the integration of Nellcor will increase revenues; however, slower growth and weaker margins will have a negative impact on earnings. Therefore, we see revenue growth of 8%-9%, and EPS growth of 10%-12% for FY 99. Although the shares are trading at a P/E ratio that offers a significant discount to that of the S&P 500, until management can demonstrate the ability to meet the challenges associated with the Nellcor acquisition, we recommend that investors avoid the shares.

Key Stock Statistics

S&P EPS Est. 1998	1.98	Tang. Bk. Value/Share	NM
P/E on S&P Est. 1998	10.5	Beta	0.52
S&P EPS Est. 1999	2.37	Shareholders	8,100
Dividend Rate/Share	0.66	Market cap. (B)	$ 1.5
Shs. outstg. (M)	73.2	Inst. holdings	81%
Avg. daily vol. (M)	0.393		

Value of $10,000 invested 5 years ago: $ 6,822

Fiscal Year Ending Jun. 30

	1998	1997	1996	1995	1994	1993
Revenues (Million $)						
1Q	—	442.0	492.1	487.7	444.9	417.0
2Q	—	453.1	528.2	516.3	466.3	441.0
3Q	—	469.7	572.6	569.1	486.7	439.9
4Q	655.3	496.4	617.3	639.0	542.2	498.4
Yr.	2,367	1,861	2,210	2,212	1,940	1,796
Earnings Per Share ($)						
1Q	—	0.47	0.46	0.45	0.45	0.36
2Q	—	0.53	0.50	0.52	0.47	0.36
3Q	—	0.65	0.67	0.62	0.55	0.39
4Q	0.14	0.84	0.88	0.78	-0.10	-2.59
Yr.	-4.89	2.47	2.50	2.37	1.38	-1.48

Next earnings report expected: late October

Dividend Data (Dividends have been paid since 1971.)

Amount ($)	Date Decl.	Ex-Div. Date	Stock of Record	Payment Date
0.165	Oct. 15	Dec. 04	Dec. 08	Dec. 31 '97
0.165	Feb. 19	Mar. 11	Mar. 13	Mar. 31 '98
0.165	Apr. 16	Jun. 10	Jun. 12	Jun. 30 '98
0.165	Aug. 12	Sep. 11	Sep. 15	Sep. 30 '98

A Division of The McGraw-Hill Companies

Business Summary - 24-AUG-98

Established in 1867 in St. Louis, Missouri, this international growth company (formerly IMCERA Group) has a long history in servicing specialty markets in human health care and chemicals. Today Mallinckrodt has a worldwide presence with over 1,000 products in more than 100 countries. Dedicated to improving health care and chemistry, MKG is a major producer of diagnostic imaging agents, medical devices, specialty pharmaceuticals, catalysts, and laboratory and microelectronic chemicals.

In August 1997, MKG completed its $1.9 billion all-cash tender offer (equivalent to $28.50 per share) for all the outstanding shares of Nellcor Puritan Bennett Inc. (NELL), a leading provider of oxygen monitoring, critical care ventilation and other respiratory products. The shares tendered represented more than 90% of NELL's outstanding shares. The company has incurred approximately $80 million in one-time charges in FY 98 related to inventory write-up, purchased R&D and integration costs. As a result of anticipated revenue enhancement and synergistic cost savings, MKG expects the transaction to be accretive to earnings in FY 99.

In June 1998, MKG announced that it would retain Mallinckrodt Baker, its specialty pharmaceutical business, and operate it as a unit of its Pharmaceutical Group. Moreover, the company announced plans to reinstitute its share repurchase program and expects to buy back $100 million worth of stock over the next two to three years.

During FY 97, MKG agreed to sell its animal health business (21% of sales and 9.5% of profits in FY 96) to Schering-Plough Corp. for $405 million in cash. It also divested its 50% interest in Tastemaker, a major flavor products manufacturer, for about $550 million, and its feed ingredients business for $44.4 million. As a result of these transactions, MKG reported earnings from discontinued operations of $0.06 per share in FY 97 and $0.19 per share in FY 98.

The company has continued with its plan to focus solely on its three major healthcare businesses, respiratory care, medical imaging and pharmaceutical specialties. In FY 98, the respiratory unit accounted for 42% of sales; the imaging agent unit accounted for 32% of sales; and the pharmaceutical specialties unit accounted for 26% of sales.

The company expects to achieve costs savings of approximately $75-$80 million in FY 99, and $20 to $25 million on an incremental basis in FY 2000. For FY 99, MKG has forecast 8%-9% top line revenue growth, reflecting synergies from the integration of Nellcor Bennett. In June 1998, the company indicated that FY 99 EPS would probably be between $2.25 and $2.35.

Per Share Data ($)

(Year Ended Jun. 30)	1998	1997	1996	1995	1994	1993	1992	1991	1990	1989
Tangible Bk. Val.	NA	11.67	7.72	15.12	6.93	5.84	16.02	14.28	11.97	11.23
Cash Flow	NA	4.17	4.47	3.99	2.73	-0.23	2.80	2.32	1.79	2.09
Earnings	-4.89	2.53	2.50	2.37	1.38	-1.48	1.65	1.37	0.84	1.40
Dividends	0.66	0.65	0.60	0.55	0.48	0.43	0.38	0.33	0.33	0.33
Payout Ratio	NM	26%	24%	23%	35%	NM	23%	26%	41%	21%
Prices - High	40	44¼	45⅞	41⅞	38½	36⅝	46⅝	43⅜	25	18½
- Low	24¾	34⅞	35⅛	29⅛	28⅜	23	28⅞	22⅜	16	12¾
P/E Ratio - High	NM	17	18	18	28	NM	28	32	30	13
- Low	NM	14	14	12	21	NM	18	16	19	9

Income Statement Analysis (Million $)

	1998	1997	1996	1995	1994	1993	1992	1991	1990	1989
Revs.	NA	1,861	2,210	2,212	1,940	1,796	1,703	1,634	1,425	983
Oper. Inc.	NA	442	465	447	390	315	306	253	173	91.0
Depr.	NA	128	149	125	105	96.0	89.0	67.0	62.0	47.0
Int. Exp.	NA	48.8	61.9	57.0	39.8	43.6	39.6	42.7	77.1	44.6
Pretax Inc.	NA	288	303	295	171	-132	203	153	87.0	132
Eff. Tax Rate	NA	36%	37%	38%	37%	NM	37%	37%	32%	16%
Net Inc.	NA	186	191	184	107	-113	129	97.0	59.0	110

Balance Sheet & Other Fin. Data (Million $)

	1998	1997	1996	1995	1994	1993	1992	1991	1990	1989
Cash	NA	809	546	62.0	88.0	51.0	68.0	362	132	444
Curr. Assets	NA	1,617	1,571	1,020	932	837	804	1,132	725	853
Total Assets	NA	2,988	3,406	2,721	2,434	2,178	2,051	2,250	2,131	1,972
Curr. Liab.	NA	654	1,212	748	671	633	452	723	414	258
LT Debt	NA	545	567	502	522	428	264	328	754	712
Common Eqty.	NA	1,240	1,221	1,161	1,005	900	1,213	1,074	815	682
Total Cap.	NA	2,045	2,051	1,750	1,575	1,364	1,530	1,460	1,632	1,643
Cap. Exp.	NA	110	169	161	172	188	150	123	173	92.0
Cash Flow	NA	313	340	309	212	-18.0	218	164	117	143
Curr. Ratio	NA	2.5	1.3	1.4	1.4	1.3	1.8	1.6	1.8	3.3
% LT Debt of Cap.	NA	26.7	27.6	28.7	33.1	31.4	17.3	22.4	46.2	43.3
% Net Inc.of Revs.	NA	10.0	8.7	8.3	5.5	NM	7.6	5.9	4.1	11.2
% Ret. on Assets	NA	6.1	6.3	7.2	4.5	NM	6.0	4.2	2.7	6.5
% Ret. on Equity	NA	15.1	15.9	17.0	11.2	NM	11.2	9.8	6.9	14.4

Data as orig. reptd.; bef. results of disc. opers. and/or spec. items. Per share data adj. for stk. divs. as of ex-div. date. Bold denotes diluted EPS (FASB 128). Bk. val. figs. in Per Share Data tbl. incl. intangibles in 1992, 1991, 1990, 1989. E-Estimated. NA-Not Available. NM-Not Meaningful. NR-Not Ranked.

Office—7733 Forsyth Blvd., St. Louis, MO 63105-1820. **Tel**—(314) 854-5200. **Fax**—(314) 854-5381. **Website**—http://www.mallinckrodt.com **Chrmn & CEO**—C. R. Holman.**Pres & COO**—M. G. Nichols. **VP & Treas**—D. A. McKinney. **SVP & CFO**—M. A. Rocca. **Dirs**—R F. Bentele, G. C. C. Chang, W. L. Davis, R. G. Evens, C. R. Holman, R. S. Karmel, C. B. Malone, M. Moskin, M. G. Nichols, B. M. Rushton, D. R. Toll, A. Viscusi. **Transfer Agent & Registrar**—First Chicago Trust Co. of New York, Jersey City, NJ. **Incorporated**—in New York in 1909. **Empl**— 12,800. **S&P Analyst:** John J. Arege

STANDARD &POOR'S
STOCK REPORTS

Manor Care

1411H
NYSE Symbol **MNR**

In S&P 500

12-SEP-98

Industry:
Health Care
(Long-Term Care)

Summary: This operator of skilled nursing and assisted living facilities has agreed to be acquired by NYSE-listed Health Care and Retirement Corp.

S&P Opinion: Hold (★★★)	Recent Price • 25	Yield • 0.4%
	52 Wk Range • 42⅜-23	12-Mo. P/E • 16.8

Quantitative Evaluations

Outlook
(1 Lowest—5 Highest)
• **5**

Fair Value
• **42⅝**

Risk
• **Average**

Earn./Div. Rank
• **A-**

Technical Eval.
• **Bearish** since 8/98

Rel. Strength Rank
(1 Lowest—99 Highest)
• **30**

Insider Activity
• **NA**

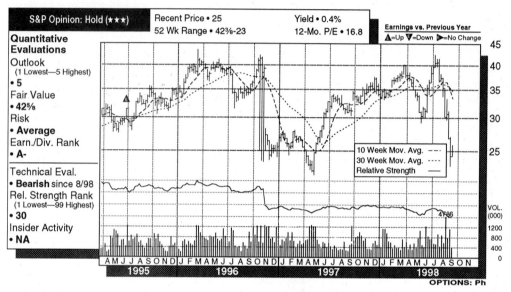

Earnings vs. Previous Year
▲=Up ▼=Down ▶=No Change

10 Week Mov. Avg. ---
30 Week Mov. Avg. ····
Relative Strength —

VOL. (000)

OPTIONS: Ph

Overview - 03-SEP-98

In June 1998, Manor Care agreed to be acquired by Health Care and Retirement Corp. (NYSE; HCR) in a share-for-share stock swap initially valued at $5.0 billion including debt assumption. The merger should be completed during the fourth quarter of calendar 1998. The combined entity, to be renamed HCR Manor Care, will have annual revenues approximating $2.5 billion, more than 50% of which will come from non-government sources, with 295 long term care facilities, 116 subacute/rehabilitation sites, 76 outpatient clinics, 47 assisted living centers, one acute care hospital and 34 home health agencies, along with four pharmacies. As a result of the agreement, MNR has terminated plans to separate its skilled nursing facility management, assisted living and home health businesses from its skilled nursing facility ownership, real estate and health care facility development businesses.

Valuation - 03-SEP-98

On a stand-alone basis, we look for MNR to generate earnings of about $1.95 in FY 99 (May), as modest growth within the skilled nursing segment is augmented by expanding contributions from the assisted living business. The company's 50% stake in Vitalink Pharmacy Services was sold to Genesis Health Ventures on August 31, 1998. Vitalink was classified as a discontinued operation since April 1998. Home health care revenue and margin trends are not encouraging, and this division will place some drag on the company's earnings going forward. The combined company can be expected to divest these operations. Management anticipates that up to $30 million of cost overlaps will be eliminated immediately following the merger, and we see pro forma combined 1998 EPS of about $1.60.

Key Stock Statistics

S&P EPS Est. 1998	NA	Tang. Bk. Value/Share	11.75
P/E on S&P Est. 1998	NA	Beta	1.13
S&P EPS Est. 1999	1.95	Shareholders	3,700
Dividend Rate/Share	0.09	Market cap. (B)	$ 1.6
Shs. outstg. (M)	63.7	Inst. holdings	51%
Avg. daily vol. (M)	0.360		

Value of $10,000 invested 5 years ago: NA

Fiscal Year Ending May 31

	1998	1997	1996	1995	1994	1993
Revenues (Million $)						
1Q	325.1	336.5	274.0	321.4	284.6	245.0
2Q	340.4	351.6	299.7	324.3	284.6	254.0
3Q	349.5	388.7	334.4	322.1	284.1	244.9
4Q	344.4	450.4	340.1	354.3	309.8	265.6
Yr.	1,359	1,527	1,248	1,322	1,163	1,010
Earnings Per Share ($)						
1Q	—	—	—	0.39	0.34	0.28
2Q	—	—	—	0.40	0.34	0.30
3Q	—	—	0.94	0.30	0.25	0.21
4Q	—	—	0.10	0.42	0.36	0.30
Yr.	**1.30**	1.98	1.04	1.51	1.29	1.09

Next earnings report expected: NA

Dividend Data (Dividends have been paid since 1975.)

Amount ($)	Date Decl.	Ex-Div. Date	Stock of Record	Payment Date
0.022	Oct. 03	Nov. 12	Nov. 14	Nov. 26 '97
0.022	Nov. 26	Feb. 11	Feb. 13	Feb. 27 '98
0.022	May. 06	May. 13	May. 15	May. 27 '98
0.022	Jun. 25	Aug. 12	Aug. 14	Aug. 27 '98

A Division of The **McGraw-Hill** *Companies*

Business Summary - 03-SEP-98

Manor Care provides a full range of health care services through 213 facilities with 28,300 beds in 29 states. It also holds a majority stake in a home health care services provider. The company has agreed to merge with NYSE-listed Health Care and Retirement Corp. in a tax-free stock swap set to close in late 1998. The lodging division, Choice Hotels International, was spun off to shareholders in November 1996.

ManorCare Health Services Inc. (MCHS) owns, operates or manages 171 skilled nursing and rehabilitation facilities and 39 assisted living facilities that provide high acuity services, long term skilled nursing care, Alzheimer's services and assisted living services, primarily for residents over the age of 65. Manor Care and its subsidiaries also own and operate a 172-bed acute care hospital in Mesquite, Texas.

Manor Care's nursing and rehabilitation centers range in bed capacity from 53 to 255 beds, and have an aggregate bed capacity of 24,170 beds, and its assisted living centers have an aggregate bed capacity of 3,935 beds, which together achieved an average occupancy rate of 88% in FY98 (May). During FY98, MNR opened

two newly-constructed skilled nursing facilities in California, and 10 assisted living facilities in Connecticut, Virginia, Maryland (2), Delaware, Georgia (2) and Florida (3). As of May 31, 1998, there were 31 nursing and assisted living facilities with a total of 2,438 beds under construction. Manor Care's nursing and assisted living centers generated 56% of revenues from private patients in FY98, with 25% coming from Medicare patients and 19% from Medicaid patients.

The company also has a 63% voting stake in In-Home Health Inc. (NASDAQ; IHHI), a provider of home health care services through offices and pharmacies located in 14 states. In Home Health offers its clients a broad range of professional and support services to meet medical and personal needs at home, including skilled nursing, infusion therapy, hospice, rehabilitation, personal care and homemaking.

In late August 1998, the company sold its 50% stake in Vitalink Pharmacy Services Inc. (NYSE, VTK) to Genesis Health Ventures (NYSE, GHV). Vitalink owns and operates 60 pharmacies located in 20 states across the U.S., providing medications, consulting, infusion and other ancillary services to 172,000 institutional beds and home infusion patients.

Per Share Data ($)

(Year Ended May 31)	1998	1997	1996	1995	1994	1993	1992	1991	1990	1989
Tangible Bk. Val.	11.75	5.25	10.40	9.01	7.52	5.13	4.09	3.03	3.83	3.49
Cash Flow	2.53	3.25	2.13	2.73	2.39	2.15	2.16	1.45	1.22	1.02
Earnings	1.30	1.98	1.04	1.51	1.29	1.09	1.16	0.56	0.46	0.40
Dividends	0.07	0.09	0.09	0.11	0.09	0.09	0.09	0.09	0.09	0.09
Payout Ratio	5%	7%	8%	7%	7%	8%	8%	16%	19%	22%
Cal. Yrs.	1997	1996	1995	1994	1993	1992	1991	1990	1989	1988
Prices - High	42³/₈	43¹/₂	35⁵/₈	29⁵/₈	26⁵/₈	24¹/₂	19	11⁷/₈	11³/₈	10¹/₄
- Low	26³/₄	23¹/₂	27¹/₂	23¹/₄	17¹/₂	14¹/₂	10³/₈	6⁷/₈	8¹/₄	6³/₈
P/E Ratio - High	33	22	34	20	21	22	16	21	25	26
- Low	21	12	26	15	14	13	9	12	18	16

Income Statement Analysis (Million $)

Revs.	1,359	1,527	1,248	1,322	1,163	1,010	916	815	709	617
Oper. Inc.	235	256	213	260	224	195	175	142	117	103
Depr.	79.3	80.4	68.0	76.2	66.5	61.0	57.0	51.1	39.1	35.8
Int. Exp.	31.5	46.4	33.4	29.0	32.0	39.7	44.9	46.0	45.6	46.6
Pretax Inc.	123	210	113	164	137	101	107	52.0	41.0	36.0
Eff. Tax Rate	41%	40%	40%	40%	43%	38%	38%	38%	35%	36%
Net Inc.	84.2	125	65.6	94.5	78.4	62.4	66.6	32.1	26.7	23.0

Balance Sheet & Other Fin. Data (Million $)

Cash	48.7	32.9	62.5	75.1	60.5	80.8	83.1	30.3	46.7	47.9
Curr. Assets	275	337	235	230	183	194	182	131	148	146
Total Assets	1,741	1,980	1,682	1,416	1,187	1,107	1,015	944	868	835
Curr. Liab.	158	228	232	201	166	180	172	119	122	104
LT Debt	534	596	491	367	277	380	374	456	419	435
Common Eqty.	779	690	708	625	534	362	305	245	222	202
Total Cap.	1,583	1,752	1,450	1,215	949	868	792	795	718	710
Cap. Exp.	238	168	136	119	91.0	90.0	63.0	64.0	81.0	91.0
Cash Flow	163	205	134	171	145	123	124	83.0	70.0	59.0
Curr. Ratio	1.7	1.5	1.0	1.1	1.1	1.1	1.1	1.1	1.2	1.4
% LT Debt of Cap.	33.7	34.0	33.9	30.3	29.2	43.8	47.2	57.4	58.3	61.3
% Net Inc.of Revs.	6.2	8.2	5.2	7.2	6.7	6.2	7.3	3.9	3.8	3.7
% Ret. on Assets	4.5	6.8	4.4	7.3	6.6	5.9	6.8	3.6	3.1	2.8
% Ret. on Equity	11.5	17.9	9.8	16.3	16.9	18.7	24.2	13.8	12.6	11.9

Data as orig. reptd.; bef. results of disc. opers. and/or spec. items. 1996 3Q EPS represents nine mos. Per share data adj. for stk. divs. as of ex-div. date. Bold denotes diluted EPS (FASB 128). E-Estimated. NA-Not Available. NM-Not Meaningful. NR-Not Ranked.

Office—11555 Darnestown Rd., Gaithersburg, MD 20878-3200. **Tel**—(301) 979-4000. **Chrmn, Pres & CEO**—S. Bainum Jr. **Vice Chrmn**—S. Bainum. **SVP & Secy**—J. H. Rempe. **SVP, CFO & Treas**—J. A. MacCutcheon. **Investor Contact**—Leigh Comas. **Dirs**—S. Bainum, S. Bainum Jr., R. E. Herzlinger, W. H. Longfield, F. V. Malek, J. E. Robertson, K. L. Simmons. **Transfer Agent & Registrar**—ChaseMellon Shareholder Services, NYC. **Incorporated**—in Delaware in 1968; reincorporated in Delaware in 1981. **Empl**— 31,481. **S&P Analyst:** Robert M. Gold

Marriott International

1420M

NYSE Symbol **MAR**

In S&P 500

12-SEP-98

Industry:
Lodging - Hotels

Summary: In March 1998, ownership of this lodging company was spun off to shareholders of the "old" Marriott International, which has been renamed Sodexho Marriott Services, Inc.

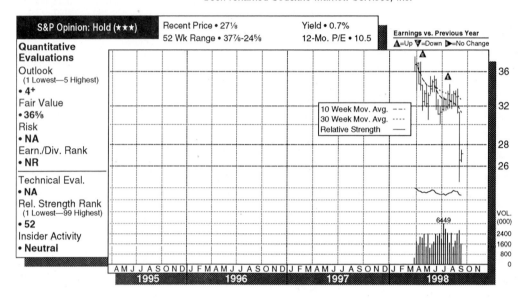

S&P Opinion: Hold (★★★)	Recent Price • 27⅛	Yield • 0.7%
	52 Wk Range • 37⅞-24⅝	12-Mo. P/E • 10.5

Quantitative Evaluations

Outlook
(1 Lowest—5 Highest)
• **4+**

Fair Value
• **36⅝**

Risk
• **NA**

Earn./Div. Rank
• **NR**

Technical Eval.
• **NA**

Rel. Strength Rank
(1 Lowest—99 Highest)
• **52**

Insider Activity
• **Neutral**

Earnings vs. Previous Year
▲=Up ▼=Down ▶=No Change

10 Week Mov. Avg. – – –
30 Week Mov. Avg. - - - -
Relative Strength ——

6449

VOL. (000)

Overview - 26-JUN-98

On March 27, 1998, common stock of this lodging and contract services company -- the "new" Marriott International -- was spun off in the form of a special dividend to shareholders of the "old" Marriott. On that same day, the "old" Marriott, which largely consisted of food service and facilities management businesses, was renamed Sodexho Marriott Services, Inc., the stock of which now trades on the New York Stock Exchange, with the ticker symbol SDH. Thus, shareholders of the "old" Marriott International ended up with stock of both the "new" Marriott and of SDH. As of March 1998, Marriott International operated or franchised more than 1,500 lodging properties, with in excess of 300,000 rooms. Also, MAR has a contract services business that includes development and operation of senior living communities and distribution of food and supplies.

Valuation - 26-JUN-98

We view the stock of this lodging company as adequately priced. We see the U.S. lodging industry as being late in the upward part of its economic or financial cycle, but look for MAR's emphasis on managing and franchising properties to provide some insulation from prospective industry overbuilding. Also, we expect MAR's senior living center business to provide good long-term growth opportunities. The stock may get some support from further share repurchases. The buyback authorization was boosted in May 1998, and as of May 20, MAR had authority to repurchase 17.2 million shares. Since MAR became a public company on March 27, 1998, the company had bought back about 2.8 million shares.

Key Stock Statistics

S&P EPS Est. 1998	1.45	Tang. Bk. Value/Share	NM
P/E on S&P Est. 1998	18.7	Beta	NA
S&P EPS Est. 1999	1.70	Shareholders	NA
Dividend Rate/Share	0.20	Market cap. (B)	$ 6.8
Shs. outstg. (M)	250.1	Inst. holdings	30%
Avg. daily vol. (M)	0.563		

Value of $10,000 invested 5 years ago: NA

Fiscal Year Ending Dec. 31

	1998	1997	1996	1995	1994	1993
Revenues (Million $)						
1Q	2,192	1,909	1,509	—	—	—
2Q	2,539	2,195	1,696	—	—	—
3Q	—	2,073	1,645	—	—	—
4Q	—	2,869	2,417	—	—	—
Yr.	—	9,046	7,267	6,255	5,746	—
Earnings Per Share ($)						
1Q	0.33	0.26	0.22	—	—	—
2Q	0.37	0.31	0.23	—	—	—
3Q	—	0.27	0.22	—	—	—
4Q	—	0.36	0.31	—	—	—
Yr.	E1.45	1.19	0.99	0.83	0.62	—

Next earnings report expected: NA

Dividend Data (Dividends have been paid since 1998.)

Amount ($)	Date Decl.	Ex-Div. Date	Stock of Record	Payment Date
0.045	Apr. 08	Apr. 16	Apr. 20	May. 01 '98
0.050	May. 20	Jun. 24	Jun. 26	Jul. 17 '98
0.050	Aug. 06	Sep. 23	Sep. 25	Oct. 16 '98

A Division of The McGraw-Hill Companies

Business Summary - 26-JUN-98

This company is largely, but not entirely, the "old" Marriott International.

On March 27, 1998, common stock of this company-- the "new" Marriott International-- was spun off in the form of a special dividend to shareholders of the "old" Marriott. On that same day, the "old" Marriott, which largely consisted of food service and facilities management businesses, was renamed Sodexho Marriott Services, Inc., the stock of which now trades on the New York Stock Exchange, with the ticker symbol SDH. Thus, shareholders of the "old" Marriott International ended up with stock of both the "new" Marriott and of SDH. Properties referred to below (operated or franchised on January 2, 1998) would essentially have been part of the "new" Marriott when the spin-off occurred in March 1998.

As of January 2, 1998, the Marriott International lodging segment included 1,478 operated or franchised hotels, with 297,086 rooms. Of these, Marriott operated 729 properties (191,214 rooms) and had 749 franchised hotels (105,872 rooms). By brand (including franchises), there were the following number of properties and rooms:

	Properties	Rooms
Marriott Hotels, Resorts and Suites	326	124,571
Ritz-Carlton	33	11,416
Renaissance	70	26,770
New World	14	6,889
Ramada International	74	14,476
Residence Inn	258	30,676
Courtyard	349	47,746
Fairfield Inn and Suites	344	32,854
TownePlace Suites	2	184
Other	8	1,504

As of January 2, 1998, the lodging segment's international presence included 235 hotels with 64,526 rooms. Of these, a total of 72 properties, with 22,930 rooms, were part of the Marriott Hotel Resorts and Suites business, 74 hotels with 14,476 rooms were part of Ramada International, and 39 properties with 12,625 rooms were part of the Renaissance business.

The Marriott Vacation Club International business develops, sells and operates vacation timeshare resorts. In 1997, this Marriott International business added 20,000 new owners, which brought its total number of timeshare owners to more than 100,000.

Marriott International also has a contract services segment that includes development and operation of senior living communities, and distribution of food and supplies. As of January 2, 1998, Marriott International operated 89 senior living communities in 24 states. The distribution business operated a nationwide network of 15 distribution centers.

Per Share Data ($)

(Year Ended Dec. 31)	1997	1996	1995	1994	1993	1992	1991	1990	1989	1988
Tangible Bk. Val.	NA	NA	NA	NA	NA	NA	NA	NA	NA	NA
Cash Flow	1.65	1.30	1.08	NA	NA	NA	NA	NA	NA	NA
Earnings	1.19	0.99	0.83	0.62	NA	NA	NA	NA	NA	NA
Dividends	NA	NA	NA	NA	NA	NA	NA	NA	NA	NA
Payout Ratio	NA	NA	NA	NA	NA	NA	NA	NA	NA	NA
Prices - High	NA	NA	NA	NA	NA	NA	NA	NA	NA	NA
- Low	NA	NA	NA	NA	NA	NA	NA	NA	NA	NA
P/E Ratio - High	NA	NA	NA	NA	NA	NA	NA	NA	NA	NA
- Low	NA	NA	NA	NA	NA	NA	NA	NA	NA	NA

Income Statement Analysis (Million $)

	1997	1996	1995	1994	1993	1992	1991	1990	1989	1988
Revs.	9,046	7,267	6,255	5,746	NA	NA	NA	NA	NA	NA
Oper. Inc.	647	525	399	NA	NA	NA	NA	NA	NA	NA
Depr.	126	89.0	67.0	NA	NA	NA	NA	NA	NA	NA
Int. Exp.	22.0	37.0	9.0	7.0	NA	NA	NA	NA	NA	NA
Pretax Inc.	531	436	362	276	NA	NA	NA	NA	NA	NA
Eff. Tax Rate	39%	38%	39%	41%	NA	NA	NA	NA	NA	NA
Net Inc.	324	271	220	163	NA	NA	NA	NA	NA	NA

Balance Sheet & Other Fin. Data (Million $)

	1997	1996	1995	1994	1993	1992	1991	1990	1989	1988
Cash	289	426	NA	NA	NA	NA	NA	NA	NA	NA
Curr. Assets	1,367	1,530	NA	NA	NA	NA	NA	NA	NA	NA
Total Assets	5,557	5,608	NA	NA	NA	NA	NA	NA	NA	NA
Curr. Liab.	1,639	1,748	NA	NA	NA	NA	NA	NA	NA	NA
LT Debt	112	413	NA	NA	NA	NA	NA	NA	NA	NA
Common Eqty.	2,586	2,549	NA	NA	NA	NA	NA	NA	NA	NA
Total Cap.	2,698	2,962	NA	NA	NA	NA	NA	NA	NA	NA
Cap. Exp.	NA	NA	NA	NA	NA	NA	NA	NA	NA	NA
Cash Flow	450	360	287	NA	NA	NA	NA	NA	NA	NA
Curr. Ratio	0.8	0.9	NA	NA	NA	NA	NA	NA	NA	NA
% LT Debt of Cap.	4.2	13.9	NA	NA	NA	NA	NA	NA	NA	NA
% Net Inc.of Revs.	3.6	3.7	3.5	2.8	NA	NA	NA	NA	NA	NA
% Ret. on Assets	6.6	NA	NA	NA	NA	NA	NA	NA	NA	NA
% Ret. on Equity	16.1	NA	NA	NA	NA	NA	NA	NA	NA	NA

Data pro forma prior to 3/27/98. Other data as orig. reptd. Data bef. results of disc. opers. and/or spec. items. Per share data adj. for stk. divs. as of ex-div. date. Bold denotes diluted EPS (FASB 128). E-Estimated. NA-Not Available. NM-Not Meaningful. NR-Not Ranked.

Office—10400 Fernwood Road, Bethesda, MD 20817. **Tel**—(301) 380-3000. **Chrmn & CEO**—J. W. Marriott, Jr. **Pres & COO**—W. J. Shaw, Jr. **EVP & CFO**—M. A. Stein. **VP & Investor Contact**—Laura E. Paugh. **Dirs**—G. M. Grosvenor, H. C. Kar-Shun, J. W. Marriott, Jr., R. E. Marriott, F. D. McKenzie, H. J. Pearce, W. M. Romney, R. W. Sant, W. J. Shaw, L. M. Small. **Transfer Agent & Registrar**—First Chicago Trust Co., Jersey City, NJ. **Incorporated**—in Delaware. **Empl**— 129,000. **S&P Analyst:** Tom Graves, CFA

12-SEP-98

Industry:
Insurance Brokers

Summary: This holding company owns Marsh & McLennan, the world's largest insurance brokerage concern. Employee benefit consulting and investment management services are also provided.

S&P Opinion: Hold (★★★)	Recent Price • 51⅜	Yield • 3.1%
	52 Wk Range • 64¼-44	12-Mo. P/E • 27.2

Quantitative Evaluations

Outlook
(1 Lowest—5 Highest)
• **2⁻**

Fair Value
• **48⅞**

Risk
• **Low**

Earn./Div. Rank
• **A**

Technical Eval.
• **Bearish** since 2/97

Rel. Strength Rank
(1 Lowest—99 Highest)
• **66**

Insider Activity
• **Neutral**

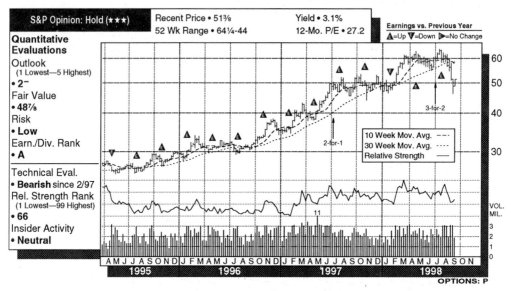

Earnings vs. Previous Year
▲=Up ▼=Down ▶=No Change

10 Week Mov. Avg. ‑ ‑ ‑
30 Week Mov. Avg. ∙ ∙ ∙ ∙
Relative Strength ——

OPTIONS: P

Overview - 12-AUG-98

Revenue growth in coming periods will be aided by contributions from the March 1997 $1.8 billion acquisition of privately held rival insurance broker Johnson & Higgins. However, underlying growth will be constrained by an intensely competitive property-casualty market environment, particularly in the U.S. Partly offsetting this is MMC's strong global franchise and dominant market position. Continued economic growth will likely spur demand for consulting services. Growth in interest income will be constrained by the relatively low interest rate environment, but this same interest rate environment has helped fuel a rise in securities markets and, in turn, profits at Putnam. Though year-to-year comparisons in coming periods could be difficult, given the strength recently seen here, Putnam will continue to be an important long-term profit contributor, as assets under management continue to grow. Stock buybacks will help EPS comparisons.

Valuation - 12-AUG-98

After generally trending upward during much of 1997, the shares plateaued in early 1998, amid renewed concerns that continuing pricing pressures would hurt insurance broking revenues. We also suspect some of the shares' weakness reflected disappointment that steps MMC recently took to retain certain Putnam key employees signaled to investors that MMC was not going to "cash in" on Putnam's value and sell the asset manager. Recently, the shares have recovered. We acknowledge MMC's franchise value as a dominant player in both the insurance brokerage and asset management arenas. However, at current levels, its shares are fairly valued.

Key Stock Statistics

S&P EPS Est. 1998	2.90	Tang. Bk. Value/Share	3.13
P/E on S&P Est. 1998	17.7	Beta	1.26
S&P EPS Est. 1999	3.35	Shareholders	17,800
Dividend Rate/Share	1.60	Market cap. (B)	$ 13.1
Shs. outstg. (M)	255.7	Inst. holdings	65%
Avg. daily vol. (M)	0.613		

Value of $10,000 invested 5 years ago: $ 20,140

Fiscal Year Ending Dec. 31

	1998	1997	1996	1995	1994	1993
Revenues (Million $)						
1Q	1,776	1,209	1,071	955.2	910.2	833.9
2Q	1,750	1,450	1,037	935.2	840.5	783.3
3Q	—	1,456	989.0	921.6	826.9	766.4
4Q	—	1,626	1,053	958.3	857.4	779.8
Yr.	—	6,009	4,149	3,770	3,435	3,163
Earnings Per Share ($)						
1Q	0.87	0.73	0.65	0.57	0.59	0.49
2Q	0.72	0.57	0.53	0.47	0.43	0.39
3Q	—	0.54	0.48	0.42	0.38	0.35
4Q	—	-0.19	0.46	0.39	0.33	0.28
Yr.	—	1.59	2.11	1.84	1.73	1.51

Next earnings report expected: late October

Dividend Data (Dividends have been paid since 1923.)

Amount ($)	Date Decl.	Ex-Div. Date	Stock of Record	Payment Date
0.500	Nov. 20	Jan. 07	Jan. 09	Feb. 13 '98
0.500	May. 19	Apr. 07	Apr. 09	May. 15 '98
3-for-2	May. 20	Jun. 29	Jun. 05	Jun. 26 '98
0.400	May. 20	Jul. 08	Jul. 10	Aug. 14 '98

A Division of The **McGraw·Hill** Companies

STANDARD
&POOR'S
STOCK REPORTS

Marsh & McLennan Companies, Inc.

1421

12-SEP-98

Business Summary - 12-AUG-98

This dominant player in the insurance brokerage arena recently reclaimed its spot as the world's largest insurance broker following its $1.8 billion acquisition of rival broker Johnson & Higgins. MMC's other strength lies in the investment management business, where its Putnam organization manages some $278 billion in assets. Revenue contributions in recent years were:

	1997	1996
Insurance services	47%	46%
Consulting	22%	28%
Investment management	31%	26%

In 1997, 53% of risk and insurance services profits were derived from international operations, up from 50% in 1996.

J&H Marsh & McLennan, Inc. advises clients in risk assessment and represents them in the design and implementation of arrangements that transfer risk to insurance underwriters or through alternative funding methods. Services include risk management counseling and administrative services for captive insurance companies. Reinsurance services are provided worldwide through Guy Carpenter & Co., Inc. Seabury & Smith, Inc. designs, distributes and administers a wide range of insurance and financial services. Frizzell Group, which designs and administers insurance programs in

the U.K., was sold in June 1996. Marsh & McLennan Risk Capital Corp. develops and invests in startup insurance and reinsurance ventures. In March 1997, MMC acquired rival insurance broker Johnson & Higgins for $1.8 billion in cash and stock. The transaction solidified MMC's position as the world's largest insurance broker. That spot was held briefly by rival Aon Corp. (NYSE: AOC) after it acquired the beleaguered brokerage firm of Alexander & Alexander Services, Inc. (AAL) in January 1997. Privately held Johnson & Higgins had 1996 revenue of about $1.2 billion. Approximately one-third of the $1.8 billion purchase price was paid in cash, with the balance in common stock.

William M. Mercer is one of the world's leading employee benefit consulting firms. Mercer Management Consulting provides management consulting services and consulting services on a broad range of microeconomic issues, including antitrust and trade regulation.

The Boston-based Putnam organization is one of the largest and fastest growing investment management firms in the U.S., offering an array of fixed-income and equity products, including more than 100 mutual funds. Assets under management totaled $278 billion as of June 30, 1998, up about 18% from 1997 year-end assets under management of $235 billion; and up 61% from 1996 year-end assets under management of $173 billion.

Per Share Data ($)

(Year Ended Dec. 31)	1997	1996	1995	1994	1993	1992	1991	1990	1989	1988
Tangible Bk. Val.	3.07	6.19	4.29	3.46	3.18	1.89	2.89	2.99	2.68	2.19
Cash Flow	2.39	2.76	2.46	2.28	2.05	1.92	1.91	1.86	1.78	1.74
Earnings	1.59	2.11	1.84	1.73	1.51	1.40	1.39	1.38	1.37	1.36
Dividends	1.10	1.10	0.99	0.93	0.90	0.88	0.87	0.85	0.85	0.81
Payout Ratio	69%	52%	54%	54%	60%	63%	61%	61%	61%	59%
Prices - High	53⅜	38¼	30	29⅝	32½	31½	29⅛	27	29⅞	19⅞
- Low	34¼	28⅛	25⅜	23¾	25⅝	23¾	23	19⅞	18⅜	15⅛
P/E Ratio - High	33	18	16	17	22	22	21	20	22	15
- Low	21	13	14	14	17	17	17	14	13	11

Income Statement Analysis (Million $)

	1997	1996	1995	1994	1993	1992	1991	1990	1989	1988
Revs.	6,009	4,149	3,770	3,435	3,163	2,937	2,779	2,723	2,428	2,272
Oper. Inc.	944	855	830	791	713	653	611	632	599	596
Depr.	199	140	135	121	120	112	113	105	89.0	81.0
Int. Exp.	106	61.6	62.8	50.6	46.1	38.3	39.1	44.2	46.6	27.8
Pretax Inc.	662	668	650	632	559	519	527	529	517	516
Eff. Tax Rate	40%	31%	38%	40%	41%	42%	42%	43%	43%	43%
Net Inc.	399	459	403	382	332	304	306	304	295	296

Balance Sheet & Other Fin. Data (Million $)

	1997	1996	1995	1994	1993	1992	1991	1990	1989	1988
Cash	424	300	328	295	332	371	349	305	293	252
Curr. Assets	2,569	1,749	1,679	1,446	1,312	1,260	1,039	1,053	911	788
Total Assets	7,914	4,545	4,330	3,831	3,547	3,088	2,382	2,411	2,035	1,830
Curr. Liab.	2,379	1,556	1,570	1,392	1,110	1,017	736	733	625	626
LT Debt	1,240	458	411	409	410	411	318	320	319	266
Common Eqty.	3,199	1,889	1,666	1,461	1,365	1,103	1,035	1,085	873	755
Total Cap.	4,439	2,347	2,077	1,870	1,775	1,525	1,358	1,417	1,206	1,038
Cap. Exp.	202	157	137	149	99	83.0	81.0	155	161	374
Cash Flow	599	599	538	503	452	416	419	409	384	377
Curr. Ratio	1.1	1.1	1.1	1.0	1.2	1.2	1.4	1.4	1.5	1.3
% LT Debt of Cap.	27.9	19.6	19.8	21.9	23.1	27.0	23.4	22.6	26.5	25.7
% Net Inc.of Revs.	6.6	11.1	10.7	11.1	10.5	10.3	11.0	11.2	12.1	13.0
% Ret. on Assets	6.4	10.4	9.9	10.4	10.0	11.0	12.9	13.6	15.2	17.4
% Ret. on Equity	15.7	25.9	25.8	27.0	26.9	28.1	29.2	30.8	36.0	38.9

Data as orig. reptd.; bef. results of disc. opers. and/or spec. items. Per share data adj. for stk. divs. as of ex-div. date. Bold denotes diluted EPS (FASB 128). E-Estimated. NA-Not Available. NM-Not Meaningful. NR-Not Ranked.

Office—1166 Ave. of the Americas, New York, NY 10036. **Tel**—(212) 345-5000. **Website**—http://www.marshmac.com **Chrmn**—A. J. C. Smith. **VP & Secy**—G. F. Van Gundy. **Sr VP & CFO**—F. J. Borelli. **Investor Contact**—J. M. Bischoff. **Dirs**—N. Barham, L. W. Bernard, R. H. Blum, F. J. Borelli, P. Coster, R. F. Erburu, J. W. Greenberg, R. J. Groves, R. S. Hickok, Lord Lang of Monkton, L. J. Lasser, R. M. Morrow , D. A. Olsen, J. D. Ong, G. Putnam, A. S. Simmons, J. T. Sinnott, A. J. C. Smith, F. J. Tasco. **Transfer Agent & Registrar**—Harris Trust Co. of New York, Chicago. **Incorporated**—in Delaware in 1923; reincorporated in Delaware in 1969. **Empl**— 36,000. **S&P Analyst:** Catherine A. Seifert

Masco Corp.

1429K

NYSE Symbol **MAS**

In S&P 500

12-SEP-98

Industry: Building Materials

Summary: Masco Corp. produces building and home improvement products, and has equity investments in other companies.

S&P Opinion: Hold (★★★)	Recent Price • 25	Yield • 1.8%
	52 Wk Range • 33-20¾	12-Mo. P/E • 19.4

Earnings vs. Previous Year
▲=Up ▼=Down ▶=No Change

Quantitative Evaluations

Outlook.
(1 Lowest—5 Highest)
• **2⁻**

Fair Value
• **24**

Risk
• **Low**

Earn./Div. Rank
• **B**

Technical Eval.
• **Bearish** since 12/96

Rel. Strength Rank
(1 Lowest—99 Highest)
• **62**

Insider Activity
• **Neutral**

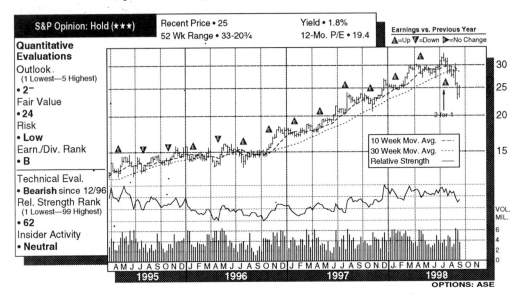

- 10 Week Mov. Avg. -----
- 30 Week Mov. Avg. ·······
- Relative Strength ———

2-for-1

VOL. MIL.

OPTIONS: ASE

Overview - 29-JUL-98

Sales from continuing operations are expected to rise solidly again in 1998, as the company continues to grow internally, as well as through acquisitions. Recent acquisitions will add about $100 million to annual sales. Further acquisitions are being sought, to keep top line growth in double digits. Despite continuing pricing pressures, margins are expected to widen, on higher volume, greater productivity, and expansion and cost reduction programs. Earnings will benefit from lower debt levels, as proceeds from the sale of the home furnishings division were used to pay down debt. The divestiture should also boost Masco's long-term growth, as it will allow the company to focus on expanding its profitable home improvement and building products business. The company expects sales to reach $4.5 billion by 2000, up from $3.2 billion in 1996. Earnings could grow nearly 15% annually over the next few years.

Valuation - 29-JUL-98

We recommend holding the shares for long-term capital gains. We believe that MAS's earnings will grow, as the company increases its market share, adds new product lines, and focuses on growing its profitable home improvement and building products business. Strength in the housing market since 1997 bodes well for MAS, as sales of building and home improvement products usually follow with a one- to two-year lag. However, producers of building products could be somewhat adversely affected by an interest rate hike or an overall economic slowdown. Management is still seeking to restore the trust of the financial community, after finally divesting its home furnishings business, which was a drag on profits for years. For the near term, the shares appear fully valued at 23X our 1998 EPS estimate of $1.35.

Key Stock Statistics

S&P EPS Est. 1998	1.35	Tang. Bk. Value/Share	4.95
P/E on S&P Est. 1998	18.5	Beta	1.22
S&P EPS Est. 1999	1.55	Shareholders	5,700
Dividend Rate/Share	0.44	Market cap. (B)	$ 8.5
Shs. outstg. (M)	340.2	Inst. holdings	98%
Avg. daily vol. (M)	1.121		

Value of $10,000 invested 5 years ago: $ 19,032

Fiscal Year Ending Dec. 31

	1998	1997	1996	1995	1994	1993
Revenues (Million $)						
1Q	1,039	854.0	764.0	721.0	1,050	946.0
2Q	1,085	913.0	787.0	714.0	1,120	948.0
3Q	—	1,003	843.0	738.0	1,150	982.0
4Q	—	990.0	843.0	754.0	1,148	1,010
Yr.	—	3,760	3,237	2,927	4,468	3,886
Earnings Per Share ($)						
1Q	**0.33**	**0.26**	0.20	0.22	0.21	0.18
2Q	**0.34**	**0.28**	0.21	0.18	0.22	0.17
3Q	**E0.35**	**0.30**	0.26	0.20	0.23	0.18
4Q	**E0.34**	**0.31**	0.26	0.03	-0.05	0.19
Yr.	**E1.35**	**1.17**	0.92	0.63	0.61	0.72

Next earnings report expected: early November

Dividend Data (Dividends have been paid since 1944.)

Amount ($)	Date Decl.	Ex-Div. Date	Stock of Record	Payment Date
0.210	Dec. 12	Jan. 07	Jan. 09	Feb. 09 '98
0.210	Mar. 20	Apr. 01	Apr. 03	May. 04 '98
2-for-1	Jun. 09	Jul. 13	Jun. 19	Jul. 10 '98
0.110	Jul. 13	Jul. 22	Jul. 24	Aug. 17 '98

A Division of The **McGraw·Hill** *Companies*

STANDARD
&POOR'S
STOCK REPORTS

Masco Corporation

1429K
12-SEP-98

Business Summary - 29-JUL-98

After a decade of disappointments, Masco (MAS) sold its home furnishings division in 1996. Between 1986 and 1989, Masco had spent $1.7 billion to acquire various furniture manufacturers, creating the world's largest home furnishings company. In August 1996, the division was sold for $1 billion, of which $500 million was used to pay down debt. Management had recognized that the expected synergies between home improvement and home furnishings were not materializing. To account for the anticipated loss from the divestiture, the company took a $650 million charge in 1995. Masco's resulting strategy is to focus on its historically successful home improvement and building products businesses.

Despite its setbacks with the home furnishings segment, the company believes it has the strongest brand name in the home improvement and building products segment. The divestiture is expected to boost the company's long-term growth potential. Several recent acquisitions should add about $100 million of annual revenues, with more acquisitions expected in the near future. Masco is one of the largest domestic manufacturers of brand name consumer products for home building and improvement. Its products are sold to consumers in over 100,000 retail outlets. MAS expects to grow to a sales level of $4.5 billion by 2000, for a compound annual growth rate of over 9%. The company

also expects $2 billion in excess cash flow over the next five years. It has benefited from a strong housing market, as well as consumer trends toward spending more time at home, which leads to spending more money on home improvement. MAS believes that consumer spending is a better indicator than housing market data in predicting future demand in the industry.

The company is the world's leading faucet manufacturer, and holds nearly a 40% market share in the U.S. of this high-margin business. Masco revolutionized faucets back in 1955 with the Delta, which is still the best-selling faucet in the U.S. The company's other faucets include Peerless, Alsons, Brass-Craft, Artistic Brass and Sherle Wagner. Masco's kitchen and bath products accounted for 78% of 1997's sales. Other product lines within this segment include plumbing supplies, such as Brass-Craft, Home Plumber and Plumb Shop; kitchen and bathroom cabinets, including Merillat, Kraftmaid, Starmark and Fieldstone; high-end kitchen appliances; bathroom and spa items, such as Aqua Glass, Watkins, Trayco, Melard, Zenith, American Shower & Bath, Huppe and Hot Spring Spa; and specialty products, including locks and builder's hardware.

Masco also has equity investments in other companies, including a 17% interest in MascoTech (formerly Masco Industries), 27% in Hans Grohe, and interests in both common and preferred shares of Furnishings International resulting from the home furnishings divestiture.

Per Share Data ($)

(Year Ended Dec. 31)	1997	1996	1995	1994	1993	1992	1991	1990	1989	1988
Tangible Bk. Val.	4.53	4.29	4.09	4.43	4.56	4.13	5.96	6.00	5.97	5.65
Cash Flow	1.48	1.23	0.91	0.99	1.10	0.98	0.49	0.76	0.99	1.32
Earnings	1.18	0.92	0.63	0.61	0.72	0.60	0.15	0.46	0.71	1.05
Dividends	0.30	0.48	0.28	0.35	0.33	0.30	0.28	0.27	0.25	0.22
Payout Ratio	26%	53%	44%	71%	45%	51%	192%	57%	35%	21%
Prices - High	26⅞	18½	15¾	20	19½	15	13¼	13⅜	15⅝	15¼
- Low	16⅞	13¼	11¼	10⅝	12¾	11	8½	7⅛	11⅞	11
P/E Ratio - High	23	20	25	33	27	25	88	29	22	14
- Low	14	14	18	17	18	18	57	16	17	10

Income Statement Analysis (Million $)

	1997	1996	1995	1994	1993	1992	1991	1990	1989	1988
Revs.	3,760	3,237	2,927	4,468	3,886	3,525	3,141	3,209	3,151	2,439
Oper. Inc.	703	580	492	630	520	473	351	456	494	471
Depr.	116	100	90.0	121	116	114	103	93.0	89.0	75.0
Int. Exp.	79.8	74.7	73.8	105	106	101	127	126	113	94.0
Pretax Inc.	631	503	352	323	363	305	98.0	236	327	421
Eff. Tax Rate	39%	41%	NM	40%	39%	40%	54%	41%	33%	32%
Net Inc.	382	295	200	194	221	183	45.0	139	221	288

Balance Sheet & Other Fin. Data (Million $)

	1997	1996	1995	1994	1993	1992	1991	1990	1989	1988
Cash	441	474	60.5	71.0	125	54.0	70.0	69.0	113	143
Curr. Assets	1,627	1,431	965	1,891	1,644	1,466	1,376	1,365	1,393	1,138
Total Assets	4,334	3,702	3,779	4,390	4,021	3,987	3,786	3,761	3,641	2,999
Curr. Liab.	620	518	446	601	490	492	514	552	540	378
LT Debt	1,322	1,236	1,577	1,593	1,418	1,487	1,369	1,334	1,153	999
Common Eqty.	2,229	1,840	1,655	2,113	1,998	1,887	1,799	1,774	1,858	1,546
Total Cap.	3,714	3,183	3,332	3,705	3,417	3,374	3,168	3,108	3,012	2,621
Cap. Exp.	167	138	165	191	167	123	119	193	193	95.0
Cash Flow	498	395	290	314	337	298	148	232	310	363
Curr. Ratio	2.6	2.8	2.2	3.1	3.4	3.0	2.7	2.5	2.6	3.0
% LT Debt of Cap.	35.6	38.8	47.3	43.0	41.5	44.1	43.2	42.9	38.3	38.1
% Net Inc.of Revs.	10.2	9.1	6.8	4.3	5.7	5.2	1.4	4.3	7.0	11.8
% Ret. on Assets	9.5	7.9	5.0	4.5	5.5	4.7	1.2	3.8	6.3	9.7
% Ret. on Equity	18.8	16.9	10.6	9.3	11.4	9.9	2.5	7.8	12.2	19.5

Data as orig. reptd.; bef. results of disc. opers. and/or spec. items. Per share data adj. for stk. divs. as of ex-div. date. Bold denotes diluted EPS (FASB 128). E-Estimated. NA-Not Available. NM-Not Meaningful. NR-Not Ranked.

Office—21001 Van Born Rd., Taylor, MI 48180. **Tel**—(313) 274-7400. **Chrmn & CEO**—R. A. Manoogian. **Pres & COO**—R. F. Kennedy. **VP & Secy**—E. A. Gargaro, Jr. **SVP-Fin**—R. G. Mosteller. **Treas & Investor Contact**—John C. Nicholls, Jr. **Dirs**—L. Bauder, E. L. Koning, W. B. Lyon, A. Manoogian (Chrmn Emeritus), R. A. Manoogian, J. A. Morgan, A. Simone, P. W. Stroh. **Transfer Agent & Registrar**—Bank of New York, NYC. **Incorporated**—in Michigan in 1929; reincorporated in Delaware in 1968. **Empl**— 28,100. **S&P Analyst:** Efraim Levy

STANDARD &POOR'S
STOCK REPORTS

Mattel, Inc.

1434

NYSE Symbol **MAT**

In S&P 500

12-SEP-98

Industry:
Leisure Time (Products)

Summary: This company, best known for its Barbie dolls, is the world's largest toy maker. In March 1997, MAT acquired Tyco Toys, Inc., the third largest U.S.-based toy maker.

| S&P Opinion: Hold (★★★) | Recent Price • 35⅜ | Yield • 0.9% |
| | 52 Wk Range • 46½-32 | 12-Mo. P/E • 21.7 |

Earnings vs. Previous Year
▲=Up ▼=Down ▷=No Change

Quantitative Evaluations

Outlook
(1 Lowest—5 Highest)
• **4**

Fair Value
• **45¼**

Risk
• **Average**

Earn./Div. Rank
• **B+**

Technical Eval.
• **Bearish** since 8/98

Rel. Strength Rank
(1 Lowest—99 Highest)
• **68**

Insider Activity
• **NA**

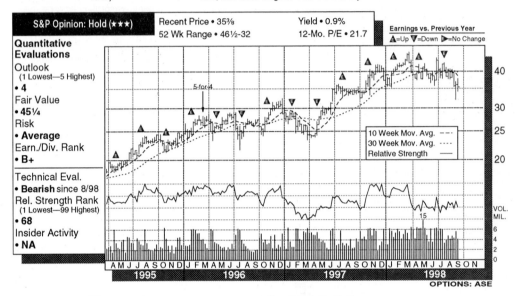

OPTIONS: ASE

Overview - 05-JUN-98

The product lines of this toy industry leader include Barbie dolls, Fisher Price and Sesame Street preschool items, Disney-related products, and Hot Wheel miniature vehicles. In 1997, Barbie-related items accounted for about 36% of MAT's overall sales. MAT's product line was expanded through the March 1997 acquisition of Tyco Toys, via an exchange of stock valued at about $755 million. Tyco, whose products include Matchbox vehicles and Sesame Street toys, reported losses in recent years. However, Mattel is making efforts to generate substantial cost savings related to the integration of Tyco and other restructuring efforts. We look for this to provide an incremental $100 million (pretax) of cost benefits in 1998. In the 1997 first quarter, MAT recorded a one-time charge of $0.73 a share, related to the Tyco merger and restructuring efforts. Excluding this charge, full-year 1997 diluted earnings per share would have been $1.65.

Valuation - 05-JUN-98

We view the stock of this major toy manufacturer as being adequately priced, and do not advise new purchases. Overall, we expect that MAT will demonstrate aggressive brand management, and that its portfolio of well-known brands and products will give the company's sales and profit levels some insulation from the changing tastes of consumers. In addition, over the long term, we look for MAT's already sizable foreign sales to become an increasingly important growth factor. In 1998, we expect the company to repurchase at least 6.5 million of its common shares. However, new MAT shares may result from exercisable options that, at year-end 1997, covered 6 million common shares at an average exercise price of $16.29 a share.

Key Stock Statistics

S&P EPS Est. 1998	1.95	Tang. Bk. Value/Share	4.39
P/E on S&P Est. 1998	18.1	Beta	0.89
S&P EPS Est. 1999	2.25	Shareholders	42,000
Dividend Rate/Share	0.32	Market cap. (B)	$ 10.4
Shs. outstg. (M)	292.7	Inst. holdings	85%
Avg. daily vol. (M)	0.987		

Value of $10,000 invested 5 years ago: $ 28,577

Fiscal Year Ending Dec. 31

	1998	1997	1996	1995	1994	1993
Revenues (Million $)						
1Q	705.2	693.5	585.9	543.6	487.3	477.2
2Q	861.5	972.7	777.4	763.5	650.3	576.6
3Q	—	1,555	1,232	1,176	1,037	896.7
4Q	—	1,613	1,191	1,155	1,030	753.9
Yr.	—	4,835	3,786	3,639	3,205	2,704
Earnings Per Share ($)						
1Q	0.04	-0.72	0.11	0.10	0.08	0.06
2Q	0.20	0.25	0.24	0.24	0.20	0.15
3Q	E0.85	0.73	0.61	0.54	0.46	0.39
4Q	E0.76	0.64	0.41	0.40	0.15	-0.11
Yr.	E1.95	0.94	1.36	1.26	0.90	0.50

Next earnings report expected: late October

Dividend Data (Dividends have been paid since 1990.)

Amount ($)	Date Decl.	Ex-Div. Date	Stock of Record	Payment Date
0.070	Nov. 07	Dec. 05	Dec. 09	Jan. 06 '98
0.070	Feb. 06	Mar. 11	Mar. 13	Apr. 03 '98
0.080	May. 06	Jun. 10	Jun. 12	Jul. 02 '98
0.080	Aug. 21	Sep. 09	Sep. 11	Oct. 02 '98

A Division of The McGraw-Hill Companies

Business Summary - 05-JUN-98

Barbie should remain the star of the show, but her supporting cast now includes Tickle Me Elmo and Doodle Bear.

In March 1997, Mattel Inc. (MAT), whose products include Barbie fashion dolls and Fisher-Price preschool items, acquired Tyco Toys via an exchange of stock valued at about $755 million. In addition to Elmo and Doodle Bear, Tyco's products include radio-controlled toys, Matchbox vehicles, Sesame Street items, and such brands as Magna Doodle and View-Master. For Mattel, already the world's largest manufacturer and marketer of toys, the acquisition brings opportunities for cost savings in comparison to what the two companies achieved separately.

In the U.S., MAT's products are distributed directly to large retailers, including discount and free-standing toy stores, chain stores, and department stores, and to other retail outlets. To a limited extent, products are distributed to wholesalers. Sales to customers within the U.S. accounted for 66% of gross sales in 1997, and were up 14% from the level of 1996 (as restated, including Tyco). Sales to customers outside the U.S. were up 3% in local currencies, but were down 5% when measured in dollars. Currency fluctuation caused

MAT's 1997 reported sales, when measured in dollars, to be reduced by about $139 million. In 1997, Toys "R" Us and Wal-Mart accounted for 18% and 15% of MAT's worldwide net sales, respectively.

MAT's largest product line is the long-lived Barbie line of fashion dolls, accessories and related products, which accounted for gross sales of $1.9 billion in 1997, up 9% in 1996. MAT's infant and preschool segment provided gross sales of $1.8 billion in 1997, up 15% from the 1996 level, as restated. This was despite a 15% decline from MAT's large Fisher-Price product line, which likely accounted for roughly half of the segment's sales. This business segment also include items related to Sesame Street and some Disney-related product. MAT's Wheels category (e.g. miniature vehicles) had about $600 million of 1997 gross sales, up 21%, while MAT's entertainment category, which includes various Disney-related products, Nickelodeon-related items, and games and puzzles, had gross sales of about $400 million, down 4%. MAT also had about $300 million of gross sales from other dolls, and roughly $200 million from products not included in other categories. Net sales reported by MAT on its income statement totaled about 94% of gross sales. Separately, since September 1997, MAT and certain other toy companies have been named as defendants in one or more antitrust actions.

Per Share Data ($)

(Year Ended Dec. 31)	1997	1996	1995	1994	1993	1992	1991	1990	1989	1988
Tangible Bk. Val.	4.06	3.84	3.09	2.25	2.46	2.14	1.77	1.45	1.00	0.74
Cash Flow	1.59	1.89	1.75	1.34	0.83	1.06	0.94	0.76	0.66	0.38
Earnings	0.94	1.36	1.26	0.90	0.49	0.73	0.63	0.49	0.44	0.20
Dividends	0.27	0.24	0.24	0.19	0.12	0.09	0.05	0.02	Nil	Nil
Payout Ratio	29%	18%	19%	21%	24%	13%	8%	5%	Nil	Nil
Prices - High	41¼	32½	24⅞	18⅞	15¾	13⅞	11⅜	7⅛	5¾	3
- Low	23⅜	21⅝	15¾	13¼	10½	10⅛	5	4¼	2½	1¹¹⁄₁₆
P/E Ratio - High	45	24	20	21	32	19	18	15	13	14
- Low	25	16	13	15	21	14	8	9	6	8

Income Statement Analysis (Million $)

Revs.	4,835	3,786	3,639	3,205	2,704	1,848	1,622	1,471	1,237	990
Oper. Inc.	1,014	796	735	673	518	325	295	233	203	131
Depr.	190	149	133	124	92.0	63.6	57.7	50.3	40.0	31.4
Int. Exp.	90.1	75.5	74.0	55.4	62.6	55.0	53.6	51.6	50.0	55.2
Pretax Inc.	425	546	533	394	237	216	189	139	108	58.0
Eff. Tax Rate	32%	31%	33%	35%	43%	33%	38%	35%	26%	38%
Net Inc.	290	378	358	256	136	144	118	91.0	80.0	36.0

Balance Sheet & Other Fin. Data (Million $)

Cash	695	501	483	260	524	295	197	198	220	104
Curr. Assets	2,462	1,771	1,691	1,544	1,471	872	709	627	603	488
Total Assets	3,804	2,894	2,696	2,459	2,000	1,260	1,061	930	830	693
Curr. Liab.	1,173	960	848	916	783	413	400	331	336	216
LT Debt	664	364	464	360	328	287	185	168	178	243
Common Eqty.	1,726	1,448	1,275	1,052	791	534	438	328	214	131
Total Cap.	2,486	1,812	1,739	1,446	1,146	823	629	566	463	456
Cap. Exp.	223	209	207	163	101	75.3	49.3	84.4	85.0	25.2
Cash Flow	469	527	491	375	223	203	176	141	120	67.0
Curr. Ratio	2.1	1.8	2.0	1.7	1.9	2.1	1.8	1.9	1.8	2.3
% LT Debt of Cap.	26.7	20.1	26.7	24.9	28.6	34.9	29.4	29.7	38.3	53.4
% Net Inc.of Revs.	6.0	10.0	9.8	8.0	5.0	7.8	7.3	6.2	6.4	3.6
% Ret. on Assets	8.7	13.5	13.9	11.3	7.2	12.3	11.7	10.3	10.4	4.9
% Ret. on Equity	17.1	27.7	30.3	26.8	16.9	28.4	30.4	33.5	46.0	30.5

Data as orig. reptd.; bef. results of disc. opers. and/or spec. items. Per share data adj. for stk. divs. as of ex-div. date. Bold denotes diluted EPS (FASB 128). E-Estimated. NA-Not Available. NM-Not Meaningful. NR-Not Ranked.

Office—333 Continental Blvd., El Segundo, CA 90245-5012. **Tel**—(310) 252-2000. **Chrmn & CEO**—J. E. Barad. **COO**—B. L. Stein. **EVP**—F. Luzuriaga. **CFO**—H. J. Pearce. **SVP & Treas**—W. Stavro. **Secy**—L. P. Smith. **Investor Contact**—Michael Salop. **Dirs**—J. E. Barad, H. Brown, T. M. Friedman, J. C. Gandolfo, R. M. Loeb, N. Mansour, W. D. Rollnick, C. A. Sinclair, B. L. Stein, J. L. Vogelstein. **Transfer Agent & Registrar**—BankBoston (c/o Boston EquiServe, L.P.). **Incorporated**—in California in 1948; reincorporated in Delaware in 1968. **Empl**— 25,000. **S&P Analyst:** Tom Graves, CFA

May Department Stores 1436

NYSE Symbol **MAY**

In S&P 500

12-SEP-98

Industry:
Retail (Department Stores)

Summary: May Department Stores is one of the largest retailing companies in the U.S., operating 370 stores in 30 states and the District of Columbia.

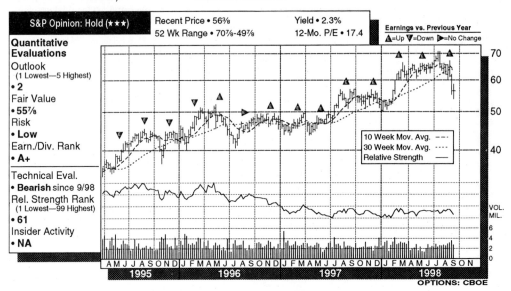

S&P Opinion: Hold (★★★)	Recent Price • 56⅜	Yield • 2.3%
	52 Wk Range • 70⅞-49⅞	12-Mo. P/E • 17.4

Earnings vs. Previous Year
▲=Up ▼=Down ▶=No Change

Quantitative Evaluations

Outlook
(1 Lowest—5 Highest)
• **2**

Fair Value
• **55⅞**

Risk
• **Low**

Earn./Div. Rank
• **A+**

Technical Eval.
• **Bearish** since 9/98

Rel. Strength Rank
(1 Lowest—99 Highest)
• **61**

Insider Activity
• **NA**

10 Week Mov. Avg. -----
30 Week Mov. Avg. ·······
Relative Strength ——

VOL. MIL.

OPTIONS: CBOE

Overview - 14-AUG-98

Sales should increase about 6% in FY 99 (Jan.), reflecting 3% growth in comparable-store sales, the opening of 19 new department stores, and sales gains resulting from the remodeling of older units. Gross margins should remain level, as any cost savings will be passed on to customers in the form of lower prices. SG&A expenses should decline at most about 20 basis points as a percentage of sales, reflecting the consolidation of functions at newly acquired stores and leverage from a larger and growing number of stores. The company has grown over the years through the addition of new stores and acquisitions. It is one of the financially strongest companies in the department store industry. The 1996 spinoff of its Payless ShoeSource subsidiary freed up capital for the expansion and acquisition of department stores via small groups of stores or possibly a large regional acquisition. In August, MAY announced the purchase of 11 department stores from Mercantile Stores Inc.

Valuation - 14-AUG-98

The shares have sold off from the 1998 high in tandem with the stock market. Second quarter earnings posted a solid 15% increase, on a 4.3% gain in same-store sales. The stock remains a worthwhile holding. May is a well managed company, and is a strong beneficiary of the consolidation of the department store industry. The company's low cost structure and growing base of stores should allow earnings to continue to advance at 10% to 12% annually over the next few years. The balance sheet should remain strong. The dividend, which was recently yielding over 2%, was raised early in 1998. However, given the expectation of only moderate earnings growth in the coming years, the shares appear fairly valued at recent levels.

Key Stock Statistics

S&P EPS Est. 1999	3.45	Tang. Bk. Value/Share	13.23
P/E on S&P Est. 1999	16.3	Beta	0.75
S&P EPS Est. 2000	3.80	Shareholders	43,100
Dividend Rate/Share	1.27	Market cap. (B)	$ 13.0
Shs. outstg. (M)	231.0	Inst. holdings	73%
Avg. daily vol. (M)	0.639		

Value of $10,000 invested 5 years ago: NA

Fiscal Year Ending Jan. 31

	1999	1998	1997	1996	1995	1994
Revenues (Million $)						
1Q	2,817	2,675	2,511	2,218	2,620	2,422
2Q	2,889	2,749	2,533	2,325	2,706	2,586
3Q	—	2,969	2,855	2,569	2,945	2,814
4Q	—	4,292	4,101	3,840	3,950	3,707
Yr.	—	12,685	12,000	10,952	12,223	11,529
Earnings Per Share ($)						
1Q	**0.44**	**0.38**	0.36	0.33	0.43	0.35
2Q	**0.53**	**0.46**	0.41	0.41	0.50	0.45
3Q	**E0.53**	**0.48**	0.44	0.42	0.54	0.51
4Q	**E1.95**	**1.79**	1.61	1.57	1.59	1.44
Yr.	**E3.45**	**3.11**	2.94	2.73	3.06	2.77

Next earnings report expected: early November

Dividend Data (Dividends have been paid since 1911.)

Amount ($)	Date Decl.	Ex-Div. Date	Stock of Record	Payment Date
0.300	Nov. 17	Nov. 26	Dec. 01	Dec. 15 '97
0.318	Feb. 12	Feb. 25	Mar. 01	Mar. 15 '98
0.318	Mar. 23	May. 28	Jun. 01	Jun. 15 '98
0.318	Aug. 21	Aug. 28	Sep. 01	Sep. 15 '98

A Division of The **McGraw·Hill** Companies

The May Department Stores Company

Business Summary - 14-AUG-98

May Department Stores is one of the leading department store companies in the U.S. At the end of FY 98 (Jan.), the company operated 369 department stores in 30 states and the District of Columbia through eight regional divisions. In May 1996, the company spun off to shareholders its Payless ShoeSource unit, the largest U.S. chain of self-service family shoe stores.

The company operates department stores in 123 markets; this constitutes most of the major markets in the U.S. Stores operate under the following trade names: Hecht's/ Strawbridge's (71; $2.3 billion in annual revenues), Lord & Taylor (63; $1.9 billion), Foley's (55; $1.9 billion), Robinsons-May (55; $1.9 billion), Kaufmann's (47; $1.5 billion), Filene's (40; $1.5 billion), Famous-Barr/ L. S. Ayres (30; $1.1 billion); and Meier & Frank (8; $0.4 billion). Sales per square foot were highest at Lord & Taylor ($243), followed by $236 at Filene's and $229 at Meier & Frank.

May's capital budget for 1998-2002 is projected at about $3.6 billion, including about $1.8 billion for new stores, $600 million to expand and remodel existing stores, and $350 million related to systems and operations. This includes 100 new department stores, totaling 16 million retail sq. ft., a 4% net annual increase in square footage. The company plans to invest more than $100 million to improve distribution centers and systems. In 1998, MAY plans to open 19 new stores and expand seven, adding 2.9 million square feet. In August 1998, the company agreed to purchase 11 department stores from Mercantile Stores Inc.

The company is repurchasing common stock; in 1996 and 1997, it repurchased a total of $900 million of stock. MAY plans to repurchase up to $500 million of stock from time to time.

In May 1996, the company distributed 0.16 of a Payless ShoeSource, Inc. common share for each May share held. Annual sales at Payless were about $2.3 billion, and it had over $1 billion in assets; it contributed $0.32 to May's fully diluted EPS in FY 95. In 1989, May sold its Caldor discount chain and its Loehmann's division. Venture, a Midwest discount chain, was spun off to shareholders in FY 91.

Per Share Data ($) (Year Ended Jan. 31)	**1998**	**1997**	**1996**	**1995**	**1994**	**1993**	**1992**	**1991**	**1990**	**1989**
Tangible Bk. Val.	13.23	12.13	15.71	14.22	12.16	10.26	7.08	7.45	8.63	8.12
Cash Flow	4.71	4.50	4.06	4.56	4.16	3.64	3.29	3.12	2.85	2.73
Earnings	3.11	2.82	2.73	3.06	2.77	2.35	2.01	1.94	1.88	1.71
Dividends	1.20	1.16	1.11	1.01	0.92	0.82	0.81	0.77	0.69	0.62
Payout Ratio	39%	41%	41%	33%	33%	35%	40%	39%	34%	37%
Cal. Yrs.	1997	1996	1995	1994	1993	1992	1991	1990	1989	1988
Prices - High	57 1/8	52 1/4	45 3/8	45 1/8	46 1/2	37 1/4	30 1/4	29 5/8	26 3/8	20
- Low	43 5/8	40	32 7/8	32 1/4	33 3/8	25 7/8	18 3/4	18 7/8	17 3/8	14 3/8
P/E Ratio - High	18	19	17	15	17	16	15	15	14	12
- Low	14	14	12	11	12	11	9	10	9	8
Income Statement Analysis (Million $)										
Revs.	12,685	12,000	10,952	12,223	11,529	11,150	10,615	10,066	9,602	11,742
Oper. Inc.	1,990	1,882	1,743	1,914	1,770	1,571	1,400	1,305	1,275	1,309
Depr.	412	373	333	374	347	321	319	294	263	300
Int. Exp.	299	277	283	257	263	306	354	314	265	254
Pretax Inc.	1,279	1,232	1,160	1,296	1,178	791	796	762	799	781
Eff. Tax Rate	39%	39%	40%	40%	40%	24%	35%	34%	36%	36%
Net Inc.	779	749	700	782	711	603	515	500	515	503
Balance Sheet & Other Fin. Data (Million $)										
Cash	199	102	159	55.0	46.0	172	207	80.0	92.0	124
Curr. Assets	4,878	5,035	5,097	4,910	4,679	4,654	4,574	4,377	4,053	4,168
Total Assets	9,930	10,059	10,122	9,472	8,800	8,545	8,728	8,295	7,802	8,144
Curr. Liab.	1,866	1,923	1,602	1,895	1,771	1,975	1,522	1,742	1,994	2,074
LT Debt	3,512	3,849	3,333	2,815	2,822	2,879	3,918	3,565	3,003	2,483
Common Eqty.	3,489	3,650	4,585	4,135	3,639	3,181	2,400	2,467	2,319	3,050
Total Cap.	8,107	8,247	8,664	7,388	6,847	6,394	7,043	6,781	6,051	5,936
Cap. Exp.	496	632	801	937	700	404	512	548	522	1,000
Cash Flow	1,173	1,122	1,014	1,137	1,039	906	816	776	763	803
Curr. Ratio	2.6	2.6	3.2	2.6	2.6	2.4	3.0	2.5	2.0	2.0
% LT Debt of Cap.	43.3	46.7	38.5	38.9	41.2	45.0	55.6	52.6	49.6	41.8
% Net Inc.of Revs.	6.1	6.2	6.4	6.4	6.2	5.4	4.9	5.0	5.4	4.3
% Ret. on Assets	7.8	7.5	7.2	8.6	8.2	7.0	6.0	6.2	7.1	7.0
% Ret. on Equity	22.4	18.1	15.6	19.6	20.3	19.6	22.1	24.3	20.6	17.4

Data as orig. reptd.; bef. results of disc. opers. and/or spec. items. Per share data adj. for stk. divs. as of ex-div. date. Bold denotes diluted EPS (FASB 128). E-Estimated. NA-Not Available. NM-Not Meaningful. NR-Not Ranked.

Office—611 Olive St., St. Louis, MO 63101-1799. **Tel**—(314) 342-6300. **Website**—http://www.maycompany.com **Chrmn** —J. T. Loeb. **Pres & CEO**—E. S. Kahn. **EVP & CFO**—J. L. Dunham. **Secy**—R. A. Brickson. **SVP, Treas & Investor Contact**—J. R. Kniffen. **Dirs**—R. L. Battram, J. L. Dunham, M. J. Evans, D. C. Farrell, E. S. Kahn, H. L. Kaplan, J. T. Loeb, E. H. Meyer, R. E. Palmer, A. E. Pearson, M. R. Quinlan, W. P. Stiritz, R. D. Storey, A. J. Torcasio, M. L. Weidenbaum, E. E. Whitacre Jr., R. D. Wolfe. **Transfer Agent & Registrar**—Bank of New York, NYC. **Incorporated**—in New York in 1910; reincorporated in Delaware in 1996. **Empl**— 119,000. **S&P Analyst:** Karen J. Sack, CFA

Maytag Corp.

1438

NYSE Symbol **MYG**

In S&P 500

12-SEP-98

Industry:
Household Furnishings
& Appliances

Summary: MYG produces appliances under the Maytag, Magic Chef, Admiral and Jenn-Air names and floor care products under the Hoover name. The Dixie-Narco division makes vending equipment.

| S&P Opinion: Hold (★★★) | Recent Price • 46⅝ | Yield • 1.5% | Earnings vs. Previous Year |
| | 52 Wk Range • 55¾-30⅜ | 12-Mo. P/E • 18.6 | ▲=Up ▼=Down ▶=No Change |

Quantitative Evaluations

Outlook
(1 Lowest—5 Highest)
• **3+**

Fair Value
• **47¼**

Risk
• **Low**

Earn./Div. Rank
• **B-**

Technical Eval.
• **Bearish** since 1/97

Rel. Strength Rank
(1 Lowest—99 Highest)
• **89**

Insider Activity
• **NA**

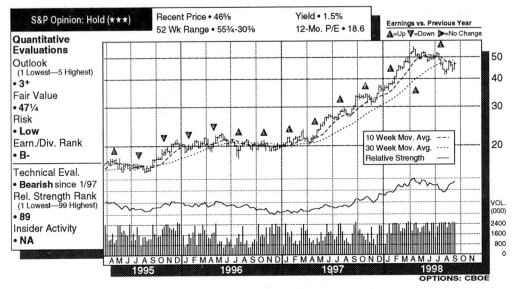

10 Week Mov. Avg. ----
30 Week Mov. Avg. ....
Relative Strength ——

VOL.
(000)
2400
1600
800
0

A M J J A S O N D J F M A M J J A S O N D J F M A M J J A S O N D J F M A M J J A S O N
1995 | 1996 | 1997 | 1998

OPTIONS: CBOE

Overview - 27-JUL-98

Sales in 1998 should benefit from new product introductions, the acquisition of the Blodgett group, and the addition of Sears as a retail outlet for Maytag products. Profits should benefit from an improved sales mix, as higher-margin sales of the higher-priced Jenn-Air and Maytag brands should exceed MYG's consolidated growth, reflecting favorable reaction to new products such as the new Neptune washer. Improved demand and backlog for vending products ahead of the spring selling season should also aid results. We also see margins expanding somewhat, on more efficient manufacturing and stable raw material prices. MYG's China joint venture, begun in late 1996, is helping to expand sales and profits; the company has become the leader (13% to 15% market share) in this fragmented market. We expect MYG to use its positive cash flow to pay dividends, repurchase common stock, and add accretive businesses.

Valuation - 27-JUL-98

The North American appliance industry is mature and highly competitive. MYG has responded by investing in new products that command higher margins, and by selectively tapping faster-growing, less mature markets. For example, MYG's recent introduction of a new refrigerator line and a horizontal axis washing machine should boost its market share in the premium appliance category. We expect income from continuing operations to increase significantly in 1998, on new product introductions, expanded distribution, cost containment efforts, more productive manufacturing. EPS comparisons should benefit from an expanded stock repurchase program. At a recent level of 15X our initial 1999 EPS estimate of $3.15, we expect MYG to perform in line with the market.

Key Stock Statistics

S&P EPS Est. 1998	2.90	Tang. Bk. Value/Share	1.19
P/E on S&P Est. 1998	16.1	Beta	0.78
S&P EPS Est. 1999	3.20	Shareholders	28,400
Dividend Rate/Share	0.72	Market cap. (B)	$ 4.3
Shs. outstg. (M)	91.5	Inst. holdings	66%
Avg. daily vol. (M)	0.674		

Value of $10,000 invested 5 years ago: $ 36,103

Fiscal Year Ending Dec. 31

	1998	1997	1996	1995	1994	1993
Revenues (Million $)						
1Q	1,040	792.5	731.3	820.1	790.6	717.0
2Q	1,022	814.5	754.6	803.5	870.4	753.3
3Q	—	855.8	742.9	726.4	848.9	770.2
4Q	—	945.1	772.9	689.5	862.6	746.7
Yr.	—	3,408	3,002	3,040	3,373	2,987
Earnings Per Share ($)						
1Q	**0.75**	**0.39**	0.15	0.37	0.29	-0.10
2Q	**0.71**	**0.44**	0.43	-0.95	0.39	0.20
3Q	**E0.72**	**0.50**	0.42	0.28	0.57	0.22
4Q	**E0.70**	**0.54**	0.36	0.16	0.17	0.16
Yr.	**E2.90**	**1.87**	1.36	-0.14	1.42	0.48

Next earnings report expected: mid October

Dividend Data (Dividends have been paid since 1946.)

Amount ($)	Date Decl.	Ex-Div. Date	Stock of Record	Payment Date
0.160	Nov. 13	Nov. 26	Dec. 01	Dec. 15 '97
0.160	Feb. 12	Feb. 26	Mar. 02	Mar. 16 '98
0.160	May. 14	May. 28	Jun. 01	Jun. 15 '98
0.180	Aug. 13	Aug. 28	Sep. 01	Sep. 15 '98

A Division of The **McGraw·Hill** *Companies*

STANDARD
&POOR'S
STOCK REPORTS

Maytag Corporation

1438

12-SEP-98

Business Summary - 27-JUL-98

Maytag is engaged in two industry segments: appliances (93% of sales and 95% of operating profits in 1997) and vending equipment (7% and 5%). Approximately 3.6% of 1997's sales were made outside of North America. In September 1996, MYG invested about $35 million (and committed an additional $35 million) for a 50.5% ownership stake in a joint venture with Hefei Rongshida, a leading manufacturer of appliances in China. In mid-1995, Maytag sold its Hoover Europe division to Candy S.p.A., a European producer of household appliances.

Home appliances include laundry equipment, gas and electric ranges, refrigerators, freezers, dishwashers, food waste disposals and floor care products. Important trademarks are Maytag, Magic Chef, Admiral, Jenn-Air, Performa, Hardwick, Norge and Hoover.

Maytag's products are sold to all major market segments, including the replacement market, the commercial laundry market, the new home and apartment building market, the manufactured housing (mobile home) market, the recreational vehicle market, the private-label market and the household/commercial floor care market. Most products are sold directly to dealers and through independent distributors, mass merchandisers and large national department stores.

Dixie-Narco produces soft-drink vending equipment and money changers. Its products are sold to all major bottlers. Maycor Appliance Parts and Service Co. provides consolidated service and parts distribution for most of Maytag's appliance brands.

In the second quarter of 1996, MYG took a one-time $40 million pretax restructuring charge associated with consolidating all aspects of product design, manufacturing, marketing and service for the four major home appliance brands and consolidating various factories.

In March 1997, MYG signed a North American supply and distribution agreement for multi-load commercial washers to bolster its commercial laundry business. The agreement calls for Primus, a Belgian company, to supply MYG with oversized front-loading commercial washers, allowing MYG to offer a complete line.

In December 1997, MYG reached an agreement with Sears, Roebuck and Co. to sell the full line of Maytag brand major appliances in 1,400 Sears Brand Central stores. As of June 30, 1998, initial channel filling at Sears was essentially completed.

In 1997, MYG's operating margins (before restructuring charges) improved to 10.5%, from 10.3%, reflecting increased sales from higher-margin new products, a rebound in vending equipment sales, and cost reductions. The company expects its new products and models to generate increased sales in coming quarters, and that some costs associated with new product initiatives will decrease.

Per Share Data ($)

(Year Ended Dec. 31)	1997	1996	1995	1994	1993	1992	1991	1990	1989	1988
Tangible Bk. Val.	1.92	1.85	2.33	3.14	2.50	2.54	6.32	6.31	5.51	6.55
Cash Flow	3.27	2.45	0.91	2.53	1.53	0.90	1.62	1.75	2.01	2.22
Earnings	1.87	1.36	-0.14	1.42	0.48	-0.08	0.75	0.94	1.27	1.77
Dividends	0.64	0.56	0.52	0.50	0.50	0.50	0.50	0.95	0.95	0.97
Payout Ratio	34%	41%	NM	35%	104%	NM	67%	102%	76%	55%
Prices - High	37½	22⅞	21½	20⅛	18⅝	20⅝	16½	20⅝	26¾	27⅝
- Low	19¾	17½	14½	14	13	12½	10⅜	9⅛	18⅞	18⅞
P/E Ratio - High	20	17	NM	14	39	NM	22	22	21	16
- Low	11	13	NM	10	27	NM	14	11	15	11

Income Statement Analysis (Million $)

	1997	1996	1995	1994	1993	1992	1991	1990	1989	1988
Revs.	3,408	3,002	3,040	3,373	2,987	3,041	2,971	3,057	3,089	1,886
Oper. Inc.	496	420	400	442	331	277	304	317	357	261
Depr.	138	111	112	119	112	103	93.0	86.0	77.0	34.0
Int. Exp.	59.0	43.0	52.1	74.6	75.4	75.0	75.2	82.0	83.4	19.7
Pretax Inc.	301	228	-60.0	241	90.0	8.0	123	159	207	215
Eff. Tax Rate	37%	39%	1.25%	37%	43%	NM	36%	38%	37%	37%
Net Inc.	183	138	-15.0	151	51.0	-8.0	79.0	99	131	136

Balance Sheet & Other Fin. Data (Million $)

	1997	1996	1995	1994	1993	1992	1991	1990	1989	1988
Cash	28.0	28.0	141	110	31.7	57.0	48.8	69.6	39.3	10.5
Curr. Assets	935	905	910	1,130	1,057	1,016	1,077	1,169	1,140	564
Total Assets	2,514	2,330	2,125	2,504	2,469	2,501	2,535	2,587	2,436	1,330
Curr. Liab.	567	570	367	534	651	563	568	556	489	246
LT Debt	550	488	537	663	725	789	809	858	877	518
Common Eqty.	616	574	637	732	587	599	1,011	1,015	938	501
Total Cap.	1,364	1,160	1,188	1,433	1,356	1,477	1,895	1,944	1,875	1,072
Cap. Exp.	230	211	148	79.0	96.0	120	143	141	128	102
Cash Flow	321	249	97.0	270	163	95.0	172	185	208	170
Curr. Ratio	1.6	1.6	2.5	2.1	1.6	1.8	1.9	2.1	2.3	2.3
% LT Debt of Cap.	40.3	42.1	45.2	46.3	53.4	53.4	42.7	44.1	46.8	48.3
% Net Inc.of Revs.	5.4	4.6	NM	4.5	1.7	NM	2.7	3.2	4.3	7.2
% Ret. on Assets	7.6	6.2	NM	6.1	2.1	NM	3.1	3.9	6.2	12.4
% Ret. on Equity	30.8	22.8	NM	22.9	8.6	NM	7.8	10.1	16.1	29.6

Data as orig. reptd.; bef. results of disc. opers. and/or spec. items. Per share data adj. for stk. divs. as of ex-div. date. Bold denotes diluted EPS (FASB 128). E-Estimated. NA-Not Available. NM-Not Meaningful. NR-Not Ranked.

Office—403 West 4th St. North, Newton, IA 50208. **Tel**—(515) 792-7000. **Fax**—(515) 787-8395. **Website**—http://www.maytagcorp.com **Chrmn & CEO**—L. A. Hadley. **Pres & COO**—Lloyd D. Ward. **EVP-CFO**—G. J. Pribanic. **Secy**—J. E. Bennett. **Treas**— D. D. Urbani. **Director, Investor Relations**—John P. Tolson (515) 787-8136. **Dirs**—B. R. Allen, H. L. Clark Jr., L. Crown, L. A. Hadley, W. R. Hicks, R. D. Ray, B. G. Rethore, W. A. Reynolds, J. A. Sivright, N.E. Stearns Jr., F. G. Steingraber, C. J. Uhrich, L. D. Ward, P. S. Wilmott. **Transfer Agent & Registrar**—Bank of Boston. **Incorporated**—in Delaware in 1925. **Empl**— 22,433. **S&P Analyst:** Efraim Levy

STANDARD &POOR'S
STOCK REPORTS

MBIA Inc.

1391M

NYSE Symbol **MBI**

In S&P 500

12-SEP-98

Industry:
Financial (Diversified)

Summary: This leading financial guarantee company is also the leading insurer of municipal bonds, based on its 36% share of the new-issue, long-term municipal bond market.

S&P Opinion: Accumulate (★★★★)	Recent Price • 53⅜	Yield • 1.5%
	52 Wk Range • 80⅞-47⅛	12-Mo. P/E • 12.2

Quantitative Evaluations

Outlook
(1 Lowest—5 Highest)
• **2⁻**

Fair Value
• **54¾**

Risk
• **Low**

Earn./Div. Rank
• **A+**

Technical Eval.
• **Bearish** since 9/98

Rel. Strength Rank
(1 Lowest—99 Highest)
• **37**

Insider Activity
• **NA**

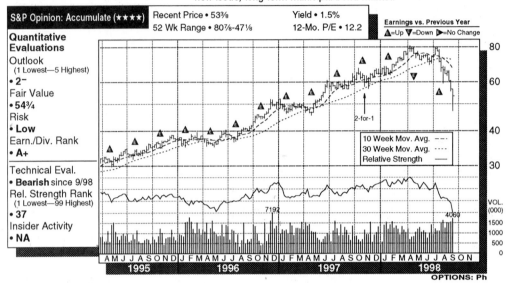

Earnings vs. Previous Year
▲=Up ▼=Down ▶=No Change

10 Week Mov. Avg. – – –
30 Week Mov. Avg. ·····
Relative Strength —

2-for-1

7192   4060

VOL. (000)

OPTIONS: Ph

Overview - 13-AUG-98

Net written premium growth will easily top 20% in coming periods, reflecting robust municipal finance activity and increased demand for bond insurance. Results over the longer term will also be aided by expansion overseas and into the structured finance arena. MBI's presence in the structured finance market will greatly expand following its $536 million acquisition of CapMAC Holdings Inc. (NYSE: KAP), which was completed in mid-February 1998. KAP is a leading insurer of structured finance securities. Contributions from asset management activities further enhance MBI's long-term prospects, although costs to expand this business may limit its near-term profit contribution. Ongoing cost shifting from the federal government to states and municipalities will increase their financing needs and likely stem any interest-rate-driven decline in municipal finance activity. During the six months ended June 30, 1998, new-issue municipal bond volume rose 59%, to $136.9 billion. The insured portion of the new-issue volume was 54%. MBI maintained its position as the leading insurer of municipal bonds, with a 36% share of the insured portion of the new issue market.

Valuation - 13-AUG-98

After plunging in December 1994 when Orange County, CA, declared bankruptcy, the shares recovered after MBI disclosed that it had no direct exposure to Orange County debt. Since then, the shares have trended steadily upward, aided by a favorable interest rate environment. We view MBI as a top notch, well managed firm with strong franchise value. Some of the shares' recent weakness is likely due to concerns over claims MBI may have to pay in connection with the bankruptcy filing of a client. We recommend investors with a long term time horizon use this correction as an opportunity to add to positions.

Key Stock Statistics

S&P EPS Est. 1998	4.50	Tang. Bk. Value/Share	35.17
P/E on S&P Est. 1998	11.9	Beta	1.05
S&P EPS Est. 1999	5.20	Shareholders	400
Dividend Rate/Share	0.78	Market cap. (B)	$ 5.3
Shs. outstg. (M)	99.3	Inst. holdings	87%
Avg. daily vol. (M)	0.460		

Value of $10,000 invested 5 years ago: $ 18,347

Fiscal Year Ending Dec. 31

	1998	1997	1996	1995	1994	1993
Revenues (Million $)						
1Q	218.5	153.9	130.2	110.8	109.6	100.3
2Q	218.0	153.0	135.0	113.9	110.1	108.9
3Q	—	166.7	140.0	118.7	110.0	103.5
4Q	—	180.4	140.3	118.8	109.8	109.5
Yr.	—	654.0	545.5	462.2	439.5	429.0
Earnings Per Share ($)						
1Q	**1.01**	1.04	0.91	0.79	0.78	0.70
2Q	**1.17**	1.02	0.92	0.80	0.77	0.75
3Q	—	1.08	0.96	0.82	0.77	0.70
4Q	—	1.08	0.94	0.81	0.77	0.74
Yr.	—	4.22	3.71	3.21	3.09	2.90

Next earnings report expected: NA

Dividend Data (Dividends have been paid since 1987.)

Amount ($)	Date Decl.	Ex-Div. Date	Stock of Record	Payment Date
0.390	Sep. 18	Sep. 25	Sep. 29	Oct. 15 '97
0.195	Dec. 11	Dec. 24	Dec. 29	Jan. 15 '98
0.195	Mar. 19	Mar. 26	Mar. 30	Apr. 15 '98
0.195	Jun. 15	Jun. 24	Jun. 26	Jul. 15 '98

A Division of The **McGraw-Hill** Companies

STANDARD
&POOR'S
STOCK REPORTS

MBIA Inc.

1391M
12-SEP-98

Business Summary - 13-AUG-98

MBIA, a dominant force in the municipal bond insurance market (based on its 36% share of the new issue market during the fist six months of 1998), is leveraging that strength and expanding into the structured finance market and into select international markets. MBIA Inc. is the successor to the Municipal Bond Insurance Association, a voluntary association formed in 1974 by five multi-line insurance companies to insure municipal bonds. The association was reorganized in 1986 with four of the original five members participating. MBI's principal business in insuring municipal bonds unconditionally and irrevocably guarantees the payment of principal and interest when due on insured municipal bonds. Composition of the insured portfolio by bond type (net insurance in force):

	1997	1996
General obligation bonds	25%	27%
Utility bonds	16%	17%
Health care bonds	13%	13%
Special revenue bonds	7%	7%
Transportation bonds	8%	7%
Other Municipal	14%	14%
Structured (asset/mortgage backed)	12%	9%
International & Other	5%	6%

As of December 31, 1997, net insurance in force equaled $483 billion (up from $411 billion at year-end 1996), of which 14% had been issued by California, 8% by New York, 7% by Florida, 5% by Pennsylvania, 5% by Texas, and 5% by New Jersey.

MBI offers insurance for new issues of municipal bonds and also for bonds traded in the secondary market, including bonds held in unit investment trusts and mutual funds. The economic value of municipal bond insurance to the governmental unit or agency offering the bonds is the saving in interest costs resulting from the difference in the yield between an insured bond and the same bond on an uninsured basis. Also, MBI's guarantee increases market acceptance for complex financings and for municipal bonds of issuers that are not well known. In addition, MBI insures asset-backed securities, as well as other non-muni obligations.

Recently, MBI expanded into the structured finance (or asset-backed) market and the international financial guarantee market. During 1997, MBI insured $28.8 billion (par value) in structured finance securities, up 42% from $20.4 billion (par value) in structured finance receivables insured during 1996. In 1995, MBI and rival municipal bond insurer AMBAC Indemnity Corp. formed a joint venture to market financial guaranty insurance in Europe. MBIA/AMBAC International jointly engage in marketing, but underwrite insurance separately.

Per Share Data ($)

(Year Ended Dec. 31)	1997	1996	1995	1994	1993	1992	1991	1990	1989	1988
Tangible Bk. Val.	32.72	27.41	25.32	19.14	17.70	15.04	12.13	10.46	8.63	8.45
Oper. Earnings	4.06	3.61	3.13	3.02	2.83	2.23	NA	NA	NA	NA
Earnings	4.22	3.71	3.21	3.09	2.90	2.31	1.87	1.67	1.37	1.23
Dividends	0.77	0.72	0.66	0.57	0.47	0.38	0.31	0.24	0.15	0.10
Payout Ratio	18%	20%	20%	18%	16%	16%	17%	14%	11%	8%
Prices - High	67⅜	52⅜	38¾	32⅝	40⅝	33¼	24¾	22¾	16⅜	10¼
- Low	45½	35	27¾	23⅝	27⅝	21⅝	11⅜	9¾	10	6½
P/E Ratio - High	16	14	12	11	14	14	13	14	12	8
- Low	11	9	9	8	10	9	6	6	7	5

Income Statement Analysis (Million $)

	1997	1996	1995	1994	1993	1992	1991	1990	1989	1988
Premium Inc.	297	252	215	218	231	163	132	107	91.0	82.0
Net Invest. Inc.	281	248	220	194	179	150	130	115	80.0	68.0
Oth. Revs.	75.1	46.0	27.0	27.4	18.8	14.5	5.1	1.8	0.7	1.1
Total Revs.	654	546	462	440	429	328	269	224	172	151
Pretax Inc.	480	408	345	329	324	244	190	165	135	118
Net Oper. Inc.	364	313	265	254	240	NA	NA	NA	NA	NA
Net Inc.	374	322	271	260	246	189	145	127	102	92.0

Balance Sheet & Other Fin. Data (Million $)

	1997	1996	1995	1994	1993	1992	1991	1990	1989	1988
Cash & Equiv.	23.2	112	110	76.4	57.3	58.8	42.1	38.5	32.1	25.0
Premiums Due	NA	1.0	6.1	0.9	31.9	2.1	2.4	0.1	3.7	4.7
Invest. Assets: Bonds	4,867	4,150	3,653	3,052	2,797	2,346	1,842	1,634	1,418	1,039
Invest. Assets: Stocks	Nil	Nil	Nil	Nil	Nil	Nil	Nil	Nil	Nil	Nil
Invest. Assets: Loans	Nil	205	212	139	105	60.8	26.0	21.8	22.9	Nil
Invest. Assets: Total	8,470	7,648	6,607	4,867	3,544	2,527	1,961	1,724	1,501	1,104
Deferred Policy Costs	154	148	140	133	120	110	97.0	89.0	77.0	64.0
Total Assets	9,811	8,562	7,267	5,456	4,106	2,885	2,278	2,024	1,786	1,283
Debt	474	374	374	299	299	299	199	200	195	Nil
Common Eqty.	3,048	2,480	2,234	1,705	1,596	1,382	1,063	932	777	705
Prop. & Cas. Loss Ratio	6.3	6.1	4.9	3.7	3.4	3.4	13.0	4.7	Nil	Nil
Prop. & Cas. Expense Ratio	26.2	28.3	29.3	28.8	27.4	33.2	32.9	33.7	40.0	39.6
Prop. & Cas. Combined Ratio	32.5	34.4	34.2	32.5	30.8	36.6	45.9	38.4	40.0	39.6
% Return On Revs.	57.2	59.1	58.7	59.2	57.4	57.5	53.8	56.6	59.6	61.1
% Ret. on Equity	13.5	13.7	13.8	15.8	17.4	15.4	14.5	14.8	13.8	13.9

Data as orig. reptd.; bef. results of disc. opers. and/or spec. items. Per share data adj. for stk. divs. as of ex-div. date. Bold denotes diluted EPS (FASB 128). E-Estimated. NA-Not Available. NM-Not Meaningful. NR-Not Ranked.

Office—113 King St., Armonk, NY 10504. **Tel**—(914) 273-4545. **Chrmn & CEO**—D. H. Elliott. **Vice Chrmn**—R. L. Weill. **SVP, CFO & Treas**—J. S. Tehrani. **VP & Investor Contact**—Judith Radasch (914-765-3014). **Secy**—L. G. Lenzi. **Dirs**—J. W. Brown Jr., D. C. Clapp, D. H. Elliott, C. L. Gaudiani, W. H. Gray III, F. S. Johnson, D. P. Kearney, J. A. Lebenthal, P-H. Richard, J. A. Rolls, R. L. Weill. **Transfer Agent & Registrar**—ChaseMellon Shareholder Services, Ridgefield Park, NJ. **Incorporated**—in Connecticut in 1986. **Empl**— 308. **S&P Analyst:** Catherine A. Seifert

STANDARD &POOR'S
STOCK REPORTS

MBNA Corp.

1391Y

NYSE Symbol **KRB**

In S&P 500

12-SEP-98

Industry:
Consumer Finance

Summary: The nation's second largest lender through bank credit cards and leading issuer of affinity cards, MBNA also provides retail deposit and financial transaction processing services.

S&P Opinion: Buy (★★★★)	Recent Price • 25½	Yield • 1.4%
	52 Wk Range • 38¾-23⅜	12-Mo. P/E • 20.1

Quantitative Evaluations

Outlook
(1 Lowest—5 Highest)
• 3

Fair Value
• 30½

Risk
• Average

Earn./Div. Rank
• A-

Technical Eval.
• Bullish since 2/95

Rel. Strength Rank
(1 Lowest—99 Highest)
• 40

Insider Activity
• Neutral

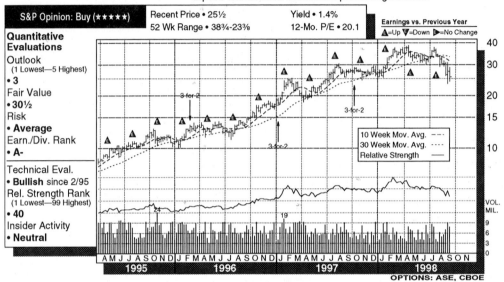

Earnings vs. Previous Year
▲=Up ▼=Down ►=No Change

10 Week Mov. Avg. - - -
30 Week Mov. Avg. ·····
Relative Strength ——

VOL.
MIL.

OPTIONS: ASE, CBOE

Overview - 06-AUG-98

A favorable industry environment, which has allowed a rapid buildup in card holder accounts, and modestly improved overall consumer credit quality should translate into solid earnings gains in 1998. MBNA's unique marketing strategy includes the targeting of individual membership organizations and developing co-branding relationships with commercial firms. Cardholders are thus encouraged to use the company's credit card over competing cards by showing support for endorsing firms or to receive various economic incentives for using the card. Aided by these factors, managed loans should increase better than 20% in 1998. Net credit losses have been slightly higher so far in 1998 as compared to last year, but have stabilized on a sequential basis and remain below peer levels, mostly a reflection of the company's ability to attract and retain high credit-scoring customers. MBNA's superior growth prospects and ability to increase market share and control credit costs should allow it to generate further strong EPS growth.

Valuation - 06-AUG-98

The shares, with a 21% rise in the first half of 1998, outperformed the S&P 500 during the period. Fundamentally, the shares remain an excellent value, based on the company's projected growth rate and earnings consistency. Delinquency levels in recent periods have increased on rapid account growth, but remain well below those of other credit card companies, reflecting the superior credit quality of MBNA's loan portfolio. Earnings should continue to be driven by a combination of exceptional credit card receivables growth, aided by successful marketing strategies and expanding market share, good control of credit costs, and greater operating efficiency. With earnings gains in excess of 20% expected in both 1998 and 1999, we continue to recommend the shares for superior capital appreciation.

Key Stock Statistics

S&P EPS Est. 1998	1.40	Tang. Bk. Value/Share	3.20
P/E on S&P Est. 1998	18.3	Beta	2.07
S&P EPS Est. 1999	1.75	Shareholders	2,400
Dividend Rate/Share	0.36	Market cap. (B)	$ 12.8
Shs. outstg. (M)	501.2	Inst. holdings	60%
Avg. daily vol. (M)	1.543		

Value of $10,000 invested 5 years ago: $ 58,722

Fiscal Year Ending Dec. 31

	1998	1997	1996	1995	1994	1993
Revenues (Million $)						
1Q	1,165	1,048	719.9	536.4	389.7	307.4
2Q	1,224	1,130	765.8	622.2	423.8	340.4
3Q	—	1,129	824.2	689.6	492.8	359.3
4Q	—	1,217	969.3	718.2	547.5	385.7
Yr.	—	4,524	3,279	2,565	1,853	1,393
Earnings Per Share ($)						
1Q	**0.28**	**0.22**	0.17	0.14	0.10	0.08
2Q	**0.32**	**0.25**	0.20	0.15	0.12	0.09
3Q	**E0.37**	**0.32**	0.24	0.19	0.15	0.11
4Q	**E0.42**	**0.35**	0.27	0.21	0.16	0.12
Yr.	**E1.40**	**1.15**	0.89	0.68	0.52	0.41

Next earnings report expected: NA

Dividend Data (Dividends have been paid since 1991.)

Amount ($)	Date Decl.	Ex-Div. Date	Stock of Record	Payment Date
0.090	Jan. 13	Mar. 12	Mar. 16	Apr. 01 '98
0.090	Apr. 14	Jun. 12	Jun. 16	Jul. 01 '98
0.090	Jul. 14	Sep. 04	Sep. 09	Oct. 01 '98
3-for-2	Jul. 14	Oct. 02	Sep. 15	Oct. 01 '98

Business Summary - 06-AUG-98

MBNA Corp. is one of the world's largest lenders through bank credit cards, and is the leading issuer of affinity credit cards, marketed primarily through endorsements of membership associations and financial institutions. Credit cards issued to affinity group members often carry custom graphics and the name and logo of the endorsing group. With a motto of "Getting the right customers and keeping them," the company has rapidly grown both the number of card accounts and receivable balances in recent years.

MBNA offers two general types of credit cards -- premium (gold) and standard -- issued under either the MasterCard or Visa name. The company markets standard and premium cards to new customers and premium cards to qualifying standard card customers. The premium card is marketed to members of endorsing organizations, customers of endorsing financial institutions and to MBNA's qualifying standard card customers. Premium card usage and average account balances are usually higher than those of standard card customers. In addition to affinity group cards, MBNA also offers co-branded cards through relationships with commercial firms, including professional sports teams.

The company also offers unsecured lines of credit and secured loans to individuals, including home equity loans and airplane loans, through its MBNA Consumer Services subsidiary, which is licensed in 42 states and the District of Columbia.

In addition, MBNA accepts deposits, primarily money market deposits and certificates of deposit, and offers credit insurance to its credit card customers. It is also licensed to provide property and casualty and life and health insurance products in about 40 states.

Loan receivables at the end of 1997 were $8.3 billion, compared to $7.7 billion a year earlier. At 1997 year end, the reserve for loan losses, which is set aside for possible loan defaults, was $162.5 million (1.46% of loan receivables), versus $118.4 million (1.17%) a year earlier. The provision for loan losses, which is added to the reserve, amounted to $260.0 million in 1997, versus $178.2 million in 1996. Net credit losses, or the amount of loans actually written off as uncollectible, were $223.8 million in 1997 (2.14% of average loans), up from $172.7 million (1.98%) in 1996.

At December 31, 1997, total managed loans, which include securitized loans and loans held for securitization, amounted to $49.4 billion, a 28% increase from year-end 1996. Delinquency on total managed loans was 4.59% in 1997 (4.28% in 1996).

Per Share Data ($)

(Year Ended Dec. 31)	1997	1996	1995	1994	1993	1992	1991	1990	1989	1988
Tangible Bk. Val.	3.20	2.97	2.42	1.73	1.42	1.21	1.10	NA	NA	NA
Earnings	1.15	0.89	0.68	0.52	0.41	0.34	0.30	0.26	0.21	0.18
Dividends	0.32	0.29	0.25	0.21	0.19	0.17	0.16	NA	NA	NA
Payout Ratio	28%	32%	36%	41%	46%	51%	53%	NA	NA	NA
Prices - High	30⅝	19½	12⅞	8⅛	7½	5	4	NA	NA	NA
- Low	17⅞	10⅛	6⅝	5¾	4¼	3½	2¼	NA	NA	NA
P/E Ratio - High	27	22	19	15	18	14	14	NA	NA	NA
- Low	16	11	10	11	10	10	8	NA	NA	NA

Income Statement Analysis (Million $)

	1997	1996	1995	1994	1993	1992	1991	1990	1989	1988
Net Int. Inc.	692	640	544	532	474	358	240	164	117	150
Tax Equiv. Adj.	1.9	1.8	1.8	1.6	1.6	1.5	1.3	Nil	Nil	Nil
Non Int. Inc.	2,813	1,896	1,425	1,014	740	577	540	452	344	255
Loan Loss Prov.	260	178	138	108	99	97.5	86.7	58.0	43.3	63.3
Exp./Op. Revs.	63%	62%	63%	64%	64%	60%	59%	58%	56%	50%
Pretax Inc.	1,022	731	585	441	190	272	235	204	159	137
Eff. Tax Rate	39%	35%	40%	40%	NM	37%	36%	37%	34%	34%
Net Inc.	623	474	353	267	208	173	149	129	104	90.0
% Net Int. Marg.	4.86	5.52	5.74	7.61	8.76	7.20	5.20	5.90	5.40	6.50

Balance Sheet & Other Fin. Data (Million $)

	1997	1996	1995	1994	1993	1992	1991	1990	1989	1988
Earning Assets:										
Money Mkt	NA	877	574	268	31.0	81.0	475	439	50.0	NA
Inv. Securities	2,509	2,318	2,096	2,002	1,409	1,265	1,293	102	102	NA
Com'l Loans	Nil	Nil	Nil	Nil	Nil	Nil	Nil	Nil	Nil	Nil
Other Loans	11,162	10,129	8,135	5,707	3,726	3,979	3,486	3,240	2,261	1,907
Total Assets	21,306	17,035	13,229	9,672	7,320	6,455	6,009	4,580	2,859	2,276
Demand Deposits	312	234	170	101	71.0	70.0	65.0	87.0	126	NA
Time Deposits	9,123	9,918	8,439	6,531	5,171	4,498	5,029	4,115	1,617	NA
LT Debt	5,479	3,950	2,658	1,564	780	471	Nil	0.6	27.4	48.8
Common Eqty.	1,970	1,704	1,265	920	769	661	592	219	262	209
% Ret. on Assets	3.2	3.1	3.1	3.2	3.1	3.0	2.8	3.9	4.1	3.5
% Ret. on Equity	33.0	32.0	35.5	32.7	30.0	28.6	37.0	49.0	37.2	38.3
% Loan Loss Resv.	2.0	1.5	2.2	1.8	2.6	2.5	2.8	3.0	3.6	3.9
% Loans/Deposits	64.0	74.3	94.5	86.0	71.1	87.1	68.4	77.1	129.7	125.3
% Equity to Assets	9.6	9.8	9.6	9.7	10.5	10.4	7.6	7.9	11.1	9.3

Data as orig. reptd.; bef. results of disc. opers. and/or spec. items. Per share data adj. for stk. divs. as of ex-div. date. Bold denotes diluted EPS (FASB 128). E-Estimated. NA-Not Available. NM-Not Meaningful. NR-Not Ranked.

Office—1100 North King St., Wilmington, DE 19884. **Tel**—(800) 362-6255; (302) 453-9930. **Website**—http://www.mbnainternational.com **Chrmn & CEO**—A. Lerner. **Pres**—C. M. Cawley. **EVP-CFO & Treas**—M. S. Kaufman. **Investor Contact**—Brian D. Dalphon (302-432-1251). **Dirs**—J. H. Berick, C. M. Cawley, B. R. Civiletti, A. Lerner, R. D. Lerner, S. L. Markowitz, M. Rosenthal. **Transfer Agent & Registrar**—National City Bank, Cleveland. **Incorporated**—in Maryland in 1990. **Empl**— 20,000. **S&P Analyst:** Stephen R. Biggar

12-SEP-98

Industry:
Engineering & Con-
struction

Summary: McDermott is engaged in the power generation systems market. It also constructs marine production and transportation structures for the oil and natural gas industry.

S&P Opinion: Sell (★)		
Recent Price • 24	Yield • 0.8%	
52 Wk Range • 43⅞-19¼	12-Mo. P/E • 6.7	

Quantitative Evaluations

Outlook
(1 Lowest—5 Highest)
• 4-

Fair Value
• 27

Risk
• Average

Earn./Div. Rank
• B-

Technical Eval.
• **Bullish** since 8/98

Rel. Strength Rank
(1 Lowest—99 Highest)
• 56

Insider Activity
• **Favorable**

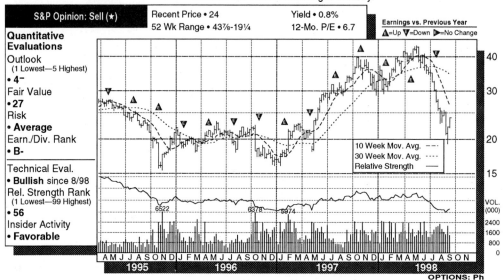

OPTIONS: Ph

Overview - 11-AUG-98

Earnings in the first quarter of FY 99 (Mar.) included $1.33 per share in non-recurring gains. Operating revenues rose and profitability was restored in FY 98 (Mar.), reflecting gains in the marine construction and power generation segments. Marine construction results benefited from stronger performance in North America and the Middle East. The power generation segment's improvement was due primarily to domestic operations. Results for FY 98 included net non-recurring gains of $1.94 per share from the sale of the company's investment in Sakhalin Energy Investment Co., Ltd. and other assets and the termination of a joint venture. Looking to FY 99, MDR will focus on continued cost cutting, increased research and development spending, and selective acquisitions. However, the economic crisis in Southeast Asia has resulted in the suspension of a power generation project in Indonesia, and another project in Pakistan appears in peril of being postponed. In addition, weak oil prices do not bode well for future bookings of marine construction projects.

Valuation - 11-AUG-98

The shares, which have been weak of late, have fallen 31% in 1998, as falling oil prices have raised the possibility of reduced oil industry spending for exploration and production, which could stall the company's turnaround. The shares are expected to be volatile in the near term, as near-term fundamentals are not promising. The company's marine construction backlog has declined, reflecting lower oil prices, and the power generation systems business is being affected by Asian economic weakness. Given the negative short term outlook for both oil prices and Asian economies, we have recently downgraded the shares to sell from hold, and believe that they will substantially underperform the broader market over the remainder of 1998.

Key Stock Statistics

S&P EPS Est. 1999	3.15	Tang. Bk. Value/Share	11.64
P/E on S&P Est. 1999	7.6	Beta	1.21
S&P EPS Est. 2000	2.00	Shareholders	6,700
Dividend Rate/Share	0.20	Market cap. (B)	$ 1.4
Shs. outstg. (M)	59.2	Inst. holdings	79%
Avg. daily vol. (M)	0.346		

Value of $10,000 invested 5 years ago: $ 12,580

Fiscal Year Ending Mar. 31

	1999	1998	1997	1996	1995	1994
Revenues (Million $)						
1Q	819.8	928.1	872.8	816.5	3,235	703.0
2Q	—	920.0	800.9	806.8	3,256	777.0
3Q	—	901.7	744.7	766.5	3,350	799.0
4Q	—	924.8	726.4	889.3	844.3	780.0
Yr.	—	3,675	3,151	3,279	3,044	3,059
Earnings Per Share ($)						
1Q	1.88	1.94	-0.26	0.12	0.02	0.48
2Q	—	0.64	-0.55	0.13	-0.10	0.52
3Q	—	0.82	0.39	0.08	0.51	0.25
4Q	—	0.25	-3.50	-0.11	-0.39	0.18
Yr.	E3.15	3.48	-3.92	0.23	0.05	1.57

Next earnings report expected: late October

Dividend Data (Dividends have been paid since 1955.)

Amount ($)	Date Decl.	Ex-Div. Date	Stock of Record	Payment Date
0.050	Nov. 21	Dec. 11	Dec. 15	Jan. 01 '98
0.050	Feb. 06	Mar. 12	Mar. 16	Apr. 01 '98
0.050	Jun. 05	Jun. 11	Jun. 15	Jul. 01 '98
0.050	Aug. 11	Sep. 11	Sep. 15	Oct. 01 '98

A Division of The **McGraw·Hill** Companies

STANDARD
&POOR'S
STOCK REPORTS

McDermott International, Inc.

1447

12-SEP-98

Business Summary - 11-AUG-98

Seeking to reverse a trend of weak earnings, McDermott International (MDR) will attempt to downsize its way to prosperity, with a strategy revolving around cost cutting and the disposal of non-core assets. The company is active in two business segments -- power generation systems and equipment and marine construction services.

Contributions to operating revenues by segment in recent fiscal years (Mar.) were:

	1998	1997
Marine construction	50%	44%
Power generation	31%	31%
Government operations	10%	12%
Other operations	9%	13%

The power generation segment, consisting primarily of the Babcock & Wilcox subsidiary, supplies fossil fuel and nuclear steam generating equipment to electric power generators and nuclear reactor components to the U.S. Navy. Marine construction services, conducted through MDR's majority-owned J. Ray McDermott subsidiary, include the design, engineering, fabrication and installation of offshore drilling and production platforms, marine pipelines and other facilities for the oil and gas

industries. The company believes that the recent trend toward offshore oil and gas production bodes well for this group's future performance.

In August 1996, MDR's chairman and CEO, Robert E. Howson, announced his retirement, apparently a casualty of the company's disappointing results during the preceding two fiscal years. In October 1996, MDR's directors recommended the implementation of several wide-ranging proposals designed to get the company back on its feet. These proposals included focusing on the core businesses of power generation, government operations and marine construction, with all other businesses to be viewed as potential divestitures. MDR also stressed the importance of lowering costs at the operating and corporate headquarters levels. Finally, the quarterly dividend was slashed 80%, to $0.05 per share, from $0.25, in January 1997.

In May 1997, the company reported a net loss of $198 million for the fourth quarter of FY 97, resulting from asset writedowns, executive severance, restructurings and various other items. For FY 97, the net loss came to about $210 million. However, MDR reported net income of $207.4 million for FY 98, including $120 million in gains from non-recurring items, including asset sales and a gain and distribution from the termination of a J. Ray McDermott joint venture.

Per Share Data ($)

(Year Ended Mar. 31)	1998	1997	1996	1995	1994	1993	1992	1991	1990	1989
Tangible Bk. Val.	7.24	NM	1.48	3.24	4.49	6.07	11.00	9.50	11.72	11.51
Cash Flow	5.48	-1.15	2.80	2.20	3.43	3.63	4.48	0.39	0.33	-0.11
Earnings	3.48	-3.92	0.23	0.05	1.57	1.29	1.75	-1.97	-2.68	-3.09
Dividends	0.20	0.60	1.00	1.00	1.00	1.00	1.00	1.00	1.00	1.40
Payout Ratio	6%	NM	NM	NM	64%	78%	57%	NM	NM	NM
Cal. Yrs.	1997	1996	1995	1994	1993	1992	1991	1990	1989	1988
Prices - High	40⅛	23¼	29⅛	27½	32⅞	26	28½	34½	26¼	21½
- Low	16	16	15⅜	19⅜	22¼	16	15¼	21⅝	14⅝	13¾
P/E Ratio - High	12	NM	NM	NM	21	20	16	NM	NM	NM
- Low	5	NM	NM	NM	14	12	9	NM	NM	NM

Income Statement Analysis (Million $)

	1998	1997	1996	1995	1994	1993	1992	1991	1990	1989
Revs.	3,675	3,151	3,279	3,044	3,060	3,173	3,524	3,136	2,645	2,423
Oper. Inc.	333	9.0	166	122	139	193	240	92.0	24.0	67.0
Depr.	142	152	140	116	99	122	126	103	113	111
Int. Exp.	81.5	95.9	86.0	60.0	64.0	92.0	105	119	139	130
Pretax Inc.	340	-219	22.0	3.0	130	126	143	-70.0	-107	-106
Eff. Tax Rate	22%	NM	4.70%	NM	19%	32%	30%	NM	NM	NM
Net Inc.	216	-205	21.0	11.0	90.0	67.0	81.0	-86.0	-100	-114

Balance Sheet & Other Fin. Data (Million $)

	1998	1997	1996	1995	1994	1993	1992	1991	1990	1989
Cash	278	334	241	219	135	319	72.0	204	135	104
Curr. Assets	1,597	1,834	1,725	1,451	1,036	1,356	1,175	1,217	1,180	1,088
Total Assets	4,501	4,599	4,387	4,752	3,209	3,093	3,126	3,314	3,336	3,294
Curr. Liab.	1,461	1,609	1,393	1,491	1,038	1,240	1,136	1,503	1,193	1,225
LT Debt	598	667	576	579	667	583	765	640	873	933
Common Eqty.	677	434	541	567	539	460	704	567	643	597
Total Cap.	1,623	1,436	1,603	1,642	1,422	1,272	1,796	1,574	1,891	1,890
Cap. Exp.	45.1	91.3	86.0	98.0	76.3	82.0	76.0	139	127	75.0
Cash Flow	350	-62.7	152	118	183	189	206	17.0	12.0	-4.0
Curr. Ratio	1.1	1.1	1.2	1.0	1.0	1.1	1.0	0.8	1.0	0.9
% LT Debt of Cap.	36.9	46.5	36.0	35.3	46.9	45.8	42.6	40.6	46.2	49.3
% Net Inc.of Revs.	5.9	NM	0.6	0.4	2.9	2.1	2.3	NM	NM	NM
% Ret. on Assets	4.7	NM	0.5	0.3	2.9	2.1	2.3	NM	NM	NM
% Ret. on Equity	37.3	NM	2.2	0.5	16.8	11.4	11.8	NM	NM	NM

Data as orig. reptd.; bef. results of disc. opers. and/or spec. items. Per share data adj. for stk. divs. as of ex-div. date. Bold denotes diluted EPS (FASB 128). E-Estimated. NA-Not Available. NM-Not Meaningful. NR-Not Ranked.

Office—1450 Poydras St., New Orleans, LA 70112-6050. **Tel**—(504) 587-5400. **Website**—http://www.mcdermott.com **Chrmn & CEO**—R. E. Tetrault. **SVP & CFO**—D. R. Gaubert. **SVP & Secy**—L. R. Purtel. **Investor Contact**—Don Washington (504-587-4080). **Dirs**—T. H. Black, P. J. Burguieres, R. E. Howson, J. W. Johnstone Jr., W. McCollam Jr., R. E. Tetrault, J. N. Turner, R. E. Woolbert. **Transfer Agent & Registrar**—First Chicago Trust Co. of New York, NYC. **Incorporated**—in Panama in 1959. **Empl**— 24,600. **S&P Analyst**: Norman Rosenberg

12-SEP-98

Industry:
Restaurants

Summary: MCD is the largest fast-food restaurant company in the U.S. and the world. Some 49% of its over 23,000 restaurants are outside the U.S.

S&P Opinion: Hold (★★★)	Recent Price • 59⅛	Yield • 0.6%
	52 Wk Range • 74⅞-42⅛	12-Mo. P/E • 26.7

Quantitative Evaluations

Outlook
(1 Lowest—5 Highest)
• **2**

Fair Value
• **56¾**

Risk
• **Low**

Earn./Div. Rank
• **A+**

Technical Eval.
• **Bullish** since 2/98

Rel. Strength Rank
(1 Lowest—99 Highest)
• **69**

Insider Activity
• **Neutral**

Earnings vs. Previous Year
▲=Up ▼=Down ▶=No Change

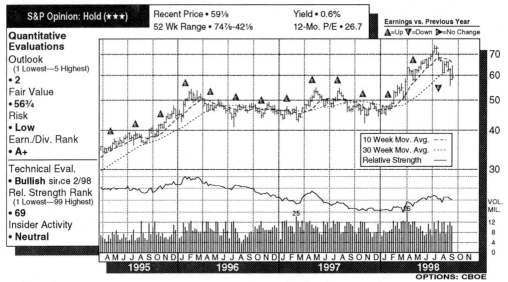

10 Week Mov. Avg. - - -
30 Week Mov. Avg. - - - -
Relative Strength ——

OPTIONS: CBOE

Overview - 27-JUL-98

In 1998 and beyond, we expect further double-digit earnings growth from the international operations of this well managed company, excluding currency fluctuations. In foreign markets, additional benefits from economies of scale are likely as MCD's presence continues to grow. Earnings from outside the U.S. have recently accounted for about 60% of operating profit. In the U.S., however, the company has faced stiff competition in a highly saturated market. As a result, the company has reexamined its domestic operations, changed management, and is focusing on increasing productivity and lowering the overall cost structure. MCD is overhauling its food preparation procedures to provide fresher, hotter food and to lower its labor costs. As a result, MCD took a $350 million pretax charge ($0.33 a share) in the second quarter of 1998. We expect at least a moderate profit increase in domestic operating earnings in 1998. Long term, we see MCD facing the challenge of an aging U.S. population increasingly shifting to casual dining restaurants that offer more amenities and a fuller menu.

Valuation - 27-JUL-98

Investors have reacted positively to MCD's announcement of strategic initiatives to improve restaurant operations and to reduce expenses. In addition, domestic operating income rose a strong 15% in the second quarter boosted by healthy sales gains. MCD cautioned that the strong level of domestic sales is not expected to continue in the second half of 1998. We expect earnings overall to grow in the 10% to 12% range in 1998 and beyond, which is already reflected in the share price. We also anticipate that the continuation of a large share repurchase program will lend support to the stock. We view the shares as an attractive holding, offering both growth and defensive characteristics.

Key Stock Statistics

S&P EPS Est. 1998	2.50	Tang. Bk. Value/Share	13.28
P/E on S&P Est. 1998	23.7	Beta	0.99
S&P EPS Est. 1999	2.80	Shareholders	925,000
Dividend Rate/Share	0.36	Market cap. (B)	$ 40.5
Shs. outstg. (M)	684.6	Inst. holdings	61%
Avg. daily vol. (M)	2.180		

Value of $10,000 invested 5 years ago: $ 25,240

Fiscal Year Ending Dec. 31

	1998	1997	1996	1995	1994	1993
Revenues (Million $)						
1Q	2,805	2,618	2,426	2,161	1,796	1,654
2Q	3,181	2,833	2,665	2,468	2,029	1,878
3Q	—	3,006	2,774	2,580	2,225	1,944
4Q	—	2,953	2,822	2,586	2,270	1,932
Yr.	—	11,409	10,688	9,795	8,321	7,408
Earnings Per Share ($)						
1Q	0.52	0.46	0.42	0.39	0.33	0.28
2Q	0.50	0.61	0.59	0.52	0.44	0.39
3Q	E0.69	0.63	0.62	0.56	0.48	0.42
4Q	E0.64	0.58	0.58	0.51	0.43	0.36
Yr.	E2.50	2.29	2.16	1.97	1.68	1.45

Next earnings report expected: mid October

Dividend Data (Dividends have been paid since 1976.)

Amount ($)	Date Decl.	Ex-Div. Date	Stock of Record	Payment Date
0.083	Oct. 29	Nov. 26	Dec. 01	Dec. 12 '97
0.083	Jan. 20	Feb. 25	Feb. 27	Mar. 13 '98
0.090	May. 21	May. 28	Jun. 01	Jun. 12 '98
0.090	Jul. 08	Aug. 27	Aug. 31	Sep. 11 '98

A Division of The McGraw-Hill Companies

Business Summary - 27-JUL-98

One of the most widely known brand names in the world, McDonald's boasts thirty-five million customers every day. The company operates and licenses more than 23,000 restaurants in over 100 countries. At December 31, 1997, there were 12,480 restaurants in the U.S. and 10,752 elsewhere.

Contributions by geographic area in 1997: U.S. (51% of revenues); Europe (23%); Asia/Pacific (17%); Latin America (4%); and other (5%). International business contributed 51% of operating income in 1997.

Restaurants offer a substantially uniform menu, including hamburgers, french fries, chicken, fish, specialty sandwiches, beverages and desserts. Most units also serve breakfast.

The company's long-term strategy is to identify and to evaluate profitable growth opportunities. The company believes that its greatest expansion opportunities are outside the U.S. While in the U.S. there are 22,000 people per McDonald's, in the rest of the world there is only one McDonald's for every 605,000 people. At the end of 1997, 85% of systemwide restaurants were in the following 11 markets - Australia, Brazil, Canada, England, France, Germany, Hong Kong, Japan, the Netherlands, Taiwan and the U.S. Some 64% of restaurant additions in 1997 were in these markets and a similar percent is expected in 1998. New and emerging markets, such as Central Europe, the Philippines, China and Africa/ Middle East, should represent a growing percentage of restaurants. Rapid expansion is expected to continue in Latin America.

The company owns or leases a substantial amount of the real estate used by franchisees in their operations. Fees from franchisees to McDonald's typically include rents and service fees, often totaling at least 11.5% of sales.

Average annual sales at U.S. restaurants in operation at least 13 months declined slightly to $1,425,000 in 1997. Average sales are affected by comparable sales, the size of new restaurants and the expansion rate. New restaurants have historically taken about four years to reach long-term volume. Average annual sales at international restaurants in operation at least 13 months fell $327,000 to $1,830,000. Nearly half of this was due to foreign currency translation, and 30% to more satellite restaurants, which typically have lower sales volumes than traditional restaurants. Average sales have also trended lower with more units opened in lower-density areas.

U.S. company unit margins were flat with 1996 at 16.5% of sales. Margins in the international division declined in 1997, to 19.1% of sales, from 19.8% in 1996. Increased food and paper costs as well as occupancy and other operating costs as a percentage of sales outweighed a decrease in payroll costs.

Per Share Data ($)

(Year Ended Dec. 31)	1997	1996	1995	1994	1993	1992	1991	1990	1989	1988
Tangible Bk. Val.	11.71	10.97	9.97	8.60	7.32	6.63	6.22	5.29	4.17	4.13
Cash Flow	3.42	3.28	3.04	2.57	2.15	1.98	1.81	1.72	1.50	1.30
Earnings	2.29	2.21	1.97	1.68	1.46	1.30	1.18	1.10	0.97	0.86
Dividends	0.32	0.29	0.26	0.23	0.21	0.20	0.18	0.17	0.15	0.14
Payout Ratio	14%	13%	13%	14%	15%	15%	15%	15%	15%	16%
Prices - High	54⅞	54¼	48	31½	29⅝	25¼	20	19¼	17½	12¾
- Low	42⅛	41	28⅝	25½	22¾	19⅛	13⅛	12½	11½	10¼
P/E Ratio - High	24	25	24	19	20	19	17	18	18	15
- Low	18	19	15	15	16	15	11	11	12	12

Income Statement Analysis (Million $)

	1997	1996	1995	1994	1993	1992	1991	1990	1989	1988
Revs.	11,409	10,687	9,795	8,321	7,408	7,133	6,695	6,640	6,065	5,521
Oper. Inc.	3,488	3,331	3,204	2,801	2,415	2,290	2,022	1,944	1,772	1,573
Depr.	794	743	709	629	493	493	457	444	390	335
Int. Exp.	363	365	363	326	336	393	418	417	332	267
Pretax Inc.	2,408	2,251	2,169	1,887	1,676	1,448	1,299	1,246	1,157	1,046
Eff. Tax Rate	32%	30%	34%	35%	35%	34%	34%	36%	37%	38%
Net Inc.	1,643	1,573	1,427	1,224	1,083	959	860	802	727	646

Balance Sheet & Other Fin. Data (Million $)

	1997	1996	1995	1994	1993	1992	1991	1990	1989	1988
Cash	341	330	335	180	186	437	220	143	137	184
Curr. Assets	1,142	1,103	956	741	663	865	646	549	495	516
Total Assets	18,242	17,386	15,415	13,592	12,035	11,681	11,349	10,668	9,175	8,159
Curr. Liab.	2,985	2,135	1,795	2,451	1,102	1,545	1,288	1,199	1,017	1,004
LT Debt	4,834	4,803	4,258	2,935	3,489	3,176	4,267	4,429	3,901	3,111
Common Eqty.	8,851	8,360	7,503	6,446	6,350	5,984	4,537	3,984	3,349	3,413
Total Cap.	15,178	15,251	12,784	10,930	10,744	9,911	9,837	9,306	8,064	7,067
Cap. Exp.	2,111	2,375	2,064	1,539	1,354	1,171	1,129	1,613	1,556	1,489
Cash Flow	2,412	2,288	2,136	1,806	1,528	1,437	1,297	1,232	1,113	981
Curr. Ratio	0.4	0.5	0.5	0.3	0.6	0.6	0.5	0.5	0.5	0.5
% LT Debt of Cap.	31.8	31.5	33.3	26.9	32.5	32.0	43.4	47.6	48.4	44.0
% Net Inc.of Revs.	14.4	14.8	14.6	14.7	14.6	13.4	12.8	12.1	12.0	11.7
% Ret. on Assets	9.2	9.6	9.9	9.6	9.3	8.3	7.8	8.1	8.5	8.6
% Ret. on Equity	18.8	19.5	20.5	19.3	17.0	17.4	19.7	21.6	21.8	20.5

Data as orig. reptd.; bef. results of disc. opers. and/or spec. items. Per share data adj. for stk. divs. as of ex-div. date. Bold denotes diluted EPS (FASB 128). E-Estimated. NA-Not Available. NM-Not Meaningful. NR-Not Ranked.

Office—McDonald's Plaza, Oak Brook, IL 60521. **Tel**—(630) 623-3000. **Chrmn & CEO**—M. R. Quinlan. **SVP & Treas**—C. D. Pearl. **Investor Contact (Broker Inquiries)**—Barbara Ven Horst (630-623-5137). **Investor Contact (Shareholder Services)**—Lynn Irwin Camp (630-623-8432). **Dirs**—H. Adams, Jr., R. M. Beavers Jr., J. R. Cantalupo, G. C. Gray, J. M. Greenberg, E. Hernandez, Jr., D. R. Keough, D. G. Lubin, A. J. McKenna, M. R. Quinlan, E. H. Rensi, T. Savage, P. D. Schrage, B. F. Smith, R. W. Stone, R. N. Thurston, F. L. Turner, B. B. Vedder Jr. **Transfer Agent & Registrar**—First Chicago Trust Co., Jersey City, NJ. **Incorporated**—in Delaware in 1965. **Empl**—212,000. **S&P Analyst:** Karen J. Sack, CFA

STANDARD &POOR'S
STOCK REPORTS

McGraw-Hill Companies
1452

NYSE Symbol **MHP**

In S&P 500

12-SEP-98

Industry: Publishing

Summary: The McGraw-Hill Companies is a leading information services organization serving worldwide markets in education, business, industry, the professions and government.

S&P Opinion: No Opinion	Recent Price • 75	Yield • 2.1%
	52 Wk Range • 87-63⅛	12-Mo. P/E • 24.3

Quantitative Evaluations

Outlook
(1 Lowest—5 Highest)
• **2**

Fair Value
• **75%**

Risk
• **Low**

Earn./Div. Rank
• **NR**

Technical Eval.
• **Bullish** since 8/98

Rel. Strength Rank
(1 Lowest—99 Highest)
• **74**

Insider Activity
• **Neutral**

Earnings vs. Previous Year
▲=Up ▼=Down ▶=No Change

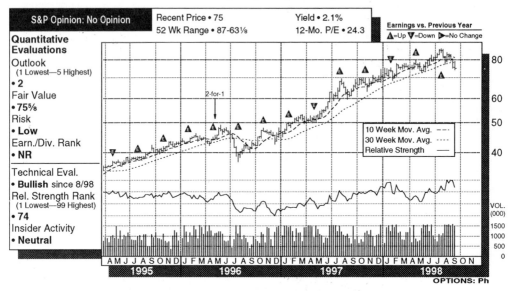

10 Week Mov. Avg. ----
30 Week Mov. Avg. ·······
Relative Strength ——

2-for-1

VOL. (000)

OPTIONS: Ph

Overview - 08-SEP-98

MHP reported a 14% gain in second quarter net income on a 17.7% revenue rise. Higher revenues anticipated for 1998, on top of a 15% advance in 1997, will reflect growth across the board. Another good year for educational publishing is expected, on top of an exceptionally strong 1997. Demand for financial services remains healthy, with revenues benefiting substantially from global growth, continued expansion in non-traditional rating services and investment in new products and markets. Information and media services revenues will continue to be bolstered by healthy demand for advertising and higher advertising rates. Profitability will benefit from the revenue growth and ongoing efficiency measures, but the improvement will be limited by the cost of investments in new products and services. The outlook for 1999 and beyond is also favorable. Standard & Poor's is a division of MHP.

Valuation - 08-SEP-98

The consensus opinion among analysts who follow MHP calls for EPS of about $3.70 for 1999 and $3.31 in 1998, up 12% from the $2.91 (diluted) reported for 1997. At 24X the consensus EPS projection for 1998, the stock currently trades at a premium to its growth rate. MHP's "growth stock" valuation stems from a number of positive factors, including the perception that the company's strong franchises have significant underlying value. Costs of expanding in international markets, acquisitions and ongoing investments in new products and services have combined with cyclical and other factors to moderate MHP's earnings gains in recent years, but the long-term outlook for each of the company's major businesses is favorable. Consistent annual increases in the cash dividend, which has been raised in each year since 1974, also support the stock.

Key Stock Statistics

S&P EPS Est. 1999	NA	Tang. Bk. Value/Share	1.28
P/E on S&P Est. 1999	NA	Beta	0.89
Dividend Rate/Share	1.56	Shareholders	5,700
Shs. outstg. (M)	99.3	Market cap. (B)	$ 7.4
Avg. daily vol. (M)	0.423	Inst. holdings	68%

Value of $10,000 invested 5 years ago: $ 28,608

Fiscal Year Ending Dec. 31

	1998	1997	1996	1995	1994	1993
Revenues (Million $)						
1Q	703.4	652.9	583.9	568.5	559.8	466.9
2Q	881.1	836.6	710.9	712.8	648.3	490.9
3Q	—	1,144	949.0	904.4	855.5	555.0
4Q	—	900.8	830.9	749.6	697.3	682.6
Yr.	—	3,534	3,075	2,935	2,761	2,195
Earnings Per Share ($)						
1Q	0.20	0.15	0.16	0.14	0.15	0.15
2Q	0.78	0.65	0.57	0.53	0.48	0.44
3Q	—	1.44	1.15	1.06	0.91	-0.94
4Q	—	0.67	3.08	0.55	0.51	0.46
Yr.	—	2.91	4.96	2.28	2.05	0.12

Next earnings report expected: mid October

Dividend Data (Dividends have been paid since 1937.)

Amount ($)	Date Decl.	Ex-Div. Date	Stock of Record	Payment Date
0.390	Jan. 28	Feb. 23	Feb. 25	Mar. 11 '98
0.390	Apr. 29	May. 22	May. 27	Jun. 10 '98
.005 Spl.	Aug. 03	Aug. 12	Aug. 14	Aug. 27 '98
0.390	Jul. 29	Aug. 24	Aug. 26	Sep. 10 '98

A Division of The **McGraw-Hill** *Companies*

Business Summary - 08-SEP-98

The McGraw-Hill Companies, Inc. is a leading provider of information products and services to business, professional and educational markets worldwide. Through acquisitions, new product and service development and a strong commitment to customer service, many of its business units have grown to be leaders in their respective fields. The McGraw-Hill group of companies includes such well known brands as Business Week, Standard & Poor's, DRI, F.W. Dodge and Sweet's.

International operations, conducted in 32 countries, accounted for 15% of revenues and 15% of operating profits in 1997.

Educational and professional publishing (44% of revenues and 34% of profits in 1997) includes college publishing, medical, international and professional book operations. This segment also contains the McGraw-Hill School Division (elementary and secondary textbooks and materials), which is benefiting from a strong state textbook adoption cycle, a healthy upturn in school enrollments and a favorable funding environment in most school districts. In October 1996, MHP completed the exchange of its Shepard's/McGraw-Hill legal publishing unit for the Times Mirror Higher Education Group (TMHE). The fourth largest college publisher in the U.S., TMHE was comprised of five well-known business

units: Richard D. Irwin, Wm. C. Brown, Brown & Benchmark, Irwin Professional Publishing and Mosby College. The acquisition makes MHP the world's largest educational publisher and the leader in 12 higher education disciplines.

Information and media services (28% and 24%) include Business Week magazine, F.W. Dodge, Sweet's Group, Tower Group International, and a number of trade magazines, newsletters, directories, and video and online products serving the construction, computer and communications, aerospace and defense, energy, health care and process industries. Also part of this segment are four network-affiliated TV stations in Denver, Indianapolis, San Diego and Bakersfield.

Financial information and services (28% and 45%) comprises Standard & Poor's Financial Information Services, which includes such leading brands as Standard & Poor's Compustat, Standard & Poor's ComStock, Standard & Poor's J.J. Kenny Drake, Standard & Poor's Marketscope, Standard & Poor's Index Services, Standard & Poor's Platt's and DRI/McGraw-Hill. This segment also includes Standard & Poor's Ratings Services, the world's leading provider of credit analysis and information. In November 1997, MHP acquired all outstanding shares of Micropal, a leading provider of mutual fund data and information.

Per Share Data ($)

(Year Ended Dec. 31)	1997	1996	1995	1994	1993	1992	1991	1990	1989	1988
Tangible Bk. Val.	1.28	0.55	0.77	-0.60	-2.00	3.62	4.30	3.74	4.80	4.28
Cash Flow	5.86	7.34	3.35	3.08	0.96	2.33	2.25	2.45	1.11	2.60
Earnings	2.91	4.96	2.28	2.05	0.12	1.56	1.51	1.76	0.41	1.92
Dividends	1.44	1.32	1.20	1.16	1.14	1.12	1.10	1.08	1.02	0.92
Payout Ratio	49%	27%	53%	57%	NM	72%	73%	61%	251%	48%
Prices - High	75⅜	49¼	43⅞	38⅝	37⅝	33¼	32⅜	30⅝	43⅛	38
- Low	44⅞	37¼	31⅞	31¼	27⅝	26½	24⅞	20	26¾	23⅜
P/E Ratio - High	26	10	19	19	NM	21	21	17	NM	20
- Low	15	8	14	15	NM	17	16	11	NM	12

Income Statement Analysis (Million $)

Revs.	3,534	3,075	2,935	2,761	2,195	2,050	1,943	1,939	1,789	1,818
Oper. Inc.	779	662	509	477	376	358	342	392	342	341
Depr.	294	239	106	102	82.9	74.3	72.1	66.8	68.9	66.2
Int. Exp.	52.5	47.7	58.8	51.7	36.3	37.6	47.0	55.6	35.0	5.3
Pretax Inc.	471	815	386	345	66.0	267	258	303	87.0	380
Eff. Tax Rate	38%	39%	41%	41%	83%	43%	43%	43%	54%	51%
Net Inc.	291	496	227	203	11.0	153	148	172	40.0	186

Balance Sheet & Other Fin. Data (Million $)

Cash	4.8	3.4	10.3	8.0	48.0	13.0	17.0	21.0	35.0	24.0
Curr. Assets	1,464	1,350	1,240	1,124	1,132	911	942	961	840	884
Total Assets	3,724	3,724	3,104	3,009	3,084	2,508	2,525	2,534	2,208	1,758
Curr. Liab.	1,206	1,219	1,046	1,008	1,069	841	819	845	793	726
LT Debt	607	557	557	658	758	359	437	508	378	2.0
Common Eqty.	1,435	1,361	1,035	913	823	909	999	954	880	923
Total Cap.	2,153	2,068	1,733	1,700	1,700	1,377	1,619	1,579	1,298	992
Cap. Exp.	78.7	63.3	58.8	77.1	49.8	55.9	51.2	95.8	58.0	44.6
Cash Flow	584	734	334	305	94.0	227	220	239	109	252
Curr. Ratio	1.2	1.1	1.2	1.1	1.1	1.1	1.2	1.1	1.1	1.2
% LT Debt of Cap.	28.2	26.9	32.2	38.7	44.6	26.0	27.0	32.1	29.1	0.2
% Net Inc.of Revs.	8.2	16.1	7.7	7.4	0.5	7.5	7.6	8.9	2.2	10.2
% Ret. on Assets	7.9	14.8	7.4	6.7	0.4	6.1	5.8	7.3	2.0	10.9
% Ret. on Equity	20.8	41.4	23.3	23.3	1.3	16.1	15.1	18.8	4.4	21.2

Data as orig. reptd.; bef. results of disc. opers. and/or spec. items. Per share data adj. for stk. divs. as of ex-div. date. Bold denotes diluted EPS (FASB 128). E-Estimated. NA-Not Available. NM-Not Meaningful. NR-Not Ranked.

Office—1221 Ave. of the Americas, New York, NY 10020. **Tel**—(212) 512-2000. **Website**—http://www.mcgraw-hill.com **Chrmn**—J. L. Dionne. **Pres & CEO**—H. W. McGraw III. **EVP & CFO**—R. J. Bahash. **EVP & Treas**—F. V. Penglase. **SVP & Gen Counsel**—K. M. Vittor. **SVP & Secy**—S. L. Bennett. **SVP & Investor Contact**—Donald S. Rubin (212-512-4321). **Dirs**—P. Aspe, J. L. Dionne, V. Gregorian, J. T. Hartley, G. B. Harvey, R. H. Jenrette, L. K. Lorimer, H. W. McGraw III, R. P. McGraw, L. D. Rice, J. H. Ross, S. Taurel, A. O. Way. **Transfer Agent**—ChaseMellon Shareholder Services, NYC. **Incorporated**—in New York in 1925. **Empl**— 15,690. **S&P Analyst:** William H. Donald

STANDARD &POOR'S
STOCK REPORTS

Mead Corp.

1464

NYSE Symbol **MEA**

In S&P 500

12-SEP-98

Industry: Paper & Forest Products

Summary: This company is a major producer of coated papers and packaging products, and also makes and distributes school and office products.

S&P Opinion: Hold (★★★)	Recent Price • 27	Yield • 2.4%
	52 Wk Range • 37¾-25⅞	12-Mo. P/E • 22.5

Quantitative Evaluations

Outlook
(1 Lowest—5 Highest)
• **3**

Fair Value
• **30½**

Risk
• **Low**

Earn./Div. Rank
• **B-**

Technical Eval.
• **Bearish** since 3/98

Rel. Strength Rank
(1 Lowest—99 Highest)
• **61**

Insider Activity
• **Neutral**

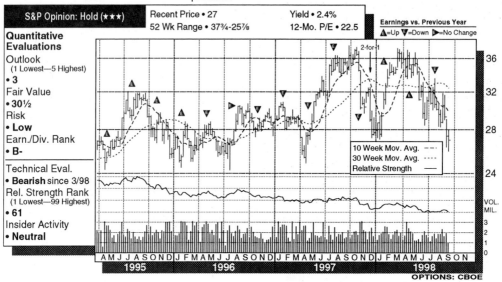

Earnings vs. Previous Year
▲=Up ▼=Down ▶=No Change

10 Week Mov. Avg. — —
30 Week Mov. Avg. ·······
Relative Strength —

OPTIONS: CBOE

Overview - 18-AUG-98

We expect sales from comparable operations to be slightly higher in 1998, on small gains in all segments. We expect gains in the paper and packaging segments to reflect somewhat higher average prices. However, the modest early 1997 to early 1998 pricing upturn for Mead's mainstay coated paper and corrugated products has recently been threatened. The current troubles reflect the negative impact of Asia's financial woes and a strong U.S. dollar on foreign trade. Sales should also pick up a bit in the school/office products area, which will face the same pricing factors as the paper and packaging segments. We expect operating margins to widen, boosted by the slightly higher average paper and packaging prices, along with cost control and productivity improvement efforts. Mead's bottom line will likely be reduced a bit by weaker results from joint ventures, given lumber oversupply and troubles in pulp markets. Our 1998 forecast excludes $0.22 a share of second quarter asset writedowns shown in EPS table, and other one-time charges to be taken.

Valuation - 18-AUG-98

The shares rebounded strongly in the spring and summer of 1997, as prices for Mead's paper and corrugated packaging grades started to recover, after a severe downturn since late 1995. They have since given back much of the gains (despite a brief upturn in early 1998), as Asia's financial woes have threatened the sector recovery since fall 1997. We presently lack enthusiasm about paper and packaging prospects, as we see troubles in the global economy limiting commodities prices for an extended period. However, we see Mead as one of the better positioned firms, given its activities in the value-added products area and its current business enhancement activities. As such, we carry a neutral opinion on the shares.

Key Stock Statistics

S&P EPS Est. 1998	1.80	Tang. Bk. Value/Share	22.09
P/E on S&P Est. 1998	15.0	Beta	0.89
S&P EPS Est. 1999	2.15	Shareholders	15,600
Dividend Rate/Share	0.64	Market cap. (B)	$ 2.8
Shs. outstg. (M)	103.8	Inst. holdings	67%
Avg. daily vol. (M)	0.361		

Value of $10,000 invested 5 years ago: $ 15,953

Fiscal Year Ending Dec. 31

	1998	1997	1996	1995	1994	1993
Revenues (Million $)						
1Q	839.0	1,136	1,067	1,241	1,008	1,136
2Q	1,051	1,322	1,259	1,442	1,166	1,263
3Q	—	1,376	1,231	1,352	1,208	1,262
4Q	—	1,244	1,150	1,144	1,176	1,130
Yr.	—	5,077	4,707	5,179	4,558	4,790
Earnings Per Share ($)						
1Q	0.32	**0.19**	0.29	0.54	0.14	0.21
2Q	**0.38**	**0.45**	0.63	0.94	0.37	0.39
3Q	—	**0.47**	0.59	0.95	0.34	0.25
4Q	—	**0.30**	0.28	0.69	-0.09	0.18
Yr.	—	**1.41**	**1.79**	3.10	0.76	1.04

Next earnings report expected: mid October

Dividend Data (Dividends have been paid since 1940.)

Amount ($)	Date Decl.	Ex-Div. Date	Stock of Record	Payment Date
2-for-1	Nov. 03	Dec. 02	Nov. 12	Dec. 01 '97
0.160	Jan. 23	Jan. 29	Feb. 02	Mar. 01 '98
0.160	Apr. 23	Apr. 30	May. 04	Jun. 01 '98
0.160	Aug. 06	Aug. 13	Aug. 17	Sep. 01 '98

 A Division of The McGraw-Hill Companies

Business Summary - 18-AUG-98

Mead Corp. is a diversified forest products company, which makes paper and packaging, and school and office products. In June 1998, Mead announced a plan to improve productivity and place further focus on its core businesses. Segment contributions in 1997 (including since disposed distribution business):

	Sales	Profits
Paper	31%	54%
Packaging & paperboard	28%	36%
Distribution & school/office products	41%	10%

Mead ranks as one of the world's largest producers of paper, with coated papers for periodicals and commercial printing accounting for most of its production. It also makes carbonless paper for business forms and a variety of specialty papers. In the packaging and paperboard area, it produces and sells beverage and food packaging materials, corrugated boxes and corrugated medium (the inner, fluted layer in corrugated boxes). The company also and makes and distributes school and office supplies. In addition, Mead has 50% stakes in two units that produce pulp and wood products.

Only a small portion of MEA's wood requirements are obtained from owned or leased timberlands, with the rest obtained from private contractors or suppliers.

In August 1998, the company sold its Zellerbach paper and packaging distribution business (annual sales of more than $1 billion) to International Paper, for $263 million. The sale was part of a program announced in

June 1998, under which Mead launched initiatives to sharpen its focus on its core businesses. The program calls for Mead to sell about $100 million in other non-strategic assets such as its packaging inks business; a hardwood sawmill and 50,000 acres of surrounding timberlands; and certain selected real estate and undeveloped mill sites. It will also combine its coated paper divisions to aid productivity.

As part of its June 1998 program, Mead announced initiatives to reduce costs and enhance operating efficiencies. It said it will implement enterprise resource planning software across the company, in an action that Mead thinks will enable it to reduce its workforce by 5%. MEA will record charges totaling about $25 million in 1998's third quarter and subsequent periods for severance costs and expenses related to the software implementation. The company expects its restructuring actions to bring annual savings of $25 million by 1999 year-end and $50 million over the longer term.

Mead also intends to reduce annual capital spending to about $300 million in both 1999 and 2000, excluding any possible acquisitions, from the $400 to $450 million level budgeted for 1998. It plans to use proceeds from asset sales to improve its balance sheet, invest strategically in core businesses and accelerate share buybacks. With 502,000 shares repurchased in 1998's first half, Mead had bought back 20 million shares since December 1995 (16%). MEA said it expects to complete its current authorized plan with the buyback of 3.4 million more shares by 1999 year-end.

Per Share Data ($)

(Year Ended Dec. 31)	1997	1996	1995	1994	1993	1992	1991	1990	1989	1988
Tangible Bk. Val.	21.35	20.84	19.69	17.93	10.39	9.89	10.59	10.88	10.49	11.97
Cash Flow	3.70	3.71	5.11	2.22	3.42	2.60	2.66	2.41	3.09	3.97
Earnings	1.41	1.78	3.10	0.76	1.04	0.32	0.65	0.85	1.67	2.77
Dividends	0.61	0.59	0.55	0.50	0.50	0.50	0.50	0.48	0.42	0.37
Payout Ratio	43%	33%	18%	66%	48%	159%	77%	53%	25%	13%
Prices - High	37¾	30¾	32⅛	26⅝	24¼	20⅞	18⅝	19¾	23⅜	24¾
- Low	24⅞	24¼	24⅜	19⅝	18¾	16⅝	12¼	9¾	17⅛	14½
P/E Ratio - High	27	17	10	35	23	66	29	23	14	9
- Low	18	14	8	26	18	53	19	11	10	5

Income Statement Analysis (Million $)

	1997	1996	1995	1994	1993	1992	1991	1990	1989	1988
Revs.	5,077	4,707	5,179	4,558	4,790	4,703	4,579	4,772	4,612	4,464
Oper. Inc.	554	542	714	370	554	521	469	498	472	547
Depr.	242	203	191	188	283	269	236	194	172	170
Int. Exp.	98.0	58.0	69.0	107	99	101	119	113	101	74.0
Pretax Inc.	233	299	527	112	202	62.0	130	159	316	582
Eff. Tax Rate	36%	37%	35%	20%	39%	39%	42%	33%	32%	38%
Net Inc.	150	190	350	89.6	124	38.0	76.0	106	216	364

Balance Sheet & Other Fin. Data (Million $)

	1997	1996	1995	1994	1993	1992	1991	1990	1989	1988
Cash	30.0	21.0	293	484	9.0	18.0	25.0	21.0	21.0	34.0
Curr. Assets	1,218	1,189	1,367	1,894	1,131	1,129	1,093	982	985	960
Total Assets	5,230	4,986	4,373	4,863	4,165	4,031	3,986	3,889	3,750	3,541
Curr. Liab.	714	758	822	1,088	712	730	746	693	700	674
LT Debt	1,428	1,240	695	958	1,369	1,332	1,316	1,257	950	924
Common Eqty.	2,289	2,246	2,160	2,183	1,578	1,495	1,478	1,531	1,681	1,568
Total Cap.	3,717	4,000	3,305	3,534	3,258	3,103	3,043	3,082	2,961	2,811
Cap. Exp.	441	433	263	365	347	271	266	455	616	631
Cash Flow	392	393	541	278	408	307	312	300	416	534
Curr. Ratio	1.7	1.6	1.7	1.7	1.6	1.5	1.5	1.4	1.4	1.4
% LT Debt of Cap.	38.4	31.0	21.0	27.1	42.0	42.9	43.2	40.8	32.1	32.9
% Net Inc.of Revs.	3.0	4.0	6.8	2.0	2.6	0.8	1.7	2.2	4.7	8.2
% Ret. on Assets	2.9	4.1	7.6	2.0	3.0	0.9	1.9	2.9	5.9	11.2
% Ret. on Equity	6.6	8.6	16.1	4.8	8.0	2.5	5.0	6.9	13.5	25.8

Data as orig. reptd.; bef. results of disc. opers. and/or spec. items. Per share data adj. for stk. divs. as of ex-div. date. Bold denotes diluted EPS (FASB 128). E-Estimated. NA-Not Available. NM-Not Meaningful. NR-Not Ranked.

Office—Courthouse Plaza N.E., Dayton, OH 45463. **Tel**—(937) 495-6323. **Website**—http://www.mead.com **Chrmn, Pres & CEO**—J. F. Tatar. **VP & CFO**—W. R. Graber. **Investor Contact**—Mark Pomerleau (937 495-3456). **Dirs**—J. C. Bogle, J. G. Breen, W. E. Hoglund, J. G. Kaiser, R. J. Kohlhepp, J. A. Krol, S. J. Kropf, C. S. Mechem Jr., L. J. Styslinger Jr., J. F. Tatar, J. L. Wilson. **Transfer Agent & Registrar**—First National Bank of Boston. **Incorporated**—in Ohio in 1930. **Empl**— 14,000. **S&P Analyst:** Michael W. Jaffe

STANDARD &POOR'S
STOCK REPORTS

MediaOne Group

2362A

NYSE Symbol **UMG**

In S&P 500

12-SEP-98

Industry:
Broadcasting (Television, Radio & Cable)

Summary: This company is the third largest domestic cable operator.

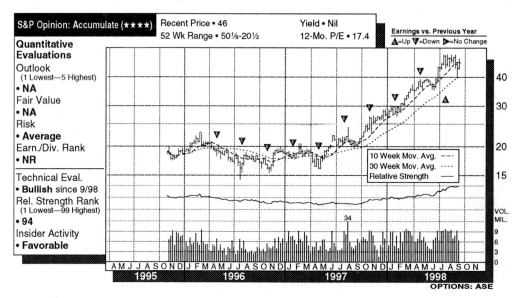

S&P Opinion: Accumulate (★★★★)

Recent Price • 46
52 Wk Range • 50⅛-20½

Yield • Nil
12-Mo. P/E • 17.4

Earnings vs. Previous Year
▲=Up ▼=Down ▷=No Change

Quantitative Evaluations

Outlook
(1 Lowest—5 Highest)
• **NA**

Fair Value
• **NA**

Risk
• **Average**

Earn./Div. Rank
• **NR**

Technical Eval.
• **Bullish** since 9/98

Rel. Strength Rank
(1 Lowest—99 Highest)
• **94**

Insider Activity
• **Favorable**

10 Week Mov. Avg. -----
30 Week Mov. Avg. ------
Relative Strength ———

40
30
20
15

VOL. MIL.
9
6
3
0

A M J J A S O N D J F M A M J J A S O N D J F M A M J J A S O N D J F M A M J J A S O N
1995   1996   1997   1998

OPTIONS: ASE

Overview - 10-AUG-98

Operating cash flows should continue their strong growth in 1998, aided by increasing demand for cable television services, and by the sale of startup wireless assets. MediaOne Group (formerly U S WEST Media Group) and U S WEST, Inc. (U S WEST Communications Group) recently split into separate public companies. UMG's November 1996 acquisition of Continental Cablevision created one of the world's largest cable operators, with 4.7 million customers in the U.S., and 16.2 million worldwide. TeleWest, UMG's joint venture in the U.K. with TCI, continues to benefit from the deregulation of the U.K. telecom market. In April 1998, AirTouch Communications (ATI) completed its $6.2 billion acquisition of UMG's domestic cellular business and its interest in PrimeCo Personal Communications Services.

Valuation - 10-AUG-98

The shares have continued to appreciate, following the recent separation of the two U.S. WEST companies, and the sale of the domestic wireless unit to AirTouch Communications. We see the shares continuing to outperform the market over the next 12 months, based on our belief that MediaOne will benefit greatly from its cable focus and corporate freedom. As the third largest cable company in the U.S., UMG's growth prospects are bolstered by an aggressive acquisition strategy. For the long term, results should benefit from the company's ability to provide customers with a bundled offering of enhanced services. UMG should gain additional strength from the reduced debt burden resulting from the sale of its domestic wireless assets, and from the nearly complete integration of Continental Cable.

Key Stock Statistics

S&P EPS Est. 1998	-0.65	Tang. Bk. Value/Share	NM
P/E on S&P Est. 1998	NM	Beta	NA
S&P EPS Est. 1999	-0.60	Shareholders	700,400
Dividend Rate/Share	Nil	Market cap. (B)	$ 28.1
Shs. outstg. (M)	609.4	Inst. holdings	61%
Avg. daily vol. (M)	1.744		

Value of $10,000 invested 5 years ago: NA

Fiscal Year Ending Dec. 31

	1998	1997	1996	1995	1994	1993
Revenues (Million $)						
1Q	1,279	1,207	613.0	536.0	--	--
2Q	641.0	1,277	658.0	585.0	877.0	--
3Q	--	1,270	694.0	604.0	482.0	--
4Q	--	1,289	990.0	649.0	549.0	--
Yr.	--	5,043	2,955	2,374	1,908	1,549
Earnings Per Share ($)						
1Q	**-0.24**	-0.20	Nil	0.03	--	--
2Q	**-0.10**	-0.17	-0.03	0.05	0.26	--
3Q	**E-0.15**	-0.26	0.04	0.07	0.11	--
4Q	**E-0.16**	-0.24	-0.16	0.15	--	--
Yr.	**E-0.65**	-0.88	-0.16	0.30	0.61	NA

Next earnings report expected: late October

Dividend Data

No cash dividends have been paid, and none are planned.

A Division of The McGraw-Hill Companies

STANDARD
&POOR'S
STOCK REPORTS

MediaOne Group, Inc.

2362A
12-SEP-98

Business Summary - 10-AUG-98

MediaOne Group (formerly U S WEST Media Group), one of America's largest broadband communications companies, is involved in domestic and international cable and telephony and directory and information services. MediaOne Group and U S WEST, Inc. (formerly U S WEST Communications Group) recently split into separate public companies.

In November 1996, UMG acquired Continental Cablevision for $5.3 billion in cash and stock plus the assumption of $5.5 billion in debt, making it the third largest cable operator in the U.S. Domestic cable operations include two cable television systems that serve 497,000 customers in Atlanta. In addition, UMG owns a 25.5% interest in Time Warner Entertainment (TWE). TWE includes HBO, Warner Brothers and Time Warner Cable.

As of December 31, 1997, the company's cable television systems passed approximately 8.4 million homes and provided service to about 4.9 million basic cable subscribers. MediaOne's systems are organized into six operating regions, including large clusters in Atlanta, eastern Massachusetts, Southern California, southern Florida, Detroit, and Minneapolis/St. Paul. At 1997 year

end, approximately 90% of UMG's total basic subscribers were located in areas with a population greater than 100,000.

In April 1998, AirTouch Communications (NYSE: ATI) completed its acquisition of UMG's domestic wireless business and its interest in PrimeCo PCS (Personal Communications Services). The $6.2 billion transaction included a tax-free distribution of ATI stock to UMG shareholders and the assumption of $1.4 billion of debt. In addition, UMG's multimedia business was transferred to U S WEST Communications Group following the merger with AirTouch.

UMG's international operations include the company's 27% interest in U.K.-based TeleWest, which is the world's largest provider of integrated cable and telephony services. MediaOne owns a 50% stake in Mercury One-2-One, which operates a wireless personal communications system in the U.K. As of December 31, 1997, the company's international wireless interests represented 76.9 million proportionate potential customers (POPs) and 1,018,000 subscribers. UMG also holds interests in other providers of cable and broadband communications services in foreign countries, including the Czech Republic, the Netherlands, Belgium, Indonesia, Singapore and Japan.

Per Share Data ($)

(Year Ended Dec. 31)	1997	1996	1995	1994	1993	1992	1991	1990	1989	1988
Tangible Bk. Val.	NM	NM	NA	NA	NA	NA	NA	NA	NA	NA
Cash Flow	1.34	0.70	0.84	0.93	NA	NA	NA	NA	NA	NA
Earnings	-0.88	-0.16	0.30	0.61	NA	NA	NA	NA	NA	NA
Dividends	Nil	Nil	Nil	Nil	Nil	Nil	Nil	Nil	Nil	Nil
Payout Ratio	Nil	Nil	Nil	Nil	Nil	Nil	Nil	Nil	Nil	Nil
Prices - High	29⅛	23	20	NA	NA	NA	NA	NA	NA	NA
- Low	16	14⅜	17⅜	NA	NA	NA	NA	NA	NA	NA
P/E Ratio - High	NM	NM	67	NA	NA	NA	NA	NA	NA	NA
- Low	NM	NM	58	NA	NA	NA	NA	NA	NA	NA

Income Statement Analysis (Million $)

	1997	1996	1995	1994	1993	1992	1991	1990	1989	1988
Revs.	5,043	2,955	2,374	1,908	1,549	1,384	1,261	1,210	NA	NA
Oper. Inc.	1,890	937	716	533	485	410	NA	NA	NA	NA
Depr.	1,294	422	249	144	127	122	NA	NA	NA	NA
Int. Exp.	680	206	100	66.0	27.0	15.0	NA	NA	NA	NA
Pretax Inc.	-641	-73.0	308	480	146	251	NA	NA	NA	NA
Eff. Tax Rate	NM	NM	53%	43%	42%	42%	NA	NA	NA	NA
Net Inc.	-479	-71.0	145	276	85.0	146	69.0	210	NA	NA

Balance Sheet & Other Fin. Data (Million $)

	1997	1996	1995	1994	1993	1992	1991	1990	1989	1988
Cash	184	179	20.0	93.0	72.0	NA	NA	NA	NA	NA
Curr. Assets	1,328	1,139	741	756	580	NA	NA	NA	NA	NA
Total Assets	22,614	24,061	8,615	7,394	5,446	3,130	3,235	2,555	NA	NA
Curr. Liab.	2,426	2,716	1,569	1,933	920	NA	NA	NA	NA	NA
LT Debt	8,228	8,772	1,265	585	1,132	NA	NA	NA	NA	NA
Common Eqty.	7,125	7,632	4,472	4,203	3,139	2,265	2,057	1,961	NA	NA
Total Cap.	19,795	21,135	6,770	5,267	4,334	NA	NA	NA	NA	NA
Cap. Exp.	1,551	652	363	343	215	169	231	195	NA	NA
Cash Flow	814	342	394	420	212	268	NA	NA	NA	NA
Curr. Ratio	0.6	0.4	0.5	0.4	0.6	NA	NA	NA	NA	NA
% LT Debt of Cap.	41.6	41.5	18.7	11.1	26.1	NA	NA	NA	NA	NA
% Net Inc.of Revs.	NM	NM	6.1	14.5	5.5	10.5	5.5	17.4	NA	NA
% Ret. on Assets	NM	NM	1.8	4.3	2.0	4.6	2.4	NA	NA	NA
% Ret. on Equity	NM	NM	3.3	7.5	3.1	6.8	3.4	NA	NA	NA

Data as orig. reptd.; bef. results of disc. opers. and/or spec. items. Per share data adj. for stk. divs. as of ex-div. date. Bold denotes diluted EPS (FASB 128). E-Estimated. NA-Not Available. NM-Not Meaningful. NR-Not Ranked.

Office—7800 E. Orchard Rd., Suite 290, Englewood, CO 80111.**Tel**—(303) 793-6356.**Website**—http://www.uswest.com **Pres & CEO**—C. M. Lillis. **VP & CFO**—D. Holmes. **Investor Contact**—Steve Lang. **Dirs**—R. L. Crandell, G. A. Dove, A. D. Gilmour, P. M. Grieve, G. J. Harad, A. F. Jacobsen, C. M. Lillis, R. D. McCormick, M. C. Nelson, F. Popoff, C. P. Russ III, L. A. Simpson, J. Slevin, S. D. Trujillo, J. O. Williams. **Transfer Agent & Registrar**—Boston Financial Data Services, Quincy, MA. **Incorporated**—in Delaware in 1995. **Empl**— 21,074. **S&P Analyst:** Philip D. Wohl

STANDARD &POOR'S
STOCK REPORTS

Medtronic, Inc.

1466P

NYSE Symbol **MDT**

In S&P 500

12-SEP-98

Industry:
Health Care (Medical Products & Supplies)

Summary: The world's leading producer of implantable cardiac pacemakers, this company also makes implantable defibrillators, heart valves, and other cardiac and neurological products.

| S&P Opinion: Accumulate (★★★★) | Recent Price • 56⅞ | Yield • 0.5% |
| | 52 Wk Range • 72¾-40½ | 12-Mo. P/E • 58.6 |

Quantitative Evaluations

Outlook (1 Lowest—5 Highest)
• **1**

Fair Value
• **52**

Risk
• **Average**

Earn./Div. Rank
• **A+**

Technical Eval.
• **NA**

Rel. Strength Rank (1 Lowest—99 Highest)
• **83**

Insider Activity
• **Unfavorable**

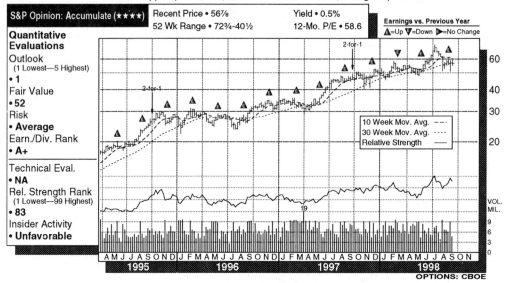

Earnings vs. Previous Year — ▲=Up ▼=Down ▶=No Change

10 Week Mov. Avg. ---
30 Week Mov. Avg. ····
Relative Strength —

OPTIONS: CBOE

Overview - 25-JUN-98

Sales are expected to rise about 12% in FY 99 (Apr.), led by continued robust gains in implantable cardioverter defibrillators used to treat tachyarrhythmia (rapid heart beating), as well as in neurological product lines. Tachyarrhythmia product sales should be augmented by the new Gem and Gem DR defibrillators (the latter has dual chamber, rate responsive capability), while strength in the SynchroMed drug infusion line and new products such as the Activa neurostimulation device to treat Parkinson's disease should boost neurological sales. Pacemaker volume is expected to be boosted by the recent launch of the Kappa 400 line. Profitability should benefit from the better volume and cost streamlining measures. Diluted EPS are projected at $1.50, up from FY 98's $0.96 (after restructuring charges of $0.29 in the third quarter).

Valuation - 25-JUN-98

The shares moved higher over the past two months, following a slightly declining trend from mid-February when the company released disappointing third quarter FY 98 earnings. EPS in that quarter included a $0.29 charge related to plant closings, personnel reductions and other writedowns at the vascular products division. MDT is not likely to achieve significant market share in key vascular categories such as coronary stents and angioplasty catheters due to strong entrenched competition in those businesses. However, Medtronic remains the world leader in pacemakers and a major player in the rapidly growing markets for implantable cardioverter defibrillators and neurostimulation devices. MDT is also working on new devices to treat atrial fibrillation, the world's most common heart rhythm disorder. Continued projected rapid earnings growth appears to justify the rich multiple enjoyed by the shares, which remain attractive for above-average long-term appreciation.

Key Stock Statistics

S&P EPS Est. 1999	1.50	Tang. Bk. Value/Share	3.36
P/E on S&P Est. 1999	37.9	Beta	1.00
Dividend Rate/Share	0.26	Shareholders	21,900
Shs. outstg. (M)	469.4	Market cap. (B)	$ 26.7
Avg. daily vol. (M)	1.397	Inst. holdings	58%

Value of $10,000 invested 5 years ago: $ 49,296

Fiscal Year Ending Apr. 30

	1999	1998	1997	1996	1995	1994
Revenues (Million $)						
1Q	653.2	646.3	600.9	523.8	403.8	331.3
2Q	—	642.1	598.1	518.5	408.1	332.1
3Q	—	631.4	598.8	529.2	413.7	344.6
4Q	—	685.0	640.5	596.1	516.7	393.0
Yr.	—	2,605	2,438	2,169	1,742	1,391
Earnings Per Share ($)						
1Q	0.32	0.31	0.27	0.21	0.14	0.11
2Q	—	0.30	0.27	0.23	0.15	0.12
3Q	—	0.02	0.27	0.23	0.15	0.12
4Q	—	0.34	0.31	0.27	0.19	0.14
Yr.	E1.50	0.96	1.11	0.94	0.64	0.51

Next earnings report expected: mid November

Dividend Data (Dividends have been paid since 1977.)

Amount ($)	Date Decl.	Ex-Div. Date	Stock of Record	Payment Date
0.055	Oct. 30	Jan. 07	Jan. 09	Jan. 30 '98
0.055	Mar. 05	Apr. 07	Apr. 10	Apr. 30 '98
0.065	Jun. 24	Jun. 30	Jul. 02	Jul. 31 '98
0.065	Aug. 26	Oct. 07	Oct. 09	Oct. 30 '98

A Division of The McGraw-Hill Companies

STANDARD
&POOR'S
STOCK REPORTS

Medtronic, Inc.

1466P
12-SEP-98

Business Summary - 25-JUN-98

Medtronic is the world's leading medical technology company, specializing in cardiac pacemakers and defibrillators. A broad line of other products such as angioplasty catheters, stents, heart valves, and neurological products are also offered. Medtronic was formed in 1949 by Earl Bakken and Palmer Hermundslie. Bakken invented the first battery-powered cardiac pacemaker in the late 1950s. Foreign operations provided 42% of sales and 35% of profits in FY 97 (Apr.). Sales by business segments in recent fiscal years were:

	FY 97	FY 96
Cardiac pacing products	66%	68%
Nonpacing cardiovascular items	22%	24%
Neurological and other products	12%	8%

The company is the world's leading producer of implantable cardiac pacemakers, with about half of the $2.5 billion worldwide bradycardia (slow or irregular heart beating) pacing market. Cardiac pacing products consist of implantable pacemakers, leads and accessories. Pacemakers, which are sold under the Thera, Elite, Kappa and other names, include models that can be noninvasively programmed by a physician to adjust sensing, electrical pulse intensity, duration, rate and other factors, as well as pacers that can sense in both the upper and lower chambers of the heart and produce appropriate impulses.

A full line of implantable defibrillators is sold under the Jewel name for the treatment of tachyarrhythmia (abnormally fast heart rhythms). These devices monitor the heart and, when a very rapid heart rhythm is detected, send either a series of electrical impulses or an electrical shock to return the heart to a normal rhythm. MDT has an estimated 40% share of this market, which is estimated at about $800 million worldwide.

Nonpacing cardiovascular products include vascular and cardiac surgical products. Vascular devices consist primarily of coronary angioplasty catheters, coronary stents and electrophysiological catheters. Cardiac surgery products include heart valves, stent-graft systems, cannulae, oxygenators and other blood management items.

Neurological and other products include implantable devices that provide spinal cord and brain stimulation to treat pain and tremor; implantable programmable drug delivery systems that are used in treating chronic intractable pain, tremor and spasticity; and a number of other neurological items such as shunt assemblies to treat hydrocephalus, other vascular access devices, trauma products, diagnostic systems and products to control urge incontinence.

Per Share Data ($)

(Year Ended Apr. 30)	1998	1997	1996	1995	1994	1993	1992	1991	1990	1989
Tangible Bk. Val.	3.36	2.69	2.81	2.89	2.27	1.82	1.68	1.44	1.25	1.11
Cash Flow	1.25	1.35	1.18	0.87	0.64	0.56	0.46	0.38	0.32	0.29
Earnings	0.96	1.11	0.94	0.64	0.51	0.45	0.34	0.28	0.25	0.23
Dividends	0.22	0.19	0.16	0.10	0.09	0.07	0.06	0.05	0.04	0.04
Payout Ratio	23%	17%	17%	16%	17%	15%	18%	18%	17%	16%
Cal. Yrs.	1997	1996	1995	1994	1993	1992	1991	1990	1989	1988
Prices - High	52³/₄	35	30	14	12	13¹/₈	11³/₄	5³/₄	4¹/₂	3¹/₈
- Low	28⁷/₈	22¹/₄	13¹/₈	8⁵/₈	6¹/₂	7⁷/₈	4⁷/₈	3³/₄	2⁷/₁₆	2¹/₈
P/E Ratio - High	55	31	32	22	24	29	35	20	18	14
- Low	30	20	14	14	13	18	14	13	10	9

Income Statement Analysis (Million $)

Revs.	2,605	2,438	2,169	1,742	1,391	1,328	1,177	1,021	837	742
Oper. Inc.	1,017	901	759	543	396	332	305	243	195	174
Depr.	138	117	112	107	63.0	54.7	59.4	37.0	30.2	26.4
Int. Exp.	8.2	9.4	8.0	9.0	8.2	10.4	13.4	13.8	10.1	8.3
Pretax Inc.	702	809	668	442	347	313	243	196	160	150
Eff. Tax Rate	35%	35%	34%	34%	33%	33%	34%	32%	32%	35%
Net Inc.	457	530	438	294	232	212	162	133	109	97.0

Balance Sheet & Other Fin. Data (Million $)

Cash	383	251	461	324	181	156	110	113	52.0	51.0
Curr. Assets	1,552	1,238	1,343	1,104	846	775	696	612	479	421
Total Assets	2,775	2,409	2,503	1,947	1,623	1,286	1,163	1,024	856	760
Curr. Liab.	572	519	525	456	439	348	309	292	260	232
LT Debt	16.2	13.9	15.3	14.2	20.2	10.9	8.6	7.9	8.0	7.8
Common Eqty.	2,044	1,746	1,789	1,335	1,053	841	796	683	541	474
Total Cap.	2,074	1,762	1,850	1,385	1,090	857	823	706	566	495
Cap. Exp.	148	171	164	96.9	86.0	87.4	77.2	73.7	58.5	56.3
Cash Flow	595	647	549	401	295	266	221	170	139	124
Curr. Ratio	2.7	2.4	2.6	2.4	1.9	2.2	2.3	2.1	1.8	1.8
% LT Debt of Cap.	0.8	0.7	1.0	1.0	1.9	1.3	1.0	1.1	1.4	1.6
% Net Inc.of Revs.	17.6	21.7	20.1	16.9	16.7	15.9	13.7	13.1	13.0	13.1
% Ret. on Assets	17.6	21.3	19.7	16.5	15.9	17.5	14.8	13.6	13.4	13.9
% Ret. on Equity	24.1	29.5	28.0	24.7	24.5	26.2	21.9	20.9	21.3	22.4

Data as orig. reptd.; bef. results of disc. opers. and/or spec. items. Per share data adj. for stk. divs. as of ex-div. date. Bold denotes diluted EPS (FASB 128). E-Estimated. NA-Not Available. NM-Not Meaningful. NR-Not Ranked.

Office—7000 Central Ave. N.E., Minneapolis, MN 55432. **Tel**—(612) 514-4000; (800) 328-2518. **Website**—http://www.medtronic.com **Chrmn & CEO**—W. W. George. **Vice Chrmn**—G. D. Nelson. **Pres & COO**—A. D. Collins, Jr. **SVP & Secy**—R. E. Lund. **SVP & CFO**—R. L. Ryan. **Investor Contact**—Christopher O'Connell (612-574-3038). **Dirs**—F. C. Blodgett, P. W. Chellgren, A. D. Collins, Jr., W. W. George, A. M. Gotto, Jr., B. P. Healy, T. E. Holloran, G. D. Nelson, R. L. Schall, J. W. Schuler, G. W. Simonson, G. M. Sprenger, R. A. Swalin. **Transfer Agent & Registrar**—Norwest Bank Minnesota, St. Paul. **Incorporated**—in Minnesota in 1957. **Empl**— 11,722. **S&P Analyst:** H.B. Saftlas

STANDARD &POOR'S
STOCK REPORTS

Mellon Bank

1467H
NYSE Symbol **MEL**

In S&P 500

12-SEP-98

Industry: Banks (Major Regional)

Summary: This Pittsburgh-based bank holding company provides a full range of banking, investment and trust products to individuals, businesses and institutions.

S&P Opinion: Accumulate (★★★★)	Recent Price • 56⅜	Yield • 2.6%
	52 Wk Range • 80⅜–47⅛	12-Mo. P/E • 18.4

Quantitative Evaluations

Outlook
(1 Lowest—5 Highest)
• 1⁻

Fair Value
• 43⅛

Risk
• **Low**

Earn./Div. Rank
• **B+**

Technical Eval.
• **Bullish** since 3/95

Rel. Strength Rank
(1 Lowest—99 Highest)
• **62**

Insider Activity
• **Neutral**

Earnings vs. Previous Year
▲=Up ▼=Down ▷=No Change

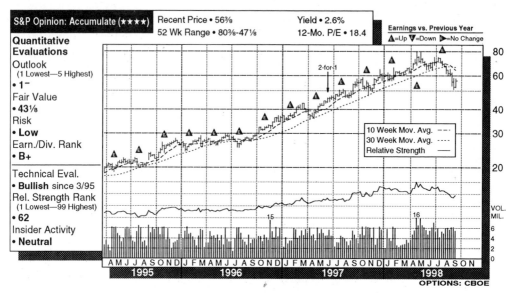

10 Week Mov. Avg. ---
30 Week Mov. Avg. ·····
Relative Strength —

OPTIONS: CBOE

Overview - 13-AUG-98

Net interest income is expected to be relatively flat in 1998, reflecting modest commercial and consumer loan growth but with some pressure on the interest margin from higher funding costs. The primary earnings driver will continue to be noninterest income, particularly trust and investment management revenues, which have benefited from several acquisitions (including Bulk Consultants and Founders Asset Management), new business, a higher market value of assets under management and continued equity inflows at the Dreyfus unit. Credit quality has improved following the disposition of an accelerated resolution portfolio of credit cards, which should relieve pressure on loan loss provisions; net charge-offs remain low compared to peers. Share earnings comparisons will continue to benefit from a significant ongoing stock repurchase program. Overall, we expect earnings growth of 12% in both 1998 and 1999.

Valuation - 13-AUG-98

The shares jumped in April 1998 following an unsolicited takeover offer from Bank of New York (BK). However, with the offer's immediate rejection from Mellon and BK's subsequent withdrawal, the shares have since trended down to the pre-offering price. A competing bid did not emerge, and Mellon has reiterated its stance of remaining independent. Nonetheless, we like Mellon's prospects as a stand alone company. Several thriving fee-based businesses should keep EPS growth at double-digit rates, and the company shares a mix of business with other regionals for which investors are willing to pay a premium valuation. Trading at 17 times estimated 1999 earnings of $3.60, we expect the shares to outperform the broader market in the year ahead.

Key Stock Statistics

S&P EPS Est. 1998	3.22	Tang. Bk. Value/Share	7.97
P/E on S&P Est. 1998	17.5	Beta	1.28
S&P EPS Est. 1999	3.60	Shareholders	23,900
Dividend Rate/Share	1.44	Market cap. (B)	$ 14.7
Shs. outstg. (M)	260.7	Inst. holdings	50%
Avg. daily vol. (M)	1.339		

Value of $10,000 invested 5 years ago: $ 38,512

Fiscal Year Ending Dec. 31

	1998	1997	1996	1995	1994	1993
Revenues (Million $)						
1Q	1,392	1,203	1,177	1,083	960.0	799.0
2Q	1,436	1,224	1,151	1,112	959.0	758.0
3Q	—	1,315	1,166	1,149	977.0	843.0
4Q	—	1,392	1,268	1,170	1,061	837.0
Yr.	—	5,134	4,762	4,515	3,957	3,237
Earnings Per Share ($)						
1Q	**0.78**	**0.69**	0.62	0.54	0.48	0.10
2Q	**0.81**	**0.71**	0.63	0.55	0.48	0.44
3Q	**E0.81**	**0.73**	0.66	0.57	0.21	0.50
4Q	**E0.82**	**0.75**	0.68	0.59	0.04	0.50
Yr.	**E3.22**	**2.88**	2.58	2.25	1.21	1.54

Next earnings report expected: mid October

Dividend Data (Dividends have been paid since 1895.)

Amount ($)	Date Decl.	Ex-Div. Date	Stock of Record	Payment Date
0.330	Oct. 21	Oct. 29	Oct. 31	Nov. 17 '97
0.330	Jan. 16	Jan. 28	Jan. 30	Feb. 17 '98
0.360	Apr. 21	Apr. 28	Apr. 30	May. 15 '98
0.360	Jul. 21	Jul. 29	Jul. 31	Aug. 17 '98

A Division of The **McGraw·Hill** *Companies*

Business Summary - 13-AUG-98

Mellon Bank Corp.'s objective is to pursue a balance among customer segments and lines of business that optimizes revenues, earnings and return on equity. Mellon has banking subsidiaries in Pennsylvania, Massachusetts, Delaware, Maryland and New Jersey. The company maintains a strong focus on market segments offering significant growth potential and on establishing multiple-product relationships with customers.

Operations are divided into four lines of business, whose contributions in 1997 were as follows:

	Revs.	Income
Consumer fee services	19%	16%
Consumer banking	29%	26%
Business fee services	38%	33%
Business banking	14%	25%

Consumer fee services include The Dreyfus Corp., where the company is the leading bank manager of mutual funds with over $93 billion of assets managed, and private asset management. Consumer banking consists of consumer lending and deposit products, business banking, credit card and mortgage banking. Business fee services include institutional asset and mutual fund management, trust and custody, securities lending and cash management. Business banking is comprised of large corporate and middle market banking, asset-based lending, leasing, real estate finance, securities underwriting and trading and international banking.

In 1997, average earning assets, from which interest income is derived, amounted to $34.8 billion and consisted mainly of loans (80%) and investment securities (16%). Average sources of funds included domestic deposits (45%), foreign deposits (6%), noninterest-bearing deposits (20%), short-term borrowings (7%), long-term debt (6%), shareholders' equity (11%) and other (5%).

At year-end 1997, nonperforming assets, consisting primarily of non-accrual and other real estate owned, were $181 million (0.62% of loans and related assets), up from $174 million (0.63%) a year earlier. The allowance for loan losses, which is set aside for possible loan defaults, was $475 million (1.63% of loans), versus $525 million (1.92%) a year earlier. Net charge-offs, or the amount of loans actually written off as uncollectible, were $136 million (0.72% of average loans) in 1997, compared to $124 million (0.46%) in 1996.

In May 1998, Bank of New York (NYSE; BK) withdrew a proposal to merge with Mellon in a stock transaction that valued each MEL share at $90 on the date the merger was announced.

Per Share Data ($)

(Year Ended Dec. 31)	1997	1996	1995	1994	1993	1992	1991	1990	1989	1988
Tangible Bk. Val.	4.54	5.58	7.05	7.74	7.43	7.61	7.09	5.73	11.17	10.08
Earnings	2.88	2.58	2.25	1.21	1.54	2.32	1.55	0.94	1.11	-1.22
Dividends	1.29	1.18	1.00	0.79	0.51	0.47	0.47	0.47	0.47	0.47
Payout Ratio	45%	46%	44%	65%	33%	20%	30%	49%	42%	NM
Prices - High	64¾	37⅜	28¼	20¼	22½	18½	12¾	10	12¾	11⅛
- Low	34½	24⅛	15⅜	15	17⅛	11¼	7¼	5⅞	8⅜	7⅝
P/E Ratio - High	23	14	13	17	15	8	8	11	11	NM
- Low	12	9	7	12	11	5	5	6	8	NM

Income Statement Analysis (Million $)

	1997	1996	1995	1994	1993	1992	1991	1990	1989	1988
Net Int. Inc.	1,467	1,478	1,548	1,508	1,307	1,154	974	867	819	838
Tax Equiv. Adj.	NA	10.0	10.0	13.0	10.0	12.0	27.0	33.0	39.0	51.0
Non Int. Inc.	2,418	2,019	1,670	1,652	1,276	851	770	814	783	720
Loan Loss Prov.	148	155	105	70.0	125	185	250	315	297	321
Exp./Op. Revs.	66%	63%	63%	75%	74%	72%	71%	69%	67%	80%
Pretax Inc.	1,169	1,151	1,092	711	600	492	308	193	204	-37.0
Eff. Tax Rate	34%	36%	37%	39%	40%	11%	9.10%	9.80%	11%	NM
Net Inc.	771	733	691	433	361	437	280	174	181	-65.0
% Net Int. Marg.	4.24	4.26	4.62	4.71	4.39	4.44	3.93	3.38	3.10	3.24

Balance Sheet & Other Fin. Data (Million $)

	1997	1996	1995	1994	1993	1992	1991	1990	1989	1988
Earning Assets:										
Money Mkt	1,083	1,076	922	883	1,583	1,376	1,240	947	4,924	5,341
Inv. Securities	4,849	6,486	5,432	5,125	5,012	5,738	5,744	4,614	3,453	3,163
Com'l Loans	12,392	11,618	11,799	10,830	9,809	8,765	8,928	8,784	9,956	8,728
Other Loans	16,750	15,775	15,891	15,903	14,664	11,191	10,175	9,954	9,442	10,256
Total Assets	44,892	42,596	40,646	38,644	36,139	31,574	29,355	28,762	31,467	31,153
Demand Deposits	7,975	8,692	6,458	5,979	6,914	5,640	4,597	5,133	4,351	4,173
Time Deposits	23,330	22,682	22,803	21,591	22,526	19,490	17,857	17,582	16,993	17,152
LT Debt	2,573	2,518	1,443	1,568	1,990	1,587	1,501	1,420	1,799	1,933
Common Eqty.	3,652	3,456	3,575	3,672	2,721	2,077	1,638	1,292	1,223	877
% Ret. on Assets	1.8	1.8	1.7	1.1	1.0	1.5	1.0	0.6	0.6	NM
% Ret. on Equity	21.1	18.4	17.9	9.5	11.9	20.4	15.4	9.0	11.5	NM
% Loan Loss Resv.	1.6	1.9	1.7	2.3	2.5	2.5	3.1	2.8	3.1	4.8
% Loans/Deposits	93.1	87.3	94.6	97.0	88.9	79.4	85.1	82.5	90.9	89.0
% Equity to Assets	8.1	9.0	9.2	9.9	7.5	6.3	5.2	4.6	3.6	2.9

Data as orig. reptd.; bef. results of disc opers. and/or spec. items. Per share data adj. for stk. divs. as of ex-div. date. Bold denotes diluted EPS (FASB 128). E-Estimated. NA-Not Available. NM-Not Meaningful. NR-Not Ranked.

Office—One Mellon Bank Center, Pittsburgh, PA 15258-0001. **Tel**—(412) 234-5000. **Website**—http://www.mellon.com **Chrmn, Pres & CEO**—F. V. Cahouet. **Vice Chrmn, CFO & Treas**—S. G. Elliott. **Secy**—C. Krasik. **Investor Contact**—Donald MacLeod. **Dirs**—D. L. Allison Jr., B. C. Borgelt, C. R. Brown, F. V. Cahouet, C. M. Condron, J. W. Connolly, C. A. Corry, C. F. Fetterolf, I. J. Gumberg, P. Hutchinson, G. W. Johnstone, R. E. Lee, A. W. Mathieson, E. J. McAniff, M. G. McGuinn, R. Mehrabian, S. P. Mellon, D. S. Shapira, W. K. Smith, J. L. Thomas, W. W. von Schack, W. J. Young. **Transfer Agent & Registrar**—ChaseMellon Shareholder Services, Ridgefield Park, NJ. **Incorporated**—in Pennsylvania in 1971; bank originally chartered in 1902. **Empl**— 27,500. **S&P Analyst:** Stephen R. Biggar

Mercantile Bancorp.

1473M

NYSE Symbol **MTL**

In S&P 500

12-SEP-98

Industry: Banks (Major Regional)

Summary: This St. Louis-based holding company, with about $35 billion in assets, operates banks throughout Missouri, Kansas, Illinois, Iowa, Kentucky and Arkansas.

S&P Opinion: Accumulate (★★★★)

Recent Price • 45⅝	Yield • 2.7%
52 Wk Range • 61⅝-42½	12-Mo. P/E • 20.8

Quantitative Evaluations

Outlook
(1 Lowest—5 Highest)
• 1⁻

Fair Value
• 40⅜

Risk
• **Low**

Earn./Div. Rank
• **A-**

Technical Eval.
• **Bearish** since 8/98

Rel. Strength Rank
(1 Lowest—99 Highest)
• 72

Insider Activity
• **NA**

Earnings vs. Previous Year
▲=Up ▼=Down ▶=No Change

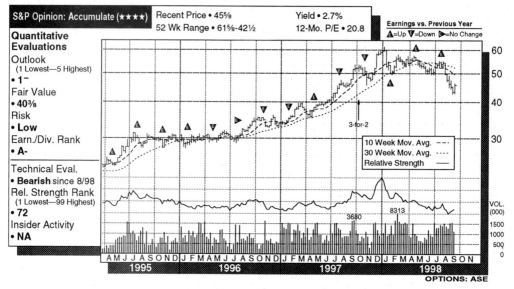

10 Week Mov. Avg. — —
30 Week Mov. Avg. ·····
Relative Strength ——

3-for-2

3680 8313

VOL. (000)

OPTIONS: ASE

Overview - 22-JUL-98

MTL reported EPS in the 1998 second quarter of $0.70, slightly ahead of expectations. Results were aided by the bank's merger with Roosevelt Financial Group (in July 1997), which was accounted for as a purchase, so that prior-period numbers were not restated. Net interest income advanced 13%, on higher loans, though margins were down reflecting refinancings and prepayments. Net interest income going forward should be modest, and driven primarily by loan volume. Noninterest income growth in the quarter was a healthy 19%. A trend we expect to continue. Other expenses should begin to trend down in coming quarters as synergies from acquisitions begin to take hold and management outsources a number of operations. MTL has been a voracious acquirer over the past few years, as management worked to expand the bank's Midwestern franchise. However, acquisition activity should slow significantly, as the bank focuses on internal growth strategies and Year 2000 issues. Net chargeoffs in the quarter were 0.13% of average loans, a level we are comfortable with going forward.

Valuation - 22-JUL-98

Mercantile's shares have underperformed the market thus far in 1998, falling about 11%, versus a more than 20% rise in the S&P 500. With its recent acquisition campaign, we believe that MTL is much better positioned to compete in key Missouri markets. Much of the company's success will hinge on its ability to meet cost savings goals, successfully integrate its acquisitions, and manage a busy consolidation schedule. We believe that the shares, recently trading at 16X our 1999 EPS estimate of $3.25, 2.9X book value, and yielding 2.3%, are an attractive long-term investment.

Key Stock Statistics

S&P EPS Est. 1998	2.95	Tang. Bk. Value/Share	13.04
P/E on S&P Est. 1998	15.5	Beta	1.13
S&P EPS Est. 1999	3.25	Shareholders	17,300
Dividend Rate/Share	1.24	Market cap. (B)	$ 6.9
Shs. outstg. (M)	152.0	Inst. holdings	29%
Avg. daily vol. (M)	0.329		

Value of $10,000 invested 5 years ago: $ 25,157

Fiscal Year Ending Dec. 31

	1998	1997	1996	1995	1994	1993
Revenues (Million $)						
1Q	657.5	415.4	384.5	337.0	248.9	225.6
2Q	645.7	499.1	408.5	341.8	249.5	225.5
3Q	—	645.8	406.6	357.5	257.9	220.8
4Q	—	625.4	421.7	362.4	267.0	221.1
Yr.	—	2,257	1,621	1,398	1,023	892.9
Earnings Per Share ($)						
1Q	**0.77**	0.64	0.05	0.62	0.61	0.52
2Q	**0.70**	0.28	0.69	0.66	0.62	0.53
3Q	**E0.73**	0.02	0.61	0.68	0.63	0.57
4Q	**E0.75**	0.71	0.73	0.70	0.63	0.59
Yr.	**E2.95**	1.65	0.69	2.67	2.49	2.21

Next earnings report expected: mid October

Dividend Data (Dividends have been paid since 1909.)

Amount ($)	Date Decl.	Ex-Div. Date	Stock of Record	Payment Date
0.278	Oct. 15	Dec. 08	Dec. 10	Jan. 02 '98
0.310	Feb. 08	Mar. 06	Mar. 10	Apr. 01 '98
0.310	May. 20	Jun. 08	Jun. 10	Jul. 01 '98
0.310	Aug. 07	Sep. 08	Sep. 10	Oct. 01 '98

A Division of The **McGraw·Hill** *Companies*

Mercantile Bancorporation Inc.

Business Summary - 22-JUL-98

Mercantile Bancorp. is building a strong banking franchise of locally managed community operations in the Midwest, primarily through an aggressive acquisition strategy. In its drive to obtain market leadership in the Midwest, MTL has created a growing six-state franchise focused on building and enhancing customer relationships. Since 1990, MTL has more than doubled its asset base, to over $30 billion. At 1997 year end, MTL was the dominant player in the St. Louis market, with a 28% share. In the second quarter of 1998, the St. Louis bank continued its acquisition strategy, announcing plans to merge with Financial Services Corporation of the Midwest, First Financial Bancorporation, and Bruno Stolze & Co. Early in 1998's third quarter, MTL completed the acquisitions of First Bank of Illinois Co. and CBT Corporation.

The majority of 1997 revenues (83%) were derived from interest income the bank generated on its earning assets. The bank's average earning assets in 1997 totaled $23.8 billion, a 22% increase from 1996 levels. Loan and leases accounted for the largest portion of average earning assets (73%), while debt and equity securities made up most of the remainder (26%).

Mercantile's average loan portfolio in 1997 amounted to $17.3 billion, up from $14.1 billion in 1996. Year to year loan growth figures were affected by $4.3 billion in loans acquired when MTL purchased Roosevelt Financial and Regional Bancshares Inc. in 1997. Residential mortgage loans accounted for 36% of the average loan portfolio in 1997, commercial loans 25%, commercial real estate loans 17%, consumer loans 11%, construction loans 4%, credit card loans 4%, and home equity loans 3%.

The average source of funds, which MTL uses to finance loan and earning asset growth, consisted mainly of core deposits (69%), short-term borrowings (11%), shareholders' equity (8%), large time deposits (5%), and long-term debt (3%).

Noninterest income in 1997 grew 12%, and accounted for 17% of revenues. Noninterest income was primarily made up of service charges (26%), trust fees (25%), investment banking and brokerage (9%), mortgage banking (6%), credit card fees (5%), securitization revenues (5%), securities gains (2%), and miscellaneous (21%).

Net chargeoffs (loans the bank deems unlikely to be collected and written off as a bad debt expense) in 1997 totaled $74,930,000, or 0.43% of average loans.

Per Share Data ($) (Year Ended Dec. 31)	1997	1996	1995	1994	1993	1992	1991	1990	1989	1988
Tangible Bk. Val.	12.28	15.79	17.55	15.53	9.69	13.72	12.12	10.96	10.37	11.07
Earnings	1.65	2.07	2.67	2.49	2.21	1.94	1.71	1.56	0.01	0.80
Dividends	1.14	1.09	0.88	0.75	0.66	0.62	0.62	0.62	0.62	0.62
Payout Ratio	69%	53%	33%	30%	30%	32%	36%	40%	NM	78%
Prices - High	$61\frac{5}{8}$	36	$31\frac{3}{8}$	$26\frac{1}{8}$	$25\frac{1}{8}$	$21\frac{1}{2}$	$16\frac{3}{4}$	$12\frac{1}{4}$	13	$13\frac{7}{8}$
- Low	$33\frac{3}{8}$	$27\frac{5}{8}$	$20\frac{7}{8}$	$19\frac{5}{8}$	$19\frac{3}{8}$	$15\frac{1}{2}$	$8\frac{1}{2}$	$7\frac{3}{4}$	$11\frac{1}{8}$	$8\frac{1}{2}$
P/E Ratio - High	37	17	12	10	11	11	10	8	NM	17
- Low	20	13	8	8	9	8	5	5	NM	11
Income Statement Analysis (Million $)										
Net Int. Inc.	921	702	595	511	446	364	292	257	241	221
Tax Equiv. Adj.	15.1	15.1	13.5	9.1	7.8	6.5	6.5	9.9	12.9	15.0
Non Int. Inc.	372	296	245	188	175	142	122	108	123	115
Loan Loss Prov.	79.3	71.0	34.7	33.5	50.4	61.0	50.0	45.0	95.0	60.0
Exp./Op. Revs.	69%	63%	56%	58%	62%	63%	64%	65%	73%	71%
Pretax Inc.	325	290	331	253	184	124	93.9	76.9	-5.7	29.8
Eff. Tax Rate	37%	34%	35%	36%	36%	32%	29%	26%	NM	3.90%
Net Inc.	205	192	217	161	117	85.0	66.6	56.7	0.5	28.7
% Net Int. Marg.	3.93	4.30	4.25	4.67	4.73	4.51	4.37	4.26	4.34	4.05
Balance Sheet & Other Fin. Data (Million $)										
Earning Assets:										
Money Mkt	603	326	196	113	344	265	406	224	150	157
Inv. Securities	7,475	4,039	3,795	3,019	2,922	2,423	1,553	1,117	1,111	889
Com'l Loans	7,471	3,337	2,559	2,120	1,886	1,741	1,697	1,892	1,888	1,968
Other Loans	11,649	9,436	7,883	5,995	4,401	4,159	3,693	3,531	3,018	2,721
Total Assets	29,955	18,987	15,934	12,242	10,513	9,476	8,089	7,617	6,942	6,459
Demand Deposits	3,586	2,584	1,852	1,529	1,562	1,244	1,147	1,267	1,187	1,114
Time Deposits	18,494	12,236	10,122	7,525	6,674	6,288	5,334	4,895	4,260	4,195
LT Debt	1,494	478	549	387	220	221	116	117	118	120
Common Eqty.	2,410	1,634	1,438	1,068	841	669	546	440	407	429
% Ret. on Assets	0.8	1.0	1.4	1.3	1.1	0.9	0.9	0.8	0.0	0.4
% Ret. on Equity	10.1	11.7	16.2	15.8	14.9	13.7	13.6	13.4	0.1	6.7
% Loan Loss Resv.	1.3	1.5	1.7	2.1	2.4	2.4	2.3	2.4	2.5	1.9
% Loans/Deposits	86.6	84.5	87.2	89.6	76.3	78.3	83.2	87.4	89.3	87.5
% Equity to Assets	8.3	8.9	8.7	8.4	7.4	6.8	6.5	6.1	6.5	6.6

Data as orig. reptd.; bef. results of disc opers. and/or spec. items. Per share data adj. for stk. divs. as of ex-div. date. Bold denotes diluted EPS (FASB 128). E-Estimated. NA-Not Available. NM-Not Meaningful. NR-Not Ranked.

Office—Mercantile Tower, P.O. Box 524, St. Louis, MO 63166-0524. **Tel**—(314) 425-2525. **Chrmn, Pres & CEO**—T. H. Jacobsen. **SEVP & CFO**—J. Q. Arnold. **Secy**—J. W. Bilstrom. **Investor Contact**—Mary Granberg (314-418-8237). **Dirs**—R. E. Beumer, H. M. Cornell Jr., Dr. H. Givens, W. A. Hall, T. H. Jacobsen, F. Lyon Jr., R.W. Murray, H. Saligman, C. D. Schnuck, A. J. Siteman, P. T. Stokes, J. A. Wright. **Transfer Agent & Registrar**—Harris Trust & Savings Bank, Chicago. **Incorporated**—in Missouri in 1970; bank founded in 1929. **Empl**— 9,770. **S&P Analyst:** Michael Schneider

STANDARD &POOR'S
STOCK REPORTS

Merck & Co.

1476

NYSE Symbol **MRK**

In S&P 500

12-SEP-98

Industry:
Health Care (Drugs - Major Pharmaceuticals)

Summary: Merck is one of the world's largest prescription pharmaceuticals concerns. Its Medco unit is the leading U.S. pharmacy benefits management company.

S&P Opinion: Buy (★★★★★)	Recent Price • 128	Yield • 1.7%
	52 Wk Range • 139⅛-82	12-Mo. P/E • 31.9

Quantitative Evaluations

Outlook
(1 Lowest—5 Highest)
• 1+

Fair Value
• 114

Risk
• Low

Earn./Div. Rank
• A+

Technical Eval.
• **Bullish** since 6/98

Rel. Strength Rank
(1 Lowest—99 Highest)
• 92

Insider Activity
• **Neutral**

Earnings vs. Previous Year
▲=Up ▼=Down ▶=No Change

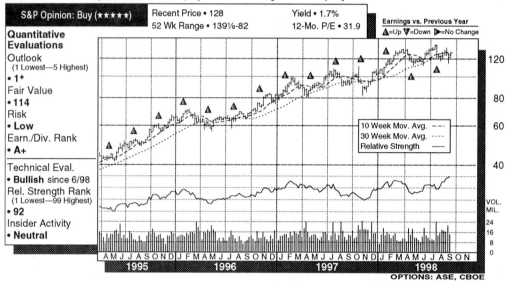

10 Week Mov. Avg. ---
30 Week Mov. Avg. ····
Relative Strength —

OPTIONS: ASE, CBOE

Overview - 04-AUG-98

Sales should rise about 9% in 1998. Growth should be paced by robust gains in Cozaar/Hyzaar and Prinivil/ Prinizide antihypertensives, Zocor cholesterol-lowering agent, Crixivan protease inhibitor AIDS drug and Fosamax for osteoporosis. Demand for Crixivan should be boosted by studies showing that Crixivan in combination with two other drugs suppressed HIV levels to below detection, while sales of Fosamax should be augmented by an expanded label that includes the prevention of osteoporosis. Other promising new drugs include Propecia for hair loss, Singulair for asthma, Aggrastat platelet blocker and Maxalt for migraine. The Medco managed care unit should also show further growth, aided by continued expansion in the membership base. Margins should benefit from the greater volume and productivity improvements.

Valuation - 04-AUG-98

The shares retreated in mid-July, after the release of second quarter EPS (which were $0.01 below consensus) and MRK's forecast that EPS for the full year would be near the lower end of the estimate range. Investors were also concerned over growing competition in Merck's cholesterol drug franchise from Warner-Lambert's Lipitor and anticipated slowing in the Medco division. However, despite patent expirations on five major drugs in 2000 and 2001, Merck should retain its premier status in the U.S. drug industry, aided by an impressive portfolio of high-quality drugs in key therapeutic classes and a strong lineup of new products. The recent divestiture of the Dupont joint venture and restructuring of the Astra/Merck unit will provide funds for R&D. Merck also recently boosted its dividend 20% and announced a $5 billion stock buyback program. The shares remain attractive for above-average appreciation.

Key Stock Statistics

S&P EPS Est. 1998	4.30	Tang. Bk. Value/Share	5.88
P/E on S&P Est. 1998	29.8	Beta	1.14
S&P EPS Est. 1999	4.95	Shareholders	247,300
Dividend Rate/Share	2.16	Market cap. (B)	$152.4
Shs. outstg. (M)	1190.9	Inst. holdings	53%
Avg. daily vol. (M)	3.594		

Value of $10,000 invested 5 years ago: $ 33,468

Fiscal Year Ending Dec. 31

	1998	1997	1996	1995	1994	1993
Revenues (Million $)						
1Q	6,059	5,568	4,530	3,817	3,514	2,380
2Q	6,470	5,909	4,909	4,136	3,792	2,574
3Q	—	5,928	4,983	4,171	3,792	2,544
4Q	—	6,232	5,406	4,557	3,872	3,001
Yr.	—	23,637	19,829	16,681	14,970	10,498
Earnings Per Share ($)						
1Q	0.95	0.82	0.70	0.61	0.54	0.54
2Q	1.07	0.93	0.80	0.69	0.61	0.15
3Q	E1.12	0.97	0.83	0.70	0.62	0.62
4Q	E1.16	1.01	0.87	0.70	0.61	0.56
Yr.	E4.30	3.74	3.12	2.70	2.38	1.87

Next earnings report expected: mid October

Dividend Data (Dividends have been paid since 1935.)

Amount ($)	Date Decl.	Ex-Div. Date	Stock of Record	Payment Date
0.450	Nov. 25	Dec. 03	Dec. 05	Jan. 02 '98
0.450	Feb. 24	Mar. 04	Mar. 06	Apr. 01 '98
0.450	May. 26	Jun. 03	Jun. 05	Jul. 01 '98
0.540	Jul. 28	Sep. 02	Sep. 04	Oct. 01 '98

A Division of The **McGraw·Hill** Companies

Business Summary - 04-AUG-98

Merck is the premier U.S.-based pharmaceutical company, manufacturing and marketing a wide range of prescription drugs in many therapeutic classes both in the U.S. and abroad. Foreign business is important, with operations outside of North America representing 25% of sales and 22% of profits in 1997. The company was originally founded in 1887 as a U.S. branch of E. Merck of Germany and grew significantly in subsequent years through aggressive new drug development and acquisition programs.

The company is the undisputed leader in the vast market for high-margin cardiovascular drugs, with five drugs generating aggregate sales of over $9 billion in 1997. Key products include cholesterol-lowering agents such as Zocor (sales of $3.6 billion) and Mevacor ($1.1 billion); and treatments for high blood pressure and congestive heart failure like Vasotec/Vaseretic ($2.5 billion), Prinivil/Prinzide ($585 million), and Cozaar/Hyzaar ($681 million), the first of a new class of antihypertensives. Merck has an estimated 40% share of the rapidly expanding worldwide cholesterol reduction market and about one-third of the moderately growing hypertension-angina market.

Other drugs exhibiting notable strength include Fosamax for osteoporosis, whose sales are being helped by recent FDA approval to market the drug for the prevention of osteoporosis (a bone-thinning disease that affects postmenopausal women); and Crixivan, a protease inhibitor AIDS drug, which in combination with other agents has been able to decrease HIV in the bloodstream to undetectable levels. Other key drugs include Pepcid antiulcer agent and Proscar for enlarged prostates.

The huge success of Merck's drugs has enabled it to support a $1.7 billion R&D program, which promises to spawn an ongoing stream of blockbuster drugs in the years ahead. Key products in late-stage clinical trials include treatments for migraine, asthma, and unstable angina. Merck recently discovered a new class of anti-infectives aimed at drug-resistant bacteria, which could revolutionize the antibiotics market.

Through a venture with Astra AB of Sweden, Merck sells Prilosec, a leading antiulcer drug. Over-the-counter medications such as Pepcid AC are offered through a venture with Johnson & Johnson. In August 1997, Merck combined its animal health units with those of Rhone-Poulenc S.A., forming the world's leading animal health business. The new firm, Merial, is owned 50/50 by Merck and Rhone-Poulenc. Merck-Medco Managed Care provides mail-order drug and related services to over 51 million people.

Per Share Data ($)

(Year Ended Dec. 31)	1997	1996	1995	1994	1993	1992	1991	1990	1989	1988
Tangible Bk. Val.	4.89	4.34	4.00	3.15	2.69	4.24	4.06	3.12	2.78	2.23
Cash Flow	4.57	3.80	3.24	2.92	2.20	2.37	2.04	1.72	1.43	1.18
Earnings	3.74	3.20	2.70	2.38	1.87	2.12	1.83	1.52	1.26	1.02
Dividends	1.74	1.48	1.28	1.16	1.06	0.96	0.79	0.67	0.57	0.46
Payout Ratio	47%	46%	47%	49%	57%	45%	43%	44%	45%	45%
Prices - High	108⅛	84¼	67¼	39½	44⅛	56⅝	55¾	30⅜	27	19⅞
- Low	78	56½	36⅜	28⅛	28⅝	40½	27⅜	22⅜	18¾	16
P/E Ratio - High	29	26	25	17	24	27	30	20	21	20
- Low	21	18	13	12	15	19	15	15	15	16

Income Statement Analysis (Million $)

	1997	1996	1995	1994	1993	1992	1991	1990	1989	1988
Revs.	23,637	19,829	16,681	14,970	10,498	9,663	8,603	7,672	6,550	5,939
Oper. Inc.	6,701	5,912	5,262	5,075	4,262	3,782	3,352	2,883	2,443	2,056
Depr.	1,034	731	667	670	377	290	243	231	206	189
Int. Exp.	130	139	99	124	84.7	72.7	68.7	69.8	53.2	76.5
Pretax Inc.	6,594	5,685	4,889	4,509	3,153	3,596	3,192	2,730	2,321	1,915
Eff. Tax Rate	28%	29%	30%	32%	30%	31%	33%	34%	34%	35%
Net Inc.	4,614	3,881	3,335	2,997	2,166	2,447	2,122	1,781	1,495	1,207

Balance Sheet & Other Fin. Data (Million $)

	1997	1996	1995	1994	1993	1992	1991	1990	1989	1988
Cash	1,125	2,181	3,349	2,270	1,542	1,094	1,412	1,197	1,144	1,550
Curr. Assets	8,213	7,727	8,618	6,922	5,735	4,400	4,311	3,766	3,410	3,389
Total Assets	25,812	24,293	23,832	21,857	19,928	11,086	9,499	8,030	6,757	6,127
Curr. Liab.	5,569	4,829	5,690	5,449	5,896	3,617	2,814	2,827	1,907	1,909
LT Debt	1,347	1,156	1,373	1,146	1,121	496	494	124	118	143
Common Eqty.	12,613	11,971	11,736	11,139	10,022	5,003	4,916	3,834	3,521	2,856
Total Cap.	16,645	15,437	13,109	14,735	12,650	6,215	6,296	4,764	4,459	3,878
Cap. Exp.	1.4	1,197	1,006	1,009	1,013	1,067	1,042	671	433	373
Cash Flow	5,648	4,612	4,002	3,667	2,543	2,737	2,364	2,013	1,702	1,396
Curr. Ratio	1.5	1.6	1.5	1.3	1.0	1.2	1.5	1.3	1.8	1.8
% LT Debt of Cap.	8.1	7.5	10.5	7.8	8.9	8.0	7.8	2.6	2.6	3.7
% Net Inc.of Revs.	19.5	19.6	20.0	20.0	20.6	25.3	24.7	23.2	22.8	20.3
% Ret. on Assets	18.4	16.1	14.6	14.4	13.5	23.9	24.2	24.3	23.3	20.4
% Ret. on Equity	37.5	33.1	29.2	28.4	27.9	49.6	48.5	48.9	47.0	48.4

Data as orig. reptd.; bef. results of disc. opers. and/or spec. items. Per share data adj. for stk. divs. as of ex-div. date. Bold denotes diluted EPS (FASB 128). E-Estimated. NA-Not Available. NM-Not Meaningful. NR-Not Ranked.

Office—One Merck Drive, P.O. Box 100, Whitehouse Station, NJ 08889. **Tel**—(908) 423-1000. **Website**—http://www.merck.com **Chrmn, Pres & CEO**—R. V. Gilmartin. **Secy**—C. A. Colbert. **VP & CFO**—J. C. Lewent. **Treas**—C. Dorsa. **Investor Contact**—Laura Jordan (908-423-5185). **Dirs**—H. B. Atwater Jr., Sir Derek Birkin, L. A. Bossidy, W. G. Bowen, J. B. Cole, C. K. Davis, L. C. Elam, C. E. Exley Jr., R. V. Gilmartin, W. N. Kelley, E. M. Scolnick, S. O. Thier, D. Weatherstone. **Transfer Agent & Registrar**—Norwest Bank Minnesota. **Incorporated**—in New Jersey in 1934. **Empl**— 53,800. **S&P Analyst:** H. B. Saftlas

12-SEP-98 Industry: Publishing

Summary: Meredith derives the bulk of its earnings from publishing magazines (primarily Better Homes and Gardens and Ladies' Home Journal) and ownership of 11 TV stations.

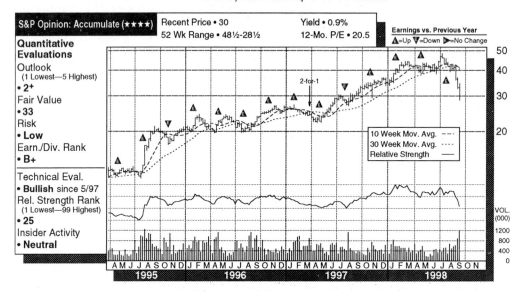

S&P Opinion: Accumulate (★★★★)

Recent Price • 30	Yield • 0.9%
52 Wk Range • 48½-28½	12-Mo. P/E • 20.5

Quantitative Evaluations

Outlook
(1 Lowest—5 Highest)
• **2+**

Fair Value
• **33**

Risk
• **Low**

Earn./Div. Rank
• **B+**

Technical Eval.
• **Bullish** since 5/97

Rel. Strength Rank
(1 Lowest—99 Highest)
• **25**

Insider Activity
• **Neutral**

10 Week Mov. Avg. ---
30 Week Mov. Avg. ·····
Relative Strength —

Earnings vs. Previous Year
▲=Up ▼=Down ▶=No Change

Overview - 08-JUN-98

Higher revenues expected through FY 99 (Jun.) will stem from stronger contributions from magazines and growth in broadcast advertising, boosted by the purchase of four TV stations from First Media in the first quarter of FY 98. Aggressive expansion in licensing and joint marketing ventures will continue. Book publishing operations are expected to improve, and real estate gains are also continuing. Ongoing revenues will continue to benefit from favorable demographics, low interest rates, and a healthy economy. Rising paper prices going forward are expected to exert only moderate pressure on operating margins. Growth in net income will be tempered, however, by costs of launching news operations at three TV stations, and increased spending on magazine promotions and start-ups.

Valuation - 08-JUN-98

With demographic trends strongly in its favor, MDP is benefiting from its position as the largest publisher of shelter magazines. Continuing expansion in licensing and joint marketing ventures, and stronger contributions from highly profitable television broadcasting enhance the longer-term outlook for revenues and margins. With the September 1997 acquisition of four TV stations, broadcast earnings equal those in publishing. The stock, which has been in a healthy uptrend for several years, was recently selling at 29X the $1.47 EPS we are projecting for FY 98 and 25X the $1.70 estimated for FY 99. Excluding unusual expense items, projected earnings gains would be in the high 20s. We believe MDP will continue to outperform the general market given the favorable outlook for revenues and earnings, as well as escalating market values of the company's assets.

Key Stock Statistics

S&P EPS Est. 1998	NA	Tang. Bk. Value/Share	NM
P/E on S&P Est. 1998	NA	Beta	0.92
S&P EPS Est. 1999	1.70	Shareholders	3,300
Dividend Rate/Share	0.28	Market cap. (B)	$ 1.2
Shs. outstg. (M)	52.8	Inst. holdings	55%
Avg. daily vol. (M)	0.171		

Value of $10,000 invested 5 years ago: $ 47,346

Fiscal Year Ending Jun. 30

	1998	1997	1996	1995	1994	1993
Revenues (Million $)						
1Q	230.9	199.2	206.6	200.2	182.3	177.0
2Q	248.9	209.8	216.1	214.9	204.6	190.0
3Q	260.2	223.0	219.4	230.4	205.8	199.0
4Q	270.0	223.2	225.0	239.1	206.8	202.6
Yr.	1,010	855.2	867.1	884.5	799.5	768.9
Earnings Per Share ($)						
1Q	0.27	0.22	0.17	0.20	0.06	0.06
2Q	**0.40**	0.31	0.28	0.16	0.20	0.08
3Q	**0.37**	0.33	0.24	0.18	0.13	0.09
4Q	**0.42**	0.36	0.27	0.18	0.09	0.09
Yr.	**1.46**	1.22	0.97	0.72	0.47	0.30

Next earnings report expected: NA

Dividend Data (Dividends have been paid since 1930.)

Amount ($)	Date Decl.	Ex-Div. Date	Stock of Record	Payment Date
0.065	Nov. 10	Nov. 25	Nov. 28	Dec. 15 '97
0.070	Feb. 02	Feb. 25	Feb. 27	Mar. 13 '98
0.070	May. 13	May. 27	May. 29	Jun. 15 '98
0.070	Aug. 12	Aug. 27	Aug. 31	Sep. 15 '98

A Division of The McGraw·Hill Companies

Business Summary - 08-JUN-98

This is an exciting time for Meredith Corp., a diversified media company with a long tradition of service to the home and family market. Operations primarily consist of publishing, broadcasting, and real estate. Branded licensing activities are also growing in importance.

Meredith goes way back. The company was founded in 1902 as an agricultural publisher, then expanded to include mass audience and special interest publications. Today, Meredith publishes 21 subscription-based magazines, including Better Homes and Gardens, Ladies' Home Journal, Successful Farming, WOOD, Country Home, Traditional Home and Midwest Living. Special-interest publications include 41 home/gardening/lifestyle products. MDP publishes 278 home and family service books, which are primarily sold through retail distribution outlets.

The company has been active in making optimal use of its famous trademarks. Retail brand licensing efforts began in 1994 when a license was granted Wal-Mart Stores to operate Better Homes and Gardens Garden Centers in all of its U.S. stores. In 1996, Wal-Mart began selling Better Homes and Gardens Floral & Na-

ture Crafts branded merchandise. Multicom Publishing is licensed to develop and publish CD-ROM titles based on MDP's editorial products. Reader's Digest Association is licensed to market MDP-trademarked products. In FY 97 (Jun.), the company contracted with third parties for the production and syndication of one year of a Better Homes and Gardens television program, which began airing in September 1997.

In 1948, Meredith entered the television broadcasting business. Today, the company owns 11 network-affiliated TV stations, including four acquired in September 1997 from First Media Television for $435 million. TV stations include KCTV (CBS), Kansas City, MO; KPHO (CBS), Phoenix, AZ; WNEM (CBS), Bay City-Saginaw-Flint, MI; WSMV (NBC), Nashville, TN; WOGX (FOX), Ocala/Gainesville, FL; KVVU (FOX), Las Vegas NV; WOFL (FOX), Orlando-Daytona Beach, FL; KPDX (FOX), Portland, OR; WHNS (FOX), Greenville, SC-Asheville, NC; KFXO (FOX), Bend, OR; and WFSB (CBS), Hartford-New Haven, CT.

MDP also operates a national real estate marketing service that licenses over 800 member real estate firms to exclusive territories in the U.S., Canada, Puerto Rico and abroad.

Per Share Data ($)

(Year Ended Jun. 30)	1998	1997	1996	1995	1994	1993	1992	1991	1990	1989
Tangible Bk. Val.	NA	1.01	NM	-3.40	-1.55	-1.44	1.46	2.44	1.78	1.97
Cash Flow	NA	1.95	1.75	1.38	1.08	0.83	0.29	0.61	0.23	0.64
Earnings	1.46	1.22	0.97	0.72	0.48	0.30	0.02	0.34	-0.02	0.44
Dividends	0.27	0.24	0.21	0.18	0.17	0.16	0.16	0.16	0.16	0.16
Payout Ratio	18%	20%	22%	25%	36%	51%	NM	47%	NM	36%
Prices - High	48½	37	26⅞	21¼	12¼	10⅞	7	7⅝	9	9⅞
- Low	34⅝	22⅛	19⅝	11⅜	9¾	6⅝	5½	5⅜	5⅛	7½
P/E Ratio - High	33	30	28	30	26	36	NM	22	NM	22
- Low	24	18	20	16	20	22	NM	16	NM	17

Income Statement Analysis (Million $)

	1998	1997	1996	1995	1994	1993	1992	1991	1990	1989
Revs.	NA	855	867	885	800	769	718	748	735	792
Oper. Inc.	NA	155	142	112	91.3	73.3	40.1	37.1	57.5	56.5
Depr.	NA	40.4	44.1	36.4	34.3	32.4	17.5	18.1	18.1	15.1
Int. Exp.	NA	1.3	5.5	15.1	5.5	9.9	0.7	2.9	4.0	5.0
Pretax Inc.	NA	118	100	77.1	54.2	33.1	1.8	37.3	-0.7	52.1
Eff. Tax Rate	NA	43%	45%	48%	50%	48%	47%	39%	NM	36%
Net Inc.	NA	67.6	54.7	39.8	27.2	18.6	1.0	22.8	-1.4	33.2

Balance Sheet & Other Fin. Data (Million $)

	1998	1997	1996	1995	1994	1993	1992	1991	1990	1989
Cash	NA	125	13.8	17.0	50.0	40.0	84.0	128	5.0	6.0
Curr. Assets	NA	337	211	262	298	287	223	309	201	191
Total Assets	NA	761	734	882	864	901	593	594	617	667
Curr. Liab.	NA	278	280	288	280	282	124	148	186	137
LT Debt	NA	Nil	35.0	166	127	132	38.0	Nil	0.3	21.1
Common Eqty.	NA	327	262	241	258	284	301	343	310	367
Total Cap.	NA	350	322	462	460	487	360	363	328	423
Cap. Exp.	NA	23.3	29.9	24.7	20.8	16.1	6.7	9.1	12.3	9.7
Cash Flow	NA	108	99	76.3	61.5	51.0	18.5	41.0	16.7	48.3
Curr. Ratio	NA	1.2	0.8	0.9	1.1	0.8	1.8	2.1	1.1	1.4
% LT Debt of Cap.	NA	Nil	10.9	36.0	27.6	27.1	10.6	Nil	0.1	5.0
% Net Inc.of Revs.	NA	7.9	6.3	4.5	3.4	2.4	0.1	3.1	NM	4.2
% Ret. on Assets	NA	9.0	7.4	4.6	3.0	2.6	0.2	3.9	NM	5.1
% Ret. on Equity	NA	23.0	21.7	16.0	10.0	6.6	0.3	7.3	NM	9.2

Data as orig. reptd.; bef. results of disc. opers. and/or spec. items. Per share data adj. for stk. divs. as of ex-div. date. Bold denotes diluted EPS (FASB 128). E-Estimated. NA-Not Available. NM-Not Meaningful. NR-Not Ranked.

Office—1716 Locust St., Des Moines, IA 50309-3023. **Tel**—(800) 284-4236. **Website**—http://home-and-family.com. **Chrmn, Pres & CEO**—W. T. Kerr. **VP-Secy**—T. L. Slaughter. **VP-CFO**—S. M. Lacy. **Investor Contact**—Jennifer S. McCoy. **Dirs**—H. M. Baum, M. S. Coleman, P. M. Grieve, F. B. Henry, J. W. Johnson, W. T. Kerr, R. E. Lee, R. S. Levitt, P. A. Marineau, E. T. Meredith III, N. L. Reding, J. D. Rehm, S. Uehling. **Transfer Agent & Registrar**—The First National Bank of Boston c/o Boston Equiserve, L.P. **Incorporated**—in Iowa in 1905. **Empl**—0. **S&P Analyst:** William H. Donald

STANDARD &POOR'S
STOCK REPORTS

Merrill Lynch

1479

NYSE Symbol **MER**

In S&P 500

12-SEP-98 | **Industry:** Investment Banking/ Brokerage | **Summary:** Merrill Lynch is one of the largest and most diversified securities firms in the world.

S&P Opinion: No Opinion	Recent Price • 56	Yield • 1.7%
	52 Wk Range • 109⅛-51½	12-Mo. P/E • 11.1

Quantitative Evaluations

Outlook
(1 Lowest—5 Highest)
• **1⁻**

Fair Value
• **55**

Risk
• **Average**

Earn./Div. Rank
• **A-**

Technical Eval.
• **Bearish** since 8/98

Rel. Strength Rank
(1 Lowest—99 Highest)
• **13**

Insider Activity
• **Neutral**

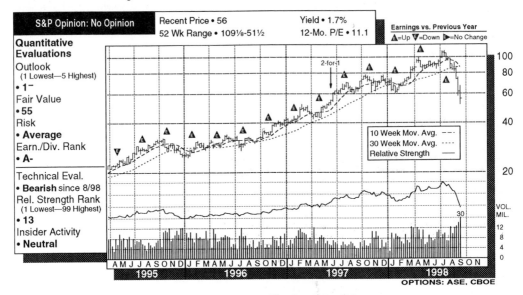

Earnings vs. Previous Year
▲=Up ▼=Down ▶=No Change

10 Week Mov. Avg. ---
30 Week Mov. Avg. ·····
Relative Strength —

2-for-1

OPTIONS: ASE, CBOE

Overview - 31-JUL-98

Profits are likely to improve slightly in 1999 on top of 1998's expected solid performance. Baby boomers appear to be aggressively saving for retirement, a development that should continue to bolster commission revenues. A sub-category of investment banking, advisory services, is benefiting from a high rate of consolidation in a number of industries. Trading income, which depends in part on the slope of the yield curve, could weaken slightly. The contribution from asset management operations is expected to rise. Higher expenses are anticipated, reflecting modest headcount growth. The company's use of variable compensation programs provides some cushion against market downturns. Cash earnings exceed reported earnings by a modest amount due to the amortization of goodwill resulting from the Mercury acquisition.

Valuation - 31-JUL-98

The stock recently hit a record high, a development we attribute to investor speculation about a potential stock split as well as recognition that the company has outperformed many of its peers in the long-standing bull market. Some investors may also have given credence to rumors Merrill was in merger discussions with a large financial firm. Our view is that management wishes to chart its own course, and that Merrill is more likely to be a buyer than a seller. Price to tangible book value has historically been the preferred valuation measure to use in assessing a brokerage stock, but given the company's relatively stable financial results, large asset management operations, and high returns, the P/E approach also has relevance. The stock has historically traded at a discount in terms of its P/E ratio to the overall market.

Key Stock Statistics

S&P EPS Est. 1998	5.10	Tang. Bk. Value/Share	11.19
P/E on S&P Est. 1998	11.0	Beta	2.07
S&P EPS Est. 1999	5.15	Shareholders	13,300
Dividend Rate/Share	0.96	Market cap. (B)	$ 19.5
Shs. outstg. (M)	348.3	Inst. holdings	57%
Avg. daily vol. (M)	4.509		

Value of $10,000 invested 5 years ago: $ 41,488

Fiscal Year Ending Dec. 31

	1998	1997	1996	1995	1994	1993
Revenues (Million $)						
1Q	9,166	7,451	6,019	5,204	4,739	3,959
2Q	9,381	8,011	6,190	5,585	4,480	3,963
3Q	—	8,146	6,201	5,431	4,530	4,140
4Q	—	8,123	6,601	5,293	4,484	4,526
Yr.	—	31,731	25,011	21,513	18,233	16,588
Earnings Per Share ($)						
1Q	**1.30**	**1.17**	1.01	0.54	0.84	0.76
2Q	**1.33**	**1.25**	1.09	0.70	0.59	0.76
3Q	**E1.25**	**1.25**	0.84	0.73	0.55	0.79
4Q	**E1.25**	**1.17**	1.15	0.74	0.38	0.77
Yr.	**E5.10**	**4.83**	**4.11**	2.72	2.38	3.07

Next earnings report expected: mid October

Dividend Data (Dividends have been paid since 1961.)

Amount ($)	Date Decl.	Ex-Div. Date	Stock of Record	Payment Date
0.200	Oct. 27	Nov. 05	Nov. 07	Nov. 26 '97
0.200	Jan. 26	Feb. 04	Feb. 06	Feb. 25 '98
0.240	Apr. 14	Apr. 29	May. 01	May. 20 '98
0.240	Jul. 27	Aug. 05	Aug. 07	Aug. 26 '98

 A Division of The McGraw·Hill Companies

STANDARD
&POOR'S
STOCK REPORTS

Merrill Lynch & Co., Inc.

1479

12-SEP-98

Business Summary - 31-JUL-98

Merrill Lynch is one of the world's leading financial management and advisory companies with offices in 45 countries and client assets of $1.4 trillion. Images that capture the essence of this company's business activities are: a trader watching a computer screen while talking to a client; an investment banker meeting with the CEO of a Fortune 500 company to discuss a takeover defense; a registered representative advising a client to set up a tax-deferred annuity; and a group of portfolio managers listening to an economist discuss the outlook for interest rates. Revenues were obtained as follows in the past two years:

	1997	1996
Commissions	30%	29%
Interest & dividends (net)	6%	8%
Principal transactions	24%	26%
Investment banking	18%	15%
Asset management	18%	17%
Other	4%	5%

Through more than 13,300 Financial Consultants in about 690 offices throughout the U. S., Merrill Lynch's U.S. private client group provides a wide array of financial products and services, including trade execution, retirement planning, first mortgage loans, and home equity- and securities-based lines of credit. The company's financial consultants have developed strong rela-

tionships with over four million households, ranging from high net worth individuals to young, "up-and-coming" clients, as well as with small and mid-sized businesses and various financial institutions. An important resource for Financial Consultants is the Financial Foundation, a sophisticated planning tool that develops tailored-made financial plans for individuals based on their assets, liabilities and other important factors.

Merrill is distinctive for its large in-house mutual fund operations. With $446 billion in assets under management, this operation, if it were a stand-alone business, would be more than four times as large as T. Rowe Price. Merrill's asset management unit generates substantial profits, reflecting the combination of an average fee we estimate at some 0.60% collected on a huge balance of funds, and expenses that amount to little more than rent for office space and salaries for the employees.

Investment bankers purchase new securities from issuers and resell them to dealers and the public, earning a spread between the purchase and selling price. Clients can be companies selling stock for the first time (initial public offerings), corporations raising additional equity capital (secondary offerings), local governments selling debt (municipal or tax-free bonds), or various others. Investment bankers in the company's advisory area, which is a highly profitable unit, offer advice on mergers and acquisitions, divestitures and the like.

Per Share Data ($)

(Year Ended Dec. 31)	1997	1996	1995	1994	1993	1992	1991	1990	1989	1988
Tangible Bk. Val.	7.31	18.93	15.74	13.84	11.63	9.77	8.03	6.73	6.89	8.07
Cash Flow	4.84	5.29	NA	NA	NA	NA	NA	NA	NA	NA
Earnings	4.83	4.10	2.72	2.38	3.07	2.09	1.50	0.40	-0.59	1.07
Dividends	0.75	0.58	0.51	0.45	0.35	0.29	0.25	0.25	0.25	0.25
Payout Ratio	16%	14%	19%	19%	11%	14%	17%	63%	NM	23%
Prices - High	78⅛	42⅝	32⅜	27⅞	25⅝	16¾	15¼	6⅞	9¼	7⅛
- Low	39¼	24¾	17⅜	16⅛	14	11⅛	4¾	4	5⅞	5½
P/E Ratio - High	16	10	12	10	8	8	10	17	NM	7
- Low	8	6	6	7	5	5	3	10	NM	5

Income Statement Analysis (Million $)

	1997	1996	1995	1994	1993	1992	1991	1990	1989	1988
Commissions	4,667	3,786	3,126	2,871	2,894	2,400	2,138	1,699	1,799	1,602
Int. Inc.	17,087	12,899	12,221	9,578	7,099	5,807	5,761	5,166	5,489	4,066
Total Revs.	9,977	25,011	21,513	18,233	16,588	13,428	12,363	11,213	11,335	10,547
Int. Exp.	16,109	11,895	11,248	8,609	6,030	4,835	5,106	4,748	5,074	3,634
Pretax Inc.	3,003	2,566	1,811	1,730	2,425	1,621	1,017	282	-157	639
Eff. Tax Rate	37%	37%	39%	41%	43%	41%	32%	32%	NM	28%
Net Inc.	1,906	1,619	1,114	1,017	1,394	952	696	192	-216	463

Balance Sheet & Other Fin. Data (Million $)

	1997	1996	1995	1994	1993	1992	1991	1990	1989	1988
Total Assets	292,819	213,016	176,857	163,749	152,910	107,024	86,259	68,130	63,942	64,403
Cash Items	17,416	9,003	8,503	7,265	5,853	4,676	4,429	5,829	4,360	4,273
Receivables	114,315	116,222	95,865	91,917	82,516	57,084	43,075	32,260	31,645	34,852
Secs. Owned	106,778	75,524	60,103	52,739	51,549	31,669	24,908	17,284	15,721	19,040
Sec. Borrowed	122,725	102,002	86,363	78,304	79,632	51,180	38,698	27,341	28,558	34,390
Due Brokers & Cust.	20,631	15,000	17,757	16,247	18,434	12,290	13,184	13,219	10,064	8,802
Other Liabs.	98,044	62,855	49,256	48,517	35,899	28,114	22,595	18,002	15,272	11,443
Capitalization:										
Debt	166,442	26,721	17,757	14,863	13,469	10,871	7,964	6,342	6,897	6,283
Equity	7,904	6,273	5,522	5,199	5,292	4,269	3,518	2,925	2,851	3,184
Total	52,046	32,994	23,481	20,681	18,955	15,140	11,483	9,267	10,048	9,768
% Return On Revs.	19.1	6.5	5.2	5.6	8.4	7.1	5.6	1.7	NM	4.4
% Ret. on Assets	0.8	0.8	0.7	0.6	1.0	0.8	0.8	0.3	NM	0.8
% Ret. on Equity	26.3	26.8	20.8	18.6	27.3	22.0	20.8	5.8	NM	14.8

Data as orig. reptd.; bef. results of disc. opers. and/or spec. items. Per share data adj. for stk. divs. as of ex-div. date. Bold denotes diluted EPS (FASB 128). E-Estimated. NA-Not Available. NM-Not Meaningful. NR-Not Ranked.

Office—World Financial Center, North Tower, New York, NY 10281-1123. **Tel**—(212) 449-1000. **Chrmn & CEO**—D. H. Komansky. **Pres & COO**—H. M. Allison Jr. **EVP & CFO**—E. S. O'Neal. **Secy**—G. T. Russo. **Dirs**—H. M. Allison Jr., W. O. Bourke, W. H. Clark, J. K. Conway, S. L. Hammerman, E. H. Harbison Jr., G. B. Harvey, W. R. Hoover, D. H. Komansky, R. P. Luciano, D. K. Newbigging, A. L. Peters, J. J. Phelan Jr., J. L. Steffens, W. L. Weiss. **Transfer Agents & Registrars**—Co.'s office; ChaseMellon Shareholder Services, NYC. **Incorporated**—in Delaware in 1973. **Empl**— 60,300. **S&P Analyst:** Paul L. Huberman, CFA

STANDARD &POOR'S

STOCK REPORTS

Fred Meyer

924J

NYSE Symbol **FMY**

In S&P 500

12-SEP-98

Industry:
Retail (General Merchandise)

Summary: This retailer, operating mainly in the Pacific Northwest, offers a wide range of food, general merchandise and jewelry through one-stop, multidepartment and specialty stores.

Quantitative Evaluations

Outlook
(1 Lowest—5 Highest)
• **1⁻**

Fair Value
• **34¼**

Risk
• **Average**

Earn./Div. Rank
• **B**

Technical Eval.
• **Bearish** since 9/98

Rel. Strength Rank
(1 Lowest—99 Highest)
• **66**

Insider Activity
• **Unfavorable**

Recent Price • 38¾
52 Wk Range • 51-25

Yield • Nil
12-Mo. P/E • NM

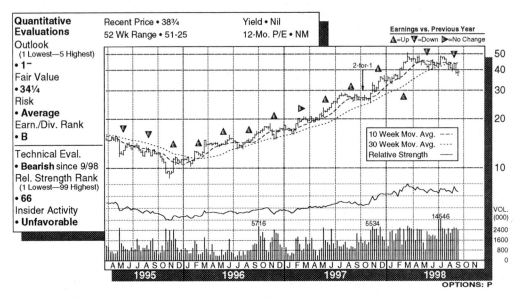

Earnings vs. Previous Year
▲=Up ▼=Down ▷=No Change

2-for-1

10 Week Mov. Avg. ---
30 Week Mov. Avg. ····
Relative Strength —

VOL. (000)

OPTIONS: P

Business Profile - 25-MAR-98

In March 1998, Fred Meyer completed mergers with Quality Food Centers, Inc. (NYSE: XQ) and Ralphs Grocery Co. in two separate transactions, creating a $15 billion multi-regional supermarket chain. The combined company is one of the largest supermarket companies in the United States, with approximately 88,000 employees and more than 800 food stores in 14 states, with the number one market share in Los Angeles, Seattle, Salt Lake City, Las Vegas and Albuquerque, and the number two share in Phoenix and Portland. As a result of the mergers, the company refinanced the majority of its debt at an annual interest rate of about 7%.

Operational Review - 25-MAR-98

Based on a preliminary report, net sales in FY 98 (Jan.) advanced 47%, reflecting the acquisition of Smith's Food & Drug Centers, Inc. and comparable-store growth of 7.4%. Comparable-store food sales increased 6.6%, while comparable nonfood sales rose 8.6%. Margins widened, and operating income rose 94%. Following 92% higher interest expense and taxes at 40.6%, versus 38.0%, net income was up 77% to $103,304,000 ($1.46 a share, on 27% more shares) from $58,545,000 ($1.05). FY 98 results exclude an extraordinary charge of $91,210,000 ($1.29) for the early retirement of debt.

Stock Performance - 11-SEP-98

In the past 30 trading days, FMY's shares have declined 11%, compared to a 10% fall in the S&P 500. Average trading volume for the past five days was 663,275 shares, compared with the 40-day moving average of 627,556 shares.

Key Stock Statistics

Dividend Rate/Share	Nil	Shareholders	1,300
Shs. outstg. (M)	154.0	Market cap. (B)	$ 6.0
Avg. daily vol. (M)	0.712	Inst. holdings	72%
Tang. Bk. Value/Share	3.89		
Beta	0.66		

Value of $10,000 invested 5 years ago: $ 24,701

Fiscal Year Ending Jan. 31

	1999	1998	1997	1996	1995	1994
Revenues (Million $)						
1Q	4,040	1,194	1,040	935.4	932.0	852.1
2Q	3,505	957.0	853.9	774.7	737.3	674.7
3Q	—	1,460	835.1	749.0	626.8	644.5
4Q	—	1,870	995.8	963.7	832.0	807.8
Yr.	—	5,481	3,725	3,429	3,128	2,979
Earnings Per Share ($)						
1Q	**-0.66**	0.24	0.17	0.06	0.28	0.25
2Q	**0.06**	0.34	0.27	0.19	0.34	0.30
3Q	—	0.22	0.12	-0.04	-0.64	0.17
4Q	—	**0.56**	0.52	0.52	0.15	0.53
Yr.	—	**1.46**	1.04	0.54	0.13	1.25

Next earnings report expected: early December

Dividend Data

No cash dividends have been paid.

*A Division of The **McGraw·Hill** Companies*

Business Summary - 25-MAR-98

Fred Meyer traveled across the U.S. from Brooklyn at age 19, and, when he opened his first store in Portland, OR, in 1922, he became a pioneer in the field of one-stop-shopping. Today, the company he founded, Fred Meyer, Inc. (FMY), is a leading regional retailer of a wide range of food, apparel, fine jewelry and products for the home. Following its recent mergers with Quality Food Centers and Ralphs Grocery Company, the company now operates more than 800 stores in 11 Western states. It also operates 259 fine jewelry stores in malls under the Fred Meyer Jewelers, Merksamer Jewelers and Fox's Jewelers banners, and five smaller specialty stores.

Larger one-stop shopping stores contain the most square footage, and are located in six states, four of which (Oregon, Washington, Idaho and Utah) are expected to grow faster than the U.S. average over the next 10 years. With a large percentage of stores situated in these states, the company's future expansion plans will focus there. FMY's primary growth strategy is to continue increasing its position in the region by opening new stores in current markets, primarily in or near well populated residential areas. Five new stores scheduled for FY 98 (Jan.) were all completed in the first quarter.

The company believes it is the only multi-department store with significant food departments in most of its markets, and feels that having a food department increases the shopping frequency of area residents, builds customer loyalty, and lets non-food department generate higher levels of sales through increased customer traffic. The food business generated 41% of total sales in FY 97.

In June 1997, the company acquired Fox Jewelry, with 44 Fox Jewelry stores located in malls in six states. More than half of the Fox stores are located in Michigan and Wisconsin, with the others in Indiana, Illinois, Iowa and Ohio. The acquisition raised to about 255 the number of company jewelry stores, in 18 states.

In September 1997, the company merged with Smith's Food & Drug Centers (SFD), a regional supermarket chain with 150 stores operating in the Intermountain and Southwest regions, in exchange for $2.0 billion in stock and assumed debt.

In March 1998, FMY completed mergers with Quality Food Centers and Ralphs Grocery. Fred Meyer exchanged 1.9 common shares (subject to adjustment) for each of Quality Food's 21 million shares, and acquired Ralphs Grocery's parent, Food 4 Less, for 21,700,000 common shares.

Per Share Data ($)

(Year Ended Jan. 31)	1998	1997	1996	1995	1994	1993	1992	1991	1990	1989
Tangible Bk. Val.	3.89	10.73	10.61	10.04	9.88	8.69	7.18	6.18	5.44	5.61
Cash Flow	3.70	3.13	2.42	1.69	2.50	2.33	1.98	1.53	0.63	1.45
Earnings	1.46	1.04	0.54	0.13	1.25	1.10	0.90	0.69	-0.14	0.75
Dividends	Nil	Nil	Nil	Nil	Nil	Nil	Nil	Nil	Nil	Nil
Payout Ratio	Nil	Nil	Nil	Nil	Nil	Nil	Nil	Nil	Nil	Nil
Cal. Yrs.	1997	1996	1995	1994	1993	1992	1991	1990	1989	1988
Prices - High	37	18⁷⁄₈	16³⁄₄	21¼	19¼	17	13¹⁄₂	9³⁄₈	11¹⁄₂	8⁵⁄₈
- Low	16¼	10¼	8³⁄₄	14⁵⁄₈	14	11³⁄₈	5⁵⁄₈	5	7⁷⁄₈	5³⁄₈
P/E Ratio - High	25	18	31	NM	15	15	15	14	NM	12
- Low	11	10	16	NM	11	10	6	7	NM	7

Income Statement Analysis (Million $)

	1998	1997	1996	1995	1994	1993	1992	1991	1990	1989
Revs.	5,481	3,725	3,429	3,128	2,979	2,854	2,703	2,476	2,285	2,074
Oper. Inc.	407	250	196	145	213	175	146	111	91.0	103
Depr.	158	117	107	89.5	70.7	67.3	54.5	41.4	38.2	34.0
Int. Exp.	75.5	40.3	40.6	31.8	24.1	12.1	19.4	21.9	19.8	9.6
Pretax Inc.	174	94.4	48.8	12.0	121	96.2	71.0	51.5	-13.1	56.9
Eff. Tax Rate	41%	38%	38%	38%	41%	37%	36%	35%	NM	36%
Net Inc.	103	58.5	30.3	7.2	70.9	60.6	45.2	33.6	-6.8	36.7

Balance Sheet & Other Fin. Data (Million $)

	1998	1997	1996	1995	1994	1993	1992	1991	1990	1989
Cash	72.6	48.8	41.8	34.9	34.1	31.9	30.0	29.0	24.9	19.0
Curr. Assets	1,415	738	633	642	592	530	487	465	452	408
Total Assets	4,431	1,693	1,672	1,563	1,319	1,079	973	906	797	689
Curr. Liab.	1,000	505	350	392	383	345	313	305	281	258
LT Debt	1,887	535	670	554	336	212	259	251	206	116
Common Eqty.	1,351	567	571	539	528	450	335	285	252	258
Total Cap.	3,278	1,137	1,272	1,115	882	679	611	550	467	401
Cap. Exp.	269	147	236	284	250	145	106	164	135	101
Cash Flow	261	175	137	97.0	142	128	100	74.9	31.3	70.7
Curr. Ratio	1.4	1.5	1.8	1.6	1.5	1.5	1.6	1.5	1.6	1.6
% LT Debt of Cap.	57.6	47.1	53.7	49.7	38.1	31.3	42.4	45.5	44.2	28.9
% Net Inc.of Revs.	1.9	1.6	0.9	0.2	2.4	2.1	1.7	1.4	NM	1.8
% Ret. on Assets	3.4	3.5	1.9	0.5	5.8	5.6	4.8	3.9	NM	5.6
% Ret. on Equity	10.8	10.3	5.5	1.3	14.3	14.7	14.5	12.5	NM	14.4

Data as orig. reptd.; bef. results of disc. opers. and/or spec. items. Per share data adj. for stk. divs. as of ex-div. date. Bold denotes diluted EPS (FASB 128). E-Estimated. NA-Not Available. NM-Not Meaningful. NR-Not Ranked.

Office—3800 S.E. 22nd Ave., Portland, OR 97202. **Tel**—(503) 232-8844. **Website**—http://www.fredmeyer.com **Chrmn & CEO**—R. G. Miller. **SVP-Fin, CFO & Investor Contact**—David R. Jessick (503-797-7900). **SVP & Secy**—R. A. Cooke. **Dirs**—V. A. Bull, J. J. Curran, A. M. Gleason, D. J. Johnson, R. S. Meier, R. G. Miller, S. R. Rogel. **Transfer Agent**—Bank of New York, NYC. **Incorporated**—in Delaware in 1981. **Empl**— 88,000 **S&P Analyst:** Ray Lam, CFA

STANDARD &POOR'S
STOCK REPORTS

MGIC Investment

1400R
NYSE Symbol **MTG**

In S&P 500

12-SEP-98

Industry:
Financial (Diversified)

Summary: Through its Mortgage Guaranty Insurance Corp. unit, this holding company is a leading U.S. provider of private mortgage insurance coverage.

S&P Opinion: Accumulate (★★★★)

Recent Price • 38⅝
52 Wk Range • 74½-37½

Yield • 0.3%
12-Mo. P/E • 12.4

Earnings vs. Previous Year
▲=Up ▼=Down ▶=No Change

Quantitative Evaluations

Outlook
(1 Lowest—5 Highest)
• **2+**

Fair Value
• **41¼**

Risk
• **Low**

Earn./Div. Rank
• **A-**

Technical Eval.
• **Bearish** since 7/98

Rel. Strength Rank
(1 Lowest—99 Highest)
• **25**

Insider Activity
• **Neutral**

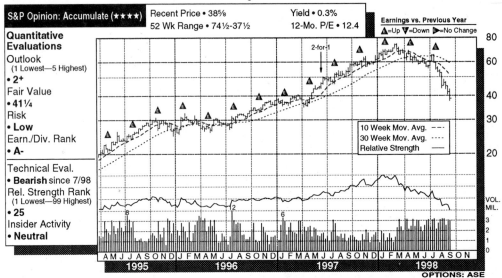

10 Week Mov. Avg. - - -
30 Week Mov. Avg. ......
Relative Strength —

OPTIONS: ASE

Overview - 15-JUL-98

MGIC recorded a 22% year-to-year increase in EPS in the second quarter of 1998. Results were driven by a 13% rise in revenues, versus only a 5.6% increase in losses and incurred expenses. We expect the positive fundamentals that have fueled demand for MTG's main product, mortgage insurance (MI), to continue for the foreseeable future. Higher numbers of first-time home buyers, a higher rate of homeownership in the U.S., and growth in the demand for housing from the immigrant population are fueling demand for mortgage insurance. Given the current interest rate and employment environment, mortgage originations in 1998 could significantly exceed 1997 levels. In addition, deeper coverage requirements (more mortgage insurance protection for a given low down payment loan) by Fannie Mae and Freddie Mac should continue to boost future premium growth. We look for investments in technology to drive operating efficiencies and keep expense growth in check. Default rates improved from year-end 1997 levels. MTG's use of sophisticated credit scoring models and the geographic diversification of its book of business should serve to keep default rates well within manageable levels.

Valuation - 15-JUL-98

While MGIC's shares have underperformed the market thus far in 1998, we believe they continue to warrant an accumulate recommendation. The economic environment remains favorable, and a number of demographic trends are fueling the demand for mortgage insurance. We feel that MTG is capable of growing earnings at a compound annual rate of 18% over the next few years through a combination of double digit revenue growth and stringent expense control. In our view, the shares remain attractive at a recent level of 17X our 1999 EPS estimate.

Key Stock Statistics

S&P EPS Est. 1998	3.30	Tang. Bk. Value/Share	14.37
P/E on S&P Est. 1998	11.7	Beta	1.22
S&P EPS Est. 1999	3.90	Shareholders	400
Dividend Rate/Share	0.10	Market cap. (B)	$ 4.4
Shs. outstg. (M)	113.3	Inst. holdings	86%
Avg. daily vol. (M)	0.861		

Value of $10,000 invested 5 years ago: $ 30,977

Fiscal Year Ending Dec. 31

	1998	1997	1996	1995	1994	1993
Revenues (Million $)						
1Q	244.0	205.1	174.6	140.2	118.0	90.70
2Q	238.0	210.9	182.3	148.6	123.0	98.05
3Q	—	223.8	189.7	159.3	127.9	105.1
4Q	—	228.5	199.1	169.8	133.4	109.7
Yr.	—	868.3	745.6	617.9	502.2	403.5
Earnings Per Share ($)						
1Q	**0.81**	0.61	0.49	0.38	0.28	0.21
2Q	**0.82**	0.67	0.53	0.42	0.33	0.27
3Q	**E0.82**	0.72	0.56	0.45	0.35	0.29
4Q	**E0.85**	0.75	0.59	0.49	0.39	0.30
Yr.	**E3.30**	2.75	2.16	1.75	1.35	1.08

Next earnings report expected: NA

Dividend Data (Dividends have been paid since 1991.)

Amount ($)	Date Decl.	Ex-Div. Date	Stock of Record	Payment Date
0.025	Oct. 23	Nov. 05	Nov. 07	Dec. 01 '97
0.025	Jan. 22	Feb. 04	Feb. 06	Mar. 02 '98
0.025	May. 07	May. 14	May. 18	Jun. 01 '98
0.025	Jul. 23	Aug. 06	Aug. 10	Sep. 01 '98

A Division of The **McGraw·Hill** *Companies*

MGIC Investment Corporation

Business Summary - 15-JUL-98

Since 1957, MGIC Investment Corp. has helped millions of Americans purchase a new home by providing insurance to mortgage lenders on low down payment loans. As a leader in the private mortgage insurance (PMI) industry, MGIC is well positioned to take advantage of favorable market trends, such as growth in affordable housing programs and increased PMI coverage requirements by the Federal Home Loan Mortgage Corp. ("Freddie Mac") and the Federal National Mortgage Association ("Fannie Mae"). In recent years, the company has parlayed its customer-service orientation and credit quality focus into consistent, strong revenue and earnings growth. In addition to mortgage insurance, MGIC provides underwriting and contract services related to home mortgage lending.

Operating through Mortgage Guarantee Insurance Corp., MGIC Investment generates the vast majority of its revenues through premiums earned on mortgage insurance. Mortgage insurance expands home ownership opportunities by enabling buyers to purchase homes with less than a 20% down payment. In the event of a home owner default, PMI reduces, and in some cases eliminates, the loss to the insured institution. Typically, mortgage lenders require the borrowers to fund the insurance premiums. Furthermore, by improving the credit quality of the underlying loans, mortgage insurance facilitates the sale of low down payment mortgage loans in the secondary market, principally to Freddie Mac and Fannie Mae.

With its close ties to the housing market, the private mortgage insurance business can be highly cyclical. MGIC, however, has reported steady, consistent revenue and earnings growth in recent years. With rising home ownership rates and the inability of many first time buyers to produce 20% down payments, this trend is likely to continue.

Since MGIC pays the coverage percentage of the claim amount on defaults (generally 6% to 30%), adequate credit controls are imperative. Losses have declined (the percentage of insured loans in default was 2.02% at June 30, 1998, versus 2.12% at December 31, 1997), and remain at a manageable level, reflecting a sound risk management policy, a geographically diverse portfolio, sophisticated credit scoring models and aggressive loss mitigation efforts.

Through investments in technology, MGIC has been able to achieve economies of scale. Total expenses as a percentage of revenues fell to 46% in 1997, from 51% in 1996.

Per Share Data ($) (Year Ended Dec. 31)	1997	1996	1995	1994	1993	1992	1991	1990	1989	1988
Tangible Bk. Val.	13.07	11.59	9.56	7.17	6.11	5.08	4.25	3.44	2.87	NA
Oper. Earnings	NA	NA	NA	NA	NA	NA	NA	NA	NA	NA
Earnings	2.75	2.17	1.75	1.35	1.08	0.87	0.67	0.56	0.26	0.14
Dividends	0.10	0.08	0.08	0.08	0.07	0.07	0.02	NA	NA	NA
Payout Ratio	4%	4%	5%	6%	7%	8%	3%	NA	NA	NA
Prices - High	66 7/8	38 7/8	31	17 1/8	17 7/8	12 7/8	10 1/2	NA	NA	NA
- Low	35	25 1/4	16 3/8	12 1/2	12 3/8	7 7/8	6 3/4	NA	NA	NA
P/E Ratio - High	24	18	18	13	17	15	16	NA	NA	NA
- Low	13	12	9	9	11	9	10	NA	NA	NA
Income Statement Analysis (Million $)										
Premium Inc.	709	617	507	404	299	226	183	168	148	137
Net Invest. Inc.	124	105	87.5	75.2	64.7	58.3	52.5	47.5	43.7	32.4
Oth. Revs.	35.0	23.2	23.8	23.0	39.5	37.4	22.5	11.7	8.4	9.6
Total Revs.	745	746	618	502	404	322	258	227	201	179
Pretax Inc.	589	365	291	217	175	142	107	88.0	38.0	16.0
Net Oper. Inc.	NA	NA	NA	NA	NA	NA	NA	NA	NA	NA
Net Inc.	447	258	208	160	127	102	75.0	60.0	29.0	15.0
Balance Sheet & Other Fin. Data (Million $)										
Cash & Equiv.	4.9	37.2	38.9	27.8	26.8	23.0	21.6	16.0	14.5	NA
Premiums Due	Nil	Nil	Nil	NA	NA	8.8	7.5	13.0	NA	NA
Invest. Assets: Bonds	2,301	2,032	1,683	1,289	1,056	893	775	603	519	NA
Invest. Assets: Stocks	116	4.0	3.8	3.6	3.4	3.1	1.3	1.3	11.2	NA
Invest. Assets: Loans	Nil	Nil	Nil	Nil	Nil	Nil	Nil	Nil	Nil	Nil
Invest. Assets: Total	231	2,036	1,687	1,293	1,100	896	777	604	531	421
Deferred Policy Costs	27.0	32.0	38.0	42.9	45.8	42.1	37.7	30.3	24.3	NA
Total Assets	2,618	2,222	1,875	1,476	1,343	1,023	894	712	649	553
Debt	238	35.4	35.8	36.1	36.5	36.7	37.0	37.2	37.4	NA
Common Eqty.	1,487	1,366	1,121	838	712	592	492	366	308	268
Prop. & Cas. Loss Ratio	34.2	38.0	37.5	37.9	35.8	38.4	44.4	29.2	39.2	30.5
Prop. & Cas. Expense Ratio	18.4	21.6	24.6	28.1	25.7	24.6	24.0	32.4	34.6	28.1
Prop. & Cas. Combined Ratio	52.6	59.6	62.1	66.0	61.5	63.0	68.4	61.6	73.8	58.6
% Return On Revs.	60.1	34.6	41.1	31.9	31.5	31.8	29.1	26.6	14.2	8.3
% Ret. on Equity	31.4	20.7	21.2	20.6	19.5	18.9	17.5	17.9	9.9	5.7

Data as orig. reptd.; bef. results of disc. opers. and/or spec. items. Per share data adj. for stk. divs. as of ex-div. date. Bold denotes diluted EPS (FASB 128). E-Estimated. NA-Not Available. NM-Not Meaningful. NR-Not Ranked.

Office—MGIC Plaza, 250 East Kilbourn Ave., Milwaukee, WI 53202. **Tel**—(414) 347-6480. **Website**—http://www.mgic.com **Pres & CEO**—W. H. Lacy. **EVP & CFO**—J. M. Lauer. **SVP & Secy**—J.H. Lane. **Dirs**—J. A. Abbott, M. K. Bush, K. E. Case, D. S. Engelman, J. D. Ericson, D. Gross, K. M. Jastrow II, W. H. Lacy, S. B. Lubar, W.A. McIntosh, L. M. Muma, P. J. Wallison, E. J. Zore. **Transfer Agent & Registrar**—Firstar Trust Co., Milwaukee. **Incorporated**—in Wisconsin in 1984. **Empl**— 1,026. **S&P Analyst:** Michael Schneider

Micron Technology

1489

NYSE Symbol **MU**

In S&P 500

12-SEP-98

Industry:
Electronics (Semiconductors)

Summary: Micron Technology is a leading manufacturer of semiconductor memories and other semiconductor components, board-level products and personal computers.

S&P Opinion: Hold (★★★)	Recent Price • 27¾	Yield • Nil
	52 Wk Range • 41⅞-20	12-Mo. P/E • NM

Quantitative Evaluations

Outlook
(1 Lowest—5 Highest)
• **NA**

Fair Value
• **NA**

Risk
• **High**

Earn./Div. Rank
• **B**

Technical Eval.
• **Bearish** since 8/98

Rel. Strength Rank
(1 Lowest—99 Highest)
• **83**

Insider Activity
• **Neutral**

Earnings vs. Previous Year
▲=Up ▼=Down ▶=No Change

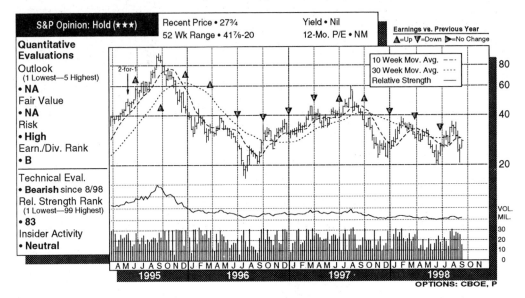

10 Week Mov. Avg. — —
30 Week Mov. Avg. - - - -
Relative Strength ——

OPTIONS: CBOE, P

Overview - 25-JUN-98

For the fourth time in as many quarters, we have significantly reduced our revenue and earnings estimates for Micron to reflect the impact of pricing pressure in the volatile DRAM market. MU is widely regarded as the lowest cost producer of this commodity product, but it has been unable to reduce unit costs fast enough to offset sharp declines in average selling prices. Given the poor pricing environment and increased costs associated with the transition to 64 meg devices, margins are likely to remain under pressure over the next few quarters. In June, MU agreed to purchase the memory chip assets of Texas Instruments for roughly $800 million in stock and assumed debt. The added capacity will allow MU to benefit when DRAM market conditions turn. Overall, however, we look for a loss per share of $0.75 in FY 99, though much will depend on the DRAM pricing environment.

Valuation - 25-JUN-98

The shares of this chip company have fallen sharply since last summer, reflecting the poor pricing environment for DRAM chips. However, we are maintaining our hold opinion, as we believe the worst may be behind the company. The Asian financial crisis has made it difficult for the "big three" Korean DRAM manufacturers to fund capital spending. As a result, there will be a lack of incremental silicon supply coming on-line. Based on continued growth in the computer market, the likelihood for improved DRAM supply/demand dynamics, and therefore improved pricing, has increased. Though near-term operating results are likely to remain weak, we believe the share price will be supported by the prospect of a turnaround in the latter part of 1999.

Key Stock Statistics

S&P EPS Est. 1998	-1.45	Tang. Bk. Value/Share	13.02
P/E on S&P Est. 1998	NM	Beta	1.46
S&P EPS Est. 1999	-0.75	Shareholders	7,400
Dividend Rate/Share	Nil	Market cap. (B)	$ 5.9
Shs. outstg. (M)	213.1	Inst. holdings	59%
Avg. daily vol. (M)	4.898		

Value of $10,000 invested 5 years ago: $ 74,619

Fiscal Year Ending Aug. 31

	1998	1997	1996	1995	1994	1993
Revenues (Million $)						
1Q	954.6	728.1	1,186	535.0	320.1	131.0
2Q	755.4	876.2	996.5	628.5	390.5	176.4
3Q	609.9	965.0	771.0	761.2	426.4	214.9
4Q	—	946.2	700.5	1,028	491.6	306.0
Yr.	—	3,516	3,654	2,953	1,629	828.3
Earnings Per Share ($)						
1Q	0.04	0.10	1.51	0.76	0.33	0.01
2Q	-0.23	0.66	0.87	0.86	0.42	0.04
3Q	-0.50	0.45	0.27	1.02	0.49	0.15
4Q	—	0.33	0.09	1.30	0.67	0.31
Yr.	—	1.54	2.76	3.95	1.91	0.52

Next earnings report expected: late September

Dividend Data

The most recent cash dividend was a payment of $0.05 a share in May 1996.

A Division of The McGraw·Hill Companies

Business Summary - 25-JUN-98

As a leading supplier of dynamic random access memory (DRAM) chips, the most widely used semiconductor memory component in personal computers (PCs), Micron Technology's (Micron's) fortunes are indelibly tied to the rise and fall of prices for this commodity memory product.

From 1993 to 1995, favorable industry dynamics, characterized by strong demand and tight supply, led to phenomenal growth in revenues and earnings at Micron. Prospects for strong profits, however, prompted a slew of competitors, primarily from Korea and Taiwan, to add significant productive capacity for DRAMs. Though the need for memory continued to grow with the PC industry, DRAM supply soon outstripped demand. As a result, prices for commodity DRAM products plummeted by more than 75% during FY 96 (Oct.), and dropped an additional 40% during FY 97. Impressively, Micron managed to achieve relatively flat revenues in FY 97, and a net profit margin of 9%, despite this difficult operating environment.

Given the commodity nature of DRAMs, the company's main product line, diligent cost control is an essential ingredient for success. Micron has earned a reputation as the industry's low-cost producer, through its advanced manufacturing processes. The company's manufacturing facility in Boise, Idaho includes two 8-inch wafer fabs, and in FY 97, Micron converted a substantial portion of its productive capacity to 0.30 micron processing. This leading-edge capability allows the company to consistently improve its manufacturing efficiency by shrinking die sizes, and thereby maximizing the number of units it can produce on a given silicon wafer.

Besides DRAMs, Micron also manufactures other semiconductor memory products, including flash memory components and static random access memory (SRAM) chips. Flash components are non-volatile devices which retain memory content when the power is turned off and are electrically erasable and reprogrammable. SRAMs perform memory functions much the same as DRAMs, but are faster and do not require memory cells to be electronically refreshed. Flash memory and SRAM components each accounted for just 1% of sales in FY 97.

Through its 64% ownership stake in Micron Electronics (MEI), Micron Technology makes and sells high performance desktop and notebook PC systems. MEI custom configures its PC products, and focuses on the direct sales channel. This strategy enables the company to avoid dealer mark-ups and limit inventory carrying costs. In July 1997, MEI acquired NetFRAME Systems, thereby expanding its product offerings to the high-end multiprocessor network server market.

In June 1998, Micron agreed to purchase the memory chip assets of Texas Instruments in a complex transaction valued at roughly $800 million in stock and assumed debt. In addition, Texas Instruments will finance facilities upgrades, allowing Micron to improve the efficiency of the plants.

Per Share Data ($)

(Year Ended Aug. 31)	1997	1996	1995	1994	1993	1992	1991	1990	1989	1988
Tangible Bk. Val.	13.64	11.98	9.19	4.91	3.19	2.67	2.65	2.62	2.60	1.75
Cash Flow	3.67	4.45	4.88	3.67	1.07	0.50	0.45	0.35	0.75	0.83
Earnings	1.54	2.76	3.95	1.92	0.52	0.03	0.03	0.03	0.57	0.68
Dividends	Nil	0.15	0.15	0.06	0.01	0.01	Nil	Nil	Nil	Nil
Payout Ratio	Nil	5%	4%	3%	2%	29%	Nil	Nil	Nil	Nil
Prices - High	60	44	94¾	22½	12¾	4½	3⅞	3¼	5⅛	5¼
- Low	22	16⅝	21¼	9	3⅝	2⅝	1⅞	1⅜	1⅞	2⅜
P/E Ratio - High	39	16	24	12	25	NM	NM	NM	9	6
- Low	14	6	5	5	5	NM	NM	NM	3	3

Income Statement Analysis (Million $)

	1997	1996	1995	1994	1993	1992	1991	1990	1989	1988
Revs.	3,516	3,654	2,953	1,629	828	506	425	333	446	301
Oper. Inc.	864	1,338	1,496	801	276	105	93.0	62.0	185	141
Depr.	462	364	199	181	110	91.0	81.4	61.0	34.6	21.9
Int. Exp.	39.9	16.1	12.2	5.8	8.2	8.6	11.2	10.6	4.2	4.5
Pretax Inc.	619	951	1,351	626	163	10.0	6.0	3.0	166	118
Eff. Tax Rate	43%	38%	38%	36%	36%	31%	14%	NM	36%	17%
Net Inc.	332	594	844	401	104	7.0	5.0	5.0	106	98.0

Balance Sheet & Other Fin. Data (Million $)

	1997	1996	1995	1994	1993	1992	1991	1990	1989	1988
Cash	988	286	128	433	186	73.0	68.0	77.0	161	164
Curr. Assets	1,972	964	1,274	793	440	227	213	198	279	250
Total Assets	4,851	3,752	2,775	1,530	966	724	706	697	625	388
Curr. Liab.	750	665	605	274	211	106	98.0	101	70.0	65.0
LT Debt	762	315	129	125	54.4	61.6	69.6	74.1	39.7	17.7
Common Eqty.	2,883	2,502	1,896	1,049	640	511	495	484	477	288
Total Cap.	3,885	3,028	2,075	1,228	740	609	598	590	547	312
Cap. Exp.	517	1,426	730	370	156	99	86.0	121	244	56.0
Cash Flow	794	957	1,043	582	214	98.0	86.0	66.0	141	120
Curr. Ratio	2.6	1.5	2.1	2.9	2.1	2.1	2.2	2.0	4.0	3.9
% LT Debt of Cap.	19.6	10.4	6.2	10.2	7.3	10.1	11.6	12.6	7.3	5.7
% Net Inc.of Revs.	9.2	16.2	28.5	24.6	12.6	1.3	1.2	1.5	23.8	32.6
% Ret. on Assets	7.7	16.4	39.2	32.1	12.1	0.9	0.7	0.7	20.0	35.4
% Ret. on Equity	12.3	27.0	57.3	47.4	17.7	1.3	1.0	1.0	26.6	51.5

Data as orig. reptd.; bef. results of disc. opers. and/or spec. items. Per share data adj. for stk./divs. as of ex-div. date. Bold denotes diluted EPS (FASB 128). E-Estimated. NA-Not Available. NM-Not Meaningful. NR-Not Ranked.

Office—8000 South Federal Way, Boise, ID 83707-0006. **Tel**—(208) 368-4400. **Website**—http://www.micron.com **Chrmn, Pres & CEO**—S. Appleton. **VP-Fin, CFO**—W. G. Stover, Jr. **Secy**—R.W. Lewis.**Investor Contact**—Kipp A. Bedard. **Dirs**—S. Appleton, J.W. Bagley, J. M. Hess, R. A. Lothrop, T. T. Nicholson, D. J. Simplot, J. R. Simplot, G. C. Smith. **Transfer Agent & Registrar**—Norwest Shareowner Services, St. Paul, MN. **Incorporated**—in Delaware in 1984 (predecessor incorporated in Idaho in 1978). **Empl**— 12,200. **S&P Analyst**: B. McGovern

Microsoft Corp. 4608M

Nasdaq Symbol **MSFT**

In S&P 500

12-SEP-98

Industry: Computer (Software & Services)

Summary: Microsoft, the world's largest software company, develops and markets PC software, including the Windows operating system and Office application suite.

S&P Opinion: Accumulate (★★★★)	Recent Price • 104¼ — Yield • Nil

Recent Price • 104¼
52 Wk Range • 119⅝-59

Yield • Nil
12-Mo. P/E • 62.4

Quantitative Evaluations

Outlook
(1 Lowest—5 Highest)
• **2⁻**

Fair Value
• **96¾**

Risk
• **Low**

Earn./Div. Rank
• **B+**

Technical Eval.
• **Bullish** since 2/96

Rel. Strength Rank
(1 Lowest—99 Highest)
• **90**

Insider Activity
• **Neutral**

Earnings vs. Previous Year
▲=Up ▼=Down ▶=No Change

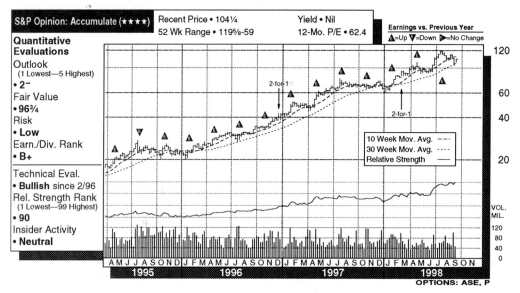

- 10 Week Mov. Avg. – – –
- 30 Week Mov. Avg. ·····
- Relative Strength —

OPTIONS: ASE, P

Overview - 22-JUL-98

Revenue growth should slow somewhat in FY 99 (Jun.), after a 28% rise in FY 98, reflecting few major product releases. However, growth will remain solid, with continued strength in operating systems, desktop applications, and enterprise software. Windows 98 was launched in late June 1998, and appears to be off to a strong start. The company's Office suite of applications, which includes Word and Excel, is the dominant force in the business application market; the next version will be released in 1999. Enterprise software products, including Windows NT, are expected to continue to gain momentum. Margins are expected to remain steady, with continued high R&D spending and a less favorable product mix offset by well controlled expenses. Results in the first quarter of FY 98 included a charge of $0.22 a share for the acquisition of WebTV Networks, Inc.

Valuation - 22-JUL-98

The shares are up sharply thus far in 1998, despite expectations of slower revenue growth in FY 99. Near-term earnings drivers include strength of Windows 98, Office 97 and Windows NT. However, nearly $3 billion spent on R&D in FY 98 will lead to several new products over the next few years, including Windows NT 5.0 (still about a year away), Office 2000 (to be launched in 1999), SQL Server 7.0 (the company's database software) and Start.com (an Internet portal site), which will be introduced later this year. While the cloud of the antitrust case still lingers over MSFT, and remains a concern, we do not expect it to have a material impact on the company's business. The shares deserve a premium market valuation, in light of MSFT's strong competitive position and future growth prospects. We recommend accumulating the shares for the long term.

Key Stock Statistics

S&P EPS Est. 1999	2.14	Tang. Bk. Value/Share	5.58
P/E on S&P Est. 1999	48.7	Beta	1.21
Dividend Rate/Share	Nil	Shareholders	53,400
Shs. outstg. (M)	2464.1	Market cap. (B)	$256.9
Avg. daily vol. (M)	15.471	Inst. holdings	34%

Value of $10,000 invested 5 years ago: $ 97,686

Fiscal Year Ending Jun. 30

	1998	1997	1996	1995	1994	1993
Revenues (Million $)						
1Q	3,130	2,295	2,016	1,247	983.0	818.0
2Q	3,585	2,680	2,195	1,482	1,129	938.0
3Q	3,774	3,208	2,205	1,587	1,244	958.0
4Q	3,995	3,175	2,255	1,621	1,293	1,039
Yr.	14,484	11,358	8,671	5,937	4,649	3,753
Earnings Per Share ($)						
1Q	0.25	0.24	0.20	0.13	0.10	0.09
2Q	**0.42**	0.28	0.23	0.15	0.12	0.10
3Q	**0.50**	0.40	0.22	0.16	0.10	0.10
4Q	**0.50**	0.40	0.22	0.14	0.15	0.11
Yr.	**1.67**	1.31	0.85	0.58	0.47	0.39

Next earnings report expected: late October

Dividend Data

Amount ($)	Date Decl.	Ex-Div. Date	Stock of Record	Payment Date
2-for-1	Jan. 26	Feb. 23	Feb. 06	Feb. 20 '98

A Division of The **McGraw·Hill** *Companies*

Business Summary - 22-JUL-98

This dominant player in the PC software market, which rose to prominence on the popularity of its operating systems software, now rules the business applications software market, and has its sights set on becoming the leading provider of software and services for the Internet. By virtue of its size, market positioning and financial strength, Microsoft (MSFT) is a formidable competitor in any market that it targets. Earnings have grown rapidly over the past several years, aided by a strong PC market in general, new product introductions, and market share gains.

MSFT is best known for its operating systems software programs, which run about 90% of the PCs currently in use. Its original DOS operating system gave way to Windows, a graphical user interface program run in conjunction with DOS, which made using a PC easier. Windows 98, MSFT's newest version of its flagship PC operating system, with sales closely tied to PC shipments, was introduced on June 25, 1998. Its predecessor, Windows 95, has an installed base of more than 100 million users. Windows NT, a network operating system providing network management and administration tools, security and operating stability, now has an installed base of more than seven million users, and continues to grow rapidly.

MSFT entered the business applications market in the early 1990s through a line-up of strong offerings combined with aggressive and innovative marketing and sales techniques. Its Office 97 suite, which includes the popular Word (word processing), Excel (spreadsheet) and PowerPoint (graphics) software programs, is now by far the number one selling application software package. The company is also devoting resources and forming alliances to offer interactive media, including children's titles, games and information products. Microsoft owns 50% of Dreamworks Interactive, MSNBC Cable, and MSNBC Interactive News. The company also recently acquired WebTV Networks, and made investments in Comcast and Apple Computer.

MSFT has rapidly repositioned itself as a major provider of software and services for the Internet. Its Explorer browser is challenging Netscape's Navigator, the market leader. In addition, MSFT's server and development tools for the Internet are being well received.

The company continues to spend heavily on research and development. Some $2.2 billion (about 20% of revenues) was spent in FY 97 (Jun.), of which about $400 million was targeted directly at the Internet. An additional $2.9 billion was spent in FY 98.

Powerful distribution channels, including strong relationships with original equipment manufacturers (OEMs, the makers of PCs), relationships with resellers, as well as guaranteed shelf space in retail stores, all give MSFT an advantage over smaller, less well established rivals.

Per Share Data ($)

(Year Ended Jun. 30)	1998	1997	1996	1995	1994	1993	1992	1991	1990	1989
Tangible Bk. Val.	NA	4.07	2.89	2.27	1.92	1.44	0.99	0.64	0.44	0.28
Cash Flow	NA	1.52	1.04	0.69	0.57	0.45	0.34	0.24	0.15	0.10
Earnings	1.67	1.31	0.86	0.58	0.47	0.39	0.30	0.21	0.13	0.08
Dividends	Nil	Nil	Nil	Nil	Nil	Nil	Nil	Nil	Nil	Nil
Payout Ratio	Nil	Nil	Nil	Nil	Nil	Nil	Nil	Nil	Nil	Nil
Prices - High	119⅝	75⅜	43⅛	27⅜	16¼	12¼	11⅞	9⅜	4½	2½
- Low	62¼	40⅜	20	14⅝	9¾	8¾	8¼	4⅛	2⁵⁄₁₆	1¼
P/E Ratio - High	72	57	50	47	35	31	39	45	35	29
- Low	37	31	23	25	21	22	27	20	18	15

Income Statement Analysis (Million $)

	1998	1997	1996	1995	1994	1993	1992	1991	1990	1989
Revs.	NA	11,358	8,671	5,937	4,649	3,753	2,759	1,843	1,183	804
Oper. Inc.	NA	5,687	3,558	2,307	1,963	1,464	1,097	714	434	260
Depr.	NA	557	480	269	237	138	101	67.0	46.0	25.0
Int. Exp.	NA	Nil	Nil	Nil	2.0	1.0	2.0	4.5	3.6	2.3
Pretax Inc.	NA	5,314	3,379	2,167	1,722	1,401	1,041	671	411	251
Eff. Tax Rate	NA	35%	35%	33%	33%	32%	32%	31%	32%	32%
Net Inc.	NA	3,439	2,195	1,453	1,146	953	708	463	279	171

Balance Sheet & Other Fin. Data (Million $)

	1998	1997	1996	1995	1994	1993	1992	1991	1990	1989
Cash	NA	8,966	6,940	4,750	3,614	2,290	1,345	686	449	301
Curr. Assets	NA	10,373	7,839	5,620	4,312	2,850	1,770	1,029	720	469
Total Assets	NA	14,387	10,093	7,210	5,363	3,805	2,640	1,644	1,105	721
Curr. Liab.	NA	3,610	2,425	1,347	913	563	447	293	187	159
LT Debt	NA	Nil	Nil	Nil	Nil	Nil	Nil	Nil	Nil	Nil
Common Eqty.	Nil	9,797	6,908	5,333	4,450	3,242	2,193	1,351	919	562
Total Cap.	NA	10,777	7,033	5,458	4,450	3,242	2,193	1,351	919	562
Cap. Exp.	NA	499	494	495	278	239	318	275	159	92.0
Cash Flow	NA	3,996	2,675	1,722	1,383	1,091	809	530	326	196
Curr. Ratio	NA	2.9	3.2	4.2	4.7	5.1	4.0	3.5	3.9	3.0
% LT Debt of Cap.	NA	Nil	Nil	Nil	Nil	Nil	Nil	Nil	Nil	Nil
% Net Inc.of Revs.	Nil	30.3	25.3	24.5	24.7	25.4	25.7	25.1	23.6	21.2
% Ret. on Assets	NA	28.2	25.4	23.1	25.0	29.1	32.5	33.4	30.1	27.9
% Ret. on Equity	NA	41.2	35.9	29.7	29.8	34.6	39.3	40.4	37.1	36.1

Data as orig. reptd.; bef. results of disc. opers. and/or spec. items. Per share data adj. for stk. divs. as of ex-div. date. Bold denotes diluted EPS (FASB 128). E-Estimated. NA-Not Available. NM-Not Meaningful. NR-Not Ranked.

Office—One Microsoft Way, Redmond, WA 98052-6399. **Tel**—(206) 882-8080.**Website**—http://www.microsoft.com **Chrmn & CEO**—W. H. Gates III. **Pres**—S. Ballmer. **EVP & COO**—R. J. Herbold. **VP-Fin & CFO**—G. B. Maffei. **Secy**—W. H. Neukom. **Investor Contact**—Carla Lewis (425-936-3703). **Dirs**—P. G. Allen, J. E. Barad, W. H. Gates III, R. Hackborn, D. F. Marquardt, R. D. O'Brien, W. G. Reed Jr., J. A. Shirley. **Transfer Agent**—ChaseMellon Shareholder Services, Ridgefield Park, NJ. **Incorporated**—in Washington in 1981; reincorporated in Delaware in 1986. **Empl**— 22,232. **S&P Analyst:** Brian Goodstadt

Millipore Corp.   1500

NYSE Symbol **MIL**

In S&P 500

12-SEP-98

Industry: Manufacturing (Specialized)

Summary: Millipore makes industrial filters, primarily for semiconductor makers, pharmaceutical companies, and academic and commercial laboratories.

S&P Opinion: Hold (★★★)	Recent Price • 20⅜ Yield • 2.2% 52 Wk Range • 52-19⅝ 12-Mo. P/E • 11.1

Quantitative Evaluations

Outlook
(1 Lowest—5 Highest)
• **1**

Fair Value
• **21⅜**

Risk
• **Average**

Earn./Div. Rank
• **B**

Technical Eval.
• **Bearish** since 3/98

Rel. Strength Rank
(1 Lowest—99 Highest)
• **34**

Insider Activity
• **NA**

Earnings vs. Previous Year
▲=Up ▼=Down ▶=No Change

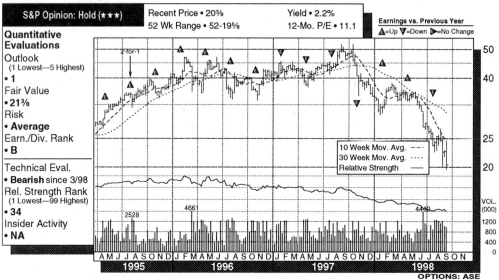

10 Week Mov. Avg. ---
30 Week Mov. Avg. ----
Relative Strength ——

OPTIONS: ASE

Overview - 23-JUL-98

This industrial and medical filter maker primarily targets the expanding semiconductor industry (35% of sales), the biopharmaceutical/health care industry (30%), and faster growing segments of the mature analytical laboratory industry (35%). Semiconductor filter sales are down from previous years, but should turn around in the second half of 1999. In the healthcare sector, U.S. population aging trends, globalization, increasing regulation, and an accelerating rate of new drug development should fuel healthy demand for medical filters. In the slower growing laboratory sector, MIL has targeted the fast-growing water purification, in-home testing kits (such as pregnancy tests) and pharmaceutical research markets. MIL's game plan is to grow by expanding its international sales, which currently represent two-thirds of total sales, and to acquire complementary businesses. However, the strong dollar will continue to dampen foreign results into 1999. Our 1998 EPS estimate excludes first quarter nonrecurring charges.

Valuation - 23-JUL-98

Revenue and profit comparisons (excluding nonrecurring charges), year to year, will continue to be unfavorable into 1999, due to the slowdown in the microelectronics industry, the strong dollar's impact on foreign operations, the deepening economic troubles in Asia/Japan, and the acquisition-related higher interest expenses. However, we believe that MIL will see revenue and earnings growth resume toward the end of 1999, supported by the semiconductor and medical filter sales businesses, aided by cost cutting initiatives and interest expense reductions. With the shares down 50% from their fourth quarter 1997 high and trading at 16X our 1999 EPS estimate of $1.60, we believe the bad news has been discounted and MIL should perform in line with the market.

Key Stock Statistics

S&P EPS Est. 1998	0.85	Tang. Bk. Value/Share	1.61
P/E on S&P Est. 1998	24.0	Beta	0.73
S&P EPS Est. 1999	1.60	Shareholders	3,400
Dividend Rate/Share	0.44	Market cap. (B)	$0.893
Shs. outstg. (M)	43.9	Inst. holdings	83%
Avg. daily vol. (M)	0.241		

Value of $10,000 invested 5 years ago: $ 12,320

Fiscal Year Ending Dec. 31

	1998	1997	1996	1995	1994	1993
Revenues (Million $)						
1Q	185.7	178.8	156.5	141.4	119.0	105.2
2Q	175.2	192.5	161.9	150.5	124.7	114.6
3Q	—	184.5	148.9	147.6	123.5	111.8
4Q	—	203.0	151.4	155.0	130.1	113.7
Yr.	—	758.9	618.7	594.5	497.3	445.4
Earnings Per Share ($)						
1Q	**0.71**	-2.25	0.57	0.45	0.27	0.17
2Q	**0.15**	0.37	0.57	0.49	0.31	0.24
3Q	—	**0.48**	0.51	0.45	0.30	0.21
4Q	—	**0.48**	-0.66	0.51	0.20	0.25
Yr.	—	**-0.89**	0.98	1.90	1.09	0.88

Next earnings report expected: NA

Dividend Data (Dividends have been paid since 1966.)

Amount ($)	Date Decl.	Ex-Div. Date	Stock of Record	Payment Date
0.100	Sep. 25	Oct. 08	Oct. 10	Oct. 28 '97
0.100	Dec. 11	Dec. 24	Dec. 29	Jan. 27 '98
0.100	Feb. 12	Mar. 11	Mar. 13	Apr. 28 '98
0.110	Jun. 18	Jun. 26	Jun. 30	Jul. 28 '98

A Division of The **McGraw-Hill** Companies

Business Summary - 23-JUL-98

In recent years, Millipore Corp. has been solidly increasing its revenue growth, by generating two-thirds of sales from overseas markets, offering a broad product line, acquiring companies that complement MIL's businesses and meet management's return on investment criteria, and targeting fast-growing markets.

MIL is primarily targeting the rapidly expanding semiconductor and pharmaceutical/healthcare industries, as well as faster growing segments of the mature analytical laboratory market. Management estimates that the semiconductor industry will grow at a compound rate of 15% over the next several years, on continued strong computer sales, and increasing use of chips in consumer products. In the healthcare sector, favorable demographic trends, increasing industry globalization, expanding regulations and new drug developments should drive accelerating demand for MIL's healthcare filters. In the slower growing laboratory sector, Millipore has identified three faster growing market niches: water purification (from increasing regulatory requirements), in-home testing kits (pregnancy, cholesterol and AIDS testing) and bio-research for the rapidly expanding pharmaceutical industry.

The company's microelectronic filters purify, deliver and monitor liquids and gases used in the production of semiconductors and other microelectronic components. Millipore's pharmaceutical/healthcare filters sterilize antibiotics, vaccines, vitamins and protein solutions. In addition, MIL's healthcare filters are used in the development of new drugs. The company's laboratory filters are used to purify proteins, cell cultures and cell structure studies, as well as to collect micro-organisms.

Segment revenue contributions and profitability statistics in recent years were:

	1997	1996	1995
SEGMENT REVENUES			
Biopharmaceutical filters	28%	31%	30%
Microelectronic filters	35%	28%	24%
Laboratory filters	37%	41%	46%
GROSS PROFIT MARGINS	55%	60%	57%
OPERATING PROFIT MARGINS	NM	9.8%	18%

Millipore places great emphasis on research and development, and performs substantially all of its own R&D. In 1997, 1996 and 1995, the company spent 7.4%, 6.2% and 6.1% of revenues on R&D, respectively. The company's principal competitors include Pall Corp. (NYSE: PLL), with nearly $1 billion in revenues; Barnstead Thermolyne Corp.; and Sartorious GmbH.

Per Share Data ($)

(Year Ended Dec. 31)	1997	1996	1995	1994	1993	1992	1991	1990	1989	1988
Tangible Bk. Val.	1.64	3.67	4.95	4.67	8.19	7.61	8.14	7.36	6.72	6.28
Cash Flow	0.04	1.70	2.51	1.59	1.30	1.31	1.61	1.01	1.39	1.40
Earnings	-0.89	1.00	1.90	1.09	0.88	0.70	1.08	0.50	0.95	0.98
Dividends	0.49	0.35	0.32	0.29	0.28	0.26	0.23	0.21	0.20	0.17
Payout Ratio	NM	35%	17%	27%	31%	36%	22%	43%	21%	18%
Prices - High	52	47⅛	41½	28½	20⅛	21	24	18⅝	18¾	20⅝
- Low	33½	33⅝	22⅞	19¼	13	13⅝	14⅞	12⅛	12⅝	16⅜
P/E Ratio - High	NM	47	22	26	23	30	22	37	20	21
- Low	NM	34	12	18	15	19	14	24	13	17

Income Statement Analysis (Million $)

	1997	1996	1995	1994	1993	1992	1991	1990	1989	1988
Revs.	759	619	594	497	445	777	748	703	658	622
Oper. Inc.	41.8	92.0	147	118	95.0	101	114	102	93.0	99
Depr.	40.7	30.6	27.5	27.6	23.8	34.0	29.2	28.7	24.8	23.5
Int. Exp.	30.5	11.5	10.6	7.9	13.3	16.3	15.1	10.3	10.3	8.1
Pretax Inc.	-18.1	57.0	110	76.9	63.2	51.5	77.9	35.4	67.4	72.7
Eff. Tax Rate	NM	24%	23%	23%	23%	23%	23%	22%	22%	25%
Net Inc.	-38.8	43.6	85.4	59.6	49.0	39.9	60.4	27.8	52.9	54.5

Balance Sheet & Other Fin. Data (Million $)

	1997	1996	1995	1994	1993	1992	1991	1990	1989	1988
Cash	2.2	46.9	23.8	30.2	40.6	70.5	76.3	55.2	57.4	36.2
Curr. Assets	352	312	262	259	357	430	442	412	376	347
Total Assets	766	683	531	528	703	787	784	734	651	576
Curr. Liab.	305	216	173	158	120	207	191	187	130	98.0
LT Debt	287	224	105	100	102	103	102	103	104	105
Common Eqty.	149	218	226	221	461	453	478	435	407	366
Total Cap.	436	442	332	322	563	556	581	538	511	471
Cap. Exp.	41.1	30.4	30.0	21.0	24.5	44.9	48.1	68.3	56.7	47.8
Cash Flow	1.9	74.2	113	87.2	72.8	73.9	89.6	56.5	77.6	78.1
Curr. Ratio	1.2	1.4	1.5	1.6	3.0	2.1	2.3	2.2	2.9	3.6
% LT Debt of Cap.	65.8	50.7	31.7	31.2	18.1	18.6	17.6	19.2	20.4	22.3
% Net Inc.of Revs.	NM	7.1	14.4	12.0	11.0	5.1	8.1	4.0	8.0	8.8
% Ret. on Assets	NM	7.2	16.0	10.8	6.6	5.1	7.9	4.0	8.6	10.3
% Ret. on Equity	NM	19.7	38.1	19.8	10.7	8.6	13.2	6.6	13.7	15.7

Data as orig. reptd.; bef. results of disc. opers. and/or spec. items. Per share data adj. for stk. divs. as of ex-div. date. Bold denotes diluted EPS (FASB 128). E-Estimated. NA-Not Available. NM-Not Meaningful. NR-Not Ranked. Operating and net operating profit margins in 1997 and 1996 include pretax acquisition-related charges of $114 million and $68 million, respectively.

Office—80 Ashby Rd., Bedford, MA 01730-2271. **Tel**—(781) 533-6000. **Fax**—(781)533-3110. **Website**—http://www.millipore.com **Chrmn, Pres & CEO**—C. W. Zadel. **VP & CFO**—F. J. Lunger. **Treas & Investor Contact**—Geoffrey E. Helliwell. **Dirs**—C. D. Baker, R. C. Bishop, S. C. Butler, R. E. Caldwell, M. A. Hendricks, M. Hoffman, T. O. Pyle, J. F. Reno, C. W. Zadel. **Transfer Agent & Registrar**—BankBoston. **Incorporated**—in Massachusetts in 1954. **Empl**—4,800. **S&P Analyst:** John A. Massey.

Minnesota Mining

1503A

NYSE Symbol **MMM**

In S&P 500

12-SEP-98

Industry: Manufacturing (Diversified)

Summary: 3-M, the well-known maker of Scotch-Tape and Post-Its, also makes a wide range of industrial adhesives and abrasives.

S&P Opinion: Avoid (★★)		
Recent Price • 71½	Yield • 3.1%	
52 Wk Range • 101⅛-65⅝	12-Mo. P/E • 14.3	

Earnings vs. Previous Year
▲=Up ▼=Down ▶=No Change

Quantitative Evaluations

Outlook
(1 Lowest—5 Highest)
• **2+**

Fair Value
• **69¾**

Risk
• **Low**

Earn./Div. Rank
• **A+**

Technical Eval.
• **Bullish** since 8/98

Rel. Strength Rank
(1 Lowest—99 Highest)
• **68**

Insider Activity
• **NA**

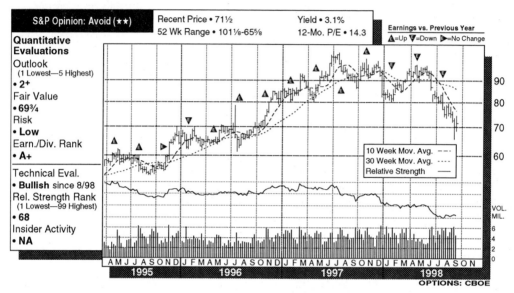

10 Week Mov. Avg. -- -
30 Week Mov. Avg. ....
Relative Strength —

VOL. MIL.

OPTIONS: CBOE

Overview - 31-JUL-98

Earnings from continuing operations are projected to increase slightly in 1998. Slower economic growth in several regions of the world, including Asia and Latin America, could limit demand for industrial products, including tapes, abrasives, and automotive and printing products, although safety and security products should fare better. Continued strong performance is expected from the life sciences division, reflecting increased sales of dental and pharmaceutical products. Productivity gains, together with favorable raw material costs, aggresive cost cutting of administrative expenses, and higher average selling prices, may be partly offset by adverse fluctuations in foreign currency valuations. Aided by large share repurchases, EPS should rise. For the longer term, company goals include increasing sales at least 10% a year, and boosting earnings at a faster rate. The company also aims to generate 30% of sales from products introduced in the preceding four years, and 10% of sales from products introduced within the last year.

Valuation - 31-JUL-98

We continue to recommend that investors avoid the shares. Although the share valuation has become more reasonable, we still think that it is high relative to the company's growth rate. In addition, MMM expects results to be hurt in 1998 by adverse fluctuations in foreign currency value versus the U.S. dollar, and by the impact of slower economic growth in Asia. Although substantial sums of cash are being directed to share repurchases, we think that this will only partially offset the impact of the currency fluctuations. The shares were recently trading at a rich P/E multiple of about 18X expected 1998 EPS. We would not add to holdings until the share valuation becomes more compelling.

Key Stock Statistics

S&P EPS Est. 1998	4.20	Tang. Bk. Value/Share	14.96
P/E on S&P Est. 1998	17.0	Beta	0.72
S&P EPS Est. 1999	4.25	Shareholders	133,100
Dividend Rate/Share	2.20	Market cap. (B)	$ 28.9
Shs. outstg. (M)	403.9	Inst. holdings	65%
Avg. daily vol. (M)	1.287		

Value of $10,000 invested 5 years ago: NA

Fiscal Year Ending Dec. 31

	1998	1997	1996	1995	1994	1993
Revenues (Million $)						
1Q	3,700	3,714	3,468	3,361	3,632	3,517
2Q	3,770	3,817	3,522	3,424	3,772	3,540
3Q	—	3,826	3,623	3,370	3,820	3,481
4Q	—	3,713	3,623	3,305	3,855	3,482
Yr.	—	15,070	14,236	13,460	15,079	14,020
Earnings Per Share ($)						
1Q	**0.98**	0.99	0.87	0.85	0.72	0.76
2Q	**0.94**	1.01	0.91	0.82	0.81	0.76
3Q	—	2.25	0.95	0.81	0.81	0.73
4Q	—	**0.89**	0.90	0.63	0.79	0.67
Yr.	—	**5.06**	3.59	3.11	3.13	2.91

Next earnings report expected: late October

Dividend Data (Dividends have been paid since 1916.)

Amount ($)	Date Decl.	Ex-Div. Date	Stock of Record	Payment Date
0.530	Nov. 10	Nov. 19	Nov. 21	Dec. 12 '97
0.550	Feb. 09	Feb. 18	Feb. 20	Mar. 12 '98
0.550	May. 12	May. 20	May. 22	Jun. 12 '98
0.550	Aug. 10	Aug. 19	Aug. 21	Sep. 12 '98

A Division of The McGraw-Hill Companies

Business Summary - 31-JUL-98

Best known for its Scotch brand adhesive tapes and Post-it Note Pads, 3-M also produces a diverse line of industrial adhesives, sandpaper, as well as medical and personal hygiene products. In recent years, the company has pruned its operations by exiting several noncore businesses. The latest divestiture involved the 1997 sale of MMM's outdoor advertising business to Outdoor Systems, Inc.

Segment revenues and operating profit margins in recent years were as follows:

	1997	1996	1995
REVENUES			
Industrial & Consumer	63%	63%	63%
Life Sciences	37%	37%	37%
PROFIT MARGINS			
Industrial & Consumer	18%	17%	16%
Life Sciences	19%	21%	21%

The company derives a majority of its revenues and operating profits from overseas markets. International sales generated 52% of 1997 revenues and 52% of 1997 operating profits. International revenues and operating profits by region in 1997 were: Europe/Middle East (24% of total revenues, 16% of total profits), Asia Pacific (18%, 23%), and Latin America/Canada/Africa (10%, 13%).

Research & development constitute an important part of 3M's internal growth. In 1997, 1996 and 1995, the company spent 6.6%, 6.7% and 6.6% of total revenues on R&D, respectively.

The Industrial and Consumer segment primarily makes a wide assortment of adhesives, tape and sandpaper, for industry as well for consumers. To a lesser extent, this segment also manufactures specialty chemicals, electronics and telecommunications equipment.

The Life Sciences segment produces products for the medical, dental, personal hygiene and highway safety markets. Medical products include tape, dressings and surgical supplies. Pharmaceutical products include anti-inflammatory, cardiovascular and respiratory products, as well as inhalers and skin patches. Dental products include adhesives, crowns, wire and brackets. Personal hygiene offerings include closures for disposable diapers. Highway safety products include reflectors used on signs and vehicles.

In late 1997, 3M was sued for damages related to allegedly defective breast implants. The company entered the breast implant business through its 1977 acquisition of McGhan Medical Corp. In 1984, 3M sold McGhan. At December 31, 1997, 3M had $292 million of breast implant liability reserves. The company also has liability insurance that 3M believes would cover substantially all of its potential breast implant liability exposure.

Per Share Data ($)

(Year Ended Dec. 31)	1997	1996	1995	1994	1993	1992	1991	1990	1989	1988
Tangible Bk. Val.	14.64	15.08	16.43	16.04	15.16	15.06	14.36	13.89	12.07	12.29
Cash Flow	7.14	5.74	5.16	5.50	5.16	5.11	4.64	4.71	4.38	3.94
Earnings	5.06	3.63	3.11	3.13	2.91	2.83	2.63	2.96	2.80	2.54
Dividends	2.12	1.92	1.88	1.76	1.66	1.60	1.56	1.46	1.30	1.06
Payout Ratio	42%	53%	60%	56%	57%	57%	59%	49%	47%	41%
Prices - High	105½	85⅞	69⅞	57⅛	58½	53½	48¾	45¾	41	33¾
- Low	80	61¼	50¾	46⅜	48⅝	42¾	39⅛	36⅞	30⅛	27⅝
P/E Ratio - High	21	24	22	18	20	19	19	15	15	13
- Low	16	17	16	15	17	15	15	12	11	11

Income Statement Analysis (Million $)

	1997	1996	1995	1994	1993	1992	1991	1990	1989	1988
Revs.	15,070	14,236	13,460	15,079	14,020	13,883	13,340	13,021	11,990	10,581
Oper. Inc.	3,545	3,374	3,159	3,254	2,985	2,984	2,843	2,972	2,850	2,515
Depr.	870	883	859	1,003	976	1,004	884	781	700	632
Int. Exp.	94.0	79.0	102	87.0	50.0	76.0	97.0	98.0	98.0	95.0
Pretax Inc.	3,440	2,479	2,168	2,154	2,002	1,947	1,877	2,135	2,099	1,882
Eff. Tax Rate	36%	36%	36%	36%	35%	35%	37%	37%	39%	39%
Net Inc.	2,121	1,516	1,306	1,322	1,263	1,236	1,154	1,308	1,244	1,154

Balance Sheet & Other Fin. Data (Million $)

	1997	1996	1995	1994	1993	1992	1991	1990	1989	1988
Cash	230	744	772	491	656	722	502	591	887	897
Curr. Assets	6,168	6,486	6,395	6,928	6,363	6,209	5,585	5,729	5,382	4,741
Total Assets	13,238	13,364	14,183	13,496	12,197	11,955	11,083	11,079	9,776	8,922
Curr. Liab.	3,983	3,789	3,724	3,605	3,282	3,241	3,236	3,339	2,721	2,371
LT Debt	1,015	851	1,203	1,031	796	687	764	760	885	406
Common Eqty.	5,926	6,294	6,884	6,734	6,512	6,599	6,293	6,110	5,378	5,514
Total Cap.	7,391	7,135	8,087	8,321	7,684	7,600	7,372	7,282	6,668	6,184
Cap. Exp.	1,406	1,109	1,088	1,148	1,112	1,318	1,326	1,337	1,187	841
Cash Flow	2,991	2,399	2,165	2,325	2,239	2,240	2,038	2,089	1,944	1,786
Curr. Ratio	1.5	1.7	1.7	1.9	1.9	1.9	1.7	1.7	2.0	2.0
% LT Debt of Cap.	13.7	11.9	14.9	12.4	10.4	9.0	10.4	10.4	13.3	6.6
% Net Inc.of Revs.	14.1	10.6	9.7	8.8	9.0	8.9	8.7	10.0	10.4	10.9
% Ret. on Assets	15.9	11.0	9.6	10.4	10.6	10.7	10.4	12.6	13.4	13.7
% Ret. on Equity	34.7	23.0	19.2	20.2	19.5	19.2	18.6	22.9	22.9	22.0

Data as orig. reptd.; bef. results of disc. opers. and/or spec. items. Per share data adj. for stk. divs. as of ex-div. date. Bold denotes diluted EPS (FASB 128). E-Estimated. NA-Not Available. NM-Not Meaningful. NR-Not Ranked.

Office—3M Center, St. Paul, MN 55144. **Tel**—(612) 733-1110. **Website**—http://www.mmm.com **Chrmn & CEO**—L. D. DeSimone. **CFO**—G. Agostini. **Secy**—R. P. Smith. **Investor Contact**—Jon Greer (612-733-8704). **Dirs**—R. O. Baukol, E. A. Brennan, L. D. DeSimone, E. R. McCracken, W. G. Meredith, R. A. Mitsch, A. E. Murray, A. L. Peters, R. L. Ridgway, F. Shrontz, E. A. Smith, L. W. Sullivan. **Transfer Agent & Registrar**—Norwest Bank Minnesota, St. Paul. **Incorporated**—in Delaware in 1929. **Empl**— 75,640. **S&P Analyst**: Robert E. Friedman, CPA

STANDARD &POOR'S
STOCK REPORTS

Mirage Resorts

1523

NYSE Symbol **MIR**

In S&P 500

12-SEP-98

Industry:
Gaming, Lottery & Pari-mutuel Cos.

Summary: This major gaming company, which owns casino/hotels in Nevada, is pursuing growth opportunities in Las Vegas, Mississippi and Atlantic City.

S&P Opinion: Hold (★★★)

Recent Price • 17⅛	Yield • Nil
52 Wk Range • 30⅜-13¾	12-Mo. P/E • 18.5

Quantitative Evaluations

Outlook
(1 Lowest—5 Highest)
• **3**

Fair Value
• **19½**

Risk
• **Average**

Earn./Div. Rank
• **B**

Technical Eval.
• **Bullish** since 11/97

Rel. Strength Rank
(1 Lowest—99 Highest)
• **59**

Insider Activity
• **NA**

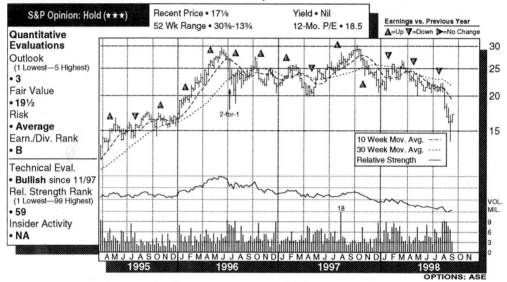

Earnings vs. Previous Year
▲=Up ▼=Down ▶=No Change

10 Week Mov. Avg. ----
30 Week Mov. Avg. ----
Relative Strength —

VOL. MIL.

OPTIONS: ASE

Overview - 24-AUG-98

This major gaming company operates five casino/hotels--four of which are in Las Vegas--and is a joint-venture partner in another Las Vegas gaming project. Also, MIR is constructing two large new casino/hotel projects, in Las Vegas and Biloxi, MS, whose combined cost (including land, capitalized interest and other preopening costs) is expected to be more than $2 billion. The Las Vegas project, called Bellagio, is scheduled to open in October 1998, and the Gulf Coast casino/hotel, called Beau Rivage, is expected to debut in the first quarter of 1999. With expansion projects under way, much of MIR's debt-related interest expense is being capitalized. Our earnings estimates exclude major preopening costs related to new facilities. Also, with the 1997-98 acquisition of Boardwalk Casino, Inc., MIR has additional land that could be used for development in Las Vegas. Longer-term MIR expansion may also include one or more MIR-related casino/hotels in Atlantic City.

Valuation - 24-AUG-98

We advise aggressive investors to hold this stock. However, we expect concern about the amount of new capacity coming on stream in Las Vegas between now and the end of 1999 (including a large MIR casino/hotel), and the prospect that problems in Asia will be hurting MIR's level of bacarrat play, to be among factors limiting investor interest in the stock during the next six to 12 months. We don't expect any new MIR-related casino/hotel in Atlantic City to debut before the year 2002. With an amended joint venture agreement, MIR has resolved a dispute with Boyd Gaming Corp. related to development of an Atlantic City casino/hotel on land owned by MIR, but a dispute continued with gaming company Circus Circus Enterprises. Also, MIR may develop a fully owned casino/hotel in Atlantic City.

Key Stock Statistics

S&P EPS Est. 1998	0.97	Tang. Bk. Value/Share	8.83
P/E on S&P Est. 1998	17.7	Beta	1.60
S&P EPS Est. 1999	1.40	Shareholders	12,400
Dividend Rate/Share	Nil	Market cap. (B)	$ 3.1
Shs. outstg. (M)	179.7	Inst. holdings	75%
Avg. daily vol. (M)	1.448		

Value of $10,000 invested 5 years ago: $ 26,239

Fiscal Year Ending Dec. 31

	1998	1997	1996	1995	1994	1993
Revenues (Million $)						
1Q	342.6	362.0	374.2	352.9	300.4	214.8
2Q	322.9	344.4	312.6	299.1	306.4	231.1
3Q	—	369.1	338.6	335.1	336.4	228.1
4Q	—	343.0	342.1	343.5	311.0	279.3
Yr.	—	1,419	1,368	1,331	1,254	953.3
Earnings Per Share ($)						
1Q	**0.22**	0.30	0.33	0.27	0.12	0.07
2Q	**0.18**	0.25	0.21	0.15	0.16	0.11
3Q	**E0.24**	0.28	0.25	0.23	0.21	0.11
4Q	**E0.33**	0.26	0.27	0.23	0.17	0.02
Yr.	**E0.97**	1.09	1.06	0.88	0.66	0.29

Next earnings report expected: NA

Dividend Data

The only cash dividend since 1972 was paid in 1978. The shares were split 5-for-2 in November 1993.

A Division of The **McGraw·Hill** *Companies*

Business Summary - 24-AUG-98

This company does things in a big way. Already one of the largest U.S. gaming companies, Mirage Resorts is now en route to investing more than $2 billion in a pair of new casino/hotel projects which are expected to open between October 1998 and spring 1999.

The flagship Mirage property, which opened on the Las Vegas Strip in 1989, has about 3,044 hotel rooms and suites and 107,200 sq. ft. of casino space. In 1997, The Mirage generated $213 million of operating profit, or more than 50% of MIR's total. MIR's pirate-themed Treasure Island, which is adjacent to The Mirage, has about 2,900 hotel rooms and 82,000 sq. ft. of casino space. Treasure Island opened in 1993.

In June 1996, the joint-venture Monte Carlo casino/hotel, which has about 3,014 rooms and a 90,000-sq.-ft. casino, opened on the Las Vegas Strip. Nearby, MIR is developing a large casino/hotel project, called Bellagio, whose design is expected to have European features. The project, which is scheduled to open in October 1998, is expected to have about 3,005 guest rooms, approximately 151,000 sq. ft. of casino space, plus a body of water inspired by Lake Como in northern Italy. The project's estimated cost (excluding art purchased for display and resale) is about $1.6 billion. Also, in June 1998, MIR completed the acquisition of Boardwalk Casino, Inc., and certain related assets, for about $112

million. Boardwalk owns and operates a Las Vegas Strip facility which has 653 hotel rooms and 33,000 sq. ft. of casino space. The acquisition boosts the amount of land that MIR has for potential future development.

In downtown Las Vegas, MIR's Golden Nugget casino/hotel has 1,907 hotel rooms and suites and about 38,000 sq. ft. of casino space. Also, the Golden Nugget in Laughlin, NV, has about 300 hotel rooms and a 32,000-sq.-ft. casino.

In Biloxi, MS, MIR is developing Beau Rivage, a beachfront resort that is expected to include about 1,780 hotel rooms and 80,000 sq. ft. of casino space. The project's estimated cost is approximately $600 million.

Also, in January 1998, pursuant to a redevelopment agreement, MIR received 181 acres of land (125 acres of which are developable) from the City of Atlantic City. In exchange, MIR has conditionally agreed to develop a casino/hotel on the site (in Atlantic City's Marina area), and would also undertake certain other obligations. Development of the casino/hotel could depend, in part, on construction of certain major road improvements, whose cost would partly be funded by MIR. Also, MIR recently entered into an amended joint venture agreement with Boyd Gaming Corp. for the development of a casino/hotel on MIR's land, but a dispute continued related to Circus Circus Enterprises' prospective involvement in development there.

Per Share Data ($)

(Year Ended Dec. 31)	1997	1996	1995	1994	1993	1992	1991	1990	1989	1988
Tangible Bk. Val.	8.43	7.24	6.59	5.67	5.03	3.71	2.74	1.46	1.06	1.33
Cash Flow	1.55	1.50	1.33	1.15	0.75	0.73	0.96	0.90	0.05	0.10
Earnings	1.09	1.06	0.89	0.66	0.29	0.26	0.40	0.31	-0.25	-0.07
Dividends	Nil	Nil	Nil	Nil	Nil	Nil	Nil	Nil	Nil	Nil
Payout Ratio	Nil	Nil	Nil	Nil	Nil	Nil	Nil	Nil	Nil	Nil
Prices - High	30³/₈	29⁵/₈	17⁵/₈	13¹/₂	12¹/₂	7³/₈	6¹/₄	8¹/₄	6³/₄	3³/₄
- Low	19⁷/₈	16⁵/₈	9⁷/₈	8³/₈	6¹/₂	4³/₈	3¹/₄	2¹/₂	3¹/₄	1¹³/₁₆
P/E Ratio - High	28	28	20	20	43	28	16	26	NM	NM
- Low	18	16	11	13	23	17	8	8	NM	NM

Income Statement Analysis (Million $)

	1997	1996	1995	1994	1993	1992	1991	1990	1989	1988
Revs.	1,419	1,368	1,331	1,254	953	833	823	909	300	175
Oper. Inc.	443	399	370	331	238	191	225	223	21.0	30.0
Depr.	88.0	86.7	86.2	93.4	77.0	64.8	61.8	55.4	25.3	18.1
Int. Exp.	7.7	31.0	33.0	52.0	89.0	103	114	116	109	68.0
Pretax Inc.	325	318	265	196	72.0	46.0	68.0	45.0	-32.0	-11.0
Eff. Tax Rate	35%	35%	36%	36%	34%	19%	34%	34%	NM	NM
Net Inc.	210	206	170	125	48.0	37.0	45.0	30.0	-21.0	-8.0

Balance Sheet & Other Fin. Data (Million $)

	1997	1996	1995	1994	1993	1992	1991	1990	1989	1988
Cash	99	82.0	48.0	47.0	57.0	143	194	134	93.0	80.0
Curr. Assets	301	236	215	180	197	260	278	243	171	101
Total Assets	3,347	2,143	1,792	1,641	1,705	1,580	1,316	1,315	1,159	1,038
Curr. Liab.	257	218	174	152	191	156	160	134	124	93.0
LT Debt	1,397	468	249	360	535	831	798	1,009	900	749
Common Eqty.	1,512	1,291	1,209	1,031	911	554	301	122	88.0	134
Total Cap.	3,077	1,914	1,607	1,481	1,506	1,416	1,150	1,175	1,032	939
Cap. Exp.	1,059	399	179	69.0	432	221	66.0	129	406	228
Cash Flow	298	293	256	218	125	102	106	85.0	4.0	11.0
Curr. Ratio	1.2	1.1	1.2	1.2	1.0	1.7	1.7	1.8	1.4	1.1
% LT Debt of Cap.	45.4	24.4	15.5	24.3	35.5	58.7	69.4	85.8	87.2	79.8
% Net Inc.of Revs.	14.8	15.1	12.8	9.9	5.0	4.4	5.4	3.3	NM	NM
% Ret. on Assets	7.6	10.5	9.9	7.4	2.7	2.2	2.9	2.4	NM	NM
% Ret. on Equity	15.0	16.5	15.2	12.8	6.1	7.7	19.3	28.3	NM	NM

Data as orig. reptd.; bef. results of disc. opers. and/or spec. items. Per share data adj. for stk. divs. as of ex-div. date. Bold denotes diluted EPS (FASB 128). E-Estimated. NA-Not Available. NM-Not Meaningful. NR-Not Ranked.

Office—3400 Las Vegas Boulevard South, Las Vegas, NV 89109. **Tel**—(702) 791-7111. **Chrmn & Pres**—S. A. Wynn. **VP & Secy**—K. R. Wynn. **SVP-Fin, CFO, Treas & Investor Contact**—Daniel R. Lee. **Dirs**—R. D. Bronson, G. S. Darman, G. J. Mason, R. M. Popeil, D. B. Wayson, M. B. Wolzinger, E. P. Wynn, K. R. Wynn, S. A. Wynn. **Transfer Agent & Registrar**—American Stock Transfer & Trust Co., NYC. **Incorporated**—in Nevada in 1949. **Empl**— 17,085. **S&P Analyst:** Tom Graves, CFA

STANDARD &POOR'S
STOCK REPORTS

Mobil Corp.

1529

NYSE Symbol **MOB**

In S&P 500

12-SEP-98

Industry:
Oil (International Integrated)

Summary: This worldwide integrated petroleum company and leading chemicals maker maintains an aggressive exploration program and focuses on high-growth retail markets.

S&P Opinion: Hold (★★★)	Recent Price • 78	Yield • 2.9%
	52 Wk Range • 83¾-62⅜	12-Mo. P/E • 21.6

Quantitative Evaluations

Outlook
(1 Lowest—5 Highest)
• 1

Fair Value
• 63¼

Risk
• **Low**

Earn./Div. Rank
• **A-**

Technical Eval.
• **Bearish** since 8/98

Rel. Strength Rank
(1 Lowest—99 Highest)
• 97

Insider Activity
• **Neutral**

Earnings vs. Previous Year
▲=Up ▼=Down ▶=No Change

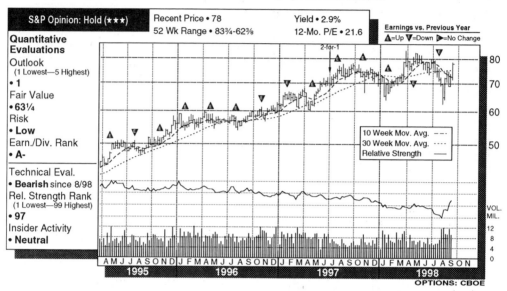

10 Week Mov. Avg. ---
30 Week Mov. Avg. ----
Relative Strength

OPTIONS: CBOE

Overview - 27-JUL-98

Operating profits, excluding special items, fell 20% in the first six months of 1998, primarily due to a drop of nearly $6.00 per barrel in average crude oil price realizations. Oil production was up slightly, while natural gas output declined nearly 5%. We now expect oil output from Nigeria, MOB's largest international producing region, to be lower than the 270,000-280,000 barrels per day we had originally expected, reflecting that country's OPEC quota reduction. In addition, a drop in Asian liquid natural gas (NGL) demand had resulted in reduced Indonesian natural gas output. Chemicals profits were lower, despite higher volumes, as polyethylene and paraxylene margins weakened. Downstream operations were a bright spot, as earnings rose strongly on higher margins and increased refined product sales. Domestic gasoline sales were particularly robust. Looking beyond 1998, we expect Mobil to achieve its goal of 4% annual production increases, aided by a growing reserve base.

Valuation - 27-JUL-98

The shares were recently down slightly in 1998, reflecting a difficult oil price environment. Worldwide crude oil prices have collapsed under the weight of a growing oversupply, and recent pledges of output cuts by some of the world's largest producers have had little positive effect to date. The shares are fairly valued, recently trading at a small discount to the P/E multiple of the S&P 500, and are at our target valuation of 20X estimated 1998 EPS of $3.50. We believe that long term fundamentals are strong for Mobil, and approve of management's focused oil and gas exploration and production plan and commitment to cost cutting. Reflecting a solid balance sheet, the dividend was increased 7.6% in January 1998.

Key Stock Statistics

S&P EPS Est. 1998	3.50	Tang. Bk. Value/Share	24.96
P/E on S&P Est. 1998	22.3	Beta	0.49
S&P EPS Est. 1999	4.20	Shareholders	185,600
Dividend Rate/Share	2.28	Market cap. (B)	$ 61.0
Shs. outstg. (M)	781.7	Inst. holdings	51%
Avg. daily vol. (M)	2.116		

Value of $10,000 invested 5 years ago: $ 30,217

Fiscal Year Ending Dec. 31

	1998	1997	1996	1995	1994	1993
Revenues (Million $)						
1Q	12,037	16,186	18,700	17,402	14,948	14,880
2Q	13,233	16,749	19,520	18,700	16,047	16,040
3Q	—	16,397	20,326	18,267	16,739	15,680
4Q	—	16,574	22,957	19,044	19,023	16,870
Yr.	—	65,906	80,365	73,413	66,757	63,474
Earnings Per Share ($)						
1Q	**0.86**	1.03	0.92	0.79	0.66	0.59
2Q	**0.79**	1.06	0.97	0.21	0.23	0.70
3Q	—	1.12	0.96	0.97	0.61	0.81
4Q	—	**0.86**	0.84	0.96	0.64	0.42
Yr.	**E3.50**	**4.01**	**3.61**	2.94	2.14	2.54

Next earnings report expected: late October

Dividend Data (Dividends have been paid since 1902.)

Amount ($)	Date Decl.	Ex-Div. Date	Stock of Record	Payment Date
0.570	Jan. 30	Feb. 05	Feb. 09	Mar. 10 '98
0.570	Apr. 24	May. 06	May. 08	Jun. 10 '98
0.570	Jul. 24	Jul. 30	Aug. 03	Sep. 10 '98
0.570	Jul. 24	Jul. 30	Aug. 03	Sep. 10 '98

A Division of The **McGraw·Hill** *Companies*

Business Summary - 27-JUL-98

Mobil Corp. (MOB), one of the world's largest oil companies, has set itself an ambitious goal. In May 1997, Lucio Noto, the chairman, president and CEO, said that Mobil aims to earn $5 billion in net income in 2001, up from nearly $3 billion in 1996. Such a gain would represent annual earnings growth in excess of 10% over the next five years. The company hopes to achieve this by increasing oil and gas production, petroleum product sales and chemicals sales, while cutting costs.

Mobil is involved in all the major segments of the oil industry, including exploration, production, refining and marketing. Mobil is also a major presence in the petrochemicals industry. The company traces its roots to the late 19th century, when it was part of John D. Rockefeller's formidable Standard Oil Trust, and then, after the Supreme Court-ordered breakup of the Trust in 1911, Standard Oil of New York.

In 1997, worldwide net crude and natural gas liquids production averaged 928,000 barrels a day (b/d), up from 854,000 b/d in 1996; the U.S. accounted for 26% of 1997 production. Net natural gas production was 4.56 billion cubic feet (Bcf) a day (4.59 Bcf in 1996), of which 25% was produced in the U.S. Refinery runs totaled 2,191,000 b/d (2,142,000), and petroleum product sales 3,337,000 b/d (3,345,000). Mobil concentrates on high-margin products where it is a leader, including synthetic lubricants and premium gasolines.

Net proved reserves at 1997 year end stood at 4,105 million barrels of crude and natural gas liquids, up from 3,782 million barrels at 1996 year end. Net proved reserves of natural gas at 1997 year end totaled 16,956 Bcf (17,105). It is estimated that Mobil is one of the world's five largest non state-owned oil companies, in terms of proved reserves.

Mobil Chemical makes and markets basic petrochemicals and is a leader in polypropylene film, a food packaging product. The plastics division was sold to Tenneco for $1.27 billion in 1995. Specialty products include synthetic lubricant base stocks and additives for fuels and lubricants. Mobil expects significant additional ethylene capacity to come on line in the U.S. in 1998; more U.S. paraxylene capacity began operations in 1997.

In January 1998, MOB announced that its capital and exploration budget for 1998 would total $5.9 billion, up from $5.3 billion in 1997. Of the total 1998 budget, $3.9 billion has been allocated for exploration & production, $1.5 billion for refining and marketing, $0.4 billion for chemicals, and $0.1 billion for corporate activities.

Per Share Data ($) (Year Ended Dec. 31)	1997	1996	1995	1994	1993	1992	1991	1990	1989	1988
Tangible Bk. Val.	23.99	23.34	21.81	21.30	21.37	20.53	21.71	21.05	19.75	19.09
Cash Flow	7.08	7.22	7.75	6.03	5.83	5.05	5.57	5.61	5.25	5.72
Earnings	4.01	3.69	2.94	2.14	2.54	1.56	2.33	2.30	2.20	2.46
Dividends	2.12	1.96	1.81	1.70	1.63	1.60	1.56	1.41	1.27	1.18
Payout Ratio	53%	53%	62%	79%	64%	102%	67%	61%	58%	48%
Prices - High	78	63	58⅜	43⅝	42⅜	34⅞	36⅝	34¾	31⅝	24⅝
- Low	60	53¾	41⅜	36	29¾	29	27⅝	28	22⅝	19⅜
P/E Ratio - High	19	17	20	20	17	22	16	15	14	10
- Low	15	15	14	17	12	18	12	12	10	8

Income Statement Analysis (Million $)

	1997	1996	1995	1994	1993	1992	1991	1990	1989	1988
Revs.	64,327	71,129	64,767	58,995	56,576	56,877	56,042	57,819	50,220	48,198
Oper. Inc.	7,768	8,153	6,649	6,611	6,467	5,755	6,459	6,875	6,271	6,012
Depr.	2,554	2,725	3,748	3,098	2,629	2,780	2,589	2,682	2,502	2,683
Int. Exp.	428	455	467	498	366	612	733	707	707	943
Pretax Inc.	6,365	6,111	4,391	3,678	4,015	2,875	4,025	4,444	3,754	3,461
Eff. Tax Rate	49%	52%	46%	52%	48%	55%	52%	57%	52%	41%
Net Inc.	3,272	2,964	2,376	1,759	2,084	1,308	1,920	1,929	1,809	2,031

Balance Sheet & Other Fin. Data (Million $)

	1997	1996	1995	1994	1993	1992	1991	1990	1989	1988
Cash	820	808	498	531	827	303	870	1,138	1,541	1,037
Curr. Assets	9,722	12,895	12,056	11,181	11,069	10,956	12,401	13,231	11,920	11,178
Total Assets	43,559	46,408	42,138	41,542	40,585	40,561	42,187	41,665	39,080	38,820
Curr. Liab.	12,421	15,248	13,054	13,418	12,203	12,629	13,602	13,653	11,216	10,255
LT Debt	3,760	4,450	4,629	4,714	5,027	5,042	4,715	4,298	5,317	6,498
Common Eqty.	18,796	18,386	17,229	16,873	17,017	16,374	17,422	17,021	16,274	15,686
Total Cap.	27,047	27,074	25,322	24,572	25,024	24,719	25,930	25,382	25,389	26,077
Cap. Exp.	4,689	4,967	4,268	3,825	3,192	4,470	4,175	3,577	2,752	3,110
Cash Flow	5,774	5,689	6,124	4,799	4,654	4,028	4,448	4,549	4,304	4,714
Curr. Ratio	0.8	0.8	0.9	0.8	0.9	0.9	0.9	1.0	1.1	1.1
% LT Debt of Cap.	13.6	16.4	18.3	19.2	20.1	20.4	18.2	16.9	20.9	24.9
% Net Inc.of Revs.	5.1	4.2	3.7	3.0	3.7	2.3	3.4	3.3	3.6	4.2
% Ret. on Assets	7.3	6.7	5.7	4.3	5.1	3.2	4.6	4.8	4.7	5.1
% Ret. on Equity	17.3	16.3	13.8	10.1	7.4	10.0	10.8	11.3	12.5	

Data as orig. reptd.; bef. results of disc. opers. and/or spec. items. Per share data adj. for stk. divs. as of ex-div. date. Bold denotes diluted EPS (FASB 128). Revs. in Inc. Statement excl. excise taxes & other revs. E-Estimated. NA-Not Available. NM-Not Meaningful. NR-Not Ranked.

Office—3225 Gallows Rd., Fairfax, VA 22037-0001. **Tel**—(703) 846-3000.**Website**—http://www.mobil.com **Chrmn & CEO**—L. A. Noto. **Pres & COO**—E. A. Renna.**SVP & CFO**—T. C. DeLoach Jr.**Secy**—C. J. Yaley.**Treas**—W. R. Arnheim. **Investor Contact**—Frank E. Hopkins (703-846-3922). **Dirs**—L. M. Branscomb, D. V. Fites, C. A. Heimbold Jr., A. F. Jacobson, S. C. Johnson, H. L. Kaplan, J. R. Munro, L. A. Noto, A. L. Peters, E. A. Renna, C. S. Sanford Jr., R. G. Schwartz, R. O. Swanson, Sir Iain Vallance. **Transfer Agent & Registrar**—ChaseMellon Shareholder Services, Ridgefield Park, NJ. **Incorporated**—in New York in 1882; reincorporated in Delaware in 1976. **Empl**— 42,700. **S&P Analyst:** Norman Rosenberg

STANDARD &POOR'S
STOCK REPORTS

Monsanto Co.

1540

NYSE Symbol **MTC**

In S&P 500

12-SEP-98

Industry: Chemicals (Diversified)

Summary: In June 1998, this company agreed to merge with American Home Products Corp.

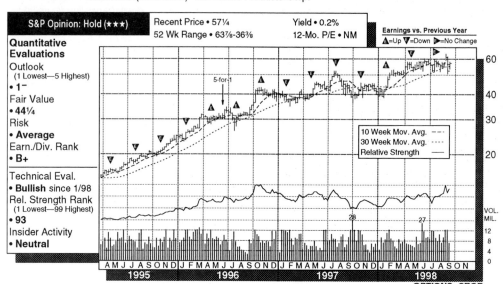

S&P Opinion: Hold (★★★)	Recent Price • 57¼	Yield • 0.2%
	52 Wk Range • 63⅞-36⅜	12-Mo. P/E • NM

Quantitative Evaluations

Outlook (1 Lowest—5 Highest)
• **1⁻**

Fair Value
• **44¼**

Risk
• **Average**

Earn./Div. Rank
• **B+**

Technical Eval.
• **Bullish** since 1/98

Rel. Strength Rank (1 Lowest—99 Highest)
• **93**

Insider Activity
• **Neutral**

Earnings vs. Previous Year
▲=Up ▼=Down ▶=No Change

10 Week Mov. Avg. - - -
30 Week Mov. Avg. ······
Relative Strength —

OPTIONS: CBOE

Overview - 04-JUN-98

On June 1, 1998, MTC agreed to merge with American Home Products Corp. (AHP), forming a new company with expected sales in 1998 of about $23 billion. MTC shareholders will receive 1.15 shares in the new company for each share of MTC currently held, thus owning about 35% of the new company. The two companies expect to realize annual cost savings of up to $1.5 billion within three years. The merger, subject to approval by shareholders of both companies, is expected to be tax-free and to be accounted for on a pooling of interests basis. AHP's share earnings will be diluted by up to 15% in the first year and become accretive in 2001. For MTC in 1998, we see agricultural operating earnings continuing to advance, on double digit volume growth of Roundup herbicide, boosted by increased worldwide applications as well as greater sales of new biotech products. Searle's sales should rise, on growth of newer products, although heavy new product testing, sales and marketing costs will limit profits. The proposed $2.5 billion purchase of the remaining 60% of DEKALB Genetics will result in EPS dilution of 20% in the first year of ownership. Results in 1997 included charges of $455 million ($0.75 a share) associated with acquisitions.

Valuation - 04-JUN-98

MTC is being acquired by AHP for about $35 billion in stock. Following the agreement, we downgraded our opinion of MTC to hold from buy. The planned merger will dilute AHP's earnings over the next three years. The merger provides MTC with deeper pockets to develop and market promising drugs in its pipeline and fund investments in agri-biotechnology. Approvals for new biotechnology products and a better profit performance by Searle helped to boost the stock in the past few years.

Key Stock Statistics

S&P EPS Est. 1998	0.95	Tang. Bk. Value/Share	3.11
P/E on S&P Est. 1998	60.3	Beta	0.56
S&P EPS Est. 1999	1.40	Shareholders	54,800
Dividend Rate/Share	0.12	Market cap. (B)	$ 34.4
Shs. outstg. (M)	600.9	Inst. holdings	63%
Avg. daily vol. (M)	2.486		

Value of $10,000 invested 5 years ago: NA

Fiscal Year Ending Dec. 31

	1998	1997	1996	1995	1994	1993
Revenues (Million $)						
1Q	2,044	1,875	2,304	2,318	2,001	1,941
2Q	2,470	2,095	2,579	2,482	2,269	2,230
3Q	—	1,724	2,176	2,048	1,912	1,849
4Q	—	1,820	2,203	2,114	2,090	1,882
Yr.	—	7,514	9,262	8,962	8,272	7,902
Earnings Per Share ($)						
1Q	0.32	0.34	0.43	0.40	0.33	0.23
2Q	0.41	0.41	0.62	0.50	0.44	0.33
3Q	E0.14	-0.28	0.28	0.24	0.20	0.16
4Q	E0.05	0.01	-0.69	0.13	0.10	0.10
Yr.	E0.95	0.48	0.69	1.27	1.06	0.82

Next earnings report expected: late October

Dividend Data (Dividends have been paid since 1925.)

Amount ($)	Date Decl.	Ex-Div. Date	Stock of Record	Payment Date
0.030	Oct. 24	Nov. 13	Nov. 17	Dec. 12 '97
0.030	Jan. 23	Feb. 12	Feb. 17	Mar. 12 '98
0.030	Apr. 24	May. 13	May. 15	Jun. 12 '98
0.030	Jul. 24	Aug. 13	Aug. 17	Sep. 11 '98

A Division of The McGraw·Hill Companies

Business Summary - 04-JUN-98

Monsanto completed a major transformation in September 1997, when it spun off its $3 billion a year chemicals business (now known as Solutia Inc.). MTC shareholders received one Solutia (SOI) common share for every five Monsanto shares held. MTC now consists of its potentially faster growing life sciences units: agricultural products, Searle pharmaceuticals, and food ingredients (combined annual sales of more than $7.5 billion). Earnings in 1997 were penalized by increased spending on R&D and marketing, and by after tax charges of $455 million associated with acquisitions.

Business segment contributions (profits in $ millions) in 1997 were:

	Sales	Profits
Agricultural products	42%	$112
Nutrition & consumer	20%	211
Pharmaceuticals	32%	318
Other	6%	-142

International operations in 1997 accounted for 42% of sales and 90% of operating income.

Monsanto's portfolio of agricultural products includes Roundup and Lasso herbicides for crop protection, seeds (Roundup Ready herbicide tolerant soybean, cotton and canola, and insect resistant Bollgard cotton and YieldGard corn), and Posilac bovine somatotropin growth hormone. Although conservation tillage (a technique that minimizes plowing to prevent soil erosion) has driven Roundup's growth in recent years, the increasing use of Roundup Ready seeds is now beginning to have a major positive impact on its use. Acquisitions completed in 1997, including Holden's Foundation Seeds, Asgrow Agronomics and Calgene, for a total of $1.7 billion, will give MTC greater market penetration for its biotechnology products.

Nutrition and consumer products consist of NutraSweet aspartame low-calorie sweeteners, Equal and Canderel brand tabletop sweeteners, food additives, and thickening and stabilizing agents for foods and pharmaceuticals. MTC has developed a new, no calorie sweetener, called neotame. The segment also includes the Solaris business, consisting of Ortho lawn and garden products and Roundup herbicide for residential use. MTC is considering alternatives for Solaris.

Searle's major pharmaceuticals include cardiovascular (Calan, Covera-HS), anti-inflammatory (Daypro, Arthrotec), gastrointestinal (Cytotec), women's health and fertility control drugs, and Ambien sleep aid. Arthrotec, used for arthritis treatment, received U.S. approval at the end of 1997. Searle's pipeline looks promising with five drugs in Phase III, including Celebra (COX-2 inhibitor) for arthritis pain, and Xemilofiban and Orbofiban anti-platelet agents. Several more products are expected to move into Phase III in 1998. Searle plans to file soon for U.S. approval for Celebra.

Per Share Data ($)

(Year Ended Dec. 31)	1997	1996	1995	1994	1993	1992	1991	1990	1989	1988
Tangible Bk. Val.	2.13	2.61	3.06	3.25	2.87	3.22	3.85	4.24	3.42	2.92
Cash Flow	1.32	1.63	2.30	1.96	1.73	0.95	1.60	1.93	1.98	1.76
Earnings	0.48	0.64	1.27	1.06	0.82	-0.20	0.47	0.85	1.00	0.83
Dividends	0.50	0.58	0.54	0.49	0.46	0.44	0.41	0.38	0.33	0.29
Payout Ratio	104%	91%	42%	46%	56%	NM	85%	44%	32%	34%
Prices - High	52¼	43¼	25	17¼	15	14¼	15¼	12	12⅜	9¼
- Low	34¾	23⅛	13⅝	13¼	9¾	10	9¼	7¾	8	7⅜
P/E Ratio - High	NM	68	20	16	18	NM	33	14	12	11
- Low	NM	36	11	13	12	NM	20	9	8	9

Income Statement Analysis (Million $)

	1997	1996	1995	1994	1993	1992	1991	1990	1989	1988
Revs.	7,514	9,262	8,962	8,272	7,902	7,763	8,864	8,995	8,681	8,293
Oper. Inc.	1,670	1,970	1,858	1,486	1,299	1,392	1,739	1,609	1,742	1,621
Depr.	487	590	598	523	550	710	723	700	664	666
Int. Exp.	170	185	208	141	141	185	193	208	204	193
Pretax Inc.	366	540	1,087	895	729	-162	458	809	1,015	893
Eff. Tax Rate	20%	29%	32%	31%	32%	NM	32%	33%	33%	34%
Net Inc.	294	385	739	622	494	-125	296	546	679	591

Balance Sheet & Other Fin. Data (Million $)

	1997	1996	1995	1994	1993	1992	1991	1990	1989	1988
Cash	134	166	297	507	273	729	189	204	253	221
Curr. Assets	4,266	4,340	4,305	3,883	3,672	4,060	3,711	3,513	3,248	3,097
Total Assets	10,774	11,191	10,611	8,891	8,640	9,085	9,227	9,236	8,604	8,461
Curr. Liab.	3,539	3,401	2,812	2,435	2,295	2,548	2,175	2,190	1,922	1,980
LT Debt	1,979	1,608	1,667	1,405	1,502	1,423	1,877	1,652	1,471	1,408
Common Eqty.	4,227	3,690	3,732	2,948	2,855	3,005	3,654	4,089	3,941	3,800
Total Cap.	6,180	5,348	5,484	4,418	4,411	4,493	6,043	6,381	6,033	5,796
Cap. Exp.	644	692	500	409	437	586	591	750	607	590
Cash Flow	781	975	1,337	1,145	1,044	584	1,019	1,246	1,343	1,257
Curr. Ratio	1.2	1.3	1.5	1.6	1.6	1.6	1.7	1.6	1.7	1.6
% LT Debt of Cap.	32.0	30.1	30.4	31.8	34.1	31.7	31.1	25.9	24.4	24.3
% Net Inc.of Revs.	3.9	4.2	8.2	7.5	6.3	NM	3.3	6.1	7.8	7.1
% Ret. on Assets	2.7	3.6	7.6	7.2	5.7	NM	3.2	6.3	8.1	7.2
% Ret. on Equity	7.3	10.4	22.1	21.8	17.2	NM	7.7	13.9	17.9	15.9

Data as orig. reptd.; bef. results of disc. opers. and/or spec. items. Per share data adj. for stk. divs. as of ex-div. date. Bold denotes diluted EPS (FASB 128). E-Estimated. NA-Not Available. NM-Not Meaningful. NR-Not Ranked.

Office—800 N. Lindbergh Blvd., St. Louis, MO 63167. **Tel**—(314) 694-1000. **Website**—http://www.monsanto.com **Chrmn & CEO**—R. B. Shapiro. **Pres**—H. Verfaillie. **CFO**—R. B. Hoffman. **SVP & Secy**—R. W. Ide, III. **Investor Contact**—Nicholas Filippello.**Dirs**—R. M. Heyssel, M. Kantor, G. S. King, P. Leder, J. F. M. Peters, N. L. Reding, J. S. Reed, J. E. Robson, W. D. Ruckelshaus, R. B. Shapiro. **Transfer Agent & Registrar**—First Chicago Trust Co., Jersey City, NJ. **Incorporated**—in Delaware in 1933. **Empl**— 21,900. **S&P Analyst:**   Richard O'Reilly, CFA

12-SEP-98

Industry:
Office Equipment &
Supplies

Summary: Moore Corp. is a major producer of business forms and related items, and also provides database management products and services, direct marketing products, and custom packaging.

| S&P Opinion: Avoid (★★) | Recent Price • 10¼ | Yield • 2.0% |
| | 52 Wk Range • 22-9⅜ | 12-Mo. P/E • NM |

Quantitative Evaluations

Outlook
(1 Lowest—5 Highest)
• **2**

Fair Value
• **9⅝**

Risk
• **Low**

Earn./Div. Rank
• **B-**

Technical Eval.
• **Neutral** since 6/98

Rel. Strength Rank
(1 Lowest—99 Highest)
• **63**

Insider Activity
• **NA**

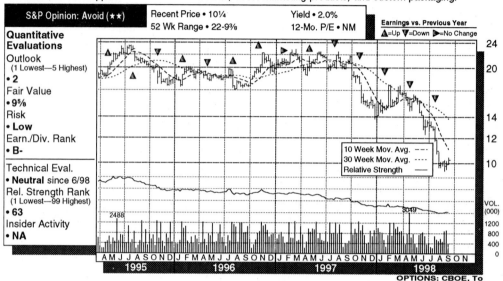

Earnings vs. Previous Year
▲=Up ▼=Down ▶=No Change

10 Week Mov. Avg. ---
30 Week Mov. Avg. ·····
Relative Strength —

OPTIONS: CBOE, To

Overview - 27-MAY-98

Acquisitions will boost reported sales for 1998. Moderately higher sales from ongoing operations will also reflect higher average paper prices. Lower unit sales of business forms, and competitive pricing will restrict revenue gains. Realignment of operations and processes to reflect lower volume began in the third quarter of 1997, and are continuing. MCL has undertaken a complete strategic review of all operations. MCL recently sold the European operations, representing some $50 million in revenues, of Peak Technologies as part of the company's strategy new strategy to focus on its North American forms and labels business, as well as its high-growth customer communications services business. MCL appears to be on the road to a sustainable recovery in earnings growth, but progress will be difficult to measure in the short term, as the new senior management team continues to streamline and refocus the business.

Valuation - 27-MAY-98

MCL is a company in transition. Its mature paper forms markets are shrinking, and, although management is aggressively seeking growth in electronic forms and services, customer communications services and joint ventures, those endeavors have been slow to pick up the slack. Moore's acquisition of four businesses in 1997 is part of its growth strategy. In late October 1997, directors elected Thomas E. Kierans as chairman of the board, and in April 1998 appointed W. Ed Tyler to the position of president and CEO. Both come to Moore from outside the company, an indication that directors are seeking fresh leadership. We are fairly optimistic about MCL's longer-term operating prospects, but the shares are likely to be underperformers in the near term. The quarterly cash dividend was recently cut to $0.05 from $0.235.

Key Stock Statistics

S&P EPS Est. 1998	-0.80	Tang. Bk. Value/Share	9.22
P/E on S&P Est. 1998	NM	Beta	1.05
S&P EPS Est. 1999	-0.80	Shareholders	7,200
Dividend Rate/Share	0.20	Market cap. (B)	$0.907
Shs. outstg. (M)	88.4	Inst. holdings	34%
Avg. daily vol. (M)	0.144		

Value of $10,000 invested 5 years ago: $ 8,117

Fiscal Year Ending Dec. 31

	1998	1997	1996	1995	1994	1993
Revenues (Million $)						
1Q	699.8	605.0	641.0	649.4	613.8	592.9
2Q	667.7	617.3	593.5	629.5	574.0	569.5
3Q	—	661.8	618.6	629.5	583.9	566.0
4Q	—	747.0	664.6	693.8	629.8	600.3
Yr.	—	2,631	2,518	2,602	2,401	2,329
Earnings Per Share ($)						
1Q	**0.06**	0.32	0.30	1.82	0.26	0.23
2Q	**-0.24**	0.31	0.36	0.34	0.26	0.21
3Q	—	-0.09	0.42	0.30	0.31	0.17
4Q	—	**0.01**	0.42	0.42	0.39	-1.39
Yr.	—	**0.59**	1.50	2.68	1.22	-0.78

Next earnings report expected: late October

Dividend Data (Dividends have been paid since 1934.)

Amount ($)	Date Decl.	Ex-Div. Date	Stock of Record	Payment Date
0.235	Oct. 22	Dec. 03	Dec. 05	Jan. 02 '98
0.235	Feb. 11	Mar. 04	Mar. 06	Apr. 01 '98
0.050	Apr. 22	Jun. 03	Jun. 05	Jul. 02 '98
0.050	Jul. 23	Sep. 02	Sep. 04	Oct. 01 '98

A Division of The **McGraw·Hill** *Companies*

Business Summary - 27-MAY-98

Moore Corp. is a company in transition. Although it is widely known as a leading multinational producer of business forms, operating in 47 countries with over 100 manufacturing plants, Moore is rapidly reducing its relative dependence on forms. Through acquisitions, greater emphasis on marketing strategies, and product and service enhancements, management is aggressively building its fully integrated direct marketing, print outsourcing, data-base management, and other high-technology services. Contributions by geographic area in 1996 (profits in millions):

	Sales	Profits
United States	65%	$81.7
Europe	12%	9.6
Latin America	8%	21.1
Asia Pacific	8%	-8.2
Canada	7%	13.2

Business forms and forms-based systems are MCL's primary focus and accounted for 79% of sales and $108.8 million of operating income in 1996, but were down to under 60% of sales by mid-year 1997. A variety of forms are manufactured, including handwritten types and complex forms for computers, optical scanners and other data processing equipment, and

multi-part interleaved carbon or carbonless forms. MCL also produces a complete line of form handling equipment.

The remaining 21% of sales and $33.5 million of operating income in 1996 were contributed by customer communication services, which include personalized mail, direct marketing program development, database management and segmentation services, response analysis services, and mail production outsourcing services. Through its strategic customer services program, MCL assumes and manages the complete business forms needs of large organizations using electronic links to track usage. Small customers are served by traditional distribution methods.

As part of its diversification strategy, Moore acquired over 90% of Colleagues Group plc, a major UK direct marketing firm, in August 1997. In July, Moore acquired Phoenix Group, a provider of direct marketing services to the automotive industry. In June 1997, Moore acquired Peak Technologies Group, the dominant integrator of data capture, printing and service solutions worldwide. Earlier, it acquired United Ad Label Co., a health care labels supplier.

In June 1997, the company commenced a one-year plan to buy back up to 5.7%, or 5.0 million shares of its outstanding common stock. A 12.0 million share buyback program was completed in May 1997.

Per Share Data ($)

(Year Ended Dec. 31)	1997	1996	1995	1994	1993	1992	1991	1990	1989	1988
Tangible Bk. Val.	9.22	15.49	14.75	13.53	13.01	14.62	15.84	15.64	14.74	13.75
Cash Flow	1.83	2.50	3.47	2.06	0.09	0.86	1.80	2.10	2.89	2.68
Earnings	0.59	1.50	2.68	1.22	-0.78	-0.02	0.91	1.27	2.15	2.01
Dividends	0.94	0.94	0.94	0.94	0.94	0.94	0.94	0.94	0.88	0.78
Payout Ratio	159%	63%	35%	77%	NM	NM	104%	75%	41%	39%
Prices - High	22⁷/₈	22¹/₄	23¹/₂	20⁷/₈	21¹/₄	22¹/₈	28¹/₂	30¹/₄	33³/₄	26⁵/₈
- Low	13¹/₂	17	17¹/₂	16¹/₄	15	14¹/₈	19	21⁵/₈	24⁷/₈	19
P/E Ratio - High	39	15	9	17	NM	NM	31	24	16	13
- Low	23	11	7	13	NM	NM	21	17	12	9

Income Statement Analysis (Million $)

	1997	1996	1995	1994	1993	1992	1991	1990	1989	1988
Revs.	2,631	2,518	2,602	2,401	2,329	2,433	2,492	2,770	2,708	2,544
Oper. Inc.	197	242	203	255	217	188	207	314	351	340
Depr.	116	100	78.9	83.4	86.5	97.6	86.9	79.3	69.7	61.7
Int. Exp.	14.2	11.0	11.8	13.1	17.2	13.5	13.2	17.2	12.8	19.0
Pretax Inc.	104	199	392	166	-95.0	26.0	137	196	301	276
Eff. Tax Rate	47%	24%	32%	26%	NM	101%	35%	38%	33%	32%
Net Inc.	55.1	150	268	121	-78.0	-2.0	88.0	121	202	186

Balance Sheet & Other Fin. Data (Million $)

	1997	1996	1995	1994	1993	1992	1991	1990	1989	1988
Cash	227	694	722	267	262	312	267	279	277	264
Curr. Assets	965	1,370	1,450	1,010	1,010	1,063	1,095	1,180	1,151	1,108
Total Assets	2,175	2,224	2,236	2,031	1,974	2,007	2,117	2,166	2,008	1,848
Curr. Liab.	790	486	542	447	451	366	332	410	376	350
LT Debt	49.1	53.8	71.5	77.0	68.0	32.0	59.0	56.0	40.0	62.0
Common Eqty.	1,186	1,550	1,488	1,365	1,313	1,476	1,585	1,538	1,441	1,292
Total Cap.	1,366	1,621	1,620	1,508	1,446	1,611	1,755	1,724	1,610	1,478
Cap. Exp.	136	120	86.6	77.0	82.0	91.0	120	166	127	88.0
Cash Flow	171	249	346	205	9.0	85.0	175	200	271	248
Curr. Ratio	1.2	2.8	2.7	2.3	2.2	2.2	3.3	2.9	3.1	3.2
% LT Debt of Cap.	3.6	3.4	4.4	5.1	4.7	2.0	3.3	3.3	2.5	4.2
% Net Inc.of Revs.	2.1	6.0	10.3	5.1	NM	NM	3.5	4.4	7.4	7.3
% Ret. on Assets	2.5	6.8	12.3	6.1	NM	NM	4.1	5.7	10.4	9.8
% Ret. on Equity	4.0	9.9	18.8	9.4	NM	NM	5.6	8.0	14.7	15.0

Data as orig. reptd. expressed in U.S. currency, based on Canadian GAAP; bef. results of disc. opers. and/or spec. items. Per share data adj. for stk. divs. as of ex-div. date. Bold denotes diluted EPS (FASB 128). E-Estimated. NA-Not Available. NM-Not Meaningful. NR-Not Ranked.

Office—1 First Canadian Place, Toronto, ON, Canada M5X 1G5. **Tel**—(416) 364-2600. **Website**—http://www.moore.com **Chrmn**—T. E. Kierans. **Pres & CEO**—W. E. Tyler. **SVP-CFO**—S. A. Holinski. **VP-Secy**—J. M. Wilson. **Treas & Investor Contact**—Shoba Khetrapal. **Dirs**—J. D. Allan, D. H. Burney, E. H. Crawford, S. A. Dawe, J. D. Farley, A. R. Haynes, T. E. Kierans, R. J. Lehmann, J. P. Lerman, C. E. Lindholm, D. R. McCamus, C. E. Ritchie, J. M. Stanford, T. M. Taylor, W. E. Tyler. **Transfer Agents**—R-M Trust Co., Toronto, Montreal, Vancouver, Winnipeg, Calgary; ChaseMellon Shareholder Services, Ridgefield Park, NJ. **Incorporated**—in Ontario in 1938. **Empl**— 20,000. **S&P Analyst:** William H. Donald

Morgan (J.P.) & Co.   1551

NYSE Symbol **JPM**

In S&P 500

12-SEP-98

Industry: Banks (Money Center)

Summary: This bank holding company emphasizes asset management and servicing, finance and advisory services, asset and liability management, and market making.

S&P Opinion: Hold (★★★)	Recent Price • 90⅛	Yield • 4.2%
	52 Wk Range • 148¾-82¾	12-Mo. P/E • 13.3

Earnings vs. Previous Year
▲=Up ▼=Down ▶=No Change

Quantitative Evaluations

Outlook (1 Lowest—5 Highest)
• 2

Fair Value
• 88⅞

Risk
• **Low**

Earn./Div. Rank
• **B+**

Technical Eval.
• **Bearish** since 8/98

Rel. Strength Rank (1 Lowest—99 Highest)
• 31

Insider Activity
• **Neutral**

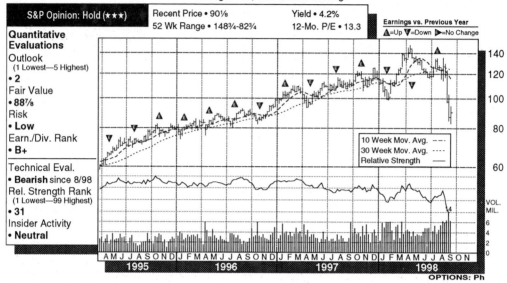

10 Week Mov. Avg. ----
30 Week Mov. Avg. ·······
Relative Strength —

VOL. MIL.

OPTIONS: Ph

Overview - 19-AUG-98

Revenues from advisory services and debt and equity underwriting, as well as asset management and servicing activities, should be the primary contributor to earnings in 1998, as efforts to earn a growing portion of clients' business have been successful. Turmoil in Asia took its toll on JPM's results in 1997, with market making revenues and nonperforming assets particularly hard hit. Accordingly, exposure to Asia was greatly curtailed in 1998's first half. Continued technology investment spending to build advisory and trading capabilities, expenses to prepare for the year 2000, and higher employee compensation and benefit costs due to a greater proportion of revenues from client-based businesses and competitive market conditions have led to high expense growth. However, an early 1998 restructuring aimed at certain sales and trading functions in Europe, refocusing the investment banking and equities business in Asia, and a workforce reduction should improve infrastructure efficiency going forward. A related charge reduced first quarter earnings by about $0.63 a share.

Valuation - 19-AUG-98

After recovering from a dip earlier in the year, the shares are now up about 13% year to date in 1998, in line with the average money center bank. Concerns about exposure to Asian turmoil should begin to ease, as exposure to emerging markets has been cut significantly since year end. Relatively high expense growth related to building client business capabilities has impacted earnings, although a recent restructuring has addressed this issue. With more than half of revenues derived from volatile trading/investment activities, earnings are inherently more difficult to predict than other banks. Based on growth assumptions, the shares appear fairly valued.

Key Stock Statistics

S&P EPS Est. 1998	7.60	Tang. Bk. Value/Share	62.38
P/E on S&P Est. 1998	11.9	Beta	1.28
S&P EPS Est. 1999	8.50	Shareholders	29,600
Dividend Rate/Share	3.80	Market cap. (B)	$ 15.9
Shs. outstg. (M)	176.6	Inst. holdings	64%
Avg. daily vol. (M)	2.223		

Value of $10,000 invested 5 years ago: $ 17,126

Fiscal Year Ending Dec. 31

	1998	1997	1996	1995	1994	1993
Revenues (Million $)						
1Q	4,923	4,275	3,898	3,358	2,831	2,884
2Q	4,969	4,325	3,923	3,346	2,957	2,945
3Q	—	4,605	3,799	3,346	3,048	3,124
4Q	—	4,496	4,246	3,639	3,079	2,988
Yr.	—	17,701	15,866	13,838	11,915	11,941
Earnings Per Share ($)						
1Q	**1.15**	**2.04**	2.13	1.27	1.69	2.16
2Q	**2.36**	**1.85**	2.14	1.56	1.73	2.12
3Q	—	**1.96**	1.32	1.78	1.63	2.30
4Q	—	**1.33**	2.04	1.80	0.96	1.92
Yr.	—	**7.17**	7.63	6.42	6.02	8.48

Next earnings report expected: mid October

Dividend Data (Dividends have been paid since 1892.)

Amount ($)	Date Decl.	Ex-Div. Date	Stock of Record	Payment Date
0.950	Dec. 10	Dec. 18	Dec. 22	Jan. 15 '98
0.950	Mar. 11	Mar. 19	Mar. 23	Apr. 15 '98
0.950	Jun. 10	Jun. 18	Jun. 22	Jul. 15 '98
0.950	Sep. 09	Sep. 17	Sep. 21	Oct. 15 '98

Business Summary - 19-AUG-98

With roots in commercial, investment and merchant banking, J.P. Morgan offers sophisticated financial services to companies, governments, institutions and individuals. It advises on corporate strategy and structure, raises equity and debt capital, manages complex investment portfolios, and provides access to developed and emerging financial markets. Revenues and pretax income in 1997 were derived:

	Revs.	Pretax Inc.
Market making	34%	20%
Finance & advisory	26%	25%
Asset management & servicing	22%	12%
Proprietary investing/trading	12%	28%
Equity investments	6%	15%

In finance and advisory, the company counsels clients on corporate strategy and structure, helping to raise capital through debt and equity underwriting and arranging credit. It offers advice on mergers, acquisitions, divestitures, privatizations and recapitalizations. Market making provides clients with access to world financial markets through dealings in securities, currencies, commodities and derivative instruments. Asset management and servicing involves managing assets for public and private pension plans, governments, endowments, foun-

dations and high net-worth individuals. Equity investments manages a portfolio invested in private equity and equity-related securities in leveraged and unleveraged acquisitions, recapitalizations, expansion financings and other special equity situations. Proprietary investing and trading involves actively managing market and credit risk positions for its own account.

In 1997, average earning assets, from which interest income is derived, amounted to $199.0 billion and consisted mainly of loans (15%), investment securities (12%), trading account assets (32%) and other temporary investments (39%). Average sources of funds included interest-bearing deposits (22%), trading account liabilities (10%), short-term borrowings (37%), long-term debt (7%), shareholders' equity (4%) and noninterest-bearing liabilities (20%).

At year-end 1997, nonperforming assets, consisting primarily of impaired loans, were $659 million (2.12% of loans), up sharply from $120 million (0.44%) a year earlier, reflecting difficulties faced by a number of Asian clients. The allowance for loan losses, which is set aside for possible loan defaults, was $1.08 billion (3.48% of loans), versus $1.12 billion (4.05%) a year earlier. Net chargeoffs, or the amount of loans actually written off as uncollectible, were $34 million (0.11% of average loans) in 1997, compared to $14 million (0.05%) in 1996.

Per Share Data ($)

(Year Ended Dec. 31)	1997	1996	1995	1994	1993	1992	1991	1990	1989	1988
Tangible Bk. Val.	60.74	58.07	53.21	46.73	48.50	34.30	29.41	25.29	21.78	30.52
Earnings	7.17	7.63	6.42	6.02	8.48	6.92	5.63	3.99	-7.04	5.38
Dividends	3.59	3.31	3.06	2.79	2.48	2.23	2.03	1.86	1.70	1.54
Payout Ratio	50%	43%	48%	46%	29%	32%	36%	47%	NM	29%
Prices - High	125¾	100⅛	82½	72	79⅜	70½	70½	47¼	48⅛	40¼
- Low	93⅛	73½	56⅛	55⅛	59⅜	51½	40½	29⅝	34	30¾
P/E Ratio - High	18	13	13	12	9	10	13	12	NM	7
- Low	13	10	9	9	7	7	7	7	NM	6

Income Statement Analysis (Million $)

	1997	1996	1995	1994	1993	1992	1991	1990	1989	1988
Net Int. Inc.	1,872	1,702	2,003	1,981	1,772	1,708	1,484	1,158	1,144	1,508
Tax Equiv. Adj.	72.0	85.0	106	120	138	161	173	197	244	271
Non Int. Inc.	5,348	5,153	3,880	3,536	4,176	2,562	2,531	2,033	1,671	1,748
Loan Loss Prov.	NA	Nil	Nil	Nil	Nil	55.0	40.0	50.0	2,045	200
Exp./Op. Revs.	70%	65%	67%	66%	59%	64%	59%	62%	63%	51%
Pretax Inc.	2,154	2,332	1,906	1,825	2,691	1,749	1,485	1,054	-1,099	1,315
Eff. Tax Rate	32%	33%	32%	33%	36%	21%	25%	27%	NM	24%
Net Inc.	1,465	1,574	1,296	1,215	1,723	1,382	1,114	775	-1,274	1,002
% Net Int. Marg.	NA	NA	1.55	1.56	1.51	1.78	1.77	1.48	1.53	2.75

Balance Sheet & Other Fin. Data (Million $)

	1997	1996	1995	1994	1993	1992	1991	1990	1989	1988
Earning Assets:										
Money Mkt	191,363	153,324	123,381	90,542	76,094	44,827	35,939	32,740	33,964	28,811
Inv. Securities	22,768	24,865	24,638	22,657	19,547	21,511	22,180	18,541	16,294	16,297
Com'l Loans	13,902	13,904	12,035	4,243	5,694	4,990	4,639	5,266	7,000	7,864
Other Loans	17,676	14,216	11,418	17,837	18,686	21,448	23,158	22,296	21,650	20,460
Total Assets	262,159	222,026	184,879	154,917	133,888	102,941	103,468	93,103	88,964	83,923
Demand Deposits	2,226	2,209	4,031	4,460	5,520	3,983	4,313	6,642	5,491	5,765
Time Deposits	56,653	50,515	42,407	38,625	34,882	28,536	32,663	30,915	33,667	36,704
LT Debt	22,989	13,103	9,327	6,802	5,276	5,443	5,395	4,723	4,690	4,052
Common Eqty.	10,710	10,738	9,957	9,074	9,365	6,572	5,574	4,695	4,001	5,534
% Ret. on Assets	0.6	0.8	0.8	0.7	1.4	1.1	1.0	0.8	NM	1.2
% Ret. on Equity	13.3	14.9	13.4	12.9	21.3	22.5	21.3	16.7	NM	19.1
% Loan Loss Resv.	1.7	2.0	4.8	4.8	4.8	4.8	5.1	6.7	9.1	5.2
% Loans/Deposits	53.6	50.3	50.5	51.3	60.3	81.3	75.2	73.4	73.2	66.7
% Equity to Assets	4.4	5.1	5.6	5.3	6.8	5.0	4.7	4.4	5.2	6.3

Data as orig. reptd.; bef. results of disc opers. and/or spec. items. Per share data adj. for stk. divs. as of ex-div. date. Bold denotes diluted EPS (FASB 128). E-Estimated. NA-Not Available. NM-Not Meaningful. NR-Not Ranked.

Formed—in 1969; bank incorporated in New York in 1864. **Office**—60 Wall St., New York, NY 10260-0060. **Tel**—(212) 483-2323. **Website**—http://www.jpmorgan.com **Chrmn & CEO**—D. A. Warner III. **CFO**—J. A. Mayer Jr. **Secy**—R. F. Robbins. **Investor Contact**—Ann B. Patton (212) 648-9446. **Dirs**—P. A. Allaire, R. P. Bechtel, L. A. Bossidy, M. Feldstein, E. V. Futter, H. H. Gray, W. A. Gubert, J. R. Houghton, J. L. Ketelsen, K. A. Krol, R. G. Mendoza, M. E. Patterson, L. R. Raymond, R. D. Simmons, K. F. Viermetz, D. A. Warner III, D. Weatherstone, D. C. Yearley. **Transfer Agent & Registrar**—First Chicago Trust Co. of New York, Jersey City, NJ. **Empl**— 16,045. **S&P Analyst:** Stephen R. Biggar

Morgan Stanley Dean Witter & Co. 1553L
NYSE Symbol MWD
In S&P 500

12-SEP-98

Industry: Financial (Diversified)

Summary: Morgan Stanley Dean Witter & Co. is a leading securities firm, with worldwide operations.

S&P Opinion: No Opinion	Recent Price • 51	Yield • 1.6%
	52 Wk Range • 97½-44	12-Mo. P/E • NM

Earnings vs. Previous Year
▲=Up ▼=Down ⬤=No Change

Quantitative Evaluations

Outlook (1 Lowest—5 Highest)
• 2

Fair Value
• 49⅞

Risk
• Average

Earn./Div. Rank
• NR

Technical Eval.
• NA

Rel. Strength Rank (1 Lowest—99 Highest)
• 14

Insider Activity
• NA

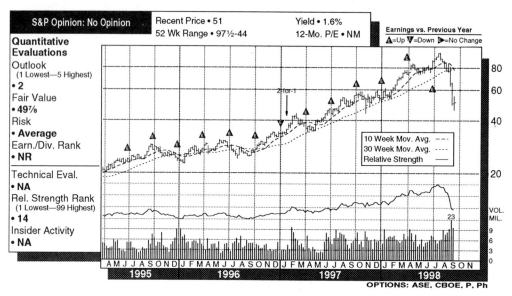

10 Week Mov. Avg. ------
30 Week Mov. Avg. ·······
Relative Strength ——

OPTIONS: ASE, CBOE, P, Ph

Overview - 23-JUN-98

Profits per share for the combined company are expected to improve in FY 99 (Nov.), primarily due to a projected decrease in credit card losses. Although the recent trend in chargeoffs has been negative, tightened underwriting standards and the use of early intervention procedures suggests reduced credit costs in the future. In the securities segments, the business outlook is good. With a number of industries rapidly consolidating, MWD is benefiting more than other brokerage firms from higher M & A fees. Asset management operations, which produce steady fee income, are growing. Trading income is hard to predict; assuming a normal level of market volatility, income from this source could be flat. Modest revenue enhancements and cost savings from the Dean Witter merger should make a positive contribution.

Valuation - 23-JUN-98

The shares, together with those of other brokers, have benefited in recent periods from heightened takeover activity, as well as from a strong market environment. While brokerage stocks have traditionally been valued on a price to book value basis, the fact that the combined company is presumably more diversified both within the securities industry and without as a result of a strong credit card presence argues for an earnings-based approach. Based on the most recent price, the stock is trading at a large discount to the market. Two factors suggesting that multiple expansion would be appropriate are the company's impressive 20% return on shareholders' equity in the latest quarter, and the large contribution to net income from asset management operations. Pure asset management firms trade at P/E ratios that approximate and in some cases exceed the P/E of the market.

Key Stock Statistics

S&P EPS Est. 1998	4.80	Tang. Bk. Value/Share	22.04
P/E on S&P Est. 1998	10.6	Beta	2.03
S&P EPS Est. 1999	4.75	Shareholders	214,300
Dividend Rate/Share	0.80	Market cap. (B)	$ 29.9
Shs. outstg. (M)	585.7	Inst. holdings	52%
Avg. daily vol. (M)	3.075		

Value of $10,000 invested 5 years ago: NA

Fiscal Year Ending Nov. 30

	1998	1997	1996	1995	1994	1993
Revenues (Million $)						
1Q	7,585	6,562	—	1,841	1,592	1,383
2Q	8,428	6,376	—	1,947	1,581	1,424
3Q	—	4,107	—	2,019	1,641	1,496
4Q	—	6,939	—	2,128	1,788	1,519
Yr.	—	27,132	22,172	7,934	6,603	5,822
Earnings Per Share ($)						
1Q	**1.10**	0.93	0.70	0.64	0.61	0.46
2Q	**1.37**	0.85	0.69	0.68	0.60	0.46
3Q	**E1.15**	1.11	0.71	0.62	0.54	0.51
4Q	**E1.18**	1.33	0.68	1.30	0.41	0.41
Yr.	**E4.80**	4.25	2.79	2.44	2.17	1.83

Next earnings report expected: late September

Dividend Data (Dividends have been paid since 1993.)

Amount ($)	Date Decl.	Ex-Div. Date	Stock of Record	Payment Date
0.140	Oct. 03	Oct. 09	Oct. 14	Oct. 31 '97
0.200	Jan. 07	Jan. 15	Jan. 20	Jan. 30 '98
0.200	Mar. 26	Apr. 13	Apr. 15	Apr. 30 '98
0.200	Jun. 26	Jul. 14	Jul. 16	Jul. 30 '98

A Division of The McGraw-Hill Companies

Business Summary - 23-JUN-98

This leading financial services firm was formed through the May 1997 merger of Dean Witter, Discover & Co. and Morgan Stanley Group. The rationale for the combination was to create an industry powerhouse with both retail and institutional distribution capabilities that could better compete in an increasingly global marketplace. Revenue contributions (pro forma) were obtained as follows in the past two fiscal years (Nov.):

	FY 97	FY 96
Securities	62%	65%
Asset Management	20%	14%
Credit & Transaction services	18%	21%

As an investment banker, the company raises capital for corporations, underwriting stock or debt or other securities, and earns a spread between the purchase and selling prices. It also advises companies purchasing other businesses or trying to fend off unwanted takeover attempts. MWD is one of the five leading players in the highly profitable mergers and acquisitions area. In its sales and trading operations, the company advises major buy-side institutions such as mutual funds

and pension funds on developments affecting their securities holdings, receiving either a commission or positive spread when the client places a buy or sell order. In its retail operations, the company's registered representatives or "stockbrokers" give financial advice to individuals, typically suggesting which stocks, bonds or mutual funds they feel are attractive. Stockbrokers might also engage in light financial planning, helping people set up savings plans for their children's education, for instance. In addition, MWD manages assets of some $338 billion, comprised of in-house mutual fund money as well as outside pension fund assets. Money management is a highly profitable business, partly because the fees are computed on assets that run into billions of dollars, while costs amount to little more than paying portfolio managers and renting office space.

Credit cards can be a very profitable business. The reason mainly relates to high interest rates. As anyone who is late in payments knows, the interest rate can be a real killer: a rate of 12.9% is considered a bargain, with most around 16%, and some over 19%. The company is a major player in this market, primarily through its Discover credit card. MWD's cardholders get rebates of up to 1% of total purchase volume.

Per Share Data ($)

(Year Ended Nov. 30)	1997	1996	1995	1994	1993	1992	1991	1990	1989	1988
Tangible Bk. Val.	21.98	17.37	13.82	11.68	9.68	7.53	NA	NA	NA	NA
Earnings	4.25	2.79	2.44	2.17	1.83	1.32	NA	NA	NA	NA
Dividends	0.56	0.44	0.32	0.25	0.15	NA	NA	NA	NA	NA
Payout Ratio	13%	16%	13%	11%	8%	NA	NA	NA	NA	NA
Prices - High	59½	34½	29⅛	21⅝	23¼	NA	NA	NA	NA	NA
- Low	32¾	22½	16¾	15¾	13½	NA	NA	NA	NA	NA
P/E Ratio - High	14	12	12	10	13	NA	NA	NA	NA	NA
- Low	8	8	7	7	7	NA	NA	NA	NA	NA

Income Statement Analysis (Million $)

	1997	1996	1995	1994	1993	1992	1991	1990	1989	1988
Net Int. Inc.	NA	2,021	1,804	1,459	1,094	1,009	965	917	NA	NA
Tax Equiv. Adj.	NA	NA	NA	NA	NA	NA	NA	NA	NA	NA
Non Int. Inc.	NA	5,441	4,615	4,095	3,912	484	2,835	2,412	NA	NA
Loan Loss Prov.	NA	1,232	744	548	458	NA	453	401	NA	NA
Non Int. Exp.	12,052	5,917	4,280	3,791	3,553	3,063	2,791	2,524	NA	NA
Exp./Op. Revs.	NA	63%	67%	82%	83%	87%	89%	91%	93%	96%
Pretax Inc.	4,274	1,545	1,396	1,215	996	703	556	404	297	150
Eff. Tax Rate	39%	38%	39%	39%	39%	38%	38%	42%	44%	43%
Net Inc.	2,586	951	856	741	604	439	345	233	166	86.0
% Net Int. Marg.	8.45	8.16	8.47	9.05	8.22	8.27	8.29	8.34	NA	NA

Balance Sheet & Other Fin. Data (Million $)

	1997	1996	1995	1994	1993	1992	1991	1990	1989	1988
Earning Assets:										
Money Mkt	6,890	4,044	3,391	2,828	22.0	2,447	1,800	NA	NA	NA
Inv. Securities	35,801	4,477	5,421	5,215	5,472	4,542	5,060	NA	NA	NA
Earn.Ass. Tot. Loans	24,499	23,177	21,557	15,608	11,711	9,459	9,525	9,441	NA	NA
Total Assets	302,287	42,414	38,208	31,859	27,662	23,822	22,751	20,839	18,945	17,598
Demand Deposits	1,210	1,716	1,552	1,166	1,157	1,362	1,264	1,290	NA	NA
Time Deposits	7,783	5,497	4,639	4,043	3,731	3,495	3,811	4,754	NA	NA
LT Debt	18,627	8,144	6,732	5,293	3,140	Nil	1,039	536	NA	NA
Common Eqty.	14,079	5,165	4,834	4,108	3,477	2,673	2,096	1,841	NA	NA
% Ret. on Assets	1.5	2.4	2.4	2.5	2.3	1.8	1.6	1.2	0.9	0.5
% Ret. on Equity	26.2	19.0	19.2	19.5	19.6	17.6	17.5	13.2	10.1	5.7
% Loan Loss Resv.	NA	3.5	3.3	3.5	3.5	3.4	3.5	3.1	NA	NA
% Loans/Deposits	NA	322.4	348.2	300.0	240.0	195.0	188.0	199.0	NA	NA
% Loans/Assets	NA	53.6	53.9	49.0	42.3	39.7	41.9	45.3	NA	NA
% Equity to Assets	5.6	12.4	12.8	12.9	12.6	11.2	9.2	NA	NA	NA

Data as orig. reptd. in annual tables for Dean Witter, Discover & Co.; bef. results of disc. opers. and/or spec. items. Per share data adj. for stk. divs. as of ex-div. date. Prior to 1997, fis. yrs. ended Dec. 31. Quarterly table rev. figure for 1996 pro forma. Bold denotes diluted EPS (FASB 128). E-Estimated. NA-Not Available. NM-Not Meaningful. NR-Not Ranked.

Office—1585 Broadway, New York, NY 10036. **Tel**—(212) 761-4000. **Chrmn & CEO**—P. J. Purcell. **Pres & COO**—J. J. Mack. **EVP & Secy**—C. A. Edwards. **Investor Contact**—John Andrews (212-762-8131). **Dirs**—R. P. Bauman, E. A. Brennan,' D. D. Brooks, D. Burke, R. B. Fisher, C. R. Kidder, J. J. Mack, M. L. Marsh, M. A. Miles, A. E. Murray, P. J. Purcell, C. B. Rogers Jr., T. C. Schneider, L. D. Tyson. **Transfer Agent & Registrar**—Dean Witter Trust FSB, Jersey City, NJ. **Incorporated**—in Delaware in 1981. **Empl**—45,000. **S&P Analyst:** Paul L. Huberman, CFA

12-SEP-98

Industry:
Chemicals (Specialty)

Summary: This worldwide producer of specialty chemicals and salt in 1997 completed the spin-off of its airbag business.

S&P Opinion: Accumulate (★★★★)	Recent Price • 23¼	Yield • 2.2%
	52 Wk Range • 35⅞-22	12-Mo. P/E • 14.8

Quantitative Evaluations

Outlook
(1 Lowest—5 Highest)
• **4+**

Fair Value
• **32¾**

Risk
• **Low**

Earn./Div. Rank
• **A-**

Technical Eval.
• **Bearish** since 5/97

Rel. Strength Rank
(1 Lowest—99 Highest)
• **69**

Insider Activity
• **Favorable**

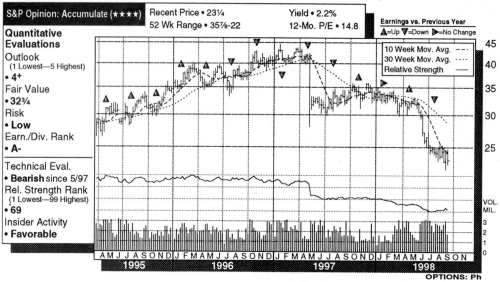

Earnings vs. Previous Year
▲=Up ▼=Down ▶=No Change

10 Week Mov. Avg. ---
30 Week Mov. Avg. ····
Relative Strength ——

OPTIONS: Ph

Overview - 08-JUL-98

MII completed a restructuring in May 1997. It merged its airbag business with Autoliv AB, creating Autoliv, Inc. (ALV). MII retained $800 million at the time of the spinoff, for use in acquisitions and stock repurchases. About $310 million was used for three acquisitions in FY 97 (Jun.), including the leading independent salt producer in Europe. MII has repurchased more than 13 million shares since the spinoff, for $427 million, and can buyback nearly another 15 million shares through April 1999. Sales of specialty chemicals should advance at a mid-single digit rate in FY 99 (Jun.), as higher volumes resulting from growing economies in the U.S. and Europe offset unfavorable currency rates and weakness from Asian markets. As part of a plan to improve the profit margins of the chemicals business closer to 20%, MII plans to sell two coatings units with annual sales totaling $50 million. MII may also further rationalize its manufacturing assets; two plants were closed recently as part of a program announced in 1996. Salt profits in FY 99 will be hurt by lower prices and early season volumes for ice control salt in North America as a result of higher-than-normal customer inventories following the mild winter in calendar 1998. The key for salt's results in FY 99 is weather conditions in the important Upper Midwest and Canadian markets. The French salt business acquired in March 1997 should make a bigger earnings contribution.

Valuation - 08-JUL-98

After a poor first half performance (down 27%), we view the stock as attractive for purchase, given the strong long-term growth prospects for the specialty chemical operations and the good cash flow of the higher margin salt business. MII plans to accelerate actions to boost chemicals segment margins closer to 20%, including divestitures of product lines and further consolidations of plants.

Key Stock Statistics

S&P EPS Est. 1999	1.80	Tang. Bk. Value/Share	10.19
P/E on S&P Est. 1999	12.9	Beta	0.45
Dividend Rate/Share	0.52	Shareholders	9,900
Shs. outstg. (M)	130.4	Market cap. (B)	$ 3.0
Avg. daily vol. (M)	0.529	Inst. holdings	65%

Value of $10,000 invested 5 years ago: $ 12,445

Fiscal Year Ending Jun. 30

	1998	1997	1996	1995	1994	1993
Revenues (Million $)						
1Q	601.3	523.0	817.9	745.5	619.6	538.0
2Q	664.9	564.2	916.1	830.9	690.9	545.0
3Q	660.5	638.5	998.4	921.0	808.3	648.3
4Q	603.4	614.9	888.4	828.5	730.8	578.2
Yr.	2,530	2,341	3,613	3,326	2,850	2,310
Earnings Per Share ($)						
1Q	0.39	0.31	0.45	0.41	0.29	0.24
2Q	**0.44**	0.35	0.66	0.49	0.36	0.23
3Q	**0.46**	0.45	0.72	0.60	0.47	0.32
4Q	**0.28**	0.37	0.41	0.46	0.39	0.06
Yr.	**1.57**	1.48	2.24	1.96	1.51	0.86

Next earnings report expected: NA

Dividend Data (Dividends have been paid since 1989.)

Amount ($)	Date Decl.	Ex-Div. Date	Stock of Record	Payment Date
0.120	Oct. 23	Nov. 20	Nov. 24	Dec. 08 '97
0.120	Jan. 22	Feb. 19	Feb. 23	Mar. 09 '98
0.120	Apr. 23	May. 13	May. 15	Jun. 08 '98
0.130	Jun. 25	Aug. 11	Aug. 13	Sep. 07 '98

A Division of The **McGraw-Hill** *Companies*

STANDARD
&POOR'S
STOCK REPORTS

Morton International, Inc.

1555T

12-SEP-98

Business Summary - 08-JUL-98

In May 1997, MII returned to its core businesses, specialty chemicals and salt. It separated these businesses from its automotive airbag operations, forming a new company that retained the Morton International name. The airbag business, which had FY 96 (Jun.) sales of $1.4 billion, was combined with Autoliv AB, forming Autoliv Inc. (ALV), with annual sales over $3 billion. MII shareholders received one new Morton common share, and 0.341 of a share of ALV, for each old Morton share held.

MII spent $310 million for three acquisitions in FY 97, using some of the $750 million of the cash given to new Morton in the spinoff. In FY 97, MII also repurchased 6.5 million common shares, including 3.2 million shares following the spinoff. Another 10 million shares were acquired in the first nine months of FY 98. In December 1997, directors authorized the purchase of up to another 10 million shares. MII would like to improve its modest Asian and Latin American positions in addition to continuing expansion in North America and Europe. Contributions by segment for the new MII in FY 97 were:

	Sales	Profits
Specialty chemicals	72%	66%
Salt	28%	34%

Foreign operations accounted for 35% of sales and 30% of operating profits in FY 97.

Specialty chemicals are produced for a wide variety of applications. Products include adhesives for flexible food packaging, industrial and automobile applications; chemical specialties (water-based polymers, thermoplastic polyurethanes, sodium borohydride, biocides, plastic additives, polymers and sealants, specialty liquid dyes, organic specialties, and advanced materials used by the construction, graphic arts, industrial, automotive and consumer goods markets); coatings (automotive and industrial finishes, coil and extrusion coatings, highway markings, powder coatings, and liquid colorants used by automotive, appliance, furniture and equipment manufacturers, and highway marking contractors); and electronic materials (photoresists and solder masks used in the manufacture of printed circuit boards).

Salt is the oldest of MII's businesses and it is the leading North American salt company. Salt is marketed under the Morton and Windsor brands for human and animal consumption; residential, municipal and industrial water conditioning; highway and residential ice control; food and meat processing; and industrial manufacturing and chemical processing. In April 1997, MII purchased for $270 million, Salins du Midi, the leading independent salt producer in Europe, with annual sales of about $270 million. The acquisition brought annual sales for MII's salt business to about $850 million.

Per Share Data ($)

(Year Ended Jun. 30)	1998	1997	1996	1995	1994	1993	1992	1991	1990	1989
Tangible Bk. Val.	NA	10.18	9.67	8.95	7.23	5.80	5.90	5.07	4.43	4.91
Cash Flow	NA	2.29	3.41	3.01	2.43	1.62	1.68	1.58	1.46	1.08
Earnings	1.57	1.48	2.24	1.96	1.51	0.86	0.98	0.95	0.93	0.68
Dividends	0.48	0.57	0.52	0.44	0.37	0.32	0.32	0.31	0.29	NA
Payout Ratio	31%	39%	23%	22%	25%	37%	32%	33%	31%	NA
Prices - High	34⅜	44⅝	43	36⅛	37¼	33½	21⅝	19½	15⅞	14
- Low	23¾	28	33¼	26¼	25½	19⅛	16⅞	12⅞	11⅛	10½
P/E Ratio - High	22	30	19	18	25	39	22	20	17	21
- Low	15	19	15	13	17	22	17	14	12	16

Income Statement Analysis (Million $)

	1998	1997	1996	1995	1994	1993	1992	1991	1990	1989
Revs.	NA	2,341	3,613	3,326	2,850	2,310	2,044	1,906	1,639	1,407
Oper. Inc.	NA	439	695	627	495	371	344	319	276	240
Depr.	NA	127	175	157	138	114	102	92.0	76.0	58.0
Int. Exp.	NA	25.6	24.6	28.4	27.8	33.7	33.8	36.4	17.3	9.1
Pretax Inc.	NA	334	539	471	358	200	231	214	215	151
Eff. Tax Rate	NA	36%	38%	38%	37%	37%	38%	36%	37%	36%
Net Inc.	NA	214	334	294	227	127	145	138	135	97.0

Balance Sheet & Other Fin. Data (Million $)

	1998	1997	1996	1995	1994	1993	1992	1991	1990	1989
Cash	NA	430	71.1	88.3	58.7	45.3	35.0	60.9	86.7	53.0
Curr. Assets	NA	1,390	1,196	1,168	996	866	816	758	730	557
Total Assets	NA	2,805	2,772	2,756	2,463	2,239	2,111	1,926	1,814	1,364
Curr. Liab.	NA	523	557	554	557	525	491	410	406	301
LT Debt	NA	224	219	219	198	218	223	256	261	44.0
Common Eqty.	NA	1,734	1,673	1,664	1,400	1,200	1,223	1,103	1,008	901
Total Cap.	NA	2,004	1,944	1,937	1,653	1,474	1,554	1,454	1,345	1,017
Cap. Exp.	NA	117	216	252	220	202	200	164	111	132
Cash Flow	NA	341	509	451	364	241	247	230	211	155
Curr. Ratio	NA	2.7	2.1	2.1	1.8	1.6	1.7	1.8	1.8	1.9
% LT Debt of Cap.	NA	11.2	11.3	11.3	12.0	14.8	14.3	17.6	19.4	4.3
% Net Inc.of Revs.	NA	9.1	9.3	8.8	7.9	5.5	7.1	7.3	8.2	6.9
% Ret. on Assets	NA	7.9	12.1	11.2	9.6	5.8	7.2	7.4	8.5	NA
% Ret. on Equity	NA	12.5	20.1	19.2	17.4	10.4	12.4	13.1	14.1	NA

Data as orig. reptd.; bef. results of disc. opers. and/or spec. items. Per share data adj. for stk. divs. as of ex-div. date. Bold denotes diluted EPS (FASB 128). E-Estimated. NA-Not Available. NM-Not Meaningful. NR-Not Ranked.

Office—100 North Riverside Plaza, Chicago, IL 60606-1596. **Tel**—(312) 807-2000. **Website**—http://www.morton.com **Chrmn & CEO**—S. J. Stewart. **Pres**—W. E. Johnston. **VP & Secy**—P. M. Phelps. **VP & CFO**—T. F. McDevitt. **VP & Investor Contact**—Nancy Hobor. **Dirs**—R. M. Barford, J. R. Cantalupo, W. T. Creson, W. J. Farrell, D. C. Fill, W. E. Johnston, R. L. Keyser, F. W. Luerssen, E. J. Mooney, G. A. Schaefer, S. J. Stewart, R. W. Stone. **Transfer Agent & Registrar**—First Chicago Trust Co. of New York, Jersey City, NJ. **Incorporated**—in Indiana in 1989. **Empl**—8,700. **S&P Analyst:** Richard O'Reilly, CFA

Motorola, Inc.

1558

NYSE Symbol **MOT**

In S&P 500

12-SEP-98

Industry:
Communications
Equipment

Summary: This leading supplier of cellular telephone systems, semi-conductors, two-way radios and paging equipment also offers information systems and other electronics products.

S&P Opinion: Hold (★★★)	Recent Price • 41⅜	Yield • 1.2%
	52 Wk Range • 75⅛-39	12-Mo. P/E • NM

Earnings vs. Previous Year
▲=Up ▼=Down ▷=No Change

Quantitative Evaluations

Outlook
(1 Lowest—5 Highest)
• **2**

Fair Value
• **39½**

Risk
• **Average**

Earn./Div. Rank
• **A+**

Technical Eval.
• **NA**

Rel. Strength Rank
(1 Lowest—99 Highest)
• **44**

Insider Activity
• **Neutral**

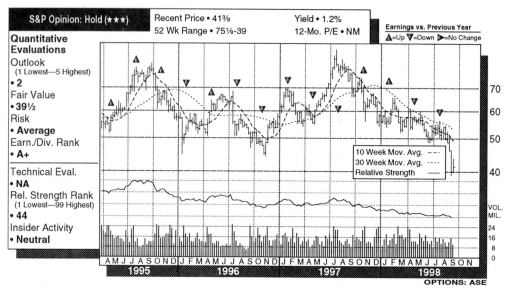

10 Week Mov. Avg. ---
30 Week Mov. Avg. ----
Relative Strength —

OPTIONS: ASE

Overview - 14-JUL-98

We now see Motorola's 1998 revenue falling 4%, based on the company's exposure to weakened Asian countries and to a global drop in demand for semiconductors. MOT announced a major restructuring program that includes approximately 15,000 layoffs, representing 10% of the workforce, and a $1.91 billion pretax charge for asset write-downs and cost reductions. Currency-influenced price competition from Asian competitors has hurt sales primarily in consumer semiconductors and analog wireless handsets. Roughly 26% of Motorola's sales are to Asian countries, with about 9% of total sales going to the weakened South East Asian countries. In July, Motorola announced plans to realign its communications businesses to allow different departments to share resources and cooperate on technology issues. The 21%-owned Iridium satellite communications system is on schedule to begin service in September 1998.

Valuation - 14-JUL-98

We lowered our EPS estimates again following weak second quarter results that included a dim operating outlook for the remainder of 1998. The shares have remained weak in 1998 as MOT has struggled with delays in new product introductions and with weakening economic conditions in key Asian markets. Conditions in the semiconductor industry have been deteriorating rapidly, and MOT's exposure to the Asian markets has negatively affected results. We lowered our 1998 EPS estimate to $0.61 from $0.85 and our 1999 estimate to $1.48, from $1.91. At 36X our 1999 EPS estimate, we feel that the shares are fully valued given the problems in Asia and the Semiconductor group.

Key Stock Statistics

S&P EPS Est. 1998	0.61	Tang. Bk. Value/Share	20.18
P/E on S&P Est. 1998	67.8	Beta	1.04
S&P EPS Est. 1999	1.48	Shareholders	71,400
Dividend Rate/Share	0.48	Market cap. (B)	$ 24.7
Shs. outstg. (M)	598.1	Inst. holdings	48%
Avg. daily vol. (M)	2.463		

Value of $10,000 invested 5 years ago: $ 16,539

Fiscal Year Ending Dec. 31

	1998	1997	1996	1995	1994	1993
Revenues (Million $)						
1Q	6,886	6,642	6,955	6,011	4,693	3,626
2Q	7,023	7,521	6,835	6,877	5,439	3,937
3Q	—	7,353	6,498	6,851	5,660	4,408
4Q	—	8,278	7,685	7,298	6,453	4,993
Yr.	—	29,794	27,973	27,037	22,245	16,963
Earnings Per Share ($)						
1Q	0.30	0.53	0.63	0.61	0.51	0.36
2Q	-2.22	0.44	0.54	0.80	0.63	0.41
3Q	—	0.44	0.34	0.81	0.65	0.44
4Q	—	0.53	0.39	0.72	0.87	0.58
Yr.	—	1.94	1.90	2.93	2.65	1.78

Next earnings report expected: early October

Dividend Data (Dividends have been paid since 1942.)

Amount ($)	Date Decl.	Ex-Div. Date	Stock of Record	Payment Date
0.120	Nov. 14	Dec. 11	Dec. 15	Jan. 16 '98
0.120	Feb. 03	Mar. 11	Mar. 13	Apr. 15 '98
0.120	May. 06	Jun. 11	Jun. 15	Jul. 15 '98
0.120	Aug. 05	Sep. 11	Sep. 15	Oct. 15 '98

A Division of The McGraw-Hill Companies

STANDARD
&POOR'S
STOCK REPORTS

Motorola, Inc.

1558
12-SEP-98

Business Summary - 14-JUL-98

As an increasing number of people all over the world use cellular telephones and pagers, Motorola has become a leading supplier to the rapidly expanding wireless industry. Although the company manufactures a variety of electronic products, it is best known for its wireless communications products. Industry segment contributions (profits in $ millions) in 1997 were:

	Sales	Profits
Cellular Products	40%	$1,380
Semiconductors	21%	332
Messaging, Information and Media	13%	80
Land Mobile	16%	588
Other Products	10%	(41)

Worldwide demand for communications and electronics products continues to surge, especially in emerging economies. Reflecting Motorola's position as a key player in the global marketplace, its international operations accounted for 58% of sales and 58% of operating profits in 1996.

The Cellular Products segment primarily develops, manufactures, sells, installs and services cellular infrastructure and cellular telephone subscriber units. The segment also includes the Network Ventures division, a joint venture partner in cellular operating systems in 16 foreign markets.

The Messaging, Information and Media products sector is composed of the Paging Products, Wireless Data, Information Systems, International Networks and Multimedia Groups. These groups provide pagers and pager systems, wireline and wireless data communication products, and modems.

The Land Mobile Product unit supplies analog and digital two-way voice and data products and systems.

While wireless communications products represent a major part of Motorola's business, they are by no means the whole story. The company is also a world leader in many key segments of the semiconductor industry. The Semiconductor Products segment manufactures a broad line of semiconductor devices for both consumer and industrial applications.

The Government and Space Technology Group provides electronic systems and products for U.S. government projects. The group's Satellite Communications division is developing the Iridium satellite-based communication system. Iridium, 21%-owned by Motorola, is expected to begin service in September 1998.

In July 1998, Motorola announced that it planned to realign its communications-related businesses under a single new organization called the Motorola Communications Enterprise. The cellular, space, land mobile and messaging groups, which together accounted for about two-thirds of 1997 sales, will be combined into the new group. The remaining one-third will consist of the Semiconductor and Automotive, Component, Computer and Energy sectors.

Per Share Data ($)

(Year Ended Dec. 31)	1997	1996	1995	1994	1993	1992	1991	1990	1989	1988
Tangible Bk. Val.	22.21	19.88	18.69	15.39	11.40	9.54	8.76	8.08	7.29	6.50
Cash Flow	5.73	5.68	6.09	5.21	3.76	2.95	2.54	2.46	2.21	1.91
Earnings	1.94	1.90	2.93	2.65	1.78	1.08	0.86	0.95	0.96	0.86
Dividends	0.48	0.46	0.40	0.27	0.22	0.20	0.21	0.19	0.19	0.17
Payout Ratio	25%	24%	14%	10%	12%	18%	22%	20%	20%	20%
Prices - High	90$^1/_2$	68$^1/_2$	82$^1/_2$	61$^1/_8$	53$^3/_4$	26$^5/_8$	17$^7/_8$	22$^1/_8$	15$^5/_8$	13$^5/_8$
- Low	54	44$^1/_8$	51$^1/_2$	42$^1/_8$	24$^3/_8$	16$^1/_8$	11$^1/_2$	12$^1/_4$	9$^7/_8$	9
P/E Ratio - High	47	36	28	23	30	25	21	23	16	16
- Low	28	23	18	16	14	15	13	13	10	10

Income Statement Analysis (Million $)

	1997	1996	1995	1994	1993	1992	1991	1990	1989	1988
Revs.	29,794	27,973	27,037	22,245	16,963	13,303	11,341	10,885	9,620	8,250
Oper. Inc.	4,276	4,268	4,850	4,119	2,848	1,968	1,636	1,597	1,446	1,269
Depr.	2,329	2,308	1,919	1,525	1,170	1,000	886	790	650	543
Int. Exp.	216	249	213	207	194	207	184	188	188	151
Pretax Inc.	1,816	1,775	2,782	2,437	1,525	800	613	666	646	612
Eff. Tax Rate	35%	35%	37%	36%	33%	28%	26%	25%	23%	27%
Net Inc.	1,180	1,154	1,781	1,560	1,022	576	454	499	498	445

Balance Sheet & Other Fin. Data (Million $)

	1997	1996	1995	1994	1993	1992	1991	1990	1989	1988
Cash	1,445	1,811	1,075	1,059	1,244	930	533	577	433	340
Curr. Assets	13,236	11,319	10,510	8,925	6,713	5,218	4,487	4,452	3,915	3,380
Total Assets	27,278	24,076	22,801	17,536	13,498	10,629	9,375	8,742	7,686	6,710
Curr. Liab.	9,055	7,995	7,793	5,917	4,389	3,335	3,063	3,048	2,751	2,691
LT Debt	2,144	1,931	1,949	1,127	1,360	1,258	954	792	755	343
Common Eqty.	13,272	11,795	11,048	9,096	6,409	5,144	4,630	4,257	3,803	3,375
Total Cap.	17,038	14,834	13,965	10,732	8,202	6,632	5,780	5,252	4,741	3,873
Cap. Exp.	2,874	2,973	4,225	3,320	2,187	1,386	1,317	1,371	1,218	965
Cash Flow	3,509	3,462	3,700	3,085	2,192	1,576	1,340	1,289	1,148	988
Curr. Ratio	1.5	1.4	1.4	1.5	1.5	1.6	1.5	1.5	1.4	1.3
% LT Debt of Cap.	12.6	13.0	14.0	10.5	16.6	19.0	16.5	15.1	15.9	8.9
% Net Inc.of Revs.	4.0	4.1	6.6	7.0	6.0	4.3	4.0	4.6	5.2	5.4
% Ret. on Assets	4.6	4.9	8.8	9.8	8.4	5.7	5.0	6.0	6.9	7.4
% Ret. on Equity	9.4	10.1	14.4	19.7	17.4	11.7	10.2	12.3	13.8	13.9

Data as orig. reptd.; bef. results of disc. opers. and/or spec. items. Per share data adj. for stk. divs. as of ex-div. date. Bold denotes diluted EPS (FASB 128). E-Estimated. NA-Not Available. NM-Not Meaningful. NR-Not Ranked.

Office—1303 E. Algonquin Rd., Schaumburg, IL 60196. **Tel**—(847) 576-5000. **Website**—http://www.mot.com **Chrmn**—G. L. Tooker.**Pres & CEO**—C. B. Galvin. **EVP & CFO**—C. F. Koenemann. **Pres & COO**—R. L. Growney. **Investor Contacts**—E. Gams, J. Stoner (800-262-8509).**Dirs**—R. C. Chan, H. L. Fuller, C. B. Galvin, R. W. Galvin, R. L. Growney, A. P. Jones, D. R. Jones, J. C. Lewent, W. E. Massey, T. J. Murrin, N. Negroponte, J. E. Pepper Jr., S. C. Scott III, G. L. Tooker, B. K. West, J. A. White.**Transfer Agent & Registrar**—Harris Trust & Savings Bank, Chicago. **Incorporated**—in Illinois in 1928; reincorporated in Delaware in 1973. **Empl**— 150,000. **S&P Analyst:** Aydin Tuncer

NACCO Industries

1572M

NYSE Symbol **NC**

In S&P 500

12-SEP-98

Industry:
Machinery (Diversified)

Summary: NC, one of the world's leading manufacturers of forklift trucks, also makes appliances through Hamilton Beach/Proctor-Silex, and is a U.S. lignite producer.

Quantitative Evaluations

Outlook
(1 Lowest—5 Highest)
• **NA**

Fair Value
• **NA**

Risk
• **Low**

Earn./Div. Rank
• **B**

Technical Eval.
• **Bearish** since 3/98

Rel. Strength Rank
(1 Lowest—99 Highest)
• **50**

Insider Activity
• **Neutral**

Recent Price • 102½
52 Wk Range • 177-93⅛

Yield • 0.8%
12-Mo. P/E • 8.9

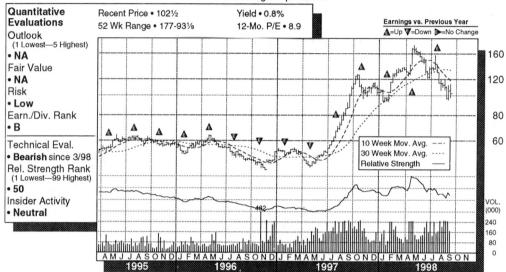

Earnings vs. Previous Year
▲=Up ▼=Down ▶=No Change

10 Week Mov. Avg. – – –
30 Week Mov. Avg. ·····
Relative Strength ——

Business Profile - 27-JUL-98

The company intends to reinvest its cash in existing business units, while seeking acquisitions that would fit well with existing operations. NC continues to focus on cost reduction efforts, and expects these programs to come to fruition in 1999. In the second quarter of 1998, NC began reporting the results of Hamilton Beach/Proctor Silex and the Kitchen Collection on a combined basis as the Housewares Group, which expects to benefit from increasing cost savings in the second half of 1998. In early 1998, the Chinese government authorized NC to manufacture lift trucks in China. NC's initial investment to build a new plant there will be $13.5 million.

Operational Review - 27-JUL-98

Total revenues in the first half of 1998 advanced 19%, year to year, led by a 22% increase at the Materials Handling Group, reflecting strong demand for lift trucks in North America, and increased volume at the Housewares Group and North American Coal. Profitability benefited mainly from strength in the Materials Handling Group; pretax income was up 162%. After taxes at 38.1%, versus 42.9%, and minority interest, net income increased 185%, to $50.4 million ($6.16 a diluted share), from $17.7 million ($2.16). NC expects lift truck shipments to remain stable in the Americas during 1998's second half due to high backlog levels, while unit shipments in Europe increase on improving economic conditions and stronger demand. Asia-Pacific shipments are expected to decline.

Stock Performance - 11-SEP-98

In the past 30 trading days, NC's shares have declined 11%, compared to a 10% fall in the S&P 500. Average trading volume for the past five days was 42,125 shares, compared with the 40-day moving average of 51,690 shares.

Key Stock Statistics

Dividend Rate/Share	0.82	Shareholders	1,300
Shs. outstg. (M)	8.2	Market cap. (B)	$0.667
Avg. daily vol. (M)	0.059	Inst. holdings	39%
Tang. Bk. Value/Share	0.37		
Beta	1.18		

Value of $10,000 invested 5 years ago: $ 21,214

Fiscal Year Ending Dec. 31

	1998	1997	1996	1995	1994	1993
Revenues (Million $)						
1Q	599.3	479.7	559.5	502.4	383.3	344.0
2Q	614.2	541.1	560.9	517.6	436.9	358.7
3Q	—	557.4	537.0	538.3	480.3	401.7
4Q	—	668.7	615.8	646.2	564.4	445.1
Yr.	—	2,247	2,273	2,205	1,865	1,549
Earnings Per Share ($)						
1Q	2.95	0.35	1.44	1.43	0.31	Nil
2Q	3.21	1.82	1.56	1.64	1.03	-0.02
3Q	—	1.78	0.85	1.53	1.23	0.23
4Q	—	3.62	1.83	2.71	2.49	1.09
Yr.	—	7.55	5.67	7.31	5.06	1.30

Next earnings report expected: mid October

Dividend Data (Dividends have been paid since 1947.)

Amount ($)	Date Decl.	Ex-Div. Date	Stock of Record	Payment Date
0.195	Feb. 11	Feb. 26	Mar. 02	Mar. 13 '98
0.205	May. 13	May. 28	Jun. 01	Jun. 15 '98
0.205	Aug. 12	Aug. 28	Sep. 01	Sep. 15 '98
0.205	Aug. 12	Aug. 28	Sep. 01	Sep. 15 '98

A Division of The McGraw-Hill Companies

Business Summary - 27-JUL-98

NACCO Industries (NC) is a holding company which owns three operating units: NACCO Materials Handling Group (NMHG), the Housewares Group and North American Coal. Following difficult market conditions in the North American lift truck industry during 1997, NC implemented a cost reduction program to offset this downturn. The company is keeping a close eye on opportunities within its markets, and expects improved margins and reduced costs to continue to have a positive impact on its results. The company also expects stronger industry demand in Europe to offset lower Asia-Pacific unit sales due to weakening currencies and economic uncertainty in that region.

The NACCO Materials Handling Group (NMHG) owns 98% of Hyster-Yale Materials Handling, Inc., one of the world's leading manufacturers of electric and internal combustion engine forklift trucks. In 1997, NMHG recorded a $16.3 million restructuring charge. This group sees a reduction in industry factory bookings for the North American market for 1998, although the lift truck market should remain strong. NC expects its new manufacturing facility in Mexico to begin production in 1999, and its cost-reduction efforts to increasingly benefit results during the next few years. NMHG accounted for 66% 1997 revenues.

As of mid-1998, the Housewares Group consisted of wholly owned Hamilton Beach/Proctor-Silex, Inc., a leading North American producer of small electric appliances, and the Kitchen Collection factory outlet stores.

Beginning in the second quarter of 1998, the results of Hamilton Beach/Proctor-Silex and the Kitchen Collection were reported on a combined basis. Motor-driven products such as blenders, food processors, mixers and electric knives are sold primarily under the Hamilton Beach name. Heat generating appliances such as toasters, irons and coffeemakers are sold under the Proctor-Silex brand. The new Saltillo facility is expected to continue to increase production capacity through 1998, with the full benefits from the plant expected in 1999. NC's retail operation consists of 143 Kitchen Collection factory outlet stores in 40 states, specializing in kitchenware and small electric appliances. During 1997, NC closed or converted 10 of its Hearthstone factory outlets to its Kitchen Collection format. NC expects a difficult factory outlet mall growth environment for the rest of 1998, and modest industry growth for small kitchen electric appliances. Houseware's sales were 22% of the 1997 total.

North American Coal is a leading producer of lignite. In 1997, it sold 29.9 million tons of lignite, versus 27.6 million in 1996. Some 80% of volume is sold to electric utilities. NC continues to study changes affecting the electric utility industry and expects a more competitive industry environment to result in growth opportunities for low-cost energy producers. The unit continues to pursue international mining opportunities and anticipates a decrease in royalty income in 1998 despite an incr ease in total lignite tons delivered. Coal sales represented 12% of the 1997 total.

Per Share Data ($)

(Year Ended Dec. 31)	1997	1996	1995	1994	1993	1992	1991	1990	1989	1988
Tangible Bk. Val.	NM	NM	-10.59	31.21	26.39	-26.83	-16.24	-17.00	-16.95	20.36
Cash Flow	18.37	15.24	16.15	13.70	9.61	9.89	9.33	10.10	11.15	8.61
Earnings	7.55	5.67	7.31	5.06	1.30	2.71	2.31	3.49	6.08	5.08
Dividends	0.77	0.74	0.71	0.68	0.66	0.64	0.61	0.59	0.57	0.55
Payout Ratio	10%	13%	10%	13%	50%	24%	27%	17%	9%	11%
Prices - High	127	64	64	64	58¼	60	56⅞	70½	56	40¾
- Low	44⅜	43⅛	46⅞	45¾	42	34¼	29	22	31¼	21¼
P/E Ratio - High	17	11	9	13	45	22	25	20	9	8
- Low	6	8	6	9	32	13	13	6	5	4

Income Statement Analysis (Million $)

	1997	1996	1995	1994	1993	1992	1991	1990	1989	1988
Revs.	2,247	2,273	2,205	1,865	1,549	1,482	1,369	1,385	1,188	616
Oper. Inc.	229	217	230	215	171	168	162	194	180	92.0
Depr.	88.6	85.3	79.3	77.3	74.3	63.8	62.3	58.7	45.0	31.2
Int. Exp.	36.6	45.9	51.9	63.4	69.6	65.8	76.3	83.9	75.5	21.9
Pretax Inc.	89.1	86.3	104	78.5	24.7	43.5	30.0	50.0	92.3	60.3
Eff. Tax Rate	30%	40%	34%	39%	55%	45%	32%	38%	42%	25%
Net Inc.	61.8	50.6	65.5	45.3	11.6	24.1	20.5	30.9	53.9	45.0

Balance Sheet & Other Fin. Data (Million $)

	1997	1996	1995	1994	1993	1992	1991	1990	1989	1988
Cash	24.1	47.8	31.0	20.0	29.0	34.0	52.0	101	172	95.0
Curr. Assets	600	592	722	587	505	496	532	658	702	357
Total Assets	1,729	1,708	1,834	1,694	1,642	1,664	1,608	1,722	1,680	837
Curr. Liab.	507	416	524	481	397	331	374	409	462	227
LT Debt	558	675	667	483	563	653	631	722	723	188
Common Eqty.	425	379	370	279	236	240	350	353	301	246
Total Cap.	1,000	1,068	1,037	802	840	934	1,016	1,111	1,030	441
Cap. Exp.	68.4	79.4	73.0	53.0	55.0	85.0	60.0	94.0	167	59.0
Cash Flow	150	136	145	123	85.9	87.9	82.8	89.7	99	76.2
Curr. Ratio	1.2	1.4	1.4	1.2	1.3	1.5	1.4	1.6	1.5	1.6
% LT Debt of Cap.	55.8	63.2	64.3	60.1	67.0	70.0	62.1	65.0	70.2	42.7
% Net Inc.of Revs.	2.8	2.2	3.0	2.4	0.7	1.6	1.5	2.2	4.5	7.3
% Ret. on Assets	3.6	2.9	3.8	2.7	0.7	1.5	1.2	1.8	4.3	5.8
% Ret. on Equity	15.4	13.5	20.2	17.6	4.9	8.1	5.8	9.5	19.7	19.9

Data as orig. reptd.; bef. results of disc. opers. and/or spec. items. Per share data adj. for stk. djvs. as of ex-div. date. Bold denotes diluted EPS (FASB 128). E-Estimated. NA-Not Available. NM-Not Meaningful. NR-Not Ranked.

Office—5875 Landerbrook Dr., Mayfield Heights, OH 44124-4017. **Tel**—(216) 449-9600.**Fax**—(216) 449-9607. **Chrmn, Pres & CEO**—A. M. Rankin Jr.**VP & Secy**—C. A. Bittenbender. **CFO**—K. C. Schilling.**Investor Contact**—Ira I. Gamm. **Dirs**—O. Brown II, R. M. Gates, L. J. Hendrix Jr., D. W. LaBarre, A. M. Rankin Jr., I. M. Ross, J. C. Sawhill, B. T. Taplin, D. F. Taplin, J. F. Turben. **Transfer Agent & Registrar**—First Chicago Trust Co., NYC. **Incorporated**—in Ohio in 1913; reincorporated in Delaware in 1986. **Empl**— 12,690. **S&P Analyst**: Stewart Scharf

Nalco Chemical — 1573

NYSE Symbol **NLC**

In S&P 500

12-SEP-98

Industry: Chemicals (Specialty)

Summary: This company is the world's largest producer of specialized service chemicals used in water and waste treatment and industrial processes.

S&P Opinion: Hold (★★★)	Recent Price • 28⅞	Yield • 3.5%	Earnings vs. Previous Year
	52 Wk Range • 42⅜-27⅜	12-Mo. P/E • 13.3	▲=Up ▼=Down ▶=No Change

Quantitative Evaluations

Outlook (1 Lowest—5 Highest)
• 3

Fair Value
• 35⅜

Risk
• Low

Earn./Div. Rank
• A

Technical Eval.
• **Neutral** since 6/98

Rel. Strength Rank (1 Lowest—99 Highest)
• 57

Insider Activity
• Neutral

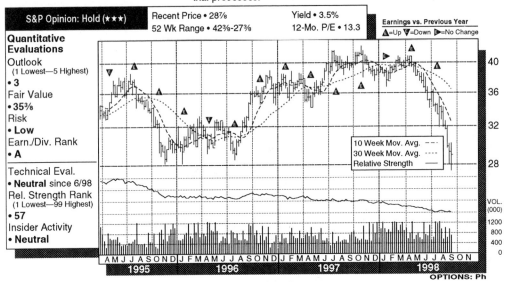

10 Week Mov. Avg.
30 Week Mov. Avg.
Relative Strength

VOL. (000)

OPTIONS: Ph

Overview - 19-AUG-98

We project that sales of this specialty chemicals company will continue to advance at a high single-digit pace for the rest of 1998 and into 1999. Domestic sales will likely continue to grow with healthy industrial markets, new products, and as NLC wins more sole-source supply contracts, although the important paper industry is being limited by the Asian economic slowdown. Most foreign markets should advance, despite the fact that Asian sales are being unfavorably affected by exchange rates. Acquisitions made in the past year will contribute to sales gains, and the selling price environment should remain favorable, following a recent round of consolidation among large competitors. Beginning with the 1997 third quarter, NLC is reporting freight revenues as a component of sales, rather than offsetting freight expenses in total costs; this change will add about two percentage points to 1998 sales growth. Sales force and raw material costs are expected to remain under good control. We expect the Exxon energy chemicals joint venture to show further profit improvement, despite low oil prices. An ongoing stock buyback program will aid EPS comparisons.

Valuation - 19-AUG-98

The stock has been a lackluster performer over the past several years, reflecting the maturing domestic water treatment industry and a poor market environment for specialty chemicals stocks. We see continuing EPS growth in 1998, as demand remains healthy, and reflecting contribution from several acquisitions that have increased NLC's presence in the growing middle market water treatment business. Industry consolidation in the past two years has improved the price environment. With the shares recently trading at a P/E multiple representing a discount to that of the overall market, we recommend holding current positions.

Key Stock Statistics

S&P EPS Est. 1998	2.25	Tang. Bk. Value/Share	5.91
P/E on S&P Est. 1998	12.9	Beta	0.65
S&P EPS Est. 1999	2.45	Shareholders	5,300
Dividend Rate/Share	1.00	Market cap. (B)	$ 1.9
Shs. outstg. (M)	65.9	Inst. holdings	79%
Avg. daily vol. (M)	0.167		

Value of $10,000 invested 5 years ago: $ 9,820

Fiscal Year Ending Dec. 31

	1998	1997	1996	1995	1994	1993
Revenues (Million $)						
1Q	367.1	334.6	301.9	292.5	336.2	339.0
2Q	403.0	354.4	318.6	302.3	352.0	347.5
3Q	—	371.0	343.3	310.0	343.4	354.0
4Q	—	373.7	339.7	309.7	314.0	348.9
Yr.	—	1,434	1,304	1,215	1,346	1,389
Earnings Per Share ($)						
1Q	**0.49**	0.46	0.40	0.44	0.45	0.46
2Q	**0.55**	0.51	0.47	0.45	0.44	0.50
3Q	E0.61	0.57	0.56	0.49	0.07	0.52
4Q	E0.60	**0.56**	0.56	0.48	0.29	0.55
Yr.	E2.25	**2.10**	1.99	1.83	1.25	2.03

Next earnings report expected: late October

Dividend Data (Dividends have been paid since 1928.)

Amount ($)	Date Decl.	Ex-Div. Date	Stock of Record	Payment Date
0.250	Oct. 16	Nov. 18	Nov. 20	Dec. 10 '97
0.250	Dec. 18	Feb. 18	Feb. 20	Mar. 10 '98
0.250	Apr. 29	May. 18	May. 20	Jun. 10 '98
0.250	Jun. 19	Aug. 18	Aug. 20	Sep. 10 '98

Business Summary - 19-AUG-98

Nalco (NLC) is the world's largest provider of specialty water treatment and process chemicals and services, which are designed to help customers maintain a high level of operating performance and efficiency or improve the quality of their products. The company has expanded its position in the growing middle market of water treatment chemicals. NLC expects 50% of its sales to be outside the U.S. by the turn of the century, versus 41% currently. Contributions to sales by business segment in recent years were:

	1997	1996
Water & waste treatment	33%	32%
Process chemicals	26%	27%
Europe	22%	22%
Latin America	8%	8%
Pacific	11%	11%

Foreign operations accounted for 31% of operating profits in 1997.

Water and waste treatment chemicals are used for water clarification, water pollution control, energy conservation and the control of corrosion, scale, foam, microbial activity and air emissions in industrial, utility, commercial, institutional and municipal boiler, cooling and process systems. Process chemicals are used during manufacturing processes to protect equipment and facilitate production in such industries as pulp and paper, steel, metals, mining and mineral processing, automotive, electronics, transportation, and food.

Since May 1996, NLC has completed acquisitions with combined annual sales of about $270 million, primarily in the growing water treatment middle market. The largest purchase was the Diversey unit of Molson Cos., for $82 million, in July 1996. The business had annual sales of about $60 million, with nearly 40% of sales outside the U.S. NLC in 1997 expanded in the metalworking fluids market with the purchase of a company with annual sales of $18 million.

The Nalco/Exxon joint venture partnership (60% owned), with sales of $456 million in 1997, is the largest supplier of petroleum chemicals used in oil and natural gas drilling and production; pipeline and transmission systems; and petroleum refining and petrochemical processing (including refined product additives). NLC had equity income in the venture of $28.2 million, versus $24.5 million in 1996. The petroleum refining industry is growing more rapidly in the less developed areas of the world than in the U.S.

Since beginning an active buyback program in 1992, NLC has acquired approximately 8 million common shares for $280 million, including 2 million shares in 1997. At the end of 1997, about 1 million shares remained authorized to be repurchased.

Per Share Data ($)

(Year Ended Dec. 31)	1997	1996	1995	1994	1993	1992	1991	1990	1989	1988
Tangible Bk. Val.	5.60	6.35	6.31	5.95	6.04	6.41	2.74	3.04	2.73	5.62
Cash Flow	3.39	3.61	3.31	2.54	3.27	3.02	2.75	2.45	2.08	1.93
Earnings	2.10	1.99	1.83	1.25	2.03	1.90	1.78	1.71	1.51	1.35
Dividends	1.00	1.00	0.99	0.94	0.89	0.84	0.83	0.76	0.68	0.65
Payout Ratio	48%	50%	54%	76%	44%	44%	47%	43%	43%	47%
Prices - High	42³⁄₈	39	38⁵⁄₈	37⁷⁄₈	37⁷⁄₈	40⁷⁄₈	42¹⁄₄	30⁵⁄₈	25	20
- Low	34¹⁄₄	28¹⁄₈	28¹⁄₈	29³⁄₄	30¹⁄₄	30³⁄₈	26¹⁄₈	22	17¹⁄₄	15⁵⁄₈
P/E Ratio - High	20	20	21	30	19	22	24	18	17	15
- Low	16	14	15	24	15	16	15	13	11	12

Income Statement Analysis (Million $)

	1997	1996	1995	1994	1993	1992	1991	1990	1989	1988
Revs.	1,434	1,304	1,215	1,346	1,389	1,375	1,237	1,212	1,071	994
Oper. Inc.	346	315	295	332	349	340	296	262	224	204
Depr.	103	98.3	89.2	89.2	86.5	79.4	69.1	51.2	43.2	45.3
Int. Exp.	15.3	14.4	16.2	21.8	27.5	40.3	27.9	15.8	14.3	11.7
Pretax Inc.	256	229	213	176	250	238	222	215	196	168
Eff. Tax Rate	36%	37%	37%	45%	39%	39%	38%	39%	39%	37%
Net Inc.	163	146	136	97.0	153	145	135	131	120	106

Balance Sheet & Other Fin. Data (Million $)

	1997	1996	1995	1994	1993	1992	1991	1990	1989	1988
Cash	49.7	38.8	38.1	45.0	78.0	222	212	120	130	85.0
Curr. Assets	409	385	370	362	375	522	518	406	387	330
Total Assets	1,441	1,395	1,370	1,282	1,212	1,351	1,324	1,037	938	839
Curr. Liab.	256	290	356	274	190	208	262	176	169	156
LT Debt	335	253	222	245	252	414	394	282	214	101
Common Eqty.	652	628	555	518	529	567	330	256	244	478
Total Cap.	992	951	855	846	861	1,097	1,014	816	720	632
Cap. Exp.	101	92.5	127	126	118	131	137	115	86.0	62.0
Cash Flow	255	244	225	175	228	214	194	174	157	151
Curr. Ratio	1.6	1.3	1.0	1.3	2.0	2.5	2.0	2.3	2.3	2.1
% LT Debt of Cap.	33.8	26.6	26.0	29.0	29.3	37.7	38.9	34.6	29.7	16.0
% Net Inc.of Revs.	11.4	11.2	11.2	7.2	11.0	10.5	10.9	10.8	11.2	10.7
% Ret. on Assets	11.5	10.6	10.3	7.8	12.0	10.8	11.4	13.5	13.9	13.5
% Ret. on Equity	23.3	24.7	25.3	16.6	26.1	24.8	42.4	49.3	32.9	23.1

Data as orig. reptd.; bef. results of disc. opers. and/or spec. items. Per share data adj. for stk. divs. as of ex-div. date. Bold denotes diluted EPS (FASB 128). E-Estimated. NA-Not Available. NM-Not Meaningful. NR-Not Ranked.

Office—One Nalco Center, Naperville, IL 60563-1198. **Tel**—(630) 305-1000. **Fax**—(630) 305-2900. **Website**—http://www.nalco.com **Chrmn, Pres & CEO**—E. J. Mooney Jr. **Secy**—Suzzanne J. Gioimo. **SVP & CFO**—W. E. Buchholz. **VP & Investor Contact**—Joseph R. Esterman. **Dirs**—J. L. Ballesteros, H. G. Bernthal, H. Corless, H. M. Dean, J. P. Frazee Jr., A. L. Kelly, B. S. Kelly, F. A. Krehbiel, E. J. Mooney Jr., S. A. Penrose, W. A. Pogue, J. J. Shea. **Transfer Agent & Registrar**—First Chicago Trust Co. of New York, Jersey City, NJ. **Incorporated**—in Delaware in 1928. **Empl**— 6,905. **S&P Analyst:** Richard O'Reilly, CFA

STANDARD &POOR'S
STOCK REPORTS

National City

1591

NYSE Symbol **NCC**

In S&P 500

12-SEP-98

Industry:
Banks (Major Regional)

Summary: The third largest bank holding company in Ohio, National City also has banking offices in Kentucky, Indiana and Pennsylvania.

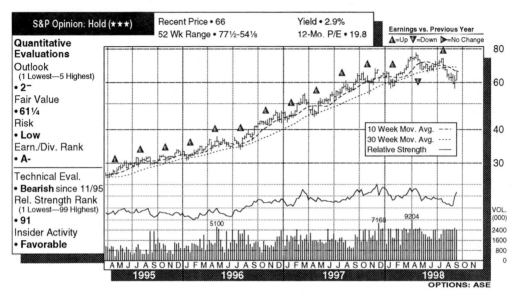

| S&P Opinion: Hold (★★★) | Recent Price • 66 | Yield • 2.9% |
| | 52 Wk Range • 77½-54⅛ | 12-Mo. P/E • 19.8 |

Quantitative Evaluations

Outlook
(1 Lowest—5 Highest)
• **2⁻**

Fair Value
• **61¼**

Risk
• **Low**

Earn./Div. Rank
• **A-**

Technical Eval.
• **Bearish** since 11/95

Rel. Strength Rank
(1 Lowest—99 Highest)
• **91**

Insider Activity
• **Favorable**

Earnings vs. Previous Year
▲=Up ▼=Down ▶=No Change

10 Week Mov. Avg. ---
30 Week Mov. Avg. ·····
Relative Strength —

OPTIONS: ASE

Overview - 28-AUG-98

Reported loan growth of about 10% is expected for 1998, as mid single-digit internal gains are enhanced by the acquisition of Fort Wayne National. Margins have been negatively impacted by the sale of the high-yielding private-label credit card portfolio, a greater mix of lower-yielding commercial loans due to healthy growth in that segment, and higher funding costs from an increasing reliance on wholesale borrowings. Noninterest income will remain a primary growth driver, benefiting from strong growth in item processing revenues and mortgage banking fees from the current robust refinancing wave. The company remains vigilant about cost control and expects noninterest expense to remain in the low single-digit range, absent merger integration charges. Integration activities will remain a primary focus throughout 1998, with both First of America and Fort Wayne National acquired in March 1998. The company made progress on several financial performance measures in 1997, notably return on equity and efficiency ratios as acquired operations were integrated.

Valuation - 28-AUG-98

With a roughly 6% decline thus far in 1998, the shares have underperformed the broader market, at least in part due to a pullback in valuations afforded regional bank stocks. In addition, investors may be taking pause as recent acquisitions are integrated. Nonetheless, fundamentals remain healthy, with strong deposit market share, good loan growth and ongoing expense control measures expected to lead to high single-digit earnings growth in 1998. Trading at about 13 times our 1999 earnings estimate of $4.65, and yielding an above-average 3.1%, the shares make a worthwhile holding.

Key Stock Statistics

S&P EPS Est. 1998	3.95	Tang. Bk. Value/Share	20.68
P/E on S&P Est. 1998	16.7	Beta	0.98
S&P EPS Est. 1999	4.65	Shareholders	36,200
Dividend Rate/Share	1.92	Market cap. (B)	$ 21.8
Shs. outstg. (M)	329.7	Inst. holdings	42%
Avg. daily vol. (M)	0.625		

Value of $10,000 invested 5 years ago: $ 32,610

Fiscal Year Ending Dec. 31

	1998	1997	1996	1995	1994	1993
Revenues (Million $)						
1Q	1,869	1,205	1,259	797.7	683.6	658.3
2Q	2,026	1,283	1,270	850.2	707.0	670.9
3Q	—	1,281	1,203	904.4	727.7	669.0
4Q	—	1,380	1,259	897.6	787.0	703.7
Yr.	—	5,152	4,928	3,450	2,905	2,702
Earnings Per Share ($)						
1Q	**0.32**	0.87	0.80	0.72	0.63	0.56
2Q	**0.99**	0.90	0.82	0.74	0.67	0.61
3Q	—	0.93	0.82	0.78	0.69	0.61
4Q	—	0.96	0.85	0.79	0.71	0.62
Yr.	—	3.66	3.29	3.03	2.70	2.41

Next earnings report expected: mid October

Dividend Data (Dividends have been paid since 1936.)

Amount ($)	Date Decl.	Ex-Div. Date	Stock of Record	Payment Date
0.425	Sep. 30	Oct. 08	Oct. 10	Nov. 01 '97
0.460	Dec. 22	Jan. 07	Jan. 09	Feb. 01 '98
0.460	Mar. 30	Apr. 07	Apr. 10	May. 01 '98
0.480	Jun. 30	Jul. 08	Jul. 10	Aug. 01 '98

A Division of The McGraw-Hill Companies

Business Summary - 28-AUG-98

Headquartered in Cleveland and operating branches throughout Ohio, Kentucky, Indiana and Pennsylvania, this bank holding company initiated a multi-year plan in 1997 to reconfigure its branch delivery system by reducing traditional, full-service branches while expanding nontraditional alternatives such as in-store locations, limited service facilities and off-site ATMs. Integration activities will be a primary focus in 1998 as the company merges Michigan-based First of America, which will enhance the franchise through the addition of three million customers in markets across Michigan, central Indiana and key Illinois cities outside Chicago.

Major business units include corporate banking, retail banking and fee-based businesses. Corporate banking involves commercial and middle-market corporate lending, commercial real estate, asset-based lending, commercial leasing, loan syndications, cash management and related services. Retail banking includes the branch franchise and lending to individual and small business with products such as mortgages, indirect and direct consumer installment loans, auto leases, home equity loans and credit card lending. Fee-based businesses include item processing, mortgage banking, institutional trust and brokerage.

In 1997, average earning assets, from which interest income is derived, amounted to $46.2 billion and consisted mainly of loans (81%) and investment securities (18%). Average sources of funds included interest-bearing deposits (59%), short-term borrowings (9%), long-term debt (8%), noninterest-bearing demand deposits (13%), shareholders' equity (9%) and other (2%).

At year-end 1997, nonperforming assets, consisting primarily of nonaccrual and other real estate owned, were $167 million (0.4% of loans and related assets), down from $168 million (0.5%) a year earlier. The allowance for loan losses, which is set aside for possible loan defaults, was $698 million (1.76% of loans), versus $706 million (1.97% of loans) a year earlier. Net chargeoffs, or the amount of loans actually written off as uncollectible, were $139 million (0.37% of average loans) in 1997, compared to $147 million (0.42%) in 1996.

The merger with Michigan-based First of America Bank Corp. (NYSE; FOA), completed in March 1998, called for each FOA common share to be exchanged for 1.2 common shares of NCC. Separately in March, the company acquired Fort Wayne National Corp., with $3.3 billion in assets and 64 branches in northern Indiana, for about $800 million in NCC common stock.

Per Share Data ($)

(Year Ended Dec. 31)	1997	1996	1995	1994	1993	1992	1991	1990	1989	1988
Tangible Bk. Val.	20.28	19.86	18.80	16.36	16.15	14.54	12.01	11.46	12.43	10.92
Earnings	3.66	3.29	3.03	2.70	2.41	2.10	1.81	1.93	2.17	1.92
Dividends	1.67	1.47	1.30	1.18	1.06	0.94	0.94	0.94	0.86	0.75
Payout Ratio	46%	45%	43%	44%	44%	45%	52%	49%	40%	39%
Prices - High	67½	47¼	33¾	29	28⅛	24⅞	21⅛	20	20¾	16⅞
- Low	42½	30⅝	25¼	23¾	23⅛	18	14	11⅜	15⅜	13⅞
P/E Ratio - High	18	14	11	11	12	12	12	10	10	9
- Low	12	9	8	9	10	9	8	6	7	7

Income Statement Analysis (Million $)

	1997	1996	1995	1994	1993	1992	1991	1990	1989	1988
Net Int. Inc.	1,943	1,943	1,321	1,237	1,200	1,153	931	898	867	805
Tax Equiv. Adj.	19.4	20.9	21.2	29.5	35.7	42.0	45.0	51.0	53.0	56.0
Non Int. Inc.	899	1,165	893	853	800	726	560	498	422	404
Loan Loss Prov.	140	146	97.5	79.4	93.1	129	191	168	125	144
Exp./Op. Revs.	71%	67%	66%	66%	66%	68%	66%	64%	61%	61%
Pretax Inc.	1,169	1,058	670	618	571	464	311	311	354	310
Eff. Tax Rate	31%	30%	31%	31%	29%	25%	26%	25%	26%	25%
Net Inc.	807	737	465	429	404	347	231	234	263	233
% Net Int. Marg.	4.25	4.44	4.44	4.65	4.80	4.65	4.60	4.59	4.80	4.86

Balance Sheet & Other Fin. Data (Million $)

	1997	1996	1995	1994	1993	1992	1991	1990	1989	1988
Earning Assets:										
Money Mkt	600	342	748	681	1,219	1,331	1,505	683	903	938
Inv. Securities	8,865	8,690	4,950	4,395	5,166	5,499	4,411	3,962	3,989	3,779
Com'l Loans	1,409	12,261	10,291	8,884	8,657	8,337	7,025	7,333	7,229	6,928
Other Loans	25,476	22,718	15,931	14,151	12,629	10,401	8,492	8,614	8,002	7,386
Total Assets	54,684	50,856	36,199	32,114	31,068	28,964	24,170	23,743	22,972	21,623
Demand Deposits	7,378	7,436	5,564	5,332	5,215	4,819	3,573	3,677	3,444	3,519
Time Deposits	29,483	14,618	19,637	19,140	17,848	17,766	14,752	14,644	13,820	13,387
LT Debt	4,810	2,994	1,215	744	510	645	644	554	397	376
Common Eqty.	4,281	4,432	2,735	2,414	2,565	2,300	1,729	1,609	1,507	1,321
% Ret. on Assets	1.5	1.5	1.4	1.4	1.4	1.2	1.0	1.0	1.2	1.2
% Ret. on Equity	18.5	17.7	18.1	17.1	16.1	15.3	12.9	15.0	18.6	18.5
% Loan Loss Resv.	1.8	2.0	1.9	2.0	2.1	2.0	1.9	1.6	1.7	1.9
% Loans/Deposits	107.4	102.0	104.0	94.1	92.3	83.0	84.7	87.0	88.2	84.7
% Equity to Assets	8.3	8.6	8.0	7.8	8.1	7.5	7.2	6.8	6.7	6.4

Data as orig. reptd.; bef. results of disc opers. and/or spec. items. Per share data adj. for stk. divs. as of ex-div. date. Bold denotes diluted EPS (FASB 128). E-Estimated. NA-Not Available. NM-Not Meaningful. NR-Not Ranked.

Office—National City Center, 1900 E. Ninth St., Cleveland, OH 44114. **Tel**—(216) 575-2000. **Website**—http://www.national-city.com **Chrmn & CEO**—D. A. Daberko.**Vice-Chrmn & CFO**—R. G. Siefers.**Sr VP & Secy**—D. L. Zoeller. **Sr VP & Treas**—T. A. Richlovshy. **Investor Contact**—Julie I. Sabroff (216) 575-2467. **Dirs**—S. H. Austin, C. H. Bowman, E. B. Brandon, J. G. Breen, J. S. Broadhurst, D. E. Collins, D. A. Daberko, D. E. Evans, O. N. Frenzel III, B. P. Healy, J. H. Lemieux, W. B. Lunsford, R. A. Paul, W. R. Robertson, W. F. Roemer, M. A. Schuler, S. A. Stitle, M. Weiss. **Transfer Agent & Registrar**—National City Bank, Cleveland. **Incorporated**—in Delaware in 1973; bank chartered in 1865. **Empl**— 29,841.
S&P Analyst: Stephen R. Biggar

National Semiconductor   1620

NYSE Symbol **NSM**

In S&P 500

12-SEP-98

Industry:
Electronics (Semicon-
ductors)

Summary: This company is a leading manufacturer of a broad line of semiconductors, including analog, digital and mixed-signal integrated circuits.

S&P Opinion: Hold (★★★)	Recent Price • 8⅞	Yield • Nil
	52 Wk Range • 42⅞-8¾	12-Mo. P/E • NM

Earnings vs. Previous Year
▲=Up ▼=Down ▶=No Change

Quantitative Evaluations

Outlook
(1 Lowest—5 Highest)
• **2⁻**

Fair Value
• **9⅛**

Risk
• **Average**

Earn./Div. Rank
• **B-**

Technical Eval.
• **Bearish** since 12/97

Rel. Strength Rank
(1 Lowest—99 Highest)
• **16**

Insider Activity
• **Neutral**

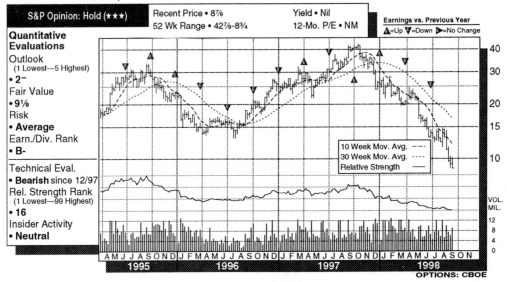

10 Week Mov. Avg. — -
30 Week Mov. Avg. - - - -
Relative Strength —

OPTIONS: CBOE

Overview - 24-AUG-98

We project revenues for FY 99 (May) about 20% below year ago levels. National Semiconductor's revenue growth has been hurt by the weak Asian demand for its chips due to the financial crisis in that area. In addition, NSM lost a design win in its LAN business with a major customer (NSM has since acquired ComCore to improve its technology in this area). While NSM's August orders reportedly strengthened compared with weak June and July levels, the company remains cautious due to the continued excess supply situation in the semiconductor industry and Asia's deepening financial crisis. In light of its reduced revenue outlook, NSM is undergoing a restructuring effort to lower costs, which includes workforce cuts, the elimination of some operations and a rationalization of research and development projects. With NSM's lower cost structure seen, once a recovery in the semiconductor industry is under way, revenue gains should flow more easily to the bottom line. In the fourth quarter of FY 98, NSM recorded a $0.29 per share restructuring charge.

Valuation - 24-AUG-98

We continue to recommend holding the shares. On a stand-alone basis, we believe that NSM should continue to benefit from demand for its analog/mixed-signal technologies from growth in networking, personal systems and communications. However, we believe that potential benefits from the combination of NSM and Cyrix Corp. could take a while to emerge. The combination promises to offer system-on-a-chip technology that would allow a sub-$500 PC offering, which NSM has long envisioned as a natural evolution of the PC toward a low-cost, omnipresent information appliance. We view the strategy as attractive in the long term, but would not add to positions near term in view of the potential for continued losses for Cyrix.

Key Stock Statistics

S&P EPS Est. 1999	-1.10	Tang. Bk. Value/Share	12.05
P/E on S&P Est. 1999	NM	Beta	0.90
Dividend Rate/Share	Nil	Shareholders	11,500
Shs. outstg. (M)	164.2	Market cap. (B)	$ 1.5
Avg. daily vol. (M)	1.636	Inst. holdings	71%

Value of $10,000 invested 5 years ago: $ 8,352

Fiscal Year Ending May 31

	1999	1998	1997	1996	1995	1994
Revenues (Million $)						
1Q	469.6	600.8	566.1	698.8	553.8	558.9
2Q	—	719.9	661.5	711.6	584.4	582.4
3Q	—	650.1	680.5	600.3	571.4	544.7
4Q	—	510.0	599.2	612.4	669.8	609.4
Yr.	—	2,537	2,507	2,623	2,379	2,295
Earnings Per Share ($)						
1Q	**-0.63**	0.47	-1.51	0.56	0.44	0.39
2Q	**E-0.48**	0.46	0.30	0.61	0.51	0.46
3Q	**E-0.05**	0.13	1.44	0.17	0.43	0.48
4Q	**E0.05**	-1.29	-0.10	0.07	0.62	0.63
Yr.	**E-1.10**	-0.60	0.19	1.36	2.02	1.98

Next earnings report expected: early December

Dividend Data

No common dividends have been paid. A "poison pill" stock purchase rights plan was adopted in 1988.

A Division of The **McGraw·Hill** Companies

Business Summary - 24-AUG-98

National Semiconductor's president and CEO, Brian Halla, has been at the helm since May 1996. Mr. Halla has headed the final stages of a restructuring that began in 1992, and he has spearheaded an effort to form a "new" National Semiconductor. The company's expertise has been primarily in analog intensive, digital and mixed-signal complex integrated circuits. In June 1996, NSM spun off its logic, memory and discrete products (considered commodity-type components) as a separate company, Fairchild Semiconductor, enabling NSM to focus on its core.

Mr. Halla is often quoted as saying that information is analog, and analog is a key strength of NSM. Analog and mixed-signal products process analog information, convert analog to digital and vice versa. Analog devices control continuously variable functions (such as light, color, sound and power), and are used in automotive, telecommunications, audio/video and industrial applications. The majority of National's sales are for its analog products.

Fitting in with its vision of the PC evolving into an information appliance, in November 1997, the company acquired Cyrix Corp., for roughly $550 million, in an exchange of shares. The strategy underlying the deal was that their combined technologies would establish all the capabilities needed to provide a complete PC system on a chip. This system on a chip would enable the introduction of a sub-$500 PC, which could later become a low-cost information appliance to provide Internet access from the bedroom to the boardroom.

In addition to supplying microprocessors for PCs, National's product line includes Super I/O (input/output) products and system logic for PCs. Super I/O refers to integrated circuits that handle system peripheral and I/O functions on the PC motherboard.

As a leading communications integrated circuit supplier, NSM concentrates on two segments: wireless communications and LAN markets. NSM's wireless circuits are used in cellular and cordless phones. In the LAN market, NSM had established itself as a leader in the 10/100 Mb Ethernet market. With the acquisition of ComCore and its advanced digital signal processing solutions, NSM hopes to expand its product line into the Gigabit Ethernet market.

NSM's most recent major investment in its wafer fab facilities is a new eight-inch fab in South Portland, ME. NSM has accelerated its transition to manufacture 8-inch wafers with .35-micron circuit geometries in order to reduce costs and rationalize production flows. NSM has three facilities in the United States and one major wafer fab facility in Scotland. NSM also has an agreement with IBM that provides for IBM Microelectronics to manufacture wafers for Cyrix through December 1999.

Per Share Data ($)

(Year Ended May 31)	1998	1997	1996	1995	1994	1993	1992	1991	1990	1989
Tangible Bk. Val.	11.24	12.05	11.52	10.31	7.60	4.92	3.90	5.14	6.70	7.06
Cash Flow	1.18	1.81	3.11	3.50	3.36	2.36	0.28	0.17	1.34	-0.11
Earnings	-0.60	0.19	1.36	2.02	1.98	0.98	-1.98	-1.55	-0.38	-2.09
Dividends	Nil	Nil	Nil	Nil	Nil	Nil	Nil	Nil	Nil	Nil
Payout Ratio	Nil	Nil	Nil	Nil	Nil	Nil	Nil	Nil	Nil	Nil
Cal. Yrs.	1997	1996	1995	1994	1993	1992	1991	1990	1989	1988
Prices - High	42⁷/₈	27⁵/₈	35⁵/₈	25	21³/₄	14¹/₈	9	8⁷/₈	10	15
- Low	21⁵/₈	13	16¹/₂	14³/₈	10¹/₈	6³/₈	3⁷/₈	3	6³/₈	8¹/₈
P/E Ratio - High	NM	NM	25	12	11	14	NM	NM	NM	NM
- Low	NM	NM	12	7	5	7	NM	NM	NM	NM

Income Statement Analysis (Million $)

	1998	1997	1996	1995	1994	1993	1992	1991	1990	1989
Revs.	2,537	2,507	2,623	2,379	2,295	2,014	1,718	1,702	1,675	1,648
Oper. Inc.	342	357	447	495	449	290	165	136	104	70.0
Depr.	292	231	233	185	167	160	160	178	177	204
Int. Exp.	26.3	13.8	16.0	6.7	3.3	4.4	3.4	5.8	5.0	21.3
Pretax Inc.	-99	57.3	247	329	304	150	-116	-148	-32.0	-198
Eff. Tax Rate	NM	52%	25%	20%	15%	13%	NM	NM	NM	NM
Net Inc.	-98.6	27.5	185	264	259	130	-119	-149	-29.0	-205

Balance Sheet & Other Fin. Data (Million $)

	1998	1997	1996	1995	1994	1993	1992	1991	1990	1989
Cash	461	890	504	467	467	332	159	193	129	228
Curr. Assets	1,308	1,553	1,256	1,178	1,016	842	595	613	625	678
Total Assets	3,101	2,914	2,658	2,236	1,748	1,477	1,149	1,191	1,378	1,416
Curr. Liab.	794	791	677	686	577	506	473	417	427	449
LT Debt	391	324	351	82.5	15.0	37.0	34.0	20.0	64.0	52.0
Common Eqty.	1,859	1,749	1,557	1,234	933	540	414	533	692	724
Total Cap.	2,254	2,082	1,940	1,509	1,139	892	588	693	895	915
Cap. Exp.	622	593	628	479	271	234	189	110	182	317
Cash Flow	194	259	412	438	408	273	30.0	18.0	138	-12.0
Curr. Ratio	1.6	2.0	1.9	1.7	1.8	1.7	1.3	1.5	1.5	1.5
% LT Debt of Cap.	17.3	15.6	18.1	5.5	1.3	4.2	5.8	2.9	7.2	5.7
% Net Inc.of Revs.	NM	1.1	7.1	11.1	11.3	6.5	NM	NM	NM	NM
% Ret. on Assets	NM	1.0	7.6	13.3	15.2	9.8	NM	NM	NM	NM
% Ret. on Equity	NM	1.7	12.8	23.4	31.3	23.4	NM	NM	NM	NM

Data as orig. reptd.; bef. results of disc. opers. and/or spec. items. Per share data adj. for stk. divs. as of ex-div. date. Bold denotes diluted EPS (FASB 128). E-Estimated. NA-Not Available. NM-Not Meaningful. NR-Not Ranked.

Office—2900 Semiconductor Dr., Santa Clara, CA 95052-8090. **Tel**—(408) 721-5000. **Website**—http://www.national.com **Chrmn, Pres & CEO**—B. Halla.**VP-Fin & CFO**—D. Macleod.**VP & Secy**—J. M. Clark III. **Investor Contact**—James Foltz. **Dirs**— G. P. Arnold, R. Beshar, B. Halla, M. A. Maidique, E. R. McCracken, J. T. O'Rourke, C. E. Sporck, D. E. Weeden. **Transfer Agent & Registrar**—First National Bank of Boston. **Incorporated**—in Delaware in 1959.**Empl**— 13,000. **S&P Analyst:** Megan Graham Hackett

12-SEP-98

Industry:
Manufacturing (Diversified)

Summary: This diversified company has interests in lighting equipment, textile rentals, specialty chemicals and envelopes.

| S&P Opinion: Hold (★★★) | Recent Price • 35¾ | Yield • 3.5% |
| | 52 Wk Range • 60¾-34⅛ | 12-Mo. P/E • 14.0 |

Quantitative Evaluations

Outlook
(1 Lowest—5 Highest)
• **1+**

Fair Value
• **34½**

Risk
• **Low**

Earn./Div. Rank
• **A**

Technical Eval.
• **NA**

Rel. Strength Rank
(1 Lowest—99 Highest)
• **24**

Insider Activity
• **NA**

Earnings vs. Previous Year
▲=Up ▼=Down ▶=No Change

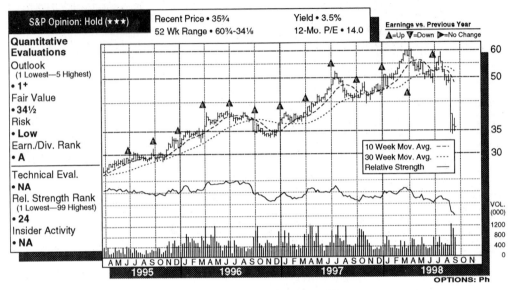

10 Week Mov. Avg. - - -
30 Week Mov. Avg. ·····
Relative Strength —

VOL.
(000)

OPTIONS: Ph

Overview - 04-SEP-98

We estimate that overall revenue growth for the remainder of FY 98 (Aug.), will be flat to slightly negative, due to the June 1997 sale of 40% of the company's textile business. The lighting division has shown the most growth, but indications are that revenues will be nowhere near as robust in FY 99 as they were in FY 98. Due to a weaker new-construction market, we now estimate that lighting revenues should grow about 3% in the next fiscal year, down from our 12% assumption. Earnings results should improve 8% for both FY 98 and FY 99, aided by acquisitions and the firm's share repurchase plan. Due to a recent preannouncement by NSI that curbed expected lighting growth and chemical division margins, we are lowering our FY 98 earnings estimate from $2.62 to $2.53, and FY 99's from $3.00 to $2.75.

Valuation - 04-SEP-98

At the end of August, NSI preannounced an expected earnings shortfall for the fourth quarter of FY 98, due to slowing lighting unit sales and increased restructuring costs in the chemical division. Expectations for the fourth quarter are now more in line with the fourth quarter of last fiscal year, as opposed to growth expectations of about 11%. The news is especially painful to digest, since the lighting division has been the real catalyst for company growth in FY 98. Although the stock is substantially off its high and we feel there is limited downside risk, the lower valuation is not compelling enough to change our current recommendation. NSI is currently trading at a P/E ratio below the overall market, but above the firm's growth rate. Given the fragility of the current market and the unforgiving attitude towards earnings blunders, we rate the shares a hold.

Key Stock Statistics

S&P EPS Est. 1998	2.53	Tang. Bk. Value/Share	11.57
P/E on S&P Est. 1998	14.1	Beta	0.99
S&P EPS Est. 1999	2.75	Shareholders	7,200
Dividend Rate/Share	1.24	Market cap. (B)	$ 1.5
Shs. outstg. (M)	41.4	Inst. holdings	58%
Avg. daily vol. (M)	0.206		

Value of $10,000 invested 5 years ago: $ 16,937

Fiscal Year Ending Aug. 31

	1998	1997	1996	1995	1994	1993
Revenues (Million $)						
1Q	487.6	511.9	492.6	481.0	459.9	434.0
2Q	479.4	499.2	482.2	465.8	439.3	427.0
3Q	521.6	515.3	516.9	505.8	481.0	460.0
4Q	—	509.8	521.9	518.0	501.6	484.0
Yr.	—	2,036	2,014	1,971	1,882	1,805
Earnings Per Share ($)						
1Q	0.61	0.54	0.48	0.43	0.39	0.38
2Q	**0.54**	0.45	0.40	0.36	0.33	0.30
3Q	**0.66**	0.65	0.58	0.53	0.46	0.41
4Q	E0.72	0.73	0.66	0.62	0.49	0.43
Yr.	**E2.53**	2.37	2.11	1.93	1.67	1.52

Next earnings report expected: late September

Dividend Data (Dividends have been paid since 1937.)

Amount ($)	Date Decl.	Ex-Div. Date	Stock of Record	Payment Date
0.300	Sep. 23	Oct. 01	Oct. 03	Oct. 14 '97
0.310	Dec. 17	Dec. 23	Dec. 26	Jan. 07 '98
0.310	Mar. 19	Apr. 01	Apr. 03	Apr. 14 '98
0.310	Jun. 23	Jun. 30	Jul. 02	Jul. 14 '98

A Division of The McGraw-Hill Companies

Business Summary - 04-SEP-98

Although you may not be aware of it, there's a good chance you've come in contact with one or more National Service Industries (NSI) products. Through four operating segments, which consist of lighting equipment, textile rentals, chemicals and envelopes, NSI products serve a variety of purposes, including lighting at evening sporting events, clothes for uniformed individuals, and packaging for business mail. Following a review of its business in FY 96 (Aug.), the company discovered eroding margins, slower sales growth, declining asset turns and acquisition programs that had not returned the cost of capital. In response, NSI is focusing on its core operating segments and concentrating on growth through acquisitions and innovation.

NSI's lighting equipment segment, known as Lithonia Lighting, is North America's largest manufacturer of lighting fixtures for commercial, industrial and residential markets, generating roughly 47% of revenues and 51% of operating income in FY 97. NSI hopes to achieve growth in this unit through advanced computer software and electronic processes, such as three-dimensional design software, electronic data interchange and Internet links.

National Linen Service, the company's textile rental division, has undergone significant changes since 1996.

NSI determined that the segment, which accounted for approximately 24% and 20% of FY 97 revenues and operating income, respectively, had serious problems with customer service, maintenance and asset management. Consequently, the company is focusing on customer retention, profitable sales growth, asset utilization and expense rationalization. In June 1997, NSI said it had agreed to sell 29 uniform plants, or roughly 40% of its textile rental volume, to G&K Services (Nasdaq: GK-SRA) for about $287 million. NSI said the sale of the plants, which were mainly dedicated uniform facilities or located outside of its southeastern focus, will allow the company to concentrate on the linen markets that offer potential for future economic profit.

Under the names Zep Manufacturing, Selig Chemical and National Chemical, NSI offers products such as cleaners, sanitizers and degreasers to the automotive, food, manufacturing, institutional and hospitality markets. The company expects significant growth in this division, which generated 20% of revenues and 23% of operating income in FY 97, aided by increased demand for environmentally friendly chemicals.

The company's smallest operating segment, Atlantic Envelope Company, experienced increases of 4.1% and 3.8% in FY 97 sales and operating profit, respectively. Fueled by acquisition activity, NSI is encouraged by this segment's potential for growth.

Per Share Data ($)

(Year Ended Aug. 31)	1997	1996	1995	1994	1993	1992	1991	1990	1989	1988
Tangible Bk. Val.	14.07	13.53	13.31	12.49	11.63	12.06	11.67	12.62	11.87	10.99
Cash Flow	3.66	3.32	3.11	2.89	2.47	2.40	1.67	2.78	2.57	2.34
Earnings	2.37	2.11	1.93	1.67	1.52	1.50	0.65	2.02	1.92	1.75
Dividends	1.19	1.15	1.11	1.07	1.03	0.99	0.97	0.90	0.82	0.73
Payout Ratio	50%	55%	58%	64%	68%	66%	149%	45%	43%	42%
Prices - High	52¼	40¼	33⅞	28⅜	27⅞	27	28¼	28¾	30⅜	24½
- Low	36¾	31⅞	24⅞	24¾	23⅛	22½	19	22⅛	21⅜	18¼
P/E Ratio - High	22	19	18	17	18	18	43	14	16	14
- Low	16	15	13	15	15	15	29	11	11	10

Income Statement Analysis (Million $)

	1997	1996	1995	1994	1993	1992	1991	1990	1989	1988
Revs.	2,036	2,014	1,971	1,882	1,805	1,634	1,602	1,648	1,540	1,414
Oper. Inc.	232	218	217	204	181	169	163	194	180	162
Depr.	58.0	58.4	57.1	60.5	47.4	44.7	50.2	37.5	36.3	31.0
Int. Exp.	1.6	1.6	3.8	3.7	5.0	2.7	3.8	3.9	5.0	4.2
Pretax Inc.	179	162	150	132	120	117	49.0	156	148	133
Eff. Tax Rate	40%	38%	38%	37%	37%	37%	34%	36%	36%	35%
Net Inc.	107	101	94.1	82.7	75.1	74.1	32.2	100	94.7	86.1

Balance Sheet & Other Fin. Data (Million $)

	1997	1996	1995	1994	1993	1992	1991	1990	1989	1988
Cash	57.1	59.1	83.0	61.0	21.0	110	88.0	125	129	134
Curr. Assets	781	606	640	608	557	568	549	576	570	552
Total Assets	1,106	1,095	1,131	1,107	1,088	1,042	1,012	962	888	825
Curr. Liab.	282	197	203	251	244	210	198	142	134	126
LT Debt	26.2	24.9	26.8	26.9	28.4	28.4	31.4	27.5	20.8	21.4
Common Eqty.	672	718	744	727	704	683	661	675	613	558
Total Cap.	732	806	771	833	817	804	792	804	736	684
Cap. Exp.	48.8	65.4	58.8	42.5	82.2	49.8	58.4	82.9	66.5	55.4
Cash Flow	165	159	151	143	123	119	82.0	137	127	115
Curr. Ratio	2.8	3.1	3.2	2.4	2.3	2.7	2.8	4.0	4.3	4.4
% LT Debt of Cap.	3.6	3.5	3.5	3.2	3.5	3.5	4.0	3.4	2.8	3.1
% Net Inc.of Revs.	5.3	5.0	4.8	4.4	4.2	4.5	2.0	6.1	6.2	6.1
% Ret. on Assets	9.7	9.1	8.5	7.6	7.1	7.2	3.3	10.8	11.1	10.9
% Ret. on Equity	15.4	13.8	12.9	11.6	10.8	11.0	4.8	15.4	16.2	16.2

Data as orig. reptd.; bef. results of disc. opers. and/or spec. items. Per share data adj. for stk. divs. as of ex-div. date. Bold denotes diluted EPS (FASB 128). E-Estimated. NA-Not Available. NM-Not Meaningful. NR-Not Ranked.

Office—1420 Peachtree St. N.E., Atlanta, GA 30309. **Tel**—(404) 853-1000. **Website**—http://www.nationalservice.com **Chrmn, Pres & CEO**—J. S. Balloun. **Exec VP & CFO**—B. A. Hattox. **Treas**—C. J. Popkowski. **Secy**—K. Murphy. **Dirs**—J. S. Balloun, J. L. Clendenin, R. M. Holder Jr., C. Kennedy, D. Levy, B. Marcus, C. W. McCall, J. G. Medlin Jr., S. Nunn, H. J. Russell, B. L. Siegel. **Transfer Agent & Registrar**—Wachovia Bank of North Carolina, Boston. **Incorporated**—in Delaware in 1928. **Empl**— 20,600. **S&P Analyst:** Jordan Horoschak

12-SEP-98

Industry: Banks (Money Center)

Summary: This bank holding company, which operates offices in 16 states and the District of Columbia, recently agreed to merge with BankAmerica Corp.

S&P Opinion: Hold (★★★)	Recent Price • 54½	Yield • 2.8%
	52 Wk Range • 88⅜-47⅞	12 Mo. P/E • 12.6

Quantitative Evaluations

Outlook (1 Lowest—5 Highest)
• **3⁻**

Fair Value
• **60¼**

Risk
• **Low**

Earn./Div. Rank
• **A-**

Technical Eval.
• **Bearish** since 2/98

Rel. Strength Rank (1 Lowest—99 Highest)
• **27**

Insider Activity
• **Neutral**

Earnings vs. Previous Year
▲=Up ▼=Down ▶=No Change

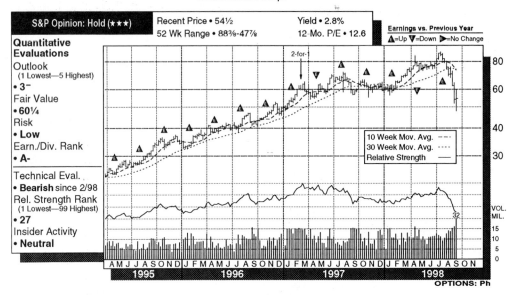

10 Week Mov. Avg. – – –
30 Week Mov. Avg. ·······
Relative Strength ———

OPTIONS: Ph

Overview - 20-JUL-98

Loan growth in 1998, prior to the pending merger with BankAmerica, is expected to benefit from the company's concentration in states with healthy regional economies, although continued competition and an overall moderation of economic growth will be limiting factors. With fairly stable lending spreads, net interest income is projected to increase about 5% in 1998. Total revenues, however, should rise a bit more, in the 6% to 7% range, led by low double-digit gains in noninterest income, with particular strength in the investment banking and brokerage businesses. Absent merger-related charges, noninterest expense is projected to be relatively flat, with higher spending for personnel and Year 2000 issues offset by flat to lower general operating costs. This should lead to strong improvement in the efficiency ratio. Overall, NB should achieve its annual target of 12% to 15% earnings growth. Earnings projections for 1998 exclude a restructuring charge of $900 million pretax, or about $0.66 a share after tax, related to the Barnett merger. The planned merger with BankAmerica, expected in the 1998 fourth quarter, will provide financial benefits in the form of operating leverage and stability of earnings.

Valuation - 20-JUL-98

The shares were recently downgraded to hold, from buy, following upward price movement in reaction to the BankAmerica merger. The merger is more about revenue enhancement potential than cost savings, with most of the incremental earnings benefit built into 2000 projections. While we are positive on the transaction itself for the long term, the shares are now trading at nearly 16X expected 1999 pro forma EPS of $5.59, and are likely only to track the broad market for the intermediate term.

Key Stock Statistics

S&P EPS Est. 1998	4.70	Tang. Bk. Value/Share	15.61
P/E on S&P Est. 1998	11.6	Beta	1.47
S&P EPS Est. 1999	5.50	Shareholders	106,300
Dividend Rate/Share	1.52	Market cap. (B)	$ 52.5
Shs. outstg. (M)	962.6	Inst. holdings	48%
Avg. daily vol. (M)	4.673		

Value of $10,000 invested 5 years ago: $ 25,024

Fiscal Year Ending Dec. 31

	1998	1997	1996	1995	1994	1993
Revenues (Million $)						
1Q	7,045	5,183	4,458	3,799	3,092	2,375
2Q	7,065	5,303	4,366	4,126	3,146	2,408
3Q	—	4,398	4,315	4,184	3,346	2,641
4Q	—	5,850	4,323	4,236	3,529	2,968
Yr.	—	21,734	17,462	16,345	13,113	10,392
Earnings Per Share ($)						
1Q	0.51	0.94	0.85	0.80	0.76	0.56
2Q	1.43	1.02	1.00	0.85	0.79	0.60
3Q	—	1.08	1.06	0.97	0.78	0.67
4Q	—	1.12	0.09	0.94	0.73	0.69
Yr.	—	4.17	4.00	3.56	3.06	2.50

Next earnings report expected: mid October

Dividend Data (Dividends have been paid since 1903.)

Amount ($)	Date Decl.	Ex-Div. Date	Stock of Record	Payment Date
0.380	Oct. 22	Dec. 03	Oct. 05	Dec. 24 '97
0.380	Jan. 28	Mar. 04	Mar. 06	Mar. 27 '98
0.380	Apr. 22	Jun. 03	Jun. 05	Jun. 26 '98
0.380	Jul. 22	Sep. 02	Sep. 04	Sep. 25 '98

A Division of The McGraw-Hill Companies

Business Summary - 20-JUL-98

In April 1998, NationsBank agreed to merge with California-based BankAmerica Corp. in a transaction that would create the second largest banking institution in the U.S., with $570 billion in assets. Having embarked on one of the banking industry's most aggressive acquisition programs (most recently NB acquired Florida-based Barnett Banks), the merger would complete NationsBank's quest for a coast-to-coast banking franchise.

For the last several years, NB has looked to increase profits through acquisitions and expansion of banking products and services to a wider variety of customers. While NB's traditional branch banking, or General Bank, segment, which operates more than 2,500 offices, still accounts for the lion's share (about 74%) of revenues, other non-traditional segments make up an increasing portion of the business. The Global Finance segment (20%) offers corporate and investment banking services such as treasury management, loan syndication, underwriting and trading. The Financial Services segment (6%) includes mainly consumer finance and commercial finance units.

In 1997, average earning assets, from which interest income is derived, amounted to $211.2 billion and consisted mainly of loans and leases (69%), investment securities (13%) and trading account securities (11%). Average sources of funds, on which the bank generally pays interest expense, included domestic deposits (38%), foreign deposits (4%), noninterest-bearing deposits (13%), short-term borrowings (21%), long-term debt (11%), shareholders' equity (8%) and other (5%).

At year-end 1997, nonperforming assets, consisting primarily of non-accrual loans and foreclosed properties, were $1.14 billion (0.79% of loans and related assets), up from $1.04 billion (0.85%) a year earlier. The allowance for loan losses, which is set aside for possible loan defaults, was $2.78 billion (1.94% of loans), versus $2.32 billion (1.89%) a year earlier. Net chargeoffs, or the amount of loans actually written off as uncollectible, were $798 million (0.54% of average loans) in 1997, compared to $598 million (0.48%) in 1996.

Terms of the transaction with BankAmerica (NYSE; BAC) call for each BAC share to be exchanged for 1.1316 shares of the new BankAmerica, while each NB share would be exchanged for one share of the new company. The transaction is expected to be completed in the fourth quarter of 1998.

Per Share Data ($)

(Year Ended Dec. 31)	1997	1996	1995	1994	1993	1992	1991	1990	1989	1988
Tangible Bk. Val.	16.66	18.42	19.09	16.62	15.51	13.43	10.94	10.39	10.47	7.44
Earnings	4.17	4.00	3.56	3.06	2.50	2.30	0.38	1.70	2.31	1.45
Dividends	1.04	1.20	1.04	0.94	0.82	0.76	0.74	0.71	0.55	0.47
Payout Ratio	25%	30%	29%	31%	33%	33%	195%	42%	24%	32%
Prices - High	71⅝	52⅝	37⅜	28¾	29	26¾	21⅜	23⅝	27½	14⅝
- Low	48	32¼	22⅜	21¾	22¼	19⅞	10¾	8½	13½	8¾
P/E Ratio - High	17	13	10	9	12	12	56	14	12	10
- Low	12	8	6	7	9	9	28	5	6	6

Income Statement Analysis (Million $)

	1997	1996	1995	1994	1993	1992	1991	1990	1989	1988
Net Int. Inc.	7,898	6,329	5,447	5,211	4,673	4,098	3,799	1,816	1,703	898
Tax Equiv. Adj.	116	94.0	113	94.0	86.0	92.0	141	39.0	76.0	82.0
Non Int. Inc.	6,351	3,646	3,078	2,597	2,101	1,913	1,742	912	623	353
Loan Loss Prov.	800	605	382	310	430	715	1,582	505	239	122
Exp./Op. Revs.	52%	57%	60%	62%	65%	68%	76%	68%	70%	61%
Pretax Inc.	4,796	3,634	2,991	2,555	1,991	1,396	109	378	516	330
Eff. Tax Rate	36%	35%	35%	34%	35%	18%	NM	3.20%	13%	24%
Net Inc.	3,077	2,452	1,950	1,690	1,301	1,145	202	366	447	252
% Net Int. Marg.	3.79	3.62	3.33	3.58	4.00	4.10	3.82	3.25	3.61	3.83

Balance Sheet & Other Fin. Data (Million $)

	1997	1996	1995	1994	1993	1992	1991	1990	1989	1988
Earning Assets:										
Money Mkt	36,095	27,491	26,393	23,212	19,133	6,110	2,436	1,052	3,580	2,467
Inv. Securities	47,203	14,387	23,847	25,825	29,054	24,729	24,879	15,894	16,170	4,727
Com'l Loans	71,442	58,796	52,101	48,109	43,538	34,478	31,164	18,937	17,735	11,154
Other Loans	69,568	61,519	66,919	55,580	50,166	38,236	37,944	18,540	16,984	7,870
Total Assets	264,562	185,794	187,298	169,604	157,686	118,059	110,319	65,285	66,191	29,848
Demand Deposits	34,674	25,738	23,414	21,380	20,719	17,701	16,270	8,939	8,439	3,914
Time Deposits	103,520	80,760	77,277	79,090	70,394	65,026	71,805	41,283	40,137	16,756
LT Debt	27,204	22,985	17,775	8,488	7,648	3,066	2,876	1,697	1,466	493
Common Eqty.	21,243	13,538	12,699	10,900	9,771	7,695	6,145	2,958	2,712	1,692
% Ret. on Assets	1.4	13.0	1.1	1.0	0.9	1.0	0.2	0.6	0.8	0.9
% Ret. on Equity	17.6	18.0	16.5	16.3	14.8	15.9	2.7	12.0	20.5	16.2
% Loan Loss Resv.	1.9	1.9	1.9	2.1	2.3	2.0	2.3	1.8	1.4	1.2
% Loans/Deposits	104.1	113.0	116.2	103.2	102.8	87.9	78.5	73.9	70.8	91.5
% Equity to Assets	7.7	7.0	6.6	6.2	6.3	6.1	5.4	4.5	3.8	5.3

Data as orig. reptd.; bef. results of disc opers. and/or spec. items. Per share data adj. for stk. divs. as of ex-div. date. Bold denotes diluted EPS (FASB 128). E-Estimated. NA-Not Available. NM-Not Meaningful. NR-Not Ranked.

Office—NationsBank Corporate Center, Charlotte, NC 28255. **Tel**—(704) 386-5000.**Website**—http://www.nationsbank.com **Chrmn**—A. B. Craig III. **CEO**—H. L. McColl Jr. **Pres**—K. D. Lewis. **Vice Chrmn & CFO**—J. H. Hance Jr. **Investor Contacts**—Kevin Stitt, Susan Carr.**Dirs**—R. C. Anderson, W. M. Barnhardt, R. Bornstein, B. A. Bridgewater Jr., T. E. Capps, A. R. Carpenter, C. W. Coker, T. G. Cousins, A. B. Craig III, A. T. Dickson, P. Fulton, C. R. Holman, W. W. Johnson, H. L. McColl Jr., K. D. Lewis, R. W. Meyer Jr., R. B. Priory,C. E. Rice, J. C. Slane, O. T. Sloan Jr.— M. R. Spangler, A. E. Suter, R. Townsend, J. M. Ward, J. A. Williams, V. R. Williams. **Transfer Agent**—ChaseMellon Shareholder Services, Ridgefield Park, NJ. **Incorporated**—in North Carolina in 1968. **Empl**— 98,961. **S&P Analyst:** Stephen R. Biggar

Navistar International   1628
NYSE Symbol **NAV**
In S&P 500

12-SEP-98   **Industry:** Trucks & Parts

Summary: This company is the largest North American maker of heavy/medium-sized trucks and school buses.

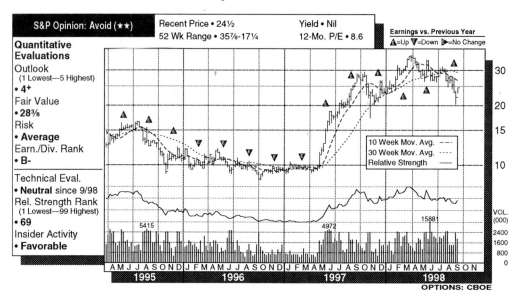

S&P Opinion: Avoid (★★)	Recent Price • 24½ Yield • Nil
	52 Wk Range • 35⅞-17¼ 12-Mo. P/E • 8.6

Earnings vs. Previous Year
▲=Up ▼=Down ▶=No Change

Quantitative Evaluations

Outlook
(1 Lowest—5 Highest)
• **4+**

Fair Value
• **28⅜**

Risk
• **Average**

Earn./Div. Rank
• **B-**

Technical Eval.
• **Neutral** since 9/98

Rel. Strength Rank
(1 Lowest—99 Highest)
• **69**

Insider Activity
• **Favorable**

10 Week Mov. Avg. ----
30 Week Mov. Avg. .....
Relative Strength ——

OPTIONS: CBOE

Overview - 14-AUG-98

Demand in the North American heavy-duty truck market has strengthened recently and the outlook for 1998 has improved. Orders rebounded in mid-1997, and although we believe there is little pent-up demand, industry sales are likely to rise about 10% in 1998. Inventories have been well controlled over the last two years and production is being modestly increased. The rise in capacity utilization relieves some of the pressure on NAV to control cost, but that is not slowing an aggressive cost control effort. The company is streamlining option packages on trucks to minimize manufacturing complexity. The company continues to benefit from growing engine sales to Ford Motor Co. Further ahead, NAV is increasing truck production in Mexico, and after reaching a new labor agreement in 1997, the company is proceeding with plans to build its next generation truck in its Springfield, Ohio, assembly plant.

Valuation - 14-AUG-98

We continue to recommend that investors avoid NAV's shares, reflecting our concern that although North American demand has strengthened recently, the improvement may be shortlived in the absence of any pent-up demand. Unit shipments in 1998 are expected to exceed 1997's levels, but sales are unlikely to rise considerably for the next several years. Following the recent spectacular run-up in the shares, we think the stock will underperform broader market averages over the next year, and advise investors to avoid the shares.

Key Stock Statistics

S&P EPS Est. 1998	3.05	Tang. Bk. Value/Share	8.60
P/E on S&P Est. 1998	8.1	Beta	1.49
S&P EPS Est. 1999	2.80	Shareholders	57,900
Dividend Rate/Share	Nil	Market cap. (B)	$ 1.6
Shs. outstg. (M)	67.1	Inst. holdings	69%
Avg. daily vol. (M)	0.372		

Value of $10,000 invested 5 years ago: $ 10,916

Fiscal Year Ending Oct. 31

	1998	1997	1996	1995	1994	1993
Revenues (Million $)						
1Q	1,727	1,296	1,432	1,416	1,139	1,033
2Q	2,042	1,551	1,480	1,640	1,392	1,238
3Q	1,874	1,586	1,391	1,514	1,251	1,123
4Q	—	1,938	1,451	1,772	1,548	1,300
Yr.	—	6,371	5,705	6,342	5,330	4,694
Earnings Per Share ($)						
1Q	**0.42**	0.10	0.20	0.21	0.12	-0.19
2Q	**0.89**	0.31	0.26	0.52	0.21	0.32
3Q	**0.72**	0.38	0.13	0.43	0.17	-9.99
4Q	**E1.02**	0.85	-0.10	0.66	0.49	0.28
Yr.	**E3.05**	1.65	0.49	1.83	0.99	-8.63

Next earnings report expected: early December

Dividend Data

Dividends on the common shares were omitted in 1981.

A Division of The **McGraw·Hill** *Companies*

Business Summary - 14-AUG-98

Navistar is the market-share leader in North America in the combined medium- and heavy-duty trucks and school buses category (Classes 5-8). The company also supplies mid-range diesel engines to other vehicle manufacturers and financial services to its dealers and customers. The company's backlog of unfilled Class 5 through 8 truck orders numbered 45,300 as of October 31, 1997, compared with 20,900 units on October 31, 1996. This rise in backlog reflects a strengthening of demand for trucks as truck buyers fears of an impending recession which led to a collapse in orders in 1996 did not materialize. Contributions to sales in recent fiscal years (Oct.) were:

	FY 97	FY 96	FY 95
Medium-duty trucks	33%	35%	32%
Heavy-duty trucks	35%	35%	42%
Parts	13%	14%	12%
Engines	16%	16%	14%
Financial Services	3%	NA	NA

NAV delivered 99,500 (28.6%) of the 347,400 medium- and heavy-duty trucks and buses produced in North America in FY 97, up from 94,000 units (27.5%) of a total market of 341,200 in FY 96. NAV is the leading supplier of school bus chassis in the U.S. and has a minority stake in American Transportation Corp., a maker of school bus bodies. Vehicles are distributed through a network of 957 dealers in the U.S. and Canada and to dealers in more than 70 countries. About 5,000 trucks are exported annually.

All NAV trucks are equipped with diesel engines. Medium-duty trucks, accounting for two-thirds of sales, are powered with NAV-built engines, while engines for heavy-duty trucks are produced primarily by outside suppliers. In FY 97, NAV sold 184,000 diesel engines to original equipment manufacturers for use in pickup trucks and vans. Some 87% of those engines are sold to Ford Motor Co. for use in its light trucks and vans under a contract expiring in 2012.

Navistar Financial finances new retail sales of NAV trucks, dealer inventories and used trucks. NAV typically finances 94% of dealer inventories and 14% of retail sales of NAV vehicles.

Per Share Data ($)

(Year Ended Oct. 31)	1997	1996	1995	1994	1993	1992	1991	1990	1989	1988
Tangible Bk. Val.	7.83	4.86	4.15	3.16	2.16	-10.90	-2.90	7.60	26.40	24.10
Cash Flow	3.26	2.24	3.29	1.94	-6.50	-3.90	-4.90	1.00	4.60	10.80
Earnings	1.65	0.49	1.83	0.99	-8.63	-7.00	-7.70	-1.60	2.30	8.90
Dividends	Nil	Nil	Nil	Nil	Nil	Nil	Nil	Nil	Nil	Nil
Payout Ratio	Nil	Nil	Nil	Nil	Nil	Nil	Nil	Nil	Nil	Nil
Prices - High	29½	12⅛	17½	26⅝	33¾	41¼	42½	46¼	70	73¾
- Low	9	8⅜	9	12¼	19¼	17½	21¼	20	32½	31¼
P/E Ratio - High	18	25	10	27	NM	NM	NM	NM	30	8
- Low	5	17	5	12	NM	NM	NM	NM	14	4

Income Statement Analysis (Million $)

Revs.	6,321	5,705	6,292	5,305	4,694	3,875	3,460	3,854	4,241	4,080
Oper. Inc.	386	240	380	289	247	20.0	-6.0	168	251	241
Depr.	120	101	81.0	72.0	75.0	77.0	71.0	66.0	60.0	49.0
Int. Exp.	74.0	83.0	87.0	91.0	105	111	134	155	167	80.0
Pretax Inc.	242	105	262	158	-440	-144	-161	-7.0	94.0	269
Eff. Tax Rate	38%	38%	37%	35%	NM	NM	NM	NM	7.40%	3.80%
Net Inc.	150	65.0	164	102	-272	-146	-164	-11.0	87.0	259

Balance Sheet & Other Fin. Data (Million $)

Cash	609	881	485	557	421	335	295	275	395	562
Curr. Assets	NM	NM	NA	NA	NA	NA	NA	NA	NA	1,280
Total Assets	5,516	5,326	5,566	5,056	5,060	3,627	3,443	3,795	3,609	2,522
Curr. Liab.	NM	NM	NA	1,810	1,338	1,152	1,145	1,579	1,731	1,126
LT Debt	1,316	1,420	1,279	696	1,194	1,291	865	682	496	178
Common Eqty.	776	672	626	544	501	93.0	332	570	664	607
Total Cap.	2,336	2,092	1,905	1,513	1,969	1,629	1,442	1,497	1,410	1,044
Cap. Exp.	172	117	139	92.0	124	55.0	77.0	182	118	127
Cash Flow	241	166	245	145	-226	-99.0	-122	26.0	118	279
Curr. Ratio	NM	NM	NA	NA	NA	NA	NA	NA	NA	1.1
% LT Debt of Cap.	56.3	67.9	67.1	46.0	60.6	79.3	60.0	45.6	35.2	17.1
% Net Inc.of Revs.	2.4	11.4	2.6	1.9	NM	NM	NM	NM	2.1	6.3
% Ret. on Assets	2.8	1.2	3.1	2.0	NM	NM	NM	NM	2.8	11.7
% Ret. on Equity	16.7	10.0	27.4	14.0	NM	NM	NM	NM	9.1	46.7

Data as orig. reptd.; bef. results of disc. opers. and/or spec. items. Per share data adj. for stk. divs. as of ex-div. date. Bold denotes diluted EPS (FASB 128). E-Estimated. NA-Not Available. NM-Not Meaningful. NR-Not Ranked.

Office—455 N. Cityfront Plaza Dr., Chicago, IL 60611. **Registrar**—First National Bank of Chicago. **Tel**—(312) 836-2000. **Website**—http://www.navistar.com **Chrmn, Pres & CEO**—J. R. Horne. **Secy**—S. K. Covey. **VP & CFO**—R. C. Lannert. **Investor Contact**—Carmen Corbett. **Dirs**—W. F. Andrews, J. D. Correnti, W. C. Craig, J. E. Dempsey, J. F. Fiedler, J. T. Grigsby, Jr., M. N. Hammes, J. R. Horne, A. J. Krowe, R. C. Lannert, W. J. Laskowski, W. F. Patient. **Transfer Agent**—Harris Trust & Savings Bank, Chicago. **Incorporated**—in New Jersey in 1918; reincorporated in Delaware in 1965. **Empl**— 14,187. **S&P Analyst:** Robert E. Friedman, CPA

New York Times

1664E

NYSE Symbol **NYT**

In S&P 500

12-SEP-98

Industry: Publishing (Newspapers)

Summary: This diversified communications company publishes newspapers and consumer magazines, operates radio and television stations and has equity holdings in newsprint and paper mills.

S&P Opinion: Hold (★★★)	Recent Price • 28⅛	Yield • 1.4%
	52 Wk Range • 40⅝-24½	12-Mo. P/E • 20.2

Quantitative Evaluations

Outlook
(1 Lowest—5 Highest)
• **2**

Fair Value
• **29⅝**

Risk
• **NA**

Earn./Div. Rank
• **B-**

Technical Eval.
• **NA**

Rel. Strength Rank
(1 Lowest—99 Highest)
• **52**

Insider Activity
• **Neutral**

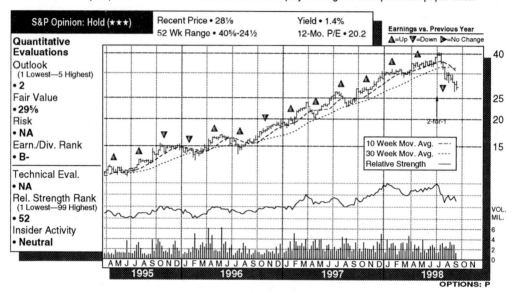

Earnings vs. Previous Year
▲=Up ▼=Down ▶=No Change

10 Week Mov. Avg. ----
30 Week Mov. Avg. ......
Relative Strength ——

2-for-1

VOL. MIL.

OPTIONS: P

Overview - 17-AUG-98

A rise in revenues of about 7% anticipated for 1998 will stem largely from continued healthy demand, higher rates charged for print and broadcast advertising, and revenue gains from other operations. Higher average cover and subscription prices for newspapers and magazines will also help. Newspaper circulation volume turned around in 1997, and should continue to gain, helped by the recent addition of color and expanded sections at The New York Times newspaper. Newsprint and coated paper prices appear to have peaked, after trending moderately higher through the first half, but the impact on operating margins has been largely offset by stable wage rates. Operating efficiencies and other conservation measures should also boost profitability. Improved earnings from newsprint affiliates should outweigh losses from startup operations.

Valuation - 17-AUG-98

The shares, recently trading at about 22X the $1.52 EPS we are projecting for 1998, deserve their generous valuation, but appear to be fully valued for now. We expect an improving operating scenario, with strong operating income gains in publishing and broadcasting partly offset by increased spending on new electronic services. The recent addition of color and expanded sections in the flagship newspaper should aid both advertising and circulation, even in a slowing economy. Combined with improving efficiencies stemming from new printing facilities and a wholly owned distribution network, this should contribute to EPS gains in the mid-teens over the next several years. NYT's attractive mix of media businesses, and management's apparent resiliency and resourcefulness in the difficult New York advertising market, also contribute to the stock's appeal.

Key Stock Statistics

S&P EPS Est. 1998	1.52	Tang. Bk. Value/Share	1.78
P/E on S&P Est. 1998	18.5	Beta	0.71
S&P EPS Est. 1999	1.82	Shareholders	16,200
Dividend Rate/Share	0.38	Market cap. (B)	$ 5.3
Shs. outstg. (M)	189.5	Inst. holdings	56%
Avg. daily vol. (M)	0.550		

Value of $10,000 invested 5 years ago: $ 23,548

Fiscal Year Ending Dec. 31

	1998	1997	1996	1995	1994	1993
Revenues (Million $)						
1Q	722.6	692.5	622.5	571.2	589.5	455.0
2Q	749.2	722.0	645.2	610.4	635.5	483.6
3Q	—	683.6	629.0	572.7	527.1	445.6
4Q	—	768.4	718.3	655.1	605.4	636.0
Yr.	—	2,866	2,615	2,409	2,358	2,020
Earnings Per Share ($)						
1Q	**0.33**	**0.26**	0.17	0.14	0.09	0.07
2Q	**0.42**	**0.43**	0.24	0.23	0.16	0.14
3Q	**E0.28**	**0.23**	-0.24	0.17	0.58	-0.02
4Q	**E0.49**	**0.41**	0.27	0.17	0.20	-0.06
Yr.	**E1.52**	**1.33**	0.43	0.70	1.02	0.04

Next earnings report expected: mid October

Dividend Data (Dividends have been paid since 1958.)

Amount ($)	Date Decl.	Ex-Div. Date	Stock of Record	Payment Date
0.170	Feb. 19	Feb. 27	Mar. 03	Mar. 20 '98
0.190	May. 20	Jun. 15	Jun. 17	Jul. 01 '98
2-for-1	May. 20	Jul. 02	Jun. 17	Jul. 01 '98
0.095	Jun. 18	Aug. 28	Sep. 01	Sep. 18 '98

A Division of The McGraw-Hill Companies

Business Summary - 17-AUG-98

The parent of what is arguably the world's most highly regarded general interest newspaper, The New York Times Company has diversified interests in newspapers, broadcasting, information services, magazines and forest products.

The Newspaper Group includes The New York Times, The Boston Globe, 21 regional newspapers, newspaper wholesalers, Information Services and a 50% interest in the International Herald Tribune. The New York Times is circulated in all 50 states, U.S. territories, and around the globe. Its average circulation in the nine months ended September 30, 1997, was 1,079,900 copies daily, while Sunday circulation was 1,653,500. The Boston Globe, New England's largest newspaper, had circulation of 472,300 daily and 756,300 Sunday. Regional newspaper circulation was 731,400 daily and 786,900 Sunday.

The Broadcasting Group, based in Memphis, includes eight network-affiliated TV stations (WNEP-TV, serving the Wilkes-Barre/Scranton area of Pennsylvania; WQAD-TV, serving the Quad-Cities area of Illinois and Iowa; KFSM-TV in Fort Smith, AR; WHNT-TV in Hunts-

ville, AL; KFOR-TV in Oklahoma City, OK; WHO-TV in Des Moines, IA; WREG-TV in Memphis, TN; and WTKR-TV, serving the Norfolk, VA, area); and two radio stations (WQXR-FM and WQEW-AM in NYC). The company also operates news, photo and graphics services; manages news and feature syndicates; has several electronic publishing and new media activities; owns a video production company; and has minority interests in a Canadian newsprint mill and in a supercalendered paper mill in Maine.

The Magazine Group currently comprises nine sports/leisure titles, but the company's holdings was to be substantially reduced with the planned sale of six sailing, tennis and ski magazines in the fourth quarter of 1997.

In 1997, newspaper publishing represented 89% of revenues and 86% of operating profits; magazine publishing accounted for 6% each, and television broadcasting accounted for 5% and 8%, respectively.

The company's Class A shares began trading on the NYSE on September 25, 1997, under the ticker symbol NYT; the shares formerly traded on the ASE under the symbol NYT.A. The Class B shares are not publicly traded.

Per Share Data ($)

(Year Ended Dec. 31)	1997	1996	1995	1994	1993	1992	1991	1990	1989	1988
Tangible Bk. Val.	1.76	0.90	1.05	0.84	0.79	NA	3.45	3.15	2.97	2.06
Cash Flow	2.21	1.20	1.37	1.76	0.56	NM	0.77	0.91	0.81	1.41
Earnings	1.33	0.43	0.70	1.02	0.04	-0.07	0.30	0.42	0.43	1.00
Dividends	0.32	0.28	0.28	0.28	0.28	0.28	0.28	0.27	0.25	0.23
Payout Ratio	24%	66%	40%	27%	NM	NM	94%	64%	57%	23%
Prices - High	33¼	20	15½	14¾	15⅝	16⅛	12⅞	13¾	17⅜	16⅜
- Low	18¼	12⅞	10⅛	10⅝	11¼	11⅜	9⅛	8½	12¼	12¼
P/E Ratio - High	25	46	22	14	NM	NM	42	32	40	16
- Low	14	30	14	10	NM	NM	30	20	28	12

Income Statement Analysis (Million $)

	1997	1996	1995	1994	1993	1992	1991	1990	1989	1988
Revs.	2,866	2,615	2,409	2,358	2,020	1,774	1,703	1,777	1,769	1,700
Oper. Inc.	629	448	368	365	216	NA	186	203	228	318
Depr.	174	148	139	154	89.3	NA	72.4	73.6	58.8	66.5
Int. Exp.	45.0	50.3	49.0	34.9	30.9	26.1	32.4	41.4	55.2	46.1
Pretax Inc.	437	198	229	383	49.0	Nil	69.0	114	132	253
Eff. Tax Rate	40%	57%	41%	45%	88%	NM	32%	43%	49%	36%
Net Inc.	262	84.5	136	213	6.0	-11.0	47.0	65.0	68.0	161

Balance Sheet & Other Fin. Data (Million $)

	1997	1996	1995	1994	1993	1992	1991	1990	1989	1988
Cash	107	39.1	91.4	41.4	42.0	119	85.0	32.0	76.0	13.0
Curr. Assets	616	479	463	412	493	433	389	338	374	331
Total Assets	3,639	3,540	3,377	3,138	3,215	1,995	2,128	2,150	2,188	1,915
Curr. Liab.	697	654	517	451	554	399	438	430	435	470
LT Debt	545	637	638	523	460	207	213	319	337	378
Common Eqty.	1,728	1,623	1,612	1,544	1,599	1,000	1,073	1,056	1,064	873
Total Cap.	2,460	2,450	2,419	2,245	2,258	1,396	1,578	1,669	1,700	1,414
Cap. Exp.	153	211	201	186	80.0	47.0	40.0	121	230	278
Cash Flow	436	232	275	368	95.0	NM	NM	138	127	227
Curr. Ratio	0.9	0.7	0.9	0.9	0.9	1.1	0.9	0.8	0.9	0.7
% LT Debt of Cap.	22.2	26.0	26.4	23.3	20.4	14.8	13.5	19.1	19.9	26.7
% Net Inc.of Revs.	9.2	3.2	5.6	9.0	0.3	NM	2.8	3.6	3.9	9.5
% Ret. on Assets	7.3	2.4	4.2	6.7	0.2	NA	2.2	3.0	3.3	9.0
% Ret. on Equity	15.6	5.2	8.6	13.6	0.4	NA	4.4	6.1	7.1	19.3

Data as orig. reptd.; bef. results of disc. opers. and/or spec. items. Per share data adj. for stk. divs. as of ex-div. date. Bold denotes diluted EPS (FASB 128). E-Estimated. NA-Not Available. NM-Not Meaningful. NR-Not Ranked.

Office—229 W. 43rd St., New York, NY 10036. **Tel**—(212) 556-1234. **Website**—http://www.nytimes.com **Chrmn & CEO**—A. O. Sulzberger. **Pres & COO**—R. T. Lewis. **Secy**—Laura J. Corwin. **SVP & CFO**—D. L. Gorham. **VP & Investor Contact**—Catherine J. Mathis (212-556-1981); mathicj@nytimes.com **Dirs**—J. F. Akers, R. L. Gelb, A. L. Higginbotham Jr., R. S. Holmberg, R. A. Lawrence, R. T. Lewis, G. B. Munroe, C. H. Price II, G. L. Shinn, D. M. Stewart, A. O. Sulzberger, A. O. Sulzberger Jr., J. P. Sulzberger, W. O. Taylor. **Transfer Agent & Registrar**—First Chicago Trust Co. of New York, NYC. **Incorporated**—in New York in 1896. **Empl**— 13,100. **S&P Analyst:** William H. Donald

STANDARD &POOR'S
STOCK REPORTS

Newell Co.

1668M

NYSE Symbol **NWL**

In S&P 500

12-SEP-98

Industry: Housewares

Summary: This leading high-volume, brand-name consumer products firm has grown through acquisitions. Major product lines include housewares, home furnishings, office products and hardware.

S&P Opinion: Accumulate (★★★★)	Recent Price • 43½	Yield • 1.7%
	52 Wk Range • 55⅛-32¾	12-Mo. P/E • 17.1

Quantitative Evaluations

Outlook
(1 Lowest—5 Highest)
• **3**

Fair Value
• **49⅜**

Risk
• **Low**

Earn./Div. Rank
• **A+**

Technical Eval.
• **Bearish** since 1/98

Rel. Strength Rank
(1 Lowest—99 Highest)
• **61**

Insider Activity
• **NA**

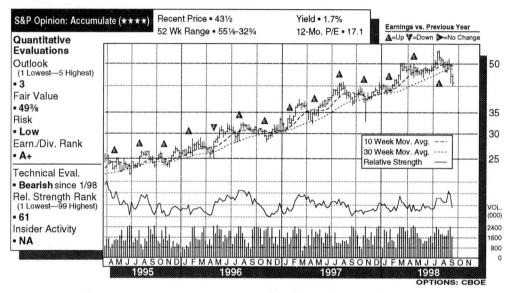

Earnings vs. Previous Year
▲=Up ▼=Down ▶=No Change

10 Week Mov. Avg. ----
30 Week Mov. Avg. ·····
Relative Strength ——

OPTIONS: CBOE

Overview - 28-JUL-98

We expect sales to increase approximately 12% to 14% in 1998. About one-half of the sales growth should come from higher volume of core businesses (businesses owned for more than two years), reflecting new product introductions, expanded distribution through new store openings at Wal-Mart and Home Depot, increased share at existing distribution outlets, and entry into new markets, including overseas markets. The remainder of the gain will reflect recent acquisitions, including the May 1997 purchases of Kirsch and Rubbermaid's office products division, and the March 1998 acquisition of Calphalon. In July 1998, NWL agreed to acquire Gardinia Group, a German window treatments supplier with annual sales of approximately $160 million. Also, the company completed its acquisition of Panex S.A. Industria e Comercia, a South American aluminum cookware manufacturer and marketer with annual sales of about $100 million.

Valuation - 28-JUL-98

Over the years, Newell has rapidly expanded its product offerings of low-ticket, higher-volume consumer products through acquisitions and new product launches. It has benefited from manufacturing and distribution leverage and synergies as it increased its product offerings, and has increased market share through discount stores, home centers, office superstores, warehouse clubs, hardware stores, department stores, and drug stores. We continue to rate the shares accumulate, based on our belief that the company will continue to achieve approximately 15% EPS growth and a 20% return on equity annually over the next several years. The shares, recently trading at 25 times estimated 1998 EPS of $2.10 (excludes $0.60 from sale of stake in Black & Decker), remain attractive.

Key Stock Statistics

S&P EPS Est. 1998	2.10	Tang. Bk. Value/Share	1.30
P/E on S&P Est. 1998	20.7	Beta	0.73
S&P EPS Est. 1999	2.40	Shareholders	14,600
Dividend Rate/Share	0.72	Market cap. (B)	$ 7.1
Shs. outstg. (M)	162.6	Inst. holdings	63%
Avg. daily vol. (M)	0.452		

Value of $10,000 invested 5 years ago: $ 23,544

Fiscal Year Ending Dec. 31

	1998	1997	1996	1995	1994	1993
Revenues (Million $)						
1Q	747.3	629.4	618.2	556.6	443.5	334.2
2Q	922.7	801.0	735.1	621.3	493.5	372.7
3Q	—	889.9	761.9	651.3	553.2	456.7
4Q	—	914.1	757.6	669.2	584.7	481.4
Yr.	—	3,234	2,873	2,498	2,075	1,645
Earnings Per Share ($)						
1Q	**0.91**	**0.24**	0.21	0.23	0.20	0.17
2Q	**0.54**	**0.49**	0.43	0.35	0.28	0.22
3Q	—	**0.53**	0.47	0.41	0.37	0.30
4Q	—	**0.56**	0.51	0.42	0.39	0.35
Yr.	—	**1.82**	1.61	1.41	1.24	1.05

Next earnings report expected: late October

Dividend Data (Dividends have been paid since 1946.)

Amount ($)	Date Decl.	Ex-Div. Date	Stock of Record	Payment Date
0.160	Nov. 06	Nov. 17	Nov. 19	Dec. 03 '97
0.180	Feb. 10	Feb. 18	Feb. 20	Mar. 06 '98
0.180	May. 14	May. 20	May. 22	Jun. 05 '98
0.180	Aug. 07	Aug. 12	Aug. 14	Aug. 28 '98

A Division of The McGraw-Hill Companies

STANDARD
&POOR'S
STOCK REPORTS

Newell Co.

1668M

12-SEP-98

Business Summary - 28-JUL-98

From a small manufacturer of drapery hardware with $20 million in sales, Newell has grown an average of nearly 20% per year over the past 25 years, into a global full service marketer of consumer products, with annual sales in excess of $3 billion and net income of nearly $300 million.

Acquisitions have been the cornerstone of Newell's growth. Since 1990, it has completed more than 15 major acquisitions, representing over $2 billion in incremental sales. Most recently, in March 1998, NWL agreed to purchase Calphalon Corp., a leading manufacturer of gourmet cookwear, which will add approximately $110 million in sales to the existing housewares unit.

Newell tries to acquire companies with branded compatible product lines that enable it to achieve critical mass in the industries in which it competes, particularly targeting those companies with unrealized profit potential. Its ability to bring newly acquired product lines up to its high standards of profitability is known as Newellization. This strategy has enabled NWL to become a market leader in many categories, including aluminum cookware, window treatments, markers and writing instruments, and picture frames.

In addition to growth provided through acquisitions, NWL has been able to sustain its strong internal growth momentum through new product introductions and a fo-

cus on a good-better-best merchandising strategy. The combination of internal growth and acquisitions allowed EPS growth of 17% on average over the past 10 years, well above the company's goal of 15%.

Until a few years ago, NWL's overseas effort was limited to a small export sales division. However, recent acquisitions, coupled with increased sales to foreign customers, pushed international contributions to almost 17% of total sales in 1997.

Products are sold through four main divisions. Major houseware brands consist of Mirro and WearEver (aluminum cookware), Anchor Hocking Glass, Anchor Hocking Plastics, Goody, Ace and Wilhold (hair accessories), and Pyrex, Pyroflam, Visions and Vitri (glassware).

Home furnishings brands include Levolor and Kirsch (window coverings), Del Mar and Joanna (window treatment hardware), Intercraft, Burnes and Decorel (picture frames), and Lee Rowan and System Works (home storage products).

Office products consists of Sanford and Berol (markers), Eberhard Faber (pencils and rolling ball pens), Stuart Hall (school & office supplies), Newell Office Products and Rogers and Keene (desktop office and computer accessories).

Hardware products include EZ Paintr (painting accessories), Amerock (cabinet hardware), BernzOmatic (hand torches), and Bulldog (home hardware products).

Per Share Data ($)

(Year Ended Dec. 31)	1997	1996	1995	1994	1993	1992	1991	1990	1989	1988
Tangible Bk. Val.	2.20	3.58	2.60	2.79	2.96	3.41	3.69	2.93	2.49	1.19
Cash Flow	2.82	2.35	2.05	1.70	1.46	1.40	1.19	1.11	1.01	0.96
Earnings	1.82	1.62	1.41	1.24	1.05	1.05	0.91	0.83	0.70	0.55
Dividends	0.64	0.56	0.46	0.39	0.34	0.30	0.30	0.25	0.21	0.14
Payout Ratio	35%	35%	33%	31%	33%	29%	33%	30%	30%	25%
Prices - High	43¾	33¾	27¼	23⅞	21½	26½	22⅞	17¾	12⅝	7½
- Low	30⅛	25	20¼	18⅞	15⅜	16½	11½	8⅞	6⅜	3½
P/E Ratio - High	24	21	19	19	20	25	25	21	18	14
- Low	17	15	14	15	15	16	13	11	9	6

Income Statement Analysis (Million $)

	1997	1996	1995	1994	1993	1992	1991	1990	1989	1988
Revs.	3,234	2,873	2,498	2,075	1,645	1,452	1,119	1,073	1,123	988
Oper. Inc.	702	602	521	415	340	301	228	208	197	160
Depr.	162	116	102	72.5	64.3	53.9	35.1	36.5	40.7	39.2
Int. Exp.	73.6	57.0	49.8	30.0	19.1	20.4	16.4	16.4	28.5	24.9
Pretax Inc.	482	425	371	329	276	278	187	171	146	104
Eff. Tax Rate	39%	40%	40%	41%	40%	41%	40%	41%	41%	41%
Net Inc.	290	256	222	196	165	163	112	101	85.0	61.0

Balance Sheet & Other Fin. Data (Million $)

	1997	1996	1995	1994	1993	1992	1991	1990	1989	1988
Cash	36.1	4.4	58.8	14.9	2.9	28.0	26.3	50.3	38.8	13.5
Curr. Assets	1,382	1,108	1,133	918	676	595	286	375	380	334
Total Assets	3,944	3,005	2,931	2,488	1,953	1,570	1,040	871	871	820
Curr. Liab.	664	637	680	784	599	375	164	181	231	192
LT Debt	784	672	762	409	218	177	177	89.0	100	154
Common Eqty.	1,714	1,492	1,300	1,125	979	859	606	500	444	249
Total Cap.	3,096	2,211	2,093	1,552	1,197	1,036	810	622	578	584
Cap. Exp.	98.4	94.2	82.6	66.0	59.0	77.6	57.1	36.6	48.7	35.3
Cash Flow	452	373	324	268	230	217	147	139	121	91.0
Curr. Ratio	2.1	1.7	1.7	1.2	1.1	1.6	1.7	2.1	1.6	1.7
% LT Debt of Cap.	25.4	30.4	36.4	26.4	18.2	17.1	21.8	14.4	17.3	26.3
% Net Inc.of Revs.	9.0	8.9	8.9	9.4	10.1	11.2	10.0	9.4	7.6	6.2
% Ret. on Assets	8.4	8.6	8.2	8.8	9.4	11.3	11.5	11.6	9.0	7.3
% Ret. on Equity	18.1	18.4	18.4	18.6	17.9	20.1	19.8	21.3	22.3	22.8

Data as orig. reptd.; bef. results of disc. opers. and/or spec. items. Per share data adj. for stk. divs. as of ex-div. date. Bold denotes diluted EPS (FASB 128). E-Estimated. NA-Not Available. NM-Not Meaningful. NR-Not Ranked.

Office—29 East Stephenson St., Freeport, IL 61032-0943. **Tel**—(815) 235-4171. **Website**—http://www.newellco.com **Chrmn**—W. P. Sovey. **Vice Chrmn & CEO**—J. J. McDonough. **Pres & COO**—T. A. Ferguson Jr. **VP-Fin**—W. T. Alldredge. **VP & Secy**—R. H. Wolff. **Investor Contact**—Ross A. Porter Jr. **Dirs**—A. F. Doody, G. H. Driggs, D. C. Ferguson, T. A. Ferguson Jr., R. L. Katz, J. J. McDonough, C. A. Montgomery, E. C. Millett, A. P. Newell, H. B. Pearsall, W. P. Sovey. **Transfer Agent & Registrar**—First Chicago Trust Co., NYC. **Incorporated**—in Delaware in 1970. **Empl**—24,600. **S&P Analyst:** Robert J. Izmirlian

12-SEP-98

Industry:
Gold & Precious Metals
Mining

Summary: This company owns a 94% interest in Newmont Gold Co., one of the world's leading gold producers, with operations in Nevada, Peru, Uzbekistan and Indonesia.

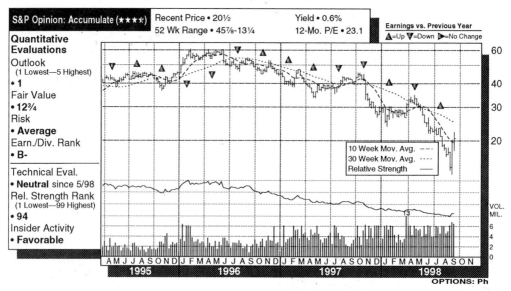

S&P Opinion: Accumulate (★★★★)	Recent Price • 20½	Yield • 0.6%
	52 Wk Range • 45⅞-13¼	12-Mo. P/E • 23.1

Quantitative Evaluations

Outlook
(1 Lowest—5 Highest)
• **1**

Fair Value
• **12¾**

Risk
• **Average**

Earn./Div. Rank
• **B-**

Technical Eval.
• **Neutral** since 5/98

Rel. Strength Rank
(1 Lowest—99 Highest)
• **94**

Insider Activity
• **Favorable**

Earnings vs. Previous Year
▲=Up ▼=Down ▶=No Change

10 Week Mov. Avg. - - -
30 Week Mov. Avg. - - - -
Relative Strength ——

VOL.
MIL.

1995   1996   1997   1998

OPTIONS: Ph

Overview - 17-AUG-98

NEM's 1998 second quarter EPS of $0.16 were in line with analyst estimates, as the company continued to demonstrate excellent operating performance. Lower costs and higher output outweighed a decline in the average price of gold to $320/oz., from $368/oz. Production rose to 1,037,700 oz., from 1,028,600 oz. in the 1997 period. Cash costs for the quarter declined to $182/oz.. from $192/oz. a year earlier; total costs declined to $247/oz., from $251/oz. NEM is on track to produce between 3.8 million oz. and 4.0 million oz. of gold in 1998, at a cash cost of under $200/oz.

Valuation - 17-AUG-98

On April 21, 1998, we upgraded NEM and most other gold stocks to accumulate, based on a more positive outlook both for the metal and the gold stocks as a group. While gold stocks have been under pressure through mid-August, we expect gold and gold stocks to begin an uptrend later in 1998 or in early 1999. Our outlook is based several factors. First, we expect central bank selling to diminish now that the new European Central Bank has announced its decision to hold 15% of its reserves in gold. Second, the rate of gain on financial investments will decline in 1998 and 1999, reducing competition for gold. Third, gold production will be flat or decline in 1999, boosting prices. Because NEM does not hedge its gold production, the stock is more highly leveraged to the price of gold than that of the company's peers. NEM's financial leverage is also higher than the group average, and the company has maintained an aggressive spending program, despite low gold prices. Consequently, the stock it has underperformed the group. However, NEM is a highly efficient producer, and the shares will outperform their rivals when gold begins a sustained uptrend.

Key Stock Statistics

S&P EPS Est. 1998	0.65	Tang. Bk. Value/Share	10.47
P/E on S&P Est. 1998	31.6	Beta	1.07
S&P EPS Est. 1999	0.95	Shareholders	5,000
Dividend Rate/Share	0.12	Market cap. (B)	$ 3.2
Shs. outstg. (M)	156.5	Inst. holdings	64%
Avg. daily vol. (M)	1.855		

Value of $10,000 invested 5 years ago: $ 6,641

Fiscal Year Ending Dec. 31

	1998	1997	1996	1995	1994	1993
Revenues (Million $)						
1Q	378.1	355.0	154.7	134.5	149.8	138.1
2Q	374.0	421.8	181.2	145.1	145.1	157.3
3Q	—	383.8	226.0	172.3	150.1	178.1
4Q	—	412.2	206.6	184.4	158.2	160.8
Yr.	—	1,628	768.5	636.2	597.4	634.3
Earnings Per Share ($)						
1Q	**0.20**	0.32	0.11	0.14	0.20	0.10
2Q	**0.16**	-0.41	0.20	0.74	0.16	0.42
3Q	**E0.14**	0.28	0.35	0.25	0.19	0.25
4Q	**E0.15**	0.25	0.20	0.05	0.15	0.15
Yr.	**E0.65**	0.44	0.86	1.17	0.70	0.92

Next earnings report expected: late October

Dividend Data (Dividends have been paid since 1934.)

Amount ($)	Date Decl.	Ex-Div. Date	Stock of Record	Payment Date
0.030	Nov. 19	Dec. 02	Dec. 04	Dec. 18 '97
0.030	Jan. 28	Feb. 09	Feb. 11	Mar. 11 '98
0.030	May. 20	Jun. 09	Jun. 11	Jun. 26 '98
0.030	Jul. 15	Jul. 27	Jul. 29	Aug. 27 '98

Newmont Mining Corporation

Business Summary - 17-AUG-98

Newmont Mining is one of the most consistently profitable North American gold companies. Following its May 1997 acquisition of Santa Fe Gold, NEM, through 94%-owned Newmont Gold (NGC), became North America's largest gold producer, and the world's second largest.

NEM plans to produce 3.8 million oz. to 4.0 million equity oz. a year at a total cash cost of under $200/oz. through 2000. To cope with low gold prices, NEM will cut 1998 capital spending $145 million, cut exploration spending $30 million from 1997's $90.4 million, and trim general and administrative expense $15 million.

As a general policy, NEM does not hedge its production, because it sees higher gold prices long term, and seeks to provide shareholders with high leverage to the price of gold. In keeping with this policy, NEM bought 1.1 million oz. of gold in July 1997, to offset a hedge position acquired in the merger with Santa Fe Gold.

Significant operating data for recent years:

	1997	1996
Gold production (oz.)	3,956,800	3,104,100
Average realized price	$354	$395
Cash cost per oz.	$187	$218
Total cost per oz.	$250	$289
Reserves at year end	52,700,000	55,200,000

U.S. operations at Carlin, NV, and the Mesquite mine in California increased production to 3,004,400 oz. in 1997, from 2,519,900 oz. in 1996, mostly reflecting improved grades and recovery rates at Carlin.

Minera Yanacocha S.A. (51% owned, up from 38% following a September 1996 court ruling), located in northern Peru, produced 530,900 equity oz. in 1997, versus 308,300 equity oz. in 1996 and 209,800 equity oz. of gold in 1995. Subsequent to the September 1996 ruling, the case was appealed to the Peruvian Supreme Court which was unable to reach a decision as of January 1998. Final resolution is pending until all judges can agree on a decision.

NGC's 50%-owned Zarafshan-Newmont venture in Uzbekistan started production in 1995. Zarafshan produced 215,000 oz. in 1997, versus 163,200 equity oz. in 1996 and 18,500 oz. in 1995.

In 1996, production commenced at the 80%-owned Minahasa project and reached 112,700 oz. for the year. Output increased to 206,500 oz. in 1997.

NEM's equity gold production in the first half of 1998 totaled 2,070,500 oz., versus 1,875,800 oz. in 1997. Cash costs declined to $183/oz., from $195/oz.; total costs declined to $248/oz., from $257/oz. The average realized gold price dropped to $322/oz., from $369/oz. in 1997.

Per Share Data ($) (Year Ended Dec. 31)	1997	1996	1995	1994	1993	1992	1991	1990	1989	1988
Tangible Bk. Val.	10.17	10.30	7.89	4.48	4.05	2.84	2.34	1.30	-2.37	-3.47
Cash Flow	2.14	2.11	2.40	1.76	2.21	2.20	2.23	3.00	2.36	1.58
Earnings	0.44	0.86	1.17	0.70	0.92	1.04	1.11	2.00	1.54	1.10
Dividends	0.39	0.48	0.48	0.48	0.48	0.48	0.48	0.48	0.48	0.48
Payout Ratio	89%	56%	41%	69%	52%	46%	43%	24%	31%	44%
Prices - High	47½	60¾	46¼	48⅛	47⅛	43⅛	35¼	43⅞	39⅞	37⅜
- Low	26½	43⅞	33⅛	33⅞	29⅝	29	26½	25⅜	25⅜	24¼
P/E Ratio - High	NM	71	40	69	51	41	32	22	26	34
- Low	NM	51	28	48	32	28	24	13	16	22
Income Statement Analysis (Million $)										
Revs.	1,573	768	639	597	634	613	623	683	582	500
Oper. Inc.	582	172	162	160	207	204	237	244	189	146
Depr.	266	125	107	91.0	111	99	94.0	84.8	69.3	40.4
Int. Exp.	77.1	49.4	36.0	10.0	21.0	15.0	13.0	42.0	90.0	123
Pretax Inc.	132	74.6	142	54.0	124	101	135	254	167	156
Eff. Tax Rate	48%	NM	8.35%	NM	15%	2.80%	21%	28%	16%	30%
Net Inc.	68.4	85.1	113	76.0	95.0	91.0	94.0	168	130	92.0
Balance Sheet & Other Fin. Data (Million $)										
Cash	146	198	71.0	174	88.0	309	35.0	149	19.0	33.0
Curr. Assets	641	456	290	370	229	409	187	274	183	183
Total Assets	3,614	2,081	1,774	1,657	1,186	1,215	818	951	1,302	1,321
Curr. Liab.	395	224	194	153	110	243	235	267	318	566
LT Debt	1,179	585	604	594	192	177	112	302	964	819
Common Eqty.	1,591	1,025	743	386	342	241	201	110	-199	-291
Total Cap.	2,938	1,716	1,429	1,347	913	830	462	600	937	729
Cap. Exp.	415	231	309	402	249	213	94.0	74.0	126	346
Cash Flow	334	210	208	151	189	188	188	253	199	132
Curr. Ratio	1.6	2.0	1.5	2.4	2.1	1.7	0.8	1.0	0.6	0.3
% LT Debt of Cap.	40.1	34.1	42.3	44.1	21.0	21.3	24.3	50.3	NM	NM
% Net Inc.of Revs.	4.3	11.1	17.7	12.7	14.9	14.8	15.1	24.7	22.2	18.4
% Ret. on Assets	2.4	4.4	6.6	5.3	7.9	8.9	10.7	14.9	9.9	5.6
% Ret. on Equity	5.2	9.6	18.0	20.9	27.1	40.1	60.6	NM	NM	NM

Data as orig. reptd.; bef. results of disc. opers. and/or spec. items, Per share data adj. for stk. divs. as of ex-div. date. Bold denotes diluted EPS (FASB 128). E-Estimated. NA-Not Available. NM-Not Meaningful. NR-Not Ranked.

Office—1700 Lincoln St., Denver, CO 80203. **Tel**—(303) 863-7414. **Chrmn, Pres & CEO**—R. C. Cambre. **EVP & CFO**—W. W. Murdy. **VP & Secy**—T. J. Schmitt. **VP & Investor Contact**—Jack H. Morris. **Dirs**—R. I. J. Agnew, J. P. Bolduc, R. C. Cambre, J. T. Curry, Jr., J. P. Flannery, D. W. Gentry, L. I. Higdon Jr., T. A. Holmes, P. M. James, G. B. Monroe, R. A. Plumbridge, R. H. Quenon, M. A. Qureshi, M. K. Reilly, J. H. Sisco, W. I. M. Turner Jr. **Transfer Agent & Registrar**—ChaseMellon Shareholder Services, Ridgefield Park, NJ. **Incorporated**—in Delaware in 1921. **Empl**— 4,100. **S&P Analyst:** Leo J. Larkin

12-SEP-98

Industry:
Telecommunications
(Cellular/Wireless)

Summary: Nextel is the leading provider of specialized mobile radio communications services.

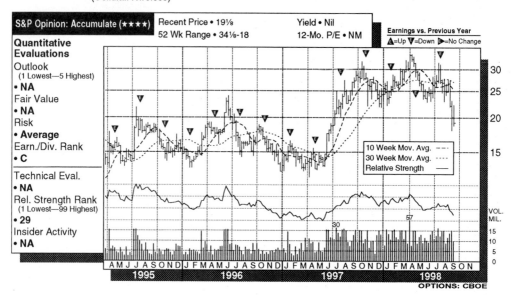

S&P Opinion: Accumulate (★★★★)	Recent Price • 19⅛	Yield • Nil
	52 Wk Range • 34⅛-18	12-Mo. P/E • NM

Earnings vs. Previous Year
▲=Up ▼=Down ▶=No Change

Quantitative Evaluations

Outlook
(1 Lowest—5 Highest)
• **NA**

Fair Value
• **NA**

Risk
• **Average**

Earn./Div. Rank
• **C**

Technical Eval.
• **NA**

Rel. Strength Rank
(1 Lowest—99 Highest)
• **29**

Insider Activity
• **NA**

10 Week Mov. Avg. ---
30 Week Mov. Avg. ·····
Relative Strength —

OPTIONS: CBOE

Overview - 03-SEP-98

The company provides enhanced dispatch services, including data services, messaging, and telephone interconnect services, to mobile workgroups. NXTL is targeting the highly competitive, but rapidly growing, cellular and PCS marketplace. In mid-1995, wireless pioneer Craig McCaw and certain members of his family agreed to invest up to $1.1 billion in the company over a period of six years. The investment, combined with a $500 million debt refinancing, provided much needed capital, which was used to purchase additional wireless spectrum. Results continue to be affected by costs associated with the digital network buildout. However, future earnings will benefit from cost savings associated with the economies of scale from a national footprint. Results in the 1998 second quarter excluded an extraordinary charge of $0.49 a share from the early extinguishment of debt.

Valuation - 03-SEP-98

In response to a recent drop in the share price from a stock market plunge, we have raised our opinion on NXTL to accumulate, from hold. With strong fundamentals, including robust revenue growth and expected positive cash flow in the third quarter, this company represents one of the few attractive pure wireless plays. Demand for digital wireless networks will continue to escalate, as users compare its superior voice and transmission quality to that provided by analog networks. Future prospects are also bolstered by the backing of wireless pioneer Craig McCaw and his family. In addition to domestic strength, the company has invested $23 million in the initial phase of a digital cellular operation in the strong Shanghai, China, market, and also owns stakes in Argentina, Japan, Brazil, and other high growth wireless markets.

Key Stock Statistics

S&P EPS Est. 1998	-5.25	Tang. Bk. Value/Share	NM
P/E on S&P Est. 1998	NM	Beta	2.15
S&P EPS Est. 1999	-3.95	Shareholders	600
Dividend Rate/Share	Nil	Market cap. (B)	$ 5.1
Shs. outstg. (M)	285.7	Inst. holdings	40%
Avg. daily vol. (M)	2.724		

Value of $10,000 invested 5 years ago: $ 13,008

Fiscal Year Ending Dec. 31

	1998	1997	1996	1995	1994	1993
Revenues (Million $)						
1Q	327.1	110.7	68.32	37.10	—	13.20
2Q	421.4	145.9	77.62	42.86	—	12.80
3Q	—	207.2	91.04	65.34	29.60	17.00
4Q	—	275.1	95.96	79.89	32.60	19.10
Yr.	—	738.9	332.9	225.2	—	--
Earnings Per Share ($)						
1Q	-1.53	-0.93	-0.56	-0.50	-0.27	-0.05
2Q	-1.45	-1.08	-0.58	-0.53	-0.35	-0.08
3Q	E-1.25	-1.26	-0.66	-0.61	-0.41	-0.17
4Q	E-1.02	-3.01	-0.70	-0.62	-0.48	-0.16
Yr.	E-5.25	-6.41	-2.50	-2.31	—	--

Next earnings report expected: mid November

Dividend Data

No cash dividends have been paid.

Business Summary - 03-SEP-98

The Nextel wireless network's footprint is being molded in the form of the U.S. The company believes that digital mobile networks will enable it to become a major provider of high-quality, enhanced mobile communications services, including two-way radio dispatch, paging, data, mobile telephone service and interconnection with the public switched telephone system. Its digital network design and technology should also significantly boost capacity of existing SMR (specialized mobile radio) channels. As of mid-April 1998, NXT's digital mobile networks reached more than 400 cities, including 79 of the 100 leading markets. By the end of 1998, the company expects its service to cover 85% of where America lives or works.

The $30 billion wireless communications market is expected to grow to about $50 billion by 2000, and $75 billion by 2005. Nextel plans to be an active participant in this healthy growth trend. The company introduced a national digital network in January 1996, and said it would not charge roaming fees for customers traveling anywhere on the digital network. The vast majority of subscribers are dispatch users using the 800/900 megahertz bands of the radio spectrum.

In March 1998, Nextel International completed a $730 million financing for selective global wireless opportunities. In February 1998, NXTL sold $1.6 billion in notes, with net proceeds of $976 million being used toward the expansion of the company's domestic wireless network.

In January 1997, Nextel acquired 81% of Wireless Ventures of Brazil, Inc., the largest specialized mobile radio (SMR) operator in Brazil, for approximately $186 million in stock. The purchase represents a price of approximately $4 for each of the 60 million potential customers Nextel may serve. The licensed coverage area includes each of the 10 leading cities in Brazil, Latin America's largest economy. Brazil reportedly has a waiting list of 1.5 million people for wireless service.

In December 1997, the company successfully bid $88.8 million for 475 of the 525 Economic Area licenses being auctioned by the FCC. On average, Nextel won rights to nearly 10 MHz of wireless spectrum in areas covering all 50 states and approximately 98% of the U.S. population. This additional capacity will be used to serve NXTL's rapidly expanding subscriber base.

In April 1995, Craig McCaw and certain members of his family agreed to purchase up to $1.1 billion of company stock over the next six years through purchases from Nextel and from Motorola, a current shareholder. Mr. McCaw became a director, with control over an operations committee.

Per Share Data ($)

(Year Ended Dec. 31)	1997	1996	1995	1994	1993	1992	1991	1990	1989	1988
Tangible Bk. Val.	NM	NM	NM	-0.98	-0.50	1.75	0.55	NA	NA	NA
Cash Flow	-4.18	-0.70	-0.66	0.01	0.02	0.28	0.30	0.76	0.26	0.09
Earnings	-6.41	-2.50	-2.31	-1.51	-0.73	-0.16	-0.65	-0.30	-0.36	-0.20
Dividends	Nil	Nil	Nil	Nil	Nil	Nil	Nil	Nil	Nil	Nil
Payout Ratio	Nil	Nil	Nil	Nil	Nil	Nil	Nil	Nil	Nil	Nil
Prices - High	32	24	21³/₄	46³/₄	54⁷/₈	18³/₄	NA	NA	NA	NA
- Low	12¹/₈	12³/₄	9³/₈	13¹/₄	17⁷/₈	9	NA	NA	NA	NA
P/E Ratio - High	NM	NM	NM	NM	NM	NM	NM	NM	NM	NM
- Low	NM	NM	NM	NM	NM	NM	NM	NM	NM	NM

Income Statement Analysis (Million $)

	1997	1996	1995	1994	1993	1992	1991	1990	1989	1988
Revs.	739	333	225	194	67.9	53.0	52.5	53.9	36.3	17.3
Oper. Inc.	-410	245	-172	-44.2	-1.8	13.0	19.1	19.3	9.6	4.7
Depr.	526	401	236	195	58.4	25.9	25.7	24.6	14.2	5.9
Int. Exp.	407	227	115	NA	37.7	2.6	12.8	14.2	7.2	3.6
Pretax Inc.	-1,308	-862	-531	-290	-78.3	-10.6	-18.9	-15.4	-13.5	-4.6
Eff. Tax Rate	NM	NM	NM	NM	NM	NM	NM	NM	NM	NM
Net Inc.	-1,567	-555	-330	-192	-56.9	-9.6	-15.7	-7.0	-8.2	-4.1

Balance Sheet & Other Fin. Data (Million $)

	1997	1996	1995	1994	1993	1992	1991	1990	1989	1988
Cash	433	140	409	474	910	31.9	13.4	0.5	3.2	0.9
Curr. Assets	840	309	505	504	922	39.9	20.2	10.1	17.9	13.2
Total Assets	9,228	6,472	5,513	2,889	2,197	334	211	212	207	100
Curr. Liab.	769	376	365	NA	103	23.3	17.5	18.2	15.8	NA
LT Debt	5,038	2,783	1,653	1,163	108	55.0	1.0	106	98.0	47.0
Common Eqty.	1,912	2,508	2,645	1,269	846	255	191	24.0	28.0	12.0
Total Cap.	8,430	6,097	5,138	2,432	2,094	310	193	161	156	78.0
Cap. Exp.	1,597	435	271	NA	241	96.8	7.8	2.7	4.2	3.3
Cash Flow	-1,051	-154	-95.0	2.1	1.5	16.3	8.2	17.7	5.9	1.8
Curr. Ratio	1.1	0.8	1.4	NA	8.9	1.7	1.2	0.6	1.1	NA
% LT Debt of Cap.	59.8	45.6	32.2	47.8	51.6	17.7	0.5	66.0	63.0	60.8
% Net Inc.of Revs.	NM	NM	NM	NM	NM	NM	NM	NM	NM	NM
% Ret. on Assets	NM	NM	NM	NM	NM	NM	NM	NM	NM	NM
% Ret. on Equity	NM	NM	NM	NM	NM	NM	NM	NM	NM	NM

Data as orig. reptd.; yrs. ended Mar. 31 of the fol. cal. yr. prior to 1994; bef. results of disc. opers. and/or spec. items. Per share data adj. for stk. divs. as of ex-div. date. Bold denotes diluted EPS (FASB 128). E-Estimated. NA-Not Available. NM-Not Meaningful. NR-Not Ranked.

Office—1505 Farm Credit Dr., Suite 100, McLean, VA 22102. **Tel**—(703) 394-3000. **Website**—http://www.nextel.com **Chrmn & CEO**—D. F. Akerson. **Vice Chrmn**—M. E. O'Brien. **Pres & COO**—T. M. Donahue. **SVP & CFO**—S. M. Shindler. **Secy**—L. Zappala. **VP & Treas**—A. J. Long. **Dirs**—D. F. Akerson, K. Bane, W. E. Conway Jr., R. Cooper, T. M. Donahue, C. O. McCaw, M. E. O'Brien, K. Nakasaki, M. Torimoto, D. Weibling. **Transfer Agent & Registrar**—First Chicago Trust Co. of New York, NYC. **Incorporated**—in Delaware in 1987. **Empl**— 3,600. **S&P Analyst:** Philip D. Wohl

Niagara Mohawk Power   1676

NYSE Symbol **NMK**

In **S&P 500**

12-SEP-98

Industry:
Electric Companies

Summary: Niagara Mohawk supplies electricity (83% of 1997 revenues) and gas (17%) to major cities in western New York and a large area in the northern part of the state.

S&P Opinion: Sell (★)	
Recent Price • 15¾	Yield • Nil
52 Wk Range • 16⅛-8⅞	12-Mo. P/E • NM

Quantitative Evaluations

Outlook
(1 Lowest—5 Highest)
• **NA**

Fair Value
• **NA**

Risk
• **Average**

Earn./Div. Rank
• **B**

Technical Eval.
• **Bullish** since 9/97

Rel. Strength Rank
(1 Lowest—99 Highest)
• **96**

Insider Activity
• **NA**

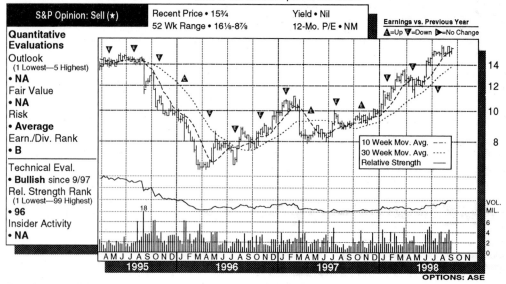

Earnings vs. Previous Year
▲=Up ▼=Down ▶=No Change

10 Week Mov. Avg. — — —
30 Week Mov. Avg. ·······
Relative Strength ———

OPTIONS: ASE

Overview - 28-JUL-98

After the closing, on June 30, 1998, of its agreement with a group of independent power producers, the company reported a second quarter non-cash charge of $1.18 a share. The charge had been previously recorded (at $0.85) in the fourth quarter of 1997, but after meetings with the staff of the Securities and Exchange Commission, it was decided to record the charge in the quarter in which the agreement (to restructure or terminate power purchase contracts representing more than 80% of NMK's above-market power costs) was closed. The difference in the charge reflects the change in the price of the stock (issued to the IPPs) on June 30 and March 26 (the date at which the fourth quarter charge was determined). In February 1998, the New York Public Service Commission approved NMK's "Power Choice" settlement, under which the company will divest all of its fossil and hydro generation assets and reduce residential and commercial rates by 3.2% over the first three years of a five-year rate plan.

Valuation - 28-JUL-98

We would continue to sell NMK stock. While the June 1998 agreement with a group of independent power producers (IPPs) is essential for NMK's long-term financial recovery, we believe that it will be several years before there is any fundamental benefit to earnings. NMK will also be impacted by its large industrial customer base, a stagnant economy, and the excess capacity in its service area. In addition to the second quarter charge, the agreement's impact on 1998 results will be an additional $240 million in interest expense and a 30% increase in the number of shares outstanding. In exchange for the restructuring of the power purchase contracts, the IPPs will be paid over $3.4 billion in debt securities and issued nearly 43 million common shares (about 23% of NMK's common stock).

Key Stock Statistics

S&P EPS Est. 1998	-0.90	Tang. Bk. Value/Share	17.04
P/E on S&P Est. 1998	NM	Beta	0.65
S&P EPS Est. 1999	0.25	Shareholders	80,500
Dividend Rate/Share	Nil	Market cap. (B)	$ 3.0
Shs. outstg. (M)	187.4	Inst. holdings	46%
Avg. daily vol. (M)	0.697		

Value of $10,000 invested 5 years ago: $ 10,375

Fiscal Year Ending Dec. 31

	1998	1997	1996	1995	1994	1993
Revenues (Million $)						
1Q	1,098	1,164	1,163	1,125	1,236	1,136
2Q	910.9	945.7	960.8	938.8	979.7	929.3
3Q	—	896.6	895.7	887.2	918.8	880.0
4Q	—	960.3	971.1	966.5	1,018	988.2
Yr.	—	3,966	3,991	3,917	4,152	3,933
Earnings Per Share ($)						
1Q	**0.08**	**0.65**	0.60	0.75	0.92	0.86
2Q	**-1.04**	**0.22**	0.30	0.31	0.42	0.41
3Q	**E0.14**	**0.15**	-0.16	0.26	0.27	0.29
4Q	**E-0.08**	**-0.86**	0.23	0.13	-0.61	0.16
Yr.	**E-0.90**	**0.16**	0.97	1.44	1.00	1.71

Next earnings report expected: late October

Dividend Data

Dividends were omitted in August 1989, reinstated with the July 1991 declaration, and omitted again in early 1996.

Business Summary - 28-JUL-98

In an attempt to resolve its problem of having to make annual payments of about $1 billion to independent power producers (IPPs), Niagara Mohawk Power (NMK) closed an agreement (on June 30, 1998) with a group of IPPs to restructure or terminate their power purchase contracts in exchange for more than $3.4 billion in debt securities and nearly 43 million NMK common shares.

Although NMK expects to realize savings of $5 billion over a 15-year period, the bulk of the savings would take place during the second half of the period, after $3.2 billion in debt has been paid off.

Niagara Mohawk supplies electricity (83% of 1997 revenues) and gas (17%) to nearly 2.1 million customers in a large area of western and upstate New York and some parts of southern Ontario. Electric revenues by customer class in recent years:

	1997	1996	1995	1994
Residential	37%	38%	37%	35%
Commercial	37%	37%	37%	36%
Industrial	18%	16%	17%	18%
Other	8%	9%	9%	11%

In February 1998, the New York State Public Service Commission (PSC) approved the company's "Power Choice" settlement. In addition to approving the agreement with the IPPs, the PSC approved the creation of a competitive wholesale electricity market that will allow full customer choice by December 31, 1999; reduce average prices slightly for residential and commercial customers and more substantially for industrial customers; and separate the non-nuclear power generation business from the rest of the business.

NMK owns 100% of the Nine Mile Point 1 nuclear unit and 41% of the Nine Mile Point 2 unit. It also owns four fossil fuel steam plants (as well as a 25% interest in the Roseton steam station) and 70 hydroelectric plants. Under "Power Choice," the non-nuclear generation business would no longer be rate-regulated. Accordingly, on December 31, 1996, the company discontinued the application of SFAS No. 71 to its fossil/hydro operations and wrote off fossil/hydro generation regulatory assets of $103.6 million ($0.47 a share).

Expenditures for construction and nuclear fuel were $291 million in 1997, down from $352 million in 1996. NMK projects expenditures of $328 million for 1998, and $269 million, $264 million, $275 million and $300 million for the respective years 1999 through 2002.

In December 1996, the PSC approved a three-year natural gas plan that resulted in a rate reduction of $10 million per year for its largest customers and a modest increase in the rates of its residential customers.

In January 1998, an ice storm caused major damage to NMK's transmission and distribution system. The restoration costs were estimated at $131 million.

Per Share Data ($)

(Year Ended Dec. 31)	1997	1996	1995	1994	1993	1992	1991	1990	1989	1988
Tangible Bk. Val.	17.63	17.45	16.78	14.25	14.39	15.25	14.73	13.53	13.17	13.59
Earnings	0.16	0.97	1.44	1.00	1.71	1.61	1.49	0.30	0.78	1.21
Dividends	Nil	Nil	1.12	1.09	0.95	0.76	0.32	Nil	0.60	1.20
Payout Ratio	Nil	Nil	78%	109%	56%	47%	21%	Nil	77%	99%
Prices - High	11⅛	10⅛	15⅝	20⅝	25½	20½	18	14¾	15	15½
- Low	7⅞	6½	9½	12	18⅞	17½	12¾	11¾	10¾	12
P/E Ratio - High	70	10	11	21	15	13	12	49	19	13
- Low	49	7	7	12	11	11	9	39	14	10

Income Statement Analysis (Million $)

	1997	1996	1995	1994	1993	1992	1991	1990	1989	1988
Revs.	3,966	3,991	3,917	4,152	3,933	3,702	3,383	3,155	2,906	2,800
Depr.	340	330	318	308	277	274	259	221	211	182
Maint.	NA	NA	203	203	236	226	228	232	206	201
Fxd. Chgs. Cov.	1.8	1.7	2.1	1.8	2.3	2.1	2.0	1.3	1.7	1.9
Constr. Credits	9.7	7.4	9.1	9.1	16.0	21.0	19.0	21.0	19.0	11.0
Eff. Tax Rate	50%	37%	39%	40%	35%	38%	36%	42%	38%	37%
Net Inc.	59.8	178	248	177	272	256	243	83.0	151	209

Balance Sheet & Other Fin. Data (Million $)

	1997	1996	1995	1994	1993	1992	1991	1990	1989	1988
Gross Prop.	11,076	10,839	10,649	10,485	10,109	9,642	9,180	8,703	8,324	7,968
Cap. Exp.	285	348	346	485	519	490	518	422	406	354
Net Prop.	6,868	6,958	7,008	7,036	6,877	6,666	6,439	6,219	6,041	5,877
Capitalization:										
LT Debt	3,417	3,478	3,582	3,298	3,259	3,491	3,325	3,313	3,249	2,996
% LT Debt	52	53	54	52	53	56	56	57	57	55
Pfd.	517	526	537	546	413	460	503	532	558	586
% Pfd.	7.90	8.00	8.10	8.70	6.70	7.40	8.50	9.20	9.70	11
Common	2,604	2,586	2,514	2,462	2,456	2,240	2,116	1,955	1,915	1,881
% Common	40	39	38	39	40	36	36	34	34	35
Total Cap.	7,859	7,922	8,022	7,565	7,442	6,947	6,643	6,431	5,961	6,025
% Oper. Ratio	87.4	89.6	86.5	89.6	86.7	85.8	84.5	85.7	85.8	82.8
% Earn. on Net Prop.	7.2	2.6	7.5	6.2	7.8	8.0	8.3	7.4	6.9	8.3
% Return On Revs.	1.5	4.5	6.3	4.3	6.9	6.9	7.2	2.6	5.2	7.5
% Return On Invest. Capital	8.1	7.0	6.8	6.1	7.7	8.0	8.3	6.1	7.5	8.0
% Return On Com. Equity	0.9	5.5	8.4	5.8	10.2	10.1	10.0	2.1	5.6	8.7

Data as orig. reptd.; bef. results of disc opers. and/or spec. items. Per share data adj. for stk. divs. as of ex-div. date. Bold denotes diluted EPS (FASB 128). E-Estimated. NA-Not Available. NM-Not Meaningful. NR-Not Ranked.

Office—300 Erie Boulevard West, Syracuse, NY 13202. **Tel**—(315) 474-1511. **Website**—http://www.nimo.com **Chrmn & CEO**—W. E. Davis. **Pres**—A. J. Budney Jr. **SVP & CFO**—W. F. Edwards. **VP & Treas**—A. W. Roos. **Secy**—K. A. Rice. **Investor Contact**—Leon T. Mazur (315-428-5876). **Dirs**—W. F. Allyn, A. J. Budney Jr., L. Burkhardt III, D. M. Costle, E. M. Davis, W. E. Davis, W. J. Donlon, A. H. Gioia, B. G. Hill, H. A. Panasci Jr., P. M. Peterson, D. B. Riefler, S. B. Schwartz. **Transfer Agent & Registrar**—Bank of New York, NYC.**Incorporated**—in New York in 1937. **Empl**— 8,500. **S&P Analyst:** Justin McCann

Nicor Inc.   1680

NYSE Symbol **GAS**

In S&P 500

12-SEP-98 **Industry:** Natural Gas

Summary: This holding company's Northern Illinois Gas subsidiary, one of the largest U.S. natural gas distributors, recently changed its name to Nicor Gas.

S&P Opinion: Hold (★★★)

Recent Price • 39⅛   Yield • 3.8%
52 Wk Range • 43⅜-36   12-Mo. P/E • 15.3

Earnings vs. Previous Year
▲=Up ▼=Down ▷=No Change

Quantitative Evaluations

Outlook
(1 Lowest—5 Highest)
• **2+**

Fair Value
• **38⅛**

Risk
• **Low**

Earn./Div. Rank
• **A-**

Technical Eval.
• **Bearish** since 7/98

Rel. Strength Rank
(1 Lowest—99 Highest)
• **91**

Insider Activity
• **Neutral**

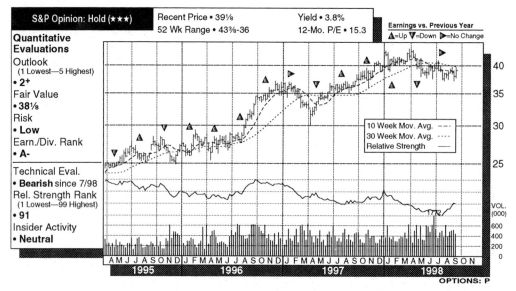

10 Week Mov. Avg. – – –
30 Week Mov. Avg. ·······
Relative Strength ——

VOL. (000)
600
400
200
0

A M J J A S O N D J F M A M J J A S O N D J F M A M J J A S O N D J F M A M J J A S O N
1995   1996   1997   1998

OPTIONS: P

Overview - 23-JUL-98

Warm weather led to 9.4% lower gas delivery in the second quarter of 1998, but greater shipping volume at Tropical, lower operating costs at the gas utility, and share buybacks drove operating cash flow and EPS higher; the company earned $0.59 in the second quarter of 1998, versus $0.58 in the year-ago period, in line with Street expectations. We believe that management will continue to reduce operating and maintenance expense at Nicor Gas, and will repurchase more shares to reduce the impact of a disappointing winter. The company should also be helped by a strong economy and a diverse industrial customer base. Although Nicor was late in entering the energy marketing industry, by joining with Dynegy Inc., a leading wholesale energy marketer, the company should be able to profit in this area as well. We also believe that the company's long term earnings growth rate will improve with a recently announced alliance with Dynegy to develop natural gas-fired wholesale electric generation and cogeneration projects in the Midwest, where more generation is needed. We still project EPS of $2.60 in 1998, and $2.80 in 1999.

Valuation - 23-JUL-98

We still recommend holding GAS stock for the near term. Long-term fundamentals and growth prospects are positive, but the stock is trading at a fair multiple of our 1998 and 1999 EPS estimates of $2.60 and $2.80. Extremely warm weather to date in 1998 will likely outweigh the benefits of a rebounding shipping unit, additional real estate sales, and customer additions. A recent dividend increase and additional stock buybacks will provide some support, so that the downside risk is small.

Key Stock Statistics

S&P EPS Est. 1998	2.60	Tang. Bk. Value/Share	15.87
P/E on S&P Est. 1998	15.0	Beta	0.42
S&P EPS Est. 1999	2.80	Shareholders	39,300
Dividend Rate/Share	1.48	Market cap. (B)	$ 1.9
Shs. outstg. (M)	47.8	Inst. holdings	50%
Avg. daily vol. (M)	0.100		

Value of $10,000 invested 5 years ago: $ 20,113

Fiscal Year Ending Dec. 31

	1998	1997	1996	1995	1994	1993
Revenues (Million $)						
1Q	562.3	900.0	700.9	609.8	780.0	673.0
2Q	271.3	303.7	336.5	246.9	268.0	278.0
3Q	—	209.2	220.4	157.1	166.0	186.0
4Q	—	579.7	592.9	466.3	395.5	538.0
Yr.	—	1,993	1,851	1,480	1,609	1,674
Earnings Per Share ($)						
1Q	**0.75**	0.82	0.90	0.80	0.95	0.83
2Q	**0.59**	0.59	0.50	0.34	0.30	0.29
3Q	—	0.40	0.30	0.12	0.14	0.16
4Q	—	**0.81**	0.71	0.71	0.67	0.68
Yr.	**E2.60**	**2.61**	**2.41**	1.96	2.07	1.97

Next earnings report expected: mid October

Dividend Data (Dividends have been paid since 1954.)

Amount ($)	Date Decl.	Ex-Div. Date	Stock of Record	Payment Date
0.350	Dec. 11	Dec. 29	Dec. 31	Feb. 01 '98
0.370	Mar. 10	Mar. 27	Mar. 31	May. 01 '98
0.370	Jun. 09	Jun. 26	Jun. 30	Aug. 01 '98
0.370	Sep. 09	Sep. 28	Sep. 30	Nov. 01 '98

A Division of The McGraw·Hill Companies

STANDARD
&POOR'S
STOCK REPORTS

Nicor Inc.

1680

12-SEP-98

Business Summary - 23-JUL-98

In preparation for increasing deregulation in the natural gas and electric utility industries, Nicor joined with Dynegy (NYSE: DYN; formerly NGC Corp.) in June 1997, forming a joint venture to offer a variety of energy services to customers in the Midwest. The joint venture, Nicor Energy L.L.C., will initially market natural gas to industrial and commercial customers in Illinois, and as deregulation of energy continues, management intends to expand the venture and offer additional energy products and services. DYN is already one of the largest U.S. wholesale energy marketers. More recently, the company and DYN formed an alliance to jointly pursue wholesale generation and cogeneration power projects in the Midwest.

While other utility companies are scurrying to cut costs and increase efficiency, Nicor can boast that it has been doing so for several years. The company owns one of the most efficient operations in the gas utility industry and a market leading shipping unit. GAS is a diversified energy company engaged in the purchase, storage, distribution, transportation and sale of natural gas; fully containerized liner shipping; and energy related services. In 1997, the company derived 87% of its revenues from gas distribution, 11% from shipping, and 2% from other sources.

Nicor Gas (formerly Northern Illinois Gas), is one of the largest U.S. gas distribution utilities, and delivers natural gas to about 1.9 million customers in a service territory that encompasses most of the northern third of Illinois, excluding Chicago. In 1997, Nicor Gas delivered 545.3 billion cubic feet (Bcf) of natural gas, 43% of which went to residential customers; this compares with 556.6 Bcf in 1996, with 44% residential. Nicor Gas has a diversified portfolio of gas supply contracts. Nicor Gas is also connected to five interstate pipelines, which supply 1.4 Bcf of gas. The company's seven underground gas storage facilities provide flexibility and can supply up to 60% of the company's peak day deliveries and approximately 30% of its normal winter deliveries.

In December 1997, the company signed an agreement with TransCanada PipeLines and Northern States Power making Nicor a 20% partner in the Viking Voyageur Gas Transmission project, a proposed $1.2 billion pipeline designed to transport natural gas from the Canadian border to the Midwest U.S. The project is awaiting regulatory and other approvals.

Tropical Shipping transports containerized freight between Florida and 26 ports in the Caribbean region. Tropical carries cargo primarily southbound to markets which are heavily dependant on the tourist industry and northbound for export trade, both of which are subject to seasonal fluctuations. Tropical transported 138,500 20-ft. equivalent units (TEUs) in 1997 (119,200 in 1996).

Per Share Data ($)

(Year Ended Dec. 31)	1997	1996	1995	1994	1993	1992	1991	1990	1989	1988
Tangible Bk. Val.	15.43	14.75	13.59	13.25	13.04	12.76	12.29	11.68	11.06	10.10
Cash Flow	5.29	4.92	4.17	4.03	3.72	4.12	3.89	3.86	3.78	3.73
Earnings	2.61	2.42	1.96	2.07	1.97	1.91	1.86	1.93	1.99	1.74
Dividends	1.40	1.32	1.28	1.26	1.22	1.17	1.12	1.06	1.00	0.94
Payout Ratio	54%	55%	65%	60%	62%	61%	60%	55%	50%	54%
Prices - High	42⁷/₈	37¹/₈	28¹/₂	29¹/₄	31⁵/₈	25³/₄	23³/₄	23¹/₂	23	16¹/₈
- Low	30	25³/₈	21³/₄	21⁷/₈	24¹/₈	19	19¹/₂	17³/₈	14⁷/₈	11⁵/₈
P/E Ratio - High	16	15	15	14	16	13	13	12	12	9
- Low	11	10	11	11	12	10	10	9	7	7

Income Statement Analysis (Million $)

	1997	1996	1995	1994	1993	1992	1991	1990	1989	1988
Revs.	1,993	1,851	1,480	1,609	1,674	1,612	1,516	1,536	1,622	1,509
Oper. Inc.	361	358	302	297	295	322	307	306	313	305
Depr.	131	125	112	103	97.0	124	118	112	106	117
Int. Exp.	49.1	47.8	41.8	40.1	41.7	47.0	42.2	42.1	44.5	44.1
Pretax Inc.	197	189	154	161	164	158	158	162	187	159
Eff. Tax Rate	35%	36%	35%	32%	33%	31%	31%	30%	36%	33%
Net Inc.	128	121	100	110	109	108	109	114	120	106

Balance Sheet & Other Fin. Data (Million $)

	1997	1996	1995	1994	1993	1992	1991	1990	1989	1988
Cash	5.2	33.2	26.4	42.3	62.1	40.0	75.9	100	82.9	60.3
Curr. Assets	535	573	390	418	509	529	488	515	529	458
Total Assets	2,395	2,439	2,259	2,210	2,222	2,339	2,280	2,180	2,137	2,100
Curr. Liab.	622	700	626	600	584	694	578	546	543	522
LT Debt	550	518	469	459	459	417	458	422	392	443
Common Eqty.	744	730	688	683	704	712	704	676	655	598
Total Cap.	1,516	1,516	1,397	1,375	1,404	1,561	1,617	1,621	1,580	1,569
Cap. Exp.	113	120	157	172	142	174	209	174	150	177
Cash Flow	259	246	212	212	205	231	225	224	224	221
Curr. Ratio	0.9	1.3	0.6	0.7	0.9	0.8	0.8	0.9	1.0	0.9
% LT Debt of Cap.	36.3	34.2	33.6	33.4	32.7	26.7	28.3	26.0	24.8	28.2
% Net Inc.of Revs.	6.4	6.5	6.5	6.8	6.5	6.7	7.2	7.4	7.4	7.0
% Ret. on Assets	5.3	5.2	4.5	5.1	4.9	4.8	4.9	5.3	5.7	5.2
% Ret. on Equity	17.3	17.1	14.5	16.1	15.3	15.3	15.6	17.0	18.9	18.0

Data as orig. reptd.; bef. results of disc. opers. and/or spec. items. Per share data adj. for stk. divs. as of ex-div. date. Bold denotes diluted EPS (FASB 128). E-Estimated. NA-Not Available. NM-Not Meaningful. NR-Not Ranked.

Office—P. O. Box 3014, Naperville, IL 60566-7014. **Tel**—(630) 305-9500. **Fax**—(630) 983-9328. **Website**—http://www.nicorinc.com **Chrmn, Pres & CEO**—T. L. Fisher. **SVP & Secy**—D. L. Cyranoski. **Treas**—D. W. Lohrentz. **Investor Contact**—Randy Horn. **Dirs**— R. M. Beavers, Jr., B. P. Bickner, J. H. Birdsall III, W. H. Clark, T. A. Donahoe, T. L. Fisher, J. E. Jones, D. J. Keller, C. S. Locke, S. R. Petersen, J. Rau, D. R. Toll, P. A. Wier. **Transfer Agent & Registrar**—Harris Trust & Savings Bank, Chicago. **Incorporated**—in Illinois in 1953. **Empl**— 3,300. **S&P Analyst**: J. Robert Cho

STANDARD &POOR'S
STOCK REPORTS

NIKE, Inc.

1681M
NYSE Symbol **NKE**
In S&P 500

12-SEP-98

Industry: Footwear

Summary: NIKE is the world's leading designer and marketer of high-quality athletic footwear, athletic apparel and accessories.

S&P Opinion: Avoid (★★)	Recent Price • 34	Yield • 1.4%
	52 Wk Range • 57⅞-31	12-Mo. P/E • 25.2

Quantitative Evaluations

Outlook (1 Lowest—5 Highest)
• **1**

Fair Value
• **31¼**

Risk
• **Average**

Earn./Div. Rank
• **A**

Technical Eval.
• **Bearish** since 7/98

Rel. Strength Rank (1 Lowest—99 Highest)
• **40**

Insider Activity
• **Neutral**

Earnings vs. Previous Year
▲=Up ▼=Down ▶=No Change

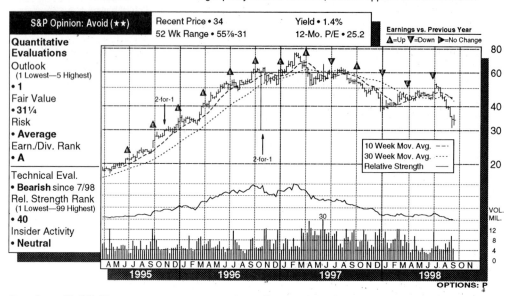

10 Week Mov. Avg. - - - -
30 Week Mov. Avg. ·······
Relative Strength ——

OPTIONS: P

Overview - 09-JUL-98

We expect total sales to decline in low single-digits during the first half of FY 99 (May), on continued weakness in the U.S. and Asia/Pacific regions. For the full year, revenues should be even with FY 98 levels, as increased sales in Europe and improvement in the U.S. during the second half of the year are offset by further declines in the Asia/Pacific region. Reported futures orders, for merchandise to be shipped between June 1998 and November 1998, declined 13% from the year-earlier level. This slowdown has been more dramatic than first anticipated. Through the first half of next year, margins will continue to be hurt by aggressive pricing of close-out sales in the U.S., Europe and Japan, as the company cuts prices in order to rid itself of excess footwear inventory. NIKE recorded a restructuring charge of $130 million in the fourth quarter of FY 98, to eliminate about 1,600 jobs and prune its cost structure.

Valuation - 09-JUL-98

We continue to rate the shares as avoid. The company is continuing to experience increased close-out sales and writedowns of slow moving inventory in the U.S., Europe and Japan. In addition, the pronounced slowdown seen in the Asia/Pacific region, particularly in Japan and South Korea, over the past few quarters shows no signs of abating. A full recovery in this region, once thought to be the catalyst of the company's sustainable profit growth for years to come, is expected to take up to five years. We expect NIKE to report at least two more quarters of lower profit comparisons, as it works through its excess inventory and begins to see some firming of its gross margins. As a result, we have lowered our EPS estimate for FY 99 to $1.70, from $2.00. We believe that investors will continue to face a bumpy road over the next six to 12 months.

Key Stock Statistics

S&P EPS Est. 1999	1.70	Tang. Bk. Value/Share	9.81
P/E on S&P Est. 1999	20.0	Beta	1.10
Dividend Rate/Share	0.48	Shareholders	17,200
Shs. outstg. (M)	287.7	Market cap. (B)	$ 6.3
Avg. daily vol. (M)	1.388	Inst. holdings	39%

Value of $10,000 invested 5 years ago: $ 17,502

Fiscal Year Ending May 31

	1998	1997	1996	1995	1994	1993
Revenues (Million $)						
1Q	2,766	2,282	1,615	1,170	1,108	1,098
2Q	2,255	2,107	1,443	1,054	805.8	876.0
3Q	2,224	2,424	1,492	1,125	871.9	972.0
4Q	2,308	2,374	1,921	1,412	1,004	983.3
Yr.	9,553	9,187	6,471	4,761	3,790	3,931
Earnings Per Share ($)						
1Q	0.85	0.77	0.56	0.36	0.37	0.40
2Q	0.48	0.60	0.40	0.29	0.17	0.24
3Q	**0.25**	0.80	0.39	0.32	0.21	0.29
4Q	**-0.23**	0.52	0.53	0.39	0.23	0.25
Yr.	**1.35**	2.68	1.88	1.36	0.99	1.19

Next earnings report expected: mid September

Dividend Data (Dividends have been paid since 1984.)

Amount ($)	Date Decl.	Ex-Div. Date	Stock of Record	Payment Date
0.120	Nov. 21	Dec. 18	Dec. 22	Jan. 05 '98
0.120	Mar. 20	Mar. 18	Mar. 20	Apr. 06 '98
0.120	May. 18	Jun. 15	Jun. 17	Jul. 03 '98
0.120	Aug. 17	Sep. 17	Sep. 21	Oct. 05 '98

A Division of The McGraw·Hill Companies

Business Summary - 09-JUL-98

NIKE's "Swoosh" design adorns athletic footwear, apparel and accessory products worn by men, women and children around the globe. As the world's largest supplier of athletic footwear, NIKE places considerable emphasis on high-quality construction and innovative design. Basketball, cross-training, running and children's shoes are currently the top selling categories and are expected to remain the top sellers in the near future. NIKE also markets shoes for tennis, golf, soccer, baseball, football, bicycling and volleyball, as well as sports apparel and athletic bags and accessory items designed to complement its athletic footwear.

Virtually all of NIKE's products are manufactured by independent contractors and are sold to approximately 19,700 accounts in the U.S. and, through a mix of independent distributors, licensees and subsidiaries, in roughly 110 countries worldwide. Most footwear is produced outside the U.S.; apparel products are produced both in the U.S. and abroad. Foot Locker, the athletic footwear and apparel chain, accounted for 12% of global net sales in FY 97 (May).

NIKE faces intense competition and rapid changes in technology and consumer preferences in the athletic footwear and apparel markets. The company believes that it is competitive in areas of performance and reliability, new product development, price, product identity through marketing and promotion and customer support and service. NIKE's research and development efforts are a key factor in its success; in FY 97, NIKE spent $73.2 million on R&D versus $46.8 million in FY 96.

NIKE recently announced plans to introduce a separate Michael Jordan brand for shoes and clothes. This new product line is expected to become its second biggest basketball brand in the U.S. during the next 12 months, after the NIKE brand itself. Mr. Jordan remains NIKE's top endorser, but the company expects big things from another spokesman, Tiger Woods, who signed on in 1996.

NIKE attributed its earnings shortfall in FY 98 to narrower gross margins resulting from a greater number of closeout sales in the U.S., Europe and Asia-Pacific regions, resulting from excess inventory. Orders for delivery between June and November 1998 totaled $4.2 billion, down 13%, year to year.

Per Share Data ($)

(Year Ended May 31)	1998	1997	1996	1995	1994	1993	1992	1991	1990	1989
Tangible Bk. Val.	9.81	9.28	6.81	5.14	5.41	4.91	4.04	3.05	2.35	1.61
Cash Flow	1.98	3.15	2.21	1.60	1.23	1.38	1.23	1.06	0.86	0.60
Earnings	1.35	2.68	1.89	1.36	0.99	1.19	1.07	0.94	0.80	0.56
Dividends	0.44	0.35	0.35	0.23	0.20	0.17	0.14	0.12	0.09	0.06
Payout Ratio	33%	13%	19%	17%	20%	15%	13%	13%	11%	11%
Cal. Yrs.	1997	1996	1995	1994	1993	1992	1991	1990	1989	1988
Prices - High	76³/₈	64	35¹/₄	19¹/₈	22³/₈	22⁵/₈	19	12	8⁵/₈	4¹/₄
- Low	37³/₄	31³/₄	17¹/₄	11⁵/₈	10³/₄	13³/₄	8³/₄	6	3¹/₈	2³/₁₆
P/E Ratio - High	57	24	19	14	23	19	18	13	11	8
- Low	28	12	9	9	11	12	8	6	4	4

Income Statement Analysis (Million $)

	1998	1997	1996	1995	1994	1993	1992	1991	1990	1989
Revs.	9,553	9,187	6,471	4,761	3,790	3,931	3,402	3,004	2,235	1,711
Oper. Inc.	1,049	1,518	1,073	757	579	672	593	516	407	291
Depr.	185	138	97.2	71.1	71.5	60.4	47.7	34.5	17.1	14.8
Int. Exp.	60.0	52.3	39.5	24.5	15.6	265	31.3	30.8	14.2	14.5
Pretax Inc.	653	1,295	899	650	491	595	522	462	393	271
Eff. Tax Rate	39%	39%	39%	39%	39%	39%	37%	38%	38%	38%
Net Inc.	400	796	553	400	299	365	329	287	243	167

Balance Sheet & Other Fin. Data (Million $)

	1998	1997	1996	1995	1994	1993	1992	1991	1990	1989
Cash	109	445	262	216	519	291	260	120	90.0	86.0
Curr. Assets	3,533	3,831	2,727	2,046	1,770	1,621	1,388	1,280	838	638
Total Assets	5,397	5,361	3,952	3,143	2,374	2,187	1,873	1,708	1,095	825
Curr. Liab.	1,704	1,867	1,467	1,108	562	453	421	628	273	216
LT Debt	379	296	9.6	10.6	12.4	15.0	69.5	30.0	25.9	34.1
Common Eqty.	3,262	3,156	2,431	1,965	1,741	1,646	1,332	1,033	784	562
Total Cap.	3,641	3,452	2,443	1,993	1,772	1,691	1,401	1,072	814	601
Cap. Exp.	506	466	216	154	95.0	97.0	106	165	87.0	42.0
Cash Flow	585	934	650	471	370	425	377	321	260	182
Curr. Ratio	2.1	2.0	1.9	1.9	3.2	3.6	3.3	2.0	3.1	3.0
% LT Debt of Cap.	10.4	8.6	0.4	0.5	0.7	0.9	5.0	2.8	3.2	5.7
% Net Inc.of Revs.	4.2	8.7	8.5	8.4	7.9	9.3	9.7	9.6	10.9	9.8
% Ret. on Assets	7.4	17.1	15.6	14.5	13.3	17.9	18.4	20.4	25.3	21.7
% Ret. on Equity	12.5	28.5	25.2	21.6	17.9	24.5	27.8	31.5	36.0	34.2

Data as orig. reptd.; bef. results of disc. opers. and/or spec. items. Per share data adj. for stk. divs. as of ex-div. date. Bold denotes diluted EPS (FASB 128). E-Estimated. NA-Not Available. NM-Not Meaningful. NR-Not Ranked.

Office—One Bowerman Drive, Beaverton, OR 97005-6453. **Tel**—(503) 671-6453. **Website**—http://www.nike.com **Chrmn & CEO**—P. H. Knight.**Pres**—T. E. Clarke. **VP & CFO**—R. S. Falcone. **Secy**—J. E. Jaqua.**Dirs**—W. J. Bowerman, T. E. Clarke, J. K. Conway, R. D. DeNunzio, R. K. Donahue, D. J. Hayes, D. G. Houser, J. E. Jaqua, P. H. Knight, K. Ohmae, R. A. Pfeiffer Jr., C. W. Robinson. J. R. Thompson Jr., A. M. Spence. **Transfer Agent & Registrar**—First Chicago Trust Co. of New York, NYC. **Incorporated**—in Oregon in 1968. **Empl**— 21,800. **S&P Analyst**: Maureen C. Carini

Nordstrom, Inc.   4793
Nasdaq Symbol **NOBE**
In S&P 500

12-SEP-98

Industry:
Retail (Department Stores)

Summary: This Seattle-based specialty retailer of apparel and accessories, widely known for its emphasis on service, operates 66 department stores in 21 states.

S&P Opinion: Hold (★★★)	Recent Price • 26⅞	Yield • 1.2%
	52 Wk Range • 40⅜-21⅜	12-Mo. P/E • 20.7

Quantitative Evaluations

Outlook
(1 Lowest—5 Highest)
• **2+**

Fair Value
• **25¾**

Risk
• **Average**

Earn./Div. Rank
• **A-**

Technical Eval.
• **NA**

Rel. Strength Rank
(1 Lowest—99 Highest)
• **38**

Insider Activity
• **Neutral**

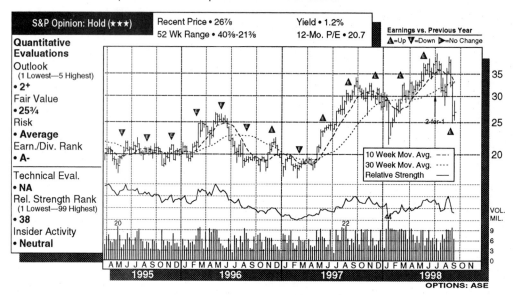

Earnings vs. Previous Year
▲=Up ▼=Down ▶=No Change

10 Week Mov. Avg. - - -
30 Week Mov. Avg. ·····
Relative Strength ——

OPTIONS: ASE

Overview - 02-JUL-98

Sales growth for FY 99 (Jan.) is projected at about 12%, with moderate same-store sales improvement of about 4% to 5%. NOBE plans to add four new full-line stores, plus additional Rack and Faconnable boutiques. Gross margins should widen, on improved merchandise margins and fewer markdowns. Expense ratios should be well controlled. Interest expense should increase, due to more long-term debt outstanding. For the longer term, square footage gains of 8% to 10% are expected annually over the next few years, as the company continues its expansion as a national retailer, enhance NOBE's long-term earnings potential. In addition, the company's growing catalog business, with newly expanded facilities for fulfillment, should make substantial contributions to earnings over time. A $400 million common stock buyback program was renewed in February 1998. Although Nordstrom has increased its borrowings to finance its share buybacks, it remains conservatively financed.

Valuation - 02-JUL-98

The shares of this long-term player in the rapidly consolidating department store sector of the retailing industry have had a strong runup so far in 1998, and now appear fairly valued. Increased square footage, systems enhancements, and new stores coming on stream should boost earnings over time. After declining for two years, EPS rebounded in FY 98, with a further gain anticipated in FY 99. Because of the company's emphasis on service, NOBE's cost structure is higher than that of other apparel retailers. As a result, income is leveraged to same-store sales, which should continue to increase moderately in the coming year.

Key Stock Statistics

S&P EPS Est. 1999	1.45	Tang. Bk. Value/Share	9.30
P/E on S&P Est. 1999	18.5	Beta	0.94
S&P EPS Est. 2000	1.65	Shareholders	74,000
Dividend Rate/Share	0.32	Market cap. (B)	$ 4.0
Shs. outstg. (M)	148.8	Inst. holdings	61%
Avg. daily vol. (M)	2.406		

Value of $10,000 invested 5 years ago: $ 14,766

Fiscal Year Ending Jan. 31

	1999	1998	1997	1996	1995	1994
Revenues (Million $)						
1Q	1,040	953.8	906.0	815.6	762.0	695.6
2Q	1,447	1,353	1,241	1,149	1,080	1,018
3Q	—	1,090	984.4	906.9	862.0	769.4
4Q	—	1,455	1,321	1,242	1,191	1,107
Yr.	—	4,852	4,453	4,114	3,894	3,590
Earnings Per Share ($)						
1Q	**0.21**	**0.20**	0.16	0.17	0.20	0.07
2Q	**0.47**	**0.38**	0.28	0.33	0.39	0.26
3Q	**E0.28**	**0.23**	0.21	0.18	0.23	0.15
4Q	**E0.47**	**0.38**	0.27	0.34	0.42	0.37
Yr.	**E1.45**	**1.20**	0.91	1.01	1.24	0.85

Next earnings report expected: mid November

Dividend Data (Dividends have been paid since 1971.)

Amount ($)	Date Decl.	Ex-Div. Date	Stock of Record	Payment Date
0.140	Feb. 17	Feb. 25	Feb. 27	Mar. 16 '98
0.140	May. 19	May. 28	Jun. 01	Jun. 15 '98
2-for-1	May. 19	Jul. 01	Jun. 08	Jun. 30 '98
0.080	Aug. 20	Aug. 27	Aug. 31	Sep. 15 '98

A Division of The McGraw-Hill Companies

Business Summary - 02-JUL-98

Nordstrom was founded by John W. Nordstrom in 1901 with his profits from the Gold Rush of 1897. The company, which began with one small shoe store in Seattle, WA, now operates 65 fashion specialty stores from Alaska to Virginia. Stores sell full lines of medium-to-upscale apparel, shoes and accessories for women, men and children. The company also operates 21 clearance and off-price stores, three men's boutiques and two freestanding shoe stores in Hawaii. The company's also has a direct sales division

Sales in FY 98 (Jan.) were derived as follows:

	FY 98
Women's apparel & accessories	56%
Shoes	20%
Men's apparel & furnishings	18%
Children's apparel & accessories	4%
Other	2%

Nordstrom is known for its emphasis on customer service, with salespersons who will go out of their way to satisfy customers. The store ambiance is upscale, with a pianist playing during most store hours. Stores feature a wide selection of style, size and color in each merchandise category. The company operates 21 clearance centers under the name Nordstrom Rack. The centers serve as outlets for clearance merchandise from the company's large specialty stores. The Racks also purchase merchandise directly from manufacturers.

The company launched its direct sales division with its first catalog mailed January 1994. The catalog division continues to grow rapidly, with sales of $156 million in FY 98. The division opened a new and larger fulfillment center in August 1997, increasing capacity for sales growth.

The company's sales by region : California 34%; East Coast 23%; Northwest 21% and Midwest 15%. Sales are Rack units account for the balance of 7%.

The company has expanded its use of information systems is providing greater flexibility in merchandising and responding to customers needs. Detailed sales information is available in all full-line stores. Automatic replenishment systems, linked directly to vendors, will be in place for about 16% of NOBE's business by the end of 1998. Internet shopping will begin in late 1998.

Nordstrom has spent about $750 million during the past three years to add new stores and facilities and to improve existing stores and technology. Over 2.6 million sq. ft. of selling space was added during this time, an increase of 26%. The company plans to spend $850 million during the next three years. Since May 1996, NOBE has repurchased 7.3 million common shares. In February 1997, directors approved a $400 million repurchase program.

Per Share Data ($)

(Year Ended Jan. 31)	1998	1997	1996	1995	1994	1993	1992	1991	1990	1989
Tangible Bk. Val.	9.67	9.25	8.77	8.17	7.11	6.42	5.74	5.05	4.50	3.93
Cash Flow	2.23	1.88	1.82	1.91	1.49	1.46	1.42	1.24	1.14	1.13
Earnings	1.20	0.91	1.01	1.24	0.85	0.83	0.83	0.71	0.70	0.76
Dividends	0.27	0.25	0.25	0.19	0.17	0.16	0.15	0.15	0.14	0.11
Payout Ratio	22%	27%	25%	16%	20%	19%	19%	21%	20%	15%
Cal. Yrs.	1997	1996	1995	1994	1993	1992	1991	1990	1989	1988
Prices - High	34⅛	26¾	22⅝	24⅞	21¾	21⅜	26½	19⅝	21¼	17
- Low	17	17⅛	17½	15½	12⅝	12¾	11	8⅝	14⅞	9⅞
P/E Ratio - High	28	29	22	20	25	26	32	28	30	23
- Low	14	19	17	13	15	15	13	12	21	13

Income Statement Analysis (Million $)

	1998	1997	1996	1995	1994	1993	1992	1991	1990	1989
Revs.	4,852	4,453	4,114	3,987	3,590	3,422	3,180	2,894	2,671	2,328
Oper. Inc.	393	310	321	475	283	283	274	232	243	241
Depr.	160	156	134	111	103	102	95.5	85.2	70.6	60.4
Int. Exp.	35.5	45.6	46.7	39.1	40.8	48.3	56.5	60.4	56.1	45.1
Pretax Inc.	307	244	272	336	231	222	217	178	179	198
Eff. Tax Rate	39%	39%	39%	40%	39%	39%	38%	35%	36%	38%
Net Inc.	186	148	165	203	140	137	136	116	115	123

Balance Sheet & Other Fin. Data (Million $)

	1998	1997	1996	1995	1994	1993	1992	1991	1990	1989
Cash	24.8	28.3	24.5	32.5	91.2	29.1	14.7	24.7	33.1	16.1
Curr. Assets	1,595	1,532	1,613	1,398	1,315	1,220	1,178	1,090	1,011	915
Total Assets	2,865	2,703	2,733	2,397	2,177	2,053	2,042	1,903	1,707	1,512
Curr. Liab.	943	787	832	690	627	511	554	552	490	448
LT Debt	320	329	366	298	336	441	502	479	441	370
Common Eqty.	1,475	1,473	1,423	1,344	1,167	1,052	939	826	733	640
Total Cap.	1,775	1,915	1,789	1,642	1,550	1,542	1,488	1,351	1,218	1,064
Cap. Exp.	260	204	253	232	125	71.0	147	200	173	153
Cash Flow	346	304	299	314	243	239	231	201	185	184
Curr. Ratio	1.7	1.9	1.9	2.0	2.1	2.4	2.1	2.0	2.1	2.0
% LT Debt of Cap.	17.8	17.2	20.5	18.1	21.7	28.6	33.8	35.4	36.2	34.7
% Net Inc.of Revs.	3.8	3.3	4.0	5.1	3.9	4.0	4.3	4.0	4.3	5.3
% Ret. on Assets	6.7	5.4	6.4	8.9	6.6	6.7	6.9	6.4	7.1	9.0
% Ret. on Equity	12.6	10.2	11.9	16.2	12.7	13.7	15.4	14.8	16.7	21.0

Data as orig. reptd.; bef. results of disc. opers. and/or spec. items. Per share data adj. for stk. divs. as of ex-div. date. Bold denotes diluted EPS (FASB 128). E-Estimated. NA-Not Available. NM-Not Meaningful. NR-Not Ranked.

Office—1501 Fifth Ave., Seattle, WA 98101-1603. **Tel**—(206) 628-2111. **Chrmn**—J. J. Whitacre. **Secy**—Karen E. Purpur. **EVP & Treas**—John A. Goesling. **Investor Contact**—Carol Gasper. **Dirs**—D. W. Gittinger, E. Hernandez, Jr., A. McLaughlin, J. A. McMillan, B. A. Nordstrom, J. N. Nordstrom, A. E. Osborne Jr., W. D. Ruckelshaus, E. C. Vaughan, J. J. Whitacre, B. Willison. **Transfer Agent & Registrar**—ChaseMellon Shareholder Services. **Incorporated**—in Washington in 1946. **Empl**—41,000. **S&P Analyst**: Karen J. Sack, CFA

STANDARD &POOR'S
STOCK REPORTS

Norfolk Southern
1686A
NYSE Symbol NSC
In S&P 500

12-SEP-98 | **Industry:** Railroads

Summary: This railroad's system expanded 50% in June 1998 with its purchase of 58% of Conrail for $5.8 billion. In March 1998, NSC sold its motor carrier unit for $200 million.

S&P Opinion: Hold (★★★)

Recent Price • 29¼	Yield • 2.7%
52 Wk Range • 41¾-27⅜	12-Mo. P/E • 13.6

Quantitative Evaluations

Outlook
(1 Lowest—5 Highest)
• 3

Fair Value
• 31⅞

Risk
• Low

Earn./Div. Rank
• A

Technical Eval.
• Bearish since 5/98

Rel. Strength Rank
(1 Lowest—99 Highest)
• 84

Insider Activity
• NA

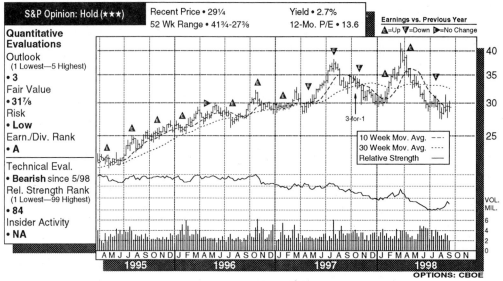

Earnings vs. Previous Year
▲=Up ▼=Down ▶=No Change

3-for-1

10 Week Mov. Avg. ---
30 Week Mov. Avg. ····
Relative Strength —

VOL. MIL.

AMJJASOND J FMAMJJASOND J FMAMJJASOND J FMAMJJASON
1995   1996   1997   1998

OPTIONS: CBOE

Overview - 30-JUN-98

Rail traffic in 1998 will benefit from the integration of Conrail routes during the third quarter. Coal traffic will rebound after being penalized in 1997 by a mild summer. Good gains are projected for intermodal shipments, reflecting new joint service with Burlington Northern and extension of "Triple Crown" service into the Southwest. Chemical traffic will benefit from a strong economy and a major expansion at Olin. NSC also will benefit from the opening of new chip mills in its territory and the ramp-up of several major steel mini-mills and melt shops. An improvement is anticipated for automobiles, reflecting a major contract to handle Ford Motor traffic and additional bi-level car capacity, limited somewhat by a lengthy strike at GM in mid-1998. Margins should widen, as fuel costs drop and casualties and claims ease reflecting improved safety performance and reduced environmental accruals. Offsetting will be increased costs to integrate Conrail and Year 2000 software expenditures. Limiting comparisons will be sharply higher interest expense.

Valuation - 30-JUN-98

The shares of this railroad have gyrated wildly during 1998. NSC first rallied when investors became convinced that the firm could smoothly execute its absorption of Conrail lines without the major service failures that accompanied Union Pacific's purchase of Southern Pacific. Later, investors bailed out, adopting a "wait-and-see" posture. With regulatory clearance in June 1998, NSC, which paid $5.8 billion in 1997 for 58% of Conrail, can now begin operation over that road's lines in late August. Should everything pan out, NSC could reap in its third year of control of Conrail some $564 million pretax (about $1.00 a share). Given its full earnings multiple, we remain neutral on NSC at this time.

Key Stock Statistics

S&P EPS Est. 1998	2.10	Tang. Bk. Value/Share	15.20
P/E on S&P Est. 1998	14.0	Beta	0.86
S&P EPS Est. 1999	2.50	Shareholders	50,700
Dividend Rate/Share	0.80	Market cap. (B)	$ 11.1
Shs. outstg. (M)	379.0	Inst. holdings	56%
Avg. daily vol. (M)	0.567		

Value of $10,000 invested 5 years ago: $ 16,753

Fiscal Year Ending Dec. 31

	1998	1997	1996	1995	1994	1993
Revenues (Million $)						
1Q	1,066	1,046	1,162	1,139	1,077	1,116
2Q	1,079	1,067	1,217	1,190	1,161	1,170
3Q	—	1,048	1,211	1,184	1,171	1,089
4Q	—	1,062	1,180	1,155	1,172	1,085
Yr.	—	4,223	4,770	4,668	4,581	4,460
Earnings Per Share ($)						
1Q	0.35	0.34	0.44	0.43	0.35	0.33
2Q	0.48	0.50	0.52	0.46	0.43	0.37
3Q	E0.55	0.47	0.54	0.47	0.41	0.23
4Q	E0.65	0.59	0.53	0.46	0.44	0.38
Yr.	E2.10	1.84	2.01	1.81	1.63	1.31

Next earnings report expected: late October

Dividend Data (Dividends have been paid since 1901.)

Amount ($)	Date Decl.	Ex-Div. Date	Stock of Record	Payment Date
0.200	Oct. 13	Nov. 05	Nov. 07	Dec. 10 '97
0.200	Jan. 27	Feb. 04	Feb. 06	Mar. 10 '98
0.200	Apr. 17	Apr. 29	May. 01	Jun. 10 '98
0.200	Jul. 28	Aug. 05	Aug. 07	Sep. 10 '98

A Division of The McGraw-Hill Companies

Business Summary - 30-JUN-98

Norfolk Southern provides rail transportation service in the eastern U.S. and specialized motor carrier services. Following a heated bidding war against CSX Corp. in early 1997 for Conrail, NSC agreed to a plan to divide Conrail. NSC, which paid $5.8 billion for 58% of Conrail's shares received regulatory clearance in June 1998 to operate Conrail. Conrail's rail routes will be integrated with those of NSC beginning in August 1998. In March 1998 NSC sold its motor carrier unit for $200 million.

Norfolk Southern's present rail network of 14,400 miles in 20 states and the Province of Ontario will be expanded 50% in August 1998 to 21,400 miles in 22 states plus Ontario with the integration of the Conrail routes. Most of the new Conrail lines being acquired are located in the Northeast and Midwest. Additionally, NSC and CSX will share Conrail lines located in New York/New Jersey, the Monongahela coal fields of Pennsylvania, and in Detroit.

The acquisition of some 58% of the Conrail system will provide greater access for Norfolk Southern into the Northeastern markets of New York City, Baltimore and Philadelphia. It also will provide NSC with better connections to western rail systems. With longer, single-system routes, NSC hopes to divert intermodal and auto shipments away from motor carriers by offering

shorter transit times between the Northeast and Southeast. In July 1997, NSC projected $423 million in net new traffic by 2000 from the Conrail routes.

In addition to new traffic, the Conrail acquisition is expected to yield cost savings of $432 million by the year 2000. These savings will be derived from the use of longer trains, more efficient equipment routing, savings in general and administrative and maintenance costs and consolidation of facilities. NSC, which paid $5.8 billion for its 58% stake in Conrail, sees the transaction diluting earnings in 1998 but being accretive to earnings by 14% in 1999 and 25% in 2000. NSC's investment in Conrail cut profits in 1997 by $0.29 a share. NSC's results in 1998's first quarter were reduced by $50 million, or $0.13, from its investment in Conrail. Conrail's operating income (before unusual items) in 1997 was $830 million on revenue of $3.8 billion.

In March 1998, NSC completed the sale of its North American Van Lines (NAVL) unit to Clayton, Dubilier and Rice, Inc. for $200 million. NAVL, which provides relocation services, the transport of high-value products, exhibits and displays, earned $22 million in 1997 on revenues of $942 million. The sale resulted in a $98 million after tax gain ($0.26 a share) in 1998's first quarter.

Non-transportation activities include the management of some 1,200,000 acres of coal, natural gas and timberland properties in six states.

Per Share Data ($)

(Year Ended Dec. 31)	1997	1996	1995	1994	1993	1992	1991	1990	1989	1988
Tangible Bk. Val.	14.44	13.27	12.48	11.73	11.12	10.05	9.55	10.52	10.15	9.58
Cash Flow	2.98	3.15	2.87	2.62	2.28	2.25	0.93	1.91	1.82	1.74
Earnings	1.84	2.03	1.81	1.63	1.31	1.31	0.07	1.14	1.16	1.17
Dividends	0.80	0.75	0.69	0.64	0.62	0.60	0.53	0.51	0.46	0.42
Payout Ratio	43%	37%	38%	39%	47%	46%	NM	43%	39%	36%
Prices - High	38⅛	32¼	27¼	24⅞	24⅛	22½	21⅞	15¾	13¾	11
- Low	28¼	25½	20⅛	19½	19¾	17¾	13¼	11⅝	10⅛	8⅛
P/E Ratio - High	21	16	15	15	18	17	NM	14	12	9
- Low	15	13	11	12	15	14	NM	10	9	7

Income Statement Analysis (Million $)

	1997	1996	1995	1994	1993	1992	1991	1990	1989	1988
Revs.	4,223	4,770	4,668	4,642	4,516	4,662	4,451	4,617	4,536	4,462
Oper. Inc.	1,645	1,626	1,500	1,519	1,360	1,330	1,173	1,181	1,165	1,251
Depr.	432	429	414	404	406	397	381	373	347	312
Int. Exp.	385	159	152	139	148	152	144	113	85.0	81.0
Pretax Inc.	998	1,197	1,115	1,049	899	875	144	875	933	1,001
Eff. Tax Rate	30%	36%	36%	36%	39%	36%	79%	37%	35%	37%
Net Inc.	699	770	713	668	549	558	30.0	556	606	635

Balance Sheet & Other Fin. Data (Million $)

	1997	1996	1995	1994	1993	1992	1991	1990	1989	1988
Cash	34.0	403	329	307	258	378	465	625	581	638
Curr. Assets	1,103	1,457	1,343	1,338	1,564	1,397	1,469	1,747	1,710	1,854
Total Assets	17,350	11,416	10,905	10,588	10,520	10,401	10,148	10,523	10,244	10,059
Curr. Liab.	1,093	1,190	1,206	1,132	1,198	1,183	1,341	1,372	1,207	1,195
LT Debt	7,398	1,800	1,553	1,548	1,482	1,566	1,300	1,030	694	676
Common Eqty.	5,445	4,978	4,829	4,685	4,621	4,233	4,093	4,912	5,169	5,153
Total Cap.	15,372	6,827	8,733	8,494	8,286	8,508	8,056	8,718	8,634	8,506
Cap. Exp.	875	688	659	713	669	716	713	697	652	529
Cash Flow	1,131	1,199	1,127	1,072	954	954	411	929	953	947
Curr. Ratio	1.0	1.2	1.1	1.2	1.3	1.2	1.1	1.3	1.4	1.6
% LT Debt of Cap.	48.1	26.4	17.8	18.2	17.9	18.4	16.1	11.8	8.0	7.9
% Net Inc.of Revs.	16.6	16.1	15.3	14.4	12.2	12.0	0.7	12.0	13.4	14.2
% Ret. on Assets	4.9	6.9	6.7	6.5	5.3	5.5	0.3	5.6	6.1	6.5
% Ret. on Equity	13.4	15.7	15.0	14.6	12.5	13.5	0.7	11.5	12.1	12.8

Data as orig. reptd.; bef. results of disc. opers. and/or spec. items. Per share data adj. for stk. divs. as of ex-div. date. Bold denotes diluted EPS (FASB 128). E-Estimated. NA-Not Available. NM-Not Meaningful. NR-Not Ranked.

Office—Three Commercial Place, Norfolk, VA 23510-2191. **Tel**—(757) 629-2680. **Website**—http://www.nscorp.com **Chrmn & Pres**—D. R. Goode. **EVP-Fin**—H. C. Wolf. **Secy**—D. M. Martin. **Investor Contact**—Deborah H. Noxon. **Dirs**—G. L. Baliles, C. A. Campbell, Jr., G. R. Carter, L. E. Coleman, D. R. Goode, T. M. Hahn, Jr., L. Hilliard, E. B. Leisenring, Jr., A. B. McKinnon, J. M. O'Brien, H. W. Pote. **Transfer Agent & Registrar**—Bank of New York, NYC. **Incorporated**—in Virginia in 1980. **Empl**—25,817. **S&P Analyst**: Stephen R. Klein

Northern States Power   1700

NYSE Symbol **NSP**

In S&P 500

12-SEP-98 Industry: Electric Companies

Summary: This utility provides electricity and gas to customers in Minnesota and the upper Midwest, and is also involved in non-regulated power and energy-related businesses.

S&P Opinion: Hold (★★★)	Recent Price • 27¼	Yield • 5.2%
	52 Wk Range • 30¼-24¼	12-Mo. P/E • 16.8

Quantitative Evaluations

Outlook
(1 Lowest—5 Highest)
• **2⁻**

Fair Value
• **27⅞**

Risk
• **Low**

Earn./Div. Rank
• **A-**

Technical Eval.
• **Bearish** since 3/98

Rel. Strength Rank
(1 Lowest—99 Highest)
• **89**

Insider Activity
• **NA**

Earnings vs. Previous Year
▲=Up ▼=Down ▶=No Change

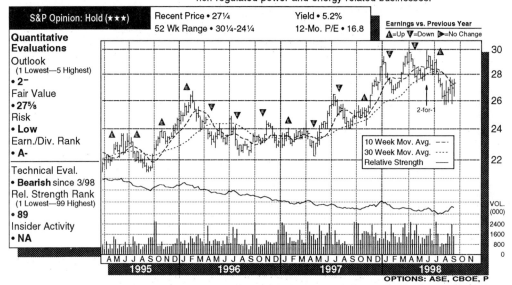

10 Week Mov. Avg. ---
30 Week Mov. Avg. ·····
Relative Strength —

2-for-1

VOL. (000)
2400
1600
800
0

1995 1996 1997 1998

OPTIONS: ASE, CBOE, P

Overview - 31-AUG-98

We expect NSP to achieve high single-digit EPS growth in 1999. Despite more shares outstanding and the adverse impact of abnormally mild weather in the first quarter, earnings in 1998 should grow about 5% from the $1.77 earned from 1997 operations. Earnings in 1997 were hurt by one-time charges of $0.17, mild weather, flooding in the Grand Forks area, and repair costs for a storm-damaged transmission system. In May 1997, NSP and Wisconsin Energy terminated a planned merger after the FERC conditioned its approval on the divestiture of generating facilities. Over the long term, we see annual earnings growth of 5%, as this low-cost producer benefits from continued growth in its service economy and the reduction of its administrative costs. NSP will also benefit from growth in its non-regulated businesses, particularly the domestic and international power generation projects, which could account for more than 20% of earnings by 2000.

Valuation - 31-AUG-98

Despite the recent underperformance of the shares, we recommend holding the stock. Although the shares were recently down about 8% year to date, this follows a strong 27% advance in 1997, in which the stock outperformed the 19.8% increase for the S&P Index of Electric Companies (electricity accounted for 81% of 1997 revenues) and the 18.6% increase for the Index of Natural Gas Companies (natural gas, 19%). In addition to benefits derived from a low interest rate environment, the shares were aided by the termination of the planned merger with Wisconsin Energy, as the market reflected investor confidence that NSP would do better on a stand-alone basis. While the shares appear fairly valued at 13X our 1999 EPS estimate of $2.05, a dividend yield of about 5.3% makes the stock an attractive holding for long-term total return.

Key Stock Statistics

S&P EPS Est. 1998	1.90	Tang. Bk. Value/Share	15.04
P/E on S&P Est. 1998	14.4	Beta	0.38
S&P EPS Est. 1999	2.05	Shareholders	86,200
Dividend Rate/Share	1.43	Market cap. (B)	$ 4.1
Shs. outstg. (M)	151.4	Inst. holdings	38%
Avg. daily vol. (M)	0.355		

Value of $10,000 invested 5 years ago: $ 17,449

Fiscal Year Ending Dec. 31

	1998	1997	1996	1995	1994	1993
Revenues (Million $)						
1Q	701.4	742.5	718.7	661.2	683.4	640.8
2Q	638.6	594.3	592.4	589.7	582.0	545.3
3Q	—	697.4	633.2	665.0	612.3	588.0
4Q	—	699.5	709.9	652.8	608.8	616.0
Yr.	—	2,734	2,654	2,569	2,487	2,404
Earnings Per Share ($)						
1Q	**0.36**	**0.46**	0.47	0.48	0.47	0.41
2Q	**0.23**	**0.12**	0.29	0.42	0.37	0.25
3Q	**E0.70**	**0.61**	0.59	0.64	0.55	0.48
4Q	**E0.61**	**0.42**	0.56	0.41	0.34	0.38
Yr.	**E1.90**	**1.60**	1.91	1.96	1.73	1.51

Next earnings report expected: late October

Dividend Data (Dividends have been paid since 1910.)

Amount ($)	Date Decl.	Ex-Div. Date	Stock of Record	Payment Date
0.705	Mar. 25	Apr. 06	Apr. 08	Apr. 20 '98
2-for-1	Apr. 22	Jun. 02	May. 18	Jun. 01 '98
0.357	Jun. 24	Jul. 07	Jul. 09	Jul. 20 '98
0.357	Aug. 26	Sep. 29	Oct. 01	Oct. 20 '98

A Division of The McGraw-Hill Companies

Business Summary - 31-AUG-98

Northern States Power and subsidiaries provide electric and gas service to a population of some three million in sections of Minnesota, Wisconsin, Michigan and North and South Dakota. Electricity contributed 81% of operating revenues in 1997, and gas 19%. Contributions to electric retail revenues in recent years were:

	1997	1996	1995	1994
Residential	36%	37%	37%	36%
Small commercial & industrial	19%	19%	18%	18%
Large commercial & industrial	43%	43%	43%	44%
Other	2%	1%	2%	2%

The Minneapolis-St. Paul area accounted for 62% of 1997 electric retail revenues and 54% of gas revenues.

Sources of fuel supply (on a Btu basis) in 1997 were coal 62%, nuclear 34%, and other 4%.

The company operates two nuclear generating plants: the single unit 543 Mw Monticello plant, and the Prairie Island plant, which has two units totaling 1,028 Mw.

In May 1997, Northern States Power and Wisconsin Energy Corp. agreed to terminate a planned merger to form a new holding company, Primergy Corp. The decision followed a refusal by the Federal Energy Regulatory Commission (FERC) to approve the merger unless the companies agreed to conditions that included the sale of certain power generating facilities.

Wholly owned Viking Gas Transmission Co. owns and operates a 500 mile interstate natural gas pipeline that serves portions of Minnesota, Wisconsin and North Dakota. Viking meets 10% of NSP's gas distribution needs and also acts as a transporter for third party shippers under authority granted (and rates regulated) by the FERC.

NRG Energy is a wholly owned non-regulated subsidiary involved in independent power projects in the U.S., Canada, Europe, Australia, the Pacific Rim and Latin America. In May 1997, NRG Energy acquired a 25.37% interest in Loy Yang A, Victoria's largest and Australia's lowest-cost electric generating facility.

NRG Energy has a 45.21% interest in Cogeneration Corporation of America (formerly NRG Generating (U.S.) Inc.), an owner of power cogeneration facilities, whose logo is CogenAmerica and which trades on the NASDAQ, under the ticker symbol CGCA.

The company's other non-regulated businesses include Eloigne, a company that invests in projects that qualify for low income housing tax credits; UltraPower Technologies, which markets non-destructive cable testing technology to companies with underground cable; and Seren Innovations, a company that offers high speed access to information through automated communications systems.

Per Share Data ($)

(Year Ended Dec. 31)	1997	1996	1995	1994	1993	1992	1991	1990	1989	1988
Tangible Bk. Val.	15.27	15.41	14.82	14.13	13.62	12.93	12.58	12.19	11.88	11.40
Earnings	1.70	1.91	1.96	1.73	1.51	1.16	1.51	1.40	1.62	1.55
Dividends	1.40	1.37	1.34	1.31	1.28	1.25	1.20	1.15	1.10	1.05
Payout Ratio	82%	72%	69%	76%	85%	108%	79%	82%	68%	67%
Prices - High	29½	26¾	24¾	23½	24	22¾	22	20¼	20	17⅛
- Low	22¼	22¼	21¼	19⅜	20⅛	19¼	15⅞	14¼	15⅛	14⅝
P/E Ratio - High	17	14	13	14	16	20	15	15	12	11
- Low	13	12	11	11	13	17	11	10	9	9

Income Statement Analysis (Million $)

	1997	1996	1995	1994	1993	1992	1991	1990	1989	1988
Revs.	2,734	2,654	2,569	2,487	2,404	2,160	2,201	2,065	1,990	2,006
Depr.	326	306	290	274	265	236	228	215	210	209
Maint.	165	156	158	170	161	181	178	170	151	172
Fxd. Chgs. Cov.	7.8	3.3	3.4	3.5	3.4	3.0	3.5	3.3	3.5	3.5
Constr. Credits	16.6	18.9	17.2	12.3	12.8	15.2	11.6	6.4	7.2	13.4
Eff. Tax Rate	29%	37%	36%	35%	38%	35%	36%	37%	34%	35%
Net Inc.	237	275	276	244	212	161	207	193	222	215

Balance Sheet & Other Fin. Data (Million $)

	1997	1996	1995	1994	1993	1992	1991	1990	1989	1988
Gross Prop.	10,460	8,741	8,407	8,109	7,776	7,349	6,979	6,703	6,476	6,211
Cap. Exp.	433	412	401	409	362	428	350	323	313	301
Net Prop.	5,759	4,338	4,310	4,274	4,214	4,126	3,997	3,955	3,896	3,859
Capitalization:										
LT Debt	1,879	1,593	1,542	1,463	1,292	1,300	1,234	1,240	1,263	1,276
% LT Debt	42	40	41	41	39	41	40	40	41	42
Pfd.	200	240	240	240	240	275	301	301	301	351
% Pfd.	4.50	6.10	6.30	6.70	7.10	8.60	9.70	9.80	9.90	12
Common	2,372	2,136	2,027	1,897	1,827	1,622	1,577	1,527	1,486	1,427
% Common	53	54	53	53	54	51	51	50	49	47
Total Cap.	5,382	4,923	4,813	4,624	4,336	4,168	4,049	4,004	3,956	4,011
% Oper. Ratio	85.0	86.2	86.5	87.6	87.4	88.1	86.1	86.0	84.6	84.9
% Earn. on Net Prop.	NA	8.5	8.1	7.3	7.3	6.3	7.7	7.3	7.9	7.8
% Return On Revs.	8.7	10.3	10.7	9.8	8.8	7.5	9.4	9.3	11.2	10.7
% Return On Invest. Capital	9.2	10.5	8.5	7.8	7.5	6.4	7.8	7.5	8.2	8.0
% Return On Com. Equity	NA	12.6	13.4	12.4	11.4	9.1	12.2	11.8	13.9	13.9

Data as orig. reptd.; bef. results of disc. opers. and/or spec. items. Per share data adj. for stk. divs. as of ex-div. date. Bold denotes diluted EPS (FASB 128). E-Estimated. NA-Not Available. NM-Not Meaningful. NR-Not Ranked.

Office—414 Nicollet Mall, Minneapolis, MN 55401. **Registrar**—Norwest Bank, Minneapolis. **Tel**—(612) 330-5500. **Website**—http://www.nspco.com **Chrmn, Pres & CEO**—J. J. Howard. **VP & CFO**—E. J. McIntyre. **Investor Contact**—R. J. Kolkmann. **Dirs**—H. L. Bretting, D. A. Christensen, W. J. Driscoll, G. Ferrari, D. L. Haakenstad, J. J. Howard, R. M. Kovacevich, D. W. Leatherdale, M. R. Preska, A. P. Sampson. **Transfer Agent**—Co.'s office. **Incorporated**—in Minnesota in 1909. **Empl**— 7,455. **S&P Analyst:** Justin McCann

Northern Telecom

1700M

NYSE Symbol **NT**

In S&P 500

12-SEP-98

Industry:
Communications
Equipment

Summary: This company (52% owned by BCE Inc.) is a leading global supplier of telecommunications equipment.

S&P Opinion: Buy (★★★★★)	Recent Price • 46½	Yield • 0.6%
	52 Wk Range • 69¼-39⅝	12-Mo. P/E • NM

Quantitative Evaluations

Outlook
(1 Lowest—5 Highest)
• **2**

Fair Value
• **51⅛**

Risk
• **Low**

Earn./Div. Rank
• **B+**

Technical Eval.
• **Bearish** since 9/98

Rel. Strength Rank
(1 Lowest—99 Highest)
• **47**

Insider Activity
• **NA**

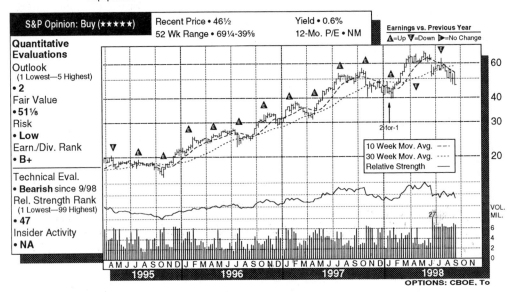

Earnings vs. Previous Year
▲=Up ▼=Down ▶=No Change

10 Week Mov. Avg. – – –
30 Week Mov. Avg. ·······
Relative Strength ——

2-for-1

VOL.
MIL.

OPTIONS: CBOE, To

Overview - 28-JUL-98

We forecast revenue growth of 15% for 1998. Nortel expects wireless equipment to account for 25% of total sales by 2000, up from 22% in 1997. Increased penetration of international markets, particularly in the Asia-Pacific and Latin American regions, will also aid growth. During the second quarter, Nortel booked a $700 million wireless infrastructure order in Mexico. In the U.S., NT signed a $1.5 billion switching deal with SBC, a Regional Bell Operating Company, and $1 billion in orders for its new 1-Megabit modem. Nortel should also benefit as worldwide deregulation and increased competition drive wireline carriers to upgrade and expand their networks. In June 1998, Nortel announced that it will acquire Bay Networks, a major data networking vendor, for approximately $9.1 billion in stock (about 134 million common shares). Bay will open up new distribution channels for NT with Internet Service Providers and enterprise customers. NT also gains leadership technology in routing switches, virtual private networks, and cable modems. NT expects the acquisition, which is scheduled to close in October 1998, to be dilutive to 1998 EPS and accretive in 1999.

Valuation - 28-JUL-98

As one of the world's largest telecommunications equipment manufacturers, NT is well positioned with a broad product line. About 50% of sales are now in high-growth wireless and broadband segments, adding balance to the company's more established network equipment franchise. Total orders were up an impressive 22% in the second quarter. Given NT's stong market position and tangible U.S. and international growth initiatives, the shares are attractive at a recent level of about 27X our 1999 EPS estimate of $2.43.

Key Stock Statistics

S&P EPS Est. 1998	1.84	Tang. Bk. Value/Share	7.61
P/E on S&P Est. 1998	25.3	Beta	1.74
S&P EPS Est. 1999	2.43	Shareholders	8,900
Dividend Rate/Share	0.30	Market cap. (B)	$ 30.4
Shs. outstg. (M)	652.1	Inst. holdings	17%
Avg. daily vol. (M)	2.269		

Value of $10,000 invested 5 years ago: $ 22,799

Fiscal Year Ending Dec. 31

	1998	1997	1996	1995	1994	1993
Revenues (Million $)						
1Q	3,510	3,353	2,596	2,247	1,999	1,942
2Q	4,156	3,787	3,010	2,442	2,123	1,868
3Q	—	3,498	3,053	2,487	2,003	1,880
4Q	—	4,811	4,188	3,496	2,749	2,458
Yr.	—	15,449	12,847	10,672	8,874	8,148
Earnings Per Share ($)						
1Q	-0.12	0.20	0.16	0.12	0.17	0.15
2Q	-0.13	0.32	0.21	0.15	0.08	-2.06
3Q	—	0.29	0.21	0.16	0.11	-0.07
4Q	—	0.74	0.61	0.49	0.44	0.21
Yr.	—	1.56	1.20	0.93	0.80	-1.77

Next earnings report expected: late October

Dividend Data (Dividends have been paid since 1965.)

Amount ($)	Date Decl.	Ex-Div. Date	Stock of Record	Payment Date
2-for-1	Oct. 30	Jan. 12	Jan. 07	Jan. 09 '98
0.075	Feb. 26	Mar. 04	Mar. 06	Mar. 31 '98
0.075	May. 28	Jun. 03	Jun. 05	Jun. 30 '98
0.075	Jul. 23	Sep. 02	Sep. 04	Sep. 30 '98

A Division of The McGraw·Hill Companies

STANDARD
&POOR'S
STOCK REPORTS

Northern Telecom Limited

1700M
12-SEP-98

Business Summary - 28-JUL-98

Northern Telecom Ltd. (Nortel) has helped create many of the major "second" or competitive networks around the globe, including the three largest competitive long distance networks in North America, and the second and third national networks in the U.K. Nortel designs, builds and integrates digital networks for customers in the information, communication, entertainment, education and commerce markets. The company works with customers in more than 150 countries and territories, creating a world of wireless, enterprise, public carrier and broadband networks. NT's wireless unit has been the fastest growing business in recent years. Nortel claimed an early lead in the deployment of digital wireless PCS (Personal Communications Services) networks in North America. Every one of the first seven PCS networks in commercial service in North America uses Nortel digital wireless infrastructure equipment. Revenue sources in recent years were:

	1997	1996
Switching networks	26%	35%
Enterprise networks	26%	30%
Wireless networks	22%	19%
Broadband networks	22%	12%

Cable & outside plant prods.	3%	4%

U.S. operations accounted for 59% of revenues in 1997, Canada for 12%, and Europe for 22%. NT is moving to penetrate markets in the Caribbean, Asia-Pacific and Latin America; these markets contributed 7% of 1997 revenues.

Principal customers are telephone companies in Canada and the U.S. Switching network products are used to interconnect access lines with transmission facilities to provide local or long-distance service. Through its enterprise networks division, NT provides private digital switching systems to businesses, including private branch exchanges (PBXs), key systems, voice messaging systems and call center solutions. NT also markets high-capacity data communications and broadband digital switching systems. NT's wireless network products include dual-mode cellular radio technology, access equipment, and products based on TDMA and CDMA technologies. Broadband network products transport voice, data, image and video communications.

In April 1998, Nortel acquired Aptis Communications, Inc. a remote-access data networking startup company, for about $305 million, comprised of 2.5 million common shares and $5 million in cash. Excluding certain charges, the acquisition is not expected to have a material impact on 1998 consolidated results of operations.

Per Share Data ($)

(Year Ended Dec. 31)	1997	1996	1995	1994	1993	1992	1991	1990	1989	1988
Tangible Bk. Val.	7.61	6.86	5.81	4.96	3.52	4.38	7.49	6.62	5.57	5.08
Cash Flow	2.60	2.23	1.92	1.61	-0.83	2.04	2.00	1.63	1.44	1.01
Earnings	1.56	1.20	0.93	0.80	-1.77	1.08	1.01	0.90	0.73	0.35
Dividends	0.29	0.25	0.21	0.18	0.18	0.17	0.16	0.15	0.14	0.13
Payout Ratio	19%	21%	23%	22%	NM	16%	16%	17%	19%	38%
Prices - High	57	33⁷⁄₈	22¹⁄₈	18⁷⁄₈	23	24⁵⁄₈	23¹⁄₈	14⁷⁄₈	12¹⁄₈	10¹⁄₈
- Low	30¹⁄₄	20³⁄₈	15³⁄₄	13	10³⁄₄	15¹⁄₄	13¹⁄₈	11¹⁄₈	7¹⁄₈	7³⁄₄
P/E Ratio - High	36	28	24	24	NM	23	23	16	16	29
- Low	19	17	17	16	NM	14	13	12	10	22

Income Statement Analysis (Million $)

	1997	1996	1995	1994	1993	1992	1991	1990	1989	1988
Revs.	15,449	12,847	10,672	8,874	8,148	8,409	8,183	6,769	6,106	5,408
Oper. Inc.	1,975	1,605	1,255	829	762	1,369	1,316	1,017	863	704
Depr.	546	525	503	408	470	474	485	352	337	313
Int. Exp.	169	175	160	195	278	251	221	80.0	97.0	67.0
Pretax Inc.	1,267	944	706	569	-1,069	756	710	619	515	235
Eff. Tax Rate	35%	34%	33%	28%	NM	28%	28%	26%	27%	22%
Net Inc.	829	623	473	408	-877	548	515	460	377	183

Balance Sheet & Other Fin. Data (Million $)

	1997	1996	1995	1994	1993	1992	1991	1990	1989	1988
Cash	1,371	730	202	1,059	138	90.0	183	105	170	79.0
Curr. Assets	8,547	6,870	5,822	5,355	4,812	4,155	3,779	3,224	3,125	2,642
Total Assets	12,554	10,903	9,442	8,785	9,485	9,379	9,534	6,842	6,375	5,878
Curr. Liab.	4,883	3,771	3,752	3,195	4,147	3,409	3,607	2,114	2,165	2,155
LT Debt	1,565	1,663	1,236	1,507	1,512	1,147	1,161	798	816	578
Common Eqty.	4,801	4,876	3,798	3,355	3,014	3,967	3,676	3,224	2,696	2,431
Total Cap.	6,667	6,636	5,262	5,293	4,954	5,681	5,498	4,688	4,130	3,636
Cap. Exp.	577	601	577	389	471	572	514	442	370	501
Cash Flow	1,358	1,148	972	812	-413	1,010	981	788	691	479
Curr. Ratio	1.8	1.8	1.6	1.7	1.2	1.2	1.0	1.5	1.4	1.2
% LT Debt of Cap.	23.5	25.1	23.5	28.5	30.5	20.2	21.1	17.0	19.8	15.9
% Net Inc.of Revs.	5.4	4.9	4.4	4.6	NM	6.5	6.3	6.8	6.2	3.4
% Ret. on Assets	7.1	6.1	5.2	4.4	NM	5.8	6.3	6.9	6.1	3.4
% Ret. on Equity	17.4	14.4	13.1	12.6	NM	14.0	14.3	14.7	13.7	6.9

Data as orig. reptd.; bef. results of disc. opers. and/or spec. items. Per share data adj. for stk. divs. as of ex-div. date. Bold denotes diluted EPS (FASB 128). E-Estimated. NA-Not Available. NM-Not Meaningful. NR-Not Ranked.

Office—8200 Dixie Road, Suite 100, Brampton, ON, Canada L6T 5P6, Canada. **Tel**—(905) 863-0000. **Website**—http://www.nortel.com **Chrmn**—D. J. Schuenke. **Pres & CEO**—J. Roth. **SVP & CFO**—P. W. Currie. **Secy**—P. J. Chilibeck. **Dirs**— R. M. Barford, Hon. J. J. Blanchard, F. C. Carlucci, G. V. Dirvin, L. Y. Fortier, E. P. Lougheed, J. C. Monty, P. F. Oreffice, J. Roth, G. Saucier, D. J. Schuenke, S. H. Smith, Jr., L. R. Wilson. **Transfer Agents & Registrars**—Montreal Trust Co. of Canada, Toronto, Montreal and Vancouver; Bank of Nova Scotia of New York Trust Co., NYC; CIBC Mellon Trust Co., Ilford, Essex, England. **Incorporated**—in Canada in 1914. **Empl**— 72,896. **S&P Analyst**: Aydin Tuncer

Northern Trust Corp.　4828

Nasdaq Symbol **NTRS**

In S&P 500

12-SEP-98　**Industry:** Banks (Major Regional)　**Summary:** Chicago-based Northern Trust Corp. is a leading provider of fiduciary, asset management and private banking services.

S&P Opinion: Hold (★★★)	Recent Price • 64	Yield • 1.3%
	52 Wk Range • 83¼-54⅝	12-Mo. P/E • 22.2

Earnings vs. Previous Year
△=Up ▽=Down ▷=No Change

Quantitative Evaluations

Outlook
(1 Lowest—5 Highest)
• **1**

Fair Value
• **56**

Risk
• **Low**

Earn./Div. Rank
• **A**

Technical Eval.
• **Bearish** since 8/98

Rel. Strength Rank
(1 Lowest—99 Highest)
• **67**

Insider Activity
• **Neutral**

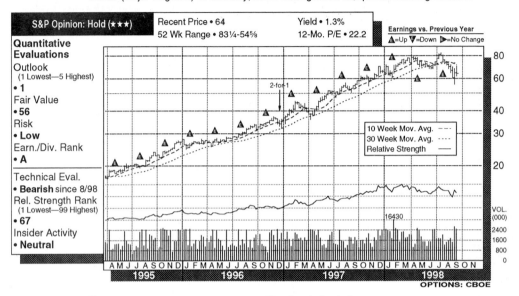

OPTIONS: CBOE

Overview - 23-JUL-98

Earnings per share increased 15%, year to year, in the second quarter of 1998, driven by increased levels of trust fees, net interest income, and treasury management revenues. Trust fees grew 20%, accounting for 76% of total noninterest income and 51% of net revenue, on good growth in assets under management and administration. This growth should continue in 1998, aided by continued geographic expansion, as well as new business originated as competition exits the corporate trust business. Average earning assets grew 12%, driven by increases in loan volume and federal agency and other securities; net interest income advanced 9%. NTRS completed the acquisition of Trust Bank of Colorado in the quarter, marking the company's entrance into the attractive Denver market as management's plan to build a national Personal Financial Services franchise continues. NTRS also recently opened an a new office in Glenview, IL, and expects to open an office in Bloomfield, MI in the third quarter.

Valuation - 23-JUL-98

The shares of this diversified bank holding company have advanced approximately 13% thus far in 1998, underperforming the broader market. NTRS continues to post strong financial results, however, buoyed by strong increases in new business and the overall health of the financial markets. Given the consistent, low-risk earnings stream produced by this blended investment management, transactions processing and bank holding company, the shares deserve a premium valuation relative to the shares of other regional banks. While Northern Trust's fundamentals remain intact, we see little room for the price/earnings multiple to expand from its current 27X our 1998 EPS estimate of $3.00 and 23X our 1999 estimate of $3.50. We expect NTRS to be a market performer over the next six to 12 months.

Key Stock Statistics

S&P EPS Est. 1998	3.00	Tang. Bk. Value/Share	16.53
P/E on S&P Est. 1998	21.3	Beta	1.25
S&P EPS Est. 1999	3.50	Shareholders	3,300
Dividend Rate/Share	0.84	Market cap. (B)	$ 7.1
Shs. outstg. (M)	111.3	Inst. holdings	62%
Avg. daily vol. (M)	0.626		

Value of $10,000 invested 5 years ago: $ 33,646

Fiscal Year Ending Dec. 31

	1998	1997	1996	1995	1994	1993
Revenues (Million $)						
1Q	613.9	414.6	472.6	422.8	333.4	308.3
2Q	636.0	555.0	481.3	439.6	378.2	312.7
3Q	—	593.9	484.2	459.2	373.4	320.2
4Q	—	703.8	491.3	460.5	393.5	317.6
Yr.	—	2,267	1,929	1,782	1,479	1,259
Earnings Per Share ($)						
1Q	**0.73**	**0.62**	0.53	0.43	0.40	0.35
2Q	**0.75**	**0.65**	0.54	0.45	0.42	0.36
3Q	**E0.75**	**0.70**	0.57	0.49	0.41	0.38
4Q	**E0.77**	**0.70**	0.58	0.51	0.34	0.38
Yr.	**E3.00**	**2.66**	2.21	1.87	1.58	1.48

Next earnings report expected: mid October

Dividend Data (Dividends have been paid since 1896.)

Amount ($)	Date Decl.	Ex-Div. Date	Stock of Record	Payment Date
0.210	Nov. 18	Dec. 08	Dec. 10	Jan. 02 '98
0.210	Feb. 17	Mar. 06	Mar. 10	Apr. 01 '98
0.210	May. 19	Jun. 08	Jun. 10	Jul. 01 '98
0.210	Jul. 21	Sep. 08	Sep. 10	Oct. 01 '98

A Division of The McGraw·Hill Companies

Business Summary - 23-JUL-98

Founded in 1889, this Chicago-based bank holding company is a leading provider of a broad array of financial services, including trust, banking, investment management and global custody services. Focusing on selected market niches, the company operates through two distinct businesses - one catering to wealthy individuals, and the other catering to corporate and institutional clients. At December 31, 1997, Northern Trust had assets totaling $25.3 billion and trust assets under administration totaling over $1.0 trillion.

Unlike most banking organizations, which derive the bulk of their revenues from net interest income (interest revenues less interest expenses), Northern garners over 65% of its income from noninterest, or fee-based, sources. This unique mix typically generates a consistent, low risk stream of revenues and earnings, and is fueled by growth in assets under management. The largest source of this noninterest income is trust fees, which accounted for approximately 50% of Northern's total revenues in 1997.

Northern's Personal Financial Services (PFS) business unit operates through over 60 offices in affluent areas

of Illinois, Florida, California, Arizona, Texas and Colorado. Through highly personalized service aimed at wealthy individuals, this unit provides fiduciary, asset custody, investment management, tax and estate planning and private banking functions. Within PFS, Northern's Wealth Management Group addresses the complex financial needs of super-rich individuals. The roughly 166 families utilizing this service have assets typically in excess of $100 million.

Northern's other key business, Corporate and Institutional Services, administers and manages global investment asset pools for corporate and institutional clients. Northern is one of a handful of dominant players in this fast consolidating business. Many second tier providers, finding it increasingly difficult to achieve economies of scale necessary to compete with the larger competitors, have exited certain businesses, allowing NTRS to grow its client base. For example, NTRS was named the preferred provider for First Chicago NBD master trust and institutional custody services. Northern intends to continue to make the necessary investments in technology to maintain its leadership role in the corporate trust and global custody businesses.

Per Share Data ($)

(Year Ended Dec. 31)	1997	1996	1995	1994	1993	1992	1991	1990	1989	1988
Tangible Bk. Val.	13.24	11.85	10.56	10.27	8.51	7.18	6.41	5.52	4.84	4.28
Earnings	2.66	2.21	1.88	1.58	1.48	1.32	1.15	1.03	1.04	1.10
Dividends	0.75	0.65	0.55	0.46	0.39	0.33	0.29	0.26	0.22	0.18
Payout Ratio	28%	29%	29%	29%	26%	25%	25%	25%	21%	16%
Prices - High	71½	37¾	28	21⅝	25¼	21⅝	17½	11¼	11⅞	8
- Low	34	24⅝	15⅞	16⅛	18½	16⅜	9	6½	7⅜	6⅛
P/E Ratio - High	27	17	15	14	17	16	15	11	11	7
- Low	13	11	8	10	13	12	8	6	7	6

Income Statement Analysis (Million $)

	1997	1996	1995	1994	1993	1992	1991	1990	1989	1988
Net Int. Inc.	438	388	358	338	329	311	282	249	237	232
Tax Equiv. Adj.	32.7	33.6	37.6	33.4	34.1	32.5	36.0	38.1	36.0	23.8
Non Int. Inc.	934	778	677	630	551	506	409	367	330	307
Loan Loss Prov.	9.0	12.0	6.0	6.0	20.0	30.0	31.0	14.0	16.0	20.0
Exp./Op. Revs.	65%	57%	66%	70%	69%	69%	69%	71%	71%	69%
Pretax Inc.	472	387	321	262	234	207	164	140	125	131
Eff. Tax Rate	34%	33%	31%	30%	28%	28%	22%	17%	9.40%	17%
Net Inc.	309	259	220	182	168	150	127	115	113	109
% Net Int. Marg.	2.18	2.25	2.30	2.36	2.65	2.96	3.00	2.80	2.95	3.20

Balance Sheet & Other Fin. Data (Million $)

	1997	1996	1995	1994	1993	1992	1991	1990	1989	1988
Earning Assets:										
Money Mkt	5,275	3,197	1,784	2,642	2,705	2,318	1,710	1,397	970	1,290
Inv. Securities	4,198	4,815	5,760	5,053	4,002	3,180	3,115	2,194	2,244	2,185
Com'l Loans	4,082	3,818	3,708	3,107	2,809	2,881	3,176	2,831	2,924	2,660
Other Loans	8,506	7,119	6,198	5,484	4,814	4,055	3,104	2,706	2,736	2,006
Total Assets	25,315	21,608	19,934	18,562	16,903	14,960	13,193	11,789	10,938	9,904
Demand Deposits	3,961	3,887	3,313	2,830	2,762	2,712	1,824	2,021	1,803	1,965
Time Deposits	12,399	9,909	9,175	8,904	7,572	7,159	6,737	6,088	5,236	4,788
LT Debt	1,225	733	352	792	1,144	545	266	172	241	175
Common Eqty.	1,619	1,424	1,282	1,111	982	841	701	589	531	410
% Ret. on Assets	1.3	1.2	1.1	1.0	1.1	1.1	1.1	1.0	1.1	1.2
% Ret. on Equity	20.0	18.8	17.7	16.7	17.9	18.3	19.0	19.8	22.8	28.9
% Loan Loss Resv.	1.2	1.4	1.5	1.7	1.9	2.1	2.3	2.7	2.6	3.2
% Loans/Deposits	76.9	79.3	79.3	73.2	73.8	70.3	73.4	68.3	80.4	69.1
% Equity to Assets	6.5	6.5	6.2	5.9	5.8	5.8	5.2	4.7	4.4	3.9

Data as orig. reptd.; bef. results of disc. opers. and/or spec. items. Per share data adj. for stk. divs. as of ex-div. date. E-Estimated. NA-Not Available. NM-Not Meaningful. NR-Not Ranked.

Office—50 S. LaSalle St., Chicago, IL 60675. **Tel**—(312) 630-6000. **Website**—http://www.northerntrust.com **Chrmn & CEO**—W. A Osborn. **Pres & COO**—B. G. Hastings. **SEVP & CFO**—P. R. Pero. **EVP & Secy**—P. L. Rossiter. **Investor Contact**—Laurie K. McMahon (312-444-7811). **Dirs**—D. L. Burnham, D. E. Cross, CS. Crown, R. S. Hamada, B. G. Hastings, R. A. Helman, A. L. Kelly, F. A. Krehbiel, W. G. Mitchell, E.J. Mooney, W. A. Osborne, H. B. Smith, W. D. Smithburg, B. L. Thomas. **Transfer Agent & Registrar**—Norwest Shareowner Services. **Incorporated**—in Delaware in 1971; bank chartered in Illinois in 1889. **Empl**— 7,553. **S&P Analyst:** Michael Schneider

12-SEP-98

Industry: Aerospace/Defense

Summary: NOC makes fighter planes, sophisticated radar equipment, and fuselages, wings and tails sections for commercial aircraft.

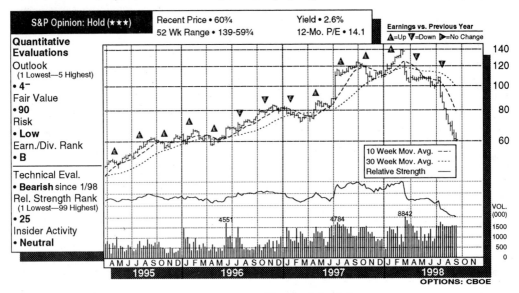

S&P Opinion: Hold (★★★)	Recent Price • 60¾ Yield • 2.6%
	52 Wk Range • 139-59¾ 12-Mo. P/E • 14.1

Quantitative Evaluations

Outlook
(1 Lowest—5 Highest)
• **4⁻**

Fair Value
• **90**

Risk
• **Low**

Earn./Div. Rank
• **B**

Technical Eval.
• **Bearish** since 1/98

Rel. Strength Rank
(1 Lowest—99 Highest)
• **25**

Insider Activity
• **Neutral**

Earnings vs. Previous Year
▲=Up ▼=Down ►=No Change

10 Week Mov. Avg. ---
30 Week Mov. Avg. ·····
Relative Strength —

VOL. (000)

OPTIONS: CBOE

Overview - 28-JUL-98

NOC, with $9 billion in revenues, is the fourth largest U.S. aerospace & defense company. Boeing (BA), with revenues nearing $50 billion, Lockheed Martin (LMT: $28 billion) and Raytheon (RTN.B: $20 billion), are #1, #2 and #3, respectively. Recently, NOC was dealt a blow after Lockheed Martin abandoned plans to merge with it. LMT dropped the proposed merger after strong Pentagon and U.S. Justice Dept. opposition. The U.S. government was very concerned the combined company would stifle competition by virtue of LMT/NOC's ability to operate as a "one-stop shop." The Pentagon feared the combined company would use only LMT/ NOC components and electronics in LMT/NOC aircraft, instead of using electronics from other military contractors. Although several smaller defense contractors still remain, it appears that mega-defense mergers may have ended.

Valuation - 28-JUL-98

Since 1993, NOC has outpaced the S&P 500, rising at an annualized rate of 31%, versus 20% for the market. We attribute NOC's past performance to strong EPS growth from acquisition-related cost cutting. However, with the defense industry consolidation winding down, we don't believe underlying industry or company fundamentals will enable NOC to consistently outpace the market going forward. The industry is capital- and R&D-intensive, operates using long-term contracts, and makes products with long lead times. Moreover, U.S. defense industry growth should remain flat in the next several years, due to tight military budgets. Also, higher margin foreign sales could come under assault as the European defense industry consolidates. So, based on average industry fundamentals and projected NOC equity returns and EPS growth, we expect NOC, at best, to perform in line with the market long term.

Key Stock Statistics

S&P EPS Est. 1998	6.60	Tang. Bk. Value/Share	NM
P/E on S&P Est. 1998	9.2	Beta	0.99
S&P EPS Est. 1999	7.50	Shareholders	10,800
Dividend Rate/Share	1.60	Market cap. (B)	$ 4.2
Shs. outstg. (M)	68.8	Inst. holdings	66%
Avg. daily vol. (M)	0.430		

Value of $10,000 invested 5 years ago: $ 20,818

Fiscal Year Ending Dec. 31

	1998	1997	1996	1995	1994	1993
Revenues (Million $)						
1Q	2,014	1,964	1,603	1,617	1,218	1,275
2Q	2,139	2,087	2,143	1,759	1,686	1,312
3Q	—	2,297	2,043	1,630	1,927	1,220
4Q	—	2,510	2,282	1,812	1,880	1,256
Yr.	—	9,153	8,071	6,818	6,711	5,063
Earnings Per Share ($)						
1Q	-0.18	1.25	1.23	1.10	1.05	1.09
2Q	1.34	1.59	1.69	1.59	1.33	1.12
3Q	—	1.44	1.21	1.25	0.79	0.54
4Q	—	1.71	0.30	1.17	-2.45	-0.73
Yr.	E6.60	5.98	4.15	5.11	0.72	1.99

Next earnings report expected: late October

Dividend Data (Dividends have been paid since 1951.)

Amount ($)	Date Decl.	Ex-Div. Date	Stock of Record	Payment Date
0.400	Nov. 19	Nov. 26	Dec. 01	Dec. 15 '97
0.400	Feb. 27	Mar. 10	Mar. 09	Mar. 31 '98
0.400	May. 15	May. 29	Jun. 02	Jun. 13 '98
0.400	Aug. 19	Aug. 27	Aug. 31	Sep. 12 '98

A Division of The **McGraw·Hill** *Companies*

Business Summary - 28-JUL-98

Formed from a series of mergers and acquisitions during the period of declining defense expenditures which followed the end of the Cold War, Northrop Grumman Corp. includes the operations of the original Northrop, Vought Aircraft Co., Grumman Corp., and the defense electronics business of Westinghouse Electric Corp. The company produces military and commercial aircraft sub-assemblies, and defense electronics systems. The company's two major customers are the U.S. government (79% of sales in 1997) and Boeing (9.4%).

NOC's major aircraft program, presently accounting for about 16% of sales, is the B-2 stealth bomber. The backlog of orders related to the B-2 was $2.8 billion at the end of 1997. One aircraft was delivered in the first quarter of 1998. In order to maintain the capability to build these aircraft in the future, the government authorized conversion of a B-2 test aircraft which will boost the B-2 fleet to 21 in 2000.

Surveillance aircraft and airborne radar accounts for 14% of sales, with programs such as J-STARS and the E-2C. J-STARS is a modified BA-707 aircraft which carries the Joint Surveillance and Target Attack Radar System. This system provides surveillance and battle management support to ground forces. the government is

planning a $1.2 billion radar technology upgrade to J-STARS. The company is exploring opportunities to network J-STARS with AWACS and other surveillance and battle management systems. NOC manufactures airframes for the E-2C Hawkeye early warning aircraft and surveillance radar for AWACS (Airborne Warning And Control Systems) deployed on BA-747 and 767 aircraft. NOC leverages its capabilities in surveillance systems by producing combat radars, electronic and infrared countermeasures, and air traffic control and air defense systems. Important programs are Longbow fire control radar and Hellfire missile systems for the Apache helicopter and GAM (GPS-aided munitions). NOC is a subcontractor on SBIRS (Space-Based Infrared System) and on the F/A-18 multi-mission plane.

Commercial aircraft including work on Boeing jetliners should rise again in 1998 due to an upswing in aircraft production. Products include engine nacelle systems, integrated tail sections and other structures for various jets.

As of March 31, 1998, the company's total funded backlog stood at $11.5 billion, with $5.9 billion for aircraft programs, $5.2 billion for electronics programs and $462 million for information technology and services contracts. New contract awards in the first quarter of 1998 totaled about $1.7 billion.

Per Share Data ($)

(Year Ended Dec. 31)	1997	1996	1995	1994	1993	1992	1991	1990	1989	1988
Tangible Bk. Val.	NA	NM	NM	-9.16	26.78	26.31	25.04	21.94	18.56	21.33
Cash Flow	12.31	11.13	10.82	6.19	6.45	5.96	9.33	8.45	2.98	4.47
Earnings	5.98	4.33	5.11	0.72	1.99	2.56	5.69	4.48	-1.71	-0.65
Dividends	1.60	1.60	1.60	1.60	1.60	1.20	1.20	1.20	1.20	1.20
Payout Ratio	27%	37%	31%	NM	80%	47%	21%	27%	NM	NM
Prices - High	127⅞	84¼	64¼	47⅜	42⅝	34⅞	31¼	20¼	29¾	35⅞
- Low	71⅜	57¾	39¾	34½	30½	22½	16½	13¾	16	25⅛
P/E Ratio - High	21	19	13	66	21	14	5	5	NM	NM
- Low	12	13	8	48	15	9	3	3	NM	NM

Income Statement Analysis (Million $)

	1997	1996	1995	1994	1993	1992	1991	1990	1989	1988
Revs.	9,153	8,071	6,818	6,711	5,062	5,550	5,694	5,490	5,248	5,797
Oper. Inc.	1,298	1,025	819	750	433	389	523	478	244	266
Depr.	418	367	283	269	214	160	171	187	221	241
Int. Exp.	257	270	137	109	38.0	47.0	80.0	95.0	124	82.0
Pretax Inc.	651	384	409	65.0	170	180	277	313	-111	-54.0
Eff. Tax Rate	37%	39%	38%	46%	44%	33%	3.20%	33%	NM	NM
Net Inc.	407	234	252	35.0	96.0	121	268	210	-81.0	-31.0

Balance Sheet & Other Fin. Data (Million $)

	1997	1996	1995	1994	1993	1992	1991	1990	1989	1988
Cash	63.0	44.0	18.0	17.0	100	230	203	173	5.0	4.0
Curr. Assets	2,936	2,597	2,072	2,431	1,560	1,760	1,807	1,785	1,747	1,615
Total Assets	9,677	9,422	5,455	6,047	2,939	3,162	3,128	3,094	3,196	3,139
Curr. Liab.	2,715	2,600	1,715	1,964	1,079	1,406	1,196	1,214	1,655	1,494
LT Debt	2,500	2,950	1,163	1,633	160	160	470	691	551	551
Common Eqty.	2,623	2,128	1,459	1,290	1,322	1,254	1,182	1,033	875	1,004
Total Cap.	5,198	5,139	2,653	2,939	1,529	1,464	1,685	1,811	1,508	1,618
Cap. Exp.	238	194	133	134	135	123	117	121	187	254
Cash Flow	825	601	535	304	310	281	440	397	140	210
Curr. Ratio	1.1	1.0	1.2	1.2	1.4	1.3	1.5	1.5	1.1	1.1
% LT Debt of Cap.	48.1	57.4	43.8	55.6	10.5	10.9	27.9	38.1	36.5	34.1
% Net Inc.of Revs.	4.4	2.9	3.7	0.5	1.9	2.2	4.7	3.8	NM	NM
% Ret. on Assets	4.3	3.1	4.4	0.8	3.1	3.8	8.6	6.7	NM	NM
% Ret. on Equity	17.1	13.0	18.3	2.7	7.3	9.9	24.2	22.1	NM	NM

Data as orig. reptd.; bef. results of disc. opers. and/or spec. items. Per share data adj. for stk. divs. as of ex-div. date. Bold denotes diluted EPS (FASB 128). E-Estimated. NA-Not Available. NM-Not Meaningful. NR-Not Ranked.

Office—1840 Century Park East, Los Angeles, CA 90067-2199. **Tel**—(310) 553-6262. **Website**—http://www.northgrum.com **Chrmn, Pres & CEO**—K. Kresa. **VP & CFO**—R. B. Waugh, Jr. **VP & Secy**—J. C. Johnson. **Investor Contact**—J. Gaston Kent, Jr. (310-201-3423). **Dirs**—J. R. Borsting, J. T. Chain, Jr. J. Edwards, P. Frost, K. Kresa, R. A. Lutz, A. L. Peters, J. E. Robson, R. M. Rosenberg, B. Scowcroft, J. B. Slaughter, R. J. Stegemeier. **Transfer Agent & Registrar**—ChaseMellon Shareholder Services, NYC. **Incorporated**—in California in 1939; reincorporated in Delaware in 1985. **Empl**— 46,600. **S&P Analyst:** Robert E. Friedman, CPA

12-SEP-98

Industry: Banks (Major Regional)

Summary: This bank holding company, which owns banks in 16 primarily upper Midwest states, recently agreed to merge with San Francisco-based Wells Fargo.

S&P Opinion: Hold (★★★)	
Recent Price • 32¼	Yield • 2.3%
52 Wk Range • 43⅞-27½	12-Mo. P/E • 17.4

Quantitative Evaluations

Outlook (1 Lowest—5 Highest)
• **1⁻**

Fair Value
• **25⅞**

Risk
• **Low**

Earn./Div. Rank
• **A+**

Technical Eval.
• **Bearish** since 8/98

Rel. Strength Rank (1 Lowest—99 Highest)
• **74**

Insider Activity
• **Neutral**

Earnings vs. Previous Year
▲=Up ▼=Down ▶=No Change

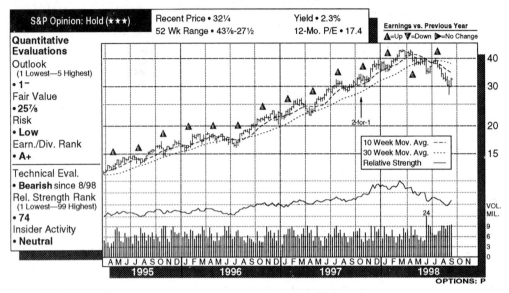

10 Week Mov. Avg. ---
30 Week Mov. Avg. ····
Relative Strength ——

2-for-1

OPTIONS: P

Overview - 23-JUL-98

Loan growth is expected to slow to the mid single digits in 1998, as the company adopts a more conservative approach to lending by maintaining risk-based pricing at this stage of the economic cycle. Margins are already well above those of the company's peer group, but have narrowed in recent quarters on a lower yielding portfolio mix. A higher provision for loan losses will be needed to cover expected growth in the loan portfolio, particularly in the consumer segment, and to maintain the company's conservative reserve position. Noninterest income should benefit from continued growth in trust fees and service charges, as well as in mortgage banking income. NOB's mortgage banking operations, the size and scope of which provide critical competitive advantages, include a $220 billion servicing portfolio, the industry's largest. Although there is not much geographic overlap, synergies from the proposed combination with Wells Fargo include $650 million of expense cuts over the next three years mostly in the areas of systems, operations and overhead functions.

Valuation - 23-JUL-98

We recently downgraded NOB from accumulate to hold following the proposed merger with Wells Fargo. The valuation in the transaction, despite the relatively low cost savings assumptions built in, was not an issue. However, we expect NOB's exceptional return on asset and return on equity parameters to be substantially diluted following the merger. In addition, the different business models of the two companies, with one focused on a thriving retail delivery platform and the other on electronic distribution, could pose integration problems. At present, we would hold the shares pending sure signs that the merger will provide tangible benefits to shareholders beyond initial cost savings projections.

Key Stock Statistics

S&P EPS Est. 1998	2.00	Tang. Bk. Value/Share	9.42
P/E on S&P Est. 1998	16.2	Beta	1.29
S&P EPS Est. 1999	2.25	Shareholders	39,100
Dividend Rate/Share	0.74	Market cap. (B)	$ 24.7
Shs. outstg. (M)	765.8	Inst. holdings	54%
Avg. daily vol. (M)	2.348		

Value of $10,000 invested 5 years ago: $ 34,489

Fiscal Year Ending Dec. 31

	1998	1997	1996	1995	1994	1993
Revenues (Million $)						
1Q	2,565	2,298	2,077	1,685	1,427	1,254
2Q	2,765	2,418	2,217	1,840	1,461	1,331
3Q	—	2,446	2,243	1,966	1,510	1,300
4Q	—	2,504	2,346	2,092	1,634	1,392
Yr.	—	9,660	8,883	7,582	6,032	5,277
Earnings Per Share ($)						
1Q	**0.47**	0.42	0.37	0.33	0.29	0.24
2Q	**0.49**	0.43	0.38	0.34	0.30	0.26
3Q	**E0.51**	0.44	0.38	0.35	0.31	0.28
4Q	**E0.53**	0.46	0.41	0.36	0.32	0.28
Yr.	**E2.00**	1.75	1.54	1.38	1.23	1.06

Next earnings report expected: mid October

Dividend Data (Dividends have been paid since 1939.)

Amount ($)	Date Decl.	Ex-Div. Date	Stock of Record	Payment Date
0.165	Oct. 23	Nov. 05	Nov. 07	Dec. 01 '97
0.165	Jan. 27	Feb. 04	Feb. 06	Mar. 01 '98
0.165	Apr. 28	May. 06	May. 08	Jun. 01 '98
0.185	Jul. 28	Aug. 05	Aug. 07	Sep. 01 '98

A Division of The McGraw·Hill Companies

Business Summary - 23-JUL-98

Norwest Corp. agreed in June 1998 to merge with Wells Fargo & Co. in a stock transaction valued at $34 billion. To retain the Wells Fargo name, the new company will have a top four market share in 16 of its 21 combined banking states in the Midwest, Rocky Mountains and Western portion of the U.S., and rank as the largest mortgage originator and servicer and bank commercial real estate lender.

Current Norwest activities are broadly divided into three distinct business segments, with operating earnings (in millions) in recent years derived as follows:

	1997	1996	1995	1994
Banking	$957	$776	$602	$507
Norwest Financial	243	264	249	223
Mortgage banking	151	125	105	71

The banking segment, operating 930 locations in 16 primarily upper Midwest states, offers retail, commercial and corporate banking, equipment leasing, and trust services, with affiliates offering insurance, securities brokerage, investment banking and venture capital investment services. Mortgage banking offers a wide range of FHA, VA and conventional loan programs through a network of 727 offices in all 50 states. Norwest Financial provides direct instalment loans to in-

dividuals, purchases sales finance contracts, provides private label and other lease and accounts receivables services, and other related products and services through 1,447 stores.

In 1997, average earning assets, from which interest income is derived, amounted to $71.5 billion and consisted mainly of loans and leases (55%) and investment securities (28%). Average sources of funds included savings and NOW accounts (12%), money market accounts (13%), savings certificates (20%), noninterest-bearing demand deposits (17%), short-term borrowings (10%), long-term debt (15%), shareholders' equity (8%) and other (5%).

At year-end 1997, nonperforming assets were $382 million (0.4% of assets), up from $311 million (0.4%) a year earlier. The allowance for loan losses, which is set aside for possible loan defaults, was $1.23 billion (2.90% of loans), versus $1.04 billion (2.64%) a year earlier. Net chargeoffs, or the amount of loans actually written off as uncollectible, were $500 million (1.23% of average loans) in 1997, versus $382 million (0.99%) in 1996.

The merger with Wells Fargo & Co. (NYSE; WFC) calls for each WFC common share to be exchanged for 10 NOB common shares. WFC operates more than 1,900 branches in 10 Western states. The deal is expected to be completed in the fourth quarter of 1998.

Per Share Data ($)

(Year Ended Dec. 31)	1997	1996	1995	1994	1993	1992	1991	1990	1989	1988
Tangible Bk. Val.	9.01	7.97	7.10	5.39	5.52	4.84	4.32	3.51	3.42	3.15
Earnings	1.75	1.53	1.38	1.23	1.06	0.71	0.74	0.68	0.63	0.56
Dividends	0.61	0.53	0.45	0.38	0.32	0.27	0.23	0.21	0.19	0.16
Payout Ratio	35%	34%	33%	31%	30%	38%	32%	31%	30%	29%
Prices - High	39½	23½	17⅜	14⅛	14½	11⅛	9¼	5⅞	6	4⅜
- Low	21⅜	15¼	11⅜	10½	10⅜	8⅜	4¾	3⅜	4	3⅛
P/E Ratio - High	23	15	13	12	14	16	13	9	10	8
- Low	12	10	8	9	10	12	6	5	6	7

Income Statement Analysis (Million $)

	1997	1996	1995	1994	1993	1992	1991	1990	1989	1988
Net Int. Inc.	4,033	3,701	3,269	2,804	2,376	2,078	1,632	1,151	958	871
Tax Equiv. Adj.	44.5	32.2	34.0	29.0	33.0	NA	34.0	30.0	27.0	32.0
Non Int. Inc.	2,924	2,612	1,901	1,718	1,406	1,166	972	700	537	464
Loan Loss Prov.	525	395	312	165	140	267	322	243	160	128
Exp./Op. Revs.	64%	65%	65%	68%	75%	NA	69%	66%	66%	71%
Pretax Inc.	2,050	1,782	1,423	1,181	938	603	475	375	318	223
Eff. Tax Rate	34%	35%	33%	32%	30%	27%	16%	25%	26%	5.10%
Net Inc.	1,351	1,154	956	800	654	440	399	281	237	211
% Net Int. Marg.	5.74	5.63	5.58	5.67	5.59	NA	5.11	4.90	4.85	4.84

Balance Sheet & Other Fin. Data (Million $)

	1997	1996	1995	1994	1993	1992	1991	1990	1989	1988
Earning Assets:										
Money Mkt	1,501	2,701	777	765	637	597	428	635	NA	NA
Inv. Securities	18,731	16,959	16,004	14,837	11,322	11,764	11,225	6,734	4,906	4,288
Com'l Loans	12,878	12,125	11,234	9,155	7,674	7,473	6,444	6,438	5,903	5,555
Other Loans	31,757	29,029	36,455	29,695	26,290	23,612	17,360	14,103	11,970	9,991
Total Assets	88,540	80,175	72,134	59,316	50,782	46,657	38,502	30,626	24,335	21,750
Demand Deposits	16,253	14,296	11,624	9,283	8,339	6,785	5,700	4,095	3,194	3,166
Time Deposits	39,204	35,834	30,405	27,141	24,234	21,919	19,739	16,029	12,012	10,736
LT Debt	12,767	13,082	13,674	9,186	6,802	4,481	3,579	2,905	2,557	2,272
Common Eqty.	6,755	5,875	5,010	3,334	3,227	2,798	2,246	1,523	1,278	1,118
% Ret. on Assets	1.6	1.5	1.4	1.4	1.3	1.0	1.1	1.1	1.1	1.0
% Ret. on Equity	21.2	20.0	21.9	22.6	20.9	12.4	18.9	20.4	20.2	19.2
% Loan Loss Resv.	2.9	2.6	2.0	2.1	3.6	2.5	2.6	2.0	1.6	1.8
% Loans/Deposits	76.7	78.6	109.5	103.6	124.3	104.8	89.8	97.6	111.8	106.6
% Equity to Assets	7.4	7.5	6.3	6.2	6.2	NA	5.6	5.2	5.2	5.1

Data as orig. reptd.; bef. results of disc opers. and/or spec. items. Per share data adj. for stk. divs. as of ex-div. date. Bold denotes diluted EPS (FASB 128). E-Estimated. NA-Not Available. NM-Not Meaningful. NR-Not Ranked.

Office—Norwest Center, Sixth and Marquette, Minneapolis, MN 55479. **Tel**—(612) 667-1234. **Website**—http://www.norwest.com **Chrmn & CEO**—R. M. Kovacevich. **Pres & COO**—L. S. Biller. **EVP & CFO**—J. T. Thornton. **SVP & Secy**—L. A. Holschuh. **VP & Investor Contact**—Robert S. Strickland (612-667-7919). **Dirs**—L. S. Biller, J. A. Blanchard, D. A. Christensen, P. M. Grieve, C. M. Harper, W. A. Hodder, L. P. Johnson, R. C. King, R. M. Kovacevich, R. S. Levitt, R. D. McCormick, C. H. Milligan, B. F. Montoya, I. M. Rolland, M. W. Wright. **Transfer Agent & Registrar**—Norwest Bank Minnesota, Minneapolis. **Incorporated**—in Delaware in 1929. **Empl**— 57,000. **S&P Analyst:** Stephen R. Biggar

STANDARD &POOR'S
STOCK REPORTS

Novell, Inc.

4842Q

Nasdaq Symbol **NOVL**

In S&P 500

12-SEP-98

Industry:
Computer (Software & Services)

Summary: Novell is a leading vendor of network operating system software with its NetWare product line and related offerings.

S&P Opinion: Hold (★★★)	Recent Price • 11⅝	Yield • Nil	Earnings vs. Previous Year
	52 Wk Range • 13⅝-6¾	12-Mo. P/E • 58.1	▲=Up ▼=Down ▶=No Change

Quantitative Evaluations

Outlook
(1 Lowest—5 Highest)
• **3⁻**

Fair Value
• **11¼**

Risk
• **Average**

Earn./Div. Rank
• **B**

Technical Eval.
• **Bearish** since 3/98

Rel. Strength Rank
(1 Lowest—99 Highest)
• **95**

Insider Activity
• **Unfavorable**

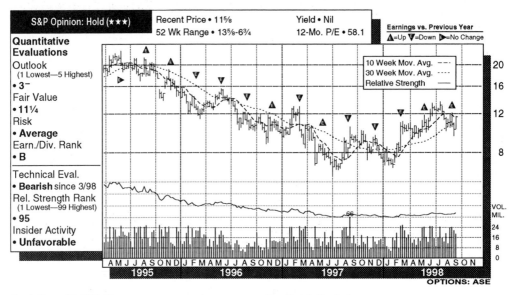

Legend: 10 Week Mov. Avg. — - —; 30 Week Mov. Avg. ·····; Relative Strength —

OPTIONS: ASE

Overview - 26-AUG-98

After a significant drop in FY 97 (Oct.), revenues should rise modestly in FY 98, as the company works to stabilize its business. Novell has been undergoing a turnaround, although it continues to suffer from competitive pressures, especially from Windows NT. Revenues should improve after the release of the company's next-generation NetWare server platform. This upgrade, which will include the company's new focus on Internet/intranet software, will be introduced in September 1998. As part of a restructuring effort, NOVL recorded a one-time charge of $55 million ($0.10 a share) in the third quarter of FY 97, for facilities consolidation and a work force reduction. These changes should produce approximately $100 million in annual cost savings. Novell returned to operating profitability in the first quarter of FY 98, and should remain profitable in FY 98, aided by the cost cutting efforts and new product introductions.

Valuation - 26-AUG-98

The shares have rebounded in 1998, as the company returned to operating profitability, and is introducing many new products. New cost controls have been put in place, which should lead to continued profitability. The company's position in large enterprise network solutions remains formidable. However, Microsoft will also be releasing its new version of Windows NT in 1999, which should put increasing pressure on Novell. Given its turnaround over the past year, the company's business is more stable, and we have upgraded the shares to hold, from avoid. In addition, Novell's $1.1 billion cash position, representing more than $3 a share, could be used for acquisitions or share buybacks, and provides some downside protection.

Key Stock Statistics

S&P EPS Est. 1998	0.24	Tang. Bk. Value/Share	4.57
P/E on S&P Est. 1998	48.4	Beta	1.30
S&P EPS Est. 1999	0.35	Shareholders	12,600
Dividend Rate/Share	Nil	Market cap. (B)	$ 4.1
Shs. outstg. (M)	353.4	Inst. holdings	39%
Avg. daily vol. (M)	4.589		

Value of $10,000 invested 5 years ago: $ 4,078

Fiscal Year Ending Oct. 31

	1998	1997	1996	1995	1994	1993
Revenues (Million $)						
1Q	252.0	374.9	437.9	493.2	488.3	260.2
2Q	262.3	273.1	188.2	529.5	534.9	280.7
3Q	272.0	90.07	365.1	537.9	488.9	272.8
4Q	—	269.3	383.7	480.5	485.9	309.2
Yr.	—	1,007	1,375	2,041	1,998	1,123
Earnings Per Share ($)						
1Q	**0.04**	0.15	0.17	0.22	0.26	0.23
2Q	**0.05**	-0.04	-0.15	0.26	0.26	0.26
3Q	**0.07**	-0.35	0.17	0.27	-0.01	-0.80
4Q	**E0.08**	0.02	0.17	0.16	0.06	0.22
Yr.	**E0.24**	-0.22	0.35	0.90	0.56	-0.11

Next earnings report expected: late November

Dividend Data

No cash has been paid.

A Division of The McGraw-Hill Companies

STANDARD
&POOR'S

STOCK REPORTS

Novell, Inc.

4842Q

12-SEP-98

Business Summary - 26-AUG-98

Novell offers a wide range of network solutions, education and support for distributed network, Internet and small-business markets. The company's products fall into three categories: server operating environments, network services and collaboration products.

Server operating environments provide the foundation of networking and network services. NetWare 3 network operating system provides users with access to data and resources controlled by a single server. NetWare 4 provides access to the resources of the entire enterprise or wide-area network and adds intranet/Internet connectivity and Web site hosting capabilities. NetWare for Small Business leverages the strengths of NetWare and GroupWise with ease of installation and administration required by small business. NetWare 5 is currently in beta testing, and is expected to begin shipping in September 1998.

Network services improve the manageability and productivity of the network and increase network efficiency. Products include NetWare Directory Services (NDS), NDS for NT, Border Manager, among others.

Collaboration products utilize NetWare network services to provide access to network-based information. GroupWise products now serve over eight million users with integrated E-Mail, group calendaring, scheduling, on-line conferencing and forms and document management.

In FY 97 (Oct.), about 45% of revenues came from international customers (50% in FY 96).

In March 1996, the company sold its personal productivity applications business to Corel Corp., and recorded a gain of $20 million ($0.04 a share) on the sale in the FY 96 second quarter. In December 1995, NOVL completed the sale to Santa Cruz Operation of its UNIX business, consisting of a full suite of UNIX operating system and UNIX connectivity products.

In April 1997, Eric Schmidt joined Novell as its new chairman and CEO. He has since instituted several key initiatives, including significant cost cutting efforts and a focus on new product introductions.

Novell did not ship any additional products to distributors in the third quarter of FY 97, leading to a 75% revenue drop. This strategy was intended to bring inventories into line with market demand. As a result, revenues were received only from license programs. In addition, NOVL recorded a $55 million restructuring charge, reflecting consolidation and a large work force reduction. These changes are expected to result in annual cost savings of about $100 million.

Per Share Data ($)

(Year Ended Oct. 31)	1997	1996	1995	1994	1993	1992	1991	1990	1989	1988
Tangible Bk. Val.	4.46	4.67	5.22	4.08	3.58	3.12	2.08	1.42	0.89	0.61
Cash Flow	0.04	0.65	1.15	0.80	0.02	0.90	0.62	0.39	0.23	0.17
Earnings	-0.22	0.35	0.90	0.56	-0.11	0.81	0.55	0.34	0.19	0.14
Dividends	Nil	Nil	Nil	Nil	Nil	Nil	Nil	Nil	Nil	Nil
Payout Ratio	Nil	Nil	Nil	Nil	Nil	Nil	Nil	Nil	Nil	Nil
Prices - High	13	15⅝	23¼	26¼	35¼	33½	32⅜	8½	4¾	4⅛
- Low	6¼	8¾	13¾	13¾	17	22½	7⅝	3⅜	3	2⅛
P/E Ratio - High	NM	45	26	47	NM	41	59	25	26	30
- Low	NM	25	15	25	NM	28	14	10	16	16

Income Statement Analysis (Million $)

	1997	1996	1995	1994	1993	1992	1991	1990	1989	1988
Revs.	1,007	1,375	2,041	1,998	1,123	933	640	498	422	281
Oper. Inc.	-53.6	232	546	547	436	386	246	148	83.0	63.0
Depr.	91.1	105	94.2	86.4	41.7	28.7	20.0	13.5	11.2	6.7
Int. Exp.	Nil	Nil	NA	NA	0.4	0.6	0.9	2.6	4.8	0.9
Pretax Inc.	-150	180	509	297	104	377	248	145	77.0	48.0
Eff. Tax Rate	NM	30%	34%	31%	134%	34%	35%	35%	37%	36%
Net Inc.	-78.3	126	338	207	-35.0	249	162	94.0	49.0	30.0

Balance Sheet & Other Fin. Data (Million $)

	1997	1996	1995	1994	1993	1992	1991	1990	1989	1988
Cash	1,033	1,025	1,321	862	664	545	347	255	130	62.0
Curr. Assets	1,470	1,591	1,925	1,453	1,052	866	553	402	270	192
Total Assets	1,911	2,049	2,417	1,963	1,344	1,097	726	494	347	227
Curr. Liab.	322	365	461	463	230	149	118	94.0	54.0	39.0
LT Debt	Nil	Nil	Nil	Nil	Nil	0.5	1.2	2.4	57.0	52.4
Common Eqty.	1,565	1,616	1,938	1,487	1,103	938	599	398	236	136
Total Cap.	1,589	1,685	1,956	1,501	1,113	947	608	401	293	188
Cap. Exp.	64.8	101	84.5	73.5	70.2	69.9	86.9	28.1	43.2	15.3
Cash Flow	12.8	231	432	293	7.0	278	182	108	60.0	37.0
Curr. Ratio	4.6	4.4	4.2	3.1	4.6	5.8	4.7	4.3	5.0	4.9
% LT Debt of Cap.	Nil	Nil	Nil	Nil	Nil	0.1	0.2	0.6	19.5	27.9
% Net Inc.of Revs.	NM	9.2	16.6	10.3	NM	26.7	25.4	19.0	11.5	10.8
% Ret. on Assets	NM	5.7	15.4	11.6	NM	26.9	26.4	21.8	15.6	16.9
% Ret. on Equity	NM	7.1	19.8	14.8	NM	31.9	32.3	29.0	24.3	25.5

Data as orig. reptd.; bef. results of disc. opers. and/or spec. items. Per share data adj. for stk. divs. as of ex-div. date. Bold denotes diluted EPS (FASB 128). E-Estimated. NA-Not Available. NM-Not Meaningful. NR-Not Ranked.

Office—122 East 1700 South, Provo, UT 84606. **Tel**—(801) 861-7000. **Website**—http://www.novell.com **Chrmn & CEO**—E. E. Schmidt. **SVP & CFO**—J. R. Tolonen. **SVP & Secy**—D. R. Bradford. **Investor Contact**—Peter Troop (408-577-8361). **Dirs**—E. R. Bond, H.-W. Hector, J. L. Messman, E. Schmidt, L. W. Sonsini, I. R. Wilson, J. A. Young. **Transfer Agent & Registrar**—ChaseMellon Shareholder Services, Ridgefield Park, NJ. **Incorporated**—in Delaware in 1983. **Empl**— 4,800. **S&P Analyst:** Brian Goodstadt

STANDARD &POOR'S
STOCK REPORTS

Nucor Corp.
1704F
NYSE Symbol **NUE**
In S&P 500

12-SEP-98

Industry: Iron & Steel

Summary: This company, the second largest U.S. steelmaker, is also the largest U.S. minimill. It is currently gaining market share in flat roll sheet and strip steel.

S&P Opinion: Hold (★★★)	Recent Price • 38¼	Yield • 1.3%
	52 Wk Range • 61¼-35¼	12-Mo. P/E • 11.5

Quantitative Evaluations

Outlook (1 Lowest—5 Highest)
• **4**

Fair Value
• **51⅜**

Risk
• **Low**

Earn./Div. Rank
• **A-**

Technical Eval.
• **Bearish** since 6/98

Rel. Strength Rank (1 Lowest—99 Highest)
• **59**

Insider Activity
• **NA**

Earnings vs. Previous Year
▲=Up ▼=Down ▷=No Change

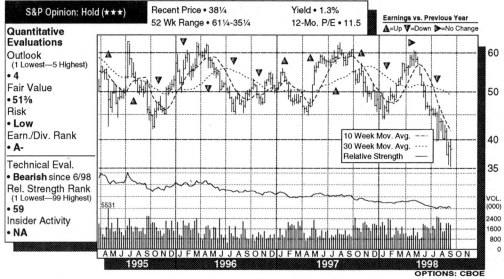

10 Week Mov. Avg. ---
30 Week Mov. Avg. ····
Relative Strength —

VOL. (000)

OPTIONS: CBOE

Overview - 18-AUG-98

We project 10% sales growth for 1998, mostly reflecting a gain in the volume of tons shipped and a better mix. We expect industry demand to be about even with that of 1997; but, with startups by other minimill plants and the re-entry of Wheeling Pittsburg Steel, steel prices will decline. The impact of lower prices on margins will outweigh decreased startup expense and a decline in scrap costs. Consequently, per ton profit and EPS will trail 1997 levels. Assuming lower imports, continued economic growth, and more stable prices, EPS should rise from 1998's depressed levels. Long-term EPS growth will be enhanced by expansion into markets for wide-flange beams, flat-rolled carbon sheet, stainless 409, and joint ventures to develop direct steelmaking.

Valuation - 18-AUG-98

We are maintaining our hold ratiing, after the release of second quarter EPS and a sharp stock price drop. Earlier, on March 23, 1998, we downgraded the stock to hold, from accumulate, based on price. Through August 14 1998, NUE was down 16.8% in 1998, versus a 17.4% decline for the S&P Steel Index and a 9.5% gain for the S&P 500. We believe that the fall reflects investor unease with the entire steel group. Rising imports and excess distributor inventories have put downward pressure on prices. The price drop will lead to unfavorable 1998 EPS comparisons for Nucor and the other steel companies. However, at a recent level of 11.7X our 1999 EPS estimate, versus 7.8X for the group, NUE is undervalued. It deserves a greater premium to its peers, based on its far superior EPS growth potential; within three years it will become the largest U.S. steel producer. Also, its EPS over the business cycle are far less volatile than those of integrated companies. Finally, a recently announced share repurchase program should help buoy the stock.

Key Stock Statistics

S&P EPS Est. 1998	3.15	Tang. Bk. Value/Share	22.66
P/E on S&P Est. 1998	12.1	Beta	0.94
S&P EPS Est. 1999	3.50	Shareholders	27,000
Dividend Rate/Share	0.48	Market cap. (B)	$ 3.4
Shs. outstg. (M)	88.1	Inst. holdings	63%
Avg. daily vol. (M)	0.383		

Value of $10,000 invested 5 years ago: $ 10,122

Fiscal Year Ending Dec. 31

	1998	1997	1996	1995	1994	1993
Revenues (Million $)						
1Q	1,139	1,010	876.1	841.7	649.7	489.8
2Q	1,128	1,035	911.1	880.1	740.1	564.9
3Q	—	1,102	937.5	860.5	786.4	587.3
4Q	—	1,037	922.4	879.6	799.4	611.8
Yr.	—	4,185	3,647	3,462	2,976	2,254
Earnings Per Share ($)						
1Q	**0.74**	**0.74**	0.60	0.77	0.40	0.25
2Q	**0.82**	**0.83**	0.63	0.80	0.57	0.35
3Q	**E0.74**	**0.91**	0.66	0.72	0.74	0.40
4Q	**E0.85**	**0.87**	0.94	0.85	0.89	0.42
Yr.	**E3.15**	**3.35**	2.83	3.14	2.60	1.42

Next earnings report expected: late October

Dividend Data (Dividends have been paid since 1973.)

Amount ($)	Date Decl.	Ex-Div. Date	Stock of Record	Payment Date
0.100	Dec. 05	Dec. 29	Dec. 31	Feb. 11 '98
0.120	Mar. 05	Mar. 27	Mar. 31	May. 12 '98
0.120	Jun. 09	Jun. 26	Jun. 30	Aug. 11 '98
0.120	Sep. 09	Sep. 28	Sep. 30	Nov. 11 '98

A Division of The McGraw-Hill Companies

STANDARD
&POOR'S
STOCK REPORTS

Nucor Corporation

1704F
12-SEP-98

Business Summary - 18-AUG-98

Nucor, the largest U.S. minimill and second biggest steelmaker, continued its aggressive expansion with the October 1996 startup of its third thin slab flat roll minimill plant. The new plant, in Berkeley County, SC, uses the same process that transforms steel scrap into a 2 inch thick slab, pioneered at NUE's Crawfordville, IN, and Hickman, AR, plants. This revolutionary process has dramatically lowered the barriers to entry in the market for flat roll carbon sheet and strip, which comprise about one-half of all domestic steel industry shipments.

Aided by increased output at the new plant in Berkeley, Nucor produced 9.7 million tons of steel in 1997, becoming the second largest U.S. steelmaker, surpassing both LTV Corp. and Bethlehem Steel. Nucor will probably add a fourth plant at the end of this decade or early in the next. With the addition of a fourth plant, Nucor will be very close to matching or exceeding USX U.S. Steel Group as the largest domestic steelmaker. Through expansion at existing mills and construction of new mills, Nucor expects to increase its annual capacity to 13 million tons over the next several years.

Although Nucor already has the broadest product line of any domestic steelmaker, commodity flat roll sheet is not the only market on which it has set its sights. In 1995, the company began making stainless 409, a commodity stainless steel product used in auto exhaust systems. While it has a lower margin than other grades of stainless steel, stainless 409 will help increase Nucor's profitability, because stainless steel carries higher margins than carbon steel.

Nucor is also positioning itself to capitalize on the growth of new flat roll minimills with its new iron carbide plant in Trinidad. The plant will lessen the company's reliance on outside purchases of scrap. Scrap is Nucor's single largest cost; its average cost of scrap was $145 a ton in 1997, versus $150 a ton in 1996 and $155 in 1995. After satisfying its own raw material needs, Nucor has the option to sell iron carbide to rival minimills that lack the capital to supply their own needs.

Shipments to outside customers were 8,435,000 tons in 1997, versus 7,252,000 tons in 1996 and 6,745,000 tons in 1995. Steel production was 9,724,000 tons in 1997, versus 8,423,000 tons in 1996.

Nucor's principal competitors for traditional minimill construction market steel products include Bayou Steel, Birmingham Steel, Chaparral Steel, Florida Steel, and Northwestern Steel & Wire.

Competition in flat roll carbon sheet includes the old line integrated companies and new minimill players such as BHP-North Star, Gallatin Steel, Steel Dynamics and Trico Steel.

On July 29, 1998, Nucor announced that directors had authorized the repurchase of up to 5,000,000 common shares. The purchases will be made from time to time at prevailing prices.

Per Share Data ($)

(Year Ended Dec. 31)	1997	1996	1995	1994	1993	1992	1991	1990	1989	1988
Tangible Bk. Val.	21.32	18.33	15.78	12.84	10.36	9.04	8.23	7.59	6.83	6.25
Cash Flow	5.83	4.91	5.15	4.41	2.83	2.04	1.83	1.86	1.57	1.50
Earnings	3.35	2.83	3.14	2.60	1.42	0.92	0.75	0.88	0.68	0.83
Dividends	0.40	0.32	0.28	0.18	0.16	0.14	0.13	0.12	0.11	0.10
Payout Ratio	12%	11%	9%	7%	11%	15%	17%	14%	16%	12%
Prices - High	62⅞	63	63¼	72	57¼	40	22⅜	20½	16⅞	12¼
- Low	44¾	45⅛	42	48¾	38	21	14¼	12⅛	11¼	9⅛
P/E Ratio - High	19	22	20	28	40	44	30	23	25	15
- Low	13	16	13	19	27	23	19	14	17	11

Income Statement Analysis (Million $)

	1997	1996	1995	1994	1993	1992	1991	1990	1989	1988
Revs.	4,184	3,647	3,462	2,976	2,254	1,619	1,465	1,482	1,269	1,061
Oper. Inc.	678	570	605	528	323	223	189	203	173	166
Depr.	218	182	174	158	122	97.8	93.6	85.0	76.6	56.3
Int. Exp.	9.3	8.1	9.3	14.6	14.3	9.0	2.6	8.1	16.9	9.2
Pretax Inc.	460	388	432	357	187	117	96.0	111	86.0	108
Eff. Tax Rate	36%	36%	37%	37%	34%	33%	33%	33%	33%	34%
Net Inc.	294	248	276	227	124	79.2	64.7	75.1	57.8	70.9

Balance Sheet & Other Fin. Data (Million $)

	1997	1996	1995	1994	1993	1992	1991	1990	1989	1988
Cash	283	104	202	102	27.0	26.0	38.0	52.0	33.0	26.0
Curr. Assets	1,126	828	831	639	468	365	334	315	280	248
Total Assets	2,984	2,620	2,296	2,002	1,829	1,490	1,182	1,038	1,034	950
Curr. Liab.	524	466	477	382	350	272	229	226	194	216
LT Debt	168	153	107	173	352	247	73.0	29.0	156	113
Common Eqty.	1,876	1,609	1,382	1,123	902	784	712	653	584	532
Total Cap.	2,321	2,028	1,710	1,535	1,428	1,190	930	813	840	734
Cap. Exp.	307	537	263	185	364	379	218	57.0	130	346
Cash Flow	512	430	449	384	246	177	158	160	134	127
Curr. Ratio	2.1	1.8	1.7	1.7	1.3	1.3	1.5	1.4	1.4	1.1
% LT Debt of Cap.	7.2	7.5	6.3	11.3	24.7	20.7	7.8	3.5	18.6	15.4
% Net Inc.of Revs.	7.0	6.8	8.0	7.6	5.5	4.9	4.4	5.1	4.6	6.7
% Ret. on Assets	10.5	10.1	12.8	11.8	7.4	5.9	5.8	7.2	5.8	8.8
% Ret. on Equity	16.9	16.6	22.0	22.4	14.6	10.6	9.5	12.1	10.3	14.7

Data as orig. reptd.; bef. results of disc. opers. and/or spec. items. Per share data adj. for stk. divs. as of ex-div. date. Bold denotes diluted EPS (FASB 128). E-Estimated. NA-Not Available. NM-Not Meaningful. NR-Not Ranked.

Office—2100 Rexford Rd., Charlotte, NC 28211. **Tel**—(704) 366-7000. **Fax**—(704) 362-4208. **Website**—http://www.nucor.com **Chrmn**—F. K. Iverson. **Vice Chrmn, Pres & CEO**—J. D. Correnti. **Vice Chrmn, CFO, Secy & Treas**—S. Siegel. **Dirs**—H. D. Aycock, J. D. Correnti, J. W. Cunningham, J. D. Hlavacek, F. K. Iverson, S. Siegel. **Transfer Agent & Registrar**—American Stock Transfer & Trust Co., NYC. **Incorporated**—in Delaware in 1958. **Empl**— 6,900. **S&P Analyst:** Leo Larkin

STANDARD &POOR'S
STOCK REPORTS

Occidental Petroleum

1712M

NYSE Symbol **OXY**

In S&P 500

12-SEP-98 **Industry:** Oil (Domestic Integrated)

Summary: This worldwide oil and natural gas and chemicals company recently divested its gas transmission business.

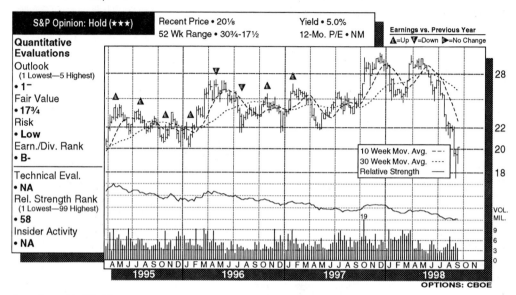

| S&P Opinion: Hold (★★★) | Recent Price • 20⅛ | Yield • 5.0% |
| | 52 Wk Range • 30¾-17½ | 12-Mo. P/E • NM |

Quantitative Evaluations

Outlook (1 Lowest—5 Highest)
• **1⁻**

Fair Value
• **17¾**

Risk
• **Low**

Earn./Div. Rank
• **B-**

Technical Eval.
• **NA**

Rel. Strength Rank (1 Lowest—99 Highest)
• **58**

Insider Activity
• **NA**

Earnings vs. Previous Year
▲=Up ▼=Down ▶=No Change

10 Week Mov. Avg. — — —
30 Week Mov. Avg. ....
Relative Strength ——

OPTIONS: CBOE

Overview - 22-JUL-98

The company made a series of announcements in early October 1997, including the purchase of the U.S. government's 78% stake in the Elk Hills field in California for $3.65 billion; the planned divestiture of the MidCon natural gas transmission subsidiary; a stock buyback program covering up to 40 million common shares; and amended employment agreements with certain top executives, which resulted in an after-tax charge of $0.16 per share in the third quarter of 1997. The divestiture of MidCon was an anticipated move, as OXY had been concerned with the unit's low-margin business environment. In early 1998, OXY sold MidCon to KN Energy for $3.49 billion. Results from MidCon were classified as discontinued operations for 1997's fourth quarter and full year. The Elk Hills purchase will add about one billion barrels equivalent of oil and gas to Occidental's reserve base, while minimizing the company's exposure to politically sensitive regions, such as Colombia. Earnings of $0.88 per share in the first half of 1998 include non-recurring gains of $0.49 resulting from asset sales.

Valuation - 22-JUL-98

OXY's shares have fallen 15% in 1998, reflecting slumping worldwide oil prices, and deteriorating chemicals industry fundamentals. We view OXY's strategic moves as positive; they should bolster production volumes, and are expected to result in higher margins. Chemicals earnings will benefit from lower feedstock costs, but will be hindered by a continued weak pricing environment, due to weak export demand. The company's restructuring, which makes OXY more of a play on oil and gas fundamentals, should boost the shares over the long term, but sluggish oil prices and the weak outlook for chemicals limit their upside now.

Key Stock Statistics

S&P EPS Est. 1998	1.90	Tang. Bk. Value/Share	9.75
P/E on S&P Est. 1998	10.6	Beta	0.98
S&P EPS Est. 1999	2.05	Shareholders	107,800
Dividend Rate/Share	1.00	Market cap. (B)	$ 7.1
Shs. outstg. (M)	353.0	Inst. holdings	66%
Avg. daily vol. (M)	0.846		

Value of $10,000 invested 5 years ago: $ 15,669

Fiscal Year Ending Dec. 31

	1998	1997	1996	1995	1994	1993
Revenues (Million $)						
1Q	1,700	—	2,522	2,714	2,106	2,169
2Q	1,543	—	2,457	2,679	2,162	2,011
3Q	—	—	2,786	2,557	2,404	1,916
4Q	—	1,934	2,792	2,473	2,564	2,020
Yr.	—	8,016	10,557	10,423	9,236	8,116
Earnings Per Share ($)						
1Q	0.38	—	0.44	0.49	-0.19	0.26
2Q	0.49	—	0.49	0.51	-0.12	0.21
3Q	—	—	0.53	0.36	0.01	-0.36
4Q	—	-0.58	0.41	-0.05	-0.06	0.02
Yr.	E1.90	0.39	1.29	1.31	-0.36	0.12

Next earnings report expected: mid October

Dividend Data (Dividends have been paid since 1975.)

Amount ($)	Date Decl.	Ex-Div. Date	Stock of Record	Payment Date
0.250	Nov. 13	Dec. 08	Dec. 10	Jan. 15 '98
0.250	Feb. 12	Mar. 06	Mar. 10	Apr. 15 '98
0.250	May. 01	Jun. 08	Jun. 10	Jul. 15 '98
0.250	Jul. 09	Sep. 08	Sep. 10	Oct. 15 '98

A Division of The **McGraw·Hill** Companies

Business Summary - 22-JUL-98

Brought back from the brink of bankruptcy by Dr. Armand Hammer, the man who would go on to dominate the company for more than 30 years until his death in 1990, Occidental Petroleum (OXY) has grown into a worldwide oil and natural gas exploration and production company with major chemical holdings. After buying OXY in 1957, the shrewd Dr. Hammer obtained oil and gas concessions in Libya in the mid-1960s. When the company found large reserves of oil on its Libyan properties, it emerged as a major factor in the oil industry. Today, OXY has oil and gas production in 10 countries and exploration projects in 21 countries.

In late 1997, OXY took several major steps to restructure the company along two major business units, oil and gas exploration and production, and chemicals. In October 1997, the company announced plans to purchase the U.S. government's 78% interest in the Elk Hills field in California for $3.65 billion. In December 1997, OXY agreed to sell its MidCon natural gas transmission and marketing unit to KN Energy for $3.49 billion in cash and the assumption of approximately $500 million in MidCon liabilities. Both deals

were completed during the first quarter of 1998. In addition, OXY began selling some non-core assets.

Production averaged 276,000 barrels of crude oil daily (bbl./d) in 1997, down from 286,000 bbl./d in 1996, and 706 million cubic feet of natural gas per day (MMcf/d) in 1997, versus 716 MMcf/d in 1996. Natural gas transportation volumes were down 10%, to 1,397 billion cubic feet (Bcf). Proved reserves at 1997 year end were 900 million bbl. of oil (897 million bbl. at year end 1996) and 2,458 Bcf of gas (2,584 Bcf). Increases in crude oil production should result from higher output from Qatar and the recently acquired Elk Hills field.

The company conducts chemical operations through OxyChem, which makes basic chemicals, petrochemicals, polymers and plastics. OxyChem operates 43 chemical product manufacturing facilities worldwide, with the most significant international concentration in Brazil. OxyChem is involved in the manufacture of basic chemicals, petrochemicals, polymers and plastics, and specialty chemicals. The company was the largest marketer of chlor-alkali chemicals in the U.S. in 1997, and is now the third largest producer of polyvinyl chloride (PVC) resins after completing an expansion project in 1997.

Per Share Data ($)

(Year Ended Dec. 31)	1997	1996	1995	1994	1993	1992	1991	1990	1989	1988
Tangible Bk. Val.	8.46	11.57	10.37	9.88	11.07	11.33	14.33	13.73	21.67	23.07
Cash Flow	2.78	5.00	4.21	2.48	2.99	3.24	3.95	-2.37	4.59	5.16
Earnings	0.39	1.86	1.31	-0.36	0.12	0.41	1.25	-5.80	0.92	1.26
Dividends	1.00	1.00	1.00	1.00	1.00	1.00	1.00	2.50	2.50	2.50
Payout Ratio	NM	54%	76%	NM	833%	244%	81%	NM	271%	219%
Prices - High	30³/₄	27¹/₄	24³/₈	22³/₈	23¹/₂	23¹/₈	25³/₈	30¹/₄	31	29
- Low	21³/₄	20¹/₈	18	15¹/₈	16⁷/₈	15³/₄	16¹/₂	17³/₄	25¹/₈	23¹/₂
P/E Ratio - High	79	15	19	NM	NM	56	20	NM	34	23
- Low	56	11	14	NM	NM	38	13	NM	27	19

Income Statement Analysis (Million $)

	1997	1996	1995	1994	1993	1992	1991	1990	1989	1988
Revs.	8,016	10,557	10,423	9,236	8,116	8,494	10,096	21,694	20,068	19,417
Oper. Inc.	1,835	2,316	2,143	1,539	1,266	1,180	1,668	2,172	2,123	1,990
Depr.	822	921	922	882	878	856	806	1,003	988	949
Int. Exp.	434	484	579	589	591	659	902	1,004	1,004	958
Pretax Inc.	528	1,152	913	109	218	325	986	-1,593	501	617
Eff. Tax Rate	59%	39%	44%	131%	66%	60%	61%	NM	44%	42%
Net Inc.	217	698	511	-36.0	74.0	126	379	-1,687	256	313

Balance Sheet & Other Fin. Data (Million $)

	1997	1996	1995	1994	1993	1992	1991	1990	1989	1988
Cash	113	279	520	129	157	90.0	276	364	303	567
Curr. Assets	1,916	2,190	2,519	2,258	1,934	2,245	2,968	4,451	3,974	3,953
Total Assets	15,282	17,634	17,815	17,989	17,123	17,877	16,115	19,743	20,741	20,747
Curr. Liab.	1,870	2,470	2,657	2,201	2,048	2,290	2,778	4,314	3,605	3,568
LT Debt	4,925	4,511	4,819	6,114	6,047	5,806	5,925	7,992	8,217	7,688
Common Eqty.	2,304	3,809	3,305	3,132	3,383	3,440	4,300	4,069	5,856	6,181
Total Cap.	10,239	12,211	12,069	13,142	12,406	11,287	10,527	13,022	15,205	14,834
Cap. Exp.	1,549	1,185	979	1,103	1,007	765	954	1,336	1,272	1,073
Cash Flow	951	1,619	1,340	770	913	979	1,178	-691	1,237	1,255
Curr. Ratio	1.0	0.9	0.9	1.0	0.9	1.0	1.1	1.0	1.1	1.1
% LT Debt of Cap.	48.1	36.9	40.0	46.5	48.7	51.4	56.3	61.4	54.0	51.8
% Net Inc.of Revs.	2.7	6.6	4.9	NM	0.9	1.5	3.8	NM	1.3	1.6
% Ret. on Assets	1.3	3.9	2.9	NM	0.4	0.7	2.1	NM	1.2	1.5
% Ret. on Equity	6.2	17.0	9.2	NM	1.0	3.2	8.8	NM	4.1	4.9

Data as orig. reptd.; bef. results of disc. opers. and/or spec. items. Per share data adj. for stk. divs. as of ex-div. date. Bold denotes diluted EPS (FASB 128). E-Estimated. NA-Not Available. NM-Not Meaningful. NR-Not Ranked.

Office—10889 Wilshire Blvd., Los Angeles, CA 90024. **Tel**—(310) 208-8800. **Website**—http://www.oxy.com **Chrmn & Pres**—R. R. Irani. **Pres & COO**—D. R. Laurance. **Exec VP & CFO**—A. R. Leach. **VP & Treas**—D. C. Yen.**VP & Investor Contact**—Kenneth J. Huffman (212-603-8183). **Dirs**—J. S. Chalsty, E. P. Djerejian, A. Gore Sr., A. Groman, J. R. Hirl, R. R. Irani, J. W. Kluge, D. R. Laurance, I. W. Maloney, G. O. Nolley, R. Segovia, A. D. Syriani, R. Tomich. **Transfer Agents & Registrars**—ChaseMellon Shareholder Services, Los Angeles, CA, and Ridgefield Park, NJ; Montreal Trust Co. **Incorporated**—in California in 1920; reincorporated in Delaware in 1986. **Empl**— 19,860. **S&P Analyst:** Norman Rosenberg

STANDARD &POOR'S
STOCK REPORTS

Omnicom Group

1717C

NYSE Symbol **OMC**

In S&P 500

12-SEP-98

Industry: Services (Advertising & Marketing)

Summary: Omnicom owns DDB Needham Worldwide, BBDO Worldwide and TBWA, three leading full-service global advertising agency networks; it also heads a diversified agency services group.

S&P Opinion: Accumulate (★★★★)	Recent Price • 48⅛	Yield • 1.0%
	52 Wk Range • 58⅜-32¾	12-Mo. P/E • 31.7

Quantitative Evaluations

Outlook
(1 Lowest—5 Highest)
• **3**⁻

Fair Value
• **48⅞**

Risk
• **Low**

Earn./Div. Rank
• **A+**

Technical Eval.
• **Bullish** since 8/96

Rel. Strength Rank
(1 Lowest—99 Highest)
• **74**

Insider Activity
• **Neutral**

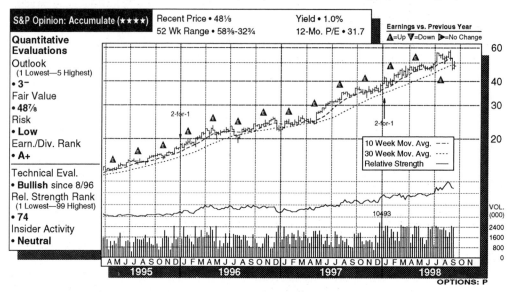

Earnings vs. Previous Year
▲=Up ▼=Down ▶=No Change

10 Week Mov. Avg. – – –
30 Week Mov. Avg. ‥‥‥
Relative Strength ——

OPTIONS: P

Overview - 23-JUN-98

Omnicom's should be able to achieve its recently stated objective, which is to grow by 15% to 20% each year on average through the year 2000. By the end of he year 2000, it expects 65% of its business to be international and 35% from the U.S. Revenues are benefiting from net new business gains in excess of $1 billion each year. Growth in marketing spending by traditional customers is also instrumental. A strong U.S. advertising market and healthy gains in Latin America and other areas are contributing factors. Economic upheavals in certain Pacific Rim and Asian nations may temper advertising gains there temporarily, but the company expects much of its expansion to occur in Asia. There should continue to be modest improvement in margins. For the longer term, Omnicom should continue to grow faster than the underlying rate of growth in advertising demand worldwide.

Valuation - 23-JUN-98

The shares, near their 52-week high, have outperformed the market in 1998, having climbed 26% through mid-June. The strong performance of the shares reflects healthy double-digit growth in revenues and earnings, and a positive outlook for the longer term. Operating results are benefiting from a healthy advertising market worldwide, and from the positive impact of acquisitions, entry into new markets, and currency translation gains. All categories of advertising look healthy in coming periods. OMC should be able to maintain earnings gains of 18% to 22% over the next several years. Favorable earnings news in the periods ahead, combined with regular dividend increases, should keep OMC ahead of the market. We are anticipating a reasonable P/E valuation, in the low to mid 20X range, over the next year or so.

Key Stock Statistics

S&P EPS Est. 1998	1.64	Tang. Bk. Value/Share	NM
P/E on S&P Est. 1998	29.4	Beta	0.91
S&P EPS Est. 1999	1.95	Shareholders	3,700
Dividend Rate/Share	0.50	Market cap. (B)	$ 8.2
Shs. outstg. (M)	169.7	Inst. holdings	76%
Avg. daily vol. (M)	0.483		

Value of $10,000 invested 5 years ago: $ 51,868

Fiscal Year Ending Dec. 31

	1998	1997	1996	1995	1994	1993
Revenues (Million $)						
1Q	861.0	696.6	591.6	499.1	376.5	339.0
2Q	1,052	786.3	666.5	570.3	425.2	382.0
3Q	—	746.8	631.8	537.7	422.3	339.5
4Q	—	895.1	751.8	650.5	532.2	456.1
Yr.	—	3,125	2,642	2,258	1,756	1,516
Earnings Per Share ($)						
1Q	**0.31**	**0.25**	0.20	0.17	0.14	0.13
2Q	**0.50**	**0.40**	0.35	0.29	0.26	0.23
3Q	**E0.31**	**0.26**	0.21	0.16	0.13	0.11
4Q	**E0.55**	**0.45**	0.38	0.32	0.26	0.24
Yr.	**E1.64**	**1.37**	1.14	0.94	0.79	0.70

Next earnings report expected: late October

Dividend Data (Dividends have been paid since 1986.)

Amount ($)	Date Decl.	Ex-Div. Date	Stock of Record	Payment Date
0.250	Dec. 01	Dec. 12	Dec. 16	Jan. 05 '98
2-for-1	Oct. 24	Dec. 30	Dec. 16	Dec. 29 '97
0.125	Feb. 02	Mar. 11	Mar. 13	Apr. 02 '98
0.125	May. 18	Jun. 10	Jun. 12	Jul. 02 '98

A Division of The McGraw-Hill Companies

Business Summary - 23-JUN-98

This global advertising and marketing services company consistently ranks near the top of its industry in the number of awards for creative excellence, such as the Clio Awards in the U.S. and Lions in Europe, and Agency of the Year awards in individual countries. For example, Omnicom agencies won 75 Lion awards at the 1997 Cannes International Advertising Festival, which was 35% of the Lions awarded at the festival, more than any other advertising group. OMC's strong reputation gives it a competitive edge in winning new assignments. Thus, in each of the five years through 1997, the company has gained net new business of $1.8 billion, providing a growth rate superior to the industry's pace, and providing for a rapid expansion in market share worldwide. At year-end 1997, OMC ranked first in worldwide gross income, up from third place in 1995, and fourth place in 1990.

Omnicom operates as three independent agency networks--the BBDO Worldwide Network, the DDB Needham Worldwide Network, and the TBWA International Network. In addition, OMC's Diversified Agency Services group includes 14 marketing services and specialized advertising agency groups with 410 offices in 55 countries. OMC's growth pace has been augmented significantly by acquisitions, including Fleishman-Hilliard in January 1998, the fifth largest public relations agency in the world, which boosted OMC to largest worldwide. In March 1998, OMC acquired GGT Group, which added particular strength to the company's position in France, the U.K. and the U.S. Other major acquisitions in recent years included TBWA International (1993), Griffin Bacal (1994), Chiat/Day (1995), Ketchum Communications Holdings and Creative Media (1996). In 1997, OMC's 10 largest clients accounted for about 20% of commissions and fees, and the company's largest client represented less than 6%. Advertising revenues represented 56% of worldwide revenues in 1997, while revenues from specialty advertising and marketing services companies accounted for the remaining 44%, up from 40% in 1996. Each of the agency networks has its own clients, and they compete with each other in the same markets.

Operations cover the major regions of North America, the U.K., Europe, the Middle East, Africa, Latin America, the Far East and Australia. Offices of subsidiaries and affiliates are located in 85 countries. In 1997, 50% of the company's commissions and fees and 46% of operating profit came from international operations.

Worldwide commission and fee income advanced 18% in 1997, to $3.125 billion. Domestic income advanced 17%, to $1.617 billion, and international revenues increased 20%, to $1.508 billion. Net new business in 1997 totaled a record $1.800 billion. Net income climbed 26%, to $222.4 million from $176.3 million.

Per Share Data ($)

(Year Ended Dec. 31)	1997	1996	1995	1994	1993	1992	1991	1990	1989	1988
Tangible Bk. Val.	NA	NM	-1.89	-1.51	-1.52	-1.49	-0.71	-1.51	-1.32	0.66
Cash Flow	1.92	1.70	1.43	1.24	1.14	1.02	0.94	0.95	0.80	0.69
Earnings	1.37	1.15	0.94	0.79	0.70	0.58	0.52	0.50	0.45	0.40
Dividends	0.45	0.38	0.33	0.31	0.31	0.30	0.28	0.27	0.24	0.24
Payout Ratio	33%	33%	35%	39%	44%	52%	55%	55%	55%	62%
Prices - High	42$^3/_8$	26$^1/_8$	18$^3/_4$	13$^1/_2$	11$^7/_8$	10$^1/_2$	8$^1/_2$	6$^7/_8$	6$^1/_2$	5$^1/_2$
- Low	22$^1/_4$	17$^3/_4$	12$^1/_2$	11	9$^1/_4$	7$^7/_8$	5$^1/_4$	4	4$^7/_8$	4$^3/_8$
P/E Ratio - High	31	23	20	17	17	18	16	14	14	14
- Low	16	16	13	14	13	14	10	8	11	11

Income Statement Analysis (Million $)

	1997	1996	1995	1994	1993	1992	1991	1990	1989	1988
Revs.	3,125	2,642	2,258	1,756	1,516	1,385	1,236	1,178	1,007	881
Oper. Inc.	506	412	343	267	223	203	181	173	138	113
Depr.	103	85.8	72.0	62.8	53.5	49.8	46.2	46.4	35.7	28.6
Int. Exp.	43.1	34.1	43.3	34.8	41.2	40.9	41.4	40.1	24.2	15.0
Pretax Inc.	411	326	243	200	156	132	121	112	99	84.0
Eff. Tax Rate	38%	38%	40%	37%	38%	40%	41%	41%	41%	42%
Net Inc.	222	176	140	108	85.3	65.5	57.1	52.0	46.8	39.2

Balance Sheet & Other Fin. Data (Million $)

	1997	1996	1995	1994	1993	1992	1991	1990	1989	1988
Cash	556	523	335	257	213	131	157	123	126	149
Curr. Assets	2,988	2,425	2,106	1,602	1,274	1,137	1,111	1,027	937	820
Total Assets	4,966	4,056	3,528	2,852	2,290	1,952	1,886	1,749	1,548	1,135
Curr. Liab.	3,579	2,863	2,502	1,987	1,524	1,311	1,197	1,106	981	761
LT Debt	342	205	290	187	278	235	245	279	267	115
Common Eqty.	981	801	552	541	402	309	366	298	238	205
Total Cap.	1,273	1,068	903	770	709	589	657	617	543	354
Cap. Exp.	76.1	48.8	49.6	38.5	33.6	34.9	32.1	32.7	33.4	28.4
Cash Flow	325	262	212	171	139	115	103	98.0	82.0	68.0
Curr. Ratio	0.8	0.8	0.8	0.8	0.8	0.9	0.9	0.9	0.9	1.1
% LT Debt of Cap.	68.1	19.2	32.2	24.3	39.3	39.9	37.3	45.2	49.2	32.4
% Net Inc.of Revs.	7.1	6.7	6.2	6.2	5.6	4.7	4.6	4.4	4.6	4.4
% Ret. on Assets	4.9	4.7	4.3	4.0	3.7	3.4	3.0	3.1	3.4	3.6
% Ret. on Equity	23.3	26.1	27.5	22.1	32.4	19.4	16.6	19.3	20.5	19.3

Data as orig. reptd.; bef. results of disc. opers. and/or spec. items. Per share data adj. for stk. divs. as of ex-div. date. Bold denotes diluted EPS (FASB 128). E-Estimated. NA-Not Available. NM-Not Meaningful. NR-Not Ranked.

Office—437 Madison Ave., New York, NY 10022. **Tel**—(212) 415-3600. **Chrmn**—B. Crawford. **Pres & CEO**—J. D. Wren. **VP & CFO**—F. J. Meyer. **Secy**—B. J. Wagner. **Investor Contact**—Louis Tripodi. **Dirs**—B. Brochand, R. J. Callander, J. A. Cannon, L. S. Coleman Jr., B. Crawford, S. S. Denison, J. R. Murphy, J. R. Purcell, K. L. Reinhard, A. Rosenshine, G. L. Roubos, Q. I. Smith Jr., W. G. Tragos, J. D. Wren, E. P. S. Zehnder. **Transfer Agent & Registrar**—ChaseMellon Shareholder Services, NYC. **Incorporated**—in New York in 1986. **Empl**—27,200. **S&P Analyst**: William H. Donald

STANDARD &POOR'S
STOCK REPORTS

ONEOK Inc.

1717R

NYSE Symbol **OKE**

In S&P 500

12-SEP-98

Industry:
Natural Gas

Summary: OKE operates natural gas utilities in Oklahoma and Kansas, as well as nonutility energy-related activities, including oil and gas exploration and natural gas liquids extraction.

S&P Opinion: Hold (★★★)	Recent Price • 34 Yield • 3.5% 52 Wk Range • 44¼-29¾ 12-Mo. P/E • 14.2

Quantitative Evaluations

Outlook
(1 Lowest—5 Highest)
• **2⁻**

Fair Value
• **32½**

Risk
• **Low**

Earn./Div. Rank
• **B+**

Technical Eval.
• **Bearish** since 6/98

Rel. Strength Rank
(1 Lowest—99 Highest)
• **84**

Insider Activity
• **Neutral**

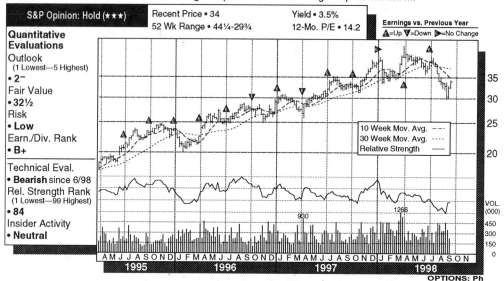

Earnings vs. Previous Year
△=Up ▽=Down ▷=No Change

10 Week Mov. Avg. – – –
30 Week Mov. Avg. ·····
Relative Strength —

VOL. (000)

OPTIONS: Ph

Overview - 22-JUN-98

ONEOK is expected to see mid-single-digit EPS growth in FY 99 (Aug.), aided by increased contributions from its non-regulated businesses and improved operating efficiencies. With the natural gas and oil reserves acquired from Oxy USA in May 1998, OKE has now doubled its reserve base. Following the November 1997 acquisition of the natural gas assets of Western Resources (WR), OKE has expanded its customer base by nearly 90% and increased its expected consolidated revenues by about 50%. The alliance involved the issuance of 3 million new OKE common shares (resulting in an 11% increase in shares outstanding), and 19.3 million shares of preferred stock with a dividend of 1.5X that of the common (or a minimum of $1.80 a share). It is expected that upon the eventual repeal of the Public Utility Holding Company Act (PUHCA), the preferred shares will be converted (share for share) into common shares. We expect the acquisition to be accretive to earnings by the first quarter of FY 99 (Aug.).

Valuation - 22-JUN-98

We would continue to hold OKE stock. The shares are down about 8.5% year to date, hurt by the overall weakness in natural gas prices. In calendar 1997, the stock gained more than 34% (outperforming both the 18.6% increase for the S&P Index of Natural Gas Companies and the 31% rise in the S&P 500). This followed a 31% gain in calendar 1996 (26%, 20%). Over the next few years, we expect OKE's nonregulated businesses to make increasing contributions to earnings. However, we do not expect a significant increase in the dividend (currently yielding around 3%), which has not been raised since a 3.4% increase in the May 1996 payment. With the stock trading at about 16X our FY 99 EPS estimate of $2.35, the shares appear fairly valued for the near term.

Key Stock Statistics

S&P EPS Est. 1998	2.25	Tang. Bk. Value/Share	17.04
P/E on S&P Est. 1998	15.1	Beta	0.77
S&P EPS Est. 1999	2.35	Shareholders	13,200
Dividend Rate/Share	1.20	Market cap. (B)	$ 1.1
Shs. outstg. (M)	31.5	Inst. holdings	41%
Avg. daily vol. (M)	0.073		

Value of $10,000 invested 5 years ago: $ 24,168

Fiscal Year Ending Aug. 31

	1998	1997	1996	1995	1994	1993
Revenues (Million $)						
1Q	314.2	248.8	238.5	166.3	177.2	159.4
2Q	722.0	473.6	464.7	287.4	295.4	314.0
3Q	444.1	231.6	289.7	304.5	190.5	188.0
4Q	—	207.9	231.5	191.8	129.3	128.2
Yr.	—	1,162	1,224	949.9	792.4	789.1
Earnings Per Share ($)						
1Q	0.44	0.44	0.31	0.29	0.29	0.22
2Q	**1.43**	1.39	1.42	1.05	0.98	1.17
3Q	**0.52**	0.49	0.42	0.33	0.21	0.10
4Q	E-0.14	-0.19	-0.22	-0.09	-0.14	-0.06
Yr.	E2.25	2.13	1.93	1.58	1.34	1.43

Next earnings report expected: late September

Dividend Data (Dividends have been paid since 1939.)

Amount ($)	Date Decl.	Ex-Div. Date	Stock of Record	Payment Date
0.300	Oct. 16	Oct. 29	Oct. 31	Nov. 14 '97
0.300	Jan. 15	Jan. 28	Jan. 30	Feb. 13 '98
0.300	Mar. 20	Apr. 28	Apr. 30	May. 15 '98
0.300	Jun. 18	Jul. 29	Jul. 31	Aug. 14 '98

A Division of The McGraw-Hill Companies

Business Summary - 22-JUN-98

With the November 1997 acquisition of the natural gas assets of NYSE-listed Western Resources (WR), ONEOK has become (in terms of customers) the eighth largest gas distribution company in the U.S.

The $660 million alliance with Western Resources (which now has a 45% interest in ONEOK) was realized through the exchange of 3 million common shares and 19.3 million shares of convertible preferred stock. The strategic transaction includes distribution properties serving 660,000 customers; a transmission and gathering system with 976 miles of pipeline; and a 42% interest in a New Mexico plant with a capacity of 200 million cubic feet per day.

In addition to gas utility operations in Oklahoma and Kansas, OKE is engaged in nonutility energy-related, marketing, processing and production activities. Segment contributions (profits in millions) in FY 97 (Aug.):

	Oper. Revs.	Oper. Profits
Distribution & transmission	51.5%	$100.4
Marketing	39.6%	7.8
Processing	6.2%	12.9
Production	2.3%	8.7
Other	0.4%	-1.0

ONEOK's regulated operations in Oklahoma are con-ducted through its Oklahoma Natural Gas Company division, an integrated transmission and distribution business. Following the alliance with WR, OKE's regulated operations in Kansas are conducted through its Kansas Gas Service Company division (which also has distribution operations in Oklahoma) and its Mid Continent Market Center, an affiliated transmission company.

ONEOK's marketing operation purchases and markets natural gas, primarily in the mid-continent area of the U.S. Formed in 1992, marketing did not have significant operations until 1995. OKE's strategy is to capitalize on day to day pricing volatility though the use of gas storage facilities, hedging and transportation arbitraging.

In February 1997, OKE acquired PSEC, Inc., an Oklahoma-based producer of oil and gas, and PSPC, Ltd., the managing general partner of an Oklahoma gas gathering system, for $25 million in cash and stock.

As of August 31, 1997, OKE had an interest in 923 gas wells and 233 oil wells, mainly in Oklahoma and Louisiana. In May 1998, ONEOK completed its acquisition (from Oxy USA) of additional natural gas and oil reserves in Oklahoma and Kansas for $135 million. The transaction included more than 400 wells with net production per day of 30 billion cubic feet of gas and 400,000 barrels of oil. Earlier, it sold its 50%-interest in 11 gas processing plants located in Western Oklahoma due to the lack of ownership in the gathering systems upstream of the plants.

Per Share Data ($)

(Year Ended Aug. 31)	1997	1996	1995	1994	1993	1992	1991	1990	1989	1988
Tangible Bk. Val.	16.48	15.19	14.38	13.88	13.63	13.28	13.03	12.51	12.11	11.34
Earnings	2.13	1.93	1.58	1.34	1.43	1.21	1.33	1.21	1.29	0.24
Dividends	1.20	1.18	1.12	1.11	1.06	0.96	0.82	0.74	0.47	0.64
Payout Ratio	56%	61%	71%	83%	74%	79%	62%	62%	37%	267%
Prices - High	40¾	30⅜	24¾	20⅜	26¼	19	16⅞	16½	17	10
- Low	25⅞	20	17⅛	15¾	17⅝	14	12½	11⅞	9¼	4⅞
P/E Ratio - High	19	16	16	15	18	16	13	14	13	41
- Low	12	10	11	12	12	12	9	10	7	20

Income Statement Analysis (Million $)

	1997	1996	1995	1994	1993	1992	1991	1990	1989	1988
Revs.	1,162	1,224	950	792	789	677	689	668	618	571
Depr.	75.0	72.9	50.4	50.8	48.0	46.8	38.2	34.3	31.2	79.5
Maint.	NA	NA	NA	6.5	7.0	6.6	6.4	6.2	6.7	7.7
Fxd. Chgs. Cov.	3.6	3.4	2.8	2.6	2.6	2.5	3.1	3.1	3.4	1.3
Constr. Credits	0.6	0.3	0.4	0.6	0.5	0.5	0.4	0.3	0.2	0.3
Eff. Tax Rate	37%	39%	37%	37%	35%	37%	38%	38%	39%	33%
Net Inc.	59.3	52.8	42.8	36.2	38.4	32.6	35.9	33.0	36.6	7.1

Balance Sheet & Other Fin. Data (Million $)

	1997	1996	1995	1994	1993	1992	1991	1990	1989	1988
Gross Prop.	1,429	1,337	1,276	1,218	1,196	1,124	1,047	952	897	1,046
Cap. Exp.	586	542	81.0	74.0	86.0	70.0	111	69.0	43.0	32.0
Net Prop.	843	795	766	737	752	684	663	591	561	616
Capitalization:										
LT Debt	328	337	351	363	376	381	283	216	144	232
% LT Debt	42	44	47	49	50	51	44	39	30	42
Pfd.	Nil	9.0	9.0	9.0	9.0	9.0	9.0	9.0	9.0	9.0
% Pfd.	Nil	1.20	1.20	1.20	1.20	1.20	1.40	1.60	1.90	1.60
Common	463	415	389	370	363	354	347	333	334	318
% Common	59	55	52	50	49	48	54	60	69	57
Total Cap.	975	761	938	940	944	926	821	731	651	713
% Oper. Ratio	92.0	92.8	91.6	91.0	90.4	90.4	90.9	91.4	90.1	92.4
% Earn. on Net Prop.	11.5	11.3	10.7	9.7	10.8	9.6	10.0	10.0	10.4	6.8
% Return On Revs.	5.1	4.3	4.5	4.6	4.9	4.8	5.2	4.9	5.9	1.2
% Return On Invest. Capital	13.4	16.0	8.6	7.5	8.1	7.4	8.0	8.3	9.0	5.8
% Return On Com. Equity	13.4	12.6	11.2	9.7	10.6	9.2	10.4	9.8	11.1	2.1

Data as orig. reptd.; bef. results of disc opers. and/or spec. items. Per share data adj. for stk. divs. as of ex-div. date. Bold denotes diluted EPS (FASB 128). E-Estimated. NA-Not Available. NM-Not Meaningful. NR-Not Ranked.

Office—100 W. Fifth St., Tulsa, OK 74103. **Tel**—(918) 588-7000. **Website**—http://www.ONEOK.com **Chrmn & CEO**—L. W. Brummett. **Pres & COO**—D. L. Kyle. **VP, CFO & Treas**—J. D. Neal. **Secy**—D. Barnes. **VP-Investor Communications**—Weldon L. Watson. **Dirs**—E. G. Anderson, W. M. Bell, L. W. Brummett, D. R. Cummings, W. L. Ford, H. R. Fricke, J. M. Graves, S. J. Jatras, S. L. Kitchen, D. L. Kyle, B. H. Mackie, D. A. Newsom, G. D. Parker, J. D. Scott, S. L. Young. **Transfer Agent & Registrar**—Bank One Trust Co., Oklahoma City. **Incorporated**—in Delaware in 1933. **Empl**—3,300. **S&P Analyst:** Justin McCann

Oracle Corporation

4876G

Nasdaq Symbol **ORCL**

In S&P 500

15-SEP-98

Industry:
Computer (Software & Services)

Summary: Oracle supplies computer software products used for database management, applications development and decision support, as well as end-user and other applications.

S&P Opinion: Hold (★★★)	Recent Price • 25½	Yield • Nil	Earnings vs. Previous Year
	52 Wk Range • 39⅝-17¾	12-Mo. P/E • 25.5	▲=Up ▼=Down ▶=No Change

Quantitative Evaluations

Outlook
(1 Lowest—5 Highest)
• **5**

Fair Value
• **46⅛**

Risk
• **Average**

Earn./Div. Rank
• **B**

Technical Eval.
• **Bearish** since 12/97

Rel. Strength Rank
(1 Lowest—99 Highest)
• **97**

Insider Activity
• **NA**

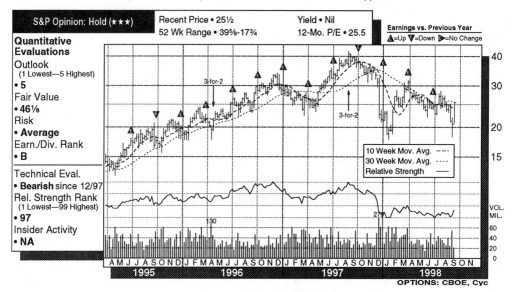

10 Week Mov. Avg. – – –
30 Week Mov. Avg. · · · ·
Relative Strength ——

3-for-2

3-for-2

VOL. MIL.

A M J J A S O N D J F M A M J J A S O N D J F M A M J J A S O N D J F M A M J J A S O N
1995   1996   1997   1998

OPTIONS: CBOE, Cyc

Overview - 15-SEP-98

Revenues grew 26% in FY 98 (May), more slowly than in previous years. Revenues should grow at a similar rate in FY 99, as database sales remain healthy, but unspectacular, after years of robust growth. Asian results have also been a drag on revenue growth. While software licence sales are only growing about 10%, services revenues should continue to be strong. However, sales of enterprise resource planning (ERP) software applications disappointingly have been flat the past two quarters, despite the high growth of competitors' revenues in this market. ORCL is shifting its focus to concentrate more on its applications business. Nevertheless, we still estimate healthy EPS gains in FY 99, to $1.22, from FY 98's $0.96 (excluding a first quarter acquisition-related charge of $0.14).

Valuation - 15-SEP-98

The shares rebounded after reporting better than expected earnings in the first quarter of FY 99, fueled by stronger database sales. However, ORCL remains still far below its year-earlier highs, due to slower overall growth. The database software segment has been slowing, and demand in Asia has declined, which should restrict future growth. We believe that the Year 2000 problem could cause some potential customers to delay both database and application purchases, but this could cause business to accelerate after 2000. ORCL maintains a leadership position in the database industry, but is losing out to more focused competitors in the higher growth applications area. ORCL is attempting to shift its focus to become an applications company. Service revenues continue to grow strongly. In light of increasing competition from Microsoft in the database area, and a difficult transition to an applications focus, we believe that the shares are fairly valued.

Key Stock Statistics

S&P EPS Est. 1999	1.22	Tang. Bk. Value/Share	3.04
P/E on S&P Est. 1999	20.9	Beta	1.09
S&P EPS Est. 2000	1.46	Shareholders	8,400
Dividend Rate/Share	Nil	Market cap. (B)	$ 25.9
Shs. outstg. (M)	973.3	Inst. holdings	41%
Avg. daily vol. (M)	8.165		

Value of $10,000 invested 5 years ago: $ 60,660

Fiscal Year Ending May 31

	1999	1998	1997	1996	1995	1994
Revenues (Million $)						
1Q	1,749	1,369	1,052	771.8	556.5	398.1
2Q	—	1,614	1,311	967.2	670.3	452.2
3Q	—	1,749	1,373	1,020	722.3	482.8
4Q	—	2,413	1,948	1,464	1,018	668.1
Yr.	—	7,144	5,684	4,223	2,967	2,001
Earnings Per Share ($)						
1Q	**0.20**	0.01	0.11	0.05	0.06	0.04
2Q	**E0.24**	0.19	0.18	0.13	0.09	0.06
3Q	**E0.27**	0.22	0.16	0.15	0.11	0.07
4Q	**E0.50**	0.41	0.36	0.27	0.18	0.12
Yr.	**E1.22**	0.81	0.81	0.60	0.45	0.28

Next earnings report expected: early December

Dividend Data

No cash has been paid. Three-for-two stock splits were effected in 1995, 1996 and 1997.

A Division of The McGraw-Hill Companies

STANDARD
&POOR'S
STOCK REPORTS

Oracle Corporation

4876G
15-SEP-98

Business Summary - 15-SEP-98

Oracle Corporation is the world's largest supplier of database software for information management. The company's principal product, Oracle8, is a multimedia, object-relational database management system (DBMS).

Oracle's products can be divided into three categories: server technologies, application development and business intelligence tools, and business applications.

Server technologies include database servers and networking products. Database management systems permit multiple users and applications to access data concurrently while protecting the data against user and program errors and against computer and network failures. DBMS are used to support the data access and data management requirements of transaction processing and decision support systems. In June 1997, Oracle introduced Oracle8, the latest version of its flagship database program. Oracle8 offered a 10-fold improvement in performance and a 10-fold increase in the number of users from the previous version.

A variety of applications development products, sold as add-ons to the Oracle relational DBMS, increase programmer productivity and allow non-programmers to design, develop and maintain their own programs. Access tools enable end users and decision support analysts to perform rapid querying, reporting and analysis of stored data.

Business applications consist of more than 30 integrated software modules for financial management, supply chain management, manufacturing, project systems, human resources, and sales force automation.

ORCL also offers consulting, education and systems integration services to assist customers in the design and development of applications based on company products.

In FY 97 (May), the company acquired the remaining shares of 13%-owned Datalogix, a vendor of process manufacturing applications, for $81 million in cash.

In September 1997, Oracle recorded a charge of $49.8 million ($0.05 a share) to write off in-process research and development associated with the merger of its Network Computer, Inc. with Netscape's Navio Communications, Inc. Separately, the company acquired Treasury Services Corp., and recorded a related charge of $91.5 million ($0.09).

Per Share Data ($)

(Year Ended May 31)	1998	1997	1996	1995	1994	1993	1992	1991	1990	1989
Tangible Bk. Val.	3.04	2.40	1.90	1.24	0.77	0.55	0.46	0.37	0.44	0.27
Cash Flow	1.14	1.07	0.82	0.59	0.35	0.20	0.12	0.05	0.17	0.11
Earnings	0.81	0.81	0.60	0.44	0.28	0.14	0.06	-0.01	0.13	0.09
Dividends	Nil	Nil	Nil	Nil	Nil	Nil	Nil	Nil	Nil	Nil
Payout Ratio	Nil	Nil	Nil	Nil	Nil	Nil	Nil	Nil	Nil	Nil
Cal. Yrs.	1997	1996	1995	1994	1993	1992	1991	1990	1989	1988
Prices - High	42⅛	34	21⅝	13¾	11⅛	4¼	2⁷/₁₆	4¼	3⅞	1⅝
- Low	20⅞	17½	11⅞	7¾	4	1¾	1³/₁₆	¾	1⅜	¹³/₁₆
P/E Ratio - High	NM	42	36	31	39	30	39	NM	30	18
- Low	NM	22	20	17	14	12	13	NM	11	9

Income Statement Analysis (Million $)

	1998	1997	1996	1995	1994	1993	1992	1991	1990	1989
Revs.	7,144	5,684	4,223	2,967	2,001	1,503	1,178	1,028	971	584
Oper. Inc.	1,740	1,565	1,124	797	485	297	165	81.0	226	143
Depr.	329	265	220	148	65.2	56.2	50.9	54.5	35.9	19.7
Int. Exp.	16.7	6.8	6.6	7.0	6.9	9.0	18.6	24.0	12.1	4.3
Pretax Inc.	1,328	1,284	920	659	423	218	96.0	-13.0	173	120
Eff. Tax Rate	39%	36%	34%	33%	33%	35%	36%	NM	32%	32%
Net Inc.	814	821	603	442	284	142	62.0	-12.0	117	82.0

Balance Sheet & Other Fin. Data (Million $)

	1998	1997	1996	1995	1994	1993	1992	1991	1990	1989
Cash	1,274	890	841	586	465	358	177	101	50.0	49.0
Curr. Assets	4,323	3,271	2,284	1,617	1,076	842	641	586	569	337
Total Assets	5,819	4,624	3,357	2,425	1,595	1,184	956	858	787	460
Curr. Liab.	2,484	1,922	1,455	1,055	682	551	406	479	284	178
LT Debt	304	300	0.9	81.7	82.8	86.4	95.9	18.0	89.1	33.5
Common Eqty.	2,958	2,370	1,870	1,211	741	528	435	345	388	231
Total Cap.	3,278	2,676	1,880	1,321	862	623	541	369	499	276
Cap. Exp.	328	391	308	262	251	41.3	46.6	60.7	89.3	68.4
Cash Flow	1,142	1,086	823	589	349	198	112	42.0	153	101
Curr. Ratio	1.7	1.7	1.6	1.5	1.6	1.5	1.6	1.2	2.0	1.9
% LT Debt of Cap.	9.3	11.2	0.1	6.2	9.6	13.9	17.7	4.9	17.9	12.1
% Net Inc.of Revs.	11.4	14.5	14.3	14.9	14.2	9.4	5.2	NM	12.1	14.0
% Ret. on Assets	15.6	20.6	20.9	22.0	20.4	13.2	6.7	NM	18.6	22.6
% Ret. on Equity	30.5	38.7	39.1	45.2	44.6	29.2	15.6	NM	37.5	43.9

Data as orig. reptd.; bef. results of disc. opers. and/or spec. items. Per share data adj. for stk. divs. as of ex-div. date. Bold denotes diluted EPS (FASB 128). E-Estimated. NA-Not Available. NM-Not Meaningful. NR-Not Ranked.

Office—500 Oracle Parkway, Redwood Shores, CA 94065. **Tel**—(415) 506-7000. **E-mail**—investor@oracle.com **Website**—http://www.oracle.com **Chrmn & CEO**—L. J. Ellison. **Pres & COO**—R. J. Lane. **EVP & CFO**—J. O. Henley. **Investor Contact**—Catherine Buan. **Dirs**—J. Berg, M. J. Boskin, L. J. Ellison, J. O. Henley, J. Kemp, R. J. Lane, D. L. Lucas, R. A. McGinn. **Transfer Agent & Registrar**—Harris Trust & Savings Bank, Chicago. **Reincorporated**—in Delaware in 1987. **Empl**— 29,431. **S&P Analyst:** Brian Goodstadt

Oryx Energy

1721D

NYSE Symbol **ORX**

In S&P 500

12-SEP-98

Industry: Oil & Gas (Exploration & Production)

Summary: Oryx is one of the world's largest independent oil and natural gas producers.

S&P Opinion: Avoid (★★)	Recent Price • 14¼	Yield • Nil
	52 Wk Range • 30⅝-10½	12-Mo. P/E • 14.8

Quantitative Evaluations

Outlook (1 Lowest—5 Highest)
• **1**

Fair Value
• **8¾**

Risk
• **Average**

Earn./Div. Rank
• **B-**

Technical Eval.
• **Bullish** since 1/98

Rel. Strength Rank (1 Lowest—99 Highest)
• **41**

Insider Activity
• **NA**

Earnings vs. Previous Year
▲=Up ▼=Down ▷=No Change

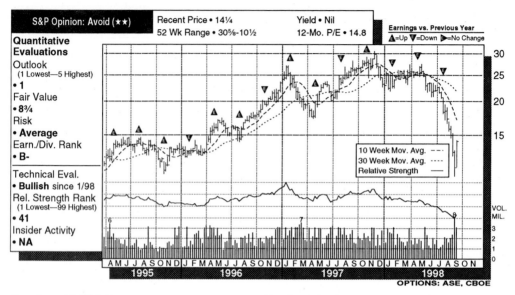

10 Week Mov. Avg. – – –
30 Week Mov. Avg. · · · · ·
Relative Strength ———

OPTIONS: ASE, CBOE

Overview - 06-AUG-98

Income and cash flow declined in the first half of 1998, reflecting lower oil prices and oil and natural gas production. Operating costs rose, but are expected to trend lower over the remainder of the year. Production of both oil and gas should be higher over the second half of 1998. ORX is beginning to see the benefits of focusing on core properties in the Gulf of Mexico, where finding and developing costs are dropping. Production from the Gulf's Baldpate field, in which Oryx has a 50% interest, is expected to begin in August 1998, and the company's share of production will reach 20,000 boe/day by year end, and 33,000 boe/day by the end of 1999's first quarter. The field boasts low per-unit production costs, and is expected to be the largest single contributor to ORX's cash flow in 1999 and beyond, and will thus have the effect of lowering the company's overall per-barrel cash operating costs.

Valuation - 06-AUG-98

Along with those of its independent energy producer peers, ORX's shares have been hurt by lower oil and gas prices, and have fallen about 29% to date in 1998. Natural gas prices have declined recently, but are expected to remain strong. The near-term outlook for oil prices, on the other hand, remains bearish, despite planned cutbacks in OPEC production, as reduced Asian demand has resulted in a worldwide oversupply condition. With oil accounting for over 60% of total estimated 1998 production, Oryx is more leveraged to oil prices than are most of its independent exploration and production company peers. Given the bearish outlook for oil prices, we recommend investors avoid the shares.

Key Stock Statistics

S&P EPS Est. 1998	0.40	Tang. Bk. Value/Share	1.74
P/E on S&P Est. 1998	35.6	Beta	1.29
S&P EPS Est. 1999	1.00	Shareholders	28,900
Dividend Rate/Share	Nil	Market cap. (B)	$ 1.5
Shs. outstg. (M)	106.2	Inst. holdings	74%
Avg. daily vol. (M)	0.835		

Value of $10,000 invested 5 years ago: $ 7,429

Fiscal Year Ending Dec. 31

	1998	1997	1996	1995	1994	1993
Revenues (Million $)						
1Q	223.0	335.0	247.0	293.0	260.0	283.0
2Q	213.0	274.0	253.0	285.0	255.0	278.0
3Q	—	287.0	289.0	345.0	273.0	264.0
4Q	—	301.0	358.0	206.0	284.0	229.0
Yr.	—	1,197	1,147	1,129	1,072	1,054
Earnings Per Share ($)						
1Q	0.02	0.61	0.31	0.13	-0.62	-0.08
2Q	0.15	0.22	0.27	0.25	-0.08	0.03
3Q	—	0.40	0.38	1.04	-0.13	-0.48
4Q	—	0.39	0.60	0.11	0.14	-0.48
Yr.	E0.40	1.62	1.55	1.54	-0.68	-1.01

Next earnings report expected: late October

Dividend Data

Common dividends, initiated in 1988, were omitted in 1994. A poison pill stock purchase rights plan was adopted in 1990.

A Division of The McGraw-Hill Companies

STANDARD
&POOR'S
STOCK REPORTS

Oryx Energy Company

1721D

12-SEP-98

Business Summary - 06-AUG-98

A major turnaround is underway at Oryx Energy Company (ORX), and the two year old program has already yielded significant results. The company, which was spun off by Sun Co. in 1988, explores for, produces and markets crude oil and condensate, natural gas and natural gas liquids, and is the managing general partner of 98%-owned Sun Energy Partners, L.P., which conducts ORX's U.S. exploration and production business. In 1995, the company sold several non-core properties, including U.K. North Sea assets (for proceeds of $390 million); all of its interests in Indonesia and Gabon ($69 million); and certain U.S. producing assets ($77 million), with the proceeds used primarily to reduce debt. With its portfolio of properties now streamlined, Oryx intends to focus its exploration spending on areas of proven success, such as the Gulf of Mexico and the North Sea.

Oryx conducts its exploration and production activities in six countries: the U.S., the U.K., Algeria, Australia, Ecuador and Kazakstan. The Gulf of Mexico remains the primary focus of the company's growth strategy. About 67% of the $520 million in capital spending in 1997 was invested in the U.S., primarily in the Gulf of Mexico, where Oryx owns 148 exploration blocks. The company's Baldpate project in the deepwater Gulf of Mexico area holds particular promise, with production

from the field expected to begin during 1998. Contributions (operating profits in millions) by geographic area in 1997 were:

	Revs.	Profits
U.S.	61%	$270
U.K.	36%	113
Other	3%	5

Net production in 1997 averaged 115,000 bbl. a day of crude oil and condensate (109,000 in 1996) and 502,000 Mcf a day of natural gas (500,000). At December 31, 1997, estimated net proved reserves were 402 million bbl. of oil (365 million) and 1,429 Bcf of natural gas (1,199 Bcf). For the five years from 1993 through 1997, ORX replaced 112% of oil and gas equivalent production with new reserves, at a cost of $4.91 per equivalent bbl.

In 1995, the company emphasized upgrading its asset base, selling assets with low margins and limited growth potential. The company shifted its priorities in 1996 from debt reduction to creation of cash flow and increasing the reserve base. The company replaced 160% of production in 1997. In 1998, production will take center stage, as ORX plans to offset declining output from existing fields with new production from recently developed areas.

Per Share Data ($)

(Year Ended Dec. 31)	1997	1996	1995	1994	1993	1992	1991	1990	1989	1988
Tangible Bk. Val.	1.48	-0.34	NM	NM	6.57	8.05	6.23	7.81	14.17	15.24
Cash Flow	4.57	4.18	4.24	2.10	3.14	5.88	6.70	8.02	4.08	NA
Earnings	1.62	1.55	1.54	-0.68	-1.01	0.74	0.08	2.26	0.51	-2.89
Dividends	Nil	Nil	Nil	Nil	0.40	0.80	1.20	1.20	1.20	0.30
Payout Ratio	Nil	Nil	Nil	Nil	NM	108%	593%	44%	233%	NM
Prices - High	30⅝	25¾	14¾	20	26¼	27¼	40⅝	54⅞	46¼	28
- Low	17¼	12⅜	9⅞	10⅝	16¼	16¾	22	34¾	25½	23⅛
P/E Ratio - High	19	17	10	NM	NM	37	NM	24	91	NM
- Low	11	8	6	NM	NM	23	NM	15	50	NM

Income Statement Analysis (Million $)

	1997	1996	1995	1994	1993	1992	1991	1990	1989	1988
Revs.	1,213	1,168	1,129	1,082	1,080	1,275	1,484	1,940	1,140	1,070
Oper. Inc.	659	655	456	424	438	544	607	952	488	52.0
Depr. Depl. & Amort.	311	276	276	271	403	444	529	581	376	416
Int. Exp.	95.0	110	144	162	163	187	217	241	115	275
Pretax Inc.	240	265	136	-99	-107	-4.0	-52.0	327	81.0	-465
Eff. Tax Rate	28%	36%	NM	NM	NM	NM	NM	31%	33%	NM
Net Inc.	172	163	158	-65.0	-93.0	73.0	19.0	225	54.0	-304

Balance Sheet & Other Fin. Data (Million $)

	1997	1996	1995	1994	1993	1992	1991	1990	1989	1988
Cash	10.0	9.0	20.0	10.0	10.0	10.0	10.0	81.0	16.0	138
Curr. Assets	238	250	181	195	205	275	397	1,184	406	363
Total Assets	2,108	1,935	1,666	2,107	3,624	3,738	4,405	5,252	4,185	4,094
Curr. Liab.	382	385	454	532	324	586	453	1,245	386	321
LT Debt	1,184	1,183	1,051	1,546	1,741	1,489	2,341	2,267	1,509	1,082
Common Eqty.	157	-0.4	-208	-346	676	817	534	622	1,485	1,611
Total Cap.	1,576	1,550	1,049	1,420	3,099	3,012	3,806	3,848	3,610	3,563
Cap. Exp.	523	484	273	281	453	372	527	1,631	428	580
Cash Flow	483	439	434	205	305	508	535	799	430	111
Curr. Ratio	0.6	0.7	0.4	0.4	0.6	0.1	0.9	1.0	1.1	1.1
% LT Debt of Cap.	75.1	76.3	100.2	108.9	56.2	49.4	61.5	58.9	41.8	30.4
% Ret. on Assets	8.5	9.1	8.4	NM	NM	1.6	0.4	5.3	1.3	NM
% Ret. on Equity	286.7	NM	NM	NM	NM	8.7	1.0	24.9	3.5	NM

Data as orig. reptd.; bef. results of disc opers. and/or spec. items. Per share data adj. for stk. divs. as of ex-div. date. Slight variances betw. revs. as stated in qtrly. tble. and Inc. tble. are due to variances in inclusion of excise taxes & other inc. Bold denotes diluted EPS (FASB 128). Estimated. NA-Not Available. NM-Not Meaningful. NR-Not Ranked.

Office—13155 Noel Rd., Dallas, TX 75240-5067. **Tel**—(972) 715-4000. **Website**—http://www.qryx.com **Chrmn & CEO**—R. L. Keiser. **Prés & COO**—J. W. Box. **EVP & CFO**—E. W. Moneypenny. **VP & Secy**—W. C. Lemmer. **Investor Contact**—John O'Keefe. **Dirs**—J. W. Box, W. E. Bradford, S. A. Earle, D. C. Genever-Watling, R. B. Gill, D. S. Hollingsworth, R. L. Keiser, E. W. Moneypenny, C. H. Pistor Jr., P. R. Seegers, I. L. White-Thomson. **Transfer Agent & Registrar**—Chase Bank, NYC. **Incorporated**—in Delaware in 1971. **Empl**—1,046. **S&P Analyst:** Norman Rosenberg

12-SEP-98

Industry: Building Materials

Summary: This leading manufacturer of glass fiber products also makes other construction and industrial products. Foreign operations account for about one-quarter of sales.

S&P Opinion: Accumulate (★★★★)	Recent Price • 34⅝ Yield • 0.9%
	52 Wk Range • 46⅝-27 12-Mo. P/E • 70.8

Quantitative Evaluations

Outlook (1 Lowest—5 Highest)
• **1⁻**

Fair Value
• **18½**

Risk
• **Low**

Earn./Div. Rank
• **B-**

Technical Eval.
• **NA**

Rel. Strength Rank (1 Lowest—99 Highest)
• **56**

Insider Activity
• **NA**

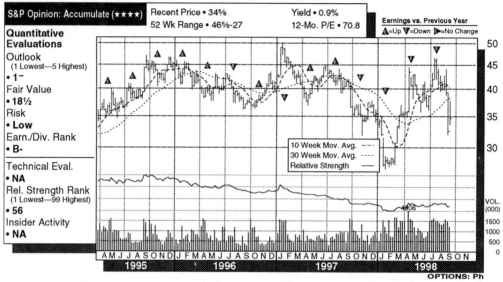

Earnings vs. Previous Year ▲=Up ▼=Down ▶=No Change

10 Week Mov. Avg. – – –
30 Week Mov. Avg. · · · ·
Relative Strength ——

OPTIONS: Ph

Overview - 29-JUL-98

Sales gains should be recorded in both divisions in 1998. Gains in building materials should be driven by the full year inclusion of recent takeovers and a return to more normal weather patterns. We also expect a small upturn in the composite materials sector, where sales volume should stay solid. Competitive pricing pressures in both sectors, which put a severe crimp in operating results in 1997, have started to ease. That factor remained a detriment in early 1998, but pricing comparisons should grow much more favorable as the year goes on. Operating results should also be helped by benefits of an early 1998 restructuring program. The program has been slated to bring $175 million of annual cost savings, with some $100 million likely in 1998. Margins should be additionally aided by the further integration of the building materials acquisitions. On the downside, interest charges should be higher, given borrowings related to acquisitions. Comparisons will be distorted by $2.12 a share of net charges recorded in 1997, with most related to the new restructuring program. Additional restructuring charges in 1998's first quarter were largely offset by credits.

Valuation - 29-JUL-98

OWC's shares had a dismal performance between the start of 1997 and early 1998, with pricing pressures in the company's businesses holding earnings far below plan. The shares have come storming back since March 1998, boosted by two price hikes for insulation and a firming of composites prices. We expect good construction and home improvement markets to allow that recovery to go on. With OWC's restructuring and cost reduction programs also progressing well, we see EPS comparisons growing much more favorable as the year goes on. Given OWC's looming business recovery, the shares should outperform over the next year.

Key Stock Statistics

S&P EPS Est. 1998	3.55	Tang. Bk. Value/Share	NM
P/E on S&P Est. 1998	9.8	Beta	1.20
S&P EPS Est. 1999	4.15	Shareholders	6,800
Dividend Rate/Share	0.30	Market cap. (B)	$ 1.9
Shs. outstg. (M)	54.0	Inst. holdings	90%
Avg. daily vol. (M)	0.334		

Value of $10,000 invested 5 years ago: $ 9,828

Fiscal Year Ending Dec. 31

	1998	1997	1996	1995	1994	1993
Revenues (Million $)						
1Q	1,137	875.0	849.0	844.0	677.0	651.0
2Q	1,286	1,017	956.0	877.0	852.0	754.0
3Q	—	1,238	1,025	927.0	936.0	785.0
4Q	—	1,243	1,002	964.0	886.0	754.0
Yr.	—	4,373	3,832	3,612	3,351	2,944
Earnings Per Share ($)						
1Q	0.16	0.76	0.75	0.71	-1.52	-0.20
2Q	1.02	1.11	-9.19	1.25	1.03	0.76
3Q	E1.25	1.05	1.53	1.35	1.19	1.09
4Q	E1.10	-2.20	1.32	1.27	0.98	0.75
Yr.	E3.55	1.17	-5.50	4.64	1.70	2.40

Next earnings report expected: late October

Dividend Data (Dividends have been paid since 1996.)

Amount ($)	Date Decl.	Ex-Div. Date	Stock of Record	Payment Date
0.075	Dec. 11	Dec. 29	Dec. 31	Jan. 15 '98
0.075	Feb. 12	Mar. 27	Mar. 31	Apr. 15 '98
0.075	Apr. 16	Jun. 26	Jun. 30	Jul. 15 '98
0.075	Jun. 18	Sep. 28	Sep. 30	Oct. 15 '98

STANDARD
&POOR'S
STOCK REPORTS

Owens Corning

1724

12-SEP-98

Business Summary - 29-JUL-98

Owens Corning (formerly Owens-Corning Fiberglas) serves consumers and industrial customers with high-performance glass composites and building materials systems. OWC has concentrated on an aggressive program of niche acquisitions, and in the second half of 1997, made two much larger takeovers in the area of exterior residential housing products (Fibreboard Corp. and AmeriMark Building Products). While OWC markets many of its products under the FIBERGLAS trademark, the company's acquisition program has expanded its product portfolio. No longer based solely on glass fiber technology, OWC's product offerings now include stryenics (extruded and expanded polystyrenes), vinyl windows, vinyl siding and fabricated products for a variety of thermal and acoustical markets.

International operations accounted for 24% of sales and only 2% of profits (before one-time items) in 1997. Europe, Canada, Latin America and Asia/Pacific now account for most of OWC's foreign operations. The company targets a goal of deriving 35% of sales outside the U.S.

The company's building materials segment (74% of sales and 54% of profits in 1997; before one-time items) sells products in the areas of insulation; roofing materials; and windows/patio doors and other specialty products for the home exterior. The division has been significantly expanded by the $657 million acquisition

(including debt assumed) of Fibreboard Corp. in July 1997, and the $310 million takeover of AmeriMark Building Products in October 1997. The two make specialty building products and give Owens the leading position in the vinyl siding market. They added a total of more than $1 billion to OWC's annual revenue base.

The composite materials segment (26% of sales and 46% of profits in 1997) is the world's leading producer of glass fiber materials used in composites. Composites are fabricated material systems made up of two or more components, which replace traditional materials such as aluminum, wood and steel.

In September 1996, Owens launched a System Thinking business strategy, which shifts its focus from a product orientation to system driven solutions. For instance, building materials for the home have typically been purchased one item at a time, one brand at a time. However, OWC's research shows that most consumers would instead prefer to purchase integrated systems that address their whole needs.

Owens launched a strategic restructuring program in January 1998. The plan has been aimed at reducing overhead, enhancing manufacturing productivity, and closing higher cost plants. OWC announced a $250 million pretax charge for the restructuring, with almost all recorded in the fourth quarter of 1997 ($143 million) and 1998's first quarter ($95 million). The plan will reduce the workforce by about 2,500 employees, or some 10% of the workforce.

Per Share Data ($)

(Year Ended Dec. 31)	1997	1996	1995	1994	1993	1992	1991	1990	1989	1988
Tangible Bk. Val.	NM	NM	-9.04	-18.80	-21.90	-25.69	-28.14	-11.06	-13.23	-15.18
Cash Flow	4.35	-2.92	7.12	4.34	4.82	4.53	-9.36	5.09	7.35	7.50
Earnings	1.17	-5.50	4.64	1.70	2.40	1.68	-12.58	1.78	4.08	4.71
Dividends	24.00	0.13	Nil	Nil	Nil	Nil	Nil	Nil	Nil	Nil
Payout Ratio	32%	NM	Nil	Nil	Nil	Nil	Nil	Nil	Nil	Nil
Prices - High	49⅞	46	47⅛	46	49¼	39¾	35½	26½	36⅞	26½
- Low	31⅞	36	30¼	27¾	34⅜	22⅜	15	13⅝	22¼	15⅞
P/E Ratio - High	43	NM	10	27	20	24	NM	15	9	6
- Low	27	NM	7	16	14	13	NM	8	5	3

Income Statement Analysis (Million $)

	1997	1996	1995	1994	1993	1992	1991	1990	1989	1988
Revs.	4,373	3,832	3,612	3,351	2,944	2,878	2,783	3,111	3,000	2,831
Oper. Inc.	451	540	547	461	372	352	304	497	597	594
Depr.	173	132	125	118	105	123	132	139	137	117
Int. Exp.	111	77.0	87.0	94.0	89.0	110	131	165	166	170
Pretax Inc.	82.0	-580	325	132	152	105	-752	133	275	324
Eff. Tax Rate	11%	NM	33%	44%	31%	31%	NM	44%	38%	39%
Net Inc.	62.0	-283	231	74.0	105	72.0	-514	75.0	172	197

Balance Sheet & Other Fin. Data (Million $)

	1997	1996	1995	1994	1993	1992	1991	1990	1989	1988
Cash	58.0	45.0	54.0	59.0	3.0	2.0	3.0	7.0	29.0	23.0
Curr. Assets	1,428	958	927	930	827	658	619	711	816	687
Total Assets	4,996	3,913	3,261	3,274	3,013	2,126	2,106	1,807	1,924	1,596
Curr. Liab.	1,307	1,121	936	1,073	876	535	448	653	791	585
LT Debt	2,098	818	794	1,037	898	1,018	1,148	1,086	1,201	1,315
Common Eqty.	-440	-483	-211	-679	-868	-1,007	-1,075	-349	-434	-609
Total Cap.	1,681	334	582	351	29.0	10.0	72.0	749	791	729
Cap. Exp.	227	325	276	258	164	130	96.0	121	125	127
Cash Flow	235	-151	356	192	210	195	-382	214	310	314
Curr. Ratio	1.1	0.9	1.0	0.9	0.9	1.2	1.4	1.1	1.0	1.2
% LT Debt of Cap.	124.8	245.0	136.5	290.5	NM	NM	NM	145.0	NM	NM
% Net Inc.of Revs.	1.4	NM	6.4	2.2	3.6	2.5	NM	2.4	5.7	7.0
% Ret. on Assets	1.4	NM	7.1	2.3	4.1	3.4	NM	4.0	9.8	12.3
% Ret. on Equity	NM	NM	NM	NM	NM	NM	NM	NM	NM	NM

Data as orig. reptd.; bef. results of disc. opers. and/or spec. items. Per share data adj. for stk. divs. as of ex-div. date. Bold denotes diluted EPS (FASB 128). E-Estimated. NA-Not Available. NM-Not Meaningful. NR-Not Ranked.

Office—One Owens Corning Pkwy., Toledo, OH 43659. **Tel**—(419) 248-8000. **Website**—http://www.owenscorning.com **Chrmn & CEO**—G. H. Hiner. **SVP & CFO**—D. Cecere. **VP & Investor Contact**—Jules L. Vinnedge. **Dirs**—N. P. Blake Jr., G. Caperton, L. S. Coleman Jr., W. W. Colville, J. H. Dasburg, L. Hilliard, G. H. Hiner, J. M. Huntsman Jr., A. Iverson, W. W. Lewis, F. C. Moseley Jr., W. A. Reynolds. **Transfer Agent & Registrar**—ChaseMellon, Ridgefield Park, NJ. **Incorporated**—in Delaware in 1938. **Empl**—24,000. **S&P Analyst:** Michael W. Jaffe

STANDARD &POOR'S
STOCK REPORTS

Owens-Illinois
1725
NYSE Symbol **OI**
In S&P 500

12-SEP-98

Industry: Containers (Metal & Glass)

Summary: This company is the leading U.S. and a major foreign maker of glass packaging containers. It also makes plastic containers, closures and labels.

S&P Opinion: Buy (★★★★★)	Recent Price • 33½	Yield • Nil
	52 Wk Range • 49-29¾	12-Mo. P/E • 15.0

Quantitative Evaluations

Outlook (1 Lowest—5 Highest)
• **3**

Fair Value
• **35⅝**

Risk
• **Low**

Earn./Div. Rank
• **NR**

Technical Eval.
• **NA**

Rel. Strength Rank (1 Lowest—99 Highest)
• **43**

Insider Activity
• **NA**

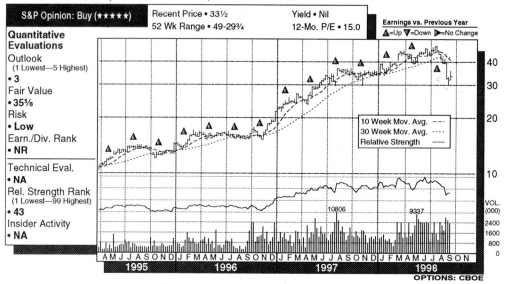

Earnings vs. Previous Year ▲=Up ▼=Down ▶=No Change

10 Week Mov. Avg. ---
30 Week Mov. Avg. ·····
Relative Strength —

VOL. (000)

OPTIONS: CBOE

Overview - 06-AUG-98

Sales from comparable operations should be moderately higher in 1998. We see improved glass container sales, with foreign sales boosted by internal growth and ongoing geographic expansion. That should outweigh market softness and currency troubles in certain nations. Domestic glass container sales should also be a bit higher, but we see gains limited by a mature market and the ongoing shift of soft-drink makers toward plastic. In plastics, solid demand should continue to boost both domestic and foreign sales. Operating margins should widen, on cost controls, productivity improvements and the further integration of recent takeovers. OI will also benefit from its major recapitalization in 1997. Comparisons will be distorted by $0.10 a share of one-time credits in 1998 and $0.06 a share of credits in 1997. The April 1998 purchase of BTR Plc's glass and plastic packaging operations will add greatly to OI's sales base, but will likely have no bottom line impact in 1998; it should be additive by 1999.

Valuation - 06-AUG-98

Absent one-time items, OI has achieved double-digit EPS gains every year since its 1991 IPO. It accomplished that feat despite the relative maturity of its domestic glass container businesses and did so by placing greater focus on overseas expansion and the more vital domestic plastic container field. OI's early 1997 takeover of Italian glass container maker AVIR and its mid-1997 refinancing were also well received, and with most lauding OI's April 1998 purchase of the packaging businesses of BTR Plc, the shares have about quadrupled since early 1995. Despite that appreciation, the shares seem well undervalued trading at only 17 times our 1998 forecast (before one-time items). Our enthusiasm reflects the belief that OI's operating strategies will allow its EPS gains to go on for an extended period.

Key Stock Statistics

S&P EPS Est. 1998	2.40	Tang. Bk. Value/Share	NM
P/E on S&P Est. 1998	14.0	Beta	1.02
S&P EPS Est. 1999	2.70	Shareholders	1,300
Dividend Rate/Share	Nil	Market cap. (B)	$ 5.2
Shs. outstg. (M)	155.3	Inst. holdings	68%
Avg. daily vol. (M)	0.772		

Value of $10,000 invested 5 years ago: $ 33,500

Fiscal Year Ending Dec. 31

	1998	1997	1996	1995	1994	1993
Revenues (Million $)						
1Q	1,099	1,056	905.8	923.6	839.0	832.1
2Q	1,385	1,225	963.7	985.0	915.4	915.0
3Q	—	1,240	1,014	962.2	927.9	914.6
4Q	—	1,138	962.1	892.4	884.8	873.3
Yr.	—	4,659	3,846	3,763	3,567	3,535
Earnings Per Share ($)						
1Q	0.56	0.44	0.33	0.28	0.23	0.18
2Q	0.75	0.65	0.55	0.49	0.43	0.39
3Q	E0.78	0.65	0.51	0.46	0.39	0.36
4Q	E0.31	0.27	0.19	0.17	-0.41	-2.64
Yr.	E2.40	2.01	1.58	1.40	0.64	-1.70

Next earnings report expected: mid October

Dividend Data

OI's bank credit agreement prohibits, and certain debt security covenants limit, the payment of cash dividends on the common stock.

A Division of The McGraw-Hill Companies

Business Summary - 06-AUG-98

Owens-Illinois ranks as the largest producer of glass containers in the U.S. and the second largest in Europe. It also makes a variety of plastic container products. The ongoing trend of consolidation in the global packaging industry has provided OI with opportunities to accelerate long-term growth. It has used those chances to significantly expand its foreign operations over the past couple of years. In early 1997, OI obtained a 99% stake in AVIR, S.p.A., a European glass bottle maker; and in April 1998, it bought the international glass and plastic packaging businesses of BTR Plc. Owens also completed a major refinancing in 1997.

OI markets glass containers in many sizes, shapes and colors for soft drinks, alcoholic beverages, food and pharmaceuticals. Owens makes about one of every two glass containers produced worldwide. Glass operations represented 76% of sales and 74% of profits in 1997.

OI greatly expanded its glass containers business through the purchase of a 99% stake in AVIR, S.p.A. in 1997 (most obtained in February). AVIR is the largest glass container maker in Italy and the Czech Republic, and also operates in Spain. Owens expects the takeover to add about $600 million to annual sales. Consideration for AVIR totaled $586 million.

Plastic containers include rigid, semi-rigid, flexible and multi-layer packages for many uses, and prescription containers. Closure products, labels and plastic carriers account for the rest of the segment's sales. At present, OI sells its plastics products almost exclusively in the U.S. Major customers include household, personal care and health care products makers, and the food and beverage industries. Plastics operations contributed 24% of sales and 26% of profits in 1997.

In April 1998, OI acquired BTR Plc's glass and plastic packaging businesses, for US$3.6 billion. The businesses had sales of US$1.2 billion in 1997, excluding UK glass operations that OI agreed to sell to meet European regulatory approval. BTR has a major presence in Australia, New Zealand and the U.K., and its leading position in the polyethylene terephthalate (PET) marks OI's entry into that vital plastic bottling market. Owens financed the purchase with bank borrowings, and right after closing announced plans to partly refinance with a total of $2 billion in public debt and equity (12.6 million common shares, seven million convertible preferred shares and $1.1 billion of debt). The new businesses should boost OI's foreign sales to about one-half of its revenue base, from 37% in 1997 and just 18% in 1991.

In October 1997, OI completed the refinancing of $1.9 billion of debt with interest rates ranging from 9.75% to 11%. Owens funded the program with $600 million of lower coupon rate notes (between 7.85% and 8.10%), the sale of 16.9 million common shares, and additional borrowings under an amended bank facility.

Per Share Data ($) (Year Ended Dec. 31)	1997	1996	1995	1994	1993	1992	1991	1990	1989	1988
Tangible Bk. Val.	0.19	-2.45	-4.32	-5.91	-6.85	-7.55	-6.19	-10.29	NA	NA
Cash Flow	4.10	3.42	2.99	2.56	0.17	2.79	4.81	1.67	NA	NA
Earnings	2.01	1.58	1.40	0.64	-1.70	0.81	-0.25	0.31	NA	NA
Dividends	Nil	Nil	Nil	Nil	Nil	Nil	Nil	Nil	Nil	Nil
Payout Ratio	Nil	Nil	Nil	Nil	Nil	Nil	Nil	Nil	Nil	Nil
Prices - High	38 3/8	22 3/4	14 3/4	13 5/8	12 3/8	14 1/2	12 1/8	NA	NA	NA
- Low	21 1/2	13 5/8	10 1/8	10 1/4	9	7 7/8	9 3/4	NA	NA	NA
P/E Ratio - High	19	14	11	21	NM	18	NM	NA	NA	NA
- Low	11	9	7	16	NM	10	NA	NA	NA	NA
Income Statement Analysis (Million $)										
Revs.	4,659	3,846	3,763	3,567	3,535	3,672	3,541	3,647	NA	NA
Oper. Inc.	984	795	760	723	707	708	704	586	NA	NA
Depr.	284	220	188	229	221	235	203	162	NA	NA
Int. Exp.	303	303	300	278	290	351	497	355	NA	NA
Pretax Inc.	452	324	310	171	-294	188	60.0	161	NA	NA
Eff. Tax Rate	33%	32%	33%	40%	NM	41%	97%	72%	NA	NA
Net Inc.	272	191	169	78.0	-200	97.0	-10.0	36.7	NA	NA
Balance Sheet & Other Fin. Data (Million $)										
Cash	218	175	162	142	94.0	106	89.0	60.0	NA	NA
Curr. Assets	1,648	1,285	1,217	1,099	960	1,059	900	1,024	NA	NA
Total Assets	6,845	6,105	5,439	5,318	4,901	5,151	4,399	4,508	NA	NA
Curr. Liab.	1,044	905	889	928	726	814	705	810	NA	NA
LT Debt	3,147	3,253	2,758	2,625	2,419	2,983	2,851	2,819	NA	NA
Common Eqty.	1,322	708	510	346	269	272	415	431	NA	NA
Total Cap.	4,964	4,379	3,591	3,173	2,838	3,438	3,353	3,336	NA	NA
Cap. Exp.	471	388	284	286	266	251	216	NA	NA	NA
Cash Flow	556	411	357	305	20.0	332	193	198	NA	NA
Curr. Ratio	1.6	1.4	1.4	1.2	1.3	1.3	1.3	1.3	NA	NA
% LT Debt of Cap.	63.3	74.3	76.8	82.7	85.2	86.8	85.0	84.5	NA	NA
% Net Inc.of Revs.	5.8	5.0	4.5	2.2	NM	2.6	NM	1.0	NA	NA
% Ret. on Assets	4.2	3.3	3.1	1.5	NM	2.0	NM	NA	NA	NA
% Ret. on Equity	26.8	31.4	39.5	24.9	NM	28.1	NM	NA	NA	NA

Data as orig. reptd.; bef. results of disc. opers. and/or spec. items. Per share data adj. for stk. divs. as of ex-div. date. Bold denotes diluted EPS (FASB 128). E-Estimated. NA-Not Available. NM-Not Meaningful. NR-Not Ranked.

Reincorporated—in Delaware in 1987. **Office**—One SeaGate, Toledo, Ohio 43666. **Tel**—(419) 247-5000. **Chrmn & CEO**—J. H. Lemieux. **Sr VP & CFO**—L. A. Wesselmann. **Exec VP & Secy**—T. L. Young. **Investor Contact**—John Hoff. **Dirs**—R. J. Dineen, E. A. Gilhuly, J. H. Greene Jr., H. R. Kravis, R. J. Lanigan, J. H. Lemieux, R. I. MacDonnell, J. J. McMackin Jr., M. W. Michelson, G. R. Roberts, L. A. Wesselmann, T. L. Young. **Transfer Agent & Registrar**—First Chicago Trust Co. of New York, Jersey City, NJ. **Empl**— 32,400. **S&P Analyst:** Robert E. Friedman, CPA

STANDARD &POOR'S
STOCK REPORTS

PACCAR Inc
Nasdaq Symbol **PCAR**

4896E

In S&P 500

12-SEP-98

Industry:
Trucks & Parts

Summary: This leading producer of heavy-duty trucks also distributes auto parts in five states.

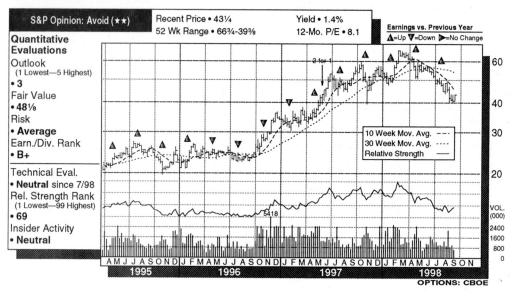

S&P Opinion: Avoid (★★)

Recent Price • 43¼
52 Wk Range • 66¾-39⅜

Yield • 1.4%
12-Mo. P/E • 8.1

Earnings vs. Previous Year
▲=Up ▼=Down ▶=No Change

Quantitative Evaluations

Outlook
(1 Lowest—5 Highest)
• **3**

Fair Value
• **48⅛**

Risk
• **Average**

Earn./Div. Rank
• **B+**

Technical Eval.
• **Neutral** since 7/98

Rel. Strength Rank
(1 Lowest—99 Highest)
• **69**

Insider Activity
• **Neutral**

10 Week Mov. Avg. – – –
30 Week Mov. Avg. · · · ·
Relative Strength ——

OPTIONS: CBOE

Overview - 23-JUL-98

Heavy-duty truck demand should increase 5% in 1998, after having fallen 20% in 1996 and risen slightly in 1997. The pace of orders picked up in recent quarters, as shippers steered more cargo traffic to truckers, due to operating problems at a major railroad. This situation may reverse over time, as the railroad breaks bottlenecks on its lines and improves throughput. There is little pent-up demand for trucks, following the strong sales cycle of the early to mid-1990s, and we expect orders and sales to flatten over the next few quarters, and then to turn down. Margins continue to benefit from the 1997 addition of DAF Trucks, with its 9% share of the European market and $1.7 billion in sales. In addition, PCAR acquired Leyland Trucks (sales of $275 million) in mid-1998. Normally, during weak periods, PCAR suffers less than its competitors, because it is less vertically integrated. However, a material decline in earnings still occurs as volume tails off. Supporting earnings through a downturn are profitable financial services and auto parts units. Income tied to the financial services unit tends to hold up well through a short downturn. However, a prolonged slowdown eventually affects that segment as well.

Valuation - 23-JUL-98

We continue to recommend that investors avoid the shares of truck makers, including PCAR. Although orders have strengthened, we believe that this is temporary. After the 1997 run-up in the shares, we think favorable market conditions are reflected in the stock price. We see considerable risk of deterioration in industry conditions, as well as a possible European downturn in 1998. Although PCAR's P/E multiple is not particularly high, we think that the economic cycle in North America is mature, and do not expect a significant expansion of the multiple.

Key Stock Statistics

S&P EPS Est. 1998	4.90	Tang. Bk. Value/Share	21.52
P/E on S&P Est. 1998	8.8	Beta	1.55
S&P EPS Est. 1999	4.60	Shareholders	3,100
Dividend Rate/Share	0.60	Market cap. (B)	$ 3.4
Shs. outstg. (M)	78.1	Inst. holdings	47%
Avg. daily vol. (M)	0.238		

Value of $10,000 invested 5 years ago: $ 22,538

Fiscal Year Ending Dec. 31

	1998	1997	1996	1995	1994	1993
Revenues (Million $)						
1Q	1,746	1,443	1,028	1,130	986.3	761.4
2Q	1,924	1,589	1,034	1,207	1,071	838.0
3Q	—	1,638	1,047	1,147	1,115	884.1
4Q	—	1,798	1,208	1,166	1,114	895.4
Yr.	—	6,468	4,332	4,894	4,285	3,379
Earnings Per Share ($)						
1Q	**1.28**	**0.74**	0.46	0.70	0.56	0.35
2Q	**1.33**	**0.92**	0.67	0.83	0.65	0.42
3Q	E1.17	1.05	0.66	0.88	0.69	0.47
4Q	E1.12	1.70	0.81	0.83	0.73	0.58
Yr.	E4.90	4.41	2.58	3.25	2.63	1.83

Next earnings report expected: mid October

Dividend Data (Dividends have been paid since 1943.)

Amount ($)	Date Decl.	Ex-Div. Date	Stock of Record	Payment Date
1.50 Ext.	Dec. 09	Dec. 18	Dec. 22	Jan. 05 '98
0.150	Dec. 09	Feb. 17	Feb. 19	Mar. 05 '98
0.150	Apr. 28	May. 19	May. 21	Jun. 05 '98
0.150	Jul. 20	Aug. 19	Aug. 21	Sep. 04 '98

A Division of The **McGraw·Hill** *Companies*

Business Summary - 23-JUL-98

If you see a brand new class 8 heavy duty truck barreling down the Interstate, there's a better than one in five chance it's a Kenworth or Peterbilt model built by PACCAR. The company is the second largest North American producer of these 33,000-pound behemoths. With the 1996 acquisition of Netherlands-based DAF Trucks for $550 million, PACCAR ranks as one of the three largest producers in the world.

Including production in the U.K. under the Foden brand, Kenworth's Australian and Mexican operations, other foreign production and sales of class 6 and 7 trucks, PACCAR produced more than 79,000 trucks in 1997. Production of medium duty class 6 and 7 trucks is a small part of PACCAR's business but is playing a larger role following the DAF acquisition. DAF also brought to PACCAR an exclusive distribution agreement in Europe covering class 3 through 5 trucks produced by British-based Leyland Trucks and production of axles and three sizes of engines. In mid-1998, PACCAR acquired Leyland. Several years ago, PACCAR formed a joint venture to produce class 8 trucks in China.

PACCAR's standard practice is to focus on the design and assembly of trucks, leaving production of major components to outside suppliers. This serves the company well when typically volatile demand for heavy trucks tails off during a cyclical downturn. The strategy of avoiding vertical integration in truck production provides PACCAR greater flexibility to reduce costs during a downturn, and has permitted an enviable record of more than 30 profitable years through even the most severe industrywide slumps. DAF's production of its own axles and engines does not mark a serious departure from the company's basic strategy.

Production of trucks and related aftermarket parts distribution businesses is PACCAR's largest business, accounting for 91% of revenues and 92% of operating income. A financial services segment accounts for 4% of revenues and 16% of operating income. Financial services provide important support to the truck business by facilitating wholesale sales to dealers, financing of retail sales and leasing of some 9,000 trucks and trailers to shippers.

Other operations include an aftermarket auto parts retailer and production of winches and planetary drives. These operations accounted for 5% of 1997 revenues, and had an operating loss. The auto parts retailer has 128 retail stores in the U.S. Northwest, and distributes replacement auto parts to an additional 430 dealers under the Al's Auto Supply and Grand Auto names in California, Nevada, Washington, Idaho and Alaska.

Per Share Data ($)

(Year Ended Dec. 31)	1997	1996	1995	1994	1993	1992	1991	1990	1989	1988
Tangible Bk. Val.	19.20	17.45	16.08	14.78	13.93	13.01	12.91	12.73	12.55	10.95
Cash Flow	5.87	3.63	4.18	3.44	2.56	1.45	1.14	1.45	3.65	2.74
Earnings	4.41	2.58	3.25	2.63	1.83	0.84	0.51	0.80	3.00	2.13
Dividends	2.08	1.25	2.00	1.50	1.00	0.57	0.48	0.43	1.09	1.04
Payout Ratio	47%	48%	62%	57%	55%	67%	94%	53%	36%	49%
Prices - High	$59^1/2$	$36^5/8$	$27^3/8$	$30^7/8$	$30^5/8$	$27^3/8$	$21^7/8$	$19^7/8$	$22^7/8$	$19^1/8$
- Low	$30^3/8$	$20^7/8$	$19^5/8$	20	$23^1/4$	$20^3/4$	$13^5/8$	$11^5/8$	$16^3/8$	$11^3/4$
P/E Ratio - High	13	14	8	12	17	33	43	25	8	9
- Low	7	8	6	8	13	25	27	15	5	6

Income Statement Analysis (Million $)

	1997	1996	1995	1994	1993	1992	1991	1990	1989	1988
Revs.	6,764	4,600	4,848	4,490	3,542	2,735	2,339	2,778	3,523	3,267
Oper. Inc.	790	516	575	471	326	185	133	226	417	379
Depr.	112	81.1	72.4	63.2	56.7	47.2	49.2	51.8	52.7	50.4
Int. Exp.	170	152	146	NA	NA	NA	96.0	120	119	96.0
Pretax Inc.	536	313	400	320	220	92.0	48.0	94.0	363	268
Eff. Tax Rate	36%	36%	37%	36%	35%	29%	18%	32%	33%	34%
Net Inc.	346	201	253	205	142	65.0	40.0	64.0	242	176

Balance Sheet & Other Fin. Data (Million $)

	1997	1996	1995	1994	1993	1992	1991	1990	1989	1988
Cash	676	508	609	553	459	465	496	478	555	381
Curr. Assets	1,756	1,548	1,137	NA	NA	NA	NA	NA	NA	NA
Total Assets	5,600	5,299	4,391	3,928	3,291	2,809	2,738	2,906	3,067	2,832
Curr. Liab.	1,214	1,352	688	NA	NA	NA	NA	NA	NA	NA
LT Debt	1,334	1,145	1,160	631	460	240	219	325	485	386
Common Eqty.	1,498	1,358	1,251	1,175	1,108	1,038	1,032	1,019	1,007	904
Total Cap.	2,987	2,655	2,562	1,838	1,567	1,278	1,251	1,344	1,492	1,290
Cap. Exp.	133	123	94.0	81.0	109	100	51.0	80.0	71.0	59.0
Cash Flow	458	282	325	268	199	112	89.0	115	295	226
Curr. Ratio	1.4	1.1	1.7	NA	NA	NA	NA	NA	NA	NA
% LT Debt of Cap.	44.7	43.1	45.3	34.3	29.3	18.7	17.5	24.2	32.5	29.9
% Net Inc.of Revs.	5.1	4.4	5.3	4.6	4.0	2.4	1.7	2.3	6.9	5.4
% Ret. on Assets	6.4	4.1	6.1	5.7	4.7	2.4	1.4	2.2	8.3	8.5
% Ret. on Equity	24.2	15.4	20.9	17.9	13.3	6.3	3.9	6.4	25.7	20.6

Data as orig. reptd.; bef. results of disc. opers. and/or spec. items. Per share data adj. for stk. divs. as of ex-div. date. Revs. in Income Statement Analysis incl. finl. svcs. Bold denotes diluted EPS (FASB 128). E-Estimated. NA-Not Available. NM-Not Meaningful. NR-Not Ranked.

Office—777 106th Ave. N.E., Bellevue, WA 98004. Tel—(425) 455-7400. Website—http://www.paccar.com Chrmn & CEO—M. C. Pigott. Pres—D. J. Hovind. Secy—J. M. D'Amato. Treas & Investor Contact—R. E. Ranheim. Dirs— J. M. Fluke, Jr., G. Grinstein, C. H. Hahn. H. J. Haynes, D. J. Hovind, C. M. Pigott, J. C. Pigott, M. C. Pigott, J. W. Pitts, W. G. Reed, M. A. Tembreull. Transfer Agent—First Chicago Trust Co. of New York, Jersey City, NJ.Incorporated—in Washington in 1924; reincorporated in Delaware in 1972. Empl— 17,000. S&P Analyst: Robert E. Friedman, CPA

PacifiCorp

1746E

NYSE Symbol **PPW**

In S&P 500

12-SEP-98

Industry: Electric Companies

Summary: This holding company, which has electric and/or natural gas operations in the U.S. and Australia, recently withdrew its bid to acquire the U.K.-based The Energy Group.

S&P Opinion: Hold (★★★)	Recent Price • 22½	Yield • 4.8%
	52 Wk Range • 27¼-20¼	12-Mo. P/E • 14.4

Quantitative Evaluations

Outlook
(1 Lowest—5 Highest)
• 1

Fair Value
• 18½

Risk
• Low

Earn./Div. Rank
• B

Technical Eval.
• **Bullish** since 7/98

Rel. Strength Rank
(1 Lowest—99 Highest)
• 93

Insider Activity
• NA

Earnings vs. Previous Year
▲=Up ▼=Down ▶=No Change

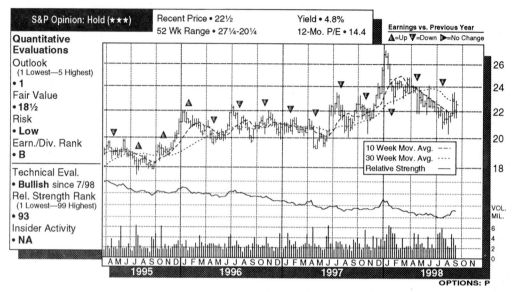

10 Week Mov. Avg. - - - -
30 Week Mov. Avg. ......
Relative Strength ——

OPTIONS: P

Overview - 19-AUG-98

PPW's failure to obtain The Energy Group (TEG) was a major disappointment; we expect the company to take its time in evaluating opportunities that would enhance its strengths in fuels management, power generation and distribution, and energy marketing. In the first quarter, PPW recorded charges of $0.18 a share related to the terminated bid, and $0.24 for a work force reduction program. In addition to special charges, 1998 EPS will be hurt by second quarter energy trading losses of $0.11. More trading losses are anticipated in the third quarter. In January 1998, PPW said it would reduce its work force about 7% in 1998, and would close a Wyoming coal mine in the second half of 1999. In order to focus on its more concentrated electric service territories, PPW intends to sell its territories in California and Montana (5.5% of its North American customers).

Valuation - 19-AUG-98

Despite recent weakness, we would continue to hold the stock. The shares were recently down about 20% in 1998, hurt by the failure to acquire The Energy Group and by losses in electricity trading operations. In addition, earnings from Australian operations have been cut back by unfavorable currency exchange rates. In 1997, PPW rose 33%, versus a 31% gain for the S&P 500, and significantly outperforming gains of 19.8% and 18.6% for peers in the S&P electric and natural gas indexes. After the termination of its bid for The Energy Group, PPW is under increased pressure to enhance shareholder value. However, we do not expect a dividend increase until it would fall within the payout ratio target of 60% to 65% of earnings. Still, there is a possibility of a share repurchase program (if another acquisition opportunity does not emerge).

Key Stock Statistics

S&P EPS Est. 1998	0.90	Tang. Bk. Value/Share	12.37
P/E on S&P Est. 1998	25.1	Beta	0.25
S&P EPS Est. 1999	1.50	Shareholders	12,700
Dividend Rate/Share	1.08	Market cap. (B)	$ 6.7
Shs. outstg. (M)	297.3	Inst. holdings	45%
Avg. daily vol. (M)	0.689		

Value of $10,000 invested 5 years ago: $ 15,495

Fiscal Year Ending Dec. 31

	1998	1997	1996	1995	1994	1993
Revenues (Million $)						
1Q	2,076	1,170	1,003	854.2	865.3	862.0
2Q	1,923	1,220	976.4	807.9	836.1	809.2
3Q	—	2,011	1,135	849.7	915.0	861.7
4Q	—	2,006	1,180	889.1	890.1	879.2
Yr.	—	6,278	4,294	3,401	3,507	3,412
Earnings Per Share ($)						
1Q	-0.07	0.32	0.42	0.37	0.39	0.38
2Q	0.12	0.24	0.31	0.29	0.28	0.30
3Q	E0.45	0.14	0.46	0.56	0.43	0.35
4Q	E0.40	-0.02	0.43	0.42	0.41	0.37
Yr.	E0.90	0.68	1.37	1.64	1.51	1.40

Next earnings report expected: late October

Dividend Data (Dividends have been paid since 1947.)

Amount ($)	Date Decl.	Ex-Div. Date	Stock of Record	Payment Date
0.270	Nov. 11	Jan. 20	Jan. 22	Feb. 17 '98
0.270	Feb. 11	Apr. 17	Apr. 21	May. 15 '98
0.270	May. 13	Jul. 20	Jul. 22	Aug. 17 '98
0.270	Aug. 04	Oct. 16	Oct. 20	Nov. 16 '98

A Division of The **McGraw-Hill** *Companies*

Business Summary - 19-AUG-98

On April 30, 1998, PacifiCorp withdrew its $11.1 billion offer for The Energy Group PLC (LSE/NYSE: TEG), a U.K. holding company with about $9.3 billion in assets. The company, which regarded its offer of 820 pence per share as the full price value, declined to outbid an offer of 840 pence per share by Texas Utilities.

PPW is a diversified energy company that provides electricity to 1.4 million customers in seven U.S. states, and to about 550,000 in Australia. It is also engaged in power production and wholesale sales. Nonregulated businesses include wholesale marketing and trading, plant and fuels management, and retail energy services. PPW acquired Utah Power & Light Co. in 1993. Revenues and profits (in million $) by business segment in 1997 were:

	Revs.	Profits
Domestic electric	59%	$601.3
Australian electric	11%	150.5
Energy Trading	28%	-8.2
Other	2%	58.9

Domestic energy revenues by customer class in 1997 were: wholesale 39%, residential 22%, industrial 20%, commercial 18% and other 1%. The domestic distribution of retail electric operating revenues in 1997 was Utah, 36%; Oregon, 33%; Wyoming, 13%; Washington, 9; Idaho, 4%; California, 3%; and Montana, 2%.

In December 1995, PPW acquired Powercor, an Australian electric distribution and marketing company, for $1.6 billion in cash. Powercor serves customers in suburban Melbourne and the west and central regions of the state of Victoria, Australia. Residential customers represented 83% of Powercor's customers, but accounted for only 35% of its 1997 electric revenues, while industrial customers, which represented only 2% of total customers, accounted for 28% of electric revenues. Commercial customers (9% of total customers) accounted for 30% of electric revenues, while farm and other customers (6%) accounted for 7%.

In April 1997, the company acquired TPC Corp., a Houston-based natural gas gathering, processing, storage and marketing company, for $288 million in cash and the assumption of about $149 million in debt. In December 1997, TPC sold its gathering and processing systems for $196 million.

In December 1997, PPW sold its Pacific Telecom (PTI) subsidiary for $1.5 billion and the assumption of PTI debt. In November 1997, PPW sold its Pacific Generation Co., for $151 million.

Per Share Data ($)

(Year Ended Dec. 31)	1997	1996	1995	1994	1993	1992	1991	1990	1989	1988
Tangible Bk. Val.	12.78	10.71	10.19	11.34	11.04	10.12	12.43	11.78	11.68	11.22
Earnings	0.68	1.62	1.64	1.51	1.40	0.42	1.86	1.85	1.81	1.73
Dividends	1.08	1.08	1.08	1.08	1.20	1.15	1.47	1.41	1.35	1.30
Payout Ratio	159%	67%	66%	72%	85%	273%	80%	79%	75%	75%
Prices - High	27¼	22½	21⅝	19½	20¾	25¼	25¼	23⅞	23⅛	18½
- Low	19¼	19½	17½	15⅞	16⅞	18⅛	20⅜	17½	16⅝	16⅛
P/E Ratio - High	40	14	13	13	15	60	14	13	13	11
- Low	28	12	11	11	12	43	11	9	9	9

Income Statement Analysis (Million $)

	1997	1996	1995	1994	1993	1992	1991	1990	1989	1988
Revs.	6,278	4,294	3,401	3,507	3,412	3,242	4,007	3,783	3,717	3,519
Depr.	477	530	444	424	405	453	576	477	456	419
Maint.	NA	309	281	292	297	288	315	297	NA	NA
Fxd. Chgs. Cov.	2.1	2.5	2.7	3.0	2.8	1.8	2.9	3.1	3.4	3.2
Constr. Credits	Nil	Nil	15.1	14.5	13.9	16.2	30.6	33.3	25.8	14.9
Eff. Tax Rate	29%	36%	32%	35%	31%	38%	29%	31%	33%	33%
Net Inc.	225	505	505	468	423	150	507	474	466	447

Balance Sheet & Other Fin. Data (Million $)

	1997	1996	1995	1994	1993	1992	1991	1990	1989	1988
Gross Prop.	13,312	14,800	14,233	12,583	12,073	11,309	12,963	11,617	10,748	10,130
Cap. Exp.	582	651	579	789	742	694	912	763	606	427
Net Prop.	9,070	10,216	9,952	8,446	8,210	7,858	9,129	8,103	7,548	7,277
Capitalization:										
LT Debt	4,415	5,324	4,968	3,768	4,028	4,349	5,195	4,672	4,395	4,347
% LT Debt	47	55	54	48	51	55	55	55	56	56
Pfd.	241	314	554	694	691	722	742	628	526	449
% Pfd.	6.30	3.20	6.00	8.80	8.80	9.00	7.80	7.40	6.60	5.80
Common	4,321	4,032	3,633	3,460	3,263	2,908	3,512	3,208	3,007	2,936
% Common	46	42	40	44	41	37	37	38	38	38
Total Cap.	11,139	11,803	11,224	9,935	9,910	9,161	10,838	9,907	9,293	8,940
% Oper. Ratio	86.3	77.6	76.2	79.0	78.7	81.1	74.7	73.8	74.1	73.2
% Earn. on Net Prop.	10.0	12.3	8.8	8.9	9.1	8.0	11.8	12.7	12.9	13.3
% Return On Revs.	3.6	11.8	14.8	13.3	12.4	4.6	12.7	12.5	12.5	12.7
% Return On Invest. Capital	NA	8.3	7.6	7.5	7.7	5.7	9.4	9.7	10.4	10.3
% Return On Com. Equity	4.9	12.4	13.2	12.8	12.4	3.5	14.1	14.3	15.0	13.9

Data as orig. reptd.; bef. results of disc. opers. and/or spec. items. Per share data adj. for stk. divs. as of ex-div. date. Bold denotes diluted EPS (FASB 128). E-Estimated. NA-Not Available. NM-Not Meaningful. NR-Not Ranked.

Office—700 N. E. Multnomah, Portland, OR 97232-4116. **Tel**—(503) 731-2000. **Website**—http://www.pacificorp.com **Chrmn**—K. R. McKennon. **Pres & CEO**—F. W. Buckman. **EVP & COO**—R. T. O'Brien. **VP & Secy**—S. A. Nofziger. **Treas**—W. E. Peressini. **Investor Contact**—Scott Hibbs. **Dirs**—W. C. Armstrong, K. A. Braun, F. W. Buckman, C. T. Conover, N. E. Karras, K. R. McKennon, R. G. Miller, A. K. Simpson, V. R. Topham, D. M. Wheeler, N. Wilgenbusch, P. I. Wold. **Transfer Agent & Registrar**—Co.'s office. **Incorporated**—in Maine in 1910; reincorporated in Oregon in 1989. **Empl**— 10,087. **S&P Analyst:** Justin McCann

STANDARD &POOR'S
STOCK REPORTS

Pall Corp.

1750

NYSE Symbol **PLL**

In S&P 500

14-SEP-98

Industry: Manufacturing (Specialized)

Summary: Pall is a leading producer of filters for the health care and aircraft industries.

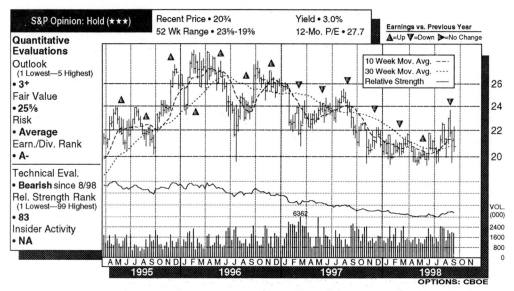

S&P Opinion: Hold (★★★)	Recent Price • 20¾	Yield • 3.0%
	52 Wk Range • 23⅝-19⅜	12-Mo. P/E • 27.7

Quantitative Evaluations

Outlook
(1 Lowest—5 Highest)
• 3+

Fair Value
• 25⅝

Risk
• Average

Earn./Div. Rank
• A-

Technical Eval.
• **Bearish** since 8/98

Rel. Strength Rank
(1 Lowest—99 Highest)
• 83

Insider Activity
• **NA**

Earnings vs. Previous Year
▲=Up ▼=Down ▶=No Change

10 Week Mov. Avg. ---
30 Week Mov. Avg. ....
Relative Strength —

OPTIONS: CBOE

Overview - 14-SEP-98

This U.S.-based global producer of health care and industrial filters is a dominant player in higher-margin niche segments (blood filtration products) of the $17 billion filter and separations market. Pall's competitive advantages include proprietary products, technological expertise, a reputation for quality and service, and global presence. The company's target is to achieve 10% revenues growth in FY 99 (Jul), reduce cost of goods sold to 40% and SG&A to 35% of sales through $10 million in cost savings. In July 1998, Britain announced its decision to begin filtering out all white blood cells, joining European neighbors Austria, France, Ireland, Norway and Portugal. Implementation of the new policy is expected in September 1998. Within two to five years the U.S. is also expected to require all blood be filtered, which should increase PLL sales by $150-$200 million annually. Excluding the $0.17 a share one-time charges (net), FY 98 earnings were $0.92.

Valuation - 14-SEP-98

Sales growth was limited in FY 98 (Jul), due to unfavorable revenue translation, microelectronics industry slump and Asia, but PLL is targeting 10% growth for FY 99. Although the microelectronic business is projected to be off 25% in the first quarter of FY 99, year to year, European prospects remain good, especially the Industrial Process division and civil aviation and blood filtrations business. Despite recent stock market weakness, PLL shares have fared relatively well because the majority of its revenue is stable, and not dependent upon economic cycles. Furthermore, its long-term fundamentals remain in place. However, we expect the shares to maintain price stability in both down and up markets; therefore, we see the shares trading in line with the overall market.

Key Stock Statistics

S&P EPS Est. 1998	0.95	Tang. Bk. Value/Share	5.86
P/E on S&P Est. 1998	21.8	Beta	0.57
Dividend Rate/Share	0.62	Shareholders	6,800
Shs. outstg. (M)	124.0	Market cap. (B)	$ 2.6
Avg. daily vol. (M)	0.404	Inst. holdings	68%

Value of $10,000 invested 5 years ago: $ 11,626

Fiscal Year Ending Jul. 31

	1998	1997	1996	1995	1994	1993
Revenues (Million $)						
1Q	237.3	207.5	191.6	159.2	141.9	148.0
2Q	259.0	234.0	239.3	192.8	169.7	167.0
3Q	289.2	275.3	247.9	217.3	177.8	173.0
4Q	301.8	290.1	281.6	253.5	211.4	198.8
Yr.	1,087	1,062	960.4	822.8	700.9	687.2
Earnings Per Share ($)						
1Q	0.15	0.18	0.16	0.12	0.10	0.09
2Q	**0.22**	0.24	0.28	0.23	0.19	0.03
3Q	**0.06**	-0.18	0.33	0.29	0.24	0.22
4Q	**0.32**	0.34	0.44	0.40	0.33	0.34
Yr.	**0.75**	0.53	1.21	1.04	0.86	0.68

Next earnings report expected: early December

Dividend Data (Dividends have been paid since 1974.)

Amount ($)	Date Decl.	Ex-Div. Date	Stock of Record	Payment Date
0.140	Oct. 06	Oct. 16	Oct. 20	Nov. 03 '97
0.155	Jan. 13	Jan. 21	Jan. 24	Feb. 07 '98
0.155	Apr. 21	Apr. 29	May. 01	May. 18 '98
0.155	Jul. 07	Jul. 16	Jul. 20	Aug. 05 '98

STANDARD
&POOR'S
STOCK REPORTS

Pall Corporation

1750
14-SEP-98

Business Summary - 14-SEP-98

In early 1997, this very profitable global producer of health care and industrial filters boosted its higher-margin health care filter sales about 25% with the acquisition of Gelman Sciences Inc. in exchange for about 10.5 million common shares. Michigan-based Gelman ($115 million annual sales) makes health care filters, primarily for the fast-growing biotech and pharmaceutical industries. Segment revenue contributions and operating margins in recent fiscal years (Jul.) were:

	FY 98	FY 97	FY 96
REVENUES			
Health care	51%	52%	49%
Aeropower	24%	23%	25%
Fluid processing	25%	25%	26%
OPERATING MARGINS			
Health care	NA	23%	31%
Aeropower	NA	24%	22%
Fluid processing	NA	19%	21%

In FY 97, sales by geographic region were: Western Hemisphere 49%, Europe 34% and Pacific Rim 17%. Gross operating profits by region were: Western Hemisphere 49%, Europe 39% and Pacific Rim 12%.

Pall's health care (HC) segment makes and sells filters and related products to four market segments. Patient protection (46% of FY 97 HC sales) includes filters for a variety of medical procedures. Pharmaceutical (37%) includes filter and separation products used in the production of drugs and biologicals. Food & beverage (10%) includes filters to produce yeast- and bacteria-free water. BioSupport & diagnostics (7%) supplies membranes used in the diagnosis and monitoring of health conditions (such as diabetes, pregnancy and infectious disease) and provides forensic testing (genetic fingerprinting).

The aeropower segment makes filters and separation products for two markets. The aerospace unit (46% of FY 97 segment sales) includes both the commercial and defense markets. The company believes it is the largest maker of filters for commercial airlines. The industrial unit (54%) includes filters made for the power industry, as well as for steel, paper, auto and heavy earthmoving equipment manufacturers.

The fluid processing (FP) segment makes filter and separation products for two markets. The electronics group (61% of FY 97 FP sales) makes products for the semiconductor, data storage and photographic film industries. The industrial processing group (39%) makes products for the oil and gas, chemical and petrochemical and power industries.

Per Share Data ($)

(Year Ended Jul. 31)	1998	1997	1996	1995	1994	1993	1992	1991	1990	1989
Tangible Bk. Val.	NA	5.84	5.73	5.13	4.71	4.42	4.51	3.98	3.67	3.23
Cash Flow	NA	1.03	1.61	1.40	1.20	0.98	1.07	0.96	0.80	0.71
Earnings	0.75	0.53	1.21	1.04	0.86	0.68	0.77	0.69	0.57	0.50
Dividends	0.60	0.54	0.47	0.41	0.36	0.31	0.26	0.21	0.18	0.15
Payout Ratio	81%	102%	39%	39%	42%	46%	33%	31%	32%	31%
Prices - High	23⅝	26⅛	29⅜	27⅞	20¼	21⅝	24⅛	21	12½	12⅛
- Low	19⅜	19½	19⅝	18⅜	13⅝	15⅝	16½	11¼	8¾	9
P/E Ratio - High	32	49	24	27	24	32	31	30	22	24
- Low	26	37	16	18	16	23	21	16	15	18

Income Statement Analysis (Million $)

Revs.	NA	1,062	960	823	701	687	685	657	564	497
Oper. Inc.	NA	182	248	212	180	170	170	157	135	121
Depr.	NA	62.8	46.8	41.7	39.5	35.2	34.4	31.9	26.8	24.7
Int. Exp.	NA	2.8	12.0	10.9	8.8	9.4	11.9	18.1	24.9	16.1
Pretax Inc.	NA	86.1	198	167	135	104	126	116	97.0	84.0
Eff. Tax Rate	NA	22%	30%	29%	27%	25%	29%	31%	32%	31%
Net Inc.	NA	67.3	139	119	99	78.3	90.2	79.9	66.2	57.7

Balance Sheet & Other Fin. Data (Million $)

Cash	NA	18.0	106	111	89.0	107	101	59.0	81.0	129
Curr. Assets	NA	607	581	525	470	470	483	385	415	433
Total Assets	NA	1,266	1,185	1,075	960	902	913	774	786	707
Curr. Liab.	NA	301	330	288	257	278	259	203	261	269
LT Debt	NA	62.1	46.7	68.8	54.1	24.5	59.0	51.6	56.3	40.4
Common Eqty.	NA	825	732	652	587	543	546	488	441	374
Total Cap.	NA	915	815	754	673	596	640	561	516	432
Cap. Exp.	NA	88.6	82.2	66.5	73.4	62.6	56.2	58.3	81.8	62.9
Cash Flow	NA	130	185	161	138	114	125	112	93.0	82.0
Curr. Ratio	NA	2.0	1.8	1.8	1.8	1.7	1.9	1.9	1.6	1.6
% LT Debt of Cap.	NA	6.8	5.7	9.1	8.0	4.1	9.2	9.2	10.9	9.4
% Net Inc.of Revs.	NA	6.3	14.4	14.5	14.1	11.4	13.2	12.2	11.7	11.6
% Ret. on Assets	NA	5.5	12.3	11.7	10.7	8.6	10.7	10.2	8.9	8.9
% Ret. on Equity	NA	8.6	20.0	19.2	17.6	14.4	17.5	17.1	16.2	16.3

Data as orig. reptd.; bef. results of disc. opers. and/or spec. items. Per share data adj. for stk. divs. as of ex-div. date. Bold denotes diluted EPS (FASB 128). E-Estimated. NA-Not Available. NM-Not Meaningful. NR-Not Ranked.

Office—2200 Northern Blvd., East Hills, NY 11548. **Tel**—(516) 484-5400. **Fax**—(516) 484-3529. **Website**—www.pall.com**Chrmn & CEO**—E. Krasnoff. **Pres, Treas & CFO**—J. Hayward-Surry. **Secy**—P. Schwartzman. **Investor Contact**—Patricia J. Iannucci. **Dirs**—A. B. Appel, John H.F.Haskell, Jr., U. Haynes Jr., J. Hayward-Surry, E. Krasnoff, E. W. Martin Jr., K. Plourde, C. F. Seibert, H. Shelley, A. B. Slifka, J. D. Watson, D. T. D. Williams. **Transfer Agent & Registrar**—Wachovia Bank of North Carolina, Winston-Salem. **Incorporated**—in New York in 1946. **Empl**— 8,500.
S&P Analyst: John A. Massey

12-SEP-98

Industry: Computer (Software & Services)

Summary: This company is a leader in the mechanical design auto- mation industry with its Pro/ENGINEER line of integrated software products.

S&P Opinion: Accumulate (★★★★)	Recent Price • 11	Yield • Nil
	52 Wk Range • 36¼-9	12-Mo. P/E • 12.6

Quantitative Evaluations

Outlook
(1 Lowest—5 Highest)
• **5**

Fair Value
• **29⅛**

Risk
• **Average**

Earn./Div. Rank
• **B+**

Technical Eval.
• **Bearish** since 7/98

Rel. Strength Rank
(1 Lowest—99 Highest)
• **12**

Insider Activity
• **Neutral**

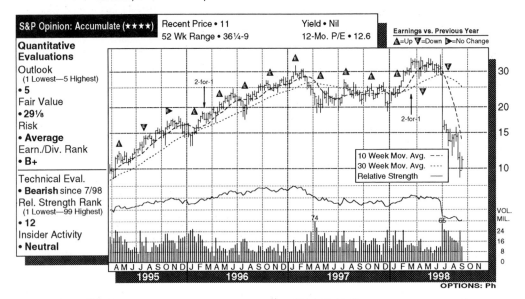

Earnings vs. Previous Year
▲=Up ▼=Down ▶=No Change

10 Week Mov. Avg. ---
30 Week Mov. Avg. ----
Relative Strength —

VOL. MIL.

OPTIONS: Ph

Overview - 22-JUL-98

We are lowering our revenue forecast for FY 98 (Sep.) and FY 99, as the company recently reported revenues that were well below expectations. The Asian economy has dragged down revenues, as has a sales force reor- ganization stemming from the recent launch of a new product and an increasing focus on major accounts. As a result of the lower revenues, margins will be con- strained. Comparisons will also be hurt as a result of the restatement of past financial statements to include the recent acquisition of Computervision. The acquisi- tion should be accretive to earnings in the second half of the fiscal year. Growth opportunities will come from the expanded customer base resulting from the acquisi- tion. The company enjoys a high level of repeat busi- ness (over 70%) and continues to gain market share. We have lowered our EPS estimates.

Valuation - 22-JUL-98

The shares of this leading developer of mechanical de- sign automation software collapsed in early July after the company announced an expected revenue shortfall. The company is suffering from some short-term transi- tional issues and needs to rebuild its credibility and consistent track record. However, in the long run, we remain positive, and expect continued market share gains as the company exploits a market that is still largely untapped. The recent launch of Windchill, a product data management software product, is crucial to the long term success of the company. We view fa- vorably the recent acquisition of Computervision, which increases the company's penetration of the automotive and aerospace industries and provides entry into the enterprise product data management industry. We have downgraded the shares to accumulate, from buy.

Key Stock Statistics

S&P EPS Est. 1998	0.72	Tang. Bk. Value/Share	1.12
P/E on S&P Est. 1998	15.3	Beta	1.65
S&P EPS Est. 1999	0.99	Shareholders	4,500
Dividend Rate/Share	Nil	Market cap. (B)	$ 3.0
Shs. outstg. (M)	272.2	Inst. holdings	84%
Avg. daily vol. (M)	3.886		

Value of $10,000 invested 5 years ago: $ 16,603

Fiscal Year Ending Sep. 30

	1998	1997	1996	1995	1994	1993
Revenues (Million $)						
1Q	223.0	183.5	125.4	72.02	53.52	32.50
2Q	264.1	198.0	140.5	83.53	58.02	38.00
3Q	245.0	207.1	157.1	97.02	63.62	43.52
4Q	—	220.2	177.1	119.2	69.09	49.01
Yr.	—	808.8	600.1	394.3	244.3	163.1
Earnings Per Share ($)						
1Q	**0.23**	0.18	0.13	0.08	0.06	0.04
2Q	**0.01**	0.20	0.14	0.09	0.07	0.04
3Q	**0.05**	0.21	0.15	0.06	0.08	0.05
4Q	—	0.23	0.10	0.08	0.08	0.06
Yr.	—	0.82	0.52	0.30	0.28	0.19

Next earnings report expected: mid October

Dividend Data

Amount ($)	Date Decl.	Ex-Div. Date	Stock of Record	Payment Date
2-for-1	Feb. 12	Mar. 09	Feb. 27	Mar. 06 '98

Business Summary - 22-JUL-98

Parametric Technology Corporation develops, markets and supports a family of fully integrated software products for the automation of the mechanical design-through-manufacturing process, a complex, iterative process encompassing a broad spectrum of distinct engineering disciplines that is essential to the development of virtually all manufactured products, from consumer items to jet aircraft.

The company's mechanical design automation (MDA) products enable end-users to reduce the time-to-market and manufacturing costs for their products and, through the easy evaluation of multiple design alternatives, to improve product quality.

Parametric's product line consists of its core product, Pro/ENGINEER, and more than 70 related application modules. Pro/ENGINEER is a parametric, feature-driven solid modeling system used in the detailed design phase of the MDA cycle. Other modules include Pro/DESIGN, a conceptual design tool; Pro/DETAIL and Pro/DRAFT, which generate detailed manufacturing drawings; and Pro/ASSEMBLY, used to design and manage very complex assemblies. The company's practice has been to issue two major releases of its product line annually, with each generally including several new products. Parametric's ability to develop new

products rapidly is facilitated by the modular structure of its software code. The company's products run on a wide range of workstations.

In January 1998, the company acquired Computervision Corp., for approximately 11.6 million (adjusted) shares of common stock. Parametric believes the acquisition will expand its business presence in the high-end of the CAD market in the automotive and aerospace industries. Computervision's products are also expected to broaden the company's enterprisewide data management product offerings.

In April 1998, PMTC announced the introduction of the Windchill product line, a family of enterprise product data management products. Customer shipments began in June.

Marketing and sales efforts are focused primarily on electronic equipment, aerospace, automotive, consumer products and telecommunications companies, with sales made directly to strategic customers and indirectly through value-added resellers and original equipment manufacturers.

End users of the company's products range from small companies to some of the world's largest manufacturing organizations.

After the acquisition, the company's products now have an installed base of over 186,000 seats (units) among approximately 21,000 customers worldwide.

Per Share Data ($)

(Year Ended Sep. 30)	1997	1996	1995	1994	1993	1992	1991	1990	1989	1988
Tangible Bk. Val.	2.52	2.01	1.48	1.06	0.67	0.38	0.21	0.15	-0.03	NA
Cash Flow	0.91	0.58	0.34	0.30	0.20	0.10	0.05	0.03	0.01	NA
Earnings	0.82	0.52	0.30	0.28	0.19	0.10	0.05	0.03	0.01	-0.01
Dividends	Nil	Nil	Nil	Nil	Nil	Nil	Nil	Nil	Nil	Nil
Payout Ratio	Nil	Nil	Nil	Nil	Nil	Nil	Nil	Nil	Nil	Nil
Prices - High	32⅛	28⅜	18⅛	10⅛	11¼	7	3⅞	1⁵⁄₁₆	¹⁵⁄₁₆	NA
- Low	18¾	13	8	5⅜	5⅝	3⅛	¹⁵⁄₁₆	⅝	½	NA
P/E Ratio - High	39	55	60	35	60	76	81	48	98	NM
- Low	23	25	27	19	30	34	20	23	72	NM

Income Statement Analysis (Million $)

	1997	1996	1995	1994	1993	1992	1991	1990	1989	1988
Revs.	809	600	394	244	163	86.7	44.7	25.5	11.0	3.3
Oper. Inc.	349	222	128	107	68.8	32.3	15.1	8.0	2.7	NA
Depr.	22.4	16.8	9.5	4.5	2.6	1.3	0.7	0.6	0.5	NA
Int. Exp.	Nil	Nil	NM	NA	NM	NM	0.1	0.1	0.1	0.1
Pretax Inc.	337	216	128	107	68.5	33.2	15.9	8.6	2.3	-0.8
Eff. Tax Rate	35%	36%	39%	37%	37%	37%	35%	35%	31%	Nil
Net Inc.	219	138	77.4	66.9	42.9	21.1	10.3	5.6	1.6	-0.8

Balance Sheet & Other Fin. Data (Million $)

	1997	1996	1995	1994	1993	1992	1991	1990	1989	1988
Cash	154	434	308	207	123	73.5	34.5	24.6	3.3	NA
Curr. Assets	691	562	400	271	165	99	48.7	33.1	6.8	NA
Total Assets	832	659	454	287	177	107	51.0	35.0	8.0	NA
Curr. Liab.	187	146	82.0	44.3	28.9	27.0	7.7	4.5	2.2	NA
LT Debt	Nil	Nil	NM	NA	NM	Nil	0.0	0.2	0.6	NA
Common Eqty.	645	512	371	242	147	78.7	42.0	28.8	-0.9	NA
Total Cap.	645	512	371	243	148	80.2	43.2	30.1	5.4	NA
Cap. Exp.	28.0	29.7	12.9	9.1	7.4	3.6	0.8	0.5	0.1	0.3
Cash Flow	242	155	86.9	71.5	45.6	22.4	11.0	6.2	1.8	NA
Curr. Ratio	3.7	3.8	4.9	6.1	5.7	3.7	6.3	7.3	3.1	NA
% LT Debt of Cap.	NM	NM	NM	NA	Nil	Nil	NM	0.7	10.3	NA
% Net Inc.of Revs.	27.1	23.0	19.6	27.4	26.3	24.3	23.1	22.0	14.5	NM
% Ret. on Assets	29.4	24.8	20.4	28.4	29.7	26.2	23.9	13.3	NA	NA
% Ret. on Equity	37.9	31.2	24.9	33.8	37.5	34.3	28.8	NM	NA	NA

Data as orig. reptd.; bef. results of disc. opers. and/or spec. items. Per share data adj. for stk. divs. as of ex-div. date. Bold denotes diluted EPS (FASB 128). E-Estimated. NA-Not Available. NM-Not Meaningful. NR-Not Ranked.

Office—128 Technology Dr., Waltham, MA 02154. **Tel**—(781) 398-5000. **Fax**—(781) 398-6000.**Chrmn & CEO**—S. C. Walske. **Pres & COO**—C. R. Harrison.**CFO**—E. Gillis. **VP & Investor Contact**—John W. Hudson. **Dirs**—R. N. Goldman, D. K. Grierson, C. R. Harrison, O. B. Marx III, M. E. Porter, N. G. Postemak, S. C. Walske. **Transfer Agent & Registrar**—American Stock Transfer & Trust Co., NYC. **Incorporated**—in Massachusetts in 1985. **Empl**— 3,432. **S&P Analyst:** Brian Goodstadt

Parker Hannifin

1764

NYSE Symbol **PH**

In S&P 500

12-SEP-98

Industry: Manufacturing (Specialized)

Summary: Parker Hannifin is a worldwide supplier of components for fluid power systems to a broad range of industrial and aerospace markets.

S&P Opinion: Sell (★)	Recent Price • 29⅞	Yield • 2.0%
	52 Wk Range • 52⅝-28¼	12-Mo. P/E • 10.4

Quantitative Evaluations

Outlook
(1 Lowest—5 Highest)
• **4+**

Fair Value
• **36¾**

Risk
• **Average**

Earn./Div. Rank
• **B+**

Technical Eval.
• **NA**

Rel. Strength Rank
(1 Lowest—99 Highest)
• **60**

Insider Activity
• **NA**

Earnings vs. Previous Year
▲=Up ▼=Down ▶=No Change

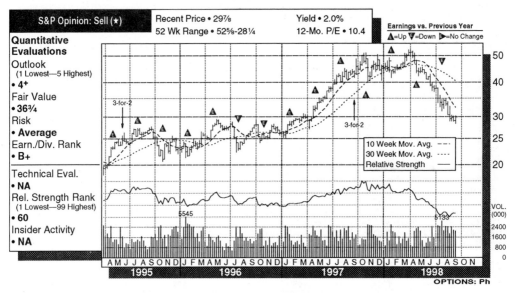

10 Week Mov. Avg. ---
30 Week Mov. Avg. ·····
Relative Strength —

OPTIONS: Ph

Overview - 05-AUG-98

Revenues are expected to advance in the high single digits through FY 99 (Jun.), as industrial and aerospace markets expand less rapidly; business conditions should continue to be affected by the economic problems in Asia, a weak semiconductor market, and the impact of the General Motors strike. The International Industrial sector is expected to benefit from an improving European economy, and from further penetration into Latin America and Asian Pacific regions. Operating margins may begin to improve somewhat, but will continue to be unfavorably affected by the Asian crisis, a sales mix favoring some lower-margin businesses, and small contributions from recent acquisitions. PH earlier revised its projection for rest of world margins from 12% for FY 99, to possibly 11%. For the long term, earnings may benefit from acquisitions, strong cash flow, new products, improved operating efficiencies, and additional share buybacks.

Valuation - 05-AUG-98

After more than doubling during 1997, and rising nearly 30% in early 1998, the shares have given back much of their gains, primarily reflecting margin pressures overseas, and a developing trend of earnings falling short of expectations. Although the shares are up somewhat from their recent 1998 lows, we see operating margins continuing to be hurt by troubles in the Far East and in some U.K. instrumentation operations. EPS could be boosted somewhat by probable stock repurchases. Despite trading recently at less than 11X our recently lowered EPS projection for FY 99 (Jun.), a discount to the projected P/E for the S&P 500 and for stock's of peer companys, we still suggest selling the stock, based on the continuing problems that we see.

Key Stock Statistics

S&P EPS Est. 1999	3.20	Tang. Bk. Value/Share	11.38
P/E on S&P Est. 1999	9.3	Beta	1.22
S&P EPS Est. 2000	3.60	Shareholders	47,400
Dividend Rate/Share	0.60	Market cap. (B)	$ 3.3
Shs. outstg. (M)	110.6	Inst. holdings	71%
Avg. daily vol. (M)	0.469		

Value of $10,000 invested 5 years ago: $ 25,445

Fiscal Year Ending Jun. 30

	1998	1997	1996	1995	1994	1993
Revenues (Million $)						
1Q	1,083	959.3	839.0	712.5	607.4	608.0
2Q	1,115	969.6	824.4	738.2	592.2	589.0
3Q	1,197	1,047	931.4	879.7	677.4	607.2
4Q	1,238	1,115	991.7	884.0	699.4	685.3
Yr.	4,633	4,091	3,586	3,214	2,576	2,489
Earnings Per Share ($)						
1Q	0.70	0.46	0.51	0.39	0.15	0.15
2Q	**0.63**	0.47	0.44	0.37	0.13	0.13
3Q	**0.75**	0.70	0.62	0.59	-0.17	0.14
4Q	**0.80**	0.83	0.58	0.61	0.37	0.18
Yr.	**2.88**	2.46	2.15	1.97	0.47	0.59

Next earnings report expected: mid October

Dividend Data (Dividends have been paid since 1949.)

Amount ($)	Date Decl.	Ex-Div. Date	Stock of Record	Payment Date
0.150	Oct. 22	Nov. 18	Nov. 20	Dec. 05 '97
0.150	Jan. 29	Feb. 17	Feb. 19	Mar. 06 '98
0.150	Apr. 09	May. 19	May. 21	Jun. 05 '98
0.150	Jul. 09	Aug. 18	Aug. 20	Sep. 04 '98

A Division of The **McGraw·Hill** *Companies*

Business Summary - 05-AUG-98

Parker Hannifin (PH) is a worldwide leader in the production of motion and control components for hundreds of industrial and aerospace markets. Contributions by segment in FY 97 (Jun.) were:

	Sales	Profits
Industrial - North America	53%	64%
Industrial - International	26%	15%
Aerospace	21%	21%

The company has been enhancing its global positioning through the expansion of its facilities in Denmark and Finland, and the construction of new facilities in Poland, the Czech Republic and South Africa. Although recent earnings have been penalized by the Asian crisis and weak margins, PH expects its European position to be a source of additional growth in the future, as economic conditions recover. In addition, the company is now in a number one or two position in most countries.

The product lines of the industrial unit cover most of the components of motion control systems. During 1997, the Motion and Control Group was divided into the Hydraulics Group and the Automation Group. Hydraulics makes components and systems for builders and users of industrial and mobile machinery and equipment, such as metering pumps, power units, control valves, accumulators, cylinders, actuators and hy-

drostatic steering components. Automation supplies pneumatic and electromechanical components and systems. The Filtration Group makes filters to remove contaminants from fuel, air, oil, water and other fluids in industrial, process and other applications. The Fluid Connectors Group makes connectors, tube and hose fittings, hoses and couplers that transmit fluid. The Seal Group makes sealing devices, gaskets and packing that ensure leak-proof connections. The Climate and Industrial Controls Group makes components for use in industrial and automotive air-conditioning and refrigeration systems, including pressure regulators, solenoid valves, expansion valves, filter-dryers and hose assemblies. In July 1997, PH formed a new instrumentation group that makes critical flow components.

Principal aerospace segment products are hydraulic, pneumatic and fuel systems and components, used on virtually every domestic commercial, military and general aviation aircraft. The segment offers complete hydraulic systems, as well as components that include hydraulic and electrohydraulic systems for precise control of aircraft rudders, elevators, and other aerodynamic control surfaces, and utility hydraulic components, such as reservoirs, accumulators and engine-driven pumps.

In September 1997, PH acquired the solenoid valve business ($100 million in sales) of Honeywell, Inc.

Backlog at March 31, 1998, totaled $1.7 billion, up from $1.5 billion a year earlier.

Per Share Data ($)

(Year Ended Jun. 30)	1998	1997	1996	1995	1994	1993	1992	1991	1990	1989
Tangible Bk. Val.	NA	11.32	9.57	9.75	8.31	9.33	7.99	8.10	7.93	7.12
Cash Flow	NA	3.98	3.43	3.06	1.51	1.60	1.53	1.45	1.84	1.76
Earnings	2.88	2.46	2.15	1.97	0.48	0.60	0.59	0.55	1.00	0.94
Dividends	0.60	0.51	0.48	0.45	0.44	0.43	0.41	0.41	0.39	0.37
Payout Ratio	21%	21%	22%	23%	92%	72%	71%	75%	39%	40%
Prices - High	52⅝	51¼	29⅜	27⅝	20⅞	17	16⅛	13¾	14½	14¼
- Low	31⅜	24⅞	21¼	18⅜	15⅛	12½	11⅝	10⅛	8¼	10⅝
P/E Ratio - High	18	21	14	14	44	28	27	25	14	15
- Low	11	10	10	9	32	19	20	18	8	11

Income Statement Analysis (Million $)

	1998	1997	1996	1995	1994	1993	1992	1991	1990	1989
Revs.	NA	4,091	3,586	3,214	2,576	2,489	2,376	2,441	2,453	2,520
Oper. Inc.	NA	633	546	502	333	283	270	273	335	320
Depr.	NA	170	141	120	113	110	103	99	92.0	90.0
Int. Exp.	NA	46.7	36.7	31.0	37.8	47.1	52.2	59.4	62.1	53.1
Pretax Inc.	NA	425	374	348	112	108	105	103	183	171
Eff. Tax Rate	NA	36%	36%	37%	54%	40%	40%	43%	40%	40%
Net Inc.	NA	274	240	218	52.2	65.0	63.0	59.0	110	103

Balance Sheet & Other Fin. Data (Million $)

	1998	1997	1996	1995	1994	1993	1992	1991	1990	1989
Cash	NA	69.0	64.0	63.8	81.6	160	100	39.0	22.0	29.0
Curr. Assets	NA	1,500	1,402	1,246	1,018	1,056	1,056	1,019	1,129	1,088
Total Assets	NA	2,999	2,886	2,302	1,913	1,964	1,921	1,890	1,996	1,923
Curr. Liab.	NA	716	767	653	504	468	359	358	438	485
LT Debt	NA	433	440	237	257	378	447	477	512	494
Common Eqty.	NA	1,547	1,384	1,192	966	933	934	943	938	841
Total Cap.	NA	2,006	1,849	1,452	1,232	1,329	1,402	1,469	1,504	1,383
Cap. Exp.	NA	189	202	152	100	91.0	85.0	112	126	153
Cash Flow	NA	444	381	338	165	175	166	158	203	193
Curr. Ratio	NA	2.1	1.8	1.9	2.0	2.3	2.9	2.8	2.6	2.2
% LT Debt of Cap.	NA	21.6	23.8	16.3	20.9	28.5	31.9	32.4	34.0	35.8
% Net Inc.of Revs.	NA	6.7	6.7	6.8	2.0	2.6	2.7	2.4	4.5	4.1
% Ret. on Assets	NA	9.3	9.2	10.3	2.7	3.3	3.3	3.1	5.6	5.6
% Ret. on Equity	NA	18.7	18.6	20.2	5.0	7.0	6.7	6.3	12.4	12.2

Data as orig. reptd.; bef. results of disc. opers. and/or spec. items. Per share data adj. for stk. divs. as of ex-div. date. Bold denotes diluted EPS (FASB 128). E-Estimated. NA-Not Available. NM-Not Meaningful. NR-Not Ranked.

Office—6035 Parkland Blvd., Cleveland, OH 44124-4141. **Tel**—(216) 896-3000. **Fax**—(216) 896-4057. **Website**—http://www.parker.com **Chrmn**—P. S. Parker. **Pres & CEO**—D. E. Collins. **VP-Fin & CFO**—M. J. Hiemstra. **VP & Secy**—J. D. Whiteman. **Treas & Investor Contact**—Timothy K. Pistell (216-896-2130). **Dirs**—J. G. Breen, D. E. Collins, P. C. Ely Jr., A. H. Ford, F. A. LePage, P. W. Likins, H. R. Ortino, A. L. Rayfield, P. G. Schloemer, W. R. Schmitt, D. L. Starnes, S. A. Streeter, D. W. Sullivan, M. A. Treschow. **Transfer Agent & Registrar**—Wachovia Bank, N.A., Boston. **Incorporated**—in Ohio in 1938. **Empl**—35,407. **S&P Analyst**: Stewart Scharf

PECO Energy

1728K

NYSE Symbol **PE**

In S&P 500

12-SEP-98

Industry:
Electric Companies

Summary: PECO Energy (formerly Philadelphia Electric) is an electric and gas utility primarily serving Philadelphia and its surrounding suburbs and two counties in northeastern Maryland.

S&P Opinion: Hold (★★★)	Recent Price • 33⅛	Yield • 3.0%
	52 Wk Range • 35⅛-18⅞	12-Mo. P/E • 21.0

Earnings vs. Previous Year
▲=Up ▼=Down ▶=No Change

Quantitative Evaluations

Outlook
(1 Lowest—5 Highest)
• **2**

Fair Value
• **31¼**

Risk
• **Low**

Earn./Div. Rank
• **B**

Technical Eval.
• **Bullish** since 5/98

Rel. Strength Rank
(1 Lowest—99 Highest)
• **98**

Insider Activity
• **Neutral**

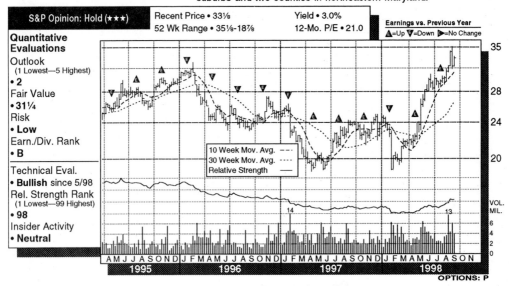

10 Week Mov. Avg. ---
30 Week Mov. Avg. ·····
Relative Strength ——

OPTIONS: P

Overview - 01-SEP-98

With its July 1998 joint venture agreement to acquire GPU's Three Mile Island Unit 1, PE has made clear its intent to become a major player in the nuclear power market. In May 1998, the Pennsylvania Public Utility Commission (PUC) approved a settlement agreement that will enable PE to recover (between 1999 and 2010) $5.26 billion in stranded costs. Earlier, in December 1997, the PUC had rejected a Partial Settlement that proposed the recovery and amortization (over 10 years) of $5.46 billion in stranded costs. In its place, the PUC would have allowed the recovery (over 8-1/2 years) of $5.02 billion in stranded costs. In January, the PUC adjusted the recovery down to $4.94 billion. For 1997, PE reported a net loss of $6.80 a share, which included an extraordinary charge of $1.8 billion ($8.24 a share) to reflect the impact of the PUC's December restructuring order. The new settlement agreement calls for rate reductions of 8% in 1999 and 6% in 2000. It will also provide choice of electric supplier to 67% of PE's customers on January 2, 1999, and the remaining 33% on January 1, 2000. In January 1998, PE reduced its quarterly dividend per share from $0.45 to $0.25.

Valuation - 01-SEP-98

We recommend holding PE stock. The shares are up 38% year to date and have rebounded 78% since the sharp drop that followed the January 26th announcement of the dividend cut. The dramatic increase primarily reflects the more favorable ruling by the PUC regarding the recovery of PE's stranded costs. While the shares were up only 4% in 1997, they had recovered more than 29% from their year low, in anticipation of the return to operation of the Salem nuclear units. With the dividend now yielding less than 3.0%, the shares appear fairly valued at around 14 times our 1999 EPS estimate of $2.45.

Key Stock Statistics

S&P EPS Est. 1998	2.25	Tang. Bk. Value/Share	12.25
P/E on S&P Est. 1998	14.7	Beta	0.17
S&P EPS Est. 1999	2.45	Shareholders	176,600
Dividend Rate/Share	1.00	Market cap. (B)	$ 7.4
Shs. outstg. (M)	222.9	Inst. holdings	48%
Avg. daily vol. (M)	1.445		

Value of $10,000 invested 5 years ago: $ 17,493

Fiscal Year Ending Dec. 31

	1998	1997	1996	1995	1994	1993
Revenues (Million $)						
1Q	1,173	1,163	1,171	1,059	1,128	1,071
2Q	1,208	1,032	989.0	959.0	951.5	901.7
3Q	—	1,278	1,110	1,125	1,041	1,073
4Q	—	1,144	1,014	1,044	919.5	941.8
Yr.	—	4,618	4,284	4,186	4,041	3,988
Earnings Per Share ($)						
1Q	0.50	0.49	0.65	0.66	0.67	0.68
2Q	0.66	0.53	0.43	0.67	0.48	0.43
3Q	E0.70	0.69	0.65	0.80	0.06	0.77
4Q	E0.39	-0.27	0.51	0.52	0.55	0.58
Yr.	E2.25	1.44	2.24	2.64	1.76	2.45

Next earnings report expected: late October

Dividend Data (Dividends have been paid since 1902.)

Amount ($)	Date Decl.	Ex-Div. Date	Stock of Record	Payment Date
0.450	Oct. 27	Nov. 12	Nov. 14	Dec. 19 '97
0.250	Jan. 26	Feb. 18	Feb. 20	Mar. 31 '98
0.250	Apr. 08	May. 20	May. 22	Jun. 30 '98
0.250	Jul. 27	Aug. 19	Aug. 21	Sep. 30 '98

A Division of The **McGraw·Hill** Companies

STANDARD
&POOR'S
STOCK REPORTS

PECO Energy Company

1728K
12-SEP-98

Business Summary - 01-SEP-98

PECO Energy (formerly Philadelphia Electric) provides electric (90% of 1997 revenues) and gas (10%) service to a population of some 3.6 million in southeastern Pennsylvania, and through a subsidiary to two northeastern Maryland counties.

Electric revenues by customer class:

	1997	1996	1995	1994
Residential	33%	36%	37%	38%
Large comm'l/ind'l	26%	28%	30%	32%
Small comm'l/ind'l	19%	19%	20%	20%
Other (including wholesale)	22%	17%	13%	10%

Sources of fuel in 1997 were nuclear 39% (43% in 1996), coal 14% (17%), purchased 44% (35%), hydro 2% (3%), and oil/internal combustion 1% (2%).

In May 1998, the Pennsylvania Public Utility Commission (PUC) approved a restructuring plan that will allow PE to recover (through an annually adjusted competitive transition charge) $5.26 billion in stranded costs from January 1, 1999 through 2010. The order permits PE to securitize $4.0 billion of the stranded costs. The new ruling followed appeals PE had filed against the PUC's December 1997 and January 1998 rulings, that would have allowed the company to recover, respec-

tively, $5.024 billion and $4.935 billion in stranded costs over an 8-1/2 year period starting in 1999.

The PUC order guarantees all electric customers of PE an 8% rate reduction in 1999 and an additional 6% reduction in 2000. It also ruled that one-third of PE's customers can choose their supplier as of January 1, 1999; another one-third on January 2, 1999, and the remainder on January 2, 2000.

The company holds a 42.6% interest in the Salem Generating Station, operated by Public Service Enterprise Group (PSEG), and has a 42.5% interest in and operates the Peach Bottom nuclear station. The two Salem units were shut down in May and June of 1995. Salem Unit 1 returned to operation in August 1997 and Salem Unit 2 was returned in April 1998. In July 1998, PE's 50%-owned AmerGen (a joint venture with British Energy) agreed to acquire the Three Mile Island Unit 1 nuclear plant from GPU for about $100 million. The regulatory approval process could take up to two years.

PE's construction work in progress (excluding nuclear fuel) totaled $611 million in 1997. For 1998, PE estimated construction capital expenditures of $450 million. It also plans to invest about $150 million in 1998 for new ventures, mainly through its Telecommunications Group. The ventures, which are expected to dilute earnings over the next several years, include the development of a digital wireless Personal Communication Services (PCS) network in partnership with AT&T Wireless.

Per Share Data ($)

(Year Ended Dec. 31)	1997	1996	1995	1994	1993	1992	1991	1990	1989	1988
Tangible Bk. Val.	12.25	20.88	20.40	19.41	19.06	18.11	17.57	16.56	17.57	17.25
Earnings	1.44	2.24	2.64	1.76	2.45	1.90	2.15	0.07	2.36	2.33
Dividends	1.80	1.75	1.65	1.54	1.43	1.32	1.23	1.45	2.20	2.20
Payout Ratio	125%	78%	62%	88%	58%	70%	57%	NM	93%	94%
Prices - High	26³/₈	32¹/₂	30¹/₄	30	33¹/₂	26³/₄	26	23¹/₂	24¹/₂	21¹/₄
- Low	18³/₄	23	24¹/₄	23⁵/₈	25¹/₂	22⁵/₈	17¹/₂	14¹/₂	19¹/₈	16⁷/₈
P/E Ratio - High	18	15	11	17	14	14	12	NM	10	9
- Low	13	10	9	13	10	12	8	NM	8	7

Income Statement Analysis (Million $)

	1997	1996	1995	1994	1993	1992	1991	1990	1989	1988
Revs.	4,618	4,284	4,186	4,041	3,988	3,962	3,976	3,705	3,406	3,229
Depr.	581	489	457	442	425	414	401	358	277	264
Maint.	NA	325	308	328	364	354	332	340	285	305
Fxd. Chgs. Cov.	2.4	3.0	3.1	2.3	2.8	2.1	2.3	1.2	2.0	2.2
Constr. Credits	21.8	19.9	27.1	22.2	23.8	20.7	23.0	55.0	271	221
Eff. Tax Rate	47%	40%	39%	37%	38%	32%	38%	30%	19%	22%
Net Inc.	337	517	610	427	591	479	535	106	590	566

Balance Sheet & Other Fin. Data (Million $)

	1997	1996	1995	1994	1993	1992	1991	1990	1989	1988
Gross Prop.	6,574	14,945	14,696	15,247	14,905	14,489	14,089	13,784	13,632	12,732
Cap. Exp.	490	549	578	571	568	594	507	541	1,038	937
Net Prop.	3,884	9,898	10,072	11,003	10,958	10,901	10,822	10,833	10,994	10,336
Capitalization:										
LT Debt	4,325	4,371	4,626	4,900	5,019	5,355	5,583	6,011	5,963	5,435
% LT Debt	59	47	49	51	51	53	55	58	56	54
Pfd.	230	292	292	370	609	654	738	753	974	991
% Pfd.	3.20	3.10	3.10	3.80	6.20	6.50	7.20	7.20	9.10	9.90
Common	3,079	4,646	4,531	4,303	4,263	4,022	3,892	3,625	3,745	3,593
% Common	37	50	48	44	43	40	38	35	35	36
Total Cap.	9,897	13,390	13,481	13,394	13,663	11,335	11,360	11,390	11,733	11,044
% Oper. Ratio	84.6	78.9	76.0	79.5	74.0	73.9	72.8	79.3	76.2	77.0
% Earn. on Net Prop.	14.4	9.1	9.9	7.6	9.5	9.5	10.0	7.0	7.6	7.4
% Return On Revs.	7.3	12.1	14.6	10.6	14.8	12.1	13.4	2.9	17.3	17.5
% Return On Invest. Capital	6.3	6.8	3.4	6.3	8.4	8.7	9.7	6.0	9.6	9.2
% Return On Com. Equity	8.0	10.9	13.3	9.1	13.1	10.6	12.5	0.4	13.5	13.4

Data as orig. reptd.; bef. results of disc. opers. and/or spec. items. Per share data adj. for stk. divs. as of ex-div. date. Bold denotes diluted EPS (FASB 128). E-Estimated. NA-Not Available. NM-Not Meaningful. NR-Not Ranked.

Office—2301 Market St., P.O. Box 8699, Philadelphia, PA 19101. **Tel**—(215) 841-4000. **Website**—http://www.peco.com. **Chrmn, Pres & CEO**—C. A. McNeill Jr. **SVP, Fin & CFO**—M. J. Egan. **Secy**—K. K. Combs. **Investor Contact**—Lisa Ewbank. **Dirs**—S. W. Catherwood, D. L. Cooper, M. W. D'Alessio, G. F. DiBona Jr., R. K. Elliot, R. G. Gilmore, R. H. Glanton, R. B. Greco, J. A. Hagen, K. R. McKee, J. J. McLaughlin, C. A. McNeill Jr., J. M. Palms, J. F. Paquette, Jr., R. Rubin, R. Subin.**Transfer Agent & Registrar**—First Chicago Trust Co. of New York, Jersey City, NJ.**Incorporated**—in Pennsylvania in 1929. **Empl**— 7,359. **S&P Analyst:** Justin McCann

STANDARD
&POOR'S
STOCK REPORTS

Penney (J.C.)

1780

NYSE Symbol **JCP**

In S&P 500

12-SEP-98

Industry:
Retail (Department
Stores)

Summary: J.C. Penney is one of the largest U.S. retailers through its department stores and catalog operations. It also operates a chain of drug stores.

S&P Opinion: Accumulate (★★★★)

| Recent Price • 50½ | Yield • 4.3% |
| 52 Wk Range • 78¾-48⅝ | 12-Mo. P/E • 25.6 |

Quantitative Evaluations

Outlook
(1 Lowest—5 Highest)
• **2⁻**

Fair Value
• **52¼**

Risk
• **Low**

Earn./Div. Rank
• **B**

Technical Eval.
• **Bearish** since 7/98

Rel. Strength Rank
(1 Lowest—99 Highest)
• **43**

Insider Activity
• **Neutral**

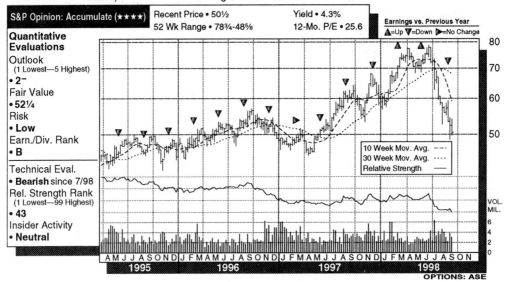

Earnings vs. Previous Year
▲=Up ▼=Down ▶=No Change

10 Week Mov. Avg. ---
30 Week Mov. Avg. ····
Relative Strength

VOL.
MIL.

OPTIONS: ASE

Overview - 17-JUL-98

Sales growth in FY 99 (Jan.) will be limited by store closures, but should reflect a modest increase in same-store sales; total sales should increase about 5%, boosted mainly by strength at the drug stores. Gross margins should be about level with those of FY 98, while SG&A expense ratios should decline. Operating income should increase moderately at retail operations and advance significantly at drug stores. Interest expense will be about level as a percentage of sales. The company's strong cash flow will be used for its $750 million a year capital expenditure program over the next three years. JCP plans to open more than 100 stores in that time. It is testing a freestanding soft goods home furnishings store, with a total of 30 locations currently. The freed-up space in department stores was replaced by expanded lines of apparel, which has higher margins. In FY 98, the company incurred over $217 million in business consolidation and restructuring costs. This included the closure of 75 Penney stores and the elimination of 1,700 management positions and 3,200 store associates.

Valuation - 17-JUL-98

Following the July 9 announcement of lower than anticipated second quarter earnings, we downgraded the shares to accumulate. Earnings will be hurt by a 2.1% drop in June same store sales at Penney stores. As a result, we have lowered our earnings estimate for FY 99 by $0.25. We still believe that the strong growth potential of the drug stores, with room for double digit operating gains over the next few years, will allow for P/E multiple expansion. We believe that the drug stores are worth about $26 a share. Cost-cutting initiatives should boost profitability at the retail operations, which we value at about $55 a share. JCP's strong cash flow and healthy dividend yield limit the downside.

Key Stock Statistics

S&P EPS Est. 1999	3.50	Tang. Bk. Value/Share	15.92
P/E on S&P Est. 1999	14.4	Beta	0.81
S&P EPS Est. 2000	4.35	Shareholders	53,000
Dividend Rate/Share	2.18	Market cap. (B)	$ 12.8
Shs. outstg. (M)	253.1	Inst. holdings	79%
Avg. daily vol. (M)	0.639		

Value of $10,000 invested 5 years ago: $ 16,323

Fiscal Year Ending Jan. 31

	1999	1998	1997	1996	1995	1994
Revenues (Million $)						
1Q	7,052	6,705	4,452	4,367	4,350	3,964
2Q	6,761	6,649	4,507	4,435	4,242	3,963
3Q	—	7,441	5,537	5,128	5,149	4,735
4Q	—	9,751	8,157	6,632	6,639	6,321
Yr.	—	30,546	22,653	20,562	20,380	18,983
Earnings Per Share ($)						
1Q	**0.64**	**0.53**	0.58	0.63	0.88	0.68
2Q	**0.08**	**0.32**	0.37	0.46	0.52	0.43
3Q	**E1.11**	**0.40**	0.98	1.00	1.11	0.88
4Q	**E1.65**	**0.85**	0.36	0.36	1.78	1.80
Yr.	**E3.50**	**2.10**	2.29	3.48	4.29	3.79

Next earnings report expected: mid November

Dividend Data (Dividends have been paid since 1922.)

Amount ($)	Date Decl.	Ex-Div. Date	Stock of Record	Payment Date
0.545	Mar. 11	Apr. 08	Apr. 13	May. 01 '98
0.545	May. 15	Jul. 08	Jul. 10	Aug. 01 '98
0.545	Sep. 09	Oct. 07	Oct. 09	Nov. 01 '98
0.545	Sep. 09	Oct. 07	Oct. 09	Nov. 01 '98

A Division of The **McGraw·Hill** *Companies*

Business Summary - 17-JUL-98

Retail giant J.C. Penney Co. (JCP) did a little shopping of its own late in FY 97 (Jan.). JCP, which has identified the rapidly consolidating drug store business as an area of strong growth potential, paid $1.2 billion in cash, plus 23 million common shares, to acquire drug chain Eckerd Corp. The combination of Eckerd's stores in the Southeast and Sunbelt with JCP's Thrift Drug and recently purchased Fay's stores in the Northeast and Mid-Atlantic created the fourth largest U.S. drug store chain, with 2,778 stores in 23 states. The Eckerd acquisition also increased the importance of drug stores in the company's overall business mix. In FY 98, drug store sales provided 32% of total revenues, up from 13% in FY 97.

While drug stores now account for a larger percentage of overall sales, JCP's main business is still the operation of its eponymous department store chain. The company's 1,203 department stores and its complementary catalog operation, the largest in the U.S., accounted for 65% of total revenues in FY 98. Major merchandise areas include women's apparel and accessories, menswear, children's apparel and home lines.

JCP has worked to shed its image as a mass merchandiser, and to be perceived instead as a department store chain, by developing such private labels as The Original Arizona Jean Company and its Worthington brand of women's career sportswear, which are offered along with many national brands. JCP is conducting a store modernization program it hopes will create a "first-class" shopping environment as well as additional selling space. JCP is combining its various labels in home lines into a single private brand, the JCP Home Collection, and plans to expand its JCPenney Home Store concept by opening additional free-standing stores under that name.

The company's JCPenney Insurance Group is the leading U.S. mass marketer of group life and health insurance products; it accounted for 4% of revenues in FY 98.

The company anticipates annual cost savings of $85 million from its 1997 early retirement program, $50 million from reduced benefit costs and improved store and home office organizations in 1998 and $100 million from the integration of its drug store operations.

The company expects second quarter FY 99 earnings to be below the $0.38 a share earned a year earlier. Lower sales levels, in part reflecting a lack of inventory for seasonal items, and higher than planned markdowns hurt sales and profitability in June.

Per Share Data ($)

(Year Ended Jan. 31)	1998	1997	1996	1995	1994	1993	1992	1991	1990	1989
Tangible Bk. Val.	15.50	15.73	23.58	23.27	21.59	20.04	15.02	15.86	15.16	13.23
Cash Flow	4.14	4.13	5.15	5.65	5.10	4.46	2.33	3.56	4.28	4.00
Earnings	2.10	2.29	3.48	4.29	3.79	3.15	0.98	2.29	3.15	3.01
Dividends	2.14	2.08	1.92	1.68	1.80	1.32	1.32	1.32	1.12	1.00
Payout Ratio	102%	91%	55%	38%	47%	42%	134%	58%	35%	31%
Cal. Yrs.	1997	1996	1995	1994	1993	1992	1991	1990	1989	1988
Prices - High	68¼	57	50	59	56⅜	40¼	29⅛	37⅞	36⅝	27⅞
- Low	44⅞	44	39⅞	41	35⅜	25⅜	21¼	18¾	25¼	19
P/E Ratio - High	32	25	14	14	15	13	30	16	12	9
- Low	21	19	11	10	9	8	22	8	8	6

Income Statement Analysis (Million $)

	1998	1997	1996	1995	1994	1993	1992	1991	1990	1989
Revs.	30,546	22,653	20,562	21,706	19,578	19,085	17,295	17,410	17,045	15,938
Oper. Inc.	2,503	1,075	1,200	2,292	1,943	1,825	1,485	1,432	1,780	1,535
Depr.	584	381	341	323	316	308	314	299	275	258
Int. Exp.	648	414	383	320	289	324	327	331	358	365
Pretax Inc.	925	909	1,341	1,699	1,554	1,259	468	832	1,170	1,192
Eff. Tax Rate	39%	38%	38%	38%	39%	38%	44%	31%	32%	32%
Net Inc.	566	565	838	1,057	944	777	264	577	802	807

Balance Sheet & Other Fin. Data (Million $)

	1998	1997	1996	1995	1994	1993	1992	1991	1990	1989
Cash	287	131	173	261	173	397	111	137	408	670
Curr. Assets	11,484	11,712	9,409	9,468	8,565	6,970	6,695	6,799	7,539	7,246
Total Assets	23,493	22,088	17,102	16,202	14,788	13,563	12,520	12,325	12,698	12,254
Curr. Liab.	6,137	7,966	4,020	4,481	3,883	3,077	2,409	2,662	3,400	2,785
LT Debt	6,986	4,565	4,080	3,335	2,929	3,171	3,354	3,135	2,755	3,064
Common Eqty.	6,831	5,526	5,509	5,292	5,096	4,486	3,504	3,697	3,649	3,251
Total Cap.	15,668	11,879	11,152	9,989	9,307	8,707	8,335	8,550	8,232	8,367
Cap. Exp.	824	704	717	550	480	453	515	637	519	487
Cash Flow	1,110	946	1,179	1,340	1,220	1,052	544	842	1,042	1,048
Curr. Ratio	1.9	1.5	2.3	2.1	2.2	2.3	2.8	2.6	2.2	2.6
% LT Debt of Cap.	44.6	38.4	36.6	33.4	31.5	36.4	40.2	36.7	33.5	36.6
% Net Inc.of Revs.	1.9	2.5	4.1	4.9	4.8	4.1	1.5	3.3	4.7	5.1
% Ret. on Assets	2.5	2.9	4.8	6.9	6.6	5.9	2.1	4.7	6.5	7.4
% Ret. on Equity	8.5	9.5	14.8	19.9	18.8	17.5	6.4	15.0	22.4	22.7

Data as orig. reptd.; bef. results of disc. opers. and/or spec. items. Per share data adj. for stk. divs. as of ex-div. date. Bold denotes diluted EPS (FASB 128). E-Estimated. NA-Not Available. NM-Not Meaningful. NR-Not Ranked.

Office—6501 Legacy Dr., Plano, TX 75024-3698. **Registrar & Transfer Agent**—Chemical Bank, NYC. **Tel**—(972) 431-1000. **Website**—http://www.jcpenney.com **Chrmn & CEO**—J. E. Oesterreicher. **EVP & CFO**—D. A. McKay. **EVP & Secy**—C. R. Lotter. **Investor Contact**—Wynn C. Watkins. **Dirs**—M. A. Burns, V. E. Jordan Jr., G. Nigh, J. E. Oesterreicher, J. C. Pfeiffer, A. W. Richards, C. S. Sanford, Jr., F. Sanchez-Loaeza, R. G. Turner, W. B. Tygart, J. D. Williams. **Transfer Agent & Registrar**—ChaseMellon Shareholder Services, S. Hackensack, NJ. **Incorporated**—in Delaware in 1924. **Empl**— 260,000. **S&P Analyst:** Karen J. Sack, CFA

Pennzoil Co.

1792

NYSE Symbol **PZL**

In S&P 500

12-SEP-98

Industry: Oil (Domestic Integrated)

Summary: This company, which engages in crude oil and natural gas production, plans to spinoff its lubricants division.

S&P Opinion: Avoid (★★)	Recent Price • 39½	Yield • 2.5%
	52 Wk Range • 82⅝-35	12-Mo. P/E • 16.3

Earnings vs. Previous Year
▲=Up ▼=Down ▶=No Change

Quantitative Evaluations

Outlook
(1 Lowest—5 Highest)
• **2⁻**

Fair Value
• **38½**

Risk
• **Low**

Earn./Div. Rank
• **B-**

Technical Eval.
• **Bullish** since 3/98

Rel. Strength Rank
(1 Lowest—99 Highest)
• **53**

Insider Activity
• **Favorable**

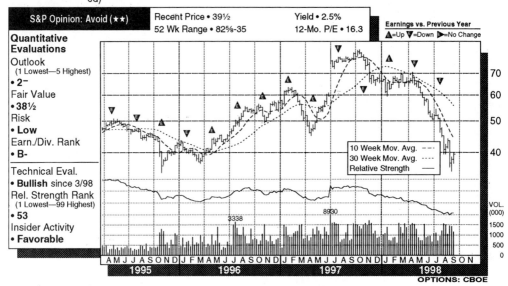

10 Week Mov. Avg. - - -
30 Week Mov. Avg. ·····
Relative Strength ——

OPTIONS: CBOE

Overview - 14-AUG-98

The company's plan to spin off its petroleum products division to shareholders represents the latest in a string of moves, made by the company and others, in an attempt to unlock the company's underlying value. In November 1997, Union Pacific Resources (UPR) withdrew its hostile takeover bid for Pennzoil. In June 1997, UPR had offered $84 in cash for 50% of PZL's common shares, with the remainder to be acquired for UPR stock. In October, UPR revised its offer to an all-cash bid. Earlier, PZL cut its dividend and instituted company-wide cost reduction programs in 1995, in an attempt to boost its profitability. Despite improved results from the motor oil and refined products segment, net income in the first half of 1998 declined significantly, due largely to a 33% drop in average oil price realizations. Production of both oil and natural gas declined, reflecting recent asset sales and normal field production declines.

Valuation - 14-AUG-98

Pennzoil believes that its planned spinoff of Pennzoil Products Co. will lead to a more favorable valuation for its remaining oil and gas exploration and production businesses, but the market appears unconvinced, as the shares are down 37% in 1998. During 1997, UPR's hostile takeover offer boosted the shares, which had been sluggish to that point in 1997. However, the shares declined sharply after UPR terminated its offer. It has yet to be determined whether the company's plan to cut expenses will be sufficient to generate consistent earnings. Oil prices will not help matters, as our projections call for an average oil price of $15.75 per barrel in 1998, down from $20.62 in 1997, the result of worldwide overproduction and reduced demand from struggling Asian economies. Based on this forecast, we project lower earnings for PZL in 1998.

Key Stock Statistics

S&P EPS Est. 1998	1.25	Tang. Bk. Value/Share	20.61
P/E on S&P Est. 1998	31.6	Beta	1.01
Dividend Rate/Share	1.00	Shareholders	18,500
Shs. outstg. (M)	47.8	Market cap. (B)	$ 1.9
Avg. daily vol. (M)	0.262	Inst. holdings	65%

Value of $10,000 invested 5 years ago: $ 9,934

Fiscal Year Ending Dec. 31

	1998	1997	1996	1995	1994	1993
Revenues (Million $)						
1Q	545.8	649.0	587.3	635.3	622.1	650.5
2Q	632.5	648.4	636.6	646.6	651.8	685.2
3Q	—	658.9	653.7	600.0	631.6	655.9
4Q	—	698.0	609.2	608.0	657.4	790.8
Yr.	—	2,654	2,487	2,490	2,563	2,782
Earnings Per Share ($)						
1Q	0.20	1.21	0.34	0.06	0.13	0.53
2Q	0.17	0.50	0.53	-0.10	0.37	0.84
3Q	—	0.78	1.40	-5.95	-6.51	0.42
4Q	—	1.27	0.61	-0.60	-0.25	2.01
Yr.	E1.25	3.76	2.88	-6.60	-6.16	3.80

Next earnings report expected: early November

Dividend Data (Dividends have been paid since 1925.)

Amount ($)	Date Decl.	Ex-Div. Date	Stock of Record	Payment Date
0.250	Nov. 07	Nov. 25	Nov. 30	Dec. 15 '97
0.250	Feb. 06	Feb. 25	Feb. 28	Mar. 15 '98
0.250	May. 07	May. 27	May. 31	Jun. 15 '98
0.250	Aug. 07	Aug. 27	Aug. 31	Sep. 15 '98

A Division of The McGraw·Hill Companies

Business Summary - 14-AUG-98

In the hopes of unlocking the underlying values of its businesses, Pennzoil (PZL) now plans to split into two companies. In April 1998, PZL announced plans to spin off its Pennzoil Products Co. (PPC) division to shareholders, with a PPC share distributed for each PZL share held. After the spinoff, expected to be completed before the end of 1998, Pennzoil Products Co. will merge with Quaker State Co., another leading automotive product company, to create a company with a 35% share of the retail motor oil market. Pennzoil Products Co. is best known for its motor oil, the #1 U.S. brand with more than 20% of the market, and its Jiffy Lube auto service franchise.

The move comes after PZL successfully fended off a hostile takeover offer. In June 1997, Union Pacific Resources (NYSE: UPR) initiated a hostile offer for PZL's shares. Under the terms of the proposed deal, UPR would pay $84 in cash for 50.1% of PZL's common stock, and would exchange UPR shares for the remaining 49.9%. Pennzoil management urged its shareholders to reject the UPR offer, despite the significant share price premium being offered. In October, UPR revised the deal to an all-cash offer of $84 per PZL share, but Pennzoil's board remained defiant. Finally, in November 1997, UPR threw in the towel, terminating its offer for PZL.

Acting as a stand-alone oil and gas exploration and production company after completion of the spinoff, Pennzoil plans to focus on development of its acreage in the Gulf of Mexico and in the former Soviet Union. The company's portfolio of properties has been pared down, with the disposition of non-core oil and gas assets over the last few years. At year-end 1997, PZL had proved crude oil reserves of 227 million bbl., versus 187 million bbl. a year earlier, and natural gas reserves of 1,059 billion cubic feet (Bcf), down from 1,277 Bcf.

PZL's 17.8 million share investment in Chevron Corp. common stock yielded about $41.3 million in dividend income in 1997 and $37.9 million in 1996. Operating profits by business unit in recent years were:

	1997	1996
Oil & gas production	71%	60%
Motor oil & auto parts	17%	13%
Franchise operations	4%	5%
Other	8%	22%

In 1997, net crude oil, condensate and natural gas liquids production averaged 56,794 barrels (bbl.) a day (down 4.7% from 1996), natural gas produced for sale 589.5 million cubic feet (Mmcf) a day (unchanged), refinery runs 55,050 bbl./day (up 3.7%), and petroleum product sales 78,201 bbl./day (up 2.5%).

Per Share Data ($) (Year Ended Dec. 31)	1997	1996	1995	1994	1993	1992	1991	1990	1989	1988
Tangible Bk. Val.	20.61	18.34	15.48	26.11	32.80	28.99	28.79	31.10	35.23	35.67
Cash Flow	9.79	8.78	0.43	5.55	12.76	6.04	4.19	7.43	11.33	10.82
Earnings	3.76	2.88	-6.60	-6.16	3.80	0.43	-1.05	2.37	6.06	-5.22
Dividends	1.00	1.00	2.50	3.00	3.00	3.00	3.00	3.00	3.00	2.60
Payout Ratio	27%	35%	NM	NM	79%	702%	NM	129%	50%	NM
Prices - High	83 7/8	58 3/4	50 7/8	56 3/8	70 3/4	57 1/2	76 1/2	89 1/2	88 7/8	79 1/8
- Low	45	36 7/8	34 5/8	43	49 3/8	43 1/8	52 1/8	61 3/4	71 5/8	65 1/4
P/E Ratio - High	22	20	NM	NM	19	NM	NM	38	15	NM
- Low	12	13	NM	NM	13	NM	NM	26	12	NM
Income Statement Analysis (Million $)										
Revs.	2,511	2,365	2,385	2,475	2,477	2,223	2,527	2,180	1,985	2,124
Oper. Inc.	614	498	337	337	472	317	329	361	346	404
Depr.	289	274	325	539	378	228	211	200	191	623
Int. Exp.	177	188	199	486	191	233	255	244	149	151
Pretax Inc.	304	169	-477	-504	219	-1.0	-77.0	102	350	-310
Eff. Tax Rate	41%	21%	NM	NM	27%	NM	NM	7.80%	33%	NM
Net Inc.	180	134	-304	-283	160	17.0	-42.0	94.0	235	-186
Balance Sheet & Other Fin. Data (Million $)										
Cash	18.6	34.4	24.0	25.0	947	21.0	112	266	469	2,128
Curr. Assets	595	538	605	728	1,544	646	783	835	1,018	2,856
Total Assets	4,406	4,124	4,308	4,716	4,886	4,457	5,231	5,261	4,882	4,480
Curr. Liab.	486	393	449	677	821	774	709	706	389	365
LT Debt	2,198	2,218	2,508	2,251	2,056	1,893	2,284	2,275	1,786	1,415
Common Eqty.	1,139	969	836	1,204	1,506	1,180	1,165	1,252	1,282	1,291
Total Cap.	3,625	3,429	3,572	3,827	3,867	3,488	4,255	4,425	4,365	3,941
Cap. Exp.	559	566	473	473	485	1,172	238	373	336	312
Cash Flow	469	408	20.0	255	538	245	169	294	411	420
Curr. Ratio	1.2	1.4	1.3	1.1	1.9	0.8	1.1	1.2	2.6	7.8
% LT Debt of Cap.	60.6	64.7	70.2	58.8	53.2	54.3	53.7	51.4	40.9	35.9
% Net Inc.of Revs.	7.2	5.7	NM	NM	6.5	0.8	NM	4.3	11.9	NM
% Ret. on Assets	4.2	3.2	NM	NM	3.2	0.4	NM	1.8	5.0	NM
% Ret. on Equity	17.1	14.8	NM	NM	11.3	1.5	NM	7.0	17.0	NM

Data as orig. reptd.; bef. results of disc. opers. and/or spec. items. Revenues in Inc. Statement table exclude excise taxes and other income. Per share data adj. for stk. divs. as of ex-div. date. E-Estimated. NA-Not Available. NM-Not Meaningful. NR-Not Ranked.

Office—Pennzoil Place, P.O. Box 2967, Houston, TX 77252-2967. **Registrars**—Society National Bank, Houston; R-M Trust Co., Toronto. **Tel**—(713) 546-4000. **Website**—http://www.Pennzoil.com **Chrmn & CEO**—J. L. Pate. **Pres & COO**—S. D. Chesebro'. **VP & Secy**—Linda F. Condit. **VP & Treas**—B. K. Misamore. **Investor Contact**—Greg Panagos. **Dirs**—H. H. Baker, Jr., W. J. Bovaird, W. L. Lyons Brown, Jr., E. H. Cockrell, H. H. Cullen, A. Fanjul, B. Lawrence, J. L. Pate, B. Scowcroft, G. B. Smith, C. Wagner, Jr. **Transfer Agents**—Co.'s office; R-M Trust Co., Toronto. **Incorporated**—in Pennsylvania in 1889; reincorporated in Delaware in 1968. **Empl**— 10,214. **S&P Analyst:** Norman Rosenberg

STANDARD &POOR'S
STOCK REPORTS

Peoples Energy
1798

NYSE Symbol **PGL**

In S&P 500

12-SEP-98

Industry:
Natural Gas

Summary: PGL operates two natural gas distribution utilities in Illinois, serving about one million customers in Chicago and the northeastern part of the state.

S&P Opinion: Hold (★★★)	Recent Price • 35⅛	Yield • 5.5%
	52 Wk Range • 39⅞-32⅛	12-Mo. P/E • 16.2

Quantitative Evaluations

Outlook
(1 Lowest—5 Highest)
• **1⁻**

Fair Value
• **27⅛**

Risk
• **Low**

Earn./Div. Rank
• **B+**

Technical Eval.
• **Bearish** since 7/98

Rel. Strength Rank
(1 Lowest—99 Highest)
• **88**

Insider Activity
• **NA**

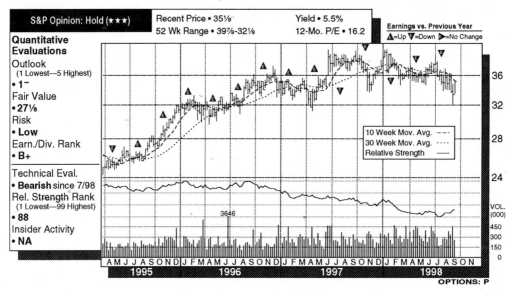

Earnings vs. Previous Year
▲=Up ▼=Down ▶=No Change

10 Week Mov. Avg. ---
30 Week Mov. Avg. ····
Relative Strength —

3646

VOL. (000)
450
300
150
0

AMJJASOND|JFMAMJJASOND|JFMAMJJASOND|JFMAMJJASON
1995   1996   1997   1998

OPTIONS: P

Overview - 06-AUG-98

Peoples Energy continued to suffer from warmer than normal weather posting EPS of $0.23 in the third quarter of 1998, versus $0.34 a year ago. The weather in the third quarter was 39% warmer than a year ago and 21% warmer than normal. Greater revenues from the company's unregulated units partly offset the drop in gas distribution sales. Because of the effect of severe weather, we dropped our 1998 and 1999 estimates to $2.40 and $2.75, from $2.80 and $3.05, respectively. Proximity to several major interstate pipeline systems provides very low cost of gas, letting the company compete effectively with alternate fuel sources. The company expects nonregulated activities, including recently formed subsidiaries Peoples Energy Resources and Peoples Energy Ventures, to account for 25% of total earnings in five years. PGL's debt to capital ratio of 42% is at a 10-year low; return on equity of 14.1%, although below the 1996 level, is above the five-year average of 11.7%; and management has brought down the dividend payout ratio to a manageable 70%, from a five-year average of 80%.

Valuation - 06-AUG-98

PGL's shares have leveled off following an interest rate driven increase in the last two months of 1997, because of the unusually warm weather across the northern U.S. and weak commodity prices. Excluding the possibility of interest rate increases or further declines in oil and gas prices, PGL stock, aided by a good dividend yield, should be able to keep up with the S&P 500 over the short term. We believe that PGL is trading at fair multiples of our revised FY 98 (Sep.) and FY 99 earnings estimates of $2.40 and $2.75, respectively.

Key Stock Statistics

S&P EPS Est. 1998	2.40	Tang. Bk. Value/Share	21.65
P/E on S&P Est. 1998	14.7	Beta	0.69
S&P EPS Est. 1999	2.75	Shareholders	27,800
Dividend Rate/Share	1.92	Market cap. (B)	$ 1.2
Shs. outstg. (M)	35.4	Inst. holdings	44%
Avg. daily vol. (M)	0.078		

Value of $10,000 invested 5 years ago: $ 16,252

Fiscal Year Ending Sep. 30

	1998	1997	1996	1995	1994	1993
Revenues (Million $)						
1Q	385.1	387.1	317.6	307.0	379.0	376.0
2Q	424.5	568.0	498.6	424.4	575.0	522.0
3Q	199.7	202.4	248.5	187.2	207.0	224.0
4Q	—	116.8	134.0	114.7	119.0	136.0
Yr.	—	1,274	1,199	1,033	1,279	1,259
Earnings Per Share ($)						
1Q	**1.01**	1.07	1.03	0.72	1.12	0.89
2Q	**1.34**	1.81	1.77	1.31	1.39	1.45
3Q	**0.23**	0.34	0.41	0.13	0.07	0.14
4Q	—	-0.40	-0.26	-0.38	-0.45	-0.38
Yr.	**E2.40**	2.81	2.96	1.78	2.13	2.11

Next earnings report expected: NA

Dividend Data (Dividends have been paid since 1937.)

Amount ($)	Date Decl.	Ex-Div. Date	Stock of Record	Payment Date
0.470	Dec. 03	Dec. 18	Dec. 22	Jan. 15 '98
0.480	Feb. 04	Mar. 18	Mar. 20	Apr. 15 '98
0.480	May. 06	Jun. 18	Jun. 22	Jul. 15 '98
0.480	Aug. 05	Sep. 18	Sep. 22	Oct. 15 '98

A Division of The McGraw·Hill Companies

STANDARD
&POOR'S
STOCK REPORTS

Peoples Energy Corporation

1798

12-SEP-98

Business Summary - 06-AUG-98

Peoples Energy is the holding company for the natural gas utility that heats the Windy City during its frigid winters (in fact, over 40% of its revenues typically come in the January-March fiscal quarter). PGL's Peoples Gas Light & Coke unit provides natural gas service to 836,000 customers within the City of Chicago. Another major subsidiary, North Shore Gas, serves about 140,000 customers in a 275 square mile area in northeastern Illinois.

The company also operates nonutility businesses. Its Peoples District Energy subsidiary provides heating and cooling services to Chicago buildings, including the largest U.S. convention center, McCormick Place. In early 1997, PGL said that, in partnership with Trigen Energy, Peoples will provide all heating, air conditioning and hot water for the new 32-story Hyatt Regency McCormick Place Hotel scheduled to open in August 1998. The Trigen-Peoples contract runs through 2021. Annual gas usage for McCormick Place, including the new south hall and the hotel, is estimated at 0.35 Bcf -- enough to heat more than 3,100 average-size homes. Other units provide fueling services for gas-powered fleet vehicles; sell and distribute CO2 detectors; and operate a plant that gasifies liquid propane and ethane.

PGL's nonregulated activities also involve wholesale services and energy investments, for which the company formed two new subsidiaries in FY 97 (Sep.): Peoples Energy Resources Corp. and Peoples Energy Ventures Corp. Peoples Energy Resources is developing other unregulated supply and storage service opportunities. Peoples Energy Ventures seeks diversified energy investments in oil and gas exploration and production, electric power generation, and gas pipelines.

The company is looking toward the future, continuing its cost containment efforts and stepping up potential expansion efforts. Today the company, which can buy supplies from nearly every major gas-production area in North America, has direct connections to four interstate pipelines and the ability to negotiate economical arrangements for transporting supplies. During the winter, both utilities (Peoples and North Shore) can tap additional supplies from Peoples' central Illinois storage facilities via company-owned pipelines. A fifth pipeline, which will connect the system with lower-priced Canadian supplies, is expected to be in place by late 1998.

In FY 97, the company sold and transported 280,728 MMcf (million cubic feet) of natural gas, down from 300,669 MMcf in FY 96. Total number of customers increased to an average of 976,238 in FY 97, up from 975,999. Residential customers accounted for nearly 74% of PGL's revenues in FY 97.

Per Share Data ($)

(Year Ended Sep. 30)	1997	1996	1995	1994	1993	1992	1991	1990	1989	1988
Tangible Bk. Val.	20.43	19.48	18.38	18.39	18.05	17.72	16.95	16.61	16.20	15.09
Earnings	2.81	2.96	1.78	2.13	2.11	2.06	2.05	2.07	2.39	2.31
Dividends	1.87	1.83	1.80	1.79	1.77	1.75	1.71	1.65	1.58	1.50
Payout Ratio	67%	62%	101%	84%	84%	85%	83%	79%	66%	65%
Prices - High	37⅞	37⅜	32	32⅛	35	31⅝	28¼	26½	26¾	21½
- Low	31¼	29⅝	24¼	23⅜	27½	24⅜	21¾	20	18⅞	15⅜
P/E Ratio - High	14	13	18	15	17	15	14	13	11	9
- Low	11	10	14	11	13	12	11	10	8	7

Income Statement Analysis (Million $)

	1997	1996	1995	1994	1993	1992	1991	1990	1989	1988
Revs.	1,274	1,199	1,033	1,279	1,259	1,097	1,104	1,165	1,188	1,117
Depr.	74.1	70.6	66.4	64.7	60.8	57.3	55.4	54.8	49.8	46.8
Maint.	47.6	45.6	41.7	37.9	35.7	36.8	36.7	34.1	33.7	33.2
Fxd. Chgs. Cov.	8.3	7.3	4.8	1.7	2.4	5.7	5.4	5.9	6.5	6.2
Constr. Credits	Nil	Nil	Nil	Nil	Nil	0.2	0.1	0.7	1.4	0.3
Eff. Tax Rate	31%	33%	30%	27%	29%	28%	28%	30%	30%	33%
Net Inc.	98.4	103	62.2	74.4	73.4	70.4	67.0	67.5	78.0	75.3

Balance Sheet & Other Fin. Data (Million $)

	1997	1996	1995	1994	1993	1992	1991	1990	1989	1988
Gross Prop.	2,134	2,046	2,088	2,019	1,951	1,844	1,747	1,668	1,593	1,472
Cap. Exp.	89.4	85.6	95.9	87.2	132	118	102	103	135	87.0
Net Prop.	1,419	1,391	1,373	1,342	1,318	1,244	1,181	1,134	1,085	1,000
Capitalization:										
LT Debt	527	527	622	626	528	490	493	502	453	460
% LT Debt	42	44	49	49	46	44	46	47	45	47
Pfd.	Nil	Nil	Nil	Nil	Nil	12.9	16.8	20.7	25.9	29.8
% Pfd.	Nil	Nil	Nil	Nil	Nil	1.10	1.60	1.90	2.50	3.00
Common	716	681	642	641	628	616	555	543	528	491
% Common	58	56	51	51	54	55	52	51	53	50
Total Cap.	1,527	1,474	1,510	1,497	1,393	1,356	1,286	1,286	1,227	1,197
% Oper. Ratio	89.7	88.9	89.8	92.0	91.0	90.2	90.5	91.2	91.3	90.6
% Earn. on Net Prop.	9.4	9.6	7.7	7.7	8.8	8.8	9.1	9.2	9.9	10.8
% Return On Revs.	7.7	8.6	6.0	5.8	5.8	6.4	6.1	5.8	6.6	6.7
% Return On Invest. Capital	6.6	9.8	17.1	8.5	8.7	8.9	9.1	9.2	10.2	10.5
% Return On Com. Equity	14.1	15.6	9.6	7.6	11.8	12.0	12.2	12.6	15.3	15.8

Data as orig. reptd.; bef. results of disc. opers. and/or spec. items. Per share data adj. for stk. divs. as of ex-div. date. Bold denotes diluted EPS (FASB 128). E-Estimated. NA-Not Available. NM-Not Meaningful. NR-Not Ranked.

Office—130 E. Randolph Dr., Chicago, IL 60601-6207. **Tel**—(312) 240-4000. **Website**—http://www.PECorp.com **Chrmn & CEO**—R. E. Terry. **Pres & COO**—J. B. Hasch. **Secy, Treas & Investor Contact**—Emmet P. Cassidy. **Dirs**—W. J. Brodsky, P. S. J. Cafferty, J. B. Hasch, F. C. Langenberg, H. J. Livingston Jr., W. G. Mitchell, E. L. Neal, R. E. Terry, R. P. Toft, A. R. Velasquez. **Transfer Agent & Registrar**—Harris Trust & Savings Bank, Chicago. **Incorporated**—in Illinois in 1855; reincorporated in Illinois in 1967. **Empl**— 2,868. **S&P Analyst:** J. Robert Cho

Pep Boys

1800

NYSE Symbol **PBY**

In S&P 500

12-SEP-98

Industry: Retail (Specialty)

Summary: This major automotive parts and accessories retailer, which also offers maintenance and parts installation services, operates more than 720 stores in 36 states.

S&P Opinion: Hold (★★★)		
Recent Price • 14⅜	Yield • 1.8%	
52 Wk Range • 28¼-12½	12-Mo. P/E • 35.1	

Quantitative Evaluations

Outlook
(1 Lowest—5 Highest)
• **4**

Fair Value
• 21¼

Risk
• **Average**

Earn./Div. Rank
• **A**

Technical Eval.
• **Bullish** since 4/98

Rel. Strength Rank
(1 Lowest—99 Highest)
• **40**

Insider Activity
• **NA**

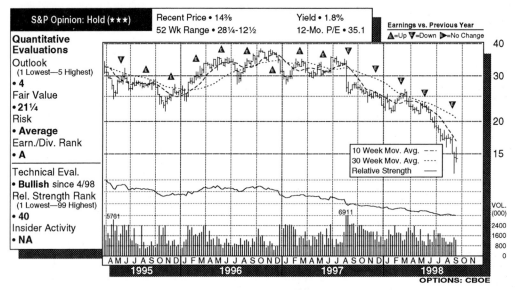

Earnings vs. Previous Year
▲=Up ▼=Down ▶=No Change

10 Week Mov. Avg. ----
30 Week Mov. Avg. ·····
Relative Strength —

VOL. (000)

OPTIONS: CBOE

Overview - 17-AUG-98

A drop in net income in FY 98 (Jan.) reflected costs from the rollout of the parts delivery program, pricing pressures, and a pretax charge of $28 million for the closure of nine stores, a reduction in the store opening plan, conversion of all Parts USA stores to the Pep Boys Express format, and other non-recurring expenses. We expect the rollout to aid revenues in FY 99, but profits will be lower, due to the costs involved, competitive pricing, higher production expenses and increased advertising and interest outlays. Ultimately, the stage should be set for a rebound in FY 2000, as rollout costs subside and store margins mature. In addition, long-term growth prospects are enhanced by PBY's ongoing expansion plans, an increase in the average vehicle age in the U.S., and the rising popularity of auto leasing (which expands vehicle servicing needs upon lease expiration).

Valuation - 17-AUG-98

PBY is a high-quality operator in the fragmented automotive parts retailing industry, and should benefit over the long-term from an active store expansion program. However, margin weakness and a reduction in the pace of new store openings have contributed to weakness in the stock price. An operating loss in the FY 98 fourth quarter, versus an anticipated profit, disappointed shareholders. We view FY 99 as a transition year, to set up a resumption of earnings growth in FY 2000, and believe that investors should focus on the long-term outlook, despite near-term difficulties. Although certain trends bode well for PBY, including high consumer debt levels and longer-lasting vehicles, which should restrain purchases of new automobiles, we expect near-term gains to be restricted by weakness in the do-it-yourself segment.

Key Stock Statistics

S&P EPS Est. 1999	1.00	Tang. Bk. Value/Share	13.03
P/E on S&P Est. 1999	14.4	Beta	1.07
Dividend Rate/Share	0.26	Shareholders	4,300
Shs. outstg. (M)	63.8	Market cap. (B)	$0.917
Avg. daily vol. (M)	0.249	Inst. holdings	55%

Value of $10,000 invested 5 years ago: $ 6,519

Fiscal Year Ending Jan. 31

	1999	1998	1997	1996	1995	1994
Revenues (Million $)						
1Q	584.2	489.3	428.6	361.2	338.0	299.0
2Q	635.3	539.3	476.7	410.8	370.4	329.1
3Q	—	525.6	478.8	411.8	363.2	316.0
4Q	—	502.4	444.4	410.5	335.7	296.8
Yr.	—	2,057	1,829	1,594	1,407	1,241
Earnings Per Share ($)						
1Q	**0.16**	0.37	0.33	0.27	0.29	0.22
2Q	**0.29**	0.47	0.49	0.41	0.39	0.31
3Q	—	0.38	0.44	0.35	0.34	0.28
4Q	—	-0.45	0.36	0.31	0.30	0.25
Yr.	**E1.00**	**0.80**	1.62	1.34	1.32	1.06

Next earnings report expected: mid November

Dividend Data (Dividends have been paid since 1950.)

Amount ($)	Date Decl.	Ex-Div. Date	Stock of Record	Payment Date
0.060	Sep. 11	Oct. 08	Oct. 13	Oct. 27 '97
0.060	Dec. 03	Jan. 08	Jan. 12	Jan. 26 '98
0.065	Mar. 31	Apr. 08	Apr. 13	Apr. 27 '98
0.065	Jun. 03	Jul. 09	Jul. 13	Jul. 27 '98

A Division of The **McGraw·Hill** *Companies*

Business Summary - 17-AUG-98

The Pep Boys - Manny, Moe & Jack is engaged primarily in the retail sale of automotive parts and accessories; automotive maintenance and service; and installation of parts. As of August 1, 1998, the company was operating a chain of 723 stores in 36 states, the District of Columbia, and Puerto Rico.

In FY 98 (Jan.), about 84% of revenues and 88% of gross profits were generated from merchandise sales, while 16% of sales and 12% of gross profits were derived from service and installation.

The company's stores occupied 13.4 million sq. ft. of retail space at the end of FY 98, up 14% from 11.8 million sq. ft. a year earlier. At FY 98 year-end, the company was operating 711 stores, including 591 SUPERCENTERS (with an average 20,800 square feet per store, and an aggregate of 6,208 service bays); one Service & Tire Center; and 119 Pep Boy Express (formerly Parts USA) stores. Pep Boy Express stores average 9,400 sq. ft., and have no service bays.

Each store carries the same basic product line, with variations based on the number and type of cars registered in different markets. A full line of a store's inventory includes about 28,000 items. A Pep Boy Express

store carries 27,000 items, reflecting the absence of tires. Products include tires; batteries; new and rebuilt parts for domestic and imported cars (including shock absorbers, struts, ignition parts, mufflers and exhaust pipes, oil and air filters, belts and hoses, and brake parts); chemicals (including oil, antifreeze, polishes, additives, cleansers and paints); and car, truck, sport utility vehicle, and van accessories (including seat covers, alarms, floor mats, gauges, mirrors and booster cables).

The company has established a commercial parts delivery business to increase its market share with the professional installer. PBY believes this will strengthen its position in the "buy-for-resale" customer segment by taking greater advantage of the breadth and quality of its parts inventory as well as its experience supplying its own service bays and mechanics. At January 31, 1998, 262 of the company's stores provide parts delivery, and by the end of the second quarter of FY 98, the company expects to provide parts delivery from all of its its suitable stores, representing about 80% of the chain.

In FY 98, sales rose 12%, year to year, but were restricted by weakness in the do-it-yourself market that led to negative comparable-store sales. Comparable-store service labor and tire revenue, however, increased 10% and 13%, respectively.

Per Share Data ($)

(Year Ended Jan. 31)	1998	1997	1996	1995	1994	1993	1992	1991	1990	1989
Tangible Bk. Val.	13.39	12.78	11.12	9.53	9.11	8.40	6.79	6.20	5.63	5.05
Cash Flow	2.15	2.58	2.16	2.05	1.69	1.50	1.28	1.17	1.04	0.99
Earnings	0.80	1.62	1.34	1.32	1.06	0.90	0.69	0.67	0.63	0.68
Dividends	0.24	0.21	0.19	0.21	0.15	0.14	0.13	0.12	0.11	0.09
Payout Ratio	30%	13%	14%	16%	14%	15%	18%	17%	17%	14%
Cal. Yrs.	1997	1996	1995	1994	1993	1992	1991	1990	1989	1988
Prices - High	35⅝	38¼	34¾	36⅞	27⅜	27⅜	19½	17¼	17¼	15⅞
- Low	22	23⅞	21⅞	25⅛	19⅞	15⅛	8⅜	8½	10½	10⅜
P/E Ratio - High	45	24	26	28	26	30	28	26	27	23
- Low	27	15	16	19	19	17	12	13	17	15

Income Statement Analysis (Million $)

	1998	1997	1996	1995	1994	1993	1992	1991	1990	1989
Revs.	2,057	1,829	1,594	1,407	1,241	1,156	1,002	885	799	656
Oper. Inc.	193	243	213	193	160	139	117	105	92.0	84.0
Depr.	82.9	65.8	53.5	44.4	39.1	36.7	33.4	27.8	22.9	17.0
Int. Exp.	39.7	31.9	33.5	27.8	21.0	21.0	25.7	21.5	19.5	13.2
Pretax Inc.	75.5	159	129	126	105	85.6	60.5	58.8	55.1	60.2
Eff. Tax Rate	34%	37%	37%	37%	37%	36%	36%	36%	36%	37%
Net Inc.	49.6	101	81.5	80.0	65.5	54.6	38.9	37.5	35.1	37.7

Balance Sheet & Other Fin. Data (Million $)

	1998	1997	1996	1995	1994	1993	1992	1991	1990	1989
Cash	10.8	2.6	11.5	11.7	12.1	11.6	14.4	15.1	14.3	20.0
Curr. Assets	770	605	466	411	342	327	259	260	187	146
Total Assets	2,161	1,818	1,500	1,291	1,079	968	857	819	676	582
Curr. Liab.	619	534	427	289	249	223	177	168	117	101
LT Debt	647	456	367	381	253	209	279	286	228	187
Common Eqty.	823	778	665	586	548	510	379	345	312	276
Total Cap.	1,543	1,284	1,073	1,002	829	745	680	651	559	481
Cap. Exp.	284	245	206	184	135	78.0	66.0	106	88.0	123
Cash Flow	132	167	135	124	105	91.3	72.3	65.4	58.0	54.7
Curr. Ratio	1.2	1.1	1.1	1.4	1.4	1.5	1.5	1.5	1.6	1.4
% LT Debt of Cap.	41.9	35.5	34.2	38.0	30.5	28.1	41.1	43.9	40.7	38.9
% Net Inc.of Revs.	2.4	5.5	5.2	5.7	5.3	4.7	3.9	4.2	4.4	5.7
% Ret. on Assets	2.5	6.1	5.9	6.7	6.4	5.7	4.6	5.0	5.5	7.2
% Ret. on Equity	6.2	14.0	13.1	14.0	12.4	11.8	10.7	11.4	11.9	14.7

Data as orig. reptd.; bef. results of disc. opers. and/or spec. items. Per share data adj. for stk. divs. as of ex-div. date. Bold denotes diluted EPS (FASB 128). E-Estimated. NA-Not Available. NM-Not Meaningful. NR-Not Ranked.

Office—3111 W. Allegheny Ave., Philadelphia, PA 19132. Tel—(215) 229-9000. Website—http://www.pepboys.com Chrmn, Pres & CEO—M. G. Leibovitz. EVP & COO—W. H. Province. EVP & CFO—Michael J. Holden. SVP & Secy—F. A. Stampone. Director, Investor Relations—Nancy R. Kyle. Dirs—L. K. Black, B. J. Korman, J. R. Leaman Jr., M. G. Leibovitz, M. D. Pryor, L. Rosenfeld, B. Strauss, M. H. Tanenbaum. Transfer Agent & Registrar—American Stock Transfer & Trust Co., NYC. Incorporated—in Pennsylvania in 1925. Empl— 24,203. S&P Analyst: Efraim Levy

STANDARD &POOR'S
STOCK REPORTS

PepsiCo

1802

NYSE Symbol **PEP**

In S&P 500

12-SEP-98

Industry:
Beverages
(Non-Alcoholic)

Summary: PepsiCo is a major international producer of branded beverage and snack food products.

S&P Opinion: Hold (★★★)		
Recent Price • 29¾	**Yield • 1.7%**	
52 Wk Range • 44¾-27½	**12-Mo. P/E • 24.0**	

Quantitative Evaluations

Outlook
(1 Lowest—5 Highest)
• **2+**

Fair Value
• **30¾**

Risk
• **Average**

Earn./Div. Rank
• **A**

Technical Eval.
• **Bearish** since 8/98

Rel. Strength Rank
(1 Lowest—99 Highest)
• **42**

Insider Activity
• **Neutral**

Earnings vs. Previous Year
▲=Up ▼=Down ▶=No Change

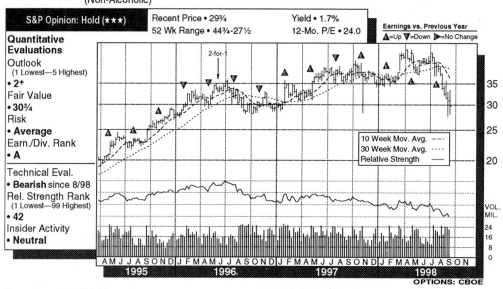

10 Week Mov. Avg. – – –
30 Week Mov. Avg. ....
Relative Strength —

OPTIONS: CBOE

Overview - 05-AUG-98

Beverage profits in 1998 (before unusual charges) are projected to rise very modestly, reflecting low single-digit growth in North America and an approximate breakeven performance for international operations (versus a $137 million loss in 1997). Profits in North America will be pressured by heavy costs incurred in accelerating the fountain channel business. Snack food profits are expected to rise at an approximate 10% rate, driven by 5% to 8% unit volume growth, higher prices, and incremental contributions from the launch of Olestra-based snacks. Lower debt levels should allow for net interest expense reduction, while excess cash generation is expected to be used for share repurchases of about 3% to 5% of shares outstanding. The acquisition of Tropicana will likely cut 1998 EPS by $0.01, and 1999 EPS by $0.02 to $0.03, due to increased amortization. In all, we look for diluted EPS of $1.29 in 1998, and $1.48 in 1999, up from 1997's $1.16 (before unusual charges).

Valuation - 05-AUG-98

The shares are expected to move in line with the S&P 500 Index over the next 12 months, given the stock's recent P/E multiple of about 30X estimated 1998 EPS of $1.29; the multiple was recently about 25% above that of the S&P 500. In the wake of PepsiCo's late 1997 spinoff of its beleaguered restaurant operations, the company's profitability levels, earnings growth consistency, and excess cash flow generation should improve. Nevertheless, we believe that investors have already built these positive factors into PEP's current premium valuation. Given the company's large market position in the growing worldwide packaged beverage and snack industries, though, the shares are suitable for conservative investors seeking above-average long-term capital appreciation.

Key Stock Statistics

S&P EPS Est. 1998	1.29	Tang. Bk. Value/Share	0.06
P/E on S&P Est. 1998	23.1	Beta	1.38
S&P EPS Est. 1999	1.48	Shareholders	207,000
Dividend Rate/Share	0.52	Market cap. (B)	$ 43.8
Shs. outstg. (M)	1472.8	Inst. holdings	55%
Avg. daily vol. (M)	4.755		

Value of $10,000 invested 5 years ago: NA

Fiscal Year Ending Dec. 31

	1998	1997	1996	1995	1994	1993
Revenues (Million $)						
1Q	4,353	4,213	6,554	6,191	5,729	5,092
2Q	5,258	5,086	7,691	7,286	6,557	5,890
3Q	—	5,362	7,867	7,693	7,064	6,316
4Q	—	6,256	9,533	9,251	9,123	7,722
Yr.	—	20,917	31,645	30,421	28,472	25,021
Earnings Per Share ($)						
1Q	**0.24**	**0.20**	0.24	0.20	0.17	0.16
2Q	**0.33**	**0.11**	0.36	0.30	0.28	0.27
3Q	**E0.41**	**0.35**	0.09	0.39	0.34	0.28
4Q	**E0.33**	**0.29**	0.03	0.11	0.32	0.28
Yr.	**E1.29**	**0.95**	0.72	1.00	1.11	0.98

Next earnings report expected: late October

Dividend Data (Dividends have been paid since 1952.)

Amount ($)	Date Decl.	Ex-Div. Date	Stock of Record	Payment Date
0.125	Nov. 13	Dec. 10	Dec. 12	Jan. 01 '98
0.125	Jan. 23	Mar. 11	Mar. 13	Mar. 31 '98
0.130	May. 06	Jun. 10	Jun. 12	Jun. 30 '98
0.130	Jul. 23	Sep. 09	Sep. 11	Sep. 30 '98

A Division of The **McGraw·Hill** *Companies*

Business Summary - 05-AUG-98

Following the October 1997 spinoff to shareholders of the restaurant division through a spinoff (named TRICON Global Restaurants, Inc., and listed on the NYSE under the symbol YUM), PepsiCo refined its focus from three large consumer businesses to two: beverages and snack foods. Business segment contributions (excluding unusual charges) in 1997 were:

	Sales	Profits
Beverages	50%	40%
Snack foods	50%	60%

International operations accounted for 29% of sales and 6% of operating profits in 1997.

Beverage operations, which operate as Pepsi-Cola Company, consist primarily of the production and distribution (to licensed bottlers) of soft drinks and soft-drink concentrates. Principal brands include Pepsi-Cola, Diet Pepsi, Mountain Dew, Slice, Mug, All-Sport and, within Canada, 7UP and Diet 7UP. The Pepsi/Lipton Tea Partnership joint venture sells tea concentrate to Pepsi-Cola bottlers under the Lipton trademark. Products are manufactured in 165 plants (PEP operates 60) throughout the U.S. and Canada and 275 plants (37 operated by PEP) outside the U.S. and Canada. Pepsi-Cola products are available in 186 countries and territories outside the U.S. and Canada.

The snack food product business is operated as The Frito-Lay Company, which produces the best-selling line of snack foods in the U.S., including Fritos brand corn chips, Lay's and Ruffles brand potato chips, Doritos and Tostitos brand tortilla chips, Chee-tos brand cheese-flavored snacks, Rold Gold pretzels, and Sun-chips brand multigrain snacks. Products are transported from Frito-Lay's manufacturing plants to major distribution centers, principally by company-owned trucks. Principal international markets include Australia, Brazil, France, Mexico, the Netherlands, Poland, Spain and the U.K. In October 1997, Frito-Lay acquired the Cracker Jack candy-coated popcorn and peanut snack business from Borden Foods.

In July 1998, the company announced plans to purchase Tropicana from The Seagram Company Ltd., for $3.3 billion cash. Tropicana is the world's largest marketer and producer of branded juices, with 1997 revenues of nearly $2 billion. In addition to Tropicana Pure Premium, Season's Best and Dole, Tropicana's portfolio includes Tropicana Pure Tropics 100% juice products and Tropicana Twister juice beverage products in the U.S., and Fruvita chilled and Hitchcock shelf-stable juices and Looza nectars and juices in Europe. The transaction is expected to close by the end of August.

Per Share Data ($)

(Year Ended Dec. 31)	1997	1996	1995	1994	1993	1992	1991	1990	1989	1988
Tangible Bk. Val.	0.72	NM	NM	-0.63	-0.99	-1.00	-0.24	-0.59	-1.00	0.36
Cash Flow	1.65	1.79	2.08	2.09	1.84	1.54	1.30	1.23	1.04	0.88
Earnings	0.95	0.72	1.00	1.11	0.98	0.81	0.68	0.69	0.56	0.48
Dividends	0.49	0.45	0.39	0.35	0.30	0.26	0.23	0.19	0.16	0.13
Payout Ratio	52%	62%	39%	32%	31%	31%	34%	28%	28%	28%
Prices - High	41¼	35⅞	29⅜	20⅝	21⅞	21¾	17⅞	14	11	7¼
- Low	28¼	27¼	17	14⅝	17¼	15¼	11¾	9	6¼	5
P/E Ratio - High	43	50	29	19	22	27	26	20	19	15
- Low	30	38	17	13	18	19	17	13	11	10

Income Statement Analysis (Million $)

	1997	1996	1995	1994	1993	1992	1991	1990	1989	1988
Revs.	20,917	31,645	30,421	28,472	25,021	21,970	19,608	17,803	15,242	13,007
Oper. Inc.	4,058	5,087	5,247	4,778	4,312	3,754	3,302	3,014	2,551	2,003
Depr.	1,106	1,719	1,740	1,577	1,405	1,189	1,009	875	760	619
Int. Exp.	478	600	682	645	573	586	616	689	613	347
Pretax Inc.	2,309	2,047	2,432	2,664	2,423	1,899	1,670	1,667	1,351	1,138
Eff. Tax Rate	35%	44%	34%	33%	35%	31%	35%	35%	33%	33%
Net Inc.	1,491	1,149	1,606	1,784	1,588	1,302	1,080	1,091	901	762

Balance Sheet & Other Fin. Data (Million $)

	1997	1996	1995	1994	1993	1992	1991	1990	1989	1988
Cash	2,883	786	1,498	1,488	1,856	2,058	2,036	1,816	1,534	1,618
Curr. Assets	6,251	5,139	5,546	5,072	5,164	4,842	4,566	4,081	3,551	3,265
Total Assets	20,101	24,512	25,432	24,792	23,706	20,951	18,775	17,143	15,127	11,135
Curr. Liab.	4,257	5,139	5,230	5,270	6,575	4,324	3,722	4,771	3,692	3,874
LT Debt	4,946	8,439	8,509	8,841	7,443	7,965	7,806	5,900	6,076	2,656
Common Eqty.	6,939	6,623	7,313	6,856	6,339	5,356	5,545	4,904	3,891	3,161
Total Cap.	13,582	16,840	17,707	17,669	15,789	15,000	14,422	11,747	10,824	6,618
Cap. Exp.	1,506	2,287	2,104	2,253	2,008	1,583	1,524	1,180	944	755
Cash Flow	2,597	2,868	3,346	3,361	2,993	2,491	2,089	1,966	1,661	1,381
Curr. Ratio	1.5	1.0	1.0	1.0	0.8	1.1	1.2	0.9	1.0	0.8
% LT Debt of Cap.	36.4	50.1	48.1	50.0	47.1	53.1	54.1	50.2	56.1	40.1
% Net Inc.of Revs.	7.1	3.6	5.3	6.3	6.3	5.9	5.5	6.1	5.9	5.9
% Ret. on Assets	7.1	4.6	6.4	7.4	7.1	6.5	6.0	6.8	6.9	7.5
% Ret. on Equity	22.0	16.5	22.7	27.2	27.2	22.0	20.7	24.8	25.5	26.8

Data as orig. reptd.; bef. results of disc. opers. and/or spec. Items. Per share data adj. for stk. divs. as of ex-div. date. EPS and estimates in bold or bold/italic follow FASB 128 definition of Diluted EPS; all other EPS and estimates generally follow earlier use of Primary EPS. 1997 3Q EPS are for 9 mos. E-Estimated. NA-Not Available. NM-Not Meaningful. NR-Not Ranked.

Office—700 Anderson Hill Rd., Purchase, NY 10577-1444. **Tel**—(914) 253-3035. **Fax**—(914) 253-2711. **Website**—http://www.pepsico.com **Chrmn & CEO**—R. A. Enrico. **Vice Chrmn & CFO**—K. M. von der Heyden. **SVP & Secy**—R. F. Sharpe, Jr. **VP & Investor Contact**—Margaret D. Moore. **Dirs**—J. F. Akers, R. E. Allen, D. W. Calloway, R. A. Enrico, P. Foy, R. L. Hunt, J. J. Murphy, S. S. Reinemund, S. P. Rockefeller, F. A. Thomas, P. R. Vagelos, K. M. von der Heyden, C. E. Weatherup, A. R. Weber. **Transfer Agent**—Bank of Boston. **Incorporated**—in Delaware in 1919; reincorporated in North Carolina in 1986. **Empl**— 142,000. **S&P Analyst**: Richard Joy

Perkin-Elmer

1803

NYSE Symbol **PKN**

In S&P 500

12-SEP-98

Industry:
Electronics (Instrumentation)

Summary: Perkin-Elmer is the leading worldwide producer of analytical instruments and life science systems.

S&P Opinion: Hold (★★★)	Recent Price • 68½	Yield • 1.0%
	52 Wk Range • 77⅞-54½	12-Mo. P/E • 61.2

Quantitative Evaluations

Outlook
(1 Lowest—5 Highest)
• **4⁻**

Fair Value
• **71¾**

Risk
• **Average**

Earn./Div. Rank
• **B**

Technical Eval.
• **Bullish** since 9/98

Rel. Strength Rank
(1 Lowest—99 Highest)
• **98**

Insider Activity
• **NA**

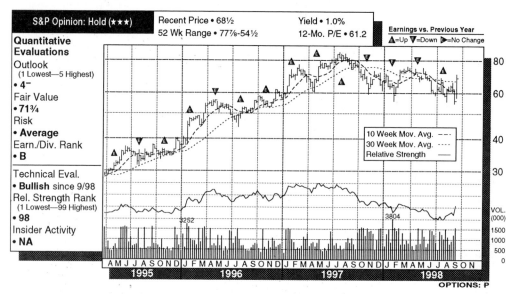

Earnings vs. Previous Year
▲=Up ▼=Down ▶=No Change

10 Week Mov. Avg. ----
30 Week Mov. Avg. ·····
Relative Strength —

OPTIONS: P

Overview - 12-AUG-98

Revenues are expected to grow by about 15% through FY 99 (Jun.), as strong life sciences volume offsets continued weakness for analytical instruments due to problems in Southeast Asia and the effects of a strong U.S. dollar overseas. PE Biosystems revenues are seen rising 20% to 25% on increased demand for new products, and contributions from PerSeptive Biosystems and Molecular Informatics. Long-term margins are expected to widen, as the global restructuring program for the AI division proceeds and synergies develop through the integration of acquired companies. Although additional pretax charges of $8 million to $10 million are seen over the next few quarters, cost savings could boost gross margins by 1% in subsequent years. EPS should grow 30% to 35%, or 25% to 30% after the effect of currency translations. The tax rate will rise to 26% from 25%.

Valuation - 12-AUG-98

With near-term results continuing to be affected by a strong U.S. dollar and weakness in Southeast Asia, we do not expect the shares to outperform the market during the next six months. The stock was recently off its lows, but was still down almost 20% since mid-May. PKN, which recorded special charges of $1.41 a share in FY 98 (Jun.) related to restructuring and other merger costs, will likely experience only modest capital gains, if any, until the currency effect softens and orders pick up in Japan when they finalize their annual budget. With unsettled worldwide markets expected to continue for the near term, and the shares trading at 19 times our EPS projection for this fiscal year, we suggest waiting before adding to positions.

Key Stock Statistics

S&P EPS Est. 1998	2.60	Tang. Bk. Value/Share	9.97
P/E on S&P Est. 1998	26.3	Beta	1.06
S&P EPS Est. 1999	3.25	Shareholders	6,900
Dividend Rate/Share	0.68	Market cap. (B)	$ 3.4
Shs. outstg. (M)	49.1	Inst. holdings	89%
Avg. daily vol. (M)	0.264		

Value of $10,000 invested 5 years ago: $ 21,857

Fiscal Year Ending Jun. 30

	1998	1997	1996	1995	1994	1993
Revenues (Million $)						
1Q	296.4	275.7	264.4	247.3	243.3	250.9
2Q	342.9	330.8	294.1	261.0	256.8	270.2
3Q	390.8	322.9	299.1	274.6	263.5	258.6
4Q	448.5	347.4	305.4	280.6	260.9	231.6
Yr.	1,531	1,277	1,163	1,064	1,024	1,011
Earnings Per Share ($)						
1Q	**0.53**	0.73	0.41	0.35	0.30	0.26
2Q	**0.18**	1.14	0.53	0.40	0.50	0.46
3Q	**-0.14**	0.23	-0.84	0.86	0.45	-0.38
4Q	**0.71**	0.48	0.22	-0.04	0.41	0.20
Yr.	**1.12**	2.58	0.32	1.57	1.66	0.54

Next earnings report expected: NA

Dividend Data (Dividends have been paid since 1971.)

Amount ($)	Date Decl.	Ex-Div. Date	Stock of Record	Payment Date
0.170	Nov. 21	Nov. 26	Dec. 01	Jan. 02 '98
0.170	Jan. 15	Feb. 26	Mar. 02	Apr. 01 '98
0.170	May. 08	May. 28	Jun. 01	Jul. 01 '98
0.170	Aug. 20	Aug. 28	Sep. 01	Oct. 01 '98

Business Summary - 12-AUG-98

Through major restructuring efforts and management changes initiated since FY 96 (Jun.), this world leader in the development and manufacture of life science and analytical instrument systems has begun to improve profitability and set its sights on aggressive growth.

Perkin Elmer (PKN) develops, manufactures, markets, sells and services analytical instrument systems and life sciences products. These include biochemical analytical instrument systems, consisting of instruments and associated consumable products for life science research and related applications. These automated systems are used for synthesis amplification, purification, isolation, analysis and sequencing of nucleic acids, proteins and other biological molecules.

During FY 96, PKN reorganized into two business segments: Life Sciences (PE Applied Biosystems division -- AB) and Analytical Instruments (AI). In late FY 98, PKN formed a third segment, Celera Genomics Corp. AB has a five year revenue growth target of more than 20% a year. The company expects AI to contribute aftertax operating cash flow of $80 million to $85 million a year by FY 99, with pretax profit margins in the mid-teens.

Life Sciences is a high growth business that will aggressively invest in technologies, products, markets and global regions. PKN is targeting genetic research, phar-

maceutical and applied and genetic testing markets for strategic investment. Between 40% and 50% of life sciences orders have been for products introduced within the prior 12 months. In FY 98, the division acquired PerSeptive Biosystems (PB) and Molecular Informatics. PB ($96 million in sales) makes consumable products and instrumentation systems. A special charge of $0.87 a diluted share was recorded in FY 98 related to the PB purchase. In early 1997, PKN formed GeneCore Biotechnologies, a DNA sequencing joint venture in Shanghai with Sequana Therapeutics, Inc.

Analytical instruments are used to analyze substances at the molecular level in a wide range of industries, from chemicals and plastics to metals and electronics. In FY 98, AI introduced a new line of atomic absorption products, reorganized its European operations and experienced 25% sales growth in Latin America.

In August 1998, PKN said it was progressing with the setup of its new Celera genomics division, and was in talks with potential pharmaceutical customers. The company noted that it is evaluating various structural alternatives for Celera, from off-balance sheet financing to targeted stock. Celera's strategy is to become the definitive source for biomedical and genomics information, derived from a plan to complete the sequencing of the human genome in three years.

International business accounted for 62% of revenues in FY 97, down from 64% in FY 96.

Per Share Data ($)

(Year Ended Jun. 30)	1998	1997	1996	1995	1994	1993	1992	1991	1990	1989
Tangible Bk. Val.	NA	9.97	7.54	7.24	6.76	1.98	9.08	7.80	11.77	14.10
Cash Flow	NA	3.38	1.29	2.52	2.61	0.39	2.70	0.82	1.82	1.70
Earnings	1.12	2.58	0.32	1.57	1.66	0.54	1.72	-0.08	1.10	1.08
Dividends	0.68	0.68	0.68	0.68	0.68	0.68	0.68	0.68	0.68	0.66
Payout Ratio	61%	26%	NM	43%	41%	126%	40%	NM	62%	61%
Prices - High	76	86⅛	56¼	40¼	39½	39¾	36	34⅜	24⅞	28¾
- Low	55½	57⅞	37⅝	25¾	26½	28½	27¼	21⅜	18⅝	20¾
P/E Ratio - High	68	33	NM	26	24	74	21	NM	23	27
- Low	50	22	NM	16	16	53	16	NM	17	19

Income Statement Analysis (Million $)

	1998	1997	1996	1995	1994	1993	1992	1991	1990	1989
Revs.	NA	1,277	1,163	1,064	1,024	1,011	911	874	838	784
Oper. Inc.	NA	189	166	132	139	129	123	103	101	112
Depr.	NA	36.0	41.2	40.7	42.7	41.3	33.7	29.8	29.1	26.9
Int. Exp.	NA	2.3	5.0	8.2	7.1	13.1	19.0	21.3	15.6	17.9
Pretax Inc.	NA	157	35.5	82.3	89.0	44.0	78.0	8.0	66.0	73.0
Eff. Tax Rate	NA	27%	61%	19%	17%	44%	25%	133%	33%	34%
Net Inc.	NA	115	13.9	66.9	74.0	24.5	58.8	-2.6	44.2	46.9

Balance Sheet & Other Fin. Data (Million $)

	1998	1997	1996	1995	1994	1993	1992	1991	1990	1989
Cash	NA	196	96.6	73.0	25.0	30.0	12.0	19.0	11.0	18.0
Curr. Assets	NA	794	641	602	515	475	491	471	537	439
Total Assets	NA	1,105	941	893	885	851	801	752	853	997
Curr. Liab.	NA	455	441	374	378	374	372	380	351	309
LT Debt	NA	33.6	0.9	34.1	34.3	7.0	57.0	54.0	60.0	33.0
Common Eqty.	NA	437	323	305	290	307	305	262	391	612
Total Cap.	NA	471	324	339	325	314	362	320	451	645
Cap. Exp.	NA	62.2	32.4	28.9	34.5	28.4	29.5	32.2	26.3	56.6
Cash Flow	NA	151	55.2	108	117	66.0	92.0	27.0	73.0	74.0
Curr. Ratio	NA	1.8	1.5	1.6	1.4	1.3	1.3	1.2	1.5	1.4
% LT Debt of Cap.	NA	7.1	0.3	10.1	10.6	2.3	15.6	17.0	13.3	5.1
% Net Inc.of Revs.	NA	9.0	1.2	6.3	7.2	2.4	6.4	NM	5.3	6.0
% Ret. on Assets	NA	11.3	1.5	7.5	8.5	2.6	7.6	NM	5.5	4.0
% Ret. on Equity	NA	30.3	4.4	22.5	24.8	6.9	20.7	NM	10.3	7.1

Data as orig. reptd.; bef. results of disc. opers. and/or spec. items. Per share data adj. for stk. divs. as of ex-div. date. Bold denotes diluted EPS (FASB 128). E-Estimated. NA-Not Available. NM-Not Meaningful. NR-Not Ranked.

Office—761 Main Ave., Norwalk, CT 06859-0001. **Tel**—(203) 762-1000. **Website**—http://www.perkin-elmer.com. **Chrmn, Pres & CEO**—T. L. White. **SVP, CFO & Treas**—D. L. Winger. **Dir of Fin**—J. S. Ostaszewski. **VP & Secy**—W. B. Sawch. **Investor Contact**—Charles Poole (203-761-5400). **Dirs**—J. F. Abely Jr., R. H. Ayers, J. Belingard, R. H. Hayes, D. R. Melville, B. R. Roberts, G. C. St. Laurent, C. W. Slayman, O. R. Smith, R. F. Tucker, T. L. White. **Transfer Agent & Registrar**—First National Bank of Boston. **Incorporated**—in New York in 1939. **Empl**— 6,500.
S&P Analyst: Stewart Scharf

STANDARD &POOR'S
STOCK REPORTS
Pfizer Inc.
1810
NYSE Symbol **PFE**

In S&P 500

12-SEP-98

Industry:
Health Care (Drugs - Major Pharmaceuticals)

Summary: This leading global pharmaceutical company also has interests in hospital products, animal health items and consumer products.

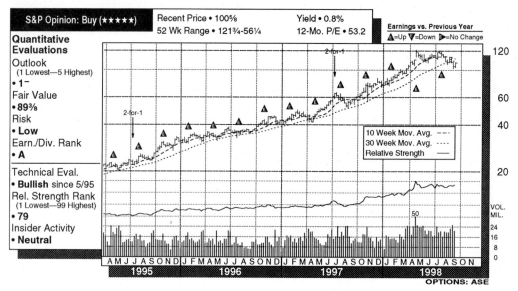

S&P Opinion: Buy (★★★★★)

Recent Price • 100⅝	Yield • 0.8%
52 Wk Range • 121¾-56¼	12-Mo. P/E • 53.2

Earnings vs. Previous Year
▲=Up ▼=Down ▶=No Change

Quantitative Evaluations

Outlook
(1 Lowest—5 Highest)
• **1⁻**

Fair Value
• **89⅜**

Risk
• **Low**

Earn./Div. Rank
• **A**

Technical Eval.
• **Bullish** since 5/95

Rel. Strength Rank
(1 Lowest—99 Highest)
• **79**

Insider Activity
• **Neutral**

10 Week Mov. Avg. – – –
30 Week Mov. Avg. - - - -
Relative Strength ——

OPTIONS: ASE

Overview - 24-JUL-98

Fueled by the strongest new drug lineup in the industry, sales growth in 1998 should exceed 20%. Principal drivers should be explosive growth in Viagra, a breakthrough therapy for male erectile dysfunction launched in April, as well as gains in established drugs such as Norvasc and Cardura cardiovasculars, Zithromax antibiotic, Zoloft antidepressant, and Glucotrol XL for diabetes. Another successful new launch has been Trovan broad-spectrum antibiotic. Volume is also being augmented by strong growth in co-marketed products such as Lipitor cholesterol-lowering agent and Aricept for Alzheimer's disease. Gains in these products should more than outweigh declining sales of older drugs and lower sales of medical devices and consumer products. Margins should widen on the better volume and an improved product mix.

Valuation - 24-JUL-98

These shares have enjoyed a sustained uptrend in recent years, reflecting the company's broad-based portfolio of blockbuster drugs coupled with a highly productive R&D platform that should continue to spawn lucrative new drugs in the years ahead. Much of the stock's recent strength is attributable to Viagra. Launched in early April, initial sales of this breakthrough therapy for male erectile dysfunction have already broken records, reflecting extremely strong pent-up demand and the lack of other competing oral products to treat this condition. Other promising new drugs presently in clinical trials include dofetilide treatment for cardiac arrhythmias, eletriptan for migraine, and droloxifene for breast cancer. PFE recently agreed to sell its Schneider angioplasty business to Boston Scientific for $2.1 billion. We recommend purchase of the shares for continued above-average appreciation.

Key Stock Statistics

S&P EPS Est. 1998	2.15	Tang. Bk. Value/Share	5.20
P/E on S&P Est. 1998	46.8	Beta	1.06
S&P EPS Est. 1999	2.60	Shareholders	65,000
Dividend Rate/Share	0.76	Market cap. (B)	$140.9
Shs. outstg. (M)	1400.2	Inst. holdings	49%
Avg. daily vol. (M)	5.256		

Value of $10,000 invested 5 years ago: $ 60,961

Fiscal Year Ending Dec. 31

	1998	1997	1996	1995	1994	1993
Revenues (Million $)						
1Q	3,339	3,002	2,682	2,338	1,983	2,338
2Q	3,633	2,913	2,661	2,401	1,923	2,401
3Q	—	3,094	2,803	2,539	2,075	1,873
4Q	—	3,496	3,160	2,744	2,300	1,989
Yr.	—	12,504	11,306	10,021	8,281	7,478
Earnings Per Share ($)						
1Q	**0.53**	0.47	0.41	0.34	0.29	0.34
2Q	**0.47**	0.35	0.30	0.24	0.21	0.24
3Q	**E0.57**	0.46	0.40	0.33	0.27	-0.16
4Q	**E0.58**	0.43	0.39	0.32	0.27	0.23
Yr.	**E2.15**	1.70	1.49	1.24	1.05	0.51

Next earnings report expected: mid October

Dividend Data (Dividends have been paid since 1901.)

Amount ($)	Date Decl.	Ex-Div. Date	Stock of Record	Payment Date
0.170	Oct. 23	Nov. 05	Nov. 07	Dec. 11 '97
0.190	Jan. 22	Feb. 04	Feb. 06	Mar. 12 '98
0.190	Apr. 23	May. 06	May. 08	Jun. 11 '98
0.190	Jun. 25	Aug. 05	Aug. 07	Sep. 10 '98

A Division of The **McGraw-Hill** *Companies*

STANDARD
&POOR'S
STOCK REPORTS

Pfizer Inc.

1810
12-SEP-98

Business Summary - 24-JUL-98

Pfizer (PFE) traces its history back to 1849, when it was founded by Charles Pfizer and Charles Erhart as a chemical products firm. Today, it is a leading global pharmaceutical firm, marketing a wide range of prescription drugs. It also holds important interests in hospital products, animal health items and consumer products. Overseas business is very significant, representing 45% of total sales and 37% of profits in 1997. Business segment contributions in 1997 were:

	Sales	Profits
Health care	85%	96%
Animal health	11%	3%
Consumer	4%	1%

Prescription pharmaceuticals, accounting for 74% of total sales in 1997, are the chief engine of PFE's growth. The company's pharmaceuticals growth has significantly exceeded that of the overall industry in recent years, bolstered by an exceptionally strong portfolio of blockbuster drugs.

Principal cardiovascular drugs include Norvasc calcium channel blocker heart drug (sales of $2.2 billion in 1997). Other heart drugs include Procardia XL ($822 million) and Cardura ($626 million). Infectious disease drugs consist of Diflucan antifungal ($881 million); Zithromax broad-spectrum quinolone antibiotic ($821

million); and other antibiotics. Other drugs include Zoloft anti-depressant ($1.5 billion), Viagra for male erectile dysfunction, Glucotrol and Glucotrol XL for diabetes, Zyrtec/Reactine antihistamine, and Feldene anti-arthritic. PFE also co-markets Lipitor cholesterol-lowering agent with Warner-Lambert and Aricept for Alzheimer's disease with Eisai Ltd.

R&D spending in 1997 totaled $1.9 billion, up from $1.7 billion in 1996. Key compounds in the pipeline include dofetilide for cardiac arrhythmias, eletriptan for migraine, several cancer treatments, and other drugs for diabetic neuropathy, fungal infections and other ailments. The company also plans to co-market Celebra, a new treatment for arthritis, with the G. D. Searle unit of Monsanto.

Medical Technology products operations (11% of sales) include Howmedica, a leading maker of reconstructive hip, knee and bone cement products and other implantable items; and Schneider angioplasty catheters (this unit is being sold to Boston Scientific for $2.1 billion). The Valleylab surgical equipment unit was sold in January 1998.

The animal health product line (11%) includes feed additives, vaccines, antibiotics, antihelmintics and other veterinary products. Consumer products (4%) include Ben-Gay ointment, Visine eye drops, Desitin ointment, Pacquin hand cream, Plax dental rinse, Bain de Soleil skin care products and Barbasol shave creams.

Per Share Data ($)

(Year Ended Dec. 31)	1997	1996	1995	1994	1993	1992	1991	1990	1989	1988
Tangible Bk. Val.	6.10	4.29	3.35	3.44	3.01	3.63	3.81	3.85	3.43	3.25
Cash Flow	2.08	1.83	1.53	1.28	0.71	1.00	0.71	0.76	0.65	0.72
Earnings	1.70	1.50	1.24	1.05	0.51	0.81	0.53	0.60	0.51	0.59
Dividends	0.68	0.60	0.52	0.47	0.42	0.37	0.33	0.30	0.28	0.25
Payout Ratio	40%	40%	42%	45%	82%	46%	60%	49%	53%	42%
Prices - High	80	45⅝	33½	19⅞	18⅞	21¾	21½	10¼	9½	7½
- Low	40⅜	30⅛	18⅝	13¼	13⅛	16¼	9¼	6⅞	6¾	5⅞
P/E Ratio - High	47	31	27	19	37	27	40	17	19	13
- Low	24	20	15	13	26	20	17	11	13	10

Income Statement Analysis (Million $)

	1997	1996	1995	1994	1993	1992	1991	1990	1989	1988
Revs.	12,504	11,306	10,021	8,281	7,478	7,230	6,950	6,406	5,671	5,385
Oper. Inc.	3,780	3,444	2,527	2,248	1,906	1,686	1,471	1,254	1,153	1,189
Depr.	502	430	374	289	254	260	238	217	201	187
Int. Exp.	147	170	205	142	121	116	138	142	131	87.0
Pretax Inc.	3,088	2,804	2,299	1,862	851	1,535	944	1,103	917	1,104
Eff. Tax Rate	28%	31%	32%	30%	23%	29%	23%	27%	25%	28%
Net Inc.	2,213	1,929	1,554	1,298	658	1,094	722	801	681	791

Balance Sheet & Other Fin. Data (Million $)

	1997	1996	1995	1994	1993	1992	1991	1990	1989	1988
Cash	877	1,637	1,512	2,019	1,177	1,704	1,548	1,068	1,058	808
Curr. Assets	6,820	6,468	6,152	5,788	4,733	5,385	4,808	4,436	4,505	4,095
Total Assets	15,336	14,667	12,729	11,099	9,331	9,590	9,635	9,052	8,325	7,638
Curr. Liab.	5,305	5,640	5,187	4,826	3,444	3,217	3,421	3,117	2,912	2,344
LT Debt	729	687	833	604	571	571	397	193	191	227
Common Eqty.	7,933	6,954	5,507	4,324	3,865	4,719	5,026	5,092	4,536	4,301
Total Cap.	8,818	7,944	6,553	5,179	4,665	5,472	5,742	5,666	5,062	4,866
Cap. Exp.	943	774	696	672	634	674	594	548	457	344
Cash Flow	2,715	2,359	1,928	1,588	912	1,353	960	1,019	882	978
Curr. Ratio	1.3	1.1	1.2	1.2	1.4	1.7	1.4	1.4	1.5	1.7
% LT Debt of Cap.	8.3	8.6	12.7	11.7	12.2	10.4	6.9	3.4	3.8	4.7
% Net Inc.of Revs.	17.7	17.1	15.5	15.7	8.8	15.1	10.4	12.5	12.0	14.7
% Ret. on Assets	14.8	14.1	13.0	12.8	7.0	11.5	7.7	9.2	8.5	10.8
% Ret. on Equity	29.7	31.0	31.6	32.0	15.4	22.6	14.3	16.7	15.4	19.3

Data as orig. reptd.; bef. results of disc. opers. and/or spec. items. Per share data adj. for stk. divs. as of ex-div. date. Bold denotes diluted EPS (FASB 128). E-Estimated. NA-Not Available. NM-Not Meaningful. NR-Not Ranked.

Office—235 E. 42nd St., New York, NY 10017. **Registrar**—ChaseMellon Shareholder Services, NYC. **Tel**—(212) 573-2323. **Website**—http://www.pfizer.com **Chrmn & CEO**—W. C. Steere, Jr. **EVP & CFO**—D. L. Shedlarz. **SVP & Secy**—C. L. Clemente. **Investor Contact**—J. R. Gardner. **Dirs**—M. S. Brown, M. A. Burns, W. D. Cornwell, G. B. Harvey, C. J. Horner, S. O. Ikenberry, H. P. Kamen, T. G. Labrecque, H. A. McKinnell, D. G. Mead, J. F. Niblack, R. J. Simmons, W. C. Steere, Jr., J.-P. Valles. **Transfer Agent & Registrar**—First Chicago Trust Co. of New York. **Incorporated**—in Delaware in 1942. **Empl**— 49,000. **S&P Analyst**: H.B. Saftlas

STANDARD &POOR'S
STOCK REPORTS

PG&E Corporation

1728P

NYSE Symbol **PCG**

In S&P 500

12-SEP-98

Industry:
Electric Companies

Summary: Subsidiaries of this California-based energy holding company include Pacific Gas and Electric Co. and Pacific Gas Transmission.

S&P Opinion: Hold (★★★)	Recent Price • 31⅞	Yield • 3.8%
	52 Wk Range • 33½-22⅝	12-Mo. P/E • 19.2

Quantitative Evaluations

Outlook
(1 Lowest—5 Highest)
• **1+**

Fair Value
• **27¾**

Risk
• **Low**

Earn./Div. Rank
• **B**

Technical Eval.
• **Bullish** since 3/97

Rel. Strength Rank
(1 Lowest—99 Highest)
• **92**

Insider Activity
• **Favorable**

Earnings vs. Previous Year
▲=Up ▼=Down ▶=No Change

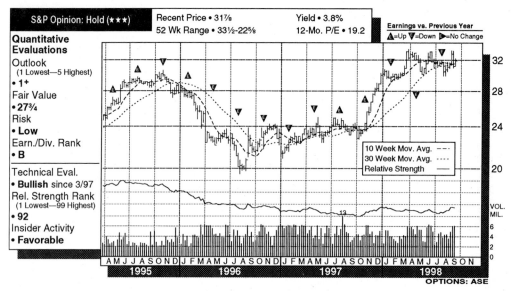

10 Week Mov. Avg. — — —
30 Week Mov. Avg. ·······
Relative Strength ——

OPTIONS: ASE

Overview - 10-AUG-98

Aided by the contribution of its non-regulated operations, we expect EPS in 1999 to advance about 20% from anticipated results in 1998. While revenues in 1998 will benefit from the acquisitions of Energy Source, Teco Pipeline and Valero Energy, EPS will remain restricted by significantly higher costs. Longer term, utility revenue and earnings growth will be limited by rate reductions and the accelerated depreciation (from 20 years to 5 years) of its Diablo Canyon costs. However, the scope of the energy management alliance with Ultramar Diamond Shamrock should give PCG a competitive edge as the industry moves toward more alliances of this kind. With the July 1998 sale of three of its California-based generating plants achieving a $120 million premium to their book value of $380 million, expect the current auction of four additional plants to obtain a significant premium to their $790 million book value.

Valuation - 10-AUG-98

We would continue to hold PCG stock. Following a strong 44% advance in 1997, the shares are up just 1.0% year to date. Still, we expect them to benefit from the growing strength of PCG's non-regulated operations. While the company paid a $500 million premium (which should be greatly offset by the premiums to be realized for the sale of its California-based plants) for New England Electric System's non-nuclear generation assets, it believes the premium will be justified. The U.S. Gen unit's northeast experience and low-cost power producing capacity should enable it to capitalize on the region's accelerated move to retail competition. Assuming an expected 1998 closing, the acquisition would be mildly dilutive in 1999 and 2000, but accretive in the years thereafter.

Key Stock Statistics

S&P EPS Est. 1998	1.75	Tang. Bk. Value/Share	21.28
P/E on S&P Est. 1998	18.2	Beta	0.46
S&P EPS Est. 1999	2.10	Shareholders	230,000
Dividend Rate/Share	1.20	Market cap. (B)	$ 12.2
Shs. outstg. (M)	382.0	Inst. holdings	54%
Avg. daily vol. (M)	1.148		

Value of $10,000 invested 5 years ago: $ 13,814

Fiscal Year Ending Dec. 31

	1998	1997	1996	1995	1994	1993
Revenues (Million $)						
1Q	4,353	3,365	2,249	2,308	2,514	2,464
2Q	4,787	3,083	2,139	2,449	2,440	2,464
3Q	—	4,063	2,522	2,638	2,855	2,947
4Q	—	4,889	2,709	2,227	2,638	2,707
Yr.	—	15,400	9,610	9,622	10,447	10,582
Earnings Per Share ($)						
1Q	**0.36**	**0.42**	0.61	0.73	0.52	0.56
2Q	**0.46**	**0.49**	0.25	0.92	0.53	0.53
3Q	**E0.58**	**0.62**	0.55	0.85	0.96	0.79
4Q	**E0.35**	**0.22**	0.34	0.48	0.21	0.45
Yr.	**E1.75**	**1.75**	1.75	2.99	2.21	2.33

Next earnings report expected: mid October

Dividend Data (Dividends have been paid since 1919.)

Amount ($)	Date Decl.	Ex-Div. Date	Stock of Record	Payment Date
0.300	Oct. 17	Dec. 11	Dec. 15	Jan. 15 '98
0.300	Feb. 18	Mar. 12	Mar. 16	Apr. 15 '98
0.300	Apr. 15	Jun. 11	Jun. 15	Jul. 15 '98
0.300	Jul. 15	Sep. 11	Sep. 15	Oct. 15 '98

A Division of The McGraw·Hill Companies

STANDARD
&POOR'S
STOCK REPORTS

PG&E Corporation

1728P
12-SEP-98

Business Summary - 10-AUG-98

Since its formation, on January 1, 1997, as the holding company for Pacific Gas and Electric Company and its subsidiaries, PG&E Corporation has moved closer to its goal of a being a national energy services company.

In July 1998, PCG agreed to manage, over a seven year period, more than $2 billion in energy purchases for Ultramar Diamond Shamrock (UDS). The alliance (which was announced in March 1998) is believed to be the largest of its kind in the energy services industry and is expected to result in savings of between 15% to 25% of UDS' gross energy costs.

In July 1997, PCG acquired the natural gas service business of Texas-based Valero Energy through a stock swap and debt assumption transaction valued at $1.5 billion. Then, in August 1997, its U.S. Gen unit agreed to acquire (in a transaction that is expected to close in 1998) a portfolio of non-nuclear electric generation assets and power supply contracts from New England Electric Systems for about $1.59 billion in cash.

Pacific Gas and Electric, which is one of the largest investor-owned gas and electric utilities in the U.S., provides electricity (81% of 1997 revenues) to some 4.5 million customers in northern and central California.

Pacific Gas Transmission Company and its affiliates own and operate natural gas transmission pipelines from the California border to Canada, Texas and the Pacific Northwest. In June 1998, it sold its Australian holdings. PG&E Enterprises and affiliates manage other energy businesses, including U.S. Generating Company (U.S. Gen), a leading power supplier in the U.S.

The company's Diablo Canyon nuclear facility consists of two units. In a move that will significantly reduce its earnings over the next few years, PCG decided to accelerate, beginning in 1997, the recovery of the facility's sunk costs from a 20-year period to a 5-year period. In 1997, the accelerated recovery resulted in an increase of $583 million in depreciation expense.

In September 1996, California passed Assembly Bill 1890, which restructured the California power market. Key elements of the bill include a nonbypassable competitive transition charge for recovery of stranded costs, and a 10% rate reduction (implemented in January 1998) for residential and small commercial customers.

In June 1998, PCG's Energy Services subsidiary entered into a multi-year agreement, valued at more than $300 million, to provide energy and energy-related services to affiliates of American Stores Company, the third largest food and drug retailer in the U.S.

In July 1998, the company completed the sale of three of its generating plants to Duke Energy for $501 million. The plants had a combined book value of about $380 million. In April 1998, PCG initiated a second auction for four generating plants with a combined book value of about $790 million.

Per Share Data ($)

(Year Ended Dec. 31)	1997	1996	1995	1994	1993	1992	1991	1990	1989	1988
Tangible Bk. Val.	21.28	20.60	19.68	20.06	18.67	18.48	18.17	17.65	17.17	16.57
Earnings	1.75	1.75	2.99	2.21	2.33	2.58	2.24	2.10	1.90	-0.10
Dividends	1.20	1.77	1.96	1.96	1.88	1.76	1.64	1.52	1.40	1.66
Payout Ratio	69%	101%	66%	89%	81%	68%	73%	72%	74%	NM
Prices - High	30⅞	28⅜	30⅝	35	36¾	34⅝	32⅝	25⅝	22	18⅜
- Low	20⅞	19½	24¼	21⅜	31¾	29	24	20	17¼	14
P/E Ratio - High	18	16	10	16	16	13	15	12	12	NM
- Low	12	11	8	10	14	11	11	10	9	NM

Income Statement Analysis (Million $)

	1997	1996	1995	1994	1993	1992	1991	1990	1989	1988
Revs.	15,400	9,610	9,622	10,447	10,582	10,296	9,778	9,470	8,588	7,646
Depr.	1,889	1,222	1,360	1,397	1,316	1,221	1,141	1,046	1,000	932
Maint.	NA	NA	NA	457	443	485	525	404	373	382
Fxd. Chgs. Cov.	2.9	2.9	3.8	3.1	3.4	3.3	3.1	2.9	2.6	0.9
Constr. Credits	Nil	Nil	31.0	32.0	120	83.6	42.0	47.0	43.0	19.0
Eff. Tax Rate	43%	42%	40%	45%	46%	43%	45%	47%	43%	NM
Net Inc.	716	755	1,339	1,007	1,065	1,171	1,026	987	901	62.0

Balance Sheet & Other Fin. Data (Million $)

	1997	1996	1995	1994	1993	1992	1991	1990	1989	1988
Gross Prop.	20,472	33,310	32,227	31,668	30,919	29,268	27,144	25,543	23,523	23,280
Cap. Exp.	1,822	1,230	932	1,107	1,842	2,352	1,771	1,517	1,423	1,317
Net Prop.	20,472	19,008	18,918	19,399	19,683	18,761	17,671	17,076	15,990	16,562
Capitalization:										
LT Debt	7,659	7,821	8,049	8,675	9,292	8,379	8,249	7,786	7,824	7,937
% LT Debt	36	46	46	48	50	48	49	48	48	50
Pfd.	539	840	840	870	883	938	987	1,101	1,152	1,190
% Pfd.	2.71	4.90	4.80	4.80	4.70	5.30	5.80	6.70	7.00	7.40
Common	8,897	8,363	8,599	8,635	8,446	8,283	7,681	7,506	7,455	6,910
% Common	42	49	49	48	45	47	45	46	45	43
Total Cap.	21,424	21,345	21,814	22,475	23,011	19,855	19,057	18,407	18,309	17,902
% Oper. Ratio	92.3	86.0	80.6	84.4	83.3	82.2	82.5	82.0	81.1	83.0
% Earn. on Net Prop.	8.8	7.1	10.5	8.4	9.2	10.1	9.9	10.1	10.2	8.2
% Return On Revs.	4.6	7.9	13.9	9.6	10.1	11.4	10.5	10.4	10.5	0.8
% Return On Invest. Capital	9.0	6.5	6.0	7.7	8.6	10.1	9.7	9.8	9.6	4.7
% Return On Com. Equity	8.3	8.5	14.7	11.1	12.0	13.7	12.3	11.9	11.1	NM

Data as orig. reptd.; bef. results of disc opers. and/or spec. items. Per share data adj. for stk. divs. as of ex-div. date. Bold denotes diluted EPS (FASB 128). E-Estimated. NA-Not Available. NM-Not Meaningful. NR-Not Ranked.

Office—77 Beale St., P.O. Box 770000, San Francisco, CA 94177. **Tel**—(415) 973-7000. **Web site**—http://www.pge.com **Chrmn, Pres & CEO**—R. D. Glynn Jr. **SVP , CFO & Treas**—M. E. Rescoe. **Secy**—L. H. Everett. **Investor Contact**—David E. Kaplan. **Dirs**—R. A. Clarke, H. M. Conger, D. A. Coulter, C. L. Cox, W. S. Davila, R. D. Glynn Jr., D. M. Lawrence, R. B. Madden, M. S. Metz, R. Q. Morgan, C. E. Reichardt, J. C. Sawhill, A. Seelenfreund, G. R. Smith, B. L. Williams. **Transfer Agent**—Company's office. **Incorporated**—in California in 1905. **Empl**— 23,500. **S&P Analyst:** Justin McCann

12-SEP-98

Industry:
Health Care (Drugs -
Major Pharmaceuticals)

Summary: Formed in 1995 through the merger of Upjohn Co. with Pharmacia AB of Sweden, this company ranks among the world's leading drugmakers.

S&P Opinion: Accumulate (★★★★)	Recent Price • 45¼	Yield • 2.4%
	52 Wk Range • 49½-28⅞	12-Mo. P/E • 83.9

Earnings vs. Previous Year
▲=Up ▼=Down ▶=No Change

Quantitative Evaluations

Outlook
(1 Lowest—5 Highest)
• **1**

Fair Value
• **39**

Risk
• **Average**

Earn./Div. Rank
• **NR**

Technical Eval.
• **Bullish** since 9/98

Rel. Strength Rank
(1 Lowest—99 Highest)
• **88**

Insider Activity
• **NA**

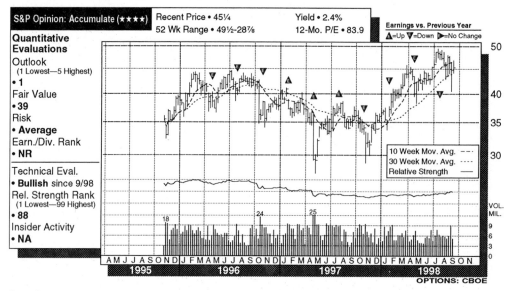

10 Week Mov. Avg. ---
30 Week Mov. Avg. ----
Relative Strength —

OPTIONS: CBOE

Overview - 28-AUG-98

Despite a first half decline, revenues for all of 1998 are likely to approximate or modestly exceed those of 1997. Sales in the second half should benefit from rising sales of new drugs such as Detrol for incontinence, Xalatan glaucoma treatment, Camptosar for colon cancer, and Edronex for depression. Gains are also seen for several older drugs, including Xanax anti-anxiety agent, Fragmin anti-clotting factor, and Depo-Provera contraceptive. Higher sales are also forecast for consumer medications, led by gains in Nicorette smoking cessation products and Rogaine baldness treatment. Modest growth is projected for animal health care products, but nutritional and diagnostic sales are likely to decline. Margins should benefit from improved volume, personnel reductions, and other restructuring measures. EPS are projected at $1.50 (after $0.08 in nonrecurring charges in the second quarter). Further progress to $1.80 is seen for 1999.

Valuation - 28-AUG-98

The shares have held up relatively well during the recent turmoil in the general market, reflecting renewed investor focus on recession-resistant drug stocks, the company's improving earnings prospects, and continuing interest in PNU as a possible takeover candidate. Despite sluggish results in the first half, significant improvement in operating results is expected for the second half, helped by a revamped U.S. sales and marketing infrastructure, other benefits from restructuring measures announced last fall, and increasing contributions from new drug products. Future prospects are enhanced by a revitalized OTC line, and by the 1997 merger of the biotech supply business with a unit of Amersham International plc. The shares merit accumulation for long-term appreciation.

Key Stock Statistics

S&P EPS Est. 1998	1.50	Tang. Bk. Value/Share	8.27
P/E on S&P Est. 1998	30.2	Beta	0.85
S&P EPS Est. 1999	1.80	Shareholders	NA
Dividend Rate/Share	1.08	Market cap. (B)	$ 23.0
Shs. outstg. (M)	508.0	Inst. holdings	66%
Avg. daily vol. (M)	1.326		

Value of $10,000 invested 5 years ago: NA

Fiscal Year Ending Dec. 31

	1998	1997	1996	1995	1994	1993
Revenues (Million $)						
1Q	1,586	1,635	1,757	1,739	--	--
2Q	1,691	1,738	1,804	1,808	--	--
3Q	--	1,587	1,741	1,722	--	--
4Q	--	1,723	1,984	1,826	--	--
Yr.	--	6,710	7,286	7,095	6,820	6,560
Earnings Per Share ($)						
1Q	**0.36**	**0.37**	0.09	0.46	--	--
2Q	**0.28**	**0.34**	0.16	0.45	--	--
3Q	**E0.41**	**0.15**	0.39	0.45	--	--
4Q	**E0.45**	**-0.26**	0.43	0.07	--	--
Yr.	**E1.50**	**0.61**	1.07	1.43	1.62	1.08

Next earnings report expected: late October

Dividend Data (Dividends have been paid since 1996.)

Amount ($)	Date Decl.	Ex-Div. Date	Stock of Record	Payment Date
0.270	Dec. 09	Jan. 05	Jan. 07	Feb. 02 '98
0.270	Feb. 16	Apr. 03	Apr. 07	May. 04 '98
0.270	Jun. 30	Jul. 08	Jul. 10	Aug. 03 '98
0.270	Aug. 31	Oct. 02	Oct. 06	Nov. 02 '98

A Division of The McGraw·Hill Companies

Pharmacia & Upjohn, Inc.

Business Summary - 28-AUG-98

This global pharmaceutical firm was formed in November 1995 through the merger of The Upjohn Company and Swedish drugmaker Pharmacia AB. The company traces its roots to Carlo Erba of Italy (established in 1853), U.S.-based Upjohn (1886), and Pharmacia (1911). Based in London, PNU maintains facilities in Italy, Sweden and the U.S., and markets its products in more than 50 countries. The U.S. accounted for 32% of 1997 sales (excluding the deconsolidated biotech business), six major European countries for 30%, Japan for 10%, and other areas for 28%. Sales in recent years (1996 pro forma) were divided as follows:

	1997	1996
Prescription drugs	64%	71%
Consumer health care	11%	10%
Animal health	8%	6%
Other	17%	13%

Principal prescription drug therapeutic classes include products for metabolic conditions (11%), such as Genotropin growth hormone, Fragmin low molecular weight heparin, and Micronase diabetes treatment; oncology drugs (9%) consisting of Farmorubicin, Adriamycin, Camtosar and others; anti-inflammatories (9%) such as Ansaid and Motrin for arthritis and Medrol and Solu-Medrol steroids; central nervous system products (8%), which include Xanax anti-anxiety, Sermion dementia treatment, and Halcion sleep-inducing agent; drugs for infectious diseases (8%) such as Cleocin, Lincocin, and Vantin antibiotics; and women's health products (8%) consisting of Depo-Provera injectable contraceptive, Ogen estrogen replacement, and Provera progestin products.

Other pharmaceutical products (11%) include ophthalmological drugs such as Xalatan for glaucoma and Healon for use in cataract surgery; Detrol treatment for incontinence; Caverject for erectile dysfunction; and various other compounds.

Consumer health care items include Nicorette nonprescription smoking cessation chewing gum and transdermal patch, Motrin IB ibuprofen analgesic, Rogaine for hair loss, and other medications. Animal health items include drugs and biological products for both food and companion animals.

Other products include nutritionals such as Intralipid fat emulsion agent, and Kabimix and Vitrimix pre-mixed supplements; reagents and chemicals for industry and research; and analytical instruments and diagnostic tests. In 1997, PNU merged its biotechnology supply business with a division of Amersham International plc, creating Amersham Pharmacia Biotech (45% owned by PNU).

Per Share Data ($)

(Year Ended Dec. 31)	1997	1996	1995	1994	1993	1992	1991	1990	1989	1988
Tangible Bk. Val.	7.94	8.72	8.63	7.51	NA	NA	NA	NA	NA	NA
Cash Flow	1.44	2.02	2.38	NA	NA	NA	NA	NA	NA	NA
Earnings	0.61	1.07	1.43	1.62	1.08	1.36	NA	NA	NA	NA
Dividends	1.08	1.08	Nil	NA	NA	NA	NA	NA	NA	NA
Payout Ratio	177%	101%	Nil	NA	NA	NA	NA	NA	NA	NA
Prices - High	41⅛	44⅝	40¼	NA	NA	NA	NA	NA	NA	NA
- Low	27½	34⅛	32⅜	NA	NA	NA	NA	NA	NA	NA
P/E Ratio - High	67	42	28	NA	NA	NA	NA	NA	NA	NA
- Low	45	32	23	NA	NA	NA	NA	NA	NA	NA

Income Statement Analysis (Million $)

	1997	1996	1995	1994	1993	1992	1991	1990	1989	1988
Revs.	6,710	7,286	7,095	6,823	6,561	5,938	NA	NA	NA	NA
Oper. Inc.	1,219	1,735	1,725	NA	NA	NA	NA	NA	NA	NA
Depr.	440	473	480	NA	NA	NA	NA	NA	NA	NA
Int. Exp.	33.0	89.0	94.0	112	183	136	NA	NA	NA	NA
Pretax Inc.	468	838	1,136	1,271	778	947	NA	NA	NA	NA
Eff. Tax Rate	31%	33%	35%	35%	28%	26%	NA	NA	NA	NA
Net Inc.	323	562	739	833	561	704	NA	NA	NA	NA

Balance Sheet & Other Fin. Data (Million $)

	1997	1996	1995	1994	1993	1992	1991	1990	1989	1988
Cash	775	1,337	1,814	1,662	NA	NA	NA	NA	NA	NA
Curr. Assets	4,327	4,895	4,974	4,872	NA	NA	NA	NA	NA	NA
Total Assets	10,380	11,173	11,461	11,137	NA	NA	NA	NA	NA	NA
Curr. Liab.	2,688	2,503	2,640	2,871	NA	NA	NA	NA	NA	NA
LT Debt	634	823	870	868	NA	NA	NA	NA	NA	NA
Common Eqty.	5,256	5,954	6,096	5,601	NA	NA	NA	NA	NA	NA
Total Cap.	6,534	7,558	7,704	6,762	NA	NA	NA	NA	NA	NA
Cap. Exp.	577	656	592	NA	NA	NA	NA	NA	NA	NA
Cash Flow	750	1,035	1,206	NA	NA	NA	NA	NA	NA	NA
Curr. Ratio	1.6	2.0	1.9	1.7	NA	NA	NA	NA	NA	NA
% LT Debt of Cap.	9.7	10.9	11.3	12.8	NA	NA	NA	NA	NA	NA
% Net Inc.of Revs.	4.8	7.7	10.4	12.2	8.6	11.9	NA	NA	NA	NA
% Ret. on Assets	3.0	5.0	6.6	NA	NA	NA	NA	NA	NA	NA
% Ret. on Equity	5.5	9.1	12.7	NA	NA	NA	NA	NA	NA	NA

Data as orig. reptd.; bef. results of disc. opers. and/or spec. items. Per share data adj. for stk. divs. as of ex-div. date. Bold denotes diluted EPS (FASB 128). E-Estimated. NA-Not Available. NM-Not Meaningful. NR-Not Ranked.

Office—95 Corporate Drive, Bridgewater, N.J. 08807. Tel—(908) 306-4452. Website—http://www.pharmacia.se Pres & CEO—F. Hassan. Secy—D. Schmitz. EVP & CFO—C. J. Coughlin. Investor Contact—Craig Tooman. Dirs—R. H. Brown, F. C. Carlucci, G. Douglas, M. K. Eickhoff, J. Ekberg, D. F. Grisham, J. F. Gyll, F. Hassan, W. E. LaMothe, R. L. B. Lindquist, O. Lund, W. D. Mullholland, W. U. Parfet, U. Reinius, B. Samuelsson. Transfer Agent & Registrar—Harris Trust & Savings Bank, Chicago. Incorporated—in Delaware in 1958. Empl—30,000. S&P Analyst: H. B. Saftlas

Phelps Dodge   1812

NYSE Symbol **PD**

In S&P 500

12-SEP-98 Industry: Metals Mining

Summary: Phelps Dodge is one of the world's largest copper producers, and one of the world's largest producers of carbon black.

S&P Opinion: Hold (★★★)	Recent Price • 46⅞	Yield • 4.3%
	52 Wk Range • 79¾-43⅞	12-Mo. P/E • 8.1

Quantitative Evaluations

Outlook
(1 Lowest—5 Highest)
• **2+**

Fair Value
• **48¾**

Risk
• **Low**

Earn./Div. Rank
• **B**

Technical Eval.
• **Bearish** since 3/98

Rel. Strength Rank
(1 Lowest—99 Highest)
• **53**

Insider Activity
• **Neutral**

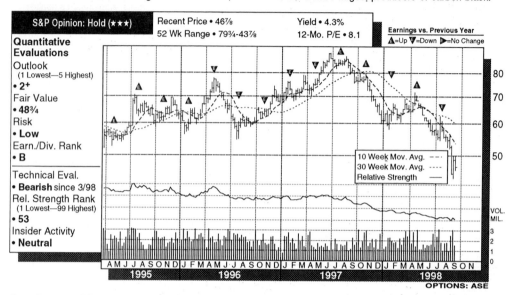

Earnings vs. Previous Year
▲=Up ▼=Down ▶=No Change

10 Week Mov. Avg. ---
30 Week Mov. Avg. ----
Relative Strength —

OPTIONS: ASE

Overview - 21-JUL-98

We project a decline in EPS in 1998 (excluding a $2.09 asset sale gain in 1998's first quarter) based mostly on our expectation of a drop in the copper unit's operating profit. Lower copper prices, along with increased interest and depreciation charges, will lead to lower income in copper despite an increase in output to 1.7 billion pounds, from 1.62 billion pounds in 1997. For modeling purposes we look for an average copper price of $0.90/lb. in 1998 versus $1.07/lb. in 1997.

Valuation - 21-JUL-98

Following 1998's second quarter EPS, we still rate PD avoid. Earlier, on March 10, 1998 we upgraded our investment opinion on PD and two other copper stocks from sell to avoid based on our expectation for short-term improvement in copper market fundamentals. Although copper prices set contract lows since our upgrade, the supply picture has improved. As of July 17, 1998 LME inventories stood at 249,100 metric tons, down from 379,235 metric tons as of February 25, 1998; similarly, inventories on the Comex totaled 53,938 metric tons, down from 116,995 metric tons on March 6, 1998. In sum, the combination of strong seasonal demand and some production cutbacks have led to a drop in supply. Notwithstanding near-term strength in the metal and a likely rebound in the stocks, we still think PD will underperform the market in 1998 and thus still rate the shares avoid. We anticipate that copper prices will begin another decline by the end of 1998's third quarter as seasonally strong demand ebbs and supply picks up. Moreover, we remain negative on the long-term outlook for copper and copper stocks due to the large expansion of mine production scheduled to come on line between now and 2000. This additional output will depress both the metal and the copper stocks.

Key Stock Statistics

S&P EPS Est. 1998	4.70	Tang. Bk. Value/Share	39.23
P/E on S&P Est. 1998	10.0	Beta	0.84
S&P EPS Est. 1999	3.00	Shareholders	11,900
Dividend Rate/Share	2.00	Market cap. (B)	$ 2.8
Shs. outstg. (M)	58.7	Inst. holdings	79%
Avg. daily vol. (M)	0.452		

Value of $10,000 invested 5 years ago: $ 11,575

Fiscal Year Ending Dec. 31

	1998	1997	1996	1995	1994	1993
Revenues (Million $)						
1Q	798.3	1,022	1,005	1,034	694.3	666.7
2Q	794.4	1,065	957.7	1,024	780.4	629.8
3Q	—	961.7	853.6	1,077	813.7	646.7
4Q	—	865.9	970.6	1,051	1,001	652.7
Yr.	—	3,914	3,787	4,185	3,289	2,596
Earnings Per Share ($)						
1Q	**2.79**	**2.13**	2.26	2.61	0.69	0.85
2Q	**0.69**	**2.16**	1.90	2.28	0.91	0.66
3Q	**E0.67**	1.72	1.22	3.03	1.33	0.56
4Q	**E0.55**	0.54	1.59	2.73	0.89	0.59
Yr.	**E4.70**	6.63	6.98	10.65	3.81	2.66

Next earnings report expected: early October

Dividend Data (Dividends have been paid since 1987.)

Amount ($)	Date Decl.	Ex-Div. Date	Stock of Record	Payment Date
.005 Spl.	Feb. 05	Feb. 20	Feb. 24	Mar. 10 '98
0.500	Feb. 04	Feb. 20	Feb. 24	Mar. 10 '98
0.500	May. 06	May. 18	May. 20	Jun. 10 '98
0.500	Jun. 24	Aug. 18	Aug. 20	Sep. 10 '98

A Division of The **McGraw·Hill** *Companies*

Business Summary - 21-JUL-98

Phelps Dodge, one of the world's largest copper producers, also makes copper rod, and is a leading manufacturer of carbon black and wire and cable. The company is seeking to expand its copper reserves and increase its market share in the non-copper businesses. Additionally, PD's strategy is to stabilize the volatility of the copper segment with the profits and cash flow from the non-copper unit. Operating profit (in millions) by segment in recent years were:

	1997	1996	1995
Copper/mining	$457.2	$526.6	$896.8
Industrial	204.9	225.8	216.5

PD's mining unit produces copper from mines in the U.S., Chile and Peru. Copper production for PD's own account was 812,100 tons in 1997, versus 770,400 tons in 1996 and 712,700 tons in 1995. As a byproduct of copper mining, in 1997 PD produced 109,000 oz. of gold, 2,577,000 oz. of silver, 1,649,000 lbs. of molybdenum and 1,052,900 tons of sulfuric acid.

In 1996, PD set a new copper production goal of 2.2 billion pounds by 2002 from existing properties. The projected production increase entails expansions at the Morenci (in Arizona), Tyrone (New Mexico) and Candelaria (Chile) operations and development of the Dos Pobres and San Juan deposits in Arizona. In October 1997, PD completed the expansion at Candelaria. The expansion will increase copper output by 130 million lbs. annually and boost PD's global copper production capability by 9%. At the same time, PD is committed to expanding its copper output and reserves through discoveries, acquisitions and joint ventures. At 1997 year end, copper reserves totaled 13.7 million tons, versus 12.1 million tons in 1996.

Copper is used principally in the electrical and electronic and construction industries. To a lesser degree, copper is used in the industrial machinery, consumer products and transportation industries. Copper prices averaged $1.04 in 1997, versus $1.06 a pound in 1996 and $1.35 a pound in 1995. PD is the world's leading producer of continuous cast copper rod, used to make electrical wire and cables. Its chief rivals in copper are Asarco Inc., Cyprus Amax Minerals and Freeport McMoran Copper & Gold.

Industrial operations include Phelps Dodge Magnet Wire, the world's leading producer of insulated magnet wire for use in motors, generators and transformers; Columbian Chemicals Co., one of the world's largest producers of carbon black; and Hudson International Conductors, a manufacturer of specialty, high-performance conductors and alloys.

According to the International Copper Study Group, world refined copper production for the first four months of 1998 increased to 4.6 million metric tons from 4.4 million metric tons in the 1997 period.

Per Share Data ($) (Year Ended Dec. 31)	1997	1996	1995	1994	1993	1992	1991	1990	1989	1988
Tangible Bk. Val.	39.23	39.92	36.58	28.87	26.35	25.69	24.24	21.94	17.02	21.17
Cash Flow	11.18	10.79	13.86	6.56	5.23	6.51	5.85	8.40	5.64	8.42
Earnings	6.63	6.97	10.65	3.81	2.66	4.28	3.93	6.56	3.80	6.58
Dividends	2.00	1.95	1.80	1.69	1.65	1.61	1.50	1.50	6.43	0.48
Payout Ratio	30%	28%	17%	44%	62%	38%	38%	23%	167%	7%
Prices - High	89⅝	77⅝	70½	65	55⅝	53	39⅝	35⅞	39⅜	26⅞
- Low	59⅞	54⅝	51⅞	47⅝	39⅛	32	26¼	23⅛	25¾	16¼
P/E Ratio - High	14	11	7	17	21	12	10	5	10	4
- Low	9	8	5	13	15	7	7	4	7	2
Income Statement Analysis (Million $)										
Revs.	3,914	3,786	4,185	3,289	2,596	2,579	2,434	2,636	2,700	2,320
Oper. Inc.	940	973	1,297	753	496	565	545	826	885	716
Depr.	284	250	223	195	182	157	134	128	129	113
Int. Exp.	62.0	68.0	65.0	57.3	54.5	47.4	47.5	51.2	55.0	50.1
Pretax Inc.	594	698	1,076	384	294	416	404	679	370	554
Eff. Tax Rate	30%	32%	30%	27%	36%	28%	33%	33%	28%	24%
Net Inc.	409	462	747	271	188	302	273	455	267	420
Balance Sheet & Other Fin. Data (Million $)										
Cash	158	471	609	287	256	251	182	162	13.0	172
Curr. Assets	1,051	1,422	1,555	1,208	987	990	818	839	691	808
Total Assets	4,965	4,816	4,646	4,134	3,721	3,441	3,051	2,827	2,505	2,755
Curr. Liab.	701	686	605	650	540	541	477	490	479	377
LT Debt	857	555	613	622	547	374	382	403	432	513
Common Eqty.	2,511	2,756	2,678	2,188	2,022	1,972	1,859	1,683	1,350	1,437
Total Cap.	3,806	3,821	3,722	3,119	2,918	2,662	2,434	2,221	1,869	2,315
Cap. Exp.	662	513	408	376	428	318	366	292	219	372
Cash Flow	693	712	970	466	370	458	406	582	395	519
Curr. Ratio	1.5	2.1	2.6	1.9	1.8	1.8	1.7	1.7	1.4	2.1
% LT Debt of Cap.	22.5	14.5	16.5	20.0	18.8	14.0	15.7	18.2	23.1	22.2
% Net Inc.of Revs.	10.4	12.2	17.8	8.2	7.2	11.7	11.2	17.3	9.9	18.1
% Ret. on Assets	8.4	9.8	17.0	6.9	5.2	9.2	9.2	17.1	9.5	16.9
% Ret. on Equity	15.5	17.0	30.7	12.9	9.4	15.7	15.3	30.1	17.9	32.2

Data as orig. reptd.; bef. results of disc. opers. and/or spec. items. Per share data adj. for stk. divs. as of ex-div. date. Bold denotes diluted EPS (FASB 128). E-Estimated. NA-Not Available. NM-Not Meaningful. NR-Not Ranked.

Office—2600 N. Central Ave., Phoenix, AZ 85004-3014.**Tel**—(602) 234-8100.**Chrmn & CEO**—D. C. Yearley.**SVP & CFO**—T. M. St. Clair.**VP & Secy**—R. C. Swan.**VP, Treas & Investor Contact**—Thomas M. Foster.**Dirs**—R. N. Burt, P. W. Douglas, W. A. Franke, P. Hazen, M. J. Iraola, M. L. Knowles, R. D. Krebs, S. J. Morcott, G. R. Parker, J. S. Whisler, D. C. Yearley.**Transfer Agent & Registrar**—ChaseMellon Shareholder Services, LLC, Ridgefield Park, NJ.**Incorporated**—in New York in 1885.**Empl**— 15,869. **S&P Analyst:** Leo J. Larkin

Philip Morris
1822

NYSE Symbol **MO**

In S&P 500

12-SEP-98

Industry:
Tobacco

Summary: Philip Morris is the world's largest cigarette producer, the largest U.S. food processor (Kraft Foods), and the second largest U.S. brewer (Miller Brewing).

S&P Opinion: Avoid (★★)	Recent Price • 43	Yield • 4.1%
	52 Wk Range • 47⅞-34¾	12-Mo. P/E • 18.1

Quantitative Evaluations

Outlook
(1 Lowest—5 Highest)
• 2

Fair Value
• 42¼

Risk
• Average

Earn./Div. Rank
• A+

Technical Eval.
• **Bullish** since 8/98

Rel. Strength Rank
(1 Lowest—99 Highest)
• 94

Insider Activity
• NA

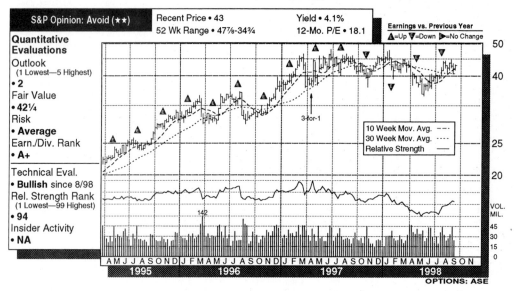

Earnings vs. Previous Year ▲=Up ▼=Down ▶=No Change

10 Week Mov. Avg. - - -
30 Week Mov. Avg. ......
Relative Strength ——

3-for-1

142

OPTIONS: ASE

Overview - 29-JUL-98

Excluding the costs of possible payments related to settling litigation during 1998, total tobacco profits are projected to rise by 10%-12%, principally reflecting middle single-digit unit volume growth and higher selling prices. Food and beer profits are expected to grow more modestly, led by an improved business mix and benefits accruing from numerous reorganization changes recently enacted in both U.S. and international operations. A stronger dollar relative to key foreign currencies may be a near-term restraining factor, but reduced interest expense and modest share repurchases should allow diluted EPS in 1998 to advance 10%, to $3.20 from 1997's $2.91 (before unusual items such as litigation settlement costs and any impact of a potential national tobacco settlement.)

Valuation - 29-JUL-98

The shares have been weak in the past few months, reflecting investor uncertainty surrounding the possibility of a national U.S. tobacco settlement, as well as the outcome of pending lawsuits brought on by various state's attorneys general. Terms of the most recently proposed national settlement, which almost doubled the industry's payments from the original deal penned in June 1997, called for the tobacco industry to pay over $600 billion over the next 25 years, without any reduction in liability risk associated with the manufacture of cigarettes. Although MO's earnings would be adversely affected by such payments, the stock's P/E multiple could benefit from the removal of significant litigation risk. Despite our positive earnings growth projections, MO's relatively modest P/E valuation, and attractive dividend yield, risks associated with recent state settlement payments make the shares unappealing over the next six to 12 months.

Key Stock Statistics

S&P EPS Est. 1998	3.20	Tang. Bk. Value/Share	NM
P/E on S&P Est. 1998	13.4	Beta	0.70
S&P EPS Est. 1999	3.60	Shareholders	139,700
Dividend Rate/Share	1.76	Market cap. (B)	$104.6
Shs. outstg. (M)	2432.1	Inst. holdings	59%
Avg. daily vol. (M)	7.024		

Value of $10,000 invested 5 years ago: $ 21,277

Fiscal Year Ending Dec. 31

	1998	1997	1996	1995	1994	1993
Revenues (Million $)						
1Q	18,383	14,093	13,734	13,300	12,727	12,570
2Q	18,978	14,290	13,760	13,763	13,532	13,160
3Q	—	13,991	13,688	13,329	13,673	12,580
4Q	—	13,740	13,371	12,747	13,844	12,320
Yr.	—	56,114	54,553	53,139	53,776	50,621
Earnings Per Share ($)						
1Q	0.57	0.72	0.63	0.53	0.45	0.46
2Q	0.71	0.75	0.66	0.56	0.47	0.40
3Q	—	0.58	0.67	0.57	0.47	0.37
4Q	—	0.53	0.60	0.51	0.42	0.13
Yr.	—	2.58	2.54	2.17	1.82	1.35

Next earnings report expected: late October

Dividend Data (Dividends have been paid since 1928.)

Amount ($)	Date Decl.	Ex-Div. Date	Stock of Record	Payment Date
0.400	Nov. 26	Dec. 11	Dec. 15	Jan. 12 '98
0.400	Feb. 25	Mar. 12	Mar. 16	Apr. 10 '98
0.400	May. 27	Jun. 11	Jun. 15	Jul. 10 '98
0.440	Aug. 26	Sep. 11	Sep. 15	Oct. 13 '98

A Division of The McGraw-Hill Companies

Business Summary - 29-JUL-98

Philip Morris Cos. is a holding company whose principal wholly owned subsidiaries are manufacturers and marketers of various consumer products, most notably Marlboro cigarettes, Kraft packaged foods, and Miller beer. The company's businesses have, in the aggregate, more than 60 brands that generate annual revenues of more than $100 million each. Business segment contributions in 1997:

	Revs.	Profits
Tobacco	55%	64%
Food	38%	30%
Brewing	6%	4%
Financial & real estate	1%	2%

International operations accounted for approximately 52% of sales (including U.S. exports) and 45% of operating profits in 1997.

Philip Morris U.S.A. is the nation's largest tobacco company, with total cigarette shipments in the U.S. amounting to 235 billion units in 1997 (an increase of 2% from 1996), accounting for about 49% of the U.S. cigarette market. PM U.S.A. contributed 19% of total company sales and 25% of operating profits in 1997. Major premium brands include Marlboro, Benson & Hedges, Merit, Virginia Slims and Parliament. Discount brands include Basic and Cambridge. In 1997, the premium and discount segments accounted for approximately 72.5% and 27.5%, respectively, of domestic cigarette industry volume. Philip Morris International's total cigarette shipments grew 8% in 1997, to 712 billion units, which equated to an approximate 14% share of the world market. PM International contributed about 37% of total company sales and 36% of operating profits in 1997.

Kraft Foods is the largest packaged food company in North America. Kraft's principal products include Kraft cheese and cheese products; Oscar Mayer and Louis Rich processed meats; Maxwell House coffee; Classen pickles, Post ready-to-eat cereals; Kraft salad dressings; and Kool-Aid, Tang, Capri Sun, Crystal Light and Country Time powdered and ready-to-drink beverages. Kraft Foods International produces a wide variety of coffee, confectionery, cheese and grocery and processed meat products in Europe, the Middle East, Africa and the Asia/Pacific region.

Miller Brewing (No. 2 U.S. brewer) holds about 22% of the U.S. beer market. Brands include Miller Lite, Miller Genuine Draft, Miller, Icehouse, Red Dog, Lowenbrau, Meister Brau and Milwaukee's Best. During 1997, Miller sold its equity interest in Molson Breweries of Canada and 49% of its ownership of Molson USA, which holds the rights to import, market and distribute the Molson and Foster's brands in the U.S.

Per Share Data ($)

(Year Ended Dec. 31)	1997	1996	1995	1994	1993	1992	1991	1990	1989	1988
Tangible Bk. Val.	NM	NM	-2.14	-2.73	-3.10	-2.24	-2.23	-2.57	-2.19	-2.67
Cash Flow	3.28	3.25	2.83	2.44	1.97	2.36	1.93	1.75	1.47	1.00
Earnings	2.58	2.56	2.17	1.82	1.35	1.82	1.41	1.28	1.06	0.74
Dividends	1.60	1.47	1.22	1.01	0.87	0.78	0.64	0.52	0.42	0.34
Payout Ratio	62%	57%	56%	56%	64%	43%	45%	40%	39%	45%
Prices - High	48$\frac{1}{8}$	39$\frac{5}{8}$	31$\frac{1}{2}$	21$\frac{1}{2}$	25$\frac{7}{8}$	28$\frac{7}{8}$	27$\frac{1}{4}$	17$\frac{3}{8}$	15$\frac{1}{4}$	8$\frac{1}{2}$
- Low	36	28$\frac{1}{2}$	18$\frac{5}{8}$	15$\frac{3}{4}$	15	23$\frac{1}{8}$	16$\frac{1}{8}$	12	8$\frac{3}{8}$	6$\frac{3}{4}$
P/E Ratio - High	19	15	14	12	19	16	19	14	14	12
- Low	14	11	9	9	11	13	11	9	8	9

Income Statement Analysis (Million $)

	1997	1996	1995	1994	1993	1992	1991	1990	1989	1988
Revs.	56,114	54,553	53,139	53,776	50,621	50,095	48,064	44,323	39,011	25,860
Oper. Inc.	14,820	13,460	12,192	11,080	9,939	11,550	10,515	9,271	7,931	5,130
Depr.	1,700	1,691	1,671	1,631	1,611	1,484	1,438	1,325	1,142	733
Int. Exp.	1,185	1,183	1,259	1,288	1,478	1,513	1,696	1,746	1,789	739
Pretax Inc.	10,611	10,683	9,347	8,216	6,196	8,608	6,971	6,311	5,058	3,727
Eff. Tax Rate	41%	41%	41%	43%	42%	43%	44%	44%	42%	45%
Net Inc.	6,310	6,303	5,478	4,725	3,568	4,939	3,927	3,540	2,946	2,064

Balance Sheet & Other Fin. Data (Million $)

	1997	1996	1995	1994	1993	1992	1991	1990	1989	1988
Cash	2,282	240	1,138	184	182	1,021	126	146	118	168
Curr. Assets	17,440	15,190	14,879	NA	NA	NA	NA	NA	NA	NA
Total Assets	55,947	54,871	53,811	52,649	51,205	50,014	47,384	46,569	38,528	36,960
Curr. Liab.	15,071	14,867	14,273	NA	NA	NA	NA	NA	NA	NA
LT Debt	11,585	11,827	13,107	14,975	15,021	14,265	14,200	16,108	14,685	17,102
Common Eqty.	14,920	14,218	13,985	12,786	11,627	12,563	12,512	11,947	9,571	7,679
Total Cap.	27,394	26,776	30,830	31,156	29,715	29,716	29,186	30,753	26,264	26,500
Cap. Exp.	1,874	1,782	1,621	1,726	1,592	1,573	1,562	1,355	1,246	3,145
Cash Flow	8,010	7,994	7,149	6,356	5,179	6,423	5,365	4,865	4,088	2,797
Curr. Ratio	1.2	1.0	1.4	NA	NA	NA	NA	NA	NA	NA
% LT Debt of Cap.	42.3	44.2	42.6	48.1	50.6	48.0	48.7	52.4	55.9	64.6
% Net Inc.of Revs.	11.2	11.6	10.3	8.8	7.0	9.9	8.2	8.0	7.6	8.0
% Ret. on Assets	11.4	11.6	10.3	9.2	7.1	10.3	8.4	8.3	7.8	7.4
% Ret. on Equity	43.3	44.7	41.0	39.2	29.8	40.0	32.2	32.9	34.1	28.8

Data as orig. reptd.; bef. results of disc. opers. and/or spec. items. Per share data adj. for stk. divs. as of ex-div. date. Bold denotes diluted EPS (FASB 128). E-Estimated. NA-Not Available. NM-Not Meaningful. NR-Not Ranked.

Office—120 Park Ave., New York, NY 10017. **Tel**—(212) 880-5000. **Chrmn & CEO**—G. C. Bible. **SVP-CFO**—L. C. Camilleri. **VP-Secy**—G. P. Holsenbeck. **Investor Contact**—Michael Kenny. **Dirs**—E. E. Bailey, G. C. Bible, M. H. Bring, H. Brown, W. H. Donaldson, J. Evans, R. E. R. Huntley, R. Murdoch, J. D. Nichols, L. A. Noto, R. D. Parsons, R. S. Penske, J. S. Reed, S. M. Wolf. **Transfer Agents & Registrars**—First Chicago Trust Co. of New York, NYC. **Incorporated**—in Virginia in 1919. **Empl**— 152,000. **S&P Analyst:** Richard Joy

Phillips Petroleum   1826

NYSE Symbol **P**

In S&P 500

12-SEP-98

Industry:
Oil (Domestic Integrated)

Summary: This integrated oil and gas company also makes plastics and petrochemicals, and is the largest U.S. producer of natural gas liquids.

| S&P Opinion: Avoid (★★) | Recent Price • 47⅝ | Yield • 2.9% |
| | 52 Wk Range • 53¼-40⅛ | 12-Mo. P/E • 15.3 |

Quantitative Evaluations

Outlook
(1 Lowest—5 Highest)
• **2⁻**

Fair Value
• **44**

Risk
• **Low**

Earn./Div. Rank
• **B+**

Technical Eval.
• **Bullish** since 8/98

Rel. Strength Rank
(1 Lowest—99 Highest)
• **95**

Insider Activity
• **Neutral**

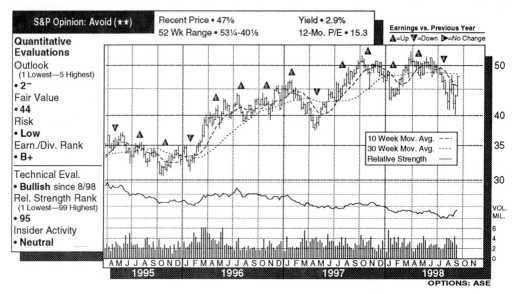

Earnings vs. Previous Year
▲=Up ▼=Down ▶=No Change

10 Week Mov. Avg. ---
30 Week Mov. Avg. ·····
Relative Strength —

OPTIONS: ASE

Overview - 04-AUG-98

Share earnings for 1997 include $0.36 in gains, primarily from a tax settlement. Share earnings in 1996 included a $2.15 gain from the interest effects of a tax settlement. Operating profits in the first half of 1998 declined 30%, despite increased worldwide production of crude oil, natural gas and natural gas liquids, reflecting lower commodity prices. Average oil price realizations fell $6.15 per barrel. The gas gathering, processing and marketing (GPM) unit was affected by lower prices for natural gas liquids. The refining, marketing and transportation (RM&T) division's profits benefited from improved refining margins. Chemicals results were hindered by lower ethylene margins. The company is aggressively developing its holdings in the Gulf of Mexico, where it has made a substantial sub-salt discovery in the Mahogany field. Phillips replaced 164% of 1997 production, and total worldwide reserves were 6% higher at year end than a year earlier.

Valuation - 04-AUG-98

The shares have declined 6.0% in 1998, as domestic integrated oil stocks continue to underperform the broader market, amid lower oil and gas prices. The outlook for the remainder of 1998 is negative, as oil prices are expected to remain weak. The company will also be hampered by weak chemicals margins, which will continue to outweigh the benefits of lower feedstock costs and higher volumes. In addition, weak natural gas liquids (NGL) prices will negatively affect the GPM unit. Despite indications that the company's long-awaited increases in oil and natural gas production are at hand, we believe that the shares will underperform the market over the remainder of 1998, given the bearish outlook for oil prices and chemicals margins.

Key Stock Statistics

S&P EPS Est. 1998	2.75	Tang. Bk. Value/Share	16.79
P/E on S&P Est. 1998	17.3	Beta	0.72
S&P EPS Est. 1999	3.25	Shareholders	61,700
Dividend Rate/Share	1.36	Market cap. (B)	$ 12.3
Shs. outstg. (M)	258.4	Inst. holdings	58%
Avg. daily vol. (M)	0.727		

Value of $10,000 invested 5 years ago: $ 22,742

Fiscal Year Ending Dec. 31

	1998	1997	1996	1995	1994	1993
Revenues (Million $)						
1Q	3,254	3,944	3,595	3,087	2,884	3,029
2Q	3,000	3,709	3,937	3,591	2,995	3,230
3Q	—	3,844	3,852	3,369	3,315	3,170
4Q	—	3,713	4,347	3,321	3,017	2,880
Yr.	—	15,424	15,731	13,368	12,211	12,309
Earnings Per Share ($)						
1Q	**0.92**	**0.86**	2.65	0.43	0.49	0.23
2Q	**0.60**	**1.15**	0.84	0.42	0.29	0.47
3Q	—	**0.81**	0.71	0.52	0.45	0.16
4Q	—	**0.79**	0.76	0.42	0.62	0.08
Yr.	**E2.75**	**3.61**	**4.91**	1.79	1.85	0.94

Next earnings report expected: late October

Dividend Data (Dividends have been paid since 1934.)

Amount ($)	Date Decl.	Ex-Div. Date	Stock of Record	Payment Date
0.340	Oct. 10	Oct. 30	Nov. 03	Dec. 01 '97
0.340	Jan. 12	Jan. 29	Feb. 02	Mar. 02 '98
0.340	Apr. 13	Apr. 29	May. 01	Jun. 01 '98
0.340	Jul. 17	Jul. 30	Aug. 03	Sep. 01 '98

A Division of The McGraw-Hill Companies

Business Summary - 04-AUG-98

Founded by Frank Phillips in Bartlesville, Oklahoma, in 1917, Phillips Petroleum (P) has grown to become one of the largest U.S.-based integrated oil companies. Phillips explores for and produces crude oil and natural gas worldwide, markets refined products in the U.S., and manufactures chemicals. In November 1927, the company opened its first refinery and its first service station. Shortly thereafter, the company's "Phillips 66" brand name and logo were introduced. These enduring symbols of the U.S. retail gasoline industry are now displayed at nearly 6,500 retail outlets nationwide.

Phillips currently holds exploration acreage in 21 countries, and produces in six nations. Aside from the U.S., the company is active in the North Sea, and was, in fact, one of the first companies to discover oil in the Norwegian sector of the North Sea, back in 1969. In 1997, crude oil production averaged 232,000 bbl. a day, up 5.9% from 1996's levels, while natural gas production fell 3.6%, to 1.47 billion cubic feet (Bcf). Worldwide crude oil proved reserves at year-end 1997 amounted to 994 million bbl.; proved natural gas reserves stood at 6,521 Bcf. Capital spending for 1997 was $2.10 billion, up from $1.54 billion in 1996. Of the funding, 66% was for projects in the upstream area. The bulk of $1,376 million expended on E&P was for international projects,

including Ekofisk II in Norway and fields in the U.K. sector of the North Sea. The company plans to spend $249 million in 1998 for North American development drilling and production-related projects. P plans to drill exploratory wells in the U.S., Algeria, Nigeria, Norway, Peru, the U.K. and Venezuela.

During 1995, P completed a restructuring of its refining and marketing (also known as "downstream") and chemical activities into two divisions: Phillips 66 Co., which includes refining, marketing and transportation; and Phillips Chemical Co., which includes natural gas liquids operations and the chemical and plastics segments. In 1997, the amount of crude oil refined fell 4.6%, while petroleum products sold fell 2.9%. Spending on chemicals amounted to $275 million in 1997, for expansions in ethylene, paraxylene and engineering plastics. Chemicals spending for 1998 is projected at $281 million.

In recent years, P has emphasized improving the financial performance of its refining and gas gathering, processing and marketing operations. It also aggressively expanded retail marketing operations, aiming at raising its marketing-to-refining ratio. This is in line with current industry conventional wisdom, which believes that marketing will be the healthier portion of the downstream segment over the next few years.

Per Share Data ($)

(Year Ended Dec. 31)	1997	1996	1995	1994	1993	1992	1991	1990	1989	1988
Tangible Bk. Val.	16.49	14.56	10.96	11.29	10.28	10.37	10.61	10.51	8.74	8.69
Cash Flow	6.88	8.53	5.12	4.89	3.98	4.13	5.03	5.33	5.96	6.81
Earnings	3.61	4.96	1.79	1.85	0.94	1.04	0.38	2.18	0.90	2.72
Dividends	1.34	1.25	1.20	1.12	1.12	1.12	1.12	1.03	1.02	0.66
Payout Ratio	37%	25%	67%	61%	119%	108%	297%	49%	114%	25%
Prices - High	52¼	45⅞	37⅛	37¼	37⅜	28⅞	29½	31⅛	30⅛	22⅜
- Low	37⅜	31⅛	29⅞	25½	24½	22	21⅞	22½	19⅛	12⅛
P/E Ratio - High	14	9	21	20	40	28	78	14	33	8
- Low	10	6	17	14	26	21	58	10	21	4

Income Statement Analysis (Million $)

	1997	1996	1995	1994	1993	1992	1991	1990	1989	1988
Revs.	15,210	15,731	13,368	12,211	12,309	11,933	12,604	13,603	12,384	11,304
Oper. Inc.	2,748	2,730	2,079	1,752	1,407	1,486	1,461	2,221	2,306	2,579
Depr.	863	941	871	794	795	804	1,208	786	1,233	962
Int. Exp.	280	250	295	265	289	392	479	628	649	720
Pretax Inc.	1,900	2,172	1,064	852	538	511	451	1,187	536	1,115
Eff. Tax Rate	50%	40%	56%	43%	55%	47%	78%	54%	59%	42%
Net Inc.	959	1,303	469	484	245	270	98.0	541	219	650

Balance Sheet & Other Fin. Data (Million $)

	1997	1996	1995	1994	1993	1992	1991	1990	1989	1988
Cash	163	615	67.0	193	119	131	114	670	708	1,079
Curr. Assets	2,648	3,306	2,409	2,465	2,193	2,349	2,459	3,322	2,876	3,062
Total Assets	13,860	13,548	11,978	11,436	10,868	11,468	11,473	12,130	11,256	11,968
Curr. Liab.	2,445	3,137	2,815	2,441	2,271	2,517	2,603	2,910	2,706	2,468
LT Debt	2,775	2,555	3,097	3,106	3,208	3,718	3,876	3,839	3,939	4,761
Common Eqty.	4,814	4,251	3,188	2,953	2,688	2,698	2,757	2,719	2,132	2,113
Total Cap.	9,497	9,286	7,584	7,354	7,159	7,438	7,828	7,841	7,792	8,748
Cap. Exp.	2,043	1,544	1,456	1,154	1,132	1,254	1,406	1,383	872	797
Cash Flow	1,822	2,244	1,340	1,278	1,040	1,074	1,306	1,327	1,452	1,601
Curr. Ratio	1.1	1.1	0.9	1.0	1.0	0.9	0.9	1.1	1.1	1.2
% LT Debt of Cap.	29.2	27.5	40.9	42.2	44.8	50.0	49.5	49.0	50.6	54.4
% Net Inc.of Revs.	6.3	8.3	3.5	4.0	2.0	2.3	0.8	4.0	1.8	5.8
% Ret. on Assets	7.0	10.2	4.0	4.3	2.2	2.4	0.8	4.5	1.9	5.2
% Ret. on Equity	21.2	35.0	15.3	17.2	9.1	9.9	3.6	21.7	10.3	33.4

Data as orig. reptd.; bef. results of disc. opers. and/or spec. items. Per share data adj. for stk. divs. as of ex-div. date. Bold denotes diluted EPS (FASB 128). E-Estimated. NA-Not Available. NM-Not Meaningful. NR-Not Ranked.

Office—Phillips Bldg., Bartlesville, OK 74004. **Tel**—(918) 661-6600. **Website**—http://www.phillips66.com**Chrmn & CEO**—W. W. Allen. **Pres & COO**—J. J. Mulva. **SVP & CFO**—T. C. Morris. **Secy**—D. J. Billam. **VP & Investor Contact**—E. K. Grigsby, 630 Fifth Ave, New York, NY 10111 (212-397-9766). **Dirs**—W. W. Allen, N. R. Augustine, G. B. Beitzel, D. L. Boren, C. L. Bowerman, R. E. Chappell, Jr., L. S. Eagleburger, J. B. Edwards, L. D. Horner, J. J. Mulva, N. L Tobias, V. J. Tschinkel, K. C. Turner. **Transfer Agent & Registrar**—ChaseMellon Shareholder Services, Ridgefield Park, NJ. **Incorporated**—in Delaware in 1917. **Empl**— 17,100. **S&P Analyst:** Norman Rosenberg

12-SEP-98

Industry: Agricultural Products

Summary: This company is the leading North American breeder and producer of hybrid seed corn, with a market share of more than 40%.

S&P Opinion: Buy (★★★★)	Recent Price • 31⅛	Yield • 1.3%
	52 Wk Range • 42⅝–29⅛	12-Mo. P/E • 28.6

Quantitative Evaluations

Outlook (1 Lowest—5 Highest)
• **1+**

Fair Value
• **22¼**

Risk
• **Low**

Earn./Div. Rank
• **A-**

Technical Eval.
• **NA**

Rel. Strength Rank (1 Lowest—99 Highest)
• **65**

Insider Activity
• **Neutral**

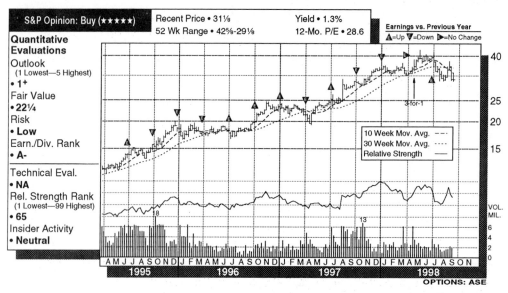

Earnings vs. Previous Year ▲=Up ▼=Down ▶=No Change

10 Week Mov. Avg. – – –
30 Week Mov. Avg. ·········
Relative Strength ———

3-for-1

OPTIONS: ASE

Overview - 07-JUL-98

Net sales in FY 98 (Aug.) are expected to rise approximately 3.0%, led by a 4% to 5% increase in prices, higher corn volumes and lower soybean volumes. Profitability is expected to benefit from these factors, as well as from a favorable product mix shift to newly developed, higher-priced hybrids. Results will be impacted by adverse currency adjustments which should lower operating income approximately $30 million or $0.07 a share. Despite strong price competition and competitor discounting, it appears that PHB will gain about 0.5% in North American corn seed market share. Looking toward FY 99, sales should benefit from the recent introduction of new products and increased demand for PHB soybean products.

Valuation - 07-JUL-98

We continue to recommend PHB for purchase given its strong market position and leading research capabilities. The shares have recently been hurt as the company announced that it expects lower FY 98 earnings resulting from increased competition and unfavorable currency adjustments. Despite the increased competition, the company has been able to increase sales, market share and margins. In addition, had it not been for the adverse currency adjustments, it appears that our original FY 98 EPS estimate of $1.15 would have been obtainable. Results in FY 99 should improve given the recent introduction of 37 new hybrid products which should enhance the company's competitiveness next year. The company should also benefit from greater sales of soybean products given their recent agreement with Monsanto (MTC) that allows them to utilize MTC's Roundup Ready gene in hybrid canola. Thus, we view the recent weakness in the shares as an opportunity to purchase the stock.

Key Stock Statistics

S&P EPS Est. 1998	1.07	Tang. Bk. Value/Share	4.39
P/E on S&P Est. 1998	29.1	Beta	0.24
S&P EPS Est. 1999	1.40	Shareholders	20,000
Dividend Rate/Share	0.40	Market cap. (B)	$ 6.0
Shs. outstg. (M)	241.6	Inst. holdings	32%
Avg. daily vol. (M)	0.374		

Value of $10,000 invested 5 years ago: $ 37,673

Fiscal Year Ending Aug. 31

	1998	1997	1996	1995	1994	1993
Revenues (Million $)						
1Q	79.00	90.00	92.00	69.00	66.67	68.00
2Q	302.0	264.0	281.0	277.0	250.0	156.7
3Q	1,317	1,288	1,168	1,049	1,039	930.9
4Q	—	142.0	180.0	137.0	123.5	187.5
Yr.	—	1,784	1,721	1,532	1,479	1,343
Earnings Per Share ($)						
1Q	-0.24	-0.18	-0.20	-0.19	-0.16	-0.14
2Q	**-0.01**	-0.01	0.02	0.04	0.06	-0.06
3Q	**1.50**	1.35	1.21	1.08	0.98	0.84
4Q	**E-0.18**	-0.17	-0.14	-0.20	-0.08	-0.14
Yr.	**E1.07**	0.98	0.89	0.72	0.80	0.51

Next earnings report expected: early October

Dividend Data (Dividends have been paid since 1935.)

Amount ($)	Date Decl.	Ex-Div. Date	Stock of Record	Payment Date
0.260	Dec. 16	Dec. 24	Dec. 29	Jan. 09 '98
0.260	Mar. 10	Mar. 25	Mar. 27	Apr. 08 '98
3-for-1	Mar. 10	Apr. 24	Mar. 27	Apr. 23 '98
0.100	Jun. 09	Jun. 24	Jun. 26	Jul. 08 '98

A Division of The McGraw·Hill Companies

Business Summary - 07-JUL-98

Pioneer Hi-Bred International is the leading North American breeder and producer of hybrid seed corn. The company's corn breeding program began in 1913, and its first actual sales of seed were made in 1924. Today, Pioneer also breeds and produces hybrid soybean, sorghum, forage and other seeds. The majority of its products are used by customers to produce feed or forage for livestock.

Since the company's success ultimately hinges on the performance of its genetically-altered seeds, PHB's primary objective is to strengthen, develop, and leverage its wide array of existing crop plant genetics, or germplasm. Consistent with this objective, the company continues to dedicate the bulk of its considerable research budget into building and maintaining its germplasm advantage over competitors.

Pioneer's product categories contributed to its FY 97 (Aug.) results as follows (profits in millions):

	Sales	Profits
Corn	77%	$402
Soybeans	12%	27
Other	11%	11

Pioneer's primary markets are the U.S. and Canada

(the North American region) and Europe. Approximately 67% of FY 97 sales were made within North America, and 23% within Europe. PHB also has operations in Latin America, Mexico, Africa, Asia, and the Middle East.

Based on company estimates, Pioneer seed corn accounted for 42% of the total North American market in FY 97. The company is also believed to have a leading position of the soybean seed market, with an estimated 17% share. In FY 97, PHB spent $146 million on research & development, up 7.4% from the level of FY 96.

The seed business is highly seasonal, with substantially all sales made in December through May. Operations in the first and fourth quarters of the fiscal year are often unprofitable.

PHB owns and operates 22 conditioning plants for commercial seed corn. The plants can handle about 55,000 bushels of ear corn an hour, on average, and condition 14,000 units an hour. In a normal year, seed conditioning is completed by early February.

In September 1997, PHB and DuPont created a broad research alliance and a separate joint venture company to speed the discovery, development, and delivery of new crops with value to farmers, livestock producers, and consumers worldwide. DuPont also acquired a 20% equity interest in PHB.

Per Share Data ($)

(Year Ended Aug. 31)	1997	1996	1995	1994	1993	1992	1991	1990	1989	1988
Tangible Bk. Val.	13.18	3.93	3.59	3.32	2.97	2.85	2.43	2.31	2.19	1.98
Cash Flow	4.03	1.20	1.01	1.03	0.70	0.75	0.59	0.44	0.45	0.38
Earnings	0.98	0.89	0.72	0.80	0.51	0.56	0.38	0.26	0.29	0.22
Dividends	0.32	0.28	0.24	0.22	0.17	0.13	0.13	0.13	0.12	0.12
Payout Ratio	32%	31%	33%	27%	33%	24%	34%	50%	43%	54%
Prices - High	36⅛	24⅝	20	13½	12⅞	10⅛	8¼	5¼	5	4⅜
- Low	19¼	16⅜	10⅞	9⅞	8	6⅝	4	3½	3¾	3¼
P/E Ratio - High	37	28	28	17	25	18	22	20	18	20
- Low	20	18	15	12	16	12	10	13	13	15

Income Statement Analysis (Million $)

	1997	1996	1995	1994	1993	1992	1991	1990	1989	1988
Revs.	1,784	1,721	1,532	1,479	1,343	1,262	1,125	964	867	875
Oper. Inc.	452	424	354	362	331	295	245	188	177	196
Depr.	89.0	77.0	74.0	60.1	52.0	51.7	56.3	52.9	49.2	49.9
Int. Exp.	8.0	11.0	13.0	11.3	17.8	16.5	22.3	16.6	12.1	14.2
Pretax Inc.	373	354	291	347	223	239	168	123	140	104
Eff. Tax Rate	34%	36%	36%	39%	38%	36%	38%	41%	40%	39%
Net Inc.	243	223	183	213	137	152	104	73.0	82.0	62.0

Balance Sheet & Other Fin. Data (Million $)

	1997	1996	1995	1994	1993	1992	1991	1990	1989	1988
Cash	97.0	99	84.0	135	92.0	97.6	62.4	48.4	54.5	43.3
Curr. Assets	901	784	770	742	717	703	605	538	474	450
Total Assets	1,603	1,422	1,293	1,253	1,221	1,216	1,086	1,006	914	865
Curr. Liab.	329	288	280	232	261	286	295	294	221	209
LT Debt	19.0	25.0	18.0	65.6	68.1	73.9	67.4	18.9	16.5	27.7
Common Eqty.	1,148	1,018	913	881	825	799	681	649	627	577
Total Cap.	1,174	1,050	938	954	900	885	754	672	650	612
Cap. Exp.	127	116	86.0	80.0	100	75.0	59.0	77.0	92.0	70.0
Cash Flow	332	300	257	273	189	204	160	126	131	112
Curr. Ratio	2.7	2.7	2.8	3.2	2.7	2.5	2.1	1.8	2.1	2.2
% LT Debt of Cap.	1.6	2.4	1.9	6.9	7.6	8.4	8.9	2.8	2.5	4.5
% Net Inc.of Revs.	13.6	13.0	11.9	14.4	10.2	12.1	9.3	7.5	9.4	7.1
% Ret. on Assets	16.1	16.4	14.3	17.5	11.3	13.2	10.1	7.6	9.2	7.1
% Ret. on Equity	22.4	23.1	20.4	25.4	17.0	20.6	15.8	11.5	13.7	11.0

Data as orig. reptd.; bef. results of disc. opers. and/or spec. items. Per share data adj. for stk. divs. as of ex-div. date. Bold denotes diluted EPS (FASB 128). E-Estimated. NA-Not Available. NM-Not Meaningful. NR-Not Ranked.

Office—700 Capital Square, 400 Locust St., Des Moines, IA 50309. **Tel**—(515) 248-4800. **Website**—http://www.pioneer.com **Chrmn & CEO**—C. S. Johnson. **VP & Treas**—D. G. Dollison. **EVP & Secy**—J. L. Chicoine. **Investor Contact**—Dirck Steimel. **Dirs**—N. Y. Bekavac, C. R. Brenton, P. Cuatrecasas, F. S. Hubbell, C. S. Johnson, L. Kaufmann, F. W. McFarlan, O. J. Newlin, T. N. Urban, V. Walbot, H. S. Wallace, F. W. Weitz, H. H. F. Wijffels. **Transfer Agent & Registrar**—Bank of Boston, Mass. **Incorporated**—in Iowa in 1926. **Empl**— 4,994. **S&P Analyst:** Robert J. Izmirlian

STANDARD &POOR'S
STOCK REPORTS

Pitney Bowes

1836

NYSE Symbol **PBI**

In S&P 500

12-SEP-98

Industry:
Office Equipment & Supplies

Summary: The world's largest manufacturer of mailing systems, this company also provides copying and facsimile systems, facilities management services and lease financing.

S&P Opinion: Hold (★★★)	Recent Price • 51¼ — Yield • 1.8%
	52 Wk Range • 55⅞-37½ — 12-Mo. P/E • 26.7

Quantitative Evaluations

Outlook
(1 Lowest—5 Highest)
• **2+**

Fair Value
• **47¾**

Risk
• **Low**

Earn./Div. Rank
• **A+**

Technical Eval.
• **Bullish** since 5/97

Rel. Strength Rank
(1 Lowest—99 Highest)
• **88**

Insider Activity
• **Neutral**

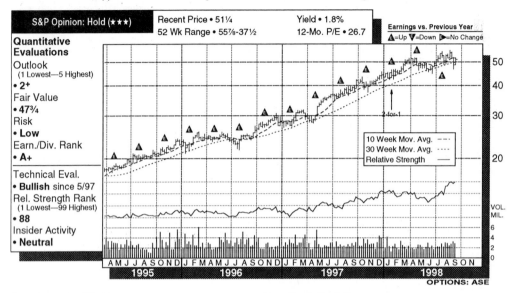

Earnings vs. Previous Year — ▲=Up ▼=Down ▶=No Change

10 Week Mov. Avg. – – –
30 Week Mov. Avg. ....
Relative Strength ——

VOL. MIL.

OPTIONS: ASE

Overview - 24-JUL-98

Revenues should rise about 9%-10% in 1998, driven by U.S. Postal Service requirements that customers migrate to digital and electronic metering, as well as increased rental and facilities management revenues and international expansion of mailing operations. The facilities management business should continue its double-digit growth. Gross margins should remain stable, and the company should be able to continue to improve its operating ratio due to tight cost controls and focus on high quality revenues. PBI's planned reduction of its large-ticket external finance portfolio by about $1.2 billion, should result in up-front cash of $1 billion which it will use to buy back shares and reduce debt. Nearly 18 million shares (post-split) were repurchased in 1997; 6.6 million shares were bought back in the first half of 1998. The stock was split 2-for-1 in January 1998.

Valuation - 24-JUL-98

PBI posted EPS of $0.51 a share in the second quarter of 1998, versus $0.45 a year earlier, beating expectations by a penny. The shares have been in a steady uptrend. This appreciation is the result of cost-cutting efforts, dividend increases, a share-buyback program, restructuring actions and strong earnings gains. PBI's operational performance has also strengthened through increased inventory and accounts receivable turns, higher net profit margins and the posting of steady and healthy return on equity of about 20% over the period. We forecast EPS to climb about 15% over the next three fiscal years. The reduction of PBI's large-ticket asset base and the use of the proceeds to buy back shares and pay down debt will enhance shareholder value. However, we see the shares, trading at 24X our 1999 EPS estimate of $2.30, as fully valued.

Key Stock Statistics

S&P EPS Est. 1998	2.05	Tang. Bk. Value/Share	5.96
P/E on S&P Est. 1998	25.0	Beta	0.69
S&P EPS Est. 1999	2.30	Shareholders	32,300
Dividend Rate/Share	0.90	Market cap. (B)	$ 14.1
Shs. outstg. (M)	274.4	Inst. holdings	77%
Avg. daily vol. (M)	0.589		

Value of $10,000 invested 5 years ago: $ 29,408

Fiscal Year Ending Dec. 31

	1998	1997	1996	1995	1994	1993
Revenues (Million $)						
1Q	1,012	961.4	906.3	839.9	876.8	833.4
2Q	1,080	1,006	942.9	862.6	954.9	874.4
3Q	—	1,013	950.7	876.1	806.4	861.2
4Q	—	1,120	1,059	977.1	900.5	973.9
Yr.	—	4,100	3,859	3,555	3,271	3,543
Earnings Per Share ($)						
1Q	**0.46**	**0.40**	0.35	0.32	0.29	0.26
2Q	**0.51**	**0.45**	0.40	0.33	0.31	0.28
3Q	**E0.50**	**0.44**	0.39	0.33	0.27	0.21
4Q	**E0.59**	**0.51**	0.42	0.37	0.30	0.36
Yr.	**E2.05**	**1.80**	1.56	1.34	1.10	1.11

Next earnings report expected: late October

Dividend Data (Dividends have been paid since 1934.)

Amount ($)	Date Decl.	Ex-Div. Date	Stock of Record	Payment Date
0.400	Nov. 10	Nov. 24	Nov. 26	Dec. 12 '97
0.225	Feb. 09	Feb. 23	Feb. 25	Mar. 12 '98
0.225	Apr. 13	May. 26	May. 28	Jun. 12 '98
0.225	Jul. 13	Aug. 26	Aug. 28	Sep. 12 '98

A Division of The **McGraw·Hill** *Companies*

Business Summary - 24-JUL-98

Pitney Bowes had its beginnings in the early 1920s, when it introduced its first postage meter devices, and over the years has built this business up to provide customers with a complete line of mail room solutions. PBI, through its business services unit, seeks to leverage this mailing expertise to offer companies not just equipment, but value-added services and solutions that allow businesses to be more efficient and reduce costs. The company also provides lease financing and other financial services to its customers and other businesses, mainly through its wholly owned subsidiary Pitney Bowes Credit Corporation.

The business equipment segment, which accounted for 77% of 1997 revenues, consists of mailing, copying and facsimile systems, and related financing. Mailing systems include postage meters, parcel registers, mailing machines, manifest systems, letter and parcel scales, mail openers, mailroom furniture, folders and paper handling and shipping equipment. The latest product is the Personal Post Office, which is a digital postage meter that offers users speed, convenience and greater security. Also sold through this business unit are high-end copying and facsimile systems and related supplies. The company's office equipment is targeted for large and medium-size businesses and recent product introductions are being targeted for the small office/home office market.

The business services segment, which accounted for 14% of 1997 revenue, consists of facilities management and mortgage servicing. Facilities management services, a natural extension of PBI's mailing system roots, provide a variety of business support functions, including correspondence mail and reprographics management and automated mail center management. Mortgage servicing provides billing, collecting, and processing services for major investors in residential first mortgages for a fee.

The commercial and industrial financing services segment provides equipment financing for non-Pitney Bowes equipment and other financial services to industrial markets. This unit accounted for the remaining revenues posted in 1997 and is currently phasing out its non-Pitney Bowes equipment financing efforts.

Overseas, PBI's strategy is to leverage its mailing know-how by aiding foreign post offices with their systems, many of which are antiquated and suffer from major inefficiencies. International operations contributed 15% of revenues in 1997, versus 16% in 1996 and 1995.

Per Share Data ($)

(Year Ended Dec. 31)	1997	1996	1995	1994	1993	1992	1991	1990	1989	1988
Tangible Bk. Val.	5.96	6.86	6.20	5.03	5.17	4.79	5.17	4.53	4.06	3.81
Cash Flow	2.21	2.48	2.23	1.96	1.93	1.76	1.65	1.34	1.18	1.27
Earnings	1.80	1.56	1.34	1.10	1.11	0.98	0.90	0.65	0.57	0.75
Dividends	0.80	0.69	0.60	0.52	0.45	0.39	0.34	0.30	0.26	0.23
Payout Ratio	44%	44%	45%	47%	41%	39%	38%	46%	45%	30%
Prices - High	45$\frac{3}{4}$	30$\frac{3}{4}$	24$\frac{1}{8}$	23$\frac{1}{4}$	22$\frac{1}{4}$	20$\frac{1}{2}$	16$\frac{3}{8}$	13$\frac{3}{8}$	13$\frac{3}{4}$	11$\frac{7}{8}$
- Low	26$\frac{7}{8}$	21	15	14$\frac{5}{8}$	18$\frac{1}{8}$	14	9$\frac{1}{2}$	6$\frac{3}{4}$	10$\frac{1}{4}$	8$\frac{1}{2}$
P/E Ratio - High	25	20	18	21	20	21	18	21	24	16
- Low	15	13	11	13	16	14	11	10	18	11

Income Statement Analysis (Million $)

	1997	1996	1995	1994	1993	1992	1991	1990	1989	1988
Revs.	4,100	3,859	3,555	3,271	3,543	3,434	3,332	3,196	2,876	2,650
Oper. Inc.	1,303	1,160	1,109	999	1,028	987	943	888	794	691
Depr.	300	278	272	268	263	251	238	221	195	166
Int. Exp.	209	204	226	194	187	227	258	265	238	166
Pretax Inc.	803	684	619	567	575	495	462	328	261	364
Eff. Tax Rate	34%	31%	34%	39%	39%	37%	38%	37%	31%	35%
Net Inc.	526	469	408	348	353	312	288	207	180	237

Balance Sheet & Other Fin. Data (Million $)

	1997	1996	1995	1994	1993	1992	1991	1990	1989	1988
Cash	139	137	88.6	76.0	56.0	73.0	118	80.0	61.0	46.0
Curr. Assets	2,464	2,222	2,101	2,084	1,937	1,839	1,936	1,799	1,699	1,519
Total Assets	7,893	8,156	7,845	7,400	6,794	6,499	6,381	6,061	5,611	4,788
Curr. Liab.	3,373	3,305	3,502	3,978	3,273	3,097	2,995	2,889	2,271	1,853
LT Debt	1,068	1,300	1,063	802	877	1,048	1,095	1,136	1,411	1,102
Common Eqty.	1,870	2,237	2,069	1,742	1,869	1,650	1,796	1,584	1,422	1,262
Total Cap.	4,146	4,260	3,947	3,001	3,158	3,037	3,385	3,170	3,305	2,935
Cap. Exp.	244	272	338	346	292	225	250	323	300	309
Cash Flow	646	747	679	616	616	563	526	427	374	403
Curr. Ratio	0.7	0.7	0.6	0.5	0.6	0.6	0.6	0.6	0.7	0.8
% LT Debt of Cap.	25.8	30.5	26.9	26.7	27.8	34.5	32.3	35.8	42.7	37.5
% Net Inc.of Revs.	12.8	12.2	11.5	10.7	10.0	9.1	8.6	6.5	6.3	8.9
% Ret. on Assets	6.6	5.9	5.3	5.0	5.3	4.9	4.6	3.5	3.5	6.5
% Ret. on Equity	25.6	21.8	21.4	19.7	20.0	18.2	16.9	13.7	13.4	20.4

Data as orig. reptd.; bef. results of disc. opers. and/or spec. items. Per share data adj. for stk. divs. as of ex-div. date. Bold denotes diluted EPS (FASB 128). E-Estimated. NA-Not Available. NM-Not Meaningful. NR-Not Ranked.

Office—1 Elmcroft Rd., Stamford, CT 06926-0700. **Tel**—(203) 356-5000. **Website**—http://www.pitneybowes.com **Chrmn & CEO**—M. J. Critelli. **Pres & COO**—M. C. Breslawsky. **VP & CFO**—M. L. Reichenstein. **Secy**—A. C. Corn. **Investor Contact**—Michael Monahan (203) 351-6349. **Dirs**—L. G. Alvarado, M. C. Breslawsky, W. E. Butler, C. G. Campbell, M. J. Critelli, E. Green, C. E. Hugel, J. H. Keyes, M. I. Roth, P. S. Sewell. **Transfer Agent & Registrar**—ChaseMellon Shareholder Services, Ridgefield, NJ. **Incorporated**—in Delaware in 1920. **Empl**— 29,901. S&P **Analyst:** Jim Corridore

STANDARD &POOR'S
STOCK REPORTS

Placer Dome

1856D

NYSE Symbol **PDG**

In S&P 500

12-SEP-98

Industry:
Gold & Precious Metals Mining

Summary: This producer of gold from properties in North and South America and the South Pacific is implementing an aggressive expansion program.

S&P Opinion: Accumulate (★★★★)	Recent Price • 12⅜	Yield • 0.8%
	52 Wk Range • 19⅞-7⅞	12-Mo. P/E • NM

Earnings vs. Previous Year
▲=Up ▼=Down ►=No Change

Quantitative Evaluations

Outlook
(1 Lowest—5 Highest)
• **1⁻**

Fair Value
• **6**

Risk
• **Average**

Earn./Div. Rank
• **B-**

Technical Eval.
• **Bearish** since 5/98

Rel. Strength Rank
(1 Lowest—99 Highest)
• **98**

Insider Activity
• **NA**

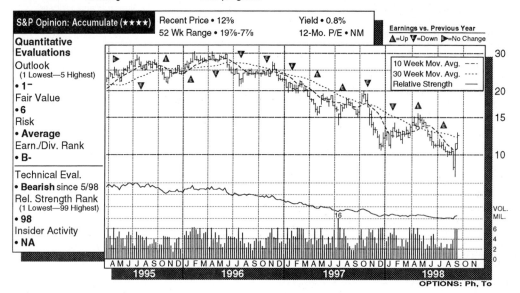

10 Week Mov. Avg. ---
30 Week Mov. Avg. ·····
Relative Strength —

OPTIONS: Ph, To

Overview - 21-AUG-98

Placer's 1998 second quarter operating results improved both year and sequentially. Equity production rose 14.8% from the 1997 second quarter level, and 13.9% from the level of the 1998 first quarter. Cash production costs declined to $150/oz., from $208/oz. in the 1997 period, and from $184/oz. in the 1998 first quarter. Total costs decreased to $218/oz., from $278/oz. in 1997 and $259/oz. in the first quarter. Improved ore grades and new low cost production helped offset lower gold prices. PDG expects to be profitable at an average gold of $300/oz. in 1998, and estimates that it will produce in excess of 2.7 million oz., at an average cash cost of $170/oz. or less.

Valuation - 21-AUG-98

On April 21, 1998, we upgraded PDG and most other gold stocks to accumulate, based on a more positive outlook both for the metal and for gold stocks as a group. Our outlook is based several factors. First, we expect central bank selling to diminish now that the new European Central Bank has announced its decision to hold 15% of its reserves in gold. Second, the rate of gain on financial investments will decline in 1998 and 1999, offering less competition for gold. Third, gold production will be flat or even decline in 1999, which should boost prices. Fourth, gold has averaged just $303/oz. through mid-August 1998, versus $331/oz. for all of 1997, but the current price of about $288/oz. is virtually dead even with the 1997 closing price. Also, despite declining fabrication demand and low inflation, gold has remained stable, in contrast to very sharp declines in such base metals as aluminum, copper, lead and zinc. This suggests that there is underlying strength in the metal. PDG and most other gold stocks are poised to rise, on stronger industry fundamentals.

Key Stock Statistics

S&P EPS Est. 1998	0.30	Tang. Bk. Value/Share	5.34
P/E on S&P Est. 1998	41.3	Beta	1.05
S&P EPS Est. 1999	0.50	Shareholders	21,000
Dividend Rate/Share	0.10	Market cap. (B)	$ 3.1
Shs. outstg. (M)	250.0	Inst. holdings	32%
Avg. daily vol. (M)	1.006		

Value of $10,000 invested 5 years ago: $ 11,534

Fiscal Year Ending Dec. 31

	1998	1997	1996	1995	1994	1993
Revenues (Million $)						
1Q	294.0	285.0	263.0	236.0	216.0	213.0
2Q	312.0	314.0	299.0	235.0	242.0	234.0
3Q	—	318.0	283.0	264.0	210.0	219.0
4Q	—	292.0	312.0	294.0	231.0	251.0
Yr.	—	1,209	1,157	1,029	899.0	917.0
Earnings Per Share ($)						
1Q	**0.06**	**0.05**	0.03	0.16	0.16	0.05
2Q	**0.08**	**0.04**	-0.13	-0.11	0.09	0.08
3Q	**E0.07**	**0.01**	0.07	0.10	0.08	0.06
4Q	**E0.09**	**-1.16**	-0.24	0.16	0.11	0.26
Yr.	**E0.30**	**-1.06**	-0.27	0.31	0.44	0.45

Next earnings report expected: late October

Dividend Data (Dividends have been paid since 1987.)

Amount ($)	Date Decl.	Ex-Div. Date	Stock of Record	Payment Date
0.075	Jul. 07	Aug. 20	Aug. 22	Sep. 22 '97
0.075	Sep. 17	Nov. 12	Nov. 14	Dec. 15 '97
0.050	Feb. 19	Mar. 04	Mar. 06	Mar. 23 '98
0.050	Jul. 22	Aug. 19	Aug. 21	Sep. 21 '98

A Division of The McGraw·Hill Companies

Placer Dome Inc.

Business Summary - 21-AUG-98

Placer Dome is engaged primarily in exploration for and production of gold, and also produces silver, copper and molybdenum. The company's main business objective is to improve financial performance by increasing its gold production to an average annual rate of 2.7 million oz. from 1998 to 2000, while reducing costs and maintaining 10 years of reserves. Nonprecious metals output is not expected to exceed 25% of gross revenue. Gross revenue from gold was 80% of the total in 1997, versus 77% in 1996 and 82% in 1995.

Placer operates as a decentralized entity, with three substantially autonomous regional business units. Hedging, finances and exploration targets are centrally managed. The company's management strategy is designed to combine the flexibility and responsiveness of small businesses with the advantages and resources of a larger company. At present, major mining operations are located in Canada, the U. S., Australia, Papua New Guinea and Chile.

PDG's exploration strategy combines the acquisition of middle to advanced stage properties with grassroots exploration to ensure a steady supply of projects with potential to maintain long term growth in gold production and reserves.

The following table presents operating and reserve data for recent years (reserve data as of year end).

	1997	1996
Gold production (oz.)	2,563,000	1,914,000
Cash cost	$208	$240
Total cost	$288	$308
Proven and probable gold reserves	31,000,000	26,518,000
Silver production (oz.)	5,900,000	7,600,000
Proven and probable silver reserves (oz.)	107,979,000	113,723,000
Copper production (lbs.)	186,700,000	182,500,000
Proven and probable copper reserves (lbs)	4,196,000,000	3,973,000,000
Molybdenum production (lbs.)	6,800,000	14,500,000

Placer's proven and probable gold reserves for 1997 were initially calculated at an average gold price of $375/oz. An assessment of the impact of a gold price at or below $375/oz. on reserves will be completed by mid-1998.

Placer anticipates consolidated gold production of 2.7 million oz. in 1998, in line with 1997. Cash and total production costs are expected to decline to about $190/oz. and $265/oz. As part of its plan to cope with lower gold prices, Placer will cut 1998 exploration spending to $115 million, from $143 million in 1997. and will defer some capital expenditures.

Equity gold production for the first half of 1998 totaled 1,402,000 oz., up from 1,235,000 oz. in the 1997 first half. Cash production costs for the period were $171/oz., versus $221/oz. in 1997; total production costs declined to $241/oz., from $295/oz.

Per Share Data ($) (Year Ended Dec. 31)	1997	1996	1995	1994	1993	1992	1991	1990	1989	1988
Tangible Bk. Val.	5.34	7.24	6.45	6.41	6.36	6.15	6.26	7.45	7.04	6.78
Cash Flow	0.01	0.56	0.98	1.01	1.15	1.26	-0.24	0.90	0.83	1.42
Earnings	-1.06	-0.27	0.31	0.44	0.45	0.47	-1.02	0.27	0.41	0.97
Dividends	0.30	0.30	0.30	0.27	0.26	0.26	0.26	0.26	0.26	0.13
Payout Ratio	NM	NM	97%	61%	58%	55%	NM	96%	63%	13%
Prices - High	22 3/8	30 5/8	29 1/2	28 1/4	25 5/8	12 3/8	16 3/4	21 1/2	19 3/4	15 3/4
- Low	10 1/2	21	18 3/8	18 1/8	11 1/4	9	9 5/8	13 3/8	12 1/8	10 7/8
P/E Ratio - High	NM	NM	95	64	57	26	NM	81	48	16
- Low	NM	NM	59	41	25	19	NM	50	30	11
Income Statement Analysis (Million $)										
Revs.	1,209	1,157	1,029	899	917	1,020	969	931	781	661
Oper. Inc.	416	403	417	286	276	321	-87.0	270	204	205
Depr.	264	199	161	136	167	187	185	148	100	102
Int. Exp.	55.0	48.0	22.0	20.0	22.0	20.0	24.9	22.7	12.2	9.4
Pretax Inc.	-268	-9.0	148	199	157	155	-237	159	201	308
Eff. Tax Rate	NM	NM	36%	33%	12%	16%	NM	40%	37%	18%
Net Inc.	-248	-65.0	74.0	105	107	111	-241	63.0	96.0	220
Balance Sheet & Other Fin. Data (Million $)										
Cash	244	417	321	312	777	477	623	785	577	637
Curr. Assets	593	760	625	565	994	757	885	1,000	1,143	874
Total Assets	2,624	2,979	2,574	2,246	2,228	2,067	2,291	2,662	2,449	2,190
Curr. Liab.	248	269	175	177	153	201	235	241	254	135
LT Debt	600	656	541	225	243	69.0	250	310	160	138
Common Eqty.	1,336	1,733	1,541	1,529	1,514	1,459	1,481	1,761	1,654	1,590
Total Cap.	2,300	2,531	2,212	1,907	1,904	1,673	1,879	2,204	1,960	1,855
Cap. Exp.	296	416	451	434	147	236	226	481	522	380
Cash Flow	2.0	133	235	241	274	298	-57.0	211	196	322
Curr. Ratio	2.4	2.8	3.6	3.2	6.5	3.8	3.8	4.1	4.5	6.5
% LT Debt of Cap.	26.1	25.9	24.5	11.8	12.8	4.1	13.3	14.1	8.1	7.4
% Net Inc.of Revs.	NM	NM	7.2	11.7	11.7	10.9	NM	6.8	12.3	33.3
% Ret. on Assets	NM	NM	3.1	4.7	5.0	5.1	NM	2.5	4.1	11.1
% Ret. on Equity	NM	NM	4.8	6.9	7.2	7.5	NM	3.7	5.9	15.6

Data as orig. reptd.; bef. results of disc. opers. and/or spec. items. Per share data adj. for stk. divs. as of ex-div. date. Bold denotes diluted EPS (FASB 128). E-Estimated. NA-Not Available. NM-Not Meaningful. NR-Not Ranked.

Offices—Suite 1600, Bentall IV, 1055 Dunsmuir St., Vancouver, BC V7X 1P1.**Tel**—(604) 682-7082.**Website**—http://www.placerdome.com **Chrmn**—R. M. Franklin. **Pres & CEO**—J. M. Willson. **SVP & CFO**—I. G. Austin. **VP & Secy**—J. D. Rose. **Investor Contact**—Earl Dunlop. **Dirs**—T. A. Buell, G. B. Coulombe, R. M. Franklin, H. J. McDonald, A. R. McFarland, C. L. Michel, R. M. Ogilvie, E. A. Parkinson-Marcoux, Vernon F. Taylor III, J. M. Willson, W. G. Wilson. **Transfer Agents & Registrars**—R-M Trust Co., Toronto, Vancouver, Montreal, Calgary; Bank of New York, NYC; Coopers & Lybrand, Sydney, Australia. **Incorporated**—in Canada in 1987.**Empl**— 8,370. **S&P Analyst:** Leo J. Larkin

STANDARD &POOR'S
STOCK REPORTS

PNC Bank

1731

NYSE Symbol **PNC**

In S&P 500

12-SEP-98

Industry: Banks (Major Regional)

Summary: This bank holding company operates bank subsidiaries in Pennsylvania, New Jersey, Indiana, Kentucky, Ohio, Delaware, Massachusetts and Florida.

S&P Opinion: Hold (★★★)	Recent Price • 45¼	Yield • 3.4%
	52 Wk Range • 66¾-41⅝	12-Mo. P/E • 13.2

Quantitative Evaluations

Outlook (1 Lowest—5 Highest)
• **1+**

Fair Value
• **41**

Risk
• **Low**

Earn./Div. Rank
• **B+**

Technical Eval.
• **Bearish** since 8/98

Rel. Strength Rank (1 Lowest—99 Highest)
• **61**

Insider Activity
• **Favorable**

Earnings vs. Previous Year
▲=Up ▼=Down ▶=No Change

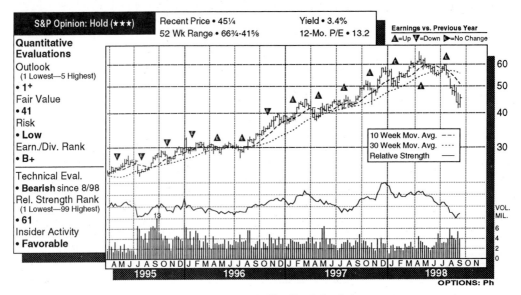

10 Week Mov. Avg. - - -
30 Week Mov. Avg. ·····
Relative Strength ——

OPTIONS: Ph

Overview - 28-AUG-98

Net interest income is expected to show low single-digit gains in 1998. The company has seen good growth in commercial and credit card lending in recent periods, although a downsizing of the indirect automobile portfolio and loan securitizations have resulted in minimal reported loan growth. Interest margins, which were impacted by a higher reliance on wholesale funds and a less favorable earning asset mix in 1998's first half, are expected to stabilize. The company has maintained considerable focus on its treasury management, capital markets and asset management activities, where expectations for future growth are higher than for traditional banking businesses. Accordingly, a majority of growth assumptions built into the 1998 earnings estimate come from these sources. Upward pressure on loan loss provisions is expected due to a growing consumer credit card portfolio. Loss reserves, however, remain in line with those of regional bank peers.

Valuation - 28-AUG-98

With a 20% drop thus far in 1998, the shares have well underperformed both the broader market and the average major regional bank. Much of this decline came in the month of August alone, a period when valuations for bank stocks in general were being reduced. The absence of takeover rumors and the likelihood of considerable competition from the recent First Union/Core-States and National City/First of America mergers also may be to blame. Although PNC still faces challenges, mostly with respect to the lending business, growth in fee-based operations should keep earnings momentum going in 1998.

Key Stock Statistics

S&P EPS Est. 1998	3.60	Tang. Bk. Value/Share	18.66
P/E on S&P Est. 1998	12.6	Beta	1.19
S&P EPS Est. 1999	3.90	Shareholders	65,900
Dividend Rate/Share	1.56	Market cap. (B)	$ 13.7
Shs. outstg. (M)	301.5	Inst. holdings	50%
Avg. daily vol. (M)	0.876		

Value of $10,000 invested 5 years ago: $ 20,028

Fiscal Year Ending Dec. 31

	1998	1997	1996	1995	1994	1993
Revenues (Million $)						
1Q	1,830	1,667	1,576	1,547	1,163	1,074
2Q	1,924	1,691	1,580	1,608	1,155	994.9
3Q	—	1,717	1,566	1,632	1,239	1,056
4Q	—	1,785	1,611	1,323	1,129	1,022
Yr.	—	6,859	6,333	6,110	4,684	4,146
Earnings Per Share ($)						
1Q	**0.87**	**0.80**	0.69	0.52	0.87	0.79
2Q	**0.90**	**0.81**	0.72	0.56	0.79	0.71
3Q	**E0.91**	**0.83**	0.69	0.62	0.79	0.92
4Q	**E0.92**	**0.85**	0.80	-0.52	0.12	0.72
Yr.	**E3.60**	**3.28**	2.90	1.19	2.57	3.14

Next earnings report expected: mid October

Dividend Data (Dividends have been paid since 1865.)

Amount ($)	Date Decl.	Ex-Div. Date	Stock of Record	Payment Date
0.390	Oct. 02	Oct. 09	Oct. 14	Oct. 24 '97
0.390	Jan. 08	Jan. 14	Jan. 16	Jan. 24 '98
0.390	Apr. 02	Apr. 09	Apr. 14	Apr. 24 '98
0.390	Jul. 02	Jul. 09	Jul. 13	Jul. 24 '98

A Division of The McGraw·Hill Companies

Business Summary - 28-AUG-98

During 1997, this Pittsburgh-based bank holding company restructured its business lines to be more focused on individual customer segments. Going forward, the traditional lending business, which includes branch and corporate banking, is expected to be less of a contributor to the overall revenue mix. PNC has made substantial investments in asset management, capital markets, treasury management, private banking and mutual fund servicing businesses, and expects noninterest income to contribute at least 50% of total revenues by the year 2000, from 42% in 1997.

Operations are currently divided into seven lines of business. National consumer banking (14% of revenues in 1997) offers consumer products and services through direct marketing and established affinity relationships. Regional community banking (36%) offers products and services to small business and retail customers. Private banking (9%) offers personalized investment management, brokerage, personal trust and estate planning services to the affluent. Secured lending (6%) includes commercial real estate banking, business credit and equipment leasing. Asset management and servicing

(9%) includes BlackRock Financial fixed-income, domestic and international equity and liquidity products, mutual fund servicing and institutional trust services. Corporate banking (16%) provides credit, capital markets and treasury management products to large and mid-size businesses, institutions and government entities. Mortgage banking (10%) includes mortgage originations and servicing.

In 1997, average earning assets, from which interest income is derived, amounted to $64.0 billion and consisted mainly of loans (83%) and investment securities (14%). Average sources of funds included interest-bearing deposits (49%), noninterest-bearing deposits (14%), short-term borrowings (11%), long-term debt (15%), shareholders' equity (8%) and other (3%).

At year-end 1997, nonperforming assets, mainly non-accrual loans and foreclosed assets, were $333 million (0.61% of loans and related assets), down from $459 million (0.88%) a year earlier. The allowance for loan losses, which is set aside for possible loan defaults, was $972 million (1.79% of loans), versus $1.17 billion (2.25%) a year earlier. Net chargeoffs (loans written off as uncollectible) were $272 million (0.51% of average loans) in 1997, versus $164 million (0.33%).

Per Share Data ($)

(Year Ended Dec. 31)	1997	1996	1995	1994	1993	1992	1991	1990	1989	1988
Tangible Bk. Val.	12.47	13.08	13.21	15.80	18.34	15.96	15.27	13.41	14.83	14.06
Earnings	3.28	2.90	1.19	2.57	3.14	2.36	1.98	0.37	1.99	2.55
Dividends	1.50	1.42	1.40	1.31	1.18	1.06	1.06	1.06	1.03	0.92
Payout Ratio	46%	49%	118%	51%	37%	45%	54%	290%	52%	36%
Prices - High	58³/₄	39³/₄	32⅜	31⅝	36³/₈	29¹/₄	24¹/₈	22¹/₈	24¹/₂	23¹/₄
- Low	36¹/₂	27¹/₂	21¹/₈	20	27	23¹/₈	9¹/₂	7⁷/₈	19¹/₄	18¹/₄
P/E Ratio - High	18	14	27	12	12	12	12	60	12	9
- Low	11	9	18	8	9	10	5	22	10	7

Income Statement Analysis (Million $)

	1997	1996	1995	1994	1993	1992	1991	1990	1989	1988
Net Int. Inc.	2,495	2,444	2,142	1,936	1,829	1,657	1,435	1,349	1,306	1,167
Tax Equiv. Adj.	99	35.0	46.6	33.5	39.5	42.8	59.0	96.0	108	94.0
Non Int. Inc.	1,759	1,373	1,240	931	945	673	742	630	546	490
Loan Loss Prov.	70.0	Nil	6.0	60.1	204	324	428	761	332	162
Exp./Op. Revs.	61%	60%	72%	61%	55%	61%	57%	59%	55%	53%
Pretax Inc.	1,618	1,527	627	902	1,117	778	548	29.0	485	590
Eff. Tax Rate	35%	35%	35%	32%	33%	32%	29%	NM	22%	25%
Net Inc.	1,052	992	408	610	745	529	390	71.0	377	443
% Net Int. Marg.	3.94	3.83	3.15	3.40	3.95	4.03	3.73	3.40	3.64	3.71

Balance Sheet & Other Fin. Data (Million $)

	1997	1996	1995	1994	1993	1992	1991	1990	1989	1988
Earning Assets:										
Money Mkt	NA	NA	NA	NA	856	1,165	1,868	1,835	553	2,746
Inv. Securities	8,522	11,917	15,839	20,921	23,060	20,742	14,173	12,189	12,867	10,401
Com'l Loans	19,989	18,062	16,812	12,445	12,463	11,751	12,211	14,870	15,965	13,344
Other Loans	34,668	33,736	32,244	23,689	20,845	14,358	13,936	13,488	12,852	11,276
Total Assets	75,120	73,260	73,404	64,145	62,080	51,380	44,892	45,534	45,661	40,811
Demand Deposits	10,158	10,937	10,707	6,992	7,057	5,889	5,095	5,380	5,096	4,759
Time Deposits	37,491	34,739	36,192	28,019	26,058	23,580	24,924	26,664	25,024	22,694
LT Debt	11,523	11,744	10,398	11,754	2,585	1,018	1,287	1,319	715	540
Common Eqty.	5,377	5,862	5,767	4,375	4,305	3,712	3,280	2,561	2,780	2,439
% Ret. on Assets	1.4	1.4	0.5	1.0	1.5	1.2	0.9	0.2	0.9	1.2
% Ret. on Equity	18.4	17.0	7.1	14.1	18.8	15.5	14.0	2.5	13.6	19.3
% Loan Loss Resv.	1.8	2.3	2.5	2.8	2.9	3.5	3.1	2.8	2.2	2.2
% Loans/Deposits	111.8	113.4	105.2	102.5	100.6	87.6	84.8	86.2	93.3	87.5
% Equity to Assets	7.6	7.9	7.6	7.1	7.9	7.6	6.4	6.0	6.5	6.1

Data as orig. reptd.; bef. results of disc opers. and/or spec. items. Per share data adj. for stk. divs. as of ex-div. date. Bold denotes diluted EPS (FASB 128). E-Estimated. NA-Not Available. NM-Not Meaningful. NR-Not Ranked.

Office—One PNC Plaza, 249 Fifth Ave., Pittsburgh, PA 15222. **Tel**—(412) 762-1553. **Website**—http://www.pncbank.com **Chrmn & CEO**—T. H. O'Brien.**Pres**—J. E. Rohr. **SVP-Fin & Admin**—W. E. Gregg Jr. **SVP & CFO**—R. L. Haunschild. **VP & Investor Contact**—William H. Callihan. **Dirs**—P. W. Chellgren, R. N. Clay, G. A. Davidson Jr., D. F. Girard-diCarlo, C. G. Grefenstette,W. R. Johnson, B. C. Lindsay, T. Marshall, W. C. McClelland, T. H. O'Brien, J. G. Pepper, J. H. Randolph, J. E. Rohr, R. H. Ross, V. A. Sarni, G. J. Scheuring, R. P. Simmons, T. J. Usher, M. A. Washington, H. H. Wehmeier. **Transfer Agent & Registrar**—Chase Manhattan Bank, Ridgefield Park. NJ. **Empl**— 25,400. **S&P Analyst**: Stephen R. Biggar

STANDARD &POOR'S
STOCK REPORTS

Polaroid Corp.

1861

NYSE Symbol **PRD**

In S&P 500

12-SEP-98

Industry:
Photography/Imaging

Summary: This company, the worldwide leader in traditional instant photography, has also developed products involving digital electronic imaging.

S&P Opinion: Hold (★★★)	Recent Price • 25 Yield • 2.4%
	52 Wk Range • 56⅛-24 12-Mo. P/E • NM

Quantitative Evaluations

Outlook
(1 Lowest—5 Highest)
• **4+**

Fair Value
• **33⅝**

Risk
• **Low**

Earn./Div. Rank
• **B-**

Technical Eval.
• **Bearish** since 7/97

Rel. Strength Rank
(1 Lowest—99 Highest)
• **19**

Insider Activity
• **Favorable**

Earnings vs. Previous Year
▲=Up ▼=Down ▶=No Change

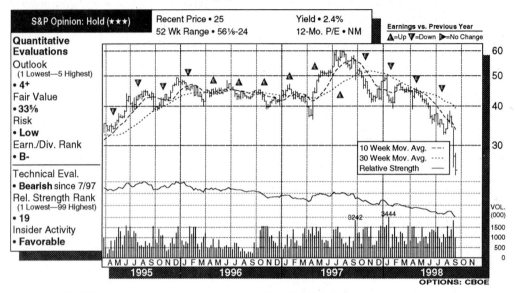

10 Week Mov. Avg. — — —
30 Week Mov. Avg. — — —
Relative Strength ——

VOL. (000)

OPTIONS: CBOE

Overview - 06-JUL-98

In June 1998, this major photography company said that second quarter 1998 profit would be reduced by efforts to reduce inventories at the dealer level and by an additional reserve related to Russian receivables. PRD expects this to be offset by a gain on the sale of real estate; however, the gain is excluded from our 1998 earnings estimate. Also, we expect that 1998 EPS will reflect some pressure from the strength of the U.S. dollar and from economic softness in Asia. Meanwhile, PRD has announced a cost cutting program from which it is looking to generate about $120 million of annual pretax savings (about $1.60 a share after tax). The program, which includes the elimination of approximately 1,800 jobs, would be fully in effect by about mid-1999. In 1997, excluding some special items (such as restructuring expense), PRD had earnings per share of about $2.22.

Valuation - 06-JUL-98

Although we recently reduced our EPS estimate for 1999, we still expect enough improvement to merit holding the stock. However, we remain concerned about the visibility and extent of longer-term earnings growth, and do not advise purchase of additional shares. Also, the extent of expected efforts to reduce inventories of Polaroid products at the dealer level makes us increasingly wary of how confident retailers are in current PRD offerings. We expect that future activity by PRD will include efforts to expand the appeal of traditional instant photography in the youth market, and that new products will include an instant single-use camera. Also, in October 1997, PRD directors authorized the repurchase of up to five million common shares (11% of the total shares outstanding) over the next three years.

Key Stock Statistics

S&P EPS Est. 1998	1.60	Tang. Bk. Value/Share	9.99
P/E on S&P Est. 1998	15.6	Beta	0.99
S&P EPS Est. 1999	3.15	Shareholders	12,100
Dividend Rate/Share	0.60	Market cap. (B)	$ 1.1
Shs. outstg. (M)	44.1	Inst. holdings	0%
Avg. daily vol. (M)	0.340		

Value of $10,000 invested 5 years ago: $ 8,809

Fiscal Year Ending Dec. 31

	1998	1997	1996	1995	1994	1993
Revenues (Million $)						
1Q	390.6	457.5	461.1	409.6	462.6	468.5
2Q	464.7	564.9	581.6	572.5	587.3	569.9
3Q	—	516.4	569.1	580.0	576.7	533.9
4Q	—	607.6	663.4	674.8	685.9	672.6
Yr.	—	2,146	2,275	2,237	2,313	2,245
Earnings Per Share ($)						
1Q	-0.39	0.35	-1.33	-1.66	0.03	-0.50
2Q	-0.27	0.76	0.63	0.50	0.62	0.61
3Q	E0.70	0.55	0.74	0.51	0.62	0.53
4Q	E1.34	-4.51	0.28	-2.44	1.23	0.83
Yr.	E1.60	-2.81	0.32	-3.09	2.49	1.45

Next earnings report expected: mid October

Dividend Data (Dividends have been paid since 1952.)

Amount ($)	Date Decl.	Ex-Div. Date	Stock of Record	Payment Date
0.150	Oct. 21	Nov. 19	Nov. 21	Dec. 20 '97
0.150	Jan. 27	Feb. 25	Feb. 27	Mar. 28 '98
0.150	May. 05	May. 27	May. 29	Jun. 27 '98
0.150	Jun. 30	Aug. 26	Aug. 28	Sep. 26 '98

A Division of The McGraw·Hill Companies

STANDARD
&POOR'S
STOCK REPORTS

Polaroid Corporation

1861

12-SEP-98

Business Summary - 06-JUL-98

For Polaroid Corp., cost reductions and product development are part of the picture, but they don't happen instantly.

PRD's earnings have been clobbered in recent years by large charges related to restructuring, including work force reductions and writedowns of asset values. Another $340 million (pretax) of restructuring and special charges was incurred in the 1997 fourth quarter. However, such charges are typically connected to cost-reduction efforts, and the latest program is expected to include the elimination of about 1,800 jobs. Through restructuring and other efforts, PRD has already made progress in reducing the large loss of its digital imaging or electronics-related businesses, which include products for medical, graphics arts and other business applications. This deficit, which totaled about $80 million in 1997 (down from about $130 million in 1996), has partially obscured the profitability of PRD's core instant photography business. Challenges facing PRD include a likely shift by consumers to new photography platforms, including digital cameras and the Advanced Photo System, which was introduced in 1996 by industry rivals. A PRD digital camera debuted in 1996, and PRD is expected to be rolling out single-use instant photography cameras in the future. Other PRD products

currently include conventional cameras and films, and videotape.

PRD's international sales in 1997 totaled $1.083 billion, down 11% from the 1996 level, largely due to the strength of the U.S. dollar. Another adverse factor was lower sales in Russia and China.

In addition to family and recreational use, PRD's photography products are used in fields such as real estate and jewelry sales, insurance, architecture, construction, theme park concessions and education. A number of PRD products are also aimed at technical and industrial customers. Included are many types of film and a broad range of application-specific imaging systems targeted for market areas such as science and medicine; office and presentation products; identification and documentation; and professional photography.

In the digital imaging area, PRD's products include film for the Helios medical imaging systems, which was developed to be a substitute for conventional transparency films used for X-rays and other medical applications. The company is also developing products for the graphic arts market.

Excluding certain one-time or special items (largely restructuring charges), PRD had 1997 earnings per share of about $2.22. Capital expenditures in 1997 totaled about $134 million, and depreciation expense was about $112 million.

Per Share Data ($)

(Year Ended Dec. 31)	1997	1996	1995	1994	1993	1992	1991	1990	1989	1988
Tangible Bk. Val.	10.88	14.69	15.76	18.79	16.39	17.33	15.80	4.15	2.86	14.12
Cash Flow	-0.34	2.89	-0.17	5.01	3.60	3.92	13.70	3.89	3.48	0.89
Earnings	-2.81	0.32	-3.09	2.49	1.45	2.06	12.54	2.20	1.96	-0.34
Dividends	0.60	0.60	0.60	0.60	0.60	0.60	0.60	0.60	0.60	0.60
Payout Ratio	NM	188%	NM	24%	41%	28%	4%	27%	28%	NM
Prices - High	60¼	48½	49⅜	36¾	38¾	35	29	48¼	50⅜	44⅛
- Low	36¼	39⅛	29	29¼	25¾	23⅝	19⅝	20¼	35⅛	21½
P/E Ratio - High	NM	NM	NM	15	27	17	2	22	26	NM
- Low	NM	NM	NM	12	18	11	1	9	18	NM

Income Statement Analysis (Million $)

	1997	1996	1995	1994	1993	1992	1991	1990	1989	1988
Revs.	2,146	2,275	2,237	2,313	2,245	2,152	2,071	1,972	1,905	1,863
Oper. Inc.	276	313	222	319	286	303	332	372	392	256
Depr.	112	118	133	118	100	89.1	85.5	87.2	87.4	81.9
Int. Exp.	47.8	52.5	56.9	56.3	60.5	68.5	65.3	85.2	89.5	31.0
Pretax Inc.	-191	31.2	-200	161	102	163	1,083	218	213	21.0
Eff. Tax Rate	NA	52%	NM	27%	33%	39%	37%	31%	32%	NM
Net Inc.	-126	15.0	-139	117	68.0	99	684	151	145	-23.0

Balance Sheet & Other Fin. Data (Million $)

	1997	1996	1995	1994	1993	1992	1991	1990	1989	1988
Cash	68.0	78.3	83.1	229	139	190	245	198	279	528
Curr. Assets	1,419	1,386	1,458	1,489	1,414	1,351	1,340	1,240	1,346	1,523
Total Assets	2,133	2,202	2,262	2,317	2,212	2,008	1,889	1,701	1,777	1,957
Curr. Liab.	863	763	719	602	580	562	645	631	704	543
LT Debt	497	490	527	566	602	637	472	514	602	402
Common Eqty.	484	658	718	864	767	809	773	208	149	1,012
Total Cap.	981	1,048	1,245	1,430	1,370	1,446	1,245	1,070	1,073	1,414
Cap. Exp.	134	122	168	147	166	202	176	121	95.0	127
Cash Flow	-15.2	133	-7.5	235	168	188	738	201	200	59.0
Curr. Ratio	1.6	1.8	2.0	2.5	2.4	2.4	2.1	2.0	1.9	2.8
% LT Debt of Cap.	50.7	46.8	NM	39.6	44.0	44.1	37.9	48.0	56.1	28.5
% Net Inc.of Revs.	NA	0.7	NM	5.1	3.0	4.6	33.0	7.7	7.6	NM
% Ret. on Assets	NM	1.2	NM	5.2	3.2	5.2	38.5	8.9	9.1	NM
% Ret. on Equity	NM	2.2	NM	14.5	8.6	12.8	133.7	64.6	25.5	NM

Data as orig. reptd.; bef. results of disc. opers. and/or spec. items. Per share data adj. for stk. divs. as of ex-div. date. Bold denotes diluted EPS (FASB 128). E-Estimated. NA-Not Available. NM-Not Meaningful. NR-Not Ranked.

Office—549 Technology Square, Cambridge, MA 02139. **Tel**—(617) 386-2000. **Website**—http://www.polaroid.com **Chrmn & CEO**—G. T. DiCamillo. **EVP & CFO**—J. G. Boynton.**EVP**—W. J. O'Neill Jr.**SVP & Secy**—T. M. Lemberg.**Investor Contact**—Philip Ruddick. **Dirs**—G. T. DiCamillo, R. Gomory, F. S. Jones, S. P. Kaufman, J. W. Loose, A. F. Moschner, R. F. Olsen, R. Z. Sorenson, C. F. St. Mark, D. C. Staley, B. D. L. Strom, A. M. Zeien. **Transfer Agent & Registrar**—First National Bank of Boston (c/o Boston EquiServe L.P). **Incorporated**—in Delaware in 1937. **Empl**— 10,011. **S&P Analyst:** Tom Graves, CFA

Potlatch Corp.

1863K

NYSE Symbol **PCH**

In S&P 500

12-SEP-98

Industry: Paper & Forest Products

Summary: This integrated forest products company is a major producer of wood products and also has interests in coated printing paper, bleached paperboard and consumer products.

S&P Opinion: Avoid (★★)	Recent Price • 33¼	Yield • 5.2%
	52 Wk Range • 52¾-31	12-Mo. P/E • 23.8

Quantitative Evaluations

Outlook
(1 Lowest—5 Highest)
• **2**

Fair Value
• **31¾**

Risk
• **Low**

Earn./Div. Rank
• **B-**

Technical Eval.
• **NA**

Rel. Strength Rank
(1 Lowest—99 Highest)
• **58**

Insider Activity
• **NA**

Earnings vs. Previous Year
▲=Up ▼=Down ▶=No Change

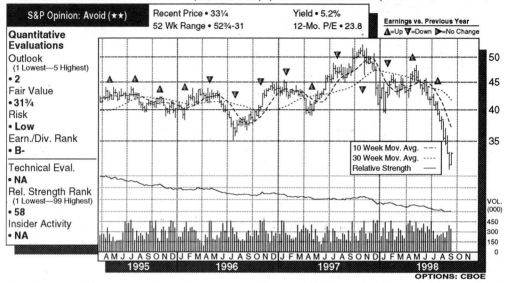

10 Week Mov. Avg. ---
30 Week Mov. Avg. ----
Relative Strength —

VOL. (000)

OPTIONS: CBOE

Overview - 29-JUL-98

Sales should be little changed in 1998, on mixed results. In other pulp-based products, we see slightly higher average prices for the division's roster of grades, on expectations of decent tissue markets and relatively flat paperboard markets (despite worries about export markets as a result of Asia's financial woes). Sales of coated papers should be little changed, as Asia's troubles and a strong U.S. dollar seem to have ended the modest recovery seen in that grade in 1997. We expect wood product sales to fall, as lumber oversupply should continue to hold down prices. We also see much added industry capacity in OSB in recent years provoking pricing pressures in the wood panels area (despite some recent strength in OSB). Margins should widen a bit, on better production efficiency, benefits of capital improvement projects and the expected easing of transportation problems stemming from Union Pacific's railroad logjam. Those factors should outweigh the projected difficulties in coated paper and wood products markets. PCH's planned formation of a timberlands REIT should have little bottom line impact in 1998.

Valuation - 29-JUL-98

The shares moved solidly higher between the spring and summer of 1997, as better interest rate trends eased worries about building markets and the troubled paper industry showed signs that it had bottomed. The shares subsequently gave back those gains, as the Asian currency crisis has caused worries about foreign trade's impact on commodities markets. We remain mostly pessimistic about Potlatch's business prospects. In wood products, we see the global economic situation leading to ongoing lumber oversupply and expect panel market difficulties to resume. We also see Asia's troubles putting any recovery in paper and paperboard on hold. Thus, we would continue to avoid the shares.

Key Stock Statistics

S&P EPS Est. 1998	1.65	Tang. Bk. Value/Share	32.59
P/E on S&P Est. 1998	20.2	Beta	0.72
S&P EPS Est. 1999	2.00	Shareholders	3,700
Dividend Rate/Share	1.74	Market cap. (B)	$0.965
Shs. outstg. (M)	29.0	Inst. holdings	51%
Avg. daily vol. (M)	0.064		

Value of $10,000 invested 5 years ago: $ 9,080

Fiscal Year Ending Dec. 31

	1998	1997	1996	1995	1994	1993
Revenues (Million $)						
1Q	402.5	399.4	388.6	394.6	365.3	361.5
2Q	400.5	394.2	386.1	397.2	345.1	326.6
3Q	—	395.5	398.2	411.2	373.3	338.2
4Q	—	379.8	381.5	402.2	387.5	342.5
Yr.	—	1,569	1,554	1,605	1,471	1,369
Earnings Per Share ($)						
1Q	0.37	0.22	0.17	0.81	0.18	0.76
2Q	0.35	0.34	0.63	0.81	0.21	0.09
3Q	E0.50	0.48	0.68	1.09	0.37	-0.07
4Q	E0.43	0.20	0.65	1.01	0.92	0.53
Yr.	E1.65	1.24	2.13	3.72	1.68	1.31

Next earnings report expected: early October

Dividend Data (Dividends have been paid since 1939.)

Amount ($)	Date Decl.	Ex-Div. Date	Stock of Record	Payment Date
0.435	Sep. 19	Nov. 07	Nov. 14	Dec. 01 '97
0.435	Jan. 22	Feb. 06	Feb. 10	Mar. 02 '98
0.435	Mar. 06	May. 08	May. 12	Jun. 01 '98
0.435	Jul. 23	Aug. 10	Aug. 12	Sep. 08 '98

A Division of The McGraw-Hill Companies

STANDARD
&POOR'S
STOCK REPORTS

Potlatch Corporation

1863K
12-SEP-98

Business Summary - 29-JUL-98

Potlatch Corp. is an integrated forest products company with significant timber resources. Its manufacturing facilities convert wood fiber into wood products, printing papers, and other pulp-based products mainly for U.S. markets. Export sales (mainly paperboard) accounted for 12% of total sales in 1997. Much of PCH's business tends to be cyclical in nature.

The wood products segment (31% of sales and 36% of profits in 1997) produced 534 million board feet of lumber, 254 million sq. ft. of plywood, 977 million sq. ft. of oriented strand board (OSB) and 67 million sq. ft. of particleboard in 1997.

At facilities in Minnesota, PCH makes high-quality coated free-sheet printing papers (28% of sales and 25% of profits in 1997) used in annual reports, catalogs, art reproductions and advertising. PCH produced 372,000 tons of printing papers in 1997.

Other pulp-based products (41% of sales and 39% of profits in 1997) include bleached kraft pulp and paperboard, tissue, towels and napkins. Bleached kraft paperboard produced by the company is used for the packaging of milk and other foods, pharmaceuticals and toiletries and for paper cups and plates. PCH ranks as one of the nation's leading producers of private-label tissue products. During 1997, PCH produced 899,000 tons of pulp (most used internally), 614,000 tons of paperboard and 150,000 tons of tissue paper.

PCH's 1.5 million acres of timberland in Idaho, Arkansas and Minnesota provided 68% of its sawlogs and plywood logs in 1997 and 46% of raw materials. In February 1998, Potlatch reached an agreement with Anderson-Tully Co. (ATCO) to form a timberlands real estate investment trust called Timberland Growth Corp. (TGC), the first publicly traded REIT of its kind. The agreement calls for PCH to combine its 514,000 acres of Arkansas timberlands with 324,000 acres of timberlands owned by ATCO in Arkansas and Mississippi (ATCO's timberlands to be purchased by TGC for about $410 million). Potlatch expects to own a majority stake in TGC, and will also enter into a long-term agreement to purchase all of the timber from TGC's timberlands at fair market value pricing. PCH thinks the formation of the REIT will enable the underlying value of all of its timberlands to be more fully realized.

In an effort to become a low-cost producer in all operations, PCH has invested in conversion and modernization projects at its plants. In late 1996, PCH completed the conversion of its plywood mills from sheathing plywood (which faces heavy competition from OSB) to industrial-grade products that offer better margins. Also in late 1996, PCH's $135 million fiber line was completed and began operating at its pulp mill in Minnesota. PCH plans to spend a total of about $245 million over the next three years to finish the plant modernization.

Per Share Data ($)

(Year Ended Dec. 31)	1997	1996	1995	1994	1993	1992	1991	1990	1989	1988
Tangible Bk. Val.	32.82	33.06	33.25	30.79	31.47	32.79	31.51	30.93	28.74	24.98
Cash Flow	6.41	7.03	8.42	5.77	5.04	6.39	5.13	6.39	7.39	6.61
Earnings	1.25	2.13	3.72	1.68	1.31	2.71	1.92	3.41	4.79	4.04
Dividends	1.71	1.67	1.61	1.57	1.51	1.43	1.34	1.23	1.08	0.95
Payout Ratio	137%	78%	43%	93%	116%	53%	70%	36%	23%	24%
Prices - High	52³/₄	44⁷/₈	44¹/₈	49¹/₂	51⁷/₈	50	47	44¹/₂	38⁵/₈	33³/₈
- Low	39	35¹/₈	37¹/₈	35¹/₂	38¹/₄	36³/₄	27³/₄	23	30³/₄	25
P/E Ratio - High	42	21	12	29	40	18	24	13	8	8
- Low	31	16	10	21	29	14	14	7	6	6

Income Statement Analysis (Million $)

	1997	1996	1995	1994	1993	1992	1991	1990	1989	1988
Revs.	1,569	1,554	1,605	1,471	1,369	1,327	1,237	1,253	1,228	1,084
Oper. Inc.	243	264	357	248	206	236	212	262	304	265
Depr.	150	142	137	120	109	107	93.0	86.2	77.3	71.7
Int. Exp.	46.1	54.1	52.1	53.9	52.6	51.5	43.3	36.2	29.4	28.1
Pretax Inc.	54.6	86.3	171	76.0	65.0	125	85.0	152	209	176
Eff. Tax Rate	34%	29%	37%	36%	41%	37%	35%	35%	34%	36%
Net Inc.	36.1	61.5	109	49.0	38.0	79.0	56.0	99	137	112

Balance Sheet & Other Fin. Data (Million $)

	1997	1996	1995	1994	1993	1992	1991	1990	1989	1988
Cash	9.0	12.3	111	56.0	8.0	13.0	22.0	1.7	221	84.6
Curr. Assets	404	378	477	371	308	324	310	292	516	345
Total Assets	2,365	2,266	2,265	2,081	2,067	1,999	1,892	1,708	1,686	1,418
Curr. Liab.	298	260	349	229	179	184	196	206	191	146
LT Debt	722	672	616	633	707	634	563	392	459	368
Common Eqty.	952	954	962	920	920	956	915	896	829	672
Total Cap.	1,911	1,850	1,759	1,705	1,767	1,815	1,696	1,502	1,495	1,272
Cap. Exp.	158	240	170	104	202	180	267	318	155	114
Cash Flow	186	203	246	169	147	186	149	185	211	178
Curr. Ratio	1.4	1.5	1.4	1.6	1.7	1.8	1.6	1.4	2.7	2.4
% LT Debt of Cap.	37.8	36.3	35.1	37.2	40.0	34.9	33.2	26.1	30.7	28.9
% Net Inc.of Revs.	2.3	4.0	6.8	3.3	2.8	5.9	4.5	7.9	11.1	10.4
% Ret. on Assets	1.6	2.7	5.0	2.4	1.9	4.0	3.1	5.8	8.5	8.2
% Ret. on Equity	3.8	6.5	11.6	5.3	4.1	8.4	6.2	11.4	17.6	17.2

Data as orig. reptd.; bef. results of disc. opers. and/or spec. items. Per share data adj. for stk. divs. as of ex-div. date. Bold denotes diluted EPS (FASB 128). E-Estimated. NA-Not Available. NM-Not Meaningful. NR-Not Ranked.

Office—601 W. Riverside Ave., Spokane, WA 99201. **Tel**—(509) 835-1500. **Website**—www.potlatchcorp.com **Chrmn & CEO**—J. M. Richards. **Pres**—L. P. Siegel. **Dirs**—R. A. Clarke, K. T. Derr, A. F. Jacobson, G. F. Jewett Jr., R. B. Madden, R. M. Morrow, V. W. Piasecki, T. Rembe, J. M. Richards, R. F. Richards, R. M. Rosenberg, R. G. Schwartz, L. P. Siegel, C. R. Weaver, F. T. Weyerhaeuser, W. T. Weyerhaeuser. **Transfer Agent & Registrar**—Harris Trust & Savings Bank, Chicago. **Incorporated**—in Delaware in 1955. **Empl**—6,700. **S&P Analyst:** Michael W. Jaffe

12-SEP-98

Industry: Chemicals (Diversified)

Summary: PPG is a leading manufacturer of coatings and resins, flat and fiber glass, and industrial and specialty chemicals.

S&P Opinion: Accumulate (★★★★)	Recent Price • 52½ Yield • 2.7% 52 Wk Range • 76⅝-49⅛ 12-Mo. P/E • 13.1

Quantitative Evaluations

Outlook
(1 Lowest—5 Highest)
• **3+**

Fair Value
• **63¾**

Risk
• **Low**

Earn./Div. Rank
• **A-**

Technical Eval.
• **Bullish** since 8/98

Rel. Strength Rank
(1 Lowest—99 Highest)
• **50**

Insider Activity
• **Neutral**

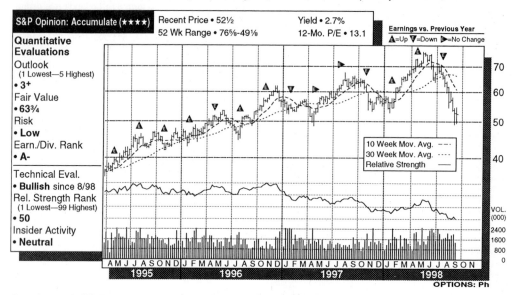

Earnings vs. Previous Year
▲=Up ▼=Down ▷=No Change

10 Week Mov. Avg. ---
30 Week Mov. Avg. ......
Relative Strength ——

1995 1996 1997 1998

VOL. (000)
2400
1600
800
0

OPTIONS: Ph

Overview - 22-JUL-98

We expect earnings of this diversified company to advance in 1998, with the growing U.S. and European economies and steady automobile and construction markets for glass and coatings. Strike related plant closings at General Motors (PPG's largest customer) will reduce third quarter EPS. Sales and profitability of the coatings segment will be helped for the rest of the year by good volume trends and recent acquisitions, while raw material costs should remain steady. Prices for U.S. flat glass could now show some strength, after dropping from 1995 through 1997, despite increased industry capacity. PPG plans to sell its marginally profitable European glass business. Specialty chemicals sales should also continue to grow, but a recent drop in chlorine prices will restrict results from commodities, offsetting higher caustic soda prices. Earnings in all segments will be boosted by continued productivity and cost reduction programs. EPS comparisons will be helped by fewer shares outstanding. PPG has slowed the pace of stock buybacks as its debt ratio is near its 40% ceiling and as it continues to make acquisitions.

Valuation - 22-JUL-98

After reaching a record high in May, the stock has been hurt by the GM strike and concerns regarding the Asian economic downturns. Our recommendation continues to be accumulate. We feel that PPG's strategy of investing globally in several growth businesses, while remaining a low-cost producer in its glass and commodity chemicals operations, enhances longer-term prospects. With the U.S. economy expected to grow at a healthy pace, better European markets and projected stable glass prices, the shares are attractive at the current multiple of our 1998 EPS estimate. Dividends, which have grown steadily over the past 27 years, should continue to advance over the long term.

Key Stock Statistics

S&P EPS Est. 1998	4.10	Tang. Bk. Value/Share	12.51
P/E on S&P Est. 1998	12.8	Beta	1.10
S&P EPS Est. 1999	4.75	Shareholders	33,200
Dividend Rate/Share	1.44	Market cap. (B)	$ 9.3
Shs. outstg. (M)	177.0	Inst. holdings	48%
Avg. daily vol. (M)	0.390		

Value of $10,000 invested 5 years ago: $ 18,471

Fiscal Year Ending Dec. 31

	1998	1997	1996	1995	1994	1993
Revenues (Million $)						
1Q	1,913	1,777	1,749	1,741	1,477	1,447
2Q	2,004	1,944	1,914	1,870	1,619	1,524
3Q	—	1,812	1,801	1,724	1,575	1,405
4Q	—	1,846	1,755	1,722	1,660	1,378
Yr.	—	7,379	7,218	7,058	6,331	5,754
Earnings Per Share ($)						
1Q	**1.07**	**0.90**	0.90	1.06	0.57	0.52
2Q	**1.11**	**1.20**	1.20	1.06	0.46	0.50
3Q	**E0.95**	**0.95**	1.03	0.85	0.68	0.12
4Q	**E0.97**	**0.89**	0.83	0.83	0.72	0.26
Yr.	**E4.10**	**3.94**	3.93	3.80	2.43	1.39

Next earnings report expected: mid October

Dividend Data (Dividends have been paid since 1899.)

Amount ($)	Date Decl.	Ex-Div. Date	Stock of Record	Payment Date
0.340	Oct. 16	Nov. 06	Nov. 10	Dec. 12 '97
0.340	Jan. 15	Feb. 12	Feb. 17	Mar. 12 '98
0.360	Apr. 16	May. 07	May. 11	Jun. 12 '98
0.360	Jul. 16	Aug. 06	Aug. 10	Sep. 11 '98

A Division of The **McGraw·Hill** Companies

Business Summary - 22-JUL-98

PPG plans to focus resources on its higher growth businesses, consisting of coatings, specialty chemicals and fiber glass, which account for about 60% of sales, in order to reach $10 billion in annual sales and to reduce cyclicality. International operations contributed 33% of sales and 22% of operating profits in 1997.

Sales and operating profits by product group in 1997:

	Sales	Profits
Coatings	42%	43%
Glass	36%	25%
Chemicals	22%	32%

PPG is the world's leading producer of original and refinish automotive and industrial coatings (used in appliance, container and industrial equipment markets) and is a major North American supplier of architectural coatings. Since September 1997, PPG has made eight automotive or industrial coatings acquisitions with combined annual sales of nearly $500 million. It plans to buy the packaging coatings and U.S. house paints business of Courtaulds for $285 million. PPG also produces metal pretreatments and adhesives and sealants for the automotive industry.

The company is one of the world's largest producers of flat glass and fabricated glass. Major markets include original and replacement glass for automobiles, com-

mercial and residential construction, aircraft transparencies, furniture and various industrial uses. These businesses aim for cash generation and earnings growth. PPG plans to sell its European flat and auto glass business (sales of $450 million) and divest interests in two glass plants in China. PPG is the world's second largest producer of continuous strand and chopped strand fiber glass, including plastic reinforcement yarns and electronic and specialty materials, for transportation, construction, electronics, recreational and industrial uses.

PPG is the world's third largest producer of chlorine and caustic soda (used in a wide variety of industrial applications), vinyl chloride monomer (for use in polyvinyl chloride resins) and chlorinated solvents. These commodity chemicals are highly cyclical. PPG has increased its chlor-alkali production for 12 consecutive years without significant new investment. Specialty chemicals (about one-third of chemical sales) include silica compounds, photochromic lenses and optical resins, and fine chemicals (phosgene derivatives and pharmaceutical intermediates). PPG plans to increase the proportion of specialty chemicals sales (which are generally less subject to cyclical business factors), with a long-term goal of equaling commodity sales.

Since 1984, stock repurchases have reduced shares outstanding by over 35%. PPG repurchased 11.9 million common shares during 1996 for $606 million and bought 5.3 million shares in 1997 for $302 million.

Per Share Data ($)

(Year Ended Dec. 31)	1997	1996	1995	1994	1993	1992	1991	1990	1989	1988
Tangible Bk. Val.	14.10	13.49	13.21	12.35	11.57	12.71	12.50	12.01	10.49	10.24
Cash Flow	6.04	5.89	5.41	3.93	2.94	3.16	2.60	3.73	3.40	3.38
Earnings	3.94	3.96	3.80	2.43	1.39	1.50	0.95	2.21	2.09	2.13
Dividends	1.33	1.26	1.18	1.12	1.04	0.94	0.86	0.82	0.74	0.64
Payout Ratio	34%	32%	31%	46%	75%	62%	91%	37%	35%	30%
Prices - High	67½	62¼	47⅞	42⅛	38⅛	34¼	29¾	27⅝	23	23½
- Low	48⅝	42⅞	34⅞	33¾	29¾	25	20¾	17¼	18½	15⅝
P/E Ratio - High	17	16	13	17	27	23	31	12	11	11
- Low	12	11	9	14	21	17	22	8	9	7

Income Statement Analysis (Million $)

	1997	1996	1995	1994	1993	1992	1991	1990	1989	1988
Revs.	7,379	7,218	7,058	6,331	5,754	5,814	5,673	6,021	5,734	5,617
Oper. Inc.	1,689	1,658	1,511	1,329	1,048	1,036	918	1,228	1,129	1,172
Depr.	373	364	352	318	331	352	351	324	292	274
Int. Exp.	105	108	94.0	91.0	109	148	169	168	148	125
Pretax Inc.	1,175	1,240	1,248	856	544	542	354	779	757	788
Eff. Tax Rate	37%	38%	39%	38%	43%	40%	42%	38%	38%	40%
Net Inc.	714	744	768	515	295	319	201	475	465	468

Balance Sheet & Other Fin. Data (Million $)

	1997	1996	1995	1994	1993	1992	1991	1990	1989	1988
Cash	129	70.0	106	62.0	112	61.0	38.0	59.0	65.0	103
Curr. Assets	2,584	2,296	2,276	2,168	2,026	1,951	2,173	2,217	2,056	1,899
Total Assets	6,868	6,441	6,194	5,894	5,652	5,662	6,056	6,108	5,645	5,154
Curr. Liab.	1,662	1,796	1,629	1,425	1,281	1,253	1,341	1,471	1,338	1,265
LT Debt	1,257	834	736	773	774	872	1,163	1,186	1,178	877
Common Eqty.	2,509	2,483	2,569	2,557	2,473	2,699	2,655	2,547	2,282	2,243
Total Cap.	4,254	3,393	3,660	3,703	3,568	4,103	4,369	4,263	3,941	3,583
Cap. Exp.	466	476	448	NA	253	279	299	564	572	402
Cash Flow	1,087	1,108	1,120	832	626	671	553	798	758	742
Curr. Ratio	1.6	1.3	1.4	1.5	1.6	1.6	1.6	1.5	1.5	1.5
% LT Debt of Cap.	29.5	24.6	20.1	20.9	21.7	21.3	26.6	27.8	29.9	24.5
% Net Inc.of Revs.	9.7	10.3	10.9	8.1	5.1	5.5	3.6	7.9	8.1	8.3
% Ret. on Assets	10.7	11.8	12.7	9.1	5.2	5.5	3.3	8.2	8.6	9.3
% Ret. on Equity	28.6	29.4	30.0	20.8	11.4	11.9	7.7	19.9	20.6	21.9

Data as orig. reptd.; bef. results of disc. opers. and/or spec. items. Per share data adj. for stk. divs. as of ex-div. date. Bold denotes diluted EPS (FASB 128). E-Estimated. NA-Not Available. NM-Not Meaningful. NR-Not Ranked.

Office—One PPG Place, Pittsburgh, PA 15272. **Tel**—(412) 434-3131. **Website**—http://www.ppg.com **Chrmn, Pres & CEO**—R. W. LeBoeuf.**VP & Secy**—H. K. Linge. **SVP-Fin**—W. H. Hernandez. **Investor Contact**—Douglas B. Atkinson. **Dirs**—E. B. Davis Jr., M. J. Hooper, A. J. Krowe, N. C. Lautenbach, R. W. LeBoeuf, S. C. Mason, R. Mehrabian, V. A. Sarni, T. J. Usher, D. G. Vice, D. R. Whitwam. **Transfer Agent & Registrar**—ChaseMellon Shareholder Services, Ridgefield Park, NJ. **Incorporated**—in Pennsylvania in 1883. **Empl**— 31,900. **S&P Analyst:** Richard O'Reilly, CFA

STANDARD &POOR'S
STOCK REPORTS

PP&L Resources

1731M

NYSE Symbol **PPL**

In S&P 500

12-SEP-98 | **Industry:** Electric Companies

Summary: This holding company owns Pennsylvania Power & Light, an electric utility with excess generating capacity serving central and eastern Pennsylvania.

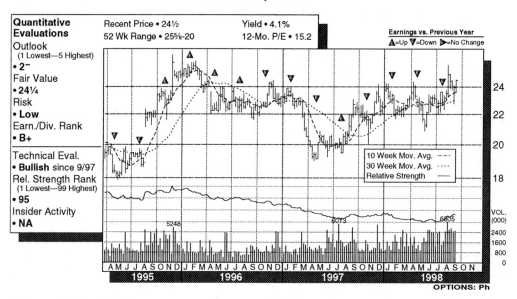

Quantitative Evaluations

Recent Price • 24½
52 Wk Range • 25⅝-20

Yield • 4.1%
12-Mo. P/E • 15.2

Outlook
(1 Lowest—5 Highest)
• **2⁻**

Fair Value
• **24¼**

Risk
• **Low**

Earn./Div. Rank
• **B+**

Technical Eval.
• **Bullish** since 9/97

Rel. Strength Rank
(1 Lowest—99 Highest)
• **95**

Insider Activity
• **NA**

OPTIONS: Ph

Business Profile - 08-SEP-98

In August 1998, PPL cut its annual dividend from $1.67 to $1.00 per share and initiated a share repurchase plan for up to 10% of its common stock. It also reported a second quarter $1.6 billion pre-tax writeoff of assets impaired by its transition to a competitive market. Also in August, PPL filed a settlement with the Pennsylvania Public Utilities Commission, under which the company would reduce rates 4% in 1999 (with the rates capped though 2004) and be allowed to recover (over an 11-year period) $2.97 billion of the $4.5 billion it had claimed in stranded costs. The PP&L Global subsidiary recently doubled its interest (51% equity, 49% voting) in U.K.-based South Western Electricity, and has now invested about $635 million in its international operations.

Operational Review - 08-SEP-98

Excluding an extraordinary charge of $5.66 a share (reflecting a $1.6 billion pre-tax writeoff), EPS in the second quarter of 1998 fell 18% to $0.32 (on 2.1% more shares) from $0.39. The impact of weather accounted for $0.03 of the decline. Operating revenues were up 21%, mainly reflecting a 90% increase in wholesale and energy trading. However, with operating expenses up 31% (driven by a 61% rise in fuel and purchased power costs), operating income was down 11%.

Stock Performance - 11-SEP-98

In the past 30 trading days, PPL's shares have increased 6%, compared to a 10% fall in the S&P 500. Average trading volume for the past five days was 918,050 shares, compared with the 40-day moving average of 752,328 shares.

Key Stock Statistics

Dividend Rate/Share	1.00	Shareholders	125,300
Shs. outstg. (M)	168.3	Market cap. (B)	$ 4.1
Avg. daily vol. (M)	1.024	Inst. holdings	33%
Tang. Bk. Value/Share	16.77		
Beta	0.29		

Value of $10,000 invested 5 years ago: $ 13,474

Fiscal Year Ending Dec. 31

	1998	1997	1996	1995	1994	1993
Revenues (Million $)						
1Q	880.2	785.8	789.2	727.5	769.0	727.0
2Q	838.0	686.0	669.1	609.2	640.0	620.0
3Q	—	777.8	714.6	682.3	661.0	683.0
4Q	—	799.2	737.4	732.9	654.0	696.0
Yr.	—	3,049	2,910	2,752	2,725	2,727
Earnings Per Share ($)						
1Q	**0.60**	**0.72**	0.73	0.65	0.70	0.70
2Q	**0.32**	**0.39**	0.38	0.28	0.31	0.40
3Q	—	**0.25**	0.49	0.55	0.46	0.49
4Q	—	**0.44**	0.45	0.56	-0.05	0.48
Yr.	—	**1.80**	2.05	2.05	1.41	2.07

Next earnings report expected: late October

Dividend Data (Dividends have been paid since 1946.)

Amount ($)	Date Decl.	Ex-Div. Date	Stock of Record	Payment Date
0.417	Nov. 26	Dec. 08	Dec. 10	Jan. 01 '98
0.417	Feb. 27	Mar. 06	Mar. 10	Apr. 01 '98
0.417	May. 22	Jun. 08	Jun. 10	Jul. 01 '98
0.250	Aug. 14	Sep. 08	Sep. 10	Oct. 01 '98

A Division of The McGraw-Hill Companies

Business Summary - 08-SEP-98

PP&L Resources is the holding company formed in April 1995 by Pennsylvania Power & Light, now its main subsidiary, which supplies electricity to some 1.2 million homes and businesses in a 10,000-square-mile area in 29 counties of central-eastern Pennsylvania. Important cities served are Allentown, Bethlehem, Harrisburg, Lancaster, Scranton, Wilkes-Barre and Williamsport.

Contributions to energy sales in recent years were:

	1997	1996	1995	1994
Residential	33%	35%	34%	35%
Commercial	27%	28%	29%	28%
Wholesale	20%	14%	12%	11%
Industrial	19%	20%	20%	20%
Other	1%	3%	5%	6%

Sources of electric generation in 1997 were 59.5% coal, 36.9% nuclear, 2.1% oil and 1.5% hydro. Peak demand in 1997 was 6,506 mw, and total generating capability at year-end was 8,257 mw, with additional firm purchases of 477 mw. During 1997, 63% of the coal delivered to PPL's generating stations was purchased under contracts, with the remainder purchased through open-market transactions.

In August 1998, PPL acquired Penn Fuel Gas, a natural gas distributor with nearly 100,000 customers in Pennsylvania and a few hundred in Maryland, for about $133 million in new stock.

PPL is also the parent of PP&L Global, which has investments in international electric energy projects. It owns a 51% equity interest (49% voting interest) in South Western Electricity in the U.K. and has holdings in Argentina, Bolivia, Chile, El Salvador, Peru, Spain and Portugal. In February 1998, it acquired a 37.5% interest in Distributidora de Electricidad del Sur, which serves 193,000 customers in El Salvador. Other unregulated businesses include: PP&L Spectrum, which markets energy-related products and services; and PP&L Capital Funding, which is engaged in financing for PPL and its subsidiaries. In January 1998, PPL acquired H. T. Lyons, a heating, ventilating and air conditioning firm.

In December 1996, Pennsylvania enacted legislation to restructure its electric utility industry. The legislation, which would phase in (over a three-year period that begins in 1999) retail customer choice, allowed utilities to recover PUC-approved transition or stranded costs through a non-bypassable transition charge. Transition bonds would be issued to refinance the stranded costs, with a transition charge on customer bills to repay the bonds. In June 1998, the PUC issued a ruling that would allow Pennsylvania Power & Light to recover (over 8-1/2 years beginning January 1, 1999) only $2.864 billion of the $4.5 billion the company had claimed in stranded costs.

Per Share Data ($) (Year Ended Dec. 31)	1997	1996	1995	1994	1993	1992	1991	1990	1989	1988
Tangible Bk. Val.	16.77	16.73	16.13	15.06	15.28	15.03	14.56	14.07	13.60	13.15
Earnings	1.80	2.05	2.05	1.41	2.07	2.02	2.01	1.98	2.03	1.87
Dividends	1.67	1.67	1.67	1.67	1.65	1.60	1.55	1.49	1.43	1.38
Payout Ratio	93%	81%	81%	118%	80%	79%	77%	76%	71%	74%
Prices - High	24¼	26	26½	27¼	31	28¼	26⅜	22¼	21½	19
- Low	19	21⅝	17⅞	18⅝	26⅛	23⅞	20⅞	19½	17⅛	16⅝
P/E Ratio - High	13	13	13	19	15	14	13	11	11	10
- Low	11	11	9	13	13	12	10	10	8	9
Income Statement Analysis (Million $)										
Revs.	3,049	2,910	2,752	2,725	2,727	2,744	2,560	2,389	2,356	2,214
Depr.	374	363	302	289	271	261	239	219	199	186
Maint.	184	191	186	180	193	201	207	224	234	224
Fxd. Chgs. Cov.	3.3	3.8	3.2	3.0	3.4	2.9	2.8	2.6	2.6	2.4
Constr. Credits	NA	NA	12.1	13.1	15.6	14.9	12.0	12.0	14.0	16.0
Eff. Tax Rate	43%	45%	43%	42%	40%	40%	38%	36%	37%	36%
Net Inc.	296	329	350	244	348	347	348	344	353	332
Balance Sheet & Other Fin. Data (Million $)										
Gross Prop.	10,336	10,242	10,235	9,998	9,684	9,054	8,758	8,553	8,340	8,150
Cap. Exp.	310	360	403	505	488	422	374	338	308	342
Net Prop.	6,766	6,905	7,122	7,127	6,997	6,855	6,754	6,699	6,653	6,616
Capitalization:										
LT Debt	2,698	2,968	2,967	3,092	2,788	2,785	2,767	2,648	2,878	2,898
% LT Debt	47	48	50	54	49	49	49	48	51	52
Pfd.	347	466	466	466	506	227	596	615	641	670
% Pfd.	6.10	7.50	7.90	7.80	8.80	9.60	11	11	11	12
Common	2,809	2,745	2,497	2,454	2,426	2,367	2,298	2,222	2,139	2,050
% Common	49	44	42	41	42	42	41	41	38	37
Total Cap.	8,075	8,075	8,356	8,290	8,232	7,037	6,972	6,741	6,836	6,677
% Oper. Ratio	82.1	80.9	79.1	81.6	79.4	79.1	77.2	75.3	73.7	72.7
% Earn. on Net Prop.	8.0	8.0	8.1	7.1	8.1	8.4	8.7	8.8	9.3	9.2
% Return On Revs.	9.7	11.3	12.7	9.0	12.8	12.6	13.6	14.4	15.0	15.0
% Return On Invest. Capital	9.4	6.5	6.8	6.6	7.6	8.5	8.7	8.9	9.3	9.3
% Return On Com. Equity	10.7	12.3	12.8	8.7	13.1	13.1	13.4	13.7	14.6	13.9

Data as orig. reptd.; bef. results of disc. opers. and/or spec. items. Per share data adj. for stk. divs. as of ex-div. date. Bold denotes diluted EPS (FASB 128). E-Estimated. NA-Not Available. NM-Not Meaningful. NR-Not Ranked.

Office—Two North Ninth St., Allentown, PA 18101. **Tel**—(610) 774-5151. **Website**—http://www.papl.com **Chrmn, Pres & CEO**—W. F. Hecht. **SVP-Fin** —J. R. Biggar. **SVP & Secy**—R. J. Grey. **Investor Contact**—T. J. Paukovits. **Dirs**—F. M. Bernthal, E. A. Deaver, N. K. Dicciani, W. J. Flood, E. D. Gates, W. F. Hecht, S. Heydt, C. L. Jones, R. Leventhal, M. W. Lewis, F. A. Long, N. Robertson. **Transfer Agents & Registrars**—Co.'s office; Norwest Bank Minnesota, South St. Paul. **Incorporated**—in Pennsylvania in 1920; reincorporated in Pennsylvania in 1994. **Empl**— 6,343. **S&P Analyst:** Justin McCann

Praxair, Inc.

1864C

NYSE Symbol **PX**

In S&P 500

12-SEP-98

Industry: Chemicals

Summary: This company is the largest producer of industrial gases in North and South America, and one of the largest worldwide. It also provides ceramic and metallic coatings.

| S&P Opinion: Hold (★★★) | Recent Price • 33⅛ | Yield • 1.5% |
| | 52 Wk Range • 55⅝-31½ | 12-Mo. P/E • 13.0 |

Quantitative Evaluations

Outlook (1 Lowest—5 Highest)
• **4**

Fair Value
• **44⅝**

Risk
• **Low**

Earn./Div. Rank
• **NR**

Technical Eval.
• **Bearish** since 8/98

Rel. Strength Rank (1 Lowest—99 Highest)
• **26**

Insider Activity
• **NA**

Earnings vs. Previous Year
▲=Up ▼=Down ▶=No Change

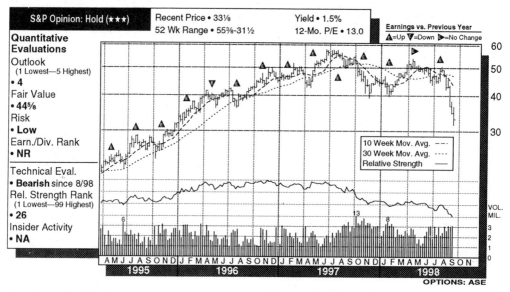

- 10 Week Mov. Avg. – – –
- 30 Week Mov. Avg. ⋯⋯
- Relative Strength —

VOL. MIL.

A M J J A S O N D J F M A M J J A S O N D J F M A M J J A S O N D J F M A M J J A S O N
1995 / 1996 / 1997 / 1998

OPTIONS: ASE

Overview - 20-AUG-98

We expect sales to advance at the high-single digit rate for the rest of 1998 and into 1999. PX should see good volume growth resulting from a high level of new business activity and projects in industrial gases in the U.S. and Europe, as well as acquisitions in the U.S. packaged gas and Surface Technologies businesses. The Surface Technologies unit should also benefit from strong aircraft engine markets and demand for specialty powders. However, austerity programs in Brazil (nearly 20% of PX's annual sales), enacted in late 1997, and unfavorable currency exchange rates will limit sales and profit growth. Operating margins should exceed PX's goal of 18%, aided by additional major productivity gains, and by further integration savings in the North American packaged gases business. PX is also implementing cost reductions in Brazil, where results have been hurt by declining industrial prices. Price increases in the U.S. will help offset higher power costs. Interest expense will begin to decline as a result of reduced capital spending; outlays in 1999 are anticipated to be 20% below 1998's $1 billion. The tax rate is projected to be about 25%. PX will continue a stock buyback program to maintain the number of shares outstanding.

Valuation - 20-AUG-98

We have a hold opinion on PX. The stock was a strong performer until mid-1997, driven by the success of the acquisition of the Liquid Carbonic unit of CBI Industries. The stock is selling at a larger than historical discount to the overall market, based upon 1998 EPS estimates, but we feel that the shares will be only average performers until economic problems in Brazil are resolved. Industrial gases fundamentals are positive, with demand growing faster than the overall economy.

Key Stock Statistics

S&P EPS Est. 1998	2.71	Tang. Bk. Value/Share	5.78
P/E on S&P Est. 1998	12.2	Beta	1.35
S&P EPS Est. 1999	3.05	Shareholders	47,200
Dividend Rate/Share	0.50	Market cap. (B)	$ 5.2
Shs. outstg. (M)	158.2	Inst. holdings	71%
Avg. daily vol. (M)	0.726		

Value of $10,000 invested 5 years ago: $ 21,149

Fiscal Year Ending Dec. 31

	1998	1997	1996	1995	1994	1993
Revenues (Million $)						
1Q	1,201	1,158	1,090	756.0	611.0	594.0
2Q	1,234	1,178	1,093	788.0	645.0	623.0
3Q	—	1,190	1,115	795.0	733.0	608.0
4Q	—	1,209	1,151	807.0	722.0	613.0
Yr.	—	4,735	4,449	3,146	2,711	2,438
Earnings Per Share ($)						
1Q	0.62	0.62	0.11	0.46	0.30	0.25
2Q	0.66	0.65	0.50	0.47	0.39	0.28
3Q	E0.70	0.65	0.54	0.44	0.36	0.24
4Q	E0.73	0.61	0.62	0.45	0.39	0.29
Yr.	E2.71	2.53	1.77	1.82	1.45	1.06

Next earnings report expected: late October

Dividend Data (Dividends have been paid since 1992.)

Amount ($)	Date Decl.	Ex-Div. Date	Stock of Record	Payment Date
0.110	Oct. 21	Dec. 03	Dec. 05	Dec. 15 '97
0.125	Jan. 27	Mar. 04	Mar. 06	Mar. 16 '98
0.125	Apr. 28	Jun. 03	Jun. 05	Jun. 15 '98
0.125	Jul. 23	Sep. 03	Sep. 08	Sep. 15 '98

A Division of The McGraw-Hill Companies

Praxair, Inc.

Business Summary - 20-AUG-98

Since its spinoff from Union Carbide Corp. in 1992, PX, the largest producer of industrial gases in North and South America, has expanded operations to 40 countries, including many high growth markets in Asia. The purchase of CBI Industries' Liquid Carbonic business in 1996 made PX the world's largest supplier of carbon dioxide. The acquisition significantly added exposure to non-cyclical food and beverage markets. PX expects to invest about $1 billion in 1998, including for acquisitions. PX continues to make acquisitions in its North American packaged gases business (with current annual sales of $960 million), although it slowed this program in 1997, due to integration problems with acquisitions made in the prior two years. Contributions in 1997 by geographical area were:

	Sales	Profits
U.S.	51%	54%
South America	21%	23%
Europe	13%	13%
Canada, Mexico & Asia	15%	10%

The industrial gases business involves the production, distribution and sale of atmospheric gases (oxygen, nitrogen, argon and rare gases), carbon dioxide, hydrogen, helium, acetylene, specialty gases and equipment for the production of industrial gases. Atmospheric gases are produced through air separation processes, primarily cryogenic, while other gases are produced by various methods. PX has also developed noncryogenic air separation processes that open new markets consisting of small users and help optimize production capacity by lowering production costs. Major customers include aerospace, beverage, chemicals, electronics, food processing, health care, glass, metal fabrication, petroleum, primary metals and pulp/paper concerns.

Industrial gases are supplied to customers through three basic methods: on-site/pipeline (19% of total 1997 sales), merchant (36%) and packaged (33%). The company has about 301 cryogenic air separation plants worldwide (164 in the U.S.), 89 carbon dioxide plants (22), and 30 hydrogen plants worldwide. S.A. White Martins (69% owned) is the leading producer of industrial gases in South America.

The Surface Technologies business (7%) applies metallic and ceramic coatings to parts and equipment provided by customers, provides aircraft engine and airframe component overhaul services, and sells specialty powders. It also manufactures thermal spray equipment. Surface Technologies sales in 1997 rose 23%, mainly due to volume growth and acquisitions. Other businesses (4%) include the sale of cylinders and products related to industrial gases.

Per Share Data ($) (Year Ended Dec. 31)	1997	1996	1995	1994	1993	1992	1991	1990	1989	1988
Tangible Bk. Val.	5.78	4.77	6.74	5.43	4.22	3.69	NA	NA	NA	NA
Cash Flow	5.24	4.43	5.60	3.40	2.93	2.52	NA	NA	NA	NA
Earnings	2.53	1.77	1.82	1.45	1.06	0.64	0.84	0.85	0.31	NA
Dividends	0.44	0.38	0.32	0.28	0.25	0.13	NA	NA	NA	NA
Payout Ratio	17%	21%	18%	19%	24%	20%	NA	NA	NA	NA
Prices - High	58	50 1/8	34 1/8	24 5/8	18 5/8	17 1/2	NA	NA	NA	NA
- Low	39 1/4	31 1/2	19 3/4	16 1/4	14 1/8	13 5/8	NA	NA	NA	NA
P/E Ratio - High	23	28	19	17	18	27	NA	NA	NA	NA
- Low	16	18	11	11	13	21	NA	NA	NA	NA
Income Statement Analysis (Million $)										
Revs.	4,735	4,449	3,146	2,711	2,438	2,604	2,469	2,420	2,073	1,826
Oper. Inc.	1,230	1,125	812	737	592	675	612	707	540	481
Depr.	444	420	279	273	253	247	236	198	175	160
Int. Exp.	216	220	125	112	108	230	177	143	138	NA
Pretax Inc.	633	350	434	346	240	166	207	266	104	115
Eff. Tax Rate	24%	31%	28%	24%	20%	22%	33%	56%	31%	32%
Net Inc.	416	282	262	203	143	84.0	107	120	43.0	54.0
Balance Sheet & Other Fin. Data (Million $)										
Cash	43.0	63.0	15.0	63.0	34.0	24.0	82.0	73.0	NA	NA
Curr. Assets	1,497	1,666	930	840	691	691	824	763	NA	NA
Total Assets	7,810	7,538	4,134	3,520	3,255	3,344	3,451	3,027	2,714	2,531
Curr. Liab.	1,366	2,550	1,029	889	831	1,210	1,862	497	NA	NA
LT Debt	2,874	1,703	933	893	967	669	176	1,275	1,242	1,245
Common Eqty.	2,122	2,122	1,121	839	635	544	650	645	527	475
Total Cap.	5,592	4,195	2,462	2,286	2,099	1,774	1,208	2,176	2,046	1,967
Cap. Exp.	902	893	600	326	240	333	417	363	243	228
Cash Flow	860	696	758	476	396	331	343	318	218	214
Curr. Ratio	1.1	0.7	0.9	0.9	0.8	0.6	0.4	1.5	NA	NA
% LT Debt of Cap.	51.4	40.6	37.9	39.1	45.9	37.7	14.6	58.6	60.7	63.3
% Net Inc.of Revs.	8.8	6.3	8.4	7.5	5.9	3.2	4.3	5.0	2.1	3.0
% Ret. on Assets	5.4	4.9	6.9	5.9	4.3	NA	3.3	4.2	1.6	2.2
% Ret. on Equity	20.6	18.5	26.8	27.2	24.0	NA	16.5	20.5	8.6	12.1

Data as orig. reptd.; bef. results of disc. opers. and/or spec. items. Per share data adj. for stk. divs. as of ex-div. date. Bold denotes diluted EPS (FASB 128). E-Estimated. NA-Not Available. NM-Not Meaningful. NR-Not Ranked.

Office—39 Old Ridgebury Rd., Danbury, CT 06810-5113. **Tel**—(203) 837-2000; (800) 879-PRAXAIR. **Website**—http://www.praxair.com **Chrmn & CEO**—H. W. Lichtenberger. **Pres**—E. G. Hotard. **EVP & CFO**—J. A. Clerico. **VP & Secy**—D. H. Chaifetz. **Investor Contact**—Joseph S. Cappello. **Dirs**—A. Achaval, J. A. Clerico, C. F. Fetterolf, D. F. Frey, C. W. Gargalli, E. G. Hotard, R. L. Kuehn Jr., R. W. LeBoeuf, H. W. Lichtenberger, B. F. Payton, G. J. Ratcliffe Jr., H. M. Watson Jr. **Transfer Agent & Registrar**—Bank of New York, NYC. **Incorporated**—in Delaware in 1988. **Empl**— 26,000. **S&P Analyst:** Richard O'Reilly, CFA

12-SEP-98

Industry:
Household Products
(Nondurables)

Summary: This leading consumer products company markets household and personal care products in more than 140 countries.

S&P Opinion: Hold (★★★)	Recent Price • 67⅞	Yield • 1.7%
	52 Wk Range • 94-62	12-Mo. P/E • 26.3

Quantitative Evaluations

Outlook
(1 Lowest—5 Highest)
• 1

Fair Value
• 56

Risk
• Low

Earn./Div. Rank
• A

Technical Eval.
• NA

Rel. Strength Rank
(1 Lowest—99 Highest)
• 40

Insider Activity
• NA

Earnings vs. Previous Year
▲=Up ▼=Down ►=No Change

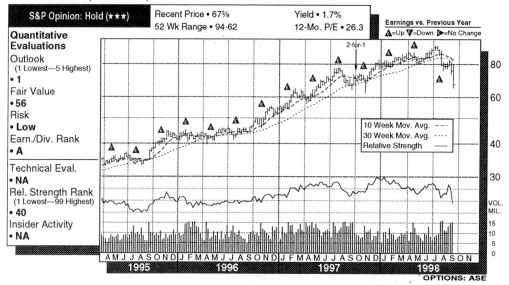

10 Week Mov. Avg. ---
30 Week Mov. Avg. ····
Relative Strength —

OPTIONS: ASE

Overview - 04-AUG-98

We expect sales to grow in the low- to mid-single digit range during FY 99 (Jun.), aided by contributions from acquisitions, including Tambrands, international volume growth, joint ventures, penetration into emerging growth markets, and new products. In the most recent period, the company's sales slowed, due to financial problems in Asia and competitive pricing pressures, as PG has selectively raised prices while competitors have not followed. Sales have also been hurt by negative currency comparisons, which may ease toward the second half of FY 99, helping to boost sales. Profitability will also be affected by investments for new product launches, which will help future results but could limit near-term profitability.

Valuation - 04-AUG-98

We recently downgraded the shares to hold, from accumulate, based on an expected difficult operating environment over the next year, as well as management's recent caution regarding earnings growth. PG's long-term goal is to increase earnings 11% to 14% annually, and it has hit the higher end of that range for the past few years. Given management's caution, it is likely that earnings will grow about 11% to 12% over the next year, restricted by financial problems in Asia, and possible price roll-backs to protect market share. Over the years, the stock has traded at a premium P/E multiple both to that of PG's peers and to the broader market, reflecting PG's steady, fairly predictable earnings growth. However, with increased uncertainty regarding earnings growth over the next year, and given an unforgiving market, we believe that investors should avoid accumulating more shares. Nevertheless, given PG's market dominance and history of solid performance, the shares remain a worthwile holding for long-term investors.

Key Stock Statistics

S&P EPS Est. 1999	2.86	Tang. Bk. Value/Share	2.68
P/E on S&P Est. 1999	23.6	Beta	0.94
Dividend Rate/Share	1.14	Shareholders	242,200
Shs. outstg. (M)	1341.0	Market cap. (B)	$ 90.3
Avg. daily vol. (M)	3.156	Inst. holdings	46%

Value of $10,000 invested 5 years ago: $ 27,729

Fiscal Year Ending Jun. 30

	1998	1997	1996	1995	1994	1993
Revenues (Million $)						
1Q	9,355	8,903	9,027	8,161	7,564	7,880
2Q	9,641	9,142	9,090	8,467	7,788	7,840
3Q	8,881	8,771	8,587	8,312	7,441	7,350
4Q	9,277	8,948	8,580	8,494	7,503	7,365
Yr.	37,154	35,764	35,284	33,434	30,296	30,433
Earnings Per Share ($)						
1Q	0.79	0.69	0.64	0.56	0.47	0.28
2Q	**0.71**	0.68	0.59	0.53	0.46	0.41
3Q	**0.65**	0.63	0.54	0.44	0.33	0.36
4Q	**0.47**	0.43	0.39	0.33	0.28	-0.92
Yr.	**2.56**	2.43	2.14	1.85	1.54	0.13

Next earnings report expected: late October

Dividend Data (Dividends have been paid since 1891.)

Amount ($)	Date Decl.	Ex-Div. Date	Stock of Record	Payment Date
0.253	Oct. 14	Oct. 22	Oct. 24	Nov. 14 '97
0.253	Jan. 13	Jan. 21	Jan. 23	Feb. 17 '98
0.253	Apr. 14	Apr. 22	Apr. 24	May. 15 '98
0.285	Jul. 14	Jul. 22	Jul. 24	Aug. 14 '98

A Division of The McGraw-Hill Companies

STANDARD
&POOR'S
STOCK REPORTS

The Procter & Gamble Company

1868

12-SEP-98

Business Summary - 04-AUG-98

With the likes of Crest toothpaste, Pampers disposable diapers and Tide detergent in its family of products, Procter & Gamble has amassed a portfolio of premier consumer brands in a variety of categories. PG manufactures and markets more than 300 brands of consumer products sold in 140 countries. Management has set some heady goals for the consumer-products giant: doubling unit volume in 10 years; growing market share in the majority of its categories; and providing total shareholder return ranking in the top third of its peer group.

Product line contributions to FY 97 (Jun.) sales and pretax profits were:

	Sales	Profits
Laundry/cleaning products	31%	38%
Beauty care products	20%	19%
Food & beverage products	12%	10%
Paper	29%	24%
Health care	8%	9%

North America contributed 49% of sales and 67% of net income in FY 97; Europe, the Middle East and Africa, 32% and 25%; Asia, 10% and 8%; and Latin America, 6% and 6%.

PG owns a long list of world-famous consumer brands. Its Laundry & Cleaning product roster includes Tide, Cascade and Dawn; the Paper group lists Bounty, Pampers, Charmin and Always; Beauty Care brands include Pantene, Vidal Sassoon, Oil of Olay, Secret and Cover Girl; Food & Beverage counts Folgers, Jif, Crisco and Pringles among its brands; and Health Care includes the Crest, Scope, Metamucil and Vicks labels.

The creation of new products and development of new performance benefits for consumers on existing products are vital to PG's continued success. Tide Ultra 2 represents the latest of more than 60 performance improvements since the brand was first introduced in 1946. Pampers Baby-Dry with breakthrough absorbing technology makes gender-specific diapers obsolete. The Food & Beverage segment is adding production capacity for Olean, a recently approved fat substitute.

PG is focusing on the successful implementation of value pricing and the maintenance of key customer relations in important developing markets such as China, Mexico, Brazil and Russia.

In July 1997, PG acquired Tambrands, the leading tampon producer in the U.S., for about $1.85 billion. PG will re-enter the tampon market with the leading Tampax brand.

Per Share Data ($)

(Year Ended Jun. 30)	1998	1997	1996	1995	1994	1993	1992	1991	1990	1989
Tangible Bk. Val.	NA	5.99	4.05	2.98	3.60	2.60	2.38	2.12	2.83	2.25
Cash Flow	NA	3.53	3.13	2.77	2.38	0.96	1.99	1.70	1.68	1.41
Earnings	2.56	2.43	2.15	1.85	1.54	0.13	1.31	1.23	1.13	0.89
Dividends	1.01	0.90	0.80	0.70	0.66	0.55	0.51	0.49	0.44	0.38
Payout Ratio	39%	37%	37%	38%	43%	449%	39%	39%	39%	41%
Prices - High	94	83³⁄₈	55¹⁄₂	44³⁄₄	32³⁄₈	29¹⁄₂	27⁷⁄₈	23⁷⁄₈	22¹⁄₈	17⁵⁄₈
- Low	77¹⁄₄	51⁷⁄₈	39³⁄₄	30³⁄₈	25⁵⁄₈	22⁵⁄₈	22⁵⁄₈	19	15¹⁄₂	10¹⁄₂
P/E Ratio - High	37	34	26	24	21	NM	21	19	20	20
- Low	30	21	19	16	17	NM	17	15	14	12

Income Statement Analysis (Million $)

	1998	1997	1996	1995	1994	1993	1992	1991	1990	1989
Revs.	NA	35,764	35,284	33,434	30,296	30,433	29,362	27,026	24,081	21,398
Oper. Inc.	NA	6,975	6,173	5,432	5,432	4,301	3,777	3,549	3,072	2,727
Depr.	NA	1,487	1,358	1,253	1,134	1,140	910	847	770	688
Int. Exp.	NA	457	484	488	482	577	535	412	445	398
Pretax Inc.	NA	5,249	4,669	4,000	3,346	349	349	2,687	2,421	1,939
Eff. Tax Rate	NA	35%	35%	34%	34%	23%	35%	34%	34%	38%
Net Inc.	NA	3,415	3,046	2,645	2,211	269	1,872	1,773	1,602	1,206

Balance Sheet & Other Fin. Data (Million $)

	1998	1997	1996	1995	1994	1993	1992	1991	1990	1989
Cash	NA	2,350	2,520	2,178	2,656	2,322	1,776	1,384	1,407	1,587
Curr. Assets	NA	10,786	10,807	10,842	9,988	9,975	9,366	8,435	7,644	6,578
Total Assets	NA	27,544	27,730	28,125	25,535	24,935	24,025	20,468	18,487	16,351
Curr. Liab.	NA	7,798	7,825	8,648	8,040	8,287	7,642	6,733	5,417	4,656
LT Debt	NA	4,143	4,670	5,161	4,980	5,174	5,223	4,111	3,588	3,698
Common Eqty.	NA	10,187	9,836	8,676	8,677	7,308	7,085	5,741	6,518	5,215
Total Cap.	NA	14,889	17,030	16,281	14,159	12,798	15,777	13,157	12,364	11,248
Cap. Exp.	NA	2,129	2,179	2,146	1,841	1,911	1,911	1,979	1,300	1,029
Cash Flow	NA	4,798	4,301	3,796	3,243	1,307	2,688	2,542	2,325	1,878
Curr. Ratio	NA	1.4	1.4	1.3	1.2	1.2	1.2	1.3	1.4	1.4
% LT Debt of Cap.	NA	27.8	27.4	31.7	35.2	40.4	33.1	31.2	29.0	32.9
% Net Inc.of Revs.	NA	9.5	8.6	7.9	7.3	0.9	6.4	6.6	6.7	5.6
% Ret. on Assets	NA	12.4	10.9	9.9	8.7	1.1	8.5	9.2	8.9	7.9
% Ret. on Equity	NA	33.1	31.8	32.7	26.3	2.0	27.7	28.0	25.7	21.1

Data as orig. reptd.; bef. results of disc. opers. and/or spec. items. Per share data adj. for stk. divs. as of ex-div. date. Bold denotes diluted EPS (FASB 128). E-Estimated. NA-Not Available. NM-Not Meaningful. NR-Not Ranked.

Office—1 Procter & Gamble Plaza, Cincinnati, OH 45202. **Registrar**—PNC Bank, Cincinnati, OH. **Tel**—(513) 983-1100. **Website**—http://www.pg.com **Chrmn & CEO**—J. E. Pepper. **Pres & COO**—D. I. Jager. **SVP & CFO**—E. G. Nelson. **Secy**—T. L. Overbey. **Treas**—C. C. Daley, Jr. **Investor Contact**—G. A. Dowdell. **Dirs**—E. L. Artzt, N. R. Augustine, D. R. Beall, G. F. Brunner, R. B. Cheney, H. Einsmann, R. J. Ferris, J. T. Gorman, D. I. Jager, C. R. Lee, L. Martin, J. E. Pepper, J. C. Sawhill, J. F. Smith, Jr., R. Snyderman, R. D. Storey, M. v.N. Whitman. **Transfer Agent**—Co. itself. **Incorporated**—in Ohio in 1905. **Empl**— 106,000. **S&P Analyst:** Robert J. Izmirlian

Progressive Corp.   1869K

NYSE Symbol **PGR**

In S&P 500

12-SEP-98

Industry: Insurance (Property-Casualty)

Summary: This leading underwriter of nonstandard auto and other specialty personal lines coverages is expanding its product line in an attempt to evolve into a full-service auto insurer.

S&P Opinion: Avoid (★★)	Recent Price • 103¾	Yield • 0.3%
	52 Wk Range • 156¾-95	12-Mo. P/E • 17.0

Quantitative Evaluations

Outlook (1 Lowest—5 Highest)
• **2**

Fair Value
• **103**

Risk
• **Low**

Earn./Div. Rank
• **B+**

Technical Eval.
• **Bearish** since 3/98

Rel. Strength Rank (1 Lowest—99 Highest)
• **48**

Insider Activity
• **Neutral**

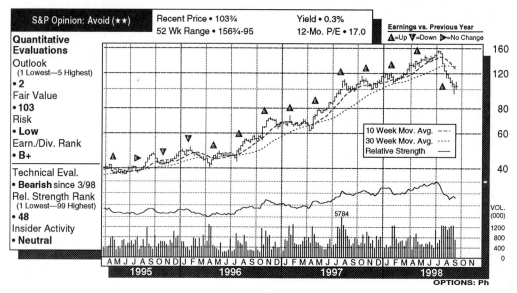

Earnings vs. Previous Year
▲=Up ▼=Down ▶=No Change

10 Week Mov. Avg. ----
30 Week Mov. Avg. ·····
Relative Strength ——

5784

VOL. (000)

OPTIONS: Ph

Overview - 28-JUL-98

Written premium growth in 1998 will likely exceed 15%, reflecting PGR's decision to aggressively price its policies and accept narrower margins in order to gain market share, as part of a plan to evolve into a full-service auto insurer, from a specialty underwriter of nonstandard coverage. The positive effects of PGR's aggressive cost cutting will also aid this effort, since well controlled costs are the key to profit growth in the price-competitive standard auto insurance market. PGR is also streamlining its operating structure, which should enhance customer service, further reduce operating expenses, and decrease the time required to implement product improvements over the long term. However, the near-term cost of these initiatives will likely restrain margins.

Valuation - 28-JUL-98

The shares trended upward during much of 1997 and early 1998, amid positive investor reaction to PGR's robust top line growth. PGR's written premium growth rates far exceed industry averages. However, these growth rates reflect PGR's decision to increase its share of the auto insurance market. Over time, underwriting results may deteriorate slightly, as more of PGR's business mix is represented by standard lines. We expected the P/E multiple of the stock to contract, as PGR evolves into a lower-margin, full-service insurer, from a niche player, since the market typically rewards niche players with higher multiples than full-service carriers. Thus far, however, the market has focused instead on PGR's above-average premium growth rates. Nevertheless, in the near term the shares will likely underperform the broader market. Note: earnings estimates are for operating earnings; historical per share data are based on net income.

Key Stock Statistics

S&P EPS Est. 1998	5.50	Tang. Bk. Value/Share	33.16
P/E on S&P Est. 1998	18.9	Beta	1.31
S&P EPS Est. 1999	6.20	Shareholders	4,200
Dividend Rate/Share	0.26	Market cap. (B)	$ 7.5
Shs. outstg. (M)	72.7	Inst. holdings	64%
Avg. daily vol. (M)	0.307		

Value of $10,000 invested 5 years ago: $ 36,457

Fiscal Year Ending Dec. 31

	1998	1997	1996	1995	1994	1993
Revenues (Million $)						
1Q	1,255	966.5	799.0	693.8	522.4	435.1
2Q	1,335	1,119	848.1	759.5	594.0	494.4
3Q	—	1,203	893.9	775.7	634.1	515.6
4Q	—	1,320	937.5	782.9	664.8	509.7
Yr.	—	4,608	3,478	3,012	2,415	1,955
Earnings Per Share ($)						
1Q	1.58	1.02	0.82	0.79	0.62	0.71
2Q	1.61	1.36	1.01	0.79	0.79	1.11
3Q	—	1.54	1.08	0.81	0.85	1.10
4Q	—	1.39	1.23	0.86	1.34	0.68
Yr.	—	5.31	4.11	3.26	3.59	3.59

Next earnings report expected: mid October

Dividend Data (Dividends have been paid since 1965.)

Amount ($)	Date Decl.	Ex-Div. Date	Stock of Record	Payment Date
0.060	Oct. 29	Dec. 10	Dec. 12	Dec. 31 '97
0.060	Feb. 09	Mar. 11	Mar. 13	Mar. 31 '98
0.060	Apr. 24	Jun. 10	Jun. 12	Jun. 30 '98
0.065	Aug. 28	Sep. 09	Sep. 11	Sep. 30 '98

A Division of The McGraw·Hill Companies

Business Summary - 28-JUL-98

This regional auto insurer is expanding into a full-service auto insurer from a specialty writer of non-standard coverage. To achieve its goal, the company has been aggressively pricing its policies and accepting narrower profit margins. Consequently, PGR's written premium growth has been much greater than that of the overall property-casualty insurance industry. Contributions to direct written premiums by division in recent years were as follows:

	1997	1996
Personal lines	90%	867
Commercial lines	10%	13%

PGR's core business (accounting for 96% of 1997's $4.7 billion in net written premiums) consists of underwriting private passenger automobile, recreational vehicle, and small commercial vehicle insurance. Historically, the bulk of PGR's core business has consisted of nonstandard insurance programs, which provide coverage for accounts rejected or canceled by other companies. The company estimates that it was the second largest insurer serving this market.

As part of a strategy to expand its share of the personal automobile insurance market, the company is selectively underwriting standard and preferred risk automobile insurance coverage. During 1997, standard and preferred risks accounted for between 20% and 25% of core premium volume. In the future, that percentage will likely increase, as the company becomes more experienced at writing and pricing preferred risks. PGR is also expanding geographically. During 1996, it increased the number of states in which it operates to 43 (from 37 in 1995). Of the $4.8 billion in direct premiums written in 1997, Florida accounted for 13.7%, Texas 10.6%, New York 9.2% and Ohio 8.4% PGR's strategy for growth also includes select acquisitions. In March 1997, the company acquired Midland Financial Group, Inc., a regional non-standard auto insurer, for about $50 million.

The company's other core personal lines products are dominated by motorcycle insurance, but also include recreational vehicle, motor home, mobile home and boat coverages. PGR's diversified division mainly provides credit-related insurance and services to lending institutions and risk management services to trade and professional organizations.

Per Share Data ($)

(Year Ended Dec. 31)	1997	1996	1995	1994	1993	1992	1991	1990	1989	1988
Tangible Bk. Val.	29.54	23.45	19.31	14.95	12.59	7.94	5.83	5.89	5.71	5.13
Oper. Earnings	4.46	4.08	2.84	2.76	2.62	1.94	NA	NA	NA	NA
Earnings	5.31	4.14	3.26	3.59	3.59	2.09	0.41	1.28	0.98	1.29
Dividends	0.24	0.23	0.22	0.21	0.20	0.19	0.17	0.16	0.15	0.13
Payout Ratio	5%	6%	7%	6%	6%	9%	43%	13%	15%	10%
Prices - High	120⅞	72¼	49½	40½	46⅛	29⅜	20¾	18⅞	14½	10¾
- Low	61½	40⅜	34¾	27¾	27½	14¾	15⅛	11	7½	7¼
P/E Ratio - High	23	17	15	11	13	14	51	15	15	8
- Low	12	10	11	8	8	7	37	9	8	6

Income Statement Analysis (Million $)

	1997	1996	1995	1994	1993	1992	1991	1990	1989	1988
Premium Inc.	4,190	3,199	2,727	2,191	1,669	1,451	1,287	1,191	1,197	1,215
Net Invest. Inc.	275	226	199	159	135	154	152	140	168	117
Oth. Revs.	144	53.0	85.6	66.0	152	134	54.0	45.0	28.0	13.0
Total Revs.	144	3,478	3,012	2,415	1,955	1,739	1,493	1,376	1,393	1,345
Pretax Inc.	579	442	346	380	373	179	33.0	88.0	86.0	132
Net Oper. Inc.	336	309	NA	NA	189	NA	NA	NA	NA	NA
Net Inc.	400	314	251	274	267	140	33.0	93.0	78.0	108

Balance Sheet & Other Fin. Data (Million $)

	1997	1996	1995	1994	1993	1992	1991	1990	1989	1988
Cash & Equiv.	23.3	62.0	56.0	56.8	42.4	50.0	48.3	52.7	54.5	36.2
Premiums Due	1,161	821	650	542	381	312	323	269	235	225
Invest. Assets: Bonds	4,301	3,568	3,076	2,704	2,333	1,988	1,955	1,908	1,885	1,601
Invest. Assets: Stocks	970	882	692	476	454	399	349	184	243	252
Invest. Assets: Loans	Nil	Nil	Nil	Nil	Nil	Nil	Nil	Nil	Nil	Nil
Invest. Assets: Total	5,270	4,450	3,768	3,180	2,785	2,386	2,304	2,093	2,128	1,853
Deferred Policy Costs	260	200	182	162	125	101	110	105	111	126
Total Assets	7,560	6,184	5,353	4,675	4,011	3,005	2,979	2,695	2,647	2,307
Debt	776	776	676	676	477	569	644	644	646	479
Common Eqty.	2,136	1,677	1,392	1,066	910	533	466	409	435	417
Prop. & Cas. Loss Ratio	71.1	70.2	71.6	NA	NA	68.3	65.7	62.1	67.9	62.9
Prop. & Cas. Expense Ratio	20.7	19.8	21.4	NA	NA	29.8	33.5	31.1	32.6	33.2
Prop. & Cas. Combined Ratio	91.8	90.0	93.0	NA	NA	98.1	99.2	93.2	100.5	96.1
% Return On Revs.	278.2	9.0	8.3	11.3	13.7	8.0	2.2	6.8	5.6	8.0
% Ret. on Equity	21.0	20.5	19.7	NA	37.0	34.7	6.7	21.5	17.4	25.9

Data as orig. reptd.; bef. results of disc. opers. and/or spec. items. Per share data adj. for stk. divs. as of ex-div. date. Bold denotes diluted EPS (FASB 128). E-Estimated. NA-Not Available. NM-Not Meaningful. NR-Not Ranked.

Office—6300 Wilson Mills Rd., Mayfield Village, OH 44143. Tel—(216) 461-5000. Website—http://www.progressive.com Chrmn, Pres & CEO—P. B. Lewis. VP, CFO, Treas & Investor Contact—Charles B. Chokel. Secy—D. M. Schneider. Dirs—M. N. Allen, B. C. Ames, C. A. Davis, S. R. Hardis, J. Hill, P. B. Lewis, N. S. Matthews, D. B. Shackelford, P. B. Sigler. Transfer Agent & Registrar—National City Bank, Cleveland.Incorporated—in Ohio in 1965. Empl— 9,557. S&P Analyst: Catherine A. Seifert

Provident Companies

1871G

NYSE Symbol **PVT**

In S&P 500

12-SEP-98

Industry: Insurance (Life & Health)

Summary: This leading provider of individual, non-cancelable disability insurance also offers group disability policies and life insurance products.

S&P Opinion: Hold (★★★)	Recent Price • 34¾	Yield • 1.2%
	52 Wk Range • 41⅛-31⅝	12-Mo. P/E • 16.8

Quantitative Evaluations

Outlook
(1 Lowest—5 Highest)
• **3**

Fair Value
• **37¾**

Risk
• **Average**

Earn./Div. Rank
• **B**

Technical Eval.
• **NA**

Rel. Strength Rank
(1 Lowest—99 Highest)
• **85**

Insider Activity
• **NA**

Earnings vs. Previous Year
▲=Up ▼=Down ▶=No Change

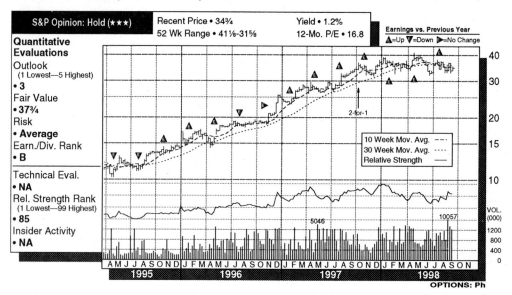

10 Week Mov. Avg. — -·
30 Week Mov. Avg. - - - -
Relative Strength ——

OPTIONS: Ph

Overview - 12-AUG-98

Operating earnings growth in 1998 will likely continue to be aided by contributions from the 1997 acquisition of The Paul Revere Corp. This purchase enhanced PVT's position in the individual disability market. PVT's results will also be aided by several restructuring moves undertaken recently. However, top line growth may be constrained by extremely competitive conditions in both the pension and disability markets. After deciding to focus on the employee benefits and individual life/disability areas, PVT moved to tighten underwriting and claims management procedures and reposition certain product lines. As part of a plan to shift its focus, the company in June 1995 sold its medical services business, and is running off its group pension business. The sale of the individual and tax sheltered annuity business to American General Corp. (NYSE: AGC) for $58 million (completed in May 1998) freed up capital that can be re-allocated toward PVT's core disability business.

Valuation - 12-AUG-98

After trending upward during much of 1997, the shares have remained in a fairly narrow range during most of 1998. The shares' strength in 1997 primarily reflected favorable investor reaction to the company's recent acquisition and restructuring actions, coupled with a relatively benign interest rate environment. We applaud PVT's recent moves, and view favorably the company's more focused approach. However, as a result of their recent strength, the shares are trading at the upper end of their historical P/E range and are fairly valued for the near term.

Key Stock Statistics

S&P EPS Est. 1998	2.20	Tang. Bk. Value/Share	19.59
P/E on S&P Est. 1998	15.8	Beta	0.49
S&P EPS Est. 1999	2.60	Shareholders	2,900
Dividend Rate/Share	0.40	Market cap. (B)	$ 4.7
Shs. outstg. (M)	135.2	Inst. holdings	53%
Avg. daily vol. (M)	0.780		

Value of $10,000 invested 5 years ago: $ 27,883

Fiscal Year Ending Dec. 31

	1998	1997	1996	1995	1994	1993
Revenues (Million $)						
1Q	993.6	571.3	591.7	713.8	689.4	698.4
2Q	983.0	993.8	569.0	644.1	688.6	785.4
3Q	—	997.1	562.7	602.7	693.2	719.3
4Q	—	989.0	568.5	594.7	691.0	734.9
Yr.	—	3,553	2,292	2,555	2,762	2,938
Earnings Per Share ($)						
1Q	**0.50**	**0.39**	0.34	0.10	0.36	0.35
2Q	**0.54**	**0.41**	0.34	0.35	0.38	0.63
3Q	—	**0.49**	0.33	0.33	0.32	-2.71
4Q	—	**0.53**	0.45	0.35	0.30	0.70
Yr.	—	**1.84**	1.46	1.14	1.35	-1.01

Next earnings report expected: late October

Dividend Data (Dividends have been paid since 1925.)

Amount ($)	Date Decl.	Ex-Div. Date	Stock of Record	Payment Date
0.100	Oct. 30	Nov. 25	Nov. 28	Dec. 10 '97
0.100	Feb. 11	Feb. 25	Feb. 27	Mar. 10 '98
0.100	May. 06	May. 22	May. 27	Jun. 10 '98
0.100	Jul. 31	Aug. 25	Aug. 27	Sep. 10 '98

A Division of The McGraw-Hill Companies

Business Summary - 12-AUG-98

This life and health insurer has chosen to focus on growing its employee benefits and individual disability businesses, sometimes via acquisitions. Coverage is offered on a group and individual basis throughout the U.S., Puerto Rico and parts of Canada. Segment contributions in 1997 (before investment gains or losses) were:

	Revenues	Pretax Profits
Individual life/disability	54%	64%
Employee benefits	25%	17%
Other operations	21%	19%

The individual life/disability division offers term and universal life insurance and single premium deferred annuities. The company is also one of the largest underwriters of individual disability insurance in the U.S. Provident greatly expanded its presence in the individual disability marketplace with the acquisition of The Paul Revere Corporation (NYSE: PRL). PVT acquired the disability insurer in March 1997 for about $1.2 billion. Zurich Insurance Group helped finance this transaction with a $300 million common stock investment,

representing about 14% of PVT's common shares. In May 1998, PVT completed the sale of its individual and tax-sheltered annuity business to American General Corp. (NYSE: AGC).

The employee benefits segment offers group long term disability, group life insurance, medical stop-loss coverage and various other related products to associations and employee groups. In February 1997, PVT acquired GENEX Services, Inc., a leading provider of case management and vocational rehabilitation services to corporations, third party administrators and insurance companies. These services are utilized in the management of disability and workers' compensation claims.

Other operations consist of guaranteed investment contracts (GICs), group single premium annuities, a closed block of corporate-owned life insurance, and a medical services unit (group health benefits on a fee for services, administrative services only and managed care basis), which was sold in June 1995.

At year end 1997, funds under management and equivalents totaled $5.6 billion (down from $7.2 billion at year end 1996), of which individual annuities accounted for 42%, traditional GICs (which are no longer being actively marketed) 29%, "synthetic" GICs 2%, group single premium annuities 21%, and other 6%.

Per Share Data ($)

(Year Ended Dec. 31)	1997	1996	1995	1994	1993	1992	1991	1990	1989	1988
Tangible Bk. Val.	17.69	17.34	16.48	11.16	13.76	15.37	14.99	14.44	12.94	11.62
Oper. Earnings	NA	1.52	1.36	1.60	-1.33	1.47	NA	NA	NA	0.92
Earnings	1.84	1.46	1.14	1.35	-1.01	1.25	1.26	1.93	1.58	0.97
Dividends	0.38	0.36	0.36	0.52	0.52	0.50	0.48	0.41	0.35	0.34
Payout Ratio	21%	25%	32%	38%	NM	40%	38%	22%	22%	35%
Prices - High	39	25¾	17	16	16	14⅝	12¼	13⅛	15⅛	11½
- Low	23¼	14¼	10¼	10¾	12⅞	10	7¼	6	9⅝	6¼
P/E Ratio - High	21	18	15	12	NM	12	10	7	10	13
- Low	13	10	9	8	NM	8	6	3	6	7

Income Statement Analysis (Million $)

	1997	1996	1995	1994	1993	1992	1991	1990	1989	1988
Life Ins. In Force	NA	102,665	98,953	81,860	78,999	79,956	82,434	82,432	80,048	81,564
Prem. Inc.: Life	1,287	646	647	NA	NA	129	131	136	112	595
Prem. Inc.: A & H	NA	501	486	1,383	1,400	1,361	1,406	1,420	1,453	1,257
Prem. Inc.: Other	145	28.0	119	NA	Nil	Nil	Nil	Nil	Nil	Nil
Net Invest. Inc.	1,355	1,090	1,221	1,239	1,319	1,242	1,195	1,088	971	889
Total Revs.	3,553	2,292	2,555	2,762	2,938	2,867	2,846	2,751	2,639	2,827
Pretax Inc.	380	226	176	201	-139	180	169	253	223	128
Net Oper. Inc.	NA	151	136	158	-119	NA	NA	NA	NA	85.0
Net Inc.	247	146	116	135	-81.0	113	117	179	148	91.0

Balance Sheet & Other Fin. Data (Million $)

	1997	1996	1995	1994	1993	1992	1991	1990	1989	1988
Cash & Equiv.	401	288	302	335	296	381	326	298	280	267
Premiums Due	73.9	72.3	75.5	63.0	65.0	93.0	102	119	127	158
Invest. Assets: Bonds	17,342	11,145	12,618	11,596	11,310	10,602	9,439	7,957	6,509	5,648
Invest. Assets: Stocks	10.0	4.9	5.3	7.0	15.0	142	167	143	103	103
Invest. Assets: Loans	1,984	1,749	1,679	2,864	2,968	3,031	3,179	3,432	3,605	3,488
Invest. Assets: Total	19,434	13,317	14,751	15,018	15,010	14,344	13,324	12,161	10,539	9,410
Deferred Policy Costs	363	422	272	638	603	561	514	464	424	380
Total Assets	23,178	14,993	16,301	17,150	16,892	15,925	14,787	13,522	11,852	10,722
Debt	725	200	200	203	248	206	207	208	215	222
Common Eqty.	3,123	1,582	1,496	1,013	1,245	1,388	1,371	1,343	1,208	1,085
% Return On Revs.	7.0	6.4	4.5	4.9	NM	3.9	4.1	6.5	5.6	3.0
% Ret. on Assets	1.3	0.9	0.7	0.8	NM	0.7	0.8	1.4	1.3	0.8
% Ret. on Equity	10.0	9.5	8.2	9.6	NM	8.3	8.6	14.1	12.0	8.1
% Invest. Yield	7.6	7.8	8.2	8.2	8.9	9.0	9.4	9.6	9.7	10.1

Data as orig. reptd.; bef. results of disc. opers. and/or spec. items. Per share data adj. for stk. divs. as of ex-div. date. Bold denotes diluted EPS (FASB 128). E-Estimated. NA-Not Available. NM-Not Meaningful. NR-Not Ranked.

Office—One Fountain Square, Chattanooga, TN 37402. **Tel**—(615) 755-1011. **Website**—http://www.providentcompanies.com **Chrmn, Pres & CEO**—J. H. Chandler. **Vice Chrmn & CFO**—T. R. Watjen. **Dirs**—W. L. Armstrong, W. H. Bolinder, J. H. Chandler, S. M. Gluckstern, C. M. Heffner, H. B. Jacks, W. B. Johnson, H. O. Maclellan Jr., A. S. Macmillan, C. W. Pollard, S. L. Probasco Jr., S. S. Reinemund, B. E. Sorensen, T. R. Watjen. **Transfer Agent & Registrar**—First Chicago Trust Co., NYC. **Incorporated**—in Tennessee in 1887. **Empl**— 4,039. **S&P Analyst:** Catherine A. Seifert

STANDARD &POOR'S
STOCK REPORTS

Providian Financial
1871N

NYSE Symbol **PVN**

In S&P 500

12-SEP-98

Industry:
Consumer Finance

Summary: This diversified consumer lender offers a broad range of lending products, including credit cards, revolving lines of credit and home equity loans.

S&P Opinion: Accumulate (★★★★)	Recent Price • 59⅜	Yield • 0.3%
	52 Wk Range • 84⅜-34½	12-Mo. P/E • 26.0

Quantitative Evaluations

Outlook
(1 Lowest—5 Highest)
• **2**

Fair Value
• **55⅝**

Risk
• **NA**

Earn./Div. Rank
• **NR**

Technical Eval.
• **NA**

Rel. Strength Rank
(1 Lowest—99 Highest)
• **44**

Insider Activity
• **NA**

Earnings vs. Previous Year
▲=Up ▼=Down ▶=No Change

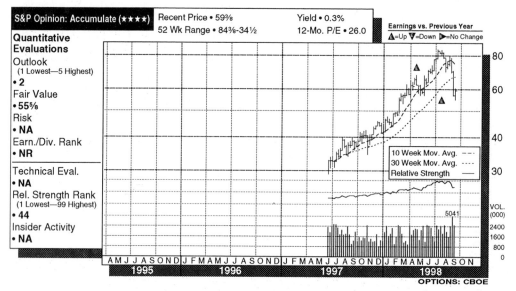

OPTIONS: CBOE

Overview - 26-JUN-98

Growth in managed loans is expected at better than 15% in 1998, as the company's proven marketing strategies continue to result in solid account expansion. The net interest margin, already enviably high, could widen modestly on the repricing of certain accounts. Gains in loan servicing income on a higher average securitized loan balance, credit product fee income on account growth and higher late fees, and sales of fee-based products will further benefit core earnings comparisons. Asset quality remains strong, despite an uptick in delinquencies and net credit losses seen recently, and loss provisions will likely closely mirror net charge-offs over the next several quarters. The integration of the two First Union credit card portfolios is progressing smoothly, and synergies should become apparent as the company leverages the use of its own profitability model on acquired accounts. Future period account growth should benefit from product development efforts that include Visa Classic and Platinum Plus credit card products and cash back reward programs.

Valuation - 26-JUN-98

The shares remain in a solid uptrend, as earnings continue to benefit from good industry fundamentals and the company's successful marketing strategies. Ongoing product development efforts that should lead to strong account growth, a focus on efficiency and asset quality, and healthy interest margins should result in earnings growth of 30% in 1998 and better than 20% in 1999. With the shares trading at 22 times our 1999 earnings estimate of $3.15 a share, selective accumulation of the shares is recommended.

Key Stock Statistics

S&P EPS Est. 1998	2.70	Tang. Bk. Value/Share	7.32
P/E on S&P Est. 1998	22.0	Beta	NA
S&P EPS Est. 1999	3.35	Shareholders	NA
Dividend Rate/Share	0.20	Market cap. (B)	$ 5.6
Shs. outstg. (M)	95.0	Inst. holdings	68%
Avg. daily vol. (M)	0.657		

Value of $10,000 invested 5 years ago: NA

Fiscal Year Ending Dec. 31

	1998	1997	1996	1995	1994	1993
Revenues (Million $)						
1Q	387.3	280.3	—	—	—	—
2Q	472.2	274.8	—	—	—	—
3Q	—	322.1	—	—	—	—
4Q	—	335.1	—	—	—	—
Yr.	—	1,217	1,008	—	—	—
Earnings Per Share ($)						
1Q	0.58	0.46	—	—	—	—
2Q	0.65	0.48	—	—	—	—
3Q	—	0.50	—	—	—	—
4Q	—	0.56	—	—	—	—
Yr.	E2.70	2.00	1.62	—	—	—

Next earnings report expected: NA

Dividend Data (Dividends have been paid since 1997.)

Amount ($)	Date Decl.	Ex-Div. Date	Stock of Record	Payment Date
0.050	Oct. 30	Nov. 26	Dec. 01	Dec. 15 '97
0.050	Feb. 17	Feb. 26	Mar. 02	Mar. 16 '98
0.050	May. 06	May. 28	Jun. 09	Jun. 15 '98
0.050	Aug. 05	Aug. 28	Sep. 01	Sep. 15 '98

Business Summary - 26-JUN-98

Spun off from Providian Corp. in June 1997, Providian Financial Corp. is a diversified consumer lender offering a broad range of lending products, including Gold Visa and MasterCard credit cards, check-access revolving lines of credit, home loans, secured credit cards, and a variety of fee-based products and services. With $8.0 billion of managed loans outstanding, the company ranks among the 15 largest credit card issuers in the U.S. Internal growth is focused on increasing the total number of customer relationships, doing more business with each customer, and expanding the number of consumer lending markets served.

Total managed loans of $9.9 billion at the end of 1997, versus $9.3 billion a year earlier, included unsecured credit card and line of credit loans (81%), home equity revolving line of credit loans (11%) and secured and partially secured credit card loans (8%).

Rather than having a branch network, the company develops customer relationships through direct mail and telephone sales. Customer and product strategy is focused on the development of universal offers designed to appeal to a broad range of consumers within target markets, using specific terms that can be customized at the time of sale to meet individual borrowing needs.

The company originates, maintains and services unsecured consumer loans generated mainly through Visa

and MasterCard credit cards. Home loan products include mainly home equity lines of credit, which are offered in 26 states to target homeowners with significant debt for use in debt consolidation. Fee-based products include prescription and other health-related discounts and referrals; emergency towing service, auto maintenance discounts and other auto and travel benefits; credit protection; shopping-related discounts; and standby letters of credit for use in case of unemployment, disability or hospitalization.

The allowance for loan losses, which is set aside for possible loan defaults, at 1997 year end was $145.3 million (4.91% of total loans), up from $114.5 million (3.88%) a year earlier. Net charge-offs, or the amount of loans deemed uncollectible, in 1997 were $591.7 million (6.32% of average managed loans), compared to $380.6 million (4.82%) in 1996. Delinquent loans, those on which minimum payments have not been received by the next billing date, amounted to $417.9 million at the end of 1997 (4.22% of managed loans), versus $405.5 million (4.36%) the year before.

In May 1998, the company acquired a $1.1 billion portfolio of unsecured credit card receivables from First Union Corp. The transaction followed a similar $1.1 billion portfolio acquisition in January 1998. Together, the transactions resulted in the addition of more than one million new unsecured accounts.

Per Share Data ($)

(Year Ended Dec. 31)	1997	1996	1995	1994	1993	1992	1991	1990	1989	1988
Tangible Bk. Val.	6.27	4.48	NA	NA	NA	NA	NA	NA	NA	NA
Earnings	2.00	1.63	NA	NA	NA	NA	NA	NA	NA	NA
Dividends	0.10	NA	NA	NA	NA	NA	NA	NA	NA	NA
Payout Ratio	5%	NA	NA	NA	NA	NA	NA	NA	NA	NA
Prices - High	46¾	NA	NA	NA	NA	NA	NA	NA	NA	NA
- Low	29⅛	NA	NA	NA	NA	NA	NA	NA	NA	NA
P/E Ratio - High	23	NA	NA	NA	NA	NA	NA	NA	NA	NA
- Low	15	NA	NA	NA	NA	NA	NA	NA	NA	NA

Income Statement Analysis (Million $)

	1997	1996	1995	1994	1993	1992	1991	1990	1989	1988
Net Int. Inc.	399	408	NA	NA	NA	NA	NA	NA	NA	NA
Tax Equiv. Adj.	NA	NA	NA	NA	NA	NA	NA	NA	NA	NA
Non Int. Inc.	635	412	NA	NA	NA	NA	NA	NA	NA	NA
Loan Loss Prov.	149	127	NA	NA	NA	NA	NA	NA	NA	NA
Exp./Op. Revs.	55%	53%	NA	NA	NA	NA	NA	NA	NA	NA
Pretax Inc.	311	262	NA	NA	NA	NA	NA	NA	NA	NA
Eff. Tax Rate	38%	38%	NA	NA	NA	NA	NA	NA	NA	NA
Net Inc.	191	162	NA	NA	NA	NA	NA	NA	NA	NA
% Net Int. Marg.	NA	NA	NA	NA	NA	NA	NA	NA	NA	NA

Balance Sheet & Other Fin. Data (Million $)

	1997	1996	1995	1994	1993	1992	1991	1990	1989	1988
Earning Assets:										
Money Mkt	115	172	NA	NA	NA	NA	NA	NA	NA	NA
Inv. Securities	173	7.2	NA	NA	NA	NA	NA	NA	NA	NA
Com'l Loans	NA	15.7	NA	NA	NA	NA	NA	NA	NA	NA
Other Loans	NA	3,680	NA	NA	NA	NA	NA	NA	NA	NA
Total Assets	4,449	4,381	NA	NA	NA	NA	NA	NA	NA	NA
Demand Deposits	32.1	28.3	NA	NA	NA	NA	NA	NA	NA	NA
Time Deposits	3,181	3,362	NA	NA	NA	NA	NA	NA	NA	NA
LT Debt	82.0	165	NA	NA	NA	NA	NA	NA	NA	NA
Common Eqty.	595	420	NA	NA	NA	NA	NA	NA	NA	NA
% Ret. on Assets	4.4	NA	NA	NA	NA	NA	NA	NA	NA	NA
% Ret. on Equity	35.5	NA	NA	NA	NA	NA	NA	NA	NA	NA
% Loan Loss Resv.	4.9	3.1	NA	NA	NA	NA	NA	NA	NA	NA
% Loans/Deposits	NA	120.9	NA	NA	NA	NA	NA	NA	NA	NA
% Equity to Assets	12.3	NA	NA	NA	NA	NA	NA	NA	NA	NA

Data as orig. reptd.; bef. results of disc. opers. and/or spec. items. Pro forma data in 1996. Per share data adj. for stk. divs. as of ex-div. date. Bold denotes diluted EPS (FASB 128). E-Estimated. NA-Not Available. NM-Not Meaningful. NR-Not Ranked.

Office—201 Mission St., San Francisco, CA 94105. Tel—(415) 543-0404. Chrmn, Pres & CEO—S. J. Mehta. SVP & CFO—D. J. Petrini. Investor Contact—Nick Colburn. Dirs—J. M. Cranor III, C. L. Darwall, J. V. Elliot, L. Everingham, J. D. Grissom, F. W. McFarlan, S. J. Mehta, R. M. Owades, L. D. Thompson, J. L. Weinberg. Transfer Agent & Registrar—First Chicago Trust Co. of New York, Jersey City, N.J. Incorporated—in Delaware in 1997. Empl— 4,016. S&P Analyst: Stephen R. Biggar

Public Service Enterprise Group 1876
NYSE Symbol PEG
In S&P 500

12-SEP-98

Industry: Electric Companies

Summary: This holding company owns Public Service Electric and Gas (PSE&G), whose service area encompasses 70% of New Jersey, and invests in energy-related businesses.

S&P Opinion: Hold (★★★)	Recent Price • 36½	Yield • 5.9%
	52 Wk Range • 37⅞-25⅛	12-Mo. P/E • 13.2

Quantitative Evaluations

Outlook (1 Lowest—5 Highest)
• 1

Fair Value
• 32¾

Risk
• Low

Earn./Div. Rank
• B+

Technical Eval.
• **Bearish** since 8/98

Rel. Strength Rank (1 Lowest—99 Highest)
• 96

Insider Activity
• Neutral

Earnings vs. Previous Year
▲=Up ▼=Down ▶=No Change

10 Week Mov. Avg. ---
30 Week Mov. Avg. ····
Relative Strength —

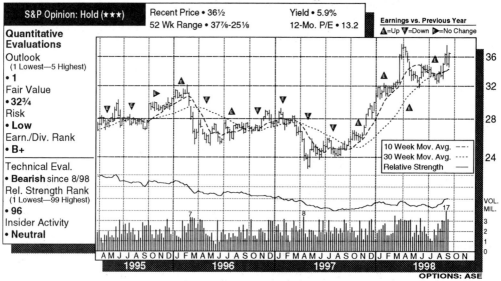

OPTIONS: ASE

Overview - 20-AUG-98

We expect EPS in 1999 to be flat with 1998 results, which are benefiting from the absence of costs related to outages at the Salem nuclear units. The Salem 1 unit was returned to service in April 1998, the Salem 2 unit in September 1997. In July 1998, the Nuclear Regulatory Commission removed both units from the NRC Watch List. In April 1997, the NJ Board of Public Utilities (BPU) issued its final Energy Master Plan, which proposed that utilities have an opportunity to recover their stranded costs, with full recovery contingent upon conditions that would include near-term rate reductions of 5% to 10%. In July 1997, PEG filed a proposal with the BPU that provided for the rate reduction requirements, a seven-year freeze on major rate components, and the recovery of $2.5 billion in stranded nuclear generation costs. The BPU is expected to submit draft legislation to the governor in the fall of 1998, with a legislative package expected to be passed by year-end.

Valuation - 20-AUG-98

We would continue to hold PEG stock. The shares were recently up 7.3% year to date (versus a 4.1% increase for the S&P Index of Electric Companies and a 2.5% decline in the Index of Natural Gas Companies). In 1997, the shares rose 16.7% (versus respective gains of 19.8% and 18.6% for the S&P Electric and Natural Gas Indexes). In addition to a still positive interest rate environment, the shares have benefited from the return of the Salem nuclear plants. EPS should benefit in the near term from a still strong economy and effective cost management; and in the longer term from the growth in nonregulated businesses. PEG's dividend (recently yielding about 6.3%) appears safe, but the high payout ratio, at 77% of our EPS estimate of $2.80 for both 1998 and 1999, limits the likelihood of an increase.

Key Stock Statistics

S&P EPS Est. 1998	2.80	Tang. Bk. Value/Share	21.98
P/E on S&P Est. 1998	13.0	Beta	0.31
S&P EPS Est. 1999	2.80	Shareholders	167,200
Dividend Rate/Share	2.16	Market cap. (B)	$ 8.5
Shs. outstg. (M)	232.0	Inst. holdings	39%
Avg. daily vol. (M)	1.450		

Value of $10,000 invested 5 years ago: $ 17,587

Fiscal Year Ending Dec. 31

	1998	1997	1996	1995	1994	1993
Revenues (Million $)						
1Q	1,901	1,733	1,797	1,676	1,794	1,595
2Q	1,557	1,323	1,336	1,329	1,278	1,246
3Q	—	1,568	1,334	1,492	1,375	1,402
4Q	—	1,746	1,574	1,667	1,468	1,462
Yr.	—	6,370	6,041	6,164	5,916	5,706
Earnings Per Share ($)						
1Q	0.82	0.60	0.79	0.87	0.94	0.89
2Q	0.53	0.39	0.55	0.45	0.53	0.49
3Q	E0.78	0.76	0.64	0.76	0.76	0.79
4Q	E0.67	0.66	0.54	0.62	0.54	0.30
Yr.	E2.80	2.41	2.42	2.71	2.78	2.48

Next earnings report expected: late October

Dividend Data (Dividends have been paid since 1907.)

Amount ($)	Date Decl.	Ex-Div. Date	Stock of Record	Payment Date
0.540	Nov. 18	Dec. 08	Dec. 10	Dec. 31 '97
0.540	Feb. 18	Mar. 06	Mar. 10	Mar. 31 '98
0.540	May. 19	Jun. 05	Jun. 09	Jun. 30 '98
0.540	Jul. 21	Sep. 04	Sep. 09	Sep. 30 '98

A Division of The McGraw-Hill Companies

Business Summary - 20-AUG-98

Public Service Enterprise Group has two wholly owned subsidiaries: Public Service Electric and Gas Co. (PSE&G), which supplies electric and gas service to the most populous area in New Jersey and accounted for 92% of 1997 earnings; and Enterprise Diversified Holdings Inc. (EDHI), which operates nonutility businesses.
Contributions to revenues in recent years were:

	1997	1996	1995
Electric	65.7%	65.3%	68.2%
Gas	30.4%	31.1%	28.6%
Non-utility	3.8%	3.6%	3.2%

PSE&G is mainly engaged in the generation, transmission, distribution and sale of electric energy service, and in the transmission, distribution and sale of gas service. Nuclear fuel comprised 34% of power generation in 1997, coal 26%, natural gas 5%, and purchased or interchanged power 35%.

PSE&G has an ownership interest in five nuclear generating units and operates three of these -- Salem Units 1 and 2 and Hope Creek. It owns 42.6% of the Salem units, which represent approximately 10% of its installed electric generating capacity. The Salem units were taken out of service in the second quarter of 1995 and, after significant changes, Unit 2 was returned to

full service in September 1997 and Unit 1 was returned to operation in April 1998. The 95%-owned Hope Creek plant successfully completed a planned refueling and maintenance outage in December 1997.

In April 1997, the New Jersey Board of Public Utilities (BPU) issued its final energy master plan policy statement on restructuring the electric power industry in New Jersey. The plan required PSE&G and the state's other public utilities to develop proposals that would allow customers to choose their electric suppliers, with 10% being allowed to choose starting in October 1998, and all remaining customers being phased in by July 2000. In July 1997, PEG proposed (instead of a phase-in) full customer choice as of January 1, 1999, but said that its ability to implement a 5% to 10% rate reduction would depend on legislation authorizing it to refinance, through securitization, about $2.5 billion of stranded costs.

PEG's non-utility businesses are operated by EDHI, and consist of three principal subsidiaries that were renamed in June 1998: PSEG Resources (formerly Public Service Resources Corp.), an investment company that contributed 10% of 1997 earnings; PSEG Global (Community Energy Alternatives), an international independent power company; and PSEG Energy Technologies (Energis Resources), which provides energy management consulting for businesses in the Northeast.

Per Share Data ($)

(Year Ended Dec. 31)	1997	1996	1995	1994	1993	1992	1991	1990	1989	1988
Tangible Bk. Val.	21.72	21.60	21.57	20.93	20.37	19.93	20.68	20.08	19.46	18.68
Earnings	2.41	2.42	2.71	2.78	2.48	2.17	2.43	2.56	2.62	2.57
Dividends	2.16	2.16	2.16	2.16	2.16	2.16	2.13	2.09	2.05	2.01
Payout Ratio	90%	89%	80%	78%	83%	100%	88%	82%	78%	78%
Prices - High	31¾	32⅛	30⅝	32	36⅛	31⅜	29⅜	29¾	29⅜	26⅞
- Low	22⅞	25⅛	26	23⅞	30	25⅜	25¼	22½	23	22
P/E Ratio - High	13	13	11	12	14	14	12	12	11	10
- Low	9	10	10	9	12	12	10	9	9	9

Income Statement Analysis (Million $)

	1997	1996	1995	1994	1993	1992	1991	1990	1989	1988
Revs.	6,370	6,041	6,164	5,916	5,706	5,357	5,093	4,800	4,805	4,395
Depr.	630	607	674	630	600	643	613	561	467	434
Maint.	282	318	312	308	304	308	315	286	316	350
Fxd. Chgs. Cov.	2.7	3.0	3.1	3.0	2.8	2.4	2.7	2.6	2.8	2.9
Constr. Credits	20.0	18.0	42.5	46.6	33.1	30.8	45.0	50.0	34.0	28.0
Eff. Tax Rate	37%	33%	35%	31%	33%	32%	32%	27%	27%	26%
Net Inc.	560	612	662	679	596	504	544	542	542	529

Balance Sheet & Other Fin. Data (Million $)

	1997	1996	1995	1994	1993	1992	1991	1990	1989	1988
Gross Prop.	17,982	16,400	16,628	16,245	15,577	14,858	14,219	13,837	12,960	12,467
Cap. Exp.	542	586	827	999	951	830	813	968	674	565
Net Prop.	11,217	11,179	11,187	11,098	10,804	10,471	10,183	9,874	9,337	9,090
Capitalization:										
LT Debt	4,925	4,622	5,243	5,234	5,209	5,031	5,182	4,722	4,348	4,000
% LT Debt	46	44	46	47	48	49	50	49	49	48
Pfd.	683	681	685	685	580	505	430	430	430	430
% Pfd.	6.30	6.50	6.00	6.10	5.30	4.90	4.10	4.50	4.80	5.10
Common	5,211	5,213	5,445	5,311	5,134	4,782	4,763	4,465	4,191	3,925
% Common	48	50	48	48	47	46	46	46	47	47
Total Cap.	14,556	14,128	14,860	14,548	14,158	12,473	12,549	11,654	10,904	10,158
% Oper. Ratio	82.5	82.5	81.0	80.0	81.0	82.0	80.4	79.7	80.4	80.8
% Earn. on Net Prop.	9.9	5.5	10.4	10.6	10.4	9.4	10.0	10.1	10.2	9.3
% Return On Revs.	8.8	10.2	10.7	11.5	10.4	9.4	10.7	11.3	11.3	12.0
% Return On Invest. Capital	10.1	7.5	10.4	8.2	8.4	8.4	8.4	8.8	9.2	9.2
% Return On Com. Equity	10.7	11.5	12.3	13.0	12.0	10.8	11.7	12.7	13.4	13.6

Data as orig. reptd.; bef. results of disc. opers. and/or spec. items. Per share data adj. for stk. divs. as of ex-div. date. Bold denotes diluted EPS (FASB 128). E-Estimated. NA-Not Available. NM-Not Meaningful. NR-Not Ranked.

Registrars—First Fidelity Bank, Newark; First Chicago Trust Co. of New York, NYC.**Office**—80 Park Plaza (P. O. Box 1171), Newark, NJ 07101-1171. **Tel**—(973) 430-7000. **Website**—http://www.pseg.com **Chrmn, Pres & CEO**—E. J. Ferland. **VP & CFO**—R. C. Murray. **Investor Contact**—Brian Smith. **Dirs**—L. R. Codey, E. H. Drew, T. J. D. Dunphy, E. J. Ferland, R. V. Gilmartin, C. K. Harper, I. Lerner, M. M. Pfaltz, F. J. Remick, R. J. Swift, J. S. Weston. **Transfer Agents & Registrars**—Co.'s office; First Chicago Trust Co. of New York, Jersey City. **Incorporated**—in New Jersey in 1924. **Empl**— 10,092. **S&P Analyst:** Justin McCann

Pulte Corp.

1882B

NYSE Symbol **PHM**

In S&P 500

12-SEP-98

Industry: Homebuilding

Summary: PHM builds moderately priced single-family homes and condominiums in 28 states, and also has a mortgage banking unit.

S&P Opinion: Hold (★★★)	Recent Price • 27⅜	Yield • 0.6%
	52 Wk Range • 36⅛-17⅛	12-Mo. P/E • 16.5

Quantitative Evaluations

Outlook
(1 Lowest—5 Highest)
• **2⁻**

Fair Value
• **29¾**

Risk
• **Low**

Earn./Div. Rank
• **B+**

Technical Eval.
• **Bearish** since 11/97

Rel. Strength Rank
(1 Lowest—99 Highest)
• **63**

Insider Activity
• **Neutral**

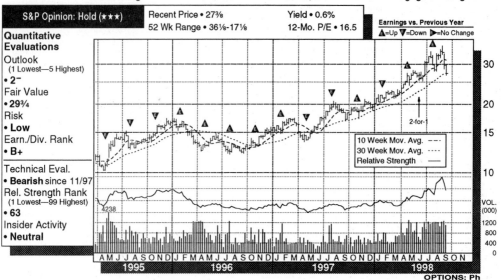

Earnings vs. Previous Year
▲=Up ▼=Down ►=No Change

10 Week Mov. Avg. — - -
30 Week Mov. Avg. ·····
Relative Strength ——

2-for-1

VOL. (000)

OPTIONS: Ph

Overview - 07-AUG-98

We expect solid sales gains in 1998. A 20% year-to-year gain in order levels in the first half of the year lifted PHM's unit order backlog to 6,152 homes at June 30, 1998, up 19% from a year earlier. A mature housing cycle presents a challenge, but we expect accommodating interest rates, strong consumer confidence, and a solid job market to allow for continued sales and order gains. Mortgage originations at the mortgage banking division should mirror home sales trends, and the big drop in interest rates over the past year should keep refinancing activity strong. Operating margins should widen, on Pulte's efforts to lower housing costs through operating efficiencies and overhead reduction. EPS comparisons should benefit from the maturation of Mexican joint-venture projects and Pulte's active adult effort. Comparisons will be distorted by $0.24 a share (adjusted) of one-time net charges in 1997. One-time adjustments in the 1998 first quarter essentially offset each other. EPS computations will be based on fewer shares in 1998, as PHM repurchased 4.6 million shares (adjusted) from its former chairman in April 1997.

Valuation - 07-AUG-98

After dropping throughout 1996, as rising interest rates dimmed investor enthusiasm for homebuilders, the shares have moved solidly higher since rates started an extended downturn in late 1996. Pulte should benefit in upcoming periods from accommodating interest rates and a cost-cutting focus. Most signs point towards ongoing strength in the housing sector, but the cycle has been getting a bit long in the tooth and would cause us to approach homebuilding investments with some caution. With the shares trading at around 14 times our 1999 forecast, which tends toward the high side for a homebuilder, we remain neutral on the shares.

Key Stock Statistics

S&P EPS Est. 1998	2.10	Tang. Bk. Value/Share	19.87
P/E on S&P Est. 1998	13.0	Beta	1.01
S&P EPS Est. 1999	2.30	Shareholders	800
Dividend Rate/Share	0.16	Market cap. (B)	$ 1.2
Shs. outstg. (M)	43.1	Inst. holdings	57%
Avg. daily vol. (M)	0.294		

Value of $10,000 invested 5 years ago: $ 18,966

Fiscal Year Ending Dec. 31

	1998	1997	1996	1995	1994	1993
Revenues (Million $)						
1Q	520.6	431.7	432.5	332.9	340.6	316.0
2Q	679.7	576.3	588.4	485.5	427.9	405.0
3Q	—	669.9	625.2	543.4	452.6	431.7
4Q	—	846.1	738.2	667.5	534.8	480.5
Yr.	—	2,524	2,384	2,029	1,756	1,633
Earnings Per Share ($)						
1Q	**0.25**	**0.03**	0.10	-0.01	0.20	0.20
2Q	**0.55**	**0.29**	0.32	0.17	0.28	0.41
3Q	**E0.56**	**0.44**	0.34	0.30	0.33	0.35
4Q	**E0.75**	**0.41**	0.54	0.43	0.31	0.43
Yr.	**E2.10**	**1.14**	**1.25**	0.90	1.12	1.39

Next earnings report expected: late October

Dividend Data (Dividends have been paid since 1977.)

Amount ($)	Date Decl.	Ex-Div. Date	Stock of Record	Payment Date
0.060	Feb. 24	Mar. 10	Mar. 12	Apr. 01 '98
2-for-1	May. 07	Jun. 02	May. 18	Jun. 01 '98
0.040	May. 07	Jun. 10	Jun. 12	Jul. 01 '98
0.040	Jul. 16	Sep. 09	Sep. 11	Oct. 01 '98

A Division of The McGraw-Hill Companies

Business Summary - 07-AUG-98

With its home sales nearly tripling since 1990, Pulte Corp. earned the distinction of being the largest U.S. homebuilder in 1997 (its third straight year in that position), based on its 15,322 unit sales during the year. The company operates in 28 states and 42 markets throughout the country, and also has operations in Mexico and Puerto Rico. Pulte targets buyers in almost all home categories, but has decided to concentrate its upcoming expansion in the affordable housing and mature buyer (age 50 and over) areas.

Pulte builds a wide variety of homes, with a focus on single-family detached homes, which account for about three-fourths of its unit volume. Sales prices for PHM's homes ranged from $45,000 to over $600,000 in 1997, but 77% fell within a range of $75,000 to $225,000; the average sales price totaled $162,000. PHM had 396 active communities at 1997 year-end (395 a year earlier). Pulte expanded its domestic operations through the July 1998 purchase of DiVosta and Co., a leading Florida builder (850 home sales in 1997 generated $134 million of revenues); and the May 1998 acquisition of Tennessee-based Radnor Homes.

The company normally designs its homes, with the construction then performed by subcontractors under supervision of PHM's on-site superintendents.

Pulte's consumer research has revealed a growing demand for reasonably priced entry-level housing, prompting the company to undertake a major expansion of its affordable housing effort. With mature age brackets expected to be the fastest growing segment of the U.S. population in coming years, PHM has also taken a leading position in active adult/retirement markets.

To assist its home sales effort, Pulte also offers mortgage banking services through its Pulte Mortgage (formerly ICM Mortgage) unit. Pulte Mortgage originates mortgage loans primarily for buyers of Pulte's homes, but also for the general public, and then sells the loans and servicing rights to outside investors.

Pulte entered the international arena through the formation of several joint ventures in Mexico in recent years. During 1996, PHM reached separate agreements with General Motors and Sony, which call for PHM to build a total of 8,000 homes for employees of those firms over a three-year period. In June 1998, Pulte formed a venture with Desarrollos Residenciales Turisticos, to construct 3,200 low- and medium-cost housing units in Central Mexico over the next 18 to 24 months. Pulte believes a prudent international diversification strategy can provide significant returns, and also act as a hedge against the cyclicality of its domestic business.

In August 1997, Pulte announced a strategic reorganization of operations, aimed at strengthening management's focus on key customer groups and generating increased operating efficiencies. Pulte recorded an after tax fourth quarter restructuring charge of $12.3 million ($0.28 a share, adjusted) for costs associated with the program. PHM sees its actions bringing $10 million of annualized cost savings starting in 1998.

Per Share Data ($)

(Year Ended Dec. 31)	1997	1996	1995	1994	1993	1992	1991	1990	1989	1988
Tangible Bk. Val.	19.11	17.82	14.08	12.94	10.10	8.78	7.21	6.71	6.04	4.72
Cash Flow	1.31	1.40	1.01	1.35	NM	NM	NM	NM	NM	NM
Earnings	1.14	1.26	0.90	1.12	1.39	1.33	0.85	0.59	1.05	0.63
Dividends	0.12	0.12	0.12	0.12	0.12	0.12	0.06	0.06	0.06	0.06
Payout Ratio	11%	10%	13%	11%	9%	9%	7%	10%	5%	10%
Prices - High	21¼	17⅜	17⅜	19⅜	20¾	15⅞	12⅝	6¼	9½	5¾
- Low	13⅝	12	10⅛	9⅛	11¾	8⅝	4⅝	3	4¾	3⅛
P/E Ratio - High	19	14	19	17	15	12	15	11	9	9
- Low	12	10	11	8	8	6	5	5	5	5

Income Statement Analysis (Million $)

	1997	1996	1995	1994	1993	1992	1991	1990	1989	1988
Revs.	2,524	2,384	2,029	1,756	1,633	1,370	1,214	1,152	1,149	1,179
Oper. Inc.	135	145	144	203	NA	NA	NA	NA	NA	NA
Depr.	7.8	6.8	6.3	13.2	NA	NA	NA	NA	NA	NA
Int. Exp.	26.6	53.3	73.0	96.6	NA	NA	NA	NA	NA	283
Pretax Inc.	81.0	102	82.0	104	113	77.9	44.9	31.6	51.7	43.4
Eff. Tax Rate	38%	38%	41%	40%	31%	7.30%	5.20%	6.00%	NM	24%
Net Inc.	49.8	63.2	48.8	62.4	77.8	72.2	42.6	29.7	55.8	33.2

Balance Sheet & Other Fin. Data (Million $)

	1997	1996	1995	1994	1993	1992	1991	1990	1989	1988
Cash	245	190	292	160	109	67.0	126	213	249	215
Curr. Assets	NA	NA	NA	NA	NA	NA	NA	NA	NA	NA
Total Assets	2,151	1,985	2,048	1,941	3,811	3,706	3,635	3,993	4,325	4,892
Curr. Liab.	NA	NA	NA	NA	NA	NA	NA	NA	NA	NA
LT Debt	584	436	589	563	876	1,202	1,751	2,220	2,536	2,810
Common Eqty.	813	829	761	711	556	481	357	316	306	255
Total Cap.	1,397	1,265	1,350	1,274	1,432	1,684	2,136	2,562	2,866	3,179
Cap. Exp.	Nil	Nil	Nil	Nil	NA	NA	NA	6.5	8.9	Nil
Cash Flow	57.6	70.0	55.2	75.6	NM	NM	NM	NM	NM	NM
Curr. Ratio	NA	NA	NA	NA	NA	NA	NA	NA	NA	NA
% LT Debt of Cap.	41.8	34.5	43.6	44.2	61.2	71.4	82.0	86.7	88.5	88.4
% Net Inc.of Revs.	2.0	2.7	2.4	3.6	4.8	5.3	3.5	2.6	4.9	2.8
% Ret. on Assets	2.4	3.2	2.4	2.2	2.1	1.9	1.1	0.7	1.3	0.7
% Ret. on Equity	6.1	8.0	6.6	9.9	15.0	16.5	12.4	9.9	20.5	13.3

Data as orig. reptd.; bef. results of disc. opers. and/or spec. items. Per share data adj. for stk. divs. as of ex-div. date. Bold denotes diluted EPS (FASB 128). E-Estimated. NA-Not Available. NM-Not Meaningful. NR-Not Ranked.

Office—33 Bloomfield Hills Pkwy., Suite 200, Bloomfield Hills, MI 48304. **Tel**—(248) 647-2750. **Website**—http://www.pulte.com **Chrmn**—W. J. Pulte. **Pres & CEO**—R. K. Burgess. **SVP & CFO**—R. A. Cregg.**VP & Investor Contact**—James P. Zeumer. **Dirs**—R. K. Burgess, D. Kelly-Ennis, D. W. McCammon, W. J. Pulte, R. L. Schlosstein, A. E. Schwartz, F. J. Sehn, J. J. Shea. **Transfer Agent & Registrar**—Boston EquiServe. **Incorporated**—in Delaware in 1969; reincorporated in Michigan in 1985. **Empl**— 4,300. **S&P Analyst:** Michael W. Jaffe

12-SEP-98

Industry: Foods

Summary: Quaker Oats is an international producer of brand name packaged food and beverage products.

S&P Opinion: Hold (★★★)	Recent Price • 54⅞	Yield • 2.1%
	52 Wk Range • 60⅜-42	12-Mo. P/E • 36.6

Earnings vs. Previous Year
▲=Up ▼=Down ►=No Change

Quantitative Evaluations

Outlook (1 Lowest—5 Highest)
• **1⁻**

Fair Value
• **36⅞**

Risk
• **Low**

Earn./Div. Rank
• **B**

Technical Eval.
• **Bearish** since 8/97

Rel. Strength Rank (1 Lowest—99 Highest)
• **89**

Insider Activity
• **Neutral**

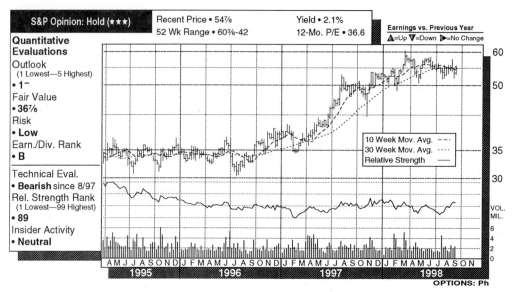

10 Week Mov. Avg. – – –
30 Week Mov. Avg. · · · · ·
Relative Strength ————

OPTIONS: Ph

Overview - 31-JUL-98

Net sales from ongoing operations in 1998 (adjusted mostly for the 1997 divestment of Snapple beverages and certain food service businesses) are projected to rise at a middle single-digit rate, paced primarily by unit volume growth for Gatorade and ready-to-eat cereals. Operating margins are expected to be relatively stable, as benefits realized from ongoing cost saving initiatives are largely offset by continued pricing pressures facing most of the company's diverse line of grocery items, particularly cereals. Cash flow, supplemented by a $240 million federal capital gains tax recovery and more than $70 million in proceeds from recent divestitures, should enable continued debt paydown and an acceleration in share repurchases. OAT has already repurchased 4.6 million common shares this year. We anticipate EPS of $2.22 in 1998, up 23% from 1997's $1.81 before nonrecurring items.

Valuation - 31-JUL-98

Despite the negative financial impact of the ill-fated Snapple acquisition over the past two years, Quaker's existing businesses remain healthy. Gatorade continues to post strong unit sales volume and profit trends, despite formidable competition from much larger rivals such as Coca-Cola and Pepsi-Cola Beverages. Food operations also continue to perform well despite intense competition in many of the markets in which OAT competes, particularly in the ready-to-eat cereal and pasta categories. In late 1997, Quaker appointed Robert Morrison as its new chairman and CEO, succeeding William Smithburg, who retired. S&P expects Mr. Morrison, a seasoned food executive (formerly at Kraft Foods), to extend Quaker's positive business trends through increased focus on core brands. The shares, which are valued (on a P/E basis) at about par with those of OAT's peers, are worthwhile holdings.

Key Stock Statistics

S&P EPS Est. 1998	2.22	Tang. Bk. Value/Share	NM
P/E on S&P Est. 1998	24.7	Beta	0.69
S&P EPS Est. 1999	2.50	Shareholders	29,700
Dividend Rate/Share	1.14	Market cap. (B)	$ 7.5
Shs. outstg. (M)	136.3	Inst. holdings	59%
Avg. daily vol. (M)	0.426		

Value of $10,000 invested 5 years ago: $ 20,132

Fiscal Year Ending Dec. 31

	1998	1997	1996	1995	1994	1993
Revenues (Million $)						
1Q	1,092	1,202	1,223	—	1,636	1,534
2Q	1,382	1,396	1,482	—	1,508	1,354
3Q	—	1,371	1,436	—	1,634	1,449
4Q	—	1,048	1,058	—	1,587	1,618
Yr.	—	5,016	5,199	2,733	6,365	5,955
Earnings Per Share ($)						
1Q	0.32	-8.15	0.23	—	0.45	0.66
2Q	0.40	0.57	0.47	—	0.25	0.32
3Q	—	0.58	0.98	—	2.73	0.54
4Q	—	0.20	0.12	—	2.75	0.17
Yr.	—	-6.80	1.80	0.09	6.00	1.68

Next earnings report expected: late October

Dividend Data (Dividends have been paid since 1906.)

Amount ($)	Date Decl.	Ex-Div. Date	Stock of Record	Payment Date
0.285	Mar. 11	Mar. 16	Mar. 18	Apr. 15 '98
0.285	May. 13	Jun. 17	Jun. 19	Jul. 15 '98
0.285	Sep. 09	Sep. 16	Sep. 18	Oct. 15 '98
0.285	Sep. 09	Sep. 16	Sep. 18	Oct. 15 '98

A Division of The **McGraw·Hill** *Companies*

Business Summary - 31-JUL-98

During 1997, Quaker Oats sold its beleaguered Snapple Beverage subsidiary at a substantial loss to Triarc Companies Inc., marking the end of the company's fruitless foray into the quirky "New Age" beverage category (OAT retained its Gatorade isotonic drink unit), and allowing it to better focus on managing its wide array of branded consumer food and beverage products. Sales and operating profit contributions (excluding special items) in 1997 were:

	Sales	Profits
Foods	68%	68%
Beverages	32%	32%

Food products include breakfast foods such as hot cereals (Quick and Old Fashioned Quaker Oats), ready-to-eat cereals (Cap'n Crunch, Life, 100% Natural, Oat Squares, Toasted Oatmeal); snacks (Quaker Chewy Granola and Quaker Rice Cakes); and rice and pasta foods (Rice-A-Roni, Pasta Roni, Near East). Beverage products consist of Gatorade brand isotonic sports drinks.

In 1997, OAT announced a plan to focus the company's management and other resources on its core businesses and growth in order to make the company more competitive. The plan included share repurchases and cost reduction programs, in addition to cost reductions resulting from the May 1997 sale of Snapple. The company is reviewing the sale of non-core businesses and the potential restructuring of certain international operations. The plan includes a goal of $30 million of cost reductions over an 18-month period (in addition to the costs related to the sale of Snapple). In 1997, earnings per share (excluding the $8.41 per share non-cash loss from the sale of Snapple, and restructuring charges of $0.27 per share) were $1.90, versus a comparable $1.34 in 1996. Separately, net financing costs declined to $89.9 million in 1997, down from $108.3 million in 1996; overall debt declined from $1.56 billion at the end of 1996 to $1.06 billion at the end of 1997.

Per Share Data ($)

(Year Ended Dec. 31)	1997	1996	1995	1994	1993	1992	1991	1990	1989	1988
Tangible Bk. Val.	NA	NM	NM	NM	-0.36	0.86	2.21	2.36	3.00	3.38
Cash Flow	-5.65	3.30	0.87	7.43	2.95	3.06	2.67	2.52	2.31	2.13
Earnings	-6.80	1.80	0.09	6.00	1.68	1.97	1.63	1.52	1.47	1.28
Dividends	1.14	1.14	1.14	1.96	1.06	0.96	0.86	0.78	0.70	0.60
Payout Ratio	NM	63%	NM	33%	63%	49%	52%	51%	47%	47%
Prices - High	55$^1/_8$	39$^1/_2$	37$^1/_2$	37$^1/_2$	42$^1/_2$	38$^1/_2$	37$^1/_4$	37$^7/_8$	29$^3/_4$	34$^1/_2$
- Low	34$^3/_8$	30$^3/_8$	30$^3/_8$	30$^3/_8$	29$^5/_8$	30$^1/_4$	25$^1/_8$	23$^1/_8$	20$^1/_2$	24$^7/_8$
P/E Ratio - High	NM	22	NM	6	25	20	23	25	20	27
- Low	NM	17	NM	5	18	15	15	16	14	19

Income Statement Analysis (Million $)

	1997	1996	1995	1994	1993	1992	1991	1990	1989	1988
Revs.	5,016	5,199	2,733	6,365	5,955	5,731	5,576	5,491	5,031	5,724
Oper. Inc.	673	612	229	571	774	724	702	659	622	700
Depr.	161	201	103	191	171	157	156	151	129	135
Int. Exp.	86.0	107	57.9	119	100	66.0	79.0	97.0	116	78.0
Pretax Inc.	-1,063	416	25.6	1,359	379	468	422	412	382	329
Eff. Tax Rate	NM	40%	47%	41%	39%	39%	41%	43%	40%	38%
Net Inc.	-930	248	13.7	806	232	287	248	236	229	203

Balance Sheet & Other Fin. Data (Million $)

	1997	1996	1995	1994	1993	1992	1991	1990	1989	1988
Cash	84.0	111	93.2	102	140	61.0	95.0	30.0	18.0	24.0
Curr. Assets	1,133	890	1,080	1,317	1,254	1,068	1,256	1,258	1,481	1,598
Total Assets	2,697	4,394	4,620	4,827	3,043	2,816	3,040	3,016	3,326	3,222
Curr. Liab.	946	1,355	1,702	1,813	1,259	1,105	1,055	927	1,139	902
LT Debt	888	993	1,052	1,103	760	633	689	701	740	767
Common Eqty.	150	1,230	1,079	1,129	446	551	752	807	919	1,037
Total Cap.	1,172	2,480	2,382	2,484	1,303	1,285	1,888	1,974	2,087	2,230
Cap. Exp.	216	243	145	276	185	187	176	241	276	298
Cash Flow	-773	445	11.7	994	399	440	400	383	353	338
Curr. Ratio	1.2	0.7	0.6	0.7	1.0	1.0	1.2	1.4	1.3	1.8
% LT Debt of Cap.	75.7	40.0	44.2	44.4	58.3	49.2	36.5	35.5	35.5	34.4
% Net Inc.of Revs.	NM	4.8	0.6	12.7	3.9	5.0	4.4	4.3	4.6	3.5
% Ret. on Assets	NM	5.5	NA	20.0	8.0	10.1	8.3	7.4	7.1	6.6
% Ret. on Equity	NM	21.1	NA	101.9	46.6	41.9	31.9	26.7	23.4	17.8

Data as orig. reptd.; bef. results of disc. opers. and/or spec. items. Per share data adj. for stk. divs. as of ex-div. date. Yrs. ended Jun. 30 of fol. cal. yr. prior to 1995 (six mos.). E-Estimated. NA-Not Available. NM-Not Meaningful. NR-Not Ranked.

Office—Quaker Tower, 321 North Clark St., Chicago, IL 60610.**Tel**—(312) 222-7111. **Website**—http://www.quakeroats.com **Chrmn, Pres & CEO**—R. S. Morrison. **SVP & CFO**—R. S. Thomason. **VP-Investor Contact**—Margaret M. Eichman. **Dirs**—F. C. Carlucci, S. C. Cathcart, K. I. Chenault, J. H. Costello, J. C. Lewent, J. M. Losh, V. R. Loucks, Jr., T. C. MacAvoy, R. S. Morrison, W. J. Salmon, W. L. Weiss. **Transfer Agent & Registrar**—Harris Trust & Savings Bank, Chicago. **Incorporated**—in New Jersey in 1901. **Empl**— 14,123. **S&P Analyst:** Richard Joy

Ralston Purina

1892K

NYSE Symbol **RAL**

In S&P 500

12-SEP-98

Industry:
Foods

Summary: This company is the world's largest producer of dry dog and cat foods (Purina), and of dry-cell battery products (Eveready, Energizer).

S&P Opinion: Accumulate (★★★★)	Recent Price • 28¾	Yield • 1.4%
	52 Wk Range • 39⅛-26	12-Mo. P/E • 8.4

Quantitative Evaluations

Outlook
(1 Lowest—5 Highest)
• **3**

Fair Value
• **28½**

Risk
• **Low**

Earn./Div. Rank
• **B+**

Technical Eval.
• **Bearish** since 10/96

Rel. Strength Rank
(1 Lowest—99 Highest)
• **70**

Insider Activity
• **NA**

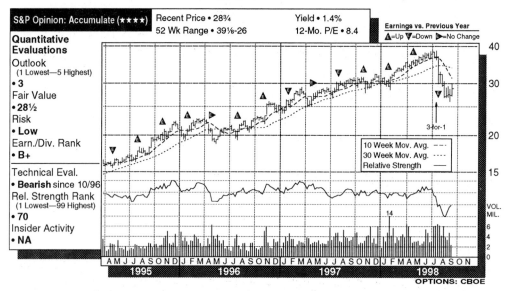

Earnings vs. Previous Year
▲=Up ▼=Down ▶=No Change

10 Week Mov. Avg. ---
30 Week Mov. Avg. ····
Relative Strength —

3-for-1

OPTIONS: CBOE

Overview - 04-AUG-98

Pet food profits in FY 98 (Sep.) are expected to advance approximately 5%, benefiting from higher volume, the inclusion of acquisitions, and possibly from lower ingredient costs (soybeans, corn). Battery division profits should rise modestly in the near term, as increased worldwide alkaline unit volume and higher selling prices may be further offset by difficult market conditions and currency devaluations in Asia Pacific markets. Including special gains of $0.16 a share (reflecting the sale of a portion of RAL's holding of IBC stock, and capital loss tax benefits), as well as a restructuring charge of $0.13 a share, we estimate EPS from continuing operations will reach $1.17 in FY 98, up 6% from FY 97's $1.10. Results in each year exclude extraordinary gains arising from the sale of discontinued businesses; in FY 98, this amounted to $2.14 a share.

Valuation - 04-AUG-98

The shares have been average performers since mid-1994, supported by positive, albeit moderate, earnings uptrends, and by expectations of a value-enhancing spinoff of Eveready. S&P believes that a possible spinoff of Eveready (worth about $18 per RAL share) would value RAL near $38 to $42. Future pet product profits should be supported by increased industry selling prices and rising U.S. pet ownership rates. Eveready prospects are bolstered by increasing global consumer usage of battery products. We believe that the shares may modestly outperform the overall market over the next 12 months, driven both by improved earnings growth momentum and by a higher P/E valuation accorded the stock because of the growing chance of a value-enhancing spinoff of Eveready. These factors should allow the shares to continue trading at a modest premium to the P/E of the S&P 500.

Key Stock Statistics

S&P EPS Est. 1998	1.17	Tang. Bk. Value/Share	4.66
P/E on S&P Est. 1998	24.6	Beta	0.96
S&P EPS Est. 1999	1.32	Shareholders	21,600
Dividend Rate/Share	0.40	Market cap. (B)	$ 9.0
Shs. outstg. (M)	312.2	Inst. holdings	55%
Avg. daily vol. (M)	0.808		

Value of $10,000 invested 5 years ago: NA

Fiscal Year Ending Sep. 30

	1998	1997	1996	1995	1994	1993
Revenues (Million $)						
1Q	1,317	1,261	1,639	1,992	1,724	1,691
2Q	1,111	1,048	1,432	1,752	1,507	1,417
3Q	1,073	1,042	1,479	1,860	1,223	1,360
4Q	—	1,136	1,564	1,607	1,304	1,448
Yr.	—	4,487	6,114	7,210	5,759	5,915
Earnings Per Share ($)						
1Q	**0.41**	0.36	0.41	0.34	0.42	0.27
2Q	**0.26**	0.18	0.18	0.18	0.23	0.24
3Q	**0.18**	0.25	0.26	0.21	0.15	0.16
4Q	—	0.30	0.28	0.25	-0.10	0.17
Yr.	—	1.10	1.14	0.92	0.71	0.85

Next earnings report expected: early December

Dividend Data (Dividends have been paid since 1934.)

Amount ($)	Date Decl.	Ex-Div. Date	Stock of Record	Payment Date
Stk.	—	Apr. 01	Apr. 01	Apr. 01 '98
0.300	Mar. 19	May. 14	May. 18	Jun. 05 '98
3-for-1	May. 28	Jul. 16	Jun. 22	Jul. 15 '98
0.100	May. 28	Aug. 20	Aug. 24	Sep. 11 '98

A Division of The McGraw-Hill Companies

Business Summary - 04-AUG-98

Incorporated in 1894 as an agricultural products company, Ralston Purina Company has in recent years evolved from a diversified conglomerate to one with significantly greater business focus. Since 1994, the company has spun off various businesses (ready to eat cereal, baby food, ski resorts, soy protein, agricultural products), and has positioned itself as a company engaged predominantly in two promising consumer businesses: the production of pet food and related products, and the manufacture of dry cell battery products. RAL derived its FY 97 (Sep.) sales and operating profits as follows:

	Sales	Profits
Pet products	51%	54%
Battery products	49%	46%

The pet products segment produces and sells dog and cat foods under the Purina name, including Dog Chow, Cat Chow, and numerous other dog and cat food brands. The division also makes and sells cat box filler and related products under the Golden Cat name. RAL operates 26 manufacturing facilities in the U.S. and abroad. Long-term pet food industry growth is supported by economic growth and social stability in the U.S. and abroad, which fosters pet ownership rates.

The battery products segment manufactures and sells primary batteries, rechargeable batteries, and battery-powered lighting products in the U.S. and worldwide, principally under the trademarks Eveready and Energizer. Battery products are manufactured in 28 facilities in the U.S. and abroad. Long-term battery product industry growth is supported by the proliferation of portable electronic products around the world that require energy sources.

In December 1997, RAL sold its Protein Technologies International subsidiary and related affiliates to DuPont Co., for $1.5 billion in DuPont stock and the assumption of certain liabilities.

In April 1998, RAL spun off to shareholders its agricultural products segment, which produces Chow brand formula feeds and animal health products in 62 facilities outside the U.S.

In July 1995, RAL sold its Continental Baking Co. subsidiary, which is engaged in the fresh bakery products business, to Interstate Bakeries Corp. (IBC). RAL retained a 45% stake immediately following the sale. As of early May 1998, RAL still held directly or indirectly approximately 31 million IBC shares, or an approximate 42% stake.

Per Share Data ($)

(Year Ended Sep. 30)	1997	1996	1995	1994	1993	1992	1991	1990	1989	1988
Tangible Bk. Val.	0.73	-0.29	-0.98	-0.55	-0.52	-1.36	-0.30	-1.13	-0.51	1.53
Cash Flow	1.72	1.75	1.95	1.87	1.47	1.74	1.78	1.66	1.38	1.33
Earnings	1.25	1.14	0.92	0.71	0.85	0.94	1.11	1.08	0.89	0.88
Dividends	0.40	0.40	0.40	0.40	0.40	0.40	0.35	0.30	0.27	0.24
Payout Ratio	36%	35%	43%	57%	47%	43%	31%	27%	29%	27%
Prices - High	32¼	26	21¼	15½	17⅜	19⅝	20	18	16⅞	14¾
- Low	23¾	18⅝	14½	11⅛	11⅛	13⅝	15⅜	13	13⅛	10⅝
P/E Ratio - High	29	23	23	22	22	21	18	17	19	17
- Low	22	16	16	16	15	14	14	12	15	12

Income Statement Analysis (Million $)

	1997	1996	1995	1994	1993	1992	1991	1990	1989	1988
Revs.	4,487	6,114	7,210	5,759	5,915	7,752	7,376	7,101	6,658	5,876
Oper. Inc.	828	1,023	1,041	946	939	1,068	1,109	1,084	980	991
Depr.	189	237	290	190	192	255	221	204	188	185
Int. Exp.	174	190	200	191	211	243	209	208	218	219
Pretax Inc.	419	562	515	451	502	542	648	655	576	606
Eff. Tax Rate	17%	38%	42%	49%	43%	41%	40%	40%	39%	40%
Net Inc.	349	362	300	231	284	321	392	396	351	363

Balance Sheet & Other Fin. Data (Million $)

	1997	1996	1995	1994	1993	1992	1991	1990	1989	1988
Cash	109	62.0	44.0	112	57.0	60.0	158	112	381	361
Curr. Assets	1,506	1,873	1,763	1,662	1,621	1,780	1,676	1,587	1,821	1,695
Total Assets	4,742	4,785	4,567	3,791	4,294	5,151	4,632	4,395	4,382	4,044
Curr. Liab.	1,216	1,896	1,741	1,520	1,370	1,745	1,194	1,340	1,316	1,082
LT Debt	1,860	1,437	1,602	1,252	1,732	2,111	2,071	1,961	1,791	1,487
Common Eqty.	854	578	494	340	436	655	784	585	832	1,090
Total Cap.	3,018	2,389	2,376	1,902	2,553	3,133	3,180	2,809	2,833	2,742
Cap. Exp.	283	314	285	267	291	376	404	470	264	303
Cash Flow	525	537	590	402	456	554	592	580	526	549
Curr. Ratio	1.2	1.0	1.0	1.1	1.2	1.0	1.4	1.2	1.4	1.6
% LT Debt of Cap.	40.3	60.1	67.5	65.8	67.8	67.4	65.1	69.8	63.2	54.2
% Net Inc.of Revs.	7.8	5.9	4.2	4.0	4.8	4.1	5.3	5.6	5.3	6.2
% Ret. on Assets	7.3	6.4	6.6	5.6	NA	6.8	8.7	9.5	8.8	9.3
% Ret. on Equity	46.9	51.7	66.2	54.1	NA	43.1	54.4	56.2	37.5	35.7

Data as orig. reptd.; bef. results of disc. opers. and/or spec. items. Per share data adj. for stk. divs. as of ex-div. date. Fiscal 1997 3Q EPS are for 9 mos. E-Estimated. NA-Not Available. NM-Not Meaningful. NR-Not Ranked.

Registrar—Boatmen's Trust Co., St. Louis. **Office**—Checkerboard Square, St. Louis, MO 63164-0001. **Tel**—(314) 982-1000. **Website**—http:// www.ralston.com **Chrmn**—W. P. Stiritz. **Co-CEO**—W. P. McGinnis. **Investor Contact**—Michael Grabel. **Dirs**—D. R. Banks, J. H. Biggs, D. Danforth, Jr., W. H. Danforth, D. C. Farrell, M. D. Ingram, R. A. Liddy, J. F. McDonnell, W. P. McGinnis, J. P. Mulcahy, K. D. Ortega, W. P. Stiritz. **Transfer Agent & Registrar**—Co.'s office; St. Louis. **Incorporated**—in Missouri in 1894. **Empl**—29,273. **S&P Analyst:** Richard Joy

Raychem Corp. 1895

NYSE Symbol **RYC**

In S&P 500

12-SEP-98

Industry: Electrical Equipment

Summary: Raychem primarily produces high-performance plastic and elastomer products and systems for customers in several industries.

S&P Opinion: Hold (★★★)	Recent Price • 29½	Yield • 1.1%
	52 Wk Range • 48½-28¼	12-Mo. P/E • 14.3

Quantitative Evaluations

Outlook
(1 Lowest—5 Highest)
• **4+**

Fair Value
• **39⅜**

Risk
• **Average**

Earn./Div. Rank
• **B-**

Technical Eval.
• **Bullish** since 8/98

Rel. Strength Rank
(1 Lowest—99 Highest)
• **70**

Insider Activity
• **Neutral**

Earnings vs. Previous Year
▲=Up ▼=Down ▶=No Change

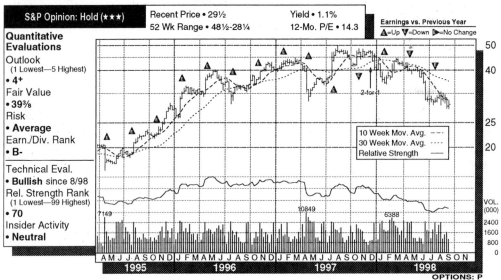

10 Week Mov. Avg. – – –
30 Week Mov. Avg. ·····
Relative Strength ——

2-for-1

7149   10849   6388

VOL. (000)
2400
1600
800
0

A M J J A S O N D | J F M A M J J A S O N D | J F M A M J J A S O N D | J F M A M J J A S O N
1995 | 1996 | 1997 | 1998

OPTIONS: P

Overview - 24-JUL-98

Revenue growth in FY 98 (Jun.) was restricted by the Asian economic crisis, decreased sales of heat tracing products and a decline in worldwide demand for electronic components. These issues should continue to hurt results in the first half of FY 99, with revenue growth projected in the mid-single digits. Gross margins should continue to be impacted by rising Miniplex sales which carry a lower gross margin than the company has historically seen. However, operating margins have benefited from restructuring activities undertaken in the past two years which have led to cost savings and higher operating efficiencies. Slightly offsetting the operating profit improvement and of some concern is the higher expected tax rate, which should rise to about 35% in FY 99. The shares are bolstered by a share repurchase program, under which RYC bought back 1.3 million shares during the fourth quarter of FY 98.

Valuation - 24-JUL-98

RYC reported EPS of $0.26 in the fourth quarter of FY 98 (Jun.), in line with recently reduced street estimates. Revenues declined 7%, year to year, reflecting a continued slowdown in Asia, where RYC gets about 20% of total revenues, and slowing sales within the electronics industry. We expect Asia to continue to affect results in the first half of FY 99, and also anticipate that near-term results will be impacted by gross margin pressures and a higher effective tax rate, as RYC's operating loss carryforwards are depleted. However, results should improve in the second half of FY 99, with growth strengthening in several product lines. Currently trading at 13X our FY 99 EPS estimate of $2.35, we expect the stock to perform in line with the market over the near term. Longer term, the shares will benefit from RYC's diverse product line, good management and growing backlog.

Key Stock Statistics

S&P EPS Est. 1999	2.35	Tang. Bk. Value/Share	9.81
P/E on S&P Est. 1999	12.6	Beta	0.75
S&P EPS Est. 2000	2.75	Shareholders	6,300
Dividend Rate/Share	0.32	Market cap. (B)	$ 2.5
Shs. outstg. (M)	83.8	Inst. holdings	81%
Avg. daily vol. (M)	0.283		

Value of $10,000 invested 5 years ago: $ 14,880

Fiscal Year Ending Jun. 30

	1998	1997	1996	1995	1994	1993
Revenues (Million $)						
1Q	455.0	430.3	410.5	368.1	355.4	348.0
2Q	467.1	441.1	411.1	382.5	353.8	352.0
3Q	445.2	427.9	417.8	368.8	361.3	324.0
4Q	431.1	465.5	432.2	411.1	391.0	361.1
Yr.	1,798	1,765	1,672	1,531	1,462	1,386
Earnings Per Share ($)						
1Q	0.70	0.79	0.36	-0.56	0.08	0.05
2Q	**0.64**	0.57	0.28	0.23	0.02	0.04
3Q	**0.46**	0.74	0.45	0.13	0.01	0.01
4Q	**0.26**	0.67	0.53	-0.05	-0.09	0.01
Yr.	**2.07**	2.77	1.61	-0.24	0.02	0.10

Next earnings report expected: mid October

Dividend Data (Dividends have been paid since 1977.)

Amount ($)	Date Decl.	Ex-Div. Date	Stock of Record	Payment Date
2-for-1	Aug. 15	Dec. 04	Nov. 17	Dec. 03 '97
0.080	Jan. 15	Feb. 09	Feb. 11	Mar. 11 '98
0.080	Apr. 15	May. 11	May. 13	Jun. 10 '98
0.080	Jul. 15	Aug. 10	Aug. 12	Sep. 09 '98

A Division of The **McGraw·Hill** *Companies*

Business Summary - 24-JUL-98

Raychem (RYC), whose name is derived from radiation chemistry, manufactures a wide variety of high-performance products based on materials science for customers in several industries. The company, founded in 1957, has built its reputation and knowledge base from years of experience by providing its customers with new and innovative products. In fact, as of June 30, 1997, RYC had in force 831 U.S. patents and 3,469 foreign patents, and had pending 255 domestic patent applications and 3,158 applications in foreign markets. The company is a large international player; overseas sales contributed about 63% of FY 97 (Jun.) revenues and accounted for 63% of operating profits.

The electronics OEM segment is RYC's largest division and represented 43% of FY 97 revenues and about 43% of operating profits. The unit produces electrical and electronic interconnection systems, wire and cable, heat-shrinkable insulation, circuit protection devices, gel protection components, identification systems, computer touchscreens, liquid crystal displays, and electromagnetic protection products for the electronics, transportation, aerospace and defense markets.

The next largest business is the telecommunications and energy networks segment which supplies a wide variety of products for telephone, electric utilities, industrial and cable companies, including fiber-optic cable systems and accessories, digital subscriber line mul-

tiplexing systems, wireless products, gel sealing products and coaxial cable connectors and accessories. This unit provided 43% of revenues and 42% of operating profits.

The final segment is the commercial and industrial division, which provided about 14% of FY 97 sales and accounted for 15% of operating profits. This segment consists of industrial process temperature maintenance systems, freeze protection systems, leak detection systems, monitoring and control systems, pipeline protection sleeves and coatings and cathodic protection systems.

Reflecting a slowdown in Asia and reduced demand for electronic components, RYC took a $28 million restructuring charge in the fourth quarter of FY 98, to cover consolidation of its newly merged telecom, energy and industrial segment, severance charges and equipment writeoffs. A $44 million restructuring charge was posted in FY 96 and a $53 million restructuring charge was taken in FY 97's third quarter, both of which included writedowns and severance charges related to employee reductions. Also included in the FY 96 charges was $2.1 million associated with the reorganization of the Ericsson Raynet joint venture. Since January 1996, RYC's interest in the joint venture is accounted for using the cost basis of accounting, and RYC no longer shares in the operating losses of the venture.

Per Share Data ($)

(Year Ended Jun. 30)	1998	1997	1996	1995	1994	1993	1992	1991	1990	1989
Tangible Bk. Val.	NA	9.84	9.39	8.59	8.52	8.23	8.88	8.53	9.48	10.42
Cash Flow	NA	3.63	2.48	0.61	1.01	1.01	0.79	0.76	-0.57	1.50
Earnings	2.07	2.77	1.61	-0.24	0.02	0.10	-0.21	-0.32	-1.56	0.52
Dividends	0.30	0.28	0.18	0.16	0.16	0.16	0.16	0.16	0.16	0.15
Payout Ratio	14%	10%	11%	NM	NM	168%	NM	NM	NM	29%
Prices - High	44⅝	50	43¼	29⅞	21¼	23⅜	22½	18½	17¾	19⅝
- Low	29¼	30¼	26	16¼	16¼	17⅛	15	10⅝	7⅞	14⅝
P/E Ratio - High	22	18	27	NM	NM	NM	NM	NM	NM	38
- Low	14	11	16	NM	NM	NM	NM	NM	NM	28

Income Statement Analysis (Million $)

	1998	1997	1996	1995	1994	1993	1992	1991	1990	1989
Revs.	NA	1,765	1,672	1,531	1,462	1,386	1,296	1,250	1,115	1,083
Oper. Inc.	NA	350	305	233	140	161	126	108	82.0	132
Depr.	NA	78.6	79.4	75.0	86.2	77.9	78.1	79.5	70.2	68.3
Int. Exp.	NA	12.1	19.0	20.0	22.0	27.0	28.4	28.1	21.0	20.5
Pretax Inc.	NA	228	146	-0.3	34.0	40.0	21.0	-3.0	-86.0	64.0
Eff. Tax Rate	NA	NM	NM	NM	95%	80%	180%	NM	NM	43%
Net Inc.	NA	253	148	-21.0	2.0	8.0	-17.0	-23.0	-110	36.0

Balance Sheet & Other Fin. Data (Million $)

	1998	1997	1996	1995	1994	1993	1992	1991	1990	1989
Cash	NA	86.6	224	118	78.0	134	149	99	137	153
Curr. Assets	NA	806	908	780	736	715	776	660	724	673
Total Assets	NA	1,509	1,551	1,455	1,399	1,332	1,393	1,235	1,271	1,173
Curr. Liab.	NA	380	451	303	324	315	335	259	456	315
LT Debt	NA	164	148	264	245	234	230	233	31.0	29.0
Common Eqty.	NA	845	841	750	733	690	715	652	690	734
Total Cap.	NA	1,044	1,019	1,053	1,009	955	1,005	937	776	816
Cap. Exp.	NA	90.5	78.6	94.0	104	90.0	93.0	137	115	101
Cash Flow	NA	332	227	54.0	88.0	86.0	61.0	56.0	-41.0	105
Curr. Ratio	NA	2.1	2.0	2.6	2.3	2.3	2.3	2.6	1.6	2.1
% LT Debt of Cap.	NA	15.7	14.5	25.1	24.2	24.5	22.9	24.9	4.0	3.6
% Net Inc.of Revs.	NA	14.4	8.9	NM	0.1	0.6	NM	NM	NM	3.4
% Ret. on Assets	NA	16.6	9.9	NM	0.1	0.6	NM	NM	NM	3.2
% Ret. on Equity	NA	30.0	18.6	NM	0.2	1.1	NM	NM	NM	5.1

Data as orig. reptd.; bef. results of disc. opers. and/or spec. items. Per share data adj. for stk. divs. as of ex-div. date. Bold denotes diluted EPS (FASB 128). E-Estimated. NA-Not Available. NM-Not Meaningful. NR-Not Ranked.

Office—300 Constitution Dr., Menlo Park, CA 94025-1164. **Tel**—(415) 361-4180. **Website**—http://www.raychem.com **Chrmn, Pres & CEO**—R. A. Kashnow. **SVP & CFO**—R. J. Simms. **VP & Secy**—K. Cottle. **Investor Contact**—Scott F. Wylie (415-361-7855). **Dirs**—R. Dulude, J. F. Gibbons, R. A. Kashnow, J. P. McTague, D. O. Morton, I. Stein, C. Tien, C. J. Yansouni. **Transfer Agent & Registrar**—Harris Trust & Savings Bank, Chicago. **Incorporated**—in California in 1957; reincorporated in Delaware in 1987. **Empl**— 9,036. **S&P Analyst:** Jim Corridore

STANDARD &POOR'S
STOCK REPORTS
Raytheon Co.
1900
NYSE Symbol **RTN.B**
In S&P 500

12-SEP-98 | **Industry:** Electronics (Defense)

Summary: One of the leading defense companies, Raytheon also produces aircraft and is a major engineering and construction services contractor.

S&P Opinion: Accumulate (★★★★)	Recent Price • 45¼	Yield • 1.8%
	52 Wk Range • 60¾-40⅝	12-Mo. P/E • 23.3

Quantitative Evaluations

Outlook
(1 Lowest—5 Highest)
• **NA**

Fair Value
• **NA**

Risk
• **Low**

Earn./Div. Rank
• **A+**

Technical Eval.
• **NA**

Rel. Strength Rank
(1 Lowest—99 Highest)
• **55**

Insider Activity
• **NA**

Earnings vs. Previous Year
▲=Up ▼=Down ▶=No Change

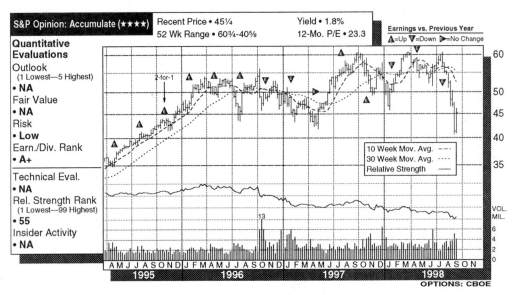

10 Week Mov. Avg. ---
30 Week Mov. Avg. ····
Relative Strength ——

OPTIONS: CBOE

Overview - 27-JUL-98

Following two major recent acquisitions and several divestitures, RTN's transition to a defense and engineering concern is nearly complete. The acquisitions reflect its aim to be a leading player in the consolidating defense industry. With the mergers complete, RTN recorded a pretax charge of $495 million in the fourth quarter of 1997, including $340 million for restructuring and melding the defense operations. Most of the remaining charge was for a 10% workforce reduction at the engineering and construction segment. Most of the costs related to the defense segment restructuring will subsequently be recovered from the U.S. government, which reimburses military contractors as cost savings are realized from mergers. The defense business formed by Raytheon is a strong competitor in missiles, surveillance and electronic warfare. Overall, Raytheon entered 1998 with a backlog of $21.3 billion, including a U.S. government backlog of $12.5 billion and an engineering backlog of $3.3 billion. RTN remains an important force in general aviation and business jets.

Valuation - 27-JUL-98

We continue our accumulate recommendation on RTN. The acquisition of the Texas Instruments and Hughes defense businesses completed RTN's plan to create a business with sufficient critical mass to compete in the consolidating defense industry. Raytheon's evolution included the divestiture of the commercial appliance business, which the company sold in May 1998 for $1.2 billion, as well as the consumer appliance business, which RTN sold in 1997. The shares continue to trade at a P/E discount to RTN's peers and the S&P 500 Index.

Key Stock Statistics

S&P EPS Est. 1998	3.55	Tang. Bk. Value/Share	NM
P/E on S&P Est. 1998	12.7	Beta	0.95
S&P EPS Est. 1999	4.10	Shareholders	21,200
Dividend Rate/Share	0.80	Market cap. (B)	$ 10.7
Shs. outstg. (M)	338.8	Inst. holdings	45%
Avg. daily vol. (M)	0.852		

Value of $10,000 invested 5 years ago: $ 19,599

Fiscal Year Ending Dec. 31

	1998	1997	1996	1995	1994	1993
Revenues (Million $)						
1Q	4,574	2,899	2,788	2,387	2,315	2,204
2Q	5,078	3,325	3,127	2,816	2,527	2,258
3Q	—	3,445	3,032	3,153	2,443	2,223
4Q	—	4,004	3,384	3,360	2,729	2,517
Yr.	—	13,673	12,331	11,716	10,013	9,201
Earnings Per Share ($)						
1Q	**0.63**	0.78	0.78	0.70	0.03	0.58
2Q	**0.79**	0.89	0.88	0.80	0.71	0.66
3Q	**E1.05**	0.89	0.80	0.82	0.72	0.63
4Q	**E1.08**	-0.31	0.75	0.92	0.81	0.69
Yr.	**E3.55**	2.18	3.21	3.25	2.25	2.56

Next earnings report expected: mid October

Dividend Data (Dividends have been paid since 1998.)

Amount ($)	Date Decl.	Ex-Div. Date	Stock of Record	Payment Date
0.200	Sep. 24	Oct. 02	Oct. 06	Oct. 27 '97
0.200	Dec. 22	Dec. 24	Dec. 29	Jan. 26 '98
0.200	Mar. 25	Mar. 31	Apr. 02	Apr. 30 '98
0.200	Jun. 24	Jun. 30	Jul. 02	Jul. 31 '98

STANDARD
&POOR'S
STOCK REPORTS

Raytheon Company

1900

12-SEP-98

Business Summary - 27-JUL-98

Following the end of the Cold War in the early 1990s, the U.S. government initiated large military spending cutbacks, which led to the subsequent consolidation of the U.S. defense industry. Raytheon capitalized on industry consolidation by acquiring several large defense businesses. Following Raytheon's latest acquisitions, the 1997 purchases of Texas Instruments' and Hughes' defense operations, Raytheon is now the third largest U.S. military contractor. Some important profitability statistics from recent years:

	1997	1996	1995
Gross profit margins	23%	21%	22%
Operating profit margins	7.9%	9.7%	9.3%
Free cash flow per share	$17.18	$5.95	$4.16

RTN derives 45% of revenues from sales to the U.S. government (principally to the U.S. Defense Department) and 30% of revenues from overseas customers.

Raytheon's electronics segment (60% of revenues) makes sophisticated electronic equipment for both the military and commercial markets. Defense electronics produces ground-based and airborne missiles (including Patriot, Hawk, Sidewinder, Sparrow, Stinger, AMRAAM, Standard and Maverick), radar systems, reconnaissance, surveillance and intelligence systems, electronic countermeasures, guidance and fire control systems, sonar, communications equipment and microwave components. Commercial electronics products are used in environmental monitoring, communications, air traffic control and transportation systems. In 1997, the electronics segment posted 14% operating profit margins.

RTN's engineering & construction (E&C) segment (20% of revenues) is one of the world's largest engineering, construction, operations and maintenance firms, undertaking responsibility for a wide variety of infrastructure, power and industrial projects. It also produces paving and mixing equipment and provides technical services and operations. In 1997, E&C generated operating profit margins of about 6%.

Raytheon's aircraft segment (20% of revenues) consists of Beech Aircraft, a leading manufacturer of general aviation aircraft, and Raytheon Corporate Jets, which makes the Hawker 800 and 1000 medium-size business jets. The segment also produces military training aircraft. In 1997, this segment posted 10% operating profit margins.

Per Share Data ($)

(Year Ended Dec. 31)	1997	1996	1995	1994	1993	1992	1991	1990	1989	1988
Tangible Bk. Val.	NM	6.44	7.26	12.92	13.97	13.95	12.15	10.28	8.85	7.93
Cash Flow	4.07	4.77	4.77	3.29	3.62	3.48	3.40	3.29	3.07	2.81
Earnings	2.20	3.21	3.25	2.25	2.56	2.36	2.24	2.13	2.00	1.84
Dividends	0.80	0.79	0.75	0.72	0.53	0.66	0.61	0.60	0.55	0.50
Payout Ratio	36%	25%	23%	32%	21%	28%	28%	28%	27%	27%
Prices - High	60½	56⅛	47¼	34½	34¼	26¾	22⅛	17⅞	21¼	18½
- Low	41¾	43⅜	31½	30¼	25¼	20⅜	16½	14½	16⅛	15¼
P/E Ratio - High	28	17	15	15	13	11	10	8	11	10
- Low	19	14	10	13	10	9	7	7	8	8

Income Statement Analysis (Million $)

Revs.	13,673	12,331	11,716	10,013	9,201	9,058	9,274	9,268	8,796	8,192
Oper. Inc.	2,036	1,602	1,584	1,353	1,207	1,196	1,128	1,102	1,027	900
Depr.	457	369	371	275	287	302	306	304	282	259
Int. Exp.	397	256	197	49.0	32.0	48.0	92.0	114	113	63.0
Pretax Inc.	790	1,083	1,192	900	1,047	956	873	837	758	706
Eff. Tax Rate	33%	30%	34%	34%	34%	34%	32%	33%	30%	31%
Net Inc.	527	761	792	597	693	635	592	557	529	490

Balance Sheet & Other Fin. Data (Million $)

Cash	296	139	210	202	190	89.0	138	138	99	108
Curr. Assets	9,233	5,604	5,275	4,985	4,609	3,776	3,748	3,603	3,104	2,844
Total Assets	28,598	11,126	9,841	7,395	7,258	6,015	6,087	6,119	5,338	4,740
Curr. Liab.	11,886	4,692	3,690	3,283	2,910	2,137	2,716	3,146	2,822	2,577
LT Debt	4,406	1,500	1,488	24.5	24.4	25.3	39.3	46.4	46.0	41.3
Common Eqty.	10,425	4,598	4,292	3,928	4,298	3,843	3,323	2,847	2,426	2,121
Total Cap.	15,617	6,098	5,780	3,953	4,322	3,869	3,363	2,893	2,472	2,162
Cap. Exp.	459	406	329	267	310	308	349	391	414	421
Cash Flow	984	1,130	1,163	872	980	937	898	861	810	749
Curr. Ratio	0.8	1.2	1.4	1.5	1.6	1.8	1.4	1.1	1.1	1.1
% LT Debt of Cap.	28.2	24.6	25.8	0.6	0.6	0.7	1.2	1.6	1.9	1.9
% Net Inc.of Revs.	3.9	6.2	6.8	6.0	7.5	7.0	6.4	6.0	6.0	6.0
% Ret. on Assets	2.7	7.3	9.2	8.5	10.5	10.4	9.6	9.7	10.6	11.2
% Ret. on Equity	7.0	17.2	19.3	15.2	17.1	17.6	19.0	21.2	23.4	24.9

Data as orig. reptd.; bef. results of disc. opers. and/or spec. items. Per share data adj. for stk. divs. as of ex-div. date. Bold denotes diluted EPS (FASB 128). E-Estimated. NA-Not Available. NM-Not Meaningful. NR-Not Ranked. Free cash flow: Net income plus depreciation/ amortization and decreases in working capital, less net capital expenditures, increases in working capital and preferred dividends.

Office—141 Spring St., Lexington, MA 02173. **Tel**—(781) 862-6600. **Website**—http://www.raytheon.com **Chrmn & CEO**—D. J. Picard. **CFO**—P. D'Angelo. **Treas**—H. Deitcher. **Secy**—C. L. Hoffmann.**Investor Contact**—Barbara L. Gasper (781-860-2303).**Dirs**—F. Colloredo-Mansfeld, S. D. Dorfman, T. L. Eliot, Jr., T. E. Everhart, J. R. Galvin, B. B. Hauptfuhrer, R. D. Hill, L. D. Kozlowski, J. N. Land, Jr., A. L. Lawson, C. H. Noski, T. L. Phillips, D. J. Picard, W. B. Rudman, A. M. Zeien. **Transfer Agent & Registrar**—Boston EquiServe, Boston. **Incorporated**—in Delaware in 1928. **Empl**— 118,200. **S&P Analyst:** Robert E. Friedman, CPA

STANDARD &POOR'S
STOCK REPORTS

Reebok International
1906F

NYSE Symbol **RBK**

In S&P 500

12-SEP-98 | Industry: Footwear

Summary: Reebok is a leading producer of athletic footwear and apparel sold in the U.S. and overseas.

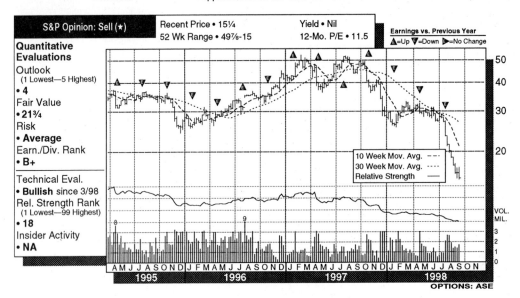

S&P Opinion: Sell (★)	Recent Price • 15¼	Yield • Nil
	52 Wk Range • 49⅞-15	12-Mo. P/E • 11.5

Earnings vs. Previous Year
▲=Up ▼=Down ▶=No Change

Quantitative Evaluations

Outlook (1 Lowest—5 Highest)
• **4**

Fair Value
• **21¾**

Risk
• **Average**

Earn./Div. Rank
• **B+**

Technical Eval.
• **Bullish** since 3/98

Rel. Strength Rank (1 Lowest—99 Highest)
• **18**

Insider Activity
• **NA**

10 Week Mov. Avg. - - -
30 Week Mov. Avg. ·····
Relative Strength ——

VOL. MIL.

1995 | 1996 | 1997 | 1998

OPTIONS: ASE

Overview - 29-JUL-98

Reebok's core athletic footwear and apparel sales are expected to fall 7.0% to 9.0% in 1998, hurt by a continued industrywide slowdown in sales of branded athletic products and continued economic problems in Asia. The two bright spots for the year should be RBK's Rockport and new Ralph Lauren line which should show solid sales gains. Unfortunately, the core Reebok footwear and apparel segments face a highly competitive domestic retail environment that is over-inventoried. Additionally, international sales comparisons will also be restricted by the negative impact of the strong dollar overseas and the economic problems in Asia. Gross margins were hurt during the first half of the year due to increased costs to launch new products, and the impact of promotional pricing. However, operating results may benefit from lower selling, general and administrative expenses, as a result of the company's recently announced restructuring initiatives, and a renewed focus on inventory controls.

Valuation - 29-JUL-98

We continue to rate the shares of RBK a sell given an industrywide slowdown in sales of branded athletic footwear in the U.S and the effect of a strong dollar on international sales. We believe management is on the right track to turn the company around, as it has reduced inventories of poor-selling product lines, redesigned its products to incorporate new cushioning technologies and improved its cost structure via a restructuring program. However, it is likely that we will have to wait until 1999 before RBK's profitability improves, since earnings continue to be restricted by a highly promotional retail selling environment which is resulting from an oversupply of inventory from major competitors.

Key Stock Statistics

S&P EPS Est. 1998	1.42	Tang. Bk. Value/Share	7.63
P/E on S&P Est. 1998	10.8	Beta	1.11
S&P EPS Est. 1999	2.00	Shareholders	7,200
Dividend Rate/Share	Nil	Market cap. (B)	$0.864
Shs. outstg. (M)	56.4	Inst. holdings	66%
Avg. daily vol. (M)	0.309		

Value of $10,000 invested 5 years ago: $ 4,664

Fiscal Year Ending Dec. 31

	1998	1997	1996	1995	1994	1993
Revenues (Million $)						
1Q	880.1	930.0	902.9	935.5	857.4	825.0
2Q	760.6	841.1	817.6	788.7	776.8	657.6
3Q	—	1,009	970.1	1,006	937.1	808.5
4Q	—	863.5	788.0	751.3	709.1	602.6
Yr.	—	3,644	3,479	3,481	3,280	2,894
Earnings Per Share ($)						
1Q	-0.06	0.69	0.64	0.80	0.77	0.74
2Q	0.11	0.35	0.27	0.26	0.60	0.46
3Q	—	1.26	0.75	0.96	1.01	0.74
4Q	—	0.01	0.35	0.02	0.64	0.59
Yr.	—	2.32	2.00	2.07	3.02	2.53

Next earnings report expected: mid October

Dividend Data

Dividends, initiated in 1987, were suspended in August 1996.

A Division of The McGraw·Hill Companies

Business Summary - 29-JUL-98

As the number two worldwide designer, marketer and distributor of sports, fitness and casual footwear, apparel and equipment, Reebok International is racing to transition itself from a company identified principally with fitness and exercise to one equally involved in sports. To accomplish this, RBK has created a host of new footwear and apparel products for football, baseball, soccer, track and field, and other sports, and signed hundreds of professional athletes, teams and federations to sponsorship contracts. Over the past several years, the Reebok brand has secured a place on major playing fields of the world and was generating significant sales in all major sports categories.

In addition to its core athletic footwear unit, Reebok designs and markets an extensive line of men's and women's apparel and accessories for sports, exercise and casual wear, carefully coordinated with the company's footwear styles. Other extensions of the Reebok brand include sports and fitness equipment such as steps and slides and heavy equipment products like the Sky Walker, marketed to both health clubs and homes.

Reebok has also formed strategic alliances with other companies to develop and market new sports products bearing Reebok's brand names or incorporating one or more Reebok technologies, and also licenses its trademarks to a limited group of strategically chosen licensees for complementary authentic sports equipment, including a line of watches, athletic gloves, sports sunglasses, basketballs and volleyballs, and weightlifting belts.

The specialty group includes the Rockport and Greg Norman brands. Rockport designs, develops and markets lightweight and comfortable casual dress and fitness walking shoes sold under the Rockport name as well as the Ralph Lauren and Polo Sport labels. Greg Norman produces a collection of golf apparel and men's casual sportswear.

The majority of company's products are manufactured through independent contractors in Southeast Asia.

In 1997, the athletic footwear and apparel industry was plagued with a worldwide glut of product as consumers' turned away from athletic footwear toward "brown shoe" or "casual" footwear products. This resulted in excessive inventories and the need for companies to discount their products. Although Reebok's inventories were in much better shape than its competitors, they were unable to increase market share due to the glut of old inventories at the retail level. Sales in 1998 will likely continue to be hurt by this phenomena as companies continue to work down their excess inventories.

Per Share Data ($)

(Year Ended Dec. 31)	1997	1996	1995	1994	1993	1992	1991	1990	1989	1988
Tangible Bk. Val.	7.83	5.58	11.11	12.24	10.12	9.38	9.05	8.71	7.42	6.12
Cash Flow	3.13	2.61	2.56	3.40	2.81	1.53	2.59	1.72	1.65	1.28
Earnings	2.32	2.00	2.07	3.02	2.53	1.24	2.37	1.54	1.53	1.20
Dividends	Nil	0.23	0.30	0.30	0.30	0.30	0.30	0.30	0.30	0.30
Payout Ratio	Nil	11%	14%	10%	12%	23%	12%	19%	20%	25%
Prices - High	52⁷/₈	45¹/₄	39⁵/₈	40¹/₄	38⁵/₈	35⁵/₈	35¹/₈	20	19⁵/₈	18³/₈
- Low	27⁵/₈	25³/₈	24¹/₈	28³/₈	23	21³/₈	10³/₄	8¹/₈	11¹/₈	9¹/₂
P/E Ratio - High	23	23	19	13	15	29	15	13	13	15
- Low	12	13	12	9	9	17	5	5	7	8

Income Statement Analysis (Million $)

	1997	1996	1995	1994	1993	1992	1991	1990	1989	1988
Revs.	3,644	3,478	3,481	3,280	2,894	3,023	2,734	2,159	1,822	1,786
Oper. Inc.	323	308	402	453	419	417	429	321	296	257
Depr.	47.4	42.9	38.6	32.2	25.2	27.2	22.0	20.2	13.5	8.9
Int. Exp.	64.4	42.2	25.7	16.5	25.0	20.1	29.4	20.4	15.9	22.8
Pretax Inc.	158	238	276	417	372	258	390	295	291	231
Eff. Tax Rate	7.90%	35%	36%	37%	38%	56%	40%	40%	40%	41%
Net Inc.	135	139	165	254	223	115	235	177	175	137

Balance Sheet & Other Fin. Data (Million $)

	1997	1996	1995	1994	1993	1992	1991	1990	1989	1988
Cash	210	232	80.4	84.0	79.0	105	85.0	227	171	99
Curr. Assets	1,465	1,463	1,343	1,337	1,127	1,060	1,027	1,030	784	714
Total Assets	1,756	1,756	1,656	1,649	1,392	1,345	1,431	1,403	1,166	1,063
Curr. Liab.	577	517	432	506	396	386	424	294	203	256
LT Debt	63.9	854	254	132	134	116	170	106	110	113
Common Eqty.	507	381	895	991	847	839	824	997	844	691
Total Cap.	1,178	1,269	1,185	1,144	995	960	1,006	1,109	963	808
Cap. Exp.	23.9	30.0	63.6	61.8	26.6	36.5	37.7	24.1	18.4	31.9
Cash Flow	183	182	203	287	249	142	257	197	189	146
Curr. Ratio	2.5	2.8	3.1	2.6	2.8	2.7	2.4	3.5	3.9	2.8
% LT Debt of Cap.	54.2	67.3	21.5	11.5	13.5	12.1	16.9	9.5	11.4	14.0
% Net Inc.of Revs.	3.7	4.0	4.8	7.8	7.7	3.8	8.6	8.2	9.6	7.7
% Ret. on Assets	7.7	8.1	10.0	17.0	16.9	8.3	18.4	13.7	15.6	14.2
% Ret. on Equity	30.4	21.8	17.5	28.1	27.4	13.9	29.0	19.1	22.7	21.4

Data as orig. reptd.; bef. results of disc. opers. and/or spec. items. Per share data adj. for stk. divs. as of ex-div. date. Bold denotes diluted EPS (FASB 128). E-Estimated. NA-Not Available. NM-Not Meaningful. NR-Not Ranked.

Office—100 Technology Center Drive, Stoughton, MA 02072. **Tel**—(781) 401-5000. **Fax**—(781) 341-5087. **Website**—http://www.reebok.com **Chrmn, CEO & Pres**—P. B. Fireman.**EVP & CFO**—K. Watchmaker.**Treas & Investor Contact**—Leo Vannoni (781-401-7259). **Dirs**—P. R. Duncan, M. K. Dwyer, P. B. Fireman, W. F. Glavin, M. L. Jackson, B. M. Lee Sr., R. G. Lesser, W. M. Marcus, R. Meers, G. Nunes **Transfer Agent & Registrar**—BankBoston N. A.**Incorporated**—in Massachusetts in 1979. **Empl**— 6,948. **S&P Analyst:** Robert J. Izmirlian

STANDARD &POOR'S
STOCK REPORTS

Regions Financial

5072M

Nasdaq Symbol **RGBK**

In S&P 500

12-SEP-98

Industry:
Banks (Major Regional)

Summary: This major southeastern bank holding company, with total assets of $27 billion, operates more than 500 offices in six southeastern states.

S&P Opinion: Hold (★★★)	Recent Price • 35½	Yield • 2.6%
	52 Wk Range • 45%–32%	12-Mo. P/E • 15.6

Quantitative Evaluations

Outlook
(1 Lowest—5 Highest)
• **1⁻**

Fair Value
• **32¼**

Risk
• **Low**

Earn./Div. Rank
• **A+**

Technical Eval.
• **Bearish** since 8/98

Rel. Strength Rank
(1 Lowest—99 Highest)
• **71**

Insider Activity
• **NA**

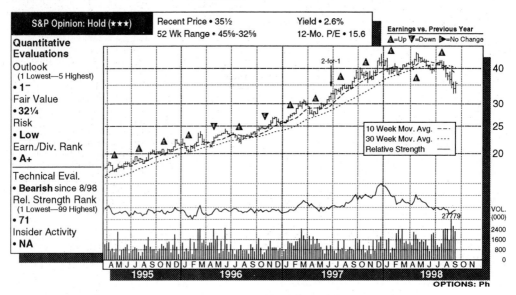

OPTIONS: Ph

Overview - 10-SEP-98

Strong growth in loans, reflecting both internal strength in commercial and real estate mortgage loans and acquisitions, as well as slightly narrower interest margins, should continue to produce double-digit gains in net interest income. The loan loss provision is expected to remain relatively flat on stable loan charge-off trends. Noninterest income continues to benefit from strength in deposit service charges and higher mortgage banking fees, and should have sustainable growth in the low double-digits. Asset quality remains strong, with loan loss reserves in line with those of the bank's peers, and a particularly low loan chargeoff rate attributable to the company's conservative business mix. Longer term plans, as contemplated by the Vision 2000 program, include getting the efficiency ratio below 50% by 2000, from 54.5% as of the 1998 second quarter, aided by a growing revenue base. Numerous pending acquisitions, which will generally be financed with stock, may be dilutive in the short-term.

Valuation - 10-SEP-98

The shares were not immune from August's market rout and registered an 18% decline in the first eight months of 1998. In addition, speculation about the company as a potential takeover candidate had given the shares a premium valuation, and the general decline in bank stock prices reduces the possibility of a strong buyout offer. Fundamentally, RGBK has come to enjoy double digit earnings growth, fueled by healthy loan growth, an aggressive acquisition strategy, and superior cost control. Despite the recent pullback, we view the shares fairly valued at 13 times our 1999 earnings estimate of $2.65 a share.

Key Stock Statistics

S&P EPS Est. 1998	2.40	Tang. Bk. Value/Share	14.63
P/E on S&P Est. 1998	14.8	Beta	0.86
S&P EPS Est. 1999	2.65	Shareholders	41,500
Dividend Rate/Share	0.92	Market cap. (B)	$ 7.6
Shs. outstg. (M)	215.0	Inst. holdings	15%
Avg. daily vol. (M)	1.945		

Value of $10,000 invested 5 years ago: $ 25,476

Fiscal Year Ending Dec. 31

	1998	1997	1996	1995	1994	1993
Revenues (Million $)						
1Q	563.0	449.0	384.7	280.1	216.4	166.3
2Q	575.7	467.9	401.1	292.0	223.3	170.4
3Q	—	490.6	406.3	302.8	237.7	173.7
4Q	—	516.8	414.7	302.3	251.8	177.2
Yr.	—	1,912	1,607	1,177	929.2	687.7
Earnings Per Share ($)						
1Q	**0.57**	**0.51**	0.42	0.46	0.40	0.37
2Q	**0.59**	**0.53**	0.49	0.46	0.42	0.38
3Q	**E0.60**	**0.55**	0.41	0.48	0.44	0.39
4Q	**E0.64**	**0.57**	0.52	0.49	0.44	0.38
Yr.	**E2.40**	**2.15**	**1.81**	1.88	1.70	1.50

Next earnings report expected: mid October

Dividend Data (Dividends have been paid since 1968.)

Amount ($)	Date Decl.	Ex-Div. Date	Stock of Record	Payment Date
0.200	Nov. 19	Dec. 11	Dec. 15	Jan. 02 '98
0.230	Jan. 21	Mar. 18	Mar. 20	Apr. 01 '98
0.230	May. 20	Jun. 15	Jun. 17	Jul. 01 '98
0.230	Jul. 29	Sep. 15	Sep. 17	Oct. 01 '98

Business Summary - 10-SEP-98

With an ambitious goal of becoming the "best performing bank in America" as the cornerstone of its Vision 2000 plan, Regions Financial Corp. (formerly First Alabama Bancshares, Inc.) has grown rapidly in recent years from both internal growth and acquisitions. Helping this growth is a quality loan portfolio and a relatively lean cost structure, which supported 435 branches in the strong regional economies of Alabama, Florida, Georgia, Louisiana, and Tennessee at the end of 1997. Regions continued to strengthen its presence in Florida, Georgia and Louisiana in 1997 through nine bank acquisitions that added $1.9 billion in assets. The company also operates nonbank subsidiaries that provide mortgage banking, credit life insurance, securities brokerage activities and commercial accounts receivable factoring.

In 1997, average earnings assets, from which interest income is derived, totaled $19.8 billion and consisted mainly of loans (76%) and investment securities (22%). Average sources of funds, used in the lending business, included interest-bearing deposits (69%), noninterest-bearing deposits (11%), short-term borrowings (8%), long-term debt (2%), shareholders' equity (9%) and other (1%)

Nonperforming assets (primarily loans where interest and principal payments are not being received as per original terms) at 1997 year end amounted to $133.5 million (0.81% of loans and other real estate), versus $101.1 million (0.76%) a year earlier. The allowance for loan losses, which is set aside for possible loan defaults, was $194.3 million (1.19% of total loans), up from $175.5 million (1.32%). Net charge-offs, or the amount of loans actually written-off as uncollectible, totaled $37.3 million (0.25% of average loans) in 1997, compared to $19.1 million (0.15%) in 1996.

As of mid-July 1998, the company had nine pending acquisitions, including five in Georgia and one each in Alabama, Arkansas, Florida and Tennessee. The largest of these was First Commercial Corp., a Little Rock, Arkansas-based bank with $7.4 billion in assets that was acquired in late July 1998 for 64.1 million RGBK common shares.

Per Share Data ($)

(Year Ended Dec. 31)	1997	1996	1995	1994	1993	1992	1991	1990	1989	1988
Tangible Bk. Val.	11.80	10.80	11.20	10.13	9.77	8.30	7.32	6.69	6.36	5.88
Earnings	2.15	1.85	1.88	1.70	1.50	1.30	1.08	0.95	0.86	0.81
Dividends	0.77	0.70	0.66	0.60	0.52	0.45	0.44	0.42	0.38	0.36
Payout Ratio	36%	38%	35%	35%	35%	35%	40%	44%	44%	45%
Prices - High	45	27	22¹/₂	18³/₈	19¹/₄	17	13⁵/₈	8¹/₂	8⁷/₈	7⁵/₈
- Low	25³/₄	20¹/₄	15¹/₂	14⁷/₈	14⁷/₈	11⁷/₈	8	6⁵/₈	6⁷/₈	6¹/₈
P/E Ratio - High	21	15	12	11	13	13	13	9	10	9
- Low	12	11	8	9	10	9	7	7	8	8

Income Statement Analysis (Million $)

	1997	1996	1995	1994	1993	1992	1991	1990	1989	1988
Net Int. Inc.	829	700	497	436	342	313	265	222	204	185
Tax Equiv. Adj.	NA	13.3	10.5	10.6	10.5	15.6	12.3	NA	NA	NA
Non Int. Inc.	258	221	160	143	132	119	102	94.0	71.0	69.0
Loan Loss Prov.	41.8	29.0	20.7	19.0	21.5	27.1	24.0	24.2	15.8	10.8
Exp./Op. Revs.	55%	59%	57%	58%	59%	59%	61%	NA	NA	NA
Pretax Inc.	445	338	258	217	166	140	112	96.0	84.0	76.0
Eff. Tax Rate	33%	32%	33%	33%	32%	32%	30%	28%	25%	23%
Net Inc.	300	230	173	146	112	95.0	78.3	68.9	62.6	58.2
% Net Int. Marg.	4.20	4.27	4.10	4.26	4.82	4.98	4.78	4.40	4.32	4.39

Balance Sheet & Other Fin. Data (Million $)

	1997	1996	1995	1994	1993	1992	1991	1990	1989	1988
Earning Assets:										
Money Mkt	127	54.0	76.4	70.6	138	85.0	156	75.0	155	278
Inv. Securities	4,451	3,901	3,025	2,609	2,368	1,670	1,576	1,489	1,133	1,222
Com'l Loans	3,856	2,830	1,992	1,871	1,498	1,437	1,328	1,376	1,169	992
Other Loans	12,572	10,505	7,665	7,277	5,658	3,964	3,158	2,925	2,607	2,246
Total Assets	23,034	18,930	13,709	12,839	10,476	7,881	6,745	6,344	5,550	5,174
Demand Deposits	2,368	1,909	1,535	1,450	1,197	1,042	875	852	836	840
Time Deposits	15,383	13,139	9,361	8,643	7,574	5,659	5,042	4,501	3,908	3,491
LT Debt	400	447	553	519	463	134	16.0	20.0	45.0	21.0
Common Eqty.	1,913	1,599	1,125	1,014	851	657	573	524	489	456
% Ret. on Assets	1.4	1.3	1.3	1.3	1.4	1.3	1.2	1.2	1.2	1.2
% Ret. on Equity	17.1	15.2	15.8	16.0	16.1	15.6	14.3	13.6	13.2	13.3
% Loan Loss Resv.	1.2	1.3	1.4	1.3	1.4	1.4	1.3	1.1	1.0	1.1
% Loans/Deposits	91.5	85.9	87.8	90.4	81.2	77.5	74.3	78.4	77.7	73.2
% Equity to Assets	8.4	8.5	8.1	8.1	8.7	8.6	8.6	9.0	9.1	9.3

Data as orig. reptd.; bef. results of disc opers. and/or spec. items. Per share data adj. for stk. divs. as of ex-div. date. Bold denotes diluted EPS (FASB 128). E-Estimated. NA-Not Available. NM-Not Meaningful. NR-Not Ranked.

Office—417 North 20th St., Birmingham, AL 35203. **Tel**—(205) 326-7100. **Website**—http://www.regionsbank.com **Chrmn & CEO**—J. S. Mackin. **Vice Chrmn**—R. D. Horsley. **Pres & COO**—C. E. Jones, Jr. **Secy**—S. E. Upchurch, Jr. **Investor Contact**—Ronald C. Jackson. **Dirs**—S. S. Blair, W. R. Boles Sr., J. B. Boone Jr., A. P. Brewer, J. S. M. French, R. D. Horsley, C. E. Jones Jr., O. B. King, J. S. Mackin, H. E. Simpson, L. J. Styslinger Jr., R. J. Williams **Transfer Agent**—First Chicago Trust Co. of New York. **Incorporated**—in Delaware in 1970. **Empl**— 8,150. **S&P Analyst:** Stephen R. Biggar

12-SEP-98

Industry: Banks (Major Regional)

Summary: This bank holding company engages in retail and commercial banking and in private banking, primarily in metropolitan New York, Florida and abroad.

| S&P Opinion: Hold (★★★) | Recent Price • 42⅛ | Yield • 2.4% |
| | 52 Wk Range • 73¼-36⅛ | 12-Mo. P/E • 10.3 |

Quantitative Evaluations

Outlook
(1 Lowest—5 Highest)
• **4**

Fair Value
• **49¼**

Risk
• **Low**

Earn./Div. Rank
• **A-**

Technical Eval.
• **Neutral** since 8/98

Rel. Strength Rank
(1 Lowest—99 Highest)
• **29**

Insider Activity
• **Neutral**

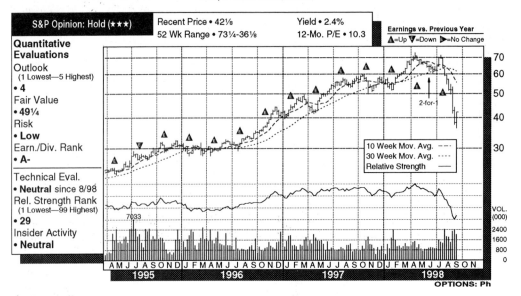

Earnings vs. Previous Year
▲=Up ▼=Down ▶=No Change

10 Week Mov. Avg. ---
30 Week Mov. Avg. ....
Relative Strength —

2-for-1

VOL. (000)

OPTIONS: Ph

Overview - 28-JUL-98

As RNB's focus remains on depositor safety, funds will continue to be invested primarily in lower-risk assets. In accordance with this low risk profile, net interest margins are well below peer levels. A modest erosion in the margin in 1997 and the first half of 1998 reflected the addition of high quality but low margin securities following efforts to lower exposure to a changing interest rate environment. RNB has been placing increasing emphasis on expanding fee income sources, particularly the domestic and international private banking business and mutual fund operations. Income from trading activities, in particular, has benefited from growth in emerging markets and the volume of derivatives trading, but will likely remain volatile. Nonperforming assets at June 30, 1998, of $89.7 million were down substantially from $128.8 million a year earlier, reflecting a lower level of nonaccrual loans and other assets and real estate owned. Given the favorable trend for underlying nonperforming assets, the allowance for loan losses will likely remain relatively steady at current levels.

Valuation - 28-JUL-98

Based on valuation and earnings growth assumptions, we remain neutral on the shares for now. Net interest income remains substantially insulated from changes in interest rates following a realignment of the investment portfolio. The launch of a corporate-wide project to improve operating efficiencies and reduce costs will benefit longer-term results. Trading at 15X our 1998 earnings estimate of $4.25 a share, the shares appear adequately valued at current levels.

Key Stock Statistics

S&P EPS Est. 1998	3.70	Tang. Bk. Value/Share	27.64
P/E on S&P Est. 1998	11.4	Beta	1.46
S&P EPS Est. 1999	4.50	Shareholders	2,900
Dividend Rate/Share	1.00	Market cap. (B)	$ 4.5
Shs. outstg. (M)	107.9	Inst. holdings	47%
Avg. daily vol. (M)	0.417		

Value of $10,000 invested 5 years ago: $ 20,390

Fiscal Year Ending Dec. 31

	1998	1997	1996	1995	1994	1993
Revenues (Million $)						
1Q	930.6	873.9	772.9	711.0	588.9	572.5
2Q	995.5	925.0	815.1	703.5	609.7	566.9
3Q	—	947.4	831.6	709.8	652.8	589.8
4Q	—	991.9	859.5	735.3	708.3	599.3
Yr.	—	3,738	3,279	2,860	2,560	2,328
Earnings Per Share ($)						
1Q	**1.03**	**0.95**	0.82	0.74	0.69	0.59
2Q	**1.05**	**0.98**	0.85	0.01	0.68	0.65
3Q	—	**0.99**	0.90	0.79	0.78	0.67
4Q	—	**1.01**	0.91	0.77	0.76	0.69
Yr.	—	**3.94**	3.54	2.33	2.90	2.60

Next earnings report expected: mid October

Dividend Data (Dividends have been paid since 1975.)

Amount ($)	Date Decl.	Ex-Div. Date	Stock of Record	Payment Date
0.500	Jan. 21	Mar. 11	Mar. 15	Apr. 01 '98
2-for-1	Apr. 15	Jun. 02	May. 01	Jun. 01 '98
0.250	Apr. 15	Jun. 11	Jun. 15	Jul. 01 '98
0.250	Jul. 15	Sep. 11	Sep. 15	Oct. 01 '98

A Division of The McGraw·Hill Companies

Business Summary - 28-JUL-98

Republic New York Corp. offers a wide variety of banking and financial services worldwide to corporations, financial institutions, governmental units and individuals through more than 80 branches in New York City and the suburban counties of Westchester, Nassau and Suffolk, and eight in southern Florida, as well as several foreign branches and representative offices. In 1997, the company continued work on Republic Profit Quest, a profitability system that will allow management to identify profitability on a consistent basis by client, product, geographic location, department and manager. It plans to implement the component pieces of Profit Quest for locations in the U.S. in 1998, with offshore locations to follow.

Through 49%-owned Safra Republic Holdings, Republic National Bank also offers a range of international private banking services to wealthy individuals and commercial banking through bank subsidiaries in Switzerland, Luxembourg, France, Guernsey, Gibraltar and Monaco. A high proportion of assets is held in liquid investments. Precious metals trading is important, as are factoring and currency trading operations. The bank is active in international banking where it operates mainly as a wholesale bank.

In 1997, average earning assets, from which interest income is derived, amounted to $45.0 billion and consisted mainly of investment securities (51%) and loans (30%). Average sources of funds, used mainly in the lending business, included interest-bearing deposits (53%), noninterest-bearing deposits (5%), short-term borrowings (16%), long-term debt (8%), shareholders' equity (6%) and other (12%).

At year-end 1997, nonperforming assets, consisting primarily of non-accrual loans and other real estate owned, were $112.7 million (0.91% of loans), down from $141.4 million (1.21%) a year earlier. The allowance for loan losses, which is set aside for possible loan defaults, was $326.5 million (2.64% of loans), versus $350.4 million (2.99%) a year earlier. Net charge-offs, or the amount of loans actually written off as uncollectible, were $11.3 million (0.08% of average loans) in 1997, compared with $25.0 million (0.21%) in 1996.

Per Share Data ($)

(Year Ended Dec. 31)	1997	1996	1995	1994	1993	1992	1991	1990	1989	1988
Tangible Bk. Val.	27.02	25.00	21.62	18.69	20.79	16.36	14.80	13.30	11.72	12.39
Earnings	3.94	3.48	2.33	2.90	2.60	2.21	1.98	1.81	0.02	1.67
Dividends	0.92	0.76	0.72	0.66	0.54	0.50	0.47	0.44	0.43	0.40
Payout Ratio	23%	22%	31%	23%	21%	23%	24%	24%	NM	24%
Prices - High	60	44³/₈	32¹/₂	26¹/₈	26⁷/₈	24¹/₈	23⁵/₈	17¹/₂	17¹/₄	16
- Low	39⁵/₈	28	22³/₈	21	22¹/₄	19	15³/₄	12³/₈	14¹/₄	13¹/₈
P/E Ratio - High	15	13	14	9	10	11	12	10	NM	10
- Low	10	8	10	7	9	9	8	7	NM	8

Income Statement Analysis (Million $)

	1997	1996	1995	1994	1993	1992	1991	1990	1989	1988
Net Int. Inc.	1,028	962	819	846	814	720	581	457	357	428
Tax Equiv. Adj.	32.2	31.9	35.3	35.5	31.0	32.0	32.0	41.0	37.0	30.0
Non Int. Inc.	493	423	387	371	388	291	267	264	275	158
Loan Loss Prov.	16.0	32.0	12.0	19.0	85.0	120	62.0	40.0	209	42.0
Exp./Op. Revs.	59%	56%	66%	58%	52%	53%	57%	61%	55%	59%
Pretax Inc.	636	591	398	492	451	347	288	223	56.0	204
Eff. Tax Rate	29%	29%	28%	31%	33%	26%	21%	9.90%	57%	17%
Net Inc.	449	419	289	340	301	259	227	201	24.0	170
% Net Int. Marg.	2.36	2.48	2.61	2.64	2.60	2.51	2.27	1.89	1.66	2.10

Balance Sheet & Other Fin. Data (Million $)

	1997	1996	1995	1994	1993	1992	1991	1990	1989	1988
Earning Assets:										
Money Mkt	12,339	14,934	13,805	15,366	8,851	12,771	9,056	8,768	9,315	10,694
Inv. Securities	25,514	21,176	16,239	11,440	14,950	12,331	9,667	7,643	5,638	4,083
Com'l Loans	3,962	2,952	3,120	2,884	2,839	2,181	2,117	2,353	1,984	1,751
Other Loans	8,398	8,770	6,759	6,076	6,765	5,975	6,664	6,880	4,698	4,106
Total Assets	55,638	52,299	43,882	41,068	39,494	37,146	31,221	29,597	25,467	24,519
Demand Deposits	NA	2,923	1,900	1,816	1,563	1,316	1,049	1,111	991	857
Time Deposits	30,466	29,252	23,020	20,910	21,239	19,787	19,334	18,875	15,534	15,490
LT Debt	4,464	3,899	3,962	4,987	4,855	4,633	3,120	2,416	2,521	2,272
Common Eqty.	2,938	2,751	2,433	1,967	2,191	1,707	1,541	1,374	1,063	1,117
% Ret. on Assets	0.8	0.9	0.7	0.8	0.8	0.8	0.7	0.7	0.1	0.7
% Ret. on Equity	14.9	14.9	11.5	21.9	21.8	20.6	19.4	19.3	0.2	20.4
% Loan Loss Resv.	2.6	3.0	3.0	3.6	3.3	3.0	2.6	2.6	4.4	3.1
% Loans/Deposits	NA	36.9	39.5	39.2	41.7	38.0	42.0	45.1	39.8	35.0
% Equity to Assets	5.3	5.4	5.2	3.4	3.4	3.4	3.4	3.4	3.0	2.9

Data as orig. reptd.; bef. results of disc opers. and/or spec. items. Per share data adj. for stk. divs. as of ex-div. date. Bold denotes diluted EPS (FASB 128). E-Estimated. NA-Not Available. NM-Not Meaningful. NR-Not Ranked.

Office—452 Fifth Ave., New York, NY 10018Tel—(212) 525-6100. Website—http://www.rnb.com Chrmn & CEO—W. H. Weiner. EVP, CFO & Treas—T. F. Robards. Investor Contact—Stephen J. Saali. Dirs—K. Andersen, R. A. Cohen, C. S. Dwek, E. Ginsberg, N. Hasson, J. C. Keil, P. Kimmelman, R. A. Kraemer, L. Lieberman, W. C. MacMillen, Jr., P. J. Mansbach, M. F. Mertz, J. L. Morice, E. D. Morris, J. L. Norwood, J. A. Pancetti, V. S. Portera, W. P. Rogers, E. Saal, D. C. Schlein, W. H. Weiner, P. White. Transfer Agent & Registrar—American Stock Transfer & Trust Co., NYC.Incorporated—in Maryland in 1973. Empl— 5,900. S&P Analyst: Stephen R. Biggar

STANDARD &POOR'S
STOCK REPORTS

Reynolds Metals
1926
NYSE Symbol **RLM**

In S&P 500

12-SEP-98 **Industry:** Aluminum

Summary: The world's third largest aluminum producer, RLM makes products for the packaging, consumer, transportation, building and construction and infrastructure markets.

S&P Opinion: Accumulate (★★★★)	Recent Price • 50	Yield • 2.8%
	52 Wk Range • 74⅝-46⅞	12-Mo. P/E • NM

Earnings vs. Previous Year
▲=Up ▼=Down ▶=No Change

Quantitative Evaluations

Outlook
(1 Lowest—5 Highest)
• **3+**

Fair Value
• **52¼**

Risk
• **Low**

Earn./Div. Rank
• **B-**

Technical Eval.
• **Bullish** since 6/98

Rel. Strength Rank
(1 Lowest—99 Highest)
• **72**

Insider Activity
• **NA**

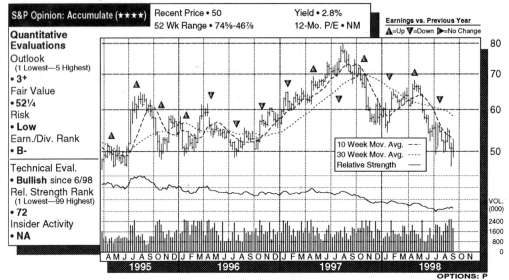

10 Week Mov. Avg. ---
30 Week Mov. Avg. ....
Relative Strength —

VOL.
(000)
2400
1600
800
0

1995 1996 1997 1998

OPTIONS: P

Overview - 11-AUG-98

We anticipate a 7% sales decline in 1998, reflecting the divestment of underperforming businesses and lower aluminum prices. However, aided by cost cutting and a more lucrative product mix, operating profit should increase. Benefiting further from an anticipated drop of 50% in interest expense, EPS excluding charges should post a sizable gain.

Valuation - 11-AUG-98

Following second quarter EPS we are maintaining our accumulate rating on RLM based on its appeal as a turnaround candidate. Excluding a $2.72 charge, second quarter EPS was $1.02, versus the consensus estimate of $0.85. Despite depressed ingot prices, margins improved both sequentially and year over year on a more lucrative product mix and strenuous cost cutting. We see continued progress in reducing operating costs and financial costs. With its restructuring program nearly complete, RLM will have much better earning power. Aided by the pending sale of substantially all of its can business, RLM will finish the 1998 third quarter with nearly $1 billion in cash. It will use the cash for debt reduction and expansion of the current share repurchase program. Also, RLM will benefit from higher aluminum prices in 1999. Aluminum prices appear to be unsustainably low, in view of the supply/demand fundamentals. As of August 6, 1998, inventories on the London Metal Exchange (LME) totaled 469,250 metric tons, versus 621,975 metric tons in August 1997. Currently, LME inventories are at their lowest level since 1991. Meanwhile, the market appears firm with lower demand in Asia being offset by strength in North America and Europe. But, aluminum prices (mid-West delivered) were $0.63/lb. as of early August 1998, versus $0.83/lb. in August 1997. We expect higher prices in 1999 to boost RLM stock.

Key Stock Statistics

S&P EPS Est. 1998	1.00	Tang. Bk. Value/Share	34.28
P/E on S&P Est. 1998	50.0	Beta	0.95
S&P EPS Est. 1999	5.00	Shareholders	9,300
Dividend Rate/Share	1.40	Market cap. (B)	$ 3.6
Shs. outstg. (M)	72.1	Inst. holdings	84%
Avg. daily vol. (M)	0.657		

Value of $10,000 invested 5 years ago: $ 10,779

Fiscal Year Ending Dec. 31

	1998	1997	1996	1995	1994	1993
Revenues (Million $)						
1Q	1,532	1,615	1,662	1,651	1,254	1,231
2Q	1,579	1,783	1,823	1,864	1,455	1,356
3Q	—	1,716	1,751	1,841	1,531	1,336
4Q	—	1,767	1,736	1,872	1,639	1,346
Yr.	—	6,881	6,972	7,252	5,879	5,269
Earnings Per Share ($)						
1Q	**0.78**	0.59	0.12	1.13	-0.46	-0.55
2Q	**-1.70**	0.75	0.81	1.51	0.05	-0.38
3Q	**E0.90**	0.73	0.26	1.56	0.86	-0.47
4Q	**E1.02**	-0.23	-0.13	1.15	0.97	-3.98
Yr.	**E1.00**	1.84	1.06	5.35	1.42	-5.38

Next earnings report expected: mid October

Dividend Data (Dividends have been paid since 1942.)

Amount ($)	Date Decl.	Ex-Div. Date	Stock of Record	Payment Date
0.350	Nov. 21	Nov. 26	Dec. 01	Jan. 02 '98
0.350	Feb. 20	Feb. 27	Mar. 03	Apr. 01 '98
0.350	May. 15	Jun. 01	Jun. 03	Jul. 01 '98
0.350	Aug. 21	Sep. 01	Sep. 03	Oct. 01 '98

A Division of The McGraw·Hill Companies

STANDARD
&POOR'S
STOCK REPORTS

Reynolds Metals Company

1926

12-SEP-98

Business Summary - 11-AUG-98

The world's third largest aluminum manufacturer, Reynolds is currently reviewing all of its plants and businesses in an effort to improve operating performance and financial returns. It is considering a number of options, including the spinoff or sale of underperforming, low rate of return businesses. In 1997, the company reduced debt by about $400 million with funds from asset sales. RLM plans to use proceeds from additional asset sales to reduce debt further and expand its stock repurchase program. Contributions by segment from continuing operations in 1997:

	Sales	Oper. Inc.
Base materials	48%	62%
Packaging and consumer	27%	28%
Construction and distribution	18%	8%
Transportation	7%	2%

Aluminum products accounted for 79% of total sales in 1997 and nonaluminum 21%. The U.S. accounted for 77% of sales in 1997, Canada 8%, and the rest of the world 15%.

The base metals segment mines bauxite and produces alumina, carbon products and primary aluminum, including value added products such as billet, foundry ingot and rod used in electrical cable. RLM's main competitors in this segment are Alcoa, Alcan, Kaiser Aluminum and Pechiney. Aluminum faces stiff competition from plastics (PET) and glass in the beverage can market and from steel and ceramics in other applications. Aluminum's brightest prospects are in motor vehicle applications where demand for weight savings is helping it replace steel.

The packaging and consumer segment makes a broad range of aluminum foil, plastic packaging and consumer products, including an extensive line of wraps and bags marketed under the Reynolds brand name.

Construction and distribution sells architectural products and distributes aluminum, stainless steel and other specialty metals products. The segment also makes polymer coated magnet wire for electrical transformers and sells infrastructure technologies.

Transportation serves the auto and truck market with cast aluminum wheels, wheel stock, door intrusion beams, bumper systems, drive shaft tubes, heat exchanger tubing, fin stock and body sheet.

Shipments in 1997 totaled 3,534,000 metric tons, versus 3,430,000 metric tons in 1996. The average realized prices for ingot was $0.83 in 1997, versus $0.74 in 1996; the average realization for fabricated products was $1.76, versus $1.79 in 1996.

On August 10, 1998, RLM announced that it had completed the sale of its North American beverage can and end assets to Ball Corp. RLM received proceeds of some $700 million and will realize an after-tax gain of $200 million on the transaction.

Per Share Data ($)

(Year Ended Dec. 31)	1997	1996	1995	1994	1993	1992	1991	1990	1989	1988
Tangible Bk. Val.	37.01	36.08	33.20	27.39	25.38	32.35	49.66	49.22	45.24	37.77
Cash Flow	6.81	7.33	9.10	6.19	-0.59	2.93	7.07	8.64	12.65	12.44
Earnings	1.84	1.06	5.35	1.42	-5.38	-1.83	2.60	5.01	9.20	9.01
Dividends	1.40	1.40	1.10	1.00	1.20	1.80	1.80	1.80	1.70	0.90
Payout Ratio	76%	132%	21%	70%	NM	NM	70%	36%	19%	10%
Prices - High	79³/₄	61⁵/₈	64³/₄	59³/₈	58⁷/₈	64³/₈	65³/₈	70	62³/₄	58
- Low	56¹/₈	48³/₄	46¹/₄	40³/₈	41¹/₈	47	46	48¹/₂	49	34
P/E Ratio - High	43	58	12	42	NM	NM	25	14	7	6
- Low	31	46	9	28	NM	NM	18	10	5	4

Income Statement Analysis (Million $)

	1997	1996	1995	1994	1993	1992	1991	1990	1989	1988
Revs.	6,881	6,972	7,213	5,879	5,269	5,593	5,730	6,022	6,143	5,567
Oper. Inc.	817	671	922	506	254	462	592	829	1,003	936
Depr.	368	365	311	295	287	284	265	214	200	184
Int. Exp.	153	173	179	156	159	167	161	96.0	122	148
Pretax Inc.	240	153	548	190	-514	-194	220	422	758	659
Eff. Tax Rate	43%	32%	29%	36%	NM	NM	30%	30%	30%	27%
Net Inc.	136	104	389	122	-321	-108	154	297	533	482

Balance Sheet & Other Fin. Data (Million $)

	1997	1996	1995	1994	1993	1992	1991	1990	1989	1988
Cash	70.0	38.0	39.0	434	19.0	80.0	67.0	90.0	71.0	331
Curr. Assets	1,994	1,873	2,014	2,322	1,590	1,757	1,780	1,816	1,763	1,864
Total Assets	7,226	7,516	7,740	7,461	6,709	6,897	6,685	6,527	5,556	5,032
Curr. Liab.	1,283	1,333	1,367	1,425	1,181	1,185	1,016	974	982	1,155
LT Debt	1,501	1,793	1,853	1,848	1,990	1,798	1,854	1,742	1,166	1,321
Common Eqty.	2,739	2,634	2,112	1,767	1,623	2,060	2,960	2,928	2,684	2,040
Total Cap.	4,509	4,689	4,706	4,303	3,769	4,024	5,219	5,094	4,257	3,630
Cap. Exp.	272	432	845	404	385	302	398	936	555	287
Cash Flow	504	469	664	382	-35.0	175	419	511	733	666
Curr. Ratio	1.6	1.4	1.5	1.6	1.3	1.5	1.8	1.9	1.8	1.6
% LT Debt of Cap.	33.2	38.2	39.4	43.0	52.8	44.7	35.5	34.2	27.4	36.4
% Net Inc.of Revs.	2.0	1.5	5.4	2.1	NM	NM	2.7	4.9	8.7	8.7
% Ret. on Assets	1.8	1.4	5.1	1.7	NM	NM	2.3	4.9	9.6	10.3
% Ret. on Equity	5.1	4.4	18.2	5.1	NM	NM	5.2	10.6	21.6	26.5

Data as orig. reptd.; bef. results of disc. opers. and/or spec. items. Per share data adj. for stk. divs. as of ex-div. date. Bold denotes diluted EPS (FASB 128). E-Estimated. NA-Not Available. NM-Not Meaningful. NR-Not Ranked.

Office—6601 W. Broad St., Richmond, VA 23261-7003. **Tel**—(804) 281-2000. **Website**—http://www.rmc.com **Chrmn & CEO**—J. J. Sheehan. **EVP-CFO**—H. S. Savedge Jr. **VP-Secy**—D. C. Dabney. **VP-Treas & Investor Contact**—Julian H. Taylor. **Dirs**—P. C. Barron, J. R. Hall, R. L. Hintz, W. H. Joyce, M. B. Mangum, D. L. Moore, R. N. Reynolds, J. M. Ringler, H. S. Savedge Jr., S. Scott, J. J. Sheehan, J. B. Wyatt. **Transfer Agent & Registrar**—ChaseMellon Shareholder Services, South Hackensack, NJ. **Incorporated**—in Delaware in 1928. **Empl**—25,500. **S&P Analyst:** Leo J. Larkin

STANDARD &POOR'S
STOCK REPORTS

Rite Aid

1937P

NYSE Symbol **RAD**

In S&P 500

12-SEP-98

Industry:
Retail (Drug Stores)

Summary: Following the acquisition of Thrifty PayLess Inc. in December 1996, Rite Aid now operates the largest chain of retail drug stores in the U.S., with nearly 4,000 units.

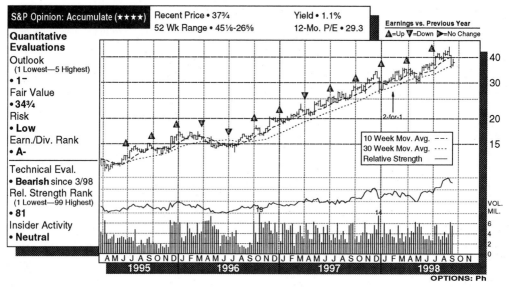

S&P Opinion: Accumulate (★★★★)

Recent Price • 37¾	Yield • 1.1%
52 Wk Range • 45⅛-26⅝	12-Mo. P/E • 29.3

Quantitative Evaluations

Outlook
 (1 Lowest—5 Highest)
• **1⁻**

Fair Value
• **34¾**

Risk
• **Low**

Earn./Div. Rank
• **A-**

Technical Eval.
• **Bearish** since 3/98

Rel. Strength Rank
 (1 Lowest—99 Highest)
• **81**

Insider Activity
• **Neutral**

Earnings vs. Previous Year
▲=Up ▼=Down ▶=No Change

10 Week Mov. Avg. ---
30 Week Mov. Avg. ·····
Relative Strength —

2-for-1

VOL. MIL.

OPTIONS: Ph

Overview - 01-JUL-98

We expect total sales to increase approximately 13% to 15% in FY 99 (Feb.), reflecting contributions from the Harco and K & B acquisitions, the addition of about 410 new stores, and same-store sales increases of approximately 6% to 8%. Gross margins should be stable as pricing pressure from third-party payment plans is offset by a more profitable front-end mix, the increased buying power from the larger store base, as well as larger stores in terms of square footage. Operating expenses should decline as a percentage of sales as RAD continues to squeeze out costs from the Thrifty PayLess stores. We also expect results to be aided by the accelerated closure of unprofitable units, the leveraging of expenses over a larger store base, and more efficient technological systems.

Valuation - 01-JUL-98

We continue to rate RAD shares "accumulate," reflecting our increased confidence in the company's ability to successfully integrate its recent acquisitions. Not only did the December 1996 acquisition of Thrifty Payless create one of the largest drug store chains in the U.S. in terms of the number of stores, but it proved management's dedication to building bargaining power with health care providers. The addition of the K & B and Harco chains further supports this. The acquisitions have extended RAD's geographical reach, giving it leading market shares in major growth markets. Earnings growth should continue to accelerate as operating leverage is achieved. We currently estimate profits will rise 15%-18% a year in the foreseeable future. The shares, which were recently selling at about 25X times FY 99 estimated per share earnings of $1.50, continue to be attractive for long-term capital gains.

Key Stock Statistics

S&P EPS Est. 1999	1.50	Tang. Bk. Value/Share	3.93
P/E on S&P Est. 1999	25.2	Beta	0.73
S&P EPS Est. 2000	1.75	Shareholders	24,000
Dividend Rate/Share	0.43	Market cap. (B)	$ 9.8
Shs. outstg. (M)	258.4	Inst. holdings	85%
Avg. daily vol. (M)	1.088		

Value of $10,000 invested 5 years ago: $ 39,937

Fiscal Year Ending Feb. 28

	1999	1998	1997	1996	1995	1994
Revenues (Million $)						
1Q	3,033	2,665	1,405	1,355	1,051	1,000
2Q	—	2,634	1,423	1,328	1,035	973.1
3Q	—	2,886	1,485	1,332	1,094	1,009
4Q	—	3,191	2,657	1,430	1,354	1,077
Yr.	—	11,375	6,970	5,446	4,534	4,059
Earnings Per Share ($)						
1Q	**0.34**	**0.27**	0.20	0.23	0.20	0.18
2Q	**E0.31**	**0.24**	0.21	0.18	0.16	0.13
3Q	**E0.32**	**0.26**	0.23	0.20	0.16	0.12
4Q	**E0.53**	**0.44**	0.23	0.23	0.32	-0.27
Yr.	**E1.50**	**1.22**	0.87	0.95	0.83	0.15

Next earnings report expected: mid September
Dividend Data (Dividends have been paid since 1968.)

Amount ($)	Date Decl.	Ex-Div. Date	Stock of Record	Payment Date
0.215	Jan. 09	Jan. 15	Jan. 20	Feb. 02 '98
2-for-1	Jan. 09	Feb. 03	Jan. 20	Feb. 02 '98
0.107	Apr. 08	Apr. 16	Apr. 20	Apr. 27 '98
0.107	Jun. 24	Jul. 16	Jul. 20	Jul. 27 '98

A Division of The **McGraw·Hill** *Companies*

Business Summary - 01-JUL-98

In December 1996, Rite Aid (RAD) completed the acquisition of Thrifty PayLess, Inc. (NYSE: TPD), the largest drug store chain in the western United States, with 1,007 stores and $4.4 billion in sales. The acquisition created a drug store chain of more than 3,600 units with FY 98 (Feb.) revenues of $11.4 billion operating in 26 states and the District of Columbia.

The integration of Thrifty Payless' pharmacy benefits management (PBM) unit into RAD's Eagle Managed Care Corp. created one of the largest PBMs owned by a drug chain, marketing prescription plans and other managed care health services to over three million people. Pharmacy volume accounted for 50% of FY 98 drug store revenues. Third-party transactions accounted for some 83% of total pharmacy sales.

During FY 98 Rite-Aid completed the vast majority of the integration of Thrifty PayLess and also purchased the two largest privately-held drugstore chains in the United States; Harco, Inc., based in Alabama; and K & B, Inc. the predominant chain in Louisiana. It is now in the process of melding the 332 stores into Rite Aid. At May 30, 1998, the company had a total of 4,010 stores in operation.

The company introduced a new 10,500-square-foot store design in FY 96, slightly larger than any of the company's existing stores. These stores offer wider aisles, more attractive lighting, expanded merchandise, one-hour photofinishing, larger pharmacy waiting areas and public restrooms. The new stores also offer expanded offerings of cosmetics, designer fragrances, frozen meals, dairy products and other convenience foods, as well as small appliances and a business service counter.

During FY 98, Rite-Aid opened 411 of these newer-format stores and closed 156 smaller units. Expansion plans call for the addition of some 1,500 new stores over the next three years, with a focus on the western and southern parts of the United States. This year, the company will also add two larger, highly sophisticated distribution centers, featuring state-of-the-art computer and materials handling equipment, which will consolidate and replace obsolete facilities.

The company is also focused on the development of information technology. During FY 98, the company completed the development of an automatic pharmacy replenishment system and is in the process of implementing a direct store delivery check-in and pricing system. A voice response units that allow customers to order prescription refills through the use of a touch-tone telephone has been rolled out to more than 1,500 stores.

Per Share Data ($)

(Year Ended Feb. 28)	1998	1997	1996	1995	1994	1993	1992	1991	1990	1989
Tangible Bk. Val.	3.85	3.44	4.57	4.50	4.82	5.05	4.58	3.71	3.29	3.17
Cash Flow	2.17	1.78	1.66	1.32	0.58	1.20	1.15	1.21	0.91	0.95
Earnings	1.22	0.87	0.95	0.83	0.15	0.76	0.71	0.65	0.49	0.57
Dividends	0.41	0.38	0.35	0.31	0.30	0.28	0.26	0.23	0.21	0.19
Payout Ratio	33%	43%	37%	37%	200%	37%	36%	36%	43%	33%
Cal. Yrs.	1997	1996	1995	1994	1993	1992	1991	1990	1989	1988
Prices - High	34¼	20½	17¼	12	10¾	12⅛	12	9⅝	10¼	10¼
- Low	18⅞	13⅝	11	7⅞	7⅝	9⅝	8⅝	7⅜	7⅜	7¼
P/E Ratio - High	28	23	18	14	72	16	17	15	21	18
- Low	15	16	12	9	51	13	12	11	15	13

Income Statement Analysis (Million $)

	1998	1997	1996	1995	1994	1993	1992	1991	1990	1989
Revs.	11,375	6,970	5,446	4,534	4,059	4,085	3,748	3,447	3,173	2,868
Oper. Inc.	964	592	443	357	300	326	318	320	279	257
Depr.	274	168	119	82.7	76.3	78.2	75.2	93.3	68.9	62.0
Int. Exp.	160	96.5	68.3	42.3	28.7	32.9	40.8	53.4	56.3	44.2
Pretax Inc.	530	259	256	231	46.0	215	202	175	134	154
Eff. Tax Rate	40%	38%	38%	39%	43%	38%	39%	39%	39%	38%
Net Inc.	316	161	159	141	26.0	132	124	107	82.0	95.0

Balance Sheet & Other Fin. Data (Million $)

	1998	1997	1996	1995	1994	1993	1992	1991	1990	1989
Cash	91.0	7.0	3.1	7.1	17.4	5.4	27.4	25.9	14.5	15.3
Curr. Assets	3,378	2,771	1,465	1,373	1,125	1,092	1,013	945	849	776
Total Assets	7,655	6,417	2,842	2,473	1,989	1,875	1,734	1,667	1,539	1,418
Curr. Liab.	1,771	1,172	630	577	362	281	290	237	216	479
LT Debt	2,551	2,416	994	806	613	489	428	585	542	228
Common Eqty.	2,916	2,489	1,104	1,012	955	1,036	951	774	704	636
Total Cap.	5,716	5,126	2,212	1,895	1,627	1,595	1,445	1,430	1,323	938
Cap. Exp.	471	371	315	183	169	125	88.0	157	177	147
Cash Flow	591	329	278	224	103	211	199	201	151	157
Curr. Ratio	1.9	2.4	2.3	2.4	3.1	3.9	3.5	4.0	3.9	1.6
% LT Debt of Cap.	44.6	47.1	45.0	42.5	37.7	30.7	29.6	40.9	41.0	24.3
% Net Inc.of Revs.	2.8	2.3	3.0	3.1	0.6	3.2	3.3	3.1	2.6	3.3
% Ret. on Assets	4.5	3.5	6.0	6.4	1.4	7.3	7.1	6.7	5.5	7.2
% Ret. on Equity	11.7	8.9	15.1	14.5	2.7	13.3	14.0	14.5	12.2	15.8

Data as orig. reptd.; bef. results of disc. opers. and/or spec. items. Per share data adj. for stk. divs. as of ex-div. date. Bold denotes diluted EPS (FASB 128). E-Estimated. NA-Not Available. NM-Not Meaningful. NR-Not Ranked.

Office—30 Hunter Lane, Camp Hill, PA 17011-2404 (P.O. Box 3165, Harrisburg, PA 17105-3165). **Tel**—(717) 761-2633. **Website**—http://www.RiteAid.com **Chrmn & CEO**—M. L. Grass. **Vice Chrmn**—F. C. Brown. **Pres & COO**—T. J. Noonan. **VP-Secy**—E. S. Gerson. **EVP, CFO & Investor Contact**—Frank Bergonzi. **Dirs**—W. J. Bratton, F. C. Brown, A. Grass, M. L. Grass, L Green, N. Lieberman, P. Neivert, T. J. Noonan, L. N. Stem. **Transfer Agent & Registrar**—Harris Trust Co. of New York, NYC. **Incorporated**—in Delaware in 1968. **Empl**—83,000. **S&P Analyst:** Maureen C. Carini

RJR Nabisco Holdings

1890H

NYSE Symbol **RN**

In S&P 500

12-SEP-98

Industry: Tobacco

Summary: This company is the second largest U.S. producer of cigarettes (R.J. Reynolds Tobacco Co.) and the leading producer of food products (80.7%-owned Nabisco Holdings Corp.).

S&P Opinion: Hold (★★★)		
Recent Price • 23⅜	Yield • 8.8%	
52 Wk Range • 38-21¼	12-Mo. P/E • NM	

Quantitative Evaluations

Outlook (1 Lowest—5 Highest)
• **3**

Fair Value
• **26¼**

Risk
• **Average**

Earn./Div. Rank
• **NR**

Technical Eval.
• **Bullish** since 5/98

Rel. Strength Rank (1 Lowest—99 Highest)
• **82**

Insider Activity
• **NA**

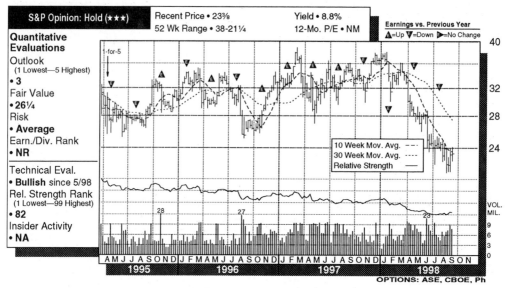

Earnings vs. Previous Year ▲=Up ▼=Down ▶=No Change

10 Week Mov. Avg. — — —
30 Week Mov. Avg. • • • •
Relative Strength ——

OPTIONS: ASE, CBOE, Ph

Overview - 31-JUL-98

We expect another difficult year for the company's tobacco unit in 1998, beset by more state settlements and possible significant consumption decline amidst higher cigarette prices. Food profits from the company's 80.7% stake in Nabisco Holdings should be down modestly from 1997's unspectacular performance, held back by significantly greater marketing spending behind core products and lackluster performance at both domestic and international food divisions. A stronger dollar relative to key foreign currencies may also be a near-term restraining factor. Controlled capital spending, though, should enable debt reduction and allow diluted EPS before unusual items to reach $2.45 in 1998, and $2.65 in 1999, from 1997's $2.95 (before an $89 million charge to restructure its international division).

Valuation - 31-JUL-98

The shares remain depressed by most valuation measurements, including P/E ratio, reflecting uninspiring tobacco profit trends, as well as investor worries concerning the challenging legal and regulatory environment facing the company's U.S. tobacco operations. The company's tobacco settlement agreements in Mississippi, Florida, Texas, and Minnesota will exact a toll on RN's cash flow in the future, and similar cases in other states are pending. Although a national tobacco accord may be reached in 1998, it is expected that significant monetary outlays by RN's tobacco operations will be required in return for little or no reduction in tobacco-related litigation risk. However, RN hopes to finalize such an accord as soon as possible, as it wishes to spin off its remaining 80.7% stake in the Nabisco food unit, which was valued at about $24 per RN share as of late July. Based on the value of this stake, we would hold RN shares for now.

Key Stock Statistics

S&P EPS Est. 1998	2.45	Tang. Bk. Value/Share	NM
P/E on S&P Est. 1998	9.5	Beta	0.75
S&P EPS Est. 1999	2.65	Shareholders	59,000
Dividend Rate/Share	2.05	Market cap. (B)	$ 7.6
Shs. outstg. (M)	324.8	Inst. holdings	70%
Avg. daily vol. (M)	1.670		

Value of $10,000 invested 5 years ago: $ 6,907

Fiscal Year Ending Dec. 31

	1998	1997	1996	1995	1994	1993
Revenues (Million $)						
1Q	3,947	3,779	3,886	3,540	3,572	3,736
2Q	4,292	4,286	4,203	4,081	3,784	3,719
3Q	—	4,409	4,349	4,063	3,966	3,598
4Q	—	4,583	4,625	4,324	4,044	4,051
Yr.	—	17,057	17,063	16,008	15,366	15,104
Earnings Per Share ($)						
1Q	-0.10	0.62	0.57	0.51	0.60	0.75
2Q	-0.44	0.71	-0.11	0.38	0.55	0.50
3Q	—	0.34	0.66	0.61	0.55	0.20
4Q	—	-0.58	0.63	0.11	0.40	-1.70
Yr.	—	1.09	1.76	1.58	2.05	-0.25

Next earnings report expected: late October

Dividend Data (Dividends have been paid since 1995.)

Amount ($)	Date Decl.	Ex-Div. Date	Stock of Record	Payment Date
0.512	Oct. 31	Dec. 11	Dec. 15	Jan. 01 '98
0.512	Feb. 06	Mar. 11	Mar. 15	Apr. 01 '98
0.512	May. 13	Jun. 11	Jun. 15	Jul. 01 '98
0.512	Sep. 09	Sep. 16	Sep. 20	Oct. 01 '98

A Division of The McGraw-Hill Companies

Business Summary - 31-JUL-98

RJR Nabisco Holdings (RN) is the indirect parent company of RJR Nabisco, Inc. (RJRN), an international producer of tobacco and food products. Business segment contributions (excluding unusual charges) in 1997 were:

	Revs.	Profits
Tobacco	49%	57%
Food	51%	43%

The U.S. tobacco business is conducted by R.J. Reynolds Tobacco Co., a wholly owned subsidiary of RJRN and the second largest manufacturer of cigarettes. In 1997, R.J. Reynolds held an approximate 25% share of the U.S. cigarette market with its brands that include Winston, Salem, Camel, Doral and Vantage. Lower priced brands include Monarch and Best Value and are intended to appeal to more cost conscious adult smokers. In May 1996, the company began testing a cigarette, called Eclipse, that primarily heats rather than burns tobacco and thereby substantially reduces second-hand smoke. Test markets were expanded in 1997 and the company is still assessing test results.

R.J. Reynolds is a defendant in a number of product-liability lawsuits related to cigarettes, particularly in the United States. As a consequence, the company has emphasized its need to establish a presence in overseas markets. Tobacco operations outside the U.S. are conducted by Reynolds International (RI), which sells more than 100 brands of cigarettes in more than 170 markets worldwide. RI has strong brand presence in Western Europe, the Middle East/Africa, Asia, the former Soviet Union and Canada. Approximately 18% of its international cigarette volume is manufactured in the U.S.

RN's food business is conducted by operating subsidiaries of 80.7%-owned Nabisco Holdings Corp. (NYSE: NA). Nabisco's subsidiaries include Nabisco Biscuit, the largest U.S. maker of cookies and crackers (Oreo, Chips Ahoy!, Ritz); Specialty Products, a maker of niche grocery products, including A.1. steak sauces, Cream of Wheat hot cereals, Grey Poupon mustards and Milk-Bone pet snacks; LifeSavers, maker of LifeSavers candy and Care-Free and Bubble Yum gum products; Planters, maker of nuts, snacks and oils; Food Service, which sells specially packaged food products for institutions; Nabisco Tablespreads Co., producer of Fleischmann's and Blue Bonnet margarines; Nabisco Brands Ltd., which conducts the company's Canadian operations; and Nabisco International, maker of powdered dessert and drink mixes.

In 1997, Nabisco Biscuit had a 40% and 54% share of the domestic cookie category and a 54% share of the domestic cracker category.

Per Share Data ($)

(Year Ended Dec. 31)	1997	1996	1995	1994	1993	1992	1991	1990	1989	1988
Tangible Bk. Val.	NM	NM	NA	-42.55	-60.60	-60.70	-63.40	-177.95	NA	NA
Cash Flow	4.62	5.34	5.50	5.60	3.70	6.65	7.00	6.30	NA	NA
Earnings	1.09	1.76	1.60	2.05	-0.25	2.75	1.10	-5.95	NA	NA
Dividends	2.05	1.85	1.50	Nil	Nil	Nil	Nil	Nil	Nil	Nil
Payout Ratio	188%	105%	94%	Nil	Nil	Nil	Nil	Nil	Nil	Nil
Prices - High	38⅞	35¼	33⅜	40⅝	46¼	58¾	65	NA	NA	NA
- Low	27	25⅛	25	26⅞	21⅞	39⅜	27½	NA	NA	NA
P/E Ratio - High	36	20	21	20	NM	21	59	NA	NA	NA
- Low	25	14	16	13	NM	14	25	NA	NA	NA

Income Statement Analysis (Million $)

	1997	1996	1995	1994	1993	1992	1991	1990	1989	1988
Revs.	17,057	17,063	16,008	15,366	15,104	15,734	14,989	13,879	NA	NA
Oper. Inc.	3,474	3,854	3,663	3,698	3,181	3,969	3,984	3,876	NA	NA
Depr.	1,138	1,174	1,171	1,083	1,073	1,071	1,050	1,058	NA	NA
Int. Exp.	912	927	899	1,065	1,209	1,449	2,217	3,176	NA	NA
Pretax Inc.	1,016	1,199	1,266	1,375	111	1,456	648	-401	NA	NA
Eff. Tax Rate	52%	49%	46%	44%	103%	47%	43%	NM	NM	NM
Net Inc.	402	611	627	764	-3.0	776	368	-461	NA	NA

Balance Sheet & Other Fin. Data (Million $)

	1997	1996	1995	1994	1993	1992	1991	1990	1989	1988
Cash	348	252	234	423	215	99	434	323	NA	NA
Curr. Assets	4,625	4,751	4,560	4,363	4,145	4,576	4,220	4,116	NA	NA
Total Assets	30,678	31,289	31,518	31,408	31,295	32,041	32,131	32,915	NA	NA
Curr. Liab.	4,145	4,306	4,124	5,594	3,943	3,846	4,055	5,205	NA	NA
LT Debt	9,456	9,256	9,429	8,883	12,005	13,353	13,149	16,955	NA	NA
Common Eqty.	9,111	9,611	9,785	9,596	7,780	8,250	8,316	2,494	NA	NA
Total Cap.	23,564	23,963	24,378	23,579	24,849	25,804	25,569	25,057	NA	NA
Cap. Exp.	763	741	744	670	623	519	459	426	NA	NA
Cash Flow	1,496	1,742	1,798	1,716	1,002	1,816	1,245	546	NA	NA
Curr. Ratio	1.1	1.1	1.1	0.8	1.1	1.2	1.0	0.8	NA	NA
% LT Debt of Cap.	40.1	38.6	38.7	37.7	48.3	51.7	51.4	67.7	NA	NA
% Net Inc.of Revs.	2.4	3.6	4.0	5.0	NM	4.9	2.5	NM	NM	NM
% Ret. on Assets	1.3	2.0	2.0	2.2	NM	2.4	0.8	NM	NM	NM
% Ret. on Equity	3.8	5.6	6.6	6.7	NM	8.9	3.0	NM	NM	NM

Data as orig. reptd.; bef. results of disc. opers. and/or spec. items. Per share data adj. for stk. divs. as of ex-div. date. Bold denotes diluted EPS (FASB 128). E-Estimated. NA-Not Available. NM-Not Meaningful. NR-Not Ranked.

Office—1301 Ave. of the Americas, New York, NY 10019. **Tel**—(212) 258-5600. **Website**—http://www.rjrnabisco.com **Chrmn & CEO**—S. Goldstone. **SVP & CFO**—D. B. Rickard. **Dirs**—J. T. Chain Jr., J. L. Chambers, J. L. Clendenin, S. F. Goldstone, R. J. Groves, F. Langhammer, H. E. Lockhart, T. E. Martin, J. G. Medlin Jr., R. L. Ridgway. **Transfer Agent**—First Chicago Trust Co. of New York, Jersey City, NJ. **Incorporated**—in Delaware in 1981. **Empl**—79,700. **S&P Analyst:** Richard Joy

Rockwell International

1943T

NYSE Symbol **ROK**

In S&P 500

12-SEP-98

Industry:
Electrical Equipment

Summary: This company, a leader in automation, avionics, communications and semiconductor systems, spun off its automotive components business in 1997.

S&P Opinion: Hold (★★★)

Recent Price • 38½
52 Wk Range • 63½-33¾

Yield • 2.6%
12-Mo. P/E • NM

Quantitative Evaluations

Outlook
(1 Lowest—5 Highest)
• **2+**

Fair Value
• **39**

Risk
• **Low**

Earn./Div. Rank
• **A-**

Technical Eval.
• **Bullish** since 9/98

Rel. Strength Rank
(1 Lowest—99 Highest)
• **66**

Insider Activity
• **Favorable**

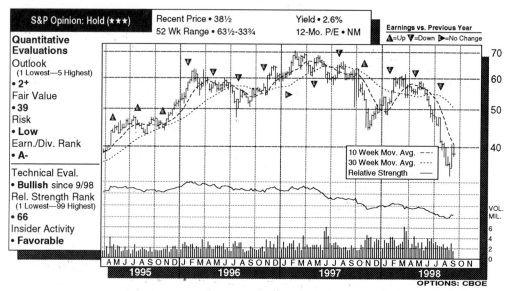

Earnings vs. Previous Year
▲=Up ▼=Down ▶=No Change

10 Week Mov. Avg. - - -
30 Week Mov. Avg. ·····
Relative Strength ——

VOL.
MIL.

OPTIONS: CBOE

Overview - 22-JUL-98

Rockwell's storied past includes the building of NASA's Space Shuttle and the U.S. Airforce's B-1 bomber, the successor to the fabled B-52 bomber. However, the end of the Cold War in the late 1980s, followed by subsequent defense cutbacks, prompted the company to sell its $2.5 billion aerospace and $1 billion defense electronics businesses in the mid-1990s. Management's desire to focus on a few core businesses prompted the divestiture of printing press operations in 1996, and the spinoff of the company's $3 billion auto parts business in 1997. In efforts to overhaul operations for the third time in three years, ROK decided to spin off its money-losing semiconductor business to shareholders by the 1998 fourth quarter. In the last several years, ROK has also made several acquisitions (with mixed results) to augment the company's remaining segments: Automation ($4.6 billion in revenues), which makes automated machinery and equipment; and Avionics ($2.2 billion in revenues), which makes navigational, communciations, and in-flight entertainment systems for aircraft manufacturers.

Valuation - 22-JUL-98

Over the last several years, ROK's earnings and ROE have materially declined, in part due to continuing restructuring, divestiture and acquisition-related charges from ongoing management efforts to overhaul the company. We believe that ROK will still face downward pressure on EPS earnings growth and ROE, primarily due to weakening Automation business (as a result of Asia's economic crisis and slowing U.S. factory investment), as well as from Automation restructuring charges. Based on our intrinsic value models, we believe that the company's stock (including the semiconductor unit) is fairly valued at recent price levels.

Key Stock Statistics

S&P EPS Est. 1998	2.40	Tang. Bk. Value/Share	12.99
P/E on S&P Est. 1998	16.1	Beta	0.99
S&P EPS Est. 1999	2.90	Shareholders	62,300
Dividend Rate/Share	1.02	Market cap. (B)	$ 7.4
Shs. outstg. (M)	191.2	Inst. holdings	39%
Avg. daily vol. (M)	0.462		

Value of $10,000 invested 5 years ago: NA

Fiscal Year Ending Sep. 30

	1998	1997	1996	1995	1994	1993
Revenues (Million $)						
1Q	1,979	1,853	2,385	2,623	2,601	2,489
2Q	1,941	1,899	2,631	3,361	2,762	2,694
3Q	1,664	1,929	2,696	3,452	2,873	2,813
4Q	—	2,081	2,661	3,545	2,889	2,844
Yr.	—	7,762	10,373	12,981	11,123	10,840
Earnings Per Share ($)						
1Q	**0.43**	0.70	0.70	0.76	0.68	0.58
2Q	**-0.53**	0.72	0.74	0.88	0.70	0.63
3Q	—	0.62	0.79	0.90	0.74	0.66
4Q	—	0.70	0.32	0.88	0.75	0.68
Yr.	—	3.01	2.55	3.42	2.87	2.55

Next earnings report expected: early November

Dividend Data (Dividends have been paid since 1948.)

Amount ($)	Date Decl.	Ex-Div. Date	Stock of Record	Payment Date
0.255	Nov. 05	Nov. 13	Nov. 17	Dec. 08 '97
0.255	Feb. 04	Feb. 12	Feb. 17	Mar. 09 '98
0.255	May. 06	May. 14	May. 18	Jun. 08 '98
0.255	Jun. 29	Aug. 13	Aug. 17	Sep. 08 '98

A Division of The McGraw-Hill Companies

Business Summary - 22-JUL-98

In the last three years, Rockwell management has been searching for a strategy that would consistently boost earnings growth and returns on investment. In the early 1990s, the company was content to utilize a diversification strategy; however, in 1995, management jettisoned this strategy in favor of a plan to focus on just a few core businesses. To this end, management either sold or spun off divisions such as ROK's $3 billion automotive parts business, $2.5 billion aerospace operations, and $1 billion defense electronics business. The company's latest divestiture involves the proposed spinoff to shareholders of ROK's $1.3 billion computer modem chip making division, the world's largest maker of semiconductor chips for personal computer and fax modems.

Some important profitability statistics from recent years are:

	1997	1996	1995
SEGMENT OP. PROFIT MARGINS			
Automation	13%	13%	13%
Avionics & Communications	15%	12%	12%
Semiconductors/Electronic Commerce	15%	21%	13%

The Automation segment makes conveyor systems, sensors, motors and related equipment, to move, control or monitor various types of industrial machinery. The segment primarily markets its offerings to the transportation, oil, drug and food industries. The company sells its automation products mostly under its Rockwell Automation, Allen-Bradley and Reliance Electric brand names. Management believes that the Automation segment, with 500,000 different offerings, is North America's largest supplier of automated machinery and related equipment.

The Avionics & Communications segment makes communications, navigation, and flight control systems for commercial aircraft manufacturers such as Boeing and Airbus. The segment also makes passenger audio and visual systems, such as small TV screens built into airplane seats. In addition, A&C is a leading worldwide producer of military communication systems. Rockwell believes that its military systems transmit and receive nearly 70% of all U.S. military airborne communications.

The Semiconductor Systems unit makes modem chips used in computers, faxes, as well as cellular and cordless phones. The segment's smaller electronic commerce unit sells computerized tracking systems to airlines and package delivery companies. ROK plans to spin off the semiconductor business, but to keep the electronic commerce operations.

Per Share Data ($)

(Year Ended Sep. 30)	1997	1996	1995	1994	1993	1992	1991	1990	1989	1988
Tangible Bk. Val.	14.67	11.17	8.08	11.77	9.69	8.80	13.98	12.58	11.50	10.07
Cash Flow	5.00	5.03	6.05	5.11	4.79	4.65	5.14	5.10	5.28	5.30
Earnings	2.74	2.55	3.42	2.87	2.55	2.16	2.57	2.56	2.87	3.04
Dividends	1.16	1.16	1.08	1.02	0.96	0.92	0.86	0.80	0.75	0.70
Payout Ratio	42%	45%	32%	36%	38%	43%	33%	31%	26%	23%
Prices - High	70⅝	64⅝	48	44⅛	38½	29⅜	29¼	28¾	27⅛	23½
- Low	44⅜	47½	35	33½	27⅞	22¼	22¾	20½	19¾	16⅛
P/E Ratio - High	26	25	14	15	15	13	11	11	9	8
- Low	16	19	10	12	11	10	9	8	7	5

Income Statement Analysis (Million $)

	1997	1996	1995	1994	1993	1992	1991	1990	1989	1988
Revs.	7,762	10,373	12,981	11,123	10,840	10,910	11,927	12,379	12,518	11,946
Oper. Inc.	1,367	1,544	1,849	1,530	1,418	1,327	1,600	1,733	1,674	1,602
Depr.	484	542	571	494	491	558	601	620	615	600
Int. Exp.	27.0	32.0	170	97.0	104	107	135	144	133	101
Pretax Inc.	923	896	1,226	1,021	904	778	1,024	1,052	1,206	1,053
Eff. Tax Rate	37%	38%	39%	38%	38%	38%	41%	41%	39%	23%
Net Inc.	586	555	742	634	562	483	601	624	735	812

Balance Sheet & Other Fin. Data (Million $)

	1997	1996	1995	1994	1993	1992	1991	1990	1989	1988
Cash	283	715	665	628	773	603	504	411	332	900
Curr. Assets	3,684	5,358	5,805	4,928	4,946	4,889	4,823	4,775	4,367	4,925
Total Assets	7,971	10,065	12,505	9,861	9,885	9,731	9,479	9,738	8,939	9,209
Curr. Liab.	1,970	4,281	4,111	3,020	2,991	3,112	3,322	3,843	3,482	3,796
LT Debt	156	161	1,776	831	1,028	1,035	740	553	552	745
Common Eqty.	4,811	4,256	3,781	3,350	2,950	2,771	4,216	4,177	3,968	3,682
Total Cap.	4,967	4,417	5,558	4,187	3,984	3,813	5,662	5,422	5,187	4,438
Cap. Exp.	683	866	685	568	433	386	484	538	609	555
Cash Flow	1,070	1,097	1,313	1,128	1,053	1,041	1,202	1,244	1,349	1,412
Curr. Ratio	1.9	1.3	1.4	1.6	1.7	1.6	1.5	1.2	1.3	1.3
% LT Debt of Cap.	3.2	3.6	31.9	19.8	25.8	27.2	13.1	10.2	10.6	16.8
% Net Inc.of Revs.	7.5	5.4	5.7	5.7	5.2	4.4	5.0	5.0	5.9	6.8
% Ret. on Assets	6.5	5.8	6.6	6.5	5.7	5.1	6.4	6.8	8.3	9.3
% Ret. on Equity	12.9	13.8	20.7	20.2	19.6	14.1	14.6	15.7	19.6	23.8

Data as orig. reptd.; bef. results of disc. opers. and/or spec. items. Per share data adj. for stk. divs. as of ex-div. date. Bold denotes diluted EPS (FASB 128). EPS in 3Q '98 includes $2.60 of restructuring charges. EPS estimates exclude special charges and discontinued ops. Free cash flow: Net income plus depr./amort. and declines in working capital, less net cap. ex., increases in working capital and preferred dividends. E-Estimated. NA-Not Available. NM-Not Meaningful. NR-Not Ranked.

Office—600 Anton Boulevard, Suite 700, P.O. Box 5090, Costa Mesa, CA 92628-5090. **Tel**—(714) 424-4546. **Website**—http://www.rockwell.com **Chrmn, Pres & CEO**—D. H. Davis Jr. **SVP-Fin & CFO**—W. M. Barnes. **SVP & Secy**—W. J. Calise Jr. **VP & Treas**—D. J. Popovec. **Investor Contact**—A. Lee Shull, Jr. (412-565-7436). **Dirs**—L. Allen Jr., R. M. Bressler, D. H. Davis Jr., J. L. Estrin, W. H. Gray III, J. C. LaForce Jr., W. T. McCormick Jr., J. D. Nichols, B. M. Rockwell, W. S. Sneath, J. F. Toot Jr. **Transfer Agent & Registrar**—ChaseMellon Shareholder Services, Ridgefield Park, NJ. **Incorporated**—in Delaware in 1928. **Empl**— 48,000. **S&P Analyst:** Robert E. Friedman, CPA

STANDARD &POOR'S
STOCK REPORTS

Rohm & Haas

1946

NYSE Symbol **ROH**

In S&P 500

12-SEP-98

Industry:
Chemicals

Summary: This company is an important producer of chemicals, plastics, pesticides and related products.

S&P Opinion: Hold (★★★)	Recent Price • 28⅝	Yield • 2.5%
	52 Wk Range • 38¾-26	12-Mo. P/E • 11.2

Quantitative Evaluations

Outlook
(1 Lowest—5 Highest)
• **3+**

Fair Value
• **31⅜**

Risk
• **Low**

Earn./Div. Rank
• **A-**

Technical Eval.
• **Bullish** since 6/98

Rel. Strength Rank
(1 Lowest—99 Highest)
• **60**

Insider Activity
• **Neutral**

Earnings vs. Previous Year
▲=Up ▽=Down ▶=No Change

10 Week Mov. Avg. — ─ ─
30 Week Mov. Avg. ─ ─ ─
Relative Strength ───

3-for-1

VOL. MIL.

OPTIONS: ASE

Overview - 14-AUG-98

In mid-August 1998, the company completed most of a recently expanded 6 million share buyback program, which is part of a recapitalization program. Since 1995, ROH has purchased more than 13 million shares (20% of the total outstanding) for more than $1 billion. ROH and The Haas Family and related trusts (owners of 40% of the shares) decided not to complete a transaction that would have exchanged four million common shares for convertible preferred stock. The stock buyback boosted ROH's low leverage (its debt to capital ratio rose to about 35% from only 17%), but it still allows the company to make a sizable acquisition. ROH is looking mostly in the electronic materials area, and the company will accept short-term EPS dilution. ROH generates good cash flow, and the recent sale of two joint ventures resulted in proceeds of $290 million. We are projecting that reported sales will decline in 1998, reflecting the absence of sales associated with one of the two ventures recently sold, as well as unfavorable currency exchange rates. Gross margins are expected to widen, on lower raw material costs and good plant operations. Profits will also benefit from continued aggressive cost reductions designed to keep overhead costs flat. The ongoing stock repurchase program will help EPS comparisons. EPS in the 1998 second quarter included a gain of $0.93 a share from the sale of 50% interests in two joint ventures.

Valuation - 14-AUG-98

We recommend holding the somewhat volatile shares of this major chemicals producer. The stock climbed to a record high in May 1998, on good earnings prospects and the possibility of a major recapitalization. ROH recently announced a three-for-one stock split and raised the dividend 8%. Dividends have been increased for 21 consecutive years, and should continue to advance over the long term.

Key Stock Statistics

S&P EPS Est. 1998	2.20	Tang. Bk. Value/Share	10.23
P/E on S&P Est. 1998	12.9	Beta	1.08
S&P EPS Est. 1999	2.33	Shareholders	4,400
Dividend Rate/Share	0.72	Market cap. (B)	$ 5.1
Shs. outstg. (M)	178.2	Inst. holdings	74%
Avg. daily vol. (M)	0.623		

Value of $10,000 invested 5 years ago: $ 18,156

Fiscal Year Ending Dec. 31

	1998	1997	1996	1995	1994	1993
Revenues (Million $)						
1Q	937.0	986.0	994.0	985.0	856.0	826.0
2Q	990.0	1,089	1,054	1,042	944.0	884.0
3Q	—	974.0	969.0	942.0	874.0	799.0
4Q	—	950.0	965.0	915.0	860.0	760.0
Yr.	—	3,999	3,982	3,884	3,534	3,269
Earnings Per Share ($)						
1Q	**0.58**	**0.53**	0.49	0.38	0.32	0.28
2Q	**0.96**	**0.61**	0.50	0.42	0.46	0.30
3Q	—	**0.48**	0.44	0.28	0.26	-0.11
4Q	—	**0.52**	0.39	0.33	0.23	0.12
Yr.	—	**2.13**	**1.79**	1.41	1.26	0.58

Next earnings report expected: mid October

Dividend Data (Dividends have been paid since 1927.)

Amount ($)	Date Decl.	Ex-Div. Date	Stock of Record	Payment Date
0.500	Feb. 02	Feb. 11	Feb. 13	Mar. 02 '98
0.500	May. 04	May. 13	May. 15	Jun. 01 '98
0.540	Jul. 27	Aug. 05	Aug. 07	Sep. 01 '98
3-for-1	Jul. 27	Sep. 02	Aug. 07	Sep. 10 '98

A Division of The **McGraw·Hill** *Companies*

Business Summary - 14-AUG-98

This chemicals company is the world's second largest producer of acrylic acid. Over two-thirds of Rohm & Haas Co.'s product portfolio is based on acrylic chemicals, which are used to make a broad range of products from paints to plastics. Its higher-growth businesses include agrichemicals, biocides, electronic chemicals and formulated chemicals; these businesses account for nearly one-third of annual sales. Contributions by product category in 1997 were:

	Sales	Income
Performance Polymers	68%	71%
Chemical Specialties	22%	18%
Electronic Materials	10%	11%

International operations accounted for 45% of sales and 37% of income in 1997.

Performance polymers consists of polymers, resins and monomers (including opaque polymers, emulsions, modifiers, water-soluble polymers, dispersants, and acrylate and methacrylate monomers) produced for paints, inks, textile and paper coatings, adhesives, sealants, nonwoven materials, construction products, leather finishes, detergents and water treatment products. It is also a global supplier of plastic additives (impact modifiers and processing aids).

In June 1998, ROH completed the sale of stakes in two joint ventures, resulting in cash proceeds of $290 million. The company sold its 50% interest in AtoHaas to Elf Atochem. AtoHaas, with annual sales of $500 million, is the leading producer of acrylic resins, plastic sheeting and molding powders (sold under the Plexiglas brand), and polycarbonate sheeting. ROH also sold its 50% interest in the RohMax lubricant additive joint venture to its partner Rohm GmbH. The venture had 1997 sales of about $220 million.

Chemical specialities consist of ion exchange and fluid process chemicals for water treatment and food and chemical processing; biocides for industrial, household cleaning and personal care products; and agricultural chemicals, including fungicides, herbicides and insecticides, primarily for specialty crops, fruits and vegetables, and turf and ornamental use.

Electronic materials (including photoresists) are used for printed wiring boards and semiconductors. ROH expects this segment will account for 20% of total sales by 2001, through a combination of internal growth and acquisition. In June 1997, the company announced $75 million in investments to acquire new technology in electronic chemicals. ROH acquired a 25% interest (raised to 31% in 1998) in Rodel, Inc., a leader in chemical mechanical polishing technology, with annual sales of $200 million. It also purchased Pratta Electronic Chemicals, a maker of solder flux for printed wiring boards

Per Share Data ($) (Year Ended Dec. 31)	1997	1996	1995	1994	1993	1992	1991	1990	1989	1988
Tangible Bk. Val.	8.51	7.84	7.58	6.70	5.79	5.64	6.24	5.75	6.28	5.74
Cash Flow	3.67	3.19	2.60	2.40	1.70	1.87	1.77	1.83	1.63	1.79
Earnings	2.13	1.82	1.41	1.26	0.58	0.84	0.82	1.03	0.88	1.15
Dividends	0.63	0.57	0.52	0.48	0.45	0.43	0.41	0.41	0.39	0.34
Payout Ratio	30%	32%	37%	38%	78%	51%	51%	39%	44%	30%
Prices - High	33¾	27½	21⅝	22⅞	20⅝	19⅞	16⅛	12⅜	12½	12½
- Low	23½	18¼	16½	17¾	15¾	14¼	10⅞	8⅛	9⅝	9⅜
P/E Ratio - High	16	15	15	18	36	24	20	12	14	11
- Low	11	10	12	14	27	17	13	8	12	8
Income Statement Analysis (Million $)										
Revs.	3,999	3,986	3,884	3,545	3,278	3,072	2,773	2,824	2,661	2,535
Oper. Inc.	896	839	765	717	560	569	442	457	421	480
Depr.	279	262	242	231	226	203	183	159	150	128
Int. Exp.	39.0	54.0	57.0	60.0	60.0	107	64.0	63.0	59.0	48.0
Pretax Inc.	616	530	441	407	194	261	240	313	251	346
Eff. Tax Rate	33%	32%	34%	35%	35%	33%	32%	34%	30%	34%
Net Inc.	410	363	292	264	126	174	163	207	176	230
Balance Sheet & Other Fin. Data (Million $)										
Cash	40.0	11.0	43.0	127	35.0	91.0	208	65.0	150	223
Curr. Assets	1,397	1,456	1,421	1,440	1,200	1,257	1,141	1,009	1,011	1,032
Total Assets	3,900	3,933	3,916	3,861	3,524	3,445	2,897	2,702	2,455	2,242
Curr. Liab.	850	886	828	932	701	713	535	585	577	547
LT Debt	509	562	606	629	690	699	718	598	359	288
Common Eqty.	1,671	1,597	1,648	1,486	1,305	1,292	1,231	1,233	1,311	1,207
Total Cap.	2,510	2,501	2,550	2,402	2,289	2,274	2,224	1,991	1,670	1,495
Cap. Exp.	254	334	417	339	382	283	265	412	385	338
Cash Flow	682	625	527	488	344	373	340	366	326	358
Curr. Ratio	1.6	1.6	1.7	1.5	1.7	1.8	2.1	1.7	1.8	1.9
% LT Debt of Cap.	20.2	22.5	23.8	26.2	30.1	30.7	32.3	30.0	21.5	19.3
% Net Inc.of Revs.	10.3	9.1	7.5	7.4	3.8	5.7	5.9	7.3	6.6	9.1
% Ret. on Assets	10.5	9.2	7.5	7.1	3.6	5.4	5.8	8.0	7.5	11.0
% Ret. on Equity	24.7	21.9	18.2	18.4	9.1	13.1	13.2	16.3	14.0	20.4

Data as orig. reptd.; bef. results of disc. opers. and/or spec. items. Per share data adj. for stk. divs. as of ex-div. date. Bold denotes diluted EPS (FASB 128). E-Estimated. NA-Not Available. NM-Not Meaningful. NR-Not Ranked.

Office—100 Independence Mall West, Philadelphia, PA 19106-2399. **Tel**—(215) 592-3000. **Website**—http://www.rohmhaas.com **Chrmn & CEO**—J. L. Wilson. **Pres**—J. P. Mulroney. **Secy**—G. P. Granoff. **VP & CFO**—B. J. Bell. **Investor Contact**—W. C. Andrews. **Dirs**—W. J. Avery, D. B. Burke, E. G. Graves, J. A. Henderson, J. H. McArthur, J. P. Montoya, S. O. Moose, J. P. Mulroney, G. S. Omenn, R. H. Schmitz, A. Schriesheim, M. C. Whittington, J. L. Wilson. **Transfer Agent & Registrar**—Wachovia Bank of North Carolina, Winston-Salem. **Incorporated**—in Delaware in 1917. **Empl**— 11,592. **S&P Analyst:** Richard O'Reilly, CFA

STANDARD &POOR'S
STOCK REPORTS

Rowan Companies

1953J

NYSE Symbol **RDC**

In S&P 500

12-SEP-98

Industry:
Oil & Gas (Drilling &
Equipment)

Summary: This company engages in contract oil and natural gas drilling, provides contract aviation services, and builds heavy equipment and offshore drilling rigs.

S&P Opinion: Avoid (★★)	Recent Price • 12⅞	Yield • Nil
	52 Wk Range • 43⅞-9	12-Mo. P/E • 5.9

Quantitative Evaluations

Outlook
(1 Lowest—5 Highest)
• **5**

Fair Value
• **26**

Risk
• **High**

Earn./Div. Rank
• **B-**

Technical Eval.
• **Bearish** since 3/98

Rel. Strength Rank
(1 Lowest—99 Highest)
• **42**

Insider Activity
• **Neutral**

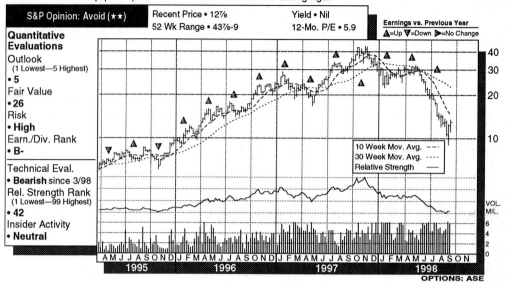

Earnings vs. Previous Year
▲=Up ▼=Down ▶=No Change

10 Week Mov. Avg. – – –
30 Week Mov. Avg. · · · ·
Relative Strength —

OPTIONS: ASE

Overview - 15-JUL-98

Earnings, which have risen significantly over the past two years, continued to climb during the first half of 1998, reflecting higher dayrates for the company's drilling fleet. However, the recent deterioration in oil prices has led to some cutbacks in exploration spending by oil companies, and demand for drilling rigs has begun to decline. Consequently, utilization rates and dayrates for jackup rigs in the Gulf of Mexico, Rowan's primary market, appear set to fall. With many of its 21 offshore rigs scheduled for contract renewals over the next 12 months, Rowan's earnings could fall short of previous expectations. Looking to the long-term, the company, through its Marathon LeTourneau subsidiary, is building three more Gorilla class rigs for use in the North Sea.

Valuation - 15-JUL-98

After rising 35% during 1997, the shares have fallen on hard times in 1998, plunging nearly 45% since the beginning of the year. The recent sharp decline in crude oil prices has raised the possibility of reductions in exploration and production capital spending by oil producers, which could hamper drilling activity. Although the offshore rig supply and demand picture currently appears healthy, any slowdown in drilling activity could stem the impressive rise in rig dayrates that has been seen over the past two years, with lower dayrates a distinct possibility. Operators of jackup rigs, such as Rowan, are seen as more vulnerable to the threat of reduced capital spending than are owners of semisubmersibles or drillships, which operate in deeper water. Shallow water oil projects have shorter cycle times than do deep water projects, and are thus more reliant on current oil prices. We have downgraded our opinion on the shares to avoid from hold, reflecting our expectation that the shares will continue to underperform the market over the remainder of 1998.

Key Stock Statistics

S&P EPS Est. 1998	1.95	Tang. Bk. Value/Share	8.50
P/E on S&P Est. 1998	6.6	Beta	1.42
S&P EPS Est. 1999	2.35	Shareholders	3,100
Dividend Rate/Share	Nil	Market cap. (B)	$ 1.1
Shs. outstg. (M)	85.2	Inst. holdings	65%
Avg. daily vol. (M)	1.282		

Value of $10,000 invested 5 years ago: $ 16,427

Fiscal Year Ending Dec. 31

	1998	1997	1996	1995	1994	1993
Revenues (Million $)						
1Q	183.9	144.8	126.8	92.80	100.7	73.54
2Q	204.2	164.8	137.2	117.4	105.4	82.09
3Q	—	195.5	154.7	134.3	129.2	106.6
4Q	—	190.3	152.5	126.8	102.9	90.93
Yr.	—	695.3	571.2	471.3	438.2	353.2
Earnings Per Share ($)						
1Q	**0.48**	0.09	0.03	-0.26	-0.07	-0.18
2Q	**0.50**	0.46	0.15	-0.04	-0.07	-0.11
3Q	—	0.61	0.26	0.01	0.07	0.10
4Q	—	0.60	0.27	0.07	-0.20	Nil
Yr.	**E1.95**	1.76	0.70	-0.22	-0.27	-0.17

Next earnings report expected: mid October

Dividend Data

Common dividends, paid since 1964, were omitted in 1986.

A Division of The McGraw-Hill Companies

STANDARD
&POOR'S
STOCK REPORTS

Rowan Companies, Inc.

1953J
12-SEP-98

Business Summary - 15-JUL-98

After an industry downturn that lasted longer than a decade, the oil and gas drilling industry has begun an impressive rebound. Rowan Companies (RDC), an international contract driller with a dominant presence in offshore markets, is betting more than half a billion dollars that the industry's good times will continue, despite lower oil prices. While dayrates, the amount paid to a contractor for a day's use of its rigs, have been rising, they have not yet reached the levels that would justify building new rigs on speculation. However, Rowan believes that dayrates will continue to advance and has plans to build three new rigs to take advantage of the growing demand for deep-water jackup rigs.

RDC currently owns 21 offshore rigs, including three heavy-duty Gorilla jackups, 17 deep-water jackups and one semisubmersible. The company sold its three submersible barge rigs in the 1995 fourth quarter for about $12 million. Work is done primarily in the Gulf of Mexico and the North Sea. Additional work is being done in Eastern Canada. At the end of 1997, utilization stood at virtually 100% for RDC's worldwide fleet.

The three new rigs will be called Gorilla V, Gorilla VI and Gorilla VII. The company has begun construction of the Rowan Gorilla V, which will be capable of operating year round in 400 ft. of water south of the 61st parallel. Total construction costs are estimated at about $175 million; completion is scheduled for the third quarter of

1998. In October 1996, directors approved the construction of two mobile offshore drilling units, to be named Gorilla VI and Gorilla VII, at an estimated combined cost of $380 million. The rigs will be constructed by the LeTourneau subsidiary, with delivery of the first rig, currently in the early stages of construction, expected in the first quarter of 1999 and delivery of the second expected in the second quarter of 2000.

The Era Aviation, Inc. unit operates a fleet of 95 helicopters, the majority of which are based in the U.S., and 21 fixed-wing aircraft that were based in Alaska. In January 1998, RDC terminated a joint venture under which it had a 49% interest in the helicopter unit of KLM Royal Dutch Airlines, which operated 15 helicopters in the North Sea.

The LeTourneau subsidiary manufactures cranes, front-end loaders and trucks used in coal, gold, copper, iron ore and other mines, and operates a mini-steel mill. Backlog at LeTourneau at February 28, 1998, amounted to $70 million. The division has built over one-third of all mobile offshore jackup drilling rigs, including all those operated by the company. Business segment contributions to consolidated revenues in recent years were:

	1997	1996
Drilling	62%	55%
Manufacturing	22%	25%
Aviation	16%	20%

Per Share Data ($)

(Year Ended Dec. 31)	1997	1996	1995	1994	1993	1992	1991	1990	1989	1988
Tangible Bk. Val.	7.53	5.80	5.06	5.21	5.44	5.08	6.06	6.63	6.58	7.09
Cash Flow	2.28	1.25	0.37	-0.33	0.49	-0.31	0.19	0.72	0.19	0.40
Earnings	1.76	0.70	-0.22	-0.27	-0.17	-1.01	-0.53	0.03	-0.52	-0.44
Dividends	Nil	Nil	Nil	Nil	Nil	Nil	Nil	Nil	Nil	Nil
Payout Ratio	Nil	Nil	Nil	Nil	Nil	Nil	Nil	Nil	Nil	Nil
Prices - High	43⁷/₈	24¹/₂	10	9¹/₄	10³/₄	9³/₈	11³/₈	15⁷/₈	11⁷/₈	8⁵/₈
- Low	16³/₄	8⁷/₈	5³/₈	5³/₄	6⁵/₈	4⁵/₈	4³/₄	9⁷/₈	5⁵/₈	4¹/₂
P/E Ratio - High	25	35	NM	NM	NM	NM	NM	NM	NM	NM
- Low	10	13	NM	NM	NM	NM	NM	NM	NM	NM

Income Statement Analysis (Million $)

	1997	1996	1995	1994	1993	1992	1991	1990	1989	1988
Revs.	695	571	471	438	353	250	272	292	226	217
Oper. Inc.	230	127	48.3	49.4	59.3	0.7	29.9	63.3	23.2	20.2
Depr.	47.1	47.9	50.6	50.8	51.9	51.4	52.7	50.4	51.8	60.0
Int. Exp.	16.2	27.5	27.7	27.5	25.4	26.3	21.4	21.6	23.7	23.9
Pretax Inc.	173	60.5	-17.7	-22.5	-13.5	-73.3	-38.0	4.0	-37.0	-32.0
Eff. Tax Rate	9.73%	NM	NM	NM	NM	NM	NM	52%	NM	NM
Net Inc.	156	61.3	-18.0	-23.0	-13.3	-73.8	-38.7	2.0	-37.8	-31.6

Balance Sheet & Other Fin. Data (Million $)

	1997	1996	1995	1994	1993	1992	1991	1990	1989	1988
Cash	108	97.2	90.0	111	117	30.0	235	108	131	74.0
Curr. Assets	412	317	273	254	216	103	303	179	184	202
Total Assets	1,122	899	802	805	765	684	896	739	738	801
Curr. Liab.	81.5	85.3	73.0	58.0	44.0	42.0	177	45.0	50.0	57.0
LT Debt	256	267	248	249	207	213	221	154	163	181
Common Eqty.	653	496	429	442	460	376	445	486	479	515
Total Cap.	984	765	681	695	672	594	671	645	649	703
Cap. Exp.	181	118	33.9	33.0	22.0	40.0	58.0	60.0	23.0	18.0
Cash Flow	204	109	32.1	27.8	38.7	-22.4	13.9	52.4	14.0	28.4
Curr. Ratio	5.1	3.7	3.8	4.4	4.9	2.5	1.7	4.0	3.7	3.5
% LT Debt of Cap.	26.0	34.9	36.4	35.7	30.8	35.9	32.9	23.8	25.2	25.8
% Net Inc.of Revs.	22.5	10.8	NM	NM	NM	NM	NM	0.7	NM	NM
% Ret. on Assets	15.5	7.2	NM	NM	NM	NM	NM	0.3	NM	NM
% Ret. on Equity	27.2	13.3	NM	NM	NM	NM	NM	0.4	NM	NM

Data as orig. reptd.; bef. results of disc. opers. and/or spec. items. Per share data adj. for stk. divs. as of ex-div. date. Bold denotes diluted EPS (FASB 128). E-Estimated. NA-Not Available. NM-Not Meaningful. NR-Not Ranked.

Office—5450 Transco Tower, 2800 Post Oak Blvd., Houston, TX 77056-6196. **Tel**—(713) 621-7800. **Chrmn, Pres & CEO**—C. R. Palmer. **VP-Fin & Treas**—E. E. Thiele. **Secy**—M.H. Hay. **VP & Investor Contact**—W. C. Provine. **Dirs**—R. E. Bailey, H. O. Boswell, R. G. Croyle, H. E. Lentz, D. F. McNease, C. B. Moynihan, C. R. Palmer, W. P. Schmoe, C. P. Siess Jr., C. W. Yeargain. **Transfer Agent & Registrar**—Harris Trust & Savings Bank, Chicago. **Incorporated**—in Delaware in 1947. **Empl**—5,250. **S&P Analyst:** Norman Rosenberg

Royal Dutch Petroleum   1954

NYSE Symbol **RD**

In S&P 500

12-SEP-98

Industry:
Oil (International Integrated)

<blockquote>**Summary:** Royal Dutch owns 60% of the Royal Dutch/Shell Group, a leading factor in the oil, natural gas and chemical industries. Shell Oil is a major U.S. integrated petroleum company.</blockquote>

S&P Opinion: Avoid (★★)

Recent Price • 50⅛   Yield • 2.7%
52 Wk Range • 60⅜-39¾   12-Mo. P/E • 25.1

Quantitative Evaluations

Outlook
  (1 Lowest—5 Highest)
• **1**

Fair Value
• **39⅜**

Risk
• **Low**

Earn./Div. Rank
• **A**

Technical Eval.
• **Bearish** since 9/96

Rel. Strength Rank
  (1 Lowest—99 Highest)
• **93**

Insider Activity
• **NA**

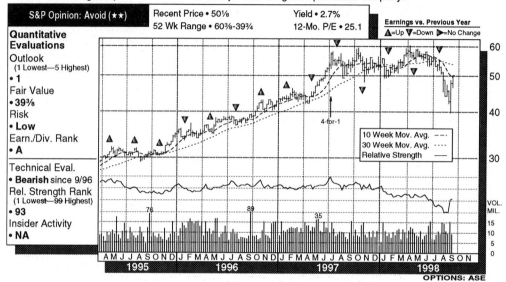

Earnings vs. Previous Year
▲=Up ▼=Down ▷=No Change

4-for-1

10 Week Mov. Avg. ---
30 Week Mov. Avg. ....
Relative Strength —

OPTIONS: ASE

Overview - 14-AUG-98

Oil and gas production was flat in 1997, but higher oil and gas production, both domestically and worldwide, is projected over the coming years. During the coming 12 months, we expect continued strength in natural gas prices, while Brent crude oil prices should remain weak, reflecting an oversupply of oil resulting from increased non-OPEC production and Iraqi exports, and spotty OPEC compliance with previously announced production cut pledges. Price realizations in 1998 will be well below 1997 levels. Chemicals profits, which tapered off in 1996, then improved in 1997, were lower in the first half of 1998, despite higher volumes, reflecting lower prices. Chemicals prices have been affected by reduced Asian demand, and the outlook for the second half of 1998 remains negative. Meanwhile, consumption of refined products in the Pacific Rim, where the group has a preeminent market share, could also be affected by the region's current economic troubles.

Valuation - 14-AUG-98

We believe that increased global demand for natural gas will aid earnings over the next several years. Excess refining industry capacity in Europe may impede 1998 earnings. However, lower crude oil prices, the result of some worldwide oversupply, bode well for margins over the next several months. Due to increasing worldwide crude oil production, Brent crude oil prices have fallen below $12 a barrel, with little upside seen in the near term. While the Royal Dutch/Shell Group's large reserves of cash and short-term investments will provide capital for an aggressive spending program, they have resulted in lower returns on capital than those of the company's peers. The shares, which were split four for one in June 1997, are expected to underperform the broader market in 1998, because of continued oil price weakness.

Key Stock Statistics

S&P EPS Est. 1998	2.25	Tang. Bk. Value/Share	29.26
P/E on S&P Est. 1998	22.3	Beta	1.07
S&P EPS Est. 1999	2.70	Shareholders	500,000
Dividend Rate/Share	1.37	Market cap. (B)	$107.6
Shs. outstg. (M)	2144.3	Inst. holdings	25%
Avg. daily vol. (M)	2.635		

Value of $10,000 invested 5 years ago: $ 29,743

Fiscal Year Ending Dec. 31

	1998	1997	1996	1995	1994	1993
Revenues (Million $)						
1Q	15,221	20,480	17,623	15,586	13,106	14,183
2Q	14,040	18,610	18,627	17,009	13,774	14,074
3Q	—	18,654	19,011	16,164	14,732	14,596
4Q	—	19,158	21,727	17,164	15,316	14,252
Yr.	—	77,911	76,988	65,923	56,898	57,105
Earnings Per Share ($)						
1Q	**0.47**	**0.68**	0.79	0.59	0.41	0.41
2Q	**0.42**	**0.51**	0.54	0.60	0.30	0.26
3Q	—	**0.61**	0.61	0.49	0.37	0.36
4Q	—	**0.51**	0.73	0.34	0.76	0.30
Yr.	**E2.25**	**2.30**	2.65	2.04	1.84	1.34

Next earnings report expected: early November

Dividend Data (Dividends have been paid since 1947.)

Amount ($)	Date Decl.	Ex-Div. Date	Stock of Record	Payment Date
0.372	—	Sep. 15	Sep. 17	Oct. 01 '97
0.765	—	May. 11	May. 13	May. 28 '98
0.060	—	Sep. 14	Sep. 16	Sep. 30 '98

Business Summary - 14-AUG-98

The Royal Dutch/Shell Group, the world's largest publicly owned oil company, is placing a large bet on deepwater exploration and production. Royal Dutch Petroleum (RD) owns 60% of the Royal Dutch/Shell Group; the other 40% is owned by Shell Transport & Trading Co. (SC). The Group owns Shell Oil Co. (U.S.) and a 79% interest in Shell Canada. In addition to being an integrated oil company, the Group has significant interests in petrochemicals, coal and metals. Segment operating profits (in million U.S.$) in recent years were:

	1997	1996	1995
Exploration & prod.	4,774	5,083	2,947
Refining and marketing	2,617	3,166	2,398
Chemicals	1,200	1,186	1,731
Other	155	18	178

During 1997, the Group's crude oil production averaged 2.3 million barrels per day (Mmbbl/d), up 1% from the 1996 level; natural gas sales 8.0 billion cubic feet a day (down 4%); refinery processing intakes 4.3 Mmbbl/d (up 7%); and crude and oil product sales 10.7 Mmbbl/d (up 1%). Net proved reserves at the end of 1997 stood at 8.4 billion bbl. of crude oil and natural gas liquids (9.1 billion in 1996) and 49.8 trillion cubic feet (Tcf) of natural gas (47.5). Official reserves numbers for

crude oil and natural gas were lowered by 1.0 million barrels and 2.6 Tcf, respectively, due to transfers of reserves to the books of associated U.S. joint venture companies.

Major initiatives to improve returns on refining assets were undertaken in 1997, including the completion of a modernization of the Pernis refinery in the Netherlands. Other projects are focused on assets in the U.S., Germany, Denmark, the Philippines, Malaysia, Thailand and China. The Chemicals division produces a large number of petrochemicals, base chemicals and solvents and is one of the world's largest producers of detergent intermediates and ethylene oxide. During 1997, basic chemicals sales volumes fell 5.4%, industrial chemicals volumes rose 1.8% and polymers volumes were up 8.2%.

The Group has stated that additions from existing fields will not be sufficient to maintain its reserve base. Instead, it will focus on exploration in new areas. Specifically, its strategy centers on finding oil and gas in deepwater areas, particularly in the Gulf of Mexico. The Group is currently the dominant player in the deepwater Gulf of Mexico, and expects to spend billions of dollars over the next few years on production from several huge fields in the area. With its large cash reserves ($3.4 billion at June 30, 1998), the Group has the financial clout to carry out its plan.

Per Share Data ($)

(Year Ended Dec. 31)	1997	1996	1995	1994	1993	1992	1991	1990	1989	1988
Tangible Bk. Val.	29.26	30.34	16.45	15.71	14.44	14.51	15.11	15.04	13.39	12.67
Cash Flow	NA	NA	4.21	3.77	3.06	3.46	3.11	3.57	3.32	2.98
Earnings	2.30	2.65	2.04	1.84	1.34	1.59	1.31	1.95	1.90	1.57
Dividends	1.06	1.23	1.16	1.13	1.00	1.05	0.94	0.90	0.82	0.70
Payout Ratio	46%	46%	57%	61%	75%	66%	72%	46%	43%	45%
Prices - High	59³⁄₈	43¹⁄₂	35¹⁄₂	29¹⁄₄	27	22⁷⁄₈	21⁵⁄₈	21³⁄₄	19³⁄₈	15¹⁄₂
- Low	42	33³⁄₈	26⁷⁄₈	24¹⁄₄	19³⁄₄	18³⁄₄	18¹⁄₄	17⁵⁄₈	14¹⁄₄	13
P/E Ratio - High	26	16	17	16	20	14	16	11	10	10
- Low	18	13	13	13	15	12	14	9	8	8

Income Statement Analysis (Million $)

	1997	1996	1995	1994	1993	1992	1991	1990	1989	1988
Revs.	129,851	136,251	65,923	56,898	57,104	57,975	61,618	63,887	51,247	47,036
Oper. Inc.	21,288	23,919	11,235	8,937	8,123	8,453	8,643	11,221	8,490	7,582
Depr.	7,282	7,764	4,864	4,138	3,710	3,932	3,854	3,500	3,001	3,055
Int. Exp.	1,274	1,345	738	716	811	911	917	966	791	734
Pretax Inc.	15,435	18,039	7,573	6,089	5,212	5,614	5,813	8,572	7,138	5,694
Eff. Tax Rate	49%	46%	44%	34%	45%	37%	52%	50%	41%	41%
Net Inc.	7,862	9,447	4,151	3,760	2,858	3,480	2,817	4,157	4,125	3,325

Balance Sheet & Other Fin. Data (Million $)

	1997	1996	1995	1994	1993	1992	1991	1990	1989	1988
Cash	5,184	12,088	6,814	6,960	5,754	5,145	5,277	5,108	3,900	4,884
Curr. Assets	33,510	42,250	23,369	21,534	18,854	19,152	20,269	22,215	17,359	16,550
Total Assets	114,784	121,590	70,561	64,711	59,898	60,491	63,320	63,859	54,116	51,168
Curr. Liab.	29,797	32,412	18,935	16,862	14,802	15,090	16,420	18,178	12,905	11,364
LT Debt	5,823	5,999	4,409	3,572	3,675	4,223	4,025	2,689	2,674	3,634
Common Eqty.	62,731	65,059	35,269	33,684	30,954	31,110	32,402	32,253	28,723	27,163
Total Cap.	79,673	83,010	46,339	42,968	41,019	41,803	43,949	42,916	38,767	37,433
Cap. Exp.	12,406	11,685	6,579	5,776	4,936	4,779	6,420	6,023	5,328	4,941
Cash Flow	15,144	17,211	9,021	8,088	6,568	7,412	6,671	7,657	7,126	6,380
Curr. Ratio	5.8	1.3	1.2	1.3	1.3	1.3	1.2	1.2	1.3	1.5
% LT Debt of Cap.	7.3	7.2	9.5	8.3	9.0	10.1	9.2	6.3	6.9	9.7
% Net Inc.of Revs.	6.1	5.2	6.3	6.9	5.0	6.0	4.6	6.5	8.0	7.1
% Ret. on Assets	6.7	7.6	6.1	6.3	4.7	5.6	4.4	7.0	7.8	6.5
% Ret. on Equity	12.3	14.4	12.0	12.2	9.2	11.0	8.7	13.6	14.8	12.6

Data as orig. reptd.; bef. results of disc. opers. and/or spec. items. Per share data adj. for stk. divs. as of ex-div. date. Revenues exclude excise taxes and other income. Prior to 1996, earnings and balance sheet data based on RD's participation in Group net income at varying exchange rates. E-Estimated. NA-Not Available. NM-Not Meaningful. NR-Not Ranked.

Office—Carel van Bylandtlaan 30, 2596 HR The Hague, The Netherlands. **Tel**—31-70-377 4540. **Managing Dirs**—C. A. J. Herkstroeter (Pres), M. A. van den Bergh, S. L. Miller, J. van der Veer. **U. S. Investor Contact**—J. C. Grapsi (212-261-5660). **Supervisory Dirs**—L. C. van Wachem (Chrmn), K. V. Cassani, J. M. H. van Engelshoven, A. G. Jacobs, J. A. A. Loudon, H. de Ruiter J. D. Timmer. **Transfer Agent & Registrar**—J.P. Morgan Service Center, Boston, (NYC drop: BancBoston Trust Corp.). **Incorporated**—in Holland in 1890. **Empl**— 105,000. **S&P Analyst:** Norman Rosenberg

STANDARD &POOR'S
STOCK REPORTS

Rubbermaid Inc.

1954M

NYSE Symbol **RBD**

In S&P 500

12-SEP-98

Industry: Housewares

Summary: This company manufactures a broad line of plastic and rubber products for the home, specialty, office and commercial markets.

S&P Opinion: Accumulate (★★★★)	Recent Price • 28¼	Yield • 2.3%
	52 Wk Range • 35⅛-23	12-Mo. P/E • 34.5

Quantitative Evaluations

Outlook (1 Lowest—5 Highest)
• **3**

Fair Value
• **32**

Risk
• **Low**

Earn./Div. Rank
• **A-**

Technical Eval.
• **Bearish** since 1/98

Rel. Strength Rank (1 Lowest—99 Highest)
• **76**

Insider Activity
• **Neutral**

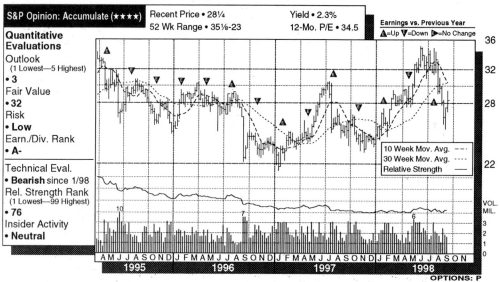

Earnings vs. Previous Year ▲=Up ▼=Down ▷=No Change

10 Week Mov. Avg. - - -
30 Week Mov. Avg. ·····
Relative Strength —

VOL. MIL.

OPTIONS: P

Overview - 27-JUL-98

We expect total sales to rise modestly during 1998, as contributions from the Curver acquisition in Europe outweigh the absence of the Office Products division, which was sold during the second quarter of 1997. Sales from core businesses should rise about 3% to 5%, aided by new products (about 30% of each year's sales are generated by products introduced in the past five years), category expansion (which should increase shelf space), and volume-building marketing programs. However, lower selling prices and the continued negative effect of a strong dollar on worldwide sales will limit gains. Gross margins should begin to improve, due to cost savings resulting from the company's recently completed two-year realignment program as well as its recently announced new restructuring initiatives and a long-awaited downturn in resin prices.

Valuation - 27-JUL-98

We continue to rate the shares of Rubbermaid "accumulate" reflecting our belief that the recent steps the company has taken to improve its cost structure have begun to have a positive effect on margin trends. Recent results continue to be helped by lower-trending resin prices and easing price competition in some of the company's more basic product lines. Going forward, RBD should begin to experience margin improvement from a more centralized procurement process and the streamlining of its global strategic management operations. In addition, the company's focus on category management and marketing should provide a boost to profitability. We expect annual earnings growth of 14% to 15% over the next several years. Although the shares are pricey on a P/E basis, a marked improvement in operations makes them attractive for accumulation. Excluding special charges, the company is expected to earn $1.20 in 1998 and $1.45 in 1999.

Key Stock Statistics

S&P EPS Est. 1998	1.20	Tang. Bk. Value/Share	4.20
P/E on S&P Est. 1998	23.6	Beta	0.72
S&P EPS Est. 1999	1.45	Shareholders	31,100
Dividend Rate/Share	0.64	Market cap. (B)	$ 4.2
Shs. outstg. (M)	149.9	Inst. holdings	62%
Avg. daily vol. (M)	0.374		

Value of $10,000 invested 5 years ago: $ 9,987

Fiscal Year Ending Dec. 31

	1998	1997	1996	1995	1994	1993
Revenues (Million $)						
1Q	649.7	601.7	533.3	563.9	491.6	484.0
2Q	658.5	640.4	573.0	556.8	531.1	488.5
3Q	—	583.4	632.7	641.5	580.3	515.2
4Q	—	574.3	616.0	582.0	566.3	472.9
Yr.	—	2,400	2,355	2,344	2,169	1,960
Earnings Per Share ($)						
1Q	**0.06**	**0.23**	0.27	0.34	0.32	0.31
2Q	**0.35**	**0.31**	0.30	0.18	0.35	0.32
3Q	—	**0.20**	0.31	0.32	0.41	0.37
4Q	—	**0.21**	0.13	-0.46	0.34	0.32
Yr.	—	**0.95**	1.01	0.38	1.42	1.32

Next earnings report expected: mid October

Dividend Data (Dividends have been paid since 1941.)

Amount ($)	Date Decl.	Ex-Div. Date	Stock of Record	Payment Date
0.160	Oct. 28	Nov. 12	Nov. 14	Dec. 01 '97
0.160	Jan. 16	Feb. 04	Feb. 06	Mar. 02 '98
0.160	Apr. 28	May. 13	May. 15	Jun. 01 '98
0.160	Jun. 23	Aug. 12	Aug. 14	Sep. 01 '98

 A Division of The McGraw·Hill Companies

Business Summary - 27-JUL-98

Over the years, Rubbermaid has evolved from a simple housewares company into a global manufacturer and marketer of an expansive array of plastic and rubber products for the consumer and commercial markets. Its key Rubbermaid, Little Tikes and Graco brands are among the most trusted consumer brands in their categories, with names that enjoy a 97% awareness rate among consumers.

The company sells a broad range of products in such categories as housewares, hardware, automotive accessories, marine, leisure and recreational, infant furnishings, commercial and industrial maintenance, home health care, sanitary maintenance, and food service.

RBD's long-term strategy is to double sales and earnings every five or six years. It expects to be able to meet these ambitious goals through the continued introduction of new products and line extensions, entry into new product categories and markets, and global expansion, supplemented by acquisitions. Its goal is to generate more than 10% of annual volume from new products, enter a new market category every 12 to 18 months, and have 30% of sales come from outside the U.S. by 2000.

During the fourth quarter of 1995, the company began a two-year strategic realignment program designed to reduce costs and improve operating efficiencies. During 1997, RBD announced an expansion of the restructuring program aimed at expanding the company's global market leadership and accelerating growth. The new program will include the centralization of global procurement, and the consolidation of manufacturing and distribution worldwide. To date, the company has eliminated under-performing product varieties, divested non-core businesses, consolidated business units with similar distribution channels, balanced manufacturing with distribution, and strengthened its global presence, particularly in Europe and the Asia Pacific region.

In June 1997, in its final realignment moves, RBD sold its office products businesses to Newell Co. for $245.6 million, and said it would combine its home and seasonal units into one operating business to further focus on competitive strengths and better align operations to meet customer needs.

The company now focuses on four leading, brand driven core businesses: Rubbermaid for its Home Products and Commercial Products businesses; Little Tikes for juvenile products; and Graco for infant products.

RBD distributes most of its products worldwide either through company-owned plants or through licensing agreements. International markets accounted for 20% of total sales in 1997. In January 1997, RBD formed a strategic alliance with Amway Japan Ltd. (NYSE: AJL) to jointly develop and sell an exclusive co-branded line of premium Rubbermaid food storage containers through AJL's 1.1 million independent distributors.

Per Share Data ($)

(Year Ended Dec. 31)	1997	1996	1995	1994	1993	1992	1991	1990	1989	1988
Tangible Bk. Val.	4.99	4.23	7.27	8.00	7.05	6.16	5.53	4.80	4.06	3.48
Cash Flow	1.74	1.73	1.03	2.00	1.82	1.48	1.41	1.25	1.16	0.97
Earnings	0.95	1.01	0.38	1.42	1.32	1.04	1.02	0.90	0.79	0.68
Dividends	0.61	0.57	0.52	0.46	0.41	0.35	0.31	0.27	0.23	0.19
Payout Ratio	61%	56%	136%	33%	31%	34%	31%	30%	29%	28%
Prices - High	30½	30⅜	34¼	35¾	37⅜	37⅜	38¼	22½	18⅞	13½
- Low	21⅜	22⅛	24¾	23⅝	27⅝	27	18½	15½	12½	10½
P/E Ratio - High	30	30	90	25	28	36	38	25	24	20
- Low	21	22	65	17	21	26	18	17	16	16

Income Statement Analysis (Million $)

	1997	1996	1995	1994	1993	1992	1991	1990	1989	1988
Revs.	2,400	2,355	2,344	2,169	1,960	1,805	1,667	1,534	1,344	1,194
Oper. Inc.	353	382	373	450	426	364	319	288	257	214
Depr.	118	109	104	93.7	80.9	69.9	62.7	55.3	54.2	43.4
Int. Exp.	37.9	26.3	13.7	7.2	7.8	7.6	8.3	8.6	8.4	7.5
Pretax Inc.	234	245	95.6	367	342	267	263	231	191	160
Eff. Tax Rate	39%	38%	38%	38%	38%	37%	38%	38%	39%	38%
Net Inc.	143	152	59.8	228	211	167	163	144	116	99

Balance Sheet & Other Fin. Data (Million $)

	1997	1996	1995	1994	1993	1992	1991	1990	1989	1988
Cash	114	27.6	51.0	151	194	122	153	77.0	97.0	34.0
Curr. Assets	816	857	851	927	830	700	664	603	516	407
Total Assets	1,924	2,054	1,692	1,709	1,513	1,327	1,245	1,114	915	782
Curr. Liab.	567	743	415	296	259	223	246	235	202	186
LT Debt	153	154	6.2	11.6	19.4	20.3	27.8	39.2	50.3	39.0
Common Eqty.	1,050	1,014	1,135	1,286	1,130	988	886	768	598	511
Total Cap.	1,203	1,168	1,142	1,297	1,150	1,010	943	837	684	581
Cap. Exp.	146	172	152	118	142	135	123	104	86.0	84.0
Cash Flow	261	261	164	322	292	237	225	199	171	143
Curr. Ratio	1.4	1.1	2.1	3.1	3.2	3.1	2.7	2.6	2.5	2.2
% LT Debt of Cap.	12.7	13.2	0.5	0.9	1.7	2.0	2.9	4.7	7.3	6.7
% Net Inc.of Revs.	5.9	6.5	2.5	10.5	10.8	9.2	9.8	9.4	8.7	8.3
% Ret. on Assets	7.2	8.1	3.5	14.1	14.9	13.0	13.8	13.6	13.7	13.2
% Ret. on Equity	13.8	14.2	4.9	18.9	20.0	17.8	19.7	20.2	21.0	20.9

Data as orig. reptd.; bef. results of disc. opers. and/or spec. items. Per share data adj. for stk. divs. as of ex-div. date. Bold denotes diluted EPS (FASB 128). E-Estimated. NA-Not Available. NM-Not Meaningful. NR-Not Ranked.

Office—1147 Akron Rd., Wooster, OH 44691-6000. **Tel**—(330) 264-6464. **Website**—http://www.Rubbermaid.com **Chrmn & CEO**—W. R. Schmitt. **Pres & COO**—C. A. Carroll. **SVP & CFO**—G. C. Weigand. **SVP & Secy**—J. A. Morgan. **VP & Investor Contact**—William H. Pfund. **Dirs**—T. H. Barrett, C. A. Carroll, S. S. Cowen, R. O. Ebert, T. J. Falk, R. M. Gerrity, K. N. Horn, W. D. Marohn, S. A. Minter, J. Nicholson, P. G. Schloemer, W. R. Schmitt, G. R. Sullivan. **Transfer Agent & Registrar**—Bank of Boston. **Incorporated**—in Ohio in 1920. **Empl**— 12,618. **S&P Analyst:** Robert J. Izmirlian

Russell Corp.

1955U

NYSE Symbol **RML**

In S&P 500

12-SEP-98

Industry: Textiles (Apparel)

Summary: Russell is a vertically integrated manufacturer and marketer of leisure apparel, athletic uniforms and woven fabrics.

S&P Opinion: Avoid (★★)

Recent Price • 30¼	Yield • 1.8%
52 Wk Range • 33⅞-23½	12-Mo. P/E • 25.7

Quantitative Evaluations

Outlook
(1 Lowest—5 Highest)
• **3**

Fair Value
• **33¼**

Risk
• **Low**

Earn./Div. Rank
• **B**

Technical Eval.
• **Bearish** since 7/98

Rel. Strength Rank
(1 Lowest—99 Highest)
• **88**

Insider Activity
• **Neutral**

Earnings vs. Previous Year
▲=Up ▼=Down ▷=No Change

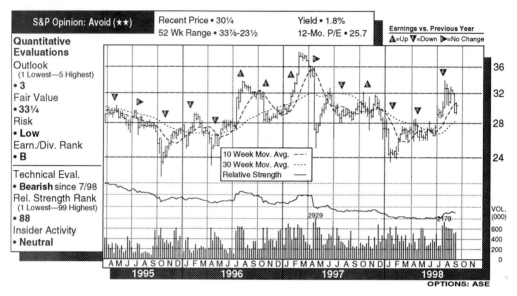

10 Week Mov. Avg. ---
30 Week Mov. Avg. ····
Relative Strength —

2929 2479

VOL. (000)

600
400
200
0

1995 1996 1997 1998

OPTIONS: ASE

Overview - 29-JUL-98

Sales were essentially flat in the first half of 1998. The lackluster sales were attributable to lower fleece sales in the Jerzees and Russell Athletic divisions, RML's two largest divisions. However, we expect sales to rise approximately 4% for the full year, primarily as a result of higher sales of fleece products in the second half of the year. In an effort to widen its margins, the company has eliminated its unprofitable Licensed Products segment, which was one of its smaller divisions. Sales from that business have been shifted to Russell Athletic and Jerzees, where cost efficiencies are possible. In addition, a major three-year restructuring initiative was announced in July 1998. The company estimates that restructuring charges will total $3.44 a share, most of which will be recorded in the third quarter of 1998.

Valuation - 29-JUL-98

Although we expect the company's restructuring plan to lead to improved efficiencies at RML, we do not anticipate any savings in the near term. Margins have been contracting, restricted by price pressures, weak revenue growth, and the effects of high inventories. Coupled with our view that the Jerzees business will continue to face a sluggish retail environment and pricing pressures, we are looking for only moderate earnings growth in 1998. In addition, RML has put its share repurchase program on hold. Reflecting the competitive environment, it is overly optimistic to expect a significant improvement in the near future. Lackluster sales and lower margins during 1997 and the first half of 1998 have tempered our enthusiasm for the company's1998 prospects. We are maintaining our avoid rating, with the shares trading recently at 19X our 1998 EPS estimate of $1.60, and at 16X our 1999 estimate of $2.00.

Key Stock Statistics

S&P EPS Est. 1998	1.60	Tang. Bk. Value/Share	18.16
P/E on S&P Est. 1998	18.9	Beta	NA
S&P EPS Est. 1999	2.00	Shareholders	12,300
Dividend Rate/Share	0.56	Market cap. (B)	$ 1.1
Shs. outstg. (M)	36.2	Inst. holdings	50%
Avg. daily vol. (M)	0.129		

Value of $10,000 invested 5 years ago: $ 10,617

Fiscal Year Ending Dec. 31

	1998	1997	1996	1995	1994	1993
Revenues (Million $)						
1Q	256.2	258.2	257.9	248.3	232.1	204.7
2Q	271.8	270.3	290.6	268.7	243.5	209.1
3Q	—	368.3	336.7	333.8	317.1	266.6
4Q	—	331.5	359.1	301.8	305.5	250.4
Yr.	—	1,228	1,244	1,153	1,098	930.8
Earnings Per Share ($)						
1Q	0.05	0.30	0.30	0.31	0.33	0.39
2Q	0.18	0.22	0.42	0.32	0.32	0.31
3Q	E0.70	0.64	0.63	0.33	0.60	-0.09
4Q	E0.67	0.32	0.76	0.42	0.71	0.59
Yr.	E1.60	1.47	2.11	1.38	1.96	1.19

Next earnings report expected: mid October

Dividend Data (Dividends have been paid since 1963.)

Amount ($)	Date Decl.	Ex-Div. Date	Stock of Record	Payment Date
0.140	Oct. 22	Oct. 30	Nov. 03	Nov. 20 '97
0.140	Jan. 28	Feb. 05	Feb. 09	Feb. 20 '98
0.140	Apr. 22	Apr. 30	May. 04	May. 20 '98
0.140	Jul. 22	Aug. 06	Aug. 10	Aug. 20 '98

A Division of The McGraw-Hill Companies

Russell Corporation

Business Summary - 29-JUL-98

With well-known brands that include Jerzees and Russell Athletic, Russell is easily recognized as a major apparel manufacturer. A vertically integrated apparel company that markets its products in nearly 90 countries, Russell designs, manufactures and markets activewear, licensed sports apparel, athletic uniforms, better knit shirts, sports and casual socks and lightweight woven fabrics.

The company believes that it is the largest U.S. manufacturer of athletic uniforms, and, under the Russell Athletic label, makes the official uniforms of major league baseball teams, as well as pro football uniforms, college basketball and other sport uniforms for professional and amateur players. Under the Jerzees label, Russell makes sweatshirts, sweatpants and lightweight sportswear. The company sells its products through four divisions: Jerzees, Athletic, International and Fabrics, as well as two wholly owned subsidiaries, Cross Creek Apparel and DeSoto Mills.

Russell has kept itself in the forefront of technology in the industry. With annual revenues surpassing $1.2 billion, the company spins enough yarn for 50 round trips to the moon each week. Spending substantially on manufacturing process technology over the years, Russell has become known for its efficiency in distribution and quick response to customer needs. In fact, the

company's Russell Athletic division has one of the top quick-response programs in its industry. The division averages a 95% on-time and complete record in season. This gives it a distinct advantage over its competitors.

Domestically, in the company's mature markets, growth will have to come from improving quality, controlling costs and aggressively servicing customers. The worldwide apparel industry was hurt in 1995 by a host of factors, including excess inventories, which influenced pricing, and higher raw material costs. The industry rebounded in 1996, with stable raw material costs, better inventory management and the benefit of the Olympics in the U.S. The strong growth was short-lived, however; in 1997, the industry was faced with overcapacity, declining prices, and weaker demand for athletic apparel. In order to enhance its growth prospects, Russell is concentrating on expanding internationally, where growth potential is greater. There has been a recent trend worldwide toward a less formal approach to living. Russell's products reflect this lifestyle of comfort and practicality. While Russell has been gaining market share in mature domestic markets, its international sales only account for about 10% of revenues. The company is therefore focusing on international expansion, and hoped to achieve double digit growth in this category in 1998.

Per Share Data ($)

(Year Ended Dec. 31)	1997	1996	1995	1994	1993	1992	1991	1990	1989	1988
Tangible Bk. Val.	17.35	16.95	15.39	14.89	13.80	13.38	11.79	10.68	9.45	8.34
Cash Flow	3.48	3.98	3.15	3.63	2.78	3.44	2.76	2.93	2.66	2.21
Earnings	1.47	2.11	1.38	1.96	1.19	1.99	1.38	1.65	1.57	1.36
Dividends	0.53	0.50	0.48	0.42	0.39	0.34	0.32	0.32	0.28	0.23
Payout Ratio	36%	24%	35%	21%	33%	17%	23%	19%	18%	17%
Prices - High	38½	33¾	31¼	32⅝	36⅞	40⅜	36¼	31	26½	17¾
- Low	25	23⅛	22	24	26	27¾	19¾	16	15⅝	11⅜
P/E Ratio - High	26	16	23	17	31	20	26	19	17	13
- Low	17	11	16	12	22	14	14	10	10	8

Income Statement Analysis (Million $)

	1997	1996	1995	1994	1993	1992	1991	1990	1989	1988
Revs.	1,228	1,244	1,153	1,098	931	899	805	714	688	531
Oper. Inc.	193	227	174	213	198	204	177	165	129
Depr.	74.4	72.2	68.0	67.0	65.3	59.7	56.6	50.6	44.6	33.3
Int. Exp.	28.2	25.7	21.7	19.4	16.9	15.8	18.1	18.9	15.6	8.8
Pretax Inc.	88.4	130	87.7	128	81.0	130	91.0	110	103	86.0
Eff. Tax Rate	38%	37%	38%	38%	39%	37%	37%	38%	37%	37%
Net Inc.	54.4	81.6	54.1	78.8	49.1	82.2	56.8	67.9	64.7	53.8

Balance Sheet & Other Fin. Data (Million $)

	1997	1996	1995	1994	1993	1992	1991	1990	1989	1988
Cash	8.6	7.4	4.5	4.1	3.9	6.1	13.4	13.2	75.6	12.6
Curr. Assets	647	600	565	511	474	428	327	334	327	210
Total Assets	1,248	1,195	1,119	1,047	1,017	965	818	795	721	561
Curr. Liab.	146	187	127	201	196	142	71.7	84.8	59.8	85.7
LT Debt	361	256	288	144	163	186	180	191	205	84.0
Common Eqty.	666	680	633	629	588	570	503	456	402	345
Total Cap.	1,076	982	969	824	800	810	737	703	656	472
Cap. Exp.	72.9	114	86.6	39.0	84.0	111	90.0	116	80.0	154
Cash Flow	129	154	122	146	114	142	113	118	109	87.0
Curr. Ratio	4.4	3.2	4.4	2.5	2.4	3.0	4.6	3.9	5.5	2.5
% LT Debt of Cap.	33.5	26.1	29.7	17.5	20.4	22.9	24.5	27.2	31.2	17.9
% Net Inc.of Revs.	4.4	6.6	4.7	7.2	5.3	9.1	7.1	9.5	9.4	10.1
% Ret. on Assets	4.5	7.1	5.0	7.7	5.0	9.2	7.0	9.0	10.1	10.5
% Ret. on Equity	8.1	12.4	8.6	13.1	8.5	15.2	11.7	15.7	17.2	16.9

Data as orig. reptd.; bef. results of disc. opers. and/or spec. items. Per share data adj. for stk. divs. as of ex-div. date. Bold denotes diluted EPS (FASB 128). E-Estimated. NA-Not Available. NM-Not Meaningful. NR-Not Ranked.

Office—755 Lee St., Alexander City, AL 35011-0272. **Tel**—(205) 329-4000. **Fax**—(205) 329-4474. **Chrmn, Pres & CEO**—J. F. Ward. **EVP & CFO**—J. D. Nabors. **Treas & Investor Contact**—K. Roger Holliday.**Secy**—S. R. Forehand. **Dirs**—H. M. Bloom, R. G. Bruno, T. Lewis, J. D. Nabors, C. V. Nalley III, M. M. Porter, B. Russell, J. R. Thomas, J. A. White. **Transfer Agent & Registrar**— Wachovia Bank of North Carolina, Winston-Salem. **Incorporated**—in Alabama in 1902. **Empl**— 17,759. **S&P Analyst**: Kathleen J. Fraser

STANDARD &POOR'S
STOCK REPORTS

Ryder System

1956M

NYSE Symbol **R**

In S&P 500

12-SEP-98

Industry:
Truckers

Summary: Ryder provides truck leasing, logistics and bus transportation services. R's auto hauling unit was sold in September 1997; its consumer truck rental unit was sold in 1996.

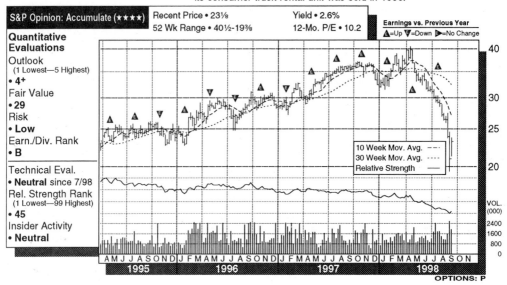

S&P Opinion: Accumulate (★★★★)	Recent Price • 23⅛ Yield • 2.6%
	52 Wk Range • 40½-19⅜ 12-Mo. P/E • 10.2

Quantitative Evaluations

Outlook
(1 Lowest—5 Highest)
• **4+**

Fair Value
• **29**

Risk
• **Low**

Earn./Div. Rank
• **B**

Technical Eval.
• **Neutral** since 7/98

Rel. Strength Rank
(1 Lowest—99 Highest)
• **45**

Insider Activity
• **Neutral**

Earnings vs. Previous Year
▲=Up ▼=Down ▶=No Change

10 Week Mov. Avg. – – –
30 Week Mov. Avg. ·····
Relative Strength —

Overview - 29-JUL-98

Profits should advance in 1998. Revenue for full service truck leasing (excluding fuel adjustments) will grow moderately as Ryder signs up new accounts, gets better rates on new contracts and expands through acquisitions. Margins will benefit from increased productivity and savings from the outsourcing of information systems. Commercial truck rental profits will advance despite a static fleet size as utilization and productivity improves. Offsetting will be lower gains from the disposition of equipment. International operations are expected to improve, aided by a new contract to provide airport ground equipment for British Airways. While logistics' top line growth will slow, profits will continue to post double-digit gains, reflecting wider margins on new contracts. Logistics growth will accelerate in late 1998 as it ramps up its new contract with Ford Motor. Bus transportation will benefit from recent acquisitions, and from increased demand for public transit and fleet management services. Limiting gains will be costs to fix Year 2000 bugs. Interest expense and depreciation charges will decline.

Valuation - 29-JUL-98

The shares have underperformed the market in 1998. Ryder turned in a decent profit performance in the first half, even though it had to spend $15 million on Year 2000 issues. Nevertheless, investors have bailed out because a whiff of recession is in the air. Meanwhile, the firm continues its aggressive share repurchases; a 3,000,000 share buyback plan was authorized in May 1998. Since late 1996, Ryder has bought 12,700,000 (or 15%) of its shares. We recommend accumulating the stock, as R's restructuring efforts have made the company less cyclical and capital intensive. We think these changes will translate into a multiple expansion for Ryder's shares.

Key Stock Statistics

S&P EPS Est. 1998	2.40	Tang. Bk. Value/Share	11.17
P/E on S&P Est. 1998	9.7	Beta	0.93
S&P EPS Est. 1999	2.80	Shareholders	18,400
Dividend Rate/Share	0.60	Market cap. (B)	$ 1.7
Shs. outstg. (M)	73.2	Inst. holdings	86%
Avg. daily vol. (M)	0.458		

Value of $10,000 invested 5 years ago: $ 9,618

Fiscal Year Ending Dec. 31

	1998	1997	1996	1995	1994	1993
Revenues (Million $)						
1Q	1,246	1,336	1,328	1,233	1,072	1,000
2Q	1,282	1,393	1,426	1,324	1,176	1,080
3Q	—	1,204	1,409	1,264	1,195	1,044
4Q	—	1,268	1,357	1,345	1,243	1,094
Yr.	—	4,894	5,519	5,167	4,686	4,217
Earnings Per Share ($)						
1Q	**0.50**	**0.41**	0.13	0.34	0.30	0.23
2Q	**0.61**	**0.55**	0.39	0.65	0.64	0.51
3Q	**E0.60**	**0.45**	0.32	0.26	0.53	0.30
4Q	**E0.70**	**0.64**	-1.21	0.71	0.48	0.39
Yr.	**E2.40**	**2.05**	-0.39	1.96	1.95	1.43

Next earnings report expected: late October

Dividend Data (Dividends have been paid since 1976.)

Amount ($)	Date Decl.	Ex-Div. Date	Stock of Record	Payment Date
0.150	Oct. 01	Nov. 18	Nov. 20	Dec. 20 '97
0.150	Feb. 19	Mar. 03	Mar. 05	Mar. 20 '98
0.150	May. 01	May. 26	May. 28	Jun. 20 '98
0.150	Jul. 30	Sep. 01	Sep. 03	Sep. 20 '98

A Division of The McGraw-Hill Companies

Business Summary - 29-JUL-98

Ryder System provides a variety of transportation and distribution-related services including truck leasing and rental, integrated logistics, bus transportation and vehicle maintenance services. The September 1997 sale of the firm's auto hauling unit was part of an ongoing streamlining process to make Ryder's earnings less cyclical and seasonal and its business less capital intensive.

Ryder is the world's largest full-service truck lessor. Its North American operation manages 102,914 vehicles, while the international division, which operates in the U.K., Germany, Poland, Mexico, Argentina and Brazil, had a fleet of 13,386 vehicles at 1997 year end. In May 1998, Ryder was reported to be seeking buyers for its U.K. operations, which accounted for 8% of total 1997 revenues. Under a full-service lease, the company provides vehicles, maintenance, supplies and emergency road service, while customers furnish drivers and control dispatching. Ryder also performs maintenance services on some 42,354 non-leased vehicles. The company also provides commercial truck rentals, using a fleet of 34,371 vehicles to meet customers' seasonal and peak needs. Gains from the disposition of vehicles accounted for 11% of this division's profits in 1997, versus 27% in 1996. Full service leasing and commercial truck rental operations generated 46% of total revenues in 1997.

Ryder's integrated logistics division (28% of revenues)

is its fastest growing unit. Logistics involves taking a system-wide management approach to a company's supply chain (i.e. from raw materials to finished product). Ryder Logistics provides clients with custom tailored distribution solutions that include dedicated transportation, warehousing and inventory control and information services. Ryder is the largest third-party logistics provider in the U.S.

Ryder's public transportation unit (11% of revenues) manages or operates 93 public transit systems in 27 states, is the second largest provider of student transportation services, operating 9,567 school buses in 25 states, and maintains 30,000 public transit vehicles. Acquisitions have been a major part of the growth strategy for this division. Additionally, continuing cost pressures in the public sector is forcing local governments to outsource transportation and fleet management services.

Ryder has streamlined its operations in recent years, selling businesses that failed to meet its minimum standards for growth, margins or cyclicality. Accordingly, Ryder sold its auto hauling unit in September 1997 and its consumer truck rental business in late 1996. The sale of both of these units reflects Ryder's strategic plan to shed businesses that are transactional in nature and have highly cyclical and seasonal earnings patterns. Ryder also wants to become less asset heavy. Proceeds from the sale of these units have helped fund the repurchase of 12,700,000 common shares (or 15% of its total) since late 1996.

Per Share Data ($)

(Year Ended Dec. 31)	1997	1996	1995	1994	1993	1992	1991	1990	1989	1988
Tangible Bk. Val.	11.17	11.00	12.30	14.33	12.81	18.23	17.47	18.04	18.22	18.68
Cash Flow	9.76	8.42	10.33	9.46	8.44	9.07	8.92	9.20	8.67	9.18
Earnings	2.05	-0.39	1.96	1.95	1.43	1.43	0.75	0.96	0.58	1.61
Dividends	0.60	0.60	0.60	0.60	0.60	0.60	0.60	0.60	0.60	0.56
Payout Ratio	29%	NM	31%	31%	42%	42%	80%	62%	103%	35%
Prices - High	37⅛	31⅛	26⅛	28	33½	28⅞	21⅝	23⅜	31⅛	32½
- Low	27⅛	22⅝	21	19⅞	24¼	19⅝	14	12¼	19¾	22⅝
P/E Ratio - High	18	NM	13	14	23	20	29	24	54	20
- Low	13	NM	11	10	17	14	19	13	34	14

Income Statement Analysis (Million $)

	1997	1996	1995	1994	1993	1992	1991	1990	1989	1988
Revs.	4,894	5,519	5,167	4,686	4,217	5,192	5,061	5,162	5,073	5,030
Oper. Inc.	1,045	877	1,118	1,000	879	941	933	981	1,043	1,151
Depr.	601	713	664	592	543	574	603	616	625	603
Int. Exp.	189	207	191	145	125	176	206	235	271	267
Pretax Inc.	264	-17.6	264	261	210	199	115	139	90.0	224
Eff. Tax Rate	39%	NM	41%	41%	45%	41%	43%	41%	42%	40%
Net Inc.	160	-31.3	155	154	115	118	66.0	82.0	52.0	135

Balance Sheet & Other Fin. Data (Million $)

	1997	1996	1995	1994	1993	1992	1991	1990	1989	1988
Cash	78.0	191	93.0	76.0	57.0	72.0	72.0	101	104	87.0
Curr. Assets	1,092	1,148	884	759	601	1,235	1,319	1,282	1,486	1,510
Total Assets	5,509	5,645	5,894	5,014	4,258	4,930	5,080	5,502	5,938	6,039
Curr. Liab.	1,090	1,155	1,120	1,093	969	1,142	1,185	1,444	1,545	1,318
LT Debt	2,268	2,237	2,411	1,795	1,375	1,529	1,777	1,923	2,193	2,415
Common Eqty.	1,061	1,106	1,240	1,129	990	1,375	1,288	1,328	1,387	1,489
Total Cap.	4,054	4,029	4,299	3,494	2,892	3,452	3,585	3,828	4,185	4,524
Cap. Exp.	1,042	1,303	2,152	1,769	1,175	1,035	580	795	1,129	1,193
Cash Flow	761	682	819	745	654	681	659	688	670	731
Curr. Ratio	1.0	1.0	0.8	0.7	0.6	1.1	1.1	0.9	1.0	1.1
% LT Debt of Cap.	55.9	55.6	56.1	51.4	47.5	44.3	49.6	50.2	52.4	53.4
% Net Inc.of Revs.	3.3	NM	3.0	3.3	2.7	2.3	1.3	1.6	1.0	2.7
% Ret. on Assets	2.9	NM	2.8	3.3	2.5	2.3	1.2	1.5	0.9	2.3
% Ret. on Equity	14.8	NM	13.1	14.4	9.3	8.0	4.2	5.4	3.2	9.1

Data as orig. reptd.; bef. results of disc. opers. and/or spec. items. Per share data adj. for stk. divs. as of ex-div. date. Bold denotes diluted EPS (FASB 128). E-Estimated. NA-Not Available. NM-Not Meaningful. NR-Not Ranked.

Office—3600 N.W. 82nd Ave., Miami, FL 33166. **Tel**—(305) 593-3726. **Website**—http://www.ryder.com **Chrmn, Pres & CEO**—M. A. Burns. **SEVP-Fin & CFO**—E. A. Huston. **Secy**—V. A. O'Meara. **Investor Contact**—Ross C. Roadman. **Dirs**—M. A. Burns, J. L. Dionne, E. T. Foote II, D. I. Fuente, J. A. Georges, V. E. Jordan Jr., D. T. Kearns, L. M. Martin, P. J. Rizzo, C. A. Varney, A. O. Way. **Transfer Agent & Registrar**—Bank Boston N.A. **Incorporated**—in Florida in 1955. **Empl**— 43,059. **S&P Analyst:** Stephen R. Klein

SAFECO Corp.

5141F

Nasdaq Symbol **SAFC**

In S&P 500

12-SEP-98

Industry:
Insurance (Property-ty-Casualty)

Summary: Mainly a property-casualty insurer, SAFECO also engages in life, health and surety insurance, investment management and commercial credit.

S&P Opinion: Hold (★★★)	Recent Price • 43½	Yield • 3.2%
	52 Wk Range • 56-38½	12-Mo. P/E • 15.6

Quantitative Evaluations

Outlook
(1 Lowest—5 Highest)
• **2⁻**

Fair Value
• **40¼**

Risk
• **Low**

Earn./Div. Rank
• **B+**

Technical Eval.
• **Bearish** since 5/98

Rel. Strength Rank
(1 Lowest—99 Highest)
• **81**

Insider Activity
• **Favorable**

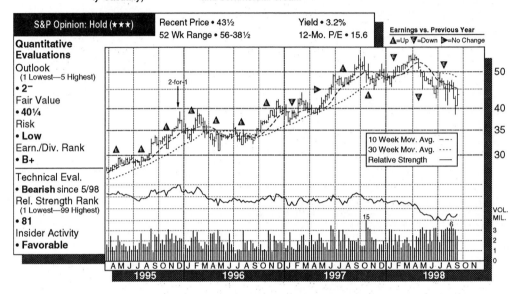

Earnings vs. Previous Year
▲=Up ▼=Down ▶=No Change

10 Week Mov. Avg. ---
30 Week Mov. Avg. ·····
Relative Strength —

Overview - 05-AUG-98

Property-casualty written premiums will likely advance 5% to 7% in 1998, reflecting modest underlying growth (especially in certain commercial lines), coupled with contributions from the October 1997 acquisition of American States Financial Corp. (NYSE: ASX). However, year to year comparisons of underwriting results will be hampered by a higher level of weather related losses expected to continue throughout 1998, particularly in the homeowners' line (SAFC's second largest). Steps recently taken here, such as premium rate hikes and higher insurance-to-value ratios, should help mitigate the impact of storm losses. Nevertheless, SAFC's exposure to heavy weather-related losses in this line remains a concern. Favorable underwriting trends should continue in the core personal auto line, but competition will limit near-term premium growth. An expanded product line (including index-linked annuities) should help life/health insurance results, though weak group results may hurt this unit's overall results. The planned sale of the real estate unit is a plus, since it will help SAFC to narrow its strategic focus.

Valuation - 05-AUG-98

After trending upward during much of 1997, the shares corrected somewhat in late 1997, after SAFC completed its $2.8 billion cash acquisition of American States in October. Once the market had digested that news, the shares began 1998 on an upward note, but have weakened, amid continued premium pricing pressures and adverse claim trends. Despite their relatively modest valuation, the shares will likely be only average performers, near term, particularly in view of the company's modest top-line growth and mixed success rate in turning around several segments.

Key Stock Statistics

S&P EPS Est. 1998	3.15	Tang. Bk. Value/Share	30.62
P/E on S&P Est. 1998	13.8	Beta	0.77
S&P EPS Est. 1999	3.65	Shareholders	4,400
Dividend Rate/Share	1.40	Market cap. (B)	$ 6.1
Shs. outstg. (M)	141.2	Inst. holdings	65%
Avg. daily vol. (M)	0.881		

Value of $10,000 invested 5 years ago: $ 18,149

Fiscal Year Ending Dec. 31

	1998	1997	1996	1995	1994	1993
Revenues (Million $)						
1Q	1,624	1,030	977.6	897.5	857.8	837.3
2Q	1,688	1,031	976.0	925.8	864.6	885.2
3Q	—	1,112	992.5	944.3	901.8	897.0
4Q	—	1,542	1,019	955.1	912.9	907.4
Yr.	—	4,770	3,965	3,723	3,537	3,517
Earnings Per Share ($)						
1Q	**0.79**	0.88	0.88	0.52	0.45	0.44
2Q	**0.49**	0.93	0.84	0.82	0.71	0.74
3Q	—	0.96	0.92	0.91	0.57	0.49
4Q	—	0.58	0.84	0.92	0.76	0.77
Yr.	—	3.31	3.48	3.17	2.50	2.44

Next earnings report expected: NA

Dividend Data (Dividends have been paid since 1933.)

Amount ($)	Date Decl.	Ex-Div. Date	Stock of Record	Payment Date
0.320	Nov. 05	Jan. 07	Jan. 09	Jan. 26 '98
0.320	Feb. 04	Apr. 07	Apr. 10	Apr. 27 '98
0.350	May. 06	Jul. 08	Jul. 10	Jul. 27 '98
0.350	Aug. 05	Oct. 07	Oct. 09	Oct. 26 '98

A Division of The McGraw·Hill Companies

STANDARD
&POOR'S
STOCK REPORTS

SAFECO Corporation

5141F
12-SEP-98

Business Summary - 05-AUG-98

This Seattle, WA-based insurer expanded its presence in the property-casualty arena by acquiring American States Financial Corp. from Lincoln National Corp.(NYSE:LNC), for $2.8 billion in cash, plus the repayment of $300 million of debt. Following the acquisition, which was completed on October 1, 1997, SAFC became the 15th largest property-casualty insurer in the U.S. Primarily a property-casualty insurer, SAFC also underwrites life and health insurance and engages in commercial credit and investment management. Real estate assets were being held for sale as of February 1998. Contributions to revenues in recent years were:

	1997	1996
Property-casualty	63%	60%
Life & health	6%	7%
Investment income (excl. cap. gains)	26%	27%
Real estate & other	5%	6%

Property-casualty insurance is the company's principal line of business. Through independent agents, most major lines of personal and commercial p-c coverage are offered in nearly all states. Net p-c premiums written in 1997 amounted to $2.45 billion ($2.31 billion in 1996), of which personal auto accounted for 48%,

homeowners 20%, other personal lines 5%, commercial lines 25% and surety 2%. Written premium growth of 6.1% during 1997 reflected 7.4% higher personal lines premiums, partly offset by only 3.4% growth in commercial lines written premiums. While overall underwritng results in 1997 (as measured by the combined loss/ expense ratio) were relatively unchanged, results varied by line. The combined ratio ended 1997 at 98.7%, versus 98.3% in 1996. This reflected improved claim trends in homeowners' and commercial property lines, offset by a deterioration in commercial auto and workers' compensation lines.

The life and health companies provide a broad range of individual and group products, pension programs and annuities, offered through independent agents in all states and the District of Columbia.

SAFECO Properties Inc.develops and manages regional shopping centers and office buildings. In February 1998, SAFC said it had retained Salomon Smith Barney to help sell this unit, which had 1997 pretax profits of $9.6 million. SAFECO Credit provides commercial credit and leasing services. SAFECO Asset Management is the investment adviser for the SAFECO family of mutual funds, for variable annuity portfolios and for outside pension accounts. At December 31, 1997, assets under management totaled $5.2 billion, up from $3.4 billion a year earlier.

Per Share Data ($)

(Year Ended Dec. 31)	1997	1996	1995	1994	1993	1992	1991	1990	1989	1988
Tangible Bk. Val.	29.28	32.58	31.61	22.48	22.05	19.48	17.70	15.75	14.63	12.44
Oper. Earnings	3.02	3.02	2.84	2.29	2.44	2.17	1.89	2.15	2.08	1.79
Earnings	3.31	3.48	3.17	2.50	3.38	2.48	2.07	2.21	2.38	2.05
Dividends	1.22	1.11	1.02	1.19	0.86	0.78	0.71	0.64	0.57	0.51
Relative Payout	37%	32%	32%	47%	25%	31%	34%	29%	24%	25%
Prices - High	55⅜	42¼	39¼	29⅞	33⅜	29¾	24⅜	21¼	19⅞	15
- Low	36½	30⅞	25⅛	23⅜	27	21	15⅝	12⅝	11⅝	11⅜
P/E Ratio - High	17	12	12	12	10	14	12	10	10	8
- Low	11	9	8	9	8	10	8	6	6	6

Income Statement Analysis (Million $)

	1997	1996	1995	1994	1993	1992	1991	1990	1989	1988
Life Ins. In Force	Nil	Nil	NA	NA	NA	NA	NA	NA	NA	NA
Prem. Inc.: Life A & H	290	266	262	277	306	329	NA	NA	NA	NA
Prem. Inc.: Cas./Prop.	2,817	2,275	2,162	2,053	1,930	1,754	NA	NA	NA	NA
Net Invest. Inc.	1,245	1,117	1,075	992	952	903	847	765	670	537
Oth. Revs.	357	307	224	215	329	309	332	303	287	257
Total Revs.	4,709	3,965	3,723	3,537	3,517	3,295	3,148	3,043	2,808	2,873
Pretax Inc.	573	578	514	390	577	403	283	294	321	277
Net Oper. Inc.	NA	380	357	288	307	272	237	272	264	235
Net Inc.	430	439	399	314	426	311	260	278	300	269

Balance Sheet & Other Fin. Data (Million $)

	1997	1996	1995	1994	1993	1992	1991	1990	1989	1988
Cash & Equiv.	728	296	300	293	278	274	248	229	206	170
Premiums Due	954	467	445	419	401	336	327	326	296	275
Invest. Assets: Bonds	19,987	14,530	11,997	9,611	10,830	9,722	8,544	7,482	6,421	5,198
Invest. Assets: Stocks	1,880	1,299	1,119	855	910	919	864	725	773	675
Invest. Assets: Loans	584	506	472	472	453	442	415	390	311	274
Invest. Assets: Total	22,451	16,889	16,132	13,467	12,641	11,477	10,272	9,052	7,953	6,564
Deferred Policy Costs	545	396	356	389	367	346	310	291	263	228
Total Assets	29,468	19,918	18,768	15,902	14,807	13,252	11,907	10,553	9,279	7,732
Debt	2,360	1,233	1,068	983	918	839	824	784	765	723
Common Eqty.	5,462	4,115	3,983	2,829	2,774	2,448	2,221	1,976	1,851	1,570
Comb. Loss-Exp. Ratio	98.7	98.3	99.7	103.8	99.5	104.1	NA	NA	NA	NA
% Return On Revs.	9.1	11.1	10.7	8.9	8.7	8.2	7.5	8.9	9.4	8.2
% Ret. on Equity	0.0	9.4	11.7	11.2	11.8	11.6	11.3	14.2	15.4	15.6
% Invest. Yield	6.5	6.7	7.4	7.6	7.9	8.3	8.8	9.0	9.2	8.9

Data as orig. reptd.; bef. results of disc. opers. and/or spec. items. Per share data adj. for stk. divs. as of ex-div. date. Bold denotes diluted EPS (FASB 128). E-Estimate. NA-Not Available. NM-Not Meaningful. NR-Not Ranked.

Registrar—Chase Manhattan Bank, Brooklyn. **Office**—SAFECO Plaza, Seattle, WA 98185. **Tel**—(206) 545-5000. **Website**—http://www.safeco.com**Chrmn & CEO**—R. H. Eigsti. **Pres & COO**—B. A. Dickey. **VP, CFO & Secy**—R. A. Pierson. **Dirs**—P. J. Campbell, R. S. Cline, B. A. Dickey, R. H. Eigsti, J. W. Ellis, W. P. Gerberding, J. Green III, W. W. Krippaehne Jr., W. G. Reed Jr., J. M. Runstad, P. W. Skinner, G. H. Weyerhaeuser. **Transfer Agent**—First Chicago Trust Co. of New York, Jersey City, NJ. **Incorporated**—in Washington in 1929. **Empl**—7,500. **S&P Analyst:** Catherine A. Seifert

STANDARD &POOR'S
STOCK REPORTS

St. Jude Medical

1974E

NYSE Symbol **STJ**

In S&P 500

12-SEP-98

Industry:
Health Care (Medical Products & Supplies)

Summary: The leading maker of mechanical heart valves, with near-ly 60% of the worldwide market, this company also produces pace-makers, defibrillators and other cardiac devices.

S&P Opinion: Accumulate (★★★★)	Recent Price • 19½	Yield • Nil
	52 Wk Range • 39⅝-19⅛	12-Mo. P/E • 18.8

Quantitative Evaluations

Outlook
(1 Lowest—5 Highest)
• **5+**

Fair Value
• **39⅝**

Risk
• **Average**

Earn./Div. Rank
• **B**

Technical Eval.
• **NA**

Rel. Strength Rank
(1 Lowest—99 Highest)
• **17**

Insider Activity
• **Neutral**

Earnings vs. Previous Year
▲=Up ▼=Down ▶=No Change

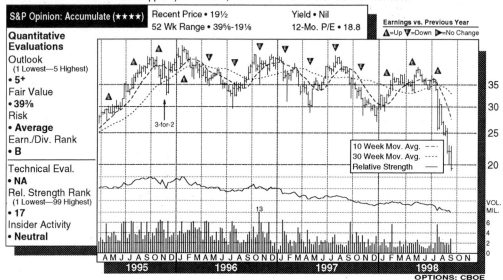

3-for-2

- 10 Week Mov. Avg. ---
- 30 Week Mov. Avg. ······
- Relative Strength ——

13

VOL.
MIL.

1995 | 1996 | 1997 | 1998

OPTIONS: CBOE

Overview - 16-JUN-98

Revenues are expected to rise about 5% in 1998. The gain should be led by higher sales of Ventritex's im-plantable cardiac defibrillators and Daig's electrophysiol-ogy catheters, bolstered by new products and a larger sales force. Further growth is also indicated for the ba-sic heart valve product line, aided by higher sales of both mechanical and tissue valves. The tissue valve line has been augmented by the acquisition of Biocor, a Brazilian maker of tissue heart valves, and by the com-pany's new Toronto SPV bioprosthetic heart valve. However, pacemaker sales are likely to remain rela-tively sluggish due to industrywide pricing pressures and new competition from Medtronic and Guidant. Mar-gins are expected to widen, on the greater volume, cost efficiencies, and improved profitability at the Ventritex and Teletronics divisions. Diluted EPS are projected at $1.43, with further progress to $1.80 seen for 1999.

Valuation - 16-JUN-98

Although still comfortably higher to date in 1998, the shares trended lower in recent weeks following the completion of the company's purchase of eight million public shares through a Dutch Auction. Part of the stock's recent weakness also reflects sluggish pace-maker sales and increasing competitive pressures in many product lines. However, the company's longer-range prospects remain bright. Ranking as the the leading producer of mechanical heart valves, St. Jude is also expanding its positions in pacers, implant-able cardioverter defibrillators (ICDs) and other growing cardiac device markets. New ICDs include the Ang-strom II, which is the smallest ICD presently available; and the Contour II, which delivers the highest energy defibrillation output of any ICD on the market. The shares are recommended for above-average apprecia-tion potential.

Key Stock Statistics

S&P EPS Est. 1998	1.50	Tang. Bk. Value/Share	8.88
P/E on S&P Est. 1998	13.0	Beta	1.05
S&P EPS Est. 1999	1.80	Shareholders	4,600
Dividend Rate/Share	Nil	Market cap. (B)	$ 1.6
Shs. outstg. (M)	84.2	Inst. holdings	55%
Avg. daily vol. (M)	0.432		

Value of $10,000 invested 5 years ago: $ 7,122

Fiscal Year Ending Dec. 31

	1998	1997	1996	1995	1994	1993
Revenues (Million $)						
1Q	257.5	250.4	201.0	180.5	66.69	68.20
2Q	261.2	261.5	203.2	185.6	66.74	66.90
3Q	—	233.2	193.8	175.9	62.47	58.95
4Q	—	249.4	212.7	181.5	163.8	58.60
Yr.	—	994.4	808.8	723.5	359.6	252.6
Earnings Per Share ($)						
1Q	**0.32**	**0.25**	0.47	0.43	0.38	0.41
2Q	**0.47**	**0.09**	0.45	0.47	0.37	0.41
3Q	E0.33	0.20	0.44	0.45	0.35	0.37
4Q	E0.38	0.05	-0.23	0.47	0.03	0.37
Yr.	E1.50	0.59	1.12	1.82	1.13	1.55

Next earnings report expected: mid October

Dividend Data

Cash dividends were terminated with the acquisition of Pacesetter in September 1994.

 A Division of The McGraw-Hill Companies

Business Summary - 16-JUN-98

Originally formed to produce mechanical heart valves, the company's business has been significantly enlarged and diversified in recent years, mainly through a number of acquisitions in the cardiac rhythm management (CRM) field. The company's growing lineup of CRM products is comprised of pacemakers, implantable cardioverter defibrillators and related specialty cardiac products. Overseas business is significant, accounting for about 41% of sales and 42% of profits in 1997. Sales by product segment in recent years were:

	1997	1996
Cardiac rhythm products	72%	69%
Heart valves	28%	31%

Pacesetter (acquired in 1994) is the world's second largest maker of pacemakers, with an estimated 25% share of the market. Consisting of pulse generators and pacing leads, implanted pacemakers treat patients with bradycardia (slow or irregular heart beating). Containing a lithium battery source and electronic circuitry, pulse generators sense and produce impulses in both the upper and lower chambers of the heart, adapt to changes in heart rate and can be non-invasively programmed by physicians. Pacesetter's products are sold under the Trilogy, Tempo, Microny and Regency names. The Tempo DR device is the world's smallest dual-chamber

rate-responsive pacemaker. The pacing business was expanded in 1996 with the acquisition of Telectronics Pacing Systems.

Through the acquisition of Ventritex in 1997, the company offers a line of implantable cardioverter defibrillators (ICDs) used to treat tachyarrhythmia (rapid heart beating). ICDs monitor the heartbeat and deliver higher energy electrical impulses, or "shocks," to terminate ventricular tachycardia and ventricular fibrillation. ICDs are sold under the Angstrom and Contour names. The interventional cardiac device line was expanded in 1996 with the acquisition of Daig, a maker of electrophysiology catheters for diagnostic mapping of the heart; bipolar temporary pacing catheters; and devices used for the ablation of malfunctioning heart tissue.

The St. Jude Medical mechanical heart valve is the most widely implanted valve in the world with over 800,000 valves implanted to date. STJ also markets the Toronto SPV stentless tissue valve, the world's leading stentless tissue valve, as well as other tissue valves. Heart valve replacement or repair is employed when a patient's natural heart valve has deteriorated, usually because of congenital defects or disease. Heart valves facilitate the one-way flow of blood in the heart and prevent significant backflow of blood into the heart. St. Jude valves account for about 60% of the world mechanical heart valve market. Annuloplasty rings are offered to repair damaged or diseased mitral heart valves.

Per Share Data ($)

(Year Ended Dec. 31)	1997	1996	1995	1994	1993	1992	1991	1990	1989	1988
Tangible Bk. Val.	6.98	5.86	5.52	7.92	6.95	6.02	4.60	3.40	2.45	1.85
Cash Flow	1.31	1.67	2.38	1.25	1.61	1.47	1.27	0.96	0.76	0.51
Earnings	0.59	1.12	1.82	1.13	1.55	1.41	1.17	0.90	0.71	0.47
Dividends	Nil	Nil	Nil	0.20	0.27	0.20	Nil	Nil	Nil	Nil
Payout Ratio	Nil	Nil	Nil	18%	17%	14%	Nil	Nil	Nil	Nil
Prices - High	42⅞	46	43¼	27⅜	28⅛	37	37	24⅜	16⅞	7⅛
- Low	27	29⅝	23⅝	16½	16⅝	18⅜	20⅛	12⅜	6⅜	3⅞
P/E Ratio - High	73	41	24	24	18	26	32	27	24	15
- Low	46	26	13	15	11	13	17	14	9	8

Income Statement Analysis (Million $)

	1997	1996	1995	1994	1993	1992	1991	1990	1989	1988
Revs.	994	809	724	360	253	240	210	175	148	114
Oper. Inc.	212	260	234	148	136	126	108	82.0	66.0	48.0
Depr.	66.1	44.9	40.3	8.3	4.5	3.6	7.2	4.3	3.4	2.0
Int. Exp.	14.4	3.5	12.9	3.7	Nil	Nil	Nil	Nil	0.0	0.1
Pretax Inc.	88.2	142	188	106	145	136	113	87.0	69.0	50.0
Eff. Tax Rate	38%	35%	31%	26%	25%	26%	26%	26%	27%	33%
Net Inc.	54.7	92.2	129	79.0	110	102	84.0	65.0	51.0	34.0

Balance Sheet & Other Fin. Data (Million $)

	1997	1996	1995	1994	1993	1992	1991	1990	1989	1988
Cash	28.5	185	166	137	369	339	263	179	121	86.0
Curr. Assets	743	665	520	434	450	416	330	241	171	125
Total Assets	1,459	1,301	1,016	920	527	470	375	278	202	143
Curr. Liab.	252	293	193	113	40.9	39.0	28.5	22.2	14.4	12.2
LT Debt	220	172	120	255	Nil	Nil	Nil	Nil	Nil	Nil
Common Eqty.	987	836	703	552	484	429	345	254	186	130
Total Cap.	1,207	1,008	823	807	486	431	347	256	187	131
Cap. Exp.	94.0	95.0	43.0	18.8	16.4	11.7	7.4	9.3	6.8	1.1
Cash Flow	121	137	169	88.0	114	105	91.0	69.0	54.0	36.0
Curr. Ratio	3.0	2.3	2.7	3.9	11.0	10.7	11.6	10.9	11.9	10.3
% LT Debt of Cap.	18.2	17.1	14.6	31.6	Nil	Nil	Nil	Nil	Nil	Nil
% Net Inc.of Revs.	5.5	11.4	17.8	22.0	43.4	42.4	40.0	36.9	34.4	29.3
% Ret. on Assets	4.0	7.9	13.3	10.9	22.2	24.0	25.6	26.9	29.4	27.1
% Ret. on Equity	6.0	11.8	20.6	15.3	24.3	26.2	28.0	29.3	32.1	29.9

Data as orig. reptd.; bef. results of disc. opers. and/or spec. items. Per share data adj. for stk. divs. as of ex-div. date. Bold denotes diluted EPS (FASB 128). E-Estimated. NA-Not Available. NM-Not Meaningful. NR-Not Ranked.

Office—One Lillehei Plaza, St. Paul, MN 55117. **Tel**—(612) 483-2000. **Website**—http://www.sjm.com **Chrmn & CEO**—R. A. Matricaria. **Pres & COO**—F. B. Parks. **VP-Fin & CFO**—R. Munzenrider. **Investor Contact**—Laura Merriam (612-766-3029). **Dirs**—P. J. Chiapparone, T. H. Garrett III, F. B. Parks, R. A. Matricaria, W. F. Mondale, W. L. Sembrowich, D. J. Starks, R. G. Stoll, G. R. Wilensky. **Transfer Agent**—American Stock Transfer & Trust Co., Brooklyn, NY. **Incorporated**—in Minnesota in 1976. **Empl**—3,772. **S&P Analyst:** H. B. Saftlas

12-SEP-98

Industry: Insurance (Property-Casualty)

Summary: This company, which owns St. Paul Fire & Marine Insurance and 77% of John Nuveen & Co., recently acquired USF&G Corp.

S&P Opinion: Hold (★★★)	Recent Price • 32⅛	Yield • 3.1%
	52 Wk Range • 47¼-28	12-Mo. P/E • 20.8

Quantitative Evaluations

Outlook
(1 Lowest—5 Highest)
• **3-**

Fair Value
• **34¾**

Risk
• **Low**

Earn./Div. Rank
• **A-**

Technical Eval.
• **Bullish** since 5/98

Rel. Strength Rank
(1 Lowest—99 Highest)
• **57**

Insider Activity
• **NA**

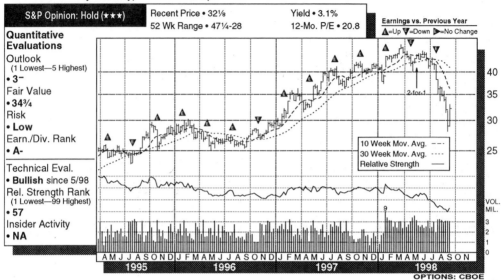

Earnings vs. Previous Year
▲=Up ▼=Down ▶=No Change

10 Week Mov. Avg. - - -
30 Week Mov. Avg. ·····
Relative Strength ——

OPTIONS: CBOE

Overview - 13-AUG-98

Growth in net written premiums and in operating earnings in 1999 will be aided somewhat by the $3.5 billion acquisition of USF&G Corp. (FG), completed April 24, 1998. The deal, which created the eighth largest U.S. property-casualty insurer, expanded SPC's product mix (particularly in non-standard auto and international lines) and geographic coverage. But underlying premium growth prospects, particularly in the near term, may be hampered by ongoing price competition in most commercial lines. Exacerbating an already difficult operating environment is the prospect that operating earnings in 1998 will be hurt by much higher year over year catastrophe losses. Profitability in 1998 will also be hurt by second quarter after-tax charges of $457.5 million ($1.95) taken to cover costs associated with the FG acquisition. (These charges are excluded from our 1998 earnings estimate.) Included in those charges was a $250 million pretax reserve boost. Additional reserve increases are likely. That aside, further profit gains are predicated on SPC's ability to wring an anticipated $200 million in annual pretax cost savings from the new entity.

Valuation - 13-AUG-98

After trading in a relatively narrow range during much of 1996, the shares strengthened during much of 1997 and into 1998. Lately, the shares have weakened, as investors display a rather tepid response to the FG deal and reassert their concern that SPC's near term profitability will be hurt by weak property-casualty pricing and adverse weather related claim trends. We share many of these concerns. Still, we applaud SPC's pro-active stance, and believe that SPC did not overpay for FG. However, neither company's growth prospects are particularly bright. As a result, we anticipate the shares will be average performers in the near term.

Key Stock Statistics

S&P EPS Est. 1998	2.35	Tang. Bk. Value/Share	24.88
P/E on S&P Est. 1998	13.7	Beta	0.94
S&P EPS Est. 1999	3.30	Shareholders	7,700
Dividend Rate/Share	1.00	Market cap. (B)	$ 7.6
Shs. outstg. (M)	236.1	Inst. holdings	76%
Avg. daily vol. (M)	0.777		

Value of $10,000 invested 5 years ago: $ 19,861

Fiscal Year Ending Dec. 31

	1998	1997	1996	1995	1994	1993
Revenues (Million $)						
1Q	1,467	1,557	1,330	1,267	1,164	1,114
2Q	2,409	1,621	1,364	1,331	1,165	1,069
3Q	—	1,497	1,476	1,365	1,199	1,105
4Q	—	1,544	1,564	1,447	1,173	1,172
Yr.	—	6,219	5,734	5,410	4,701	4,460
Earnings Per Share ($)						
1Q	0.83	1.05	0.84	0.64	0.36	0.51
2Q	-1.28	1.25	0.79	0.65	0.74	0.63
3Q	—	0.89	0.67	0.82	0.76	0.82
4Q	—	1.01	0.95	0.89	0.70	0.89
Yr.	—	4.20	3.06	3.00	2.56	3.00

Next earnings report expected: NA

Dividend Data (Dividends have been paid since 1872.)

Amount ($)	Date Decl.	Ex-Div. Date	Stock of Record	Payment Date
0.500	Feb. 03	Mar. 27	Mar. 31	Apr. 17 '98
2-for-1	Feb. 03	May. 12	May. 06	May. 11 '98
0.250	May. 05	Jun. 26	Jun. 30	Jul. 17 '98
0.250	Aug. 04	Sep. 28	Sep. 30	Oct. 16 '98

A Division of The McGraw·Hill Companies

Business Summary - 13-AUG-98

Founded in Saint Paul, MN, in 1853, the St. Paul Companies is that state's oldest business corporation, and a leading property-casualty insurer with several important franchises. The principal operating subsidiary is St. Paul Fire & Marine Insurance Co., a leading property-casualty insurer and the largest medical liability insurer in the world. St. Paul Re, another subsidiary, is the eighth largest reinsurance underwriter in the U.S., and sells reinsurance worldwide. SPC also has a 77% ownership interest in John Nuveen & Co., a municipal bond underwriter that traces its roots back to the 19th century. On April 24, 1998, SPC expanded its presence in the property-casualty market by acquiring Baltimore-based USF&G Corp. for $3.5 billion in stock and assumption of debt. As a result of the transaction, the combined entities became the eighth largest property-casualty company in the U.S. (based on latest available industry statistics).

Contributions to revenues in recent years were:

	1997	1996
Insurance underwriting	62%	65%
Reinsurance underwriting	12%	13%
Investment income/realized inv. gains	21%	17%
Investment banking & other	5%	5%

The company writes most lines of property-liability insurance. Of $4.5 billion in written premiums in 1997 ($4.4 billion in 1996), specialized commercial accounted for 29%, standard commercial 19%, personal insurance 17%, reinsurance 17%, medical services 12% (SPC is the largest medical liability insurer in the U.S.) and international 6%. During the first six months of 1998, extremely competitive premium pricing, combined with higher pretax catastrophe losses of $157 million versus $70 million, led to sharply lower operating earnings. Operating earnings (which exclude realized investment gains or losses) amounted to $0.21 a share, versus $0.71 a share in the 1997 interim. Results in the 1998 period exclude a $457.7 million ($1.95 a share) after-tax charge taken to cover costs associated with the April 1998 acquisition of USF&G Corp.

John Nuveen & Co., 77%-owned as of year-end 1997, underwrites and trades municipal bonds and tax-exempt unit investment trusts and markets tax-exempt open-end and closed-end bond funds. At year-end 1997, assets under management totaled $49 billion.

London-based Minet Group, the world's 10th largest insurance broker, was sold to Aon Corp. in the second quarter of 1997.

Per Share Data ($)

(Year Ended Dec. 31)	1997	1996	1995	1994	1993	1992	1991	1990	1989	1988
Tangible Bk. Val.	50.19	22.96	20.27	14.57	16.06	12.37	12.05	9.93	9.38	8.00
Oper. Earnings	2.88	2.27	2.67	2.39	2.22	-1.64	2.19	2.11	1.73	1.81
Earnings	4.20	3.25	3.00	2.56	2.46	-1.42	2.34	2.14	2.03	1.83
Dividends	0.94	0.88	0.80	0.75	0.70	0.68	0.65	0.60	0.55	0.50
Payout Ratio	22%	27%	27%	29%	28%	NM	28%	28%	27%	27%
Prices - High	43¾	30⅜	29¾	22¾	24½	20¼	18⅝	16½	15⅞	12¾
- Low	28⅞	25⅛	21¾	18⅞	18¾	16⅝	14¼	11¾	10¾	9⅝
P/E Ratio - High	10	13	10	9	10	NM	8	8	8	7
- Low	7	11	7	7	8	NM	6	5	5	5

Income Statement Analysis (Million $)

	1997	1996	1995	1994	1993	1992	1991	1990	1989	1988
Premium Inc.	4,616	4,448	3,971	3,412	3,178	3,143	3,146	2,894	2,668	2,706
Net Invest. Inc.	886	807	772	695	661	666	676	670	662	592
Oth. Revs.	717	479	667	595	621	690	530	441	459	333
Total Revs.	5,333	5,734	5,410	4,701	4,460	4,499	4,352	4,005	3,789	3,631
Pretax Inc.	1,019	699	656	564	523	-224	528	504	489	422
Net Oper. Inc.	531	415	465	414	387	-256	381	385	338	349
Net Inc.	773	558	521	443	428	-232	405	391	398	352

Balance Sheet & Other Fin. Data (Million $)

	1997	1996	1995	1994	1993	1992	1991	1990	1989	1988
Cash & Equiv.	23.0	181	232	230	200	195	189	174	185	179
Premiums Due	1,503	1,559	1,969	2,000	1,813	1,759	1,761	1,676	1,179	1,210
Invest. Assets: Bonds	12,450	11,944	10,373	8,829	9,148	8,361	7,833	7,405	6,828	6,345
Invest. Assets: Stocks	2,991	1,394	1,100	861	847	725	687	591	773	679
Invest. Assets: Loans	Nil	Nil	Nil	Nil	Nil	Nil	Nil	Nil	Nil	Nil
Invest. Assets: Total	15,036	14,366	13,067	11,163	11,256	9,577	8,973	8,468	8,107	7,467
Deferred Policy Costs	404	402	372	324	295	280	293	286	264	251
Total Assets	21,501	20,681	19,657	17,496	17,149	13,597	12,982	12,204	11,030	10,382
Debt	869	689	704	623	640	567	487	460	263	288
Common Eqty.	4,611	3,988	3,719	2,733	3,005	2,202	2,533	2,196	2,349	2,015
Prop. & Cas. Loss Ratio	70.9	74.6	72.1	72.1	72.5	85.6	75.2	73.2	75.7	73.6
Prop. & Cas. Expense Ratio	33.8	30.9	29.7	30.2	32.0	32.2	29.4	30.0	30.5	30.0
Prop. & Cas. Combined Ratio	104.7	105.5	101.8	102.3	104.5	117.8	104.6	103.2	106.2	103.6
% Return On Revs.	14.5	9.7	9.6	9.4	9.6	NM	9.3	9.8	10.5	9.6
% Ret. on Equity	17.8	14.3	15.9	16.4	NM	16.9	17.0	18.4	20.4

Data as orig. reptd.; bef. results of disc. opers. and/or spec. items. Per share data adj. for stk. divs. as of ex-div. date. Bold denotes diluted EPS (FASB 128). E-Estimated. NA-Not Available. NM-Not Meaningful. NR-Not Ranked.

Office—385 Washington St., St. Paul, MN 55102. **Tel**—(612) 221-7911. **Website**—http://www.stpaul.com **Chrmn, CEO & Pres**—D. W. Leatherdale. **Vice Chrmn**—N. P. Blake, Jr. **VP- CFO**— P. J. Liska. **VP & Investor Contact**—James L. Boudreau. **Secy**—S. U. Wiese. **Dirs**— N. P. Blake, Jr., M. R. Bonsignore, J. H. Dasburg, W. J. Driscoll, P. M. Grieve, R. James, W. H. Kling, D. W. Leatherdale, B. K. MacLaury, G. D. Nelson, A. M. Pampusch, G. Sprenger, P. A. Thiele. **Transfer Agent & Registrar**—First Chicago Trust Co. of New York, NYC. **Incorporated**—in Minnesota in 1853; reincorporated in 1968. **Empl**— 10,000. **S&P Analyst:** Catherine A. Seifert

Sara Lee

1982

NYSE Symbol **SLE**

In S&P 500

12-SEP-98

Industry: Foods

Summary: Sara Lee is a diversified producer of branded products (meats, fresh and frozen baked goods and coffee products) and personal apparel and household care products.

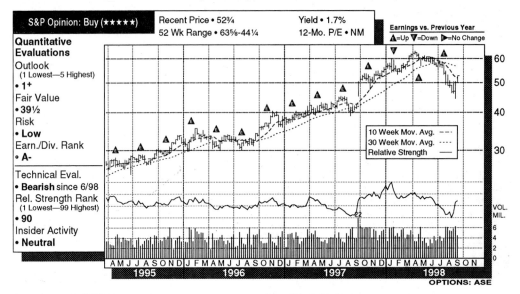

S&P Opinion: Buy (★★★★★)	Recent Price • 52¾	Yield • 1.7%
	52 Wk Range • 63⅝-44¼	12-Mo. P/E • NM

Quantitative Evaluations

Outlook (1 Lowest—5 Highest)
• 1+

Fair Value
• 39½

Risk
• **Low**

Earn./Div. Rank
• A-

Technical Eval.
• **Bearish** since 6/98

Rel. Strength Rank (1 Lowest—99 Highest)
• **90**

Insider Activity
• **Neutral**

Earnings vs. Previous Year ▲=Up ▼=Down ▶=No Change

10 Week Mov. Avg. — - —
30 Week Mov. Avg. - - - -
Relative Strength ———

OPTIONS: ASE

Overview - 01-MAY-98

Sales are projected to rise at a low single-digit rate in FY 98 (Jun.), led by broad-based, but modest, unit volume growth for existing operations. Profit margins should improve, helped by growing benefits expected to be realized from SLE's recent restructuring initiatives and increasing de-emphasis of certain low-margin manufacturing functions, such as its U.S. yarn and textile operations (most of which were sold in January 1998). The sale of certain other capital-intensive assets over the next few years should also generate funds that are likely to be used for debt reduction and share repurchases. Improving margins and returns on invested capital should boost EPS growth from 10% in recent years to about 12% to 14% over the next three years. In FY 98, we look for EPS of $2.28 (excluding charges), up 12% from FY 97's $2.03.

Valuation - 01-MAY-98

We view SLE's recent enactment of its three-year plan to improve its financial returns by shedding various capital-intensive manufacturing assets very positively. SLE's increasing reliance on outsourced production should improve the company's sub-par profit margins and historically high capital requirements in coming years. In addition, proceeds realized from the sale of these assets should allow SLE to enact its ambitious $3 billion share repurchase plan over the next three years. The January 1998 sale of the majority of the company's yarn and textile plants is expected to contribute $600 million in cash flow benefits over the next three years. Given the prospects of enhanced EPS growth, the stock's valuation should improve. Despite their recent strength, we view the shares as attractive, at only a modest P/E premium to that of the S&P 500.

Key Stock Statistics

S&P EPS Est. 1998	NA	Tang. Bk. Value/Share	NM
P/E on S&P Est. 1998	NA	Beta	0.90
S&P EPS Est. 1999	2.51	Shareholders	89,000
Dividend Rate/Share	0.92	Market cap. (B)	$ 24.6
Shs. outstg. (M)	467.1	Inst. holdings	51%
Avg. daily vol. (M)	1.222		

Value of $10,000 invested 5 years ago: $ 19,850

Fiscal Year Ending Jun. 30

	1998	1997	1996	1995	1994	1993
Revenues (Million $)						
1Q	4,893	4,886	4,656	4,290	3,796	3,580
2Q	5,279	5,269	4,898	4,648	4,010	3,840
3Q	4,736	4,649	4,443	4,193	3,664	3,308
4Q	5,103	4,930	4,627	4,588	4,066	3,849
Yr.	20,011	19,734	18,624	17,719	15,536	14,580
Earnings Per Share ($)						
1Q	0.46	0.41	0.37	0.33	0.31	0.28
2Q	-2.71	0.62	0.57	0.51	0.48	0.44
3Q	0.46	0.41	0.37	0.33	0.30	0.30
4Q	0.62	0.57	0.52	0.45	-0.65	0.38
Yr.	-1.14	2.03	1.83	1.62	0.44	1.40

Next earnings report expected: NA

Dividend Data (Dividends have been paid since 1946.)

Amount ($)	Date Decl.	Ex-Div. Date	Stock of Record	Payment Date
0.230	Oct. 30	Nov. 26	Dec. 01	Jan. 02 '98
0.230	Jan. 29	Feb. 26	Mar. 02	Apr. 01 '98
0.230	Apr. 30	May. 28	Jun. 01	Jul. 01 '98
0.230	Jun. 25	Aug. 28	Sep. 01	Oct. 01 '98

A Division of The McGraw·Hill Companies

Business Summary - 01-MAY-98

Best known for its familiar baked goods, Sara Lee boasts many other branded food and non-food products--ranging from Ball Park franks to the Wonderbra. The company incurred an after-tax charge of $1.6 billion in its second quarter of FY 98 (Jun.) related to the writedown and sale of assets included in a strategic restructuring program aimed at raising $3 billion over the next three years through the divestment of certain assets and cost reduction programs.

Segment contributions in FY 97 (Jun.) were:

	Sales	Profits
Packaged foods:		
Packaged meats & bakery	39%	25%
Coffee & grocery	14%	23%
Packaged consumer products:		
Personal products	38%	40%
Household & body care	9%	12%

The Packaged Meats division makes pork, poultry and beef products sold to supermarkets, warehouse clubs and other customers in the U.S., Europe and Mexico. Brands include Ball Park, Best's, Kahn's, and Hillshire Farm. The Bakery division produces fresh and frozen Sara Lee brand baked goods and specialty items

throughout the U.S., the U.K., France, Mexico, Australia and many Pacific Rim countries. Foodservice business is conducted principally under the PYA/Monarch name. Coffee and Grocery products (Douwe Egberts coffee, Pickwick tea) are sold mainly in Europe.

Consumer products include such personal products as hosiery (Hanes, L'eggs, Sheer Energy, Underalls, Dim, Pretty Polly); activewear (Beefy-T, Champion, Hanes Her Way); underwear and intimate apparel (Bali, Dim, Hanes, Playtex); and household and personal care items (Kiwi shoecare, Sanex skin-care products).

Foreign operations in FY 97 accounted for 42% of sales (34% Western/Central Europe, 6% Asia Pacific/Latin America, 2% other) and 47% of pretax profits (38% Western/Central Europe, 7% Asia Pacific/Latin America, 2% other).

The company's longstanding financial goals include: inflation-adjusted EPS growth of 8%; return on equity of 20%; and a total debt to capital ratio below 40%. Management recently added another financial goal: an aftertax return on invested capital above 15%. Through the first nine months of FY 98, SLE repurchased more than 19 million shares of its common stock for a total of $1.028 billion. At the end of the FY 98 third quarter, approximately 30 million shares remained under a current share repurchase authorization.

Per Share Data ($)

(Year Ended Jun. 30)	1998	1997	1996	1995	1994	1993	1992	1991	1990	1989
Tangible Bk. Val.	NA	0.69	0.91	NM	NM	7.32	6.37	4.76	4.23	3.45
Cash Flow	NA	3.43	3.14	2.74	1.56	2.45	2.51	1.71	1.52	1.35
Earnings	-1.14	2.03	1.83	1.62	0.44	1.40	1.54	1.08	0.96	0.88
Dividends	0.90	0.82	0.74	0.67	0.63	0.56	0.61	0.46	0.41	0.34
Payout Ratio	NM	40%	40%	41%	142%	40%	41%	44%	43%	40%
Prices - High	63⅝	57¾	40½	33¾	26	32⅜	31⅛	29⅛	16¾	16⅞
- Low	47⅞	36½	29⅞	24¼	19⅜	21	21	14⅞	12⅛	10¾
P/E Ratio - High	NM	28	22	21	59	23	22	27	17	19
- Low	NM	18	16	15	44	15	17	14	13	12

Income Statement Analysis (Million $)

	1998	1997	1996	1995	1994	1993	1992	1991	1990	1989
Revs.	NA	19,734	18,624	17,719	15,536	14,580	13,243	12,381	11,606	11,718
Oper. Inc.	NA	2,323	2,185	2,010	1,834	1,686	1,518	1,252	1,127	956
Depr.	NA	680	634	606	568	522	472	302	268	215
Int. Exp.	NA	202	228	243	188	162	172	195	192	154
Pretax Inc.	NA	1,484	1,378	1,219	389	1,082	1,174	830	713	639
Eff. Tax Rate	NA	32%	34%	34%	40%	35%	35%	36%	34%	36%
Net Inc.	NA	1,009	916	804	234	704	761	535	470	410

Balance Sheet & Other Fin. Data (Million $)

	1998	1997	1996	1995	1994	1993	1992	1991	1990	1989
Cash	NA	272	243	202	189	325	198	125	169	117
Curr. Assets	NA	5,391	5,081	4,928	4,469	3,976	3,695	2,920	2,868	2,500
Total Assets	NA	12,953	12,602	12,431	11,665	10,862	9,989	8,122	7,636	6,523
Curr. Liab.	NA	5,016	4,642	4,844	4,919	4,269	3,300	2,526	2,483	2,275
LT Debt	NA	1,933	1,842	1,817	1,496	1,164	1,389	1,399	1,524	1,486
Common Eqty.	NA	4,280	4,320	3,939	3,326	3,551	3,055	2,215	1,949	1,567
Total Cap.	NA	7,394	7,356	6,882	5,963	5,888	5,913	5,174	4,816	3,944
Cap. Exp.	NA	547	542	480	628	728	509	640	673	789
Cash Flow	NA	1,663	1,523	1,372	778	1,190	1,194	791	699	611
Curr. Ratio	NA	1.1	1.1	1.0	0.9	0.9	1.1	1.2	1.2	1.1
% LT Debt of Cap.	NA	26.1	25.1	26.4	25.0	19.8	23.5	27.0	31.6	37.7
% Net Inc.of Revs.	NA	5.1	5.0	4.5	1.5	4.8	5.7	4.3	4.1	3.5
% Ret. on Assets	NA	7.9	7.1	6.7	2.0	6.7	8.3	6.8	6.6	7.0
% Ret. on Equity	NA	22.9	21.6	21.2	6.1	19.2	27.0	23.4	24.3	24.9

Data as orig. reptd.; bef. results of disc. opers. and/or spec. items. Per share data adj. for stk. divs. as of ex-div. date. Bold denotes diluted EPS (FASB 128). E-Estimated. NA-Not Available. NM-Not Meaningful. NR-Not Ranked.

Office—3 First National Plaza, Chicago, IL 60602-4260. **Registrar**—First National Bank of Chicago. **Tel**—(312) 726-2600. **Chrmn & CEO**—J. H. Bryan. **Vice Chrmn**—D. J. Franceschini. **SVP & CFO**—Judith A. Sprieser. **SVP & Secy**—J. L. Kelly. **VP & Investor Contact**—Janet E. Bergman (312-558-4966). **Dirs**—P. A. Allaire, F. H. Andriessen, J. H. Bryan, D. L. Burnham, C. W. Coker, W. D. Davis, D. J. Franceschini, A. F. Jacobson, V. E. Jordan Jr., J. L. Ketelsen, H. B. van Liemt, J. D. Manley, C. S. McMillan, F. L. Meysman, N. M. Minow, M. E. Murphy, Sir Arvi H. Parbo, R. L. Ridgway, R. L. Thomas. **Transfer Agent**—Co. itself. **Incorporated**—in Maryland in 1941. **Empl**— 141,000. **S&P Analyst:** Kenneth A. Shea

SBC Communications Inc. 1958

NYSE Symbol **SBC**

In S&P 500

12-SEP-98

Industry: Telephone

Summary: This telephone holding company holds investments in cellular telephone service, cable television and international ventures.

S&P Opinion: Hold (★★★)

Recent Price • 40	Yield • 2.3%
52 Wk Range • 46½-28⅝	12-Mo. P/E • 22.6

Quantitative Evaluations

Outlook
(1 Lowest—5 Highest)
• **1**

Fair Value
• **35⅞**

Risk
• **Low**

Earn./Div. Rank
• **A-**

Technical Eval.
• **Bullish** since 12/96

Rel. Strength Rank
(1 Lowest—99 Highest)
• **91**

Insider Activity
• **Neutral**

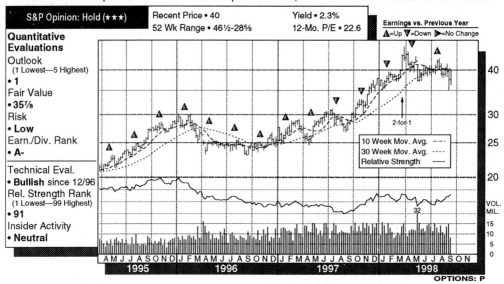

Earnings vs. Previous Year
▲=Up ▼=Down ▷=No Change

10 Week Mov. Avg. ---
30 Week Mov. Avg. ----
Relative Strength —

2-for-1

OPTIONS: P

Overview - 22-JUL-98

In May 1998, SBC agreed to acquire Ameritech Corp. (NYSE: AIT) in a $62 billion stock transaction expected to be completed in mid-1999. AIT shareholders would receive 1.316 SBC shares for each AIT share held (currently about 1.1 billion shares outstanding). Following the transaction, current SBC shareholders would own 56% of the combined company, and current AIT shareholders would own 44%. In January 1998, SBC signed a definitive agreement to acquire Southern New England Telecommunications Corp. (NYSE: SNG) in a $4.4 billion transaction via an exchange of stock (0.8784 of a SBC share for each SNG share). The transaction is expected to be completed by the end of 1998. SBC currently serves seven of the 10 leading U.S. markets, with more than 34.2 million access lines, and revenues of more than $25 billion. With two of the biggest U.S. markets (Texas and California), SBC is well positioned to exploit the fast growing international telecommunications market. Over 50% of all international traffic to Mexico and 20% to Asia originates in its combined territory.

Valuation - 22-JUL-98

The shares have continued to move in line with the market recovery, following the completion of SBC's merger with Pacific Telesis and subsequent agreements to purchase Southern New England Telephone and Ameritech. As a result of the slow process of adjusting to the rapidly changing telecommunications industry, we believe that the shares, which yield an average 2.4%, are likely to continue to be only market performers over the next year. We see the company receiving the green light to offer long-distance services in its own markets by late 1998 or early 1999 at the latest. However, we view the proposed acquisition of fellow Baby Bell Ameritech as having little chance of receiving the necessary regulatory approvals.

Key Stock Statistics

S&P EPS Est. 1998	2.10	Tang. Bk. Value/Share	4.17
P/E on S&P Est. 1998	19.0	Beta	0.61
S&P EPS Est. 1999	2.30	Shareholders	800,500
Dividend Rate/Share	0.94	Market cap. (B)	$ 73.5
Shs. outstg. (M)	1837.3	Inst. holdings	43%
Avg. daily vol. (M)	2.402		

Value of $10,000 invested 5 years ago: $ 25,763

Fiscal Year Ending Dec. 31

	1998	1997	1996	1995	1994	1993
Revenues (Million $)						
1Q	6,424	5,991	3,197	2,910	2,650	2,460
2Q	6,591	5,936	3,333	3,025	2,760	2,540
3Q	—	6,345	3,600	3,292	3,000	2,800
4Q	—	6,633	3,768	3,443	3,210	2,900
Yr.	—	24,856	13,898	12,670	11,620	10,690
Earnings Per Share ($)						
1Q	**0.45**	0.47	0.38	0.33	0.29	0.26
2Q	**0.52**	-0.43	0.41	0.36	0.32	0.28
3Q	**E0.55**	0.45	0.48	0.44	0.40	0.34
4Q	**E0.58**	0.32	0.45	0.42	0.35	0.32
Yr.	**E2.10**	0.80	1.73	1.55	1.37	1.20

Next earnings report expected: late October

Dividend Data (Dividends have been paid since 1984.)

Amount ($)	Date Decl.	Ex-Div. Date	Stock of Record	Payment Date
0.448	Dec. 19	Jan. 07	Jan. 10	Feb. 02 '98
2-for-1	Jan. 30	Mar. 20	Feb. 20	Mar. 19 '98
0.234	Jan. 30	Apr. 07	Apr. 10	May. 01 '98
0.234	Jun. 29	Jul. 08	Jul. 10	Aug. 03 '98

A Division of The **McGraw·Hill** Companies

Business Summary - 22-JUL-98

In May 1998, SBC agreed to acquire fellow Baby Bell Ameritech Corp. (NYSE: AIT) in a $62 billion stock transaction expected to be completed in mid-1999. Current SBC shareholders would own 56% of the combined company, and current AIT shareholders 44%.

In January 1998, the company signed a definitive agreement to acquire Southern New England Telecommunications Corp. (NYSE: SNG) in a $4.4 billion exchange of stock, expected to be completed by the end of 1998.

In April 1997, SBC Communications (formerly Southwestern Bell), the eighth largest U.S. telephone holding company, merged its operations with fellow RBOC (regional bell operating company) Pacific Telesis Group. As a result, SBC holds 25% of the local domestic telephony market. SBC serves two the largest states, California and Texas, as well as 16 of the 50 leading U.S. markets. It also provides service for seven non-U.S. growth markets, including Mexico, Chile, South Korea, France, South Africa, and Israel. SBC believes that cost savings from the merger could add about $1 billion annually to net income by 2000.

SBC serves more than 34 million domestic access lines in high-growth areas and reaches more than 87 million potential domestic wireless customers. Outside the U.S., SBC has equity stakes in telecommunications businesses reaching more than 260 million potential customers.

SBC believes that the potential for revenue growth and cost savings that it identified during the merger integration give it the opportunity to add $1 billion in net income annually by 2000. In addition, it expects to be able to offer long-distance service in its markets during 1998, subject to FCC approval.

The company owns two cable television systems in the Washington, DC, area, serving 278,000 customers. During 1995, SBC became an equal partner in a venture with Ameritech, BellSouth, GTE and Walt Disney. The venture, Americast, will design, market and deliver video programming and interactive services.

International operations include a nearly 10% interest in Telefonos de Mexico, cable and telecommunications operations in the U.K. and Chile, wireless interests in France, South Korea and South Africa, a long-distance alliance and cable television operations in Israel, and Australian directory services. Ventures formed in 1997 included Switzerland, South Korea and Taiwan, and SBC has joined with 13 other international companies to build a trans-Pacific fiber-optic cable for long-distance traffic between the U.S. and China.

Per Share Data ($)

(Year Ended Dec. 31)	1997	1996	1995	1994	1993	1992	1991	1990	1989	1988
Tangible Bk. Val.	3.60	3.59	2.89	4.68	5.35	6.51	6.07	5.92	5.71	5.79
Cash Flow	3.47	3.58	3.33	3.06	2.87	2.62	2.44	2.33	2.48	2.42
Earnings	0.80	1.73	1.55	1.37	1.20	1.08	0.96	0.92	0.91	0.89
Dividends	0.89	0.85	0.81	0.78	0.75	0.72	0.70	0.68	0.64	0.61
Payout Ratio	111%	49%	53%	57%	63%	67%	73%	74%	71%	69%
Prices - High	38⅛	30⅛	29¼	22¼	23½	18¾	16½	16¼	16⅛	10⅝
- Low	24⅝	23	19⅞	18⅜	17⅛	14⅛	12¼	11⅞	9¾	8¼
P/E Ratio - High	48	17	19	16	20	17	17	18	18	12
- Low	31	13	13	13	14	13	13	13	11	9

Income Statement Analysis (Million $)

	1997	1996	1995	1994	1993	1992	1991	1990	1989	1988
Revs.	24,856	13,898	12,670	11,619	10,690	10,015	9,332	9,113	8,730	8,453
Depr.	4,922	2,240	2,170	2,038	2,007	1,842	1,765	1,691	1,891	1,845
Maint.	NA	NA	NA	NA	NA	NA	1,535	1,553	1,450	1,469
Constr. Credits	NA	NA	11.2	NA	NA	NA	34.1	26.1	14.8	15.3
Eff. Tax Rate	37%	36%	32%	32%	30%	30%	30%	29%	26%	25%
Net Inc.	1,474	2,101	1,889	1,649	1,435	1,302	1,157	1,101	1,093	1,060

Balance Sheet & Other Fin. Data (Million $)

	1997	1996	1995	1994	1993	1992	1991	1990	1989	1988
Gross Prop.	65,286	31,595	29,256	29,256	28,171	26,978	25,755	24,670	24,529	23,651
Net Prop.	27,339	14,007	12,988	17,317	17,092	16,899	16,510	16,322	16,078	16,304
Cap. Exp.	5,766	3,027	2,336	2,350	2,221	2,144	1,826	1,778	1,483	1,222
Total Cap.	21,911	12,340	11,928	16,893	15,885	19,044	18,622	18,224	18,051	17,792
Fxd. Chgs. Cov.	3.2	7.4	4.6	4.4	5.1	4.5	4.0	3.7	3.6	3.4
Capitalization:										
LT Debt	12,019	5,505	5,672	5,848	5,459	5,716	5,675	5,483	5,456	5,039
Pfd.	Nil	Nil	Nil	Nil	Nil	Nil	Nil	Nil	Nil	Nil
Common	10,075	6,835	6,256	8,356	7,609	9,304	8,859	8,581	8,367	8,504
% Return On Revs.	5.9	15.2	14.9	14.2	13.4	13.0	12.4	12.1	12.5	12.5
% Return On Invest. Capital	NA	28.5	15.9	13.0	11.1	9.7	9.2	9.1	9.3	9.1
% Return On Com. Equity	17.2	32.1	25.9	20.7	19.2	14.3	13.0	12.9	12.9	12.7
% Earn. on Net Prop.	15.3	15.6	20.0	11.6	10.3	9.8	10.0	10.0	10.0	9.7
% LT Debt of Cap.	54.9	44.7	47.6	41.2	41.8	38.1	39.0	39.0	39.5	37.2
Capital. % Pfd.	Nil	Nil	Nil	Nil	Nil	Nil	Nil	Nil	Nil	Nil
Capital. % Common	45.1	55.4	52.4	58.8	58.2	61.9	61.0	61.0	60.5	62.8

Data as orig. reptd.; bef. results of disc. opers. and/or spec. items. Per share data adj. for stk. divs. as of ex-div. date. Bold denotes diluted EPS (FASB 128). E-Estimated. NA-Not Available. NM-Not Meaningful. NR-Not Ranked..

Office—175 E. Houston, San Antonio, TX 78205. **Tel**—(210) 821-4105. **Website**—http://www.sbc.com **Chrmn & CEO**—E. E. Whitacre Jr. **SVP, Treas & CFO**—D. E. Kiernan. **Secy**—J. M. Sahm. **Investor Contact**—William B. McCullough. **Dirs**—C. C. Barksdale, J. E. Barnes, A. A. Busch III, R. S. Caldwell, R. R. Cardenas, W. P. Clark, M. K. Eby Jr., H. E. Gallegos, J. T. Hay, B. R. Inman, C. F. Knight, M. S. Metz, H. M. Monroe Jr., T. Rembe, S. D. Ritchey, R. M. Rosenberg, P. P. Upton, E. E. Whitacre Jr. **Transfer Agent & Registrar**—Bank of New York, NYC. **Incorporated**—in Delaware in 1983. **Empl**— 119,062. **S&P Analyst:** Philip D. Wohl

STANDARD &POOR'S
STOCK REPORTS

Schering-Plough

1985J

NYSE Symbol **SGP**

In S&P 500

12-SEP-98

Industry:
Health Care (Drugs - Major Pharmaceuticals)

Summary: This company is a leading producer of prescription and OTC pharmaceuticals and has important interests in sun care, animal health and foot care products.

| S&P Opinion: Accumulate (★★★★) | Recent Price • 94⅝ | Yield • 0.9% |
| | 52 Wk Range • 105½-48¼ | 12-Mo. P/E • 43.8 |

Quantitative Evaluations

Outlook
(1 Lowest—5 Highest)
• 1

Fair Value
• 83⅝

Risk
• Low

Earn./Div. Rank
• A+

Technical Eval.
• **Bullish** since 5/96

Rel. Strength Rank
(1 Lowest—99 Highest)
• 91

Insider Activity
• Neutral

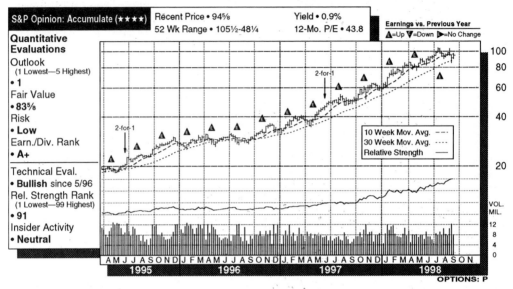

Earnings vs. Previous Year
▲=Up ▼=Down ▶=No Change

10 Week Mov. Avg. ---
30 Week Mov. Avg. ----
Relative Strength —

OPTIONS: P

Overview - 31-JUL-98

Sales should post another high double-digit gain in 1998. Despite ongoing generic erosion in the Proventil anti-asthma line, volume should benefit from continued strong gains in Claritin and Claritin-D nonsedating antihistamine agents, Intron A anticancer/anti-infective agent and other drugs. Claritin should benefit from expansion in the large Japanese market, while new indications should boost Intron A volume. New products such as Cedax antibiotic, Integrelin heart drug and Fareston breast cancer treatment should also augment sales. Last year's acquisition of Mallinckrodt's veterinary product lines has substantially expanded SGP's animal health products business. Consumer products sales should show modest growth. Margins should be well maintained, on improved volume and cost efficiencies.

Valuation - 31-JUL-98

The shares have been outstanding performers over the past few years, driven by superior earnings growth (EPS gains equaled 20% or better in each of the past four quarters) and prospects for more of the same over the coming quarters. Near-term results should continue to benefit from gains in Claritin, the worldwide leading antihistamine; Intron A, an important antiviral/anticancer agent; and Vancenase, an inhaled steroid for allergies. Promising new products include Rebetol, a combination of Intron A and ribavarin to treat chronic hepatitis C; Integrilin heart drug; and Prandin anti-diabetic agent. SGP's mix of popular prescription drugs and OTC medications, its highly productive R&D program, and strict cost controls should provide the basis for continued strong earnings growth in coming years. The R&D pipeline includes new drugs for asthma, cancer, infections, arthritis, and erectile dysfunction. The shares remain attractive for above-average long-term total return.

Key Stock Statistics

S&P EPS Est. 1998	2.33	Tang. Bk. Value/Share	3.92
P/E on S&P Est. 1998	40.6	Beta	1.15
S&P EPS Est. 1999	2.73	Shareholders	35,000
Dividend Rate/Share	0.88	Market cap. (B)	$ 69.5
Shs. outstg. (M)	734.0	Inst. holdings	62%
Avg. daily vol. (M)	2.124		

Value of $10,000 invested 5 years ago: $ 66,394

Fiscal Year Ending Dec. 31

	1998	1997	1996	1995	1994	1993
Revenues (Million $)						
1Q	1,908	1,568	1,383	1,224	1,162	1,090
2Q	2,124	1,720	1,477	1,333	1,190	1,123
3Q	—	1,709	1,382	1,257	1,126	1,062
4Q	—	1,781	1,414	1,291	1,180	1,066
Yr.	—	6,778	5,656	5,104	4,657	4,341
Earnings Per Share ($)						
1Q	0.61	0.51	0.45	0.39	0.33	0.28
2Q	0.61	0.50	0.43	0.37	0.31	0.27
3Q	E0.56	0.48	0.40	0.34	0.29	0.26
4Q	E0.55	0.46	0.38	0.33	0.27	0.24
Yr.	E2.33	1.95	1.63	1.43	1.21	1.06

Next earnings report expected: late October

Dividend Data (Dividends have been paid since 1952.)

Amount ($)	Date Decl.	Ex-Div. Date	Stock of Record	Payment Date
0.190	Oct. 28	Nov. 05	Nov. 07	Nov. 28 '97
0.190	Jan. 27	Feb. 04	Feb. 06	Feb. 27 '98
0.220	Apr. 28	May. 06	May. 08	May. 29 '98
0.220	Jun. 23	Aug. 05	Aug. 07	Aug. 31 '98

A Division of The McGraw-Hill Companies

Business Summary - 31-JUL-98

Schering-Plough is a leading maker of niche-oriented prescription pharmaceuticals. Interests are also held in animal health products, over-the-counter (OTC) medications, and consumer products. The company traces its history to Ernst Schering, a Berlin chemist who founded the company in 1864. International operations accounted for 39% of sales and 27% of profits in 1997. Schering is also a leader in biotechnology, with strong positions in genomics and gene therapy. Contributions by business segment in 1997 were:

	Sales	Profits
Pharmaceutical products	90%	93%
Health care products	10%	7%

Respiratory/allergy drugs are Schering's largest product category, accounting for about 40% of total 1997 sales. SGP is the U.S. leader in allergy/respiratory products, as well as a principal factor in these markets overseas. The lead products are Claritin nonsedating antihistamine and Claritin D combination decongestant, the world's largest selling antihistamines with 1997 sales of $1.7 billion. Claritin has over 40% of the U.S. market. Other allergy/respiratory drugs include Proventil, Theo-Dur, and Uni-Dur asthma treatments; and

Vancenase allergy nasal products and Vanceril asthma inhaler.

Anti-infectives and anticancer products (17% of 1997 sales) consist of Intron-A, the leading alpha interferon marketed for several anticancer and antiviral indications; Eulexin, a treatment for prostatic cancer; Cedax, a third-generation cephalosporin antibiotic; Leucomax, a granulocyte macrophage colony stimulating factor; Netromycin, an aminoglycoside antibiotic; and Ethyol, a cytoprotective agent.

Dermatological products (8%) include high-potency steroids such as Diprolene and Diprosone; Elocon, a topical steroid cream and ointment; and Lotrisone, a topical antifungal and anti-inflammatory cream. Cardiovasculars (9%) consist of Imdur, an oral nitrate; Nitro-Dur, a transdermal nitroglycerin patch for angina pectoris; Normodyne, an anti-hypertensive; and K-Dur, a potassium supplement. Other drugs (10%) include Losec anti-ulcer drug, Fibre Trim diet aid products and other items. SGP is also a leading maker of animal health products (6%).

Health care products (10%) encompass OTC medicines such as Afrin nasal spray, Chlor-Trimeton allergy tablets, Coricidin and Drixoral cold medications, and Gyne-Lotrimin for vaginal yeast infections; foot care items sold under Dr. Scholl's and other names; and Coppertone and other sun care products.

Per Share Data ($)

(Year Ended Dec. 31)	1997	1996	1995	1994	1993	1992	1991	1990	1989	1988
Tangible Bk. Val.	3.19	2.82	2.23	1.89	1.81	1.76	1.43	2.15	1.97	1.65
Cash Flow	2.22	1.89	1.64	1.41	1.22	1.05	0.89	0.74	0.63	0.54
Earnings	1.95	1.65	1.43	1.21	1.06	0.90	0.75	0.63	0.52	0.43
Dividends	1.09	0.64	0.58	0.49	0.43	0.38	0.32	0.27	0.22	0.17
Payout Ratio	56%	39%	41%	41%	41%	42%	40%	42%	43%	40%
Prices - High	64	36⅝	30⅜	19	17¾	17½	16¾	12¾	10¾	7½
- Low	31¾	25¼	17¾	13⅝	13	12½	10¼	9¼	7	5⅝
P/E Ratio - High	33	22	21	16	17	19	22	20	21	17
- Low	16	15	12	11	12	14	14	15	13	13

Income Statement Analysis (Million $)

	1997	1996	1995	1994	1993	1992	1991	1990	1989	1988
Revs.	6,778	5,656	5,104	4,657	4,341	4,056	3,616	3,323	3,158	2,969
Oper. Inc.	2,159	1,820	1,609	1,407	1,234	1,124	1,003	832	767	684
Depr.	200	173	157	158	127	120	115	109	99	95.0
Int. Exp.	40.0	56.0	69.0	68.0	61.0	71.0	77.0	89.0	100	124
Pretax Inc.	1,913	1,606	1,395	1,213	1,078	954	861	769	646	534
Eff. Tax Rate	25%	25%	25%	24%	24%	25%	25%	27%	27%	27%
Net Inc.	1,444	1,213	1,053	922	825	720	646	565	471	390

Balance Sheet & Other Fin. Data (Million $)

	1997	1996	1995	1994	1993	1992	1991	1990	1989	1988
Cash	714	536	322	161	429	529	927	920	935	808
Curr. Assets	2,920	2,365	1,956	1,739	1,901	2,013	2,102	2,000	2,047	1,914
Total Assets	6,507	5,398	4,665	4,326	4,317	4,157	4,013	4,103	3,614	3,426
Curr. Liab.	2,891	2,599	2,362	2,029	2,132	1,969	1,528	1,530	1,214	1,336
LT Debt	46.0	47.0	87.0	186	182	184	754	183	186	190
Common Eqty.	2,821	2,060	1,623	1,574	1,582	1,597	1,346	2,081	1,955	1,677
Total Cap.	3,145	2,374	1,965	2,006	1,940	1,980	2,286	2,436	2,271	1,988
Cap. Exp.	405	325	294	272	365	403	339	243	186	156
Cash Flow	1,644	1,386	1,210	1,080	952	840	760	674	571	485
Curr. Ratio	1.0	0.9	0.8	0.9	0.9	1.0	1.4	1.3	1.7	1.4
% LT Debt of Cap.	1.4	2.0	4.4	9.3	9.4	9.3	33.0	7.5	8.2	9.5
% Net Inc.of Revs.	21.3	21.5	20.6	19.8	19.0	17.8	17.9	17.0	14.9	13.1
% Ret. on Assets	24.3	24.1	23.4	21.8	19.8	17.7	16.7	14.8	13.4	11.8
% Ret. on Equity	59.2	65.9	65.9	59.6	52.7	49.2	39.9	28.3	25.9	24.9

Data as orig. reptd.; bef. results of disc. opers. and/or spec. items. Per share data adj. for stk. divs. as of ex-div. date. Bold denotes diluted EPS (FASB 128). E-Estimated. NA-Not Available. NM-Not Meaningful. NR-Not Ranked.

Office—One Giralda Farms, Madison, NJ 07940-1000. **Tel**—(973) 822-7000. **Fax**—(973) 822-7048. **Website**—http://www.sch-plough.com **Chrmn**—R. P. Luciano. **Pres & CEO**—R. J. Kogan. **Sr VP & Investor Contact**—Geraldine U. Foster. **VP & Secy**—W. J. Silbey. **VP-Fin**—J. L. Wyszomierski. **VP & Treas**—E. K. Moore. **Dirs**—H. W. Becherer, H. A. D'Andrade, D. C. Garfield, R. E. Herzlinger, R. J. Kogan, R. P. Luciano, D. L. Miller, H. B. Morley, C. E. Mundy, Jr., R. de J. Osborne, P. F. Russo, W. A. Schreyer, R. F. W. van Oordt, J. Wood. **Transfer Agent & Registrar**—Bank of New York, NYC. **Incorporated**—in New Jersey in 1970. **Empl**— 22,700. **S&P Analyst:** H. B. Saftlas

12-SEP-98

Industry:
Oil & Gas (Drilling & Equipment)

Summary: This worldwide leader in wellsite and drilling services for the oil and natural gas industry also manufactures meters and measurement instruments.

S&P Opinion: Hold (★★★)		
Recent Price • 51⅛	Yield • 1.5%	
52 Wk Range • 94⅜-43⅜	12-Mo. P/E • 18.4	

Quantitative Evaluations

Outlook
(1 Lowest—5 Highest)
• **4**

Fair Value
• **60¾**

Risk
• **Average**

Earn./Div. Rank
• **A-**

Technical Eval.
• **Bearish** since 11/96

Rel. Strength Rank
(1 Lowest—99 Highest)
• **53**

Insider Activity
• **Neutral**

Earnings vs. Previous Year
△=Up ▽=Down ▷=No Change

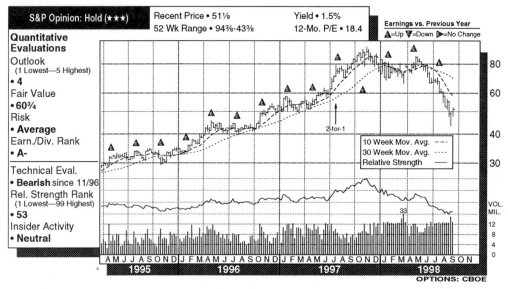

2-for-1

10 Week Mov. Avg. – – –
30 Week Mov. Avg. · · · ·
Relative Strength ——

80
60
40
30

33

VOL. MIL.
12
8
4
0

A M J J A S O N D J F M A M J J A S O N D J F M A M J J A S O N D J F M A M J J A S O N
1995 1996 1997 1998

OPTIONS: CBOE

Overview - 22-JUL-98

The recent slide in crude oil prices has tempered our enthusiasm for Schlumberger's shares, which we now expect only to perform in line with the market over the next six to 12 months. Over the longer term, earnings growth will be bolstered by SLB's increasing market share in the fastest growing segments of the oil services market. Seismic profits should increase at a more rapid pace, since the company made significant upgrades to three of its offshore seismic streamer vessels during 1996, while the backlog for land seismic is seeing impressive growth. SLB has also been able to capitalize on demand for well-logging equipment that lowers finding and producing costs via reduced drilling time. Sharply higher day rates for Sedco Forex's offshore rig fleet provided a boost to earnings in the first half of 1998, but we expect offshore rig dayrates to level off during the second half of the year, reflecting lower levels of drilling activity.

Valuation - 22-JUL-98

SLB's shares are often cited as bellwethers for the entire oil services industry, which now faces the prospect of slower than anticipated growth in capital spending by oil companies, due to the deterioration in oil prices. We project world oil demand growth of less than 2.0% in 1998. We believe that OPEC's increased production, as well as slower demand growth from floundering Asian economies will continue to put some downward pressure on prices. Oil prices should rebound from current levels, but are not expected to approach $20.00 per barrel over the next year. Our projections now call for an average crude oil price of $15.75 a bbl. and natural gas prices of $2.10 per Mcf in 1998. We now expect a much smaller increase in capital spending in 1998 than the 10% called for in our original forecast.

Key Stock Statistics

S&P EPS Est. 1998	2.95	Tang. Bk. Value/Share	12.22
P/E on S&P Est. 1998	17.3	Beta	1.19
S&P EPS Est. 1999	3.35	Shareholders	25,000
Dividend Rate/Share	0.75	Market cap. (B)	$ 27.8
Shs. outstg. (M)	544.3	Inst. holdings	54%
Avg. daily vol. (M)	4.603		

Value of $10,000 invested 5 years ago: $ 19,771

Fiscal Year Ending Dec. 31

	1998	1997	1996	1995	1994	1993
Revenues (Million $)						
1Q	2,934	2,426	2,028	1,762	1,640	1,624
2Q	2,889	2,602	2,151	1,877	1,639	1,745
3Q	—	2,736	2,262	1,919	1,637	1,665
4Q	—	2,908	2,515	2,064	1,781	1,746
Yr.	—	10,648	8,956	7,622	6,697	6,705
Earnings Per Share ($)						
1Q	**0.68**	0.53	0.35	0.30	0.25	0.28
2Q	**0.69**	0.62	0.40	0.34	0.26	0.34
3Q	—	0.72	0.47	0.35	0.28	0.34
4Q	—	**0.72**	0.52	0.34	0.32	0.26
Yr.	**E2.95**	2.52	1.70	1.34	1.10	1.20

Next earnings report expected: mid October

Dividend Data (Dividends have been paid since 1957.)

Amount ($)	Date Decl.	Ex-Div. Date	Stock of Record	Payment Date
0.188	Oct. 22	Dec. 24	Dec. 29	Jan. 09 '98
0.188	Jan. 21	Feb. 19	Feb. 23	Apr. 03 '98
0.188	Apr. 15	May. 29	Jun. 02	Jul. 10 '98
0.188	Jul. 16	Aug. 31	Sep. 02	Oct. 09 '98

A Division of The McGraw-Hill Companies

Business Summary - 22-JUL-98

Schlumberger (SLB) stands out as the dominant player in the generally fragmented oil and gas equipment and services industry. The company is a world leader in providing drilling services and fully computerized wireline and interpretation services to the petroleum industry. Through its Measurement & Systems business, SLB also makes computer-aided systems and electronic products.

Segment contributions in 1997 were as follows:

	Revs.	Profits
Oilfield services	72%	91%
Measurement & systems	28%	9%

During the oil industry downturn in the late 1980s, SLB continued to invest heavily in research and development. Now, as the industry has bounced back, Schlumberger is benefiting from its commitment to technology. The company has introduced several new products and services over the past two years, designed to increase efficiency and lower costs when exploring for, developing and producing oil and natural gas. SLB also seeks to take advantage of the trend among oil companies to outsource oilfield services functions, by becoming a "one-stop shop," offering a complete package of oilfield management products and services.

Within oilfield services, the Geco-Prakla division provides acquisition, processing and interpretation of land, transition zone and marine seismic data. Dowell provides cementing, stimulation, coiled tubing and drilling fluids services to enhance well productivity. SLB has a leading wireline services market share throughout the major exploration regions of the world. SLB also offers measurement-while-drilling and logging-while-drilling services. The Sedco Forex unit operates 53 offshore and 32 land drilling rigs.

The Measurement & Systems segment consists of two business units: Tests & Transactions, and Resource Management Services. Tests & Transactions provides technology, products, services and systems to various industries, including semiconductors, banking, telecommunication, retail petroleum, transportation and health care. The division also designs and manufactures smart cards and magnetic stripe cards for use in electronic transactions. Resource Management Services provides meters and other products to the electricity, water and gas industries.

Aided by strong performances from the Geco-Prakla seismic unit, the Wireline and Testing division, and the Sedco Forex drilling division, net income advanced 51% in 1997, on a 19% rise in revenues. The company said that it benefited from continued strength in the level of worldwide drilling activity, which occurred despite a decline in commodity prices during the period.

Per Share Data ($)

(Year Ended Dec. 31)	1997	1996	1995	1994	1993	1992	1991	1990	1989	1988
Tangible Bk. Val.	11.10	8.91	7.47	6.97	6.77	7.58	7.11	5.99	5.52	5.29
Cash Flow	4.41	3.54	3.04	2.69	2.73	2.77	3.02	2.29	1.92	1.86
Earnings	2.52	1.74	1.34	1.10	1.20	1.38	1.71	1.20	0.89	0.86
Dividends	1.13	0.75	0.71	0.60	0.60	0.60	0.60	0.60	0.60	0.60
Payout Ratio	45%	43%	53%	54%	50%	44%	35%	50%	68%	63%
Prices - High	94³/₈	54¹/₈	35¹/₄	31¹/₂	34¹/₂	35³/₈	37	35	25¹/₄	19³/₈
- Low	49	32³/₄	25¹/₈	25	27³/₄	26³/₈	25¹/₄	21³/₄	16	14¹/₄
P/E Ratio - High	37	31	26	29	29	26	22	29	29	23
- Low	19	19	19	23	23	19	15	18	18	17

Income Statement Analysis (Million $)

	1997	1996	1995	1994	1993	1992	1991	1990	1989	1988
Revs.	10,648	8,956	7,622	6,697	6,705	6,332	6,145	5,306	4,686	4,925
Oper. Inc.	2,622	1,895	1,581	1,373	1,373	1,373	1,358	1,210	962	997
Depr.	973	885	820	776	739	671	627	552	493	531
Int. Exp.	87.0	0.7	82.0	63.0	69.0	77.0	102	87.0	96.0	129
Pretax Inc.	1,669	675	770	617	664	748	982	698	531	589
Eff. Tax Rate	22%	NM	17%	13%	12%	12%	17%	18%	21%	23%
Net Inc.	1,296	851	649	536	583	662	816	570	420	454

Balance Sheet & Other Fin. Data (Million $)

	1997	1996	1995	1994	1993	1992	1991	1990	1989	1988
Cash	1,761	1,359	1,121	1,232	1,186	1,345	1,466	1,324	1,353	1,449
Curr. Assets	6,071	5,043	4,024	3,824	3,476	3,453	3,566	3,247	3,031	3,223
Total Assets	12,097	10,325	8,910	8,322	7,917	7,007	6,854	6,176	5,482	5,600
Curr. Liab.	3,630	3,474	2,765	2,787	2,568	2,211	2,472	2,435	2,147	2,512
LT Debt	1,069	637	613	394	447	374	341	332	292	191
Common Eqty.	6,695	5,626	4,964	4,583	4,406	4,231	3,853	3,255	2,898	2,755
Total Cap.	7,764	6,263	5,577	4,977	4,853	4,605	4,194	3,587	3,190	2,946
Cap. Exp.	1,496	1,158	939	783	691	809	921	675	549	455
Cash Flow	2,269	1,736	1,469	1,312	1,322	1,333	1,442	1,090	913	985
Curr. Ratio	1.7	1.4	1.5	1.4	1.4	1.6	1.4	1.3	1.4	1.3
% LT Debt of Cap.	13.8	10.1	11.0	7.9	9.2	8.1	8.1	9.2	9.2	6.5
% Net Inc.of Revs.	12.2	9.5	8.5	8.0	8.7	10.4	13.3	10.7	9.0	9.2
% Ret. on Assets	11.6	8.8	7.5	6.6	7.8	9.5	12.5	9.8	7.6	7.9
% Ret. on Equity	21.0	16.0	13.6	12.0	13.4	16.3	22.9	18.5	14.9	14.9

Data as orig. reptd.; bef. results of disc. opers. and/or spec. items. Per share data adj. for stk. divs. as of ex-div. date. Bold denotes diluted EPS (FASB 128). E-Estimated. NA-Not Available. NM-Not Meaningful. NR-Not Ranked.

Offices—277 Park Ave., New York, NY 10172. **Tel**—(212) 350-9400. **Website**—http://www.slb.com **Chrmn & CEO**—D. E. Baird. **EVP-Fin & CFO**—A. Lindenauer. **Secy**—D. S. Browning. **Investor Contact**—Simone Crook. **Dirs**—D. E. Ackerman, D. E. Baird, J. Deutch, Sir Denys Henderson, A. Levy-Lang, W. T. McCormick, Jr., D. Primat, N. Seydoux, L. G. Stuntz, S. Ullring, Y. Wakumoto. **Transfer Agent & Registrar**—First National Bank of Boston. **Incorporated**—in Netherlands Antilles in 1956. **Empl**— 63,500. **S&P Analyst:** Norman Rosenberg

Schwab (Charles)

1986F

NYSE Symbol **SCH**

In S&P 500

12-SEP-98

Industry: Investment Banking/ Brokerage

Summary: This company's Charles Schwab & Co. subsidiary is the largest discount brokerage firm in the U.S.

S&P Opinion: No Opinion	Recent Price • 34	Yield • 0.5%
	52 Wk Range • 46-27¾	12-Mo. P/E • 32.7

Quantitative Evaluations

Outlook
(1 Lowest—5 Highest)
• **2**

Fair Value
• **29⅝**

Risk
• **Average**

Earn./Div. Rank
• **A-**

Technical Eval.
• **Bearish** since 8/98

Rel. Strength Rank
(1 Lowest—99 Highest)
• **82**

Insider Activity
• **Neutral**

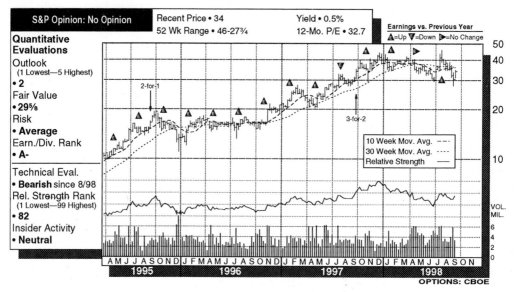

Earnings vs. Previous Year
△=Up ▽=Down ▷=No Change

10 Week Mov. Avg. – – –
30 Week Mov. Avg. ‥‥
Relative Strength ——

OPTIONS: CBOE

Overview - 20-JUL-98

Subject to market conditions, Schwab's revenues appear to be in a long-term uptrend. Commissions should benefit from a secular trend toward increased trading volume on the major exchanges, the internationalization of the world's equity markets, likely increases in saving, new branches, and the company's dominant market position. One caveat is that trading by individuals can be volatile on a quarterly basis. Fees are increasing, aided by the growth of in-house mutual fund assets and the popularity of the Mutual Fund OneSource product, which allows investors to choose among a variety of mutual funds without transaction fees. The company is continually introducing new products. Margins could widen slightly, aided by a high degree of automation and a central phone system. Stock buybacks could help EPS comparisons.

Valuation - 20-JUL-98

A host of factors should be considered in valuing this brokerage/special situation stock. On a P/E basis, the stock was recently trading at a hefty premium to that of the overall market, to the company's estimated 1998 growth rate, and to the P/E ratios of other brokers, which, given a lack of truly comparable companies, could be roughly regarded as peers. The shares, however, deserve a premium to those of the general brokerage group, because of Schwab's growth record over the past five years, as well as its leading market position. Other distinguishing features of the company include its impressive return on shareholders' equity (over 20%), and a high level of insider ownership. In addition, unlike certain other brokers, the company's somewhat flexible cost structure could partially mitigate the impact of a market downturn.

Key Stock Statistics

S&P EPS Est. 1998	1.15	Tang. Bk. Value/Share	4.37
P/E on S&P Est. 1998	29.6	Beta	1.80
S&P EPS Est. 1999	1.25	Shareholders	2,700
Dividend Rate/Share	0.16	Market cap. (B)	$ 9.1
Shs. outstg. (M)	266.9	Inst. holdings	40%
Avg. daily vol. (M)	0.858		

Value of $10,000 invested 5 years ago: $ 90,922

Fiscal Year Ending Dec. 31

	1998	1997	1996	1995	1994	1993
Revenues (Million $)						
1Q	604.4	535.6	446.8	296.9	287.9	236.3
2Q	638.0	530.8	491.8	342.7	258.2	232.4
3Q	—	611.8	430.0	385.6	248.1	238.8
4Q	—	620.6	482.3	394.8	270.4	257.5
Yr.	—	2,300	1,851	1,420	1,065	965.0
Earnings Per Share ($)						
1Q	**0.25**	**0.25**	0.17	0.15	0.14	0.13
2Q	**0.28**	**0.23**	0.26	0.17	0.12	0.12
3Q	**E0.30**	**0.28**	0.21	0.17	0.12	0.11
4Q	**E0.32**	**0.23**	0.22	0.16	0.13	0.11
Yr.	**E1.15**	**0.99**	0.87	0.65	0.51	0.46

Next earnings report expected: mid October

Dividend Data (Dividends have been paid since 1989.)

Amount ($)	Date Decl.	Ex-Div. Date	Stock of Record	Payment Date
0.040	Oct. 22	Nov. 12	Nov. 14	Nov. 28 '97
0.040	Jan. 20	Feb. 11	Feb. 13	Feb. 27 '98
0.040	Apr. 21	May. 11	May. 13	May. 27 '98
0.040	Jul. 24	Aug. 11	Aug. 13	Aug. 27 '98

A Division of The McGraw-Hill Companies

The Charles Schwab Corporation

Business Summary - 20-JUL-98

As America's largest discount broker, with a 55% share of the overall market, Charles Schwab executes buy and sell orders for various securities for millions of individual investors throughout the country. Schwab operates in the discount brokerage segment of the industry, where firms offer some research, back office and other support, which contrasts with the deep-discount segment, where the emphasis is on bare bones trade execution for a minimal price. The discount brokerage industry was born in 1975, when the Securities & Exchange Commission dismantled the old system of fixed commission rates, a throwback to the old clubby days of Wall Street. Operating revenues in recent years were derived as follows:

	1997	1996	1995
Commissions	51%	51%	53%
Interest	15%	14%	15%
Principal transactions	11%	14%	13%
Mutual fund service fees	19%	17%	15%
Other	4%	4%	4%

A snapshot profile of the firm's typical customer would be: a professionally employed or retired individual, with substantial income or assets, who for one reason or another became disenchanted with a full-service broker or did not want to pay full-service commission rates.

Financial planners, or people who devise complex investment, savings and insurance plans for others based on their unique risk, return, liquidity, regulatory and other considerations, are also an important constituent, making up about 30% of the customer base. Financial planners are drawn to Schwab because of its record-keeping services, reputation for independence and ability to offer a wide range of products.

Schwab is one of the financial services industry's leading innovators. It was the first to open a mutual fund supermarket, called Mutual Fund OneSource, which allows investors to choose from 825 no-load mutual funds without a transaction fee, and to receive a single monthly statement. The company has also devised a wide range of software products to track portfolio holdings and market information, a service that helps investors locate investment managers, and was one of the first brokers to offer trade execution via computer.

Growth is an important part of Schwab's corporate culture. Factors expected to aid the company over the next several years include a large number of individuals entering their peak savings and investing years, the company's goal of attaining a greater share of the retirement savings market, an ongoing emphasis on opening new branches, and expansion into limited forms of investment advice. Schwab's long-term annual objective is to increase revenues 20%, and to attain a 20% return on stockholders' equity.

Per Share Data ($) (Year Ended Dec. 31)	1997	1996	1995	1994	1993	1992	1991	1990	1989	1988
Tangible Bk. Val.	4.10	2.99	2.11	1.72	1.31	0.82	0.52	0.28	0.24	0.21
Cash Flow	1.45	1.23	NA	NA	NA	NA	NA	NA	NA	NA
Earnings	0.99	0.87	0.65	0.51	0.46	0.31	0.19	0.06	0.07	0.03
Dividends	0.13	0.12	0.09	0.06	0.04	0.03	0.02	0.01	0.01	Nil
Payout Ratio	13%	14%	13%	12%	9%	11%	10%	21%	13%	Nil
Prices - High	44 1/4	21 7/8	19 3/8	8 1/4	8 1/2	5 5/8	4 3/4	1 3/4	1 11/16	15/16
- Low	20 1/4	12	7 3/8	5 1/4	3 5/8	2 7/16	1 1/8	1 1/16	11/16	9/16
P/E Ratio - High	45	25	30	16	18	18	25	29	25	36
- Low	20	14	11	10	8	8	6	17	10	22
Income Statement Analysis (Million $)										
Commissions	1,174	954	751	546	552	441	349	244	229	205
Int. Inc.	NA	681	568	363	252	251	302	310	273	168
Total Revs.	2,299	1,851	1,420	1,065	965	909	795	626	553	392
Int. Exp.	546	426	357	198	132	159	226	238	207	126
Pretax Inc.	447	394	277	224	206	146	88.1	29.1	33.2	13.3
Eff. Tax Rate	40%	41%	38%	40%	40%	45%	44%	42%	43%	44%
Net Inc.	270	234	173	135	124	81.2	49.5	16.8	18.9	7.4
Balance Sheet & Other Fin. Data (Million $)										
Total Assets	16,482	13,779	10,552	7,918	6,897	5,905	5,026	4,188	3,480	2,533
Cash Items	7,541	7,869	5,856	4,587	3,956	3,714	3,467	3,141	2,335	1,572
Receivables	8,019	5,244	4,088	3,010	2,625	1,952	1,350	842	932	745
Secs. Owned	283	128	114	Nil	Nil	Nil	Nil	Nil	Nil	Nil
Sec. Borrowed	Nil	Nil	Nil	Nil	Nil	Nil	Nil	Nil	Nil	Nil
Due Brokers & Cust.	14,498	12,280	9,346	7,084	6,173	5,376	4,605	3,856	3,121	2,201
Other Liabs.	478	361	327	195	159	118	102	52.0	57.0	41.0
Capitalization:										
Debt	361	284	246	171	185	152	119	126	131	132
Equity	1,145	855	633	467	379	259	200	154	172	159
Total	1,506	1,139	879	638	565	410	319	280	302	291
% Return On Revs.	9.5	12.7	12.2	12.7	12.9	8.9	6.2	2.7	3.4	1.9
% Ret. on Assets	1.8	2.0	1.9	1.8	1.9	1.5	1.1	0.4	0.6	0.3
% Ret. on Equity	27.0	31.5	31.4	32.0	39.0	35.4	28.0	10.3	11.4	4.8

Data as orig. reptd.; bef. results of disc opers. and/or spec. items. Per share data adj. for stk. divs. as of ex-div. date. Bold denotes diluted EPS (FASB 128). E-Estimated. NA-Not Available. NM-Not Meaningful. NR-Not Ranked.

Office—101 Montgomery St., San Francisco, CA 94104. **Tel**—(415) 627-7000. **E-Mail**—SCH stock@aol.com **Website**—www.sch.com **Chrmn & CEO**—C. R. Schwab. **Pres**—D. S. Pottruck. **EVP-Fin & CFO**—S. L. Scheid. **Secy**—M. B. Templeton. **Investor Contact**—Rich Fowler. **Dirs**—N. H. Bechtle, C. P. Butcher, D. G. Fisher, A. M. Frank, F. C. Herringer, S. T. McLin, D. S. Pottruck, G. Schultz, C. R. Schwab, L. J. Stupski, R. O. Walther. **Transfer Agent & Registrar**—Norwest Bank Minnesota, St. Paul. **Incorporated**—in California in 1971. **Empl**— 12,700. **S&P Analyst:** Paul L. Huberman, CFA

STANDARD &POOR'S
STOCK REPORTS
Scientific-Atlanta
1987D
NYSE Symbol **SFA**
In S&P 500

12-SEP-98

Industry: Communications Equipment

Summary: This company manufactures broadband communications systems and satellite-based video, voice and data communications networks.

S&P Opinion: Hold (★★★)	Recent Price • 19⅛	Yield • 0.3%
	52 Wk Range • 27⅞-14	12-Mo. P/E • 18.6

Quantitative Evaluations

Outlook (1 Lowest—5 Highest)
• **4⁻**

Fair Value
• **27⅝**

Risk
• **Average**

Earn./Div. Rank
• **B+**

Technical Eval.
• **Bullish** since 8/98

Rel. Strength Rank (1 Lowest—99 Highest)
• **49**

Insider Activity
• **NA**

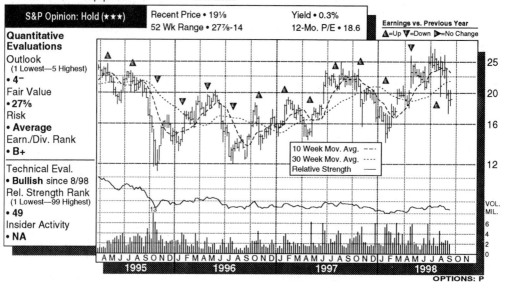

Earnings vs. Previous Year
▲=Up ▼=Down ▶=No Change

10 Week Mov. Avg. ─ ─ ─
30 Week Mov. Avg. · · · · ·
Relative Strength ──

OPTIONS: P

Overview - 26-AUG-98

In August 1998, the company said that Tele-Communications, Inc. (TCI) had agreed to purchase substantial quantities of SFA's advanced digital set-top devices, marking TCI's first commitment to use SFA's products. At the same time, Time-Warner Cable agreed to expand deployment of SFA's digital systems and set-top boxes in preparation for a major rollout in calendar 1999. Revenues in FY 98 (Jun.) grew only about 1%, reflecting a severe slowdown in Asian markets. We expect FY 99 sales to rise about 15%, in part aided by easy comparisons. Broadband transmission sales should be a solid contributor, reflecting increased capital spending by cable operators and local telephone companies seeking to provide video, voice and data services. SFA is ramping up production of its Explorer 2000 digital set-top box, which can enable two-way, interactive consumer applications such as Internet access and video-on-demand.

Valuation - 26-AUG-98

We continue to recommend holding the shares. The stock has rebounded from its 1998 lows, but has been stuck in a trading range for the past several months. FY 98 fourth quarter results, excluding charges, were slightly above analyst expectations, despite a 6% drop in revenues that reflected the continuing slowdown in Asia. However, gross margins widened sequentially, and operating expenses were well controlled. The long-term outlook for SFA's digital set-top boxes is compelling, as cable companies plan the conversion of their systems to digital, from advanced analog and analog. Nevertheless, based on SFA's long-term growth rate of 18%, and concerns over diminished revenue visibility for the near-term, we view the shares as fairly valued at a recent level of 19X our calendar 1999 EPS estimate of $1.19.

Key Stock Statistics

S&P EPS Est. 1998	NA	Tang. Bk. Value/Share	7.39
P/E on S&P Est. 1998	NA	Beta	1.77
S&P EPS Est. 1999	1.10	Shareholders	6,500
Dividend Rate/Share	0.06	Market cap. (B)	$ 1.5
Shs. outstg. (M)	78.8	Inst. holdings	53%
Avg. daily vol. (M)	0.497		

Value of $10,000 invested 5 years ago: $ 15,383

Fiscal Year Ending Jun. 30

	1998	1997	1996	1995	1994	1993
Revenues (Million $)						
1Q	294.5	261.7	242.2	232.3	170.3	171.0
2Q	294.5	282.2	261.1	277.4	178.0	730.6
3Q	288.7	301.7	271.9	313.5	204.1	184.1
4Q	303.6	322.7	272.7	323.3	259.4	188.6
Yr.	1,181	1,168	1,048	1,147	811.6	730.6
Earnings Per Share ($)						
1Q	0.21	0.14	0.05	0.16	0.10	0.10
2Q	**0.19**	0.18	0.09	0.19	-0.06	0.02
3Q	**0.22**	0.21	0.15	0.21	0.15	0.09
4Q	**0.40**	0.25	-0.20	0.27	0.27	0.13
Yr.	**1.03**	0.78	0.09	0.83	0.45	0.33

Next earnings report expected: NA

Dividend Data (Dividends have been paid since 1976.)

Amount ($)	Date Decl.	Ex-Div. Date	Stock of Record	Payment Date
0.015	Nov. 12	Nov. 28	Dec. 02	Dec. 17 '97
0.015	Mar. 03	Mar. 06	Mar. 10	Mar. 25 '98
0.015	May. 15	May. 29	Jun. 02	Jun. 17 '98
0.015	Aug. 20	Aug. 31	Sep. 02	Sep. 16 '98

A Division of The McGraw·Hill Companies

Business Summary - 26-AUG-98

Every day millions of people around the globe rely on Scientific-Atlanta to access entertainment, information and communications networks. Time Warner, TCI, and Comcast, among others, utilize SFA's analog and fiber optic set-top boxes for cable TV service. These companies also use SFA "headends" to build cable infrastructure. SFA has been an industry leader in pioneering satellite technology to deliver programming for entertainment giants such as Disney, HBO, and Viacom. In the information arena, SFA helps businesses, government agencies, and other customers access information via coaxial cable or fiber optic equipment. SFA also offers alternative communication equipment for emerging technologies such as telephony-over-cable and satellite service.

The company's products include set-top terminals that allow subscribers to receive cable TV (CATV) signals, receivers, transmitters, digital audio terminals, digital video compression and transmission equipment, satellite earth station antennas and headend systems that allow CATV operators to receive and process television signals. These products, and integrated systems and networks using these and other products, are sold to a variety of customers, including CATV operators, telephone companies, communications network operators and utility companies. Sales of set-top terminals ac-

counted for 30% of revenues in FY 97 (Jun.), up from 27% in FY 96.

SFA's transmission products, which include radio frequency amplifiers and line extenders, transmit signals via coaxial cable or fiber optics from a cable operator to the customer. The company's transmission products enable operators to transmit telephony, video and data over the same network, with a reverse path for customers to communicate back to the operator. The company's satellite earth stations receive and transmit signals for video, voice and data and are utilized in satellite-band telephone, data and television distribution networks.

SFA has actively sought to increase its penetration of international markets; international sales represented 37% of total sales in FY 97, up from 36% in FY 96.

SFA's Communications and Tracking Systems division is under contract to build 57 earth terminals for IRID-IUM, a worldwide wireless telecommunications network being designed to provide telephone, paging, facsimile and data services to registered subscribers using handheld telephones and pagers. In December 1997, Iridium LLC launched five satellites into orbit. The launch, Iridium's ninth in eight months, brought the total number of orbiting IRIDIUM satellites to 46. Worldwide commercial service availability is planned for September 1998, when the entire 66-satellite network is scheduled to be operational.

Per Share Data ($)

(Year Ended Jun. 30)	1998	1997	1996	1995	1994	1993	1992	1991	1990	1989
Tangible Bk. Val.	NA	6.70	5.94	6.07	5.14	4.63	4.20	3.98	3.99	3.54
Cash Flow	NA	1.33	0.57	1.22	0.72	0.58	0.46	0.27	0.82	0.69
Earnings	1.03	0.78	0.09	0.83	0.46	0.33	0.23	0.02	0.64	0.51
Dividends	0.06	0.06	0.06	0.06	0.06	0.06	0.05	0.05	0.05	0.04
Payout Ratio	6%	8%	67%	7%	13%	18%	23%	344%	8%	8%
Prices - High	27$7/8$	24$7/8$	20$3/8$	24$7/8$	23$1/4$	19$3/8$	13$3/4$	6	9$3/4$	8$3/8$
- Low	14	14$1/4$	12	11$3/8$	12$1/2$	8$7/8$	5$1/8$	3$7/8$	3	4$1/4$
P/E Ratio - High	27	32	NM	30	51	59	54	NM	15	16
- Low	14	18	NM	14	27	27	22	NM	5	8

Income Statement Analysis (Million $)

	1998	1997	1996	1995	1994	1993	1992	1991	1990	1989
Revs.	NA	1,168	1,048	1,147	812	731	581	494	614	547
Oper. Inc.	NA	127	74.0	120	87.8	49.3	33.7	25.1	79.7	65.6
Depr.	NA	43.2	36.6	29.8	20.9	19.1	16.1	16.8	13.3	13.2
Int. Exp.	NA	0.5	0.7	0.8	1.1	0.9	0.6	1.1	1.5	1.3
Pretax Inc.	NA	89.2	10.6	93.4	51.5	32.9	21.7	1.5	64.2	56.7
Eff. Tax Rate	NA	32%	32%	32%	32%	25%	25%	31%	31%	36%
Net Inc.	NA	60.6	7.2	63.5	35.0	24.7	16.3	1.1	44.3	36.3

Balance Sheet & Other Fin. Data (Million $)

	1998	1997	1996	1995	1994	1993	1992	1991	1990	1989
Cash	NA	107	21.0	80.0	123	104	91.0	112	91.0	80.0
Curr. Assets	NA	597	563	615	505	406	343	311	310	294
Total Assets	NA	824	763	785	640	524	441	394	389	356
Curr. Liab.	NA	250	262	276	202	130	112	87.0	87.0	74.0
LT Debt	NA	1.8	0.4	0.8	1.1	1.4	1.7	2.0	2.3	2.6
Common Eqty.	NA	533	464	474	396	353	300	282	279	257
Total Cap.	NA	534	464	475	397	354	307	288	285	268
Cap. Exp.	NA	53.1	60.8	64.8	34.9	24.0	18.5	19.9	27.4	15.6
Cash Flow	NA	104	43.8	93.3	55.9	43.7	32.4	17.9	57.6	49.5
Curr. Ratio	NA	2.4	2.1	2.2	2.5	3.1	3.1	3.6	3.6	4.0
% LT Debt of Cap.	NA	0.3	0.1	0.2	0.2	0.4	0.6	0.7	0.8	1.0
% Net Inc.of Revs.	NA	5.2	0.7	5.6	4.3	3.4	2.8	0.2	7.2	6.6
% Ret. on Assets	NA	7.6	1.0	8.9	6.0	4.9	3.9	0.3	12.1	11.0
% Ret. on Equity	NA	12.2	1.6	14.0	9.3	7.3	5.6	0.4	16.7	15.0

Data as orig. reptd.; bef. results of disc. opers. and/or spec. items. Per share data adj. for stk. divs. as of ex-div. date. Bold denotes diluted EPS (FASB 128). E-Estimated. NA-Not Available. NM-Not Meaningful. NR-Not Ranked.

Office—One Technology Parkway, South, Norcross, GA 30092-2967. **Tel**—(770) 903-5000. **Website**—http://www.sciatl.com **Chrmn**—J. V. Napier. **Pres & CEO**—J. F. McDonald. **SVP, CFO & Treas**—W. Haislip. **SVP & Secy**—W. E. Eason Jr. **Investor Contact**—Robert S. Meyers. **Dirs**—M. H. Antonini, W. E. Kassling, W. B. King, M. B. Mangum, A. L. McDonald, J. F. McDonald, D. J. McLaughlin, J. V. Napier, S. Nunn, S. Topol. **Transfer Agent & Registrar**—Bank of New York, NYC. **Incorporated**—in Georgia in 1951. **Empl**—5,343. **S&P Analyst**: Mark Cavallone

STANDARD &POOR'S
STOCK REPORTS

Seagate Technology

1996

NYSE Symbol **SEG**

In S&P 500

12-SEP-98

Industry:
Computers (Peripherals)

Summary: This leading manufacturer of disc drives for systems ranging from PCs to workstations also makes disc drive components, tape drives and software.

S&P Opinion: Hold (★★★)	Recent Price • 22⅞	Yield • Nil
	52 Wk Range • 40⅝-16⅛	12-Mo. P/E • NM

Quantitative Evaluations

Outlook
(1 Lowest—5 Highest)
• **4+**

Fair Value
• **23¾**

Risk
• **High**

Earn./Div. Rank
• **B**

Technical Eval.
• **NA**

Rel. Strength Rank
(1 Lowest—99 Highest)
• **90**

Insider Activity
• **NA**

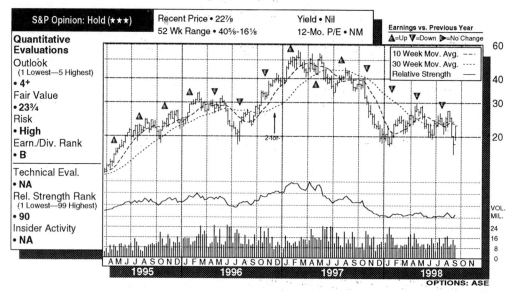

Earnings vs. Previous Year
▲=Up ▼=Down ▶=No Change

10 Week Mov. Avg. – – –
30 Week Mov. Avg. – – –
Relative Strength ——

OPTIONS: ASE

Overview - 22-JUL-98

Sales should rebound slightly in FY 99 (Jun.), after a 24% decline in FY 98. Revenues continue to be restricted by intense pricing pressures in the disc drive industry. In addition, demand for the company's enterprise-class disc drives has been weak. Overall demand also continues to be weak in Asia. Margins have narrowed, due to the price erosion, as well as the under-utilization of manufacturing facilities due to weaker demand. Although market share has declined significantly, due to competitive pressures, Seagate has regained its focus on product quality and efficiency. Margins should widen in the longer term, on volume efficiencies, manufacturing cost reductions, and increased contributions from software offerings. Earnings should improve in FY 99. FY 98 earnings include $2.19 of nonrecurring charges.

Valuation - 22-JUL-98

The shares of this highly regarded disc drive maker have fallen significantly from their high, due to soft demand and intense pricing pressures. However, SEG remains well positioned, particularly in the high capacity/high performance (and higher margin) segment of the market, and still boasts wider margins than its competitors. We believe that the industry's supply and demand balance is moving toward equilibrium, which could help restore a more normal pricing environment in the near future. However, due to increased competition, Seagate lost significant market share in 1997. As a result, the company needs to improve its product quality and efficiency; we believe that this is occurring. The recent acquisition of Quinta should result in new product offerings by late this year. SEG's software business should also help improve revenue growth. We would hold the shares for their longer term potential.

Key Stock Statistics

S&P EPS Est. 1999	1.20	Tang. Bk. Value/Share	11.13
P/E on S&P Est. 1999	19.1	Beta	1.56
Dividend Rate/Share	Nil	Shareholders	6,400
Shs. outstg. (M)	243.1	Market cap. (B)	$ 5.6
Avg. daily vol. (M)	2.656	Inst. holdings	66%

Value of $10,000 invested 5 years ago: $ 23,375

Fiscal Year Ending Jun. 30

	1998	1997	1996	1995	1994	1993
Revenues (Million $)						
1Q	1,896	2,061	2,141	933.1	773.9	742.6
2Q	1,673	2,400	2,340	1,130	815.9	776.6
3Q	1,675	2,502	2,093	1,185	909.3	754.1
4Q	1,575	1,977	2,015	1,292	1,001	770.2
Yr.	6,819	8,940	8,588	4,540	3,500	3,044
Earnings Per Share ($)						
1Q	-0.98	0.59	0.61	0.15	0.26	0.43
2Q	**-0.75**	0.91	0.74	0.54	0.29	0.46
3Q	**-0.53**	1.01	-0.79	0.48	0.46	0.28
4Q	**0.09**	0.61	0.46	0.59	0.54	0.24
Yr.	**-2.17**	2.73	1.03	1.76	1.54	1.40

Next earnings report expected: mid October

Dividend Data

No cash dividends have been paid. The shares were split two-for-one in November 1996.

Seagate Technology, Inc.

1996

Business Summary - 22-JUL-98

The largest independent provider of mass storage products for computers and related equipment, Seagate's core business is in disc drives. Seagate is the most diversified of the disc drive vendors, offering more than 50 drive models with form factors (a measure of the disc size accommodated) of 2.5, 3.5 and 5.25 inches, and capacities ranging from one gigabyte to 23 gigabytes. Products are differentiated by form factor and on a price/performance basis.

The company pursues a strategy of vertical integration, meaning it makes many of the component parts for its drives itself. Seagate is a major designer and manufacturer of major disc drive components, including thin film and magnetoresistive recording heads, head stack assemblies, media and motors. SEG believes its vertical integration provides a competitive advantage. However, it entails a high level of fixed costs and requires a high volume of production to be successful.

Pricing has always been an issue in the disc drive industry. Prices for the same capacity class of disc drives trend only one way -- down. However, industry-wide disc drive capacity increases approximately 60% per year, resulting in continual new product introductions.

In addition to its core disc drive business, SEG continues to broaden its strategy to more fully address the markets for the storage, retrieval and management of data. Seagate offers a complete line of mini-cartridge and DAT tape drive products used primarily for system backup purposes. Through its fast growing Seagate Software unit, SEG also provides storage management and information management software solutions.

The company has strong relationships with its customers, primarily major original equipment manufacturers (OEMs), and has proven itself able to manage the industry's increasingly short product cycles. Shipments to OEMs were 64% of net sales in FY 98 (71% in FY 97).

Capital expenditures were $698 million in FY 98, after approximately $935 million in FY 97. The company's products are primarily manufactured in the Far East.

In June 1997, the company invested in Gadzoox Networks, Inc., a manufacturer of Fibre Channel based storage network connectivity products. In August 1997, Seagate acquired Quinta Corp., a developer of optically assisted Winchester (OAW) disc drives.

Nonrecurring charges in FY 97 included $153 million as a result of an adverse judgment in the Amstrad PLC litigation and $2.5 million for restructuring costs at the company's Seagate Software subsidiary. Excluding these charges, earnings per share would have been $3.05.

Per Share Data ($)

(Year Ended Jun. 30)	1998	1997	1996	1995	1994	1993	1992	1991	1990	1989
Tangible Bk. Val.	NA	13.40	10.27	9.39	9.12	7.67	6.32	5.88	5.32	4.42
Cash Flow	NA	5.25	3.04	3.02	2.48	2.51	1.69	1.52	1.92	0.78
Earnings	-2.17	2.73	1.03	1.76	1.54	1.40	0.46	0.47	0.96	0.01
Dividends	Nil	Nil	Nil	Nil	Nil	Nil	Nil	Nil	Nil	Nil
Payout Ratio	Nil	Nil	Nil	Nil	Nil	Nil	Nil	Nil	Nil	Nil
Prices - High	29⅝	56¼	42¾	27⅜	14⅜	12⅝	11¼	10	9⅞	8⅛
- Low	17¾	18⅜	18⅛	11⅞	9⅜	6⅝	4½	3⅝	2⅞	4¼
P/E Ratio - High	NM	21	42	16	9	9	24	21	10	NM
- Low	NM	7	18	7	6	5	10	8	3	NM

Income Statement Analysis (Million $)

	1998	1997	1996	1995	1994	1993	1992	1991	1990	1989
Revs.	NM	8,940	8,588	4,540	3,500	3,044	2,875	2,677	2,413	1,372
Oper. Inc.	NA	1,627	1,044	630	449	439	309	256	297	91.0
Depr.	NA	607	417	187	138	155	169	138	118	78.0
Int. Exp.	NA	34.8	55.8	33.0	26.3	23.5	34.0	42.5	48.7	24.1
Pretax Inc.	NA	891	331	409	322	271	85.0	82.0	150	NM
Eff. Tax Rate	NM	26%	36%	37%	30%	28%	26%	23%	22%	26%
Net Inc.	NA	658	213	260	225	195	63.0	63.0	117	NM

Balance Sheet & Other Fin. Data (Million $)

	1998	1997	1996	1995	1994	1993	1992	1991	1990	1989
Cash	NM	2,283	1,174	1,247	1,334	629	504	252	263	190
Curr. Assets	NA	4,552	3,399	2,445	2,246	1,471	1,259	1,184	1,139	652
Total Assets	NA	6,723	5,240	3,361	2,878	2,031	1,817	1,880	1,851	1,077
Curr. Liab.	NA	1,836	1,438	910	703	544	502	591	550	265
LT Debt	NA	702	798	540	549	281	321	393	510	305
Common Eqty.	NA	3,476	2,466	1,542	1,328	1,045	862	766	675	442
Total Cap.	NA	4,657	3,616	2,326	2,097	1,450	1,280	1,254	1,269	812
Cap. Exp.	NA	890	907	353	198	174	82.0	99	58.0	63.0
Cash Flow	NA	1,265	630	447	363	350	232	201	235	78.0
Curr. Ratio	NA	2.5	2.4	2.7	3.2	2.7	2.5	2.0	2.1	2.5
% LT Debt of Cap.	NA	15.1	22.1	23.2	26.2	19.4	25.0	31.4	40.2	37.6
% Net Inc.of Revs.	NA	7.4	2.5	5.7	6.4	6.4	2.2	2.3	4.9	NM
% Ret. on Assets	NM	11.0	4.2	8.4	8.9	10.2	3.3	3.3	7.3	NM
% Ret. on Equity	NM	22.2	9.7	18.2	18.4	20.5	7.6	8.6	19.0	0.1

Data as orig. reptd.; bef. results of disc. opers. and/or spec. items. Per share data adj. for stk. divs. as of ex-div. date. Bold denotes diluted EPS (FASB 128). E-Estimated. NA-Not Available. NM-Not Meaningful. NR-Not Ranked.

Office—920 Disc Drive, Scotts Valley, CA 95066. **Tel**—(831) 438-6550. **Website**—http://www.seagate.com **Pres & CEO**—S. J. Luczo. **COO**—W. D. Watkins. **EVP & CAO**—D. L. Waite. **SVP & CFO**—C. C. Pope. **Investor Contact**—Nancy E. Hamm (831-439-2371). **Dirs**—G. B. Filler, K. E. Haughton, R. A. Kleist, S. J. Luczo, L. Perlman, T. P. Stafford, L. L. Wilkening. **Transfer Agent & Registrar**—Harris Trust Co of California. **Incorporated**—in California in 1978; reincorporated in Delaware in 1986. **Empl**— 101,486. **S&P Analyst:** Brian Goodstadt

STANDARD &POOR'S
STOCK REPORTS

Seagram Co.

1999M

NYSE Symbol **VO**

In S&P 500

12-SEP-98

Industry: Beverages (Alcoholic)

Summary: Seagram is a leading global producer of distilled spirits, wines and fruit juices. In 1995, it acquired an 80% interest in entertainment concern MCA Inc.

S&P Opinion: Hold (★★★)	Recent Price • 32⅜	Yield • 2.0%
	52 Wk Range • 46⅝-30¼	12-Mo. P/E • 12.1

Quantitative Evaluations

Outlook (1 Lowest—5 Highest)
• **1+**

Fair Value
• **26¾**

Risk
• **Low**

Earn./Div. Rank
• **B+**

Technical Eval.
• **NA**

Rel. Strength Rank (1 Lowest—99 Highest)
• **64**

Insider Activity
• **Neutral**

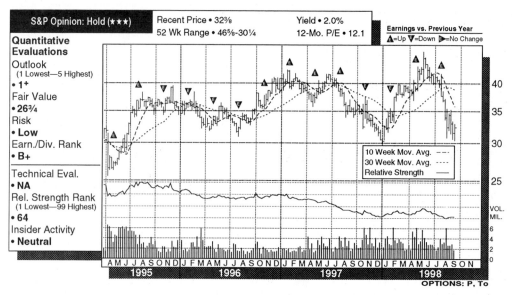

Earnings vs. Previous Year ▲=Up ▼=Down ▷=No Change

10 Week Mov. Avg. ----
30 Week Mov. Avg. ----
Relative Strength —

OPTIONS: P, To

Overview - 27-MAY-98

In May 1998, VO said it plans to acquire music company PolyGram N.V. (PLG) for $10.6 billion, and also plans to sell its Tropicana Products business through an IPO. These moves should result in a significantly larger portion of VO's asset base and cash flow being related to entertainment businesses. The acquisition price is expected to include the issuance of about 47.9 million VO common shares. Ownership of PLG, which could involve large non-cash goodwill charges, is not reflected in our earnings estimates. VO currently owns 84% of Universal Pictures Inc. (formerly MCA Inc.), and 45% of cable programming and broadcast company USA Networks, Inc. (formerly HSN, Inc.). VO also remains a major spirits and wine company; results of that business are being hurt by weakness in Asian markets. Thus far in FY 98 (Jun.), EPS included a charge of $0.14 a share for the writedown of assets and severance in Asia, and about $1.32 a share of third-quarter gains from asset sales. VO already has some non-cash charges related to acquisitions.

Valuation - 27-MAY-98

In late May 1998, we raised our opinion on VO to accumulate, from hold. We look for the stock to benefit further from the expected acquisition of PolyGram N.V. (PLG). The addition of PLG would bring a further shift in VO's asset base. toward more glamorous, potentially faster growing businesses. However, with greater emphasis on entertainment businesses, we also see added risk, or less smoothness, in VO's cash flow stream. We look for VO to sell Time Warner stock that it owns, and also to sell PLG's film unit, to help pay the $10.6 billion acquisition cost for PLG. We have a low $50s price target for VO stock in the next six to 12 months.

Key Stock Statistics

S&P EPS Est. 1998	NA	Tang. Bk. Value/Share	14.20
P/E on S&P Est. 1998	NA	Beta	0.90
Dividend Rate/Share	0.66	Shareholders	7,600
Shs. outstg. (M)	346.3	Market cap. (B)	$ 11.2
Avg. daily vol. (M)	0.535	Inst. holdings	30%

Value of $10,000 invested 5 years ago: $ 14,228

Fiscal Year Ending Jun. 30

	1998	1997	1996	1995	1994	1993
Revenues (Million $)						
1Q	2,939	2,944	1,282	1,211	1,195	1,238
2Q	3,541	3,749	1,883	1,448	1,441	1,411
3Q	2,534	2,847	2,917	1,513	1,417	1,445
4Q	2,168	3,020	3,665	2,227	1,985	2,007
Yr.	9,714	12,560	9,787	6,399	6,038	6,101
Earnings Per Share ($)						
1Q	0.37	0.45	0.16	0.53	0.43	0.41
2Q	**0.08**	0.43	0.24	0.60	0.46	0.29
3Q	**1.32**	0.07	-0.15	0.53	-0.27	0.44
4Q	**0.88**	0.40	0.21	0.52	0.40	0.12
Yr.	**2.49**	1.36	0.46	2.18	1.02	1.26

Next earnings report expected: early November

Dividend Data (Dividends have been paid since 1937.)

Amount ($)	Date Decl.	Ex-Div. Date	Stock of Record	Payment Date
0.165	Nov. 05	Nov. 26	Dec. 01	Dec. 15 '97
0.165	Feb. 04	Feb. 25	Feb. 27	Mar. 13 '98
0.165	May. 06	May. 28	Jun. 01	Jun. 15 '98
0.165	Aug. 12	Aug. 28	Sep. 01	Sep. 15 '98

A Division of The **McGraw-Hill** *Companies*

Business Summary - 27-MAY-98

This major producer of distilled spirits and wine is also one of the world's largest investors in entertainment and media companies. Seagram Co. now owns about 84% of Universal Studios, Inc. (formerly known as MCA Inc.), whose operations include the Universal movie business, various record labels, and several theme parks. In May 1998, VO announced plans to acquire music company PolyGram N.V. for about $10.6 billion, and also to divest VO's ownership of fruit juice company Tropicana Products Inc.

Beverage operations, which include spirits, wine, and fruit juices, still account for the majority of the operating cash flow reported by VO. In the spirits and wine business, some of VO's best-known brand names include Crown Royal and Seagram's VO Canadian whiskies; Seagram's 7 Crown blended whiskey; Four Roses bourbon; Chivas Regal, Royal Salute and Passport Scotch whiskies; Glenlivet and Glen Grant single malt Scotch whiskies; Martell Cognacs; Seagram's Extra Dry Gin; and Captain Morgan and Myer's Rum. In total, either directly or through affiliates and joint ventures, VO distributes more than 400 brands of distilled spirits, wines, champagnes, ports and sherries.

Fruit juice operations include products sold under the Tropicana, Dole, Juice Bowl, Fruvita and Looza brands. The Tropicana business, acquired in 1988, has various juice-related products; VO says that Tropicana is the world's leading chilled orange juice brand. In May 1995, VO acquired Dole Food's juice business.

In 1995, VO bought an 80% equity interest in MCA Inc. (now called Universal Studios, Inc.) from Matsushita Electric Industrial Co.,for $5.7 billion. Universal's Putnam Berkley Group publishing division was sold in December 1996, for $336 million. Universal's longer-term growth is expected to include expansion of the Universal theme park business in Florida, and development of a Universal park in Japan. Universal would have an equity interest in each business.

Prior to acquiring its ownership of MCA, VO was a major investor in DuPont (DD). However, in April 1995, DD bought 156 million of its common shares from VO, in a transaction valued at about $8.8 billion. In July 1996, DD repurchased 156 million equity warrants from VO for $500 million. VO continued to own 8.2 million DD shares. In 1996, VO changed its fiscal year end to June 30, from January 31.

Per Share Data ($)

(Year Ended Jun. 30)	1998	1997	1996	1995	1994	1993	1992	1991	1990	1989
Tangible Bk. Val.	NA	14.20	13.45	10.58	9.28	9.09	13.01	11.72	10.04	8.81
Cash Flow	NA	2.89	1.45	2.67	1.46	1.70	2.32	2.37	2.15	1.82
Earnings	2.49	1.36	0.46	2.18	1.02	1.26	1.92	2.01	1.84	1.53
Dividends	0.66	0.65	0.60	0.58	0.56	0.55	0.50	0.46	0.35	0.29
Payout Ratio	27%	47%	130%	27%	55%	43%	26%	23%	19%	20%
Prices - High	46⅝	42¾	39½	32⅝	30⅜	30⅞	29½	23½	22⅞	15½
- Low	30¾	30¼	25½	26¼	24½	25⅛	20⅜	18⅛	15⅛	12½
P/E Ratio - High	19	31	86	15	30	25	15	12	12	10
- Low	12	22	55	12	24	20	11	9	8	8

Income Statement Analysis (Million $)

	1998	1997	1996	1995	1994	1993	1992	1991	1990	1989
Revs.	NA	12,560	8,935	5,563	5,227	5,214	5,278	5,031	4,508	3,935
Oper. Inc.	NA	1,480	952	909	920	926	910	843	694	559
Depr.	NA	547	368	184	166	164	150	135	118	113
Int. Exp.	NA	326	378	408	351	341	345	347	325	270
Pretax Inc.	NA	899	349	1,000	550	650	952	912	839	676
Eff. Tax Rate	NA	43%	44%	19%	31%	27%	24%	17%	15%	12%
Net Inc.	NA	502	174	811	379	474	727	756	711	589

Balance Sheet & Other Fin. Data (Million $)

	1998	1997	1996	1995	1994	1993	1992	1991	1990	1989
Cash	NA	504	254	157	131	116	266	131	138	235
Curr. Assets	NA	6,954	6,640	4,176	3,794	3,836	4,327	3,970	3,289	3,182
Total Assets	NA	20,936	21,355	12,956	11,718	10,104	11,876	11,477	10,213	9,697
Curr. Liab.	NA	3,517	3,854	4,091	2,996	2,003	1,896	3,130	2,491	1,994
LT Debt	NA	2,494	2,889	2,841	3,053	2,559	3,013	2,038	2,011	2,329
Common Eqty.	NA	9,422	9,328	5,509	5,001	4,930	6,483	5,952	5,357	4,974
Total Cap.	NA	16,228	1,624	8,377	8,295	7,689	9,684	8,166	7,538	7,532
Cap. Exp.	NA	507	433	172	163	168	215	309	206	142
Cash Flow	NA	1,049	542	995	545	638	877	891	828	703
Curr. Ratio	NA	2.0	1.7	1.0	1.3	1.9	2.3	1.3	1.3	1.6
% LT Debt of Cap.	NA	15.4	17.8	33.9	36.8	33.3	31.1	25.0	26.7	30.9
% Net Inc.of Revs.	NA	4.0	1.9	14.6	7.3	9.1	13.8	15.0	15.8	15.0
% Ret. on Assets	NA	2.4	1.0	6.6	3.5	4.3	6.2	7.0	7.2	6.7
% Ret. on Equity	NA	5.4	2.3	15.4	7.6	11.6	8.4	11.6	13.5	12.3

Data as orig. reptd.; bef. results of disc. opers. and/or spec. items. Per share data adj. for stk. divs. as of ex-div. date. Prior to FY 97, annual data are for fiscal years ended Jan., and Revs. in Income Statement Analysis excl. excise taxes. E-Estimated. NA-Not Available. NM-Not Meaningful. NR-Not Ranked.

Office—1430 Peel St., Montreal, QC, Canada H3A 1S9. Tel—(514) 849-5271. Website—http://www.seagram.com Chrmn—E. M. Bronfman. Co-Chrmn—C. R. Bronfman. Pres & CEO—E. Bronfman Jr. Vice Chrmn & CFO—R. W. Matschullat.Secy—M. C. L. Hallows. Investor Contacts—J. M. Fitzgerald (VP), 212-572-7282; Maureen S. Hannan (Sr. Dir.), 212-572-1397. Dirs—M. W. Barrett, F. J. Biondi, Jr., C. R. Bronfman, E. M. Bronfman, E. Bronfman Jr., S. Bronfman II, D. M. Culver, W. G. Davis, P, Desmarais, M. J. Hooper, D. L. Johnston, E. L. Kolber, M.-J. Kravis, R. W. Matschullat, C. E. Medland, S. Minzberg, J. L. Weinberg, J. S. Weinberg. Transfer Agents & Registrars—ChaseMellon Shareholder Services, Ridgefield Park, NJ; CIBC Mellon Trust Co., Montreal, Toronto, Calgary & Vancouver. Incorporated—in Canada in 1928.Empl— 30,000. S&P Analyst: Tom Graves, CFA

STANDARD &POOR'S
STOCK REPORTS

Sealed Air

2000H
NYSE Symbol SEE
In S&P 500

12-SEP-98

Industry: Manufacturing (Specialized)

Summary: This maker of protective packing materials and systems and selected food packaging products, recently merged with W.R. Grace's Cryovac packaging unit.

S&P Opinion: Hold (★★★)	Recent Price • 33⅞	Yield • Nil
	52 Wk Range • 68-32⅝	12-Mo. P/E • NM

Quantitative Evaluations

Outlook
(1 Lowest—5 Highest)
• **3⁻**

Fair Value
• **40¾**

Risk
• **NA**

Earn./Div. Rank
• **NR**

Technical Eval.
• **NA**

Rel. Strength Rank
(1 Lowest—99 Highest)
• **38**

Insider Activity
• **Favorable**

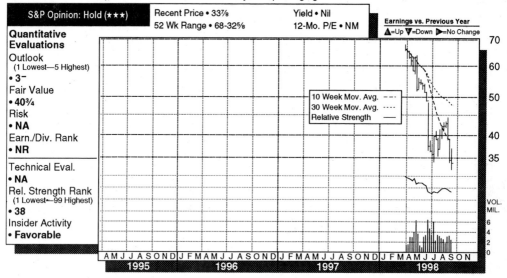

Earnings vs. Previous Year
▲=Up ▼=Down ▶=No Change

10 Week Mov. Avg. ---
30 Week Mov. Avg. ----
Relative Strength —

Overview - 05-AUG-98

Although we expect the company's recent merger with W.R. Grace's Cryovac packaging unit to have a positive effect on earnings down the road, at least for the balance of 1998 and into 1999, results will be adversely affected by the strong U.S. dollar against foreign currencies, especially in the Asia-Pacific region. In addition, SEE will incur restructuring and integration charges, and a one-time charge for income taxes on the accumulated earnings of the Cryovac business outside the U.S. Sales are expected to rise in single digits, while gross margins will likely range from 36% to 37% through 1999, well below their normal 38% level. SEE plans to offset the sales shortfall by cutting costs through work force reductions, minimizing capital spending, and controlling working capital. Expected annual cost savings of $45 million should begin to be fully realized by late 1999.

Valuation - 05-AUG-98

The new common shares, which began trading on the NYSE in early April 1998, fell 50% in recent months, before starting to rebound in late July. We believe that the stock has the potential to return to its past steady growth trend, as synergies from the merger with Cryovac are realized. However, weak foreign currencies and Asian markets are likely to continue, and the effective tax rate will remain high, ranging from 45% to 46%, due to the non-deductibility of goodwill. SEE continues to increase cash generation, and directors recently authorized the repurchase of 5% of the common and Series A preferred shares. We recently reduced our 1998 EPS estimate (excluding charges of $1.08 to $1.15), but raised our projection for 1999. However, will still do not expect the shares to outperform the market. SEE will report basic EPS this year, as diluted EPS would be higher than basic.

Key Stock Statistics

S&P EPS Est. 1998	1.15	Tang. Bk. Value/Share	NM
P/E on S&P Est. 1998	29.5	Beta	0.58
S&P EPS Est. 1999	1.80	Shareholders	NA
Dividend Rate/Share	Nil	Market cap. (B)	$ 2.8
Shs. outstg. (M)	83.3	Inst. holdings	60%
Avg. daily vol. (M)	0.571		

Value of $10,000 invested 5 years ago: NA

Fiscal Year Ending Dec. 31

	1998	1997	1996	1995	1994	1993
Revenues (Million $)						
1Q	431.0	—	—	—	—	—
2Q	670.0	—	—	—	—	—
3Q	—	—	—	—	—	—
4Q	—	—	—	—	—	—
Yr.	—	NA	—	—	—	—
Earnings Per Share ($)						
1Q	0.18	—	—	—	—	—
2Q	0.27	—	—	—	—	—
3Q	—	—	—	—	—	—
4Q	—	—	—	—	—	—
Yr.	—	NA	NA	NA	NA	NA

Next earnings report expected: late October

Dividend Data

Dividends, initiated in 1975, were discontinued in 1989. A two-for-one stock split was effected in 1995.

A Division of The McGraw-Hill Companies

STANDARD
&POOR'S
STOCK REPORTS

Sealed Air

2000H
12-SEP-98

Business Summary - 05-AUG-98

With its diverse mix of protective packaging materials and systems, it has been hard to determine whether Sealed Air (SEE) is a packaging company or a specialty chemicals company. However, with its recent merger with W.R. Grace's packaging business, SEE became the world's leading protective and specialty packaging company, with annual sales expected to exceed $2.5 billion.

Although SEE has begun to experience growing pains following the Cryovac merger, it has established itself as a steady growth company over the years, through acquisitions, expansion overseas, and the development of new products. In March 1998, SEE completed a merger with the Cryovac packaging business of W.R. Grace (NYSE: GRA), acquired for about $5 billion in cash and stock. SEE shareholders received one new Sealed Air share for each share they had owned. GRA shareholders received 0.536 of a new SEE common share, and 0.475 of a new SEE convertible preferred share. Subsequently, SEE declared a $0.50 a share quarterly cash dividend on the Series A convertible preferred stock. SEE shareholders owned 63% of the new company, and GRA shareholders 37%.

With its broadened global presence, SEE expects more of its sales to come from outside the U.S. On a pro forma basis, assuming that Sealed Air and Cryovac were combined for all of 1997, 48% of sales would have been generated outside the U.S.

The company's surface protection and other cushioning products include its air cellular packaging materials, which are plastic sheets containing encapsulated air bubbles that protect products from damage through shock or vibration during shipment.

SEE's engineered products consist of its Instapak foam-in-place packaging systems, which provide protection packaging for a variety of products, including computer, electronic and communications equipment, and void-fill packaging of office supplies, books and other small products.

Food packaging products consist of absorbent pads, produce bags and flexible films, bags, pouches and related equipment.

The company's other products consist primarily of specialty adhesive products, loose-fill polystyrene packaging and paper products.

The company expects to incur pretax restructuring charges of $135 million to $145 million ($1.08 to $1.15 a share, after taxes) in the 1998 third quarter. It expects this to reduce annual operating costs by $45 million by the end of 1999. The restructuring will include the elimination of 5% of the work force, combining or closing of certain facilities, leveraging Cryovac's infrastructure in Latin America and Asia, and streamlining Cryovac's manufacturing organization.

Per Share Data ($)

(Year Ended Dec. 31)	1997	1996	1995	1994	1993	1992	1991	1990	1989	1988
Tangible Bk. Val.	5.69	NA	NA	NA	NA	NA	NA	NA	NA	NA
Cash Flow	2.38	NA	NA	NA	NA	NA	NA	NA	NA	NA
Earnings	NA	NA	NA	NA	NA	NA	NA	NA	NA	NA
Dividends	NA	NA	NA	NA	NA	NA	NA	NA	NA	NA
Payout Ratio	NA	NA	NA	NA	NA	NA	NA	NA	NA	NA
Prices - High	NA	NA	NA	NA	NA	NA	NA	NA	NA	NA
- Low	NA	NA	NA	NA	NA	NA	NA	NA	NA	NA
P/E Ratio - High	NA	NA	NA	NA	NA	NA	NA	NA	NA	NA
- Low	NA	NA	NA	NA	NA	NA	NA	NA	NA	NA

Income Statement Analysis (Million $)

	1997	1996	1995	1994	1993	1992	1991	1990	1989	1988
Revs.	1,480	NA	NA	NA	NA	NA	NA	NA	NA	NA
Oper. Inc.	155	NA	NA	NA	NA	NA	NA	NA	NA	NA
Depr.	93.0	NA	NA	NA	NA	NA	NA	NA	NA	NA
Int. Exp.	19.0	NA	NA	NA	NA	NA	NA	NA	NA	NA
Pretax Inc.	143	NA	NA	NA	NA	NA	NA	NA	NA	NA
Eff. Tax Rate	38%	NA	NA	NA	NA	NA	NA	NA	NA	NA
Net Inc.	88.0	NA	NA	NA	NA	NA	NA	NA	NA	NA

Balance Sheet & Other Fin. Data (Million $)

	1997	1996	1995	1994	1993	1992	1991	1990	1989	1988
Cash	48.0	NA	NA	NA	NA	NA	NA	NA	NA	NA
Curr. Assets	2,176	NA	NA	NA	NA	NA	NA	NA	NA	NA
Total Assets	3,773	NA	NA	NA	NA	NA	NA	NA	NA	NA
Curr. Liab.	1,358	NA	NA	NA	NA	NA	NA	NA	NA	NA
LT Debt	48.5	NA	NA	NA	NA	NA	NA	NA	NA	NA
Common Eqty.	468	NA	NA	NA	NA	NA	NA	NA	NA	NA
Total Cap.	322	NA	NA	NA	NA	NA	NA	NA	NA	NA
Cap. Exp.	24.3	NA	NA	NA	NA	NA	NA	NA	NA	NA
Cash Flow	181	NA	NA	NA	NA	NA	NA	NA	NA	NA
Curr. Ratio	1.6	NA	NA	NA	NA	NA	NA	NA	NA	NA
% LT Debt of Cap.	15.1	NA	NA	NA	NA	NA	NA	NA	NA	NA
% Net Inc.of Revs.	5.9	NA	NA	NA	NA	NA	NA	NA	NA	NA
% Ret. on Assets	2.0	NA	NA	NA	NA	NA	NA	NA	NA	NA
% Ret. on Equity	16.0	NA	NA	NA	NA	NA	NA	NA	NA	NA

Data as orig. reptd.; bef. results of disc. opers. and/or spec. items. Per share data adj. for stk. divs. as of ex-div. date. Bold denotes diluted EPS (FASB 128). E-Estimated. NA-Not Available. NM-Not Meaningful. NR-Not Ranked.

Office—Park 80 East, Saddle Brook, NJ 07662-5291. **Tel**—(201) 791-7600. **Website**—http://www.cfonews.com/see **Chrmn & CEO**—T. J. D. Dunphy. **Pres & COO**—W. V. Hickey. **CFO**—D. S. Van Riper. **Secy**—H. K. White. **VP & Investor Contact**—Mary A. Coventry. **Dirs**—H. Brown, J. K. Castle, C. Cheng, L. R. Codey, T. J. D. Dunphy, C. F. Farell Jr., D. Freeman, V. A. Kamsky, A. H. Miller, J. E. Phipps, R. L. San Soucie. **Transfer Agent**—First Chicago Trust Co. of New York, Jersey City, NJ. **Incorporated**—in New Jersey in 1960; reincorporated in Delaware in 1969. **Empl**—14,500. **S&P Analyst:** Stewart Scharf

12-SEP-98

Industry:
Retail (General Merchandise)

Summary: This multi-line retailer provides a wide array of merchandise and services in the U.S. and Canada.

S&P Opinion: Hold (★★★)

| Recent Price • 45⅛ | Yield • 2.0% |
| 52 Wk Range • 65-38¾ | 12-Mo. P/E • 13.2 |

Quantitative Evaluations

Outlook
(1 Lowest—5 Highest)
• **NA**

Fair Value
• **NA**

Risk
• **Average**

Earn./Div. Rank
• **B**

Technical Eval.
• **Bearish** since 3/98

Rel. Strength Rank
(1 Lowest—99 Highest)
• **51**

Insider Activity
• **NA**

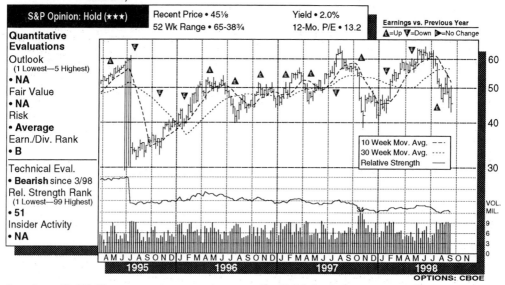

Earnings vs. Previous Year
▲=Up ▼=Down ▶=No Change

10 Week Mov. Avg. -- --
30 Week Mov. Avg. ....
Relative Strength ——

OPTIONS: CBOE

Overview - 29-JUL-98

Sales at the merchandise group should increase about 6% in 1998, aided by the remodeling of units, and by gains of about 3% in same-store sales. Credit revenues should also have a healthy advance. Gross margins should widen slightly, reflecting increased retail square footage of higher-margin apparel, and improved logistics and sourcing. Apparel should show strong same-store sales gains. Costs and expenses should continue to decline as a percentage of sales, reflecting successful cost cutting and leverage from the strong sales gains. The company's strategy calls for remodeling the mall stores, increasing the assortment of apparel, opening freestanding hardware and furniture stores and cutting costs. By 2000, S expects to be operating about 5,000 stores, including 860 department stores, 560 off-the-mall hardware stores, 540 tire stores, 800 dealer stores, 180 HomeLife units, and 2,000 Parts America units. The company is also expanding its home services operations, currently a $3 billion business; it believes that this business could grow to $10 billion by the end of the decade.

Valuation - 29-JUL-98

We remain optimistic regarding the company's growth prospects for the next few years, based on its operating strategies. We recommend retaining the shares for capital gains. Second quarter earnings were slightly better than anticipated, but weak apparel sales hurt gross margins, and the shares fell. Although a continuing trend of increased delinquencies in the payment of credit card debt led to a higher provision for uncollectible accounts in the quarter, the rate of growth has slowed from the end of 1997. With a better handle on the problem and an easing of delinquencies in the later part of the year, S will be back on track to resume posting 12% to 14% annual earnings gains.

Key Stock Statistics

S&P EPS Est. 1998	3.50	Tang. Bk. Value/Share	15.76
P/E on S&P Est. 1998	12.9	Beta	1.31
S&P EPS Est. 1999	3.95	Shareholders	244,000
Dividend Rate/Share	0.92	Market cap. (B)	$ 17.7
Shs. outstg. (M)	392.4	Inst. holdings	72%
Avg. daily vol. (M)	2.144		

Value of $10,000 invested 5 years ago: NA

Fiscal Year Ending Dec. 31

	1998	1997	1996	1995	1994	1993
Revenues (Million $)						
1Q	9,163	8,733	7,995	7,449	12,440	11,298
2Q	10,247	9,701	9,132	8,204	13,151	12,157
3Q	—	9,781	9,067	8,418	13,342	12,719
4Q	—	13,081	12,042	10,854	15,626	14,664
Yr.	—	41,296	38,236	34,925	54,559	50,838
Earnings Per Share ($)						
1Q	**0.34**	**0.46**	0.36	0.30	-0.28	0.82
2Q	**0.85**	**0.29**	0.67	0.54	1.30	2.86
3Q	**E0.74**	**0.89**	0.68	0.56	0.87	1.15
4Q	**E1.57**	**1.35**	1.42	1.13	1.23	1.39
Yr.	**E3.50**	**2.99**	3.12	2.53	3.12	6.22

Next earnings report expected: mid October

Dividend Data (Dividends have been paid since 1935.)

Amount ($)	Date Decl.	Ex-Div. Date	Stock of Record	Payment Date
0.230	Oct. 08	Nov. 25	Nov. 28	Jan. 02 '98
0.230	Feb. 03	Feb. 25	Feb. 27	Apr. 01 '98
0.230	May. 14	May. 27	May. 29	Jul. 01 '98
0.230	Aug. 12	Aug. 26	Aug. 28	Oct. 01 '98

STANDARD
&POOR'S
STOCK REPORTS

Sears, Roebuck and Co.

2002

12-SEP-98

Business Summary - 29-JUL-98

Through a renewed focus on its retailing business, Sears, Roebuck and Co. has transformed itself from an industry laggard into a growing, innovative company. It is a leading retailer of apparel, home and automotive products and related services.

In 1993, Sears announced a plan to streamline the merchandise group by discontinuing money-losing catalog operations, closing unprofitable stores and offering an early-retirement program. The company is now focused on its three core retail operations: apparel; home, including home appliances and electronics, home improvement and furniture; and automotive, including Sears Auto Centers and Western Auto. About 75% of the company's $4 billion store remodeling program has been completed.

At the end of 1997, merchandising operations included 833 full-line stores, averaging 86,000 square feet, mostly in malls. There were 129 HomeLife furniture stores, 255 hardware stores, and 576 dealer stores. Sears Auto Centers included 576 auto parts stores and 808 independently owned and operated Western Auto stores in small and rural markets. Direct response marketing includes specialty catalogs. Foreign operations are conducted through 54.8%-owned Sears Canada and 15%-owned Sears Mexico. Sears sold a 60% interest in Sears Mexico for $103 million and took a $36 million charge in the 1997 first quarter.

Sears also realizes significant income from its credit portfolio, which consists primarily of Sears credit card customer receivables ($28.9 billion at the end of 1997).

Sears plans to take a bigger bite out of the $165 billion home services industry in the next few years. Sears already holds the leading market share, with annual revenues around $3 billion, consisting of service contracts for repairs, home product installations and improvements.

As part of its effort to focus on its core merchandising business, Sears exited a number of non-retail businesses in the past few years. Dean Witter, Discover & Co. was spun off to shareholders in June 1993; Coldwell Banker Residential Services and the Sears Mortgage Banking Group were sold in 1993. Sears spun off its 80% stake in Allstate Corp. to shareholders in mid-1995. The company divested its 50% interest in Prodigy Services in 1996 and its 30% stake in the Advantis data services business in 1997.

During the second quarter of 1997, S reached an agreement with debtor class action plaintiffs and Attorneys General in 50 states. S agreed to return amounts with interest to Chapter 7 bankruptcy debtors whose reaffirmations of debt were not filed with the court as required by law. As a result, S incurred a charge of $475 million ($320 million after tax, or $0.80 a share) for the settlement and related expenses.

Per Share Data ($)

(Year Ended Dec. 31)	1997	1996	1995	1994	1993	1992	1991	1990	1989	1988
Tangible Bk. Val.	15.00	12.63	10.40	26.18	28.80	25.94	38.70	35.77	38.15	36.06
Cash Flow	4.96	4.87	3.93	NM	NM	NM	NM	NM	NM	NM
Earnings	2.99	3.12	2.53	3.16	6.22	-7.02	3.71	2.60	4.12	2.72
Dividends	0.92	0.92	1.26	1.60	1.60	2.00	2.00	2.00	2.00	2.00
Payout Ratio	31%	29%	50%	51%	26%	NM	54%	77%	47%	72%
Prices - High	65¼	53⅞	61¼	55⅛	60⅛	48	43½	41⅞	48⅛	46
- Low	38¾	38¼	29⅜	42⅛	38½	37	24⅜	22	36½	32¼
P/E Ratio - High	22	17	24	17	10	NM	12	16	12	17
- Low	13	12	12	13	6	NM	7	8	9	12

Income Statement Analysis (Million $)

Revs.	41,296	38,236	34,925	54,559	50,838	52,345	57,242	55,972	53,794	50,251
Oper. Inc.	4,664	4,145	3,707	3,818	NA	NA	NA	NA	NA	NA
Depr.	786	697	578	649	NA	NA	NA	NA	NA	NA
Int. Exp.	1,409	1,370	1,377	1,340	1,531	1,559	3,309	3,413	3,263	2,978
Pretax Inc.	2,138	2.0	1,728	1,712	2,810	-4,680	1,471	671	1,799	1,086
Eff. Tax Rate	43%	40%	41%	21%	14%	NM	13%	NM	20%	4.90%
Net Inc.	1,188	1,271	1,025	1,244	2,409	-2,566	1,279	892	1,446	1,032

Balance Sheet & Other Fin. Data (Million $)

Cash	358	660	606	1,421	1,864	2,627	5,984	5,217	3,281	3,458
Curr. Assets	30,682	28,447	26,441	NA	NA	NA	NA	NA	NA	NA
Total Assets	38,700	36,167	33,130	91,896	90,808	83,533	106,434	96,253	86,972	77,952
Curr. Liab.	15,790	14,950	14,607	NA	NA	NA	NA	NA	NA	NA
LT Debt	13,071	12,170	10,044	9,713	10,265	11,467	17,680	12,493	9,443	8,903
Common Eqty.	5,862	4,945	4,060	9,240	10,103	9,212	13,863	12,824	13,622	14,055
Total Cap.	18,933	17,115	14,429	22,448	24,263	22,240	31,868	25,316	23,498	24,501
Cap. Exp.	1,328	1,189	1,183	1,120	670	967	1,228	1,219	1,040	889
Cash Flow	1,974	1,943	1,550	NM	NM	NM	NM	NM	NM	NM
Curr. Ratio	1.9	1.9	1.8	NA	NA	NA	NA	NA	NA	NA
% LT Debt of Cap.	69.0	71.1	28.1	43.3	42.3	51.6	55.5	49.3	40.2	37.9
% Net Inc.of Revs.	2.9	3.3	2.9	2.3	4.7	NM	2.2	1.6	2.7	2.1
% Ret. on Assets	3.2	3.7	2.9	1.4	2.7	NM	1.3	1.0	1.8	1.4
% Ret. on Equity	22.0	27.7	14.6	12.5	24.5	NM	9.5	6.7	10.9	7.5

Data as orig. reptd.; bef. results of disc. opers. and/or spec. items. Per share data adj. for stk. divs. as of ex-div. date. Bold denotes diluted EPS (FASB 128). E-Estimated. NA-Not Available. NM-Not Meaningful. NR-Not Ranked.

Office—3333 Beverly Rd., Hoffman Estates, IL 60179. **Tel**—(847) 286-2500. **Website**—http://www.sears.com **Chrmn & CEO**—A. C. Martinez. **SVP-Fin**—A. J. Lacy. **SVP & Secy**—M. D. Levin **Investor Contact**—Jerome J. Leshne (847-286-1468). **Dirs**—H. Adams Jr., W. L. Batts, B. C. Barnes, A. D. Correll, Jr., A. C. Martinez, M. A. Miles, R. C. Notebaert, H. B. Price, C. B. Rogers Jr., P. G. Ryan, D. A. Terrell. **Transfer Agent & Registrar**—First Chicago Trust Co. of New York, Jersey City, NJ. **Incorporated**—in New York in 1906. **Empl**— 296,000. **S&P Analyst:** Karen J. Sack, CFA

Sempra Energy

2007
NYSE Symbol **SRE**

In S&P 500

12-SEP-98

Industry:
Natural Gas

Summary: This energy holding company was formed through the mid-1998 merger of Pacific Enterprises and Enova Corp.

S&P Opinion: Accumulate (★★★★)	Recent Price • 25⅜	Yield • 6.1%
	52 Wk Range • 28⅞-23¾	12-Mo. P/E • NM

Quantitative Evaluations

Outlook
(1 Lowest—5 Highest)
• **2**

Fair Value
• **24¾**

Risk
• **NA**

Earn./Div. Rank
• **NR**

Technical Eval.
• **NA**

Rel. Strength Rank
(1 Lowest—99 Highest)
• **NA**

Insider Activity
• **Favorable**

Earnings vs. Previous Year
▲=Up ▼=Down ▶=No Change

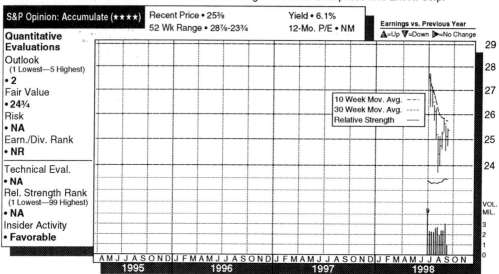

10 Week Mov. Avg. ---
30 Week Mov. Avg. ....
Relative Strength —

VOL. MIL.

Overview - 14-JUL-98

With a combined customer base of nearly six million, Sempra Energy is well positioned to compete in California's restructured energy market. Still, we expect EPS in 1998 to decline about 9% from 1997's pro forma results. The July 1997 Performance Based Regulation (PBR) decision by the California Public Utility Commission (CPUC), which requires sharing with ratepayers a percentage of earnings above the authorized rate of return, will make it difficult for SoCalGas to achieve the level of returns earned prior to the August 1997 implementation of the rate reduction. However, we expect results to improve in 1999, as SRE starts to benefit from anticipated turnarounds in several of its non-regulated operations. For the next two years, we expect Sempra Energy's earnings to grow at an annual rate of 5% to 6%. Thereafter, we foresee a higher rate of annual earnings growth, fueled by significant operating synergies and increased contributions from the unregulated businesses.

Valuation - 14-JUL-98

We recommend the accumulation of SRE shares. While the July 1997 PBR decision by the CPUC will restrict the rate of SoCalGas's earnings growth, it should also enable Sempra Energy to benefit from the emergence of a more competitive market environment. SRE will also benefit from San Diego Gas & Electric having the lowest electric rates of California's three major utilities, a small concentration of industrial customers and a low level of stranded assets. Although it may take a couple of years for some of the non-regulated operations to become significantly profitable, we expect them to make a major contribution to long-term earnings growth. With the stock trading at less than 16 times our 1999 EPS estimate of $1.75, and the planned annual dividend of $1.56 yielding around 5.6%, the shares are attractive for long-term total return.

Key Stock Statistics

S&P EPS Est. 1998	1.35	Tang. Bk. Value/Share	NM
P/E on S&P Est. 1998	18.8	Beta	0.41
S&P EPS Est. 1999	1.75	Shareholders	NA
Dividend Rate/Share	1.56	Market cap. (B)	$ 6.1
Shs. outstg. (M)	240.8	Inst. holdings	7%
Avg. daily vol. (M)	0.480		

Value of $10,000 invested 5 years ago: NA

Fiscal Year Ending Dec. 31

	1998	1997	1996	1995	1994	1993
Revenues (Million $)						
1Q	1,335	—	—	—	—	—
2Q	1,335	—	—	—	—	—
3Q	—	—	—	—	—	—
4Q	—	—	—	—	—	—
Yr.	—	5,069	4,496	4,166	—	—
Earnings Per Share ($)						
1Q	0.37	—	—	—	—	—
2Q	0.13	—	—	—	—	—
3Q	E0.45	—	—	—	—	—
4Q	E0.13	—	—	—	—	—
Yr.	E1.35	1.82	1.77	1.67	—	—

Next earnings report expected: NA

Dividend Data (Dividends have been paid since 1998.)

Amount ($)	Date Decl.	Ex-Div. Date	Stock of Record	Payment Date
0.390	Sep. 01	Sep. 17	Sep. 21	Oct. 15 '98

A Division of The McGraw·Hill Companies

Business Summary - 14-JUL-98

Sempra Energy is an energy holding company that was formed on June 26, 1998, through the merger of Pacific Enterprises, the holding company for Southern California Gas (SoCalGas), and Enova Corp., the holding company for San Diego Gas & Electric (SDG&E).

SoCalGas is the largest natural gas distribution utility in the U.S., serving approximately 4.8 million customers throughout most of Southern California and part of central California. San Diego Gas & Electric provides electric service to 1.2 million customers and gas service to around 720,000 customers in Southern California.

In July 1997, the California Public Utility Commission (CPUC) granted SoCalGas performance based regulation (PBR), under which earnings will become more dependent on operational efficiencies. The PBR decision ordered a net rate reduction of $164 million and determined that earnings up to 25 basis points (b.p.) above the authorized rate of return on the rate base (the total investment in the facilities required to provide utility service) are 100% retained by shareholder. Earnings 25 b.p. above the authorized return are shared between customers and shareholders on a sliding scale that begins with a customer return of 75% declining to 0% as earnings approach 300 b.p. above the authorized return. In 1998, SoCalGas was authorized a 9.49% return on a rate base of approximately $2.7 billion.

SDG&E has a 20% stake in the San Onofre nuclear generating plants (SONGS), which began operating in 1983. In late 1992, regulators ordered SONGS 1 permanently shut down. The unit's costs have been fully recovered and it will be decommissioned. In January 1996, the CPUC approved the accelerated recovery of SONGS 2 and 3. As of December 31, 1997, about $600 million was not recovered. California legislation requires that all generation-related stranded assets, which includes SONGS 2 and 3, be recovered by 2001.

Sempra Energy Solutions provides energy-related products and services for all customer classes. It owns CES/Way International, a Houston-based provider of energy services. Sempra Energy Trading is a wholesale marketer and trader of physical and financial energy products, including natural gas, power, crude oil and other associated commodities.

Sempra Energy Resources acquires and develops power plants, as well as natural gas storage, production and transportation assets. Sempra Energy Utility Ventures acquires and develops small to medium size domestic energy utilities. Sempra Energy Financial invests in tax-advantaged investments, such as affordable housing limited partnerships.

Sempra Energy International develops and operates SRE's energy infrastructure projects outside the U.S., including natural gas distribution systems and power generation facilities. It is currently involved in gas distribution partnerships in Mexico, Argentina and Uruguay.

Per Share Data ($)

(Year Ended Dec. 31)	1997	1996	1995	1994	1993	1992	1991	1990	1989	1988
Tangible Bk. Val.	12.56	12.21	NA	NA	NA	NA	NA	NA	NA	NA
Earnings	1.82	1.77	1.67	NA	NA	NA	NA	NA	NA	NA
Dividends	1.27	1.24	1.22	NA	NA	NA	NA	NA	NA	NA
Payout Ratio	NA	NA	NA	NA	NA	NA	NA	NA	NA	NA
Prices - High	NA	NA	NA	NA	NA	NA	NA	NA	NA	NA
- Low	NA	NA	NA	NA	NA	NA	NA	NA	NA	NA
P/E Ratio - High	NA	NA	NA	NA	NA	NA	NA	NA	NA	NA
- Low	NA	NA	NA	NA	NA	NA	NA	NA	NA	NA

Income Statement Analysis (Million $)

	1997	1996	1995	1994	1993	1992	1991	1990	1989	1988
Revs.	5,069	4,496	4,166	NA	NA	NA	NA	NA	NA	NA
Depr.	604	586	521	NA	NA	NA	NA	NA	NA	NA
Maint.	NA	NA	NA	NA	NA	NA	NA	NA	NA	NA
Fxd. Chgs. Cov.	4.3	4.3	3.6	NA	NA	NA	NA	NA	NA	NA
Constr. Credits	Nil	Nil	Nil	Nil	Nil	Nil	Nil	Nil	Nil	Nil
Eff. Tax Rate	41%	41%	40%	NA	NA	NA	NA	NA	NA	NA
Net Inc.	432	427	401	NA	NA	NA	NA	NA	NA	NA

Balance Sheet & Other Fin. Data (Million $)

	1997	1996	1995	1994	1993	1992	1991	1990	1989	1988
Gross Prop.	12,040	11,835	NA	NA	NA	NA	NA	NA	NA	NA
Cap. Exp.	397	413	NA	NA	NA	NA	NA	NA	NA	NA
Net Prop.	6,119	6,343	NA	NA	NA	NA	NA	NA	NA	NA
Capitalization:										
LT Debt	3,175	2,704	NA	NA	NA	NA	NA	NA	NA	NA
% LT Debt	50	45	NA	NA	NA	NA	NA	NA	NA	NA
Pfd.	279	279	NA	NA	NA	NA	NA	NA	NA	NA
% Pfd.	4.40	4.70	NA	NA	NA	NA	NA	NA	NA	NA
Common	2,959	2,930	NA	NA	NA	NA	NA	NA	NA	NA
% Common	46	50	NA	NA	NA	NA	NA	NA	NA	NA
Total Cap.	7,309	6,859	NA	NA	NA	NA	NA	NA	NA	NA
% Oper. Ratio	82.3	79.5	78.8	NA	NA	NA	NA	NA	NA	NA
% Earn. on Net Prop.	9.3	NA	NA	NA	NA	NA	NA	NA	NA	NA
% Return On Revs.	8.5	9.5	9.6	NA	NA	NA	NA	NA	NA	NA
% Return On Invest. Capital	9.0	NA	NA	NA	NA	NA	NA	NA	NA	NA
% Return On Com. Equity	14.7	NA	NA	NA	NA	NA	NA	NA	NA	NA

Data as orig. reptd.; bef. results of disc opers. and/or spec. items. Per share data adj. for stk. divs. as of ex-div. date. Bold denotes diluted EPS (FASB 128). E-Estimated. NA-Not Available. NM-Not Meaningful. NR-Not Ranked.

Office—101 Ash St., San Diego, CA 92101-3017 **Tel**—(619) 696-2034. **Website**—http://www.sempra.com **Chrmn & CEO**—R. D. Farman. **Vice Chrmn, Pres & COO**—S. L. Baum. **EVP & CFO**—N. E. Schmale. **Investor Contact**—Clem Teng. **Dirs**—S. L. Baum, H. H. Bertea, A. Burr, H. L. Carter, R. A. Collato, D. W. Derbes, R. D. Farman, W. D. Godbold, R. H. Goldsmith, W. D. Jones, I. E. Lozano, Jr., R. R. Ocampo, W. G. Ouchi, R. J. Stegemeier, T. C. Stickel, D. L. Walker. **Transfer Agent & Registrar**—First Chicago Trust, Jersey City NJ. **Incorporated**—in California in 1998. **Empl**— 12,000. **S&P Analyst:** Justin McCann

STANDARD &POOR'S
STOCK REPORTS

Service Corp. Int'l
2010
NYSE Symbol SRV
In S&P 500

12-SEP-98

Industry:
Services (Commercial & Consumer)

Summary: This company, the world's largest funeral and cemetery operator, has reached an agreement to acquire Equity Corp. International.

S&P Opinion: Accumulate (★★★★)	Recent Price • 35⅝	Yield • 1.0%
	52 Wk Range • 47⅛-27⅞	12-Mo. P/E • 25.3

Quantitative Evaluations

Outlook
(1 Lowest—5 Highest)
• **4⁻**

Fair Value
• **46⅛**

Risk
• **Low**

Earn./Div. Rank
• **A**

Technical Eval.
• **Bullish** since 6/94

Rel. Strength Rank
(1 Lowest—99 Highest)
• **72**

Insider Activity
• **NA**

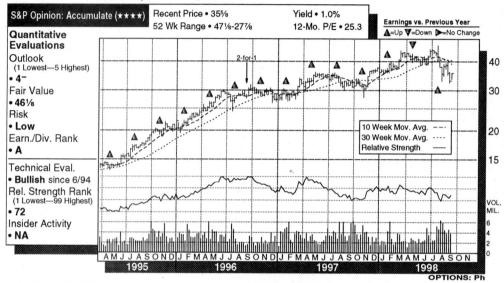

Earnings vs. Previous Year
▲=Up ▼=Down ▶=No Change

10 Week Mov. Avg. ---
30 Week Mov. Avg. ----
Relative Strength —

OPTIONS: Ph

Overview - 12-AUG-98

Total revenues are expected to advance about 9% in 1998, reflecting an unusually weak funeral service segment offset by increasingly profitable cemetery operations. Growth should improve in the second half of 1998 as a result of the pending acquisition of Equity Corp. International (EQU) and a return to more favorable death rates. The cemetery unit should put in a stellar performance due to acquisitions and higher pre-need sales. SRV management has had excellent success expanding margins in the past, and the size of the pending acquisition pipeline leaves tremendous opportunity for operational improvements. Conservatively, we anticipate 1998 EPS to rise 15% (before investment gains), to $1.52, and look for 1999 EPS of $1.80.

Valuation - 12-AUG-98

We recently upgraded SRV to accumulate from hold based on the stock's attractive price and the planned acquisition of Equity Corp. International (EQU). The second quarter of 1998 was extremely difficult for funeral service providers, due to an unusually low death rate during the period. The mortality environment has begun to normalize, and we anticipate same-stores sales will return to historic levels in the second half of the year. SRV's proposed acquisition of EQU, the nation's fourth largest publicly traded death care provider, would create an industry behemoth with $3 billion in annual sales. EQU was spun-off from SRV in 1990, which should allow for a smooth integration that will be accretive and without customer base overlap. SRV has had superb success with consolidation and margin expansion in the past, and we expect that the EQU deal will be no less rewarding to shareholders. SRV shares are substantially off 52-week highs, and we recommend investors accumulate the stock and take advantage of the weakness.

Key Stock Statistics

S&P EPS Est. 1998	1.52	Tang. Bk. Value/Share	4.79
P/E on S&P Est. 1998	23.4	Beta	0.79
S&P EPS Est. 1999	1.80	Shareholders	7,700
Dividend Rate/Share	0.36	Market cap. (B)	$ 9.2
Shs. outstg. (M)	257.3	Inst. holdings	71%
Avg. daily vol. (M)	0.860		

Value of $10,000 invested 5 years ago: $ 41,692

Fiscal Year Ending Dec. 31

	1998	1997	1996	1995	1994	1993
Revenues (Million $)						
1Q	682.7	638.5	575.5	348.1	261.3	224.4
2Q	671.9	601.1	564.8	353.6	262.9	217.1
3Q	—	584.8	544.5	403.5	277.8	211.4
4Q	—	644.0	609.5	546.9	315.2	246.3
Yr.	—	2,468	2,294	1,652	1,117	899.2
Earnings Per Share ($)						
1Q	0.42	0.54	0.30	0.24	0.22	0.18
2Q	**0.35**	0.32	0.26	0.21	0.17	0.14
3Q	**E0.33**	0.28	0.24	0.20	0.17	0.12
4Q	**E0.42**	**0.36**	0.30	0.24	0.20	0.17
Yr.	**E1.52**	**1.47**	1.10	0.90	0.76	0.62

Next earnings report expected: late October

Dividend Data (Dividends have been paid since 1973.)

Amount ($)	Date Decl.	Ex-Div. Date	Stock of Record	Payment Date
0.075	Nov. 13	Jan. 13	Jan. 15	Jan. 30 '98
0.090	Feb. 12	Apr. 13	Apr. 15	Apr. 30 '98
0.090	May. 14	Jul. 13	Jul. 15	Jul. 31 '98
0.090	Aug. 14	Oct. 13	Oct. 15	Oct. 30 '98

A Division of The McGraw-Hill Companies

STANDARD
&POOR'S
STOCK REPORTS

Service Corporation International

2010
12-SEP-98

Business Summary - 12-AUG-98

Since its founding in 1962, Service Corporation International (NYSE: SRV) has grown into the largest death care provider in the world. The company is regarded as the original consolidator (i.e., a company that grows through the acquisition of smaller firms) in the funeral home and cemetery business. SRV was operating 3,292 funeral service locations, 422 cemeteries and 174 crematoria in 18 countries at June 30, 1998.

SRV's funeral segment sells caskets, burial vaults, cremation receptacles, flowers and burial garments, and also offers the use of facilities and motor vehicles. In recent years, the funeral industry has suffered from a slowing mortality rate, but as the baby-boomer generation approaches its "golden years," demand for SRV's services should increase. In 1997, the funeral division generated 70% of revenues.

The company's cemetery operations include the selling of cemetery plot rights and certain merchandise, such as stone and bronze memorials and burials vaults. The cemetery segment accounted for 29% of 1997 revenues.

In recent years, SRV has benefited from increasing demand for prearranged funeral and cemetery services. This option provides customers with the opportunity to take advantage of current prices for property, merchandise and services that may not be needed for years and also allows families to avoid making important decisions during trying emotional times. In 1997, prearranged funeral services produced about $561 million in future revenues. In the second quarter of 1998, prearranged funeral contracts generated $139 million in revenues. At June 30, 1998, the aggregate value of all prearranged services totaled more than $3.3 billion, which for accounting purposes is recognized when the services are provided.

Although SRV and large competitors such as Loewen Group and Stewart Enterprises have achieved significant growth by acquiring smaller "mom and pop" service providers, the industry is still highly fragmented. Worldwide, 54 million individuals are expected to pass away in 1998. However, with SRV providing funeral services to just 600,000 (1.1%) of these individuals, the company believes there is a significant opportunity to grow through consolidation. In 1997, the company acquired 364 funeral locations, cemeteries and crematoria at a cost of $643 million. As of June 30, 1998, SRV had acquired, or agreed to acquire, 271 funeral service locations, 39 cemeteries and 12 crematoria, for an aggregate purchase price of $562 million. In addition, SRV has reached a definitive agreement to merge with Equity Corp. International (EQU), the nation's fourth largest publicly traded death care provider. The combination would generate $3 billion in annual revenues, and reunite the company with EQU, which was spun-off in 1990. EQU focuses on the rural market, while SRV concentrates on the metropolitan market.

Per Share Data ($)

(Year Ended Dec. 31)	1997	1996	1995	1994	1993	1992	1991	1990	1989	1988
Tangible Bk. Val.	4.85	3.64	3.51	2.04	2.60	1.71	1.93	2.31	3.17	2.54
Cash Flow	2.06	1.64	1.38	1.04	0.84	0.79	0.69	0.57	0.46	NM
Earnings	1.47	1.10	0.90	0.76	0.62	0.56	0.52	0.42	0.33	0.03
Dividends	0.28	0.24	0.22	0.21	0.20	0.19	0.19	0.19	0.17	0.08
Payout Ratio	19%	22%	24%	28%	32%	34%	39%	43%	54%	267%
Prices - High	38	31³/₄	22	14	13¹/₄	9³/₈	9¹/₄	8¹/₈	7³/₈	8⁵/₈
- Low	26⁷/₈	19¹/₂	13¹/₈	11¹/₄	9	7⁷/₈	6³/₄	4³/₈	4¹/₄	5¹/₄
P/E Ratio - High	26	29	24	19	21	17	18	19	23	NM
- Low	18	18	15	15	14	14	13	10	13	NM

Income Statement Analysis (Million $)

	1997	1996	1995	1994	1993	1992	1991	1990	1989	1988
Revs.	2,468	2,294	1,652	1,117	899	772	643	563	519	463
Oper. Inc.	778	671	510	341	257	217	169	143	124	40.0
Depr.	158	130	98.4	51.0	37.1	34.1	25.9	21.0	19.8	17.1
Int. Exp.	141	139	118	80.1	59.6	54.4	43.1	36.6	33.0	23.5
Pretax Inc.	580	414	294	219	173	139	109	99	85.0	6.0
Eff. Tax Rate	35%	36%	38%	40%	41%	38%	33%	36%	37%	22%
Net Inc.	375	265	184	131	103	86.5	73.4	63.5	53.6	4.5

Balance Sheet & Other Fin. Data (Million $)

	1997	1996	1995	1994	1993	1992	1991	1990	1989	1988
Cash	46.9	44.1	29.7	218	21.0	31.0	38.0	18.0	37.0	38.0
Curr. Assets	811	714	630	592	312	259	237	180	179	NA
Total Assets	10,307	8,870	7,664	5,162	3,683	2,611	2,123	1,654	1,601	1,872
Curr. Liab.	535	608	584	472	141	107	80.2	66.8	58.3	76.9
LT Debt	2,635	2,049	1,732	1,330	1,062	980	787	577	486	466
Common Eqty.	2,726	2,235	1,975	1,197	885	683	616	434	558	516
Total Cap.	6,062	4,984	4,145	2,937	2,094	1,762	1,472	1,073	1,094	1,054
Cap. Exp.	231	193	125	81.0	60.0	67.0	38.0	30.0	26.0	32.0
Cash Flow	532	395	282	182	140	121	99	81.2	66.5	NM
Curr. Ratio	1.5	1.8	1.1	1.3	2.2	2.4	2.9	2.7	3.1	NA
% LT Debt of Cap.	43.5	41.1	41.8	45.3	50.7	55.6	53.5	53.8	44.4	44.2
% Net Inc.of Revs.	15.2	11.6	11.1	11.7	11.5	11.2	11.4	11.3	10.3	1.0
% Ret. on Assets	3.9	3.2	2.9	2.8	3.1	3.6	3.7	4.0	3.1	NA
% Ret. on Equity	15.1	12.6	11.6	12.0	12.6	13.2	13.4	12.5	8.7	NA

Data as orig. reptd.; bef. results of disc. opers. and/or spec. items. Per share data adj. for stk. divs. as of ex-div. date. Bold denotes diluted EPS (FASB 128). E-Estimated. NA-Not Available. NM-Not Meaningful. NR-Not Ranked.

Office—1929 Allen Pkwy., Houston, TX 77019. **Tel**—(713) 522-5141. **Website**—http://www.sci-corp.com **Chrmn & CEO**—R. L. Waltrip. **Pres & COO**—L. W. Heiligbrodt. **SVP & CFO**—G. R. Champagne. **Secy**—J.M. Shelger **VP & Investor Contact**—Todd Matherne. **Dirs**—A. L. Coelho, J. Finkelstein, A. J. Foyt Jr., J. H. Greer, L. W. Heiligbrodt, B. D. Hunter, J. W. Mecom Jr., C. H. Morris Jr., E. H. Thornton Jr., R. L. Waltrip, W. B. Waltrip, E. E. Williams. **Transfer Agent & Registrar**—Society National Bank, Houston. **Incorporated**—in Texas in 1962. **Empl**— 24,072. **S&P Analyst:** Jordan Horoschak

Shared Medical Systems   2017B

NYSE Symbol **SMS**

In S&P 500

12-SEP-98

Industry:
Services (Computer Systems)

Summary: Shared Medical is a leading provider of computer-based information systems and related services to hospitals, clinics and physician groups.

S&P Opinion: Hold (★★★)	Recent Price • 55⅛	Yield • 1.5%
	52 Wk Range • 86½-51	12-Mo. P/E • 20.9

Quantitative Evaluations

Outlook
(1 Lowest—5 Highest)
• 3⁻

Fair Value
• 61⅜

Risk
• **Average**

Earn./Div. Rank
• **A-**

Technical Eval.
• **NA**

Rel. Strength Rank
(1 Lowest—99 Highest)
• 47

Insider Activity
• **NA**

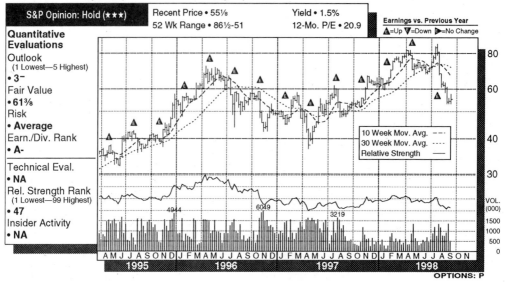

Earnings vs. Previous Year
▲=Up ▼=Down ▶=No Change

10 Week Mov. Avg. ---
30 Week Mov. Avg. ----
Relative Strength —

OPTIONS: P

Overview - 29-JUL-98

Revenue growth should be in the mid-teens in 1998, reflecting continued demand for SMS's products in the hospital systems market, and benefits from acquisitions. Revenues derived from hardware sales should remain somewhat flat, while service and system revenues should increase strongly. European business has performed below expectations recently, and could hamper overall growth. Nevertheless, we expect margins to improve, aided by volume efficiencies and well controlled costs. SMS's goal is for pretax margins to reach 11.7% to 12.0% in 1998, while its longer term target is 13% to 15%. Changes in the delivery of health care services, including the advent of managed care and the vertical integration of services at multiple treatment locations, will demand more complex and specific health care information systems. Earnings should benefit from the higher revenues and improved margins, and should grow about 20% in 1998.

Valuation - 29-JUL-98

The shares have risen nicely in 1998, on solid growth, widening margins, and prospects for improved international growth. Revenues rose 15% in 1997, and pretax margins reached 10.9%. We believe that the company can achieve its 1998 target of 14% service and system revenue growth. It is also likely that European operations will rebound somewhat in the second half of 1998, aided by recent acquisitions. The company's business backlog exceeded $2.1 billion at year-end 1997. The shares rightly command a premium valuation to the market P/E, reflecting above-market earnings growth, a steady revenue stream, and a conservative balance sheet. The company's customer retention rate exceeds 99%. However, with its premium valuation, we expect the stock only to perform in line with the market in coming months.

Key Stock Statistics

S&P EPS Est. 1998	2.82	Tang. Bk. Value/Share	14.08
P/E on S&P Est. 1998	19.6	Beta	1.06
S&P EPS Est. 1999	3.40	Shareholders	5,600
Dividend Rate/Share	0.84	Market cap. (B)	$ 1.5
Shs. outstg. (M)	26.5	Inst. holdings	74%
Avg. daily vol. (M)	0.184		

Value of $10,000 invested 5 years ago: $ 27,664

Fiscal Year Ending Dec. 31

	1998	1997	1996	1995	1994	1993
Revenues (Million $)						
1Q	255.5	209.9	170.3	145.3	125.2	117.2
2Q	257.0	213.4	191.0	155.3	132.6	124.2
3Q	—	224.7	186.9	169.2	138.8	123.7
4Q	—	248.2	219.2	180.8	154.2	136.2
Yr.	—	896.2	767.4	650.6	550.8	501.3
Earnings Per Share ($)						
1Q	**0.66**	0.56	0.45	0.41	0.37	0.33
2Q	**0.67**	0.57	0.47	0.41	0.37	0.34
3Q	E0.69	0.59	0.48	0.42	0.38	0.31
4Q	E0.80	**0.65**	0.55	0.44	0.39	0.37
Yr.	**E2.82**	**2.37**	1.95	1.68	1.51	1.35

Next earnings report expected: late October

Dividend Data (Dividends have been paid since 1977.)

Amount ($)	Date Decl.	Ex-Div. Date	Stock of Record	Payment Date
0.210	Sep. 11	Sep. 26	Sep. 30	Oct. 15 '97
0.210	Dec. 09	Dec. 29	Dec. 31	Jan. 15 '98
0.210	Mar. 09	Mar. 27	Mar. 31	Apr. 15 '98
0.210	Jun. 11	Jun. 26	Jun. 30	Jul. 15 '98

Business Summary - 29-JUL-98

Founded in 1969, Shared Medical Systems (SMS) is meeting the information needs of health care providers by providing computer-based information systems and related services mainly in North America and Europe. These systems and services include clinical, financial, patient management, electronic data interchange, managed care, management solutions and integrated multimedia solutions. SMS also provides system installation and support, consulting and customer education.

Despite a decline in the number of stand-alone acute-care hospital beds in recent years, the demand for health information systems has grown, because of consolidation in the health care industry, cost containment pressures, and increases in information requirements. SMS's customers include integrated health networks, multi-entity health corporations, community health information networks, hospitals, physician groups, clinics, and other health providers.

SMS's systems include clinical systems providing point-of-care data entry and access to clinical information; financial systems providing accounting for both hospitals and physicians; patient management systems to support functions such as admissions, outpatient visits and medical records; ambulatory care systems; management solutions, which provide information from clinical, financial and patient management systems;

physician information systems, providing information processing and administrative support; and integrated health network systems, which connect all points of care. SMS's Novius.ihn client/server health information system allows the flow of clinical, financial and demographic data throughout an integrated health network consisting of a variety of allied health care providers. The company also offers electronic data interchange services which facilitate the sharing and standardization of information between health providers and payers.

In January 1998, SMS acquired Data-Plan Software GmbH, a provider of client/server clinical, financial, and administrative health information services in Germany. The company also purchased the remaining 50% of Delta Health Systems which it did not own.

In March 1998, PeopleSoft, Inc. attempted to terminate a multi-year distribution agreement. SMS has filed for an injunction in connection with this move.

In February 1997, SMS acquired American Healthware Systems, Inc., a provider of financial information systems and facilities management services to New York health organizations. In November 1997, SMS teamed up with Cisco Systems, Inc. to provide high performance networking solutions to the health industry. The company also announced a joint venture with Orbis Broadcast Group to provide online health information and Internet services.

Per Share Data ($)

(Year Ended Dec. 31)	1997	1996	1995	1994	1993	1992	1991	1990	1989	1988
Tangible Bk. Val.	12.01	10.74	9.39	8.68	8.71	8.27	7.89	7.69	7.45	7.36
Cash Flow	3.87	3.54	3.23	2.62	2.45	2.32	2.39	2.22	1.84	2.28
Earnings	2.37	1.95	1.68	1.51	1.35	1.24	1.11	1.01	0.79	1.25
Dividends	0.84	0.84	0.84	0.84	0.84	0.84	0.84	0.84	0.84	0.81
Payout Ratio	35%	43%	50%	56%	62%	67%	76%	83%	106%	63%
Prices - High	66¾	72⅛	57⅝	34½	26	24⅜	23⅜	18⅜	19⅜	27⅛
- Low	36¾	42¼	30⅞	22⅛	17½	16⅞	13⅞	12	12	14⅜
P/E Ratio - High	28	37	34	23	19	20	21	18	25	22
- Low	16	22	18	15	13	14	13	12	15	12

Income Statement Analysis (Million $)

	1997	1996	1995	1994	1993	1992	1991	1990	1989	1988
Revs.	896	767	651	550	501	468	438	403	388	377
Oper. Inc.	140	118	105	84.0	78.0	69.0	69.0	57.0	51.0	69.0
Depr.	38.2	38.4	36.8	25.8	25.4	24.7	29.0	22.3	24.0	24.2
Int. Exp.	3.9	3.6	3.0	1.4	1.4	1.1	1.0	0.9	1.3	1.4
Pretax Inc.	97.5	76.4	65.2	57.5	51.7	45.0	39.5	33.8	27.0	45.0
Eff. Tax Rate	38%	38%	39%	39%	40%	37%	36%	33%	33%	35%
Net Inc.	60.4	47.0	39.8	35.1	31.0	28.4	25.3	22.7	18.1	29.4

Balance Sheet & Other Fin. Data (Million $)

	1997	1996	1995	1994	1993	1992	1991	1990	1989	1988
Cash	29.2	36.6	23.3	21.2	35.8	30.9	27.3	10.7	18.3	32.2
Curr. Assets	307	271	221	177	166	156	151	140	133	136
Total Assets	600	499	435	380	341	306	293	286	278	285
Curr. Liab.	218	168	133	117	92.8	87.9	82.0	82.2	75.1	60.2
LT Debt	16.3	15.4	17.0	5.0	6.4	2.3	4.2	4.4	4.8	7.7
Common Eqty.	328	281	249	219	198	187	177	172	168	169
Total Cap.	374	323	266	246	227	205	198	193	188	205
Cap. Exp.	27.0	28.2	18.8	20.3	24.9	18.4	21.6	22.6	22.5	24.1
Cash Flow	99	85.4	76.6	60.9	56.4	53.1	54.3	45.0	42.1	53.6
Curr. Ratio	1.4	1.6	1.7	1.5	1.8	1.8	1.8	1.7	1.8	2.3
% LT Debt of Cap.	4.4	4.8	6.4	2.0	2.8	1.1	2.1	2.3	2.6	3.8
% Net Inc.of Revs.	6.7	6.1	6.2	6.4	6.2	6.1	5.8	5.6	4.7	7.8
% Ret. on Assets	11.0	10.1	9.8	9.7	9.5	9.5	8.7	8.1	6.5	10.2
% Ret. on Equity	19.8	17.7	17.0	16.8	16.1	15.6	14.5	13.4	10.9	17.1

Data as orig. reptd.; bef. results of disc. opers. and/or spec. items. Per share data adj. for stk. divs. as of ex-div. date. Bold denotes diluted EPS (FASB 128). E-Estimated. NA-Not Available. NM-Not Meaningful. NR-Not Ranked.

Office—51 Valley Stream Parkway, Malvern, PA 19355. **Tel**—(610) 219-6300. **Website**—http://www.SMS.com **Chrmn**—R. J. Macaleer. **Pres & CEO**—M. S. Cadwell. **VP-Fin, Treas & Investor Contact**—Terrence W. Kyle. **Secy**—J. C. Kelly. **Dirs**—M. S. Cadwell, R. K. Denworth, Jr., F. W. DeTurk, R. J. Macaleer, J. S. Rubin, J. S. Weston, G. R. Wilensky. **Transfer Agent**—ChaseMellon Shareholder Services, Ridgefield Park, NJ. **Incorporated**—in Delaware in 1969. **Empl**— 4,826. **S&P Analyst:** Brian Goodstadt

Sherwin-Williams

2030

NYSE Symbol **SHW**

In S&P 500

14-SEP-98

Industry: Retail (Building Supplies)

Summary: Sherwin-Williams, the largest U.S. producer of paints, is also a major seller of wallcoverings and related products.

S&P Opinion: Avoid (★★)	Recent Price • 22¼	Yield • 2.0%
	52 Wk Range • 37⅞-19⅜	12-Mo. P/E • 14.4

Quantitative Evaluations

Outlook
(1 Lowest—5 Highest)
• **4**

Fair Value
• **29⅞**

Risk
• **Low**

Earn./Div. Rank
• **A+**

Technical Eval.
• **Bearish** since 8/98

Rel. Strength Rank
(1 Lowest—99 Highest)
• **25**

Insider Activity
• **Neutral**

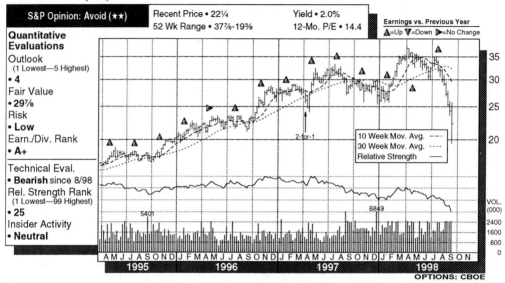

Earnings vs. Previous Year
▲=Up ▼=Down ■=No Change

10 Week Mov. Avg. - - -
30 Week Mov. Avg. ----
Relative Strength —

OPTIONS: CBOE

Overview - 16-SEP-98

Sherwin-Williams has expanded rapidly in recent years, purchasing Thompson Minwax in early 1997, following the 1996 acquisition of Pratt & Lambert. After initial difficulties with the integration of the acquired business, the company appears to be back on track. We expect mid-teens sales growth in 1998, reflecting 55 net new stores, continued strength in housing starts, and new product introductions. The paints segment plans 20 new products, including a new line of volatile organic compounds (VOC)-compliant interior stains, sealers and varnishes. The coatings segment will introduce new exterior and interior coatings product lines under the Dutch Boy label. Martha Stewart Everyday Colors, a recently launched line of paints, was rolled out in Sears stores in March 1998, following a successful launch in Kmart stores in 1997. SHW will also develop its powder technologies, a potentially high growth area.

Valuation - 16-SEP-98

We recently lowered our opinion of Sherwin-Williams to underperform from market perform due to reduced earnings visibility following news that third quarter results would be below expectations, primarily reflecting weakness in the do-it-yourself coatings segment. Prior to the announcement, the coatings segment had experienced a decline in sales in recent periods, primarily due to the loss of about $60 million of annual sales to Home Depot's Northeast division beginning with the 1997 third quarter. Still, sales comparisons for the coatings segment should improve in 1998's second half, as the lost sales are anniversaried. However, margins for the coatings segment may come under pressure later this year as raw material costs, particularly titanium dioxide, are expected to rise. Although SHW plans to pass on the increase to consumers through selective price hikes, market forces may dictate otherwise.

Key Stock Statistics

S&P EPS Est. 1998	1.55	Tang. Bk. Value/Share	1.24
P/E on S&P Est. 1998	14.4	Beta	1.26
Dividend Rate/Share	0.45	Shareholders	11,900
Shs. outstg. (M)	172.9	Market cap. (B)	$ 3.8
Avg. daily vol. (M)	0.644	Inst. holdings	63%

Value of $10,000 invested 5 years ago: $ 15,867

Fiscal Year Ending Dec. 31

	1998	1997	1996	1995	1994	1993
Revenues (Million $)						
1Q	1,104	1,070	857.8	716.8	639.2	618.3
2Q	1,378	1,373	1,145	904.7	880.5	824.2
3Q	—	1,347	1,171	911.4	876.7	838.8
4Q	—	1,091	958.8	740.9	703.6	668.0
Yr.	—	4,881	4,133	3,274	3,100	2,949
Earnings Per Share ($)						
1Q	**0.14**	**0.13**	0.12	0.11	0.09	0.08
2Q	**0.57**	**0.54**	0.48	0.42	0.40	0.34
3Q	**E0.57**	**0.57**	0.51	0.43	0.41	0.36
4Q	**E0.27**	**0.26**	0.23	0.20	0.18	0.15
Yr.	**E1.55**	**1.50**	1.33	1.17	1.07	0.93

Next earnings report expected: mid October

Dividend Data (Dividends have been paid since 1979.)

Amount ($)	Date Decl.	Ex-Div. Date	Stock of Record	Payment Date
0.100	Oct. 17	Nov. 12	Nov. 14	Nov. 28 '97
0.113	Feb. 04	Feb. 26	Mar. 02	Mar. 16 '98
0.113	Apr. 22	May. 20	May. 22	Jun. 05 '98
0.113	Jul. 22	Aug. 19	Aug. 21	Sep. 04 '98

Business Summary - 16-SEP-98

With several acquisitions over the past two years, Sherwin-Williams continues its quest to become "America's Paint Company." Already the largest producer and distributor of paints and varnishes in the U.S. and third largest worldwide, the company has more than 2,150 paint stores operating in 48 states, Puerto Rico and Canada. The U.S. paint industry has over $14.5 billion in revenues, and sells 1.2 billion gallons of paint annually. However, annual unit growth has been a sluggish 1.5% to 2.0% over the past few years. With that in mind, SHW's strategy is clearly to expand its business through acquisitions in the fragmented paint industry. The largest acquisitions to date include Pratt & Lambert United, Inc. (1996), enhancing SHW's access to the independent dealer and mass merchandising distribution channels in the U.S.; and Thompson Minwax Holding Corp. (1997), providing leading brands in the stain and varnish category.

The company has been selling paint for 130 years, and has consistently been on the leading edge of technology in the paint industry. In April 1996, the American Chemical Society awarded SHW its prestigious National Historic Chemical Landmarks designation for a milestone technological innovation. This actually took place during World War II, when a team of SHW chemists created the first durable, washable waterborne paint, called Kem-Tone, which led to the expansion of do-it-yourself painting in the post-war period. Today, with the consistent introduction of new products, the company is continuing to meet technological challenges. In 1997, SHW posted its 19th consecutive year of earnings and dividend growth, and continued to gain market share.

SHW consists of two main business segments: Paint Stores (53% of sales in 1997; 59% in 1996) and Coatings (46%; 42%). In the Paint Store segment, the company sells paint, wallcoverings, floor coverings, window treatments, industrial maintenance products and finishes, and assorted tools. These products are marketed to the do-it-yourself, professional painting, industrial maintenance and home building markets, as well as to manufacturers of products that require a factory finish. This segment is still expanding. In 1997, the company opened 39 net new stores, and it expects to open 50 to 60 more in 1998. The Coatings segment manufactures, distributes and sells paints, varnishes, lacquers and allied products under the brand names Sherwin-Williams, Dutch Boy, Kem-Tone, Martin Senour, Cuprinol, Acme, Krylon and others. Within this segment, there are four divisions, each one selling the company's products to different market segments: Consumer Brands, Automotive, Diversified Brands, and Transportation Services.

Per Share Data ($)

(Year Ended Dec. 31)	1997	1996	1995	1994	1993	1992	1991	1990	1989	1988
Tangible Bk. Val.	0.86	2.19	3.19	5.58	5.18	4.40	4.13	3.67	3.79	3.41
Cash Flow	2.48	1.08	0.77	1.50	1.31	1.19	1.06	1.00	0.89	0.80
Earnings	1.50	1.33	1.17	1.07	0.93	0.81	0.72	0.70	0.63	0.57
Dividends	0.50	0.35	0.32	0.28	0.25	0.22	0.21	0.19	0.17	0.16
Payout Ratio	33%	26%	27%	25%	27%	27%	29%	27%	28%	27%
Prices - High	33⅜	28⅞	20¾	17⅞	18¾	16½	13⅞	10½	9	7⅞
- Low	24⅛	19½	16	14¾	15	12¾	8⅞	7½	6¼	6
P/E Ratio - High	22	22	18	17	20	20	19	15	14	14
- Low	16	15	14	14	16	16	12	11	10	10

Income Statement Analysis (Million $)

	1997	1996	1995	1994	1993	1992	1991	1990	1989	1988
Revs.	4,881	4,133	3,274	3,100	2,949	2,748	2,541	2,267	2,123	1,950
Oper. Inc.	613	495	384	383	340	310	275	235	207	174
Depr.	90.2	76.0	63.0	73.7	68.8	66.3	59.9	51.5	44.3	39.1
Int. Exp.	80.8	25.0	3.0	3.2	6.5	8.6	12.3	10.9	13.1	14.3
Pretax Inc.	427	375	318	299	264	226	199	187	170	163
Eff. Tax Rate	39%	39%	37%	38%	38%	36%	36%	35%	36%	38%
Net Inc.	261	229	201	187	165	145	128	123	109	101

Balance Sheet & Other Fin. Data (Million $)

	1997	1996	1995	1994	1993	1992	1991	1990	1989	1988
Cash	3.5	1.9	269	251	270	168	101	99	202	154
Curr. Assets	1,532	1,416	1,239	1,189	1,151	988	887	824	846	766
Total Assets	4,036	2,995	2,141	1,962	1,915	1,730	1,612	1,504	1,375	1,259
Curr. Liab.	1,116	1,051	619	597	568	506	488	432	433	378
LT Debt	844	143	24.0	20.0	38.0	60.0	72.0	138	105	130
Common Eqty.	1,592	1,401	1,212	1,053	1,033	906	868	764	668	601
Total Cap.	2,436	1,544	1,236	1,074	1,089	982	1,040	1,000	866	823
Cap. Exp.	164	123	108	78.7	63.0	68.8	51.0	64.4	66.9	71.6
Cash Flow	351	305	264	260	234	NA	188	174	153	140
Curr. Ratio	1.4	1.4	2.0	2.0	2.0	2.0	1.8	1.9	2.0	2.0
% LT Debt of Cap.	34.6	9.3	1.9	1.9	3.5	6.1	6.9	13.8	12.1	15.7
% Net Inc.of Revs.	5.3	5.5	6.1	6.0	5.6	NA	5.0	5.4	5.1	5.2
% Ret. on Assets	7.4	8.9	9.8	9.8	9.1	8.6	8.2	8.5	8.3	8.5
% Ret. on Equity	17.4	17.5	17.7	18.3	17.0	16.2	15.6	17.1	17.2	17.7

Data as orig. reptd.; bef. results of disc. opers. and/or spec. items. Per share data adj. for stk. divs. as of ex-div. date. Bold denotes diluted EPS (FASB 128). E-Estimated. NA-Not Available. NM-Not Meaningful. NR-Not Ranked.

Office—101 Prospect Ave., N.W., Cleveland, OH 44115-1075. **Tel**—(216) 566-2000. **Website**—www.sherwin.com **Chrmn & CEO**—J. G. Breen. **Pres & COO**—T. A. Commes. **SVP-Fin, Treas & CFO**—L. J. Pitorak. **VP & Secy**—L. E. Stellato. **VP & Investor Contact**—Conway G. Ivy. **Dirs**—J. M. Biggar, J. G. Breen, D. E. Collins, T. A. Commes, D. E. Evans, R. W. Mahoney, W. G. Mitchell, A. M. Mixon, III, C. E. Moll, H. O. Petrauskas, R. K. Smucker. **Transfer Agent & Registrar**—Bank of New York, NYC. **Incorporated**—in Ohio in 1884. **Empl**—25,000. **S&P Analyst:** Efraim Levy

Sigma-Aldrich Corp. 5216

Nasdaq Symbol **SIAL**

In S&P 500

12-SEP-98

Industry: Chemicals (Specialty)

Summary: This company makes and sells a wide range of biochemicals, organic chemicals, chromatography products and diagnostic reagents. It also produces metal components.

S&P Opinion: Accumulate (★★★★)	Recent Price • 30 — Yield • 0.9%
	52 Wk Range • 42¾-25¾ — 12-Mo. P/E • 18.1

Quantitative Evaluations

Outlook (1 Lowest—5 Highest)
• **1**

Fair Value
• **19⅞**

Risk
• **Low**

Earn./Div. Rank
• **A+**

Technical Eval.
• **Bearish** since 7/98

Rel. Strength Rank (1 Lowest—99 Highest)
• **82**

Insider Activity
• **Neutral**

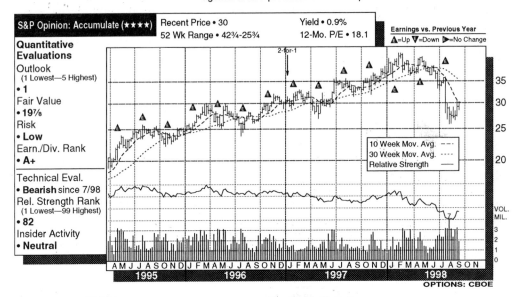

Earnings vs. Previous Year
▲=Up ▼=Down ▶=No Change

10 Week Mov. Avg. ---
30 Week Mov. Avg. ·····
Relative Strength —

OPTIONS: CBOE

Overview - 19-AUG-98

S&P projects that sales will increase about 7% to 8% for SIAL in 1998, reflecting continued good growth in research and fine chemicals (about 75% of total sales), despite a slowdown in some Asian and European markets. The introduction of new products and applications, and further geographical expansion (SIAL opened offices in four countries during 1997), will continue to spur growth. Research chemicals sales will benefit from the increased customer contact of a new sales force that supplements SIAL's existing catalog business, but diagnostic sales may remain lower, on reduced sales of coagulation analyzers. Currency exchange rates will also continue to be modestly unfavorable. Margins for the chemicals segment will narrow, due to higher spending for information systems and product development. For the rest of 1998, the metals segment should grow at a faster rate than the first half's 4.4%, reflecting stronger demand for telecommunications products, continued good construction markets, and expanded manufacturing and distribution capacity. Metal margins should show some recovery with the ending of startup costs for a new plant in Texas. The tax rate is projected at 34.0%.

Valuation - 19-AUG-98

Following a 27% increase in 1997, the stock was recently down nearly 30% in 1998, in response to disappointing earnings. The shares were trading at a modest discount to the P/E of the overall market, below historical levels. We continue to feel that the shares are a worthwhile investment to accumulate, in view of our projections for the company's long-term growth of 10% to 12% a year (excluding possible acquisitions). In addition, dividends have been raised each year since 1975.

Key Stock Statistics

S&P EPS Est. 1998	1.66	Tang. Bk. Value/Share	11.24
P/E on S&P Est. 1998	18.1	Beta	0.43
S&P EPS Est. 1999	1.85	Shareholders	2,100
Dividend Rate/Share	0.28	Market cap. (B)	$ 3.0
Shs. outstg. (M)	100.6	Inst. holdings	68%
Avg. daily vol. (M)	0.639		

Value of $10,000 invested 5 years ago: $ 10,955

Fiscal Year Ending Dec. 31

	1998	1997	1996	1995	1994	1993
Revenues (Million $)						
1Q	306.2	279.1	262.4	244.8	208.5	180.0
2Q	294.6	278.6	258.8	243.3	212.4	183.8
3Q	—	286.1	255.8	239.1	217.4	190.8
4Q	—	283.4	257.5	232.6	212.9	184.8
Yr.	—	1,127	1,035	959.8	851.2	739.4
Earnings Per Share ($)						
1Q	**0.43**	**0.40**	0.37	0.33	0.30	0.27
2Q	**0.41**	**0.40**	0.37	0.34	0.27	0.27
3Q	**E0.41**	**0.41**	0.37	0.33	0.27	0.27
4Q	**E0.41**	**0.41**	0.37	0.33	0.27	0.27
Yr.	**E1.66**	**1.62**	1.48	1.32	1.10	1.07

Next earnings report expected: NA

Dividend Data (Dividends have been paid since 1970.)

Amount ($)	Date Decl.	Ex-Div. Date	Stock of Record	Payment Date
0.070	Nov. 11	Dec. 11	Dec. 15	Jan. 02 '98
0.070	Feb. 17	Feb. 26	Mar. 02	Mar. 16 '98
0.070	May. 05	May. 28	Jun. 01	Jun. 15 '98
0.070	Aug. 11	Aug. 28	Sep. 01	Sep. 15 '98

A Division of The McGraw-Hill Companies

Business Summary - 19-AUG-98

Well known through its extensive catalog business, Sigma-Aldrich is the world's largest provider of research chemicals, diagnostic reagents, chromatography products and related products. It also manufactures metal components for strut, cable tray, pipe support and telecommunication systems and electrical enclosures. SIAL intends to grow through the continued global expansion of its chemicals businesses by entering new countries (sales offices were opened in Argentina, Ireland, Greece, and Finland in 1997), as well as acquisitions, joint ventures and partnerships related to all current product lines. Segment contributions in 1997 were:

	Sales	Profits
Chemical products	80%	88%
Metal products	20%	12%

Foreign operations accounted for 37% of sales and 11% of pretax income in 1997. In 1997, 55% of sales of chemical products were to customers outside the U.S.

The company distributes 83,000 chemical products for use primarily in research and development, in the diagnosis of disease and as specialty chemicals for manufacturing. In laboratory applications, its products are used in biochemistry, synthetic chemistry, quality control and testing, immunology, hematology, pharmacology, microbiology, neurology and endocrinology and in studies of life processes. In June 1997, SIAL formed a 75%-owned laboratory chemicals partnership comprising Allied Signal Inc.'s Riedel-de Haen unit, which has annual sales of $40 million. Diagnostic products are used to detect heart, liver and kidney diseases and metabolic disorders. Through a partnership with Amelung (a German manufacturer), the company also offers analyzers that measure blood clotting. Supelco Inc. (acquired in 1993) is a global supplier of chromatography products used in chemical research and production.

SIAL also offers about 75,000 esoteric chemicals (less than 1% of total sales) as a special service to customers that screen them for potential applications.

SIAL itself produces about 35,000 products, which accounted for 46% of 1997 net sales of chemical products. The remainder were purchased from outside sources.

In the metals business, B-Line Systems makes and markets a line of products for use in electrical, mechanical and telecommunication applications. These products include strut, cable tray and pipe support systems and telecommunication racks and cable runways. Circle AW Products (acquired in 1993) produces enclosure boxes used to protect electric meters, fuse and circuit breaker boards and electrical panels. Electronic Metal Products, a manufacturer of electronics enclosures, was acquired during 1996.

Per Share Data ($)

(Year Ended Dec. 31)	1997	1996	1995	1994	1993	1992	1991	1990	1989	1988
Tangible Bk. Val.	10.56	9.42	8.27	7.02	5.93	5.14	4.43	3.71	3.02	2.47
Cash Flow	2.08	1.93	1.73	1.48	1.38	1.24	1.06	0.95	0.81	0.70
Earnings	1.62	1.48	1.32	1.10	1.07	0.96	0.80	0.72	0.65	0.57
Dividends	0.26	0.23	0.19	0.17	0.11	0.13	0.11	0.10	0.09	0.08
Payout Ratio	16%	16%	14%	15%	11%	14%	14%	14%	14%	14%
Prices - High	41¹/₈	32¹/₈	25⁷/₈	27⁵/₈	29	29⁵/₈	26³/₄	18	14⁷/₈	12⁷/₈
- Low	26⁷/₈	23³/₄	16¹/₄	15	22¹/₄	20³/₄	13⁷/₈	12¹/₂	11	10
P/E Ratio - High	25	22	20	25	27	31	33	25	23	22
- Low	17	16	12	14	21	22	17	17	17	17

Income Statement Analysis (Million $)

	1997	1996	1995	1994	1993	1992	1991	1990	1989	1988
Revs.	1,127	1,035	960	851	739	654	589	529	441	375
Oper. Inc.	302	277	247	210	198	180	158	142	123	105
Depr.	48.1	45.2	40.9	36.7	29.7	27.4	25.8	23.6	16.1	12.6
Int. Exp.	0.7	1.8	1.6	2.9	2.4	5.4	8.0	8.3	6.8	3.8
Pretax Inc.	253	230	204	170	166	147	124	110	100	89.0
Eff. Tax Rate	34%	36%	36%	35%	35%	35%	36%	35%	36%	36%
Net Inc.	166	148	132	110	107	95.5	79.8	71.2	64.0	56.5

Balance Sheet & Other Fin. Data (Million $)

	1997	1996	1995	1994	1993	1992	1991	1990	1989	1988
Cash	46.2	104	84.0	9.7	10.3	44.9	28.1	6.6	9.7	5.7
Curr. Assets	707	667	610	502	451	416	391	341	284	233
Total Assets	1,244	1,100	985	852	753	616	597	546	472	360
Curr. Liab.	119	110	108	105	111	66.2	70.9	92.9	99	88.2
LT Debt	0.6	3.8	13.8	14.5	17.3	18.7	69.3	70.8	61.5	15.7
Common Eqty.	1,073	942	825	700	591	512	441	368	299	244
Total Cap.	1,061	946	839	714	608	543	520	448	367	265
Cap. Exp.	109	93.8	60.2	72.0	102	30.9	26.1	32.5	51.7	35.6
Cash Flow	214	193	173	147	137	123	106	95.0	80.0	69.0
Curr. Ratio	5.9	6.0	5.6	4.8	4.0	6.3	5.5	3.7	2.9	2.6
% LT Debt of Cap.	0.0	0.4	1.6	2.0	2.8	3.5	13.3	15.8	16.7	5.9
% Net Inc.of Revs.	14.7	14.3	13.7	13.0	14.5	14.6	13.5	13.5	14.5	15.0
% Ret. on Assets	14.2	14.2	14.3	13.7	15.6	15.7	14.0	14.0	15.3	17.5
% Ret. on Equity	16.4	16.7	17.3	17.1	19.4	20.0	19.7	21.3	23.5	25.7

Data as orig. reptd.; bef. results of disc. opers. and/or spec. items. Per share data adj. for stk. divs. as of ex-div. date. Bold denotes diluted EPS (FASB 128). E-Estimated. NA-Not Available. NM-Not Meaningful. NR-Not Ranked.

Office—3050 Spruce St., St. Louis, MO 63103. **Tel**—(314) 771-5765; (800) 521-8956. **E-mail**—sig-ald@sial.com **Website**—http://www.sial.com/ sig-ald **Chrmn & CEO**—C. T. Cori. **Pres & COO**—D. R. Harvey. **VP & Secy**—T. M. Tallarico. **VP & CFO**—P. A. Gleich. **Treas & Investor Contact**—Kirk A. Richter. **Dirs**—C. T. Cori, N. V. Fedoroff, D. R. Harvey, D. M. Kipnis, A. E. Newman, W. C. O'Neil Jr., J. W. Sandweiss, D. D. Spatz, T. N. Urban. **Transfer Agent**—Harris Trust and Savings Bank, Chicago. **Incorporated**—in Delaware in 1975. **Empl**—6,666. **S&P Analyst:** Richard O'Reilly, CFA

STANDARD &POOR'S
STOCK REPORTS

Silicon Graphics

2039

NYSE Symbol **SGI**

In S&P 500

12-SEP-98

Industry: Computers (Hardware)

Summary: This company manufactures workstations, servers and supercomputers that incorporate interactive 3-D graphics, digital media and multiprocessing technologies.

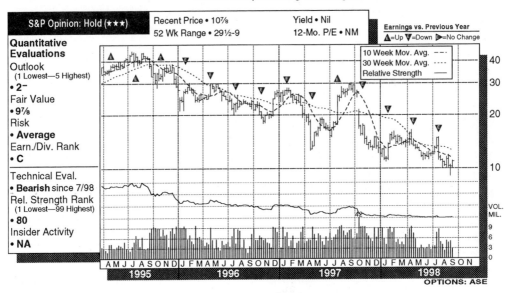

S&P Opinion: Hold (★★★)	Recent Price • 10⅞ 52 Wk Range • 29½-9

Yield • Nil
12-Mo. P/E • NM

Quantitative Evaluations

Outlook
(1 Lowest—5 Highest)
• **2⁻**

Fair Value
• **9⅞**

Risk
• **Average**

Earn./Div. Rank
• **C**

Technical Eval.
• **Bearish** since 7/98

Rel. Strength Rank
(1 Lowest—99 Highest)
• **80**

Insider Activity
• **NA**

Earnings vs. Previous Year
▲=Up ▼=Down ▶=No Change

10 Week Mov. Avg. ---
30 Week Mov. Avg. ·····
Relative Strength —

OPTIONS: ASE

Overview - 27-JUL-98

We project FY 99 (Jun.) revenues will be roughly flat with those of FY 98. First half results will continue to be challenged by the stiff competition in SGI's workstation stronghold, as NT Workstations (based on Intel microprocessors and Microsoft's Windows NT operating system) have proved overwhelming to SGI's results. However, SGI's product offering in this area should begin to benefit results in the second half of the year. In addition, recent results have shown a solid improvement in demand for SGI's servers. We project gross margins of around 42% for FY 99, with improvement in the second half. SGI has cautioned that its gross margins at least in the near term will also be challenged by low-margin supercomputer sales. SGI is targeting lower operating expenses, helped by several rounds of restructuring programs. We project FY 99 earnings per share of $0.10.

Valuation - 27-JUL-98

We continue to recommend holding SGI. The shares fell dramatically after the company preannounced a large and unexpected operating loss in the first quarter of FY 98. SGI's EPS consistency was believed to have improved, based on the strength of its FY 97 fourth quarter, when both revenue growth and gross margins far exceeded expectations. Losses since then have shown that SGI has not yet turned the corner on execution. The shares recovered briefly on the naming of well-regarded former Hewlett-Packard computer unit head Richard Belluzzo as chairman and CEO, replacing SGI's longtime CEO, Ed McCracken, who resigned. Based on current valuation, we see little downside risk in the stock, and see upside potential, given planned new products and new management. We thus recommend holding the shares.

Key Stock Statistics

S&P EPS Est. 1999	0.10	Tang. Bk. Value/Share	10.18
P/E on S&P Est. 1999	NM	Beta	1.06
Dividend Rate/Share	Nil	Shareholders	9,800
Shs. outstg. (M)	188.8	Market cap. (B)	$ 2.1
Avg. daily vol. (M)	0.928	Inst. holdings	52%

Value of $10,000 invested 5 years ago: $ 7,641

Fiscal Year Ending Jun. 30

	1998	1997	1996	1995	1994	1993
Revenues (Million $)						
1Q	768.0	765.6	595.3	448.5	301.6	231.1
2Q	850.8	825.3	671.7	549.6	370.4	270.2
3Q	708.3	909.4	676.9	577.0	376.3	270.7
4Q	773.6	1,162	977.4	653.2	433.3	319.3
Yr.	3,101	3,663	2,921	2,228	1,482	1,091
Earnings Per Share ($)						
1Q	-0.31	-0.13	0.33	0.26	0.17	0.10
2Q	-0.17	-0.07	0.31	0.34	0.24	0.15
3Q	-0.81	0.06	0.31	0.38	0.23	0.14
4Q	-1.17	0.56	-0.30	0.30	0.28	0.21
Yr.	-2.47	0.43	0.65	1.28	0.91	0.60

Next earnings report expected: NA

Dividend Data

No cash dividends have been paid. The shares were split two for one in 1993 and 1992.

A Division of The McGraw-Hill Companies

Business Summary - 27-JUL-98

Silicon Graphics (SGI) computers created the dinosaurs used to make Jurassic Park. The Silicon Graphics family of workstation, server and supercomputer systems incorporates interactive three-dimensional graphics, digital media and multiprocessing supercomputing technologies.

Formerly, all SGI computers used MIPS RISC microprocessors, developed by its MIPS Technologies subsidiary (acquired in 1992), rather than Intel Corp.'s CISC microprocessors, and used SGI's UNIX operating system, IRIX, instead of Microsoft's popular Windows NT. However, in April 1998, SGI announced a dual platform strategy. Under a strategic arrangement with Intel, SGI will also provide, beginning in the second half of 1998, workstations based on Intel architecture and Windows NT. In addition, both Intel and SGI will work further on 64-bit systems, as Intel's Merced chip becomes available in 1999 and SGI ports IRIX to Merced.

This strategy is the latest effort to improve SGI's competitive market position after a string of disappointing earnings results. Partly at fault was that most of SGI's product line had undergone a significant product transition in a short period of time. In October 1996, SGI announced the new O2, Origin and Onyx2 families, and, in January 1997, it announced the Octane workstation line, thus replacing a large portion of its product line.

SGI's servers and high-performance computing systems (primarily the Origin, POWER CHALLENGE, CHALLENGE, Onyx and Cray families) account for about 60% of revenues. Servers are general-purpose computers with the same computational performance as workstations, but without graphics capabilities. SGI's supercomputing servers, introduced in 1994, are meant to replace or augment aging mainframes. SGI acquired Cray Research, the world's leading provider of advanced computers, in 1996, for $576 million cash and 7 million common shares. Cray's business model introduced a new dynamic to SGI, as Cray's products have much longer sales cycles than those of SGI.

Workstations provide 40% of SGI's revenues (including the O2, Indy and Indigo2 families). Workstations are used primarily by technical, scientific and creative professionals to analyze, develop and display complex 3-D objects. While SGI has benefited from its niche position in graphics, personal computers have emerged as competitors. Intel's high performance Pentium chips and graphics accelerator chips combined with Windows NT have raised the graphics performance of PCs, and their ability to display 3-D.

In April 1998, SGI announced that its MIPS Technologies subsidiary would offer up to 20% of its outstanding shares in an initial public offering. Proceeds from the offering are expected to benefit SGI's FY99 September quarter results.

Per Share Data ($)

(Year Ended Jun. 30)	1998	1997	1996	1995	1994	1993	1992	1991	1990	1989
Tangible Bk. Val.	NA	10.18	9.62	8.28	6.37	4.56	3.60	3.97	3.02	2.43
Cash Flow	NA	2.37	1.78	1.89	1.45	0.97	-0.54	0.68	0.68	0.39
Earnings	-2.47	0.43	0.65	1.28	0.91	0.60	-1.09	0.36	0.42	0.17
Dividends	Nil	Nil	Nil	Nil	Nil	Nil	Nil	Nil	Nil	Nil
Payout Ratio	Nil	Nil	Nil	Nil	Nil	Nil	Nil	Nil	Nil	Nil
Prices - High	16½	30⅜	30⅜	45⅝	33⅛	24¾	14⅞	12¼	10¼	7⅜
- Low	10⅞	11⅝	17⅞	26⅞	18¾	11¾	7⅛	5⅝	4½	3⅝
P/E Ratio - High	NM	70	47	36	36	41	NM	33	24	44
- Low	NM	27	28	21	21	20	NM	15	11	21

Income Statement Analysis (Million $)

	1998	1997	1996	1995	1994	1993	1992	1991	1990	1989
Revs.	NA	3,663	2,921	2,228	1,482	1,091	867	550	420	264
Oper. Inc.	NA	477	475	436	277	180	88.2	74.8	69.3	29.7
Depr.	NA	354	198	107	84.2	54.8	63.4	31.3	22.3	15.1
Int. Exp.	NA	24.8	22.4	18.2	8.3	2.9	2.8	3.2	5.6	2.3
Pretax Inc.	NA	98.2	185	317	198	125	-102	48.0	48.0	16.0
Eff. Tax Rate	NA	20%	40%	29%	29%	30%	NM	31%	33%	30%
Net Inc.	NA	78.6	115	225	141	88.0	-117	33.0	32.0	11.0

Balance Sheet & Other Fin. Data (Million $)

	1998	1997	1996	1995	1994	1993	1992	1991	1990	1989
Cash	NA	287	295	516	401	155	183	196	86.0	94.0
Curr. Assets	NA	2,316	2,096	1,509	1,024	676	578	480	298	238
Total Assets	NA	3,345	3,158	2,207	1,519	946	758	642	364	291
Curr. Liab.	NA	106	1,101	573	356	268	217	116	83.0	46.0
LT Debt	NA	419	381	287	230	26.0	27.3	27.8	36.4	87.8
Common Eqty.	NA	1,822	1,658	1,329	887	600	446	329	210	157
Total Cap.	NA	2,258	2,057	1,633	1,151	660	507	523	281	245
Cap. Exp.	NA	215	189	148	89.4	83.6	67.0	47.2	29.6	23.3
Cash Flow	NA	432	312	332	224	142	-60.3	62.5	54.3	26.6
Curr. Ratio	NA	2.1	1.9	2.6	2.8	2.5	2.7	4.1	3.6	5.1
% LT Debt of Cap.	NA	18.6	18.5	17.5	20.0	3.9	5.4	5.3	13.0	35.9
% Net Inc.of Revs.	NA	2.1	3.9	10.0	9.5	8.0	NM	6.0	7.7	4.4
% Ret. on Assets	NA	2.4	4.3	11.9	11.1	10.0	NM	6.1	9.5	4.6
% Ret. on Equity	NA	4.5	7.7	20.1	18.3	16.3	NM	10.8	16.9	7.6

Data as orig. reptd.; bef. results of disc. opers. and/or spec. items. Per share data adj. for stk. divs. as of ex-div. date. Bold denotes diluted EPS (FASB 128). E-Estimated. NA-Not Available. NM-Not Meaningful. NR-Not Ranked.

Office—2011 N. Shoreline Blvd., Mountain View, CA 94039-7311. **Tel**—(415) 960-1980. **Website**—http://www.sgi.com **Chrmn & CEO**—R. E. Belluzzo. **SVP, Corp. Operations**—W. L. Kelly. **VP & CFO**—S. J. Gomo. **Investor Contact**—Michael Look. **Dirs**—R. E. Belluzzo, R. R. Bishop, A. F. Jacobson, C. R. Kramlich, R. A. Lutz, E. R. McCracken, J. A. McDivitt, L. Shapiro, R. B. Shapiro, J. G. Treybig. **Transfer Agent & Registrar**—Boston EquiServe, LP. **Incorporated**—in California in 1981; reincorporated in Delaware in 1990. **Empl**— 10,930. **S&P Analyst:** Megan Graham Hackett

SLM Holding

1965H

NYSE Symbol **SLM**

In S&P 500

12-SEP-98 **Industry:** Financial (Diversified)

Summary: This company is the leading U.S. provider of post-secondary educational financial services.

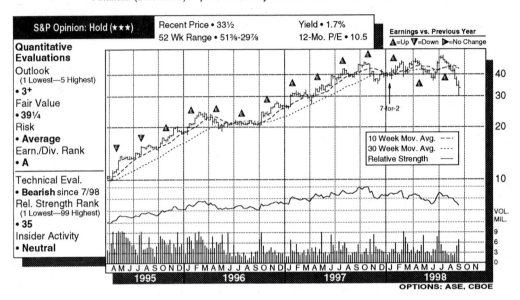

S&P Opinion: Hold (★★★)	Recent Price • 33½ 52 Wk Range • 51⅜-29⅞	Yield • 1.7% 12-Mo. P/E • 10.5

Earnings vs. Previous Year
▲=Up ▼=Down ▶=No Change

Quantitative Evaluations

Outlook
(1 Lowest—5 Highest)
• **3+**

Fair Value
• **39¼**

Risk
• **Average**

Earn./Div. Rank
• **A**

Technical Eval.
• **Bearish** since 7/98

Rel. Strength Rank
(1 Lowest—99 Highest)
• **35**

Insider Activity
• **Neutral**

7-for-2

10 Week Mov. Avg. – – –
30 Week Mov. Avg. ⋯⋯
Relative Strength ——

VOL.
MIL.

1995   1996   1997   1998

OPTIONS: ASE, CBOE

Overview - 17-JUL-98

Earnings are expected to improve in 1999. Student loan purchases could grow to $9.0 billion, from the $8.0 billion expected for 1998, reflecting greater penetration of the school market, as well as growth in the size of the overall market, partly offset by the company's exit from the loan consolidation business. Margins on student loans are likely to be lower. The outlook for floor income, or income that SLM realizes on certain loans in a low rate environment, is uncertain, but will depend on the interest rate environment. Warehousing advances should decline, as the company has chosen to de-emphasize this low-margin business. Flat income from loan securitization is anticipated. Considerable cost savings are expected from staff reductions in servicing and technology areas. Credit losses should remain negligible, because nearly all of SLM's student loans are backed directly or indirectly by the government. EPS should continue to benefit from share repurchases.

Valuation - 17-JUL-98

The stock is expected to be an average performer for the foreseeable future. Although the shares were recently trading at a P/E ratio well below the market average, we have several concerns about SLM. First, it is not clear whether the company would be successful in generating healthy returns in any new lines of business it chose to enter. Second, the pending reauthorization of the Higher Education Act means that Congress is likely to reduce margins for student loan lenders and holders on the order of some 0.30%. Finally, with a large percentage of earnings coming from gains on loan sales, as opposed to more recurring sources, the quality of the company's earnings is not as high as that of some other financial firms.

Key Stock Statistics

S&P EPS Est. 1998	3.40	Tang. Bk. Value/Share	3.76
P/E on S&P Est. 1998	9.9	Beta	1.69
S&P EPS Est. 1999	3.80	Shareholders	25,000
Dividend Rate/Share	0.56	Market cap. (B)	$ 5.6
Shs. outstg. (M)	167.5	Inst. holdings	92%
Avg. daily vol. (M)	0.837		

Value of $10,000 invested 5 years ago: $ 19,497

Fiscal Year Ending Dec. 31

	1998	1997	1996	1995	1994	1993
Revenues (Million $)						
1Q	840.8	922.1	840.6	915.8	595.0	624.6
2Q	805.7	937.7	821.1	924.0	660.7	591.2
3Q	—	1,034	820.5	926.7	753.1	588.6
4Q	—	884.7	905.3	927.1	842.8	613.1
Yr.	—	3,785	3,590	3,694	2,852	2,417
Earnings Per Share ($)						
1Q	**0.80**	0.62	0.52	0.33	0.41	0.46
2Q	**0.84**	0.63	0.51	0.34	0.37	0.45
3Q	**E0.86**	0.79	0.51	0.37	0.34	0.44
4Q	**E0.90**	**0.76**	0.57	0.50	0.31	0.49
Yr.	**E3.40**	**2.80**	2.12	1.53	1.44	1.83

Next earnings report expected: early October

Dividend Data (Dividends have been paid since 1983.)

Amount ($)	Date Decl.	Ex-Div. Date	Stock of Record	Payment Date
7-for-2	Nov. 21	Jan. 05	Dec. 12	Jan. 02 '98
0.140	Jan. 23	Feb. 25	Feb. 27	Mar. 13 '98
0.140	May. 21	Jun. 03	Jun. 05	Jun. 19 '98
0.140	Jul. 17	Sep. 02	Sep. 04	Sep. 18 '98

A Division of The McGraw·Hill Companies

STANDARD
&POOR'S
STOCK REPORTS

SLM Holding Corporation

1965H
12-SEP-98

Business Summary - 17-JUL-98

SLM Holding (formerly Student Loan Marketing Association) is the nation's leading provider of financial services for postsecondary education needs and the country's largest source of funding for education loans. It also finances academic plant and equipment. The company's original mission was to improve the access of the average citizen to a college education, thereby contributing to a better informed electorate, a more skilled workforce, etc. The former Student Loan Marketing Association (known as Sallie Mae), a government sponsored enterprise, is a subsidiary of the company.

The company makes a secondary market for student loans by buying such loans from various lenders. Student loans consist principally of loans originated under the Federal Family Education Loan Program (FFELP) and the Health Education Assistance Loan Program (HEAL). On most FFELP loans, the U.S. pays interest on loans while the student is in school, including a special allowance. This allowance, together with stated interest on the loans, provides for an interest rate of 3.25% to 3.50% over the 91-day treasury bill rate. SLM buys most loans after borrowers graduate. In 1997, Sallie Mae purchased $9.0 billion of student loans, versus $9.9 billion in 1996.

Warehousing advances are secured loans made by

Sallie Mae to financial and educational institutions to fund certain student loans and other forms of education-related credit. Warehousing advances totaled $1.9 billion at December 31, 1997, down from $2.8 billion a year earlier.

In late 1997, Congress began discussions concerning the reauthorization of the Higher Education Act. One risk is the possibility Congress may reduce margins on student loans, which could harm SLM and other companies that originate and hold student loans. In 1997, the company rechartered as a private sector corporation, and new management assumed control of the board following an extended proxy battle. The threat of direct lending by the U. S. government had abated considerably.

Under a complex insurance and reinsurance system involving both the U. S. Department of Education and various state agencies, the company is able to file claims for loan defaults, which are reimbursed nearly 100% provided the loan documentation was in accordance with certain highly specific rules. Thus, investors generally regard the company as having virtually no credit risk. Default rates typically peak shortly after the student has graduated or left school. One reason for the uptick in delinquencies at this time is that it is more difficult for SLM to service the loan with the individual often changing addresses.

Per Share Data ($)

(Year Ended Dec. 31)	1997	1996	1995	1994	1993	1992	1991	1990	1989	1988
Tangible Bk. Val.	3.89	4.44	4.29	4.89	3.63	3.21	2.88	2.67	2.39	1.84
Earnings	2.80	2.12	1.53	1.44	1.83	1.50	1.01	0.85	0.72	0.61
Dividends	1.81	0.49	0.43	0.41	0.36	0.30	0.24	0.17	0.12	0.07
Payout Ratio	65%	23%	28%	28%	20%	20%	24%	20%	16%	11%
Prices - High	47⅛	28⅛	20¼	14¼	21½	21¾	21¾	16⅛	15¼	9⅞
- Low	25⅜	18⅛	9⅜	8⅞	11⅜	16⅞	12½	9⅜	9½	8
P/E Ratio - High	17	13	13	10	12	15	21	19	22	16
- Low	9	9	6	6	6	11	12	11	13	13

Income Statement Analysis (Million $)

	1997	1996	1995	1994	1993	1992	1991	1990	1989	1988
Interest On: Mtges.	2,711	2,900	2,974	2,351	2,031	2,072	2,268	3,503	2,275	1,729
Interest On: Invest.	573	543	719	500	387	543	854	922	894	443
Int. Exp.	2,526	2,577	3,021	2,142	1,481	1,812	2,562	3,024	2,751	1,799
Guaranty Fees	Nil	Nil	Nil	Nil	Nil	Nil	Nil	Nil	Nil	Nil
Loan Loss Prov.	Nil	Nil	Nil	17.0	16.5	36.2	53.2	31.1	16.9	NA
Admin. Exp.	269	199	161	130	109	101	31.1	79.0	70.0	62.0
Pretax Inc.	765	608	512	579	827	701	469	400	348	310
Eff. Tax Rate	32%	30%	28%	29%	31%	31%	27%	25%	26%	27%
Net Inc.	511	424	371	412	567	487	345	301	258	225

Balance Sheet & Other Fin. Data (Million $)

	1997	1996	1995	1994	1993	1992	1991	1990	1989	1988
Mtges.	32,765	38,016	39,514	38,951	35,197	33,447	31,801	28,770	24,630	21,191
Invest.	5,076	7,436	7,614	10,435	9,157	10,094	6,337	4,221	2,522	3,104
Cash & Equiv.	54.0	271	1,253	2,262	1,113	1,974	6,040	7,030	7,317	3,464
Total Assets	39,909	47,630	50,002	52,961	46,509	46,621	45,320	41,124	35,488	28,628
ST Debt	23,176	22,517	17,447	16,016	13,619	13,716	11,986	14,801	14,965	9,820
LT Debt	14,541	22,606	30,083	34,319	30,925	30,724	31,153	24,243	18,623	17,163
Equity	675	834	867	1,257	1,066	1,006	936	879	823	581
% Ret. on Assets	1.2	0.9	0.8	0.8	1.2	1.1	0.8	0.8	0.8	0.9
% Ret. on Equity	67.7	49.9	35.0	35.5	53.7	49.1	36.5	32.9	31.7	41.0
Equity/Assets Ratio	1.7	1.7	2.1	2.7	2.2	2.1	2.1	2.2	2.2	NA
Price Times Book Value:										
Hi	12.1	6.3	4.7	2.9	5.9	6.8	7.5	6.0	6.4	5.3
Low	6.5	4.1	2.2	1.8	3.1	5.2	4.3	3.5	4.0	4.3

Data as orig. reptd.; bef. results of disc. opers. and/or spec. items. Per share data adj. for stk. divs. as of ex-div. date. Bold denotes diluted EPS (FASB 128). E-Estimated. NA-Not Available. NM-Not Meaningful. NR-Not Ranked.

Established—in 1972 by a 1965 Act of Congress, as amended. **Office**—1050 Thomas Jefferson St., N.W., Washington, DC 20007. **Tel**—(202) 333-8000. **Chrmn**— E. A. Fox. **Vice Chrmn & CEO**—A. L. Lord. **EVP**—J. P. Carey. **VP & Investor Contact**—Michael Arthur (703-810-7600). **Dirs**— J. E. Brandon, C. L. Daley, T. J. Fitzpatrick, E. A. Fox, D. S. Gilleland, A. T. Grant, R. F. Hunt, R. J. Lambert, III, A. L. Lord, M. V. McDemmond, B. A. Munitz, A. A. Porter, W. Schoelkopf, S. L. Shapiro, R. H. Waterfield, Jr. **Transfer Agent & Registrar**—Chase Manhattan Bank, NYC. **Empl**— 4,608. **S&P Analyst:** Paul L. Huberman, CFA

Snap-on Inc.

2051G

NYSE Symbol **SNA**

In S&P 500

12-SEP-98

Industry: Auto Parts & Equipment

Summary: Snap-on is the largest manufacturer and distributor of hand tools, storage units and diagnostic equipment for professional mechanics and industry.

S&P Opinion: Hold (★★★)	Recent Price • 29⅜ Yield • 3.0% 52 Wk Range • 46⅜-25½ 12-Mo. P/E • 13.4

Quantitative Evaluations

Outlook
(1 Lowest—5 Highest)
• **4+**

Fair Value
• **36¼**

Risk
• **Low**

Earn./Div. Rank
• **B+**

Technical Eval.
• **Bullish** since 2/98

Rel. Strength Rank
(1 Lowest—99 Highest)
• **52**

Insider Activity
• **Favorable**

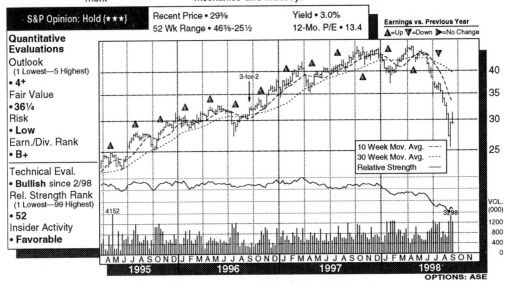

Earnings vs. Previous Year
▲=Up ▼=Down ▷=No Change

10 Week Mov. Avg. ——
30 Week Mov. Avg. - - - -
Relative Strength ——

OPTIONS: ASE

Overview - 30-JUL-98

SNA's string of five consecutive years of record sales, net earnings and EPS is in jeopardy. The company recently warned that earnings would decline in the 1998 second and third quarters, primarily due to difficulties related to its newly installed computer system. SNA also announced a restructuring that is expected to result in a third quarter charge of about $175 million, but is also expected to yield annual savings of $60 millions by 2000, and to boost the likelihood of meeting a targeted return on equity of 20% by 2000. Other financial goals include increasing sales 10% annually, including acquisitions, and increasing EPS at a 15% annual rate. We see sales rising in high-single digits in 1998, reflecting acquisitions and growth in tool demand related to a projected increase in the automotive aftermarket for vehicle repair services. Most of the dilution from a German acquisition, plus a disproportionate portion of a reduction in finance income, was incurred in the first quarter.

Valuation - 30-JUL-98

We lowered our rating on the shares to avoid, from hold, on news of flat first quarter earnings, versus anticipated double-digit gains. In June, we further reduced our 1998 EPS estimate from $2.70 to $2.15, versus 1997's $2.44. For the longer term, growth, although at a reduced pace, will come despite softness in the overall motor vehicle aftermarket, as results are aided by acquisitions and strong North American markets. A Congressional threat to reopen the Clean Air Act of 1990 resulted in delays in the planned 1994-95 startup of new emissions testing standards, and the EPA eventually changed the way the new standards were to be implemented. However, delays are easing, and it appears that the result will be a larger overall market for emissions test, diagnostic and repair equipment.

Key Stock Statistics

S&P EPS Est. 1998	2.00	Tang. Bk. Value/Share	9.64
P/E on S&P Est. 1998	14.7	Beta	0.94
Dividend Rate/Share	0.88	Shareholders	10,600
Shs. outstg. (M)	59.1	Market cap. (B)	$ 1.7
Avg. daily vol. (M)	0.354	Inst. holdings	70%

Value of $10,000 invested 5 years ago: $ 16,234

Fiscal Year Ending Dec. 31

	1998	1997	1996	1995	1994	1993
Revenues (Million $)						
1Q	426.4	375.3	344.4	309.1	298.8	270.7
2Q	442.2	409.2	384.6	326.8	298.8	272.7
3Q	—	391.2	347.2	309.1	278.4	271.1
4Q	—	496.5	409.2	347.1	318.4	317.5
Yr.	—	1,672	1,485	1,292	1,194	1,132
Earnings Per Share ($)						
1Q	**0.56**	0.55	0.49	0.41	0.36	0.29
2Q	**0.38**	0.63	0.57	0.49	0.41	0.35
3Q	**E0.38**	0.58	0.51	0.43	0.35	0.32
4Q	**E0.68**	0.68	0.60	0.51	0.41	0.39
Yr.	**E2.00**	2.44	2.16	1.84	1.53	1.35

Next earnings report expected: mid October

Dividend Data (Dividends have been paid since 1939.)

Amount ($)	Date Decl.	Ex-Div. Date	Stock of Record	Payment Date
0.210	Oct. 24	Nov. 17	Nov. 19	Dec. 10 '97
0.210	Jan. 23	Feb. 12	Feb. 17	Mar. 10 '98
0.210	Apr. 24	May. 18	May. 20	Jun. 10 '98
0.220	Jun. 26	Aug. 18	Aug. 20	Sep. 10 '98

A Division of The McGraw-Hill Companies

Business Summary - 30-JUL-98

In 1996, as part of its effort to become a complete solutions provider to the transportation and industrial service markets worldwide, Snap-on Inc. (formerly Snap-on Tools) acquired the John Bean Co., a producer of wheel and brake service equipment. In early 1997, it bought a 50% interest in The Thomson Corp.'s Mitchell Repair Information business, a provider of vehicle repair information for service establishments. In March 1997, SNA acquired Computer Aided Service, Inc., a developer of repair shop management and point of sale systems and diagnostics equipment. In late 1997, it purchased Hofman Werkstatt-Technik, a European leader in under-car equipment technology. In April 1998, SNA agreed to acquire Hein-Werner Corp., a leading worldwide manufacturer and marketer of automotive collision repair equipment, for about $36 million.

SNA produces a line of 15,000 high-quality professional mechanic tools, diagnostic equipment and tool chests. Products are sold to mechanics, industrial accounts and foreign distributors for use in automotive service, manufacturing and other repair and maintenance.

SNA makes hand tools (wrenches, screwdrivers, sockets, pliers and similar items), power tools (pneumatic impact wrenches, ratchets, power drills, sanders and polishers), tool storage units (tool chests and roll cabinets), and electronic tools and shop equipment (automotive diagnostic equipment, wheel balancing and aligning equipment, battery chargers and other items). Acquisitions expanded product lines, especially in electronic diagnostics and emissions test and repair equipment, and opened new distribution channels.

SNA manages mobile van sales to automotive technicians who are serviced by about 6,000 mostly franchised dealers worldwide. Industrial products are sold by more than 500 company salesmen. Dealers operate out of walk-in vans that carry an inventory of products. Snap-on Diagnostics employs a company salesforce to sell equipment, diagnostics and software to repair shops and original equipment manufacturers. Snap-on Financial Services provides financing to facilitate the sale or lease of products, with a particular focus on more expensive electronic equipment.

In 1996, John Bean with to provide Pep Boys (NYSE: PBY) with PC-based alignment systems at 140 existing stores and 150 locations expected to open over three years.

Sales by product category in recent years were:

	1997	1996	1995
Hand tools	38%	40%	40%
Power tools	8%	8%	10%
Tool storage	9%	10%	10%
Equipment & related services	45%	42%	40%

Per Share Data ($) (Year Ended Dec. 31)	1997	1996	1995	1994	1993	1992	1991	1990	1989	1988
Tangible Bk. Val.	12.74	12.30	11.07	11.08	10.19	10.45	10.31	10.28	9.29	8.23
Cash Flow	3.06	2.68	2.35	2.00	1.84	1.44	1.57	2.03	2.05	2.11
Earnings	2.44	2.16	1.84	1.53	1.35	1.04	1.17	1.63	1.70	1.81
Dividends	0.82	0.76	0.72	0.72	0.72	0.72	0.72	0.72	0.69	0.59
Payout Ratio	34%	35%	39%	47%	53%	69%	62%	44%	41%	32%
Prices - High	46¼	38¼	31½	29⅝	29⅝	26⅝	23	25⅜	27⅞	29⅞
- Low	34¼	27⅜	20⅝	19⅜	20⅜	18	18¼	17½	19¼	21¾
P/E Ratio - High	19	18	17	19	22	26	20	16	16	16
- Low	14	13	11	13	15	17	16	11	11	12
Income Statement Analysis (Million $)										
Revs.	1,672	1,485	1,292	1,254	1,193	1,047	938	985	938	893
Oper. Inc.	232	188	157	188	179	141	149	187	189	201
Depr.	38.4	31.9	31.5	30.1	31.8	25.5	25.6	24.4	21.9	18.7
Int. Exp.	17.7	12.6	13.3	10.8	11.2	6.0	5.3	6.8	3.8	2.6
Pretax Inc.	239	209	180	154	136	110	119	160	166	183
Eff. Tax Rate	37%	37%	37%	36%	37%	40%	38%	37%	37%	38%
Net Inc.	150	131	113	98.0	86.0	66.0	73.0	101	105	113
Balance Sheet & Other Fin. Data (Million $)										
Cash	25.7	15.4	16.2	9.0	6.7	59.0	10.9	6.6	5.1	16.9
Curr. Assets	1,022	1,017	947	873	855	838	667	675	565	505
Total Assets	1,641	1,521	1,361	1,235	1,219	1,177	915	908	778	668
Curr. Liab.	353	341	336	238	308	322	177	237	179	142
LT Debt	151	150	144	109	100	93.1	7.2	7.3	7.7	8.1
Common Eqty.	892	828	751	766	702	665	653	636	573	505
Total Cap.	1,055	985	899	882	809	763	660	656	591	525
Cap. Exp.	55.4	52.3	31.6	41.8	33.2	21.1	23.4	44.1	71.4	37.3
Cash Flow	189	163	145	128	118	91.0	99	125	127	132
Curr. Ratio	2.9	3.0	2.8	3.7	2.8	2.6	3.8	2.9	3.1	3.5
% LT Debt of Cap.	14.3	15.2	16.0	12.4	12.3	12.2	1.1	1.1	1.3	1.5
% Net Inc.of Revs.	9.0	8.9	8.7	7.8	7.2	6.3	7.8	10.2	11.2	12.7
% Ret. on Assets	9.5	9.1	8.7	8.0	7.1	6.3	7.9	11.9	14.5	17.8
% Ret. on Equity	17.5	16.7	14.9	13.3	12.5	10.0	11.2	16.6	19.4	23.8

Data as orig. reptd.; bef. results of disc. opers. and/or spec. items. Per share data adj. for stk. divs. as of ex-div. date. Bold denotes diluted EPS (FASB 128). E-Estimated. NA-Not Available. NM-Not Meaningful. NR-Not Ranked.

Office—10801 Corporate Drive, Kenosha, WI 53141-1410. **Tel**—(414) 656-5200. **Chrmn, CEO & Pres**—R. A. Cornog. **VP & Secy**—S. F. Marrinan. **SVP & CFO**—D. J. Huml. **Treas**—Denis J. Loverine. **Investor Contact**—Lynn L. McHugh. **Dirs**—B. M. Beronja, D. W. Brinckman, B. S. Chelberg, R. A. Cornog, R. J. Decyk, A. L. Kelly, L. A. Hadley, G. W. Mead, J. D. Michaels, E. H. Rensi, R. F. Teerlink. **Transfer Agent & Registrar**—First Chicago Trust Co. of New York, Jersey City, NJ. **Incorporated**—in Delaware in 1930. **Empl**— 11,200. **S&P Analyst:** Efraim Levy

12-SEP-98 | **Industry:** Natural Gas

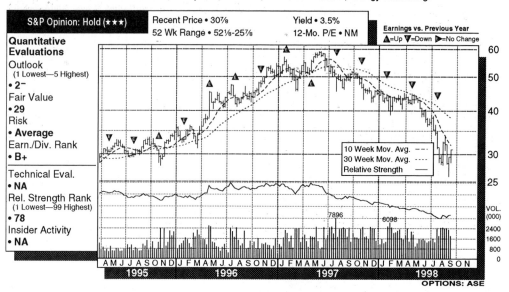

Summary: This energy company operates a natural gas pipeline serving eight southeastern states, and is involved in exploration and production and, to a lesser extent, energy marketing.

S&P Opinion: Hold (★★★)	Recent Price • 30⅞	Yield • 3.5%
	52 Wk Range • 52⅛-25⅞	12-Mo. P/E • NM

Earnings vs. Previous Year
▲=Up ▼=Down ▶=No Change

Quantitative Evaluations

Outlook
(1 Lowest—5 Highest)
• **2⁻**

Fair Value
• **29**

Risk
• **Average**

Earn./Div. Rank
• **B+**

Technical Eval.
• **NA**

Rel. Strength Rank
(1 Lowest—99 Highest)
• **78**

Insider Activity
• **NA**

10 Week Mov. Avg. —·—
30 Week Mov. Avg. ----
Relative Strength ——

OPTIONS: ASE

Overview - 15-MAY-98

Sonat posted 1998 first quarter EPS of $0.34, down from $0.62 in the 1997 period, and below analyst expectations. Results were hurt by lower oil and gas prices, and higher costs at Sonat Exploration. There is a silver lining, however, as the company announced a restructuring plan under which it will sell about 19% of its total proven oil and gas reserves and 24% of current daily production. SNT also intends to consolidate business units from the current seven to three, and to reduce its Sonat Exploration work force by 25%. The company expects to incur an after tax charge of $250 milion to $275 million in the second quarter of 1998, to save $55 million in annual G&A and operating costs, and to cut $20 million in annual interest expense. In addition, the per unit amortization rate is expected to decline from the current $1.01 per thousand cubic feet (Mcf) of natural gas equivalent to about $0.75 per Mcf. This is encouraging, as it should help improve the company's earnings and lower the debt ratio, since proceeds of the divestiture program will be used to repay debt.

Valuation - 15-MAY-98

Although the acquisition of Houston-based Zilkha must be seen as positive for SNT's increasingly serious efforts to become an exploration and production player, current weakness in commodity prices, related to mild winter weather conditions, will be difficult to overcome. Pipeline returns are also weather related, although volumes remain respectable. We believe that restructuring and cost cutting measures will add value over the long term, but advise investors to wait for further details, expected by the end of May 1998, before considering purchases. We see the stock currently as only a market performer.

Key Stock Statistics

S&P EPS Est. 1998	2.25	Tang. Bk. Value/Share	12.18
P/E on S&P Est. 1998	13.7	Beta	0.46
S&P EPS Est. 1999	2.40	Shareholders	12,000
Dividend Rate/Share	1.08	Market cap. (B)	$ 3.4
Shs. outstg. (M)	110.0	Inst. holdings	48%
Avg. daily vol. (M)	0.516		

Value of $10,000 invested 5 years ago: $ 15,285

Fiscal Year Ending Dec. 31

	1998	1997	1996	1995	1994	1993
Revenues (Million $)						
1Q	1,109	1,122	734.4	425.0	479.5	496.9
2Q	925.2	815.3	847.1	476.3	415.0	356.5
3Q	—	1,024	788.2	509.4	411.8	324.6
4Q	—	1,264	1,025	579.3	467.6	563.2
Yr.	—	4,175	3,395	1,990	1,774	1,741
Earnings Per Share ($)						
1Q	0.34	0.76	0.53	0.44	0.57	0.80
2Q	-2.32	0.41	0.47	0.20	0.40	1.46
3Q	—	0.15	0.56	1.51	0.40	0.23
4Q	—	0.69	0.78	0.09	0.25	0.57
Yr.	E2.25	2.01	2.30	2.24	1.62	3.05

Next earnings report expected: NA

Dividend Data (Dividends have been paid since 1936.)

Amount ($)	Date Decl.	Ex-Div. Date	Stock of Record	Payment Date
0.270	Oct. 23	Nov. 25	Nov. 28	Dec. 12 '97
0.270	Jan. 22	Feb. 25	Feb. 27	Mar. 13 '98
0.270	Apr. 23	May. 27	May. 29	Jun. 12 '98
0.270	Jul. 23	Aug. 27	Aug. 31	Sep. 14 '98

A Division of The McGraw·Hill Companies

Business Summary - 15-MAY-98

Sonat Inc. (SNT), through its three operating segments, explores for, develops and produces oil and natural gas, transmits natural gas, and markets natural gas and electric power. SNT's management has aggressive goals for the future, and is focusing on creating strategic alliances and partnerships in the energy services business in order to grow.

In order to improve the company's ability to earn returns in excess of its cost of capital, management has decided to initiate a restructuring program in 1998. The restructuring involves property divestitures, a reduction in the number of business units, and substantial cost reduction initiatives. The divestiture will include all of SNT's Austin Chalk, Arkoma Basin Properties, and substantially all onshore Gulf Coast properties, as well as certain properties from other units. SNT expects to substantially complete its divestiture program by the end of the third quarter of 1998, with proceeds to be used to reduce debt. The company will consolidate its business units from seven to three, and will reduce its work force by about 220 people.

SNT's Sonat Exploration Co. subsidiary is a large independent oil and natural gas exploration and production company. Its oil and gas properties are principally located onshore in the southern coastal states, in various states in the Southwest and Midwest, and in federal waters located offshore Louisiana and Texas. In 1997, SNT replaced 200% of production. As of December 31, 1997, the company had working interests in approximately 3.1 million gross (2.4 million net) acres.

The Southern Natural Gas Co. unit operates a 9,055 mile interstate pipeline system serving markets in seven states in the Southeast. Southern Natural spent much of 1997 expanding its pipeline system and cutting costs. However, due to warm weather, its market-area throughput declined to 611 billion cubic feet (Bcf), from 630 Bcf in 1996. SNT made three market-area expansions, and it reached an agreement with Amoco Pipeline Co. and Shell Gas Pipeline Co. to build a $300 million pipeline to transport natural gas supplies from the deepwater Gulf of Mexico to five interstate pipelines, including Southern Natural and Florida Gas Transmission, which is the primary pipeline transporter of natural gas in the state of Florida and is owned by Citrus Corp. (50%-owned by SNT). Florida Gas's 4,500 mile pipeline system extends from South Texas to a point near Miami, FL. Total 1997 volume was 471 Bcf of natural gas, versus 457 Bcf in 1996.

Sonat Energy Services acts as a holding company for SNT's subsidiaries engaged in unregulated natural gas and electric power marketing, power generation, and intrastate natural gas transmission. In 1997 the company sold 1,288 Bcf of gas and 8,768,000 Megawatt-hours (Mwh) of electricity, both up from 968 Bcf and 2,969,000 Mwh in 1996.

Per Share Data ($) (Year Ended Dec. 31)	1997	1996	1995	1994	1993	1992	1991	1990	1989	1988
Tangible Bk. Val.	19.06	18.34	17.21	16.11	15.64	13.62	12.14	13.59	13.66	13.32
Cash Flow	5.74	5.68	5.70	4.58	5.66	3.79	3.48	3.66	3.33	2.92
Earnings	2.01	2.33	2.24	1.62	3.05	1.18	0.91	1.29	1.33	1.04
Dividends	1.08	1.08	1.08	1.08	1.04	1.00	1.00	1.00	1.00	1.00
Payout Ratio	54%	46%	48%	67%	34%	85%	110%	77%	75%	96%
Prices - High	59 1/8	54 3/4	36 1/4	34 7/8	9 1/4	24 1/8	23 3/4	28	25 1/4	15 5/8
- Low	42 1/4	31 1/8	26	26	2 3/8	14 1/2	15 1/2	21 1/2	14 3/8	11 5/8
P/E Ratio - High	29	23	16	22	12	21	26	22	19	15
- Low	21	13	12	16	8	12	17	17	11	11
Income Statement Analysis (Million $)										
Revs.	4,175	3,395	1,990	1,774	1,741	1,484	1,421	1,509	1,778	1,392
Oper. Inc.	623	629	488	484	459	436	424	406	371	327
Depr.	326	288	299	258	226	225	187	202	163	152
Int. Exp.	90.0	92.0	103	87.0	91.0	116	137	133	110	98.0
Pretax Inc.	261	294	288	157	368	137	100	162	171	125
Eff. Tax Rate	31%	32%	33%	10%	28%	26%	23%	32%	36%	33%
Net Inc.	176	201	193	141	265	101	78.0	111	109	85.0
Balance Sheet & Other Fin. Data (Million $)										
Cash	129	29.6	37.3	9.0	11.0	58.0	24.0	22.0	15.0	19.0
Curr. Assets	938	752	494	387	464	649	632	643	682	591
Total Assets	4,432	3,775	3,511	3,531	3,214	3,165	3,208	3,196	3,084	3,138
Curr. Liab.	1,250	849	640	570	633	448	484	535	606	432
LT Debt	1,043	873	770	963	741	1,176	1,315	1,086	928	858
Common Eqty.	1,635	1,584	1,483	1,392	1,363	1,172	1,043	1,165	1,123	1,082
Total Cap.	3,023	2,742	2,466	2,543	2,297	2,556	2,552	2,507	2,331	2,182
Cap. Exp.	699	510	488	448	516	226	478	592	426	382
Cash Flow	502	489	492	399	491	326	298	313	272	237
Curr. Ratio	0.8	0.9	0.8	0.7	0.7	1.4	1.3	1.2	1.1	1.4
% LT Debt of Cap.	34.5	31.9	31.3	37.9	32.3	46.0	51.5	43.3	39.8	39.3
% Net Inc.of Revs.	4.2	6.0	9.7	8.0	15.2	6.8	5.5	7.3	6.1	6.1
% Ret. on Assets	4.3	5.6	5.5	4.2	8.3	3.2	2.4	3.5	3.5	2.7
% Ret. on Equity	10.9	13.2	13.5	10.3	20.8	9.1	7.1	9.5	9.8	8.1

Data as orig. reptd.; bef. results of disc. opers. and/or spec. items. Per share data adj. for stk. divs. as of ex-div. date. Bold denotes diluted EPS (FASB 128). E-Estimated. NA-Not Available. NM-Not Meaningful. NR-Not Ranked.

Office—AmSouth-Sonat Tower, Birmingham, AL 35203. **Tel**—(205) 325-3800. **Website**—http://www.sonat.com **Chrmn, Pres & CEO**—R. L. Kuehn, Jr. **Vice Chrmn**—D. G. Russell. **SVP & CFO**—J. E. Moylan, Jr. **VP & Secy**—Beverley T. Krannich. **Investor Contact**—Bruce L. Connery. **Dirs**—W. O. Bourke, R. L. Kuehn, Jr., R. J. Lanigan, M. L. Lukens, C. Marshall, B. F. Payton, J. J. Phelan, Jr., J. J. Richardson, D. G. Russell, A. M. Tocklin, J. B. Williams, J. B. Wyatt, M. S. Zilkha, S. K. Zilkha. **Transfer Agent & Registrar**—ChaseMellon Shareholder Services, Ridgefield Park, NJ. **Incorporated**—in Delaware in 1935. **Empl**— 2,110. **S&P Analyst:** J. Robert Cho

STANDARD &POOR'S
STOCK REPORTS

Southern Co.
2066
NYSE Symbol **SO**

In S&P 500

12-SEP-98

Industry:
Electric Companies

Summary: This major electric utility holding company serves the U.S. Southeast and southwestern England, and has a 99.9% interest in one of the world's largest independent power producers.

S&P Opinion: Hold (★★★)	Recent Price • 27⅝	Yield • 4.9%
	52 Wk Range • 29¼-22	12-Mo. P/E • 17.7

Earnings vs. Previous Year
▲=Up ▼=Down ►=No Change

Quantitative Evaluations

Outlook
(1 Lowest—5 Highest)
• **2⁻**

Fair Value
• **26⅝**

Risk
• **Low**

Earn./Div. Rank
• **A-**

Technical Eval.
• **NA**

Rel. Strength Rank
(1 Lowest—99 Highest)
• **94**

Insider Activity
• **Neutral**

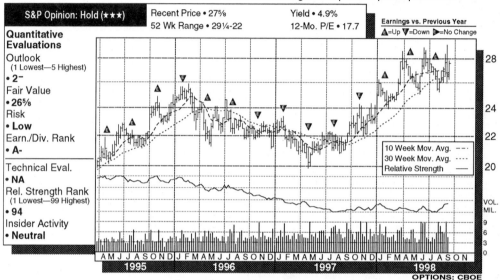

10 Week Mov. Avg. — –·
30 Week Mov. Avg. ----
Relative Strength —

VOL. MIL.

OPTIONS: CBOE

Overview - 26-AUG-98

We expect SO to achieve mid-single digit EPS growth in 1999. The company should continue to benefit from solid 2% growth in its domestic customer base. With the completion of a May 1998 agreement to acquire electric generating plants in New England, SO will be able to significantly strengthen its trading and marketing operations in that region. From the international operations, we expect SO's reduced interest in its U.K.-based subsidiary, South Western Electricity plc, to lower EPS contributions from about $0.09 in 1998 to $0.06 in 1999. SO's 3.6% interest (with an 8.25% voting share) in the Brazilian utility CEMIG, South America's largest electricity distributor, should add about $0.01 to both 1998 and 1999 results. The company's 26% interest in Bewag, a vertically integrated electric utility in Berlin, should add about $0.05 in 1998 and $0.06 in 1999, while SO's 99% ownership of Hong Kong-based Consolidated Electric Power Asia (CEPA) could dilute EPS about $0.02 in 1998, but add about $0.07 in 1999 and $0.15 in 2000.

Valuation - 26-AUG-98

We recommend holding the shares. After a 14% increase in 1997 (versus a 19.8% gain for the S&P Index of Electric Companies), the shares were recently up about 6% in 1998. With the stock trading at nearly 15X our 1999 EPS estimate of $1.85, the shares appear fairly valued. For the long term, however, we expect the shares to benefit from expansion of international and non-regulated operations. SO intends to be one of the five leading U.S. energy marketers by 2000, and expects non-core operations to grow to about 30% of net income by 2003. While we believe that the stock will offer only modest gains over the near term, the dividend (yielding about 4.9%) could provide long-term investors with a solid total return.

Key Stock Statistics

S&P EPS Est. 1998	1.75	Tang. Bk. Value/Share	10.52
P/E on S&P Est. 1998	15.8	Beta	0.17
S&P EPS Est. 1999	1.85	Shareholders	215,200
Dividend Rate/Share	1.34	Market cap. (B)	$ 19.3
Shs. outstg. (M)	697.8	Inst. holdings	36%
Avg. daily vol. (M)	1.403		

Value of $10,000 invested 5 years ago: $ 19,049

Fiscal Year Ending Dec. 31

	1998	1997	1996	1995	1994	1993
Revenues (Million $)						
1Q	2,514	2,585	2,416	1,929	1,932	1,840
2Q	2,913	2,717	2,534	2,184	2,069	2,068
3Q	—	4,071	2,917	2,759	2,381	2,636
4Q	—	3,238	2,453	2,308	1,915	1,945
Yr.	—	12,611	10,358	9,180	8,297	8,489
Earnings Per Share ($)						
1Q	**0.35**	0.28	0.35	0.31	0.22	0.28
2Q	**0.39**	0.31	0.43	0.40	0.39	0.40
3Q	**E0.72**	0.55	0.69	0.71	0.64	0.69
4Q	**E0.29**	0.28	0.21	0.24	0.27	0.21
Yr.	**E1.75**	1.42	1.68	1.66	1.52	0.09

Next earnings report expected: mid October

Dividend Data (Dividends have been paid since 1948.)

Amount ($)	Date Decl.	Ex-Div. Date	Stock of Record	Payment Date
0.325	Oct. 20	Oct. 30	Nov. 03	Dec. 06 '97
0.335	Jan. 19	Jan. 29	Feb. 02	Mar. 06 '98
0.335	Apr. 20	Apr. 30	May. 04	Jun. 06 '98

A Division of The **McGraw·Hill** *Companies*

Business Summary - 26-AUG-98

With the 1997 acquisition of more than 99.9% of Consolidated Electric Power Asia (CEPA) for about $2.7 billion, The Southern Company, already the largest U.S. electricity producer, has become one of the largest independent power producers in the world.

This utility holding company serves 3.7 million customers in the southeastern U.S. through its domestic subsidiaries: Alabama Power, Georgia Power, Gulf Power, Mississippi Power and Savannah Electric & Power. It also serves 1.3 million customers in southwestern England through 49%-owned South Western Electricity, of which 100% was acquired in October 1995. Electric revenues by customer class in recent years were:

	1997	1996	1995
Residential	33.2%	34.0%	33.7%
Commercial	30.4%	30.1%	29.5%
Industrial	25.1%	25.1%	26.2%
Other	11.3%	10.8%	10.6%

CEPA is the fifth largest independent power producer in the world. The Hong Kong-based company has electric power generating projects either completed or under development in China, the Philippines, Indonesia, Pakistan and India. SO will hold its CEPA interest through wholly owned Southern Energy, which builds, owns and operates domestic and international cogeneration and independent power projects.

In September 1997, Southern Energy acquired 26% of Berliner Kraft und Licht AG (commonly known as Bewag), a vertically integrated electric utility serving 2.1 million customers in Berlin, for approximately $820 million in cash. The transaction provided Southern with an entry into a strong and growing economy and access to transmission lines connecting to other parts of Europe.

The company has budgeted construction expenditures of $2.0 billion for each of 1998 and 1999, and $1.6 billion for 2000. Current construction costs related to Phase II compliance of the Clean Air Act Amendments of 1990 (required by 2000) are estimated to be around $70 million, of which $15 million has already been spent.

In May 1998, Southern Energy agreed to acquire power generation plants in New England for $537 million. In August 1997, Southern Energy agreed to form Southern Company Energy Marketing with Vastar Resources. Southern Energy's 60% interest in the venture will grow to 75% by July 1, 2001.

In June 1998, Southern Energy sold an additional 26% interest in SWEB Holdings (the parent of U.K.-based South Western Electricity) to PP&L Global, for $170 million. Although this increased PP&L's interest in SWEB to 51%, Southern Energy will retain a majority of both the directors and the voting shares.

Per Share Data ($) (Year Ended Dec. 31)	1997	1996	1995	1994	1993	1992	1991	1990	1989	1988
Tangible Bk. Val.	10.52	12.49	11.99	12.46	NA	11.05	10.71	10.57	10.54	10.29
Earnings	1.42	1.68	1.66	1.52	1.57	1.51	1.39	0.95	1.34	1.36
Dividends	1.30	1.26	1.22	1.18	1.14	1.10	1.07	1.07	1.07	1.07
Payout Ratio	92%	75%	73%	78%	73%	73%	77%	112%	80%	79%
Prices - High	26¼	25⅞	25	22⅛	23⅝	19⅝	17⅜	14¾	14⅞	12⅛
- Low	19⅞	21⅛	19⅜	17	18½	15¼	12⅞	11½	11	10¼
P/E Ratio - High	18	15	15	15	15	13	13	15	11	9
- Low	14	13	12	11	12	10	9	12	8	7

Income Statement Analysis (Million $)

	1997	1996	1995	1994	1993	1992	1991	1990	1989	1988
Revs.	12,611	10,358	9,180	8,297	8,489	8,073	8,050	7,975	7,492	7,235
Depr.	1,246	996	904	821	793	768	763	749	698	632
Maint.	763	782	683	660	653	613	637	602	542	547
Fxd. Chgs. Cov.	2.7	3.8	3.3	3.3	4.0	2.9	2.6	2.1	2.5	2.5
Constr. Credits	20.0	23.0	25.0	29.0	22.0	22.0	31.0	67.0	134	268
Eff. Tax Rate	43%	40%	39%	39%	35%	37%	34%	34%	30%	26%
Net Inc.	972	1,127	1,103	989	1,002	953	876	604	846	846

Balance Sheet & Other Fin. Data (Million $)

	1997	1996	1995	1994	1993	1992	1991	1990	1989	1988
Gross Prop.	34,044	34,190	33,093	30,694	28,947	27,955	27,313	26,809	26,532	25,579
Cap. Exp.	1,859	1,229	1,401	1,536	1,441	1,105	1,123	1,185	1,346	1,754
Net Prop.	22,110	23,269	23,026	21,117	20,013	16,489	16,609	16,811	16,998	16,849
Capitalization:										
LT Debt	10,274	7,935	8,306	7,593	7,411	7,241	7,992	8,458	8,575	8,433
% LT Debt	46	43	45	44	45	46	49	51	51	51
Pfd.	2,237	1,402	1,432	1,432	1,333	1,359	1,333	1,358	1,400	1,465
% Pfd.	10	7.60	7.70	8.30	8.10	8.60	8.20	8.20	8.30	8.80
Common	9,647	9,216	8,772	8,186	7,684	7,234	6,976	6,783	6,861	6,686
% Common	44	50	47	48	47	46	43	41	41	40
Total Cap.	27,997	24,454	24,877	23,063	22,358	16,791	17,305	17,662	17,947	17,745
% Oper. Ratio	84.6	82.1	79.5	79.3	79.2	78.2	78.4	79.6	78.5	80.7
% Earn. on Net Prop.	8.6	8.0	8.5	8.3	9.7	10.6	10.4	9.6	9.5	8.4
% Return On Revs.	7.7	10.9	12.0	11.9	11.8	11.8	10.9	7.6	11.3	11.7
% Return On Invest. Capital	10.4	7.9	7.9	7.6	9.3	10.5	10.2	8.6	9.7	9.6
% Return On Com. Equity	10.3	12.5	13.0	12.5	13.4	13.4	12.7	8.9	12.5	13.0

Data as orig. reptd.; bef. results of disc. opers. and/or spec. items. Per share data adj. for stk. divs. as of ex-div. date. E-Estimated. NA-Not Available. NM-Not Meaningful. NR-Not Ranked.

Office—270 Peachtree St. N.W., Atlanta, GA 30303. **Tel**—(404) 506-5000. **Website**—www.southernco.com **Chrmn, Pres & CEO**—A. W. Dahlberg. **VP-Fin, CFO & Treas**—W. L. Westbrook. **Secy**—T. Chisholm. **Investor Contact**—Timothy J. Perrótt (212-269-8842). **Dirs**—J. C. Adams, A. D. Correll, A. W. Dahlberg, P. J. DeNicola, J. Edwards, H. A. Franklin, B. S. Gordon, L. G. Hardman III, E. B. Harris, W. A. Parker Jr., W. J. Rushton III, G. M. Shatto, G. J. St. Pe, H. Stockham. **Transfer Agent & Registrar**—SCS Stockholder Services, Atlanta. **Incorporated**—in Delaware in 1945. **Empl**— 29,246. **S&P Analyst:** Justin McCann

12-SEP-98   Industry:
Airlines

Summary: LUV, the seventh largest U.S. airline, offers discounted fares, primarily for short-haul, point-to-point flights; it also recently expanded its service into Eastern markets.

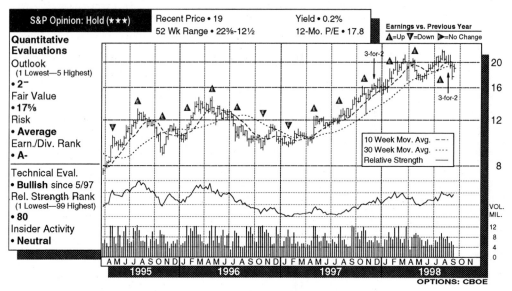

S&P Opinion: Hold (★★★)	Recent Price • 19	Yield • 0.2%	Earnings vs. Previous Year
	52 Wk Range • 22⅜-12½	12-Mo. P/E • 17.8	▲=Up ▼=Down ▶=No Change

Quantitative Evaluations

Outlook
(1 Lowest—5 Highest)
• **2⁻**

Fair Value
• **17⅞**

Risk
• **Average**

Earn./Div. Rank
• **A-**

Technical Eval.
• **Bullish** since 5/97

Rel. Strength Rank
(1 Lowest—99 Highest)
• **80**

Insider Activity
• **Neutral**

10 Week Mov. Avg. – – –
30 Week Mov. Avg. ⋯⋯
Relative Strength ——

OPTIONS: CBOE

Overview - 24-AUG-98

Traffic growth in 1998 is projected at 12% to 14%, well above 1997's 4.7%. The improvement in traffic reflects the offering of longer-haul flights, such Nashville-San Diego and Providence-Kansas City. LUV is also benefiting from continued expansion of service into Florida, the lifting of flight restrictions from Love Field in Dallas, the introduction of service from Manchester, NH, in June 1998, and increased frequencies on existing routes. The load factor will improve, as capacity expansion is estimated at 7%. Margins will continue to widen, as LUV benefits from lower fuel prices, flat commissions, and stable landing and jet rental costs. Offsetting, labor costs could increase faster than revenues, reflecting increases wages and health care benefits, and profit sharing payments. Advertising, depreciation and credit card processing costs will increase. Yields could slip, reflecting the flying of longer-haul routes, rather than competitive pressure on fares. Net interest expense will drop. LUV will record penalty payments from Boeing as non-operating income.

Valuation - 24-AUG-98

The shares of this leading low-fare airline rallied to all-time highs in July 1998, buoyed by falling fuel costs and double-digit traffic gains. While other airline issues slumped during the summer, LUV has held firm. Southwest has no exposure to weakness that is spreading in international markets. While we believe that LUV is one of the best managed carriers, offering outstanding value to customers, and possessing a fairly clean balance sheet, we think that the shares will be only average market performers over the next six to 12 months, as the P/E multiple is excessive relative to that of other airline issues.

Key Stock Statistics

S&P EPS Est. 1998	1.25	Tang. Bk. Value/Share	6.26
P/E on S&P Est. 1998	15.2	Beta	1.43
S&P EPS Est. 1999	1.35	Shareholders	9,500
Dividend Rate/Share	0.03	Market cap. (B)	$ 6.4
Shs. outstg. (M)	335.8	Inst. holdings	59%
Avg. daily vol. (M)	1.333		

Value of $10,000 invested 5 years ago: $ 21,938

Fiscal Year Ending Dec. 31

	1998	1997	1996	1995	1994	1993
Revenues (Million $)						
1Q	942.6	887.1	772.5	621.0	619.4	499.0
2Q	1,079	956.9	910.3	738.2	661.1	568.0
3Q	—	997.2	891.5	765.0	685.3	621.0
4Q	—	975.6	831.8	748.6	626.2	608.6
Yr.	—	3,817	3,406	2,873	2,592	2,297
Earnings Per Share ($)						
1Q	**0.20**	**0.15**	0.10	0.04	0.12	0.08
2Q	**0.38**	**0.28**	0.25	0.18	0.18	0.13
3Q	**E0.35**	**0.27**	0.18	0.20	0.18	0.15
4Q	**E0.32**	**0.23**	0.08	0.13	0.06	0.12
Yr.	**E1.25**	**0.93**	0.61	0.55	0.54	0.47

Next earnings report expected: late October

Dividend Data (Dividends have been paid since 1976.)

Amount ($)	Date Decl.	Ex-Div. Date	Stock of Record	Payment Date
0.010	Jan. 22	Mar. 04	Mar. 06	Mar. 31 '98
0.010	May. 22	Jun. 03	Jun. 05	Jun. 30 '98
3-for-2	Jul. 23	Aug. 21	Jul. 31	Aug. 20 '98
0.010	Jul. 20	Aug. 31	Sep. 02	Sep. 23 '98

A Division of The McGraw·Hill Companies

Southwest Airlines Co.

Business Summary - 24-AUG-98

Southwest Airlines was the seventh largest U.S. airline in 1997, based on revenue passenger miles. In 1996, it expanded into the Florida and New England markets. At 1997 year end, it offered flights between 51 cities in 25 states. Service to Manchester, NH, began in June 1998.

LUV's focus is on short-haul, high-frequency, point-to-point service. The average trip length in 1997 was 425 miles. Unlike all other major airlines, LUV does not operate through a hub-and-spoke structure that involves gathering passengers to central hubs from feeder airlines. However, 20% to 25% of LUV's passengers make connections to second flights on its system. Southwest avoids interlining to keep its aircraft turnaround times low. In addition, by primarily serving short-haul markets, LUV avoids food costs, as well as ground service that keeps aircraft out of service and requires leasing more airport gate space.

In 1997, the International Air Transportation Competition Act of 1979 was amended to permit service from Southwest's Love Field in Dallas to points in Alabama, Mississippi and Kansas. Previously, Southwest could only serve markets in Arkansas, Louisiana, New Mexico and Oklahoma from its base airport. These restrictions were imposed to shield the significantly larger Dallas-Fort Worth International Airport from competition.

Part of Southwest's strategy to control costs is to fly only one aircraft type. As a result, scheduling, maintenance and pilot training are simplified. At 1997 year end, LUV operated 261 Boeing 737s, of which 142 were owned. The average age of LUV's fleet was 8.3 years, one of the industry's youngest. At July 31 1998, LUV had on order 114 B737-700 aircraft, for delivery between 1998 and 2004. The new aircraft are quieter, more fuel efficient, and have greater range than LUV's existing aircraft.

Southwest has one of the industry's lowest cost structures; it spent 7.4 cents per seat-mile in 1997. Savings are realized by offering only unrestricted coach seats. This greatly reduces ticketing costs. In addition, LUV books 60% of its customers electronically, and, since 1996, has allowed passengers to book flights through its Internet site. Since 1995, LUV has been developing its own computer reservation system (CRS), dubbed SWAT. Because of anticipated delays in implementing SWAT, in July 1998, LUV chose to extend its contract for CRS services with Sabre Group for at least two more years, Despite its low costs, Southwest delivers consistently high levels of service, and ranks high in on-time performance, baggage handling, and overall customer satisfaction in the Department of Transportation's survey of air travelers.

Some 84% of employees are covered by collective bargaining agreements. LUV's flight attendants approved a new six-year pact in December 1997. Contracts with customer service representatives and flight dispatchers became amendable in November 1997, and were still being negotiated in August 1998.

Per Share Data ($) (Year Ended Dec. 31)	1997	1996	1995	1994	1993	1992	1991	1990	1989	1988
Tangible Bk. Val.	6.05	5.04	4.39	3.84	3.28	2.74	2.21	2.13	1.99	1.79
Cash Flow	1.50	1.14	1.01	1.00	0.86	0.63	0.39	0.44	0.47	0.39
Earnings	0.93	0.61	0.55	0.54	0.47	0.29	0.09	0.16	0.23	0.18
Dividends	0.02	0.02	0.02	0.02	0.02	0.02	0.01	0.01	0.01	0.01
Payout Ratio	2%	3%	3%	3%	4%	5%	16%	9%	6%	7%
Prices - High	17 1/2	14 3/4	13 1/4	17 3/8	16 3/4	8 7/8	5 1/8	3	3	2 1/16
- Low	9 1/2	9 1/8	7 1/4	6 7/8	8 1/8	4 3/4	2 7/16	1 7/8	1 15/16	1 5/16
P/E Ratio - High	19	24	24	32	36	31	56	18	13	11
- Low	10	15	13	13	17	17	26	12	8	7
Income Statement Analysis (Million $)										
Revs.	3,817	3,406	2,873	2,592	2,297	1,685	1,314	1,187	1,015	860
Oper. Inc.	720	534	470	470	434	291	149	161	170	152
Depr.	196	183	157	153	131	108	86.2	79.4	72.3	66.2
Int. Exp.	43.7	59.3	58.8	53.4	58.5	58.9	43.9	32.0	33.5	29.2
Pretax Inc.	517	341	305	300	260	147	44.0	75.0	111	85.0
Eff. Tax Rate	39%	39%	40%	40%	41%	38%	39%	37%	36%	32%
Net Inc.	318	207	183	179	154	91.0	26.9	47.1	71.6	58.0
Balance Sheet & Other Fin. Data (Million $)										
Cash	623	582	317	175	296	411	261	88.0	146	210
Curr. Assets	806	751	473	315	432	506	340	158	204	265
Total Assets	4,246	3,723	3,256	2,823	2,576	2,293	1,837	1,471	1,415	1,308
Curr. Liab.	869	765	611	522	479	368	260	225	196	153
LT Debt	628	650	661	583	639	699	617	327	354	370
Common Eqty.	2,009	1,648	1,427	1,239	1,054	854	629	605	587	567
Total Cap.	3,076	2,749	2,370	2,055	1,877	1,687	1,351	1,041	1,060	1,038
Cap. Exp.	689	677	729	789	530	533	341	318	262	389
Cash Flow	513	391	339	333	285	199	113	127	144	124
Curr. Ratio	0.9	1.0	0.8	0.6	0.9	1.4	1.3	0.7	1.0	1.7
% LT Debt of Cap.	20.4	24.5	27.9	28.4	34.1	41.4	45.7	31.4	33.4	35.6
% Net Inc.of Revs.	8.3	6.1	6.4	6.9	6.7	5.4	2.0	4.0	7.0	6.7
% Ret. on Assets	8.0	5.9	6.0	6.6	6.3	4.2	1.6	3.3	5.4	4.9
% Ret. on Equity	17.4	13.5	13.7	15.6	16.0	11.8	4.4	8.1	12.8	10.7

Data as orig. reptd.; bef. results of disc. opers. and/or spec. items. Per share data adj. for stk. divs. as of ex-div. date. Bold denotes diluted EPS (FASB 128). E-Estimated. NA-Not Available. NM-Not Meaningful. NR-Not Ranked.

Office—P.O. Box 36611, Dallas, TX 75235-1611. **Tel**—(214) 792-4000. **Website**—http://www.iflyswa.com **Chrmn, Pres & CEO**—H. D. Kelleher. **EVP & Secy**—C. C. Barrett. **VP & CFO**—G. C. Kelly. **Investor Contact**—Tammy Romo (214-792-4415).**Dirs**—S. E. Barshop, G. H. Bishop, C. W. Crockett, W. P. Hobby Jr., T. C. Johnson, H. D. Kelleher, R. W. King, W. M. Mischer Sr., J. M. Morris. **Transfer Agent & Registrar**—Continental Stock Transfer & Trust Co., NYC. **Incorporated**—in Texas in 1967. **Empl**— 23,974. **S&P Analyst:** Stephen R. Klein

STANDARD &POOR'S
STOCK REPORTS

Springs Industries
2095
NYSE Symbol **SMI**
In S&P 500

12-SEP-98

Industry: Textiles (Home Furnishings)

Summary: This company is a major manufacturer of home furnishings and finished fabrics.

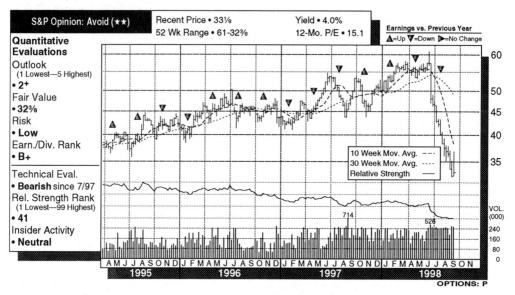

S&P Opinion: Avoid (★★)	Recent Price • 33⅛	Yield • 4.0%
	52 Wk Range • 61-32⅜	12-Mo. P/E • 15.1

Earnings vs. Previous Year
▲=Up ▼=Down ▶=No Change

Quantitative Evaluations

Outlook
(1 Lowest—5 Highest)
• **2+**

Fair Value
• **32⅜**

Risk
• **Low**

Earn./Div. Rank
• **B+**

Technical Eval.
• **Bearish** since 7/97

Rel. Strength Rank
(1 Lowest—99 Highest)
• **41**

Insider Activity
• **Neutral**

10 Week Mov. Avg. ---
30 Week Mov. Avg. ····
Relative Strength —

VOL. (000)

OPTIONS: P

Overview - 27-JUL-98

We expect sales from the home furnishings business (85% of sales) to advance approximately 2% in 1998. However, we project no top line growth in the specialty fabrics segment (15%). We expect gross margins to contract, as a result of less favorable results in the bed fashions business, which has recently seen a decrease in volume, coupled with pricing pressures. In the 1998 second quarter, SMI recorded a charge of $7.5 million ($0.24 a share, after tax) for increased provisions for bad debt in the windows fashion business. We remain concerned about excess inventories in the bedding division, and about the company's inability to deliver strong results. In October 1997, directors authorized the repurchase of up to 2 million common shares; about 600,000 shares had been purchased through February 3, 1998.

Valuation - 27-JUL-98

In an effort to improve production and efficiencies, in the first quarter of 1998, the company announced plans to modernize its towel manufacturing facility and consolidate its printing and finishing plant. As a result of these initiatives, SMI recorded pretax charges of $24.85 million in the first quarter and $1.24 million in the second quarter. The company plans to spend approximately $15 million for Year 2000 issues during 1998 and 1999; in the second half of 1998, restructuring charges are expected to be approximately $8 to 10 million. These factors, as well as problems with the bed fashions business will continue to restrict earnings. We have lowered our 1998 EPS estimate to $2.61 (excluding unusual charges), from $2.90. Considering SMI's poor record of EPS growth, and the small likelihood of a turnaround in the near future, we advise avoiding the shares at their recent valuation of 15X projected 1998 EPS.

Key Stock Statistics

S&P EPS Est. 1998	2.61	Tang. Bk. Value/Share	39.69
P/E on S&P Est. 1998	12.7	Beta	0.64
S&P EPS Est. 1999	3.80	Shareholders	3,200
Dividend Rate/Share	1.32	Market cap. (B)	$0.373
Shs. outstg. (M)	18.5	Inst. holdings	44%
Avg. daily vol. (M)	0.070		

Value of $10,000 invested 5 years ago: $ 11,053

Fiscal Year Ending Dec. 31

	1998	1997	1996	1995	1994	1993
Revenues (Million $)						
1Q	556.7	543.0	583.5	483.1	485.2	502.0
2Q	537.1	528.9	545.0	532.7	515.3	483.9
3Q	—	579.2	569.2	623.7	535.3	514.5
4Q	—	574.9	545.6	593.5	533.2	522.7
Yr.	—	2,226	2,243	2,233	2,069	2,023
Earnings Per Share ($)						
1Q	**-0.16**	0.55	0.60	0.55	0.33	0.51
2Q	**0.28**	0.73	2.10	0.78	0.73	0.50
3Q	**E0.70**	1.34	1.11	1.08	1.10	0.77
4Q	**E0.85**	0.74	0.51	1.30	1.34	0.87
Yr.	**E2.61**	3.43	4.32	3.71	3.50	2.65

Next earnings report expected: mid October

Dividend Data (Dividends have been paid since 1898.)

Amount ($)	Date Decl.	Ex-Div. Date	Stock of Record	Payment Date
0.330	Dec. 11	Dec. 18	Dec. 22	Jan. 05 '98
0.330	Feb. 12	Mar. 11	Mar. 13	Mar. 27 '98
0.330	Apr. 20	Jun. 10	Jun. 12	Jun. 26 '98
0.330	Aug. 13	Sep. 09	Sep. 11	Sep. 25 '98

A Division of The McGraw-Hill Companies

Business Summary - 27-JUL-98

Springs Industries, Inc. has undergone major changes throughout the organization over the past two years. In April 1996, the company sold its Clark-Schwebel fiberglass division for nearly $200 million. In 1995, SMI made three significant acquisitions: Dundee Mills, a producer of towels, baby products and health care products; Dawson Home Fashions, a maker of shower curtain and bath accessories; and Nanik Window Coverings, a manufacturer of wood blinds and interior shutters. These acquisitions expanded the product line, and added approximately $350 million to annual revenues.

In the first quarter of 1998, the company announced plans to modernize its towel manufacturing facility and consolidate its printing and finishing plant. As a result of these initiatives, SMI recorded a pretax charge of $24.85 million in the 1998 first quarter.

Springs is a leading maker of home furnishings (which contributes about 85% of total sales) and specialty fabrics (15%). The home furnishings group makes sheets, pillowcases, bedspreads, comforters, infant and toddler bedding, towels, shower curtains, bath and accent rugs, other bath fashion accessories, knitted infant apparel, baby and healthcare products, juvenile novel-

ties, drapery hardware and hard and soft decorative window furnishings. Bed and bath products are sold under the brand names Springmaid, Wamsutta, Performance, and Dundee. Decorative widow products are sold under brand names including Graber, Bali, Nanik, FashionPleat, Maestro and CrystalPleat.

Specialty fabrics are sold under the brand names Springmaid, Wamsutta and Ultrasuede. Fabrics are used for various applications to manufacturers of apparel and decorative home furnishings, and retailers of home sewing fabrics. This division also offers protective and fire retardant fabrics for both industrial and commercial use.

Internally, SMI has restructured its businesses into three operating groups. The company closed three older manufacturing plants and updated the technology in other plants. It also invested in information and operating systems development. As a result of these initiatives, SMI incurred several restructuring charges in 1996. The company has been experiencing execution delays related to its cost reduction plans, and anticipated savings failed to materialize in 1997.

In the second quarter of 1998, SMI recorded a charge of $7.5 million ($0.24 a share, after taxes), reflecting a larger than anticipated increase in the provision for bad debt in the windows fashion business.

Per Share Data ($)

(Year Ended Dec. 31)	1997	1996	1995	1994	1993	1992	1991	1990	1989	1988
Tangible Bk. Val.	40.69	38.75	36.48	33.20	30.89	33.47	32.39	32.05	33.08	30.67
Cash Flow	7.43	8.50	8.82	7.98	7.03	6.87	5.77	3.72	7.43	6.49
Earnings	3.43	4.32	3.71	3.50	2.65	2.50	1.53	-0.39	3.64	2.98
Dividends	1.32	1.32	1.26	1.20	1.20	1.20	1.20	1.20	1.20	1.02
Payout Ratio	38%	31%	34%	34%	45%	47%	78%	NM	33%	34%
Prices - High	54¾	50½	44¾	41	49	43⅞	36¼	39½	45¼	38¾
- Low	41	38⅜	35¼	29¼	33½	30½	21¼	16⅞	30½	27
P/E Ratio - High	16	12	12	12	18	18	24	NM	12	13
- Low	12	9	10	8	13	12	14	NM	8	9

Income Statement Analysis (Million $)

	1997	1996	1995	1994	1993	1992	1991	1990	1989	1988
Revs.	2,226	2,243	2,233	2,069	2,023	1,976	1,890	1,878	1,909	1,825
Oper. Inc.	211	203	232	216	200	191	155	165	190	184
Depr.	84.6	89.4	99	79.7	78.1	77.7	75.2	72.6	67.5	62.1
Int. Exp.	18.6	22.1	32.0	29.3	30.3	31.4	32.3	30.6	28.1	26.9
Pretax Inc.	103	105	111	107	84.0	80.0	50.0	-7.0	101	85.0
Eff. Tax Rate	33%	15%	36%	42%	44%	44%	45%	NM	36%	38%
Net Inc.	69.0	84.9	71.6	62.2	47.3	44.5	27.1	-6.8	64.9	52.8

Balance Sheet & Other Fin. Data (Million $)

	1997	1996	1995	1994	1993	1992	1991	1990	1989	1988
Cash	0.4	30.7	2.6	1.0	3.0	4.0	6.0	5.0	6.0	67.0
Curr. Assets	787	790	769	617	627	603	596	588	607	619
Total Assets	1,409	1,398	1,528	1,289	1,292	1,250	1,251	1,201	1,188	1,118
Curr. Liab.	240	252	263	244	273	275	266	231	252	229
LT Debt	164	178	327	265	293	274	288	260	228	238
Common Eqty.	978	781	735	584	543	588	569	561	585	542
Total Cap.	969	975	1,088	880	864	896	902	865	878	837
Cap. Exp.	99	75.1	75.0	93.0	88.0	80.0	137	118	119	102
Cash Flow	154	174	170	142	125	122	102	66.0	132	115
Curr. Ratio	3.3	3.1	2.9	2.5	2.3	2.2	2.2	2.5	2.4	2.7
% LT Debt of Cap.	20.4	18.3	30.1	30.2	33.9	30.5	31.9	30.1	25.9	28.5
% Net Inc.of Revs.	3.1	3.8	3.2	3.0	2.3	2.3	1.4	NM	3.4	2.9
% Ret. on Assets	4.9	5.8	5.1	4.8	3.7	3.6	2.2	NM	5.6	4.8
% Ret. on Equity	7.2	11.2	10.9	11.0	8.4	7.7	4.8	NM	11.5	10.1

Data as orig. reptd.; bef. results of disc. opers. and/or spec. items. Per share data adj. for stk. divs. as of ex-div. date. Bold denotes diluted EPS (FASB 128). E-Estimated. NA-Not Available. NM-Not Meaningful. NR-Not Ranked.

Office—205 North White St., Fort Mill, SC 29715. **Tel**—(803) 547-1500. **Website**—www.springs.com**Chrmn, CEO, Pres**—C. C. Bowles. **EVP & CFO**—J. F. Zahm. **SVP & Secy**—C. P. Dorsett. **Dirs**—J. F. Akers, C. C. Bowles, J. L. Clendenin, L. S. Close, C. W. Coker, J. H. McArthur, A. Papone, D. S. Perkins, R. B. Smith, S. H. Smith Jr., S. Turley. **Transfer Agent & Registrar**—Wachovia Bank of North Carolina, Winston-Salem. **Incorporated**—in South Carolina in 1895. **Empl**— 19,500. **S&P Analyst:** Kathleen J. Fraser

STANDARD &POOR'S
STOCK REPORTS

Sprint Corp.

2095M

NYSE Symbol **FON**

In S&P 500

12-SEP-98

Industry: Telecommunications (Long Distance)

Summary: Sprint is the third largest U.S. long-distance carrier.

S&P Opinion: Accumulate (★★★★)	Recent Price • 69⅛	Yield • 1.4%
	52 Wk Range • 75⅝-46⅛	12-Mo. P/E • 36.2

Quantitative Evaluations

Outlook (1 Lowest—5 Highest)
• **1**

Fair Value
• **54¾**

Risk
• **Average**

Earn./Div. Rank
• **B**

Technical Eval.
• **Bearish** since 3/98

Rel. Strength Rank (1 Lowest—99 Highest)
• **86**

Insider Activity
• **Neutral**

Earnings vs. Previous Year
▲=Up ▼=Down ▷=No Change

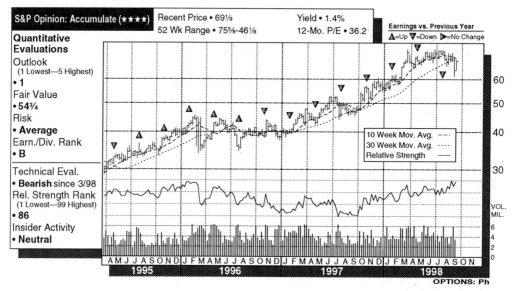

10 Week Mov. Avg. - - -
30 Week Mov. Avg. · · · ·
Relative Strength ——

VOL. MIL.

OPTIONS: Ph

Overview - 24-JUL-98

Through alliances with other industry members, FON is seeking to capitalize on the opening of telecommunications markets worldwide. The Sprint PCS network has been quite successful in its just over a year of operations, as the company has already signed up nearly 1.4 million customers. Sprint utilizes cutting edge CDMA technology in its wireless digital system, which has grown to be the largest PCS network in the U.S. in both number of customers and markets served. The company recently said that it plans to assume ownership and management control of Sprint PCS, which is now majority owned by three major cable companies. Sprint will also issue a new common stock that tracks its wireless operations. Conversely, the Global One alliance the company formed with French and German telephone companies continued to underperform expectations. Recent earnings have been restricted by losses from Global One and the buildout of the Sprint PCS network.

Valuation - 24-JUL-98

The shares have continued to outperform the market in recent months, reflecting the success of the company's wireless PCS network. Sprint is also leveraging key investments in emerging businesses such as Internet access, international development, and competitive local exchange carrier services. These areas will serve to round out the company's bundling strategy, creating a one-stop-shopping environment for customers. We have a very favorable view of the long-distance market, as its companies are well positioned to excel in an increasingly competitive environment. We maintain our positive view of the shares, with the expectation that they will outperform the S&P 500 over the next 12 months.

Key Stock Statistics

S&P EPS Est. 1998	2.00	Tang. Bk. Value/Share	21.44
P/E on S&P Est. 1998	34.6	Beta	0.66
S&P EPS Est. 1999	2.55	Shareholders	100,000
Dividend Rate/Share	1.00	Market cap. (B)	$ 23.8
Shs. outstg. (M)	430.1	Inst. holdings	50%
Avg. daily vol. (M)	0.867		

Value of $10,000 invested 5 years ago: NA

Fiscal Year Ending Dec. 31

	1998	1997	1996	1995	1994	1993
Revenues (Million $)						
1Q	3,911	3,579	3,372	3,079	3,033	2,718
2Q	3,967	3,668	3,506	3,142	3,150	2,801
3Q	—	3,779	3,544	3,205	3,234	2,868
4Q	—	3,849	3,622	3,339	3,244	2,981
Yr.	—	14,874	14,045	12,765	12,662	11,368
Earnings Per Share ($)						
1Q	**0.49**	**0.67**	0.77	0.64	0.65	-0.03
2Q	**0.49**	**0.59**	0.73	0.69	0.63	0.48
3Q	**E0.52**	**0.49**	0.73	0.76	0.66	0.39
4Q	**E0.50**	**0.45**	0.57	0.61	0.59	0.55
Yr.	**E2.00**	**2.18**	2.79	2.69	2.53	1.39

Next earnings report expected: mid October

Dividend Data (Dividends have been paid since 1939.)

Amount ($)	Date Decl.	Ex-Div. Date	Stock of Record	Payment Date
0.250	Oct. 14	Dec. 04	Dec. 08	Dec. 29 '97
0.250	Feb. 10	Mar. 06	Mar. 10	Mar. 31 '98
0.250	Apr. 21	Jun. 05	Jun. 09	Jun. 30 '98
0.250	Aug. 11	Sep. 04	Sep. 09	Sep. 30 '98

A Division of The McGraw-Hill Companies

STANDARD
&POOR'S
STOCK REPORTS

Sprint Corporation

2095M
12-SEP-98

Business Summary - 24-JUL-98

Sprint, the third largest long-distance carrier, is off to a running start in providing digital wireless PCS (personal communications services). Revenue contributions in recent years were:

	1997	1996
Long-distance services	57%	57%
Local services	33%	35%
Product distribution/Directory publishing	9%	8%
Emerging business	1%	---

The company's strategy includes key strategic alliances, which will enable it to compete for the long run. Sprint's long-distance operations control about 10% of the domestic market, behind industry leaders AT&T and MCI and ahead of rising WorldCom, which is in the process of acquiring MCI. At December 31, 1997, local telephone units served more than 7.4 million access lines in 19 states. Complementary businesses include directory publishing and distribution of telecommunications and security and alarm products.

Sprint and cable operators Tele-Communications Inc. (TCI), Comcast Corporation and Cox Communications formed a joint venture called Sprint Spectrum LP. The venture's plans include the provision of nationwide wireless communications services in the U.S. using personal communications services (PCS) licenses acquired in FCC auctions. However, In May 1998, the company said that it plans to assume ownership and management control of Sprint PCS, and issue a stock that will track the wireless operations in late 1998.

In January 1997, Sprint won the right to PCS licenses in 39 states, for $545 million, in an FCC auction. FON paid an average of $7.78 per person for each 10 Mhz license, which will reach a total population of 70 million in cities across the contiguous U.S., Hawaii, Alaska, Puerto Rico and the Virgin Islands. In addition, the venture plans to offer competitive local telecommunications services on a national basis using the facilities of the cable partners. Sprint PCS is the first single-technology, 100%-digital, state-of-the-art wireless network to provide personal communications services across the U.S. By year-end, Sprint PCS had initiated service in 134 metropolitan markets, and plans to add another 100 markets by early 1999.

In January 1996, FON, Deutsche Telekom and France Telecom launched Global One, a new international telecommunications venture serving business, consumer and carrier markets in more than 55 countries. Sprint also plans to create a seamless platform of crossborder services through its interest in Sprint Canada and a separate strategic alliance with Telefonos de Mexico.

Per Share Data ($)

(Year Ended Dec. 31)	1997	1996	1995	1994	1993	1992	1991	1990	1989	1988
Tangible Bk. Val.	21.04	19.81	13.30	10.96	9.26	12.75	11.54	10.30	9.42	8.58
Cash Flow	6.14	6.53	6.89	6.77	5.35	7.35	7.04	6.21	6.14	4.97
Earnings	2.18	2.79	2.73	2.53	1.39	1.93	1.68	1.43	1.72	0.68
Dividends	1.00	1.00	1.00	1.00	1.00	1.00	1.00	1.00	0.97	0.96
Payout Ratio	46%	36%	37%	40%	72%	52%	60%	70%	56%	142%
Prices - High	60⅝	45½	41⅛	40⅛	40¼	26¾	31½	46⅜	43¾	23⅞
- Low	38⅜	33⅞	25⅞	26⅛	25½	20¾	21¼	20⅝	22	12⅛
P/E Ratio - High	28	16	15	16	29	14	19	32	25	35
- Low	18	12	9	10	18	11	13	14	13	18

Income Statement Analysis (Million $)

	1997	1996	1995	1994	1993	1992	1991	1990	1989	1988
Revs.	14,874	14,045	12,765	12,662	11,368	9,230	8,780	8,345	7,549	6,493
Oper. Inc.	4,178	3,858	3,388	3,266	2,609	2,248	2,177	1,877	1,834	1,300
Depr.	1,726	1,591	1,466	1,478	1,359	1,192	1,164	1,023	924	877
Int. Exp.	280	301	318	407	452	395	421	414	381	346
Pretax Inc.	1,583	1,912	1,480	1,404	776	656	607	470	562	-92.0
Eff. Tax Rate	40%	38%	36%	36%	38%	35%	32%	33%	29%	NM
Net Inc.	953	1,191	946	884	481	427	368	309	363	142

Balance Sheet & Other Fin. Data (Million $)

	1997	1996	1995	1994	1993	1992	1991	1990	1989	1988
Cash	102	1,151	124	123	207	109	74.0	119	115	617
Curr. Assets	3,773	4,353	3,619	2,189	1,978	1,444	1,618	1,777	1,509	2,125
Total Assets	18,185	16,953	15,196	14,936	14,149	10,188	10,464	10,553	9,821	9,817
Curr. Liab.	3,077	3,314	5,142	3,055	3,069	2,507	2,326	2,438	2,279	2,149
LT Debt	3,755	2,981	3,253	4,605	4,571	3,535	3,696	3,974	3,747	3,675
Common Eqty.	9,025	8,520	4,643	4,525	3,918	2,814	2,519	2,296	2,073	1,875
Total Cap.	13,809	12,360	8,772	10,426	9,711	7,339	7,910	7,896	7,416	7,518
Cap. Exp.	2,863	2,434	1,857	2,016	1,595	1,151	1,244	1,566	1,730	4,461
Cash Flow	2,678	2,781	2,412	2,359	1,839	1,617	1,529	1,389	1,284	1,015
Curr. Ratio	1.2	1.3	0.7	0.7	0.6	0.6	0.7	0.7	0.7	1.0
% LT Debt of Cap.	27.1	24.1	37.1	44.2	47.1	48.2	46.7	50.3	50.5	48.9
% Net Inc.of Revs.	6.4	8.5	7.4	7.0	4.2	4.6	4.2	3.7	4.8	2.2
% Ret. on Assets	5.4	7.4	6.4	6.0	3.5	4.1	3.5	3.0	3.7	1.7
% Ret. on Equity	10.8	18.1	20.6	20.7	12.1	15.8	15.0	13.8	18.2	8.1

Data as orig. reptd.; bef. results of disc. opers. and/or spec. items. Per share data adj. for stk. divs. as of ex-div. date. Bold denotes diluted EPS (FASB 128). E-Estimated. NA-Not Available. NM-Not Meaningful. NR-Not Ranked.

Office—2330 Shawnee Mission Pkwy., Westwood, KS 66205 (P.O. Box 11315, Kansas City, MO 64112). **Tel**—(913) 624-3000. **Website**—http://www.sprint.com **Chrmn & CEO**—W. T. Esrey. **Pres & COO**—R. T. LeMay.**EVP & CFO**—A. B. Krause. **SVP & Treas**—M. J. Strandjord.**VP, & Secy**—D. A. Jensen. **Dirs**—D. Ausley, W. L. Batts, M. Bon, W. T. Esrey, I. O. Hockaday, Jr., H. S. Hook, R. T. LeMay, L. Koch Lorimer, C. E. Rice, R. Sommer, S. Turley. **Transfer Agents & Registrars**—UMB Bank, Kansas City, MO; ChaseMellon Shareholder Services, NYC. **Incorporated**—in Kansas in 1938. **Empl**— 50,602. **S&P Analyst:** Philip D. Wohl

STANDARD &POOR'S
STOCK REPORTS

Stanley Works

2124K

NYSE Symbol **SWK**

In S&P 500

12-SEP-98

Industry: Hardware & Tools

Summary: This company is a worldwide producer of tools, hardware and specialty hardware for home improvement, consumer, industrial and professional use.

| S&P Opinion: Hold (★★★) | Recent Price • 38⅛ | Yield • 2.3% |
| | 52 Wk Range • 57¼-37⅝ | 12-Mo. P/E • 53.8 |

Quantitative Evaluations

Outlook
(1 Lowest—5 Highest)
• **1**

Fair Value
• **35⅞**

Risk
• **Average**

Earn./Div. Rank
• **B**

Technical Eval.
• **Bullish** since 7/98

Rel. Strength Rank
(1 Lowest—99 Highest)
• **61**

Insider Activity
• **Neutral**

Earnings vs. Previous Year
▲=Up ▼=Down ▶=No Change

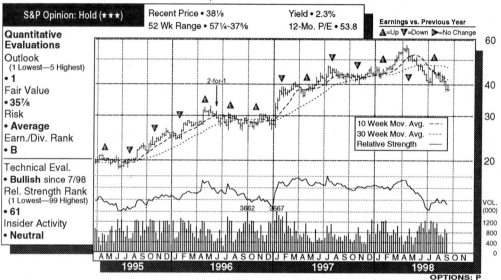

10 Week Mov. Avg. ----
30 Week Mov. Avg. ·····
Relative Strength ——

OPTIONS: P

Overview - 30-JUL-98

In July 1997, SWK's new CEO, John Trani, outlined a bold new strategy. He emphasized that, given the fragmented nature of the hard goods industry, SWK's greatest asset, its well recognized and respected brand name, was not being fully utilized, and said he would triple the advertising budget. Also, recognizing product innovation as the life blood of a manufacturing company, SWK would invest much more in developing new products and product extensions. This should help make SWK a one-stop shop for its customers, the consolidating domestic "big box" (e.g. Home Depot) retail channel. In addition, SWK expects to foster growth via acquisitions; by entering related markets through brand name and distribution leverage; and by pursuing global expansion opportunities. To help pay for these initiatives and attain low-cost producer status, the company is aggressively streamlining operations, and is focusing on improving working capital turnover. SWK will incur $340 million in restructuring and related transition charges ($239 million in 1997) to reduce facility locations from 123 to 70, and to cut employment about 23%.

Valuation - 30-JUL-98

The shares have nearly tripled since early 1995, following the unveiling of aggressive growth and cost-cutting programs in July 1995, and the December 1996 appointment of a new CEO. The pricing environment remains competitive, but revenues should benefit from new growth strategies, industry outsourcing trends, and strong sales of existing homes over the past two years. Margins should expand over the next few years, aided by cost-cutting programs, but until it consistently improves customer service, SWK will not realize its potential. Despite its difficulties, pro forma core operations are showing gains, and SWK remains a good long-term holding.

Key Stock Statistics

S&P EPS Est. 1998	2.30	Tang. Bk. Value/Share	6.11
P/E on S&P Est. 1998	16.6	Beta	1.04
Dividend Rate/Share	0.86	Shareholders	16,200
Shs. outstg. (M)	88.8	Market cap. (B)	$ 3.4
Avg. daily vol. (M)	0.162	Inst. holdings	62%

Value of $10,000 invested 5 years ago: $ 20,953

Fiscal Year Ending Dec. 31

	1998	1997	1996	1995	1994	1993
Revenues (Million $)						
1Q	671.9	646.6	635.3	643.3	585.7	553.4
2Q	691.8	673.6	677.2	655.5	628.8	565.2
3Q	—	650.5	672.9	655.7	632.6	576.3
4Q	—	698.8	685.4	669.8	663.8	578.2
Yr.	—	2,670	2,671	2,624	2,511	2,273
Earnings Per Share ($)						
1Q	0.40	0.41	0.34	0.33	0.28	0.26
2Q	0.47	-0.72	0.37	0.35	0.38	0.30
3Q	—	-0.46	0.42	-0.02	0.36	0.28
4Q	—	0.29	-0.03	0.01	0.38	0.20
Yr.	E2.30	-0.47	1.09	0.66	1.40	1.03

Next earnings report expected: mid October

Dividend Data (Dividends have been paid since 1877.)

Amount ($)	Date Decl.	Ex-Div. Date	Stock of Record	Payment Date
0.200	Oct. 22	Nov. 25	Nov. 28	Dec. 26 '97
0.200	Feb. 25	Mar. 05	Mar. 09	Mar. 27 '98
0.200	May. 20	Jun. 04	Jun. 08	Jun. 29 '98
0.215	Jul. 15	Sep. 03	Sep. 08	Sep. 29 '98

A Division of The McGraw-Hill Companies

Business Summary - 30-JUL-98

The Stanley Works makes hand tools and hardware products for the home improvement, consumer, industrial and professional markets. Contributions by industry segment (profits in millions) in 1997 were:

	Sales	Profits
Tools	76%	$29.2
Hardware	13%	10.5
Specialty hardware	11%	-4.6

Foreign operations, a large portion of which are in Europe, accounted for 28% of sales in each of 1996 and 1997.

The Tools segment produces consumer hand tools such as measuring instruments, planes, hammers, knives and blades, wrenches, sockets, screwdrivers, saws, chisels, boring tools, masonry, tile and drywall tools, and paint preparation and application tools. The company also makes industrial and mechanics hand tools and high-density industrial storage and retrieval systems. In addition, SWK manufactures engineered tools, including fastening tools and fasteners used for commercial, industrial, construction, packaging and consumer use; hydraulic tools used in heavy construction; and precision air tools used chiefly by vehicle manufacturers.

The Hardware segment makes hinges, hasps, shelf brackets, bolts and latches; closet organizing systems; and residential door hardware, wall mirrors and mirrored closet doors.

Specialty hardware includes residential insulated steel and reinforced fiberglass door systems and automatic doors.

In 1996, Stanley took a number of significant restructuring actions, continuing a program begun in 1995. These moves resulted in a net pretax restructuring charge of $47.8 million (versus $85.5 million in 1995) from a net loss of $3 million on the sale of five businesses, the writedown of impaired assets, the closure of 13 plants and severance; in addition, related transition costs of $32.9 million ($9.5 million) were incurred and expensed as operating items.

These 1995-96 restructuring actions resulted in a total of $400 million of savings, including $250 million from asset divestitures and inventory reductions. Improved procurement and other operational savings rendered the remaining $150 million in savings, of which about half is targeted for promotional activities to expand market share; the other half will flow directly to the bottom line.

With the sale of the garage-related products business in February 1997, SWK completed a divestiture program announced in early 1996. New restructuring initiatives announced in July 1997 should bring an additional $145 million annual benefit, most of which will be reinvested into new products and brand development.

Per Share Data ($)

(Year Ended Dec. 31)	1997	1996	1995	1994	1993	1992	1991	1990	1989	1988
Tangible Bk. Val.	5.67	7.68	6.79	6.52	5.70	5.74	6.28	7.19	6.58	7.00
Cash Flow	0.34	1.93	1.58	2.10	1.74	1.75	1.81	1.97	2.00	1.78
Earnings	-0.47	1.09	0.67	1.40	1.03	1.07	1.16	1.26	1.35	1.20
Dividends	0.77	0.73	0.71	0.69	0.67	0.64	0.61	0.57	0.51	0.46
Payout Ratio	NM	67%	107%	49%	65%	60%	58%	44%	37%	38%
Prices - High	47³/₈	32⁷/₈	26³/₄	22¹/₂	24	24¹/₄	22	20	19⁵/₈	15⁷/₈
- Low	28	23⁵/₈	17⁷/₈	17¹/₂	19	16¹/₄	13	13¹/₄	13³/₄	11⁷/₈
P/E Ratio - High	NM	30	40	16	23	22	19	16	14	13
- Low	NM	22	27	12	18	15	11	10	10	10

Income Statement Analysis (Million $)

	1997	1996	1995	1994	1993	1992	1991	1990	1989	1988
Revs.	2,670	2,671	2,624	2,511	2,273	2,218	1,962	1,977	1,972	1,909
Oper. Inc.	331	342	324	330	271	270	266	274	292	269
Depr.	72.4	74.7	81.2	63.3	63.1	62.4	61.4	59.5	55.9	50.3
Int. Exp.	24.7	28.0	35.6	33.6	32.0	33.1	38.0	37.6	35.5	39.7
Pretax Inc.	-18.6	174	113	202	148	158	157	172	194	172
Eff. Tax Rate	NM	44%	48%	38%	37%	38%	39%	38%	39%	40%
Net Inc.	-41.9	96.9	59.1	125	93.0	98.0	95.0	107	118	103

Balance Sheet & Other Fin. Data (Million $)

	1997	1996	1995	1994	1993	1992	1991	1990	1989	1988
Cash	152	84.0	75.4	69.3	43.7	81.1	58.3	94.7	55.4	36.6
Curr. Assets	1,005	911	915	889	759	779	744	744	760	710
Total Assets	1,759	1,660	1,670	1,701	1,577	1,608	1,548	1,494	1,491	1,405
Curr. Liab.	623	382	388	422	357	330	309	282	284	267
LT Debt	284	343	391	387	377	438	397	398	416	339
Common Eqty.	608	780	735	744	681	696	706	697	674	698
Total Cap.	892	1,123	1,142	1,146	1,094	1,189	1,159	1,152	1,146	1,083
Cap. Exp.	73.3	78.7	66.5	66.0	70.0	65.0	92.0	78.0	84.0	90.0
Cash Flow	30.5	172	140	189	156	161	157	166	174	154
Curr. Ratio	1.6	2.4	2.4	2.1	2.1	2.4	2.4	2.6	2.7	2.7
% LT Debt of Cap.	31.8	30.6	34.2	33.8	34.5	36.8	34.2	34.6	36.3	31.3
% Net Inc.of Revs.	NM	3.7	2.3	5.0	4.1	4.4	4.8	5.4	6.0	5.4
% Ret. on Assets	NM	5.9	3.5	7.7	5.9	6.2	6.0	7.3	8.1	7.4
% Ret. on Equity	NM	12.8	8.0	17.6	13.6	14.0	12.9	15.9	17.1	15.5

Data as orig. reptd.; bef. results of disc. opers. and/or spec. items. Per share data adj. for stk. divs. as of ex-div. date. Bold denotes diluted EPS (FASB 128). E-Estimated. NA-Not Available. NM-Not Meaningful. NR-Not Ranked.

Office—1000 Stanley Dr., New Britain, CT 06053. **Tel**—(860) 225-5111. **Website**—http://www.stanleyworks.com **Chrmn & CEO**—J. M. Trani. **VP & Secy**—S. S. Weddle. **VP & CFO**—R. Huck. **Investor Contact**—Gerard J. Gould (860-827-3833). **Dirs**—S. B. Brown, E. R. Fiedler, M. L. Jackson, J. G. Kaiser, E. S. Kraus, J. M. Trani, H. E. Uyterhoeven, W. W. Williams, K. D. Wriston. **Transfer Agent & Registrar**—Boston EquiServe. **Incorporated**—in Connecticut in 1852. **Empl**— 18,903. **S&P Analyst:** Efraim Levy

STANDARD &POOR'S
STOCK REPORTS

State Street Corp.

2132C

NYSE Symbol **STT**

In S&P 500

12-SEP-98

Industry: Banks (Major Regional)

Summary: This bank holding company, with $4.5 trillion in assets under custody and $459 billion in assets under management, is a leading servicer of financial assets worldwide.

S&P Opinion: Accumulate (★★★★)	Recent Price • 50⅝	Yield • 1.0%
	52 Wk Range • 74¼-48½	12-Mo. P/E • 19.9

Quantitative Evaluations

Outlook
(1 Lowest—5 Highest)
• **1**

Fair Value
• **47¾**

Risk
• **Low**

Earn./Div. Rank
• **A+**

Technical Eval.
• **Bearish** since 8/98

Rel. Strength Rank
(1 Lowest—99 Highest)
• **37**

Insider Activity
• **Neutral**

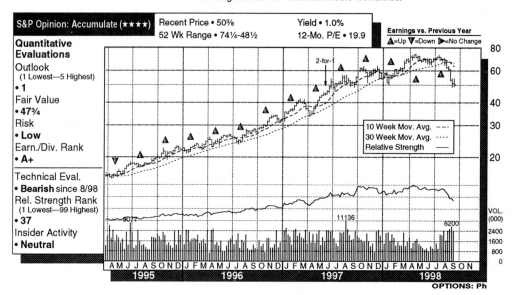

Earnings vs. Previous Year
▲=Up ▼=Down ▶=No Change

10 Week Mov. Avg. ---
30 Week Mov. Avg. ----
Relative Strength —

OPTIONS: Ph

Overview - 29-JUL-98

Fee revenue growth should continue at better than 20% in 1998, led mainly by rising fiduciary compensation resulting from new business and expanded customer relationships, appreciated assets serviced, and additional non-U.S. fund services. A concurrent rise in operating expenses to support business expansion needed to handle the greater revenue volume will limit the overall effect on the bottom line. Nevertheless, the company intends to achieve a growth rate of revenues greater than the growth rate of expenses through several streamlining initiatives. Volatile currency markets and higher foreign deposit levels due to investor uncertainty have had a near term positive impact on earnings. Following an exceptionally strong 1997, results in 1998 are expected to return to more sustainable 15% growth rates, due to a slowdown in underlying asset appreciation from recent years and somewhat less volatile currency markets.

Valuation - 29-JUL-98

Earnings continue to benefit from a strong equity market and mutual fund inflow activity. The company's strategy of technology investment, global expansion and product enhancement is continuing to pay off. Favorable business conditions include rising mutual fund assets, substantial growth in non-U.S. business and consolidation among financial asset servicing companies. The company's dominant industry position, which has made it a preferred provider, and good long-term prospects make the shares worthwhile to accumulate for long-term accounts. A substantial portion of revenues is derived from noninterest (i.e., fee-based) income sources. Thus, STT's shares typically trade at a premium valuation to those of other regional banks.

Key Stock Statistics

S&P EPS Est. 1998	2.70	Tang. Bk. Value/Share	13.39
P/E on S&P Est. 1998	18.7	Beta	1.70
S&P EPS Est. 1999	3.10	Shareholders	5,800
Dividend Rate/Share	0.52	Market cap. (B)	$ 8.1
Shs. outstg. (M)	161.5	Inst. holdings	66%
Avg. daily vol. (M)	0.790		

Value of $10,000 invested 5 years ago: $ 24,791

Fiscal Year Ending Dec. 31

	1998	1997	1996	1995	1994	1993
Revenues (Million $)						
1Q	960.0	772.0	653.0	580.5	440.7	357.4
2Q	1,043	829.0	665.0	606.9	442.7	377.1
3Q	—	894.0	693.0	625.1	479.6	388.3
4Q	—	933.0	734.0	643.3	522.8	409.5
Yr.	—	3,428	2,745	2,456	1,886	1,532
Earnings Per Share ($)						
1Q	**0.64**	**0.53**	0.42	0.33	0.34	0.28
2Q	**0.66**	**0.56**	0.43	0.38	0.33	0.28
3Q	**E0.69**	**0.62**	0.46	0.39	0.34	0.30
4Q	**E0.71**	**0.61**	0.48	0.40	0.35	0.31
Yr.	**E2.70**	**2.32**	1.79	1.49	1.35	1.18

Next earnings report expected: mid October

Dividend Data (Dividends have been paid since 1910.)

Amount ($)	Date Decl.	Ex-Div. Date	Stock of Record	Payment Date
0.110	Sep. 18	Sep. 29	Oct. 01	Oct. 15 '97
0.120	Dec. 18	Dec. 30	Jan. 02	Jan. 15 '98
0.120	Mar. 19	Mar. 30	Apr. 01	Apr. 15 '98
0.130	Jun. 18	Jun. 29	Jul. 01	Jul. 15 '98

A Division of The McGraw-Hill Companies

State Street Corporation

Business Summary - 29-JUL-98

Best known as a leading provider of services in the post-trade phase of the investment process, which includes custody, accounting, fund administration and performance, State Street Corp. is one of largest providers of trust services in the U.S., with $3.9 trillion of assets under custody and $390 billion of assets under management at 1997 year-end. Its strategy for growth revolves around enhancing and adding products and services, redesigning business processes and expanding globally. The company seeks to take advantage of certain long-term trends that should increase the overall demand for its products, such as an aging world population, greater cross-border investing and the need for complex global investment strategies. Acquisitions may be made for strategic purposes, though the focus remains on internal growth.

Operations are conducted through three lines of business: services for institutional investors (64% of operating profits in 1997), investment management (15%) and commercial lending (21%). Services for institutional investors are primarily accounting, custody, daily pricing and information services for large pools of invested assets such as mutual funds and pension plans and corporate trusteeship. State Street is the leading mutual fund custodian in the U.S., with $1.7 trillion of mutual fund assets under custody. Investment management services are provided for financial assets worldwide for both institutions and individuals and include passive and active equity, money market and fixed income strategies. Commercial lending provides loans and other banking services for regional middle market companies and for broker/dealers; it also includes leasing and international trade finance.

In 1997, average earning assets, from which interest income is derived, amounted to $31.4 billion and consisted mainly of loans (17%), investment securities (33%), interest-bearing deposits (27%), and federal funds sold, securities purchased under resale agreements and trading account assets (23%). Average sources of funds included interest-bearing deposits (6%), foreign deposits (36%), noninterest-bearing demand deposits (15%), short-term borrowings (30%), long-term debt (2%), shareholders' equity (5%) and other (6%).

At year-end 1997, nonaccrual loans were $2 million (0.04% of total loans), down from $12 million (0.25%) a year earlier. The allowance for loan losses, which is set aside for possible loan defaults, was $83 million (1.49% of loans), versus $73 million (1.55%) a year earlier. There were net charge-offs of $6 million in 1997, compared to net recoveries of $2 million in 1996.

Per Share Data ($) (Year Ended Dec. 31)	1997	1996	1995	1994	1993	1992	1991	1990	1989	1988
Tangible Bk. Val.	12.40	10.94	9.63	8.05	7.28	6.35	5.49	4.75	4.14	3.61
Earnings	2.32	1.79	1.49	1.35	1.18	1.05	0.93	0.80	0.71	0.63
Dividends	0.44	0.38	0.33	0.30	0.26	0.23	0.20	0.17	0.15	0.13
Payout Ratio	19%	21%	22%	22%	22%	22%	21%	21%	21%	21%
Prices - High	$63\frac{5}{8}$	$34\frac{1}{4}$	$23\frac{1}{8}$	$21\frac{5}{8}$	$24\frac{5}{8}$	$22\frac{1}{2}$	$16\frac{1}{8}$	$10\frac{7}{8}$	$10\frac{1}{4}$	7
- Low	$31\frac{3}{8}$	$20\frac{7}{8}$	14	$13\frac{7}{8}$	$14\frac{5}{8}$	$14\frac{5}{8}$	$7\frac{3}{4}$	$5\frac{1}{2}$	$6\frac{3}{8}$	$4\frac{7}{8}$
P/E Ratio - High	27	19	16	16	21	21	17	14	14	11
- Low	13	12	9	10	12	14	8	7	9	8
Income Statement Analysis (Million $)										
Net Int. Inc.	641	551	429	367	318	282	274	271	217	200
Tax Equiv. Adj.	44.0	37.0	34.9	23.8	20.2	13.6	18.8	20.8	15.5	16.1
Non Int. Inc.	1,673	1,292	1,107	982	818	691	617	503	447	396
Loan Loss Prov.	16.0	8.0	8.0	11.6	11.3	12.2	60.0	45.7	19.4	15.6
Exp./Op. Revs.	74%	74%	75%	74%	75%	73%	67%	69%	70%	71%
Pretax Inc.	564	447	367	320	277	257	225	183	163	145
Eff. Tax Rate	33%	35%	33%	35%	35%	38%	38%	36%	36%	36%
Net Inc.	380	293	247	207	180	160	139	117	104	92.3
% Net Int. Marg.	2.18	2.23	2.01	NA	2.08	2.14	2.89	3.26	3.34	3.51
Balance Sheet & Other Fin. Data (Million $)										
Earning Assets:										
Money Mkt	16,450	16,952	12,233	7,615	7,763	8,224	8,113	4,278	3,262	2,481
Inv. Securities	10,375	9,387	6,360	8,414	5,701	4,092	3,250	2,842	2,515	2,367
Com'l Loans	3,919	3,701	3,144	2,522	2,215	1,771	1,623	1,738	1,632	1,472
Other Loans	1,643	1,012	842	711	466	233	282	803	833	707
Total Assets	37,975	36,524	25,785	21,730	18,720	16,490	15,046	11,651	9,983	8,372
Demand Deposits	7,785	6,395	5,082	4,212	5,450	4,374	3,564	3,236	3,263	2,775
Time Deposits	17,093	13,124	11,565	9,691	7,568	6,687	5,168	4,422	2,915	2,613
LT Debt	774	511	175	128	129	146	147	112	115	123
Common Eqty.	1,995	1,775	1,588	1,231	1,105	953	817	695	597	506
% Ret. on Assets	1.1	1.1	1.0	1.0	1.0	1.0	1.2	1.1	1.3	1.3
% Ret. on Equity	20.2	17.5	16.9	17.8	17.4	18.1	18.0	18.1	18.7	18.7
% Loan Loss Resv.	1.5	1.6	1.6	1.8	2.0	2.9	3.5	2.0	2.0	2.3
% Loans/Deposits	22.4	24.2	23.9	23.3	20.6	18.1	21.8	33.2	39.9	40.4
% Equity to Assets	5.4	5.9	6.1	5.7	5.7	5.7	6.7	6.3	6.9	6.8

Data as orig. reptd.; bef. results of disc. opers. and/or spec. items. Per share data adj. for stk. divs. as of ex-div. date. Bold denotes diluted EPS (FASB 128). E-Estimated. NA-Not Available. NM-Not Meaningful. NR-Not Ranked.

Formed—in 1970; bank incorporated in Massachusetts in 1891. **Office**—225 Franklin St., Boston, MA 02110. **Tel**—(617) 786-3000. **Website**—http://www.statestreet.com **Chrmn & CEO**—M. N. Carter. **Pres & COO**—D. A. Spina. **EVP, CFO & Treas**—R. L. O'Kelley. **Investor Contact**—Karen Wharton (617) 664-3477. **Dirs**—T. E. Albright, J. A. Baute, I. M. Booth, M. N. Carter, J. I. Cash Jr., T. S. Casner, N. F. Darehshori, A. L. Goldstein, D. P. Gruber, C. F. Kaye, J. M. Kucharski, C. R. LaMantia, D. B. Perini, D. J. Picard, A. Poe, B. W. Reznicek, D. A. Spina, D. Walsh, R. E. Weissman. **Transfer Agent**—State Street Bank and Trust Co., Boston. **Empl**— 14,199. **S&P Analyst:** Stephen R. Biggar

12-SEP-98

Industry:
Containers and Packaging (Paper)

Summary: This unbleached paper and packaging maker agreed in May 1998 to be bought by Jefferson Smurfit Corp. The combination will be the world's largest paper-based packaging firm.

| S&P Opinion: Hold (★★★) | Recent Price • 9¼ | Yield • Nil |
| | 52 Wk Range • 21⅛-9 | 12-Mo. P/E • NM |

Quantitative Evaluations

Outlook
 (1 Lowest—5 Highest)
• 1

Fair Value
• 6⅝

Risk
• **Average**

Earn./Div. Rank
• C

Technical Eval.
• **Bearish** since 8/98

Rel. Strength Rank
 (1 Lowest—99 Highest)
• **18**

Insider Activity
• **Unfavorable**

Earnings vs. Previous Year
▲=Up ▼=Down ▶=No Change

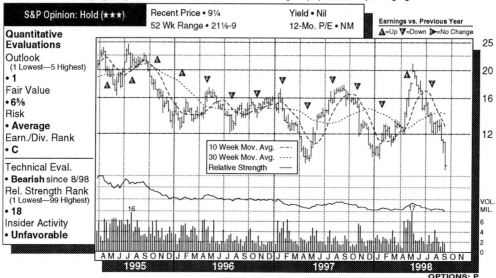

10 Week Mov. Avg. ---
30 Week Mov. Avg. ·····
Relative Strength —

1995 1996 1997 1998

OPTIONS: P

Overview - 24-AUG-98

Jefferson Smurfit's (JJSC) planned purchase of Stone is expected to take place in the fall of 1998. We think STO's sales will be modestly higher to that point, on slightly higher average prices. However, Asia's financial crisis and a strong U.S. dollar have drastically slowed industry exports over the past few months, causing a setback in the packaging recovery seen in 1997. Given the difficult trends and Stone's huge debt load, we see substantial losses continuing. The EPS table includes $0.95 a share of second quarter charges for the writeoff of a pulp mill investment and exchange losses, but we have taken them out of our full year 1998 estimate. Forecasts shown are for STO alone. We see the merger as slightly additive to 1999 EPS of the duo. Stone's huge debt load worries us, but JJSC has a reputation for fast, successful cost cutting steps. It plans to reduce debt by carrying out Stone's earlier announced plan to dispose of non-core assets, and sees $350 million of merger synergies within two years of closing.

Valuation - 24-AUG-98

The shares have seesawed in 1998. They rose sharply early on, when investors relaxed about Asia's woes and expected the corrugated recovery to go on. Rumors about Jefferson Smurfit's May 1998 agreement to buy Stone provided further fuel. They have since given back most of the gains, as difficult global economies set back the corrugated recovery. We view the combination favorably. The dominant corrugated share of the combined firm should be a big plus during better industry times. The partners have also identified major cost saving synergies. Stone carries a huge debt load into the package, but JJSC's fine management team should make the merger work. However, given our belief that sector troubles will go on for an extended period, we would not presently add to our STO stake.

Key Stock Statistics

S&P EPS Est. 1998	-2.20	Tang. Bk. Value/Share	NM
P/E on S&P Est. 1998	NM	Beta	1.13
S&P EPS Est. 1999	0.40	Shareholders	6,400
Dividend Rate/Share	Nil	Market cap. (B)	$0.978
Shs. outstg. (M)	105.0	Inst. holdings	67%
Avg. daily vol. (M)	0.362		

Value of $10,000 invested 5 years ago: $ 5,904

Fiscal Year Ending Dec. 31

	1998	1997	1996	1995	1994	1993
Revenues (Million $)						
1Q	1,265	1,181	1,322	1,819	1,291	1,306
2Q	1,274	1,200	1,282	1,964	1,354	1,268
3Q	—	1,183	1,295	1,924	1,482	1,243
4Q	—	1,285	1,243	1,644	1,621	1,243
Yr.	—	4,849	5,142	7,351	5,749	5,060
Earnings Per Share ($)						
1Q	-0.71	-0.99	0.31	1.04	-0.99	-0.91
2Q	-1.59	-1.10	-0.23	1.42	-0.58	-1.03
3Q	—	-1.01	-0.50	1.32	-0.38	-1.42
4Q	—	-1.04	-0.89	0.86	0.31	-1.23
Yr.	—	-4.16	-1.32	4.64	-1.60	-4.59

Next earnings report expected: late October

Dividend Data

After being paid since 1995, cash dividends were omitted in January 1997.

 A Division of The McGraw·Hill Companies

STANDARD
&POOR'S
STOCK REPORTS

Stone Container Corporation

2151

12-SEP-98

Business Summary - 24-AUG-98

Stone Container Corp. reached an agreement in May 1998 to be acquired by Jefferson Smurfit Corp. (JJSC). The combined firm will be the number one paper-based packaging company in the world. STO is the world's leading manufacturer of containerboard (the outside and inside coatings of a cardboard box) and corrugated containers, and holds the same position in the area of kraft paper (used for grocery bags) and bags and sacks. Jefferson (47%-owned by Jefferson Smurfit Group PLC; JSG), ranks as the largest U.S. producer of recycled paperboard and packaging products, and also makes recycled newsprint.

The merger agreement with Jefferson calls for STO holders to receive 0.99 JJSC shares for each STO share held. Upon closing, JJSC's name will be changed to Smurfit-Stone Container Corp. Holders of Stone's convertible debt and preferred shares will have the right to convert such securities into Smurfit-Stone common shares under the same terms and conditions (adjusted for the exchange ratio of 0.99 to one).

Smurfit-Stone will have annual production capacity of 5.5 million tons of linerboard, 1.9 million tons of corrugated medium (the wavy center part of a corrugated box) and 700,000 tons of kraft paper. It will also be among the world's largest collectors and processors of recovered fiber. JJSC thinks the merger will generate

more than $350 million of annual cost savings, before any planned asset divestitures. It expects to achieve the savings through optimization of production, elimination of redundant overhead costs, reduction of STO's working capital needs, and lower interest charges from a planned refinancing. JJSC expects these synergies within the first 24 months of the merger.

A major goal of Smurfit-Stone will be a reduction of some $2.5 billion in debt through the planned divestiture of non-core businesses and assets; pro forma debt of the two companies stood at $6.4 billion at 1997 year-end. Smurfit-Stone will initially focus on the asset disposal program announced by Stone in October 1997. It includes STO's 25% interest in Abitibi-Consolidated, the largest publications paper company in the world; and newsprint and market pulp operations. Smurfit-Stone will also consider the monetization of JJSC's one million acres of owned or leased southern timberlands, and its newsprint operations.

The parties expect the merger to close in the fall of 1998. The transaction remains subject to shareholder approval. Dr. M. Smurfit, chairman of JJSC and JSG will be chairman of Smurfit-Stone, and R. Stone, chairman, president and CEO of Stone, will be president and CEO.

In May 1997, STO implemented a $700 million funding program to address its near-term capital, financing and debt amortization needs.

Per Share Data ($)

(Year Ended Dec. 31)	1997	1996	1995	1994	1993	1992	1991	1990	1989	1988
Tangible Bk. Val.	NA	1.96	3.48	-3.90	-6.59	0.78	5.55	4.67	4.02	17.39
Cash Flow	-1.06	1.86	8.61	2.47	0.27	1.29	3.55	5.75	8.11	7.85
Earnings	-4.16	-1.32	4.64	-1.60	-4.59	-2.50	-0.77	1.56	4.67	5.58
Dividends	Nil	0.60	0.30	Nil	Nil	0.36	0.71	0.71	0.71	0.35
Payout Ratio	Nil	NM	6%	Nil	Nil	NM	NM	45%	15%	6%
Prices - High	17³/₄	17³/₈	24⁵/₈	21¹/₈	19¹/₂	32	25¹/₂	24³/₄	35⁵/₈	38³/₄
- Low	9¹/₂	12¹/₈	12¹/₂	9⁵/₈	6³/₈	12¹/₂	8⁷/₈	8	21³/₄	20¹/₄
P/E Ratio - High	NM	NM	5	NM	NM	NM	NM	16	8	7
- Low	NM	NM	3	NM	NM	NM	NM	5	5	4

Income Statement Analysis (Million $)

	1997	1996	1995	1994	1993	1992	1991	1990	1989	1988
Revs.	4,849	5,142	7,351	5,749	5,060	5,521	5,384	5,756	5,330	3,742
Oper. Inc.	212	460	1,573	616	324	468	576	839	935	762
Depr.	301	315	372	359	347	269	274	257	210	139
Int. Exp.	457	425	473	461	438	434	479	487	402	111
Pretax Inc.	-604	-188	795	-162	-462	-194	-12.0	194	482	549
Eff. Tax Rate	NM	NM	40%	NM	NM	NM	NM	48%	41%	38%
Net Inc.	-403	-122	445	-128	-318	-170	-49.0	95.0	286	342

Balance Sheet & Other Fin. Data (Million $)

	1997	1996	1995	1994	1993	1992	1991	1990	1989	1988
Cash	113	113	40.0	109	247	58.9	64.1	53.9	22.9	8.5
Curr. Assets	1,596	1,561	1,683	1,817	1,753	1,679	1,685	1,586	1,687	866
Total Assets	5,824	6,354	6,399	7,005	6,837	6,682	6,903	6,690	6,254	2,395
Curr. Liab.	1,089	889	702	1,032	944	939	915	1,147	1,073	426
LT Debt	3,935	3,951	3,885	4,432	4,268	4,105	4,046	3,681	3,537	765
Common Eqty.	162	680	890	533	471	1,070	1,521	1,447	1,335	1,064
Total Cap.	4,428	5,156	5,384	5,683	5,623	5,590	5,883	5,438	5,102	1,969
Cap. Exp.	137	251	387	233	150	281	430	552	502	137
Cash Flow	-104	184	817	218	20.0	92.0	224	352	496	481
Curr. Ratio	1.5	1.8	2.4	1.8	1.9	1.8	1.8	1.4	1.6	2.0
% LT Debt of Cap.	88.9	76.6	72.2	78.0	75.9	73.4	68.8	67.7	69.3	38.9
% Net Inc.of Revs.	NM	NM	6.1	NM	NM	NM	NM	1.7	5.4	9.1
% Ret. on Assets	NM	NM	6.6	NM	NM	NM	NM	1.5	6.6	14.6
% Ret. on Equity	NM	NM	61.3	NM	NM	NM	NM	6.9	23.8	37.8

Data as orig. reptd.; bef. results of disc. opers. and/or spec. items. Per share data adj. for stk. divs. as of ex-div. date. Bold denotes diluted EPS (FASB 128). E-Estimated. NA-Not Available. NM-Not Meaningful. NR-Not Ranked.

Office—150 North Michigan Ave., Chicago, IL 60601. **Tel**—(312) 346-6600. **Chrmn, Pres & CEO**—R. W. Stone. **SVP & CFO**—R. C. Read. **Investor Contact**—Bruce Byots. **Dirs**—W. F. Aldinger, III, D. Garza, R. A. Giesen, J. J. Glasser, J. M. Greenberg, J. D. Nichols, J. K. Pearlman, R. J. Raskin, P. B. Rooney, A. Stone, I. N. Stone, J. H. Stone, R. W. Stone. **Transfer Agent & Registrar**—First Chicago Trust Co. of New York, Jersey City, NJ. **Incorporated**—in Illinois in 1945; reincorporated in Delaware in 1987. **Empl**— 24,600. **S&P Analyst:** Michael W. Jaffe

STANDARD &POOR'S
STOCK REPORTS

Summit Bancorp

2157T

NYSE Symbol **SUB**

In S&P 500

12-SEP-98

Industry: Banks (Major Regional)

Summary: This $30 billion bank holding company, the largest in New Jersey, operates member banks with about 430 offices in New Jersey and eastern Pennsylvania.

S&P Opinion: Hold (★★★)

Recent Price • 36¾	Yield • 3.3%
52 Wk Range • 53⅞-32¾	12-Mo. P/E • 15.8

Quantitative Evaluations

Outlook (1 Lowest—5 Highest)
• **1⁻**

Fair Value
• **32**

Risk
• **Low**

Earn./Div. Rank
• **B+**

Technical Eval.
• **NA**

Rel. Strength Rank (1 Lowest—99 Highest)
• **52**

Insider Activity
• **Neutral**

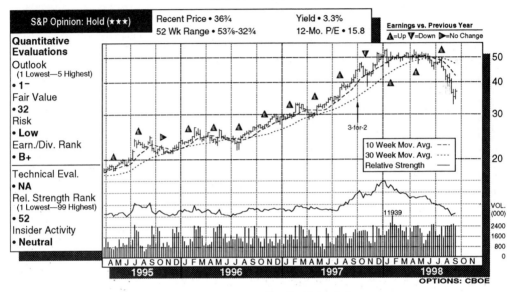

Earnings vs. Previous Year
▲=Up ▼=Down ▶=No Change

3-for-2

10 Week Mov. Avg. − − −
30 Week Mov. Avg. · · · ·
Relative Strength —

11939

VOL. (000)

OPTIONS: CBOE

Overview - 15-JUL-98

We are maintaining our hold opinion on the shares for now, mainly based on our belief that the company's growth may slow in coming years. Although Summit still holds strong positions in the affluent markets of northern New Jersey and eastern Pennsylvania, recent mergers in the region threaten lending volume growth, and intensify pricing pressure. Net interest income rose only 3.0% in the first half of 1998, as 5.9% loan growth, primarily in commercial and consumer loans, was partly offset by a narrower net interest margin. In the future, we see flat deposit growth continuing to raise the cost of funding, and subsequently narrowing the overall lending spread. On the bright side, noninterest income, currently about 23% of net revenue, advanced 26%, on increases in loan fees and trust income, including mutual fund sales. The company continues to boast enviable credit quality and well controlled expenses, as shown by a better than average operating efficiency ratio (noninterest expenses divided by net revenue) of 49.8%.

Valuation - 15-JUL-98

After a stellar performance in 1997, the shares have retreated about 8.0% thus far in 1998, versus a 20% return for the S&P 500. We believe that, although Summit has tremendous takeover appeal, its decision to remain independent in the face of slowing growth, while its peers merge into stronger institutions, has hurt investor confidence. Despite Summit's solid management and franchise reputation, increasing competition for customers and narrowing net interest margins should slow core growth. In light of this, we recommend only holding the shares, recently trading at about 18X our 1998 operating EPS estimate of $2.67, and at 17X the $2.92 we see for 1999.

Key Stock Statistics

S&P EPS Est. 1998	2.65	Tang. Bk. Value/Share	13.82
P/E on S&P Est. 1998	13.9	Beta	1.12
S&P EPS Est. 1999	2.92	Shareholders	20,300
Dividend Rate/Share	1.20	Market cap. (B)	$ 6.4
Shs. outstg. (M)	173.8	Inst. holdings	42%
Avg. daily vol. (M)	0.673		

Value of $10,000 invested 5 years ago: $ 27,003

Fiscal Year Ending Dec. 31

	1998	1997	1996	1995	1994	1993
Revenues (Million $)						
1Q	607.2	570.7	446.0	415.1	305.3	270.7
2Q	628.5	588.4	435.6	429.8	293.3	266.6
3Q	—	591.7	447.8	435.6	276.3	265.6
4Q	—	615.9	455.8	439.2	263.4	259.6
Yr.	—	2,368	1,798	1,720	1,138	1,062
Earnings Per Share ($)						
1Q	0.63	0.56	-0.02	0.44	0.34	0.21
2Q	0.66	0.59	0.53	0.45	0.35	0.29
3Q	E0.68	0.40	0.53	0.47	0.47	0.15
4Q	E0.69	0.63	0.59	0.49	0.41	0.30
Yr.	E2.65	2.09	1.63	1.85	1.59	0.95

Next earnings report expected: mid October

Dividend Data (Dividends have been paid since 1935.)

Amount ($)	Date Decl.	Ex-Div. Date	Stock of Record	Payment Date
0.270	Dec. 17	Jan. 06	Jan. 08	Feb. 02 '98
0.270	Feb. 18	Apr. 07	Apr. 09	May. 01 '98
0.300	Apr. 16	Jul. 07	Jul. 09	Aug. 03 '98
0.300	Aug. 19	Oct. 06	Oct. 08	Nov. 02 '98

Business Summary - 15-JUL-98

Summit Bancorp holds the leading market share position for deposits in New Jersey, and has strong positions in eastern Pennsylvania. This Princeton, NJ-based regional bank, with nearly $31 billion in assets (primarily loans and investments), continued its aggressive expansion with the acquisition of Collective Bancorp in mid-1997, strengthening its presence in the southern portion of New Jersey. It also plans to open additional supermarket branches as a lower-cost means of expansion. Through subsidiaries, SUB provides a range of banking and certain nonbanking services, including asset management (SUB has its own family of mutual funds) and discount brokerage.

The company derives the majority of its revenue from net interest income, which is the interest income it receives on loans and other investments less the interest expense it pays for the use of funds (deposits and other borrowed funds). Loans at December 31, 1997, totaled $18.9 billion (up 8.6% from 1996 year-end), comprised of 33% commercial, industrial and construction loans, 14% commercial mortgage, 30% residential mortgage and 23% consumer (mostly home equity).

The net interest margin, a common measure of lending profitability, is obtained by dividing net interest income by average interest-earning assets. In 1997, the net interest margin increased to 4.26%, from 4.21% in 1996, largely on an increase in interest-free demand deposits.

Asset quality improved in 1997. This was especially impressive, considering the integration of some significant acquisitions. Thanks to a stable real estate market and SUB's aggressive loan workout strategies, nonperforming loans, where interest and principal are not being received as per original terms, totaled $85.1 million (0.45% of total loans) at year-end 1997, down from $139.1 million (0.80%) in 1996. Similarly, net chargeoffs (the amount of loans actually written off as uncollectible, less any recoveries) fell to 0.28% of average loans outstanding, from 0.50%.

Noninterest income, derived from activities other than lending, is also a key to profit growth, accounting for 21% of total net revenues in 1997. It was derived 38% from service charges on accounts, 27% from ATM access fees and other, 16% from trust income, 17% from service and loan fee income, and 2% from securities gains.

Per Share Data ($)

(Year Ended Dec. 31)	1997	1996	1995	1994	1993	1992	1991	1990	1989	1988
Tangible Bk. Val.	13.73	12.62	12.36	12.44	11.85	11.25	.10.84	10.97	12.19	11.07
Earnings	2.09	1.63	1.85	1.59	0.95	0.73	0.30	-0.11	1.75	1.72
Dividends	0.99	0.88	0.79	0.63	0.46	0.40	0.40	0.77	0.55	0.67
Payout Ratio	47%	54%	43%	39%	49%	55%	133%	NM	31%	39%
Prices - High	53³/₈	30¹/₈	24⁷/₈	19¹/₂	22³/₈	16³/₈	11⁵/₈	13³/₈	19¹/₄	15⁷/₈
- Low	28¹/₂	21³/₄	16¹/₈	15	14³/₈	9³/₈	4⁵/₈	4³/₈	12	12⁵/₈
P/E Ratio - High	26	18	13	12	24	23	39	NM	11	9
- Low	14	13	9	9	15	13	15	NM	7	7

Income Statement Analysis (Million $)

	1997	1996	1995	1994	1993	1992	1991	1990	1989	1988
Net Int. Inc.	1,145	912	869	616	563	538	491	485	470	431
Tax Equiv. Adj.	14.4	13.6	17.3	15.3	16.7	19.1	23.0	27.0	31.0	32.0
Non Int. Inc.	296	242	216	175	178	158	136	171	108	112
Loan Loss Prov.	59.1	62.0	71.9	84.0	96.0	139	167	246	53.0	40.0
Exp./Op. Revs.	57%	64%	59%	63%	73%	70%	69%	63%	62%	61%
Pretax Inc.	571	349	379	204	99	71.9	25.0	-22.0	160	154
Eff. Tax Rate	35%	34%	36%	35%	25%	25%	11%	NM	26%	25%
Net Inc.	371	229	243	132	74.2	53.8	22.0	-6.0	119	116
% Net Int. Marg.	4.26	4.52	4.60	4.63	4.64	4.52	4.22	4.33	4.84	4.93

Balance Sheet & Other Fin. Data (Million $)

	1997	1996	1995	1994	1993	1992	1991	1990	1989	1988
Earning Assets:										
Money Mkt	53.7	162	209	97.0	149	270	72.0	95.0	156	312
Inv. Securities	9,232	5,882	5,455	4,294	3,619	3,515	3,377	2,944	2,589	2,204
Com'l Loans	8,957	4,795	4,751	4,627	4,236	3,314	4,586	3,358	3,327	2,826
Other Loans	9,931	10,025	8,990	5,029	4,371	5,468	4,183	5,325	5,032	4,513
Total Assets	29,964	22,668	21,537	15,429	13,411	13,771	13,378	12,818	12,172	10,888
Demand Deposits	4,531	3,984	3,874	3,261	2,802	2,587	2,097	2,008	2,043	2,156
Time Deposits	17,799	14,391	14,081	9,307	8,654	9,200	9,217	8,621	7,293	6,738
LT Debt	1,048	690	425	205	208	216	66.6	72.2	81.1	87.9
Common Eqty.	2,612	1,927	1,760	1,074	946	890	782	777	823	740
% Ret. on Assets	1.4	1.0	1.3	0.9	0.6	0.4	0.2	NM	1.1	1.1
% Ret. on Equity	16.3	12.4	15.0	12.6	8.2	6.3	2.6	NM	14.3	15.9
% Loan Loss Resv.	1.6	1.8	2.0	2.2	2.8	3.1	3.3	3.0	1.5	1.5
% Loans/Deposits	84.6	80.7	78.1	76.8	75.1	74.5	77.5	81.5	89.3	82.3
% Equity to Assets	8.6	8.3	8.8	7.1	6.8	6.1	5.9	6.5	7.1	6.8

Data as orig. reptd.; bef. results of disc. opers. and/or spec. items. Per share data adj. for stk. divs. as of ex-div. date. Bold denotes diluted EPS (FASB 128). E-Estimated. NA-Not Available. NM-Not Meaningful. NR-Not Ranked.

Office—301 Carnegie Center, P.O. Box 2066, Princeton, NJ 08543-2066. **Registrar**—First Chicago Trust Co. of New York, NYC. **Tel**—(609) 987-3200. **Website**—www.summitbank.com **Chrmn & CEO**—T. J. Semrod. **Pres**—R. G. Cox. **Vice Chrmn**—J. G. Collins, J. R. Howell. **SEVP**—J. R. Haggerty. **SVP & Investor Contact**—Kerry K. Calaiaro (609-987-3226). **Dirs**—S. R. Benjamin, R. L. Boyle, J. C. Brady Jr., J. G. Collins, R. G. Cox, T. J. D. Dunphy, A. E. Estabrook, E. J. Ferdon, T. H. Hamilton, F. G. Harvey, J. R. Howell, F. J. Mertz, G. L. Miles Jr., W. R. Miller, H. S. Patterson II, T. J. Semrod,—R. Silverstein, O. R. Smith, J. M. Tabak, D. G. Watson. **Transfer Agent & Registrar**—First Chicago Trust Co. of New York, NYC. **Incorporated**—in New Jersey in 1969. **Empl**— 7,613. **S&P Analyst:** Lee A. Olive

Sun Co.

2160

NYSE Symbol **SUN**

In S&P 500

12-SEP-98

Industry:
Oil & Gas (Refining & Marketing)

Summary: Sun is primarily a petroleum refiner and marketer serving much of the Northeast and the Midwest through its Sunoco brand.

S&P Opinion: Hold (★★★)	Recent Price • 32⅜ Yield • 3.1%
	52 Wk Range • 46⅝-30¾ 12-Mo. P/E • 10.8

Quantitative Evaluations

Outlook
(1 Lowest—5 Highest)
• **1⁻**

Fair Value
• **30¼**

Risk
• **Low**

Earn./Div. Rank
• **B**

Technical Eval.
• **Neutral** since 9/98

Rel. Strength Rank
(1 Lowest—99 Highest)
• **57**

Insider Activity
• **Neutral**

Earnings vs. Previous Year
▲=Up ▼=Down ▶=No Change

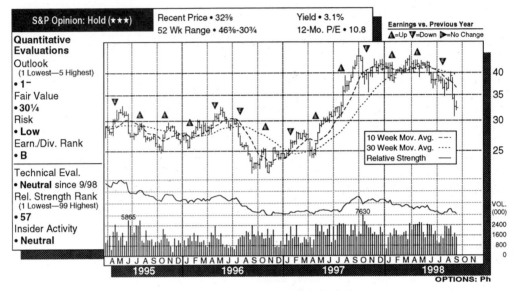

10 Week Mov. Avg. - - - -
30 Week Mov. Avg. ·······
Relative Strength —

OPTIONS: Ph

Overview - 28-JUL-98

An impressive earnings turnaround was accomplished in 1997, with lower crude oil prices leading to wider refining margins in the second and third quarters of the year. However, margins weakened considerably during the fourth quarter, as a sharp drop in crude oil prices was accompanied by an equally dramatic decline in retail gasoline prices, and a full margin recovery will not be at hand until retail marketing margins improve. Despite increased refinery downtime and lower retail gasoline and petrochemicals margins, net income was higher during the first six months of 1998 than in the prior year period. Results were aided by improved lubricants results and healthy wholesale margins at Sun MidAmerica Refining. With refinery maintenance projects in the company's Northeast division now complete, we expect higher production volumes over the second half of the year. Strong demand for petroleum products in the Northeast, Sun's main market, bodes well for the future.

Valuation - 28-JUL-98

The shares have fallen 17% in 1998 to date. We expect oil prices, which have fallen sharply from 1997 third quarter levels, to remain sluggish, aiding refined product margins in 1998. Despite sluggish current demand for heating oil, due to a warmer than normal fall/winter season in the Northeast, refining margins are expected to benefit from healthy demand for refined products, particularly for gasoline, and from high industry capacity utilization rates, which are now above 90%. However, gasoline demand during the current driving season has been somewhat disappointing so far, and the Northeast U.S., SUN's primary market, remains particularly vulnerable to refined product imports. As such, we maintain our neutral opinion on the shares.

Key Stock Statistics

S&P EPS Est. 1998	3.20	Tang. Bk. Value/Share	10.85
P/E on S&P Est. 1998	10.1	Beta	0.78
S&P EPS Est. 1999	3.50	Shareholders	42,000
Dividend Rate/Share	1.00	Market cap. (B)	$ 2.3
Shs. outstg. (M)	93.5	Inst. holdings	58%
Avg. daily vol. (M)	0.364		

Value of $10,000 invested 5 years ago: $ 14,946

Fiscal Year Ending Dec. 31

	1998	1997	1996	1995	1994	1993
Revenues (Million $)						
1Q	2,118	2,744	2,545	2,588	2,070	2,304
2Q	2,190	2,593	2,903	2,915	2,250	2,439
3Q	—	2,649	2,898	2,415	2,730	2,384
4Q	—	1,545	3,027	2,501	1,631	2,290
Yr.	—	10,531	11,300	8,370	7,702	7,297
Earnings Per Share ($)						
1Q	**0.58**	0.10	-0.22	-0.07	0.32	0.32
2Q	**0.97**	1.29	-0.19	1.29	0.11	0.66
3Q	—	1.38	1.46	0.87	0.45	1.07
4Q	—	0.25	-3.22	0.09	0.03	0.60
Yr.	**E3.20**	2.70	-4.43	2.24	0.91	2.65

Next earnings report expected: late October

Dividend Data (Dividends have been paid since 1904.)

Amount ($)	Date Decl.	Ex-Div. Date	Stock of Record	Payment Date
0.250	Oct. 07	Nov. 06	Nov. 10	Dec. 10 '97
0.250	Jan. 08	Feb. 06	Feb. 10	Mar. 10 '98
0.250	Apr. 02	May. 06	May. 08	Jun. 10 '98
0.250	Jul. 02	Aug. 06	Aug. 10	Sep. 10 '98

 A Division of The **McGraw·Hill** *Companies*

Business Summary - 28-JUL-98

As millions of highway travelers in the Northeast and Midwest can attest, Sun Company (SUN) is a leading petroleum refiner and marketer. As of December 31, 1997, the company's familiar Sunoco brand gasoline was sold in 3,789 retail gasoline outlets (most independently owned) in 17 states. SUN is the sole gasoline supplier to service stations on the New Jersey Turnpike, the Pennsylvania Turnpike, and the Ohio Turnpike, and supplies most service stations on the New York Thruway.

SUN is also involved in chemicals, lubricants, coal and pipeline transportation of crude oil and refined products. With the sale of its international oil and gas production business for $278 million in cash in September 1996, SUN completed its withdrawal from the oil and gas exploration and production arena. In June 1995, the company divested its 55% stake in Suncor, a Canadian integrated oil company, receiving $770 million in cash.

Refining capacity at the company's five domestic refineries as of December 31, 1997, totaled 692,000 barrels per day (bbl./d), making the company the second largest independent refiner in the U.S. at the time (second only to Tosco Corp., which supplanted SUN as the leading independent refiner in the U.S. during 1996, due to acquisitions), with a total refining capacity of about 950,000 bbl./d. Gasoline sales in 1997 accounted

for 46% of manufactured products; middle distillate heating oil 31%; residual fuel 10%; petrochemicals 4%; and other 9%.

While SUN's decision to exit the profitable oil and gas production business in order to focus on the difficult refining and operations businesses seemed odd at the time, the company feels that it will benefit in the long run by concentrating on its core businesses. SUN's current strategy involves upgrading its product offerings, improving the reliability and efficiency of refining facilities and reducing operating and administrative costs. During 1996, the company wrote off refinery assets and cut its work force, in moves designed to carry out its strategy.

Earnings in recent years (in millions) were derived as follows:

	1997	1996
Northeast Refining	$ 75	-$60
Northeast Marketing	73	1
Lubricants	1	-14
MidAmerica Marketing & Refining	40	-3
Chemicals	77	40
Coal and Coke	38	31
Logistics	51	48
International production	---	41

Per Share Data ($)

(Year Ended Dec. 31)	1997	1996	1995	1994	1993	1992	1991	1990	1989	1988
Tangible Bk. Val.	10.41	9.45	12.82	17.07	18.10	17.37	25.41	30.83	30.50	31.24
Cash Flow	4.93	-0.80	5.99	4.26	6.02	0.68	3.28	6.46	4.76	6.87
Earnings	2.70	-4.43	2.24	0.91	2.65	-2.98	-1.25	1.86	0.92	0.06
Dividends	1.00	1.00	1.40	1.40	1.80	1.80	1.80	1.80	1.80	2.70
Payout Ratio	37%	NM	63%	198%	68%	NM	NM	96%	196%	NM
Prices - High	46³/₈	32⁵/₈	32⁷/₈	35¼	32³/₄	30³/₄	35³/₄	41⁷/₈	43¼	61³/₄
- Low	24	21⁷/₈	24³/₄	25¹/₈	22¼	22½	25³/₄	25³/₄	31³/₈	28
P/E Ratio - High	17	NM	15	39	12	NM	NM	23	47	NM
- Low	9	NM	11	28	8	NM	NM	14	34	NM

Income Statement Analysis (Million $)

	1997	1996	1995	1994	1993	1992	1991	1990	1989	1988
Revs.	10,464	11,233	8,370	7,702	7,297	8,626	10,184	11,812	9,805	8,612
Oper. Inc.	680	225	575	562	671	221	670	941	697	769
Depr.	259	267	341	359	359	389	480	491	411	723
Int. Exp.	71.0	79.0	105	97.0	81.0	97.0	112	208	227	296
Pretax Inc.	385	-407	319	155	453	-431	-128	390	211	-43.0
Eff. Tax Rate	32%	NM	29%	15%	32%	NM	NM	49%	54%	NM
Net Inc.	263	-280	227	97.0	283	-316	-131	199	98.0	7.0

Balance Sheet & Other Fin. Data (Million $)

	1997	1996	1995	1994	1993	1992	1991	1990	1989	1988
Cash	33.0	67.0	14.0	117	118	179	366	298	416	848
Curr. Assets	1,248	1,535	1,460	1,508	1,277	1,331	1,694	2,503	2,368	2,455
Total Assets	4,667	5,025	5,184	6,465	5,900	6,071	7,143	9,000	8,699	8,616
Curr. Liab.	1,464	1,817	1,530	1,915	1,505	1,746	1,965	2,613	2,429	2,279
LT Debt	824	835	888	1,073	726	792	853	1,459	1,377	1,491
Common Eqty.	739	690	949	1,863	1,984	1,896	2,696	3,274	3,254	3,325
Total Cap.	2,359	2,273	2,709	3,606	3,451	3,347	4,625	6,028	5,912	6,070
Cap. Exp.	380	408	545	848	612	530	674	788	763	1,258
Cash Flow	478	-59.0	545	456	642	72.0	348	690	509	729
Curr. Ratio	0.9	0.8	0.9	0.8	0.8	0.8	0.9	1.0	1.0	1.1
% LT Debt of Cap.	34.9	36.8	32.8	29.8	21.0	23.7	18.4	24.2	23.3	24.6
% Net Inc.of Revs.	2.5	NM	2.7	1.3	3.9	NM	NM	1.7	1.0	0.1
% Ret. on Assets	5.4	NM	3.9	1.6	4.7	NM	NM	2.3	1.1	0.1
% Ret. on Equity	30.7	NM	14.5	5.0	14.6	NM	NM	6.1	3.0	0.1

Data as orig. reptd.; bef. results of disc. opers. and/or spec. items. Per share data adj. for stk. divs. as of ex-div. date. Bold denotes diluted EPS (FASB 128). E-Estimated. NA-Not Available. NM-Not Meaningful. NR-Not Ranked.

Office—Ten Penn Center, 1801 Market St., Philadelphia, PA 19103-1699. **Tel**—(215) 977-3000. **Chrmn & CEO**—R. H. Campbell. **Pres & COO**—J. G. Drosdick.**EVP & CFO**—R. M. Aiken Jr. **Treas**—M. I. Ruddock.**Secy**—A. C. Mule. **Investor Contact**—Terry Delaney. **Dirs**—R. H. Campbell, R. E. Cartledge, R. E. Cawthorn, J. G. Drosdick, M. J. Evans, T. P. Gerrity, J. G. Kaiser, R. D. Kennedy, R. A. Pew, W. F. Pounds, A. B. Trowbridge. **Transfer Agent & Registrar**—First Chicago Trust Co., NYC. **Incorporated**—in New Jersey in 1901; reincorporated in Pennsylvania in 1971. **Empl**— 10,900. **S&P Analyst:** Norman Rosenberg

Sun Microsystems
5343M

Nasdaq Symbol **SUNW**

In S&P 500

12-SEP-98

Industry:
Computers (Hardware)

Summary: Sun makes high-performance workstations for engineering, scientific and technical markets, and also sells servers and operating system software.

S&P Opinion: Accumulate (★★★★)	Recent Price • 48⅜	Yield • Nil
	52 Wk Range • 52¾-30⅜	12-Mo. P/E • 25.1

Quantitative Evaluations

Outlook
(1 Lowest—5 Highest)
• **4⁻**

Fair Value
• **55¼**

Risk
• **Average**

Earn./Div. Rank
• **B+**

Technical Eval.
• **Bearish** since 2/98

Rel. Strength Rank
(1 Lowest—99 Highest)
• **97**

Insider Activity
• **Neutral**

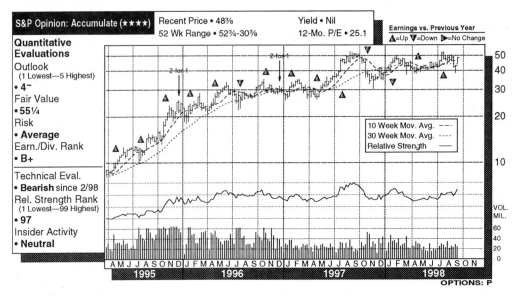

Earnings vs. Previous Year
▲=Up ▼=Down ▶=No Change

10 Week Mov. Avg. - - -
30 Week Mov. Avg. ·····
Relative Strength —

OPTIONS: P

Overview - 22-JUL-98

We expect revenue growth of 17% in FY 99 (Jun.). Strength in Sun's high- and mid-range servers spurred revenue growth of 14% in FY 98, despite a difficult pricing environment and the negative impact of weak Asian markets. While these factors should continue to impact FY 99 revenues, we expect growth from new low-end workstations and high-end storage products to more than offset. While gross margins have continued above 50% in recent quarters, we believe these levels could trend down in FY 99, due to the competitive pricing environment and the addition of several low-end platforms to Sun's product lines. Expense growth should at a minimum keep pace with revenue growth, as Sun continues to build up its commercial enterprise infrastructure and invest in R&D initiatives. Based on these assumptions, we project FY 99 EPS of $2.75.

Valuation - 22-JUL-98

Sun shares have started to gain momentum after several months of weakness, as the company has continued to post healthy EPS growth despite worries over the future of UNIX platforms (in the face of Microsoft's Windows NT success) and weakness in Asia. While NT has been successful, it has yet to prove it can challenge the performance of UNIX servers in high-end computing tasks. In addition, Sun's success in launching new products and in penetrating large customer accounts has offset the downturn in Asia. Meanwhile, Sun has maintained healthy gross margins that have exceeded expectations. We continue to believe Sun will achieve EPS growth of 15% over the next few years, and, based on their current attractive valuation, believe the shares should be accumulated.

Key Stock Statistics

S&P EPS Est. 1999	2.75	Tang. Bk. Value/Share	8.51
P/E on S&P Est. 1999	17.6	Beta	1.04
Dividend Rate/Share	Nil	Shareholders	8,500
Shs. outstg. (M)	378.8	Market cap. (B)	$ 18.3
Avg. daily vol. (M)	5.161	Inst. holdings	55%

Value of $10,000 invested 5 years ago: $ 57,546

Fiscal Year Ending Jun. 30

	1998	1997	1996	1995	1994	1993
Revenues (Million $)						
1Q	2,099	1,859	1,485	1,273	960.5	856.0
2Q	2,450	2,082	1,751	1,475	1,131	1,051
3Q	2,361	2,115	1,840	1,505	1,196	1,141
4Q	2,881	2,543	2,018	1,648	1,403	1,261
Yr.	9,791	8,598	7,095	5,902	4,690	4,309
Earnings Per Share ($)						
1Q	0.27	0.32	0.21	0.10	0.04	0.01
2Q	**0.38**	0.46	0.33	0.21	0.12	0.06
3Q	**0.59**	0.58	0.36	0.27	0.15	0.12
4Q	**0.69**	0.61	0.31	0.32	0.20	0.18
Yr.	**1.93**	1.96	1.21	0.90	0.51	0.37

Next earnings report expected: mid October

Dividend Data

No cash dividends have been paid. A two-for-one stock split was effected in December 1996.

A Division of The **McGraw·Hill** *Companies*

STANDARD
&POOR'S
STOCK REPORTS

Sun Microsystems, Inc.

5343M
12-SEP-98

Business Summary - 22-JUL-98

Sun Microsystems, which invented the workstation, is a leading supplier of these networked computing products, as well as servers, software, microprocessors and a full range of services and support. Sun's hardware incorporates its Scaleable Processor Architecture ("SPARC") microprocessors and the Solaris software environment, an open client-server UNIX system software environment offered on both SPARC and Intel platforms.

Workstations are a type of computer used for engineering applications (CAD/CAM), desktop publishing, software development, and other types of applications that require a moderate amount of computing power and relatively high quality graphics capabilities. In terms of computing power, workstations are somewhere in between personal computers and minicomputers, although the line is fuzzy on both ends. High-end personal computers, helped by the ever-faster speeds of microprocessors, are now equivalent to low-end workstations. High-end workstations are comparable to minicomputers. The most common operating system for workstations is UNIX, although Microsoft's Windows NT Workstation is posing a healthy challenge.

Sun's workstations range from low cost SPARCstations to high performance color graphics systems. Current desktops include the low-end SPARCstation 5, and the new family of Ultra workstations. The company's servers can be used for file sharing, enabling users to access data distributed across multiple storage devices and networks, or as compute resources, to distribute compute-intensive applications across multiple processors. Sun's servers range from the low-end Ultra Enterprise 1 Server to the Ultra Enterprise 10000, a highly scaleable, enterprise-wide symmetric multiprocessor server. Netra servers provide preconfigured solutions for Internet and intranet publishing.

Sun formed JavaSoft to develop, market and support Java, an object-oriented programming language. The Java programming language has attracted tremendous interest in the software development industry because of its portability; software created in Java can run on any type of system, including PCs, workstations and World Wide Web browsers. It is expected to be popular as a tool for designing software for distribution over the Internet, because anyone can access and use it. In October 1997, Sun filed suit against software giant Microsoft for violating its licensing agreement with Sun regarding Java. Reportedly, Microsoft did not include certain Java features in its new version of Internet Explorer, while incorporating new features that make it run better on Windows platforms. This violates Sun's "write once, run anywhere" basis for Java.

In 1996, Sun acquired supercomputer maker Cray Research, and SPARC/Solaris assets, from Silicon Graphics.

Per Share Data ($)

(Year Ended Jun. 30)	1998	1997	1996	1995	1994	1993	1992	1991	1990	1989
Tangible Bk. Val.	NA	7.40	6.05	5.39	4.34	4.02	3.71	3.15	2.50	1.97
Cash Flow	NA	2.84	1.94	1.51	1.15	0.93	0.95	1.00	0.78	0.48
Earnings	1.93	1.96	1.21	0.90	0.51	0.37	0.43	0.46	0.30	0.19
Dividends	Nil	Nil	Nil	Nil	Nil	Nil	Nil	Nil	Nil	Nil
Payout Ratio	Nil	Nil	Nil	Nil	Nil	Nil	Nil	Nil	Nil	Nil
Prices - High	52¾	53¼	35⅛	20	9⅜	10¼	9	9⅝	9⅜	5¾
- Low	37⅝	25⅞	18	7½	4⅝	5¼	5⅝	5¼	3¾	3⅜
P/E Ratio - High	27	27	29	22	19	28	21	21	31	30
- Low	19	13	15	8	9	14	13	11	12	18

Income Statement Analysis (Million $)

	1998	1997	1996	1995	1994	1993	1992	1991	1990	1989
Revs.	NA	8,598	7,095	5,902	4,690	4,309	3,589	3,221	2,466	1,765
Oper. Inc.	NA	1,391	1,017	741	526	473	477	516	361	191
Depr.	NA	342	284	241	248	232	215	221	184	103
Int. Exp.	NA	7.5	9.1	17.8	21.8	34.9	45.2	49.4	37.4	14.3
Pretax Inc.	NA	1,121	709	523	283	224	255	284	154	78.0
Eff. Tax Rate	NA	32%	33%	32%	31%	30%	32%	33%	28%	22%
Net Inc.	NA	762	476	356	196	157	173	190	111	61.0

Balance Sheet & Other Fin. Data (Million $)

	1998	1997	1996	1995	1994	1993	1992	1991	1990	1989
Cash	NA	660	990	1,228	883	1,139	1,220	834	394	54.0
Curr. Assets	NA	3,728	3,034	2,934	2,305	2,272	2,148	1,801	1,297	880
Total Assets	NA	4,697	3,801	3,545	2,898	2,768	2,672	2,326	1,779	1,269
Curr. Liab.	NA	1,849	1,489	1,331	1,148	947	839	713	493	463
LT Debt	NA	106	60.2	91.0	116	154	313	351	359	143
Common Eqty.	NA	2,742	2,251	2,123	1,628	1,643	1,485	1,213	927	662
Total Cap.	NA	2,848	2,312	2,214	1,745	1,797	1,798	1,564	1,286	805
Cap. Exp.	NA	554	296	242	213	196	186	192	213	205
Cash Flow	NA	1,104	760	596	444	389	389	411	295	164
Curr. Ratio	NA	2.0	2.0	2.2	2.0	2.4	2.6	2.5	2.6	1.9
% LT Debt of Cap.	NA	3.9	2.6	4.1	6.7	8.6	17.4	22.5	27.9	17.7
% Net Inc.of Revs.	NA	8.9	6.7	6.0	4.2	3.6	4.8	5.9	4.5	3.4
% Ret. on Assets	NA	17.9	13.0	11.0	7.2	5.7	6.7	8.9	7.3	5.7
% Ret. on Equity	NA	30.5	21.8	18.9	12.5	9.9	12.6	17.5	13.4	11.2

Data as orig. reptd.; bef. results of disc. opers. and/or spec. items. Per share data adj. for stk. divs. as of ex-div. date. Bold denotes diluted EPS (FASB 128). E-Estimated. NA-Not Available. NM-Not Meaningful. NR-Not Ranked.

Office—2550 Garcia Ave., Mountain View, CA 94043-1100. **Tel**—(415) 960-1300. **Website**—http://www.sun.com **Chrmn & CEO**—S. G. McNealy. **VP & CFO**—M. Lehman. **VP & Secy**—M. H. Morris. **Investor Contact**—M. Paisley. **Dirs**—L. J. Doerr, J. Estrin, R. J. Fisher, W. R. Hearst III, R. L. Long, S. G. McNealy, M. K. Oshman, A. M. Spence. **Transfer Agent & Registrar**—Bank of Boston. **Incorporated**—in California in 1982. **Empl**—26,343. **S&P Analyst:** Megan Graham Hackett

SunAmerica Inc.

2161T

NYSE Symbol **SAI**

In S&P 500

12-SEP-98   **Industry:** Financial (Diversified)   **Summary:** SAI specializes in selling tax-deferred, long-term savings products for the pre-retirement market.

S&P Opinion: Accumulate (★★★★)	Recent Price • 63⅝ Yield • 0.9% 52 Wk Range • 76¼-32 12-Mo. P/E • 27.1

Quantitative Evaluations

Outlook
(1 Lowest—5 Highest)
• 1⁻

Fair Value
• 55¾

Risk
• **Average**

Earn./Div. Rank
• **A**

Technical Eval.
• **Bullish** since 7/95

Rel. Strength Rank
(1 Lowest—99 Highest)
• **95**

Insider Activity
• **Neutral**

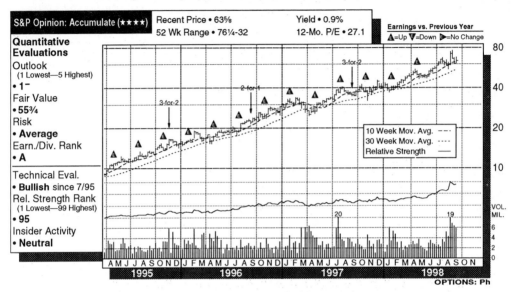

Earnings vs. Previous Year   ▲=Up ▼=Down ▷=No Change

10 Week Mov. Avg. — ·—
30 Week Mov. Avg. · · · ·
Relative Strength ——

OPTIONS: Ph

Overview - 13-AUG-98

Operating earnings growth in coming periods will reflect the company's ability to gain market share in a rapidly expanding market. Capitalizing on booming demand for pre-retirement savings products, SunAmerica continues to offer new products, expand its broker-dealer network, and strengthen its brand name. Operating EPS in the nine months ended June 30, 1998, advanced 31%, to $1.79, from $1.37 in the year ago period, driven by 31% higher variable annuity sales, the accretive effects of selective acquisitions, a favorable interest rate environment, and robust demand for the flexibility offered by company products. SAI's share of the variable annuity market has grown rapidly in the last two years. Despite the impact of a lower capital gains tax, SunAmerica's ability to sell a diverse mix of innovative retirement savings products, in addition to both variable and fixed annuities, offers fuel for continued growth.

Valuation - 13-AUG-98

SAI shares handily outperfomed the broader market during 1997, and continue to outperform in 1998, as investors rewarded SAI's growth strategy and consistent earnings performance. With the addition of the Polaris II and Seasons variable annuities and the Style Select Series of mutual funds, the company has recently expanded its already wide range of retirement savings products. SunAmerica continues to place emphasis on distribution and marketing, nearly tripling its sales force to 9,400 since 1993, and improving brand recognition through an extensive TV ad campaign. Given the company's potential for significant long-term growth, including the effects of potential acquisitions of managed assets or distribution networks, the shares remain attractively valued. Despite their fairly lofty P/E multiple of 21X our FY 99 operating EPS estimate of $2.85, the shares have additional upside.

Key Stock Statistics

S&P EPS Est. 1998	2.40	Tang. Bk. Value/Share	13.30
P/E on S&P Est. 1998	26.5	Beta	1.16
S&P EPS Est. 1999	2.85	Shareholders	2,300
Dividend Rate/Share	0.60	Market cap. (B)	$ 11.4
Shs. outstg. (M)	195.7	Inst. holdings	65%
Avg. daily vol. (M)	2.450		

Value of $10,000 invested 5 years ago: $ 114,388

Fiscal Year Ending Sep. 30

	1998	1997	1996	1995	1994	1993
Revenues (Million $)						
1Q	621.1	431.3	303.8	155.0	228.6	210.8
2Q	633.5	459.1	342.9	259.3	222.3	214.9
3Q	—	576.6	404.7	279.7	225.8	225.5
4Q	—	603.3	422.9	254.9	232.2	233.1
Yr.	—	2,114	1,475	1,064	905.8	884.2
Earnings Per Share ($)						
1Q	**0.56**	0.39	0.31	0.22	0.19	0.14
2Q	**0.60**	0.41	0.32	0.23	0.19	0.15
3Q	—	0.45	0.33	0.23	0.20	0.16
4Q	—	0.53	0.34	0.27	0.21	0.17
Yr.	—	1.80	1.30	0.95	0.80	0.61

Next earnings report expected: late October

Dividend Data (Dividends have been paid since 1962.)

Amount ($)	Date Decl.	Ex-Div. Date	Stock of Record	Payment Date
0.100	Nov. 21	Nov. 26	Dec. 01	Dec. 05 '97
0.100	Feb. 13	Feb. 19	Feb. 23	Mar. 02 '98
0.100	May. 01	May. 07	May. 11	May. 18 '98
0.150	Jul. 31	Aug. 06	Aug. 10	Aug. 17 '98

SunAmerica Inc.

Business Summary - 13-AUG-98

This leading financial services firm is well positioned to capture an ever-increasing share of the rapidly growing pre-retirement market. Growth in this segment of the financial services industry has been fueled by demographics (i.e. aging baby boomers), and by a shift in pension trends from defined benefit plans to defined contributions plans (401K, 403B plans). SAI has focused its efforts on the sale of annuities and guaranteed investment contracts (GICs), and now ranks among the largest U.S. issuers of tax-deferred fixed and variable annuities and guaranteed investment contracts. Other subsidiaries provide asset management, financial planning and investment services. During FY 1997 (Sep.), annuity operations accounted for 91% of revenues and pretax profits.

Much of SunAmerica's recent success is due to its innovative and diverse product line of variable annuities, which are increasingly popular with aging baby boomers looking for a tax-deferred means of building up their assets. Products can be structured in a variety of ways and allow the investor to capture more stock market-oriented (or bond, money market, or guaranteed fixed rate) returns than other retirement products available. The company augments the sale of its retail annuity products with a line of institutional guaranteed investment contracts (GICs). At September 30, 1997, SAI had $5.6 billion of GIC obligations, of which 67% were

fixed rate and 33% were variable rate obligations. SunAmerica asset management, with over $3 billion of assets under management at FY end 1997, offers a diverse and growing family of mutual funds.

For many insurers, annuities have been a vehicle for growth, a way to offset sluggish sales of traditional life insurance products. But this growth has come at the price of razor-thin margins from these fee-based products. Consequently, economies of scale and cost effective distribution strategies are crucial to a firm's long term success. SAI is effectively addressing both issues. In April 1998, it expanded its already formidable sales team by acquiring two more broker-dealers. As a result, SAI's six wholly owned broker-dealers (and 9,400 registered representatives) comprise the largest network of independent registered reps and the fifth largest retail securities sales force in the U.S. SAI also sells its products through an array of other financial service distribution channels, including registered representatives of unaffiliated broker-dealers, independent general insurance agents and financial institutions.

SAI continues to augment its internal growth through acquisitions. In mid-July 1998, SAI agreed to acquire about 380,000 universal life insurance and annuity policies for $130 million in cash from MBL Life Assurance Corp., the successor to the failed Mutual Benefit Life. SAI estimates that $300 million of capital will be required to support the acquired business.

Per Share Data ($)

(Year Ended Sep. 30)	1997	1996	1995	1994	1993	1992	1991	1990	1989	1988
Tangible Bk. Val.	11.43	7.41	5.17	3.64	4.03	3.00	2.48	1.97	2.40	2.64
Earnings	1.80	1.30	0.95	0.80	0.61	0.40	0.29	0.23	0.18	0.17
Dividends	0.27	0.20	0.13	0.09	0.04	0.04	0.04	0.04	0.03	0.07
Payout Ratio	15%	15%	14%	11%	7%	10%	15%	17%	16%	44%
Prices - High	45$^5/_8$	30$^7/_8$	16$^5/_8$	10$^1/_4$	10$^3/_8$	6$^1/_8$	4$^3/_8$	2$^5/_8$	3$^1/_2$	3$^1/_2$
- Low	24$^5/_8$	14$^3/_4$	8	7$^1/_2$	5$^5/_8$	3$^3/_8$	1	$^3/_4$	1$^7/_{16}$	2$^5/_{16}$
P/E Ratio - High	25	24	16	13	17	15	15	12	20	21
- Low	14	11	18	9	9	8	4	3	8	14

Income Statement Analysis (Million $)

	1997	1996	1995	1994	1993	1992	1991	1990	1989	1988
Premium Inc.	141	105	84.6	79.5	67.5	57.7	48.5	34.7	31.2	73.1
Invest. Inc.	1,796	1,254	906	758	754	763	741	671	490	431
Oth. Revs.	139	107	76.4	86.9	83.7	71.8	71.1	146	60.8	64.2
Total Revs.	2,076	1,466	1,067	903	884	837	815	818	551	496
Int. Exp.	1,075	741	539	464	491	544	579	538	380	341
Exp./Op. Revs.	73%	74%	74%	73%	79%	87%	92%	93%	92%	104%
Pretax Inc.	537	392	280	240	184	107	68.0	55.5	43.2	-19.4
Eff. Tax Rate	29%	30%	31%	31%	31%	32%	38%	40%	40%	NM
Net Inc.	379	274	194	165	127	72.2	42.1	33.4	26.1	-20.4

Balance Sheet & Other Fin. Data (Million $)

	1997	1996	1995	1994	1993	1992	1991	1990	1989	1988
Receivables	Nil	Nil	Nil	0.1	0.1	0.1	113	112	92.4	97.2
Cash & Invest.	21,187	16,199	10,809	9,280	10,312	9,422	7,583	7,275	5,887	5,690
Loans	3,139	Nil	Nil	Nil	Nil	Nil	Nil	Nil	Nil	Nil
Total Assets	35,637	23,727	16,844	14,656	15,214	13,398	11,001	10,079	7,020	6,610
Capitalization:										
Debt	1,136	573	525	501	508	434	455	532	459	742
Equity	2,336	1,276	891	587	631	463	385	319	365	156
Total	3,856	2,234	1,738	1,463	1,618	1,164	905	916	889	912
Price Times Bk. Val.: High	3.7	3.6	3.0	2.8	2.6	2.1	1.8	1.4	1.4	1.3
Price Times Bk. Val.: Low	2.2	2.0	1.5	2.0	1.4	1.1	0.4	0.4	0.6	0.9
% Return On Revs.	18.3	18.7	18.1	18.3	14.4	8.6	5.2	4.1	4.8	NM
% Ret. on Assets	1.3	1.4	1.2	1.1	0.9	0.6	0.4	0.4	0.4	NM
% Ret. on Equity	19.9	25.3	26.0	16.9	19.7	15.2	11.9	9.8	10.0	NM
Loans/Equity	1.3	Nil	Nil	Nil	Nil	Nil	Nil	Nil	Nil	Nil

Data as orig. reptd.; bef. results of disc opers. and/or spec. items. Per share data adj. for stk. divs. as of ex-div. date. Bold denotes diluted EPS (FASB 128). E-Estimated. NA-Not Available. NM-Not Meaningful. NR-Not Ranked.

Office—1 SunAmerica Center, Century City, Los Angeles, CA 90067-6022. **Tel**—(310) 772-6000. **Website**—http://www.sunamerica.com **Chrmn, Pres & CEO**—E. Broad. **VP & Treas**—D. R. Bechtel. **VP & Secy**—S. L. Harris. **Investor Contact**—Karel Carnohan (310-772-6535). **Dirs**—W. F. Aldinger, R. J. Arnault, E. Broad, K. Hastie-Williams, P. G. Heasley, D. O. Maxwell, B. Munitz, L. Pollack, C. E. Reichardt, R. D. Rohr, S. C. Sigoloff, H. M. Williams. **Transfer Agent & Registrar**—ChaseMellon Shareholder Services, LA. **Incorporated**—in Maryland in 1961. **Empl**— 2,000. **S&P Analyst:** Catherine A. Seifert

SunTrust Banks

2168M

NYSE Symbol **STI**

In S&P 500

12-SEP-98

Industry: Banks (Major Regional)

Summary: This bank holding company, the 19th largest in the U.S., operates about 700 full-service branch offices in Florida, Georgia, Tennessee and Alabama.

S&P Opinion: Accumulate (★★★★)

Recent Price • 58
52 Wk Range • 87¾-54

Yield • 1.7%
12-Mo. P/E • 17.3

Quantitative Evaluations

Outlook (1 Lowest—5 Highest)
• **1+**

Fair Value
• **51¼**

Risk
• **Low**

Earn./Div. Rank
• **A+**

Technical Eval.
• **Bearish** since 8/98

Rel. Strength Rank (1 Lowest—99 Highest)
• **47**

Insider Activity
• **Neutral**

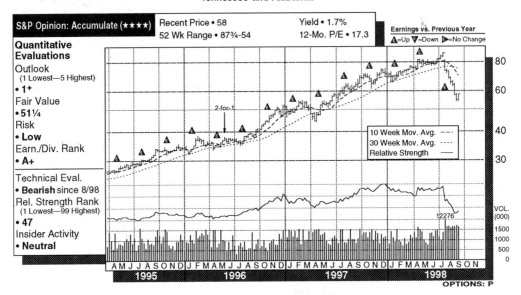

Earnings vs. Previous Year: △=Up ▽=Down ▷=No Change

10 Week Mov. Avg.
30 Week Mov. Avg.
Relative Strength

VOL. (000)

OPTIONS: P

Overview - 21-JUL-98

With a regional service territory among the healthiest in the nation, earning asset growth is expected to remain at about 10% in 1998. The net interest margin may narrow further mainly due to a shift to more expensive sources of funds to support loan growth, but also to a less favorable mix of earning assets. Credit quality is strong, with the allowance for loan losses at 558% of nonperforming loans at June 30, 1998. Demonstrating STI's conservative loss reserve posture, the loan loss provision in the first half of 1998 exceeded the level of net charge-offs by a wide margin, leading to a further build-up of loss reserves. Growth in noninterest income, led by trust income and mortgage fees during the latest refinancing wave, reflects further success of the company's growth initiatives. The early 1998 acquisition of Equitable Securities Corp. added equity research, underwriting, sales and trading capabilities and compliments the company's debt capital markets activities. However, the transaction is having a neutral impact on 1998 earnings due to dilution from shares issued.

Valuation - 21-JUL-98

Based on continued strong operating fundamentals, the shares remain near record levels. Earnings should continue to benefit from above average loan growth from an attractive service territory and strong gains in several fee-based services, somewhat offset by expenses to support growth initiatives. Due to its significant stake in Coca-Cola Co., which provides hefty dividend income, the shares typically trade at a premium valuation to other regional banks. With the current cost-cutting wave running out of steam, we see banks with good revenue generation having an easier time maintaining earnings momentum, and recommend selective accumulation of the shares.

Key Stock Statistics

S&P EPS Est. 1998	3.50	Tang. Bk. Value/Share	26.22
P/E on S&P Est. 1998	16.6	Beta	1.28
S&P EPS Est. 1999	3.90	Shareholders	29,000
Dividend Rate/Share	1.00	Market cap. (B)	$ 12.1
Shs. outstg. (M)	208.9	Inst. holdings	46%
Avg. daily vol. (M)	0.805		

Value of $10,000 invested 5 years ago: $ 29,788

Fiscal Year Ending Dec. 31

	1998	1997	1996	1995	1994	1993
Revenues (Million $)						
1Q	1,246	1,089	994.2	903.4	767.2	774.4
2Q	1,273	1,127	998.6	932.6	798.3	770.8
3Q	—	1,168	1,018	942.5	825.8	772.8
4Q	—	1,202	1,054	961.8	860.9	770.7
Yr.	—	4,585	4,064	3,740	3,252	3,089
Earnings Per Share ($)						
1Q	**0.85**	0.74	0.66	0.59	0.52	0.45
2Q	**0.88**	0.77	0.68	0.61	0.55	0.47
3Q	**E0.88**	0.80	0.70	0.63	0.56	0.48
4Q	**E0.89**	0.82	0.72	0.64	0.56	0.48
Yr.	**E3.50**	3.13	2.76	2.47	2.19	1.89

Next earnings report expected: mid October

Dividend Data (Dividends have been paid since 1985.)

Amount ($)	Date Decl.	Ex-Div. Date	Stock of Record	Payment Date
0.250	Nov. 11	Nov. 26	Dec. 01	Dec. 15 '97
0.250	Feb. 10	Feb. 26	Mar. 02	Mar. 16 '98
0.250	Apr. 21	May. 28	Jun. 01	Jun. 15 '98
0.250	Aug. 11	Aug. 28	Sep. 01	Sep. 15 '98

A Division of The McGraw·Hill Companies

STANDARD
&POOR'S
STOCK REPORTS

SunTrust Banks, Inc.

2168M
12-SEP-98

Business Summary - 21-JUL-98

SunTrust Banks, Inc. operates about 700 full-service banking offices in Florida, Georgia, Tennessee and Alabama. Part of the company's strategy is to capitalize on the opportunities and demands presented by the strong economic growth of the Southeast region. Primary businesses include traditional deposit and credit services as well as trust and investment services. The company also provides mortgage banking, corporate finance, credit cards, factoring, discount brokerage, credit-related insurance, and data processing and information services. At 1997 year-end, it had discretionary trust assets of $67.4 billion and a mortgage servicing portfolio of $16.9 billion.

Contributions by the company's principal banking subsidiaries ($ million) in 1997 were:

	Net Inc.	Return on Assets
SunTrust Banks of Florida	$371.5	1.44%
SunTrust Banks of Georgia	281.5	1.54%
SunTrust Banks of Tennessee	110.1	1.45%

Average earning assets, from which interest income is derived, amounted to $47.0 billion in 1997 and consisted mainly of loans (80%) and investment securities

(17%). Average sources of funds, which the bank uses to fund its lending business, included mainly time deposits (23%), NOW/money market accounts (19%), savings deposits (10%), short-term borrowings (15%), long-term debt (5%), shareholders' equity (6%) and certain noninterest-bearing deposits (14%).

At year-end 1997, nonperforming assets, which include mainly non-accrual and restructured loans and other real estate owned, were $150.6 million (0.37% of loans and other real estate owned), down from $255.8 million (0.72%) a year earlier. The company made a $117 million provision for possible loan losses in 1997, up from $116 million a year earlier. The provision is added to a reserve for loan losses and held in anticipation of actual losses. The reserve was 1.87% of loans at the end of 1997, versus 2.05% at the end of 1996. Net charge-offs, or the amount of loans actually written off as uncollectible, were $91.0 million in 1997 (0.24% of average loans), compared to $90.2 million (0.27%) the year before.

The company owns 48,266,496 shares of common stock of Coca-Cola Co., which had a market value of about $3.22 billion at 1997 year-end.

In January 1998, STI acquired Equitable Securities Corp., an investment banking, securities brokerage and investment advisory firm, for 1,305,000 common shares.

Per Share Data ($)

(Year Ended Dec. 31)	1997	1996	1995	1994	1993	1992	1991	1990	1989	1988
Tangible Bk. Val.	23.38	20.88	17.66	13.90	13.89	10.09	9.24	8.37	7.42	6.51
Earnings	3.13	2.76	2.47	2.19	1.89	1.64	1.45	1.38	1.30	1.19
Dividends	0.93	0.82	0.74	0.66	0.58	0.52	0.47	0.43	0.39	0.35
Payout Ratio	30%	30%	29%	30%	31%	31%	32%	31%	30%	29%
Prices - High	75¼	52½	35½	25¾	24⅞	22⅞	20	12⅛	13½	12¼
- Low	44⅛	32	23⅝	21¾	20¾	16¾	10¼	8¼	9⅞	9¼
P/E Ratio - High	24	19	14	12	13	14	14	9	10	10
- Low	14	12	10	10	11	10	7	6	8	8

Income Statement Analysis (Million $)

	1997	1996	1995	1994	1993	1992	1991	1990	1989	1988
Net Int. Inc.	1,894	1,784	1,676	1,620	1,572	1,515	1,352	1,265	1,216	1,146
Tax Equiv. Adj.	36.6	40.1	49.6	55.7	62.7	68.6	76.0	88.0	93.0	96.0
Non Int. Inc.	933	804	720	703	726	658	601	548	510	464
Loan Loss Prov.	117	116	112	138	189	220	206	197	178	186
Exp./Op. Revs.	60%	62%	60%	59%	60%	61%	61%	62%	61%	62%
Pretax Inc.	1,026	903	826	782	701	589	503	444	441	372
Eff. Tax Rate	35%	32%	32%	33%	32%	30%	26%	21%	24%	17%
Net Inc.	667	617	565	523	474	413	371	350	337	309
% Net Int. Marg.	4.11	4.40	4.50	4.60	4.80	5.11	4.83	4.88	5.05	5.13

Balance Sheet & Other Fin. Data (Million $)

	1997	1996	1995	1994	1993	1992	1991	1990	1989	1988
Earning Assets:										
Money Mkt	1,180	1,815	1,425	1,095	1,204	1,920	1,987	1,165	1,642	1,225
Inv. Securities	11,729	10,551	9,677	9,319	10,644	8,384	7,257	6,012	4,643	4,051
Com'l Loans	14,387	11,966	10,560	9,552	8,570	8,158	7,570	7,907	7,322	7,037
Other Loans	25,749	23,428	20,741	18,996	16,722	14,740	14,144	14,404	14,058	13,399
Total Assets	57,983	52,468	46,471	42,709	40,728	36,649	34,554	33,411	31,044	29,177
Demand Deposits	8,928	8,900	7,821	7,654	7,611	6,935	5,944	5,848	5,529	5,531
Time Deposits	29,270	27,990	25,362	24,565	22,875	21,909	22,044	20,978	19,433	18,413
LT Debt	3,172	1,565	1,002	930	630	545	475	480	485	491
Common Eqty.	5,199	4,880	4,270	3,453	3,610	2,704	2,546	2,305	2,089	1,880
% Ret. on Assets	1.2	1.2	1.3	1.3	1.3	1.2	1.1	1.1	1.2	1.1
% Ret. on Equity	13.2	13.5	14.6	14.8	16.5	15.8	15.2	16.0	16.9	17.4
% Loan Loss Resv.	1.9	2.0	2.2	2.3	2.2	2.0	1.7	1.6	1.6	1.5
% Loans/Deposits	137.1	96.0	94.3	88.6	83.0	79.0	77.1	82.4	84.6	84.0
% Equity to Assets	9.1	9.3	8.7	8.5	8.9	7.7	7.4	7.1	6.7	6.5

Data as orig. reptd.; bef. results of disc. opers. and/or spec. items. Per share data adj. for stk. divs. as of ex-div. date. Bold denotes diluted EPS (FASB 128). E-Estimated. NA-Not Available. NM-Not Meaningful. NR-Not Ranked.

Office—303 Peachtree St., Atlanta, GA 30308; P.O. Box 4418, Center 645, Atlanta, GA 30302. **Tel**—(404) 588-7711. **Website**—http://www.SunTrust.com **Chrmn, Pres & CEO**—L. P. Humann. **Exec VP & CFO**—J. W. Spiegel. **Investor Contact**—James C. Armstrong. **Dirs**—J. H. Brown, J. D. Camp, Jr., A. D. Correll, A. W. Dahlberg, D. H. Hughes, L. P. Humann, S. K. Johnton, Jr., J. L. Lanier Jr., L. L. Prince, S. L. Probasco Jr., R. R. Rollins, J. B. Williams. **Transfer Agent**—SunTrust Bank, Atlanta. **Incorporated**—in Georgia in 1984. **Empl**— 21,227. **S&P Analyst:** Stephen R. Biggar

Supervalu Inc.

2172M

NYSE Symbol **SVU**

In S&P 500

12-SEP-98

Industry:
Distributors (Food & Health)

Summary: This company, one of the largest food wholesalers in the U.S., also operates more than 330 supermarkets under various names and formats.

S&P Opinion: Hold (★★★)	
Recent Price • 21⅜	Yield • 2.5%
52 Wk Range • 25¼-16¾	12-Mo. P/E • 11.4

Earnings vs. Previous Year
▲=Up ▼=Down ▶=No Change

Quantitative Evaluations

Outlook
(1 Lowest—5 Highest)
• **3**

Fair Value
• **23⅝**

Risk
• **Low**

Earn./Div. Rank
• **A-**

Technical Eval.
• **Bullish** since 9/98

Rel. Strength Rank
(1 Lowest—99 Highest)
• **78**

Insider Activity
• **Neutral**

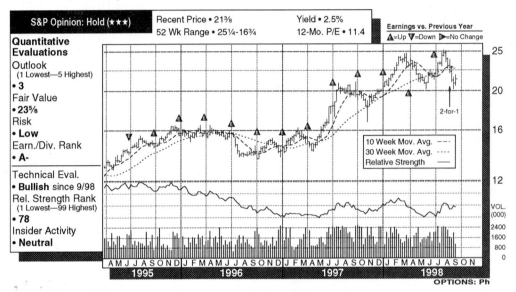

OPTIONS: Ph

Overview - 10-JUL-98

We expect sales to advance about 2%-4% in FY 99 (Feb.), which represents a solid rise in an industry characterized by sluggish top-line growth. Revenue gains should be spread evenly between the wholesale unit, which will benefit from customer additions, and the retail division, which is expected to open a significant number of stores during FY 99. Margins should expand on the revenue increase, as well as efficiencies achieved through an ongoing restructuring program. Over the next twelve months, we expect the company to roll out an improved pricing system and continue its plan to regionalize its distribution system. We believe both initiatives will enable SVU to improve profitability. We see FY 99 EPS rising approximately 9%, to $3.08, from FY 98's $2.83, which excludes an $0.82 a share gain related SVU's sale of its ShopKo investment.

Valuation - 10-JUL-98

Shares of SVU have risen rapidly since mid-1997 and are currently trading at 14 times our calendar 1998 EPS estimate of $3.08, which is at the high end of their historical range, but at a significant discount to the P/E of the broader market. Despite a recent pullback over the past several months, we believe the shares are reasonably valued. As a result we are maintaining our hold recommendation for the shares. Despite a non-inflationary environment, which is generally unfavorable for the supermarket industry, we expect SVU to achieve revenue gains by marketing its improved distribution systems and continuing to open retail stores. We are encouraged by management's commitment to investing in the business, evidenced by a 32% increase in budgeted capital expenditures for fiscal 1999. In addition, SVU's above average dividend yield provides added value to the conservative investor.

Key Stock Statistics

S&P EPS Est. 1999	1.54	Tang. Bk. Value/Share	5.81
P/E on S&P Est. 1999	13.9	Beta	1.10
S&P EPS Est. 2000	1.70	Shareholders	7,500
Dividend Rate/Share	0.53	Market cap. (B)	$ 2.6
Shs. outstg. (M)	121.0	Inst. holdings	64%
Avg. daily vol. (M)	0.336		

Value of $10,000 invested 5 years ago: $ 16,212

Fiscal Year Ending Feb. 28

	1999	1998	1997	1996	1995	1994
Revenues (Million $)						
1Q	5,203	5,033	4,979	4,973	4,991	4,876
2Q	—	3,866	3,779	3,779	3,774	3,704
3Q	—	4,005	3,905	3,887	3,908	3,670
4Q	—	4,297	3,890	3,847	3,891	3,687
Yr.	—	17,201	16,552	16,486	16,564	15,937
Earnings Per Share ($)						
1Q	0.42	0.37	0.34	0.33	0.35	0.35
2Q	E0.32	0.71	0.27	0.24	0.23	0.26
3Q	E0.36	0.33	0.30	0.28	-0.59	0.32
4Q	E0.43	0.42	0.40	0.36	0.30	0.36
Yr.	E1.54	1.82	1.30	1.22	0.30	1.29

Next earnings report expected: mid September

Dividend Data (Dividends have been paid since 1936.)

Amount ($)	Date Decl.	Ex-Div. Date	Stock of Record	Payment Date
0.260	Dec. 10	Feb. 26	Mar. 02	Mar. 15 '98
0.260	Apr. 08	May. 28	Jun. 01	Jun. 15 '98
2-for-1	Jul. 01	Aug. 19	Jul. 20	Aug. 18 '98
0.265	Jul. 01	Aug. 26	Sep. 01	Sep. 15 '98

A Division of The McGraw-Hill Companies

Supervalu Inc.

2172M
12-SEP-98

Business Summary - 10-JUL-98

To better cope with slow growth and intense competition in the food wholesale and distribution industry, Supervalu Inc. (formerly Super Value Stores) is reorganizing its operations. During FY 95 (Feb.), the company announced plans for the sale, closure and restructuring of certain retail businesses and for a fundamental change in business processes (the ADVANTAGE project). SVU aims to create a more efficient, low-cost logistics network; to develop marketing capabilities for independent retailers; and to adopt a new approach to pricing.

In FY 98 the company continued to incur additional costs associated with implementation of the ADVANTAGE program. However, Information Technology expenditures, a large portion of these added costs, are expected to plateau in FY 99.

Supervalu is the largest U.S. food wholesaler, and the company estimates that it is also the 13th largest food retailer. It serves approximately 4,600 retail stores and 730 limited-assortment stores in 48 states. SVU operated 32 retail food stores at July 1, 1998. The company recently sold its 46% stake in the common stock of ShopKo Stores through a public stock offering and a private sale to ShopKo itself; proceeds were used to repurchase 10% of SVU stock.

Sales and operating profit by business segment in FY 98 were:

	Sales	Profits
Wholesale foods	76%	73%
Retail foods	24%	27%

Supervalu supplies its retail food stores with an increasing variety and selection of products, including national and regional brands and the company's own lines of private-label products.

In addition to supplying merchandise, the company offers retail stores a wide variety of support services, including advertising, promotional and merchandising assistance, computerized inventory control and many other services.

SVU's retail stores operate under formats and names that include Cub Foods, Hornbachers, Scott's Foods, bigg's, Laneco, Save-a-Lot and Shop 'n Save.

Per Share Data ($)

(Year Ended Feb. 28)	1998	1997	1996	1995	1994	1993	1992	1991	1990	1989
Tangible Bk. Val.	5.81	6.04	5.26	4.79	5.84	4.88	7.17	6.50	5.79	5.20
Cash Flow	3.66	3.04	2.83	1.70	2.50	2.14	2.13	1.94	1.80	1.68
Earnings	1.82	1.30	1.22	0.30	1.29	1.16	1.39	1.03	0.98	0.91
Dividends	0.52	0.50	0.48	0.57	0.43	0.38	0.35	0.32	0.29	0.24
Payout Ratio	28%	38%	40%	188%	33%	33%	24%	31%	30%	27%
Cal. Yrs.	1997	1996	1995	1994	1993	1992	1991	1990	1989	1988
Prices - High	21⅛	16½	16½	20⅛	19	17½	15⅛	14½	15⅛	13¼
- Low	14⅛	13⅝	11¼	11	14¾	11¾	10⅞	10⅞	11⅜	8½
P/E Ratio - High	12	13	13	66	15	15	11	14	15	15
- Low	8	10	9	36	11	10	8	11	11	9

Income Statement Analysis (Million $)

	1998	1997	1996	1995	1994	1993	1992	1991	1990	1989
Revs.	17,201	16,552	16,486	16,564	15,937	12,568	10,632	11,612	11,136	10,296
Oper. Inc.	636	613	585	553	543	431	352	443	419	391
Depr.	230	232	219	199	174	141	111	137	131	118
Int. Exp.	134	137	140	138	123	87.1	75.1	81.4	79.9	72.9
Pretax Inc.	385	281	268	16.0	294	259	323	254	243	224
Eff. Tax Rate	40%	38%	38%	NM	37%	36%	36%	39%	30%	40%
Net Inc.	231	175	166	43.0	185	165	208	155	148	135

Balance Sheet & Other Fin. Data (Million $)

	1998	1997	1996	1995	1994	1993	1992	1991	1990	1989
Cash	6.0	6.5	5.0	4.8	2.9	1.8	1.5	2.7	2.2	2.2
Curr. Assets	1,612	1,601	1,554	1,646	1,563	1,574	1,163	1,144	1,081	1,045
Total Assets	4,093	4,283	4,283	4,305	4,042	4,064	2,484	2,615	2,429	2,305
Curr. Liab.	1,457	1,369	1,327	1,447	1,224	1,326	745	998	951	906
LT Debt	1,261	1,420	1,446	1,460	1,263	1,347	608	577	561	571
Common Eqty.	1,196	1,301	1,210	1,187	1,270	1,135	1,031	979	870	778
Total Cap.	2,499	2,765	2,699	2,653	2,638	2,568	1,690	1,591	1,473	1,395
Cap. Exp.	231	245	236	298	240	152	158	262	223	293
Cash Flow	461	407	385	242	359	305	319	292	270	251
Curr. Ratio	1.1	1.2	1.2	1.1	1.3	1.2	1.6	1.1	1.1	1.2
% LT Debt of Cap.	50.5	51.4	53.6	55.0	47.9	52.5	36.0	36.3	38.1	40.9
% Net Inc.of Revs.	1.3	1.1	1.0	0.3	1.2	1.3	2.0	1.3	1.3	1.3
% Ret. on Assets	5.5	4.2	3.9	1.1	4.6	5.0	8.3	6.1	6.2	6.3
% Ret. on Equity	18.5	14.0	13.8	3.6	15.4	15.2	21.1	16.8	17.9	18.6

Data as orig. reptd.; bef. results of disc. opers. and/or spec. items. Per share data adj. for stk. divs. as of ex-div. date. Bold denotes diluted EPS (FASB 128). E-Estimated. NA-Not Available. NM-Not Meaningful. NR-Not Ranked.

Office—11840 Valley View Rd., Eden Prairie, MN 55344 (P.O. Box 990, Minneapolis, MN 55440). **Tel**—(612) 828-4000. **Website**—http://www.supervalu.com **Chrmn, Pres & CEO**—M. W. Wright. **Exec VP & CFO**—P. Knous. **VP & Treas**—K. M. Erickson. **Secy**—J. P. Breedlove. **Investor Contact**—Beth A. Heming (612) 828-4540. **Dirs**—H. Cain, L. A. Del Santo, E. C. Gage, W. A. Hodder, G. L. Keith Jr., R. L. Knowlton, C. M. Lillis, H. K. Perlmutter, S. S. Rogers, C. F. St. Mark, M. W. Wright. **Transfer Agent & Registrar**—Norwest Shareowner Services, South St. Paul. **Incorporated**—in Delaware in 1925. **Empl**—48,600. **S&P Analyst:** Maureen C. Carini

STANDARD &POOR'S
STOCK REPORTS

Synovus Financial

2178F

NYSE Symbol **SNV**

In S&P 500

12-SEP-98

Industry: Banks (Major Regional)

Summary: This company owns 34 community banks, in Georgia, Florida, Alabama and South Carolina, and has an 81% interest in one of the world's largest bankcard processing companies.

S&P Opinion: Hold (★★★)	Recent Price • 19½	Yield • 1.5%
	52 Wk Range • 25⅞-13⅜	12-Mo. P/E • 29.6

Quantitative Evaluations

Outlook (1 Lowest—5 Highest)
• **1**

Fair Value
• **15⅛**

Risk
• **Low**

Earn./Div. Rank
• **A+**

Technical Eval.
• **Bearish** since 8/98

Rel. Strength Rank (1 Lowest—99 Highest)
• **69**

Insider Activity
• **Neutral**

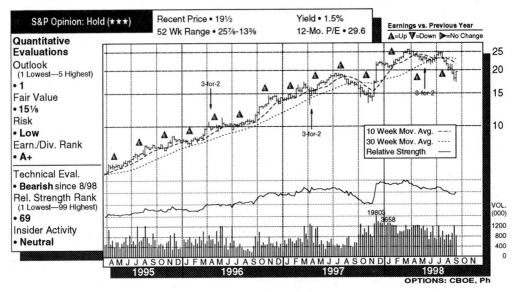

Earnings vs. Previous Year: ▲=Up ▼=Down ▶=No Change

10 Week Mov. Avg. — • —
30 Week Mov. Avg. - - - -
Relative Strength ———

OPTIONS: CBOE, Ph

Overview - 05-AUG-98

Loan growth in the mid-single digits, a stable net interest margin, and strong contributions from noninterest income are expected to provide for earnings growth of about 15% in 1998. The loan portfolio continues to benefit from a dynamic service territory, which consists of states in the Southeast with economic growth well above the national average. Healthy growth in the deposit base has offset some pressure on asset yields, leading to steady margins. Revenues and profits from the company's 81%-owned bankcard data processing subsidiary, Total System Services (TSS), are growing rapidly, aided by agreements to provide additional processing services for customers. Asset quality remains strong, but with the company's conservative reserve policy, the provision for loan losses will likely remain modestly above the level of net chargeoffs.

Valuation - 05-AUG-98

SNV remains well positioned for the future, aided by the growing revenue base of its TSS data processing subsidiary, and by its relatively healthy service territory. The company's ability to attract core deposits is impressive, especially considering competition, and bodes well for the bank's funding cost picture. With a higher than normal proportion of the bank's profits derived from noninterest income sources, SNV's shares typically trade at a premium to those of other regional banks, but at a recent level of 30X our $0.71 EPS estimate for 1998, we regard the shares, which were split three for two in May 1998, as being fully valued.

Key Stock Statistics

S&P EPS Est. 1998	0.71	Tang. Bk. Value/Share	3.62
P/E on S&P Est. 1998	27.4	Beta	1.18
S&P EPS Est. 1999	0.80	Shareholders	16,300
Dividend Rate/Share	0.29	Market cap. (B)	$ 5.2
Shs. outstg. (M)	263.4	Inst. holdings	29%
Avg. daily vol. (M)	0.197		

Value of $10,000 invested 5 years ago: $ 47,071

Fiscal Year Ending Dec. 31

	1998	1997	1996	1995	1994	1993
Revenues (Million $)						
1Q	319.3	284.6	256.6	217.8	158.6	148.1
2Q	318.5	301.3	266.5	234.4	168.4	151.4
3Q	—	309.4	278.0	247.2	175.9	155.8
4Q	—	319.6	287.2	257.2	190.4	160.1
Yr.	—	1,215	1,089	956.6	693.4	615.4
Earnings Per Share ($)						
1Q	**0.15**	**0.13**	0.12	0.09	0.08	0.07
2Q	**0.17**	**0.15**	0.13	0.10	0.09	0.08
3Q	E0.19	**0.17**	0.13	0.12	0.10	0.09
4Q	E0.20	**0.17**	0.16	0.13	0.11	0.09
Yr.	E0.71	**0.62**	0.53	0.44	0.38	0.33

Next earnings report expected: mid October

Dividend Data (Dividends have been paid since 1930.)

Amount ($)	Date Decl.	Ex-Div. Date	Stock of Record	Payment Date
0.090	Nov. 10	Dec. 17	Dec. 19	Jan. 02 '98
0.110	Mar. 09	Mar. 18	Mar. 20	Apr. 01 '98
3-for-2	Apr. 23	May. 22	May. 07	May. 21 '98
0.073	May. 11	Jun. 16	Jun. 18	Jul. 01 '98

A Division of The **McGraw·Hill** Companies

Synovus Financial Corp.

2178F
12-SEP-98

Business Summary - 05-AUG-98

Synovus Financial Corp., whose name was created by combining the words synergy (interaction of separate components such that the result is greater than the sum of its parts) and novus (of superior quality and different from others in the same category), operates with a decentralized, community-focused management structure that allows it to offer tailored financial services to its customers. The company's 34 bank subsidiaries in Georgia, Florida, Alabama and South Carolina are involved mainly in commercial banking, as well as trust operations, mortgage banking and broker/dealer activities. SNV also holds an 81% interest in Total System Services, Inc., one of the world's largest bankcard data processing concerns.

Gross loans of $6.62 billion at 1997 year-end ($6.08 billion a year earlier) were divided: commercial, financial and agricultural 35%, commercial real estate 32% and consumer 33%.

In 1997, average earning assets, from which interest income is derived, amounted to $7.9 billion and consisted mainly of loans (79%) and investment securities (21%). Average sources of funds, used in the lending business, included interest-bearing deposits (70%), non-interest-bearing deposits (13%), borrowings (6%), shareholders' equity (9%) and other (2%).

At year-end 1997, nonperforming assets, consisting primarily of nonaccrual loans and other real estate owned, were $28.8 million (0.44% of loans and related assets), down from $36.1 million (0.59%) a year earlier. The allowance for loan losses, which is set aside for possible loan defaults, was $103.1 million (1.56% of loans), versus $94.7 million (1.56%) a year earlier. Net chargeoffs, or the amount of loans actually written off as uncollectible, were $23.9 million (0.38% of average loans) in 1997, compared with $18.7 million (0.32%) in 1996.

Synovus holds an 81% interest in Total System Services (TSS), one of the world's largest credit, debit, commercial and private-label card processing companies. TSS provides card production, electronic clearing, statement preparation, customer support, merchant accounting and other services throughout the U.S., Puerto Rico, Canada and Mexico, representing more than 93 million cardholder accounts. TSS accounted for 30% of consolidated revenues in 1997.

Per Share Data ($)

(Year Ended Dec. 31)	1997	1996	1995	1994	1993	1992	1991	1990	1989	1988
Tangible Bk. Val.	3.43	3.00	2.66	2.22	2.12	1.85	1.56	1.33	1.21	1.05
Earnings	0.62	0.53	0.44	0.38	0.33	0.27	0.22	0.21	0.20	0.17
Dividends	0.24	0.20	0.16	0.13	0.11	0.09	0.08	0.07	0.07	0.06
Payout Ratio	39%	37%	36%	35%	34%	34%	36%	35%	33%	33%
Prices - High	22³/₈	14⁷/₈	9	5⁷/₈	6	4⁷/₈	3³/₄	3³/₄	3⁷/₈	3
- Low	13¹/₄	7³/₄	5¹/₄	4⁷/₈	4¹/₂	3¹/₄	2⁵/₈	2⁷/₁₆	2¹/₄	2⁵/₁₆
P/E Ratio - High	36	28	20	15	18	18	17	18	19	17
- Low	21	15	12	13	14	12	12	12	11	13

Income Statement Analysis (Million $)

	1997	1996	1995	1994	1993	1992	1991	1990	1989	1988
Net Int. Inc.	412	375	342	260	229	211	144	118	95.0	86.0
Tax Equiv. Adj.	4.4	4.6	5.1	5.0	5.9	7.2	6.5	6.8	7.2	7.8
Non Int. Inc.	489	426	340	264	225	195	161	121	92.0	74.0
Loan Loss Prov.	32.3	31.8	25.8	22.1	23.5	30.5	21.3	12.3	8.6	8.3
Exp./Op. Revs.	67%	67%	70%	69%	68%	68%	72%	71%	69%	69%
Pretax Inc.	268	219	179	134	118	95.6	62.1	52.1	44.9	36.3
Eff. Tax Rate	35%	36%	36%	36%	34%	33%	30%	28%	NA	NA
Net Inc.	165	140	115	86.4	74.1	61.2	40.5	35.1	31.4	26.8
% Net Int. Marg.	5.26	5.19	5.15	5.11	4.84	4.79	4.84	5.21	5.52	5.81

Balance Sheet & Other Fin. Data (Million $)

	1997	1996	1995	1994	1993	1992	1991	1990	1989	1988
Earning Assets:										
Money Mkt	93.3	38.2	125	33.5	84.2	107	18.2	47.6	84.0	50.3
Inv. Securities	1,655	1,639	1,487	1,147	1,120	1,014	787	497	435	348
Com'l Loans	4,411	4,002	3,670	1,589	1,558	1,304	1,012	728	NA	NA
Other Loans	2,204	2,073	1,857	2,741	2,291	2,269	2,826	2,014	1,615	1,342
Total Assets	9,260	8,612	7,928	6,115	5,627	5,184	4,070	2,921	2,410	1,957
Demand Deposits	2,385	2,212	2,074	809	734	661	449	410	392	358
Time Deposits	5,323	4,991	4,654	4,219	3,940	3,745	3,032	2,095	1,672	1,315
LT Debt	126	97.0	107	120	128	128	106	24.0	21.0	8.0
Common Eqty.	904	784	694	580	476	416	297	225	194	163
% Ret. on Assets	1.8	1.7	1.5	1.5	1.4	1.2	1.2	1.3	1.5	1.5
% Ret. on Equity	19.6	19.1	18.0	17.5	16.8	15.5	15.3	16.4	18.0	17.6
% Loan Loss Resv.	1.6	1.6	1.5	1.5	1.6	1.6	1.5	1.5	1.7	1.6
% Loans/Deposits	85.8	82.9	81.9	86.1	82.0	80.5	80.6	79.5	77.2	79.0
% Equity to Assets	9.4	8.9	8.4	8.4	7.9	7.6	7.6	8.0	8.3	8.4

Data as orig. reptd.; bef. results of disc opers. and/or spec. items. Per share data adj. for stk. divs. as of ex-div. date. Bold denotes diluted EPS (FASB 128). E-Estimated. NA-Not Available. NM-Not Meaningful. NR-Not Ranked.

Office—901 Front Ave., P.O. Box 120, Columbus, GA 31902. **Tel**—(706) 649-2197. **Website**—http://www.synovus.com **Chrmn & CEO**—J. H. Blanchard. **Pres**—S. L. Burts Jr. **EVP & CFO**—T. J. Prescott. **VP & Investor Contact**—Patrick A. Reynolds. **Dirs**—R. E. Anthony, J. E. Beverly, J. H. Blanchard, R. Y. Bradley, S. L. Burts Jr., W. M. Deriso Jr., C. E. Floyd, G. W. Garrard Jr., V. N. Hansford, J. P. Illges III, M. H. Lampton, E. C. Ogie, J. T. Oliver Jr., H. L. Page, R. V. Royall Jr., M. T. Stith, W. B. Turner, G. C. Woodruff Jr., J. D. Yancey. **Transfer Agent & Registrar**—State Street Bank & Trust Co., Canton, MA. **Incorporated**—in Georgia in 1972. **Empl**— 8,149. **S&P Analyst:** Stephen R. Biggar

Sysco Corp.

2179M

NYSE Symbol **SYY**

In S&P 500

12-SEP-98

Industry: Distributors (Food & Health)

Summary: Sysco is the largest marketer and distributor of foodservice products in the U.S., serving approximately 270,000 customers.

S&P Opinion: Avoid (★★)	Recent Price • 23⅜	Yield • 1.5%
	52 Wk Range • 26¾-17⅞	12-Mo. P/E • 24.6

Quantitative Evaluations

Outlook (1 Lowest—5 Highest)
• **4+**

Fair Value
• 27⅛

Risk
• **Low**

Earn./Div. Rank
• **A+**

Technical Eval.
• **Bullish** since 8/98

Rel. Strength Rank (1 Lowest—99 Highest)
• **90**

Insider Activity
• **Neutral**

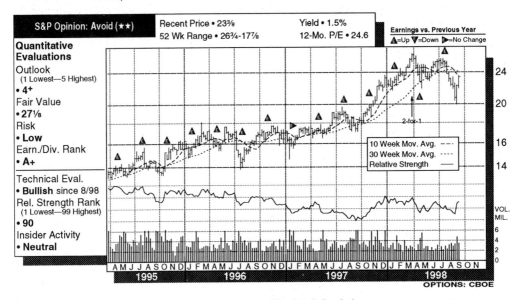

Earnings vs. Previous Year
▲=Up ▼=Down ▷=No Change

- 10 Week Mov. Avg. – – –
- 30 Week Mov. Avg. ⋯⋯
- Relative Strength ——

OPTIONS: CBOE

Overview - 30-JUL-98

Sales are expected to advance at a mid-single-digit pace through FY 99 (Jun.), reflecting 5% to 6% volume growth and, to a lesser extent, acquisition contributions. Our volume expectations assume further 3% annual growth in the approximate $140 billion U.S. foodservice distribution market. SYY's solid balance sheet, coupled with the highly fragmented nature of the U.S. foodservice industry, should allow Sysco to continue its selective acquisition policy. Furthermore, the current economic environment, characterized by high consumer confidence and low unemployment, should drive demand for "away from home meals."

Valuation - 30-JUL-98

We recently downgraded the shares of SYY to avoid from hold, reflecting limited upside potential given the sharp rise in the shares since since mid-1997. Industry fundamentals remain decent, as economic prosperity is likely to keep many consumers out of the kitchen and in restaurants. However, the current non-inflationary environment makes it difficult for SYY to raise prices. The shares have been buoyed by management's consistent repurchase program. Although gross margins have benefited from the addition of new independent customers, this benefit is somewhat offset by higher operating expenses associated with independent customers relative to chain restaurant customers. We see FY 99 EPS rising 11%, to $1.05, from FY 98's $0.95. Despite SYY's solid outlook and the company's somewhat recession-resistant nature, we believe investors would do best to avoid the shares as they are trading at a multiple more than twice its growth rate. As such, it appears that the risk is greater to the downside.

Key Stock Statistics

S&P EPS Est. 1999	1.05	Tang. Bk. Value/Share	3.35
P/E on S&P Est. 1999	22.3	Beta	0.82
Dividend Rate/Share	0.36	Shareholders	17,900
Shs. outstg. (M)	337.6	Market cap. (B)	$ 7.9
Avg. daily vol. (M)	0.733	Inst. holdings	63%

Value of $10,000 invested 5 years ago: $ 19,217

Fiscal Year Ending Jun. 30

	1998	1997	1996	1995	1994	1993
Revenues (Million $)						
1Q	3,828	3,679	3,292	2,983	2,710	2,416
2Q	3,786	3,610	3,302	3,007	2,666	2,392
3Q	3,712	3,470	3,257	2,966	2,685	2,399
4Q	4,001	3,695	3,545	3,162	2,882	2,814
Yr.	15,328	14,455	13,395	12,118	10,943	10,022
Earnings Per Share ($)						
1Q	0.23	0.20	0.18	0.16	0.13	0.12
2Q	**0.24**	0.21	0.21	0.17	0.15	0.13
3Q	**0.19**	0.17	0.15	0.14	0.13	0.12
4Q	**0.29**	0.26	0.23	0.21	0.18	0.17
Yr.	**0.95**	0.85	0.76	0.69	0.59	0.54

Next earnings report expected: mid October

Dividend Data (Dividends have been paid since 1970.)

Amount ($)	Date Decl.	Ex-Div. Date	Stock of Record	Payment Date
0.170	Nov. 07	Dec. 30	Jan. 02	Jan. 23 '98
2-for-1	Feb. 11	Mar. 23	Feb. 27	Mar. 20 '98
0.090	May. 13	Jun. 30	Jul. 02	Jul. 24 '98
0.090	Sep. 04	Sep. 30	Oct. 02	Oct. 23 '98

A Division of The McGraw-Hill Companies

Business Summary - 30-JUL-98

Sysco Corporation is the largest marketer and distributor of foodservice products in North America. Operating from 69 distribution centers throughout the continental United States, Alaska and parts of Canada, the company provides products and services to approximately 270,000 restaurants, hotels, schools, hospitals, retirement homes and other foodservice operations--almost wherever a meal is prepared away from home. The approximate $140 billion foodservice distribution market is expected to grow at an approximate 3% annual real (ex-inflation) rate over the next few years. Sales contributions by type of customer in recent fiscal years (Jun.) were:

	FY 97	FY 96	FY 95
Restaurants	61%	61%	60%
Hospitals & nursing homes	11%	11%	12%
Schools & colleges	7%	7%	7%
Hotels & motels	6%	6%	6%
Other	15%	15%	15%

Traditional foodservice products distributed by the company to businesses and organizations include a full line of frozen foods, such as meats, fully prepared entrees, fruits, vegetables and desserts, and a full line of canned and dry goods, fresh meats, imported specialties and fresh produce. The company also provides a wide variety of nonfood items, including paper products (disposable napkins, plates and cups); tableware (china and silverware); restaurant and kitchen equipment and supplies; medical/surgical supplies; and cleaning supplies. Products include both nationally branded merchandise and items packed under Sysco's private label. No single traditional foodservice customer accounted for as much as 5% of the company's total sales in FY 97.

Sysco's SYGMA Network subsidiary specializes in customized service to chain restaurants, whose sales consist of a variety of food products necessitated by the increasingly broad menus of chain restaurants. No chain restaurant customer accounted for as much as 3% of total sales in FY 97.

The company estimates that it purchases from thousands of independent sources, none of which represents more than 5% of its purchases.

Per Share Data ($)

(Year Ended Jun. 30)	1998	1997	1996	1995	1994	1993	1992	1991	1990	1989
Tangible Bk. Val.	NA	3.35	3.40	3.13	2.67	2.36	2.13	1.74	1.36	1.01
Cash Flow	NA	1.31	1.16	1.04	0.88	0.80	0.73	0.67	0.59	0.51
Earnings	0.95	0.85	0.76	0.69	0.59	0.54	0.47	0.41	0.36	0.30
Dividends	0.34	0.28	0.24	0.20	0.16	0.13	0.09	0.06	0.05	0.04
Payout Ratio	36%	33%	32%	29%	27%	24%	18%	14%	14%	14%
Prices - High	35	23⅝	18⅛	16¼	14⅝	15½	13¾	11⅞	9⅝	8⅜
- Low	21⅝	14⅝	13⅞	12½	10⅝	11⅛	10⅜	7½	6⅜	4⅝
P/E Ratio - High	28	28	24	24	25	29	29	28	26	28
- Low	23	17	18	18	18	21	22	18	18	15

Income Statement Analysis (Million $)

	1998	1997	1996	1995	1994	1993	1992	1991	1990	1989
Revs.	NA	14,455	13,395	12,118	10,942	10,022	8,893	8,150	7,591	6,851
Oper. Inc.	NA	703	639	586	509	464	418	385	347	306
Depr.	NA	160	145	131	107	95.0	100	81.5	81.8	74.3
Int. Exp.	NA	47.0	44.0	38.6	37.6	40.3	45.6	52.9	60.7	61.3
Pretax Inc.	NA	496	454	418	368	332	282	251	216	177
Eff. Tax Rate	NA	39%	39%	40%	41%	39%	39%	39%	39%	39%
Net Inc.	NA	303	277	252	217	202	172	154	132	108

Balance Sheet & Other Fin. Data (Million $)

	1998	1997	1996	1995	1994	1993	1992	1991	1990	1989
Cash	NA	118	108	134	86.7	68.8	74.4	70.2	56.0	55.5
Curr. Assets	NA	1,964	1,922	1,787	1,600	1,420	1,240	1,144	1,047	1,022
Total Assets	NA	3,437	3,325	3,095	2,812	2,530	2,302	2,160	1,992	1,869
Curr. Liab.	NA	1,114	1,038	945	847	746	655	612	574	566
LT Debt	NA	686	582	542	539	494	489	543	583	620
Common Eqty.	NA	1,400	1,475	1,404	1,241	1,137	1,057	919	771	643
Total Cap.	NA	2,323	2,288	2,151	1,965	1,784	1,646	1,548	1,418	1,303
Cap. Exp.	NA	211	236	202	161	128	134	135	182	159
Cash Flow	NA	463	422	383	324	297	272	246	214	182
Curr. Ratio	NA	1.8	1.9	1.9	1.9	1.9	1.9	1.9	1.8	1.8
% LT Debt of Cap.	NA	29.6	25.4	25.2	27.4	27.7	29.7	35.1	41.1	47.6
% Net Inc.of Revs.	NA	2.1	2.1	2.1	2.0	2.0	2.0	1.9	1.7	1.6
% Ret. on Assets	NA	9.0	8.6	8.5	8.1	8.4	8.1	7.4	6.8	7.4
% Ret. on Equity	NA	21.1	19.2	19.1	18.2	18.5	17.4	18.1	18.7	18.1

Data as orig. reptd.; bef. results of disc. opers. and/or spec. items. Per share data adj. for stk. divs. as of ex-div. date. Bold denotes diluted EPS (FASB 128). E-Estimated. NA-Not Available. NM-Not Meaningful. NR-Not Ranked.

Office—1390 Enclave Parkway, Houston, TX 77077-2099. **Tel**—(281) 584-1390. **Website**—http://www.sysco.com **Chrmn**—J. F. Woodhouse. **Pres & CEO**—B. M. Lindig. **VP, Treas & Investor Contact**—Diane Day Sanders. **Secy**—C. Mitchell. **Dirs**—J. W. Anderson, J. F. Baugh, C. G. Campbell, C. H. Cotros, J. Craven, F. A. Godchaux III, J. Golden, D. J. Keller, B. M. Lindig, R. G. Merrill, F. H. Richardson, R. J. Schnieders, P. S. Sewell, A. J. Swenka, —T. B. Walker Jr., J. F. Woodhouse. **Transfer Agent & Registrar**—Boston EquiServe, L.P., Boston. **Incorporated**—in Delaware in 1969. **Empl**— 32,000. **S&P Analyst:**   Robert J. Izmirlian

STANDARD &POOR'S
STOCK REPORTS

Tandy Corp.

2191

NYSE Symbol **TAN**

In S&P 500

12-SEP-98

Industry: Retail (Computers & Electronics)

Summary: This leading retailer of consumer electronics sells its products through about 6,900 RadioShack and 100 Computer City stores.

| S&P Opinion: Hold (★★★) | Recent Price • 56⅛ | Yield • 0.7% |
| | 52 Wk Range • 63⅜-30⅜ | 12-Mo. P/E • 42.8 |

Quantitative Evaluations

Outlook (1 Lowest—5 Highest)
• **1+**

Fair Value
• **49⅛**

Risk
• **Average**

Earn./Div. Rank
• **B**

Technical Eval.
• **Bearish** since 3/98

Rel. Strength Rank (1 Lowest—99 Highest)
• **94**

Insider Activity
• **Neutral**

Earnings vs. Previous Year
▲=Up ▼=Down ▶=No Change

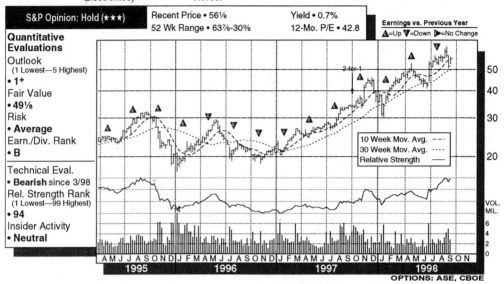

10 Week Mov. Avg. ----
30 Week Mov. Avg. ·······
Relative Strength ——

OPTIONS: ASE, CBOE

Overview - 25-JUN-98

Good sales growth is seen for RadioShack in 1998, aided by new store openings, and strong growth for the telecommunications business. We expect a favorable impact from the September 1997 rollout of a Sprint Store at RadioShack units. Also, a recent agreement in which Compaq Presario personal computers will be the exclusive computer line sold at many RadioShack stores may help PC sales. In June 1998, TAN said that it had agreed to sell its Computer City business, which was unprofitable in 1997, to CompUSA Inc. for about $275 million, payable in cash and a note. TAN has already largely exited the Incredible Universe retail business, which had incurred significant losses. A prospective one-time charge related to divestiture of the Computer City business is excluded from our 1998 EPS estimate.

Valuation - 25-JUN-98

In late June 1998, we lowered our opinion on this stock to "hold," from accumulate. The stock was up sharply after news of TAN's agreement to sell its Computer City business. We have a 6-to-12 month price target for the stock of the low $50s. Earlier, TAN's first quarter 1998 earnings comparisons benefited from the absence of some stores which were closed as part of restructuring activity. Those closed stores had $129 million of revenues and a loss of $15 million ($0.08 a share after-tax) in the year-ago quarter. In full-year 1997, stores closed pursuant to restructuring plans had a loss of $30 million (about $0.16 a share). Also, between December 1995 and March 31, 1998, TAN repurchased about 22 million (adjusted) common shares for $569 million. This was in addition to shares required for employee plans. At March 31, 1998, authorization remained for TAN to buy back eight million additional shares. The stock was split two-for-one in September 1997.

Key Stock Statistics

S&P EPS Est. 1998	2.25	Tang. Bk. Value/Share	8.62
P/E on S&P Est. 1998	24.9	Beta	0.58
S&P EPS Est. 1999	2.65	Shareholders	27,000
Dividend Rate/Share	0.40	Market cap. (B)	$ 5.6
Shs. outstg. (M)	100.4	Inst. holdings	65%
Avg. daily vol. (M)	0.773		

Value of $10,000 invested 5 years ago: $ 40,735

Fiscal Year Ending Dec. 31

	1998	1997	1996	1995	1994	1993
Revenues (Million $)						
1Q	1,258	1,292	1,447	1,227	992.0	865.0
2Q	1,193	1,146	1,353	1,185	1,009	843.0
3Q	—	1,228	1,435	1,340	1,119	940.0
4Q	—	1,707	2,051	2,087	1,823	1,455
Yr.	—	5,372	6,286	5,839	4,944	4,103
Earnings Per Share ($)						
1Q	0.34	0.21	0.10	0.28	0.27	0.25
2Q	-0.21	0.24	0.07	0.28	0.22	0.19
3Q	E0.45	0.32	0.17	0.33	0.29	0.26
4Q	E1.11	0.88	-1.20	0.69	0.69	0.52
Yr.	E2.25	1.63	-0.82	1.56	1.46	1.24

Next earnings report expected: late October

Dividend Data (Dividends have been paid since 1987.)

Amount ($)	Date Decl.	Ex-Div. Date	Stock of Record	Payment Date
0.100	Dec. 01	Dec. 29	Jan. 01	Jan. 20 '98
0.100	Feb. 25	Mar. 30	Apr. 01	Apr. 21 '98
0.100	May. 26	Jun. 29	Jul. 01	Jul. 21 '98
0.100	Aug. 21	Sep. 29	Oct. 01	Oct. 20 '98

A Division of The McGraw-Hill Companies

STANDARD
&POOR'S

STOCK REPORTS

Tandy Corporation

2191

12-SEP-98

Business Summary - 25-JUN-98

Tandy Corp. is a retailer of consumer electronics and personal computers, including the large RadioShack business. TAN recently agreed to divest its Computer City retail business.

At December 31, 1997, the RadioShack division had 4,972 company-owned stores, located throughout the U.S., largely in metropolitan markets. RadioShack also had a network of 1,934 dealer/franchise stores to service smaller communities. Company-owned stores average approximately 2,200 sq. ft. and carry an assortment of electronic parts and accessories, audio/video equipment, digital satellite systems, personal computers and cellular and conventional telephones, as well as specialized products such as scanners, electronic toys and batteries. Personal computers and related items account for about 11% of the RadioShack division's sales. RadioShack also provides access to third party services, such as cellular phone, PCS, direct satellite programming and pager service. In 1997, the TAN had sales from its Radio Shack business of $3.2 billion.

In February 1998, TAN signed an agreement under which Compaq will replace IBM as the sole supplier of computers sold through all of RadioShack's company-owned stores and at dealer/franchise outlets

which choose to participate. Also, TAN has developed a Sprint Store at RadioShack concept, which features telecommunications products and services.

Also, at year-end 1997, TAN's Computer City retail chain had 96 stores open, including seven in Canada. In June 1998, TAN said that it had agreed to sell the Computer City business, to CompUSA Inc., for about $275 million. TAN currently owns 100% of this business, after recently reacquiring a 19.9% interest which it had sold in 1997 to Eureka Venture Partners III LLP for what was likely a price of $24,9 million , largely in the form of a note. Operating primarily in a superstore format, Computer City units averaged, at year-end 1997, about 21,050 sq. ft. Computer City offers thousands of products, including personal computer hardware and software, and related items. Also, service centers were located within each of the 89 U.S. stores. In 1997, the Computer City business had sales of $1.9 billion and an operating loss of $15 million.

Also, TAN recorded one-time restructuring charges of $1.70 a share (adjusted) in 1996's fourth quarter stemming from its plan to exit the unprofitable Incredible Universe business, reduce the number of stores and markets in the Computer City chain, and eliminate the remaining McDuff stores.

Per Share Data ($)

(Year Ended Dec. 31)	1997	1996	1995	1994	1993	1992	1991	1990	1989	1988
Tangible Bk. Val.	9.37	10.21	12.05	11.64	11.44	10.50	9.06	9.53	9.37	9.58
Cash Flow	2.48	0.14	2.31	1.80	1.55	0.24	1.69	1.93	2.33	2.23
Earnings	1.63	-0.82	1.56	1.46	1.24	0.01	1.12	1.29	1.77	1.82
Dividends	0.40	0.40	0.37	0.32	0.30	0.15	0.30	0.30	0.30	0.30
Payout Ratio	25%	NM	24%	22%	24%	NM	27%	23%	16%	16%
Prices - High	46	29⅝	32¼	25⅜	25⅜	15⅞	15⅞	18¼	20⅝	24⅜
- Low	20⅜	17⅛	18¼	15⅜	12⅜	11⅛	11⅛	11¾	11¾	19⅛
P/E Ratio - High	28	NM	21	17	20	NM	14	14	12	13
- Low	12	NM	12	11	10	NM	10	9	7	10

Income Statement Analysis (Million $)

	1997	1996	1995	1994	1993	1992	1991	1990	1989	1988
Revs.	5,372	6,286	5,839	4,991	4,160	2,228	4,742	4,656	4,500	4,181
Oper. Inc.	434	261	428	440	423	163	435	549	572	591
Depr.	97.2	109	92.0	84.8	79.9	37.0	103	100	92.1	75.4
Int. Exp.	46.1	36.0	33.7	30.0	39.7	25.5	59.4	91.2	78.4	47.8
Pretax Inc.	304	-145	343	360	311	33.0	300	339	474	527
Eff. Tax Rate	38%	NM	38%	38%	37%	89%	39%	39%	39%	39%
Net Inc.	187	-91.6	212	224	196	4.0	184	206	290	324

Balance Sheet & Other Fin. Data (Million $)

	1997	1996	1995	1994	1993	1992	1991	1990	1989	1988
Cash	106	122	143	206	213	84.0	106	186	135	58.0
Curr. Assets	1,716	1,940	2,048	2,556	2,160	1,954	2,340	2,262	2,485	1,942
Total Assets	2,318	2,583	2,722	3,244	3,219	3,151	3,165	3,078	3,240	2,574
Curr. Liab.	976	1,194	960	1,206	1,032	880	784	711	1,172	569
LT Debt	236	104	141	153	187	307	358	428	253	141
Common Eqty.	959	1,165	1,501	1,370	1,481	1,346	1,388	1,747	1,723	1,783
Total Cap.	1,295	1,369	1,742	2,004	2,137	2,223	2,349	2,337	2,045	1,985
Cap. Exp.	118	175	227	181	129	55.0	123	139	113	133
Cash Flow	278	17.0	304	270	236	38.0	270	301	382	395
Curr. Ratio	1.8	1.6	2.1	2.1	2.1	2.2	3.0	3.2	2.1	3.4
% LT Debt of Cap.	18.2	7.6	8.1	7.7	8.7	13.8	15.2	18.3	12.3	7.1
% Net Inc.of Revs.	3.5	NM	3.7	4.5	4.7	0.2	3.9	4.4	6.5	7.7
% Ret. on Assets	7.6	NM	7.1	7.3	6.1	NM	6.5	6.6	10.4	12.8
% Ret. on Equity	17.0	NM	12.3	13.6	10.5	NM	11.9	11.7	17.3	19.3

Data as orig. reptd.; bef. results of disc. opers. and/or spec. items. Per share data adj. for stk. divs. as of ex-div. date. Bold denotes diluted EPS (FASB 128). E-Estimated. NA-Not Available. NM-Not Meaningful. NR-Not Ranked.

Office—100 Throckmorton St., Suite 1800, Fort Worth, TX 76102. **Tel**—(817) 415-3700. **Website**—http://www.tandy.com **Chrmn & CEO**—J. V. Roach. **Pres**—L. H. Roberts. **SVP & CFO**—D. H. Hughes. **VP & Secy**—M. C. Hill. **VP & Treas**—L. K. Jensen. **VP & Investor Contact**—Martin O. Moad. **Dirs**—J. I. Cash Jr., R. E. Elmquist, L. F. Kornfeld Jr., J. L. Messman, W. G. Morton Jr., T. G. Plaskett, J. V. Roach, L. H. Roberts, A. J. Stein, W. E. Tucker, E. D. Woodbury. **Transfer Agent & Registrar**—First National Bank of Boston. **Incorporated**—in New Jersey in 1899; reincorporated in Delaware in 1967. **Empl**—48,400. **S&P Analyst:** Tom Graves, CFA.

STANDARD &POOR'S
STOCK REPORTS

Tektronix, Inc.

2195

NYSE Symbol **TEK**

In S&P 500

12-SEP-98

Industry: Electronics (Instrumentation)

Summary: The world's leading producer of oscilloscopes, this company also makes printers, X terminals and television systems.

S&P Opinion: Avoid (★★)	Recent Price • 17¼
	52 Wk Range • 48⅛-15⅛

Yield • 2.8%

12-Mo. P/E • 10.8

Quantitative Evaluations

Outlook (1 Lowest—5 Highest)
• **5**

Fair Value
• **31½**

Risk
• **Average**

Earn./Div. Rank
• **B**

Technical Eval.
• **Bearish** since 4/98

Rel. Strength Rank (1 Lowest—99 Highest)
• **10**

Insider Activity
• **Neutral**

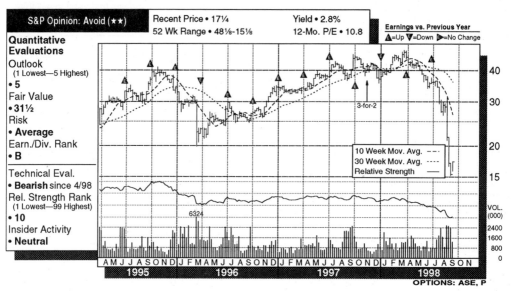

Earnings vs. Previous Year
▲=Up ▼=Down ▶=No Change

10 Week Mov. Avg. – – –
30 Week Mov. Avg. · · · ·
Relative Strength —

3-for-2

OPTIONS: ASE, P

Overview - 25-AUG-98

Sales for FY 99 (May) are expected to be flat, primarily reflecting weak demand for TEK's measurement and video products resulting from the fallout in the Asian markets; color printer sales should remain strong, and results should improve sequentially in the second half of the fiscal year as new products are introduced. However, EPS will be hurt by the weak sales, and losses at TEK's 27%-owned circuit board maker Merix Corp. (MERX; NASDAQ). Additionally, softer than expected conditions in Japan will continue to affect product sales there. Sales in Asia/Pacific accounted for 12% of TEK's FY 98 total, down from 19% in FY 97. EPS for FY 99's second half should match those of the FY 98 period. We see long-term results benefiting from increased demand in Europe and the Americas for color printers, with unit growth ranging from 30% to 50%. TEK still remains committed to Asia's long-term potential and will continue to make strategic investments while cutting costs through a 10% workforce reduction in that region.

Valuation - 25-AUG-98

The shares have fallen 60% from their March 1998 high, and 18% since we downgraded our opinion recently to avoid from hold following TEK's lower than expected EPS forecast for the FY 99 first quarter. WE also revised our EPS projections for both FY 99 and FY 00, and recommend steering clear of TEK's stock until conditions in the Far East improve. TEK is focused on enhancing shareholder value through new product introductions, improved productivity and a stronger position in its growth markets, as well as through further share repurchases (2.3 million shares available under its current authorization). However, given the lack of strength in certain markets and an erratic stock market, we suggest avoiding purchase of the shares.

Key Stock Statistics

S&P EPS Est. 1999	1.80	Tang. Bk. Value/Share	14.35
P/E on S&P Est. 1999	9.6	Beta	1.65
S&P EPS Est. 2000	2.25	Shareholders	4,400
Dividend Rate/Share	0.48	Market cap. (B)	$0.872
Shs. outstg. (M)	50.3	Inst. holdings	84%
Avg. daily vol. (M)	0.616		

Value of $10,000 invested 5 years ago: $ 14,224

Fiscal Year Ending May 31

	1998	1997	1996	1995	1994	1993
Revenues (Million $)						
1Q	481.3	440.1	401.0	314.7	290.1	305.0
2Q	529.0	477.2	443.6	350.3	317.2	333.0
3Q	517.6	478.9	433.5	367.2	332.8	311.2
4Q	557.9	543.9	490.7	439.5	377.9	353.0
Yr.	2,086	1,940	1,769	1,472	1,318	1,302
Earnings Per Share ($)						
1Q	0.53	0.46	0.45	0.35	0.21	0.14
2Q	-0.42	0.54	0.53	0.39	0.25	0.19
3Q	**0.67**	0.58	0.45	0.47	0.34	0.20
4Q	**0.83**	0.74	0.57	0.55	0.53	-1.82
Yr.	**1.60**	2.32	2.00	1.75	1.33	-1.29

Next earnings report expected: mid September

Dividend Data (Dividends have been paid since 1972.)

Amount ($)	Date Decl.	Ex-Div. Date	Stock of Record	Payment Date
0.120	Sep. 24	Oct. 08	Oct. 10	Oct. 31 '97
0.120	Dec. 17	Jan. 14	Jan. 16	Feb. 02 '98
0.120	Mar. 19	Apr. 07	Apr. 10	Apr. 27 '98
0.120	Jun. 25	Jul. 08	Jul. 10	Jul. 27 '98

A Division of The McGraw-Hill Companies

Business Summary - 25-AUG-98

Tektronix (TEK), a leading supplier of electronic products and systems in the areas of test and measurement, computer graphics and communications, has been focusing on its three core businesses -- measurement, color printing, and video and networking -- and implementing strategies to create sustainable annual sales growth, control costs and enhance shareholder value. The company has been emphasizing growing markets, expansion in key geographic areas, innovative products, and strategic alliances and acquisitions. In June 1998, TEK acquired a manufacturing facility in Malaysia for $10 million. TEK plans to begin producing solid ink color printers there within the next 12 months. Sales by product line in recent fiscal years (May) were:

	FY 98	FY 97
Measurement	46%	44%
Color printing & imaging	35%	33%
Video and networking	19%	23%

Foreign sales were 48% of revenues in FY 98.

The oscilloscope is TEK's primary measurement product. Oscilloscopes measure an electrical event and display the measurement on the screen of a cathode ray tube. Other instrument products include logic analyzers, digitizers, curve tracers, signal sources and a modular line of general-purpose test instruments. The company

has improved this business in recent years by focusing on high-growth markets such as electronic tools, communications and TV test.

Color printing and imaging sales are led by the company's line of color Phaser printers aimed at the office market. While the market for color printers is growing rapidly, it is still much smaller than the market for monochrome printers.

Video systems and network display products consist mainly of television systems products used primarily by the television industry to test and display the quality of video signals. Communications products also include cable and fiber optic testers and data communications analyzers. Network display sales consist primarily of the company's line of X terminals.

In September 1997, TEK acquired the Communications Test Equipment business ($60 million in sales) of Germany-based Siemens AG. TEK recorded a charge of $19 million in the FY 98 second quarter to write off R&D projects currently under way at the Siemens unit.

In August 1998, TEK said it expects earnings of $0.07 to $0.12 a share for the FY 99 first quarter, down from $0.52 a year ago, on 8% to 10% lower sales. The shortfall reflects weaker than anticipated demand for measurement and video products, and an operating loss at its Merix unit, which will account for $0.10 of the EPS drop. TEK sees earnings of $0.20 to $0.25 for the second quarter on 5% to 7% lower sales.

Per Share Data ($)

(Year Ended May 31)	1998	1997	1996	1995	1994	1993	1992	1991	1990	1989
Tangible Bk. Val.	14.35	15.39	13.77	12.78	9.95	8.89	9.82	9.61	8.63	11.18
Cash Flow	2.89	3.53	2.95	2.63	2.53	0.11	1.93	2.81	-0.45	2.20
Earnings	1.60	2.32	2.00	1.75	1.33	-1.29	0.45	1.11	-2.13	0.44
Dividends	0.46	0.40	0.40	0.40	0.40	0.40	0.40	0.40	0.40	0.40
Payout Ratio	29%	17%	20%	23%	30%	NM	90%	36%	NM	92%
Cal. Yrs.	1997	1996	1995	1994	1993	1992	1991	1990	1989	1988
Prices - High	46³/₈	34⁷/₈	41¹/₄	27	18⁵/₈	15¹/₄	20⁵/₈	12⁷/₈	16¹/₈	20¹/₈
- Low	32¹/₈	19⁷/₈	20⁷/₈	15³/₄	13³/₈	11	10⁵/₈	7³/₄	10³/₄	12⁵/₈
P/E Ratio - High	29	15	21	15	14	NM	46	12	NM	46
- Low	20	9	10	9	10	NM	24	7	NM	29

Income Statement Analysis (Million $)

	1998	1997	1996	1995	1994	1993	1992	1991	1990	1989
Revs.	2,086	1,940	1,769	1,940	1,318	1,302	1,297	1,331	1,408	1,433
Oper. Inc.	219	223	185	152	143	136	132	165	106	144
Depr.	65.9	59.6	47.0	40.7	54.9	63.1	65.6	74.6	73.1	75.4
Int. Exp.	10.1	12.1	14.0	10.1	10.0	10.3	11.3	16.5	23.9	23.2
Pretax Inc.	123	169	142	110	86.0	-99.0	30.0	78.0	-70.0	57.0
Eff. Tax Rate	33%	32%	30%	26%	29%	NM	34%	38%	NM	67%
Net Inc.	82.3	115	100	81.2	60.7	-58.0	20.0	48.0	-93.0	19.0

Balance Sheet & Other Fin. Data (Million $)

	1998	1997	1996	1995	1994	1993	1992	1991	1990	1989
Cash	121	143	37.0	32.0	43.0	30.0	18.0	33.0	71.0	71.0
Curr. Assets	749	752	754	651	591	516	447	461	523	549
Total Assets	1,377	1,317	1,328	1,210	991	985	877	900	973	1,023
Curr. Liab.	350	304	365	381	276	334	295	309	340	357
LT Debt	151	152	202	105	104	70.0	84.0	89.0	175	114
Common Eqty.	785	771	675	603	469	435	440	428	385	497
Total Cap.	936	923	877	708	574	505	530	548	591	642
Cap. Exp.	155	112	107	102	70.3	57.8	66.0	68.0	97.0	85.0
Cash Flow	148	174	147	122	116	5.0	85.0	123	-19.0	94.0
Curr. Ratio	2.1	2.5	2.1	1.7	2.0	1.5	1.5	1.5	1.5	1.5
% LT Debt of Cap.	19.2	16.5	23.0	14.8	18.2	13.9	15.9	16.3	29.7	17.7
% Net Inc.of Revs.	3.9	5.9	5.6	5.5	4.6	NM	1.5	3.6	NM	1.3
% Ret. on Assets	6.1	8.7	7.8	7.4	6.2	NM	2.2	5.1	NM	1.8
% Ret. on Equity	10.6	15.9	15.6	15.2	13.5	NM	4.5	11.9	NM	3.7

Data as orig. reptd.; bef. results of disc. opers. and/or spec. items. Per share data adj. for stk. divs. as of ex-div. date. Bold denotes diluted EPS (FASB 128). E-Estimated. NA-Not Available. NM-Not Meaningful. NR-Not Ranked.

Office—26600 S.W. Parkway (P.O. Box 1000, M/S 63-858), Wilsonville, OR 97070-1000. **Tel**—(503) 627-7111. **Website**—http://www.tek.com **Chrmn, Pres & CEO**—J. J. Meyer.**SVP & CFO**—C. W. Neun. **SVP & Secy**—J. P. Karalis.**Treas & Investor Contact**—Douglas Shafer. **Dirs**—P. Lo Alker, A. G. Ames, G. B. Cameron, P. C. Ely Jr., A. M. Gleason, W. R. Hicks, M. A. McPeak, J. J. Meyer, W. D. Walker. **Transfer Agent & Registrar**—ChaseMellon Shareholder Services, South Hackensack, NJ. **Incorporated**—in Oregon in 1946. **Empl**— 8,392. **S&P Analyst:** Stewart Scharf

12-SEP-98

Industry:
Broadcasting (Television, Radio & Cable)

Summary: This cable TV system operator, which also engages in programming through Liberty Media Group, has agreed to be acquired by AT&T.

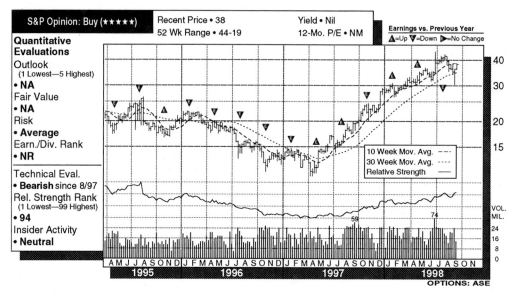

S&P Opinion: Buy (★★★★)	Recent Price • 38	Yield • Nil
	52 Wk Range • 44-19	12-Mo. P/E • NM

Quantitative Evaluations

Outlook
(1 Lowest—5 Highest)
• **NA**

Fair Value
• **NA**

Risk
• **Average**

Earn./Div. Rank
• **NR**

Technical Eval.
• **Bearish** since 8/97

Rel. Strength Rank
(1 Lowest—99 Highest)
• **94**

Insider Activity
• **Neutral**

Earnings vs. Previous Year
▲=Up ▼=Down ▷=No Change

10 Week Mov. Avg. ---
30 Week Mov. Avg. ....
Relative Strength —

OPTIONS: ASE

Overview - 17-AUG-98

Revenues and cash flow from continuing cable operations in 1998 will reflect the positive effect of price hikes instituted in early 1997 and early 1998, as well as other measures. TCI has also sharply curtailed its capital spending plans over the past year. The number of shares outstanding will continue to rise. The outlook for cash flow in 1998 is strongly positive. In June 1998, the company agreed to be acquired by AT&T through an exchange of stock. Under terms of the agreement, each TCOMA share will be exchanged for 0.7757 of an AT&T common share (recent price about $60), and each TCOMB share will be exchanged for 0.8533 of an AT&T share. The agreement marks the culmination of a strategy, announced in the fall of 1996, to enhance earnings power, asset values, and the health of the balance sheet.

Valuation - 17-AUG-98

TCI's management proved true to its word when in late 1996 it embarked on a strategy to maximize shareholder value. That strategy culminated in the June 24, 1998, announcement that AT&T would acquire TCI's cable, telecommunications and high-speed Internet interests, in a transaction to be effected via an exchange of stock, and expected to be completed during the first half of 1999. Current shareholders of Liberty Media and TCI Ventures will maintain their interests, but under a new structure and through a new tracking stock. TCI's shares still have strong upside potential, inasmuch as we believe that T shares will outperform the market over the next year. In addition, TCI's Class A and Class B shares were recently trading at significant discounts to the projected value of the transaction.

Key Stock Statistics

S&P EPS Est. 1998	-0.60	Tang. Bk. Value/Share	NM
P/E on S&P Est. 1998	NM	Beta	1.19
Dividend Rate/Share	Nil	Shareholders	9,000
Shs. outstg. (M)	523.3	Market cap. (B)	$ 18.0
Avg. daily vol. (M)	4.756	Inst. holdings	64%

Value of $10,000 invested 5 years ago: NA

Fiscal Year Ending Dec. 31

	1998	1997	1996	1995	1994	1993
Revenues (Million $)						
1Q	1,577	1,791	1,861	1,524	1,060	1,018
2Q	1,504	1,851	1,948	1,660	1,081	1,042
3Q	—	1,934	2,058	1,761	1,286	1,044
4Q	—	1,922	2,155	1,906	1,509	1,049
Yr.	—	6,429	8,022	6,851	4,936	4,153
Earnings Per Share ($)						
1Q	**0.38**	-0.12	-0.22	-0.08	0.07	0.11
2Q	**-0.28**	-0.25	-0.30	-0.14	0.01	0.07
3Q	—	-0.33	-0.25	0.12	0.04	-0.13
4Q	—	**-0.11**	-0.46	-0.12	-0.02	-0.07
Yr.	**E-0.60**	**-0.85**	-1.22	-0.26	0.09	-0.02

Next earnings report expected: NA

Dividend Data

No cash dividends have been paid. The shares (both classes) were split two for one in 1989, three for two in 1987 and two for one in 1986.

*A Division of The **McGraw·Hill** Companies*

Business Summary - 17-AUG-98

Tele-Communications, Inc. (TCI), the largest U.S. owner and operator of cable TV systems, unsettled the order of the telecommunications universe, and gave cable stocks an additional boost, when it announced on June 24, 1998, an agreement to be acquired by AT&T via an exchange of stock, in a transaction valued at the time at $48 billion. Immediately following the closing, expected in the first half of 1999, AT&T will combine its current consumer long distance, wireless and Internet services units with TCI's cable, telecommunications (Teleport) and high-speed Internet (At Home) interests to create a new subsidiary, AT&T Consumer Services. Each TCOMA common share wil be exchanged for 0.7757 of an AT&T common share, and each supervoting TCOMB share will be exchanged for 0.8533 of an AT&T share. AT&T said at the time of the announcement that in its opinion it was paying 13X estimated 1999 cash flow for TCI, or $2,970 per cable subscriber. Current TCI holders will continue to hold their interests in Liberty and TCI Ventures separately, but the structure will change. TCI Ventures will be merged into Liberty Media, and current holders will receive new tracking stock representing their holdings in the new entity, valued by AT&T at $20 billion.

TCI began to dismantle and restructure its far-flung empire in the fall of 1996, as part of a strategy to remake itself into a profit-oriented business with a healthier balance sheet. The new strategy included the re-structuring of cable operations into more manageable, regional units; the swap of large blocs of cable subscribers for equity interests in other cablers, and the completion of its plan to restructure worldwide operations into three publicly held and separately traded entities.

TCI Group (Nasdaq: TCOMA, TCOMB) is largely comprised of TCI's U.S. cable system operations, serving about 14.4 million subscribers as of December 31, 1997. In March 1998, TCI swapped systems serving 820,000 subscribers, plus $675 million of debt, for a 33% equity interest in Cablevision Systems, as part of a plan to swap up to 4 million subscribers for equity in other cable companies, and to reduce debt by a total of $4.5 billion.

Liberty Media Group (Nasdaq: LBTYA, LBTYB) has significant equity interests in the likes of such powerhouses as Fox Kids Worldwide; Fox/Liberty (sports) Networks; QVC; Court TV; BET; Discovery Communications; Time Warner Inc.; and dozens more.

TCI Ventures (Nasdaq: TCIVA, TCIVB) was created in September 1997 to hold investments in telecommunications ventures. Consolidated investments include At Home Corp.; ETC w/tci, Inc.; Tele-Communications International; United Video Satellite Group; National Digital Television Center, and Western Tele-Communications. Equity interests are also held in Sprint Spectrum; Teleport Communications Group; and Flextech p.l.c.

Per Share Data ($)

(Year Ended Dec. 31)	1997	1996	1995	1994	1993	1992	1991	1990	1989	1988
Tangible Bk. Val.	NM	NM	NM	-11.24	-15.75	-11.42	-10.23	-12.60	-10.60	-5.49
Cash Flow	0.71	2.80	1.19	1.38	2.01	1.45	1.63	1.01	0.76	1.14
Earnings	-0.85	-1.22	-0.26	0.09	-0.02	-0.08	-0.28	-0.81	-0.73	0.15
Dividends	Nil	Nil	Nil	Nil	Nil	Nil	Nil	Nil	Nil	Nil
Payout Ratio	Nil	Nil	Nil	Nil	Nil	Nil	Nil	Nil	Nil	Nil
Prices - High	29⅛	22⅜	26¼	30¼	33¼	22	17½	18½	21⅝	14
- Low	10¾	11¼	16⅝	18¼	17½	15⅜	11⅝	8⅜	12⅝	10¼
P/E Ratio - High	NM	NM	NM	NM	NM	NM	NM	NM	NM	90
- Low	NM	NM	NM	NM	NM	NM	NM	NM	NM	66

Income Statement Analysis (Million $)

	1997	1996	1995	1994	1993	1992	1991	1990	1989	1988
Revs.	7,570	8,022	6,851	4,936	4,153	3,574	3,827	3,625	3,026	2,282
Oper. Inc.	2,975	2,276	1,931	1,488	1,817	1,614	1,491	1,326	1,094	872
Depr.	1,614	1,616	1,372	700	880	650	687	646	525	382
Int. Exp.	1,160	1,096	1,010	785	731	718	877	918	817	574
Pretax Inc.	-804	596	-290	169	166	172	-9.0	-325	-334	99
Eff. Tax Rate	NM	44%	NM	69%	101%	87%	NM	NM	NM	44%
Net Inc.	-625	278	-170	55.0	-7.0	-19.0	-101	-286	-256	56.0

Balance Sheet & Other Fin. Data (Million $)

	1997	1996	1995	1994	1993	1992	1991	1990	1989	1988
Cash	284	394	118	74.0	1.0	34.0	35.0	31.0	19.0	20.4
Curr. Assets	NA	NA	NA	NA	NA	NA	NA	NA	NA	NA
Total Assets	32,323	30,244	25,130	19,528	16,520	13,164	13,010	12,310	11,432	8,574
Curr. Liab.	NA	NA	NA	2,399	1,777	1,300	1,242	814	1,402	1,151
LT Debt	15,250	14,926	13,211	9,956	8,904	9,640	9,286	9,300	7,356	5,440
Common Eqty.	4,432	4,253	4,550	2,971	2,112	1,486	1,439	622	908	1,206
Total Cap.	29,530	28,342	23,420	16,969	14,629	11,808	11,585	11,265	9,705	7,279
Cap. Exp.	709	2,055	1,782	1,264	1,020	1,209	694	990	1,511	1,061
Cash Flow	946	1,859	1,201	747	871	616	585	359	268	438
Curr. Ratio	NA	NA	NA	NA	NA	NA	NA	NA	NA	NA
% LT Debt of Cap.	51.6	52.7	56.4	58.7	60.9	81.6	80.2	82.6	75.8	74.7
% Net Inc.of Revs.	NM	3.5	NM	1.1	NM	NM	NM	NM	NM	2.5
% Ret. on Assets	NM	1.0	NM	0.3	NM	NM	NM	NM	NM	0.7
% Ret. on Equity	NM	5.5	NM	1.7	NM	NM	NM	NM	NM	5.3

Data as orig. reptd.; bef. results of disc. opers. and/or spec. items. Per share data adj. for stk. divs. as of ex-div. date. Bold denotes diluted EPS (FASB 128). E-Estimated. NA-Not Available. NM-Not Meaningful. NR-Not Ranked.

Office—5619 DTC Parkway, Englewood, CO 80111-3000. **Tel**—(303) 267-5500. **Website**—http://www.tci.com **Chrmn**—J. C. Malone. **Pres**—L. Hindery. **SVP & CFO**—B. Clouston. **SVP, Treas & Investor Contact**—Bernard W. Schotters. **Secy**—P. J. O'Brien. **Dirs**—D. F. Fisher, J. W. Gallivan, P. A. Gould, J. H. Kern, K. Magness, J. C. Malone, R. A. Naify, J. C. Sparkman. **Transfer Agents & Registrars**—First Security Bank of Utah, Salt Lake City; Bank of New York, NYC. **Incorporated**—in Delaware in 1968. **Empl**— 24,000. **S&P Analyst:** William H. Donald

STANDARD & POOR'S
STOCK REPORTS

Tellabs, Inc.

5376R

Nasdaq Symbol **TLAB**

In S&P 500

16-SEP-98

Industry:
Communications
Equipment

Summary: This company designs, makes, markets and services voice and data equipment used in public and private communications networks worldwide.

S&P Opinion: Accumulate (★★★★)

Recent Price • 45	Yield • Nil
52 Wk Range • 93⅛-39¾	12-Mo. P/E • 25.6

Quantitative Evaluations

Outlook
(1 Lowest—5 Highest)
• **5**

Fair Value
• **75**

Risk
• **Average**

Earn./Div. Rank
• **B**

Technical Eval.
• **Bearish** since 8/98

Rel. Strength Rank
(1 Lowest—99 Highest)
• **18**

Insider Activity
• **Neutral**

Earnings vs. Previous Year
▲=Up ▼=Down ▶=No Change

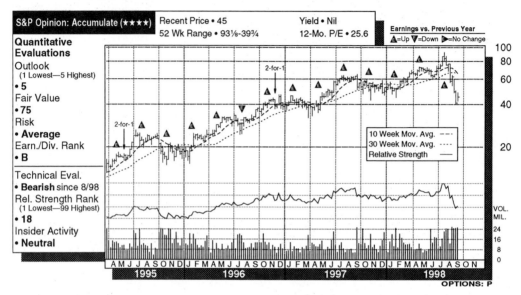

10 Week Mov. Avg. — — —
30 Week Mov. Avg. · · · · · ·
Relative Strength ———

OPTIONS: P

Overview - 16-SEP-98

Following a series of negative announcements from Ciena (CIEN) that dragged down the stock prices of both TLAB and CIEN, the planned merger of the two companies was terminated in September. Shareholders of Tellabs had been concerned that TLAB was overpaying for a company with uncertain prospects. While the failure of the merger now leaves Tellabs without an optical networking product, other options are being considered to remedy the situation. Further acquisition attempts are possible, although for the present, Tellabs will likely just build in-house products or form partnerships. We expect revenues for Tellabs to expand by about 30% in each of the next two years, reflecting higher sales of SONET-based TITAN digital cross-connects, Martis DXX systems, and echo-cancelling equipment.

Valuation - 16-SEP-98

We upgraded the shares to accumulate, from hold, following the termination of the company's merger agreement with Ciena. On the day of the announcement, TLAB shares dropped sharply, reflecting management's cautions about third quarter earnings. Despite this warning, earnings in the third quarter should only be slightly below analyst expectations, and business looks strong for the fourth quarter and for 1999. We are optimistic about continued growth for the TITAN digital cross-connect and Martis broadband multiplexer in 1998 and beyond, especially with expanding international opportunities for Martis. We expect TLAB to earn $2.34 a share in 1999, with solid gross margins, in excess of 60%. Based on TLAB's 30% growth rate, and with the stock recently trading at only 16X our 1999 EPS estimate, we would accumulate the shares.

Key Stock Statistics

S&P EPS Est. 1998	1.82	Tang. Bk. Value/Share	5.59
P/E on S&P Est. 1998	24.7	Beta	1.68
S&P EPS Est. 1999	2.34	Shareholders	3,000
Dividend Rate/Share	Nil	Market cap. (B)	$ 8.0
Shs. outstg. (M)	193.7	Inst. holdings	69%
Avg. daily vol. (M)	11.386		

Value of $10,000 invested 5 years ago: $ 218,181

Fiscal Year Ending Dec. 31

	1998	1997	1996	1995	1994	1993
Revenues (Million $)						
1Q	327.5	247.1	172.3	142.2	99.5	64.70
2Q	387.7	292.7	189.5	159.9	123.0	71.50
3Q	—	309.4	234.3	151.8	123.0	77.10
4Q	—	354.3	272.9	181.3	148.6	107.2
Yr.	—	1,204	869.0	635.2	494.2	320.5
Earnings Per Share ($)						
1Q	**0.37**	**0.34**	0.17	0.13	0.06	0.03
2Q	**0.63**	**0.32**	-0.10	0.15	0.10	0.03
3Q	—	**0.34**	0.25	0.15	0.10	0.04
4Q	—	**0.42**	0.32	0.21	0.14	0.09
Yr.	—	**1.42**	**0.64**	0.63	0.40	0.17

Next earnings report expected: early October

Dividend Data

No cash dividends have been paid. A two-for-one common stock split was effected in November 1996.

A Division of The **McGraw·Hill** Companies

STANDARD
&POOR'S
STOCK REPORTS

Tellabs, Inc.

5376R
16-SEP-98

Business Summary - 16-SEP-98

Tellabs, Inc. has evolved from a manufacturer of analog-based products intended for the North American telecommunications industry, to a global supplier of digital systems to service providers. The company's voice and data transport and network access systems are used by telephone companies, long distance carriers, alternate service providers, wireless service providers, cable operators, government agencies, utilities and businesses. Its products include digital cross-connect systems, managed digital networks and network access products. Tellabs is in an enviable position to capitalize on the global trend for these service providers to upgrade their systems to high-capacity digital technology.

Network access products (10% of sales in 1997) include digital signal processing (DSP) products, special service products and local access products such as echo cancellers and T-coders; special service products (SSP) such as voice frequency products; and local access products such as high bit digital subscriber line (HDSL) products and the CABLESPAN system.

Managed digital networks (28%) include the Martis DXX multiplexer, statistical multiplexers, packet switches, T1 multiplexers and network management systems. These products are used to combine voice, data and video applications for transmission over T1, FT1, E1, Nx56 and Nx64 facilities. The products pro-vide for more efficient utilization of the bandwidth and access to dedicated servers.

Digital cross-connect systems (57%) include the company's TITAN 5500 series, which consists of software intensive digital cross-connect systems and network management platforms. These systems are typically used to build the wideband and broadband transmission infrastructure of telecommunication service providers. In 1998, Tellabs plans to leverage its TITAN product line to introduce voice over ATM (asynchronous transfer mode) systems.

The Wireless Systems division is developing products for two target markets: the wireless local loop and wideband base stations. Wireless local loop technology uses radio technology to provide residential and small business customers with telephony service, providing an economical alternative to the installation of wireline infrastructure. Wideband microcell base stations provide wireless coverage in harder to cover areas such as inside buildings and congested areas such as airports and downtown locations.

In August 1998, Tellabs acquired Coherent Communications Systems Corp. for approximately $670 million in stock. Modest EPS accretion is expected in 1998 and 1999. Coherent's focus on international echo cancellation markets augments TLAB's North American echo canceller activity. Coherent had sales of $73.6 million in 1997.

Per Share Data ($)

(Year Ended Dec. 31)	1997	1996	1995	1994	1993	1992	1991	1990	1989	1988
Tangible Bk. Val.	4.80	2.93	2.19	1.43	0.94	1.01	0.90	0.85	0.80	0.74
Cash Flow	1.67	0.82	0.76	0.51	0.23	0.15	0.10	0.11	0.10	0.13
Earnings	1.42	0.64	0.63	0.40	0.17	0.10	0.05	0.06	0.05	0.09
Dividends	Nil	Nil	Nil	Nil	Nil	Nil	Nil	Nil	Nil	Nil
Payout Ratio	Nil	Nil	Nil	Nil	Nil	Nil	Nil	Nil	Nil	Nil
Prices - High	65	46¾	26⅜	14	6¾	2³⁄₁₆	1¹³⁄₁₆	1¼	1¼	1⁵⁄₁₆
- Low	32	15¼	11¾	5½	1⁹⁄₁₆	1⁵⁄₁₆	1	¹¹⁄₁₆	¹¹⁄₁₆	¹⁵⁄₁₆
P/E Ratio - High	46	73	42	35	39	22	43	24	26	15
- Low	23	24	19	14	9	13	24	13	15	11

Income Statement Analysis (Million $)

	1997	1996	1995	1994	1993	1992	1991	1990	1989	1988
Revs.	1,204	869	635	494	320	259	213	211	181	155
Oper. Inc.	410	276	180	119	43.0	25.0	14.0	17.0	19.0	20.0
Depr.	46.9	32.6	24.0	19.5	10.7	8.6	8.4	8.3	8.2	5.5
Int. Exp.	0.4	1.2	0.1	1.8	0.5	0.1	0.4	0.9	0.5	0.3
Pretax Inc.	400	175	163	97.8	35.8	19.2	7.0	10.7	9.3	17.6
Eff. Tax Rate	34%	33%	29%	26%	15%	12%	5.60%	25%	25%	23%
Net Inc.	264	118	116	72.4	30.5	16.9	6.6	8.1	7.1	13.5

Balance Sheet & Other Fin. Data (Million $)

	1997	1996	1995	1994	1993	1992	1991	1990	1989	1988
Cash	109	90.4	162	74.7	45.6	49.4	44.3	38.5	42.4	44.8
Curr. Assets	863	475	366	221	176	144	128	111	106	97.0
Total Assets	1,183	744	552	390	329	211	186	172	158	141
Curr. Liab.	226	132	99	82.0	112	35.0	32.0	32.0	27.0	19.0
LT Debt	2.9	2.9	2.9	2.9	2.9	3.8	4.0	4.2	4.4	4.4
Common Eqty.	933	591	433	293	207	167	145	130	120	112
Total Cap.	936	601	447	297	210	174	154	139	131	122
Cap. Exp.	84.7	64.8	35.0	23.0	40.1	18.8	7.2	13.9	15.4	10.9
Cash Flow	311	151	139	91.9	41.2	25.5	15.0	16.4	15.3	18.9
Curr. Ratio	3.8	5.6	3.7	2.7	1.6	4.1	4.0	3.4	3.9	5.2
% LT Debt of Cap.	0.0	0.5	1.0	1.0	1.4	2.2	2.6	3.0	3.3	3.6
% Net Inc.of Revs.	21.9	13.6	18.3	14.6	9.5	6.5	3.1	3.8	3.9	8.7
% Ret. on Assets	27.4	18.2	24.5	20.1	11.1	8.4	3.6	4.9	4.7	10.1
% Ret. on Equity	34.6	23.0	32.0	29.0	16.0	10.6	4.7	6.4	6.1	12.7

Data as orig. reptd.; bef. results of disc. opers. and/or spec. items. Per share data adj. for stk. divs. as of ex-div. date. Bold denotes diluted EPS (FASB 128). E-Estimated. NA-Not Available. NM-Not Meaningful. NR-Not Ranked.

Office—4951 Indiana Ave., Lisle, IL 60532. **Tel**—(630) 378-8800. **Website**—www.tellabs.com **Pres & CEO**—M. J. Birck. **EVP, CFO, Treas & Investor Contact**—Peter A. Guglielmi (630-378-6111). **VP & Secy**—C. C. Gavin. **Dirs**—M. J. Birck, J. D. Foulkes, P. A. Guglielmi, B. J. Jackman, F. A. Krehbiel, S. P. Marshall, W. F. Souders, J. H. Suwinski. **Transfer Agent**—Harris Trust & Savings Bank, Chicago. **Incorporated**—in Delaware in 1992. **Empl**— 4,087. **S&P Analyst:** Mark Cavallone

Temple-Inland

2198M

NYSE Symbol **TIN**

In S&P 500

12-SEP-98

Industry:
Containers and Packaging (Paper)

Summary: This major producer of corrugated containers and containerboard also makes paperboard and building products, and has expanded into financial services as well.

S&P Opinion: Hold (★★★)	Recent Price • 43⅞ Yield • 2.9%
	52 Wk Range • 67½-42⅝ 12-Mo. P/E • 29.8

Quantitative Evaluations

Outlook
(1 Lowest—5 Highest)
• **2+**

Fair Value
• **43¾**

Risk
• **Low**

Earn./Div. Rank
• **B**

Technical Eval.
• **Neutral** since 6/98

Rel. Strength Rank
(1 Lowest—99 Highest)
• **50**

Insider Activity
• **Neutral**

Earnings vs. Previous Year
▲=Up ▼=Down ▶=No Change

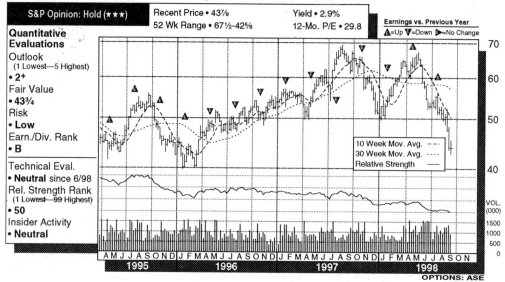

10 Week Mov. Avg. ---
30 Week Mov. Avg. ·····
Relative Strength —

1995 1996 1997 1998

VOL. (000)

OPTIONS: ASE

Overview - 06-AUG-98

We expect moderately higher sales in 1998, on mixed sector trends. Sales in the paper area should improve, as the pricing upturn seen during 1997 leads us to expect higher average containerboard prices for full-year 1998. However, the Asian financial crisis and strong U.S. dollar have hurt foreign trade and started to set back the recovery. On top of its battles with global economic woes, paper sector sales will also be limited by the recent struggle in paperboard markets. Building products sales should fall a bit, hurt by oversupply conditions in lumber markets. Financial services revenues seem likely to climb, on aggressive efforts to increase lending activity and the full year inclusion of two mid-1997 purchases. Operating margins should widen, aided by the higher average container prices and the expected solid performance in financial services. Those factors should far outweigh the more difficult conditions we see in building products and some likely latter year troubles in the now struggling corrugated sector. We also do not expect TIN's unusually high effective tax rate in 1997 (46.5%) to be revisited.

Valuation - 06-AUG-98

The shares seesawed in recent days. They headed upward in early 1998, as investors grew relaxed about Asia's financial woes and acted like the corrugated recovery would go on. The shares reversed in spring 1998, when it looked like the opposite had occurred. We have a mixed outlook for TIN's businesses. We remain quite positive on its financial sector, given healthy industry conditions and Temple's aggressive growth efforts. However, our current belief that troubles in the global economy will hurt forest products markets for a while offsets that enthusiasm. We still expect a modest earnings revival through 1999, but the conflicting trends in TIN's businesses leave us neutral on the shares.

Key Stock Statistics

S&P EPS Est. 1998	2.30	Tang. Bk. Value/Share	36.51
P/E on S&P Est. 1998	19.1	Beta	0.97
S&P EPS Est. 1999	2.70	Shareholders	7,300
Dividend Rate/Share	1.28	Market cap. (B)	$ 2.4
Shs. outstg. (M)	55.6	Inst. holdings	73%
Avg. daily vol. (M)	0.249		

Value of $10,000 invested 5 years ago: $ 9,761

Fiscal Year Ending Dec. 31

	1998	1997	1996	1995	1994	1993
Revenues (Million $)						
1Q	944.6	850.9	868.7	834.7	706.3	682.8
2Q	940.7	907.9	883.4	889.0	725.1	702.6
3Q	—	938.4	862.5	869.7	755.0	681.0
4Q	—	928.2	845.7	867.1	751.1	669.4
Yr.	—	3,625	3,460	3,461	2,938	2,736
Earnings Per Share ($)						
1Q	**0.47**	0.24	0.84	1.04	0.41	0.50
2Q	**0.62**	0.28	0.63	1.30	0.48	0.38
3Q	**E0.58**	0.22	0.59	1.51	0.59	0.21
4Q	**E0.63**	0.17	0.33	1.16	0.87	0.12
Yr.	**E2.30**	0.90	2.39	5.01	2.35	1.21

Next earnings report expected: mid October

Dividend Data (Dividends have been paid since 1984.)

Amount ($)	Date Decl.	Ex-Div. Date	Stock of Record	Payment Date
0.320	Nov. 07	Nov. 26	Dec. 01	Dec. 15 '97
0.320	Feb. 06	Feb. 25	Feb. 27	Mar. 13 '98
0.320	May. 01	May. 28	Jun. 01	Jun. 15 '98
0.320	Aug. 07	Aug. 28	Sep. 01	Sep. 15 '98

A Division of The **McGraw·Hill** Companies

STANDARD
&POOR'S
STOCK REPORTS

Temple-Inland Inc.

2198M
12-SEP-98

Business Summary - 06-AUG-98

Temple-Inland has diverse operations in the areas of forest products and financial services. In forest products, TIN makes both paper products and building materials. Financial services operations include savings bank and related activities, with the segment expanded by the June 1997 purchases of Stockton Savings Bank F.S.B. and Knutson Mortgage Corp. Segment contributions in 1997 (operating profits in millions):

	Revs.	Profits
Paper	57%	-$39.0
Building products	17%	131.1
Financial services	26%	132.1

The company's paper division produces containerboard, the material used to make corrugated boxes. Temple-Inland converts more than 80% of the containerboard it produces into corrugated boxes and sells the rest on the open market. The division also makes bleached paperboard, which gets sold to other paper companies for conversion into items such as paper cups and plates, file folders and paperback book covers. In the building materials area, the company makes wood products including lumber, plywood, particleboard, gypsum wallboard, and fiberboard, which are primarily used in home construction, remodeling and repair, and the production of cabinets and furniture.

TIN owned 2.2 million acres of timberland in Texas, Louisiana, Georgia and Alabama at 1997 year end. TIN estimates that these sources can provide more than 55% of its total fiber needs.

Temple-Inland modernized two particleboard plants in 1997, had one new plant come fully on stream during the year and modernized one additional particleboard plant in 1996. That capital spending effort boosted TIN's particleboard production capacity by 50%.

Financial services include savings and loan activities, mortgage banking, real estate development and insurance. Guaranty Federal Bank, F.S.B., operates 110 branches in the eastern part of Texas. In June 1997, TIN purchased California Financial Holding Co., the parent of Stockton Savings Bank, for $143 million in cash and stock; now operating as Guaranty, it has 25 branches in the Central Valley of California. TIN also bought Knutson Mortgage Corp. (also in June), a Minneapolis-based mortgage banking organization that services over $6 billion in mortgage loans -- bringing total loans serviced by TIN's mortgage banking operations to more than $26 billion at 1997 year-end.

In April 1998, the SEC terminated its investigation of the company, which stemmed from allegations made by a former employee of TIN in a wrongful termination lawsuit. The former employee will continue his lawsuit. It alleges that TIN knowingly underpaid federal income taxes and submitted false financial reports to its shareholders at some point while the claimant worked there.

Per Share Data ($)

(Year Ended Dec. 31)	1997	1996	1995	1994	1993	1992	1991	1990	1989	1988
Tangible Bk. Val.	36.30	36.34	35.48	31.83	30.64	29.55	27.89	26.37	22.02	19.39
Cash Flow	5.68	6.97	8.88	6.07	4.76	5.75	5.43	6.81	6.08	5.65
Earnings	0.90	2.39	5.01	2.35	1.21	2.65	2.51	4.20	3.75	3.58
Dividends	1.28	1.24	1.14	1.02	1.00	0.96	0.88	0.80	0.58	0.42
Payout Ratio	142%	52%	23%	43%	83%	36%	35%	19%	15%	12%
Prices - High	69⅜	55⅜	55¾	56¾	52½	57½	51½	38⅝	35½	28⅜
- Low	49⅝	39¾	41½	43	37¼	43⅞	28½	24⅛	23⅜	20⅛
P/E Ratio - High	77	23	11	24	43	22	21	9	9	8
- Low	55	17	8	18	31	17	11	6	6	6

Income Statement Analysis (Million $)

	1997	1996	1995	1994	1993	1992	1991	1990	1989	1988
Revs.	3,625	3,460	3,460	2,938	2,736	2,713	2,507	2,401	2,124	2,099
Oper. Inc.	467	515	716	545	459	443	392	501	489	434
Depr.	268	254	216	208	197	172	162	145	129	115
Int. Exp.	110	113	95.4	176	181	121	86.0	106	55.0	48.0
Pretax Inc.	95.0	156	431	193	96.0	177	167	269	314	302
Eff. Tax Rate	46%	15%	35%	32%	30%	17%	17%	14%	34%	34%
Net Inc.	51.0	133	281	131	67.0	147	138	232	207	199

Balance Sheet & Other Fin. Data (Million $)

	1997	1996	1995	1994	1993	1992	1991	1990	1989	1988
Cash	188	228	358	315	165	125	171	180	93.0	110
Curr. Assets	NA	NM	NM	NA	NA	NA	NA	NA	NA	NA
Total Assets	14,364	12,947	12,764	12,251	11,959	10,766	10,068	7,834	7,249	3,370
Curr. Liab.	NA	NM	NM	NA	NA	NA	NA	NA	NA	428
LT Debt	1,605	1,791	1,734	1,531	1,267	2,569	997	652	1,502	435
Common Eqty.	2,045	2,015	1,975	1,783	1,700	1,633	1,532	1,439	1,259	1,096
Total Cap.	3,873	3,871	3,926	3,477	3,083	4,542	2,828	2,400	3,069	1,804
Cap. Exp.	251	290	420	483	354	370	387	328	273	224
Cash Flow	319	387	497	339	264	319	300	377	336	314
Curr. Ratio	NA	NM	NM	NA	NA	NA	NA	NA	NA	NA
% LT Debt of Cap.	41.4	42.8	44.2	44.0	41.1	56.6	35.3	27.2	49.0	24.1
% Net Inc.of Revs.	1.4	3.9	8.1	4.5	2.5	5.4	5.5	9.7	9.8	9.5
% Ret. on Assets	0.4	1.1	2.2	1.1	0.6	1.4	1.5	3.1	3.9	7.7
% Ret. on Equity	2.5	6.7	15.0	7.5	4.0	9.3	9.3	17.3	17.7	19.7

Data as orig. reptd.; bef. results of disc. opers. and/or spec. items. Per share data adj. for stk. divs. as of ex-div. date. Bold denotes diluted EPS (FASB 128). E-Estimated. NA-Not Available. NM-Not Meaningful. NR-Not Ranked.

Office—303 South Temple Drive, Diboll, TX 75941. **Tel**—(409) 829-5511. **Chrmn & CEO**—C. J. Grum. **Pres, COO & CFO**—K. M. Jastrow II. **VP & Secy**—M. R. Warner. **Investor Contact**—Doyle R. Simons (409-829-1378). **Dirs**—P. M. Anderson, R. Cizik, A. M. Frank, C. J. Grum, W. B. Howes, B. R. Inman, K. M. Jastrow II, H. A. Sklenar, W. P. Stern, A. Temple III, C. Temple, L. E. Temple. **Transfer Agent & Registrar**—First Chicago Trust Co. of New York, Jersey City, NJ. **Incorporated**—in Delaware in 1983. **Empl**— 15,000. **S&P Analyst:** Michael W. Jaffe

Tenet Healthcare

2200H

NYSE Symbol **THC**

In S&P 500

12-SEP-98

Industry:
Health Care (Hospital Management)

Summary: The second largest for-profit hospital manager, with 122 acute care facilities in 18 states, Tenet also operates home health-care, rehabilitation and psychiatric facilities.

S&P Opinion: Accumulate (★★★★)	Recent Price • 29½	Yield • Nil
	52 Wk Range • 40⅞-25¼	12-Mo. P/E • 24.2

Earnings vs. Previous Year
▲=Up ▼=Down ►=No Change

Quantitative Evaluations

Outlook
(1 Lowest—5 Highest)
• **4-**

Fair Value
• **33⅝**

Risk
• **Average**

Earn./Div. Rank
• **B-**

Technical Eval.
• **NA**

Rel. Strength Rank
(1 Lowest—99 Highest)
• **93**

Insider Activity
• **Neutral**

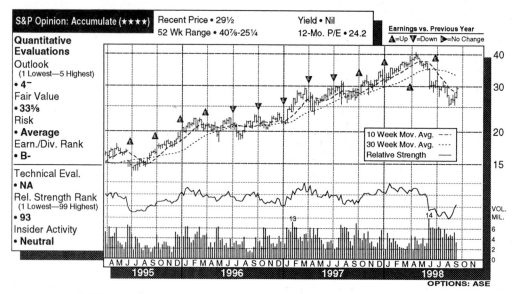

10 Week Mov. Avg. ---
30 Week Mov. Avg. .....
Relative Strength —

VOL. MIL.

OPTIONS: ASE

Overview - 04-AUG-98

Net operating revenues in FY 99 (May) should rise about 7%, to approximately $10.5 billion, as increased managed care admissions and modest Medicare volume gains help to mitigate some of the negative impact stemming from continued pricing pressures across customer lines. Acquisitions may provide some incremental revenue growth, but we do not anticipate any significant transactions in the coming year. Much of the company's earnings gains in recent quarters reflected a more streamlined operating cost structure, as well as the successful integration of facilities acquired from OrNda Healthcorp; EBITDA margins reached 18.6% in the fourth quarter of FY 98, up from 17.8% in the FY 97 quarter. Assuming that EBITDA margins can reach 19%, we look for FY 99 EPS of $2.05, and see a gain to $2.30 for FY 2000.

Valuation - 04-AUG-98

We are maintaining our accumulate rating on the shares, and believe that recent weakness presents investors with a buying opportunity, with THC recently trading at a P/E under 15X our FY 99 EPS estimate. We attribute the weakness in the stock to fears regarding continued pressure on pricing within both the Medicare and HMO payors, as well as lingering fears regarding the aggressive fraud and abuse investigations that continue to plague the healthcare services group. We are not aware that Tenet has been targeted for any investigation, but investor concern may restrict upside movement of the stock. Although THC is not among our top selections in the healthcare services sector, the stock is compelling on a valuation basis, and we look for modest out-performance in the coming six months.

Key Stock Statistics

S&P EPS Est. 1999	2.05	Tang. Bk. Value/Share	0.26
P/E on S&P Est. 1999	14.4	Beta	0.98
S&P EPS Est. 2000	2.30	Shareholders	15,700
Dividend Rate/Share	Nil	Market cap. (B)	$ 9.1
Shs. outstg. (M)	308.3	Inst. holdings	82%
Avg. daily vol. (M)	0.957		

Value of $10,000 invested 5 years ago: $ 24,502

Fiscal Year Ending May 31

	1998	1997	1996	1995	1994	1993
Revenues (Million $)						
1Q	2,331	1,439	1,284	662.8	775.0	942.0
2Q	2,429	1,476	1,371	638.8	770.0	933.0
3Q	2,564	2,237	1,432	660.5	720.3	933.0
4Q	2,571	2,351	1,472	1,356	701.8	956.0
Yr.	9,895	8,691	5,559	3,318	2,967	3,762
Earnings Per Share ($)						
1Q	0.38	0.33	0.59	0.38	-0.32	0.30
2Q	0.44	0.35	0.90	0.27	0.37	0.32
3Q	**0.47**	-0.21	0.33	0.29	0.55	0.33
4Q	**-0.08**	-0.67	0.12	0.17	0.07	0.02
Yr.	**1.22**	-0.24	1.90	1.10	1.29	0.96

Next earnings report expected: early October

Dividend Data

Dividends, initiated in 1973, were omitted in 1993.

A Division of The McGraw-Hill Companies

Business Summary - 04-AUG-98

Tenet's $3.2 billion purchase of OrNda HealthCorp in January 1997 solidified its standing as the second largest U.S. for-profit hospital management company after Columbia/HCA Healthcare Corp. At the end of FY 98 (May), Tenet owned or operated 122 acute care hospitals containing 27,867 licensed beds. Geographically, these facilities were concentrated primarily in California (46), Texas (22), Florida (19), Louisianna (12) and Arizona (7). The hospitals offer acute care services, and most offer operating and recovery rooms, radiology services, intensive care and coronary care nursing units, pharmacies, clinical labs, respiratory and physical therapy services and outpatient facilities. Several hospitals also offer services such as open-heart surgery, neonatal intensive care, neurosciences, orthopedic services and oncology services. In addition, Tenet has been developing a variety of subacute inpatient services to enhance occupancy levels.

Tenet also owns and operates a small number of rehabilitation hospitals, specialty hospitals, long-term care facilities and psychiatric facilities, as well as various ancillary healthcare businesses, including outpatient surgery centers, home healthcare programs, ambulatory, occupational and rural healthcare clinics, a health maintenance organization (HMO), a preferred provider organization (PPO) and a managed care insurance company.

Hospital net patient revenues in FY 98 were generated from Medicare (38%), managed care (34%), Medicaid (8%) and indemnity /other (20%).

On a same-facility basis (those under THC management for at least one year), admissions rose 2.5% in FY 98 (771,443, versus 752,336), net inpatient revenue per patient day advanced 1.0% ($1,290, versus $1,277) and net inpatient revenue per admission edged up 0.3% ($6,689, versus $6,667). The average length of stay was flat at 5.2 days, while the number of outpatient visits fell 4.7%, to 9,129,446.

At FY 98 year-end, Tenet held an 11.3% equity interest in TRC, an operator of kidney dialysis units and certain related healthcare businesses; and a 23% stake in HCPP, a partnership from which it leases two general acute care hospitals. Tenet's 12% equity stake in NYSE-listed Vencor Inc. was sold in the fourth quarter of FY 98, following that company's separation from Ventas Inc. (now a real estate investment trust), as required by the indenture agreement covering Tenet's 6% exchangeable subordinated notes.

Per Share Data ($)

(Year Ended May 31)	1998	1997	1996	1995	1994	1993	1992	1991	1990	1989
Tangible Bk. Val.	NA	0.26	0.07	9.93	7.95	10.56	10.03	10.08	7.97	7.45
Cash Flow	NA	1.21	3.43	2.20	2.15	1.97	1.68	2.59	2.37	2.07
Earnings	1.22	-0.24	1.90	1.10	1.29	0.96	0.77	1.73	1.52	1.29
Dividends	Nil	Nil	Nil	Nil	0.12	0.48	0.46	0.40	0.36	0.34
Payout Ratio	Nil	Nil	Nil	Nil	9%	50%	60%	25%	23%	26%
Cal. Yrs.	1997	1996	1995	1994	1993	1992	1991	1990	1989	1988
Prices - High	34⅞	23¾	20¾	19½	14⅜	18⅛	25⅞	20⅛	19½	12⅜
- Low	21⅜	18⅛	13⅜	12½	6½	9⅝	12⅝	14⅝	10¾	8⅞
P/E Ratio - High	29	NM	11	18	11	19	34	12	13	10
- Low	18	NM	7	11	5	10	16	8	7	7

Income Statement Analysis (Million $)

	1998	1997	1996	1995	1994	1993	1992	1991	1990	1989
Revs.	NA	8,691	5,559	3,318	2,967	3,762	3,951	3,806	3,935	3,679
Oper. Inc.	NA	1,597	1,099	623	534	581	644	707	650	558
Depr.	NA	443	321	195	143	168	156	138	137	129
Int. Exp.	NA	417	312	138	74.0	88.0	105	149	162	157
Pretax Inc.	NA	-21.0	746	338	360	272	239	472	405	316
Eff. Tax Rate	NA	NM	47%	40%	40%	36%	41%	41%	40%	39%
Net Inc.	NA	-73.0	-73.0	194	216	160	133	277	242	192

Balance Sheet & Other Fin. Data (Million $)

	1998	1997	1996	1995	1994	1993	1992	1991	1990	1989
Cash	NA	151	201	294	373	239	200	197	170	109
Curr. Assets	NA	2,391	1,545	1,624	1,444	1,068	1,097	941	935	998
Total Assets	NA	11,705	8,332	7,918	3,697	4,173	4,236	4,060	3,807	3,877
Curr. Liab.	NA	1,869	1,134	1,356	1,640	913	874	595	686	552
LT Debt	NA	5,022	3,191	3,273	223	892	1,066	1,140	1,361	1,671
Common Eqty.	NA	3,224	2,636	1,986	1,320	1,752	1,674	1,762	1,257	1,101
Total Cap.	NA	8,678	6,221	5,560	1,668	2,961	3,072	3,289	2,992	3,127
Cap. Exp.	NA	406	370	264	185	306	509	403	494	448
Cash Flow	NA	370	719	389	359	328	289	415	379	321
Curr. Ratio	NA	1.3	1.4	1.2	0.9	1.2	1.3	1.6	1.4	1.8
% LT Debt of Cap.	NA	57.9	51.3	58.9	13.4	30.1	34.7	34.7	45.5	53.4
% Net Inc.of Revs.	NA	NM	7.2	5.9	7.3	4.3	3.4	7.3	6.2	5.2
% Ret. on Assets	NA	NM	4.9	3.4	5.5	3.8	3.3	6.7	6.1	5.2
% Ret. on Equity	NA	NM	17.3	11.8	14.1	9.4	7.9	17.6	20.0	18.5

Data as orig. reptd.; bef. results of disc. opers. and/or spec. items. Per share data adj. for stk. divs. as of ex-div. date. E-Estimated. NA-Not Available. NM-Not Meaningful. NR-Not Ranked.

Office—3820 State St., Santa Barbara, CA 93105. **Tel**—(805) 563-7000. **Chrmn & CEO**—J. C. Barbakow. **Pres & COO**—M. H. Focht Sr. **EVP & CFO**—T. Fetter. **VP-Fin**—S. D. Farber. **SVP & Secy**—S. M. Brown. **VP & Treas**—T. P. McMullen. **Investor Contact**—Paul J. Russell (805-563-7188). **Dirs**—J. C. Barbakow, B. B. Bratter, M. J. DeWald, P. de Wetter, E. Egbert, M. H. Focht, R. A. Hay, L. P. Korn, R. S. Schweiker. **Transfer Agent & Registrar**—Bank of New York, NYC. **Incorporated**—in California in 1968; reincorporated in Nevada in 1976. **Empl**—105,000. **S&P Analyst:** Robert M. Gold

STANDARD &POOR'S
STOCK REPORTS

Tenneco Inc.

2201

NYSE Symbol **TEN**

In S&P 500

12-SEP-98

Industry:
Manufacturing (Diversified)

Summary: This holding company is focusing on its auto parts and packaging businesses, following the divestiture of its natural gas pipeline and shipbuilding units.

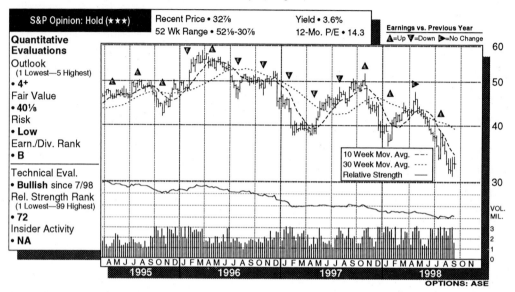

S&P Opinion: Hold (★★★)	Recent Price • 32⅞	Yield • 3.6%
	52 Wk Range • 52⅛-30⅞	12-Mo. P/E • 14.3

Quantitative Evaluations

Outlook
(1 Lowest—5 Highest)
• **4+**

Fair Value
• **40⅛**

Risk
• **Low**

Earn./Div. Rank
• **B**

Technical Eval.
• **Bullish** since 7/98

Rel. Strength Rank
(1 Lowest—99 Highest)
• **72**

Insider Activity
• **NA**

Earnings vs. Previous Year
▲=Up ▼=Down ▷=No Change

10 Week Mov. Avg. ---
30 Week Mov. Avg. ····
Relative Strength —

OPTIONS: ASE

Overview - 04-AUG-98

Having divested its shipbuilding and energy units, Tenneco is now focusing its efforts on packaging and auto parts. The company recently announced a strategic review that may include the separation of its automotive and packaging businesses into stand alone entities; the separation of its containerboard packaging business from its specialty packaging business; and the reduction of overhead and operating expenses. Further details are expected over the next several months. Prior to the announcement, Tenneco had grow in recent years, in part, through acquisitions that diversified the group into less cyclical, faster growing segments of packaging, such as food containers and wrappings. The specialty packaging division should benefit from volume gains, new product introductions, and cost reductions. The paperboard business should be aided by lower containerboard inventories and solid demand for corrugated boxes. Despite expectations of flat vehicle production in 1998, Tenneco's automotive OE business should see growth aided by participation in 40 promising major launches. Auto parts remains focused on exhaust and ride control products. Seeking global expansion in faster growing regions of the world such as India and East Asia, Tenneco Automotive has undertaken 18 acquisitions and joint ventures in the past several years.

Valuation - 04-AUG-98

TEN recently traded at 12 times our 1998 EPS estimate of $3.05. Given its well seasoned management, an above-average yield, and potential to leverage its technical expertise in emerging markets, TEN is an attractive long-term holding. While the company has generally positioned itself in faster growing, less cyclical niches within the auto parts and packaging industries, it is still vulnerable to economic downturns.

Key Stock Statistics

S&P EPS Est. 1998	3.05	Tang. Bk. Value/Share	5.50
P/E on S&P Est. 1998	10.8	Beta	0.70
Dividend Rate/Share	1.20	Shareholders	95,600
Shs. outstg. (M)	169.6	Market cap. (B)	$ 5.6
Avg. daily vol. (M)	0.598	Inst. holdings	77%

Value of $10,000 invested 5 years ago: NA

Fiscal Year Ending Dec. 31

	1998	1997	1996	1995	1994	1993
Revenues (Million $)						
1Q	1,825	1,629	1,539	2,163	3,049	3,250
2Q	1,996	1,892	1,694	2,198	3,258	3,482
3Q	—	1,831	1,653	2,136	3,049	3,150
4Q	—	31.15	1,686	2,402	2,818	3,376
Yr.	—	7,220	6,572	8,899	12,174	13,255
Earnings Per Share ($)						
1Q	**0.44**	**0.44**	0.34	0.84	0.66	0.46
2Q	**0.81**	**0.61**	0.70	1.05	0.88	0.63
3Q	—	**0.62**	0.45	1.23	0.81	0.64
4Q	—	**0.44**	-0.21	1.05	1.14	0.83
Yr.	**E3.05**	**2.11**	1.28	4.16	3.49	2.59

Next earnings report expected: late October

Dividend Data (Dividends have been paid since 1948.)

Amount ($)	Date Decl.	Ex-Div. Date	Stock of Record	Payment Date
0.300	Oct. 14	Nov. 19	Nov. 21	Dec. 09 '97
0.300	Jan. 13	Feb. 25	Feb. 27	Mar. 10 '98
0.300	May. 12	May. 20	May. 22	Jun. 09 '98
0.300	Jul. 14	Aug. 26	Aug. 28	Sep. 08 '98

A Division of The McGraw-Hill Companies

Business Summary - 04-AUG-98

Following a major restructuring in 1996, Tenneco is focusing on two major business segments, packaging and auto parts. The packaging unit, having made a dozen acquisitions valued at more than $1.6 billion in the last several years, has doubled its size to $4.0 billion in revenues; it now ranks as the fourth largest packaging company in the U.S. and tenth largest in the world. The segment includes the largest domestic producer of single-use food containers made from clear plastic, aluminum foil, pressed paperboard, and polystyrene foam, and the sixth largest domestic supplier of corrugated containers. Numerous other packaging and related products are also produced. The cyclical paperboard business in 1997 accounted for about 35% of the unit's revenues, versus 65% derived from less cyclical specialty packaging applications. In April 1997, Tenneco acquired the packaging operations of KNP BT, a Dutch concern with $540 million in annual sales, for about $380 million.

Automotive produces exhaust and ride-controls products, with sales of $3.2 billion split between the aftermarket and original equipment markets. Walker Manufacturing produces mufflers, pipe, catalytic converters, tubular manifolds, headers and electronic noise control technology. Monroe Auto Equipment makes shock absorbers, struts, cartridges, load levelers and adjustable electronic suspensions. Plans call for additional expansion in India, China and other high growth Far East regions, and in Europe. In December 1996, Tenneco Automotive acquired approximately 94% of Fric-Rot S.A.I.C., its fifteenth acquisition or joint venture in two years; subsequently three additional transactions were completed. Fric-Rot is Argentina's leading ride control manufacturer.

Segment contributions (profits in million $) in 1997 were:

	Revs.	Profits
Packaging	55%	$371
Automotive	45%	407

TEN completed a major restructuring in December 1996 by spinning off its Newport News Shipbuilding (NNS) unit to its shareholders, and selling Tenneco Energy to El Paso Energy; TEN shareholders received stock in El Paso worth a total of about $750 million. El Paso assumed TEN debt, liabilities and preferred stock worth $3.25 billion.

In the first quarter of 1997, TEN announced a new stock repurchase program that allows the company to buy up to 5%, or nearly 8.6 million of its outstanding shares. In 1997, Tenneco repurchased $132 million in common stock, partly offset by the issuance of $48 million in stock, related to employee benefit plans.

Per Share Data ($)

(Year Ended Dec. 31)	1997	1996	1995	1994	1993	1992	1991	1990	1989	1988
Tangible Bk. Val.	5.61	6.66	17.93	13.67	12.78	5.21	18.07	23.92	22.82	21.86
Cash Flow	4.25	3.01	6.80	5.88	5.69	-0.83	-1.03	8.29	8.47	3.39
Earnings	2.11	1.28	4.16	3.49	2.59	-4.85	-5.62	4.37	4.46	-0.18
Dividends	1.20	1.80	1.60	1.60	1.60	1.60	2.80	3.12	3.04	3.04
Payout Ratio	57%	141%	38%	46%	62%	NM	NM	70%	68%	NM
Prices - High	52⅛	58½	50⅜	58¾	55	46	52	71	64¼	51
- Low	37¼	43⅜	41⅞	37	39⅛	31¼	27⅜	40	46⅞	38¼
P/E Ratio - High	25	46	12	17	21	NM	NM	16	14	NM
- Low	18	34	10	11	15	NM	NM	9	11	NM

Income Statement Analysis (Million $)

	1997	1996	1995	1994	1993	1992	1991	1990	1989	1988
Revs.	7,220	6,572	8,899	12,174	13,255	13,139	13,662	14,511	14,083	13,234
Oper. Inc.	1,031	861	1,403	1,681	1,455	1,348	696	1,728	1,761	1,236
Depr.	365	309	449	429	509	579	563	488	509	519
Int. Exp.	216	195	422	568	718	902	1,045	972	905	903
Pretax Inc.	548	412	1,020	972	636	-606	-682	857	825	84.0
Eff. Tax Rate	30%	47%	26%	31%	23%	NM	NM	35%	29%	101%
Net Inc.	361	646	735	641	451	-682	-673	561	584	-1.0

Balance Sheet & Other Fin. Data (Million $)

	1997	1996	1995	1994	1993	1992	1991	1990	1989	1988
Cash	41.0	62.0	354	405	218	111	231	147	276	328
Curr. Assets	2,115	1,923	3,582	3,895	5,417	6,283	6,968	7,945	7,523	7,454
Total Assets	8,332	7,587	13,451	12,542	15,373	16,584	18,696	19,034	17,381	17,376
Curr. Liab.	1,661	1,621	3,836	3,054	4,910	5,680	6,848	7,234	6,201	6,442
LT Debt	2,633	2,067	3,751	3,570	4,799	6,400	6,837	5,976	5,573	5,612
Common Eqty.	2,528	2,646	3,148	2,900	2,592	1,321	2,765	3,367	3,277	3,161
Total Cap.	6,199	5,493	8,788	8,396	8,941	9,272	10,972	11,057	10,507	10,329
Cap. Exp.	558	930	976	736	587	595	894	920	663	688
Cash Flow	726	515	1,184	1,058	960	-119	-126	1,031	1,075	493
Curr. Ratio	1.3	1.2	0.9	1.3	1.1	1.1	1.0	1.1	1.2	1.2
% LT Debt of Cap.	37.6	37.7	42.7	42.5	54.0	69.0	62.3	54.0	53.0	54.3
% Net Inc.of Revs.	5.0	9.9	8.3	5.3	3.4	NM	NM	3.9	4.1	NM
% Ret. on Assets	4.5	29.1	5.7	4.3	2.8	NM	NM	3.1	3.4	NM
% Ret. on Equity	14.0	7.2	24.3	21.8	22.3	NM	NM	16.6	17.6	NM

Data as orig. reptd.; bef. results of disc. opers. and/or spec. items. Per share data adj. for stk. divs. as of ex-div. date. Bold denotes diluted EPS (FASB 128). E-Estimated. NA-Not Available. NM-Not Meaningful. NR-Not Ranked.

Office—1275 King Street, Greenwich, CT 06831. **Tel**—(203) 863-1000. **Website**—http://www.tenneco.com **Chrmn & CEO**—D. G. Mead. **COO**—P. T. Stecko. **EVP & CFO**—R. T. Blakely. **VP & Secy**—K. A. Stewart. **VP & Treas**—K. R. Osar. **VP & Investor Contact**—Stanley R. March.**Dirs**—M. Andrews, W. M. Blumenthal, L. D. Brady, M. K. Eickhoff, P. T. Flawn, H. U. Harris, Jr., B. K. Johnson, J. B. McCoy, D. G. Mead, D. Plastow, R. B. Porter, W. L. Weiss, C. R. Wharton, Jr. **Transfer Agent & Registrar**—First Chicago Trust Co. of New York, Jersey City, NJ. **Incorporated**—in Delaware in 1947. **Empl**— 49,000. **S&P Analyst:** Efraim Levy

STANDARD &POOR'S
STOCK REPORTS

Texaco Inc.

2205

NYSE Symbol **TX**

In S&P 500

12-SEP-98

Industry: Oil (International Integrated)

Summary: This leading international oil and natural gas company is engaged in exploration, refining and marketing operations.

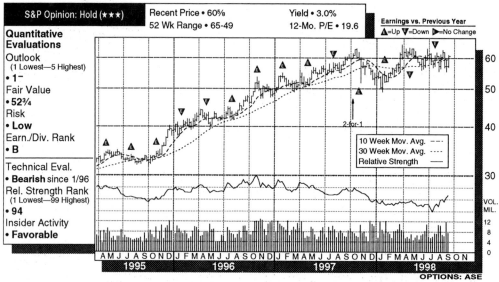

| **S&P Opinion: Hold (★★★)** | Recent Price • 60⅝ | Yield • 3.0% | **Earnings vs. Previous Year** |
| | 52 Wk Range • 65-49 | 12-Mo. P/E • 19.6 | ▲=Up ▼=Down ▶=No Change |

Quantitative Evaluations

Outlook
(1 Lowest—5 Highest)
• **1⁻**

Fair Value
• **52¾**

Risk
• **Low**

Earn./Div. Rank
• **B**

Technical Eval.
• **Bearish** since 1/96

Rel. Strength Rank
(1 Lowest—99 Highest)
• **94**

Insider Activity
• **Favorable**

10 Week Mov. Avg. – – –
30 Week Mov. Avg. · · · ·
Relative Strength ———

2-for-1

VOL. MIL.

OPTIONS: ASE

Overview - 27-JUL-98

Operating earnings rose significantly in 1997, despite lower oil prices, aided by increased volumes and significantly improved refining results. As reported, EPS in 1997 included several nonrecurring items, including a tax refund that resulted in a credit of $1.88 a share in the first quarter. For the full year, EPS before nonrecurring items were $3.52. Earnings in the first half of 1998 were restrained by sharply lower oil and gas prices, which outweighed a 13% rise in worldwide oil and gas production and a reduction in per barrel cash operating expenses. Refining and marketing results improved during the first half of 1998, on improved margins and increased refined product sales. Texaco is often seen as having an advantage relative to its international integrated oil peers, as it no longer has a chemicals unit, and is therefore not exposed to the fundamentally weak petrochemicals industry.

Valuation - 27-JUL-98

The shares have appreciated 12% in 1998, underperforming the overall market. TX plans to double earnings over the next five years, and will likely boost its total oil and gas production 40% from 1995 to 2000. Future capital spending will focus on a promising Gulf of Mexico and Latin American asset base, and on strong prospects in the North Sea. However, spending in 1998 will be below original plans, as sharply lower oil prices have led TX to defer certain projects. Despite this, we expect TX to post double-digit gains in overall production volumes in 1998, a growth rate well in excess of those of the company's major oil peers. However, despite the company's positive long-term production growth outlook, the shares currently appear fully valued, based both on earnings and on cash flow multiples, and they are expected to be only market performers over the remainder of 1998.

Key Stock Statistics

S&P EPS Est. 1998	2.80	Tang. Bk. Value/Share	23.35
P/E on S&P Est. 1998	21.7	Beta	0.56
S&P EPS Est. 1999	3.35	Shareholders	195,700
Dividend Rate/Share	1.80	Market cap. (B)	$ 32.5
Shs. outstg. (M)	535.9	Inst. holdings	60%
Avg. daily vol. (M)	1.707		

Value of $10,000 invested 5 years ago: $ 25,490

Fiscal Year Ending Dec. 31

	1998	1997	1996	1995	1994	1993
Revenues (Million $)						
1Q	8,147	11,813	10,271	8,585	7,230	8,585
2Q	8,044	10,983	11,261	9,031	7,865	9,031
3Q	—	10,834	11,097	8,621	8,725	8,621
4Q	—	11,557	11,932	9,314	8,718	9,652
Yr.	—	45,187	44,561	35,551	32,540	33,245
Earnings Per Share ($)						
1Q	0.46	1.80	0.71	0.78	0.34	0.49
2Q	0.61	1.05	1.29	0.49	0.17	0.56
3Q	—	0.90	0.81	0.53	0.49	0.56
4Q	—	1.12	0.95	-0.51	0.71	0.63
Yr.	E2.80	4.87	3.68	1.28	1.72	2.23

Next earnings report expected: late October

Dividend Data (Dividends have been paid since 1903.)

Amount ($)	Date Decl.	Ex-Div. Date	Stock of Record	Payment Date
0.450	Oct. 24	Nov. 03	Nov. 05	Dec. 10 '97
0.450	Jan. 23	Feb. 03	Feb. 05	Mar. 10 '98
0.450	Apr. 28	May. 06	May. 08	Jun. 10 '98
0.450	Jul. 24	Aug. 03	Aug. 05	Sep. 10 '98

A Division of The **McGraw-Hill** *Companies*

Business Summary - 27-JUL-98

Born in 1902 out of the oil craze surrounding "Spindletop," the hill that produced the nation's first true "gusher" and represented the beginning of the oil industry in Texas, Texaco (TX) has emerged as one of the world's largest international integrated oil companies.

The company has extensive international interests, including 50%-owned Caltex (Chevron Corp. holds the other 50%). Caltex operates in 58 countries, including some of the world's fastest growing economies. In 1988, TX and Saudi Arabian Oil Co. (the world's largest oil company) formed Star Enterprise, a U.S.-based joint venture that refines, distributes and markets Texaco-brand petroleum products in 26 East and Gulf Coast states and the District of Columbia. Operating profits (in millions) in recent years were:

	1997	1996
U.S. exploration & production	$1,031	$1,123
Intl. exploration & production	438	451
U.S. manufacturing & marketing	305	233
Intl. manufacturing & marketing	530	252

TX's 1997 capital and exploratory spending amounted to $4.5 billion, with about 71% used for worldwide exploration and production projects. Emphasis was on adding reserves and developing projects in the deep water Gulf of Mexico, the North Sea, West Africa, Indonesia and the Neutral Zone between Saudi Arabia and Kuwait. Spending in 1998 will also include projects in Kazakhstan, Venezuela and Western Australia. In November 1997, TX acquired Monterey Resources, an independent oil and gas producer operating primarily in California, for a total of $1.4 billion in TX common stock and debt assumption.

In 1997, net production of crude oil and natural gas liquids averaged 833,000 barrels (bbl.) a day (787,000 bbl. in 1996), natural gas production was 2.18 billion cubic feet (Bcf) a day (2.06), natural gas sales 4.18 Bcf a day (3.65), refinery input 1,551,000 bbl./day (1,486,000), and petroleum product sales 2,585,000 bbl./day (2,558,000). Net proved reserves at the end of 1997 were 3.3 billion bbl. of crude oil and natural gas liquids, and 6,242 Bcf of natural gas.

In January 1998, Texaco and Shell Oil merged their midwestern and western U.S. refining and marketing businesses, creating Equilon Enterprises, a refining and marketing giant with a nearly 15% share of the markets in which it competes. Shell owns 56% and Texaco owns 44% of the venture. In July, the two companies and Saudi Refining Inc. (SRI) merged Star Enterprises, a 50/50 joint venture between TX and SRI in the eastern U.S., with Shell's eastern U.S. refining and marketing business, forming Motiva Enterprises.

Per Share Data ($)

(Year Ended Dec. 31)	1997	1996	1995	1994	1993	1992	1991	1990	1989	1988
Tangible Bk. Val.	22.87	18.91	17.35	17.75	17.63	17.14	17.54	16.79	16.04	15.56
Cash Flow	7.81	6.54	5.89	5.07	5.26	4.91	5.33	5.78	7.78	6.97
Earnings	4.87	3.76	1.28	1.72	2.23	1.76	2.31	2.59	4.56	2.67
Dividends	1.75	1.65	1.60	1.60	1.60	1.60	1.60	1.52	5.00	1.13
Payout Ratio	36%	44%	125%	93%	72%	91%	69%	58%	114%	42%
Prices - High	63³/₈	53⁵/₈	40¹/₄	34¹/₈	34³/₄	33¹/₂	35	34¹/₄	29¹/₂	26¹/₄
- Low	48⁷/₈	37³/₄	29⁷/₈	29¹/₈	28⁷/₈	28¹/₈	27³/₄	27¹/₂	24¹/₄	17⁷/₈
P/E Ratio - High	13	14	31	20	16	19	15	13	6	10
- Low	10	10	23	17	13	16	12	11	5	7

Income Statement Analysis (Million $)

	1997	1996	1995	1994	1993	1992	1991	1990	1989	1988
Revs.	45,187	44,561	35,551	32,540	33,245	36,812	37,271	40,899	32,416	33,544
Oper. Inc.	3,960	4,005	2,672	2,668	2,390	2,581	2,503	3,490	2,573	4,064
Depr.	1,633	1,455	2,385	1,735	1,568	1,627	1,560	1,658	1,662	2,094
Int. Exp.	412	446	503	511	508	565	624	609	735	1,068
Pretax Inc.	3,395	2,911	986	1,248	1,189	1,323	1,436	2,187	3,086	2,474
Eff. Tax Rate	20%	33%	26%	18%	NM	22%	8.80%	33%	22%	44%
Net Inc.	2,664	2,018	728	979	1,259	1,012	1,294	1,450	2,413	1,304

Balance Sheet & Other Fin. Data (Million $)

	1997	1996	1995	1994	1993	1992	1991	1990	1989	1988
Cash	311	552	536	464	536	482	883	829	2,320	1,485
Curr. Assets	6,432	7,665	6,458	6,019	6,865	5,611	6,581	7,256	7,730	6,770
Total Assets	29,600	26,963	24,937	25,505	26,626	25,992	26,182	25,975	25,636	26,337
Curr. Liab.	5,994	6,188	5,206	5,015	4,756	4,225	6,290	6,968	6,409	6,174
LT Debt	5,507	5,125	5,503	5,564	6,157	6,441	5,173	4,485	4,714	6,655
Common Eqty.	12,009	9,975	9,161	9,216	9,132	8,867	9,068	8,667	8,498	7,605
Total Cap.	20,743	16,950	16,323	16,802	18,130	17,972	16,848	15,700	15,560	16,411
Cap. Exp.	3,628	2,897	2,386	2,050	1,844	2,076	2,346	2,270	1,975	1,757
Cash Flow	4,242	3,415	3,053	2,623	2,726	2,540	2,751	3,006	4,011	3,397
Curr. Ratio	1.1	1.2	1.2	1.2	1.4	1.3	1.0	1.0	1.2	1.1
% LT Debt of Cap.	26.5	30.2	33.7	33.1	34.0	35.8	30.7	28.6	30.3	40.6
% Net Inc.of Revs.	5.9	4.5	2.0	3.0	3.8	2.7	3.5	3.5	7.4	3.9
% Ret. on Assets	9.4	7.8	2.9	3.8	4.8	3.9	5.0	5.7	8.9	4.3
% Ret. on Equity	24.1	20.5	7.3	9.7	12.9	10.2	13.4	15.9	28.1	15.5

Data as orig. reptd.; bef. results of disc. opers. and/or spec. items. Per share data adj. for stk. divs. as of ex-div. date. Bold denotes diluted EPS (FASB 128). E-Estimated. NA-Not Available. NM-Not Meaningful. NR-Not Ranked.

Office—2000 Westchester Ave., White Plains, NY 10650. **Tel**—(914) 253-4000. **Website**—http://www.texaco.com **Chrmn & CEO**—Peter I. Bijur. **Vice Chrmn**—A. J. Krowe. **SVP & CFO**—P. J. Lynch. **VP & Secy**—C. B. Davidson. **VP & Investor Contact**—Elizabeth P. Smith. **Dirs**—P. I. Bijur, J. Brademas, M. K. Bush, W. C. Butcher, E. M. Carpenter, M. C. Hawley, F. G. Jenifer, T. S. Murphy, S. Nunn, C. H. Price II, R. B. Smith, W. C. Steere, Jr., T. A. Vanderslice, W. Wrigley. **Transfer Agents**—Co.'s office; ChaseMellon Shareholder Services, NYC. **Incorporated**—in Delaware in 1926 (original co. in 1902). **Empl**— 29,313. **S&P Analyst:** Norman Rosenberg

STANDARD &POOR'S
STOCK REPORTS

Texas Instruments
2208
NYSE Symbol **TXN**
In S&P 500

12-SEP-98

Industry: Electronics (Semiconductors)

Summary: One of the world's largest manufacturers of semiconductors, Texas Instruments also produces digital products.

S&P Opinion: Accumulate (★★★★)	Recent Price • 52¾	Yield • 0.6%
	52 Wk Range • 71¼-39⅝	12-Mo. P/E • 14.0

Quantitative Evaluations

Outlook (1 Lowest—5 Highest)
• 3⁻

Fair Value
• 53⅞

Risk
• Average

Earn./Div. Rank
• B

Technical Eval.
• NA

Rel. Strength Rank (1 Lowest—99 Highest)
• 74

Insider Activity
• Neutral

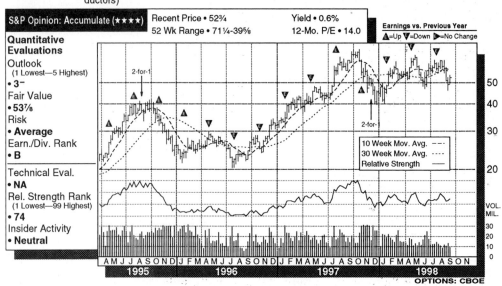

Earnings vs. Previous Year ▲=Up ▼=Down ▶=No Change

10 Week Mov. Avg. ---
30 Week Mov. Avg. ····
Relative Strength —

OPTIONS: CBOE

Overview - 23-JUL-98

We expect revenues to be down about 10% in 1998. Weak DRAM prices have limited revenue growth in recent quarters, but in June, the company agreed to sell its underperforming memory assets to Micron Technology. TXN is now squarely focused on the market for digital signal processing solutions (DSPS). This segment was particularly strong through most of 1997, driven by demand from the wireless communications and networking end-markets. However, economic turmoil in Asia has limited near-term growth in these DSP-intensive segments. As a result, order trends have slipped in recent quarters, and revenues are expected to decline sequentially in the near term. However, gross margins should improve over the next few quarters, reflecting a more favorable product mix, and continued manufacturing efficiencies. In 1999, we expect EPS to rise to $3.00 from our projection of $1.65 in 1998 (before extraordinary items), reflecting the absence of DRAM losses.

Valuation - 23-JUL-98

Despite evidence of a near-term slow-down, due primarily to economic weakness in Asia, we are maintaining our accumulate rating on the shares. TXN has a commanding share (nearly 45%) of the fast growing DSP market. DSPs have a broad base of applications, primarily in communications, and TXN's leadership position in this market will provide it with significant opportunities to boost revenues and earnings. We view favorably the company's decision to exit the commodity DRAM market. While the sale will result in a material loss, the company is now focused on the fast growing DSP segment. The shares, recently trading at 20X our 1999 EPS estimate of $3.00, were at a discount to TXN's long-term growth prospects of 20% to 25%, and offer significant potential for capital appreciation.

Key Stock Statistics

S&P EPS Est. 1998	1.65	Tang. Bk. Value/Share	15.27
P/E on S&P Est. 1998	32.0	Beta	1.77
S&P EPS Est. 1999	3.00	Shareholders	32,800
Dividend Rate/Share	0.34	Market cap. (B)	$ 20.6
Shs. outstg. (M)	390.1	Inst. holdings	66%
Avg. daily vol. (M)	2.283		

Value of $10,000 invested 5 years ago: $ 47,967

Fiscal Year Ending Dec. 31

	1998	1997	1996	1995	1994	1993
Revenues (Million $)						
1Q	2,187	2,263	2,675	2,862	2,449	1,884
2Q	2,167	2,559	2,399	3,238	2,510	2,105
3Q	—	2,500	2,407	3,425	2,574	2,161
4Q	—	2,428	2,459	3,603	2,782	2,374
Yr.	—	9,750	9,940	13,128	10,315	8,523
Earnings Per Share ($)						
1Q	0.03	0.26	0.34	0.60	0.35	0.22
2Q	0.11	0.56	0.10	0.72	0.48	0.29
3Q	—	0.60	-0.47	0.74	0.48	0.39
4Q	—	-0.67	-0.10	0.75	0.49	0.35
Yr.	—	0.76	-0.12	2.81	1.82	1.27

Next earnings report expected: mid October

Dividend Data (Dividends have been paid since 1962.)

Amount ($)	Date Decl.	Ex-Div. Date	Stock of Record	Payment Date
2-for-1	Sep. 18	Nov. 24	Oct. 24	Nov. 21 '97
0.085	Dec. 04	Dec. 29	Dec. 31	Jan. 26 '98
0.085	Apr. 15	Apr. 28	Apr. 30	May. 18 '98
0.085	Jul. 16	Jul. 29	Jul. 31	Aug. 17 '98

A Division of The McGraw-Hill Companies

Business Summary - 23-JUL-98

Texas Instruments is one of the world's leading high technology companies, with sales or manufacturing operations in over 30 countries. The company has recently sold off many of its non-core operations to concentrate more resources in its electronic component (semiconductor) business, especially its rapidly growing digital signal processing solutions (DSPS) unit.

The DSPS unit is the most important part of the company's growth strategy. The unit's sales have grown dramatically, to approximately $1.8 billion in 1997. Digital signal processing devices translate "real-world" signals such as speed, temperature and pressure into the "zeros and ones" of the digital world. TXN feels that DSPS revenues can grow up to 30% annually, and the company has a commanding 45% market share in the digital signal processing market. TXN has made strategic acquisitions to enhance is digital signal processing capabilities, including the 1997 purchase of Amati Communications Corp. Also in 1997, the company introduced the C6x, the industry's most powerful digital signal processor. TXN believes that this device offers significantly better performance than any other DSP on the market today. Among its uses will be to make Internet connection and surfing much faster.

Electronic components currently account for about 80% of revenues from continuing operations. In addition to the DSPS unit, which includes mixed signal and analog circuits, TXN also manufactures microprocessors/ microcontrollers, application processors, and digital circuits. These components are used in a wide variety of applications, including computer and peripheral equipment, cellular phones, telecommunications equipment, automobiles, instrumentation, and industrial automation controls.

TXN has successfully expanded its product portfolio in recent years to include more differentiated devices like DSPS and mixed-signal circuits, which has made the company less dependent on commodity products like DRAM. The company feels that this will add more stability to future results.

Digital products, which make up the bulk of non-component revenues, include electronic calculators and other electronic systems. Recent divestitures in this segment include the company's mobile computing and software businesses.

In July 1997, the company sold its defense electronics business to Raytheon Co. for $2.95 billion in cash. In June 1998, TXN agreed to sell its struggling dynamic random access memory (DRAM) operations to Micron Technology .

Per Share Data ($)

(Year Ended Dec. 31)	1997	1996	1995	1994	1993	1992	1991	1990	1989	1988
Tangible Bk. Val.	15.18	10.77	10.81	8.20	6.37	4.46	4.06	5.62	6.03	5.34
Cash Flow	3.55	2.23	4.75	3.55	2.87	2.40	0.45	1.43	2.08	2.14
Earnings	0.76	-0.12	2.81	1.82	1.27	0.63	-1.35	-0.23	0.76	1.01
Dividends	0.34	0.34	0.32	0.23	0.18	0.18	0.18	0.18	0.18	0.18
Payout Ratio	45%	NM	11%	13%	14%	28%	NM	NM	23%	17%
Prices - High	71¼	34¼	41⅞	22⅜	21⅛	13⅛	11⅞	11	11¾	15
- Low	31⅛	20¼	17¼	15¼	11½	7½	6½	5⅝	7	8⅝
P/E Ratio - High	94	NM	15	12	17	21	NM	NM	15	15
- Low	41	NM	6	8	9	12	NM	NM	9	9

Income Statement Analysis (Million $)

	1997	1996	1995	1994	1993	1992	1991	1990	1989	1988
Revs.	9,750	9,940	13,128	10,315	8,523	7,440	6,784	6,567	6,522	6,295
Oper. Inc.	1,724	878	2,350	1,748	1,345	1,030	341	515	773	758
Depr.	1,109	904	756	665	617	610	590	541	454	390
Int. Exp.	94.0	108	69.0	58.0	55.0	57.0	59.0	47.0	38.4	48.3
Pretax Inc.	713	-23.0	1,619	1,042	696	369	-303	-21.0	355	516
Eff. Tax Rate	58%	NM	33%	34%	32%	33%	NM	NM	18%	29%
Net Inc.	302	-46.0	1,088	691	476	247	-408	-39.0	292	366

Balance Sheet & Other Fin. Data (Million $)

	1997	1996	1995	1994	1993	1992	1991	1990	1989	1988
Cash	1,015	978	1,553	1,290	888	859	601	412	637	780
Curr. Assets	6,103	4,454	5,518	4,017	3,314	2,626	2,381	2,305	2,446	2,549
Total Assets	10,849	9,360	9,215	6,989	5,993	5,185	5,009	5,048	4,804	4,427
Curr. Liab.	2,496	2,486	3,188	2,199	2,001	1,665	1,568	1,479	1,303	1,199
LT Debt	1,286	1,697	804	808	694	909	896	715	618	624
Common Eqty.	5,914	4,097	4,095	3,039	2,315	1,473	1,335	1,837	1,964	1,723
Total Cap.	7,200	5,794	4,899	3,847	3,009	2,856	2,851	3,073	3,102	2,867
Cap. Exp.	1,238	2,063	1,439	1,076	730	429	504	909	863	656
Cash Flow	1,411	858	1,844	1,356	1,073	820	147	466	707	726
Curr. Ratio	2.4	1.8	1.7	1.8	1.7	1.6	1.5	1.6	1.9	2.1
% LT Debt of Cap.	17.9	29.3	16.4	21.0	23.1	31.8	31.4	23.3	19.9	21.8
% Net Inc.of Revs.	3.1	NM	8.3	6.7	5.6	3.3	NM	NM	4.5	5.8
% Ret. on Assets	3.0	NM	13.4	10.5	8.1	4.8	NM	NM	6.3	8.3
% Ret. on Equity	6.0	NM	30.5	25.6	23.2	14.9	NM	NM	13.6	19.2

Data as orig. reptd.; bef. results of disc. opers. and/or spec. items. Per share data adj. for stk. divs. as of ex-div. date. Bold denotes diluted EPS (FASB 128). E-Estimated. NA-Not Available. NM-Not Meaningful. NR-Not Ranked.

Office—8505 Forest Lane P.O. Box 660199, Dallas, TX 75243-4136. **Tel**—(972) 995-2011. **Website**—http://www.ti.com **Chrmn**—J. R. Adams. **Vice Chrmn**—W. P. Weber. **Pres & CEO**—T. J. Engibous. **SVP, Treas & CFO**—W. A. Aylesworth. **SVP & Secy**—R. J. Agnich. **Investor Contact**—Max Post or Dick Greiner (972-995-3773). **Dirs**—J. R. Adams, D. L. Boren, J. B. Busey IV, D.A. Carp, T. J. Engibous, G. W. Fronterhouse, D. R. Goode, W.R. Sanders, G. M. Shatto, W. P. Weber, C. K. Yeutter. **Transfer Agent & Registrar**—Harris Trust & Savings Bank, Chicago. **Incorporated**—in Delaware in 1938. **Empl**— 59,927. **S&P Analyst**: B. McGovern

STANDARD
&POOR'S
STOCK REPORTS

Texas Utilities
2216

NYSE Symbol **TXU**

In S&P 500

12-SEP-98

Industry:
Electric Companies

Summary: This Dallas-based energy holding company recently acquired the U.K.-based The Eastern Group.

| S&P Opinion: Accumulate (★★★★) | Recent Price • 42¼ | Yield • 5.2% |
| | 52 Wk Range • 44⅜-34⅛ | 12-Mo. P/E • 17.3 |

Quantitative Evaluations

Outlook (1 Lowest—5 Highest)
• **2⁻**

Fair Value
• **41%**

Risk
• **Low**

Earn./Div. Rank
• **B**

Technical Eval.
• **NA**

Rel. Strength Rank (1 Lowest—99 Highest)
• **94**

Insider Activity
• **Neutral**

Earnings vs. Previous Year
▲=Up ▼=Down ▶=No Change

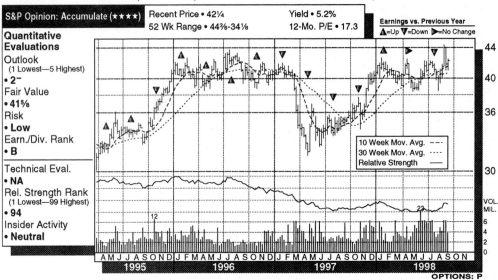

10 Week Mov. Avg. – – –
30 Week Mov. Avg. ·····
Relative Strength ——

OPTIONS: P

Overview - 28-AUG-98

TXU's acquisition of The Eastern Group (TEG) will provide it with a strong presence in the U.K., a strategic base for European expansion, and strength in natural gas and energy trading. TEG sold its Peabody Coal unit for $2.5 billion. Following an expected decline in 1998 EPS (reflecting acquisition-related charges, higher interest expense, reduced rates and the slower realization of cost reductions), we expect EPS to advance around 16% in 1999, with TEG adding about $0.10 to the increase. Customer growth of about 2% and a good service area economy will help to offset the rate reductions, but utility revenues will see only a fractional increase for the next several years. Contributions from the Texas Utilities Australia subsidiary should add about $0.07 to 1999 EPS. For the longer term, the ENSERCH companies acquired will let TXU deliver comprehensive energy services and provide significant operating synergies. However, for the short term, the acquisition will dilute EPS about $0.15 in 1998 and $0.05 in 1999.

Valuation - 28-AUG-98

We would continue to accumulate TXU stock. Since the company completed its May 1998 acquisition of The Eastern Group, the shares have risen about 10%. TXU's offer of 840 pence ($13.86) a share totaled $7.3 billion. After the assumption of $3.2 billion of TEG debt, less $2.5 billion received for the sale of Peabody coal, the acquisition will cost about $8.0 billion. To help reduce debt, TXU may issue up to $1.5 billion in common stock and about $1.3 billion in convertible securities and preferred stock. In April 1998, the Public Utility Commission of Texas approved a rate reduction agreement (implemented at the start of 1998) that will cut revenues $118 million in 1998 and $145 million in 1999. With the dividend yielding more than 5%, and the stock trading at around 13X our 1999 EPS estimate of $3.20, the shares are attractive for long-term total return.

Key Stock Statistics

S&P EPS Est. 1998	2.75	Tang. Bk. Value/Share	22.19
P/E on S&P Est. 1998	15.4	Beta	0.15
S&P EPS Est. 1999	3.20	Shareholders	87,300
Dividend Rate/Share	2.20	Market cap. (B)	$ 11.8
Shs. outstg. (M)	279.5	Inst. holdings	52%
Avg. daily vol. (M)	1.282		

Value of $10,000 invested 5 years ago: $ 14,550

Fiscal Year Ending Dec. 31

	1998	1997	1996	1995	1994	1993
Revenues (Million $)						
1Q	2,499	1,494	1,464	1,244	1,301	1,142
2Q	3,236	1,588	1,691	1,354	1,430	1,256
3Q	—	2,265	1,930	1,776	1,702	1,786
4Q	—	2,598	1,466	1,265	1,230	1,250
Yr.	—	7,946	6,551	5,639	5,664	5,435
Earnings Per Share ($)						
1Q	**0.51**	0.51	0.56	0.33	0.30	0.70
2Q	**0.33**	0.72	0.90	0.66	0.65	0.74
3Q	**E1.42**	1.24	1.59	-1.96	1.30	0.23
4Q	**E0.49**	0.39	0.30	0.35	0.16	0.01
Yr.	**E2.75**	2.85	3.35	-0.61	2.40	1.66

Next earnings report expected: late October

Dividend Data (Dividends have been paid since 1917.)

Amount ($)	Date Decl.	Ex-Div. Date	Stock of Record	Payment Date
0.550	Nov. 21	Dec. 04	Dec. 08	Jan. 02 '98
0.550	Feb. 20	Mar. 04	Mar. 06	Apr. 01 '98
0.550	May. 08	Jun. 03	Jun. 05	Jul. 01 '98
0.550	Aug. 21	Sep. 02	Sep. 04	Oct. 01 '98

Business Summary - 28-AUG-98

In May 1998, this Dallas-based energy holding company acquired, for about $8 billion, the U.K.-based The Eastern Group (formerly The Energy Group), which has holdings that include Eastern, a British regional electric company with more than 3 million customers.

In August 1997, the company acquired Lone Star Gas and Lone Star Pipeline, the local distribution and pipeline companies of ENSERCH Corp., for about $1.7 billion of stock and assumed debt.

The company's main subsidiary, Texas Utilities Electric Co., provides electricity and related services to a population of 6.0 million in the Dallas/Ft. Worth area, about one-third of the state's population. The area has seen significant growth in high technology enterprises, particularly in telecommunications and electronics. In 1997, there was a 2.0% increase in electric customers.

In November 1997, TXU acquired Lufkin-Conroe Communications, the fourth largest telephone provider in Texas with nearly 100,000 telephone lines in southeast Texas.

In late 1995, the company ventured into the rapidly evolving global energy market by acquiring Eastern Energy Ltd., an electricity distribution company serving more than 480,000 customers in southeastern Australia.

The company's diverse fuel mix provides generating flexibility and reduces the risk of fluctuations in the cost or availability of any one fuel source. TU Electric owns and operates two nuclear-fueled generating units at the Comanche Peak nuclear generating station, each with a net capacity of 1,150 megawatts. Sources of power generation in recent years were:

	1997	1996	1995
Lignite/coal	38.9%	39.6%	37.4%
Gas/oil	32.9%	33.0%	33.4%
Nuclear	17.1%	15.0%	17.9%
Purchased power	11.1%	12.4%	11.3%

The acquisition of Lone Star Gas and Lone Star Pipeline expanded TXU's customer base and its ability to deliver comprehensive energy services to one of the most economically attractive areas in the U.S. Lone Star Gas is one of the largest gas distribution companies in the U.S., and the largest in Texas, providing service to more than 1.35 million customers through over 23,800 miles of distribution mains. Lone Star Pipeline has one of the largest pipelines in the U.S., with 7,600 miles of gathering and transmission pipelines in Texas. The combination of the companies is expected to save at least $850 million over the next decade.

Per Share Data ($)

(Year Ended Dec. 31)	1997	1996	1995	1994	1993	1992	1991	1990	1989	1988
Tangible Bk. Val.	21.96	26.64	25.10	28.74	29.29	30.06	29.55	34.38	34.26	33.07
Earnings	NA	3.35	-0.61	2.40	1.66	2.88	-1.98	4.40	4.44	4.00
Dividends	2.13	2.02	2.81	3.08	3.08	3.04	3.00	2.96	2.92	2.88
Payout Ratio	NM	60%	NM	128%	186%	106%	NM	67%	66%	72%
Prices - High	42	43¾	41¼	43⅛	49¾	43¾	43	39	37½	30⅝
- Low	31½	38½	30⅛	29⅝	41⅝	37	34⅛	32	27¾	24⅝
P/E Ratio - High	NM	13	NM	18	30	15	NM	9	8	8
- Low	NM	11	NM	12	25	13	NM	7	6	6

Income Statement Analysis (Million $)

	1997	1996	1995	1994	1993	1992	1991	1990	1989	1988
Revs.	7,946	6,551	5,639	5,664	5,435	4,908	4,893	4,543	4,321	4,154
Depr.	667	621	564	550	440	421	437	328	251	242
Maint.	Nil	Nil	290	305	350	301	309	297	265	295
Fxd. Chgs. Cov.	2.2	2.3	2.3	2.0	1.8	2.0	0.2	2.5	2.6	2.4
Constr. Credits	8.9	11.0	15.0	22.0	263	304	364	618	506	387
Eff. Tax Rate	36%	31%	30%	33%	29%	22%	45%	11%	14%	15%
Net Inc.	660	754	-138	543	369	619	-409	851	779	643

Balance Sheet & Other Fin. Data (Million $)

	1997	1996	1995	1994	1993	1992	1991	1990	1989	1988
Gross Prop.	25,287	25,562	24,616	24,001	23,722	22,994	21,902	20,715	19,137	17,391
Cap. Exp.	446	434	434	444	871	1,137	1,232	1,454	1,812	1,563
Net Prop.	18,571	17,599	17,746	17,669	17,818	17,484	16,768	17,280	15,989	14,460
Capitalization:										
LT Debt	8,759	8,668	9,175	7,888	8,380	7,932	7,951	7,381	6,417	6,343
% LT Debt	52	55	57	50	51	50	51	47	46	48
Pfd.	1,200	1,084	1,134	1,258	1,480	1,328	1,433	1,434	1,337	1,238
% Pfd.	7.20	6.90	7.10	8.00	9.00	8.40	9.20	9.20	9.50	9.40
Common	6,843	6,033	5,732	6,490	6,571	6,591	6,284	6,828	6,330	5,641
% Common	41	38	36	42	40	42	40	44	45	43
Total Cap.	20,362	19,226	19,393	19,168	19,823	17,613	17,228	17,496	15,881	14,985
% Oper. Ratio	80.7	69.4	68.3	76.5	78.2	76.3	76.8	76.1	76.1	77.0
% Earn. on Net Prop.	10.5	11.3	10.1	7.5	6.7	6.8	6.7	6.5	6.8	7.1
% Return On Revs.	8.3	11.5	NM	9.6	6.8	12.6	NM	18.7	18.0	15.5
% Return On Invest. Capital	9.6	10.4	NM	7.0	6.0	7.9	2.4	9.0	8.8	8.7
% Return On Com. Equity	10.3	12.8	NM	8.3	6.3	9.6	NM	12.9	13.0	12.0

Data as orig. reptd.; bef. results of disc opers. and/or spec. items. Per share data adj. for stk. divs. as of ex-div. date. Bold denotes diluted EPS (FASB 128). E-Estimated. NA-Not Available. NM-Not Meaningful. NR-Not Ranked.

Office—Energy Plaza, 1601 Bryan Street, Dallas, TX 75201-3411. **Tel**—(214) 812-4600. **Website**—http://www.tu.com **Chrmn & CEO**—E. Nye. **Pres & COO**—D. W. Biegler. **EVP & CFO**—M. J. McNally. **Secy**—P. B. Tinkham. **Treas**—R. S. Shapard. **Investor Contact**—David Anderson. **Dirs**—J. Farrington, B. H. Friedman, W. M. Griffin, K. Laday, M. N. Maxey, J. A. Middleton, E. Nye, J. E. Oesterreicher, C. R. Perry, H. H. Richardson. **Transfer Agent & Registrar**—Texas Utilities Shareholder Services, Dallas. **Incorporated**—in Texas in 1945. **Empl**— 14,751. **S&P Analyst:** Justin McCann

STANDARD &POOR'S
STOCK REPORTS

Textron Inc.

2218

NYSE Symbol **TXT**

In S&P 500

12-SEP-98

Industry: Manufacturing (Diversified)

Summary: This diversified company conducts operations in aircraft, automotive and other industrial markets, as well as in financial services.

S&P Opinion: Hold (★★★)	Recent Price • 61⅞	Yield • 1.8%
	52 Wk Range • 80⅞-54	12-Mo. P/E • 17.5

Earnings vs. Previous Year
▲=Up ▼=Down ▶=No Change

Quantitative Evaluations

Outlook (1 Lowest—5 Highest)
• **1**

Fair Value
• **45⅝**

Risk
• **Low**

Earn./Div. Rank
• **A**

Technical Eval.
• **Bearish** since 8/98

Rel. Strength Rank (1 Lowest—99 Highest)
• **58**

Insider Activity
• **Neutral**

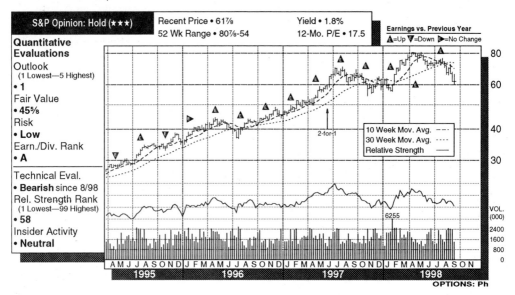

10 Week Mov. Avg. ---
30 Week Mov. Avg. ·····
Relative Strength —

2-for-1

6255

VOL. (000)
2400
1600
800
0

1995 1996 1997 1998

OPTIONS: Ph

Overview - 22-JUL-98

Revenues are expected to rise about 6% in 1998. Aircraft sales should benefit from increased commercial aircraft deliveries, funding for the AH-1 helicopter upgrade and the V-22 Osprey program, and a continued rise in single-engine aircraft production at Cessna. Sales by the systems and components division may continue to decline, reflecting lower military shipments. Results in the industrial division are expected to expand, due primarily to acquisitions, with a focus on international markets. Automotive sales should be up slightly, aided by acquisitions and a favorable product mix, partially offset by pricing pressures. Results for financial services should improve modestly, on growth in global consumer markets, offset by a slowdown in domestic consumer markets. Earnings will benefit from cost reduction efforts. Comparisons will also be aided by a stock repurchase program funded by the company's strong cash flow. For the longer term, the company will continue its international expansion, aimed at boosting foreign revenues to 40% of the total, from 35% in 1996.

Valuation - 22-JUL-98

We continue our accumulate recommendation on TXT, based on the attractive valuation of the stock relative to its peers. We expect strength in several divisions of this well managed conglomerate to outweigh weakness in others, and anticipate another year of solid earnings improvement. The dividend was increased in 1998 for the seventh consecutive year. For the long term, we expect investors to benefit from continued steady earnings and dividend growth.

Key Stock Statistics

S&P EPS Est. 1998	3.75	Tang. Bk. Value/Share	8.93
P/E on S&P Est. 1998	16.5	Beta	1.16
S&P EPS Est. 1999	4.20	Shareholders	25,000
Dividend Rate/Share	1.14	Market cap. (B)	$ 10.1
Shs. outstg. (M)	163.9	Inst. holdings	73%
Avg. daily vol. (M)	0.501		

Value of $10,000 invested 5 years ago: $ 31,214

Fiscal Year Ending Dec. 31

	1998	1997	1996	1995	1994	1993
Revenues (Million $)						
1Q	2,718	2,551	2,214	2,029	2,408	2,165
2Q	2,953	2,667	2,384	2,138	2,517	2,253
3Q	2,953	2,508	2,248	2,057	2,381	2,233
4Q	—	2,818	2,428	2,229	2,377	2,427
Yr.	—	10,544	9,274	8,453	9,683	9,078
Earnings Per Share ($)						
1Q	0.85	0.73	0.63	0.55	0.55	0.46
2Q	0.98	0.86	0.72	0.61	0.61	0.53
3Q	E0.91	0.81	0.70	0.60	0.61	0.55
4Q	E1.01	0.89	0.75	0.63	0.63	0.56
Yr.	E3.75	3.29	2.81	2.40	2.40	2.10

Next earnings report expected: mid October

Dividend Data (Dividends have been paid since 1942.)

Amount ($)	Date Decl.	Ex-Div. Date	Stock of Record	Payment Date
0.250	Oct. 22	Dec. 10	Dec. 12	Jan. 01 '98
0.285	Feb. 25	Mar. 11	Mar. 13	Apr. 01 '98
0.285	May. 27	Jun. 10	Jun. 12	Jul. 01 '98
0.285	Jul. 22	Sep. 09	Sep. 11	Oct. 01 '98

A Division of The **McGraw·Hill** Companies

STANDARD
&POOR'S
STOCK REPORTS

Textron Inc.

2218

12-SEP-98

Business Summary - 22-JUL-98

Textron is a diversified company with operations in manufacturing and financial services. Among the company's businesses are such venerable names as Bell Helicopter, Cessna Aircraft, Lycoming and Avco Financial Services. In 1997, the company sold its 83% interest in Paul Revere Corp. for $800 million to Provident Companies. In 1996, TXT sold its aerostructures unit for $180 million. Contributions by segment (profits based on $1,218 million) in 1997 were:

	Sales	Oper. Profits
Aircraft	30%	27%
Automotive	20%	12%
Industrial	29%	27%
Finance	21%	34%

Foreign operations accounted for 29% of revenues and 31% of income in 1997. An additional 10% of revenues was derived from exports, raising total foreign transactions to 39% of revenues.

Aircraft consists of Bell Helicopter and Cessna Aircraft. Bell is an international helicopter company with a 60% share of the worldwide market for commercial helicopters and a leading position in military markets. Cessna Aircraft is the world's largest producer of light and mid-size business jets and utility turboprops and the largest manufacturer of single engine aircraft. Among important new projects are two tiltrotor aircraft -- the Bell Boeing 609 civilian and the V-22 Osprey military programs. TXT is acquiring full control of the 609 project from Boeing, which had been Bell's partner.

The automotive segment, a global full-service supplier of automotive interior and exterior plastic components, has been the company's weakest performing division in recent years. New management was installed in 1997 with orders to boost earnings.

The industrial segment consists of four major business groups: fastening systems, golf and turf-care equipment, diversified products and fluid power systems and industrial components. This group includes Textron Lycoming which is the leading producer of piston aircraft engines. Since 1992 this segment has completed 17 acquisitions, 10 of which are located abroad. These will account for about $1.5 billion of 1998 revenues.

Finance consists of Avco Financial Services, a global consumer finance company, and Textron Financial Corp., a diversified commercial finance company that finances the sale of Textron and third-party products. In mid-1998, TXT announced that it was evaluating the fate of its Avco financial unit. Possibilities include a third-party sale or spin-off to shareholders. A decision is expected during the third quarter.

Per Share Data ($)

(Year Ended Dec. 31)	1997	1996	1995	1994	1993	1992	1991	1990	1989	1988
Tangible Bk. Val.	9.10	9.42	11.17	7.76	7.18	6.07	11.02	9.39	8.07	7.28
Cash Flow	5.84	5.05	4.36	4.61	3.25	3.31	2.98	2.82	2.71	2.71
Earnings	3.29	2.80	2.40	2.40	2.10	1.83	1.71	1.59	1.51	1.55
Dividends	1.00	0.88	0.78	0.70	0.62	0.56	0.52	0.50	0.50	0.50
Payout Ratio	30%	31%	33%	29%	29%	30%	30%	30%	33%	31%
Prices - High	70¾	48⅞	38¾	30⅜	29½	22½	20⅛	13⅞	14¾	15
- Low	45	34⅝	24⅜	23¼	20¼	16⅞	12⅛	9⅜	11⅜	10⅜
P/E Ratio - High	22	17	16	13	14	12	12	9	10	10
- Low	14	12	10	10	10	9	7	6	7	7

Income Statement Analysis (Million $)

	1997	1996	1995	1994	1993	1992	1991	1990	1989	1988
Revs.	10,544	9,274	8,453	9,681	9,075	8,344	7,823	7,915	7,431	7,279
Oper. Inc.	2,109	1,945	2,248	1,815	1,483	1,530	1,455	1,451	1,348	1,234
Depr.	435	387	342	398	206	264	223	220	214	205
Int. Exp.	726	731	812	665	668	742	754	775	733	602
Pretax Inc.	922	827	690	754	614	527	495	459	410	433
Eff. Tax Rate	39%	39%	40%	41%	38%	39%	40%	38%	35%	37%
Net Inc.	558	482	416	433	379	324	300	283	269	272

Balance Sheet & Other Fin. Data (Million $)

	1997	1996	1995	1994	1993	1992	1991	1990	1989	1988
Cash	87.0	47.0	84.0	49.0	26.2	31.0	50.0	66.0	29.0	16.0
Curr. Assets	NA	NA	NA	NA	NA	NA	NA	NA	NA	NA
Total Assets	18,610	18,235	17,347	20,925	19,658	18,367	15,737	14,892	13,790	12,554
Curr. Liab.	NA	NA	NA	NA	NA	NA	NA	NA	NA	NA
LT Debt	10,496	10,346	10,211	8,137	7,789	7,543	6,219	6,449	5,942	5,462
Common Eqty.	3,215	3,169	3,388	2,866	2,763	2,467	2,905	2,637	2,520	2,353
Total Cap.	14,207	14,012	13,623	11,019	10,569	10,030	9,147	9,111	8,489	7,847
Cap. Exp.	412	343	279	302	252	217	156	191	240	218
Cash Flow	992	869	757	830	584	588	521	502	482	475
Curr. Ratio	NA	NA	NA	NA	NA	NA	NA	NA	NA	NA
% LT Debt of Cap.	73.9	73.8	75.0	73.8	73.7	75.2	68.0	70.8	70.0	69.6
% Net Inc.of Revs.	5.3	2.0	4.9	4.5	4.2	3.9	3.8	3.6	3.6	3.7
% Ret. on Assets	3.0	2.7	2.5	2.2	2.0	1.9	1.9	2.0	2.0	3.1
% Ret. on Equity	17.4	14.7	13.3	15.6	14.4	11.9	10.7	11.2	10.7	12.0

Data as orig. reptd.; bef. results of disc. opers. and/or spec. items. Per share data adj. for stk. divs. as of ex-div. date. Bold denotes diluted EPS (FASB 128). E-Estimated. NA-Not Available. NM-Not Meaningful. NR-Not Ranked.

Office—40 Westminster St., P.O. Box 878, Providence, RI 02903. **Tel**—(401) 421-2800. **Website**—http://www.textron.com **Chrmn & CEO**—J. F. Hardymon. **Pres & COO**—L. B. Campbell. **EVP & CFO**—S. L. Key. **VP & Secy**—F. K. Butler. **VP & Investor Contact**—Mary F. Lovejoy (401-457-6009). **Dirs**—H. J. Arnelle, T. Beck, L. B. Campbell, R. S. Dickson, P. E. Gagne, J. F. Hardymon, J. D. Macomber, D. Mead, B. H. Rowe, S. F. Segnar, J. H. Sisco, J. W. Snow, M. D. Walker, T. B. Wheeler. **Transfer Agent & Registrar**—First Chicago Trust Co. of New York, Jersey City, NJ. **Incorporated**—in Rhode Island in 1928; reincorporated in Delaware in 1967. **Empl**— 64,000. **S&P Analyst:** Robert E. Friedman, CPA

12-SEP-98

Industry:
Manufacturing (Diversified)

Summary: This maker of analytical instruments, biomedical equipment, cogeneration systems, and process equipment has sold minority interests in several publicly traded subsidiaries.

S&P Opinion: Hold (★★★)	Recent Price • 16½	Yield • Nil
	52 Wk Range • 44½-14⅛	12-Mo. P/E • 11.4

Earnings vs. Previous Year
▲=Up ▼=Down ▶=No Change

Quantitative Evaluations

Outlook
(1 Lowest—5 Highest)
• 5

Fair Value
• 27⅜

Risk
• Average

Earn./Div. Rank
• B+

Technical Eval.
• **Bearish** since 5/98

Rel. Strength Rank
(1 Lowest—99 Highest)
• 16

Insider Activity
• NA

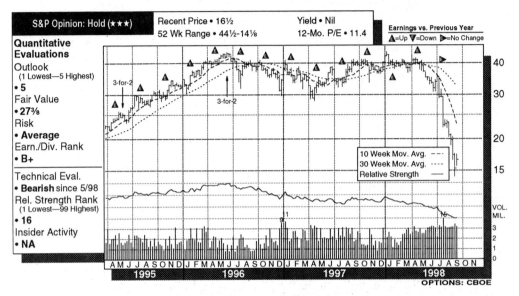

10 Week Mov. Avg. - - -
30 Week Mov. Avg. ⋯⋯
Relative Strength —

VOL.
MIL.

OPTIONS: CBOE

Overview - 19-AUG-98

TMO's earnings in the first half of 1998 were well below our expectation, principally due to economic troubles in Asia (9% of sales), slowdowns in certain industrial markets and negative currency translations. In August 1998, the company announced a major corporate reorganization intended to simply its structure by consolidating and realigning its 23 majority owned public subsidiaries into 15. The long-term results should be stronger, more competitive subsidiaries with higher market valuations and liquidity. The reorganization is expected to take two years. The divestiture of some businesses that no longer fit long-term growth plans is expected to reduce revenue by $100 million.

Valuation - 19-AUG-98

TMO's shares slid nearly 40% following its early July warning of a second quarter earnings shortfall. The disappointing results stemmed largely from delays in orders received at its Thermo Instrument subsidiary. The company has grown successfully through acquisitions, however, with fewer acquisitions expected and a major reorganization announced, TMO must prove that it can generate growth internally. The reorganization aims to simplify the corporate structure by consolidating and realigning business, but TMO does not expect any benefits near term. These actions are long overdue and should improve efficiency. Given the impact of slowing international economies (24% of sales) and management's focus on the reorganization, we expect earnings growth below the 18% consensus five-year forecast. Although the shares are currently trading modestly at 14 times our 1998 EPS estimate, we believe TMO's shares will perform in line with the broader market.

Key Stock Statistics

S&P EPS Est. 1998	1.50	Tang. Bk. Value/Share	3.31
P/E on S&P Est. 1998	11.0	Beta	0.90
S&P EPS Est. 1999	1.70	Shareholders	9,200
Dividend Rate/Share	Nil	Market cap. (B)	$ 2.8
Shs. outstg. (M)	166.1	Inst. holdings	68%
Avg. daily vol. (M)	1.154		

Value of $10,000 invested 5 years ago: $ 11,863

Fiscal Year Ending Dec. 31

	1998	1997	1996	1995	1994	1993
Revenues (Million $)						
1Q	944.3	763.5	652.4	478.6	350.5	292.8
2Q	947.8	875.0	745.8	528.7	395.0	300.4
3Q	—	909.9	740.0	570.4	406.4	318.4
4Q	—	1,010	794.4	629.8	433.4	338.1
Yr.	—	3,558	2,933	2,207	1,585	1,250
Earnings Per Share ($)						
1Q	0.37	0.31	0.31	0.25	0.21	0.17
2Q	0.34	0.34	0.32	0.26	0.22	0.19
3Q	E0.36	0.36	0.36	0.30	0.25	0.20
4Q	E0.43	0.40	0.36	0.31	0.25	0.21
Yr.	E1.50	1.41	1.35	1.11	0.93	0.78

Next earnings report expected: early November

Dividend Data

No cash dividends have been paid. A shareholder rights plan was adopted in 1988.

 A Division of The McGraw·Hill *Companies*

Thermo Electron Corporation

Business Summary - 19-AUG-98

Thermo Electron's growth strategy has focused on developing and acquiring technologies complementary to existing businesses, commercializing the technology or service, spinning off the business as a subsidiary and selling a minority equity interest to the public, and realizing the cash and accounting gain from such sale. The company believes that this "spin out" approach allows it to fund development of new ventures and provides additional motivation and incentive for management of the subsidiaries to maximize shareholder value.

In August 1998, management announced a major corporate reorganization. The principal aim of the reorganization is to simplify its corporate structure by consolidating and realigning its businesses into 15 majority-owned publicly traded subsidiaries from the current 23. These actions are intended to align similar market focused businesses together to create stronger and more competitive subsidiaries. Additionally, TMO expects the surviving publicly traded companies' shares will benefit from better exposure and an increase in liquidity due to their larger size. Management expects to divest non-strategic business with annual revenues of approximately $100 million. The pace of spinouts should slow during the two year reorganization.

Upon completion of the reorganization, TMO plans to

have seven majority-owned public subsidiaries and eight indirect public subsidiaries ("grandchildren"). The seven majority-owned subsidiaries will include: Thermo Instrument Systems Inc. (currently 82% owned), which makes instruments to detect and measure air pollution, nuclear radioactivity and toxic substances; Thermo Fibertek (84%), a maker of processing machinery for the paper-making and recycling industries; Thermo TerraTech (81%), which produces thermal processing systems to treat primary metals and metal parts; ThermoQuest (90%), a maker of commercial mass spectrometers; Thermo Ecotek (82%), which operates alternative energy power systems; Thermedics Inc. (55%), which makes biomedical products and instruments used to detect explosives and narcotics; and ThermoTrex (51%), which does research in electro-optical and advanced laser systems, thermodynamics and parallel and signal processing.

Other notable changes include the privatization of Thermo Power (64%) as a wholly owned subsidiary of TMO. Thermo Power develops and makes packaged cogeneration and cooling systems and intelligent traffic control systems. Alternatively, Thermo Coleman, a private subsidiary of TMO that provides systems integration, systems engineering, and analytical services to government and commercial customers, will be merged into ThermoTrex.

Per Share Data ($)

(Year Ended Dec. 31)	1997	1996	1995	1994	1993	1992	1991	1990	1989	1988
Tangible Bk. Val.	1.60	1.60	3.59	8.63	7.96	6.07	5.52	4.34	2.33	2.06
Cash Flow	2.13	2.13	1.79	1.50	1.21	1.00	0.87	0.76	0.61	0.51
Earnings	1.41	1.35	1.11	0.93	0.78	0.67	0.58	0.49	0.40	0.34
Dividends	Nil	Nil	Nil	Nil	Nil	Nil	Nil	Nil	Nil	Nil
Payout Ratio	Nil	Nil	Nil	Nil	Nil	Nil	Nil	Nil	Nil	Nil
Prices - High	44½	44⅜	34⅝	21¼	19¼	14⅛	13⅞	10½	11¼	6⅛
- Low	28⅜	29¾	19½	16	13⅞	11⅛	7⅝	6½	5⅝	3¾
P/E Ratio - High	32	33	31	23	25	21	24	21	28	18
- Low	20	22	18	17	18	17	13	13	14	11

Income Statement Analysis (Million $)

Revs.	3,558	3,558	2,207	1,585	1,247	947	805	708	579	501
Oper. Inc.	543	543	332	242	163	95.5	65.3	56.9	32.6	30.0
Depr.	136	136	84.9	62.3	42.4	29.2	23.4	18.8	12.7	9.9
Int. Exp.	93.1	93.1	76.9	61.7	40.0	31.4	18.3	13.9	11.6	10.2
Pretax Inc.	488	488	299	204	131	102	79.0	58.0	37.0	29.0
Eff. Tax Rate	36%	36%	33%	34%	26%	27%	31%	30%	26%	25%
Net Inc.	239	239	140	103	76.6	60.6	47.1	33.9	24.6	20.1

Balance Sheet & Other Fin. Data (Million $)

Cash	594	594	462	998	700	369	422	178	210	136
Curr. Assets	3,094	3,094	22,021	1,683	1,245	830	763	494	416	331
Total Assets	5,796	5,796	3,745	3,020	2,474	1,818	1,199	898	624	490
Curr. Liab.	1,092	1,092	715	537	416	326	297	254	153	123
LT Debt	1,743	1,550	1,116	1,050	790	694	255	210	172	148
Common Eqty.	1,998	1,998	1,299	990	859	553	481	307	211	182
Total Cap.	3,925	4,065	2,947	2,426	1,989	1,451	869	614	450	357
Cap. Exp.	112	125	63.0	60.0	60.0	193	33.0	24.0	20.0	24.0
Cash Flow	375	375	225	166	119	89.8	70.4	52.6	37.3	30.0
Curr. Ratio	2.8	2.8	2.8	3.1	3.0	2.5	2.6	1.9	2.7	2.7
% LT Debt of Cap.	44.4	38.1	37.9	43.3	39.7	47.8	29.4	34.2	38.2	41.6
% Net Inc.of Revs.	6.7	6.7	6.3	6.5	6.1	6.4	5.8	4.8	4.2	4.0
% Ret. on Assets	4.1	5.0	4.1	3.7	3.3	3.9	4.1	4.2	4.3	4.4
% Ret. on Equity	12.0	14.5	12.0	10.9	10.1	11.5	10.9	12.3	12.3	11.7

Data as orig. reptd.; bef. results of disc. opers. and/or spec. items. Per share data adj. for stk. divs. as of ex-div. date. Bold denotes diluted EPS (FASB 128). E-Estimated. NA-Not Available. NM-Not Meaningful. NR-Not Ranked.

Office—81 Wyman St., P.O. Box 9046, Waltham, MA 02254-9046. **Tel**—(781) 622-1000. **Website**—http://www.thermo.com **Chrmn**—G. N. Hatsopoulos. **Pres, CFO & Investor Contact**—John N. Hatsopoulos (781-622-1111). **VP-Fin**—P. F. Kelleher. **Secy**—Sandra L. Lambert. **Dirs**—J. M. Albertine, P. O. Crisp, E. P. Gyftopoulos, G. N. Hatsopoulos, J. N. Hatsopoulos, F. Jungers, R. A. McCabe, F. E. Morris, D. E. Noble, H. S. Olayan, R. F. Syron, R. D. Wellington. **Transfer Agent & Registrar**—BankBoston, N. A. **Incorporated**—in Delaware in 1956; reincorporated in 1960. **Empl**— 22,000. **S&P Analyst:** John A. Massey

STANDARD &POOR'S
STOCK REPORTS

Thomas & Betts
NYSE Symbol **TNB**

2227

In S&P 500

12-SEP-98

Industry: Electrical Equipment

Summary: This company is a leading manufacturer of electrical and electronic components.

| S&P Opinion: Hold (★★★) | Recent Price • 35⅞ | Yield • 3.1% |
| | 52 Wk Range • 64-33¼ | 12-Mo. P/E • 12.3 |

Quantitative Evaluations

Outlook
(1 Lowest—5 Highest)
• **4**

Fair Value
• **51**

Risk
• **Low**

Earn./Div. Rank
• **B+**

Technical Eval.
• **Neutral** since 7/98

Rel. Strength Rank
(1 Lowest—99 Highest)
• **48**

Insider Activity
• **NA**

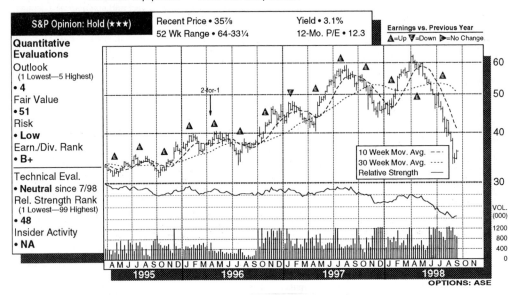

Earnings vs. Previous Year
▲=Up ▼=Down ▶=No Change

10 Week Mov. Avg. ---
30 Week Mov. Avg. -----
Relative Strength —

OPTIONS: ASE

Overview - 06-AUG-98

TNB's second quarter EPS were $0.05 below the street's consensus estimate of $0.78. Earnings were depressed by the continuing downturn in the electronic connector industry and Asia. Revenues declined 4.8%, due to the deconsolidation of automotive electronics businesses contributed to the Exemplar joint venture, a planned phase-out of certain automotive lines and foreign currency translations; excluding these items, revenue rose 1%. However, improved margins led to a small year-to-year gain in EPS. We expect single-digit sales growth in 1998 for the Electrical segment (54% or total revenue), well below 1997's gain, from volume improvements in the U.S. and Europe. The OEM segment (32% of sales), which includes Telecommunications Devices, Inc., will likely have a decline in sales in 1998 due to the transfer of some business. The Communications segment should register growth for the full year, despite a 4% decline for the first half. Third quarter 1998 earnings are expected to be similar to the $0.73 a share a year earlier. The third quarter 1998 EPS projection excludes one-time charges totaling $90 - $110 million related to plant and product line relocations and other actions.

Valuation - 06-AUG-98

The stock market's momentum helped drive TNB's share price up 40% during the first quarter of 1998, but as Asian worries resurfaced and earnings growth stagnated, TNB's shares gave up all of their gains and more. Revenues should be flat to up modestly in the second half of 1998. Although the shares currently sell at about 14X our 1998 EPS estimate of $2.95 (excluding large third quarter nonrecurring charges), we believe foreign competition will cut growth in the important connector segment. Therefore, we recommend holding the shares until the connector market improves.

Key Stock Statistics

S&P EPS Est. 1998	2.95	Tang. Bk. Value/Share	8.55
P/E on S&P Est. 1998	12.2	Beta	1.07
S&P EPS Est. 1999	3.50	Shareholders	5,600
Dividend Rate/Share	1.12	Market cap. (B)	$ 2.0
Shs. outstg. (M)	56.7	Inst. holdings	76%
Avg. daily vol. (M)	0.241		

Value of $10,000 invested 5 years ago: $ 12,945

Fiscal Year Ending Dec. 31

	1998	1997	1996	1995	1994	1993
Revenues (Million $)						
1Q	501.3	504.3	486.7	310.3	248.3	267.1
2Q	553.3	537.8	499.8	307.8	261.7	264.8
3Q	—	520.4	497.1	307.8	277.4	268.5
4Q	—	532.6	501.6	310.9	288.8	275.6
Yr.	—	2,115	1,985	1,237	1,076	1,076
Earnings Per Share ($)						
1Q	**0.64**	0.55	0.49	0.42	0.27	0.35
2Q	**0.73**	0.70	0.58	0.48	0.34	0.33
3Q	—	0.73	0.63	0.53	-1.05	0.35
4Q	—	**0.83**	-0.57	0.58	0.50	0.43
Yr.	**E2.95**	**2.81**	1.13	2.02	0.05	1.46

Next earnings report expected: NA

Dividend Data (Dividends have been paid since 1934.)

Amount ($)	Date Decl.	Ex-Div. Date	Stock of Record	Payment Date
0.280	Dec. 03	Dec. 11	Dec. 15	Jan. 02 '98
0.280	Feb. 04	Mar. 05	Mar. 09	Apr. 01 '98
0.280	May. 06	Jun. 11	Jun. 15	Jul. 01 '98
0.280	Sep. 02	Sep. 11	Sep. 15	Oct. 05 '98

A Division of The **McGraw·Hill** *Companies*

Business Summary - 06-AUG-98

Thomas & Betts, a leading producer of connectors and components for worldwide electrical and electronic markets, established itself as one of the top five electronic connector manufacturers in the world with the December 1996 acquisition of Augat, Inc. With 1996 sales of approximately $580 million, Augat's product lines strengthened TNB's positions in the automotive and communications industries, especially the cable components business.

TNB's operating segments made the following contributions in 1997:

	Revs.	Profits
Electrical components	36.1%	45.1%
Electronic components	42.3%	37.5%
Other products	21.6%	17.4%

In 1997, international operations accounted for 23% of sales and 24% of operating profits.

The electrical construction and maintenance components segment manufactures products that connect, terminate, protect and manage raceways, wires and cables for the distribution of electrical power. These products include fittings and accessories for electrical raceways, fastening products, terminals, power connectors, switch and outlet boxes, covers and accessories, floor boxes, metal framing, ground rods and clamps,

products for outdoor security, roadway and adverse and hazardous location lighting, circuit breakers, safety switches and metal centers. In North America, components are sold through distributors and retail outlets such as home centers and mass merchants.

The electronic/OEM components segment is a worldwide designer, manufacturer and marketer of printed circuit connectors, IDC connectors, flexible interconnects, flat cable and assemblies, cable ties, terminals, D-subminiature connectors, modular voice and data connectors and other components. Products are sold through electronic distributors and directly to end users and major OEMs.

Other products and components include heating products, utility poles and transmission towers, telecommunications components and other components. Products are sold through distributors and directly to end users.

TNB completed six acquisitions in 1997, representing a total cost of $62 million in cash and stock, including the January 1997 purchase of the Taylor Wiring Duct business from Gould-Shawmut. Taylor supplies wiring duct and accessories to the industrial OEM market.

In July 1998, TNB said that it will begin implementing expense reduction programs and accelerating plant and product line relocations to lower-cost regions, resulting in nonrecurring restructuring charges of $90 - $110 million in 1998's third quarter. It expected to realize savings from its actions at an annualized rate in excess of $50 million by year-end 1999.

Per Share Data ($)

(Year Ended Dec. 31)	1997	1996	1995	1994	1993	1992	1991	1990	1989	1988
Tangible Bk. Val.	8.58	6.55	7.14	5.86	4.50	3.96	9.88	9.43	8.87	8.63
Cash Flow	4.54	2.85	3.40	1.44	3.00	2.82	2.45	2.44	2.42	2.52
Earnings	2.75	1.13	2.02	0.05	1.46	1.36	1.42	1.42	1.58	1.73
Dividends	1.12	1.12	1.12	1.12	1.12	1.12	1.10	1.04	0.98	0.90
Payout Ratio	41%	99%	55%	NM	77%	82%	78%	73%	62%	52%
Prices - High	59¼	47¼	38⅛	35⅝	36	34½	30½	30¾	27⅞	30⅜
- Low	40⅜	33¼	31	29⅛	28½	27⅜	22½	20⅛	23	22¾
P/E Ratio - High	22	42	19	NM	25	25	21	22	18	18
- Low	15	29	15	NM	20	20	16	14	15	13

Income Statement Analysis (Million $)

	1997	1996	1995	1994	1993	1992	1991	1990	1989	1988
Revs.	2,115	1,985	1,237	1,076	1,076	1,051	566	599	544	515
Oper. Inc.	354	277	192	168	163	173	109	125	113	120
Depr.	95.3	91.6	54.7	53.5	57.9	54.7	35.1	34.9	28.6	26.8
Int. Exp.	51.6	48.7	27.6	26.9	30.2	33.4	12.4	13.0	10.2	7.7
Pretax Inc.	224	90.9	117	0.5	78.4	69.8	68.0	74.4	78.9	87.4
Eff. Tax Rate	31%	34%	31%	NM	30%	27%	29%	35%	32%	33%
Net Inc.	155	59.9	80.9	1.9	54.9	50.9	48.5	48.4	53.7	58.7

Balance Sheet & Other Fin. Data (Million $)

	1997	1996	1995	1994	1993	1992	1991	1990	1989	1988
Cash	43.9	162	105	122	104	98.0	101	90.0	98.0	50.0
Curr. Assets	796	957	528	534	489	463	335	337	336	264
Total Assets	2,039	2,131	1,259	1,208	1,133	1,117	600	586	564	493
Curr. Liab.	440	492	283	280	205	199	152	167	160	124
LT Debt	503	645	328	320	394	420	68.3	48.8	57.6	40.6
Common Eqty.	977	868	601	553	481	463	363	351	336	315
Total Cap.	1,507	1,538	941	887	899	893	440	409	401	366
Cap. Exp.	117	108	102	59.1	38.6	47.4	40.3	47.9	44.9	53.9
Cash Flow	250	151	136	55.0	113	106	83.5	83.3	82.4	85.4
Curr. Ratio	1.8	1.9	1.9	1.9	2.4	2.3	2.2	2.0	2.1	2.1
% LT Debt of Cap.	33.4	41.9	34.8	36.0	43.8	47.1	15.5	11.9	14.4	11.1
% Net Inc.of Revs.	7.3	3.0	6.5	0.2	5.1	4.8	8.6	8.1	9.9	11.4
% Ret. on Assets	7.4	3.2	6.6	0.2	4.9	5.7	8.2	8.4	10.1	13.0
% Ret. on Equity	16.8	7.0	14.0	0.4	11.6	11.8	13.5	14.1	16.5	19.4

Data as orig. reptd.; bef. results of disc. opers. and/or spec. items. Per share data adj. for stk. divs. as of ex-div. date. Bold denotes diluted EPS (FASB 128). E-Estimated. NA-Not Available. NM-Not Meaningful. NR-Not Ranked.

Office—1555 Lynnfield Rd., Memphis, TN 38119. **Tel**—(901) 682-7766. **Chrmn**—T. K. Dunnigan. **Pres & CEO**—C. R. Moore. **VP-Fin & Treas**—F. R. Jones. **Secy**—J. Kronenberg. **Dir. of Investor Relations**—Renee Johansen. **Dirs**—E. H. Drew, T. K. Dunnigan, J. K. Hauswald, T. W. Jones, R. A. Kenkel, J. N. Lemasters, K. R. Masterson, T. C. McDermott, C. R. Moore, J.-P. Richard, I. M. Ross, W. H. Waltrip. **Transfer Agent & Registrar**—First Chicago Trust Co. of New York, Jersey City, NJ. **Incorporated**—in New Jersey in 1917; reincorporated in Tennessee in 1996. **Empl**— 16,400. **S&P Analyst:** John A. Massey

STANDARD &POOR'S
STOCK REPORTS

3Com Corp.

5417K
Nasdaq Symbol **COMS**

In S&P 500

12-SEP-98

Industry: Computers (Networking)

Summary: This computer networking company makes a range of products, including adapters, hubs and routers for Ethernet, Token Ring and high-speed networks.

S&P Opinion: Accumulate (★★★★)	Recent Price • 28⅜	Yield • Nil	Earnings vs. Previous Year
	52 Wk Range • 56¾-22⅞	12-Mo. P/E • NM	▲=Up ▼=Down ▶=No Change

Quantitative Evaluations

Outlook
(1 Lowest—5 Highest)
• **5**

Fair Value
• **42⅞**

Risk
• **High**

Earn./Div. Rank
• **B-**

Technical Eval.
• **Bearish** since 10/97

Rel. Strength Rank
(1 Lowest—99 Highest)
• **93**

Insider Activity
• **Neutral**

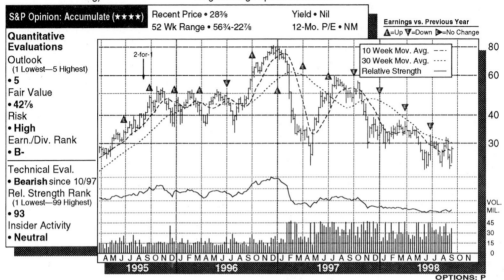

OPTIONS: P

Overview - 29-JUN-98

We see revenues increasing 17% in FY 99 (May) as 3Com appears to have stabilized its inventory management procedures. A buildup of excess inventory occurred in the fall of 1997 because of weak demand from troubled Asian economies and a delay in the industry standard for the company's new high-speed (56K) modem. A 56K standard was ratified in February, improving visibility for this key product line. As of June 1998, one-third of 3Com's Internet Service Provider customers had upgraded to 56K, and the company expects 80% of its ISPs to offer the faster service by early fall. We believe that weakness in Asia-Pacific (10% of revenues) could prove a longer-term issue, and could hold growth to a 20% to 40% rate, versus prior expectations of 30% to 50%. Still, new product launches (specifically, the Corebuilder 9000) could take off faster than we predict. Gross margins will be about 44% to 46%, until improving to a 47% goal in FY 2000.

Valuation - 29-JUN-98

We upgraded 3Com shares to accumulate, from hold, in late June following solid fourth quarter results. COMS has completed a transition to a new channel inventory model and already is showing improved revenue visibility. Gross margins improved 100 basis points sequentially and operating costs fell significantly, signaling potential margin improvements going forward. Given COMS's strong position in cable modems, we are encouraged by AT&T's bid to acquire TCI, the largest cable company in the U.S. Although we are concerned about 3Com's exposure to Asia, the majority of the company's international sales are to the booming European markets. We have raised our FY 99 EPS to $1.38, from $1.23. At 16X our $1.74 calendar 1999 estimate, we view the shares as attractively valued, given a 20% growth rate and the stabilization of the business.

Key Stock Statistics

S&P EPS Est. 1999	1.38	Tang. Bk. Value/Share	7.82
P/E on S&P Est. 1999	20.6	Beta	1.32
S&P EPS Est. 2000	1.98	Shareholders	4,900
Dividend Rate/Share	Nil	Market cap. (B)	$ 10.2
Shs. outstg. (M)	358.9	Inst. holdings	46%
Avg. daily vol. (M)	6.869		

Value of $10,000 invested 5 years ago: $ 38,312

Fiscal Year Ending May 31

	1998	1997	1996	1995	1994	1993
Revenues (Million $)						
1Q	1,598	710.1	497.3	249.3	162.1	135.6
2Q	1,197	820.3	563.5	304.8	205.3	152.7
3Q	1,250	786.8	606.0	338.7	218.2	161.4
4Q	1,375	829.9	660.3	402.5	241.5	167.5
Yr.	5,420	3,147	2,327	1,295	827.0	617.2
Earnings Per Share ($)						
1Q	-0.15	0.50	0.33	0.20	0.20	0.05
2Q	0.01	0.56	0.09	0.02	0.16	0.07
3Q	**0.04**	0.47	0.42	0.32	-0.82	0.08
4Q	**0.17**	0.48	0.17	0.33	0.20	0.10
Yr.	**0.08**	2.02	1.01	0.86	-0.23	0.31

Next earnings report expected: late September

Dividend Data

No cash has been paid. Two-for-one stock splits were effected in 1994 and 1995.

STANDARD
&POOR'S
STOCK REPORTS

3Com Corporation

5417K
12-SEP-98

Business Summary - 29-JUN-98

3Com's June 1997 merger with U.S. Robotics (for 3Com stock valued at roughly $8 billion) created a networking leader with $5.5 billion in annual revenues. The company believes this will help it participate fully in the strong industry growth of 30%-50% expected in the years ahead. COMS and USR have complementary sales channels, which should help expand distribution. More than half of 3Com's sales are from outside the U.S., while the majority of U.S. Robotics revenues are in North American and European markets. 3Com is a leading global data networking company providing a range of networking solutions that include modems, remote access products, adapters, hubs, routers and switches for Ethernet, Token Ring and other high-speed networks.

3Com's sales are mostly divided between network adapters (42% of the total in FY 97) and systems products (57%).

Network adapters, or network interface cards (NICs), are add-in printed circuit boards that allow desktop computers to connect to the local area network (LAN). 3Com is the world's largest supplier of Ethernet adapters, and had an estimated 59% market share for

fast-Ethernet adapters as of 1997's first quarter. 3Com has been battling with Intel Corp. in a price war to gain share in this segment.

3Com's systems products include hubs, bridges/routers, LAN switches, network management and servers. Hubs provide the physical connection between network elements. Bridges and routers control the flow of data between LANs, allowing connectivity between networks. LAN switches provide high-speed links between multiple network segments. 3Com's Transcend network management architecture allows network administrators to monitor traffic and diagnose problems from a single remote location.

Over the past five years, 3Com has completed business combinations with and corporate acquisitions of 12 companies. Recent acquisitions included: OnStream Networks, a leading provider of Asynchronous Transfer Mode (ATM) and broadband WAN and access products; Axon Networks Inc., a leader in remote monitoring data network traffic; and Chipcom Corp., a leader in high-end hubs.

In June 1998, 3Com directors authorized the repurchase of up to 10 million shares of the company's common stock. Such purchases will be made in the open market from time to time, with no termination date.

Per Share Data ($)

(Year Ended May 31)	1998	1997	1996	1995	1994	1993	1992	1991	1990	1989
Tangible Bk. Val.	7.82	8.51	5.80	3.36	2.16	2.09	1.80	1.75	1.91	1.67
Cash Flow	0.92	2.78	1.52	1.19	0.02	0.50	0.23	-0.05	0.37	0.44
Earnings	0.08	2.02	1.01	0.86	-0.23	0.31	0.04	-0.24	0.18	0.29
Dividends	Nil	Nil	Nil	Nil	Nil	Nil	Nil	Nil	Nil	Nil
Payout Ratio	Nil	Nil	Nil	Nil	Nil	Nil	Nil	Nil	Nil	Nil
Cal. Yrs.	1997	1996	1995	1994	1993	1992	1991	1990	1989	1988
Prices - High	78¼	81⅜	53⅝	26⅝	12⅛	7½	3⅛	4¾	7¼	6
- Low	24	33½	22¼	10⅛	4⅞	2⁷/₁₆	1⅜	1⅜	2½	3⅞
P/E Ratio - High	NM	40	53	31	NM	24	84	NM	40	20
- Low	NM	17	22	12	NM	8	37	NM	14	13

Income Statement Analysis (Million $)

Revs.	5,420	3,147	2,327	1,295	827	617	408	399	419	386
Oper. Inc.	662	711	515	306	164	85.4	33.9	41.5	55.9	68.9
Depr.	300	141	91.0	46.7	30.6	25.1	21.6	22.7	22.5	16.7
Int. Exp.	Nil	11.8	12.6	6.9	NA	NA	NA	NA	NA	NA
Pretax Inc.	116	584	308	198	19.5	60.2	5.2	-44.6	32.8	54.2
Eff. Tax Rate	74%	36%	42%	37%	247%	36%	49%	NM	38%	37%
Net Inc.	30.2	374	178	126	-28.7	38.6	4.2	-27.7	20.5	34.3

Balance Sheet & Other Fin. Data (Million $)

Cash	529	890	499	324	130	117	78.7	97.5	86.7	43.1
Curr. Assets	3,135	1,831	1,240	708	361	304	229	218	229	188
Total Assets	4,081	2,266	1,525	840	444	368	294	271	294	247
Curr. Liab.	1,184	598	415	264	163	108	87.1	71.4	59.0	36.4
LT Debt	35.8	110	110	111	1.1	0.6	1.5	0.3	0.8	3.4
Common Eqty.	2,807	1,518	979	465	281	258	199	190	232	206
Total Cap.	2,892	1,664	1,105	576	282	259	200	192	235	211
Cap. Exp.	508	248	180	76.2	36.5	22.3	21.5	26.6	25.8	23.7
Cash Flow	330	514	269	172	1.9	63.7	25.7	-5.0	43.0	51.0
Curr. Ratio	2.6	3.1	3.0	2.7	2.2	2.8	2.6	3.1	3.9	5.2
% LT Debt of Cap.	1.2	6.6	10.0	19.3	0.4	0.2	0.7	0.2	0.4	1.6
% Net Inc.of Revs.	0.6	11.9	7.6	9.7	NM	6.2	1.0	NM	4.9	8.9
% Ret. on Assets	1.0	19.7	13.7	19.6	NM	11.1	1.5	NM	7.5	15.2
% Ret. on Equity	1.4	30.0	22.1	33.7	NM	16.0	2.1	NM	9.3	18.6

Data as orig. reptd.; bef. results of disc. opers. and/or spec. items. Per share data adj. for stk. divs. as of ex-div. date. Bold denotes diluted EPS (FASB 128). E-Estimated. NA-Not Available. NM-Not Meaningful. NR-Not Ranked.

Office—P.O. Box 58145, 5400 Bayfront Plaza, Santa Clara, CA 95052-8145. **Tels**—(408) 764-5000; (800) NET-3Com. **Fax**—(408) 764-5001. **Website**—http://www.3com.com **Chrmn, Pres & CEO**—E. A. Benhamou. **SVP-Fin & CFO**—C. B. Paisley. **SVP & Secy**—M. D. Michael. **Investor Contacts**—Bill Slakey, Shirly Stacy. **Dirs**—J. L. Barksdale, E. A. Benhamou, G. A. Campbell, C. Cowell, J. E. Cowie, D. W. Dorman, J.-L. Gassee, S. C. Johnson, P. C. Kantz, P. G. Yovovich, W. F. Zuendt. **Transfer Agent**—Boston EquiServe. **Incorporated**—in California in 1979. **Empl**—13,000. **S&P Analyst:** Aydin Tuncer

STANDARD &POOR'S
STOCK REPORTS

Time Warner

2236

NYSE Symbol **TWX**

In S&P 500

12-SEP-98

Industry: Entertainment	**Summary:** Time Warner is one of the world's largest media/entertainment companies, with major interests in publishing, music, filmed entertainment, and cable TV systems and programming.

S&P Opinion: Buy (★★★★★)

Recent Price • 84⅞	Yield • 0.4%
52 Wk Range • 100-52⅝	12-Mo. P/E • NM

Quantitative Evaluations

Outlook
(1 Lowest—5 Highest)
• **1⁻**

Fair Value
• **41¾**

Risk
• **Average**

Earn./Div. Rank
• **B-**

Technical Eval.
• **Bullish** since 3/98

Rel. Strength Rank
(1 Lowest—99 Highest)
• **85**

Insider Activity
• **Neutral**

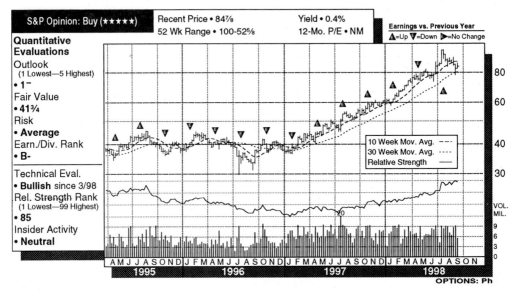

Earnings vs. Previous Year
▲=Up ▼=Down ▶=No Change

10 Week Mov. Avg. ---
30 Week Mov. Avg. ····
Relative Strength —

OPTIONS: Ph

Overview - 24-AUG-98

Time Warner is one of the world's premier communications and entertainment companies, with leading ownership positions in such areas as magazines, movie and TV show distribution, recorded music, cable TV networks, and cable TV systems. A partnership called Time Warner Entertainment (TWE), in which TWX has a majority interest, owns a sizable portion of the filmed entertainment-related operations. Meanwhile, TWX's earnings per share are limited by non-cash charges and interest expense related to acquisitions. Also, the company's earnings for the first half of 1998 and for full-year 1997 include gains from the sale or exchange of assets.

Valuation - 24-AUG-98

We recommend purchase of this stock. We look for the shares to benefit from the prospect of at least mid-teens growth in future cash flow (as measured and approximated by earnings before interest, taxes and amortization). This would include cash flow of the majority-owned Time Warner Entertainment business, whose assets include Warner Bros. movie and television business, the HBO pay-TV channel, and various cable systems. However, TWX does not fully consolidate the income statement and balance sheet of TWE for financial reporting purposes. Also, we expect investors to anticipate lower borrowing costs for TWX, and to like the idea that TWX will use free cash flow to buy back more stock. In addition, there may be some support from the speculative prospect of other companies using TWX's cable TV wires as telephony pipelines. During 1997, the stock price climbed 65%, and it has also risen considerably in 1998.

Key Stock Statistics

S&P EPS Est. 1998	-0.10	Tang. Bk. Value/Share	NM
P/E on S&P Est. 1998	NM	Beta	0.91
S&P EPS Est. 1999	0.55	Shareholders	26,000
Dividend Rate/Share	0.36	Market cap. (B)	$ 46.1
Shs. outstg. (M)	599.3	Inst. holdings	60%
Avg. daily vol. (M)	1.627		

Value of $10,000 invested 5 years ago: $ 30,371

Fiscal Year Ending Dec. 31

	1998	1997	1996	1995	1994	1993
Revenues (Million $)						
1Q	3,137	3,034	2,068	1,817	1,558	—
2Q	3,672	3,193	2,139	1,907	1,667	—
3Q	—	3,231	2,157	1,981	1,884	4,620
4Q	—	3,836	3,700	2,362	2,287	1,960
Yr.	—	13,294	10,064	8,067	7,396	14,544
Earnings Per Share ($)						
1Q	**-0.25**	**-0.05**	-0.32	-0.13	-0.14	-0.33
2Q	**0.04**	**-0.09**	-0.26	-0.03	-0.06	-0.13
3Q	—	**-0.19**	-0.43	-0.30	-0.09	-0.30
4Q	—	**0.28**	-0.03	0.01	0.02	-0.01
Yr.	**E-0.10**	**-0.03**	-0.95	-0.46	-0.27	-0.75

Next earnings report expected: mid October

Dividend Data (Dividends have been paid since 1930.)

Amount ($)	Date Decl.	Ex-Div. Date	Stock of Record	Payment Date
0.090	Nov. 20	Nov. 26	Dec. 01	Dec. 15 '97
0.090	Jan. 15	Feb. 26	Mar. 02	Mar. 16 '98
0.090	May. 14	May. 28	Jun. 01	Jun. 15 '98
0.090	Jul. 16	Aug. 28	Sep. 01	Sep. 15 '98

A Division of The McGraw-Hill Companies

Business Summary - 24-AUG-98

With a stable of household names ranging from HBO to Time magazine and Bugs Bunny to Batman, Time Warner holds leading market positions across a broad spectrum of the entertainment and information world, including television programming, magazines, movies, cable TV and recorded music.

After a decade of megamergers, entertainment industry assets are increasingly concentrated in the hands of conglomerates such as TWX, Viacom, Disney, News Corp., Sony and Seagram (84% owner of Universal Studios, Inc.). In October 1996, TWX added to its distribution and brand-name power by acquiring Turner Broadcasting System, the owner of such cable TV networks as CNN, Superstation TBS, and the Cartoon Channel. Media maverick Ted Turner is now vice chairman of TWX, and one of TWX's largest shareholders.

TWX's diverse assets and consumer franchises offer opportunities to build value. Movie blockbusters such as Batman can be leveraged into sequels, with related merchandise sold through the Warner Bros. retail chain. In addition, the cash flow from TWX's large library of older movies and TV shows helps to finance the substantial up-front costs for new productions, giving TWX a competitive advantage over new and smaller entrants.

However, TWX's vast collection of content and distribution outlets came at a price. Time Inc.'s acquisition of Warner Communications in 1989-90 added more than

$10 billion of debt, and the Turner merger in 1996 included the issuance of TWX common stock valued at more than $6 billion.

A majority-owned partnership, known as Time Warner Entertainment Co., L.P. (TWE), owns much of the filmed entertainment operations which are likely to be associated with TWX ownership, including the Warner Bros. movie and television businesses, the HBO pay-TV channel, and various cable systems. MediaOne Group, Inc. (formerly U S WEST, Inc.) owns 25.5% limited partnership interests in portions of TWE's capital. Also, TWE has an equity interest in the Primestar direct broadcast satellite business. TWX does not fully consolidate the income statement and balance sheet of TWE for financial reporting purposes. In 1997, TWE had revenues of $11.3 billion that are not included in the $13.3 billion of revenues reported by TWX.

TWX (including TWE's operations) is one of the largest U.S. operators of cable TV systems. TWX is also one of six companies that dominate the worldwide market for recorded music and it publishes various magazines. In 1998, TWE sold its 49% equity interest in the Six Flags theme-park chain. Also, TWX, TWE and a partnership that includes TWE each owns an equity interest in the Road Runner joint venture, which is involved in seeking to offer high-speed Internet access. Other partners (including holders of convertible preferred equity) include MediaOne, Microsoft and Compaq Computer.

Per Share Data ($)

(Year Ended Dec. 31)	1997	1996	1995	1994	1993	1992	1991	1990	1989	1988
Tangible Bk. Val.	NM	NM	NM	2.66	3.25	4.40	6.05	1.57	5.11	1.65
Cash Flow	2.25	1.93	1.13	0.88	0.38	1.70	1.45	1.53	1.17	2.22
Earnings	-0.03	-0.95	-0.46	-0.27	-0.75	-1.46	-2.40	-3.42	-1.09	1.25
Dividends	0.36	0.36	0.36	0.35	0.31	0.27	0.26	0.25	0.25	0.25
Payout Ratio	NM	NM	NM	NM	NM	NM	NM	NM	NM	20%
Prices - High	62	45¼	45⅝	44¼	46⅞	29⅝	31¼	31¼	45¾	30⅝
- Low	36⅜	29¾	33⅝	31½	28¾	21½	19½	16⅝	26	19¾
P/E Ratio - High	NM	NM	NM	NM	NM	NM	NM	NM	NM	24
- Low	NM	NM	NM	NM	NM	NM	NM	NM	NM	16

Income Statement Analysis (Million $)

	1997	1996	1995	1994	1993	1992	1991	1990	1989	1988
Revs.	13,294	10,064	8,067	7,396	6,581	13,070	12,021	11,517	7,642	4,507
Oper. Inc.	2,484	1,876	1,182	1,074	942	2,374	2,127	2,126	1,294	897
Depr.	1,294	988	559	437	424	1,172	1,109	1,138	531	224
Int. Exp.	1,008	1,141	877	769	698	729	912	1,096	965	111
Pretax Inc.	832	4.0	2.0	89.0	81.0	320	52.0	-144	-241	529
Eff. Tax Rate	64%	NM	NM	202%	303%	73%	290%	NM	NM	45%
Net Inc.	301	-155	-123	-91.0	-163	86.0	-99.0	-226	-255	289

Balance Sheet & Other Fin. Data (Million $)

	1997	1996	1995	1994	1993	1992	1991	1990	1989	1988
Cash	645	452	628	282	200	942	199	172	234	121
Curr. Assets	5,011	4,821	3,720	2,817	2,534	5,117	3,890	3,946	3,834	1,321
Total Assets	34,163	35,064	22,132	16,716	16,892	27,366	24,889	25,337	24,791	4,913
Curr. Liab.	4,371	4,012	3,027	2,972	2,225	3,912	3,576	3,651	3,270	905
LT Debt	11,833	12,713	9,907	8,839	9,291	10,068	8,716	11,184	10,838	1,485
Common Eqty.	5,817	5,943	679	1,008	1,230	1,635	2,242	360	1,172	1,359
Total Cap.	28,114	29,406	17,943	12,687	13,659	22,025	19,730	20,135	20,140	3,402
Cap. Exp.	574	481	266	164	198	574	527	574	522	355
Cash Flow	1,276	832	435	333	142	630	417	352	275	513
Curr. Ratio	1.1	1.2	1.2	0.9	1.1	1.3	1.1	1.1	1.2	1.5
% LT Debt of Cap.	42.1	43.2	55.2	69.7	68.0	45.7	44.2	55.5	53.8	43.7
% Net Inc.of Revs.	2.3	NM	NM	NM	NM	0.7	NM	NM	NM	6.4
% Ret. on Assets	0.9	NM	NM	NM	NM	0.3	NM	NM	NM	6.2
% Ret. on Equity	NM	NM	NM	NM	NM	NM	NM	NM	NM	22.4

Data as orig. reptd.; bef. results of disc. opers. and/or spec. items. Per share data adj. for stk. divs. as of ex-div. date. Bold denotes diluted EPS (FASB 128). E-Estimated. NA-Not Available. NM-Not Meaningful. NR-Not Ranked.

Office—75 Rockefeller Plaza, New York, NY 10019. **Tel**—(212) 484-8000. **Website**—http://www.timewarner.com. **Chrmn & CEO**—G. M. Levin. **Vice Chrmn**—R. E. Turner. **Pres**—R. D. Parsons. **EVP & CFO**—R. J. Bressler. **EVP & Secy**—P. R. Haje. **Investor Contact**—Joan Nicolais Sumner (212-484-8718). **Dirs**—M. Adelson, J. C. Bacot, S. F. Bollenbach, J. C. Danforth, B. S. Greenough, G. Greenwald, C. A. Hills, G. M. Levin, R. Mark, M. A. Miles, R. D. Parsons, R. E. Turner, F. T. Vincent, Jr. **Transfer Agent**—ChaseMellon Shareholder Services, L. L. C., Ridgefield Park, NJ. **Incorporated**—in New York in 1922; reincorporated in Delaware in 1983. **Empl**— 67,900. **S&P Analyst:** Tom Graves, CFA

STANDARD &POOR'S

STOCK REPORTS

Times Mirror

2237

NYSE Symbol **TMC**

In S&P 500

12-SEP-98

Industry:
Publishing

Summary: This major information company is primarily a publisher of newspapers, professional information and magazines.

S&P Opinion: Hold (★★★)	Recent Price • 54¾	Yield • 1.3%	
	52 Wk Range • 65¾-52⅛	12-Mo. P/E • 24.1	Earnings vs. Previous Year

▲=Up ▼=Down ▶=No Change

Quantitative Evaluations

Outlook
(1 Lowest—5 Highest)
• **1+**

Fair Value
• **44½**

Risk
• **Low**

Earn./Div. Rank
• **B**

Technical Eval.
• **NA**

Rel. Strength Rank
(1 Lowest—99 Highest)
• **64**

Insider Activity
• **NA**

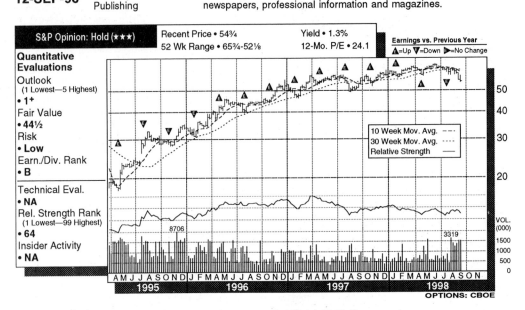

10 Week Mov. Avg. ---
30 Week Mov. Avg. ·····
Relative Strength —

8706

3319

VOL. (000)

1500
1000
500
0

A M J J A S O N D | J F M A M J J A S O N D | J F M A M J J A S O N D | J F M A M J J A S O N
1995 | 1996 | 1997 | 1998

OPTIONS: CBOE

Overview - 08-JUN-98

We expect moderate growth in revenues from newspapers in 1998, largely due to continued healthy gains in advertising demand at the Los Angeles Times and at Newsday. Circulation revenues will benefit from rising circulation, in spite of lower average cover prices in the early part of the year. Operating expenses will continue to be tightly controlled, but operating margins will be restrained by higher newsprint costs, reflecting higher prices and greater consumption. Nevertheless, newspaper profits are likely to rise roughly 10%. Magazine publishing will also benefit from healthy advertising and rising circulation, but here again, paper costs will restrain profits. TMC expects to report a gain of $1 billion, or $10.50 a share, on the sale of its legal publishing operations to Reed Elsevier plc for $1.65 billion. TMC is continuing the divestiture process for its health sciences publisher Mosby.

Valuation - 08-JUN-98

The stock, selling close to its historical high, remains an attractive holding for the near term. The pending sale of legal publishing businesses will put $1 billion on the balance sheet, and the planned sale of health science publishing should also be lucrative. Much of the proceeds will probably be utilized in shoring up and expanding TMC's newspaper business. Even if the re-investment program proves successful, management expects its strategies to take several years to bear significant fruits. And that adds a degree of uncertainty at a time when cost pressures, particularly for paper, are increasing. Nevertheless, we applaud management's strategies. With these considerations in mind, we are maintaining our "hold" recommendation on TMC as an attractive stock for potential longer-term capital gains.

Key Stock Statistics

S&P EPS Est. 1998	2.80	Tang. Bk. Value/Share	NM
P/E on S&P Est. 1998	19.6	Beta	0.65
S&P EPS Est. 1999	3.15	Shareholders	3,700
Dividend Rate/Share	0.72	Market cap. (B)	$ 3.4
Shs. outstg. (M)	86.7	Inst. holdings	43%
Avg. daily vol. (M)	0.316		

Value of $10,000 invested 5 years ago: $ 19,477

Fiscal Year Ending Dec. 31

	1998	1997	1996	1995	1994	1993
Revenues (Million $)						
1Q	803.9	773.9	806.8	773.7	733.7	868.0
2Q	760.6	811.8	837.3	843.1	807.6	903.0
3Q	—	814.5	885.6	864.8	858.7	924.0
4Q	—	918.4	871.4	966.7	957.4	1,019
Yr.	—	3,319	3,401	3,448	3,357	3,714
Earnings Per Share ($)						
1Q	**0.44**	**0.36**	0.14	0.09	0.06	0.21
2Q	—	**0.58**	0.33	0.14	0.25	0.31
3Q	—	**0.62**	0.43	-2.48	0.31	0.57
4Q	—	**0.73**	0.67	-1.62	0.36	0.18
Yr.	—	**2.29**	1.55	-3.74	0.98	1.27

Next earnings report expected: late October

Dividend Data (Dividends have been paid since 1892.)

Amount ($)	Date Decl.	Ex-Div. Date	Stock of Record	Payment Date
0.150	Oct. 09	Nov. 24	Nov. 26	Dec. 10 '97
0.180	Feb. 05	Feb. 18	Feb. 20	Mar. 10 '98
0.180	May. 07	May. 27	May. 29	Jun. 10 '98
0.180	Jul. 09	Aug. 26	Aug. 28	Sep. 10 '98

Business Summary - 08-JUN-98

The Times Mirror Company is a Los Angeles-based news and information company with business interests in newspaper publishing, professional information and consumer media. For the past several years, the company has been undertaking a number of strategic moves to re-emphasize its newspaper publishing business. In April 1998, TMC agreed to sell its legal publishing holdings to Reed Elsevier Plc (Reed) in a deal valued at $1.65 billion. Reed will buy TMC's Matthew Bender & Co. unit as well as its 50% stake in Shepard's. TMC expects to report a gain on the Reed sale of about $1 billion, or $10.50 per share, when the deal closes in the summer of 1998. TMC is continuing with the divestiture process for its health sciences publishing unit, Mosby. Divestiture of these assets will boost newspapers to 76% of revenues, up from 61% in 1996 and 50% five years ago.

Newspaper publishing (66% of revenues and 70% of profits in 1997) includes five metropolitan and two suburban daily newspapers: Los Angeles Times, serving the nation's second largest metropolitan area; Newsday, serving Nassau and Suffolk counties on Long Island and the borough of Queens, New York; The Baltimore Sun, Maryland's largest newspaper; The Hartford Courant, largest in Connecticut; The Morning Call, serving eastern Pennsylvania's Lehigh Valley; and The (Stamford) Advocate and Greenwich Time, serving Connecticut's affluent Fairfield County.

Following the divestitures of Matthew Bender, Shepard's and Mosby, the Professional Information segment (26% and 26%) will consist of StayWell, consumer health information provider; Jeppesen Sanderson, flight information provider; AchieveGlobal, skills training and consulting solutions provider; and Allen Communications, software developer.

The Magazine Publishing group (8% and 4%) publishes 18 titles, including Field & Stream, Outdoor Life, Popular Science, Golf Magazine, Today's Homeowner, The Sporting News, Ski, Skiing, Salt Water Sportsman, Yachting, Transworld Skateboarding, TransWorld Snowboarding, Verge, Freeze, Warp, Ride BMX, SNAP and Snowboard Life.

TMC sold art book publisher Harry N. Abrams in April 1997, and its cable TV operations in February 1995. TMC divested its college publishing business in October 1997.

Per Share Data ($) (Year Ended Dec. 31)	1997	1996	1995	1994	1993	1992	1991	1990	1989	1988
Tangible Bk. Val.	NA	3.58	4.67	8.56	6.33	4.35	6.90	5.61	5.16	4.17
Cash Flow	3.80	2.77	-1.46	2.30	3.26	2.33	2.54	3.29	3.96	4.08
Earnings	2.29	1.55	-3.74	0.98	1.27	0.44	0.64	1.40	2.30	2.58
Dividends	0.55	0.32	0.45	Nil	1.08	1.08	1.08	1.08	1.00	0.92
Payout Ratio	24%	21%	NM	Nil	85%	245%	169%	77%	43%	36%
Prices - High	61¾	56	35¼	37⅛	35¼	38⅜	32⅝	39⅜	45	40¼
- Low	46⅛	30⅝	17¼	28¾	28¼	28½	25½	21¼	32⅜	29
P/E Ratio - High	27	36	NM	38	28	87	51	28	20	16
- Low	20	20	NM	29	22	65	40	15	14	11
Income Statement Analysis (Million $)										
Revs.	3,319	3,401	3,449	3,357	3,714	3,702	3,614	3,621	3,475	3,259
Oper. Inc.	616	525	351	464	632	622	550	614	712	662
Depr.	155	162	173	170	256	243	252	244	215	194
Int. Exp.	53.4	27.0	30.0	70.6	85.6	78.5	90.9	94.2	77.4	69.2
Pretax Inc.	417	404	-454	248	302	120	166	307	494	542
Eff. Tax Rate	40%	49%	NM	49%	46%	53%	51%	41%	40%	39%
Net Inc.	250	206	-338	126	164	57.0	82.0	180	298	332
Balance Sheet & Other Fin. Data (Million $)										
Cash	57.0	177	256	81.9	5.0	24.8	34.0	37.0	38.0	37.0
Curr. Assets	764	870	1,248	1,533	1,217	903	839	860	824	771
Total Assets	3,416	3,730	3,817	4,265	4,606	4,327	4,052	4,193	3,947	3,476
Curr. Liab.	922	809	1,035	1,486	1,162	902	665	692	695	472
LT Debt	925	459	248	246	795	1,114	978	1,068	892	877
Common Eqty.	519	922	510	1,957	1,899	1,701	1,884	1,917	1,877	1,687
Total Cap.	1,964	2,087	2,194	2,335	2,975	2,951	3,119	3,255	3,022	2,802
Cap. Exp.	130	147	129	128	229	198	209	340	452	332
Cash Flow	373	368	-165	296	420	300	327	424	513	526
Curr. Ratio	0.8	1.1	1.2	1.0	1.0	1.0	1.3	1.2	1.2	1.6
% LT Debt of Cap.	47.1	22.0	11.3	10.6	26.7	37.8	31.4	32.8	29.5	31.3
% Net Inc.of Revs.	7.5	6.1	NM	3.8	4.4	1.5	2.3	5.0	8.6	10.2
% Ret. on Assets	7.2	5.6	NM	2.8	3.7	1.4	2.0	4.4	8.0	10.1
% Ret. on Equity	34.8	15.1	NM	6.5	9.1	3.2	4.3	9.5	16.7	21.1

Data as orig. reptd.; bef. results of disc. opers. and/or spec. items. Per share data adj. for stk. divs. as of ex-div. date. Bold denotes diluted EPS (FASB 128). E-Estimated. NA-Not Available. NM-Not Meaningful. NR-Not Ranked.

Office—Times Mirror Square, Los Angeles, CA 90053. **Tel**—(213) 237-3700. **Website**—http://www.tm-investor.com **Chrmn, Pres & CEO**—M. H. Willes. **EVP & CFO**—T. Unterman. **Secy**—S. C. Meier. **Treas**—S. J. Scoch. **Investor Contact**—Jean M. Jarvis (213-237-3955). **Dirs**—G. G. Babcock, D. R. Beall, J. E. Bryson, B. Chandler, C. W. Frye Jr., A. E. Osborne Jr., J. A. Payden, W. Stinehart Jr., M. H. Willes, W. B. Williamson, E. Zapanta. **Transfer Agent & Registrar**—Harris Trust Company of California, Chicago. **Incorporated**—in California in 1884; reincorporated in Delaware in 1986. **Empl**— 21,877. **S&P Analyst:** William H. Donald

12-SEP-98

Industry: Machinery (Diversified)

Summary: Timken is a leading manufacturer of highly engineered bearings and alloy steels for the auto, machinery, railroad, aerospace and agricultural industries.

S&P Opinion: Avoid (★★)	Recent Price • 17⅝ 52 Wk Range • 41⅞-17	Yield • 4.1% 12-Mo. P/E • 6.5

Quantitative Evaluations

Outlook
(1 Lowest—5 Highest)
• **3+**

Fair Value
• **19⅜**

Risk
• **Low**

Earn./Div. Rank
• **B**

Technical Eval.
• **Bearish** since 3/98

Rel. Strength Rank
(1 Lowest—99 Highest)
• **18**

Insider Activity
• **Favorable**

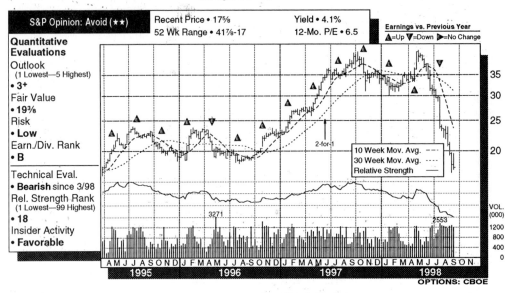

Earnings vs. Previous Year
▲=Up ▼=Down ▷=No Change

10 Week Mov. Avg. ---
30 Week Mov. Avg. .....
Relative Strength —

2-for-1

3271   2553

VOL. (000)
1200
800
400
0

A M J J A S O N D | J F M A M J J A S O N D | J F M A M J J A S O N D | J F M A M J J A S O N
1995   1996   1997   1998

OPTIONS: CBOE

Overview - 25-AUG-98

We look for 3% sales growth in 1998, reflecting gains in both segments. Bearings will benefit from new products, continued strong U. S. markets, and improvement in European demand. Steel sales will continue to rise, mostly reflecting strong industrial demand in the U. S. However, as a result of unplanned outages, the impact of the GM strike and plant start-up costs, operating income and EPS will decline from 1997's levels. Assuming more stable conditions in Asia, continued economic growth in the U. S. and Europe and the absence of outages, EPS should increase in 1999.

Valuation - 25-AUG-98

On August 20, 1998, we downgraded TKR to avoid from hold based on a less optimistic EPS outlook. As a result of unplanned outages at the Faircrest melt shop, the impact of the GM strike and start-up costs for a new mill, 1998's third quarter operating income will decline by some $15 million. While we expect sequential improvement in the fourth quarter, EPS will trail 1997. The disappointing EPS, combined with a general aversion to cyclical stocks, increases the near-term vulnerability of the stock. Based on our 1999 EPS, TKR appears reasonably valued at a P/E of 8.4. However, we would still rate the shares avoid intermediate term because we think the consensus estimate of $2.96 for 1999 is too optimistic. Consequently, there is ample room for EPS disappointment next year. Even if the 1999 consensus estimate declines toward the level of our estimate, we doubt the market will place a very high multiple on the stock given the length of the current cycle. On a much longer term basis we like TKR based on its strong market position in bearings, its generally conservative finances and its highly profitable steel business.

Key Stock Statistics

S&P EPS Est. 1998	2.35	Tang. Bk. Value/Share	14.66
P/E on S&P Est. 1998	7.5	Beta	1.13
S&P EPS Est. 1999	2.70	Shareholders	9,600
Dividend Rate/Share	0.72	Market cap. (B)	$ 1.1
Shs. outstg. (M)	62.3	Inst. holdings	67%
Avg. daily vol. (M)	0.314		

Value of $10,000 invested 5 years ago: $ 15,678

Fiscal Year Ending Dec. 31

	1998	1997	1996	1995	1994	1993
Revenues (Million $)						
1Q	707.4	640.6	596.0	568.9	466.5	422.0
2Q	701.8	676.0	601.5	585.8	494.1	441.2
3Q	—	629.9	581.4	519.5	466.3	405.5
4Q	—	671.1	615.8	556.4	503.5	439.5
Yr.	—	2,618	2,395	2,231	1,930	1,709
Earnings Per Share ($)						
1Q	**0.78**	**0.64**	0.54	0.55	0.13	0.05
2Q	**0.61**	**0.70**	0.55	0.50	0.34	0.15
3Q	**E0.41**	**0.59**	0.51	0.30	0.23	-0.01
4Q	**E0.55**	**0.74**	0.63	0.45	0.41	-0.48
Yr.	**E2.35**	**2.69**	2.21	1.80	1.10	-0.28

Next earnings report expected: late October

Dividend Data (Dividends have been paid since 1922.)

Amount ($)	Date Decl.	Ex-Div. Date	Stock of Record	Payment Date
0.165	Nov. 07	Nov. 19	Nov. 21	Dec. 08 '97
0.180	Feb. 06	Feb. 18	Feb. 20	Mar. 09 '98
0.180	Apr. 21	May. 13	May. 15	Jun. 01 '98
0.180	Aug. 07	Aug. 19	Aug. 21	Sep. 08 '98

Business Summary - 25-AUG-98

Timken Co. is the world's largest producer of tapered roller bearings, with about 130 tapered bearing types in some 26,000 combinations. Sales and operating profits in 1997 were:

	Sales	Profits
Bearings	66%	56%
Steel	34%	44%

International operations accounted for 21% of sales and 15% of operating income in 1997.

Tapered roller anti-friction bearings reduce friction where shafts, gears or wheels are used. They consist of four components: the cone or inner race, the cup or outer race, the tapered rollers that roll between the cup and the cone and the cage, which serves as a retainer and maintains proper spacing between the rollers. The four components are made and sold in a wide variety of configurations and sizes. TKR's bearings are used in general industry and a wide variety of products, including passenger cars, aircraft, trucks, railroad cars and locomotives, machine tools, rolling mills, and farm and construction equipment. Through MBP Corp., TKR makes super-precision ball and roller bearings for high-end applications for the aerospace, defense, com-

puter peripherals and medical instruments markets. Most bearings sales are made to original equipment manufacturers (OEMs). The company's main competitors are Ingersoll-Rand, SKF of Sweden, FAG of Germany, and Japanese companies Koyo, NSK and NTN.

In 1997, TKR acquired Gnutti Carlo, S.p.A., an bearings maker located near Brescia, Italy whose principal markets include the trucking, railroad and industrial sectors. Additionally, the company acquired the aerospace bearings operations of The Torrington Co. Ltd. located in Wolverhampton, England. In 1996, TKR expanded its bearings business with the acquisition of FLT Prema Milmet S. A. in Poland and the formation of a joint venture in China with Yantai Bearing Factory to serve the Chinese auto and agricultural markets in Shandong Province.

Steel products include carbon and alloy seamless tubing, carbon and alloy steel solid bars and various solid shapes, tool steels and other custom-made specialty steel products. A principal use for TKR's steel is in its bearings operations. Sales are also made to other anti-friction bearing companies and to the aircraft, automotive, forging, oil and gas well drilling, tooling and steel warehouse industries. Sales are made to OEMs and distributors. TKR's principal competitors in the steel bar business are Quanex Corp. and Republic Engineered Steel.

Per Share Data ($)

(Year Ended Dec. 31)	1997	1996	1995	1994	1993	1992	1991	1990	1989	1988
Tangible Bk. Val.	14.20	12.72	11.46	10.33	9.65	14.56	15.39	16.58	17.43	17.16
Cash Flow	4.79	4.23	3.78	3.04	1.64	1.97	1.24	2.62	2.29	2.74
Earnings	2.69	2.21	1.80	1.10	-0.28	0.08	-0.60	0.93	0.94	1.17
Dividends	0.66	0.60	0.56	0.50	0.50	0.50	0.50	0.49	0.46	0.35
Payout Ratio	25%	27%	31%	45%	NM	NM	NM	52%	51%	30%
Prices - High	41½	23⅞	24	19⅝	17½	15¼	15	18⅛	19⅝	20¾
- Low	22⅝	18¼	16¼	15⅝	13¼	11⅝	10⅜	10	12¾	13⅜
P/E Ratio - High	15	11	13	18	NM	NM	NM	20	21	18
- Low	8	8	9	14	NM	NM	NM	11	14	11

Income Statement Analysis (Million $)

	1997	1996	1995	1994	1993	1992	1991	1990	1989	1988
Revs.	2,618	2,395	2,231	1,930	1,709	1,642	1,647	1,701	1,533	1,554
Oper. Inc.	424	384	334	258	187	163	149	231	205	229
Depr.	134	126	123	119	118	114	109	101	80.0	89.0
Int. Exp.	21.4	17.9	20.0	28.0	31.3	30.9	28.7	26.3	17.2	20.9
Pretax Inc.	267	225	180	111	-21.0	13.0	-42.0	99	96.0	112
Eff. Tax Rate	36%	38%	38%	39%	NM	67%	NM	44%	43%	41%
Net Inc.	171	139	112	68.5	-17.7	4.5	-36.0	55.0	55.0	66.0

Balance Sheet & Other Fin. Data (Million $)

	1997	1996	1995	1994	1993	1992	1991	1990	1989	1988
Cash	9.8	5.3	7.3	12.1	5.3	7.9	2.0	23.0	42.0	35.0
Curr. Assets	855	794	710	657	586	556	562	658	608	619
Total Assets	2,327	2,071	1,926	1,859	1,790	1,738	1,759	1,815	1,566	1,593
Curr. Liab.	580	528	462	479	432	390	414	419	248	271
LT Debt	203	166	151	151	181	173	135	114	48.0	158
Common Eqty.	1,032	922	821	733	685	985	1,019	1,075	1,065	974
Total Cap.	1,235	1,088	972	884	866	1,247	1,256	1,301	1,220	1,213
Cap. Exp.	233	151	129	114	89.0	136	146	181	92.0	79.0
Cash Flow	306	265	236	188	101	119	73.0	157	135	155
Curr. Ratio	1.5	1.5	1.5	1.4	1.4	1.4	1.4	1.6	2.4	2.3
% LT Debt of Cap.	19.7	15.3	15.5	17.1	20.9	13.9	10.7	8.7	3.9	13.1
% Net Inc.of Revs.	6.5	5.8	5.0	35.0	NM	0.3	NM	3.2	3.6	4.2
% Ret. on Assets	7.8	7.0	5.9	3.7	NM	0.3	NM	3.3	3.4	4.3
% Ret. on Equity	17.5	16.0	14.5	9.6	NM	0.4	NM	5.3	5.2	6.9

Data as orig. reptd.; bef. results of disc. opers. and/or spec. items. Per share data adj. for stk. divs. as of ex-div. date. Bold denotes diluted EPS (FASB 128). E-Estimated. NA-Not Available. NM-Not Meaningful. NR-Not Ranked.

Registrars—First Chicago Trust Co. of New York, Jersey City, NJ; United National Bank & Trust Co., Canton, OH. **Office**—1835 Dueber Ave., S.W., Canton, OH 44706. **Tel**—(330) 438-3000. **Website**—http://www.timken.com **Chrmn, CEO & Pres**—W. R. Timken Jr. **SVP-Fin**—G. E. Little. **Investor Contact**—Richard J. Mertes. **Dirs**—R. Anderson, S. C. Gault, J. C. La Force, Jr., R. W. Mahony, J. A. Precourt, J. M. Timken Jr., W. J. Timken, W. R. Timken Jr., F. Toot, Jr., M. D. Walker, C. H. West, A. W. Whitehouse. **Transfer Agent & Registrar**—First Chicago Trust Co. of New York, Jersey City, NJ. **Incorporated**—in Ohio in 1904. **Empl**— 20,994. **S&P Analyst:** Leo Larkin

STANDARD &POOR'S
STOCK REPORTS

TJX Companies

2185G
NYSE Symbol **TJX**

In S&P 500

12-SEP-98

Industry:
Retail (Special-
ty-Apparel)

Summary: TJX primarily operates off-price apparel specialty stores in the U.S., Canada and the U.K.

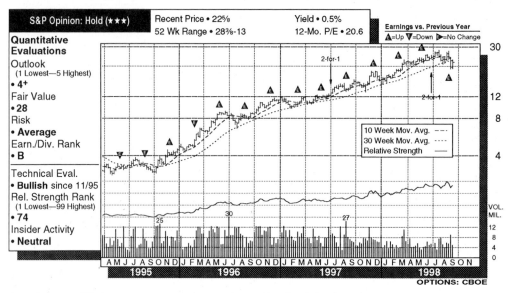

S&P Opinion: Hold (★★★)	Recent Price • 22⅝	Yield • 0.5%
	52 Wk Range • 28⅜-13	12-Mo. P/E • 20.6

Quantitative Evaluations

Outlook
(1 Lowest—5 Highest)
• **4+**

Fair Value
• **28**

Risk
• **Average**

Earn./Div. Rank
• **B**

Technical Eval.
• **Bullish** since 11/95

Rel. Strength Rank
(1 Lowest—99 Highest)
• **74**

Insider Activity
• **Neutral**

Earnings vs. Previous Year
▲=Up ▼=Down ▶=No Change

10 Week Mov. Avg. - - - -
30 Week Mov. Avg. ....
Relative Strength ———

OPTIONS: CBOE

Overview - 08-JUL-98

The November 1995 acquisition of Marshalls doubled the company's revenues. The increased size of the combined company, with over 1,040 T.J. Maxx and Marshalls units, has resulted in improved buying power. This also means a much reduced cost structure, allowing TJX to lower prices for customers, while boosting operating margins for the company. Same-store sales in FY 99 should increase about 6%. Operating profits should increase significantly, reflecting higher gross margins and lower expense ratios. Winners Apparel should continue to achieve strong sales gains and increases in operating profit. Interest expense will decline substantially as the company uses its ample cash flow to pay down debt. TJX plans to add about 12 to 15 stores in Canada. TJX's U.K. venture, T.K. Maxx, is expanding, and is a prelude to expanding the off-price retail concept overseas.

Valuation - 08-JUL-98

The shares have steadily increased in price for three years and are near their all-time high. We continue to recommend that they be held. TJX is deriving benefits from the acquisition of Marshalls and healthy sales gains. The company's strong and revitalized management team, larger store base (giving it buying clout), and ability to leverage costs from this larger base have put earnings on a growth track for the next few years. We see earnings advancing at a more modest pace in the future and at least 15% in each of the following two years. The company's strong cash flow generation and proceeds from the sale of Chadwick's have allowed TJX to pay down debt. Capital expenditures will be financed from internally generated funds and, with excess cash flow, a share buyback has been authorized.

Key Stock Statistics

S&P EPS Est. 1999	1.10	Tang. Bk. Value/Share	2.75
P/E on S&P Est. 1999	20.6	Beta	0.97
S&P EPS Est. 2000	1.25	Shareholders	22,700
Dividend Rate/Share	0.12	Market cap. (B)	$ 7.2
Shs. outstg. (M)	317.2	Inst. holdings	81%
Avg. daily vol. (M)	1.296		

Value of $10,000 invested 5 years ago: $ 35,400

Fiscal Year Ending Jan. 31

	1999	1998	1997	1996	1995	1994
Revenues (Million $)						
1Q	1,776	1,560	1,472	830.4	851.0	785.6
2Q	1,864	1,698	1,548	848.9	866.7	841.0
3Q	—	1,888	1,722	1,013	1,012	959.7
4Q	—	2,243	1,946	1,756	1,113	1,040
Yr.	—	7,389	6,689	4,448	3,843	3,627
Earnings Per Share ($)						
1Q	**0.26**	0.14	0.06	0.03	0.06	0.07
2Q	**0.25**	0.14	0.09	0.02	0.06	0.08
3Q	E0.37	0.30	0.23	0.11	0.10	0.15
4Q	E0.29	**0.29**	0.21	0.03	0.04	0.10
Yr.	E1.10	**0.87**	0.59	0.18	0.26	0.41

Next earnings report expected: mid November

Dividend Data (Dividends have been paid since 1980.)

Amount ($)	Date Decl.	Ex-Div. Date	Stock of Record	Payment Date
0.060	Apr. 08	May. 12	May. 14	Jun. 04 '98
2-for-1	Apr. 08	Jun. 26	Jun. 11	Jun. 25 '98
0.030	Jun. 02	Aug. 11	Aug. 13	Sep. 03 '98
0.030	Sep. 10	Nov. 09	Nov. 12	Dec. 03 '98

A Division of The McGraw-Hill Companies

Business Summary - 08-JUL-98

TJX Companies' November 1995 acquisition of the 496-store Marshalls chain created the largest off-price family apparel chain in the U.S. Although the company now operates 580 stores in 47 states under the T.J. Maxx banner and 461 Marshalls in 37 states and Puerto Rico, it has combined buying and merchandise functions, giving it the ability to purchase merchandise at favorable prices and to operate with a low cost structure. This is essential to TJX's strategy of providing brand-name merchandise at 20% to 60% below department and specialty store prices. The company has expanded to the U.K. and Ireland, operating 31 T. K. Maxx off-price stores.

The operations and strategies of T.J. Maxx and Marshalls are similar. The target customers fit a similar profile: women between 25 and 50 years of age and in the middle to upper-middle income range. Marshalls stores average 32,000 gross square feet, slightly larger than T.J. Maxx's average of 29,000 sq. ft. In recent years, T.J. Maxx has enlarged a number of its stores to 30,000 to 40,000 sq. ft., and plans to continue boosting the size of other successful stores. Although the merchandise is similar in both Marshalls and T.J. Maxx, Marshalls offers a full-line shoe department, a larger

men's department and costume jewelry, rather than fine jewelry.

The company acquires large quantities of merchandise at significant discounts from initial wholesale prices. Purchases can be closeouts of current season fashions and out-of-season purchases of basic seasonal items. Highly automated storage and distribution systems track, allocate and deliver an average of 10,000 items per week to each store.

TJX acquired Winners Apparel Ltd. in 1990. This provided an opportunity to introduce the off-price concept to the Canadian market. Since the acquisition, the company has increased the number of stores from five to 76. Home Goods is a chain of off-price home fashion stores, started by the company in 1992; it currently operates 23 stores.

The company sold its Chadwick's of Boston catalog to Brylane, Inc. in December 1996 and sold its Hit or Miss division to that unit's management in October 1995. In 1989, the company changed its name from Zayre Corp. following a major restructuring. TJX remains contingently liable for leases on most former Zayre stores still operated by Ames, a number of leases of BJ's Wholesale Club, Inc. and leases of the Hit or Miss division. It has available $17.8 million in reserves to meet these liabilities. TJX also has $99 million in capital loss carryforwards.

Per Share Data ($)

(Year Ended Jan. 31)	1998	1997	1996	1995	1994	1993	1992	1991	1990	1989
Tangible Bk. Val.	2.77	2.39	0.85	1.41	1.32	1.03	0.58	0.61	0.46	2.42
Cash Flow	1.20	0.94	0.48	0.52	0.63	0.55	0.45	0.42	0.43	0.40
Earnings	0.87	0.59	0.18	0.26	0.41	0.35	0.25	0.27	0.29	0.24
Dividends	0.14	0.07	0.14	0.14	0.09	0.12	0.14	0.11	0.10	0.10
Payout Ratio	15%	12%	76%	53%	23%	33%	57%	42%	34%	41%
Cal. Yrs.	1997	1996	1995	1994	1993	1992	1991	1990	1989	1988
Prices - High	19¼	12⅛	4¾	7⅜	8⅝	7¼	5⅛	4½	7½	6¾
- Low	9⅝	4¼	2¾	3⅝	6⅛	3⅞	2⁷⁄₁₆	2³⁄₁₆	3½	3⅝
P/E Ratio - High	22	20	26	29	91	21	20	17	26	28
- Low	11	7	15	14	65	11	10	8	12	15

Income Statement Analysis (Million $)

	1998	1997	1996	1995	1994	1993	1992	1991	1990	1989
Revs.	7,389	6,689	4,448	3,843	3,627	3,261	2,758	2,446	2,149	1,921
Oper. Inc.	652	530	274	244	297	262	205	197	190	163
Depr.	125	127	85.9	76.5	67.2	62.7	56.5	48.2	41.0	35.7
Int. Exp.	4.5	37.4	44.2	26.2	19.2	26.6	27.3	26.5	23.5	9.0
Pretax Inc.	522	366	109	142	211	173	121	124	134	116
Eff. Tax Rate	41%	42%	42%	42%	40%	40%	42%	40%	40%	40%
Net Inc.	307	214	63.6	83.0	127	104	70.0	74.0	76.0	55.0

Balance Sheet & Other Fin. Data (Million $)

	1998	1997	1996	1995	1994	1993	1992	1991	1990	1989
Cash	404	475	209	42.0	58.0	107	67.0	83.0	54.0	123
Curr. Assets	1,683	1,662	1,687	1,046	882	821	656	631	563	935
Total Assets	2,610	2,561	2,746	1,638	1,427	1,305	1,105	1,047	949	1,462
Curr. Liab.	1,218	1,182	1,278	758	592	576	485	401	369	453
LT Debt	221	244	691	239	211	180	307	309	296	312
Common Eqty.	1,091	977	482	498	482	398	261	271	228	543
Total Cap.	1,392	1,379	1,186	880	836	729	621	646	580	1,009
Cap. Exp.	192	119	112	128	126	112	90.0	79.0	67.0	75.0
Cash Flow	420	341	140	152	187	163	127	122	117	91.0
Curr. Ratio	1.4	1.4	1.3	1.4	1.5	1.4	1.4	1.6	1.5	2.1
% LT Debt of Cap.	15.8	17.7	58.2	27.2	25.2	24.7	49.5	47.7	51.0	30.9
% Net Inc.of Revs.	4.1	3.2	1.4	2.2	3.5	3.2	2.5	3.0	3.5	2.9
% Ret. on Assets	11.9	8.2	2.9	5.4	9.3	8.4	6.5	7.4	5.5	3.0
% Ret. on Equity	28.5	29.3	13.1	15.5	27.3	29.8	26.4	29.7	16.8	8.6

Data as orig. reptd.; bef. results of disc. opers. and/or spec. items. Per share data adj. for stk. divs. as of ex-div. date. Bold denotes diluted EPS (FASB 128). E-Estimated. NA-Not Available. NM-Not Meaningful. NR-Not Ranked.

Office—770 Cochituate Rd., Framingham, MA 01701. Tel—(508) 390-1000. Website—http://www.tjx.comChrmn—J. M. Nelson. Pres & CEO—B. Cammarata. EVP-Fin & CFO—D. G. Campbell. Treas—S. Wishner. Investor Relations—Sherry Lang. SVP & Secy—J. H. Meltzer. Dirs—B. Cammarata, P. B. Davis, D. F. Hightower, R. Lesser, A. F. Loewy, J. M. Nelson, J. F. O'Brien, R. F. Shapiro, W. B. Shire, F. H. Wiley. Transfer Agent & Registrar—Boston EquiServe, Canton, MA. Incorporated—in Delaware in 1962. Empl—59,000. S&P Analyst: Karen J. Sack, CFA

Torchmark Corp.

2242K

NYSE Symbol **TMK**

In S&P 500

12-SEP-98

Industry: Insurance (Life & Health)

Summary: This financial services company derives most of its earnings from life and health insurance operations. A mutual fund subsidiary is being spun off.

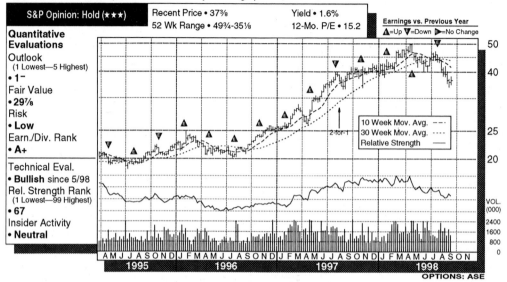

S&P Opinion: Hold (★★★)	Recent Price • 37⅜	Yield • 1.6%
	52 Wk Range • 49¾-35⅛	12-Mo. P/E • 15.2

Earnings vs. Previous Year
▲=Up ▼=Down ▶=No Change

Quantitative Evaluations

Outlook
(1 Lowest—5 Highest)
• **1⁻**

Fair Value
• **29⅞**

Risk
• **Low**

Earn./Div. Rank
• **A+**

Technical Eval.
• **Bullish** since 5/98

Rel. Strength Rank
(1 Lowest—99 Highest)
• **67**

Insider Activity
• **Neutral**

10 Week Mov. Avg. - - - -
30 Week Mov. Avg. ······
Relative Strength ——

OPTIONS: ASE

Overview - 27-JUL-98

Earnings growth in coming periods is predicated on TMK's ability to offset margin contraction in the health area with growth in the core life insurance line. Earnings estimates exclude gains from the anticipated sale of the Waddell & Reed (W&R) mutual fund unit. In March 1998, W&R completed an initial public offering of 36% of its common stock. TMK owns the remaining 64% of the shares, and plans to distribute them to its shareholders in a tax-free spinoff in late 1998. The sale of W&R is part of TMK's long-term stategy to enhance shareholder value. A decision reached in 1996 not to divide into separate, publicly traded companies, and to divest energy operations, was also part of that plan. Life insurance margins should be aided by steps taken to enhance agent productivity and increase persistency rates. (Improved policy persistency rates lower policy acquisition costs.) Health insurance margins will remain under pressure from a declining premium base and from continuing litigation expense.

Valuation - 27-JUL-98

After bottoming in mid-1996, when TMK said that it no longer planned to divide into separate publicly traded companies, the shares have climbed steadily upward, thanks to favorable market conditions for most financial stocks, and to positive investor reaction to several steps recently taken. The ascent was halted briefly in mid-1998, when 38%-owned Vesta Insurance Group announced certain accounting irregularities. Having recently recovered, the shares were trading at the upper end of their historical valuation range, and are fairly valued for the near term. Earnings estimates are based on operating profits (which exclude net realized investment gains or losses); historical EPS numbers are presented as net income (including realized investment gains or losses).

Key Stock Statistics

S&P EPS Est. 1998	2.80	Tang. Bk. Value/Share	14.04
P/E on S&P Est. 1998	13.4	Beta	1.17
S&P EPS Est. 1999	3.15	Shareholders	7,300
Dividend Rate/Share	0.60	Market cap. (B)	$ 5.3
Shs. outstg. (M)	140.3	Inst. holdings	58%
Avg. daily vol. (M)	0.322		

Value of $10,000 invested 5 years ago: $ 14,903

Fiscal Year Ending Dec. 31

	1998	1997	1996	1995	1994	1993
Revenues (Million $)						
1Q	601.5	557.1	550.8	517.7	498.7	525.0
2Q	622.0	554.2	552.0	515.6	464.4	543.3
3Q	—	584.1	550.4	501.4	463.3	531.2
4Q	—	589.9	552.6	532.8	496.2	577.1
Yr.	—	2,282	2,206	2,067	1,923	2,177
Earnings Per Share ($)						
1Q	**0.66**	**0.55**	0.53	0.48	0.52	0.34
2Q	**0.48**	**0.53**	0.55	0.48	0.45	0.53
3Q	—	**0.66**	0.56	0.41	0.45	0.43
4Q	—	**0.66**	0.58	0.53	0.45	0.58
Yr.	**E2.80**	**2.39**	2.23	1.90	1.86	1.88

Next earnings report expected: mid October

Dividend Data (Dividends have been paid since 1933.)

Amount ($)	Date Decl.	Ex-Div. Date	Stock of Record	Payment Date
0.150	Jul. 25	Oct. 01	Oct. 03	Oct. 31 '97
0.150	Oct. 23	Dec. 30	Jan. 02	Jan. 31 '98
0.150	Mar. 23	Apr. 07	Apr. 10	May. 01 '98
0.150	Apr. 29	Jul. 08	Jul. 10	Jul. 31 '98

A Division of The McGraw-Hill Companies

STANDARD
&POOR'S
STOCK REPORTS

Torchmark Corporation

2242K

12-SEP-98

Business Summary - 27-JUL-98

As part of a long term plan to enhance shareholder value and narrow its scope of focus, in early 1998, Torchmark sold 36% of Waddell & Reed (W&R), its mutual fund/asset management unit, in an initial public offering. TMK shareholders are set to receive the remaining 64% of W&R in a tax-free spinoff set for late 1998. In late 1996, TMK decided not to divide into separate publicly traded companies and instead sold Torch Energy Advisors, its energy unit. As a result, TMK's core lines of business consist primarily of individual of life and health insurance and, to a lesser degree, annuities.

TMK's principal operating subsidiaries are Liberty National Life Insurance Co., Globe Life and Accident Insurance Co., United American Insurance Co., Family Service Life Insurance Co., United Investors Life Insurance Co. and Waddell & Reed, Inc. Revenue sources (from continuing operations) in recent years were:

	1997	1996
Life insurance premiums	40%	39%
Health insurance & other premiums	34%	34%
Financial services	9%	8%
Net investment income & investment gains/losses	17%	19%

TMK's subsidiaries offer a full line of nonparticipating ordinary individual life products and health insurance (primarily Medicare supplemental coverage). Fixed and variable annuities are also offered. The subsidiaries are licensed to sell insurance in all 50 states, the District of Columbia, Puerto Rico, Guam, the Virgin Islands, New Zealand, and Canada. Distribution is through home service agents, independent and exclusive agents and direct solicitation.

Annualized life and health insurance premiums in force at year-end 1997 equaled $1.8 billion, of which traditional life accounted for 31%, Medicare supplemental 31%, term life 15%, interest-sensitive life 9%, cancer 8%, and other life and health policies 7%. Annuity deposits at year-end 1997 were $2.8 billion, of which 36% were fixed and 64% variable.

Waddell & Reed, Inc., 64%-owned as of March 6, 1998, markets and manages mutual funds under the following names: United Group of Mutual Funds (17 funds), Waddell & Reed Fund (eight funds), and TMK/United Fund (11 funds). At December 31, 1997, assets under management totaled $23.4 billion, of which United Funds accounted for 76%, various institutional and private accounts 12%, TMK/United Funds 8%, and Waddell & Reed funds 4%. On March 5, 1998, W&R sold 23.9 million class A shares in an initial public offering that netted $516 million.

Per Share Data ($)

(Year Ended Dec. 31)	1997	1996	1995	1994	1993	1992	1991	1990	1989	1988
Tangible Bk. Val.	10.05	7.81	7.21	4.70	8.38	7.24	6.74	5.76	5.21	4.58
Oper. Earnings	NA	2.21	1.97	1.91	1.84	1.79	1.55	1.41	1.29	1.06
Earnings	2.56	2.23	1.90	1.86	1.88	1.79	1.56	1.43	1.29	1.03
Dividends	0.59	0.58	0.56	0.56	0.54	0.53	0.50	0.47	0.42	0.37
Payout Ratio	23%	26%	30%	30%	29%	30%	32%	33%	32%	35%
Prices - High	42¾	26⅛	22⅝	24¾	32⅜	29¼	19¾	19⅛	19⅝	11¼
- Low	25	20⅛	17⅛	16¼	20⅝	18	15½	12¾	10	8
P/E Ratio - High	17	12	12	13	17	16	13	13	15	10
- Low	10	9	9	9	11	10	10	9	8	7

Income Statement Analysis (Million $)

	1997	1996	1995	1994	1993	1992	1991	1990	1989	1988
Life Ins. In Force	91,870	86,948	80,391	74,835	61,367	58,306	56,111	54,774	53,743	52,901
Prem. Inc.: Life	910	855	772	602	556	544	524	488	432	NA
Prem. Inc.: A & H	NA	733	751	768	800	798	770	738	683	NA
Prem. Inc.: Other	NA	23.0	23.0	19.0	137	112	72.0	65.0	70.0	NA
Net Invest. Inc.	434	405	382	330	372	383	364	348	308	266
Total Revs.	1,849	2,206	2,067	1,923	2,177	2,046	1,932	1,796	1,634	1,670
Pretax Inc.	516	495	428	387	441	418	381	353	324	282
Net Oper. Inc.	336	316	281	275	272	266	243	226	211	185
Net Inc.	338	319	272	269	280	265	246	229	211	180

Balance Sheet & Other Fin. Data (Million $)

	1997	1996	1995	1994	1993	1992	1991	1990	1989	1988
Cash & Equiv.	126	110	95.2	70.0	110	68.9	63.9	56.1	53.0	54.6
Premiums Due	127	112	122	224	153	131	95.0	81.0	108	77.0
Invest. Assets: Bonds	5,860	5,328	5,210	4,505	4,762	4,193	3,889	3,597	3,091	2,771
Invest. Assets: Stocks	12.0	8.9	10.6	32.0	41.0	54.0	38.0	40.0	27.0	22.0
Invest. Assets: Loans	301	271	246	202	154	152	151	146	190	204
Invest. Assets: Total	6,538	5,940	5,779	5,236	5,441	4,926	4,542	4,100	3,507	3,712
Deferred Policy Costs	1,371	1,254	1,121	1,017	902	904	1,028	1,024	942	772
Total Assets	10,967	9,801	9,364	8,404	7,646	6,770	6,161	5,536	4,921	4,428
Debt	564	792	792	793	792	498	667	529	498	497
Common Eqty.	1,933	1,629	1,589	1,243	1,416	1,115	1,078	943	894	807
% Return On Revs.	18.3	14.4	13.2	14.0	12.8	13.0	12.8	12.8	12.9	11.1
% Ret. on Assets	3.3	3.3	3.1	3.4	3.9	4.1	4.2	4.4	4.5	4.3
% Ret. on Equity	19.0	19.8	19.2	20.2	21.8	23.9	23.8	24.2	24.1	20.5
% Invest. Yield	7.0	6.9	7.1	7.1	7.2	8.1	8.4	9.2	9.2	8.6

Data as orig. reptd.; bef. results of disc. opers. and/or spec. items. Per share data adj. for stk. divs. as of ex-div. date. Bold denotes diluted EPS (FASB 128). E-Estimated. NA-Not Available. NM-Not Meaningful. NR-Not Ranked.

Office—2001 Third Avenue South, Birmingham, AL 35233. **Tel**—(205) 325-4200. **Chrmn & CEO**—R. K. Richey. **COO**—C. B. Hudson. **Investor Contact**—Joyce Lane. **Dirs**—D. L. Boren, J. M. Farley, L. T. Hagopian, C. B. Hudson, J. L. Lanier Jr., H. T. McCormick, G. J. Records, R. K. Richey. **Transfer Agent & Registrar**—First Chicago Trust Co. of New York, Jersey City, NJ.**Incorporated**—in Alabama in 1929; reincorporated in Delaware in 1979. **Empl**— 4,781. **S&P Analyst:** Catherine A. Seifert

STANDARD &POOR'S
STOCK REPORTS

Toys "R" Us

2243J

NYSE Symbol **TOY**

In S&P 500

12-SEP-98

Industry: Retail (Specialty)

Summary: This company is the world's largest toy retailer, and also operates a children's retail clothing business. In early 1997, it acquired retailer Baby Superstores, Inc.

S&P Opinion: Hold (★★★)		
Recent Price • 17⅞	Yield • Nil	
52 Wk Range • 36½-17½	12-Mo. P/E • 11.2	

Quantitative Evaluations

Outlook (1 Lowest—5 Highest)
• **4+**

Fair Value
• **25¼**

Risk
• **Average**

Earn./Div. Rank
• **B+**

Technical Eval.
• **Neutral** since 6/98

Rel. Strength Rank (1 Lowest—99 Highest)
• **40**

Insider Activity
• **Neutral**

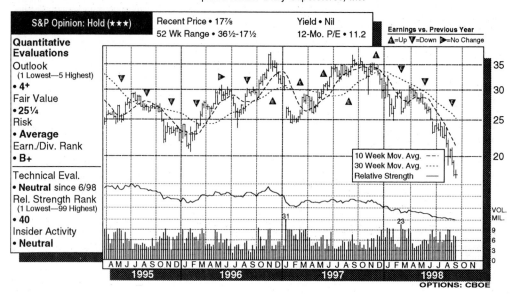

Earnings vs. Previous Year
▲=Up ▼=Down ▶=No Change

10 Week Mov. Avg. — – –
30 Week Mov. Avg. · · · ·
Relative Strength ——

OPTIONS: CBOE

Overview - 24-AUG-98

This specialty retailer operates or franchises more than 1,400 stores, with an emphasis on products for children. The stores include the flagship Toys "R" Us chain, the Kids "R" Us clothing stores, and the newer Babies "R" Us chain. We expect a nine-store test of a new toy store format to start soon, which would be followed by retrofits of at least 200 units in the fiscal year ending January 2000. The new format is likely to include various changes, including an expanded electronics department, the addition of children's apparel, and a greater emphasis on lower-priced, close-out or promotional items. However, sales results from earlier redesign efforts were disappointing. Also, the company has been reducing comparable-store inventory at U.S. toy stores; in FY 99's first half, the value of such inventory dropped by about $220 million from the year-earlier level. This could help boost future asset productivity.

Valuation - 24-AUG-98

We view the stock's appeal as largely coming from the extent of its below-market P/E multiple. However, we don't expect much near-term enthusiasm for the shares. We have reduced our expectations for the pace of sales and earnings gains from a new U.S. toy store format, changes in toy store product mix, and better inventory turnover. We recently lowered our earnings per share estimate for the fiscal year ending January 2000 to $1.85, from $2.00. Also, we have become more cautious about the 1998 holiday season, and trimmed our FY 99 EPS earnings estimate to $1.65, from $1.70. In the current fiscal year, through August 14, the company repurchased nearly 19 million of its common shares, at a cost of about $480 million. Meanwhile, we do not expect anti-trust charges related to the company's toy business to be a major negative factor.

Key Stock Statistics

S&P EPS Est. 1999	1.65	Tang. Bk. Value/Share	14.48
P/E on S&P Est. 1999	10.8	Beta	0.66
S&P EPS Est. 2000	1.85	Shareholders	32,300
Dividend Rate/Share	Nil	Market cap. (B)	$ 4.9
Shs. outstg. (M)	275.8	Inst. holdings	84%
Avg. daily vol. (M)	1.542		

Value of $10,000 invested 5 years ago: $ 4,454

Fiscal Year Ending Jan. 31

	1999	1998	1997	1996	1995	1994
Revenues (Million $)						
1Q	2,043	1,924	1,646	1,493	1,462	1,286
2Q	2,020	1,989	1,736	1,614	1,452	1,317
3Q	—	2,142	1,883	1,715	1,631	1,449
4Q	—	4,983	4,668	4,605	4,200	3,893
Yr.	—	11,038	9,932	9,427	8,746	7,946
Earnings Per Share ($)						
1Q	**0.07**	**0.10**	0.07	0.07	0.13	0.12
2Q	**0.05**	**0.13**	-0.03	0.06	0.13	0.12
3Q	**E0.10**	**0.16**	0.12	0.08	0.17	0.13
4Q	**E1.42**	**1.32**	1.38	0.34	1.46	1.27
Yr.	**E1.65**	**1.70**	1.54	0.53	1.85	1.63

Next earnings report expected: mid November

Dividend Data

No cash dividends have every been paid.

Business Summary - 24-AUG-98

This company thinks young. Toys "R" Us operates or franchises more than 1,400 stores that focus on providing toys, clothing or other items for children. The company's presence in the market for infant and toddler products was significantly expanded in February 1997, when it acquired retailer Baby Superstore, Inc.

The company's merchandising philosophy includes developing strong consumer recognition and acceptance of its name through the use of mass media advertising that promotes its selection and prices. TOY uses a computer inventory system that allows management to constantly monitor current activity and inventory. The company has been reducing comparable-unit inventory at U.S. toy stores; in FY 99's first half, the value of such inventory dropped by about $220 million from the year-earlier level. This could help boost future asset productivity. Retailers that compete with TOY include Wal-Mart, Kmart, Target and Consolidated Stores' K*B toy business.

As of August 1998, the flagship Toys "R" Us chain included 697 company-operated stores in the U.S. In October 1998, TOY is expected to begin testing a new toy store format in nine existing stores. This would be followed by retrofits of at least 200 units in the year

ending January 2000. Also, as of August 1998, including franchises, the company had 446 toy stores outside the U.S.

As of August 1998, TOY's Kids "R" Us clothing store chain included 214 units. This business features brand name and private label items. Also, including the acquisition of Baby Superstore, which added 77 units, the Babies "R" Us business had 101 stores in August 1998. To acquire Baby Superstore, TOY issued about 13 million common shares. Also, TOY was operating two KidsWorld superstores, which combine all three of the "R" Us concepts under one roof.

In January 1998, TOY said directors had authorized an additional $1 billion repurchase of common stock over the next several years. TOY still had about $94 million remaining under a $1 billion buyback plan announced in 1994. At January 31, 1998, TOY had cash and equivalents totaling $214 million, and short-term borrowings of $134 million. TOY's FY 97 (Jan.) EPS included a charge of $0.14 related to an unfavorable arbitration award, which was being contested by TOY. In FY 96, TOY had a restructuring charge of $0.98 a share. Also, in February 1998, according to a Reuters news report, TOY was appealing a Federal Trade Commission administrative judge ruling related to alleged unacceptable anti-competitive behavior by the company.

Per Share Data ($)

(Year Ended Jan. 31)	1998	1997	1996	1995	1994	1993	1992	1991	1990	1989
Tangible Bk. Val.	14.44	13.29	12.57	12.26	10.87	9.86	8.39	7.11	5.95	4.94
Cash Flow	2.58	2.28	1.16	2.41	2.08	1.87	1.49	1.37	1.32	1.09
Earnings	1.70	1.54	0.53	1.85	1.63	1.47	1.15	1.11	1.09	0.91
Dividends	Nil	Nil	Nil	Nil	Nil	Nil	Nil	Nil	Nil	Nil
Payout Ratio	Nil	Nil	Nil	Nil	Nil	Nil	Nil	Nil	Nil	Nil
Cal. Yrs.	1997	1996	1995	1994	1993	1992	1991	1990	1989	1988
Prices - High	37¹/₈	37⁵/₈	30⁷/₈	40⁷/₈	42⁷/₈	41	36	35	26³/₄	18
- Low	24³/₈	20¹/₂	21⁵/₈	29⁵/₈	32³/₈	30³/₈	22	19⁷/₈	16	13³/₈
P/E Ratio - High	22	24	58	22	26	28	31	32	25	20
- Low	14	13	41	16	20	21	19	18	15	15

Income Statement Analysis (Million $)

	1998	1997	1996	1995	1994	1993	1992	1991	1990	1989
Revs.	11,038	9,932	9,427	8,746	7,924	7,169	6,124	5,510	4,788	4,000
Oper. Inc.	1,097	1,020	940	1,073	954	858	684	664	612	497
Depr.	253	206	192	161	133	119	101	79.0	66.0	55.0
Int. Exp.	85.0	102	109	90.9	79.6	77.5	70.1	82.7	52.8	32.9
Pretax Inc.	772	673	265	844	773	689	539	523	514	429
Eff. Tax Rate	37%	37%	44%	37%	38%	37%	37%	38%	38%	38%
Net Inc.	490	427	148	532	483	438	340	326	321	268

Balance Sheet & Other Fin. Data (Million $)

	1998	1997	1996	1995	1994	1993	1992	1991	1990	1989
Cash	214	761	203	370	792	764	445	35.0	41.0	123
Curr. Assets	2,904	3,160	2,419	2,531	2,708	2,385	1,927	1,404	1,338	1,133
Total Assets	7,963	8,023	6,738	6,571	6,150	5,323	4,548	3,582	3,075	2,555
Curr. Liab.	2,325	2,541	2,093	2,137	2,075	1,588	1,594	1,228	1,100	878
LT Debt	851	409	827	785	724	671	391	195	173	174
Common Eqty.	4,428	4,191	3,432	3,429	3,148	2,889	2,426	2,046	1,705	1,424
Total Cap.	5,498	5,322	4,487	4,434	4,075	3,735	2,954	2,355	1,975	1,677
Cap. Exp.	494	415	468	586	557	422	549	486	374	339
Cash Flow	743	633	340	693	616	557	440	405	387	323
Curr. Ratio	1.3	1.2	1.2	1.2	1.3	1.5	1.2	1.1	1.2	1.3
% LT Debt of Cap.	15.4	17.1	18.4	17.7	17.8	18.0	13.2	8.3	8.8	10.4
% Net Inc.of Revs.	4.4	4.3	1.6	6.1	6.1	6.1	5.5	5.9	6.7	6.7
% Ret. on Assets	6.1	5.8	2.2	8.5	8.5	8.8	8.3	9.8	11.4	11.7
% Ret. on Equity	11.4	11.2	4.3	16.4	16.1	16.4	15.1	17.3	20.6	20.9

Data as orig. reptd.; bef. results of disc. opers. and/or spec. items. Per share data adj. for stk. divs. as of ex-div. date. Bold denotes diluted EPS (FASB 128). E-Estimated. NA-Not Available. NM-Not Meaningful. NR-Not Ranked.

Office—461 From Rd., Paramus, NJ 07652. Tel—(201) 262-7800. Website—http://www.toysrus.com Chrmn—M. Goldstein. CEO—R. C. Nakasone. Pres & COO—B. W. Krysiak. EVP, CFO & Investor Contact—Louis Lipschitz (201-368-5548). Dirs—R. A. Bernhard, R. Costin, M. Goldstein, C. Hill, S. S. Kenny, B. W. Krysiak, C. Lazarus, N. S. Matthews, H. W. Moore, R.C. Nakasone, A. B. Newman. Transfer Agent & Registrar—American Stock Transfer & Trust Co., NYC. Incorporated—in Delaware in 1928. Empl— 68,000. S&P Analyst: Tom Graves, CFA

STANDARD &POOR'S
STOCK REPORTS

Transamerica Corp.

2246

NYSE Symbol **TA**

In S&P 500

12-SEP-98

Industry:
Insurance (Life & Health)

Summary: This diversified financial services organization is involved primarily in life insurance and finance-related operations. It is also the second largest lessor of containers.

S&P Opinion: Hold (★★★)	Recent Price • 106¼	Yield • 1.9%
	52 Wk Range • 126½-96⅜	12-Mo. P/E • 11.0

Quantitative Evaluations

Outlook
(1 Lowest—5 Highest)
• **3+**

Fair Value
• **107**

Risk
• **Low**

Earn./Div. Rank
• **B+**

Technical Eval.
• **Bullish** since 11/96

Rel. Strength Rank
(1 Lowest—99 Highest)
• **75**

Insider Activity
• **NA**

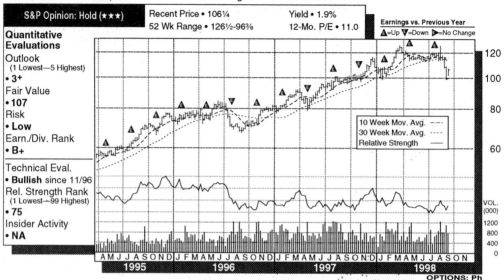

Earnings vs. Previous Year
▲=Up ▼=Down ▶=No Change

10 Week Mov. Avg. ----
30 Week Mov. Avg. ·····
Relative Strength ——

VOL. (000)

OPTIONS: Ph

Overview - 13-AUG-98

Operating earnings in 1998 will likely be flat to slightly lower, largely due to weakness in the leasing and life sectors. Partly offsetting this is the positive impact on year-to-year comparisons from the absence of a $20.1 million charge taken in early 1997 to settle a class action lawsuit in the life unit. Like most life insurers, TA is seeing a shift in its product mix away from traditional life insurance products (which are slower growing but have wider margins) and to fee based annuity and asset management products (which are growing faster but have narrower margins). However, we remain concerned about TA's ability to successfully roll out its variable annuity line and keep its cost structure competitive. The relatively lower interest rate environment that has existed over the last few years triggered higher refinancing activity, which helped real estate profits. This trend will likely continue into 1998, though year-to-year comparisons could be difficult. Margins in the leasing segment will likely come under continued pressure in 1998, largely due to worldwide overcapacity. Commercial lending profit growth will be aided by continued receivables growth as TA builds critical mass in three core areas: distribution finance, business credit and insurance premium finance. The sale of the consumer finance unit, for $1.1 billion, is a positive move, since proceeds were earmarked to pay down debt and buy back shares. Please note, EPS estimates exclude realized investment gains/losses; actual EPS are based on net income.

Valuation - 13-AUG-98

After a mixed performance during much of 1998, the shares strengthened in mid-August after published reports speculated TA might restructure. Such a move would strengthen the stock. But, if nothing materializes, the shares will be average performers.

Key Stock Statistics

S&P EPS Est. 1998	7.20	Tang. Bk. Value/Share	74.91
P/E on S&P Est. 1998	14.8	Beta	0.84
S&P EPS Est. 1999	8.10	Shareholders	45,900
Dividend Rate/Share	2.00	Market cap. (B)	$ 6.6
Shs. outstg. (M)	62.6	Inst. holdings	56%
Avg. daily vol. (M)	0.185		

Value of $10,000 invested 5 years ago: $ 25,943

Fiscal Year Ending Dec. 31

	1998	1997	1996	1995	1994	1993
Revenues (Million $)						
1Q	1,559	1,539	1,494	1,421	1,235	1,150
2Q	1,543	2,100	1,515	1,581	1,363	1,229
3Q	—	1,561	1,592	1,581	1,371	1,210
4Q	—	1,500	1,627	1,518	1,385	1,245
Yr.	—	5,727	6,228	6,101	5,355	4,833
Earnings Per Share ($)						
1Q	**2.34**	1.10	1.63	1.33	1.29	1.08
2Q	**2.33**	1.65	1.52	1.63	1.34	1.49
3Q	—	2.28	1.67	2.08	1.40	1.70
4Q	—	2.90	1.77	1.54	1.43	1.17
Yr.	—	7.87	7.10	6.58	5.46	5.44

Next earnings report expected: mid October

Dividend Data (Dividends have been paid since 1934.)

Amount ($)	Date Decl.	Ex-Div. Date	Stock of Record	Payment Date
0.500	Sep. 18	Oct. 02	Oct. 06	Oct. 31 '97
0.500	Dec. 18	Dec. 29	Dec. 31	Jan. 30 '98
0.500	Mar. 19	Apr. 02	Apr. 06	Apr. 30 '98
0.500	Jun. 18	Jun. 30	Jul. 03	Jul. 31 '98

A Division of The McGraw-Hill Companies

Business Summary - 13-AUG-98

This San Francisco-based financial services concern- noted for its pyramid shaped headquarters office- is carving out selective niches for itself in the life insurance, real estate services, leasing and finance marketplaces. In mid-October 1997, TA expanded its presence in the commercial finance arena through its acquisition of about $1.23 billion in net receivables and other assets from Whirlpool Financial Corp. (a unit of Whirlpool Corp.), for about $1.35 billion. During the second quarter of 1997, TA sold its branch-based consumer finance subsidiary to Household International (NYSE: HI) for $1.1 billion, or about 2.3X that unit's book value. Proceeds from the sale were earmarked to repay debt and repurchase common stock.

The Transamerica Life Companies market an array of life insurance (including term and universal), annuity (such as fixed, variable and structured settlement), group pension and life/health reinsurance products. Premiums and equivalents totaled $1.8 billion in 1997, of which interest-sensitive policy charges contributed 30%, reinsurance 34%, traditional life insurance 20%, Canadian lines 6%, annuities 4%, and other 6%.

Contributions to operating income from continuing operations (in millions) in recent years were:

	1997	1996
Life insurance	$306.4	$325.4
Commercial finance	81.0	58.2
Real estate services	73.9	44.3
Leasing	64.3	78.7

Transamerica Commercial Finance provides inventory, asset-based and insurance premium financing and is one of the leading commercial finance firms in North America, with $5.0 billion in receivables outstanding (owned and serviced) at year-end 1997. Real estate services include real estate tax, information and other services. The leasing unit leases and manages intermodal transportation equipment, including refrigerator and tank containers.

In 1997, TA sold its consumer finance unit, Transamerica Financial Services ($4.2 billion of net finance receivables outstanding at year end 1996, of which more than 88% were secured by residential real estate).

Per Share Data ($)

(Year Ended Dec. 31)	1997	1996	1995	1994	1993	1992	1991	1990	1989	1988
Tangible Bk. Val.	70.87	52.09	52.69	28.48	31.98	29.86	29.04	28.83	28.11	27.71
Oper. Earnings	7.22	6.21	6.08	5.25	5.12	4.05	1.10	3.11	3.65	4.27
Earnings	7.87	6.59	6.58	5.46	5.44	4.11	1.14	3.29	4.18	4.42
Dividends	2.00	2.00	2.00	2.00	2.00	2.00	1.98	1.94	1.90	1.86
Payout Ratio	25%	30%	30%	37%	37%	49%	174%	59%	45%	42%
Prices - High	116½	84½	77½	57⅝	62⅜	50½	40	44⅝	48	36¾
- Low	77⅛	67	49½	46¼	45⅝	37⅛	29⅝	23¼	32¾	29¾
P/E Ratio - High	15	13	12	11	11	12	35	14	11	9
- Low	10	10	8	8	8	9	26	7	8	7

Income Statement Analysis (Million $)

	1997	1996	1995	1994	1993	1992	1991	1990	1989	1988
Life Ins. In Force	241,380	220,163	206,723	NA	NA	306,800	288,852	272,657	251,700	23,600
Prem. Inc.: Life	1,818	1,848	1,863	1,495	1,256	1,590	1,440	1,362	1,568	3,104
Prem. Inc.: A & H	Nil	Nil	Nil	Nil	Nil	Nil	Nil	Nil	Nil	Nil
Prem. Inc.: Other	Nil	Nil	Nil	Nil	19.7	29.0	1,920	1,895	1,716	1,661
Net Invest. Inc.	2,191	2,102	1,990	1,783	1,750	1,600	1,777	1,652	1,430	1,216
Total Revs.	5,727	6,228	6,101	5,355	4,833	4,988	6,815	6,703	6,834	7,879
Pretax Inc.	662	585	705	690	601	560	143	369	454	380
Net Oper. Inc.	NA	431	436	413	425	338	96.0	253	292	336
Net Inc.	532	456	471	428	451	343	99	266	332	346

Balance Sheet & Other Fin. Data (Million $)

	1997	1996	1995	1994	1993	1992	1991	1990	1989	1988
Cash & Equiv.	133	472	68.0	64.0	93.0	22.0	43.0	40.0	74.0	235
Premiums Due	3,903	2,383	3,130	2,610	2,015	885	1,621	1,535	1,444	1,222
Invest. Assets: Bonds	29,211	26,986	26,076	21,037	19,616	18,546	18,546	1,703	14,884	12,292
Invest. Assets: Stocks	1,608	1,046	703	427	466	342	615	401	397	294
Invest. Assets: Loans	1,201	1,188	1,021	868	890	948	1,020	1,074	1,163	1,409
Invest. Assets: Total	32,356	29,385	28,027	22,496	20,972	18,294	20,181	18,548	16,444	13,995
Deferred Policy Costs	2,103	2,138	1,974	2,481	1,929	1,706	1,754	1,724	1,590	1,255
Total Assets	51,173	49,875	47,945	40,394	36,051	32,298	33,682	31,784	29,840	26,759
Debt	5,236	9,087	9,342	7,489	5,681	6,511	7,000	6,641	6,960	5,842
Common Eqty.	4,881	3,826	3,985	2,602	2,939	2,875	2,801	2,792	2,704	2,604
% Return On Revs.	9.3	7.3	7.7	8.0	9.3	6.9	1.5	4.0	4.9	4.3
% Ret. on Assets	1.1	0.9	1.1	1.1	1.3	1.1	0.3	0.9	1.2	1.4
% Ret. on Equity	11.8	11.2	14.1	15.0	14.7	11.3	3.1	9.1	12.2	13.3
% Invest. Yield	7.1	7.3	7.9	8.2	8.9	9.1	9.2	9.4	9.4	9.4

Data as orig. reptd.; bef. results of disc. opers. and/or spec. items. Per share data adj. for stk. divs. as of ex-div. date. Bold denotes diluted EPS (FASB 128). E-Estimated. NA-Not Available. NM-Not Meaningful. NR-Not Ranked.

Office—600 Montgomery St., San Francisco, CA 94111. **Tel**—(415) 983-4000.**Website**—http://www.transamerica.com **Chrmn & CEO**—F. C. Herringer.**EVP-CFO**—E. H. Grubb.**SVP & Secy**—S. H. Buccieri.**VP & Investor Contact**—James F. McArdle.**Dirs**—S. L. Ginn, F. C. Herringer, R. W. Matschullat, G. E. Moore, T. Rembe, C. Rice, C. R. Schwab, F. N. Shumway, P. V. Ueberroth. **Transfer Agent & Registrar**—First Chicago Trust Co. of New York, Jersey City, NJ. **Incorporated**—in Delaware in 1928. **Empl**— 8,700. **S&P Analyst:** Catherine A. Seifert

12-SEP-98   **Industry:** Insurance (Multi-Line)   **Summary:** TRV offers investment services through Salomon Smith Barney Inc., consumer finance services, and insurance through the Travelers. A merger with Citicorp is pending.

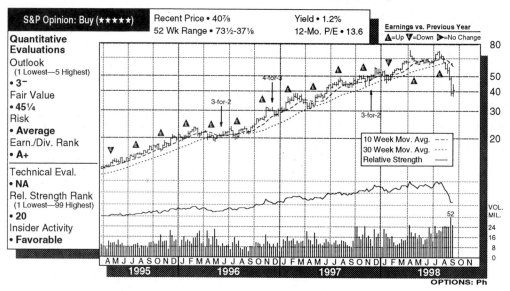

S&P Opinion: Buy (★★★★)

Recent Price • 40⅞	Yield • 1.2%
52 Wk Range • 73½-37⅛	12-Mo. P/E • 13.6

Quantitative Evaluations

Outlook
(1 Lowest—5 Highest)
• **3⁻**

Fair Value
• **45¼**

Risk
• **Average**

Earn./Div. Rank
• **A+**

Technical Eval.
• **NA**

Rel. Strength Rank
(1 Lowest—99 Highest)
• **20**

Insider Activity
• **Favorable**

Earnings vs. Previous Year
▲=Up ▼=Down ▶=No Change

10 Week Mov. Avg. ---
30 Week Mov. Avg. ····
Relative Strength —

OPTIONS: Ph

Overview - 28-JUL-98

Earnings growth in 1998 and beyond will likely be aided by contributions from the pending merger with Citicorp (NYSE: CCI). The deal -- termed a "merger of equals," set to close in the third quarter of 1998 -- would create an unmatched global financial services franchise with 1997 pro forma assets of almost $700 billion, shareholders' equity of over $44 billion, operating earnings (before restructuring charges) of over $7.5 billion and a market capitalization of about $135 billion. Terms of the transaction call for TRV to issue 2.5 shares for every share of CCI in a tax-free exchange. The combined company, renamed Citigroup Inc., would be owned equally by existing CCI and TRV shareholders. While current law prohibits a bank holding company from engaging in insurance underwriting activities, TRV has applied for the appropriate waivers, including a two-year waiver, which may be extended for three additional one-year periods. Following this deal, TRV will have a presence in virtually every financial services segment: banking, brokerage, asset management and insurance. However, the success of the deal is predicated upon Citigroup's ability to leverage the potential for expense savings, economies of scale and cross selling opportunities.

Valuation - 28-JUL-98

After trending generally upward during late 1997 and early 1998, the shares ticked up amid favorable investor reaction to the Citicorp merger. Since then, they have settled back into a trading range, which is where they will likely remain until the deal is completed later in 1998. We view the deal positively, and believe investors with a longer term time horizon should use any near term weakness in the share price to add to positions.

Key Stock Statistics

S&P EPS Est. 1998	3.25	Tang. Bk. Value/Share	15.27
P/E on S&P Est. 1998	12.6	Beta	1.90
S&P EPS Est. 1999	3.80	Shareholders	55,100
Dividend Rate/Share	0.50	Market cap. (B)	$ 47.3
Shs. outstg. (M)	1156.2	Inst. holdings	61%
Avg. daily vol. (M)	9.005		

Value of $10,000 invested 5 years ago: NA

Fiscal Year Ending Dec. 31

	1998	1997	1996	1995	1994	1993
Revenues (Million $)						
1Q	10,368	8,700	4,515	3,960	4,769	1,302
2Q	10,096	9,184	5,426	4,172	4,601	1,284
3Q	—	9,961	5,622	4,290	4,714	2,016
4Q	—	9,765	5,782	4,161	4,381	2,195
Yr.	—	37,609	21,345	16,583	18,465	6,797
Earnings Per Share ($)						
1Q	0.91	0.67	0.51	0.30	0.33	0.30
2Q	0.95	0.77	0.59	0.37	0.31	0.26
3Q	—	0.85	0.56	0.46	0.32	0.34
4Q	—	0.30	0.65	0.49	0.33	0.40
Yr.	—	2.54	2.42	1.62	1.29	1.29

Next earnings report expected: mid October

Dividend Data (Dividends have been paid since 1986.)

Amount ($)	Date Decl.	Ex-Div. Date	Stock of Record	Payment Date
0.100	Oct. 22	Oct. 30	Nov. 03	Nov. 26 '97
0.125	Jan. 28	Feb. 05	Feb. 09	Feb. 27 '98
0.125	Apr. 22	Apr. 30	May. 04	May. 22 '98
0.125	Jul. 22	Jul. 30	Aug. 03	Aug. 28 '98

STANDARD
&POOR'S
STOCK REPORTS

Travelers Group Incorporated

2254A
12-SEP-98

Business Summary - 28-JUL-98

Travelers Group Inc. (formerly Travelers Inc. and, before that, Primerica Corp.) is a diversified financial services holding company that has successfully transformed itself from a slow growing, multiline insurance company into a leading financial services entity. Contributions to pro forma revenues:

	1997	1996
Investment services	57%	58%
Life insurance services	12%	12%
Property-casualty insurance services	26%	25%
Consumer finance & other	5%	5%

Investment services consist of Salomon Smith Barney Inc., an investment banking and securities brokerage firm that was formed through the November 28, 1997 acquisition of Salomon Inc. for more than $9 billion. The transaction, accounted for as a pooling of interests, propelled TRV into the top tier of securities brokers. Based on 1997 data, Salomon Smith Barney was the number one municipal debt underwriter, and the number two global debt and equity underwriter, according to Securities Data Corp. On a pro forma basis, net revenues for

1997 approached $11 billion, up slightly from $10.7 billion in 1996 (restated). Operating earnings, though, declined to $1.6 billion from $1.8 billion (restated), largely due to certain trading-related losses at Salomon. At year-end 1997, third party assets under management equaled $164 billion, up from $134 billion at year-end 1996. On June 1, 1998, TRV extended this unit's global reach by acquiring a 25% equity interest in Tokyo-based Nikko Securities Co. for $1.6 billion.

Insurance services include life, accident and health, and property-casualty insurance. Travelers Life and Annuities and Primerica Financial Services and its affiliates underwrite individual life insurance and market annuities and mutual funds. At year-end 1997, life and annuity assets under management equaled $23.8 billion, and life insurance in force totaled $422 billion. Property-casualty insurance operations are conducted by 83%-owned Travelers Property-Casualty Corp. (TAP), the fourth largest p-c insurer. TAP was formed in 1996 after TRV acquired the domestic p-c operations of Aetna Life and Casualty for $4.0 billion.

Consumer finance services include real estate-secured loans, personal loans, credit cards and other personal loans. Net consumer finance receivables were $10.8 billion at year-end 1997.

Per Share Data ($)

(Year Ended Dec. 31)	1997	1996	1995	1994	1993	1992	1991	1990	1989	1988
Tangible Bk. Val.	13.97	9.93	8.16	6.15	6.48	3.82	2.87	2.13	1.87	1.50
Earnings	2.54	2.33	1.62	1.29	1.29	1.11	0.71	0.55	0.48	0.60
Dividends	0.40	0.30	0.27	0.19	0.16	0.12	0.08	0.06	0.05	0.05
Payout Ratio	16%	13%	16%	15%	13%	11%	10%	11%	10%	7%
Prices - High	57⅜	31⅝	21¼	14⅜	16½	8⅜	6¾	6¼	5	4⅞
- Low	29⅛	18⅞	10¾	10⅛	8	6	3⅝	2⅞	3⅜	3⅜
P/E Ratio - High	23	14	11	11	13	7	9	12	10	8
- Low	11	8	7	8	6	5	5	5	7	6

Income Statement Analysis (Million $)

	1997	1996	1995	1994	1993	1992	1991	1990	1989	1988
Premium Inc.	8,995	7,633	4,977	7,590	1,480	1,694	1,783	1,922	1,816	307
Invest. Inc.	16,214	5,549	4,355	3,637	718	605	688	839	873	82.0
Oth. Revs.	12,400	8,163	7,251	7,238	4,599	2,826	4,138	3,433	3,007	614
Total Revs.	37,609	21,345	16,583	18,465	6,797	5,125	6,608	6,194	5,695	1,004
Int. Exp.	11,443	2,259	1,956	1,284	707	674	876	1,027	1,001	244
Exp./Op. Revs.	87%	86%	85%	90%	78%	81%	89%	91%	91%	76%
Pretax Inc.	5,012	3,398	2,521	2,149	1,523	1,188	791	602	513	238
Eff. Tax Rate	34%	31%	35%	38%	36%	36%	36%	36%	35%	32%
Net Inc.	3,104	2,300	1,628	1,326	951	756	479	373	289	162

Balance Sheet & Other Fin. Data (Million $)

	1997	1996	1995	1994	1993	1992	1991	1990	1989	1988
Receivables	16,549	12,174	10,123	12,256	10,477	3,220	3,263	Nil	Nil	Nil
Cash & Invest.	65,867	56,745	42,831	40,347	43,725	3,618	3,696	3,522	3,511	3,377
Loans	10,816	5,722	5,936	6,746	6,216	5,655	6,772	8,301	7,348	5,282
Total Assets	386,555	151,067	114,475	115,297	101,360	23,397	21,561	19,689	17,955	14,435
Capitalization:										
Debt	28,352	12,884	10,658	9,555	9,526	6,584	8,044	7,022	6,276	6,357
Equity	19,533	12,460	10,910	7,840	8,526	3,929	3,280	2,859	2,603	1,947
Total	51,906	25,294	21,568	18,333	18,052	10,813	11,323	9,881	8,878	8,514
Price Times Bk. Val.: High	4.1	3.2	2.6	2.3	2.5	2.1	2.3	3.0	2.7	3.2
Price Times Bk. Val.: Low	2.1	1.9	1.3	1.6	1.2	1.5	1.3	1.3	1.8	2.3
% Return On Revs.	8.3	10.8	9.8	7.2	14.0	14.8	7.2	6.0	5.1	16.1
% Ret. on Assets	1.2	1.7	1.4	1.2	1.5	3.4	2.3	2.0	1.8	1.7
% Ret. on Equity	18.6	18.9	16.4	15.2	15.5	20.8	15.6	13.7	12.7	12.5
Loans/Equity	51.7	50.0	54.4	0.8	1.0	1.6	1.8	2.9	2.8	3.2

Data as orig. reptd.; bef. results of disc. opers. and/or spec. items. Per share data adj. for stk. divs. as of ex-div. date. Bold denotes diluted EPS (FASB 128). E-Estimated. NA-Not Available. NM-Not Meaningful. NR-Not Ranked.

Office—388 Greenwich St., New York, NY 10013.**Tel**—(212) 816-8000. **Chrmn & CEO**—S. I. Weill. **Vice Chrmn**—M. A. Carpenter, T. W. Jones, J. B. Lane, R. I. Lipp, J. C. Madonna, D. C. Maughan, J. J. Plumeri, R. B. Willumstad. **Pres & COO**—J. Dimon.**VP-CFO**—H. G. Miller.**VP-Secy**—C. O. Prince III. **VP-Treas**—R. Matza.**VP-Investor Contact**—Bill Pike (212-816-8874).**Dirs**—C. M. Armstrong, J. Arron, K. J. Bialkin, J. A. Califano Jr., J. Dimon, L. B. Disharoon, G. R. Ford, T. W. Jones, A. D. Jordan, R. I. Lipp, M. T. Masdin, D. C. Maughan, D. C. Mecum, A. E. Pearson, F. J. Tasco, L. J. Wachner, S. I. Weill, J. R. Wright, Jr., A. Zankel.**Transfer Agent & Registrar**—The Bank of New York. **Incorporated**—in Delaware in 1968.**Empl**— 67,250. **S&P Analyst:** Catherine A. Seifert

STANDARD &POOR'S
STOCK REPORTS

Tribune Co.

2255L

NYSE Symbol **TRB**

In S&P 500

12-SEP-98

Industry:
Publishing (Newspapers)

Summary: Tribune is a leading information, entertainment and education company, with interests including newspaper publishing and radio and TV broadcasting.

S&P Opinion: Hold (★★★)	Recent Price • 60¼	Yield • 1.1%
	52 Wk Range • 75-50	12-Mo. P/E • 19.3

Quantitative Evaluations

Outlook
(1 Lowest—5 Highest)
• **2+**

Fair Value
• **61¾**

Risk
• **Low**

Earn./Div. Rank
• **A-**

Technical Eval.
• **Bullish** since 9/98

Rel. Strength Rank
(1 Lowest—99 Highest)
• **64**

Insider Activity
• **Favorable**

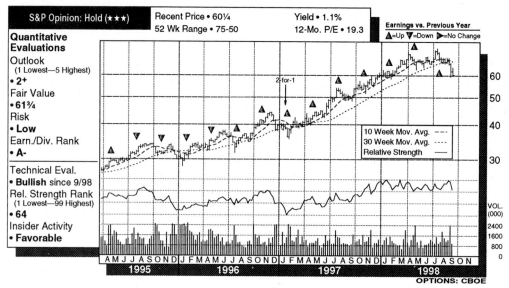

Earnings vs. Previous Year
▲=Up ▼=Down ▷=No Change

10 Week Mov. Avg. ---
30 Week Mov. Avg. ·····
Relative Strength ——

OPTIONS: CBOE

Overview - 01-APR-98

Higher revenues in 1998 will largely reflect gains from publishing, broadcasting and entertainment operations. Acquired TV stations will also contribute. Operating margins will be under pressure from gradually rising newsprint prices and greater newsprint consumption. Continued startup and acquisition costs will continue to restrain education group operating profits. Dilution from the Renaissance acquisition should be reduced, particularly after the first quarter. Higher losses are expected from cable programming/development activities and from equity interests in the WB network. In spite of the negative-sounding outlook, profitability will be aided nonetheless by the very healthy revenue gains, cost controls, and higher margins at acquired stations. Share net will benefit from ongoing repurchases. Our $2.65 estimate is 15% over the $2.30 of 1997, excluding nonrecurring items.

Valuation - 01-APR-98

The shares, at about 25X the $2.65 EPS we are projecting for 1998 are fully valued on a short-term basis, having appreciated more than 80% from their 1997 low, and trading at a premium to the market. TRB should be a market performer in the short term, but the shares remain an attractive holding for long-term capital appreciation, based on the company's long-term record for building asset value and a positive long-term earnings outlook. The acquisition of Renaissance Communications' six TV stations boosts TRB to the second largest television group in audience reach, with positive implications for revenue growth and profitability, notwithstanding initial dilution. TRB's low-risk commitment of its TV stations to the WB network provides a means to hike profitability and asset values. The stock's attractiveness is augmented by rising dividend income.

Key Stock Statistics

S&P EPS Est. 1998	2.65	Tang. Bk. Value/Share	NM
P/E on S&P Est. 1998	22.8	Beta	0.63
Dividend Rate/Share	0.68	Shareholders	5,200
Shs. outstg. (M)	121.9	Market cap. (B)	$ 7.4
Avg. daily vol. (M)	0.318	Inst. holdings	52%

Value of $10,000 invested 5 years ago: $ 27,402

Fiscal Year Ending Dec. 31

	1998	1997	1996	1995	1994	1993
Revenues (Million $)						
1Q	672.7	593.9	537.1	521.4	482.8	521.4
2Q	785.6	719.7	641.9	577.2	573.8	577.2
3Q	—	695.3	618.3	552.2	513.3	552.2
4Q	—	710.8	608.3	593.8	591.1	513.9
Yr.	—	2,720	2,406	2,245	2,155	1,953
Earnings Per Share ($)						
1Q	**0.49**	**0.45**	0.37	0.45	0.27	0.45
2Q	**1.07**	**0.80**	0.65	0.53	0.59	0.53
3Q	—	**0.75**	0.50	0.30	0.32	0.30
4Q	—	**0.81**	0.63	0.47	0.48	0.40
Yr.	**E2.65**	**2.81**	1.98	1.75	1.66	1.28

Next earnings report expected: mid October

Dividend Data (Dividends have been paid since 1902.)

Amount ($)	Date Decl.	Ex-Div. Date	Stock of Record	Payment Date
0.160	Oct. 21	Nov. 25	Nov. 28	Dec. 11 '97
0.170	Feb. 17	Feb. 25	Feb. 27	Mar. 12 '98
0.170	May. 19	May. 27	May. 29	Jun. 11 '98
0.170	Jul. 28	Aug. 26	Aug. 28	Sep. 10 '98

Tribune Company

Business Summary - 01-APR-98

Tribune Company is a leading information, entertainment and education company with businesses in 12 of the nation's largest markets. Through newspapers, broadcasting, education and new media, the company reaches some 75% of U.S. households daily. One would expect stodginess from a company that has been around for over 150 years, but not Tribune Company. In recent years the company has aggressively expanded its size and scope, and significantly changed its business mix. In December, 1997, TRB purchased 80.5% of Landoll Inc., the eighth largest publisher of children's books. In February 1997, TRB acquired Renaissance Communications Corp., owner of six TV stations. During 1996, the company sold off its substantial interests in newsprint producer, QUNO Corp., acquired several education companies, and merged its Compton's unit into Softkey International.

TRB is the nation's second largest TV group broadcaster, whose 18 TV stations reach nearly 35% of television households in the U.S. TV stations are located in New York City, Los Angeles, Chicago, Philadelphia, Dallas, Atlanta, Houston, Miami, Denver, Sacramento, Indianapolis, San Diego, Hartford, New Orleans, Seattle, Grand Rapids, Harrisburg and Boston. Eleven stations are affiliated with The WB Network, in which TRB owns a 25% minority interest, five are Fox affiliates,

and one each CBS and ABC. TRB owns four radio stations: WGN-AM, Chicago; and KVOD-FM, KOSI-FM & KEZW-AM, Denver. The company owns 33% of Qwest Broadcasting LLC; 31% of the TV Food Network; 50% of Central Florida News 13; 33% of Classified Ventures LLC; 20% of Digital City, Inc.; 23% of Image Builders Software Inc.; and 25% of Interealty Corp. Tribune Entertainment develops, produces and syndicates first-run television programming, including such well-known programs as "The Geraldo Rivera Show" and "Soul Train." The company owns the Chicago Cubs Baseball team.

Tribune Publishing includes four daily newspapers: The Chicago Tribune, The Fort Lauderdale Sun-Sentinel, The Orlando Sentinel and the Newport News, VA, Daily Press.

The educational publishing division, formed in 1993, has grown rapidly to become the nation's leading publisher of supplemental education and core curriculum materials, and is a leader in providing multimedia products and services for the school and consumer markets. TRB has a 16% equity interest in SoftKey International, one of the world's largest publishers and distributors of multimedia software. TRB has a number of minority interests in emerging media businesses with emphasis on interactive services and Internet businesses. These include Excite, Inc., The Learning Company, Inc., Peapod, Inc., CareerPath.com, Discourse Technologies, Inc. and others.

Per Share Data ($)

(Year Ended Dec. 31)	1997	1996	1995	1994	1993	1992	1991	1990	1989	1988
Tangible Bk. Val.	NA	-1.62	0.53	NM	NM	NM	NM	NM	NM	1.17
Cash Flow	4.04	4.04	3.08	2.70	2.06	1.99	1.89	0.33	2.33	2.16
Earnings	2.81	2.15	1.75	1.66	1.28	0.91	0.97	-0.61	1.58	1.39
Dividends	0.64	0.60	0.56	0.52	0.48	0.48	0.48	0.48	0.44	0.38
Payout Ratio	23%	28%	32%	31%	38%	53%	50%	NM	26%	27%
Prices - High	62⅝	44⅛	34½	32¼	30⅝	25⅜	24¼	24⅛	31⅝	21½
- Low	35½	28⅜	25⅜	24½	24	19⅜	16⅝	15⅝	18¼	16⅞
P/E Ratio - High	22	21	20	19	24	28	25	NM	20	15
- Low	13	13	14	15	19	21	17	NM	11	12

Income Statement Analysis (Million $)

	1997	1996	1995	1994	1993	1992	1991	1990	1989	1988
Revs.	2,720	2,406	2,245	2,155	1,953	2,096	2,035	2,353	2,455	2,335
Oper. Inc.	815	633	526	512	459	411	406	362	551	535
Depr.	173	143	121	115	103	140	119	124	108	117
Int. Exp.	86.5	47.8	21.8	20.6	25.8	52.7	65.1	62.3	61.5	67.6
Pretax Inc.	659	474	413	429	332	233	242	-94.0	411	378
Eff. Tax Rate	40%	40%	41%	44%	43%	41%	41%	NM	41%	44%
Net Inc.	394	283	245	242	189	137	142	-64.0	242	210

Balance Sheet & Other Fin. Data (Million $)

	1997	1996	1995	1994	1993	1992	1991	1990	1989	1988
Cash	66.6	274	22.9	21.8	18.5	16.8	17.0	13.6	27.7	15.1
Curr. Assets	848	887	546	544	491	574	589	618	657	646
Total Assets	4,778	3,701	3,288	2,786	2,536	2,752	2,795	2,826	3,051	2,942
Curr. Liab.	706	673	557	530	505	680	599	616	631	625
LT Debt	1,521	980	757	411	511	741	898	999	881	650
Common Eqty.	1,522	1,227	1,056	1,262	1,040	871	504	415	728	1,188
Total Cap.	3,710	2,397	2,361	1,894	1,695	1,720	1,920	1,962	2,194	2,045
Cap. Exp.	104	93.3	118	92.0	76.0	130	94.0	149	243	231
Cash Flow	547	496	399	339	273	258	244	43.0	338	327
Curr. Ratio	1.2	1.3	1.0	1.0	1.0	0.8	1.0	1.0	1.0	1.0
% LT Debt of Cap.	41.0	40.9	32.1	21.7	30.1	43.1	46.8	50.9	40.1	31.8
% Net Inc.of Revs.	14.5	11.8	11.0	11.2	9.7	6.5	7.0	NM	9.9	9.0
% Ret. on Assets	9.3	8.1	8.1	9.1	7.0	4.9	5.0	NM	8.4	7.5
% Ret. on Equity	27.3	23.2	18.4	19.5	17.6	13.9	27.1	NM	25.3	18.6

Data as orig. reptd.; bef. results of disc. opers. and/or spec. items. Per share data adj. for stk. divs. as of ex-div. date. E-Estimated. Bold denotes diluted EPS (FASB 128). NA-Not Available. NM-Not Meaningful. NR-Not Ranked.

Office—435 N. Michigan Ave., Chicago, IL 60611. **Tel**—(312) 222-9100. **Website**—http://www.tribune.com **Chrmn, Pres & CEO**—J. W. Madigan. **Sr VP & CFO**—D. C. Grenesko. **VP & Secy**—C. H. Kenney. **VP & Treas**—D. J. Granat. **VP & Investor Contact**—Ruthellyn Musil (312) 222-3787. **Dirs**—J. C. Dowdle, D. E. Hernandez, R. E. LaBlanc, J. W. Madigan, N. H. Maynard, A. J. McKenna, K. Miller, J. J. O'Connor, D. H. Rumsfeld, D. S. Taft, A. R. Weber. **Transfer Agent & Registrar**—First Chicago Trust Co. of New York, Jersey City, NJ. **Incorporated**—in Illinois in 1861; reincorporated in Delaware in 1968. **Empl**—11,600. **S&P Analyst**: William H. Donald

12-SEP-98   Industry: Restaurants

Summary: YUM is the world's largest fast-food business with some 30,000 KFC, Pizza Hut and Taco Bell units.

S&P Opinion: Hold (★★★)	Recent Price • 38	Yield • Nil
	52 Wk Range • 40¾-25	12-Mo. P/E • NM

Quantitative Evaluations

Outlook
(1 Lowest—5 Highest)
• **NA**

Fair Value
• **NA**

Risk
• **NA**

Earn./Div. Rank
• **NR**

Technical Eval.
• **NA**

Rel. Strength Rank
(1 Lowest—99 Highest)
• **97**

Insider Activity
• **Favorable**

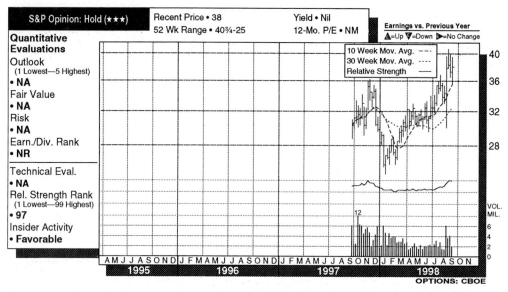

Earnings vs. Previous Year
▲=Up ▼=Down ▷=No Change

10 Week Mov. Avg. —·—
30 Week Mov. Avg. ----
Relative Strength ——

OPTIONS: CBOE

Overview - 11-AUG-98

Since mid-1995, the company's strategy has been focused on closing underperforming units and refranchising others to new and current franchisees. In 1998, this should generate some $400 million which will be used to pay down debt. The emphasis will be on international expansion given the high saturation level of fast-food restaurants in the U.S. Currently about one-third of restaurants are overseas. Operating profit should advance some 12% with strongest gains from international operations (before currency translation). The refranchising strategy is expected to generate high levels of cash flow over the next few years. This will be earmarked to service and to pay down the company's high debt level. In addition, the company's capital needs are kept low by a reduced level of new openings. The quarterly variations in the gains from refranchising units are difficult to estimate and could cause large deviations from estimated earnings. In the first half of 1998, the company posted a $108 million pretax gain ($0.37 a share) from the refranchising of units. Excluding refranchising gains, earnings per share were $0.70.

Valuation - 11-AUG-98

The shares have had a runup in price since the February 1998 low as investors began to look at restaurant companies more favorably. We remain neutral on the stock. The fast-food industry in the U.S. will remain highly competitive over the next few years and international expansion will be the focus. We anticipate that YUM can generate modest double-digit earnings growth over the next few years. Based on this assumption, the shares appear fairly valued at 18 times estimated 1998 operating earnings per share of $2.05. Over time as the company aggressively pays down its high debt level with excess cash flow, earnings growth could exceed this level.

Key Stock Statistics

S&P EPS Est. 1998	2.40	Tang. Bk. Value/Share	NM
P/E on S&P Est. 1998	15.8	Beta	NA
Dividend Rate/Share	Nil	Shareholders	NA
Shs. outstg. (M)	152.5	Market cap. (B)	$ 5.8
Avg. daily vol. (M)	0.811	Inst. holdings	60%

Value of $10,000 invested 5 years ago: NA

Fiscal Year Ending Dec. 31

	1998	1997	1996	1995	1994	1993
Revenues (Million $)						
1Q	1,921	--	--	--	--	--
2Q	2,001	--	--	--	--	--
3Q	--	6,638	—	—	—	—
4Q	—	—	—	—	—	—
Yr.	—	9,681	9,838	—	—	—
Earnings Per Share ($)						
1Q	0.35	—	—	—	—	—
2Q	0.72	--	--	--	--	--
3Q	E0.68	1.64	—	—	—	—
4Q	E0.65	—	—	—	—	—
Yr.	E2.40	-0.77	0.85	—	—	—

Next earnings report expected: late October

Dividend Data

No cash dividends have been paid.

STANDARD
&POOR'S
STOCK REPORTS

TRICON Global Restaurants, Inc.

2255N

12-SEP-98

Business Summary - 11-AUG-98

The highways, strip malls and streets are dotted with fast-food units operated by this company. TRICON Global Restaurants is the world's largest quick service restaurant business in number of units, with almost 30,000 KFC, Pizza Hut and Taco Bell system units generating over $20 billion in worldwide system sales. Formerly a wholly owned subsidiary of PepsiCo, Inc., the company was spun off to PepsiCo shareholders, with one YUM common share distributed for every 10 PepsiCo shares held as of September 19, 1997.

Each of YUM's divisions operates, develops, licenses and franchises a system of both traditional and non-traditional quick service restaurant units. Nontraditional units include express units and kiosks which have a more limited menu and operate in nontraditional locations like airports, gas and convenience stores, where a full-scale traditional outlet would not be practical or efficient. Also, there are about 349 units housing more than one concept.

KFC (originally Kentucky Fried Chicken) operates more than 5,100 units in the U.S. and over 5,100 units in 78 countries and territories internationally. In 1997, KFC's worldwide system sales exceeded $8 billion, of which $4 billion were in the U.S. In 1997, average U.S. system sales per traditional unit were $786,000. At the end of 1997, KFC was the leader in the U. S. chicken quick service segment with 5% market share, well ahead of its closest national competitor.

Pizza Hut operates over 8,600 units in the U.S. and more than 3,800 units in 88 countries and territories throughout the world under the Pizza Hut name. Units feature a variety of pizzas with different toppings as well as pasta salads, sandwiches and other food items and beverages. In 1997, worldwide system sales exceeded $7.3 billion, of which $4.7 billion were in the U.S. Average U. S. system sales per traditional unit in 1997 were $630,000. At the end of 1997, Pizza Hut was the leader in the U.S. pizza quick service segment with a 22% market share, almost double its closest national competitor.

Taco Bell specializes in Mexican style food products, including various types of tacos and burritos, salads, nachos and other related items. At year-end 1997, there were more than 6,700 units in the U.S. and 170 units internationally. In 1997, worldwide system sales exceeded $4.9 billion, of which $4.8 billion were in the U.S.

In 1997, Tricon International accounted for 34% of the company's total system sales and 24% of the company's revenues. These sales have grown at a compounded rate of 8% over the past five years. About 38% of worldwide units were operated by the company, 51% by franchisees and 11% by licensees.

Per Share Data ($)

(Year Ended Dec. 31)	1997	1996	1995	1994	1993	1992	1991	1990	1989	1988
Tangible Bk. Val.	NA	NM	NM	NM	NM	NM	NM	NM	NM	NM
Cash Flow	2.80	NM	NM	NM	NM	NM	NM	NM	NM	NM
Earnings	-0.77	0.85	NA	NA	NA	NA	NA	NA	NA	NA
Dividends	Nil	Nil	Nil	Nil	Nil	Nil	Nil	Nil	Nil	Nil
Payout Ratio	Nil	Nil	Nil	Nil	Nil	Nil	Nil	Nil	Nil	Nil
Prices - High	36¼	NA	NA	NA	NA	NA	NA	NA	NA	NA
- Low	27⅞	NA	NA	NA	NA	NA	NA	NA	NA	NA
P/E Ratio - High	NM	NM	NM	NM	NM	NM	NM	NM	NM	NM
- Low	NM	NM	NM	NM	NM	NM	NM	NM	NM	NM

Income Statement Analysis (Million $)

	1997	1996	1995	1994	1993	1992	1991	1990	1989	1988
Revs.	9,681	9,838	NA	NA	NA	NA	NA	NA	NA	NA
Oper. Inc.	1,198	NA	NA	NA	NA	NA	NA	NA	NA	NA
Depr.	536	NA	NA	NA	NA	NA	NA	NA	NA	NA
Int. Exp.	276	NA	NA	NA	NA	NA	NA	NA	NA	NA
Pretax Inc.	-35.0	308	NA	NA	NA	NA	NA	NA	NA	NA
Eff. Tax Rate	NM	58%	NA	NA	NA	NA	NA	NA	NA	NA
Net Inc.	-110	131	NA	NA	NA	NA	NA	NA	NA	NA

Balance Sheet & Other Fin. Data (Million $)

	1997	1996	1995	1994	1993	1992	1991	1990	1989	1988
Cash	268	157	NA	NA	NA	NA	NA	NA	NA	NA
Curr. Assets	683	819	NA	NA	NA	NA	NA	NA	NA	NA
Total Assets	5,098	5,976	NA	NA	NA	NA	NA	NA	NA	NA
Curr. Liab.	1,579	1,382	NA	NA	NA	NA	NA	NA	NA	NA
LT Debt	4,551	4,674	NA	NA	NA	NA	NA	NA	NA	NA
Common Eqty.	-1,619	-834	NA	NA	NA	NA	NA	NA	NA	NA
Total Cap.	2,964	4,139	NA	NA	NA	NA	NA	NA	NA	NA
Cap. Exp.	541	NA	NA	NA	NA	NA	NA	NA	NA	NA
Cash Flow	425	NA	NA	NA	NA	NA	NA	NA	NA	NA
Curr. Ratio	0.4	0.6	NA	NA	NA	NA	NA	NA	NA	NA
% LT Debt of Cap.	153.5	113.0	NA	NA	NA	NA	NA	NA	NA	NA
% Net Inc.of Revs.	NM	1.3	NA	NA	NA	NA	NA	NA	NA	NA
% Ret. on Assets	NM	NM	NM	NM	NM	NM	NM	NM	NM	NM
% Ret. on Equity	NM	NM	NM	NM	NM	NM	NM	NM	NM	NM

Data as orig. reptd. (pro forma in 1996; balance sheet as of June 14, 1997); bef. results of disc. opers. and/or spec. items. 3Q 1997 data for 36 wks. Per share data adj. for stk. divs. as of ex-div. date. Bold denotes diluted EPS (FASB 128). E-Estimated. NA-Not Available. NM-Not Meaningful. NR-Not Ranked.

Office—1441 Gardiner Lane, Louisville, KY 40213**Tel**—(502) 456-8300.**Website**—http://www.triconglobal.com**Chrmn**—A. E. Pearson.**Vice-Chrmn & Pres**—D. C. Novak.**CFO**—R. C. Lowes.**Treas**—S. S. Wijnberg.**Dirs**—D. R. Daniel, J. Dimon, M. Ferragamo, R. Holland Jr., S. Kohl, K. G. Langone, D. C. Novak, A. E. Pearson, J. Trujillo, R. J. Ulrich, J. S. Wagner, J. L. Weinberg.**Transfer Agent & Registrar**—BankBoston, Boston, MA**Incorporated**—in North Carolina in 1997.**Empl**— 350,000. **S&P Analyst:** Karen J. Sack, CFA

TRW Inc.

2186K
NYSE Symbol **TRW**

In S&P 500

12-SEP-98

Industry: Auto Parts & Equipment

Summary: TRW provides high-technology products and services to the automotive and space and defense markets.

S&P Opinion: Accumulate (★★★★)	Recent Price • 45¼	Yield • 2.7%
	52 Wk Range • 61⅛-42⅝	12-Mo. P/E • NM

Earnings vs. Previous Year
▲=Up ▼=Down ▷=No Change

Quantitative Evaluations

Outlook (1 Lowest—5 Highest)
• 3

Fair Value
• 46¾

Risk
• **Low**

Earn./Div. Rank
• **B**

Technical Eval.
• **Neutral** since 8/98

Rel. Strength Rank (1 Lowest—99 Highest)
• 62

Insider Activity
• **Neutral**

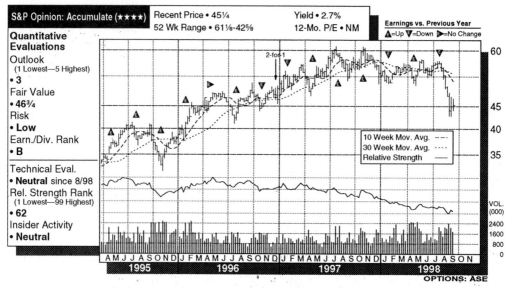

- 10 Week Mov. Avg. ----
- 30 Week Mov. Avg. ......
- Relative Strength ——

2-for-1

VOL. (000)

OPTIONS: ASE

Overview - 28-JUL-98

Sales and profits before acquisitions should rise in 1998, despite expectations of only modest economic growth. The automotive segment will benefit from increased demand for airbags, engine valves, and rack and pinion power steering in North America and Europe, and from recent acquisitions. Domestic operations should benefit from improved efficiency, and from growing sales to Japanese automakers assembling vehicles in the U.S. Space and defense revenues are rising, on new contract awards for both government defense projects and commercial projects, and the acquisition of BDM International. The sale of the information systems unit will let TRW concentrate its assets and efforts on its core automotive and space and defense businesses. The company has been seeking automotive acquisitions; some promising joint ventures have been established. Over the next few years, TRW should benefit from receipt of contracts to supply side impact airbags for more than 50 vehicle models.

Valuation - 28-JUL-98

TRW is positioned to capitalize on its status as a space and defense technology leader, providing innovative products to civilian and commercial markets. With proceeds from the sale of the information services unit, we look for the company to step up efforts to leverage its expertise in automotive electronics. TRW has achieved 20% annual growth in its content per vehicle produced worldwide since 1985. We expect this increase in market penetration to continue, as side airbag markets develop in the next few years. Major long-term initiatives include establishing a satellite-driven global cellular telephone system, called Odyssey. The stock remains modestly valued, at about 13X our 1998 EPS estimate, and is a worthwhile portfolio addition.

Key Stock Statistics

S&P EPS Est. 1998	4.35	Tang. Bk. Value/Share	7.22
P/E on S&P Est. 1998	10.4	Beta	0.97
Dividend Rate/Share	1.24	Shareholders	26,400
Shs. outstg. (M)	121.9	Market cap. (B)	$ 5.5
Avg. daily vol. (M)	0.437	Inst. holdings	54%

Value of $10,000 invested 5 years ago: $ 18,248

Fiscal Year Ending Dec. 31

	1998	1997	1996	1995	1994	1993
Revenues (Million $)						
1Q	3,095	2,660	2,514	2,596	2,159	2,029
2Q	3,028	2,852	2,729	2,712	2,317	2,011
3Q	—	2,521	2,572	2,401	2,164	1,903
4Q	—	2,799	2,514	2,463	2,447	2,005
Yr.	—	10,831	9,857	10,172	9,087	7,948
Earnings Per Share ($)						
1Q	**1.03**	0.92	0.87	0.87	0.48	0.40
2Q	**1.00**	1.05	0.98	0.92	0.67	0.42
3Q	—	0.85	-1.13	0.69	0.63	0.39
4Q	—	**-3.34**	0.85	0.86	0.74	0.49
Yr.	**E4.35**	**-0.40**	1.38	3.34	2.52	1.70

Next earnings report expected: mid October

Dividend Data (Dividends have been paid since 1936.)

Amount ($)	Date Decl.	Ex-Div. Date	Stock of Record	Payment Date
0.310	Oct. 22	Nov. 12	Nov. 14	Dec. 15 '97
0.310	Dec. 10	Feb. 11	Feb. 13	Mar. 15 '98
0.310	Apr. 29	May. 06	May. 08	Jun. 15 '98
0.310	Jul. 22	Aug. 12	Aug. 14	Sep. 15 '98

A Division of The McGraw-Hill Companies

TRW Inc.

Business Summary - 28-JUL-98

TRW is a leader in auto parts, space and defense systems and information systems. Segment contributions in 1997 were:

	Sales	Profits
Automotive parts	65%	66%
Space & defense	35%	34%

TRW manufactures a broad range of automotive product lines for cars, trucks, buses and off-highway vehicles. Products include, occupant safety restraint systems, steering & suspension products, engine valves and valve train part components, electrical and electronic products and controls, and fasteners. Parts are sold primarily to the original equipment market. Sales to Ford, Volkswagen AG and Chrysler, accounted for 21%, 12% and 9%, respectively of sales of the automotive segment. Key growth areas include inflatable restraints (airbags), engine valves, power rack and pinion steering systems, and remote keyless entry systems. Growth in airbags is being fueled by increased sales of passenger-side airbags in cars and driver-side airbags in light trucks in the U.S. and increased foreign shipments for both occupant positions. Further growth in the next few years should be derived from the addition of side-impact airbags and the development of smart airbags.

Space and defense includes spacecraft; propulsion systems; electro-optical and instrument systems; spacecraft payloads; lasers; space and defense mission software and systems engineering services; communications and avionics systems, and other electronic technologies for space, defense and commercial uses.

In December 1997, TRW purchased BDM International for nearly $1 billion. The acquisition should aid the company in its expansion in the information technology markets. The transaction significantly increased TRW's debt, and resulted in a 1997 fourth quarter non-cash charge of $548 million for in-process research and development, but it is only expected to be slightly dilutive or EPS neutral in 1998.

In February 1997, TRW acquired for about $450 million an 80% equity interest in two Magna International Inc. (NYSE: MGA) European air-bag automotive operations, as part of a strategic alliance to serve the global market; TRW purchased the remaining 20% in January 1998. The initial agreement also included the creation of a joint technical center. These operations were initially expected to add about $500 million in annual net sales to TRW's occupant safety systems business.

Per Share Data ($) (Year Ended Dec. 31)	1997	1996	1995	1994	1993	1992	1991	1990	1989	1988
Tangible Bk. Val.	7.22	16.56	11.47	8.96	6.63	5.47	7.81	9.30	8.04	10.36
Cash Flow	3.44	4.80	7.13	6.14	5.23	4.70	2.05	4.82	5.03	4.84
Earnings	-0.40	1.38	3.31	2.52	1.70	1.54	-1.15	1.70	2.15	2.15
Dividends	1.24	1.14	1.02	0.97	0.94	0.91	0.90	0.87	0.86	0.81
Payout Ratio	NM	83%	31%	38%	55%	59%	NM	50%	39%	38%
Prices - High	61 1/4	52	41 3/8	38 3/4	35 1/8	30 1/8	23 1/8	25 7/8	25	27
- Low	47 3/8	37 1/2	30 7/8	30 1/2	26 1/4	20 1/2	17 1/4	15 3/4	20 5/8	20 3/8
P/E Ratio - High	NM	38	12	15	21	19	NM	15	12	13
- Low	NM	27	9	12	15	13	NM	9	10	9
Income Statement Analysis (Million $)										
Revs.	10,831	9,857	10,172	9,087	7,948	8,311	7,913	8,169	7,340	6,982
Oper. Inc.	802	908	1,323	1,125	953	967	811	932	874	831
Depr.	490	452	510	476	458	392	392	381	349	349
Int. Exp.	75.0	88.0	100	112	146	176	200	195	142	136
Pretax Inc.	260	302	708	535	359	348	-128	343	399	420
Eff. Tax Rate	111%	40%	37%	38%	39%	44%	NM	39%	34%	38%
Net Inc.	-49.0	182	446	333	220	194	-139	208	263	261
Balance Sheet & Other Fin. Data (Million $)										
Cash	70.0	386	59.0	109	79.0	66.0	75.0	72.0	114	127
Curr. Assets	2,435	2,781	2,336	2,215	1,994	2,116	2,262	2,237	2,295	2,105
Total Assets	6,410	5,899	5,890	5,636	5,336	5,458	5,635	5,555	5,259	4,442
Curr. Liab.	2,719	2,157	2,012	1,986	1,826	2,012	1,982	1,947	1,794	1,396
LT Debt	1,117	458	541	694	870	941	1,213	1,042	1,063	863
Common Eqty.	1,623	2,181	2,171	1,812	1,523	1,404	1,671	1,893	1,734	1,548
Total Cap.	2,903	2,703	3,099	2,954	2,707	2,642	3,402	3,472	3,310	2,873
Cap. Exp.	549	500	485	506	482	530	537	587	452	417
Cash Flow	440	634	956	808	677	585	251	588	611	586
Curr. Ratio	0.9	1.3	1.2	1.1	1.1	1.1	1.1	1.1	1.3	1.5
% LT Debt of Cap.	38.4	16.9	17.5	24.3	32.1	35.6	35.7	30.0	32.1	30.0
% Net Inc.of Revs.	NM	1.8	4.4	3.7	2.8	2.3	NM	2.5	3.6	3.7
% Ret. on Assets	NM	3.1	7.8	6.0	4.0	3.5	NM	3.8	5.4	5.9
% Ret. on Equity	NM	8.3	22.4	19.8	14.9	12.4	NM	11.4	15.9	17.6

Data as orig. reptd.; bef. results of disc. opers. and/or spec. items. Per share data adj. for stk. divs. as of ex-div. date. Bold denotes diluted EPS (FASB 128). E-Estimated. NA-Not Available. NM-Not Meaningful. NR-Not Ranked.

Registrars—First Chicago Trust Co. of New York, Jersey City, NJ; National City Bank, Cleveland. **Office**—1900 Richmond Rd., Cleveland, OH 44124. **Registrar**—National City Bank, Cleveland. **Tel**—(216) 291-7000. **Website**—http://www.trw.co **Chrmn & CEO**—J. T. Gorman. **Pres & COO**—P. S. Hellman. **EVP & CFO**—C. G. Miller. **EVP & Secy**—W. B. Lawrence. **Investor Contact**—Thomas A. Myers. **Dirs**—M. H. Armacost, M. Feldstein, R. M. Gates, J. T. Gorman, C. H. Hahn, G. H. Heilmeier, P. S. Hellman, K. N. Horn, E. B. Jones, W. S. Kiser, D. B. Lewis, J. T. Lynn, L. M. Martin, J. D. Ong, R. W. Pogue. **Transfer Agents and Registrars**—National City Bank, Cleveland; Co.'s office: First Chicago Trust Co. of New York, Jersey City, NJ.**Incorporated**—in Ohio in 1916. **Empl**— 65,200. **S&P Analyst:** Efraim Levy

Tupperware Corp.

2260C

NYSE Symbol **TUP**

In S&P 500

12-SEP-98 **Industry:** Housewares

Summary: This well-known manufacturer of plastic food storage products was spun off by Premark International Inc. in May 1996.

S&P Opinion: Hold (★★★)

Recent Price • 18¾	Yield • 4.7%
52 Wk Range • 29-18⅛	12-Mo. P/E • 19.5

Quantitative Evaluations

Outlook
(1 Lowest—5 Highest)
• **3+**

Fair Value
• **21⅞**

Risk
• **NA**

Earn./Div. Rank
• **NR**

Technical Eval.
• **NA**

Rel. Strength Rank
(1 Lowest—99 Highest)
• **31**

Insider Activity
• **Neutral**

Earnings vs. Previous Year
▲=Up ▼=Down ▶=No Change

10 Week Mov. Avg. ---
30 Week Mov. Avg. ·····
Relative Strength ——

OPTIONS: CBOE, Ph

Overview - 22-JUL-98

We expect sales to advance slightly in 1998, as continued strength in Europe and a turnaround in U.S. operations are largely offset by weaker sales in Asia and Latin America. Sales will also be restricted by negative foreign exchange rates. Margins will narrow, on the lower volume and a more promotional sales environment. Operating earnings for 1998, excluding a negative currency effect, are likely to be flat to down slightly. For FY 99, sales and EPS gains will be driven by Tupperware's expansion into overseas markets, particularly in Eastern Europe, Latin America and Southeast Asia. In more mature markets, including those in Europe and North America, sales growth will depend on rapid new product introductions and efforts to expand the company's network of distributors, as well as a focus on increasing the business of existing distributors. The sales mix is expected to become less profitable, however, as the company expands into emerging growth markets where demand is for less expensive products than in mature markets.

Valuation - 22-JUL-98

We recently upgraded the stock to hold, from avoid, based on recent share price stability and the likelihood that profitability will improve in the second half of 1998, after a weak 1997. U.S. operations should benefit from a more efficient distributor network, and European operations should be aided by stronger recruiting efforts in the second half of the year. Although sales in Latin America are expected to be soft for the remainder of the year, results in 1999 should improve, as the company rebuilds its distributor network there. Second half results should also see a modest boost to sales from new product introductions. At a recent level of 16X our 1998 EPS estimate of $1.70, the shares should perform in line with the market, as TUP's profitability begins to improve.

Key Stock Statistics

S&P EPS Est. 1998	1.70	Tang. Bk. Value/Share	2.39
P/E on S&P Est. 1998	11.0	Beta	NA
S&P EPS Est. 1999	1.90	Shareholders	NA
Dividend Rate/Share	0.88	Market cap. (B)	$ 1.1
Shs. outstg. (M)	57.7	Inst. holdings	77%
Avg. daily vol. (M)	0.135		

Value of $10,000 invested 5 years ago: NA

Fiscal Year Ending Dec. 31

	1998	1997	1996	1995	1994	1993
Revenues (Million $)						
1Q	268.8	315.3	329.0	—	—	—
2Q	282.9	342.5	379.0	—	—	—
3Q	—	251.4	290.6	—	—	—
4Q	—	320.1	370.7	—	—	—
Yr.	—	1,229	1,369	1,359	—	—
Earnings Per Share ($)						
1Q	**0.26**	**0.40**	0.47	—	—	—
2Q	**0.39**	**0.61**	0.77	—	—	—
3Q	**E0.15**	**0.06**	0.29	—	—	—
4Q	**E0.90**	**0.25**	1.17	—	—	—
Yr.	**E1.70**	**1.32**	**2.71**	2.57	—	—

Next earnings report expected: late October

Dividend Data (Dividends have been paid since 1996.)

Amount ($)	Date Decl.	Ex-Div. Date	Stock of Record	Payment Date
0.220	Nov. 12	Dec. 11	Dec. 15	Jan. 06 '98
0.220	Mar. 05	Mar. 19	Mar. 23	Apr. 08 '98
0.220	May. 08	Jun. 12	Jun. 16	Jul. 06 '98
0.220	Aug. 06	Sep. 10	Sep. 14	Oct. 02 '98

A Division of The McGraw-Hill Companies

Business Summary - 22-JUL-98

With annual sales of over $1.2 billion in 1997, this multinational company is one of the world's leading direct sellers of consumer products for the home and personal use. Tupperware's scope is truly global; it has operations in more than 74 countries, and its products are sold in the U.S. and more than 100 foreign countries. Foreign operations generated about 84% of TUP's 1997 sales, and all of its profits.

TUP's core product line includes food storage containers that preserve food freshness through the well-known Tupperware seals. The company also has an established line of children's educational toys, serving products and gifts. The line of products has expanded over the years into kitchen, home storage and organizing uses with products such as Modular Mates, Fridge Stackables, OneTouch canisters and many specialized containers.

New product development continues to be an important part of TUP's growth strategy as it strives to generate about 20% of annual sales from new products. The development of new products differs in various markets, due to dissimilarities in cultures, lifestyles and needs.

Tupperware's products are distributed worldwide through the direct selling method, via consultants (independent contractors who are not company employees). The sales force relies primarily on the demonstration method of sales, sometimes referred to as Tupperware parties, in homes, offices, social clubs and other locations. More than 17.3 million demonstrations were held worldwide in 1997.

Because there is a strong correlation between sales growth and the number of people selling, a key element of Tupperware's growth strategy includes expanding its number of distributors and consultants. As of December 27, 1996, the worldwide Tupperware distribution system had over 1,800 distributors, 50,400 managers and 950,000 consultants. With the exception of 1997, the company has increased its sales force by an average of 19% a year over the past five years, and hopes to double its current size to about two million over the next several years.

Europe, which in TUP's organizational structure also includes Africa and the Middle East, is the company's largest market, accounting for 44% of sales in 1997. Asia Pacific, Latin America and the U.S. accounted for 23%, 20% and 13% of sales, respectively. Reflecting large emerging middle classes, undeveloped retail infrastructures, and shortages of jobs for women who want to work, TUP believes that there is tremendous potential for expansion into new countries and underserved markets. Over the past two years, the company has entered China, India, Poland, the Czech Republic and Estonia, Turkey, Latvia, Lithuania, Russia, Colombia, Peru, and Central America.

Per Share Data ($)

(Year Ended Dec. 31)	1997	1996	1995	1994	1993	1992	1991	1990	1989	1988
Tangible Bk. Val.	3.51	4.90	3.27	NA	NA	NA	NA	NA	NA	NA
Cash Flow	2.40	3.80	3.53	NA	NA	NA	NA	NA	NA	NA
Earnings	1.32	2.70	2.57	NA	NA	NA	NA	NA	NA	NA
Dividends	0.88	0.44	Nil	Nil	Nil	Nil	Nil	Nil	Nil	Nil
Payout Ratio	67%	16%	Nil	Nil	Nil	Nil	Nil	Nil	Nil	Nil
Prices - High	54½	55½	NA	NA	NA	NA	NA	NA	NA	NA
- Low	22½	38¼	NA	NA	NA	NA	NA	NA	NA	NA
P/E Ratio - High	41	21	NA	NA	NA	NA	NA	NA	NA	NA
- Low	17	14	NA	NA	NA	NA	NA	NA	NA	NA

Income Statement Analysis (Million $)

	1997	1996	1995	1994	1993	1992	1991	1990	1989	1988
Revs.	1,229	1,369	1,359	NA	NA	NA	NA	NA	NA	NA
Oper. Inc.	201	320	286	NA	NA	NA	NA	NA	NA	NA
Depr.	66.1	65.3	61.3	NA	NA	NA	NA	NA	NA	NA
Int. Exp.	24.1	13.2	15.3	NA	NA	NA	NA	NA	NA	NA
Pretax Inc.	111	235	213	NA	NA	NA	NA	NA	NA	NA
Eff. Tax Rate	26%	26%	23%	NA	NA	NA	NA	NA	NA	NA
Net Inc.	82.0	175	164	NA	NA	NA	NA	NA	NA	NA

Balance Sheet & Other Fin. Data (Million $)

	1997	1996	1995	1994	1993	1992	1991	1990	1989	1988
Cash	22.1	53.0	97.3	NA	NA	NA	NA	NA	NA	NA
Curr. Assets	403	523	526	NA	NA	NA	NA	NA	NA	NA
Total Assets	847	979	944	NA	NA	NA	NA	NA	NA	NA
Curr. Liab.	300	380	545	NA	NA	NA	NA	NA	NA	NA
LT Debt	237	215	100	NA	NA	NA	NA	NA	NA	NA
Common Eqty.	214	306	209	NA	NA	NA	NA	NA	NA	NA
Total Cap.	451	521	309	NA	NA	NA	NA	NA	NA	NA
Cap. Exp.	67.5	96.0	69.3	NA	NA	NA	NA	NA	NA	NA
Cash Flow	148	240	225	NA	NA	NA	NA	NA	NA	NA
Curr. Ratio	1.3	1.4	1.0	NA	NA	NA	NA	NA	NA	NA
% LT Debt of Cap.	52.5	41.3	32.4	NA	NA	NA	NA	NA	NA	NA
% Net Inc.of Revs.	6.7	12.8	12.1	NA	NA	NA	NA	NA	NA	NA
% Ret. on Assets	9.0	18.2	NA	NA	NA	NA	NA	NA	NA	NA
% Ret. on Equity	31.6	48.5	NA	NA	NA	NA	NA	NA	NA	NA

Data as orig. reptd.; bef. results of disc. opers. and/or spec. items. Per share data adj. for stk. divs. as of ex-div. date. Bold denotes diluted EPS (FASB 128). E-Estimated. NA-Not Available. NM-Not Meaningful. NR-Not Ranked.

Office—P.O. Box 2353, Orlando, FL 32802-2353. **Tel**—(407) 826-5050. **Website**—http://www.tupperware.com **Chrmn & CEO**—E. V. Goings. **Pres** —A. D. Kennedy. **SVP & CFO**—T. O'Neill. **VP & Treas**—J. M. Moline. **SVP & Secy**—T. M. Roehlk. **Investor Contact**—Christine J. Hanneman. **Dirs**—Dr. R. Bornstein, W. O. Bourke, R. M. Davis, L. C. Elam, E. V. Goings, C. J. Grum, J.R. Lee, B. Marbut, D. Parker, R. M. Price, J. M. Roche. **Transfer Agent & Registrar**—Norwest Bank Minnesota. **Incorporated**—in Delaware in 1996. **Empl**— 6,800. **S&P Analyst:** Robert J. Izmirlian

12-SEP-98

Industry: Manufacturing (Diversi- fied)

Summary: This leading maker of fire protection systems also pro- vides electronic security services and makes disposable medical products, flow control products, and electrical components.

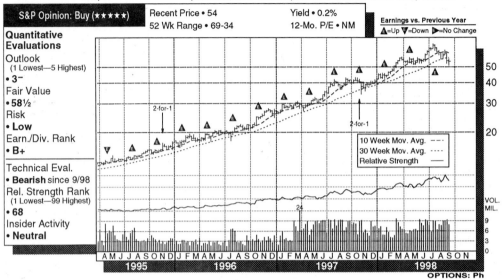

S&P Opinion: Buy (★★★★★)	Recent Price • 54	Yield • 0.2%
	52 Wk Range • 69-34	12-Mo. P/E • NM

Quantitative Evaluations

Outlook
(1 Lowest—5 Highest)
• **3⁻**

Fair Value
• **58½**

Risk
• **Low**

Earn./Div. Rank
• **B+**

Technical Eval.
• **Bearish** since 9/98

Rel. Strength Rank
(1 Lowest—99 Highest)
• **68**

Insider Activity
• **Neutral**

Earnings vs. Previous Year
▲=Up ▼=Down ▶=No Change

10 Week Mov. Avg. - - - -
30 Week Mov. Avg. ·······
Relative Strength ——

OPTIONS: Ph

Overview - 20-AUG-98

During the September 1997 quarter, Tyco changed its reporting period to a September 30 fiscal year. Solid sales gains from comparable operations should con- tinue through FY 99, with gains likely in all segments. Strong internal growth and favorable economies in global markets served by TYC should aid sales. The full-year inclusion of Sherwood-Davis & Geck (bought in March 1998) and the addition of several other recent acquisitions will also boost Tyco's top line. Operating margins should widen, on a better sales mix, production efficiencies, reduced overhead costs and benefits of fur- ther integration of recent takeovers. Tyco only acquires companies that can immediately add to EPS, and we expect noticeable contributions from recent additions; the planned purchase of U.S. Surgical Corp. should also work. Tyco has embarked on a major integration program for a variety of large takeovers completed in the second half of calendar 1997, which includes the shutdown of offices and plants and workforce reduc- tions. It recorded $1.27 billion of related after-tax charges in the September 1997 quarter (not shown in EPS table). TYC's aggressive integration plans will also continue with its more recent acquisitions.

Valuation - 20-AUG-98

The shares have been in a strong uptrend since late 1994, driven by Tyco's favorable earnings reports and prospects, and investor excitement about TYC's savvy acquisition program. Given our enthusiasm for TYC's operating strategy and business sectors, we expect its earnings momentum to continue for an extended pe- riod. That outlook leads us to anticipate ongoing appre- ciation for the stock. The shares should also continue to get a boost from the variety of major acquisitions com- pleted since mid-1997, which all seem to be fitting in quite well in the Tyco organization.

Key Stock Statistics

S&P EPS Est. 1998	2.02	Tang. Bk. Value/Share	NM
P/E on S&P Est. 1998	26.8	Beta	1.06
S&P EPS Est. 1999	2.65	Shareholders	7,700
Dividend Rate/Share	0.10	Market cap. (B)	$ 31.7
Shs. outstg. (M)	585.6	Inst. holdings	82%
Avg. daily vol. (M)	2.032		

Value of $10,000 invested 5 years ago: $ 53,807

Fiscal Year Ending Sep. 30

	1998	1997	1996	1995	1994	1993
Revenues (Million $)						
1Q	2,688	2,290	1,216	1,054	790.0	809.0
2Q	2,852	2,333	1,244	1,098	802.9	765.1
3Q	3,235	2,548	1,258	1,135	809.9	744.2
4Q	—	2,709	1,372	1,248	860.1	796.4
Yr.	—	—	5,090	4,535	3,263	3,115
Earnings Per Share ($)						
1Q	**0.43**	0.30	0.22	0.18	0.15	0.13
2Q	**0.48**	0.31	0.23	0.09	0.16	0.14
3Q	**0.54**	—	0.26	0.21	0.17	0.14
4Q	**E0.57**	—	0.31	0.23	0.19	-0.02
Yr.	**E2.02**	--	1.02	0.72	0.68	0.40

Next earnings report expected: late October

Dividend Data (Dividends have been paid since 1975.)

Amount ($)	Date Decl.	Ex-Div. Date	Stock of Record	Payment Date
0.025	Aug. 21	Sep. 29	Oct. 01	Nov. 11 '97
0.025	Dec. 16	Dec. 30	Jan. 02	Feb. 02 '98
0.025	Mar. 23	Apr. 01	Apr. 03	May. 04 '98
0.025	Jun. 15	Jun. 30	Jul. 03	Aug. 03 '98

A Division of The McGraw-Hill Companies

STANDARD
&POOR'S
STOCK REPORTS

Tyco International Ltd.

2262F

12-SEP-98

Business Summary - 20-AUG-98

Tyco International is a global conglomerate, with operations in four core areas: disposable and specialty products (30% of sales and 44% of operating profits in FY 97 (Jun.; since changed to September 30), fire and safety services (39% and 24%, respectively), flow control (22% and 19%) and electrical and electronic components (9% and 13%). Tyco has been very aggressive in the takeover arena, closing more than 10 acquisitions between July 1996 and August 1997, for a combined value in excess of $10 billion. Each met Tyco's established acquisition criteria, where the acquired firm must make an immediate positive contribution to earnings and strengthen a core business in a strategic way. The program continued into FY 98, and has included a May 1998 agreement to buy U.S. Surgical Corp. (NYSE: USS) for some 59 million TYC shares; the March 1998 purchase of an American Home Products Corp. unit for $1.8 billion in cash; plus several smaller transactions.

In the fire and safety area, Tyco ranks as the world's largest contractor for the design and installation of fire detection, suppression and sprinkler systems, and for the servicing of such systems. These systems get placed in buildings and other installations. Through TYC's July 1997 merger with ADT Ltd. (annual revenues of about $1.7 billion), the division also became the leading provider of electronic security services in North America and the U.K. TYC merged with ADT under a complex stock swap valued at around $6 billion.

Flow control products consist of pipe, fittings, valves, meters and related products, which are used to transport, control and measure the flow of liquids and gases. TYC expanded this division through the August 1997 acquisition of Keystone International (annual revenues of $675 million), a maker of industrial valves, for about $1.3 billion in TYC stock.

The electrical and electronic components sector makes underwater communications cable, cable assemblies, printed circuit boards, electrical conduit and related components. It also assembles backplanes for the electronics field. In July 1997, Tyco bought AT&T's submarine systems business (annual revenues of $1 billion) for $850 million. The unit makes, installs and maintains undersea fiber optic telecommunications systems.

The disposable and specialty products segment produces medical supplies, adhesive products and tapes, disposable medical products, and various other products. In May 1998, TYC agreed to buy U.S. Surgical (sales of $1.2 billion in 1997), a leading maker of surgical wound closure products and advanced surgical products. When added to its March 1998 purchase of the Sherwood-Davis & Geck unit (annual sales of about $1 billion) of American Home Products, and its prior operations in that area, TYC will be one of the world's leaders in disposable medical devices.

Per Share Data ($)

(Year Ended Sep. 30)	1997	1996	1995	1994	1993	1992	1991	1990	1989	1988
Tangible Bk. Val.	2.60	2.31	2.08	1.16	0.47	0.61	0.24	1.46	0.75	1.40
Cash Flow	1.68	1.28	1.16	1.03	0.74	0.87	0.99	NA	0.99	0.83
Earnings	1.30	1.01	0.72	0.68	0.40	0.52	0.64	0.72	0.58	0.48
Dividends	0.10	0.10	0.10	0.13	0.07	0.11	0.09	0.08	0.08	0.06
Payout Ratio	8%	10%	14%	19%	19%	22%	14%	11%	15%	12%
Prices - High	45½	28	17⅞	13⅞	13	10⅝	13⅛	16½	13½	9⅝
- Low	25⅞	16¼	11⅝	10¾	9⅜	7⅝	2	9¼	8⅛	5¼
P/E Ratio - High	35	28	18	20	33	21	20	23	23	20
- Low	20	16	11	16	24	15	11	13	14	11

Income Statement Analysis (Million $)

	1997	1996	1995	1994	1993	1992	1991	1990	1989	1988
Revs.	6,598	5,090	4,535	3,263	3,115	3,066	3,108	2,103	1,971	1,575
Oper. Inc.	899	666	618	312	282	261	328	287	234	168
Depr.	120	83.0	133	66.2	63.1	66.5	64.8	43.7	40.6	33.2
Int. Exp.	90.8	62.0	63.0	45.0	50.5	63.3	73.9	41.3	45.0	25.8
Pretax Inc.	688	524	385	201	129	131	189	202	146	105
Eff. Tax Rate	39%	41%	44%	38%	44%	28%	38%	41%	38%	37%
Net Inc.	419	310	217	125	72.0	95.0	117	119	91.0	66.0

Balance Sheet & Other Fin. Data (Million $)

	1997	1996	1995	1994	1993	1992	1991	1990	1989	1988
Cash	171	69.4	66.0	6.2	32.9	32.1	22.7	15.8	9.9	7.4
Curr. Assets	2,447	1,696	1,452	1,048	1,133	1,107	1,098	732	728	605
Total Assets	5,888	3,954	3,381	2,416	2,459	2,452	2,393	1,417	1,399	941
Curr. Liab.	1,735	1,292	1,085	811	869	833	855	513	436	302
LT Debt	919	512	506	413	562	535	609	270	445	324
Common Eqty.	73,052	1,938	1,635	1,079	920	1,041	905	607	491	293
Total Cap.	3,996	2,469	2,151	1,506	1,490	1,602	1,538	904	963	640
Cap. Exp.	199	123	119	73.0	80.0	68.0	67.0	55.0	121	110
Cash Flow	539	393	350	191	135	162	182	NA	NA	132
Curr. Ratio	1.4	1.3	1.3	1.3	1.3	1.3	1.3	1.4	1.7	2.0
% LT Debt of Cap.	23.0	20.7	23.5	27.4	37.7	33.4	39.6	29.8	46.2	50.7
% Net Inc.of Revs.	6.4	6.1	4.8	3.8	2.3	3.1	3.8	5.7	4.6	4.2
% Ret. on Assets	8.5	8.5	6.6	5.1	3.0	3.9	NA	8.5	7.3	8.7
% Ret. on Equity	16.8	17.4	14.4	12.5	7.4	9.8	NA	21.7	21.9	25.3

Data as orig. reptd.; bef. results of disc. opers. and/or spec. items. Per share data adj. for stk. divs. as of ex-div. date. Yrs. ended Jun. 30 prior to 1997 on Rev. and EPS tables, and through 1997 on Per Share Data, Income Statement and Balance Sheet tables; 1997 Rev. and EPS tables restated for pooling-of-int. acqs. Bold denotes diluted EPS (FASB 128). E-Estimated. NA-Not Available. NM-Not Meaningful.

Office—The Gibbons Building, 10 Queen Street, Suite 301, Hamilton HM11 Bermuda. **Tel**—(441) 292-8674. **Website**—http://www.tycoint.com **Chrmn, Pres & CEO**—L. D. Kozlowski. **SVP & Investor Contact**—J. Brad McGee (603-778-9700). **Dirs**—M. A. Ashcroft, J. M. Berman, R. S. Bodman, J. F. Fort, III, S. W. Foss, R. A. Gilleland, P. M. Hampton, L. D. Kozlowski, J. S. Pasman Jr., W. P. Slusser, F. E. Walsh, Jr. **Transfer Agents & Registrars**—AS&K Services Ltd., Hamilton, Bermuda; ChaseMellon Shareholder Services, Ridgefield Park, NJ, and Essex, U.K. **Incorporated**—in Bermuda in 1984. **Empl**—75,000. **S&P Analyst**: Michael W. Jaffe

Unicom

2270R

NYSE Symbol **UCM**

In S&P 500

12-SEP-98

Industry:
Electric Companies

Summary: This electric utility holding company (formerly Commonwealth Edison) serves more than 3.4 million customers in the diverse economy of northern Illinois.

S&P Opinion: Hold (★★★)	Recent Price • 36⅛	Yield • 4.4%
	52 Wk Range • 36⅞-22½	12-Mo. P/E • NM

Quantitative Evaluations

Outlook
(1 Lowest—5 Highest)
• **2**

Fair Value
• **33¾**

Risk
• **Average**

Earn./Div. Rank
• **B**

Technical Eval.
• **Bearish** since 4/98

Rel. Strength Rank
(1 Lowest—99 Highest)
• **95**

Insider Activity
• **NA**

Earnings vs. Previous Year
▲=Up ▼=Down ▷=No Change

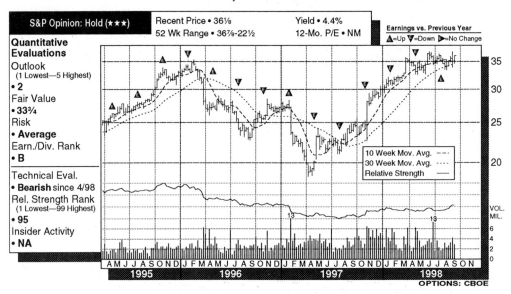

10 Week Mov. Avg. ----
30 Week Mov. Avg. ·······
Relative Strength ——

OPTIONS: CBOE

Overview - 26-AUG-98

We expect EPS to grow about 16% in 1999. Aided by reduced operating and maintenance expenses tied to the impressive restoration of UCM's nuclear program, 1998 EPS will recover from their 1997 decline. Excluding one-time items, UCM earned $1.99 in 1997. In July 1998, the NRC removed the Dresden nuclear plant from its Watch List, and has allowed the restart of LaSalle Unit 1. While results in 1999 should also benefit from a reduced level of purchased power expenses, earnings will continue to be restricted by accelerated depreciation of nuclear facilities. In December 1997, Illinois enacted legislation that calls for a 15% rate reduction as of August 1, 1998. However, it also provides UCM with the means to recover a significant portion of its substantial stranded costs. For the longer term, earnings should benefit from the improved performance of UCM's nuclear plants, and from greater cost efficiencies in its non-nuclear operations.

Valuation - 26-AUG-98

We would continue to hold the stock. Reflecting continuing improvement of UCM's nuclear program, the shares were recently up about 16% in 1998, compared to an approximate 4% increase for the S&P Index of Electric Companies. The shares have gained more than 90% since hitting their low in early 1997, when the Nuclear Regulatory Commission placed two more of UCM's nuclear plants on its watch list. The shares then recovered, benefiting from the low interest rate environment, and from anticipation (and subsequent enactment) of legislation that, despite its call for sharp rate reductions, would provide for a relatively smooth transition to a more competitive market environment. While the dividend remains secure, we do not expect an increase for the foreseeable future.

Key Stock Statistics

S&P EPS Est. 1998	2.20	Tang. Bk. Value/Share	22.51
P/E on S&P Est. 1998	16.4	Beta	0.33
S&P EPS Est. 1999	2.55	Shareholders	171,900
Dividend Rate/Share	1.60	Market cap. (B)	$ 7.8
Shs. outstg. (M)	217.0	Inst. holdings	61%
Avg. daily vol. (M)	0.664		

Value of $10,000 invested 5 years ago: $ 21,374

Fiscal Year Ending Dec. 31

	1998	1997	1996	1995	1994	1993
Revenues (Million $)						
1Q	1,712	1,750	1,684	1,578	1,525	1,483
2Q	1,779	1,651	1,548	1,560	1,432	1,431
3Q	—	2,107	2,068	2,191	1,855	1,872
4Q	—	1,655	1,637	1,582	1,465	474.1
Yr.	—	7,083	6,937	6,910	6,278	5,260
Earnings Per Share ($)						
1Q	**0.25**	0.51	0.64	0.41	0.17	0.23
2Q	**0.37**	-0.08	0.47	0.51	-0.11	0.27
3Q	**E1.16**	1.23	1.55	1.90	1.23	1.27
4Q	**E0.42**	-2.54	0.44	0.25	0.37	-1.60
Yr.	**E2.20**	-1.10	3.09	3.07	1.66	0.17

Next earnings report expected: NA

Dividend Data (Dividends have been paid since 1890.)

Amount ($)	Date Decl.	Ex-Div. Date	Stock of Record	Payment Date
0.400	Dec. 10	Dec. 29	Dec. 31	Feb. 01 '98
0.400	Mar. 11	Mar. 27	Mar. 31	May. 01 '98
0.400	May. 29	Jun. 26	Jun. 30	Aug. 01 '98
0.400	Sep. 10	Sep. 28	Sep. 30	Nov. 01 '98

A Division of The McGraw·Hill Companies

STANDARD
&POOR'S
STOCK REPORTS

Unicom Corporation

2270R
12-SEP-98

Business Summary - 26-AUG-98

Unicom (formerly Commonwealth Edison) is an electric utility holding company that, through its ComEd subsidiary, serves 3.4 million customers in Chicago and northern Illinois. It is also the owner and operator of the largest network of nuclear plants in the U.S.

Contributions to electric revenues by customer class in recent years:

	1997	1996	1995
Residential	38%	37%	38%
Small commercial & industrial	32%	30%	30%
Large commercial & industrial	22%	21%	21%
Other	8%	12%	11%

Sources of power generation in 1997 were nuclear, 57% (67% in 1996); coal, 39% (30%); natural gas, 4% (2%) and oil, nil (1%).

In December 1997, Illinois enacted legislation that will reduce residential rates 15% as of August 1, 1998 and an additional 5% as of May 1, 2002. The bill provides for the phase in of customer choice of supplier, with all customers able to choose as of May 1, 2002. UCM will be able to securitize revenues to mitigate stranded costs (cost commitments above asset market value) and to collect a "Competitive Transition Charge" from customers who select an alternate supplier.

In January 1997, the Nuclear Regulatory Commission (NRC) added ComEd's LaSalle and Zion nuclear plants to its "Watch List" of problem plants and said that the Dresden plant would remain on the list. UCM responded to the NRC concerns and initiated an 11% increase in the 1997 operating and maintenance expenditures for its nuclear program.

In July 1998, the NRC removed the Dresden plant from its Watch List, but kept the LaSalle plant on the list. However, the NRC did allow LaSalle Unit 1 to be restarted, and it is expected that, after an extensive testing operation, it will be returned to operation. LaSalle Unit 2 has been scheduled for restart in the spring of 1999. Earlier, in January 1998, ComEd announced the retirement of its Zion nuclear plant, after determining that it would not be able to produce competitively priced power over its remaining licensed life (2013).

UCM's construction expenditures in 1997 totaled $970 million, and it expected to spend $930 million in 1998 (not including nuclear fuel expenditures of $160 million), mainly for improvements to existing facilities.

Unicom Enterprises, an unregulated subsidiary, provides district cooling services to office and other buildings in Chicago through wholly owned Unicom Thermal. The company's other wholly owned subsidiary, Unicom Technology Development, is involved in the commercial application of advanced technologies for the power industry.

Per Share Data ($)

(Year Ended Dec. 31)	1997	1996	1995	1994	1993	1992	1991	1990	1989	1988
Tangible Bk. Val.	22.49	28.03	26.58	25.15	25.02	26.43	26.72	29.63	32.46	32.63
Earnings	-1.10	3.09	3.07	1.66	0.17	2.08	0.08	0.22	2.83	3.01
Dividends	1.60	1.60	1.60	1.60	1.60	2.30	3.00	3.00	3.00	3.00
Payout Ratio	NM	52%	52%	96%	NM	111%	NM	NM	106%	100%
Prices - High	30¾	35⅜	33⅞	28¾	31⅝	40⅛	42⅝	37⅞	40¾	33⅜
- Low	18½	22⅝	23¼	20⅝	22⅞	21¾	33⅝	27¼	32⅛	22¾
P/E Ratio - High	NM	11	11	17	NM	19	NM	NM	14	11
- Low	NM	7	8	12	NM	10	NM	NM	11	8

Income Statement Analysis (Million $)

	1997	1996	1995	1994	1993	1992	1991	1990	1989	1988
Revs.	7,083	6,937	6,910	6,278	5,260	6,026	6,276	5,262	5,751	5,613
Depr.	1,005	954	898	887	863	835	825	879	865	844
Maint.	NA	NA	NA	561	582	588	527	489	436	434
Fxd. Chgs. Cov.	1.9	2.8	2.7	1.8	1.1	2.0	1.5	1.3	2.5	2.5
Constr. Credits	42.3	40.2	24.0	42.0	38.0	37.0	32.0	36.0	43.0	135
Eff. Tax Rate	767%	41%	40%	40%	26%	34%	79%	60%	38%	36%
Net Inc.	-239	666	660	355	103	514	95.0	128	694	738

Balance Sheet & Other Fin. Data (Million $)

	1997	1996	1995	1994	1993	1992	1991	1990	1989	1988
Gross Prop.	28,424	28,706	27,788	26,947	26,760	26,291	25,164	24,963	24,436	21,447
Cap. Exp.	1,229	1,264	1,216	997	1,102	1,216	1,212	959	1,051	965
Net Prop.	16,778	17,226	17,222	17,323	17,892	15,283	15,003	15,506	15,783	16,127
Capitalization:										
LT Debt	5,737	6,070	6,549	7,886	7,872	7,948	7,123	7,306	6,964	6,896
% LT Debt	49	46	49	56	56	55	52	50	47	47
Pfd.	1,031	925	969	800	751	755	797	866	896	979
% Pfd.	8.80	7.10	7.30	5.70	5.30	5.20	5.80	6.00	6.10	6.60
Common	4,919	6,104	5,770	5,448	5,422	5,708	5,738	6,345	6,923	6,949
% Common	42	47	43	39	39	40	42	44	47	47
Total Cap.	16,140	18,806	18,859	19,236	14,792	15,188	14,469	15,373	15,667	15,793
% Oper. Ratio	87.0	81.8	80.6	82.7	92.3	80.1	79.0	82.5	76.6	77.9
% Earn. on Net Prop.	5.4	7.3	7.8	6.2	2.3	7.9	8.6	5.9	8.5	7.6
% Return On Revs.	NA	9.6	9.6	5.7	2.0	8.5	1.5	2.4	12.1	13.1
% Return On Invest. Capital	6.3	8.9	6.9	5.4	0.5	7.8	5.0	4.9	8.3	8.5
% Return On Com. Equity	NA	11.2	11.4	6.5	0.8	7.7	0.3	0.7	8.6	9.2

Data as orig. reptd.; bef. results of disc opers. and/or spec. items. Per share data adj. for stk. divs. as of ex-div. date. Bold denotes diluted EPS (FASB 128). E-Estimated. NA-Not Available. NM-Not Meaningful. NR-Not Ranked.

Office—10 South Dearborn St., 37th Fl., P.O. Box A-3005, Chicago, IL 60690-3005. **Tel**—(312) 394-7399. **Website**—http://www.ucm.com **Chrmn, Pres & CEO**—J. W. Rowe. **SVP & CFO**—J. C. Bukovski. **Secy**—D. A. Scholz. **Investor Contact**—Eunice Collins (8354). **Dirs**—E. A. Brennan, C. H. Cantu, J. W. Compton, B. DeMars, S. L. Gin, D. P. Jacobs, E. D. Janotta, G. E. Johnson, J. W. Rowe, R. L. Thomas. **Transfer Agent & Registrar**—First Chicago Trust Co. of New York, Jersey City and Chicago. **Incorporated**—in Illinois in 1913. **Empl**—16,704. **S&P Analyst:** Justin McCann

STANDARD &POOR'S
STOCK REPORTS

Unilever N.V.

2271K

NYSE Symbol **UN**

In S&P 500

12-SEP-98

Industry: Foods

Summary: This company and Unilever PLC constitute a vast international organization that is a world leader in brand name consumer goods, mainly foods, detergents and toiletries.

S&P Opinion: Hold (★★★)	Recent Price • 67⅛ Yield • 1.4% 52 Wk Range • 83⅞-48⅜ 12-Mo. P/E • 33.1

Quantitative Evaluations

Outlook
(1 Lowest—5 Highest)
• **1+**

Fair Value
• **62¼**

Risk
• **Low**

Earn./Div. Rank
• **A**

Technical Eval.
• **Bullish** since 7/98

Rel. Strength Rank
(1 Lowest—99 Highest)
• **74**

Insider Activity
• **NA**

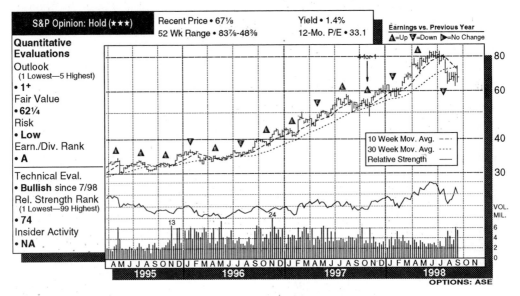

Earnings vs. Previous Year ▲=Up ▼=Down ▷=No Change

10 Week Mov. Avg. - - -
30 Week Mov. Avg. ·····
Relative Strength —

VOL. MIL.

OPTIONS: ASE

Overview - 10-AUG-98

We expect 1998 sales to be flat or to decline slightly, as the absence of sales from discontinued or disposed businesses outweighs contributions from acquisitions and modest price and volume increases. This should result in sales from continuing operations increasing at a mid-single digit pace. Growth in developing markets should increase due to price and volume increases. Operating margins are likely to slip given heavy promotional spending in the Americas and Europe. Additionally, Asia-Pacific margins may be hurt by the financial problems in that region. Strong cash flows, coupled with profits from divestitures, will permit additional acquisitions. In addition, UN's accelerated restructuring program, as well as its decision to focus on the consumer goods operations, particularly in emerging markets, should further boost long-term profitability. For the short term, however, a rising dollar versus the Dutch guilder is likely to restrict dollar-denominated earnings.

Valuation - 10-AUG-98

We recently downgraded the shares to hold, from accumulate. UN has many vast opportunities to grow in developing countries, which should help fuel future results. However, in order to gain market share in the Americas and Europe, the company has had to increase its advertising and promotional expenses considerably. It is likely that Procter & Gamble and Colgate-Palmolive may retaliate to protect market share. Given expected margin weakness from the promotional spending and expected retaliation by competitors, we are reducing our 1998 EPS estimate by U.S. $0.05, to $2.60, and rate the shares a hold until there is some certainty that market share gains can be retained without more promotional spending.

Key Stock Statistics

S&P EPS Est. 1998	2.60	Tang. Bk. Value/Share	NM
P/E on S&P Est. 1998	25.8	Beta	0.83
S&P EPS Est. 1999	3.00	Shareholders	78,800
Dividend Rate/Share	0.97	Market cap. (B)	$ 43.0
Shs. outstg. (M)	640.2	Inst. holdings	26%
Avg. daily vol. (M)	0.987		

Value of $10,000 invested 5 years ago: $ 28,529

Fiscal Year Ending Dec. 31

	1998	1997	1996	1995	1994	1993
Revenues (Million $)						
1Q	11,577	12,429	13,893	10,902	10,172	9,675
2Q	12,128	13,740	13,893	12,235	11,650	10,647
3Q	—	12,842	13,802	12,487	11,737	10,649
4Q	—	11,717	13,687	14,107	11,860	10,907
Yr.	—	48,721	52,161	49,732	45,419	41,878
Earnings Per Share ($)						
1Q	**0.62**	0.43	0.44	0.42	0.39	0.39
2Q	**0.65**	3.77	0.49	0.58	0.51	0.53
3Q	**E0.73**	0.76	0.69	0.69	0.62	0.55
4Q	**E0.60**	Nil	0.60	0.38	0.61	0.27
Yr.	**E2.60**	4.96	2.23	2.07	2.13	1.74

Next earnings report expected: early November

Dividend Data (Dividends have been paid since 1955.)

Amount ($)	Date Decl.	Ex-Div. Date	Stock of Record	Payment Date
4-for-1	—	Oct. 21	Oct. 10	Oct. 20 '97
0.327	—	Nov. 13	Nov. 17	Dec. 19 '97
0.635	—	May. 11	May. 13	Jun. 01 '98

A Division of The **McGraw·Hill** *Companies*

STANDARD
&POOR'S
STOCK REPORTS

Unilever N.V.

2271K
12-SEP-98

Business Summary - 10-AUG-98

With a portfolio of more than 1,000 brands in three key product categories (foods, home and personal care products), Unilever touches the lives of more than half of the families around the globe. Its products include local, regional and international brands that take into account the differences among various consumers.

Unilever continues to expand its businesses through geographic expansion as well as via the development of existing business and new product extensions, particularly concentrating on the fastest growing markets outside Europe and North America, where sales have grown from 19% to more than 30% of total sales in the past 10 years. On average, the company launches a new product or processing method nearly every day. In categories like shampoo, toothpaste and prestige fragrances, for example, more than 40% of sales come from products created in the past three years.

In the past three years, Unilever has added Bolivia, Israel, Russia, Romania, Lebanon, Paraguay, Peru, Syria, Zambia and Vietnam to the list of more than 160 countries in which its products are sold. It plans to concentrate its new investments in five priority regions: Central and Eastern Europe, China, India, Southeast Asia, and South Latin America. In 1997, it acquired 23 businesses, most notably Kibon, Monthelado and Ho-

landa ice cream businesses in Latin America, and disposed of 19 others.

The foods divisions, which account for about half of Unilever's business, focus on six main areas: margarine, tea, ice cream, culinary products, frozen foods and bakery products. The company tries to develop global brands for products with an international reach, like ice cream and tea, and provide strong local and regional brands for other products.

The household products business, encompassing products for cleaning fabrics, surfaces and people, operates in every country in which UN has a presence. Products range from basic hard soap bars for hand washing, to high-end concentrated detergents for washing machines.

In the personal care category, UN covers the spectrum, from mass market toiletries to the most sophisticated cosmetics and fragrances. Strictly a toothpaste, hair care and deodorants business until just a few years ago, UN now offers skin care, cosmetics and fragrances, covering both the mass and prestige markets.

In July 1997, Unilever sold its specialty chemicals businesses (National Starch and Chemical Co., Quest International, Unichema International, and Crosfield) to Imperial Chemical Industries, PLC, in order to concentrate on its consumer goods operations.

Per Share Data ($)

(Year Ended Dec. 31)	1997	1996	1995	1994	1993	1992	1991	1990	1989	1988
Tangible Bk. Val.	NA	NA	NA	NA	NA	NA	NA	NA	NA	NA
Cash Flow	NA	NA	NA	NA	NA	NA	NA	NA	NA	NA
Earnings	4.96	2.23	2.07	2.13	1.74	2.04	1.81	1.76	1.50	1.35
Dividends	0.84	0.77	0.85	0.69	0.67	0.69	0.64	0.60	0.52	0.44
Payout Ratio	17%	35%	41%	32%	38%	34%	35%	34%	34%	32%
Prices - High	62⅞	44	35½	30⅛	29⅞	29¼	26⅝	22¾	21¼	15⅞
- Low	40⅞	32½	28⅝	25	23⅞	24¼	18½	18	14½	12½
P/E Ratio - High	13	20	17	14	17	14	15	13	14	12
- Low	8	15	14	12	14	12	10	10	10	9

Income Statement Analysis (Million $)

	1997	1996	1995	1994	1993	1992	1991	1990	1989	1988
Revs.	NA	87,795	49,732	45,419	41,878	43,719	40,767	39,620	34,434	30,980
Oper. Inc.	NA	10,372	NA	4,977	3,918	4,742	4,439	4,467	3,836	3,356
Depr.	NA	2,224	NA	1,121	1,013	986	922	816	672	612
Int. Exp.	NA	969	NA	537	526	627	792	842	670	424
Pretax Inc.	NA	6,960	3,659	3,648	2,915	3,591	3,154	3,172	2,883	2,631
Eff. Tax Rate	NA	36%	34%	32%	30%	34%	33%	34%	38%	40%
Net Inc.	NA	4,215	2,324	2,386	1,949	2,286	2,028	1,980	1,687	1,510

Balance Sheet & Other Fin. Data (Million $)

	1997	1996	1995	1994	1993	1992	1991	1990	1989	1988
Cash	NA	3,893	2,313	2,327	1,731	2,204	1,838	1,609	854	2,560
Curr. Assets	NA	30,138	16,314	15,337	13,133	13,140	13,834	13,654	11,539	11,951
Total Assets	NA	54,040	30,067	28,393	24,735	24,267	25,394	24,737	20,618	19,909
Curr. Liab.	NA	21,076	11,668	11,029	10,200	10,054	10,530	10,418	9,388	8,381
LT Debt	NA	3,650	3,407	3,230	2,176	2,548	3,158	3,383	2,384	1,655
Common Eqty.	NA	16,877	8,729	8,188	6,813	6,789	6,367	5,389	4,262	5,676
Total Cap.	NA	NA	NA	12,233	10,091	10,795	10,991	10,174	7,966	8,841
Cap. Exp.	NA	NA	1,780	2,185	2,031	1,678	1,978	2,104	1,734	1,506
Cash Flow	NA	6,424	NA	3,499	2,950	3,262	2,943	2,788	2,351	2,114
Curr. Ratio	NA	1.4	1.4	1.4	1.3	1.3	1.3	1.3	1.2	1.4
% LT Debt of Cap.	NA	NA	NA	26.4	21.6	23.6	28.7	33.3	29.9	18.7
% Net Inc.of Revs.	NA	4.8	4.7	5.3	4.7	5.2	5.0	5.0	4.9	4.9
% Ret. on Assets	NA	8.2	8.0	9.0	7.9	9.2	8.1	8.7	8.3	7.8
% Ret. on Equity	NA	26.0	27.5	31.7	28.5	34.6	34.4	40.9	33.8	26.8

Data as orig. reptd.; Unilever PLC and Unilever N.V. combined; bef. results of disc. opers. and/or spec. items. Per New York sh. data (equiv. to one ord. sh.); adj. for stk. divs. as of ex-div. date. Quarterly data based on varying exch. rates; quarters will not add to yr. end totals. E-Estimated. NA-Not Available. NM-Not Meaningful. NR-Not Ranked.

Office—Weena 455 (P.O. Box 760) 3000 DK Rotterdam, The Netherlands. **Registrar**—Morgan Guaranty Trust Co., NYC.**Tel**—(212) 906-4694.**Website**—http://www.unilever.com**U.S. Investor Contact**—Mike Miller, 390 Park Ave., New York, NY 10022. **Dirs**—M. Tabaksblat (Chrmn), N. W. A. FitzGerald (Vice Chrmn), J. I. W. Anderson, R. D. Brown, A. Burgmans, A. C. Butler, H. Eggerstedt, A. Kemner, J. Peelen, R. Phillips. **Secys**—J. W. B. Westerburgen, S. G. Williams. **Transfer Agent & Registrar**—New York Shares: Morgan Guaranty Trust Co., NYC. **Incorporated**—in the Netherlands in 1927. **Empl**— 270,000. **S&P Analyst:** Robert J. Izmirlian

STANDARD &POOR'S
STOCK REPORTS

Union Camp

2274

NYSE Symbol **UCC**

In S&P 500

12-SEP-98

Industry:
Containers and Packaging (Paper)

Summary: This major producer of paper, paperboard and packaging also has interests in wood products and chemicals.

| S&P Opinion: Hold (★★★) | Recent Price • 35⅝ | Yield • 5.1% |
| | 52 Wk Range • 64½-34 | 12-Mo. P/E • 23.4 |

Quantitative Evaluations

Outlook
(1 Lowest—5 Highest)
• **2**

Fair Value
• **35⅞**

Risk
• **Low**

Earn./Div. Rank
• **B-**

Technical Eval.
• **Neutral** since 6/98

Rel. Strength Rank
(1 Lowest—99 Highest)
• **39**

Insider Activity
• **NA**

Earnings vs. Previous Year
▲=Up ▼=Down ▶=No Change

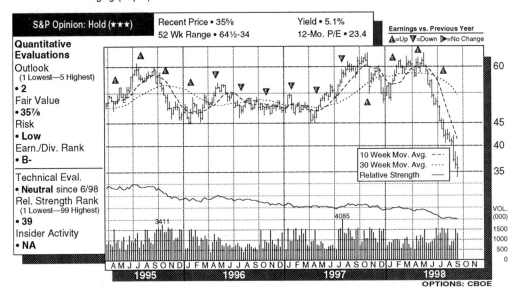

10 Week Mov. Avg. — — —
30 Week Mov. Avg. - - - -
Relative Strength —

OPTIONS: CBOE

Overview - 18-AUG-98

Slight sales gains should be recorded in 1998, on a small increase in average paper and packaging prices. However, the modest pricing recovery seen since early 1997 in UCC's mainstay containerboard and uncoated papers have recently suffered a setback. The troubles stem mostly from foreign trade difficulties related to Asia's financial woes and a strong U.S. dollar. Margins should be about flat. On the positive side, we see Union aided by the maturation of a profit enhancement program introduced in late 1996. UCC has already started to benefit from the product mix enhancements, cost reductions, asset realignments and business process improvements introduced in that program. However, those benefits will likely be offset by the impact of downtime being taken by UCC in recognition of the recent setback in the paper and packaging recovery.

Valuation - 18-AUG-98

Union Camp's shares have seesawed over the past year. The shares headed downward in the fall of 1997, when investors began to realize that the Far Eastern currency crisis might place the previously expected paper industry recovery on hold. They then rebounded in early 1998, as investors seemingly grew more relaxed about the Asian situation. However, the shares have given back those gains and more since May, when the worries about the Far Eastern impact proved to be founded. We have lacked enthusiasm about the forest products industry throughout, and see the global economic troubles holding back commodities markets for an extended period. However, given our enthusiasm for UCC's ongoing actions to enhance its operating position, we have a neutral investment stance on the shares.

Key Stock Statistics

S&P EPS Est. 1998	1.20	Tang. Bk. Value/Share	27.55
P/E on S&P Est. 1998	29.7	Beta	0.84
S&P EPS Est. 1999	1.65	Shareholders	8,800
Dividend Rate/Share	1.80	Market cap. (B)	$ 2.5
Shs. outstg. (M)	69.3	Inst. holdings	77%
Avg. daily vol. (M)	0.245		

Value of $10,000 invested 5 years ago: $ 9,492

Fiscal Year Ending Dec. 31

	1998	1997	1996	1995	1994	1993
Revenues (Million $)						
1Q	1,145	1,057	978.3	1,021	790.1	761.5
2Q	1,134	1,106	934.0	1,109	827.2	786.5
3Q	—	1,127	1,017	1,073	856.3	778.7
4Q	—	1,187	1,084	1,008	922.2	793.8
Yr.	—	4,477	4,013	4,212	3,396	3,120
Earnings Per Share ($)						
1Q	**0.38**	**0.14**	0.85	1.50	0.16	0.18
2Q	**0.27**	**0.15**	0.26	1.90	0.37	0.22
3Q	**E0.27**	**0.40**	0.21	1.85	0.31	0.07
4Q	**E0.28**	**0.47**	-0.09	1.20	0.83	0.25
Yr.	**E1.20**	**1.16**	**1.23**	6.45	1.67	0.72

Next earnings report expected: mid October

Dividend Data (Dividends have been paid since 1940.)

Amount ($)	Date Decl.	Ex-Div. Date	Stock of Record	Payment Date
0.450	Oct. 28	Dec. 02	Dec. 04	Dec. 15 '97
0.450	Jan. 27	Mar. 02	Mar. 04	Mar. 13 '98
0.450	Apr. 28	Jun. 02	Jun. 04	Jun. 15 '98
0.450	Jun. 29	Sep. 02	Sep. 04	Sep. 14 '98

A Division of The McGraw-Hill Companies

Business Summary - 18-AUG-98

Union Camp was created in 1956 through the merger of Union Bag and Paper Corp. and Camp Mfg. Co. Today, UCC is an integrated manufacturer of paper, packaging, chemicals and wood products.

UCC's paper and paperboard segment (45% of sales in 1997) produced 3,700,000 tons of paper and paperboard in 1997. The company's unbleached kraft paper is used mainly in the production of multiwall bags, and unbleached kraft linerboard for use in corrugated shipping containers. UCC sells bleached uncoated free sheet for conversion into envelopes and forms and for use in business and printing papers. Union sold about 20% of its paper and paperboard production in export markets in 1997.

Alling & Cory Co., acquired in August 1996 for $88.5 million, distributes business communications and printing papers, industrial packaging and business products.

Packaging products (30% of sales in 1997) include multiwall bags used to package cement, feed, fertilizer, clay, pet food, chemicals and mineral products; and specialty bags and plastic packaging. UCC also makes corrugated and solid-fibre containers and makes folding cartons used for shelf packaging.

UCC owns or controls 1,605,000 acres of timberland in the Southeast, with 39% of its requirements obtained from its own timberlands in 1997. The wood products segment (8% of sales in 1997) also produces southern pine lumber, plywood and particleboard.

In chemicals (17% of sales in 1997), UCC owns 68% of Bush Boake Allen, a maker of flavors, fragrances and aroma chemicals. The segment also converts chemical byproducts from the paper pulping process into chemicals used in inks, coatings and adhesives.

In the fourth quarter of 1996, UCC initiated a program aimed at boosting pretax earnings by $100 million over the following 24 months. It expected to derive two-thirds of the gain from cost reductions and asset realignments, with the rest from shifts in product and business mix. UCC is targeting the fast-growing small office/home office business paper segment; targeting specialty lightweight and heavyweight packaging products where growth is accelerating due to world trade flows; and broadening its product line in the engineered wood products markets. In reporting 1998 second quarter results, UCC said that with the program nearing completion, it has started to develop plans for further profitability enhancements with an emphasis on structural cost improvements.

The highly cyclical paper and packaging industry tends to be greatly influenced by global economic conditions and industry capacity. After suffering from sharp price declines since the latter part of 1995, UCC's operating performance finally started to pick up in the last half of 1997. However, with economic difficulties in Asia contributing to a softer pricing environment, the recovery has suffered something of a setback recently.

Per Share Data ($)

(Year Ended Dec. 31)	1997	1996	1995	1994	1993	1992	1991	1990	1989	1988
Tangible Bk. Val.	27.55	28.76	30.23	25.68	25.41	26.93	27.38	27.81	25.19	22.66
Cash Flow	5.64	5.54	10.56	5.30	4.20	4.03	4.82	6.52	7.32	7.00
Earnings	1.17	1.23	6.45	1.67	0.72	0.61	1.80	3.35	4.35	4.25
Dividends	1.80	1.80	1.66	1.56	1.56	1.56	1.56	1.54	1.42	1.22
Payout Ratio	154%	146%	26%	93%	218%	255%	87%	45%	33%	28%
Prices - High	64¹/₂	55³/₈	61¹/₄	50⁷/₈	49¹/₈	55¹/₈	51¹/₂	39³/₄	41³/₈	38⁵/₈
- Low	45¹/₈	44⁷/₈	45³/₄	42¹/₄	38³/₄	40¹/₈	34⁵/₈	30¹/₂	33¹/₂	31
P/E Ratio - High	55	45	9	30	68	90	29	12	10	9
- Low	39	36	7	25	54	66	19	9	8	7

Income Statement Analysis (Million $)

	1997	1996	1995	1994	1993	1992	1991	1990	1989	1988
Revs.	4,477	4,013	4,212	3,396	3,120	3,064	2,967	2,840	2,761	2,661
Oper. Inc.	568	586	1,111	542	455	477	486	588	699	685
Depr.	311	298	288	253	243	238	209	217	205	191
Int. Exp.	117	117	123	131	133	150	144	100	70.0	64.0
Pretax Inc.	144	151	731	195	100	65.0	200	366	469	468
Eff. Tax Rate	36%	37%	37%	37%	50%	35%	38%	37%	36%	37%
Net Inc.	81.1	85.3	451	117	50.0	43.0	125	230	299	295

Balance Sheet & Other Fin. Data (Million $)

	1997	1996	1995	1994	1993	1992	1991	1990	1989	1988
Cash	34.9	45.0	30.0	13.0	38.0	68.0	61.0	52.0	56.0	128
Curr. Assets	1,212	1,134	1,034	951	911	1,024	910	860	721	774
Total Assets	5,242	5,096	4,838	4,777	4,685	4,739	4,698	4,400	3,417	3,094
Curr. Liab.	803	780	574	884	909	892	765	643	367	326
LT Debt	1,367	1,252	1,198	1,252	1,245	1,290	1,348	1,222	693	628
Common Eqty.	2,036	2,094	2,122	1,836	1,816	1,882	1,936	1,911	1,755	1,559
Total Cap.	4,250	4,156	4,030	3,758	3,644	3,725	3,912	3,722	3,030	2,768
Cap. Exp.	337	386	267	325	323	220	483	1,026	563	359
Cash Flow	392	384	739	371	293	280	334	447	504	486
Curr. Ratio	1.5	1.5	1.8	1.1	1.0	1.1	1.2	1.3	2.0	2.4
% LT Debt of Cap.	32.2	30.1	29.7	33.3	34.2	34.6	34.5	32.8	22.9	22.7
% Net Inc.of Revs.	1.8	2.1	10.7	3.5	1.6	1.4	4.2	8.1	10.8	11.1
% Ret. on Assets	1.6	1.7	9.4	2.5	1.1	0.9	2.7	5.9	9.2	10.1
% Ret. on Equity	3.9	4.0	22.8	6.4	2.7	2.2	6.4	12.7	18.1	20.0

Data as orig. reptd.; bef. results of disc. opers. and/or spec. items. Per share data adj. for stk. divs. as of ex-div. date. Bold denotes diluted EPS (FASB 128). E-Estimated. NA-Not Available. NM-Not Meaningful. NR-Not Ranked.

Office—1600 Valley Rd., Wayne, NJ 07470. **Tel**—(973) 628-2000. **Website**—http://www.unioncamp.com **Chrmn & CEO**—W. C. McClelland. **Pres & COO**—J. H. Ballengee. **EVP & CFO**—A. W. Hamill. **Investor Contact**—Patricia A. Spinella. **Dirs**—J. H. Ballengee, G. D. Busbee, R. E. Cartledge, Sir C. R. Corness, R. D. Kennedy, G. E. MacDougal, W. C. McClelland, A. D. McLaughlin, G. J. Sella Jr., J. J. Sheehan, T. D. Simmons. **Transfer Agent**—Bank of New York, NYC. **Incorporated**—in Virginia in 1956. **Empl**— 19,000. **S&P Analyst:** Michael W. Jaffe

STANDARD &POOR'S
STOCK REPORTS

Union Carbide

2276

NYSE Symbol **UK**

In S&P 500

12-SEP-98 | Industry: Chemicals

Summary: This company is a leading producer of petrochemicals, plastics, solvents and resins, and specialty chemicals, including ethylene oxide and its derivatives and polyethylene resins.

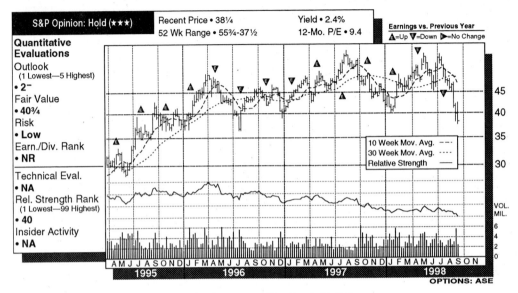

S&P Opinion: Hold (★★★)

Recent Price • 38¼
52 Wk Range • 55¾-37½

Yield • 2.4%
12-Mo. P/E • 9.4

Earnings vs. Previous Year
▲=Up ▼=Down ▶=No Change

Quantitative Evaluations

Outlook (1 Lowest—5 Highest)
• **2⁻**

Fair Value
• **40¾**

Risk
• **Low**

Earn./Div. Rank
• **NR**

Technical Eval.
• **NA**

Rel. Strength Rank (1 Lowest—99 Highest)
• **40**

Insider Activity
• **NA**

10 Week Mov. Avg. ---
30 Week Mov. Avg. ·····
Relative Strength —

OPTIONS: ASE

Overview - 20-MAY-98

We see earnings declining in 1998, on further softness in polyethylene prices resulting from the addition of major new ethylene industry capacity. Polyethylene prices have declined since mid-1997. Prices and profitability for ethylene glycol climbed for most of 1997, on improving demand from polyester markets, but are now under downward pressure, largely due to economic problems in the Far East. The less cyclical specialties and intermediates segment should return to a growth track, on price increases for solvents and lower raw material costs, although currency exchange rates will remain unfavorable. Incremental savings from UK's $1.1 billion cost reduction program will be about $180 million in 1998. Losses of a Kuwaiti petrochemical joint venture will soon end, as it increased output following its startup in late 1997, but a new ethylene/propylene rubber plant may not turn profitable until 1999, due to plant problems. UK's after tax share of preoperating expenses for the Kuwaiti venture was about $43 million in 1997, while the rubber plant had pretax losses of about $50 million. An aggressive stock repurchase program will boost share earnings.

Valuation - 20-MAY-98

S&P is maintaining its hold opinion on the shares, in view of a further downturn expected in the petrochemicals and plastics industries. We see the specialties businesses remaining healthy, however, and UK recently announced a larger cost reduction target designed to help its commodity chemicals and polymers business to achieve it goal of at least break-even performance at the bottom of the next chemicals cycle. The stock jumped recently, on rumors of a potential merger with an international oil company.

Key Stock Statistics

S&P EPS Est. 1998	3.30	Tang. Bk. Value/Share	18.11
P/E on S&P Est. 1998	11.6	Beta	1.19
S&P EPS Est. 1999	3.50	Shareholders	51,000
Dividend Rate/Share	0.90	Market cap. (B)	$ 5.2
Shs. outstg. (M)	135.3	Inst. holdings	64%
Avg. daily vol. (M)	0.709		

Value of $10,000 invested 5 years ago: $ 26,249

Fiscal Year Ending Dec. 31

	1998	1997	1996	1995	1994	1993
Revenues (Million $)						
1Q	1,561	1,638	1,501	1,453	1,126	1,193
2Q	1,459	1,666	1,559	1,541	1,177	1,244
3Q	—	1,659	1,538	1,495	1,252	1,130
4Q	—	1,539	1,508	1,399	1,310	1,073
Yr.	—	6,502	6,106	5,888	4,865	4,640
Earnings Per Share ($)						
1Q	**1.01**	**1.03**	1.11	1.57	0.39	0.28
2Q	**0.85**	**1.27**	1.23	1.59	0.44	0.24
3Q	**E0.74**	**1.18**	1.19	1.96	0.61	0.23
4Q	**E0.70**	**1.04**	0.74	1.33	1.01	0.26
Yr.	**E3.30**	**4.53**	3.90	6.44	2.44	1.00

Next earnings report expected: mid October

Dividend Data (Dividends have been paid since 1918.)

Amount ($)	Date Decl.	Ex-Div. Date	Stock of Record	Payment Date
0.225	Sep. 24	Nov. 14	Nov. 18	Dec. 01 '97
0.225	Jan. 28	Feb. 13	Feb. 18	Mar. 02 '98
0.225	Apr. 22	May. 15	May. 19	Jun. 01 '98
0.225	Jul. 22	Aug. 17	Aug. 19	Sep. 01 '98

A Division of The McGraw·Hill Companies

STANDARD
&POOR'S
STOCK REPORTS

Union Carbide Corporation

2276

12-SEP-98

Business Summary - 20-MAY-98

Top managers of UK are putting their money where their mouths are by putting a portion of their base pay (a full year's in the case of CEO Bill Joyce) at risk as part of their commitment to earn fully diluted share earnings of at least $4.00 in 1999 and 2000, which are anticipated to be trough years for the petrochemicals industry. UK has targeted $1.1 billion in annual cost savings by 2000 to help achieve its goal. UK achieved its earlier cost saving target of $637 million threeyears ahead of schedule. Since the start of a common share buyback program in 1993, the company has repurchased 50.4 million shares for $1.76 billion, under a total authorization of 60 million shares. Segment contributions in 1997 were:

	Sales	Profits
Specialties & intermediates	65%	64%
Basic chemicals & polymers	35%	37%
Other	Nil	-1%

Foreign operations accounted for 29% of sales and 9% of operating income in 1997.

Specialties and intermediates consist of ethylene oxide derivatives (polyethylene glycols, surfactants, amines, deicing fluids, heat transfer fluids, lubricants and solvents); solvents and emulsion systems (alcohols, ac-

rylics, vinyl acetate, latexes and modifiers) for use in paints, adhesives and household products; specialty polyolefins; UNIPOL technology licensing for polyethylene and polypropylene; speciality polymers and products (biocides, water soluble resins, coating materials, resins, plastic additives and modifiers), and the UOP partnership (catalysts, molecular sieves).

The company is a leading manufacturer of polyethylene, the world's most widely used plastic for films, bags, bottles and electrical insulation, and is a technology leader in this industry, and of polypropylene, one of the world's fastest growing plastics. UK is the world's largest producer of ethylene oxide and derivatives, used for antifreeze and polyester fibers, resins and films. UK manufactures about two-thirds of its ethylene requirement, and nearly one-third of its propylene needs. These are the key raw materials for many of its businesses. UK and NOVA Corp. plan to build an equally owned, 2 billion pound per year ethylene facility in Alberta, Canada, with completion expected in 2000. The company's share of the ethylene production will be used for a 1 billion pound per year polyethylene plant to be built nearby.

Startup of a petrochemical joint venture in Kuwait began production in late 1997. The world scale complex will make ethylene, polyethylene and ethylene glycol, primarily for Asian markets.

Per Share Data ($)

(Year Ended Dec. 31)	1997	1996	1995	1994	1993	1992	1991	1990	1989	1988
Tangible Bk. Val.	16.45	15.83	15.15	10.19	9.19	8.68	16.60	17.72	16.39	12.96
Cash Flow	7.88	6.58	8.67	4.24	2.85	2.98	1.20	5.56	7.61	8.36
Earnings	4.53	4.28	6.44	2.44	1.00	0.76	-1.06	2.19	4.07	4.88
Dividends	0.79	0.75	0.75	0.75	0.75	0.88	1.00	1.00	1.00	1.15
Payout Ratio	17%	18%	12%	31%	75%	114%	NM	41%	25%	24%
Prices - High	56³/₄	49⁷/₈	42³/₄	35⁷/₈	23¹/₈	29⁵/₈	22⁵/₈	24⁷/₈	33¹/₄	28³/₈
- Low	40¹/₂	36³/₈	25¹/₂	21¹/₂	16	10³/₄	15³/₈	14¹/₈	22³/₄	17
P/E Ratio - High	13	12	7	15	23	39	NM	11	8	6
- Low	9	8	4	9	16	14	NM	6	6	3

Income Statement Analysis (Million $)

	1997	1996	1995	1994	1993	1992	1991	1990	1989	1988
Revs.	6,502	6,106	5,888	4,865	4,640	4,872	4,877	7,621	8,744	8,324
Oper. Inc.	1,215	1,058	1,257	766	572	584	542	1,450	1,764	1,878
Depr.	340	312	306	274	276	293	287	476	498	473
Int. Exp.	79.0	121	113	93.0	84.0	164	245	467	432	419
Pretax Inc.	969	829	1,367	526	243	164	-167	626	916	1,165
Eff. Tax Rate	29%	28%	28%	26%	32%	27%	NM	45%	31%	38%
Net Inc.	676	593	925	389	165	119	-115	308	573	662

Balance Sheet & Other Fin. Data (Million $)

	1997	1996	1995	1994	1993	1992	1991	1990	1989	1988
Cash	68.0	94.0	449	109	108	171	64.0	127	142	146
Curr. Assets	1,866	1,873	2,196	1,614	1,429	1,579	2,641	2,930	2,787	2,883
Total Assets	6,964	6,546	6,256	5,028	4,689	4,941	6,826	8,733	8,546	8,441
Curr. Liab.	1,504	1,278	1,338	1,285	1,196	1,477	2,432	2,539	2,328	2,455
LT Debt	1,458	1,487	1,285	899	931	1,113	1,160	2,340	2,080	2,295
Common Eqty.	2,348	2,114	2,045	1,509	1,428	1,238	2,239	2,373	2,383	1,836
Total Cap.	3,839	3,683	3,354	2,567	2,474	2,488	3,801	5,992	5,703	5,448
Cap. Exp.	755	721	542	409	395	359	400	744	785	671
Cash Flow	1,009	895	1,231	653	431	395	152	784	1,071	1,135
Curr. Ratio	1.2	1.5	1.6	1.3	1.2	1.1	1.1	1.2	1.2	1.2
% LT Debt of Cap.	38.0	40.4	38.3	35.0	37.6	44.7	30.5	41.3	36.5	42.1
% Net Inc.of Revs.	10.4	9.7	15.7	8.0	3.6	2.4	NM	4.0	6.6	8.0
% Ret. on Assets	10.0	9.3	16.4	8.2	3.2	2.0	NM	3.8	6.7	8.0
% Ret. on Equity	29.6	28.0	52.0	26.3	11.0	5.7	NM	13.7	26.8	42.3

Data as orig. reptd.; bef. results of disc. opers. and/or spec. items. Per share data adj. for stk. divs. as of ex-div. date. Bold denotes diluted EPS (FASB 128). E-Estimated. NA-Not Available. NM-Not Meaningful. NR-Not Ranked.

Office—39 Old Ridgebury Rd., Danbury, CT 06817-0001. **Registrar**—ChaseMellon Shareholder Services. **Tel**—(203) 794-2000. **Transfer Agent**—Co.'s office. **Website**—http://www.unioncarbide.com **Chrmn, Pres & CEO**—W. H. Joyce. **VP & CFO**—J.K. Wulff. **VP & Secy**—J. E. Geoghan. **Investor Contact**—D. Nicholas Thold (203-794-6440). **Dirs**—C. F. Fetterolf, J. E. Geoghan, R. E. Gut, V. E. Jordan, Jr., W. H. Joyce, R. D. Kennedy, R. L. Kuehn, Jr., R. L. Ridgway, J. M. Ringler. **Incorporated**—in New York in 1917. **Empl**— 11,813. **S&P Analyst:** Richard O'Reilly, CFA

STANDARD &POOR'S
STOCK REPORTS

Union Pacific

2286

NYSE Symbol **UNP**

In S&P 500

12-SEP-98

Industry: Railroads

Summary: The purchase of Southern Pacific for $4.1 billion in September 1996 made UNP the largest U.S. railroad. UNP plans to sell its trucking unit in 1998 via a public offering.

S&P Opinion: Avoid (★★)	Recent Price • 39	Yield • 2.1%
	52 Wk Range • 66⅜-37¼	12-Mo. P/E • NM

Quantitative Evaluations

Outlook (1 Lowest—5 Highest)
• 2

Fair Value
• 40½

Risk
• Low

Earn./Div. Rank
• B+

Technical Eval.
• **Bearish** since 9/97

Rel. Strength Rank (1 Lowest—99 Highest)
• 68

Insider Activity
• Neutral

Earnings vs. Previous Year
▲=Up ▼=Down ▶=No Change

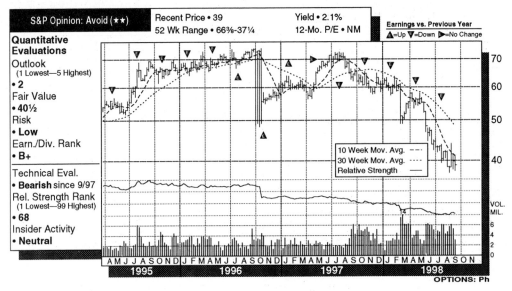

10 Week Mov. Avg. —-—
30 Week Mov. Avg. ------
Relative Strength

VOL. MIL.

OPTIONS: Ph

Overview - 29-JUN-98

Rail traffic in 1998 could fall an additional 4%, versus a 2.4% decline in 1997 as UNP's congestion problems have persisted through 1998's first half. Union Pacific is attacking the problem on several fronts, adding crews and equipment, shifting traffic to rival carriers, and sharing dispatching and track with Burlington Northern. Coal shipments should rebound after being penalized by mild weather in 1997. Grain traffic may slip as the strong dollar hurt our nation's ability to compete in export markets. Auto shipments may be hurt by the strike at General Motors. Intermodal traffic will be off, reflecting a loss of market share to other railroads and diversion to motor carriers. Supporting comparisons will be lower fuel costs and the absence of some $60 million in nonrecurring merger-related costs charged to 1997 first half pretax profits. Interest expense will increase and UNP will have to pay preferred dividends on recently issued convertible preferred securities. Our earnings model excludes Overnite Transportation.

Valuation - 29-JUN-98

The shares of this transportation firm have sunk as rail congestion problems have led to pools of red ink. UNP has been plagued by a spate of accidents, crew shortages, and poor communication between parts of its system. UNP has been directed to open its lines to competitors through August 2, and could see permanent losses in market share. UNP's chief financial officer resigned in June under clouded circumstances. UNP's financial condition has deteriorated; in February the dividend was cut in half following the sale of $1.5 billion of convertible preferred stock in April 1998. An IPO is planned in 1998's third quarter for its trucking unit. We advise continuing to avoid these shares until a long-term base is built.

Key Stock Statistics

S&P EPS Est. 1998	-0.10	Tang. Bk. Value/Share	30.86
P/E on S&P Est. 1998	NM	Beta	0.58
S&P EPS Est. 1999	2.90	Shareholders	52,900
Dividend Rate/Share	0.80	Market cap. (B)	$ 9.6
Shs. outstg. (M)	247.3	Inst. holdings	68%
Avg. daily vol. (M)	1.118		

Value of $10,000 invested 5 years ago: NA

Fiscal Year Ending Dec. 31

	1998	1997	1996	1995	1994	1993
Revenues (Million $)						
1Q	2,586	2,810	1,968	1,664	1,860	1,830
2Q	2,362	2,883	2,012	1,874	1,988	1,848
3Q	—	2,825	1,996	1,974	1,958	1,901
4Q	—	2,561	2,810	1,974	1,992	1,982
Yr.	—	11,079	8,786	7,486	7,798	7,561
Earnings Per Share ($)						
1Q	-0.25	0.52	0.52	0.63	1.39	0.80
2Q	-0.64	0.87	0.90	0.73	1.11	0.96
3Q	E0.35	0.96	1.00	0.78	1.02	0.53
4Q	E0.46	-0.62	0.93	0.87	1.14	1.14
Yr.	E-0.10	1.74	3.36	3.01	4.66	3.43

Next earnings report expected: late October

Dividend Data (Dividends have been paid since 1900.)

Amount ($)	Date Decl.	Ex-Div. Date	Stock of Record	Payment Date
0.430	Nov. 20	Dec. 08	Dec. 10	Jan. 02 '98
0.200	Feb. 26	Mar. 09	Mar. 11	Apr. 01 '98
0.200	May. 28	Jun. 08	Jun. 10	Jul. 01 '98
0.200	Jul. 30	Sep. 04	Sep. 09	Oct. 01 '98

A Division of The McGraw-Hill Companies

Business Summary - 29-JUN-98

Failing to win the Santa Fe railroad in 1995, Union Pacific (UNP) turned instead to the financially ailing Southern Pacific Railroad, which it acquired in September 1996 for $4.1 billion in cash and stock. The merger restored UNP's position as North America's largest railroad (35,000 route miles in 23 western and midwestern states), and was intended to deliver significant profit savings in several years. Those savings may not be realized on the original timetable as UNP has been overwhelmed with congestion problems, which began in mid-1997 and have persisted into mid-1998. UNP's other business, trucking, which has turned around following several years of losses, is slated for sale in 1998's third quarter via a public offering. UNP completed its withdrawal from all non-transportation activities in 1996.

Since mid-1997, UNP has incurred serious operating problems on its rail system. Most of the congestion has been in Texas and Louisiana. UNP blames its problems on deficient infrastructure, crew and equipment shortages, derailments, track washouts and abnormally high demand. To address the capacity shortfall, UNP is buying new locomotives and wants to double and triple track certain lines. To generate the capital for these investments, UNP placed privately in April 1998 $1.5 billion in preferred stock that is convertible into common at $68.90 a share. Additionally, to conserve cash, the quarterly dividend was cut 53%. Other steps taken to cure its ills include joint dispatching in the Gulf Coast with Burlington Northern (BN) and the creation of a jointly owned line with BN between Houston and New Orleans. The Surface Transportation Board issued an emergency service order covering UP's system in October 1997 which has been extended through August 2, 1998. The order allows competing rail lines to divert freight to their lines and suspends shippers' contracts with Union Pacific. UNP estimates that its service problems cost it $450 million in losses in 1997. Service problems contributed to further losses in 1998's first quarter. Citing costs to litigate and settle shippers' claims, management in May 1998 predicted additional losses for the second quarter.

Overnite Transportation (8.5% of 1997 revenues) primarily offers less-than-truckload (LTL) service in the U.S. and in parts of Canada and Mexico. LTL is a premium rated service involving the consolidation of small shipments from several locations. Few players compete in the LTL market since it requires an expensive network of terminals. Overnite's edge is its non-union status. However, the Teamsters have waged an organizing drive at Overnite since early 1995. Through December 1997, the Teamsters had been certified at 19 of Overnite's 164 service centers. In May 1998 UNP announced that it planned to sell 100% of Overnite via an initial public offering during 1998's third quarter. Management no longer views trucking as part of its core business.

Per Share Data ($) (Year Ended Dec. 31)	1997	1996	1995	1994	1993	1992	1991	1990	1989	1988
Tangible Bk. Val.	30.79	30.51	26.62	20.36	17.38	16.43	14.02	14.62	12.82	13.82
Cash Flow	5.97	6.86	6.15	9.55	7.77	7.71	3.74	6.56	5.38	4.56
Earnings	1.74	3.36	3.01	4.66	3.43	3.57	0.31	3.09	2.81	2.45
Dividends	1.72	1.72	1.72	1.66	1.54	1.42	1.30	1.18	1.11	1.05
Payout Ratio	99%	51%	57%	36%	45%	40%	414%	38%	38%	43%
Prices - High	73	74½	70⅛	67⅛	67	60½	51¾	39⅞	40½	35⅛
- Low	56¼	48¼	45⅝	43¾	56⅞	44⅜	32⅝	30⅝	31⅝	25½
P/E Ratio - High	42	22	23	14	20	17	NM	13	14	14
- Low	32	14	15	9	17	12	NM	10	11	10
Income Statement Analysis (Million $)										
Revs.	11,079	8,786	7,486	7,798	7,561	7,294	7,029	6,964	6,492	6,068
Oper. Inc.	2,296	2,295	1,983	2,501	2,282	2,119	1,939	1,853	1,711	1,605
Depr.	1,043	762	642	1,005	892	843	691	616	543	486
Int. Exp.	605	501	450	337	335	369	394	383	376	324
Pretax Inc.	676	1,113	933	1,419	1,155	1,101	112	952	893	872
Eff. Tax Rate	36%	34%	34%	33%	39%	34%	43%	35%	33%	36%
Net Inc.	432	733	619	958	705	728	64.0	618	595	559
Balance Sheet & Other Fin. Data (Million $)										
Cash	90.0	191	230	121	113	245	144	169	187	439
Curr. Assets	1,415	1,334	1,679	1,822	1,382	1,381	1,168	1,255	1,255	1,667
Total Assets	28,764	27,914	19,446	15,942	15,001	14,098	13,326	13,078	12,459	12,228
Curr. Liab.	3,247	3,056	1,899	2,505	2,089	2,084	1,868	1,814	1,868	1,860
LT Debt	8,285	7,900	6,232	4,090	4,069	3,989	3,913	3,883	3,837	3,222
Common Eqty.	8,225	8,225	6,364	5,131	4,885	4,639	4,163	4,277	3,911	4,482
Total Cap.	22,762	22,064	16,310	12,077	11,630	11,004	10,206	10,417	9,821	9,608
Cap. Exp.	2,101	1,360	1,058	1,597	1,520	1,525	1,191	1,229	1,137	1,126
Cash Flow	1,475	1,495	1,261	1,963	1,597	1,571	755	1,234	1,138	1,038
Curr. Ratio	0.4	0.4	0.9	0.7	0.7	0.7	0.6	0.7	0.7	0.9
% LT Debt of Cap.	36.3	35.8	38.2	33.9	35.0	36.3	38.3	37.3	39.1	33.5
% Net Inc.of Revs.	3.9	8.3	8.3	12.8	9.3	10.0	0.9	8.9	9.2	9.2
% Ret. on Assets	1.5	3.1	3.7	6.2	4.8	5.3	0.5	4.8	5.1	4.7
% Ret. on Equity	5.3	10.0	10.8	19.1	14.8	16.5	1.5	15.1	15.1	13.0

Data as orig. reptd.; bef. results of disc. opers. and/or spec. items. Per share data adj. for stk. divs. as of ex-div. date. Bold denotes diluted EPS (FASB 128). E-Estimated. NA-Not Available. NM-Not Meaningful. NR-Not Ranked.

Office—1717 Main St., Suite 5900, Dallas, TX 75201-4605.**Tel**—(214) 743-5600. **Website**—http://www.up.com **Chrmn, CEO & Pres**—R. K. Davidson.**VP & Secy**—C. W. von Bernuth. **VP-CFO & Investor Contact**—Gary M. Stuart. **Dirs**—P. F. Anschutz, R. Bauman, R. Cheney, E. V. Conway, R. K. Davidson, S. F. Eccles, E. T. Gerry, Jr., W. H. Gray III, J. R. Hope, R. J. Mahoney, J. R. Meyer, T. A. Reynolds, Jr., R. D. Simmons. **Transfer Agent & Registrar**—Harris Trust and Savings Bank, Chicago. **Incorporated**—in Utah in 1969; R.R. incorporated in 1897. **Empl**— 65,600. **S&P Analyst:** Stephen R. Klein

12-SEP-98

Industry:
Oil & Gas (Exploration & Production)

Summary: This company is one of the largest independent oil and gas exploration and production companies in th U.S.

S&P Opinion: Hold (★★★)	Recent Price • 12⅜ 52 Wk Range • 27¾-8¼
Yield • 1.6% 12-Mo. P/E • 19.7	

Quantitative Evaluations

Outlook
(1 Lowest—5 Highest)
• **1⁺**

Fair Value
• **7⅝**

Risk
• **Average**

Earn./Div. Rank
• **NR**

Technical Eval.
• **Neutral** since 5/98

Rel. Strength Rank
(1 Lowest—99 Highest)
• **59**

Insider Activity
• **Favorable**

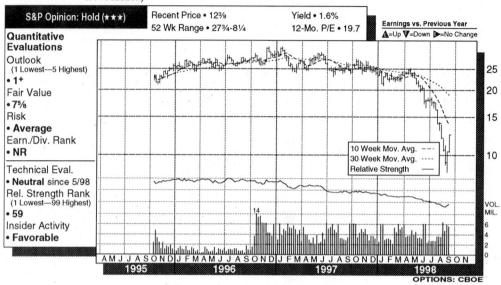

Earnings vs. Previous Year
▲=Up ▼=Down ▷=No Change

10 Week Mov. Avg. ----
30 Week Mov. Avg. ·····
Relative Strength ——

OPTIONS: CBOE

Overview - 04-SEP-98

Foiled in its attempts to acquire Pennzoil Co. (NYSE: PZL) in the second half of 1997, UPR succeeded in acquiring Norcen Energy Resources Ltd. in March 1998 for $2.6 billion. Although the acquisition has benefited revenues and has expanded UPR's property base outside the U.S., the debt used to fund the transaction resulted in a substantially higher debt to equity ratio, and lower credit rating. In response, the company has began a deleveraging program aimed at reducing debt. Specifically, the company has earmarked some $600 million of properties, representing less than 10% of UPR's production, to be sold by the end of 1998; the company has made some progress toward this goal. In addition, the program calls for the "monetization" of the gas, processing and marketing segment (GPM), a unit which is a significant contributor to operating income. Earnings estimates for 1998 assume the sale of this division during the third quarter of this year.

Valuation - 04-SEP-98

UPR's shares have not been spared in the recent downturn in the oil and gas sector; shares are down 70% from their high. Weak oil prices directly affect UPR's revenues, and until prices improve we would not add to positions. Also, the company has repeatedly touted its GPM segment as a contributor to the "gas value chain"; to this effect, UPR acquired Highlands Gas Corp. in August 1997 for $180 million. Yet in an about face, UPR may sell the entire GPM division. Although gas prices are strong, the general perception of a weak commodity price environment may negatively affect the sale price. However, UPR's shares are trading at a significant discount to our estimated present value of reserves, and should prove of longer term interest, especially when potentially significant recent discoveries become commercial.

Key Stock Statistics

S&P EPS Est. 1998	0.40	Tang. Bk. Value/Share	7.03
P/E on S&P Est. 1998	31.1	Beta	NA
S&P EPS Est. 1999	1.15	Shareholders	58,000
Dividend Rate/Share	0.20	Market cap. (B)	$ 3.1
Shs. outstg. (M)	251.1	Inst. holdings	71%
Avg. daily vol. (M)	1.404		

Value of $10,000 invested 5 years ago: NA

Fiscal Year Ending Dec. 31

	1998	1997	1996	1995	1994	1993
Revenues (Million $)						
1Q	499.0	531.7	389.7	321.3	—	—
2Q	621.1	444.6	427.9	336.7	—	—
3Q	—	449.0	447.1	331.3	—	—
4Q	—	499.4	566.3	466.5	—	—
Yr.	—	1,925	1,831	1,456	1,333	—
Earnings Per Share ($)						
1Q	0.13	0.47	0.24	—	—	—
2Q	-0.07	0.30	0.28	—	—	—
3Q	—	0.27	0.31	—	—	—
4Q	—	0.30	0.46	—	—	—
Yr.	E0.40	1.33	1.28	1.25	1.33	—

Next earnings report expected: mid October

Dividend Data (Dividends have been paid since 1996.)

Amount ($)	Date Decl.	Ex-Div. Date	Stock of Record	Payment Date
0.050	Oct. 02	Dec. 15	Dec. 17	Jan. 02 '98
0.050	Jan. 26	Mar. 09	Mar. 11	Apr. 01 '98
0.050	Apr. 17	Jun. 08	Jun. 10	Jul. 01 '98
0.050	Jul. 14	Sep. 04	Sep. 09	Oct. 01 '98

A Division of The McGraw·Hill Companies

STANDARD
&POOR'S
STOCK REPORTS

Union Pacific Resources Group Inc.

2286F
12-SEP-98

Business Summary - 04-SEP-98

Union Pacific Resources Group (UPR), is one of the largest independent oil and gas exploration and production companies in the U.S. Following the March 1998, $2.6 billion purchase of Norcen Energy Resources, UPR's presence was expanded in western Canada, Guatemala, Venezuela, and other international areas. Domestically, the company reorganized its exploration and production units during the second quarter of 1998 into five business units: a) the Austin Chalk trend in Texas and Louisiana, b) the East/West Texas unit, c) the Western Region, consisting of the Land Grant Area in Colorado, Wyoming and Utah, as well as additional properties in Kansas, d) the Gulf Coast Onshore unit, and e) the Offshore unit, which includes the Gulf of Mexico.

On April 20, 1998, the company announced a deleveraging program aimed at reducing the company's indebtedness and improving its credit rating within 18 months. The program involves the sale of approximately $600 million of producing properties by the end of 1998, as well as the monetization of the gathering, processing, and marketing division. The properties identified for sale represent less than 10% of UPR's reserves, cash flow, and production. As part of this program, in May, UPR sold its interest in certain DJ Basin properties for $41 million, as well as its interest in Canada's Superior Propane for $47 million. In August, the company announced the sale of its interest in a Texas Gulf field for $158 million.

In November 1997, Union Pacific Resources formally withdrew its $6.4 billion unsolicited bid to acquire Pennzoil Co. (NYSE: PZL) due to the determined opposition of Pennzoil directors and management, even though over 60% of PZL shareholders expressed support by tendering their shares.

UPR emphasizes natural gas in its exploration and production activities; as of December 31, 1997, natural gas constituted 64% of the 4.1 Bcfe in reserves, and 60% of the 1.9 Tcfe UPR produced per day. The company owns assets in proximity to its primary producing properties that are dedicated to gas value chain activities, which consist of the gathering, processing, transportation, and marketing of natural gas and natural gas liquids. The company markets most of its gas and liquids through its wholly owned Union Pacific Fuels subsidiary.

The company also has a hard minerals business unit, whose objective is to increase royalty income and income from investments in nonoperated ventures in several coal and trona (natural soda ash) mines on lands within and adjacent to its Land Grant holdings in Wyoming.

Per Share Data ($)

(Year Ended Dec. 31)	1997	1996	1995	1994	1993	1992	1991	1990	1989	1988
Tangible Bk. Val.	7.06	6.06	5.26	4.01	NA	NA	NA	NA	NA	NA
Cash Flow	3.59	3.42	3.25	3.08	NA	NA	NA	NA	NA	NA
Earnings	1.33	1.28	1.25	1.33	NA	NA	NA	NA	NA	NA
Dividends	0.20	0.20	0.05	NA	NA	NA	NA	NA	NA	NA
Payout Ratio	15%	16%	NM	NA	NA	NA	NA	NA	NA	NA
Prices - High	31⅝	31⅝	26¼	NA	NA	NA	NA	NA	NA	NA
- Low	23	24⅛	21	NA	NA	NA	NA	NA	NA	NA
P/E Ratio - High	24	25	NM	NA	NA	NA	NA	NA	NA	NA
- Low	17	19	NM	NA	NA	NA	NA	NA	NA	NA

Income Statement Analysis (Million $)

	1997	1996	1995	1994	1993	1992	1991	1990	1989	1988
Revs.	1,925	1,831	1,456	1,333	NA	NA	NA	NA	NA	NA
Oper. Inc.	1,063	1,060	929	760	NA	NA	NA	NA	NA	NA
Depr.	568	534	459	426	NA	NA	NA	NA	NA	NA
Int. Exp.	53.1	50.6	19.1	74.1	NA	NA	NA	NA	NA	NA
Pretax Inc.	466	473	458	417	NA	NA	NA	NA	NA	NA
Eff. Tax Rate	29%	32%	23%	22%	NA	NA	NA	NA	NA	NA
Net Inc.	333	321	351	325	NA	NA	NA	NA	NA	NA

Balance Sheet & Other Fin. Data (Million $)

	1997	1996	1995	1994	1993	1992	1991	1990	1989	1988
Cash	70.6	119	27.6	19.7	NA	NA	NA	NA	NA	NA
Curr. Assets	577	586	420	357	NA	NA	NA	NA	NA	NA
Total Assets	4,472	3,649	3,309	3,158	NA	NA	NA	NA	NA	NA
Curr. Liab.	558	613	1,067	1,059	NA	NA	NA	NA	NA	NA
LT Debt	1,231	671	102	216	NA	NA	NA	NA	NA	NA
Common Eqty.	1,761	1,514	1,312	978	NA	NA	NA	NA	NA	NA
Total Cap.	3,544	2,620	1,852	1,633	NA	NA	NA	NA	NA	NA
Cap. Exp.	1,352	880	560	NA	NA	NA	NA	NA	NA	NA
Cash Flow	901	855	810	752	NA	NA	NA	NA	NA	NA
Curr. Ratio	1.0	1.0	0.4	0.3	NA	NA	NA	NA	NA	NA
% LT Debt of Cap.	34.7	25.6	5.5	13.2	NA	NA	NA	NA	NA	NA
% Net Inc.of Revs.	17.3	17.6	24.1	24.4	NA	NA	NA	NA	NA	NA
% Ret. on Assets	8.2	9.3	10.7	NA	NA	NA	NA	NA	NA	NA
% Ret. on Equity	20.3	22.7	22.3	NA	NA	NA	NA	NA	NA	NA

Data as orig. reptd.; bef. results of disc. opers. and/or spec. items. Per share data adj. for stk. divs. as of ex-div. date. Bold denotes diluted EPS (FASB 128). E-Estimated. NA-Not Available. NM-Not Meaningful. NR-Not Ranked.

Office—801 Cherry St., Fort Worth, TX 76102-6803. **Tel**—(817) 877-6000. **Website**—http://www.upr.com **Chrmn & CEO**—J. L. Messman. **Pres & COO**—G. Lindahl, III. **VP & CFO**—M. B. Smith. **VP & Secy**—J. A. LaSala, Jr. **Investor Contact**—David R. Larson. **Dirs**—H. J. Arnelle, L. V. Cheney, P. M. Geren III, L. M. Jones, D. Lewis, C. B. Malone, J. L. Messman, J. W. Poduska Sr., M. E. Rossi, S. K. Skinner, J. R. Thompson. **Transfer Agent & Registrar**—Harris Trust & Savings Bank, Chicago. **Incorporated**—in Utah in 1969. **Empl**—1,907. **S&P Analyst:** Ephraim Juskowicz

12-SEP-98

Industry:
Computer (Software & Services)

Summary: Unisys is a leading worldwide supplier of information services and technology solutions to more than 60,000 customers in 100 countries.

S&P Opinion: Accumulate (★★★★)

| Recent Price • 22⅝ | Yield • Nil |
| 52 Wk Range • 30⅝-11 | 12-Mo. P/E • NM |

Earnings vs. Previous Year
▲=Up ▼=Down ▶=No Change

Quantitative Evaluations

Outlook
(1 Lowest—5 Highest)
• **2⁻**

Fair Value
• **19¼**

Risk
• **Average**

Earn./Div. Rank
• **C**

Technical Eval.
• **NA**

Rel. Strength Rank
(1 Lowest—99 Highest)
• **72**

Insider Activity
• **Neutral**

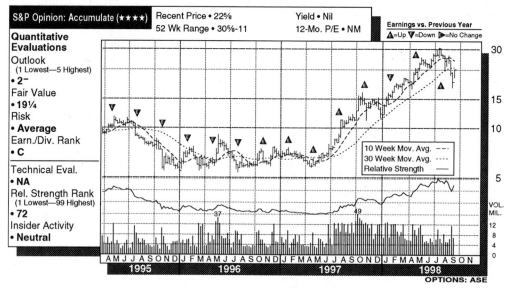

10 Week Mov. Avg. - - - -
30 Week Mov. Avg. ......
Relative Strength ——

OPTIONS: ASE

Overview - 05-AUG-98

Since Lawrence Weinbach became CEO in September 1997, he has cut debt by $1 billion, without adversely impacting the balance sheet. UIS intends to focus on its high-end enterprise servers, and on its service and consulting businesses, areas in which the company feels it can grow profitably. UIS will outsource the manufacture of low-end servers and PCs to Hewlett-Packard. The company recorded a $1.1 billion charge in the 1997 fourth quarter, to discontinue the manufacture of PCs, write down $900 million of goodwill, and reduce debt. Information services group revenues are projected to grow about 10% in 1998; global customer services should increase about 4%, and computer systems revenues should be down slightly. Earnings growth should come from improved margins, decreased interest expense and amortization charges, and a lower tax rate.

Valuation - 05-AUG-98

UIS posted EPS of $0.24 in the second quarter of 1998, beating expectations. Revenues grew a strong 9%, and the operating margin improved to 10.7%, from 8.1%, due to cost cutting and improvement at the information services group. We project 1998 EPS of $1.00, reflecting high single-digit revenue growth, continued cost savings, improved gross margins, and lower amortization charges and interest expense. Demand for the company's Clearpath enterprise servers, which lets clients run Windows NT and UNIX on the same platform, continues strong, and the information services group will grow profitably in 1998. The long-term outlook for UIS is positive, aided by its improved balance sheet and focus on its strengths. The shares, up over 100% since we upgraded UIS to its current four star ranking, still warrant accumulation at 22 times our 1999 EPS estimate of $1.30.

Key Stock Statistics

S&P EPS Est. 1998	1.02	Tang. Bk. Value/Share	NM
P/E on S&P Est. 1998	22.2	Beta	1.84
S&P EPS Est. 1999	1.30	Shareholders	41,500
Dividend Rate/Share	Nil	Market cap. (B)	$ 5.8
Shs. outstg. (M)	254.3	Inst. holdings	56%
Avg. daily vol. (M)	1.541		

Value of $10,000 invested 5 years ago: $ 22,406

Fiscal Year Ending Dec. 31

	1998	1997	1996	1995	1994	1993
Revenues (Million $)						
1Q	1,650	1,531	1,423	1,407	1,689	1,908
2Q	1,729	1,585	1,505	1,496	1,799	1,927
3Q	—	1,621	1,631	1,461	1,788	1,807
4Q	—	1,899	1,812	1,839	2,124	2,101
Yr.	—	6,636	6,371	6,202	7,400	7,743
Earnings Per Share ($)						
1Q	0.14	-0.06	-0.25	0.02	0.21	0.16
2Q	0.24	0.08	-0.14	0.06	0.12	0.44
3Q	E0.23	0.13	-0.09	-0.36	0.08	0.33
4Q	E0.41	-4.75	0.15	-4.06	-0.48	0.53
Yr.	E1.02	-5.30	0.34	-4.37	-0.07	1.46

Next earnings report expected: mid October

Dividend Data

Common dividends, paid since 1895, were omitted in September 1990. Preferred dividends were reinstated in January 1993, following suspension in February 1991. In February 1994, UIS retired the dividend arrearage on its Series A preferred shares with an $80 million payment. A "poison pill" stock purchase rights plan was adopted in 1986.

A Division of The McGraw-Hill Companies

Business Summary - 05-AUG-98

Unisys, a provider of information services, technology, software and customer support worldwide, was formed when one-time computer giants Sperry and Burroughs combined in 1986. Like many other marriages, the union has seen plenty of rocky times, including a staggering $1.4 billion loss in 1991. In response, UIS has launched a number of restructurings, most recently in late 1995. In late 1997, the company incurred a $1.1 billion charge, including $900 million to write off goodwill associated with the 1986 merger, with the remainder for debt reduction and to discontinue the manufacture of PCs and low-end servers, which will now be outsourced but will continue to be sold under the Unisys name. This move, coupled with other recent debt reductions, leaves UIS with a healthier balance sheet and reduces interest expense and amortization charges significantly.

UIS operates through three business units: computer systems, global customer service and information services. Segment revenues in recent years were:

	1997	1996
Computer Systems Group	37%	41%
Global Customer Services	32%	30%
Information Services Group	31%	29%

The computer systems group offers hardware and software technologies that serve as building blocks of advanced information management solutions. Global customer service provides network integration, desktop services, and other support services that help clients maximize the availability and effectiveness of their computing environments. The information services group provides systems integration, outsourcing services, application development, information planning and education as well as in-depth market sector expertise to help clients use information to enhance their competitiveness and better serve customers.

UIS's products include enterprise systems and servers that comprise a complete line of small to large processors and related communications and peripheral products, such as printers, storage devices and document handling processors and equipment. Servers and desktop systems include UNIX servers, workstations, personal computers and terminals. UIS also provides equipment and preventive maintenance, spare parts and other repair activities.

Unisys is a large international player; export sales provided about 51% of 1997 revenues. UIS is also a significant U.S. government contractor, with sales to that market accounting for 12% of 1997 revenues, up from 8.5% in 1996.

Per Share Data ($)

(Year Ended Dec. 31)	1997	1996	1995	1994	1993	1992	1991	1990	1989	1988
Tangible Bk. Val.	NA	NM	NM	-0.63	-0.98	-3.45	-5.72	2.41	5.52	12.15
Cash Flow	1.39	0.91	-2.24	1.69	3.47	4.30	-4.98	0.25	-0.97	7.49
Earnings	-5.30	-0.34	-4.37	-0.07	1.46	1.06	-9.37	-3.45	-4.71	3.58
Dividends	Nil	Nil	Nil	Nil	Nil	Nil	Nil	0.50	1.00	0.98
Payout Ratio	Nil	Nil	Nil	Nil	Nil	Nil	Nil	NM	NM	27%
Prices - High	16½	9⅛	11¾	16½	13⅞	11¾	7	17⅛	30½	39
- Low	5¾	5⅜	5½	8¼	9⅞	4⅛	2⅛	1¾	12⅜	25
P/E Ratio - High	NM	NM	NM	NM	10	11	NM	NM	NM	11
- Low	NM	NM	NM	NM	7	4	NM	NM	NM	7

Income Statement Analysis (Million $)

	1997	1996	1995	1994	1993	1992	1991	1990	1989	1988
Revs.	6,636	6,371	6,202	7,400	7,743	8,422	8,687	10,111	10,097	9,902
Oper. Inc.	1,722	556	-453	791	1,066	1,251	123	635	383	1,701
Depr.	1,218	228	244	300	332	530	711	591	593	628
Int. Exp.	233	250	202	204	242	341	408	447	426	305
Pretax Inc.	-758	93.7	-780	153	503	436	-1,287	-336	-553	959
Eff. Tax Rate	NA	34%	NM	29%	28%	32%	NM	NM	NM	29%
Net Inc.	-853	61.8	-626	108	362	296	-1,392	-436	-638	681

Balance Sheet & Other Fin. Data (Million $)

	1997	1996	1995	1994	1993	1992	1991	1990	1989	1988
Cash	803	1,035	1,120	885	951	809	814	403	9.0	26.0
Curr. Assets	2,887	3,133	3,219	3,142	3,200	3,868	4,296	4,870	5,083	5,815
Total Assets	5,591	6,967	7,113	7,324	7,519	7,509	8,432	10,289	10,751	11,535
Curr. Liab.	2,577	2,465	3,147	2,509	2,366	3,044	3,663	4,210	3,537	3,432
LT Debt	1,438	2,271	1,533	1,864	2,025	2,173	2,695	2,495	3,248	3,078
Common Eqty.	-213	187	290	1,034	1,017	666	436	1,907	2,453	3,526
Total Cap.	2,644	4,027	3,393	4,469	4,720	4,465	4,863	6,079	7,214	8,103
Cap. Exp.	302	162	195	226	197	252	248	460	615	670
Cash Flow	253	157	-382	288	572	704	-803	40.0	-153	1,202
Curr. Ratio	1.1	1.3	1.0	1.3	1.4	1.3	1.2	1.2	1.4	1.7
% LT Debt of Cap.	54.4	56.4	45.2	41.7	42.9	48.7	55.4	41.0	45.0	38.0
% Net Inc.of Revs.	NA	0.1	NM	1.5	4.7	3.5	NM	NM	NM	6.9
% Ret. on Assets	NA	NM	NM	1.5	4.7	2.2	NM	NM	NM	6.2
% Ret. on Equity	NA	NM	NM	NM	31.2	31.6	NM	NM	NM	16.8

Data as orig. reptd.; bef. results of disc. opers. and/or spec. items. Per share data adj. for stk. divs. as of ex-div. date. Bold denotes diluted EPS (FASB 128). E-Estimated. NA-Not Available. NM-Not Meaningful. NR-Not Ranked.

Office—Township Line and Union Meeting Roads, Blue Bell, PA 19424. **Tel**—(215) 986-4011. **Website**—http://www.unisys.com **Chrmn, Pres & CEO**—L. A. Weinbach. **SVP & Secy**—H. S. Barron. **SVP & CFO**—R. H. Brust. **VP & Investor Contact**—J. F. McHale (215-986-6999). **Dirs**—J. P. Bolduc, J. J. Duderstadt, H. C. Duques, G. D. Fosler, M. R. Goodes, E. A. Huston, K. A. Macke, T. E. Martin, R. McClements Jr., A. E. Schwartz, L. A. Weinbach. **Transfer Agent & Registrar**—Harris Trust Co. of New York, NYC. **Incorporated**—in Michigan in 1905; reincorporated in Delaware in 1984. **Empl**— 32,600. **S&P Analyst:** Jim Corridore

12-SEP-98

Industry:
Health Care (Managed Care)

Summary: This leading health care services company recently agreed to terminate a planned acquisition of rival Humana Inc.

S&P Opinion: Hold (★★★)	Recent Price • 36	Yield • 0.1%
	52 Wk Range • 73⅞-29½	12-Mo. P/E • NM

Quantitative Evaluations

Outlook
(1 Lowest—5 Highest)
• **5**

Fair Value
• **66⅜**

Risk
• **Average**

Earn./Div. Rank
• **B+**

Technical Eval.
• **Bearish** since 7/98

Rel. Strength Rank
(1 Lowest—99 Highest)
• **27**

Insider Activity
• **Neutral**

Earnings vs. Previous Year
▲=Up ▼=Down ▷=No Change

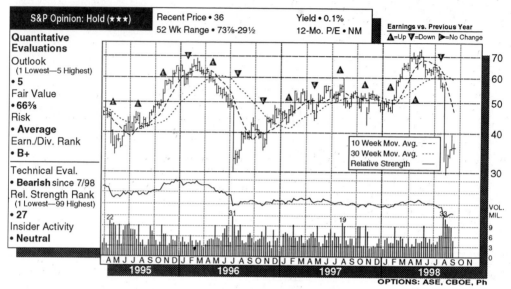

10 Week Mov. Avg. - - - -
30 Week Mov. Avg. ·······
Relative Strength ——

OPTIONS: ASE, CBOE, Ph

Overview - 13-AUG-98

Following a surprisingly weak second quarter earnings release that included special charges of $900 million ($3.62 a share) related to an operational realignment, United lost nearly $3.0 billion in market capitalization as investors feared another earnings meltdown was in store for the most recent HMO darling. As a result of the decline, the company's all-stock merger deal with Humana Inc. was terminated. On a stand-alone basis, we look for 1998 premium revenues in the $16 billion range, aided by commercial rate hikes of about 6%, modest Medicare rate increases and the inclusion of a contract with the American Association of Retired Persons. The Medicare business, however, will likely be curtailed as the company is experiencing significantly higher-than-anticipated medical costs in many new geographic markets. Excluding the second quarter charges, we look for 1998 EPS of $2.65 and see 1999 EPS of $3.05.

Valuation - 13-AUG-98

We lowered our opinion to hold from accumulate to reflect our concerns regarding a possible margin squeeze in the second half of 1998. Although operating earnings of $0.66 a share in the second quarter of 1998 were in line with estimates, the earnings report raised doubts regarding United's ability to meet analyst projections with Medicare and commercial medical costs on the rise and start-up markets performing well below management's expectations. We viewed the Humana deal as a long term strategic plus for United, and the deal's collapse has removed much of the stock's allure. Over the coming six months, we expect UNH to provide returns about in line with the S&P 500, but note that upcoming earnings reports will be choppy and the stock carries some additional downside risk at current levels.

Key Stock Statistics

S&P EPS Est. 1998	-0.97	Tang. Bk. Value/Share	10.81
P/E on S&P Est. 1998	NM	Beta	1.85
S&P EPS Est. 1999	3.05	Shareholders	14,900
Dividend Rate/Share	0.03	Market cap. (B)	$ 7.0
Shs. outstg. (M)	195.3	Inst. holdings	83%
Avg. daily vol. (M)	2.320		

Value of $10,000 invested 5 years ago: $ 12,705

Fiscal Year Ending Dec. 31

	1998	1997	1996	1995	1994	1993
Revenues (Million $)						
1Q	4,115	2,851	2,318	1,104	713.5	580.2
2Q	4,235	2,931	2,492	1,158	939.5	627.1
3Q	—	2,959	2,587	1,216	956.8	649.3
4Q	—	3,054	2,676	2,194	969.0	670.8
Yr.	—	11,794	10,074	5,671	3,769	2,527
Earnings Per Share ($)						
1Q	**0.63**	**0.54**	0.62	0.51	0.40	0.27
2Q	**-2.96**	**0.57**	0.23	0.51	0.30	0.29
3Q	**E0.66**	**0.57**	0.45	0.53	0.46	0.32
4Q	**E0.70**	**0.58**	0.47	0.03	0.48	0.35
Yr.	**E-0.97**	**2.26**	1.76	1.57	1.64	1.24

Next earnings report expected: NA

Dividend Data (Dividends have been paid since 1990.)

Amount ($)	Date Decl.	Ex-Div. Date	Stock of Record	Payment Date
0.030	Feb. 12	Mar. 30	Apr. 01	Apr. 15 '98

Business Summary - 13-AUG-98

This Minnesota-based company is a national leader in health care management, providing a range of health care products and services including health maintenance organizations (HMOs), point-of-service (POS) plans, preferred provider organizations (PPOs) and managed fee-for-service programs. It also offers managed behavioral health services, utilization management, workers' compensation and disability management services, specialized provider networks, and third-party administration services.

The company's products and services use a number of core competencies, including medical information management, health care delivery management, health benefit administration, risk assessment and pricing, health benefit design and provider contracting and risk sharing. These capabilities allow UNH to provide comprehensive managed care services such as health maintenance organization, insurance and self-funded health care coverage products, as well as unbundled health care management and cost containment products such as mental health and substance abuse services, utilization review services, specialized provider networks and employee assistance programs.

At 1997 year end, United held a majority stake in HMOs operating in about 40 markets nationwide and in Puerto Rico, where it assumes the financial risks for providing health care services. These plans charge members a fixed annual premium while entering into contractual arrangements with independent health care providers to help manage medical and hospital use, quality and costs. A few of these plans employ health care providers and directly deliver health care services to members. UNH also provides administrative and management services to a few plans in which it has no ownership stake. In return, it receives an administrative fee and generally assumes no responsibility for health care costs. At June 30, 1998, health plan enrollment totaled 6,657,000, including commercial (5,719,000), Medicare (427,000) and Medicaid (511,000) members.

Under a 10-year agreement with the American Association of Retired Persons (AARP), United began delivering Medicare supplement health insurance products to over 4.0 million AARP members in January 1998. This contract is expected to generate annual premiums of approximately $3.5 billion.

United also develops and markets specialty services to HMOs, PPOs, insurers, providers, Blue Cross/Blue Shield plans, third-party administrators, employers, labor unions and/or government agencies. These include care management and benefit administration; transplant networks; workers' compensation and disability management; demand management; geriatric care management; behavioral health; and third-party administration.

Per Share Data ($)

(Year Ended Dec. 31)	1997	1996	1995	1994	1993	1992	1991	1990	1989	1988
Tangible Bk. Val.	11.79	9.11	8.34	14.42	4.92	3.81	2.07	0.94	0.52	0.09
Cash Flow	3.02	2.48	2.14	2.01	1.54	1.02	0.71	0.68	0.26	-0.45
Earnings	2.26	1.76	1.57	1.64	1.24	0.82	0.60	0.33	0.16	-0.57
Dividends	0.03	0.03	0.03	0.03	0.02	0.01	0.01	0.01	Nil	Nil
Payout Ratio	1%	2%	2%	2%	1%	1%	1%	2%	Nil	Nil
Prices - High	60⅛	69	65⅝	55⅜	39⅜	29¼	19⅝	6	3¼	1⅜
- Low	42⅜	30	34⅛	37¼	20	17⅛	5	1¹⁵/₁₆	1¼	⅞
P/E Ratio - High	27	39	42	34	32	35	33	18	20	NM
- Low	19	17	22	23	16	21	8	6	8	NM

Income Statement Analysis (Million $)

	1997	1996	1995	1994	1993	1992	1991	1990	1989	1988
Revs.	11,563	9,889	5,511	3,769	2,527	1,442	847	605	412	440
Oper. Inc.	657	544	549	570	352	205	129	66.0	34.0	19.0
Depr.	146	133	94.5	64.1	45.7	27.0	14.3	10.6	7.8	8.3
Int. Exp.	Nil	0.6	0.8	2.2	1.1	0.9	1.3	3.3	4.3	4.5
Pretax Inc.	742	581	460	468	305	177	114	52.0	22.0	-34.0
Eff. Tax Rate	38%	39%	37%	38%	36%	35%	34%	34%	36%	NM
Net Inc.	460	356	286	288	195	114	74.8	33.9	13.7	-36.8

Balance Sheet & Other Fin. Data (Million $)

	1997	1996	1995	1994	1993	1992	1991	1990	1989	1988
Cash	1,256	1,647	1,804	1,654	250	242	251	113	152	95.0
Curr. Assets	2,193	2,740	2,867	1,908	431	320	301	142	175	113
Total Assets	7,623	6,997	6,161	3,489	1,494	994	574	293	237	169
Curr. Liab.	2,570	2,643	2,434	664	513	333	235	139	103	81.0
LT Debt	19.0	31.0	39.0	24.3	0.7	0.4	3.4	7.0	58.3	60.0
Common Eqty.	4,534	3,823	3,188	2,795	959	656	319	126	50.0	5.0
Total Cap.	4,553	4,354	3,227	2,825	971	658	331	145	127	81.0
Cap. Exp.	187	165	109	79.6	55.3	22.4	15.1	2.7	3.7	4.4
Cash Flow	577	460	380	352	240	141	89.2	44.6	21.5	-28.4
Curr. Ratio	0.9	1.0	1.2	2.9	0.8	1.0	1.3	1.0	1.7	1.4
% LT Debt of Cap.	0.4	0.7	1.2	0.9	0.1	0.1	1.0	4.8	46.0	73.9
% Net Inc.of Revs.	4.0	3.6	5.2	7.6	7.7	7.9	8.8	5.6	3.3	NM
% Ret. on Assets	6.3	5.4	5.9	11.2	15.0	14.1	16.4	10.9	6.2	NM
% Ret. on Equity	10.3	9.3	9.4	14.9	23.0	22.7	32.2	34.5	48.0	NM

Data as orig. reptd.; bef. results of disc. opers. and/or spec. items. Per share data adj. for stk. divs. as of ex-div. date. Quarterly revs. incl. other income. Bold denotes diluted EPS (FASB 128). E-Estimated. NA-Not Available. NM-Not Meaningful. NR-Not Ranked.

Office—300 Opus Center, 9900 Bren Road East, Minnetonka, MN 55343. **Tel**—(612) 936-1300. **Website**—http://www.unitedhealthcare.com **Chrmn, Pres & CEO**—W. W. McGuire. **VP-Treas & CFO**—David P. Koppe. **Secy**—D. J. Lubben. **VP-Investor Contact**—Bernard McDonagh (612-936-7214). **Dirs**—W. C. Ballard Jr., R. T. Burke, J. A. Johnson, T. H. Kean. D. W. Leatherdale, W. F. Mondale, W. W. McGuire, M. O. Mundinger, R. L. Ryan, K. L. Simmons, W. G. Spears, G. R. Wilensky. **Transfer Agent & Registrar**—Norwest Bank Minnesota, Minneapolis. **Incorporated**—in Minnesota in 1977. **Empl**—29,600. **S&P Analyst:** Robert M. Gold

U.S. Bancorp

2331V

NYSE Symbol **USB**

In S&P 500

12-SEP-98

Industry: Banks (Major Regional)

Summary: Following its merger with First Bank System, this Minneapolis-based bank holding company now operates about 1,000 banking offices in 17 states.

S&P Opinion: Buy (★★★★★)

Recent Price • 41¾	Yield • 1.7%
52 Wk Range • 47¼-30⅛	12-Mo. P/E • 35.7

Quantitative Evaluations

Outlook
(1 Lowest—5 Highest)
• **1** −

Fair Value
• **33⅜**

Risk
• **Low**

Earn./Div. Rank
• **B**

Technical Eval.
• **NA**

Rel. Strength Rank
(1 Lowest—99 Highest)
• **91**

Insider Activity
• **Favorable**

Earnings vs. Previous Year
▲=Up ▼=Down ⯈=No Change

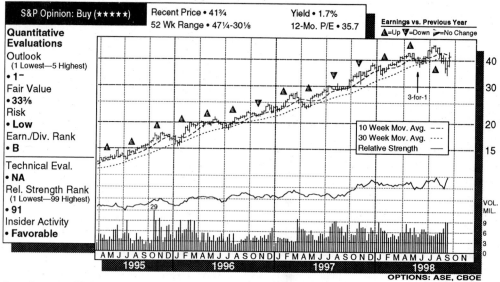

10 Week Mov. Avg. ---
30 Week Mov. Avg. ····
Relative Strength —

3-for-1

OPTIONS: ASE, CBOE

Overview - 31-JUL-98

Earnings in 1998 are expected to benefit from overall loan growth in the mid single-digits, expanding noninterest income, and particularly well controlled operating expenses as benefits from the First Bank System merger begin to have a strong impact. Margins remain well above average, but are expected to trend down slightly to about the 4.85% level on a shifting asset mix and continued competition for lending. Strong growth in noninterest income is expected in the form of higher credit card fees and trust/investment management income, as well as the addition of investment banking revenues and higher investment product fees following the Piper Jaffray acquisition. Loss provisions are expected to closely track the level of net chargeoffs, which have been fairly stable since late 1997. Loss reserves remain more than adequate at 359% of nonperforming loans at June 30, 1998. A substantial share buyback program recently announced will provide additional leverage to earnings.

Valuation - 31-JUL-98

Following in the footsteps of other large super-regionals, USB has substantially expanded its fee-based capabilities in the areas of equity underwriting, retail brokerage and merger/advisory services with the May 1998 acquisition of Piper Jaffray, which has already contributed to earnings. Substantial cost savings are expected in 1998 from a standardization of products and other efficiencies in the First Bank System combination. Improved earnings from the company's strong fee-generating businesses, excellent cost structure, and opportunities for expansion of market share in core banking segments should propel the shares higher in the coming year. With expectations that merger benefits will become increasingly apparent in earnings, purchase of the shares is recommended.

Key Stock Statistics

S&P EPS Est. 1998	2.05	Tang. Bk. Value/Share	8.27
P/E on S&P Est. 1998	20.4	Beta	1.13
S&P EPS Est. 1999	2.45	Shareholders	22,300
Dividend Rate/Share	0.70	Market cap. (B)	$ 30.9
Shs. outstg. (M)	739.9	Inst. holdings	48%
Avg. daily vol. (M)	1.676		

Value of $10,000 invested 5 years ago: $ 51,637

Fiscal Year Ending Dec. 31

	1998	1997	1996	1995	1994	1993
Revenues (Million $)						
1Q	1,784	1,660	1,038	805.2	544.3	559.7
2Q	1,924	1,734	1,025	829.6	579.6	557.9
3Q	—	1,732	886.9	854.0	611.3	556.9
4Q	—	1,769	890.0	839.5	639.9	556.9
Yr.	—	6,909	3,840	3,328	2,375	2,231
Earnings Per Share ($)						
1Q	**0.44**	**0.39**	0.43	0.32	0.28	0.20
2Q	**0.43**	**0.41**	0.60	0.33	0.29	0.08
3Q	—	**-0.07**	0.33	0.36	0.30	0.25
4Q	—	**0.39**	0.42	0.38	0.32	0.27
Yr.	—	**1.11**	**1.57**	1.40	1.19	0.80

Next earnings report expected: mid October

Dividend Data (Dividends have been paid since 1930.)

Amount ($)	Date Decl.	Ex-Div. Date	Stock of Record	Payment Date
0.525	Feb. 18	Feb. 26	Mar. 02	Mar. 15 '98
3-for-1	Feb. 18	May. 19	May. 04	May. 18 '98
0.175	Apr. 24	May. 28	Jun. 01	Jul. 15 '98
0.175	Jul. 15	Aug. 28	Sep. 01	Sep. 15 '98

A Division of The McGraw-Hill Companies

Business Summary - 31-JUL-98

U.S. Bancorp is a multi-state bank holding company formed through the August 1997 merger of Minneapolis-based First Bank System and Portland-based U.S. Bancorp. With $74 billion in assets, the company is now the 14th largest U.S. bank holding company. The combined company operates about 1,000 banking offices in 17 states: Minnesota, Oregon, Washington, Colorado, California, Idaho, Nebraska, North Dakota, Nevada, South Dakota, Montana, Iowa, Illinois, Utah, Wisconsin, Kansas and Wyoming. USB provides comprehensive banking, trust, investment and payment systems products and services to consumers, businesses and institutions. It is the world's largest provider of VISA corporate and purchasing cards, and one of the largest U.S. providers of corporate trust services.

In 1997, average earning assets amounted to $61.7 billion and consisted mainly of loans (87%) and investment securities (10%). Average sources of funds included checking accounts (8%), savings and money market accounts (19%), savings certificates (23%), non-interest-bearing deposits (18%), short-term borrowings (11%), long-term debt (8%), shareholders' equity (8%) and other (5%).

At year-end 1997, nonperforming assets, consisting primarily of nonperforming loans and other real estate owned, were $340 million (0.62% of loans and related assets), up from $320 million (0.61%) a year earlier. The allowance for loan losses, which is set aside for possible loan defaults, was $1.01 billion (1.84% of loans), versus $993 million (1.90%) a year earlier. Net chargeoffs, or the amount of loans actually written off as uncollectible, were $450 million (0.84% of average loans) in 1997, versus $262 million (0.51%) in 1996.

Terms of the August 1997 merger between First Bank System (FBS) and the old U.S. Bancorp (USBC) called for each outstanding USBC common share to be exchanged for 0.755 shares of FBS common stock. The resulting company immediately changed its name to U.S. Bancorp.

In May 1998, the company acquired Piper Jaffray Companies Inc., a full-service investment banker and securities broker, for $738 million in cash. The acquisition added retail brokerage, investment banking and merger and acquisition capabilities to USB's platform of services.

In June 1998, directors authorized the repurchase of up to $2.5 billion of common stock through March 2000. During 1998's second quarter, 6.6 million shares were repurchased for $275.2 million.

Per Share Data ($)

(Year Ended Dec. 31)	1997	1996	1995	1994	1993	1992	1991	1990	1989	1988
Tangible Bk. Val.	7.96	7.55	6.86	4.81	5.04	5.26	3.97	3.76	3.36	4.79
Earnings	1.11	1.78	1.40	1.19	0.80	0.37	0.71	0.51	-0.09	-1.75
Dividends	0.62	0.55	0.48	0.39	0.33	0.29	0.27	0.27	0.48	0.55
Payout Ratio	56%	31%	35%	32%	42%	80%	39%	54%	NM	NM
Prices - High	38$^{7}/_8$	24$^{5}/_8$	17$^{7}/_8$	13	11$^{3}/_8$	9$^{1}/_2$	8$^{1}/_4$	5$^{5}/_8$	9	8$^{1}/_8$
- Low	22$^{1}/_2$	15$^{3}/_8$	10$^{7}/_8$	9$^{3}/_4$	8$^{5}/_8$	7$^{3}/_4$	4$^{1}/_4$	3$^{1}/_4$	5$^{1}/_4$	6$^{1}/_4$
P/E Ratio - High	35	14	13	11	14	26	12	11	NM	NM
- Low	20	9	8	8	11	21	6	6	NM	NM

Income Statement Analysis (Million $)

	1997	1996	1995	1994	1993	1992	1991	1990	1989	1988
Net Int. Inc.	3,048	1,533	1,440	1,195	1,133	846	710	639	654	539
Tax Equiv. Adj.	57.9	20.6	13.8	15.1	17.7	21.7	32.0	43.0	59.0	87.0
Non Int. Inc.	1,612	1,171	783	632	569	410	344	326	357	325
Loan Loss Prov.	460	136	115	93.0	125	164	153	133	254	76.0
Exp./Op. Revs.	60%	51%	54%	57%	64%	71%	64%	68%	72%	66%
Pretax Inc.	1,391	1,195	902	677	477	183	213	144	-1.0	-334
Eff. Tax Rate	40%	38%	37%	38%	38%	32%	11%	9.60%	NM	NM
Net Inc.	839	740	568	420	298	124	190	131	2.0	-309
% Net Int. Marg.	5.04	4.89	4.91	5.28	5.07	4.73	4.67	3.79	3.52	2.60

Balance Sheet & Other Fin. Data (Million $)

	1997	1996	1995	1994	1993	1992	1991	1990	1989	1988
Earning Assets:										
Money Mkt	887	973	351	548	1,393	1,896	1,652	1,591	567	1,501
Inv. Securities	6,885	3,555	3,256	3,148	3,319	3,327	1,546	1,780	1,984	2,916
Com'l Loans	33,783	10,361	9,331	8,266	8,363	6,674	6,589	7,262	9,075	9,823
Other Loans	20,925	16,767	17,069	11,015	10,416	8,768	6,563	6,196	6,639	6,308
Total Assets	71,295	36,489	33,874	26,129	26,385	23,527	18,301	19,001	20,820	24,248
Demand Deposits	14,544	7,871	6,357	5,777	7,409	5,215	4,020	3,648	3,437	3,369
Time Deposits	34,483	16,508	16,157	13,014	13,542	13,328	10,459	10,985	12,316	13,835
LT Debt	10,247	3,553	3,201	1,483	1,058	822	681	1,202	1,433	1,545
Common Eqty.	5,890	3,053	2,622	2,169	1,979	1,697	1,151	1,031	793	879
% Ret. on Assets	1.6	2.1	1.7	1.6	1.2	0.6	1.1	0.7	0.0	NM
% Ret. on Equity	18.5	23.8	21.9	21.1	16.5	8.4	21.7	12.0	NM	NM
% Loan Loss Resv.	1.8	1.9	1.4	2.3	2.3	2.5	2.6	2.7	2.5	2.8
% Loans/Deposits	158.7	111.0	117.3	102.6	89.3	83.3	90.8	92.0	99.8	93.8
% Equity to Assets	8.3	8.1	7.5	7.5	6.4	5.5	4.4	4.6	4.2	4.8

Data as orig. reptd.; bef. results of disc opers. and/or spec. items. Per share data adj. for stk. divs. as of ex-div. date. Bold denotes diluted EPS (FASB 128). E-Estimated. NA-Not Available. NM-Not Meaningful. NR-Not Ranked.

Office—First Bank Place, 601 Second Ave. South, Minneapolis, MN 55402-4302. **Tel**—(612) 973-1111. **Website**—http://www.usbank.com **Chrmn**—G. B. Cameron. **Pres & CEO**—J. F. Grundhofer. **EVP & CFO**—S. E. Lester. **Investor Contact**—John R. Danielson, Judith T. Murphy. **Dirs**—L. Ahlers, H. L. Bettis, G. B. Cameron, C. Silva Chambers, A. D. Collins, P. H.Coors, F. G. Drake, R. L. Dryden, J. B. Fery, J. Green III, J. F. Grundhofer, R. L. Hale, D. W. Johnson, N. M. Jones,—R. L. Knowlton, J. W. Levin, K. A. Mcke, A. T. Noble, E. J. Phillips, P. A. Redmond, S. W. Richey, R. L. Robinson, N. S. Rogers, R. L. Schall, W. Scott, Jr., B. R. Whiteley. **Transfer Agent & Registrar**—First Chicago Trust Co. of New York, Jersey City, NJ. **Incorporated**—in Delaware in 1929. **Empl**—27,031. **S&P Analyst:** Stephen R. Biggar

12-SEP-98

Industry:
Health Care (Medical Products & Supplies)

Summary: This leading manufacturer of surgical stapling devices and minimally invasive laparoscopic surgical products has agreed to be acquired by Tyco International.

S&P Opinion: Accumulate (★★★★)	Recent Price • 40½ Yield • 0.4%
	52 Wk Range • 50-23¼ 12-Mo. P/E • 31.2

Quantitative Evaluations

Outlook
(1 Lowest—5 Highest)
• **4‾**

Fair Value
• **58⅜**

Risk
• **Average**

Earn./Div. Rank
• **B**

Technical Eval.
• **Bullish** since 5/98

Rel. Strength Rank
(1 Lowest—99 Highest)
• **76**

Insider Activity
• **NA**

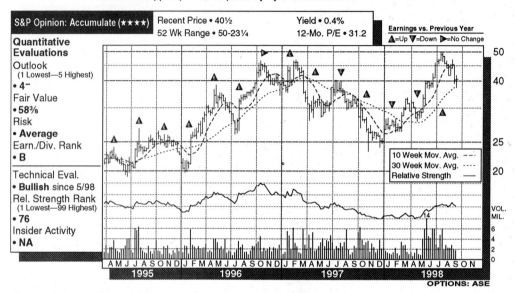

Earnings vs. Previous Year
▲=Up ▼=Down ▶=No Change

10 Week Mov. Avg. -- -
30 Week Mov. Avg. ······
Relative Strength ——

OPTIONS: ASE

Overview - 24-JUN-98

Sales in 1998 (for U.S. Surgical alone) are expected to rise about 20%, bolstered by the January 1998 acquisition of Pfizer's Valleylab division, and by rising contributions from new products. Valleylab, a leader in electrosurgical and ultrasonic products, has annual sales of about $200 million. New products contributing importantly to sales include new breast biopsy instruments, advanced suturing devices, minimally invasive coronary bypass surgical instruments, and a fusion spinal cage for patients with degenerative disc disease. However, sales in core surgical stapling and laparoscopic product lines are likely to remain under competitive pressure from Johnson & Johnson. Although dilution from Valleylab and negative foreign exchange are expected to restrict earnings for the first half, a strong showing is projected for the second half. EPS are projected at $1.65, up from 1997's $1.21 (after net nonrecurring charges of $0.44).

Valuation - 24-JUN-98

In late May, USS agreed to be acquired by Tyco International (NYSE: TYC), with each USS common share to be exchanged for 0.7606 of a TYC share (recent price $60.50). Merging with Tyco's disposable medical businesses would create a more formidable competitor in USS's core surgical stapling, laparoscopic and suture businesses, which have been under intensified competition from Johnson & Johnson. For TYC, acquiring USS will provide important cost synergies, and should be immediately accretive to earnings. TYC, a diversified manufacturing and service firm with annual revenues estimated at $13 billion, is expected to maintain strong EPS momentum in coming years. We view the expected takeover by TYC as a positive development for USS; the shares merit accumulation.

Key Stock Statistics

S&P EPS Est. 1998	1.65	Tang. Bk. Value/Share	11.80
P/E on S&P Est. 1998	24.5	Beta	0.97
S&P EPS Est. 1999	1.90	Shareholders	8,700
Dividend Rate/Share	0.16	Market cap. (B)	$ 3.1
Shs. outstg. (M)	77.1	Inst. holdings	62%
Avg. daily vol. (M)	0.485		

Value of $10,000 invested 5 years ago: $ 6,065

Fiscal Year Ending Dec. 31

	1998	1997	1996	1995	1994	1993
Revenues (Million $)						
1Q	317.3	284.6	266.0	240.6	226.0	326.0
2Q	363.9	290.0	283.6	263.6	232.0	229.0
3Q	—	295.0	280.0	254.8	234.2	238.0
4Q	—	302.5	283.1	263.3	226.5	244.0
Yr.	—	1,172	1,113	1,022	918.7	1,037
Earnings Per Share ($)						
1Q	**0.32**	**0.38**	0.28	0.17	-0.14	0.61
2Q	**0.37**	**0.24**	0.38	0.25	0.05	-0.39
3Q	**E0.45**	**0.41**	0.39	0.37	0.15	-0.26
4Q	**E0.48**	**0.19**	0.43	0.26	0.02	-2.46
Yr.	**E1.65**	**1.21**	1.48	1.05	0.08	-2.48

Next earnings report expected: late October

Dividend Data (Dividends have been paid since 1985.)

Amount ($)	Date Decl.	Ex-Div. Date	Stock of Record	Payment Date
0.040	Oct. 21	Nov. 25	Nov. 28	Dec. 12 '97
0.040	Feb. 03	Feb. 25	Feb. 27	Mar. 13 '98
0.040	Apr. 28	May. 27	May. 29	Jun. 12 '98
0.040	Jul. 29	Aug. 19	Aug. 21	Sep. 11 '98

A Division of The McGraw·Hill Companies

Business Summary - 24-JUN-98

U.S. Surgical was founded by Leon Hirsch in 1964 to develop and commercialize the surgical stapler. Today, the company ranks as a leading manufacturer of technologically advanced surgical staplers, as well as a major producer of minimally invasive, disposable laparoscopic surgical products. USS is also a growing factor in the suture market. Foreign operations (including sales to international distributors) accounted for 47% of total sales in 1997 (50% in 1996).

Surgical stapling products, sold under the Auto Suture name, include disposable and reusable staplers, disposable surgical clip appliers and presterilized disposable loading units for use with the reusable stapling instruments. These instruments are analternative to manual suturing techniques utilizing needle/suture combinations and enable surgeons to reduce blood loss, tissue trauma and operating time while joining internal tissue, reconstructing or sealing off organs, removing diseased tissue, occluding blood vessels and closing skin. Products are made from titanium,stainless steel and proprietary absorbable copolymer materials.

A wide array of disposable products is also manufactured for use in laparoscopic (also referred to as endoscopic) surgical procedures. A minimally invasive surgical technique that requires incisions of less than one-half inch in diameter, laparoscopy is used extensively in gall bladder removals and is being applied to other procedures such as hernia repair, appendectomy, hysterectomy and breast surgery. It offers important reductions in patient trauma and hospital stays vis-a-vis conventional methods. USS products serving this market include laparoscopes for viewing inside the body cavity; laparoscopic surgical clip appliers and stapling instruments; trocars that provide entry ports to the body; and a line of instruments that allow the surgeon to see, cut, clamp, retract, suction, irrigate or otherwise manipulate tissue during a laparoscopic procedure.

Suture products include both absorbable and nonabsorbable sutures. The company's sutures are designed to come out of the package without kinking, and offer other competitive advantages.

Other products include the MIBB and ABBI devices for minimally invasive breast biopsy; the VCS clip applier, which holds a blood vessel together without penetrating it; and the Mini-CABG instruments used in cardiac bypass procedures. USS also has an option to commercialize new coronary stent and aneurysm repair products developed by EndoTex Interventional Systems. In January 1998, USS acquired the Valleylab division of Pfizer for $425 million in cash. Valleylab is the world leader in electrosurgical and ultrasonic products, with sales of about $200 million.

Per Share Data ($)

(Year Ended Dec. 31)	1997	1996	1995	1994	1993	1992	1991	1990	1989	1988
Tangible Bk. Val.	11.80	10.96	6.74	7.03	7.89	10.61	6.30	4.62	3.60	2.85
Cash Flow	2.49	3.23	3.01	1.66	-0.99	3.03	2.09	1.32	1.11	0.96
Earnings	1.47	1.48	1.05	0.08	-2.48	2.32	1.58	0.89	0.66	0.50
Dividends	0.16	0.08	0.08	0.08	0.24	0.30	0.29	0.24	0.17	0.15
Payout Ratio	11%	5%	8%	100%	NM	13%	17%	25%	27%	30%
Prices - High	47	46⅝	27¾	32½	79½	134½	116⅜	35⅞	15⅜	8⅝
- Low	23¼	19¾	18¾	15⅞	19⅞	53¾	31¼	12⅛	7⅝	6⅝
P/E Ratio - High	32	32	26	NM	NM	58	74	41	23	17
- Low	16	13	18	NM	NM	23	20	14	12	13

Income Statement Analysis (Million $)

	1997	1996	1995	1994	1993	1992	1991	1990	1989	1988
Revs.	1,172	1,113	1,022	919	1,037	1,197	844	514	345	291
Oper. Inc.	258	237	202	140	102	250	172	99	69.0	61.0
Depr.	93.8	86.7	91.7	89.4	83.2	42.3	29.4	22.6	21.5	21.4
Int. Exp.	1.2	9.0	20.7	18.2	28.0	14.7	12.0	9.8	7.8	7.7
Pretax Inc.	121	142	89.8	33.0	-136	193	130	66.0	44.0	32.0
Eff. Tax Rate	22%	23%	12%	41%	NM	28%	30%	31%	30%	27%
Net Inc.	94.1	109	79.2	19.0	-138	139	91.2	46.0	30.6	23.2

Balance Sheet & Other Fin. Data (Million $)

	1997	1996	1995	1994	1993	1992	1991	1990	1989	1988
Cash	18.3	107	10.5	11.3	0.9	2.5	2.6	3.0	1.9	1.8
Curr. Assets	677	691	507	440	465	517	386	219	147	114
Total Assets	1,726	1,515	1,266	1,104	1,171	1,168	742	461	327	264
Curr. Liab.	313	295	260	184	217	163	122	90.0	58.0	43.0
LT Debt	131	142	257	249	505	395	252	131	97.0	90.0
Common Eqty.	1,257	1,054	541	462	444	590	330	225	168	130
Total Cap.	1,413	1,219	805	919	954	1,005	619	371	269	221
Cap. Exp.	55.6	42.3	33.6	47.0	216	272	145	72.0	44.0	32.0
Cash Flow	183	196	171	94.0	-56.0	181	121	69.0	52.0	45.0
Curr. Ratio	2.2	2.3	1.9	2.4	2.1	3.2	3.2	2.4	2.5	2.6
% LT Debt of Cap.	9.3	11.6	31.9	27.0	53.0	39.3	40.6	35.3	36.0	40.5
% Net Inc.of Revs.	8.0	9.8	7.7	2.1	NM	11.6	10.8	9.0	8.9	8.0
% Ret. on Assets	5.8	7.8	6.7	1.7	NM	14.2	14.7	11.5	10.3	9.2
% Ret. on Equity	7.7	12.1	16.1	0.9	NM	29.5	31.9	23.0	20.4	18.9

Data as orig. reptd.; bef. results of disc. opers. and/or spec. items. Per share data adj. for stk. divs. as of ex-div. date. Bold denotes diluted EPS (FASB 128). E-Estimated. NA-Not Available. NM-Not Meaningful. NR-Not Ranked.

Office—150 Glover Ave., Norwalk, CT 06856. **Reincorporated**—in Delaware in 1990. **Tel**—(203) 845-1000. **Website**—http://www.ussurg.com **Chrmn**—L. C. Hirsch. **Pres & COO**—H. M. Rosenkrantz. **VP & CFO**—R. A. Douville. **Secy**—P. Komenda. **VP & Investor Contact**—Marianne Scipione (203-845-1404). **Dirs**—J. K. Blake, J. A. Bogardus Jr., T. R. Bremer, L. C. Hirsch, T. Josefsen, D. L. King, R. A. Knarr, J. R. Mellor, W. F. May, B. D. Romeril, H. M. Rosenkrantz, M. Scipione, J. R. Silber. **Transfer Agent & Registrar**—First Chicago Trust Co. of New York, NYC. **Empl**—6,133. **S&P Analyst:** H. B. Saftlas

STANDARD &POOR'S
STOCK REPORTS
U S WEST
2362
NYSE Symbol **USW**

In S&P 500

12-SEP-98

Industry: Telephone

Summary: This regional Bell operating company operates in 14 western and midwestern states.

S&P Opinion: Hold (★★★)	Recent Price • 52¼	Yield • 4.1%
	52 Wk Range • 58-36½	12-Mo. P/E • 23.1

Quantitative Evaluations

Outlook
(1 Lowest—5 Highest)
• **1**

Fair Value
• **44**

Risk
• **Low**

Earn./Div. Rank
• **B**

Technical Eval.
• **Bullish** since 9/98

Rel. Strength Rank
(1 Lowest—99 Highest)
• **93**

Insider Activity
• **Neutral**

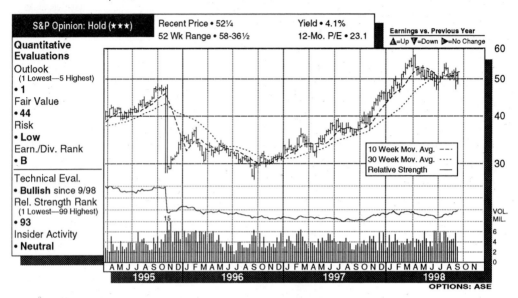

Earnings vs. Previous Year
▲=Up ▼=Down ▶=No Change

10 Week Mov. Avg. ----
30 Week Mov. Avg. ·····
Relative Strength ——

OPTIONS: ASE

Overview - 10-AUG-98

U S WEST recently split U S WEST, Inc. (formerly U S WEST Communications Group) and MediaOne Group (formerly U S WEST Media Group) into separate public companies. USW now consists of the core local telephone operations, combined with growth opportunities in data, wireless and long distance, and continues to pay the dividend. While legislation has opened local telephone markets to competition, USW was initially only allowed to offer long-distance service outside its region. Under terms of the legislation, USW will likely begin offering in-region long-distance services by the end of 1999. Reduced earnings in the second quarter of 1998 resulted from a one-time after-tax charge of $89 million ($0.17 a share) related to the split from MediaOne Group.

Valuation - 10-AUG-98

The shares have continued to rise in line with the market, and should continue this pattern over the next 12 months. While USW will likely lose customers as new competitors enter its local markets, the rural nature of much of its operating territory means that many new competitors will likely be purchasing local service from USW to resell to customers. Therefore, USW will still have most of these customers on the wholesale level. Its eventual entry into the in-region long-distance market will not materially affect results over the next few years. However, as a result of the targeted stock plan, the company's fastest-growing businesses are now tracked by the MediaOne Group shares, which will benefit from the recent split. For the near term, we see the shares as market performers, but, with a very healthy dividend, they provide adequate long-term total-return prospects.

Key Stock Statistics

S&P EPS Est. 1998	2.75	Tang. Bk. Value/Share		9.57
P/E on S&P Est. 1998	19.0	Beta		0.29
S&P EPS Est. 1999	3.00	Shareholders		722,200
Dividend Rate/Share	2.14	Market cap. (B)		$ 26.2
Shs. outstg. (M)	501.7	Inst. holdings		56%
Avg. daily vol. (M)	0.923			

Value of $10,000 invested 5 years ago: NA

Fiscal Year Ending Dec. 31

	1998	1997	1996	1995	1994	1993
Revenues (Million $)						
1Q	2,710	2,587	2,465	2,318	--	--
2Q	3,053	2,543	2,500	2,338	4,534	--
3Q	--	2,673	2,515	2,389	2,316	--
4Q	--	2,516	2,599	2,375	2,839	--
Yr.	--	10,319	10,079	9,284	9,176	8,870
Earnings Per Share ($)						
1Q	**0.71**	**0.70**	0.62	--	--	--
2Q	**0.67**	**0.69**	0.68	1.29	1.30	—
3Q	**E0.70**	**0.70**	0.60	0.62	0.59	—
4Q	**E0.64**	**0.35**	0.65	0.60	0.65	--
Yr.	**E2.75**	**2.42**	2.55	2.52	2.53	--

Next earnings report expected: late October

Dividend Data (Dividends have been paid since 1984.)

Amount ($)	Date Decl.	Ex-Div. Date	Stock of Record	Payment Date
0.535	Sep. 19	Oct. 08	Oct. 10	Nov. 03 '97
0.535	Jan. 02	Jan. 08	Jan. 12	Feb. 02 '98
0.535	Mar. 13	Apr. 07	Apr. 10	May. 01 '98
0.535	Jun. 11	Jul. 08	Jul. 10	Aug. 01 '98

*A Division of The **McGraw·Hill** Companies*

Business Summary - 10-AUG-98

Based on 1997 U.S. access lines, U S WEST, Inc. is the seventh largest U.S. telephone holding company. It is also one of the original Baby Bells, spun off from AT&T in 1984.

U S WEST recently split MediaOne Group (formerly U S WEST Media Group) and U S WEST, Inc. (formerly U S WEST Communications Group) into separate public companies.

On November 1, 1995, U S WEST replaced its common shares with two classes of common stock. The shares of U S WEST, Inc. tracked the company's core telephone operations. Telephone operations provide local telephone and exchange access service to 16.2 million customer access lines in 14 states. The company serves approximately 80% of the region's population and about 40% of its geographic area.

The Communications Group has three major business units: Markets, Carrier Services and Operations and Technologies. The Markets organization has product, marketing and sales and service units that work together to develop, market and deliver innovative and targeted communications packages to various customer groups.

The Carrier unit is responsible for providing network access and services primarily to long-distance and wireless companies, as well as telecommunications services to independent local exchange telephone companies.

The Operations and Technologies unit provides research and development, underlying network services, and systems development for U S WEST Communications.

U S WEST owns jointly, with the four other Regional Bell holding companies, Bell Communications Research, which provides technical assistance and consulting services to the companies.

USW added 609,000 access lines in 1997, and now has more than 16.0 million access lines in service. The company is also exploring new opportunities in data, wireless, long distance and video.

In early 1998, U S WEST formed partnerships with Williams Communications, Intermedia, Qwest Communications, Cisco Systems, Digital Equipment, Hewlett Packard, Novell, Oracle and Sun Microsystems to create a next-generation data network.

The company's Access2 Advanced PCS (personal communications services) wireless service operates in eight states, covering 6.5 million POPs (population equivalents), and encompasses more than 20% of the population in USW's 14-state territory.

Per Share Data ($)

(Year Ended Dec. 31)	1997	1996	1995	1994	1993	1992	1991	1990	1989	1988
Tangible Bk. Val.	8.67	6.81	NA	NA	NA	NA	NA	NA	NA	NA
Cash Flow	6.66	6.98	6.88	6.75	NA	NA	NA	NA	NA	NA
Earnings	2.42	2.55	2.52	2.53	NA	NA	NA	NA	NA	NA
Dividends	2.14	2.14	2.14	NA	NA	NA	NA	NA	NA	NA
Payout Ratio	88%	84%	85%	NA	NA	NA	NA	NA	NA	NA
Prices - High	46⁷/₈	37¹/₂	48³/₈	46¹/₄	50³/₄	40	40³/₄	40¹/₂	40³/₈	NA
- Low	31¹/₈	27¹/₄	28³/₈	34⁵/₈	37³/₄	32⁷/₈	33³/₄	32³/₈	28³/₈	NA
P/E Ratio - High	19	15	19	NM	NA	NA	NA	NA	NA	NA
- Low	13	11	11	NM	NA	NA	NA	NA	NA	NA

Income Statement Analysis (Million $)

Revs.	10,083	9,831	9,284	9,176	8,870	8,530	8,345	8,235	NA	NA
Depr.	2,103	2,101	2,022	1,908	1,828	1,759	NA	NA	NA	NA
Maint.	NA	NA	NA	NA	NA	NA	NA	NA	NA	NA
Constr. Credits	NA	NA	NA	NA	NA	NA	NA	NA	NA	NA
Eff. Tax Rate	38%	38%	36%	36%	35%	29%	NA	NA	NA	NA
Net Inc.	1,252	5,375	1,219	1,150	391	930	771	935	NA	NA

Balance Sheet & Other Fin. Data (Million $)

Gross Prop.	33,182	32,451	30,988	29,578	28,173	NA	NA	NA	NA	NA
Net Prop.	14,141	13,929	13,448	13,041	12,631	NA	NA	NA	NA	NA
Cap. Exp.	2,101	2,392	2,437	2,254	2,234	NA	NA	NA	NA	NA
Total Cap.	10,478	10,415	10,105	8,473	7,549	NA	NA	NA	NA	NA
Fxd. Chgs. Cov.	6.0	5.6	5.1	5.5	4.6	4.1	NA	NA	NA	NA
Capitalization:										
LT Debt	5,020	6,311	5,411	4,516	4,291	NA	NA	NA	NA	NA
Pfd.	Nil	Nil	Nil	Nil	Nil	NA	NA	NA	NA	NA
Common	4,400	4,060	3,746	3,179	2,722	NA	NA	NA	NA	NA
% Return On Revs.	12.4	12.5	13.1	12.5	4.4	10.9	9.2	11.4	NA	NA
% Return On Invest. Capital	14.3	15.5	16.2	19.0	NA	NA	NA	NA	NA	NA
% Return On Com. Equity	29.6	31.6	32.8	39.0	39.0	13.7	10.4	NA	NA	NA
% Earn. on Net Prop.	11.2	11.9	11.6	11.4	NA	NA	NA	NA	NA	NA
% LT Debt of Cap.	53.3	57.0	59.1	58.7	61.2	NA	NA	NA	NA	NA
Capital. % Pfd.	Nil	Nil	Nil	Nil	Nil	NA	NA	NA	NA	NA
Capital. % Common	46.7	43.0	40.9	41.3	38.8	NA	NA	NA	NA	NA

Data as orig. reptd.; bef. results of disc. opers. and/or spec. items. Per share data adj. for stk. divs. as of ex-div. date. Bold denotes diluted EPS (FASB 128). E-Estimated. NA-Not Available. NM-Not Meaningful. NR-Not Ranked.

Office—7800 E. Orchard Rd., Englewood, CO 80111-2526. **Tel**—(303) 793-6500. **Chrmn**—R. D. McCormick. **Pres & CEO**—S. Trujillo. **EVP & CFO**—M. Glinsky.**VP & Treas**—J. T. Anderson.**Investor Contact**—Sara Stratton. **Dirs**—R. L. Crandell, G. A. Dove, A. D. Gilmour, P. M. Grieve, G. J. Harad, A. F. Jacobsen, C. M. Lillis, R. D. McCormick, M. C. Nelson, F. Popoff, C. P. Russ III, L. A. Simpson, J. Slevin, S. D. Trujillo, J. O. Williams. **Transfer Agent & Registrar**—Boston Financial Data Services, Quincy, MA. **Incorporated**—in Colorado in 1983. **Empl**— 48,551. **S&P Analyst:** Philip D. Wohl

12-SEP-98

Industry:
Manufacturing (Diversified)

Summary: This company is a major producer of aircraft jet engines, helicopters, flight systems, air-conditioning equipment, elevators and escalators, and automotive products.

| S&P Opinion: Accumulate (★★★★) | Recent Price • 76⅝ | Yield • 1.9% |
| | 52 Wk Range • 100⅛-66¾ | 12-Mo. P/E • 16.5 |

Quantitative Evaluations

Outlook
(1 Lowest—5 Highest)
• **2+**

Fair Value
• **77⅞**

Risk
• **Low**

Earn./Div. Rank
• **B**

Technical Eval.
• **Bullish** since 6/98

Rel. Strength Rank
(1 Lowest—99 Highest)
• **56**

Insider Activity
• **Favorable**

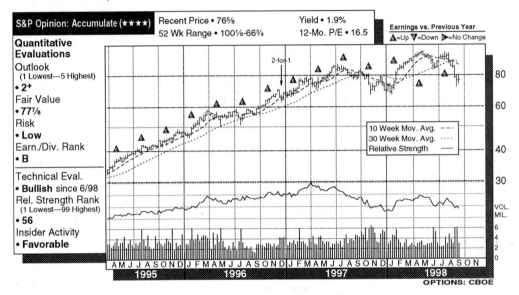

Earnings vs. Previous Year
▲=Up ▼=Down ▶=No Change

10 Week Mov. Avg. ----
30 Week Mov. Avg. ·····
Relative Strength ——

OPTIONS: CBOE

Overview - 24-JUL-98

Revenues are projected to increase 5% in 1998. Pratt & Whitney will be the strongest segment due to a sharp rise in demand for new commercial aircraft, which drives demand for aircraft engines. Otis has undertaken a major restructuring which will eliminate redundant research centers and smaller production plants. Carrier also began restructuring operations at its rotary chiller unit and plans to reduce costs in Asia and Europe. Absent these charges, Carrier's margins are expanding. UT Automotive is in a turnaround, with profit margins continuing to widen. Opportunities for growth are developing in the integration of interior components with electronic controls. Flight systems profits may drop due to timing of Sikorsky helicopter deliveries. Overall, earnings are expected to benefit from strong productivity improvement initiatives and cost reduction efforts. Share earnings will be supported by an active stock repurchase program. Over the long term, UTX will continue its efforts to enter new foreign markets and to deepen penetration in existing ones. Acquisitions will continue to play a role in this gradual foreign expansion.

Valuation - 24-JUL-98

We continue to rank the shares as attractive. Over the long term, high exposure to foreign markets is a company strength, as domestic markets are slower growing, on average. The shares remain modestly valued compared to recent multiples for the S&P 400 Industrial Index. With modest debt levels, the company is using its strong cash flow to finance an active share repurchase program, to pay a growing dividend and to complete modest acquisitions--all of which should lead to further increases in shareholder value.

Key Stock Statistics

S&P EPS Est. 1998	4.85	Tang. Bk. Value/Share	13.49
P/E on S&P Est. 1998	15.8	Beta	1.19
S&P EPS Est. 1999	5.60	Shareholders	23,000
Dividend Rate/Share	1.44	Market cap. (B)	$ 17.5
Shs. outstg. (M)	228.0	Inst. holdings	74%
Avg. daily vol. (M)	1.021		

Value of $10,000 invested 5 years ago: $ 36,166

Fiscal Year Ending Dec. 31

	1998	1997	1996	1995	1994	1993
Revenues (Million $)						
1Q	6,111	5,934	5,348	5,344	4,838	4,864
2Q	6,665	6,483	6,002	5,840	5,489	5,570
3Q	—	5,979	5,908	5,651	5,253	5,128
4Q	—	6,317	6,015	5,967	5,675	5,519
Yr.	—	24,713	23,273	22,802	21,197	21,081
Earnings Per Share ($)						
1Q	1.04	0.87	0.62	0.52	0.25	0.21
2Q	1.44	1.19	0.98	0.82	0.61	0.47
3Q	—	1.18	0.97	0.80	0.70	0.58
4Q	—	0.97	0.87	0.71	0.63	0.49
Yr.	E4.85	4.21	3.48	2.85	2.20	1.76

Next earnings report expected: late October

Dividend Data (Dividends have been paid since 1936.)

Amount ($)	Date Decl.	Ex-Div. Date	Stock of Record	Payment Date
0.310	Oct. 06	Nov. 19	Nov. 21	Dec. 10 '97
0.310	Feb. 09	Feb. 18	Feb. 20	Mar. 10 '98
0.360	Apr. 30	May. 20	May. 22	Jun. 10 '98
0.360	Jul. 29	Aug. 19	Aug. 21	Sep. 10 '98

A Division of The **McGraw·Hill** Companies

Business Summary - 24-JUL-98

With well known brands such as Pratt & Whitney, Otis, Carrier and Sikorsky, United Technologies is expanding its diverse operations into emerging foreign markets. Overseas operations, including exports, already account for 56% of revenues, so UTX's new market initiatives are focused in China, Russia and India. Besides its stable of brands, UTX counts among its resources strong cash flow, which permits payment of a growing dividend, share buybacks and investment in acquisitions, new products and new markets. Segment contributions in 1997 (based on profit of $2.2 billion) were:

	Revs.	Profits
Pratt & Whitney	30%	37%
Carrier	24%	21%
Otis	22%	21%
Flight systems	12%	13%
Automotive	12%	8%

Pratt & Whitney manufactures engines and spare parts for commercial, general aviation and military aircraft, and also provides maintenance, overhaul and repair services. In 1997, P&W delivered its most powerful commercial engine, a 90,000 pound-thrust engine for Boeing 777s. In early 1998, a new geared turbofan engine was unveiled which reduces operating costs 10%, fuel consumption 9% and noise levels 30 decibels. P&W's F-119 engine will be the only engine used on the U.S. government's two new fighter programs: the F-22, which is in production, and the Joint Strike Fighter, which is in development.

Carrier's heating, ventilating and air-conditioning equipment and transport and commercial refrigeration equipment are used worldwide by a diverse customer base. In 1998, Carrier began restructuring its rotary chiller operation and reducing costs in Asia and Europe.

Otis is the leading producer of elevators and escalators. Maintenance and repair work accounts for 50% of segment revenues, new equipment for 35% and modernization services for 15%. In 1998, Otis will step up its cost cutting efforts. Plans call for closing of more than half of Otis's 19 research centers and up to 10 of 43 production facilities around the world.

UT Automotive has begun to turnaround with margins beginning to widen in recent quarters. Growth opportunities lie in the integration of interior components and vehicle controls.

Flight systems includes Sikorsky helicopters and Hamilton Standard. Sikorsky is compensating for flat military orders by offering civilian versions of its helicopters. Sikorsky is also developing the U.S. government's "Stealth" copter for the post-2000 period. Hamilton Standard is benefiting from an upswing in orders for environmental control systems for commercial aircraft.

Per Share Data ($)

(Year Ended Dec. 31)	1997	1996	1995	1994	1993	1992	1991	1990	1989	1988
Tangible Bk. Val.	13.49	15.23	14.06	12.35	11.55	10.64	10.69	15.95	14.09	17.44
Cash Flow	7.43	6.72	6.00	5.14	5.00	3.43	-1.31	5.86	5.08	4.67
Earnings	4.21	3.45	2.85	2.20	1.76	-0.03	-4.46	2.96	2.67	2.52
Dividends	1.24	1.10	1.02	0.95	0.90	0.95	0.90	0.90	0.80	0.78
Payout Ratio	29%	32%	36%	43%	51%	NM	NM	31%	28%	31%
Prices - High	88⅞	70½	48⅞	36	33⅛	29	27¼	31¼	28¾	21⅜
- Low	65⅛	45¼	31⅛	27½	21⅞	20¾	21⅛	20⅛	20	16½
P/E Ratio - High	21	20	17	16	19	NM	NM	11	11	8
- Low	15	13	11	13	12	NM	NM	7	7	7

Income Statement Analysis (Million $)

	1997	1996	1995	1994	1993	1992	1991	1990	1989	1988
Revs.	24,495	23,273	22,624	21,161	21,081	22,032	20,953	21,550	19,614	18,088
Oper. Inc.	2,598	2,395	2,254	2,108	1,975	1,028	1,178	2,119	2,084	1,758
Depr.	848	853	844	793	815	852	764	700	620	562
Int. Exp.	195	237	260	294	280	334	409	422	407	370
Pretax Inc.	1,764	1,560	1,344	1,076	909	200	-890	1,291	1,260	1,165
Eff. Tax Rate	32%	34%	35%	36%	37%	39%	NM	37%	40%	40%
Net Inc.	1,072	906	750	585	487	35.0	-1,020	751	702	659

Balance Sheet & Other Fin. Data (Million $)

	1997	1996	1995	1994	1993	1992	1991	1990	1989	1988
Cash	755	1,127	900	386	421	354	523	201	267	243
Curr. Assets	9,248	9,611	8,952	8,228	7,706	8,101	8,931	9,012	8,507	7,989
Total Assets	16,719	16,745	15,958	15,624	15,618	15,928	15,985	15,918	14,598	12,748
Curr. Liab.	7,311	7,390	6,659	6,553	6,920	7,037	6,577	5,951	6,376	4,948
LT Debt	1,275	1,437	1,649	1,885	1,939	2,358	2,903	2,902	1,960	1,643
Common Eqty.	3,658	4,306	4,021	3,752	3,598	3,370	3,961	5,343	4,739	4,822
Total Cap.	6,362	6,810	7,031	6,572	6,259	6,411	7,555	9,002	7,381	7,073
Cap. Exp.	843	794	780	759	846	920	1,193	1,208	1,251	877
Cash Flow	1,888	1,753	1,567	1,356	1,259	845	-318	1,415	1,308	1,221
Curr. Ratio	1.3	1.3	1.3	1.3	1.1	1.2	1.4	1.5	1.3	1.6
% LT Debt of Cap.	20.0	21.1	23.5	28.7	31.0	36.8	38.4	32.2	26.6	23.2
% Net Inc.of Revs.	4.4	3.9	3.3	2.8	2.3	0.2	NM	3.5	3.6	3.6
% Ret. on Assets	6.4	5.5	4.7	3.8	3.1	0.2	NM	4.9	5.3	5.3
% Ret. on Equity	27.7	21.6	18.6	15.5	12.0	NM	NM	14.2	14.9	14.4

Data as orig. reptd.; bef. results of disc. opers. and/or spec. items. Per share data adj. for stk. divs. as of ex-div. date. Bold denotes diluted EPS (FASB 128). E-Estimated. NA-Not Available. NM-Not Meaningful. NR-Not Ranked.

Office—United Technologies Bldg., Hartford, CT 06101. **Tel**—(203) 728-7000. **Website**—http://www.utc.com **Chrmn & CEO**—G. David. **Acting CFO**—J. Haberland.**VP & Secy**—W. H. Trachsel. **Investor Contact**—Angelo J. Messina (203-728-7575). **Dirs**—A. H. Chayes, G. David, C. W. Duncan Jr., J. P. Garnier, P. G. Gyllenhammar, K. J. Krapek, C. R. Lee, R. H. Malott, W. J. Perry, F. P. Popoff, A. Villeneuve, H. A. Wagner, J. G. Wexler. **Transfer Agent & Registrar**—First Chicago Trust Co. of New York, Jersey City, NJ. **Incorporated**—in Delaware in 1934. **Empl**— 180,100.
S&P Analyst: Robert E. Friedman, CPA

Unocal Corp.

2374M

NYSE Symbol **UCL**

In S&P 500

12-SEP-98

Industry:
Oil (Domestic Integrated)

Summary: Unocal is the world's largest independent exploration and production company, with major oil and gas production activities in Asia and the U.S. Gulf of Mexico.

S&P Opinion: Sell (★)

Recent Price • 35¾	Yield • 2.2%
52 Wk Range • 45¼-30⅛	12-Mo. P/E • 20.1

Quantitative Evaluations

Outlook
(1 Lowest—5 Highest)
• **1+**

Fair Value
• **29⅜**

Risk
• **Low**

Earn./Div. Rank
• **B+**

Technical Eval.
• **Bullish** since 1/98

Rel. Strength Rank
(1 Lowest—99 Highest)
• **95**

Insider Activity
• **NA**

Earnings vs. Previous Year
▲=Up ▼=Down ▶=No Change

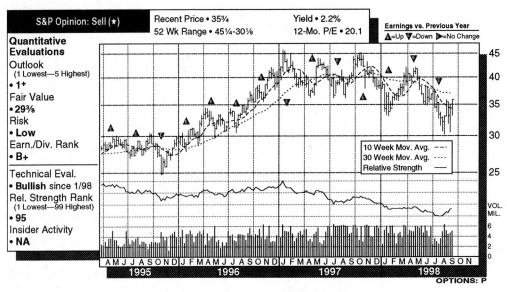

10 Week Mov. Avg. - - -
30 Week Mov. Avg. ----
Relative Strength —

VOL.
MIL.

OPTIONS: P

Overview - 05-AUG-98

Operating profits in the first half of 1998 were restrained by sharply lower crude oil prices, which outweighed the positive effects of lower production costs. Oil and natural gas production levels were lower. In early 1997, UCL sold its refining and marketing business to Tosco Corp., for total consideration of about $2 billion. Proceeds from the sale were used to fund investments in international exploration and production projects, and for a share repurchase program and debt reduction. In this way, the company hopes to divert funds from low-return downstream businesses to high-return upstream projects. Upon completion of the sale of its downstream assets in 1997, UCL became the world's largest independent oil and gas company. Recently announced oil price-related cutbacks in capital spending will result in lower domestic oil and gas production than we had originally anticipated.

Valuation - 05-AUG-98

The shares have fallen about 16% in 1998 to date, as lower oil prices have taken their toll on shares of energy producers. UCL's recent decision to dispose of its downstream business, which had been producing low returns on investment in recent years, in order to focus on international exploration and production projects, seemed destined to produce improved operating results. Over the longer term, the company's strategy of becoming the low-cost producer of natural gas in Asia is expected to pay off. However, the current economic crisis in Asia, a region that accounts for some 45% of UCL's total production, has put the viability of several major energy projects in the region in doubt. And, with world oil prices expected to remain weak, we expect the shares to significantly underperform the market over the rest of 1998.

Key Stock Statistics

S&P EPS Est. 1998	1.25	Tang. Bk. Value/Share	9.54
P/E on S&P Est. 1998	28.6	Beta	0.75
S&P EPS Est. 1999	1.90	Shareholders	32,600
Dividend Rate/Share	0.80	Market cap. (B)	$ 8.6
Shs. outstg. (M)	241.4	Inst. holdings	65%
Avg. daily vol. (M)	1.032		

Value of $10,000 invested 5 years ago: $ 16,124

Fiscal Year Ending Dec. 31

	1998	1997	1996	1995	1994	1993
Revenues (Million $)						
1Q	1,207	1,456	1,201	1,906	1,830	2,200
2Q	1,397	1,654	1,405	2,290	2,020	2,040
3Q	—	1,397	1,337	2,005	—	1,910
4Q	—	1,557	1,385	2,224	1,984	1,930
Yr.	—	6,064	5,328	8,425	7,965	8,080
Earnings Per Share ($)						
1Q	**0.07**	0.75	0.50	0.27	0.22	0.55
2Q	**0.43**	0.63	0.72	0.28	0.21	0.33
3Q	—	0.71	0.54	0.20	0.25	0.25
4Q	—	**0.59**	0.01	0.16	-0.32	0.14
Yr.	**E1.25**	2.65	1.76	0.91	0.36	1.27

Next earnings report expected: late October

Dividend Data (Dividends have been paid since 1916.)

Amount ($)	Date Decl.	Ex-Div. Date	Stock of Record	Payment Date
0.200	Sep. 29	Oct. 08	Oct. 10	Nov. 10 '97
0.200	Dec. 08	Jan. 07	Jan. 09	Feb. 10 '98
0.200	Mar. 30	Apr. 07	Apr. 09	May. 08 '98
0.200	Jun. 01	Jul. 08	Jul. 10	Aug. 10 '98

A Division of The McGraw-Hill Companies

Unocal Corporation

Business Summary - 05-AUG-98

After nearly 80 years, Unocal (UCL) recently handed over the keys to its well-known "Union 76" gas stations and pulled out of the petroleum refining and marketing business to concentrate on exploration and production. In March 1997, UCL completed the sale of its West Coast refining and marketing business, 76 Products (known for its distinctive blue and orange "76" logo), to Tosco Corp. for approximately $1.8 billion and additional considerations. Upon completion of the deal, UCL became the largest independent oil and gas exploration and production company in the world, in terms of both reserves and production volumes.

Unocal's reserves at the end of 1997 amounted to 533 million barrels of crude oil (versus 513 million barrels at year-end 1996) and 6.6 trillion cubic feet (Tcf) of natural gas (6.8 Tcf). Reserves have declined in recent years, reflecting asset sales; in addition, new U.S. reserves have not fully replaced production in recent years.

The company is also involved in a number of diversified businesses, including agricultural products, carbon and minerals, pipelines and geothermal and power operations. These businesses contributed 19% of UCL's total operating income in 1997, down from 23% in 1996.

During 1997, UCL's earnings from continuing operations before special items were 11% lower than in 1996. Exploration and production earnings declined 13%, on lower oil production and weaker oil prices. Net crude oil production declined 4.4%, while natural gas production was up 2.0%. The company's average worldwide oil price was $18.11 per barrel in 1997, down from $19.20 in 1996. The average worldwide gas price came to $2.34 per Mcf in 1997, up from $2.27 in 1996.

During 1997, UCL used the cash from the sale of its refining and marketing business for debt reduction, a share repurchase program and investment in promising international exploration and production projects. By reinvesting refining and marketing assets in international projects, UCL hopes to replace a business that typically produced returns of about 5.0% with one that has traditionally achieved returns in excess of 15%. UCL's experience in dealing with non-U.S. governments will help the company navigate the often-treacherous foreign political terrain.

During 1997, UCL backed-up its commitment to international expansion with stepped-up capital spending. International exploration and production capital expenditures rose nearly 60%, and accounted for 58% of the total in 1997, up from 43% in 1996. Overall capital expenditures came to $1.38 billion in 1997, up from $1.17 billion in 1996. Capital spending plans for 1998 were recently revised to $1.30 billion, down about 10% from original plans, reflecting the current weak crude oil price environment.

Per Share Data ($) (Year Ended Dec. 31)	1997	1996	1995	1994	1993	1992	1991	1990	1989	1988
Tangible Bk. Val.	9.92	9.08	9.77	9.43	10.84	10.88	10.50	10.87	9.83	9.26
Cash Flow	622.52	5.43	5.05	4.27	5.27	4.80	4.14	5.54	5.00	3.60
Earnings	2.65	1.76	0.91	0.36	1.27	0.75	0.31	1.71	1.53	0.11
Dividends	0.80	0.80	0.80	0.80	0.72	0.70	0.70	0.70	0.55	0.50
Payout Ratio	30%	45%	88%	NM	57%	93%	225%	41%	36%	NM
Prices - High	45 7/8	42 1/8	30 1/2	30 3/4	32 5/8	28 7/8	29 1/2	34 1/2	31 1/4	20 1/4
- Low	36 1/8	27 3/4	24 3/4	24 3/8	23 1/2	20 1/4	20 5/8	24 5/8	18 5/8	14 1/4
P/E Ratio - High	17	24	34	85	26	39	95	20	20	NM
- Low	14	16	27	68	19	27	67	14	12	NM
Income Statement Analysis (Million $)										
Revs.	5,781	5,101	8,425	6,904	7,261	8,895	9,685	10,645	10,056	8,853
Oper. Inc.	1,633	1,724	1,776	1,348	1,611	1,523	1,458	1,649	1,558	1,568
Depr.	962	914	1,022	947	963	964	899	897	811	816
Int. Exp.	183	294	326	308	334	413	435	429	444	473
Pretax Inc.	771	758	463	294	611	354	218	506	589	46.0
Eff. Tax Rate	13%	40%	44%	58%	44%	43%	64%	17%	37%	28%
Net Inc.	669	456	260	124	343	196	73.0	401	358	24.0
Balance Sheet & Other Fin. Data (Million $)										
Cash	338	217	94.0	148	205	157	175	130	348	391
Curr. Assets	1,501	3,228	1,576	1,528	1,578	1,660	1,896	2,071	1,993	1,879
Total Assets	7,530	9,123	9,891	9,337	9,254	9,452	9,836	9,762	9,257	9,508
Curr. Liab.	1,160	1,622	1,316	1,257	1,196	1,436	1,543	1,846	1,475	1,368
LT Debt	2,169	2,940	3,698	3,461	3,468	3,546	4,563	4,047	3,887	4,341
Common Eqty.	2,314	2,275	2,417	2,302	2,616	2,618	2,464	2,550	2,300	2,161
Total Cap.	5,142	6,085	6,837	6,919	7,472	7,596	7,928	7,711	7,512	7,885
Cap. Exp.	1,427	1,398	1,459	1,272	1,249	959	1,470	1,316	1,050	1,100
Cash Flow	1,631	1,352	1,246	1,035	1,270	1,143	972	1,298	1,169	840
Curr. Ratio	1.3	2.0	1.2	1.2	1.3	1.2	1.2	1.1	1.4	1.4
% LT Debt of Cap.	42.2	48.3	54.1	50.0	46.4	46.7	57.6	52.5	51.7	55.1
% Net Inc.of Revs.	11.6	8.9	3.1	1.8	4.7	2.2	0.8	3.8	3.6	0.3
% Ret. on Assets	8.0	48.0	2.7	1.3	3.7	2.0	0.7	4.2	3.8	0.2
% Ret. on Equity	29.2	18.7	9.5	3.6	11.7	7.0	2.9	16.5	16.0	1.2

Data as orig. reptd.; bef. results of disc. opers. and/or spec. items. Per share data adj. for stk. divs. as of ex-div. date. Revs.in quarterly table incl. oth. inc. E-Estimated. NA-Not Available. NM-Not Meaningful. NR-Not Ranked.

Office—2141 Rosecrans Avenue, Suite 4000, El Segundo, CA 90245. **Tel**—(310) 726-7600.**Web site**—http://www.unocal.com**Chrmn & CEO**—R. C. Beach. **Pres**—J. F. Imle, Jr. **CFO**—T. H. Ling.. **VP & Investor Contact**—Robert Wright (310-726-7665). **Dirs**—J. W. Amerman, R. C. Beach, J. W. Creighton, M. R. Currie, F. C. Herringer, J. F. Imle, Jr., D. P. Jacobs, K. W. Sharer, C. R. Weaver, M. v. N. Whitman. **Transfer Agent & Registrar**—ChaseMellon Shareholder Services, Ridgefield Park, NJ. **Incorporated**— in California in 1890; reincorporated in Delaware in 1983. **Empl**— 8,394. **S&P Analyst:** Norman Rosenberg

STANDARD &POOR'S
STOCK REPORTS

UNUM Corp.

2267

NYSE Symbol **UNM**

In S&P 500

12-SEP-98

Industry:
Insurance (Life & Health)

Summary: This company offers a broad range of disability, health and life insurance and group pension products; it is a leading provider of group long-term disability insurance.

S&P Opinion: Hold (★★★)

Recent Price • 47
52 Wk Range • 59⅝-41⅝

Yield • 1.3%
12-Mo. P/E • 18.5

Earnings vs. Previous Year
▲=Up ▼=Down ▶=No Change

Quantitative Evaluations

Outlook
(1 Lowest—5 Highest)
• **1**

Fair Value
• **43¼**

Risk
• **Low**

Earn./Div. Rank
• **A-**

Technical Eval.
• **Bearish** since 7/96

Rel. Strength Rank
(1 Lowest—99 Highest)
• **70**

Insider Activity
• **NA**

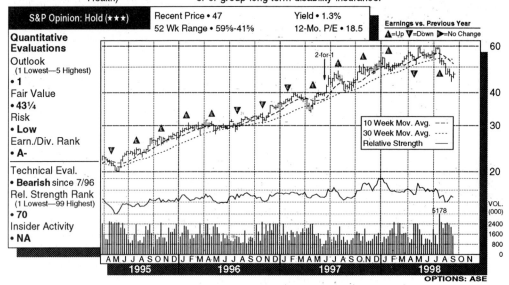

10 Week Mov. Avg. – – –
30 Week Mov. Avg. ——
Relative Strength

OPTIONS: ASE

Overview - 28-JUL-98

Operating earnings growth in 1998 is predicated on UNM's ability to continue the positive sales and policy retention trends begun in late 1996. Results will also benefit from a decision to stop selling fixed-price, non-cancelable individual disability insurance. UNM remains a dominant underwriter of disability insurance, with a more than one-third share of the group long-term disability (LTD) market, and is therefore afforded a certain degree of pricing control. Expansion into supplemental insurance products will also aid results, as UNM leverages its strength in the LTD market to expand its presence in the short term disability and other specialty markets. The sale of the tax sheltered annuity business in late 1996 and the reinsurance of a block of certain non-cancelable individual disability policy reserves freed up more than $350 million of capital that can be allocated to other activities, including the repurchase of shares. During 1997, UNM reacquired approximately 7.1 million of its common shares. The company repurchased more than 1.2 million of its shares during the first six months of 1998. At June 30, 1998, 5.3 million shares were authorized for repurchase.

Valuation - 28-JUL-98

Since plunging in late 1994, when the adverse claim development in individual disability lines began to emerge, the shares have trended steadily upward. Their ascent was briefly interrupted in early 1997 amid fears of higher interest rates. Once those fears subsided, the shares resumed their climb. We believe that UNM's market dominance and high degree of specialization merit a slightly higher P/E multiple than that of a standard lines insurer. Nevertheless, at current levels, the shares are trading at the upper end of their historical P/E range, and thus seem fairly valued over the near term.

Key Stock Statistics

S&P EPS Est. 1998	2.80	Tang. Bk. Value/Share	18.69
P/E on S&P Est. 1998	16.8	Beta	0.99
S&P EPS Est. 1999	3.30	Shareholders	23,300
Dividend Rate/Share	0.59	Market cap. (B)	$ 6.5
Shs. outstg. (M)	138.3	Inst. holdings	73%
Avg. daily vol. (M)	0.503		

Value of $10,000 invested 5 years ago: $ 19,440

Fiscal Year Ending Dec. 31

	1998	1997	1996	1995	1994	1993
Revenues (Million $)						
1Q	1,122	1,043	1,003	955.1	877.4	822.6
2Q	1,160	974.5	1,024	1,156	928.0	854.6
3Q	—	1,025	1,024	967.6	890.5	850.3
4Q	—	1,034	1,028	1,044	927.8	869.5
Yr.	—	4,077	4,043	4,123	3,624	3,397
Earnings Per Share ($)						
1Q	**0.66**	**0.79**	0.49	0.43	0.51	0.48
2Q	**0.70**	**0.62**	0.51	0.61	0.57	0.51
3Q	—	**0.64**	0.30	0.46	-0.42	0.46
4Q	—	**0.54**	0.33	0.42	0.38	0.54
Yr.	—	**2.59**	1.63	1.94	1.04	1.98

Next earnings report expected: late October

Dividend Data (Dividends have been paid since 1987.)

Amount ($)	Date Decl.	Ex-Div. Date	Stock of Record	Payment Date
0.142	Oct. 10	Oct. 23	Oct. 27	Nov. 21 '97
0.142	Jan. 09	Jan. 22	Jan. 26	Feb. 20 '98
0.147	Mar. 13	Apr. 23	Apr. 27	May. 15 '98
0.147	Jul. 10	Jul. 23	Jul. 27	Aug. 21 '98

A Division of The **McGraw-Hill** *Companies*

Business Summary - 28-JUL-98

This innovative insurer is leveraging its strength as the leading writer of disability insurance -- particularly group long term disability insurance -- and is focusing on an array of other specialty life and health insurance products. UNUM Corp. was formed in 1986 when Union Mutual converted from a mutual to a stock company. Contributions to pretax income (in millions) in recent years were:

	1997	1996	1995
Disability	$312.7	$215.3	$217.0
Special Risk	101.3	79.2	60.3
Colonial Products	98.8	92.4	87.7
Retirement Products	76.2	1.4	45.5
Corporate	-52.6	-28.6	-28.2

The Disability Insurance segment markets group long- and short-term disability, individual disability, long-term care, long-term disability reinsurance, and association group disability products; it also includes a Japanese accident and disability subsidiary. Individual disability products, which were sold on a noncancelable basis, are being discontinued, and are being replaced with a new line of individual disability products.

Special Risk insurance includes group life, accidental death and dismemberment, reinsurance pools and special risk products. The Colonial Products segment offers accident and sickness, cancer and life products through payroll deductions.

The Retirement Products segment consists of the tax sheltered annuity (TSA) operations, which were sold to Lincoln National (NYSE: LNC) for about $171 million in October 1996, as well as several other products (such as guaranteed investment contracts) that are no longer being actively marketed. The rebound in 1997 was due, in part, to the absence of aftertax charges of $66 million ($0.46 a share, adjusted) taken in 1996 to cover the estimated future costs incurred to reinsure the active life reserves of existing U.S. non-cancellable individual disability business (which is no longer being marketed); and to cover charges taken to cover certain other restructuring actions that were taken to cut costs and streamline operations around the core disability, special risk, and select health lines.

Per Share Data ($)

(Year Ended Dec. 31)	1997	1996	1995	1994	1993	1992	1991	1990	1989	1988
Tangible Bk. Val.	17.61	15.76	15.77	13.22	13.84	12.46	11.05	9.31	8.54	7.92
Oper. Earnings	2.39	2.04	0.91	0.83	1.77	1.68	1.48	1.30	0.93	0.71
Earnings	2.59	1.63	1.94	1.04	1.98	1.85	1.54	1.34	0.97	0.74
Dividends	0.56	0.55	0.52	0.46	0.38	0.31	0.24	0.19	0.14	0.12
Payout Ratio	22%	33%	27%	44%	19%	17%	16%	14%	15%	15%
Prices - High	54³⁄₈	36³⁄₄	28¹⁄₄	29	30¹⁄₈	27¹⁄₄	20¹⁄₄	14¹⁄₄	12¹⁄₄	7
- Low	33⁵⁄₈	27³⁄₈	18⁷⁄₈	17⁵⁄₈	23⁷⁄₈	16	10³⁄₈	8	6⁵⁄₈	4¹⁄₂
P/E Ratio - High	21	23	15	28	15	15	13	11	13	10
- Low	13	17	10	23	12	9	7	6	7	6

Income Statement Analysis (Million $)

	1997	1996	1995	1994	1993	1992	1991	1990	1989	1988
Life Ins. In Force	260,015	199,019	164,478	145,426	130,323	98,657	84,794	65,243	52,351	38,633
Prem. Inc.: Life	626	523	554	504	477	370	322	277	231	NA
Prem. Inc.: A & H	2,560	2,582	2,441	2,207	1,972	1,376	1,270	1,121	962	NA
Prem. Inc.: Other	3.0	15.0	23.1	21.3	25.7	32.1	24.2	23.1	26.6	NA
Net Invest. Inc.	658	802	806	770	790	779	773	726	694	630
Total Revs.	4,080	4,043	4,123	3,624	3,397	2,641	2,421	2,170	1,934	2,199
Pretax Inc.	536	342	382	199	460	338	262	232	194	147
Net Oper. Inc.	342	302	NA	NA	NA	225	196	179	149	129
Net Inc.	370	238	281	155	312	249	205	185	155	135

Balance Sheet & Other Fin. Data (Million $)

	1997	1996	1995	1994	1993	1992	1991	1990	1989	1988
Cash & Equiv.	208	243	251	232	205	195	203	166	133	132
Premiums Due	308	252	224	190	166	142	130	106	85.0	70.0
Invest. Assets: Bonds	7,311	6,943	9,135	7,868	7,433	6,837	6,309	5,535	4,779	4,587
Invest. Assets: Stocks	30.7	31.3	25.2	628	730	572	545	466	464	323
Invest. Assets: Loans	1,260	1,365	1,383	1,417	1,611	1,830	2,006	2,142	2,243	2,317
Invest. Assets: Total	8,703	8,725	11,693	10,434	10,096	9,516	9,147	8,450	7,650	7,370
Deferred Policy Costs	984	844	1,142	1,035	879	568	482	401	350	292
Total Assets	13,200	15,468	14,788	13,127	12,437	11,214	10,668	9,514	8,556	8,127
Debt	509	409	457	182	129	75.8	50.0	75.7	Nil	Nil
Common Eqty.	2,435	2,263	2,303	1,915	2,103	1,687	1,468	1,237	1,213	1,360
% Return On Revs.	9.1	5.9	6.8	4.3	9.2	9.4	8.5	8.5	8.0	5.9
% Ret. on Assets	2.6	1.6	2.0	1.2	2.6	2.3	2.0	2.0	1.9	1.7
% Ret. on Equity	15.8	10.4	13.3	7.7	15.2	15.8	15.1	15.1	12.3	9.6
% Invest. Yield	7.6	7.9	3.5	7.5	7.9	8.4	8.8	9.0	9.2	9.0

Data as orig. reptd.; bef. results of disc. opers. and/or spec. items. Per share data adj. for stk. divs. as of ex-div. date. Historical EPS data incl. realized inv. gains & losses; estimates do not. E-Estimated. NA-Not Available. NM-Not Meaningful. NR-Not Ranked.

Office—2211 Congress St., Portland, ME 04122. **Tel**—(207) 770-2211. **Website**—http://www.unum.com **Chrmn & CEO**—J. F. Orr III. **EVP & CFO**—R. W. Crispin. **Secy**—K. J. Tierney. **VP & Investor Contact**—Kent W. Mohnkern (207-770-4330). **Dirs**—G. O. Averyt, R. E. Dillon Jr., G. H. Gillespie, R. E. Goldsberry, D. W. Harward, G. J. Mitchell, C. A. Montgomery, J. L. Moody Jr., J. F. Orr III, L. R. Pugh, L. D. Rice, J. W. Rowe. **Transfer Agent & Registrar**—First Chicago Trust Co.of New York, Jersey City, NJ. **Incorporated**—in Delaware in 1985. **Empl**— 7,800. **S&P Analyst:** Catherine A. Seifert

STANDARD &POOR'S
STOCK REPORTS

US Airways Group

2377P

NYSE Symbol **U**

In S&P 500

12-SEP-98 | Industry: Airlines

Summary: Based in the eastern U.S., this airline is expanding its international flights, launched a low-fare carrier in mid-1998 and has formed a marketing alliance with American Airlines.

S&P Opinion: Accumulate (★★★★)	Recent Price • 50⅞	Yield • Nil
	52 Wk Range • 83¼-36¾	12-Mo. P/E • 5.4

Quantitative Evaluations

Outlook (1 Lowest—5 Highest)
• **1⁻**

Fair Value
• **34¼**

Risk
• **Average**

Earn./Div. Rank
• **B-**

Technical Eval.
• **Bearish** since 2/98

Rel. Strength Rank (1 Lowest—99 Highest)
• **26**

Insider Activity
• **Neutral**

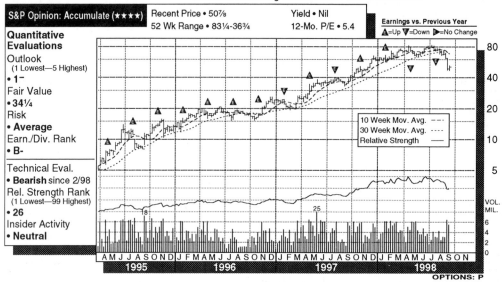

Earnings vs. Previous Year ▲=Up ▼=Down ▶=No Change

10 Week Mov. Avg. ---
30 Week Mov. Avg. ·····
Relative Strength —

OPTIONS: P

Overview - 29-JUN-98

Total traffic growth is expected to slow to 1% in 1998, from 6.8% in 1997, largely reflecting an anticipated 2.4% decline in capacity as U won't take delivery of new aircraft until late 1998. International travel growth will slow to 10%-12% in 1998, from a 35% growth rate, as U won't be able to maintain 1997's aggressive pace of new route offerings. In April 1998, it launched service between Philadelphia and London and Amsterdam. Domestic traffic will be flat as traffic gains at MetroJet and new jet service at US Express offset lower capacity. Margins will widen in 1998, reflecting an expected $90 million in savings from U's new pilot contract, the termination of flights to unprofitable markets, and the consolidation of reservation and maintenance facilities and crew bases. Savings will also come from lower fuel prices, outsourcing information technology services, and lower agents' commissions. Offsetting will be start-up costs for MetroJet and to integrate U's new Airbus jets. Yields will remain under pressure. Overall profit comparisons will be negative, as lower interest and preferred dividend payments are outweighed by the absence of a 1997 gain on the sale of interests in two computer reservation systems and a large tax credit.

Valuation - 29-JUN-98

Despite strong gains over the past 12 months, U remains attractively priced. A new pilots' contract, approved in October 1997, paved the way for launch in June 1998 of a low-fare offering, MetroJet, which will halt inroads into U's markets by carriers such as Southwest Airlines. The new pact gives U the green light to buy up to 400 new planes, and to become a more aggressive player in the international market. In April 1998, U formed a marketing alliance with American Airlines. With its balance sheet purged of high cost preferred stock and debt, U is still worth accumulating.

Key Stock Statistics

S&P EPS Est. 1998	5.25	Tang. Bk. Value/Share	2.51
P/E on S&P Est. 1998	9.7	Beta	1.88
S&P EPS Est. 1999	6.00	Shareholders	32,400
Dividend Rate/Share	Nil	Market cap. (B)	$ 4.8
Shs. outstg. (M)	93.9	Inst. holdings	71%
Avg. daily vol. (M)	1.158		

Value of $10,000 invested 5 years ago: $ 39,950

Fiscal Year Ending Dec. 31

	1998	1997	1996	1995	1994	1993
Revenues (Million $)						
1Q	2,063	2,101	1,868	1,763	1,686	1,716
2Q	2,297	2,213	2,149	1,983	1,880	1,816
3Q	—	2,115	2,073	1,873	1,751	1,749
4Q	—	2,085	2,052	1,855	1,681	1,802
Yr.	—	8,514	8,142	7,474	6,997	7,083
Earnings Per Share ($)						
1Q	**0.96**	2.00	-0.86	-1.91	-3.64	-1.65
2Q	**1.95**	2.46	2.71	1.47	-0.09	-0.23
3Q	—	2.04	0.69	0.35	-3.32	-3.33
4Q	—	**4.66**	0.08	0.61	-5.63	-2.29
Yr.	**E5.25**	9.87	2.69	0.55	-12.73	-7.68

Next earnings report expected: late October

Dividend Data

Common dividends, paid since 1980, were omitted in 1990. Preferred dividends, omitted in 1994, were resumed in July 1996. A "poison pill" stock purchase rights plan was adopted in 1989.

A Division of The **McGraw·Hill** *Companies*

Business Summary - 29-JUN-98

US Airways Group (formerly USAir Group) operates the sixth largest U.S. air carrier, US Airways (92% of revenues). The bulk of U's flights are concentrated in the eastern U.S., where the airline faces considerable competition from lower-cost airlines. With the signing of a new pilots' contract in October 1997, U hopes to fend off the competition with its own low-fare offering, MetroJet, and to more aggressively expand its international route network. The new pilots' contract also paves the way for a major aircraft order, which should lead to a simpler fleet in the future. A marketing alliance was formed with American Airlines in April 1998.

US Airways operates an air network harnessing hubs at Philadelphia, Charlotte, Pittsburgh and Baltimore. Short-haul feeder service, under the name US Airways Express, is provided by 10 regional airlines, of which U owns three: Allegheny Airlines, Piedmont Airlines and PSA Airlines. The company also operates an air shuttle service between New York and Boston and Washington DC. In December 1997, U bought the 53% of the shuttle held by several banks for $285 million.

With one of the highest cost structures among major airlines, U has faced a steady erosion in market share on routes where it competes against low-cost competition. To address this competitive deficiency, U successfully negotiated a new contract with its pilots in October 1997, allowing the launch in June 1998 of a new carrier, MetroJet, that will pay pilots about one-third less

than main line pilots. MetroJet, to be based in Baltimore, will operate 20 planes by 1998 year end but may eventually account for up to 25% of U's total flying time. U's new pilots' contract also contains a formula that will reduce pilots' pay through 2001, until their pay reaches parity (plus 1%) with pilots at other major carriers. In return, U will issue stock options on 11,500,000 common shares to pilots, and will guarantee no furloughs for five years.

U launched a major international push in 1996, adding routes to Munich, Rome and Madrid. At 1997 year end, 9% of US Airways' capacity (measured by available seat miles) was in international service. The bulk of U's growth over the next few years will be from international routes. The airline ended a marketing arrangement with British Airways (BAB) in March 1997. BAB, which came to US Airways' rescue in 1993, sold its 22.5% voting stake in U in May 1997. U began direct service to Amsterdam in April 1998. Service to London was postponed after U failed to obtain acceptable landing and takeoff times.

A key element of management's cost reduction program is to simplify the aircraft fleet. At 1997 year end, US Airways operated 376 aircraft, manufactured by three firms. By limiting its fleet to a single aircraft type, U could realize savings in pilot training and maintenance. In keeping with this strategy, U ordered up to 400 narrowbody planes in late 1996 from Airbus Industrie.

Per Share Data ($)

(Year Ended Dec. 31)	1997	1996	1995	1994	1993	1992	1991	1990	1989	1988
Tangible Bk. Val.	NM	NM	-24.58	-18.71	-21.36	-23.11	7.24	15.43	25.07	28.69
Cash Flow	13.23	7.54	7.60	-6.90	-1.90	-6.94	-0.86	-3.35	4.29	9.54
Earnings	9.87	2.69	0.55	-12.73	-7.68	-13.88	-7.62	-10.89	-1.73	3.81
Dividends	Nil	Nil	Nil	Nil	Nil	Nil	Nil	0.09	0.12	0.12
Payout Ratio	Nil	Nil	Nil	Nil	Nil	Nil	Nil	NM	NM	3%
Prices - High	65¾	25⅞	15⅞	15⅜	24¾	18⅜	24½	33¾	54¾	40⅛
- Low	19¼	11¾	4¼	3⅞	11⅛	10½	7	12⅝	30⅝	28
P/E Ratio - High	7	10	29	NM	NM	NM	NM	NM	NM	11
- Low	2	4	8	NM	NM	NM	NM	NM	NM	7

Income Statement Analysis (Million $)

	1997	1996	1995	1994	1993	1992	1991	1990	1989	1988
Revs.	8,514	8,142	7,474	6,997	7,083	6,686	6,514	6,559	6,252	5,707
Oper. Inc.	985	753	673	113	753	97.0	72.0	-12.0	287	704
Depr.	401	316	352	350	318	326	310	338	266	248
Int. Exp.	244	267	363	284	250	249	259	226	172	168
Pretax Inc.	672	275	128	-684	-348	-600	-414	-654	-72.0	270
Eff. Tax Rate	NM	4.40%	7.00%	NM	NM	NM	NM	NM	NM	39%
Net Inc.	1,025	263	119	-684	-348	-600	-304	-453	-63.0	165

Balance Sheet & Other Fin. Data (Million $)

	1997	1996	1995	1994	1993	1992	1991	1990	1989	1988
Cash	1,094	1,587	902	452	368	296	320	408	15.0	78.0
Curr. Assets	2,777	2,310	1,583	1,117	1,178	988	1,029	1,253	936	822
Total Assets	8,372	7,531	6,955	6,808	6,878	6,595	6,454	6,574	6,069	5,349
Curr. Liab.	2,528	2,849	2,485	2,260	2,237	2,433	1,943	1,892	1,578	1,209
LT Debt	2,426	2,616	2,717	2,895	2,444	2,265	2,115	2,263	1,468	1,333
Common Eqty.	725	-797	-1,048	-1,142	-425	-168	1,105	1,434	1,893	2,070
Total Cap.	3,509	2,790	1,881	2,757	2,990	2,667	3,902	4,239	4,075	3,743
Cap. Exp.	280	181	147	180	816	440	499	1,245	1,078	581
Cash Flow	1,363	490	471	-412	-104	-325	-39.0	-149	189	413
Curr. Ratio	1.1	0.8	0.6	0.5	0.5	0.4	0.5	0.7	0.6	0.7
% LT Debt of Cap.	69.1	93.8	144.4	105.0	81.7	84.9	54.2	53.4	36.0	35.6
% Net Inc.of Revs.	12.0	3.2	1.6	NM	NM	NM	NM	NM	NM	2.9
% Ret. on Assets	12.9	3.6	1.7	NM	NM	NM	NM	NM	NM	3.1
% Ret. on Equity	NM	NM	NM	NM	NM	NM	NM	NM	NM	8.3

Data as orig. reptd.; bef. results of disc. opers. and/or spec. items. Per share data adj. for stk. divs. as of ex-div. date. Bold denotes diluted EPS (FASB 128). E-Estimated. NA-Not Available. NM-Not Meaningful. NR-Not Ranked.

Office—2345 Crystal Dr., Arlington, VA 22227. **Tel**—(703) 872-5306. **Website**—http://www.usairways.com **Chrmn & CEO**—S. M. Wolf. **Pres & COO**—R. Gangwal. **Secy**—M. V. Bryan. **SVP & CFO**—T. L. Hall.**Investor Contact**—Laura F. Smith (703-872-5009). **Dirs**—M. J. DeVito, R. Gangwal, G. J. W. Goodman, J. W. Harris, E. A. Horrigan Jr., R. L. Johnson, R. LeBuhn, J. G. Medlin Jr., H. M. Merriman, R. W. Smith, S. M. Wolf. **Transfer Agent & Registrar**—Bank of New York, NYC. **Incorporated**—in Delaware in 1937. **Empl**— 38,500. **S&P Analyst:** Stephen R. Klein

STANDARD &POOR'S
STOCK REPORTS

UST Inc.

2269U

NYSE Symbol **UST**

In S&P 500

12-SEP-98 | **Industry:** Tobacco

Summary: This company is a leading producer of moist smokeless tobacco products, marketed under such leading brand names as Copenhagen and Skoal.

S&P Opinion: Avoid (★★)	Recent Price • 27⅞	Yield • 5.8%
	52 Wk Range • 36⅞-24½	12-Mo. P/E • 11.5

Quantitative Evaluations

Outlook
(1 Lowest—5 Highest)
• **3**

Fair Value
• **29¼**

Risk
• **Low**

Earn./Div. Rank
• **A+**

Technical Eval.
• **Bullish** since 7/98

Rel. Strength Rank
(1 Lowest—99 Highest)
• **93**

Insider Activity
• **Neutral**

Earnings vs. Previous Year
▲=Up ▼=Down ▶=No Change

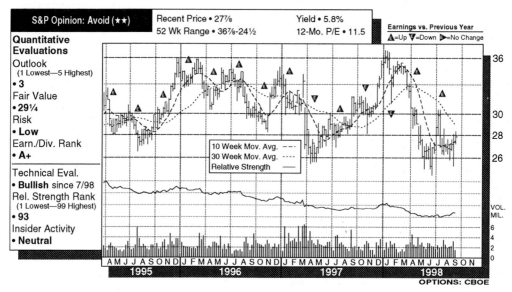

10 Week Mov. Avg. ---
30 Week Mov. Avg. ----
Relative Strength —

VOL. MIL.

1995 1996 1997 1998

OPTIONS: CBOE

Overview - 29-JUL-98

We project net sales rising at a mid-single-digit pace in 1998, led by modestly higher moist smokeless tobacco unit volumes. In mid-1997, in response to market share erosion in its important tobacco segment, UST introduced a low-priced tobacco brand, Red Seal, to help it better compete against price competition. Although this action could stall further market share loss, operating margins are likely to suffer in coming quarters. Reflecting the suspension of its stock repurchase program (due to the pending national tobacco industry settlement), EPS are also expected to rise at a mid single-digit pace. We anticipate EPS of $2.50 in 1998, up 5% from 1997's $2.37. For 1999, we expect EPS to rise 8%, to $2.70. These EPS estimates do not reflect any possible settlement payments related to the pending tobacco industry settlement.

Valuation - 29-JUL-98

Based on the poor unit volume and net pricing trends for UST's important moist smokeless tobacco products in recent years, the shares are expected to be market underperformers for the near term. Despite UST's dominant presence (about 77% market share) and more aggressive new product initiatives in the highly profitable moist smokeless tobacco market, recent inroads by increasingly aggressive price value brand competition will likely restrict profit margins for the foreseeable future. Still, given the company's strong balance sheet and the stock's low valuation, the shares have some downside protection. Investors should note, however, that the company's high dividend payout ratio (65%) suggests that future dividend hikes will likely be very modest. The shares are also very sensitive to tobacco-related regulatory and legal developments.

Key Stock Statistics

S&P EPS Est. 1998	2.50	Tang. Bk. Value/Share	2.85
P/E on S&P Est. 1998	11.2	Beta	0.43
S&P EPS Est. 1999	2.70	Shareholders	11,800
Dividend Rate/Share	1.62	Market cap. (B)	$ 5.2
Shs. outstg. (M)	185.7	Inst. holdings	67%
Avg. daily vol. (M)	0.481		

Value of $10,000 invested 5 years ago: $ 11,094

Fiscal Year Ending Dec. 31

	1998	1997	1996	1995	1994	1993
Revenues (Million $)						
1Q	340.2	340.5	327.8	306.1	280.4	265.0
2Q	357.4	365.1	350.5	340.2	310.2	279.9
3Q	—	360.6	366.0	334.3	310.4	279.0
4Q	—	350.8	352.5	344.9	322.1	286.7
Yr.	—	1,402	1,397	1,325	1,223	1,110
Earnings Per Share ($)						
1Q	**0.60**	**0.54**	0.55	0.49	0.42	0.47
2Q	**0.64**	**0.63**	0.62	0.55	0.48	0.41
3Q	**E0.64**	**0.62**	0.65	0.55	0.48	0.41
4Q	**E0.62**	**0.57**	0.61	0.56	0.49	0.41
Yr.	**E2.50**	**2.37**	**2.44**	2.16	1.87	1.71

Next earnings report expected: mid October

Dividend Data (Dividends have been paid since 1912.)

Amount ($)	Date Decl.	Ex-Div. Date	Stock of Record	Payment Date
0.405	Oct. 23	Dec. 02	Dec. 04	Dec. 15 '97
0.405	Feb. 18	Mar. 02	Mar. 04	Mar. 16 '98
0.405	May. 05	Jun. 01	Jun. 03	Jun. 15 '98
0.405	Jul. 23	Sep. 01	Sep. 03	Sep. 15 '98

A Division of The McGraw-Hill Companies

Business Summary - 29-JUL-98

The leading U.S. producer of smokeless tobacco has found its profit growth slowed by intensified price competition. In recent years, UST's smokeless tobacco sales volumes (down 1.5% in 1997, to 624 million cans), market share and earnings have been under pressure from increasing competitive actions by rivals, who generally sell their smokeless tobacco products at substantially lower prices than UST's products. In July 1997, management addressed these pressures by introducing a low-priced tobacco product, Red Seal, in areas where price competition was the fiercest.

In addition to its smokeless tobacco offerings, UST is also a significant importer and producer of wines, and has other operations including a small but growing premium cigar business. Segment contributions (profits in millions) in 1997 were:

	Sales	Profits
Tobacco	85%	$712.2
Wine	10%	29.2
Other	5%	-5.7

UST still holds a formidable 79% share of the highly profitable U.S. smokeless tobacco market, but it has seen this measure shrink from 86% in 1991. The company's moist smokeless tobacco products include Copenhagen and Skoal, which are the world's two largest selling brands of moist smokeless tobacco. Moist brands also include Skoal Long Cut and Skoal Bandits. Other tobacco products carry the names Bruton, CC, Red Seal and WB Cut. The company sells tobacco products throughout the U.S., principally to chain stores and tobacco and grocery wholesalers. In 1986, federal legislation was enacted regulating smokeless tobacco products by requiring health warning notices on smokeless tobacco packages and advertising and by prohibiting the advertising of smokeless tobacco products on electronic media. In recent years, other proposals have been made at the federal, state and local levels for additional regulation of tobacco products including the requirement of additional warning notices on cigar products, a significant increase in federal excise taxes, a ban or further restriction of all advertising and promotion, regulation of environmental tobacco smoke and increased regulation of the manufacturing and marketing of tobacco products.

Wines consist of premium varietal and blended wines dominated by Washington State-produced Chateau Ste. Michelle and Columbia Crest and Villa Mt. Eden, a premium-quality California wine. In 1997, overall wine case volume increased 6.8%, to 2.5 million cases.

Other company businesses include UST's international operation which markets moist smokeless tobacco; the manufacture and marketing of cigars (Don Tomas, Astral); a microbrewery; a video entertainment business (Cabin Fever Entertainment Inc.); and the operation of agricultural properties.

Per Share Data ($)

(Year Ended Dec. 31)	1997	1996	1995	1994	1993	1992	1991	1990	1989	1988
Tangible Bk. Val.	2.37	1.53	1.53	1.79	2.20	2.38	2.22	2.19	2.19	2.05
Cash Flow	2.53	2.57	2.30	2.00	1.83	1.51	1.28	1.07	0.89	0.78
Earnings	2.37	2.42	2.16	1.87	1.71	1.41	1.18	0.98	0.82	0.71
Dividends	1.62	1.48	1.30	1.12	0.96	0.80	0.66	0.55	0.46	0.37
Payout Ratio	68%	61%	60%	60%	56%	54%	52%	52%	53%	50%
Prices - High	$36^7/_8$	$35^7/_8$	36	$31^1/_2$	$32^3/_4$	$35^3/_8$	34	$18^1/_4$	$15^3/_8$	$10^5/_8$
- Low	$25^1/_2$	$28^1/_4$	$26^1/_2$	$23^3/_8$	$24^3/_8$	$25^1/_4$	$16^3/_8$	$12^3/_8$	$9^3/_4$	$6^1/_8$
P/E Ratio - High	16	15	17	17	19	25	29	19	19	15
- Low	11	12	12	13	14	18	14	13	12	9

Income Statement Analysis (Million $)

	1997	1996	1995	1994	1993	1992	1991	1990	1989	1988
Revs.	1,402	1,397	1,325	1,198	1,080	1,013	880	751	670	607
Oper. Inc.	742	779	737	669	591	524	446	369	319	281
Depr.	30.5	28.3	29.1	28.2	25.9	23.6	22.3	19.5	16.4	16.6
Int. Exp.	8.4	7.3	4.8	4.6	1.2	0.7	0.7	1.6	3.1	4.4
Pretax Inc.	704	745	705	641	602	503	426	352	302	261
Eff. Tax Rate	38%	38%	39%	40%	39%	38%	38%	37%	37%	38%
Net Inc.	439	464	430	388	369	313	266	223	190	162

Balance Sheet & Other Fin. Data (Million $)

	1997	1996	1995	1994	1993	1992	1991	1990	1989	1988
Cash	6.9	54.5	69.4	50.7	25.3	36.4	41.5	46.6	54.6	72.7
Curr. Assets	442	444	426	382	335	330	305	266	280	291
Total Assets	827	807	785	741	706	674	657	623	636	598
Curr. Liab.	167	307	281	161	107	81.2	95.5	68.7	92.1	69.9
LT Debt	100	100	100	125	40.0	Nil	Nil	3.1	6.8	21.8
Common Eqty.	438	282	294	362	463	517	483	474	482	453
Total Cap.	538	382	394	492	511	563	534	530	544	528
Cap. Exp.	58.1	44.7	35.3	27.7	54.5	34.0	41.5	26.9	35.8	17.7
Cash Flow	470	492	459	416	395	336	288	243	207	179
Curr. Ratio	2.7	1.4	1.5	2.4	3.1	4.1	3.2	3.9	3.0	4.2
% LT Debt of Cap.	18.6	26.2	25.4	25.4	7.8	Nil	Nil	0.6	1.2	4.1
% Net Inc.of Revs.	31.3	33.2	32.4	32.4	34.1	30.9	30.2	29.7	28.4	26.7
% Ret. on Assets	53.7	58.3	56.3	54.7	54.2	47.0	41.8	35.9	31.0	28.3
% Ret. on Equity	122.0	161.2	131.0	96.3	76.5	62.5	55.8	47.3	40.9	38.0

Data as orig. reptd.; bef. results of disc. opers. and/or spec. items. Per share data adj. for stk. divs. as of ex-div. date. Bold denotes diluted EPS (FASB 128). E-Estimated. NA-Not Available. NM-Not Meaningful. NR-Not Ranked.

Office—100 W. Putnam Ave., Greenwich, CT 06830. **Tel**—(203) 661-1100. **Chrmn, Pres & CEO**—V. A. Gierer Jr. **Secy**—Debra A. Baker. **Investor Contact**—Mark A. Rozelle (203-622-3520). **Dirs**—J. W. Chapin, J. P. Clancey, E. H. DeHority Jr., E. J. Eisenman, E. T. Fogerty, V. A. Gierer Jr., P. X. Kelley, P. J. Neff, L. P. Weicker Jr. **Transfer Agent & Registrar**—First National Bank of Boston. **Incorporated**—in New Jersey in 1911; reincorporated in Delaware in 1986. **Empl**— 4,677. **S&P Analyst:** Richard Joy

STANDARD &POOR'S
STOCK REPORTS

USX-Marathon Group
NYSE Symbol MRO

2269Y
In S&P 500

12-SEP-98

Industry:
Oil (Domestic Integrated)

Summary: This company, comprising the energy operations of USX Corp., engages in worldwide exploration and production, and domestic refining and marketing.

S&P Opinion: Hold (★★★)		
Recent Price • 34⅝	**Yield • 2.4%**	
52 Wk Range • 40½-25	12-Mo. P/E • 17.4	

Quantitative Evaluations

Outlook (1 Lowest—5 Highest)
• **3**

Fair Value
• **33⅞**

Risk
• **Low**

Earn./Div. Rank
• **NR**

Technical Eval.
• **Bearish** since 3/98

Rel. Strength Rank (1 Lowest—99 Highest)
• **98**

Insider Activity
• **NA**

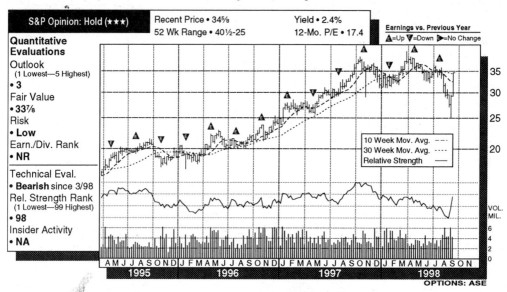

Earnings vs. Previous Year
▲=Up ▼=Down ▶=No Change

10 Week Mov. Avg. – – –
30 Week Mov. Avg. · · · ·
Relative Strength ——

VOL. MIL.

OPTIONS: ASE

Overview - 04-AUG-98

Several non-operating items added a net of $0.37 to EPS in 1998's first half. Inventory market valuation (IMV) reserve adjustments lowered EPS in 1997 by about $0.60. MRO's rate of worldwide reserve replacement has risen recently, aided by major discoveries in the Gulf of Mexico and the North Sea. The company replaced 146% of 1997 production, and has now replaced 103% of the last five years' production. Recent property sales will let Marathon focus on its highly profitable international upstream operations, which have benefited from expense reductions, as well as the company's growing inventory of Gulf of Mexico prospects. In May, MRO announced plans to acquire Tarragon Oil & Gas. The deal is expected to increase MRO's total reserve base by 20%. Looking ahead, we expect solid production growth for the company through 2000, with oil accounting for most of the gains. With a continued slide in oil prices so far in 1998, and given our forecast for weak oil prices throughout 1998, we expect continued downstream margin improvement.

Valuation - 04-AUG-98

An increased focus on domestic upstream opportunities should boost the shares over the next 12 months, as will the company's recently completed merger of its downstream operations with those of Ashland Inc. The company has achieved the highest downstream return on assets of its peer group over the past five years, and is well positioned to benefit from the continued rebound in refining margins expected this year. However, given the current oil price weakness, we believe the shares are now fairly valued, and should generate returns in line with the overall market over the next six months. The shares remain attractive to investors with a longer-term focus.

Key Stock Statistics

S&P EPS Est. 1998	2.10	Tang. Bk. Value/Share	13.40
P/E on S&P Est. 1998	16.5	Beta	0.96
S&P EPS Est. 1999	2.35	Shareholders	91,400
Dividend Rate/Share	0.84	Market cap. (B)	$ 10.1
Shs. outstg. (M)	290.6	Inst. holdings	72%
Avg. daily vol. (M)	1.101		

Value of $10,000 invested 5 years ago: $ 24,140

Fiscal Year Ending Dec. 31

	1998	1997	1996	1995	1994	1993
Revenues (Million $)						
1Q	5,498	4,103	3,627	3,337	2,747	2,954
2Q	5,562	3,787	4,071	3,528	3,105	3,103
3Q	—	3,944	4,195	3,492	3,497	2,983
4Q	—	3,920	4,439	3,514	3,408	2,922
Yr.	—	15,754	16,332	13,871	12,757	11,962
Earnings Per Share ($)						
1Q	0.63	0.37	0.75	0.26	0.38	0.10
2Q	0.56	0.41	0.43	0.37	0.25	0.07
3Q	—	0.66	0.57	0.33	0.35	0.10
4Q	—	0.13	0.58	-1.27	0.12	-0.31
Yr.	E2.10	1.58	2.31	-0.31	1.10	-0.04

Next earnings report expected: late October

Dividend Data (Dividends have been paid since 1991.)

Amount ($)	Date Decl.	Ex-Div. Date	Stock of Record	Payment Date
0.190	Oct. 28	Nov. 17	Nov. 19	Dec. 10 '97
0.210	Jan. 27	Feb. 13	Feb. 18	Mar. 10 '98
0.210	Apr. 28	May. 18	May. 20	Jun. 10 '98
0.210	Jul. 28	Aug. 17	Aug. 19	Sep. 10 '98

A Division of The McGraw-Hill Companies

Business Summary - 04-AUG-98

A wave of consolidation is sweeping the U.S. oil refining and marketing industry, and Marathon Group (MRO), which consists of the energy segment of USX Corp., has joined the movement. Effective January 1, 1998, Marathon and Ashland Inc. merged their refining, marketing and transportation operations to form Marathon Ashland Petroleum (MAP). Marathon owns 62% and Ashland 38% of the new venture, which has a combined refining capacity of 930,000 barrels per day (representing 6% of total U.S. refining capacity) and approximately 5,400 retail gasoline outlets in 20 states.

In 1997, worldwide crude oil production averaged 164,200 bbl. per day (180,700 b/d in 1996), and natural gas production totaled 1,176,700 Mcf per day (1,206,500 Mcf/d). International oil output represented some 30% of total crude production. Total natural gas output was divided 61% domestic and 39% international. Foreign gas volumes fell 14% in 1997, while crude oil volumes declined 16%. Proved reserves at 1997 year end were 878 million bbl. of oil (792 million bbl. in 1996) and 3,402 Bcf of natural gas (3,570 Bcf). About 69% of the company's total oil reserves and 65% of total natural gas reserves are located in the U.S.

The Gulf of Mexico represents one of Marathon's core exploration and production areas. The Troika (Green Canyon 244) oil and gas field in the Gulf of Mexico, in which MRO has a 33% interest, began production in November 1997, and the company plans to begin production from its Green Canyon blocks 112/113 in 1999. Other promising fields in the Gulf include Viosca Knoll 786 and Ewing Bank 873. Internationally, during 1997, Marathon increased its interest in the Sakhalin Energy Investment Co., formed to develop two fields offshore Sakhalin Island in the former Soviet Union, to 37.5% from 30%.

Marathon's refined product sales in 1997 were 775,400 b/d (775,500 b/d), all in the U.S. Prior to the joint venture with Ashland, Marathon was the ninth largest U.S.-based refiner in terms of refined product sales volumes, and had a 570,000 b/d capacity. The refining system consists of a five-facility refining complex designed to convert low-cost, high-sulfur, heavy crude oil into high-value gasoline and diesel fuels. A network of 51 terminals in the Midwest and South serves 2,465 independently owned Marathon-brand gasoline service stations. The company also sells refined products to independent unbranded retail outlets. With a combined refining capacity of 935,000 b/d, representing 6% of total U.S. refining capacity, the new Marathon/Ashland venture is one of the largest U.S. refiners.

Per Share Data ($)

(Year Ended Dec. 31)	1997	1996	1995	1994	1993	1992	1991	1990	1989	1988
Tangible Bk. Val.	12.52	11.62	10.01	11.01	10.57	11.35	12.44	13.14	13.25	13.12
Cash Flow	3.89	4.74	2.56	3.61	2.48	3.23	3.12	5.95	5.47	3.89
Earnings	1.58	2.33	-0.31	1.10	-0.04	0.37	-0.31	1.94	1.49	0.05
Dividends	0.76	0.70	0.68	0.68	0.68	1.22	0.70	NM	NM	NM
Payout Ratio	48%	30%	NM	62%	NM	330%	NM	NM	NM	NM
Prices - High	38⁷/₈	25¹/₂	21¹/₂	19¹/₈	20⁵/₈	24³/₄	33¹/₈	NA	NA	NA
- Low	23³/₄	17¹/₄	15³/₄	15³/₈	16³/₈	15³/₄	20⁷/₈	NA	NA	NA
P/E Ratio - High	25	11	NM	17	NM	67	NM	NA	NA	NA
- Low	15	7	NM	14	NM	43	NA	NA	NA	NA

Income Statement Analysis (Million $)

	1997	1996	1995	1994	1993	1992	1991	1990	1989	1988
Revs.	15,668	16,332	13,871	10,215	10,035	11,127	12,313	13,283	11,080	8,864
Oper. Inc.	1,510	1,927	1,581	1,305	892	1,197	1,236	2,106	1,954	1,439
Depr.	664	693	817	721	723	812	874	1,025	1,024	1,006
Int. Exp.	285	308	357	384	389	359	407	447	634	570
Pretax Inc.	672	991	-189	476	-55.0	201	65.0	779	571	88.0
Eff. Tax Rate	32%	32%	NM	33%	NM	46%	209%	35%	26%	40%
Net Inc.	456	671	-83.0	321	-6.0	109	-71.0	508	425	53.0

Balance Sheet & Other Fin. Data (Million $)

	1997	1996	1995	1994	1993	1992	1991	1990	1989	1988
Cash	36.0	32.0	77.0	28.0	185	35.0	200	193	490	NA
Curr. Assets	2,018	2,046	1,888	1,737	1,598	1,934	2,153	2,357	2,381	NA
Total Assets	10,565	10,151	10,109	10,951	10,806	11,141	11,644	11,931	12,622	NA
Curr. Liab.	2,262	2,142	2,025	1,712	1,668	2,278	2,467	2,527	2,148	NA
LT Debt	2,476	2,642	3,367	3,983	4,239	3,743	4,084	3,986	4,586	NA
Common Eqty.	3,618	3,340	2,872	3,163	3,032	3,257	3,215	3,542	3,387	NA
Total Cap.	7,596	7,342	7,493	8,676	8,572	8,307	8,856	9,091	10,162	NA
Cap. Exp.	1,038	751	642	753	910	1,193	960	1,000	1,033	871
Cash Flow	1,120	1,364	734	1,036	711	915	796	1,519	1,408	1,020
Curr. Ratio	0.9	1.0	0.9	1.0	1.0	0.8	0.9	0.9	1.1	NA
% LT Debt of Cap.	32.6	36.0	44.9	45.9	49.5	45.1	46.1	43.8	45.1	NA
% Net Inc.of Revs.	2.9	4.1	NM	3.1	NM	1.0	NM	3.8	3.8	0.6
% Ret. on Assets	4.4	6.6	NM	2.9	NM	0.9	NM	4.1	3.3	NA
% Ret. on Equity	13.1	21.6	NM	10.2	NM	3.0	NM	13.9	11.4	NA

Data as orig. reptd.; bef. results of disc. opers. and/or spec. items. Per share data adj. for stk. divs. as of ex-div. date. Revs. in quarterly table incl. oth. inc. E-Estimated. NA-Not Available. NM-Not Meaningful. NR-Not Ranked.

Office—USX Corp., 600 Grant St., Pittsburgh, PA 15219-4776. **Registrar**—Mellon Bank, Pittsburgh. **Tel**—(412) 433-1121. **Marathon Oil**—5555 San Felipe Rd., P.O. Box 3128, Houston, TX 77253-3128. **Tel**—(713) 629-6600. **Website**—www.usx.com **Chrmn & CEO**—T. J. Usher. **Vice Chrmn-Marathon Group**—V. G. Beghini. **Vice Chrmn & CFO**—R. M. Hernandez. **SVP & Secy**—D. D. Sandman. **VP & Treas**—E. F. Guna.**VP & Investor Contact**—George Fredericks (212-826-8418). **Dirs**—N. A. Armstrong, V. G. Beghini, J. G. Brown, C. A. Corry, R. M. Hernandez, C. R. Lee, P. E. Lego, R. Marshall, J. F. McGillicuddy, J. M. Richman, S. E. Schofield, J. W. Snow, T. J. Usher, P. J. Wilhelm, D. C. Yearley. **Transfer Agent**—USX Corp., 600 Grant St., Pittsburgh. **Incorporated**—in New Jersey in 1901; reincorporated in Delaware in 1965. **Empl**— 20,695. **S&P Analyst**: Norman Rosenberg

STANDARD &POOR'S
STOCK REPORTS

USX-U.S. Steel Group

2269Z

NYSE Symbol **X**

In S&P 500

12-SEP-98

Industry: Iron & Steel

Summary: Shares of USX-U.S. Steel Group track the results of USX Corp.'s steel segment, which is the largest U.S. integrated steelmaker.

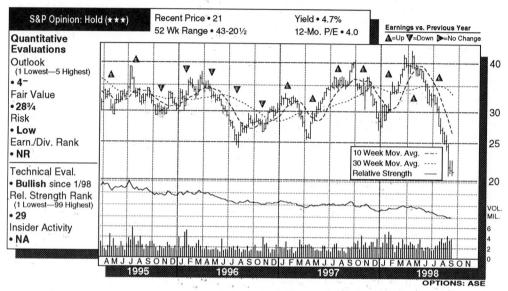

S&P Opinion: Hold (★★★)	Recent Price • 21	Yield • 4.7%
	52 Wk Range • 43-20½	12-Mo. P/E • 4.0

Quantitative Evaluations

Outlook (1 Lowest—5 Highest)
• **4⁻**

Fair Value
• **28¾**

Risk
• **Low**

Earn./Div. Rank
• **NR**

Technical Eval.
• **Bullish** since 1/98

Rel. Strength Rank (1 Lowest—99 Highest)
• **29**

Insider Activity
• **NA**

Earnings vs. Previous Year ▲=Up ▼=Down ▶=No Change

10 Week Mov. Avg. - - -
30 Week Mov. Avg. - - -
Relative Strength ——

OPTIONS: ASE

Overview - 10-AUG-98

We project a 1.4% sales decline in 1998, reflecting a 1.3% decrease in revenue per ton and a 1.7% decline in the volume of tons shipped. Our forecast assumes flat overall steel demand in 1998. However, we see lower prices, as a result of increased supply from new minimill startups, the re-entry of Wheeling Pittsburgh Steel into the market, and weakness in oil country tubular goods. Planned and unplanned outages will also reduce volume and lead to higher costs per ton. Consequently, we anticipate lower EPS in 1998.

Valuation - 10-AUG-98

After posting a large gain through the first quarter of 1998, X has declined sharply ever since. Through early August, the shares were down 16.7%, versus an 11.4% decline in the S&P Steel Index and a 12.3% gain for the S&P 500. X's poor performance relative to its peers reflects a deterioration in profit prospects for 1998. Earlier in 1998, analysts were projecting flat to slightly lower EPS. However, because of a sharp decline in demand for oil country tubuar goods and lower volume resulting from an unplanned outage, EPS will fall substantially in 1998. We think that this accounts for the large drop since April. We believe that X is oversold at current levels, and are maintaining our hold recommendation, based on valuation. X was recently trading at 6.3X our 1999 estimate, versus a multiple of 8.2X for the group. X still compares very favorably with its competitors in terms of its per ton profit, a key industry benchmark, and its strong balance sheet. On that basis, X's large discount to the group is unwarranted. Our estimate for 1999 is based on modest assumptions. We see higher volume, a small decline in prices, and a minimum gain of $4 in profit per ton, in the absence of outages, in 1999.

Key Stock Statistics

S&P EPS Est. 1998	4.05	Tang. Bk. Value/Share	18.78
P/E on S&P Est. 1998	5.2	Beta	1.24
S&P EPS Est. 1999	4.25	Shareholders	70,500
Dividend Rate/Share	1.00	Market cap. (B)	$ 1.9
Shs. outstg. (M)	88.1	Inst. holdings	79%
Avg. daily vol. (M)	0.767		

Value of $10,000 invested 5 years ago: $ 7,420

Fiscal Year Ending Dec. 31

	1998	1997	1996	1995	1994	1993
Revenues (Million $)						
1Q	1,696	1,631	1,591	1,577	1,384	1,208
2Q	1,733	1,737	1,580	1,623	1,534	1,427
3Q	—	1,735	1,611	1,609	1,505	1,429
4Q	—	1,838	1,765	1,647	1,643	1,548
Yr.	—	6,941	6,547	6,456	6,066	5,612
Earnings Per Share ($)						
1Q	**0.95**	**0.93**	0.49	0.89	-0.56	0.13
2Q	**1.46**	**1.06**	0.32	0.99	0.65	-5.71
3Q	**E0.74**	**1.25**	0.76	0.99	1.11	0.41
4Q	**E0.90**	**1.64**	1.43	0.68	1.11	1.67
Yr.	**E4.05**	**4.88**	2.97	3.53	2.35	-2.96

Next earnings report expected: late October

Dividend Data (Dividends have been paid since 1991.)

Amount ($)	Date Decl.	Ex-Div. Date	Stock of Record	Payment Date
0.250	Oct. 28	Nov. 17	Nov. 19	Dec. 10 '97
0.250	Jan. 27	Feb. 13	Feb. 18	Mar. 10 '98
0.250	Apr. 28	May. 18	May. 20	Jun. 10 '98
0.250	Jul. 28	Aug. 17	Aug. 19	Sep. 10 '98

A Division of The **McGraw·Hill** *Companies*

Business Summary - 10-AUG-98

Faced with fierce competition, USX's U.S. Steel Group, the largest U.S. steelmaker, has been concentrating mightily on cost reduction and product mix improvement. A growing number of low cost minimill steel plants in the U.S., coupled with continued high levels of imported steel, poses a serious challenge to X and the other old line integrated steelmakers. Steel itself faces increased competition from other materials such as aluminum, glass, plastics and ceramics.

Through its focused efforts to become more efficient, X was able to increase its annual raw steelmaking capacity by 300,000 tons in 1995 without adding new steelmaking plants. This has enabled it to reduce its unit costs by spreading more volume over a fixed amount of plant and equipment. X's operating cost per ton, a widely used benchmark for measuring efficiency, is one of the best in the industry. In addition, X has been steadily strengthening its balance sheet by paying down debt.

Via joint ventures, X is increasing its sales of higher-margin coated steel as a way of insulating itself from commodity grades of steel which are the staple of the low cost minimill steel companies. In addition, through a joint venture with Nucor Corp. and Praxair, X is researching the development of new methods of steelmaking.

In 1997, X shipped 11.6 million tons of steel, versus 11.4 million tons in 1996 and 1995. Earnings rose sharply in 1997, reflecting higher revenue per ton and the absence of a $24 increase in operating cost per ton stemming from a large outage at one of X's key plants in 1996. Revenue per ton was $479 in 1997, versus $467 in 1996. Operating profit per ton rose to $41, from $15 in 1996.

X's steel is transformed into components for a wide variety of consumer and producer durable goods. Cars, household appliances, earthmoving equipment and oil drilling rigs use X's steel. X sells its steel both to original equipment manufacturers and distributors.

In addition to steel, X is a major producer and seller of coke, coal and iron ore pellets, the principal raw materials for integrated steelmaking. X is the only domestic steel company totally self sufficient in raw materials; this is one of the reasons for its low operating costs.

Direct domestic competition in the market for higher margin coated steel for automotive and appliance applications includes AKS Steel Holding, Bethlehem Steel, Inland Steel Industries, LTV Corp., National Steel and Rouge Steel. In commodity grades, X competes against Nucor, Gallatin Steel, Trico Steel and Steel Dynamics.

Results in the1998 second quarter included special gains totaling $0.30 a share. As a result of one scheduled reline, an unscheduled outage, and lower prices, shipments in the quarter declined to 2,857,000 tons, from 2,943,000 tons in 1997, and per ton profit decreased to $29, from $43.

Per Share Data ($) (Year Ended Dec. 31)	1997	1996	1995	1994	1993	1992	1991	1990	1989	1988
Tangible Bk. Val.	18.78	14.38	16.11	11.25	7.22	3.18	32.01	40.62	38.03	28.95
Cash Flow	7.89	6.49	7.86	6.52	1.93	0.25	-5.02	11.44	16.13	19.74
Earnings	4.88	3.00	3.53	2.35	-2.96	-4.92	-10.00	6.00	10.17	12.83
Dividends	1.00	1.00	1.00	1.00	1.00	1.00	0.50	NM	NM	NM
Payout Ratio	20%	33%	28%	43%	34%	NM	NM	NM	NM	NM
Prices - High	40¾	37⅞	39⅛	45⅝	46	34⅜	30¼	NA	NA	NA
- Low	25⅜	24⅛	29⅛	30¼	27½	22⅛	20	NA	NA	NA
P/E Ratio - High	8	13	11	19	NM	NM	NM	NA	NA	NA
- Low	5	8	8	13	NM	NM	NM	NM	NM	NM
Income Statement Analysis (Million $)										
Revs.	6,814	6,547	6,456	6,066	5,612	4,947	4,864	6,073	6,509	6,996
Oper. Inc.	949	652	815	627	549	85.0	38.0	754	948	1,295
Depr.	303	292	318	314	314	288	253	279	308	363
Int. Exp.	98.0	128	142	160	336	189	192	215	248	340
Pretax Inc.	686	367	453	248	-209	-393	-755	437	787	904
Eff. Tax Rate	34%	25%	33%	19%	NM	NM	NM	29%	31%	22%
Net Inc.	452	275	303	201	-168	-270	-506	310	540	703
Balance Sheet & Other Fin. Data (Million $)										
Cash	18.0	23.0	52.0	20.0	79.0	22.0	79.0	70.0	296	NA
Curr. Assets	1,531	1,428	1,444	1,780	1,575	1,321	1,292	1,541	1,217	NA
Total Assets	6,694	6,580	6,521	6,480	6,616	6,251	5,627	5,582	5,499	NA
Curr. Liab.	1,334	1,299	1,519	1,267	1,621	1,263	1,193	1,020	1,177	NA
LT Debt	456	1,014	923	1,432	1,540	2,132	1,848	1,404	1,393	NA
Common Eqty.	1,634	1,559	1,337	913	585	222	1,667	2,219	1,968	NA
Total Cap.	2,486	2,644	2,331	2,441	2,162	2,395	3,577	3,738	3,448	NA
Cap. Exp.	261	337	324	248	198	298	432	574	399	411
Cash Flow	742	545	621	490	124	14.0	-255	585	831	1,035
Curr. Ratio	1.1	1.1	0.9	1.4	1.0	1.0	1.1	1.5	1.0	NA
% LT Debt of Cap.	18.3	38.4	39.6	58.7	71.2	89.0	51.7	37.6	40.4	NA
% Net Inc.of Revs.	6.6	4.2	4.7	3.3	NM	NM	NM	5.1	8.3	10.0
% Ret. on Assets	6.8	4.2	4.7	3.0	NM	NM	NM	5.4	9.4	NA
% Ret. on Equity	31.7	17.5	12.4	22.8	NM	NM	NM	14.3	30.3	NA

Data as orig. reptd.; bef. results of disc. opers. and/or spec. items. Per share data adj. for stk. divs. as of ex-div. date. E-Estimated. NA-Not Available. NM-Not Meaningful. NR-Not Ranked. EPS diluted from 4Q 1997.

Office—600 Grant St., Pittsburgh, PA 15219-4776. **Registrar**—Mellon Bank, Pittsburgh. **Tel**—(412) 433-1121. **Website**—http://www.usx.com **Chrmn & CEO**—T. J. Usher. **Vice Chrmn & CFO**—R. M. Hernandez. **Secy**—D. A. Sandman. **Pres U.S. Steel Group**—P. J. Wilhelm. **Investor Contact**—Charles D. Williams. **Dirs**—N. A. Armstrong, V. G. Beghini, J. G. Brown, C. A. Corry, R. M. Hernandez, C. R. Lee, P. E. Lego, R. Marshall, J. F. McGillicuddy, J. M. Richman, S. E. Schofield, J. W. Snow, T. J. Usher, P. J. Wilhelm, D. C. Yearley. **Transfer Agent**—Co.'s office. **Incorporated**—in New Jersey in 1901; reincorporated in Delaware in 1965. **Empl**— 20,683. **S&P Analyst:** Leo Larkin

Venator Group

2499

NYSE Symbol **Z**

In S&P 500

12-SEP-98

Industry: Retail (Specialty)

Summary: Z, which changed its name from Woolworth Corp. in June 1998, operates specialty stores under a number of formats worldwide.

S&P Opinion: Hold (★★★)	Recent Price • 9¼	Yield • Nil
	52 Wk Range • 27¼-8⅜	12-Mo. P/E • 8.3

Quantitative Evaluations

Outlook
(1 Lowest—5 Highest)
• 4

Fair Value
• 12¼

Risk
• Average

Earn./Div. Rank
• B-

Technical Eval.
• **Bearish** since 3/98

Rel. Strength Rank
(1 Lowest—99 Highest)
• 12

Insider Activity
• **Neutral**

Earnings vs. Previous Year
▲=Up ▼=Down ▶=No Change

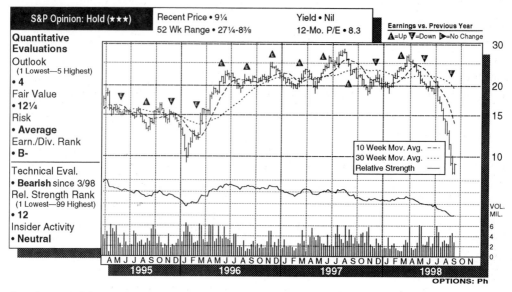

10 Week Mov. Avg. – – –
30 Week Mov. Avg. ········
Relative Strength ——

OPTIONS: Ph

Overview - 01-JUL-98

Since 1994, the company has sold or closed 19 formats or 1,237 stores and closed 1,180 stores in existing formats. During 1997, Z discontinued its 442 store U.S. and Mexican general merchandise operations. About 130 of the U.S. locations are being converted to Foot Lockers, a new larger Champs Sports and other athletic or specialty formats. The company has improved its balance sheet and is funding a $1 billion capital expenditure program through the year 2000. This includes about 4,300 new and remodeled stores domestically and internationally, most earmarked for the athletic businesses. Same-store sales should increase modestly in FY 99. Operating income should rise, fueled by lower expense ratios. Interest expense should decline with lower debt levels. The company made three acquisitions in 1997 - Eastbay, Inc., Koenig Sporting Goods and Athletic Fitters. In May Z announced plans to acquire The Sports Authority, Inc. (TSA) for $570 million in stock (0.8 share of Z common for each TSA share). TSA operates 202 superstores with annual revenues of $1.5 billion. The company has signed an agreement to sell its 1913 landmark corporate headquarters in lower Manhattan.

Valuation - 01-JUL-98

We remain neutral on the shares for the near term. Sales in the athletic shoe market have been weak; in the first quarter of FY 99 (Jan.), same-unit sales fell 6.4%. Moderate gains in same-store sales are needed to put the company on a more sustainable earnings growth track. In addition, the retail landscape remains overcrowded and we anticipate smaller gains in consumer spending in the second half of 1998 with slower growth in the economy. The Sports Authority acquisition will be accretive to earnings beginning in the year 2000.

Key Stock Statistics

S&P EPS Est. 1999	1.10	Tang. Bk. Value/Share	7.97
P/E on S&P Est. 1999	8.5	Beta	1.79
Dividend Rate/Share	Nil	Shareholders	42,900
Shs. outstg. (M)	135.3	Market cap. (B)	$ 1.3
Avg. daily vol. (M)	0.722	Inst. holdings	88%

Value of $10,000 invested 5 years ago: $ 3,296

Fiscal Year Ending Jan. 31

	1999	1998	1997	1996	1995	1994
Revenues (Million $)						
1Q	1,466	1,766	1,820	1,794	1,760	2,135
2Q	1,465	1,500	1,856	1,922	1,876	2,288
3Q	—	1,583	2,048	2,071	2,097	2,387
4Q	—	2,002	2,368	2,437	2,560	2,816
Yr.	—	6,624	8,092	8,224	8,293	9,626
Earnings Per Share ($)						
1Q	**-0.04**	0.01	-0.17	-0.60	-0.29	-0.18
2Q	**-0.09**	0.19	0.17	-0.09	-0.32	-0.08
3Q	**E0.38**	0.41	0.52	0.26	0.28	-2.66
4Q	**E0.86**	0.85	0.74	-0.80	0.69	-0.84
Yr.	**E1.10**	1.57	1.26	-1.23	0.36	-3.76

Next earnings report expected: mid November

Dividend Data

Prior to omission in April 1995, dividends had been paid since 1912. A dividend reinvestment plan is available. A "poison pill" stock purchase rights plan was adopted in 1988.

A Division of The **McGraw·Hill** *Companies*

Business Summary - 01-JUL-98

Venator Group, Inc. (formerly Woolworth Corp.) has moved a long way from its five and dime store origins and its recent name change reflects this. The company has eliminated and downsized its mature formats (Woolworth general merchandise and Kinney shoe stores) in order to focus on its high-return, specialty retailing formats. At the end of FY 98 (Jan.), Z operated 7,237 stores in North America, Europe, Asia and Australia.

The company's retailing business is conducted via two major segments: specialty stores; and international general merchandise stores. The specialty segment includes: the athletic group, the Northern group, specialty footwear and other specialty stores. The international general merchandise segment includes operations in Germany and Canada.

The athletic group is comprised of the Foot Locker family of businesses and Champs Sports, totaling 3,394 units at the end of January 1998. The Northern Group consists of Northern Reflections, Northern Getaway, Northern Elements, and Northern Traditions, totaling 760 stores. The specialty footwear group, consisting of 1,199 stores, includes formats in the U.S., Canada, Germany and Australia, the largest of which is the Kinney shoe store chain. There are 1,405 other specialty units, of which 834 are Afterthoughts stores. The 546

international general merchandise stores consists of German general merchandise and The Bargain! Shop in Canada units.

The company's new management team has undertaken a host of initiatives to strengthen the company and to plan a course for long-term growth. A new strategic planning process has been developed with a three-year comprehensive plan.

Venator has improved its financial position in a number of ways. Z had been relying on short-term debt for financing and has converted $290 million of short-term debt to intermediate-term debt. Total debt, net of cash, has been reduced by almost $800 million in the past two years. Underperforming divisions and excess real estate have been sold off. The cash proceeds from dispositions and real estate were $222 million.

Venator has also improved its inventory management. Total inventory has been reduced by $353 million (22%) since 1994. Inventory aging standards have been adopted to keep merchandise in the stores fresh and current with the season. Some $200 million in cost reductions have been extracted from the business by centralizing functions and reducing payroll expenses.

In July 1997, the company announced that despite its best efforts, the general merchandise division continued to lose money. Management decided to close the 400-store division and took an aftertax charge of $207 million or $1.54 a share in the second quarter of FY 98.

Per Share Data ($)

(Year Ended Jan. 31)	1998	1997	1996	1995	1994	1993	1992	1991	1990	1989
Tangible Bk. Val.	7.97	9.19	8.41	9.15	9.05	14.44	14.22	16.78	14.78	13.10
Cash Flow	2.80	2.66	0.56	2.12	-1.81	4.03	1.56	4.22	4.12	3.62
Earnings	1.57	1.26	-1.23	0.36	-3.76	2.14	-0.41	2.45	2.55	2.24
Dividends	Nil	Nil	Nil	0.74	1.16	1.12	1.08	1.04	0.94	0.82
Payout Ratio	Nil	Nil	Nil	NM	NM	52%	NM	43%	37%	37%
Cal. Yrs.	1997	1996	1995	1994	1993	1992	1991	1990	1989	1988
Prices - High	28¾	25¼	19⅜	26¼	32¾	35	36⅜	36½	36⅛	30⅜
- Low	18¼	9⅜	12¼	12⅞	20½	26	23½	27⅞	24⅛	17
P/E Ratio - High	18	20	NM	73	NM	16	NM	15	14	14
- Low	12	7	NM	36	NM	12	NM	9	9	8

Income Statement Analysis (Million $)

Revs.	6,624	8,092	8,224	8,293	9,626	9,962	9,914	9,789	8,820	8,088
Oper. Inc.	521	505	323	466	264	773	650	822	816	692
Depr.	168	187	239	233	257	249	256	234	201	177
Int. Exp.	44.0	73.0	119	110	84.0	94.0	99	104	104	75.0
Pretax Inc.	338	280	-232	96.0	-797	437	-83.0	493	514	444
Eff. Tax Rate	37%	40%	NM	51%	NM	36%	NM	36%	36%	35%
Net Inc.	213	169	-163	47.0	-494	280	-53.0	317	329	288

Balance Sheet & Other Fin. Data (Million $)

Cash	116	321	13.0	72.0	57.0	49.0	69.0	50.0	56.0	81.0
Curr. Assets	1,459	1,823	1,618	2,069	2,494	2,654	2,590	2,391	2,235	1,949
Total Assets	3,182	3,476	3,506	4,173	4,593	4,692	4,618	4,305	3,907	3,535
Curr. Liab.	756	856	841	1,710	2,081	1,658	1,592	1,436	1,299	1,166
LT Debt	535	580	619	309	336	372	425	269	306	347
Common Eqty.	1,271	1,334	1,229	1,353	1,344	2,054	2,025	2,334	2,069	1,836
Total Cap.	1,854	1,972	1,936	1,767	1,767	2,536	2,545	2,713	2,476	2,265
Cap. Exp.	284	134	167	218	359	333	387	396	317	343
Cash Flow	381	356	75.0	280	-237	529	203	551	530	465
Curr. Ratio	1.9	2.1	1.9	1.2	1.2	1.6	1.6	1.7	1.7	1.7
% LT Debt of Cap.	28.9	29.4	32.0	17.5	19.0	14.7	16.7	9.9	12.4	15.3
% Net Inc.of Revs.	3.2	2.1	NM	0.6	NM	2.8	NM	3.2	3.7	3.6
% Ret. on Assets	6.4	4.8	NM	1.1	NM	6.0	NM	7.7	8.8	8.4
% Ret. on Equity	16.4	13.2	NM	3.5	NM	13.7	NM	14.4	16.8	16.3

Data as orig. reptd.; bef. results of disc. opers. and/or spec. items. Per share data adj. for stk. divs. as of ex-div. date. Bold denotes diluted EPS (FASB 128). E-Estimated. NA-Not Available. NM-Not Meaningful. NR-Not Ranked.

Office—233 Broadway, New York, NY 10279-0003. **Tel**—(212) 553-2000. **Website**—http://www.venatorgroup.com **Chrmn & CEO**—R. N. Farah. **Pres & COO**—D. W. Hilpert. **VP & Treas**—J. H. Cannon. **VP & Secy**—G. M. Bahler. **VP - Investor Relations**—Juris Pagrabs. **Dirs**—J. C. Bacot, P. Crawford, R. N. Farah, P. H. Geier, Jr., J. Gilbert, Jr., D. W. Hilpert, A. Loren, M. P. MacKimm, J. J. Mackowski, J. E. Preston, C. Sinclair. **Transfer Agents & Registrars**—First Chicago Trust Co. of New York, Jersey City, NJ; R-M Trust Co., Toronto. **Incorporated**—in New York in 1911. **Empl**—75,000. **S&P Analyst:** Karen. J. Sack, CFA

STANDARD &POOR'S
STOCK REPORTS

V. F. Corp.

2378K
NYSE Symbol **VFC**
In S&P 500

12-SEP-98

Industry:
Textiles (Apparel)

Summary: This global apparel company produces jeans, decorated knitwear and sportswear, intimate apparel, children's playwear and specialty apparel under various well-known brand names.

S&P Opinion: Hold (★★★)	Recent Price • 39	Yield • 2.1%
	52 Wk Range • 54⅝-36⅜	12-Mo. P/E • 13.5

Quantitative Evaluations

Outlook
(1 Lowest—5 Highest)
• **2+**

Fair Value
• **38⅞**

Risk
• **Low**

Earn./Div. Rank
• **A-**

Technical Eval.
• **Bearish** since 8/98

Rel. Strength Rank
(1 Lowest—99 Highest)
• **51**

Insider Activity
• **Neutral**

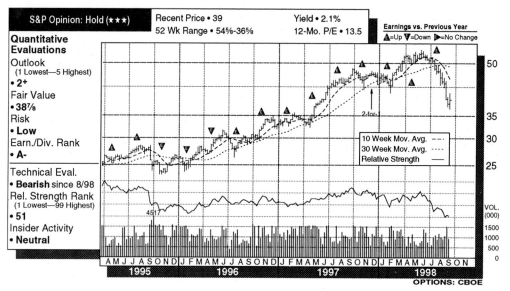

Earnings vs. Previous Year
▲=Up ▼=Down ▶=No Change

10 Week Mov. Avg. ---
30 Week Mov. Avg. ·····
Relative Strength —

OPTIONS: CBOE

Overview - 27-JUL-98

Aided by a 1997 restructuring of operating divisions, VFC's net income rose 11% year to year in the first half of 1998, on a 6.3% increase in sales. In addition, an aggressive share repurchase program boosted EPS 16%. We project sales growth of 4% to 5% for the second half of the year, reflecting the continued success of VFC's popular Lee, Riders and Wrangler jeans, and the inclusion of sales from the January 1998 acquisition of Bestform Group. These gains should offset sluggish sales of knitwear, which has been hurt like the rest of the industry, and has excess inventories. However, we believe that margins should continue to widen, due to improved operating efficiencies and an increase of off-shore manufacturing. With the continuation of VFC's stock buyback program, we expect to see EPS rise approximately 12% in 1998.

Valuation - 27-JUL-98

The 1998 second quarter marked the ninth consecutive quarter of year to year earnings growth for VFC. However, we are maintaining our hold opinion on the shares. Although we continue to see margin improvement during 1998, much of the easy cost savings from the company's restructuring initiatives have already been realized. Slower margin expansion, coupled with only modest sales gains, are likely to limit investor enthusiasm for the near term. As a result, we believe that the stock, recently trading at 16X our revised 1998 EPS estimate of $3.02, is fairly valued. For the longer term, however, the company's renewed focus on its core brands, and its efforts to reduce its cost structure, should continue to translate into higher sales and earnings. A strong level of cash flow and a low debt-to-capital ratio will also allow VFC to make acquisitions and repurchase shares.

Key Stock Statistics

S&P EPS Est. 1998	3.02	Tang. Bk. Value/Share	8.54
P/E on S&P Est. 1998	12.9	Beta	0.92
S&P EPS Est. 1999	3.25	Shareholders	7,600
Dividend Rate/Share	0.80	Market cap. (B)	$ 4.7
Shs. outstg. (M)	121.5	Inst. holdings	81%
Avg. daily vol. (M)	0.241		

Value of $10,000 invested 5 years ago: $ 16,704

Fiscal Year Ending Dec. 31

	1998	1997	1996	1995	1994	1993
Revenues (Million $)						
1Q	1,326	1,263	1,158	1,188	1,123	1,017
2Q	1,350	1,256	1,221	1,272	1,186	1,053
3Q	—	1,417	1,381	1,332	1,373	1,153
4Q	—	1,287	1,377	1,271	1,289	1,098
Yr.	—	5,222	5,137	5,062	4,972	4,320
Earnings Per Share ($)						
1Q	**0.62**	**0.53**	0.43	0.45	0.41	0.41
2Q	**0.69**	**0.60**	0.54	0.51	0.45	0.42
3Q	**E0.93**	**0.84**	0.71	0.54	0.67	0.59
4Q	**E0.78**	**0.74**	0.64	-0.28	0.57	0.47
Yr.	**E3.02**	**2.70**	2.32	1.21	2.10	1.90

Next earnings report expected: mid October

Dividend Data (Dividends have been paid since 1941.)

Amount ($)	Date Decl.	Ex-Div. Date	Stock of Record	Payment Date
2-for-1	Oct. 15	Nov. 25	Nov. 04	Nov. 24 '97
0.200	Feb. 10	Mar. 06	Mar. 10	Mar. 20 '98
0.200	Apr. 21	Jun. 05	Jun. 09	Jun. 19 '98
0.200	Jul. 21	Sep. 03	Sep. 08	Sep. 18 '98

Business Summary - 27-JUL-98

This international apparel company's ambitious goals are to achieve $7 billion in new sales over the next several years, and to increase earnings 8% to 10% annually over the long term.

V.F. Corporation bases its plans on its strong established brands and leading market shares throughout the world in most of its key categories. The company's principal brands include Lee, Wrangler, Rustler, Riders, Brittania, Maverick, Vanity Fair, Vassarette, Healthtex, Lee Sport, Red Kap, JanSport and Jantzen. Its European intimate apparel brands include Lou, Bolero, Variance, Carina, Siltex, Belcor, Intima Cherry and Gemma. Jantzen also produces women's sportswear and swimwear under the Nike trademark.

The bulk of sales growth is expected to come from a higher degree of international penetration. Over 16% of 1997 sales and operating income were derived from overseas markets. Most international sales to date have come from Western Europe, but sales are increasing in Eastern Europe. Lee jeans are also manufactured and marketed in China.

Realizing the need to capitalize on its strengths in order to achieve its goals, management has focused on four key categories: jeanswear, intimate apparel, workwear and daypacks. VFC believes that these categories present the areas of greatest strength and opportunity for future growth. In fact, after implementing this plan, these divisions had sales growth that outpaced the company's overall sales growth in 1997.

In a further move, beginning in late 1996, VFC embarked on the most extensive reorganization in its history, aimed at reducing operating redundancies. During 1997, the company consolidated 17 different operating divisions into five streamlined consumer-focused marketing coalitions: Jeanswear, Intimate Apparel, Knitwear, Playwear, and International. Although the marketing functions remain separate, allowing marketing specialists to focus on specific brands, most sourcing, manufacturing and administrative functions are carried out on either a coalition or company-wide basis. The bulk of production will be moved to lower-cost offshore locations. VFC will also make additional investments in consumer research, product development, in-store marketing programs and advertising. The company estimates that it will invest $1.25 billion in brand marketing over the next several years. In addition, VFC plans to update its computer system to a common system at cost of approximately $150 million. It expects to achieve long-term benefits from these investments.

The company expanded its intimate apparel business with the January 1998 acquisition of Bestform Group, a leading designer, marketer and manufacturer of women's intimate apparel. As a result of the acquisition, VFC became the second largest manufacturer of intimate apparel in the U.S.

Per Share Data ($)

(Year Ended Dec. 31)	1997	1996	1995	1994	1993	1992	1991	1990	1989	1988
Tangible Bk. Val.	8.69	8.67	6.97	6.41	7.54	5.04	4.47	3.47	3.35	4.73
Cash Flow	3.87	3.57	2.51	3.33	2.88	2.91	2.17	1.53	2.06	1.93
Earnings	2.70	2.32	1.21	2.10	1.90	1.99	1.38	0.68	1.36	1.27
Dividends	0.77	0.73	0.69	0.65	0.61	0.56	0.51	0.50	0.46	0.42
Payout Ratio	29%	31%	57%	31%	32%	28%	37%	74%	30%	33%
Prices - High	48¼	35	28⅝	26⅞	28¼	28¾	20¾	17⅛	19¼	17
- Low	32¼	23⅞	23⅜	22⅛	19¾	19¼	8⅞	5⅞	13⅞	12⅜
P/E Ratio - High	18	15	24	13	15	14	15	25	14	13
- Low	12	10	19	11	10	10	6	9	10	10

Income Statement Analysis (Million $)

	1997	1996	1995	1994	1993	1992	1991	1990	1989	1988
Revs.	5,222	5,137	5,062	4,972	4,320	3,824	2,952	2,613	2,533	2,516
Oper. Inc.	761	718	522	697	558	538	395	347	404	399
Depr.	156	161	168	159	126	108	91.0	97.9	91.0	88.9
Int. Exp.	50.0	62.8	77.0	80.3	72.7	71.1	68.6	76.4	46.2	46.9
Pretax Inc.	585	508	284	456	400	376	263	143	284	275
Eff. Tax Rate	40%	41%	45%	40%	38%	37%	39%	43%	38%	37%
Net Inc.	351	300	157	275	246	237	161	81.0	176	174

Balance Sheet & Other Fin. Data (Million $)

	1997	1996	1995	1994	1993	1992	1991	1990	1989	1988
Cash	124	271	84.0	60.0	152	86.0	162	62.0	36.0	87.0
Curr. Assets	1,601	1,706	1,668	1,551	1,500	1,366	1,071	824	874	786
Total Assets	3,323	3,450	3,447	3,336	2,877	2,712	2,127	1,853	1,890	1,760
Curr. Liab.	766	766	868	912	660	684	511	351	325	231
LT Debt	516	519	614	517	528	768	583	585	638	302
Common Eqty.	1,841	1,974	1,772	1,734	1,547	1,154	938	823	820	1,095
Total Cap.	2,439	2,562	2,469	2,335	2,151	1,985	1,591	1,535	1,535	1,468
Cap. Exp.	154	139	155	133	209	207	111	110	125	64.0
Cash Flow	503	457	321	429	368	341	248	175	267	263
Curr. Ratio	2.1	2.2	1.9	1.7	2.3	2.0	2.1	2.3	2.7	3.4
% LT Debt of Cap.	21.1	20.3	24.9	22.1	24.5	38.7	36.7	38.1	41.5	20.6
% Net Inc.of Revs.	6.7	5.9	3.1	5.5	5.7	6.2	5.5	3.1	6.9	6.9
% Ret. on Assets	10.4	8.6	4.6	8.9	8.5	9.7	8.1	4.4	10.4	9.4
% Ret. on Equity	18.3	15.8	8.7	16.5	17.3	21.9	17.7	9.5	20.1	16.7

Data as orig. reptd.; bef. results of disc. opers. and/or spec. items. Per share data adj. for stk. divs. as of ex-div. date. Bold denotes diluted EPS (FASB 128). E-Estimated. NA-Not Available. NM-Not Meaningful. NR-Not Ranked.

Office—1047 North Park Rd., Wyomissing, PA 19610. **Tel**—(610) 378-1151. **Website**—http://www.vfc.com **Chrmn & CEO**—L. R. Pugh.**Pres**—M. J. McDonald. **VP-Fin & CFO**—R. K. Shearer.**VP & Secy**—Lori M. Tarnoski. **Investor Contact**—Cindy Knoebel (212-782-0276). **Dirs**—R. D. Buzzell, E. E. Crutchfield Jr., U. Fairbairn, B. S. Feigin, G. Fellows, R. J. Hurst, M. J. McDonald. W. E. Pike, L. R. Pugh, M. R. Sharp, L. D. Walker. **Transfer Agent & Registrar**—First Chicago Trust Co. of New York, Jersey City, NJ. **Incorporated**—in Pennsylvania in 1899. **Empl**—63,400. **S&P Analyst:** Kathleen J. Fraser

STANDARD &POOR'S
STOCK REPORTS

Viacom Inc.

9499K
ASE Symbol **VIA.B**
In S&P 500

12-SEP-98

Industry:
Entertainment

Summary: This major entertainment company now includes certain businesses of Paramount Communications and Blockbuster Entertainment, acquired in 1994.

S&P Opinion: Accumulate (★★★★)	Recent Price • 60⅛	Yield • Nil
	52 Wk Range • 70-26½	12-Mo. P/E • 31.8

Quantitative Evaluations

Outlook
(1 Lowest—5 Highest)
• **NA**

Fair Value
• **NA**

Risk
• **NA**

Earn./Div. Rank
• **B-**

Technical Eval.
• **Bullish** since 11/96

Rel. Strength Rank
(1 Lowest—99 Highest)
• **90**

Insider Activity
• **NA**

Earnings vs. Previous Year
▲=Up ▼=Down ▶=No Change

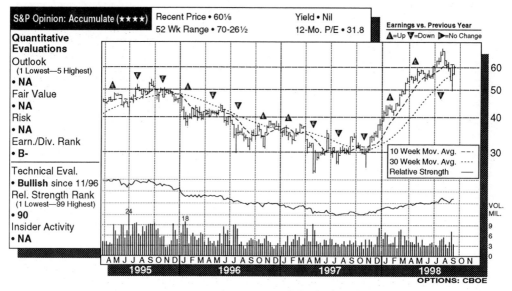

10 Week Mov. Avg. - - -
30 Week Mov. Avg. ·····
Relative Strength —

OPTIONS: CBOE

Overview - 24-AUG-98

Viacom is one of the world's leading entertainment and media companies. Operations include the Paramount movie business, Blockbuster Video, TV stations, and such U.S. cable networks as MTV, Nickelodeon and Showtime. In 1997, divestitures generated gross proceeds of more than $2.7 billion, and the company is expected to sell much of its publishing business, for over $4 billion. In the 1998 second quarter, VIA's earnings include a large non-cash charge, related to inventory revaluation at the company's Blockbuster retail business. This revaluation was connected to new revenue-sharing programs with Hollywood studios. Earlier, results in the 1997 second quarter included a large charge related to VIA's retail operations. Our earnings estimates exclude the 1998 charge, and also exclude the results of the publishing operations, which VIA is expected to sell.

Valuation - 24-AUG-98

We see some appeal in holding this stock, but do not recommend new purchases. VIA owns assets that are difficult to duplicate, and we expect that there will be further cross-promotional and growth opportunities ahead. In addition, at VIA's Blockbuster Video business, we look for cash flow and profit benefits from revenue-sharing arrangements with Hollywood studios to be more apparent in future quarters. We expect that an initial public offering of Blockbuster stock and/or a spinoff of Blockbuster equity will occur within the next couple years. Because of non-cash charges, particularly goodwill expense related to acquisitions made in 1994, we believe that it is better to value the stock on the basis of cash flow, rather than on reported EPS. We see the recent stock price as adequately valuing a favorable outlook for EPS and cash flow growth.

Key Stock Statistics

S&P EPS Est. 1998	0.22	Tang. Bk. Value/Share	NM
P/E on S&P Est. 1998	NM	Beta	1.13
S&P EPS Est. 1999	0.85	Shareholders	33,500
Dividend Rate/Share	Nil	Market cap. (B)	$ 17.3
Shs. outstg. (M)	358.0	Inst. holdings	51%
Avg. daily vol. (M)	0.892		

Value of $10,000 invested 5 years ago: $ 14,373

Fiscal Year Ending Dec. 31

	1998	1997	1996	1995	1994	1993
Revenues (Million $)						
1Q	3,088	2,918	2,623	2,696	878.0	471.0
2Q	3,324	3,031	2,785	2,865	1,728	496.0
3Q	—	3,647	3,266	3,062	2,131	508.0
4Q	—	3,610	3,409	3,066	2,777	530.0
Yr.	—	13,206	12,084	11,689	7,363	2,005
Earnings Per Share ($)						
1Q	-0.04	-0.11	0.01	0.13	-3.59	0.59
2Q	-0.83	-0.66	0.03	0.10	1.69	0.35
3Q	—	0.01	0.26	0.21	1.45	0.25
4Q	—	1.65	0.01	-0.03	-0.14	0.11
Yr.	—	0.89	0.30	0.41	0.25	1.30

Next earnings report expected: late October

Dividend Data

No cash dividends have been paid since Viacom's predecessor was acquired in 1987 by National Amusements, Inc. In 1990, one share of nonvoting common stock (otherwise identical to ordinary common) was distributed for each common share held.

A Division of The **McGraw·Hill** *Companies*

Business Summary - 24-AUG-98

The shape of this major entertainment company was changed dramatically in 1994, when it spent about $17.5 billion to acquire Paramount Communications and Blockbuster Entertainment. In so doing, VIA added businesses that ranged from Paramount's moviemaking operations to the vast network of video stores operating under the Blockbuster name. In 1997, segment contributions (profits in millions of dollars, including depreciation) from continuing operations were:

	Revs.	Profits
Networks & broadcasting	20.6%	$747.5
Entertainment	29.2%	233.4
Video, music & theme parks	32.5%	-248.3
Publishing	18.7%	221.7
Intercompany revenue, or corporate expense	-1.0%	-201.5

VIA's mix of businesses has continued to change. In mid-1997, the company sold its 10 radio stations for $1.075 billion (gross), with net proceeds targeted for debt reduction. Also, in October 1997, VIA sold its 50% interest in the cable channel USA Networks business for $1.7 billion, and has agreed to sell much of its publishing business for more than $4 billion.

VIA's network and broadcasting segment includes both advertiser-supported basic cable programming (e.g.,

MTV: Music Television; Nickelodeon; and VH-1) and premium subscription TV programming (Showtime; The Movie Channel; and Flix). The company also owns 15 television stations, and has 50% ownership of the United Paramount Network. VIA's Entertainment segment includes the production and distribution of movies and television shows, largely done through Paramount and majority-owned Spelling Entertainment.

VIA owns the Blockbuster Video business, which as of mid-1998 had 6,153 stores (including 994 franchises). In August 1998, VIA said it had agreed to sell its Blockbuster Music business, which had about 380 stores, for $115 million. VIA also has six theme parks and a large publishing segment, which were largely acquired through the Paramount merger. VIA is expected to sell much of its publishing business. There are also other assets in which VIA owns less than a majority equity interest. Revenue and profit from such assets is not included in segment data above.

In the 1998 second quarter, earnings included a $437 million pretax non-cash charge related to inventory revaluation at the Blockbuster Videol business. The revaluation was connected to new revenue-sharing programs with Hollywood studios. Results in the 1997 second quarter included a $323 million charge related to retail operations, largely for a reduction in value of what VIA termed excess inventory, and reorganizing and closing underperforming stores in certain international markets.

Per Share Data ($)

(Year Ended Dec. 31)	1997	1996	1995	1994	1993	1992	1991	1990	1989	1988
Tangible Bk. Val.	NM	NM	-14.22	-15.39	-10.45	-11.95	-13.16	-18.03	-16.60	-19.97
Cash Flow	3.55	2.53	2.60	1.23	2.07	1.23	0.21	-0.13	1.77	-1.06
Earnings	0.89	0.30	0.41	0.25	1.30	0.55	-0.41	-0.84	1.07	-1.77
Dividends	Nil	Nil	Nil	Nil	Nil	Nil	Nil	Nil	Nil	Nil
Payout Ratio	Nil	Nil	Nil	Nil	Nil	Nil	Nil	Nil	Nil	Nil
Prices - High	42¼	47⅝	54¼	45	67½	44	35⅜	29⅝	32⅝	15⅝
- Low	25¼	29¾	40¼	21¾	37⅛	28⅛	23½	15⅝	15¼	8⅞
P/E Ratio - High	47	NM	NM	NM	52	80	NM	NM	31	NM
- Low	28	NM	NM	NM	29	51	NM	NM	14	NM

Income Statement Analysis (Million $)

	1997	1996	1995	1994	1993	1992	1991	1990	1989	1988
Revs.	13,206	12,084	11,689	7,363	2,005	1,865	1,712	1,600	1,436	1,259
Oper. Inc.	1,696	2,181	2,314	824	478	429	382	300	219	221
Depr.	943	818	821	216	92.8	81.5	70.1	75.7	75.0	76.0
Int. Exp.	782	832	868	536	155	196	299	296	314	278
Pretax Inc.	1,060	468	632	395	299	151	-4.0	-69.0	152	-111
Eff. Tax Rate	65%	63%	66%	71%	43%	56%	NM	NM	14%	NM
Net Inc.	375	171	215	131	169	66.0	-47.0	-90.0	131	-122

Balance Sheet & Other Fin. Data (Million $)

	1997	1996	1995	1994	1993	1992	1991	1990	1989	1988
Cash	292	209	464	598	1,882	48.4	28.7	43.1	12.4	16.4
Curr. Assets	5,714	5,718	5,199	5,255	2,686	797	718	654	591	553
Total Assets	28,289	28,834	29,026	28,274	6,417	4,317	4,188	4,028	3,753	3,980
Curr. Liab.	5,053	4,269	4,099	4,131	966	911	876	799	713	787
LT Debt	7,423	9,856	10,712	10,402	2,441	2,423	2,321	2,537	2,283	2,186
Common Eqty.	12,184	11,394	10,894	10,592	918	757	699	366	456	337
Total Cap.	19,607	22,450	22,806	22,194	5,159	3,179	3,020	2,903	2,739	2,974
Cap. Exp.	530	599	731	365	135	110	57.0	76.0	57.0	54.0
Cash Flow	1,318	929	976	271	250	148	24.0	-14.0	189	-112
Curr. Ratio	1.1	1.3	1.3	1.3	2.8	0.9	0.8	0.8	0.8	0.7
% LT Debt of Cap.	37.8	43.9	47.0	46.9	47.3	76.2	76.8	87.4	83.4	73.5
% Net Inc.of Revs.	2.8	1.4	1.9	1.8	8.5	3.5	NM	NM	9.1	NM
% Ret. on Assets	1.3	0.6	0.8	0.6	3.2	1.6	NM	NM	3.4	NM
% Ret. on Equity	2.7	0.9	1.3	0.8	18.7	9.1	NM	NM	28.6	NM

Data as orig. reptd.; bef. results of disc. opers. and/or spec. items. However, first nine mos. of 1996 (and earlier periods) incl. some businesses which are now considered discontinued. Per share data adj. for stk. divs. as of ex-div. date. Bold denotes diluted EPS (FASB 128). E-Estimated. NA-Not Available. NM-Not Meaningful. NR-Not Ranked.

Office—1515 Broadway, New York, NY 10036. **Tel**—(212) 258-6000. **Chrmn & CEO**—S. M. Redstone. **Dep Chrmn, EVP & Secy**—P. P. Dauman. **Dep Chrmn & EVP**—T. E. Dooley. **SVP & CFO**—G. S. Smith, Jr. **SVP & Treas**—V. A. Clarke. **Shareholder Relations**—(212-258-6700). **Dirs**—G. S. Abrams, P. P. Dauman, T. E. Dooley, K. H. Miller, B. D. Redstone, S. M. Redstone, S. Redstone, F. V. Salerno, W. Schwartz, I. Seidenberg. **Transfer Agent & Registrar**—First Chicago Trust Co. of New York, NYC. **Incorporated**—in Delaware in 1986. **Empl**— 116,700. **S&P Analyst:** Tom Graves, CFA

12-SEP-98

Industry: Banks (Major Regional)

Summary: This bank holding company operates 830 branches in North Carolina, Virginia, South Carolina, Georgia and Florida.

S&P Opinion: Hold (★★★)	Recent Price • 82¼	Yield • 2.4%
	52 Wk Range • 90⅛-66¾	12-Mo. P/E • 28.1

Quantitative Evaluations

Outlook
(1 Lowest—5 Highest)
• **1⁻**

Fair Value
• **71¾**

Risk
• **Low**

Earn./Div. Rank
• **A-**

Technical Eval.
• **NA**

Rel. Strength Rank
(1 Lowest—99 Highest)
• **90**

Insider Activity
• **NA**

Earnings vs. Previous Year
▲=Up ▼=Down ▶=No Change

10 Week Mov. Avg. ----
30 Week Mov. Avg. ·····
Relative Strength ——

OPTIONS: P

Overview - 27-JUL-98

Healthy demand for loans in WB's service territory, particularly from commercial customers, should result in low double-digit loan growth in 1998. A relatively stable net interest margin at about 4.20% on similar asset yields and funding costs will likely lead to net interest income gains also in the low double-digits. Recent efforts to move into attractive markets in Virginia and Florida fit well with growth initiatives and will help broaden the customer base, although they are not expected to contribute to earnings until late in 1998 and will be modestly dilutive until then. Noninterest income should continue to benefit from gains in service charges, credit card fee income, trust fees and capital markets income. The company has placed particular emphasis on controlling core operating expenses, though Year 2000 project costs and incentive pay tied to revenue growth in certain business lines will hurt comparisons with 1997. Asset quality remains among the best of the major regional banks, with the allowance for loan losses at 4.3 times nonperforming loans at June 30, 1998.

Valuation - 27-JUL-98

The shares were up only about 4% in the first half of 1998, well below both the average major regional bank and the broader market. Concerns about the dilutive effects of two Virginia acquisitions in 1997, which were priced at the high end of recent bank merger valuations, appear to be holding back the shares. Though some investors may have viewed WB itself as a takeover target, the company appears to be embarking on a strategy of independence. Recent acquisitions, meanwhile, should provide good revenue growth opportunities as well as the usual cost savings objectives over the long-term, though near-term earnings will be hurt by share dilution while operations are integrated. We continue to view the shares as fully valued at present.

Key Stock Statistics

S&P EPS Est. 1998	4.40	Tang. Bk. Value/Share	26.02
P/E on S&P Est. 1998	18.7	Beta	0.98
S&P EPS Est. 1999	5.05	Shareholders	32,600
Dividend Rate/Share	1.96	Market cap. (B)	$ 17.0
Shs. outstg. (M)	206.6	Inst. holdings	49%
Avg. daily vol. (M)	0.544		

Value of $10,000 invested 5 years ago: $ 28,399

Fiscal Year Ending Dec. 31

	1998	1997	1996	1995	1994	1993
Revenues (Million $)						
1Q	1,435	1,247	968.0	848.9	679.3	689.5
2Q	1,488	1,312	991.1	995.4	723.3	674.9
3Q	—	1,330	1,023	956.9	759.4	682.4
4Q	—	1,381	1,030	977.6	808.0	703.7
Yr.	—	5,270	4,011	3,779	2,970	2,750
Earnings Per Share ($)						
1Q	**0.93**	**0.95**	0.87	0.83	0.72	0.70
2Q	**1.00**	**0.98**	0.94	0.94	0.78	0.71
3Q	**E1.15**	**1.00**	0.98	0.88	0.80	0.71
4Q	**E1.32**	**0.02**	1.02	0.85	0.83	0.71
Yr.	**E4.40**	**2.94**	**3.65**	3.50	3.13	2.83

Next earnings report expected: mid October

Dividend Data (Dividends have been paid since 1936.)

Amount ($)	Date Decl.	Ex-Div. Date	Stock of Record	Payment Date
0.440	Oct. 24	Nov. 04	Nov. 06	Dec. 01 '97
0.440	Jan. 23	Feb. 03	Feb. 05	Mar. 02 '98
0.440	Apr. 24	May. 05	May. 07	Jun. 01 '98
0.490	Jul. 24	Aug. 04	Aug. 06	Sep. 01 '98

A Division of The McGraw·Hill Companies

STANDARD
&POOR'S
STOCK REPORTS

Wachovia Corporation

2407D

12-SEP-98

Business Summary - 27-JUL-98

Operating through dual headquarters in Atlanta, GA, and Winston-Salem, NC, this bank holding company has 201 branch offices in North Carolina, 341 in Virginia, 130 in Georgia, 125 in South Carolina and 33 in Florida. Its single most important strategic development in 1997 was expansion into Virginia and Florida through the acquisition of Jefferson Bankshares, Central Fidelity Banks and 1st United Bancorp. The company believes that the mergers position it in significant new markets with attractive customer households.

Principal business lines include credit and deposit services, insurance, investment and trust products, and information services to consumers in five states and corporations domestically and internationally. Wachovia also serves consumers nationwide through its credit card business. At 1997 year-end, the company had $33.6 billion of trust assets under discretionary management.

In 1997, average earning assets, from which interest income is derived, amounted to $52.0 billion and consisted mainly of loans and leases (76%) and investment securities (21%). Average sources of funds included savings and money market accounts (18%), savings certificates (23%), interest-bearing demand deposits (7%), foreign deposits (3%), noninterest-bearing demand deposits (12%), short-term borrowings (16%), long-term debt (11%), shareholders' equity (8%) and other (2%).

At year-end 1997, nonperforming assets, consisting primarily of non-accrual loans and foreclosed property, were $129.5 million (0.29% of loans and related assets), down from $131.5 million (0.35%) a year earlier. The allowance for loan losses, which is set aside for possible loan defaults, was $544.7 million (1.23% of loans), versus $519.3 million (1.37%) a year earlier. Net chargeoffs, or the amount of loans actually written off as uncollectible, were $264.2 million (0.67% of average loans) in 1997, compared to $193.5 million (0.53%) in 1996.

In April 1998, Wachovia acquired Ameribank Bancshares, a $280 million-asset Florida bank with seven branches in Broward County, for about $71 million in WB common stock.

Per Share Data ($)

(Year Ended Dec. 31)	1997	1996	1995	1994	1993	1992	1991	1990	1989	1988
Tangible Bk. Val.	25.13	22.90	22.11	18.77	17.61	15.58	13.84	13.23	12.12	10.94
Earnings	2.94	3.81	3.49	3.13	2.83	2.51	1.34	2.13	1.94	1.81
Dividends	1.68	1.52	1.38	1.23	1.11	1.00	0.92	0.82	0.70	0.58
Payout Ratio	57%	40%	40%	39%	39%	40%	69%	39%	36%	32%
Prices - High	83⁷/₈	60¹/₄	48¹/₄	35³/₈	40¹/₂	34³/₄	30	22³/₈	22³/₄	17
- Low	53¹/₂	39⁵/₈	32	30¹/₈	31⁷/₈	28¹/₄	20¹/₄	16¹/₄	15¹/₂	13⁷/₈
P/E Ratio - High	29	16	14	11	14	14	22	11	12	9
- Low	18	10	9	10	11	11	15	8	8	8

Income Statement Analysis (Million $)

	1997	1996	1995	1994	1993	1992	1991	1990	1989	1988
Net Int. Inc.	2,094	1,555	1,441	1,324	1,284	1,255	1,169	817	771	736
Tax Equiv. Adj.	68.2	69.9	99	100	99	79.0	95.0	93.0	85.0	75.0
Non Int. Inc.	1,006	784	759	604	628	555	490	375	335	297
Loan Loss Prov.	265	150	104	72.0	93.0	119	293	86.0	62.0	61.0
Exp./Op. Revs.	63%	52%	52%	54%	57%	58%	63%	58%	60%	60%
Pretax Inc.	869	935	869	761	688	596	281	371	338	315
Eff. Tax Rate	32%	31%	31%	29%	28%	27%	18%	20%	21%	23%
Net Inc.	593	645	602	539	492	433	230	297	269	244
% Net Int. Marg.	4.14	4.02	4.16	4.34	4.64	4.75	4.50	4.33	4.39	4.72

Balance Sheet & Other Fin. Data (Million $)

	1997	1996	1995	1994	1993	1992	1991	1990	1989	1988
Earning Assets:										
Money Mkt	2,721	1,393	1,710	1,098	1,492	1,565	2,399	1,663	1,692	1,352
Inv. Securities	10,419	8,112	9,029	7,723	7,879	6,486	6,265	3,779	3,598	3,309
Com'l Loans	15,136	12,421	12,486	10,376	8,843	8,442	8,505	7,307	6,703	5,934
Other Loans	29,059	18,862	16,366	15,515	14,134	12,644	12,112	9,329	8,594	7,819
Total Assets	65,397	46,905	44,981	39,188	36,526	33,367	33,158	26,271	24,050	21,815
Demand Deposits	8,598	9,578	9,329	5,663	6,144	5,627	4,758	4,988	4,377	4,276
Time Deposits	29,552	17,672	17,040	17,406	17,209	17,749	18,248	13,225	13,010	12,216
LT Debt	5,934	6,477	5,430	4,790	590	439	171	113	171	179
Common Eqty.	5,174	3,762	3,774	3,287	3,018	2,775	2,484	1,929	1,740	1,557
% Ret. on Assets	1.1	1.4	1.4	1.5	1.5	1.4	0.7	1.2	1.2	1.2
% Ret. on Equity	13.3	17.1	17.1	17.4	17.1	16.7	9.3	16.4	16.5	17.2
% Loan Loss Resv.	1.2	1.3	1.4	1.6	1.8	1.8	1.8	1.1	1.1	1.1
% Loans/Deposits	378.4	114.8	114.3	112.2	98.4	90.2	89.6	91.3	87.8	83.2
% Equity to Assets	8.0	8.2	8.4	8.4	8.5	8.2	7.7	7.5	7.3	7.1

Data as orig. reptd.; bef. results of disc. opers. and/or spec. items. Per share data adj. for stk. divs. as of ex-div. date. E-Estimated. NA-Not Available. NM-Not Meaningful. NR-Not Ranked.

Offices—100 N. Main St., Winston-Salem, NC 27150; 191 Peachtree St., N.E., Atlanta, GA 30303. **Tels**—(336) 770-5000; (404) 332-5000. **Website**—http://www.wachovia.com **Chrmn**—J. G. Medlin Jr. **Pres & CEO**—L. M. Baker Jr. **EVP & CFO**—R. S. McCoy Jr. **Investor Contact**—James C. Mabry (336-732-5788). **Dirs**—L. M. Baker Jr., J. S. Balloun, J. F. Betts, P. C. Browning, J. T. Casteen III, J. L. Clendenin, L. M. Gressette Jr., T. K. Hearn Jr., G. W. Henderson III, W. H. Hipp, R. M. Holder Jr., R. A. Ingram, J. W. Johnston, G. R. Lewis, J. G. Medlin Jr., L. U. Noland III, W. Robertson, H. J. Russell, S. H. Smith Jr., J. C. Whitaker, Jr. **Transfer Agent**—Wachovia Bank, Winston-Salem. **Incorporated**—in North Carolina in 1985. **Empl**– 21,652. **S&P Analyst:** Stephen R. Biggar

Wal-Mart Stores

2413

NYSE Symbol **WMT**

In S&P 500

12-SEP-98

Industry:
Retail (General Merchandise)

Summary: Wal-Mart is the largest retailer in North America, operating a chain of discount department stores, wholesale clubs and combination discount stores and supermarkets.

S&P Opinion: Hold (★★★)	Recent Price • 60%	Yield • 0.5%
	52 Wk Range • 69¾-30¼	12-Mo. P/E • 34.6

Quantitative Evaluations

Outlook
(1 Lowest—5 Highest)
• **1+**

Fair Value
• **45¾**

Risk
• **Low**

Earn./Div. Rank
• **A+**

Technical Eval.
• **Bearish** since 3/98

Rel. Strength Rank
(1 Lowest—99 Highest)
• **85**

Insider Activity
• **Neutral**

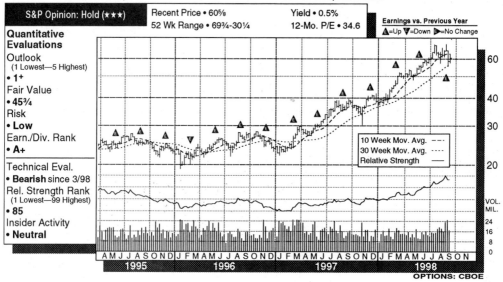

Earnings vs. Previous Year
▲=Up ▼=Down ▷=No Change

10 Week Mov. Avg. - - -
30 Week Mov. Avg. ·······
Relative Strength ——

OPTIONS: CBOE

Overview - 02-JUN-98

In FY 99 (Jan.), same-store sales at discount stores should increase some 5%, while same-store sales at Sam's should show a modest increase of about 2%. Higher volume and continued efforts to pare costs should result in a widening of gross margins. Operating profit should increase about 8%. Further out, the supercenter format, which includes groceries and general merchandise, is the key to the company's long-term domestic growth. The company operates over 340 of these units, generating some $60 million per unit annually, and plans an additional 120 units in FY 99, mostly replacing smaller discount units. International expansion through joint ventures in China, Hong Kong, Indonesia and South America enhances the company's long-term growth prospects. In December 1997, WMT completed the acquisition of the Wertkauf chain of 21 hypermarkets in Germany. WMT plans to repurchase $1.6 billion to $2.0 billion of its common shares from time to time.

Valuation - 02-JUN-98

The shares are a worthwhile holding as the company continues to gain market share from less-well-managed retailers and through extensive global expansion. Focusing on international growth, notably in Mexico, Canada, Latin America and Germany, and its supercenter general merchandise and supermarket format, Wal-Mart is on track for solid earnings gains in the 15% range over the next few years. After years of reinvesting in its business for new store growth and new technology, these investments are paying off and the company is reinvesting its ample cash flow. WMT has also paid down some debt and is repurchasing its shares. Wal-Mart should benefit from consolidation in the U.S. retail marketplace, resulting in fewer players and easing of the competitive landscape.

Key Stock Statistics

S&P EPS Est. 1999	1.80	Tang. Bk. Value/Share	8.42
P/E on S&P Est. 1999	33.7	Beta	0.75
S&P EPS Est. 2000	2.05	Shareholders	257,200
Dividend Rate/Share	0.31	Market cap. (B)	$135.5
Shs. outstg. (M)	2235.7	Inst. holdings	36%
Avg. daily vol. (M)	4.648		

Value of $10,000 invested 5 years ago: $ 19,747

Fiscal Year Ending Jan. 31

	1999	1998	1997	1996	1995	1994
Revenues (Million $)						
1Q	30,157	25,409	22,772	20,440	17,690	13,920
2Q	33,521	28,386	25,587	22,723	19,942	16,237
3Q	—	28,777	25,644	22,913	20,418	16,827
4Q	—	35,386	30,856	27,550	24,448	20,361
Yr.	—	117,958	104,859	93,627	82,494	67,345
Earnings Per Share ($)						
1Q	**0.37**	0.29	0.25	0.24	0.22	0.20
2Q	**0.46**	0.35	0.31	0.28	0.25	0.22
3Q	**E0.40**	0.35	0.30	0.27	0.26	0.23
4Q	**E0.63**	**0.57**	0.48	0.41	0.45	0.38
Yr.	**E1.80**	**1.56**	1.33	1.19	1.17	1.02

Next earnings report expected: mid November

Dividend Data (Dividends have been paid since 1973.)

Amount ($)	Date Decl.	Ex-Div. Date	Stock of Record	Payment Date
0.068	Nov. 13	Dec. 17	Dec. 19	Jan. 12 '98
0.078	Mar. 05	Mar. 18	Mar. 20	Apr. 06 '98
0.078	Jun. 04	Jun. 17	Jun. 19	Jul. 13 '98
0.078	Aug. 13	Sep. 16	Sep. 18	Oct. 12 '98

A Division of The McGraw-Hill Companies

STANDARD
&POOR'S
STOCK REPORTS

Wal-Mart Stores, Inc.

2413
12-SEP-98

Business Summary - 02-JUN-98

Wal-Mart, now the largest retailer in North America, has set its sights on the rest of the world. Faced with limited expansion opportunities in the U.S., growth into Latin America and the Far East has become a top priority. As of April 30, 1998, the company operated stores Germany (21 units), Argentina (11), Brazil (9), and China (3) under a joint venture agreement. In North America, Wal-Mart operated 1,908 Wal-Mart stores, 458 supercenters and 444 Sam's Clubs in the U.S. and 404 units in Mexico and 14 in Puerto Rico.

The average Wal-Mart discount store is 93,400 sq. ft. in size; store sizes range from 30,000 to 150,000 sq. ft. Wal-Mart stores are organized with 36 departments and offer a wide variety of merchandise, about 25% of which is soft goods and 25% hardware, housewares, auto supplies and small appliances. A typical discount store has more than 70,000 items in stock. Nationally advertised merchandise accounts for a majority of sales. WMT markets limited lines of merchandise under brand names including "Sam's American Choice." The company also operates Wal-Mart supercenters in 28 states, averaging 182,200 sq. ft. A typical supercenter carries more than 20,000 grocery items in addition to general merchandise.

Sam's Clubs are membership-only, cash-and-carry wholesale warehouses operating in 48 states and Puerto Rico, averaging 120,900 sq. ft.

Capital expenditures for FY 99 are projected at $4 billion, up from $2.6 billion in FY 98. WMT plans to add 50 Wal-Mart and between 120 and 125 supercenters domestically in FY 99 and to open ten new Sam's Clubs. Expansion should include a total of 50 to 60 units in Argentina, Brazil, China, Germany, Mexico and Canada. The company plans to finance these new units primarily from internally generated cash flows.

Wal-Mart has long been the leader in developing and implementing retail information technology. The company boasts an annual technology and communications budget of $500 million. The company is intent on increasing productivity to pass on cost reductions to customers via an everyday low pricing strategy and to provide a more complete assortment of merchandise in the stores. The Retail Link system, for example, provides sales data, by item, by store, by day, to vendors. These suppliers use this information in planning their production and merchandise replenishment can be accomplished via electronic data interchange in an efficient, low cost way.

Per Share Data ($)

(Year Ended Jan. 31)	1998	1997	1996	1995	1994	1993	1992	1991	1990	1989
Tangible Bk. Val.	8.26	7.50	6.43	5.54	4.68	3.81	3.04	2.35	1.74	1.32
Cash Flow	2.30	1.97	1.76	1.63	1.37	1.14	0.91	0.72	0.60	0.47
Earnings	1.56	1.33	1.19	1.17	1.02	0.87	0.70	0.57	0.48	0.37
Dividends	0.27	0.21	0.20	0.17	0.13	0.10	0.09	0.07	0.06	0.04
Payout Ratio	17%	16%	17%	15%	13%	11%	12%	12%	12%	11%
Cal. Yrs.	1997	1996	1995	1994	1993	1992	1991	1990	1989	1988
Prices - High	41⁷/₈	28¹/₄	27⁵/₈	29¹/₄	34¹/₈	33	30	18³/₈	11¹/₄	8¹/₂
- Low	22	19¹/₈	20¹/₂	21	23	25¹/₈	14¹/₄	10¹/₈	7¹/₂	6¹/₈
P/E Ratio - High	27	21	23	25	33	38	43	32	24	23
- Low	14	14	17	18	23	29	20	18	16	16

Income Statement Analysis (Million $)

	1998	1997	1996	1995	1994	1993	1992	1991	1990	1989
Revs.	117,958	104,859	93,627	82,494	67,345	55,484	43,887	32,602	25,811	20,649
Oper. Inc.	6,796	5,871	5,416	5,120	4,389	3,615	2,892	2,296	1,940	1,538
Depr.	1,634	1,463	1,304	1,070	822	627	475	347	269	214
Int. Exp.	784	889	938	776	582	403	302	194	155	144
Pretax Inc.	5,719	4,850	4,346	4,262	3,692	3,166	2,553	2,043	1,708	1,325
Eff. Tax Rate	37%	37%	37%	37%	37%	37%	37%	37%	37%	37%
Net Inc.	3,526	3,056	2,740	2,681	2,333	1,995	1,608	1,291	1,076	837

Balance Sheet & Other Fin. Data (Million $)

	1998	1997	1996	1995	1994	1993	1992	1991	1990	1989
Cash	1,447	883	83.0	45.0	20.0	12.0	31.0	13.0	13.0	13.0
Curr. Assets	19,352	17,993	17,331	15,338	12,115	10,198	8,575	6,415	4,713	3,631
Total Assets	45,384	39,604	37,541	32,819	26,441	20,565	15,443	11,389	8,198	6,360
Curr. Liab.	14,460	10,957	11,454	9,973	7,406	6,754	5,004	3,990	2,845	2,066
LT Debt	9,674	10,016	10,600	9,709	7,960	4,845	3,278	1,899	1,273	1,193
Common Eqty.	18,503	17,143	14,756	12,726	10,752	8,759	6,990	5,366	3,966	3,008
Total Cap.	30,115	28,647	26,087	22,846	19,035	13,811	10,440	7,398	5,353	4,294
Cap. Exp.	2,636	2,643	3,566	3,734	4,371	4,043	1,805	1,388	955	593
Cash Flow	5,160	4,519	4,044	3,751	3,155	2,622	2,084	1,638	1,345	1,051
Curr. Ratio	1.3	1.6	1.5	1.5	1.6	1.5	1.7	1.6	1.7	1.8
% LT Debt of Cap.	32.1	35.0	40.6	40.6	41.8	35.1	31.4	25.7	23.8	27.8
% Net Inc.of Revs.	3.0	2.9	2.9	3.3	3.5	3.6	3.7	4.0	4.2	4.1
% Ret. on Assets	8.3	7.9	7.8	9.1	9.9	11.1	12.0	13.1	14.8	14.6
% Ret. on Equity	19.8	19.2	19.9	19.9	23.9	25.3	26.0	27.6	30.8	31.8

Data as orig. reptd.; bef. results of disc. opers. and/or spec. items. Per share data adj. for stk. divs. as of ex-div. date. Bold denotes diluted EPS (FASB 128). E-Estimated. NA-Not Available. NM-Not Meaningful. NR-Not Ranked.

Office—702 Southwest 8th St. (P.O. Box 116), Bentonville, AR 72716-8611.**Tel**—(501) 273-4000. **Website**—http://www.wal-mart.com **Chrmn**—S. R. Walton. **Pres & CEO**—D. D. Glass. **Vice Chrmn & COO**—D. G. Soderquist. **Secy**—R. K. Rhoads. **Dirs**—P. R. Carter, J. A. Cooper Jr., S. Friedman, S. C. Gault, D. D. Glass, F. S. Humphries, F. K. Iverson, E. S. Kroenke, E. A. Sanders, J. Shewmaker, D. G. Soderquist, P. Stern, J. T. Walton, S. R. Walton. **Transfer Agent & Registrar**—First Chicago Trust Co. of NY, Jersey City, NJ. **Incorporated**—in Delaware in 1969. **Empl**—835,000. **S&P Analyst:** Karen J. Sack, CFA

STANDARD &POOR'S
STOCK REPORTS

Walgreen Co.

2408

NYSE Symbol **WAG**

In S&P 500

12-SEP-98

Industry: Retail (Drug Stores)

Summary: The largest U.S. retail drug chain in terms of revenues, this company operates over 2,400 drug stores in 34 states and Puerto Rico.

S&P Opinion: Accumulate (★★★★)	Recent Price • 43⅞	Yield • 0.6%
	52 Wk Range • 49⅞-24⅛	12-Mo. P/E • 44.3

Quantitative Evaluations

Outlook (1 Lowest—5 Highest)
• **1⁻**

Fair Value
• **34⅜**

Risk
• **Low**

Earn./Div. Rank
• **A+**

Technical Eval.
• **Bullish** since 9/98

Rel. Strength Rank (1 Lowest—99 Highest)
• **92**

Insider Activity
• **Neutral**

Earnings vs. Previous Year
▲=Up ▼=Down ▷=No Change

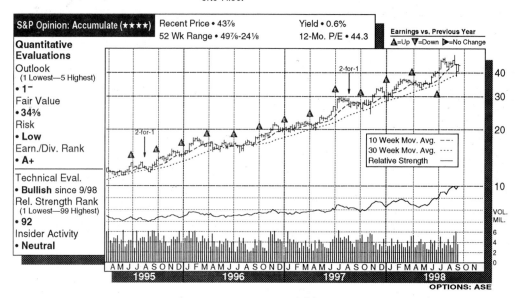

10 Week Mov. Avg. –––
30 Week Mov. Avg. ----
Relative Strength ——

OPTIONS: ASE

Overview - 01-JUL-98

Sales growth for the remainder of FY 98 (Aug.) is projected in the 13% to 15% range, fueled by strong gains for prescription sales; same-store prescription sales should continue to increase at a double-digit pace. We expect the company to continue to gain market share as it accelerates its store expansion program and enters several new markets. Competitive pricing and increased third-party programs will restrict gross margins, but expense ratios should improve, aided by cost containment and better inventory management. The company plans to reduce costs to 20% of sales by 2000. Annual EPS growth should approximate 18% to 20% for the next few years. Over the long term, continued productivity gains, superior pharmacy operations and new-store growth should sustain the company's strong industry position. WAG is conservatively financed, with no long term debt. Ample cash flow generation allows internal funds to be used for capital spending.

Valuation - 01-JUL-98

With strong sales gains, particularly in prescriptions, the share price has risen solidly since late 1994, and was recently trading near its all-time high. WAG is one of the premier drug store chains in a rapidly consolidating industry, with a relatively high ROE, a strong balance sheet, and one of the highest returns on sales in the industry. As a result, the shares trade at a premium to the P/E multiple accorded the shares of other drug store chains. WAG's prospects continue bright, as it expands its market share in existing markets, enters new markets, and reduces its cost structure. We continue to believe that the stock, recently trading at 34X estimated FY 99 EPS of $1.20, will provide above-average appreciation potential for long-term investors.

Key Stock Statistics

S&P EPS Est. 1998	1.00	Tang. Bk. Value/Share	5.44
P/E on S&P Est. 1998	43.9	Beta	0.88
S&P EPS Est. 1999	1.20	Shareholders	53,300
Dividend Rate/Share	0.25	Market cap. (B)	$ 21.8
Shs. outstg. (M)	497.5	Inst. holdings	48%
Avg. daily vol. (M)	0.967		

Value of $10,000 invested 5 years ago: $ 43,040

Fiscal Year Ending Aug. 31

	1998	1997	1996	1995	1994	1993
Revenues (Million $)						
1Q	3,485	3,054	2,693	2,406	2,118	1,915
2Q	4,094	3,603	3,179	2,807	2,499	2,258
3Q	3,887	3,403	2,990	2,617	2,336	2,085
4Q	—	3,303	2,918	2,565	2,283	2,037
Yr.	—	13,363	11,778	10,395	9,235	8,295
Earnings Per Share ($)						
1Q	0.18	0.15	0.13	0.11	0.09	0.08
2Q	**0.34**	0.30	0.26	0.23	0.20	0.17
3Q	**0.25**	0.21	0.18	0.16	0.14	0.13
4Q	E0.23	0.22	0.18	0.15	0.14	0.12
Yr.	E1.00	0.88	0.75	0.65	0.57	0.49

Next earnings report expected: late September

Dividend Data (Dividends have been paid since 1933.)

Amount ($)	Date Decl.	Ex-Div. Date	Stock of Record	Payment Date
0.063	Oct. 08	Nov. 13	Nov. 17	Dec. 12 '97
0.063	Jan. 14	Feb. 18	Feb. 20	Mar. 12 '98
0.063	Apr. 08	May. 20	May. 22	Jun. 12 '98
0.063	Jul. 08	Aug. 19	Aug. 21	Sep. 12 '98

A Division of The McGraw-Hill Companies

STANDARD
&POOR'S
STOCK REPORTS

Walgreen Co.

2408

12-SEP-98

Business Summary - 01-JUL-98

Walgreen Co. (WAG) certainly has the prescription for success. In 1997, Chicago-based WAG, the largest U.S. retail drug store chain in terms of revenues, reported its 23rd consecutive year of record sales and earnings. Sales in FY 97 (Aug.) increased 13.5%, to $13.4 billion, making the company the 16th largest U.S. retailer. Net earnings were $436 million, up 17.2%.

In 1909, founder Charles Rudolph Walgreen Sr. purchased one of the busiest drug stores on Chicago's South Side and transformed it by constructing an ice cream fountain featuring his own brand of ice cream. This ice cream fountain was the forerunner of Walgreen's famous soda fountain which became the main attraction of customers from the 1920s through the 1950s. People lined up to buy a product that WAG invented in the early 1920s - the milkshake.

Recently, WAG has resisted the merger fever that has taken over the drug store industry. The company has instead stressed internal growth strategies - large-scale infiltrations of new markets and relocations of units to freestanding stores; and "convenience," including 24-hour operations and drive-thru pharmacy service.

At August 31, 1997, WAG operated 2,358 drug stores in 34 states and Puerto Rico, with large concentrations of stores in Florida, Illinois and Texas. WAG, which is growing faster than any other drug store chain, opened a total of 251 new drug stores during FY 97, including

71 stores that were relocated. All of the company's new stores are freestanding buildings located at major intersections, as opposed to shopping centers and strip malls. More than half of the chain (over 1,300 stores) are now freestanding stores and nearly 1,000 offer drive-thru prescription service. WAG plans to open 280 new drug stores across the country in FY 98 (including units in the new markets of Kansas City and Detroit), and 360 in FY 99, with a goal of 3,000 stores by the year 2000.

Pharmacy sales represent the largest part of the company's sales. Already the leading dispenser of prescriptions in the country, WAG boosted pharmacy sales 18% during FY 97 (13% for comparable stores).

Recent technological advances include satellite linkage to all stores and facilities, point-of-sale scanning and implementation of the strategic inventory management system (SIMS), uniting all elements of the purchasing, distribution and sales cycle. This will reduce inventory, improve in-stock positions and provide quicker reaction to sales trends. The Intercom on-line pharmacy system links all stores with headquarters and one another.

Healthcare Plus, WAG's pharmacy mail-order subsidiary, offers sales, marketing and operational support for third-party retail and mail-order prescriptions through two facilities. WAG has also formed a pharmacy benefits manager, WHP Health Initiatives, targeting small to medium-size employers and HMOs.

Per Share Data ($)

(Year Ended Aug. 31)	1997	1996	1995	1994	1993	1992	1991	1990	1989	1988
Tangible Bk. Val.	4.80	4.16	3.65	3.20	2.80	2.50	2.19	1.93	1.67	1.45
Cash Flow	1.20	1.04	0.92	0.81	0.71	0.63	0.56	0.49	0.44	0.38
Earnings	0.88	0.75	0.65	0.57	0.49	0.45	0.40	0.35	0.31	0.26
Dividends	0.24	0.22	0.20	0.17	0.15	0.13	0.12	0.10	0.09	0.08
Payout Ratio	27%	29%	30%	30%	30%	29%	29%	28%	27%	29%
Prices - High	33⅝	21⅞	15¾	11½	11⅛	11⅛	9⅝	6⅝	6¼	4⅝
- Low	19¼	14⅝	10⅞	8½	8⅞	7⅝	6⅛	5	3¾	3⅜
P/E Ratio - High	38	29	24	20	23	25	24	19	20	18
- Low	22	19	17	15	18	17	16	14	12	13

Income Statement Analysis (Million $)

Revs.	13,363	11,778	10,395	9,235	8,295	7,475	6,733	6,047	5,380	4,884
Oper. Inc.	872	750	652	574	511	451	405	355	317	284
Depr.	164	147	132	118	105	92.1	84.3	70.4	63.8	59.4
Int. Exp.	2.0	2.0	2.0	3.1	6.8	16.2	19.1	19.3	18.9	20.0
Pretax Inc.	712	607	524	458	400	353	312	281	244	209
Eff. Tax Rate	39%	39%	39%	39%	39%	38%	38%	38%	37%	38%
Net Inc.	436	372	321	282	245	221	195	175	154	129

Balance Sheet & Other Fin. Data (Million $)

Cash	73.0	9.0	22.0	108	121	226	135	214	226	209
Curr. Assets	2,326	2,019	1,813	1,673	1,463	1,439	1,247	1,187	1,083	974
Total Assets	4,207	3,634	3,253	2,909	2,535	2,374	2,095	1,914	1,681	1,512
Curr. Liab.	1,439	1,182	1,078	1,051	884	889	684	632	545	489
LT Debt	Nil	Nil	Nil	11.0	17.0	31.0	136	163	168	191
Common Eqty.	2,373	3,634	1,793	1,574	1,379	1,233	1,081	947	823	713
Total Cap.	2,486	3,779	1,935	1,758	1,569	1,462	1,393	1,266	1,124	1,023
Cap. Exp.	485	365	310	290	185	145	202	192	121	114
Cash Flow	600	519	453	400	350	313	279	245	218	188
Curr. Ratio	1.6	1.7	1.7	1.6	1.7	1.6	1.8	1.9	2.0	2.0
% LT Debt of Cap.	Nil	Nil	Nil	0.6	1.1	2.1	9.8	12.9	14.9	18.7
% Net Inc.of Revs.	3.3	3.2	3.0	3.1	3.0	3.0	2.9	2.9	2.9	2.6
% Ret. on Assets	11.1	10.8	10.4	10.4	10.0	9.9	9.7	9.7	9.7	9.0
% Ret. on Equity	19.7	10.8	10.4	19.1	18.8	19.1	19.2	19.7	20.1	19.3

Data as orig. reptd.; bef. results of disc. opers. and/or spec. items. Per share data adj. for stk. divs. as of ex-div. date. Bold denotes diluted EPS (FASB 128). E-Estimated. NA-Not Available. NM-Not Meaningful. NR-Not Ranked.

Office—200 Wilmot Rd., Deerfield, IL 60015. **Tel**—(708) 940-2500. **Website**—http://www.walgreens.com **Chrmn & CEO**—C. R. Walgreen III. **Pres**—L. D. Jorndt. **SVP & CFO**—R. L. Polark. **Secy**—J. A. Oettinger. **Investor Contact**—John M. Palizza. **Dirs**—T. Dimitriou, J. J. Howard, C. D. Hunter, L. D. Jorndt, C. Reed, J. B. Schwemm, W. H. Springer, M. M. von Ferstel, C. R. Walgreen III. **Transfer Agent & Registrar**—Harris Trust & Savings Bank, Chicago. **Incorporated**—in Illinois in 1909. **Empl**—77,000. **S&P Analyst:** Maureen C. Carini

STANDARD &POOR'S
STOCK REPORTS

Warner-Lambert
2420
NYSE Symbol **WLA**

In S&P 500

12-SEP-98

Industry:
Health Care (Diversi-fied)

Summary: This company is a leading producer of prescription pharmaceuticals and OTC medications, with interests in gums and mints and other consumer products.

S&P Opinion: Buy (★★★★★)	Recent Price • 69⅞	Yield • 0.9%
	52 Wk Range • 85⅞-36⅛	12-Mo. P/E • 55.9

Quantitative Evaluations

Outlook
(1 Lowest—5 Highest)
• **1**

Fair Value
• **61**

Risk
• **Low**

Earn./Div. Rank
• **A-**

Technical Eval.
• **Bullish** since 9/98

Rel. Strength Rank
(1 Lowest—99 Highest)
• **85**

Insider Activity
• **Neutral**

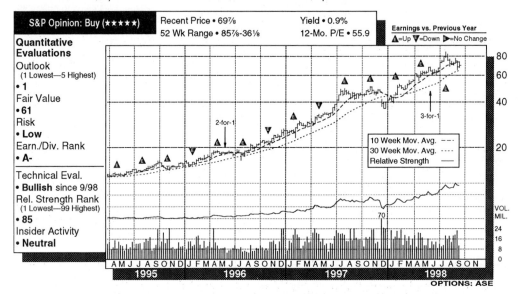

Earnings vs. Previous Year
▲=Up ▼=Down ▶=No Change

10 Week Mov. Avg. - - -
30 Week Mov. Avg. ·····
Relative Strength —

VOL. MIL.

OPTIONS: ASE

Overview - 14-AUG-98

Largely reflecting a huge gain in sales of WLA's new Lipitor cholesterol lowering drug, revenues should rise about 30% in 1998. Bolstered by further rollout over-seas and greater penetration of existing markets, Lipitor sales could reach $2.3 billion this year, up from $865 million in 1997. Well tolerated with minimal side effects, Lipitor continues to benefit from high efficacy in lower-ing both cholesterol and triglycerides. Sales of the new Rezulin treatment for Type II diabetes are also ex-pected to rise, although the gain will be tempered by a more restrictive label. Further gains are also seen for older drugs such as Accupril cardiovascular and Dilan-tin and Neurontin anticonvulsants. Modest growth is seen for the consumer products businesses. Margins should widen on a much improved product mix. Diluted EPS are projected to rise 42% to $1.48, with further progress to $1.90 seen for 1999.

Valuation - 14-AUG-98

The shares pulled back somewhat over the past few weeks, reflecting the general market slump and reports of several fatalities of patients using WLA's Rezulin dia-betes drug. The company responded by tightening phy-sician monitoring guidelines for the drug. WLA main-tains Rezulin is safe and effective when used as indicated. The FDA also agreed that Rezulin should re-main on the market and sales of the drug should con-tinue to grow in the years ahead. However, much more impressive growth is seen for WLA's new breakthrough Lipitor cholesterol-lowering drug, which could eventually achieve peak annual sales of over $5 billion. WLA's new drug pipeline includes promising new treatments for prostate cancer, Alzheimer's disease, infection, ar-thritis and other conditions. The shares continue to offer appeal for above-average total return.

Key Stock Statistics

S&P EPS Est. 1998	1.48	Tang. Bk. Value/Share	1.84
P/E on S&P Est. 1998	47.2	Beta	0.97
S&P EPS Est. 1999	1.90	Shareholders	40,000
Dividend Rate/Share	0.64	Market cap. (B)	$ 57.4
Shs. outstg. (M)	820.9	Inst. holdings	67%
Avg. daily vol. (M)	3.627		

Value of $10,000 invested 5 years ago: $ 68,938

Fiscal Year Ending Dec. 31

	1998	1997	1996	1995	1994	1993
Revenues (Million $)						
1Q	2,219	1,777	1,829	1,605	1,473	1,332
2Q	2,557	1,967	1,791	1,800	1,552	1,450
3Q	—	2,108	1,768	1,776	1,671	1,479
4Q	—	2,327	1,843	1,860	1,721	1,534
Yr.	—	8,180	7,231	7,040	6,417	5,794
Earnings Per Share ($)						
1Q	**0.33**	0.25	0.31	0.25	0.24	0.17
2Q	**0.40**	0.28	0.26	0.25	0.24	0.23
3Q	**E0.36**	0.24	0.19	0.26	0.21	0.19
4Q	**E0.39**	**0.28**	0.21	0.15	0.17	-0.24
Yr.	**E1.48**	**1.04**	**0.95**	0.91	0.86	0.35

Next earnings report expected: late October

Dividend Data (Dividends have been paid since 1926.)

Amount ($)	Date Decl.	Ex-Div. Date	Stock of Record	Payment Date
0.480	Jan. 27	Feb. 04	Feb. 06	Mar. 10 '98
0.160	Apr. 28	May. 06	May. 08	Jun. 10 '98
3-for-1	Nov. 25	May. 26	May. 08	May. 22 '98
0.160	Jun. 29	Aug. 05	Aug. 07	Sep. 10 '98

Business Summary - 14-AUG-98

Well known for popular consumer brands such as Listerine mouthwash, Halls cough drops and Trident chewing gum, Warner-Lambert ranks among the world's leading makers of prescription drugs, over-the-counter (OTC) medications, and gums and mints. The company traces its beginnings to a small botanical medicines firm formed in 1866 by H. C. Parke and G. S. Davis. Foreign business is significant, accounting for 53% of sales and 52% of operating profits in 1997. Segment contributions in 1997 were:

	Sales	Profits
Pharmaceuticals	44%	62%
Consumer health care	33%	28%
Gums & mints	23%	10%

The company's extensive and growing prescription pharmaceutical business is operated by the Parke-Davis division. Principal products include Lipitor cholesterol-lowering agent (sales of $865 million in 1997), Rezulin treatment for Type II diabetes ($420 million), Accupril antihypertensive ($378 million), Neurontin ($291 million) and Dilantin ($222 million) anticonvulsants, and Loestrin oral contraceptive ($126 million). Other ethical drugs include Vanquin anti-parasitic; Chloromycetin and other anti-infectives; Ponstan and other analgesics; Fempatch estrogen replacement therapy; Estrostep oral contraceptive; Procanbid antiarrhythmia agent; Cognex for Alzheimer's disease; and treatments for respiratory disorders, dermatological conditions, mental illness and other ailments. Empty hard-gelatin drug capsules are also sold under the Capsugel name.

A wide variety of popular OTC products is offered. These include Rolaids and Gelusil antacids; Sudafed and Sinutabs cold and sinus products; Benadryl and Actifed allergy treatments; Halls cough tablets; Replens vaginal moisturizer; Myadec vitamins; Listerine mouthwashes; and Efferdent denture adhesives. WLA's OTC business affords the opportunity to extend prescription drug franchises after patent expirations. Other consumer lines include Schick and Wilkinson Sword razors and blades; and Tetra home aquarium products.

The company plans to complete the dissolution of its OTC joint venture with Glaxo-Wellcome by the end of 1998. Following the split, WLA will retain exclusive rights to the OTC Zantac heartburn medication in the U.S. and Canada, while Glaxo will have rights to Zantac in all other world markets, as well rights to Zovirax cold sore cream and Beconase hayfever medicine.

Gums and mints include Dentyne, Trident, Freshen-Up, Bubblicious, Mondo, Chiclets, Cinn-A-Burst and Mint-A-Burst gums; and Clorets, Dynamints and Certs mints. The company also markets Fruitwaves hard candies, Saila and Koldt'tm specialty candies, and a line of throat drops sold under the Celestial Seasonings Soothers name.

Per Share Data ($)

(Year Ended Dec. 31)	1997	1996	1995	1994	1993	1992	1991	1990	1989	1988
Tangible Bk. Val.	4.13	1.38	2.27	1.78	1.34	1.69	1.25	1.54	1.22	1.04
Cash Flow	4.09	1.25	1.16	1.09	0.56	0.99	0.34	0.75	0.64	0.54
Earnings	1.04	0.97	0.91	0.86	0.35	0.80	0.17	0.60	0.51	0.42
Dividends	0.51	0.46	0.43	0.41	0.38	0.34	0.29	0.25	0.21	0.18
Payout Ratio	49%	48%	47%	47%	108%	43%	168%	42%	42%	43%
Prices - High	50$^7/_8$	26$^5/_8$	16$^3/_8$	14$^1/_2$	12$^3/_4$	13$^1/_4$	13$^3/_4$	11$^3/_4$	9$^7/_8$	6$^5/_8$
- Low	23$^1/_8$	14$^7/_8$	12$^1/_4$	10	10	9$^3/_4$	10$^1/_4$	8$^1/_4$	6$^1/_4$	5
P/E Ratio - High	49	28	18	17	36	17	78	19	19	16
- Low	22	15	13	12	28	12	59	14	12	12

Income Statement Analysis (Million $)

	1997	1996	1995	1994	1993	1992	1991	1990	1989	1988
Revs.	8,180	7,231	7,040	6,417	5,794	5,598	5,059	4,687	4,196	3,908
Oper. Inc.	1,700	1,499	1,270	1,192	985	989	852	782	676	641
Depr.	276	231	202	181	170	156	136	120	105	96.0
Int. Exp.	167	156	133	103	72.8	88.9	67.6	73.9	61.9	74.2
Pretax Inc.	1,234	1,177	1,149	1,005	319	858	222	681	592	538
Eff. Tax Rate	29%	27%	24%	22%	11%	25%	36%	29%	30%	37%
Net Inc.	870	787	740	694	285	644	141	485	413	340

Balance Sheet & Other Fin. Data (Million $)

	1997	1996	1995	1994	1993	1992	1991	1990	1989	1988
Cash	757	492	563	465	441	718	536	306	253	177
Curr. Assets	3,297	2,785	2,778	2,515	2,219	2,176	1,844	1,559	1,367	1,265
Total Assets	8,031	7,197	6,101	5,533	4,828	4,077	3,602	3,261	2,860	2,703
Curr. Liab.	2,589	2,137	2,425	2,353	2,016	1,333	1,250	1,101	1,031	1,025
LT Debt	1,831	1,721	635	535	546	565	448	307	303	318
Common Eqty.	2,836	2,581	2,246	1,816	1,390	1,529	1,171	1,402	1,130	999
Total Cap.	4,839	4,446	3,064	2,461	2,005	2,145	1,656	1,890	1,596	1,452
Cap. Exp.	495	389	387	406	347	334	326	240	219	190
Cash Flow	1,146	1,018	942	875	455	799	276	605	518	437
Curr. Ratio	1.3	1.3	1.1	1.1	1.1	1.6	1.5	1.4	1.3	1.2
% LT Debt of Cap.	37.8	38.7	20.8	21.7	27.5	26.3	27.0	16.2	19.0	21.9
% Net Inc.of Revs.	10.6	10.9	10.6	10.8	4.9	11.5	2.8	10.3	9.8	8.7
% Ret. on Assets	11.4	11.9	12.9	13.4	6.4	16.7	4.1	15.9	14.9	13.2
% Ret. on Equity	32.1	32.6	36.5	43.2	19.6	47.6	10.9	38.4	38.9	36.5

Data as orig. reptd.; bef. results of disc. opers. and/or spec. items. Per share data adj. for stk. divs. as of ex-div. date. Bold denotes diluted EPS (FASB 128). E-Estimated. NA-Not Available. NM-Not Meaningful. NR-Not Ranked.

Office—201 Tabor Rd., Morris Plains, NJ 07950. **Tel**—(973) 540-2000. **Website**—http://www.warner-lambert.com **Chrmn & CEO**—M. R. Goodes. **Pres & COO**—L. J. R. de Vink. **VP & CFO**—E. J. Larini. **Secy**—R. G. Paltiel. **Investor Contact**—George Shields. **Dirs**—R. N. Burt, D. C. Clark, L. J. R. de Vink, J. A. Georges, M. R. Goodes, W. H. Gray III, W. R. Howell, L. D. Leffall, Jr., G. A. Lorch, A. Mandl, L. G. Rawl, M. I. Sovern. **Transfer Agent & Registrar**—First Chicago Trust Co. of New York, NYC. **Incorporated**—in Delaware in 1920. **Empl**— 40,000. **S&P Analyst:** H.B. Saftlas

STANDARD &POOR'S
STOCK REPORTS

Washington Mutual
Nasdaq Symbol **WAMU**

5590M

In S&P 500

12-SEP-98

Industry:
Savings & Loan Companies

Summary: In March 1998, Washington Mutual agreed to buy H. F. Ahmanson, forming the seventh largest U.S. banking organization.

| S&P Opinion: Hold (★★★) | Recent Price • 33 | Yield • 2.5% |
| | 52 Wk Range • 51⅝-30 | 12-Mo. P/E • 20.3 |

Quantitative Evaluations

Outlook
(1 Lowest—5 Highest)
• **1⁻**

Fair Value
• **29⅝**

Risk
• **Average**

Earn./Div. Rank
• **B+**

Technical Eval.
• **Bearish** since 7/98

Rel. Strength Rank
(1 Lowest—99 Highest)
• **49**

Insider Activity
• **Favorable**

Earnings vs. Previous Year
▲=Up ▼=Down ▶=No Change

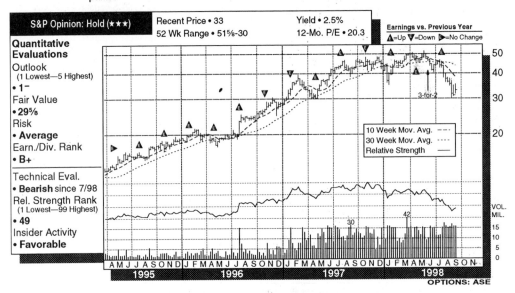

10 Week Mov. Avg. - - -
30 Week Mov. Avg. ·······
Relative Strength ——

OPTIONS: ASE

Overview - 24-JUL-98

Profits in 1999 are expected to improve from the level of 1998, which included several small transaction-related charges. Loan growth is the major factor contributing to the anticipated gain. In the first half of 1998, the company expanded its loan portfolio nearly 10% on an annualized basis, aided by a strong housing market in California and an emphasis on high yielding consumer loans. With California's economy strengthening even further, the growth should continue. The spread between loan rates and funding costs may narrow slightly, reflecting the tight yield curve, partially offset by growth in the checking account base. A flat to lower credit provision is anticipated, as reserves cover over 100% of non-accrual loans. Additional gains in non-interest income, mainly depositor fees, are likely with continued build-up in transaction accounts. Flat costs are expected.

Valuation - 24-JUL-98

The shares are expected to perform in line with market averages for the foreseeable future. Valuation considerations are the main reason for our hold opinion. The stock was recently trading at a price to book value multiple well in excess of the thrift industry average. The stock's P/E ratio on projected 1999 EPS is in line with peer averages. The company's risk profile is also an issue. Over the past year, WAMU acquired two large thrifts, Great Western and American Savings, and it plans to complete the purchase of another large thrift, H. F. Ahmanson (which acquired Coast Savings), later this year. All told, the purchases will triple the company's size. It should be noted that Washington Mutual is a good performer, typically posting return on assets and return on shareholders' equity figures much higher than the industry average.

Key Stock Statistics

S&P EPS Est. 1998	2.90	Tang. Bk. Value/Share	13.58
P/E on S&P Est. 1998	11.4	Beta	1.26
S&P EPS Est. 1999	3.55	Shareholders	16,000
Dividend Rate/Share	0.83	Market cap. (B)	$ 12.8
Shs. outstg. (M)	387.2	Inst. holdings	77%
Avg. daily vol. (M)	5.244		

Value of $10,000 invested 5 years ago: $ 25,484

Fiscal Year Ending Dec. 31

	1998	1997	1996	1995	1994	1993
Revenues (Million $)						
1Q	2,020	1,804	821.6	380.0	304.5	237.8
2Q	2,151	1,858	834.9	402.1	315.5	320.0
3Q	—	1,840	865.9	415.7	334.2	304.6
4Q	—	2,023	886.1	427.7	361.4	317.4
Yr.	—	7,524	3,409	1,625	1,316	1,180
Earnings Per Share ($)						
1Q	**0.68**	**0.47**	0.50	0.41	0.41	0.37
2Q	**0.69**	**0.50**	0.56	0.43	0.41	0.49
3Q	**E0.74**	-0.36	0.05	0.45	0.43	0.48
4Q	**E0.79**	0.63	-0.54	0.49	0.43	0.49
Yr.	**E2.90**	1.24	0.57	1.79	1.69	1.83

Next earnings report expected: NA

Dividend Data (Dividends have been paid since 1986.)

Amount ($)	Date Decl.	Ex-Div. Date	Stock of Record	Payment Date
0.290	Jan. 20	Jan. 28	Jan. 30	Feb. 13 '98
0.300	Apr. 21	Apr. 28	Apr. 30	May. 15 '98
3-for-2	Apr. 21	Jun. 02	May. 18	Jun. 01 '98
0.207	Jul. 21	Jul. 29	Jul. 31	Aug. 14 '98

A Division of The **McGraw·Hill** *Companies*

Business Summary - 24-JUL-98

Washington Mutual, Inc. is the largest U.S. savings institution, and the 11th largest banking organization, following its July 1997 acquisition of Great Western Financial, a California-based thrift with $43 billion in assets. Assuming completion of the H. F. Ahmanson (assets of $54.5 billion) merger for some $9.9 billion in stock, it will become the seventh largest U.S. banking company. At December 31, 1997, the company had assets of $96.7 billion and operated over 1,900 offices throughout the U.S. Loans outstanding (not giving effect to the Ahmanson merger) totaled $67.8 billion and $61.8 billion at the end of 1997 and 1996, respectively, and were divided:

	1997	1996
Residential real estate	79%	79%
Commercial real estate	10%	10%
Mfd. housing, second mortgage, other consumer	6%	6%
Residential construction & other	5%	5%

Residential real estate loans basically consist of mortgages extended to homebuyers for the purchase of a 1-4 family house. Both 30-year and 15-year fixed rate mortgages are offered, as are a variety of adjustable rate products. Mortgages can also be issued to refinance an existing debt. Commercial real estate loans are mortgages extended to individuals or corporations to buy or refinance properties such as apartments, office buildings, warehouses, etc. Second mortgages are loans made primarily for debt consolidation purposes to individuals with substantial equity in their home. In the event of a default, a second mortgage has a lower claim than a first mortgage. Construction loans, which tend to be risky, are made to developers.

Primarily because of the relative health of housing markets in the Pacific Northwest over the past several years, as well as the company's historical focus on low-risk residential loans, asset quality has been excellent. At year-end 1997, loans 90 days or more delinquent, restructured loans and foreclosed real estate amounted to only $83 per $10,000 of loans.

Services also include mutual fund management, securities brokerage, annuities and insurance. Aristar, Inc. makes direct consumer installment loans and purchases retail installment contracts.

Savings products offered include checking accounts, certificates of deposit of various maturities and regular savings accounts. The company is attempting to build up its checking account base as a means to lower its cost of funds and generate fee income. In addition, checking accounts, which are viewed as constituting the customers' primary relationship to the bank, can be utilized to cross sell other products.

Per Share Data ($)

(Year Ended Dec. 31)	1997	1996	1995	1994	1993	1992	1991	1990	1989	1988
Tangible Bk. Val.	13.64	11.97	14.40	11.97	10.79	8.03	7.93	6.96	7.52	6.12
Earnings	1.24	0.57	1.79	1.69	1.83	1.45	1.12	-0.08	0.36	0.73
Dividends	0.71	0.60	0.51	0.47	0.33	0.22	0.16	0.12	0.12	0.12
Payout Ratio	57%	106%	29%	28%	18%	15%	14%	NM	33%	16%
Prices - High	48³/₈	30⁵/₈	19⁵/₈	16⁵/₈	18⁷/₈	15	10⁵/₈	5³/₄	8	5⁷/₈
- Low	28¹/₈	17³/₈	11¹/₈	10¹/₂	12	7⁷/₈	3¹/₂	2⁵/₈	4¹/₈	3⁷/₈
P/E Ratio - High	39	54	11	10	10	10	10	NM	22	8
- Low	23	31	6	6	7	5	3	NM	11	5

Income Statement Analysis (Million $)

	1997	1996	1995	1994	1993	1992	1991	1990	1989	1988
Net Int. Inc.	2,656	1,191	578	571	529	295	205	168	136	131
Loan Loss Prov.	207	202	10.0	20.0	35.0	13.5	20.5	61.4	3.4	10.9
Non Int. Inc.	751	259	107	108	144	88.5	92.9	59.8	36.9	65.4
Non Int. Exp.	2,300	1,025	382	384	369	217	174	150	142	130
Pretax Inc.	901	223	292	275	269	153	103	16.0	27.0	55.0
Eff. Tax Rate	47%	43%	35%	37%	35%	35%	35%	94%	28%	32%
Net Inc.	482	114	191	172	175	100	67.5	0.9	19.8	37.3
% Net Int. Marg.	3.03	2.89	3.05	3.60	4.12	3.97	3.17	2.61	NA	NA

Balance Sheet & Other Fin. Data (Million $)

	1997	1996	1995	1994	1993	1992	1991	1990	1989	1988
Total Assets	96,981	44,552	21,633	18,458	15,827	8,980	7,118	6,922	6,594	6,364
Loans	67,140	30,467	12,536	12,555	13,868	8,065	6,302	6,148	5,825	5,272
Deposits	50,986	24,080	10,597	9,778	9,351	5,383	4,802	4,501	3,967	3,771
Capitalization:										
Debt	23,791	7,918	3,936	3,817	2,164	964	498	797	1,138	1,687
Equity	5,191	2,398	1,592	1,305	1,190	877	558	414	423	350
Total	29,100	10,316	5,527	5,122	3,359	1,841	1,056	1,211	1,563	2,037
% Ret. on Assets	0.5	0.3	1.0	1.0	1.4	1.2	1.0	NM	0.3	0.6
% Ret. on Equity	9.3	3.9	11.9	13.7	14.8	13.9	13.1	NM	4.8	11.2
% Loan Loss Resv.	1.0	1.2	1.1	1.0	0.8	0.6	0.8	0.8	0.2	0.3
% Risk Based Capital	NA	NA	11.5	14.9	10.6	16.5	14.2	NA	NA	NA
Price Times Book Value:										
Hi	3.9	2.6	1.4	1.4	1.8	1.9	1.3	0.8	1.1	1.0
Low	2.3	1.5	0.8	0.9	1.1	1.0	0.4	0.4	0.5	0.6

Data as orig. reptd.; bef. results of disc. opers. and/or spec. items. Per share data adj. for stk. divs. as of ex-div. date. Bold denotes diluted EPS (FASB 128). E-Estimated. NA-Not Available. NM-Not Meaningful. NR-Not Ranked.

Office—1201 Third Ave., Seattle, WA 98101. **Tel**—(206) 461-2000.**Chrmn, Pres & CEO**—K. K. Killinger. **Contr & Investor Contact**—Douglas G. Wisdorf (206-461-3805). **Secy**—W. L. Lynch. **Dirs**—D. P. Beighle, D. Bonderman, J. T. Crandall, R. H. Eigsti, J. W. Ellis, D. J. Evans, A. V. Farrell, S. E. Frank, W. P. Gerberding, E. Hernandez, Jr., K. K. Killinger, S. B. McKinney, M. K. Murphy, W. G. Reed Jr., J. H. Stever, W. B. Wood, Jr. **Transfer Agent & Registrar**—ChaseMellon Shareholder Services, South Hackensack, NJ. **Incorporated**—in Washington in 1983. **Empl**— 19,880. **S&P Analyst:** Paul L. Huberman, CFA

Waste Management, Inc.   2268R

NYSE Symbol **WMI**
In S&P 500

12-SEP-98 **Industry:** Waste Management

Summary: This company is the third largest U.S. trash hauling/disposal concern.

S&P Opinion: Hold (★★★)	Recent Price • 47⅜	Yield • Nil
	52 Wk Range • 58⅛-32⅝	12-Mo. P/E • 29.3

Earnings vs. Previous Year
▲=Up ▼=Down ▶=No Change

Quantitative Evaluations

Outlook (1 Lowest—5 Highest)
• **4⁻**

Fair Value
• **61⅛**

Risk
• **Average**

Earn./Div. Rank
• **B**

Technical Eval.
• **NA**

Rel. Strength Rank (1 Lowest—99 Highest)
• **78**

Insider Activity
• **Neutral**

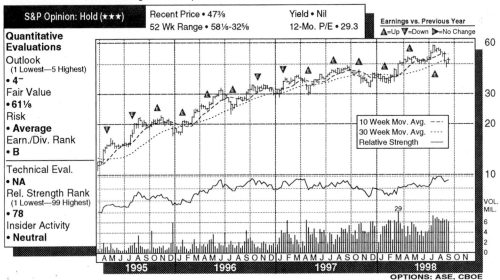

10 Week Mov. Avg. ---
30 Week Mov. Avg. ·····
Relative Strength —

OPTIONS: ASE, CBOE

Overview - 20-AUG-98

Waste Management Inc. was formed through the July 1998 merger of industry giants USA Waste Services (UW) and the old Waste Management (WMX). The transaction was effectively a takeover of WMX by UW's management team, led by CEO John Drury. The new WMI believes that it will be the low cost provider, and expects to realize $800 million in annual cost savings from the combination. Corporate G&A reductions should account for about $224 million, including the elimination of WMX's corporate headquarters staff. The company also intends to save approximately $175 million through an improved internalization rate of 65% to 70%, up from a current rate of about 56%. The remaining $400 million of cost reductions should result from field synergies, including route reductions and the elimination of duplicate facilities.

Valuation - 20-AUG-98

We are maintaining our neutral rating on the shares. Through its aggressive acquisition strategy, WMI has achieved critical mass in the rapidly consolidating municipal solid waste industry. However, we believe that this trend will ultimately lead to increased competition for customers and 'tuck-in' acquisitions. With an established infrastructure in a given market, the incremental cost of adding new routes is minimal. As in any commodity business, customers will ultimately choose the lowest cost hauler. Cut-throat price competition could result, as the few surviving players attempt to maximize their infrastructures. Similar reasoning also leads us to believe that 'tuck-in' acquisitions will become increasingly expensive, leading to a lower return on investment. We expect WMI to achieve its merger-related cost savings goals, but believe that EPS growth will slow in future years, as acquisitions account for a shrinking percentage of revenues. We see the shares performing only in line with the overall market.

Key Stock Statistics

S&P EPS Est. 1998	2.15	Tang. Bk. Value/Share	5.16
P/E on S&P Est. 1998	22.1	Beta	1.15
S&P EPS Est. 1999	3.00	Shareholders	3,700
Dividend Rate/Share	Nil	Market cap. (B)	$ 27.1
Shs. outstg. (M)	571.8	Inst. holdings	31%
Avg. daily vol. (M)	2.169		

Value of $10,000 invested 5 years ago: $ 32,715

Fiscal Year Ending Dec. 31

	1998	1997	1996	1995	1994	1993
Revenues (Million $)						
1Q	769.4	364.9	282.5	101.2	38.21	15.76
2Q	882.0	535.2	327.7	111.2	44.87	18.34
3Q	—	761.8	352.8	120.0	47.13	19.55
4Q	—	735.3	350.4	124.7	59.50	24.49
Yr.	—	2,614	1,313	457.1	176.2	78.14
Earnings Per Share ($)						
1Q	0.52	0.29	0.21	Nil	0.11	0.19
2Q	0.53	0.40	-0.01	-0.54	0.04	0.20
3Q	—	0.09	-0.27	0.35	0.21	0.20
4Q	—	0.45	0.31	0.60	0.27	0.21
Yr.	—	1.26	0.24	0.55	0.61	0.80

Next earnings report expected: mid November

Dividend Data

No cash dividends have been paid.

A Division of The McGraw-Hill Companies

Business Summary - 20-AUG-98

Waste Management Inc. (WMI) was formed through the July, 1998 merger of industry giants USA Waste Services (UW) and the old Waste Management (WMX). This transaction was effectively a takeover of WMX by UW's management team, led by CEO John Drury. Over the past several years, UW embarked on an aggressive acquisition strategy, capitalizing on the consolidation of the fragmented municipal solid waste (MSW) industry. In the past six years, UW's MSW revenues grew at a compound annual rate of 130%, to $2.6 billion in 1997. Today, WMI's acquisition strategy is focused on non-hazardous MSW collection and landfill operations in North America; the company is not pursuing recycling, environmental cleanup or overseas operations.

UW generated among the highest profit margins in the industry. However, the cost has been high. From 1994 through 1997, UW posted $440 million in cumulative merger and restructuring charges. Some important profitability statistics for UW recent years were (restated results for the UW-WMX merger are not yet available):

	1997	1996	1995
Gross profit margins	49%	46%	44%
Operating profit margins	26%	22%	18%
Free cash flow per share	$1.36	-$0.54	-$0.72

In August 1998, WMI announced that it would acquire Eastern Environmental Services in a $1.3 billion stock swap. The company views this deal as a large 'tuck-in' acquisition, given the strategic geographic overlap of Eastern's operations. Annual cost savings are expected to be $75 million, resulting from corporate eliminations and field synergies.

WMI operates in an otherwise slow-growing, highly competitive and capital-intensive billion municipal solid waste (MSW) industry. In recent years, the MSW industry has been consolidating, primarily due to increasingly stringent state and federal regulations. These costly regulations have forced many small waste companies to go out of business, or to sell their operations to large, financially stronger, publicly traded MSW companies such as WMI. Despite significant industry consolidation, 66% of the municipal solid waste industry consists equally of municipally managed and small, privately owed MSW operations.

The company primarily competes with Browning Ferris, Republic Services (the July 1998 MSW spinoff from automotive concern Republic Industries), many mid-sized and small MSW concerns, and many municipalities that handle their own waste operations. Municipalities are often able to offer lower direct charges, because municipal MSW operations are often subsidized by tax revenues and tax-exempt bonds.

Per Share Data ($) (Year Ended Dec. 31)	1997	1996	1995	1994	1993	1992	1991	1990	1989	1988
Tangible Bk. Val.	4.51	4.57	4.32	0.90	4.04	3.79	2.59	2.07	1.84	1.86
Cash Flow	2.47	1.33	1.57	1.47	1.48	1.07	0.49	0.32	0.18	0.15
Earnings	1.26	0.24	0.55	0.61	0.80	0.65	0.32	0.08	0.03	0.07
Dividends	Nil	Nil	Nil	Nil	Nil	Nil	Nil	Nil	Nil	Nil
Payout Ratio	Nil	Nil	Nil	Nil	Nil	Nil	Nil	Nil	Nil	Nil
Prices - High	$44\frac{1}{8}$	$34\frac{1}{4}$	$22\frac{1}{2}$	$15\frac{1}{8}$	15	$18\frac{1}{2}$	18	6	$3\frac{1}{8}$	$5\frac{1}{8}$
- Low	$28\frac{5}{8}$	$17\frac{1}{4}$	10	$10\frac{3}{8}$	$9\frac{3}{4}$	$10\frac{1}{2}$	$5\frac{3}{8}$	$1\frac{3}{8}$	$1\frac{1}{2}$	$2\frac{1}{4}$
P/E Ratio - High	35	NM	41	25	19	28	56	75	NM	73
- Low	23	NM	18	17	12	16	17	17	NM	32

Income Statement Analysis (Million $)	1997	1996	1995	1994	1993	1992	1991	1990	1989	1988
Revs.	2,614	1,313	457	176	78.1	52.2	18.3	3.7	2.6	1.9
Oper. Inc.	983	448	141	51.7	27.9	19.1	7.2	1.0	0.3	0.4
Depr.	303	153	56.4	18.8	8.2	4.8	1.6	0.7	0.4	0.2
Int. Exp.	104	45.5	41.3	11.4	6.0	3.5	1.9	0.2	0.2	0.1
Pretax Inc.	463	78.1	18.9	21.6	15.0	11.8	4.4	0.2	0.1	0.3
Eff. Tax Rate	41%	58%	60%	36%	36%	35%	32%	Nil	Nil	36%
Net Inc.	273	32.9	30.3	13.8	9.6	7.3	3.0	0.2	0.1	0.2

Balance Sheet & Other Fin. Data (Million $)	1997	1996	1995	1994	1993	1992	1991	1990	1989	1988
Cash	51.2	23.5	13.2	6.6	3.2	11.7	3.9	2.3	1.2	3.0
Curr. Assets	655	340	120	37.0	15.1	20.3	7.5	2.9	1.5	3.3
Total Assets	6,623	2,831	908	323	166	110	60.0	14.0	7.0	7.0
Curr. Liab.	569	320	105	28.4	14.9	10.9	4.7	1.4	0.4	0.6
LT Debt	2,724	1,158	335	154	93.6	49.3	22.8	2.6	0.7	0.7
Common Eqty.	2,629	1,155	403	108	46.7	39.9	25.6	9.9	5.3	5.2
Total Cap.	5,674	2,322	738	278	146	96.4	54.0	12.7	6.3	6.2
Cap. Exp.	436	348	84.6	40.9	49.1	29.6	23.5	3.4	2.3	1.9
Cash Flow	577	186	86.6	32.1	17.8	12.2	4.6	0.9	0.5	0.4
Curr. Ratio	1.2	1.1	1.1	1.3	1.0	1.9	1.6	2.1	3.3	5.1
% LT Debt of Cap.	48.0	49.9	45.4	55.4	64.3	51.1	42.3	20.2	11.6	11.9
% Net Inc.of Revs.	10.5	2.5	6.7	7.8	12.3	14.1	16.2	6.2	3.5	8.8
% Ret. on Assets	4.1	1.4	3.6	4.3	6.7	8.5	6.3	1.9	1.3	3.2
% Ret. on Equity	10.4	3.2	10.7	13.3	21.2	21.9	11.8	2.6	1.7	5.3

Data as orig. reptd.; bef. results of disc. opers. and/or spec. items. Per share data adj. for stk. divs. as of ex-div. date. Bold denotes diluted EPS (FASB 128). E-Estimated. NA-Not Available. NM-Not Meaningful. NR-Not Ranked. EPS estimates exclude special charges.

Office—1001 Fannin St., Suite 4000, Houston, TX 77002. **Tel**—(713) 512-6200. **Chrmn & CEO**—J. E. Drury. **Pres & COO**—R. R. Proto. **EVP & CFO**—E. E. Defrates. **Investor Contact**—Lew Nevins. **Dirs**—G. L. Ball, J. E. Drury, P. J. Gibbons, R. J. Heckmann, W. E Moffett, D. F. Moorehead, Jr., R. R. Proto, A. W. Rangos, J. G. Rangos, Sr., K. Shirvanian, D. Sutherland-Yoest. **Transfer Agent & Registrar**—First National Bank of Boston. **Incorporated**—in Oklahoma in 1987, reincorporated in Delaware in 1995. **Empl**— 9,800. **S&P Analyst:** Eric J. Hunter

Wells Fargo

2442

NYSE Symbol **WFC**

In S&P 500

12-SEP-98

Industry: Banks (Major Regional)

Summary: This California-based bank holding company recently agreed to merge with Minneapolis-based Norwest Corp.

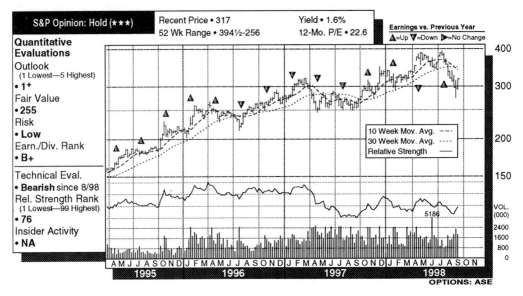

S&P Opinion: Hold (★★★)	Recent Price • 317	Yield • 1.6%
	52 Wk Range • 394½-256	12-Mo. P/E • 22.6

Earnings vs. Previous Year
△=Up ▽=Down ▷=No Change

Quantitative Evaluations

Outlook
(1 Lowest—5 Highest)
• **1+**

Fair Value
• **255**

Risk
• **Low**

Earn./Div. Rank
• **B+**

Technical Eval.
• **Bearish** since 8/98

Rel. Strength Rank
(1 Lowest—99 Highest)
• **76**

Insider Activity
• **NA**

10 Week Mov. Avg. - - -
30 Week Mov. Avg. · · · · ·
Relative Strength ——

OPTIONS: ASE

Overview - 11-AUG-98

Net interest income is expected to be relatively flat in 1998, following declines in recent periods, as a runoff in both the loan and deposit portfolios following the First Interstate merger appears to have abated. Loss provisions have caught up with the level of charge-offs and should now remain stable. Overall revenue growth continues to improve, with gains particularly in the small business, middle market lending and capital markets segments. Margins have and should continue to turn upward, reflecting an improved outlook for deposit balances. Looking longer term, the pending merger with Norwest Corp. will provide opportunities for expense savings in the areas of systems, operations and overhead functions, while the absence of branch closures given the lack of geographic overlap should minimize customer attrition.

Valuation - 11-AUG-98

We maintained our hold recommendation following the proposed merger with Norwest Corp. The valuation, despite the relatively low cost savings assumptions due to lack of geographic overlap, was not really an issue in our assessment of the transaction. After enduring several missteps related to its First Interstate integration, Wells is likely to maintain a strong focus on how to keep customers through the Norwest merger process. And we suspect management is being conservative this time around in assumptions for cost savings. Still, the differing business models of the two companies, with Norwest focused on its thriving retail delivery platform and Wells on its electronic distribution, could pose integration issues. For now, we would hold the shares pending signs that the merger will provide tangible benefits to shareholders beyond initial cost savings projections.

Key Stock Statistics

S&P EPS Est. 1998	15.25	Tang. Bk. Value/Share	68.60
P/E on S&P Est. 1998	20.8	Beta	0.85
S&P EPS Est. 1999	17.40	Shareholders	42,300
Dividend Rate/Share	5.20	Market cap. (B)	$ 27.0
Shs. outstg. (M)	85.1	Inst. holdings	59%
Avg. daily vol. (M)	0.391		

Value of $10,000 invested 5 years ago: $ 46,427

Fiscal Year Ending Dec. 31

	1998	1997	1996	1995	1994	1993
Revenues (Million $)						
1Q	2,410	2,413	1,360	1,267	1,195	1,229
2Q	2,411	2,395	2,497	1,341	1,231	1,211
3Q	—	2,384	2,490	1,358	1,261	1,189
4Q	—	2,416	2,376	1,444	1,278	1,225
Yr.	—	9,608	8,723	5,409	4,965	4,854
Earnings Per Share ($)						
1Q	**3.58**	3.62	5.39	4.41	3.41	1.72
2Q	**3.87**	2.49	3.61	4.51	3.57	2.46
3Q	—	3.26	3.23	5.23	3.86	2.74
4Q	—	**3.36**	1.12	6.29	3.96	3.18
Yr.	**E15.25**	**12.64**	**12.05**	20.37	14.78	10.10

Next earnings report expected: late October

Dividend Data (Dividends have been paid since 1936.)

Amount ($)	Date Decl.	Ex-Div. Date	Stock of Record	Payment Date
1.300	Oct. 21	Oct. 29	Oct. 31	Nov. 20 '97
1.300	Jan. 20	Jan. 28	Jan. 30	Feb. 20 '98
1.300	Apr. 21	Apr. 28	Apr. 30	May. 20 '98
1.300	Jul. 21	Jul. 29	Jul. 31	Aug. 20 '98

A Division of The **McGraw·Hill** *Companies*

Business Summary - 11-AUG-98

Wells Fargo & Co., fresh from completing the integration of its April 1996 acquisition of First Interstate Bancorp, agreed in June 1998 to merge with Minneapolis-based Norwest Corp. Billed as the creation of the Western Hemisphere's most extensive and diversified financial services network, the combined company would have an estimated 20 million customers, nearly 5,800 financial services stores in all 50 states, Canada, the Caribbean, Latin America and elsewhere internationally.

Current Wells operations are largely divided into six principal business lines. The retail distribution group sells and services retail financial products for consumers and small businesses. The business banking group provides credit products and financial services to small businesses and their owners. The investment group sells and manages savings and investment products, and investment management and fiduciary and brokerage services. The real estate group supports the commercial real estate market with construction loans, land acquisition and development loans, and secured and unsecured lines of credit. The wholesale products group serves larger businesses with products and services such as commercial loans, letters of credit, international trade facilities, foreign exchange services and cash management products. The consumer lending division offers credit cards, transportation loans and leases, home equity lines and instalment loans.

In 1997, average earning assets, from which interest income is derived, amounted to $77.3 billion and consisted mainly of loans and leases (84%) and investment securities (15%). Average sources of funds, on which the bank generally pays interest, included interest-bearing deposits (50%), noninterest-bearing deposits (18%), short-term borrowings (3%), long-term debt (6%), shareholders' equity (13%) and other (10%).

At year-end 1997, non-accrual and restructured loans were $537 million (0.8% of loans), down from $724 million (1.1%) a year earlier. The allowance for loan losses, which is set aside for possible loan defaults, was $1.83 billion (2.78% of loans), versus $2.02 billion (3.00%) a year earlier. Net chargeoffs, or the amount of loans actually written off as uncollectible, were $805 million (1.25% of average loans) in 1997, versus $640 million (1.05%) in 1996.

The merger with Norwest Corp. (NYSE; NOB) calls for each WFC share to be exchanged for 10 NOB common shares. Norwest owns banks in 16 primarily upper Midwest states. The deal is expected to be completed in the fourth quarter of 1998.

Per Share Data ($)

(Year Ended Dec. 31)	1997	1996	1995	1994	1993	1992	1991	1990	1989	1988
Tangible Bk. Val.	64.80	67.67	67.75	51.08	50.63	40.70	33.61	37.20	41.18	34.27
Earnings	12.64	12.21	20.37	14.78	10.10	4.44	0.04	13.39	11.02	9.20
Dividends	5.20	5.20	4.60	4.00	2.25	2.00	3.50	3.90	3.30	2.45
Payout Ratio	41%	43%	23%	27%	22%	45%	NM	29%	30%	27%
Prices - High	350	292½	230¼	160¾	133½	86⅜	98¾	86	87½	71¼
- Low	245	202¾	141	127⅛	74¾	56⅜	48	41¼	59	43⅛
P/E Ratio - High	28	24	11	11	13	19	NM	6	8	8
- Low	19	17	7	9	7	13	NM	3	5	5

Income Statement Analysis (Million $)

	1997	1996	1995	1994	1993	1992	1991	1990	1989	1988
Net Int. Inc.	4,614	4,521	2,654	2,610	2,657	2,691	2,520	2,314	2,159	1,976
Tax Equiv. Adj.	13.0	11.0	5.0	NA	3.0	5.0	20.0	23.0	22.0	36.0
Non Int. Inc.	2,684	2,190	1,341	1,192	1,093	1,014	895	909	781	683
Loan Loss Prov.	615	105	Nil	200	550	1,215	1,335	310	362	300
Exp./Op. Revs.	62%	69%	55%	57%	58%	55%	59%	53%	53%	56%
Pretax Inc.	2,154	1,979	1,777	1,454	1,038	500	54.0	1,195	1,001	835
Eff. Tax Rate	46%	46%	42%	42%	41%	43%	61%	41%	40%	39%
Net Inc.	1,155	1,071	1,032	841	612	283	21.0	712	601	512
% Net Int. Marg.	5.99	6.11	5.74	5.55	5.74	5.70	5.17	5.11	5.09	4.94

Balance Sheet & Other Fin. Data (Million $)

	1997	1996	1995	1994	1993	1992	1991	1990	1989	1988
Earning Assets:										
Money Mkt	82.0	187	177	260	1,668	NA	NA	NA	11.0	349
Inv. Securities	9,888	13,505	8,920	11,608	13,058	9,338	3,833	1,387	1,738	3,970
Com'l Loans	24,191	22,518	11,539	9,492	8,124	9,381	12,440	15,800	15,544	14,501
Other Loans	41,543	44,871	24,043	26,855	24,975	27,512	31,659	33,176	26,183	23,170
Total Assets	97,456	97,456	50,316	53,374	52,513	52,537	53,547	56,199	48,737	46,617
Demand Deposits	23,953	29,073	10,391	10,145	9,719	9,190	8,216	8,130	8,003	7,113
Time Deposits	48,246	52,748	28,591	32,187	31,925	33,054	35,503	34,555	28,427	27,956
LT Debt	5,867	6,210	3,049	2,853	4,221	4,040	4,220	2,417	2,541	2,917
Common Eqty.	12,614	13,512	3,566	3,422	3,676	3,170	2,808	2,955	2,456	2,174
% Ret. on Assets	1.1	1.3	2.0	1.6	1.2	0.5	0.0	1.4	1.3	1.1
% Ret. on Equity	8.7	11.8	28.3	26.6	20.7	9.7	0.1	29.4	29.6	30.0
% Loan Loss Resv.	2.8	3.0	5.0	5.7	6.4	5.6	3.7	1.8	1.8	2.0
% Loans/Deposits	91.0	82.1	91.3	85.9	79.5	87.4	100.9	114.7	114.5	107.4
% Equity to Assets	12.7	10.7	6.7	5.8	5.3	4.6	4.8	4.5	4.1	3.6

Data as orig. reptd.; bef. results of disc opers. and/or spec. items. Per share data adj. for stk. divs. as of ex-div. date. Bold denotes diluted EPS (FASB 128). E-Estimated. NA-Not Available. NM-Not Meaningful. NR-Not Ranked.

Office—420 Montgomery St., San Francisco, CA 94163. **Tel**—(415) 477-1000. **Website**—http://www.wellsfargo.com **Chrmn & CEO**—P. Hazen. **Vice Chrmn & CFO**—R. L. Jacobs. **Secy**—G. Rounsaville Jr. **Investor Contact**—Cindy Koehn (415-396-3099). **Dirs**—H. J. Arnelle, M. R. Bowlin, E. Carson, W. S. Davila, R. S. Dezember, P. Hazen, R. K. Jaedicke, T. Lee, E. M. Newman, P. J. Quigley, C. E. Reichardt, D. B. Rice, R. Stegemeier, S. G. Swenson, D. Tellep, C. L. Tien, J. A. Young. **Transfer Agent & Registrar**—First Chicago Trust Co. of New York, Jersey City, NJ. **Incorporated**—in California in 1968; reincorporated in Delaware in 1987; bank incorporated in 1899. **Empl**— 31,620. **S&P Analyst:** Stephen R. Biggar

12-SEP-98

Industry: Restaurants

Summary: This company operates or franchises more than 5,200 Wendy's restaurants, and has also acquired the breakfast-oriented Tim Hortons food-service chain.

S&P Opinion: Accumulate (★★★★)	Recent Price • 21¾
	52 Wk Range • 25⅛-19⅝

Yield • 1.1%
12-Mo. P/E • 24.4

Quantitative Evaluations

Outlook
(1 Lowest—5 Highest)
• **4+**

Fair Value
• **27**

Risk
• **Low**

Earn./Div. Rank
• **A-**

Technical Eval.
• **Bearish** since 7/98

Rel. Strength Rank
(1 Lowest—99 Highest)
• **86**

Insider Activity
• **NA**

Earnings vs. Previous Year
▲=Up ▼=Down ▶=No Change

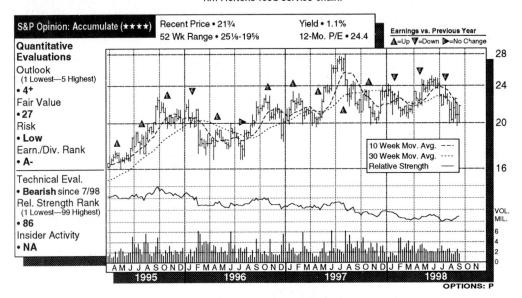

10 Week Mov. Avg. ---
30 Week Mov. Avg. ····
Relative Strength ―

OPTIONS: P

Overview - 03-JUN-98

WEN's sales growth in 1998 is expected to be fueled by some 575 new units; same-unit sales should rise moderately. In the Wendy's chain, we look for the company to continue its successful strategy of offering a diversified menu, including both relatively low-cost items and special premium sandwiches. The closure of 64 unprofitable stores and writedown of 18 others in addition to cost reduction initiatives should offset continued higher labor costs. Over the longer term, the company is accelerating its restaurant development in international markets, and increasing openings of Tim Hortons in the U.S., as well as combination Tim Hortons/Wendy's units both in Canada and the U.S. As consolidation in the restaurant industry continues, we expect the company to make additional strategic acquisitions of units. The company took a charge of $73 million in the fourth quarter of 1997 for the closures, writedown of assets and other items.

Valuation - 03-JUN-98

We recommend accumulating the shares of this strong player in the consolidating fast-food industry. It has continued to gain market share in spite of intense competition in the restaurant industry. The company has ample growth opportunities, both domestically and abroad. Over the past few years, the company has had gains from the sale of company operated stores to franchisees and real estate. Beginning in 1998, the gains should drop to $10 million to $15 million (pretax) annually, from $81 million ($0.33 a share after tax) in 1997. Wendy's is projecting 13% to 15% increases in earnings from operations over the next few years. A $200 million share repurchase program gives support to the shares.

Key Stock Statistics

S&P EPS Est. 1998	1.15	Tang. Bk. Value/Share	9.56
P/E on S&P Est. 1998	18.9	Beta	0.61
S&P EPS Est. 1999	1.35	Shareholders	82,000
Dividend Rate/Share	0.24	Market cap. (B)	$ 2.8
Shs. outstg. (M)	127.2	Inst. holdings	54%
Avg. daily vol. (M)	0.393		

Value of $10,000 invested 5 years ago: $ 18,501

Fiscal Year Ending Dec. 31

	1998	1997	1996	1995	1994	1993
Revenues (Million $)						
1Q	455.6	458.9	409.9	398.0	319.8	310.4
2Q	530.0	540.2	491.9	437.4	367.2	345.2
3Q	—	525.5	506.6	451.5	359.4	338.9
4Q	—	512.7	488.8	459.4	351.5	325.7
Yr.	—	2,037	1,897	1,746	1,398	1,320
Earnings Per Share ($)						
1Q	**0.18**	0.19	0.16	0.15	0.12	0.10
2Q	**0.34**	0.42	0.38	0.38	0.32	0.27
3Q	**E0.33**	0.39	0.36	0.34	0.29	0.24
4Q	**E0.29**	-0.03	0.30	0.15	0.21	0.17
Yr.	**E1.15**	0.97	1.20	0.90	0.93	0.77

Next earnings report expected: late October

Dividend Data (Dividends have been paid since 1976.)

Amount ($)	Date Decl.	Ex-Div. Date	Stock of Record	Payment Date
0.060	Oct. 30	Nov. 06	Nov. 10	Nov. 24 '97
0.060	Feb. 19	Feb. 26	Mar. 02	Mar. 16 '98
0.060	Apr. 29	May. 07	May. 11	May. 26 '98
0.060	Jul. 30	Aug. 06	Aug. 10	Aug. 28 '98

A Division of The McGraw·Hill Companies

Business Summary - 03-JUN-98

Wendy's International, Inc. is the third largest quick-service restaurant chain in the world. It was founded by Dave Thomas, the company's ubiquitous spokesperson, as Wendy's Old Fashioned Hamburgers in 1969. Annual 1997 systemwide sales of the Wendy's and Tim Hortons (the second largest quick-service chain in Canada) totaled $6.0 billion.

In 1997, average net sales at domestic company operated restaurants in the Wendy's chain were $1.11 million, up 5.9% from the year before. Average net sales per domestic Wendy's franchise totaled $1.0 million. The number of Wendy's units in operation at the end of recent years was:

	1997	1996
Company-owned	1,202	1,315
Franchised	4,005	3,618
Total	5,207	4,933

The company plans to continue its domestic expansion and aggressively grow outside the U.S. In December 1995, Wendy's purchased Tim Hortons, Canada's largest chain featuring coffee and freshly baked goods. The company plans to expand the number of Tim Hortons in Canada from 1,499 in 1997 to 2,000 by the end of this decade, and to develop and expand the number of Wendy's-Tim Hortons combination units in the U.S. New unit development in the U.S. and Canada is expected at 575 units in 1998; the company plans to accelerate unit development in 1999 to about 675 units.

International expansion represents a long-term growth opportunity for the company. It operated only 632 units outside of the U.S. in 1997. Canada is the largest international market with 245 Wendy's at the end of 1997. Since Tim Hortons is widely known in Canada, there are strong opportunities for expansion in that country as outlined above. The company is also focusing its growth strategy on three other regions: Latin America/Caribbean (with a total of 86 units in operation); Europe/Middle East (66); and Asia/Pacific (235).

Capital expenditures in 1997 totaled about $294.6 million and were projected to approximate $285 million in 1998. The company plans to repurchase up to $200 million worth of shares over the next 18 to 24 months.

Per Share Data ($)

(Year Ended Dec. 31)	1997	1996	1995	1994	1993	1992	1991	1990	1989	1988
Tangible Bk. Val.	9.78	8.89	7.47	6.37	5.70	5.07	4.61	4.31	4.16	4.07
Cash Flow	1.68	1.91	1.56	1.59	1.41	1.25	1.08	0.97	0.83	0.88
Earnings	0.97	1.20	0.90	0.93	0.77	0.64	0.52	0.40	0.25	0.30
Dividends	0.24	0.24	0.24	0.24	0.24	0.24	0.24	0.24	0.24	0.24
Payout Ratio	25%	20%	27%	26%	31%	37%	45%	60%	96%	81%
Prices - High	27⅞	23	22¾	18½	17⅜	14¼	11	7½	7	8
- Low	19⅝	16¾	14⅜	13¼	12⅜	9⅝	5⅞	3⅞	4½	5⅛
P/E Ratio - High	29	19	25	20	23	22	21	19	28	27
- Low	20	14	16	14	16	15	11	10	18	17

Income Statement Analysis (Million $)

	1997	1996	1995	1994	1993	1992	1991	1990	1989	1988
Revs.	2,037	1,897	1,746	1,370	1,303	1,220	1,048	1,002	1,051	1,046
Oper. Inc.	335	356	306	199	176	157	135	120	89.0	100
Depr.	105	95.0	84.4	68.1	65.7	61.7	56.1	55.1	56.4	55.7
Int. Exp.	18.9	20.3	20.4	18.7	21.6	22.5	23.3	21.4	22.3	22.4
Pretax Inc.	219	255	165	149	116	101	78.0	61.0	37.0	44.0
Eff. Tax Rate	41%	39%	33%	35%	31%	36%	34%	37%	36%	35%
Net Inc.	131	156	110	97.2	79.3	64.7	51.7	38.6	23.7	28.5

Balance Sheet & Other Fin. Data (Million $)

	1997	1996	1995	1994	1993	1992	1991	1990	1989	1988
Cash	234	224	214	135	112	112	135	55.0	74.0	48.0
Curr. Assets	382	337	321	203	179	162	176	98.0	122	110
Total Assets	1,942	1,781	1,509	1,086	996	920	880	758	780	777
Curr. Liab.	213	208	296	207	143	128	133	109	129	110
LT Debt	250	242	337	145	201	234	240	168	179	193
Common Eqty.	1,184	1,057	822	681	601	529	478	447	429	420
Total Cap.	1,715	1,562	1,207	866	842	786	742	646	647	665
Cap. Exp.	295	307	218	142	117	120	69.0	42.0	39.0	56.0
Cash Flow	236	251	191	165	145	126	108	94.0	80.0	84.0
Curr. Ratio	1.8	1.6	1.1	1.0	1.2	1.3	1.3	0.9	0.9	1.0
% LT Debt of Cap.	14.6	15.5	27.9	16.7	23.8	29.7	32.3	26.0	27.7	28.9
% Net Inc.of Revs.	6.4	8.2	6.3	7.1	6.1	5.3	4.9	3.9	2.3	2.7
% Ret. on Assets	7.0	9.5	8.1	9.3	8.2	7.1	6.3	5.0	3.0	3.7
% Ret. on Equity	11.7	16.6	14.4	15.1	13.9	12.8	11.2	8.8	5.6	6.8

Data as orig. reptd.; bef. results of disc. opers. and/or spec. items. Per share data adj. for stk. divs. as of ex-div. date. Bold denotes diluted EPS (FASB 128). E-Estimated. NA-Not Available. NM-Not Meaningful. NR-Not Ranked.

Office—4288 West Dublin-Granville Rd., P.O. Box 256, Dublin, OH 43017-0256. **Tel**—(614) 764-3100. **Website**—www.wendys.com **Chrmn, Pres & CEO**—G. F. Teter. **Treas**—J. Brownley. **Investor Contacts**—John D. Barker (614-764-3044) for analysts and portfolio managers; Marsha Gordon (614-764-3019) for general inquiries. **Dirs**—W. C. Hamner, E. S. Hayeck, J. Hill, P. D. House, R. V. Joyce, F. Keller, T. H. Knowles, A. G. McCaughey, R. E. Musick, F. B. Nutter Sr., J. V. Pickett, F. R. Reed, T. R. Shackelford, G. F. Teter, R. D. Thomas. **Transfer Agent & Registrar**—American Stock Transfer & Trust Co., NYC. **Incorporated**—in Ohio in 1969. **Empl**— 47,000. **S&P Analyst:** Karen J.Sack, CFA

STANDARD &POOR'S
STOCK REPORTS

Westvaco Corp.

2470D

NYSE Symbol **W**

In S&P 500

12-SEP-98

Industry:
Paper & Forest Products

Summary: One of the largest integrated producers of bleached board and white printing and converting papers, this company is also an important factor in corrugated packaging.

S&P Opinion: Hold (★★★)

Recent Price • 22¼
52 Wk Range • 37½-21

Yield • 3.9%
12-Mo. P/E • 15.0

Quantitative Evaluations

Outlook
(1 Lowest—5 Highest)
• **2**

Fair Value
• **22¼**

Risk
• **Low**

Earn./Div. Rank
• **B**

Technical Eval.
• **Neutral** since 6/98

Rel. Strength Rank
(1 Lowest—99 Highest)
• **60**

Insider Activity
• **Neutral**

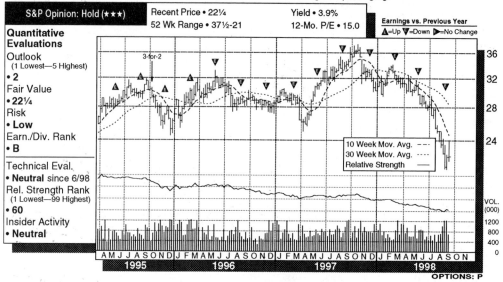

Earnings vs. Previous Year
▲=Up ▼=Down ▶=No Change

10 Week Mov. Avg. – – –
30 Week Mov. Avg. · · · ·
Relative Strength —

VOL.
(000)

OPTIONS: P

Overview - 18-JUN-98

Sales should be slightly higher in FY 98 (Oct.). Following a downturn that extended about 18 months, prices for the company's paper and packaging grades finally reversed over the course of 1997. However, we see the recovery being quite subdued. Our lukewarm forecast mostly reflects the belief that the Asian financial crisis and strong U.S. dollar will slow exports. When combined with added industry capacity in certain areas, this will likely limit the level of price hikes. In addition, W has been battling against an economic slowdown in Brazil (despite some stabilization in recent days), where it has a major position in packaging. Margins should be about flat. On the positive side, margins should be aided by the higher pricing trends and the company's ongoing cost management initiatives. Those factors will be offset by the impact of economic troubles in certain of the company's global markets, competitive conditions in several product grades, a second quarter FY 98 strike at the envelope business, and a planned machine rebuild at a production facility.

Valuation - 18-JUN-98

The shares moved sharply higher in the spring and summer of 1997, when indications grew strong that industry trends had finally bottomed. However, much of those gains have been erased since the Asian financial crisis became leading news in the fall. We still expect the paper and packaging recovery to continue to a modest extent, and with Westvaco's differentiated products strategy also offering assistance, expect W's operating performance to improve a bit. However, the Asian crisis and strong U.S. dollar will likely slow the domestic industry's export shipments, thus tapping the brakes on any major recovery. With Westvaco's major Brazilian market also posing a problem, we would not currently be interested in adding to positions in the company.

Key Stock Statistics

S&P EPS Est. 1998	1.30	Tang. Bk. Value/Share	22.26
P/E on S&P Est. 1998	17.2	Beta	0.92
S&P EPS Est. 1999	1.50	Shareholders	7,800
Dividend Rate/Share	0.88	Market cap. (B)	$ 2.3
Shs. outstg. (M)	101.3	Inst. holdings	65%
Avg. daily vol. (M)	0.246		

Value of $10,000 invested 5 years ago: $ 11,635

Fiscal Year Ending Oct. 31

	1998	1997	1996	1995	1994	1993
Revenues (Million $)						
1Q	702.1	736.4	748.7	741.7	577.3	561.0
2Q	724.2	724.6	760.3	804.6	626.4	579.5
3Q	727.8	738.2	757.7	854.6	641.3	586.0
4Q	—	783.1	778.7	871.6	762.5	618.0
Yr.	—	2,982	3,045	3,272	2,607	2,345
Earnings Per Share ($)						
1Q	**0.32**	0.35	0.61	0.49	0.16	0.21
2Q	**0.34**	0.37	0.50	0.65	0.16	0.20
3Q	**0.31**	0.37	0.43	0.79	0.20	0.22
4Q	**E0.33**	0.51	0.55	0.88	0.51	-0.06
Yr.	**E1.30**	1.60	2.09	2.80	1.03	0.57

Next earnings report expected: mid November

Dividend Data (Dividends have been paid since 1892.)

Amount ($)	Date Decl.	Ex-Div. Date	Stock of Record	Payment Date
0.220	Nov. 25	Dec. 03	Dec. 05	Jan. 02 '98
0.220	Feb. 24	Mar. 04	Mar. 06	Apr. 01 '98
0.220	May. 26	Jun. 03	Jun. 05	Jul. 01 '98
0.220	Aug. 25	Sep. 02	Sep. 04	Oct. 01 '98

A Division of The McGraw·Hill Companies

STANDARD
&POOR'S
STOCK REPORTS

Westvaco Corporation

2470D
12-SEP-98

Business Summary - 18-JUN-98

Westvaco Corp. ranks as one of the largest U.S. producers of paper and paperboard. It also has a substantial international presence, with foreign business accounting for about one-quarter of Westvaco's sales base. The company derives its international sales from a major paperboard and corrugated packaging position in Brazil, as well as from exports to more than 70 nations.

The paper and forest products industry tends to be extremely cyclical in nature. The principal factors influencing Westvaco's businesses include the level of economic growth in domestic and international markets, and the industry capacity situation. However, W believes its emphasis on distinctive products and services enables it to record far more stable earnings than most of its competitors during industry downturns.

W produced 3,058,000 tons of paper, paperboard and market pulp in FY 97 (95.6% of capacity), up a bit from 3,001,000 tons in FY 96. The company makes bleached products (68% of sales in FY 97) at four domestic mills, and markets them as pulp, printing-grade papers and board, envelopes, food containers, folding cartons and cartons for liquid products and tobacco. Overall, sales of printing-grade papers and board accounted for 43% of W's sales total in FY 97, folding cartons 11% and envelopes 10%.

W also manufactures unbleached products (21% of sales in FY 97) at four mills, including two in Brazil, with the products marketed as kraft paper and board and corrugated shipping containers. The company's specialty in unbleached paper is saturating kraft, of which W is the largest supplier in the world. Made by only a few companies, saturating kraft is treated to make decorative laminates such as countertops, furniture, flooring and wall paneling as well as compact laminates for wall dividers and stadium seats.

At October 31, 1997, W owned 1,461,000 acres of timberland in the U.S. and Brazil. In FY 97, 39% of wood needed was harvested from its own forests.

In the specialty chemicals segment (11% of sales in FY 97), W is the leading supplier of activated carbons to U.S. manufacturers of cars and trucks for automated emission controls; and also sells activated carbon for solvent recovery systems. By-products from W's pulp production, are used to produce additives for fabric dyes, inks, soap and agricultural chemicals.

In reporting second quarter FY 98 earnings, W spoke with cautious optimism about upcoming prospects. It cited improving markets for most of its products and some stabilization of the troubled Brazilian economy. However, it also noted that a complete recovery of its Brazilian packaging business would take some time, and that it remained very cautious in its outlook for Asian markets.

Per Share Data ($)

(Year Ended Oct. 31)	1997	1996	1995	1994	1993	1992	1991	1990	1989	1988
Tangible Bk. Val.	22.35	21.69	20.49	18.48	18.18	17.84	17.21	16.53	15.27	13.59
Cash Flow	4.25	4.45	5.08	3.21	2.51	3.21	3.22	3.65	3.89	3.49
Earnings	1.60	2.09	2.80	1.03	0.57	1.37	1.40	1.93	2.30	2.07
Dividends	0.88	0.88	0.77	0.73	0.73	0.73	0.71	0.68	0.63	0.55
Payout Ratio	55%	42%	28%	71%	129%	53%	51%	35%	27%	27%
Prices - High	37¹/₂	33¹/₈	31⁷/₈	26¹/₂	25³/₈	27¹/₂	26¹/₂	21	22¹/₄	21³/₈
- Low	25	25³/₈	24¹/₈	19³/₄	20	21³/₈	17¹/₈	14⁵/₈	17⁷/₈	16¹/₈
P/E Ratio - High	23	16	11	26	45	20	19	11	10	10
- Low	16	12	9	19	35	16	12	8	8	8

Income Statement Analysis (Million $)

	1997	1996	1995	1994	1993	1992	1991	1990	1989	1988
Revs.	2,982	3,045	3,272	2,607	2,345	2,336	2,301	2,411	2,284	2,134
Oper. Inc.	580	637	771	485	429	471	481	521	527	478
Depr.	269	240	230	219	195	183	179	168	155	139
Int. Exp.	93.3	105	108	115	115	102	100	90.3	72.7	54.7
Pretax Inc.	247	336	470	162	92.9	206	226	327	373	313
Eff. Tax Rate	34%	37%	40%	36%	39%	34%	39%	42%	40%	36%
Net Inc.	163	212	283	104	56.5	136	137	188	223	200

Balance Sheet & Other Fin. Data (Million $)

	1997	1996	1995	1994	1993	1992	1991	1990	1989	1988
Cash	175	115	152	75.0	57.0	191	172	184	185	187
Curr. Assets	805	716	787	631	609	671	624	668	624	589
Total Assets	4,899	4,437	4,253	3,983	3,928	3,704	3,462	3,332	2,961	2,513
Curr. Liab.	406	419	429	362	365	353	314	298	296	271
LT Debt	1,513	1,153	1,147	1,234	1,258	1,055	970	961	768	577
Common Eqty.	2,279	2,210	2,081	1,862	1,824	1,777	1,699	1,619	1,488	1,318
Total Cap.	4,494	4,018	3,824	3,621	3,563	3,351	3,148	3,034	2,665	2,242
Cap. Exp.	621	522	290	215	433	318	303	472	537	393
Cash Flow	432	453	514	323	252	319	317	357	378	339
Curr. Ratio	2.0	1.7	1.8	1.7	1.7	1.9	2.0	2.2	2.1	2.2
% LT Debt of Cap.	33.7	28.7	30.0	34.1	35.3	31.5	30.8	31.7	28.8	25.7
% Net Inc.of Revs.	5.5	7.0	8.7	4.0	2.4	5.8	6.0	7.8	9.8	9.4
% Ret. on Assets	3.5	4.9	6.9	2.6	1.5	3.8	4.0	6.0	8.1	8.5
% Ret. on Equity	7.3	9.9	14.4	5.6	3.1	7.8	8.2	12.1	15.9	16.1

Data as orig. reptd.; bef. results of disc. opers. and/or spec. items. Per share data adj. for stk. divs. as of ex-div. date. Bold denotes diluted EPS (FASB 128). E-Estimated. NA-Not Available. NM-Not Meaningful. NR-Not Ranked.

Office—299 Park Ave., New York, NY 10171. **Tel**—(212) 688-5000. **Chrmn, Pres & CEO**—J. A. Luke Jr. **VP & Secy**—J. W. Hetherington. **Sr VP & CFO**—J. E. Stoveken Jr. **Investor Contact**—Roger A. Holmes (212) 318-5288. **Dirs**—S. W. Bodman III, W. L. L. Brown Jr., T. W. Cole Jr., D. L. Hopkins Jr., R. G. Johnstone Jr., D. S. Luke, J. A. Luke, J. A. Luke Jr., W. R. Miller, K. G. Peden, J. L. Warner, R. A. Zimmerman. **Transfer Agent & Registrar**—Bank of New York, NYC. **Incorporated**—in Delaware in 1899. **Empl**— 13,370. **S&P Analyst:** Michael W. Jaffe

STANDARD &POOR'S
STOCK REPORTS

Weyerhaeuser Co.

2471

NYSE Symbol **WY**

In S&P 500

12-SEP-98

Industry:
Paper & Forest Products

Summary: WY is the world's largest private owner of marketable softwood timber and a major producer of pulp and paper products.

S&P Opinion: Avoid (★★)	Recent Price • 39	Yield • 4.1%
	52 Wk Range • 62⅛-36¾	12-Mo. P/E • 21.3

Quantitative Evaluations

Outlook
(1 Lowest—5 Highest)
• **2**

Fair Value
• **37⅜**

Risk
• **Low**

Earn./Div. Rank
• **B+**

Technical Eval.
• **Bearish** since 3/98

Rel. Strength Rank
(1 Lowest—99 Highest)
• **68**

Insider Activity
• **NA**

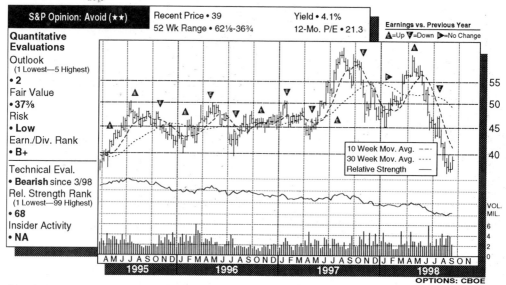

Earnings vs. Previous Year
▲=Up ▼=Down ▷=No Change

10 Week Mov. Avg. — —
30 Week Mov. Avg. - - -
Relative Strength —

OPTIONS: CBOE

Overview - 04-AUG-98

Sales from comparable operations should be slightly lower in 1998, on mixed trends. We expect lower wood products sales. On the domestic side, WY's mainstay lumber products have been battling oversupply, and we see major recent industry capacity additions in oriented strand board (OSB) hindering panels markets (despite some recent strength in OSB). On the foreign side, the housing market slowdown in Japan will likely limit wood products demand in WY's leading export market for a while. We see those reductions partly offset by a tiny increase in paper and packaging sales. With Asia's financial woes and a strong U.S. dollar impacting foreign trade, the recovery of paper and packaging prices seems to have been put on hold. However, with prices turning around a bit in 1997 and early 1998 (following a steep downturn), we expect slightly higher average 1998 full year prices. Margins should be about flat, as the benefits of slightly higher paper and packaging prices and business improvement efforts, will be offset by the ongoing troubles we see in wood products.

Valuation - 04-AUG-98

The shares have seesawed over the past year or so. A downturn in the fall of 1997 reflected investors' belief that Asia's financial troubles, particularly the slowdown in Japan's housing markets, would hurt WY's results for a while. The shares then reversed in early 1998, when a strong domestic economy made investors more relaxed about Asia. However, they headed down again in the spring, when most admitted that global economic woes would not disappear too quickly. Given current trends, we expect troubles in wood products to persist for a lengthy period. Coupled with our belief that any further recovery in paper markets will be limited at best in coming periods, we would still find a better place for our funds.

Key Stock Statistics

S&P EPS Est. 1998	1.55	Tang. Bk. Value/Share	23.09
P/E on S&P Est. 1998	25.2	Beta	0.97
S&P EPS Est. 1999	2.00	Shareholders	23,400
Dividend Rate/Share	1.60	Market cap. (B)	$ 7.8
Shs. outstg. (M)	199.0	Inst. holdings	60%
Avg. daily vol. (M)	0.717		

Value of $10,000 invested 5 years ago: $ 12,760

Fiscal Year Ending Dec. 31

	1998	1997	1996	1995	1994	1993
Revenues (Million $)						
1Q	2,603	2,608	2,605	2,686	2,386	2,340
2Q	2,676	2,909	2,886	3,009	2,598	2,388
3Q	—	2,823	2,852	3,037	2,681	2,225
4Q	—	2,870	2,771	3,056	2,733	2,591
Yr.	—	11,210	11,114	11,788	10,398	9,545
Earnings Per Share ($)						
1Q	0.43	0.10	0.72	1.00	0.62	0.87
2Q	0.34	0.55	0.52	1.21	0.62	0.89
3Q	E0.40	0.57	0.60	0.47	0.71	0.32
4Q	E0.38	0.49	0.50	1.25	0.91	0.50
Yr.	E1.55	1.71	2.33	3.93	2.86	2.58

Next earnings report expected: mid October

Dividend Data (Dividends have been paid since 1933.)

Amount ($)	Date Decl.	Ex-Div. Date	Stock of Record	Payment Date
0.400	Oct. 16	Oct. 29	Oct. 31	Dec. 01 '97
0.400	Jan. 08	Jan. 28	Jan. 30	Mar. 02 '98
0.400	Apr. 21	Apr. 29	May. 01	Jun. 01 '98
0.400	Jul. 07	Jul. 29	Jul. 31	Aug. 31 '98

A Division of The McGraw-Hill Companies

Business Summary - 04-AUG-98

Weyerhaeuser Co. grows and harvests timber, and produces, distributes and sells wood and paper products. WY ranks as the world's largest private owner of marketable softwood timber and its largest producer of softwood lumber and market pulp. The company also has a real estate development division. Weyerhaeuser's businesses tend to be highly cyclical, influenced by economic factors such as interest rates, housing starts, industrial production and GDP growth in the U.S. Because the company is a large exporter, it is also affected by foreign economic activity (particularly in Japan, its largest export market), and by changes in currency exchange rates. Sales outside the U.S., including exports, accounted for 26% of the total in 1997.

Since 1990, WY has narrowed its business focus to concentrate on core operations. Toward this goal, WY has divested non-core businesses such as its milk carton, diaper, insurance and nursery products concerns. Also, to strengthen its primary operations, WY has acquired timberlands, timber licenses, and a number of mills and corrugated packaging plants. In the second quarter of 1997, WY sold Weyerhaeuser Mortgage Co., its principal financial services business, for about $192 million; it sold its Saskatoon Chemicals unit in July.

WY manages 5.2 million acres of company-owned and 0.2 million acres of leased commercial forestland in the U.S. (60% in the South and 40% in the Pacific North-

west), and also has long-term license arrangements in Canada covering about 23.7 million acres. Of WY's total timber inventory, about 75% is softwood, the principal wood used for building construction. WY's wood products businesses produce lumber, plywood and veneer, composite panels, oriented strand board, doors, treated products, logs, chips and timber. The timberlands and wood products division accounted for 48% of sales in 1997.

Products made by WY's pulp, paper and packaging segment (41% of sales in 1997) include chemical wood pulp for world markets; newsprint, for sale to West Coast and Japanese newspaper publishers; coated and uncoated paper; linerboard, corrugating medium and corrugated shipping containers; and bleached paperboard used to produce liquid containers.

To reduce the capital required to sustain and grow its core assets, WY has entered into strategic ventures with a number of domestic and international partners.

In reporting 1998 second quarter results, the company said it has been battling weaker demand for its products in Asia, and the increased competitiveness of imports caused by the strong U.S. dollar. Weyerhaeuser also noted that it had seen some minor signs of improved results in recent days. However, WY said that with markets remaining unsettled, it will stay focused on cutting costs and effectively managing capital expenditures.

Per Share Data ($) (Year Ended Dec. 31)	1997	1996	1995	1994	1993	1992	1991	1990	1989	1988
Tangible Bk. Val.	23.31	23.25	22.54	20.86	19.34	17.85	17.25	19.21	18.55	18.14
Cash Flow	4.85	5.45	6.96	5.46	4.87	4.23	1.99	4.34	3.85	4.56
Earnings	1.71	2.34	3.93	2.86	2.58	1.83	-0.50	1.87	1.56	2.68
Dividends	1.60	1.60	1.50	1.20	1.20	1.20	1.20	1.20	1.20	1.15
Payout Ratio	94%	68%	38%	42%	47%	66%	NM	63%	77%	43%
Prices - High	63⅞	49⅞	50⅜	51¼	46½	39¼	30⅝	28⅜	32¾	29⅝
- Low	42⅝	39½	36⅞	35¾	36¼	26⅝	20⅛	17⅜	24½	23⅛
P/E Ratio - High	37	21	13	18	18	21	NM	15	21	11
- Low	25	17	9	12	14	15	NM	9	16	9

Income Statement Analysis (Million $)

	1997	1996	1995	1994	1993	1992	1991	1990	1989	1988
Revs.	11,210	11,114	11,788	10,398	9,545	9,219	8,702	9,024	10,106	10,004
Oper. Inc.	1,486	1,687	2,514	1,754	1,452	1,294	1,122	1,506	1,816	1,694
Depr.	628	617	621	534	471	489	501	503	467	401
Int. Exp.	297	405	411	391	388	410	478	516	641	529
Pretax Inc.	539	720	1,244	920	808	563	-177	600	514	849
Eff. Tax Rate	37%	36%	36%	36%	35%	34%	NM	34%	34%	34%
Net Inc.	342	463	799	589	527	372	-100	394	341	564

Balance Sheet & Other Fin. Data (Million $)

	1997	1996	1995	1994	1993	1992	1991	1990	1989	1988
Cash	122	33.0	34.0	112	160	524	616	215	261	204
Curr. Assets	2,294	2,225	2,235	NA	NA	NA	NA	NA	NA	NA
Total Assets	13,075	13,596	13,253	13,007	12,638	18,158	16,928	16,356	15,976	15,387
Curr. Liab.	1,384	1,483	1,603	NA	NA	NA	NA	NA	NA	NA
LT Debt	4,743	5,328	4,736	4,586	5,082	5,449	5,013	5,209	3,374	4,197
Common Eqty.	4,649	4,604	4,486	4,290	3,966	3,646	3,489	3,864	3,798	3,695
Total Cap.	10,931	11,369	10,529	9,965	10,062	9,949	8,592	9,988	8,689	9,076
Cap. Exp.	656	879	996	1,102	948	1,174	663	977	954	846
Cash Flow	970	1,080	1,420	1,123	998	861	400	883	786	947
Curr. Ratio	1.7	1.5	1.4	NA	NA	NA	NA	NA	NA	NA
% LT Debt of Cap.	43.4	40.5	45.0	46.0	50.5	54.8	58.3	52.1	43.0	46.2
% Net Inc.of Revs.	3.1	4.2	6.8	5.7	5.5	4.0	NM	4.4	3.4	5.6
% Ret. on Assets	2.6	3.5	6.1	4.6	3.4	2.1	NM	2.5	2.2	5.0
% Ret. on Equity	7.4	10.2	18.2	14.3	13.8	10.4	NM	10.0	8.5	15.5

Data as orig. reptd.; bef. results of disc. opers. and/or spec. items. Per share data adj. for stk. divs. as of ex-div. date. Ratios are affected by inclusion of non-forest products opers. E-Estimated. NA-Not Available. NM-Not Meaningful. NR-Not Ranked.

Office—CH 2E32, P.O. Box 2999, Tacoma, WA 98477-2999. **Tel**—(253) 924-2345. **Website**—http://www.weyerhaeuser.com **Chrmn**—G. H. Weyerhaeuser. **Pres & CEO**—S. R. Rogel. **EVP & CFO**—W. C. Stivers. **Investor Contact**—Richard J. Taggart. **Dirs**—W. J. Driscoll, P. M. Hawley, M. R. Ingram, J. I. Kieckhefer, D. F. Mazankowski, S. R. Rogel, W. D. Ruckelshaus, R. H. Sinkfield, J. N. Sullivan, G. H. Weyerhaeuser. **Transfer Agent**—ChaseMellon, Ridgefield Park, NJ. **Incorporated**—in Washington in 1900. **Empl**— 35,800. **S&P Analyst:** Michael W. Jaffe

12-SEP-98

Industry: Household Furnishings & Appliances

Summary: Whirlpool is the world's second largest manufacturer of home appliances. Sears, Roebuck is its largest customer.

S&P Opinion: Hold (★★★)	Recent Price • 45⅞ 52 Wk Range • 75¼-45
	Yield • 3.0% 12-Mo. P/E • 99.9

Quantitative Evaluations

Outlook
(1 Lowest—5 Highest)
• **4⁻**

Fair Value
• **59¼**

Risk
• **Low**

Earn./Div. Rank
• **B**

Technical Eval.
• **NA**

Rel. Strength Rank
(1 Lowest—99 Highest)
• **33**

Insider Activity
• **Neutral**

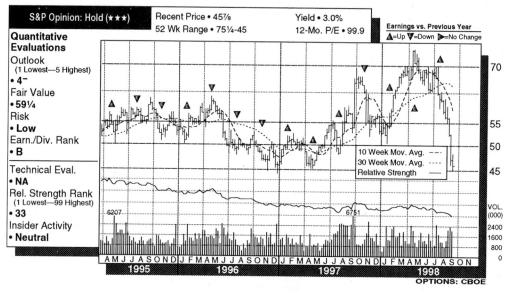

Earnings vs. Previous Year ▲=Up ▼=Down ▷=No Change

10 Week Mov. Avg. — ——
30 Week Mov. Avg. - - - -
Relative Strength ——

OPTIONS: CBOE

Overview - 27-JUL-98

Net sales fell 4.5% in the first nine months of 1997, but rose in the fourth quarter and full year, due to the consolidation of an acquisition. Comparable sales will likely remain under pressure in 1998, reflecting increased competitive pressure in India and Asia. In addition, devaluations and market turmoil will slow growth in Asia and Latin America. Sales in overseas markets should eventually benefit from expanded operations in Asia, including contributions from acquisitions and joint ventures. In North America, 1998 results should be aided by new products, a more favorable mix and efficiencies arising from restructurings. Despite recent volatility, in the longer term, results should benefit from global expansion, particularly in Asian and Latin American markets, where economies are growing and saturation levels for many appliance categories are low.

Valuation - 27-JUL-98

After rising in the summer of 1997, in anticipation that WHR would turn around its long-troubled Asian ventures within the next one to two years, investors were dealt a blow by currency turmoil that began in Asia and roiled markets around the globe. However, the shares rebounded to new highs as investors calmed down. While the company's long-term outlook should benefit from its investments in both European and emerging markets, we feel that it is still too early to describe these operations as beneficial to its medium-term earnings outlook. After a favorable 1998 first half and muted fallout from the Asian crisis, we recently raised our 1998 EPS estimate to $4.00. In a highly competitive environment, the shares, recently trading at about 16X estimated 1998 EPS, appear fairly valued.

Key Stock Statistics

S&P EPS Est. 1998	4.00	Tang. Bk. Value/Share	12.88
P/E on S&P Est. 1998	11.5	Beta	0.93
Dividend Rate/Share	1.36	Shareholders	10,900
Shs. outstg. (M)	76.0	Market cap. (B)	$ 3.5
Avg. daily vol. (M)	0.391	Inst. holdings	79%

Value of $10,000 invested 5 years ago: $ 11,865

Fiscal Year Ending Dec. 31

	1998	1997	1996	1995	1994	1993
Revenues (Million $)						
1Q	2,464	2,038	2,059	1,985	1,870	1,808
2Q	2,585	2,117	2,272	2,115	2,050	1,912
3Q	—	2,043	2,200	2,154	2,085	1,909
4Q	—	2,510	2,165	2,093	2,099	1,904
Yr.	—	8,617	8,696	8,347	8,104	7,533
Earnings Per Share ($)						
1Q	0.90	0.57	0.50	1.00	0.90	0.25
2Q	1.05	0.81	0.70	0.70	1.10	1.04
3Q	—	-2.68	0.28	0.85	1.30	0.96
4Q	—	0.66	0.60	0.25	-1.20	0.94
Yr.	E4.00	-0.62	2.08	2.80	2.10	3.19

Next earnings report expected: mid October

Dividend Data (Dividends have been paid since 1929.)

Amount ($)	Date Decl.	Ex-Div. Date	Stock of Record	Payment Date
0.340	Oct. 21	Nov. 26	Dec. 01	Dec. 31 '97
0.340	Feb. 17	Feb. 26	Mar. 02	Mar. 15 '98
0.340	Apr. 21	May. 19	May. 21	Jun. 15 '98
0.340	Aug. 18	Aug. 28	Sep. 01	Sep. 15 '98

A Division of The McGraw-Hill Companies

Business Summary - 27-JUL-98

Whirlpool Corporation manufactures a full line of household appliances and other products for home and commercial use. Products are manufactured in 13 countries and marketed in approximately 140. Growth in recent years has been aided by acquisitions, including the purchase of the appliance business of N.V. Philips Electronics of the Netherlands in the early 1990s. In Latin America and Asia, growth is primarily being fueled by partnerships with existing local appliance companies.

In November 1994, WHR restructured its North American and European operations, resulting in a pretax charge of $250 million. The move, which eliminated 3,200 positions and two plants, was aimed at improving productivity and is expected to result in annual cost savings of $150 million. A $30 million pretax charge was incurred in 1996 to restructure additional North American and Asian operations.

Major appliances produced include home laundry equipment (31% of 1997 sales); home refrigeration and room air conditioning equipment (34%); and various other appliances, including dishwashers and cooking equipment (35%). Whirlpool Financial Corp., which provides financing for distributors, dealers, and consumers, was sold to Transamerica Distribution Finance Corp. in late 1997, for approximately $927 million.

In 1997, 61% of total sales were made in North America. Major brands in the U.S. include Whirlpool, KitchenAid, Roper, Kenmore, Estate, Chambers and Coolerator. Major brands in Canada are Inglis, Admiral, Speed Queen, Estate, Roper, Whirlpool and KitchenAid. About 27% of total sales were made by Whirlpool Europe, B.V. under the Algor, Bauknecht, Fides, Ignis, Laden and Whirlpool brand names.

Other markets include Latin America and Asia. Approximately 7% of total sales were made in Latin America. Most sales in Latin America take place through six joint ventures in Brazil and Argentina. About 5% of total sales were made in Asia. The company is also involved in five joint ventures in China and three joint ventures in India.

In 1997, product shipments in North America were essentially flat, primarily reflecting weak air conditioning sales stemming from a cool summer season, but margins widened on a combination of improved product mix, manufacturing efficiencies and lower material costs. European shipments, counter to the industry, were higher; sales rose in local currency, but fell when translated into dollars. Latin American operating profits declined, and Asia produced a loss, on slightly lower revenues.

Per Share Data ($)

(Year Ended Dec. 31)	1997	1996	1995	1994	1993	1992	1991	1990	1989	1988
Tangible Bk. Val.	11.25	14.08	12.61	13.38	12.63	11.50	8.70	14.21	15.44	17.46
Cash Flow	4.13	6.32	6.55	5.62	6.88	7.19	6.18	4.59	5.90	4.39
Earnings	-0.62	2.08	2.80	2.10	3.19	2.90	2.45	1.04	2.70	2.33
Dividends	1.36	1.36	1.36	1.22	1.19	1.10	1.10	1.10	1.10	1.10
Payout Ratio	NM	65%	49%	58%	37%	38%	45%	106%	41%	47%
Prices - High	69$^1/_2$	61$^3/_8$	60$^7/_8$	73$^1/_2$	68	48$^7/_8$	41	33$^1/_2$	33$^1/_4$	29$^7/_8$
- Low	45$^1/_4$	44$^1/_4$	49$^1/_4$	44$^5/_8$	43$^1/_4$	34$^1/_2$	19$^7/_8$	17$^1/_2$	24$^1/_4$	23$^1/_8$
P/E Ratio - High	NM	30	22	35	21	17	17	32	12	13
- Low	NM	21	18	21	14	12	8	17	9	10

Income Statement Analysis (Million $)

	1997	1996	1995	1994	1993	1992	1991	1990	1989	1988
Revs.	8,617	8,696	8,163	8,104	7,533	7,301	6,770	6,623	6,289	4,421
Oper. Inc.	710	754	775	904	838	888	779	696	696	452
Depr.	356	318	282	266	266	302	260	247	222	143
Int. Exp.	168	236	207	165	172	227	229	231	187	101
Pretax Inc.	-103	223	314	351	391	359	300	187	350	252
Eff. Tax Rate	NM	36%	32%	50%	38%	43%	43%	59%	39%	36%
Net Inc.	-46.0	156	209	158	231	205	170	72.0	187	161

Balance Sheet & Other Fin. Data (Million $)

	1997	1996	1995	1994	1993	1992	1991	1990	1989	1988
Cash	578	129	149	72.0	88.0	66.0	42.0	80.0	141	143
Curr. Assets	4,281	3,812	3,541	3,078	2,708	2,740	2,920	2,900	2,889	1,827
Total Assets	8,270	8,015	7,800	6,655	6,047	6,118	6,445	5,614	5,354	3,410
Curr. Liab.	3,676	4,022	3,829	2,988	2,763	2,887	2,931	2,651	2,251	1,399
LT Debt	1,074	955	983	885	840	1,215	1,528	874	982	474
Common Eqty.	1,771	1,926	1,877	1,723	1,648	1,600	1,515	1,424	1,421	1,321
Total Cap.	3,035	3,269	3,273	2,924	2,747	3,028	3,211	2,641	2,809	1,998
Cap. Exp.	378	336	483	418	309	288	287	272	693	180
Cash Flow	310	474	491	424	497	507	430	319	409	304
Curr. Ratio	1.2	0.9	0.9	1.0	1.0	0.9	1.0	1.1	1.3	1.3
% LT Debt of Cap.	35.4	29.3	30.0	30.3	30.6	40.1	47.6	33.1	35.0	23.7
% Net Inc.of Revs.	NM	NM	2.6	1.9	3.1	2.8	2.5	1.1	3.0	3.6
% Ret. on Assets	NM	2.0	2.9	2.5	3.7	3.3	2.8	1.3	4.3	5.5
% Ret. on Equity	NM	8.2	11.6	9.3	13.9	13.1	11.6	5.1	13.6	12.3

Data as orig. reptd.; bef. results of disc. opers. and/or spec. items. Per share data adj. for stk. divs. as of ex-div. date. Bold denotes diluted EPS (FASB 128). E-Estimated. NA-Not Available. NM-Not Meaningful. NR-Not Ranked.

Office—2000 North M-63, Benton Harbor, MI 49022-2692. **Tel**—(616) 923-5000. **Website**—http://www.whirlpool.com **Chrmn & CEO**—D. R. Whitwam. **Vice Chrmn**—W. D. Marohn. **EVP & CFO**—R. F. Hake. **Secy**—D. F. Hopp. **Investor Contact**—Thomas C. Filstrup.**Dirs**—R. A. Burnett, H. Cain, G. T. DiCamillo, H. M. Etchenique A. D. Gilmour, K. J. Hempel, A. G. Langbo, W. D. Marohn, M. L. Marsh, P. L. Smith, P. G. Stern, J. D. Stoney, D. R. Whitwam. **Transfer Agent & Registrar**—Harris Trust & Savings Bank, Chicago. **Incorporated**—in Delaware in 1955. **Empl**— 61,370.
S&P Analyst: Efraim Levy

Willamette Industries   2483N

NYSE Symbol **WLL**

In S&P 500

12-SEP-98

Industry: Paper & Forest Products

Summary: This integrated forest products company manufactures a wide variety of paper and building products and owns or controls 1.8 million acres of forests.

S&P Opinion: Accumulate (★★★★)

Recent Price • 24⅛	Yield • 2.7%
52 Wk Range • 43½-23	12-Mo. P/E • 30.9

Quantitative Evaluations

Outlook (1 Lowest—5 Highest)
• **3**

Fair Value
• **25½**

Risk
• **Low**

Earn./Div. Rank
• **B+**

Technical Eval.
• **NA**

Rel. Strength Rank (1 Lowest—99 Highest)
• **46**

Insider Activity
• **Neutral**

Earnings vs. Previous Year
▲=Up ▼=Down ▶=No Change

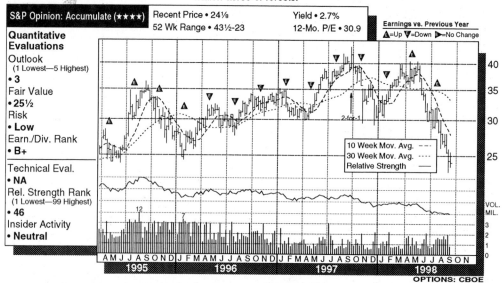

10 Week Mov. Avg. ---
30 Week Mov. Avg. .....
Relative Strength —

OPTIONS: CBOE

Overview - 29-JUL-98

We expect moderately higher sales in 1998, on mixed sector trends. Sales gains should be recorded in the paper segment. With Asia's financial woes and a strong U.S. dollar impacting foreign trade, the recovery of paper and packaging prices seems to have been put on hold. However, we see modestly higher average prices for the full year, boosted by the pricing turnaround seen between early 1997 and early 1998 (following a steep downturn that started in late 1995). We expect those gains to be partly offset by lower sales in the smaller building products division. In that area, we see much recent OSB capacity additions restricting structural panel pricing (despite some significant strength in OSB in recent days), and oversupply and Asian troubles holding down lumber prices. Margins will likely widen, on higher average paper and packaging prices, cost control efforts and the ongoing benefits of WLL's ambitious capital spending program.

Valuation - 29-JUL-98

The shares have seesawed over the past year or so. They came tumbling down in the fall of 1997, when the Asian currency crisis made it appear that the expected recovery of paper and packaging markets would not come to pass. The shares then rebounded in early 1998 when investors seemingly grew more relaxed about Asia. However, they reversed once more in the spring of 1998, when it began to appear that Asia's troubles would be here for a while. We remain relatively bearish on the forest products industry, as we see troubles in the global economy continuing to impact commodities markets. Given that modest outlook, we would not take a major sector position. However, WLL stands as one of the industry's lowest cost producers, and would be a good choice for one who wants exposure to the forest products industry.

Key Stock Statistics

S&P EPS Est. 1998	1.00	Tang. Bk. Value/Share	18.01
P/E on S&P Est. 1998	24.1	Beta	0.85
S&P EPS Est. 1999	1.60	Shareholders	6,500
Dividend Rate/Share	0.64	Market cap. (B)	$ 2.7
Shs. outstg. (M)	111.4	Inst. holdings	48%
Avg. daily vol. (M)	0.332		

Value of $10,000 invested 5 years ago: $ 13,119

Fiscal Year Ending Dec. 31

	1998	1997	1996	1995	1994	1993
Revenues (Million $)						
1Q	900.1	837.7	866.1	900.6	679.7	633.0
2Q	946.4	857.7	858.8	1,004	728.7	654.1
3Q	—	872.8	862.7	1,019	780.8	677.1
4Q	—	870.4	837.6	950.0	818.7	658.0
Yr.	—	3,439	3,425	3,874	3,008	2,622
Earnings Per Share ($)						
1Q	**0.20**	0.12	0.67	0.90	0.30	0.28
2Q	**0.21**	0.16	0.43	1.22	0.27	0.24
3Q	**E0.29**	0.19	0.39	1.36	0.34	0.19
4Q	**E0.30**	0.19	0.25	1.19	0.70	0.29
Yr.	**E1.00**	0.65	1.74	4.67	1.61	1.01

Next earnings report expected: early October

Dividend Data (Dividends have been paid since 1962.)

Amount ($)	Date Decl.	Ex-Div. Date	Stock of Record	Payment Date
0.160	Nov. 13	Nov. 20	Nov. 24	Dec. 12 '97
0.160	Feb. 12	Feb. 19	Feb. 23	Mar. 13 '98
0.160	Apr. 21	May. 20	May. 25	Jun. 12 '98
0.160	Aug. 06	Aug. 27	Aug. 31	Sep. 14 '98

A Division of The **McGraw-Hill** *Companies*

Business Summary - 29-JUL-98

Willamette Industries' two main businesses, paper and building materials, are both highly cyclical. Paper results tend to reflect the strength of the general economy and industry capacity. Factors having the greatest influence on the building materials sector include the level of new housing starts, remodeling activity and terms of construction financing. The costs of timber and recycled fiber, the basic raw materials for both sectors, react to various supply and demand factors. WLL sells 90% of its products in the U.S. Segment contributions in 1997:

	Sales	Profits
Paper	65%	50%
Building materials	35%	50%

Willamette's pulp and paper business makes market pulp, fine paper and unbleached paper. Hardwood market pulp, one of the primary raw materials in the production of paper, is sold to outside customers (WLL produced 4% of the nation's hardwood market pulp in 1997). Uses for WLL's fine paper (8%) include copy paper, computer forms, tablets and envelopes. Its unbleached paper includes linerboard, which is the inner and outer seals of a corrugated box; corrugating medium, the brown wavy center of the wall of a corrugated box; and bag paper. WLL uses nearly all of its unbleached paper at its box and bag manufacturing plants or trades it for their needs.

Converted paper products include office papers, corrugated containers and sheets, and bags. WLL's office papers consist mostly of long-run continuous computer forms (WLL made 14% of all U.S. forms in 1997) and photocopy and cut-sheet printer paper (representing 12% of U.S. cut-sheet production). WLL's corrugated containers and sheets range from colorful store displays to the plain brown box, and represented 6% of the nation's corrugated box production in 1997. It also produced 12% of the nation's paper bags in 1997.

In building products, WLL makes structural panels, consisting of plywood (3% of plywood produced in the U.S. in 1997) and oriented strand board, or OSB (5%), a structural panel made of engineered wood used in applications such as roof, wall and floor sheathing. The division also makes lumber (accounting for only a modest 2% of industry production in the U.S. in 1997), and produces composite board and non-OSB engineered wood products.

With timber supply from federal lands increasingly curtailed as a result of environmental regulations, the company has made fiber self-sufficiency a top priority. In May 1996, WLL purchased 1.1 million acres of timberland in Louisiana and the Pacific Northwest, and an Oregon sawmill, from a unit of Hanson PLC for $1.6 billion. It concurrently sold about half of the acreage for a total of $640 million. The net effect boosted WLL's timber base by more than 40%, to 1.8 million acres, which now supply about 56% of the company's log needs.

Per Share Data ($)

(Year Ended Dec. 31)	1997	1996	1995	1994	1993	1992	1991	1990	1989	1988
Tangible Bk. Val.	17.91	17.85	16.72	12.61	11.46	10.63	9.76	9.71	8.86	7.34
Cash Flow	3.06	3.97	6.65	3.59	2.78	2.38	1.94	2.33	2.91	2.53
Earnings	0.66	1.74	4.67	1.61	1.01	0.76	0.45	1.27	1.88	1.58
Dividends	0.64	0.62	0.57	0.48	0.44	0.42	0.40	0.40	0.36	0.30
Payout Ratio	97%	36%	12%	30%	44%	56%	89%	31%	19%	19%
Prices - High	43½	35⅛	36⅜	29¾	25	21¼	15¼	14⅜	13⅞	13⅜
- Low	29¼	24⅜	23⅜	19¾	17	14½	9¾	7½	10¼	9⅝
P/E Ratio - High	66	20	8	18	25	28	34	11	7	8
- Low	44	14	5	12	18	19	22	6	5	6

Income Statement Analysis (Million $)

	1997	1996	1995	1994	1993	1992	1991	1990	1989	1988
Revs.	3,439	3,425	3,874	3,008	2,622	2,372	2,005	1,905	1,892	1,716
Oper. Inc.	494	642	1,113	584	451	371	295	347	439	382
Depr.	268	247	219	217	194	174	151	108	104	95.0
Int. Exp.	117	103	77.0	80.8	79.2	73.8	64.0	52.0	42.1	35.1
Pretax Inc.	111	306	824	289	189	129	74.0	209	308	255
Eff. Tax Rate	34%	37%	38%	39%	42%	37%	38%	38%	38%	37%
Net Inc.	73.0	192	515	178	111	82.0	46.0	130	191	161

Balance Sheet & Other Fin. Data (Million $)

	1997	1996	1995	1994	1993	1992	1991	1990	1989	1988
Cash	27.6	22.2	18.0	12.8	9.5	9.0	2.2	21.1	11.4	33.2
Curr. Assets	766	860	775	605	533	481	439	402	349	344
Total Assets	4,811	4,721	3,414	3,033	2,805	2,527	2,219	1,965	1,604	1,430
Curr. Liab.	458	570	416	466	376	323	292	246	167	152
LT Debt	1,916	1,767	790	916	942	844	747	565	388	391
Common Eqty.	1,994	1,976	1,847	1,388	1,258	1,165	994	987	901	747
Total Cap.	4,313	4,117	2,967	2,535	2,398	2,191	1,912	1,717	1,437	1,275
Cap. Exp.	528	486	454	393	387	367	244	347	280	278
Cash Flow	341	439	734	395	305	255	197	237	296	257
Curr. Ratio	1.7	1.5	1.9	1.3	1.4	1.5	1.5	1.6	2.1	2.3
% LT Debt of Cap.	44.4	43.0	26.6	36.1	39.3	38.5	39.0	32.9	27.0	30.7
% Net Inc.of Revs.	2.1	5.6	13.3	5.9	4.2	3.4	2.3	6.8	10.1	9.4
% Ret. on Assets	1.5	4.8	16.0	6.1	4.1	3.3	2.2	7.3	12.6	12.3
% Ret. on Equity	3.7	10.1	31.8	13.4	9.1	7.3	4.6	13.7	23.2	23.6

Data as orig. reptd.; bef. results of disc. opers. and/or spec. items. Per share data adj. for stk. divs. as of ex-div. date. Bold denotes diluted EPS (FASB 128). E-Estimated. NA-Not Available. NM-Not Meaningful. NR-Not Ranked.

Office—1300 S.W. Fifth Ave., Portland, OR 97201. **Tel**—(503) 227-5581.**Website**—http://www.wii.com **Chrmn & CEO**—W. Swindells. **Pres**—D. C. McDougall. **EVP, CFO, Secy & Treas**—J. A. Parsons. **Investor Contact**—E. Jane Sinnema. **Dirs**—G. K. Drummond, K. W. Hergenhan, C. W. Knodell, P. N. McCracken, G. J. Prendergast, S. J. Shelk Jr., R. M. Smelick, W. Swindells, S. C. Wheeler, B. R. Whiteley. **Transfer Agent & Registrar**—ChaseMellon Shareholder Services, NJ.**Incorporated**—in Oregon in 1906. **Empl**— 13,800. **S&P Analyst:** Michael W. Jaffe

Williams Companies

2486

NYSE Symbol **WMB**

In S&P 500

12-SEP-98

Industry: Natural Gas

Summary: WMB owns and operates interstate natural gas and petroleum products pipeline systems, operates a national fiber-optic network, and provides telecommunications services.

S&P Opinion: Accumulate (★★★★)

Recent Price • 26½	Yield • 2.3%
52 Wk Range • 36⅞-20	12-Mo. P/E • 40.9

Quantitative Evaluations

Outlook
(1 Lowest—5 Highest)
• **1⁻**

Fair Value
• **17¾**

Risk
• **Low**

Earn./Div. Rank
• **B+**

Technical Eval.
• **Bullish** since 8/96

Rel. Strength Rank
(1 Lowest—99 Highest)
• **64**

Insider Activity
• **Neutral**

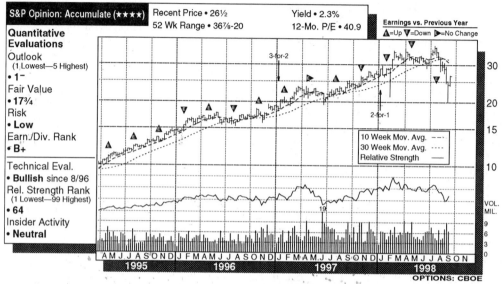

Earnings vs. Previous Year
▲=Up ▼=Down ▶=No Change

10 Week Mov. Avg. ---
30 Week Mov. Avg. ·····
Relative Strength —

OPTIONS: CBOE

Overview - 06-MAY-98

Excluding one-time charges, MAPCO-related expenses and debt restructuring costs, Williams's results for the first quarter of 1998 would have been approximately $0.26 per share, down from $0.42 the previous year, meeting Wall Street's expectations. The company's gas pipeline operation was the only segment that saw an improvement in operating profit, due primarily to the impact of three expansion projects. Energy Services was hit by reduced trading profit, lower per-unit natural gas liquids margins and increased operating and administrative expenses, on top of the costs related to the MAPCO acquisition. The communications unit increased revenues 79%, primarily because of the addition of Nortel Communications Systems, which merged with Williams in the second quarter of 1997, but operating profit declined because of the costs of expanding the infrastructure of the communications unit. The company's rapid expansion of Energy Services and the communications unit will add to the company's growth prospects and will make it less dependent on the regulated pipeline operations. Although it may be some time before profits from communications operations make a substantial positive impact on the bottom line.

Valuation - 06-MAY-98

Long-term growth prospects continue to be quite strong, especially with the addition of MAPCO. The energy services sector should become a major source of income, outdistancing the regulated pipeline business. Also, in the current atmosphere, the communications segment can be expected to grow. Williams is very well run, and management's focus on shareholder value is encouraging. Finally, the P/E ratio is reasonable considering WMB's projected EPS growth rate, leading us to recommend accumulation of the stock.

Key Stock Statistics

S&P EPS Est. 1998	1.15	Tang. Bk. Value/Share	8.60
P/E on S&P Est. 1998	23.1	Beta	1.01
S&P EPS Est. 1999	1.40	Shareholders	12,400
Dividend Rate/Share	0.60	Market cap. (B)	$ 11.3
Shs. outstg. (M)	424.9	Inst. holdings	56%
Avg. daily vol. (M)	1.457		

Value of $10,000 invested 5 years ago: $ 47,129

Fiscal Year Ending Dec. 31

	1998	1997	1996	1995	1994	1993
Revenues (Million $)						
1Q	1,960	1,001	893.7	642.4	386.6	750.8
2Q	1,781	1,021	837.5	663.9	419.9	541.9
3Q	—	1,121	842.2	712.4	467.3	541.8
4Q	—	1,267	957.8	837.0	477.3	603.7
Yr.	—	4,410	3,531	2,856	1,751	2,438
Earnings Per Share ($)						
1Q	0.16	0.31	0.32	0.28	0.16	0.43
2Q	0.14	0.32	0.24	0.26	0.23	0.11
3Q	—	0.19	0.21	0.19	0.17	0.05
4Q	—	0.19	0.32	0.19	0.26	0.16
Yr.	E1.15	1.04	1.08	0.93	0.82	0.73

Next earnings report expected: mid October

Dividend Data (Dividends have been paid since 1974.)

Amount ($)	Date Decl.	Ex-Div. Date	Stock of Record	Payment Date
2-for-1	Nov. 24	Dec. 30	Dec. 05	Dec. 29 '97
0.150	Jan. 26	Mar. 12	Mar. 16	Mar. 30 '98
0.150	May. 21	Jun. 03	Jun. 05	Jun. 29 '98
0.150	Jul. 27	Aug. 26	Aug. 28	Sep. 14 '98

A Division of The **McGraw·Hill** *Companies*

Business Summary - 06-MAY-98

The Williams Companies (WMB) is engaged in pipeline transportation of natural gas and petroleum products, natural gas trading, production, gathering and processing, and nationwide telecommunications and network services. In March 1998, the company completed its acquisition of MAPCO Inc., a Tulsa, Oklahoma-based diversified energy company. MAPCO's subsidiaries engage in the transportation by pipeline of natural gas liquids (NGLs), anhydrous ammonia, crude oil, and refined petroleum products; the transportation by truck and rail of NGLs and refined petroleum products, the refining of crude oil, the marketing and trading of NGLs, refined petroleum products, and crude oil; NGL storage; and the marketing of motor fuel and merchandise through convenience stores.

The company's interstate natural gas pipeline group, comprised of Williams Interstate Natural Gas Systems, Inc. and its subsidiaries, owns and operates a combined total of approximately 27,000 miles of pipelines with a total annual throughput of approximately 3,700 trillion Btu of natural gas and peak-day delivery capacity of approximately 15 billion cubic feet (Bcf) of natural gas. The interstate natural gas pipeline group consists of Transcontinental Gas Pipe Line Crop., Northwest Pipeline Corp., Kern River Gas Transmission Co., Texas Gas Transmission Corp. and Williams Gas Pipelines Central, Inc. The pipeline group also holds minority interests in joint venture interstate natural gas pipeline systems.

Williams Holdings of Delaware, Inc.'s energy subsidiaries are engaged in exploration and production; natural gas gathering, processing and treating activities; petroleum products transportation and terminaling; ethanol production and marketing; and energy commodity marketing and trading and price risk management and energy finance services. In addition, these subsidiaries provide a variety of other products and services to the energy industry. Williams Holdings' communications subsidiaries offer data-, voice-, and video-related products and services and customer premise voice and data equipment, including installation, maintenance, and integration, nationwide.

In 1997, the gas pipelines accounted for 36% of revenues ($614.2 million in operating profit), energy services made up 32% of revenues ($360.9 million), and 31% of revenues was derived from the communications operations ($55.7 million operating loss).

Per Share Data ($)

(Year Ended Dec. 31)	1997	1996	1995	1994	1993	1992	1991	1990	1989	1988
Tangible Bk. Val.	9.35	10.35	9.68	5.15	5.25	4.58	4.27	4.10	4.05	4.94
Cash Flow	2.49	2.35	2.19	1.00	1.44	1.09	1.08	0.91	0.81	0.64
Earnings	1.04	1.08	0.93	0.82	0.75	0.42	0.39	0.26	0.20	-0.02
Dividends	0.54	0.47	0.36	0.28	0.26	0.25	0.23	0.23	0.23	0.23
Payout Ratio	52%	43%	39%	34%	35%	62%	59%	89%	120%	NM
Prices - High	28⅝	19½	14⅞	11⅛	10⅝	6⅞	6½	6¾	7½	6⅜
- Low	18⅛	14⅛	8⅛	7⅜	6	4⅝	4¼	3⅞	5	3¾
P/E Ratio - High	28	18	16	14	14	16	17	26	38	NM
- Low	17	13	9	9	8	11	11	15	25	NM

Income Statement Analysis (Million $)

	1997	1996	1995	1994	1993	1992	1991	1990	1989	1988
Revs.	4,410	3,531	2,856	1,751	2,438	2,448	2,092	1,822	1,717	1,673
Oper. Inc.	1,414	1,271	998	465	584	452	436	376	348	312
Depr.	500	411	369	150	211	184	172	161	141	126
Int. Exp.	389	360	278	146	166	162	163	142	163	126
Pretax Inc.	543	545	401	247	377	172	151	102	76.0	6.0
Eff. Tax Rate	33%	34%	25%	33%	38%	26%	27%	25%	31%	182%
Net Inc.	351	362	299	165	185	128	110	77.0	53.0	-5.0

Balance Sheet & Other Fin. Data (Million $)

	1997	1996	1995	1994	1993	1992	1991	1990	1989	1988
Cash	81.3	115	90.0	36.0	64.0	212	48.0	51.0	65.0	110
Curr. Assets	2,256	1,890	1,344	1,457	627	743	448	512	471	610
Total Assets	13,879	12,419	10,495	5,226	5,020	4,982	4,247	4,034	3,900	3,567
Curr. Liab.	3,027	2,199	2,050	1,474	733	978	687	717	713	729
LT Debt	4,565	4,377	2,874	1,308	1,605	1,683	1,540	1,368	1,285	1,159
Common Eqty.	3,430	3,260	3,014	1,406	1,624	1,268	1,070	1,017	998	1,128
Total Cap.	9,973	9,425	7,456	3,476	3,954	3,772	3,325	3,106	2,976	2,678
Cap. Exp.	1,162	819	828	326	529	586	317	254	198	202
Cash Flow	840	763	669	306	431	298	271	227	186	147
Curr. Ratio	0.7	0.9	0.7	1.0	0.9	0.8	0.7	0.7	0.7	0.8
% LT Debt of Cap.	45.8	46.4	38.5	37.6	40.6	44.6	46.3	44.0	43.2	43.3
% Net Inc.of Revs.	7.9	10.3	46.1	9.4	9.5	5.2	5.3	4.2	3.1	NM
% Ret. on Assets	2.7	3.2	16.8	3.4	4.4	2.7	2.6	1.9	1.4	NM
% Ret. on Equity	10.2	11.2	13.5	11.0	14.5	9.3	9.4	6.5	4.6	NM

Data as orig. reptd.; bef. results of disc. opers. and/or spec. items. Per share data adj. for stk. divs. as of ex-div. date. Bold denotes diluted EPS (FASB 128). E-Estimated. NA-Not Available. NM-Not Meaningful. NR-Not Ranked.

Office—One Williams Center, Tulsa, OK 74172. **Tel**—(918) 588-2000. **Website**—http://www.twc.com **Chrmn, Pres & CEO**—K. E. Bailey. **SVP-Fin & CFO**—J. D. McCarthy. **Secy**—D. M. Higbee. **VP & Investor Contact**—Mark Husband. **Dirs**—K. E. Bailey, G. A. Cox, T. H. Cruikshank, W. E. Green, P. L. Higgins, W. R. Howell, R. J. LaFortune, J. C. Lewis, J. A. MacAllister, P. C. Meinig, K. A. Orr, G. R. Parker, J. H. Williams. **Transfer Agent & Registrar**—First Chicago Trust Co. of New York, Jersey City, NJ. **Incorporated**—in Nevada in 1949; reincorporated in Delaware in 1987. **Empl**—15,000. **S&P Analyst:** J. Robert Cho

Winn-Dixie Stores

2490

NYSE Symbol **WIN**

In S&P 500

12-SEP-98

Industry: Retail (Food Chains)

Summary: Winn-Dixie, based in Jacksonville, FL, is the largest supermarket operator in the highly competitive Sunbelt.

S&P Opinion: Hold (★★★)	Recent Price • 37⅝	Yield • 2.7%
	52 Wk Range • 62¾-34½	12-Mo. P/E • 28.3

Earnings vs. Previous Year
▲=Up ▼=Down ▶=No Change

Quantitative Evaluations

Outlook
(1 Lowest—5 Highest)
• **1**

Fair Value
• **32**

Risk
• **Low**

Earn./Div. Rank
• **A**

Technical Eval.
• **Bearish** since 8/98

Rel. Strength Rank
(1 Lowest—99 Highest)
• **65**

Insider Activity
• **NA**

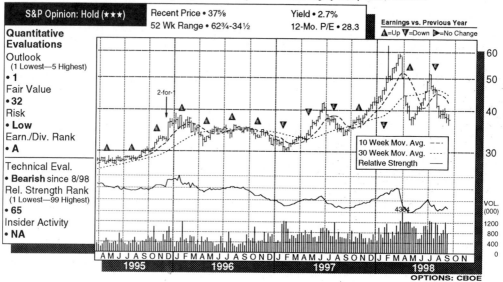

10 Week Mov. Avg. - - - -
30 Week Mov. Avg. ·······
Relative Strength ——

VOL.
(000)

OPTIONS: CBOE

Overview - 30-JUL-98

We expect total sales to advance modestly in FY 99 (Jun.), aided by the remodeling of 80 to 90 stores and the addition of 80 new stores. Despite favorable food prices in the past few years, margins are likely to be restricted early in the year as the company focuses on its top-line revenue growth in favor of maintaining margins. However, margins should begin to improve as the year unfolds as the company shifts its focus to its operations. Longer term, the company should benefit from store remodelings and increasing average store square footage. This should help boost future profitability as larger stores with higher volume account for a greater percentage of WIN's store base, because these stores carry a wider-margin product, including service departments and more general merchandise. Although the larger stores tend to have higher operating and administrative expenses, reflecting higher employee benefit costs, improved buying should help to offset some of the higher operating costs.

Valuation - 30-JUL-98

We maintain our hold opinion on Winn-Dixie despite expected margin weakness early in FY 99. Recent results have been hurt by sluggish food inflation and the company's promotional strategy to help boost sales. Thus far, the company has been successful in increasing sales, but margins have suffered. We expect the company to continue to be competitive in its pricing, which should hurt margins for the next few quarters. As a result, we are lowering our FY 99 EPS estimate $0.10 to $1.55. Although the shares are pricey at the moment, WIN's aggressive store expansion and refurbishment program should help to boost future profitability. Further, the company's balance sheet is one of the strongest in the supermarket industry, and WIN's returns on sales, assets and equity are among the highest in its peer group.

Key Stock Statistics

S&P EPS Est. 1999	1.55	Tang. Bk. Value/Share	9.19
P/E on S&P Est. 1999	24.3	Beta	0.55
Dividend Rate/Share	1.02	Shareholders	55,200
Shs. outstg. (M)	148.5	Market cap. (B)	$ 5.6
Avg. daily vol. (M)	0.197	Inst. holdings	21%

Value of $10,000 invested 5 years ago: $ 11,400

Fiscal Year Ending Jun. 30

	1998	1997	1996	1995	1994	1993
Revenues (Million $)						
1Q	3,056	2,986	2,935	2,590	2,464	2,390
2Q	4,150	4,057	3,973	3,538	3,381	3,240
3Q	3,161	3,114	3,035	2,776	2,651	2,504
4Q	3,250	3,062	3,013	2,884	2,585	2,691
Yr.	13,617	13,219	12,955	11,788	11,082	10,832
Earnings Per Share ($)						
1Q	0.32	0.31	0.30	0.27	0.24	0.22
2Q	**0.22**	0.32	0.48	0.46	0.42	0.41
3Q	**0.41**	0.38	0.42	0.38	0.35	0.38
4Q	**0.22**	0.35	0.49	0.45	0.43	0.55
Yr.	**1.33**	1.36	1.69	1.55	1.45	1.55

Next earnings report expected: early October

Dividend Data (Dividends have been paid since 1934.)

Amount ($)	Date Decl.	Ex-Div. Date	Stock of Record	Payment Date
0.085	Apr. 01	Jun. 11	Jun. 15	Jul. 01 '98
0.085	Jul. 01	Jul. 13	Jul. 15	Aug. 03 '98
0.085	Jul. 01	Aug. 12	Aug. 14	Sep. 01 '98
0.085	Jul. 01	Sep. 11	Sep. 15	Oct. 01 '98

A Division of The **McGraw·Hill** *Companies*

Winn-Dixie Stores, Inc.

Business Summary - 30-JUL-98

Winn-Dixie is the largest food retailer in the Sunbelt, and the fifth largest in the U.S. in terms of supermarket sales. At September 17, 1997, the company operated 1,174 stores in the U.S. and the Bahamas, distributed as follows: Florida (424), North Carolina (130), Georgia (123), Alabama (96), South Carolina (79), Louisiana (76), Texas (69), Kentucky (61), Virginia (34), Tennessee (24), Ohio (20), Mississippi (16), the Bahamas (13), Oklahoma (7) and Indiana (2). WIN aims to maintain low price leadership by offering high food quality and variety at the lowest prices possible.

Since 1993, the company has been increasing average store size, adding new food products, as well as more fresh, prepared foods. As of the end of FY 97 (Jun.), 68% of WIN stores were either new, in the process of being enlarged, or had been remodeled within the last five years. In FY 97, the company opened and acquired 83 new store locations, averaging 49,700 sq. ft., and closed 87 older store locations averaging 29,300 sq. ft. An additional 79 stores were enlarged or remodeled. Total average square footage per store for FY 97 was 40,700. Store data as of the end of recent fiscal years were:

	FY 97	FY 96	FY 95	FY 94
Number of stores	1,178	1,178	1,175	1,159
Total store square footage (million)	47.8	45.7	43.8	40.7

WIN stores operate under the names Winn-Dixie, Marketplace, Thriftway, The City Meat Markets, and Buddies. The company's labor force is predominantly nonunion.

Store sales in FY 97 totaled $13.2 billion, up 2% from those of FY 96. This represented WIN's 63rd consecutive year of sales increases. In FY 97, average store sales increased 1.8%, while same-store sales decreased 0.9%. Gross profits rose $69.0 million, to 26% of sales, from 24% in 1996; the increase was a result of an improved inventory mix in larger stores. Operating and administrative expenses were 24.1% of sales, versus 21.5%, reflecting higher payroll and occupancy costs in larger stores, and a more competitive, promotional sales environment.

In support of WIN's stores, the company operates 22 manufacturing facilities and 17 warehouses and distribution centers. WIN's manufacturing facilities produce dairy products, including ice cream, yogurt, oleomargarine; canned and bottled carbonated beverages; jams, jellies, peanut butter, condiments, frozen pizza, crackers, cookies and snacks. Warehouse and distribution centers, including perishable facilities, are spread throughout the southeastern U.S.

Per Share Data ($) (Year Ended Jun. 30)	**1998**	**1997**	**1996**	**1995**	**1994**	**1993**	**1992**	**1991**	**1990**	**1989**
Tangible Bk. Val.	9.19	8.97	8.84	8.16	7.13	6.57	6.20	5.58	5.20	4.91
Cash Flow	3.55	3.30	3.30	2.88	2.49	2.48	2.23	1.82	1.71	1.69
Earnings	1.33	1.36	1.69	1.55	1.45	1.55	1.41	1.10	0.96	0.84
Dividends	1.02	0.96	0.89	0.78	0.72	0.66	0.60	0.54	0.49	0.48
Payout Ratio	77%	71%	53%	50%	50%	42%	43%	49%	51%	57%
Prices - High	62 3/4	44	39	37 5/8	29 1/4	39 7/8	39 3/4	20 5/8	19 3/8	16 1/4
- Low	36 1/4	29 7/8	31	25 5/8	21 3/8	26 3/8	17 7/8	14 7/8	14 1/4	10 3/4
P/E Ratio - High	47	32	23	24	20	26	28	19	20	19
- Low	27	22	18	16	15	17	13	14	15	13
Income Statement Analysis (Million $)										
Revs.	13,617	13,219	12,955	11,788	11,082	10,832	10,337	10,074	9,744	9,151
Oper. Inc.	579	513	538	463	422	391	361	282	247	248
Depr.	330	291	247	201	157	141	127	113	118	136
Int. Exp.	28.0	22.0	21.0	14.3	14.3	18.1	25.2	21.6	17.8	24.8
Pretax Inc.	318	319	387	354	348	364	328	259	224	198
Eff. Tax Rate	37%	36%	34%	34%	38%	35%	34%	34%	32%	32%
Net Inc.	199	204	256	232	216	236	216	171	153	135
Balance Sheet & Other Fin. Data (Million $)										
Cash	24.0	14.1	32.0	30.4	31.5	108	204	103	198	128
Curr. Assets	1,736	1,588	1,501	1,456	1,361	1,413	1,363	1,203	1,169	1,031
Total Assets	3,069	2,921	2,649	2,483	2,147	2,063	1,977	1,817	1,733	1,575
Curr. Liab.	1,507	1,393	1,112	1,030	873	869	813	767	742	635
LT Debt	49.0	54.0	54.0	78.0	85.0	87.0	90.0	97.0	83.0	72.0
Common Eqty.	1,369	1,337	1,343	1,241	1,057	985	952	860	813	783
Total Cap.	1,418	1,391	1,404	1,319	1,143	1,072	1,042	957	897	856
Cap. Exp.	370	423	362	372	278	209	164	179	133	140
Cash Flow	529	495	503	433	374	378	343	284	271	271
Curr. Ratio	1.2	1.1	1.4	1.4	1.6	1.6	1.7	1.6	1.6	1.6
% LT Debt of Cap.	3.5	3.9	4.3	5.9	7.5	8.1	8.7	10.1	9.3	8.5
% Net Inc.of Revs.	1.5	1.5	2.0	2.0	2.0	2.2	2.1	1.7	1.6	1.5
% Ret. on Assets	6.6	7.3	10.0	10.0	10.3	11.8	11.4	9.7	9.3	8.7
% Ret. on Equity	14.7	15.2	19.9	20.2	21.2	24.7	23.9	20.6	19.3	17.8

Data as orig. reptd.; bef. results of disc. opers. and/or spec. items. Per share data adj. for stk. divs. as of ex-div. date. Bold denotes diluted EPS (FASB 128). E-Estimated. NA-Not Available. NM-Not Meaningful. NR-Not Ranked.

Office—5050 Edgewood Court, Jacksonville, FL 32254-3699. **Tel**—(904) 783-5000. **Chrmn & CEO**—A. Dano Davis. **Pres**—J. Kufeldt. **Secy**—J. W. Dixon. **VP-Fin & Investor Contact**—Richard P. McCook. **Dirs**—A. M. Codina, A. D. Davis, R. D. Davis, T. W. Davis, J. Kufeldt, R. D. Lovett, C. H. McKellar, D. F. Miller, J. B. North, C. T. Rider, C. P. Stephens. **Transfer Agent & Registrar**—First Chicago Trust Co. of New York. **Incorporated**—in Florida in 1928. **Empl**— 136,000. **S&P Analyst:** Robert J. Izmirlian

STANDARD &POOR'S
STOCK REPORTS

WorldCom Inc.   5669
Nasdaq Symbol **WCOM**
In S&P 500

12-SEP-98

Industry:
Telecommunications
(Long Distance)

Summary: WorldCom, the fourth largest U.S. long-distance carrier, has agreed to acquire MCI Communications, the second largest long-distance provider.

S&P Opinion: Buy (★★★★★)	Recent Price • 47	Yield • Nil
	52 Wk Range • 57⅞-28	12-Mo. P/E • NM

Earnings vs. Previous Year
▲=Up ▼=Down ▶=No Change

Quantitative Evaluations

Outlook
(1 Lowest—5 Highest)
• **1⁻**

Fair Value
• **42½**

Risk
• **Average**

Earn./Div. Rank
• **B**

Technical Eval.
• **Bullish** since 1/98

Rel. Strength Rank
(1 Lowest—99 Highest)
• **80**

Insider Activity
• **Neutral**

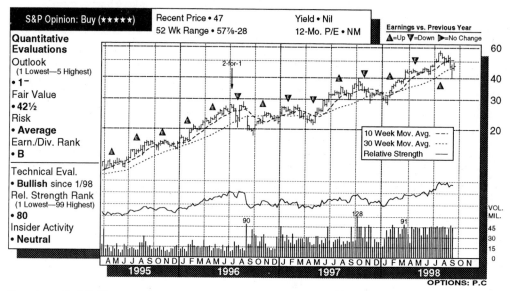

10 Week Mov. Avg. ---
30 Week Mov. Avg. ·····
Relative Strength —

OPTIONS: P.C

Overview - 28-JUL-98

November 10, 1997, could go down as one of the most important days in WCOM's history. On that date, the company announced that its revised $37 billion offer to acquire MCI Communications (Nasdaq: MCIC) for $51 a share in stock had been accepted. WCOM recently received approvals for the deal from the European Commission and the U.S. Justice Department, and it expects to get the go ahead from the FCC by the end of the summer. In January 1998, the company acquired Brooks Fiber Properties, Inc. (Nasdaq: BFPT) through an exchange of stock valued at over $2 billion, plus the assumption of debt. Subsequently, WCOM completed a three-way transaction with Compuserve and America Online, further strengthening its Internet infrastructure. Results in the 1998 first quarter included non-recurring charges of $0.46 a share.

Valuation - 28-JUL-98

WorldCom is one of only a few companies that offer full local and long-distance services. Together, MCI and WorldCom control about half of the world's Internet traffic, and we expect MCI to have to divest its wholesale customers before the merger is approved in Europe. We do not see this as significant, and continue to be bullish on WCOM's long-term prospects, both pre- and post-MCI merger. The power of the combined company, with more than $30 billion in revenues and an international presence in more than 200 countries, will rival that of the industry's largest player, AT&T. The WorldCom-MCI merger's synergies are expected to add about $2.5 billion to earnings in 1999, rising to about $5.2 billion by 2002. With revenues and cash flows expected to grow at more than 25% and 35% a year, respectively, this company is primed to become the next telecommunications giant.

Key Stock Statistics

S&P EPS Est. 1998	0.85	Tang. Bk. Value/Share	NM
P/E on S&P Est. 1998	55.4	Beta	1.42
S&P EPS Est. 1999	1.90	Shareholders	8,800
Dividend Rate/Share	Nil	Market cap. (B)	$ 50.4
Shs. outstg. (M)	1071.3	Inst. holdings	67%
Avg. daily vol. (M)	12.926		

Value of $10,000 invested 5 years ago: $ 62,924

Fiscal Year Ending Dec. 31

	1998	1997	1996	1995	1994	1993
Revenues (Million $)						
1Q	2,350	1,677	1,034	865.0	411.3	219.0
2Q	2,610	1,770	1,074	894.7	424.5	251.5
3Q	—	1,901	1,143	933.6	439.8	281.8
4Q	—	2,003	1,234	946.6	573.0	392.4
Yr.	—	7,351	4,485	3,640	2,221	1,145
Earnings Per Share ($)						
1Q	-0.28	0.05	0.21	0.14	0.12	0.08
2Q	0.21	0.08	-0.69	0.17	0.13	0.10
3Q	E0.21	0.12	0.27	0.14	0.14	0.13
4Q	E0.25	0.15	-5.22	0.20	-0.24	0.12
Yr.	E0.85	0.40	-5.50	0.65	-0.47	0.42

Next earnings report expected: late October

Dividend Data

No cash has been paid.

A Division of The **McGraw·Hill** *Companies*

STANDARD
&POOR'S
STOCK REPORTS

WorldCom Inc.

5669

12-SEP-98

Business Summary - 28-JUL-98

This worldwide communications company is the fourth largest domestic long-distance carrier, the world's largest Internet services provider, a premier provider of competitive local communications services, and a leading participant in the international telecommunications market. In November 1997, WCOM said that its revised $37 billion unsolicited offer to acquire MCI Communications (Nasdaq: MCIC) for $51 a share in stock had been accepted.

In January 1998, WorldCom acquired Brooks Fiber Properties, Inc. (Nasdaq: BFPT) in exchange for stock, in a transaction valued at over $2 billion, plus the assumption of debt. Subsequently, the company completed a three-way deal with Compuserve and America Online (AOL), which included the acquisition of ANS Communications, Inc. from AOL.

Operating in more than 50 countries, the company serves the telecommunications needs of business and government organizations by offering private line services, special access communications services, high speed data communications services, and a variety of switched services. All services are provided over WorldCom's city and long-distance fiber-optic networks in the U.S. and Europe. The company also provides business and residential local and long distance service, equipment and equipment maintenance, and a variety of enhanced services including voice mail, calling card, 800/888 number services, and customized billing services.

Internationally, the company owns fiber optic facilities on most major international cable systems in the Pacific and Atlantic Ocean regions, providing fiber optic cable connections between the U.S. and the Pacific Rim, Europe, Latin America, South America and the former Soviet Union. The company also offers certain international services over leased facilities in Japan, Hong Kong and Singapore. WorldCom recently placed into service, with joint venture partner Cable & Wireless (NYSE: CWP), a high capacity fiber optic undersea cable between the U.S. and the U.K. The cable was designed so that, without removing it from the ocean floor, it will be possible to upgrade its capacity to meet increased demand. The two companies plan to use the same technology used by WorldCom to extract increased capacity from its domestic long-distance cable.

In December 1996, WCOM completed its merger with telecommunications services provider MFS Communications. Results in 1996 were penalized by nonrecurring charges of $2.63 billion, mainly related to the merger. Excluding charges, 1996 income was $415,716,000 ($1.02 a share), versus $266,271,000 ($0.64) in 1995, as restated for acquisitions.

Per Share Data ($)

(Year Ended Dec. 31)	1997	1996	1995	1994	1993	1992	1991	1990	1989	1988
Tangible Bk. Val.	NM	NM	NM	-0.77	-0.51	-0.56	-1.39	-0.99	-0.99	NA
Cash Flow	1.33	-4.74	1.41	0.05	0.79	0.27	0.40	0.26	0.19	-0.01
Earnings	0.40	-5.50	0.65	-0.47	0.42	-0.01	0.21	0.13	0.07	-0.04
Dividends	Nil	Nil	Nil	Nil	Nil	Nil	Nil	Nil	Nil	Nil
Payout Ratio	Nil	Nil	Nil	Nil	Nil	Nil	Nil	Nil	Nil	Nil
Prices - High	39⅞	28⅞	18	14¾	13¼	7⅝	5	2¹/₁₆	1¹¹/₁₆	1⁹/₁₆
- Low	21¼	16¼	9⅝	7	7⅛	4⅛	1¹⁵/₁₆	1	⁹/₁₆	¹¹/₁₆
P/E Ratio - High	NM	NM	28	NM	31	NM	23	16	26	NM
- Low	NM	NM	15	NM	17	NM	9	8	9	NM

Income Statement Analysis (Million $)

	1997	1996	1995	1994	1993	1992	1991	1990	1989	1988
Revs.	7,351	4,485	3,640	2,221	1,145	801	263	154	110	21.0
Oper. Inc.	2,019	1,100	987	341	278	172	58.2	36.1	23.1	1.4
Depr.	921	303	311	164	79.9	53.9	15.4	9.4	6.4	1.4
Int. Exp.	320	222	249	47.3	27.0	23.8	13.1	10.5	9.4	1.4
Pretax Inc.	799	-2,058	439	-48.0	175	8.2	31.1	17.6	7.8	-2.0
Eff. Tax Rate	52%	NM	39%	NM	41%	102%	43%	44%	45%	NM
Net Inc.	384	-2,188	268	-121	104	-0.2	17.7	9.8	4.3	-2.0

Balance Sheet & Other Fin. Data (Million $)

	1997	1996	1995	1994	1993	1992	1991	1990	1989	1988
Cash	66.9	996	41.7	20.3	6.2	4.2	4.1	1.1	0.6	0.5
Curr. Assets	1,683	2,296	655	589	322	178	56.0	22.6	16.4	4.8
Total Assets	22,390	19,862	6,635	3,430	2,515	870	337	169	129	27.0
Curr. Liab.	2,048	1,911	1,979	711	309	164	72.0	28.4	21.4	7.5
LT Debt	6,527	4,804	2,278	788	526	334	151	94.0	77.0	14.0
Common Eqty.	13,510	12,947	2,187	1,827	1,621	296	100	39.0	29.0	6.0
Total Cap.	19,037	17,764	4,465	2,615	2,148	704	263	140	108	20.0
Cap. Exp.	2,645	657	356	192	35.6	57.7	19.0	13.1	9.5	1.2
Cash Flow	1,278	-1,885	546	14.0	174	51.6	33.1	19.2	10.7	-0.7
Curr. Ratio	0.8	1.2	0.3	0.8	1.0	1.1	0.8	0.8	0.8	0.6
% LT Debt of Cap.	34.3	27.0	51.0	30.1	24.5	47.4	57.2	67.0	71.2	69.2
% Net Inc.of Revs.	5.2	NM	7.2	NM	9.1	NM	6.7	6.3	3.9	NM
% Ret. on Assets	1.8	NM	5.3	NM	5.8	NM	6.6	6.1	NA	NA
% Ret. on Equity	2.7	NM	11.7	NM	9.4	NM	24.0	26.4	NA	NA

Data as orig. reptd.; bef. results of disc. opers. and/or spec. items. Per share data adj. for stk. divs. as of ex-div. date. Bold denotes diluted EPS (FASB 128). E-Estimated. NA-Not Available. NM-Not Meaningful. NR-Not Ranked.

Office—515 E. Amite St., Jackson, MS 39201-2702. **Tel**—(601) 360-8600. **Fax**—(601) 974-8350. **Website**—http://www.wcom.com **Vice Chrmn & COO**—J. W. Sidgmore. **Pres & CEO**—B. J. Ebbers. **CFO & Secy**—S. D. Sullivan. **Investor Contact**—Gary Brandt. **Dirs**—J. C. Allen, C. J. Aycock, M. E. Bobbit, S. M. Case, B. J. Ebbers, F. Galesi, S. A. Kellett Jr., J. A. Porter, J. W. Sidgmore, S. D. Sullivan, L. C. Tucker. **Transfer Agent & Registrar**—Bank of New York. **Incorporated**—in Mississippi in 1983; reincorporated in Georgia in 1993. **Empl**— 20,300. **S&P Analyst:** Philip D. Wohl

12-SEP-98

Industry: Iron & Steel

Summary: This leading processor of close-tolerance steel intends to divest its custom plastic and cast product segments.

S&P Opinion: Hold (★★★)	Recent Price • 11½	Yield • 4.9%
	52 Wk Range • 20⅞-10⅜	12-Mo. P/E • 11.2

Quantitative Evaluations

Outlook
(1 Lowest—5 Highest)
• **3**

Fair Value
• **14**

Risk
• **Low**

Earn./Div. Rank
• **A-**

Technical Eval.
• **Bullish** since 10/96

Rel. Strength Rank
(1 Lowest—99 Highest)
• **36**

Insider Activity
• **Favorable**

Earnings vs. Previous Year
△=Up ▽=Down ▷=No Change

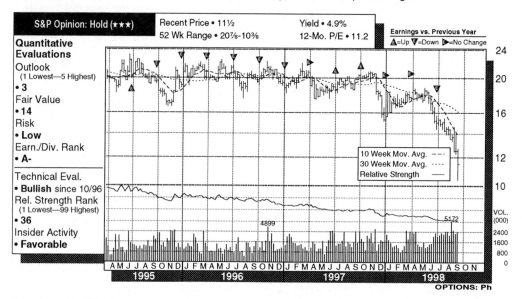

10 Week Mov. Avg. ---
30 Week Mov. Avg. ----
Relative Strength —

OPTIONS: Ph

Overview - 29-JUN-98

We anticipate 8% sales growth in FY 99 (May) from continuing operations, mostly reflecting continued, albeit less vibrant, economic growth. Some growth will result from acquisitions, but they are not likely to be a major factor, in contrast to FY 98's sales gains. Margins should improve, as operating problems at key plants are resolved and startup delays and costs become less of a factor. Benefiting further from another solid gain in equity income, EPS should increase from FY 98's depressed levels.

Valuation - 29-JUN-98

Although FY 98 (May) fourth quarter EPS from continuing operations beat the consensus estimate, the shares dropped sharply subsequent to the EPS release and conference call. WTHG expects to achieve 5% to 7% EPS growth in 1998 but alerted analysts that start-up costs for two new ventures would cost it $0.04 in the first quarter. We believe this disclosure along with fears that the strike at General Motors could also hurt profits led the market to overlook the strong fourth quarter. The market also ignored WTHG's decision to sell its custom and cast products units. Earlier, on April 1, WTHG said it had retained investment banking firms to explore strategic options for these operations. WTHG intends to apply the proceeds to acquisitions of steel related businesses, stock repurchases or debt repayment. In recent years these business segments have had either high, erratic returns or low single digit returns on investment. By narrowing its focus to steel processing and related businesses, WTHG should be better able to boost its EPS and return on equity. Currently selling at under 17X our FY 99 estimate and yielding over 3.5%, the shares are worth holding for their turn-around potential.

Key Stock Statistics

S&P EPS Est. 1999	0.90	Tang. Bk. Value/Share	7.08
P/E on S&P Est. 1999	12.8	Beta	0.67
Dividend Rate/Share	0.56	Shareholders	9,200
Shs. outstg. (M)	96.7	Market cap. (B)	$ 1.1
Avg. daily vol. (M)	0.697	Inst. holdings	49%

Value of $10,000 invested 5 years ago: $ 8,786

Fiscal Year Ending May 31

	1998	1997	1996	1995	1994	1993
Revenues (Million $)						
1Q	500.4	430.3	325.7	346.3	289.9	250.0
2Q	520.3	458.4	354.5	363.3	295.9	262.0
3Q	518.5	486.6	360.2	370.1	323.1	276.1
4Q	446.7	536.5	437.3	403.9	376.2	327.2
Yr.	1,624	1,912	1,478	1,484	1,285	1,116
Earnings Per Share ($)						
1Q	0.24	0.23	0.24	0.28	0.22	0.15
2Q	0.23	0.23	0.29	0.31	0.21	0.17
3Q	**0.23**	0.23	0.23	0.32	0.22	0.17
4Q	**0.26**	0.28	0.25	0.38	0.29	0.25
Yr.	**0.85**	0.97	1.01	1.29	0.94	0.74

Next earnings report expected: mid September

Dividend Data (Dividends have been paid since 1968.)

Amount ($)	Date Decl.	Ex-Div. Date	Stock of Record	Payment Date
0.130	Nov. 20	Dec. 05	Dec. 09	Dec. 29 '97
0.130	Feb. 27	Mar. 06	Mar. 10	Mar. 30 '98
0.140	May. 27	Jun. 08	Jun. 10	Jun. 26 '98
0.140	Aug. 27	Sep. 08	Sep. 10	Sep. 29 '98

A Division of The McGraw-Hill Companies

Business Summary - 29-JUN-98

Since mid-1995, Worthington Industries, Inc. (WTHG), the largest independent U.S. steel processor, has implemented an aggressive expansion strategy designed to increase sales and profit growth. Initiatives include startup of eight new plants, five acquisitions, formation of two joint ventures, and 10 internal expansion projects. As a result, WTHG's debt to capitalization ratio increased from 7.4% at the end of FY 95 (May) to 28% at the end of FY 97. In addition to processing flat-rolled steel, WTHG manufactures pressure cylinders and makes a broad line of cast steel products and precision parts, but these operations are to be divested. Sales and profits in FY 97 were derived as follows:

	Sales	Profits
Processed steel products	74%	78%
Custom plastic products	20%	17%
Cast products	6%	15%

The processed steel products segment consists of four different businesses. Processed steel products buys coils of wide, open-tolerance sheet steel from major steel mills and processes it to the orders of more than 1,700 industrial customers in the automotive, appliance, electrical, machinery, communication, leisure time and other industries. Worthington Cylinders produces disposable and reusable steel and aluminum cylinders, sold primarily to producers and distributors of refrigerant gases, and refillable steel and aluminum cylinders, used to hold liquefied petroleum gas. Dietrich Industries, makes metal framing products for the commercial and residential building industries. Gerstenlager Co. manufactures automotive after-market body panels for the U. S. market.

Custom products include injection-molded plastic component parts and assemblies, primarily for customers in automotive original equipment markets. Custom products also include precision metal components for power steering, transmission, brake and other mechanical systems.

Cast products consist of a broad line of cast steel products ranging in size from 100 pounds to 30 tons. The products are sold to the railroad, mass transit, construction and off-highway markets.

WTHG participates in six joint ventures that are accounted for by the equity method: Worthington Armstrong, Worthington Specialty Processing, TWB Co., London Industries, Acerex, S.A. de C.V. and Worthington S.A.

Per Share Data ($)

(Year Ended May 31)	1998	1997	1996	1995	1994	1993	1992	1991	1990	1989
Tangible Bk. Val.	7.08	6.38	6.32	6.49	5.56	4.80	4.35	4.00	3.84	3.55
Cash Flow	1.48	1.50	1.44	1.66	1.30	1.07	0.93	0.77	0.85	0.93
Earnings	0.85	0.97	1.01	1.29	0.94	0.74	0.63	0.50	0.61	0.70
Dividends	0.52	0.36	0.56	0.40	0.36	0.33	0.30	0.27	0.25	0.20
Payout Ratio	61%	37%	55%	31%	38%	0%	49%	54%	41%	29%
Cal. Yrs.	1997	1996	1995	1994	1993	1992	1991	1990	1989	1988
Prices - High	22	22¹/₂	23¹/₄	23¹/₂	21⁵/₈	17⁵/₈	15⁵/₈	11	11³/₈	11
- Low	15¹/₈	17¹/₂	16⁵/₈	17¹/₂	15	12³/₈	9¹/₈	8³/₈	9¹/₈	7¹/₂
P/E Ratio - High	26	23	23	18	23	24	25	22	18	16
- Low	18	18	16	14	16	17	14	17	15	11

Income Statement Analysis (Million $)

	1998	1997	1996	1995	1994	1993	1992	1991	1990	1989
Revs.	1,624	1,912	1,478	1,484	1,285	1,116	974	875	916	1,006
Oper. Inc.	197	206	166	188	152	138	118	99	113	127
Depr.	61.5	51.4	39.2	34.1	32.4	29.2	26.9	23.8	20.8	20.4
Int. Exp.	25.6	18.4	8.3	6.0	3.0	3.4	4.4	6.3	4.7	4.8
Pretax Inc.	131	151	148	187	136	105	87.0	70.0	88.0	102
Eff. Tax Rate	37%	38%	38%	38%	37%	37%	36%	36%	37%	37%
Net Inc.	82.3	93.3	91.3	117	84.9	66.2	55.5	44.6	55.2	64.2

Balance Sheet & Other Fin. Data (Million $)

	1998	1997	1996	1995	1994	1993	1992	1991	1990	1989
Cash	3.8	7.2	19.0	2.0	13.3	17.6	6.0	9.0	50.0	43.1
Curr. Assets	643	594	476	452	413	364	311	276	313	333
Total Assets	1,842	1,561	1,220	917	799	686	622	564	561	558
Curr. Liab.	410	247	151	179	181	147	131	107	133	150
LT Debt	440	450	299	53.5	54.1	55.6	57.3	59.0	42.5	46.9
Common Eqty.	780	716	640	590	504	433	389	355	344	320
Total Cap.	1,407	1,296	1,052	720	617	539	490	455	426	406
Cap. Exp.	309	173	109	61.5	47.0	29.1	45.1	63.3	54.6	45.1
Cash Flow	144	145	131	151	117	95.4	82.4	68.4	76.0	84.5
Curr. Ratio	1.6	2.4	3.1	2.5	2.3	2.5	2.4	2.6	2.3	2.2
% LT Debt of Cap.	31.3	34.8	28.4	7.4	8.8	10.3	11.7	13.0	10.0	11.5
% Net Inc.of Revs.	5.1	4.9	6.2	7.9	6.6	5.9	5.7	5.1	6.0	6.4
% Ret. on Assets	4.8	6.6	8.5	13.6	11.4	10.1	9.3	8.0	9.9	12.1
% Ret. on Equity	11.0	13.5	14.8	21.3	18.1	16.0	14.9	12.8	16.7	21.3

Data as orig. reptd.; bef. results of disc. opers. and/or spec. items. Per share data adj. for stk. divs. as of ex-div. date. Bold denotes diluted EPS (FASB 128). E-Estimated. NA-Not Available. NM-Not Meaningful. NR-Not Ranked.

Office—1205 Dearborn Dr., Columbus, OH 43085. **Tel**—(614) 438-3210. **Website**—http://www.stockprofiles.com/wthg **Chrmn & CEO**—J. P. McConnell. **Pres & COO**—D. H. Malenick. **VP & CFO**—D. G. Barger Jr.**Secy**—C. D. Minor. **Investor Contact**—Todd Rollins (614-438-3133). **Dirs**—C. R. Carson, W. S. Dietrich, J. E. Fisher, J. F. Havens, P. A. Klisares, K. S. LeVeque, D. H. Malenick, J. H. McConnell, J. P. McConnell, R. B. McCurry, C. D. Minor, G. B. Mitchell, J. Petropoulos. **Transfer Agent & Registrar**—Bank of Boston. **Incorporated**—in Ohio in 1955; reincorporated in Delaware in 1986. **Empl**—12,000. **S&P Analyst:** Leo J. Larkin

Wrigley (Wm.) Jr. 2506

NYSE Symbol **WWY**

In S&P 500

12-SEP-98

Industry: Foods

Summary: This company is the world's largest producer of chewing gum, with about 50% of the U.S. market. The Wrigley family controls 51% of the supervoting Class B stock.

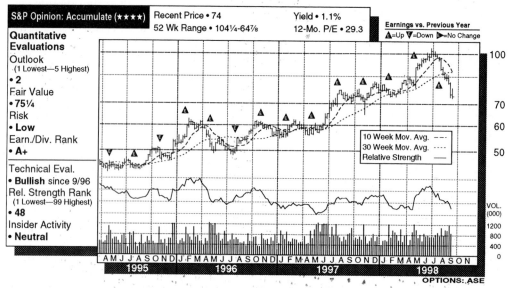

S&P Opinion: Accumulate (★★★★)

Recent Price • 74	Yield • 1.1%
52 Wk Range • 104¼-64⅞	12-Mo. P/E • 29.3

Quantitative Evaluations

Outlook (1 Lowest—5 Highest)
• **2**

Fair Value
• **75¼**

Risk
• **Low**

Earn./Div. Rank
• **A+**

Technical Eval.
• **Bullish** since 9/96

Rel. Strength Rank (1 Lowest—99 Highest)
• **48**

Insider Activity
• **Neutral**

Earnings vs. Previous Year ▲=Up ▼=Down ▶=No Change

10 Week Mov. Avg. - - - -
30 Week Mov. Avg. ·········
Relative Strength ——

OPTIONS: ASE

Overview - 04-AUG-98

Net sales in 1998 are projected to rise at a high single-digit annual pace, as a nearly 10% rise in sales volume growth (1% to 2% in the U.S.; approximately 15% outside the U.S.) is slightly offset by unfavorable currency exchange translations. WWY's relatively high operating profitability should benefit near term from cost savings realized from the 1997 realignment of production facilities and from the projected pickup in more profitable U.S. sales. However, heavy capital spending devoted to further penetrating high-potential foreign markets (China, Russia, Central Europe) is likely to continue. We expect EPS (including a $0.06 special gain) to rise 12% in 1998, to $2.63, from 1997's $2.34. We expect longer-term annual EPS to grow at a 10% to 14% pace.

Valuation - 04-AUG-98

Earnings growth has clearly slowed in recent years for this once reliable mid-teen EPS grower. This is primarily a result of increased competition in the highly mature U.S. marketplace for gum-related products and the high costs of expanding the business worldwide. However, with benefits beginning to accrue from the recent cost cutting actions taken in the U.S., together with improving profitability abroad, our near-term earnings growth expectations could prove conservative. Longer term, we expect Wrigley to reap generous rewards for its past and present investment in developing high-potential markets. This, together with the company's already-dominant position in the U.S. and a very strong balance sheet, will allow for earnings growth well into the future. The shares are attractive for low-risk accounts seeking long-term capital appreciation.

Key Stock Statistics

S&P EPS Est. 1998	2.63	Tang. Bk. Value/Share	9.40
P/E on S&P Est. 1998	28.2	Beta	0.64
S&P EPS Est. 1999	2.95	Shareholders	35,000
Dividend Rate/Share	0.80	Market cap. (B)	$ 6.9
Shs. outstg. (M)	116.2	Inst. holdings	27%
Avg. daily vol. (M)	0.216		

Value of $10,000 invested 5 years ago: $ 25,060

Fiscal Year Ending Dec. 31

	1998	1997	1996	1995	1994	1993
Revenues (Million $)						
1Q	473.2	451.2	426.7	410.2	378.6	332.0
2Q	541.2	521.3	483.6	470.6	423.1	386.2
3Q	—	481.9	462.4	431.5	404.1	360.5
4Q	—	486.2	463.3	442.6	390.9	349.5
Yr.	—	1,937	1,836	1,755	1,597	1,429
Earnings Per Share ($)						
1Q	**0.66**	0.54	0.50	0.48	0.65	0.36
2Q	**0.73**	0.66	0.49	0.55	0.50	0.46
3Q	**E0.67**	0.60	0.53	0.50	0.53	0.42
4Q	**E0.57**	0.54	0.47	0.40	0.30	0.26
Yr.	**E2.63**	2.34	1.99	1.93	1.98	1.50

Next earnings report expected: late October

Dividend Data (Dividends have been paid since 1913.)

Amount ($)	Date Decl.	Ex-Div. Date	Stock of Record	Payment Date
0.190	Oct. 29	Jan. 13	Jan. 15	Feb. 02 '98
0.200	Mar. 03	Apr. 13	Apr. 15	May. 01 '98
0.200	May. 27	Jul. 13	Jul. 15	Aug. 03 '98
0.200	Aug. 26	Oct. 13	Oct. 15	Nov. 02 '98

STANDARD
&POOR'S
STOCK REPORTS

Wm. Wrigley Jr. Company

2506

12-SEP-98

Business Summary - 04-AUG-98

Since 1891, Wrigley has concentrated its operations essentially on one line of business: the manufacture and marketing of chewing gum. Today, the company is the world's largest gum manufacturer, accounting for about 50% of total chewing gum sales volume in the U.S. Principal products include Wrigley's Spearmint, Doublemint, Juicy Fruit, Big Red, Winterfresh and Extra. Other products include Freedent, Orbit, P.K. and Hubba Bubba (bubble gum). Chewing gum accounts for over 90% of total sales and earnings.

By geographical area, sales and profit contributions in 1997 were derived as follows:

	Sales	Profits
North America	46%	45%
Europe	41%	45%
Asia, Pacific & other	13%	10%

Finished gum is manufactured in two factories in the U.S. and 11 factories in other countries. Three wholly owned associated domestic companies also manufacture products other than finished chewing gum: L. A. Dreyfus Co. produces chewing gum base for Wrigley and other customers; Northwestern Flavors, Inc. processes flavorings and rectifies mint oil for Wrigley and ingredients for other food-related industries; and The Wrico Packaging division produces a large portion of the company's domestic printed and other wrapping supplies. WWY's 10 largest markets outside of the U.S. in 1997 were Australia, Canada, China, France, Germany, the Philippines, Poland, Russia, Taiwan and the U.K. WWY brands are sold in more than 140 countries and territories.

WWY's Amurol Confections subsidiary, in addition to manufacturing and marketing children's bubble gum items (Big League Chew, Bubble Tape) and other uniquely packaged confections, has various non-gum items, such as a line of suckers, dextrose candy, liquid gel candy and hard roll candies as an important part of its total business. Amurol is also developing export markets, currently the largest being Canada, Brazil and Japan. Separately, WWY paid an extra dividend of $0.43 per share in December 1997 (up from $0.34 in 1996), bringing the full-year 1997 dividend to $1.17.

Per Share Data ($)

(Year Ended Dec. 31)	1997	1996	1995	1994	1993	1992	1991	1990	1989	1988
Tangible Bk. Val.	8.50	7.74	6.87	5.92	4.94	4.27	3.95	3.42	2.91	2.59
Cash Flow	2.78	2.39	2.31	2.33	1.80	1.52	1.34	1.22	1.11	0.92
Earnings	2.34	1.99	1.93	1.98	1.50	1.27	1.09	1.00	0.90	0.73
Dividends	1.17	1.02	0.96	0.90	0.75	0.62	0.55	0.49	0.45	0.36
Payout Ratio	50%	51%	50%	45%	50%	49%	50%	49%	50%	50%
Prices - High	82	$62^7/_8$	54	$53^7/_8$	$46^1/_8$	$39^7/_8$	27	$19^3/_4$	18	$13^3/_4$
- Low	$54^1/_2$	$48^3/_8$	$42^7/_8$	$38^1/_8$	$29^1/_2$	$22^1/_8$	$16^3/_8$	$14^5/_8$	$11^7/_8$	$10^3/_4$
P/E Ratio - High	35	32	28	27	31	31	25	20	20	19
- Low	23	24	22	19	20	17	15	15	13	15

Income Statement Analysis (Million $)

	1997	1996	1995	1994	1993	1992	1991	1990	1989	1988
Revs.	1,937	1,836	1,754	1,597	1,429	1,287	1,149	1,111	993	891
Oper. Inc.	432	412	381	331	303	249	227	203	178	154
Depr.	50.4	47.3	43.8	41.1	34.6	29.8	28.7	26.9	24.6	23.2
Int. Exp.	1.0	1.1	2.0	1.5	1.5	1.2	1.4	1.1	0.8	0.5
Pretax Inc.	394	359	350	353	279	232	208	188	170	141
Eff. Tax Rate	31%	36%	36%	35%	37%	36%	38%	38%	38%	38%
Net Inc.	272	230	224	231	175	149	129	117	106	87.0

Balance Sheet & Other Fin. Data (Million $)

	1997	1996	1995	1994	1993	1992	1991	1990	1989	1988
Cash	207	301	232	230	190	182	145	114	109	115
Curr. Assets	798	729	672	623	502	449	403	357	308	269
Total Assets	1,343	1,234	1,099	979	815	711	625	564	499	440
Curr. Liab.	226	218	213	210	159	149	127	127	148	125
LT Debt	Nil	Nil	Nil	Nil	Nil	Nil	Nil	Nil	Nil	Nil
Common Eqty.	985	897	797	688	575	499	463	401	343	309
Total Cap.	1,016	922	816	704	598	512	471	410	351	315
Cap. Exp.	127	102	103	87.0	63.1	66.7	45.2	45.5	45.4	29.8
Cash Flow	322	278	268	272	209	178	157	144	131	110
Curr. Ratio	3.5	3.3	3.2	3.0	3.2	3.0	3.2	2.8	2.1	2.1
% LT Debt of Cap.	Nil	Nil	Nil	Nil	Nil	Nil	Nil	Nil	Nil	Nil
% Net Inc.of Revs.	14.0	12.5	12.8	14.4	12.2	11.5	11.2	10.6	10.7	9.8
% Ret. on Assets	21.1	19.7	21.5	25.7	23.0	22.3	21.7	22.1	22.7	20.7
% Ret. on Equity	28.9	27.2	30.1	36.5	31.0	31.0	29.8	31.6	32.8	29.4

Data as orig. reptd.; bef. results of disc. opers. and/or spec. items. Per share data adj. for stk. divs. as of ex-div. date. Bold denotes diluted EPS (FASB 128). E-Estimated. NA-Not Available. NM-Not Meaningful. NR-Not Ranked.

Office—410 N. Michigan Ave., Chicago, IL 60611. **Tel**—(312) 644-2121. **Pres & CEO**—W. Wrigley. **Treas**—A. J. Schneider. **Investor Contact**—Christopher J. Perille. **Dirs**—C. F. Allison III, D. S. Barrie, L. P. Bell, T. A. Knowlton, P. S. Pritzker, S. B. Sample, A. Shumate, R. K. Smucker, W. Wrigley, W. Wrigley Jr. **Transfer Agent & Registrar**—First Chicago Trust Co. of New York, NYC. **Incorporated**—in Delaware in 1927. **Empl**—8,200. **S&P Analyst:** Richard Joy

STANDARD &POOR'S
STOCK REPORTS

Xerox Corp.

2509

NYSE Symbol **XRX**

In S&P 500

12-SEP-98

Industry: Photography/Imaging

Summary: Xerox serves the document processing market worldwide, offering a complete line of copiers, electronic printers, and other office and computer equipment.

S&P Opinion: Accumulate (★★★★)	Recent Price • 84⅝	Yield • 1.7%
	52 Wk Range • 116½-66⅛	12-Mo. P/E • NM

Quantitative Evaluations

Outlook (1 Lowest—5 Highest)
• **2**

Fair Value
• **90¼**

Risk
• **Average**

Earn./Div. Rank
• **B**

Technical Eval.
• **Bullish** since 6/98

Rel. Strength Rank (1 Lowest—99 Highest)
• **46**

Insider Activity
• **Unfavorable**

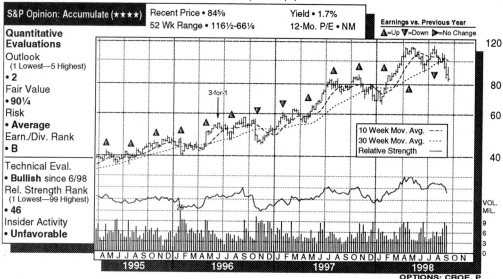

Earnings vs. Previous Year
▲=Up ▼=Down ▷=No Change

10 Week Mov. Avg. ---
30 Week Mov. Avg. ·····
Relative Strength ——

OPTIONS: CBOE, P

Overview - 24-JUL-98

XRX recorded a $1.1 billion restructuring charge in the 1998 second quarter, covering the elimination of about 9,000 jobs, the closing and consolidation of facilities, and the writeoff of certain assets. Once the restructuring is fully implemented, the company hopes to realize $1 billion in annual cost savings. Sales should grow about 8% in 1998, spurred by growing demand for XRX's digital black and white copiers and color publishing products, as well as growth in outsourcing, as companies increasingly look to Xerox to manage their document facilities. Negative currency translations and Asia/Pacific troubles will continue to prove a challenge, and will hold down sales growth slightly. Operating expenses should benefit from efforts to reduce SG&A expense as a percentage of revenues. XRX recently reinstated its $1 billion stock repurchase program. The company bought back 470,000 common shares in the second quarter.

Valuation - 24-JUL-98

XRX had EPS of $1.09 (before a $3.28 restructuring charge) in the 1998 second quarter, versus $0.94 in the 1997 period, exceeding expectations. Revenues rose 9%. Gross margins narrowed, but operating margins improved, on tight cost controls. We expect XRX to have another excellent year in 1998, driven by its digital product superiority, the growing market for digital copiers, and strong acceptance of new product lines. Partly offsetting these gains will be a decline in traditional light lens copying. Gross margins should narrow, due to price competition, but operating margins should benefit from efforts to control costs. We expect XRX's restructuring program to begin to help in 1999. The shares, recently trading at 20X our 1999 EPS estimate of $5.50, are attractive for accumulation, based on XRX's long-term growth potential.

Key Stock Statistics

S&P EPS Est. 1998	4.70	Tang. Bk. Value/Share	6.74
P/E on S&P Est. 1998	18.0	Beta	1.11
S&P EPS Est. 1999	5.50	Shareholders	55,900
Dividend Rate/Share	1.44	Market cap. (B)	$ 27.8
Shs. outstg. (M)	328.6	Inst. holdings	77%
Avg. daily vol. (M)	1.534		

Value of $10,000 invested 5 years ago: $ 36,830

Fiscal Year Ending Dec. 31

	1998	1997	1996	1995	1994	1993
Revenues (Million $)						
1Q	4,304	4,022	3,928	3,770	3,271	3,230
2Q	4,742	4,356	4,217	4,054	3,584	3,430
3Q	—	4,376	4,158	4,027	3,636	3,490
4Q	—	5,412	5,075	4,760	4,597	4,080
Yr.	—	18,166	17,378	16,611	15,088	14,230
Earnings Per Share ($)						
1Q	0.84	0.75	0.68	0.53	0.35	0.33
2Q	-2.19	0.94	0.85	0.74	0.44	0.29
3Q	E1.07	0.89	0.71	0.74	0.54	0.50
4Q	E1.70	1.46	1.25	1.39	0.92	-1.87
Yr.	E4.70	4.04	3.32	3.40	2.24	-0.82

Next earnings report expected: late October

Dividend Data (Dividends have been paid since 1930.)

Amount ($)	Date Decl.	Ex-Div. Date	Stock of Record	Payment Date
0.320	Oct. 13	Dec. 03	Dec. 05	Jan. 01 '98
0.360	Jan. 23	Mar. 04	Mar. 06	Apr. 01 '98
0.360	May. 20	Jun. 03	Jun. 05	Jul. 01 '98
0.360	Jul. 13	Sep. 02	Sep. 04	Oct. 01 '98

A Division of The McGraw·Hill Companies

STANDARD
&POOR'S
STOCK REPORTS

Xerox Corporation

2509

12-SEP-98

Business Summary - 24-JUL-98

Long known as the photocopier company, Xerox has shifted its focus toward serving the global document market with newer, digital, multifunction products. As the copier market in the U.S. has matured, and with the office environment becoming more digitized, XRX has needed to develop newer products with cutting edge technologies to remain competitive. In April 1998, the company said it would incur a $1 billion after tax restructuring charge in the 1998 second quarter, to cut about 9,000 jobs, close and consolidate facilities, and write off certain assets.

XRX's product lines consist of digital products (37% of 1997 sales), light-lens copiers (53%) and paper and other products (10%). Digital products consist of black and white production publishing, black and white production printing, color laser copying and black and white digital copiers. Production publishing is done through DocuTech digital publishers, which scan hard copy and convert it to a digital format and also accept input directly from PCs. Production printing includes high-end, host connected, high speed printers and low-end desktop printers.

Color laser copying and printing is an accelerating business for XRX, with revenues growing 46% in 1997 to $1.5 billion. The standout products in this field include the Docucolor 70, which produces 70 high-quality, full color impressions per minute, and the Docucolor 40, which produces 40- pages per minute. Black and white digital copiers can be connected to a customer's network so they can be used as high-speed network printers and can ultimately replace desktop printers, single-purpose copiers and fax machines.

Revenues from traditional light-lens copiers declined 2% in 1997, reflecting the transition to digital products. The company expects light-lens copiers to continue to decline as a percentage of the company's revenues. XRX also sells paper and other consumables to the installed base, and provides printing, publishing, duplicating and related services at more than 5,000 customer locations in 40 countries.

The company operates globally through wholly owned Xerox Ltd. (formerly Rank Xerox) and Fuji Xerox, which Xerox co-owns with Fuji Photo Film of Japan. In June 1997, XRX acquired the remaining 20% interest in Rank Xerox for about $1.5 billion. Xerox Ltd. markets products and supplies in more than 80 countries in Europe, Asia and Africa. International revenues were about 51% of total 1997 sales.

Customer financing is provided through Xerox Credit Corp. in the U.S., and through subsidiaries in Europe, Canada and Latin America. Approximately 75% to 80% of all equipment sales are financed through Xerox.

Per Share Data ($)

(Year Ended Dec. 31)	1997	1996	1995	1994	1993	1992	1991	1990	1989	1988
Tangible Bk. Val.	11.07	11.57	10.03	12.24	11.78	12.09	12.31	11.81	11.32	13.88
Cash Flow	5.91	5.89	5.66	4.31	1.25	1.22	3.73	4.28	4.75	3.73
Earnings	4.04	3.49	3.40	2.24	-0.82	-1.11	1.30	1.84	2.19	1.17
Dividends	1.28	1.16	1.00	1.00	1.00	1.00	1.00	1.00	1.00	1.00
Payout Ratio	32%	33%	29%	45%	NM	NM	76%	53%	43%	87%
Prices - High	88	58¹/₄	48¹/₄	37⁵/₈	30	27³/₈	23¹/₄	19⁵/₈	23	21
- Low	51¹/₂	39³/₄	32¹/₈	29¹/₄	23¹/₄	22¹/₈	11³/₄	9⁵/₈	18¹/₈	16³/₄
P/E Ratio - High	22	17	14	17	NM	NM	18	11	11	18
- Low	13	11	9	13	NM	NM	9	5	8	14

Income Statement Analysis (Million $)

	1997	1996	1995	1994	1993	1992	1991	1990	1989	1988
Revs.	18,166	17,378	16,611	16,831	16,193	17,040	16,745	16,951	16,806	15,994
Oper. Inc.	3,400	3,161	3,016	1,961	1,434	512	1,615	1,467	2,031	2,154
Depr.	739	715	660	681	655	739	695	691	765	784
Int. Exp.	520	513	509	714	755	862	821	855	882	643
Pretax Inc.	2,268	1,821	1,847	1,558	-226	171	963	1,103	1,240	1,005
Eff. Tax Rate	32%	38%	33%	35%	NM	162%	36%	28%	31%	47%
Net Inc.	1,452	1,206	1,174	794	-188	-255	454	605	704	388

Balance Sheet & Other Fin. Data (Million $)

	1997	1996	1995	1994	1993	1992	1991	1990	1989	1988
Cash	75.0	104	130	1,058	1,796	657	797	1,407	1,219	1,365
Curr. Assets	10,766	10,152	9,833	NA	NA	NA	NA	NA	NA	NA
Total Assets	27,732	26,818	25,969	38,585	38,750	34,051	31,658	31,495	30,088	26,441
Curr. Liab.	7,692	7,204	6,999	NA	NA	NA	NA	NA	NA	NA
LT Debt	8,779	8,424	7,867	7,780	7,386	8,105	6,247	7,108	7,511	5,379
Common Eqty.	4,985	4,985	3,878	4,177	3,972	3,875	5,140	5,051	5,035	5,371
Total Cap.	15,233	14,355	12,490	13,214	12,627	13,256	12,870	13,595	13,807	12,003
Cap. Exp.	520	510	438	389	470	582	498	444	436	508
Cash Flow	2,134	1,921	1,834	1,402	381	398	1,063	1,210	1,419	1,140
Curr. Ratio	1.4	1.4	1.4	NA	NA	NA	NA	NA	NA	NA
% LT Debt of Cap.	57.6	58.7	63.0	58.9	59.5	61.1	48.5	52.3	54.4	44.8
% Net Inc.of Revs.	8.0	6.9	7.1	4.7	NM	NM	2.7	3.6	4.2	2.4
% Ret. on Assets	5.3	4.6	4.4	2.0	NM	NM	1.4	2.0	2.6	2.0
% Ret. on Equity	29.8	27.8	29.2	17.5	NM	NM	7.2	10.3	13.3	6.7

Data as orig. reptd.; bef. results of disc. opers. and/or spec. items. Per share data adj. for stk. divs. as of ex-div. date. Bold denotes diluted EPS (FASB 128). E-Estimated. NA-Not Available. NM-Not Meaningful. NR-Not Ranked.

Office—800 Long Ridge Rd., P.O. Box 1600, Stamford, CT 06904-1600. Tel—(203) 968-3000. Fax—(203) 968-3944. Website—http:// www.xerox.com Chrmn & CEO—P. A. Allaire. Pres & COO—G. R. Thoman. EVP & CFO—B. D. Romeril.VP, Secy & Treas—E. M. Filter. Investor Contacts—Charles K. Wessendorf. Dirs—P. A. Allaire, B. R. Inman, A. A. Johnson, V. E. Jordan Jr., Y. Kobayashi, H. Kopper, R. S. Larsen, J. D. Macomber, G. J. Mitchell, N. J. Nicholas Jr., J. E. Pepper, P. F. Russo, M. R. Seger, T. C. Theobald G. R. Thoman. Transfer Agent and Registrar—First National Bank of Boston. Incorporated—in New York in 1906. Empl— 91,400. S&P Analyst: Jim Corridore